WALFORD'S GUIDE TO REFERENCE MATERIAL

EIGHTH EDITION

WALFORD'S GUIDE TO REFERENCE MATERIAL

Volume 1

Science and Technology

Edited by

Marilyn Mullay MA ALA
Senior Librarian, Edinburgh School of Agriculture

and

Priscilla Schlicke BA DipLib ALA

LIBRARY ASSOCIATION PUBLISHING
LONDON

Published by
Library Association Publishing
7 Ridgmount Street
London WC1E 7AE

Library Association Publishing is wholly owned by The
Library Association.

First published 1959
Supplement 1963
Second edition 1966
Third edition 1973
Fourth edition 1980
Fifth edition 1989
Sixth edition 1993
Seventh edition 1996
This eighth edition 1999

British Library Cataloguing in Publication Data
A catalogue record for this book is available from
The British Library

ISBN 1-85604-341-X

Computer production software and typesetting by LIBPAC
(Computer Services) Ltd, Whittle le Woods, Lancs.
Printed and made in Great Britain by MPG Books Ltd,
Bodmin, Cornwall.

Contents

Contents

Introduction

Background

From its first edition the purpose of *Walford* has been to identify and evaluate the widest possible range of reference materials. In addition to the expected bibliographies, indexes, dictionaries, encyclopaedias, directories, etc, a number of important textbooks and manuals of general practice are included. While the majority of items are reference 'books', *Walford* is a guide to reference 'material'. Thus periodical articles, microforms, online, CD-ROM and Internet sources are all represented. The objective is for *Walford* to provide a 'one-stop' source of information on all types of reference material, regardless of form. Targeted users include librarians developing and revising reference collections, staff on enquiry desks needing advice on further sources when local stock has been checked, research workers in the preliminary stages of projects, and students of library and information studies.

To be of manageable proportions a guide such as this must inevitably be selective. Most major reference tools are included, whenever originally published, provided they remain useful. Geographic scope is international, but with an emphasis on English-language material. A special effort has been made to ensure that the output of small and specialist publishers is not neglected.

Subject arrangement and indexing

Entries in *Walford* follow a subject arrangement based on the Universal Decimal Classification International Medium Edition of 1985 (BS1000M). Subject access for users unfamiliar with UDC can be gained either by checking the contents page to find the relevant section and then browsing through the entries, which are subdivided by form, place, etc, or by using the subject index. The first level of subheading within each broad subject class is typographically highlighted by the use of rules (see sample entry overleaf).

Terms in the subject index are generated by the classification numbers given to the entries. Each entry has been allocated a running serial number in the text to provide easy access from both the subject and author/title indexes. There is an index of online, Internet and database services. Full instruction on the structure and use of the indexes can be found in their introductions.

Compilation

Individual entries in *Walford* are wherever possible based on examination of the actual item and include full bibliographical details, ISBN, ISSN and, if in print, the price when it can be ascertained. Brief critical annotations are provided in most cases, giving summary publishing history, outline of contents, comparison with other works, especially notable features and a brief general assessment of overall value, often illustrated by quotations from or references to reviews. The example overleaf shows the general layout of entries.

Work on this volume was completed in mid-1999. Although no cut-off date for new material was specified, the aim has been to include as many 1998 publications as possible, together with some items published early in 1999. Intimation of planned new and revised editions is also given where possible.

This volume includes almost 700 new items, with every existing entry checked and, if necessary revised. A special effort has been made to include a selection of websites and electronic reference sources throughout. All URLs were checked and correct at the time of compilation. In all sections out-of-date or superseded materials have been deleted.

New and expanding subject areas in this volume include telecommunications, multimedia and digitization technology, building and construction, alternative medicine, sports medicine and emerging subdisciplines of palaentology, such as palaeopathology and palaeosols.

This volume is the work of two compilers: Marilyn Mullay was responsible for Classes 5/6, 52/529, 55, 56, 572, 573, 58/59, 61, 63, 64, and 654/656. Priscilla Schlicke was responsible for Classes 51, 53, 54, 6, 608, 62, 629, 66, 67/68 and 69. The whole project was overseen by Kathryn Beecroft of Library Association Publishing. Joan Bibby ably constructed a thesaurus based on the

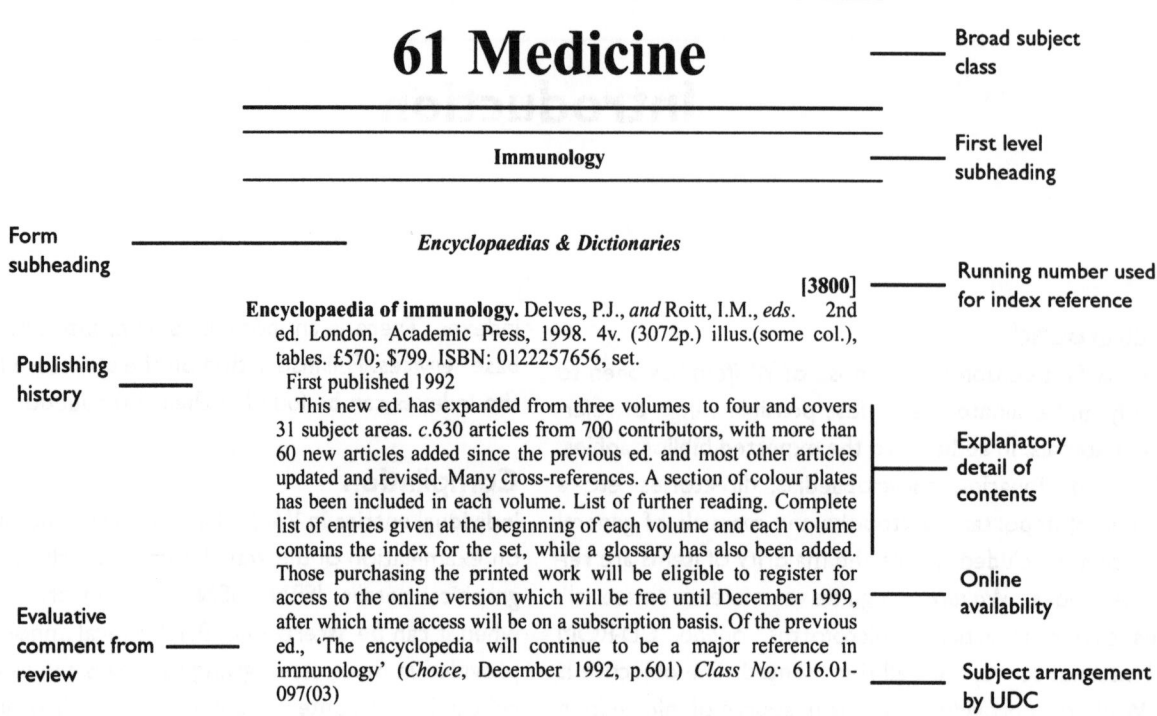

61 Medicine — Broad subject class

Immunology — First level subheading

Form subheading — *Encyclopaedias & Dictionaries*

[3800] — Running number used for index reference

Encyclopaedia of immunology. Delves, P.J., *and* Roitt, I.M., *eds*. 2nd ed. London, Academic Press, 1998. 4v. (3072p.) illus.(some col.), tables. £570; $799. ISBN: 0122257656, set.

Publishing history — First published 1992

This new ed. has expanded from three volumes to four and covers 31 subject areas. *c.*630 articles from 700 contributors, with more than 60 new articles added since the previous ed. and most other articles updated and revised. Many cross-references. A section of colour plates has been included in each volume. List of further reading. Complete list of entries given at the beginning of each volume and each volume contains the index for the set, while a glossary has also been added. Those purchasing the printed work will be eligible to register for access to the online version which will be free until December 1999, after which time access will be on a subscription basis. Of the previous ed., 'The encyclopedia will continue to be a major reference in immunology' (*Choice*, December 1992, p.601) *Class No:* 616.01-097(03)

Explanatory detail of contents

Online availability

Evaluative comment from review — Subject arrangement by UDC

UDC classification scheme. Martin Harrison of LIBPAC Computer Services automated the data capture, indexing and typesetting.

Acknowledgments

The compilers are indebted to John Walford for his continuing interest in this work and his contributions in the form of advice and notes on new material. They would also like to thank Joan Walford, Jennie Doyle (BPIF Marketing Communications), John Flanagan (Royal Botanic Gardens, Kew), A. J. Mullay, Ray Prytherch, Ted Schlicke and the staff of the National Library of Scotland for assistance in the compilation of this volume.

Libraries consulted

General and academic libraries
British Library
British Library Document Supply Centre
Heriot-Watt University Library
London Library
National Library of Scotland
University of Cambridge Library
University of Edinburgh Library
University of Glasgow Library
University of Leeds Library
University of London Library
University of York Library.

Public libraries
Bishopsgate
Cambridge
Edinburgh City Libraries
Holborn
Kensington
Leeds City Libraries
Marylebone
Mitchell Library (Glasgow)
St Pancras
Westminster
York City Libraries.

Special libraries
British Geological Survey
British Library Science Reference and Information Service (Holborn; Aldwych)
Bush Agriculture Library and Information Centre
Chartered Institute of Surveyors
Darwin Library (University of Edinburgh)
Department of Health and Social Security
Department of Energy
Department of Trade (Export Promotion)
Departments of the Environment and Transport

Edinburgh School of Agriculture Library and
   Information Centre
Erskine Medical Library
Imperial War Museum
Imperial College (Lyon Playfair Library)
Institute of Geological Science
Institution of Electrical Engineers
Institution of Civil Engineers
Marine Laboratory (Aberdeen)
Ministry of Agriculture, Fisheries and Food
Ministry of Defence
National Railway Museum Library
National Sports Medicine Institute of the UK
Royal Anthropological Society
Royal Astronomical Society
Royal Botanic Garden (Edinburgh)
Royal Chemical Society
Royal College of Veterinary Surgeons

Royal Dick Veterinary College
Royal Institute of British Architects
Royal Institute of Internal Affairs
Royal Institution of Chartered Surveyors
Royal Observatory (Edinburgh)
Science Museum Library
Scottish Natural Heritage
Scottish Office Agriculture and Fisheries Department
Scottish Science Library
Sports Council
United Nations Information Centre
Watford College (on Printing).

E-mail discussion lists and Internet sites too numerous to
mention have also been used.

Marilyn Mullay
Priscilla Schlicke

Abbreviations

Listed below are the chief bibliographical abbreviations used in the *Guide*. Generally accepted abbreviations such as Co., Corpn. e.g., i.e., Inc., Ltd. and q.v. are not included.

AG [German] – Aktiengesellschaft: Co.
ALA – American Library Association
Abt. [German] – Abteiling: part
ampl. [Italian] – ampliata: enlarged
ampl. [Spanish] – ampliado: enlarged
Aufl. [German] – Auflage: edition
augm. [French] – augmenté: enlarged
aum. [Portuguese] – aumentada: enlarged
aum. [Spanish] – aumentado: enlarged
Ausg. [German] – Ausgabe: printing, edition

BS – British Standard
Bd [German] – Band: volume
BFr – Belgian francs
bearb. [German] – bearbeitet: compiled, edited
Belg. – Belgian

c – copyright date
C. Cd. Cmd. Cmnd. – Command papers
ch. – chapter(s)
chron. – chronology
col. – colour, coloured
cols. – columns
comp. – compiler
corr. – corrected
corr. – [French] – corrigé: corrected
corr. – [Spanish] – corregido: corrected
corr. – [Portuguese] – corrigida: corrected

DFl – Dutch florins
Dan. – Danish
diagrs. – diagrams
distr. – distributed
DM [German] – Deutschmark
druk [Dutch] – edition

ea. – each

ed. – edition, editor(s)
ed. – [Italian] – edizione
ed. – [Spanish] – edición
ed. – [French] – édition
ed. – [Portuguese] – ediçáo: edition
enl. – enlarged
erw., erweit. [German] – erweiterte: enlarged
exp. – expanded

FID – Fédération Internationale de Documentation
facsim(s) – facsimile(s)
fasc(s) – fascicule(s)
fig. – figures
fldg. – folding
FFr – French francs
front. – frontispiece

ganz. [German] – gänzlich: complete
glav.red. [Russian] – glavnyi redaktor: editor-in-chief
Gld. [Dutch] – guilders
GmbH [German] – Gesellschaft mit beschränkter Haftung: Ltd
Gosud. [Russian] – Gosudarstvo: State

HMSO – Her Majesty's Stationery Office
Hft [German] – Heft: part number
hrsg. [German] – herausgegeben: edited, published

illus. – illustrations, illustrated
imp. [French] – imprimé, imprimerie: printed, printing firm
izd. [Russian] – izdanie: edition
izd. [Serbo-Croat] – izdanje: edition
Izdat. [Russian] – Izdatel': publisher

Jahrg. [German] – Jahrgang: annual publication
kiad. [Hungarian] – kiadás: edition

Kr [Danish, Norwegian, Swedish] – kroner

L. [Italian] – lire
l. – leaves
Lfg. [German] – Lieferung: number, part

m. fl. [Danish] – med flere: and others

n.d. – no date
neubearb. [German] – neubearbeitet:: revised
no. – number
Nor. – Norwegian
nouv. [French] – nouvelle: new (edition)
n.p. – no place of publication
Nr [Danish, German] – Nummer: number
n.s. – new series
NV [Dutch] – naamloze vennootschap: limited company

o.p. – out of print
omarb. [Swedish] – omarbetad: revised
opl. [Danish] – oplag: edition

p. – page(s)
pl. – plate(s)
port. – portrait(s)
pt(s) – part(s)
pub. – publisher
pubn. – publication

réd. [French] – rédigé: edited, compiled
repr. – reprinted
rev. – revised, revision
rev. – [French] – révisé: revised
rev. – [Portuguese] – revistada: revised
riv. [Italian] – riveduto: revised
R. [South Africa] – rands

Rs – rupees

Sch – Schillings
ser. – series
sér. [French] – série: series
SFr – Swiss francs
supp. – supplementary, supplement(s)
Sw. – Swiss
Swed. – Swedish

t. [French] – tome(s): volume(s)
T. [German] – Teil(e): part(s)

u. [German] – und: and
UDC – Universal Decimal Classification
udg. [Danish] – udgave: edition
uit. [Dutch] – uitgaaf: publication
uitg. [Dutch] – uitgegeven: published
umgearb. [German] – umbearbeitete: revised
Univ. – University
unveränd. [German] – unverändert: unaltered
uppl. [Swedish] – upplaga: edition
utg. [Norwegian] – utgave: edition

v. – volume(s)
v. p. – various pagings
VEB [German] – Volkseigener Betrieb: People's
   Concern
verand. [German] – verandert: revised
verb. [German] – verbesserte: improved
verm [German] – vermehrte: enlarged
vyd. [Czech] – vydání: edition
vyd. [Slovak] – vydanie: edition

wyd. [Polish] – wydanie: edition

5/6 Science & Technology

Government Policies

Dictionaries

[1]

Wörterbuch der Wirtschaftswissenschaft: russisch, deutsch, englisch.
Dobrov, G., *and others*. 2 überarb & erweit. Aufl. Berlin, Verlag der
Wirtschaft, 1984. 560p.

Dictionary of science policy studies. About 8,000 Russian-base
terms, with German and English equivalents and indexes.
Class No: 5/6.0(038)

Worldwide

[2]

Cartermill guides to science and technology. London, Cartermill
Publishing, 1996-.

Formerly published as *Longman guide to world science and
technology* (Harlow, Essex, Longman Group, 1982-1996).

Science and technology in Africa, by J.W. Forje. 1989. 281p. £85.
ISBN 0582000866.

*Science and technology in Australasia, Antarctica and the Pacific
Islands*. 1989. 335p. £85. ISBN 0582900603.

Science and technology in Canada, edited by P. Dufour and J. de la
Mothe. 1993. xiv,331p. ISBN 0582101068.

Science and technology in China, by T.B. Tang. 1984. 278p. £85.
ISBN 0582900565.

Science and technology in Eastern Europe, edited by G. Darvas.
1988. xx,283p. £85. ISBN 0582900549.

Science and technology in France and Belgium, by E.W. Kellerman.
1988. 140p. £85. ISBN 058290084X.

Science and technology in Germany, edited by W. Krull and F.
Meyer-Krahmer. 1996. ix,237p. £45. ISBN 1860671462.

*Science and technology in India, Pakistan, Bangladesh and Sri
Lanka*, by A. Rahman. 1990. xviii,245p. £95. ISBN 0582064694.

Science and technology in Japan, by J. Sigurdson. 3rd ed. 1995.
xviii,356p.illus. £45. ISBN 1860670121.

Science and technology in Latin America, by Latin American
Newsletters, Ltd. 1983. 373p. £85. ISBN 0582900573.

Science and technology in the Middle East, by Z. Sardar. 1982.
335p. ISBN 0582900522.

Science and technology in Scandinavia, by G. Férne. 1988. 175p.
£85. ISBN 0582018927.

*Science and technology in southern Europe: Spain, Portugal, Greece
and Italy*, by C.O. Hidalgo. 1997. xvi,309p. £49.50. ISBN
1860671853.

Science and technology in the USSR, edited by M.J. Berry. 1988.
424p. £85. ISBN 0582900530.

Science and technology in the United Kingdom, by R. Nicholson.
1991. xv,312p. £95. ISBN 0582900514.

Science and technology in the USA, by A.H. Teich and J.H. Pace.
1986. 427p. £85. ISBN 0582900611.

Chapters in each volume concern the organizational sectors,
followed by specific areas (*e.g.* agriculture). Appended directory of
sources. Establishments and subject index. *Class No:* 5/6.0(100)

[3]

Megascience policy issues. Paris, OECD, 1995. 237p. figs.,tables.
ISBN: 9264145575.

Contains issues discussed by the OECD's Megascience Forum. 5
chapters: 1. Generic megascience policy issues - 2. Megascience and
national decision-making processes ... 5. Cost, funding, and budget
issues in megascience projects: the case of the United States.
Bibliography, p.232-34. Short list of acronyms, p.235.
Class No: 5/6.0(100)

[4]

Outlook on science policy. Guildford, Surrey, published for the
International Science Policy Foundation by Beech Tree Publishing,
1967-. 12pa. £117 pa. ISSN: 01650262.

Covers national and international science and technology policy.
Issue for v.20(11), December, 1998 includes items on: Innovation and
technology in Hong Kong ... Major increase in Portuguese research ...
UK S & T policy: online. *Class No:* 5/6.0(100)

[5]

Reviews of national science and technology policy. Paris, OECD,
1965-.

Australia. 1986. £7.50. *Austria.* 1988. *Belgium.* 1966. *Canada.*
1969. *China.* 1979. *Finland.* 1987. £9.50. *France.* 1966. *German
Democratic Republic.* 1986. *Greece.* 1984. *Iceland.* 1984. *Ireland.*
1974. *Italy.* 1992. £14. *Japan.* 1967. *Mexico.* 1994. *Netherlands.*
1987. £9.50. *New Zealand.* 1987. *Norway.* 1985. *Poland.* 1996. £19.
Portugal. 1993. *Spain.* 1971. *Sweden.* 1987. £6. *Switzerland.* 1989.
£12. *Turkey.* 1995. £19. *United Kingdom and Germany.* 1967. *USA.*
1968. *Yugoslavia.* 1976.

Finland (154p.) is OECD's first evaluation of science and
technology policy in that country. Sections: Reasons for decision
making; Planning; Inputs from university research; Interactions
between R & D and industrial policy. *Class No:* 5/6.0(100)

[6]

Science and technology policy in the 1980s and beyond.
Gibbons, M., *and others eds*. London & New York, Longman, 1984.
xxvi, 346p. ISBN: 0582902002.

18 chapters: 1. Science and technology in India: policy,
management implications (with 11 notes) - 2. Science policy in the
UK; a view from the centre ... 10. The problematic relationship
between research and policy ... 17. Some science and technology
issues in global disarmament and development - 18. Science and
technology in the New International Economic Order (with 32 notes
and references). Assembles some of the papers presented at a
workshop held in Manchester, 27-29 April 1983.
Class No: 5/6.0(100)

[7]

Science, technology and industry outlook. Paris, OECD, 1998. 296p.
tables,charts. £40. ISBN: 9264161090.

Published every two years, the 1998 ed. discusses recent trends in
science, technology and industry and, among other things, gives an
overview of policy in these areas in OECD countries. This ed. includes
chapters on the impact of advanced technologies in traditional
industries and recent changes in R & D expenditure and their impact
on innovation and growth. 50-page appendix gives statistics in 83
tables and 132 charts, alongwith information on the main OECD
databases covering these areas. *Class No:* 5/6.0(100)

[8]

Science, technology, and innovation : a review of recent policy
developments. London, British Library Science Reference and
Information Service, 1995-. 6pa. £110. ISSN: 09529616.

Formerly *Science and technology policy: a review of recent
developments*.

Reviews current UK and international press comment and
specialized reports on scientific policy matters. Contents of December
1995 issue: News and views - Conference report - Internet news -
World views - Recent publications (237 annotated entries). Author and
subject indexes for 'Recent publications'. *Class No:* 5/6.0(100)

Europe

[9]

**BRAZIER, P.C. and SHOULTS, T.A.S. Guide to European
collaboration in science and technology.** London, Science and Energy
Policy Studies Unit; Royal Society; Fellowship of Engineering, 1990.
213+4p. insert. £30. ISBN: 0854034293.

First published 1987 as *European collaboration in science and
technology*.

3 parts (104 entries): 1. European Community programmes - 2.
Non-EC multinational organizations, programmes and facilities - 3.
Grant schemes for exchange, fellowships. Appendix: Computer
networks, online databases and other sources of information. Detailed
index, p.201-13. *Class No:* 5/6.0(4)

[10]

Science policies in Europe: unity and diversity. Proceedings of a
symposium sponsored and organised by the Scottish Agricultural
Science Agency, as part of the Edinburgh International Science
Festival 1994. Hay, R.K.M., *ed*. Edinburgh, HMSO, 1994. xiii,102p.
tables. ISBN: 0114952604.

Seven papers precede the symposium: 1. The need for directed
national science and technology policies ... 3. Germany: new
challenges - infrastructure and innovation crisis ... 7. EC science
policies: competitiveness, subsidiary and cohesion. *Class No:* 5/6.0(4)

Europe—Eastern

[11]

Science and technology in Eastern Europe. Darvas, G., *ed.* Harlow, Essex, Longman Group, 1988. xx,283p. £85. (*Longman guide to world science and technology.*) ISBN: 0582900549.

Science and technology policy in each of seven former Eastern bloc countries: Bulgaria, Czechoslavakia, German Democratic Republic, Hungary, Poland, Romania and Yugoslavia. Includes data on relevant associations and bodies. *Class No: 5/6.0(401)*

Great Britain

[12]

Science and technology in the United Kingdom. Nicholson, R., *Sir, and others, eds.* Harlow, Essex, Longman, 1991. xv,312p. £95. (*Longman guide to world science and technology, v.14.*) ISBN: 0582900514.

13 sections: 1. Overview of the UK economy, society and politics and the role of S & T - 2. History, development and organization of UK science and technology up to 1982 - 3. Central government organization and policy making for UK science and technology since 1982 ... 7. Agriculture and food - 8. Environmental and natural resources ... 11. Science and technology in sectors dominated by the private sector ... 13. International collaboration. 'Directory of selected research establishments', p.287-312. Short bibliography appended to each chapter. *Class No: 5/6.0(410)*

[13]

UK science policy: a critical review of policies for publicly funded research. Goldsmith, M., *ed.* Harlow, Essex, Longman Group, 1984. xxii, 275p. ISBN: 0582902568.

Two parts. 1. Critical, documented reviews (1. Agricultural research policy; 9. Transport research) - 2 . Comparative studies (10. France: a logical attitude to science; 11. The Netherlands: towards a national science policy). Acronyms. Biographical notes. Index, p.267-75. *Class No: 5/6.0(410)*

Federal Republic of Germany

[14]

Science and technology in Germany. Krull, W. *and* Meyer-Krahmer, F., *eds.* London, Cartermill Publishing, 1996. ix,237p. figs.,tables. £45. (*Cartermill guides to science and technology.*) ISBN: 1860671462.

First published in 1990 as *Science and technology in the Federal Republic of Germany.*

Five sections (13 chapters): Introduction and review - Science and technology in Germany: trends and perspectives - Changing roles of science and technology institutions - Technological change and industrial R & D management - Statistical surveys of scientific output, research and development. Brief index. Each chapter has a list of references appended. *Class No: 5/6.0(430.1)*

France

[15]

Science and technology in France and Belgium. Kellermann, E.W., *ed.* Harlow, Essex, Longman Group, 1988. viii, 131p. £85. (*Longman guide to world science and technology, v.7.*) ISBN: 058290084x.

Two parts: France; Belgium. Separate chapers on each concern science policy, industrial R & D, institutions, etc., followed by specific chapters on individual sectors of science and technology, and a list of useful addresses. *Class No: 5/6.0(44)*

Russia

[16]

FORTESCUE, S. **Science policy in the Soviet Union.** London, Routledge, 1990. xi,230p. tables. £42.50. ISBN: 0415023793.

10 chapters (3. The Academy of Sciences ... 6. The research establishment ... 10. Main themes and current developments). Chapter notes, p.187-213. Glossary and abbreviations. References, p.217-25. Detailed, analytical index. Author is a professor of politics. *Class No: 5/6.0(47)*

[17]

Science and technology in the USSR. Berry, M.J., *ed.* Harlow, Essex, Longman Group, 1988. xvi, 405p. diagrs., maps. £85. (*Longman guide to world science and technology, v.6.*) ISBN: 0582900530.

27 chapters, of which the initial 12 provide historical background, organizational structure fostering Soviet scientific research, etc. Chapters 13-27, by specialists, concern individual branches of science in the USSR, scientific associations and the like. Index of establishments. *Class No: 5/6.0(47)*

[18]

Science, technology and innovation policies: Federation of Russia. Paris, OECD, 1994. 2v. ISBN: 9264140816, v.1; 9264142398, v.2.
    v.1. *Evaluation report.* 115p. figs., tables.
    v.2. *Background report.* 256p. figs., tables.
    V.1 contains six chapters: 1. Major issues ... 3. The science base ... 6. Principal recommendations. Two appendices: 1. Tables - 2. Summary of the discussion of the evaluation report. V.2 is a detailed report of the organization and current directions of Russian science and technology in 10 chapters (*e.g.* 7. The climate for innovation ... 10. Russian science and technology in the international community). *Class No: 5/6.0(47)*

Scandinavia

[19]

FERNE, G. **Science and technology in Scandinavia.** Harlow, Essex, Longman, 1989. 175p. £85. (*Longman guide to world science and technology, v.9.*) ISBN: 0582018927.

8 sections: 1. Introduction - 2. Decision-making ... 4. Research in higher education - 5. Research in the service of collective needs ... 7. International dimension - 8. Conclusion. Each section covers Denmark, Finland, Iceland, Norway and Sweden. Bibliography, p.155-57. Appendix, 'Directory of major research establishments', p.158-70. Index of establishments. *Class No: 5/6.0(48)*

China

[20]

Guide to China's science and technology policy. 1989. Beijing, International Academic Publications, 1991. xii,472p. diagrs., tables. (*White paper on science and technology, no.4.*) ISBN: 7800031357.

7 parts. 2 appendices (A: State laws and regulations). *Class No: 5/6.0(510)*

[21]

Science and technology in China. Tang, T.B., *ed.* Harlow, Essex, Longman Group, 1984. xii, 269p. £85. (*Longman guide to world science and technology, v.3.*) ISBN: 0582900565.

The main chapters focus on specific branches of Chinese science and technology, with a separate chapter on Taiwan. Statistical appendices are followed by a directory of major research establishments. Indexes of establishments and subjects. Presentation is 'clear, concise and in general easily readable' (*Nature*, 13 December 1986, p.649). It nicely complements *Science in contemporary China*, edited by L.A. Orleans (Stanford Univ. Press, 1980), which goes to the end of 1974. *Class No: 5/6.0(510)*

Japan

[22]

SIGURDSON, J. **Science and technology in Japan.** 3rd ed. London, Cartermill Publishing, 1995. xviii,356p. illus. £45. ISBN: 1860670121.

First published 1984.

Contents include an overview, science and government, universities and academic research, government programmes in science and technology, research in life sciences, marine and environment research, etc. Good value. *Class No: 5/6.0(52)*

India

[23]

Modern India and progress in science and technology. New Delhi, Vikas Publishing House, 1979. [vii], 164p. ISBN: 0706907434.

9 chapters (2. The role of universities - 3. Scientific surveys and research - 4. Learned societies and institutions - 5. Medical education and research - 6. Engineering and industry - 7. Technical education and research - 8. Agricultural education and research - 9. Conclusion). Non-analytical index, p. 161-4. *Class No: 5/6.0(540)*

Indian Subcontinent States

[24]

Science and technology in India, Pakistan, Bangladesh and Sri Lanka. Rahman, A., *and others, eds.* Harlow, Essex, Longman, 1990. xviii,259p. tables. £95. (*Longman guide to world science and technology, v.13.*) ISBN: 0582064694.

Gives an overview of science in each country. Part 1. India (1. Introduction ... 6. New technologies ... 8. Scientific societies and periodicals ... 10. Epilogue) - Part 2. Pakistan (11. Introduction ... 14. National science and technology policy ... 16. Status and progress in important areas - 17. Conclusions) - Part 3. Bangladesh (18. Introduction ... 23. International cooperation in science and technology) - Part 4. Sri Lanka. Short bibliographies throughout. 2 appendices: 1. Directory of selected establishments - 2. Organizational chart of science and technology in India. No index. *Class No: 5/6.0(54.)*

Islamic World

[25]

Science and technology in the Middle East: a guide to issues, organizations and institutions. Sardar, Z., *ed.* Harlow, Essex, Longman Group, 1982. x, 324p. tables, map. (*Longman guide to world science and technology, v.1.*) ISBN: 0582900522.

Part 1: Overview - Part 2: Regional organizations (*e.g.* Arab League Educational, Cultural and Scientific Organization (ALESCO)), p.83-115 - Part 3: Country profiles (19; Afghanistan ... People's Democratic Republic of Yemen), p.119-285. Appendix: 'Directory of major establishments in the Middle East'. Index of establishments. Detailed, analytical index, with country subdivisions. Omits Israel. *Class No: 5/6.0(5.297)*

Africa

[26]

FORJE, J.W. Science and technology in Africa. Harlow, Essex, Longman, 1989. xiii,281p. tables. £85. (*Longman guide to world science and technology, v.10.*) ISBN: 0582000866.

16 sections: 1. The continent and its people ... 3. Science and government - 4. National science and technology policy ... 9. Industrial research and development ... 13. Cooperation in science and technology - 14. Militarization: technology and development ... 16. Transport and communications. 3 appendices (*e.g.* 'Directory of research establishments'). A bibliography is appended to each chapter. *Class No: 5/6.0(6)*

USA

[27]

The Fragile contract: university science and federal government. Guston, D.H. *and* Keniston, K., *eds.* Cambridge, Mass., MIT Press, 1994. 244p. ISBN: 0262071614.

11 chapters: 1. Introduction: the social contract for science ... 4. Integrity and accountability in research ... 6. How large an R & D enterprise? ... 8. Financing science after the Cold War ... 11. Conclusion. Bibliographies appended to each chapter. *Class No: 5/6.0(73)*

[28]

Science and technology in the USA. Teich, A. *and* Pace, J.H., *eds.* Harlow, Essex, Longman Group, 1986. xix, 408p. tables. £85. (*Longman guide to world science and technology, v.5.*) ISBN: 0582900611.

18 chapters: 1. Demographic, economic and political overview ... 4. Government science and policy ... 6. Industrial research and development ... 8. Agricultural science and technology ... 9. Biomedical research and devlopment ... 14. Associations, societies and academies in science, engineering and higher education ... 17. International cooperation in science and technology - 18. Scientific and technical information. Appendix 1: Sources of information in US science and technology (p.359-64; grouped); 2. Federal research establishments and index. Non-analytical subject index, p.396-408. The result of a team effort. *Class No: 5/6.0(73)*

[29]

Science, technology, and the Federal Government national goals for a new era. United States. National Research Council. Washington, D.C., National Academy Press, 1993. x,54p. ISBN: 0716713454.

Five sections: The changing context for science and technology - Science and technology in modern society ... The Federal role in the adoption and development of technology - Conclusion and next steps. Appendix: Federal funding of research and technology in the United States. *Class No: 5/6.0(73)*

America—South

[30]

Science and technology in Latin America. Roper, C. *and* Silva, J., *eds.* Harlow, Essex, Longman Group, 1983. ix, 363p. diagrs., tables, map. £85. (*Longman guide to world science and technology.*) ISBN: 0582900573.

25 country chapters (Argentina ... Venezuela), p.1-248. Each chapter has sections on societies and organizations, information sources in science and technology. Index of establishments, p.314-51. Analytical subject index, p.352-63. *Class No: 5/6.0(8)*

Australasia & Oceania

[31]

RONAYNE, J. *and* BOAG, C. Science and technology in Australasia, Antarctica and the Pacific Islands. Harlow, Essex, Longman, 1989. xi,335p. tables, graphs. £85. (*Longman guide to world science and technology, v.11.*) ISBN: 0582900603.

4 sections: 1. Australia (1. Geography, demography, politics and economics ... 8. State and territory governments ... 10. Academic science and research ... 12. Learned and professional societies) - 2. New Zealand (13. Demographic, political and economic background

.... (contd.)
... 17. Health and medical science ... 20. Other scientific activities) - 3. The South Pacific - 4. Antarctica (22. Geography, resources, climate and politics ... 24. Scientific and research activities). Brief list of references appended to each chapter, 'Directory of selected establishments', p.307-335. *Class No: 5/6.0(9)*

Thesauri

[32]

UNITED NATIONS. Educational, Scientific and Cultural Organization. **SPINES thesaurus:** a controlled and structured vocabulary of science and technology. Rev. ed. Paris, Unesco, 1988. 2v. (xxii,1122p.). £38.

The *Thesaurus* contains *c.*10,500 terms, of which some two-thirds are descriptors linked by a network of more than 74,000 semantic relations. *Class No: 5/6.0:025.43*

Science

Abbreviations & Symbols

[33]

ABBR: abbreviations for scientific and engineering terms. Montreal, Canadian Standards Association, [*c.*1983]. 280p.

Consists of 2 main A-Z sequences: 7,000 terms; 6,800 abbreviations. Appended: a list of 250 symbols and a bibliography. Excludes abbreviations for organizations, agencies, computer-language etc., concentrating on 'abbreviations for words and word combinations for use in drawings and in engineering and scientific writing'. *Class No: 5(003)*

[34]

Abbreviations dictionary. De Sola, R., *and others.* 9th ed. Boca Raton, CRC Press, 1995. xvii,1347p. £49.95. ISBN: 0849389445.

Over 270,000 entries, 14,000 new to this ed. Not a specialist science and technology abbreviations dictionary but contains many terms encountered by the scientist. Includes non-English abbreviations. Abbreviations are followed by sections which include: Airlines of the world; Chemical element symbols, atomic numbers, and discovery data; Earthquake data (Richter Scale); Numeration; Winds of the world. *Class No: 5(003)*

[35]

Acronyms, initialisms, and abbreviations dictionary: a guide to acronyms, abbreviations, contractions, alphabetic symbols, and similar condensed appellations. Bonk, M.R., *ed.* New York, Gale, 1960- . Annual. $305. ISSN: 02704404.

First published 1960 as *Acronyms dictionary*, then issued irregularly, but now published annually in 2v.

23rd edition (1997) comprises Vol.1, 3166p., Vol.2, 179p. giving a highly comprehensive listing of abbreviations and acronyms, (Vol. 1. Pt.1. A-F; 2. Pt.2. G-O; Pt. 3. P-Z; Vol.2. contains 10,000 'newly coined or newly found terms'). United States bias. Covers aerospace, biochemistry, data processing, electronics, genetics, information technology, medicine, pharmacy, physiology, science, technical drawings and specifications, telecommunications, and transportation. AIDS is given 51 different definitions. *Class No: 5(003)*

[36]

BRITISH STANDARDS INSTITUTION. Specification for quantities, units and symbols. London, BSI, 1993. 14 pts. (*BS 5775.*)

Replaces BS 1991: *Letter symbols, signs and abbreviations* (1961).

0. *General principles.* 1993. 28p. £50. 1. *Space and time.* 1993. 20p. £50. 2. *Periodic and related phenomena.* 1979. 16p. £36. 3. *Mechanics.* 1993. 28p. £50. 4. *Heat.* 1993. 24p. £50. 5. *Electricity and magnetism.* 1993. 42p. £66. 6. *Light and related electromagnetic radiations.* 1993. 28p. £50. 7. *Acoustics.* 1993. 20p. £50. 8. *Physical chemistry and molecular physics.* 1993. 36p. £66. 9. *Atomic and nuclear physics.* 1993. 32p. £50. 10. *Nuclear reactions and ionizing radiations.* 1993. 36p. £66. 11. *Mathematical signs and symbols for use in the physical sciences and technology.* 1993. 36p. £66. 12. *Characteristic numbers.* 1993. 16p. £36. 13. *Solid state physics.* 1982. 28p. £50. *Class No: 5(003)*

[37]

—ROYAL SOCIETY. Quantities, units and symbols: a report by the Symbols Committee of the Royal Society, representing the Royal Society, the Chemical Society, the Institute of Physics. 2nd ed. London, Royal Society, 1975. 54p. Addendum, 1981. 2p. £1. ISBN: 0854030719.

Has 14 sections: 1. Introduction - 2. Physical quantities and symbols for physical quantities - 3. Units and symbols for units... 6. Chemical elements, nuclides and particles... 7. Quantum states... 8. Nuclear physics... 12. Recommended values of physical constants... 13. Sources - 14. Bibliography (p.50-54). 'A very useful summary' (*RSR*, v.5(2), April/June 1977, p.18). *Class No: 5(003)*

[38]

Glossary of Russian abbreviations and acronyms. Washington, Library of Congress, 1967. x, 806p.

First published 1952.

23,600 entries selected from 40,000 abbreviations and acronyms in files of the Lexicography and Terminology Section, Aerospace Technology Division. Restricted to abbreviated words in general use by 20th-century authors, scientists, journalists, teachers, editors, librarians and archivists, and acronyms used in Soviet publications since World War II, emphazising aerospace, scientific and technical literature. *Class No:* 5(003)

[39]

LIUNGMAN, C.G. Thought signs: the semiotics of symbols - western non-pictorial ideograms. Amsterdam, IOS Press, 1995. 698p. figs. £47.50. ISBN: 9051991975.

Previously published as *Dictionary of symbols* (Gale Research, 1993).

Contains more than 2,500 Western signs, arranged into 54 groupings. Has 1,600 brief articles discussing the history and meaning of the ideograms. Internet version is *Symbols.com* at http://www.SYMBOLS.com/. Two main access points: Graphic index; Word index. An offline version, *SYMBOLS '98 encyclopedia*, is available for downloading from this site. *Class No:* 5(003)

[40]

MURITH, J. *and* **BOCABEILLE, J.-M. Dictionnaire des abréviations et acronymes scientifiques, techniques, médicaux, économiques, juridiques.** [Dictionary of scientific, technical, medical, economic, legal abbreviations and acronyms.] Paris, Technique et Documentation, 1992. 949p. £110;FFr950. ISBN: 2852066815.

About 25,000 abbreviations and acronyms, including those of organizations and companies, with their names and addresses. In French and English. *Class No:* 5(003)

[41]

OCRAN, E.B. Ocran's acronyms: a dictionary of abbreviations and acronyms used in scientific and technical writing. London, Routledge & Kegan Paul, 1978. xiv, 262p. (reprinted with corrections, 1980).

About 7,000 entries in the main A-Z sequence, p.1-184, followed by 47 subject sections (Aeronautics... Transportation). Excludes most associations and government bodies. Aeronautics and computer services figure prominently. 'Compiled to fulfil a subject approach' (*Introduction*). 'Reference librarians will find this volume very useful' (*Choice*, v.16(1), March 1979, p.58). *Class No:* 5(003)

[42]

Pugh's dictionary of acronyms and abbreviations: abbreviations in management, technology and information science. Pugh, E., *comp.* 5th ed. London, Library Association Publishing, 1987. v, 366p. £60. (£48 to LA members). ISBN: 0853655375.

First published 1968.

More than 34,000 entries, stating country of origin or organization, as considered necessary. Unlike the wide-ranging *Acronyms, initialisms and abbreviations dictionary* (q.v.), with its 500,000 odd terms, plus *International acronyms, initialisms & abbreviations dictionary* (4th ed. Gale, 1997), for terms of foreign origin, Pugh concentrates largely on management, technology and information science. *Class No:* 5(003)

[43]

SHEPHERD, W. Shepherd's glossary of graphic signs and symbols. London, Dent, 1971. x, 599p.

About 5,000 signs and symbols, covering engineering, mathematics, electricity, physics, numismatics, meteorology, etc., are interpreted. Bibliography, p.583-90. Index of signs with names, p.591-7. 'Believed to be the first extensive treatment of the subject to be published' (*Preface*). *Class No:* 5(003)

[44]

—**ARNELL, A. Standard graphical symbols:** a comprehensive guide for use in industry, engineering and science. New York, etc., McGraw-Hill, 1963. x, 534p. diagrs.

A compendium of symbols approved as standards by leading US engineering and scientific institutions. Some 9,000 illustration-symbols, with descriptive captions, numbers and titles of official standards. Symbols are grouped in 13 sections, each with a detailed contents-list: Electro-electronic ... Flags and pennants. Appendix 1: Symbols available from typographers and printers; 2: Abbreviations to be used on drawings (but only one page on topographical features). Lists of abbreviations and subject index, p.527-34. *Class No:* 5(003)

[45]

Units, symbols, and abbreviations: a guide for medical and scientific editors and authors. Baron, D.N., *ed.* 5th ed. London, Royal Society of Medicine Services, 1994. 64p. £5. ISBN: 0905958780.

First published 1971.

Sections: 1. Metrication and SI units - 2. Symbols and nomenclature (p.21-51; 23 references) - 3. Layout of references - 4. Proof correction. 'Many journals quote this booklet as a guide in their Instructions to Authors', (*Introduction*). *Class No:* 5(003)

[46]

WENNRICH, P. Anglo-American and German abbreviations in science and technology. [Anglo-amerikanische und deutsche Abkürzungen in Wissenschaft und Technik.] New York, Bowker; Munich, K.G. Saur, 1976-77, 1980. 3v. (xx, 2276p.) and Supplement (vi, 618p.). $125. (*Handbook of international documentation and information, v.14.*)

V.1-3 form a single sequence (A-E, F-O, P-Z) of over 150,000 Anglo-American and German abbreviations. Although entries for journals are categorized as such, plus country of origin, this is an exception to the general rule. The abbreviation 'U' occupies 2 columns. Number of entries is somewhat inflated (*e.g.* 'WHTHS': William Howard Taft High School'!). *Class No:* 5(003)

[47]

ZALUCKI, H. Dictionary of Russian technical and scientific abbreviations, in Russian, English and German. Amsterdam, etc., Zalucki, 1968. xii, 387p. $92. ISBN: 0444406573.

About 7,300 entries. Primarily intended for readers of Russian scientific publications. *Class No:* 5(003)

Databases

[48]

Gale directory of databases. Andover, Hants., Gale Research, 1998. 2v. £200; $260, set. ISBN: 0787622982, set.

Formed by the merger of *Computer readable databases*, *Directory of online databases*, and *Directory of portable databases*.

V.1. *Online databases.* V.2. *CD-ROM, diskette, magnetic tape, handheld, and batch access database products*.

Over 13,000 databases are described. Each entry includes address; telephone and fax numbers; contact name; subjects covered; languages used; size; format; availability; price; vendors and suppliers. Subject, master, and geographical indexes. Also includes details of more than 3,900 producers, 2,400 online services and vendors/distributors. Available online through Data-Star, Questel-ORBIT, and DIALOG. Also available on CD-ROM (£300; $390), and on the Internet at http://www.thomson.com/gale/gale.html. *Class No:* 5(003.4)

[49]

The Internet for scientists and engineers: online tools and resources. Thomas, B.J., *ed.* 3rd ed. Bellingham, Wash., SPIE (International Society for Optical Engineering)/Oxford University Press, 1998. 498p. ISBN: 019856547x.

Part I: Internet access, tools, and navigation, p.3-207, including: 1. Introduction - 2. Getting online - 3. Your first logon ... 13. World Wide Web. Part II covers Internet resources in 21 technical (although not exclusively scientific) fields from aeronautics to virtual reality, p.208-454. Appendix: Personal computer basics, p.455-71; glossary, bibliography, and index, p.488-97. Helpful 'screen' illustrations. A detailed work, but written in a light, accessible style. *Class No:* 5(003.4)

[50]

NTIS. Springfield, National Technical Information Service, US Department of Commerce, 1964-.

Has *c.*1,500,000 records, covering government-sponsored research, development, and reports prepared by state and federal agencies. Multidisciplinary, subject areas include agriculture; chemistry; civil engineering; medicine; biology; transport. Updated every 2 weeks and also available on CD-ROM (1983-. Updated quarterly). *Class No:* 5(003.4)

[51]

PASCAL. Vandoeuvre-Les-Nancy, Institue de l'Information Scientifique et Technique (IIST), Centre National de la Recherche Scientifique, 1973-.

Formerly in print format as *Bulletin signalétique*.

Multidisciplinary database containing *c.*12 million records, with *c.*450,000 citations being added each year. 8,000 periodical titles are covered, with conference proceedings, technical reports, and books also included. Most abstracts are in French but coverage is international, with documents in more than 100 languages included, although emphasis is given to French and European literature. Coverage of subjects can be patchy, *e.g.* areas such as earth sciences are covered exhaustively, while nuclear physics and animal husbandry are not included. Available online via Dialog, EINS and Questel-Orbit, and also on CD-ROM. *Class No:* 5(003.4)

CD-ROM

[52]

Magill's survey of science CD-ROM. Englewood Cliffs, N.J., Salem Press, 1998. 1 disc. $750. ISBN: 0893562718.

Contains 1,509 articles published in the four volumes of the *Magill's survey of science* series: *Earth science series (q.v.)*; *Life science series (q.v.)*; *Physical science series (q.v.)*; *Applied science series (q.v.)*. Includes *c.*1,000 images (not of the highest quality), bibliographies (which are more up-to-date than in the printed version), and hyperlinks to related topics. Criticized in *Reference books bulletin*, August 1998,

....(contd.)
p.2051 for being unable to open two or more chapters simultaneously, with the reviewer unable to see that an electronic version has any advantage over the print version apart from the price. Updates in CD-ROM are cheaper ($250) than those for the paper versions ($360), while the CD-ROM may be networked for no extra charge. Can be used on both Macintosh and Windows PCs. *Class No:* 5(003.40)

Bibliographies of Bibliographies

[53]

CONRAD, E.. **'LC science tracer bullet: an index'.** In *Reference services review,* v.16(3), 1988, p.49-56. Washington, D.C., Library of Congress, 1972 -. Irregular. ISSN: 00907324.

The *Tracer bullet* series (Library of Congress, Science and Technology Division) has appeared since 1972. It covers a wide variety of subjects in the natural and physical sciences and technology - two *Tracer bullet* publications published in 1998 were entitled *Cryptology* and *Biodiversity*. In the form of 'library pathfinder' handouts (about 10pa. and each about 4p. in length), it lists texts, handbooks, encyclopedias, dictionaries, bibliographies, government documents, and journal articles, *plus* addresses and telephone numbers of relevant organizations.

An earlier list may be found in *Reference services review,* v.11, Winter 1983, p.75-80. A database of all *Tracer bullets* from 1989, and selected older *Tracer bullets,* can be found on *SCTB online* on the Internet at http://lcweb2.loc.gov/sctb/. *Class No:* 5(009)

[54]

Internationale Bibliographie der Fachbibliographien für Technik, Wissenschaft und Wirtschaft. [International bibliography of bibliographies in technology, science and economics.] 9.-2. Ausg. Munich, K.G. Saur, 1969. 2v. (*Handbuch für Dokumentation, 3.*)

A. *Einmalig erscheinende Bibliographien.* 9. Ausg. viii, 887p. B. *Periodisch erscheinende Bibliographien.* 2. Ausg. viii, 817p. Volume A lists *c.*2,200 systematically arranged entries (in 10 classes) for non-periodical bibliographies, catalogues and other lists covering science, technology and economics. The indexes, which precede, are a feature: authors and editors, countries (subdivided by subjects), subjects, and publishers. *Class No:* 5(009)

[55]

—BESTERMAN, T. **Physical sciences: a bibliography of bibliographies.** Totowa, N.J., Rowman & Littlefield, 1971. 2v. (672p.).

A reprint of appropriate sections (*e.g.* Astronomy, Atomic energy, Chemistry, Electricity, Geology, Hydrography, Mathematics, Meteorology, Physics, Science, Statistics) of Besterman's *World bibliography of bibliographies* (4th ed. 1965-66. 4v. & index). No index. *Class No:* 5(009)

[56]

SCIENCE MUSEUM LIBRARY. London. **Science Library bibliographical series.** Permuted key word index to the titles of the Science Museum Library's bibliographical series. London, Science Museum Library, 1980. 25 sheets. (*Science Museum Bibliographical series, no. 808.*)

The index covers bibliographies no.1-807 (1931-1978). An ad hoc mimeographed series of lists, prepared on request in a variety of scientific and technology fields. No.807, *Some references on lipids in the lungs of vertebrates, including man, 1958 to 1976* (1978) ran to 26p. *Class No:* 5(009)

Bibliographies

[57]

A **Bibliography of the philosophy of science, 1945-1981.** Blackwell, R.J., *comp.* Westport, Conn., Greenwood Press, 1983. 585p. $95. ISBN: 0313231249.

Cites more than 7,000 books, papers, symposia and review articles on 47 topics. Excludes doctoral theses. Index of personal names, but not of subjects. *Class No:* 5(01)

[58]

Bibliotheca chemico-mathematica: catalogue of works in many tongues on exact and pure science, with a subject index. Zeitlinger, H. *and* Sotheran, H.C., *comps.* London, Sotheran, 1921. 2v. Supplements, 1931, 1937, 1952. illus.

53,489 annotated entries in all. Compiled from Sotheran's sale catalogues of scientific and technical works. Details on each item include author, full title, description, date, sale price. Under authors, A-Z, with a detailed subject index. Records many old and rare books important in the history of science. *Class No:* 5(01)

[59]

Books for college libraries: a core collection of 50,000 titles. V.5: Psychology, science, technology, bibliography. 3rd ed. Chicago, American Library Association, 1988. 422p. $90. ISBN: 0838933580.

Lists over 7,500 books, arranged by LC classifications. Omits textbooks unless considered essential. *Class No:* 5(01)

[60]

CAMBRIDGE UNIVERSITY. Scientific Periodicals Library. **Union catalogue of scientific libraries in the University of Cambridge: Books published before 1801.** London, Mansell, 1977. 9 fiches.

Author index, with *c.*5,800 entries, plus a chronological index of authors and short titles, covering 1478-1800. *Class No:* 5(01)

[61]

CHEN, C.-C. **Scientific and technical information sources.** 2nd ed. Cambridge, Mass., and London, M.I.T. Press, 1987. xxx, [1], 824p. £76.50. ISBN: 0262031205.

3,650 entries, grouped into 23 form categories (1. Selection tools ... 4. Encyclopedias ... 15. Abstracts and indexes, and current awareness services ... 19. Patents and standards ... 21. Non-print materials ... 22. Professional societies and their publications ... 23. Data bases). Brief annotations; citations to *c.*150 review sources. General index to authors only. Omits medicine. Patchy coverage of certain fields (*e.g.* geology, agriculture). Admits to a heavy U.S. emphasis; very few non-English titles. 'Intended primarily as a reference guide for science and engineering librarians and their assistants and as a textbook for library school students engaged in the study of the structure, properties and output of science literature' (*Preface*). Lack of an analytical subject index is a definite drawback. *Class No:* 5(01)

[62]

Encyclopedia of physical sciences and engineering information sources: a bibliographic guide to approximately 16,000 citations for publications, organizations, and other sources of information on 425 subjects relating to the physical sciences and engineering. Wasserman, S., *and others, eds.* Detroit, Gale, 1989. 736p. $140. ISBN: 0810324989.

Information sources listed include abstracts; yearbooks; bibliographies; monographs; professional associations; handbooks; databases; periodicals. Prices are given but there are no comments on level and extent of coverage. Many cross-references in the index and throughout. Some primary sources are omitted. 'Nevertheless, the directory is a helpful supplement' (*Science and technology libraries,* v.11(1), Fall 1990, p.141). *Class No:* 5(01)

[63]

GROGAN, D. **Science and technology: an introduction to the literature.** 4th ed. London, Bingley, 1982. 400p. £9.95. ISBN: 0851573150.

First published 1970.

Concerns the kinds of sources. 22 chapters (usually with 'Further reading'): 1. The literature - 2. Guides to the literature - 3. Encyclopedias - 4. Dictionaries - 5. Handbooks - 6. Directories and yearbooks - 7. Books 'in the field' - 8. Bibliographies - 9. Periodicals - 10. Indexing and abstracting services - 11. Computerized databases - 12. Reviews of progress - 13. Conference proceedings - 14. Research reports - 15. Patents and trademarks - 16. Standards - 17. Translations - 18. Trade literature - 19. Theses and research in progress - 20. Non-print media - 21. Microforms - 22. Biographical sources. Analytical index of subjects and forms; titles mentioned in text - merely examples of their kind - are not included. An impressive survey, 'written primarily for students, not practitioners' (*Introduction*). Rather dated now and mainly of historical interest. *Class No:* 5(01)

[64]

Handbooks and tables in science and technology. Powell, R.H., *ed.* 3rd ed. Phoenix, Oryx, 1994. viii,359p. $95. ISBN: 0897745345.

First published 1970.

Covers 3,662 handbooks and tables (mainly in English) in science, technology, and medicine. Almost 400 titles have been dropped from this edition and 650 new ones added. Annotations are between 50-75 words in length. Data on each has complete bibliographic citation and many annotations which briefly describe the intellectual content of the handbook and tables. Keyword, author/editor, and title indexes. *Class No:* 5(01)

[65]

HURT, C.D. **Information sources in science and technology.** 3rd ed. Englewood, Colo., Libraries Unlimited, 1998. xvi,346p. $55. ISBN: 1563085313.

First published 1988.

Most pre-1991 material has been dropped from this edition and more electronic and Internet sources have been included. Gives brief citations and annotations for *c.*1,500 mainly English-language reference sources. Four main sections (21 chapters): Multidisciplinary sources of information; The biological sciences (2. Biology ... 4. Zoology); The physical sciences and mathematics (5. Astronomy ... 8. Geosciences ... 10. Mathematics); Engineering (11. General engineering ... 18. Transportation engineering). Followed by chapters on computer and information technology; agriculture, food sciences, and veterinary sciences; health sciences. Author, title, and subject indexes. For academic and public libraries. *Class No:* 5(01)

[66]
International catalogue of scientific literature, 1st - 14th annual. Published for the International Council by the Royal Society of London. London, Harrison, 1902-21. 238v. Reprinted New York, Johnson Reprint Corpn.; London, Johnson Reprint Co., Ltd., 1968. 32v.

Unique coverage for 1901-14 (some sections to 1920). Each annual issue consists of 17v.: A. Mathematics; B. Mechanics; C. Physics; D. Chemistry; E. Astronomy; F. Meteorology; G. Mineralogy; H. Geology; J. Geography; K. Palaeontology; L. General biology; M. Botany; N. Zoology; O. Human anatomy; P. Anthropology; Q. Physiology; R. Bacteriology. Each volume has (1) schedules of the classification and subject indexes in English, French, German and Italian; (2) an author catalogue; (3) a classified subject catalogue. Like the Royal Society's *Catalogue of scientific papers, 1800-1900 (qv)*, of which it is a continuation, *International catalogue* also indexes papers in pamphlets, memoirs and books. 4,673 journals were indexed in the 1903 annual volumes, as against 1,535 journals indexed in the Royal Society's *Catalogue*. The only part of the *International catalogue* with a continued existence is Zoology, as covered in *Zoological record*. The *Bibliographie scientifique française* (monthly, 1900-42), included in the *International catalogue,* carried on until 1942 on its own. The *List of journals with abbreviations used in the Catalogue as references* (1903, 312p.; Supplement, 1904, 680p.) includes over 5,500 periodicals from more than 20 countries. *Class No:* 5(01)

[67]
JOHN CRERAR LIBRARY. Catalog. [John Crerar Library]. Boston, Mass., G.K. Hall, 1967. 77v.

Author-title catalog. 35v. $3,800 *Classified subject catalog.* 42v. $4,560. Subject index. 1967. 66p. The John Crerar Library collections (including Illinois Institute of Technology holdings) comprised more than 1,100,000 v. of current and historical research materials in pure and applied sciences. The *Author-title catalog* (563,000 cards, photolithographically reproduced) includes titles of 13,000 current serials. The *Classified subject catalog* (704,000 cards) includes a subject index of 47,000 entries. *Class No:* 5(01)

[68]
McGraw-Hill basic bibliography of science and technology. Recent titles on more than 7000 subjects, compiled and annotated by the editors of the *McGraw-Hill Encyclopedia of science and technology*. New York, etc., McGraw-Hill, 1966. ix, 738p. $25. ISBN: 0070452180.

Aims to direct the purposive reader with an enquiring mind 'to reading beyond the articles in the *McGraw-Hill Encyclopedia of science and technology...*' (*Foreword*). More than 8,000 briefly annotated entries for books; items starred are recommended for young people and school science collections. Annotations state contents and level. Cross-references. 'Topical guide to subject areas' (p.699-738) lacks precision. (eg, 'Animal pathology' has over 600 unspecified references). Replaces R.R. Hawkins '*Scientific, medical and technical books*' (2nd ed. Washington, National Research Council, 1958). Valuable, but dated. No author index. *Class No:* 5(01)

[69]
MALCLÈS, L.-N. Les Sources du travail bibliographique. Geneva, Droz, 1950-58. 3v. in 4. $22.50, v.1; $46.50, v.2; $22.50, v.3.

1-2. 1950-52. 3. *Bibliographies spécialisées (sciences exactes et techniques).* 1958. x, 575, [1]p. V.3 still has importance for the specialist in pure and applied science and medicine. Mlle. Malclès contributed 6 of the 13 chapters. Others deal with chemistry, earth sciences, general and animal biology, medical sciences, zoology, botany and plant physiology, and pharmacy. No chapter on agriculture, and certain aspects of engineering are also wanting (*Journal of documentation*, v.15(3), September 1959, p.156-9). The index (p.521-75) has *c*.10,000 entries. Some of the chapters still constitute our best and most detailed conspectus of the scientific and technical literature of the 19th and earlier 20th-century in their fields. *Class No:* 5(01)

[70]
MALINOWSKY, H.R. Best science and technology reference books for young people. Phoenix, Ariz., Oryx, 1991. 216p. $24.95. ISBN: 0897745809.

669 reference books for the age group 5-18 are listed. Arranged, in 12 chapters, by subject, *e.g.* 'Astronomy'; 'Physics'; 'Science'; 'Chemistry', the annotated entries provide full bibliographic information, review citation and recommended age group. 4 indexes: title; author; subject; grade level. The author is bibliographer for science and technology at the University of Illinois-Chicago library. *Class No:* 5(01)

[71]
—SOSA, M. *and* MALCOLM, S.M. 'Science books & films' best books for children: 1992-95. Washington, D.C., Directorate for Education and Human Resources Programs, American Association for the Advancement of Science, 1996. £20.95; $24. (*AAAS publication, 96-4S*.)

Lists hundreds of books deemed suitable for children. For all those involved in choosing books and resource materials for children. *Class No:* 5(01)

[72]
MALINOWSKY, H.R. Reference sources in science, engineering, medicine, and agriculture. Phoenix, Ariz., Oryx, 1994. 355p. $49.95; £39.95. ISBN: 0897747429.

An introductory guide to the core literature, covering about 2,400 titles. The first section looks at current issues in library science: serial prices; scientific communication; finding scientific literature. The second section lists encyclopaedias, indexes, core periodicals, dictionaries, etc. Author, title, and subject indexes. Essentially broader in scope than, and there is some duplication with, *Information sources in science and technology* by C.D. Hurt (2nd ed. 1988) (*q.v.*) but the separate subject, title and authors indexes appear to be less thorough. Recommended as an ideal 'one-stop' source. *Class No:* 5(01)

[73]
The Museum of Science and Industry basic list of children's science books, 1973-1984. Richter, B. *and* Wenzel, D., *comps*. Chicago, Ill., & London, American Library Association, 1985. xi, 154p.

1st supp. 1986. 80p. $6.95; 2nd supp. 1987. 84p. $8.95; 3rd supp. 1988. 80p. $11.95.

The parent list covers 1,400 children's science books up to junior high-school level, in 17 broad subject areas (*e.g.* Earth sciences). Ratings range from recommended to not recommended. 10-30 word annotations indicate reading level and price; other reviews are cited. Appended directory of publishers, list of children's science magazines and review journals, and an annotated bibliography of source books for teachers. Author and title indexes. The 1986 supplement adds 500 titles in 16 subject areas. An excellent US 'buying guide and reference tool' (*Reference books bulletin*, 1985/1986. p.87). *Class No:* 5(01)

[74]
PARKER, C.C. *and* **TURLEY, R.V. Information sources in science and technology:** a practical guide to traditional and online use. 2nd ed. London, etc., Butterworths, 1986. [viii], 328p. diagrs., tables, charts. £35. ISBN: 0408014679.

First published 1975.

Main sections: Choosing sources of information and their guides - People - Organizations - The literature (p.37-138) - Information services (p.139-210) - Searching: the literature and computer databases - Obtaining literature in a usable form - Organizing and presenting information - Current awareness. Appendix: Helping the library user. Detailed, analytical index. A feature is the graphic use of charts for comparison and rating purposes (*e.g.* chart 1, Information sources and guides versus coverage). The index (p.302-28) includes authors and titles. Good use of bold type. Admirably meets the authors' objective: 'to produce a text which is suitable for beginners, but which will also serve as a handy reference work for the more experienced' (*Preface*). *Class No:* 5(01)

[75]
PRIMACK, A.L. Finding answers in science and technology. New York, Van Nostrand Reinhold, 1984. 364p. facsims. ISBN: 0442282279.

13 chapters: 1. Finding the answers. Search strategy. Getting the materials - 2. Computer searching - 3. General science... 13. Engineering. Energy. Appendix: Libraries (large science and technology libraries in the U.S.); U.S. government depository libraries; NASA information centers; U.S. publications depository libraries. Detailed subject index, p.339-62. Not a bibliography, but a discussion of literature-searching techniques, followed by running commentary on sources. *Class No:* 5(01)

[76]
Pure and applied science books, 1876-1982: subject index; author index. New York & London, Bowker, [1982]. 6v. (7784p.). $345, set. ISBN: 0835214370.

Lists *c*.220,000 titles. V.1-5: Subject index, using over 56,000 Library of Congress subject headings; v.6: author and title indexes. Despite the dates of coverage cited, over 5,000 titles are pre-1876. Coverage: all areas of physical and biological sciences, omitting introductory level textbooks and government publications. Medicine is allotted a separate listing, - *Health science books, 1876-1982* ([1982]. 4v.) (*q.v.*). The first comprehensive retrospective bibliography in the area of science publishing. *Class No:* 5(01)

[77]

REUSS, J.D. Repertorium commentationum a societatibus litterariis editarum. Secundum disciplinarum ordinem digessit I.D. Reuss. Göttingen, Dieterich, 1801-21. 16v. Reprinted New York, B. Franklin, 1963.

1. *Historia naturalis, generalis et zoologia.* 2. *Botanica et mineralogia.* 3. *Chemia et res metallicae.* 4. *Physica.* 5. *Astronomia.* 6. *Oeconomia.* 7. *Mathesis; mechanica; hydrostatica; hydraulica; hydrotechnia; aerostatica; pneumatica; technologia; architectura civilis; scientia navalis; scientia militaris.* 8. *Historia.* 9. *Philologia; linguae; scriptores graeci; scriptores latini; litterae elegantiores; poesis; rhetorica; ars antiqua; pictura; musica.* 10-16. *Scientia et ars medica et chirurgica.* A valuable classified index to publications of scientific, historical, literary and medical learned societies from their inception in the 17th century, to 1800. The Royal Society's *Catalogue of scientific papers, 1800-1900 (qv)* provides a continuation, for the sciences. *Class No:* 5(01)

[78]

ROYAL SOCIETY. Book catalogue of the library of the Royal Society. Clark, A.J. Frederick, Md., University Publication of America, 1982. 5v. $550. ISBN: 0890935203.

About 62,500 entries for *c.*45,000 books and pamphlets. Basically an author catalogue, with numerous cross-references from names of editors, of scientists as biographers, etc. Pagination is omitted, but locations are given, with a list of 50 named classes and groupings shelves. Entries have been photographically reproduced from catalogue cards. A particularly significant collection for study of the history of science during the Society's first two centuries (1660-). *Class No:* 5(01)

[79]

ROYAL SOCIETY. Catalogue of scientific papers, 1800-1900. London, HMSO, 1867-72; London, Clay, 1877-1902; Cambridge Univ. Press, 1914-25. 19v. Reprinted New York, Johnson Reprint Corpn.; London, Johnson Reprint Co., Ltd., 1968.

V.1-6. 1st series, 1800-63; v.7-8. 2nd series, 1864-73; v.9-11. 3rd series, 1874-83; v.12. Supplementary v., 1800-83; v.13-19. 4th series, 1884-1900.

The standard index to 19th-century scientific papers. An author index to 1,555 periodicals, including transactions of European academies and other learned societies. A separate A-Z sequence runs through each series. Includes medical but excludes purely technical papers. Titles of papers appear in the original language; Russian titles are followed by English, French or German translation. *Class No:* 5(01)

[80]

—ROYAL SOCIETY. Catalogue of scientific papers, 1800-1900. Subject index. Cambridge, Cambridge University Press, 1908-14. 3v. in 4.

V.1: *Pure mathematics.* V.2: *Mechanics.* V.3: *Physics.* (2pts).

Indexes papers for the entire period in each volume. Classified as in the *International catalogue of scientific literature,* although only 3v. of the 17v. planned were published. Details given for each paper are much abbreviated but sufficiently indicative for the subject index to be used independently of the *Catalogue.* Each volume carries a classification schedule, a list of serials (with abbreviations used) and locations in 23 major British libraries. *Class No:* 5(01)

[81]

Sale catalogues of libraries of eminent persons. Volume 11: Scientists. Feisenberger, H.A., *ed.* London, Mansell/Sotheby Parke Bernet, 1975. 302p.

The scientists concerned: Elias Ashmole, Edmund Halley, Robert Hooke, John Ray. This is the final volume in a series of facsimile reprints of catalogues of the libraries and effects of persons prominent in their respective fields. *Class No:* 5(01)

[82]

SCICAT: Science Reference and Information Service Catalogue. London, British Library, Science Reference and Information Service, 1990-. 4 issues pa. Negative microfiche. £326.

Author/title catalogue. Classified catalogue.

Contains additions to SRIS stock from 1974, plus many items published earlier, including all serials held by SRIS. Contains references to 300,000 items of scientific and business interest, *e.g.* 25,000 journals. The *Classified catalogue* is arranged according to the SRIS classification scheme and has an index. Available on CD-ROM (£300 pa.). *Class No:* 5(01)

[83]

SUBRAMANYAM, K. Scientific and technical information resources. New York, Dekker, 1981. 416p. (*Books on library and information science, 33.*)

Sections on indexes, primary journals, bibliographies, congresses, theses and technical reports; also on secondary journals, commercial catalogues, patents and standards. Bibliography, p.361-81; index, p.387-416. For library and information science students, librarians and documentalists. A development, to some extent, of his lengthy

....(contd.)

contribution to *Encyclopedia of library and information science* v.26 (1979), p.376-548, on 'Scientific literature', with its 271 references and bibliography, p.522-416. *Class No:* 5(01)

[84]

UNITED STATES. Department of the Interior. **Dictionary catalog of the Department Library.** Boston, Mass., G.K. Hall, 1967. 37v. (29,573p.). Supplements, 1968-. $4,000, set; $910, 4th supp. ISBN: 0816107157, set; 0816100160, 4th supp.

The main catalogue and supplements 1-4 (1968-75) total 992,200 photolithographed catalogue cards. The largest specialised collection in the U.S.A. on mines, minerals, petroleum and coal, plus a good working collection on geology, and unequalled holdings on fish, fisheries and wildlife. *Class No:* 5(01)

Encyclopaedias

[85]

The Encyclopaedia of ignorance: everything you ever wanted to know about the unknown. Duncan, R. *and* Weston-Smith, M., *eds.* Oxford, Pergamon Press, 1977. 2v. in 1. £17. ISBN: 0080224241.

1. *The physical sciences.* 203, xiiip.

2. *Life sciences and earth sciences.* p.208-433, xiiip.

51 scientific theories discussed. V.1. has 23 contributors. The essay, 'Is space curved?', p.85-91, has 7 references. V.2 with 27 contributors, includes 'The limitations of evolutionary theory', p.235-42; 9 references. Each volume has an analytical index. 'The usual encyclopaedia states what we know. This one contains papers on what one does not know or matters which lie on the edge of knowledge' (*Editorial preface*). *Class No:* 5(031)

[86]

Encyclopedia of physical science and technology. Meyers, R.A.M., *ed.* 2nd ed. San Diego, Academic Press, 1992. 18v. 14000p. £1,550. ISBN: 0122269306.

First published 1987-88.

Coverage includes chemistry, physics, geology, astronomy, computer science, meteorology and mineralogy. 85% of the articles from the previous edition have been re-written with 155 new ones added. 4,200 glossaries accompany the articles. Includes 6,000 figures and 2,000 tables. Bibliographies consist of 4,000 titles. V.18. *Subject index* contains 70,000 entries. A scholarly encyclopaedia, recommended for academic, rather than school, libraries. 2nd ed. contains 155 new articles and 85% of existing ones re-written. Available on CD-ROM ($2,995).

Encyclopedia of physical science and technology yearbook (1991 ed. £126) updates between editions. *Class No:* 5(031)

[87]

Illustrated dictionary of science. Allaby, M., *ed.* New York, Facts on File, 1995. 256p. illus. $29.95. ISBN: 081603253x.

First published in 1988 as *The Encyclopedic dictionary of science* (Edited by C.Hunt. Facts on File).

Explains and defines *c.*5,000 terms. Descriptive entries vary from one to three paragraphs in length. Outstanding feature is 34 pages of full-colour illustrations. Includes over 700 brief biographies. Popular dictionary intended for school and public libraries. *Class No:* 5(031)

[88]

McGraw-Hill encyclopedia of science and technology. Parker, S.P., *ed.* 8th ed. New York, etc., McGraw-Hill, 1997. 20v. & index. illus. (some col. pl.), diagrs., tables, maps. $1,995. ISBN: 0079115047, set.

About 3,500 contributors, 19 of them Nobel laureates. 7,100 entries (some 400 fewer than in the previous edition) arranged A-Z, on all branches of pure and applied science, with many topics being combined to aid explanation and discussion. Subjects which are decreasing in importance are given less space, while currently important topics are given greater prominence. 1,600 articles are either new or totally revised, with an additional 1,750 new illustrations bringing the total to *c.*13,000. The quality of illustrations in this edition is greatly improved from previous eds. Signed contributions, normally with short bibliographies appended. 'It is *the* recommended multivolume encyclopedia for science and technology' (*Reference books bulletin*, 15 September 1997, p.268).

Now available on CD-ROM as the *McGraw-Hill multimedia encyclopedia of science and technology (q.v.)* (version 2.0, 1998) which also includes the full text of the *McGraw-Hill dictionary of scientific and technical terms (q.v.).*

Annual updates, between editions: *McGraw-Hill yearbook of science and technology (q.v.). Class No:* 5(031)

[89]

—McGraw-Hill concise encyclopedia of science and technology. Parker, S.P., *ed*. 4th ed. New York, McGraw-Hill, 1998. 2318p. illus., figs., diagrs., tables. £108.99; $150. ISBN: 0070526591.

First published 1984.

Based on the 20v. *McGraw-Hill encyclopedia of science and technology* (8th ed.). Features more than 8,100 articles relevant to over 75 disciplines, although there are 100 fewer entries than in the previous ed. Many new illustrations and updated bibliographies. Available on the CD-ROM, *Science navigator*, which also contains *McGraw-Hill dictionary of scientific and technical terms* (5th ed. 1998. $150 (single-user); $295 (network)). *Class No:* 5(031)

[90]

Macmillan encyclopedia of science. Kerrod, R., *ed*. Rev. ed. New York, Macmillan Reference, 1997. 12v.(1184p.) illus. £300; $325. ISBN: 0028645561.

First published in 1991.

Each volume is dedicated to a specific topic, *e.g.* The heavens; Body and health. Arrangement is by subject, with some being revised since the previous edition to reflect current trends. Each volume includes an index for that volume, while v.12 contains a cumulative index. Many illustrations. Designed specifically for younger teenagers. *Class No:* 5(031)

[91]

Magill's survey of science: applied science series. Magill, F.N., *ed*. Englewood Cliffs, N.J., Salem Press, 1993. 7v.(including *Supplement* (1998. 448p.)). $475; $90 (Supplement). ISBN: 0893567051.

More than 380 signed articles, averaging seven pages in length, alphabetically arranged by topic, and also including many emerging disciplines, such as hazardous wastes and biotechnology. 190 contributors. Each entry has appended a glossary, cross-references, and annotated bibliography. V.6 contains a general index. For public and academic libraries. *Class No:* 5(031)

[92]

Magill's survey of science: life science series. Magill, F.N., *ed*. Pasadena, Calif., Salem Press, 1992. 7v.(including *Supplement* (1998. 448p.)). $475; $90 (Supplement). ISBN: 0893566128.

163 academic contributors. 370 articles on topics covering plant anatomy, genetics, biology, ecology, physiology, and biochemistry, arranged A-Z. Data in each article include: definitions of key terms; methods of study; context in relation to other aspects of the life sciences; annotated bibliography; cross-references. Cumulated glossary in the final volume, followed by a detailed index. No illustrations. Suitable for those with some basic knowledge. 'A solid contribution' (*Library journal*, 15th September 1992, p.62).

The *Supplement* updates and expands the original volumes. *Class No:* 5(031)

[93]

Van Nostrand's scientific encyclopedia. Considine, D.M. *and* Considine, G., *eds*. 8th ed. New York, Van Nostrand, 1995. 2v. 3455p. illus., diagrs., graphs, tables, maps. $199.95 set. ISBN: 0442018657, v.1; 0442018681, v.2; 0442018649, set.

First published 1938.

Contributions from *c*.250 scientists. Approximately 7,300 entries arranged alphabetically (AAAS-Zymolytic reaction), increasing this edition by about 500 entries and by 200 pages from the 7th ed. Subject coverage includes life sciences, physics and chemistry, earth and space sciences, environmental sciences, materials science, and mathematics and information sciences. Many black-and-white illustrations of variable quality. A useful feature is the index at the end of each of the two volumes. Brief bibliographies at the end of the longer articles. Twice as long as the *McGraw-Hill concise encyclopedia of science and technology (q.v.)* and with longer entries, this publication's index is not so extensive, has inferior quality illustrations, and does not have in depth coverage of databases. For academic and public libraries.

A revised 8th ed. in CD-ROM format was due to be published in 1999. *Class No:* 5(031)

CD-ROM

[94]

McGraw-Hill multimedia encyclopedia of science and technology. Version 2.0. New York, McGraw-Hill, 1998. CD-ROM. $795(single user); $995(LAN user); $1,295(WAN user).

Over 7,100 articles taken from *McGraw-Hill encyclopedia of science and technology* and *McGraw-Hill dictionary of scientific and technical terms*, with 250 short biographies added. Fewer illustrations and graphics than in the print version (13,000 in printed work; 1,400 on the CD-ROM); animation is used in 66 entries. Hotlinks only apply to relevant entries within each section so it is not possible to link between the dictionary and the encyclopaedia. Searches may be expanded to the Internet but this is done awkwardly by using three search engines. A somewhat disappointing electronic product which falls short of the printed versions of these works. *Class No:* 5(031)(003.40)

Handbooks & Manuals

[95]

COLEMAN, G.J. *and* **DEWAR, D. The Addison-Wesley science handbook.** Don Mills, Ontario, Addison-Wesley, 1997. 281p. illus.,charts. $18. ISBN: 0201766523.

Covers 'key concepts, formulas, illustrations and tables' (*Preface*) in biology, chemistry, geology, physics, and mathematics. For schools and public libraries. Good value. *Class No:* 5(035)

[96]

Composite index for CRC handbooks. 3rd ed. Boca Raton, Fla., CRC Press, Inc., 1991. 3v. [vii], 1111p. $1,295. ISBN: 0849302846.

First published 1971.

Covers over 300 *CRC handbooks* published up to 1990 and contains over 600,000 entries. Subject areas include life, physical, engineering, mathematical, and environmental sciences. This set includes a computer laser optical disk, a CD-ROM user's guide, and 2 computer disks. Annual supplements are available on a subscription basis. *Class No:* 5(035)

[97]

COTTERILL, R.M.J. The Cambridge guide to the material world. Cambridge Univ. Press, 1985. vii, 352p. illus., diagrs., tables, chemical formulas. ISBN: 0521246407.

18 chapters, on electrons, nuclei and quanta, the chemical bond, states of matter, crystals, water, minerals, ceramics, metals, conductors and insulators, glass, carbon, liquid crystals, polymers, biopolymers, the cell, the plant, the animal. Chapter bibliographies, p.348; detailed index (in tiny type), p.320-2. Intended primarily for the non-specialist. 'A reliable first resource for a student at any level' (*Scientific American,* September 1985, p.22). *Class No:* 5(035)

[98]

HARRÉ, R. The Philosophies of science: an introductory survey. 2nd ed. Oxford, University Press, 1985. [viii], 203p. diagrs. £7.99. (*An OPUS book.*) ISBN: 0192892010.

First published 1972.

7 chapters: 1. The philosophy of science - 2. The forms of reasoning in science - 3. Scientific knowledge - 4. Metaphysical theories - 5. The corpuscularian inheritance - 6. Explanation - 7. Science and society. Further reading, p.196-8 (by chapters). Partly analytical index. Aims 'to bring out the way problems which appear specific to science are actually species of wider philosophical issues' (*Preface to the second edition*). *Class No:* 5(035)

[99]

Science and technology desk reference. 2nd ed. Andover, Hants, Gale Research, 1996. xxxvi, 795p. figs., maps. £46; $60. ISBN: 0810391767.

First published 1993.

c.1,800 answers to frequently asked or difficult-to-answer questions, with 400 questions not in previous ed. Question and answer entries, divided into 20 broad subject categories, *e.g.* 'Chemistry'; 'Medicine'. The sources where the answers were found are also listed. *c*.100 line drawings. Bibliography, p.685-719. Subject index. Useful for school and public libraries as a quick, low-cost, reference tool. Scheduled for 3-yearly publication. *Class No:* 5(035)

[100]

The World Book encyclopedia of science. Rev. ed. Chicago, Ill., World Book, Inc., 1997. 8v. (1200p.) col. illus., diagrs., chemical structures. ISBN: 0716633949, set.

Originally published by Verlagsgruppe Bertelsmann International GmbH, Munich 1984. First English ed., 1985.

8v. (ea.140-160p.): v.1. *Astronomy;* v.2. *Physics;* v.3. *Chemistry;* v.4. *The planet earth;* v.5. *The plant world;* v.6. *The animal world;* v.7. *The human body;* v.8. *Men and women of science; index.* There is a new section on careers in each volume and a new cumulative index. Expanded biography section; 90 new photographs, 25 new diagrams. v.3. *Chemistry* has been completely re-written. *Class No:* 5(035)

Dictionaries

[101]

Catalogue of the Translator's Library of the Department of Trade and Industry: dictionaries, glossaries, encyclopedias, books about Europe. Hamilton, G.E., *ed*. Dobbs Ferry, New York, Oceana, 1975. 3v. $270. ISBN: 0379003759.

1. *Authors.* xxxvii, [1], 319p. 2. *Subjects.* vii,[1], 540p. 3. *Languages.* vii,[1], 555p.

About 5,000 items, covering 68 languages, figure in v.1. V.2 arranges the items under subjects, Abbreviations ... Zoology. V.3 features entry under languages, Afrikaans ... Yiddish. *Class No:* 5(038)

[102]
The Dictionary catalogue. Molho, E., *ed.* New York & Los Angeles, The French & Spanish Book Corpn., 1988. xviii, 174p. $14.95. ISBN: 0828801509.
'Pure and applied sciences' section, p.78-138, lists *c.*1,800 entries, with pagination and prices. Sections: General works - Abbreviations, symbols and units - Agricultural sciences - Astronomy - Biological sciences - Chemistry - Data processing & information systems - Earth sciences - Engineering - Mathematics - Medical sciences - Miscellaneous technologies - Physics - Psychology & psychiatry.
Class No: 5(038)

[103]
International bibliography of specialized dictionaries. Lengenfelder, H., *ed.* 6th ed. Munich, K.G. Saur, 1979. xxi, 470p. ISBN: 3598205015.
Not to be confused with E. Wüster's *International bibliography of standardized vocabularies.* Its 5,719 numbered entries concern monolingual and multilingual dictionaries that have appeared since 1970. Three of the 9 sections concern science and technology: 1. Science and medicine - 2. Applied science, technology - 3. Agriculture. Selected bibliography, p.373-7. Indexes of names and subjects; directory of publishers. *Class No:* 5(038)

[104]
McGraw-Hill dictionary of scientific and technical terms. Parker, S.P., *ed.* 5th ed. New York, McGraw-Hill, 1994. xvii,2194p. illus., figs., diagrs. disk. $110.50. ISBN: 0070423334.
First published 1974.
Contains *c.*105,100 terms (5,000 new to this edition) and 122,600 brief definitions. Pronunciation given for all terms. Entries include synonyms, abbreviations and acronyms. Brief definitions. *c.*3,000 illustrations in the margins. Appendices include SI conversion tables, the Greek alphabet, the periodic table of the elements, schematic electronic symbols and the classification of living organisms. The last appendix is a biographical dictionary of over 1,500 eminent historical and contemporary scientists. Has provided several encyclopaedia spin-offs, *e.g. McGraw-Hill dictionary of earth science (q.v.).* A new edition is due to be published in 1999.
Included in the *McGraw-Hill multimedia encyclopedia of science and technology* CD-ROM *(q.v.)* (1994. $1,300) and the *Science navigator* CD-ROM (1998. $150). *Class No:* 5(038)

[105]
UNITED NATIONS. Service Linguistique. Section de Terminologie et de Documentation Technique. **Catalogue des ouvrages disponibles au service linguistique.** 5th ed. Geneva, United Nations, 1987.
Lists *c.*5,000 titles of language dictionaries, etc. Two parts: General works (abbreviations; general monolingual dictionaries; general bilingual; atlases; encyclopedias; science and technology dictionaries: monolingual, bilingual; linguistics; translation and related subjects; miscellaneous - Specialized works (aerospace ... transport), p.69-506. Subject indexes (French; English). One of the few relatively recent lists of language dictionaries. *Class No:* 5(038)

[106]
World dictionaries in print, 1983: a guide to general and subject dictionaries in world languages. New York, Bowker, 1983. xii, 579p. $99.50. ISBN: 0835216152.
Lists over 13,600 in-print dictionaries, wordbooks, glossaries and thesauri in more than 235 languages. Four indexes: Subject index (using *c.*2,000 Library of Congress subject headings); Title index (with equally full information); Language index (grouping titles by language); Author, editor, compiler index. A key to publishers and distributors concludes. The fullest list of its kind, but confined to in-print dictionaries. Still useful although the information may now be rather out-of-date. *Class No:* 5(038)

[107]
WÜSTER, E. International bibliography of standardized vocabularies. 2nd ed., rev. and edited by INFOTERM. Munich, etc., K.G. Saur, 1979. 540p. ISBN: 3598055021.
First published 1955, as *Bibliography of monolingual scientific and technical glossaries,* by E. Wüster (Paris, Unesco), v.1: *National standards.* 219p.
More than 11,000 references to standardized nomenclature: definitions and symbols. *Class No:* 5(038)

Polyglot

[108]
BUECKEN, F.J. Vocabulário técnico: portugués-inglés-francês-alemão. 5. ed. São Paulo, Ediçoes Melhoramentos, 1979. 600p.
First published 1946; 4th ed. [1961] (600p.).
Portuguese terms (*c.*15,000 entries), with English, French and German equivalents, p.15-241. Combined English, French and German index, giving the Portuguese equivalents. Appended glossary of motor-vehicle terms, similarly arranged. *Class No:* 5(038)=00

[109]
ETTINGEN, S.G. Dictionary of technical terms in five languages: Hebrew-English-French-German-Russian. Tel-Aviv, Yavneh Publishing House, 1961 (reprinted 1983). 2v. (64, 1188p.). illus.
The dictionary has reverse indexes in English, French, German and Russian. Introduction and explanatory notes are in Hebrew.
Class No: 5(038)=00

[110]
FEUTRY, M. Technological dictionary/ Dictionnaire technologique/ Technologisches Wörterbuch. Paris, La Maison du Dictionnaire, 1976-78. 3v.
1. *Mechanics, metallurgy, hydraulics and related industries.* 1976. *Supplemento español.* 1976. 2. *Les ressorts.* 1978. 3. *Aeronautique.* 1978.
V.1 has 14,051 numbered entries, English-French-German, in 3 columns, with French and German indexes. Well spoken of.
Class No: 5(038)=00

[111]
HOYER, E. von *and* **KREUTER, F. Technologisches Wörterbuch.** 6. vollkommen neubearb. Aufl., hrsg. von A. Schlomann. Berlin, Springer, 1932 (reprinted New York, Ungar, 1944). 3v.
1. *Deutsch-Englisch-Französisch.* 2. *English-German-French.* 3. *French-German-English.*
About 100,000 terms in each of three languages. Coverage: technology and allied subjects such as trade and banking. Overdue for revision, but a thorough and reliable set of dictionaries.
Class No: 5(038)=00

[112]
MEDEIROS, M.F. da S. de. Dicionário técnico poliglota: portugues, espanhol, francés, italiano, inglés, alemão. Lisbon, Gomez & Rodrigues, 1949-53. 8v.
V.1-3 (1949-51) comprise 68,193 numbered Portuguese base terms and synonyms, with equivalents in Spanish, French, Italian, English and German. V.4-8 comprise the Spanish, French, Italian, English and German equivalents, plus Latin. An ambitious project, coverage of the Romance languages being particularly generous.
Class No: 5(038)=00

[113]
—Dictionary of scientific and technical terminology: English, French, Dutch, Russian. Markov, A.S., *ed.* The Hague, Nijhoff, 1984. 496p. £35.95; $34.50. ISBN: 0318016613.
Has *c.*9,000 English-base terms, with equivalents in the other languages. Intended for 'scientists and engineers'. But too many concepts are introduced for the dictionary 'to be of more than partial use to anyone but a professional translator, who would, presumably, prefer a specialized dictionary for each topic' (*Nature,* v.312, 13 December 1986, p.670). *Class No:* 5(038)=00

[114]
QUÉMADA, G. Dictionnaire de termes nouveaux des sciences et des techniques. [Dictionary of new scientific and technical terms.] Paris, Conseil International de la Langue Française (CILF), [1983]. xix, 602p. £57.50. ISBN: 2853191117.
Part 1 provides *c.*7,000 French-base terms, with equivalents (where available) in German, English and Spanish. The French terms are then grouped (p.325-87), followed by a single A/Z sequence of English, German and Spanish equivalents. Part 2, 'Répertoire des formants morphosémantiques' (French prefixes and suffixes), p.523-602.
Class No: 5(038)=00

English

[115]
Academic Press dictionary of science and technology. San Diego, Academic Press, 1991. xxxii,2432p. illus., diagrs., tables. £68; $102. ISBN: 0122004000.
Contains 133,007 fully-defined entries in 122 areas of science. Claims to include more medical terms overall than any other general science dictionary presently available. 122 essays give concise information on each scientific discipline. Over 2,000 illustrations, with 24 colour plates. Pronunciation guides for difficult or phonetically irregular terms. Data in appendix include standard weights and measures periodical table, and chronology of science. Claims to be 'the largest scientific dictionary ever compiled in the English language' (*Preface*). However, criticized in *Nature,* v.361 (no.6411), 4th February 1993 for inconsistencies and poor illustrations.
The CD-ROM version ($79.95; 1996) includes spoken pronunciation for 3,500 difficult terms and more than 200 additional illustrations. The science chronology from the print version has been updated until the end of 1994. 'The chief difficulty in using this dictionary is the lack of clear documentation' (*Choice,* November 1996, p.440). Note that the electronic version is cheaper than the print version.
Class No: 5(038)=20

[116]
BALLENTYNE, D.W.G. *and* LOVETT, D.R. **A Dictionary of named effects and laws in chemistry, physics and mathematics.** 4th ed. London, Chapman & Hall, 1980. viii,346p. diagrs., tables, chemical structures £17.95. ISBN: 0412223902.

First published 1958.

*c.*1,500 entries, A-Z, for effects and laws best known by the name of the person(s) who discovered or propounded them. Formulas and chemical structures; cross-references. Definitions are clearly stated, but omit biographical data and bibliographies.

Ruffner, J.A. *Eponyms dictionaries index* (Detroit, Mich., Gale, 1977. xxxi, [1], 734p. Supplement no.1, 1985. 248p.) covers a much wider field. *Class No:* 5(038)=20

[117]
BRAGONIER, R. *and* FISHER, D. **What's what: a visual glossary of the physical world.** Rev. ed. Maplewood, N.J., Hammond Inc., 1990. viii,581p. illus. $14.95. ISBN: 0843733225.

First published 1981.

Displays thousands of clear illus. of physical objects, duly keyed. Arrangement is by broad categories (*e.g.* Earth; Living things). The 1981 ed. was considered an improvement on the *Oxford Duden pictorial English dictionary* series (*Choice*, v.19(7), March 1982, p.888). *Class No:* 5(038)=20

[118]
—CRISPIN, F.S. **Dictionary of technical terms.** 11th ed. New York, Bryce Publishing Co., 1970. vi, 455p. diagrs.

Provides 10,000 brief definitions of technical terms 'in use in all sections of the United States' (*Preface*). Intended for students, draughtsmen, mechanics, builders, electricians, and workmen generally. Syllabification, hyphenation, stress and capitalization shown. Terms are categorized. About 1 diagram per page. *Class No:* 5(038)=20

[119]
BRENNAN, R.P. **Dictionary of scientific literacy.** New York, John Wiley, 1992. xiv,334p. illus., diagrs., tables. £14.95. ISBN: 0471532142.

Lists *c.*700 terms, A-Z (Absolute zero ... Zygote), of current interest. Many clear illustrations and diagrams. Cross-references in bold, upper-case type within the text. Pronunciation is given for some terms. Aimed at 'the intelligent non-scientist' (*Preface*) who wishes to understand scientific terminology which is now part of everyday life. *Class No:* 5(038)=20

[120]
—Harrap's illustrated dictionary of science. London, Harrap, 1988. 256p. figs., diagrs. £19.95. ISBN: 0245547800.

Covers *c.*7,500 terms (Aa ... Zymase). 34 colour illustrations: 1. Nobel Prizes in science, 1901-1987 ... 14. Hormones ... 27. Senses ... 34. Universe-scale and distance. Short biographies, *e.g.* Mendel (¼ column), Darwin (1/3 column). American spelling, with cross-references from that of the English. Written in clear, non-specialist language. 'Reference book for those wanting to understand scientific terms and the meanings behind them' (*British book news*, February 1991, p.103). *Class No:* 5(038)=20

[121]
Code names dictionary: a guide to code names, slang, nicknames, journalese and similar terms,- aviation, rockets and missiles, military, aerospace, meteorology, atomic energy, communications, and others. Ruffner, F.G. *and* Thomas, R.C., *eds.* Detroit, Mich., Gale, 1963. 555p. $55. ISBN: 0810306859.

Deciphers more than 8,500 code names (including acronyms), mainly drawn from government publications and originating from World War II, the Korean War, space probes, etc. Chief use is for identifying passwords, operations and projects, not for defining terms. *Class No:* 5(038)=20

[122]
Concise science dictionary. Isaacs, A., *and others*, *eds.* 2nd ed. Oxford, University Press, 1991. vi, 758p. illus., tables. £17.50; £7.99. ISBN: 0198661673.

About 7,500 definitions of terms and concepts in physics, chemistry, biology, the earth sciences, and astronomy. Aims 'to provide school and first-year university students with explanations of unfamiliar words they might come across' (*Preface*). 7 appendices (*e.g.* 4. Geological time scale). Criticized in *Choice* (v.22(9), May 1985, p.1303) for inadequate coverage of agriculture, engineering, medicine and the applied sciences in general. However, it may be assumed that 'science' concerns the physical, earth and biological sciences, in the strict sense of the word. A good general-purpose science dictionary. *Class No:* 5(038)=20

[123]
EMILIANI, E. **Dictionary of the physical sciences:** terms, formulas, data-physics, chemistry, geology, cosmology. New York, Oxford University Press, 1987. 416p. illus., tables. £27.50; £17.50. ISBN: 0195036514.

Over 5,000 definitions of fundamental terms. 70 tables (p.233-365; 'Isotope chart', p.288-300). *Class No:* 5(038)=20

[124]
FLOOD, W.E. **Scientific words, their structure and meaning:** an explanatory glossary of about 1,150 word elements (roots, prefixes, affixes) which enter into the formation of scientific terms. London, Greenwood Press, 1960. xix, 220p. £32.50. ISBN: 0837175410.

Word elements, A-Z 'Hecter, hetero-': 1 column; 'Pyro, pyr-': 1½ columns. Entries state the meaning of each word and also its origin, usually Latin or Greek. Chemical formulas are given whenever they serve a useful purpose. *Class No:* 5(038)=20

[125]
The Hutchinson dictionary of science. Lafferty, P. *and* Rowe, S., *eds.* London, Hutchinson, 1993. 678p. illus. £20. ISBN: 009177151x.

Published in the US as *The Dictionary of science* (Simon and Schuster, 1994).

5,000 entries ranging from a few lines to over a page in length. More than 400 black-and-white diagrams. Many cross-references. Includes chronologies of important scientific events; the periodic table; lists of scientists complete with birth and death dates; thematic indexes. For public and school libraries looking for a current, moderately-priced dictionary. *Class No:* 5(038)=20

[126]
—The Longman dictionary of scientific usage. Godman, A. *and* Payne, E.M.F. Harlow, Essex, Longman, 1979. xxxx, 684p. diagrs., graphs, tables, chemical structures. ISBN: 058252587x.

Definitions of over 10,000 terms in two main sections. The first handles over 1,300 basic terms. The second treats 8,500 'special terms' grouped in thesaurus fashion into *c.*100 subject sets in biology, chemistry, physics etc. 12 appendices. Index, p.615-84. The non-technical definitions (not always accurate) and many illus. give it some appeal to schools and general readers. *Class No:* 5(038)=20

[127]
—The New Penguin dictionary of science. Clugston, M.J., *ed.* London, Penguin Books, 1998. xiv,845p. illus. £7.99. ISBN: 0140512713.

Includes basic terms in areas such as physics, chemistry, biology, etc. For school, public, and academic libraries with undergraduate reference collections. *Class No:* 5(038)=20

[128]
KNIGHT, D. **A Companion to the physical sciences.** London, Routledge, 1989. 177p. £7.50. ISBN: 0415009014.

Dictionary of 125 terms, varying in length from a quarter to two pages. Numerous cross-references. 4-page list of individuals discussed in the main sequence is appended. Supplements Bynum, W.F., *The Dictionary of the history of science* (Princeton, 1981). Undergraduate level. *Class No:* 5(038)=20

[129]
Larousse dictionary of science and technology. Muir, H., *eds and* Walker, P.M.B. Edinburgh, Larousse, 1995. 1248p. figs., tables. £45; £19.99; $45. ISBN: 0752300105.

First published as *Chambers technical dictionary* in 1940 and as *Chambers science and technology dictionary* in 1988.

49,000 entries. Some major changes from the previous ed.; now covers food science and includes over 500 drawings and illustrations. Many cross-references; appendices include the periodic table, geologic eras, mathematical symbols, etc. 'An impressive work' (*New scientist*, 8 July 1995, p.47). Aimed at general readers and useful as a quick reference tool.

For students and personal libraries, *The Cassell dictionary of science* (Cassell, 1998. 512p. illus. $35. ISBN: 0304344834) has *c.*10,000 alphabetically arranged entries. *Class No:* 5(038)=20

[130]
A List of scientific terms with Scottish connections. Edinburgh, Scottish National Dictionary Association, 1976.

Supplement to *Scottish national dictionary*, v.10, pt.iv, 1976, p.575-91. *Class No:* 5(038)=20

German

[131]
DE VRIES, L. *and* HERRMANN, T.M. **English-German technical and engineering dictionary.** 2nd ed. New York, London, etc., McGraw-Hill, 1966. [xv], 1154p.

First published 1954.

More than 200,000 entries, including compounds. Lengthy entries are sectionalized. 76 specialist collaborators. New subjects added include: astronautics, automation, climatology, control engineering,

....(contd.)
data processing, inertial navigation, measurement systems, sail mechanics. 51 categories. Abbreviations figure in main sequence. Badly needs updating. *Class No:* 5(038)=30

[132]
DE VRIES, L. German-English science dictionary, updated and expanded by L. Jacolev and P.L. Bolton. 4th ed. New York, London, etc., McGraw-Hill, 1978. xxxviii, 628p. $37.95. ISBN: 0070166021.
First published 1939.
About 65,000 entries; Addendum, p.559-628: *c.*7,000 entries. Coverage: mathematics, physics, chemistry, biology, botany, zoology, anatomy, agronomy, horticulture. Sub-entries in bold type. 'Keim' (germ) and compounds: 1½ columns. Preliminary essay: 'Suggestions for translators'. Appended lists of geographical names, abbreviations, chemical elements, weights and measures, etc. *Class No:* 5(038)=30

[133]
DE VRIES, L. *and* **HERRMANN, T.M. German-English technical and engineering dictionary.** 2nd ed., completely rev. and enl. New York, London, etc., McGraw-Hill, 1965. ix, 1178p. £74.95. ISBN: 0070166315.
First published 1950; supp., 1959.
Over 225,000 entries, 100,000 more than in 1st ed. Terms are categorized. Medicine and agriculture are not covered in any depth. Lengthy entries are sectionalized (*e.g.* 'Festigkeit' has 32 compounds, in 3 groups). Includes *c.*25,000 new terms in such fields as nuclear physics, space flight and plastics. Badly needs updating. *Class No:* 5(038)=30

[134]
DORIAN, A.F. Dictionary of science and technology, German-English. 2nd rev. ed. Amsterdam, etc., Elsevier, 1981. x, 1119p. £150; $202.75. ISBN: 0444419977.
First published 1970.
About 100,000 entries. Terms in the 1st ed. 'regarded as ballast' have been dropped and 20,000 new headwords added. *Class No:* 5(038)=30

[135]
—**DORIAN, A.F.** Dictionary of science and technology, English-German. 2nd rev. ed. Amsterdam, etc., Elsevier, 1978. xii, 1402p. £150; $195. ISBN: 0444416498.
First published 1967.
Has *c.*100,000 entries, with definitions and explanations of many of the English terms. Well thought of by translators, although the tendency to enter under the qualifying adjective and not the noun qualified should be noted. *Class No:* 5(038)=30

[136]
ERNST, R. Wörterbuch der industriellen Technik. [Dictionary of engineering and technology.] 5. Aufl. Wiesbaden, Brandstetter, 1985-89. 2v. £80.35ea.
First published 1948.
1. *Deutsch-Englisch.* 5. Aufl. 1989. 1258p. 2. *Englisch-Deutsch.* 5. Aufl. 1985. 1422p.
V.1 has *c.*157,000 entries. V.2 has an introduction on 'The nature of technical English'. Also available on CD-ROM (£119.95). Regarded as the standard work in the field. *Class No:* 5(038)=30

[137]
KUČERA, A. Compact Wörterbuch der exakten Naturwissenschaften und der Technik. [The Compact dictionary of exact science and technology.] Wiesbaden, Brandstetter, 1982-89. 2v. DM140, v.1; DM95, v.2. ISBN: 0685483045, v.1; 387097088x, v.2.
1. *English-German.* 2nd ed. 1989. xxxi,1460p., £61.70. 2. *German-English.* 1982. xiv,826p.
V.1 offers *c.*50,000 headword entries; v.2, over 67,000. Gives not merely equivalents but also frequently refers to *Chambers dictionary of science and technology* (for fuller definitions) and to the German DIN standards. Appendices on German, British and US standards, etc. 'Few dictionaries succeed in putting so much solid, reliable information in so little space. Invaluable not only for anyone working in the field, but also can serve as a model for other bilingual terminological dictionaries' (*ARBA,* 1984, entry 1232). *Class No:* 5(038)=30

[138]
Routledge German technical dictionary. [Universal-Wörterbuch der technik Englisch.] London, Routledge, 1995. 2 vols. (850p.; 750p.). £90 (vol.). ISBN: 0415093929.
Vol. 1: German-English; vol. 2: English-German.
About 100,000 entries per language in 63 technical subject areas (*e.g.* acoustics, electricity, opticsmechanics, quality assurance, textiles, etc.). Appended list of over 3,000 abbreviations; details of inflexion; cross references. A major dictionary. An electronic version is available on CD-ROM (£199) and computer diskette. *Class No:* 5(038)=30

[139]
WALTHER, R. Dictionary of technology. 5th ed. Amsterdam, etc., Elsevier, 1985. 2v. $187.25ea. ISBN: 0444995919, v.1; 0444995900, v.2.
Rev. ed. of *Polytechnisches Wörterbuch.*
1. *English-German.* 1985. 1126p. 2. *German-English.* 1985. viii, 1046p.
Each volume has *c.*100,000 entries for terms in technology and industrial production. Subentries are given separate lines. 40 categories apply to terms. German genders given. Appendices list abbreviations. 'This fundamental work' (*New technical books,* v.70(8), October 1985, item 1051). *Class No:* 5(038)=30

Dutch
[140]
JANSONIUS, H. Technish Engels woordenboek: Nederlands-Engels en Engels-Nederlands. Leiden, Nederlandsche Uit., 1976. 555p. £42.85; $109.25. ISBN: 9061100291.
Dutch-English (p.7-406): *c.*4,000 headwords (many subentries); English-Dutch (p.409-55): *c.*1,500 headwords. *Class No:* 5(038)=393

[141]
STEKHOVEN, G.S. Kluwer's universal engineering dictionary. Deventer, Antwerp, Kluwer Technische Boeken B.V., 1971-77. 2v. ISBN: 9020106023, v.1; 9020106058, v.2.
A continuation of *Ten Bosch technisch woordenboek.*
v.1 *English-Dutch.* v.2 *Dutch-English.*
V.1 contains about 50,000 entry-words, including abbreviations. Many compounds, usually given separate entries. Language areas: British and American English, Flemish, Dutch and Afrikaans. *Class No:* 5(038)=393

Norwegian
[142]
ANSTEINSSON, J. English-Norwegian technical dictionary. [Engelsk-norsk teknisk ordbok.] 6th rev. ed. Trondheim, Brun, 1996. 581p. £37.90. ISBN: 8270284920.
First published 1948.
About 20,000 entries. Clear layout; compounds are picked out in bold type. *Class No:* 5(038)=396

[143]
ANSTEINSSON, J. Norsk-engelsk teknisk ordbok. 4th ed. Trondheim, Brun, 1994. 514p. £37.90. ISBN: 8270284904.
About 25,000 entries for Norwegian terms, with English equivalents.
The two dictionaries are intended for Norwegian technical colleges and do not cater for the foreigner's lack of knowledge of stress, pronunciation or syllabification of Norwegian words. The specialized vocabularies are, however, recommended by translators.
Class No: 5(038)=396

Swedish
[144]
ENGSTRÖM, E. Engelsk-svensk teknisk ordbok. 14. uppl. Stockholm, Travaru-Tidning Förlaget, 1997. 1026, [2]p. £49.50 ISBN: 0828806756, US ed.
Over 100,000 entries (including subentries). 'Safety': nearly 2 columns. Includes abbreviations. About 200 categories, etc. are applied to terms. American technical terms receive special attention. Also available electronically. *Class No:* 5(038)=397

[145]
ENGSTRÖM, E. Svensk-engelsk teknisk ordbok. [Swedish-English technical dictionary.] 10. uppl. Stockholm, Svensk Trävarutidning Förlaget, 1977 (reprinted 1998). 973, [1]p. £49.50.
About 100,000 entries and subentries. 'Kraft' (power): 3 columns. Appended list of sources. Also available electronically. *Class No:* 5(038)=397

[146]
GULLBERG, I.F. Svensk-engelsk fackordbok för näringsliv, fövaltning, undevisning och forskning. [A Swedish-English dictionary of technical terms used in business, industry, administration, education and research.] 2. revid. uppl., med suppl. Stockholm, Norstedt, 1977. xix, [1], 1722p. $225. ISBN: 9117750520.
First published 1964 (xvi, 1246p.).
The 2nd ed. has an extensive supplement of *c.*40,000 new terms, giving a total of *c.*175,000 categorized terms, A/Z. Rich in idioms. Includes many proper names ('Internationella...': nearly 36 columns). British and US usages not differentiated. Includes abbreviations. List of important dictionaries in 50 languages. Well-produced and a fine example of its kind. *Class No:* 5(038)=397

Danish

[147]
WARRERN, A. **Dansk-Engelsk teknisk ordbog.** 6. udg. Copenhagen, Clausen Bøger, 1981. 393p. ISBN: 8711040270.
First published 1949; 5th ed., 1976 (385p.).
About 15,000 word-for-word entries. Many compounds. British and US usage differentiated; terms categorized. Entry under qualifying adjective. Abbreviations not included. *Class No:* 5(038)=398

[148]
WARRERN, A. **Engelsk-dansk teknisk ordbog.** 9. udg. Copenhagen, Clausen Bøger, 1986. 400p. $75. ISBN: 8711041544.
15,000 word-for-word entries, compounds being given separate entries. *Class No:* 5(038)=398

French

[149]
CUSSET, F. **Vocabulaire technique, anglais-français, français-anglais:** électricité, mécanique, industries extractives et annexes, métallurgie, sciences. 9. éd. Paris, Berger-Levrault. 1977. 434p.
First published 1946 as *English-French, French-English* dictionary. 8th ed. 1968 (434p.).
About 7,000 entry-words in each half. English-French, p.5-220; French-English, p.221-424. Compiled by a mining engineer. Terms are strictly technical, with separate entries for compounds. Conversion tables, p.427-34. *Class No:* 5(038)=40

[150]
DE VRIES, L. **French-English science and technology dictionary.** 4th ed., rev. and enl. by S. Hochman. New York, etc., McGraw-Hill, 1976. xiii, 683p. $46.10. ISBN: 0070166293.
First published 1940; 3rd ed; 1962.
About 52,500 entries, including a supplement of *c.*4,500 new terms added to 3rd ed. Emphasises new developments (*e.g.* in automotive technology, astronautics, electronics, electronic data processing). 'All the terms published by the French Ministry of National Education, in January 1973 have been included' (*Library journal,* v.101(13), July 1976, p.1516). *Class No:* 5(038)=40

[151]
Dictionnaire des racines scientifiques. Cailleux, A. *and* Komorn, J., *eds.* 3. éd., rev. et augm. Paris, Société d'Éditions d'Enseignement Supérieur [S.E.D.E.S.], 1981. 263p.
First published 1961 (246p.).
Explains more than one thousand scientific word roots. Could be used in conjunction with W.E. Flood's *Scientific words* (*qv*). *Class No:* 5(038)=40

[152]
DORIAN, A.F. **Dictionary of science and technology, French-English.** Amsterdam, etc., Elsevier, 1980. x, 1085p. £150.
Claims to have over 150,000 terms relating to more than 150 differing fields. *Class No:* 5(038)=40

[153]
—**Dictionary of science and technology, English-French.** Dorian, A.F., *comp.* Amsterdam, etc., Elsevier, 1979. [x], 1586p. £150. ISBN: 0444418296.
Covers *c.*150,000 terms, including trivia. Some 100 categories are applied. Entry under qualifying adjective (*e.g.* 'mobile crane' - entered under 'mobile', but not under 'crane'). Criticized for errors of commission and omission. 'It is considered of only marginal use to the professional linguist' (Picken, C. *The Translator's handbook,* p.208, 1983). *Class No:* 5(038)=40

[154]
ERNST, R. **Comprehensive dictionary of engineering and technology,** with extensive treatment of the most modern techniques and processes. Cambridge, University Press; New York, French and European, 1982-1984. 2v. $135ea. ISBN: 052130377x, v.1; 0521303788, v.2; 082880611x, v.1, US ed; 0828806101, v.2, US ed.
1. *Français-Anglais,* viii, 1085p. 2. *English-French.* xxiii, 1399p.
V.1 has 159,142 entries; v.2 195,546 entries. Each term is categorized. 'Deals with all branches of modern industry involving chemistry, electrical engineering, electronics, commerce, space travel, telecommunications, data processing, & microprocessors. 'Though expensive, the set belongs in all comprehensive science and technology collections and in the hands of serious translators' (*New technical books,* v.70(8), October 1985, item 1056). *Class No:* 5(038)=40

[155]
Harrap's French and English science dictionary. Hathway, D.E., *consultant ed.* London, Harrap, 1985. ix, 320 + 302p. £25. ISBN: 0245540725.
About 30,000 headwords, with *c.*100 categories applied. Part 1: English-French; part 2: French-English. Mostly equivalents. 'Nucleus': 11 sub-entries. 'Selected subject-matter contains terms in the physical and earth sciences, including chemistry, biochemistry, physics, mineralogy, geology and meteorology, as well as the broad sweep of the life sciences ...' (*Preface*). *Class No:* 5(038)=40

[156]
—**Harrap's visual French-English dictionary.** London, Harrap, 1987. 924p. £14.95. ISBN: 0245545964.
Has 28 sections (Astronomy ... Symbols), a number of which concern science and technology. Thus, 'offshore platform' is illustrated on p.643, with 18 keyed parts. General, thematic and specialized indexes in both English and French. *Class No:* 5(038)=40

[157]
KETTRIDGE, J.O. **French-English and English-French dictionary of technical terms and phrases** used in civil, mechanical, electrical and mining engineering, and allied sciences and industries; with a method of telegraphic coding. Rev. ed., with suppt. by Y.R. Arden. London, Routledge & Kegan Paul, 1980. (reprinted 1989). 2v. £60, set; £35, ea. ISBN: 0415043093, v.1; 0415027683, v.2.
First published 1959.
1. *French-English.* 640p. 2. *English-French.* 672p.
About 100,000 entries for terms and phrases, covering both volumes. Each volume has a supplement and an appendix of abbreviations, symbols and conversion tables. *Class No:* 5(038)=40

[158]
Routledge French technical dictionary. [Routledge Dictionnaire technique anglais.] London, Routledge, 1994. 2 vols. (xxiv, 777p.; xxxiv, 841p.) £92.50 (vol.). ISBN: 0415056705.
Vol. 1: French-English; vol. 2: English-French.
34 contributors. About 100,000 entries per language in 70 technical subject areas (*e.g.* acoustics, mechanics, quality assurance, recycling, etc.). Appended list of abbreviations, chemical elements, conversion tables. A major dictionary. An electronic version is available on CD-ROM and computer diskette. *Class No:* 5(038)=40

Italian

[159]
DENTI, R. **Dizionario tecnico, italiano-inglese, inglese-italiano.** 11. ed. riv., ampliata ed aggiornata. Milan, S.F. Vanni, 1985. [xvi], 2023p. £38.90. ISBN: 882031052x.
First published 1946.
About 105,500 entries. Italian-English, p.1-835; English-Italian, p.837-1916. Many sub-entries are given separate entries. 'Leva' (lever), over 1½ columns. Appendices include technical abbreviations in common use, conversion factors, mathematical symbols, British and American measures and metric equivalents. *Class No:* 5(038)=50

[160]
—RAGAZINI, G. *and* RUSSI, D. Nuovissimo dizionario tecnico, inglese-italiano, italiano-inglese. [Milan], Mursia, 1983. 1278p.
Has *c.*50,000 headwords. Italian-English, p.1-641; English-Italian, p.679-1278. About 150 subject categories are applied. Appended list of abbreviations and tables. *Class No:* 5(038)=50

[161]
MAROLLI, G. **Dizionario tecnico, inglese-italiano, italiano-inglese.** [Technical dictionary, English-Italian, Italian-English.] 13a. ed. interamente riv. ed ampl. Milan, U. Hoepli editore, 1996. xx, 1848p. illus., tables.
About 130,000 technical terms, including abbreviations. Some 200 categories are applied to terms. Whereas Denti sets out compounds as separate entries, Marolli masses them under the headwords and is less easy to use. A separate folder of plates is included. Also available on CD-ROM (£65.52). *Class No:* 5(038)=50

[162]
—Dizionario enciclopédico scientifico e tecnico, inglese-italiano, italiano-inglese. Bologna, Zanichelli, 1980. 1650p.
Based on the *McGraw-Hill dictionary of scientific and technical terms (q.v.).* 102 categories are applied to its 96,000 terms. *Class No:* 5(038)=50

[163]
—GATTO, S. Dizionario tecnico scientifico illustrato italiano-inglese, inglese-italiano. 2. ed., riv. e coretta. Milan, Ceschina, 1965. xx, [1], [1], 1381p. illus.
Intended for Italians. About 60,000 terms, with separate entry for each application. About 150 categories feature. The small line-drawings are infrequent and hardly merit inclusion. Bibliography, p.vii-viii. *Class No:* 5(038)=50

Rumanian

[164]
Dictionar tehnic: englez-român. Dumitrescu, D., *and others.* Bucharest, Editura Tehnicâ; New York, Irvington, 1967. xi, 1301p. $124.50. ISBN: 0829009876, US ed.
About 115,000 Rumanian equivalents of English scientific and technical terms. *Class No:* 5(038)=590

[165]

Dictionar tehnic: român-englez. Dumitrescu, D., *and others.* Bucharest, Editura Tehnicâ, 1970. xi, 1118p.

About 120,000 Rumanian entry-words, with English equivalents. 51 categories applied. Bibliography of 21 items, p.1118.

Class No: 5(038)=590

Spanish

[166]

[Castilla's] Diccionario politécnico de las linguas española e inglesa. 3. ed. aumentada y actualizada. Madrid, Ediciones Castilla, S.A., 1965. 2v.

First published 1958; 2nd ed. 1961. Original Spanish as *Diccionario politécnico de las linguas española e inglesa.*

1. *Inglés-español.* xii, 1755p. 2. *Español-inglés.* [v], 1464p.

Although concentrating on engineering technology, the 3rd ed. claims to cover latest developments in industry and commerce, banking and jurisprudence. V.1 has *c.*200,000 entries, with separate lines for sub-entries. Many idioms are compounds. Appendices of conversion tables, signs and symbols. V.2 has under 200,000 entries. Conversion tables appended. *Class No:* 5(038)=60

[167]

Chambers diccionario cientifico y tecnológico i español / inglés / francés / alemán. Collocott, T.C. Barcelona, Omega, 1979. 2v. (xii, 1739p.; 1007p.). ISBN: 8428205310.

V.1 consists of *c.*40,000 Spanish terms and explanations, plus English, French and German equivalents. About 65 categories are applied. V.2 has 3 sequences, - English-Spanish, French-Spanish, German-Spanish. *Class No:* 5(038)=60

[168]

COLLAZO, J.L. English-Spanish, Spanish-English encyclopedic dictionary of technical terms. 3v. New York, McGraw-Hill, 1980. £99.99; $195.

1. (2pts). *English-Spanish.* lxcxxv, 1187p. 2. *Spanish-English.* [xv], 430p.

V.1 has *c.*100,000 extended entries with definitions, phrases, synonyms, variant expressions, etc. V.2 has Spanish terms and their English equivalents. *Class No:* 5(038)=60

[169]

—GUINLE, R.L. A Modern Spanish-English and English-Spanish technical & engineering dictionary, suitable for Spain and all the Spanish-speaking countries of Central America and South America. Mexico, Continental, 1980. xv, [2], 311p. $27.95.

First published 1938 and frequently reprinted, is by a consulting engineer. *Class No:* 5(038)=60

[170]

Diccionario de términos cientificos y técnicos. Lapedes, D.N., *redactor jefe.* Barcelona, Marcombo; New York, French and European, 1981. 5v. illus. ISBN: 0070791724; 0828806683, US ed.

Spanish translation of *McGraw-Hill Dictionary of scientific and technical terms* (2nd ed., 1978), with its categorized 108,000 entries. V.1-4 provide the translation, adding English term. V.5 provides the English original, with Spanish equivalent. *Class No:* 5(038)=60

[171]

Routledge Spanish technical dictionary. [Routledge diccionario técnico inglés.] London, Routledge, 1997. 2v. £90; $140 (v.1); £90; $140 (v.2); £180; $280 (set). ISBN: 0415112729, v.1; 0415112737, v.2; 0415112745, set.

V.1: Spanish-English; v.2: English-Spanish.

Over 100,000 headwords and more than 70 subject areas. Covers basic technical terms and principles, as well as emerging and new topics, *e.g.* safety assurance. Entries include noun gender, parts of speech, and abbreviations and, in some cases, the use of the term in context is shown. For academic libraries. Also available on CD-ROM (£199). *Class No:* 5(038)=60

[172]

SELL, L.L. Spanish-English technical dictionary of aircraft - automobile - railways - highways - electricity - electronics - radio - television - machine tools - agricultural implements - paints and dyes - petroleum - steel products. New York, etc., McGraw-Hill, 1949. xi, 1706p.

700,000 Spanish and English technical terms, entries being set solid under headwords (*e.g.* 'conducts' (passageway): 5½ columns (somewhat relieved by use of bold type for the Spanish)). About 120 categories are applied. Many idioms. *Class No:* 5(038)=60

[173]

—SELL, L.L. English-Spanish comprehensive technical dictionary. New York & London, McGraw-Hill, 1944. xii, 1478p.

Contains 525,000 Spanish and English technical terms. 20 subject-categories are applied. Distinguishes between British and American English. Forbidding layout of type, set solid. *Class No:* 5(038)=60

[174]

—SELL, L.L. English-Spanish comprehensive technical dictionary... Section 2. New York, McGraw-Hill, 1959. [3], iv, 1079p.

Adds a further 400,000 entries, including a supplement, p.933-1079. 'Extensive, but rather difficult to use' (Finch, C.A. *An Approach to technical translation* (1970), p.58). *Class No:* 5(038)=60

Portuguese

[175]

DE PINA ARAÚJO, A. De Pina's technical dictionary / Dicionário técnico. São Paulo, McGraw-Hill do Brasil, 1978. 2v. (616p. + 495p.).

1. *English-Portuguese.* 616p. 2. *Portuguese-English.* 493p. Reprint of the 1964 ed.

About 75,000 translated terms in all, mostly equivalents. American English used (*e.g.* 'aluminium'). Tendency to enter under qualifying word instead of noun (*e.g.* 'high tide' - under 'high' and not 'tide'). No fewer than *c.*500 categories applied to terms.

Class No: 5(038)=690

[176]

FÜRSTENAU, E. Dicionário de termos técnicos (inglés-portugués). 20. ed. Porto Alegre, Brazil, Editora Globo, 1996. 2v., 1413p. illus.

First published 1947.

*c.*30,000 new, revised, and updated terms from previous ed. Includes bibliographical references, p.1407-13.

Class No: 5(038)=690

Greek

[177]

PAPANIKOLAOU, E.N. Tehnikon ellēno-agglikon kai agglo-ellēnikon lexikon meta proforas. Piraeus, Multilēnaiou, 1962. 684p. tables.

'Greek-English and English-Greek technical dictionary'. About 20,000 entries and sub-entries in each half. Coverage: mechanics, electricity, radio, mathematics, physics and chemistry.

Class No: 5(038)=77

Russian

[178]

Anglo-russkiĭ politekhnicheskiĭ slovar': 87,000 terminov. Chernukhin, A.E., *ed.* Izd. 4. Moscow, Ruskiĭ Iazyk, 1979. 687p. ISBN: 0080219365.

3rd ed. 1976 (647p.).

'English-Russian polytechnical dictionary' has entries for *c.*87,000 terms. Coverage excludes medicine, mathematics, pure and natural sciences. Appendices: abbreviations; conversion tables.

Class No: 5(038)=82

[179]

CALLAHAM, L.I. Callaham's Russian-English dictionary of science and technology. 3th ed. New York, London, etc., Wiley, 1996. xxxiv, 814p. £120. ISBN: 0471129984.

First published 1947; 2nd ed., 1962. Previously published under title *Russian-English chemical and polytechnical dictionary.*

About 100,000 Russian entries and sub-entries. Terms are categorized, genders given; abbreviations, prefixes and common Russian word-endings included. Good typography for cyrillic characters. Particularly helpful on pure and applied chemistry.

Class No: 5(038)=82

[180]

—ALFORD, M.H.T. and ALFORD, V.L. Russian-English scientific and technical dictionary. Oxford, Pergamon, 1970. 2v. (xxxvi, [1], 764p.; vii, 765-1423p.).

Over 100,000 entries, drawn from 94 different disciplines. Stress shown. Endings of certain cases provided, to illustrate their paradigms. All irregular forms are shown with, where necessary, their own alphabetical entries. Separate entry-lines for compounds, etc. 'Supplementary dictionary of Russian word endings', v.2, p.1809-23. 'Reference sources', v.1, p.xxi-xxiii. Specially designed for people with weak or moderate knowledge of Russian grammar.

Class No: 5(038)=82

[181]

Russian-English dictionary of scientific and technical usage. Kuznetsov, B.V., *and others.* [Moscow], Russky Yazyk (distributed by Pergamon), 1986. 655p. $175. ISBN: 0080325513.

About 30,000 entry-words. Not confined to providing English equivalents to Russian terms. Emphasises usage in everyday language as well as giving examples of specialized application.

Class No: 5(038)=82

[182]
Russko-angliiskiĭ politekhnicheskiĭ slovar'. Chernukhin, A.E., *ed.* Moscow, Ministerstvo Oborony, 1971. 1027p.

Companion volume to the English-Russian polytechnical dictionary and also carrying *c.*80,000 entries. Separate lines for sub-entries. Wide coverage of military terms, reflecting the nature of the publishing body, - Ministry of Defence. *Class No:* 5(038)=82

[183]
UNITED STATES. Library of Congress. Reference Department. Aerospace Information Division. **Soviet Russian scientific and technical terms:** a selective list. Washington, Library of Congress, 1963. [v], 668p.

26,000 entries. 'Generally speaking, those terms are included which cannot be found in standard dictionaries, or which have a special meaning when used in a particular field' *(Introduction)*. Incorporates frequently used and important abbreviations, including names of Russian organizations. 31 categories are applied to terms. *Class No:* 5(038)=82

[184]
ZIMMERMAN, M. *and* **VEDENEEVA, C. Russko-angliĭskiĭ nauchno-tekhnicheskiĭ slovar perevodchika.** [Russian-English translator's dictionary: a guide to scientific and technical usage.] 3rd ed. Moscow, Nauka Publishers; Chichester, Wiley, 1992. 735p. £65. ISBN: 0471933163.

First published 1967 (294p.).

Not a dictionary of terms, but a collection of *c.*9,000 typical examples from scientific and technical sources, *i.e.,* to give equivalents in full context. Of the 2nd ed., 'This new, updated edition will come as a boon to the younger generation of translators' *(Nature,* v.312, 13 December 1984, p.670). *Class No:* 5(038)=82

Polish

[185]
English-Polish dictionary of science and technology. Czerni, S., *and others.* 11th ed. Warsaw, Wydawnictwa Naukowo-Techniczne, 1997. 1032p. £35.

First published 1962.

Has *c.*77,000 categorized entry-words; different applications are numbered. English terms that have no Polish equivalents are explained. Appended list of abbreviations of technical terms. organizations, etc. *Class No:* 5(038)=84

[186]
Polish-English dictionary of science and technology. Czerni, S., *and others.* 8th ed. Warsaw, Wydawnictwa Naukowo-Techniczne, 1994. 831p. £35.

About 63,000 entry-words. List of abbreviations appended.

'These two dictionaries are of high standing; accurate, up-to-date and with well-balanced coverage of a wide range of subject fields' *(Library journal,* v.89(16), 15 September 1964, p.3296, on the 1962 ed.). *Class No:* 5(038)=84

Czech

[187]
Česko-anglický technický slovník. [Czech-English technical dictionary.] 5th ed. Prague, SNTL, 1992. 2v. (944p.; 1026p.). £18.25; £19.55. ISBN: 8003004438.

About 55,000 entries for each language; arranged in some 40 categories. *Class No:* 5(038)=850

[188]
NOVÁK, J. *and* **BINDER, R. Vreckový anglicko-slovenský a slovensko-anglický technický slovník.** 2. prep. vyd. Bratislava, Slovenskó Vydavetel'stvo Technickej Literatury, [1964]. 610p.

'Concise English-Slovak and Slovak-English dictionary'. *Class No:* 5(038)=850

[189]
Velký anglicko-ceský technický slovník. Pĕkarek, O., *and others.* Prague, Státni Nakladatelství Technické Literatury, 1956-70. 3v. (*c.*3000p.).

'Large English-Czech technical dictionary'. Over 100,000 English entry-words. *Class No:* 5(038)=850

Serbo-Croat

[190]
Rečnik technićkih 13 izrago srpskohrvatso-engleski, francuski-nemaćki; englesko-francusko-nemaćko-srpskohrvatso. Ristić, S., *and others.* 3.izd. Belgrade, Tehnicka Knjica, 1971. 2v. ([iv], 612p. + [ii], 633p.). illus.

'Dictionary of technical terms, Serbo-Croatian/English/French/German, English/French/German/Serbo-Croatian'. V.1 has *c.*25,000 Serbo-Croatian entry-words, with equivalents in the other languages.

....(contd.)
V.2 *c.*30,000 English entry-words, with equivalents. About 50 categories are applied to terms. V.1 only has small illus.
Class No: 5(038)=86

Arabic

[191]
A New dictionary of scientific and technical terms, English-Arabic, with illustrations. Al-Khatib, A.Sh., *comp. and ed.* 6th ed. Beirut, Librairie du Liban, 1987. xv, 751p. illus., tables.

First published 1971 (xv, 751p).

About 50,000 entries; 3 columns, with about one illus. per column. 17 appendices (conversion tables, etc.). Bibliography, p.750. A reprint of the 1971 edition in quarto format. *Class No:* 5(038)=927

Turkish

[192]
ÖZBALKAN, N. English-Turkish dictionary. Istanbul, Ozbalkan Yayinlari, 1972. 952p. *Class No:* 5(038)=943.5

[193]
ÖZBALKAN, N. Turkçe-Ingilizce teknik terimler sözlügü. [Turkish-English dictionary of technical terminology.] 2. bask. Istanbul, Ozbalkan Yayinlari, 1984. 1152p. $150. *Class No:* 5(038)=943.5

Hungarian

[194]
Angol-magyar müszaki szótár. Nagy, E. *and* Klar, J., *eds.* 5. vaitozotlan kiad. Budapest, Akadémiai Kiadó; New York, French and European, 1980. viii, 791p. $65. ISBN: 9630523310; 0828806748, US ed.

A reprint of the 2nd ed. (1959).

'English-Hungarian technical dictionary'. About 100,000 entry-words, including meanings in common use. Many compounds. Appendix: English technical abbreviations, p.743-79; weights and measures, p.780-91. *Class No:* 5(038)=945

[195]
Magyar-angol müszaki szótár. Nagy, E., *and others, eds.* 5th ed. Budapest, Akadémiai Kiadó, 1983. viii, 752p. ISBN: 9630532735.

Reprint of the 1957 ed.

Companion to the English-Hungarian dictionary. Concerning these two Nagy dictionaries, C.A. Finch (*An approach to technical translation* (1970), p.58) states: 'Of doubtful technical accuracy in some subjects. L. Orzagh's *Angol-magyar szótár* (9th ed. 1979) and *Magyar-angol szótár* (5th ed. 1977. 2v.), both published by Akadémiai Kiadó, can also be consulted with profit for technical terms.' *Class No:* 5(038)=945

Finnish

[196]
Suomalais-englantilainin teknikan ja kaupan sanakorjo. Talvitie, J.K., *and others.* 4. uusittu laitos. Espoo, Tietoteos, 1995. 1136p. £119. ISBN: 9519035818.

About 50,000 Finnish technical and commercial terms, with equivalents in English. Also available in electronic format.
Class No: 5(038)=945.41

Chinese

[197]
Han ying kung cheng chi shu tzu hui. [Chinese-English dictionary of engineering technology.] Pei-ching, Hai yang chu pan she, 1986. 892p.

Includes *c.*107,000 terms on technological subjects, including astronautics and telecommunications. Radical index, p.7-13 and index of syllables of Hanyupinyin, p.14-21. *Class No:* 5(038)=951

[198]
Modern Chinese-English technical and general dictionary. New York, etc., McGraw-Hill, 1963. 3v.

1. *Tables* (Wade-Giles - Pinyin conversion table, etc.). Radical stroke index, in alphabetical sequence, - the real key to the dictionary. 2. *Standard telegraphic code, in numerical sequence.* 1900p. 3. *Pinyin romanization in alphabetical sequence* (permuted index). 188p.

About 212,000 entries, over 80% of them common scientific and technical terms. 'The main emphasis is on information not readily available in existing dictionaries' *(Introduction)*. Proper names and vocabulary of Chinese Communism are included. Each Chinese character is represented by a 4-digit code (0001-), adapted from the Standard Telegraphic Code. V.2-3 both give English equivalents. Recent linguistic reforms are included. *Class No:* 5(038)=951

[199]

—A Chinese-English dictionary of scientific and technical terms. Harbin, Heilongjang Renmin Chuban She, 1985. 2v. (1976p.).

Has *c*.100,000 entries for terms in Chinese characters, with English equivalents. *Class No:* 5(038)=951

Japanese

[200]

Inter-Press dictionary of science and engineering. English-Japanese; Japanese-English. [Tokyo], Inter-Press, 1984. 2v. (1927p. + 1888p.). ISBN: 4870870010.

About 120,000 entries in each volume. *Class No:* 5(038)=956

[201]

TUNG, L.W. Japanese/English, English/Japanese glossary of scientific and technical terms. New York, John Wiley, 1993. xxi,1146p. £90. ISBN: 0471574635.

Includes 120 subject areas, with *c*.3,000 chemical terms, 1,600 mathematical terms, 900 computer and logic terms, 3,200 engineering terms, and 3,700 biological terms. *Class No:* 5(038)=956

Theses

[202]

Comprehensive dissertation index, 1861-1972. Ann Arbor, Mich., Xerox Univ. Microfilms. 1973. 37v. Annual supplements, 1973-. *(1983-87 cumulation. 22v.)*

V.1-16 concern science and technology:
1-4. *Chemistry.*
5. *Mathematics and statistics.*
6-7. *Astronomy and physics.*
8-10. *Engineering.*
11-13. *Biological sciences.*
14. *Health and environmental sciences.*
15. *Agriculture.*
16. *Geography and geology.*

V.11. *Biological sciences: Biology and zoology* (1973. xix, 1210p.) has prelims.: 'Sources consulted', 'How to obtain dissertation copies'. Biology, p.1-218; Zoology, p.219-1210, - under subjects A-Z. About 80,000 entries. Subject index. *Class No:* 5(043)

[203]

Dissertation abstracts international. B: Physical sciences and engineering. Abstracts of dissertations available on microfilm or as xerographic reproductions. Ann Arbor, Mich., University Microfilms, 1969-. 12pa. $395. ISSN: 04194217.

Originally as *Microfilm abstracts* (v.1-11, 1938-51), then *Dissertation abstracts* (1952-69). As from 1966, the latter appeared in two sections: A. *Humanities and social sciences;* B. *The sciences and engineering,* - both 12pa. In 1977, C. *European abstracts* followed.

The title, *Dissertation abstracts international,* reflects inclusion of disssertations from foreign universities. The abstracts are in subject groups, A-Z (*e.g.* Aerospace studies ... Zoology). Keyword, title and author indexes pa. Available online and on CD-ROM. On microfilm. *Class No:* 5(043)

[204]

Masters theses in the pure and applied sciences accepted by colleges and universities of the United States and Canada. New York & London, Plenum Press, 1974-. v.18-. Annual. Price varies. ISSN: 02442861.

V. 1-17 (1957-73) published by Thermophysical Properties Research Center, Purdue Univ., Lafayette, Ind., covering US colleges and univs. only.

Over 10,000 titles of masters theses pa., covering mainly chemistry, physics and engineering subjects. Arranged under major study disciplines, A-Z, subdivided by universities. *Class No:* 5(043)

[205]

Retrospective index to theses of Great Britain and Ireland, 1716-1950. Bilboul, R.R. *and* Kent, F.L., *eds.* Santa Barbara, Calif., ABC-Clio, 1975-77. 5v.

1. *Social sciences and humanities.* 1975. ix, 393p.
2. *Applied sciences and technology.* 1976. xi, 159p.
3. *Life sciences.* 1977. xi, 327p.
4. *Physical sciences.* 1976. xi, 99p.
5. *Chemical sciences.* 1976. xx, 251p.

A checklist, up to 1950 (continued in *Aslib index to theses accepted for higher degrees by the universities of Great Britain and Ireland ...* v.1, 1950-51- (1953-)). 2pa. Subject and author sections for each volume. Available on microfiche and online. *Class No:* 5(043)

Reports Literature

[206]

AUGER, C.P. Information sources in grey literature. 3rd ed. London, Bowker-Saur, 1994. ix,170p. figs. £35; $65. (*Guides to information sources.*) ISBN: 1857390075.

First published 1975 as *Use of reports literature* (London, Butterworths). Fourth edition announced by Bowker-Saur, 1998.

12 chapters: 1. The nature and development of grey literature ... 4. Report writing - 5. Theses, translations and meetings papers ... 7. Aerospace - 8. Life sciences ... 11. Energy - 12. Science and technology. 3 appendices: A. Keys to report series codes - B. Trade literature - C. Addresses of organizations mentioned in the text. Short bibliography appended to each chapter. This edition is actually shorter than the previous ed. (1989) and it presents little that is new, so 'libraries that own the 2nd edition will not need this one' (*Choice*, May 1994, p.1407). *Class No:* 5(047)

[207]

Dictionary of report series codes. Godfrey, L.E. *and* Redman, H.F., *eds.* 2nd ed. New York, Special Libraries Association, 1973. vi, [1], 645p.

First published 1962.

Relates technical report series codes to US Department of Defense agencies, Atomic Energy Commission, their contractors and other US government agencies. Also lists agencies and the codes they use. Includes a bibliography on the report code literature. *Class No:* 5(047)

[208]

Government reports announcements & index. Springfield, Va., National Technical Information Service (NTIS), 1975-. Semi-monthly. $535 (US); $725 (non US). ISSN: 00979007.

Succeeds *Government research announcements* (1971-75). Orignally as *Bibliography of scientific and industrial reports* (1946-49), then as *Bibliography of technical reports* (1949-54), then as *US government research reports* (1954-64) and then as *US government research and development reports* (1965-71). Title and frequency vary.

About 2,500 abstracts per issue, including patents. 22 subject fields, further divided. Indexes: subject, personal author, corporate author, contract number, accession/report number. Covers government sponsored R & D reports, government analyses, etc. The annual index incorporates the cumulative index for 1968-87. NTIS database is available online and CD-ROM. *Class No:* 5(047)

[209]

Information work with unpublished reports. Holloway, A., *and others.* London, Deutsch, in association with the Institute of Information Scientists, 1976. 302p. illus.

Part 1: Work in large national information centres. Part 2: Work in company-based information units. 15 chapters, each with select bibliography appended. 'Other relevant literature', p.287. Index 'Will surely become a basic text of work in this field for many years to come'. *Class No:* 5(047)

Reviews & Abstracts

[210]

Aslib book guide: an international guide to scientific and technical books in English. London, Aslib, 1992-. v.57-. 12pa. £120 pa. ISSN: 00012521.

Quarterly until March 1948. Formerly *Aslib book list* (1935-91).

V.63(12), December 1998 contains 124 short reviews, by subject specialists, in DC order. Books are graded: 'A', elementary level; general readership; 'B', intermediate level; university textbook; 'C', advanced level; specific readership; 'D', reference books. Broad subject index and author or title index per issue and cumulated annually. A reliable current book-selection tool, normally restricted to books in English. *Class No:* 5(048)

[211]

CHEN, C.C. Biomedical, scientific & technical book reviewing. Metuchen, N.J., Scarecrow Press, 1976. xv, 186p.

Identifies and assesses 500 major biomedical, scientific and technical reviewing journals as quantitative sources of book reviews. One finding was that 9 general science reviewing journals provided reviews of more than 50% of the total output of new science books in the period studied, - 1970 or 1971. *Class No:* 5(048)

[212]

COPLEY, E.J. A Guide to 'Referativnyĭ zhurnal'. 3rd ed. London, British Library, Science Reference Library, 1975. [ii], 26p. facsim. (*Occasional publication*).

First published 1970.

Lists 65 titles in the *Referativnyĭ zhurnal* series and includes an A-Z subject index. An example is given of a *Referativnyĭ Zhurnal* abstract. Sub-series of *RZh* are not listed. On these, see the more detailed *Rubrikatov referativnykh izdanii SSSR* (Moscow, VINITI), -updated at intervals.

For details of translations from *RZh*, consult announcements in the

....*(contd.)*
British Library's *British reports, translations and theses* and US *Government reports, announcements and index* (with NTIS as its database). *Class No:* 5(048)

[213]

Current contents. Philadephia, Pa., Institute for Scientific Information, 1958-. (6 series.)
Current contents: Social and behavioral sciences. Weekly. $730.
Current contents: Physical, chemical and earth sciences. Weekly. $730.
Current contents: Life sciences. Weekly. $1015.
Current contents: Clinical medicine. Weekly. $730.
Current contents: Engineering, computing and technology. Weekly. $730.
Current contents: Agriculture, biology and environmental sciences. Weekly. $730.
Each of the series provides facsimiles of contents pages of current issues of journals in its field. Accompanying these is a list of journal issues covered, title-word index, author index and address directory, publishers address directory, plus the customary request-a-print form. Although offering prompt current awareness, these services do depend for their adequacy on sufficient detail being provided on the various contents pages. Online, CURRENT CONTENTS SEARCH database, containing 950,000 records, with 18,000 records added weekly, and on diskette. CD-ROM editions of each of the series also available. Internet access as *Current Contents Connect* at http://connect.isihost.com. *Class No:* 5(048)

[214]

Current contents: Physical, chemical and earth sciences. Philadelphia, Pa., Institute for Scientific Information, 1979-. v.19-. Weekly. $730. ISSN: 01632574.
Previously as *Current contents: Physical and chemical sciences* (formed by the merger of *Current contents: Physical sciences* and *Current contents: Chemical sciences*), 1961-78.
Reproduces contents pages of more than 900 journals in the fields concerned. Each weekly number covers *c.*100 journal issues. Online in CURRENT CONTENTS SEARCH, CD-ROM and available on diskette. Internet access as *Current Contents Connect* at http://connect.isihost.com. *Class No:* 5(048)

[215]

General science index. New York, H.W. Wilson, 1978- 10pa., with annual cumulative index. ISSN: 01621963.
Covers *c.*150 general English-language science journals, mostly indexed in the more comprehensive *Applied science and technology index* and *Biological and agricultural index*. Adds more than 40,000 records annually. Arranged under subjects, A-Z, with appended 'Book reviews'. Mainly US journals. Online via Wilsonline, BRS, CD-ROM (May 1984-. 12pa. $1,495pa). *Class No:* 5(048)

[216]

A Guide to the culture of science, technology and medicine. Durbin, R.T., *ed.* New York, Free Press. 1980 (reprinted 1984, with a bibliographic update). xl,723p. $75; $24.95.
Nine documented state-of-the-art contributions by specialists. More than 3,200 citations. For graduate students and scholars. 'One of the most important references of its kind for integrating the cross-disciplinary approaches necessary in their endeavours' (*Choice*, v.18, November 1980, p.416). *Class No:* 5(048)

[217]

Index to scientific book contents. Philadelphia, Pa., Institute for Scientific Information, 1985-. 4pa. Annual cumulation. $1,840. ISSN: 08848440.
Compiled in 2v.: 1. Contents of books; 2. Author/editor index; Corporate index; Permuterm subject index. The author/editor index is a key to specific book editors and chapter authors. 'Corporate index' is the term used for geographic and organization sections. Online via DIMDI. *Class No:* 5(048)

[218]

New technical books: a selective list with descriptive annotations. New York Public Library, Science & Technology Research Center, 1915-. 6pa. $30 (US); $35 (non US). ISSN: 00286869.
Each issue contains *c.*500 annotated entries for noteworthy books, mostly in English. Entries, in broad Dewey Decimal Classes feature two paragraphs: 'Content' and 'Note', the latter indicating readership, level and standing. Parts of continuing multi-volume works (*e.g.* Kirk-Othmer) and annual review series (*e.g. Advances in ...*) receive attention. The annual author and catchword indexes occupy middle pages of the December issue each year. A valuable selection tool, although somewhat late in appearance. *Class No:* 5(048)

[219]

Referativnyĭ zhurnal. Moscow, Akademiya Nauk SSSR, (Institut Nauchnoi Informatsii, VINITI), 1953-. Frequency varies. Annual, etc. indexes.
The most comprehensive of abstracting services, producing over 1,000,000 abstracts and references pa., in *c.*90 main series. Coverage: periodical articles, monographic series, patents, standards and specifications. Originals may be in any of some 70 languages. (In fact, one disadvantage for the Western reader may be inability to see originals). Time lag in appearance of abstracts may average 6-7 months. Diagrams and maps are sometimes used to elucidate abstracts. Duplication between the various series is sensibly permitted.
Topics covered in the present series include (in UDC order) Information ... Mathematics ... Energy ... Automation ... Air transport ... Food industry machinery ... Photography and cinematography. Those selected for inclusion in this volume of the *Guide* can be traced by consulting *Referativnyi zhurnal* in the Author/Title index. *Class No:* 5(048)

[220]

Science abstracts. London, INSPEC (Institution of Electrical Engineers), 1898-. V.1-.
V.1-5 (1898-1902), reprinted London, Butterworth, 1964, entitled *Science abstracts: Physics and electrical engineering*. From 1903 as Section A: *Physics abstracts* and B: *Electrical engineering abstracts*. Now in three sections: *Physics abstracts*. 24pa. £2,135pa. *Electrical and electronics abstracts*. 12pa. £1680pa. *Computer and control abstracts*, 1966-, *(q.v.)* 12pa. £1115pa.
Available online as INSPEC, and on CD-ROM. *Class No:* 5(048)

[221]

Science citation index. Philadelphia, Pa., Institute for Scientific Information, 1961-. 6pa., with annual and 5-yearly cumulations for the period 1969-79. $15,020. ISSN: 0036827x.
Citation index. Source index. Permuterm subject index.
The *Citation index* records, A-Z, authors of papers, monographs, etc., followed by a list of later writers who have cited/quoted those originals. The *Source index* has entries for those citing/quoting writers, while the *Permuterm subject index* based on relevant words in titles of papers etc., provides the subject approach. *SCI* covers *c.*3,800 journals, monographs etc.
Available online via DIALOG, Data-Star, and on the *Web of science*; CD-ROM (Institute for Scientific Information). *Class No:* 5(048)

[222]

Science tracer bullets. Washington, Library of Congress, Science and Technology Division, Reference Section, 1972-. Irregular. Free.
A series of brief guides to information sources (bibliographies; organizations; persons) on specific topics of current interest. Two titles published in 1998 are *Cryptology* and *Biodiversity*. Sections include: Scope, Introductory text - Subject headings - Basic texts ... Bibliographies - Government publications ... Journal articles - Primary journals - Reports - Selected technical reports - Selected materials.
Compilation volume, containing 173 of these guides published between 1972 and 1989, entitled *Science tracer bullets: a reference guide to scientific, technological, health, and environmental information sources* (H. Henderson, *ed.* Omnigraphics, 1990. 4v. 1687p. $160).
A database of all *Tracer bullets* from 1989, and selected older *Tracer bullets*, can be found on *SCTB online* on the Internet at http://lcweb2.loc.gov/sctb/. *Class No:* 5(048)

Bibliographies

[223]

Abstracting services. Vol.1: Sciences, technology, medicine, agriculture. 2nd ed. The Hague, International Federation for Documentation, 1969. 284p. *(FID pubn. 455.)*
First published 1965. V. 2: *Social sciences and humanities* (1965; 2nd ed., 1969).
About 1,300 abstracting services (journals and cards), plus *c.*100 primary journals with important abstracts sections. Section 1: A/Z list of abstracting services - Section 2: UDC arrangement by subjects. A/Z list of subjects in English, French, Russian and Spanish. Titles, under 39 countries, A/Z. Data on each title: frequency, price, number of abstracts pa., arrangement, indexed, journal and subject coverage. *Class No:* 5(048)(01)

[224]

Index to scientific reviews: an international interdisciplinary index to the review literature of science, medicine, agriculture, technology and the behavioral sciences. Philadephia, Pa., Institute for Scientific Information, 1974-. 2pa. $1,300. ISSN: 03606661.
The two major parts are: *Source index*, listing review articles (*not* book reviews as such) under authors, and *Permuterm subject index* (running to 4872 columns of tiny print in the 1986 first semiannual). More specialized review material is covered by Research front speciality index. Sources, *c.*2,200 journals and over 200 series, are

....*(contd.)*

listed in 'Guide and list of source publications' (on blue pages). Based on review articles included in *Science citation index*.
Class No: 5(048)(01)

[225]

OWEN, D.B. Abstracts and indexes in science and technology: a descriptive guide. 2nd ed. Metuchen, N.J., Scarecrow Press, 1985. ix, 235p. £17.50; $22.50. ISBN: 0810817128.
First published 1974.
223 abstracting and indexing services. 11 sections, in Dewey order: General - Mathematics, statistics and computer science - Astronomy - Chemistry and physics - Nuclear science and space science - Earth sciences, archaeology, and anthropology - Engineering and technology - Energy and environment - Biological sciences - Agricultural engineering - Health science. Data on each service: arrangement; coverage; scope (*e.g.* international); locating material (entry numbering); abstracts (language, etc.); indexes; other material (*e.g.* review articles); periodicals scanned (lists); databases. Title index, p.215-35. *Class No:* 5(048)(01)

[226]

Scientific abstracting and indexing periodicals in the British Library: a guide to SRIS holdings and their use. 4th ed. London, British Library, Science Reference and Information Service, 1991. [iii],64p. £20. ISBN: 071230780x.
3rd ed. 1985 (iii,149p.).
404 entries in all, with emphasis on abstracting services. Introductory matter highlights major abstracting periodicals (nos.1-27). The main sequence (nos.28-389), conforming to the SRS classification scheme (not outline), is followed by a section on research projects and reprints, citing nos.390-404. The necessary title and subject indexes follow. The drop in the number of entries from 1,880 in the 3rd ed. to 404 in this ed. is a cause for concern. Even allowing for cessations, cuts in titles must have been drastic. Roads and road transport are poorly represented, and the user will miss such titles as *Meteorological and geoastrophysical abstracts, Military science index,* and *Photographic abstracts*. Nevertheless, this 4th ed. records much of the basic scientific abstracting material. *Class No:* 5(048)(01)

[227]

STEPHENS, J. Inventory of abstracting and indexing services produced in the UK. 3rd ed. London, British Library, 1986. viii, 238p. £29. (*British Library Information guide,* 2.) ISBN: 0712330801.
Previous eds., 1978, 1983.
430 numbered entries, with titles of services, A-Z. Systematic data on each include subject, scope, sources, language, cost, start, frequency, number of entries, online-access, availability, indexes. Science and technology services are prominent (agriculture: 51 entries; biology: 39; medicine: 36). Broad subject and specific subject indexes; index of authorities (issuing bodies); index of online databases according to processor. Specimen report form questionnaire. Omits ISBN/ISSNs. A valuable research tool. *Class No:* 5(048)(01)

Periodicals

[228]

Nature. Basingstoke, Hants., Macmillan Journals, 1869-. V.1-. Weekly. £245. ISSN: 00280836.
The leading science journal, carrying articles, news and views, short reports of research ('Letters to Nature'), correspondence, and reviews. V.398, 4 March 1999 issue contains 5 signed book reviews. Spring and autumn book supplements provide some 30 signed reviews apiece, prefaced by introductory articles. Contents pages, available on the Internet (http://www.nature.com/), can also be delivered by e-mail to subscribers. Available on CD-ROM - the 1992-1994 archive contains 153 issues (5,500 articles and 16,000 images). Full-text online access is also available to those who subscribe to the paper edition.
Class No: 5(051)

[229]

Science & technology libraries. Binghamton, N.Y., Haworth Press, 1980-. 4pa. $160 (US), $224 (non US). ISSN: 0194262x.
Each issue has contributions on a particular theme (*e.g.* 'Role of computers in sci-tech libraries', v.6(4); 'Role of translations in sci-tech libraries', v.3(2)). Also featured are special papers, *e.g.* 'Information sources in laser science and technology'. A regular section is 'New reference works in science and technology', while v.15(2), 1995 devotes 14p. to 'Electronic sources in science and technology: world wide web'. Reviews are descriptive but do indicate readership.
Class No: 5(051)

[230]

The Scientific journal. Meadows, A.J., *ed.* London, Aslib, 1979. [vii], 300p. graphs, charts, tables. £18; £11. (*Aslib Reader series,* v.2.) ISBN: 0851421180.
50 contributors. 7 parts (24 documented contributions): 1. The development of the scientific journal [1665-1798] - 2. Economics of journal publication (*e.g.* 'Some effects of delay in publication of information in medical journals and implications for the future', with 26 references) ... 4. The refereeing of scientific journals - 5. Characteristics and interrelationships of journals - 6. An alternative viewpoint (*e.g.* 'The deposition of scientific works (the experience of VINITI)') - 7. The future of the scientific journal (*e.g.* 'An on-line scientific journal'). 'Further reading', p.297-8. 'Author index' (*i.e.,* list of contributors). No subject index. An impressive and authoritative survey. *Class No:* 5(051)

Abbreviations & Symbols

[231]

Bibliographic guide for editors & authors. Prepared through the combined efforts of BIOSIS, Chemical Abstracts Service, and Engineering Index, Inc. Washington, American Chemical Society, 1974. 23,362p.
3 sections: 1. Guidelines for the use of the coded bibliographic strip - 2. Bibliographic standards - 3 (362p.). Serial titles, abbreviations and codes (complete titles, title abbreviations and ASTM CODEN abbreviations for *c.*27,700 scientific and technical serials).
Class No: 5(051)(003)

[232]

International CODEN directory. Columbus, Ohio, Chemical Abstracts Service, 1980-. Five yearly (with annual supplements). $1,080 (plus $315 per supplement). ISSN: 03643670.
First published 1963 as *CODEN for periodical titles* (including non-periodical titles and deleted CODEN).
CODEN - a six-character code, the first five characters being letters (*e.g., Government research announcements*: GVRAA; *Technical book review index*: TBRIA), designed for titles of periodicals for computer retrieval, etc. *Class No:* 5(051)(003)

CD-ROM

[233]

ROMULUS. Version 5. Ottawa, Canada Institute for Scientific and Technical Information/National Library of Canada, 1997.
A CD-ROM system for locating serials and ordering documents from Canadian libraries. Contains *c.*14,000 titles, with 65% of the titles covering science, technology, and medicine. 90% of these titles are held by CISTI. Contents pages are added to the database on a weekly basis, while the journal titles are updated 4 times per year, with *c.*400 new titles added each quarter. *Class No:* 5(051)(003.40)

Bibliographies

[234]

BOLTON, H.C. Catalogue of scientific and technical periodicals, 1665-1895, together with chronological tables and a library check-list. 2nd ed. Washington, Smithsonian Institution, 1897 (reprinted New York, Johnson Reprint Corporation, 1965). vii, 1247p. (*Smithsonian Misc. Coll.,* v.40, no.1076.)
First published 1885.
An A-Z title catalogue; pt. 1, a corrected reprint of the 1st ed., listing 4,954 titles; pt. 2, listing over 3,600 new titles. Entry is under earliest title, with later titles listed in chronological order, plus cross-references from later titles, well-known short titles, and names of principal editors. Excludes transactions of learned societies unless later as an independent periodical. Appended chronological table giving publication date of each volume of several hundred journals, 1728-1895. Title index; general subject index; location list for 3,000 titles in *c.*200 US libraries. A valuable checklist for early periodicals not included in the *World list*. *Class No:* 5(051)(01)

[235]

—**SCUDDER, S.H. Catalogue of scientific serials of all countries,** including the transactions of learned societies in the natural, physical and mathematical sciences, 1633-1876. Cambridge, Mass., Harvard Univ., 1879. xii, 358p.
Reprinted New York, Kraus Reprints, 1965.
Lists over 4,400 titles, arranged by country and town of origin, with indexes of towns and titles, and a brief subject index. Excludes serials devoted entirely to medicine, agriculture or technology. Less complete than, but complementary to, H.C. Bolton's *Catalogue*, which includes applied sciences but not publications of learned societies.
Class No: 5(051)(01)

[236]
Current serials received. Boston Spa, British Library Document Supply Centre, [and] London, Science Reference and Information Service. 1986-. Annual. ISSN: 09594914.

First published 1965 as *Current serials received by the N.L.L.*.

1999 ed. (£64) lists *c.*64,000 titles, differentiating (by symbols) between those received at the Document Supply Centre (Boston Spa) and those received at SRIS (London). 3 parts: 1. Current serial titles, except for cyrillic; 2. Cyrillic titles; 3. Cover-to-cover translations of cyrillic serials. *Class No:* 5(051)(01)

[237]
INTERNATIONAL COUNCIL OF SCIENTIFIC UNIONS. Abstracting Board. **International serials catalogue.** Paris, International Council of Scientific Unions Abstracting Board, 1978. 2v. ([x], 521p.).

1. *Catalogue.* 2. *Index/concordance.*

A/Z list of titles of over 25,000 scientific and technical journals 'abstracted and indexed by the member services of the International Council of Scientific Unions Abstracting Board'. Entries include CODEN, ISSN and initials of issuing service, Pt. 2 provides ISSN-CODEN and CODEN-ISSN indexes to the titles in pt. 1. *Class No:* 5(051)(01)

[238]
Journals in translation. Delft, International Translations Centre, 1996. 128, 21p.

First published 1976; 2nd ed. 1978.

'This is a printout of the fully revised diskette version of *Journals in translation*, originally published in book form between 1976 (1st ed.) and 1991 (5th ed.) (*Preface*). Original titles are mostly Russian, plus some Japanese, Chinese, etc. Data on each: start; holdings; brief description; frequency; publisher; former title(s); to be ordered from; held by. Keyword index; Original titles index; Key to publishers and/or distributors. *Class No:* 5(051)(01)

[239]
Journals with translations held at the Science Reference Library. Alexander, B.A. London, Science Reference Library, 1985. [iii], 65p. ISBN: 0712307176.

List of 542 titles held, with subject index and index of original titles. Shelf marks indicated. *Class No:* 5(051)(01)

[240]
Keyword index to serial titles (KIST). Boston Spa, British Library Document Supply Centre, 1980-. 4pa. Set of 48x microfiche. £330pa. plus VAT. ISSN: 01439553.

A keyword union list of current and non-current holdings of serials at the BLDSC, Boston Spa, and at the Science Reference and Information Service, plus the Science Museum, London. Other libraries' holdings are to be included. *Class No:* 5(051)(01)

[241]
OXFORD UNIVERSITY. Bodleian Library. **Union list of serials in the science area, Oxford.** Stage II (incorporating Stage I). Oxford, Bodleian Library, 1970. xvii, 598p. (*1st supplement 1971. v, 240p.*)

Stage I, 1968.

Stage II lists *c.*15,000 titles in 50 Oxford libraries. 'This stage of the *Union list* does NOT record all the serials in the Radcliffe Science Library (RSL) but those on the open shelves together with a considerable proportion of those on the stack' (prefatory note). Planned in 3 stages, each to include and amplify its predecessor.

The four richest collections of scientific serials in the UK are cited as the Radcliffe Science Library, BLLD, Science Museum Library and Science Reference Library. *Class No:* 5(051)(01)

[242]
Scientific serials in Australian libraries. Conochie, J.A., *ed.* Melbourne, Commonwealth Scientific and industrial Research Organization [CSIRO], 1976. 3v. Loose-leaf.

Supersedes *Union catalogue of scientific and technical periodicals in the libraries of Australia* (2nd ed., edited by E.R. Pitt. 1951) and *New titles: 1946-52 supplement* (compiled by A.L. Kent. 1954).

Lists *c.*60,000 scientific and technical periodicals and serial titles held in 180 Australian libraries. *Class No:* 5(051)(01)

[243]
Ulrich's international periodicals directory. New Providence, N.J., etc., Bowker. Annual. ISSN: 00000175.

First published 1932. Incorporates *Ulrich's irregular series and annuals*.

The 36th ed., 1998 (5v. 11,000p. $460) is an international directory of *c.*160,000 periodicals arranged A-Z under 869 subject headings, with 7,000 titles new to this edition. Much detail given in concise form, including presence of book reviews, whether indexed/abstracted or online. Also an appended section, 'Cessations' (*c.*9,586 entries) and a full title index. Scientific and technical titles figure prominently. Gives addresses for *c.*80,000 publishers from 200 countries. Available on CD-ROM ($595), microfiche, and online via DIALOG. A vital reference tool, updated by supplements 3 times a year. *Class No:* 5(051)(01)

[244]
World list of scientific periodicals published in the years 1900-1960. 4th ed. London, Butterworth, 1963-65.

First published in 1925-27.

The 4th ed. 'the last to appear in this format' listed 59,961 numbered titles (A-E, F-P, Q-Z, plus 'Periodic international congresses'). Although thereafter incorporated into *British union-catalogue: New periodical titles*; the *World list* appeared as an annual supplement for a time, with 1960-68 (1970) and 1969-73 (1976).

Entry is under title as published, with adequate cross-references. Holdings of nearly 300 libraries, including BLDSC, Boston Spa. Unlocated items are also listed. A major location list in its day. *Class No:* 5(051)(01)

Histories

[245]
HOUGHTON, B. Scientific periodicals: their historical development, characteristics and control. London, Bingley, 1975. 156p. diagrs.

In 3 parts: 1. History and development of scientific periodicals, 1663 to the present day - 2. Select list of periodicals current, grouped by subject area and international in origin - 3. Evaluation of select list by reference to usage, citations and length of useful life. 'Scientific periodical literature has not hitherto been analysed from the librarian's point of view on a comparable scale' (*British book news*, July 1975, p.480). *Class No:* 5(051)(091)

[246]
KRONICK, D.A. A History of scientific and technical periodicals: the origin and development of the scientific and technical press, 1665-1790. 2nd ed. Metuchen, N.J., Scarecrow Press, 1976. xvi, 356p.

First published 1962.

A study of origins and development in the social and intellectual setting of the time, as well as treating the various types of periodical, - the substantive journal, proceedings of scientific societies, abstracts and review journals, plus the bibliographical apparatus affording access to them. Bibliography. Subject and title indexes. *Class No:* 5(051)(091)

Progress Reports

[247]
UNITED NATIONS. Educational, Scientific and Cultural Organization. **List of annual reviews of progress in science and technology.** [Liste de "mises au point" annuelles sur les progrès de la science et de la technologie.] 3rd ed. Paris, Unesco, 1981. 43p.

First published 1965.

Classed arrangement of several hundred 'annual series containing papers which review fairly narrow topics within the broader subject designated by the serial title' (*Introduction*). Appended list of publishers. No index. *Class No:* 5(055)

Yearbooks & Directories

[248]
Consultants and consulting organizations directory: a reference guide to concerns and individuals engaged in consultation for business, industry, and government. Detroit, Mich., Gale. Annual. ISSN: 01961292.

First published 1966.

1996 ed. gives details of more than 23,000 firms and individuals. Arranged alphabetically under 14 general subject areas, with more than 400 specialties represented. Available online.

New consultants (2pa.) is issued between editions of the main directory. *Class No:* 5(058)

[249]
Directory of technical and scientific directories: a world bibliographic guide to medical, agricultural, industrial and natural science directories. 6th ed. London, Longman; Phoenix, Ariz., Oryx Press, 1989. 302p. £99. (*Reference on research.*) ISBN: 0582044294; 0897746376, US ed.

First published as *Directory of scientific directories* in 1969.

In addition to directories, dictionaries, yearbooks, encyclopaedias, handbooks and bibliographies are included. Grouped according to subject headings: general science and technology; agriculture and the environment, chemical and materials technology; computer and electronic sciences; earth and space studies; engineering; industry; medical and biological sciences; physics and energy technology. 3 indexes: author, editor and compiler; directory titles; publishers' addresses. The entries have been compiled from information gleaned from questionnaires, publishers' catalogues and direct enquiries. Where contents of directories are listed there is no evaluative comment. *Class No:* 5(058)

[250]
Guide to directories at the Science Reference and Information Service. 3rd ed. London, British Library, SRIS, 1992. v,137p. £39. ISBN: 071230777x.

First published 1986.

Over 2,500 entries covering 'sciences, professional trades, business people and telecommunications' (*Introduction*). Classified listing; title and subject indexes. *Class No:* 5(058)

[251]
INTERNATIONAL COUNCIL OF SCIENTIFIC UNIONS. Year book. Paris, ICSU Secretariat, 1954-. Annual. £42.50. ISSN: 00744387.

Provides historical and descriptive data of very ICSU member body, with names and contact details of *c.*2,000 office-bearers. Sections include: Standing committees and ad hoc groups - National participation ... Interdisciplinary ICSU bodies - Joint programmes. Addresses of international organizations... Alphabetical address list. Index. *Class No:* 5(058)

[252]
McGraw-Hill yearbook of science and technology: comprehensive coverage of the important events of the year, as compiled by the staff of the McGraw-Hill Encyclopedia of Science and Technology. New York, etc., McGraw-Hill, 1961-. Annual. illus., diagrs., graphs, tables, maps. ISSN: 00762016.

The 1999 annual (1998. 464p. $125) has *c.*250 contributors; *c.*250 illustrations. Updates the *McGraw-Hill encyclopedia of science and technology* (*q.v.*) by presenting new developments and topics, *e.g.* Genetically modified crops. Detailed, analytical index.
Class No: 5(058)

[253]
Science year: the World Book science annual - a review of science and technology during the ... school year. Chicago, Ill., World Book-Childcraft International, Inc., 1965-. illus. (mostly col.). Price varies. ISSN: 00807621.

First published 1965.

Science year, 1986 (1985. 400p. $29.95) has 14 'special reports' (*e.g.* 'Cleaning up the River Thames'), followed by 'Science file', - 39 articles, A-Z, plus 6 'close-ups' (*e.g.* 'Compact disk players'). Appendices include 'People in science' and 'World Book supplement' (2 reviewed articles from the 1985 ed. of *World Book encyclopedia*). Detailed index, p.385-396. Fully illustrated and captioned.

Review of the year in science aimed at the younger reader, with a good index. *Class No:* 5(058)

[254]
Yearbook of science and the future. Chicago, Ill., London, etc., Encyclopaedia Britannica, Inc., 1972-. col. illus., diagrs., tables. £75 (1999 ed.). ISSN: 00963291.

First half of the *Yearbook* contains lengthy feature articles on current scientific topics (*e.g.* 'Star maps of the ancient orient'; 'The great consciousness debate'; 'Science for the soldier; the US Army's Natick Labs.' in the 1999 edition). The second half concentrates on the main scientific events and achievements of the year. Many illustrations, most of them in colour. Three-year cumulative index. *Class No:* 5(058)

Teaching Materials

[255]
The New illustrated science and invention encyclopedia : how it works. New York, Stuttman, 1994. 28v. illus. (incl. col.). ISBN: 086307491x.

Based on *How it works: the illustrated encyclopedia of science and technology* (1978), but simplified and Americanized for children. Formerly *Growing up with science: the illustrated encyclopedia of inventions* (1984. 25v.). 'Revised' ed., 1988.

Concerns the 'hows', 'whats' and 'whys' of the scientific world in an A-Z sequence covering all aspects of natural science, engineering and mechanics. Of a previous ed., 'An up-to-date inviting set of scientific and technical information for elementary and junior high school children, with a good emphasis on graphics' (*Reference books bulletin*, 1984/1985, p.66). *Class No:* 5(072)

[256]
Oxford illustrated encyclopedia. Oxford, University Press, 1985-93. 8v. illus. (mostly col.).

8v. 1. *The physical world;* edited by V. Fuchs. 1985. 384p. £19.50. 2. *The natural world;* edited by M. Coe. 1985. 384p. £19.50. 3. *World history - from earliest times to 1800.* 400p. 1988. £22.50. 4. *World history - from 1800 to the present day.* 400p. 1988. £22.50. 5. *The arts.* 512p. 1990. £25. 6. *Invention and technology.* 392p. 1992. £25. 7. *Peoples and cultures.* 392p. 1992. £25. 8. *The universe.* 300p. 1993. £19.95.

V.1-2 each carry *c.*2,500 entries, A-Z. V.1 concerns mathematics, chemistry, physics, geology and physical geography. V.2, living and extinct animal and plant species, plus specific representative organisms. Biographical entries figure; cross-references. Very well illustrated. No index or bibliographies. Aimed at parents and their

....(contd.)
children of 15 or over. For school library reference collections, easing the load of demand for articles in general encyclopedias.

Replaces *Oxford junior encyclopaedia* (2nd ed. OUP, 1964. Corrected reprint, 1974. 13v.). *Class No:* 5(072)

[257]
PILGER, M.A. Science experiments index for young people. 2nd ed. Englewood, Colo., Libraries Unlimited, 1996. 504p. $60. ISBN: 1563083418.

First published 1988.

1,527 titles are included in this index providing subject access to experiments and demonstrations found in elementary and intermediate-level science books. Standard bibliographic information is given, with about two-thirds of the entries published in the 1980s and 1990s. For school and public libraries. *Class No:* 5(072)

[258]
Science experiments on file experiments, demonstrations and projects for school and home. Bruce, K., *and others*. New York, Facts on File, 1989. 100p. illus., looseleaf. $145. ISBN: 081601888x.

Contains 84 science experiments, demonstrations and projects written by science teachers. 4 sections: earth sciences, biology, physical science/chemistry, and physics. Description of each experiment contains: introduction, time and materials required, safety precautions, step-by-step procedure and analysis. Many line drawings and charts. Appendices index the experiments by grade level, supervision requirements, setting (school or home), number of participants and lists experiments which can be completed in less than an hour. List of sources of materials and equipment. Subject index (no cross-references). For public and school libraries. *Class No:* 5(072)

[259]
—**Junior science experiments on file.** New York, Facts on File, 1994. loose-leaf. illus. charts. tables. $155. ISBN: 0816029210.

Same format as *Science experiments on file*, aimed at primary and elementary school libraries. *Class No:* 5(072)

Bibliographies

[260]
Appraisal: science books for young people. Boston, Mass., Children's Science Book Review Committee, 1967-. v.1-. 4pa. $46 (US), $57 (non US). ISSN: 00037052.

Critical reviews of 40-50 books per issue, on both pure and applied science. Each book is assessed by a subject specialist as well as a librarian; ratings extend from 'excellent' to 'unsatisfactory'. Age range is also indicated. A special section deals with series. v.28(4), Fall 1995 includes 'Supporting environmental education through poetry'. 'Candid authoritative and scrupulous analysis' (*RQ*, v. 7(4), Summer 1968, p.187-8). Addressed to children's librarians, teachers and other providers of books for young people. *Class No:* 5(072)(01)

[261]
School science review. Hatfield (Herts.), Association for Science Education, 1920-. v.1-. 4pa. £60 (UK), £84 (abroad). ISSN: 00366811.

No. 290, 1998 includes articles such as 'The corporate infiltration of science education', 'Experiments with zeolites', and 'Some of Bunsen's other inventions'. 'Reviews of books', p.127-31, which gives indication as to level of readership, *e.g.* primary class teacher, students, young readers, is followed by a review of computer software. Recent issues are available on the Internet at: http://www.ase.org.uk/publish/jnews/ssr/index.html. *Class No:* 5(072)(01)

[262]
Science & technology in fact and fiction: a guide to children's books. Kennedy, D.M., *and others*. New Providence, N.J., Bowker, 1990. 319p. $35. ISBN: 0835227081.

*c.*350 fiction and non-fiction books for children are listed. Entries arranged alphabetically by the author's surname. Bibliographic details and an authoritative evaluation are given. Five indexes: author; title; illustrator; subject; readability. Contains fewer entries than *Museum of Science and Technology basic list of children's science books* but includes fiction, items for younger children and has lengthier annotations.

By the same author, *Science & technology in fact and fiction: a guide to children's books and young adult books* (1990. 2v. 331p. $59.95) and *Science & technology in fact and fiction: a guide to young adult books* (1990. 363p. $36). *Class No:* 5(072)(01)

Handbooks & Manuals

[263]

ASE secondary science teachers' handbook. Hemel Hempstead, Simon and Schuster Education, 1993. 380p. diagrs., charts, tables. £18. ISBN: 0748722041.

Gives practical information for science teachers, including advice on the practical side of teaching science using different methods, assessment and evaluation, and cross-curricular themes. For those teaching 11-18 year-olds. *Class No:* 5(072)(035)

[264]

—**ASE primary science teachers' handbook.** 2nd ed. Cheltenham, Stanley Thornes, 1995. viii,262p. diagrs., charts, tables. ISBN: 074872270x.

First published 1993.

Gives practical information for science teachers teaching young school children. *Class No:* 5(072)(035)

Reviews & Abstracts

[265]

Science books & films. Washington, American Association for the Advancement of Science, 1975-. V.11-. 9pa. ISSN: 0098342x.

Continues *AAAS science books: a quarterly review* (V.1-10, 1965-75), with assessments and ratings of scientific and technical books, audio-visual material, and software. *Class No:* 5(072)(048)

Yearbooks & Directories

[266]

Sourcebook for out-of-school science and technology education. Paris, UNESCO, 1986. 202p. illus. ISBN: 9231023861.

Translated into 27 languages.

Describes 'various activities and programmes in out-of-school science and technology education, including clubs, societies and congresses for young scientists, science fairs, project work, olympiads and other contests, visits, science camps and excursions' (*Unesco Publications catalogue Supplement* 1986, p.18).
Class No: 5(072)(058)

Quotations

[267]

Isaac Asimov's book of science and nature quotations. Asimov, I. *and* Shulman, J.A., *eds.* New York, Weidenfeld and Nicolson, 1988. 360p. £12.95. ISBN: 1555841112.

*c.*2,000 quotations in 86 different subject areas (Aeronautics ... Zoology). Quotations arranged chronologically within each subject by the date of the quotation or, if unavailable, by the date of birth of the speaker. Brief description of the speaker is also given. Index of speaker names. *Class No:* 5(082.2)

[268]

MacKAY, A.L. A Dictionary of scientific quotations. Bristol, Adam Hilger, 1991. xii,297p. £9.50. ISBN: 0750301066.

Second and expanded edition of *A Harvest of a quiet eye* (Institute of Physics, 1977).

2,130 quotations, epigrams and aphorisms, under authors, Abelson ... Zuckerman, plus entries for 'Anonymous' and 'Bible'. Authors' dates and sources are given. Quotations in foreign languages appear in translation, with or without the original. Subject and first word of title index. *Class No:* 5(082.2)

Tables & Data Books

[269]

BALLENTYNE, D.W.G. *and* **LOVETT, D.R. A Dictionary of named effects and laws in chemistry, physics and mathematics.** 4th ed. London, Chapman & Hall, 1980. viii, 346p. diagrs., tables, chemical structures. £17.95. ISBN: 0412223902.

First published 1958.

Defines and describes precisely *c.*1,500 effects, laws, units and other phenomena. The dictionary, p.1-320 (Abbe number ... Zinkl's Rule). 'Mossbauer effect': ½p. Appendix: A list of named units; Table of organic compounds. In this edition most entries have received some revision. In particular, units are now in SI units, wherever possible. *Class No:* 5(083)

[270]

Basic science and technology statistics. [Statistiques de base de la science et de la technologie.] Paris, OECD, 1997. 536p. tables. ISBN: 926405538x.

Published every two years.

Contains '22 country tables giving the main basic statistical series selected from the OECD Scientific and Technological Indicators data bases, of which 18 concern resources devoted to research and experimental development and four indicators of the output of scientific and technological activities' (*Foreword*). Available on diskette (annual), while the complete database is available on magnetic tape. *Class No:* 5(083)

[271]

BRITISH STANDARDS INSTITUTION. Conversion factors and tables. Basis of tables. Conversion factors. Part 1. London, BSI, 1974. 104p. AMD 4153. 1974. Supplement, no. 1. 1967. AMD 342,1255. £52; £52, supp. (*BS 350. Part 1: 1974.*)

Part 1 provides conversion factors for metrology, mechanics, heat, extended basic information units (including SI, metric technical, imperial). Tables of conversion factors showing inter-relationship of units. Letter symbols for avery units. Omits purely electrical units. *Supplement no. 1* adds tables for 51 conversions, plus 36 tables for conversion to conversion to and from SI units. BS 350. Part 2 withdrawn. *Class No:* 5(083)

[272]

CODATA. Inventory of data sources in science and technology: a preliminary survey. Paris, Unesco, 1983. [vii], 229p. $14. ISBN: 923102048x.

An inventory of 652 international sources in 94 countries. 6 sections: 1. Renewable energy sources - 2. Fertilizers - 3. Hydrological sciences and water resources - 4. Nutrition - 5. Pesticides - 6. Soil science. Indexes to institutions, centres, etc.; to centres by country; to personal names; to subjects. Aimed at scientists, engineers and information specialists, particularly those in developing countries.

CODATA bulletin (Oxford, Pergamon Press, 1984. 6pa.) incorporates the *Inventory*.

CODATA international conferences (*e.g.* 10th Conference, on generation, compilation, evaluation and dissemination of data for science and technology. *Proceedings*. North Holland, 1987) are fruitful sources of new data. *Class No:* 5(083)

[273]

Data activities: a guide to scientific and technical data collection in the United Kingdom. Reynard, K.W., *ed.* London, Aslib, 1993. ix,89p. £23. ISBN: 0851422942.

306 entries, including computerized and hard copy data collections. Details for each entry include name, address, telex, fax, and telephone numbers, acronym, type of organization, subject, coverage, access. Acronyms, p.79-81. Index, p.83-9. *Class No:* 5(083)

[274]

Handbooks and tables in science and technology. Powell, R.H., *ed.* 3rd ed. Phoenix, Oryx, 1994. viii,359p. $95. ISBN: 0897745345.

First published 1970.

Covers 3,662 handbooks and tables (mainly in English) in science, technology, and medicine. Almost 400 titles have been dropped from this edition and 650 new ones added. Annotations are between 50-75 words in length. Data on each has complete bibliographic citation and many annotations which briefly describe the intellectual content of the handbook and tables. Keyword, author/editor, and title indexes. *Class No:* 5(083)

[275]

International critical tables of numerical data, physics, chemistry and technology; prepared under the auspices of the International Research Council and the National Academy of Sciences. New York, etc., McGraw-Hill, 1926-33. 7v. and index. tables, graphs, charts.

Each volume has explanatory text and contents lists in four languages, English, French, German and Italian. Data are selected from v. 1-7 (1910-26) of *Tables annuelles de constants et données numériques de chimie, de physique et de technologie* (Paris, Gauthier-Villars; Chicago, Univ. of Chicago Press (v. 1-11, pt. 1. 1912-37). Now largely obsolete and incomplete, but important as the work of experts who critically examined the data before including it. The accompanying index covers subject data in detail. *Class No:* 5(083)

[276]

JERRARD, H.G. *and* **McNEILL, D.B. Dictionary of scientific units,** including dimensionless numbers and scales. 6th ed. London, Chapman & Hall, 1992. 255p. tables. £15.95. ISBN: 0412467208.

First published 1963.

Contains *c.*950 units, supported by *c.*650 references. The dictionary, Abampere ... Zhubov scale, p.9-190. 'Beaufort scale': nearly 1p. 5 appendices (*e.g.* 1. Fundamental physical constants; 2. Standardization committees and conferences). References, p.221-39. Detailed analytical index, p.241-55. *Class No:* 5(083)

[277]

LANDOLF, H.H. *and* **BÖRNSTEIN, R. Zahlenwerte und Funktionen aus Naturwissenschaften und Technik.** Neue Serie. [Numerical data and functional relationships in science and technology.] Berlin, Springer Verlag, 1961-. tables, graphs.

Continues Landolf-Börnstein's *Zahlenwerte und Funktionen aus Physik, Chemie, Astronomie, Geophysik und Technik* (6. Aufl. 1950-80. 4v. in 26).

The *Neue Serie* runs to 7 groups, compared with the previous four. Also, the text is in English (but sometimes in both German and English): 1. *Nuclear and particle physics*. 2. *Atomic and nucleic physics*. 3. *Crystal and solid state physics*. 4. *Macroscopic and technical properties of matter*. 5. *Geophysics and space research*. 6. *Astronomy, astrophysics and space research*. 7. *Biophysics*.

....*(contd.)*

Tabular and graphic data on the grand scale, the series now running to about 100v., with new volumes appearing as subjects develop or new fields arise. *Class No:* 5(083)

[278]

MOSES, A.J. The Practicing scientist's tables: a guide for physical and terrestrial scientists and engineers. New York, London, etc., Van Nostrand Reinhold, 1978. x, [i], 1292p. tables. ISBN: 0442255845.

12 chapters (1. Introduction - 2. Properties of the elements - 3. Properties of organic compounds ... 10. Properties of superconductors - 11. Properties of the environment - 12. Properties of miscellaneous materials (*e.g.* man-made organic fibres)). Appendix A. List of registered trademarks; B. Table of isotopes. Virtually all the text is in tabular data form. Analytical index. *Class No:* 5(083)

[279]

Tables of physical and chemical constants. Kaye, G.W.C. *and* Laby, T.H., *comps.* 16th ed. London & New York, Longman, 1995. [xi], 611p. graphs, tables. ISBN: 0582226295.

75 contributors. 8 main sections: 1. Units and fundamental constants - 2. General physics - 3. Chemistry - 4. Atomic and nuclear physics - 5. Miscellaneous engineering data - 6. Statistical methods for the treatment of experimental data - 7. Laboratory safety - 8. Introduction to quality assurance of measurements. Analytical index. Subsection references. All tabulated values appear in SI units. Originally compiled by G.W.C. Kaye and T.H. Laby (cover title is 'Kaye and Laby'), but this edition prepared by an editorial committee. Essential for any reference library. *Class No:* 5(083)

Illustrations

[280]

The Guild handbook of scientific illustration. Hodges, E.R.S., *ed.* New York, Van Nostrand Reinhold, 1989. 575p. illus. $85.95. ISBN: 0442236816.

Book sponsored by the Guild of Natural Science Illustrators. Includes illustration techniques using various media, *e.g.* ink, watercolour, pencil and acrylics. Suggestions on how to handle, measure, preserve and draw various subjects, *e.g.* plants, mammals, birds, fossils, amphibians and reptiles. List of material and equipment suppliers is given. Lengthy bibliography. Well illustrated. *Class No:* 5(084.1)

Chronologies

[281]

ASIMOV, I. Asimov's chronology of science and discovery. 2nd ed. New York, Harper Collins, 1994. 790p. £25.00. ISBN: 0062701134.

1,500 entries listed in chronological order (Bipedality, 4,000,000 BC ... Very Long Baseline Array, 1993). Entries vary from a few lines to two pages - in general, longer than those in *Milestones in science and technology*, by E. Mount and B.A. List (Phoenix, Ariz., Oryx Press, 1987. 141p.) Subject and name indexes. No bibliographies but 65 line drawings added for this edition. *Class No:* 5(090)

[282]

HELLEMANS, A. *and* BUNCH, B. The Timetables of science: a chronology of the most important people and events in the history of science. London, Sidgwick & Jackson, 1989. vii,656p. tables. ISBN: 0283999268.

Records *c.*10,000 separate events, arranged chronologically, under broad subject areas, *e.g.* astronomy, life science, mathematics, physical science, technology. Nine broad overviews: Science before there were scientists: 2,400,000-599 BC ... The Newtonian epoch: 1660-1734 ... Science after World War II: 1946-1988. Name and subject indexes. *Class No:* 5(090)

[283]

PARKINSON, C. Breakthroughs: a chronology of great achievements in science and mathematics 1200-1930. London, Mansell, 1985. xi,576p. ISBN: 072011800x.

Records several thousand events chronologically, by year, under broad subject areas. Chronology, p.1-511. Sources, p.512-21. Name and subject indexes. *Class No:* 5(090)

Histories

Bibliographies

[284]

AMERICAN PHILOSOPHICAL SOCIETY. Library. Catalog of books in the American Philosophical Society Library. Westport, Conn., Greenwood Press, [1970]. 28v. ISBN: 0837132665.

Photolithographed reproduction of the Library's card catalogue. Concentrates 'on particular aspects of the history of science and selected fields' (*Introduction*). *Class No:* 5(091)(01)

[285]

CORSI, P. *and* WEINDLING, P. Information sources in the history of science and medicine. London, Butterworth Scientific, 1983. xvi, 531p. facsims., diagrs. £43. (*Butterworths guides to information sources.*) ISBN: 0408107642.

21 contributors; 24 documented chapters, in 4 parts. Part 1 consists of general chapters on the history of science and relations with associated areas (*e.g.* anthropology, religion). Part 2, on major institutions and research methods. Part 3 (chapters 11-19), historical range of modern sciences and developments. Part 4 reviews status of non-European developments - US, Indian, Islamic and Chinese, African. Chapter 8: 'Guide to bibliographical sources', p.137-56; Chapter 19: Medicine since 1500, p.378-407, has bibliography, p.393-407. List of journals, p.501-8. Analytical subject index, including names of authors and institutions, p.509-31. 'Highly recommended' (*Choice*, v. 21 (1), September 1983, p.64). *Class No:* 5(091)(01)

[286]

Horus: a guide to the history of science: a first guide for the study of the history of science, with introductory essays on science and tradition. Sarton, G., *comp.* Waltham, Mass., Chronica Botanica Co., 1952. xviii, 316p.

Greatly expanded from the bibliography in his *Study of the history of science* (Cambridge, Mass., Harvard Univ. Press, 1936), p.53-70, with annotations in Sarton's characteristic style.

Includes sections for the history of science in special countries, in special cultural groups, and for the history of special sciences. Also a list of journals on the history and philosophy of science, and lists of institutes, museums, libraries and international congresses. An important bibliographic guide, not least for the introductory notes to each chapter. Well documented. *Class No:* 5(091)(01)

[287]

ISIS cumulative bibliography: a bibliography of the history of science, formed from *ISIS* critical bibliographies, 1-90, 1913-65. Whitrow, M., *ed.* London, Mansell, in conjunction with the History of Science Society, 1971-84. 6v. £270.

1. *Personalities, A-J.* 1971. £90.
2. *Personalities, K-Z, and institutions, A-Z.* 1971.
3. *Subjects.* 1976. 772p. £90.
4. *Civilizations and periods, Prehistory to Middle Ages.* 1982.
5. *Civilizations and periods, 18th to 19th centuries. Addenda to v.1-3,* 1982. £176 (v.4/5).
6. *Author index.* 1984. 350p. £70.

'The result of weeding, tidying and sorting the *ISIS* Critical Bibliographies 1-90' (Jayawardene, S.A. *Reference books for the historian of science*). The *Personalities* section has nearly 40,000 entries for 10,000 individuals. 'Aristotle': *c.*450 entries; 'Royal Society': 123 entries. 'The whole series will be an essential purchase for any library catering for the needs of historians of events' (*British book news*, August 1977, p.598). *Class No:* 5(091)(01)

[288]

—ISIS cumulative bibliography, 1966-75: a bibliography of the history of science formed from ISIS critical bibliographies 91-100, indexing literature published from 1965 through 1974. Neu, J., *ed.* London, Mansell, in conjunction with the History of Science Society, 1980-85. 2v.

1. *Personalities and institutions.* 1980. 514p. £90.
2. *Subjects, periods and civilizations.* 1985. 720p. £90.

Follows the pattern of the earlier set. V.2 includes a bibliographic index to book reviews. 'Its thoroughness, coupled with its layout and indexes, confirm both its scholarly standing and its usefulness for more general enquiries' (*Library review*, v.35(2), Summer 1986, p.149). *Class No:* 5(091)(01)

[289]

—ISIS cumulative bibliography, 1976-85: a bibliography of the history of science formed from ISIS critical bibliographies 101-110, indexing literature published from 1975 through 1984. Neu, J., *ed.* London, Mansell in conjunction with the History of Science Society, 1990. 2v.

V.1. *Persons and institutions.* 800p. £60. V.2. *Subjects, periods, and civilizations.* 80p. £60.

Continues this essential work. *Isis current bibliography of the history of science and its cultural influences: 1994* (300p.) was published as a supplement to *Isis*, v.85. *Class No:* 5(091)(01)

[290]

—ISIS cumulative bibliography, 1986-95. Whitrow, M., *ed.* London, Mansell in conjunction with the History of Science Society, 1997. 4v. (2,355p.) £190; $249.95. ISBN: 0881351318.

V.1. *Persons: A-L.* 496p. V.2. *Persons: M-Z; Institutions.* 480p. V.3 *Subjects, time periods: antiquity-18th century.* 640p. V.4 *Time periods: 19th-20th centuries, book reviews.* 739p.

Continues this essential work. Cumulates material listed listed from 1986-1995. A huge increase in literature has necessitated a 4v. work. *Class No:* 5(091)(01)

[291]
JAYAWARDENE, S.A., *comp.* **Reference books for the historian of science:** a handlist. London, Science Museum, 1982. xi, 229p. £2.50. (*Science Museum Library, Occasional publications, 2.*) ISBN: 0901805149.

1,034 numbered entries, some of them annotated, in 3 parts (44 chapters): 1. The history of sciences and its sources - 2. History related subjects - 3. General reference. Author/title index; analytical subject index. Wide-ranging, *e.g.* on catalogues of scientific books, manuscripts and archives, societies. Based on Science Museum Library holdings. 'This handlist provides an invaluable foundation for researchers' (*Natural history book reviews*, v.6 (3/4), 1983, p.145). *Class No:* 5(091)(01)

[292]
—RIDER, K.J. History of science and technology: a select bibliography for students. 2nd ed. London, Library Association, 1970. 75p.
First published 1967.

Includes 353 numbered and annotated entries. 'History of science', items 1-173; 'History of technology', items 174-353; systematic subdivision by periods and subjects. Includes medicine for the first time, but excludes commercial history of industry. Scarcity of material on agricultural and textile history. Index, p.71-75. Largely material in English. *Class No:* 5(091)(01)

[293]
ROLLER, D.H.D. *and* GOODMAN, M.M. **The Catalogue of the history of science collections of the University of Oklahoma Libraries.** London, Mansell, 1976. 2v. (1212p).

39,000 main entries; under authors, A-Z; also subject entries and cross-references. 'A very important list for the history of science' (*British book news*, December 1976, p.900). *Class No:* 5(091)(01)

[294]
SUMMERS, A. **How to find source materials: British Library collections on the history and culture of science, technology and medicine.** London, British Library, 1996. 37p. £10. (*How to find series.*) ISBN: 0712308350.

Guide to the resources of the British Library - printed books, newspapers, etc., and special collections. Includes the Document Supply Centre, Map Library, etc. Well laid out. *Class No:* 5(091)(01)

[295]
THORNTON, J.L. *and* TULLY, R.I.J. **Scientific books, libraries and collectors:** a study of bibliography and the book trade in relation to science. 3rd rev. ed. London, Library Association Publishing, 1971. iv, 508p. Supplement to third edition, 1969-75, 1978, vi, 172p. ISBN: 0853654247; 0853659206.
First published 1954.

12 chapters, providing 'an introductory history of the production, distribution and storage of scientific literature from the earliest times' (*Preface*, 1954). The rise of scientific societies, growth of periodical literature, scientific publishing and bookselling, and scientific libraries. Extensive author bibliography, p.381-465; detailed index, p.467-508.

The 1969-75 *Supplement* updates, in 12 chapters. Bibliography, p.117-56 (*c.*800 items). Detailed index. 'A marvel of compression and orderly discipline' (*Annals of science*, v.36, 1979, p.417), although almost restricted to Western science (especially British and American authors and collections) and medicine. *Class No:* 5(091)(01)

Encyclopaedias & Dictionaries

[296]
Dictionary of the history of science. Bynum, W.F., *ed.* Princeton, N.J., Princeton Univ. Press; London, Macmillan, 1981. xxxi, 494p. $75; $17.95. ISBN: 0691023840.

700 articles by 95 scholars, plus 10 subject editors, mostly British. Coverage: pure science, human science and medicine. Basically a dictionary of the leading ideas and concepts of Western science developed over the last five centuries. Entries usually carry brief references. Appended list of 800 scientists, cross-referenced to entries. Bibliography of 130 reference works and monographs. 'This scholarly, high quality dictionary' (*Wilson library bulletin*, March 1982, p.542). *Class No:* 5(091)(03)

[297]
Encyclopaedia of the history of science, technology and medicine in non-Western cultures. Selin, H., *ed.* Boston, Kluwer, 1996. 1117p. illus. £285; $420. ISBN: 0792340663.

*c.*600 entries, 270 contributors. Entries, arranged A-Z, can be brief or in-depth essays several pages in length. Further reading lists are attached to each entry. For public and academic libraries. *Class No:* 5(091)(03)

[298]
MAYERHÖFER, J. **Lexikon der Geschichte der Naturwissenschaften:** Biographien, Sachwörter and Bibliographien. Vienna, Hollinek, 1959-76. Lfg.1-8.
Bd.1 (Lfg.1-6), Lfg.7-8. A - Edelstein.

Lfg.1. has a 110p. introduction to the age of scientific research, with appended bibliography. Signed and documented articles follow, on scientists and scientific topics (*e.g.* 'Aristotle' p.259-75, with 7p. of bibliography, in small type; 'Darwin', p.718-26, with 4p. of bibliography). Numerous cross-references. The final article, on 'Edelstein', left unfinished, was completed in the continuation to the *Lexikon*. *Class No:* 5(091)(03)

[299]
—Archiv der Geschichte der Naturwissenschaften: Biographien, Sachwörter, und Bibliographien. Vienna, Hollinek, 1980-. Heft 1-. Loose-leaf. Irreg.

The continuation of the *Lexikon*. *Class No:* 5(091)(03)

Handbooks & Manuals

[300]
Album of science. New York, Scribner's, 1978-89. 5v.(1789p.) illus., facsims. ISBN: 0684190745, set.

1. *Album of science: Antiquity and the Middle Ages*, by J.E. Murdoch. 1984. xii, 402p. $80.

2. *Album of science: From Leonardo to Lavoisier, 1450-1800,* I.B. Cohen, general editor. 1980. xiii, 333p. $80.

3. *Album of science: The nineteenth century*, by L.P. Williams. 1978. xv, 413p. $80.

Album of science: The biological sciences in the twentieth century, by M. Borrell. 1989. 306p. $80.

Album of science: The physical sciences in the twentieth century, by O. Gingerich. 1989. 306p. $80.

V.3 has 6 parts: 1. The environment of science - 2. The world of nineteenth century science - 3. Man - 4. The living world - 5. Atoms and molecules and sources - 6. The marvels of science. Bibliography, p.383. Index (to text & illus.), p.389-413. Essentially a pictorial record, with nearly 600 illus. (the 5v. set contains more than 2,300 illustrations), and facsims. *Class No:* 5(091)(035)

[301]
BRUNO, L.C. **Science & technology firsts.** New York, Gale, 1997. 636p. illus. £50; $65. ISBN: 0787602566.

*c.*4,000 entries arranged by subject, *e.g.* agriculture, physics, transport. Within each subject the brief entries are arranged chronologically. *c.*200 photographs. Subject and name index. Bibliography. Does not claim to be a comprehensive history of science, often ignoring important scientific events and people because they weren't 'firsts', but a useful addition to public and academic library reference sections.

A 2v. abridged version, *Science and technology breakthroughs: from the wheel to the world wide web* , aimed at school children, was published in 1998 (£39.50; $55). *Class No:* 5(091)(035)

[302]
BRUNO, L.C. **The Tradition of science:** landmarks of Western Science in the collection of the Library of Congress. Washington, Library of Congress, 1987. xi,351p. illus., facsims. $30. ISBN: 0844405280.

8 chapters: Astronomy - Botany - Zoology - Medicine - Chemistry - Geology - Mathematics - Physics. Epilogue. Chapter bibliographies, p.299-333. Detailed, analytical index, p.385-51. *Class No:* 5(091)(035)

[303]
DARMSTAEDTER, L. **Ludwig Darmstaedter's Handbuch zur Geschichte der Naturwissenschaften** und der Technik in chronologischer Darstellung. 2. ungearb. und verm. aufl. Berlin, Springer, 1908. x,ii, 1262. 127p. (Reprinted New York, Kraus, 1960).

Brief descriptions, chronologically arranged, of 13,000 scientific discoveries and inventions, from 3500 BC to the year of publication. Name and subject indexes. *Class No:* 5(091)(035)

[304]
—WEISS, B. Wie finde ich Literatur zur Geschichte der Naturwissenschaften und Technik. Berlin, Verlag Arno Spitz, 1985. 289p. front., charts. ISBN: 3870612118.

A guide to the history of the literature on the natural sciences and technology. 7 sections deal with types of libraries and organizations, catalogues, bibliographies, directories, histories, leading journals and reference material. 1,653 unannotated entries. Detailed index. Some slant towards German-language countries, but not confined to the historical aspects of scientific and technical literature. *Class No:* 5(091)(01)

[305]

A General history of the sciences. Translated by A.J. Pomerans. Taton, R., *ed.* London, Thames & Hudson, 1963-66. 4v. illus. (incl. pl.), diagrs.

Translated from *Histoire générale des sciences* (Paris, Presses Universitaires de France, 1957-64. 3v. in 4).

1. *Ancient and medieval science, from pre-history to A.D. 1450.* 1963. xvi, 552p.

2. *The beginnings of modern science, from 1450 to 1800.* 1964. xx, 665p.

3. *Science in the nineteenth century.* [1965]. xix, 623p.

4. *Science in the twentieth century.* 1966. xxiv, 638p.

V.1 has 21 notable French contributors. 3 pts.: Ancient science in the East - Science in the Greco-Roman world - The Middle Ages. Chapter bibliographies; name and subject indexes. Covers developments in Phoenicia, pre-Columbian America and medieval India, - all subjects frequently neglected in general histories of science. Readable and well illustrated (v.1: 52 plates; 43 figures). *British book news* (April 1971, p.261) refers to the *General history* as a 'collaborative work which has come under heavy fire'. *Class No:* 5(091)(035)

[306]

HUFF, T.E. The Rise of early modern science: Islam, China and the West. Cambridge, University Press, 1993. xiv,409p. ISBN: 0521434963.

9 sections: 1. Comparative study of science ... 2. Arab science and the Islamic world ... 4. The European legal revolution ... 9. The rise of early modern science. Bibliography, p.365-86. Index, p.387-409. *Class No:* 5(091)(035)

[307]

LOSEE, J. A Historical introduction to the philosophy of science. 3rd ed. Oxford, University Press, 1993. [viii], 323p. ISBN: 0192892479.

First published 1972.

19 documented chapters. 1. Aristotle's philosophy of science ... 7. The seventeenth century attack on Aristotelian philosophy (Galileo; Francis Bacon; Descartes) - 8. Newton's axiomatic method - 9. Analysis of the implications of the new science for a theory of scientific method ... 14. Theories of scientific progress ... 19. Descriptive philosophies of science. Selected chapter bibliographies, p.286-313. Indexes, p.314-23. 'The third edition includes new material on theories of scientific progress, causal explanation, Bayesian confirmation theory, scientific realism, and alternatives to prescriptive philosophy of science' (*Preface*). *Class No:* 5(091)(035)

[308]

RONAN, C.A. The Cambridge illustrated history of the world's science. Cambridge, University Press; London, Newnes, 1983. 543p. illus., facsims, maps. ISBN: 0521258448.

10 chapters: 1. The origins of science - 2. Greek science - 3. Chinese science - 4. Hindu and Indian science - 5. Arabian science - 6. Roman and medieval science - 7. From Renaissance to scientific revolution ... 10. Twentieth-century science. Bibliography (by chapters), p.528-9. Index, p.532-43, includes references to the illus. *Class No:* 5(091)(035)

[309]

SARTON, G. A History of science. Cambridge, Mass., Harvard Univ. Press; London, Oxford Univ. Press, 1953. 2v. illus.

1. *Ancient Greece through the golden age of Greece.* 1953. xxvi. 646p.

2. *Hellenistic science and culture in the last three centuries BC.* 1959. xxvi, 554p.

V. 1 'is not written for classical philologists, but rather for students of science whose knowledge of antiquity is rudimentary, who may never have studied Greek ...'. V. 2, despite its title, 'deals with Roman culture and Latin letters as well as with Greek letters and the culture of Eastern Europe, Egypt and Western Asia' (*Preface*). Both volumes are well illustrated and amply documented. *Class No:* 5(091)(035)

[310]

SARTON, G. Introduction to the history of science. Baltimore, Md., Williams and Wilkins, for Carnegie Institution of Washington, 1927-48 (reprinted, Krieger, 1975). 3v. in 5. $425, set. (*Carnegie Institution publication 376.*) ISBN: 0882751727.

1. *Homer to Omar Khayyam.* xi, 839p.

2. (2 pts.). *From Rabbi ben Ezra to Roger Bacon.* xxxv, xvi, 1251p.

3. (2 pts.). *Science and learning in the 14th century.* xxxv, xi, 2155p.

Treatment is by time-periods. Each chapter normally surveys a half-century, summarizing events in science and learning, with notes on lives and works, criticism and bibliographical history of the principal personalities concerned. Each volume has an index, combined in v.3. A monumental bibliographical history, embracing all branches of knowledge. Invaluable source book for students of the early history of science.

Addenda and errata are included in the *ISIS 'Critical bibliography of the history and philosophy of science'*. *Class No:* 5(091)(035)

[311]

SINGER, C. A Short history of scientific ideas to 1900. Oxford, Clarendon Press, 1959. xviii, [2], 525p. illus.

'Based on *A short history of science*, first drafted in 1929 and published in 1941' (*Preface*).

A concisely written, straight-forward history, with 188 illus., and many brief biographical notes. Chapters 1-4 (p.6-136) concern scientific ideas in ancient times; chapters 7-9 (p.218 onwards), the 17th-19th centuries. Index of names, p.517-25. The best of the short histories of science. *Class No:* 5(091)(035)

[312]

THORNDIKE, L. History of magic and experimental science. New York, Columbia Univ. Press, 1923-58. 8v. $93ea.

1-2 *First 13 centuries.* 3-4. *14th-15 centuries.* 5-6. *16th century.* 7-8. *17th century.*

'Based on an examination of the original MSS and documents of the early writers, scientists and historians in library collections all over the world'. The word 'magic' as used in the title 'is understood in its broadest sense as including all occult arts and sciences, superstitions and folklore' (Hawkins, R.R. *Scientific, medical and technical Books ... 1930-44*, p.4). Well documented. V. 1-2 include a general index, bibliographical index, and index of MSS; v. 3-4 and 5-6, general index, index of MSS and index of incipits; v. 7-8, general index and index of MSS. A monumental survey. *Class No:* 5(091)(035)

Periodicals

[313]

Archive for history of exact sciences. Berlin, etc., Springer Verlag, 1960-. 4pa. DM1061.90 ISSN: 00039519.

Focuses mainly on mathematics and natural philosophy, but also includes the physical sciences. V.49(5), 1995 includes an article, 'Ptolemy and Maslama on the transformation of circles into circles in stereographic projection'. Languages used may be English, French, German, Italian, Latin and Spanish. *Class No:* 5(091)(051)

[314]

British journal for the history of science. Cambridge, University Press, for the British Society of the History of Sciences, 1962-. 4pa. £91. ISSN: 00070874.

V.36(4), December 1998, carries three well-documented articles (e.g. 'The transformation of medicine in England', followed by 134 refs.). Book reviews (affiliations of reviewers are stated); also 'Books received'. 'Long recognized as a prominent publication in the history of science' (*Magazines for libraries*, 5th ed., 1986, p.883). *Class No:* 5(091)(051)

[315]

History of science. Cambridge, Science History Publications, Ltd., 1962-. 4pa. £71 ISSN: 00732753.

Originally as *History of science: an annual review of literature research and teaching* (Cambridge, Heffer, 1962-71. v.1-10. Annual; v.11-. 4pa.).

V.37(1), March 1999, has 4 well-documented articles (*e.g.* 'The Scientific Revolution: has there been a British view? - a personal assessment', p.79-106). Annual index of authors-titles. Book reviews, notices of books and notes on contributors. 'Aims to provide analysis, review, and assessment, of specific topics in the history of science, medicine, and technology'. *Class No:* 5(091)(051)

Films

[316]

Discovery & invention: a review of films & videos on the history of science and technology. Grant, C. *and* Ballantyne, J., *eds.* London, British Universities Film & Video Council, 1985. £7 (£3.50, to members). ISBN: 0901299391.

53 reviewers, listing 283 items currently available in the UK. 43 subject sections (Agriculture ... Transport - Water); 3 appendices: 1. Late additions; 2. Materials not yet reviewed; 3. Some materials for secondary education. Title index. Distributors' index. *Class No:* 5(091)(084.122)

[317]

EASTWOOD, B. Directory of audio-visual sources: history of science, medicine, and technology. New York, Science History Publications, 1979. v.p. $20. ISBN: 0882021850.

Audio-visual directory of 543 numbered entries, under titles A-Z. List of major academic rental libraries; list of distributors cited. Brief descriptions plus technical data on each title and order number. Topical index. An all-American directory. Perhaps rather dated now, but the list of titles will still be of use. *Class No:* 5(091)(084.122)

Middle Ages

[318]

KREN, C. **Medieval science and technology:** a selected, annotated bibliography. New York & London, Garland, 1985. xix, 369p. $53. (*Bibliography of the history of science and technology, v.11. Garland reference library of humanities, v. 492.*) ISBN: 0824089693.

1,470 briefly annotated entries in 13 sections. Included: Physical science and natural philosophy - Philosophy, metaphysics, methodological consideration, logic - Mathematics - Medicine and Veterinary medicine - Psychology - Natural history - Technology - Education: schools and universities - Quasiscience (*e.g.* alchemy). Appended: Reports on manuscripts. Detailed, non-analytical index, p.341-69. *Class No:* 5(091)"01/14"

[319]

Science in the Middle Ages. Lindberg, D.C., *ed.* Chicago, Ill., & London, Univ. of Chicago Press. 1978. 549p. illus., facsims. $40. ISBN: 0226452324.

16 contributors. 15 chapters: 1. Science, technology and progress in the early Middle Ages - 2. The transmission of Greek and Arabic learning to the West ... 5. Mathematics (with 84 references) ... 9. Astronomy ... 12. Medicine ... 13. Natural history - 14. The nature, scope and classification of the sciences - 15. Science and magic (with 52 references). 'Suggestions for further reading' (by chapters), p.507-15. Notes on contributors. A well documented and illustrated textbook by the author of *A catalogue of medieval and Renaissance optical manuscripts* (1975). *Class No:* 5(091)"01/14"

[320]

—GRANT, E. Physical science in the Middle Ages. Cambridge, University Press, 1977. xi, [1], 128p. diagrs. £10.50. ISBN: 0521292948.

First published 1971 (Wiley).

In 6 chapters, plus a 'Bibliographical essay' (p.91-116), - a grouped running commentary, emphasizing the topics covered, but including other aspects of medieval science. Analytical index. Supports his earlier *A Source book in mediaeval science* (Cambridge, Mass., Harvard Univ. Press, 1974. xviii, 864p.), in 'Source books in the history of science' series. *Class No:* 5(091)"01/14"

[321]

STILLWELL, M.B. **The Awakening interest in science during the first century of printing:** an annotated checklist of first editions viewed from the angle of their subject content: astronomy, mathematics, medicine, natural science, physics, technology. New York, Bibliographical Society of America, 1970. xxix, 390p. $25. ISBN: 0914930001.

Pt.1 has lengthy, valuable annotations on 900 numbered items (plus interpolations). Abbreviations of sources cited, p.xvii-xxvi. Pt.2A: Analytical lists (commentators; editors; places of printing; printers and publishers; translators). Pt. 2B: Chronologies (author, by periods; chronological table of first editions). Detailed index. Well produced. *Class No:* 5(091)"01/14"

Modern Times

[322]

Companion to the history of modern science. Olby, R.C., *and others, eds.* London, Routledge, 1990. 1081p. £85; $79.95. ISBN: 0415019885.

61 contributors; 67 documented essays present a guide to Western science from 1500 onwards. Part 1 describes methods and problems of research. Part 2 applies those methods to a wide range of fields, from Newton to relativity, and genetic engineering. Subject and name indexes which are described as 'adequate' in *Choice*, October 1990, p.332. Some typographical errors. *Class No:* 5(091)"15/19"

[323]

KNIGHT, D. **Sources for the history of science, 1660-1914.** London, Sources of History, Ltd., 1975. 223p.

A bibliographical essay. Chapters: 1. The history of science - 2. Histories of science - 3. Manuscripts - 4. Journals - 5. Scientific books - 6. Non-scientific books - 7. Surviving physical objects. Many footnotes. Non-analytical index. Focuses on materials available in Britain, and particularly helpful on 19th century. *Class No:* 5(091)"15/19"

[324]

PLEDGE, H.T. **Science since 1500:** a short history of mathematics, physics, chemistry, biology. Ministry of Education, Science Museum. 2nd ed. London, HMSO, 1966. 360p. illus., (pl.), graphs, maps.

First published 1939.

2nd ed. adds a prefatory note on the period 1939-59 and provides further dates. A brief but handy survey of modern science, mainly intended as a background study for the manuals on the history of special science subjects published by the Science Museum. Footnotes and a note on further reading. Valuable name and subject indexes. 16p. of plates. *Class No:* 5(091)"15/19"

20th Century

[325]

Harrap's illustrated history of the 20th century - Science: invention and discovery in the 20th century. London, Harrap, 1990. 236p. illus., ports. £18.95. ISBN: 0245600248.

Covers 6 periods: 1900/1919 ... 1973/1989. Appended: Biographies; Glossary; Further reading; Index, p.252-6. About 350 illus. (incl. col.). Quarto format. Succinct; clearly presented for the layperson. *Class No:* 5(091)"19"

[326]

Scientific thought, 1900-1960: a selective survey. Harré, R., *ed.* Oxford, Clarendon Press, 1969. viii, 277p. illus., diagrs. £11.95. ISBN: 0198581262.

13 contributors; 12 surveys: 1. Logic - 2. Relativity and cosmology - 3. Matter and radiation - 4. Geophysics - 5. Chemistry - 6. Biochemistry - 7. Molecular biology - 8. Ecological genetics - 9. Hormones and transmitters - 10. Cell biophysics - 11. The viruses - 12 Ethnology. Each survey carries appended references. Author and subject indexes. 8 plates. Aims 'to capture something of the main movements of scientific thought since the beginning of this century' (*Preface*). *Class No:* 5(091)"19"

Libraries

[327]

'Library and archive resources in the history of science'. In *British journal for the history of science,* v.6, 1972-3. p.336-7, 459-61; v.7, 1974. p.100-103, 201-2; v.8, 1975. p.94-99; v.10, 1977. p.89-92; v.11, 1978. p.191-5.

1. 'The Turner Collection of the history of mathematics at the University of Keele'. 2. 'The Crawford Collection of books and manuscripts on the history of astronomy, mathematics, etc., at the Royal Observatory, Edinburgh'. 3. The Mathematical Association Library at the University of Leicester'. 4. 'Private manuscript collections in Scotland'. 5. 'History of science in Durham libraries'. 6. 'Manchester'. 7. 'University College, London'.

The contribution on Durham libraries (*British journal ...,* v.8, 1975, p.94-99) is by A.J. Burnett and D.M. King. Sections: Introduction - University library - Other local libraries - Conclusion. 16 footnotes. *Class No:* 5(091):061:026/027

Biographies

[328]

ASIMOV, I. **Asimov's biographical encyclopedia of science and technology:** the lives of 1510 great scientists from ancient times to the present, chronologically arranged. 2nd rev. ed. Garden City, N.Y., Doubleday, 1982. 941p. illus. $29.95. ISBN: 0385177712.

First published 1967 (revised 1972).

The 2nd ed. adds 310 biographies (half of them contemporaries) to the 1,200 of the 1972 ed. The chronological sequence begins with Imhotep (fl. 2980-2950 BC). Two-thirds of entries cover 19th-20th century scientists. The index, p.901-41, finds a place for names of individuals other than the 1,510 whose biographies are included. No bibliographies. Very readable; for the layman. *Class No:* 5(092)

[329]

The Biographical dictionary of scientists. Porter, R., *ed.* 2nd ed. Oxford, University Press, 1994. 891p. $85.

First ed. published in 6v. as: *Mathematicians.* 1984. [vii], 175p.; *Astronomers.* 1984. 204p.; *Physicists.* 1984. 212p.; *Chemists.* 1984. 203p.; *Biologists.* 1984. 194p.; *Engineers and inventors.* 1985. 188p.

Arranged A-Z and lists more than 1,200 scientists, deceased and for the first time, those still alive. Historical essays provide background information. Includes lists of Nobel Prize winners and a glossary of more than 2,000 terms. *Class No:* 5(092)

[330]

A **Biographical dictionary of scientists.** 4th. ed. Glasgow, Harper Collins, 1994. xviii, 602p. ISBN: 0004701097.

First published 1969.

A-Z sequence of entries for *c.*1,600 deceased scientists, p.1-545; Nobel Laureates in science, p.546-48; anniversaries, p.549-78. Appended list of scientists referred to but not given entries. Bibliographical references to sources. Subject index. 86 contributors. 250 entries added since 1982 ed. Designed for the general reader as well as for the serious student. *Class No:* 5(092)

[331]

Biographical encyclopaedia of scientists. Daintith, J., *and others.* 2nd ed. Bristol, Institute of Physics Publishing, 1994. 1075p. 2v. $150;£95. ISBN: 0750302879, set; 0750302852, v.1; 0750302860, v.2.

First published 1981.

This edition contains over 200 new entries and revisions of the remainder. Concentrates mainly on British and European scientists. Almost 2,000 concise entries with data including place and date of birth, date of death, relevant posts held, and the subject's main scientific contributions. Other sections comprise: chronology;

....(contd.)

institutions; book lists; name and subject indexes. The indexes are criticized by the reviewer in *Reference reviews*, v.8(6), 1994 as being erratic and less than comprehensive, although he concludes, 'this is a very major work'. *Class No:* 5(092)

[332]

Biographical encyclopedia of scientists. New York, Marshall Cavendish, 1998. 5v.(lv,1,460,lxxxp.) $299.95. ISBN: 0761470646, set.

V.1. *Abbott-Copernicus*; v.2. *Cori-Heisenberg*; v.3. *Helmholtz-McCormick*; v.4. *Mach-Schrödinger*; v.5. *Schwarzschild-Zworykin*.

Arranged A-Z, coverage of almost 500 scientists, with entries 750-1,250 words in length. Sidebars list most important scientific discoveries. Text includes personal and professional information. Index for the complete set in each volume. Three indexes: General; Nationality; Scientific discovery. For school and public libraries. *Class No:* 5(092)

[333]

The Cambridge dictionary of scientists. Millar, D., *and others*. Cambridge, University Press, 1996. 387p. illus., diagrs. £10.95; $16.95. ISBN: 052156185x.

First published as *Chambers concise dictionary of scientists* (Chambers, 1989).

1,300 entries arranged alphabetically by surname, Abbe ... Zworykin. Concisely written entries, which vary in length from a paragraph to several pages, give dates of birth and death, nationality, field of study, significance and a brief biography (more emphasis on women scientists in this edition). Portraits of the individuals (included in *Chambers concise dictionary of scientists*) have been dropped in this revision. Cross-references in bold and italic type. *c.*30 information boxes. Includes a chronology and a list of Nobel Prizewinners. Name and subject index. No bibliographies. Recommended for school libraries or those libraries which need a general overview. *Class No:* 5(092)

[334]

Chambers biographical encyclopedia of scientists. Daintith, J., *and others, eds*. Edinburgh, Chambers, 1983. viii, 599p. $125.

A large format version of *A Biographical encyclopedia of scientists*; edited by J. Mitchell and others (New York, Facts on File, 1981. 2v.).

15 contributors. About 2,000 entries on important scientists - or on people who have made important contributions to science - from the earliest times to the present day. 'Leibig': nearly 2 columns; 'Lysenko': nearly 1 column; 'Hippocrates': 1 column. Notes works *by*, but not *on* the person concerned. Appended chronology (of their discoveries and publications). Book list, under titles, A-Z, p.581-8. Index of subjects, followed by names of persons. 'As much about science itself as about scientists' (*Preface*). More comprehensive than *Asimov's biographical encyclopedia of scientists (q.v.)*, with its 1,500 entries, but at nearly four times the price. *Class No:* 5(092)

[335]

Concise dictionary of scientific biography. New York, Scribner's, 1981. 773p. $95. ISBN: 068416630x.

Based on the parent *Dictionary of scientific biography (q.v.)*. Retains entries for the 5,000 scientists, but with a text reduced to about 10% of the original. 'Highly recommended' (*Choice*, January 1982, p.603). *Class No:* 5(092)

[336]

Dictionary of scientific biography. Gillespie, C.C., *ed*. New York, Scribner's, 1970-80. 16v. (8v. reprint, 1981). $1,080, set; $80ea. ISBN: 0684169622, set.

Edited under the auspices of the American Council of Learned Societies.

1-14. A-Z. 1970-76.

15. *Supplement 1. Biographies and topical essays.* 1978. xi, [1], 518p.

Supplement II. 1990. 2v.

16. *Index.* 1980. 510p.

Bibliographical entries for *c.*5,000 deceased scientists, from Thales to Bernal. A panel of 39 consultants for the main volumes; several hundred contributors per volume. Contributions focus on the biographee's place in the history of science rather than on his or her life story. All entries are signed and fully documented. 'Bacon, Francis': v.1, p.372-85, with 51 references (bibliography of 2½ columns: 1. Original works; 2. Secondary); 'Wallace, Alfred Russell': v.14, p.133-40; 1½ columns bibliography. V.15 includes 6 topical essays on Indian, Babylonian, Assyrian, Egyptian, early Japanese and Mayan science. *Supplement II* adds more 20th-century figures; v.2 has an index for both volumes. V.16, name and subject index, includes persons not the subject of biographical articles, mustering 45,000 names in all. Separate lists of contributors and biographies, societies, periodicals, scientists (by field). At least comparable, for the historiographer of science, to the *Dictionary of American biography* and *Dictionary of national biography*. The 'single most valuable reference work in the history of science' (Jayawardene, S.A. *Reference books for the historian of science* (1982), p.19). *Class No:* 5(092)

[337]

Eponyms dictionaries index: a reference guide to persons, both real and imaginary, and the terms derived from their names, providing basic biographical identification, and citing dictionaries, encyclopaedias, word books, journal articles, and other sources for additional information. Ruffner, J.H., *and others, eds*. Detroit, Mich., Gale, 1977. Supplements, 1984-. 760p. $135; $94, 1st supp. ISBN: 0810306883; 0810306891, 1st supp.

About 20,000 eponym entries and 13,000 personal names on which they are based, in one sequence, A-Z. Over 500 biographical sources are cited in all. Fields include agriculture, anthropology, botany, chemistry, engineering and industry, fine arts, law, linguistics, mathematics, mythology, politics, religion, weaponry and zoology. 'The definitive source for eponyms' (*Library journal*, 15 April 1978, p.816). Supplements (1984-.) each carry *c.*9,000 new entries. (1st supp. 1984. 248p.). *Class No:* 5(092)

[338]

FELDMAN, A. *and* **FORD, B. Scientists and inventors.** New York, Facts on File, 1986. 352p. illus. (incl. col.), ports, facsims, diagrs.

More than 150 biographies, each with a two-page spread. Chronological order, from Empedocles (*c.*490-430 BC.) to Christian Barnard (1922-). Index of names; detailed subject index. About 3 illus. per page. An attractive quarto pictorial record, for schools and the general public. *Class No:* 5(092)

[339]

Larousse dictionary of scientists. Muir, H., *ed*. Edinburgh, Larousse, 1994. ix,595p. £30. ISBN: 0752300024.

*c.*2,200 unsigned entries from 33 contributors. No cross-references. Includes a list of Nobel Prize winners arranged by subject. Subject index, p.577-95. 'Schools and public libraries will find it very good value, although it probably lacks the depth and detail needed by serious researchers' (*The Year in reference* 1994, no.246). *Class No:* 5(092)

[340]

McGraw-Hill modern scientists and engineers. 2nd ed. New York, London, etc., McGraw-Hill, 1980. 3v. (1366p). ISBN: 0070452660.

Revised and updated ed. of *McGraw-Hill modern men of science* (1966-68. 2v.).

1,140 biographies of scientists, both living and deceased (A-G, H-Q, R-Z and index). 'Mead, Margaret': 3½ colums. Include references to the parent work, *McGraw-Hill encyclopedia of science and technology*, to which it functions as a biographical supplement. V.3 includes a field-of-interest index, p.375-85 (Aeronautical engineering ... Zoology). *Class No:* 5(092)

[341]

Notable twentieth-century scientists. McMurray, E.J., *and others, eds*. Detroit, Gale, 1995. 4v.(2397p. illus.) $295. ISBN: 0810391813.

Includes data for almost 1,300 scientists, living and deceased; only about 70 scientists are from outside North America. Many of the entries (750-2,500 words in length) are accompanied by a photograph. The final volume includes indexes by fields of specialization, subject, gender, and nationality/ethnicity. The reviewer in *Choice*, March 1995 comments 'these indexes are marred by inconsistencies and errors' but also notes 'the comprehensiveness of the coverage' and 'the excellence of the research'.

A supplement (1998. 617p. $85) adds 234 profiles. *Class No:* 5(092)

[342]

POGGENDORFF, J.C. Poggendorff's biographisch-literarisches Handwörterbuch zur Geschichte der exakten Wissenschaften. Leipzig, Barth, 1863-1904; Verlag Chemie, 1923-40; Berlin, Akademie-Verlag, 1955-. (Reprint of v.1-6. Ann Arbor, Mich., Edwards, 1945).

Bd.1-2, to 1857; Bd.3, 1858-83; Bd.4, 1883-1904; Bd.5, 1904-22; Bd.6, 1923-31, Bd.7, 1932-.

Interprets the 'exact' sciences in a broad sense, to cover mathematics, astronomy, physics and geophysics, chemistry, crystallography, mineralogy, and the like. Arrangement under periods is A-Z. Author entries comprise short biography and full bibliography embracing contributions to journals. Living scientists included. Bd.7A carries biobibliographies of German, Austrian and Swiss scientists, technologists and medical men for the period 1932-53. Bd.7B, non-German language scientists, 1932-62 (*e.g.* Needham, Othmer, Bertrand Russell). Bd.7D. Teil 8, Lfg.1-3, 1985-87, has reached Tiselius (p.5482). A most valuable source on the lives and writings of scientists of all countries. *Class No:* 5(092)

[343]

ROYAL SOCIETY. Biographical memoirs of Fellows of the Royal Society. London, Royal Society of London, 1955-. v. 1-. ports. (*A new series, continuing Obituary notices of Fellows of the Royal Society*, v. 1-9, 1932-54. 9v.) ISBN: 0854032584.

Before 1860 the obituary notices were published annually in the Society's *Proceedings*; during 1860-99 they appeared there irregularly. *Proceedings*, v.5, 'contains obituaries of deceased Fellows chiefly for the period 1898-1904', with a general index to obituaries in *Proceedings*, v.10-64, 1880-99. From 1900 they appeared in the *Yearbook*, as well as in *Proceedings*. In 1932 they began separate issue as *Obituary notices*.

Lengthy, authoritative signed articles on deceased Fellows, including foreign members, and with a portrait of each subject. V. 40, 1994 ([v], 445,), includes 24 contributions arranged alphabetically, some, but not all, followed by bibliographical references (*e.g.* on G.F.J. Temple, followed by 64 scientific papers; 7 books written by him, and 13 references to other authors of scientific papers, books and articles about Temple). Also contains Subject Index for V 37-40, 1991-94. *Class No:* 5(092)

[344]

Scienziate e tecnologi contemporairei. Milan, Mondadori, 1968-74. 3v. illus. (incl. col.), ports.

1. *Adams, Roger to Hodgkin, Dorothy.* 1968. 527p.
2. *Hoffman, Samuel K. to Stanley, Wendell M.* 1974. 527p.
3. *Starr, Chauncey to Zworykin, Vladimir K.* 1974. 738p.

The bulk of v.3 is devoted to 'Annali della scienza e della tecnica contemporanee, 1875-1975' (p.209-705; by decades). 'Teilhard de Chardin,Pierre': 2p., with 2 references and cross-references. V.3 also carries an index to authors and their works in all 3 volumes. A well-illustrated set. *Class No:* 5(092)

[345]

Who's who in science and engineering, 1992-1993. Wilmette, Ill., Reed Publishing, 1992. 1084p. ISBN: 0837957516.

Covers 22,000 scientists and engineers from 70 countries, although the majority are from the US. Data include date and place of birth, current address, awards, publications, and significant professional achievements. Geographic and discipline indexes. Review in *Booklist*, 1 November, 1992 compared this source with the larger (over 120,000 entries) and more expensive *American men and women of science (q.v.)* and found remarkably few areas of overlap. Recommended for those libraries who receive requests for this type of information but which cannot afford the more expensive work. *Class No:* 5(092)

[346]

The Who's who of Nobel Prize winners, 1901-1995. Schlessinger, B.S. *and* Schlessinger, J.H., *eds.* 2nd ed. Phoenix, Ariz., Oryx, 1995. 251p. $49.95. ISBN: 0897748999.

First published 1986.

Previous edition (1991) covered prizewinners from 1901 to 1990. 181 contributors. Entries have been updated, *e.g.* death dates have been added, publications list extended. Each entry consists of up to 15 categories. this edition includes organizational winners. Indexes of nationality, name, religion, and educational institution make this a useful addition to reference collections. *Class No:* 5(092)

Bibliographies

[347]

BARR, E.S. An Index to biographical fragments in unspecialized specific journals. Alabama, Univ. of Alabama Press, 1973. vii, [1], 294p. ISBN: 0817396039.

Notes on *c.*7,000 individuals, - 'distinguished persons who, prior to about 1920, were active in the sciences' (*Foreword*). Arranged A-Z (d'Abbadie ... Zarhellen, W). Data: name; specialization; dates; country. About 15,000 citations. 8 coded sources (*e.g. Nature, Philosophical magazine, Popular science monthly, Science*). *Class No:* 5(092)(01)

[348]

GASCOIGNE, R.M. A Historical catalogue of scientists and scientific books. New York, Garland, 1984. 1177p. (*Garland Reference Library of the humanities, v.495.*) ISBN: 0824087526.

More than 13,000 authors are identified. 3 main sections (further subdivided): Classical and medieval periods (p.3-68) - Early modern period, *c.*1450-1700 (p.71-222) - Eighteenth and nineteenth centuries. Main index: individuals; index of selected titles; index of dictionaries and encyclopedias; index of bibliographies and book catalogues. Titles are based on a survey of holdings in Australian libraries, with an English-language slant. Includes most periodical material. 'A must for any history of science collection' (*Reference books bulletin, 1984-1985*, p.132). *Class No:* 5(092)(01)

[349]

IRELAND, N.O. Index to scientists of the world, from ancient to modern times: biographies and portraits, 1988-99. 4th ed. Boston, Mass., Faxon, 1997. xxxiv, 1638p. $259.95. ISBN: 0837957567.

A greatly-expanded index to biographies, portraits and chief scientific contributions of over 31,000 scientists from 125 countries as contained in biographical dictionaries (*e.g. Chambers's dictionary of scientists, Current biography, Biography index*). Entries, A-Z, state name, dates, description, source and page number. 'Ampère': 26 references; 'Galileo': 60 references; 'Réamur': 12 references; 'Cockroft, Sir J.D.': 4 references. Many entries muster 1 or 2 references only. References are asterisked if sources are especially suitable for younger readers. 80% US bias. Also available on *Complete Marquis who's who on CD-ROM. Class No:* 5(092)(01)

[350]

JAYAWARDENE, S.A. *and* **LAWES, J. 'Biographical notices of historians of science: a checklist'.** *Annals of science.* v.36, 1979, p.315-94.

'This is a first attempt at consolidating and extending the lists of biographies of historians of science compiled by George Sarton, Aldo Mieli and Francis Russo.' Lists *c.*3,000 biographical notices (800 of them historians of science), drawn from obituaries, bibliographies, articles in biographical dictionaries, monographs, etc. *Class No:* 5(092)(01)

[351]

Prominent scientists: an index to collective biographies. Pelletier, P.A., *ed.* 3rd ed. New York, Neal-Schuman, 1994. 353p. $49.95. ISBN: 1555701140.

Lists *c.*10,500 scientists, representing the contents of *c.*330 sources. Coded list of collective works in English published primarily between 1960 and 1992. Indexes of scientists by surnames and by fields (Aeronautics ... Zoology). *Class No:* 5(092)(01)

[352]

SMITH, R. Biographies of scientists: an annotated bibliography. Lanham, Md., Scarecrow, 1998. 293p. £34.20; $36. (*A Magill bibliography..*) ISBN: 0810833840.

Nine chapters: 1. Multidisciplinary sources ... 3. Chemistry ... 6. Mathematics ... 9. Related fields. Discusses 736 biographical and autobiographical publications about scientists from all ages and nations. Selective - *e.g.* omits Koestler's biographical work on Kammerer - but readable and interesting. Also provides a list of Web sites about scientists. Bibliography is not comprehensive but concentrates on more recent works. Name and subject indexes. For public and academic libraries. *Class No:* 5(092)(01)

Women

[353]

BAILEY, M. American women in science: a biographical dictionary. Santa Barbara, Calif., ABC-Clio, 1994. xxi,463p. illus. $60. ISBN: 0874367409.

Includes details of 304 women in the social, medical, and physical sciences (78 professions in all) who began their careers before 1950. Data include date of birth, education, employment history, and achievements. Bibliographies of alternative sources of information for each scientist is given, p.437.39. Black-and-white photographs accompany 52 of the entries. For academic and public libraries. *Class No:* 5(092)-0055.2

[354]

—**BAILEY, M.J. American women in science, 1950 to the present.** Santa Barbara, Calif., ABC-Clio, 1998. 455p. illus. $60. ISBN: 0874367409.

Supplements *American women in science: a bibliography* (Santa Barbara, Calif., ABC-Clio, 1994) (*q.v.*)

Includes details of more than 300 women in the social, medical, and physical sciences. Arranged in A-Z order. The entries for this volume are longer and more evaluative than for the previous volume. Data include date of birth, education, employment history, and achievements. There is also personal information in addition to professional details. Bibliographies of alternative sources of information for each scientist is given. Black-and-white photographs accompany some of the entries. For academic and public libraries. *Class No:* 5(092)-0055.2

[355]

CREESE, M.R.S. *and* **CREESE, T.M. Ladies in the laboratory?** American and British women in science, 1800-1900: a survey of their contributions to research. Lanham, Md., Scarecrow, 1998. xiii, 453p., tables. $98.50. ISBN: 0810832879.

3 sections: 1. Life sciences (botanists, lepidopterists, etc.) - 2. Mathematical, physical and earth sciences - 3. Social sciences 'plus others'. Bibliography of papers by women 1800-1900, p.371-427. Index. Title is misleading, many of the subjects having been born before 1900 but still active well into mid-20th century (*e.g.* Alice Hamilton, toxicologist, 1869-1970). Division of each chapter into American and British sections prevents chronological treatment of

....(contd.)

subject, otherwise text is comprehensive and sympathetically written. 'An incredibly well informed and well written history of the women and the science to which they contributed' (*Choice*, October 1998, p.339). *Class No:* 5(092)-0055.2

[356]

HERZENBERG, C.L. **Women scientists from antiquity to the present:** an index, an international reference listing and biographical dictionary. West Cornwall, Conn., Locust Hill, 1986. 200p. $30. ISBN: 0933951019.

Purports to be a name index of more than 2,500 women who have made their mark as zoologists, chemists, mechanical engineers, inventors, cartographers, nurses, midwives, sociologists, etc. Draws on 130 biographical sources. Entries are very brief and, at times, risible. 'Cleopatra, cosmetic chemist' raises doubts. 'Many of the sources are notoriously unreliable' (*Choice*, v.23 (11/12), July/August 1986, p.1656). *Class No:* 5(092)-0055.2

[357]

HØYRUP, E. **Women of science, technology and medicine:** a bibliography. Roskilde, Denmark, Roskilde Univ. Library, [1987]. viii, 132p. (*Skriftserie fra Roskilde Universitetsbibliotek, 15.*) ISBN: 8773490962.

About 1,000 biographies of women scientists, and to a lesser extent women technologists (inventors and engineers), women physicians, and a few nurses. Entries A-Z; data: dates; claim to fame. Appended groups: women in mathematics, science, psychology and medicine, respectively. General reference works, p.1-4. *Class No:* 5(092)-0055.2

[358]

OGILVIE, M.B. **Women and science:** an annotated bibliography. New York, Garland, 1996. 556p. £77;$95. ISBN: 0815309295.

2,700 entries covering women scientists and also the effect of science on women's lives. More up-to-date and wider in scope than the same author's *Women in science: antiquity through the nineteenth century (q.v.)*. Useful indexes. For public and academic libraries. *Class No:* 5(092)-0055.2

[359]

—OGILVIE, M.B. Women in science: antiquity through the nineteenth century; a biographical dictionary, with annotated bibliography. Cambridge, Mass., & London, MIT Press, 1986. xi, [1], 254p. $12.50. ISBN: 026265038x.

Biographical accounts of more than 150 women scientists, p.22-187. The annotated bibliography has sections A-G (A. Bibliographies and reference works; abstracts, bibliographies, catalogues, guides and biographical dictionaries and encyclopedias, p.189-96 ... G. Nineteenth and early twentieth centuries, p.225-9). List of subjects of biographical accounts, p.240-5. Detailed index, p.246-54. Supplements the major multi-volume biographical dictionaries. *Class No:* 5(092)-0055.2

[360]

SIEGEL, P.J. *and* FINLEY, K.T. **Women in the scientific search:** an American bio-bibliography, 1724-1979. Metuchen, N.J., & London, Scarecrow, 1985. xvii, 399p. ISBN: 0810817551.

1,517 bio-bibliographies. 1-49: General biographies of women in science. 50-1,517: Specialists, in 29 classes (Archaeologists, anthropologists, ethnologists, and folklorists ... Zoologists). Chronological sub arrangements. Detailed index, p.379-99. *Class No:* 5(092)-0055.2

Manuscripts & Incunabula

[361]

AMERICAN PHILOSOPHICAL SOCIETY. Library. **Catalog of manuscripts in the American Philosophical Society Library,** including the archival shelflist. Westport, Conn., Greenwood Press, [1970]. 10v. ISBN: 0837149754.

Photographed reproduction of the Library's card catalogue of manuscripts. *Class No:* 5(093)

[362]

HARPER, P. **Guide to the manuscript papers of British scientists,** catalogued by the Contemporary Scientific Archives Centre and the National Cataloguing Unit for the Archives of Contemporary Scientists, 1973-93. Bath, NCUAS at the University of Bath, 1993. xv, 111p. £10. ISBN: 0952200902.

A-Z listing of 158 scientists who died during 1973-93 (or whose papers came into the public domain in that period), arranged by full name, biographical outline, date-span of papers, place of deposit, description of papers, language, and provenance. *Supplement, 1993-98* from the same author and publisher in 1998 (viii, 46p. 0952200953, £10) contains a further 34 entries. Both publications have indexes of persons and places of deposit, but a cumulated index in the supplement would have been helpful. *Class No:* 5(093)

[363]

JAYAWARDENE, S.A. **'Western scientific manuscripts before 1900: a check list of published catalogues'.** In *Annals of science*, v.35, 1978, p.148-72.

386 numbered entries in 10 sections: 1. Science (general) ... 7. Medicine - 8. Miscellaneous (technology; geography; metrology) ... Index of names of persons; index of cities. Uses of P.O. Kristeller's *Latin manuscripts before 1600* (New York, 1965) as a guide.

A supplement to Thorndike and Kibre (*q.v.*). *Class No:* 5(093)

[364]

THORNDIKE, L. *and* KIBRE, P. **A Catalogue of incipits of mediaeval scientific writings in Latin.** Rev. and augm. ed. London, The Mediaeval Academy of America, 1963. xxiip., 1938 cols. (*Mediaeval Academy of America publication no. 29.*)

First published 1937.

Entries are arranged A-Z under the initial word. In each case, a brief indication of author and title of the work to which the incipit belongs, plus a note of 'one or more manuscripts or editors where it may be found, or some secondary work giving this information, or some other sources for the incipit'. Abbreviations of sources, p.ix-xxii. Detailed, analytical index, cols. 1718-1938. *Class No:* 5(093)

Developing Countries

[365]

Science, technology, and society in the Third World: an annotated bibliography. Shrum, W., *and others*. Metuchen, N.J., Scarecrow Press, 1995. 399p. ISBN: 0810828715.

978 annotated entries in 14 sections: 1. General materials ... 6. Agriculture ... 8. Politics and policy ... 14. Development of science and technology. Author and subject indexes. *Class No:* 5(4/9-77)

Europe

[366]

Scientific Europe: research and technology in 20 countries. Maastricht, Formation Science Europe, 1990. 508p. illus. (incl. col.), diagrs., maps. ISBN: 9073035066.

9 parts: 1. Europe on the move - 2. New partnerships ... 8. Machinery of life - 9. Heirs of Galileo. 17 editors; 80 contributors from 20 countries. Fully illustrated and well captioned. No bibliography. Detailed index. *Class No:* 5(4)

[367]

Who's who in science in Europe: a biographical guide to science, technology, agriculture and medicine. 9th ed. London, Cartermill International, 1995. 2v (A-K, L-Z). (2084p). ISBN: 1860670237.

First published 1967; 3rd ed. (Hodgson), 1978; 8th ed., 1993.

About 22,000 biographical entries for scientists from 36 countries (Albania: only 2 names; no entry found for Russia). Data include titles of major publications and research interests. Some entries, indicated by an asterisk, are very brief, and appear to have been prepared without the subject's co-operation. The main sequence is supported by a country and subject index, in which the scientists feature under the country in which they work, subdivided into subject specializations. Available on the CD-ROM *Current research in Europe*. *Class No:* 5(4)

Europe—Southern

[368]

HIDALGO, C.O. **Science and technology in southern Europe:** Spain, Portugal, Greece and Italy. London, Cartermill Publishing, 1997. xvi,309p. figs.,maps,tables. £49.50. (*Cartermill guides to science and technology.*) ISBN: 1860671853.

A chapter is devoted to science and technology in each country. Issues discussed include funding, research programmes, and co-operation. References are listed at the end of each chapter. Three appendices: 1. General information - 2. Relevant addresses - 3. Acronyms. An index would have been useful. *Class No:* 5(403)

Great Britain

Theses

[369]

British reports, translations and theses: a current awareness bibliography. Boston Spa, British Library Document Supply Centre, 1981-. Monthly. £98pa. ISSN: 09594922.

Supersedes *BLLD announcement bulletin*.

About 1,200 items per issue. Includes Canadian and Australian technical reports. Monthly and quarterly keyterm and author indexes on microform. European SIGLE database (1981-), available online through BLAISE-LINE. *Class No:* 5(410)(043)

Reports Literature

[370]

British reports, translations and theses: a current awareness bibliography. Boston Spa, British Library Document Supply Centre 1981-. Monthly. £98pa. ISSN: 09594922.

Supersedes *BLLD announcement bulletin*.

Each issue lists over 1,200 British reports and translations produced by British government organizations, industry, universities and learned bodies, plus doctoral theses (1970-), etc. Includes reports and unpublished translations from Eire. Classes 01 Aeronautics ... 22 Space technology. Key term index per issue. Quarterly cumulating microfiche insert, providing author, report number and key term indexes. Includes Canadian and Australian reports. European SIGLE database (1981-), available through BLAISE. *Class No:* 5(410)(047)

Biographies

[371]

MacLEOD, R.M. *and* **FRIDAY, J.R. Archives of British men of science.** London, Mansell, 1972. 65 fiches (COSATI 60 frame format) plus printed index and guide. ISBN: 0720102812.

Each microfiche has biographical data on 60 scientists, A-Z by name. An accompanying booklet indexes the complete work. This venture represents 'the first stage of a survey of the biographical and conceptual history of science carried out at Sussex University' (*Library of Congress information bulletin*, v.31 (11), 17 March 1972, p.121-2). *Class No:* 5(410)(092)

[372]

Who's who of British scientists, 1980/81. Boff, S., *ed.* 3rd ed. Dorking, Simon Book Directories 1980. xv,[1], 589p. ISBN: 0882290015.

First published by Longman, 1971.

The 1980/81 ed. has entries for *c.*5,500 British scientists working in British universities, polytechnics, research establishments and industry (Lovell, Sir Bernard: 13½ lines). Of historical interest. *Class No:* 5(410)(092)

Boyle

[373]

FULTON, J.F. A Bibliography of the Honourable Robert Boyle, Fellow of the Royal Society. 2nd ed. Oxford, Clarendon Press, 1961. xxvi, 217, [ii]p. port., facsims.

First published 1932. Originally in Oxford Bibliographical Society *Proceedings and papers* (v.3 (1), 1932, p.1-172; v.3 (3), 1933, p. 339-65.

Sections: A. Separate works (42); chronological order - B. Contributions to other works - C. Collected works - D. Biography and criticism (p. 155-96). Locations in *c.*100 libraries in USA, Britain, Canada, Sweden, etc. 26 facsims. *Class No:* 5(410)(092)BOY

Dalton

[374]

SMYTH, A.L. John Dalton, 1760-1844: a bibliography of works by and about him. Manchester, Univ. Press, 1966. xvi, 114p. facsims.

Part 1: Works by Dalton (separately published works; translations and edited texts; scientific manuscripts ... lectures) - Part 2: Works (including periodical articles) about Dalton, p.74-104. 771 numbered items, with bibliographical notes. Locations in 14 libraries. *Class No:* 5(410)(092)DAL

Faraday

[375]

JEFFREYS, A.E. Michael Faraday: a list of his lectures and published writings. London, Chapman & Hall, on behalf of the Royal Institution of Great Britain, 1960. xxviii, [1], 86p. front., illus. (pl.).

489 numbered items, in one chronological sequence. Covers (i) all books and separate publications, including later editions and reprints; (ii) all articles, papers, etc., in journals, including letters to *The Times*; (iii) all lectures; (iv) all the manuscript lecture notes in the Faraday Collection at the Royal Institution. Brief bibliographical notes. Biographical references, p.xxv-xxvi. Analytical index. *Class No:* 5(410)(092)FAR

Hooke

[376]

KEYNES, G. A Bibliography of Dr Robert Hooke. Oxford, Clarendon Press, 1960. xiv, [1], [1], 115p. illus., facsims.

40 sections, - Individual works; Cutlerian lectures; Philosophical collections; Posthumous works; contributions to books; Hooke's Diaries. 25 libraries were consulted. 4 appendices (3. Biography and criticism, p.87-96). *Class No:* 5(410)(092)HOO

Newton

[377]

GJERTSEN, D. The Newton handbook. London & New York, Routledge & Kegan Paul, 1986. xiv, 665p. $59.95. ISBN: 0710202792.

A dictionary of topics, personalities and works, Aberration ... Young, Thomas, p.1-613 (over 500 entries). '*Principia*': p.455-502; 'Priority dispute': p.502-7. Works: (Newton's more important contributions; 119 items). Bibliography, p.626-9. Analytical index, p.648-65. 'A quite thorough research' (*Choice*, v.24(9), May 1987, p.1378). *Class No:* 5(410)(092)NEW

[378]

WALLIS, P. *and* **WALLIS, R. Newton and Newtoniana, 1672-1975:** a bibliography. Folkestone, Kent, Dawson, 1977. xxiv, 362p. £40. ISBN: 0712907696.

About 5,000 entries: *c.*600 library locations. 10 sections (1. Collected works, correspondence, bibliography - 2. The *Principia* ... 8. Report on coinage - 9. Works edited by Newton - 10. Biographies and general works, including Newton's minor scientific papers). Includes material on Newton. Indexes of names; anonyma; printers, publishers and booksellers; places of publication. List of authorities, p.xvii. *Class No:* 5(410)(092)NEW

Priestley

[379]

CROOK, R.E. A Bibliography of Joseph Priestley, 1733-1804. London, Library Association, 1966. xiv, 201p.

Based on a thesis for the LA Fellowship in 1965. 7 sections: theological and religious; political and social; educational and psychological; philosophical and metaphysical; historical; scientific; and 'Works about Priestley' (636 items, mostly biographical). The published work adds a section 8: 'Periodical works of Priestley' (items 637-686). A valuable contribution. *Class No:* 5(410)(092)PRI

Manuscripts & Incunabula

[380]

ROYAL COMMISSION ON HISTORICAL MANUSCRIPTS. The Manuscript papers of British scientists, 1600-1940. London, HMSO, 1982. 118p. £3.95. (*Guides to sources for British history*.) ISBN: 0114401225.

Inventory of extant manuscript papers of 635 British scientists, including mathematicians, astronomers, physicists, botanists, medical men and engineers. The papers range from personal correspondence and diaries to laboratory notebooks and other working papers. Index of locations. *Class No:* 5(410)(093)

Germany

Biographies

[381]

Kürschners deutschen Gelehrten-Kalender. Bio-bibliographisches Verzeichnis deutschsprachiger Wissenschaftler der Gegenwart. Berlin & New York, de Gruyter, 1925-. About 4-yearly. ISBN: 3110104962.

First published 1925.

The 16th ed. (1992. (xii,4808p.) DM948) has *c.*35,000 *Who's who*-style entries for contemporary German, Austrian and Swiss scholars, with some prominence given to their writings. Includes appended obituaries, anniversary calendar, subject categories of biographees, and list of publishers. *Class No:* 5(430)(092)

France

Biographies

[382]

ACADÉMIE DES SCIENCES. Paris. Index biographique des membres et correspondents de l'Académie des Sciences, du 22 décembre 1666 au 1 Octobre 1978. Paris, Gauthier-Villars, 1979. 515p.

A complete list of names of all who have appeared on the rolls of the Academy since its inception. Gives dates of birth and death, election to and offices held in the Academy, details of career, and main scientific interests; indicates biographical notices read or deposited and documents, portraits, etc. held at the Academy. *Class No:* 5(44)(092)

Italy

[383]

Scientific books in Italy: subject guide. Milan, Editrice Bibliografica, 1989. lxv,1004p. ISBN: 8870752267.

2 sections: 1. Contributions - 2. Subject guide. Part 1 contains several badly translated articles on research, libraries, publishing, and science in Italy. Part 2 begins with a 42-page list of Italian publishers'

....(contd.)
addresses and telephone numbers. A list of books arranged alphabetically by subject follows. Author, title, date of publication, pagination, price and publisher are given for each. *Class No:* 5(450)

Russia

Bibliographies

[384]
Bibliografiia izdanii Akademii Nauk SSSR. Ezhegodnik, 1956-. [Bibliography of publications of the Academy of Sciences of the USSR.] Moscow, Izd-vo Akad. Nauk SSSR; Rockville, Md., Victor Kamkin Inc., 1957-. Annual. ISSN: 05685222.
Annual bibliography of publications of the Soviet Academy of Sciences. 'The most useful Russian bibliography of science available' (*Library trends*, v.15(4), April 1967, p.800). *Class No:* 5(47)(01)

[385]
Guide to Russian reference books. Volume 5: Science, technology and medicine. Maichel, K., *and others*. Stanford, Calif., Hoover Institution Press, Stanford Univ., 1967. 387p. (*Hoover Institution, Bibliographical series, 32.*) ISBN: 0817923217.
Nearly 3,000 items in Russian, English, French and German. Systematically arranged, mainly subjects A-Z. General science - General technology - Agriculture - Astronomy - Mathematics - Physics - Medicine (p.256-302: Bibliographies of bibliographies; bibliographies; bibliographies of periodicals; abstracts and indexes; congresses; encyclopedias; dictionaries; biographies; handbooks; legislation). Index, p.303-84. Excellent annotations; introductory notes to sections. *Class No:* 5(47)(01)

CD-ROM

[386]
Access Russia - science and technology. Access Innovations, Inc., 1993-. 4pa. CD-ROM. $1,500pa.
Gives bibliographic citations and abstracts of science and technical subjects in 20 areas including geology, physical sciences, mathematics, astronomy, environmental studies, materials sciences, transport, etc. Material covered includes periodicals, monographs, patents, theses, and conference proceedings published in 38 former Soviet bloc countries. The full text of the original documents can be obtained in microform format. *Class No:* 5(47)(01)(003.40)

Reviews & Abstracts

[387]
USSR report. Foreign Broadcast Information Service. Springfield., Va., National Technical Information Service, 1975-. 12pa. (*Joint Publications Research Service/JPRS.*)
Formerly *USSR and East European scientific abstracts* service.
USSR report: Chemistry. Cybernetics, computers and automation technology. Earth sciences. Engineering and equipment. Life sciences. Biomedical and behavioral sciences. Materials sciences and metallurgy. Space biology and aerospace medicine.
About 100 abstracts per service, monthly, from Soviet sources. 'JPRS publications contain information primarily from foreign newspapers, periodicals and books, but also from news agency transmissions and broadcasts. Materials from foreign-language sources are translated or reprinted with the original phrasing and other characteristics retained' (*Note*). Some of the series are available in microform.
Current JPRS publications are announced in *Government reports announcements* and index (*q.v.*), issued semi-monthly by National Technical Information Service, and are listed in *Monthly catalog of US Government publications. Class No:* 5(47)(048)

Periodicals

[388]
Scientific and technical serial publications of the Soviet Union, 1945-1960. Zikeev, N.T. Washington, Library of Congress, 1963. [vii], 347p.
5,091 numbered titles, A-Z. Entries state issuing body, title romanized and translated, date first received by the Library, frequency and Library of Congress call number. Cover-to-cover English translations are included. Keyword index to institutes. The 'Guide to subject content' needs to be far more specific. As it is, under 'Medicine' is a sequence of about 500 numbers, with no titles specified or subject breakdown. *Class No:* 5(47)(051)

Histories

[389]
GRAHAM, L.E. Science in Russia and the Soviet Union: a short history. Cambridge, University Press, 1993. xxvii,321p. ISBN: 0521245664.
3 sections: I. The Tsarist period. II. Russian science and the Marxist revolution. III. Science and Soviet society. Appendices, p.207-59. Bibliography, p.293-306. Index, p.307-21. Americanized text. *Class No:* 5(47)(091)

Biographies

[390]
Biograficheskiĭ slovar' deyatelei estestvoznaniya i tekhnicki. Zvorykin, A.A., *ed.* Moscow, Bol'shaya Sovetskaya Entsiklopediya, 1958-59. 2v. (A-Lm, M-Ya).
'Biographical dictionary of scientists in the natural and technical sciences.' Based on material in *Bol'shaya Sovetskaya Entsiklopediya* (2nd ed. 1949-60), revised and expanded. V.2 (p.427-642) includes *c.*4,500 additional biographies, as well as a review and bibliography of Russian and foreign biographical dictionaries. (Based on Maichel, K. *Guide to Russian reference books*, v.5, entry ST47).
Class No: 5(47)(092)

[391]
Lycedi russkoĭ nauki: ocherki o vydayushchikaya deyatelya'kh estestvoznaniya i tekniki. Kuznetsov, I.V., *ed.* Moscow, Gos. Izd-vo Fiziko-Matematicheskoĭ Literatury, 1961-65. 4v. ports.
1. *Matematika, mekhanika, astronomiya, fizika, kimiya.* 1961. 2. *Geologiya, geografiya.* 1962. 3. *Biologiya, meditsina, sel'skokhozyaistvennie. 1963.* 4. *Tekhnika* 1965.
'Brief biographies of prominent workers in the field of natural science and technology'. Covers only deceased scientists. V.1.(599p.) contains 55 signed biographical sketches, 20 of them chemists. The article on S.V. Lebedev (1874-1934), p.582-94 has a bibliography and portrait; that on A.S. Favorskii, p.516-29, has 1 page of bibliography with material on him as well as by him. *Class No:* 5(47)(092)

China

[392]
Chinese science abstracts. Beijing, Science Press (distributed by Elsevier), 1982-. 12pa. $564(A), $504(B). ISSN: 02545179.
Part A (issued in odd-numbered months) covers mathematics, mechanics, astronomy, physics and technical sciences. *Part B* (issued in even-numbered months) covers chemistry, life sciences and earth sciences.
Part A, v.14 no.6, November 1995 carried 637 abstracts. More than 120 Chinese scientific periodicals are used in CSA. Keyword and author indexes at the end of each issue of both parts. *Class No:* 5(510)

[393]
Periodicals current in mainland China held by the Science Reference Library. Kyang, R.K., *comp.* 2nd ed. London, Science Reference Library, 1984. [ii], 91p. £4.50. ISBN: 0712307117.
First published 1982 as *Periodicals from mainland China.*
A/Z subject and title lists of *c.*450 periodicals held, plus a list of periodicals consisting of abstracts of translations. 'Unless otherwise stated, all journals are in Chinese. English summaries or contents lists are separately noted' (*Introduction*). *Class No:* 5(510)

[394]
Science and civilization in China. Needham, J., *and others.* Cambridge, University Press, 1956-.
1. *Introductory orientations.* 1988. xxxviii, 318p. £55.
2. *History of scientific thought.* 1956. xxiv. 697p. £85.
3. *Mathematics and the sciences of the heavens and the earth.* 1959. xlvii, 877p. £110.
4. *Physics and physical technology.* Pt.1. *Physics.* 1962. xxxiv, 434p. £70. - Pt.2. *Mechanical engineering.* 1965. iv. 759p. £100 - Pt.3. *Civil engineering and nautics.* 1971. vii. 931p. £110.
5. *Chemistry and chemical technology.* Pt.1. *Paper and printing* by T. Tsuen-Hsuin 1980. 512p. £75. - Pts.2-5. *Spagyrical discovery and invention.* 4v. £335. - Pt.6. *Military technology - missiles and sieges.* 1995. 552p. £80. - Pt.9. *Textile technology: Spinning and reeling,* by Dieter Kunn. 1988. xxxiv, 520p. £75.
6. *Biology and biological technology.* Pt.1. *Botany.* 1986. xxxii, 718p. £80. - Pt.2. *Agriculture.,* by F. Bray. 1984. 760p. £80.
A comprehensive, well-produced history of Chinese science, scientific thought and technology in relation to the history of civilization, and especially comparative development of Asia and Europe. V.1 concerns geographical and historical background, the Chinese language and cultural contacts with the West. Valuable annotated bibliographies of Chinese and Western books and articles are a feature. Thus, the bibliography in v.4, pt.3 occupies p.700-830, with general index, p.831-905. Profusely footnoted. (An interim list of editions of Chinese texts used for v.1-4 is available gratis.) 'A

....(contd.)

monumental work of great importance to history of science collections and oriental history collections' (*New technical books*, October 1976, entry 1059). *Class No:* 5(510)

[395]

—RONAN, C.A. The Shorter 'Science and civilization in China': an abridgement by C.A. Ronan of J. Needham's original text. Cambridge Univ. Press, 1978-. V.1-. illus., diagrs. £15.95, v.1; £19.95, v.2 £42.50; £17.95, v.3. ISBN: 0521292867, v.1; 0521315360, v.2; 0521315603, v.3.

The work so far has reached v.1-3, covering v.1-2,3 and parts 4-1 and 4-3 of the major series. V.3 (1986. [xi], 298p.) includes a table of Chinese dynasties and a bibliography, p.274-82. This abridgement has been prepared with a general non-scientific readership in view. 'This set cannot be praised too highly' (*New technical books*, March 1987, p.324). *Class No:* 5(510)

Japan

[396]

Directory of Japanese scientific periodicals. Tokyo, National Diet Library, 1984. 1861p. ISBN: 4875820860.

Previous ed. 1974 (1000p.).

Classed arrangement of *c.*12,000 titles of current serials in science and technology published in Japan. *Class No:* 5(52)

[397]

GIBSON, R.W. *and* KUNKEL, B.K. Japanese scientific and technical literature: a subject guide. Westport, Conn., Greenwood Press, 1981. 560p. $125. ISBN: 0313229295.

Part 1 analyses information activities and bibliographical control of scientific and technical literature in Japan. Part 2 is a subject guide (using modified UDC scheme) to 9,116 journals. Data on each item: title and publisher's imprint (romanized Japanese plus English translation), language, and where abstracted/indexed. *Class No:* 5(52)

[398]

Information from Japan. Papers presented at a seminar on Japanese scientific, technical and commercial information. King, S.V., *ed.* London, British Library, Science Reference Library, 1985. [1], [1], [1], 128p. £12. ISBN: 0712307206.

8 papers (*e.g.* 'The scientific and technical information sciences in Japan: recent trends and development'), plus discussion, conclusions and recommendations. General bibliography, p.115-28 (1. Books; 2. Serials from the Western world; 3. Japanese serials; 4. Grey literature; 5. Translations and the language barrier; 6. Dictionaries and guides to the Japanese language). *Class No:* 5(52)

[399]

Japanese journals in English: scientific, technical and commercial journals held by the British Library. Science Reference Library and/or the British Library Lending Division. Smith, B. *and* King, S.V., *comps*. Boston Spa, BLLD & London, SRL, 1985. [vii], 138p. £12. ISBN: 0712307214.

Contents: 1. Subject keyword list of English-language journals published in Japan, p.1-118 (*c.*1,000 titles) - 2. Subject keyword list of translated journals and journals with translations - 3. Original titles of Japanese journals appearing in (2), above. Covers titles published 1960-84. The main groups of translated journals are: 1. Cover-to-cover translations; 2. Journals containing selected articles. *Class No:* 5(52)

[400]

SMITH, B. The Scientific and technical serial literature of Japan: a study and bibliography. [Thesis for Library Association diploma], 1975. [xi], 7, 812p., 12l.

Pts. 1-2: 10 preliminary chapters. Pt. 3: main A-Z listing of over 2,000 titles, under actual/Englished title, p.93-485, plus keyword-in-context index. Pt. 4: identification of Japanese language serial titles (including glossary of words used). Pt. 3 includes annuals and ceased journals; it states frequency and notes whether periodicals carry review articles and the like; many cross-references. *Class No:* 5(52)

India

[401]

Indian science abstracts. New Delhi, Indian National Documentation Centre, 1965-. 24pa. $600. ISSN: 00196339.

Each issue contains *c.*1,000 abstracts and references in UDC order (340.6, Forensic science; 51, Mathematics ... 67/68, Manufactures). Author and keyword index per issue and annually. *Class No:* 5(540)

[402]

JAGGI, O.P. History of science and technology in India. Delhi, Atma Ram and Sons, 1969-80. illus. (pl.), facsims., tables.

1. *Dawn of Indian technology.* 1969. 160p. 2. *Dawn of Indian science.* 1969. 264p. 3. *Folk medicine.* 1973. 276p. 4. *Indian system of medicine.* 1973. 276p. 5. *Yogic and Tantric medicine.* 1973. 190p. 6. *Indian astronomy and mathematics.* 7. *Science and technology in medieval India.* 8. *Medicine in medieval India.* 1977. 9. *Science in modern India.* 10. *Technology in modern India.* 11. *Impact of science and technology in modern India.* 12/15. *Western medicine in India.* 1980. 214p.

A detailed survey. V.15, Social impact (1980, 214p.) has 10 documented chapters. 8 appendices. Bibliography, p.204-7. Analytical index. *Class No:* 5(540)

[403]

Science and technology in medieval India: a bibliography of source materials in Sanskrit, Arabic and Persian. Rahman, A., *and others.* New Delhi, Indian National Science Academy, 1982. xxxi, 719p.

13 chapters: 1. Medicine - 2. Astronomy - 3. Mathematics - 4. Alchemy - 5. Physics - 6. Agriculture - 7. Botany - 8. Zoology - 9. Geography - 10. Gemology - 11. Architecture - 12. Encyclopaedia - 13. Dictionary. Chronological arrangement within chapters. Many works are usually allotted annotations. Numerous cross-references. A detailed survey of manuscripts and books. Unfortunately, no index. *Class No:* 5(540)

Islamic World

[404]

An Annotated bibliography of Islamic science. Nasr, S.H., *and others.* Tehran, Imperial Iranian Academy of Philosophy, 1975-78 (paperback ed. 1985). 2v. (432p. + xxiii, 317p.).

V.1 has entries for 2,770 items, in 2 parts: 1. General works - 2. Biographical and bibliographical studies of Muslim men of science. V.2 (parts 3-7): 3. Sciences influential in the formation of the Islamic sciences - 4. Translation of scientific texts into Islamic languages - 5. Classification of the sciences, scientific encyclopedias and bio-bibliographies - 6. Cosmology and cosmography - 7. Logic. Both volumes have an index of writers. *Class No:* 5(5.297)

[405]

Encyclopedia of the history of Arabic science. Rashed, R., *ed.* London, Routledge, 1996. 3v. (1105p.) illus.,figs. $250. ISBN: 0415020638.

V.1. *Astronomy - theoretical and applied*; v.2. *Mathematics and the physical sciences*; v.3. *Technology, alchemy and life sciences.*

Six broad subject areas, covering seven centuries: Astronomy; Mathematics; Physics; Technology; Alchemy; Life sciences. Bibliography, p.1045-66. Proper name, treatise, and subject indexes. *Class No:* 5(5.297)

[406]

NASR, S.H. Islamic science: an illustrated study. London, World of Islam Festival Publishing, 1976. 288p. illus. £15.

A well-documented, finely illustrated coverage of 'the entire spectrum of the subject from mathematics, astronomy, physics and medicine to astrology and alchemy' (*British book news*, August 1976, p.584). An excellent introduction for both students and scientists to medieval Islamic science. *Class No:* 5(5.297)

[407]

NASR, S.H. Science and civilisation in Islam. 2nd ed. Cambridge, Islamic Texts Society, 1987. xvi,388p. figs. £14.95. ISBN: 094662111x.

First published by Harvard University Press, 1968.

13 chapters: 1. The universal figures of Islamic science ... 4. Physics ... 7. Medicine, p.184-229 - 8. The sciences of Man ... 13. The gnostic tradition. Selected bibliography, p.355-66. Index. *Class No:* 5(5.297)

[408]

SEZGIN, F. Geschichte des arabischen Schrifttum. Leiden, Brill, 1967-79. 7v.

1. Qur'an-Wissenschafter. 1967. xiii, [1], 936p.

2. Poesie. 1975. cxii, 807p.

3. Medizin. Pharmazie. Zoologie. Tierheilkunde, bis ca. 430H. 1970. 520p.

4. Alchemie-chemie. Botanik-Agrikultur, bis ca. 430H. 1971. 411p.

5. Mathematik, bis ca. 430H. 531p.

6. Astronomie, bis ca. 430H. 1978. 536p.

7. Astrologie, Meteorologie and Verwandtes, bis ca. 430H. 1979. 502p.

8. Lexikographie, bis 430H.

9. Grammatik, bis ca. 430H.

A detailed analysis of Arabic writings, chiefly scientific, up to about AD 1052 (430 Hegira). V.7, on astrology, meterorology and kindred subjects, concerns the works of 54 authors. Bibliography, p.417-22. Indexes to authors and titles. A major survey in its field. *Class No:* 5(5.297)

Africa
[409]

Profiles of African scientists. Nairobi, African Academy of Sciences, 1991. xi,661p. ISBN: 996683107x.

2nd ed.

Companion volume to *Profiles of African scientific institutions (q.v.)*. *Class No:* 5(6)

America—North
[410]

American men and women of science 1998-99: a biographical directory of today's leaders in physical, biological and related sciences. 20th ed. New Providence, N.J., Bowker, 1998. 8v. $900. ISSN: 00001287.

First published 1906, as *American men of science*.

Covers 190 fields in 10 major areas of study. 119,600 scientists and engineers are listed, with 4,300 profiled for the first time. Each entry comprises name, subject area, current position, previous posts held, personal data, degrees and honorary degrees, honours and awards, concurrent positions held, research interests, mailing address. Separate discipline index (A-Z by specialty). Updated every three years. Also available online via DIALOG and on CD-ROM. *Class No:* 5(71+73)

[411]

American men and women of science. Editions 1-14. Cumulative index. Press, J.C., *comp.* New York, Bowker, 1984. 847p. ISBN: 0835212386.

Forms an index of over 270,000 scientists, living and dead, who appeared in editions 1-14 (1906-79). Editions 10-13 were in 2 sections: *The physical and biological sciences* and *The social and behavorial sciences*. Of the latter section only psychiatry, public health and statistics were retained in edition 14. *Class No:* 5(71+73)

[412]

Who's who in frontiers of science and technology. 2nd ed. Chicago, Ill., Marquis Who's who, 1985. xvi,606p. $84.50. ISBN: 0837957028.

Approx. 14,000 entries for scientists and technologists 'currently working in North America in the frontier areas of their respective specialities' (*Preface*). Index of 420 subspecialties arranged under 23 major fields (*e.g.* biology, mathematics, engineering). Available on *Marquis Who's who* database. *Class No:* 5(71+73)

USA

Bibliographies
[413]

BATSCHELET, M.W. Early American scientific and technical literature: an annotated bibliography of books, pamphlets, and broadsides. Metuchen, N.J., Scarecrow Press, 1990. xi,136p. $20. ISBN: 0810823187.

Lists scientific material published in the US between 1665 and 1799. Excludes periodicals, almanacs, some government documents and legislative acts. 3 sections: 1. Medical titles - 2. Technical science titles - 3. Natural and physical science titles. 833 entries. Arranged chronologically within each section. Author and subject indexes. 'A useful research tool, though it falls short of being the authoritative reference work on the subject' (*Choice*, v.28(3), November 1990, p.450). *Class No:* 5(73)(01)

Periodicals
[414]

Encyclopedia of associations: Association periodicals. V.2: Science, medicine, and technology. Detroit, Mich., Gale, 1987. 495p. ISBN: 0810340622.

Information on 2,717 US association periodicals arranged under subject categories, A-Z. Data include description of contents, special issues, where indexed/abstracted, circulation, year established, former title(s), frequency, price, ISSN, online or microform availability, whether advertising is accepted ... Title/keyword Association indexes. Some areas of this publication will now be out-of-date,*e.g.* price, but still a good basic starting point for organizational publications. *Class No:* 5(73)(051)

Histories
[415]

CLARK, C.A. History of science in the United States: a chronology and research guide. New York, Garland, 1996. x,543p. £80;$83. ISBN: 0815313098.

Time-scale covered is from Colonial days to 1990 and focuses on life and physical sciences. The detailed chronology makes up the major part of the work but this leads to fragmentation of the information. Useful essay reviewing reference tools. Index. For academic libraries. *Class No:* 5(73)(091)

[416]

—ROTHENBERG, M. The History of science and technology in the United States: a critical and selective bibliography. New York, Garland, 1982. 262p. $56. (*Bibliography of the history of science and technology, 2. Garland reference library of the humanities, 308.*) ISBN: 0824092783.

832 annotated entries in 6 sections, on bibliographies and general studies; the physical sciences; the biological sciences; the social sciences; technology and agriculture. Most of the references concern items published 1940-80. Author and subject indexes. 'An excellent overview of the role science and technology have played in American history' (*Choice*, v.20(8), April 1983, p.114). *Class No:* 5(73)(091)

Biographies
[417]

ELLIOTT, C.A. Biographical dictionary of American science: the seventeenth through the nineteenth centuries. Westport, Conn., Greenwood Press, 1979. xvii, 360, [1]p. tables. ISBN: 0313204195.

About 900 entries, including nearly 600 scientists never included in *American men of science* (11th ed., 1968), to which it serves as a retrospective companion. Most of the scientists died before 1906. Appendices provide data under 5 heads, A-E: year of birth; place of birth; education; occupation; fields of science. 'This tool fills an important gap for all science collections' (*Choice*, v.16(8), October 1979, p.992). *Class No:* 5(73)(092)

[418]

ELLIOTT, C.A. Biographical index to American science: the seventeenth century to 1920. Westport, Conn., Greenwood Press, 1990. 300p. $55. (*Bibliographies and indexes in American history, no. 16.*) ISBN: 0313265666.

Lists *c.*2,800 American scientists who died prior to 1920. Data include occupation, field of study, birth and death dates, and citations to other sources of biographical information. Supplements *Biographical dictionary of American science: the seventeenth through the nineteenth centuries* (Greenwood Press, 1979) (*q.v.*) which provides actual biographies. Covers some less obvious collections of biographies. Useful for research collections in the history of science. *Class No:* 5(73)(092)

[419]

NATIONAL ACADEMY OF SCIENCES OF THE UNITED STATES OF AMERICA. Biographical memoirs. Washington, National Academy Press (Initially, New York, Columbia Univ. Press), 1877-. ports. ISBN: 0309032873.

Contains memoirs of deceased members of the National Academy, each with a portrait and bibliography of his, or her, published scientific contributions. Clearly written statements on each scientist's achievements. Reminiscent of the Royal Society's *Biographical memoirs*, but less formal. 'The goal of the Academy is to have these memoirs serve as a contribution towards the history of American science' (*Preface*). *Class No:* 5(73)(092)

Australia
[420]

Australian men and women of science, engineering and technology. Port Melbourne, Reed Reference Australia, 1995. 661p. £102. ISBN: 1875589643.

Lists 3,500 scientists with an average age of 52. Also includes some non-Australians working in Australia. Two indexes - the first lists entrants by area of specialization, the second by location and discipline. Also available on CD-ROM. *Class No:* 5(94)

Translations
[421]

British reports, translations and theses: a current awareness bibliography. Boston Spa, British Library Document Supply Centre, 1981-. 12pa. £98pa. ISSN: 09594922.

Supersedes *BLLD announcement bulletin*.

Each issue lists over 1,200 British reports and translations produced by British government organizations, industry, universities and learned bodies, plus docotoral theses (1970-), etc. Includes reports and unpublished translations from Eire. Classes 01, Aeronautics ... 22, Space technology. Key term index per issue. Quarterly cumulating microfiche insert, providing author, report number and key term indexes. Includes Canadian and Australian reports. European SIGLE database (1981-), available through BLAISE. *Class No:* 5=03

[422]

Directory of translators and interpreters. 6th ed. London, Institute of Translation and Interpreting, 1994. ISSN: 09612084.

Lists members of the Institute. Also available on the Internet at: http://www.iti.org.uk. *Class No:* 5=03

[423]
Internationale Bibliographie der Übersetzung. [International bibliography of translations.] Hoof, H. van, *[comp]*. Munich, K.G. Saur, 1973. xv, 591p.

Contents: A. Bibliography of translation (p.3-521), including theory of tanslation; teaching in translation; translator's profession; typology of translation; bibliographies - B. Organizations (translators' associations; study and research centres; terminology control) - C. Publications (journals; publications on mechanical translation; technological publications; bibliographical publications). Indexes of authors and periodicals. Now of limited use. *Class No:* 5=03

[424]
Scientific and technical translation. Wright, S.E. *and* Wright, L.D., *eds*. Philadelphia, John Benjamins Publishing Co., 1993. 298p. illus. ISBN: 1556196253.

Covers all aspects of translating scientific and technical material. A useful handbook. *Class No:* 5=03

[425]
Technical translation bulletin. Oxford, Learned Information Ltd, 1961-. 3pa. $39. ISSN: 04970489.

Originally Aslib Engineering Group's *Electrical translators' bulletin* (1955-60).

Articles concern machine translation, role of translators, language teaching and research, the foreign-language barrier, etc. Bibliography section (bilingual, multilingual and monolingual dictionaries); terminology section; book reviews. *Class No:* 5=03

[426]
Transdex index. Ann Arbor, Mich., University Microfilms International, 1975-. 12pa. Annual cumulation on microfiche. ISSN: 00411116.

Replaces *Transindex: bibliography and index to the United States Joint Publications Research Services (JPRS) translations* (v.9-12. 1970/71-74), which continues *Bibliography-index to current US JPRS translations* (v.1-8. 1962-70).

The key to US JPRS translations. 4 divisions: a series and ad hoc title section; a bibliographic section; a keyword index section; and a personal names section. The JPRS series are mainly translations from Communist Bloc countries' publications. *Class No:* 5=03

[427]
The Translator's handbook. Owens, R. 3rd ed. London, Aslib, 1996. viii,328p. £38. ISBN: 0851423523.

First published 1983.

5 sections: Introductory survey - Training/development - Quality - 'The personal touch' — Machine translation and translation rules. Index, p.309-326. Unfortunately, shows signs of hasty publication; full-page erratum included and mis-spelt contributors' headings. *Class No:* 5=03

[428]
World translations index. Delft, International Translations Centre, 1987-. 10pa. DF11,600. ISSN: 02598264.

Continues *Translations register index* and *World transindex*.

Announces translations of literature relating to all fields of science and technology. Source and author indexes per issue and annually. Translations announced from 1977 can be searched on the *World translations index* database on ESA/IRS. *Class No:* 5=03

Writing & Lecturing

[429]
BEACH, D.P. *and* **ALVAGER, T.K. Handbook for scientific and technical research.** Englewood Cliffs., N.J., Prentice-Hall, 1992. xi,255p. diagrs., tables, graphs. $40. ISBN: 0134310403.

5 units (15 sections, further divided): 1. What is research? - 2. Research planning and design - 2. Methodologies of research design ... 4. Measurement, data analysis, and models - 5. Presenting the results of research. Appendices: A. Grant proposal guidance - B. A sample research report (with bibliography), p.228-46. Index, p.247-55. 'For students in scientific or technical disciplines' (*Preface*). *Class No:* 5:001.81

[430]
BRITISH STANDARDS INSTITUTION. Specification for the presentation of research and documentation reports. London, BSI, 1972. AMDs 1121, 2694 (1978). 20p. £26. (*BS 4811 1972*.)

Sections: Presentation - Format - Production. *Class No:* 5:001.81

[431]
DAY, R.A. How to write and publish a scientific paper. 5th ed. Cambridge, University Press, 1998. xvi,275p. £12.95. ISBN: 0521658799.

First published 1979.

A publication which is regularly revised (4th ed., 1995) to reflect changes in scientific writing styles. This edition reflects the impact IT, and particularly the Internet, is having on scientific publication, with no fewer than seven new chapters devoted to this area, *e.g.* publishing

....(contd.)
in electronic journals. Appendices include coverage of common misspellings andthe correct use of abbreviations. Glossary. Well-written, and easy to read. For all scientists. *Class No:* 5:001.81

[432]
EBEL, H.F. The Art of scientific writing, from student reports to professional publications in chemistry and related fields. Weinheim, VCH, 1987. xix, 493p. diagrs., graphs, tables. ISBN: 3527264698.

Part 1. Scientific writing: aims and forms (reports, theses, papers (journal articles), books) - Part 2. Scientific writing: materials, tools and methods. Appendices A-K (A. Oral presentations, organization and vital materials). References and further reading, p.441-8, 450. Index, p.451-93. *Class No:* 5:001.81

[433]
—**KATZ, M.J.** Elements of the scientific paper: a step-by-step guide for students and professionals. New York & London, Yale Univ. Press, 1985. xii, [1], 130p. tables. $25. ISBN: 0300035322.

20 short chapters, with examples (*e.g.* 4. Writing with a computer; 8. Organizing the new material; 9. Results; 16. References; 19 Gestation and rewriting; 20. Editors, referees and revisions). Appendices A-I, include 'Books for further reading'. Brief index. *Class No:* 5:001.81

[434]
Handbook of technical writing practices. Jordan, S., *and others, eds*. New York, London, etc., Wiley; Interscience 1971. 2v. (1374 + 25p.). illus., diagrs., tables. $160ea. ISBN: 0317108654, v.1; 0317108662, v.2.

32 chapters (6. Technical reports, p.345-423; bibliography of 16 items). V.2 has a lengthy glossary (p.1035-65) and a selected bibliography of 32 items on technical and scientific writing. Each volume carries an index. A comprehensive manual. *Class No:* 5:001.81

[435]
HUTH, E.J. Scientific style and format: the CBE manual for authors, editors, and publishers. 6th ed. Cambridge, University Press for the Council of Biology Editors, 1994. xv,825p. tables. £19.95; $34.95. ISBN: 0521471540.

First published 1960.

Greatly expanded edition covering all scientific disciplines. 33 chapters in 5 sections: Introduction; General style conventions; Special scientific conventions; Journals and books; Publishing process. Appendices contain information on journal title abbreviations and publishers' names. Index, p769-825p. Recommended for academic libraries. *Class No:* 5:001.81

[436]
The ISTC handbook of technical writing and publication techniques: a practical guide for managers, engineers, scientists and technical publishers. Austin, M., *ed*. London, Heinemann, 1985. 213p. ISBN: 043490354x.

8 contributors. Chapter 1: 'Choosing language for effective technical writing'. Other chapters on preparation for writing, editing , illustration, translations and printing. British Standard requirements are considered. Index. 'A work which should be available in all scientific and professional libraries' (*Library review*, v.35(2), Summer 1986, p.149-50). *Class No:* 5:001.81

[437]
—**ISTC** bibliography on technical communication. Kirkman, J. *and* Peake, J., *eds*. Hatfield, Herts., Institute of Scientific and Technical Communications, 1978. 72p.

Lists 1,300 references in 17 sections, on editing, typography, copyright, style, standards (BSI, ISO, etc). Includes information retrieval. *Class No:* 5:001.81

[438]
KIRKMAN, J. Good style: writing for science and technology. London, E. & F.N. Spon, 1992. viii,221p. £10.95. ISBN: 0419171908.

8 chapters: 1. Which style do technical readers prefer? - 2. On style in general ... 7. Writing for international audiences - 8. On avoiding ambiguity. Appendices A-E. 38 references, p.217-8. Index, p.219-21. *Class No:* 5:001.81

[439]
The McGraw-Hill style manual: a concise guide for writers and editors. Longyear, M., *ed*. New York, McGraw-Hill, 1989. 333p. $17.95. ISBN: 0070886846.

Guidelines for creating publishable manuscripts, with hints on grammatical points such as capitalization, hyphenation, split infinitives. Includes chapters on technical writing in mathematics, electronics, computer science, chemistry, and the life sciences. *Class No:* 5:001.81

[440]

Text and graphics in the electronic age: desktop publishing for scientists. Russey, W.E., *and others*. Weinheim, VCH, 1995. xv,359p. figs. ISBN: 3527285199.

Three sections (1. Basic principles - 2. Hardware - 3. Software) subdivided into 12 chapters: 1. Electronic manuscripts and desktop publishing ... 5. Data analysis ... 8. Scanners ... 10. Page-layout programs ... 12. Miscellaneous software. Addresses of suppliers, p.339-45. A useful guide. *Class No:* 5:001.81

[441]

WILKINSON, A.M. The Scientist's handbook for writing papers and dissertations. Englewood Cliffs, N.J., Prentice Hall, 1991. 522p. illus., tables. $45. ISBN: 0139694110.

Gives writing examples and techniques for the physical, biological, and social sciences. Describes common errors; includes writing abstracts, and the printing process. 'Thoroughly recommended for inclusion in the science reference collection of all libraries' (*New technical books*, May/June 1991, item 619). *Class No:* 5:001.81

Equipment & Instruments

[442]

Instruments of science: an historical encyclopedia. Bud, R., *and others*, *eds*. New York, Garland, 1998. 725p. illus.,tables. £110; $138. (*Garland encyclopedias in the history of science, 2; Garland reference library of social science, v.936.*) ISBN: 0815315619.

327 signed entries (*c*.2,000-3,500 words), arranged A-Z (Abacus ... X-ray), from more than 200 contributors giving information on instruments currently being used but also those of only historical interest, *e.g.* astrolabes. Short bibliographies are attached to each entry which is usually illustrated by a photograph or small diagram. Many cross-references. Subject/name index. A collaboration between the Science Museum (London) and the National Museum of American History, Smithsonian Institution (Washington). Well laid out. A useful addition to any reference section. *Class No:* 5:002.50

Thesauri

[443]

Cambridge illustrated thesaurus of science & technology. Godman, A. *and* Denney, R. Cambridge, University Press, 1985. 256p. col. illus., tables. £7.95. ISBN: 032126362x.

One of a series of thesauruses, on physics, chemistry, computer science, etc. This thesaurus concentrates on physical sciences and technology, and biological sciences. 'Physical sciences and technology' (p.8-137) has 4 sections and 22 subsections, within each of which are grouped definitions of terms related to the same topic. About 2,000 definitions in all, with cross-references and an index. A feature is the plentiful use of coloured diagrams. Small format. Might prove helpful to 'O' and 'A' level students. *Class No:* 5:025.43

[444]

Thesaurus of scientific, technical, and engineering terms. Science Information Resource Center. Cambridge, Mass., etc., Hemisphere Publishing, 1988. xix,841,376p. $125. ISBN: 0891167943.

Based primarily on the NASA *Thesaurus* and the *DOD Thesaurus of scientific and engineering terms*. 2 v. (in one). V. 1. *Hierarchical listing* contains subject terms and USE cross references; V. 2. *Access vocabulary* lists permuted terms, embedded terms, postable and nonpostable terms and other word entries. *Class No:* 5:025.43

Information Services

[445]

European sources of scientific and technical information. 11th ed. London, Cartermill, 1995. 398p. £180. (*Reference on research*.) ISBN: 058224966x.

First published 1957.

A guide to more than 1,500 organizations in 35 European countries, including patent and standard offices, national and special bodies and their library facilities. 26 subject sections, subdivided under countries. New to this edition is a section on Euroinformation centres. Subject index; organization and keyword index. Includes Eastern Europe but excludes the former USSR. Available online and on CD-ROM. *Class No:* 5:061:025.5

Libraries

Worldwide

[446]

KLESHCHUK, S.E. *and* KORENEVA, S.B. Directory of libraries and information centers of the Academies of Sciences of Socialist countries. Moscow, Nauka Publishers, 1986. 120p.

At head of title-page: 'Library of the USSR Academy of Sciences'. Russian ed., 1984.

Directory of 37 libraries: Bulgaria (1); Hungary (1); Vietnam (1); German Democratic Republic (2); Mongolia (1); Poland (6); Romania

....(contd.)

(1); USSR (20); Czechoslovakia (2); Yugoslavia (2). Data on each library under 15 heads, *e.g.* date of establishment; present status and functions; stock; catalogues; reader services; library publications; activities/programmes. Small format. Now mainly of historical interest. *Class No:* 5:061:026/027(100)

[447]

Libraries, information centres and databases in science and technology: a world guide. Lengenfelder, H., *ed*. 2nd ed. Munich, K.G. Saur, 1988. [xxi], 665p.

First published 1984 as a supplement to *World guide to special libraries* (1983), also edited by H. Lengenfelder.

Contains 13,687 brief entries, arranged A-Z by country and then alphabetically by body. Data include address, subject coverage, holdings, publications, databases. Data bank, organization, and subject indexes. Not comprehensive, but would be useful in a reference library. *Class No:* 5:061:026/027(100)

Europe

[448]

Guide to libraries in central and eastern Europe. Hughes, M., *ed*. London, British Library, Science Reference and Information Service, 1992. 82p. ISBN: 0712307958.

Deals entirely with major libraries in former Soviet Bloc countries arranged A-Z (Albania - Uzbekistan; 227 entries on p.1-68). Also lists 8 UK libraries with east European collections, followed by subject and geographical indexes (p.75-82). No contents page. *Class No:* 5:061:026/027(4)

[449]

Guide to libraries in Western Europe: national, international and government libraries. Dale, P., *ed*. 2nd ed. London, British Library, Science Research and Information Service, 1994. 160p. £36. (*Key resource series*.) ISBN: 0712308105.

First ed. published 1991.

Includes details of libraries in 17 countries. Data include full address and contact details; stock coverage; opening hours; services for outside enquirers; publications. Subject and name indexes. *Class No:* 5:061:026/027(4)

[450]

LEWANSKI, R.C. Subject collections in European libraries. 2nd ed. New York & London, Bowker, 1978. xiii, 495p. ISBN: 0859350118.

First published 1965.

Arranged by subject, based on the 18th ed. of Dewey Decimal Cl. Usual directory information on type of collection, availability, facilities. Subject index, p.483-95. Derived from a mailing of 10,000 libraries, of which *c*.25% responded, with best results from Great Britain, Scandinavia, Low Countries, and Germany, (1965 ed. had data on *c*.6,000 libraries). Intended as a companion to L. Ash's *Subject collections* (5th ed. 1978), covering USA and Canada. *Class No:* 5:061:026/027(4)

Great Britain

[451]

The Aslib directory of information sources in the United Kingdom. Reynard, K.W. *and* Reynard, J.M.E., *eds*. 10th ed. London, Aslib, 1998. 1,508p. £295. ISBN: 0851424090.

First published 1928.

Includes details of over 10,000 organizations, arranged A-Z. Data include: Enquiries to ...; Subject coverage; Special collections; Information services (*e.g.* online searching, own databases); Publications; Electronic and video products. Now includes over 3,000 e-mail addresses and *c*.3,200 Web sites. Many cross-references. Index of acronyms and abbreviations. Subject index. CD-ROM version has 7,000 hotlinks to Web sites. *Class No:* 5:061:026/027(410)

[452]

Guide to libraries and information units in government departments and other organisations. Dale, P., *ed*. 32nd ed. London, British Library, Science Reference and Information Service, 1996. Annual. (*Key resource series*.) ISBN: 0712308288. ISSN: 90525416.

Formerly *Guide to government departments and other libraries* (1948-88).

682 entries arranged A-Z (*c*.150 more than in the previous ed.). Data for each library include address, telephone/fax number, staff, stock and subject coverage, hours of opening, services, publications. E-mail and WWW addresses are included where available. Subject and organization indexes. Typeface used does not clearly differentiate between full and sub-entries and some of the information is obviously out of date. However, useful as a starting point. *Class No:* 5:061:026/027(410)

[453]
Guide to libraries in key UK companies. Dale, P., *ed*. London, British Library, Science Reference and Information Service, 1993. 169p. ISBN: 0712307966.

Arranged A-Z by company name (p.1-136) and including those companies in fields such as biotechnology, nuclear power, etc., detailing address, phone/fax numbers, stock, hours, availability (often company use only), and services. Also lists companies by industry sector, and in organization and subject indexes (p.149-57). Organization index merely duplicates main alphabetical core of the book. *Class No:* 5:061:026/027(410)

Ireland

[454]
Directory of libraries and information centres in Ireland. 5th ed. Dublin & Belfast, Library Association of Ireland and Library Association, Northern Ireland Branch, 1996. 277p. £10. ISBN: 0946037337.

Supersedes *Directory of Northern Ireland libraries* (LA, N. Ireland Branch, 2nd ed., 1977) and *Directory of libraries in Ireland* (2nd ed., 1988).

c.200 entries. Indexes to libraries and special collections and subjects. Similar format to LA/RSIS *Regional guides to library resources*. *Class No:* 5:061:026/027(415)

Federal Republic of Germany

[455]
GERMANY. Federal Republic. Arbeitsgemeinschaft der Spezialbibliotheken. **Verzeichnis der Spezialbibliotheken in der Bundesrepublik Deutschland, einschliesslich West-Berlin.** 2. erw. Aufl., neu bearb. von F. Meyen. Braunschweig, Vieweg, 1970. [viii], 207p.

First published 1965.

Directory of *c*.500 special libraries in the Federal Republic of Germany, and West-Berlin. Dewey Classification grouping. Data: name, address, name of librarian, stock, facilities, co-operation. Many cross-references. Subject, locality and name indexes. Needs to be updated. *Class No:* 5:061:026/027(430.1)

France

[456]
CHAULEUR, A. Bibliothèques et archives: comment se documenter? Guide pratique à l'usage pratique à des étudiants, des professeurs, des documentalistes et archivistes, des chercheurs... 2. éd. Paris, Economica, 1980. 334p.

First published 1978.

Separate parts for libraries and archives, each part with addresses. 'Introduction bibliographique' precedes. Extensive subject index; index of names, book titles and places. Selective listing, with a bias towards the humanities. *Class No:* 5:061:026/027(44)

Japan

[457]
Directory of information sources in Japan, 1986. Tokyo, Nichigai Association, 1986. xiii,378p. ISBN: 4816905537.

Guide to *c*.1,500 libraries and services of all kinds, excluding many smaller public libraries, but including non-library information sources. In Japanese and English. Index of libraries in English and Japanese. Subject index. *Class No:* 5:061:026/027(52)

Egypt

[458]
ARAB REPUBLIC OF EGYPT. National Information and Documentation Centre. **Directory of scientific and technical libraries in the United Arab Republic.** Cairo, the Centre, 1970. 242p.

Data on 208 libraries in Egypt. *Class No:* 5:061:026/027(620)

America—North & Central

[459]
Directory of special libraries and information centers 1999. 23rd ed. Detroit, Mich., Gale, 1998. Annual. 2v. £445; $580, v.1; £479; $365, v.2. ISSN: 0731633x.

First published 1963.

1. *Directory*. 2. *Geographic and personnel indexes*.

V.1 has over 23,300 entries (A-Z, by name) for special libraries in US, Canada, plus more than 380 special libraries in over 80 other countries. Subject index (3,500 subjects). Appendices (*eg*, Networks and consortia). V.2 consists of two separate indexes - geographic and personnel. Expanded international coverage includes *c*.300 entries for libraries outside the US and Canada. Also includes an appendix of EC depository libraries in the US.

....(contd.)
Subject directory of special libraries (3v. 23rd ed. 1999. £670) contains the contents of *Directory of special libraries and information centers*, arranged A-Z by subject. *Class No:* 5:061:026/027(71/73)

[460]
—ASH, L. Subject collections: a guide to special book collections and subject emphases as reported by university, college, public and special librarians and museums in the United States and Canada. 6th ed. New York, Bowker, 1985. 2v. (2144p.). $175. ISBN: 0835219178.

First published 1958; 5th ed. (xi, 1184p.), 1978.

A directory of 20,000 collections, adding *c*.5,000 to entries in the 5th ed. Arranged under Library of Congress subject-headings, A-Z subdivided by US states and Canadian provinces. Less easy to use than *Subject directory of special libraries and information centers*, V.3 & 5, supported as they are by v.2 (Geographic and personnel indexes) of the parent *Directory of special libraries and information centers* (*q.v.*).

7th ed., revised by W.G. Miller, (Bowker, 1993. 2v. 2466p. $275; £145). *Class No:* 5:061:026/027(71/73)

[461]
—Sci-tech libraries in museums and aquariums. New York, Columbia Univ., School of Library Service; London, Haworth Press, 1986. xiv,204p. ISBN: 0866564845.

Has also been published as *Science & technology libraries*, v.6(1/2), Fall 1985/Winter 1985/86.

Highlights 'some outstanding sci-tech libraries serving museums and aquariums around the country'. Data on each include history and functions, collections, services to users, catalogue and classification, special features, policies and programmes.
Class No: 5:061:026/027(73)

Australia

[462]
Directory of special libraries in Australia. Cree, J., *ed*. 7th ed. Ultimo, New South Wales, Library Association of Australia, Special Libraries Section, 1988. 552p. ISBN: 0868040592.

First published 1954.

Lists *c*.1,000 special libraries, arranged by area. Index of names, subjects. *Class No:* 5:061:026/027(94)

Institutions & Associations

Worldwide

[463]
Scientific and technical organizations and agencies directory: a guide to approximately 25,000 organizations and agencies providing information in the physical sciences, engineering and technology. Dresser, P.D., *ed*. 3rd ed. Detroit, Mich., Gale, 1994. 2v. ISBN: 0810354640, set.

First published 1985.

Chapters on US, Canadian, and international scientific and technical organizations and agencies. Each chapter deals with a particular type of organization. Master name and keyword index.
Class No: 5:061:061.2(100)

[464]
World guide to scientific associations and learned societies. [Internationales Verzeichnis wissenschaftlicher Verbände und Gesellschaften.] Zils, M., *ed*. 7th ed. Munich, K.G. Saur, 1998. xiv, 529p. (*Handbook of international documentation and information, v.13*.) ISBN: 3598205813.

First published 1974, as *World guide to scientific organizations*.

A guide to more than 17,100 associations and societies, with 1,400 added since the 6th ed. Contains information on national and regional associations from 167 countries, in addition to international organizations. Data include name/abbreviation; address; year founded; areas of activity; membership; chief officials. Coverage: science, technology, humanities, and social sciences. Subject index with 177 headings. An alphabetical index to associations' names (including abbreviations) is included. Other indexes: German-English concordance to areas of specialization; subject index; publications index (16,056 periodicals, annuals, bulletins, etc.). Some overlap with *World of learning*. *Class No:* 5:061:061.2(100)

Great Britain

[465]
Centres & bureaux: a directory of concentrations of effort, information and expertise. Sellar, L., *ed*. Beckenham, Kent, CBD Research, Ltd., 1987. ix, 214p. £42. (*CBD Research publication*.) ISBN: 0900246472.

Nearly 1,000 entries for specialist bodies - self-styled 'centre', 'bureau' and otherwise - in the UK and Ireland (*e.g.* Centre for Medical Research, Waste Management Information Bureau, CAB International). A-Z directory and addenda, p.1-172. Index of sponsors

....*(contd.)*
and participating oranizations. Subject index (Abortion ... Youth studies), p.195-214. Fills a gap in the CBD series.
Class No: 5:061:061.2(410)

Federal Republic of Germany
[466]
Directory of international cooperation in science and technology: index of institutions in the Federal Republic of Germany cooperating with developing countries. Gottstein, K., *ed.* 2nd enl. and rev. ed. Munich, K.G. Saur, 1989. 256p. £55. ISBN: 3598106262.
595 institutions involved in transfer of information in science, technology or the arts. Partner countries/institutions are listed separately, after the description of activities for each institution.
Class No: 5:061:061.2(430.1)

China
[467]
Directory of selected scientific institutions in mainland China. Prepared by Surveys and Research Corpn. Stanford, Calif., Hoover Institution Press, for the National Science Foundation, 1976. xxii, 469p.
The directory, p.1-374 (1. Chinese Academy of Sciences ... 490. Yünnan University). 3 appendices include 'A supplementary list of 1,127 additional research and development institutions', p.381-424. 7 indexes, - of institutions (by English translation; by Wade-Giles and P'in Yin romanizations), scientists and other key personnel, fields and sub-fields, major publications, and geographic (province or city).
Class No: 5:061:061.2(510)

Africa
[468]
Profiles of African scientific institutions. Nairobi, African Academy of Sciences and Network of African Scientific Organizations, 1992. xiii,282p. ISBN: 9966831118.
Gives details of 186 organizations in 36 nations. Almost half are research institutions, with the remainder private or government agencies. Data include short history, contact details, publications, etc. Companion volume to *Profiles of African scientists* (2nd ed. 1992) *(q.v.)*. *Class No:* 5:061:061.2(6)

South Africa
[469]
Scientific and technical societies in South Africa. Pretoria, South African Council for Scientific and Industrial Research, 1967-. Annual.
Includes data on aims, membership requirements, meetings, branches and publications. *Class No:* 5:061:061.2(680)

America—North
[470]
Research centers directory: a guide to approximately 13,400 university-related and other non-profit research organizations established on a permanent basis and carrying on continuing research programs. Piccirelli, A., *ed.* Detroit, Mich., Gale, Annual. 2v. ISSN: 00801518.
First published 1960.
Entries for over 13,000 research units in the US and Canada arranged in subject sections under 5 broad headings (Life sciences; Physical sciences and engineering; Private and public policy and affairs; Social and cultural studies; Multidisciplinary and coordinating centers). 5 indexes: detailed subject, alphabetical, acronyms, institutional, and special capabilities (*e.g.* facilities, collections, databases). Available online via DIALOG File 115. Supplemented between editions by *New research centers*.
Class No: 5:061:061.2(71+73)

USA
[471]
BATES, R.S. Scientific societies in the United States. 3rd ed. Cambridge, Mass., M.I.T. Press; Oxford, etc., Pergamon Press, 1965. [xv], 326p.
First published 1945; 2nd ed. 1958.
'The history and influence of the scientific societies of the United States' (*Preface*, 1st ed.). Historical survey in 7 chapters: 1. Scientific societies in eighteenth century America ... 6. The atomic age - 7. Scientific societies in the space age. Chronology; bibliography, p.245-93 (systematically arranged, including 'Special references to American scientific agencies other than scientific societies'). Index, p.295-326.
Class No: 5:061:061.2(73)

Brazil
[472]
Guia des sociedades e associacões científicas e technológicas do Brasil. Brasília, Instituto Brasileiro de Informacão en Ciencia e Tecnologia, 1984. 293p.
Directory of nearly 230 organizations, plus *c.*40 universities. Subject groups: General - Geology - Biological science - Engineering - Medicine - Agriculture - Applied social sciences - Humanities - Linguistics - Literature & arts. Index of societies and associations.
Class No: 5:061:061.2(81)

Australia
[473]
Directory of Australian professional associations, 1996. Carlton, Victoria, CRNet, 1996. 300p. ISBN: 0646289861.
Cover title (*Australian science and technology associations 1996*) makes this volume the logical successor to CSIRO's *Australian scientific societies and professional associations*, 2nd ed. 1978. Available on the Internet at http://crnet.com.au/Australian science and technology online. *Class No:* 5:061:061.2(94)

Conferences
[474]
EPPLE, A. Organizing scientific meetings. Cambridge, University Press, 1997. xiv, 184p. £32.50. ISBN: 0521563518.
19 chapters: 1. Introduction: what can go wrong ... 7. Dates of the meeting: you can't win ... 12. Office and staff: don't take chances ... 18. Design of forms, name tags etc. 18 appendices (*e.g.* A: Poster presentation). Index. The author's light-hearted approach does not detract from this handbook's considerable value to any conference organizer. *Class No:* 5:061:061.3

[475]
Forthcoming international scientific and technical conferences. London, Aslib, 1924-. 4pa. (Main list is in February, updated by supplement in May and cumulative supplements in August and November). £204. ISSN: 00464686.
Records more than 1,000 conferences pa., arranged in chronological order. Data on each: date; title of conference; location; address for enquiries. Subject, location and organization indexes.
Class No: 5:061:061.3

[476]
Mind: the meetings index: Series SEMT, science, engineering, medicine, technology. Harrison, N.Y., InterDok, 1984-. 4pa. $460 (US), $485 (non US). ISSN: 07395914.
Lists forthcoming SEMT meetings, under keywords. Supporting indexes of sponsors, locations and dates. Details of contacts. *Interdok* (*q.v.*) lists the resultant published proceedings. *Class No:* 5:061:061.3

[477]
Science and engineering conference proceedings: a guide to sources for identification and verification. DeFelice, B., *ed.* Chicago, Ill., Association of College and Research Libraries, 1995. 80p. $16.50. ISBN: 0838977901.
Lists 62 abstracting and indexing services which cover conference proceedings in science and technology, excluding medicine. Useful feature is the discussion of the problems of conference proceedings, *e.g.* lack of bibliographic control. For trainee librarians and those unfamiliar with scientific literature. *Class No:* 5:061:061.3

[478]
Scientific meetings; describing future meetings of technical, scientific, medical, and management organizations and universities. San Diego, Calif., Scientific Meetings Publications, 1957-. 4pa. $75 (US); $82.50 (non US). ISSN: 04878965.
Meetings A-Z, with chronological and keyword indexes. Details of contacts. Pronounced US slant. Available on microfilm from University Microfilms International. *Class No:* 5:061:061.3

[479]
TORRENCE, S.R. How to run scientific and technical meetings. New York, Van Nostrand Reinhold, 1991. xix,887p. figs., tables. $39.95. ISBN: 0442236751.
19 documented chapters: 1. Defining and conceptualizing the technical meeting - 2. Organization ... 5. Selecting your meeting site ... 7. Liability, insurance, and the law ... 17. Enhancing your meeting with exhibitions... 19. International meetings. 45 appendices (*e.g.* 14. Sample contract with a hotel; 24. Creating good visuals). Glossary, p.835-54. Index. US-slant, but useful for anyone involved in organizing a technical meeting. *Class No:* 5:061:061.3

[480]
World meetings: outside United States and Canada. New York, Macmillan Publishing, 1968-. 4pa. $200. ISSN: 00438677.
A two-year-span register of future medical, scientific and technical meetings. Data include information on availability of abstracts or papers. Indexes: by date of meeting, keyword, location, deadline for abstracts or papers and sponsors. *Class No:* 5:061:061.3

[481]
World meetings: United States and Canada. New York, Macmillan Publishing, 1963-. 4pa. $200. ISSN: 00438693.
Like its companion register, *World meetings: outside United States and Canada*, provides a two-year-span record of future medical, scientific and technical meetings. Similar data. *Class No:* 5:061:061.3

Bibliographies

[482]
Bibliographic guide to conference publications, 1975-. Thorndike, ME., Hall, 1974-. Annual. $410. ISSN: 03602729.
Annual dictionary catalogue compiled by the Research Libraries of the New York Public Library, plus Library of Congress MARC tapes additional entries. Indexes *c.*26,000 private and government conference publications. *Class No:* 5:061:061.3(01)

[483]
CAMBRIDGE UNIVERSITY LIBRARY. Union catalogue of scientific libraries in the University of Cambridge: Scientific proceedings, 1644-1974. London, Mansell, 1975. 2v. (1232p).
About 25,000 entries for the proceedings of some 6,000 conferences, symposia and lecture meetings. Arranged by name and keyword. *Class No:* 5:061:061.3(01)

[484]
Conference papers index. Bethesda, Md., Cambridge Scientific Abstracts, 1978-. v.6-. 24pa. $985; $1,015 (non US). ISSN: 0162704x.
Formerly *Current programs* (v.1-5, 1973-77).
Lists authors and titles of papers given at scientific conferences. Available online via DIALOG and ESA. *Class No:* 5:061:061.3(01)

[485]
Directory of published proceedings. Harrison, N.Y., InterDok Corpn., 1966-.
Series SEMT - *Science/Engineering/Medicine/Technology.* 1967-. 10pa. $575.
Series SSH - *Social sciences/Humanities.* 1968-. 4pa. $375.
Series PCE - *Pollution Control/Ecology.* 1974-. 2pa. Annual. $150.
The directory records preprints and published proceedings of congresses, conferences, symposia, meetings seminars and summer schools that have been held from 1964 to date.
Series SEMT (September-June) - like the other two series - lists entries chronologically by date of conference and of proceedings, with publishers' and distributors' addresses. Editor, location and subject/sponsor indexes. The annual cumulative volume includes cumulating indexes. *Class No:* 5:061:061.3(01)

[486]
Index to scientific & technical proceedings. Philadelphia, Pa., Institute for Scientific Information, 1978-. 12pa., cumulated annually, $2060. ISSN: 01498088.
Indexes over 180,000 conference papers pa. Each issue contains category index (Acoustics ... Zoology); contents of proceedings; author and editor index; sponsor index; meetings location index; permuterm subject index; corporate index (geographic section; organization section). Online via DIALOG and on CD-ROM. *Class No:* 5:061:061.3(01)

[487]
Proceedings in print. Halifax, Mass., Proceedings in Print, Inc., 1964-. 6pa. $615 (US); $680 (non US). ISSN: 00329568.
About 2,500 entries pa. under title of conference, A-Z. Author and subject index. The December issue includes cumulative annual index. *Class No:* 5:061:061.3(01)

[488]
Scientific, engineering and medical societies publications in print. New York, Bowker, 1974-. Two-yearly. $65. ISSN: 02777355.
An in-print service listing societies' available publications. *Class No:* 5:061:061.3(01)

Research Establishments

Worldwide

[489]
International research centers directory. Detroit, Mich., Gale, 1982-. Biennial. ISSN: 02782731.
8th ed. 1996-97 (1995. Gerring, A.L., *ed.* xv,1674p.). A guide to *c.*8,000 research facilities in approx. *c.*150 countries. Entries are arranged by country, with an international section. Name and keyword index; country index; subject index. *Class No:* 5:061:061.62(100)

Europe

[490]
European research centres: a directory of scientific, technological, agricultural and biomedical laboratories. 10th ed. London, Cartermill, 1995. 1246p. £375. ISBN: 0582256925.
Directory of over 14,000 research laboratories in over 30 European countries, with *c.*2,000 new entries added since 9th ed. Data include organization title, address, director's name, graduate research staff, annual expenditure and lists of organizational activities and publications. Major laboratories are highlighted with a star before the title. Subject and establishment indexes. Available on the CD-ROM *Current research in Europe*. *Class No:* 5:061:061.62(4)

Great Britain

[491]
Industrial research in the United Kingdom: a guide to organizations and programmes. 16th ed. London, Cartermill, 1995. 592p. £240.
First published 1946 as *Industrial research in Britain*. 15th ed. 1993.
Details of 4,250 laboratories active in agricultural and environmental sciences, chemical and materials sciences, earth and astronomical sciences, electronics and computer sciences, pharmaceutical, biomedical and biological sciences, and engineering and transportation. 6 Sections: 1. Industrial firms - 2. Research associations and consultancies - 3. Government departments, and their laboratories - 4. Universities and polytechnics - 5. Trade and development associations - 6. Learned and professional societies. Indexes: personal name; title of establishments; subject; establishments by subject. Data is a subset of *World research database*, available online via ESA-IRS and on CD-ROM. *Class No:* 5:061:061.62(410)

Russia

[492]
Russian research institutions and scientists directory. Washington, Russian Information and Business Center, 1997-.
A useful listing which, it is intended, will be revised and updated at regular intervals. *Class No:* 5:061:061.62(47)

Asia—Far East

[493]
Pacific research centres: a directory of scientific, industrial, agricultural, and biomedical laboratories. 4th ed. Harlow, Essex, Longman Group, 1993. vi,392p. ISBN: 0582216699.
First published 1986.
Arranged alphabetically by country and including details of 3,500 organizations. 950 new entries since previous edition (1990). Countries covered include Australia, People's Republic of China, Indonesia, Japan, Malaysia, New Zealand, Philippines, Singapore, Taiwan, Thailand, Vietnam. Data note size of organization, key personnel, main research activities, and trade associations and societies. Indexes arranged by titles and subjects of establishments, and general subjects. *Class No:* 5:061:061.62(51/52+57)

China

[494]
WANNACK-NUNN, S. Directory of scientific research institutes in the People's Republic of China. Washington, National Council for US - China Trade, 1977-78. 3v.
1. Agriculture, fisheries, forestry 2. Chemicals, construction 3. (2pts). Electrical and electronics; light industry; machinery, including metals and mining; transportation.
Entries under subject areas. Does not claim to be definitive and omits universities. *Class No:* 5:061:061.62(510)

Israel

[495]
ISRAEL. National Centre of Scientific and Technical Information. Directory of research institutes and industrial laboratories in Israel. 3rd ed. Tel Aviv, COSTI, 1980. 230p.
Data on 175 institutions. In Hebrew and English. *Class No:* 5:061:061.62(569.4)

USA

[496]
Government research directory. Batten, D., *ed.* 12th ed. Detroit, Mich., Gale, 1999. xiv, 805p. ISBN: 0787621919.
First published 1980.
Described as *a descriptive guide to more than 4,400 U.S. and Canadian government research and development centers, institutes, laboratories, bureaux, test facilities, experiment stations, data collection and analysis centers, and grants management and research*

....(contd.)

coordinating offices in agriculture, commerce, education, energy, engineering, environment, the Humanities, medicine, military science, and basic and applied sciences. Indexed. *Class No:* 5:061:061.62(73)

[503]

TEREK, F. **Scientific expeditions.** Jamaica, N.Y., Queens Borough Public Library, 1952. xvii, 176p.

Lists major scientific expeditions, with data on objectives, personnel, equipment, sponsorship, location and the like. Bibliography of source material; index of members and sponsors of expeditions. *Class No:* 5:061:910.4

Research Projects

[497]

Current research in Britain. 10th ed. London, Cartermill, 1995. Annual. 4v in 6. £350, set. ISBN: 1860670628, set.

Previously as *Research in British universities, polytechnics and colleges* (RBUPC).

1. *Physical sciences.* 1995. 2v. (1088p) £135.
2. *Biological sciences.* 1995. 2v. (1061p) £135.
3. *Social sciences.* 1995. £99.
4. *The humanities.* 1995. £80.

Register of current research in all British universities, many colleges and other academic institutions, and government departments and other centres. Indexes for names, study area, and keywords. A basic research tool, now also available on CD-ROM.

Physical sciences covers mathematics, astronomy, physics, chemistry and technology (*e.g.* engineering, accountancy). Details of 57,000 projects from 400 institutions. Includes list of new universities. *Class No:* 5:061:061.62.005

[498]

SMITHSONIAN SCIENCE INFORMATION EXCHANGE, Inc. **Information services on research in progress:** a world inventory. 2nd ed. Paris, Unesco, 1982. 330p. illus. $20. ISBN: 9231020714.

First published 1978.

Profiles of 230 individual information systems, with international, regional or national coverage. Five indexes, - of subjects, countries, organizations, information systems, and individual names. *Class No:* 5:061:061.62.005

Museums

[499]

DANILOV, V.J. **America's science museums.** Westport, Conn., Greenwood Press, 1990. 496p. $65. ISBN: 0313258651.

Contains entries for 587 museums, covering areas such as space and aviation, transport and botany. 12 sections, arranged alphabetically by subject, with museums listed alphabetically within each section. Data include address, hours and days of operation, admission fees, history and collection description. Bibliography and index. More detailed than the *Official museum directory* (American Association of Museums, 1980-. Annual). *Class No:* 5:061:069

[500]

GOLDBECK, G. **Museen in Deutschland (West): Technische Museen.** Führer zu der Museen für die Geschichte von Naturwissenschaft, Technik, Gewerbe und Industrie in den Bundesrepublik Deutschland und West Berlin. Stuttgart, J. Fink Verlag, 1975. 71p. illus. ISBN: 3771801974.

West German science/technology museums devoted to the history of natural history, technology, business and industry. Arranged under places, Altera ... Wuppertal. Appended notes on railway historical museums, and list of 8 other museums. Name and subject indexes. *Class No:* 5:061:069

[501]

HUDSON, K. *and* NICHOLLS, A. **The Cambridge guide to the museums of Britain and Ireland.** Cambridge, University Press, 1989. x,452p. illus. (some col.) maps. ISBN: 0521378923.

First published 1987.

Covers over 2,000 collections, arranged A/Z (Abbots Bromley ... Wollaston). Separate section on museums new to this edition. Data on each collection include hours of opening; facilities for the disabled; refreshments; tours; parking. Index of museum names; index of subjects (*e.g.* agriculture; botany; medicine); index of museums associated with individuals (*e.g.* Charles Darwin). 16 pages of location maps. 400 illustrations. *Class No:* 5:061:069

Education Institutions

[502]

Croner's manual for heads of science. Kingston upon Thames, Croner, 1993-. Loose-leaf. ISBN: 1855241560.

12 contributors; six sections: 1. The curriculum - 2. Safety in the school laboratory ... 5. Services out of schools - 6. Further information. Also available on floppy disk or CD-ROM. *Class No:* 5:061:37

51 Mathematics

Mathematics

Databases

[504]

Mathematics abstracts. Karlsruhe, Fachinformationszentrum Karlsruhe.

The database equivalent of *Zentralblatt für Mathematik und ihre Grenzgebiete*. Includes citations, with abstracts since 1984; international coverage. 1,000,000 records, updated monthly. Available online via STN International and on CD-ROM (Springer-Verlag). *Class No:* 510(003.4)

[505]

MathSci. Providence, R.I., American Mathematical Society.

MATHSCI is a database equivalent of *Mathematical reviews*, and other subfiles, including *Current mathematical publications*, *ACM guide to computing literature*, *Current index to statistics*. 1,700,000 records. Available on DIALOG (file 239) and other hosts. Available on CD-ROM (SilverPlatter) as *MathSci Disc* (1940-), and on magentic tape. Also available, as MathSciNet, at the web site of the American Mathematical Society (URL: http://www.ams.org). *Class No:* 510(003.4)

[506]

World databases in physics and mathematics. Armstrong, C.J., *ed*. London, Bowker-Saur, 1995. [xii], 1085p. £150. (*World database series*.) ISBN: 1857390385.

The series 'aims to become the de facto authority on electronically published databases' (*Introduction*). Lists about 1,200 electronically published databases in 9 sections: 1. Science/Technology - 2. Science/General - 3. Astronomy - 4. Mathematics - 5. Meterology - 6. Nuclear Science - 7. Materials Science - 8. Physics - 9. Domestic Sciences. Entries include a brief description of contents and coverage, online hosts, CD-ROM and internet availability, etc. Database 'families' and subsets identified. Indexes: addresses; database name; subject. Claims to be comprehensive but the coverage of European databases is fuller than that of North American. Clumsy and awkward to use, partly because some substantial entries appear in several sections (*e.g. Science citation index*). *Class No:* 510(003.4)

Internet

[507]

Math archives. University of Tennessee Knoxville. URL: http://archives.math.utk.edu.

A resource for students and teachers. Topics are organized by major categories (*e.g.* algebra; calculus; fractals; history; number theory, etc.). Includes links to software and teaching materials. *Class No:* 510(003.41)

[508]

MathGuide. Lower Saxony State and University Library, Göttingen, Germany. URL: http://www.sub.uni-goettingen.de/ssgfi/math/singleindex.html.

The web site offers links to electronic archives and journals, factual printed reference works and bibliographic sources. Searches can be conducted by author, title or primary American Mathematical Society Subject Classification. 'A useful gateway site for access to university level mathematics' (*Choice*, January 1999, p.924). *Class No:* 510(003.41)

Software

[509]

Guide to available mathematical software (GAMS). Washington, D.C., National Institute of Standards and Technology. URL: http://math.nist.gov/

An online cross index of about 10,000 publicly accessible mathematical software modules. Focus is on mathematical problems for computational sciences and engineering. *Class No:* 510(003.42)

Bibliographies

[510]

DEAN, N. 'Mathematics and statistics for engineers'. *Information sources in engineering*. K.W. Mildren and P.J. Hicks, eds. (3rd ed., 1996), p.451-66. 3rd ed. London, Bowker Saur, 1996. £80. ISBN: 1857390571.

A brief survey of information sources. Covers software, organizations, books (by topic, *e.g.* catastrophe theory), conference proceedings, periodicals. References, p.461-66. *Class No:* 510(01)

[511]

DORLING, A.R., *ed*. **Use of mathematical literature.** London, Butterworths, 1977. xii, 260p. (*Butterworths Guides to information sources*.)

16 contributors. 14 Documented chapters: 1. The role of the literature in mathematics - 2. Major organisations and journals - 3. Reference material (encyclopedias; handbooks; abstracting journals) - 4. Mathematical education - 5. History of mathematics - 6. Logic and foundations - 7. Combinations - 8. Rings and algebras - 9. Group theory - 10. Measure and probability - 11. Complex analysis and special functions - 12. Convexity - 13. Topology - 14. Mathematical programming (88 references). Each chapter provides running commentary on items. Author index; subject and title index. 'A valuable guide to the subject for students and scientists' (*New technical books*, March 1978, entry 334). *Class No:* 510(01)

[512]

—**GAFFNEY, M.P.** *and* **STERN, L.A.** Annotated bibliography of expository writing in the mathematical sciences. Washington, D.C., Mathematical Association of America, 1976. xi, 282p.

Includes 'over 1,000 articles and a few books of general interest' (*Preface*). Sections: 1. General - 2. Foundations - 3. Algebra - 4. Analysis - 5. Geometry - 6. Statistics and computing - 7. Applications. Author index. *Class No:* 510(01)

[513]

—**HØYRUP, L.** Books about mathematics: history, philosophy. education, models, system theory and works of reference, etc. Roskilde, Denmark, Roskilde Univ. Center, 1979. viii, 182p.

A bibliography [unannotated] of 'books ABOUT mathematics - and not "technical" textbooks or research monographs on mathematics ...' (*Preface*). Pt.1: History and philosophy of mathematics and mathematics education, etc. - Pt.2: Models and systems theory - Pt.3: Works of reference (1. Bibliographies...Addresses). Author index. *Class No:* 510(01)

[514]

PARKE, N.G. Guide to the literature of mathematics and physics, including related works on engineering science. 2nd rev. ed. New York, Dover, 1958; London, Constable, 1959. xviii, 436p.

First published 1947.

The 2nd ed. is double the size, although Pt.1 'General considerations' (p.3-74; including principles of making a literature search) remains unrevised. In Pt.2 'The literature', over 5,000 entries appear under *c.*120 subject headings (Acoustics ... Writing-technical), in double columns. One heading is 'Bibliographic aids', p.132-42. Subject headings are defined and notes provided on some titles. Emphasis is on applied mathematics. Mathematics and physics often figure together, but not always (*eg*, 'Tables (mathematical)'; 'History - Mathematics'). Peripheral fields include chemistry, machine and general engineering. Author and subject indexes, p.383-436. Dates of many of the references do not go beyond 1955. *Class No:* 510(01)

[515]

PEMBERTON, J.E. How to find out in mathematics: a guide to sources of information. 2nd ed. Oxford, etc., Pergamon Press, 1969. xiv, 193p. facsims. (*The Commonwealth and international library of science, technology, engineering and liberal studies*.)

First published 1964.

Chapters: 1. Careers for mathematics - 2. The organisation of mathematical information - 3. Mathematical dictionaries, encyclopedias and theses - 4. Mathematical periodicals and abstracts - 5. Mathematical societies - 6. Mathematical education - 7. Computers and mathematical tables - 8. Mathematical history and biography - 9/10. Mathematical books (bibliographies; evaluation and acquisition) - 11. Probability and statistics - 12. Operational research and related techniques. Exercises are appended to chapters. Appendices (*e.g.* Sources of Russian mathematical information). The index, p.181-93, covers authors of works cited. A helpful, comprehensive survey, mainly in the form of a running commentary. *Class No:* 510(01)

Indexes

[516]

CompuMath citation index: an international, interdisciplinary index to the literature of applied mathematics, computer science statistics, operations research and related disciplines. Phildealphia, Pa., Institute for Scientific Information, 1981-. 2pa. ISSN: 07306199.

CMCI consists of 5 indexes: Research front specialty index; Citation index; Corporate index; Source index; Permuterm subject index. Also, annual *Guide and list of source publications*. Available online as part of Scisearch. *Class No:* 510(014)

Encyclopaedias

[517]

Encyclopaedia of mathematics. Hazewinkel, M., *ed.* Dordrecht, Netherlands, Reidel, 1988-94. 10v. formulas; equations. ISBN: 0155608010, set.

A translation, with updates and editorial comments, of The Soviet *Mathematical encyclopaedia* ('Soviet Encyclopaedia Publishing House', 1977-85. 5v.).

Three kinds of articles: 1. Surveys of main directions in mathematics - 2. Detailed discussion of concrete problems, results and techniques - 3. Short (reference) definitions. Many include annotations or editorial comment and references (to both Soviet and Western literature). Entries classified by AMS numbers from the 1980 scheme. A CD-ROM version is available (Kluwer Academic, 1997; $235 (stand alond version); $1775 (network version); ISBN: 0792348079).

Class No: 510(031)

[518]

Encyclopedic dictionary of mathematics. Mathematical Society of Japan. 2nd ed., edited by K. Itó. Cambridge, Mass., & London, MIT Press, 1987. 4v. (2,120p.). diagrs, graphs, tables, formulas. $350. ISBN: 0262090260.

First published 1934. 2nd ed. is English translation of the 3rd Japanese ed. (1985), with references to English-language textbooks in place of the original Japanese textbooks.

V.1-3 (A-E, F-N, O-Z) comprise 450 articles (Abel ... Zeta functions). V.4 includes 23 appendices (1. Algebraic functions ... 23. Statistical estimation and statistical hypothesis testing), as well as numerical and statistical tables, a list of journals, systematic and A-Z lists of the articles. Name index; detailed, analytical subject index (p.1917-2148). 'An essential buy for every library and for many private bookdealers' (*Nature*, v.330, 26 November 1987 p.322).

Class No: 510(031)

[519]

GELLERT, W., *and others, eds.* **The VNR concise encyclopedia of mathematics.** 2nd ed. New York, etc., Van Nostrand Reinhold, 1989. 776+56p. illus. (partly col.), diagrs., graphs, tables. $30. ISBN: 0442205902.

First published by VEB Bibliographisches Institut (Leipzig, 1973) as *Kleine Enzyklopädie der Mathematik.*

Three parts (42 sections): 1. Elementary mathematics - 2. Steps towards higher mathematics - 3. Brief reports on selected topics (*e.g.* topology, game theory). Closely written, colours being used extensively to help the reader (yellow background for important definitions and groups of formulae; blue, for examples; red, for theorems); red arrows indicate more complicated calculations. The reviewer in *Choice* (October 1990, p.289) found 'almost no change' from the 1977 edition and concluded that the work was 'much more like a reprint than a new edition'. But the *New Scientist* urged readers to 'save up your pennies for a few months and buy' (2 February 1991, p.66). *Class No:* 510(031)

[520]

NAAS, H. *and* **SCHMID, H.L. Mathematisches Wörterbuch,** mit Einbeziehung der theoretischen Physik. Im Auftrag des Instituts für Reine Mathematik an der Deutschen Akademie für Wissenschaft zu Berlin. Berlin, Akademie Verlag GmbH; London & New York, Pergamon Press, 1961. 2v. (A.-K. xi, 1043p.; L-Z. vi, 952p).

127 contributors, 96 of them German. Entries concern terms, phrases, methods and trends of research plus brief biographies of 400 deceased mathematicians and the history of mathematics. Some articles carry short bibliographies of texts and papers. Treatment in depth (*e.g.* 'Legendre functions': 18p.). Many formulae. V.2 has appended list of more common symbols and of 82 branches and applications of mathematics. Very favourably reviewed in *Nature*, v.196, no.4855, 17 November 1962. *Class No:* 510(031)

[521]

—**Enzyklopädie der Mathematischen Wissenchaften,** mit Einschluss ihrer Anwendungen, Hrsg. im Auftrage der Akademien der Wissenschaften zu Berlin: 2 völlig neubarb. Aufl. Leipzig, Teubner, 1960-. v.1-.

First published 1898-1935 (6v. in 23: 1. *Arithmetik und Algebra* (2 pts.) - 2. *Analyse* (2 pts.) - 3. *Geometrie* (6 pts.) - 4. *Mechanik* (4 pts.) - 5. *Physik* (3 pts.) - 6. *Geodäsie und Geophysik. Astronomie*). Noted for its comprehensive treatment and well-documented, scholarly articles, aimed at the specialist. Detailed attention to applications in mechanics, physics, geodesy, geophysics and astronomy. The 2nd ed. is only slowly replacing the 1st ed. *Class No:* 510(031)

[522]

The Prentice-Hall encyclopedia of mathematics. West, B.H., *and others, eds.* Englewood Cliffs, NJ., Prentice-Hall, 1983. 638p. diagrs., graphs. £42.25. ISBN: 0136960138.

An encyclopedia of 'basic definitions, forumlas, examples, applications and occasional projects' (*Preface*). 8 broad topics (*e.g.* algebra; infinity; rational and irrational numbers; probability; zero). For scientists, teachers and non-professionals. *Class No:* 510(031)

[523]

SNEDDON, I.N., *ed.* **Encyclopaedic dictionary of mathematics for engineers and applied scientists.** Oxford etc., Pergamon Press, 1976. viii, 800p. diagrs., tables. ISBN: 0080167675.

More than 2,000 entries, A-Z; over 150 contributors. Longer articles are signed, with short bibliographies (*e.g.* 'Phase-integral methods': 9 columns; 8 references). Numerous cross-references. Appendix: includes addenda, 'Calculators, Electronic'. Editor: Professor of Mathematics, Glasgow University. Full index and good layout, - 'a boon to the librarian as well as the pressured engineer, researcher or student' (*RSR*, v.6(3), July/September 1978, p.19). *Class No:* 510(031)

Handbooks & Manuals

[524]

CRC handbook of mathematical sciences. Beyer, W.H., *ed.* 6th ed. Boca Raton, Florida, CRC Press, 1987. 860p. diagrs., graphs, tables, formulas. £52.

5th ed. 1978, and formerly as *CRC Handbook of tables for mathematics.*

Compendium on mathematical and statistical functions, logically arranged in 13 sections. 1. Constants and conversion factors - 2. Algebra - 3. Combinatorial analysis - 4. Geometry - 5. Trigonometry - 6. Logarithmic exponential and hyperbolic functions - 7. Analytical geometry - 8. Calculus - 9. Differential equations - 10. Special functions - 11. Numerical methods 12. - Probability and statistics - 13. Aerodynamics. Appendix: Mathematic symbols and abbreviations. Detailed index, p.849-60. *Class No:* 510(035)

[525]

DUNHAM, W. The Mathematical universe: an alphabetical journey through the great proofs, problems, and personalities. New York, Wiley, 1994. vi, 314p. illus., graphs, mathematical formulas. $22.95. ISBN: 0471536563.

25 topics, Arithmetic - Z (complex numbers). A narrative rather than a highly mathematical treatment. Index, p.309-14. Selected by *Choice* as an outstanding academic book for 1995. *Class No:* 510(035)

[526]

LEDERMANN, W. Handbook of applicable mathematics. New York, etc., Wiley, 1980-84. 6v. in 8.

1. *Algebra.* 2. *Probability.* 3. *Numerical methods.* 4. *Analysis,* edited by W. Ledermann and S. Vajda. 1982. 5. (2 pts.): *Combinations and geometry*, edited by W. Ledermann and S. Vajda. 1984-. 6 (2 pts.): *Statistics*, edited by E. Lloyd. 1984.

Each volume has chapter bibliographies and an analytical index. The set is designed specifically for the needs of the professional, although 'it aims to cater for all levels' (*The plan of the handbook*).

V. 7, *Supplement,* appeared in 1990; *Contents and general index* in 1991. *Class No:* 510(035)

[527]

PEARSON, C.E., *ed.* **Handbook of applied mathematics:** selected results and methods. 2nd ed. New York, Van Nostrand Reinhold, 1983. 1307p. ISBN: 0442238665.

First published 1974 (1266p.).

20 contributors. 21 documented chapters (2. Elements of analysis ... 7. Special functions ... 12. Asymptotic methods ... 18. Numerical analysis ... 21. Probability with statistics). Worked examples. The topics dealt with 'involve results and techniques which experience has shown to be of utility in a very broad survey of applications' (*Preface*). Detailed index. *Class No:* 510(035)

[528]

TUMA, J.J. **Engineering mathematics handbook.** 4th ed. New York, etc., McGraw-Hill, 1998. 566p. illus., tables. $79.95. ISBN: 0070655294.

First published 1970; 3rd ed. 1987.

22 chapters. Main parts: Algebra; geometry; trigonometry; plane analytical geometry; space analytical geometry; elementary functions. Differential calculus; sequences of series; integral calculus; vector analysis; functions of a complex variable; Fourier series; ordinary differential equations; partial differential equations; Laplace transforms. Numerical methods; probability and statistics. Tables of indefinite integrals; tables of definite integrals; plane curves and areas; space curves and surfaces. Aims to serve as a desk-top reference book for engineers, scientists and architects. 'A gold mine of information' (*Choice*, September 1998, p.163). *Class No:* 510(035)

[529]

—ASM handbook of engineering mathematics, by Faculty members of the Dept. of Mechanical Engineering, Univ. of Akron, Metals Park, Ohio, American Society for Metals. Ohio, ASM, 1983. 697p. illus. ISBN: 087176157x.

In 2 parts. Pt.1 contains basic operations and theories of algebra, trigonometry, geometry, analytical geometry, calculus, etc. in ascending order of difficulty. Pt.2 gives mathematical equations, focusing on those equations of practical problems in mechanical analysis and design. Index. *Class No:* 510(035)

Dictionaries

Polyglot

[530]

EISENREICH, G. *and* SUBE, R. **Dictionary of mathematics in four languages:** English, German, French, Russian. 4th ed. Amsterdam, etc., Elsevier, in co-edition with VEB Verlag, Berlin, 1996. 2v. (1458p.). $146.25. £100. ISBN: 0444997067.

1: English-German-French-Russian. 2: German, French and Russian indexes.

About 25,000 base terms. The thesaurus-type approach involves major subject-category groupings: fundamentals of mathematics; logic; algebra; topology; mathematical analysis; calculus; statistics; geometry. Each term is assigned to a subject category (about 60 in all). The emphasis is on 'pure' mathematics; logic, algebra and topography are covered in particularly full detail. *Class No:* 510(038)=00

[531]

—MESCHKOWSKI, H. Mehrsprachen Wörterbuch Matematischer Begriffe. Mannheim, Bibliographisches Institut, 1972. 131, [4]p.

Lists *c.*2,500 German terms, with English-German, French-German, Russian-German and Italian-German equivalents. Genders are stated. *Class No:* 510(038)=00

[532]

Elsevier's dictionary of computer science and mathematics in English, German, French, and Russian. Peeva, K. *and* Delijska, B., *comps.* Amsterdam, etc., Elsevier, 1995. 785p. $220.50. ISBN: 0444818162.

9,594 English-base terms, followed by equivalents in the other languages. Index; appendix of mathematical symbols. *Class No:* 510(038)=00

English

[533]

BOROWSKI, E.J. *and* BORWEIN, J.M. **Collins dictionary of mathematics.** London, Harper Collins, 1989. xi,659p. diagrs., graphs. £7.99. ISBN: 0004343476.

Over 9,000 terms, briefly defined (*e.g.* 'epicycloid': 7 lines). 400 diagrams. Cross-references. 3 appendices: 1. Symbols and convention - 2. Derivatives and integrals - 3. Hilbert problems. Undergraduate level; good value. *Class No:* 510(038)=20

[534]

CLAPHAM, C. **Concise Oxford dictionary of mathematics.** 2nd ed. Oxford Univ. Press, 1996. 320p. illus., formulas. £15; $29.95. ISBN: 0192800418.

First published 1990.

About 1,200 terms, briefly defined. Includes brief biographical sketches of leading mathematicians. Cross-references. A basic, general-purpose dictionary. *Class No:* 510(038)=20

[535]

DAINTITH, J. *and* NELSON, R.D. **Penguin dictionary of mathematics.** Harmondsworth, Penguin, 1986. 304p. £4.99. ISBN: 0140511199.

Covers mathematical terms and theories in both pure and applied mathematics. *Class No:* 510(038)=20

[536]

GLENN, J. *and* LITTLER, G., *ed.* **A Dictionary of mathematics.** London, etc., Harper & Row, 1984. [viii], 230p. diagrs., graphs. ISBN: 0063182920.

Defines *c.*2,500 terms, half of them being combinations of two or more words, as found in mathematics textbooks of today. 2 appendixes (2. The symbols of mathematics). Aimed at sixth-formers and undergraduates. *Class No:* 510(038)=20

[537]

—HORRILL, P.J.F. Mathematics A-Z. Harlow, Essex, Longman Group, 1986. vi, 166p. diagrs., tables, formulas. ISBN: 0582555854.

Explains more than 1,000 terms and concepts 'encountered in public examinations in mathematics' (*Foreword*). Appended 'Mathematical notations', p.163-6. Intended chiefly for those studying the subject at school or college. *Class No:* 510(038)=20

[538]

JAMES, G. *and* JAMES, R.C. **Mathematics dictionary.** 5th ed. New York, etc., Van Nostrand Reinhold, 1992. viii,548p. diagrs., equations. £19.95. ISBN: 0442012411.

First published 1942; 4th ed. 1976.

8 contributors. Over 4000 terms, some defined at length (*e.g.* logarithm: 2 cols.). Numerous topics (*e.g.* fractals, fuzzy sets, robust statistics) have been updated. Multilingual index: French, German, Spanish, Russian. Appendices include denominate numbers, mathematical symbols, differential formulas, integral tables, Greek alphabet. *Class No:* 510(038)=20

[539]

McGraw-Hill dictionary of mathematics. Parker, S.P., *ed.* New York, etc., McGraw-Hill, 1997. 306p. $12.95. ISBN: 0070524335.

About 4,000 terms briefly defined and drawn from the *Mcgraw-Hill dictionary of scientific and technical terms* (5th ed., 1994). Covers all branches of mathematics; gives variant spellings and mathematical notations with definitions. *Class No:* 510(038)=20

[540]

The Pan dictionary of mathematics. Gibson, C., *ed.* Rev. ed. London, Pan, 1990. [vi],234p. diagrs., graphs. £6.99. ISBN: 0330314556.

First published 1981. This ed. published in the US as *Facts on File Dictionary of mathematics*, 1988.

About 1,500 terms, briefly defined (*e.g.* 'great circle': 5 lines). Cross-references. 12 appendices. Secondary school level. *Class No:* 510(038)=20

[541]

SELKIRK, K. **Longman mathematics handbook:** the language and concepts of mathematics explained. Harlow, Essex, Longman; Beirut, York Press, 1990. 312p. diagrs. (col.). £6.99. ISBN: 0582012618.

About 3,000 terms, briefly defined (*e.g.* 'integral norm': 9 lines). Arranged by subject (*e.g.* algebra; vectors; probability, etc.), with terms listed in index. Effective use of colour in diagrams. For senior secondary pupils and undergraduates. *Class No:* 510(038)=20

[542]

Webster's new world dictionary of mathematics. Karush, W., *ed.* New York, Prentice-Hall, 1989. 317p. illus., diagrs., graphs, tables. $11.95. ISBN: 0131926675.

Defines over 1400 mathematical terms. Includes arithmetic, algebra, geometry, trigonometry and analytical geometry. Appended: Brief biographies of famous mathematicians, a chart of mathematical symbols and tables of powers, roots, logarithms and trigonometric functions. Much overlap with *Facts on file dictionary of mathematics* (2nd ed., 1988). 'For high school and college students' ('Reference books bulletin', *Book list,* December 15, 1989, p.860). *Class No:* 510(038)=20

German

[543]

HERLAND, L. **Dictionary of mathematical sciences.** 2nd ed., rev. and enl. London, Hafner, 1965. 2v. (323p.; 349p.).

First published 1951-54. 1: *German-English.* 2: *English-German.*

Each volume covers *c.*9,000 terms, with many subentries. Areas include mathematical logic, statistics and commercial arithmetic, plus mathematics as applied to physics and astronomy. Two features: generous use of cross-references, and abundance of model usages. V.1 introduces more than 4,000 revised entries and additions; v.2 has a supplement of new words. *Class No:* 510(038)=30

[544]

—MACINTYRE, S. *and* WITTLE, E. German-English mathematical vocabulary. 2nd ed. Edinburgh & London, Oliver & Boyd, 1966. ix, 95p.

First published 1956.

Includes *c.*1,500 German terms, with English equivalents. Irregular verbs are asterisked. Abbreviations; sketch of grammar. Confined to pure mathematics. 'Designed to help English-speaking mathematicians to read German' (*Preface*). *Class No:* 510(038)=30

French

[545]

BOUVIER, A., *and others*. **Dictionnaire des mathématiques.** Paris, Presses Universitaire de France, 1983. xiv, 834p. illus. ISBN: 2130354270.

7,600 terms are defined, covering geometry, analysis, algebra, arithmetic, topology, probability, etc. Supporting line drawings. Intended for a wide range of users (*Bulletin critique du livre français*, no.410, February 1980, entry 10459). *Class No:* 510(038)=40

[546]

—LYLE, W.D. Dictionnaire français et anglais de terminologie mathématique. Ottawa, Didier, 1970. xiv, 137p.

In two parts, French-English and English-French, each with *c.*1,500 entry-words. Appended list of cardinals, ordinals, fractions, decimals and larger numbers. *Class No:* 510(038)=40

Spanish

[547]

GARCÍA-RODRIGUEZ, M. **Diccionario matemático, español-inglés/ inglés-español.** [Mathematics dictionary, Spanish-English, English-Spanish.] New York, Hobbs, Dorman, 1965. [x], 78p.

About 1,500 entry-words in each half. Spanish-English, p.1-40; English-Spanish. p.41-78. *Class No:* 510(038)=60

Russian

[548]

LOHWATER, A.J. **A.J. Lohwater's Russian-English dictionary of the mathematical sciences.** Boas, R.P., *ed.* 2nd ed. Providence, R.I., American Mathematical Society, 1990. 343p. $50. ISBN: 0821801233.

First published 1961.

More than 10,000 entries, preceded by a short Russian grammar. Idiomatic translations, with stress markings. Includes a listing of Russian versions of mathematician's names. Good use of bold cyrillic type. 'Highly recommended as a reference source' (*New technical books*, Sept./Oct. 1991). *Class No:* 510(038)=82

[549]

—ALEXANDROV, P.S., *and others*. Anglo-russkiĭ slovar' matematicheskiĭ terminov. Akademiya Nauk SSR. Matematicheskiĭ Institut. Moscow, Izd-vo Inostr. Library, 1962. 369p.

The English-Russian counterpart of Lohwater and Gould's *Russian-English dictionary of the mathematical sciences*. *Class No:* 510(038)=82

[550]

—MILNE-THOMSON, L.M. Russian-English mathematical dictionary: Words and phrases in pure and applied mathematics, with roots and accents arranged for easy reference. Madison, Univ. of Wisconsin Press, 1962. xiv, 191p.

Includes *c.*10,000 entries (p.3-160), plus outline of Russian grammar and brief list of Russian abbreviations. Good use of bold type; welcome indication of Russian roots of foreign derivation. Not confined to purely mathematical terms. *Class No:* 510(038)=82

Arabic

[551]

LEAGUE OF ARAB STATES. Education, Culture and Sciences Organization. Permanent Bureau of Arabisation. **Lexicon of mathematics:** English-French-Arabic. Rabat, Morocco, Bureau Permanent de Coordination de l'Arabisation, 1971. 192, xxivp.

1,862 English-base terms, with French equivalents and Arabic equivalents/explanations. French and Arabic indexes. *Class No:* 510(038)=927

Chinese

[552]

DE FRANCIS, J. **Chinese-English glossary of the mathematical sciences.** Providence, R.I., American Mathematical Society, 1964. iv, 275, [1]p.

16,540 terms. 'Characters are arranged on the basis of first, the radical of a character and second, the number of strokes in the character, apart from the radical' (*Preface*). The author is Research Professor of Chinese, Seton Hall Univ., N.J. *Class No:* 510(038)=951

Glossaries

[553]

SCHWARTZMAN, S. **The Words of mathematics:** an etymological dictionary of mathematical terms used in English. Washington, D.C., Mathematical Association of America, 1994. vii, 261p. diagrs. ISBN: 0083855114.

Describes the origins and derivations of about 1,500 mathematical terms used in English. Cross references. Appendix: 'Mathematical entries that are etymologically related, grouped by roots'. An unusual approach to the language of mathematics; will complement rather than replace more standard dictionaries. *Class No:* 510(038.1)

Reviews & Abstracts

[554]

Current mathematical publications. Providence, R.I., American Mathematical Society, 1969-. v.1(1)-. Every 3 weeks. $200 pa. ISSN: 03614794.

Formerly *Contents of contemporary mathematical journals and new publications*.

About 5,000 references per issue. Classified by a modified AMS scheme (00. General ... 08. General mathematical systems ... 20. Group theory and generalizations ... 40. Sequences, series ... 51. Geometry ... 60. Probability theory and stochastic processes ... 70. Mechanics of particles and systems ... 90. Information and communication circuits). Entries for book items are asterisked. Appended list of serials represented per issue; serial additions and changes; etc. Author and keyword indexes per issue, cumulated half-yearly. *Class No:* 510(048)

[555]

Mathematical reviews. Providence, R.I., American Mathematical Society, 1940-. v.1-. Monthly. $5025 pa. ISSN: 00255629.

About 45,000 abstracts pa. 94 sections (as in *Zentralblatt für Mathematik*): 00. General ... 01. History and biography ... 03. Mathematical logic and foundations ... 11. Number theory ... 20. Group theory and generalizations ... 26. Real functions ... 40. Sequences, series ... 51. Geometry ... 60. Probability theory and stochastic processes ... 70. Mechanics of particles and systems ... 80. Chemical thermodynamics, heat transfer ... 90. Economics, operational research, programming games ... 94. Information and communication, circuits. Author index; keyword index; serial additions and changes. Annual index: *Index of mathematical papers* (1973-). *Mathematical reviews cumulative index, 1973-1979* covers v.45-58 in 12v., with *c.*300,000 entries. The basic reviewing service in mathematics. Database: MATHSCI; CD-ROM: *MathSci Disc*. *Class No:* 510(048)

German

[556]

Zentralblatt für Mathematik und ihre Grenzgebiete. [Mathematical abstracts.] Berlin, etc., Springer., 1931-. Irregular. DM 166 per Bd. ISSN: 00444235.

Preceded by *Jahrbuch über die Forschritte der Mathematik* (Berlin, de Gruyter, 1868-1942).

About 2,000 abstracts pa. 94 sections (00-94), as in *Mathematical reviews (qv)*. Abstracts range in length from 1½ lines to 20 lines, signed, and in English, French or German. Author and subject indexes per issue; cumulated. Online database. *Class No:* 510(048)=30

Russian

[557]

Referativnyĭ zhurnal. Matematika. Akademiya Nauk SSSR. Nauchoi Informatsii. Moscow, VINITI, 1953-. Monthly.

About 25,000 abstracts pa. Three main sections: General. Mathematical logic. Theory of numbers. Algebra. Topology. Geometry - Mathematical anlysis - Numerical methods. Probability theory and mathematical statistics. Cybernetics. Monthly author index, and English translation of contents of main sections. Three separate parts are also available. *Class No:* 510(048)=82

Periodicals

[558]

LONDON UNIVERSITY. Library. **Union list of periodicals on mathematics and allied subjects in London libraries.** 2nd ed. London, the University Library, 1968. [viii], 139p.

First published 1958.

926 titles in 45 libraries in London, 15 of the libraries not connected with the University. Entry is under latest title. *World list of periodicals* (3rd ed.) numbers are cited. Appendix: List of abbreviated and alternative titles sometimes found in references. Excludes ephemera, congress proceedings and mongraph series, 'and journals primarily devoted to the teaching of mathematics at the lower level' (*Introduction*). Supplement lists 45 titles held by the Science Reference Library. *Class No:* 510(051)

[559]

—BRITISH LIBRARY. Science Reference Library. Mathematics and statistics periodicals held by Science Reference Library. London, SRL, 1977. vii, 47p.

In two sections: Mathematics and statistical periodicals (p.1-46; *c*.500 titles) - Abstracting and indexing periodicals. Call numbers are given, with a summary of the classification used. *Class No:* 510(051)

Bibliographies

[560]

LIANG, D.F. **Mathematical journals:** an annotated guide. Metuchen, NJ, Scarecrow Press, 1992. 235p. $29.50. ISBN: 0810825856.

About 350 primary English-language periodicals. Data include bibliographic information, price, indexing, publication history, editor, manuscript submission requirements and short annotation (usually descriptive). Index of publishers and ISSNs, but not subjects. *Class No:* 510(051)(01)

Progress Reports

[561]

Progress in mathematics. Boston, Mass., Birkhaüser, 1967-. v.1.

Each volume deals with a specific area. Thus, v.128 (1955, 310p.) covers dynamical systems of algegraic origins and v.133 (1955, 685p.) is 'The Floer memorial volume'. All are the work of several contributors and include extensive references. *Class No:* 510(055)

Yearbooks & Directories

[562]

Mathematical sciences professional directory. Providence, R.I., American Mathematical Society, 1995. 226p. $50. ISBN: 0821801929. ISSN: 07374356.

Includes personal members, academic institutions, government agencies and other professional organizations (*e.g.* Society of Actuaries). Data include name, title, research interests, address, e-mail, etc. Worldwide coverage. *Class No:* 510(058)

[563]

—Combined membership list 1996-1997: American Mathematical Society, American Mathematical Association of Two-Year Colleges, Mathematical Association of America, Society for Industral and Applied Mathematics. Providence, R.I., American Mathematical Society, 1996. 389p. $59. ISBN: 0821801864.

Over 60,000 entries in 2 sections: alphabetical list of individual, institutional and corporate members; geographical list (US; Canada; other countries). *Class No:* 510(058)

[564]

World directory of mathematicians. 8th ed. Helsinki, the University, 1986. (Distributed by the American Mathematical Society). xix, 950p.

Published under the auspices of the International Mathematical Union. 7th ed., 1982.

Lists *c*.30,000 mathematicians from 93 countries. Data on each include posts held, university and its address. List of mathematical organizations precedes the A-Z directory (p.1-789). Geographical list (Algeria ... Zimbabwe). *Class No:* 510(058)

Teaching Materials

[565]

Handbook of research on mathematics, teaching, and learning. Grouws, D.A., *ed.* New York, Macmillan, 1992. 771p. $65. ISBN: 0029223814.

29 chapters covering the history of research in mathematics education, teaching methods and the international view. Produced by the National Council of Teachers of Mathematics (US). *Class No:* 510(072)

Quotations

[566]

GAITHER, C.C. *and* CAVAZOS-GAITHER, A. **Mathematically speaking:** a dictionary of quotations. Bristol, Institute of Physics, 1998. 484p. illus. £19.95; $39. ISBN: 0750305037.

A wide-ranging and often amusing collection of quotations from scientists and lay people (*e.g.* Lewis Carroll). Arranged by subject; indexes. *Class No:* 510(082.2)

[567]

MORITZ, R.E. **Memorabilia Mathematica,** or, The philosopher's quotation book. New York, Macmillan Co., 1914. (Reprinted American Mathematical Association, 1993. $24. ISBN: 0883853213). xiii, 410p. diagrs.

Over 2,000 quotations, some of them lengthy, with sources cited. Foreign quotations usually appear only in translation. 21 chapters (*e.g.* 1. Definitions and objects of mathematics; 9/10. Persons and anecdotes; 21. Paradoxes and curiosities). Detailed, analytical index, p.385-410 (*e.g.* 'Liebnitz': ½ column). Still a valuable work. *Class No:* 510(082.2)

Tables & Data Books

[568]

BARTLETT, B.R. *and* FYFE, D.J. **Handbook of mathematical formulae for engineers and scientists.** London, Denny Publications, Ltd., 1974. [ix], 216p. tables. ISBN: 0950315400.

Over 1,600 mathematical formulas, definitions and methods. Main sections: Mathematics - Statistics - Numerical methods. 'Intended to cover, in standard notation, the definitions and formulae relating to the Mathematical techniques which are required by students in Technical Colleges, Polytechnics and Universities' (*Preface*). *Class No:* 510(083)

[569]

COOK, J.L. **Conversion factors.** Oxford Univ. Press, 1992. 160p. tables. $12.95. ISBN: 0198563523.

More than 3,500 conversion factors, arranged by areas of application. SI units. 'Well formatted ... reasonably priced ... a valuable addition to a reference collection' (*Choice*, September 1992, p.74). *Class No:* 510(083)

Models

[570]

Mathematical modelling: a source book of case studies. Huntley, I.D. *and* James, D.J.G. Oxford Univ. Press, 1990. xiv,462p. £40. ISBN: 0198536577.

28 case studies (some with references) in 4 parts: 1. Simple illustrative examples - 2. Models for class development - 3. Extended problems - 4. Further problem statements. Intended for application to undergraduate mathematics teaching, with suggestions made for adaptation, changes to problems. *Class No:* 510(086.48)

Histories

[571]

BOYER, C.B. A History of mathematics. 2nd ed. New York, London, etc. Wiley. 1989. 762p. illus., ports., diagrs., maps. $53.95. ISBN: 0471097632.

First published 1968. This ed. revised by U.C. Merzbach.

27 chapters (1. Primitive origins - 2. Egypt ... 26. The rise of abstract algebra - 27. Aspects of the twentieth century), each with appended references and graded exercises, plus footnote references. Few changes have been made to the material in this new edition, but coverage of the twentieth century has been expanded and the bibliographies and references have been updated. A well-written and admirably documented survey. *Class No:* 510(091)

[572]

Companion encyclopedia of the history and philosophy of the mathematical sciences. Grattan-Guinness, I., *ed.* London, Routledge, 1994. 2 v. (xiii, 1806p.) diagrs. £200. ISBN: 0415037859.

In 13 parts (1. Ancient and non-Western traditions . . . 3. Calculus and mathematical analysis . . . 7. Geometrics and topology . . . 11. Higher education and institutions - 12. Mathematics and culture - 13. Reference and information). Part 0 is an introduction outlining the range and scope of the work and detailing omissions (*e.g.* biographies, all original notations). Parts include several contributions, by different hands, each with bibliography, sometimes annotated. Detailed, analytical index, p.1721-1806. 'A truly excellent publication' (*Reference Reviews*, vol. 8, 7, 1994, p.21). *Class No:* 510(091)

[573]

—GRATTAN-GUINNESS, I. The Norton history of the mathematical sciences: the rainbow of mathematics. New York, Norton, 1998. 817p. $35. ISBN: 0393046508.

Concentrates on mathematics from post-Renaissance Europe, with briefer accounts of progress outside Europe. Extremely good value. 'A great place to begin; it deserves a place in every library' (*Choice*, May 1999, p.1638). *Class No:* 510(091)

[574]

DUNHAM, W. **Journey through genius:** the great theorems of mathematics. New York, Wiley, 1990. xiv, 300p. illus., diagrs. $19.95; £14.95. ISBN: 0471500305.

Provides an historical, biographical and 'creative' treatment of mathematical proofs. 12 chapters covering Hippocrates, Euclid, Archimedes, Heron, Cardano, Newton, Euler and Cantor. Index, p.295-300. *Class No:* 510(091)

[575]

EVES, H. **An Introduction to the history of mathematics.** 5th ed. New York, Saunders College Publishing, 1982. xviii, 593p. illus., port., diagrs., formulas. ISBN: 0030620643.

First published 1953.

Pt. 1: Before the seventeenth century (chapters 1-8; 1. Numerical systems - 2. Babylonian and Egyptian mathematics ... 7. Chinese, Hindu and Arabian mathematics - 8. European mathematics, 500-1600). Pt.2 The seventeenth century and after (chapters 9-15; 10. Analytic geometry and other precalculus developments ... 15. Abstraction and the transition into the twentieth century). Each chapter features 'Problem studies', 'Essay topics' and 'Bibliography'. General bibliography, p.512-3; chronological table. Answers and suggestions for the solution of the problem studies. Analytical index, p.553-93. A standard textbook for undergraduates. *Class No:* 510(091)

[576]

HEIJENOORT, J. van. **From Frege to Gödel:** a sourcebook in mathematical logic, 1879-1931. Cambridge, Mass., Harvard Univ. Press, 1967. c.665p. (*Source books in the history of the sciences.*)

51 papers (some of them translated) and letters between mathematicians (*e.g.* Hilbert's lecture, 'The foundations of mathematics' (1927)). References, p.629-55. Detailed, non-analytical index. The series aims to provide 'collections of classical papers that have changed the structure of the various sciences'. *Class No:* 510(091)

[577]

—STRUIK, D.J., *ed.* A source book in mathematics, 1200-1800. Cambridge, Mass., Harvard Univ. Press., 1969. xiv, 427p.

Includes 75 excerpts from the writings of Western mathematicians, with references. Criticized in Dorling's *Use of mathematical literature* (*qv*), p.65, for attempting to cover too much ground, leaving a blurred impression, and compared unfavourably to Heijenoort's selection of core papers. *Class No:* 510(091)

[578]

—The World of mathematics: a small library of the literature of mathematics, from A'h-mosé the Scribe to Albert Einstein, presented with commentaries and notes. Newman, J.R., *comp.* New York, Simon & Schuster, 1956; London, Allen & Unwin, 1960. 4v. illus., diagrs.

Covers in popular fashion the whole literature of mathematics, although extracts are inevitably arbitrary in their selection. Footnote references. Detailed, analytical index (v.4, p.2471-2535). *Class No:* 510(091)

[579]

KLINE, M. **Mathematical thought:** from ancient to modern times. Oxford Univ. Press, 1972. xvii, 1238p. diagrs. (*£45..*)

Two-thirds of this impressive history is devoted to concepts that acquired significance after 1700. Includes bibliographies. Despite its length, 'even his [Kline's] 1250 pages are silent on many things' (Dorling, A.E., ed. *Use of mathematical literature* (1977), p.64). *Class No:* 510(091)

[580]

SMITH, D.E. **History of mathematics.** New York, Dover; London, Constable, 1958 (reprint). 2v. (xxxiv, 1321p.). illus., tables.

Originally published 1923-5 (Boston, Ginn). 1. *General survey ...* 2. *Special topics of elementary mathematics.*

A textbook on the history of elementary mathematics 'through the first stages in the calculus' (*Preface*). V.1 contains many brief biographical sketches, chronological tables (to 1850) and a selective bibliography. V.2 has numerous footnote references. 510 illus. in all. *Class No:* 510(091)

[581]

—TEMPLE, S. 100 years in mathematics. London, Duckworth, 1981. xvi, 316p. ISBN: 0715611305.

In 3 parts: 1. Number - 2. Space - 3. Analysis. 17 chapters (10. The concept of functionality; 11. Derivative integrals; 12. Distributions; 13. Ordinary differential equations; 14. Calculus of variations; 15. Potential theory; 16. Mathematical logic; 17. Conclusion). Bibliography, p.283. References, p.285-307. Index of authors; analytical general index. Detailed contents. 'This account is, of necessity, a personal selection of its [mathematics'] major developments' (*Preface*). *Class No:* 510(091)

[582]

STILLWELL, J. **Mathematics and its history.** New York, etc., Springer-Verlag, 1989. x,371p. illus., diagrs. $49.80. ISBN: 0387969810.

Approaches mathematics 'through its history' (*Preface*). 20 chapters, each with 'Biographical notes' (*e.g.* 9. 'Infinite series' includes notes on James Gregory and Leonhard Euler). References, p.333-62. Index, p.362-71. *Class No:* 510(091)

Bibliographies

[583]

DAUBEN, J.W. **The History of mathematics, from antiquity to the present:** a selective bibliography. New York & London, Garland, 1985. xxxv, 467p. $80. ISBN: 0824092848.

2,400 entries, mostly annotated, with numerous cross-references. 6 sections: 1. General reference works - 2. Source materials - 3. General histories of mathematics - 4. The history of mathematics: chronological periods (p.29-215) - 5. The history of mathematics: sub-disciplines (algebra ... topology) - 6. The history of mathematics: selected topics (*e.g.,* Mathematics education; Regional studies; Women in mathematics). Author and subject (non-analytical) indexes. 'An excellent addition to existing bibliographical sources in the history of mathematics' (*ISIS*, v.76, December 1985, p.595). The author is editor of *Historia mathematica. Class No:* 510(091)(01)

[584]

LORIA, G. **Guida allo studio della storia delle matematiche;** generalità didattica, bibliografia. Appendice: Questioni stouche concernenti le scienze esatte. 2.ed., rif & aum. Milan, Hoepli, 1946. xix, 385p.

About 1,600 titles, with comments. 10 chapters (2. survey of histories of mathematics; 3. analysis of the contents of the leading journals for the history of mathematics). 4 appendices (*e.g.* research aids, - manuscripts, biographies, treatise). Index of persons cited. Full contents list, p.355-81. Addressed to students. *Class No:* 510(091)(01)

[585]

MAY, K.O. **Bibliography and research material of the history of mathematics.** Toronto, Univ. of Toronto Press, 1973. [ix] 818p.

Two parts: 1. Research manual (Information retrieval; Personal information retrieval; Historical analysis and writing) - 2. Bibliography (Biography; Mathematical topics; Epimathematical topics; Historical classifications; Information retrieval). About 30,000 unannotated entries in all. Many cross-references. Appendix 2: 'Coded list of serials' (p.709-818). International in scope. 'This bountiful and authoritative guide' (*Choice*, v.10(10), December 1973, p.1531). Weak on the literature before 1868 and on Oriental studies (*ISIS*, v.65, 1974, p.514-6). *Class No:* 510(091)(01)

[586]

—Historia mathematica. Toronto, Univ, of Toronto Press, 1974-. 4pa.

A publication of the International Commission on the History of Mathematics.

Carries articles, reports on meetings, reviews, and abstracts of current literature on the history of mathematics. Thus, V.13(2), May 1986, has abstracts on p.196-209. Annual index of authors of works reviewed and abstracted. *Class No:* 510(091)(01)

Ancient Greece

[587]

GERICKE, N. **Mathematik in Antike und Orient.** Berlin, etc., Springer, 1984. xii, 292p. diagrs., tables, maps. ISBN: 0387110478.

Four parts: 1. Pre-Greek mathematics (*e.g.* Babylonia; Egypt) - 2. Greek mathematics (p.70-168) - 3. Mathematics in the East (China; India; Islam) - 4. Biography. Biographical notes. Chronology and maps follow. Short catchword index. 140 figures and tables; 4 maps. *Class No:* 510(091)(37)

[588]

HEATH, Sir T.L. **A History of Greek mathematics.** Oxford, Clarendon Press, 1921. 2v. diagrs., formulas.

1. *From Thales to Euclid.* xv, 446p. 2. *From Aristarchus to Diophantus.* xi, 586p.

21 chapters, the major mathematicians (*e.g.* Euclid, Archimedes) being given a chapter apiece. The final chapter deals with commentators. Careful exposition is allotted to the main writings; many formulas. V.2 carries an index of Greek words as well as an English index. The standard work in English. *Class No:* 510(091)(37)

Biographies

[589]

ABBOTT, D., *ed*. **Mathematicians.** London, Blond Educational, 1985. [vii], 175p. (*The Biographical dictionary of scientists*.) ISBN: 0584700059.

About 200 entries, Abel ... Zermerlo. Historical introduction precedes. Glossary, p.145-60. Grouped index, with references to name entries, p.161-75. Criticised in *Choice* (July/August 1986, p.1651) for lack of criteria in selection of entries and also for lack of citation of sources. *Class No:* 510(092)

[590]

Biographical dictionary of mathematicians. New York, Scribner's, 1991. 4v. illus. $200. ISBN: 0684192829.

Entries 'borrowed' from the *Dictionary of scientific biography* and its two supplements (Scribner's, 1970-90). Includes illus. Bibliographies not updated. Simple but serviceable index. *Class No:* 510(092)

[591]

Biographical encyclopedia of mathematicians. Franceschetti, D.R., *ed*. London, Marshall Cavendish, 1998. 2v. (640p.). illus. $149.95. ISBN: 0761470697.

About 170 entries, A-Z, 2-4p. in length. Sidebars highlight significant achievements and give brief bibliographies. Indexes; chronology; list of mathematicians by country. 'Recommended for public libraries' ('Reference books bulletin', *Booklist*, December 15, 1998, p.762). *Class No:* 510(092)

[592]

HOWSON, A.G. **A History of mathematics education in England.** Cambridge Univ. Press, 1982. x, 294p. tables. £27.50. ISBN: 0512124061.

9 chapters: 1. Robert Recorde - 2. Samuel Pepys - 3. Philip Doddridge - 4. Charles Hutton - 5. Augustus De Morgan - 6. Thomas Tate - 7. James Wilson - 8. Charles Godfrey - 9. Elizabeth Williams. Appendix: 'A selection of examination papers, syllabus, etc.' Notes p.239-80. Name and subject indexes. A biographical account, 'even though it requires frequent scenic changes and "flashbacks"' (*Preface*). *Class No:* 510(092)

[593]

MESCHKOWSKI, H. **Mathematiker - Lexikon.** 3., überarb. & eng. Aufl. Mannheim, Bibliographischer Institut, 1980. 342p. ports. ISBN: 3411015764.

First published 1968.

Entries, 'Abel, Niels Henrik'...'Zu Chong-zhi'; 'Newton': 3½p., 'Laplace': 2p. Bibliography, p.311-42 (A. Works by the mathematicians; B. Literature on individual works; C. General works on the history of mathematics). *Class No:* 510(092)

[594]

Notable mathematicians: from ancient times to the present. Young, R.V. *and* Minderovic, Z., *eds*. Detroit, Mi., Gale, 1998. 612p. illus. $85. ISBN: 0787619302.

Over 300 mathematicians, including 60 women and 15 from American ethnic minorities; about 30 from countries outside North America and Western Europe. Data include name, dates, nationality and fields of specialization, followed by a biographical essay. Chronology; indexes: specialization, gender, nationality, subject. Selected as an outstanding academic book for 1998 by *Choice*, January 1999. *Class No:* 510(092)

Bibliographies

[595]

DIODATO, V. *and* TOLAN, M. 'Mathematical biographies: profiles and sources of information on eighteen mathematicians'. In *Science and technology libraries*, V.11(4), Winter 1991, p.9-42. ISSN: 0194262x.

Brief, non-scholarly and mostly twentieth-century; 6 or 7 references for each mathematician. *Class No:* 510(092)(01)

England

[596]

TAYLOR, E.G.R. **The Mathematical practitioners of Tudor and Stuart England.** Cambridge Univ. Press, for the Institute of Navigation, 1954. xv, 443p. illus.

Three parts: 1. description of the progress and work of practical mathematicians, 1485-1715; 2. short biographical notes on 582 mathematical practitioners; 3. chronological annotated bibliography of 628 mathematical treatises published during the period. An essential reference work on the history of science and mathematics. *Class No:* 510(092)(420)

[597]

—TAYLOR, E.G.R. An Index to 'The mathematical practitioners of Hanoverian England, 1714-1800'; compiled by K. Bostok [and others]. Cambridge Univ. Press; London, H. Wynter, 1980. 23p.

Acts as a selective A-Z index of major practitioners, complementing the grouping of names into 14 period sections in the main volume. *Class No:* 510(092)(420)

[598]

—TAYLOR, E.G.R. The Mathematical practitioners of Hanoverian England, 1714-1800: a sequel to *The mathematical practitioners of Tudor and Stuart England*. Cambridge Univ. Press, for the Institute of Navigation, 1966. xv, 503p. illus.

Two parts. 1. Narrative (p.5-106) - 2. Biographies of inventors, makers and users of mathematical instruments, teachers, writers and theorists, by decades (p.107-483). Indexes: 1. General; 2. Secondary practitioners. 'Sources and references', p.xiv-xvi. *The Marine observer* (v.37(46), April 1967, p.88) offers a minor criticism: the grouping of names in 14 separate periods in the biographies, and the two methods of indexing names. *Class No:* 510(092)(420)

Women

[599]

GRINSTEIN, L.S. *and* CAMPBELL, P.J., *eds*. **Women of mathematics:** a bibliographic sourcebook. Westport, Conn., Greenwood Press, 1987. 288p. ISBN: 0313248494.

Bibliographical studies of 43 women mathematicians, from antiquity to the 20th century, in A/Z order. *Library journal* (1 September 1987, p.175) queries selection policy, -'more often attainment of an advanced mathematics degree'. Entries vary in content and quality. Nevertheless, considered (*ibid*) 'a major contribution to the history of mathematics and of women'. *Class No:* 510(092)-0055.2

[600]

Notable women in mathematics: a biographical dictionary. Morrow, C. *and* Perl, Teri, *eds*. Westport, Ct., Greenwood, 1998. 196p. $49.95. ISBN: 0313291314.

Gives biographical details (usually 5-6p.) of 59 mathematicians who lived between the third century BC and the twentieth. Information includes childhood, education, family life, obstacles overcome and achievements. *Class No:* 510(092)-0055.2

Writing & Lecturing

[601]

HIGHAM, N.J. **Handbook of writing for the mathematical sciences.** Philadelphia, Pa., Society for Industrial and Applied Mathematics, 1993. xii, 241p. $21.50. ISBN: 0898713145.

10 chapters (10. Computer aids for writing and research). Glossary; bibliography (225 items); index. *Class No:* 510:001.81

Conferences

[602]

Conferences in energy, physics and mathematics. Karlsruhe, Fachinformationszentrum Karlsruhe.

Database of conferences, past, present and future. Data include title, sponsoring organization, location and dates, notes on related publications, etc. 100,000 records; updated weekly. Available online via STN International and on the internet. *Class No:* 510:061:061.3

Computation Devices

[603]

MADDISON, F. 'Early astronomical and mathematical instruments - a brief survey of sources and modern studies'. In *History of science*, v.2, 1963, p.17-50.

Includes a lengthy bibliography, p.35-50. *Class No:* 510-3

Recreational Mathematics

[604]

EISS, H.E. **Dictionary of mathematical games, puzzles and amusements.** New York, Greenwood Press, 1988. xiv, 278p. illus. $49.95. ISBN: 0313247145.

A-Z sequence of mathematical games, both classical and modern, with detailed explanations, line drawings and cross-references. Mathematic theories, underlying the games, feature throughout; chapters include brief bibliographies. Criticized in *Choice* (July/August, 1988, p.1273) for omission of 'significant terms' and poor illustrations. *Class No:* 510-8

[605]

SCHAAF, W.L. A Bibliography of recreational mathematics. Washington, National Council of Teachers of Mathematics, 1970-78. 4v. facsims., diagrs. ISBN: 0873531209.

First published 1955.

V.4 (1978. xii, [ii], 172p.) has 12 chapters: 1. Arithmetical and algebraic recreations - 2. Number theory as recreation - 3. Geometric recreations - 4. Topological recreations - 5. Magic squares and related configurations - 6. Pythagorean recreations - 7. Classical recreations - 8. Combinatorial recreations - 9. Games and puzzles - 10. Miscellaneous mathematical recreations - 11. Mathematics in the arts - 12. Mathematical recreations and education. 3 appendices (A: Contemporary general works on mathematical recreations). Supplementary glossary, p.146-72. Fills a gap. *Class No:* 510-8

[606]

WELLS, D. The Penguin book of curious and interesting puzzles. Harmondsworth, Penguin, 1992. viii,382p. illus., diagrs. £6.99. ISBN: 0140148752.

568 puzzles, with solutions, from ancient times, the nineteenth and twentieth centuries. Bibliography, p.373-77; index, p.379-82. *Class No:* 510-8

Logic

[607]

GREENSTEIN, C.H. Dictionary of logical terms and symbols. New York, Van Nostrand Reinhold, 1978. xii, [1], 188p. diagrs., tables.

Contains 'a list of technical terms and expressions most likely to be encountered in currently studied works, along with the ways in which they are commonly characterized, used or defined' (*Preface*). Another aim is 'to reduce the difficulty in formalizing key English expressions in alternative ways'. The notational systems are arranged by functions. Glossary of logical terms. Bibliography (authors, A-Z), p.179-88. *Class No:* 510.6

Arithmetic

[608]

SMITH, D.E. Rara arithmetica: a catalogue of the arithmetics written before the year MDCI, with a description of those in the library of George Arthur Plumpton of New York. Boston, Mass., & London, Ginn, 1908. xiii, [ii] 507p. facsims.

Addenda. 1939. x 52p. facsims.

The main work lists *c.*750 items published 1478 - *c.* 1600, giving bibliographical descriptions plus brief notes. Index of dates (of printed books); index of names, places and subjects.

Reprinted 1970. *Class No:* 511.1

[609]

—DE MORGAN, A. Arithmetical books, from the invention of printing to the present time, being brief notices of a large number of works drawn up from actual inspection. London, Taylor & Walton, 1847. [xiii], xxviii, 124p.

About 300 titles covering the period 1491-1800. Chronologically arranged and annotated. *Class No:* 511.1

Number Theory

[610]

BORWEIN, J.M. and BORWEIN, P. A Dictionary of real numbers. New York, Brooks/Cole, 1990. 424p. $69.95. ISBN: 0534128408.

Over 100,000 entries indicating classical computations which have approximately the same outcome as the entry. 'The first book of its kind' (*Choice*, July/Aug. 1990, p.,1855). *Class No:* 511.2

[611]

FLEGG, G. Numbers, their history and meaning. London, Deutsch, 1983. 294p. illus., facsims. ISBN: 0023397282.

9 chapters: 2. Counting with numbers - 3. Writing with numbers - 4. Calculating with numbers - 5. Computing with numbers ... 7. Recreational numbers ... 9. Teaching and learning numbers. Bibliographic note, p.291. Indexes (in tiny print): (a) Names quoted; (b) Works quoted; (c) General. Gives interesting examples of the ways in which numerals were represented through the ages. *Class No:* 511.2

[612]

HOPKINS, N.J., *and others.* **The Numbers you need.** Detroit, Mi., Gale, 1992. 354p. illus., tables. $29.95. ISBN: 081038373x.

9 chapters, closely subdivided (*e.g.* health; gambling; sports; weather (temperature scales, pollution, earthquakes, etc.)). 3 appendices: 1. Units of measurement - 2. Money matters - 3. Use of tables, graphs and statistics. 'Further reading' at end of each chapter. Index. 'A welcome addition to general reference collections' ('Reference books bulletin', in *Booklist,* September 1, 1992, p.90). *Class No:* 511.2

[613]

IFRAH, G. Histoire universelle des chiffres. Paris, Seghers, 1981. [viii], 568p. illus., diagrs., charts, tables.

Published with the assistance of the Centre National de la Recherche Scientifique.

6 parts (30 chapters), following an introduction: 1. La conscience des nombres - 2. Les comptes concretes - 3. L'invention des chiffres - 4. Les chiffres et les lettres - 5. Les hybrides - 6. Le stade ultime de la notation numérique (including chapter 30: L'origine des chiffres 'arabes'). Appended: Répertoire chronologique; Orientation et notes bibliographiques (by parts and chapters), p.527-65, - 508 numbered references. A scholarly study of the history of numerals, ancient and modern, East and West. *Class No:* 511.2

[614]

SPENCER, D.D. Key dates in number theory history: from 10,529 B.C. to the present. Ormond Beach, Fl., Camelot, 1995. 126p. illus. $18.95. ISBN: 0892183187.

Charts the progress and achievements in mathematics, computer science and number theory over nearly 12,000 years. 'Fascinating and accessible ... indispensable' (*American reference books annual*, 1996, p.768). *Class No:* 511.2

Algebra

[615]

HOWSON, A.G., *comp.* **A Handbook of terms used in algebra and analysis.** Cambridge Univ. Press, 1972. ix, 238p. £20; £8.

38 sections (2. Sets and functions ... 21. Topological spaces and continuity ... 37. Measure and Lebesque integration - 38. Fourier series). Appendix 1: Some named theorems and perspectives; 2: Alphabets used in mathematics. Index of symbols. Analytical subject index ('Function(s)': 2/3column), p.225-38. *Class No:* 512

[616]

LÜTKEPOHL, H. Handbook of matrices. Chichester, Wiley, 1996. xvi, 304p. formulas. ISBN: 047196686x.

A collection of matrix results for quick reference. Definitions and results only are given; no proofs. 11 chapters (*e.g.* 10: 'Vector and matrix derivatives'). Appendix A (p.225-86) comprises a dictionary of matrices and related terms. *Class No:* 512

[617]

VARADARAJAN, V.S. Algebra in ancient and modern times. Providence, R.I., American Mathematical Society, 1998. *c.*200p. £15. ISBN: 082180989x.

Provides a historical exposition of topics from algebra, with emphasis on the ideas of ancient Indian mathematicians. Extensive bibliography. 'Recommended' (*Choice*, March 1999, p. 1299). *Class No:* 512

Geometry

[618]

BIX, R. Topics in geometry. San Diego, Ca., Academic Press, 1994. 538p. $59.95. ISBN: 0121027406.

Topics: elementary Euclidean geometry, transformation geometry, projective geometry, conic section and non-Euclidean geometry. Includes an historical context and numerous examples. Detailed, analytical index. *Class No:* 514

Analysis

Differentials

[619]

COHEN, M.S., *and others.* **Student research projects in calculus.** Washington, D.C., Mathematical Association of America, 1992. 216p. $20. ISBN: 0883855038.

Includes a list of more than 100 project problems, most class tested, with level of difficulty indicated. *Class No:* 517.2

[620]

POLYANIN, A.D. *and* **ZAITSEV, V.F. Handbook of exact solutions for ordinary differential equations.** Boca Raton, Fl., 1995. 707p. $95. ISBN: 0849394384.

About 5,000 equations with solutions, 2,000 of them of the second order or higher. Appendices cover types of functions and their properties. 'Highly recommended' (*Choice*, February 1996, p.985). *Class No:* 517.2

Integrals

[621]

GRADSHTEYN, I.S. *and* **RYZHIK, I.M. Table of integrals, series, and products.** 5th ed. New York & London, Academic Press, 1980, reprinted with corrections, 1994. 1204p. £40. ISBN: 012294755x.

Translated from the Russian by Scripta Technica, Inc. Incorporates the 4th ed., 1965 (xiv, 1086p.).

Translation of a standard Russian compendium on functions and integrals (about 20,000), plus Fourier and Laplace transforms, etc. To the original Russian bibliography - 'much of which is likely to be inaccessible to the user of these tables' - has been added 'Classified supplementary references'. 'Rich in useful formulae' (Norris, W.T., in *Information sources in engineering.* 2nd ed., 1986, p.372). *Class No:* 517.3

[622]

—**DWIGHT, H.B. Tables of integrals and other mathematical data.** 4th ed. New York, Macmillan, 1961. 335p. tables, formulas. ISBN: 0023311703.

First published 1934.

Includes over 1,000 tables of types of functions. Appended tables of numerical values. Bibliography; index. A handy companion to *Barlow's Tables of squares, cubes, square roots, cube roots, and reciprocals* (qv). *Class No:* 517.3

[623]

PRUDNIKOV, A.P., *and others.* **Integrals and series.** New York, Gordon and Breach, 1986-1992. 5v. ISBN: 2881240976.

V.1: *Elementary functions.*
V.2: *Special functions.*
V.3: *More special functions.*
V.4: *Direct Laplace transforms.*
V.5: *Inverse Laplace transforms.*

Each v. includes a bibliography. *Class No:* 517.3

[624]

SLOANE, N.J.A. *and* **PLOUFFE, S. The Encyclopedia of integer sequences.** Orlando, Fl., Academic Press, 1995. 587p. $44.95. ISBN: 0125586302.

Supercedes *Handbook of integer sequences* (1973) by N.J.A. Sloane.

Catalogue of sequences with detailed, analytical index. An electronic version of the work is available on the internet. *Class No:* 517.3

[625]

TALLARIDA, R.J. Pocket book of integrals and mathematical formulas. 2nd ed. Boca Raton, Fl., CRC Press, 1992. [xiv], 225p. graphs, mathematical formulas. £12.40. ISBN: 0849301424.

11 chapters: 1. Elementary algebra and geometry ... 3. Trigonometry ... 7. Integral calculus ... 9. Special functions ... 11. Statistics. Table of derivatives; table of integrals. 5 Appendices: A.2: 'Poisson distribution'. Index, p.219-25. Handy format, 'a companion to the calculator and the computer' (*Preface to the first edition*). *Class No:* 517.3

Functions

[626]

ABRAMOWITZ, M. *and* **STEGUN, I.A. Handbook of mathematical functions,** with formulas, graphs, and mathematical tables. US National Bureau of Standards. Washington, US Government Printing Office; New York, Dover, 1964. xiv, 1045p. graphs, tables, formulas. (*National Bureau of Standards, Applied mathematics series, no. 55.*) ISBN: 0486612724.

29 chapters by 26 specialists. Bibliographies are brief, but helpful; 'a little more annotation would not have come amiss' (*Nature*, v.205, 2 January 1965, p.9). 'Here, for the first time, the numerical tables of

....(contd.)

mathematical functions normally useful to engineers, physicists, chemists etc., are found in one text that is authoritative' (*The Military engineer*, no. 373, September/October 1964, p.390). *Class No:* 517.5

[627]

HANSEN, E.R. A Table of series and products. Englewood Cliffs, N.J., Prentice-Hall, 1975. 523p. tables. ISBN: 0138819386.

Systematic collection of tables of mathematical series and infinite products (*e.g.* trigonometric series; logarithmic functions). Bibliography for further reading. Index. *Class No:* 517.5

Probabilities

[628]

BOROVKOV, K.A. Russian-English English-Russian dictionary on probability, statistics, and combinatorics. Philadelphia, Pa., Moscow, Society for Industrial and Applied Mathematics, TVP Science, 1994. viii, 154p. £49.90. ISBN: 0898713161.

About 7,500 head words for each language. *Class No:* 519.2

[629]

CRC handbook of tables for probability and statistics. Beyer, W.H., *ed.* 2nd ed. Cleveland, Ohio, Chemical Rubber Co., 1987. xiv, 642p. ISBN: 0849306922.

First published 1966.

'Many of the tables have been expanded and increased in effectiveness' (*Preface*). 13 parts: 1. Probability and statistics - 2. Normal distribution - 3. Binominal, Poisson, hypergeometric and negative binominal distributions ... 10. Non-parametric statistics - 11. Quality control - 12. Miscellaneous statistical tables - 13. Miscellaneous mathematical tables. Index, p.637-40. *Class No:* 519.2

Statistics

Bibliographies

[630]

KENDALL, M.G. *and* **DOIG, A.G. Bibliography of statistical literature pre-1940,** with supplements to the volumes for 1940-49 and 1950-58. Edinburgh & London, Oliver and Boyd, 1968; reprinted New York, Arno Press, 1981. vi, [1], 356p. ISBN: 0405138822.

Four parts: 1. Pre-1900 - 2. 1900-1939 - 3. Supplement to the 1940-49 volume - 4. Supplement to the 1950-58 volume. About 10,000 entries, under authors A-Z. To avoid confusion, the reference numbers of entries in the pre-1900 section are given in prefix A. In the supplementary section, prefix S is used. Part 3 begins at 7,001 and part 4 at 10,000. No subject index. The 3v. in all contain over 27,000 entries, up to 1958. *Class No:* 519.22(01)

[631]

—**KENDALL, M.G.** *and* **DOIG, A.G.** Bibliography of statistical literature, 1940-49. Edinburgh & London, Oliver & Boyd, 1965. [vi], 190p.

Lists 6,036 items under authors A-Z, then chronologically. Full bibliographical details. Two defects: lack of a subject index and failure to translate many of the titles in foreign languages. *Class No:* 519.22(01)

[632]

—**KENDALL, M.G.** *and* **DOIG, A.G.** Bibliography of statistical literature, 1950-58. Edinburgh & London, Oliver & Boyd, 1962. xii, 297p.

Lists 9,802 items, under authors A-Z. 26 contributors. For 12 journals almost all the articles are indexed; for 42 others, relevant articles only. On its limitations as a finding tool, see *Librarian-statistician relations in the field of economic statistics* (London, Library Association, 1965) p.42-44. The 3v. set was reprinted in 1981 (New York, Arno). Coverage of the literature is continued in *Statistical theory and method abstracts* (qv). *Class No:* 519.22(01)

[633]

LANCASTER, H.O. 'Problems in the bibliography of statistics'. Royal Statistical Society. *Journal*, series A, v.144, 1970. pt.3, p.409-41.

Part 1: Aims and techniques of statistical bibliography. Part 2: Bibliography and information retrieval (74 references appended). A basic bibliographical survey. *Class No:* 519.22(01)

[634]
—LANCASTER, H.O. Bibliography of statistical bibliographies. Edinburgh & London, Oliver & Boyd, for the International Statistical Institute, 1968. ix, 103p.

Comprises: 1. Personal bibliographies - 2. Subject bibliographies (up to 1965, with some for 1966) - 3. National bibliographies. Subject index to 'Personal bibliographies'; author index to subject and national bibliographies. Aims to cover the theory of statistics at university level. *Class No:* 519.22(01)

Indexes

[635]
Current index to statistics: applications, methods and theory. Washington, American Statistical Association and Institute of Mathematical Statistics, 1976-. v.1-. Annual.

Articles from *c.*60 core journals, selected monographs and conference proceedings of the previous year. 'This annual series aspires to provide comprehensive index coverage on a timely basis' (*Introduction*). About 1,500 items are listed annually. Author index; subject index; index of journal and publisher abbreviations. International coverage. *Class No:* 519.22(014)

[636]
JOINER, P.L., *and others*. **An Author and permuted title index to selected statistical journals.** U.S. National Bureau of Standards. Washington, U.S. Government Printing Office, 1970. iv, 506p.

About 30,000 entries in permuted title index, p.1-354; author index. Appended contents-lists of selected handbooks of mathematical tables. 'This volume must be one of the most comprehensive works of indexing ever undertaken in scientific work' (*Nature*, v.202, 25 April 1964, p.330). *Class No:* 519.22(014)

Encyclopaedias

[637]
KOTZ, S. *and* JOHNSON, N.L., *eds.* **Encyclopaedia of statistical sciences.** New York, Chichester, etc., Wiley, 1982-88. 9v. + supplement. illus., diagrs., formulas. £850 (set).

V.1. *A - Circular probable error.* 1982. V.9. *Strata chart - Zyskind.* 1988.

V.1 has 100 contributors. Signed articles, including biographies (*e.g.* Bienaymé I.J.: 3½ columns; 10 references; 14 cross-references). The final article in v.3, 'Hypothesis testing', occupies p.712-22, with 17 references, 15 cross-references. Included are entries for leading organizations and core journals. A scholarly encyclopaedia on theoretical and applied statistics.

Supplements published 1989, 1998. The 1998 supplement (745p. $195. ISBN: 0471119393) provides detailed coverage of recent developments and a cumulative index. Annual updates are also published. V.1 (896p. 1997. $195. ISBN:0471118362) covers, among other topics, asymptotic expansions, classical discrete distributions, statistical graphics and nonlinear time series. *Class No:* 519.22(031)

Handbooks & Manuals

[638]
TIETJEN, G.L. **A Topical dictionary of statistics.** London, Chapman & Hall, 1986. ix, [i] 171p. £17.50. ISBN: 0412012014.

15 topical chapters, each with short annotated bibliography: Summarizing data - Random variables and probability distribution - Some useful distributions - Estimation and some hypothesis testing - Regression - The design of experiments and the analysis of variants - Reliability and survival analysis - Order statistics - Stochastic processes - Time series - Categorical data - Epidemiology - Quality control and acceptance sampling - Multivariate analysis - Survey sampling. Index of specific terms. Detailed, analytical index. *Class No:* 519.22(035)

[639]
—WALL, J.J. Statistical data analysis handbook. New York, etc., McGraw-Hill, 1986. 136+[2]+[8]p. tables. £49.50. ISBN: 0070679312.

In 5 parts: 1. Simple comparison - 2. Linear relationship - 3. Comparison of relationships - 4. Supporting Topics - 5. Tables, A-T (*e.g.* T: Random digits). 2-page bibliography. 8-page index. *Class No:* 519.22(035)

Dictionaries

Polyglot

[640]
HUNGARY. Központi Statisztikai Hivatel. **Statisztikal szótái.** 1700 stativztikai kifejezés hat nyelven. [Statistical dictionary. 1700 statistical terms in seven languages.] [2 kaid]. Budapest, Statisztikai Kiadá Vállalat, 1961. viii, 171p.

First published 1960.

....(contd.)
The basic sequence is of Russian terms, with Bulgarian, Czech, English, German, Hungarian and Polish equivalents and indexes. *Class No:* 519.22(038)=00

[641]
PAENSON, I., *with others*. **Glossaire systématique, anglais-français-espagnol-russe de la terminologie des methodes statistiques.** Oxford, etc., Pergamon Press, 1970. xxxviii, 517p. tables.

About 1,200 statistical terms are given in context over 20 subject chapters (p.2-413). English, French, Spanish and Russian indexes, p.415-7. Bibliography of sources, p.xxiv. 26 tables. A companion to I. Paenson's *Systematic glossary, English/French/Spanish/Russian of selected economic and second terms* (1963). *Class No:* 519.22(038)=00

English

[642]
EVERITT, B.S. **The Cambridge dictionary of statistics.** Cambridge Univ. Press, 1998. 360p. illus., diagrs., graphs, formulas. $39.95. ISBN: 0521593468.

Defines about 3,000 terms, clearly and distinctly, with examples and references for many of them. Includes brief biographies of about 100 statisticians. 'Highly recommended' (*Choice*, February 1999, p.1043). *Class No:* 519.22(038)=20

[643]
KENDALL, M.G. *and* BUCKLAND, W.R. **A Dictionary of statistical terms.** 5th ed. by F.H.C. Marriott. London, Longman, for International Statistical Institute, 1990. [viii],223p. tables, formulas. ISBN: 0582019052.

First published 1957 by M.G. Kendall and W.R. Buckland. 4th ed. 1982.

Defines about 3,400 terms, with some 400 new additions. Entries range from 25 to 150 words. Author and date citations are given for more recent terms. Formulae and cross-references figure. *Class No:* 519.22(038)=20

[644]
KURTZ, A.K. *and* EDGERTON, H.A. **Statistical dictionary of terms and symbols.** New York, Wiley, 1939; London, Chapman & Hall, 1940. xiii, 191p. (Reprinted New York, Hafner, 1967).

Concise definitions of *c.*2000 terms. Aimed primarily 'to provide the user with clear and accurate definitions of each of the various meanings of the statistical terms which he encounters in his reading of scientific literature' (*Preface*). 'Multiple ratio correlation', *c.*250 words. *Class No:* 519.22(038)=20

[645]
PORKESS, R. **Dictionary of statistics.** London, Collins, 1988. xii, 267p. £3.95. (*Collins reference.*) ISBN: 0004343549.

Definitions of 426 terms, some 'encyclopedic' (*Preface*, p.xi); includes worked examples. Appendices: symbols; formulas; tables. *Class No:* 519.22(038)=20

Russian

[646]
KOTZ, S. **Russian-English/English-Russian glossary of statistical terms.** London, Oliver & Boyd, for the International Statistical Institute, 1972. 88p.

Russian equivalents of *c.*2,500 terms included in the 3rd ed. of Kendal & Buckland's *A dictionary of statistical terms*, etc. Some terms are given brief explanations. 'Not a book for the beginner, either in statistics or in Russian' (*Nature*, v.239, 8 September 1972, p.114-5). *Class No:* 519.22(038)=82

Reviews & Abstracts

[647]
Statistical theory and method abstracts. Voorburg, Netherlands, International Statistical Institute, 1959-. v.1(1)-. Quarterly. £46 ($65) pa. ISSN: 00390518.

Continues *International journal of abstracts: Statistical theory and method* (1954-63. 10v. Annual). Incorporates *International journal of abstracts: Application of statistical methods in industry*.

About 3,000 abstracts pa. Classification scheme (00 ... 15), closely subdivided: 00. Mathematical methods - 01. Probability theory ... 08. Analyses of variance - 09. Sampling ... 12. Statistical inference for stochastic processes - 13. Operations research and related topics ... 15. General features. Brief abstracts (20-150 words). Author index precedes in each issue. Annual author index and index to book reviews. Continues Kendall and Doig bibliographies (*qv*). *Class No:* 519.22(048)

Tables & Data Books

[648]

GREENWOOD, J.A. *and* **HARTLEY, H.O. Guide to tables in mathematical statistics.** Princeton, N.J., Princeton Univ. Press; London, Oxford Univ. Press, 1962. lxii, 1014p. diagrs.

Sponsored by the Committee on Statistics of the Division of National Academy of Sciences, National Research Council (USA).

A descriptive catalogue in 16 main sections. Appendices: 1. Supplement to the descriptive catalogue - 2. Contents of books of tables - 3. Mathematical tables listed in this *Guide*, and in Fletcher, etc. Author and subject indexes. Near-printed; a bulky volume. *Class No:* 519.22(083)

[649]

LINDLEY, D.V. *and* **SCOTT, W.F. New Cambridge statistical tables.** 2nd ed. Cambridge Univ. Press, 1995. 96p. tables. $12.95. ISBN: 0521484855.

First published 1984 as *New Cambridge elementary statistical tables*. Includes tables for common elementary statistical functions and tests of significance. Good value. *Class No:* 519.22(083)

[650]

NEAVE, H.R. Statistical tables for mathematicians, engineers, economists and the behavioural and management sciences. London, Allen & Unwin, 1978. 87, [1]p. tables.

9 sections: 1. Discrete probability distributions - 2. The normal distribution - 3. Continuous probability distributions - 4. Analysis of variance - 5. Non-parametric tests - 6. Correlation - 7. Random numbers - 8. Quality control - 9. Miscellaneous. References to appropriate books or articles figure for the less familiar tables. *Class No:* 519.22(083)

[651]

PEARSON, E.S. *and* **HARTLEY, H.O.,** *eds.* **Biometrika tables for statisticians.** London, Biometrika Trust, 1976. 2v. tables.

First published 1954-72. Based on *Tables for statisticians and biometricians*, edited by K. Pearson (1924; 3rd ed., 1948).

Tables in applied statistics, v.2 covering more specialised functions, with examples. (Biometrics is concerned with the statistical study of biological problems). *Class No:* 519.22(083)

Stochastic Processes

[652]

WOLD, H.O.A. Bibliography on time series and stochastic processes. Edinburgh & London, Oliver & Boyd, for the International Statistical Institute, 1965. xv, 516p.

Nearly 6,000 entries, limited - for the period up to 1930 and to a lesser extent 1931-50 - to items with a basic value for further developments. No abstracts, although each entry carries a 6-category code (including 'field of application'). The bibliography, ending with 1959, continues in *International journal of abstracts: Statistical theory and method* (1954-63) and *Statistical theory and method abstracts* (1959-) (*qv*). *Class No:* 519.246

Computation

[653]

FISHER, D., *ed.* **Rules of thumb for engineers and scientists.** Rev. ed. Houston, Tx., Gulf, 1991. 242p. tables. $28.95. ISBN: 0872017869.

Several hundred published rules, by proponent, A-Z. Indexes of dependent and independent variables. *Class No:* 519.254

[654]

Handbook of evolutionary computation. Bäck, T., *and others, eds.* Oxford Univ. Press; Bristol, Institute of Physics, 1997. 1096p. illus. $395. ISBN: 0750303921.

Covers computation in a number of application areas including computer and information science, engineering, physics, chemistry, biology, medicine, economics, finance, business, cognition and operations research. In 8 parts: A. Introduction - B. Fundamental concepts - C. Evolutionary computation models - D. Hybrid approaches - E. Evolutionary computation implementations - F. Applications - G. Case studies - H. Research. Glossary; detailed, analytical index. Updates (2pa.) are planned. Also available on the World Wide Web (URL: http://www.oup-usa.org/acadref/compint.html). *Class No:* 519.254

[655]

HARRIS, J.W. *and* **STÖCKER, H. Handbook of mathematics and computational science.** Berlin, Springer, 1998. 1028p. graphs. £19.50; $29.95. ISBN: 0387947469.

Covers a range of mathematical topics including analytics, geometry, derivatives, integrals, vector analysis, differential equations and transforms. The well-organized table of contents makes it 'easy to use' (*Choice*, January 1999, p.923.) *Class No:* 519.254

[656]

KANJI, G.K. 100 statistical tests. Beverly Hills, Ca., Sage, 1993. 216p. tables. $59.95. ISBN: 0803987048.

Mostly elementary tests in a brief standardized format: 1. Object of the test - 2. Limitations of the test - 3. Detailed formulas - 4. Numerical example. No proofs included. *Class No:* 519.254

[657]

Mathematics of computation: a journal devoted to advances in numerical analysis, the application of computational methods, mathematical tables, high-speed calculators, and other aids to computation. Washington, National Research Council, National Academy of Sciences, 1941-. Quarterly. ISSN: 00255718.

Previously (1943-59) as *Mathematical tables and other aids to compilation*.

This journal (*MTAC*) 'serves as a clearing house for all sorts of mathematical work, containing articles, reviews of new books and reviews of new tables'. Lists of errors in old and new tables are published as received from contributors worldwide. The journal's editorial office also maintains a repository of unpublished mathematical tables (UMT). 'An excellent tool' (*Information sources in science and technology*, 3rd. ed., 1998, p.237). *Class No:* 519.254

Mathematical Tables

[658]

BARLOW, P. Barlow's Tables of squares, cubes, square roots, cube roots, and reciprocals of all integers up to 12,000. 4th ed., edited by L.J. Comrie. London, Spon, 1941. xii, 258p.

First published 1814. 'In 1840 De Morgan edited a new edition, the stereo plates for which were used for all subsequent editions' (*Preface to the third edition*).

Invaluable to the mathematician and designed to facilitate mathematical processes. Essential for any scientific reference library and decidedly cheaper than the *CRC Handbook of mathematical sciences (qv)*. *Class No:* 519.66

[659]

BRITISH ASSOCIATION FOR THE ADVANCEMENT OF SCIENCE. Mathematical tables. Cambridge Univ. Press, 1931-52. v.1-10.

Under the auspices of the Royal Society.

1. *Circular and hyperbolic functions.* 3rd ed. 1951. 2. *Emden functions.* 1932. 3. *Minimum decompositions into fifth powers.* 1933. 4. *Cycles of reduced ideals in quadratic fields.* 1934. 5. *Factor table.* 1935. 6. *Bessel functions.* pt.1. 1937. 7. *The probability integral.* 1939. 8. *Number-division tables.* 1940. 9. *Tables of powers giving integral powers of integers.* 1940. 10. *Bessel functions.* pt.2. 1952. Part Vol.A: *Legendre polynomials.* 1946; B. *The Airy integrals.* 1946. *Auxiliary tables,* nos. 1-2. 1946. Continued in the Royal Society mathematical tables (*qv*). *Class No:* 519.66

[660]

BURINGTON, R.S. Handbook of mathematical tables and formulas. 5th ed. New York, etc., McGraw-Hill, 1973. x, [2], 500p. diagrs., tables. $24.50.

Part 1 summarizes the more important formulas, definitions and theorems. Part 2: 5-place logarithmic and trigonometric tables and more specialised tables. References, p.450-1. Glossary of symbols. Index of numerical tables. Analytical subject index, p.459-500. Aims to meet the needs of students and workers in mathematics, engineering, physics, chemistry, science. A well-known handbook. *Class No:* 519.66

[661]

COMRIE, L.J. Chambers six-figure mathematical tables. Edinburgh & London, Chambers, 1948-49. 2v.

V.1: Logarithmic tables; V.2: Natural values (trigonometrical functions of angles in degrees; circular volume; functions; exponential and hyperbolic functions). Each volume has an appendix of physical and other constants, plus a bibliography of more extended tables (p.568-73). *Class No:* 519.66

[662]

CRC standard mathematical tables and formulae. Zwillinger, D., *ed.* 30th ed. Boca Raton, Fl., CRC Press, 1996. [xii], 812p. diagrs., graphs, tables. $39.95. ISBN: 0849324793.

First published 1964; 29th ed., 1991.

Sections: Analysis - Algebra - Discrete mathematics - Geometry - Continuous mathematics - Special functions - Probability and statistics - Scientific computing - Financial analysis - Miscellaneous (*e.g.* electronic mathematical resources, with URLs; professional societies; biographies). Detailed index. New and revised topics for this ed. include partial differential equations, scientific computing, integral equations, group theory and graph theory. 'A must' (*Choice*, October 1996, p.318). *Class No:* 519.66

[663]

FLETCHER, A., *and others, eds.* **An Index of mathematical tables.** 2nd ed. Oxford, Blackwell, for Scientific Computing Service, Ltd., 1962. 2v. (994p.).

First published 1946 (London, Scientific Computing Service, Ltd).

V.1, pt.1: Historical introduction. Index of mathematical tables (with descriptions and comparisons), according to functions (24 series) - V.2, pt.2: Bibliography (p.609-780; over 4,000 references; under authors, A-Z) - pt.3: Errors (in published tables) - pt.4: Index to introduction and pt.1. The 2nd ed., more than twice the size of the 1st, adds the feature, the list of errors. 'This standard work of reference became an indispensable classic from the moment of its publication in 1946' (*Nature,* v.201, 8 February 1964, p.537). *Class No:* 519.66

[664]

LEBEDEV, A.V. *and* **FEDEROVA, R.M. A Guide to mathematical tables.** English ed., prepared from the Russian by D.G. Fry. Oxford, etc., Pergamon Press, 1960. xlvi, 586p. *Supplement* no. 1. 1960. xxxviii, 190p.

Translated from the Russian ed. of 1956.

Tables are arranged by mathematical function or type of operation. International coverage, but its emphasis on Russian tables makes it complementary to Fletcher's *An index of mathematical tables (qv).* *Class No:* 519.66

[665]

ROYAL SOCIETY. Mathematical Tables Committee. **Royal Society mathematical tables.** Cambridge Univ. Press, for the Royal Society, 1950-68. 11v.

Continuation of the British Association for the Advancement of Science's *Mathematical tables* (Cambridge Univ. Press, 1931-52. 10v.) *(qv).*

1. *The Forey series of order 1025.* 1950. 2. *Rectangular-polar conversion tables.* 1956. 3. *Tables of binomial coefficients.* 1953. 4. *Tables of partitions.* 1958. 5. *Representation of primes by quadratic forms.* 1960. 6. *Tables of the Riemann zeta function.* 1960. 7. *Bessel functions.* pt.3: *Zeros.* 1960. 8. *Tables of natural and common logarithms to 110 decimals.* 1964. 9. *Tables of indices and primitive roots.* 1968. 10. *Bessel functions.* pt.4: *Kelvin functions.* 1964. 11. *Coulomb wave functions.* 1964. *Auxiliary tables.* 1950. *Class No:* 519.66

Logarithms

[666]

THOMPSON, A.J. Logarithmetica Britannica, being a standard table of logarithms to twenty decimal places of the numbers 10,000 to 100,000. Cambridge, Univ. Press, 1952. 2v.

Issued by the Department of Statistics, University College, London, to commemorate the tercentenary of Henry Briggs' publication of *Arithmetica logarithmica,* 1624.

V.1: Numbers 10,000 to 50,000; v.2: Numbers 50,000 to 100,000. V.1 contains a lengthy general introduction (p.xii-lxxxiii), including a list of errors in Briggs. *Class No:* 519.662

52/529 Astronomy & Surveying

Astronomy

Databases

[667]

INSPEC. Stevenage, Herts., Institution of Electrical Engineers, 1969-. Updated weekly.

Although not dealing exclusively with astronomy, INSPEC is one of the best databases available online because of the close relationship between astronomy and physics. Coverage embraces periodical articles, conference proceedings, books, technical reports, theses, etc. Also available on CD-ROM, magnetic tape, and Batch Access.

Other databases that contain astronomical information are: Astronomy Forum, accessible via Compuserve (ASTROFORUM), PASCAL B on DIALOG and CD-ROM, NASA Database (although access limited to NASA itself, US government departments and some university libraries), and *Meteorological and geoastrophysical abstracts,* on DIALOG. *Class No:* 520(003.4)

Bibliographies

[668]

HOUZEAU, J.C. *and* **LANCASTER, A. Bibliographie générale de l'astronomie,** ou, Catalogue méthodique des ouvrages, des memoires et des observations astronomiques publiés depuis l'origine de l'imprimerie jusqu'en 1880. Brussels, Hayez. 1882-89. 2v. in 3.

Reprinted London, Holland Press, 1964.

V.1: *Ouvrages imprimés et manuscrits* (1887-89): 15,880 items, systematically arranged; bibliographical notes; locations of MSS are given. The lengthy introduction (to p.310) covers the historical background. V.2: *Mémoires et notices insérés dans les collections académiques et les périodiques* (1882) concerns articles in periodicals, prefixed by a list of periodicals scanned. Systematically arranged; author index, citing short titles of articles. The primary bibliographical science for the history of astronomy. The 1964 reprint includes an author index to v.1. *Class No:* 520(01)

[669]

—Astronomischer Jahresbericht. Berlin, de Gruyter, 1900-68. v.1-68.

Continues Houzeau and Lancaster, with a gap for 1880-98. The unpublished material for those years - over 60,000 slips - has been microfilmed by University Microfilms, Ltd. on 18 reels of 35mm. film (1970), the original being at the Observatoire Royale de Belgique, Brussels. *Class No:* 520(01)

[670]

—LALANDE, J.J.F. de. Bibliographie astronomique, avec l'histoire de l'astronomie depuis 1781 jusqu'à 1802. Paris, Imprimerie de la République, 1803. viii, 966p.

Lists 5,000 titles and is arranged chronologically, with author and subject indexes (unlike v.1) of Houzeau and Lancaster. Reprinted 1970 (Amsterdam, Gieben). *Class No:* 520(01)

[671]

KEMP, D.A. Astronomy and astrophysics: a bibliographical guide. London, Macdonald, 1970. xxiii, 584p. (*Macdonald bibliographical guides.*) ISBN: 0356030113.

Annotated entries for 3,642 numbered items (with interpolations). 75 sections, systematically arranged (1. Reference media - 2. Star catalogues, ephemerides, etc.... 25. Origin of the solar system... 49. Stellar evolution... 73. Cosmology - 74. Abundance and origin of the elements. - 75. Cosmic rays and gamma - and X-ray astronomy). Periodical articles are included. Entries (in column form): running number, title, author, etc; number of items and years covered; annotations (sometimes evaluative). Entries go up to 1969. Author and subject indexes, p.533-84. The author was at one time librarian of the Royal Observatory, Edinburgh. 'An invaluable reference source for astronomers, other scientists working in the fringe areas of astronomy, and librarians' (*The Recorder,* no.271, 15 February 1971, p.2). *Class No:* 520(01)

[672]

—SEAL, R.A. *and* MARTIN, S.S. A Bibliography of astronomy, 1970-1979. Littleton, Colo., Libraries Unlimited, 1982. 407p. ISBN: 0872872807.

Provides a ten-year continuation to Kemp. The 2,119 entries are in 4 parts (18 sections): Reference works - Subject sections - Appendices (International Astronomical Union Colloquia; I.A.U. symposia, 1969-1979; Abbreviations) - Indexes (author; monographic title or conference proceeding index; subject). Annotations average 50 words, conference proceedings being labelled 'C'. Periodical articles are included. Coverage is based on 15 U.S. and Canadian libraries' holdings. Intended as an introductory overview and selection tool for all types of libraries and users, not as a comprehensive reference tool for the decade of the 1970s. *Class No:* 520(01)

[673]

LUSIS, A. Astronomy and aeronautics: an enthusiast's guide to books and periodicals. London, Mansell, 1986. xx, 292p. ISBN: 072011795x.

968 annotated and numbered entries. 7 sections: 1. General astronomy - 2. Practical astronomy - 3. History of astronomy - 4. Astronomy plus ... (multi-and interdisciplinary works) - 5. Astrophysics - 6. The solar system - 7. Astronautics (p.198-255). Items asterisked were not available for inspection. Author index; Title index: books; Title index: periodicals; Subject index (analytical). Annotations are often evaluative and may cite reviews in *Sky and telescope,* etc. Attempts to provide a comprehensive annotated list in English 'for anyone ... below professional or undergraduate level' (*Introduction*). Claims to be in some ways a successor to Seal's *Guide* (*q.v.*). *Class No:* 520(01)

[674]

SEAL, R.A. A Guide to the literature of astronomy. Littleton, Colo., Libraries Unlimited, 1977. 306p.

578 numbered entries, with evaluative comments of a high standard. 4 sections: 1. Reference material in astronomy - 2. General materials (*e.g.* history; textbooks) - 3. Descriptive astronomy - 4. Special topics (*e.g.* space science and aerodynamics). Appended 'Bibliography of basic reference material in astronomy' (p.238-9) - 80 items, including 31 atlases and star catalogues. Items are coded as recommended for A. Astronomy libraries; B. Public libraries; C. College/university libraries. Author-title and subject indexes. Excludes astronautics. For the non-specialist. *Class No:* 520(01)

[675]

—ROYAL ASTRONOMICAL SOCIETY. Catalogue of the Library. [Royal Astronomical Society]. London, the Society, 1886-1924. 3pts.

An author catalogue. Pt.1 (1886) includes entries for much early material. Included are form headings for 'Bibliographies', 'Ephemerides' and sea charts. *Class No:* 520(01)

[676]

SMITH, R. Popular physics and astronomy: an annotated bibliography. Metuchen, N.J., Scarecrow, 1996. 507p., illus. $64. ISBN: 081084149x.

Lists 886 books, with annotations of about 200 words. Excludes works which depend on an understanding of mathematics, but includes a special section for juvenile works. A popular approach. *Class No:* 520(01)

[677]

UNITED STATES. Naval Observatory Library, Washington. **Catalog of the Naval Observatory Library.** Boston, Mass., G.K. Hall, 1976. 6v. (4118p.). $655. ISBN: 0816100314.

89,300 photolithographed catalogue-cards, representing a collection of 75,000 items in astronomy and mathematics. The Library was founded in 1842, and the catalogue includes entries for pre-1960 periodical articles. *Class No:* 520(01)

Encyclopaedias

[678]

The Astronomy and astrophysics encyclopaedia. Maran, S.P., *ed.* New York, Van Nostrand Reinhold, 1992. xxix,1002p. illus., figs., tables. £60. ISBN: 0521417449.

403 entries arranged A-Z, written by more than 400 contributors. The articles are very technical and go into great detail. Extensive cross-references. Bibliographies appended to each chapter. Black-and-white illustrations. Index. Attractively presented. 'This volume is now the premier encyclopedia of astronomy' (*Choice,* March 1992,

....(contd.)

p.1037), although the reviewer in *Reference reviews,* v.6(3) 1992, p.6 thinks more illustrations would have been useful. For the academic library. *Class No:* 520(031)

[679]

The Astronomy encyclopaedia. Moore, P., *ed.* London, Mitchell Beazley, 1987. 464p. illus. (incl. col.), ports., diagrs., tables. ISBN: 0855336048.

Published as *The International encyclopedia of astronomy* (Crown, 1987).

About 100 contributors. A-Z sequence of 2,500 entries (50-3,000 words in length), including 7 essays on major topics (*e.g.* 'The big bang'; 'Exploring space'; 'Interstellar matter'; 'Pulsars'). 570 illus. (170 in colour), well captioned. Cross-references. No bibliographies. 'A volume that will remain a popular reference source for many years to come' (*New scientist,* no.1589, 3 December 1987, p.67). For school and public libraries. *Class No:* 520(031)

[680]

Encyclopedia of astronomy and astrophysics. Meyers, R.A., *ed.* San Diego, Academic Press, 1989. xiv,807p. illus., diagrs., tables. $59.95. ISBN: 0122266900.

41 articles, arranged A-Z (Astronomy, Infrared ... X-ray Astronomy), averaging 20 pages in length. Each article has a glossary and bibliography appended. *c.*300 photographs and illustrations. Cross-references and analytical index. *Class No:* 520(031)

[681]

McGraw-Hill encyclopedia of astronomy. Parker, S.P. *and* Pasachoff, J.M., *eds.* 2nd ed. New York, McGraw-Hill, 1993. 531p. illus. (incl. col. pl.), tables. ISBN: 0070453144.

230 articles, A-Z and briefly documented, drawn unabridged from the parent *McGraw-Hill encyclopedia of science and technology* (7th ed., 1992). 103 contributors; extensive cross-references; detailed index. 402 illus., with 13 colour plates. 21 new articles added to this edition, and 20 articles rewritten. Some, but not all, articles are followed by bibliographical references. Well and attractively produced, although the emphasis is on theoretical and experimental aspects of astronomy. *Class No:* 520(031)

[682]

WEIGERT, A. *and* **ZIMMERMAN, H. Concise encyclopedia of astronomy.** Dickson, J.H., *trans.* 2nd English ed., revised by H. Zimmerman. Bristol, Hilger, 1975. 532p. illus., diagrs., tables.

Based on *ABC of astronomy* (translated from the 2nd ed. of *ABC der Astronomie).*

About 2,000 entries (A ... Zone time), with many cross-references. Includes brief biographies (Kepler: 2 columns; Galileo: 2/3column). 66 plates appended. 'For the advanced amateur and is also an excellent reference book' (*Nature,* v.264, 9 December 1976, p.591-2). *New scientist* (9 December 1976, p.609) finds the photography 'still poorly produced'. *Class No:* 520(031)

[683]

—The Encyclopaedia of astronomy and space. Ridpath, I., *ed.* London, Macmillan, 1976 (rev. ed. 1980).

Over 1,000 short but adequate entries, including brief biographies, as well as more than 100 tables, charts and photographs, many in colour. Decidedly more simple text than Weigert and 'seems aimed at people in their early teens' (*Nature,* v.264, 9 December 1976, p.591-2). *Class No:* 520(031)

Handbooks & Manuals

[684]

ABELL, G.O. Exploration of the universe. 5th ed. Philadelphia, Pa., Saunders College Publishing, 1987. x,748p. (incl. col.), ports., diagrs., tables, star charts. ISBN: 0030051436.

First published 1964.

38 chapters, descriptive and historical, with exercises appended. 21 appendices (1. Bibliography; 2. Glossary (p.699-721)... 21. Star maps). Double-column page; analytical index (in tiny print). An attractively produced text-book, well organised and clearly written. Aimed at the average college student, taking a one-year or even a one-semester course. Highly regarded by R.A. Seal (*A Guide to the literature of astronomy*). 6th ed., 1991. 682p. $37.50. *Class No:* 520(035)

[685]

The Cambridge encyclopaedia of astronomy. Mitton, S., *editor-in-chief.* London, Cape, 1977. 481, [14]p. illus., sky maps. Page size, 25 x 25cm. £60. ISBN: 0517528061.

16 contributors. 23 chapters (1. A survey of the universe... 9. The solar system... 15. Our local group of galaxies... 20. Life in the universe. 21. Major trends in the history of astronomy... 23. Astronomy in space). Appendix 1: Star atlas of Smithsonian Astrophysical Observatory sky maps (p.457-71). 'Material has been gathered into cohesive theories in order to present a more accurate and understandable guide to the new universe' (*Introduction*). Analytical index, in tiny type. Over 500 illus. (150 in full colour), with

....(contd.)

descriptive captions. Data up to 1975. No supplementary readings or bibliography. Written primarily for readers in the northern hemisphere. However, the volume has a wealth of astronomical data and fine illustrations, with a detailed index. The editor-in-chief was then Secretary of the Institute of Univ. of Cambridge and most of the contributors were associated with the Institute. *Class No:* 520(035)

[686]

Encyclopedia of astronomy: a comprehensive survey of our solar system, galaxy and beyond. Ronan, C., *ed.* London, New York, etc., Hamlyn, 1979. 240p. illus. (incl. coloured), star charts, diagrs., graphs.

6 contributors. Chapters : Introduction - The stars - The solar system - Extragalactic astronomy - Theories of the universe - Observing the universe - The amateur observer - Star charts. 13 appendices (6. Star catalogues; 10. Comparative data on the planets; 12. Names of stars). Appended glossary, short bibliography and index (in tiny print). Like the *Cambridge Encyclopedia of astronomy,* fully illustrated, making good use of a large format. Praised in *New scientist* (29 November 1979, p.710) for its in-depth treatment of galaxies. 'The pictures and diagrams are as good as the text'. *Class No:* 520(035)

[687]

GIBSON, B. The Astronomer's sourcebook: the complete guide to astronomical equipment, publications, planetariums, organizations, events, and more. Rockville, Md., Woodbine House, 1992. iv,302p. illus. ISBN: 0933149433.

10 sections: 1. Armchair astronomy ... 5. Astro-photography ... 10. Astronomy education. Well-organized directory which includes data on organizations, telescopes, accessories, museums, scholarships, useful publications, etc. Indexes for corporations, publications, and subjects. US-slant. 'Enthusiastically recommended for popular science collections in public and academic collections' (*Library journal,* 15 April 1992, p.86). Good value. *Class No:* 520(035)

[688]

HARTUNG, E.J. Astronomical objects for southern telescopes: with an addendum for northern observatories. Cambridge, University Press, 1968 (reprinted 1984). 238p. illus. tables. £13.95. ISBN: 0521318874.

5 introductory chapters: 1. Radiation - 2. Stars - 3. Star clusters - 4. Galactic nebulae - 5. Extra-galactic systems - 6. Amateur observing. Followed by: General list of telescopic objects for southern observers; Description of constellations and objects (p.66-227) (over 1,000 objects). Addendum for northern observatories (80 objects). Bibliography. Index. 16p. of black-and-white plates. For the amateur observer. *Class No:* 520(035)

[689]

Larousse astronomy. Morris, M.R., *ed.* Twickenham, Middx., Hamlyn, 1987. 326p. illus. (incl. col.). facsims., diagrs., tables, star charts. ISBN: 0600501086.

A revised translation of *Astronomie, les astres, l'univers,* originally published by Larousse in 1948 and subsequently, with supplement, in 1956. Previous ed. *Larousse encyclopedia of astronomy* (1966).

4 sections (25 chapters): 1. Man and the sky - 2. The empire of the sun - 3. The realm of the stars - 4. Toward infinity. Well written and lavishly illustrated, with numerous plates, diagrams, etc. Bibliography, p.321-2. Index (tiny print). Essentially for the lay person. *Class No:* 520(035)

[690]

MOORE, P. The Guinness book of astronomy. 5th ed. Enfield, Guinness Publishing, 1995. 288p. illus. (incl. col.), star charts, tables. ISBN: 085112643x.

First published 1979. Before 3rd edition, known as *The Guinness book of astronomy facts and feats.*

Sections: The solar system (p.5-138) - The stars - The star catalogue (p.167-255) - Telescopes and observatories - The history of astronomy - Astronomers - Glossary - Index. Clearly and attractively produced, and kept commendably up-to-date (Comet Shoemaker-Levy's collision with Jupiter is described). A good introduction for the beginner. *Class No:* 520(035)

[691]

MOORE, P. The Observer's year. London, Springer, 1998. xii,368p. figs.,tables. £19. (*Practical astronomy series*.) ISBN: 3540761470.

Takes each day of the year and points out items of interest in the night sky at that time. Small side panels give anniversaries or points of interest on the same day in coming years. Three appendices: A. The 88 constellations - B. Glossary - C. The Greek alphabet. Index. For the amateur astronomer. *Class No:* 520(035)

[692]

MOORE, P. Philip's guide to stars and planets. London, George Philip, 1997. 256p. illus. (col.), charts. £9.99. ISBN: 0540072354.

First published 1980 as *Patrick Moore's pocket guide to the stars and planets.*

Covers solar system p.22-83. and more distant objects p.84-243. Index p.251-56. Good, cheaply-priced introduction to astronomy, with star charts by Wil Tirion. *Class No:* 520(035)

[693]

MUIRDEN, J. **The Amateur astronomer's handbook.** 3rd ed. New York, Harper & Row, 1983. [viii], 472p. illus., diagrs., tables. $16.95; £7.95. ISBN: 0061816221.

First published 1968.

5 parts (29 chapters). 1. Equipment - 2. The solar system - 3. The stars and nebulae - 4. Autobiography - 5. Optical work for amateurs (a major new section). 8 appendices (*e.g.* Tables of precision for ten years). Glossary; chapter bibliographies, p.457-62; analytical index. p.463-72. Written primarily for readers in the northern hemisphere, and for the novice who wants to make telescope observations on his or her own. It tries 'to bridge the gap between works that deal with the spectacular 'wonders of the sky' and the formal handbook full of facts'. Not to be confused with Sidgwick's similarly titled book. *Class No:* 520(035)

[694]

NEWTON, J. *and* TEECE, P. **The Guide to amateur astronomy.** 2nd ed. Cambridge, University Press, 1995. 335p. illus., diagrs. £24.95. ISBN: 0521444926.

First edition published 1988.

Written by amateur astronomers and intended mainly for the beginner. 6 sections:- 1. First discoveries; the adventure begins. 2. Solar system voyages. 3. A deep sky guide. 4. The night sky on film; astrophotography. 5. Amateur astronomy in the electronic age. 6. The build-it-yourself astronomer. 5 appendices. Good illustrations and diagrams. *Class No:* 520(035)

[695]

The Observer's guide to astronomy. Martinez, P., *ed.* Cambridge, University Press, 1994. 2v.(1148p.) $34.95ea. (*Practical astronomy handbooks 4.*) ISBN: 052137068x, v.1; 0521452651, v.2.

Translation of work done by French and Belgian professional astronomers. Basically a reference tool meticulously describing various aspects of astronomy, *e.g.* sun, solar eclipses, moon, planetary surfaces, as well as such observation techniques as plate comparators, astrometry, spectroscopy, and photoelectronic photometry. Prior knowledge is assumed and, although the work lacks an index or glossary, the detailed contents pages are adequate substitutes. 'For serious amateur astronomers and students with access to telescopes, this set is a necessity' (*Choice*, September 1995, p.152). Recommended for academic and large public libraries. *Class No:* 520(035)

[696]

SIDGWICK, J.B. **Amateur astronomer's handbook.** 4th ed., prepared by J. Muirden. London, Pelham Books, 1979. xxix, 508p. diagrs., tables. ISBN: 0720711649.

1st ed., 1955.

41 sections on the instrumental and theoretical background of practical astronomy (40. Manufacturers and suppliers; 41. Bibliography, p.521-52, under 29 heads). Index, partly analytical, p.555-68. A classic in its field. Although the 4th ed. shows extensive revision, the text retains its original flavour. *Class No:* 520(035)

[697]

—SIDGWICK, J.B. **Observational astronomy for amateurs.** 4th ed., prepared by J. Muirden. London, Pelham Books, 1982. xix, 348p. ISBN: 0720713781.

Intended as a sequel to Sidgwick's *Amateur astronomer's handbook*, and first published in 1957. The 19 sections (1. Solar observation... 19. Nebulae and clusters) are followed by a lengthy bibliography (p.299-337) under 27 heads, and an analytical index. 'It is a sound reference for established and would-be practising astronomers, even if they have an earlier edition, and also for all amateurs interested in the real basics of solar system astronomy' (*Sky and telescope*, v.65, January 1983, p.40). *Class No:* 520(035)

[698]

A Source book in astronomy and astrophysics, 1900-1975. Lang, K.R. *and* Gingerich, O., *eds.* Cambridge, Mass., & London, Harvard Univ. Press, 1979. xx, 922p. £63.95. ISBN: 0674822005.

Collects 132 seminar papers in astronomy and astrophysics, - reproduced as originally published, but with editorial comments. 8 chapters. 1. New windows on the universe - 2. The solar system - 3. Stellar atmospheres and stellar spectra - 4. Stellar evolution and nucleosynthesis - 5. Variable stars and dying stars - 6. The distribution of stars and the space between them - 7. Normal galaxies, radio galaxies and quasars - 8. Relativity and cosmology. Author and analytical subject indexes. 'Some papers are technical but well within the purview of the undergraduate science major' (*Choice*, v.19(1), September 1981, p.34). *Class No:* 520(035)

Dictionaries

[699]

A Dictionary of astronomy. Ridpath, I., *ed.* Oxford, University Press, 1997. 523p. illus.,tables. £7.99. ISBN: 0192115960.

21 contributors; 4,000 entries, including cross-references. The entries are shorter than *The Penguin dictionary of astronomy*, but it does include biographical entries, *e.g.* 200 words on Edwin Hubble. For public and academic libraries. *Class No:* 520(038)

[700]

Glossary of astronomy and astrophysics. Hopkins, J., *ed.* 2nd ed. Chicago, Ill., & London, Univ. of Chicago Press, 1980. ix, 196p. £19.95; £10.50. ISBN: 0226351718.

1st ed., 1976. Published under the auspices of *Astronautical journal*. Briefly defines *c.*2000 of the astronomical and astrophysical terms used in current research. Eponyms and abbreviations also figure. Variant definitions given by different authors are included. A handy compendium. *Class No:* 520(038)

[701]

KLECZEK, J. **Astronomical dictionary.** New York & London, Academic Press; Prague, Publishing House of the Czechoslovak Academy of Sciences, 1962. 972p. ISBN: 0124119506.

Originally published in Prague, 1961.

An English-Russian-German-French-Italian-Czech dictionary of *c.*10,000 terms in astronomy and related sciences (*e.g.* mathematics, spectroscopy). The main part (p.16-574) consists of English base terms, with equivalents across the double page, in 34 sections. English, Russian, German, French, Italian and Czech indexes, p.577-972. British and American usages are not differentiated, but genders of nouns in the foreign languages are given. *Class No:* 520(038)

[702]

The Macmillan dictionary of astronomy. Illingworth, V., *ed.* 2nd ed., (1st ed., 1979, has U.S. title *The Facts on File dictionary of astronomy*). London, Macmillan, 1985. [v], 437p. diagrs., tables. £30; £12.99. (*Macmillan reference books.*) ISBN: 0333390628.

1st ed., 1979.

19 contributors. Over 2,300 entries, generous in length (*e.g.* 'Saturn' : 2 columns; 'Black hole' : 2½ columns). Ample cross-references. 12 appended tables (*e.g.* 'Planetary satellites; 12. Recent successful planetary probes). 'The book walks the fine line between dictionary and encyclopaedia, but it does it very well' (*New scientist*, 5 September 1985, p.57). *Class No:* 520(038)

[703]

MEL'NIKOV, A.O. **Anglo-russkiĭ astronomicheskiĭ slovar'.** Moscow, Izdat. 'Sovetskaya Entisklopediya'. 1971. 504p.

English-Russian astronomical dictionary. About 20,000 entry-words. *Class No:* 520(038)

[704]

MITTON, J. **A Concise dictionary of astronomy.** Oxford, University Press, 1991. vii,423p. figs., tables. £12.95. ISBN: 0198539673.

Contains *c.*2,500 entries. Includes acronyms and many cross-references. Bibliography, p.410-12. 7 tables (*e.g.* 'The characteristics of planetary ring systems'). Aimed mainly at the amateur and the general reader. Author is editor of the *Journal of the British Astronomical Association*. *Class No:* 520(038)

[705]

The Penguin dictionary of astronomy. Mitton, J., *ed.* 3rd ed. Harmondsworth, Middx., Penguin, 1998. 422p., tables. £7.99. ISBN: 0140513752.

About 2,800 entries, covering all aspects of historical and modern astronomy, names of stars, observatories, etc. Lacks biographical information on astronomers. *Class No:* 520(038)

[706]

PLANT, M. **Dictionary of space.** Harlow, Essex, Longman Group, 1986. xi, 270p. illus. £7.95. ISBN: 0582892953.

Over 2,500 entries, including brief biographical sketches, 'Aberration'... 'Zond'. 'Hubble space telescope': 1p., plus cross-references; 'Galileo' : 2/3p. : 'Mars' : ½p. : 'Mission 41B'... 'Mission 61C', p. 143-8. 22 keyed line-drawings. Intended for 'casual readers or keen expert' (*Introduction*). *Class No:* 520(038)

[707]

ROOM, A. **Dictionary of astronomical names.** London, Routledge, 1988. [vi],282p. illus. £19.99. ISBN: 0415012988.

*c.*600 entries on stars, minor planets, constellations, planets, planetary constellations, and lunar features. 3 sections: 1. Introduction - 2. Astronomical glossary - 3. Dictionary of astronomical names (Asteroid ... Zubeneschamali). 2 appendices: 1. Names of craters on the moon - 2. Names of minor planets (1,000 are listed). Entries in the dictionary are variable in length. 2-page bibliography. Profuse cross-references. A valuable introduction. *Class No:* 520(038)

Reviews & Abstracts

[708]

Astronomy and astrophysics abstracts. New York, Springer-Verlag for Astronomisches Rechen-Institut, Heidelberg, 1969-. v.1(1)-. irregular. Price varies.

Prepared under the auspices of the International Astronomical Union. Continues *Astronomisches Jahresbericht* (v.1-68, 1900-68).

V.51B: Literature, 1990, pt.1 has 566p. of entries. Parts A and B of v.51 comprise together 11,423 brief abstracts and references. The 13 main classes (001-161) comprise: 001-015: Periodicals, proceedings, books, activities - 021-022: Applied mathematics, physics - 031-036: Astronomical instruments and techniques - 041-046: Positional astronomy, celestial mechanics - 051-053: Space research - 061-067: Theoretical astrophysics - 071-080: Sun - 081-085: Earth - 091-107: Planetary system - 111-126: Stars - 131-134: Interstellar matter, nebulae - 041-144: Radio sources, X-ray sources, cosmic rays - 151-161: Stellar systems, galaxy, extragalactic objects, cosmology. Author, subject and object indexes. A major abstracting and indexing service. *Class No:* 520(048)

[709]

Referativnyǐ zhurnal. 51. Astronomiia. Moscow, Akademiia Nauk SSSR, Institut Nauchnoǐ Informatsii, VINITI, 1953-. 12pa. $674. ISSN: 04862236.

Previously part of *Referativnyǐ zhurnal. Astronomiia i geodeziia* (1953-62. Monthly).

Each issue contains *c.*1,000 indicative and informative abstracts. Sections: General astronomy - Theoretical astronomy - Astronometry - Astrophysics - Theoretical astrophysics - Stellar astronomy - Radio astronomy - The sun - Solar system - Cosmogony and cosmology - Astronomical optics, telescopes and observations. Exploration of space. Monthly author index. Annual author and subject indexes. *Class No:* 520(048)

[710]

Vistas in astronomy: an international review journal. Kidlington, Oxon., Elsevier Science, 1955-. v.1-. (Annual; quarterly, 1976-). $601 (1998) pa. ISSN: 00836656.

Incorporated *Astronomy quarterly*, 1977-91.

Coverage: history and philosphy; instrumentation; solar system; nearby stars; stellar spectra; astrophysics; galaxies; galactic clusters; cosmic rays. V.28(4), 1985 carries an editorial and 3 documented contributions (*e.g.* 'The accuracy of Halley's cometary orbit', 18 references) and list of contents for v.22-27. Special issues are a feature (*e.g.* v.17: 'Copernicus, yesterday and today': v.18 : 'Kepler : four hundred years'; v.28(1/2): 'The longitude zero symposium, 1984'). *Class No:* 520(048)

Periodicals & Progress Reports

[711]

Annual review of astronomy and astrophysics. Palo Alto, Calif., Annual Reviews, Inc., 1963-. v.1-. illus., port. $140 (US); $150 (non US). ISSN: 00664146.

V.36, 1998 has 21 contributors (680p.). 14 well-documented articles (*e.g.* 'Simulations of structure formation in the universe'; 'Modeling extragalactic jets'; 'Astronomical searches for earth-like planets and signs of life'). Analytical subject index; cumulative index of contributing authors; v.26-36; cumulative index of chapter titles, v.26-36. One virtue of this annual review is the regular inclusion of an introductory autobiographical sketch (*e.g.* 'A half-century of astronomy'. by A.E. Whitford, in v.24, 1986), throwing light on the current state of the art and providing biographical data on a personality. *Class No:* 520(05)

[712]

Sky and telescope. Cambridge, Mass., Sky Publishing, 1941-. 12pa. $37.95 (US); $54.95 (non US). ISSN: 00376604.

Formerly *Telescope: drama of the skies* and *Sky*.

Monthly, with appeal for serious amateur and professional astronomers. May 1999 issue contains ten illustrated articles ('The rise and fall of quasars', p.40-48 ... 'Pluto reconsidered', p.49-54) plus short features ('Guide to the evening sky'), reviews, calendar of events. Well-produced; North American bias. *Class No:* 520(05)

Periodicals

[713]

Union list of astronomy serials. URL: http://sesame.stsci.edu/lib/union.html.

Lists *c.*2,300 titles, with holdings and bibligraphic information, from 42 contributing libraries. Emphasis is on North American collections but there is also material from Europe, South America, China, and India. *Class No:* 520(051)

Yearbooks & Directories

[714]

The Air & space catalog: the complete sourcebook to everything in the universe. Makower, J., *ed*. New York, Random/Vintage, 1989. 336p. illus. $27.50; $16.95. ISBN: 0394583272.

Lists organizations, equipment, software and activities in the fields of astronomy, aviation meteorology and space flight. Useful for public libraries. *Class No:* 520(058)

[715]

BRITISH ASTRONOMICAL ASSOCIATION. The Handbook of the British Astronomical Association 1996. London, the Association, 1996. 104p. graphs, tables. Annual. ISSN: 0068130x.

Contents include: Visibility of planets ... Eclipses ... Time ... Radio signals ... Earth and Sun ... Moon. Lunar occultations - Planets ... Comets - Meteor diary ... Ephemerides of double stars ... Variable stars ... Bright stars ... Elements of the planetary orbits - Satellites - Astronomical and physical constants - Miscellaneous data and telescope data - Conversion formulae. List of articles in earlier editions of the *Handbook*, on back cover. *Class No:* 520(058)

[716]

Yearbook of astronomy. Moore, P., *ed*. London, Sidgwick & Jackson, 1961-. Annual. illus., graphs, star charts. ISBN: 0337721209.

The *1999 Yearbook* (1998. 242p.) has eight contributors. 3 parts: 1. Monthly charts and astronomical phenomena (*e.g.* 'Some events in 1994')- 2. Eight articles (*e.g.* 'The invasion threat of cosmic impact and planetary defence'; 'The astronomer's microscope'). Appended: 'Astronomical societies in Great Britain', p.234-42. Small format. *Class No:* 520(058)

Tables & Data Books

[717]

CURTIS, A.R. Space almanac: facts, figures, names, dates, places, lists, charts, tables, maps covering space from Earth to the edge of the universe. Woodsboro, Md., Arcsoft Publishers, 1990. 955p. illus., tables, charts, maps. $19.95. ISBN: 0866680659.

8 major sections: Astronauts - Space stations - Shuttles - Rockets - Satellites - Solar system - Deep space - Calendar of events. 33-page index. Many photographs, drawings and illustrations, although these are of variable quality. However, full of useful information, and a handy reference tool. A smaller 2nd ed. (746p.) was published in 1992 (Houston, Gulf Publishing). *Class No:* 520(083)

[718]

JASCHEK, C. Data in astronomy. Cambridge, University Press, 1989. x,198p. tables. £35. ISBN: 0521340942.

Aimed at all those who handle astronomical data. 13 sections: 1. Observations ... 4. Archiving of observations ... 6. Designation of astronomical objects ... 9. Data banks and data bases - 20. Data centres - 11. The publication of scientific information ... 13. International data organizations. Particularly useful are the bibliographies appended to each section. (*e.g.* 7. Catalogues (4p. of references)). Index. *Class No:* 520(083)

Films

[719]

A Catalogue of videos and films on astronomy. Zucker, E., *comp*. Dewsbury, West Yorks., Association for Astronomy Education, 1988. 35p.

Lists *c.*300 titles, arranged by distributor, Each entry gives title; format; duration; level; details of whether the item may be hired or bought. Brief subject index. Supplementary lists, updating this catalogue, appear in the Association's newsletter, *Gnomon*. *Class No:* 520(084.122)

Histories

[720]

Astronomy before the telescope. Walker, C., *ed*. London, British Museum Press, 1996. 352p. illus.(some col.),figs.,maps. £25. ISBN: 0714117463.

19 contributors, 17 chapters: Archaeoastronomy in Europe ... Later Greek and Byzantine astronomy ... Traditional astronomical knowledge in Africa ... Modern uses of ancient astronomy. Brief bibliography appended to each chapter. Glossary and index. For public and academic libraries. *Class No:* 520(091)

[721]
Cambridge illustrated history of astronomy. Hoskin, M., *ed.*
Cambridge, University Press, 1997. x,392p. illus.,figs. £24.95. ISBN:
0521411580.
Nine chapters: 1. Astronomy before history ... 4. Medieval Latin
astronomy ... 6. Newton and Newtonianism ... 9. Astronomy's
widening horizons. Reference guide contains a chronology, glossary,
and further reading. Panels give short biographies of famous
astronomers and details of specific topics, *e.g.* 'Longitude and the
moons of Jupiter'. Index, p.384-92. For specialists and the general
reader. *Class No:* 520(091)

[722]
—MOORE, P. Patrick Moore's history of astronomy. 6th rev. ed.
London, Macdonald, 1983. 327p. illus. (mostly black-and-white),
facsims. ISBN: 0356086070.
First published 1961.
6 parts (40 chapters): 1. General - 2. Useful tables - 3. The solar
system - 4. Stars, nebulas and galaxies - 5. Telescopes and accessories.
Appendix : Useful addresses - 6. Star charts (data on backs).
Appendix: Some landmarks in the history of astronomy (B.C.585-
A.D.1982); List of illustrations; Acknowledgements. Non-analytical
index. Well-captioned illus. *Class No:* 520(091)

[723]
EVANS, D.S. **Under Capricorn:** a history of southern hemisphere
astronomy. Bristol, Philadelphia, Adam Hilger, 1988. x,376p. illus.
£35. ISBN: 082564384x.
Covers astronomy in the area from 1600. 11 sections: 1. The
expeditionary era (17th and 18th centuries) ... 3. Some international
projects ... 6. The new century: Africa ... 8. The post-war renaissance
... 11. Coda. 2 appendices: 1. Some frequently mentioned instruments
- 2. Southern hemisphere observatories. References and bibliography,
p.329-52. Index. Many black-and-white illustrations. Lines in the text
are double-spaced, making the publication bulkier than it needs to be.
A good, general introduction. *Class No:* 520(091)

[724]
The General history of astronomy. Cambridge, University Press, 1984-
. ISBN: 0521242568, v.4A.
V.2. *Planetary astronomy from the Renaissance to the rise of
astrophysics: Pt. A. Tycho Brahe to Newton,* edited by R. Taton and
C. Wilson. 1989. ix,274p.; Pt. B. *Planetary astronomy from the
Renaissance to the rise of astrophysics: the eighteenth and nineteenth
centuries,* edited by R. Taton and C. Wilson. 1995. xiv,345p.
v.4A. *Astrophysics and twentieth-century astronomy to 1950.* 1984.
198, lvip.
V.4A has two parts (11 sections, each with further reading): 1. The
birth of astrophysics and other late nineteenth century trends (*c.*1850-
*c.*1950) - 2. Observatories and instrumentation. Appendix: The world's
largest telescopes, 1850-1950. Index, p.li-lvi. Well illustrated, and
intended for a wide audience. 'These are going to be books that every
astronomer and many non-astronomers will wish to possess for
themselves'. (*History of science,* v.23(1), no. 59, March 1985, p.122).
Class No: 520(091)

[725]
HERRMANN, D.B. **The History of astronomy from Herschel to
Hertzsprung.** Krisciunas, K., *trans. & rev.* English ed. Cambridge,
University Press, 1984. x, 220p. illus., ports., diagrs. £22.95. ISBN:
0521257336.
Original German as *Geschichte der Astronomie von Herschel bis
Hertzsprung* (1973).
4 sections: 1. Construction and motion of the heavens - Classical
astronomy - 2. The origin of astrophysics - 3. Microcosmos -
Macrocosmos - 4. Technology and the organization of research. The
author is director of the Archenhold Observatory, Berlin Treplow.
Class No: 520(091)

[726]
The History of modern astronomy and astrophysics: a selected,
annotated bibliography. DeVorkin, D.H., *ed.* New York, Garland.
1982. 434p. illus. $102. (*Bibliographies of the history of science &
technology, v.1.*)
Over 1,400 annotated entries, in subject categories, with numerous
cross-references. Emphasis is on English-language material, and range
of items extends from the popular to the scholarly; also on mid-19th to
mid-20th century literature. Index. 'Imperfect, but a useful starting
point' (*Journal of the history of astronomy,* v.4, 1983, p.146).
Class No: 520(091)

[727]
History of oriental astronomy: proceedings of International
Astronomical Union colloquium no. 91, held in New Delhi, India, 13-
16 November 1985. Swarup, G., *and others, eds.* Cambridge,
University Press, 1987. 288p. illus., tables. ISBN: 0521346592.
3 sections (Ancient astronomy and its characteristics; Ancient
elements and planetary models; Medieval astronomy), comprising 36
papers, *e.g.* 'The characteristics of ancient China's astronomy'; 'Greek
astronomers and their neighbours'; 'Indian calendars'; 'An unknown

....(contd.)
Arabic source for star names'. 4 indexes: subject; manuscript;
astronomers; author. Brief bibliographies appended to some of the
papers. *Class No:* 520(091)

[728]
NORTH, J. **The Fontana history of astronomy and cosmology.**
London, Fontana Press, 1994. xxvii,697p. illus., figs. $35. ISBN:
0006861776, UK; 0393036561, US.
Published in the US by W.W. Norton, 1995 as *The Norton history of
astronomy and cosmology.*
Covers 5,000 years of astronomy and includes discussion of
technological improvements. 20 sections: 1. Prehistory - 2. Ancient
Egypt ... 11. Copernicus' planetary theory ... 18. Radio astronomy ...
20. Macrocosm and microcosm. Bibliographical essay, p.624-58. Brief
biographies of famous astronomers. Author is Professor of History of
the Exact Sciences at the University of Groningen. 'A valuable
reference tool exploding with information' (*Choice,* September 1995,
p.152). *Class No:* 520(091)

[729]
SHEEHAN, W. **Worlds in the sky:** planetary discovery from earliest
times through Voyager and Magellan Tucson, University of Arizona
Press, 1992. xv,243p. $35. ISBN: 0816512906.
Sections: Wandering stars - Through the telescope - Rockets into
space - The moon - Mercury - Venus - Mars - Asteroids - Jupiter -
Saturn - Uranus - Neptune - Pluto — Comets and meteors. Appendices
list planetary statistics. Eight-page bibliography. Excellent drawings
and photographs. Recommended for any would-be astronomer and
good for general reading. *Class No:* 520(091)

[730]
World archaeoastronomy: selected papers from the 2nd Oxford
International Conference on Archaeoastronomy, held in Merida,
Yucatan, Mexico, 13-17 January 1986. Aveni, A.F., *ed.* Cambridge,
University Press, 1989. xiii,504p. illus., figs., tables. £80.
4 sections: 1. The boundaries of archaeoastronomy: overviews and
syntheses (11 papers, *e.g.* 7. The cosmic temples of old Beijing) - 2.
Archaeoastronomy: the textual basis (16 papers, *e.g.* 13. Comets and
meteors in the last Assyrian Empire) - 3. Archaeoastronomy: an
interdiscipline in practice (11 papers, *e.g.* 38. Star walking - the
preliminary report) - 4. Additional abstracts submitted. Each of the 38
papers has a short bibliography appended. *Class No:* 520(091)

Biographies
[731]
BARANOWSKI, H., *comp.* **Bibliografia Kopernikowska, 1509-1955.**
Warsaw, Państwowe Wydawnictwo Naukowe. 1958. 449p. illus.
3,750 entries for works by Copernicus and for books and articles
about him in many languages, including specific papers on him in
more general works. Sections: 1. Works of Copernicus (chronological
order, with descriptive notes and locations) - 2. Bibliographies - 3.
Monographs - 4. Biographies - 5. On his work and activities - 6. On
his significance - 7. Copernicus in literature - 8. Copernicus in the
plastic arts - 9. On Copernicus museums and exhibitions - 10. On
anniversary celebrations. Indexes of Copernicus' writings and of
proper names. List of abbreviations and libraries cited.
Class No: 520(092)

[732]
Bibliography of astronomers: books and pamphlets in English by and
about astronomers. Luther, P., *comp.* Richmond, Va., Willmann-Bell,
1990-. ISBN: 094339628x.
V.1. *The Spirit of the nineteenth century.* 208p. $34.95.
A projected 3v. set. V.1 covers nearly 30% of all 19th century
books with a planned v.2 continuing in that period, adding over 3,000
entries. V.3 will include an index plus an essay on collecting
secondhand books, bookseller terminology, and the secondhand book
trade. A useful reference source. *Class No:* 520(092)

Institutions & Associations
[733]
Earth and astronomical sciences research centres: a world directory of
organizations and programmes. 4th ed. London, Cartermill, 1995. x,
465p. £250. ISBN: 1860670180.
First published 1984.
Guide to over 5,000 technology and research laboratories in 147
countries, arranged A-Z (Algeria ... Zimbabwe). Subject coverage
includes artificial satellites, cartography and surveying, geology,
meteorology, mineralogy, natural resources, oceanography, petrology,
space technology. Data include title of establishment in original
language, acronym and English translation; telecommunication contact
nos., senior staff; research expenditure; publications; research
activities; affiliation. Titles of establishments index; subject index.
Personal name and acronym indexes would also be useful.
Class No: 520:061:061.2

[734]
Handbook for astronomical societies. Jones, B., *ed.* Plymouth, Federation of Astronomical Societies, 1977-. Annual. diagrs. tables.

Contents of the 12th ed., 1989: 4 articles - FAS list of officers - The Federation of Astronomical Societies - FAS slide list - Other astronomical organizations - List of local astronomical societies - Regional groups - Periodicals (26) - Equipment suppliers - Places to visit - Speakers - Information sources - Visual aid sources - Sources of astronomical software - Additions and amendments - Index to articles in previous handbooks. A very useful quick-reference tool.
Class No: 520:061:061.2

[735]
History of the Royal Astronomical Society. Dreyer, J.L.E. *and* Turner, H.H., eds. Oxford, Blackwell Scientific Publications, 1987. 2v. illus. ISBN: 063202173x, v.1; 0632017910, v.2.

V.1. *1820-1920,* edited by J.L.E. Dreyer and H.H. Turner, vii,258p. V.2. *1920-1980,* edited by R.J. Tayler. vii,262p.

Each decade of the Society's existence is covered by a chapter written by various contributors and this is therefore a strictly chronological account with little to give an overall view. V.2 has 5 appendices: 1. Officers of the Society, 1920-80 ... 3. The Society's medallists 1920-80 ... 5. Statistical information 1920-80. Index.
Class No: 520:061:061.2

[736]
International directory of astronomical associations and societies together with related items of interest. [Répertoire international d'associations et de societés astronomiques ainsi que d'autres entrées d'intérêts général.] Heck, A., *comp.* 8th ed. Strasbourg, Observatoire Astronomique, 1989. 707p. (*Observatoire Astronomique de Strasbourg publication spéciale du CDS, no. 13.*) ISBN: 2908064111. ISSN: 07649614.

7th edition published in 1987.

Intended to complement *International directory of professional astronomical institutions 1990 (IDPAI 1990) (q.v.).* Lists *c.*3,200 entries from 87 countries, Algeria ... Zimbabwe. Data include date of foundation, membership, activities, publications observatories, coordinates and awards. Index (yellow pages, p.599-707).
Class No: 520:061:061.2

[737]
International directory of professional astronomical institutions together with related items of interest. [Répertoire international des institutions astronomiques professionnelles ainsi que d'autres entrées d'intérêt général.] Heck, A., *comp.* Strasbourg, Observatoire Astronomique, 1989. 649p. (*Observatoire Astronomique de Strasbourg publication spéciale du CDS, no. 14.*) ISBN: 290806412x. ISSN: 07649614.

First published 1983.

Entries under 87 countries, Algeria ... Zimbabwe (USA, by states, p.319-479). *c.*3,500 entries listed alphabetically. Data on each include date of foundation, activities, staff, publications and coordinates. Index (yellow pages, p.545-650). A greatly enlarged revision.
Class No: 520:061:061.2

Conferences

[738]
INTERNATIONAL ASTRONOMICAL UNION. Transactions of the General Assembly. Pt.A. Reports on astronomy. v.1-. Dordrecht, Kluwer, 1922-. 3-yearly. Price varies. ISSN: 00801372.

Reports on astronomy form one part of the I.A.U. *Transactions,* the other part being the *Proceedings of the General Assembly. Reports,* covering a wide range, are sectionalized, with valuable bibliographical notes. *Class No:* 520:061:061.3

Astrophysics

[739]
ALLEN, C.W. Astrophysical quantities. 3rd ed. London, Athlone Press, 1973. 310p. tables. £50. ISBN: 0485111500.

First published 1955.

15 sections, data being largely numerical and tabular: 2. General constants and units - 3. Atoms - 4. Spectra - 5. Radiation - 6. Earth - 7. Planets and satellites - 8. Interplanetary matter - 9. Sun - 10. Normal stars - 11. Stars with special characteristics - 12. Star population and the solar neighbourhood - 13. Nebulae, sources and interstellar space - 14. Clusters and galaxies - 15. Incidental tables (*e.g.* annual variations). Analytical index, p.303-30. 'The most widely used source of astrophysical data' (Coblans, H., *ed. Use of physics literature* (1975), p.124). Allen : Emeritus Professor of Astronomy, Univ. of London. *Class No:* 520-1

[740]
LANG, K.R. Astrophysical formulae: a compendium for the physicist and astrophysicist. 2nd ed. Berlin & New York, Springer, 1980. 759p. $49. ISBN: 0387099336.

5 major sections: Continuum radiation - Monochrome (Line) radiation - Gas processes - Nuclear astrophysics and high energy particles - Astrometry and cosmology. References are cited for each formula and its derivatives, - 'a total of well over 2,000 references' (Seal, R.A., and Martin, S.S. *A bibliography of astronomy, 1970-1979,* p.49). *Class No:* 520-1

Astronomical Instruments

[741]
BENNETT, J.A. The Divided circle: a history of instruments for astronomy, navigation and surveying. Oxford, Phaidon Christie's, 1987. 224p. illus. (some col.), figs. ISBN: 0714880388.

14 chapters: 1. Foundations in astronomy - 2. The beginnings of oceanic navigation ... 6. The heroic age - 7. The growth of observatories ... 11. Astronomical circles ... 14. A practical postscript. Bibliography, p.215-17. Index of makers; index of technical terms; general index. *Class No:* 520.0

[742]
—**MADDISON, F.** 'Early astronomical and mathematical instruments: a brief survey of sources and modern studies.' in *History of science,* v.2, 1963, p.17-50.

Includes a lengthy bibliography, p.34-50. *Class No:* 520.0

Observatories

[743]
Directory of European observatories 1988. Vercoutter, P.A.J., *comp.* 3rd ed. Ieper, Astronomical Contact Group, 1988. 432p. tables. (*Philippe's astronomical series, v.3.*) ISBN: 907247001x. ISSN: 07757085.

729 entries for observatories and institutions (1. Austria ... 27. Yugoslavia). 'Great Britain', 42 entries; 'France', 57 entries. Omits the former USSR. 6 types of observatory are differentiated. Data on each observatory appear under 19 heads (*e.g.* library; regular publications; observatory information; instruments). *Class No:* 520.1

[744]
GREENWICH OBSERVATORY. The Royal Observatory at Greenwich and Herstmonceux, 1675-1975. London, Taylor and Francis, 1975. 3v. £70. ISBN: 0850660939.

V.1: *Origins and early history (1675-1835),* by E.G. Forbes. v.2: *Recent history (1836-1975),* by A.J. Meadows. v.3: *The buildings and instruments,* by D. Howse. *Class No:* 520.1

[745]
—**SHENTON, D.E.** The Royal Greenwich Observatory and the Astronomers Royal, 1675-1976: a bibliography. London, Library Association, 1977. xxv, 723p.

Library Association F.L.A. thesis, accepted 27 September 1977.

Chiefly concerned with bio-bibliographies of the Astronomers Royal. Subject and author indexes. *Class No:* 520.1

[746]
KIRBY-SMITH, H.T. US observatories: a directory and travel guide. Princeton, N.J., Van Nostrand Reinhold, 1976. 173p. ISBN: 0442244517.

Data, state by state, on 300 observatories and planetaria: brief description; equipment; public access. 15 of the largest observatories have more detailed treatment. Two brief bibliographies. Index of institutions. *Class No:* 520.1

[747]
KRISCIUNAS, K. Astronomical centers of the world. Cambridge, University Press, 1988. x,320p. illus. £20. ISBN: 0521302781.

A selection of 'the observatories and dynamic individuals that were involved in the collaborative progress of institutionalized astronomy' (*Preface*). 9 sections 1. The Alexandrian Museum - 2. Astronomical capitals of the Moslem world ... 4. Paris and Greenwich - 5. Pulkovo Observatory ... 7. Mt. Wilson and Palomar - 8. The present - 9. The future. Appendix: The electromagnetic spectrum. Notes, p.281-310, is a list of references. Index. *Class No:* 520.1

[748]
MARX, S. *and* **PFAU, W. Observatories of the world.** Mitton, S., *ed. & rev.* English ed. Poole, Dorset, Blandford Press, 1982. 200p. illus. (incl. col.), diagrs., maps. ISBN: 0713711914.

Originally as *Sternwarten der Welt* (Leipzig, 1979).

Describes 40 selected telescopes from around the world, Abastumani Astrophysical Observatory... Special Astrophysical Observatory, Zelenchukskaya, USSR; plus NASA's 24-metre telescope. Bibliography, p.195-7; non-analytical index; sources of illus. Fully illustrated, with 40 colour plates, 76 black-and-white illus. and 18 line-drawings. *Class No:* 520.1

[749]

RIGAUX, F. Les Observatoires astronomiques et les astronomes. Brussels, Observatoire Royal de Belgique, for the International Astronomical Union, 1959. 452p.

Provisional ed., 1955.

Observatories are listed by country and town. Entries give information on personnel, publications, instruments and type of work carried out by each observatory. No longer current, but would now be of historical interest. *Class No:* 520.1

Telescopes

[750]

LEARNER, R. Astronomy through the telescope. London, Evans, 1982. 224p. illus. (incl. col.), facsims., ports. ISBN: 0217456443.

Devotes 17 chapters to 500 years' progress of astronomy, as seen in the use and development of the telescope. The book (written by a senior lecturer at the Imperial College of Science and Technology, London) is well illustrated, with an analytical index. For the layman; for reading rather than reference (*New scientist,* 28 January 1982, p.251). *Class No:* 520.2

[751]

—**BARLOW, B.V. The Astronomical telescope.** London, Wykeham Publications (London), 1975. viii, 213p. illus., tables. ISBN: 0851094600.

11 chapters (11: New developments). Chapter references; short glossary. Half-tone illus. and good line-drawings. 'He is very basic in his description of this mainstay of astronomical observation' (*Choice,* v.19(1), September 1981, p.34). 'The astronomy community has needed a book like this for a long time' (*Nature,* v.255(no.5507), 1975, p.432). *Class No:* 520.2

Solar System

[752]

The Encyclopedia of the solar system. Weissman, P.R., *and others, eds.* San Diego, Academic Press, 1999. 992p. illus.(some col.) £60; $99.95. ISBN: 0122268059.

Essays arranged by proceeding outwards from the sun. Each chapter has a glossary, brief bibliography. Web site includes links recommended by the contributors. Detailed subject index of 4,500 terms. An Internet site at http://www.academicpress.com/solar/ features author-recommended links to subjects discussed in the chapters. 'An excellent summary' (*Choice,* February 1999, p.1043). For academic and large public libraries. *Class No:* 523

[753]

GREELEY, R. *and* **BATSON, R. The NASA atlas of the solar system.** Cambridge, University Press, 1997. 369p. illus.(some col.),maps. £100; $150. ISBN: 0521561272.

Maps, derived from digital images taken by electronic cameras, contain geological, topographical, geophysical, and geochemical data, and are accompanied by short descriptive text. Includes a glossary, gazetteer, and further reading. 'This spectacular atlas' (*Reference books bulletin,* August 1997, p.1928). *Class No:* 523

[754]

SMITH, R. The Solar system. Pasadena, Calif., Salem Press, 1998. 3v.(1,151p.) illus. $175. ISBN: 0893569593.

126 articles, each averaging 3,000-3,5000 words, are drawn from three other Magill publications: *Magill's survey of science: space exploration series; Earth science series; Physical science series.* These are supplemented by nine articles specially commissioned for this work, *e.g.* space-based telescopes. Each article has a bibliography appended containing basic titles and important current work. Glossary. *Class No:* 523

[755]

The Solar system. Kuiper, G.P. *and* Middlehurst, B.M., *eds.* Chicago, Ill. (and later, London), Univ. of Chicago Press, 1953-63. 4v. illus., diagrs., maps, charts, tables. ISBN: 0685157520, v.2; 0226459276, v.3; 0226459284, v.4.

V.1: *The sun.* 1953. xx, 746p. v.2: *The earth as a planet.* 1955. xviii, 752p. $160. v.3: *Planets and satellites.* 1961. xx, 601p. $50. v.4: *The moon, meteorites and comets.* 1963. xxii, 820p. $60.

V.4 has 22 chapters, each with its own contributors; references appended. Thus, chapter 1: 'The lunar surface: introduction (p.1-56) has references (p.47-50) up to 1960. The analytical 'index of subjects and definitions' (p.799-810) has 76 sub-entries under 'Lunar craters'. A standard work of reference, now somewhat dated. *Class No:* 523

Handbooks & Manuals

[756]

Planetary exploration. Hughes, D., *ed.* New York, Facts on File, 1990. 6v. $65, set $13.95ea.

V.1: *The distant planets.* v.2: *Jupiter.* v.3: *Mars.* v.4: *The moon.* v.5: *Our sun and the inner planets.* v.6: *Saturn.*

Aimed at children aged 10-14. Many colour illustrations based on recent NASA photographs and scientific knowledge. Index in each volume. Clearly and attractively presented. *Class No:* 523(035)

Moon

[757]

Lunar sourcebook: a user's guide to the moon. Heiken, G., *and others.* Cambridge, University Press, 1991. xix,736p. illus. (some col. pl.), figs., tables. £50. ISBN: 0521334446.

11 chapters: 1. Introduction - 2. Exploration, samples, and recent concepts of the moon - 3. The lunar environment ... 5. Lunar minerals ... 8. Chemistry ... - 11. Afterword. Bibliography, p.655-715. Sample and subject indexes. 'Summarizes what we know about the Moon as a result of US and USSR lunar missions' (*Preface*). *Class No:* 523.3

[758]

RÜKL, A. Atlas of the moon. Rackham, T.W., *ed.* London, Hamlyn, 1991. 224p. maps. ISBN: 0600571904.

76 maps of sections of the near-side of the moon. Each map is accompanied by summaries giving brief biographical details of the eminent people whose names have been given to lunar formations and a brief description of the formations themselves. Nomenclature is as authorized by the International Astronomical Union. Intended for observers and amateur astronomers. *Class No:* 523.3

[759]

—**KOPAL, Z. A New photographic atlas of the moon.** London, Hale, 1971. vii, 311p. illus., tables. ISBN: 0709123701.

First published 1965.

3 parts: 1. The moon, an alien world - 2. Atlas of the moon and description of the plates (p.63-293) - 3. Appendices (Tables: 1. List of lunar aircraft (1959-1969) ... 3. Kinematic characteristics of the artificial lunar satellites). Bibliographical notes; glossary; index. Magnificent close-up photographs, some taken from spacecraft. *Class No:* 523.3

[760]

—**The Times atlas of the moon.** Lewis, H.A.G., *ed.* London, Times Newspapers, Ltd., 1969. xxxvii,110p. illus. (incl. col.), maps.

The introductory articles: 'The moon; 'The far side'; 'Mapping the moon'; 'The lunar landscape'; 'Techniques of lunar flight'. 'Index to names' and 'Key to the maps' (*c.*800 entries, with separate lists of promontories, peaks, mountain ranges, bays, marshes, lakes, oceans and seas, rilles (clefts), rimae, valleys) are followed by the maps, p.1-110. The atlas is essentially a reproduction of the US Air Force 1: 1,000,000 lunar charts of pre-Apollo vintage; the most serious weakness is the quality of reproduction of some photographs (*The Listener,* v.83(2134), 19 February 1970, p.256). Page size, 30 x 32.5cm. *Class No:* 523.3

Planets

[761]

BODECHTEL, J. *and* **GIERLOFF-EMDEN, H.G. The Earth from space.** Mayhew, M. *and* Evans, L., *trans.* Newton Abbot, Devon, David & Charles, 1974. 176p. illus. (mostly col.), maps. ISBN: 0715360760.

Sections: Space experiments as milestones in geography, geology, meteorology and cartography - Satellite techniques and technology - Flying spies [satellites] - Pictures of the earth: atmosphere, oceans, continents - Satellites in meteorological research and weather forecasting - The movements of the earth's crust - Landscape types on earth's deserts, mountains, coasts, islands - Our environment in relation to its surroundings - The moon, satellite of the earth. No index, but detailed contents list. A fine production. *Class No:* 523.4

[762]

The Cambridge photographic atlas of the planets. Briggs, G.A. *and* Taylor, F.W. Cambridge University Press, 1982. 255p. ISBN: 0521239761.

6 sections: Mercury - Venus - Earth and moon - Mars - The Jovian system - The Saturnian system. Some 200 photographs (*c.*50% in full colour) obtained from space vehicles over the past two decades. Draws on the NASA collection of photographs, many of them not previously published in books. 'An annotated snapshot album of the planets and their satellites' (*New scientist,* 18 November 1983, p.455). 'The style is highly readable and intended for an educated general public' (*Geology,* v.15, September 1987, p.882). *Class No:* 523.4

[763]

CARR, M.H. The Surface of Mars. New Haven, Conn., Yale Univ. Press, 1981. 232p. $29.95. ISBN: 0300032420.

An historical perspective is followed by chapters on Martian craters, atmosphere, volcanoes, sections, surface chemistry, and the two Martian moons (Phobos and Deinos). Aimed at 'the informed scientific reader', and assumes some knowledge of geology, physics and chemistry. 'Science at its very best' (*American scientist*, v.70 March/April 1982, p.274). *Class No: 523.4*

[764]

The Geology of the terrestrial planets. Carr, M.H., *ed*. Washington, NASA, 1984. 317p. $16. (*Special publication SP 469.*) ISBN: 0160041627.

Takes the terrestrial planets (Venus, Mars, Mercury, Moon, Earth) in solar system order. Data: orbit, magnetic fields (if any), surface characteristics, craters, tectonics, etc., summarizing what has been learned since 1962. The Earth is given a brief chapter. 'Intended for the interested layman' (*Astronomy*, v.13, October 1985, p.88). *Class No: 523.4*

[765]

Mars. Kieffer, H.H., *and others, eds*. Tucson, University of Arizona Press, 1992. xv,1498p. diagrs. maps. plates (col.) $65. ISBN: 0816512575.

Based on information received by spacecraft. Seven sections: Introduction; Solid body geophysics; Bedrock geology and geologic units; Surface properties and processes; Current atmospheres; Biology; Martian satellites. Appendix of Martian nomenclature. Glossary (41p.) and 85-page bibliography, p.1361-1455. Excellent value. *Class No: 523.4*

[766]

MINER, D. Uranus: the planet, rings and satellites. 2nd ed. Chichester, Wiley, 1998. 360p. illus., figs., tables. (*Wiley-Praxis series in astronomy and astrophysics*.) ISBN: 047197398x.

13 sections: 1. The discovery of Uranus ... 4. The discovery of the rings of Uranus ... 6. The saga of Voyager 2 ... 10. The magnetosphere of Uranus ... 13. Post-Voyager observations of Uranus. Incorporates data from the Voyager 2 space mission. Notes, references and bibliographies appended to each chapter. Index, p.349-360. The author worked on the Voyager project. *Class No: 523.4*

[767]

The New solar system. Beatty, J.K., *and others*. 4th ed. Cambridge, University Press; Cambridge, Mass., Sky Publishing Corporation, 1999. vii,421p. illus. (incl. col.), maps (incl. col.). £24.95. ISBN: 0521641837.

First published 1982. 3rd edition, 1990.

Attractively-illustrated work, edited by experts and aimed at amateur (but adult) readership. 28 chapters: 1. Exploring the solar system ... 6. The role of collisions ... 12. Surfaces and interiors of the terrestrial planets ... 16. Planetary rings ... 24. Comets ... 28. Other planetary systems. Includes descriptions of the Earth and Moon. 'This fourth edition is nearly twice the length of the first' (*Preface*). *Class No: 523.4*

Comets

[768]

Comet Halley: investigations, results, interpretations. Mason, J.W., *ed*. Chichester, Ellis Horwood, 1990. 2v. (*Ellis Horwood library of space science and space technology*.) ISBN: 0131710753, v.1; 0131710834, v.2.

V.1. *Organization, plasma, gas*. xix,295p. V.2. *Dust, nucleus, evolution*. xix,275p.

A selection of review articles dealing with cometary research conducted during the 1985/86 return of Halley's Comet. 39 chapters, 54 contributors. Chapter titles include: 'The dust trail of comet Halley'; 'Models of cometary nuclei'; 'The ageing of comet Halley and other periodic comets'; 'The International Halley Watch'. Each volume contains a list of names, acronyms and abbreviations and a bibliography is appended to each chapter. Many figures, tables and some coloured plates. *Class No: 523.64*

[769]

FREITAG, R.S. Halley's comet: a bibliography. Washington, Library of Congress, 1984. 555p. $26. ISBN: 0844404594.

Annotated bibliography of over 3,200 entries, based on Library of Congress holdings to mid-1974. English- and European-language material. Arrangement is by authors A-Z, with author and subject indexes. Entries cite Library of Congress numbers and library locations. Bibliographical sources are listed. As to the entries themselves, 'daily cartoons jostle thick tomes of dry calculations' (*Scientific American*, v.235(5), November 1985, p.22). *Class No: 523.64*

[770]

—**MORTON, B. Halley's comet, 1755-1984: a bibliography.** Westport, Conn., Greenwood, 1985. 280p. $36.95. ISBN: 0313240221.

Has 1,301 annotated entries, arranged chronologically, Such an arrangement - complementary to Freitag's - sets 'citations in relation to others as part of the cultural response of its time... *Halley's Comet* is recommended for college, university, and large public libraries' (*RQ*, v.25(2), Winter 1985, p.259). *Class No: 523.64*

[771]

KRONK, G.W. Comets: a descriptive catalogue. Hillside, N.J., Enslow, 1984. viii, 331p.

First section: Long-period and non-periodic comets (over 500, listed in order of discovery). Second section: Short period comets (A/Z by common names). Notes on comet watching. References to books and periodical articles (years: -371 to 1800; years 1800 to 1982). Index to common names of comets, p.331. *Class No: 523.64*

[772]

YEOMAN, D.K. Comets: a chronological history of observation, science, myth and folklore. New York, Wiley, 1991. x,485p. illus., figs., tables. £24.95. ISBN: 0471610119.

11 sections: 1. The origin of cometary thought - 2. Medieval views ... 6. The return of comet Halley ... 9. The physics of comets ... 11. The births and deaths of comets. Appendix: Naked-eye comets reported through A.D. 1700, p.361-424. Extensive bibliography, p.425-74. Detailed index. *Class No: 523.64*

Sun

[773]

Illustrated glossary for solar and solar-terrestrial physics. Bruzek, A. *and* Durrant, C.J., *eds*. Norwell, Mass., Kluwer, 1977. xviii, 204p. illus., diagrs. $67. ISBN: 9027708258.

14 contributors. 14 sections (1. Solar interior ... 4. Quiet photosphere and chromosphere ... 6. Solar corona ... 11. Solar radio emission ... 14. Solar-terrestrial physics). Sub-section references. Striking illus. Subject index. *Class No: 523.9*

[774]

ZIRIN, H. Astrophysics of the sun. Cambridge, University Press, 1988. x,433p. illus., tables, graphs. £45; £15.95. ISBN: 0521302684.

A new edition of *The solar atmosphere* (1966).

12 sections: 1. Looking at the sun - 2. Observing the sun ... 5. Atomic spectra - 6. The interior and the photosphere ... 9. Prominences - 10. Solar activity ... 12. Questions. Abbreviations, p.411. Bibliography, p.412-28. Index. Many black-and-white illustrations. Aimed at the academic and amateur astronomer. *Class No: 523.9*

Stars & Galaxies

Handbooks & Manuals

[775]

BAKICH, M. Cambridge guide to the constellations. Cambridge, University Press, 1995. xiii, 320p. ISBN: 0521465206.

Alphabetical list of constellations, p.136-311, with details of each, including modern star diagram and historic celestial map. Preceded by 'Lists', p.1-132, of constellations, names in different languages, bordering constellations, biblical references, 200 nearest stars, overall brightness of the constellations. References p.319-20. The illustrations let the book down. *Class No: 524(035)*

[776]

HODGE, P.W. Galaxies. Cambridge, Md., Harvard Univ. Press, 1986. 174p. illus., maps. $25.50. ISBN: 0674340655.

Contents: Galactic structure - The formation and evolution of galaxies - The missing mass - The nearest spirals - Clusters and superclusters of galaxies - Disturbed galaxies - Quasars. About 100 photographs and maps. Index. A compendium of facts and problems, with highly readable text. *Class No: 524(035)*

[777]

MOTZ, L. and NATHANSON, C. The Constellations: an enthusiast's guide to the night sky. London, Aurum Press, 1988. xix,411p. illus., diagrs. £19.95. ISBN: 1854100882.

Looks at the myths attached to the constellations, in addition to giving details of galaxies, nebulae, variable stars, quasars, etc. 6 sections, subdivided in 15 chapters: 1. Two bears and a dragon ... 4. The hunter ... 8. Three tragic myths ... 14. Phoenix to Antlia - 15. South circumpolar constellations. Bibliography. Index. *Class No: 524(035)*

[778]

RIDPATH, I. and TIRION, W. Collins' pocket guide to stars and planets. 2nd ed. London, Collins, 1993. 384p. illus., (incl. colour), star charts. £9.99. ISBN: 0002199793.

88 star charts by W. Tirion, depicting the constellations A-Z (Andromeda to Vulpecula), form the core of this pocket-sized volume, with descriptive text facing. A further section provides over 35 coloured plates, and there are sky charts for observers in both northern and southern hemispheres for every month of the year. Analytical index. Author and illustrator are highly regarded in their field.

The Night sky, by I. Ridpath and W. Tirion (London, Collins, 1985. 240p.) also makes good use of the 88 constellation charts. *Class No:* 524(035)

[779]

—**EICHER, D.J. The Universe from your backyard:** a guide to deep-sky objects from *Astronomy* magazine. Cambridge, University Press; Milwaukee, Wis., Astromedia, 1988. 188p. illus. (some col.), tables, maps. £15.95. ISBN: 0913135054, US ed; 0521362997, UK ed.

46 articles, each covering a constellation, giving details of 690 deep-sky objects. Arrangement is alphabetical (Andromeda, Triangulum ... Virgo). Many colour illustrations. Bibliography. Index. For school and public libraries. *Class No:* 524(035)

[780]

—**MENZEL, D.H. and PASACHOFF, J.M. A Field guide to the stars and planets.** 2nd ed. Boston, Mass., Houghton Mifflin, 1983. 473p. illus., star charts, maps. $19.95. *(Peterson Field guides no.15.)* ISBN: 039534641x.

Tight-packed, pocket-sized manual - comprises 10 moon maps, 72 monthly sky maps and 52 crowded charts (for the use of observers equipped with a small telescope). 83 full-colour photographs, 10 moon maps, and 11 graphic annual timetables (tracking paths of planets, 1984-89). 'Has much to recommend it' *(Astronomy,* October 1984, p.39).

3rd ed. (viii,502p.) published in 1992, edited by J.M. Pasachoff. *Class No:* 524(035)

[781]

—**MURDIN, P. and ALLEN, D. Catalogue of the universe,** with original photographs by D. Malin. Cambridge, University Press. 1979. 288p. illus. (incl. col. pl.). $29.95. ISBN: 052122859x.

Comprises 3 parts: 1. The universe of galaxies - 2. Stars and nebulae - 3. The solar system. Appendix: Messier catalogue. Notes on special photographic techniques; Glossary. Partly analytical index, p.253-6. 53 colour subjects, 200 half-tones and line subjects. Aims 'to illustrate a comprehensive selection of objects in the Universe and to write about the examples chosen, bringing the basic principles out of the objects themselves' *(Preface). Class No:* 524(035)

[782]

Stars and stellar systems: compendium of astronomy and astrophysics. Kuiper, G.P. and Middlehurst, B.M., *eds.* Chicago, Ill., & London, Univ. of Chicago Press, 1961-75. 9v. illus., tables, maps.

V.1: *Telescopes.* 1961 (reprinted 1977). v.2: *Astronomical techniques.* 1962. v.3: *Basic astronomical data.* 1963. v.4: *Clusters and binaries.* (Cancelled). v.5: *Galactic structures.* 1965. v.6: *Stellar atmospheres.* 1960. v.7: *Nebulae and interstellar matters.* 1968. v.8: *Stellar structure.* 1965. v.9: *Galaxies and the universe.* 1975.

Intended as an extension to the 4-v. *Solar system* series *(qv),* to cover astrophysics and stellar astronomy. Separate editors are appointed for each volume. V.2 has 24 main chapters, each by an expert, with extensive references (chapter 17, 'Photographic photometry', has 111 references). Subject index. 'The aim of the series is to present stellar astronomy and astrophysics as basically empirical sciences, co-ordinated and illustrated by the application of theory' *(Preface to the Series).* 'A landmark series' *(New technical books,* July 1978, entry 777). Supported in part by the National Science Foundation. *Class No:* 524(035)

[783]

The Webb Society deep sky observer's handbook. Hillside, N.J., Enslow, 1980-90. 8v. ISBN: 0894901222, v.1; 0894900285, v.2; 089490034x, v.3; 0894900501, v.4; 0894900668, v.5; 0894901338, v.6; 0894901346, v.7; 0894902083, v.8.

1. *Double stars.* 2nd ed. 1986. £14.95; $18.95. 2. *Planetary and gaseous nebulae.* 1980. £13.95; $17.95. 3. *Open and globular clusters,* 1980. £15.95; $19.95. 4. *Galaxies.* 1982. £16.95; $21.95. 5. *Clusters of galaxies.* 1982. £16.95; $21.95. 6. *Anonymous galaxies.* 1987. £13.95; $17.95. 7. *The southern sky.* 1987. £15.97; $21.95. 8. *Variable stars.* 1990. £15.95; $19.95.

The *Handbook's* aim is 'to provide a series of observer's manuals that do justice to the equipment that is available today and to cover fields that have not been adequately covered by other organizations of amateurs. The manuals are designed primarily for the more experienced amateur' *(General preface).* Intended to replace Revd. T.W. Webb's classic *Celestial objects for common telescopes* (first published 1839, reaching 6 editions by 1917, and still in print). The new *Handbook,* with its appendices and bibliographies, 'will justly have a special place in any amateur's bookshelf as the most

....(contd.)

comprehensive guide' *(British book news,* August 1982, p.466).

Periodical, *The Deep sky observer* 1992- (2pa. Windlesham, Surrey.), aimed at the enthusiast. *Class No:* 524(035)

[784]

—**CORLISS, W.R. Mysterious universe:** handbook of astronomical anomalies. Glen Arm, Md., The Sourcebook Project, 1979. 710p. $19.95. ISBN: 0915554054.

Assembles over 500 short contributions, 'anomalies' ranging from auroras in comet tails to zodiacal light-rifts and black and white holes to X-ray bursts. 'It is strong meat... but in short bursts the book is a joy... The book is to be highly recommended. It has been well produced, extremely well indexed and is excellent value for money' *(Nature,* v.280 (5717), 5 July 1979, p.92). *Class No:* 524(035)

[785]

ZOMBECK, Martin V. Handbook of space astronomy and astrophysics. 2nd ed. Cambridge, University Press, 1990. [viii],440p. graphs, diagrs., tables. £50; £20. ISBN: 0521314550.

First published 1982.

19 chapters: 1. General data - 2. Astronomy and astrophysics ... 6. X-ray astronomy - 7. Gamma-ray astronomy ... 13. Plasma physics ... 19. Astronomical catalogs. Aims 'to provide a ready reference and working tool for the practicing *[sic]* space astronomer and astrophysicist' *(Preface).* A standard handbook. *Class No:* 524(035)

Tables & Data Books

[786]

HIRSHFELD, A. and SINNOTT, R., eds. Sky catalogue 2000.0: stars to visual magnitude 2000.0. Cambridge, University Press, 1982-5. 2v. (604 + 385p.). tables. £45; £25, v.1; £60; £35, v.2. ISBN: 0521417430, v.1; 0521258189, v.2.

1: *Stars to magnitude 8.0.* 2nd ed. 1991. 2: *Double stars, variable stars and nonstellar objects.* 1985.

Companion volumes to Tirion's *Sky atlas 2000.0.* V.1 tabulates 50,071 stars, listed in order of increasing sight ascension. 91% of the stars in the catalogue have their distances given, apart from other data. Both the *Sky atlas* and the *Catalogue* (v.1) are considered 'essential acquisitions for all active astronomical observers' *(Nature,* v.298, 5 August 1982, p.588). V.2 (15 main data sections) covers more than 28,000 celestial objects not in the previous ed. of v.1. Useful for both amateur and professional astronomers. *Class No:* 524(083)

[787]

JONES, K.G. Messier's nebulae and star clusters. 2nd ed. Cambridge, University Press, 1991. xvii,427p. illus., diagrs., tables, maps. $49.50. ISBN: 0521370795.

First published 1968.

Covers the 102 nebulous objects in Messier's catalogue of 1771, plus 7 additional objects. Very well illustrated. 5 sections: 1. Astronomical background to the Messier Objects: the 'missing' and 'additional' objects ... 4. The Messier Objects in detail (p.51-306) - 5. Biographical and historical. 6 appendices, *e.g.* 'Catalogue of stars in the Pleiades'; 'Bibliography'. Indexes of names; objects; subjects. Of the earlier ed., 'An excellent aid for the observer' (Seal, R.A. *A Guide to the literature of astronomy* (1977), p.50). 'The revised edition is tighter than the first' *(Sky and telescope,* v.84(1), July 1992, p.45). *Class No:* 524(083)

[788]

A Master list of nonstellar optical astronomical objects. Dixon, R.S. and Sonneborn, G., *comps.* [Athens], Ohio State University Press, 1980. 835p. tables. ISBN: 0814202500.

Includes *c.*185,000 listings from 270 catalogues. Data for each object include 1950.0 position, angular diameter, magnitude and description. Bibliography (p.39-47) is under authors A-Z. Appendices A & B (A: 'The Luyten search for faint blue stars'). *Class No:* 524(083)

[789]

—**BURNHAM, R., Jr.** Burnham's celestial handbook: an observer's guide to the universe beyond the solar system. New York, Dover, 1978. 3v.(2138p.) illus., diagrs., graphs. £14.95 per vol. ISBN: 048623567x, v.1; 0486235688, v.2; 0486236730, v.3.

Lists over 7,000 objects available to observers with telescopes in the 2-inch to 12-inch range. Objects are arranged A-Z. Appended to v.3 'Index to the Messier objects'; 'The brightest stars'; 'Index to the 25 nearest stars'; 'Bibliography - a partial list of works consulted'. Intended to be a standard catalogue and detailed descriptive handbook. *Class No:* 524(083)

[790]

NGC 2000.0: the complete new general catalogue and index catalogues of nebulae and star clusters by J.L.E. Dreyer. Sinnott, R.W., *ed.* Cambridge, University Press; Cambridge, Mass., Sky Publishing Corporation, 1988. xxiv,273p. tables. $19.95. ISBN: 0933346514, US ed; 0521378133, UK ed.

An update of J.L.E. Dreyer's *New general catalogue of nebulae and clusters of stars (1888), Index catalogue (1895)* and *Second index catalogue (1908).*

3 sections: 1. NGC 2000.0 - 2. Right ascensions of NGC objects - 3. Right ascensions of IC objects. Information about specific objects not as detailed as Hirshfeld's *Sky catalogue 2000.0* but covers all 13,226 NGC and IC objects, while *Sky catalogue 2000.0* covers fewer than 3,500 of those studied most. 'This volume is certain to be a standard reference for professional and amateur astronomers for years to come' (*Science and technology libraries,* v.11(1), Fall 1990, p.139). *Class No:* 524(083)

[791]

Second reference catalogue of bright galaxies: containing information on 4,364 galaxies, with references to papers published between 1964-1975. De Vaucouleurs, G., *and others.* Austin, Texas, Univ. of Texas Press, 1976. 396p. $101.

Supplement to *Reference catalogue of bright galaxies,* by G. and A. De Vaucouleurs (Univ. of Texas Press, 1964. 268p. $40).

175p. of catalogue data and 147p. of notes, reference and source material for the period January 1, 1964 to July 1, 1975 (covering 4,364 bright galaxies). 66p. of introduction and explanatory matter are added. Recommended for the relatively large and specialized science library. Continued by: *Class No:* 524(083)

[792]

—Third reference catalogue of bright galaxies. Berlin, Springer-Verlag, 1991. 3v. $198, set; $69, v.1; $79, v.2; $79, v.3. ISBN: 0387975497, v.1; 0387955008, v.2; 0387955109, v.3.

V.1 *Introduction, references, notes and appendices.* 714p. V.2 *Data for galaxies between 0h and 12h.* 723p. V.3. *Data for galaxies between 12h and 24h.* 632p. *Class No:* 524(083)

[793]

SMITHSONIAN INSTITUTION ASTROPHYSICAL OBSERVATORY. Star catalog. Washington, Smithsonian Institution, 1966 (reprinted 1974). 4v.

Data on the proper position and motion of 258,997 stars of the epoch 1950.0 A comprehensive catalogue that combines earlier star catalogues of that epoch, including the FK4, FK3, AGK2, AGK1 and GC. Available on magnetic tape. 'An indispensable tool for the working astronomer' (Seal, R.A. *A guide to the literature of astronomy,* entry 103). *Class No:* 524(083)

Illustrations

[794]

The Cambridge atlas of astronomy. Audouze, J. *and* Israël, G., *eds.* 3rd ed. Cambridge, University Press, 1994. 470p. illus., charts, tables. ISBN: 0521434386.

Translation of *Le grand atlas de l'astronomie* (Encyclopaedia Universalis, 1986).

30 contributors, plus 3 consultant editors. Main sections: Sun (33p.); The solar system (189p.); Stars and the Galaxy (91p.); The extragalactic domain (69p.). 770 photographs (350 in colour) and 350 colour diagrams. There are no major changes from the second edition (1988), apart from the addition of a new section 'The scientific perspective' (38p.) which includes articles on 'The extraterrestrial life debate', 'The Hubble Space telescope', and 'The history of astronomy'. There are only 2p. of maps covering the entire sky, treatment being in the form of 2, 4 or 6-page topics. A major reference work. Page size: 36.8 x 26.8cm. *Class No:* 524(084.1)

[795]

HENBEST, N. *and* **MARTEN, M. The New astronomy.** 2nd ed. Cambridge, University Press, 1996. 240p. £55; £19.95. ISBN: 0521403243; 0521408717, pbk.

First published 1983.

12 chapters. Using 323 illustrations, nearly all in colour, this work examines almost all forms of radiation from celestial bodies, including gamma and X-rays, UV, optical, infrared and radio waves. Index, p.238-240. 'Clear and interesting text ... the hardback is rather expensive for individuals, but the paperback is excellent value' (*Observatory,* v.117, April 1997, p.118-119). *Class No:* 524(084.1)

[796]

LAUSTSEN, S. Exploring the southern sky: a pictorial atlas from the European Southern Observatory (ESO). Berlin & New York, Springer, 1987. 274p. illus. $49. ISBN: 0387177353.

Observations taken at ESO, La Silla, Chile. Well over 200 excellent photgraphs, well captioned. 'A valuable reference guide to the southern sky for its organization and completeness. This atlas deserves a wide audience' (*Sky and telescope,* December 1987, p.608). *Class No:* 524(084.1)

Maps & Atlases

[797]

NORTON, A.P. Norton's star atlas and reference handbook (epoch 2000.0). Ridpath, I., *ed.* 19th ed. Harlow, Essex, Addison Wesley Longman, 1998. xii,180p. maps, diagrs., tables. £25. ISBN: 0582312833.

First published 1910. 18th ed., 1989, published as *Norton's 2000.0.*

5 sections: 1. Star charts (37 charts indicate the position of *c.*8,800 stars and 600 deep-sky nebulae) - 2. Position and time - 3. Practical astronomy - 4. The solar system - 5. Stars, nebulae and galaxies. Appendix includes units and notation, astronomical constants, symbols and abbreviations and useful addresses. Text has been almost entirely rewritten for this edition. The best atlas for amateurs. *Class No:* 524(084.3)

[798]

—MOORE, P. Philip's atlas of the universe. London, George Philip, 1997. 288p. illus. (col.), charts, diagrs., maps. £25. ISBN: 0540072613.

First published as *New Atlas of the universe* in 1994.

Profusely illustrated; addressed to the amateur astronomer. 'Explaining the universe' p.10-29. 'The solar system' p.30-149. 'The sun' p.150-161. 'The stars' p.162-89. 'The universe' p.190-207. Star maps. p.208-59. 'The practical astronomer' p.260-7. Index p.278-87. 'Little of the last edition remains' (*Introduction*). *Class No:* 524(084.3)

[799]

—SMITHSONIAN INSTITUTION ASTROPHYSICAL OBSERVATORY. Star atlas of reference stars and nonstellar objects. Cambridge, Mass., MIT Press, 1969. 13p. charts.

Intended for use with the Observatory's *Star catalog.* There are 152 boxed charts, with a transparent location grid. *Class No:* 524(084.3)

[800]

—TIRION, W. Sky atlas 2000.0. Cambridge, Cambridge University Press, 1982. 26 star colour charts. £25. ISBN: 0521244676.

Competes with Norton for the quality of its star maps and its recency, including *c.*43,000 stars down to the 8th magnitude for epoch 2000. *Class No:* 524(084.3)

[801]

SANDAGE, A. *and* **BEDKE, J. The Carnegie atlas of galaxies.** Washington, D.C., Carnegie Institution of Washington/Flintridge Foundation, 1994. 2v.(750p.) illus. $92. ISBN: 0872796671, set.

The result of a 25-year project to catalogue and classify the brightest galaxies over the entire sky. Each of the 1,168 galaxies listed is accompanied by a black-and-white photograph and a description. An explanation of the classification scheme is given in volume 1. The subsidized printing means that this is an affordable reference tool for both astronomy researchers and students. *Class No:* 524(084.3)

[802]

SINNOTT, R.W. *and* **PERRYMAN, M.A.C. Millennium star atlas:** an all-sky atlas comprising one million stars to visual magnitude eleven from the Hipparcos and Tycho catalogues and ten thousand non-stellar objects. Cambridge, Mass., Sky Publishing Corporation/European Space Agency, 1997. 3v. £249.95; $249.95. ISBN: 0933346840.

The largest star atlas ever produced. Includes 1,548 charts and data from the Hipparchos satellite. Most up-to-date data on star positions, distances, proper motions, and magnitude. For public and academic libraries. *Class No:* 524(084.3)

[803]

TIRION, W. The Cambridge star atlas. 2nd ed. Cambridge, University Press, 1996. vi, 90p. tables, maps. $19.95. ISBN: 0521560985.

First published 1991.

A 'not-too-complicated' moon map is added to 12 monthly sky-maps, star-charts (include 9,500 stars to magnitude 6.5 plus 866 nonstellar objects), all-sky maps, sources and references (1p.). Clear explanations of maps and charts. Designed for use in both hemispheres, and for the amateur or more advanced observer. Well-produced and good value. For public, school and academic libraries. *Class No:* 524(084.3)

[804]

Uranometria 2000.0. Tirion, W., *and others.* Richmond, Va., Willmann-Bell, 1987. 2v. $39.95ea. ISBN: 094339614x, v.1; 0993396158, v.2.

V.1: *The Northern hemisphere to -6 degrees.* xliii,259p. maps. V.2: *The Southern hemisphere to +6 degrees.*

473 star charts in all, showing stars to 9.5 magnitude. A three-volume companion star catalog is planned. *Class No:* 524(084.3)

[805]

WRAY, J.D. The Color atlas of galaxies. Cambridge, University Press, 1988. xii,189p. col.pl. £60. ISBN: 0521322367.

Colour images of more than 600 galaxies, in 94 plates. Table of galaxies illustrated in the atlas, p.189. *Class No:* 524(084.3)

Navigation

Handbooks & Manuals

[806]

Admiralty manual of navigation. Rev. ed. London, HMSO, 1954-73. 5v. illus., diagrs., tables, maps. (*B.R.45.*) ISBN: 0117707686; 0117714674.

First published 1914.

V.1 is a practical guide for executive officers; v.2 (rev. ed. 1973) provides a textbook of nautical astronomy and off-shore navigation; v.3 (1954) is based on the navigation syllabus for officers qualifying in navigation and direction, and deals with advanced subjects and mathematical proofs not included in v.1-2. Admiralty charts and publications are covered in v.1, chapter 2. V.4 (1962), on certain navigational equipment and techniques used by H.M. ships, is not available to the public. V.5 (6 bound parts) provides exercises on the use of tables (*e.g.* astronomical, Great Circle, tidal and tidal streams, time and chronometer, relative velocity questions).

The 1987 revised ed. of v.1 (xviii, 697p.) is entitled *General navigation, coastal navigation and pilotage*, with 19 chapters, a bibliography (p.675-7) and index (p.677-97).

The Admiralty issues updates and amendments for mariners in its weekly publication, *Admiralty notices to mariners*, now also available in electronic and CD-ROM/floppy disk forms. *Class No: 527(035)*

[807]

—Brown's star atlas, showing all the bright stars, with instructions how to find and use them for navigational purposes and Board of Trade examinations. New and rev. ed. Glasgow, Brown, Son and Ferguson, 1977. [v], 49p. charts, tables. ISBN: 0851742718.

2 parts: 1. How to find the stars; 2. Star problems. *Class No: 527(035)*

[808]

—COTTER, C.H. 'A Brief historical survey of British navigational manuals', *Journal of navigation*, v.36, May 1983, p.237-48.

47 references appended. *Class No: 527(035)*

[809]

Air navigation plans. 12th-30th ed. Montreal, International Civil Aviation Organization, 1983-95. 5v. loose-leaf in binders, figs., charts, tables.

European region. 23rd ed. 1985, reprinted 1995 with amendments (Doc. 7754). *Middle East and South East Asia region.* 15th ed. 1989 (Doc. 8700). *Africa-Indian Ocean region.* 26th ed. 1989, reprinted 1995 with amendments (Doc. 7474). *North Atlantic, North American, and Pacific regions.* 13th ed. 1990, (Doc. 8755). *North Atlantic Region.* Trial ed. 1995 (Doc. 9634). *Caribbean and South American regions.* 30th ed. 1985. (Doc. 8733/13).

European region has 10 parts: 1. Assumed operating parameters - 2. General planning aspects - 3. Aerodrome operations - 4. ATS routes and associated navigation means - 5. Air traffic management - 6. Air traffic services - 7. Aeronautical information services - 8. Meteorological services - 9. Search and rescue services - 10. Aeronautical communications. *Class No: 527(035)*

[810]

COTTER, C.H. The Elements of navigation and nautical astronomy. 2nd ed. Glasgow, Brown, Son, and Ferguson, 1992. xviii, 463p. ISBN: 0851745431.

First published 1977.

48 chapters in six sections: 1. Mathematics of navigation and nautical astronomy - 2. The sailings - 3. Introduction to chartwork - 4. General astronomy - 5. Nautical astronomy - 6. The instruments of navigation. Exercises after each chapter, with answers, p.443-52. Index, p.453-63. *Class No: 527(035)*

Dictionaries

[811]

HARBORD, J.B. Glossary of navigation. 4th ed., rev. and enl. by C.W.T. Layton. Glasgow, Brown, Son & Ferguson, 1938 (reprinted 1977). x, [1], 451p. diagrs. £10. ISBN: 085174277.

First published 1862.

Defines *c*.1,000 terms, some at length. Entries are grouped under the qualified noun (*e.g.* types of 'log' - 'Dutchman's log'. 'ground log', 'current log', 'screw log' - under 'Log'). *Class No: 527(038)*

Almanacs

[812]

The Astronomical almanac for the year 1998: data for astronomy, space sciences, geodesy, surveying, navigation and other applications. Washington, US Government Printing Office; London, Stationery Office, 1997. tables. Annual. tables. ISBN: 0118873024. ISSN: 07376421.

'Beginning with the edition for 1981, the title *The Astronomical almanac* replaced both the title *The American ephemeris and nautical almanac* and the title *The Astronomical ephemeris,* unifying the two series' (*Preface, 1998*).

'The principal ephemerides in this Almanac have been computed from fundamental ephemerides of the planets and the moon prepared at the Jet Propulsion Laboratory, California, in cooperation with the U.S. Naval Observatory' (*Preface 1998*). Sections A-N. (D. Moon, 1998 ... E. Major planets, 1998 ... J. Observatories, 1998 ... N. Index. Corrections for years 1992-1996). *Class No: 527(059)*

[813]

—Astronomical phenomena for the year 1999. Washington, US Government Printing Office; London, Stationery Office, 1996. Annual. 81p. ISBN: 0118873059. ISSN: 00832421.

Prepared jointly by the Nautical Almanac Office, US Naval Observatory, and HM Nautical Almanac Office, Royal Greenwich Observatory. Printed in advance of the main volume, this contains extracts from *The Astronomical almanac,* including movements and visibility of planetary and lunar phenomena, etc. 12 sections: Phenomena; International time zones, Sunrise and sunset tables, Moonrise and moonset tables, and Eclipses. From 2000 will no longer be published in the UK, but still available from HM Nautical Almanac Office. *Class No: 527(059)*

[814]

—Planetary and lunar co-ordinates for the years 1984-2000. London, HMSO, 1983. 336p. £10. ISBN: 0118669175.

Issued by HM Nautical Almanac Office in advance of the annual *Astronomical almanac,* to provide low-precision data for planning purposes. *Class No: 527(059)*

[815]

—YALLOP, B.D. *and* HOHENKERK, C.Y. Compact data for navigation and astronomy 1996-2000. London, Stationery Office, 1995. ix,122p. tables. ISBN: 011772467x.

Prepared by HM Nautical Almanac Office at the Royal Greenwich Observatory and intended primarily for use in the practice of astronomical navigation. 9 sections: 1. Introduction - 2. Sun and planets ... 6. Refraction and dip - 7. Sight reduction formulae - 8. Times of rising and setting and transit - 9. Hints for programmers. 7 tables: 1. Sun and planets ... 4. Phases of the moon and seasons ... 7. Alphabetical list of star names. Includes IBM-compatible computer disk with NAVPAC software, with manual (p.94-122) on its use. Convenient summary of basic astronomical information needed for navigation at sea. *Class No: 527(059)*

Histories

[816]

WATERS, D.W. The Art of navigation in England in Elizabethan and early Stuart times. 2nd ed. Greenwich, Trustees of the National Maritime Museum, 1978. 3v. facsims.

First published 1958.

A specialized study, well supported by illustrations, bibliography and index. Chart reproductions. Bibliography; index of navigational MSS. and works printed before 1640. Detailed index. *Class No: 527(091)*

Biographies

[817]

TAYLOR, E.G.R. The Mathematical practitioners of Hanoverian England, 1714-1800: a sequel to *The mathematical practitioners of Tudor and Stuart England.* Cambridge, University Press, for the Institute of Navigation, 1966. xv,503p. illus.

2 parts: 1. Narrative - 2. Biographies of inventors, makers and users of mathematical instruments, teachers, writers and theorists, by decades. Indexes: 1. General; 2. Secondary practitioners. 'Sources and references', p.xiv-xvi. *Class No: 527(092)*

[818]

TAYLOR, E.G.R. The Mathematical practitioners of Tudor and Stuart England. Cambridge, University Press, for the Institute of Navigation, 1954. xv,443p. illus.

3 parts: 1. Description of the progress and work of practical mathematicians, 1485-1715; 2. Short biographical notes on 582 mathematical practitioners; 3. Chronological annotated bibliography of 628 mathematical treatises published during the period. An essential work. *Class No: 527(092)*

Air & Nautical Almanacs

[819]

Brown's nautical almanac; daily tide tables for 1999. Brown, T.N., *ed.* Glasgow, Brown, Son and Ferguson, Ltd., 1998. 921 + 39p. tables. £40. ISBN: 0851746659.

First published 1858.

Has as main contents: Nautical information - Planetary information - Tables of navigable distances - Legal section, meteorology, beacons, buoys, etc. *Class No:* 527.05

[820]

The Nautical almanac for the year 2000. London, H.M. Nautical Almanac Office; Washington, Nautical Almanac Office, U.S. Naval Observatory, 1999. 318p. + 36p. £27. ISSN: 0077619x.

The detailed calendar of tables for the sun, moon, eclipses, planets, and stars for the year is followed by 'Explanation', standard times, star charts, etc. 'This Almanac, with minor modifications and changes of language, has been adopted for the Brazilian, Danish, Greek, Indian, Indonesian, Italian, Korean, Mexican and Norwegian almanacs' (*Preface*). *Class No:* 527.05

[821]

Olsen's fisherman's nautical almanack, 1999, containing tide tables and directory of British fishing vessels, (also suitable for yacht and small boat operators). Scarborough, Dennis, 1998. 680p. tables, maps. £21.95. ISBN: 0952767848.

Includes, in an impressive compendium of marine facts, a guide to lighthouses & light vessels (UK, Eire, and 5 continental countries), daily tide tables, port facilities and a list of British fishing vessels 'over 10 meters'. Preceded by a useful index described as 'Contents'. *Class No:* 527.05

[822]

UK air almanac. London, The Stationery Office, 1933-. Now annual. 80p. £18. (*A.P. 1602.*)

Produced by H.M. Nautical Almanac Office, Royal Greenwich Observatory.

'This can be regarded as an abridged version of *The Air almanac* which is no longer published in the UK' (*Preface*). 'Contains data useful in planning activities where the level of illumination is important', providing tables on rising and setting of sun and moon. Meets requirements of RAF and can be used in latitudes between N72 and S60 degrees, and at altitudes up to 60,000 feet. *Class No:* 527.05

Tide Tables

[823]

Tide tables for the year ... London, Hydrographic Department, 1977-83. 3v. illus., forms, tables, maps. (*NP 201-203.*)

First published 1833.

V.1: *European waters, including Mediterranean Sea.* 1983. 1, 434p. v.2: *Atlantic and Indian Oceans, including tidal stream tables.* 1980. xlviiip. v.3: *Pacific Ocean and adjacent seas, including tidal stream tables.* 1981. [469]p.

V.1 has 3 parts: 1. Prediction of high and low water for standard ports; 2. Non-harmonic data; 3. Harmonic constants. Geographical index, p.415-20. List of tidal publications. *Class No:* 527.08

Surveying. Geodesy

Bibliographies

[824]

NATIONAL MARITIME MUSEUM. Catalogue of the Library. v.3: *Atlases & cartography.* London, HMSO, 1971. 2v. (catalogue; index).

V.1, p.597-654, 'Cartography & historiography' comprises 188 entries, with appended contents-listing of *Imago mundi: yearbook of old cartography,* v.1-21 (1935-67) and the Map Collectors Circle series. *Class No:* 528(01)

Handbooks & Manuals

[825]

BOMFORD, G. Geodesy. 4th ed. Oxford, Clarendon Press, 1980. vii, 855p. diagrs., tables. ISBN: 019851946x.

First published 1952.

7 chapters: 1. Triangulation, traverse and trilateration (field work) - 2. Computation of triangulation, traverse and trilateration - 3. Heights above sea-level - 4. Geodetic astronomy - 5. Gravity observations - 6. Physical geodesy - 7. Artificial satellites. 10 appendices. Bibliography (620 items), p.800-28. Analytical index. Chapter 7, on satellite geodesy, because of the great advances during the last ten years, has been much expanded. A standard text. *Class No:* 528(035)

[826]

Surveying. Bannister, A., *and others.* 7th ed. Harlow, Essex, Longman, 1998. x,502p. illus., diagrs., tables. £21.95. ISBN: 0582302498.

For this edition some traditional techniques have been withdrawn and a new chapter on satellite surveying has been included. 13 chapters: 1. Introductory ... 4. The theodolite and its use ... 6. Satellite positioning systems ... 11. Curve ranging ... 13. Photogrammetry. Chapter exercises. References, p.496-7. Partly analytical index. Many photographs and diagrams. Emphasizes modern equipment and techniques. A standard text. *Class No:* 528(035)

Dictionaries

[827]

FÉDÉRATION INTERNATIONALE DES GÉOMÈTRES. Commission de Dictionnaire Technique. **Dictionnaire multilingue de la Fédération International de Géomètres.** Edition trilingue: français-alemand-anglais. Amsterdam, 'Argus', [1963]. xix, 501p.

Prepared with Unesco financial aid and technical aid of the Institut Géographique National, Paris, the Institut für Angewandte Geodäsie, Frankfurt/Main, and the Royal Institute of Chartered Surveyors, London.

About 5,500 terms in French, with definitions and examples of usage, followed by German and English/American equivalents. Genders are stated. French, German and English indexes. Bibliography p.xviii-xix.

Dutch index: *Dictionnaire multilingue. Index néerlandais* (The Hague, Rijkscommisie voor Geodesie, 1966, 92p.). *Class No:* 528(038)

[828]

Glossaries for surveyors. Minnick, R., *comp.* Rancho Cordova, Calif., Landmark Enterprises, [1985]. [xi], 517p.

Consists of 4 glossaries: *Glossary of mapping, charting and geodetic terms* (U.S. Dept. of Defense, 3rd ed. 1973. p.1-281); *Definitions of terms used in geodetic and other surveys* (U.S. Dept. of Commerce. H.C. Mitchell, 1945); *Tide and current glossary* (U.S. Dept. of Commerce. P. Schureman; revised by S.D. Hicks, 1975, p.283-371); and *Glossary of BLM surveying and mapping terms* (U.S. Dept. of Interior. Bureau of Land Management). Prepared by Cadastral Survey Training Staff, Denver Service Center, 1978).

2nd ed., 1989. 607p. $30. *Class No:* 528(038)

[829]

MARTON, G. Dictionar poliglot de geodezie, fotogrammetrie si cartografie: engleză, române, germâne, franceză, rusă. Bucharest, Editura Tehnica, 1976. xv, 325, [2]p.

About 4,000 English-base terms, with equivalents and indexes in Rumanian, German, French and Russian. Appended bibliography. *Class No:* 528(038)

[830]

MITCHELL, H.C. Definitions of terms used in geodetic and other surveys. Washington, US Coast and Geodetic Survey, 1945 (reprinted 1969). 121p.

Includes definitions compiled by the Committee on Definitions of the Federal Board of Surveys and Maps. *Class No:* 528(038)

Reviews & Abstracts

[831]

Referativnyĭ zhurnal. 52. Geodeziia i aeros'emka. Akademiia Nauk SSSR, Institut Nauchnoĭ Informatsii. Moscow, VINITI, 1963-. 12pa. $213. ISSN: 03759717.

Formerly *Referativnyi zhurnal. Geodeziia, 1963-69,* previously part of *Referativnyi zhurnal. Astronomiia i geodeziia* (1953-).

About 3,000 indicative and informative abstracts pa. on geodesy and aerial surveying, in 15 sections. Monthly author index; annual author and subject indexes. *Class No:* 528(048)

[832]

RICS Library Information Service abstracts and reviews. London, Royal Institution of Chartered Surveyors, 1965-. v.1(1)-. 12pa. £265pa., to non-members. ISSN: 00336939.

Contains *c.*1,500 abstracts pa. Abstracts, 50-400 words in length are arranged under subject A-Z. Items include films and videos. Headings include Arbitration - Auctions - Buildings and construction... Landlord and tenant... Property... Taxation... Water. On back cover: Statistical data (Financial indicators... Agricultural wages). Annual indexes. Also available in microform. 'A monthly bulletin of selected references for Chartered Surveyors'. *Class No:* 528(048)

[833]

—RICS Library Information Service Weekly briefing: a digest of news selected from the press. London, Royal Institution of Chartered Surveyors, 1965-. Weekly. £265. ISSN: 00336947.

Uses arrangement and headings as in *RICS Library Information Service abstracts and reviews* (*q.v.*), plus 'Departmental circulars', 'Statutory Instruments', 'Bills in progress' and 'Forthcoming conferences'. Also available in microform. *Class No:* 528(048)

Yearbooks & Directories

[834]

ROYAL INSTITUTION OF CHARTERED SURVEYORS. **Directory** 1998. Basingstoke, Hants., Macmillan, 1997. 2v.(2200p.). £91. ISBN: 0333575150, set.

Formerly RICS *Yearbook.*

V.1 contains a list of 73,000 members, A-Z. V.2 is a geographical directory, arranged A-Z by town/city. *Class No:* 528(058)

Great Britain

[835]

GREAT BRITAIN. Ordnance Survey. **The History of the retriangulation of Great Britain, 1935-1962...** London, HMSO, 1968. 446p. diagrs., graphs. tables. £15.75. ISBN: 0117004936.

Provides a detailed technical account of the retriangulation. 26 illus., 20 diagrs. Bibliography of 51 items. 20 folded diagrs. Well produced. *Class No:* 528(410)

Land

Handbooks & Manuals

[836]

Textbook of topographical surveying. London, HMSO, 1965. 388p. + 16pl. illus., diagrs., forms, maps.

First published 1905.

19 chapters (19. British and foreign maps). Appendices A-J. Detailed analytical index. *Class No:* 528.4(035)

Almanacs

[837]

GREAT BRITAIN. Nautical Almanac Office. **The Star almanac for land surveyors...** 1999; prepared by HM Nautical Almanac Office on behalf of the Particle Physics and Astronomy Research Council. London, Stationery Office, 1999. xvi, 80p. tables, star charts. £12.50. ISBN: 0118873091. ISSN: 00814377.

Includes ephemeris of the sun, sunrise, sunset, moon's phases; apparent places of 650 stars; radio time signals, auxiliary tables and star charts. Index of star names and numbers. Also available on diskette. *Class No:* 528.4(059)

Biographies

[838]

Dictionary of land surveyors and local map-makers of Great Britain and Ireland, 1530-1850; compiled from a variety of sources... Bendall, S., *ed.* London, British Library, 1997. 2v. £75; $150. ISBN: 0712345582, v.1; 0712345590, v.2; 0712345094, set.

1st ed. published 1975/76 as *Dictionary of land surveyors and local cartographers of Great Britain and Ireland, 1550-1850.*

V.1. *Introductory guide to the use of the dictionary and indexes.* (xi, 312p. illus.(col.),tables). V.2. *Dictionary.* (578p.).

Biographical entries in v.2 cross-refer to sources, printed and archival, in v.1. which includes indexes of surveyors by date, area covered, type of map produced and places of surveyors' residence. Number of entries is increased by more than 4,000 from previous ed. to document 13,744 surveyors and mapmakers. General index p.257-312. Chronological coverage extended retrospectively an extra 20 years from 1st ed. For academic and large public libraries. *Class No:* 528.4(092)

[839]

—Dictionary of land surveyors and local cartographers of Great Britain and Ireland, 1550-1850. Supplement. Eden, P., *ed.* Folkestone, Dawson, 1979. p.[vi], 379-528. ISBN: 0712908994.

A project supported by the Social Science Research Council.

Similarly arranged. 3,010 entries, bringing the total for the *Dictionary* to *c.*10,000. Appendix 2: 'Dictionary of surveyors (Irish Plantation surveyors)'. General index and topographical index to the *Supplement. Class No:* 528.4(092)

Hydrographic Surveying

Handbooks & Manuals

[840]

GREAT BRITAIN. Hydrographic Department. **Admiralty manual of hydrographic surveying. 1965-73.** [New ed.]. London, Hydrographer of the Navy, 1973. 2v.

Previously published 1938 and 1948.

V.1 covers principally the theory and the practical mathematics necessary to enable the surveyor to carry out this work. V.2 deals more specifically with the hydrographic surveyor's practical work and the special methods applicable to marine surveying (*Foreword*). V.1 has 9 chapters (2. Geodesy - 3. The measurement of distance... 9. Heights and levelling; bibliography and analytical index). Of v.2 (1969-) only chapters 1-5 have apparently been published (1969-73). *Class No:* 528.47(035)

Photogrammetry

Handbooks & Manuals

[841]

A **Dictionary of photogrammetry.** Slama, C.C., *ed.* 4th ed. Falls Church, Va., American Society for Photogrammetry and Remote Sensing, 1980. 1056p. $40. ISBN: 0937294012.

'The definitive work on the use of photogrammetric techniques to extract quantitative information from vertical and oblique aerial photography' (Harris, C.D. *ed. Geographical bibliography for American libraries* (1985), entry 375). *Class No:* 528.7(035)

Dictionaries

[842]

INTERNATIONAL SOCIETY OF PHOTOGRAMMETRY. **Multilingual dictionary for photogrammetry.** Amsterdam, 'Argus', [1969]. 6v.

One volume for each of the 6 languages,- English, French, German, Italian, Polish and Swedish. Cross-references between volumes. *Class No:* 528.7(038)

Remote Sensing

Databases

[843]

RESORS (Remote Sensing On-line Retrieval System). Ottawa, Canada, Centre for Remote Sensing.

Covers 1900 to date. A bibliographic and referral database providing references to the literature of remote sensing, photogrammetry and image analysis and processing, with emphasis on instrumentation techniques and applications. Sources: English- and French-language reports, periodical articles and conference papers. File size: 78,000 documents and 8,000 35mm slides. Updated monthly. 5,000-6,000 additions pa. Available via the Centre. Also available as RESORS Microfiche and on CD-ROM (updated twice pa.). *Class No:* 528.71(003.4)

Bibliographies

[844]

HYATT, E. **Keyguide to information sources in remote sensing.** London, Mansell, 1988. xiv, 274p. £40. ISBN: 0720118549.

The largest and most up-to-date English-language guide to its subject. 3 parts: 1. Survey of remote sensing and its literature. 2 chapters outline the development of remote sensing, the technology, the systems and the satellites, in general and regionally by continent. 2 further chapters provide an in-depth analysis of the literature of the subject, covering the conventional categories (books, reports, trade literature, etc.) and the secondary sources (bibliographies, abstracts, reviews, databases). Chapter 5 covers language factors and dictionaries; chapter 6 details sources of remotely sensed imagery; chapter 7, 'Audio-visual material', includes slides, videocassettes, maps and atlases). Part 2 (p.127-249) is an annotated bibliography of 819 items. Of the 493 published information sources, over 100 journals and 100 books are listed, and more than 20 entries each for literature guides, abstracts and indexes and databases. Finally, 326 organizations, grouped under 81 countries, with addresses, are listed. This is an immensely impressive guide, well written, clearly set out - the work of an information specialist in a remote sensing research unit. *Class No:* 528.71(01)

[845]

—BRYAN, M.L. Remote sensing of earth resources: a guide to information sources. Detroit, Mich., Gale, 1979. xv,188p. $68. (*Geography and travel information guides, v.1*.) ISBN: 0810314134.

378 annotated entries, with extensive cross-references, covering general literature, journals, bibliographies, maps, guides and education and training facilities. Acronyms and abbreviations list. Indexes of author, title, subject. *Class No:* 528.71(01)

Handbooks & Manuals

[846]

LILLESAND, T.M. *and* KIEFER, R.W. **Remote sensing and image interpretation.** 3rd ed. New York, John Wiley & Sons, 1994. xiv,750p., illus. (some col.), figs., diagrs., maps, tables. £19.95. ISBN: 0471577839.

First published 1979.

Provides a broad introduction to remote sensing. 8 sections: 1. Concepts and foundations of remote sensing - 2. Elements of photographic systems (p.49-147) ... 4. Photogrammetry ... 7. Digital image processing - 8. Microwave sensing ... Appendices on remote sensing data sources and periodicals. Selected bibliography after every chapter (204 refs. for chapter 7). Index, p.727-750. Many black-and-white illustrations and 24 excellent colour plates. 'At the very good price of £19.95, every college library should have a reference copy and it must be a very strong contender for inclusion as the course reader on college remote sensing courses' (*Geological journal* v.30(2), 1995, p.204). *Class No:* 528.71(035)

[847]

Manual of remote sensing. Colwell, R.N., *ed.* 2nd ed. Falls Church, Va., American Society of Photogrammetry and Remote Sensing, 1983. 2v. (xxxiii, 2440p.) illus., diagrs., (mostly col.). ISBN: 0937294527.

The classic manual. More than 200 contributors. 36 chapters in 2v., with theoretical and systems material in v.1 and practical applications in v.2. Comprehensive coverage of core subject and related fields, with full attention to the technology and equipment. Extensive bibliographies. Glossary, p.1183-98. Combined index, p.1209-32. *Class No:* 528.71(035)

Dictionaries

[848]

Multilingual dictionary of remote sensing and photogrammetry: English glossary and dictionary, equivalent terms in French, German, Italian, Portuguese, Spanish, Russian. Rabchevsky, G.A., *ed.* Falls Church, Va., American Society of Photogrammetry, 1984. xx,[1],343p. $20. ISBN: 0937294462.

1,717 numbered terms defined in English, with equivalents in French, German, Italian, Spanish, Portuguese and Russian. Indexes in other languages refer to English base. Bibliography and acronyms list. *Class No:* 528.71(038)

Yearbooks & Directories

[849]

CARTER, D.J. **The Remote sensing source book: a guide to remote sensing products, services, facilities, publications and other materials.** London, McCarta/Kogan Page, 1986. 175p. diagrs., maps. ISBN: 1850910340.

Provides detailed guidance on the main products, services and facilities available in the UK and gives details of equipment, imagery collections and personnel in commercial, government and academic institutions. Also covers educational material and maps. Bibliography (p.65-93) is a guide to the current literature.

'Fills a gap in the remote sensing literature that has become conspicuous since the recent explosion... in the volume of remotely sensed data gathered on a global basis... In addition to providing a comprehensive index to the remotely sensed data available within Europe and North America, it provides a reference to textbooks and journals on different applications of remote sensing...' (*Journal of physics - E. Scientific instruments*, v.19, October 1986, p.757).

'It is unfortunately let down by a poor layout that tends to obscure the substantial amount of information contained; this problem is compounded by a scanty index and lack of accurate cross-referencing... [but] the volume is quite informative and fairly comprehensive, especially on British products ... (E. Hyatt, *Keyguide to information sources on remote sensing*. (Mansell, 1988), p.169). It needs to be updated soon if it is to retain its usefulness. *Class No:* 528.71(058)

[850]

Remote sensing yearbook 1990. Cracknell, A. *and* Hayes, L., *eds.* London, Taylor & Francis, 1990. Annual. vii,330p. figs., maps, tables. £50. ISBN: 0850668085. ISSN: 02676133.

First published 1986.

4 sections: 1. Developments in remote sensing - 2. Remote sensing societies, p.139-52 - 3. Satellite data - 4. Directory, p.175-330, (12 sections: Establishments receiving and supplying satellite data ... Consultants ... Research establishments ... Societies ... Directory index). The section, Bibliography, which was in previous issues, has been excluded from this edition. *Class No:* 528.71(058)

[851]

United Kingdom remote sensing directory. Farnborough, Hants., National Remote Sensing Centre (Royal Aircraft Establishment), 1986.

An update of the Department of Industry's *Remote sensing of earth resources* (3rd ed., 1976).

Facilities and activities of over 200 organizations in 5 sections: academic, commercial, industrial, consultancy, government and learned bodies. Lists staff and their geographical or subject interests. *Class No:* 528.71(058)

Cartography

Bibliographies

[852]

Bibliographia cartographica ... Hrsg. von der Staatsbibliothek Preussischer Kulturbesitz in Verbindung mit der Deutschen Gesellschaft für Kartographie. [International documentation of cartographical literature.] Munich, etc., K.G. Saur, 1974-. v.1-. Annual. Price varies. ISSN: 03400409.

Supersedes *Bibliotheca cartographica* (v.1-29/30. 1946/47).

Contains *c.*2,500 numbered items. 12 sections: 1. Bibliographies. Map collection. Documentation - 2. General publications - 3. History of cartography - 4. Institutions and organizations of cartography - 5. Theoretical cartography - 6. Cartographic technology - 7. Topographic and landscape cartography - 8. Thematic maps and cartograms - 9. Atlas cartography - 10. Use and application of maps. General purpose maps - 11. Reliefs and other forms of cartographic representation - 12. Globes. List of periodicals (*c.*300); List of abbreviations; Concordance of the UDC and of the chapter headings of the *Bibliotheca cartographica*. Index of authors. *Class No:* 528.9(01)

[853]

Catalogue of cartographic materials in the British Library 1975-1988. London, Saur, 1989. 3v. ISBN: 0862917654, set; 0862917662, v.1; 0862917670, v.2; 0862917689, v.3.

'Contains bibliographic records for atlases, single-sheet maps, map series, maritime charts, plans, globes and related reference materials acquired by the British Library Map Library since 1974 ... includes a number of pre-1974 and antiquarian items' (Explanatory note by publisher). V.1 and 2 contain names/titles, while v.3 lists geographic names and subjects. Also available on microfiche. *Class No:* 528.9(01)

[854]

HODGKISS, A.G. *and* TATHAM, A.F. **Keyguide to information sources in cartography.** London, Mansell, 1986. x, 253p. £40. (*Keyguides*.) ISBN: 0720117682.

4 parts: 1. Cartography and maps: the subject and its literature - 2. Annotated bibliography of reference sources: history of cartography - 3. Annotated bibliography of reference sources: contemporary cartography - 4. Directory of organizations (nos.797-1397). Detailed analytical index. Items 1-796, in parts 2-3, are usually annotated, frequently indicating readership. A refreshing approach. Aimed at curators of map collections, libraries, cartographers, students and other map-users. *Class No:* 528.9(01)

[855]

Information sources in cartography. Perkins, C.F. *and* Parry, R.B., *eds.* London, Bowker-Saur, 1990. xiii,540p. illus., maps. $96. ISBN: 0408024585.

33 contributors; 6 parts (30 well-documented chapters): 1. General - 2. The history of cartography - 3. Map production - 4. Map librarianship - 5. Types of mapping - 6. Map use and promotion. 3 appendices: 1. Cartographic periodicals - 2. Cartographic societies - 3. Map publishers. Subject and, unlike the other volumes in this series, name indexes. An outstanding volume. *Class No:* 528.9(01)

[856]

PARRY, R.B. *and* PERKINS, C.R. **World mapping today.** London, Butterworths, 1987. [x],583p. diagrs., maps. £145. ISBN: 0408028505.

7 General chapters (*e.g.* 2. The state of world mapping - 3. Map acquisition - 4. Map evaluation - 5, Maps and remote sensing - 6. Digital mapping - 7. Future trends in digital mapping). World mapping, p.61-568: The world; Africa; The Americas; Australia; Europe; The oceans. ('Philippines', p.340-2: Mapping - Further information - Addresses; Catalogue; Atlases and gazetteers; General. 2

....(contd.)

map keys, 1:50,000). 'List of geographic indexes' [*i.e.,* of 200 map keys] precedes text. Glossary, p.569-72. Geographical index. Publishers index. Well organized and well produced. For all map libraries as well as for most non-specialist libraries. 2nd ed. planned for 1999. *Class No:* 528.9(01)

[857]
UNITED STATES. Library of Congress. Geography and Map Division. **The Bibliography of cartography.** Boston, Mass., G.K. Hall, 1973, 5v.; First supplement, 1980. $615, set; $285, supp. ISBN: 0816102597.

The main work reproduces 91,600 photolithographed catalogue cards. Author, title and subject entries for books and periodical articles on maps, mapmakers, and the history of cartography. Particularly strong on history of cartography and cartobibliography for 1895-1922. Available on microfilm. *Class No:* 528.9(01)

Encyclopaedias

[858]
STEFOFF, R. The British Library companion to maps and mapmaking. London, British Library, 1995. 303p. illus. (some col.), maps. ISBN: 0712306501.

Arranged A-Z (Académie des Sciences ... Zorsi, Alessandro), containing more than 350 entries. Many cross-references, with many entries listing further reading. Three appendices: 1. Important dates in the history of mapmaking - 2. Organizations and publications related to maps - 3. Collections and exhibits of maps. Bibliography, p.295-7. Index *Class No:* 528.9(031)

Handbooks & Manuals

[859]
CANTERS, F. *and* **DECLEIR, H. The World in perspective:** a directory of world map projections. Chichester, New York, John Wiley, 1989. x,181p. maps. $74.95; £69. ISBN: 0471921475.

Illustrated overview of 68 different projections for world maps. Part 1. Principles of map projections and their application (The mathematical theory of map projections; The classification of map projections; The evaluation and choice of a map projection) - Part 2. Directory of world map projections, p.39-176 (Introduction; Polyconic projections; Pseudocylindrical projections; Pseudoconical projections; Cylindrical projections). References, p.177-78. Index. *Class No:* 528.9(035)

[860]
Elements of cartography. Robinson, A.H., *and others.* 6th ed. New York, Wiley, 1995. 674p. illus. (incl. col.), facsims., diagrs., graphs, tables. 2.95. ISBN: 0471555797.

First published 1953.

7 pts. (31 chapters) systematically covering nature and history of cartography, basic geography, map projections, remote sensing, data processing, digital databases, cartographic design, map compilation and reproduction, etc. References after each chapter. Appendices A-F; analytical index. The standard work for students in cartography. *Class No:* 528.9(035)

[861]
LOCK, C.B.M. Modern maps and atlases: an outline guide to twentieth century production. London, Bingley, 1969. 619p. ISBN: 0851570720.

A manual in five sections: 1. The techniques of modern cartography - 2. International maps and atlases - 3. National and regional maps and atlases (p.109-403) - 4. Thematic maps and atlases - 5. Map librarianship. The detailed analytical index has *c.*6,000 main entries. A solid contribution on 20th-century mapping (despite absence of map specimens) and an essential reference.

Modern maps and atlases is not fully incorporated into Dr. Lock's later *Geography and cartography* (Bingley, 1976); 'only a few entries (*i.e.,* map librarianship) have been included' (*RQ,* v.16(3), Spring 1977, p.259). *Class No:* 528.9(035)

[862]
Manual of map reading and land navigation. 2nd ed. London, HMSO, 1989. various pagings, 5 folding maps. £7.95. (*Army code 70947.*) ISBN: 0117726117.

1st ed. published as *Manual of map reading,* 1973.

13 chapters: 1. Introduction - 2. Scale - 3. Marginal information - 4. Representation of detail - 5. Representation of relief - 6. Referencing systems - 7. Direction - 8. Compasses and their use - 9. Land navigation - 10. Tactical information printing systems - 11. Map substitutes - 12. Special maps - 13. Map supply. 'Produced primarily to provide instructors in the Armed Services with a comprehensive source of reference on which to base training' (*Publisher's description*). *Class No:* 528.9(035)

[863]
Planetary mapping. Greeley, R. *and* Batson, R.M., *eds.* Cambridge, University Press, 1990. ix,296p. illus., diagrs., tables, maps. (*Cambridge planetary science series.*) ISBN: 0521307740.

Outlines methods and techniques used in making maps of planetary objects. 7 sections: 1. Introduction - 2. History of planetary cartography ... 4. Planetary nomenclature ... 6. Topographic mapping - 7. Geologic mapping. 3 appendices: 1. Map formats and projections used in planetary cartography - 2. Halftone processes for planetary maps - 3. Digital planetary cartography. Bibliography appended to each section. *Class No:* 528.9(035)

[864]
Surveying and mapping for field scientists. Ritchie, W., *and others.* Harlow, Essex; New York, John Wiley, 1988. ix,180p. illus., diagrs. £14.99. ISBN: 058230086x.

New edition of *Mapping for field scientists* (David & Charles, 1977).

5 chapters: 1. The problem and how to approach a solution - 2. Ground surveying techniques - 3. Aerial surveying techniques - 4. Remote sensing techniques - 5. Cartographic presentation. 2 appendices: 1. Examples of Ordnance Survey information - 2. Sources of aerial photography and earth satellite imagery. Bibliography, p.173-75. Index. 'This book is designed as a comprehensive practical introduction and guide to a range of sources and techniques that can be used by a wide group of people' (*Preface*). *Class No:* 528.9(035)

Dictionaries

[865]
Anglo-russkiĭ slovar' po kartografii, geodezii, aerofototopografii. Galperin, G.L., *comp.* Moscow, Gos. Izd-vo Fiziko-matem. Literatury, 1958. 548p.

An English-Russian dictionary on cartography, geodesy and aerial photography, with an index of Russian terms. *Class No:* 528.9(038)

[866]
BARGILLIAT, A. Vocabulaire pratique, anglais-français et français-anglais des termes techniques concernant la cartographie (géodesie, topographie, dessin, photomécanique, impression). Paris, Institut Géographique National, 1944. 397p

Part 1: Anglais-français (p.38-217); pt.2: Français-anglais (p.220-397). Conversion tables, p.12-35. *Class No:* 528.9(038)

[867]
BONACKER, W. **Karten-Wörterbuch:** eine Verdeutschung fremdsprachiger Kartersignatur-Bezeichnungen... Bonn, Kirschbaum, 1970. xx, 276p. $59.95. ISBN: 3781207048.

This ed. is a facsimile of 1941 ed.

A polyglot glossary of terms (physical features, etc.) occurring on maps. No fewer than 56 languages are involved, including Breton, Cambodian, Asset and Tatar. Under each language: *c.*450 words are given in the native tongue, first translated and then in the original script, plus German meaning and notes on pronouncing the original. About 21,000 terms are so covered. *Class No:* 528.9(038)

[868]
DE OLIVEIRA, C. Dicionário cartográfico. 3rd ed. Rio de Janeiro, Instituto Brasileiro de Geografia e Estastica, 1987. xv,645p.illus.(some col.pl.),figs.,maps. ISBN: 8524002484.

First published 1980.

Brief definitions of terms are given. Includes short biographies of cartographers and details of important maps and atlases. 2 appendices, *e.g.* 2. Brazilian cartographic legislation. *Class No:* 528.9(038)

[869]
Dictionary of mapping, charting and geodetic terms. Madison, Wisc., Map Division IV, 1978. [i], 271p.

About 5,000 technical terms are defined, with numerous cross-references. *Class No:* 528.9(038)

[870]
Glossary of technical terms in computer assisted cartography. [Glossaire des termes techniques en cartographie assistée par ordinateur.] Edson, D.T., *ed.* 2nd ed. Falls Church, Va., American Congress on Surveying and Mapping, for the International Cartographic Association's Commission on Cartographic Terminology, 1980. 157p.

English/French glossary. *Class No:* 528.9(038)

[871]
Multilingual dictionary of technical terms in cartography. Meynen, E., *comp.* Wiesbaden, Steiner Verlag GmbH.; New York, French and European Publications, 1984. 700p. maps. $135. ISBN: 0828814643, US ed.

First published 1973.

Defines *c.*1,000 cartographic terms in German, English, Spanish, French and Russian, with equivalents in 9 other languages (Czech, Italian, Japanese, Hungarian, Dutch, Portuguese, Polish, Swedish and Slovak). 2 appendices list names (in the 5 major languages) of individual grouped map projections. 3 sample maps illustrate some of

....*(contd.)*

the more important terms. Bibliography. Of the 1973 ed., 'The production of this dictionary has itself done much to standardise cartographic terms' (*Geographical journal*, v.140(2), June 1974, p.339). *Class No:* 528.9(038)

[872]

—Glossary of cartographic terms and manual of symbols and abbreviations used on latest navigational charts of the various countries... 3rd ed. Monaco, International Hydrographic Bureau, 1951. 186p. Amendments, 1951-.

French and English text. Covers 17 languages.

Class No: 528.9(038)

[873]

—UNITED STATES. Department of Defense. Army Topographic Command. Glossary of mapping, charting and geodetic terms. 3rd ed. Washington, 1973. 281p.

First published by Defense Intelligence Agency in 1967 as a 'DOD glossary'.

About 5,000 entries. *Class No:* 528.9(038)

Periodicals & Progress Reports

[874]

The Cartographic journal. University of Aberdeen, British Cartographic Society, 1964-. v.1(1)-. 2pa. £25pa. ISSN: 00087041.

V.32(2), December 1995 issue carries 9 papers, *e.g.* 'The rendering of relief images from digital contour data'; 'A study of point symbol design for computer based large scale tourist maps'; 'The International Cartographic Association - progress during 1991-95'. Also includes book reviews, software review, recent literature, recent maps and atlases, etc. A major journal in its highly specialized field.

Class No: 528.9(05)

[875]

Progress in contemporary cartography. Taylor, D.R.F., *general ed.* New York, Wiley, 1980-85. v.1-3. illus., diagrs., maps. ISBN: 0471276995; 0471103160; 0471903051.

V.1. *The computer in contemporary cartography.* 1980. xv, 252p. V.2. *Graphic communication and design in contemporary cartography.* 1983. xviii, 314p. £29.50. V.3 *Education and training in contemporary cartography.* 1985. 324p.

V.3 has 19 contributors. 3 sections: 1. Emerging trends and challenges - 2. Specific responses to education for a new cartography - 3. Cartography and the developing nations, (*e.g.* 'Remote sensing, remote development and education in Africa', p.189-225. 71 references). Author and subject indexes. *Class No:* 528.9(05)

[876]

World cartography. New York, United Nations, Dept. of Technical Co-operation and Development, 1951-. irregular. Price varies. ISSN: 00841471.

Contains statistics, analyses and reports on recent and planned activities in cartography. V.21, 1990 has 2 parts: 1. Local data banks - 2. Organization and functions of a national geographical names standardization programme. Very specialized, but poorly printed in places. *Class No:* 528.9(05)

Yearbooks & Directories

[877]

MAIZLISH, A. *and* **TEFFT, W. The World map directory, 1992-1993.** Santa Barbara, Map Link, 1992. 335p. maps. $29.95. ISBN: 0929591089.

A commercial catalogue of maps available from this publisher. Lists *c*50,000 titles, including thematic and topographic maps. International in scope though not all-inclusive, but includes Antartica and the Universe. Each entry includes sheet name, Map Link code, price, scale, date and an estimation of the quality of the map. Annotations of variable length are provided for most maps. Contains a list of publisher abbreviations (no addresses) and a geographic index. '*The World Map Directory* is a must for all map collections and map libraries' (*Reference books bulletin*, 1 May 1989, p.1531).

Class No: 528.9(058)

Maps & Atlases

[878]

A Directory of UK map collections. Chibnall, J. 3rd ed. Kingston upon Thames, British Cartographic Society, [1995]. viii, 324p. (*Map Curators Group publication no.4.*) ISBN: 0904482111.

Now rearranged geographically; after list of copyright libraries, there follows arrangement by England (Avon-West Yorkshire), Wales, Scotland, Northern Ireland, Channel Islands. Data: address, contact person, phone, opening hours, brief contents of collection, services available. Indexes: General, and Special collections. Small handy format, with 17 additions to previous complement of *c*.400 collections. Now requires updating, particularly following local government reorganisation. *Class No:* 528.9(084.3)

[879]

Guide to U.S. map resources. Cobb, D.A., *comp.* 2nd ed. Chicago, Ill., American Library Association, 1990. 495p. $65. ISBN: 0838905470.

First published 1986.

Covers 975 map collections in academic, public, private, geoscience, federal and state libraries. Arranged alphabetically by state, city and institution. Data include special collections, hours, holdings and chronological coverage. 128 pages of indexes, *e.g.* Library/Institution Index, Collection Strengths Index. Appendices: 1. Earth science national information centers - 2. State information resources - 3. State mapping advisory committees. Page layout is better than that of the previous edition and there is more information on each collection than in *Map collections in the United States and Canada (q.v.)* 'With the improvements in this edition, ALA's *Guide to U.S. map resources* is the preferred directory to U.S. map collections and cartographic resources' (*Booklist*, v.87(4), 15 December 1990, p.881).

Class No: 528.9(084.3)

[880]

Map collections in the United States and Canada: a directory. Carrington, D.K. *and* Stephenson, R.W., *eds.* 4th ed. New York, Special Libraries Association, 1985. 178p. $35. ISBN: 0871113066.

First published 1954, 3rd ed., 1978.

Details of 804 map collections: USA (states, A-Z); Canada (by provinces). Data include size of collection, annual accessions, special collections, availability, publications. Detailed index.

Class No: 528.9(084.3)

[881]

World directory of map collections. Compiled by the [IFLA] Section of Geography and Map Libraries. Dubreuil, L., *ed.* 2nd ed. Munich & London, K.G. Saur, 1993. ix, 310p. (*IFLA publication, v.63.*) ISBN: 3598217919.

Lists 522 collections, in 67 countries (previous ed. covered 670 in 65). Arrangement is by countries (Argentina-Zimbabwe). Data on each collection include size and nature, the type and availability of catalogues. Name index of institutions and person in charge.

Class No: 528.9(084.3)

Histories

[882]

BAGROW, L. History of cartography. Revised and enlarged by R.A. Skelton. Translated from German by D.L. Paisey. 2nd ed. Chicago, Precedent Publishing, 1985. 312p. illus., facsims.

Originally *Die Geschichte der Kartographie* (Berlin, Safari Verlag, 1951.). 1st English-language ed. 1964.

2nd ed. includes maps and illustrations excluded from previous edition. Comprises an extensive list of cartographers who practised before 1750 (p.225-80). Select bibliography (278 grouped references), p.281-300. 158 plates (26 in colour). 76 line-drawings in text. A handsome volume. 'The mapping of the New World is largely ignored in this work' (Harris, C.D., ed. *Geographical bibliography for American libraries* (1985), entry 325). *Class No:* 528.9(091)

[883]

Cartographical innovations: an international handbook of mapping terms to 1900. Wallis, H.M. *and* Robinson, A.H., *eds.* Tring, Herts., Map Collector Publications (1982), Ltd., in association with the International Cartographic Association, 1987. 353p. facsims., maps. £42. ISBN: 0906430046.

Terms and their history feature in 8 groups (1. Types of maps... 8. Atlases). 'Tidal map', p.134-6, has 1 facsimile and 11 references. General index, p.328-48. Index to bibliographies, p.347-53. Aims to identify on a worldwide scale the main points of advance and change in the science and art of cartography. *Class No:* 528.9(091)

[884]

CRONE, G.R. Maps and their makers: an introduction to the history of cartography. 5th ed. Folkestone, Kent, Dawson, 1978. [v], 152p. facsims., maps. £16. ISBN: 0712907564.

First published 1953.

14 brief chapters (*e.g.* 1. The Classical and medieval heritage - 2. The evolution of the medieval seachart - 3. The cartography of the great discoveries - 8. Hydrographic charts and atlases - 11. The British contribution - 12. National surveys and world maps, 1800-1975 - 13. Atlases and thematic maps - 14. Contemporary cartography). Bibliography, p.144-6 (1. General works on cartography, cartographical periodicals and map catalogues; 2. Reproductions of early maps and charts). Detailed, non-analytical index. Larger format and well illustrated (unlike editions 1-4). 'A good overview of the history of cartography' (*Special libraries*, v.70(7), July 1979, p.309) by the former Librarian and Map Curator of the Royal Geographical Society. *Class No:* 528.9(091)

[885]

The History of cartography. Chicago, Ill., Univ. of Chicago Press, 1987-. v.1-. illus., maps. ISBN: 0226316335, v.1; 0226316351, v.2(1); 0226316378, v.2(2); 0226907287, v.2(3).

1. *Cartography in prehistoric, ancient and medieval Europe, and the Mediterranean.* 1987. 599p. £79.95. 2, Bk. 1. *Cartography in the traditional Islamic and south Asian societies.*; 704p. £99.95. Bk.2. *Cartography in the traditional east and southeast Asian societies.*; 970p. £119.95. 1992-94. Bk.3. *Cartography in the traditional African, American, Arctic, Australian, and Pacific societies*; 500p. 1998.

V.2 now complete; series to be complete in 6v. V.1 carries the narrative up to *c.*1470. V.2-6 are to extend coverage both chronologically and geographically. 'No large library can afford to be without this' (*Library journal,* 15 September 1987, p.79). *Class No:* 528.9(091)

[886]

Imago mundi: the journal of the International Society for the History of Cartography. Haywards Heath, Sussex, I.M. Ltd. London, 1935-. Annual. $60. ISSN: 03085694.

V.46 (1994) has 10 contributors, 10 documented papers, *e.g.* 'The Forlani map of North America'; 'A nineteenth century Burmese map relating to French colonial expansion in southeast Asia'. 16 book reviews. 'Chronicle for 1993' includes information on conferences and meetings, notable acquisitions, etc. 'Bibliography of literature in the history of cartography 1991-93', p.205-13. *Class No:* 528.9(091)

[887]

RISTOW, W.W. Guide to the history of cartography: an annotated list of references on the history of maps and mapmaking. Washington, Library of Congress, Geography and Map Division, 1973. iii, 96p.

Expansion of *A guide to historical cartography,* by W.W. Ristow and C.F. LeGear (1954; 2nd ed., 1960).

398 numbered entries, under authors, A-Z. Includes works on individual countries and specialised aspects of cartography. Index to subjects, geographical areas, etc. *Class No:* 528.9(091)

[888]

TOOLEY, R.V. Maps and map-makers. 7th ed. London, Batsford, 1987. xii, 140p. illus., facsims. ISBN: 0713413956.

First published 1949. 6th ed. 1978 (ISBN also 0713413956).

Treatment is by schools of geography. Chapters: Pre-Christian geography - The Arabs and medieval Europe - Italy - Germany - Holland and Belgium - French cartography - English map-makers. English marine atlases - The county maps of England and Wales - Scotland and Ireland - Africa - Asia - America - Australia - Scandinavia. Extensive chapter bibliographies; many reproductions of maps. 104 illus. Detailed index. A popular work on the history of cartography, whose 7th 'edition' is identical to the 6th. *Class No:* 528.9(091)

[889]

Who's who in the history of cartography: the international guide to the subject. Lowenthal, M.A., *ed.* D8. Tring, Herts., Map Collector Publications, 1995. ISBN: 0906430151.

First published 1974; 3rd ed. 1981. Editions D1-6 were entitled *International directory of current research in the history of cartography and in carto-bibliography.*

D(for directory)8, 1995, lists 508 researchers working in 39 countries, UK and USA predominating. Indexes. 'This is the major reference source into current work in the field of carto-bibliography and the history of cartography' (Hodgkiss, A.G., and Tatham, A.F. *Cartography* (1986), p.53). *Class No:* 528.9(091)

Biographies

[890]

TOOLEY, R.V. Tooley's dictionary of mapmakers. Tring, Herts., Map Collector Publications, 1979. xii, 684p. Supplement, 1985. ISBN: 0845117012; 0845117033, supp.

Brief biographical data on over 20,000 mapmakers, from earliest times to 1900: name; date of birth and death (when known), titles of honour (if any), working address and changes of address (which often enables the user to establish the approximate date of publication of a map), main output of maps or atlases, with dates and editions whenever known. Includes a list of 'Works consulted', revealing surprising omissions. The *Supplement* adds *c.*4,000 names to the dictionary. Nevertheless, a standard work and attractively produced. *Class No:* 528.9(092)

[891]

—SKELTON, R.A. Maps: a historical survey of their study and collecting. Chicago, Ill., & London, University of Chicago Press, 1972. 138p. $15. ISBN: 0266761665.

Consists of 4 lectures at the Newberry Library, Chicago. 'Unsurpassed as the best general introduction' (*RQ,* v.12(4), Summer 1973, p.409). Included is a list of R.A. Skelton's published works. *Class No:* 528.9(092)

Worldwide

[892]

Cartography, past, present and future: a Festschrift for F.J. Ormeling. Rhind, D.W. *and* Taylor, D.R.F., *eds.* London, New York, Published on behalf of the International Cartographic Association by Elsevier Applied Science Publishers, 1989. xx,193p. $63. ISBN: 1851663363.

A short biography of F.J. Ormeling is followed by 2 main sections: 1. Contemporary regional issues in cartography - 2. Thematic issues in cartography. Section 1 consists of 7 documented chapters covering cartography in specific countries, *e.g.* 'The status of cartography in Nigeria'; 'China's cartography: the present situation and future perspectives'. The 7 chapters in section 2 cover major issues and developments in cartography, *e.g.* 'Cartography as an art'; 'Education and training and cartography'; 'The revolution in cartography in the 1980s'. *Class No:* 528.9(100)

Space

[893]

WHITFIELD, P. The Mapping of the heavens. London, British Library, 1995. 134p. illus. ISBN: 0712304029.

Narrates and illustrates the history of celestial mapping from palaeolithic times to the present in a colourful, well-produced large-size book. Further reading, p.133; index p.134. *Class No:* 528.9(15)

Marine Environment

[894]

ROBINSON, A.H. Marine cartography in Britain: a history of the sea chart to 1855. Leicester Univ. Press, 1962. 222p. diagrs., charts.

Sub-title should read: 'a history of British marine cartography of the British Isles down to 1855'. Appendix A: 'Additional biographical notes on some of the sixteenth century surveyors and chart-makers'; B to L: lists of charts and hydrographic surveys (p.152-202). The authoritative text is marred by a disappointing short bibliography and inadequate index. *Class No:* 528.9(26)

Great Britain

[895]

A History of the Ordnance Survey. Seymour, W.A., *ed.* Folkestone, Dawson, 1980. xiv, 394p. maps. £35. ISBN: 0712909796.

35 chapters by various hands (1. The origins of the Ordnance Survey... 35. The restoration of the Survey - a new home and new aims). 6 appendices (*e.g.* Recommendations of the Davidson Committee (1938). Analytical index, p.379-94. A handsome tribute. *Class No:* 528.9(410)

[896]

OLIVER, R. Ordnance Survey maps: a concise guide for historians. London, the Charles Close Society, 1993. 192p. tables. £12.95. ISBN: 087059813x.

Eight sections: 1. The development of the Ordnance Survey - 2. Scales and characteristics of Ordnance Survey maps ... 6. Air photographs and air photo mosaics ... Select bibliography. Index to subjects and people. *Class No:* 528.9(410)

Africa

[897]

McILWAINE, J. Maps and mapping of Africa: a resource guide. London, Hans Zell Publishers, 1997. xxviii,391p. £60. ISBN: 1873836767.

Claims to be 'the first comprehensive guide to maps and map-making across the whole of the African continent and its Atlantic and Indian Ocean island groups'. Three parts: 1. Africa in general - 2. Africa as mapped by colonial and overseas agencies - 3. Africa by region and country. Covers mapping up to the end of 1995, with a few from 1996. The 3,131 entries (many with annotations) include bibliographies and catalogues, individual works of cartographic reference, writings on maps and survey, map collections, etc. Name index, p.353-85. Subject index, p.386-91. *Class No:* 528.9(6)

Libraries

[898]

LONDON UNIVERSITY. Library Resources Co-ordinating Committee. Geography Sub-committee. **A Guide to geography and map collections.** London, the University, 1985 (2nd ed., 1990. 40p.). [i], 40p. ISBN: 0718797125.

1. Geography collections (12 libraries) - 2. Map collections (10 libraries. Data: name and address; telephone no.; location; hours of openings; access; readers places; name of map curator; staff availability; catalogue(s); classification; holdings; special collections or strengths; publications; additional facilities). *Class No:* 528.9:061:026/027

Map Printing

[899]

WOODWARD, D., *ed*. **Five centuries of map printing.** Chicago, Ill., & London, Univ. of Chicago Press, for the Hermon Dunlop Smith Center for the History of Cartography, the Newberry Library, 1975. xi, 177p. illus., facsims., maps. $7.95. ISBN: 0226907244.

8 contributions, all by American geographers, although developments in Britain and other European countries are well covered. Select bibliography, p.167-70. 'The first book to be devoted to the technical history of the processes used for printing maps'. (*Aslib proceedings*, v.28(6/7), June/July 1976, p.252). Well received in *Cartographic journal*, v.13(2), 1976, p.197-8. *Class No: 528.9:655.1*

Time

[900]

AVENI, A.F. Empires of time: calendars, clocks and cultures. London, I.B. Taurus & Co, 1990. ix,371p. £19.95. ISBN: 1850432155.

4 parts: 1. Serving and marking time - 2. Our time: the imposition of order - 3. Their time: following the order of the skies (Maya, Aztec, Inca, Chinese) - 4. A world of time (building on the basic rhythms). Notes, p.343-58. Detailed, analytical index, p.359-71. *Class No: 529*

[901]

The Book of calendars. Parise, F., *ed*. New York, Facts on File, 1982. [vii], 387p. tables. $35. ISBN: 0871964678.

Main sections: Ancient calendars (p.1-122) - Africa - Modern Near East - India - Southeast Asia - Far East - Central America - Western calendars (p.291-379, including Calendar of saints; French Revolutionary calendar; Soviet calendar [discontinued in 1940]). Non-analytical index. A handbook that offers basic information on the structure of the calendar and extensive tables for quick conversions. More than 40 ancient peoples' calendars; over 60 calendars 'enabling the reader to translate one calendar date to its appropriate Julian or Gregorian date' (*Introduction*). *Class No: 529*

[902]

Encyclopedia of time. Macey, S.L., *ed*. New York, Garland, 1994. 699p. illus. diagrs. tables $95. (*Garland reference library of social science, 810*.) ISBN: 0815306156.

About 360 articles on the interdisciplinary field of time studies by *c*.200 contributors, with brief lists of further reading. Many cross-references. For academic and public libraries. *Class No: 529*

[903]

MACEY, S.L. Time: a bibliographic guide. New York, Garland, 1991. xxi,426p. £62. (*Garland reference library of the humanities, v.1506*.) ISBN: 0815306466.

Contains *c*.6,000 entries for English and non-English language time-related books in 25 academic disciplines. Author and subject indexes. Does not aim to be comprehensive but is well presented and easy to use.

For older references, *Time: a bibliography* (London Information Retrieval, 1977) by E.S Krudy *and others* is recommended. This contains *c*.3,000 references from the late 1950s to 1970s. *Class No: 529*

[904]

SAMUEL, A.E. Greek and Roman chronology: calendars and years in Classical antiquity. Munich, Beck, 1972. 325p. (*Handbuch der Altertumswissenschaft. 1. Abt. 7. Teil*.)

A monograph-section of the massive co-operative work on Classical antiquity and part of section 1: *Einleitende und Hilfsdisziplinen*. Well documented. *Class No: 529*

[905]

—**FREEMAN-GRENVILLE, G.S.P.** The Islamic and Christian calendars AD 622-2222 (AH1-1650); a complete guide for converting Christian and Islamic dates, and dates of festivals. 3rd ed. Reading, Garnet, 1995. 113p. tables. £12.95. ISBN: 1859640664.

First published 1963 as *The Muslim and Christian calendars*.

Enables the user to ascertain the corresponding days of the week. Tables 6-8 cover the principal Muslim festivals and the principal fixed and movable Christian festivals. Previous bias in favour of East African readers has been removed. *Class No: 529*

53 Physics

Physics

Abbreviations & Symbols

[906]

GABCOM & GABNET: acronyms of compounds and methods in chemistry and physics. Gmelin-Institut. Berlin, Springer-Verlag, 1993. [vi], 380p. ISBN: 354093653x.

About 4,000 acronyms of chemical compounds and 4,200 acronyms of physicochemical or physical methods and notations. *Class No:* 530(003)

[907]

INTERNATIONAL UNION OF PURE AND APPLIED PHYSICS. Commission for Symbols, Units and Nomenclature. **Symbols, units, nomenclature and fundamental constants in physics.** London, The Union, through the Royal Society of London, 1987. 67p. tables. (*Document IUPAP 25.*)

First published 1978 as *Symbols, units and nomenclature in physics.*

As well as thoroughly covering physics, lists embrace mathematical terminology and symbols. 'Strongly recommended for libraries serving physical sciences' (*Science and technology libraries,* V.11(1), Fall 1990, p.740). *Class No:* 530(003)

[908]

POLON, D.D., ** *ed.* **DPMA: Dictionary of physics and mathematical abbreviations, signs and symbols. New York, Odyssey Press, 1965. xvii,333p.

One of a series, each with numerous sequences, A-Z plus definitions. Abbreviations for use in text - Letter symbols - Mathematical signs and symbols - Abbreviations for scientific and learned societies - Abbreviations for government annd military departments, agencies and offices. Generous use of white space. Of value to the specialist in one field who must become familiar with publications in another (*The Recorder,* no. 170, 1 December 1966, p.6). *Class No:* 530(003)

Databases

[909]

INSPEC. Stevenage, Herts., Institution of Electrical Engineers, 1969-. Updated weekly.

INSPEC database provides online access to *Physics abstracts, Electrical and electronic abstracts, Computer and control abstracts* and *Information technology.* About 6,000,000 records. D.T. Hawkins notes both bibliographic (INSPEC, PHYS, SPIN, Atomicindex and Nuclear science) and numeric (Superindex, PHYSCOMP, OECD Nuclear Energy Agency database, and GAPHYOR) databases covering physics (*Database,* v.8(1), February 1985, p.15-16, with a comparison table and references, p.17-18). Available online via DataStar, DIALOG, EINS, FIZ-TECHNIK, OCLC, Ovid, Orbit, STIC and STN International and on CD-ROM. *Class No:* 530(003.4)

[910]

SPIN (Searchable physics information notices). New York, American Institute of Physics.

Coverage of AIP journals, Russian translations and some additional journals. Author-prepared abstracts. About 750,000 records; updated monthly. Available on DIALOG, file 62. *Class No:* 530(003.4)

[911]

World databases in physics and mathematics. Armstrong, C.J., *ed.* London, Bowker-Saur, 1995. [xii], 1085p. £150. (*World database series.*) ISBN: 1857390385.

The series 'aims to become the de facto authority on electronically published databases' (*Introduction*). Lists about 1,200 electronically published databases in 9 sections: 1. Science/Technology - 2. Science/General - 3. Astronomy - 4. Mathematics - 5. Meterology - 6. Nuclear Science - 7. Materials Science - 8. Physics - 9. Domestic Sciences. Entries include a brief description of contents and coverage, online hosts, CD-ROM and internet availability, etc. Database 'families' and subsets identified. Indexes: addresses; database name; subject. Claims to be comprehensive but the coverage of European databases is fuller than that of North American. Clumsy and awkward to use, partly because some substantial entries appear in several sections (*e.g. Science citation index*). INSPEC, on the other hand, does not appear in the Physics section. *Class No:* 530(003.4)

Internet

[912]

PhysLINK: the ultimate physics resource. Skorucak, A., *ed.* URL: http://www.physlink.com

An Internet site, created in 1966, for students, teachers and researchers. Numerous links to academic physics departments and sources of information, including reference, journals, history, news, companies, software and societies. Includes listings of jobs and facilities for interactive communication. Easy navigation; frequently updated. Received the 1997 Award for Education from the Academy of Web Design. *Class No:* 530(003.41)

[913]

PINETPlus College Park, Md., American Institute of Physics. 1999-. URL: www.aip.org/pinet.

A subscription-based web site offering acces to the research library (bibliographic databases, tables of contents, abstracts), online journals, newsroom, communications, resources and conferences. *Class No:* 530(003.41)

Bibliographies

[914]

SHAW, D.F., ** *ed.* **Information sources in physics. London, Bowker Saur, 1994. xxv, 507p. graphics, tables. £40.00. (*Guides to information sources.*) ISBN: 0408014741.

First published 1975; 2nd ed. 1985.

20 contributors; 20 documented chapters. 1. Introduction - 2. The scope and control of physics and its literature - 3. Science libraries, reference material and general treatises - 4. Atomic and molecular physics ... 8. Crystallography ... 12. Geophysics, astrophysics and meteorological physics ... 15. Nuclear and particle physics ... 19. Grey literature (*e.g.* reports) - 20. Patent literature. 3 appendices (A: the most important physics journals according to INSPEC; C: Publishers; abbreviations and addresses). Subject and title index. Editor is Keeper of Scientific Books, Radcliffe Science Library, Oxford University. In this edition, references to digitally-stored information sources have been incorporated into appropriate subjects areas rather than in a separate treatment of online services. *Class No:* 530(01)

Encyclopaedias & Dictionaries

[915]

KNIGHT, D. A Companion to the physical sciences. London, Routledge, 1989. 177p. £7.50. ISBN: 0415009014.

An encyclopedic dictionary (terms, concepts, theories and individuals). Includes some citations to additional in-depth readings. *Class No:* 530(03)

[916]

THEWLIS, J., ** *ed.* **Encyclopaedic dictionary of physics: general, nuclear, solid state, molecular, chemical, metal and vacuum physics, geophysics, biophysics and related subjects. Oxford, Pergamon Press, 1961-64; 1966-75. 9v.,+Supplementary v.1-5. illus., diagrs.

V.1-8: A-Z and index; v.9: *Multilingual glossary* (see entry at 530(038)=00).

A major work, covering not only physics but other sciences that have a physical basis. V.1 has over 100 contributors, longer signed articles carrying bibliographies. 'Alpharay, Measurement techniques for' runs to 5½ columns, is in 3 sections and has 5 references. Historical background figures when considered necessary. The subject index in v.8 (p.1-481) has *c.*45,000 entries; author index, p.485-95; errata, p.497-8. References to articles of 500 words or more are given volume number in bold type. 'The articles are, in general, of graduate or near-graduate level' (*Foreword*). An essay-review in *Chemistry and industry* (3 August 1963, p.1273-5) pointed out errors, misprints and insufficiency of diagrams. Compared with Sir. R. Glazebrook's *Dictionary of applied physics* (1922-23. 5v; reprinted Gloucester, Mass., Smith, 1950 - now of historical value only - Thewlis's set lacked adequate planning; the Glazebrook volumes each dealt with a group of subjects and were self-indexing. *Class No:* 530(03)

Encyclopaedias

[917]

BESANÇON, R.M., *ed*. **The Encyclopedia of physics.** 3rd ed. New York, Van Nostrand Reinhold, 1985. [xix], 1378p. diagrs., graphs, formulas. ISBN: 0442257783.

First published 1966; 2nd ed., 1974 (xv, 1067p.).

More than 300 A-Z entries, by *c*.250 contributors. 'Quantum theory': p.985-1000, with 21 references, 7 cross-references. Detailed index, p.1347-78. A substantial revision, aimed at a wide public: physicists, teachers and librarians, students, engineers and scientists. Handy for basic, up-to-date information. *Class No:* 530(031)

[918]

—**LERNER, R.G.** *and* **TRIGG, G.L.,** *eds*. Encyclopedia of physics. 2nd ed. New York, VCH, 1991. 1408p. illus. $150. ISBN: 0895737523.

First published 1981.

Contains 509 signed articles by specialist contributors, including Nobel prize winners. Bibliographies usually indicate readership level. Numerous illus. Complementary to Besançon, according to the reviewer in 'Reference books bulletin' (*Booklist*, August 1991, p.2171). *Class No:* 530(031)

[919]

Encyclopedia of applied physics. Trigg, G.L. New York, VCH, 1991-. V.1-. $255; £160.

V.1. 'Accelerators linear' to 'Analytic methods'. 1991. 666p, ISBN: 156081521.

V.16: 'Raman spectroscopy to Schottky barriers'. 1996. 600p. ISBN: 1560810750.

A major work, with 20v. planned. Articles are subdivided and frequently include glossary, bibliography and 'Additional' readings. Indexes are projected after every third volume. *Class No:* 530(031)

[920]

Encyclopedia of modern physics. Meyers, R.A.M., *ed*. San Diego, Ca., Academic Press, 1990. 773p. $89.50. ISBN: 0122266927.

34 entries, A-Z, surveying the state-of-the-art, traditional and applied physics (*e.g.* holography, quasi-crystals and superconductivity). Each entry has cross-references; brief glossary; index. 'Suitable for advanced undergraduate and graduate students as well as professional scientists and engineers' (*New technical books*, Jan/Feb, 1991, p.1045). *Class No:* 530(031)

[921]

Encyclopedia of physical science and technology. Meyers, R.A.M., *ed*. 2nd ed. San Diego, Ca., Academic Press, 1992. 18v. illus., diagrs., graphs, tables. £1500. ISBN: 0122269306.

First published 1987.

Over 750 contributors. 705 documented articles covering aeronautics; space technology; earth sciences; physical sciences; computer science and tellecommunication; electronics; mathematics; nuclear technology. Available on CD-ROM as *Academic Press encyclopedia of physical science and technology* (Knight-Ridder OnDisc; $3000). *Class No:* 530(031)

[922]

McGraw-Hill encyclopedia of physics. Parker, S.P., *ed*. 2nd ed. New York, etc., McGraw-Hill, 1992. [viii], 1624p. illus., graphs, charts. £82.95 ISBN: 0070514003.

First published 1984.

Selects 828 signed articles from the parent *McGraw-Hill encyclopedia of science and technology* (7th ed., 1992, 15v.) ranging from 'A15 phases' to 'Zeeman effect'. Extensive index, p.1386-1624. Aimed at high schools and colleges. *Class No:* 530(031)

[923]

Macmillan encyclopedia of physics. Rigden, J.S., *ed*. New York, Macmillan, 1996. 4v. $400. ISBN: 0028973593.

Broad-based coverage of concepts and principles, laws and theories, phenomena and effects. No living physicts are included. Suitable for public and school libraries; for non-specialists. *Class No:* 530(031)

[924]

Magill's survey of science: physical science series. Magill, F.N., *ed*. Pasadena, Ca., Salem Press, 1992. 6v. 2796p. $475. ISBN: 0893566187.

380 entries on classical mechanics, unified field theory, molecular structure, chaos, black holes, expert systems, methodologies of computing and mathematics. Articles are 7 to 8p. and most are written by US academics. Cross-references. Volume indexes; glossary (*c*.500 terms), V. 6. 'Readable ... should be eminently useful' (*Choice*, July/August 1992, p.1659). Supplement V.7 was published in 1998 ($90; ISBN: 0893569356). The series is also available on CD-ROM ($750; ISBN 0893562718). *Class No:* 530(031)

Handbooks & Manuals

[925]

American Institute of Physics handbook. Gray, D.E., *ed*. 3rd ed. New York, the Institute, 1972. [2342]p. illus., tables. ISBN: 007001485x.

First published 1957.

About 120 contributors. 9 sections, each with its own editor: 1. Mathematics (with bibliography of 71 annotated entries) - 2. Mechanics - 3. Acoustics - 4. Heat - 5. Electricity and magnetism - 6. Optics - 7. Atomic and nuclear physics - 8. Nuclear physics - 9. Solid-state physics. Many tables (*e.g.* Properties of nuclides, p.8-6 to 8-91). An authoritative compendium. While the *CRC handbook of chemistry and physics* is to be preferred as a first choice, the AIP *Handbook* has a stronger focus on theoretical summaries and references (*Choice*, March 1973, p.55). 'One of the most respected handbooks in all science' (*Information sources in science and technology*, 3rd ed., 1998, p.155). *Class No:* 530(035)

[926]

FLÜGGE, S., *ed*. **Handbuch der Physik.** [Encyclopedia of physics.] [2.Aufl.]. Berlin, Springer, 1955-.

First published 1926-29 (24v. and index).

Over 70v. have so far been published of the 2nd ed. 1-2: *Mathematical methods*. 1955-56. 3: *Principles of classical mechanics and field theory*. 1956-65. 3 pts. 4: *Principles of thermodynamics and relativity*. 1962. 5: *Principles of quantum theory*. 1958-. pt.1-. 6: *Elasticity and plasticity*. 1958. 6a: *Mechanics of solids*. 1972-74. 4v. 7: *Crystal physics*. 1955-58. 2 pts. 8: *Fluid dynamics*. 1960-63. 2 pts. 9: *Fluid mechanics*. 3v. 1960. 10: *Structure of fluids*. 1960. 11: *Acoustics*. 1961-62. 2 pts. 12: *Thermodynamics of gases*. 1958. 13: *Thermodynamics of liquids and solids*. 1962. 14-15: *Low-temperature physics*. 1956. 16: *Electric fields and waves*. 1958. 17: *Dielectrics*. 1956. 18: *Magnetism. Ferromagnetics*. 1966-68. 2 pts. 19-20: *Electrical conductivity*. 1956-57. 21-22: *Electron emission. Gas discharges*. 1956. 23: *Electrical instruments*. 1967. 25/1: *Crystal optics. Diffraction*. 1961-. pt. 1-. 25/2,26: *Light and matter*. 1958-. 27-28: *Spectroscopy*. 1957-64. 29: *Optical instruments*. 1967. 30: *X-rays*. 1957. 31: *Corpuscles and radiation in matter*. pt.1. 1982. 32: *Structural research*. 1957

A systematic treatise, the only major current work covering the whole field of physics. Contributions may be in English, German or French, with full references. Thus V.27: *Spectroscopy*, pt.1 (1964. vi, 507p.) has 2 contributions in English, on Line width and Atomic spectra, and one, on Electronic nuclear spectroscopy, in French, with 133 references. The 'numerous beautifully drawn figures' are praised in *Nature* (v.204, 10th October 1964, p.114). Subject indexes act as German and English glossaries. An authorative series. *Class No:* 530(035)

[927]

LANDAU, L.D. *and* **LIFSHITZ, E.M. Course of theoretical physics.** Oxford, Pergamon Press, 1959-73. 9v. in 10.

Translation of *Teoreticheskaya fizika* (Moscow, Nauka, 1954-67).

1. *Mechanics* 2. *Classical theory of fields*. 3. *Quantum mechanics*. 4. (1-2). *Relativistic quantum theory*. 5. *Statistical physics*. pt.1. 6. *Fluid mechanics*. 7. *Theory of elasticity*. 8. *Electrodynamics of continuous media*. 9. *Statistical physics*. pt.2. 'A magnificent work, written with great clarity and emphasizing the unity of the physical ideas that interweave the whole set. The course can be started at the advanced undergraduate level' (Shaw, D.F. *Information sources in physics* (2nd ed., 1985. p.343)). *Class No:* 530(035)

[928]

A Physicist's desk reference. Anderson, H.L., *ed*. New York, American Institute of Physics, 1989. 356p. $60. ISBN: 0883186202.

Updated edition of *Physics vade mecum*. (1981).

22 fields of physics (*e.g.* acoustics, cryogenics, crystallography, elementary particles, fluid dynamics, spectroscopy and structure, nuclear physics, optics, plasma physics, surface physics). Chapters on fundamental constants, conversion factors, basic mathematical and physics formulas. Each chapter by an expert. 'An indispensable handbook for all libraries serving readers who need physics information' (*Science and technology libraries*, v.11(1), Fall 1990, p.139). *Class No:* 530(035)

[929]

—**COHEN, E.R.** The Physics quick reference guide. New York, American Institute of Physics, 1996. x, 209p. illus., tables. $30. ISBN: 1563961431.

Material taken from *A Physicist's desk reference*, updated and suppplemented. Contents: 1. Physical quantities, symbols, and units - 2. The international system of units - 3. Recommended symbols for physical quantities - 4. Precise physical constants - 5. Physics formulary - 6. Engineering physics - 7. Properties of matter - 8. Mathematical formulas - 9. Probability and statistics. *Class No:* 530(035)

Dictionaries

Polyglot

[930]
RYDNIK, V.J., *and others, eds*. **Dictionary of physics in four languages:** Russian, English, German and French. Amsterdam, Elsevier, 1989. 392p. £106.50. ISBN: 0444704906.

About 3,000 English-base terms, with equivalents and indexes in the other languages. *Class No:* 530(038)=00

[931]
SUBE, R. *and* EISENREICH, G. **Wörterbuch Physik:** Englisch/Deutsch/Französisch/Russisch. Berlin, VEB Verlag-Technik, 1973. 3v. (2895p.).

About 75,000 English-base entry-words, with German, French and Russian equivalents. V.3 is the German, French and Russian index volume. Scope includes astrophysics, biophysics, geophysics and mathematical affinities of physics. *Class No:* 530(038)=00

[932]
—THEWLIS, J. Multilingual glossary: English, French, German, Spanish, Russian, Japanese. Oxford, Pergamon Press, 1964. xvi, 988p.

Lists 13,675 numbered terms in English, mostly drawn from titles of articles in the *Encyclopaedic dictionary of physics* (*qv*). The English terms carry number references to French, German, Spanish, Russian and Japanese equivalents, separately listed A-Z, with back-references to the numbered English base-terms. A cumbersome departure from the normal layout of polyglot dictionaries. *Class No:* 530(038)=00

English

[933]
DAINTITH, J. **The Pan dictionary of physics.** London, Pan, 1990. 240p. illus. £6.99. ISBN: 0330314521.

Defines 3000 commonly used physics terms.
Class No: 530(038)=20

[934]
Dictionary of physics. Gray, H.J. *and* Isaacs, A., *eds*. 3rd ed. Harlow, Essex, Longman, 1991. [iv], 635p. diagrs., graphs, tables. £29.50. ISBN: 0582037972.

First published 1958; 2nd ed. 1975.

About 6,000 terms, some defined at length (*e.g.* 'diffraction of light': 5 columns; 7 diagrs.). 14 tables (14: Nobel prizewinners in physics). A standard dictionary. *Class No:* 530(038)=20

[935]
HARRISON, P. **The Cassell dictionary of physics.** London, Cassell, 1998. vii, 216p. diagrs., graphs, tables. ISBN: 0304350346.

About 2,000 terms, briefly defined. Appendices include SI units, electromagnetic spectrum, etc. A basic dictionary.
Class No: 530(038)=20

[936]
ILLINGWORTH, V., *ed*. **The Penguin dictionary of physics.** Harmondsworth, Penguin, 1991. 544p. illus., diagrs., graphs, tables. £5.99. ISBN: 0140512365.

An abridgement of the *Dictionary of physics* (Harlow, Essex, Longman, 1991).

About 4,500 entries, some defined at length (*e.g.* 'mass': 1 col.). 11 tables appended (7: 'Long-lived elementary particles').
Class No: 530(038)=20

[937]
LORD, M.P. **Macmillan dictionary of physics.** London, Macmillan, 1986. xx, 330,[1]p. diagrs., tables. £29.50; £12.95. ISBN: 0333390660, HB; 0333423771, PB.

Enlarged and updated version of the physics content of *Dictionary of physical science*, edited by J. Daintith (Pan Books, 1978).

Over 4,000 entries, averaging *c.*50 words but occasionally of column length (*e.g.* 'Laser'). 7 tables precede (*e.g.* 'Symbols and SI units for some physical quantities'). 'Further reading suggestions' (undergraduate level: 2 items; pre-postgraduate level: 2). Adequate cross-references; *c.*200 small diagrams. 'Will be of use to Physics students at first year undergraduate and lower levels, and also to amateur enthusiasts and lay persons' (*Preface*).
Class No: 530(038)=20

[938]
McGraw-Hill dictionary of physics. Parker, S.P., *ed*. 2nd ed. New York, etc., McGraw-Hill, 1997. xiii, 498. $16.95; £12.99. ISBN: 0070524297.

First published 1985.

Lists about 9,000 physics terms from *McGraw-Hill dictionary of scientific and technical terms* (5th ed., 1994). Includes acronyms and abbreviations; appendix gives tables of data and information (*e.g.* 'Primary thermometry methods'). For students and public libraries.
Class No: 530(038)=20

[939]
SCHUBERT, J. **Dictionary of effects and phenomena in physics:** descriptions, applications, tables. Weinheim, New York, VCH, 1987. 140p. $25. ISBN: 0895734877.

Concise descriptions of *c.*400 physical effects, with references. Eponymous terms carry biographical notes on originators. Appendices comprise tables (*e.g.* Cluster courses, effects). More detailed in its field than *Dictionary of named effects and laws in chemistry, physics and mathematics* by D.W.G. Ballentyne and D.R. Lovett (4th ed. 1980). 'Recommended for all physics collections' (*Science and technology libraries*, v.10(3), Spring 1990, p.113).
Class No: 530(038)=20

German

[940]
HYMAN, C.J. *and* IDLIN, R., *eds*. **Dictionary of physics and allied sciences.** [Wörterbuch für Physik und verwandter Wissenschafterv.] New York, Ungar, 1978. 2v.

1. *German-English*, by C.J. Hyman. 696p. 2. *English-German*, by R. Idlin. 663p. First published 1958/62.

V.1 has *c.*30,000 entries, employing some 70 categories. Translations are mostly equivalents. V.2, 'by no means an inversion of the first volume' (*Preface*), has *c.*25,000 entries, with sample phrases and sentences. German genders are shown. The 1978 ed. of the 2 volumes simply adds a supplement at the end of each dictionary.
Class No: 530(038)=30

[941]
—DE VRIES, L. *and* CLASON, W.E., *comps*. Dictionary of pure and applied physics. Amsterdam etc., Elsevier, 1963-64. 2v.

V.1: *German-English*. 1963. viii, 367p. V.2: *English-German*. 1964. viii, 341p.

Includes *c.*31,000 entries per volume, including terms from related fields as well as words in common use. Normally gives equivalents only. 'De Vries's habit of omitting any distinction of meanings, although mitigated by the restriction to physics, is still in evidence' (*Nature*, v.207, 28 August 1965, p.905). *Class No:* 530(038)=30

French

[942]
MATHIEU, J.-P., *and others*. **Dictionnaire de physique.** Paris, Masson/Eyrolles, 1983. 568p. diagrs., graphs. F250. ISBN: 2225744483.

Several thousand entries for terms in fundamental physics, omitting technical aspects, history and biography. Clearly written and well illustrated. Earmarked in *Bulletin critique du livre français* (no.460, April 1984, item 126179) as suitable for specialists and those on graduate and post-graduate courses. *Class No:* 530(038)=40

Russian

[943]
TOLSTOI, D.M., *ed*. **Anglo-russkiĭ fizicheskiĭ slovar'.** Moscow, Izdat. 'Sovetskaya Entsiklopediya', 1968; Oxford, Pergamon, 1978. 848p.

About 60,000 English entry-words, with Russian equivalents; separate lines for sub-entries. The Dictionary needs using with care; 'principle of entropy increase' appears under 'Principle' and not under 'Entropy'. Abbreviations, p.832-48. Bibliography of sources, p.9-10. *Class No:* 530(038)=82

[944]
—ERNIN, L., *and others*. Russian-English physics dictionary. New York, etc., Wiley, 1963. xxx, 554p.

Lists 25,000 entries, including terms in allied fields and in common usage, abbreviations and also proper names. Word-for-word entries. Where many compounds are massed under an entry-word, the entry is sectionized. Layout is clear, with bold type for sub-entries, as in Callaham's *Russian-English chemical and polytechnical dictionary* (*qv*). The helpful reference section (p.xviii-xxix) contains notes on the alphabet, common Russian technical word endings, verb formation, and the like. Sources (dictionaries, encyclopaedias, etc.) p.ix-xii. Ernin's collaborators were the Consultant Bureau of Physicists - Translators. Well produced; 'edge' index. *Class No:* 530(038)=82

Arabic

[945]
LEAGUE OF ARAB STATES. Education, Culture and Sciences Organization. Permanent Bureau of Arabisation. **Lexicon of physics.** [Lexique de physique. English-French-Arabic.] Rabat, Morocco, Bureau Permanent de Coordination de l'Arabisation, 1971. 190, xlvii p.

2,062 numbered English base-terms, with French and Arabic equivalents or explanations. French-terms index to numbered English entries. *Class No:* 530(038)=927

Reviews & Abstracts

[946]

Contemporary physics: a review of physics and its applications. London, New York etc., Taylor & Francis, 1960-. v.1-. 6 pa. ISSN: 00107514.

Volumes include lengthy review articles, with extensive bibliographies, as well as book reviews, shorter notices and list of books received. *Class No:* 530(048)

[947]

Current contents: Physical, chemical and earth sciences. Philadelphia, Pa., Institute for Scientific Information, 1979-. v.19-. Weekly. ISSN: 01632574.

Previously as *Current contents: Physical and chemical sciences* (formed by the merger of *Current contents: Physical sciences* and *Current contents: Chemical sciences*), 1961-78.

Reproduces contents pages of more than 900 journals in the fields concerned. Each weekly number covers *c*.100 journal issues. Online in CURRENT CONTENTS SEARCH, CD-ROM and available on diskette. *Class No:* 530(048)

[948]

Current papers in physics. London, INSPEC (The Institution of Electrical Engineers), 1966-. Bi-weekly. £370. ISSN: 00113786.

About 75,000 references pa., using the INSPEC classification scheme. A current awareness service, without indexes, that aims 'to provide a convenient means for engineers and scientists to keep abreast of newly published information'. Companion to *Current papers in electrical and electronic engineering* (CPE) and *Current papers in computers and control* (CPC) *(qqv)*. *Class No:* 530(048)

[949]

Current physics index. New York, American Institute of Physics, 1975-. Quarterly. $1410. ISSN: 00989819.

Replaces *Current physics advance abstracts* and *Current physics titles* (1972-).

About 9,000 abstracts per quarter of articles in the primary journals published by the American Institute of Physics. Uses the INSPEC classification scheme (outlined in the *Physics Abstracts* entry). Profuse cross-references. Author index per issue; annual subject and author indexes. Available online through SPIN and through PINET Plus, the Physics Information Network. *Class No:* 530(048)

[950]

Physics abstracts. Science abstracts. Section A. Stevenage, Herts, Institution of Electrical Engineers, 1898-. Twice monthly. £2430. ISSN: 00368091.

About 180,000 abstracts and references pa. Main sections (Closely subdivided): 0000 General - 1000 The physics of elementary particles and fields - 2000 Nuclear physics - 3000 Atomic and molecular physics - 4000 Classical areas of phenomenology (*e.g.* electricity and magnetism) - 5000 Fluids, plasmas and electric discharges - 6000 Condensed matter: structure, thermal and mechanical properties - 7000 Condensed matter: electronic structure, electrical, magnetic, and optical properties - 8000 Cross-disciplinary physics and related areas of science and technology - 9000 Geophysics, astronomy and astrophysics. Author index: subsidiary indexes: bibliography; book; conference; corporate author. Subject indexes, 2pa. List of journals scanned in half-yearly author index. Four or five-yearly cumulative indexes. The major English-language physics abstracting service. Available online as part of the INSPEC database; CD-ROM. *Class No:* 530(048)

[951]

Physics briefs. [Physikalische Berichte. Edited by Deutscher Physikalische Gesellschaft & Fachinformationszentrum Energie, Physik, Mathematik, in cooperation with American Institute of Physics.] New York, American Institute of Physics, 1979-94. Bimonthly. ISSN: 01707434.

Succeeds *Physikalische Berichte* (v.1-57. 1920-78. Monthly), originally (1845-1918) as *Fortschritte der Physik*.

Originally about 125,000 abstracts and references pa, covering all fields of physics and related topics. Ceased publication December 1994, but available online as part of the INSPEC database. *Class No:* 530(048)

[952]

Referativnyǐ zhurnal. Fizika. Akademiya Nauk SSSR, Institut Nauchnoi Informatsii. Moscow, VINITI, 1954-. Monthly. ISSN: 00342343.

About 80,000 abstracts pa. in 11 sections (General aspects of Physics ... Acoustics). Covers over 20,000 journals in various languages, as well as theses, reports, patents and some conferences. Author index per issue; annual cumulated author and classified subject index. Parts are available separately. *Class No:* 530(048)

[953]

Reviews of modern physics. New York, American Physical Society, 1929-. v.1-. 4 pa. $405. ISSN: 00346861.

Includes scholarly reviews and turtorials and a series of shorter papers which present current research interest to a broad audience of physicists. Also available on CD-ROM ($45 per disk with print subscription). *Class No:* 530(048)

Periodicals

[954]

PRIMACK, A.L. Journal literature of the physical sciences: a manual. Metuchen, N.J., Scarecrow Press, 1992. x, 209p. facsims. $29.50; £25. ISBN: 0810825929.

7 chapters (2. Searching the journal literature ... 3. Leading indexing and abtracting services ... 5. Writing scientific journal articles ... 7. Directory of core journals). Two appendices (units; standards). Index. *Class No:* 530(051)

Progress Reports

[955]

Reports on progress in physics. Bristol, Institute of Physics, 1934-. Monthly. £876 pa. ISSN: 00344885.

Covers all branches of physics and includes review articles that adopt a broad, long term perspective. V.62 (1999) has papers on quantum computing, neural networks, Jovian aurorae, and the ferromagnetic resonance of ultra thin metallic layers. Available on the World Wide Web (URL: http://www.iop.org/Journals/rp). *Class No:* 530(055)

Quotations

[956]

GAITHER, C.C. *and* **CAVAZOS-GAITHER, A. Physically speaking:** a dictionary of quotations on physics and astronomy. Bristol, Institute of Physics, 1997. xii, 492p. illus. £19.95. ISBN: 0750304707.

A wide-ranging and often amusing collection of quotations from scientists and lay people. Arranged by subject; indexes. *Class No:* 530(082.2)

Anthologies

[957]

MAGIE, W.F. A Source book in physics. Cambridge, Mass., Harvard Univ. Press. xiv, 620p. (*Source books in the history of science*.)

More than 100 examples from the writings of physicists in the period 1600-1900. Sections: Mechanics - Properties of matter - Sound - Heat - Light - Magnetism and electricity. Biographical notes precede excerpts. *Class No:* 530(082.21)

[958]

The New physics. Davies, P., *ed.* Cambridge Univ. Press, 1989. ix,516p. illus., col. pl., diagrs., graphs. £16.94 (Pbk). ISBN: 0521304202; 0521438314, Pbk.

19 international contributors. 18 chapters survey recent developments in physics. Chaper 1 provides a synthesis of these; other chapters cover general relativity, low temperature physics, astrophysics, chaos, quantum optics, etc. Detailed, analytical index, p.505-16. *Class No:* 530(082.21)

[959]

SAMBURSKY, S., *ed.* **Physical thought from the Presocratic to the quantum theory:** an anthology. London, Hutchinson, 1974. xv, 584p. ISBN: 0091028507.

6 sections: 1. Antiquity - 2. The Middle Ages - 3. Copernicus to Pascal - 4. The Royal Society to Laplace - 5. Dalton to Mach - 6. Planck to Pauli. Each section comprises introduction and extracts. List of sources (by sections). Index of authors (bio-bibliographies). Analytical subject index; general index. Aims to depict the development of physical thought 'as a chapter in the history of ideas' (*General introduction*). *Class No:* 530(082.21)

Tables & Data Books

[960]

CRC handbook of chemistry and physics. Lide, D.R., *ed.* 79th ed. Boca Raton, Fl., CRC Press, 1998. v.p. diagrs., charts, tables, chemical structures. $99.95, £85. ISBN: 0849304792.

First published 1914; updated annually.

The 79th ed. includes numerous new or revised tables.In addition to physics and chemistry also covers conversion factors, laboratory safety, geology, astronomy and pure mathematics. An invaluable mine of information which 'remains the first choice of sources for scientific data—as it has for most of this century' ('Reference books bulletin', *Booklist*, December 1, 1998, p.689). Available on CD-ROM as *Handbook of chemistry and physics CRCnetBASE 1999* (1999; ISBN: 0849397200). *Class No:* 530(083)

[961]
FISCHBECK, H.J. *and* **FISCHBECK, K.H. Formulas, facts and constants** for students and professionals in engineering, chemistry and physics. 2nd rev. and enlgd. ed. Berlin, etc., Springer, 1987. x, 260p. diagrs., graphs, tables. ISBN: 3540176106.
First published 1972.
5 sections: 1. Basic mathematical facts and figures - 2. Units, conversion factors and constants - 3. Spectroscopy and atomic structures - 4. Basic wave mathematics - 5. Facts, figures and data. Useful in the laboratory. Detailed, analytical subject index.
Class No: 530(083)

[962]
Handbook of physical quantities. Griogoriev, I.S. *and* Meilikhov, E.Z., *eds.* Boca Raton, Fl., CRC Press, 1997. [xix], 1548p. graphs, tables. $99. ISBN: 0849328616.
Translated from Russian by A.A. Radzig.
53 Russian contributors. 45 chapters, each with a short introduction, then tables, figures, references (*e.g.* ch.3 'The Mechanical properties of materials' has 62 tables, 28 figures, 42 references). Detailed subject index. 'Highly recommended for any science collection' (*American reference books annual* 1998, p.711). *Class No:* 530(083)

[963]
JAMES, A.M. *and* **LORD, M.P. Macmillan's chemical and physical data.** London, Macmillan, 1992. 448p. tables. £35. ISBN: 0333511670.
15 subject areas. About 430 tables, most with references for further information and/or additional data. *Class No:* 530(083)

[964]
JERRARD, H.G. *and* **McNEILL, D.B. Dictionary of scientific units,** including dimensionless numbers and scales. 6th ed. London, Chapman & Hall, 1992. 255p. tables £15.95. ISBN: 0412467208.
First published 1963.
Contains *c.*950 units, supported by *c.*650 references. The dictionary, Abampere ... Zhubov scale, p.9-190. 'Beaufort scale': nearly 1p. 5 appendices (*e.g.* 1. Fundamental committees and conferences). References, p.221-39. Detailed, analytical index, p.241-55.
Class No: 530(083)

[965]
NORDLING, C. *and* **ÖSTERMAN, J. Physics handbook for science and engineering.** 5th ed. Lund, Studentlitteratur; Bromley, Kent, Chartwell-Brett, 1996. 402p. diagrs., graphs, tables, forumlas. ISBN: 0862384451.
Four parts: CU. Constants and units - T. Physical tables - F. Physical formulae and diagrams - M. Mathematical formulae. Addenda. Detailed, analytical index. 'It has been used [in Sweden] as a standard source of numerical data and formulae for exercise, problems and ... as a companion in problem solving by both students and teachers' (*Foreword*). *Class No:* 530(083)

[966]
Tables of physical and chemical constants. Kaye, G.W.C. *and* Laby, T.H., *comps.* 16th ed. London & New York, Longman, 1995. [xi], 611p. graphs, tables. ISBN: 0582226295.
75 contributors. 8 main sections: 1. Units and fundamental constants - 2. General physics - 3. Chemistry - 4. Atomic and nuclear physics - 5. Miscellaneous engineering data - 6. Statistical methods for the treatment of experimental data - 7. Laboratory safety - 8. Introduction to quality assurance of measurements. Analytical index. Subsection references. All tabulated values appear in SI units. Originally compiled by G.W.C. Kaye and T.H. Laby (cover title is 'Kaye and Laby'), but this edition prepared by an editorial committee. Essential for any reference library. *Class No:* 530(083)

[967]
TUMA, J.J. Handbook of physical calculations. 2nd ed. New York, McGraw-Hill, 1983. 512p. illus., diagrs., tables, changes. ISBN: 0070654395.
First published 1976 (x,370p).
10 sections of definitions, formulas, charts and tables of elementary and intermediate technological physics, with revised data in appendices. 'It serves as a referencee source for practicing engineers, architects and technologists' (*New technical books*, October 1983, item 915). *Class No:* 530(083)

Audio-Visual Materials

[968]
Video encyclopedia of physics demonstrations. Seattle, Wa., University of Washington, 1994. 25 CD-ROMs. £2226.
About 600 interactive physics demonstrations linked to popular physics textbooks. *Class No:* 530(086)

Histories

[969]
CAJORI, F. A History of physics in its elementary branches, including the evolution of physical laboratories. Rev. and enl. ed. New York, Macmillan Co., 1929. xiii 424p. illus.
First published 1899.
Arranged chronologically under periods, each subdivided by the main divisions of physics. Concentrates mainly on period from 17th to 20th century (up to 1925). Includes a bibliography. Intended mainly for students and teachers of physics. *Class No:* 530(091)

[970]
JUNGNICKEL, C. *and* **McCORMMACH, R. Intellectual mastery of nature:** theoretical physics from Ohm to Einstein. Chicago, Univ. of Chicago Press, 1986. 2 v. (xxviii, 350p.; xx, 435p.).
V.1. *The Torch of mathematics 1800-1870.* ISBN: 0226415813.
V.2. *The Now mighty theoretical physics 1870-1925.* ISBN: 0226415848.
A scholarly treatment concentrating on German universities and research laboratories. Extensive notes and bibliography. Analytical index. *Class No:* 530(091)

[971]
PEDERSEN, O. *and* **PIHL, M. Early physics and astronomy:** a historical introduction. New York, American Elsevier, 1974. 413p.
Revised and updated version of the original Danish.
Stresses major aspects of ancient and medieval science history. Numerous sub-sections. Praised in *Nature* (v.252, 8 November 1974, p.130) for its clear and scholarly style; an excellent translation. 'Will generally appeal to science undergraduates reading the books as a part of an introductory survey course in the history of the exact sciences'. *Class No:* 530(091)

[972]
Physicists look back: studies in the history of physics. Roche, L.J., *ed.* Bristol, Hilger, 1990. xii, 393p. illus. $90. ISBN: 0852740018.
20 chapters in 3 parts: 1. Method in the history of physics - 2. Applying the history of physics - 3. Physicists look back. Chapter 1, by D.F. Shaw, author of *Information sources in physics*, considers the resources of research libraries worldwide. *Class No:* 530(091)

Bibliographies

[973]
BRUSH, S.G. *and* **BELLONI, E. The History of modern physics:** an international bibliography. New York, Garland, 1983. xviii, [1], 334p. (*Bibliographies of the history of science and technology, 4. Garland reference library of the humanities, 420.*) ISBN: 0824091175.
About 2,300 entries. Section A covers general and miscellaneous works on the history of modern physics. Section M, research on the history and its use in education, etc., Name index; partly analytical subject index; institutional index. 'Modern physics' is defined here as physics since the discovery of X-rays in 1895. Intended as a companion to both the *ISIS cumulative bibliography* (1913-65) and to Heilbron and Wheaton (*qv.*). *Class No:* 530(091)(01)

[974]
—Resources for the history of physics. Brush, S.G., *ed.* Hanover, N.H., The University Press of New England, 1972. 202p.
In 2 sections, - a guide to books and audio visual material; and a guide to original texts of importance and their translations into other languages. Intended primarily for teachers of physics.
Class No: 530(091)(01)

[975]
HEILBRON, J.L. *and* **WHEATON, B.R. Literature on the history of physics in the twentieth century.** Berkeley, Calif., Office for History of Science and Technology, Univ. of California, 1981. ix, 485p. $20. (*Berkeley Papers on history of science, v.5.*) ISBN: 0918102057.
Contents: General - Biography - Institutions - Mechanics - Electricity and magnetism - Relativity - Radiation - Atomic physics - Nuclear physics - Particles and beams - Quantum physics - Solid states - Geo-, astro-, and biophysics - Physical chemistry - Techniques and apparatus - Physics and society - Philosophy of physics. Useful abbreviations for major sources. Index. For university librarians, doctoral candidates and readers with a serious interest in this subject.
Class No: 530(091)(01)

[976]
HOME, R.W. The History of classical physics: a selected, annotated bibliography. New York & London, Garland, 1984. xix, 324p. (*Bibliographies of the history of science and technology, 8.*)
1,210 briefly annotated entries. 7 chapters: 1. General bibliographical works, biographical dictionaries - 2. Biographies of individual scientists - 3. Collected works, correspondence and bibliographies of individual scientists - 4. General histories - 5. Eighteenth-century physics - 6. Physics in transition, 1790-1820-. 7. Nineteenth-century physics. Non-analytical index, p.293-324.
Class No: 530(091)(01)

Anthologies
[977]

WEAVER, J.H. The World of physics: a small library of the literature of physics from antiquity to the present. New York, Simon & Schuster, 1987. 3v. $30 each.

V.1. *The Aristotelian cosmos and the Newtonian system.* 889p. ISBN: 0671499262.

V.2. *The Einstein universe and the Bohr atom.* 941p. ISBN: 0671499309.

V.3. *The evolutionary cosmos and the limits of science.* 1118p. ISBN: 0671499319.

A collection for the general reader of the major writings in physics. Explanatory introductions help to define the discipline and trace its history. Occasionally heavy going for non-mathematicians, but 'a greater understanding of current physics is to be gained here than could be obtained from works of lesser scope ... a standard' (*Choice,* January 1988, p.793). *Class No:* 530(091)(082.21)

Biographies
[978]

The Biographical dictionary of scientists: physicists. Abbott, D., *ed.* London, Blond Educational, 1984. [vii], 212p. $18.95. ISBN: 0584700032.

Lists *c.*200 biographies of varying length (*e.g.* 'Maxwell, James Clark': 6 columns; 'Galileo': 3½ columns). Glossary, p.179-193. Analytical index (subjects only), p.195-212. *Class No:* 530(092)

[979]

GAMOW, G. The Great physicists, from Galileo to Einstein. New York, Dekker, 1988. 338p. illus., diagrs. $7.95. ISBN: 0486257673.

A reprint of the 1961 ed.

Each chapter consists of a biography of a seminal figure in physics history. Source index. Primary aim: 'to inspire young readers to study physics' (*Introduction*). *Class No:* 530(092)

[980]

HERMANN, A. Lexikon Geschichte der Physik, A-Z: Biographien, Sachwörter, Originalschriften und Sekundärliteratur. Cologne, Deubner, 1972. [vi], 423p. illus., diagrs., facsims.

Signed articles. Particularly valuable for biographical entries. 'Leibniz': 7½ columns (1 column of bibliography; works by; material on); 'Newton': 10 columns (3½ columns of bibliography; works by; material on, *ie*, commentaries, biographies, periodical articles, bibliographies). 'Relativitätstheorie': nearly 8 columns (2/3 column of bibliographic sources, references, bibliographies). *Class No:* 530(092)

[981]

The Nobel prize winners: physics. Magill, F.N., *ed.* Pasadena, Ca., Salem Press, 1989. 3v., 1346p. ports. $210. ISBN: 0893565571.

Winners are arranged chronologically, with a 6-10p. article for each. Includes: summaries of presentation and acceptance speeches, account of scientific reputation, personal and scientific biography, 'incomplete' (*Choice,* February 1990, p.934-5) list of publications. For undergraduates. *Class No:* 530(092)

Bibliographies
[982]

CROMER, D.E. 'Biographies of physicists': an annotated bibliography. In *Science and technology libraries,* V.11(4), Winter 1991, p.75-98. ISSN: 0194262x.

16 physicists, mostly twentieth-century; excludes Einstein. *Class No:* 530(092)(01)

Women
[983]

Notable women in the physical sciences: a biographical dictionary. Shearer, B.F. *and* Shearer, B., *eds.* Westport, Ct., Greenwood, 1997. 496p. illus. $49.95. ISBN: 0313293031.

Readable essays (*c.*1,000-1,500 words), some illus., on women who worked in the physical sciences (physics; astronomy; chemistry). Covers childhood, education, family life, obstacles overcome and achievements. Appendixes list specialties and prize winners. *Class No:* 530(092)-0055.2

20th Century
[984]

GINGERICH, O. The Physical sciences in the twentieth century. New York, Scribner, 1989. 306p. illus. $75. (*Album of science.*) ISBN: 0684154978.

Covers physics, chemistry, astronomy, geology and computers. Includes brief outline of major discoveries, principles and participants within each discipline and numerous captioned illustrations, about 400 in all. Bibliography of science histories; Nobel prize winners in

....(contd.)

physics and chemistry to 1988. A 'well-conceived and handsomly-executed volume'. (*Choice,* January, 1990, p.826). *Class No:* 530"19"

[985]

Twentieth century physics. Brown, L.M., *and others, eds.* Bristol, Institute of Physics; New York, American Institute of Physics, 1995. 3v. (2059p.) illus., graphs. £275; $375 ISBN: 0750303107.

A survey of the ideas and developments in physics over the last century, written for the interested student and lay-person. 28 contributors; 27 well-documented chapters (*e.g.* 'History of relativity' includes 368 references and notes). Vol. 1 considers developments in physics over the century as a whole; vols. 2 and 3 cover more recent, specialized topics (*e.g.* nuclear dynamics, plasma physics, etc.). Subject and name indexes. An admirable and serious attempt to popularize physics and make it more accessible to non-physicists. *Class No:* 530"19"

Writing & Lecturing
[986]

AMERICAN INSTITUTE OF PHYSICS. AIP Style manual. 4th ed. New York, American Institute of Physics, 1990. 64p. illus.

3rd ed., 1978, as *Style manual for guidance in the preparation of papers for journals published by the American Institute of Physics.*

Guide to authors in physics by the AIP Publication Board. *Class No:* 530:001.81

[987]

NOBEL FOUNDATION. Nobel lectures including speeches and laureates' biographies. Physics. Amsterdam, etc., Elsevier, for the Nobel Foundation, 1942-64. 3v. illus., diagrs., tables.

1. *1901-21.* 1942. xii, 500p. 2. *1922-41.* xii, 458p. 3. *1942-62.* 1964. xiii, 621p.

The Nobel lectures are followed by brief biographies (*e.g.* v.1, p.417-90: Einstein lecture; p.491-2: biography). Each volume has name and subject indexes, plus index of biographies. *Class No:* 530:001.81

Thesauri
[988]

Thesaurus 1999. London, Institution of Electrical Engineers, 1999. 752, 95p. ISBN: 085296966x.

Formerly published as INSPEC Thesuarus; 1st ed. 1973.

The thesaurus remains the subject key to the INSPEC database. Contains about 16,000 terms, of which 8,300 are preferred and 7,700 lead-ins. In two sections: alphabetical display; hierarchical display. *Class No:* 530:025.43

Classification Systems
[989]

Classification 1995: a classification scheme for the INSPEC database. London, Institution of Electrical Engineers, 1995. ix, 136p. + index, 36p. ISBN: 0852969651.

A new version of the scheme designed for use with the INSPEC 2 version of the database. Includes classification codes (in order, A ... to D ...) and textual headings. Invaluable for a careful, structured search of the database or the printed indexes. *Class No:* 530:025.44

Conferences
[990]

Conferences in energy, physics and mathematics. Karlsruhe, Fachinformationszentrum Karlsruhe.

Database of conferences, past, present and future. Data include title, sponsoring organization, location and dates, notes on related publications, etc. 100,000 records; updated weekly. Available online via STN International and on the internet. *Class No:* 530:061:061.3

Research Establishments
[991]

CROWTHER, J.G. The Cavendish Laboratory, 1874-1974. London, Macmillan, 1974. xvi, 464p. illus.

33 short chapters on the history of the Cavendish Physics Laboratory, Cambridge. Includes valuable biographical material. References, p.447-53 (Maxwell; Rayleigh; J.J. Thomson; Rutherford; Bragg; Mott; Pollard). *Class No:* 530:061:061.62

[992]
PYATT, E. **The National Physical Laboratory.** Bristol, Hilger, 1983. x, 270p. illus., ports., graphs, tables.

4 parts: 1. The founding of NPL [1900] - 2. Early development of NPL - 3. The inter-war period - 4. The post-war period. Each part has appended notes. 6 appendices (1. Biographical notes of principal characters; 2. Calendar of events, 1900 ... 4. Highlights in the history of standards). Detailed, non-analytical index, p.264-70.
Class No: 530:061:061.62

Research Projects

[993]
Current research in Britain: physical sciences. 14th ed. London, Cartermill; The British Library, 1998. 2v. (xxiii, 936p.). £150. ISBN: 1860673988.

First published 1985.

Part I: Research; Part II: Indexes. A register of current research being carried out in the UK universities, colleges and other institutions.
Class No: 530:061:061.62.005

[994]
INSTITUTE OF PHYSICS. **Research fields in physics.** 10th ed. Bristol, the Institute, 1997. 201p. £84; $168. ISBN: 0750304731.

First published 1970; 9th ed. 1994.

About 75 institutions, most of them universities in Britain and Ireland, but also industrial and government research laboratories. Data on each: research fields, academic personnel; higher degrees and diplomas; scholarship and fellowship sources; correspondence (contact). Name and subject indexes. Does not record completed work.
Class No: 530:061:061.62.005

Physical Measurement

Encyclopaedias

[995]
LORD, J. **Sizes: the illustrated encyclopedia.** New York, Harper Perennial, 1995. 374p. illus., diagrs., tables. $15. ISBN: 0062732285.

Provides information on the measurement of a wide range of substances, products and goods. Well illustrated; conversion charts.
Class No: 530.08(031)

Handbooks & Manuals

[996]
The Economist desk companion: how to measure, convert, calculate and define practically anything. London, Century Business, 1992. 272p. tables. ISBN: 0712698167.

Published in association with The Economist Books.

Gives the methods of measurement appropriate in a large number of fields, *e.g.* agriculture, chemistry, construction, energy, engineering, economics and finance, transport, weapons, etc. 4 parts: I. Systems of measurement - II. A-Z of definitions, terms and special measurements - III. Conversion tables - IV. Appendices (*e.g.* Rough conversions). A wealth of information, well presented. *Class No:* 530.08(035)

[997]
Sensors: a comprehensive survey. Göpel, W., *and others, eds.* New York, VCH, 1989-. V. 1-. illus., diagrs., graphs, tables. £164 each.
1. *Fundamentals and general aspects.* 1989. ISBN: 3527267670. xiii,641p.
2/3. *Chemical and biochemical sensors.*
4. *Thermal sensors.*
5. *Magnetic sensors.*
6. *Optical sensors.*
7. *Mechanical sensors.*
8. *Micro-and nanosensors/Sensors: market trends.*

V.1 has 23 contributors, 22 documented chapters in 4 sections: I. Sensor fundamentals - II. Basic sensor technologies - III. Sensor interfaces - IV. Sensor applications. Detailed, analytical index, p.603-29. An update vol. is planned for 1996. *Class No:* 530.08(035)

[998]
SYDENHAM, P.H., *and others.* **Handbook of measurement science.** New York, Wiley, 1982-92. 3v.
1. *Theoretical fundamentals.* 1982. xxiv, 654p.
2. *Practical fundamentals.* 1983. xxii, p.655-1413.
3. *Elements of change.* 1992. 584p.

V.1 has 18 contributors; v.2, 17. 32 documented chapters, in all (*e.g.* 7. Pattern recognition (6 contributors), v.1, p.277-330, including 5p. of references; 32. Sources of information measurement, v.2, p.1363-89, with 7 references). V.3 concentrates on factors responsible for the emergence of new measurement systems. Index. 'No measurement or control enquirer should be without it' (*Measurement and control,* v.16, February 1983, p.47-48). *Class No:* 530.08(035)

Dictionaries

[999]
DARTEN, M. *and* CLARK, J.O.E. **The Dent dictionary of measurement.** London, Dent, 1994. vi, 538p. ISBN: 0460861379.

About 5,000 terms, briefly defined. Covers a large number of disciplines, in particular science and mathematics, but also analytical linguistics, music, paper, military ranks, etc. *Class No:* 530.08(038)

[1000]
DRAZIL, J.V. **Quantities and units of measurement:** a dictionary and handbook. London, Mansell; Wiesbaden, Brandstetter, 1983. [v], 313p. £15; £8.95. ISBN: 0720116651.

Supersedes his *Directory of quantities and units* (London, L. Hill, 1971).

3 parts: 1. A dictionary of units of measurements, their symbols and abbreviations - 2. A dictionary of quantities and selected constants - 3. Symbols denoting quantities and constants. 4 appendices (2. UK and US units; 4. Bibliography, p. 287-94). French and German indexes, with references to corresponding English terms in pt. 2. 'The book is comprehensive and all scientists should have access to a copy' (*New Scientist,* 2 April 1984, p.48). *Class No:* 530.08(038)

[1001]
MELARAGNO, M. **Quantification in science:** the VNR dictionary of engineering units and measures. New York, Van Nostrand Reinhold, 1991. 333p. illus., tables. $42.95. ISBN: 0442006411.

Covers historical background of measurement and systems of units. Non-technical language. Includes chapter on conversion of units. A 'wealth of information' (*Choice,* September 1992, p.84).
Class No: 530.08(038)

Glossaries

[1002]
International vocabulary of basic and general terms in metrology. [Vacabulaire international des termes fondamentaux et généraux de métrologie.] 2nd ed. Geneva, International Organization for Standardization, 1993. 59p. ISBN: 9267010751.

First ed. 1984, ammended 1987.

Definitions and examples of 125 terms used in measurement. 6 parts: 1. Quantities and units ... 4. Measuring instruments ... 6. Measurement standards. Bibliography; English, French indexes.
Class No: 530.08(038.1)

Reviews & Abstracts

[1003]
Key abstracts: measurements in physics. London, INSPEC, 1990-. Monthly. $116l; £70 pa. (*Key abstracts.*) ISSN: 09504818.

About 250 abstracts per issue. 8 major sections: 1.0. Measurement science - 2.0 Sensors - 3.0 Nonelectric variables measurement - 4.0 Thermal techniques - 5.0 Electrical and magnetic measurements - 6.0 Optical instrumentation - 7.0 Nuclear instrumentation - 8.0 Other instruments and experimental techniques (*e.g.* X-ray and gamma ray techniques). Subject index per issue. *Class No:* 530.08(048)

Relativity & Einstein

[1004]
D'INVENO, R.A. **Introducing Einstein's relativity.** Oxford, Clarendon Press, 1991. 540p. illus. £50. ISBN: 0198596537.

Main topics: black holes, gravitational waves, cosmology. 213 illus.
Class No: 530.12

Quantum Theory

[1005]
KUHN, T.S., *and others, eds.* **Sources for the history of quantum physics:** an inventory and report. Philadelphia, Pa., American Philosophical Society, 1967. Supplement, 1973. [xi], 176p. + 7p. (Supplement, 1973). (*A.P.S. Memoirs, v.68.*)

Funded by the National Science Foundation.

Inventory of materials on the history of quantum physics and related developments in theoretical physics. Sections: 1. Activities and procedures - 2. Author catalogue of principle sources (Abraham, Max ... Zeeman) - 3. Inventory of oral records - 4. Inventory of microfilm records. 3 appendices (1. Sample biographies). Indexes: Source materials by type; Index of names; Index of Institutions; Depositories of relevant sources (p.176). The result of three years intensive work locating unpublished papers, notebooks and letters of more than 250 physicists. *Class No:* 530.145

Mechanics

[1006]

POLSKA KOMITET NORMALIZACY. **Vocabulary of mechanics in five languages:** English, German, French, Polish, Russian. Oxford, etc., Pergamon Press; Warsaw, Wydawnictwa Naukowo - Techniczne, 1962-67. 2v. (viii, 190.; x,452p.) diagrs.
Group 05: *Theoretical mechanics.* 10: *Strength of materials.* 15: *Mechanics of fluids.*
About 3,000 specialized terms in classified order (in line with ISO/TC37 recommendations). The English entry is defined, with equivalents in German, French, Polish and Russian. 5 language indexes. Well produced. *Class No: 531/534*

[1007]

Three hundred years of gravitation. Hawking, S.F. *and* Israel, W., *eds.* Cambridge Univ. Press, 1987. xiii,684p. diagrs., tables. £45. ISBN: 0521343127.
16 contributions with extensive references from celebrated physicists to mark the anniversary of the publication of Newton's *Principia.* Most of the articles 'review current developments and future prospects' (*Preface*). Topics covered include 'Dark stars' (W. Israel), 'Astrophysical black holes' (R.D. Blandford), 'Gravitational radiation' (K. Thorne), 'Superstring unification' (J.H. Schwarz). Not for the beginner in physics, but lucid accounts of the forefront of research. *No index,* a serious drawback in a work of this nature. 'A guide to current thinking on gravity' (*New Scientist,* 17 September 1987, p.77). *Class No: 531/534*

Solids

Kinematics

[1008]

DRUCE, G. 'Kinematics, dynamics and machines'. *Information sources in engineering.* K.W. Mildren and P.J. Hicks, eds. (3rd ed., 1996), p.151-97. 3rd ed. London, Bowker Saur, 1996. £80. ISBN: 1857390571.
Sections: Organizations - Abstracts and databases - Glossary - Historical background - Design process ... Conferences - Machine components ... Methodologies of mechanism design ... Tribology ... Quality and reliability ... Noise. Sections list useful sources of information (journals; standards, etc.). Extensive list of references, p.184-97. *Class No: 531.1*

[1009]

SINGER, L., *comp.* **Russian-English-French-German kinematics dictionary.** London, Scientific Information Consultants, Ltd., 1966. [ii], 128p.
1,169 numbered entry-words in Russian, with English, French and German equivalents and indexes. Genders are not given. *Class No: 531.1*

Barometers

[1010]

MIDDLETON, W.E.K. **The History of the barometer.** Baltimore, MD., Johns Hopkins Univ. Press; London, Oxford Univ. Press, 1964. xx, 489p. illus. $127.80. ISBN: 0317084461.
Broadly chronological order of chapters, with footnote references. 'A detailed and wide-ranging account of an instrument whose use now extends far beyond the simple measurement of barometric pressure ... A well-documented and well-written account' (*Geographical journal,* v.131(4), December 1965, p.567-8). *Class No: 531.78*

Fluids

[1011]

Annual review of fluid mechanics. Palo Alto, Ca., Annual Reviews, Inc. 1969-. ISSN: 00664189.
V.26, (1995. 704p. $52) contains several documented articles, *e.g.* 'Wave evolution on a falling film'; 'Vortex reconnection'; 'The Physics of supersonic turbulent boundary layers', etc. Subject index. Cumulative indexes: Contributing authors, v. 1-26; chapter titles, v. 1-26. *Class No: 532*

[1012]

Encyclopedia of fluid mechanics. Cheremisinoff, N.P. Houston, Texas, Gulf Publishing Co., 1985-. V.1-. supplements. graphs, formulas. ISBN: 0872015130.
1. *Flow phenomena and movement.* 1985. 2. *Dynamics and single-fluid flows and mixing.* 1985. 3. *Gas-liquid flows.* 1986. 4. *Solids and gas-solids flows.* 1986. 5. *Slurry flow technology.* 1987. 6. *Complex flow phenomena and modeling.* 1987. 7. *Rheology and non-Newtonian flows.* 1988. 8. *Aerodynamics and compressible flows.* 1989. 9. *Polymer flow engineering.* 1990. 10. *Surface and ground water flow phenomena.* 1990. Supplement 1. *Applied mathematics in fluid*

....*(contd.)*
dynamics. 1993. Supplement 2. *Advances in multiphase flow.* 1993.
V.8 (xiii,1216p.) has 45 contributors. 2 parts: 1. Turbulence phenomena and modelling - 2. Selected engineering problems. 29 documented chapters (*e.g.* 'Wind wave phenomena', p.589-635, 176 references). Detailed, analytical index, p.1203-16. For the specialist. *Class No: 532*

[1013]

NOVECK, S. **Russian-English glossary of physics of fluids and meteorology.** New York, Interlanguage Dictionaries Publishing Corp., 1969. [iii], 93p.
More than 4,000 Russian entry-words, with English equivalents. *Class No: 532*

Rheology

[1014]

BRITISH STANDARDS INSTITUTION. **Glossary of rheological terms.** London, BSI, 1996. 18p. (*BS 5168: 1996.*)
About 300 terms on deformation and flow of matter are defined, 'Activation energy' ... 'Young's modules'. *Class No: 532.135*

[1015]

Rheology abstracts: a survey of world literature. Oxford, Pergamon Press, for the British Society of Rheology, 1958-. 4pa. $380; £255 pa. ISSN: 0035452x.
About 800 abstracts pa. Sections: Theoretical - Instruments and techniques - Polymers and viscoelastic materials - Dispersions and liquids - Special topics. Subject indexes per issue. *Class No: 532.135*

[1016]

Solid liquid flow abstracts. Cranfield, Beds., British Hydromechanics Research Association, 1973-91.
Originally published by Gordon and Breach (v.1-3, 1969-1972). Included informative abstracts on hydraulic and pneumatic transport of solids, fluid mechanics of flow, equipment and applications and industrial processes. Now comprises part of *Fluid abstracts: process engineering;* available online via FLUIDEX. *Class No: 532.135*

Hydrodynamics

[1017]

Fluid flow measurements abstracts. Cranfield, Beds., British Hydromechanics Research Association, 1974-91. ISSN: 00412694.
Included about 600 informative abstracts pa. of items drawn from 1000 journals, plus reports, conference papers, books and selected British patents. Also included measurements of physical properties of fluids. Now comprises part of *Fluid abstracts: process engineering;* accessible on-line via FLUIDEX. *Class No: 532.5*

[1018]

Surface wave abstracts. Brentwood, Essex, Multi-Science Publishing Co., Ltd., 1970-. 4 pa. ISSN: 00492639.
About 250 abstracts pa. 13 sections: Generation and reception - Propagation, guidance and interaction - Reflection - Measurements - Amplification - Materials and fabrication - Devices - Applications - Acoustic optics - Non-destructive testing - General surface wave physics - Signal processing - Miscellaneous and reviews. Coverage of the world's major periodical literature, conference proceedings and unpublished reports. No index. *Class No: 532.5*

Aerodynamics

[1019]

GUNSTON, B. **The Guinness book of speed.** Enfield, Middx., Guinness, 1984. 192p. illus. ISBN: 0851122671.
Pt.1: The living world. Pt.2: The technical world. Index to text and illus., p.189-92. *Class No: 533.6*

[1020]

Industrial aerodynamics abstracts: world literature of non-aeronautical aerodynamics. Cranfield, Beds., British Hydromechanics Research Association, Fluid Engineering Centre, 1970-91.
Published about 1,200 abstracts pa. Coverage included fluid mechanics; the atmosphere; wind structure; air pollution; aerodynamics of surface features; instrumentation. Annual reviews. Now part of *Fluid abstracts: civil engineering.* Accessible online via FLUIDEX. *Class No: 533.6*

Plasma Physics

[1021]

PRINCETON UNIVERSITY. Plasma Physics Laboratory Library. **Dictionary catalog.** Boston, Mass., G.K. Hall, 1971. 4v.
Photolithographic reproduction of *c.*62,000 cards - 21 cards per page. The catalogue lists journal articles, reports, reprints and books, plus microfiches of all USAEC reports on controlled thermonuclear fusion and dissertations of the Plasma Physics Laboratory doctoral candidates. *Class No: 533.9*

Sound. Vibrations

Bibliographies

[1022]

'References to contemporary papers on acoustics'. Stern, R., ed. *The Journal of the Acoustical Society of America*, v.90, No., 2, Pt.2, August 1991, 560p.

Published since v.11 as a supplement.

Cites papers published between 1988 and early 1990. Broad classified sequence; topics include non-linear acoustics, ultrasonics, noise effect and control, physiological and psychological acoustics, speech communication, measurement and instrumentation, and transduction. Entries derived from INSPEC database.
Class No: 534(01)

Encyclopaedias

[1023]

Encyclopedia of acoustics. Crocker, M.J., ed. New York, Willey, 1997. 4v. (xxv, 2017p.) illus., diagrs., graphs, tables, formulas. $475. ISBN: 0471804657.

About 200 contributors. 166 sections in 18 main parts: I. General linear acoustics ... IV. Underwater sound ... VIII. Noise: its effects and control ... X. Acoustical signal processing ... XIII. Speech communication ... XVIII. Transducers. Detailed, analytical index, p.1993-2017. A definitive work; selected as an outstanding academic book for 1998 by *Choice*, January 1999. *Class No: 534(031)*

Handbooks & Manuals

[1024]

Acoustics source book. Parker, S.P., ed. New York, etc., McGraw-Hill, 1988. [viii],333p. illus., diagrs., graphs, tables. £35. (*McGraw-Hill science reference series*.) ISBN: 0070455082.

All material previously appeared in *McGraw-Hill encyclopedia of science and technology*, 6th ed. (1987). 9 chapters: 3. Physics of sound ... 5. Sound transducers ... 8. Sound reproduction. A basic treatment, more suitable for schools and beginning students. An unnecessary purchase for libraries holding the full encyclopedia.
Class No: 534(035)

[1025]

Handbook of acoustics. Crocker, M.J., ed. New York, Wiley, 1998. xviii, 1461p. diagrs., graphs, tables. £135. ISBN: 047125293x.

113 chapters in 16 parts: I. General linear acoustics ... IV. Underwater sound ... X. Acoustical signal processing ... XIV. Music and musical acoustics ... XVI. Transducers. Much of the content is derived from the *Encyclopedia of acoustics* (Wiley, 1997. 4v.).
Class No: 534(035)

[1026]

HARRIS, C.M., ed. Shock and vibration handbook. 4th ed. New York, etc., McGraw-Hill, 1995. v.p. diagrs., graphs, tables. ISBN: 0070269203.

First published 1961; 3rd ed. 1987.

44 sections, each with references; 54 contributors. Section 44: Effects of shock and vibration (65p.; 39 references). Index. Particularly intended 'as a working reference for those engaged in acoustical, aeronautical, air-conditioning, civil, electrical, mechanical and transportation engineering' (*Preface*). *Class No: 534(035)*

Dictionaries

[1027]

PIRAUX, H. Dictionnaire général d'acoustique et d'electroacoustique. Paris, Eyrolles, 1964. 330p. illus., diagrs.,tables.

Defines nearly 1,000 French terms, arranged A-Z. Not confined to acoustics and electroacoustics. Terms that are loosely or inaccurately applied are also listed, together with the correct words. One of the longest entries is 'Caracteristiques des tubes électroniques' (4p.; 8 diagrs.). English equivalents are given. Appendix tables.
Class No: 534(038)

[1028]

STEPHENS, R.W.B., ed. Sound. London, Crosby, Lockwood, Staples, 1975. 854p. (*International dictionaries of science and technology*.)

3,556 English-base terms (with definitions), and equivalents and indexes in German, French, Italian, Dutch, Portuguese, Russian and Spanish. 'The definitions appear accurate and they are certainly crisp and informative' (*New scientist*, 15 May 1975, p.404). Stresses applied and technical aspects of sound. *Class No: 534(038)*

[1029]

WEISSING, H. Fachwörterbuch akustick: Englisch-Deutsch - Deutsch-Englisch. [Dictionary of acoustics: English-German, German-English] Berlin, Paris, Verlag Hatier, 1992. 260p. £39.90. ISBN: 3861190842.

About 10,000 headwords in each all. *Class No: 534(038)*

Glossaries

[1030]

BRITISH STANDARDS INSTITUTION. Glossary of electrotechnical, power, telecommunication, electronics, lighting and colour terms. Part 3. Terms particular to telecommunications and electronics. Group 08. Acoustics and electroacoustics terminology. London, BSI, 1995. 43p. (*BS 4727: Part 3: Group 08: 1995*.)

Supercedes BS 661: 1969.

Terms in a systematic order. Alphabetical index.
Class No: 534(038.1)

Reviews & Abstracts

[1031]

Acoustics abstracts. Brentwood, Essex, Multi-Science Publishing Co., Ltd., 1967-. Monthly. ISSN: 00014974.

About 3,700 abstracts pa. Sections: Fundamental acoustics - Solid state acoustics - Liquid state acoustics - Gaseous state acoustics ... Ultrasonic applications - Audio frequencies - Noise - Architectural acoustics - Vibration and shock - Reviews and miscellaneous. Annual indexes. *Class No: 534(048)*

Histories

[1032]

HUNT, F.V. Origins in acoustics: the science of sound from antiquity to the age of Newton. New Haven, Conn., Yale Univ. Press, 1978. 197p.

A major feature of the book is its detailed account of the Arab contribution to the science of acoustics during Western Europe's Dark Ages. An appendix considers the contribution of Newton and his followers. Notes and references. Detailed index. A scholarly text.
Class No: 534(091)

Optics

Bibliographies

[1033]

BRITISH OPTICAL ASSOCIATION. Library catalogue. [British Optical Association]. Mitchell, M., ed. London, the Association, 1932-57. 3v.

V.1-2 (1932-35) had the title *Library and Museum Catalogue* and included facsimiles of title-pages. V.3 (1957) is an annotated author catalogue (p.1-226), plus a list of journals, a broad subject index (p.229-55) and 'Books for professional and honours examinations'. The BOA Library contains practically every work on opthalmic optics in English, and many on ocular pathology, anatomy, physiology and related topics, plus foreign works. *Class No: 535(01)*

Handbooks & Manuals

[1034]

Handbook of optics. Bass, M., ed. 2nd ed. New York, London etc., McGraw-Hill, 1995. 2v. (v.p.) illus., diagrs., graphs, tables. ISBN: 007047740x.

First published 1978; sponsored by the Optical Society of America.

V.1: *Fundamentals, techniques and designs*.

V.2: *Devices, measurements and properties*.

Intended 'to serve as a general purpose desktop reference' with 'archival, tutorial articles which contain not only useful data but also descriptive materials and references' (*Preface*). 83 chapters, closely subdivided and with extensive references (*e.g.* 'Polarizers': 70p., 12 parts, 332 references), in 17 parts: 1. Geometric optics - 2. Physical optics ... 6. Imaging detectors ... 9. Optical design techniques ... 12. Terrestrial optics ... . Selected by *Choice* as an outstanding academic book for 1995. *Class No: 535(035)*

[1035]

HAWKES, P.W. *and* KASPER, E. Principles of electron optics. London, etc., Academic Press, 1989-94. diagrs. 3 vols.

Vol. 1: *Basic geometrical optics*. 1989. ISBN: 0123333512.

Vol. 2: *Applied geometrical optics*.

Vol. 3: *Wave optics*. 1994 ISBN: 0123333547.

An update of *Grundlagen der Elektronenoptik* (1952) and *Handbuch der Physik*, (1955-, *qv*). Vol. 1 contains 34 chapters in 6 parts: 1. Classical mechanics - 2. Calculation of static fields - 3. The paraxial

.... *(contd.)*

approximation - 4. Abbreviations - 5. Deflection systems - 6. Computer-aided electron optics. Notes and references, p.577-623. Detailed, analytical index. A scholarly treatment. *Class No:* 535(035)

[1036]

PALIK, E.D., *ed.* Handbook of optical constants of solids. San Diego, Ca., Academic Press, 1985-. 5v. diagrs., graphs, tables. *(Academic Press Handbook.)* ISBN: 012544415x.

V.5 (*Handbook of thermo-optic coefficients of optical materials with applications*; G. Ghosh, ed.; 1997; 325p.; £99.95; ISBN: 0122818555) contains refractive indexes and thermo-optic coefficients for nonlinear crystals, semiconductors, optical and fibre glasses. Extensive references throughout the set of 5 vols. *Class No:* 535(035)

Dictionaries

Polyglot

[1037]

SCHULZ, E. Wörterbuch der Optik und Feinmechanik. [Dictionary of optics and precision engineering.] Wiesbaden, Brandstetter; London, Pitman, 1960-61. 3v. £9.20 each.

1. *German-English-French.* 1960. 112p. 2. *English-French-German.* 1961. 124p. 3. *French-German-English.* 1961. 110p.

V.1 covers *c.*3,000 terms in optics and precision mechanics and gives compounds and phrases, with German and French genders. A section of general terms is followed by specialised chapters (each with subdivisions): The eye - Eyeglass optics - Instruments and apparatus of precision mechanics and optics (*e.g.* barometer, compass, microscope) - The workshop. Little on spectroscopy, no general index. Sources, p.vi. 'Clearly directed towards opticians and optical instrument makers' (*Science reference notes*, v.10 (3/4), July/October 1963, item 92). *Class No:* 535(038)=00

English

[1038]

Dictionary of visual science Cline, D., *and others.* 3rd ed. Radnor, Pa., Chilton Book Co., 1980. xviii, 711p. illus., diagrs., charts.

2nd ed., 1968, edited by M. Schapero, and others.

68 contributors. About 20,000 entries, some of them lengthy (*e.g.* 'Lens': p.346-65). Coverage spans illumination and physical optics. Entries include eponyms, organizations and abbreviations.

4th ed., 1989 (xxi,820p. $55). *Class No:* 535(038)=20

German

[1039]

BINDMANN, W. Fachwörterbuch Optic und Optischer Gerätebau: Englisch-Deutsch, Deutsch-Englisch. [Dictionary of optics and optical instrument making: English-German, German-English.] 2nd ed. Berlin, Paris, Verlag Hatier, 1992. 832p. £70. ISBN: 3801170306.

First published 1975.

Technical dictionary of optics and optical instrument making. 22,000 terms in each part. According to the preface, not a 'complete revision' but several 'inaccuracies' from the earlier ed. have been removed. *Class No:* 535(038)=30

Progress Reports

[1040]

Progress in optics. Amsterdam, North-Holland Publishing Co., 1961-. illus., tables. ISBN: 0444898360.

V.31 (1993. 450p. £101.25) covers multiphoton ionization of atoms in intense radiation fields; properties of light diffracted by gratings; optical amplifiers; adaptive multilayer optical networks; two- and four-level atoms; and free electron lasers. *Class No:* 535(055)

Tables & Data Books

[1041]

CRC handbook of tables of functions for applied optics. Levi, L. Cleveland, Ohio, Chemical Rubber Co., 1974. [x], 624p. tables.

31 tables, in sections: A. Elementary functions - B. Error functions. Fresnel integrals - C,D,E. Blackbody radiation tables - F,G. Functions for perfect lens, circular aperature, monochromatic radiation - H. Miscellaneous tables. 'A good reference book at the college level' (*Choice*, April 1977, p.198). *Class No:* 535(083)

Infra-Red Rays

[1042]

The Infrared handbook. Wolfe, W.L. *and* Zissis, G.J., *eds.* Rev. ed. Washington, Office of Naval Research, Dept. of the Navy, 1985; reprinted 1993. v.p. diagrs., graphs, tables, forumlas. ISBN: 0906359015.

Prepared by the Infrared Information and Analysis (IRIA) Center, Environmental Research Institute of Michigan.

First published 1978.

25 documented chapters (1. Radiation theory ... 25. Ranging, communication and simulation systems). Detailed analytical index of 42p . 'Both a comprehensive review of the field and a detailed reference work' (Shaw D.F., *ed. Information sources in physics.* 2nd ed., 1985, p.307). *Class No:* 535-1

Microscopy

[1043]

Advances in optical and electron microscopy. Orlando, Fl., & London, Academic Press. 1966-. illus., diagrs., tables. ISBN: 0120299143. ISSN: 00653012.

V.14 (1994. xii, 340p. £65) has 7 contributors. The 4 documented articles include 'Microspectrofluorimetry' (5p. of references). Author and subject (analytical) indexes. *Class No:* 535.083.98

[1044]

Dictionary of light microscopy. Bradbury, S., *and others, comps.* Oxford Univ. Press; Royal Microscopical Society, 1989. x,139p. diagrs., tables. £6.95 (pbk). *(Microscopy handbooks 15.)* ISBN: 0198564139, pbk.

Covers *c.*1250 terms: A (symbol for absorbance, etc.) ... Zoom. Entries range from 2 to *c.*15 lines. Non-preferred terms are indicated as such. Numerous cross-references. Appendices give equivalent terms in English, French and German. Compiled by the Nomenclature Committee of the Royal Microscopical Society. Well-produced. *Class No:* 535.083.98

[1045]

FREUND, H. *and* BERG, A., *eds.* Geschichte der Mikroskopie. Frankfurt am Main, Umschau Verlag, 1963-66. 3v. illus.

1. *Biologie.* 1963. xv, 375p. 2. *Medizin.* 1964. xv, 506p. 3. *Angewandte Naturwissenschaft und Technik.* 1966. xvi, 550p.

History of microscopy, stressing applications. Well documented. *Class No:* 535.083.98

[1046]

LOCQUIN, H. *and* LANGERON, M. Handbook of microscopy. [Manuel de microscopie.] London, Butterworths, 1983. xii, 322p. illus., diagrs., tables, chemical structures. ISBN: 0408106794.

Originally published Paris, Masson, 1978. This translation edited by H. Hillman.

6 parts: 1. Instruments and techniques - 2. Methods of fixation, examination, cutting and mounting - 3. Stains - 4. Staining and impregnation - 5. Topological stains - 6. Non-specific cytological stains. Appendix 1: Physicochemical constants. Glossary of stains and dyes, p.179-87. Bibliography, p.303-8 (covering 1981/82-1948, in reverse chronological order). Detailed analytical index. Adds about 60 new techniques to the original ed., including a lengthy section on organic matter in microfossils. *Class No:* 535.083.98

Light

[1047]

DITCHBURN, R.W. Light. 3rd ed. London, New York etc., Plenum Press, 1976. xxv, 775, 19p. illus. (incl. col.), diagrs.

Chapters 1-12 provide a course on physical optics for students reading for a first degree in physics; chapters 13-20, - for the postgraduate worker. The chapters include: 2/3. Wave theory; 12. Polarized light; 13. The electromagnetic theory; 20. The limitations of optical instruments. No bibliographies, 19p. index. 6 plates. *Class No:* 535.1

Reflection. Emission.

[1048]

Advances in imaging and electron physics. London, Academic Press, 1995-. v.90-. 4 or 5 pa., with supplements. illus., diagrs., graphs, tables. ISSN: 00652539.

Previously *Advances in electronics,* v. 1-5, 1948-1953; then *Advances in electronics and electron physics,* v.7-89, 1954-1994.

Several major reviews in each vol. V.106 (1999; 346p.; £89.95; ISBN: 0120147483). has lengthy articles on optics at high and low energies, microlithography, image science and digital image processing and electron microscopy. *Class No:* 535.3

[1049]

CSELT (Centro Studi e Laboratori Telecommunicazioni), Turin. **Optical fibre communication.** New York etc., McGraw-Hill, 1981. xxxv, 883p. illus., ports. ISBN: 0070148821.

15 documented chapters in 5 parts, by specialists: 1. The transmission medium - 2. Sources and detectors - 3. Cables and connections - 4. Systems - 5. Integrated optics. 'Light propagation theory in optical fibres', p.47-144: 108 references. Detailed, analytical index, p.871-83. *Class No: 535.3*

Holography

[1050]

LEHMANN, M. **Holography:** technique and practice. London & New York, Focal Press, 1970. 148p. illus. (pl). diagrs. (*Focal library*.)

9 documented chapters: 1. Introduction and history - 2. Basic principles of optics - 3. Principles of holography - 4. The practice of holography - 5. Holographic systems - 6. Devices and instruments - 7. Special techniques - 8. Applications (*e.g.* 8.3: Data storage and retrieval systems) - 9. The future of holography. 'The emphasis is on practical detail, the theoretical and mathematical content being minimal' (*Aslib book list*, v.36(5), May 1971, entry No. 190). *Class No: 535.32*

Lasers

[1051]

Encyclopedia of lasers and optical technology. Meyers, R.A., *ed*. San Diego, Ca., Academic Press, 1991. xii,764p. illus., diagrs., graphs, tables. $69.95. ISBN: 0122266935.

56 contributors. 38 documented entries, A-Z ('Chemical lasers' ... 'Ultrashort laser pulse chemistry and spectroscopy'). Each article begins with brief glossary (*e.g.* 'Micro optics': 6 terms). Cross-references; detailed, analytical index, p.741-64. *Class No: 535.33*

Spectral Data

[1052]

BRITISH LIBRARY. Science Reference Library. **A Guide to the published collections of spectral data held by the SRL.** de Hamel, C., *comp*. London, Science Reference Library. 1983. iii, 52p. £3. ISBN: 0712307087.

Supersedes the 1977 ed., by R. Coman.

Grouped, first by spectroscopic technique (17 sections) and then by chemical class (subsections). The sections (Compendia of spectral data ... Mass spectral data) are usually subdivided: indexes and bibliographies; collections of spectral data. Index of subjects. *Class No: 535.330*

[1053]

CRC atlas of spectral data and physical constants for organic compounds. Grasselli, J.G. *and* Ritchey, W.M. 2nd ed. Cleveland, Ohio, CRC Press, 1975. 6v. (4688p.). tables, formulas. ISBN: 0878193170.

First published 1973.

1. *Name. Synonym directory. Structures. Spectroscopic aids. Special cross-correlation tables. 2/4. Data tables: Compounds , A-B, C-D, P-Z. 5. Indexes* for molecular formulas, molecular weights, physical constants, WLN [Wiswesser Line Notation], Mass spectra 6. *Special data indexes.*

Spectral data and physical constraints for *c*.21,000 organic compounds. Bibliographic references, for further reading. *Class No: 535.330*

[1054]

MASS SPECTROMETRY DATA CENTRE. **Eight peak index of mass spectra.** 4th ed. Cambridge, Royal Society of Chemistry, 1991. 3v. (in 8; 4332p.). tables. £1295. ISBN: 0851864171.

First published 1970; 3rd ed. 1983.

81,123 mass spectra covering 65,600 compounds. Includes data from the American Petroleum Institute, Thermodynamics Research Center, American Society for Testing and Materials, DOW Chemical Company and Downstream data colletions. Data tabulated include mass to charge ratios, molecular weight, intensities, compound name, CAS registry number. *Class No: 535.330*

[1055]

ODEGARD, G. *and* HURD, J.M. **'Spectra: a bibliography of sources'.** In *Science and technology libraries*. V.11(4), Winter 1991, p.173-208. ISSN: 0194262x.

About 125 briefly annotated entries. Sections: Books - Carbon-13 NMR - Infrared - Mass - Nuclear Magnetic Resonance - Ultraviolet - Miscellaneous. *Class No: 535.330*

Colours

Encyclopaedias

[1056]

HOPE, A. *and* WALCH, M. **The Color compendium.** New York, etc., Van Nostrand Reinhold, 1990. 360p. illus. $49.95.

An encyclopedia of topics on colour, ranging from art and history to the social sciences and technology. Each entry is cross-referenced. Includes bibliographies. Colour illus. and photographs throughout. Wide appeal. *Class No: 535.6(031)*

Tables & Data Books

[1057]

Colour index. 3rd ed. (2nd revision). Bradford, Society of Dyers and Colourists, 1971-82. Additions and amendments, 4pa. 7v. (7304p). tables.

First published 1924-28.

V.1-5 (1971 ed.) record 7,898 generic names of individual dyes and pigments. V.1-3: Colorants classified according to their usage; v.4: Colorants classified according to their chemical constitution; index of intermediate compounds; index of formulae. V.5: Code letters for colorant manufacturers; index of *Colour index* generic names, with colorants listed under each; index of commercial names of colorants. V.6-7 are supplements to V.1-4, 6. Supplement 1988: Pigments and solvent dyes. Also available on CD-ROM. *Class No: 535.6(083)*

[1058]

SMITHE, F.B. **Naturalist's color guide.** New York, American Museum of Natural History, 1974-81. 3 parts. ISBN: 0913474056.

Part 1 (24p., loose-leaf) comprises 86 named and numbered colour samples/swatches. Part 2 (229p.) acts as a supplement, analyses each colour and correlates it to other colours. A further supplement appeared in 1981. *Class No: 535.6(083)*

[1059]

WYSZECKI, G. *and* STILES, W.S. **Colour science:** concepts and methods, quantitative data and formulae. 2nd ed. New York, etc., Wiley, 1982. 950p. graphs, charts, tables.

First published 1967 (xiv, [1], 628p.).

Contents: Physical data - The eye - Colorimetry - Photometry - Visual equivalence and visual matching - Uniform colour scales - Visual thresholds - Theories and models of colour vision. Appendix. References. Author and subject indexes. *Class No: 535.6(083)*

Maps & Atlases

[1060]

ICI colour atlas. London, Butterworths, 1971. Loose-leaf.

Previously limited availability through ICI Dyestuffs Division.

Illustrates 1,379 colours, permuted into 27,580 by using a provided set of 20 optically graded filters. Page size, 35 x 30cm. *Class No: 535.6(084.3)*

Heat

Heat Transfer

[1061]

Advances in heat transfer. San Diego, Ca., Academic Press. 1969-. illus., diagrs., tables. ISSN: 01200313.

V.31 (1998, xi, 416p.) has 5 review articles covering drying, hydraulic systems, heat exchangers, Monte Carlo strategies and mitigation of water fouling. *Class No: 536.2*

[1062]

BEGELL, W., *ed*. **Glossary of terms in heat transfer, fluid flow, and related topics.** Washington, Hemisphere, 1983. 176p. $37.95. ISBN: 0891162615.

304 English base terms (plus concise definitions), with equivalents and indexes in Russian, German, French and Japanese. Included are a recommended nomenclature and list of recommended journal title abbreviations. *Class No: 536.2*

[1063]

HTFS digest. Heat Transfer and Fluid Flow Service. Harwell, Oxon HTFS, 1968-. 6pa. ISSN: 03091953.

A current awareness service in 23 sections (1. Boilers and evaporation ... 7. Enhanced heat and mass transfer ... 10. Heat exchanges ... 13. Instruments and techniques - 14. Multiphase fluid systems ... 21. Single phase fluid systems ... 23. Miscellaneous). Index per issue. HTFS Library database. Available online as *Heatflo* (74,000 records) via ESA-IRS. *Class No: 536.2*

[1064]

ROHSENOW, W.M. *and* HARTNETT, J.P., *eds*. **Handbook of heat transfer applications.** 3rd ed. New York, etc., McGraw-Hill, 1998. v.p. illus., diagrs. graphs, tables. $140. ISBN: 0070535558.

First published 1975; 2nd ed. 1985.

Main sections: Basic concepts of heat transfer - Conduction - Convection - Radiation - Microscale transport - Heat transfer in porous media - Non-Newtonian fluid mechanics and heat transfer - Enhanced heat transfer - Heat pipes - Condensation - Boiling - Measurement methods - Heat exchangers - Materials processing heat transfer. Numerous references; extensively illustrated. 'Strongly recommended' (*Choice*, February 1999, p.1088). *Class No:* 536.2

Heat Effects on Bodies

[1065]

BARIN, I. **Thermochemical data of pure substances.** 2nd ed. Weinheim, VCH, 1993. 2v. (1738p.). tables. ISBN: 3527285318, (set).

First published 1989.

Data on thermochemical functions for 2,372 substances tabulated at temperature intervals of 100k. 5 indexes (*e.g.* 'Symbols and abbreviations used in the tables'). *Class No:* 536.4

[1066]

CHANEY, J.F., *and others, eds*. **Thermophysical properties research literature retrieval guide, 1900-1980.** New York, Plenum Press, 1982. 7v. tables. (*First published 1964-70. 2v.*)

1. Elements. 2. Inorganic compounds. 3. Organic compounds and polymeric materials. 4. Alloys, intermetallic compounds and cermets. 5. Oxide mixtures and minerals. 6. Mixtures and solutions. 7. Coatings, systems, composites, foods, animal & vegetable products.

Covers world literature on 14 thermodynamic and physical properties of 44,300 substances. Over 75,000 references. Each volume has a materials directory (A-Z), search parameters (substances, numerically), a bibliography and author index. An important research tool for the physical chemist. *Class No:* 536.4

[1067]

CRC handbook of thermophysical and thermochemical data. Lide, D.R. *and* Kehiain, H.V., *eds*. Boca Raton, Fl., CRC Press, 1994. tables.. $149.95, £125. ISBN: 0849301971.

5 sections: 1. Introduction - 2. Thermodynamic properties of pure substances - 3. Properties of mixtures - 4. Transport properties (viscosity; conductivity; diffusion) - 5. Tables of properties of individual substances. Appended: substance list. Index. 'The editorial work is excellent in this valuable reference' (*Choice*, May 1995, p.1488). *Class No:* 536.4

[1068]

TOULOUKIAN, Y.S., *and others*. **Thermophysical properties of matter:** a comprehensive compilation of data by the Thermophysical Properties Research Center. New York, IFI/Plenum Press, 1970-. 14v. graphs, tables.

1-3. Thermal conductivity. 1970. *4-6. Specific heat.* 1970. *7-9. Thermal radiative properties ...* 1970-72. *10. Thermal diffusivity.* 1974. *11. Viscosity.* 1972. *12-13. Thermal expansion.* 1974. *14. Master index to materials and properties.* 1979.

Each volume contains introductory text, the body of numerical data (with source references) and a materials index. Primarily intended for designers, researchers, experimentalists and theoreticians. Each volume was to be revised and updated every fifth year. *Class No:* 536.4

Low Temperatures

[1069]

AMERICAN INSTITUTE OF PHYSICS. **Glossary of terms frequently used in cryogenics.** New York, the Institute, [1966]. [8], 46, [1]p.

About 100 terms are defined ('Entropy': 1p.). 13 references to books and *Scientific American* articles. *Class No:* 536.48

[1070]

Handbook of applied superconductivity. Seeber, B., *ed*. Bristol, Institute of Physics, 1998. 2 vols. (c.2000p.). illus., diagrs. graphs, tables. £350; $545. ISBN: 0750303778.

V.1: *Fundamental theory, basic hardware and low temperature science and technology*; V.2: *Applications*.

9 sections: A. Introduction - B. Superconducting wires and cables - C. Superconducting magnets - D. Cooling technology for superconductors - E. Instrumentation - F. Materials at low temperatures - G. Present applications - H. Power applications - I. Superconducting electronics. Glossary; detailed, analytical index. *Class No:* 536.48

[1071]

Progress in low temperature physics. Amsterdam, North Holland Publishing Co, 1955-. diagrs., tables. ISBN: 0444852107, set.

V.14 (1995. xvi, 466p.) has 9 contributors. 5 reviews (*e.g.* 'The Landau critical velocity') each with numerous references. Author and subject indexes. *Class No:* 536.48

Measurements

[1072]

WHITEHOUSE, D.J. **Handbook of surface metrology.** Bristol, Institute of Physics, 1994. xxiv, 988p. illus., diagrs., graphs, tables. ISBN: 0750300396.

8 lengthy chapters, closely sub-divided; thus chapter 4 'Instrumentation', p.355-578, has some 120 sections and nearly 200 references. Author is Professor of engineering at Warwick University. *Class No:* 536.5

Thermodynamics

[1073]

O'CALLAGHAN, P.W. 'Thermodynamics and thermal systems'. *Information sources in engineering.* K.W. Mildren and P.J. Hicks, eds. (3rd ed., 1996), p.199-222. 3rd ed. London, Bowker Saur, 1996. £80. ISBN: 1857390571.

Covers properties, availability and exergy, thermal systems, heat transfer and fluid mechanics, cooling systems, fans and pumps, electricity generation, new technologies and alternative energy systems. *Class No:* 536.7

[1074]

PERROT, P. **A to Z of thermodynamics.** Oxford Univ. Press, 1998. vi, 329p. diagrs., graphs, formulas. £35. ISBN: 0198565569.

Original French ed. *Dictionnaire de thermodynamique*, Paris, Intereditions, 1994.

About 800 terms, defined and explained, with some worked examples. After some 20 years a new dictionary in this field is welcome, but the editors at OUP would have done well to soften some of the 'purple prose' in the preface (*e.g.* '... mathematical and physical baggage ... whose weight does not exceed that which honest scientists can support when life is so burdened as to make them forget everything.'). *Class No:* 536.7

[1075]

RAZNJEVIC, K. **Handbook of thermodynamic tables and charts.** New York, Hemisphere Publishing Corpn., McGraw-Hill, 1976. viii, 392p. tables, charts. ISBN: 0070812701.

Sections: Solids - Liquids - Vapors - Gases - Units and measures. More than 100 tables (SI units) on solids, liquids, vapour. 16 folded charts. Includes steam tables up to 1000 degrees and 1000 bar. Comprehensive treatment of basic data for engineering thermodynamics as well as practical and theoretical thermodynamics. *Class No:* 536.7

Electricity

[1076]

CONNOLLY, T.F., *ed*. **Electrical properties of solids, surface preparation and methods of measurement.** New York & London, IFI/Plenum, 1972. xxiv, 96p. (*Solid state literature guides, v.4.*)

A comprehensive work of reference, covering semiconductors, metals, alloys, insulators and dielectrics. International scope, up to 1971, in 5 sections. For the scientific and industrial research worker. *Class No:* 537

[1077]

HEILBRON, J.L. **Electricity in the 17th and 18th centuries.** Berkeley, etc., Univ. of California Press, 1979. xiv, 606p. illus., facsims., diagrs. ISBN: 0520034783.

5 footnoted parts (21 chapters): 1. Early modern physics and its cultivators - 2. Electricity in the seventeenth century - 3. The great discoveries - 4. The age of Franklin - 5. Quantification. Bibliography (A-Z authors), p.501-69. Analytical index, p.571-606. Outstanding scholarly history of the period. *Class No:* 537

[1078]

MOTTELAY, P.F., *comp*. **Bibliographical history of electricity & magnetism,** chronologically arranged. Researches into the domain of the early sciences, especially from the period of the revival of scholasticism, with biographical and other accounts of the most distinguished philosophers throughout the Middle Ages. London, Griffin, 1922. xvii, 678p. illus.(pl.), facisms.

Covers the period 2637 B.C.-A.D. 1821. Faraday: p.483-99, with biographical data, including 1p. of references. 6 appendices (4. 'Names of additional electrical and magnetic works, published up to

....*(contd.)*
1800'). Detailed index, p.565-678. A valuable source that can be used to supplement F. Cajori's *History of physics* (*qv*), but the chronological sequence needs to be revised. *Class No:* 537

[1079]
WHITTAKER, Sir E.T. A History of the theories of aether and electricity. London, Nelson, 1951-53. 2v.
V.1 (1951) deals with the classical physics theories up to 1900. V.2 (rev. and enl. ed., 1953), with the modern theories, 1900-1926. The standard history on the subject for physicists. *Class No:* 537

Measurements

[1080]
Key abstracts: electronic instrumentation. London, INSPEC; New York, Institute of Electrical and Electronic Engineers, 1976-. Monthly. (*Key abstracts.*) ISSN: 0950480x.
Formerly *Key abstracts: Electrical measurements and instrumentation.*
About 200 abstracts per issue. 6 main sections: 1. Measurement systems - 2. Displays - 3. Signal processing equipment - 4. Sensors and transducers - 5. Bench instruments - 6. Measurement of electric and magnetic variables. No indexes. A selection from the INSPEC database offered as a current awareness service. *Class No:* 537.083

Radiation. Discharges

Radiology

[1081]
BRITISH STANDARDS INSTITUTION. Glossary of electrotechnical, power, telecommunication, electronics, lighting and colour terms. Part 5: Terms particular to electromedical equipment. Group 01: Radiology and radiological physics terminology. London, BSI, 1985. 58p. (*BS 4727, Part 5. Group 01: 1985.*) ISBN: 0580146146.
Supersedes BS 2597: 1955, withdrawn. Corresponds to IEC Publication 50(881): 1984.
Some 660 numbered terms and definitions. Main sections: General terms - Ionizing radiations - Radiological apparatus and techniques - Dosimetry - Radiation protection - Biological effects. Index. *Class No:* 537.53

X-rays

[1082]
CLARK, G.L., *ed.* **The Encyclopedia of X-rays and gamma-rays.** New York, Reinhold; London, Chapman & Hall, 1963. xxvii, 1149p. illus., diagrs., tables.
302 contributors; about 350 signed articles, A-Z (entry-word being the keyword in the title, *e.g.* 'Historical milestones for X-rays and gamma rays 1600-1962', - under 'Historical'). References appended to articles are nummbered (*e.g.* 'Microradiography in biology': p.607-18; 78 references; 26 illus. and diagrs.). Occasional uneven coverage (*e.g.* 12p. on 'Portland cement compounds'; under 3p. on 'Biological consequences of exposure to ionizing radiation'). Cross-references; index. *Class No:* 537.531

Thermionics

[1083]
ORGANIZATION FOR ECONOMIC COOPERATION AND DEVELOPMENT. Joint ENEA-IAEA Liaison Group on Thermionic Electrical Power Generation. **Glossary of terms and symbols in thermionic conversion.** Paris, O.E.C.D., 1971. 115p.
Internationally agreed definitions of more than 200 technical terms and expressions. List of preferred symbols. Index of terms in English, French and Russian. *Class No:* 537.58

Magnetism

[1084]
RADO, G.T. *and* **SUHL, H.,** *eds.* **Magnetism.** New York & London, Academic Press, 1963-73. 5v. illus., diagrs., tables.
1, *Magnetic ions in insulators, their interactions, resonances and optical properties.* 1963. xv, 688p. 2. *Statistical models, magnetic symmetry, hyperfine interactions and metals.* 1965-66. 2pts. 3. *Spin arrangement and crystal structure, domains and micromagenetics.* 1963. 623p. 4. *Exchange interactions among itinerant electrons* 1966. 407p. 5. *Magnetic properties of metallic alloys.* 1973. [xvi], 400p.
V.5 of this general treatise has 16 chapters by specialists, with chapter references, and author and subject indexes. *Class No:* 537.6

Nuclear Magnetic Resonance

[1085]
Encyclopedia of nuclear magnetic resonance. Grant, D.M. *and* Harris, R.K., *eds.* New York, Wiley, 1995. 8v. (5323p.). illus., diagrs., graphs. $3500; £1750. ISBN: 0471938718.
V.1: Historical perspectives; V.2-8: A-Z + indexes.
About 600 contributors in all. V.1 includes about 200 'personal recollections' in the development of NMR. V.2-8 carry about 800 technical articles with extensive references in 5 broad areas of NMR applications: inorganic - physics - biological - instrumentation; organic - biomedical. These areas are each closely subdivided and the articles listed in the Foreword. Imaging and medical glossary, p.5073-83; detailed, analytical index, p.5119-5323. *Class No:* 537.635

[1086]
HOMANS, S.W. A Dictionary of concepts in NMR. Rev. ed. Oxford, Clarendon Press, 1992. 380p. illus., diagrs., graphs. £22.50. ISBN: 019854765x.
A-Z (*Absolute-value mode* to *Zero-quantum coherence*), detailed (*c.*1-page) definitions. Emphasis is towards two-dimensional NMR methods in liquids reflecting 'present experimental trends' (*Preface*). Cross references; 'further reading' after many entries. 4 appendices: Properties of cartesian product operators; Trigonometric identities; Matrix algebra; Rotation operators. *Class No:* 537.635

Solid State Physics

[1087]
CONNOLLY, T.F., *ed.* **Solid state physics literature guides.** Prepared under the auspices of the Research Materials Information Center, Oak Ridge National Laboratory. New York, IFI/Plenum, 1970-79. 10v. in 11.
1. *Ferro-electric materials and ferro-electricity.* 1970.
2. *Semiconductors - Preparation, crystal growth, and selected properties.* 1972.
3. *Groups iv,v and vi transition metals and compounds - Preparation and properties.* 1972.
4. *Electrical properties of solids - Surface preparation and methods of measurement.* 1972.
5. *Bibliography of magnetic materials and tabulation of magnetic transition temperatures.* 1972.
6. *Ferroelectric literature index.* 1974.
7. *Scattering of thermal neutrons: a bibliography.* 1974.
8. *Bibliography of microwave optical technology.* 1976.
9. *Laser window and mirror materials.* 1977.
10a,b. *Crystal growth bibliography.* 1979.
V.10a: *Bibliography* carries more than 5,000 references on the crystal growth of organic materials covering 1972-77. V.10b provides permuted title index and author index (ix, 430p.). *Class No:* 538.9

[1088]
LERNER, R.G. *and* **TRIGG, G.L.,** *eds.* **Concise encyclopedia of solid state physics.** Reading, Mass., Addison-Wesley Publishing Co., Inc., 1983. [xv], 311p. illus., diagrs., graphs, tables. $39.50. ISBN: 020114204x.
About 140 contributors; *c.*120 documented main entries (Acoustoelectric effect ... Work function). The article 'Liquid Crystals' (5½p.) has 14 notes and references and 4 figures. Analytical index, p.305-11. Aims 'to provide in one volume, a convenient and readily accessible set of resource materials in the area of sold state physics' (*Preface*). The articles are drawn from the Lerner and Trigg *Encyclopedia of physics* (1st ed.). *Class No:* 538.9

[1089]
Solid state physics: advances in research and applications. San Diego, Ca., Academic Press, 1948-. diagrs., graphs, tables. ISBN: 0126077495. ISSN: 00811947.
V.52 (1999; 400p.; £90; ISBN: 0126607533) focuses on the optical and electronic properties and applications of semiconductors. Author and subject index. Cumulative author and subject index, v.1-51. *Class No:* 538.9

[1090]
Solid state/superconductivity abstracts. Bethesda, Md., Cambridge Science Abstracts, Engineering Information, Inc. 1960-. 6pa + index. $628 pa. ISSN: 08965900.
Incorporates *Science research abstracts journal* (six titles); formerly *Solid state abstracts journal.*
About 8,000 abstracts pa. 6 broad engineering groups (civil; mining; mechanical, etc.). Also available on the Internet (URL: http://www/ csa/com). *Class No:* 538.9

Structure of Matter

[1091]

Advances in atomic, molecular and optical physics. San Diego, Ca., Academic Press, 1965-. Annual. ISSN: 1049250x.

V.38 (1997. 400p.) has extensively documented review articles. Index. *Class No:* 539

Nuclear Physics

[1092]

Advances in nuclear physics. New York etc., Plenum Press. 1968-. Annual. ISSN: 00652970.

V.23 (1996. 315p.) has review articles with extensive references. Contents of earlier volumes. *Class No:* 539.1

[1093]

Annual review of nuclear and particle science. Palo Alto, Ca., Annual Reviews Inc., 1978-. v. 28-. ISSN: 01638998.

Formerly (1952-77) as *Annual review of nuclear science*.

V.46 (1996. 658p.) includes review articles with extensive references. Indexes. *Class No:* 539.1

[1094]

MLADJENOVIĆ, M. The Defining years in nuclear physics, 1932-1960s. Bristol, Institute of Physics, 1998. 464p. £85; $150. ISBN: 0750304723.

Covers the significant nuclear physics discoveries during the period under consideration. Extensive quotations and bibliography. *Class No:* 539.1

Particles

[1095]

CINDA 97 (1988-1997): the index to literature and computer files in microscopic neutron data. Vienna, International Atomic Energy Agency, 1997. 24, 494, 43p. tables. ISBN: 9201018975. ISSN: 10112545.

Supersedes previous issues. CINDA = Computer index of neutron data.

Prelims. include 'Selected literature scanned for the present edition'; 'Neutron data handbooks'. Entries, p.1-484; a. Elements or isotopes; c. Molecules and mixtures. Annex (A1-A43) of 5 tables (*e.g.* Abbreviations for molecules and mixtures). Online. *Class No:* 539.12

[1096]

Current awareness in particle technology. Particle Science and Technology Information Service, Univ. of Technology, Loughborough, 1976-. Monthly. ISSN: 03764842.

Continues *Particulate information*, 1974-75.

About 9,000 references pa, covering the world literature of particle science and technology: journal articles, conference papers, reports, patents, theses, books. 18 subject sections (Particle properties ... Powder and compact properties ... Aerosols ... Gas filtration ... Crystallisation ... Granulation and pelletisation - Miscellaneous applications). General; Books; Conference index. Appended: 'Forthcoming conference meetings and exhibitions'. Quarterly author and subject indexes, cumulated annually. *Class No:* 539.12

[1097]

McCRANE, W.C. *and* **DELLY, J.C. The Particle atlas:** an encyclopedia of techniques for small particle identification. 2nd ed. Ann Arbor, Mich., Ann Arbor Science Publishers, 1973-80. 6v. (1703p.). micrographs. ISBN: 0250400189.

First published 1967.

1. *Principles and techniques.* 1973. 2. *The light microscopy atlas.* 1973. 3. *The electron microscopy atlas.* 1973. 4. *The particle analyst's handbook.* 1979. 5. *Light microscopy techniques and atlas.* 1979. 6. *Electron-optical techniques and atlas.* 1980.

4,500 micrographs, for the identification of 1,020 substances, *e.g.* fertilizers, insecticides, pigments, industrial chemicals, explosives, minerals. V.3 has 9 illus. of micrographs per page. Each volume carries an index, cumulating. *Class No:* 539.12

[1098]

The Particle century. Fraser, G., *ed*. Bristol, Institute of Physics, 1998. 232p. illus. £45; $59.50. ISBN: 0750305436.

The 19 essays, each with a brief editorial introduction, present a review of the status of particle physics at the end of the century. Glossary; bibliographies; detailed, analytical index. A useful overview, appropriate for both scientists and lay persons. *Class No:* 539.12

[1099]

Particle physics: one hundred years of discoveries: an annotated chronological bibliography. Ezhela, V.V., *and others, eds*. New York, American Institute of Physics, 1996. 328p. $49. ISBN: 1563966425.

Includes important papers in the field published from 1895 to 1905, with an abstract or brief excerpt for each, references and comments desribing its contribution. Author and subject indexes. *Class No:* 539.12

Atoms

[1100]

Atomic, molecular, and optical physics handbook. Drake, G.W.F., *ed.* New York, American Institute of Physics, 1996. 1095p. $130. ISBN: 156396242x.

Provides access to an extensive range of published material (journals articles, etc.) required by researchers and postgraduate students. 7 sections: Mathematical methods - Atoms - Molecules - Scattering theory - Scattering experiments - Quantum optics - Applications. Bibliographic information is minimal. *Class No:* 539.18

[1101]

BOORSE, H.A., *and others*. **The Atomic scientists:** a biographical history. New York, Wiley, 1989. viii,472p. ports. £19.95. ISBN: 0471504556.

Brief (*e.g.* Max Planck (1858-1947), p.123-30) narrative biographies of significant contributors to atomic science. Chronological. Index, p.469-72 'Highly readable' (*New technical books,* v.23(2), March/April 1990, p.394). *Class No:* 539.18

Energy Levels

[1102]

High energy physics index. Compiled at Deutsches Elektronen-Synchroton DESY, Hamburg. [Hochenergiephysik index.] Karlsruhe, Fachinformationszentrum, 1963-. Bi-monthly. ISSN: 00181447.

About 15,000 references pa. 3 sections: Experimental physics - Instrumental physics - Theoretical physics. Book index. Conference index. Author and affiliation index. Preprint and report number index. Subject index. Available online (230,000 records) from Deutsches Elektronen-Synchrotron. *Class No:* 539.184

[1103]

SUBE, R. Dictionary of high-energy physics, in English, German, French, Russian. Amsterdam etc., Elsevier, 1987. 164p. £99.90. ISBN: 0444989838.

About 5,000 English-base terms, with equivalents and indexes in German, French and Russian. *Class No:* 539.184

54 Chemistry

Chemistry

Abbreviations & Symbols

[1104]

WOHLAUER, G.E.M. *and* **GHOLSTON, H.D.**, *comps. and eds*. **German chemical abbreviations.** New York, Special Libraries Association, 1965. iv, 63p.

About 3,000 abbreviations, mostly taken from *Chemisches Zentralblatt*, Beilstein, Lenk-Börner, Hunnius (*Pharmazeutisches Wörterbuch*, 1959) and De Vries. Entries state German abbreviations, full form and English translation. Includes abbreviations for technical terms not specifically confined to chemistry. *Class No:* 540(003)

Databases

[1105]

CA [Chemical abstracts]. Columbus, Ohio, American Chemical Society, Chemical Abstracts Service; 1967-.

CA is a major database, derived from the weekly *Chemical abstracts*. About 14,000,000 records, updated weekly. Available from a number of online hosts, but the file on STN International (owned by Chemical Abstracts Service) is the most comprehensive. Numerous sub-files and closed files are also available, as are a number of data subsets on CD-ROM; see *World databases in chemistry* (ed. C.J. Armstrong, Bowker Saur, 1995, p.47-57) for a discussion of these. *Class No:* 540(003.4)

[1106]

—**CA Registry** Columbus, Ohio, American Chemical Society, Chemical Abstracts Service.

Lists CA Registry Numbers of chemical substances; a companion to other CA databases. 16,800,000 substances. Available online via STN International and on the internet. *Class No:* 540(003.4)

[1107]

SCHULZ, H. *and* **GEORGY, U. From CA to CAS online:** databases in chemistry. [Von CA bis CAS online: datenbanken in der chemie.] 2nd ed. Berlin, etc., Springer-Verlag, 1994. xv, 311p. diagrs., tables, chemical formulas and structures. £50; $86.95. ISBN: 0387574832.

Covers the contents of CAS ONLINE and search techniques appropriate to various hosts. Includes other online chemical information sources: patents; business and industry; Beilstein; Gmelin. Glossary (*c.* 200 terms), p.293-302; keyword index, p.303-11. *Class No:* 540(003.4)

[1108]

World databases in chemistry. Armstrong, C.J., *ed*. London, Bowker-Saur, 1995. xii, 1200p. £145. (*World database series*.) ISBN: 1857391012.

The series aims 'to list databases completely, and group databases logically' (*Introduction*). Treats chemistry in its broadest sense and covers agrochemistry, forensic chemistry, thermochemistry, pharmacology, materials science, chemical engineering, manufacturing chemistry and patents. About 1,300 electronically published databases in 10 sections: 1. Chemistry - 2. Chemistry general - 3. Organic, organometallic, petrochemistry - 4. Inorganic chemistry - 5. Analytical chemistry - 6. Toxicology, pollution, waste treatment - 7. Pharmaceuticals, cosmetics - 8. Surface chemistry, materials chemistry - 9. Chemical engineering, manufacture - 10. Patents - chemistry. Full-text journals, directories, educational software, etc. are included. Entries include a brief description of contents and coverage, online hosts, CD-ROM and internet availability, etc. Database 'families' and subsets identified. Indexes: addresses; database name; subject. Claims to be comprehensive but the coverage of European databases is fuller than that of North American. Clumsy and awkward to use, partly because some substantial entries appear in several sections (*e.g. Compendex*). Overall, a valuable source of information. *Class No:* 540(003.4)

Internet

[1109]

ChemConnect: chemistry journals.

The Web site provides a guide to the chemistry literature available on the Internet, including full-text journals, those partially available and tables of contents. *Class No:* 540(003.41)

[1110]

ChemWeb. Oxford, Elsevier, 1997-. URL: http://www.chemweb.co.uk.

The web site offers access to around 200 journals and 20 databases; a fee is charged for these. Also offers free access to a wide range of services, including notice boards, product directories, jobs and exchanges, conferences and meetings, etc. *Class No:* 540(003.41)

Software

[1111]

Directory of chemistry software, 1992. Warr, W., *and others, eds*. Washington, D.C., Cherwell Scientific/American Chemical Society, 1992. 204p. $34.95. ISBN: 0951823604.

Over 170 software packages, A-Z by program name. Categories: structure drawing, DBMS, expert systems, 3-D molecular modeling, quantum mechanics, utility packages, terminal emulators for on-line searching, communications and off-line query formulation. Data include product description, features and capabilities; company and distributor contact; hardware and software requirements; level of support; price; references to product reviews. 'Recommended' (*Choice*, October 1992. p.270). *Class No:* 540(003.42)

Bibliographies

[1112]

BOLTON, H.C. A Select bibliography of chemistry, 1492-1902. Washington, Smithsonian Institution, 1893-1904. 4v. (*Smithsonian Miscellaneous Collections, v.35, 39, 41(3), 44(5).*)

Reprinted New York, Kraus, 1969.

About 18,000 items. The main two volumes (1893. ix. 1,212p.) have 7 sections (Bibliography - Dictionaries and tables - History of chemistry - Biography - Chemistry, pure & applied - Alchemy - Periodicals). Section 8, an international list of academic dissertations, appeared in the 3rd volume (1st suppt.). Some entries have brief, usually bibliographical, annotations. Subject indexes. *Class No:* 540(01)

[1113]

—**COLE, W.A. Chemical literature, 1700-1860:** a bibliography with annotations, detailed descriptions, comparisons and locations. London, Mansell, 1988. *c.*600p. £98. ISBN: 0720119677.

Records *c.*1,450 items, chosen as major contributions to the period of 'chemical revolution'. Bibliographical descriptions, annotations and references. Brief biographies for most authors. Library locations in USA, Canada, UK and France. *Class No:* 540(01)

[1114]

—**DUVEEN, D.I.** Bibliotheca alchemica et chemica: an annotated catalogue of printed books. London, Weil, 1949. vii, 609p. illus.

Facsimile reprint. London, Dawsons, 1965.

Another valuable private collection catalogue. *Class No:* 540(01)

[1115]

—**FERGUSON, J.** Bibliotheca chemica: a catalogue of the alchemical, chemical and pharmaceutical books in the collection of the late James Young of Kelly & Davis. Glasgow, Maclehose, 1906. 2v.

More than a catalogue of 2,500 items. It contains concise and critical biographical accounts of the authors, and appraisals of their works, making it an encyclopaedia of the history, biography and bibliography of early chemistry. *Class No:* 540(01)

[1116]

BOTTLE, R.T. *and* **ROWLAND, J.F.B.**, *eds*. **Information sources in chemistry.** 4th ed. New York, London, Bowker-Saur, 1992. xvi, 341p. $75; £40. (*Guides to information sources*.) ISBN: 1857390164.

First published 1962 as *Use of chemical literature*. 3rd ed. 1979.

17 contributors; 17 chapters in 4 sections: A. General sources - B. Pure chemistry - C. Industrial chemistry - D. Conclusion (practical use of chemical information sources). Glossary of acronyms; databases (p.325-34); analytical subject index (p. 335-41). Special attention to and guidance for the complexities of handling chemical structures in electronic searching. *Class No:* 540(01)

[1117]

LEES, N. How to find information: chemistry - a guide to searching in published services. London, British Library, Science Reference and Information Service, 1995. 30p. £5. ISBN: 0712308067.

A brief guide, intended for undergraduates, on sources of chemical information. Covers printed sources (nomenclature, etc.), abstracts and indexes, theses, online searching, chemical business sources. Numerous worked examples. Excellent value. *Class No:* 540(01)

[1118]

MAIZELL, R.E. **How to find chemical information:** a guide for practicing chemists, educators and students. 3rd ed. New York, Chichester, etc., Wiley, 1998. 515p. £64.95. ISBN: 0471125792.

First published 1979; 2nd ed. 1987.

18 sections covering current awareness and document delivery; Chemical Abstracts Service; other abstracting and indexing services; US government technical information sources; electronic media, including the Internet; critical literature reviews; major reference works; journals and patents; physical property data; health and safety information; marketing and business information; analytical chemistry. New to this ed. is the section on CD-ROM portable databases and appendices listing major chemical information awards and online databases for particular users. A practical approach, with 'pros and cons' for many sources described. 'Indispensable' (*Choice*, November 1998). *Class No:* 540(01)

[1119]

MELLON, M.G. **Chemical publications, their nature and use.** 5th ed. New York, etc., McGraw-Hill, 1982. xii, 419p. ISBN: 0070415145.

First published 1958.

Part 1 (chapters 1-12): Publications, kinds and nature (Primary sources - periodicals; technical reports; patents; etc.; Secondary sources - periodicals; *Chemical abstracts*; bibliographies; reference works; Tertiary sources - guides and directories). Part 2 (chapters 13-16): Publications, storage and use; Libraries and information centers (US slanted); Searches, manual and computer; Library problems. Author and analytical subject indexes, p.395-419. Well-documented chapters. *Class No:* 540(01)

[1120]

SKOLNIK, H. **The Literature matrix of chemistry.** New York, etc., Wiley, 1982. xi, [1], 297p. ISBN: 0471705453.

11 chapters: 1. Books -2. Encyclopedias and treatises - 3. Numerical data compilations - 4. Patents - 5. The journal literature - 6. Secondary publication - 7. Chemical Abstracts Service - 8. Other indexing/ abstracting services - 9. Computer-based information services - 10. Evolution of the literature, from antiquity to the early twentieth century - 11. Contributions of American chemists to the literature. Name and analytical subject indexes. 'Aimed at students majoring in chemistry and chemical engineering and to scientists and engineers employed by the chemical industry in research and development and in plant operations' (*Preface*). *Class No:* 540(01)

[1121]

—WOLMAN, Y. **Chemical information:** a practical guide to utilization. 2nd ed. New York, Wiley, 1988. xiv, 291p. $44.95.

First published 1983.

16 sections (2. The scientific journal; 3. The library; 4. Keeping updated - the current awareness programme; 5. How to conduct a literature search; 6. Obtaining numerical data; 7. Chemical reactions and concepts; 8. Selecting a bibliographical database; 9. Synthetic reaction search; 10. Structural and substructural searches; 11. Environmental impact and control; 12. The patent literature; 13. Chemical marketing, processes and engineering information; 14. Gathering information about individuals and organizations; 15. Expert systems; 16. Perspectives. A 'very good publication' according to *Choice* (May 1989, p.1547), which also noted that 'many subjects are treated too briefly'. Glossary of acronyms. Detailed index, partly analytical. *Class No:* 540(01)

[1122]

—WOODBURN, H.M. Using the chemical literature: a practical guide. New York, Dekker, 1974. viii, 362p.

In 18 sections: 3. US government publications ... 6. Collections of physical data ... 10. *Gmelin's Handbuch der organische Chimie* - 11. Abstracting services - 12. Scope and use of indexes on *Chemical abstracts* ... 15. Microform publications - 16. The availability of translations - 17. Patent literature - 18. Computer-readable material. Glossary of acronyms, p.279-81. Index of subjects, forms, titles. 'A practical guide, not a bibliography of sources' (*Preface*). Compared with Mellon, Skolnik, and Bottle (3rd ed.), this guide is considered fullest on major reference books (*Choice*, v.21(6), February 1984, p.808). *Class No:* 540(01)

[1123]

WIGGINS, G. **Chemical information sources.** New York, McGraw-Hill, 1991. 352p. 2 disks (IBM-PC). $42.35. ISBN: 0079099394.

Covers databases including citation, subject and patent searching, with emphasis on online sources. Includes more traditional printed ones (dictionaries, handbooks, etc.) as well. An innovation in this type of work is the floppy disks (3.5 inch) containing over 2100 records with citations for, among other things, the complete reference collection of the Indiana University Chemical Library. 'Recommended very highly' (*Choice,* February 1992, p.920). *Class No:* 540(01)

Teaching Materials

[1124]

JENKINS, E.W. **References for chemistry teachers.** Leeds, Centre for Studies in Science and Mathematics Education, Univ. of Leeds, [1984]. [1], [1], 110p. £1.65.

A sequel to his *Bibliography of resources for chemistry teachers* (1973).

Lists under 36 heads (Analytical chemistry and stoichiometry ... Structure and bonding) 'some of the material that has appeared in three journals': - *Education in chemistry*, *The Journal of chemical education* and *The School science review*. It covers the period ending June 1983. *Class No:* 540(01)(072)

Indexes

[1125]

Index chemicus. Philaldelphia, Pa., ISI/Institute for Scientific Information, 1970-. Weekly. chemical structures. ISSN: 0161455x.

Formerly *Current abstracts of chemistry and index chemicus.*

Concentrates on *c.*100 key research journals (*c.*25 titles per issue), chemical structure accompanying each abstract. The synthesis, isolation and identification of new compounds are thus reported. 5 indexes: Journal - Keyword - Biological activity - Labeled compound - Corporate. Back cover lists the journals covered each week. Quarterly and annual cumulated indexes. 'This is one of the most important keys to the recent literature of organic chemistry' (Katz, B. and L.S. *Magazines for libraries* (5th ed. 1986), p.13). *Class No:* 540(014)

Encyclopaedias

[1126]

Concise encyclopedia chemistry. Jakubke, H-D. *and* Jeschkeit, H., *eds.* Rev. ed. Berlin, Walter de Gruyter, 1994. [viii], 1201p. diagrs., tables, chemical structures. $69.95. ISBN: 3110114518.

First published 1987; this ed. rev. and translated by M. Eagleson.

About 12,000 entries, A-Z, covering general, organic, inorganic, physical and technical chemistry; omits biochemistry. No index, but numerous *see* references. 'Good, reasonably priced' ('Reference books bulletin', *Booklist*, Setpember 1, 1994, p.66). *Class No:* 540(031)

[1127]

CONSIDINE, D.M. *and* CONSIDINE, G.D., *eds*. **Van Nostrand encyclopedia of chemistry.** 4th ed. Princeton, N.J., Van Nostrand Reinhold, 1984. [viii], 1082p. diagrs., tables. $89.50. ISBN: 0442225725.

About 1,300 entries, 'Absolute zero' ... 'Zymolytic reaction'. 112 contributors, although entries are not usually signed. Longer articles are documented (*e.g.* 'Phosphorous': 9½ columns, with 7 references). Analytical index, p.1039-82. Nearly 80% of the text is completely new. 'Designed for ready comprehension by anyone with a general background in chemistry' (*Journal of chemical education*, December 1984). *Class No:* 540(031)

[1128]

FALBE, J. *and* REGITZ, M. **Römpp's Chemie-Lexikon.** 9, erweiterte und bearbeitete Auf. Stuttgart, Thieme, 1989-. illus., diagrs., tables, chemical structures.

First published 1947; 8th ed., 1979-88.

To be compiled in 9v. Well-documented (*e.g.* 'Recycling', p.3808-10, with 1 column bibliography). Includes brief biographies and some trade names. Cross references. Etymology given. The major German general encyclopedia of chemistry and chemical products. *Class No:* 540(031)

[1129]

McGraw-Hill encyclopedia of chemistry. Parker, S.P., *ed.* 2nd ed. New York, etc., McGraw-Hill, 1993. x, 1230p. illus., diagrs., tables, charts. 82.95. ISBN: 0070454558.

First published 1984.

About 850 articles, A-Z, extracted intact from the parent work, *McGraw-Hill encyclopedia of science and technology* (7th ed. 1993. 15v.). Cross-references; index. A comprehensive and up-to-date treatment intended for high schools and colleges. *Class No:* 540(031)

[1130]

Macmillan encyclopedia of chemistry. Lagowski, J.J., *ed.* New York, Macmillan, 1997. 4v. (1696p.). illus., diagrs., graphs, tables. $400. ISBN: 0028972252.

Short articles (*c.*2p.) focusing closely on chemical aspects rather than on social or environmental issues. Suitable for secondary schools. An 'important new addition to chemical reference sources ... comprehensive, well-organized, and up to date' ('Reference books bulletin', *Booklist*, March 15, 1998, p.1266). *Class No:* 540(031)

Dictionaries

Polyglot

[1131]

Dictionary of chemistry and chemical technology. Huimin, C. *and* Wenchu, B., *eds*. Beijing, Chemical Industry Press; Amsterdam, Elsevier, 1989. 1716p. £151.

Terms in English, Chinese, Japanese. *Class No:* 540(038)=00

[1132]

DORIAN, A.F. Elsevier's dictionary of chemistry, including terms from biochemistry, in English, French, Spanish, Italian and German. Amsterdam, etc., Elsevier, 1983. vi, 586p. £141. ISBN: 0444442307.

9,013 numbered English-base chemical terms, with equivalents and indexes in French, Spanish, Italian and German. Genders are omitted. The inclusion of biochemical terms provides a link between organic chemistry, physiology, genetics and medicine.
Class No: 540(038)=00

[1133]

—KRYT, D., *ed*. Dictionary of chemical terminology, in English, German, French, Polish and Russian. Amsterdam, etc., Elsevier, 1980. [xiii], 600p. £103. ISBN: 0444997681.

Lists 3,805 English-base terms and definitions, with equivalents and indexes (on tinted paper) in German, French, Polish and Russian. 15 Contributors. Nearly 100 categories, plus symbols denoting the pure substance, standard state, and activated complex. Omits nomenclature of chemical compounds and terms from chemical terminology and technology. Intended for students, researchers, scientists and engineers. *Class No:* 540(038)=00

[1134]

SOBECKA, Z. *and* **CHOINSKI, W.,** *eds*. **Dictionary of chemistry and chemical technology in six languages:** English, German, Spanish, French, Polish, Russian. Oxford, etc., Pergamon Press; Warsaw, Wydawnictwa Naukowo-Techniczne, 1966. vii, 1325p. £125. ISBN: 0080116000

First published 1962.

11,987 numbered entries in English, with German, Spanish, French, Polish and Russian equivalents across the double page, and German, etc., indexes, on tinted paper. Categorizes terms, notes differences in meaning and gives genders of nouns. It omits current English terms that have no corresponding expressions in one or other of the foreign languages. No abbreviations. 'An excellent work of reference for any European chemist' (*Chemistry & industry,* 3 December 1966, p.2035).
Class No: 540(038)=00

English

[1135]

BENNETT, H., *ed*. **Concise chemical and technical dictionary.** 4th ed. London, E. Arnold, 1986. xxxviii, 1271p. £95. ISBN: 0713135840.

First published 1974.

Some 85,000 brief definitions, with many cross-references. Includes abbreviations and chemical structures. Prelims. on nomenclature, pronunciation, names and formulas of radicals occurring in organic compounds. The 4th ed. is enlarged with definitions of new trademark products, chemicals, drugs and terms coined to cover the latest technical developments. Prelims. have a section, 'The pronunciation of chemical words'. Intended for use by both professionals and laymen.
Class No: 540(038)=20

[1136]

—BEVAN, S.C., *and others*. Concise etymological dictionary of chemistry. London, Applied Science Publishers, Ltd., 1976. ix, 140p.

Defines *c*.2,500 chemical terms. Brief historical notes (*e.g.* where words were coined or proposed, and by whom). Eponyms included. 8 appendices on prefixes, formation of plurals, etc. Helpful introduction, including list of works consulted. Intended for a wide public.
Class No: 540(038)=20

[1137]

GODMAN, A. Longman chemistry handbook. Harlow, Essex, Longman; Beirut, York Press, 1992. 256p. diagrs., (col.). £5.99. ISBN: 0582088100.

About 1,500 terms, briefly defined (*e.g.* 'equilibrium': 13 lines). Arranged by subject (*e.g.* chemical reactions; colloids; electrolysis; organic reactions, etc.), with terms listed in index. 6 appendices. Effective use of colour in diagrams. For senior secondary pupils and undergraduates. *Class No:* 540(038)=20

[1138]

Grant and Hackh's chemical dictionary. Grant, R.L. *and* Grant, A.C., *eds*. 5th ed. New York, etc., McGraw-Hill, 1987. xii, 641p. diagrs., charts, tables. £74.

First published 1929; 4th ed. 1969.

More than 55,000 entries, including terms in such related fields as physics, medicine, biology, agriculture, pharmacy and mineralogy. Emphasis on chemical nomenclature. A standard chemical dictionary.
Class No: 540(038)=20

[1139]

HAMPEL, C.A. *and* **HAWLEY, G.C., eds. Glossary of chemical terms.** 2nd ed. New York, Van Nostrand Reinhold, 1982. ix [1], 306p. $25.50. ISBN: 0442238711.

First published 1968 (vi, 281p.).

Definitions, by many hands, of *c*.2,000 'essential terms used in chemistry and the process industries' (*Preface to second edition*). 'Oxygen': nearly 1 column; 'Nomenclature': 2/3 column. Includes brief biographical sketches. Cross-references. Intended for students and a wide public. *Class No:* 540(038)=20

[1140]

Hawley's condensed chemical dictionary. 13th ed., revised by R.J. Lewis, Sr. New York, etc. Wiley, 1997. xiii, 1229p. chemical structures. ISBN: 0471292052.

First published 1919; 12th ed. 1993.

'A compendium of technical data and descriptive information covering many thousand chemicals' (*Introduction*). Data for chemical and raw materials include name; synonym; CAS registry number; formula; source or occurrence; derivation; grade; hazard; use; shipping regulations. 3 appendices (3. Manufacturers of trademarked products). For this edition 'all trademarked entries were revised' (*Introduction*). Also available on CD-ROM with *Sax's dangerous properties of industrial materials*. A standard dictionary.
Class No: 540(038)=20

[1141]

HIBBERT, D.B. *and* **JAMES, A.M. Macmillan dictionary of chemistry.** London, Macmillan, 1987. viii, 532p. diagrs., tables. £45; £14.95. ISBN: 0333390814.

5,200 chemical terms and concepts, with emphasis on physical chemistry. Omits extensive lists of organic and inorganic compounds and also physical data of compounds. Entries range in length from 15 words to 1p. Appendices: SI units; tables of atomic masses of elements. Intended for students of science, researchers and lay persons. *Class No:* 540(038)=20

[1142]

—McGraw-Hill dictionary of chemistry. Parker, S.P., *ed*. New York, etc., McGraw-Hill, 1997. 454p. $16.95. ISBN: 0070524289.

Entries for *c*.8,500 terms in both theoretical and applied chemistry from six disciplines (general, inorganic, organic, physical, analytic and spectroscopy). Terms and definitions were selected from the *McGraw-Hill dictionary of scientific and technical terms* (5th ed., 1994). 'User-friendly' (*American reference books annual*, 1998, p.703).
Class No: 540(038)=20

[1143]

Miall's dictionary of chemistry. Sharp, D.W.A., *ed*. 5th ed. London, Longman, 1981. ix, 501p. diagrs., tables, chemical structures & formulas. £25. ISBN: 0582351529.

First published 1940; 4th ed. edited by L.M. Miall and D.W.A. Sharp, with others.

8 contributors. About 8,000 entries. 'Chromatography': nearly 1 column; 'Molecular distillation': ½ column. Cross-references. Explains terms, 'with brief accounts of important substances, chemical operations and chemists themselves' (*Preface to the fifth edition*). Special attention is paid to industrial processes and the use of particular chemicals. Intended for use in schools, colleges and universities, etc.
Class No: 540(038)=20

Children

[1144]

WERTHEM, J., *and others*. **The Usborne illustrated dictionary of chemistry.** London, Usborne, 1987. 128p. illus., chemical structures. £3.95. ISBN: 0860208214.

Introductory dictionary with useful information arranged thematically so that words are defined in context. 2 indexes: substances, symbols and formulae; terms. Good for schools.
Class No: 540(038)=20-0053

German

[1145]

DE VRIES, L. *and* **KOLB, H. Wörterbuch der Chemie und der chemischen Vefahrenstechnik.** [Dictionary of chemistry and chemical engineering.] 2., überarb. & erw. Aufl. Weinheim/Bergstr., Verlag Chemie; New York & London, Academic Press, 1978-79. 2v. ISBN: 3527256350; 3527257810.

First published 1970-72.

1. *Deutsch-Englisch*. 1978. iv, 849, [1]p.
2. *Englisch-Deutsch*. 1979. ix, 779, [1]p.

V.1 has *c*.80,000 German entry-words, with English equivalents. About 80 categories are applied and German genders given. In v.2 the entry for 'Water' and its compounds occupies 3½ columns. Each volume has appendices of conversion tables, abbreviations, etc.
Class No: 540(038)=30

[1146]

—ERNST, R. *and* MORGENSTERN, I.E.V. Dictionary of chemistry, including chemical engineering and fundamental allied science. London, Pitman, 1961-63. 3v.

1: *German-English.* 1961. 727p. 2: *English-German.* 1963. 1056p.

Later reprinted without revision.

V.1 has nearly 45,000 entry-words. 'Ambiguous words are in every case explained by synonyms.' (*Foreword*). About 40 of the many categories apply to chemistry and chemical engineering. British and US usages are differentiated. Many compounds; genders of German nouns are stated. V.2 has 65,000 entry words; abbreviations, p.1047-56. *Class No:* 540(038)=30

[1147]

—NEVILLE, H.H., *and others*. A New German-English dictionary for chemists. London, Blackie, 1964. xviii, 330p.

Lists *c*.42,000 terms and equivalents, including a large selection of non-technical words. Differentiates between British and US usage. Abbreviations included. Adequate cross-references. Small but clear type. Includes terms in general technology and chemical engineering. *Class No:* 540(38)=30

[1148]

Dictionary of chemistry and chemical technology: English-German. Gross, H., *ed.* 4th ed. Amsterdam, Elsevier; Berlin, VEB Verlag Technik, 1989. 752p. £97.40. ISBN: 0444988637.

English into German only. About 60,000 terms. Coverage is claimed for all branches of chemistry, chemical technology and related fields of science. *Class No:* 540(038)=30

[1149]

—Fachwörterbuch chemie und chemische: Deutsch-Englisch. 4th ed. Berlin; Verlag Alexandre Hatier, 1992. 760p. ISBN: 3861170353.

German into English only. About 62,000 terms. The English-German volume [see above] appeared in 1989.

Class No: 540(038)=30

[1150]

PATTERSON, A.M. Patterson's German-English dictonary for chemists. Cox, J. *and* Condoyannis, G., *eds.* 4th ed. New York, etc., Wiley, 1992. liii, 890p. £90. ISBN: 0471669911.

First published 1917; 3rd ed. 1950.

About 65,000 German terms with their English equivalents. A welcome new edition (after 40 years) of a standard dictionary, with increased emphasis on recent developments (*e.g.* biochemistry, food processing, the environment). Excellent editorial guidance on use. 'Highly recommended ... Welcome back, old friend' (*Choice,* July/August 1992, p.1659). *Class No:* 540(038)=30

[1151]

WENSKE, G. Wörterbuch chemie: Englisch/Deutsch. [Dictionary of chemistry: English/German.] Weinheim, VCH, 1992. xiv,1546p. £153. (*Parat.*) ISBN: 3527264280. ISSN: 09306862.

About 100,000 entries, English into German. Genders given and obsolete terms and phrases are indicated. Preference is for American rather than British spelling. A major dictionary. Available on CD-ROM. *Class No:* 540(038)=30

[1152]

—WENSKE, G. Wörterbuch chemie: Deutsch/Englisch. [Dictionary of chemistry: German/English.] Weinheim, VCH, 1994. xiv, 2041p. £138. (*Parat.*) ISBN: 3527264299.

The 'German/English' volume of this major dictionary. About 100,000 words. Available on CD-ROM. *Class No:* 540(038)=30

Afrikaans

[1153]

SUD-AFRIKAANSE AKADEMIE VIR VETENSKAP EN KUNS. Chemiewoordeboek. [Chemical dictionary. Edited by the Vaktaalburo and a Committee for Chemical Terms.] Voortrekkerpers, 1968. 418p.

About 15,000 terms: English-Afrikaans, p.1-196; Afrikaans-English, p.197-395. Equivalents; no genders. Appended list of institutional abbreviations. *Class No:* 540(038)=393.6

French

[1154]

DUVAL, C *and* DUVAL, R. Dictionnaire de la chimie et de ses applications. Paris, Technique et Documentation, 1978. 1087p.

The leading French chemical dictionary. *Class No:* 540(038)=40

[1155]

PATTERSON, A.M. A French-English dictionary for chemists. 2nd ed. New York, Wiley, 1954. 476p.

First published 1921.

'The vocabulary has grown from 35,000 terms to an estimated 42,000, in spite of the fact that many terms having the same spelling and meaning in French and English have been omitted in order to save time and space' (*Preface* to 2nd ed). Some of the technical vocabularies consulted are mentioned in the Preface. Well spoken of. *Class No:* 540(038)=40

[1156]

—CORNUBERT, R. Dictionnaire chimique: anglais-français; mots et locutions fréquemment rencontrés dans les textes anglais et américains. 6th ed. Paris, Dunod, 1977. 215p.

5th ed. 1970.

Includes nearly 6,000 entry-words. Appendices of abbreviations, weights and measures. *Class No:* 540(038)=40

[1157]

—FROMHERZ, H. *and* KING, A. French-English chemical terminology: an introduction to chemistry in French and English. Translated by J. Jousset. Weinheim/Bergstrasse, Verlag-Chemie GmbH; Paris, Gauthier-Villars, 1968. xix, 2-561p.

Similar in layout to their *Englische und deutsche chemische Fachausdrücke* (5th ed. 1958). Index of French terms (*c*.8,000), p.463-508; index of English terms, p.509-61. Intended for students, research scientists, industrial chemists and translators. *Class No:* 540(038)=40

Spanish

[1158]

Diccionario de química y de productos químicos. Español-inglés, inglés-español. 2nd. ed. Barcelona, Omega, 1975. 1017p.

First published 1959.

The 2nd ed. is based on *The Condensed chemical industry* (then in its 8th ed., 1966, revised by G.G. Hawley) and translated by G. Ramos.

The 1959 ed. (1080p. + 130p.) has *c*.30,000 entries. The Spanish-English section (p.29-1080) gives explanations (properties; analysis; uses), with cross-references, whereas the 130-p. English-Spanish section acts as an index of entry-words. *Class No:* 540(038)=60

[1159]

KAPLAN, S.M. Wiley's English-Spanish Spanish-English chemistry dictionary. Chichester, Wiley, 1998. viii, 530p. £70 (Hbk); £32.50 (Pbk). ISBN: 0471192880, (Hbk); 0471249238, (Pbk).

About 20,000 terms in each half. *Class No:* 540(038)=60

Russian

[1160]

HOSEH, M. *and* HOSEH, M.I. Russian-English dictionary of chemistry and chemical technology. New York, Reinhold; London, Chapman & Hall, 1964. xiii, [1], 522p.

About 40,000 entries, many of them compounds. Multiword terms are grouped under the keyword, with the modifier following, A-Z. Abbreviations are included. Categories (and sometimes explanations) appear italicized, in parentheses. Genders of Russian nouns given, but not stress. Well produced on good paper, in clear cyrillic type. Compared with Callaham (also with 40,000 entries, but with compounds subsumed), Hoseh gives more strictly chemical meanings and not the wider annotations that make Callaham such a valuable general technical Russian-English dictionary. *Class No:* 540(038)=82

[1161]

—CARPOVICH, E.A. *and* CARPOVICH, V.V. The Russian-English chemical dictionary. 2nd ed. New York, Technical Dictionaries Co., 1963. 352p. £31.50.

First published 1961.

About 24,000 Russian entry-words. Coverage extends not only to chemistry and chemical engineering but also to fuels, foods and pharmacology. Includes many formulas and adopts US nomenclature. Good layout but considered less reliable than Callaham (*qv*) by Neiswender (*Guide to Russian reference and language aids,* p.29). *Class No:* 540(038)=82

[1162]

—DIVSIC, L.B. *and* MIKHAILOV, V.V., *eds.* Anglo-russkii Khimiko-tekhnologiches Kiĭ. 7th ed. Moscow, 1971. 756p.

English-Russian dictionary of pure and applied chemistry. 30,000 English entry-words, with Russian equivalents. *Class No:* 540(038)=82

[1163]

MACURA, P. Elsevier's dictionary of chemistry: Russian/English. Amsterdam, Elsevier, 1993. [xi], 929p. £139.25. ISBN: 0444896287.

About 10,000 entries; most equivalents. Short bibliography and list of abbreviations precede. *Class No:* 540(038)=82

Arabic

[1164]

LEAGUE OF ARAB STATES. Education, Culture and Sciences Organization. Permanent Bureau of Arabisation. **Lexicon of chemistry.** [Lexique de chimie.] Rabat, Bureau Permanent de Coordination de l'Arabisation, 1971. [1] xv, 141p.

985 Arabic terms, with English and French equivalents, plus indexes to numbered Arabic entries. *Class No:* 540(038)=927

Oriental

[1165]

Chinese-English-Japanese glossary of chemical terms. Hong Kong, Joint Publishing Co., 1980. 611p. ISBN: 9620400263.

About 10,000 Chinese-character entry-words, with English and Japanese equivalents and indexes. *Class No:* 540(038)=95

Japanese

[1166]

JAPAN: Ministry of Education. **Japanese-English scientific terms: chemistry.** 4th ed. Tokyo, Chemical Society of Japan, 1987. 689p.

Part 1: Japanese-English (romanised form; Japanese character; English equivalent) - Part 2: English-Japanese (English-Japanese; romanised form). About 8,000 terms. *Class No:* 540(038)=956

Reviews & Abstracts

[1167]

British abstracts. London, Bureau of Abstracts, 1945-53. pts.A; B (12pa.); C (4pa.).

Previous titles: *Abstracts of chemical papers.* A: *Pure chemistry* (1924-25); *British chemical abstracts* (1926-37); *British chemical and physiological abstracts* (1938-44). As *British abstracts,* totalled *c.*50,000 abstracts pa. Of value on BIOS and FIAT reports on World War II German chemical industry (see *Guide to reference material* (3rd ed.), v.1, p.58).

British abstracts, now superseded as an overall service by *Chemical abstracts,* is being continued as follows: A I-II, - by lists of papers in pure chemistry in *Current chemical papers* (Chemical Society, 1954-69). A III, - by *British abstracts of medical science,* 1954-56; subsequently *International abstracts of biological sciences,* 1956-c.82; later *Current awareness in the biological sciences,* 1983- (*qv*). B I-II, - by abstracts in *Journal of applied chemistry,* 1954-71. B III, - by abstracts in *Journal of the science of food and agriculture,* 1954-. C, - by *Analytical abstracts,* 1954- (*qv*). *Class No:* 540(048)

[1168]

Chemical abstracts. Columbus, Ohio, American Chemical Society, 1907-. v.1 Weekly. $10,000pa. ISSN: 00092258.

Chemical abstracts provides over 700,000 abstracts pa., taken from over 8,000 journals worldwide, plus patents, conference proceedings, government research reports, books and dissertations. Coverage in 80 sections. Odd-numbered weekly issues feature organic and biochemical sections; even-numbered issues cover applied chemistry, chemical engineering. Weekly keyword, patent and author indexes; half-yearly author, general subject, chemical substance, formula and patent indexes. The earlier 10-yearly cumulative indexes (1907-56) became 5-yearly 1957-; The 13th Collective index, for 1992-96, occupied 24v., with extremely detailed indexing, - *c.*650 entry-words per 1,000 words in the abstracts).

Chemical abstracts is also available in 5 fortnightly index groupings (1963-): *Applied chemistry and chemical engineering* sections (CAAS), *Biochemical sections* (CABS), *Macramolecular sections* (CAMS), *Organic chemistry* sections (CAOS), and *Physical, inorganic and analytical chemistry* sections (CAPS). (No volume indexes are included in section subscriptions). Other features available: *Index guide; Ring index handbook;* and a chemical-compound *Registry,* assigning CAS Registry Numbers to unique compounds. *Using chemical abstracts* comprises a cassette and workbook.

CA selects offers a current-awareness service, reproducing 100-200 CA abstracts per bi-weekly issue in 36 areas (*e.g. Chemical hazards, Forensic chemistry, Liquid crystals,* and *New books in chemistry*). *Chemical Abstracts Service source index* (CASSI) lists periodicals abstracted. Other titles include *Chemical titles.*

Chemical abstracts is the most widely used abstracting service in English that covers the whole field of chemistry, pure and applied, and including biochemistry. All science libraries should provide at least some parts of the Chemical Abstracts Service.

CA corresponds as a database to *Chemical abstracts.* *Class No:* 540(048)

[1169]

—Chemical titles. Columbus, Ohio, Chemical Abstracts Service, 1961-. Bi-weekly. $320 pa.

A current awareness service listing *c.*5,000 research papers from some 750 periodicals worldwide on pure and applied chemistry. A keyword-in-context index precedes a 'Bibliography' of the 'contents tables' of journals A-Z. Appended author index. A list of journals covered appears on the inside cover of each issue, with CODEN and abbreviated titles. *Class No:* 540(048)

[1170]

Chemischer Informationsdienst. Weinheim/Bergstrasse, Verlag Chemie GmbH, 1970-. 2 series, ea. weekly. ISSN: 00012975.

An abstracting service in 2 parts: *Organische Chemie* and *Anorganische und physikalische Chemie,* together covering *c.*40,000 research papers in organic, inorganic and physical chemistry. Systematically arranged. Abstracts appear about 2 months after the original publication. Replaces *Chemischer Zentralblatt* (*qv*). *Class No:* 540(048)

[1171]

—Chemischer Zentralblatt. Berlin, Akademie Verlag GmbH; Weinheim/ Bergstrasse, Verlag Chemie, 1856-1969. Weekly.

Initially *Pharmaceutisches Centralblatt* (1830-49); subsequently *Chemisch-pharmaceutisches Centralblatt* (1850-55).

In its heyday it carried *c.*100,00 indicative abstracts pa., - fuller than *Chemical abstracts,* its rival in world coverage of chemistry and allied subjects, particularly for pre-1937 material. Available on microfilm from Princeton Microfilm Corp., Princeton, N.J. *Class No:* 540(048)

[1172]

Current contents: Physical, chemical and earth sciences. Philadelphia, Pa., Institute for Scientific Information, 1979-. v.19-. Weekly.

Previously as *Current contents: Physical and chemical sciences* (formed by the merger of *Current contents: Physical sciences* and *Current contents: Chemical sciences*), 1961-78.

Reproduces contents pages of more than 900 journals in the fields concerned. Each weekly number covers *c.*100 journal issues. Online in CURRENT CONTENTS SEARCH, CD-ROM and available on diskette. *Class No:* 540(048)

[1173]

Referativnyi zhurnal. Khimiya. Moscow, Izdat. Akademii Nauk SSSR, 1953-. 24pa. ISSN: 04862325.

About 100,000 abstracts pa. from world literature. Sections (in Russian): General problems of chemistry - Physical chemistry - Inorganic chemistry - Analytical chemistry - Laboratory equipment - Chemistry of earth and space - Organic chemistry - General problems of chemical technology - Corrosion and corrosion protection - Technology of inorganic substances - Chemistry of processing wood - Natural fuels and natural gases - Chemistry and technology of high polymers. Author index per issue; annual author, subject, patent and formula indexes. Also available in separate parts. *Class No:* 540(048)

Periodicals

[1174]

BRITISH LIBRARY. Science Reference Library. **Periodicals on chemistry held by the Science Reference Library.** Compiled by C.L. de Hamel. 2nd ed. London, Science Reference Library, 1983. 73p. £5. ISBN: 0712307001.

About 2,400 titles, in A-Z, word-by-word sequence. Reports, bulletins, etc., are listed under names of issuing bodies. Entries give starting dates of holdings and SRL classification number. *Class No:* 540(051)

[1175]

—ROYAL SOCIETY OF CHEMISTRY. Periodicals in the library of the Royal Society of Chemistry. 4th ed. London, the Society, 1986. [i], [i], 82p. £2.50. ISBN: 0851864694.

Lists *c.*1,600 title entries, A-Z, with cross-references. Includes amendments up to March 1986. *Class No:* 540(051)

Bibliographies

[1176]

Chemical Abstracts Service source index [CASSI], 1907-1994 cumulative. Columbus, Ohio, Chemical Abstracts Service, 1990. 3v. (A-L,M-Z); Quarterly supplements, cumulated annually.

Formerly as *Chemical abstracts list of periodicals.*

About 70,000 entries, drawn from 65,000 serials and other sources. Data include former titles, language, history, frequency, price, publisher. CASSI is also available on CD-ROM and online. *Class No:* 540(051)(01)

Progress Reports

[1177]

Annual reports on the progress of chemistry. London, Royal Society of Chemistry, 1905-. 3 sections, each annual. ISSN: 02601818; 00693030; 02601826.

A. *Inorganic chemistry.* £144. B. *Organic chemistry.* £136. C. *Physical chemistry.* £144.

Each annual section volume comprises about a dozen well-documented, authoritative contributions, with author index. Provides for the general reader critical coverage of the significant advances in the major areas of chemistry during the previous year.

Available electronically over the Internet as part of the *Electronic journals from the RSC* database. *Class No:* 540(055)

[1178]

ROYAL SOCIETY OF CHEMISTRY. Specialist periodical reports: reviews of the chemical literature. London, the Society [formerly Chemical Society], 1967-. 45 series, usually annual.

Alicyclic chemistry.
Aliphatic, alicyclic and saturated heterocyclic chemistry.
Aliphatic and related natural product chemistry.
Aliphatic chemistry.
The alkaloids.
Amino-acids, peptides and proteins.
Aromatic and heteroaromatic chemistry.
Biosynthesis.
Carbohydrate chemistry.
Catalysis.
Chemical physics of solids and their surfaces.
Chemical thermodynamics.
Colloid science.
Dielectric and related molecular processes.
Electrochemistry.
Electron paramagnetic resonance.
Electronic structure and magnetism of inorganic compounds.
Environmental chemistry.
Fluorocarbon and related chemistry.
Foreign compound metabolism in mammals.
Gas Kinetics and energy transfer.
General and synthetic methods.
Heterocyclic chemistry.
Inorganic biochemistry.
Inorganic chemistry of the main group elements.
Inorganic chemistry of the transition elements.
Inorganic reaction mechanisms.
Macromolecular chemistry.
Mass spectroscopy.
Molecular spectroscopy.
Molecular structure by diffraction methods.
Nuclear magnetic resonance.
Organic compounds of sulphur, selenium and tellurium.
Organometallic chemistry.
Organophosphorous chemistry.
Photochemistry.
Radiochemistry.
Reaction kinetics.
Saturated hetrocyclic chemistry.
Spectroscopic properties of inorganic and organometallic compounds.
Statistical mechanics.
Surface and defect properties of solids.
Terpenoids and steroids.
Theoretical chemistry.

The reports are critical in-depth accounts of the progress in specific areas by acknowledged authorities, normally appearing within 12 months after the period of literature coverage. From 1988 the reports are available on the Internet; URL: http://www.rsc.org/spr.

Class No: 540(055)

[1179]

Survey of progress in chemistry. New York, London, Etc., Academic Press, 1974—. Annual. illus., graphs, chemical structures. ISBN: 0126105103.

Volumes include documented articles by specialists.
Class No: 540(055)

Yearbooks & Directories

[1180]

Chemocyclopedia: the manual of commercially available chemicals. Global ed. Washington, D.C., American Chemical Society, 1995. 472p. ISBN: 0841230900.

Global directory provides names and addresses of about 100 companies worldwide. Chemical directory gives chemical name, CAS Registry number, name of supplier, grades and physical forms, and special shipping or handling requirements. *Class No:* 540(058)

[1181]

ROYAL SOCIETY OF CHEMISTRY. Directory of consulting practices in chemistry and related subjects. London, the Society, [1986?]. 162p.

Part 1: Guide to services (Abrasives ... Yeast and yeast products) - 2. Subject guide - 3. Alphabetical index of consulting practices. Coverage includes related fields such as physics, engineering, computers, biological sciences, medicine, metallurgy. Consulting practices are those 'in which Professional Members of the Royal Society of Chemistry are principals'. *Class No:* 540(058)

Anthologies

[1182]

LEICESTER, H.M. *and* **KLICKSTEIN, H.S. A Source book in chemistry, 1400-1900.** New York, etc., Wiley, 1952. xvi, 554p. (*Source books in the history of science.*)

Selections of writings of famous chemists; restricted to material that illustrates the development of chemical theory only. Each section, documented, contains explanatory matter on the period concerned, followed by material on the chemists. *Class No:* 540(082.21)

[1183]

LEICESTER, H.M., ed. A Source book in chemistry, 1900-1950. Cambridge, Mass., Harvard Univ. Press, 1968. xvii, [1], 408p.

A collection of chemical papers that have shaped the structures of the various sciences (*General editor's preface*). Four parts (subdivided); 1. Techniques - 2. General and physical chemistry - 3. Organic chemistry - 4. Biochemistry. Bibliography of 63 biographies, p.393-402. Index, p.403-8. *Class No:* 540(082.21)

Tables & Data Books

[1184]

CRC handbook of chemistry and physics. Lide, D.R., *ed.* 79th ed. Boca Raton, Fl., CRC Press, 1998. v.p. diagrs., charts, tables, chemical structures. $99.95, £85. ISBN: 0849304792.

First published 1914; updated annually.

The 79th ed. includes numerous new or revised tables.In addition to physics and chemistry also covers conversion factors, laboratory safety, geology, astronomy and pure mathematics. An invaluable mine of information which 'remains the first choice of sources for scientific data—as it has for most of this century' ('Reference books bulletin', *Booklist*, December 1, 1998, p.689). Available on CD-ROM as *Handbook of chemistry and physics CRCnetBASE 1999* (1999; ISBN: 0849397200). *Class No:* 540(083)

[1185]

—Basic laboratory and industrial chemicals: a CRC quick reference handbook. Lide, D.R., *ed.* Boca Raton, Fl., CRC Press, 1993. 370p. diagrs., charts, tables. $39.95. ISBN: 0849344980.

About 1,000 organic and inorganic compounds, A-Z. Data include physical constants; phase transition properties; thermodynamic and transport properties; hazards. 'A convenient and inexpensive reference' (*Choice*, February 1994, p.958). *Class No:* 540(083)

[1186]

JAMES, A.M. *and* **LORD, M.P. Macmillan's chemical and physical data.** London, Macmillan, 1992. 448p. tables. £35. ISBN: 0333511670.

15 subject areas. About 430 tables, most with references for further information and/or additional data. *Class No:* 540(083)

[1187]

Lange's handbook of chemistry. Dean, J.A., *ed.* 15th ed. New York, etc., McGraw-Hill, 1998. v.p. tables, chemical structures. $120. ISBN: 0070163847.

First published 1934; 14th ed. 1992.

Mainly tables. Numerous sections covering: organic compounds; general information, conversion tables and mathematics; inorganic chemistry; properties of atoms, radicals and bonds; physical properties; thermodynamic properties; spectroscopy; electrolytes, electromotive force, and chemical equilibrium; physicochemical relationships; polymers, rubbers, fats, oils and waxes; practical laboratory information. Notable changes in this edition include a new section on separation methods and analytical chemistry. A standard work. *Class No:* 540(083)

[1188]

SHUGAR, G.J., *and others, eds.* **Chemical technicians' ready reference handbook.** 4th ed. New York, etc., McGraw-Hill, 1997. c.900p. illus., diagrs., tables. $85. ISBN: 0070571864.

First published 1973 (463p.). 3rd ed. 1990.

Emphasis on step-by-step procedures. Explains frequently-used laboratory and spectroscopy techniques with concern for laboratory safety. *Class No:* 540(083)

[1189]
—SHUGAR, G.J. *and* DEAN, J.A. The Chemist's ready reference handbook. New York, McGraw-Hill, 1990. xiv,640p. illus., diagrs., tables. £63.50. ISBN: 0070571783.

Concentrates on the actual questions and problems faced in the chemical laboratory. While deriving relevant material from Shugar's *Chemical technicians' ready reference handbook* (3rd ed.), a major portion is new, with sections on chromatography, thermal methods, determination of physical properties and much else, plus practical checklists and trouble-shooting hints. 288 illus. *Class No:* 540(083)

[1190]
Tables of physical and chemical constants. Kaye, G.W.C. *and* Laby, T.H., *comps.* 16th ed. London & New York, Longman, 1995. [xi], 611p. graphs, tables. ISBN: 0582226295.

75 contributors. 8 main sections: 1. Units and fundamental constants - 2. General physics - 3. Chemistry - 4. Atomic and nuclear physics - 5. Miscellaneous engineering data - 6. Statistical methods for the treatment of experimental data - 7. Laboratory safety - 8. Introduction to quality assurance of measurements. Analytical index. Subsection references. All tabulated values appear in SI units. Originally compiled by G.W.C. Kaye and T.H. Laby (cover title is 'Kaye and Laby'), but this edition prepared by an editorial committee. Essential for any reference library. *Class No:* 540(083)

Libraries

[1191]
SWEENEY, J.M. A Guide to sources of physical property data held by the Science Reference and Information Service. London, British Library, 1988. iv,128p. ISBN: 0712307508.

Sources of data, largely chemical. Classified arrangement. Entries include author, title, date of publication and brief annotation. *Class No:* 540(083):061:026/027

Nomenclatures

[1192]
HOWARD, P.H. *and* NEAL, M. Dictionary of chemical names and synonyms. Boca Raton Fl., Lewis Publishers, 1992. v.p. $149.95. ISBN: 0873713966.

About 20,000 chemicals in all, in 3 sections: chemicals in CAS Registry number order with synonyms, A-Z; about 130,000 chemical names, A-Z; index of formulas by the Hill system. Valuable for libraries lacking full *Chemical abstracts* or without access to chemical databases. *Class No:* 540(083.72)

[1193]
INTERNATIONAL UNION OF PURE AND APPLIED CHEMISTRY. Compendium of chemical terminology: IUPAC recommendations. McNaught, A.D. *and* Wilkinson, A., *eds.* 2nd ed. Oxford, Blackwell Scientific, for IUPAC, 1997. 464p. diagrs., chemical structures. £39.50. ISBN: 0865426848.

First published 1987.

Definitions of *c.*3,000 terms ('Absolute zero' ... 'Z value'), with references to sources 'published up to the end of 1995 from the Physical, Inorganic, Organic, Macromolecular and Analytical Chemistry Divisions of IUPAC' (*Preface*). Source documents. Chemical structures are a feature. *Class No:* 540(083.72)

[1194]
—LEES, R. *and* SMITH, A.F. Chemical nomenclature usage. Chichester, E. Horwood for the Laboratory of the Government Chemist, 1983. 172p.

With 22 contributors. 18 chapters (*e.g.* 1. Problems of use of chemical nomenclature in specialized areas; 8. The use of chemical nomenclature in *Chemical abstracts*; 11. Biochemical nomenclature; 18. Nomenclature, the way ahead). Further reading, p.164-8. Index, p.169-72. *Class No:* 540(083.72)

Films

[1195]
ROYAL SOCIETY OF CHEMISTRY. Index of chemistry films, 1984. 7th ed. London, the Society, 1984. 480p. £21. ISBN: 0851864996.

First published 1959.

Comprehensive list of *c.*2,500 films, filmstrips, filmloops, videotapes, slides, soundtapes and overhead transparancies. 7 parts: 1. Physical chemistry - 2. Inorganic chemistry - 3. Organic chemistry - 4. Energy - 5. Biochemical topics - 6. Applied chemistry - 7. Miscellaneous topics. A-Z indexes. Classified index precedes parts. Appended addresses of distributors. *Class No:* 540(084.122)

Patents

[1196]
GRUBB, P.W. Patents in chemistry and biotechnology. 2nd ed. Oxford, Clarendon Press, 1986. xii, 335p. £40; £20. ISBN: 019855222x, HB; 0198552211, PB.

First published 1982 as *Patents for chemists*.

A guide to the lay reader of the patent systems of the UK, US and Europe. Contains sections on general principles of patenting, inventions in chemistry, pharmaceuticals and biotechnology, patenting for the chemical inventor and the politics of patents. Also has a glossary of terms and list of cases. *Class No:* 540(088.8)

Chronologies

[1197]
NEUFELDT, S. Chronologie Chemie, 1800-1970. Weinheim & New York, Verlag Chemie, 1977. vi, 359p. ports., tables. DM78. ISBN: 3527256768.

Includes 19 portraits, 4 tables. *Class No:* 540(090)

Histories

[1198]
BROCK, W.H. The Fontana history of chemistry. London, Fontana, 1992. xxiii,744p. illus., tables. £8.99. (*Fontana history of science.*) ISBN: 0006861733.

16 chapters, subdivided: 1. On the nature of the universe and the hermetic museum ... 3. Elements of chemistry ... 6. Chemical method ... 12. The chemical news ... 16. At the sign of the hexagon. Extensive 'Bibliographical Essay', chapter-by-chapter, p.674-714, a useful feature. Detailed, analytical index, p.715-44. An early volume in a new series, intended for non-specialists. *Class No:* 540(091)

[1199]
HUDSON, J. The History of chemistry. London, Macmillan, 1992. 320p. £40. ISBN: 0333535502.

Includes results of recent research into the history of chemistry. Concentrates on chemistry in the nineteenth century. *Class No:* 540(091)

[1200]
PARTINGTON, J.R. A History of chemistry. London, Macmillan, 1961-70. v.1 (pt.1), v.2-4. illus., ports.

Enlargement of his *A short history of chemistry* (2nd ed. London, Macmillan, 1948. xiv, 386p.).

V.1 (pt.1. 1970. xiv, 370p.) has 20 chapters (1. Early Greek philosphy ... 20. The Quabalah); name and subject indexes. Final stages of the manuscript were left incomplete when the author died, in 1965. V.2-4 (1961-64) concern the period from 1500 to the 20th century and assess achievements and influence of individual chemists. Practically the whole text is based on primary sources and is profusely footnoted. V.4, on the development of chemistry in the 19th and part of the 20th century, is in 5 parts (electrochemistry; physics, organic and inorganic chemistry; and radioactivity and atomic structure). Each volume has name and subject indexes. Publication of v.1 (pt.2) has been abandoned. *Class No:* 540(091)

[1201]
RUSSELL, C.A., *ed.* Recent developments in the history of chemistry. London, Royal Society of Chemistry, 1985. x, 333p. ISBN: 0851869173.

12 chapters: 1. Introduction - 2. Chemical biographies - 3. Chemical education and chemical institutions - 4. Chemistry to 1800 - 5. General and inorganic chemistry - 6. Organic chemistry - 7. Physical chemistry - 8. Analytical chemistry - 9. Biochemistry - 10. Instruments and apparatus - 11. Industrial chemistry - 12. Chemistry by location in Western and Central Europe (with 187 footnotes). Appendices: 1. Periodicals for the history of chemistry: 2. Some useful addresses. Author index; subject index - people; subject index - theories. *Class No:* 540(091)

Bibliographies

[1202]
PENNSYLVANIA UNIVERSITY. Catalog of the Edgar Fahs Smith Memorial Collection in the History of Chemistry. Boston, Mass., G.K. Hall, 1960. 524p. ISBN: 0816105227.

Photolithographic reproduction of the author-title catalogue of 11,000 cards. This collection, began by Edgar Fahs Smith, Professor of Chemistry and Provost of the University of Pennsylvania, comprises more than 13,000 volumes, prints and manuscripts. *Class No:* 540(091)(01)

Biographies

[1203]

Chemistry: Who's who. Agarwal, R.K., *ed*. Sahibabad, India, Chemico Publishing Co, 1987. 336p. ports. $60.

Over 200 entries on chemists in 14 countries: Austria, Brazil, China, Denmark, Egypt, Greece, Hong Kong, Hungary, India, Japan, Saudi Arabia, Spain, UAE, Yugoslavia. Entries include a list of biographers' publications. Index, p.335-6. *Class No:* 540(092)

[1204]

FARBER, E. Great chemists. New York & London, Interscience, 1961. xxvi, 1642p. illus., ports.

Nearly 100 contributors; more than biographies. 59 sections (1. Babylonian chemists - 2. Arabic chemists ... 9. Robert Boyle ... 20. Antoine Laurent Lavoisier ... 34. Leopold Gmelin ... 52. Dmitrii Ivanovitch Mendeleev ... 58. American chemists at the turn of the century - 59. Otto Wallach). Some sections have brief references. Index, p.1619-42. *Class No:* 540(092)

[1205]

—**ABBOTT, D.,** *ed*. **The Biographical dictionary of scientists: chemists.** London, Blond Education, 1983. [vi], 203p. £8.50. ISBN: 0058470008.

Contains *c*.200 readable biographies (*e.g.* Bunsen, Robert Wilhelm: 1½ columns). The series is designed for school and first-year University students who need quick reference information. Criteria for inclusion are not stated. *Class No:* 540(092)

[1206]

Nobel laureates in chemistry, 1901-1992. James, L.K., *ed*. Washington, D.C., American Chemical Society/Chemical Heritage Foundation, 1993. 798p. illus., diagrs., formulas. $34.95. (*History of modern chemical sciences*.) ISBN: 0841226903.

Detailed biographies (*c*.5-7p.) of 116 Nobel laureates, each with references and bibliography. Information includes education, family background, employment history, research interests. Arranged chronologically. 'Recommended' (*Choice*, March 1994, p.1102). *Class No:* 540(092)

[1207]

—**Nobel prize winners: chemistry.** Magill, F.N., *ed*. Pasadena, Ca., Salem Press, 1990. 3v. ports. $210.

Winners are arranged chronologically from 1901 to 1989, with a 6-10p. article for each. Includes summaries of presentation and acceptance speeches, account of scientific reputation, personal and scientific biography, and list of publications. *Class No:* 540(092)

Great Britain

[1208]

CAMPBELL, W.A. *and* **GREENWOOD, N.N. Contemporary British scientists.** Londona, Taylor & Francis, 1971. [viii], 286p. illus., ports.

Summarizes the life and achievements of *c*.130 distinguished contemporary British chemists. *Class No:* 540(092)(410)

USA

[1209]

MILES, W.B., *ed*. **American chemists and chemical engineers.** Washington, American Chemical Society, 1976. x, [1], 544p.

V.2 was published by Gould Books, 1994 ($20; ISBN: 0964025507).

517 biographical sketches of deceased chemists and chemical engineers, including editors of journals, writers of influential texts and founders of chemical companies. 162 contributors. Entries, signed, average *c*.700 words; references appended. V.2 includes 269 sketches and a table of contents. *Class No:* 540(092)(73)

Women

[1210]

Notable women in the physical sciences: a biographical dictionary. Shearer, B.F. *and* Shearer, B., *eds*. Westport, Ct., Greenwood, 1997. 496p. $49.95. ISBN: 0313293031.

Readable essays (*c*.1,000-1,500 words), some illus., on women who worked in the physical sciences (physics; astronomy; chemistry). Covers childhood, education, family life, obstacles overcome and achievements. Appendixes list specialties and prize winners. *Class No:* 540(092)-0055.2

[1211]

RAYNER-CANHAM, M.F. *and* **RAYNER-CANHAM, G.W. Women in chemistry:** their changing roles from alchemical times to the mid-twentieth century. Philadelphia, Pa., Chemical Heritage Foundation, 1998. 240p. illus. $34.95. (*History of modern chemical sciences*.)

Co-published with the American Chemical Society.

Considers the role of women chemists and the prejudices they faced. Emphasis is on professional women chemists from the 1850s onwards. *Class No:* 540(092)-0055.2

[1212]

Women in chemistry and physics: a biobibliographic sourcebook. Grinstein, L.S., *and others, eds*. Westport, Ct., Greenwood Press, 1993. 721p. $99.50. ISBN: 0313273820.

75 scientific careers, all women born before 1933 and over half deceased. Entries comprise biiography, scientific contributions and list of works by and about the subject. Clearly written. One aim of the work is 'to inspire young women to pursue careers in chemistry and physics' (*Wilson library bulletin*, February 1994, p.84). *Class No:* 540(092)-0055.2

20th Century

[1213]

GINGERICH, O. The Physical sciences in the twentieth century. New York, Scribner, 1989. 306p. illus. $75. (*Album of science*.) ISBN: 0684154978.

Covers physics, chemistry, astronomy, geology and computers. Includes brief outline of major discoveries, principles and participants within each discipline and numerous captioned illustrations, about 400 in all. Bibliography of science histories; Nobel prize winners in physics and chemistry to 1988. A 'well-conceived and handsomly-executed volume'. (*Choice*, January, 1990, p.826). *Class No:* 540"19"

Writing & Lecturing

[1214]

DODD, J.S., *ed*. **The ACS style guide:** a manual for authors and editors. Washington, American Chemical Society, 1986. 264p. diagrs., tables. ISBN: 0841209170.

Contents: The scientific paper - Grammar, style and usage - Illustrations and tables - Copyright and permissions - Manuscripts submissions in machine-readable form - The literal literature: becoming part of it and using it - Making effective oral presentations. 'This is a true *vade mecum*, in the best sense of the word' (*New technical books*, January 1986, entry 831).

The ACS also publishes *Handbook for authors of papers in American Chemical Society publications* (Washington, 1978, vi, 122p). *Class No:* 540:001.81

[1215]

Nobel lectures including presentation speeches and laureates' biographies. Chemistry. Amsterdam, etc., Elsevier, for the Nobel Foundation, 1964-72. 4v. illus., diagrs., tables.

1. *1901-1921*. 1966. xii, 411p.
2. *1922-1941*. 1966. xii, 508p.
3. *1941-62*. 1964. xiii, 712p.
4. *1963-70*. 1972. x, 271p.

The 1963-70 volume contains 8 lectures (*e.g.* 'Recent advances in the chemistry of natural products', by R.B. Woodward, p.100-121, with 8 references), plus biography (p.122-3). 11 biographies in all. Name index; subject index; index of biographies. The Nobel lectures subsequently appear in the annual publication of *Les prix Nobel*. *Class No:* 540:001.81

Information Management

[1216]

ASH, J., *and others*. **Communication, storage and retrieval of chemical information.** Chichester, E. Horwood; New York, Halsted Press: Wiley, 1985. 297p. ISBN: 0853125716.

11 chapters (1. The information need of chemists - 2. Classical methods of communicating non-structural chemical information - 3. Online access to the chemical literature - 4. Databanks - 5. Methods of structure representation and registration ... 8. Reaction indexing - 9. Techniques of structure manipulation - 10. Developments in computing - 11. Trends in the communication of chemical information. Appendices: 1. Glossary of acronyms, trade and product names; 2. Organization addresses. Analytical index, p.278-97. *Class No:* 540:025.4

[1217]

WARR, W. *and* **SUHR, C. Chemical information management.** Weinheim, VCH, 1992. xix, 260p. $90. ISBN: 1560811803.

25 sections, closely subdivided: 1. The scientific journal - 2. Abstracting and indexing services - 3. Tertiary literature - 4. Business and economic information ... 7. Information technology — software and environments - 8. Records management - 9. Data banks - 10. Chemical structure handling ... 13. Functions of patent literature ... . References, p.208-35; index, p.237-61. Expanded from the authors' article 'Information and documentation' for Uhlmann's *Encyclopedia of industrial chemistry*, v.B1, p.12-1 to 12-119. A comprehensive treatment with the emphasis on chemical information in a business context. 'Ranks with other major players in the chemical literature field ... Recommended' (*Choice*, May 1993, p.1496). *Class No:* 540:025.4

Institutions & Associations

[1218]
INTERNATIONAL UNION OF PURE AND APPLIED CHEMISTRY. **IUPAC handbook 1998/99.** Oxford, Blackwell, 1998. 240p. £29.50. ISBN: 0632052767. ISSN: 02698757.

Extensive information and data on the structure, activities, officers, etc. of the Union. *Class No:* 540:061:061.2

Research Establishments

[1219]
AMERICAN CHEMICAL SOCIETY. Committee on Professional Training. **Directory of graduate research:** faculties, publications, and doctoral and master's theses in departments or divisions of chemistry, chemical technology, biochemistry, pharmaceutical/medicinal chemistry, clinical chemistry, and polymer science at universitites in the United States and Canada. Washington, the Society, 1953-. Biennial. xxv, 1632p. (1993 ed.). £65. ISBN: 0841227233. ISSN: 01935011.

Includes names of faculty members, biographical data, their research interests, and titles of their recent publications. Also, statistics of numbers of faculty, postdoctoral appointments, graduate enrolments and masters and Ph.D. degrees granted. Faculty index, p.1A-25A. *Class No:* 540:061:061.62

[1220]
Chemical research faculties: an international directory. 3rd ed. Washington, American Chemical Society, 1996. 1248p. $199.95. ISBN: 0841233012.

First published 1984; 2nd ed. 1988
Information on institutions in countries other than the US and Canada (for which see the ACS *Directory of graduate research*). Chemical disciplines (*e.g.* chemistry, chemical engineering, biochemistry, etc.) are subdivided by country, then by individual university departments. Data include staff, contact details, specializations and citations of recent publications. Also available on CD-ROM (*Directories on disc*, American Chemical Society). *Class No:* 540:061:061.62

Research Projects

[1221]
Current research in Britain: physical sciences. 14th ed. London, Cartermill; The British Library, 1998. 2v. (xxiii, 936p.). £150. ISBN: 1860673988.

First published 1985.
Part 1: Research; Part II: Indexes. A register of current research being carried out in the UK universities, colleges and other institutions. *Class No:* 540:061:061.62.005

Women

[1222]
ROSCHER, N.M. **Women chemists, 1990:** a supplementary report by the American Chemical Society's 1990 survey of members' salary and employment. 5th ed. Washington, D.C., American Chemical Society, 1990. 418p. tables. $39.95. ISBN: 0841219095.

First report 1950; 4th ed. 1980.
Narrative summary (150p.) and over 200p. of tabular data. Hightlights the professional status of women chemists. *Class No:* 540-0055.2

State of Substances

[1223]
Dictionary of substances and their effects. Richardson, M.L., *and others, eds.* Cambridge, Royal Society of Chemistry, 1992-95. 7v. (6200p.) chemical formulas. £1050. ISBN: 0851863817.

About 5,000 chemicals. Data: identifiers; uses; occupational exposure limits; ecotoxicity; mamallian toxicity; status in legislation worldwide; physical properties; effects on sewage works processes; references. Known as DOSE. Available online via DIALOG and on CD-ROM.

The 2nd ed. is due for publication October 1999. *Class No:* 540-1/-4

Solids

[1224]
HANNAY, N.B., *ed.* **Treatise on solid state chemistry.** New York & London, Plenum Press, 1976. 6v. graphs, tables. ISBN: 0306350505.

1. *The chemical structure of solids.* xv, 540p. 2. *Defects in solids.* xiii, 527p. 3. *Crystalline and noncrystalline solids.* xvi, 774p. 4. *Reactivity of solids.* xiii, 721p. 5. *Changes of state.* xvi, 600p. 6. A,B. *Surfaces.* xii, 491p.; xiii, 418p.

A well-documented text. V.1, chapter 8: 'Structural characterization of solids', has 115 references. *Class No:* 540-16

Reagents

[1225]
100 modern reagents. Simpkins, N.S. Nottingham, Moss Publishing for the Royal Society of Chemistry, 1989. ix,203p. chemical structures. £24 ISBN: 0851868932.

Reagents, A-Z. Data include CAS Registry name and number; molecular formula and weight; reactions; safety and handling; availability; preparation. Examples of reaction schemes and literature references for each reagent. *Class No:* 540-4

[1226]
AMERICAN CHEMICAL SOCIETY. **Reagent chemicals.** American Chemical Society Specifications: official from January 1, 1993. 8th ed. Washington, the Society, 1993. ix, 806p. $149.95. (*American Chemical Society Specifications.*) ISBN: 0841225028.

First published 1950; 7th ed. 1986.
Definitions, test procedures, and standards support the actual specifications, of which 24 are new. CAS Registry numbers are included to aid online searching. Index, p.794-806. At least one formal supplement is planned before the next ed. *Class No:* 540-4

[1227]
FIESER, L.F. *and* FIESER, M. **Reagents for organic synthesis.** New York, etc., Wiley, 1967-. V.1-.

Data on each reagent include structural formula, atomic weight, preparation, uses, sources of supply, critical comments and references. Index of reagents according to use; author and subject indexes per volume. A comprehensive treatise. *Class No:* 540-4

[1228]
MUNDY, B.P. *and* ELLERD, M.G. **Name reactions and reagents in organic synthesis.** New York, Wiley, 1988. 546p. $39.95. ISBN: 0471836365.

Data on over 120 common named reactions and over 145 of the most commonly used reagents in organic synthesis. Journal references for the examples and to Feisers's *Reagents for organic synthesis*. 'This indispensable volume' (*Science and technology libraries,* V.10(3), Winter 1989, p.140). *Class No:* 540-4

Quantum Chemistry

[1229]
Advances in quantum chemistry. San Diego, Ca., Academic Press, 1967-. Annual. ISBN: 0120348268. ISSN: 00653276.

V.26 (1995. 367p.) has 5 reviews including 'Valence bond mixing and curve crossing diagrams in chemical reactivity and bonding' (85 references) and 'Quantum groups: application to nuclear and molecular spectroscopy' (120 references). *Class No:* 540.062

[1230]
ATKINS, P.W. **Quanta: a handbook of concepts.** 2nd ed. Oxford Univ. Press, 1991. 434p. diagrs., tables. $95. ISBN: 0198555725.

First published 1974.
Brief explanations (most about 1p.) of over 200 quantum concepts, A-Z. Detailed, analytical index; extensive bibliography (with references to 1991 publications). *Class No:* 540.062

Theoretical Chemistry

Physical Chemistry

[1231]
Advances in chemical physics. New York, Interscience: Wiley, 1925-. Annual. ISBN: 0471120022.

V.91 (1995. 600p.) has 12 contributors. The 7 papers include 'Predicting rare events in molecular dynamics' with 157 references. *Class No:* 541.1

[1232]
Annual reports on the progress of chemistry. Section C: Physical chemistry. London, Royal Society of Chemistry (formerly Chemical Society). £144. ISBN: 0854049037. ISSN: 02601826.

Each annual volume comprises about a dozen well-documented, authoritative contributions, with author index. Provides for the general reader critical coverage of the significant advances in physical chemistry during the previous year.

Available electronically over the Internet as part of the *Electronic journals from the RSC* database. *Class No:* 541.1

[1233]
Annual review of physical chemistry. Palo Alto, Ca., Annual Reviews, Inc., 1950-. illus., graphs, tables, chemical structures. ISSN: 0066426x.
V.45 (1994 (799p. $56) has several documented articles, *e.g.* 'Multiphoton spectroscopy of molecular species'; 'Surface photochemistry'; 'Orientation and alignment of reaction products', etc. Author and subject indexes. *Class No:* 541.1

[1234]
ATKINS, P.W. Physical chemistry. 6th ed. Oxford Univ. Press, 1998. 1032p. illus., diagrs., tables. £60 (Hbk); £26.95 (Pbk). ISBN: 0198501021, (Hbk); 0198501013, (Pbk).
First published 1978; 5th ed. 1995.
Some 30 chapters, each with 'further reading' and problems, in 3 parts: 1. Equilibrium - 2. Structure - 3. Change. Index. This ed. includes a CD-ROM with hyper-text links, all illus. from the text, animations, interactive graphs, and tools for problem solving and graph plotting. A standard, comprehensive textbook. *Class No:* 541.1

[1235]
BORG, R.J. *and* **DIENES, G.J. The Physical chemistry of solids.** Boston, Mass., Academic Press, 1992. xii,584p. diagrs., graphs, tables. £46.50. ISBN: 012118420x.
14 chapters (closely subdivided), each with 'additional reading'. Appendices, A-H. Author and subject indexes. 'For university chemistry and materials science departments' (*Preface*). *Class No:* 541.1

[1236]
Comprehensive dictionary of physical chemistry. Ulický, L. *and* Kemp, T.J., *eds.* New York, etc., Ellis Horwood; Bratislava, ALFA Publishers, 1992. 472p. diagrs., tables. £49.95. ISBN: 0131517473.
About 2,000 terms, A-Z, signed by contributors. Bibliography, p. 467-72. *Class No:* 541.1

[1237]
INTERNATIONAL UNION OF PURE AND APPLIED CHEMISTRY. Recommended reference materials for the realization of physicochemical properties. Marsh, K.N., *ed.* Oxford, etc., Blackwell Scientific, 1987. x, 500p. ISBN: 063201718x.
20 contributors. 18 sections (2. Density; 5. Pressure, volume, temperature; 9. Enthalpy; 10. Thermal conductivity; 15. Optical refraction; 18. Relative molecular mass (19 references)). Subentry references and sources. 'Reference materials with known properties that can be used as references for checking the correct operation of or for the calibration of equipment used for physicochemical measurement'. *Class No:* 541.1

[1238]
MILLS, I. Quantities, units and symbols in physical chemistry. 2nd ed. Oxford, Blackwell Scientific, 1993. ix, 166p. tables. £18.50. ISBN: 0632035838.
First published 1970 as *Manual of symbols and terminology for physicochemical quantities and units.* First ed. of this title 1988.
9 sections: 1. Physical quantities and units - 2. Tables of physical quantities - 3. Definitions and symbols for units - 4. Recommended mathematical symbols - 5. Fundamental physical constants - 6. Properties of particles and nuclides - 7. Conversion of units - 8. Abbreviations and acronyms - 9. References. Index of symbols, p.143-56. *Class No:* 541.1

Kinetics

[1239]
BAMFORD, C.H., *and others, eds.* **Comprehensive chemical kinetics.** Amsterdam, etc., Elsevier, 1969-. graphs, tables, formulas.
1. *The practice and theory of kinetics.* 3v.
2. *Homogeneous decompostion and isomerization reactions.* 2v.
3. *Inorganic reactions.* 2v.
4. *Organic reactions.* 6v.
5. *Polymerization reactions.* 2v.
6. *Oxidation and combustion reactions.* 2v.
7. *Selected elementary reactions.*
8. *Heterogeneous reactions.* 4v.
9. *Kinetics and chemical technology.*
10. *Modern methods, theory and data.* 3v. (*i.e.,* v.24-26).
V.29 is entitled *New techniques for the study of electrodes and their reactions.* 1989. 504p. £137. *Class No:* 541.124

[1240]
HOCHSTIM, A.R., *ed.* **Bibliography of chemical kinetics and collision processes:** an annotated bibliography of gas-phase reaction rates and low energy cross sections of atoms, ions and small molecules ... Prepared by M. Berman [and others]. New York, Plenum Press, 1969. ix, 953p. tables.
'About 20,000 entries, each specifying the study of a collision process, drawn from about 7,000 selected articles' (*Preface*). Covers the literature 1900-66. Main index, supplement; reviews. 'List of sources used in the literature search', p.22. Computer-compiled. *Class No:* 541.124

[1241]
JACOBSON, C.A. *and* **HAMPEL, C.A. Encyclopedia of chemical reactions.** New York, Reinhold; London, Chapman & Hall, 1946-59. 8v.
Records more than 15,000 reactions of the elements (excluding carbon and oxygen). Arranged A-Z, first as to the formulas of the reactants, and then as to the reagents. Each volume has lists of abstractors and journals used by them; also indexes to reagents and to substances obtained. Addendum volumes were planned. *Class No:* 541.124

Electrochemistry

[1242]
Advances in electrochemical science and engineering. Gerischer, H. *and* Tobias, C.W., *eds.* Weinheim; New York, VCH, 1990-.
A new series, formerly published by Wiley as *Advances in electrochemistry and electrochemical engineering.*
V. 2 (1992, 269p.) has 4 articles, all extensively documented. 'Progress in cathode activation', p.1-85, carries 594 references. Detailed, analytical index, p.265-69. *Class No:* 541.13

[1243]
CRC handbook series in organic electrochemistry. Meites, L. *and* Zeiman, P. Cleveland, Ohio (later Boca Raton, Fla.), CRC Press, 1977-83. 6v. tables, chemical structures. ISBN: 0849372208.
V.6 ([viii], 538p.) is largely tabular, - 11 main tables (1. Electrotechnical data, p.5-333), including a key to literature citations. Author index. 'Although these six volumes contain the largest collection of organic electrochemical data ever made, ... they include only a fraction of the data that have appeared in the original literature' (*Preface, v.6*). Thus, electrochemical techniques are excluded. *Class No:* 541.13

[1244]
Encyclopedia of electrochemistry of the elements. Bard, A.J., *ed.* New York, Dekker, 1973-. graphs, tables.
V.1-10: Inorganic chemistry; v.11-: Organic chemistry.
V.9, pt.B (1986, xvi, [1], 674p.) has 13 contributors. 5 chapters: Alkali metals - Bismuth - Zirconium and hafnium - Chromium - Uranium. Systematic treatment of each element: 1. Introduction and standard potential; 2. Voltametric characteristics; 3. Kinetic parameters and double-layer properties; 4. Electrochemical studies; 5. Applied electrochemistry. Well-documented (Chromium: 396 references). Detailed, analytical index, p.667-74. Aims 'to provide a critical, systematic, and comprehensive review of the electrochemical behavior of the elements and their compounds' (*Introduction*). *Class No:* 541.13

[1245]
HIBBERT, D.B. *and* **JAMES, A.M. Dictionary of electrochemistry.** 2nd ed. London, Macmillan, 1984. ix, 308p. diagrs., graphs, tables, chemical structures. ISBN: 0333349830.
First published 1976.
Several hundred electrochemical terms and concepts. 'pH': 3½p. Numerous cross-references. 'References and methods', p.298-9; 'Electrochemical journals', p.300; 'Tables of useful data', p.301-8. Further reading, on occasion. Eponyms. 130 diagrams. *Class No:* 541.13

[1246]
KUHN, A.T., *ed.* **Techniques in electrochemistry, corrosion and metal finishing:** a handbook. Chichester, Wiley, 1987. xviii,567p. illus., tables. ISBN: 047191407x.
8 contributors. In 3 parts: A. Introduction to experimental methods - B. Specialized techniques (Section I: Methods based on light; Section II: Spectroscopic methods; Section III: Other methods (*e.g.* physiochemical; radio-chemical; acoustic emission; dyes, etc.) - C. The literature (37p. bibliography of post-1960 monographs, most from the British Library Science Reference and Information Service). 28 chapters, most with extensive references (*e.g.* 'Raman spectroscopy', p.237-49, includes 166). Subject index. Dedicated - gracefully - to the 'Library' and its 'staff'. *Class No:* 541.13

Photochemistry

[1247]
RABEK, J.F. Photochemistry and photophysics. Boca Raton, Fl., CRC Press, 1994. 2v. (183p.; 200p.). chemical formulas. ISBN: 0849940419.
V.1, 3 chapters; v.2, 5 chapters, each closely subdivided with extensive references (*e.g.* v.2, chapter 5: 'photoelectrochemical utilization of solar energy'). *Class No:* 541.14

Radiation Chemistry

[1248]

CRC handbook of radiation chemistry. Tabata, V., *and others*. Boca Raton, Fl., CRC Press, 1990. 936p. graphs, tables. £228.50. ISBN: 0849429957.

18 chapters, some with references. Much tabular data. Index, p.921-36. *Class No:* 541.15

Colloids

[1249]

BECKER, P. Dictionary of colloid and surface science. New York, M. Dekker, 1990. 202p. $80. ISBN: 0824783263.

Brief definitions (2 lines ... 1/3 page) of terms not found in general chemical dictionaries. Features names of chemists, plus concise biographical data, who have contributed to the fields over the last 200 years. *Class No:* 541.18

Aerosols

[1250]

SANDERS, P.A. Handbook of aerosol technology. 2nd ed. New York, etc., Van Nostrand Reinhold, 1979; reprinted 1989. xi, 528p. illus., diagrs., micrographs, graphs, tables. ISBN: 0442273487.

First published 1970.

3 main parts: 1. Homogeneous systems and their properties - 2. Emulsions, foams and suspensions - 3. Miscellaneous. 25 documented sections (23. Toxicity of fluorocarbon propellants: 189 references, plus 4½p. of supplementary references). Detailed, analytical index, p.513-28. An extensive revision. *Class No:* 541.182.2

Chemical Compounds

[1251]

Comprehensive coordination chemistry: the synthesis, reactions, properties and applications of coordinate compounds. Wilkinson, Sir G., *ed*. Oxford, etc., Pergamon Press, 1987. 7v. ISBN: 0080262325.

1. *Theory and background.*
2. *Linards.*
3. *Main group & early transition elements.*
4. *Middle transition elements.*
5. *Late transition elements.*
6. *Applications.*
7. *Index.*

V.1 has 18 contributors. Well-documented articles (*e.g.* 'substitution reactions', p.281-329.; 559 references). V.7 (xi, 642p.) comprises 'Index of review articles and specialist texts' (1,707 entries); detailed and analytical cumulative subject index; and formula index. (Co-ordination compounds are compounds in which the atoms or groups are united by co-ordinate bonds). *Class No:* 541.4

[1252]

GABCOM & GABNET: acronyms of compounds and methods in chemistry and physics. Gmelin-Institut. Berlin, Springer-Verlag, 1993. [vi], 380p. ISBN: 354093653x.

About 4,000 acronyms of chemical compounds and 4,200 acronyms of physicochemical or physical methods and notations. *Class No:* 541.4

[1253]

Handbook of existing and new chemical substances. Chemical Products Safety Division [Japan], *ed*. 5th ed. Tokyo, The Chemical Daily Co., Ltd., 1992. [iv], 833p.

Lists about 20,000 substances registered for import and manufacture in Japan. Includes an English translation of the 'Law, Enforcement Order, Ministerial orders and notifications which we hope will be helpful to business' ('Recommendation', p.(1)). *Class No:* 541.4

Oxides

[1254]

SAMSONOV, G.V., ed. The Oxide handbook. Translated from Russian by R.K. Johnston. 2nd ed. New York, Plenum Press, 1982. 463p. tables. $75. ISBN: 0306651777.

First published 1973 (xi, 524p.).

Sections: General data, stoichiometry and crystal-chemical properties - Thermodynamics and thermal properties - Molecular properties - Mechanical properties - Electrical and magnetic properties - Optical properties - Nuclear properties and radiation effects - Clinical and catalytic properties - Refractory properties - Phase diagrams and binary element - Oxygen systems. References. Index of elements and their oxides. The oxides in the tables are listed in increasing order of atomic

....(contd.)
number of the element. 644 reference citations, mainly from Russian literature. 'Excellent' (*New technical books,* October 1982, item 984). *Class No:* 541.45

Chemical Structures

Solubility

[1255]

STEPHEN, H. *and* STEPHEN, T., eds. Solubilities of inorganic and organic compounds. Oxford, etc., Pergamon Press, 1963. 3v. in 7 (7300p.). tables.

1. (2pts.) *Binary systems.*
2. (2pts.) *Ternary systems.*
3. (3pts.) *Multi component systems.*

Translated from Russian. Over 27,000 tables in all, the data - uncritically presented - being based on a survey of periodical literature in all languages, on the solubility of elements, inorganic compounds, metallo-organic and organic compounds. References; index of chemical component formulas and table numbers. *Class No:* 541.8

Laboratory Tools & Techniques

CD-ROM

[1256]

Safe use of chemicals: a training package. Hamilton, Ont., Canadian Centre for Occupational Health and Safety, 1994. 1 disc. $1000.

Ver 2.0.

A multi-media training programme with 8 modules on receiving, storing, using and disposing of chemicals. Includes the CCINFO database which gives access to chemical profiles and hazard classificiations and access to the worldwide occupational health and safety community. Includes trainer's guide. *Class No:* 542(003.40)

Handbooks & Manuals

[1257]

COYNE, G.S. The Laboratory companion: a practical guide to materials, equipment, and technique. Rev. ed. New York, etc., Wiley, 1997. 527p. illus., tables. $60. ISBN: 0471184225.

First published 1992 as *The Laboratory handbook of materials, equipment, and technique.*

A guide to laboratory, research equipment and supplies, and measurement and operational techniques. Much emphasis on laboratory safety. 'Up to date, practical ... Highly recommended' (*Choice*, September 1998, p.159). *Class No:* 542(035)

[1258]

ROYAL SOCIETY OF CHEMISTRY. Working Party. Guidance on laboratory fume cupboards. London, Royal Society of Chemistry, 1990. 35p. £15. ISBN: 0851863299.

Provides practical guidance for users in accordance with Control of Substances Hazardous to Health (COSHH) Regulations (UK). Includes a review of the literature on factors affecting the efficiency of fume cupboard systems. *Class No:* 542(035)

[1259]

YOUNG, J.A., ed. Improving safety in the chemical laboratory : a practical guide. 2nd ed. New York, Wiley, 1991. 406p. $75. ISBN: 0471530360.

Chapters cover safety organization, labels and safety data sheets, summary of causes of accidents, inspection, chemical hygiene planning. 5 appendices: hazards; safety regulations (US, Canada, UK); personal protection; design; resources. 'A plainly written, thorough guide ... [which] should be in the hands of every manager responsible for laboratory safety' (*Choice*, March 1992, p.1109). *Class No:* 542(035)

Dictionaries

[1260]

JUNGE, H.D., ed. Pocket dictionary of laboratory equipment, English/German. Weinheim, VCH Verlagsgesellschaft, 1987. viii, 201p.

Two parts: German-English; English-German. Includes combinations of words in basic expressions. American spelling. 'A useful work' (*Chemistry and industry*, 2 November 1987). For students, research workers, technicians. *Class No:* 542(038)

[1261]

OCKERMAN, H.W. Illustrated chemistry laboratory terminology. Boca Raton, Fl., CRC Press, 1991. 211p. illus. $22.50. ISBN: 0849301521.

Lists several hundred items, most of them standard pieces of equipment. Table of contents and index in English, Chinese, French, German, Polish, Spanish and Turkish. *Class No:* 542(038)

Education Institutions

[1262]

Croner's manual for heads of science. Rev. ed. Kingston-upon-Thames, Croner, 1995. Looseleaf. ISBN: 0900319631.

The school science laboratory, its management and safety; emphasis is on chemistry. 6 sections (5. Science out of school - 6. Further information). Regular updates are planned. *Class No:* 542:061:37

Work with High Temperatures

[1263]

KOSOLAPOVA, T.Y., ed. Handbook of high temperature compounds: properties, production, applications. Translated from Russian by S.N. Gorin and others. New York, Hemisphere, 1990. xxvi,933p. tables. £132. ISBN: 0891168494.

Originally published as *Svoïstva, poluchemie i primenenie tugoplavkika soedineni,* Moscow, Mettalurgiya, 1986.

Covers borides, carbides, nitrides, silicides, sulfides, selenides and tellurides. 11 chapters, each with brief introduction and numerous tables: 1. Crystal chemical properties - 2. Thermodynamic - 3. Electrical, thermophysical, and magnetic - 4. Optical - 5. Mechanical - 6. Chemical - 7. Preparation of powders - 8. Production of materials - 9. Powder ignition and explosion hazards - 10. Toxicity - 11. Applications. 1138 references, many from Russian literature. A wealth of data. *Class No:* 542.46

Work with Liquids

[1264]

Science and practice of liquid-liquid extraction. Thornton, J.D., *ed.* Oxford, Clarendon Press, 1992. 2v. diagrs., graphs, tables. (*Oxford engineering science.*) ISBN: 0198561784, set.

1. *Phase equilibria; Mass transfer and interfacial phenomena; Extractor Hydrodynamics, selection and design.* xviii,603p. £60. ISBN: 0198562365.

2. *Process chemistry and extraction operations in the hydrometallurgical, nuclear, pharmaceutical, and food industries.* xviii,436p. £60. ISBN: 0198562373.

12 contributors, 13 chapters, closely subdivided, with extensive references (*e.g.* v.2, chapter 1 has 10 sections, 9p. of references). Volume indexes. A scholarly treatment. *Class No:* 542.6

[1265]

VISWANATH, D.S. *and* **NATARAJAN, G. Data book on the viscosity of fluids.** New York, Hemisphere, 1989. 990p. $275. ISBN: 0891167781.

Includes organic compounds, inorganic liquids, liquid metals, plasticizers and foods like soybean oil. For each compound one primary journal reference and *Chemical abstracts* CAS Registry number are given. Common name index. 'A major source for viscosity data' (*Science and technology libraries,* v.10(2), Winter 1989, p.138). *Class No:* 542.6

Work with Gases

[1266]

HAAR, L., *and others.* **NBS/NRC steam tables:** thermodynamic and transport properties and computer programs for vapor and liquid states of water in SI units. Washington, New York, McGraw-Hill, Hemisphere Publishing Corpn., 1984. xii, 320p. $34.50 ISBN: 0891163549.

Contents: Thermodynamic property values - Transport and other themophysical property values. Appendices, A-C (C. Equations for transport and other themophysical properties). 70 references, p.317-20. *Class No:* 542.7

Catalysis

[1267]

Advances in catalysis. San Diego, Ca., Academic Press, 1953-. diagrams, graphs, tables.

V.41 (1996. 416p.) includes documented articles with extensive references. Detailed analytical index. *Class No:* 542.97

[1268]

—**Catalysts in chemistry.** Braintree, Essex, R.H. Chandler, 1976-. Monthly. £170pa. ISSN: 03095770.

An alerting service, with *c.*4,000 entries pa., monitoring journals, monographs, patents and conference proceedings in several languages. *Class No:* 542.97

[1269]

EMMETT, P.H., *ed.* **Catalysis.** New York, Reinhold; London, Chapman & Hall, 1954-60. 7v. diagrs., tables.

1/2. *Fundamental principles.* 1954-55.

3. *Hydrogenation and dehydrogenation.* 1955.

4. *Hydrocarbon synthesis hydrogenation and cyclisation.* 1956.

5. *Hydrogenation ...* 1957.

6. *Alkylation, isomerization, polymerization, cracking and hydroreforming.* 1958.

7. *Oxidation, hydration, dehydration and cracking catalysts.* 1960.

A comprehensive and authoritative treatise for research chemists, fully documented. Thus v.7 (with 7 chapters by specialists) has 183 references for chapter 1, 'Cracking catalysis'. Author index (including references) and brief subject indexes. *Class No:* 542.97

[1270]

TWIGG, M.V., *ed.* **Catalyst handbook.** 2nd ed. London, Wolfe, 1989. 608p. illus., diagrs., graphs, tables. £50. ISBN: 0723408572.

First published 1970.

15 contributors. 10 chapters: 1. Fundamental principles - 2. Process design, rating and performance ... 4. Feedstock purification - 5. Steam reforming ... 8. Ammonia synthesis - 9. Methanol synthesis - 10. Catalytic oxidations. 21 appendices (1. 'Further reading'; 16. 'Specific heats of catalysts'). Extensive references; analytical subject index (18p.). Intended 'primarily for people working in the chemical industry' (*Preface,* p.16). *Class No:* 542.97

Analytical Chemistry

Encyclopaedias

[1271]

Encyclopedia of analytical science. Townshend, A., *ed.* London, Academic Press, 1995. 10v. (6059p.) illus., diagrs., graphs, tables, chemical structures. $1950. ISBN: 0122267001, Set.

The primary focus is on chemistry but also include analysis within physics, electronics, computer science, mathematics and biochemistry. Covers 3 broad areas: techniques; field or material of application; analysis. About 750 articles, A-Z, some lengthy, most with bibliographies (*e.g.* 'Arsenic': 17p.; 17 readings). V.10 is a detailed, analytical index. *Class No:* 543(031)

Handbooks & Manuals

[1272]

CRC handbook of basic tables for chemical analysis. Bruno, T.J. *and* Svornos, P.D.N. Boca Raton, Fl., 1989. [viii],517p. tables, chemical structures, graphs. £84.50. ISBN: 0849339359.

11 chapters, closely sub-divided (*e.g.* 'Thin layer chromatography' (p.129-59): 5 sections; 243 references). Index, 28p. *Class No:* 543(035)

[1273]

A Guide to materials characterization and chemical analysis. Sibilia, J.P., *ed.* New York, VCH, 1988. x,318p. illus., diagrs., graphs, tables. ISBN: 0895732696.

Includes over 100 materials methodologies including evaluation, chemical analysis and physical testing techniques. 13 chapters, closely subdivided: 2. Molecular spectroscopy ... 6. X-ray analysis - 7. Microscopy ... 9. Thermal analysis ... 13. Scientific computation. Index, non-analytical, p.307-18. *Class No:* 543(035)

[1274]

KOLTHOFF, I.M., *and others, eds.* **Treatise on analytical chemistry.** New York, London, etc., Interscience: Wiley, 1959-. illus., diagrs., graphs, tables.

1. *Theory and practice.* 1959-76. 11v. & index.

2. *Analytical chemistry of inorganic and organic compounds.* 1959-76. 15v.

3. *Analytical chemistry in industry.* 1967-.

Comprehensive. Pt.3(4), 1977 (xxxviii, [1], 686p.) has 14 contributors. It contains section D, 'Physical testing methods for the characterization of materials: Surface properties', p.167-227, with 91 referencs. Each part has cumulative author and subject indexes. Thorough treatment of the elements, one by one. 'Valuable as a source book of ideas as well as facts' (*Chemistry & industry,* no. 47, 23 November 1963, p.1867).

The 2nd rev. ed. (1978-) reflects the extensive development (*e.g.* in computing) and increased specialization of analytical chemists. Pt.1, v.1-14, so far. *Class No:* 543(035)

[1275]
POTTS, L.W. **Quantitative analysis:** theory and practice. New York, etc., Harper & Row, 1987. 710p. diagrs., graphs, tables, formulas. ISBN: 0060452714.

18 chapters (2. Errors in chemical analysis and the standard treatment of data; 8. Solubility equilibria; 9. Precipitation; 13. UV-visible absorption spectrometry and colorimetric methods and anlysis; 15. Potentiometry; 18. Chromographic equipment). 7 appendices, p.645-89 (*e.g.* 7. Some compounds of analytical importance). Answers, by chapters, to selected problems. Detailed, analytical index. Aimed at 'second and third-year undergraduate chemistry, biology, pre-medicine and engineering majors' (*Preface*). *Class No:* 543(035)

[1276]
WILSON, C.L. *and* WILSON, D.W., *eds*. **Wilson and Wilson's Comprehesive analytical chemistry.** Amsterdam, etc. Elsevier, 1959-. illus., diagrs., graphs, tables. ISBN: 0444417354.

V.29 (1992. xvi, 293p.) is on 'Chemical immunossay' and has about 280 references. Analytical index. The series 'aims to provide a work which, in many instances, should be a self-sufficient reference work; but where this is not possible, it should at least be a starting point for any analytical investigation' (*Preface*). *Class No:* 543(035)

Dictionaries

[1277]
MALUDZINSKA, G., *ed*. **Dictionary of analytical chemistry:** English, German, French, Polish, Russian. Amsterdam, etc., Elsevier, 1990. x,391p. diagrs., graphs. £86.35. ISBN: 0444987290.

7 contributors. About 2,000 English-base entries, with equivalents and indexes in other languages. Cross-references. About 300 symbols applied. Genders shown. *Class No:* 543(038)

Reviews & Abstracts

[1278]
Analytical abstracts. London, Royal Society of Chemistry, 1954-. 12pa. £868; $1432. ISSN: 00032689.

About 14,000 abstracts pa. Classes A-H: A. General analytical chemistry - B. Inorganic chemistry - C. Organic chemistry - D. Biochemistry - E. Pharmaceutical chemistry - F. Food - G. Agriculture - H. Environmental chemistry. Cross-references. Subject index. Annual subject and author indexes. Available online from DataStar, DIALOG, STN International, Orbit; on CD-ROM (1980-; SilverPlatter); and on the Internet from ChemWeb (URL: http://www.chemWeb.com). *Class No:* 543(048)

Nomenclatures

[1279]
INTERNATIONAL UNION OF PURE AND APPLIED CHEMISTRY. Analytical Chemistry Division. **Compendium of analytical nomenclature:** definitive rules. Freiser, H. *and* Nancollas, G.H., *eds*. 2nd ed. Oxford, Blackwell Scientific Publications, 1987. vii, 279p. graphs, tables, formulas. ISBN: 0632019077.

Recommendations based on individual PAC reports. The IUPAC's 'Orange book'. *Class No:* 543(083.72)

Gas & Air

[1280]
Encyclopédie des gas. [Gas encyclopaedia.] Amsterdam, Elsevier, for L'Air Liquide, 1976. viii, 1150p. graphs, tables. ISBN: 0444414924.

5 chapters on physical properties and flammability of gases, their safe handling, general metrology, symbols and units. Over 100 monographs (p.61-1150), each with bibliography appended. 'Ammonia' (p.951-72; 26 references) has data under 6 heads: physical properties; flammability; biological properties; precautions in handling and storage; materials of construction; uses. *Class No:* 543.27

[1281]
—KEENAN, J.H., *and others*. **Gas tables.** 2nd ed. New York, London, etc., Wiley, 1985. 2v. tables. $82. ISBN: 0471842400.

First published 1948.

The main tables include: Air at low pressures (for one pound) ... Standard atmosphere ... Physical constants ... Conversion factors. Sources of data and calculation methods. Examples provided to illustrate the use of the tables. Bibliography. *Class No:* 543.27

Optical Methods

Spectroscopy

Abbreviations & Symbols

[1282]
WENDISCH, D.A.W. **Acronyms and abbreviations in molecular spectroscopy:** an encyclopedic dictionary. Berlin, Springer Verlag, 1990. v,315p. $60; £35. ISBN: 3540513485.

Definitions (¼p. to 2p.). Readable, but more compressed than Honan's *Dictionary of concepts in NMR*. Each entry has at least one reference for further reading (many have 5 or even 10 such references). 'This is the most extensive listing of spectroscopic acronyms' (*Science and technology libraries*, v.11(1), Spring 1991, p.148). *Class No:* 543.42(003)

Encyclopaedias

[1283]
PERKAMPUS, H.-H. **Encyclopedia of spectroscopy.** Weinheim, VCH, 1995. [vi], 669p. diagrs., graphs, tables. £60. ISBN: 3527292810.

First published 1993 as *Parat lexicon spektroscopie*; translated by H.-C. and R. Grinter.

About 1,000 terms defined and briefly discussed (*e.g.* 'Dual-wavelength spectroscopy', 2½p). German equivalents are given for English entry words. The translators have attempted to replace the original citations (mostly to German material) with similar sources in English. Selected by *Choice* as an outstanding academic book for 1995. *Class No:* 543.42(031)

Handbooks & Manuals

[1284]
CRC handbook of spectroscopy. Robinson, J.W., *ed*. Cleveland, Ohio, Chemical Rubber Co., 1974-75. 2v. ([xi], 913p. [ix], 578p.). diagrs., charts, graphs, tables.

30 contributors. Aims to cover the major areas of spectroscopy, - 'NMR, IR, Raman, UV (absorption and fluorescence), ESCA, X-ray (absorption, diffraction, fluorescence), mass spectrometry, atomic absorption, flame photometry, emission spectrography, and flame spectroscopy' (*Preface*). V.1 carries 9 tables and detailed index; v.2: 139 tables and detailed index. References are appended to tables. *Class No:* 543.42(035)

Dictionaries

[1285]
DENNEY, R.C. **A Dictionary of spectroscopy.** 2nd ed. New York, Macmillan, 1982. xiii, 205p. diagrs., graphs, tables, chemical structures. ISBN: 0333138805.

First published 1972.

Defines c.1,000 terms; 10 categories. 'Fluorescence' : ½p.; 'Lasers' : over 1p. + diagr. 275 references, p.194-205. 55 diagrs. Usefully 'deals with some of the newer electron spectroscopies - such as Mossbauer and Auger spectroscopy - that are less well covered in other dictionaries which tend to concentrate exclusively on the more familiar molecular, atomic and electron spectroscopy techniques' (*Nature*, v.300, 3 November 1982, p. 464). *Class No:* 543.42(038)

[1286]
MORITZ, H. *and* TÖRÖK, T. **Technical dictionary of spectroscopy and spectral analysis.** Oxford, etc., Pergamon Press; Berlin, VEB Verlag Technik, 1971. 188p. illus. (pl.).

An English-French-German-Russian dictionary of c.3,500 specialist terms. Adds a 5-page supplement in Spanish. German, French and Russian indexes. *Class No:* 543.42(038)

[1287]
—INTERNATIONAL UNION OF PURE AND APPLIED CHEMISTRY. Commission on Molecular Structure and Spectroscopy. **Multilingual dictionary of important terms in molecular spectroscopy.** Ottawa, National Research Council of Canada, 1966. 221p.

Languages covered: English, French, German, Japanese, Russian. *Class No:* 543.42(038)

Reviews & Abstracts

[1288]
Mass spectrometry bulletin. Cambridge, Royal Society of Chemistry, 1966-. Monthly. £788; $1318. ISSN: 00254738.

About 7,000 references pa., 8 sections (*e.g.* 2. Isotopic analysis, precision mass measurement, isotope separation and age determination - 3. Chemical analysis - 4. Organic chemistry - 5. Atomic and molecular processes - 6. Surface phenomena and solid state studies - 7. Thermodynamics and reaction kinetics - 8. Other references). 3 indexes: subject, general, author. Cumulated subject and author indexes, 2pa. Also available on the World Wide Web (URL: http://www.rsc.org/msb). *Class No:* 543.42(048)

Progress Reports

[1289]

Annual reports on NMR spectroscopy. New York, London, etc., Academic Press, 1968-. graphs, tables, chemical structures.

V.1-2 as *Annual review of NMR spectroscopy.*

V.37 (1999; 400p.; £84.95; ISBN: 0125053371) has 6 documented articles covering a range of polymer science topics. Analytical subject index. State-of-the art accounts of aspects of nuclear magnetic resonance. *Class No:* 543.42(055)

Chromatography

Handbooks & Manuals

[1290]

Chromatography: fundamentals and applications of chromatography and related differential systems methods. Heftmann, E., *ed.* Amsterdam, Elsevier, 1992. 2v. (*Journal of chromatography library, V.51A,51B.*)

Pt.A. *Fundamentals and techniques.* 547p. ISBN: 0444882367. £76.

Pt.B. *Applications.* 564p. ISBN: 0444882375. £120.

Chapters carry extensive references, most upwards of 200.

Class No: 543.54(035)

[1291]

POOLE, C.F. and POOLE, S.K. Chromatography today. Amsterdam, Elsevier, 1991. x,1026p. illus., diagrs., graphs, tables. £91 (HB); £46.50 (PB). ISBN: 0444884920; 0444891617, Pbk.

9 chapters, with sub-chapter references. Subject index. Near print. *Class No:* 543.54(035)

Dictionaries

[1292]

ANGELÉ, H.P. Dictionary of chromatography, English, German, French and Russian. Heidelberg, Hutheg, 1984. 132p. $27.

First ed. as *Technical dictionary of chromatography in four languages* (Pergamon, 1970. 119p.).

About 3,000 technical terms in English, with German, French and Russian equivalents and indexes. German and French genders are given. Considered a useful and well-produced dictionary, although there are surprising omissions. *Class No:* 543.54(038)

[1293]

DENNEY, R.C. A Dictionary of chromatography. 2nd ed. London, Macmillan, 1982. [xiv], 229p. diagrs., formulas. £15. ISBN: 0333316673.

First published 1976.

About 1,000 entries ('Absolute detector sensitivity' ... 'Zwitterions'). 'Refractive index detector': 1½p., including 2 keyed diagrams. 55 diagrams in all. Adequate cross-references. 506 references. Aims 'to provide a source of reference for students, technicians and those newly interested in these particular areas of science' (*Introduction*). 'Gives the impression of being more sure-footed than that [his dictionary] on spectroscopy' (*Nature*, v.300, 2 December 1982, p.464). *Class No:* 543.54(038)

[1294]

SERRE, R. Dictionnaire contextuel anglais-français de la chromatographie. Ottawa, the Author, 1981. 106p. £19.95.

375 English terms used in chromatography are defined, with sources. The French equivalents are shown in correct context, using sentence form, plus references to further readings. 'This dictionary was prepared for translators and aims to give all the information necessary for a correct translation' (*Journal of chromatography*, v. 236, 5 February 1982, p.262). *Class No:* 543.54(038)

Reviews & Abstracts

[1295]

Chromatography abstracts. Cambridge, The Royal Society of Chemistry, 1986-. 12 pa. £726; $1198. ISSN: 02686287.

Formerly *Gas and liquid chromatography abstracts* (1958-84).

About 5,000 abstracts pa. Sections: General - Gas chromatography - Liquid chromatography - Electrophoresis. Annual cumulative indexes. *Class No:* 543.54(048)

Progress Reports

[1296]

Advances in chromatography. New York, Marcel Dekker, 1962-. Annual. ISBN: 0824793617.

V.35 (1995. xviii, 425p.) has 15 contributors. The 8 articles include 'Chromatographic characterization of gasolines' (202 references). Contents of other volumes [v.11-34]. Author and subject indexes. *Class No:* 543.54(055)

[1297]

Recent advances in thin-layer chromatography. Dallas, F.A.A., *and others, eds.* New York, Plenum, 1988. xiii,247p. illus., graphs, tables. ISBN: 0306429349.

26 chapters in 4 sections: Instrumentation - Radio-thin-layer chromatography: instruments and applications - Sorbents and modifiers - Applications. Compound and subject indexes. *Class No:* 543.54(055)

Tables & Data Books

[1298]

CRC handbook of chromatography. Zwieg, G. *and* Sherma, J., *eds.* Cleveland, Ohio, CRC Press, 1972. 2v. tables. ISBN: 0849305615; 0878195629.

Chromatographic data for *c.*12,000 chemical components in all. Tables cover gas, liquid, paper and thin-layer chromatography, plus compound index, in v.1. V.2 has 2 sections: Principles and techniques; Practical applications. Appended: International chromatography book directory. Detailed, analytical subject index. *Class No:* 543.54(083)

Biological Reactions

[1299]

Chemoreception abstracts: chemical senses & applied techniques. Bethesda, Md., Cambridge Scientific Abstracts, 1973-. 4pa. $275pa. ISSN: 03001261.

About 1,500 abstracts pa., drawing on *c.*5,000 primary journals, etc. Sections: Peripheral & central sensory mechanisms ... Animal behavior & chemical communication, including phenomenes ... Special products (*e.g.* perfumery) - Odor control - Chemosensory aspects of food ... Miscellaneous - Book notices - Notification of proceedings. Author and analytical subject indexes, cumulated annually. Also available via the internet (http://www.csa.com). *Class No:* 543.9

Inorganic Chemistry

Encyclopaedias

[1300]

Encyclopedia of inorganic chemistry. King, R.B., *ed.* Chichester, Wiley, 1994. 8v (4819p.) diagrs., graphs, tables, chemical formulas and structures. $2500. ISBN: 0478936206.

About 260 main articles and 850 definition entries. V.1 carries detailed list of the contents. V.8 covers T-Z and the index ('Tungsten: inorganic and coordination chemistry', p.4240-58; 212 references). Aimed 'at a wide range of readers' (*Preface*, v.1). Aslo available on CD-ROM (1997; £1600; $2500; ISBN: 0471967798x). *Class No:* 546(031)

[1301]

Inorganic reacitons and methods. Zuckerman, J.J., *and others, eds.* New York, VCH, 1986-. V.1-. £148 each. ISBN: 3527262598, V.1.

To be complete in 18 v. V.16 *Reactions catalyzed by inorganic compounds* (1993. 655p.) has 8 chapters, closely subdivided, each with extensive references. List of abbreviations. Indexes: author; compound; subject. *Class No:* 546(031)

Handbooks & Manuals

[1302]

Comprehensive inorganic chemistry. Bailou, J.C., *Jr., and others, eds.* Oxford, etc., Pergamon, 1973. 5v. diagrs., tables. ISBN: 008017275x.

1. H. Noble gases. Group IA, IIB, IIIB, C and Si.

2. Ge, Sn, Pb. Group VB, VIB, VIIB.

3. Groups IB, IIB, IIIA, IVA, VA, VIA, VIII.

4. Lenthanides. Transition metal compounds.

5. Actinides. Master index..

Data on physical, chemical and biological properties of elements. V.2 (xvii, 1613p.) has 13 contributors. Section 23: Sulphur (p.798-933) carries 579 footnote references. Analytical index, p.1594-1613. 'Highly recommended, even with its age' (*Information sources in science and technology*, 3rd ed., 1998, p.113). *Class No:* 546(035)

[1303]

GMELIN-INSTITUT. Gmelin's Handbuch der anorganischen chemie. 8. vollig neu bearb. Aufl. Leipzig, Berlin, Weinheim/ Bergstrasse,Verlag chemie GmbH, 1922-.

First published as Gmelin's *Handbuch der theoretischen Chemie* (1817-1819). 8th ed. under auspices of the German Chemical Society until 1945; then by the Gmelin-Institut.

More than 70v. have appeared, plus a new supplement series. Thus, the main volume 'Water desalting' (1974) had Supplement 1 in 1979. The classification system is based on the Gmelin system of the

....*(contd.)*

numerical sequence of elements (system number). Each element has a systematic monograph (history, occurrence, formation, preparation, with a summary of latest information, plus a full bibliography of source material). 'Biel'(Lead): C4. System-Nummer 47 (xix, p.1213-1851) covers literature up to 1969. Index. Formula index AC-NS(11.), 1975-79.

Available online, with over 1,000,000 records (from 1817 to 1975 for the *Handbook* and 1970 to date for selected journals), via STN International and on the Internet. *Class No:* 546(035)

[1304]
Inorganic chemistry handbook. McKetta, J.J., *ed.* New York, Dekker, 1993. v.1-. diagrs., graphs, tables. ISBN: 0824766873.

V.1: *Aluminium - Chloralkali and chlorine.*

To be in 3v. Documented entries, but no separate volume indexes. Articles originally published in *Encyclopedia of chemical processing* (*q.v.*). *Class No:* 546(035)

[1305]
MELLOR, J.W. A Comprehensive treatise on inorganic and theoretical chemistry. London, Longmans, Green, 1922-37. 16v. Supplements 1-7, 1956-80. 16v. illus., diagrs., tables.

Surveys the elements in periodic-table order. V.1 is mainly theoretical; v. 16 consists largely of the general index. The scope of articles on each element is similar to that in Gmelin. The Supplements update, with copious literature references (*e.g.* v.8, Suppt. 2, final section, 'Determination of nitrogen in natural products', occupies p.655-73, with 683 references). Indispensable in all chemistry libraries. *Class No:* 546(035)

Progress Reports

[1306]
Advances in inorganic chemistry. New York, London, etc. Academic Press, 1957-. v.1-. Annual. chemical structures. ISSN: 08988838.

Formerly *Advances in inorganic chemistry and radiochemistry.*

V.43 (1995. vii, 452p. £73.) has 9 contributors. The 7 papers include 'Diron-oxygen proteins' (186 references) and 'Reactions between metal complexes and DNA' (202 references). Subject index. *Class No:* 546(055)

[1307]
Annual reports on the progress of chemistry. Section A: Inorganic chemistry. Cambridge, Royal Society of Chemistry, 1905-. V.1-. Annual. £144. ISSN: 02601818.

Each annual volume comprises about a dozen well-documented, authoritative contributions, with author index. Provides for the general reader critical coverage of the significant advances in inorganic chemistry during the previous year.

Available electronically over the Internet as part of the *Electronic journals from the RSC* database. *Class No:* 546(055)

[1308]
Progress in inorganic chemistry. New York, etc., Wiley, 1959-. v.1-. Annual. graphs, tables, chemical structures.

V.46 (1997. 496p.) includes review articles with extensive bibliographies. Analytical subject index; cumulative author index, v.1-46. *Class No:* 546(055)

Tables & Data Books

[1309]
CRC handbook series in inorganic electrochemistry. Meites, L., *and others, eds.* Boca Raton, Florida, CRC Press, 1980-81. 2v. ISBN: 0849303613.

13 tables of data on the electrochemical behaviour of ions in solvents, etc. Key to citations. Companion set: *CRC Handbook series in organic electrochemistry* (*qv*). *Class No:* 546(083)

[1310]
Handbook of inorganic compounds. Perry, D.L. *and* Phillip, S.L., *eds.* Boca Raton, Fl., CRC Press, 1995. v.p. chemical formulas. £95. ISBN: 0849386713.

3,326 compounds, A-Z. Data: name; synonyms; formula; molecular formula and weight; CAS registry no.; properties; solubility; reactions, etc. Indexes: CAS registry no.; molecular formula; name/synonym. *Class No:* 546(083)

Nomenclatures

[1311]
Inorganic chemical nomenclature: principles and practice. Block, B.P., *and others.* Washington, DC, American Chemical Society, 1990. 210p. tables. $59.95; $39.95. ISBN: 0841216975; 0841216983, Pbk.

16 chapters, from single-atom species to inorganic polymers. 13 tables. 'Sufficient for nearly all uses' (*Choice,* February 1991, p.958). *Class No:* 546(083.72)

[1312]
Nomenclature of inorganic chemistry: recommendations 1990. Leigh, G.J., *ed.* Oxford, Blackwell for the International Union of Pure and Applied Chemistry, 1990. xxi,289p. ISBN: 0632023198; 0632024941, Pbk.

First published 1959; 2nd ed. 1972 known as IUPAC's 'Red book'.

States the 1990 recommendations on nomenclature, including formulas and names of compounds in general, names for ions and radicals. Tables note prefixes or affixes used in the inorganic nomenclature index. 'More comprehensive than the ACS volume on the subjects covered' (*Choice,* February 1991, p.958). *Class No:* 546(083.72)

Non-metals

[1313]
REID, R.C., *and others.* The Properties of gases and liquids. 4th ed. New York, etc., McGraw-Hill, 1987. x. 742p. illus. ISBN: 0070517991.

First published 1958.

12 sections: 1. The estimation of physical properties -2. Pure-component constants -3. Pressure-volume-temperature relations of pure gases and liquids -4. Volumetric properties and mixtures -5. Thermodynamic properties -6. Thermodynamic properties of ideal gases -7 Vapour pressures and enthalpies of vaporization of pure fluids 8. Fluid-phase equilibria in multicomponent systems -9 Viscosity -10. Thermal conductivity -11. Diffusion coefficients -12. Surface tension. 2. appendices (A. Property data bank: property data values for over 600 pure chemicals). Detailed, analytical index. *Class No:* 546.1/.2

Fluorine

[1314]
SIMONS, J.H., *ed.* Fluorine chemistry. New York & London, Academic Press, 1950-64. 5v. tables.

V.4 (1964. xv, 505p.) has 4 contributors (all US). 4 chapters: 1. General chemistry of fluorine-containing compounds - 2. Physical chemistry of fluorocarbons - 3. Radiochemistry and radiation chemistry of fluorine - 4. Industrial and utilitarian aspects of fluorine chemistry (190 references). Analytical subject index. *Class No:* 546.16

Oxygen

[1315]
Advances in oxygenated processes. Greenwich, Ct., London, JAI Press, 1989-. diagrs., tables. ISBN: 1559384514.

V.4 (1995. x, 249p. £62.50.) has 11 contributors. The 7 documented articles include 'Oxidation of lignin' with 145 references. *Class No:* 546.21

Water

[1316]
AMMON, F. von. Wörterbuch der Wasserchemie. [Dictionary of water chemistry. Dictionnaire de la chimie de l'eau.] Deerfield Beach, Florida, VCH Verlagsgesellschaft, 1985. 203p. $58. ISBN: 0895734966.

A German-English-French dictionary, promoted by the German Chemical Society's Water Chemistry Section. Main coverage: Water composition and quality, water purification, and all aspects of water chemistry. US terms are cross-referenced to British. *Class No:* 546.212

[1317]
FRANKS, F., *ed.* Water: a comprehensive treatise. New York, etc., Plenum Press, 1972-. diagrs., tables.

1. *The physics and physical chemistry of water.* 1972. xx, 596p.

2. *Water in crystalline hydrates, aqueous solutions of simple non-electrolytes.* 1973. xix, 683p.

3. *Aqueous solutions of simple electrolytes.* 1973. vii, 472p.

4. *Aqueous solutions of amphiphiles and macromolecules.* 1975. xxi, 839p.

5. *Water in disperse systems.* 1975. xvi, 366p.

6. *Recent advances.* 1979. 466p.

7. *Water and aqueous solutions at subzero temperature.* 1982. 400p.

Each volume carries its own bibliography of references (*e.g.* v.1, p.545-78) and index. V.6 concerns recently-developed methods of testing chemistry and physics of aqueous systems, solutions and hydrates. 'This treatise should be available to all serious research workers with chemical or biological problems in a primarily aqueous world' (*Nature,* v.261, 24 June 1976, p.729, on v.4-5). *Class No:* 546.212

[1318]
TEKNISKA NOMENKLATURCENTRALEN. Vattenordlista.
[Glossary of water.] Stockholm, the Centre, 1968-74. 3v. (*TNC 41, 45, 54.*) ISBN: 9171960414.

Swedish-base terms and definitions, with French, German and English equivalents and indexes for this water glossary, covering hydrological terms. *Class No:* 546.212

Carbons

[1319]
RODD, E.H., *ed.* **Rodd's chemistry of carbon compounds:** a modern comprehensive treatise. 2nd ed., edited by S. Coffey. Amsterdam, etc., Elsevier, 1964-77. Supplements, 1973-. 4v. and suppts. illus., tables.

First published 1951-62 (10v.).
1. *General introduction. Aliphatic compounds.* 11v.
2. *Aliphatic compounds.* 6v.
3. *Aromatic compounds.* 11v.
4. *Heterocyclic compounds.* v.1-10.
5. *Miscellaneous. General index.*

Full references to original sources. Each volume has an index of compounds, named reactions, reagents and methods. Part E, *Six-membered monohetrocyclic compounds ...* was published as a supplement to Vol. 4 in 1990. Second supplements to the 2nd ed. have been published in 5 vols. (v.3, 1995, xvi, 354p.).

The 1st ed. bridged the gap between the encyclopaedic surveys like Beilstein (*qv*) and textbooks. *Class No:* 546.26

Metals

[1320]
ROBB, C. Metals databook. London, The Institute of Metals, 1987. [xvi],500p. diagrs., tables. £90. ISBN: 0904357694.

Data, largely in tabular form, on the chemical, physical and mechanical properties of commercially available metallic materials. Much of the data is specific to British Standards. Covers welding, heat treatment, test house and laboratory data. 4 appendices: 1. S.I. units - 2. Hardness testing - 3. Material specifications - 4. Equilibrium diagrams. No index, but detailed contents list. Small, handy format, but very expensive. *Class No:* 546.3/.9

Rare Earths

[1321]
GSCHNEIDNER, K.A., *Jr* and **EYRING, Le R.,** *eds..* **Handbook of the physics and chemistry of rare earths.** Amsterdam, etc., North-Holland Co., 1978-. graphs, tables.
1. *Metals.* 1978, xxv, 894p.
2. *Alloys and intermetallics.* 1979. xiii, 628p. £110.
3./4. *Non-metallic compounds.* 1979. xiii, 604p; xiii, 602p. £115; £105.
5. *Rare earth alloys and compounds.* 1982. x, 701p. £132.
10. *High energy spectroscopy.* 1987. 611p. £113.
11. *Two hundred year impact of rare earth on science.* 1988. xiv, 594p. £113.
13. *Rare earth elements.* 1990. xii,473p.
19. *Lanthanides/Actinides: Physics-II.* 1994. xvii, 700p.

Each volume carries documented chapters by specialists. V.19 includes chapters 130 to 134, by various hands, each with extensive bibliography. 'Indispensible for academic libraries and chemistry collections' (*New technical books,* June 1980, item 273).
Class No: 546.65

[1322]
—**Rare earth bulletin: an interdisciplinary abstracts journal.** London, Multi-Science Publishing Co., 1972-. 6 pa. £165pa. ISSN: 03078531.

Includes *c.*700 abstracts pa. Sections: Extraction; Chemical properties; Crystallography; Nuclear properties; Solid state; Mechanical and accoustic properties; Applications. Subject index. *Class No:* 546.65

[1323]
JEZOWSKA-TRZEBIATOWSKA, B., *and others.* **The Rare elements:** occurrence and technology. Amsterdam, Elsevier; Warszawa, PWN-Polish Scientific Publishers, 1990. x,536p. diagrs., graphs, tables. £131.25. (*Topics in inorganic and general chemistry, 23.*) ISBN: 0444988777.

Rev. and enlarged translation of the 1976 Polish original.

7 chapters, each with appended bibliography (6: The technology of rare elements, p.238-496 (copper ... uranium; each element, with references)). Indexes (subject; name), p.523-36. *Class No:* 546.65

Organic Chemistry

Databases

[1324]
Beilstein online. Frankfurt, Beilstein Institute.

The online version of *Handbuch der organischen chemie.* Coverage: 1779-. (*c.*7,000,000 records). Available via DIALOG and STN International; updated 2-4 times per year. Since 1990 available on CD-ROM (DM5,680). *Class No:* 547(003.4)

[1325]
—'Beilstein online.' *Science & technology libraries,* v.10(4) Summer 1990, p.125-7.

A discussion of *Beilstein online. Class No:* 547(003.4)

[1326]
—The Beilstein system : strategies for effective searching. Heller, S.R., *ed.* Washington, DC, American Chemical Society, 1998. 208p. graphs, tables, chemical structures. $74.95. ISBN: 0841235236.

Updates and expands the author's earlier book *The Beilstein online database: implementation, content, and retrieval.*

Invaluable guide to 'Beilstein online'. Provides an introduction and overview of the database and hints for search techniques and strategies. Compares and contrasts *Beilstein* with *Chemical abstracts,* and includes discussion of numerous recent *Beilstein* products (*e.g.* Aautonom; Netfire; Crossfire; Gmelin; Current facts in chemistry, etc.). *Class No:* 547(003.4)

[1327]
Chapman & Hall chemical database. London, Chapman & Hall.
Formerly *HEILBRON.*

Data on over 230,000 substances, drawn from the publisher's sources, *e.g. Dictionary of organic compounds, Dictionary of organometallic compounds, carbohydrates, amino acids and peptides,* and other publications. Updated semi-annually. Available online via DIALOG, file 303, and Questel SA. Subsets of the data are available on CD-ROM from the publisher. *Class No:* 547(003.4)

CD-ROM

[1328]
The Chapman & Hall chemical database: the natural products on CD-ROM. London, Chapman & Hall, 1992. £2950, full subscription; £1750, renewal. ISSN: 09662146.

Includes the natural products in the following printed publications: *Dictionary of organic compounds, Dictionary of alkaloids, Dictionary of antibiotics, Dictionary of steroids, Dictionary of Terpenoids* and others.

Over 80,000 substances in 33,000 entries. Data: name; synonyms; structure display; hazards; toxicity; CAS Registry number; colour; melting/boiling points; refractive index; pharmacological and other uses, etc. Each entry carries a bibliography. IBM PC-AT or compatible micro. *Class No:* 547(003.40)

Encyclopaedias

[1329]
Dictionary of organic compounds. Buckingham, J., *ed.* 6th ed. London, Chapman & Hall, 1996. 9v. £2,950. ISBN: 0412540908.

First published 1934-37; 3rd ed., edited by Sir I. Heilbron and H.M. Bunbury (1953. 4v.); 5th ed (7v. + supplements), 1983.

The main work (v.1-6) has data on 170,000 of the most common and important organic compounds for chemists, biochemists, pharmacologists and biologists. Documented. Three indexes: name; molecular formula; Chemical Abstracts Service Registry number. Known as 'DOC 6'. 'An essential adjunct wherever organic compounds are used' (*Nature,* v.300, 25 November 1982, p.336, on the 5th ed.).

Available online in the *Chapman and Hall Chemical database* (formerly *HEILBRON*), DIALOG file 303; CD-ROM (ISSN: 09676686). *Class No:* 547(031)

[1330]
—**RHODES, P.H.** The Organic chemist's desk reference: a companion volume to the *Dictionary of organic compounds,* sixth edition. London, Chapman & Hall, 1995. xi, 170p. formulas, tables. ISBN: 041264410x.

Issued as a companion volume to the new 6th ed. of *DOC* and includes 'a wide variety of the miscellaneous facts that organic chemists need but which would be out of place in *DOC 6* itself' (*Preface*). 17 chapters (*e.g.* history of *DOC*; organic chemistry journals; molecular formulae; hazard information; spectroscopy, etc.); index. A useful volume. *Class No:* 547(031)

Handbooks & Manuals

[1331]

Beilstein's Handbuch der organischen chemie. 4. Aufl. hrsg. und bearb. von F. Richter (from 1948; previously by Deutsch Chemische Gesellschaft). Berlin, etc., Springer-verlag, 1918-.

The 4th ed. of the definitive work (*Hauptwerk*) covered the literature on *c*.200,000 compounds up to the end of 1909. Supplements (*Ergänzungswerke*): 1-4 cover 1910-19, 1920-29, 1930-49 and 1950-59 respectively. A 5th supplement, for 1960-69 began publication in English in 1964. Each supplement consists of 27v. Subject and formula indexes to both main work and supplements are proceeding. Data (where applicable): name(s), formula, structure(s), history, occurrence, formation, preparation, properties (physical, chemical and physiological), technology, analysis, etc. Each volume contains indexes, list of abbreviations for sources, and classifed table of contents. Beilstein is the most extensive reference work to the literature of organic chemistry, including patents. *Class No:* 547(035)

[1332]

—BRITISH LIBRARY. Science Reference Library. An Introduction to Beilstein's Handbuch der organischen Chemie. Rev. ed. London, SRL, 1985. 9p. *Gratis.* ISSN: 03064301.

In 6 sections: 1. Introduction - 2. Information given in Beilstein - 3. Structure - 4. Indexes - 5. Search procedures: based on the indexes - 6. Future developments. Appendix 1: List of the more common abbreviations used in Beilstein and their meaning in English - 2. A bibliography of guidebooks to Beilstein's Handbook. *Class No:* 547(035)

[1333]

—How to use Beilstein: Beilstein's Handbook of organic chemistry. Berlin etc., Springer, [1984]. 34p. chemical structures. *gratis.*

In 4 sections: 1. Questions about Beilstein; 2. How to search for and find compounds in Beilstein; 3. The history of Beilstein; 4. Literature on Beilstein, p.34. *Class No:* 547(035)

[1334]

CRC handbook of organic photochemistry and photobiology. Horspool, W.M. *and* Song, P.-S., *eds.* Boca Raton, Fl., 1995. 1636p. tables. $149.95. ISBN: 0849386349.

Covers the impact of irradiation on a variety of substances, e.g. oxygen, sulfur, nitorgen, halogens, DNA, etc. Includes extensive references current to 1994. *Class No:* 547(035)

[1335]

ELIEL, E.L. *and* **WILEN, S.L. Stereochemistry of organic compounds.** Chichester, Wiley, 1994. xiii, 1267p. chemical formulas. £57. ISBN: 0471016705.

14 well-documented chapters (*e.g.* ch.1 has *c*.160 references). Glossary. Index. *Class No:* 547(035)

[1336]

HOUBEN, J. *and* **WEYL, T. Methoden der organischen Chemie.** 4. vollig neue gestaltete Aufl., hrsg. von E. Müller. Stuttgart, Thieme, 1952. illus., tables.

1, pt.1: *Allgemeine Laboratorium spraxis.* 1958.
2: *Analytische Methoden.* 1953.
3, pt.1: *Physikalische Forchungsmethoden.* 1955.
4, pt.1: a-b: *Oxidation.* 1981; c-d: *Reduktion.* 1980.
4, pt.2: *Allgemeine chemische Methoden.* 1955.
4, pt.3: *Carbocyclische Driering-Verbindungen.* 1971.
4, pt4: *Isocyclische Driering-Verbindungen.* 1971.
5, pt.1: a-d *Kohlenwasserstoffe.* 1970-72.
5, pt.2a: *Alkine d-und Polyine Allene, Kumulene.* 1977.
5, pt.2b: *Arene und Arine.* 1951.
5, pt.3-4: *Halogen-Verbindungen.* 1962, 1960.
6, pt.1, a-b: *Alkohole.* 1979-84.
6, pt.1, c: *Phenole.* 1976.
6, pt.1, d: *Enole.* 1978.
6, pt.2-4; 7, pt.1,4; 8: *Sauerstoff-Verbindungen.* 1963-66, 1954, 1968, 1952.
7, pt.2, a-c: *Ketone.* 1973-77.
7, pt.3, a-c: *Chinone.* 1977-79.
9: *Schwefel-, Selen-, Tellur-Verbindungen.* 1955.
10, pt.1-4; 11, pt. 1-2: *Stickstoff-Verbindungen.* 1965-71.
12, pt.1-2; E, pt. 1-2: *Organische Phosphor-Verbindungen.* 1963-64, 1982.
13, pt. 1-2a, pt. 4-8, pt. 9b: *Metallorganische-Verbindungen.* 1970-84.
13, pt. 3 a-c: *Organobor-Verbindungen.* 1982-83.
14, pt. 1-2: *Makromolekulare Stoffe.* 1961-63.
E 3: *Aldehyde.* 1983.
E 4: *Kohlinsaure Derivate.* 1983.
E 5, pt.1-2: *Carbonsauron and Carbonsäure Derivative.* 1965.
E 11, pt.1-2: *Organische Schwefel-Verbindungen.* 1985.
Subject index for v. E4: author index for v. E4, E5, E11, (1987).
The 4th ed. is to be in 16v. (v.16 index), comprising 57 parts by 1987, with supplementary volumes (Erweiterungs- und Folgebände), *i.e.,* v.E3,4,5,11, to cover developments of the past two decades. *Class No:* 547(035)

[1337]

MARCH, J. Advanced organic chemistry: reactions, mechanisms, and structure. 4th ed. New York, Wiley, 1992. xv,1495p. diagrs., tables, chemical formulas. £45. ISBN: 0471601802.

19 chapters; 2 appendices: A: 'The Literature of organic chemistry' (p.1239-68); B: 'Classification of reactions by type of compound synthesized' (p.1269-1300). Indexes: Author (p.1301-1431); Subject (p.1433-95). Primarily a textbook, but valuable for the more than 10,000 references included. *Class No:* 547(035)

[1338]

SCHWARZENBACH, R.P., *and others.* **Environmental organic chemistry.** Chichester, Wiley, 1993. x, 681p. diagrs. graphs, tables, chemical structures. £54. ISBN: 0471839418.

15 chapters, closely subdivided. Bibliography (A-Z authors), p.626-55. Detailed, analytical index, p.657-81. *Class No:* 547(035)

[1339]

—SCHWARZENBACH, R.P., *and others.* Environmental organic chemistry: illustrative examples, problems and case studies. Chichester, Wiley, 1995. 388p. diagrs., graphs, tables, chemical structures. £19.95. ISBN: 0471125881.

Provides much supplementary material to the above work. *Class No:* 547(035)

Dictionaries

[1340]

GOLD, V., *ed.* **'Glossary of terms used in physical organic chemistry'.** Provisonal ed., 1979. In *Pure and applied chemistry*, v.51, 1979, p.1725-1801. diagrs., chemical structures.

About 130 contributors. A dagger against the title of an entry 'implies that we recommend discontinuation of use'. 2½p. of references appended. *Class No:* 547(038)

[1341]

PATAL, S. Glossary of organic chemistry including physical organic chemistry. New York & London, Interscience: Wiley, 1962. xiv, 227p. chemical structures.

Concise definitions; references frequent. Many structural formulas; also, reactions. Deliberately omits most analytical methods. 'Writen mainly for ... those who are not specialists (or not yet specialists) in Organic and Physical Organic Chemistry, but who have need and occasion to use the relevant literature' *(Preface)*. *Class No:* 547(038)

Progress Reports

[1342]

Advances in physical organic chemistry. New York, London etc., Academic Press, 1965-, v.1-. Annual. ISSN: 00653160.

V.30 (1995. ix, 242p.) has 7 contributors. The 4 papers cover spectroscopy, acid-base behaviour, diolefin crystals and hydrocarbon salts. Author index, to references. Cumulative indexes of authors and titles, v.1-30. *Class No:* 547(055)

[1343]

Progress in physical organic chemistry. New York, Wiley: Interscience, 1971-. v.1-. ISBN: 0471524425.

V.19 (1993. ix, 349p. £103.) has 12 contributors. The 4 papers include one on the Menshutkin reaction (306 references). Author and subject indexes; cumulative index (titles of articles), v.1-19. *Class No:* 547(055)

Tables & Data Books

[1344]

CRC handbook series in organic electrochemistry. Meites, L. *and* Zeiman, P. Cleveland, Ohio (later Boca Raton, Fla.), CRC Press, 1977-83. 6v. tables, chemical structures. ISBN: 0849372208.

V.6 ([viii], 538p.) is largely tabular, - 11 main tables (1. Electrotechnical data, p.5-333), including a key to literature citations. Author index. 'Although these six volumes contain the largest collection of organic electrochemical data ever made, ... they include only a fraction of the data that have appeared in the original literature' *(Preface, v.6)*. Thus, electrochemical techniques are excluded. *Class No:* 547(083)

[1345]

VERSCHUEREN, K. Handbook of environmental data on organic chemistry. 3rd ed. New York, Wiley, 1996. vi, 2064p. £155. ISBN: 0471286591.

First published 1977; 2nd ed. 1983..

Lists chemicals, A-Z, and gives data on properties, air, water and soil pollution factors, biological effects and toxicity. 'Explanatory notes' interpret the data. Bibliography of over 5,700 items; molecular formula cross index. Also published on CD-ROM (Wiley, 1998; $215). 'Highly recommended' (*Choice*, January 1997, p.824).

The 4th ed is due October 1999. *Class No:* 547(083)

Nomenclatures

[1346]

INTERNATIONAL UNION OF PURE AND APPLIED CHEMISTRY. **Nomenclature of organic chemistry.** 4th ed. Oxford, etc., Pergamon Press, 1979. xix, 359p. tables, chemical structures. ISBN: 0080223699.

Sections, A,B,C,D,E,F and H. (Sections A and B were first published in 1958, section C, in 1965, and sections D,E,F,H, in 1979).

Sections: A Hydrocarbons - B. Fundamental heterocyclic systems … D. Conductivity … H. Isotopically modified compounds.
Class No: 547(083.72)

[1347]

NICKON, A. *and* SILVERSMITH, E.F. **Organic chemistry: the name game:** modern coined terms and their origins. New York, etc., Pergamon, 1987. xii,347p. illus., chemical structures. ISBN: 008034481x; 0080351573, Pbk.

Covers several hundred distinctively named reactions and structures. 20 chapters, each on a common theme; *e.g.* 9. 'Join organic and see the world' discusses, among others, the plant alkaloid 'istanbulamine' (collected in western Anatolia, Turkey), and 'manxane' (synthesized by researchers in Northern Ireland and Scotland, who were struck by its structural similarity to the coat of arms of the Isle of Man). Extensive chapter references. 6 appendices (A. Etymology of some traditional chemical names … F. Nobel prizes in the sciences). Name index, 9p. An unusual, humorous treatment. Highly recommended in *Choice*, May 1988, p.1429. *Class No:* 547(083.72)

Reactions

[1348]

GOWAN, J.E. *and* WHEELER, T.S. **Name index of organic reactions.** 2nd ed. London, Longmans, 1960. v, 293p. diagrs.

First published 1950, by The Society of Chemical Industry.

739 named and numbered reactions, A-Z, showing chemical structures. Colour reactions are not shown (see *Merck index* for these). For each reaction, reference to the original literature, *Organic reactions, Organic syntheses,* etc. Type of reaction index; general (analytical index). No biographical data (for which see A.R. Surrey's *Name reactions in organic chemistry* (2nd ed. New York, Academic Press, 1961). Considered singularly free from mistakes (*Chemistry & Industry,* 24 June 1961, p. 937-8). *Class No:* 547.03

[1349]

Organic reactions. New York, Wiley, 1942-. Chemical formulas.

V.50 (1997. 700p.) has reviews with extensive references, covering limitations, interfering influences, structural effects and experimental techniques. Indexes to vols. 1-50: author; chapter and topic.
Class No: 547.03

Synthesis

[1350]

Comprehensive organic synthesis: selectivity, strategy and efficiency in modern oroganic chemistry. Trost, B.M., *ed.* Oxford, Pergamon Press, 1991. 9v. tables, chemical formulas. $3000. ISBN: 0080359229, set.

V. 1-2. *Additions to C-X -bonds.* xxi,989p.; xxiii,1233p.
V. 3. *Carbon-carbon -Bond formation.* xxi,1186p.
V. 4. *Additions to and substitutions at C-C -bonds.* xxi,1299p.
V. 5. *Combining C-C -bonds.* xxv,1333p.
V. 6. *Heteroatom manipulation.* xxi,1194p.
V. 7. *Oxidation.* xxv,1012p.
V. 8. *Reduction.* xxv,1139p.
V. 9. *Cumulative indexes.* xv,811p.

Over 250 international contributors. V. 1 has 22 closely subdivided chapters, each with extensive references. A major work.
Class No: 547.057

[1351]

Organic syntheses; an annual publication of satisfactory methods for the preparation of organic chemicals. New York, Wiley; London, Chapman & Hall, 1971-.

The series' main object is to state the most convenient laboratory methods for preparing various substances in ½ to 5lb. lots, but as far as possible also adaptable to large-scale development. V.71 (1993) records '30 checked procedures of value to the modern practicing chemist'. Important in all areas of analytical chemistry as reference sources.

Collective volumes, with cumulative indexes, act as revised editions of v.1-9, 10-19, etc. *Class No:* 547.057

[1352]

The Total synthesis of natural products. Ap Simion, J., *ed.* New York, Wiley, 1973-.

10 vols. have appeared so far (V.10, 1997, ISBN: 0471596795). Each contains one or more articles on an aspect of organic synthesis. V.9 (1992. ISBN: 0471551899. £98) contains 'The synthesis of insect pheromones, 1979-1989', by K. Mori of 534p. and 1,229 references. *Class No:* 547.057

Ring Index

[1353]

Ring systems handbook. Columbus, Ohio, American Chemical Society Chemical Abstracts Service, 1998. v.p. \$585. ISSN: 07425996.

Previously published as *The Ring index.*

Includes over 100,000 ring and cage systems with entries in ring analysis order and ring systems indexed by molecular formula and CA index name. New editions appear every 5 years. *Class No:* 547.12

Compounds

[1354]

BARTON, Sir D. *and* OLLIS, W.D. **Comprehensive organic chemistry;** the synthesis and reactions of organic compounds. Oxford, etc., Pergamon Press, 1979. 6v. (*c.*8,000p). ISBN: 0080213197.

1. Stereochemistry, hydrocarbons, halo compounds, oxygen compounds. 2. Nitrogen compounds, carboxylic acids, phosphorous compounds. 3. Sulphur, silenium, silicon, boron, organometallic compounds. 4. Heterocyclic compounds. 5. Biological compounds. 6. Author, formula, subject, reagent, reaction indexes.

Emphasises throughout the properties and reactions of all the important classes of organic compounds, including those compounds prepared by synthesis as well as natural products created by biosynthesis. Over 100 contributors; over 20,000 literature references. Actual coverage of v.6 (xii, 1,628 p.): formula, subject, author, reaction and reagent. 'A must for all chemistry collections of importance' (*New technical books,* v.64(10), December 1979, entry 1493). 'Highly recommended' (*Information sources in science and technology,* 3rd ed., 1998, p.113). *Class No:* 547.2

[1355]

CRC handbook of data on organic compounds. Lide, D.R. *and* Milne, G.W.A., *eds.* 3rd ed. Boca Raton, Fl., CRC Press, 1994. 7v. tables. £1876. ISBN: 0849304202.

First published 1985; 2nd ed. 1989.

Physical properties and spectral data for 30,000 of the most common organic compounds. Data: molecular weight, boiling point, melting point, density, refractive index, specific rotation, colour, solubility. Spectral data include infra-red, Raman, ultraviolet, nuclear magnetic resonance, mass spectroscopy, plus CAS Registry Number, CAS index no., synonyms, chemical structure, line and molecular entries. Indexes for melting points, etc. Available online via STN International. *Class No:* 547.2

[1356]

—**Handbook of data on common organic compounds.** Lide, D.R. *and* Milne, G.W.A., *eds.* Boca Raton, Fl., CRC Press, 1995. 3v. (2229p.). tables. \$995. ISBN: 0849304040.

Contains a selection of 12,000 compounds from the 3rd ed. of *CRC handbook of data on organic coumpounds. Class No:* 547.2

[1357]

—**Properties of organic compounds.** Boca Raton, Fa., CRC Press, 1993. CD-ROM + user manual. \$2795.

The electronic counterpart of *CRC handbook of data on organic compounds.* Focuses on 27,500 commonly used compounds. Allows searching by range, Boolean logic, CAS registry numbers. Runs on Windows. 'Highly recommended' (*Choice,* February 1994, p.924). *Class No:* 547.2

[1358]

DREISBACH, R.R., *comp.* **Physical properties of chemical compounds.** Washington, American Chemical Society, 1957-61. 3v. tables.

Treats 1,421 substances. V.1 has sub-title: 'A systematic tabular representation of accurate data on the physical properties of 511 cyclic compounds'. V.2 continues the survey, dealing with 476 organic straight-chain compounds. V.3 presents data on the physical properties of 414 alipathic compounds, 22 miscellaneous compounds and elements of these. Each volume has an index, cumulating in v.3. *Class No:* 547.2

[1359]

UTERMARK, W. *and* SCHICKE, W. **Melting point tables of organic compounds.** 2nd new and supplemented ed. New York, Interscience, 1963. xxxii, 715p.

Tabulates names, formulas, molecular weights, specific gravity and boiling points of 3,213 compounds, arranged in order of melting points. *Class No:* 547.2

Hydrocarbons

[1360]
GALLANT, R.W. *and* YATES, C.L. **Physical properties of hydrocarbons and other chemicals.** 2nd ed. Houston, Texas, Gulf Publishing, 1992-95. 4v. Mainly graphs. ISBN: 088415176x.

First published 1968-70

Aims 'to provide the working engineer with all the essential data to design and run production facilities' (*Preface*). About 800 references. Vol.4 (1995, $75, ISBN: 0884152723) includes the properties of other chemicals as well and has 264 charts covering vapour pressure, liquid density, surface tension, viscosity, heat thermal conductivity, etc. for each group of hydrocarbons. *Class No:* 547.21

Organometallic Compounds

[1361]
Advances in organometallic chemistry. San Diego, Ca., Academic Press, 1963-. diagrs., chemical structure, tables.

V.41 (1997. 400p.) covers boron atoms in transition metal clusters and the analogy between structure and bonding in parent hydrides and multiple bonded silicon and germanium compounds. *Class No:* 547.25

[1362]
Dictionary of organometallic compounds. McIntyre, J.E., *ed.* 2nd ed. London, etc., Chapman & Hall, 1995. 5v. £2950. ISBN: 0412430606.

About 26,000 entries describing about 50,000 compounds. Data include chemical structure, chemical and physical properties and literature references. The work is designed as a companion to the *Dictionary of organic compounds* and the *Dictionary of inorganic compounds*. 'It may be regarded as the Red Bible' (*Nature,* v.314, 21 March 1985, p.296, on the first ed.). Available online as part of the Chapman & Hall database. *Class No:* 547.25

[1363]
Organometallic compounds: abstracts of literature and patents relating to compounds which contain at least metal, carbon and hydrogen atoms. Braintree, Essex, R.H. Chandler, Ltd., 1961-. Biweekly. tables, chemical structures. ISSN: 00305138.

About 8,500 abstracts (mostly brief) pa., under compounds A-Z. Author index per issue. Six-monthly subject, author and patent name indexes. *Class No:* 547.25

[1364]
Organometallics in synthesis: a manual. Schlosser, M., *ed.* New York, Wiley, 1994. 603p. chemical formulas and structures. $100. ISBN: 0471936375.

8 chapters, each with extensive references, by various hands. Substances covered include lithium, titanium, copper, palladium, boron, aluminium, among others. Numerous recipes. Indexes: subject; formula. 'An outstanding contribution to the practicing chemist' (*Choice,* May 1995, p.1478). *Class No:* 547.25

Carbohydrates

[1365]
Carbohydrates. Collins, P.M. London, Chapman & Hall, 1987. xi,720p. chemical structures. £95. (*Chapman & Hall chemistry sourcebooks.*) ISBN: 0412269600.

Data largely derived from the *Dictionary of organic compounds* (5th ed. 1982) and supplements, but with revision and update. Indexes: Name; Molecular formula; CAS Registry number; Type of compound. *Class No:* 547.454

Amino Acids

Organophosphorous

[1366]
EDMUNDSON, R.S., *ed. and comp.* **Dictionary of organophosphorus compounds.** London, Chapman & Hall, 1988. xxi, 1347p. tables, chemical structures.

Entries (p.1-880) in alphanumeric order. Introduction includes 'Sources of further information', p.xiii-xxii. Name index, p.881-987; Molecular formula index, p.989-1118; CAS Registry Number index, p.1119-120. Type of compound index, p.1203-1347. Many compounds are included as derivatives of main-entry compounds. Heilbron (file 303) available online via DIALOG. *Class No:* 547.5

Heterocyclic Compounds

[1367]
Advances in heterocyclic chemistry. San Diego, Ca., Academic Press. 1949- Annual.

V.69 (1997. 480p.) has review articles with extensive references Cumulative indexes (author, title, subject) for recent volumes. *Class No:* 547.7

[1368]
Comprehensive heterocyclic chemistry: the structure, reactions, synthesis and uses of hetrocyclic compounds. Katritzky, A.R. *and* Rees, C.W., *eds.* Oxford, etc., Pergamon, 1984-85. 9 vols. + indexes. diagrs., tables. ISBN: 0080262008, set.

The aim of the work is two-fold: to give an up-to-date overview of the subject as a whole and to provide enough detail to answer specific questions and to direct attention to detailed reviews. Numerous contributors. Contents include general reviews of the literature and monograph studies of specialist topics. Indexes: physical data, authors, subjects, rings. V.9, *Handbook,* is a digest of the general chapters in V.1-8, and therefore suitable for libraries not requiring the full text. Vols.10 and 11 are indexes. Also available on CD-ROM (Elsevier Science). *Class No:* 547.7

Natural Substances

[1369]
Dictionary of natural products. Buckingham, J., *ed.* London, Chapman & Hall, 1993. 11v. (*c.*11,000p.). £3500. ISBN: 0412466201.

About 1130,000 natural products grouped within about 36,000 entries. Data include uses, physical properties, structures, references. Available online as part of the Chapman & Hall database and on CD—ROM. *Class No:* 547.9

Fats

[1370]
The Lipid handbook. Gunstone, F.D., *and others, eds.* 2nd ed. London, Chapman & Hall, 1994. xiii, 722p + 551p. ISBN: 0412433206.

First published 1986.

A major compendium on the occurrence, isolation, chemical identification and technical applications of fatty acids. 3 editors, 17 contributors. 12 sections, p.1-721: 1. Fatty acid structure - 2. Lipid structure - 6. Analytical methods - 11. Lipid metabolism - 12. Medical and agricultural aspects of lipids. Dictionary Section follows *p.1-432,* compound name index, *p.433-470,* formula index, *p.471-510,* CAS Registry Number index, *p.511-551* For more advanced students in chemistry, biochemistry, food science, etc. *Class No:* 547.915

Alkaloids

[1371]
Dictionary of alkaloids. Southon, I.W. *and* Buckingham, J., *eds.* London, Chapman & Hall, 1989. 2v. (xlvi, 1161, 620p.) chemical formulas, structures. ISBN: 0412249103.

V.1: *Dictionary*; V.2 *Indexes.*

About 10,000 alkaloids, A-Z, described, frequently with references (to 1988). Indexes: name; molecular formula; CAS registry number; type of compound; species. Available online as part of the Chapman & Hall database. *Class No:* 547.94

[1372]
GLASBY, J.S. **Encyclopedia of the alkaloids.** New York & London, Plenum Press, 1975-83. 4v. ISBN: 0306308452.

V.1-2 (A-H, I-Z. 1423p.) provide data on the occurrence, structure and physical constants of more than 3,000 alkaloids, their salts and derivatives, chemical structure; references. V.3 (1977) and v.4 (1983), both A-Z, record compounds reported in the literature (to the end of October 1976 and for 1977-81 respectively). V.3 includes a formula index for v. 1-3 and v. 4 also carries a formula index. *Class No:* 547.94

Proteins

[1373]
Advances in protein chemistry. San Diego, Ca., Academic Press, 1949-. Annual.

V.49 (1996. 544p.) has papers on Antigen binding molecules - Antibodies and T-cell receptors. Extensive references. *Class No:* 547.96

Crystallography

Bibliographies

[1374]
MEGAW, H.D., *with others.* **Crystallographic book list.** Cambridge, H.D. Megaw, c/o Cavendish Laboratory, 1965. Supplement, 1966. xii, 83p.

5 lists: 1. Books, in English, French, German, Spanish and Russian, - but not Japanese - (authors, A-Z; data include reviews; subject reference; teaching level) -2. Conferences (in chronological order) -3.

....(contd.)

Serial publications (titles, A-Z) -4. Subject classification of books -5. Appendix (additional items).

Second supplement in *Journal of applied crystallography* (v.5, 1972, p. 148-62). Latest supplement, - in the same journal (v.15, 1982, p.640-76) as 'Current crystallographic books, 1970 through 1981', edited by J.H. Robertson. *Class No:* 548(01)

Handbooks & Manuals

[1375]

HAMMOND, C. **Introduction to crystallography.** Oxford Univ. Press, 1990. 104p. £9.95. ISBN: 0198364236.

A step-by-step, user-friendly approach to the basics of crystallography. Includes biographical notes, a further reading list and exercises. 'For microscopists and science students'(*New technical books*, March/April 1991, entry 393). *Class No:* 548(035)

[1376]

Handbook of crystal growth. Hurle, D.T.J., *ed.* Amsterdam, North-Holland, 1993. 3v. (in 6). ISBN: 0444899332.

V.1: *Fundamentals* (£242).

V.2: *Bulk crystal growth* (£695).

V.3: *Thin films and epitaxy* (£695).

V. 3 contains 22 closely subdivided and well-documented chapters by 29 contributers. No indexes. A scholarly treatment.

Class No: 548(035)

[1377]

VAINSTEIN, B.K., *and others, eds.* **Modern crystallography.** Berlin, etc., Springer, 1979-84. 4v.

First published Moscow, Nauka, 1979.

1. *Symmetry of crystals, methods of structural crystallography*, by B.K. Vainstein.

2. *Structure of crystals*, by B.K. Vainstein, and others.

3. *Crystal growth*, by A.A. Chemov, and others.

4. *Physical properties of crystals*, by L.A. Shumov, and others.

By 3 members of the Institute of Crystallography of the USSR Academy of Sciences. Describes all branches of crystallography in their interrelation, presenting 'a unified science' (*Foreword*). Each volume carries bibliography, references and subject index. Chapters vary in length (*e.g.* 'Crystalline state', v.1, p. 1-26; 'Structure analysis of crystals', v.1, p. 223-376). Intended for research workers, scientists, engineers and students. *Class No:* 548(035)

Dictionaries

[1378]

BACKHAUS, K.O. **Technik-Wörterbuch Kristallographie:** Englisch-Deutsch-Französisch-Russisch. [Dictionary of crystallography: English-German-French-Russian.] Berlin, VEB Verlag Technik, 1983. 132p. £15.70.

About 3,600 English-base terms, with German, French and Russian equivalent and indexes. Coverage: geometric crystallography, physico-chemical crystallography, crystal chemistry and physics.

Class No: 548(038)

Reviews & Abstracts

[1379]

Zentralblatt für Mineralogie. Stuttgart, E. Schweizerbart'sche Verlagsbuchhandlung, 1950-. Monthly. ISSN: 05147123.

Preceded by *Jahrbuch für Mineralogie* (1830-32), *Neues Jahrbuch für Mineralogie* (1833-1942) and *Zentralblatt für Mineralogie, Geologie und Paläontologie* (1943-49).

Teil 1: *Kristalographie und Mineralogie*.

2: *Petrographie, techische Mineralogie, Geochemie und Lagerstättenkunde*.

Teil 1 (7pa., pt.7: annual author & subject indexes) has *c*.3,000 abstracts and references pa, in sections. Teil 2 (13pa., pt.13: annual author & subject indexes) has *c*.5,000 abstracts and references pa., in sections A-N. *Class No:* 548(048)

Yearbooks & Directories

[1380]

World directory of crystallographers, and of other scientists employing cyrstallographic methods. Epelboin, Y., *ed.* 9th ed. Kingston upon Thames, Kluwer, 1995. 318p. £18. ISBN: 9027720940.

First published 1957; 8th ed., 1986.

A directory of *c*.9,000 crystallographers in 69 countries, A-Z (Algeria ... Zimbabwe). Data include name, address, year of birth, status, and major fields of scientific interest. Name index.

Class No: 548(058)

Tables & Data Books

[1381]

International tables for crystallography. 2nd rev. ed. Dordrecht, Reidel, for the International Union of Crystallography, 1987-. (*3rd series of International tables*; 1st series, 1935.) ISBN: 0792321898.

V.A. *Space group symmetry.* 1987. xvi, 878p. Brief teaching edition (156p.) was published in 1993.

V.B. *Reciprocal space.* 1993. 506p.

V.C. *Mathematical and physical tables.* 1992. 500p.

V.A (pt.1: Tables for plane groups and space groups has 15 documented sections, plus subsections) treats the symmetries of one-, two- and three-dimensional space groups and point groups in direct space. Detailed features of each space group appear under 13 heads.

Class No: 548(083)

[1382]

International tables for X-ray crystallography. Dordrecht, Reidel, 1952-83. 4v. tables. ISBN: 902271956x, v.2.

1. *Symmetry groups*; edited by N.F.M. Hendry and K. Lonsdale. 1952.

2. *Mathematical tables*; edited by J.B. Kasper and K. Lonsdale. 1982.

3. *Physical and chemical tables*; edited by C.H. MacGillavry and other 1983.

4. *Revised and supplementary tables*; edited by J.A. Ivers and W.C. Hamiton 1982.

Each volume carries a dictionary of crystallographic terms/phrases in English with equivalents in French, German, Russian and Spanish. V.3 has a subject index; v.4 applies to tables in v. 2-3. 'The crystallographer's Bible' (Coblans, H., ed., *Use of physics literature* (1975), p.237).

Will gradually be replaced by the 2nd rev. ed. *Class No:* 548(083)

[1383]

PORTER, M.W. and SPILLER, R.C. **The Barker index of crystals:** a method for the identification of crystalline substances. Cambridge, Heffer, for the Barker Index Committee, 1951-65. 3v. (7 pts.).

1. (2 pts.). *Crystals of the tetragonal, hexagonal, trigonal and orthorhombic systems.* 1951.

2. (3 pts.). *Crystals of monoclinic systems.* 1956.

3. (2 pts.). *Crystals of the anorthic systems.* 1965.

An index based on geometric form rather than on crystal structure as described in T.V. Barker's *Systematic crystallography* (London, Murby, 1930). V.1 describes 2,991 compounds; v.2, *c*.3,500.

Class No: 548(083)

Maps & Atlases

[1384]

LIMA-DE-FARIA, J., *ed.* **Historical atlas of crystallography.** Boston, Kluwer Academic, 1990. 158p. $36. ISBN: 079230649x.

Includes bibliography on the history of crystallography. Indexes. 'An important contribution ... particularly useful for the teaching of crystallography' (*Choice*, April 1991, p.1339). *Class No:* 548(084.3)

Crystal Structure

[1385]

Structure reports: a critical guide to papers on crystallography of metal alloys and compounds. Utrecht, Oostboek, for the International Union of Crystallography, 1940/41-.v.8-. Annual. ISSN: 01667033.

Continues *Strukturbericht*, 1913-39 (Leipzig, Akademie Verlagsgesellschaft, 1931-43. 7v.).

Each annual from 1965 has 2 parts: A. Metals and inorganic sections; B. Organic compounds (including organometallic compounds). The 2-part *Report* v.48, for 1981 (1852p.) appeared in 1986. Data normally cover name, formula, papers reported, unit cell and space group, analysis, atomic positions, plus detailed description and discussion of the structure. Subject, formula and author indexes. Cumulative subject/formula indexes (1913-1980); ten-year author index (1971-1980). 60-year structure index (1913-1973).

Class No: 548.7

[1386]

—WYCKOFF, R.W.G. Crystal Structures. 2nd ed. New York, London, etc., Interscience; Wiley. 6v. diagrs., tables.

First published 1948 (4v.).

V.2-3 (1964-66) cover inorganic compounds. The volumes contain data on each structure, plus a bibliography and name and formula indexes. Now somewhat dated. *Class No:* 548.7

Mineralogy

Bibliographies

[1387]

O'DONOGHUE, M. **The Literature of mineralogy.** London, British Library, Science Reference and Information Service, 1986. 85p. diagrs. £12. ISBN: 0712307370.

10 sections: Major reference monographs - Abstracts - Databases - Current awareness publications and review literature - General comprehensive surveys - Crystals - Mineral formation and deposits - Mineral identification - Journals: general; for the collector - Regional mineralogy - Clay minerals - Mineral names - Glossaries and dictionaries - Directories - Maps - Addresses. Detailed index, p.78-85. 9p. of line-drawings (142 figures). A valuable, up-to-date reference tool, with concise annotations. *Class No:* 549(01)

Encyclopaedias & Dictionaries

[1388]

CARR, D.D. *and* HERZ, N., *eds*. **Concise encyclopedia of mineral resources.** Oxford, Pergamon Press, 1989. xxiii,426p. diagrs., tables. £80; $145. (*Advances in materials science and engineering, v.8.*) ISBN: 0080347347, UK; 0262031558, US.

Mainly a compilation of articles from the *Encyclopedia of materials science and engineering* (Pergamon Press, 1986), arranged A-Z (Abrasives ... Zirconium and hafnium resources). Larger topics are subdivided, *e.g.* coal: geology; mining; world resources. Short bibliographies are appended to the articles. Subject index. *Class No:* 549(03)

Encyclopaedias

[1389]

The Encyclopedia of gemstones and minerals. Holden, U. *and* Mathez, E.A., *eds*. New York, Facts on File, 1992. 320p. illus. £24.95. ISBN: 0876021775.

Properties/values of over 200 rocks, stones, jewels and other mineral substances. 400 illus. Data on characteristic form, specific gravity, symmetry, system, refraction, location, use and commercial value. 'Highly recommended for all types of libraries' (*Library Journal,* 15 February 1992, p.160). *Class No:* 549(031)

[1390]

FRYE, K., *ed*. **The Encyclopedia of mineralogy.** Stroudsburg, Pa., Hutchinson Ross, 1982. xxi, 794p. $95. (*Encyclopedia of earth sciences, v.4B.*)

Comprises 148 articles by over 100 specialists, with an A-Z mineral glossary of *c*.3,000 entries. Readership is likely to be mainly professional scientists and technologists; 'too complex for the non-mineralogist' (*Nature,* v.297, 24 June 1982, p.710). *Class No:* 549(031)

[1391]

ROBERTS, W.L., *and others*. **Encyclopedia of minerals.** 2nd ed. New York, Van Nostrand Reinhold, 1990. xxiii,979p. illus. (some col. pl.). £77; $99.95. ISBN: 0442276818.

First published 1974.

Item-by-item description of more than 2,500 minerals, Abelsonite ... Zykaite. Data include crystal system, space group, lattice constants, hardness, density, cleavage, habit, colour-lustre, mode of occurrence, strongest diffraction lines and selected references. Glossary, p.xix-xxiii. 237 colour photos. 'The first place to turn for information on the third kingdom of the natural world' ('Reference books bulletin', *Booklist,* December 1, 1998, p.689). *Class No:* 549(031)

Handbooks & Manuals

[1392]

DANA, J.D. *and* DANA, E.S. **The System of mineralogy.** 7th ed., entirely rewritten and greatly enl. by C. Palache [and others]. New York & London, Wiley, 1944-62. 3v.

First published 1837; 6th ed. 1892.

1. *Elements; sulfides; sulfosalts; oxides.*

2. *Halides; nitrates; borates; carbonates; sulphates; phosphates; arsenates; tungstates; molybdates, etc.*

3. *Silica minerals.*

Systematic and detailed descriptions of minerals, with references to the literature in each case. Minerals are arranged in 50 classes. Each volume carries a subject index. Authoritative classification of minerals. *Class No:* 549(035)

[1393]

DEER, W.A. **Rock-forming minerals.** 2nd ed. Harlow, Essex, Longman Group, 1979-. illus. (incl col.), diagr., graphs, tables.

1A. *Orthosilicates.* 2nd ed. 1982. 936p. £85.

1B. *Disilicates and ring silicates.* 2nd ed. 1986. £91.

2A. *Chain silicates.* 1978. 668p. £34.

3. *Sheet-silicates.*

4. *Framework silicates.*

5. *Non-silicates.*

V.2A has two parts: Pyroxenes (p.3-543; including 19p. of references) - Non-pyroxenes (Wollastonite ... Serendibite). The monograph on ilmenite in v.5 (p.28-33) covers properties, structure, chemistry, optical and physical properties, distinguishing features, paragenesis; 31 references. Non-analytical index. *Class No:* 549(035)

[1394]

—Elsevier's mineral and rock table. Amsterdam, Elsevier, 1982. 70 x 133 cm. coloured wall chart.

Illustrates 74 rock-forming minerals and 40 ore minerals. 'A wealth of information concerning the microscopic properties of igneous, metamorphic, sedimentary and ore-containing rocks' (*Nature,* v.302, 10 March 1983, p.183). *Class No:* 549(035)

[1395]

GERMAIN, G. *and* SCHUBNEL, H.J. **Larousse des minéraux.** Paris, Larousse, 1981. 384p. F235. ISBN: 2035182018.

Concise description of 2,900 species of minerals, A/Z. Data include notes on stratigraphy and nomenclature. Numerous quality photographs. The introduction states the basics of mineralogy and its history. Favourably reviewed in *Bulletin critique des livres français,* no. 432, December 1981, entry 117183. *Class No:* 549(035)

[1396]

Industrial minerals and rocks (nonmetallics other than fuels). Lefond, S.J., *ed*. 5th ed. New York, American Institute of Mining, Metallurgical and Petroleum Engineers, 1983. 2v. (1,446p.). illus.

First published 1937.

4 parts (with extensive chapter references by specialists): 1. Introduction - 2. Industrial minerals grouped by uses - 3. Sources of information for industrial minerals - 4. Commodities. Concerns the origin, occurrence, nature, properties, winning and uses of commercially important minerals. Statistics mostly relate to USA. Each volume carries an index. *Class No:* 549(035)

[1397]

KLEIN, C. *and* HURLBUT, C.S. **Manual of mineralogy:** (after James D Dana). 21st ed. New York, Wiley. 1993. xii, 681p. illus., diagrs., tables. ISBN: 047157452x.

First published 1848; 20th ed. 1989..

Sections cover crystallography (structure, chemistry, etc.) and minerals (physical and optical properties). Systematic mineralogy and determinative tables for some 200 common minerals. Mineral and subject indexes; extensively illustrated. A classic text. *Class No:* 549(035)

[1398]

NICKEL, E.H. *and* NICHOLS, M.C. **Mineral reference manual.** New York, Van Nostrand Reinhold, 1991. 250p. $14.95. ISBN: 0442003447.

A-Z listing of valid minerals. Data: name, formula, current status, crystal system, appearance, hardness, measured and calculated density, type, locality, mineral classification, name origin, indication of related species and selected literature references for each species; also, crystal structure determination, when available. 'An excellent reference addition to mineralogical collections in all libraries' (*New technical books,* May/June 1991, 722). *Choice* (June 1991, p.1620) was less enthusiastic: 'merely a listing allowing someone in mineralogy to put a few pieces of information onto a name'. *Class No:* 549(035)

[1399]

O'DONOGHUE, M., *ed*. **The Encyclopedia of minerals and gemstones.** London, Orbis, 1985. 330p. illus. (incl. col.), ports, facsims, tables. £9. ISBN: 0856232092.

8 chapters: The chemistry of minerals - The crystalline state - Geology for the collector - Minerals valuable to man - Identifying minerals - The fashioning of stones - Conserving and displaying minerals - The mineral kingdom (p.148-287; data on over 1,000 different minerals). Appendix: Some organic materials (*e.g.* amber). Glossary, p.288. Mineral identification tables. Conversion tables. Bibliography, p.296-7 (grouped). Detailed, non-analytical index. Superb illus., a number in full-page colour. 'The general public and many professionals will welcome this technically precise and aesthetically pleasing introduction to the world of minerals' (*Library journal,* 15 November 1976, p.2359). *Class No:* 549(035)

[1400]

O'DONOGHUE, M. An Illustrated guide to rocks and minerals. Limpsfield, Surrey, Dragon's World, 1991. 192p. col. illus., diagrs. £6.95. ISBN: 1850251114.

Part 1: Rocks. Part 2: Minerals (including 'Mineral descriptions', p.71-169). Appended: Deposits; Museums. Bibliography. Glossary. Detailed index. About 100 minerals are covered, with superb coloured photographs. 'This book is intended to introduce some of the major rock and mineral species' (*Preface*). *Class No: 549(035)*

[1401]

PASCAL, P. Nouveau traité de chimie minérale. Paris, Masson, 1956-64. 33v. illus. (pl.), diagrs., tables.

Previous ed. as *Traité de chimie minérale* (1931-34. 13v.).

A massive, comprehensive treatise, fully documented, and running to well over 20,000 pages of text. Fasc. 2 of v.17, 'Cobalt, nickel' (1963. xi, 896p.) carries 8,422 references to the literature.

Compléments au Nouveau traité de chimie minérale, by P. Pascal, began publication in 1974. *Class No: 549(035)*

[1402]

PELLANT, C. Rocks, minerals and fossils of the world. Boston, Mass., Little, Brown, 1990. 175p. illus. $17.95. ISBN: 0316697966.

Contents: Glossary - Geological time scale - Igneous rocks - Metamorphic rocks - Sedimentary rocks - Fossils. Further reading. Index. Over 300 colour illus. 'A basic reference work for college and research libraries' (*New Technical Books,* Nov./Dec. 1990, 1734).

Class No: 549(035)

Children

[1403]

COOK, D. *and* KIRK, W. Field guide to the rocks and minerals of the world. London, Kingfisher Books, 1991. 192p. col. illus., tables. £7.95. ISBN: 088272699x.

A general overview of rocks and minerals, their formation and the qualities for identification. Glossary; further reading (p.192); index. Suitable for school libraries. *Class No: 549(035)-0053*

Dictionaries

[1404]

NAKHIMIZHAN, O.E., *comp.* Pyatiyazychnyĭ slovar' mineralogicheskikh nazvanii. Moscow, Glav. Redakt. Inostr. Naucho-Tekh. Slovarei Fizmatgiz, 1962. 347p.

Polyglot dictionary of mineralogical species and varieties, in five languages. English, French, German and Spanish terms are given in one sequence, with Russian equivalents. No Russian language index. *Class No: 549(038)*

[1405]

THRUSH, P.W., *ed.* A Dictionary of mining, minerals, and related terms. Washington, US Dept. of the Interior, 1968. vii, [1], 1269p.

About 55,000 terms (including abbreviations), with *c.*150,000 definitions. Quotes sources (listed on p.1259-68). Cross-references. Compared with A.H. Fay's *A glossary of the mining and mineral industry* (Washington, USGPO, 1920. 745p.), which Thrush revises and enlarges. Fay (*c.*20,000 terms) should be retained for its several thousand Spanish American mining terms. *Class No: 549(038)*

Reviews & Abstracts

[1406]

Mineralogical abstracts. London, Mineralogical Society of Great Britain, and Mineralogical Society of America, 1920-. 4pa. £165; $200. ISSN: 37915002.

Earlier (1920-58) published in *The mineralogical magazine.*

About 5,000 abstracts and references pa. 17 sections, A-V: Age determination - Apparatus and techniques - Book notices ... Economic minerals and mineral deposits ... Experimental mineralogy ... Geochemistry ... Meteorites and tektites - Mineral data ... Petrology. Index of authors per issue; annual author and subject indexes. Also available on CD-ROM. *Class No: 549(048)*

[1407]

Zentralblatt für Mineralogie. Stuttgart, E. Schweizerbart'sche Verlagsbuchhandlung, 1950-. Monthly. ISSN: 05147123.

Preceded by *Jahrbuch für Mineralogie* (1830-32), *Neues Jahrbuch für Mineralogie* (1833-1942) and *Zentralblatt für Mineralogie, Geologie und Paläontologie* (1943-49).

Teil 1: *Kristalographie und Mineralogie.*

2: *Petrographie, techische Mineralogie, Geochemie und Lagerstättenkunde.*

Teil 1 (7pa., pt.7: annual author & subject indexes) has *c.*3,000 abstracts and references pa, in sections. Teil 2 (13pa., pt.13: annual author & subject indexes) has *c.*5,000 abstracts and references pa., in sections A-N. *Class No: 549(048)*

Yearbooks & Directories

[1408]

United Kingdom minerals yearbook, 1995. Lofty, G.J. *and* Highley, D.E., *comps.* Nottingham, British Geological Survey, 1996. *c.*80p. tables, maps. £30. ISBN: 0852722702.

Includes statistics to 1994. 5 parts: Minerals in the national economy - Energy minerals - Construction and industrial minerals - Metals - Commodity summaries. No index, but detailed table of contents. *Class No: 549(058)*

[1409]

World directory of mineralogists. Cesbon, F., *ed.* Orléans, Bureau de Recherches Géologiques et Minières; Marburg, West Germany, International Mineralogical Association, 1985. 361p. illus. ISBN: 2531509001.

First published 1962.

Compiled with the help of the representatives of the national mineralogical societies. *Class No: 549(058)*

Nomenclatures

[1410]

CLARK, A.M. Hey's mineral index: mineral species, varieties and synonyms. 3rd ed. London, Chapman & Hall, 1993. xiii, 852p. (*Natural History Museum publications.*) ISBN: 0412399504.

First published 1950; 2nd ed. 1955 (appendices published 1963, 1974).

A long-awaited revision of a standard text. About 3,500 mineral species, A-Z, with chemical formulas and literature references. Chemical classification (32 sections), p.783-852.

Class No: 549(083.72)

[1411]

EMBERY, P.G. *and* FULLER, J.P., *eds.* A Manual of new mineral names, 1892-1978. London, British Museum (Natural History) and Oxford Univ. Press, 1980. x, 467p. £32. ISBN: 0198585012.

A compilation from 30 lists published in the *Mineralogical magazines,* 1897-1976. About 5,500 'new' mineral names, A-Z, followed by an author list. Complements J.D. Dana's *System of mineralogy (qv). Class No: 549(083.72)*

[1412]

FLEISCHER, M. Glossary of mineral species. [4th] ed. Tuscon, Arizona, Mineralogical Record, 1983. [vi], 202p. $8.

First published 1971; previous ed. 1980.

About 2,000 one or two line entries. An A-Z list of names, symmetry and chemical compositions of mineral species. Includes only the most commonly used synonyms and obsolete names. Cross-references. Lists all known minerals, with their chemical composition, crystal system, colour, grouping by mineral family, plus references. *Class No: 549(083.72)*

[1413]

—**MITCHELL, R.S. *and* HENRY, J.R. Mineral names: what do they mean?.** New York, Van Nostrand Reinhold, 1979. xv, [1], 229p.

In two parts: 1. Mineral names: a discussion (*e.g.* names from persons, places) - 2. Mineral names: an alphabetical list. 3 appendices (1. Glossary). General bibliography, p.235-7 (authors, A-Z). Aims 'to bring together the derivations of all minerals' (*Preface*). *Class No: 549(083.72)*

Worldwide

[1414]

DUDA, R. *and* REIJL, L. Minerals of the World. London, Hamlyn, 1986. 520p. col. illus. ISBN: 0600333762.

602 minerals. Descriptive text and diagram, facing col. illus. (plates, p.31-479). Identification tables (p.482-508). List of reference books (p.511-13). Non-analytical index (p.514-20). Over 500 col. photographs and 300 line drawings. *Class No: 549(100)*

Marine Environment

[1415]

MERO, J.L. The Mineral resources of the sea. Amsterdam, etc., Elsevier, 1965. xiii, 312p. illus., maps.

8 chapters. 1. Introduction - 2. Marine beaches - 3. Minerals from sea water - 4. The continental shelves - 5. Strata underlying the soft sea-floor sediments - 6. The deep sea-floor - 7. Ocean mining methods - 8. Some economic and legal aspects of ocean mining. References, p.296-304. Non-analytic index. *Class No: 549(26)*

Europe

[1416]

BOISSONNAS, J. *and* OMENETTO, P. **Mineral deposits within the European Community.** Berlin, Springer-Verlag, 1988. xxiii,558p. illus., maps. $144. ISBN: 0387182012.

3 parts: 1. Tungsten (tin, lithium, etc.) - 2. Platinum-group elements - 3. Base metals. *Class No:* 549(4)

Great Britain

[1417]

PATTRICK, R.A.D. *and* POLYA, D.A. **Mineralization in the British Isles.** London, Chapman & Hall, 1993. 499p. illus., diagrs., tables, graphs, maps. ISBN: 041231200x.

12 contributors. 9 parts, each with ample references (1. The mineralization and geological evolution in the British Isles ... 9. Sedimentary iron ore). Detailed, analytical index. *Class No:* 549(410)

France

[1418]

Inventaire minéralogique de la France. Paris, Bureau de Recherches Géologiques et Minières, 1977-. v.1. maps.

Arranged by départements (*e.g.* 2. Hautes Alpes; 3. Finistére 4. Alpes Maritimes; 5. Côtes du Nord ...). Details of mineralogical excursions, with maps, access points, types of deposit, and mineralogy. Each guide has general and mineral indexes, plus a bibliography. *Class No:* 549(44)

USA

[1419]

CHESTERMAN, C.W. **The Audubon Society field guide to North American rocks and minerals.** New York, Knopf, 1979. 850p. illus. (col. pl.), diagrs., tables. $17.95. ISBN: 0394502698.

A pocket-sized guide to 232 mineral species and 40 types of rocks, in 4 parts. Pt.1, Minerals and pt.2, Rocks, both include a guide to identification, a visual key, and colour plates 1-702 and 703-94 respectively. Pt.3, Mineral collecting; pt.4, Appendices (Glossary, p.785-97; Bibliography, p.799-801; Rock forming minerals; localities; etc.). Index, p.831-50. *Class No:* 549(73)

Museums

[1420]

World directory of mineral collections. International Mineralogical Association. 2nd ed. Copenhagen, Geological Museum, 1977. n.p.

Lists collections in 32 countries. Data: name of collection (in original and in English), address, name of person in charge, total number of specimens (usually divided into minerals, rocks, ores, gems, meteorites/tektites), uses of the collection, speciality, loan facilities, exchange arrangements, catalogue, times of admission. *Class No:* 549:061:069

Gemmology

Bibliographies

[1421]

GILL, J.O. **Gill's Index to journals, articles and books relating to gems and jewelry:** works in the English language, arranged chronologically and by type. Santa Monica, Calif., Gemological Society of America, 1978. vii, 420p. tables. ISBN: 0873110099.

7 sections: 1. *Minerals yearbook* (chapters on gemstones) - 2. *The Gemmologist* (August 1931 - December 1962) - 3. *Gems & Geology* - 4. *The Journal and Gemmology* - 5. *Lapidary journal* - 6. *The Australian Gemmologist* - 7. *Gem Library bibliography (1652-1978)*. Table of subjects (Gems & gem materials; Gem locations; Gemology; Jewelry). *Class No:* 549.091(01)

[1422]

O'DONOGHUE, M. **The Literature of gemstones.** London, British Library, Science Reference and Information Service, 1986. [ii], 75, [2]p. £12. ISBN: 0712307389.

16 Sections: Encyclopedic works - General comprehensive surveys - Gem testing - Gem testing instruments - Quick reference publications and tables - Textbooks - Synthetic stones - Gemstones - Fashioning - Works on individual species - Jewelry - Gemstones of particular localities - Bibliographies - Abstracts - Journals - Gemstone prices - Guide to collections - Regalia. A list 'based largely on the collection of Science Reference and Information Service of the British Library' (*Preface*). *Class No:* 549.091(01)

Encyclopaedias

[1423]

AREM, J.E. **Color encyclopedia of gemstones.** 2nd ed. New York, Van Nostrand Reinhold, 1987. 288p. illus. $53.95. ISBN: 0442208332.

Data on all mineral species (organic, occurrence, size) which are cut and polished for ornamental purposes. Over 360 col. illus. Index. *Class No:* 549.091(031)

[1424]

BARIAND, P. *and* POIROT, J.P. **Larousse des pierres précieuses, fines, ornamentales, organiques.** Paris, Larousse, 1985. 264p. illus. (col.), diagrs.

The bulk of this attractive record of precious stones, A-Z, is preceded by chapters on symbolism of gemstones, their origin and historical use, their properties, fashioning and synthesis. 350 col. illus. (some of them previously published). 'The book is worth buying for its illustrations alone' (*Journal of gemmology*, v.20, January 1986, p.57).

An English translation was published by Van Nostrand Reinhold, 1992 ($45; ISBN: 0442302894). 'Highly recommended' (*Choice*, September 1992, p.72). *Class No:* 549.091(031)

Handbooks & Manuals

[1425]

CAVENARGO-BIGNAMI MONETA, S. **Gemmologia.** 4th ed. 3v. illus., tables.

First published 1958.

Extensive coverage of all types of precious stones, including artificial types,. V.3 concerns gem testing, identification tables and a bibliography. Fully illustrated and well presented, though not made for easy handling. 'As with the Webster book the term gemstones is widely interpreted' (O'Donoghue, M. *The literature of gemstones*, p.10). *Class No:* 549.091(035)

[1426]

CIPRIANI, C. **The Macdonald encyclopedia of precious stones.** 3rd ed. London, Macdonald, 1986. 384p. illus. (col.), diagrs., table. £7.95.

English translation of the Italian (Milan, Mondadori, 1984).

Three parts: Natural stones (introduction, p.10-72; gem descriptions) - Organic gems - Synthetic and artificial products. Synoptic table. Glossary. Bibliography, p.381. Analytical index. A handy, small-format guide, with over 300 well-coloured illus. *Class No:* 549.091(035)

[1427]

HURLBUT, C.S. *and* KAMMERLING, R.C. **Gemology.** 2nd ed. Chichester, Wiley, 1991. 336p. illus., diagrs., tables. $58. ISBN: 0471526673.

First published 1979.

Covers the occurrence, mineralogy, identification and fashioning of gemstones. Gem determinative tables. Chapter references and detailed, analytical index. *Class No:* 549.091(035)

[1428]

SMITH, G.F.H. **Gemstones.** Revised by F.C. Phillips. 14th ed. London, Chapman & Hall, 1972. xii, 580p. illus. (incl. col.), diagrs., tables. ISBN: 0412108909.

First published 1912.

Four parts (41 footnoted chapters): 1. Physical character - 2. Technology and history - 3. Description (A. Principle stones; B. Other gem materials; C. Ornamental stones; D. Organic products, *e.g.* pearl, ivory, resin) - 4. Classification tables. Appendices include bibliography (12 groups), p.544-56. Index, p.559-80. Still the most complete scholarly work in English. *Class No:* 549.091(035)

[1429]

WEBSTER, R. **Gems:** their sources, descriptions and identification. 4th ed., revised by B.W. Anderson. London, etc., Butterworths, 1983. xxii, 1,006p. illus. (incl. col. pl.), diagrs., tables. ISBN: 0408011485.

First published 1962.

Two parts (38 chapters), Pt. 1 (1-24): Description of gemstones (diamond ... ivory and tortoise shell) - Pt. 2 (25-38): (How gemstones are identified, *e.g.* crystals: specific gravity, colour, measurement of refraction index, luminescence. Identification, p.895-929. Appendices (*e.g.* 'Famous diamonds and those large diamonds to which names have been applied'. 'Suggested list of permissive names for gemstones'). Bibliography, p.965-70. Name and subject (partly analytical) indexes. 16 colour plates. *Class No:* 549.091(035)

Dictionaries

[1430]

READ, P.G. **Dictionary of gemmology.** 2nd ed. Oxford, Butterworth, 1988. 256p. illus., diagrs., tables. £25. ISBN: 0408029520.

First published 1982.

About 3,000 entries, giving concise descriptions of the principal gem materials, plus definitions of associated scientific terms, and notes on gemmological instruments. Includes trade names of natural and man-

....*(contd.)*
made materials. Cross-references from disused/misleading terms. Aimed at both professional gemmologist and the student. *Class No:* 549.091(038)

Tables & Data Books

[1431]

SCHUMANN, W. **Gemstones of the world.** Rev. ed. New York, Sterling Publishing Co., 1997. 272p. col. illus., tables. $24.95. ISBN: 0806994614.

German original published by BLV Verlagsgesellschaft mbH. Munich. First English ed. 1977.

About 1,400 gemstones. Descriptive text faces colour plates in 4 sections: Minerals (function and structure; properties; classification; rock-forming minerals. 11 colour plates) - Precious stones and gemstones (characteristics; descriptions; trade names and mineralogical names; cutting of stones. 8 colour plates) - Rocks (igneous; sedimentary; metamorphic rocks; meteorites. 38 colour plates) - Ore deposits (12 colour plates). Fossils. Hints to collectors. Mineral identification tables. Aids to identification. A concise compendium in small format. *Class No:* 549.091(083)

[1432]

SINKANKAS, J. **Gemstones and mineral data book:** a compilation of data, recipes, formulas, and the instructions for the mineralogist, gemologist, lapidary, jeweller, craftsman and collector. New York, Winchester Press, 1972. vi, 346p. tables. ISBN: 0876910673.

Data on *c.*1,000 gems, stones and ornamental minerals, their characteristics and chemical properties. 12 sections. Much use of tables. 'An excellent reference book for the "rock hound" and lapidary, it will be very useful in a mineralogy laboratory or museum' (*Choice,* v.9(11), January 1973, p.1435). *Class No:* 549.091(083)

Elements

[1433]

EMSLEY, J. **The Elements.** 3rd ed. Oxford Univ. Press, 1998. 292. tables. £40; £15.95(Pbk); $78; $29.95(Pbk). ISBN: 0198558198; 019855818x, Pbk.

First published 1988; 2nd ed. 1992.

Key facts (discovery, names, formulae, properties, etc.) about the chemical elements (A-Z). The 3rd ed. includes new information on health hazards, mineral sources, electron binding energies, and elements discoverd since the 2nd ed. A handy book; 'strongly recommended' (*Choice,* January 1999, p.915). *Class No:* 549.2/.9

[1434]

FERGUSON, J.E. **The Heavy elements:** chemistry, environmental impact and health effects. Oxford, Pergamon Press, 1990. vii,614p. diagrs., graphs, tables. ISBN: 0080348602; 0080402755, Pbk.

4 parts (16 documented chapters): 1. Introduction and history - 2. Chemistry - 3. Heavy elements in the environment - 4. Heavy elements in human beings. 10 heavy elements: antimony, arsenic, bismuth, cadmium, indicum, lead, mercury, selenium, tellurium, thallium. About 1400 references; detailed, analytical index, p.599-614. *Class No:* 549.2/.9

[1435]

KREBS, R.E. **The History and use of our earth's chemical elements:** a reference guide. Westport, Ct., Greenwood, 1998. 346p. formulas. $39.95. ISBN: 0313301239.

Provides clear and concise informtion on the uses of elements; information on biological roles is limited. Entries include symbol, valence, atomic weight, physical properties and isotopes. Glossary; index. 'A marvelous reference' (*Choice,* July/August 1998, p.1880). *Class No:* 549.2/.9

[1436]

The Periodic table of elements compendium. Eccles, H., *comp.* London, Royal Society of Chemistry, Education Division, 1994. n.p., diagrs., tables. ISBN: 1870343271.

The elements, hydrogen to zirconium, with information on appearance, general reactivity, physical and chemical properties, industrial uses, etc. For school pupils. *Class No:* 549.2/.9

[1437]

PUDDEPHATT, R.J., *and* MONAGHAN, P.K. **The Periodic table of elements.** 2nd ed. Oxford, Clarendon Press, 1986. x, 102p. diagrs., graphs, tables. £15; £7.50. (*Oxford chemistry series.*) ISBN: 0198555156.

First published 1972.

8 Chapters, on atomic structure; building the periodic table; periodicity of main group elements (atomic, bonding, physical and structural properties); transition elements; lanthanides and actinides. Most chapters have problems appended, with answers on p.97. Bibliograpy of 5 items; subject index. Presents 'the periodic behaviour of the elements in a non-theoretical way' (*Preface*). Suitable for senior secondary pupils and first-year undergraduates. *Class No:* 549.2/.9

[1438]

—WILLIAMS, R.A. Handbook of the atomic elements. London, Vision Press, 1971. 124, [1]p. tables.

First published New York, Philosophical Library, 1970.

Provides more than 30 data on 100 elements (Actinium ... Zirconium), p.13-115. Details include principal quantum number, atomic number, x-ray notation, density, melting point, ground state, electron configuration, radioactive isotopes. Such information is based on Carbon-12 and values released by IUPAC. 5 appended tables (*e.g.* 1. Percentage composition of the elements in the earth's surface). *Class No:* 549.2/.9

55 Earth Sciences

Earth Sciences

Databases

[1439]

GeoArchive. Didcot, Oxon., Geosystems, 1974-.

Contains *c.*800,000 records, adding more than 100,000 records pa. Indexes more than 5,000 serials, books, conferences, technical reports, and doctoral dissertations. Subject coverage includes geophysics; geology; palaeontology; geochemistry; while also providing coverage of mineral and petroleum production and resources, names of new taxa, new minerals, and new stratigraphic names. Also available on CD-ROM. *Class No:* 550(003.4)

[1440]

GEOBASE. Amsterdam, Elsevier, 1980-.

Over 600,000 references on geography, geology, ecology and related disciplines, with 50,000 additional records each year. Includes abstracts as well as bibliographic citations. Covers 3,000 science and technology journals, as well as 2,000 other sources such as books; reports; monographs; theses. Includes *International development abstracts; Geographical abstracts; Mineralogical abstracts; Ecological abstracts.* Available via DIALOG, ESA/IRS, OCLC, and on CD-ROM. *Class No:* 550(003.4)

[1441]

GeoGuide. URL:http://www.sub.uni-goettingen.de/ssgfi/geo/singleindex.html.

Internet site based at Lower Saxony State and University Library, Goettingen, Germany, with more than 1,400 information resources, printed and online in the earth sciences. Arrangement is by type, *e.g.* data collections, bibliographies. Web sites are evaluated with regard to clarity, index, and links. Appears to be updated regularly. *Class No:* 550(003.4)

[1442]

GeoRef. Alexandria, Va., American Geological Institute; GeoRef Information System, 1785-.

Contains over 1.9 million records, adding 80,000 annually, and scans *c.*4,500 serials and other publications, such as theses and dissertations; state, federal and non-US government documents; technical reports. Covers the geology of America from 1785 and the geology of the rest of the world since 1933. Corresponds to the print publications *Bibliography and index of North American geology, Bibliography of theses in geology, Geophysical abstracts, Bibliography and index of geology exclusive of North America,* and *Bibliography and index of geology (q.v.).* Up-dated monthly. Available on CD-ROM. *Class No:* 550(003.4)

[1443]

RITTER, M.E. Earth online: an Internet guide for earth science. Belmont, Calif., Wadsworth, 1997. xvi, 264p. £14.99. ISBN: 0534517072.

Handbook for Web site operated by this publisher at http://www.brookscale.com/geo/ritter, but also contains information about other home pages on 41 related subjects. 10 chapters: 1. Getting to know the Internet ... 4. File transfer over the Internet ... 6. Searching the Internet ... 10. Internet resources (Astronomy - Wetlands). Glossary, references, index. Light, accessible style. *Class No:* 550(003.4)

[1444]

World databases in geography and geology. Armstrong, C.J., *ed.* London, Bowker Saur, 1995. xii, 1255p. £120. ISBN: 185739111x.

Two sections: Geography, p.1-586; Geology, p.587-882. Listing of databases within each subject area - details of master record, keywords, online and CD-ROM availability. Addresses p.883-918. Indexes of database names and subjects, p.919-1255. *Class No:* 550(003.4)

Bibliographies

[1445]

Bibliography and index of geology. Alexandria, Va., American Geological Institute, 1969-. 17pa. $1,345. ISSN: 00982784.

Succeeds *Bibliography of North American geology* (U.S. Geological Survey, 1931-72, which included literature 1785-1970), and *Bibliography and index of geology exclusive of North America* (Geological Society of America), 1933-68. 32v.

....(contd.)

References photocomposed from citations in GeoRef. *(q.v.),* the AGI database. 29 fields of interest (01. Mineralogy and crystallography - 02. Geochemistry - 03. Geochronology - 04. Extraterrestrial geology - 05/06. Petrology - 07. Marine geology and oceanography - 08/11. Paleontology - 12. Stratigraphy, historical geology and paleoecology... 16. Structural geology - 17/20. Geophysics - 21. Hydrogeology and hydrology - 22. Engineering and environmental geology - 23/25. Surficial geology - 26/29. Economic geology). Profuse cross-references. Omits geography and meteorology, both well covered elsewhere. List of serials precedes. Analytical subject and author indexes; annual cumulative index in 4 pts. Available on microfiche, online (CISTI; DIALOG) and CD-ROM. The major indexing service for geology. *Class No:* 550(01)

[1446]

—User guide to the *Bibliography and index of geology.* Mulvihill, J., *ed.* Falls Church, Va., American Geological Institute, 1982. 160p. $8.95.

Has 6 sections: 1. Scanning and searching - 2. Documents covered - 3. Fields of interest - 4. Subject indexing - 5. Alphabetical term list ... (p.24-57) - 6. Special lists (*e.g.* Commodities; Fossils; Soils; Geographic terms). Analytical index, p.139-60. *Class No:* 550(01)

[1447]

Books in the earth sciences and related topics: a bibliography and index of non-periodical literature (base-line January 1976). Worthing, Sussex, Bibliographic Press, 1977-. no.1-. 4pa. £50pa; $75. ISSN: 01407805.

About 700 author entries, with full bibliographical details. Coverage extends to economics of minerals and energy resources. Subject index, index to conference symposia volumes, and title-keyword index per issue. Annual author index. A helpful check-list that cites items in press and indicates readership (*e.g.* professional/research/reference).

A complementary serials index from the same publishers is *British geological literature (q.v.). Class No:* 550(01)

[1448]

Geologic reference sources: a subject and regional bibliography of publications and maps in the geological sciences. Ward, D.C., *and others.* 2nd ed. Metuchen, N.J., Scarecrow Press, 1981. $49.50. ISBN: 0810814285.

First published 1972.

Contains 4,324 entries, - mostly references. Three main sections; General (in which some of the principal information sources are discussed); Subject (p.75-318): earth sciences; physical geography; environmental geology; Regional (World; North America ... Antarctic). Computer databases are identified in the General section. Non-analytical subject index; geographic index. Intended as a ready-reference guide, although the subject index falls short here. *Class No:* 550(01)

[1449]

Information sources in the earth sciences. Wood, D.N., *and others, eds.* 2nd ed. London, Bowker Saur, 1989. 518p. £45. (*Guides to information sources.*)

First published as *Use of earth sciences literature* (Butterworth, 1973).

20 chapters: 1. Introduction - 2. Earth science libraries and their use ... 6. Computerized information services and geological databases/databanks ... 9. Palaeontology ... 12. Petrology ... 16. Engineering and environment geology ... 18. Meteorology and climatology ... 20. History of geology. The chapter on computerized bibliographic and data retrieval is new to this edition. Aimed at students and practising geologists. *Class No:* 550(01)

[1450]

—GUELPA, P.M. 'Sciences de la terre'. In Malclès, L.-N. *Les sources du travail bibliographique,* v.3. Geneva, Droz; Paris, Librairie Minard, 1958. p.236-96.

Systematically surveys the chief reference material, bibliographies and periodicals in the earth sciences. Contents lists and annotations are given for the most important items. Regional geology covers p.272-87. Still of value. *Class No:* 550(01)

[1451]

UNITED STATES. Department of the Interior. **Dictionary catalog of the Department [of the Interior].** Boston, Mass., G.K. Hall, 1967-. 37v.; Supplements 1-4. 1968-75. 18v. $4,000, set; $910, supp. 4 (8v.). ISBN: 0816107157, set; 0816100160, supp. 4.

724,000 + 268,200 catalogue cards, reproduced photolithographically on 29,573 + 12,818p. The Department of the Interior has the largest specialized collection in the US on mines, minerals, petroleum and coal, as well as a good working collection on geology. The collection covers both published and unpublished material. *Class No:* 550(01)

[1452]

UNITED STATES. Geological Survey. Library. **Catalog of the United States Geological Survey Library.** Boston, Mass., G.K. Hall, 1970. 25v. Supplements 1-3. 1972-76. 21v. $2,720, set; $950, supp.1 (11v.); $475, supp.2 (4v.); $690, supp.3 (6v.). ISBN: 0816107122, set; 0816108765, supp.1; 081611031x, supp.2; 0816100519, supp.3.

416,000 + 350,000 catalogue cards reproduced photolithographically. The largest geological library in the world, intended to be as complete as possible in geology, palaeontology, petrology, mineralogy, ground and surface water, cartography and mineral resources. In general only books and monographs are individually catalogued, under authors, titles (including periodical titles) and subject. Included are a number of old or rare items. *Class No:* 550(01)

Encyclopaedias

[1453]

Encyclopedia of earth sciences. Fairbridge, R.W., *ed.* New York, Van Nostrand Reinhold.

1. *The Encyclopedia of oceanography.* 1966. 2. *The Encyclopedia of atmospheric sciences and astrogeology.* 1967. 3. *The Encyclopedia of geomorphology.* 1968. 4A. *The Encyclopedia of geochemistry and environmental sciences.* 1972. 4B. *The Encyclopedia of mineralogy,* edited by K. Frye. 1981. 6. *The Encyclopedia of sedimentology,* edited by R.W. Fairbridge and J. Bourgeois. 1978. 7. *The Encyclopedia of paleontology,* edited by R.W. Fairbridge and D. Jablanski. 1979. 8(1). *The Encyclopedia of world regional geology: Western hemisphere.* 1975. 11. *The Encyclopedia of climatology,* edited by R.W. Fairbridge and J.E. Oliver. 1987. 12(1). *The Encyclopedia of soil science: Physics, chemistry, biology, fertility and technology,* edited by R.W. Fairbridge and C.W. Finkl, Jr. 1979. 14. *The Encyclopedia of field and general geology,* edited by C.W. Finkl, Jr. 1988. 15. *The Encyclopedia of beaches and coastal environments,* edited by M.L. Schwartz. 1982. 16. *The Encyclopedia of solid earth geophysics,* edited by D.E. James. 1989.

The following vols. are unnumbered: *The Encyclopedia of igneous and metamorphic petrology,* edited by D.R. Bowes. 1989. *The Encyclopedia of European and Asian regional geology,* edited by E.M. Moores and R.W. Fairbridge. (Chapman & Hall, 1997).

Planned in 24v. An ambitious, comprehensive series of encyclopaedias, alphabetically-arranged. Lengthy, documented articles preponderate, each beginning with a simple explanation, expanding into detailed treatment. Inter-volume cross-references. Detailed indexes. *Class No:* 550(031)

[1454]

Encyclopedia of earth sciences. Dasch, E.J., *ed.* New York, Macmillan, 1996. 2v.(1273p.) illus.,tables. $190. ISBN: 0028830008.

A-Z arrangement of 360 entries, many of them biographical and all followed by useful references. Cross-references and illustrations. 81-page index. The mixture of technical articles and those which are accesible to laypersons make this an ideal resource for academic and public libraries. Criticized in *Choice* (January 1997, p.768) for some lack of focus and inconsistencies but 'this set provides in a single place a significant amount of information and offers some very interesting and well-written entries'. *Class No:* 550(031)

[1455]

Encyclopedia of earth system science. Nierenberg, W.A., *ed.* San Diego, Academic Press, 1992. 4v. (2500p.). illus., diagrs., graphs, tables. $950, set. ISBN: 0122267222, set; 0122267206, v.1-2; 0122267214, v.3-4.

257 international contributors. 229 entries, A-Z. Each article includes a bibliography containing books and journal articles, and a glossary. Useful cross-references. The excellent illustrations consist of colour plates and several thousand black-and-white photographs, maps, graphs, charts, and tables. V.4 contains a 170-page, double column, subject index and a 12-page (15,000 entries), relational index linking closely related articles. This is a basic overview, aimed at students, the public, and professionals. While *The Encyclopedia of earth sciences (q.v.)* has greater depth, this has longer articles than *McGraw-Hill encyclopedia of the geological sciences (q.v.).* For academic libraries, although the reviewer in *Library journal,* 15 February 1992, p.156 comments, 'small undergraduate and public libraries can skip this and make do nicely with a more general encyclopedia such as the *McGraw-Hill encyclopedia of science and technology*'. *Class No:* 550(031)

[1456]

The Encyclopedia of the solid earth sciences. Kearey, P., *ed.* Oxford, Blackwell Scientific, 1993. ix, 713p. £27.50. ISBN: 0632025778.

Contains 2,700 headwords and over 8,000 index entries. 3 formats: brief definitions; longer entries of about 200 words; detailed entries of up to 1,500 words. 8 subject editors, 66 contributors. References after some entries. Index, p.673-713. For those libraries which do not have the *Encyclopedia of earth sciences (q.v.). Class No:* 550(031)

[1457]

FARNDON, J. **Concise encyclopedia earth.** London, Dorling Kindersley, 1998. 192p., illus.(col.) £7.99. ISBN: 0751352489.

Previously published as *Dictionary of the earth* by Dorling Kindersley, 1994.

14 sections: Studying the earth ... Changing landscape ... Living world. Index, p.182-92. Attractively illustrated, aimed at senior school pupils. For public and school libraries. *Class No:* 550(031)

[1458]

McGraw-Hill encyclopedia of the geological sciences. Parker, S.P., *ed.* 2nd ed. New York, McGraw-Hill, 1988. 722p. illus. $85. ISBN: 0070455007.

First published 1978.

Derived from *McGraw-Hill encyclopedia of science and technology* (6th ed. 1987). 520 signed articles, with 235 revised since the first edition. Subject coverage includes mineralogy, geochemistry, geology, geophysics and petrology. A-Z arrangement, with cross-references. Length of entries varies from one paragraph to several pages. *c.*600 illustrations. Includes list of contributors. Subject index. For large public, and university, libraries. *Class No:* 550(031)

[1459]

The Marshall Cavendish illustrated encyclopedia of plants and earth sciences. Moore, D.M., *ed.* London, Marshall Cavendish, 1988. 10v. ISBN: 0863079016.

V.1-2: *Dictionary of plants.* V.3-5: *Flowering plant families.* V.6-7: *Plant ecology.* V.8-9: *Earth sciences.* V.10 includes indexes, glossary and bibliography. International in scope though the majority of the 120 contributors are British or European. Numerous colour photographs and diagrams throughout. Many cross-references. For school and public libraries. *Class No:* 550(031)

[1460]

Sciences of the earth: an encyclopedia of events, people, and phenomena. Good, G.A., *ed.* New York, Garland, 1998. 2v.(901p.) illus.,maps. £110; $150. (*Garland encyclopedia in the history of science, v.3.*) ISBN: 081530062x.

More than 230 articles written by 135 contributors. Bias is towards Western science. Discusses ideas and research, with some articles on relevant institutions and groups. No biographies. Name and subject indexes. Listing of the entries by subject. Bibliographies. 'Highly recommended for all academic libraries and larger public libraries' (*Reference books bulletin,* 1 December 1998, p.702). *Class No:* 550(031)

Handbooks & Manuals

[1461]

The Cambridge encyclopedia of earth sciences. Smith, D.C., *editor-in-chief.* Cambridge Univ. Press, 1982. 496p. illus., (mostly col.), diagrs., graphs, tables, maps. ISBN: 0521239001.

32 contributors. 6 parts (27 chapters): 1. The earth sciences in perspective - 2. Physics and chemistry of the earth - 3. Crustal processes and evolution - 4. Surface processes and environments - 5. Evaluation of earth resources and hazards - 6. Extraterrestrial geology (chapter 27: 'The geology of the solar system'). Glossary, p.468-78; Further reading, by chapters. Analytical index, p.481-94. Concentrates on those aspects in which the most significant advances have recently been made. 'The aim is to provide ready access to the wealth of geological information which has been gleaned over the years and to show how it fits into the framework of plate tectonics' (*Foreword*). *Class No:* 550(035)

[1462]

—The New Larousse encyclopedia of the earth. Bertin, L., *ed.* Rev. ed. London, Hamlyn, 1972. 424p. illus. (incl. col.), maps.

First published 1961.

Has 3 parts: 1. The present; 2. Earth in the service of man - 3. The past (geological history and former life on earth; fossil man). Over 500 black-and-white illus.; 30 col. plates. Despite some misspellings and errors, 'the book is in all senses good value' (*Geographical magazine,* February 1973, p.396-7). For the general reader. *Class No:* 550(035)

[1463]
Magill's survey of science: earth science series. Magill, F.N., *ed.*
Englewood Cliffs, N.J., Salem Press, 1990. 6v.(including *Supplement*
(1998. 448p.)). $400; $90 (Supplement). ISBN: 0893566063.

377 articles, written by professional geologists. Each chapter
contains cross-references and a short bibliography. Subject index and
glossary appear in the final volume. Not so detailed as *Encyclopedia of
earth sciences* (Van Nostrand Reinhold. 1966-) (*q.v.*). Aimed at the
layperson.
The *Supplement* updates and expands the original volumes.
Class No: 550(035)

Dictionaries

English

[1464]
Chambers earth sciences dictionary. Edinburgh, Chambers, 1991.
vi,250p. figs., tables. £20; £9.99. ISBN: 0550132449.

Over 6,000 definitions based on entries in *Chambers science and
technology dictionary (q.v.).* Subject coverage includes geology,
mineralogy, crystallography, chemistry, physics and biology. Major
feature is special articles which give fuller treatments of important
topics, *e.g.* 'Bivalves'; 'Iron'; 'Quaternary'. Alternative forms and
cross-references are indicated. *Class No:* 550(038)=20

[1465]
The Concise Oxford dictionary of earth sciences. Allaby, A. *and*
Allaby, M., *eds.* Oxford, University Press, 1990. xxi,410p. £6.99.
ISBN: 0198661460.

One-third of the *c.*8,000 entries are taken from *The Oxford
dictionary of natural history,* (1985). Entries, AA ...
Zosterophyllophytina, include abbreviations, *e.g.* FFT, and short
biographies, *e.g.* Holmes, Buffon, Thomson. Many cross-references.
11-page bibliography. 'A mine of information' (*Nature*, v.344, 29
March 1990, p.391). *Class No:* 550(038)=20

[1466]
McGraw-Hill dictionary of earth science. Parker, S.P., *editor-in-chief.*
5th ed. New York, London, etc., McGraw-Hill, 1997. [xii], 468p.
$17.95. ISBN: 0071149201.

Brief definitions of *c.*10,400 terms, most of the entries having been
previously published in the *McGraw-Hill dictionary of scientific and
technical terms* (5th ed., 1994). Terms are categorized in nine fields:
climatology, geochemistry, geodesy, geography, geology, geophysics,
hydrology, meteorology, oceanography. Slight change of title, with
many terms moved into new companion vol. *McGraw-Hill dictionary
of geology and mineralogy*(q.v.). No illus. Appendices, p.445-68,
include 100 highest mountain-peaks. *Class No:* 550(038)=20

[1467]
McNEIL, M. Earth sciences reference. Carlsbad, Calif., Flamingo
Press, 1991. 709p. $52. ISBN: 0938905015.

Concise, informative definitions covering geology, geophysics,
ecology, geography, meteorology and oceanography. Biographies
included. Subject and geographical indexes. *Class No:* 550(038)=20

German

[1468]
Dictionary of geosciences. English/German, German/English.
[Wörterbuch Geowissenschaft.] Watznauer, A., *ed.* 3rd ed.
Amsterdam, etc., Elsevier, with Berlin, VEB Verlag Technik; New
York, French and European, 1987-88. 2v. (388p. + 372p.). tables,
charts, formulas. $95ea.; £52.50ea. ISBN: 3871441392, v.1;
3871441406, v.2.
First published 1973.
Each volume carries *c.*38,000 terms. Omits hydrogeology and soil
mechanics, - the subject of two other Elsevier dictionaries.
Class No: 550(038)=30

[1469]
MURAWSKI, H. Geologisches Wörterbuch. Erklärung der
geologischen Fachausdrücke der deutschen literatur für Geologen,
Paläontologen, Mineralogen, Geographen, Geophysiker,
Bodenkundler, Bau-und Bodeningenieure, Studierende und alle
Freunde der Geologie. 7. erg. und. erw. Aufl. Stuttgart, Enke; New
York, French and European, 1977. 280p. diagrs., tables. $29.95.
ISBN: 3432841078, US ed.
First published 1937.
The standard German-German dictionary of terms in geology and
allied fields. About 2,000 entries, some of them definitions, others,
fuller explanations. Complicated terms are dealt with in simple
language, plus diagrs. Many cross-references.
Class No: 550(038)=30

French

[1470]
MICHEL, J.P. Dictionary of earth sciences: English-French, French-
English. [Dictionnaire des sciences de la terre: anglais-français,
français-anglais.] 3rd ed. Chichester, John Wiley; Paris, Masson,
1997. xvii, 346p. £50. ISBN: 0471966037, UK ed; 2225853142.
First published 1980.
Wider in scope than previous editions (the English-French section
has increased by 24p.; the French-English section has increased by
19), with additions in the fields of environmental sciences,
meteorology, and petrology. Lists the most common terms in the
geological sciences and related disciplines. French section contains
*c.*17,500 terms, while the English-French part lists *c.*27,000. Brief
bibliography. A useful list of equivalents. *Class No:* 550(038)=40

Russian

[1471]
Anglo-russkiĭ geologicheskiĭ slovar': okolo 52,000 terminov [English-
Russian dictionary of geology.] Timofeev, P.P., *and others.* Moscow,
Russkiiiazyk, 1988 (reprinted 1995). 540p. £29.95. ISBN:
5200002842.
52,000 terms, covering geology, geophysics, hydrogeology,
mineralogy, stratigraphy, tectonics, palaeontology, geochemistry, etc.
Short list of abbreviations and a list of the Russian spelling of the
names of foreign geologists that frequently occur in the literature.
Appended tables for geological time periods, etc.
Class No: 550(038)=82

[1472]
—SOFIANO, T.A., *comp.* Russko-angliiskiĭ geologicheskiĭ slovar'. Pod
red. A.P. Ledeva i V.E. Khaina. Moscow, Glav. Red. Inostr.
Nauchno-Tekhn. Slovarei Fizmatgiza, 1960. 559p.
American supplement. New York, Telberg, 1964. 148p.
35,000 Russian-English entries, with similar coverage to the
foregoing. *Class No:* 550(038)=82

[1473]
BHATNAGAR, K.P. Elsevier's dictionary of geosciences: Russian-
English. Amsterdam, Elsevier, 1991. xii,1023p. £130.25. ISBN:
0444884254.
Contains *c.*56,000 terms used in geology, meteorology,
palaeontology, sedimentology, geochemistry, etc. Brief list of
abbreviations. *Class No:* 550(038)=82

[1474]
USSR. Vsesoyuznyi Nauchno-Issledovatel'skii Geologicheskii Institut
(VSE-GEI) Ministerstva Geologii i Okhrany Nedr SSSR.
Geologicheskiĭ slovar'. 2nd ed. Moscow, Gosud. Nauchno-
Tekhnicheskoe Izdat. Lit. po Geologii i Okhrane Nedr, 1960. 2v.
(402p. + 445p.). tables.
First published 1955.
Entries for over 12,000 Russian geological terms, stating origins.
Coverage includes volcanology, geomorphology, geochemistry,
hydrogeology, crystallography, mineralogy, palaeontology, petrology,
as well as economic geology. Entries are included for individual
minerals. *Class No:* 550(038)=82

Reviews & Abstracts

[1475]
Current contents: Physical, chemical and earth sciences. Philadelphia,
Pa., Institute for Scientific Information, 1979-. v.19-. Weekly. $730.
ISSN: 01632574.
Previously as *Current contents: Physical and chemical sciences*
(formed by the merger of *Current contents: Physical sciences* and
Current contents: Chemical sciences), 1961-78.
Reproduces contents pages of more than 900 journals in the fields
concerned. Each weekly number covers *c.*100 journal issues. Online in
CURRENT CONTENTS SEARCH, CD-ROM and available on
diskette. Internet access as *Current Contents Connect* at http://
connect.isihost.com. *Class No:* 550(048)

[1476]
Geoscience documentation: a bi-monthly journal for the study of
geoscience literature. Didcot, Oxon., Geosystems Publications, 1969-.
6pa. £60. ISSN: 00168483.
Each issue contains *c.*250 references. Classes 100000-900000:
Regional geology; Applied geology; Mineral deposits; General geology
(including mineralogy, palaeontology); Geochemistry; Physical
geology (including geomorphology, history of geology); Methodology
(including equipment and instrumentation); Geoscience information.
Subject, stratigraphical, geophysical and author indexes. Available
online and on CD-ROM. *Class No:* 550(048)

[1477]

—GeoSciTech citation index: an international interdisciplinary index to the literature of geology, earth science, mineralogy atmospheric sciences and related disciplines. Philadelphia, Pa., Institute for Scientific Information, 1976-. Annual, with 2 interim issues pa.; 5 year cumulation, 1976-80. ISSN: 07320558.

Consists of 3 parts: 1. Citation index (authors; anonymous; patents) - 2. Corporate index; geographic sections; source index - 3. Permuterms. Subject index. *Class No:* 550(048)

[1478]

Geotitles: geoscience bibliography. Didcot, Oxon., Geosystems Publications, 1960-. 12pa. £425; $800. ISSN: 09522700.

Each issue contains *c.*3,000 references in a closely classified sequence, 100000-900000 (General publications - Regional geology... Equipment and instrumentation - Geoscience information). Stratigraphic, geophysical, and author indexes. Online via DIALOG. *Class No:* 550(048)

[1479]

Referativnyĭ zhurnal. 08. Geologiia. Moscow, VINITI; Rockville, Md. Victor Kamkin Inc., 1982-. 12pa. $1,905. ISSN: 04862309.

Formerly part of *Referativnyi zhurnal. Geologiya, geografiya,* 1954-55. *Referativnyi zhurnal. Geologiia/Akademiia Nauk SSSR, Institut Nauchnoi Informatsii,* 1956-81.

About 35,000 abstracts pa. 10 sections: General geology - Stratigraphy. Palaeontology - Anthropogene period and geomorphology of land and sea bed - Geochemistry. Mineralogy. Petrography - Ore deposits - Nonmetalliferous deposits - Geological and geochemical methods of research for minerals - Exploration methods and valuation of mineral deposits - Exploration geophysics and logging - Techniques of geological prospecting - Hydrogeology. Engineering geology. Frost action research. Annual author and subject indexes. *Class No:* 550(048)

Progress Reports

[1480]

Annual review of earth and planetary sciences. illus., diagrs., charts, maps. Palo Alto, Calif., Annual Reviews, Ltd., 1973-. Annual. $140 (US); $150 (non US). ISSN: 00846597.

V.26, 1998 (760p.) has 35 contributors. The 21 documented papers include 'Volcanism and tectonics on Venus'; 'The importance of pahoehoe'; 'Isotopic reconstruction of past continental environments'. Subject index. Cumulative indexes of contributing authors, v.14-26, and chapter titles, v.14-26. Prelims. list 'some selected articles in other *Annual reviews*'. Abstracts of papers available online 3 months before publication date at http://www.AnnualReviews.org. *Class No:* 550(055)

Yearbooks & Directories

[1481]

GIS world geodirectory. Fort Collins, Colorado, GeoInformation International, 1996. 3v. ISBN: 1862420041, v.1; 186242005x, v.2; 1862420068, v.3.

v.1. *Products and services* (341p. $69.95); v.2. *Academic institutions* (97p. $49.95); v.3. *Data sources* (126p. $69.95).

Coverage includes digital data, GIS, mining, natural resource management, mapping. V.1, arranged A-Z, with data including address details, URL, ownership, markets, applications. V.2 is arranged A-Z by country, then by institution and includes details of courses and contacts. V.3, arranged A-Z, includes data on addresses and information on datasets, *e.g.* common name, collecting period, updating policy, data keywords. Also available on CD-ROM as *GeoSourceCD*. *Class No:* 550(058)

Tables & Data Books

[1482]

CORLISS, W.R., *comp.* **Handbook of unusual natural phenomena.** Glen Aron, Md., The Sourcebook Project, 1977 (reprinted 1988, New York, Outlet). [vi], 542p. illus.

8 chapters: 1. Luminous phenomena - 2. Optical and radio anomalies in the atmosphere - 3. Unusual weather phenomena - 4. Mysterious natural sounds - 5. The strange phenomena of earthquakes - 6. Phenomena of the hydrosphere - 7. Falling material (*e.g.* dust, thunderstorms, and sundry inorganic matter) - 8. Magnetic disturbances. Cites journal article in each case. Subject and source indexes. Aims to provide 'a comprehensive collection of reliable eye accounts of unusual natural phenomena' (*Preface*). *Class No:* 550(083)

Photographs

[1483]

The Home planet. Kelley, K.W., *comp.* London, Queen Anne Press; Reading, Mass., Addison-Wesley, 1988. 149p. illus. (col.). $22.95. ISBN: 0356159481.

A stunning collection of colour photographs of Earth taken from space vehicles and satellites. *Class No:* 550(084.12)

Histories

[1484]

PORTER, R. The Earth sciences: an annotated bibliography. New York & London, Garland, 1983. xxxiv, 192p. illus. $37. (*Bibliography of the history of science and technology, v.3.*) ISBN: 0824092678.

808 briefly annotated entries in 10 sections: 1. Bibliography and reference works - 2. General histories - 3. Specialist histories (C. Geomorphology; D. Palaeontology; I. Mineralogy) - 4. Cognate sciences (*e.g.* Natural history) - 5. Studies by area - 6. Biographical studies - 7. Institutional histories - 8. The social dimension - 9. Geology, culture and the arts. Entries average *c.*50 words. Author and subject index. 'A valuable bibliographical source book... About 1/3 of titles are in a major Western language other than English' (*Natural history book reviews,* v.7(3), 1984, p.171). *Class No:* 550(091)

Information Services

[1485]

Keeping current with geoscience information. Proceedings of the 15th meeting of the Geoscience Information Society, November 16-20, 1980 (*Proceedings,* v.11, 1981). Pruett, N.J., *ed.* Alexandria, Va., Geoscience Information Society, c/o American Geological Institute, 1981. v, 214p. $20. ISBN: 0934485089.

Part 1. Symposium: Keeping current with geoscience information (7 papers, *e.g.* 'GeoRef coverage and improvements in the *Bibliography and Index of Geology',* by J.G. Mulvihill, p.55-64) - Part 2. Contributed papers (*e.g.* 'A directory of information resources in the United States: geosciences and oceanography', by J.F. Price, p.81-88). *Class No:* 550:061:025.5

Libraries

[1486]

Directory of geoscience libraries, North America. 5th ed. Alexandria, Va., Geoscience Information Society, 1997. v,113p.

3rd ed. (1986) published as *Directory of geoscience libraries, United States and Canada.*

Data on *c.*400 libraries. Entries are arranged A-Z by US states, then by Canadian provinces. Asterisked entries are for libraries making no returns. Organization index. Of the 3rd ed., 'This is a timely, comprehensive and relatively inexpensive directory, especially useful for geoscience collections in industry, academic, government and the larger public libraries' (*Science & technology libraries,* v.7(4), Summer 1987, p.98). *Class No:* 550:061:026/027

Institutions & Associations

[1487]

Earth and astronomical sciences research centres: a world directory of organizations and programmes. 4th ed. London, Cartermill, 1995. x, 465p. £250. ISBN: 1860670180.

First published 1984.

Guide to over 5,000 technology and research laboratories in 147 countries, arranged A-Z (Algeria ... Zimbabwe). Subject coverage includes artificial satellites, cartography and surveying, geology, meteorology, mineralogy, natural resources, oceanography, petrology, space technology. Data include title of establishment in original language, acronym and English translation; telecommunication contact nos., senior staff; research expenditure; publications; research activities; affiliation. Titles of establishments index; subject index. Personal name and acronym indexes would also be useful. *Class No:* 550:061:061.2

[1488]

UNITED STATES. National Referral Center for Science and Technology. **Geosciences and oceanography:** a directory of information resources in the United States. Washington, Library of Congress, 1981. xx, 375p.

Contents; Organization locator - Directory, A/Z (p.1-275). Data on each body include area of interest, holdings, publications and information services. Extensive analytical subject index, p.277-375. 'For the purpose of this directory, "geoscience" and "oceanography" have been defined quite broadly' (*Preface*). Thus, palaeontology and astronomy both figure in the index. *Class No:* 550:061:061.2

Geophysics

Encyclopaedias

[1489]

The Encyclopedia of solid earth geophysics. James, D.E., *ed*. New York, Van Nostrand Reinhold, 1989. xvi,1328p. figs. $124.95. (*Encyclopedia of earth sciences, 16*.) ISBN: 0442243669.

160 articles, arranged A-Z (Absolute age determination: radiometric ... Viscous remanent magnetization (VRM) and viscous remagnetization) covering seismology, gravity, geodesy tectonophysics, geomagnetism and related subjects. Short bibliographies and cross-referenced list of related entries. Subject and author citation indexes. Aimed at both the academic and layperson. *Class No:* 550.3(031)

[1490]

Encyclopedic dictionary of exploration geophysics. Sheriff, R.E., *comp*. 3rd ed. Tulsa, Oklahoma, Society of Exploration Geophysicists, 1991. 376p. illus., diagrs., graphs, tables, maps, formulas. $59. ISBN: 1560800186.

First published 1972.

About 5,000 brief unsigned entries, 'ABC method' ... 'Z transform'. 'Satellite navigation': ½ column. Cross-references. Appendices A-N (*e.g.* C. Symbols used in geophysical exploration; N. Publishing houses). References, p.375-6. 'Compiled for "practical" geophysicists rather than for researchers or other specialists' (*Excerpts from the preface to the first edition*). *Class No:* 550.3(031)

[1491]

International dictionary of geophysics, seismology, geomagnetism, aeronomy, oceanography, geodesy, gravity, marine geophysics, meteorology, the earth as a planet, and its evolution. Runcorn, S.K., *and others, eds*. Oxford, etc. Pergamon Press, 1967. 2v. (1728p.). illus., diagrs., charts, maps. $740, set; £315, set. ISBN: 0080118348, set.

220 contributors: over 700 signed articles, A-Z. An encyclopaedic dictionary that omits biographies but includes eponyms (*e.g.* Kepler's laws). Entries vary in length - and quality - from 20-word definitions to lengthy articles (*e.g.* 'Magnetic properties of minerals', p.861-75, with 21 figures, 3 tables and 3 columns of references). Many cross-references. Index in v.2 (p.1689-1728). 'The dictionary provides an authoritative source of reference for students and for scientists and engineers working in unfamiliar areas of geophysics' (*Science journal*, v.4(6), June 1968, p.94). *Class No:* 550.3(031)

Handbooks & Manuals

[1492]

FOWLER, C.M.R. The Solid earth: an introduction to global geophysics. Cambridge, University Press, 1990. xviii,472p. tables, diagrs. £40. ISBN: 0521370256.

9 chapters, each with appended 'problems and bibliography'. Glossary, p.454-62. 7 appendices. A textbook intended for students and geologists. 'Well-written, accurate, comprehensive and up-to-date ... a book to be used in conjunction with a course, not given to the average student to read for himself' (*Geophysical journal international*, v.105(2), May 1991, p.557). *Class No:* 550.3(035)

Dictionaries

[1493]

GUSEV, B.V., *and others*. English-Russian dictionary of applied geophysics. Moscow, Russkii Vazyk', Pergamon Press; New York, State Mutual, 1984. ix, 488p. £43; $50. ISBN: 0080281680, UK ed; 0317594192, US ed.

About 25,000 English terms with Russian equivalents. Abbreviations included. Appendices 1-2: Trade names for main types of geophysical equipment. Index of Russian terms, p.479-88. *Class No:* 550.3(038)

Reviews & Abstracts

[1494]

Meteorological and geoastrophysical abstracts. Littleton, Mass., American Meteorological Society, 1960-. v.1(1)-. 12pa. $1,120; CD-ROM $5,200. ISSN: 00261130.

Formerly *Meteorological abstracts and bibliography*, 1950-59.

Indexes over 200 sources, including technical journals, monographs, proceedings, reviews, and annual publications. Each issue has *c*.600 abstracts and references. 6 sections: A. Environmental sciences - B. Meteorology - C. Astrophysics - D. Hydrosphere. Hydrology - E. Glaciology - F. Physical oceanography. Author, subject and geographic indexes. Available online, 1972-, with database containing *c*.150,000 records. CD-ROM also available, with coverage from 1974-. *Class No:* 550.3(048)

Progress Reports

[1495]

Advances in geophysics. San Diego, etc., Academic Press, 1952-. v.1-. Irregular. ISSN: 00652687.

V.38, 1996 has ten contributors and contains 3 papers (*e.g.* 'Dissipation of tidal energy paleotides, and evolution of the earth-moon system', p.179-266), each followed by a considerable number of references. Detailed, analytical index, p.267-75. *Class No:* 550.3(055)

Yearbooks & Directories

[1496]

The Geophysical directory. 54th ed. Houston, Texas, The Geophysical Directory, Inc., 1999. 500p.

Lists *c*.7,000 companies providing geophysical equipment, supplies or services, plus mining and petroleum companies using geophysical techniques. Also, a list of *c*.18,000 geophysicists and geologists directly involved with geophysical operations - plus a company name cross-reference section. Separate listings on the activities of national and international geophysical societies. Extensive company index. *Class No:* 550.3(058)

Published Series

[1497]

Annals of the IQSY. International Years of the Quiet Sun. Cambridge, Mass., & London, MIT Press, 1968-70. 7v.

1. *Geophysical measurements: techniques, observation schedules, and treatment of data.* 1968.
2. *Solar and geophysical events, 1960-65 (Calendar record).* 1968.
3. *The Proton flare project (The July 1966 event).* 1969.
4. *Solar-terrestrial physics: solar aspects.* 1969.
5. *Solar-terrestrial physics: terrestrial aspects.* 1969.
6. *Survey of IQSY observations and bibliography.* 1970. 608p.
7. *Sources and availability of IQSY data.* 1970. 368p.

Annals of an international programme of scientific research and study aimed at investigating how the sun's 11-yearly quiet cycle influences the solar system.

Annals of the International Geophysical Year (Oxford, Pergamon Press, 1957-70. 48v. illus., diagrs., tables) record studies of the sun at maximum activity during the 1957-78 IGY of the International Council of Scientific Unions. *Class No:* 550.3(082.1)

Tables & Data Books

[1498]

Global earth physics: a handbook of physical constants. Ahrens, T.J., *ed*. Washington, D.C., American Geophysical Union, 1995. vii,376p. diagrs., charts. $60. (*AGU reference shelf, 1*.) ISBN: 0875908519.

V.1 of a series of three publications expanding and revising *Handbook of physical constants*, edited by S. Clark (Geological Society of America, 1966). Covers basic global physics with chapters on geodetic properties of the earth and planets; structure of the mantle, crust, and tectonic plates; global magnetic fields. Described in *Choice*, February 1996 as being 'more definitive and advanced than D.E. James's *Encyclopedia of solid earth geophysics, (q.v.)*'. Many charts, diagrams, and an extensive index and bibliography. *Class No:* 550.3(083)

[1499]

UNITED STATES. Air Force. Air Force Geophysics Laboratory, Air Force Systems Command. **Handbook of geophysics and the space environment.** Jursa, A.S., *scientific editor*. 4th ed. Hanscom Air Force Base, Air Force Geophysics Laboratory, 1983. vp. illus., diagrs., tables, maps.

88 contributing editors. 25 documented chapters (1. The sun... 25. Infrared astronomy). Chapter 21: 'Atmospheric composition': 67p., includes 10p. of references. Appendix: units, constants and conversion factors. Aims 'to provide Air Force designers, engineers and systems operators with facts and data about the environment in which the Air Force operates' (*Preface*). *Class No:* 550.3(083)

Histories

[1500]

BRUSH, S.G. and LANDSBERG, H.E. The History of geophysics and meteorology: an annotated bibliography. New York & London, Garland, 1985. 450p. ISBN: 0824091167.

'Geophysics' is here interpreted to include the origin and development of the solar system and the formation of the earth's surface features. About 2,000 annotated entries in sections A-W (A. General histories; B. Biographies ... G. Geodesy, terrestrial gravitation, size and shape of the earth - H. Formation of the earth's surface features ... M. Meteorology: general histories ... R. Atmospheric dynamics and thermodynamics ... V. Upper atmosphere, ionosphere, magnetosphere, aurora). Author and subject indexes. *Class No:* 550.3(091)

Marine Environment

[1501]

CRC handbook of geophysical exploration at sea. Geyer, R.A., *ed*. 2nd ed. Boca Raton, Florida, CRC Press, 1992. 2v. illus., diagrs., graphs, tables, maps. ISBN: 084934252x, v.1; 0849342538, v.2.
First published in 1983.
V.1. *Hydrocarbons*. 496p. V.2. *Hard minerals*. 544p.
Class No: 550.3(26)

Research Projects

[1502]

O'REILLY, W., *comp.* **International directory to geophysical research.** Amsterdam, etc., Elsevier, 1986. [v], 122p. £32.81; $48.75. ISBN: 0444425918.
About 2,700 entries, A-Z (name, address, specialization). Subject index in 8 sections (1. Solid earth and core - 2. The oceans - 3. Terrestrial atmosphere and magnetosphere - 4. Extra-terrestrial - 5. Engineering, resources and exploration - 6. Physical properties of materials - 7. Methods, techniques and instrumentation - 8. Mathematical/computational techniques and theoretical geophysics). Aims 'to provide a means of reaching geoscientists who have certain general or specific scientific interests' (*Preface*).
Class No: 550.3:061:061.62.005

Earthquakes (Seismology)

Bibliographies

[1503]

HOLLIS, E.P. Bibliography of earthquake engineering. 3rd ed. [Oakland, Calif.], Earthquake Engineering Research Institute, 1971. x, 247p. $5. ISBN: 0318163179.
First published 1954 as *Bibliography of engineering seismology*.
4 parts: Miscellaneous sources of data (bibliographies, periodicals, maps, directories, etc.) - Seismology, seismic geology and seismometry (by country) - Dynamics of soils, rocks and structures - Design and construction in seismic regions. Author index.
Class No: 550.34(01)

[1504]

TYCKSON, D.A. Earthquake prediction. Phoenix, Ariz., Oryx, 1986. 67p. $18.75. ISBN: 0897742281.
246 annotated entries for material published between 1976-1983. English-language items only. Author index. Aimed at the general public. *Class No:* 550.34(01)

Encyclopaedias

[1505]

RITCHIE, D. The Encyclopedia of earthquakes and volcanoes. New York, Facts on File, 1994. 232p. illus. ISBN: 0816026599.
A-Z listing of *c*.800 terms for earthquakes and vulcanology, including names of individual volcanoes, and short biographies of scientists working in the field. Chronology of earthquakes and eruptions. Bibliography, p.217-9. Index. For school and public libraries. *Class No:* 550.34(031)

Handbooks & Manuals

[1506]

BRYANT, E. Natural hazards. Cambridge, University Press, 1991. xviii,294p. illus., figs., tables, maps. £40; £14.95. ISBN: 052137295x.
3 documented sections: Section 1 examines storms; wind; the oceans; drought and flood; precipitation; fires: Section 2, earthquakes; volcanoes; tsunami; land instability: Section 3 looks at responses to hazards. Many small illustrations. Glossary, p.275-86. Index. *Class No:* 550.34(035)

[1507]

CORNELL, J. The Great international disaster book. 3rd ed. New York, Scribner's, 1982. 472p. illus. $5. ISBN: 068417345x.
First published 1976.
Claims to cover all types of disasters, both natural and man-made (but not war or holocausts) throughout history. Each chapter concerns a particular kind of catastrophe. 'One of the most comprehensive sources of its kind', the author being 'press liaison for the Smithsonian Institution Center for Short-lived Phenomena' (*Reference services review*, v.12(2), Summer 1984, p.83-84). *Class No:* 550.34(035)

[1508]

HARRIS, S.L. Agents of chaos: earthquakes, volcanoes, and other natural disasters. Missoula, Mont., Mountain Press Publishing Company, 1990. 260p. illus., maps. $12.95. ISBN: 0878422439.
3 sections: 1. Earthquake hazards in the US - 2. Volcanic hazards in the West - 3. Ice and fire, myth and reality. Each of the 30 chapters has a bibliography appended. Glossary. Good illustrations. *Class No:* 550.34(035)

[1509]

WHITTOW, J. Disasters: the anatomy of environmental hazards. Harmondsworth, Middlesex, Penguin Books, 1980. 411p. illus., diagrs. (*Pelican Books*.)
5 parts: 1. Introduction (environmental hazards) - 2. Subterranean stress (2. Earthquakes; 3. Volcanoes, Sinking coastlines) - 3. Surface instability (5. Landslides and avalanches; 6. Ground surface collapse) - 4. The restless atmosphere (7. High winds; 8. Floods; 9. Drought; 10. Snow and fog) - 5. Will we ever learn? (11. Hazard city: a case study of Los Angeles; 12. Disaster research). Chapter references, p.399-402. Further reading, p.403-5, Analytical index, p.406-11. Praised, especially for its illus. and index, in *Geographical journal*, v.152(2). July 1986, p.258. *Class No:* 550.34(035)

Dictionaries

[1510]

JAPAN: Ministry of Education. Japanese scientific terms: Seismology. [Tokyo], Japanese Society for the Promotion of Science, 1974. 182, [1]p.
About 5,000 entries. Appendices: Magnetic scale; Seismic intensity scale. *Class No:* 550.34(038)

Reviews & Abstracts

[1511]

Abstract journal in earthquake engineering. Berkeley, Calif., Earthquake Engineering Research Center, Univ. of California, 1971-. Semi-annual. $100 (US); $125 (non US). ISSN: 03635732.
About 800 abstracts per issue. 9 sections: 1. General topics of conference proceedings - 2. Selected topics in seismology - 3. Engineering seismology - 4. Strong motion seismetry - 5. Dynamics of soils, rocks and foundations - 6. Dynamics of structures - 7. Earthquake-resistant construction and hazard reduction - 8. Earthquake effects - 9. Earthquakes and natural disasters. Title, author and analytical subject indexes. Abstracts cover technical papers, research reports, books, codes and conference proceedings.
Class No: 550.34(048)

[1512]

Bibliography of seismology / Bibliographie de séismologie / Bibliographia seismologii. Newbury, Berks., International Seismological Centre, 1965-. 2pa. £90.
Published with Unesco financial assistance.
About 2,000 references per issue. 3 parts: Subject index; author index; list of citations to important events. Appended: 'A cumulative list of source abbreviations' (*c*.500 sources). *Class No:* 550.34(048)

Geochemistry

[1513]

CHESTER, R. Marine geochemistry. London, Unwin Hyman, 1990. xviii,698p. diagrs., tables, maps. £92; £34.95. ISBN: 004551108x.
17 chapters: 1. Introduction - 2. The input of material to the ocean reservoir ... 8. Dissolved gases in sea water ... 12. Down-column fluxes and the benthic boundry layer ... 17. Marine geochemistry: an overview. Bibliography appended for each chapter. Aimed at intermediate and advanced students of chemical oceanography, marine geochemistry and the earth sciences. Criticized in *Choice*, January 1991 for badly reproduced tables due to poor paper quality, but 'provides the best descriptive survey of ocean geochemistry since the 1970s'. The author is Professor of Oceanography at the University of Liverpool. *Class No:* 550.4

[1514]

The Encyclopedia of geochemistry and environmental sciences. Fairbridge, R.W., *ed.* New York, etc., Van Nostrand Reinhold, 1972. xxi, 1321p. diagrs., graphs, tables, maps. (*Encyclopedia of earth sciences, v.4A.*)
378 articles, A-Z, by 237 specialists. Broad scope, embracing all elements in nature, all the more important cycles and processes, mineral groups, and all economic ore deposits. Each contribution has references and cross-references (*e.g.* 'Groundwater motion in draining basins', p.478-87, has 3 columns of references, plus cross-references to other volumes in the series. 'Hydrocarbons', p.495-503; 2p. of references). A major reference source. *Class No:* 550.4

[1515]

Geochemical reference material compositions: rocks, minerals, sediments, soils, carbonates, refractions & ores used in research & industry. Potts, P.J., *and others*. Latheronwheel, Caithness, Whittles Publishing; Boca Raton, Fla., CRC Press, 1992. xiv,313p. tables. £60. ISBN: 1870325400.

Sections: 1. Reference materials indexed by sample name - 2. Reference materials indexed by sample description - 3. Compilation tables (p.22-189) - 4. Concentration ladders - 5. References to source data. For the analyst, geochemist, and those in the mining and metallurgical industries involved in the exploitation of raw materials. *Class No:* 550.4

[1516]

Handbook of geochemistry. Wedepohl, K.M., *ed.* Berlin, New York, Springer-Verlag, 1969-74. 2v. in 6. diagrs., graphs, tables, Loose-leaf.

About 70 contributors. V.1 'contains fundamental facts of geochemistry, geophysics and cosmochemistry, together with definitions, dimensions, methods of evaluation, etc.' (*Preface*). V.2 (5v., *c.*3300p.) has data on 'each element, with the exception of the noble gases, the lanthanides and the platinum elements'. *Class No:* 550.4

[1517]

INSTITUTE OF GEOLOGICAL SCIENCES. Regional geochemical atlases. British Geological Survey. Oxford, Blackwell, 1978-84. (Keyworth, Notts., British Geological Survey, 1987-)

Shetland. 1978. *Orkney.* 1979. *South Orkney and Caithness.* 1980. *Sutherland.* 1982. *Hebrides.* 1984. *Great Glen.* 1987. *Argyll.* 1990. *East Grampians.* £75. *Lake District.* £50. *Southern Scotland and part of Northern England.* £100.

Each vol. comprises up to 30 folding maps and 12p. of text, and each atlas of maps covers *c.*16 elements (barium ... zirconium). Originally designed to provide systematic data on trace element levels in stream sediments as a basis for mineral exploration, the later publications lay more emphasis on monitoring contamination from these natural sources. Authoritative, but too unwieldy for field use. *Class No:* 550.4

[1518]

The Wolfson geochemical atlas of England and Wales. Compiled by the Applied Geochemistry Research Group, Imperial College of Science and Technology, London. Webb, J.S., *and others.* Oxford, University Press, 1978. 70p. maps. £90. ISBN: 0198911130.

55 maps (48 in colour) plus 3 maps in back cover. Scale: 1:2,000,000. The computer-produced maps depict data on 21 elements from the analysis of 50,000 stream samples. Introductory text provides examples of potential uses of the atlas in agriculture, ecology and public health, as well as mineral exploration. *Class No:* 550.4

Prospecting & Exploration

[1519]

Applied geology for engineers. Great Britain. Ministry of Defence. London, HMSO, 1976. xxxv, 378p. illus., diagrs., graphs, tables, maps. £9. (*Military engineering, v.15.*) ISBN: 0117715972.

Sponsored jointly by the Ministry of Defence and the Institution of Civil Engineers.

11 chapters: 1. The scope of geology - 2. General geological theory - 3. The formation of rocks - 4. Properties and identification of rock types - 5. Landforms and rocks - 6. Geophysical methods - 7. Geological maps and other information sources (p.147-70)- 8. Terrain evaluation - 9. Site selection and evaluation - 10. Engineering in rocks and soil - 10. Construction materials - 11. Groundwater and its exploitation. Annex A: Unified classification system for soils. Detailed index, p.364-78. *Class No:* 550.8

[1520]

McLEAN, A.C. *and* **GRIBBLE, C.D. Geology for civil engineers.** 2nd ed., reprinted 1992. London, Allen & Unwin, 1985. xviii, 314p. illus., diagrs., tables, maps. £23.50. ISBN: 0046240055.

8 chapters: 1. Introduction - 2. Minerals and rocks - 3. Superficial deposits - 4. Distribution of rocks at and below the surface - 5. Subsurface (ground) water - 6. Geological exploitation of an engineering site - 7. Rocks and civil engineering - 8. Principal geological factors affecting certain geological projects. 'References and selected reading' appended to each chapter. Appendices A-H (A. Descriptions of some important soil groups; F. Quality of aggregates). Analytical index, p.305-14. Well tailored to meet the needs of qualified engineers. *Class No:* 550.8

[1521]

NELSON, A. *and* **NELSON, K.D. Dictionary of applied geology, mining and civil engineering.** London, Newnes, 1967. vii, 421p. diagrs.

Concise definitions, with cross-references. Detailed list of minerals, gemstones and rock types. Other topics include building materials, rock structures in relation to civil engineering projects, water resources and supplies, soil mechanics and site investigation, geophysics, exploratory drilling and sampling. Appendix 1: 'Recommended symbols for rock and soils'. 'Intended primarily for school and college students, and engineers in the mining and civil engineering professions' (*Preface*). *Class No:* 550.8

Remote Sensing

[1522]

BRYAN, M.L. Remote sensing of earth resources: a guide to information sources. Detroit, Mich., Gale, 1979. xv, 188p. $68. (*Geography and travel information guides, v.1.*) ISBN: 0810314134.

Carries 378 annotated entries in 8 chapters: 1. General literature; 2. Proceedings; 3. Manuals and guides; 4. Catalogs; 5. Maps; 6. Bibliographies; 7. Journals; 8. Workshops, university and training courses; [U.S.]. Each chapter has an introduction. Author, title and subject index; NTIS (National Technical Information Service, Springfield, Va.); Series index. *Class No:* 550.81

[1523]

DRURY, S.A. Images of the earth: a guide to remote sensing. 2nd ed. Oxford, University Press, 1998. viii, 203p. illus.(many col.). £50. ISBN: 0198549989.

First published 1990 as *A Guide to remote sensing.*

5 chapters: 1. The problems (water, food, natural disasters etc.) - 2. Getting the information - 3. Interpreting the information - 4. Using the information - 5. Operational issues. Two appendices. Glossary. Index, p.199-203. Attractive presentation. *Class No:* 550.81

[1524]

HYATT, E. Keyguide to information sources in remote sensing. London, Mansell, 1988. xiv,274p. £40. ISBN: 0720118549.

3 parts: 1. Survey of remote sensing and its literature - 2. is an annotated bibliography of 819 items which includes books, journals, literature guides, abstracts and indexes, and databases - 3. is a list of 326 organizations, grouped under 81 countries, with addresses. Index. A well-presented, impressive guide. *Class No:* 550.81

[1525]

Manual of remote sensing. Colwell, R.N., *ed.* 2nd ed. Falls Church, Va., American Society of Photogrammetry, 1983. 2v. (xvii, xvii, 2440p.). illus. (incl. col.). ISBN: 0937294527.

First published 1975.

V.1: Theory, instruments and techniques; v.2: Interpretation and applications. 36 documented chapters; 279 col. plates. 'The most comprehensive work on remote sensing to date' (Harris, C.D. *Geographical bibliography for American libraries* (1985, item 356)). *Class No:* 550.81

[1526]

Multilingual dictionary of remote sensing and photogrammetry: English glossary and dictionary, equivalent terms in French, German, Italian, Portuguese, Spanish, Russian. Rabchevsky, G.A., *ed.* Falls Church, Va., American Society of Photogrammetry, 1984. xx, [1], 343p. $20. ISBN: 0937294462.

7 parts, Part 1: English glossary and dictionary (1,716 numbered terms, with equivalents and indexes in the other 6 languages). Appended selected bibliography, p.341-3. *Class No:* 550.81

Geothermal Exploration

[1527]

ARMSTEAD, H.C. Geothermal energy: its past, present and future contributions to the energy needs of man. 2nd ed. London & New York, Spon, 1983. xxxviii, 404p. illus., diagrs., tables. £49; $59.95. ISBN: 0419122206.

First published 1978.

19 chapters (1. Historical note... 4. The heat energy of the earth - 5. The nature and occurrence of geothermal fields - 6. Exploration - 7. Drilling - 8. Bore characteristics and their measurement - 9. Fluid collection and transmission - 10. Electric power generation from geothermal energy - 11. Direct applications of earth heat... 14. Some economic considerations... 18. The future - 19. Epilogue: the frame of the geothermal picture). 257 references, p.377-88. Detailed, partly analytical index, p.389-404. A comprehensive treatment; the standard textbook. *Class No:* 550.836

[1528]
BOWEN, R. **Geothermal resources.** 2nd ed. London, New York, Elsevier, 1989. xii,485p. illus., figs., maps, tables. £74; $52. ISBN: 1851662871.
First published 1979.
7 well-documented chapters: 12. The origins of earth heat - 2. Geothermal systems and models - 3. Geothermal exploration ... 6. Environmental impact - 7. Uses of geothermal energy. Brief glossary. 4 appendices: 1. Geothermal miscellanea - 2. Companies of geothermal interest - 3. Organizations of geothermal interest - 4. World geothermal localities. Author and subject indexes. *Class No:* 550.836

[1529]
Geothermal energy: a current awareness bulletin. Springfield, Va., Office of Scientific and Technical Information, US Dept. of Energy, 1983-. Semi-monthly. $145pa. (US), $290 (non US & Canada). ISSN: 08966257.
Formerly *Geothermal energy update,* 1977-82.
International in scope, each issue carries *c.*20 abstracts. General coverage: Resource status and assessment - Geology and hydrology of geothermal systems - Geothermal exploration - Legal and institutional aspects - Environmental aspects and waste disposal - By-products - Geothermal power plants - Geothermal engineering - Direct energy utilization - Geothermal data and theory. Energy database.
Class No: 550.836

[1530]
Geothermal energy - the potential in the United Kingdom. Downing, R.A. *and* Gray, D.A., *eds.* London, HMSO, 1986. xiii, 187p. diagrs., charts, graphs, tables, maps. ISBN: 0118843663.
Programme sponsored by the Department of Energy and the Commission of the European Communities.
11 contributors. Assessment of results of an investigation of Britain's geothermal potential by the British Geological Survey, 1977-84. 10 chapters (*e.g.* 6. 'Geochemistry of geothermal craters in the UK'; 9. 'Engineering and economic aspects of low anthalopy development'). References, p.162-70. 4 appendices (3. Glossary of technical terms). Partly analytical index. Geological map of the UK, in back pocket. The first comprehensive review of its kind for the UK.
Class No: 550.836

[1531]
Handbook of geothermal energy. Edwards, L.M., *and others, eds.* Houston, Texas, Gulf Publishing Co., 1982. ix, 613p. illus., diagrs., graphs, tables. £67; $89. ISBN: 0872013227.
15 contributors. 10 chapters: 1. Introduction - 2. Worldwide geothermal resources - 3. Geology of geothermal systems - 4. Exploration for geothermal energy - 5. Geothermal well drilling and completion - 6. Casing and tubular design concepts - 7. Geothermal cementing - 8. Formation evaluation - 9. Reservoir engineering concepts - 10. Energy conversion and economic issues for geothermal energy. Statistics, to 1982. Detailed, analytical index, p.599-610. Aims at 'a comprehensive review of significant developments in the location and production of geothermal energy' (*Foreword*). Complementary to Armstead in stressing practical aspects.
Class No: 550.836

[1532]
SUMMERS, W.K. **Annotated and indexed bibliography of geothermal phenomena.** Socarro, New Mexico, New Mexico State Bureau of Mines and Mineral Resources, 1971. [vi, 665p.].
14,177 references, some with abstracts, to all the natural, physical and chemical aspects of the earth's heat. Claimed to be 95% complete to December 1969, with selected references from 1970. Computer-produced bibliography, in rundown order. Manually produced subject index; also geographic and author indexes. *Class No:* 550.836

Geology

Bibliographies

[1533]
'Geological literature'. In *Encyclopedia of library and information science* v.9, 1973, p.309-44. Lea, G, *and others*.
A survey of geology documentation. Sections on the primary literature, nomenclature and terminology, secondary sources (p.324-52). Detailed accounts of international, national and regional, and specialized services, guides to literature and reference works (75 items, unannotated); select list of 180 abbreviations. 74 references. 'Geological libraries and collections' (*Encyclopedia,* v.9, p.283-309) describes the development of geological libraries and collections, with references and bibliography (21 items). Of historical interest only. For more current information, the reader should consult the relevant chapters in D.N. Wood's *Information sources in the earth sciences (q.v.)* (London, Bowker Saur, 1989). *Class No:* 551(01)

[1534]
—MACKAY, J.W. Sources of information for the literature of geology: an introductory guide. 2nd ed. Edinburgh, Scottish Academic Press, 1974. v, 59p.
Originally (1971) prepared for internal use in the University College, London, Department of Geology; now 'slightly revised and edited for a more general audience' (*Preface*). 9 chapters (2. General bibliographical services ... 4. Special subject services (*e.g., Mineralogical abstracts*)- 5. Regional and minor subject bibliographies in geology ... 8. A miscellany of useful sources of information (*e.g.* library catalogues; theses; maps) - 9. Using information services. 13 references. Valuable commentary on abstracting and indexing services. Admits to a bias towards metropolitan sources. *Class No:* 551(01)

[1535]
—MARGERIE, E. de. Catalogue des bibliographies géologiques. Paris, Gauthier-Villars, 1896. (Reprinted Amsterdam, Meridian, 1968. 2v.). xx, 733p.
1,667 numbered entries for bibliographies, in general and regional sections. Author, subject and geographical indexes. A major source for bibliographies "hidden" in books, as appendices, or in periodicals. *Class No:* 551(01)

[1536]
—MATTHEWS, E.B. Catalogue of published bibliographies in geology, 1898-1920. Washington, National Research Council, 1923. 228p. Bulletin of the National Research Council, v.6(5), October 1923.
Continues Margerie in part, omitting regional bibliographies. Subject arrangement; author index. *Class No:* 551(01)

Encyclopaedias

[1537]
The Encyclopedia of applied geology. Finkl, C.W., *ed.* Princeton, N.J., Van Nostrand Reinhold, 1984. xxviii, 832p. illus., diagrs., graphs, tables, maps. $122.95. (*Encyclopedia of earth sciences, v.13.*) ISBN: 0442225377.
82 contributors. 87 main entries, well subheaded and documented (*e.g.* 'Geochronology': 8p.; subsections, 3 tables, 3 graphs; 55 references. 'Geomorphology, applied': p.243-70; nearly 5p. of references). Valuable preface, with sections on abstracting and indexing services, computerised databanks,. periodicals, texts and reference works. Adequate cross-references. Samples a wide range of interrelated topics in geology in the service of man.
Class No: 551(031)

[1538]
Encyclopedia of field and general geology. Finkl, C.W., *ed.* New York, Van Nostrand Reinhold, 1988. 911p. $89.95. (*Encyclopedia of earth sciences, v.14.*) ISBN: 0442224900.
Intended as a companion volume to *Encyclopedia of applied geology (q.v.),* this volume includes biogeochemistry, geoanthropology, and geobotany. As with the other volumes in the series, there are many internal cross-references, and to v.13. Good index. 'A must in any geology collection at all levels' (*New technical books,* Nov/Dec, 1988, item 1579). *Class No:* 551(031)

Europe

[1539]
Encyclopedia of European and Asian regional geology. Moores, E.M. *and* Fairbridge, R.W., *eds.* London, Chapman & Hall, 1997. xxi,804p. illus.,maps. $309.50. $d Encyclopedia of earth science series ISBN: 0412740400.
Multi-authored, with chapters on national geology written by native experts, including nations previously part of the USSR. International subjects on land-mass and mountain ranges are also included in this important review of European and Asian geology. Assumes some previous knowledge. *Class No:* 551(031)(4)

Asia

[1540]
Encyclopedia of European and Asian regional geology. Moores, E.M. *and* Fairbridge, R.W., *eds.* London, Chapman & Hall, 1997. xxi,804p. illus.,maps. $309.50. $d Encyclopedia of earth science series ISBN: 0412740400.
Multi-authored, with chapters on national geology written by native experts, including nations previously part of the USSR. International subjects on land-mass and mountain ranges are also included in this important review of European and Asian geology. Assumes some previous knowledge. *Class No:* 551(031)(5)

Handbooks & Manuals

[1541]
LAMBERT, D. *and* THE DIAGRAM GROUP. **The Field guide to geology.** New York, Facts on File, 1988. 256p. diagrs., maps. $22.95. ISBN: 0816016976.

Contains many illustrations with over 500 maps, diagrams, and charts. Appendices list achievements of famous geologists, and geological displays around the world. Brief bibliography. Subject index. For public libraries. *Class No:* 551(035)

[1542]
PUTNAM, W.C. **Putnam's geology.** Birkeland, P.W. *and* Larson, E.E.
5th ed. New York, Oxford University Press, 1989. 646p. illus. (incl. col.), diagrs., maps. $49.95; $28.95; £22.50. ISBN: 0195056302.

First published 1964.

19 chapters: 1. The planetary system ... 8. Volcanism ... 11. Mass movements and related geological hazards ... 15. Shore processes and landforms ... 19. Resources and energy. References appended to each chapter. Conversion table and glossary. Analytical index, p.635-46. A detailed textbook, with numerous black-and-white illustrations. *Class No:* 551(035)

[1543]
WILHELMS, D.E. **The Geologic history of the moon.** Washington, US Government Printing Office, 1987. 302p. illus. (some col. pl.).

A review of lunar science from the viewpoint of historical geology. 14 chapters: 1. General features ... 3. Crater materials ... 6. Structure - 7. Relative ages ... 9. Nectarian system ... 12. Eratostherian system ... 14. Summary. References cited, p.283-94. Index. 12 colour plates and many black-and-white illustrations. For geoscientists, planetologists and geologists. *Class No:* 551(035)

Dictionaries

Polyglot

[1544]
Geostatistical glossary and multilingual dictionary. Olea, R.A., *ed.* New York, Oxford University Press, 1991. 177p. $39.95. ISBN: 0195066898.

Part 1: The glossary (Absolute dispersion ... Z-score). Part 2: The multilingual dictionary (English, Chinese, French, German, Greek, Portuguese, Russian, Spanish). Selected bibliography, p.85-88. *Class No:* 551(038)=00

[1545]
ZYLKA, R. **Geological dictionary:** English, Polish, Russian, French, German. Warsaw, Wydawnictwa Geologiczne, 1970. 1439p.

About 25,000 numbered English-base entries, with Polish, Russian, French and German equivalents (and synonyms) and indexes. 'One of those rare multilingual dictionaries of technical terms that will please a geologist, a translator, and a graduate student faced with any important piece of geological literature from Europe' (*Choice,* v.9, November 1972, p.1116). *Class No:* 551(038)=00

[1546]
—Multilingual thesaurus of geosciences. Rassam, G.M., *and others, eds.* Oxford, etc., Pergamon Press, 1987. 500p. £115; $120. ISBN: 0080364314.

A six-language geological dictionary, with *c.*5,000 terms, mostly taken from the American Geological Institute's *Glossary of geology (q.v.),* in English, French, German, Italian, Spanish and Russian. Has a field index listing terms by subfields within geology. *Class No:* 551(038)=00

English

[1547]
BATES, R.L. *and* JACKSON, J.A. **Glossary of geology.** 3rd ed. Amsterdam, Elsevier, 1987. 754p. £60. ISBN: 0913312894.

First published 1957. Published in the US and Canada by the American Geological Institute.

Contains *c.*37,000 terms, covering subject areas which include geology; geophysics, sedimentology; hydrogeology; mineralogy; plate tectonics. For the first time, pronunciation is given. Includes abbreviations and dates when terms were first used. There are *c.*2,000 bibliographic references. The definitive geology glossary. *Class No:* 551(038)=20

[1548]
CHALLINOR, J. **Challinor's dictionary of geology.** 6th ed., edited by A. Wyatt. Cardiff, Univ. of Wales Press, 1986. xviii, 374p. £25; £9.95. ISBN: 0708509135.

First published 1961.

Defines over 2,000 terms, many at length. Numerous quotations; valuable commentary. 'Landslide': nearly 1 columm. 63 categories are applied. Classified index, p.345-74. Probably the most comprehensive source of geologic terminology for the general public. Sources of quotations are chiefly British in origin. *Class No:* 551(038)=20

[1549]
—WATT, A. Longman illustrated dictionary of geology: the principles of geology explained and illustrated. Harlow, Essex, Longman Group, 1982. 192p. col. illus., diagrs., tables, maps. £5.99. ISBN: 0582555493.

Over 1,500 entries, supported by more than 350 illus. Adequate cross-references. Appendix: Common abbreviations in geology; International system of units; Understanding scientific words. Detailed analytical index, p.171-82. 'It is an ideal book for first-year undergraduate students' (*Bulletin of the American Association of Petroleum Geologists,* v.67, June 1983, p.1045). *Class No:* 551(038)=20

[1550]
LAPIDUS, D.F. **Collins dictionary of geology.** London, Harper Collins, 1990. 565p. figs. £5.95. ISBN: 0004341481.

First published as *Facts on File dictionary of geology and geophysics* (Facts on File Publications, 1987).

Contains over 4,500 entries, Aa ... Zweikanter. Length of entries varies from a few words, *e.g.* 'Dorsum' to several pages, *e.g.* 'Carboniferous'. Many cross-references. 5 appendices: 1. SI units ... 4. Some techniques used in the analysis of rocks and minerals - 5. Suggested further reading. Useful for school, public and academic libraries, and complements *Challinor's dictionary of geology (qv).* *Class No:* 551(038)=20

[1551]
McGraw-Hill dictionary of geology and mineralogy. Parker, S.P., *ed.* New York, McGraw-Hill, 1997. xi, 346p. £16.95. ISBN: 0070524327.

8,700 terms drawn from the *McGraw-Hill dictionary of scientific and technical terms* (5th ed., 1994), and intended 'as a major compendium to the special language essential to understand these fields'. Includes petrology. New companion vol. to *McGraw-Hill dictionary of earth science.* *Class No:* 551(038)=20

[1552]
The New Penguin dictionary of geology. Kearey, P. London, Penguin, 1996. 366p. £6.99 ISBN: 0140512772.

7,606 entries arranged A-Z, but no attempt to cover all minerals and lacks biographical entries. Bibliography p.352-66. Rendered more valuable by the rival McGraw-Hill publication splitting into *McGraw-Hill dictionary of earth science (q.v.)* and *McGraw-Hill dictionary of geology and mineralogy (q.v.).* *Class No:* 551(038)=20

Czech

[1553]
ZEMAN, O.S. **Anglicko-Český geologický slovník s rejstříken Českých Názvů.** 2nd ed. Prague, Academia Praha, 1985. 367p.

English-Czech dictionary of geological terms, with Czech reverse index. 18,241 numbered English entries. Czech index, p.307-479. List of sources, p.9-11. *Class No:* 551(038)=850

Arabic

[1554]
ARAB LEAGUE EDUCATIONAL, CULTURAL AND SCIENTIFIC ORGANIZATION. **Lexicon of geology: English-French-Arabic.** Rabat, Morocco, Bureau Permanent de Co-ordination de l'Arabisation, 1971. 238, xlvp. *Class No:* 551(038)=927

Theses

[1555]
Comprehensive dissertation index, 1861-1972. Volume 15: Geography and geology. Ann Arbor, Mich., Xerox: Univ. Microfilms, 1973. xxi, 728p. Cumulation for 1973-77, with annual suppts. ISBN: 0835700941.

Arranged by subject keyword. Data: title, author, degree, university, number of pages, date of degree, *Dissertation abstracts international* citation, order number. No indexes. Difficult to use. *Class No:* 551(043)

Reviews & Abstracts

[1556]
Geological abstracts. Norwich, Elsevier, Geo Abstracts, 1989-. 12pa. $1,413. ISSN: 09540512.

Previously *Geophysics and tectonic abstracts* (1982-85), originally *Geophysical abstracts* (1977-81).

1986-1988, split into 4 series: *Economic geology; Sedimentary geology; Palaeontology & stratigraphy; Geophysics & tectonics.*

Divided into 16 subject areas: Mineralogy - Geochemistry - Geochronology - Igneous and metamorphic geology - Sedimentary geology - Stratigraphy - Quaternary geology - Palaeontology - Regional geology - Geophysics - Structural geology and tectonics - Seismology - Engineering and environmental geology - Economic geology - Extra-terrestrial geology - General texts. Monthly, annual

....*(contd.)*
and regional indexes. Available online (DIALOG; QUESTEL-ORBIT) and on CD-ROM on the GEOBASE database and CD-ROM. Also available on microfilm. *Class No:* 551(048)

[1557]
Zentralblatt für Geologie und Paläontologie. Teil 1 : Allgemeine, angewandte, regionale und historische Geologie. Stuttgart, E. Schweizerbart'sche Verlagsbuchhandlung, 1807-. 13pa. Price varies. ISSN: 03405109.
Each issue carries 1,400 references. 6 sections: 1. General geology; 2. Applied geology; 3. Regional geology; 4. Historical geology; 5. Miscellaneous; 6. Geophysics. Entries include descriptors. Keyword index; geographical index; index of topographical maps. Annual catchword and geographical indexes; topographic index for maps. Teil 2: *Paläontologie (q.v.).* *Class No:* 551(048)

Periodicals

[1558]
GEOLOGICAL SOCIETY. London. **Serial titles held in the Geological Society Library.** Bath, the Society, 1996. 30p. £5. ISBN: 0903317230.
Lists over 4,500 titles of serial publications, alongwith holdings details, received up to 1996, including discontinued titles. A list of the titles currently received may also be obtained from the Library although title details are given on the Internet at http://www.geolsoc.org.uk/lib/gs3lbsls.htm *Class No:* 551(051)

Yearbooks & Directories

[1559]
Directory of geo-analytical facilities in British universities, colleges, polytechnics and research institutions. Potts, P.J. *and* Tindle, A.G., *comps.* Latheronwheel, Caithness, Whittles Publishing, 1990. 153p. tables. £40. ISBN: 1870325451.
Directory tables, p.2-124. Index of specialists; index of techniques. Addresses of contributing departments. References, p.145-53.
Class No: 551(058)

[1560]
The Geologist's directory: a guide to the earth sciences in Britain, geological services, equipment and sources of geological information. Reeves, G.M., *comp.* 8th ed. London, Geological Society, 1996. Biennial. [viii], 568p. ISBN: 1897799373.
6th ed., 1992.
10 sections: 1. The Geological Society - 2. Chartered geologists (p.21-112) - 3. Geology in government (*e.g.*, 'Local government in England') - 4. The water industry - 5. Education - 6. Extractive industries - 7. Consultants - 8. Specialist services - 9. Buyer's guide - 10. Information services. Includes list of 350 schools where geology is taught as an A-level subject (p.186-199). *Class No:* 551(058)

[1561]
—Geological directory of the British Isles: a guide to information sources, 1978. Diment, J.A., *ed.* London, Geological Society of London, Geological Information Group, 1978. 109p. £3. ISBN: 0903317206.
Previously published 1970.
3 sections: 1. Geographical index - 2. Directory of organizations (p.18-98) - 3. Name index. Data on organizations (Aberdeen ... Zennor): name and address; telephone; date founded; library (including main subjects; special collections); publications.
Class No: 551(058)

Tables & Data Books

[1562]
The Geology of the terrestrial planets. Carr, M.H., *ed.* Washington, NASA, 1984. 317p. $16. (*Special publication SP 469.*) ISBN: 0160041627.
Takes the terrestrial planets (Venus, Mars, Mercury, Moon, Earth) in solar system order. Data: orbit, magnetic fields (if any), surface characteristics, craters, tectonics, etc., summarizing what has been learned since 1962. The Earth is given a brief chapter. 'Intended for the interested layman' (*Astronomy,* v.13, October 1985, p.88).
Class No: 551(083)

Nomenclatures

[1563]
Geological nomenclature: English-Dutch-French-German. Schieferdecker, A.A.G., *ed.* Gorinchem, J. Noorduijn, for the Royal Geological and Mining Society of the Netherlands, 1959. xvi, 523p.
First published 1929.
5,409 numbered English-base terms, with explanations in English and equivalents in Dutch, French and German. Classified arrangement: 10 sections, with subdivisions. Combined index in all four languages. A valuable polyglot dictionary. *Class No:* 551(083.72)

[1564]
—Geological nomenclature. Visser, W.A., *ed.* Utrecht, Bohn, Scheltema & Holkema; Norwell, Md., Kluwer, 1980. xxvi, [1], 540p. tables. $164.50. ISBN: 9024724031.
A later edition of Schieferdecker's *Geological nomenclature,* includes Spanish in the languages covered. 4,876 numbered English-base terms, with equivalents in Dutch, French, German and Spanish. Thematic arrangement. 5 language indexes, 14 indexes.
Class No: 551(083.72)

Films

[1565]
AMERICAN ASSOCIATION OF PETROLEUM GEOLOGISTS. **Index to films related to geology and energy exploration.** Tulsa, Oklahoma, the Association, 1976. 74p. *Class No:* 551(084.122)

Maps & Atlases

[1566]
DERRY, D.R. **World atlas of geology and mineral deposits.** London, Mining Journal Books, 1980. [iv], 110p. diagrs., tables, maps. ISBN: 0470269960.
3 parts: the text (Introduction; Landscape and geology; Structure and history of the earth; Distribution of earthquakes and volcanoes; Distribution of mineral deposits) - the world atlas (p.25-88; mostly in colour: The Americas ... Arctic) - Tables: world mineral resources production and reserves. Suggested reading, p.102. Sources of additional information. Glossary, p.108-10. 'Written for the layman' (*Geological magazine,* v.118, July 1981, p.436).
Class No: 551(084.3)

[1567]
—Geological world atlas. Compiled for Unesco and the Commission for the Geological Map of the World by the International Geological Mapping Office, 1984. 22 sheets.
On the scale of 1:10,000,000 (1:16,000,000 in the case of ocean sheets). Sheet 1: General; Sheets 2-15, 17; Continents; Sheets 16, 18-22; Oceans. Each sheet or group of sheets has brief explanatory note in English and French. *Class No:* 551(084.3)

[1568]
—Index to maps in earth science publications, 1963-1983. Van Balen, J., *comp.* Westport, Conn., Greenwood Press, 1985. 400p. $55; £58.50. ISBN: 0313249636.
Aims at listing *c*.4,900 geological maps in serials and monographs published during the period. Maps are recorded A-Z, with author index. Periodicals were searched for the years 1951-82, but only 60 monographs selected for 1963-83. The lack of selection criteria, the absence of scales in the source index, and the emphasis on larger-area rather than smaller-area maps are criticised in *Choice,* v.23(4), December 1985, p.587. *Class No:* 551(084.3)

[1569]
MALTMAN, A. **Geological maps:** an introduction. 2nd ed. Chichester, Wiley, 1998. x,260p. illus. (col. pl.), figs., maps. £19.99. ISBN: 0471976962.
Covers fundamental principles, with data on sources of geological maps, a short history, new techniques and forms of geology maps. 15 documented chapters: 1. Some fundamentals of geological maps ... 5. Geological cross-sections - 6. Visual assessment of outcrop patterns - 7. Unconformities ... 11. Geological history from maps ... 15. The production of geological maps. For first-year geology undergraduates but could also be useful for the more advanced student. A knowledge of rocks and geological processes is assumed. *Class No:* 551(084.3)

Chronologies

[1570]
THOMPSON, S. **A Chronology of geological thinking from antiquity to 1899.** Metuchen, N.J., Scarecrow Press, 1988. vii,320p. $29.50. ISBN: 0810821214.
Chronology, p.1-270. List of sources cited and their abbreviations. Bibliography of sources cited, followed by an author index. A subject index would have been useful. *Class No:* 551(090)

Histories

[1571]
ADAMS, F.D. **The Birth and development of the geological sciences.** Baltimore, Md., Williams & Wilkins, 1938; reprinted, New York, Dover, 1954. v. 506p., facsims., ports. $10.95. ISBN: 048626372x.
A history in 14 footnoted chapters 'to the earlier part of the nineteenth century'. Chapter 1. Introduction, bibliography and sources; 2. Geological science in Classical times ... 3/5. Middle Ages (p.51-169); 10. The origin of mountains (p.329-98, with 75 references); 13. Quaint stories and beliefs. Profuse quotations. Analytical index, p.495-

....*(contd.)*

506. 'In preparing the present history the writer has in all cases gone back for his material to the original authorities' (*Introduction*). By no means superseded. *Class No:* 551(091)

[1572]

—LAUDAN, R. From mineralogy to geology: the foundations of a science, 1650-1860. Chicago, Ill., Univ. of Chicago Press, 1987. 278p. illus., facsims. $27.50; £21.95. ISBN: 0226469506.

10 chapters (*e.g.* 2. Mineralogy and cosmogony in the late seventeenth century; 4. The botanical model rejected; 7. Historical geology; 9. Lyell's geological logic). Chapter notes, p.229-35. Extensive bibliography, p.236-68. Detailed, analytical index, p.269-78. Stresses concepts. '...it deserves to be widely read' (*TLS*, no.4442, 20 May 1988, p.562).

2nd ed., 1993 (University of Chicago Press. xii, 278p.) *Class No:* 551(091)

[1573]

ZITTEL, K.A. von. **Geschichte der Geologie und Paläontologie bis Ende des XIX Jahrhunderts.** [History of geology and palaeontology.] Munich, Oldenbourg, 1899. vii, 868p. $35.

English translation by M.M. Ogilvie-Gordon (London, Walter Scott, 1905; reprinted New York, Hafner, 1962).

A masterly survey of ancient, medieval and early modern geology in four parts. 'Most complete history of geology' (Smith, H.W. 'Guide to geological literature', in *Journal of geological education,* v.18(1), January 1970, p.25). *Class No:* 551(091)

Biographies

[1574]

LA ROCQUE, A. **Contributions to the history of geology.** Columbus, Ohio, State Univ., Dept. of Geology, 1964. 3v. Mimeographed.

Publication began in parts. 1. *Biographies of geologists.* 2. *Bibliography of the history of geology.* 3. *Biographic index.*

V.3 [iii], 217p.) has *c.*20,000 very brief entries, giving name; dates; description; nationality; specialization; post held. List of sources. *Class No:* 551(092)

[1575]

SARJEANT, W.A.S. **Geologists and the history of geology:** an international bibliography from the origins to 1978. London, Macmillan, 1980. 7v. in 6 (4526p.) + Supplement, 1979-84. 2v. (1691p.) and additions (Malabar, Fla., Krieger, 1987); Supplement 2: 1985-1993 (1996). $450; $175, Supp. 1; £275, Supp. 2. ISBN: 0333293638, set.

V.1 (5 sections) provides an introduction and records histories of geology and related sciences; v.2-3 (sections 6-7): The individual geologists, A-Z; v.4 (sections 8-9): Index of geologists by nationality and country; index of geologists by speciality; v.5 (section 10): Index of authors, editors and translators, p.3535-4515. 'This bibliography attempts to bring together details of all those works in languages using the Latin alphabet which deal with the history of geology' (section 1, *General introduction*). Bibliographies of about 10,000 geologists, - a mammoth undertaking. 'It merits unqualified recommendation to those libraries serving users interested in the history of science' (*Choice,* v.18(4), December 1980, p.510). New supplements are planned at 5-yearly intervals. *Class No:* 551(092)

[1576]

—GUNTAU, M. Biographien bedeutender Geowissenschaftler der Sowjetunion. Berlin, Akademie Verlag, 1979. 199p. illus., facsims., ports., diagrs. (*Schriftenreihe für geologische Wissenschaften, Heft 14.*)

Provides 19 biographical sketches of Russian and Soviet geologists of the 18th-20th centuries, with summaries in Russian and English (*e.g.* M.V. Lomonosov (1711-1765): p.7-18. 1 port., 1 facsim. 1p. of bibliography - material by and on). 36 illus. in all. Supplements Sarjeant regarding Soviet geoscientists. *Class No:* 551(092)

Worldwide

[1577]

Beiträge zur regionalen Geologie der Erde. Berlin & Stuttgart, Borntraeger; New York, Lubrecht & Cramer, 1961-. illus., maps.

1. *Die Geologie Mittelamerikas.* R. Weyl. 1961. xvi, 226p.
2. *Die Geologie von Paraguay.* H. Poutzer. 1962, xii, 184p.
3. *Geologie von Chile.* W. Zeil. 1964. xi. 233p.
4. *Geologie der Antillen.* R. Weyl. 1966. viii, 410p.
5. *Rocky Mountains.* D.H. Roeder. 1966. xiv, 316p. $99.50.
6. *Geologie von Syrien und dem Libanon.* R. Wohlfart. 1967. xii, 326p.
7. *Geologie von Jordanien.* F. Bender, 1968. xi, 230p. Supplementary ed. in English, with revisions. 1974, xi, 196p. $110.95.
8. *Geologie von Ungarn.* L. Trunko. 1969. x, 258p.
9. *Geologie von Brasilien.* K. Beurlen. 1970. viii, 444p.
10. *Geology of the South Atlantic Islands,* R.C. Mitchell-Thomé. 1970. x, 368p. $105.

....*(contd.)*

11. *Geologie von Ecuador.* W. Sauer. 1971. ix, 316p.
12. *Geology of the Middle Atlantic Islands.* R.C. Mitchell-Thomé, 1976. ix, 382p. $138.60.

Volumes 13-19 deal with the Andes (1979), Afghanistan (1980), Central America (2nd ed. 1980. $105), Burma (1983), the USSR (1985), N.W. Germany (1986) and Greece (1986), respectively. An excellent series of regional geologies. *Class No:* 551(100)

[1578]

The **Encyclopedia of world regional geology.** Part 1: Western Hemisphere (including Antarctica and Australia). Fairbridge, R.W., *ed.* Stroudsburg, Pa., Dowden, Hutchinson & Ross, 1975. xv,704p. illus., tables, maps. $129. (*Encyclopedia of earth sciences, v.8.*) ISBN: 012786461x.

88 contributors; *c.*150 signed entries, with references and cross-references. Entries are under countries A-Z. 'United States of America', p.502-641 ('Alaksa', p.513-22: climatology and biogeography; physiography and geomorphology; tectonic framework; stratigraphy; geological history; mineral resources. 52 references, 2 illus., 2 maps). 'West Indies', p.658-66; 20 cross-references. Author and subject indexes. Well illustrated. A major work of reference of considerable value to all levels of enquirer. *Class No:* 551(100)

[1579]

Overseas geology and mineral resources. London, HMSO, 1950-.

New series in print: nos.41-63 (1973-86). Some of the original series (v.1 1950-71) were entitled *Colonial geology and mineral resources.* The range is now worldwide (*e.g.* no.49: *Outline of the geology and mineral deposits of the Democratic Republic of the Sudan and adjacent areas,* by J.R. Vail. 1978. no.58: *An annotated bibliography of Ecuadorian geology,* by C.R. Bristow. 1981.).

The *Overseas memoirs* series (no.1-. 1976-) supplements the above as more specialised monographs (*e.g. The geology of Guadalcanal, Solomon Islands,* by B.D. Hackman. 1980.). *Class No:* 551(100)

Marine Environment

[1580]

BROOKS, J.R.V. *and* THOMAS, P. **'A Selected bibliography of North Sea geology (up to 1974)'.** In *Proceedings, Geologists Association,* v.85, 1974. p.103-11.

141 items, under 12 subject headings (*e.g.* Forties Field). Updated by their 'A classified bibliography of northwest European continental shelf geology, 1974 and 1975' (*Scottish journal of geology,* v.13(1), 1977, p.1-10). *Class No:* 551(26)

[1581]

KENNETT, J.P. **Marine geology.** Englewood Cliffs, N.J., Prentice-Hall, 1982. xv, 813p. illus., diagrs., graphs, tables, maps. ISBN: 0135569362.

Introduction: History of marine geology - 1. The structural and oceanographic setting - 2. The ocean margins - 3. Oceanic sediments and microfossils - 4. Ocean history. References, p.752-87. Author index; analytical subject index (p.795-813). The text, 'intended for a first course in maritime geology at the advanced undergraduate or graduate level, assumes little background in oceanography' (*Preface*). *Class No:* 551(26)

[1582]

The **Sea ... v.3: The earth beneath the sea.** History. Hill, M.N., *ed.* New York & London, Interscience: Wiley, 1963 (Reprinted 1980. Melbourne, Fla., Krieger. $88). xvi, 963p. ISBN: 0898740991. *Class No:* 551(26)

[1583]

—SHEPARD, F.P. **Geological oceanography.** New York, Crane Russak & Co., 1977. 214p. illus. (some col.), diagrs.

'Written for students beginning to study geology or anyone interested in important developments' in oceanography, - this text provides 'a clear and simple account, by an authoritative author' (*Marine geology,* v.28(3/4), 1978, p.293). *Class No:* 551(26)

[1584]

SHEPARD, F.P. **Submarine geology.** 3rd ed. New York, Evanston, 1973. x, 517p. illus., diagrs., fldg. chart, maps.

First published 1948.

14 chapters: 1. Introduction and history. 3. Waves and currents. 5. Plate tectonics. 9. Continental terraces. 12. Coral reefs. Deep-sea deposits and stratigraphy. References (authors, A-Z), p.483-490. Index. Emphasis is on shore and nearshore aspects of the subject. *Class No:* 551(26)

Europe

[1585]

AGER, D.V. **The Geology of Europe.** New York, London, etc. McGraw-Hill, 1980. xix, 535p. diagrs., table, maps. $27.95. ISBN: 0070841152.

4 parts (17 chapters): 1. Eo-Europe - 2. Palaeo-Europe - 3. Meso-Europe - 4. Neo-Europe. Prelims. include 'Keys to the geological divisions of Europe; Stratigraphical table; General references'. Each chapter has selected references (*e.g.* 16. Southern Alpides: 2¼p. of grouped references). Non-analytical index. 'It is Europe as seen by a stratigraphic palaeontologist' (*Preface*). Author, at University College, Swansea. *Class No:* 551(4)

[1586]

GEOLOGICAL SOCIETY. London. **Sources of information on the geology of the continental EEC countries.** London, the Society, 1980. [1], [1], 150p. (*Miscellaneous paper no. 12.*)

European Economic Community countries, Belgium ... Netherlands (*e.g.* 'Geological mapping and geological surveys of France', p.48-63). Appended: 'Selected bibliography of references, available in London geological libraries on the geology and mineral resources of the continental EEC countries', p.129-36. *Class No:* 551(4)

[1587]

RUTTEN, M.G. **The Geology of Western Europe.** Amsterdam, etc., Elsevier, 1969. xviii, 520p. illus., diagrs., tables, maps.

18 documented chapters, closely subdivided: 1. The main divisions; 2/3. Northern Europe; 4/7. Hercynian Europe; 8. The Massif Central; 9/16. Alpine Europe; 17, Lowlands and low plateaus; 18. Younger volcanoes. Addendum: Sources for geological information on Western Europe, p.475-6. Reference [names] index; detailed, non-analytical subject index, p.485-520. Helpful introduction, with 15 references. A well-produced survey. *Class No:* 551(4)

[1588]

ZIEGLER, P.A. **Geological atlas of western and central Europe.** 2nd ed. The Hague, Shell Internationale Petroleum Maatschappij BV, 1990. 239p. figs., maps. 56 enclosures. £50. (*International Lithosphere Program publication, no.148.*) ISBN: 9066441259.

First published 1982.

9 chapters: 1. Introduction ... 3. Caledonian suturing of Laurussia ... 5. Permo-Triassic development of Pangaea ... 9. Plate tectonics and basin evolution: geodynamics processes. References, p.195-233. Geographic index, p.234-37. Geodynamic processes, p.238-39. A major revision, with 56 enclosures in this edition, compared to 40 in the previous. The number of text figures has increased from 29 to 100. A standard work. *Class No:* 551(4)

Great Britain

[1589]

BRITISH GEOLOGICAL SURVEY. **British regional geology.** 2nd-4th ed. London, HMSO, 1935-.

Scotland:
Orkney and Shetland, by W. Mykura. 1976.
The Northern Highlands of Scotland, by G.S. Johnstone and W. Mykura. 4th ed. 1989. £6.
Grampian Highlands. 4th ed., by D. Stephenson and D. Gould, 1995.
The Tertiary volcanic districts. 4th ed., by J.E. Richey. 1987.
The Midland Valley of Scotland. 3rd ed., by I.B. Cameron and D. Stephenson. 1985. £5.
The South of Scotland. 3rd ed., by D.C. Greig and others. 1972.
England:
Northern England. 4th ed., rev. by B.J. Taylor, and others. 1971.
The Pennines and adjacent areas. 3rd ed. by W. Edwards and F.M. Trotter. 1954.
Eastern England from the Tees to the Wash, 2nd ed., by P. Kent, 1980.
Central England. 3rd ed., by B. Hains and A. Horton. 1969.
East Anglia and adjoining areas. 4th ed., by C.P. Chatwin, 1961.
Bristol and Gloucester Region. 3rd ed., by G.W. Green, 1993. (Previous editions entitled *Bristol and Gloucester district).*
London and Thames valley. 3rd ed., by R.L. Sherlock, 1930. (4th ed. due to be published 1996).
The Wealden district. 4th ed., by R.W. Gallois. 1965.
The Hampshire basin and adjoining areas, 4th ed. by R.V. Melville and E.C. Freshney. 1982.
South-west England. 4th ed., by E.A. Edmonds and others. 1975.
Wales:
North Wales. 3rd ed., by B. Smith and T.N. George. 1961.
South Wales. 3rd ed., by T.N. George. 1970.
The Welsh Borderland. 3rd ed., by J.B. Earp and B.A. Hains. 1971.
A series of pamphlets and handbooks that include maps based on the 1:250,000 scale maps of the Geological Survey.
Regional geology of Northern Ireland by H.E. Wilson (Belfast Ministry of Commerce and Geological Survey of Northern Ireland. 1972. xiiv,maps.). *Class No:* 551(410)

Bibliographies

[1590]

British geological literature (new series): a bibliography and index of geology (and related topics) of the British Isles and adjacent sea areas. Worthing, Sussex, Bibliographic Press, 1972-. 4pa. £62; $95 pa. ISSN: 01407813.

In original form, last appeared in 1968.

About 500 abstracts pa. (each *c.*60 words in length). The 26 sections (History of geology ... Engineering geology) include geomorphology and palaeontology. Quarterly author index; annual author, subject and locality indexes. *Class No:* 551(410)(01)

Handbooks & Manuals

[1591]

ANDERSON, J.G.C. **Field geology in the British Isles:** a guide to regional excursions. Oxford, etc., Pergamon, 1983. xi, 324p. maps. £16. ISBN: 0080220541.

10 chapters (*e.g.* 4. Precambrian terrains; 5/6 Caledonian terrains; 7. Hercynian terrains; 8. Alpine terrains). 3 appendices (1. Stratigraphical grouping of excursions). Detailed index, p.320-4. Describes 194 geological itineraries, complementing J.G.C. Anderson's and T.R. Owen's *The structure of the British Isles* (2nd ed. Pergamon, 1980) by providing local data. *Class No:* 551(410)(035)

Theses

[1592]

HODGSON, A.V. *and* LAMING, D.J.C., *comps.* **Titles of research theses, 1960-1975: Geology of the British Isles and offshore areas,** with classified subdiscipline/regional list. 2nd ed. Worthing, Sussex, Bibliographic Press, 1976. [iii], 128p.

Compiled in co-operation with Computer Centre, Sunderland Polytechnic.

About 1,350 titles. Chronological author list; classified subdiscipline list (arranged by year of award, then by authors A-Z); author index. 2-letter code for geological systems; 4-letter code for geophysical subdisciplines. *Class No:* 551(410)(043)

Government Publications

[1593]

Government publications. Sectional list 45, revised January 1996. British Geological Survey. London, HMSO, 1996. 67p. + xviii. *Gratis.*

Lists 'Bulletins of the Geological Survey of Great Britain' and other BGS publications, as well as material produced by other agencies such as the National Rivers Authority and the Natural History Museum. *Class No:* 551(410)(061.1)

Maps & Atlases

[1594]

BRITISH GEOLOGICAL SURVEY. **1:50,000 maps** [England & Wales; Scotland; Northern Ireland]. Southampton, Ordnance Survey, for the British Geological Survey.

Replaces the 1:63,360 (one inch to one mile) map series.

The 1:50,000 series of maps appears in two forms: 'solid' (showing the solid rocks at, or immediately beneath, the earth's surface), and 'drift' (showing detritus or drift materials such as broken rock, sand, gravel, alluvium and glacial clays). Some sheets combine the 'solid' and 'drift'. National Grid is given.

Other scales include the 1:250,000, covering the UK and its continental shelf.

A series of 1:50,000 sheet memoirs accompanies the geological maps. Those in print are listed in HMSO's sectional list 45: *Government Publications (q.v.). Class No:* 551(410)(084.3)

Histories

[1595]

CHALLINOR, J. **The History of British geology:** a bibliographical study. Newton Abbot, Devon, David & Charles, 1971. 224p.

Part 1: The primary literature: a chronological listing (to 1969), 659 items - 2. The major themes (86; *e.g.* 16. The Western counties of England; 74. Pleistocene geology; 86. Some recent collaborative volumes). Appendices: A. Secondary and associated literature; B. Index of authors, with some biographical detail; C. Index of names: places, counties, stratigraphical divisions, fossils. Well-documented and providing 'lively and most interesting reading' (*TLS,* no.3645, 7 January 1972, p.21). *Class No:* 551(410)(091)

Institutions & Associations

[1596]

WILSON, H.E. Down to earth: one hundred and fifty years of the British Geological Survey [1835-1985]. Edinburgh & London, Scottish Academic Press, 1985. [iv], 190p. illus., ports., facsims. ISBN: 0701304733.

18 chapters, on the origins, development and expansion of the British Geological Survey, at home and overseas. Chapter 18: 'What next: the future of the Geological Survey'. References, p.159; Index, p.190. A personal, not an official account.
Class No: 551(410):061:061.2

Scotland

[1597]

Geology of Scotland. Craig, G.Y., *ed.* 3rd ed. London, Geological Society, 1991. xii,612p. illus., diagrs., charts, tables, maps. £65; £29. ISBN: 090331763x.

First published 1965.

19 contributors. 16 chapters: 1. The growth and structure of Scotland - 2. The Lewisian complex ... 4. Moine ... 12. Permian and Triassic (p.421-38; nearly 5p. of references) ... 16. Economic geology. Partly analytical index, p.597-612. Well produced, with over 200 illustrations. For all those with an interest in geology.
Class No: 551(411)

Ireland

[1598]

CHARLESWORTH, J.K. Historical geology of Ireland. Edinburgh & London, Oliver & Boyd, 1963. vii, 565p. diagrs., maps.

18 chapters; 140 maps and diagrams. Lengthy bibliography (authors, A-Z), p.500-30. Non-analytical index 'A most important and carefully compiled work, and will hold the field as a standard reference for many a day' (*Nature*, v.199, 7 September 1963, p.941). 'The Irish equivalent of the "Handbooks on the regional geology of Great Britain". (*Geographical journal*, v.129(4), December 1963, p.514-5). Criticised in *Geography* (v.49(4), November 1964, p.447) for lack of a large coloured geological map of Ireland and indifferent illus. Designed for the advanced student of Irish geology or the professional geologist. *Class No:* 551(415)

[1599]

A Geology of Ireland. Holland, C.H., *ed.* Edinburgh, Scottish Academic Press, 1981. x, 335p. illus., diagrs., graphs, maps. £15. ISBN: 0707302692.

9 contributing authors. 19 documented chapters (*e.g.* 3. The Orthotectonic Caledonides; 12. Permiam and Mesozoic; 16. The Quaternary - until 10,000 BP; 18. Economic geology; 19. The history of Irish geology). Analytical index, p.317-35. Deals primarily with historical geology, but also offers a short survey of geophysical evidence, of Ireland's now very important economic geology and 'the fascination of Irish geology itself' (*Preface*). *Class No:* 551(415)

England & Wales

[1600]

Geology of England and Wales. Duff, P.McL.D. *and* Smith, A.J., *eds.* London, The Geological Society, 1992. xix,651p. illus., figs., tables. £75; £34. ISBN: 0903317702.

22 contributors. Comprehensive account including recent advances in offshore drilling, plate tectonics, age dating, structure geology and sedimentary environments. 19 documented sections: 1. The growth and structure of England and Wales - 2. Precambrian ... 8. Silesian - 9. Permian ... 12. Cretaceous - 13. Tertiary ... 15. Offshore geology - 16. Igneous rocks ... 18. Deep geology - 19. Economic geology. Many black-and-white illustrations and figures. Index, p.639-51, is in very small print. *Class No:* 551(42)

Wales

[1601]

BASSETT, D.A. Bibliography and index of geology and allied sciences for Wales and the Welsh borders, 1536-1896. Cardiff, National Museum of Wales, 1963. [x], 246p. £4.

7 sections: 1. Introduction; 2. Publications of the Geological Survey and Museum; 3. Palaeontological Society monographs; 4. List of books, papers, etc. (p.12-126; chronological order of publication); 5. List of books and papers written in Welsh; 6. Author index; 7. Analytical subject index. *Class No:* 551(429)

[1602]

—**BASSETT, D.A.** Bibliography and index of geology and allied sciences for Wales and the Welsh borders, 1897-1958. Cardiff, National Museum of Wales, 1961. 376p. £4.

8 sections, including 2: Reference books, bibliographies, indexes, etc., plus papers and books containing comprehensive lists of references; and 6: Theses accepted for higher degrees. Author and detailed, analytical subject indexes.

Updated in issues of *Geological journal* and *Welsh geological quarterly*. *Class No:* 551(429)

China

[1603]

The Geology of China. Zunyi, Y., *and others.* Oxford Univ. Press, 1986. 303p. tables, maps. £55. (*Oxford Geological Science series.*) ISBN: 019854460x.

Sections: Background - Stratigraphy - Magnetic and metamorphic rocks of China since 1939 - Geotectonic development of China. Includes regional stratigraphical tables. Selected references. Stratigraphic index. Subject index. *Class No:* 551(510)

Asia—Middle & Near East

[1604]

AVNIMELECH, M.A. Bibliography of Levant geology. Jerusalem, Israel Program for Scientific Translations, 1965-69. 2v.

Covers the 'Fertile Crescent', including Cyprus, Hatay, Israel, Jordan, Lebanon, Sinai and Syria. V.1: *c.*4,500, up to 1963; v.2 adds *c.*900 pre-1963 references and 1,100 for 1963-68. A-Z list, with chronological and subject indexes. List of quoted periodicals and serials.

Current bibliography of Middle East geology (Jerusalem, Geological Survey of Israel, 1976-) supplements Avnimelech.
Class No: 551(53+56)

Asia—South East

[1605]

HUTCHISON, C.S. Geological evolution of south-east Asia. Oxford, Clarendon Press, 1989. xv,368p. illus., diagrs., maps. £77.50. (*Oxford monographs on geology and geophysics, 13.*) ISBN: 0198544391.

9 sections: 1. Introduction - 2. Late Mesozoic and Cainozoic tectonic features ... 5. Terrains of Cathaysian affinity (p.133-200) ... 7. Ophiolites and sutures ... 9. Granite and associated plutonic rocks. Many maps and figures. References, p.318-49. Index.
Class No: 551(59)

Africa

[1606]

FURON, R. The Geology of Africa. Hallam, A. *and* Stevens, L.A., *trans.* Edinburgh & London, Oliver & Boyd, 1963. xii, 377p. illus., maps.

French original first published 1950; 2nd ed. (Paris, Payot, 1960), - used for this translation.

Part 1: General stratigraphy; part 2: Regional ecology (25 chapters on individual regions, exclusive of North Africa). Numerous footnotes reference. Combined author and subject index (inadequate on subjects). 'Highly useful for scholars and students. The volume, though dated, remains the best source available' (Harris, C.D. *ed., Geographical bibliography for American libraries* (1985), entry 2613).
Class No: 551(6)

[1607]

—Bulletin d'information et de liaison. [Information and liaison bulletin.] Orleans, Association of African Geological Surveys, 1976-. no.1-. 4pa. FFr550. ISSN: 03968863.

Has a major feature, - 'Bibliographie analytique africaine' (*e.g.* issue 1, p.11-127: literature, 1973-1975). Extensive abstracts, arranged by country, then topic. Issue 1 also contains reports on progress in geology in African countries, international project meetings. No index.
Class No: 551(6)

Africa—West

[1608]

Geology and mineral resources of West Africa. Wright, J.B., *and others.* London, Allen & Unwin, 1985. xiii, 187p. diagrs., maps. £54. ISBN: 0045560013.

4 sections (18 chapters): 1. The Precambrian of West Africa. 2. Sedimentary basins in West Africa - 3. Mesozoic to Cenozoic igneous activity in West Africa - 4. The Quaternary of West Africa. Glossary, p.163-71. Index of place names. Subject index and bibliographies. 'The principal aim is to provide a broad view of West African geology as a whole' (*Preface*). *Class No:* 551(66)

America—North

[1609]

Archaeological geology of North America. Lasca, N.P. *and* Donahue, J., *eds*. Boulder, Colo., Geological Society of America, 1990. 633p. illus., diagrs., tables, maps. $62.50. (*Centennial special volume, 4*.) ISBN: 081375304x.

Published as part of the celebration of the centenary of the Society. Parts: Eastern Canada - Western Canada - Eastern United States - Central United States - Costa Rica and Mexico - North America general - Techniques. Documented chapters range from site specifics to regional studies. Some look at laboratory and field methodology, applications of geophysics to archaeological investigations, and isotope chemistry. Detailed, analytical index, p.619-33. For research and academic libraries. *Class No:* 551(71+73)

[1610]

GEOSCIENCE INFORMATION SOCIETY. Guidebooks Committee. **Union list of geologic field trip guidebooks of North America.** 5th ed. Washington, American Geological Institute, 1989. xxix, 201p. $60. ISBN: 0913312975.

Union list, p.1-172 (Abilene Geological Society (Texas) ... Wyoming Geological Association. Miscellaneous guide books). Participating libraries, p.xiii-xvi. Geographic index. *Class No:* 551(71+73)

Australasia & Oceania

[1611]

The Geological evolution of Australia & New Zealand. Brown, D.A., *and others*. Oxford, etc., Pergamon Press, 1968. x, 409p. diagrs., charts, map. ISBN: 008203186x.

12 sections (*e.g.* The Precambrian system ... The Quaternary system). References, p.365-86; unpublished references, p.387-8. Map references, p.389-92. Detailed, non-analytical index. Aims to be an 'update teaching aid in the stratigraphy of Australia and New Zealand' (*Preface*). *Class No:* 551(9)

Greenland

[1612]

Geology of Greenland. Escher, A.S. *and* Watt, W.S., *eds*. Copenhagen, Grønlands Geologiske undesøgelse [Geological Survey of Greenland], 1976. 603p. illus., diagrs., tables, maps. ISBN: 8798040405.

29 contributors. 21 documented sections (*e.g.* Economic minerals; Petroleum geology; Coal geology; Fossil flora of Greenland). Detailed, analytical index. Fully illustrated and mapped. Aerial photographs are a feature. An admirable example of a country geological survey. *Class No:* 551(988)

Antarctic

[1613]

Geological evolution of Antarctica. Thomson, M.R.A., *and others, eds*. Cambridge, University Press, 1991. xi,722p. illus., diagrs., graphs, tables, maps. £55. ISBN: 0521372666.

The text of 138 papers presented at the 5th International Symposium on Antarctic Earth Sciences, in Cambridge, UK, 23-28 August 1987.

6 topics: 1. Crustal development: the craton - 2. Crustal development: the Transantarctic Mountains - 3. Crustal development: Weddell Sea-Ross Sea region - 4. Crustal development: the Pacific margin - 5. Crustal development: Gondwana break-up - 6. Evolution of Cenozoic palaeo-environments. Papers carry references. Analytical index, p.707-22. Many illustrations with clearly written captions. A valuable compendium. *Class No:* 551(99)

Thesauri

[1614]

GeoRef thesaurus and guide to indexing. Shimomura, R., *ed*. 5th ed. Alexandria, Va., American Geological Institute, 1989. 752p. Also available in microfiche. $75; $25, microfiche. ISBN: 091331983x.

First published 1977.

Thesaurus of 20,242 terms, A-Z, 4,284 of the new to this ed. A 'guide to indexing', provides a three-level hierarchical index. Categories: A. First order terms; F. Fossils; H. Igneous rocks; M. Soils; N. Sediments; O. Areas. Appended lists of authorities and abbreviations. *Class No:* 551:025.43

Libraries

[1615]

ROBINSON, E., *comp*. **A Guide to geology libraries in London.** 3rd ed. London, Geology Subject Sub-committee of the Library Resources Committee, Univ. of London, 1982. 24p.

First published 1974 as *Libraries for the geologist in and around London* (London, Imperial College, Lyon Playfair Library, 1974).

A student's guide to 22 libraries, including 3 public libraries. Entries

....(contd.)

are in narrative from, outlining facilities available (*e.g.* reference/loan, seating, photocopying, postal address, hours of opening, name of librarian, etc.). No index. A companion guide covers geography and map collections. *Class No:* 551:061:026/027

Museums

[1616]

Directory of British geological museums. Bath, Geological Society, 1994. vii,141p. £14.95. (*Geological Society of London miscellaneous paper, no.18*.) ISBN: 189779908x.

Contains data on around 100 public collections throughout the UK. Each entry includes address, administration, times of opening, major strengths, etc. Results of a survey undertaken between 1991 and 1993. *Class No:* 551:061:069

[1617]

Geology in museums: a bibliography and index. Sharpe, T., *comp*. Cardiff, National Museum of Wales, 1983. 128p. (*Geological series, no. 6*.) ISBN: 0720002818.

'Over one thousand references relating to geological curation' (*Introduction*). Under authors, A/Z. Keywords appended to entries. Keyword index ('Palaeontology': 8½ columns). *Class No:* 551:061:069

Earth Structure

[1618]

HOLMES, A. Holmes' principles of physical geology. Duff, P.McL.D., *ed*. 4th ed. London, Chapman and Hall, 1992. xvi,791p. illus. (some col.), diagrs., maps. ISBN: 0412438305.

First published 1944.

31 sections, each with selected references (*e.g.* 5. Igneous rocks: volcanic and plutonic ... 12. Igneous intrusions (p.176-206), 46 illus. and diagrs.; 3 references ... 21. Ice Ages and climatic change ... 31. Orogenic belts). Analytical index. Very well illustrated. Excellent value; standard text. *Class No:* 551.1

[1619]

Hutchinson encyclopedia of the earth. Smith, P.J., *ed*. London, etc., Hutchinson, 1986. 248 + 8p. illus. (incl. col.), diagrs., maps. £14.95. ISBN: 0091658608.

Has 6 parts (23 chapters): The earth today - The solid earth - The fluid earth - Shaping the earth (*e.g.* climate and climate change) - Surface environment - Geology and man (*e.g.* engineering geology). Further reading and credits, p.24. Glossary of geological terms. Index. Fully illustrated in colour. 'In this book we see the Earth in the exciting light of the plate-tectonic revolution' (*Introduction*). A popular treatment. *Class No:* 551.1

[1620]

JEFFREYS, Sir H. The Earth: its origin, history and physical constitution. 6th ed. Cambridge Univ. Press, 1976. x, [2], 574p. illus. (pl.), diagrs., tables, maps. £70. ISBN: 0521206480.

First published 1924.

12 chapters (1. The mechanical properties of rocks ... 3. Observational seismology - 4. The theory of the figures of the earth and moon ... 9. The age of the earth ... 11. The origin of the earth's surface features). Appendices A-H (G. Statistical methods). Bibliography and author index, p.535-66. Undergraduate level. *Class No:* 551.1

[1621]

LAMBERT, D. *and* **THE DIAGRAM GROUP. The Cambridge guide to the earth.** Cambridge, University Press, 1988. 256p. figs., diagrs., maps. £27.95; £4.49. ISBN: 0521333652.

12 chapters: 1. Sizing up the earth - 2. The restless coast - 3. Fiery rocks ... 7. How rivers shape the land - 8. The work of the sea ... 11. The last 600 million years - 12. Rocks and man. 1-page bibliography. Index. Large type face and many diagrams, figs., etc. For those with no previous knowledge of the subject. *Class No:* 551.1

[1622]

Planet earth: an encyclopaedia of geology. Hallam, A., *ed*. Oxford, Elsevier-Phaidon, 1977. 320p. illus. (incl. col.), diagrs., tables, maps.

9 sections: The earth and its neighbours - Processes that shape the earth - Landscapes - The ocean floor - Economic geology - The rocks of the earth - Geological history - History of life - Making of geology. Glossary. Index. Most chapters consist of a narrative account, but there is A-Z order for minerals, rocks, fossils and biographies. Authoritative text; readable, with excellent illus. and art work. 'A long and impressive list of contributors... A good general introduction to earth sciences for the layman, and is well worth reading by the professional' (*Journal of natural history,* v.19(1), January/February 1979, p.128). *Class No:* 551.1

[1623]
SKINNER, B.J. *and* PORTER, S.C. **Physical geology.** New York, John Wiley, 1988. xii,750p. illus. (many col.), figs., diagrs. $51.95. ISBN: 0471056685.

5 sections: 1. Planet earth and its materials - 2. Time and the changing landscape - 3. The dynamic earth - 4. The earth's resources - 5. Beyond planet earth. Brief list of references appended to each chapter. 5 appendices: A. Organization of matter - B. Identification of common minerals - C. Identification of common rocks - D. Maps, cross sections, field measurements, interpretations - E. Units and their conversions. Glossary, p.723-38. Index. Many colour illustrations. *Class No:* 551.1

Geodynamics

Volcanoes

[1624]
FRANCIS, P. **Volcanoes: a planetary perspective.** Oxford, Clarendon Press, 1993. viii,443p. illus. £50 ISBN: 0198544529.

Lively book for both scientists and general readers. Many attractive illustrations. Useful bibliographies. *Class No:* 551.21

[1625]
INTERNATIONAL ASSOCIATION OF VOLCANOLOGY. **Catalogue of the active volcanoes of the world,** including Solfatara fields. Rome, the Association, 1951-. pt.1-. 22v. illus., tables, maps.
  1. *Indonesia.* 1951.
  2. *Philippine Islands and Cochin China.* 1953.
  3. *Hawaiian Islands.* 1955.
  4. *Africa and the Red Sea.* 1957.
  5. *Melanesia.* 1957.
  6. *Central America.* 1958.
  7. *Kurile Islands.* 1958.
  8. *Kamchatka and continental areas of Asia.* 1959.
  9. *United States of America.* 1960.
  10. *Antarctica.* 1960.
  11. *Japan, Taiwan and Marianas.* 1962.
  12. *Greece.* 1962.
  13. *Kermadec, Tonga and Samoa.* 1962.
  14. *Archipelago de Colón, Isla San Felix and Islas Juan Fernández.* 1962.
  15. *The Chilean continent.* 1963.
  16. *Arabia and the Indian Ocean.* 1963.
  17. *Caucasus. Turkey.* 1963.
  18. *Italy.* 1965.
  19. *Colombia, Ecuador and Peru.* 1966.
  20. *West Indies.* 1966.
  21. *Atlantic Ocean.* 1967.
  22. *New Zealand.* 1975.

Partly financed by Unesco. Pt.16 (xvii, 64p.) includes for each volcano: 1. Name and location - 2. Form and structure - 3. Volcanic activity - 4. Petrography - 5. Bibliography (chronologically arranged). The entry on Piton de la Fournaise (p.39-52) includes a list of outbursts (with symbols indicating lava flows, normal explosions, etc.), 2 maps and 1½p. bibliography. Pt. 16 also has a general bibliography for the area (p.xv-xvii).

Updates appear in *Bulletin of volcanic eruptions* (Tokyo, Volcanological Society of Japan, 1961-. no. 1-), which provides an 'Annual report of the world volcanic eruptions'. *Class No:* 551.21

[1626]
Volcanoes of North America: United States and Canada. Wood, C.A. *and* Kienle, J., *eds.* Cambridge, University Press, 1990. 354p. illus., maps. $70. ISBN: 0521364698.

81 contributors give short, but detailed entries on 262 volcanoes in the region. Data include volcano type; elevation; location; eruptive history; composition; selected references; maps and photographs. 'Loaded with pertinent, very helpful information for the scientist as well as for the intelligent general reader' (*Choice*, v.28(7), March 1991, p.1110). *Class No:* 551.21

[1627]
Volcanoes of the world: a regional directory gazetteer and chronology of volcanism during the last 10,000 years. Simkin, T., *and others.* Stroudsburg, Pa., Hutchinson Ross, and the Smithsonian Institution, 1981. vii, 233p. ISBN: 0879334088.

3 parts: a directory of volcanoes (1,343 active; 5,564 dead); chronology of eruptions; gazetteer. Based on the computerized database at the Smithsonian Institution. The 30p. introduction outlines the catalogues' background, sources and significance of the various categories of information utilised. 709 references. 'This is a truly monumental work which, it is hoped, will be updated from time to time' (*Natural history book reviews,* v.7(4), 1985, p.258).

2nd ed. published 1994 (Tucson, Ariz., Geoscience Press. x,349p.) *Class No:* 551.21

Tectonics

[1628]
DENNIS, J.G., *ed.* **International tectonic dictionary: English terminology.** Tulsa, Okla., American Association of Petroloeum Geologists, Committee on Structural Nomenclature, 1967. xi, 196p. illus. (*A.A.P.G. memoir 7.*)

At head of title: International Geological Congress, Committee for the Geological Map of the World.

About 400 terms are dealt with (*e.g.* Nappe, p.111-2: derivation; definitions; history and usage; recommendation; synonyms and partial synonyms). Bibliography, p.164-84 (A-Z authors). *Class No:* 551.24

[1629]
The Encyclopedia of structural geology and plate tectonics. Seyfert, C.K., *ed.* New York, Van Nostrand Reinhold, 1987. 912p. illus., diagrs., graphs, maps. $114.95. (*Encyclopedia of earth sciences, v.10.*) ISBN: 0442281250.

About 90 contributors. 119 main entries, A-Z, Many cross-references 'Gondwanaland', p.309-14; 6 references. 'Rift valleys', p.671-88; 3 columns of references. Author citation index. Detailed, non-analytical subject index. A well-organized treatment, typical of this continuing series. 'Highly recommended' (*Choice* v.23(7), March 1988, p.1062). *Class No:* 551.24

[1630]
—DE SITTER, L.U. Structural geology. 2nd ed. New York, etc., McGraw-Hill, 1964. xii, 511p. diagrs.

3 parts (36 chapters): 1. Theoretical structural geology - 2. Comparative structural geology - 3. Geotechnics. References. 'It stands apart from most other books dealing with this subject in presenting facts and hypotheses with distinctive clarity' (*Geological journal,* v.123(2), June 1957, on the 1st ed.). It makes great use of comparative aspects, whereas other books have a distinctive regional slant. *Class No:* 551.24

[1631]
KASBEER, T. **Bibliography of continental drift and plate tectonics.** Boulder, Colo., Geological Society of America, 1972-75. xi, 96p. + vi, 151p. (*GSA Special papers no.142, 164.*) ISBN: 0515711628.

2,784 references, in all. V.1 has 2 sections: 1. Origin and development (chronological order; selected cross-references; author index), citing general articles as well as material on sea floor spreading and mid-ocean ridges, paleomagnetism and rock magnetism. Section 2: Convection currents, other lines of evidence (glacial, evaporites, palaeontological) expansion theory, monographs and symposia. Author index. V.2 provides a similar sequence, citing older references as well as new items. *Class No:* 551.24

Sedimentation

[1632]
The Encyclopedia of sedimentology. Fairbridge, R.W. *and* Bourgeois, J., *eds.* Stroudsburg, Pa., Dowden, Hutchinson & Ross, Inc., 1978. xvi, [1], 901p. illus., graphs, tables, maps. (*Encyclopedia of earth sciences, v.6.*) ISBN: 0879331526.

193 contributors from 23 countries. Entries. 'Abrasion pH' ... 'Zebra dolomite' - each signed, with references and cross-references. 'Estuarine sedimentation': p.288-93, with 11/3 cols. of bibliography and 6 drawings. Analytical index, p.875-90. 'An essential reference book for geologists, oceanographers, and scientists, hydrologists and others in related fields' (*Choice,* v.16(2), April 1979, p.202). *Class No:* 551.3

[1633]
PETTIJOHN, F.J. *and* POTTER, P.E. **Atlas and glossary of primary sedimentary structures.** New York, Springer-Verlag, 1964. ISBN: 0387963502.

198 excellent photographs. Facing each are title, location, geological age and explanatory statement in English, German, French and Spanish. 70-page glossary of 300 terms, with definitions in English, and equivalents and indexes in German, French and Spanish. *Class No:* 551.3

Floods

[1634]
WARD, R. **Floods: a geographical perspective.** London, Macmillan, 1978. 244p. illus., diagrs., graphs, maps. (*Focal problems in geography series.*) ISBN: 0333148924.

12 chapters (*e.g.* 2/3. Floods caused by precipitation; 6. Flood problems; 8/10. Human response to the flood hazard; 11. Economic response to the flood hazard; 12. Prospect). Bibliography of works cited. Detailed, analytical index, p.234-44. *Class No:* 551.311

Glaciology

Bibliographies

[1635]

AMERICAN GEOGRAPHICAL SOCIETY. Department of Exploration and Field Research. **Author/title, subject and geographic catalogs of the Glaciology Collection.** Boston, Mass., G.K. Hall, 1971. 3v. $330. ISBN: 0816109222.

About 48,900 author, subject and regional catalogue cards, photolithographically reproduced. Classified order, based on the Scott Polar Research Institute's *Universal decimal classification for use in Polar libraries*. *Class No:* 551.32(01)

[1636]

SCOTT POLAR RESEARCH INSTITUTE. Cambridge. **The Library catalogue of the Scott Polar Research Institute, Cambridge.** Boston, Mass., G.K. Hall, 1976. Supplement. 1981. 19v.; 5v. ISBN: 0816112169.

The main catalogue has 300,000 photolithographed catalogue cards. Three separate catalogues; author, subject (UDC order, with special regional classification) and regional. The largest collection of its kind. *Class No:* 551.32(01)

Handbooks & Manuals

[1637]

BENN, D.I. *and* EVANS, D.J.A. **Glaciers and glaciation.** London, Arnold, 1998. 734p. illus.(some col.) £55. ISBN: 0340653035.

Incorporating recent research, covers all aspects of glaciers, *e.g.* glacier motion, erosion forms and landscapes, megageomorphology, etc. *c.*300 black-and-white photographs. 86-page bibliography. A well-written account, suitable for undergraduates. Excellent value. 'This is a masterpiece' (*Choice*, July/August 1998, p.1881).
Class No: 551.32(035)

[1638]

LLIBOUTRY, L. **Traité de glaciologie.** Paris, Masson, 1964-65. 2v. (iv, 1040p.). illus. (incl. pl.), graphs, maps.

1. *Glace, neige, hydrologie, nivale.* 1964. 2. *Glaciers, variations du climat, sols gelés.* 1965.

23 chapters in all, with appended bibliographies (Ch. 20: Variations séculaires et millénaires du climat, p.824-72; references, p.870-2). 'A complete and critical review of glaciology, these volumes will be equally useful to the geomorphologist and the engineer, to the ski instructor and the meteorologist' (*Nature and resources*, v.2(3), September 1966, p.19). *Class No:* 551.32(035)

Dictionaries

Polyglot

[1639]

Elsevier's dictionary of glaciology in four languages: English (with definitions), Russian (with definitions), French and German. Kotlyakov, V.M. *and* Smolyarova, N.A., *comps.* Amsterdam, Elsevier, 1990. 336p. £62; $114.50.

*c.*1,200 terms, with French, German, and Russian equivalents and indexes. *Class No:* 551.32(038)=00

[1640]

Illustrated glossary of snow and ice. Armstrong, T., *and others.* 2nd ed. Cambridge, Scott Polar Research Institute, 1973. v, 60p. illus. £2.50. ISBN: 0901021016.

First published 1966. Issued with UNESCO support.

Classified summary of terms, p.7-8. Definitions and linguistic equivalents (Ablation ... Young ice) in English, Danish, Finnish, French, German, Icelandic, Norwegian, Russian and Spanish. Language indexes. 78 illus. *Class No:* 551.32(038)=00

Progress Reports

[1641]

Advances in periglacial geomorphology. Edited by M.J. Clark, for the International Geophysical Union Commission on the Significance of Periglacial Phenomena. Chichester, Wiley, 1988. xxiv, 481p. illus., diagrs., graphs, maps. £90. ISBN: 0471909815.

18 contributors. 4 parts (17 documented chapters): 1. Weathering, erosion and related sedimentary features - 2. Frozen ground and active layer processes - 3. Process and form: the example of frost mounds - 4. Perspectives on the periglacial system. Chapter 6.: Ground ice and permafrost; p.113-49, has 6½p. of references. Abstracts in English, French and German precede each chapter text. Detailed, analytical index, p.475-81. Well organized; authoritative.
Class No: 551.32(055)

[1642]

Periglacial geomorphology; proceedings of the 22nd Annual Binghamton Symposium in Geomorphology. Dixon, J.C. *and* Abrahams, A.D., *eds.* Chichester, John Wiley, 1992. xii,354p. illus., graphs, tables. ISBN: 0471933422.

23 contributors. 14 documented papers: 1. Periglacial geomorphology: what, where, when? ... 5. Mechanical weathering in the Antarctic: a maritime perspective (with 3p. of references) ... 14. Recent ground warming inferred from the temperature in permafrost near Mayo, Yukon Territory. Brief index. *Class No:* 551.32(055)

Nomenclatures

[1643]

WORLD METEOROLOGICAL ORGANIZATION. **WMO sea-ice nomenclature:** terminology, codes and illustrated glossary. Geneva, WMO, 1970. 147p. illus.

Terms are arranged first by subject, then in A-Z order. 162 supporting illus. Quality of paper, illus. and binding are criticized in *The Polar record*, v.16(101), 1972, p.279-80.
Class No: 551.32(083.72)

Great Britain

[1644]

BALLANTYNE, C.K. *and* HARRIS, C. **The Periglaciation of Great Britain.** Cambridge, University Press, 1994. x,330p. illus.,diagrs.,graphs,maps. ISBN: 0521324599.

Four parts (14 chapters): 1. Introduction and context; 2. The periglaciation of lowland Britain; 3. The periglaciation of upland Britain; 4. Periglacial environments. References, p.299-323. Detailed index. *Class No:* 551.32(410)

Polar Regions

[1645]

DARTMOUTH COLLEGE LIBRARY. Hanover, N.H. **Dictionary catalogue of the Stefansson Collection on the Polar regions.** Boston, Mass., G.K. Hall, 1967. 8v. $790. ISBN: 0816106762.

About 115,000 photolithographed catalogue cards, representing *c.*20,000 volumes and *c.*20,000 pamphlets and many manuscript items. The collection's main emphasis is now historical, with primary concern for the history of Polar exploration. *Class No:* 551.32(98/99)

[1646]

KOSACK, H.P. **Die Polarforschung.** Ein Datenbuch über die Natur-Kultur-Wirtschaftsverhältnisse und die Erforschungsgeschichte der Polarregionen. Braunschweig, Vieweg, 1967. xvi, 472p. tables, maps.

Tables list Polar organizations and scientific stations; chronology of expeditions. Cartographic display of basic data; short bibliography; comprehensive index. 'A remarkable condensation into a single volume of all the general data relating to both polar regions' (*Geographical journal*, v.134(2), June 1968, p.290).
Class No: 551.32(98/99)

[1647]

MILLS, W. *and* SPEAK, P. **Keyguide to information sources in the polar and cold regions.** London, Mansell, 1998. xiv,330p. £70. ISBN: 0720121760.

Three parts: 1. Survey of the polar and cold regions and information sources relating to them - 2. Bibliography - 3. Directory of related organizations. In all, lists 1,781 sources including texts, national organizations, electronic resources, etc. Part 2 is split into regional and general sources, and subject sources. Index, p.301-30. Both authors are at the Scott Polar Research Institute. An up-to-date and comprehensive review of this subject. *Class No:* 551.32(98/99)

[1648]

Polar and glaciological abstracts. Compiled by the Scott Polar Research Institute Library and Information Service, Cambridge. Cambridge, University Press, 1990-. 4pa. £90; $158pa. ISSN: 09575073.

Continues *Recent Polar and glaciological literature* (1981-89).

Each issue contains *c.*1,300 abstracts, each 30-100 words in length. Class A-Z (A. Geophysical sciences (General) ... E. Glaciology ... T. Social anthropology and ethnography ... Z. Miscellaneous). Contains subject-geographic and author indexes. Annual cumulative index. Available online via QL Systems Ltd. For the research library.
Class No: 551.32(98/99)

Arctic

[1649]

Arctic bibliography. Prepared by the Arctic Institute of North America with the support of government agencies in the United States and Canada. Montreal & London, McGill-Queen's Univ. Press, v.1-16, 1953-75. 16v.

V.1-16 carried 108,723 signed abstracts of books, periodical articles, government reports, etc., covering all aspects of the Arctic-administration and governments. Eskimos, archaeology, economic and

....(contd.)

social conditions, physics, geology, life sciences, mapping, population, communications, psychology, education, colonization, transportation and ethnography. Of the 8,011 entries in v.13, 43% are Russian, 42% English, and 5% Scandinavian in origin. Arrangement is by authors A-Z, with a very detailed subject and locality index (*c*.35,000 entries in v.12 index). 'It would be difficult to imagine polar research today without this scholarly resource' (*Polar record*, v.14(88), January 1968, p.71). *Class No:* 551.32(98)

[1650]

ARCTIC INSTITUTE OF NORTH AMERICA Library. **Catalogue.** [Arctic Institute of North America Library]. Boston, Mass., G.K. Hall, 1969. Supplements, 1971-. 4v. $410, set; $130, supp. 1; $265, supp. 2; $455, supp. 3. ISBN: 0816108234, set; 0816108307, supp. 1; 0816110301, supp. 2; 0816111626, supp. 3.

The main catalogue has *c*.70,000 author and subject catalogue cards, photolithographically reproduced. Entries cover books, pamphlets and reprints, as well as microfilms, audio-tapes and recordings, but not current Arctic maps. Analytical entries for *c*.4,500 articles in non-polar serials. Concentrates on the Polar regions, especially the Arctic or sub-Arctic, plus cold weather research, snow and ice studies. Supplements 1-3 (1971-80) add *c*.70,000 cards. *Class No:* 551.32(98)

[1651]

ASTIS current awareness bulletin. Calgary, Alberta, ASTIS, Arctic Institute of North America; Univ. of Calgary, 1979-. 6pa. $85Can. ISSN: 07058454.

About 2,500 abstracts (each 25-300 words) pa. 22 classes (A. Geography, geomorphology, and cartography - B. Geology, mineralogy, geochemistry, and palaeontology - C. Soils and permafrost... G. Ice (except glacier and ground ice)... Q. Petroleum, natural gas and pipelines... T. Native people (except archaeology)- U. Archaeology - V. History - X. General). Broad geographic index. Author index.

Annual cumulation, *ASTIS bibliography*, on microfiche and on CD-ROM (1978-). *Class No:* 551.32(98)

Antarctic

[1652]

AMERICAN GEOPHYSICAL UNION. Antarctic research book series. Washington, American Geophysical Union, 1964-. v.2-. irreg. Formerly *Antarctic research series*.

Provides a major series of research reports (*e.g.* no.55, 1992: Stilwell, J.D., ed. *Molluscan systematics and biostratigraphy* (202p.)). *Class No:* 551.32(99)

[1653]

Antarctic bibliography. Prepared by the Library of Congress. Washington, Library of Congress, 1965-. v.1-. Annual (irregular). Price varies. ISSN: 00664626.

Each issue contains *c*.2,000 abstracts. 13 subject areas: A. General - B. Biological sciences - C. Cartography - D. Expeditions - E. Geological sciences - F. Ice and snow - G. Logistics, equipment and supplies - H. Medical scientists - I. Meteorology - J. Oceanography - K. Atmospheric physics - L. Terrestrial physics - M. Political geography. Author-title, analytical subject, geographic and grantee indexes. Available online (Orbit) and on CD-ROM (NISC).

The *Antarctic bibliography, 1951-1961 (1970)* extends cover retrospectively.

Antarctic bibliography (1962-) is the printed version of COLD database (Cold Regions Research and Engineering Laboratory). *Class No:* 551.32(99)

[1654]

Antarctic earth science. Oliver, R.L., *and others*. Cambridge, University Press, 1983. 719p. illus., diagrs., graphs, tables, maps. £55. ISBN: 0521258367.

The text (full or abstracted) of 174 papers presented at the 4th International Symposium on Antarctic Earth Sciences in Adelaide, South Australia, 16-20 August 1982.

15 Symposium topics: Precambrian East Antarctic craton; East Antarctica; West Antarctica boundary and the Ross Orogen, including Northern Victoria Land; ... Maritime geology; Antarctic resources; ... Crustal structure of Antarctica; ... Subantarctic islands; Canozoic igneous activity. Papers carry references. Analytical index, p.681-97. Illus. are well captioned. A valuable compendium. *Class No:* 551.32(99)

[1655]

Antarctic science. Walton, D.W.H., *ed*. Cambridge, University Press, 1987. viii, 280p. illus, (incl. col.), graphs, tables, maps. £7.99. ISBN: 052126233x.

6 contributors. 5 parts (18 chapters): 1. Geography, politics and science - 2. Life in a cold environment - 3. Antarctic ice and rocks - 4. The Antarctic atmosphere - 5. Cooperation or confrontation. Select bibliography, p.272-3. Detailed, analytical index, p.274-8. Striking illus. Reflects contributors' experience of British Antarctic findings. *Class No:* 551.32(99)

[1656]

Current Antarctic literature. Prepared by Cold Regions Bibliography Project, Science and Technology Division, Library of Congress, for the Office of Polar Programs, National Science Foundation. Washington, Library of Congress, 1961-. 12pa. *Gratis.* ISSN: 0096879x.

'Prepared for later formal publication in the *Antarctic bibliography*' Over 3,000 abstracts (50-250 words) pa. 13 classes: A. General - B. Biological sciences - C. Cartography - D. Expeditions - E. Geological sciences - F. Ice & snow - G Logistics, equipment and supplies - H. Medical sciences - I. Meteorology - J. Oceanography - K. Atmospheric physics - L. Terrestrial physics - M. Political geography. Available on CD-ROM. *Class No:* 551.32(99)

[1657]

FOGG, G.E. A History of Antarctic science. Cambridge, University Press, 1992. xxi,483p. illus., figs., maps. £55. (*Studies in polar research.*) ISBN: 0521361133.

Coverage spans 3 centuries, beginning with Halley. 13 sections: 1. Introduction - 2. The science of the early explorations - 3. The national expeditions of 1828 to 1843 ... 7. The sciences of the Antarctic seas - 8. The earth sciences ... 11. Man and the Antarctic environment ... 13. Postscript. Extensive bibliography, p.425-63. Index, p.464-83. *Class No:* 551.32(99)

[1658]

HEADLAND, R.K. Chronological list of Antarctic expeditions and related historical events. Cambridge, University Press, 1989. 730p. illus., graphs, maps. £75. (*Studies in Polar research.*) ISBN: 0521309034.

A revision of Roberts, B. 'Chronological list of Antarctic expeditions'. In *Polar record*, v.9(60), September 1958.

Gives information on 3,342 expeditions. 8 sections: 1. Introduction - 2. Structure - 3. Observations - 4. Statistical examination - 5. Information - 6. Chronological list (p.51-603) - 7. Bibliography - 8. Index (27,000 entries). For all libraries concerned with Antarctic science. *Class No:* 551.32(99)

[1659]

Report on United Kingdom Antarctic research, 1994 report. London, Royal Society, 1995. vii,72p.

Covers the period April 1993 - September 1994: Record of activities; October 1994 - September 1995: Planned activities. Sections: BAS science highlights - List of permits for entry into SPAs and SSSIs - University research in Antarctica - Prospectus of field activities planned for 1994/95 - Principal investigators and addresses - Hydrography - Antarctic research by the SPRI Sea Ice Group - Science highlights - NERC funded research - Bibliography, p.50-72. *Class No:* 551.32(99)

Geomorphology (Earth's physical forms)

Bibliographies

[1660]

AMERICAN GEOGRAPHICAL SOCIETY. Research catalogue of the American Geographical Society. Boston, Mass., G.K. Hall, 1962. 15v. (10436p.) and map supplement. Supplements 1-2, 1972-78. 6v. $1,595, 15v. set. ISBN: 0816106282, set.

1-2. *General.*

3. *Regional. North America.*

4-5. *United States.*

6. *Mexico, Central America, Bermuda, West Indies, South America.*

7. *South America.*

8-10. *Europe.*

11. *Africa.*

12-13. *Asia.*

14. *Australasia.*

15. *Polar regions, Oceania, Tropics.*

219,000 entries (21 card entries per page). A photolithographic reproduction of the largest geographical collection in the Western hemisphere, and the *Research catalogue* is particularly strong in periodical article references. The 'Map supplement' ([i], 24p.) is a map key to the classification key used.

First supplement (1972-74. 4v.) and *Second supplement* (1978. 2v.) each divide into regional and topical catalogues. *Class No:* 551.4(01)

[1661]

—Current geographical publications: additions to the 'Research catalogue of the American Geographical Society'. Milwaukee, the Society, 1938-. v.1-. 12pa., omitting July and August. $70pa. ($93pa. overseas). ISSN: 00113514.

5 sections: 1. Topical (aids to geographical research: biogeography; climatology; economic geography...politcal geography) - 2. Regional - 3. Selected maps - 4. Selected books and monographs - 5. Selected reviews. About 750 references per issue. A major current-awareness source in its field. Available on microfilm. *Class No:* 551.4(01)

[1662]

—VAN BALEN, J. Geography and earth science publications: an author, title and subject guide to books reviewed, and an index to the reviews. Ann Arbor, Mich., Pierian Press, 1978. 2v. (313p. + 232p.). $62.50, set; $39.50ea. ISBN: 0876500904, v.1; 0876500912, v.2; 0685040429, set.

Devotes v.1 to years 1968-72 (3,400 author entries, 4,900 citations to book reviews from 21 geographical journals), v.2: 1973-75 (2,500 author entires, 3,700 citations to book reviews). *Class No:* 551.4(01)

[1663]

A Geographical bibliography for American libraries. Harris, C.D., *and others, eds.* Washington, Association of American Geographers, 1985. xxiii, 437p. $20. ISBN: 089291193x.

A joint project of the Association of American Geographers and the National Geographic Society.

71 contributors. 7 parts: 1. General aids and sources - 2. History, philosophy and methodology, - 3. Systematic fields of physical geography - 4. Systematic fields of human geography - 5. Applied geography (*e.g.* Planning; Military geography) - 6. Regional geography (worldwide) - 7. Publications suitable for school libraries. 2,903 concise, well-annotated entries. Analytical index, p.384-437. An important aid, 'to assist libraries in the United States, Canada, and other countries to identify, select and secure publications of value in geography that are appropriate to the purposes and resources of each collection' (*Introduction*). *Class No:* 551.4(01)

[1664]

—GODDARD, S. A Guide to information sources in the geographical sciences. London, Croom Helm, 1983. xiii, 273p. diagrs., tables, maps. ISBN: 038920403x.

13 contributors. Chapters 1-9 concern 'The communication of man's spatial experience', 'The systematic approach' (*e.g.* geomorphology) and 'Sources of regional information'. Chapters 10-13, on 'Tools for the geographer' cover cartographic items, aerial photographs and satellite information, statistics, and archives. Running commentary. No index. *Class No:* 551.4(01)

[1665]

—WRIGHT, J.K. and PLATT, E.T. Aids to geographical research: bibliographies, periodicals, atlases, gazetteers and other reference books. 2nd ed., completely revised. New York, Columbia Univ. Press, for the American Geographical Society, 1947. xii, 331p. $38.50. (*A.G.S. Research series, no.22.*) ISBN: 083713384x.

Reprinted Westport, Conn., Greenwood Press, [1971] and was first published 1921.

1,174 numbered entries, with detailed, evaluative annotations. Sections: Introduction - General aids - Topical aids - Regional aids (by areas and countries) and general geographical periodicals. Detailed index of systems cited. A valuable tool for items published up to 1945, but now rather dated. *Class No:* 551.4(01)

[1666]

HARRIS, C.D. Bibliography of geography. Chicago, Ill., Univ. of Chicago, 1976-. ISBN: 0890650861, v.1; 0890651124, v.2.

Pt.1. *Introduction to general aids.* 1976. ix, 276p. $12. 2. *Regional.* v.1: *The United States of America.* 1984. viii, 178p. $12.(v.2-4 are to deal with Soviet Union, Europe; and Africa, Asia, Australia and the Pacific).

Pt.1 has 585 annotated entries in 16 sections (1. Bibliographies of bibliographies... 5. Books - 6. Serials... 10. Maps and atlases... 13. Dictionaries - 14. Encyclopedias - 15. Statistics - 16. Methodology in geography). Appendix 2: 'A small geographical reference collection' (entries 530-580). Non-analytical index. V.2 (974 entries, some briefly annotated) opens with a general section: 'World-wide bibliographies and guides'. 'The Americas as a whole. North America as a whole. The United States of America' has 4 sections: 1. General aids - 2. Physical geography, related earth sciences, the environment and resources - 3. Human geography and related social sciences - 4. Regions of the United States. Index of subjects, authors and short titles. *Class No:* 551.4(01)

Encyclopaedias

[1667]

The Encyclopedia of geomorphology. Fairbridge, R.W., *ed.* New York, London, etc., Van Nostrand Reinhold, 1968 (reprinted 1982). xvi, 1298p. illus. diagrs., tables, maps. $126.95. (*Encyclopedia of earth sciences, v.3.*)

About 410 entries, A-Z; 150 contributors from 20 countries. Each article has an appended list of references. 'Geography: concept, growth and status', p.384-8 with 6 references. 'Submarine geomorphology', p.1079-97; with 10 references. 12½ lines of cross-references. Index of *c.*6,000 terms. A standard source, now in need of revision. *Class No:* 551.4(031)

Handbooks & Manuals

[1668]

BELL, M. *and* BOARDMAN, J. Soil erosion past and present: archaeological and geographical perspectives. Oxford, Oxbow Books, 1992. vii,250p. illus., diagrs., tables, maps. (*Oxbow monograph 22..*) ISBN: 0946897488.

31 contributors. Four sections (20 documented subsections): A. Field studies in lowland Britain; B. Field structures in continental north west Europe; C. Mediterranean erosion; D. Analytical techniques and modelling. Detailed, analytical index. *Class No:* 551.4(035)

[1669]

BRIDGES, E.M. World geomorphology. Cambridge, University Press, 1990. x,260p. illus., diagrs., maps. £37.50; £14.95. ISBN: 0521383439.

10 chapters (*e.g.* 2. Continental drift and plate tectonics ... 9. The Pacific Ocean basin - 10. Geographical implications of major geomorphological features). Further reading, p.253-5. Index. Textbook, aimed at undergraduates. *Class No:* 551.4(035)

[1670]

CHORLEY, R.J. *and* SUGDEN, D.E. Geomorphology. London, Chapman & Hall, 1984. 632p. illus., diagrs., charts, tables, maps. £18.99. (*Geographies for advanced studies.*) ISBN: 0416325904.

4 parts (20 sections each with references): 1. Introduction - 2. Geological geomorphology - 3. Geomorphic processes and landforms - 4. Climatic geomorphology. Appendix: Applied geomorphology. Index. A textbook, well illustrated and documented, for sixth-formers and undergraduates. R.J. Chorley is Professor of Geography, Univ. of Cambridge. *Class No:* 551.4(035)

[1671]

OLLIER, C. Ancient landforms. London, Belhaven, 1991. 233p. maps. ISBN: 1852930748.

Topics include erosion surfaces, rivers and valleys, oceans and coasts, continental margins, faults and rifts, and the history of geomorphic theory. Many maps and photographs. Lengthy bibliography, p.214-29. A concise and well written treatment of the geology of landscape evolution. *Class No:* 551.4(035)

[1672]

SPARKS, B.W. Geomorphology. 3rd ed. London, Longman, 1986. xxi, 561p. illus., diagrs, tables. £16.99. ISBN: 0582306711.

First published 1960.

17 chapters (*e.g.* 3. Weathering - 7. The effects of rocks as relief - 12. Landforms in the humid tropics - 17. The estimation of denudation). References (by chapters), p.521-43. Index, p.547-61. About 250 illus. 'Written as a university textbook' (Brewer, J.G. *The literature of geography.* 2nd ed. 1978, p.169). *Class No:* 551.4(035)

[1673]

STRAHLER, A. *and* STRAHLER, A.N. Introducing physical geography. New York, Wiley, 1998. xviii, 567p. illus.(col.) £95. ISBN: 0471147133.

Aimed at undergraduate readers and written in lively manner with all-colour illustrations and supporting CD-ROM. 18 chapters: 1. Our place in the sun ... 5. Winds and global circulation ... 10. Earth materials ... 18. Glacial landforms. Index p.527-37. US bias. *Class No:* 551.4(035)

[1674]

The Student's companion to geography. Rogers, A., *and others, eds.* Oxford, Blackwell, 1992. 386p. illus., tables. £50; £14.95. ISBN: 063117088x.

50 contributors. 6 sections: 1. Introductory essays - 2. What is geography? Past, present and future - 3. How to study geography (*e.g.* 'Remote sensing') - 4. What's what and who's who in geography (*e.g.* 'The literature of physical geography'; 'Biographical dictionary') 5. A geographical directory (*e.g.* 'World libraries and museums'; 'On-line data sources') - 6. What next? (*e.g* 'Postgraduate studies in Australia'; 'Overseas work and independent travel'). Index. A good overview of the subject. Suitable for those beginning, or contemplating, a career in geography. *Class No:* 551.4(035)

[1675]

SUMMERFIELD, M.A. Global geomorphology: an introduction to the study of landforms. Harlow, Essex, Longman Scientific and Technical, 1991. xiv,537p. illus., diagrs., maps. ISBN: 0582301564.

5 parts (19 chapters): 1. Introduction - 2. Endogenic processes and landforms - 3. Exogenic processes and landforms - 4. Endogenic-exogenic interactions - 5. Extraterrestrial landforms. Bibliographies appended to each chapter. Good photographs and over 500 line drawings. Useful appendices (E. Behaviour of materials). Aimed at undergraduates. An up-to-date treatment. *Class No:* 551.4(035)

Dictionaries

[1676]

Bibliography of mono- and multilingual dictionaries and glossaries of technical terms used in geography, as well as in related natural and social sciences. Meynen, E., *comp.* Wiesbaden, Steiner, for International Geographical Union, Commission on International Geographical Terminology, 1974. xx, 246p. $58.50. ISBN: 3515018468.

Lists 3,211 dictionaries, arranged by fields of geography and related disciplines. *Class No: 551.4(038)*

[1677]

Dictionary of concepts in physical geography. Huber, T.P., *and others.* New York, Greenwood Press, 1988. 301p. $49.95. (*Reference sources for the social sciences and humanities no.5.*) ISBN: 0313253692.

Contains 88 entries. Definitions are in the style of bibliographic essays, averaging 3 pages in length. Bibliography and list of sources (many annotated) follow the entries. Includes 'Outline of concepts', listing 185 terms. Index. Numerous cross-references.
Class No: 551.4(038)

Polyglot

[1678]

Chertyrekyh' yazychuyy entsiklopedicheskiy slovar' torminov po fiziacheskoy geografii: Russko-Anglo-Nemetsko-Frantsuzskiy. [Four language encyclopaedic dictionary of terms in physical geography: Russian-English-German-French.] Shehukin, I.S. Moskva, Sovetskaya Entsiklopediya, 1980. 703p.

'Compared with an English-language counterpart, *The Encyclopaedic dictionary of physical geography (q.v.)* edited by Andrew S. Goudie, it includes nearly three times as many terms (5,700 compared with 2,000) and thus substantially more definitions, but has less full treatment of some of the current research, concepts, or methods in physical geography' (C.D. Harris, *'Recent Soviet geographical dictionaries',* in *Soviet geography,* v.29, no.8 October 1988, p.775-782). *Class No: 551.4(038)=00*

[1679]

International geographical glossary. [Internationale geographische Terminologie.] Meynen, E., *ed.* Deutsche Ausgabe. Wiesbaden, F. Steiner; New York, French and European, 1985. 1479p. $350. ISBN: 0828809577, US ed.

About 2,400 German-base geographical terms, with equivalents in English, French, Italian, Spanish, Russian and Japanese. Terms are also grouped by categories for English, German and French. 'The product of international collaboration' (*A Geographical bibliography for American libraries;* edited by C.D. Harris, 1985, entry 102).
Class No: 551.4(038)=00

English

[1680]

CLARK, A.N. Longman dictionary of geography, human and physical. Harlow, Essex, Longman, 1985. ix, 724p. £33; £12.50.

About 8,000 shortish entries for terms 'commonly used in geographical writing over the past 100 years' (*Preface*), with claims to be the first dictionary to deal with the major aspects of geography in one volume. Entries for terms covered by Stamp and Clark are cited as 'G' and those in Chisholm's *Handbook of commercial geography* (20th ed. Longman, 1980) as 'C'. Includes terms for commodities; also, brief biographies. 'The book is a valuable addition to geographical literature and will be an asset to many people, by no means only geographers' (*Geographical journal,* v.152(2), July 1986, p.257).

There is an abridged and revised 1990 ed., published by Penguin. *Class No: 551.4(038)=20*

[1681]

The Encyclopaedic dictionary of physical geography. Goudie, A., *ed.* 2nd ed. Oxford, Blackwell Reference, 1994. xii, 611p. illus., diagrs., tables. ISBN: 0631186085.

First published 1985.

58 contributors. About 3,200 entries (including cross references), ranging from 10-word definitions to articles of 3 columns. All but very brief entries are documented (*e.g.* Hydrology: 10 'Reading and references'), but sources of terms are not included - unlike Stamp's *Glossary* (*q.v.*). Adequate cross-references and a fully analytical index, p.569-611. 'Abbreviations in physical geography', p.xii-xxvi. 'We have designed this dictionary for professional geographers and for earth, environmental and life scientists who work on the boundaries of our discipline. It is also intended for use by tertiary-level students and secondary/school teachers' (*Editor's Introduction*). Companion to *The Dictionary of human geography,* edited by R.J. Johnston, and others (Blackwell, 1981). *Class No: 551.4(038)=20*

[1682]

A Glossary of geographical terms, based on a list prepared by a Committee of the British Association for the Advancement of Science. Stamp, Sir D. *and* Clark, A.N., *eds.* 3rd ed. London, Longman, 1979. xxix, [1], 571p.

First published 1961.

57 correspondents and collaborators. Coverage: physical, human, economic and political geography. Terms are given various definitions, drawn freely from leading works, with acknowledgements, and 'Comment' added, as necessary. Thus the entry 'Savannah, Savanna, Savana' cites 6 sources plus comments on derivation, spelling, meaning etc. Appendix 2 lists words in foreign languages that have been absorbed into English literature; Appendix 3: 'Some stratigraphical terms'. 'List of standard works', p.xvii-xxv. 'A valuable work of reference, with its most useful features preserved' (*Geographical magazine,* January 1980, p.316).
Class No: 551.4(038)=20

[1683]

—**The Penguin dictionary of physical geography.** Whittow, J.B., *ed.* London, Lane, 1984. 591p. diagrs., tables, maps. £7.99. ISBN: 014051094x.

Claims to have over 5,000 entries, differentiating between British and US usage wherever they occur. 'Dry Valley': nearly 1 column; 'Tornado': ¾ column. 'See' and 'see also' reference to other Penguin science dictionaries. No bibliography. Aims to include all the terms currently used by physical geographers working within the 16-19-age school groups. A few photographs would have helped.
Class No: 551.4(038)=20

[1684]

LOCK, C.B.M. Geography and cartography: a reference handbook. 3rd ed. London, Bingley, 1976. 720p.

An integration of *Geography: a reference handbook* (1968; 2nd ed. 1972) and *Modern maps and atlases* (1969).

1,400 entries, A/Z (titles of works, forms of literature, biographies, topics), with a strong bibliographical and cartobibliographical slant. Extended entries on 'Cartography', (p.159-95), 'Audio-visual aids', 'Bibliographies, national', 'Classification', 'Education in geography and cartography', 'Globes', 'Map librarianship', 'Maps (historical)', 'Abstracts'. Detailed index, p.635-762. The work does not fully integrate *Modern maps and atlases,* which retain for its coverage of national, regional and thematic maps and atlases (*RQ,* v.15(3), Spring 1977, p.258-9). A/Z order is apt to scatter related material and choice of entry-words can be capricious (*e.g.* 'Man and wildlife'). Illus. and samples would have been appreciated. A bulky but rewarding volume.
Class No: 551.4(038)=20

[1685]

SMALL, J. *and* **WITHERICK, M. A Modern dictionary of geography.** 3rd ed. London, Edward Arnold, 1995. 265p. diagrs., graphs, charts. ISBN: 0340603399.

Has well over 2,000 entries, - definitions plus commentary - covering both physical and human geography. It thus supplements Goudie (*q.v.*) and also *The Dictionary of human geography,* edited by R.J. Johnston and others (1981). Adequate cross-references, but no index. For 'A'-level students and first-year undergraduates.
Class No: 551.4(038)=20

French

[1686]

Dictionnaire de la géographie. George, P., *ed.* 4e éd. Paris, Presses Universitaires de France, 1990. 520p. diagrs. FFr320. (*Grands dictionnaires.*) ISBN: 2130429815.

1970 ed.: 448p.

More than 3,000 clear definitions of terms used in French geography. About two-thirds of the terms concern physical geography. References are appended to lengthier entries.
Class No: 551.4(038)=40

Russian

[1687]

KALESNIK, S.V., *ed.* **Entsiklopedicheskiĭ slovar' geograficheskikh terminov.** Moscow, Sovetskaya Entsiklopediia, 1968. 435p.

'Encyclopaedia dictionary of geographical terms'. A Russian-Russian dictionary defining *c*.4,200 terms, with special emphasis on physical geography. *Class No: 551.4(038)=82*

Reviews & Abstracts

[1688]

Bibliographie géographique internationale. Paris, Centre National de la Recherche Scientifique, Laboratoire d'Information et de Documentation en Géographie (INTERGEO), 1891-. v.1-. Annual. FFr648; FFr665 (abroad). ISSN: 12749249.

About 6,500 abstracts pa. 11 sections: 01. General - 02. Historical - 03. Physical geography - 04. Human geography - 05. World.

....*(contd.)*

Multiregional geography - 06. Europe - 07. Asia - 08. Africa - 09. America - 10. Oceania - 11. Polar regions. Appended: Index of periodicals. List of principal English terms. Subject index. Place index. Author index. Online via Questel, and on CD-ROM. 'It is unexcelled in its coverage of the field of geography since the rise of this field as an academic and research discipline' (Harris, C.D. *Bibliography of geography*, Pt.1. Univ. of Chicago, Dept. of Geography, 1976, p.29). *Class No:* 551.4(048)

[1689]
Geographical abstracts. Physical geography. Norwich, Elsevier; Geo Abstracts, Ltd., 1989-. 12pa. fl.1,239; $1,378. ISSN: 09540504.

Formerly *Geo abstracts. A. Landforms and the Quaternary*, 1966-85 and *Geographical abstracts. A. Landforms and the Quaternary*, 1986-88. Merged with other titles in the series - B. *Climatology and hydrology*; E. *Sedimentology*; G. *Remote sensing, photogrammetry and cartography*. Continues *Geological abstracts: palaeontology and stratigraphy*.

Covers 'over 1,000 leading geographical journals, plus books, conference proceedings, reports and theses' (*Editorial introduction*). Subject areas covered include sedimentology; landforms and the Quaternary; hydrology; meteorology and climatology; remote sensing, photogrammetry and cartography. Each issue contains a regional index, and there is a separately published index issue arranged by subject, author, and geographical area. Included in the GEOBASE (*q.v.*) database via DIALOG, and on CD-ROM. *Class No:* 551.4(048)

[1690]
Referativnyǐ zhurnal. Geografiia. Moscow, VINITI, 1956-. 12pa. $1,815. ISSN: 00342378.

About 50,000 abstracts pa. 10 sections, each with an editor: Theoretical - Cartography - Anthropology. Geomorphology - Oceanography. Hydrology - Meteorology - Biogeography - Geography: USSR - Geography: Europe - Geography: Asia and Africa - Geography: America, Australia, Oceania and Antarctica. Annual author, subject and geographical indexes. The definitive Soviet bibliographic source of geographical material. International coverage, with an estimated 25% of abstracted items being Eastern European in origin. *Class No:* 551.4(048)

Periodicals & Progress Reports

[1691]
International list of geographical serials. Harris, C.D. *and* Fellmann, J.D., *comps.* 3rd ed. Chicago, Ill., University of Chicago, Dept. of Geography, 1980. [iv], 457p. $12. (*Research paper no.193.*) ISBN: 0890651000.

First published 1960.

'A comprehensive retrospective inventory of 3,445 geographical serials from 107 countries [International. Afghanistan ... Zimbabwe] in 55 languages with locations in union lists' (sub-title). A list of principal sources precedes and 'Lists of titles in non-Roman scripts' follows the definitive inventory. Index and cross-reference, p.399-457. *Class No:* 551.4(05)

[1692]
—HARRIS, C.D. Annotated world list of selected current geographical serials. 4th ed. Chicago, Ill., Univ. of Chicago, Dept. of Geography, 1980. [iv], 165p. $12. (*Research paper no.194.*) ISBN: 0890651019.

Records '443 current geographical serials from 72 countries with a study of serials most cited in geographical bibliographies' (sub-title). Criteria for selection included 'frequency, regularity, and longevity of publication, availability in major libraries, linguistic accessibility and frequency of citation in major geographic bibliographies'. Index, p.143-85. Location maps on inside covers. A valuable check-list. *Class No:* 551.4(05)

[1693]
Progress in physical geography: an international review of geographical work in the natural and environmental sciences. London, Edward Arnold, 1969-. v.1-. diagrs., tables, maps, 4pa. £154. ISSN: 03091333.

Initially annual (v.1-9, 1969-76).

Most recent volume, V.23, 1999, contains documented articles (*e.g.* 'Erosion, flooding and channel management in Mediterranean environments of southern Europe'; 'Atmospheric transport of aerosols and trace gases over southern Africa'). *Class No:* 551.4(05)

Teaching Materials

[1694]
Geography teachers handbook. Bailey, P. *and* Fox, P., *eds.* London, Geographical Association, 1996. ix,341p. illus. £26.95. ISBN: 1899085106. *Class No:* 551.4(072)

Maps & Atlases

[1695]
BLUME, H. Das Relief der Erde: ein Bildatlas. [Colour atlas of the surface forms of the earth.] Stuttgart, Ferdinand Enke Verlag, 1992. 140p. illus. (mostly col.), figs., maps. DM98. ISBN: 1852932066, English ed; 3432992416.

English translation published by Belhaven Press, London.

Describes and illustrates the most important processes and forms in geomorphology. 11 sections: 1. General classification - 2. Processes: weathering and erosion ... 4. Volcanic landforms ... 8. Glacial landforms ... 11. Anthropogenic landforms. Bibliography and sources of figures and tables, p.138-39. Index. Many colour illustrations. For the layman and geoscience student. *Class No:* 551.4(084.3)

[1696]
Fiziko-geograficheskiĭ atlas mira. Moscow, Akademiya Nauk SSSR, 1964. 298p. ISBN: 0471800708.

A physico-geographical atlas of the world, with 240p. of maps and 45p. of text. Pt.1 devotes more than 70 maps to geology, geomorphology, and soils of the world. Pt.2, on the continents; pt.3 concentrates on the USSR (over 60 maps). Page size, 50 x 35cm. Unsurpassed as a physical world atlas. *Class No:* 551.4(084.3)

Histories

[1697]
History of geomorphology: from Hutton to Hack. Tinkler, K.J., *ed.* Boston, Unwin Hyman, 1989. xi,344p. figs., maps. $75. (*Binghamton symposia in geomorphology: international series, no. 19.*) ISBN: 0045511381.

15 well-documented essays: 1. On the nature of geo-history, with reflections on the historiography of geomorphology ... 3. Worlds apart: eighteenth century writings on rivers, lakes and the terraqueous globe ... 12. Different aspects of Polish geomorphology: palaeogeographic, dynamic and applied ... 15. Afterword. Analytical index, p.333-44. *Class No:* 551.4(091)

[1698]
—TINKLER, K.J. A Short history of geomorphology. London & Sydney, Croom Helm, 1985. xviii, 317p. ISBN: 0709924410.

Four parts: 1. Introduction. The frames of reference - 2. Birthpangs of a discipline - 3. The principles: a century [19th] of debate - 4. A system and its feedback - 5. One more century: making the system work. Bibliography (authors, A-Z), p.241-79. Analytical index ('Weathering': nearly 1 column), p.281-317. Written for students and earth science professionals. *Class No:* 551.4(091)

[1699]
The History of the study of landforms or, The development of geomorphology. Chorley, R.J., *and others.* London, Methuen; Routledge, 1964-91. 3v. illus., ports., facsims. ISBN: 0416268900, v.2; 0415056268, v.3.

1. *Geomorphology before Davis.* 1964. xvi, 678p. 2. *The life and work of William Morris Davis.* 1973. xxii, 874p. £65. 3. *Historical and regional geomorphology*, 1890-1950. 1991. xxiii,496p. £65.

V.1 has 4 pts. (2. The age of Lyell: 1820-1845 - 3. Marine versus subaerial erosionists: 1846-1875 - 4. The western explorations). Many questions; 26p. of references; 133 illus. and maps, and an excellent 'Informative index', p.649-78. V.2 has a bibliography of Davis (p.793-825), general references, p.828-39, and a bibliography. Subject and place index, plus an index of persons. *Class No:* 551.4(091)

Worldwide

[1700]
The Evolution of geomorphology: a nation by nation summary of development. Walker, H.T. *and* Graham, W.E., *eds.* New York, Wiley, 1993. n.p. illus. £85. ISBN: 0471938580.

Covers 53 countries and describes each country's national policy on landscapes. *Class No:* 551.4(100)

Tropics

[1701]
THOMAS, M.F. Geomorphology in the tropics: a study of weathering and denudation in low latitudes. Chichester, Wiley, 1994. xix,460p. illus., diagrs., maps. £85. ISBN: 0471330350.

Four parts, *e.g.* 4. The evolution of tropical landscapes. References, p.389-433. Author and subject indexes. *Class No:* 551.4(213)

Arid Zones

[1702]
Arid zone geomorphology: process, form and change in drylands. Thomas, D.S.G. 2nd ed. Chichester, Wiley, 1997. xviii,713p. illus., figs., tables. £65; ISBN: 047197160x.

34 contributors. Six sections, made up of 30 chapters: 1. Framework - 2. Surface processes and characteristics - 3. The work of water - 4.

....(contd.)

The work of the wind - 5. Geomorphology of the world's arid zones - 6. Extensions and change in the arid realm. References are appended to each chapter. Index, p.697-713. *Class No:* 551.4(213.52)

[1703]
HOPKINS, S.T. *and* **JONES, T.E. Research guide to the arid lands of the world.** Phoenix, Arizona, Oryx, 1983. 391p. maps. ISBN: 0897746661.

3,199 entries, arranged geographically and by subject, (further subdivided). Descriptive rather than evaluative annotations. Author and subject index. *Class No:* 551.4(213.52)

Europe
[1704]
Geomorphology of Europe. Embleton, C., *ed.* New York, Wiley; London, Macmillan. 1984. [x], 465p. illus., maps. £25. ISBN: 0471800708, US ed; 0333379632, UK ed.

20 chapters by members of the Commission on Geomorphological Survey and Mapping of the International Geographical Union. 1. Structural and tectonic framework of the continent of Europe - 2. Principal structural and tectonic features of ocean floors around Europe - 3. Exogenic landforms of Europe - 4. Iceland ... 16. Balkan Peninsula ... 19. Ural mountains - 20. Submarine morphology around Europe (8 maps; 1 cross-section). References (A-Z authors), p.431-47. Detailed, analytical index, p.449-65. 'The first comprehensive survey of the geomorphology of Europe' (*New technical books*, February 1986, item 285). *Class No:* 551.4(4)

Great Britain
[1705]
The Geomorphology of the British Isles. Brown, E.H. *and* Clayton, K., *general eds.* London, Methuen, 1976-81. 5v. illus., tables, maps. ISBN: 0416839908.

Scotland, by J.B. Sissons. 1976. *Ireland*, by G.L.H. Davies and N. Stephens 1978. *Southeast and Southern England*, by D.K.C. Jones. 1981. *Eastern and Central England*, by A. Straw and K. Clayton. 1979. *North England*, by C.A.M. King. 1976.

The *Ireland* volume (xii, 250p.) has 7 chapters (7. Coastline), has references on p.222-42 and a non-analytical index. Volumes on the *Midlands* and *Wales and Southwest England* have not so far appeared. *Class No:* 551.4(410)

Information Management
[1706]
Geographic information systems. Antenucci, J.C., *and others.* New York, Van Nostrand Reinhold, 1991. xiii,301p. illus. (some col. pl.), figs., diagrs., tables. $59.95. ISBN: 0442007566.

3 sections: 1. Technology for the information age (Introduction ... Applications; Benefits and costs) - 2. System components (Data base concepts; Data types ... Geographic information system software; System configurations and data communications) - 3. Managing change (Implementation; Legal issues; Horizons). Glossary, p.276-92. Index. References appended to each chapter.

New ed. planned for 1999. *Class No:* 551.4:025.4

Libraries
[1707]
LONDON UNIVERSITY. Library Resources Co-ordinating Committee. Geography Sub-committee. **A Guide to geography and map collections.** London, the University, 1985 (2nd ed., 1990. 40p.). [i], 40p. ISBN: 0718707125.

1. Geography collections (12 libraries) - 2. Map collections (10 libraries. Data: name and address; telephone no.; location; hours of opening; access; readers' places; name of map curator; staff availability; catalogue(s); classification; holdings; special collections or strengths; publications; additional facilities). An important guide. *Class No:* 551.4:061:026/027

Islands
[1708]
Oceans and islands. Talbot, F.H. *and* Stevenson, R.E., *eds.* London, Merehurst, 1991. 240p. illus. (col.), figs., maps. ISBN: 1853911569.

40 contributors. 3 sections: 1. The miracle of the sea - 2. Islands: worlds apart - 3. The future of oceans and islands. Facts about oceans and islands, p.228-29. Glossary. Further reading. Index. Many colour illustrations. For school and public libraries. *Class No:* 551.42

[1709]
Standard encyclopedia of the world's oceans and islands. Huxley, A., *ed.* London, Weidenfeld & Nicolson, 1962. 383p. illus. (incl. col.), maps.

A-Z sequence of more than 350 articles (Aden ... Zuyder Zee), with geographical and background data on the world's oceans, channels, straits, gulfs, currents, islands, capes, etc. (Greenland is ranked as an island, but Australia not). 'Galapagos Islands': location, area, map reference, plus 1½ columns of description. Gazetteer of c.2,000 entries, p.325-64. 10 location maps; 16 col. plates. No bibliographies. Evidently for popular consumption. *Class No:* 551.42

Mountains
[1710]
Geology of the Himalayas. Beijing, Geological Publishing House, 1991. 2v. illus., diagrs., tables, graphs, maps. ISBN: 7116007385, v.1; 7116007482, v.2.

V.1. *Papers on geophysics.* v,298p. V.2. *Papers on geology.* v,544p.

Based on an International Symposium of the Geology of the Himalayas. V.1 has 21 documented chapters. It contains 'achievements of earth sciences research on the Himalayas and its adjacent areas since 1980' (*Foreword*). *Class No:* 551.432

[1711]
Standard encyclopedia of the world's mountains. Huxley, A., *ed.* London, Weidenfeld & Nicolson, 1962. 383p. illus. (incl. col.), maps.

Introductory essays, a brief glossary and location maps precede an A-Z sequence of unsigned articles on 'The world's mountains' (p.55-320). Gazetteer of over 1,500 entries (p.323-57) plus acknowledgements and index. 'Aconcagua', 'Eiger', - each 2½ columns. Entries comprise a brief statement, location, height, map reference, description, history. Stresses human rather than physical aspects. Article on the Andes (3p.) is less extensive and informative than that in the *Columbia-Lippincott gazetteer*. No bibliography. *Class No:* 551.432

Coastlines
[1712]
CARTER, R.W.G. Coastal environments: an introduction to the physical, ecological and cultural systems of coastlines. London, San Diego, Academic Press, 1988. xv,617p. illus., figs., tables, maps. £50; $95. ISBN: 0121618552.

An overview of the subject. Sections include: Waves and wave dominated coasts - Shoreline morphodynamics ... Sea-level changes ... Structures and organization ... Coastal hazards. References, p.561-609. For academic libraries. *Class No:* 551.435.36

[1713]
Dunes of the European coasts: geomorphology-hydrology-soils. Cremlingen-Destedt, CATENA Verlag, 1990. vi,223p. illus., facsims., diagrs., graphs, tables, maps. DM139. (*CATENA supp., 18.*) ISBN: 3923381239.

20 contributors, each with references. 6 sections ('Geohydrology', p.109-83). Profuse maps. No index. *Class No:* 551.435.36

[1714]
The Geology of continental margins. Burk, C.A. *and* Drake, C.L., *eds.* New York, Springer, 1974. 1009p. $69.30. ISBN: 038706866x.

Over 100 contributors. 'An indispensable reference for those specializing in the geology of continental margins'. *Class No:* 551.435.36

[1715]
KING, C.A.M. Beaches and coasts. 2nd ed. London, Edward Arnold, 1972. 570p. £25. ISBN: 0713156090.

First published 1959.

A comprehensive and systematic survey of coastal geomorphology. 'Incorporates quantitative approaches in coastal engineering with exploratory descriptions of coastal landforms and beach features. Provides the best coverage of international literature' (Harris, C.D. ed., *A geographical bibliography for American libraries* (1985), item 687). *Class No:* 551.435.36

[1716]
SCHWARTZ, H.L. The Encyclopedia of beaches and coastal environments. Stroudsburg, Pa., Van Nostrand Reinhold, 1982. 940p. illus., maps. $149.95; £109. (*Encyclopedia of earth sciences, v.15.*) ISBN: 0879332131.

184 contributors. Articles A-Z, usually documented. Cross-references. Coverage: geomorphology; ecology; coastal engineering; continental, regional and specific types of coast. Well illustrated. 'The most thorough glossary of its kind' (*A geographical bibliography for American libraries,* edited by C.D. Harris (1985), p.96). *Class No:* 551.435.36

[1717]
STEERS, J.A. **The Coastline of England and Wales.** 2nd ed. Cambridge, University Press, 1964. xxviii, 762p. diagrs., tables, maps.

First published 1946.

8 of the initial 19 chapters give detailed geomorphological data on the coast, working anticlockwise from 'The Solway to the Dee', and ending with 'The North-East Coast'. Chapters 20-27 add data on the same regional pattern, noting the great damage done to the east coast on 31 January and 1 February 1933. 163 diagrs., tables and maps. Numerous footnotes, including references to the plates in Steers' *The coast of England and Wales in pictures* (2nd ed., 1960). Index, p.721-50. 'He has given us what is, perhaps, the most important physiographic monograph since geography attained full status in the British universities' (*Geographical journal*, v.109(1/3), July 1947, p.109, on the 1946 ed.).

The Coastline of Scotland, by J.A. Steers (C.U.P., 1973. xvi, 325p. illus., maps) is the companion volume. *Class No:* 551.435.36

Deserts

[1718]
Desertification: a world bibliography. Prepared for the 22nd International Congress, Moscow, 1976. Paylore, P., *comp. and ed.* Tucson, Arizona, Office of Arid Lands Studies, Univ. of Arizona, 1976. 644p.

1,409 references (often annotated) in English, French and German, plus 217 Russian references (translated). Geographical arrangement, by continent then country.

Followed by *Desertification world bibliography update, 1976-1980* (with imprint as above), adding 400 annotated entries. (Based on C.D. Harris's *A geographical bibliography for American libraries* (1985), entries 2762-3). *Class No:* 551.435.77

[1719]
MIDDLETON, N.J. *and* THOMAS, D.S.G. **World atlas of desertification.** 2nd ed. London, Edward Arnold for United Nations Environment Program, 1997. 138p. illus.(col.) £125. ISBN: 0340691662.

First published 1992.

Large-format atlas which shows the extent and severity of desertification throughout the world's arid regions. 4 sections: 1. Global view - 2. Africa - 3. ASSOD: New assessment of soil degradation in South and South-east Asia - 4. Desertification studies and issues. For academic and research libraries covering earth sciences, climatology, geography, and environmental sciences. Second edition is substantially more detailed than the first.
Class No: 551.435.77

[1720]
PETROV, M.P. **Deserts of the world.** Translated from the Russian by the IPST staff. Jerusalem, Israel Program for Scientific Translations; New York, etc., Wiley, 1976. viii, 647p. illus., diagrs., tables, maps.

Russian edition, 1973.

A global survey of arid regions. Three parts: 1. Physical features of world deserts - 2. Specific environmental features of deserts; 3. Natural resources of deserts and prospects for their investigation and exploitation. Each part carries a bibliography. General index. Illus. are helpful but lack precision. 'The book should be easily available, because it contains so much of value to university and sixth-form students, as well as to the general reader' (*Geographical journal*, v.144, March 1978, p.137). *Class No:* 551.435.77

Coral Reefs

[1721]
Coral reefs of the world. Nairobi, United Nations Environment Programme; Gland, International Union for Conservation of Nature and Natural Resources, 1988. 3v. $100, set; $55ea. ISBN: 2880329434, v.1; 2880329442, v.2; 2880329450, v.3.

V.1. *Atlantic and eastern Pacific.* xlvii,373p. maps. V.2. *Indian Ocean, Red Sea and Gulf.* l389p. maps. V.3. *Central and western Pacific.* xlix,329p. maps.

Arrangement is by country within each volume. Data for each reef include geographical location; area, depth, altitude; physical features; reef structures and corals; scientific importance and research. Lists of references are given for each section. An excellent, well presented work which, although biased towards environmental aspects of coral reefs, also gives much useful information about their physical features.
Class No: 551.438

[1722]
GUILCHER, A. **Coral reef geomorphology.** Chichester, John Wiley, 1988. vi,228p. illus., figs., maps. $89.95. ISBN: 0471917559.

5 sections: 1. Distribution and ecology - 2. Surface features of coral reefs - 3. The origin of coral reefs - 4. Types of reefs - 5. Reef and man. Bibliography, p.203-22. Location index. The many black-and-white illustrations could be of better quality. *Class No:* 551.438

Caves

[1723]
Atlas of the great caves of the world. Courbon, P., *and others*. St. Louis, Mo., Cave Books, 1989. 369p. maps. $30. ISBN: 0939748215. Translation and revision of *Atlas des grands gouffres du monde* (1986).

Gives statistics and maps of all the major caves throughout the world. Information up to date as of 1988. Maps can be of variable quality. However, packed with useful information. The definitive work. *Class No:* 551.44

[1724]
Current titles in speleology: bibliographical details of papers published throughout the world on caving topics. London, British Cave Research Association, 1972-. Annual.

Continues *Speleological abstracts* (1964-70).

No. 25: The literature of 1992 (1993. xi,137p.) has 3,639 entries in 6 main sections: Generalia - Africa (Algeria ... Zimbabwe) - America (Anguilla ... Venezuela) - Asia (China ... Vietnam) - Australasia and Pacifica (Australia ... Solomon Islands) - Europe (Albania ... former Yugoslavia). A list of periodicals consulted and addresses precedes the sections. *Class No:* 551.44

[1725]
FORD, T.D. *and* CULLINGFORD, C.H.D. **The Science of speleology.** New York & London, Academic Press, 1976. xiv, 593p. illus., diagrs., graphs, tables. $99.95. ISBN: 0122625501.

22 contributors. 14 chapters (*e.g.* 2. The geology of caves; 8. Cave minerals and speleotherms; 10. Cave faunas; 11. Cave flora; 12. Bats in caves; 14. The computer in speleology). Cave and fissure index. Subject index. The standard work. 'Reference of inestimable value to anyone engaged in speleological research ... a primer of caving' (*Palaeogeography, palaeoclimatology, palaeoecology*, v.24(4), 1978, p.568-9). *Class No:* 551.44

[1726]
A Guide to speleological literature of the English language, 1794-1996. Northup, D.E., *and others, eds.* St. Louis, Cave Books, 1998. xviii,539p. $34.95. ISBN: 0939748517; 0939748525, pbk.

Includes over 3,800 items. Material ranges from children's books to scientific literature. Excludes material on bats - due to shortage of space - and periodical literature. Geographic index. 'For anyone interested in caves ... this book is worth its weight in gold' (*Choice*, April 1999, p.1436). *Class No:* 551.44

[1727]
MIDDLETON, J. *and* WALTHAM, T. **The Underground atlas:** a gazetteer of the world's cave region. London, Hale, 1986. 239p. illus., tables, maps. $16.95. ISBN: 0709027982.

Main sections: The continents - The countries (Afghanistan ... Zimbabwe, p.25-228). Appendices: 1. Longest, deepest and largest caves - 2. National caving organizations - 3. Further reading (running commentary, p.234-5) - 4. Cave map credits. Glossary, p.238-9. A popular account, by the Senior Lecturer in Geology at Trent Polytechnic. *Class No:* 551.44

Oceanography

CD-ROM

[1728]
Oceanographic and marine resources. Baltimore, Md., National Information Services Corporation, 1992. 2v. $970, v.1; $445, v.2.

V.1 of this 2v. CD-ROM set contains *Oceanographic literature review*, (1976 to present; 110,000 abstracts and citations); Institute of Oceanographic Sciences Deacon Laboratory; Proudman Oceanographic Laboratory; Plymouth Marine Laboratory (1985 to present; 240,000 records from this consortium of 3 major oceanographic institutes). V.2 has *Sea Grant abstracts* (1968 to present; over 30,000 bibliographic records) and *c.*135,000 records from the National Oceanic and Atmospheric Administration's collection covering hydrographic surveying, oceanography, meteorology, hydrology, living marine resources, and meteorological satellite applications. *Class No:* 551.46(003.40)

Bibliographies

[1729]
FREEMAN, C. **A Guide to the literature of oceanography** and an enquiry into the density, distribution, and use of the periodical literature of the discipline. A thesis presented for the degree of Master of Science in Information Studies, University of Sheffield, Postgraduate School of Librarianship and Information Science. University of Sheffield, 1971. 306p.

14 chapters (3. Information flow in the marine sciences - 4. Guides to the literature (13 items, briefly annotated) - 5. Directories - 6. Guide to meetings - 7. Abstracting and indexing services (p.64-132) - 8. Bibliographies - 9. Concentration of information (*e.g.* Encyclopaedias; Tables and handbooks) - 10. Information analysis entries - 11.

....(contd.)

Translations ... 14. Literature use). 4 appendices (*e.g.* Institutions involved in the marine sciences and contacted for information - 28). *Class No:* 551.46(01)

[1730]

Oceanographic index. Woods Hole Oceanographic Institution, Mass. Sears, M., *comp.* Boston, Mass., G.K. Hall, 1971-72.

Author cumulation, 1946-1970. 3v. 58,600 cards. $330. *Author cumulation, 1972-1974.* 1v. 18,100 cards. $130. *Regional cumulation, 1946-1970.* 1v. 28,900 cards. $110. *Regional cumulation, 1971-1974.* 1v. 11,500 cards. $120. *Subject cumulation, 1946-1971.* 4v. 95,500 cards. $420. *Subject cumulation, 1971-1974.* 2v. 40,000 cards. $265. *Organismal cumulation, 1946-1973.* 3v. 48,400 cards. $240.

These cumulative indexes are working guides to journal articles, monographs, etc. on the marine sciences held at the Library of the Marine Biological Laboratory and at the Woods Hole Oceanographic Institution. They also serve as cumulative indexes to the bibliographic abstracts section of *Deep sea research (qv).* *Class No:* 551.46(01)

[1731]

SCRIPPS INSTITUTION OF OCEANOGRAPHY. Library. **Catalogs of the Scripps Institution of Oceanography Library. University of California at San Diego.** Boston, Mass., G.K. Hall, 1970. 12v. Supplement 1-. 1973-. $270.

Author/title catalog. 7v. (5212p.). $730.
Subject catalog. 2v. (1759p.). $220.
Shelf list. 2v. (1299p.). $205.
Shelf list of documents, reports and translations collection. 592p. $105.

The 12v. comprise 175,500 photolithographically reproduced card catalogue entries for 80,000 bound volumes and 13,000 reports. *Class No:* 551.46(01)

[1732]

WOODS HOLE OCEANOGRAPHIC INSTITUTION. Catalog of the Library of the Marine Biological Laboratory and the Woods Hole Oceanographic Institution. Boston, Mass., G.K. Hall, 1971. 12v. (9339p.). ISBN: 0816109370.

About 339,000 author-catalogue cards for books, reports of expeditions, and articles, photolithographically reproduced. V.12, *Journal catalog* (418p.), lists over 4,000 titles. Coverage includes biology, zoology, botany, physiology, microbiology, medicine, physics, chemistry, mathematics, geology, meteorology, fisheries and oceanography. *Class No:* 551.46(01)

Encyclopaedias

[1733]

The Encyclopedia of oceanography. Fairbridge, R.W., *ed.* New York, Van Nostrand Reinhold, 1966. 1056p. illus. (incl.pl.), diagrs., tables, maps. (*Encyclopedia of earth sciences, v.1.*)

245 signed articles, A-Z, by 135 specialists, on all aspects of oceanography and submarine geology. 'Atlantic Ocean': 30p.; 'Sea ice': 5p.; 'Mineral potential of the oceans': 8p.; 'Gulf Stream': 5p.). Short selected bibliograhies follow most articles; well illustrated. The first of a series, each volume being autonomous but cross-indexed. The general editor is Professor of Geology, Columbia Univ. Aimed at high-school students, teachers and specialists. *Class No:* 551.46(031)

[1734]

GROVES, D.G. *and* **HUNT, L.M. Ocean world encyclopedia.** New York, etc., McGraw-Hill, 1980. xv, 443p. illus., facsims, maps. $54.50. ISBN: 0070250103.

Over 400 entries. Coverage: physical, geological, chemical, biological, meteorological and oceanographic aspects. Entries: 'Abalone (molluscs)' ... 'Yellow Sea'. The sectionalized article 'Instrumentation, oceanographic', p.165-78, has 16 illus. Striking, well-captioned photographs, but no bibliographies. Detailed, analytical index, p.419-43. Aimed at being 'both useful and interesting to high school, and college students as well as to interested nonspecialists from many walks of life' (*Preface*). Both authors are on the professional staff of the National Academy of Sciences. *Class No:* 551.46(031)

[1735]

McGraw-Hill encyclopedia of ocean and atmospheric sciences. Parker, S.P., *editor-in-chief.* New York etc., McGraw-Hill, 1980. [ix], 580p. £65; $79.95. ISBN: 0070452679.

230 articles; much of the material in them was previously published in the *McGraw-Hill Encyclopedia of science and technology* (4th ed. 1979). Over 200 contributors. 'Marine sediments': p.254-68; 9 references; 17 illus., diagrs., graphs, maps. About 500 illus. in all. Analytical index. Some US slant. *Class No:* 551.46(031)

[1736]

Standard encyclopedia of the world's oceans and islands. Huxley, A., *ed.* London, Weidenfeld & Nicolson, 1962. 383p. illus. (incl. col.), maps.

A-Z sequence of more than 350 articles (Aden ... Zuyder Zee), with geographical and background data on the world's oceans, channels, straits, gulfs, currents, islands, capes, etc. (Greenland is ranked as an island, but Australia not). 'Galapagos Islands': location, area, map reference, plus 1½ columns of description. Gazetteer of *c*.2,000 entries, p.325-64. 10 location maps; 16 col. plates. No bibliographies. Evidently for popular consumption. *Class No:* 551.46(031)

Handbooks & Manuals

[1737]

GROSS, M.G. *and* **GROSS, E. Oceanography:** a view of the earth. 7th ed. Englewood Cliffs, N.J., Prentice-Hall, 1996. xi, 472p. illus. (incl. col.), diagrs., maps. ISBN: 0132317885.

First published 1972. 4th ed., 1987.

15 chapters: 1. Origins of oceanography ... 3. Plate tectonics ... 5. Sediments ... 7. Ocean and climate ... 9. Waves ... 15. The ocean on a changing earth. Chapter questions and references. Seven appendices (*e.g.* 2. Useful data about the earth and ocean). Glossary and index. *Class No:* 551.46(035)

[1738]

MILLERO, F.J. Chemical oceanography. 2nd ed. Boca Raton, Fla., CRC Press, 1996. 469p.,illus., maps. £67. (*Marine science series.*) ISBN: 0849384230.

First published 1992.

10 chapters: 1. Descriptive oceanography - 2. Composition of the major components of seawater ... 7. The carbonate system ... 9. Primary production in the oceans - 10. Processes in the oceans. Appendices; glossary; index. Contains much up-to-date data although the quality of the illustrations could be improved. *Class No:* 551.46(035)

[1739]

The Ocean basins and margins. Nairn, A.E.M. *and* Stehli, F.G., *eds.* New York, Plenum Press, 1973-85. 7v. illus., diagrs., graphs, maps. $110ea.

1. *The South Atlantic.* 1973. xv, 583p.
2. *The North Atlantic.* 1974. xiv, 598p.
3. *The Gulf of Mexico and the Caribbean.* 1975. xvi, 503p.
4a. *The Eastern Mediterranean.* 1977. xv, 503p.
4b. *The Western Mediterranean.* 1978. xiv, 447p.
5. *The Arctic Ocean.* 1981. xiv, 447p.
6. *The Indian Ocean.* 1982. xvii, 796p.
7. *The Pacific Ocean.* 1985. xiv, 733p.

V.6, *The Indian Ocean,* has 21 contributors. The 15 documented chapters include: 1. Sedimentation and sedimentary deposits; 5. The Red Sea Region; 10. South East Asia; 15. The Antarctic margin (with 1½p. of references). Partly analytical index. Each volume includes authoritative reviews by specialists. Detailed geological and geophysical coverage. *Class No:* 551.46(035)

[1740]

The Sea: ideas and observations in progress in the study of the sea. Hill, M.N., *ed.* New York, Interscience: Wiley, 1962-. illus., diagrs., tables, maps.

1. *Physical oceanography.* 1962. xv, 564p.
2. *The composition of sea water. Comparative and descriptive oceanography.* 1963. xv, 554p.
3. *The earth beneath the sea. History* 1963. xvi, 963p.
4.(2pts.) *New concepts of sea floor evolution* edited by A.E. Maxwell. 1971.
5. *Marine chemistry,* edited by E.D. Goldberg. 1974. xiv, 895p.
6. *Marine modeling;* edited by E.D. Goldberg. 1977. xxv, 1045p.
7.(2pts.) *The oceanic lithosphere,* edited by C. Emiliane. xii, [i], 1728p.
8. *Deep-sea biology,* edited by G.T. Rowe. 1983. ix[i], 560p. $95. *(qv).*
9. *Ocean engineering science,*edited by B. Le Méhauté and D.M. Hanes. 1990. 2v. xii,1317p.
10. *The global coastal ocean: processes and methods,* edited by K.H. Brink and A.R. Robinson. 1998. xii,604p.
11. *The global coastal ocean: regional studies and syntheses,* edited by K.H. Brink and A.R. Robinson. 1998. xvii,1062p.

V.1 has 33 contributors. v.2:29. V.3 (39 contributors) is the first comprhensive work of its kind. 3 sections: 1. Geophysical exploration - 2. Topography and structure - 3. Sedimentation. Chapter 34, 'The Pleistocene period' has 6½p. of references. Well illustrated throughout. Each volume has author and subject indexes. An authoritative, critical and detailed survey that attempts to be 'a balanced account of how oceanography and the thoughts of oceanographers were moving' (*Preface*). *Class No:* 551.46(035)

[1741]

SHEPARD, F.P. **Geological oceanography.** New York, Crane Russak & Co., 1977. 214p. illus., (some col.), diagrs.

'Written for students beginning to study geology or anyone interested in important developments' in oceanography, - this text provides 'a clear and simple account, by an authoritative author' (*Marine geology,* v.28(3/4), 1978, p.293). *Class No:* 551.46(035)

Dictionaries

[1742]

AGENCE DE COOPÉRATION CULTURELLE ET TECHNIQUE *and* CONSEIL INTERNATIONAL DE LA LANGUE FRANÇAISE. **Vocabulaire de l'océanologie.** Paris, the Agence; C.I.L.F.; New York, French and European, 1976. 431p. $49.95.

French-base terms, with definitions and eqivalents and indexes in English, German and Russian. Genders are shown. Appended are classification tables. *Class No:* 551.46(038)

[1743]

—Dictionnaire technique illustré en six langues. [Illustrated technical dictionary in six languages.] Brussels, Permanent International Association of Navigation Congresses, [1957]-. illus., diagrs.

La mer/The sea... by A. Rouville. [1957]. 272p.

A systematically arranged dictionary of 2,284 French terms, with equivalents and reverse indexes in English, German, Spanish and Italian. 6 sections: 1. Sea-water - 2. Conditions of sea-waves - 3. Tides. Currents - 4. Winds - 5. Meteorology - 6. Marine charts. Soundings. Appendix, on charts, etc., p.181-98.
Class No: 551.46(038)

[1744]

FISCHER, K. **Fachwörterbuch der Meereskunde-Meerestechnik.** Deutsch-Englisch, Englisch-Deutsch. 2. erw. Aufl. Rostock-Warnemünde, Institut für Meereskunst der AdW der DDR, 1979. 329p.

An East German dictionary (German and English) of oceanography and ocean technology. *Class No:* 551.46(038)

[1745]

Glossary of oceanographic terms. Baker, B.B. *Jr, and others, eds..* 2nd ed. Washington, US Naval Oceanographic Office, 1966. vi, 204p. diagrs. (*US Naval Oceanographic Office, Special publication SR35.*)

First published 1960 (US Hydrographic Office).

Definitions of *c*.4,500 terms (*e.g.* 'ship motion') - List of 74 sources. Appendix A: Abbreviations and acronyms; B: List of oceanographic institutions, agencies, activities and groups (mostly US). *Class No:* 551.46(038)

Reviews & Abstracts

[1746]

Aquatic sciences and fisheries abstracts. Bethesda, Md., Cambridge Scientific Abstracts, 1978-. 6pa. 3pts. $1,045 (US); $1,195 (non US), pt.1; $815; ($945), pt. 2, $350; ($385) pt. 3 (7pa.).

Formerly part of *Aquatic sciences and fisheries abstracts,* 1971-77.

Pt.1: *Biological sciences and living resources.*
Pt.2: *Ocean technology, policy and non-living resources.*
Pt.3: *Aquatic pollution and environmental quality.*

Pt.2 carries *c*.8,800 abstracts pa. Coverage: oceanography, limnology, geochemistry, underwater optics and acoustics, geology and geophysics, marine technology and engineering resources (including oil, minerals, desalination and energy, pollution policy and sea law, documentation). Monthly and annual subject and author indexes. Magnetic tapes available. ASFA database available on CD-ROM. Available online via DIALOG, and to subscribers via the Internet. *Class No:* 551.46(048)

[1747]

Oceanic abstracts. Bethesda, Md., Cambridge Science Abstracts, 1972-. 12pa. $1,045 (US); $1085 (non US). ISSN: 07481489.

Supersedes *Oceanic Index* and *Oceanic Citation Index.*

c.12,000 abstracts pa. 8 sections: Marine biology, oceanography, ecology - Physical and chemical oceanography and meteorology - Marine geology, geophysics and geochemistry - Marine pollution, environmental protection - Marine resources, living - Marine resources, non-living - Ships and shipping - Books and conferences. Subject, organism, geographic and author indexes. An essential bibliographical tool in its field. Online and available on CD-ROM.

McCusig, H. 'Navigating your way through *Oceanic abstracts* database' (*Database,* v.1(1), December 1978, p.26-41) describes the system as 'the foremost database in the oceanographic field'. *Class No:* 551.46(048)

[1748]

Oceanographic literature review. Oxford. etc., Elsevier, 1993-. 12pa. Dfl.2,772; $1,593. ISSN: 09670653.

Formerly *Oceanographic abstracts and bibliography,*(1977-78), and *Deep-sea research,* Pt. B, (1979-93).

About 7,000 abstracts and references pa. Sections A-G: A. Physical oceanography - B. Marine meteorology - C. Chemical oceanography - D. Submarine geology and geophysics - E. Biological oceanography - F. General - G. New patents. Sections are closely subdivided. Annual author and subject indexes. An authoritative source, scanning *c*.3,500 journals. Available online and on CD-ROM. *Class No:* 551.46(048)

Periodicals & Progress Reports

[1749]

INSTITUTE OF OCEANOGRAPHIC SCIENCES. **Serial holdings of UK marine and freshwater sciences libraries.** Godalming, Surrey, the Institute, [1977]. 185p.

Lists 6,000 serials by titles, A-Z. Data: library location (9 UK libraries) and years of holdings. *Class No:* 551.46(05)

[1750]

Oceanography and marine biology: an annual review. Aberdeen, Aberdeen University Press, 1963-. Annual. Price varies. ISSN: 00783218.

V.34, 1996 has eight articles with extensive lists of references appended. They include 'Beach clam fisheries' and 'Coastal fisheries in the Pacific islands'. Author, systematic and analytical subject indexes. *Class No:* 551.46(05)

Almanacs

[1751]

MANGONE, G.J. **Mangone's concise marine almanac.** 2nd rev. and expanded ed. New York, Taylor & Francis, 1991. viii,199p. tables. ISBN: 0844816744.

7 sections: 1. Measurements of marine forms - 2. Physical-political marine features (*e.g.* 'Warships of the minor powers') - 4. Merchant marines and ports (*e.g.* 'Major ports of the world by tonnage') - 5. Fisheries - 6. Marine and seabed minerals - 7. Pollution of the marine environment (*e.g.* 'Biologic agents'). Index. Many statistical tables. Useful as a quick reference tool. *Class No:* 551.46(059)

Festschriften

[1752]

The Ocean floor: a Bruce Heezen commemorative volume. Scrutton, R.A. *and* Talwani, M., *eds.* New York, etc., Wiley, 1982. 318p. illus., diagrs., maps. $250. ISBN: 0471100919.

A Festschrift by 38 authors, the 18 papers covering aspects of most oceans, from global to microscopic scale. A tribute to Heezen and a bibliography of his writings (over 300) precede. Index. 'Largely a reference book and will be of great value in many libraries' (*Geographical journal,* v.149(2), July 1982, p.231). *Class No:* 551.46(082.20)

Tables & Data Books

[1753]

CRC handbook of geophysical exploration at sea. Geyer, R.A. 2nd ed. Boca Raton, Florida, CRC Press, 1992. 2v. illus., diagrs., graphs, tables, maps. ISBN: 084934252x, v.1; 0849342538, v.2.

First published in 1983.

V.1. *Hydrocarbons.* 496p. V.2. *Hard minerals.* 544p. *Class No:* 551.46(083)

[1754]

CRC handbook of marine science. Cleveland, Ohio, CRC Press, 1974. 2v. ([viii], 627p. + [viii], 390p.). graphs, tables, maps. $149, v.1; $75, v.2. ISBN: 0849302110, v.1; 0878193901, v.2.

V.1 (mainly tabular data), edited by F.G.W. Smith, has six sections, on chemical and physical oceanography, atmospheric science, geology, ocean engineering, tables of conversion and constants. Analytical index. V.2, edited by F.G.W. Smith and F.A. Kalber, has four sections: 1. Primary productivity; 2. Fishery statistics; 3. Zooplankton populations; 4. Phytoplankton populations. 4 folding maps. Analytical index.

A third volume was to deal with other facets of marine productivity. *Class No:* 551.46(083)

[1755]

International oceanographic tables. Paris, UNESCO, 1968-73. 2v. ISBN: 9230009067, v.1; 9230010448, v.2.

Prepared by a Joint Panel on Oceanographic Tables and Standards, and published, with Unesco, by the National Institute of Oceanography, Wormley, Godalming, Surrey. V.1 appeared in loose-leaf form, with English, French, Spanish and Russian text, in 1968. V.2 (in binder, xvi, 141p.), 1973. *Class No:* 551.46(083)

Gazetteers

[1756]

UNITED STATES. Board on Geographic Names. **Gazetteer of undersea features.** 4th ed. Washington, Defense Mapping Agency, 1990. xi,146,152p.

2nd ed., 1971.

Official standard names approved by the Board on Geographic Names. Includes index.

Standardization of undersea features, produced by GEBCO (General Bathymetric Chart of the Oceans) [c.1983], is in English/French, English/Russian and English/Spanish versions.

Class No: 551.46(083.86)

Maps & Atlases

[1757]

Atlas of the seas round the British Isles. Lee, A. *and* Ramster, J., *eds.* Lowestoft, MAFF, Directorate of Fisheries Research, 1981. Loose-leaf. £10. ISBN: 0907545001.

75 large coloured charts, including explanatory text, sources used and further sources available. Coverage: water movements, seabed features, dissolved chemicals, plankton, fisheries, oil and gas deposits, ferry routes, telephone cables, dumping areas, marine safety systems. 'Brings together for the first time the nature of the seas themselves' - resources, pollution, dangers and safety measures (*Library review,* v.31, Summer 1982, p.158-9). *Class No:* 551.46(084.3)

[1758]

INTERNATIONAL HYDROGRAPHIC ORGANIZATION. **The General bathymetric chart of the oceans.** (GEBCO). 5th ed. [Monaco], International Hydrographic Organization, the Intergovernmental Oceanographic Commission, 1983.

Co-sponsored by the International Hydrographic Organization, and the Intergovernmental Oceanographic Commission.

GEBCO (5th ed.) comprises 16 sheets, Mercator projection, on a scale of 1:10 million at the equator, plus 2 Polar sheets on a scale of 1:6 million at 75° latitude. The 18 map sheets are available boxed, with a reduced world map (1:35 million) and a supporting manual, (Based on review in *Geographical journal,* November 1986, p.86, p.430-1). *Class No:* 551.46(084.3)

[1759]

The Mitchell Beazley atlas of the oceans. London, Mitchell Beazley, 1977. 208p. illus., diagrs., maps.

Sections: The ocean realm (geomorphology) - Man's ocean quest (history) - Life in the oceans - The great resource (fish, oil, minerals, energy) - The face of the deep (60p. of coloured maps, mineral resources; living resources) - Encyclopedia of marine life (p.172-86). Tables. Glossary. Index, c.1,000 entries. 'The weakness of this book lies not with the material presented but in the presentation' (*Library journal,* 1 February 1978, p.355). A lavishly illustrated account, but not an atlas. *Class No:* 551.46(084.3)

[1760]

STOMMEL, H. *and* FIEUX, M. **Oceanographic atlases:** a guide to their geographic coverage and contents. Woods Hole, Mass., Woods Hole Press, 1978. vi, [114p.]. $15; $7.50. ISBN: 091517622x.

Examines 97 atlases (usually 1 per page) as to scope, scale, measurements, data plotted and contours, sources of data; dates. 5 areas: Antarctic Ocean, Atlantic Ocean and adjacent seas; Indian Ocean and adjacent seas; Pacific Ocean and adjacent seas; Whole ocean studies. Small key maps show area of ocean covered. For oceanographers, hydrographers and geographers.

Class No: 551.46(084.3)

[1761]

The Times atlas and encyclopaedia of the sea. Couper, A.D. 2nd ed. London, Times Books, 1989. 272p. illus. (col.), diagrs., tables, maps. ISBN: 0723003181.

First published as *The Times atlas of the oceans* (Times Books, 1983).

Comprehensive but unconventional (neither a detailed atlas nor an alphabetically-arranged encyclopaedia) treatment of the world's oceans, written and cartographed by 28 contributors. 5 sections: The ocean environment (incl. the ocean basins, p.26-43) - Resources of the ocean (incl. fisheries, p.90-101) - Ocean trade (incl. shipping routes, p.146-59) - The world ocean (incl. strategic use of the oceans, p.178-91). 11 appendices, glossary, index, p.258-72. With c.400 illustrations and maps, all in colour, it should serve a wide readership.

Class No: 551.46(084.3)

[1762]

World ocean atlas. Translated from Russian by D.A. Brown. Gorshkov, S.G., *ed.* Oxford, etc., Pergamon Press, 1975-83. 3v. illus., maps. £90, v.1; £310; $620, v.2; £380; $760, v.3. ISBN: 0080199992, v.1; 0080219535, v.2; 0080287352, v.3.

1 *Pacific Ocean.* 1975. 350p. 2. *Atlantic and Indian Oceans.* 1978. 350p. 3. *Arctic Ocean.* 1983. 184pl.

Presents oceanological and meteorological data. Contents of v.2: History of ocean exploration; Ocean bed; Climate; Hydrology;

....(contd.)

Hydrochemistry; Biogeography; Reference and navigation geographical charts. V.3 has 184 plates and a 4-page index. Introduction and index in English; map plates in Russian. Highly priced, but important. *Class No:* 551.46(084.3)

Biographies

[1763]

FOOD AND AGRICULTURE ORGANIZATION. **International directory of marine scientists.** Rome, F.A.O., 1977. [viii], 33p. $25. ISBN: 9250003676.

Computer-prepared guide. Names are arranged under countries (A-Z), plus statement on specialization. Name index.

3rd ed., 1983, while in 1986 *Supplement 1: Directory of Chinese marine scientists* (Tianjin, China Ocean Press) was published.

Class No: 551.46(092)

Great Britain

[1764]

Estuaries and coastal waters of the British Isles: an annual bibliography of recent scientific papers. Noble, L. Plymouth, Marine Biological Association of the United Kingdom, Library and Information Services, 1979-. Annual (irregular). maps. £32. ISSN: 02610663.

Formerly *Estuaries of the British Isles: a bibliography of recent scientific papers,* 1977-78.

48 sea areas, plus British Isles (general), England (general), Ireland (general), Scotland (general) and Wales (general). No.16, 1992, carries 1,223 references. Subjects include biology, geochemistry, sedimentation, fisheries. Author index. *Class No:* 551.46(410)

Polar Regions

[1765]

Polar oceanography. Smith, W.O., *Jr., ed.* San Diego, Academic Press, 1990. 2v. $69.50, Pt.A; $65, Pt.B. ISBN: 0126530319, pt.A; 0126530327, pt.B.

Pt.A. *Physical science.* xviii,406p. Pt.B. *Chemistry, biology, and geology.* xvi,354p.

13 chapters in the set: 1. Meteorology - 2. Sea ice in the Polar regions ... 6. Small-scale processes ... 10. Polar zooplankton ... 13. Particle fluxes and modern sedimentation in the Polar oceans. A bibliography is appended to each chapter. *Class No:* 551.46(98/99)

Equipment & Instruments

[1766]

McCONNELL, A. **Historical instruments in oceanography:** background to the Oceanography Collection at the Science Museum. London, HMSO, 1981. [iv], 52p. illus., facsim., map. £3.95. ISBN: 011290324x.

Sections: 1. General introduction (seas and oceans) - 2. Historical investigations (p.4-46; *e.g.* 'Sounding voyages for laying telegraph cables. 1850-1900'; 'International fisheries research') - 3. Modern oceanography. 'Further reading', p.51. End-paper maps.

Class No: 551.46:002.50

Institutions & Associations

[1767]

Annotated acronyms and abbreviations of marine science related international organizations. Ashby, C.M. *and* Flesh, A.R., *eds.* 3rd ed. Washington, US Dept. of Commerce, National Oceanic & Atmospheric Administration, Environmental Data and Information Service; National Oceanographic Data Center, 1981. 349p.

First published 1969. *Class No:* 551.46:061:061.2

[1768]

UNITED STATES. National Referral Center for Science and Technology. **Geosciences and oceanography:** a directory of information resources in the United States. Washington, Library of Congress, 1981. xx, 375p.

Contents; Organization locator - Directory, A/Z (p.1-275). Data on each body include area of interest, holdings, publications and information services. Extensive analytical subject index, p.277-375. 'For the purpose of this directory, "geoscience" and "oceanography" have been defined quite broadly' (*Preface*). Thus, palaeontology and astronomy both figure in the index. *Class No:* 551.46:061:061.2

Meteorology

Encyclopaedias

[1769]

The Encyclopedia of atmospheric sciences and astrogeology.
Fairbridge, R.W., *ed.* New York, London etc., Reinhold, 1967. xv,
1200p. illus., diagrs., tables, maps. (*Encyclopedia of earth sciences,*
v.2.) ISBN: 012786458x.
About 150 contributors. Signed articles, A-Z, with references
appended. Lengthier articles preponderate, beginning with a simple
explanation and proceeding to detailed technical data (*e.g.* 'Radar
astronomy', p.786-91; 3 figures, 1 table, ½ col. of references, 25
cross-references). Well illustrated. Intended for all scientists, for those
still in high school to the emeritus professor (*Preface*). A
comprehensive reference work on astronomy, climatology,
meteorological and related sciences. *Class No:* 551.5(031)

Handbooks & Manuals

[1770]

Handbook of applied meteorology. Houghton, D.D., *ed.* New York,
etc., Wiley, 1985. xv, 1461p. illus., diagrs., graphs, charts, tables,
maps. $105; £102. ISBN: 0471084042.
54 contributors. 5 parts: 1. Fundamentals - 2. Measurements - 3.
Applications - 4. Societal impacts - 5. Resources (data; books and
journals; education; research centers and libraries; directory sources).
46 documented chapters in all (*e.g.* ch. 4: 'Weather forecasting',
p.205-79, including 4p. of references and bibliography). Appendices:
A. Glossary and units; B. Climatic data (monthly; 147 locations,
worldwide), p.1369-1431. A massive compendium; North American
slant. 'Designed for professionals and technicians outside the
meteorological profession.' (*New technical books,* January 1986,
p.101). *Class No:* 551.5(035)

[1771]

Handbook of aviation meteorology. 3rd ed. London, HMSO, 1994. xi,
401p. (*Met. O. 1016.*)
Five parts, comprising 21 chapters: 1. Physical principles; 2.
Meteorological observations; 3. Synoptic meteorology; 4. General
circulation and world climate; 5. Meteorological information for
aviators. 2 appendices and an annex (p.360-390). Index, p.391-401.
'An elementary knowledge of meteorology on the part of the reader
will be an advantage' (*Preface*). *Class No:* 551.5(035)

[1772]

HEASTIE, H. A Course in elementary meteorology. 2nd ed. London,
HMSO, 1978. xii, 208p. illus. (pl.) diagrs. £7.50. (*Met. O. 911.*)
ISBN: 0114003122.
First published 1962.
Part 1: Physical meteorology; part 2: Synoptic meteorology. 12
documented chapters. Appendices: A. Radar and meteorology; B.
Weather satellites. 'Books for further reading', p.402. Analytical
index. An introductory textbook of theoretical meteorology, 'intended
for the reader whose knowledge of physics is roughly equivalent to
those of upper science forms in schools, although parts ... are of a
rather higher standard' (*Preface to the first edition*).
Class No: 551.5(035)

[1773]

The Marine observer's handbook. 11th ed. London, HMSO, 1995.
227p. illus. (some col.), diagrs., tables. £23. (*Met. O. 1016.*) ISBN:
011400367x.
Has 4 parts (14 chapters): 1. Instrumental observations - 2. Non-
instrumental observations - 3. Phenomena - 4. Summary of
meteorological work at sea. 'State of sea photographs, Force 0 to 12',
p.40-7, plus cloud pl. in col., p.63-93. Analytical index, p.222-7. First
revised edition for 18 years. *Class No:* 551.5(035)

[1774]

Meteorology source book. Parker, S.P., *ed.* New York, McGraw-Hill,
1988. 304p. figs., maps. $45. (*McGraw-Hill Science reference series.*)
ISBN: 0070455112.
Derived from the *McGraw-Hill encyclopedia of science and*
technology (q.v.). Introduction, followed by 8 sections: 1. The
atmosphere - 2. Atmospheric electrical phenomena ... 7.
Instrumentation, observation and forecasts - 8. Weather modification.
Brief chapter bibliographies. Numerous illustrations and charts. Subject
index. For public and academic libraries. *Class No:* 551.5(035)

[1775]

Observer's handbook. 4th ed. London, HMSO, 1982. vi, 220p. illus.,
diagrs. £13.95. (*Met. O. 933.*) ISBN: 0114003297.
First published 1952.
11 chapters of instructions in the exposure of meteorological
instruments and in the making of weather observations, both
instrumental and non-instrumental, at all types of stations. 1.
Observational routine - 2. Clouds - 3. Visibility - 4. Weather - 5. Wind
- 6. State of ground and concrete slab - 7. Atmospheric pressure - 8.
Temperature and humidity - 9. Precipitation - 10. Sunshine - 11.
Special phenomena (*e.g.* electrometeors). 3 appendices (*e.g.* Recording
of observations ...). Bibliography, p.213. Analytical index, p.214-20,
31 pl., 23d. Well organized; for both amateur and professional
meteorologists. *Class No:* 551.5(035)

[1776]

—Meteorology for mariners: a text-book of elementary theoretical
meteorology for Merchant Navy officers which also presents the
practical application of meteorology to safe and economic ship
operations. 3rd ed. London, HMSO, 1978. x, 215p. diagrs., graphs,
maps. £14.70. ISBN: 0114003114.
First published 1957 (19 chapters).
6 parts: 1. The meteorological elements - 2. Climatology - 3.
Weather systems - 4. Weather forecasting - 5. Ocean surface currents -
6. Ice and exchange of energy between sea and atmosphere. Appended
bibliography of 10 items. *Class No:* 551.5(035)

Dictionaries

[1777]

Anglo-russkii meteorologicheskii slovar'. Ainbinder, M.I., *and others.*
Moscow, Fizmetgiz, 1959. 244p.
An English-Russian meteorological dictionary of *c.*7,000 terms, with
a Russian index. Covers 'general, synoptic and (in part) dynamical
meteorology, and also climatology' (Maichel, K. *Guide to Russian*
reference books, v.2, edited by J.S.G. Simmons (1964), entry F353).
Class No: 551.5(038)

[1778]

Dictionnaire encyclopédique d'agrométéorologie: française-anglais-
espagnol. [Encyclopaedic dictionary of agrometeorology: French-
English-Spanish.] Versailles, INRA Editions, 1990. 323p.
Gives definitions of *c.*500 currently used agrometeorological terms.
Related expressions are given. English-French and Spanish-French
indexes of main terms and a French index of all terms.
Class No: 551.5(038)

[1779]

Glossaire de météorologie et de climatologie. Villeneuve, G.-O., *and*
others. 2nd ed. Quebec, Presses de l'Université Laval, 1980.
xix,626p. tables. ISBN: 2763768962.
About 6,000 French terms defined in 10-40 words, with English
equivalents and categorized. English-French index. List of works
consulted, p.xv-xix. *Class No:* 551.5(038)

[1780]

Glossary of meteorology. Hüschke, R.E., *ed.* Boston, Mass. American
Meteorological Society, 1959. viii, 638p. $25. ISBN: 0933876351.
Sponsored by the US Weather Bureau, and others.
Attempts to define *c.*7,000 terms, - 'Every important meteorological
term likely to be found in the literature today' - in words 'that are
understandable to the generalist and yet palatable to the specialist'
(*Preface*). Cites short phrases to illustrate usage. Includes mathematical
approach. *Class No:* 551.5(038)

[1781]

Meteorological glossary. Lewis, R.P.W., *comp.* 6th ed. London,
HMSO, 1991. 335p. illus. (incl. col. pl.). £20. ISBN: 0114003637.
About 2,300 technical terms used in meteorology are concisely
defined and discussed, with profuse cross-references. The publisher
claims that 'many new terms and definitions have been introduced as a
result of research and developments in meteorology, climatology,
hydrology and from increasing research into the greenhouse effect
(given 110 words) and global warming', (although there is no entry for
latter term). Attractively produced, although the use of lower case
typeface slightly irritates.
The 3rd ed., (1938-39) carried tables of equivalents in English,
Danish, Dutch, French, German, Italian, Norwegian, Portuguese,
Spanish, and Swedish. *Class No:* 551.5(038)

[1782]

ROGOYSKI, D.A., *comp*. Glossary of Polish-English meteorological
terms. Washington, Library of Congress, 1968. vi, 301p.
Prepared by the Aerospace Technology Division, Library of
Congress.
About 10,000 terms and phrases. Patterned after the American
Meteorological Society's *Glossary of meteorology,* edited by R.H.
Hübschke (1959) (*qv*). *Class No:* 551.5(038)

[1783]
WORLD METEOROLOGICAL ORGANIZATION. International meteorological vocabulary. 2nd ed. Geneva, Secretariat of the WMO, 1992. xv, 784p. ISBN: 9263021821.

First published 1966.

Multilingual meteorological nomenclature; international meteorological definitions. English, French, Spanish and Russian indexes. Substantially enlarged since first edition (276p.).
Class No: 551.5(038)

Reviews & Abstracts

[1784]
Meteorological and geoastrophysical abstracts. Littleton, Mass., American Meteorological Society, 1960-. v.1(1)-. 12pa. $1,120; CD-ROM $5,200. ISSN: 00261130.

Formerly *Meteorological abstracts and bibliography, 1950-59.*

Each issue contains *c.*600 abstracts and references. 6 sections: A. Environmental sciences - B. Meteorology - C. Astrophysics - D. Hydrosphere. Hydrology - E. Glaciology - F. Physical oceanography. Author subject and geographic indexes, cumulated annually and at longer intervals, *e.g.* for v.21-26. Online on DIALOG; CD-ROM also available, with coverage from 1974-.

Cumulated bibliography and index to 'Meteorological and geoastrophysical abstracts', 1950-1969: classified subject and author arrangements (Boston, Mass., G.K. Hall, 1972. 8v.) is made up of a 4-v. subject sequence of 138,000 entries, classified by UDC and a corresponding 4-v. author sequence. *Class No: 551.5(048)*

Tables & Data Books

[1785]
Smithsonian meteorological tables. List, R.J., *ed.* 6th rev. ed. Washington, Smithsonian Institution, 1966 (reprinted 1984). 540p. $30. (*Smithsonian Miscellaneous collections, 114.*) ISBN: 0874741157.

The most comprehensive available set of tables for meteorological calculations. Supplementary conversion tables, etc.
Class No: 551.5(083)

Maps & Atlases

[1786]
Atlas of meteorology: a series of over four hundred maps. Under the patronage of the Royal Geographical Society. Buchan, A., *ed.* Edinburgh, Bartholomew, 1889. 40, xivp. with 34pl. of maps.

Formed v.3 Bartholomew's *Physical atlas*. Text: 1. General introduction - 2. Description of the maps in the atlas - 3. Appendices (meteorological services and societies, their publications; bibliography; glossary; meteorological tables). The 400 maps comprise world maps, with insets for Britain, France, Europe, etc. Index to letterpress and maps. Page size: 45 x 30cm. Of historical value.
Class No: 551.5(084.3)

Histories

[1787]
BRUSH, S.G. *and* **LANDSBERG, H.E. The History of geophysics and meteorology:** an annotated bibliography. New York & London, Garland, 1985. 450p. ISBN: 0824091167.

'Geophysics' is here interpreted to include the origin and development of the solar system and the formation of the earth's surface features. About 2,000 annotated entries in sections A-W (A. General histories; B. Biographies ... G. Geodesy, terrestrial gravitation, size and shape of the earth - H. Formation of the earth's surface features ... M. Meteorology: general histories ... R. Atmospheric dynamics and thermodynamics ... V. Upper atmosphere, ionosphere, magnetosphere, aurora). Author and subject indexes.
Class No: 551.5(091)

Practical Work

Instruments

[1788]
Handbook of meteorological instruments. 2nd ed. London, HMSO, 1980-82. 7v. illus., diagrs., graphs, tables. (*Met. O. 919.*)

1. *Measurement of atmospheric pressure.* 1980.
2. *Measurement of temperature.* 1980, vii. 70p.
3. *Measurement of humidity.* 1981.
4. *Measurement of surface wind.* 1981.
5. *Measurement of precipitation and evaporation.* 1981.
6. *Measurement of sunshine and solar and terrestrial radiation.* 1982.
7. *Measurement of velocity and cloud height.* 1982.

Booklets intended primarily for Met. Office personnel about the

....(contd.)

instruments used at official stations. 'Particulars of some other types are included to illustrate different principles' (*Introduction*). Each volume has bibliography, glossary and index. *Class No: 551.508*

[1789]
MIDDLETON, W.E.K. The History of the barometer. Baltimore, Md., Johns Hopkins Press, 1964. xx, 489p. illus. $127.80. ISBN: 0317084461.

Broadly chronological order of chapters, with footnote references. 'A well documented and well written account' (*Geographical journal*, v.131(4), December 1965, p.568). A new edition was announced by Baros Books in 1995, (0948382082). *Class No: 551.508*

Wind

[1790]
LONGSHORE, D. Encyclopedia of hurricanes, typhoons, and cyclones. New York, Facts on File, 1998. 372p. illus.,maps,charts. £36; $45. ISBN: 0816033986.

Over 350 entries covering hurricanes, typhoons and cyclones by name; storm-related terms; locations where storms frequently occur; biographies; related topics. Numerous cross-references. Appendices include a list of the names, locations, and dates of hurricanes, typhoons, cyclones, and tropical storms and a chronology of all major storms since 1281 which have caused damage to property or death. Bibliography and index. For public and school libraries.
Class No: 551.55

Vapours

Clouds

[1791]
International cloud atlas. Geneva, WMO, 1956-87. 2v. illus. (pl.). $78, v.2.

Replaces *International atlas on clouds and types of sky* (1934).

V.1 provides a comprehensive text, with detailed descriptive study of clouds, and the methods and techniques of observing them. V.2 is a collection of 224 excellent plates, 103 in colour, supporting the v.1 text.

International cloud atlas - abridged atlas (Geneva, WMO, 1956. 210p.) selects 72 plates from v.2, plus 'brief description and explanatory text to meet day-by-day needs of meteorological observers at surface stations' (*Weatherwise*, v.16(4), August 1963, p.182).
Class No: 551.576

[1792]
—**Cloud types for observers.** Rev. ed. London, HMSO, 1982. 38p. col. illus. £11. ISBN: 0114003343.

Explains the classification, based on 10 main groups of clouds (divided into 3 levels, - low, medium and high). Each level is accorded a section. *Class No: 551.576*

[1793]
SCORER, R. Clouds of the world: a complete colour encyclopedia. Melbourne, Victoria, Lothian Publishing Co. (Pty.), Ltd.; Newton Abbot, Devon, David & Charles, 1972. 176p. illus. (incl. col. pl.).

14 sections (1. Cumulus ... 4. Cirrus ... 7. Altocirrus (p.100-5; 4 black-and-white illus.; 14 col. illus.) ... 8. Warm sector cloud ... 11. Condensation trails ... 13. Optical phenomena - 14. Rotation. Appendix: Photogrammetry and stereoscopic photography. Bibliography, p.172. Detailed, non-analytical index. 14 col. plates, each with 5-8 photos., lengthy descriptive captions facing. 'The text is admirably clear ... The book can be heartily recommended to all those whose business involves clouds, particularly meteorologists and aviators' (*British book news*, January 1973, p.35). *Class No: 551.576*

Droughts

[1794]
Drought in Africa. 2. [Sécheresse en Afrique. 2.] Dalby, D. *and* Church, R.J.H., *eds.* 2nd rev. and expanded ed. London, International African Institute, in association with the Environment Training Programme, UNEP-IDEP-SIDA, 1977. viii, 200p. diagrs., tables, maps. $54.10. (*African Environment Special report 6.*) ISBN: 0853020566.

First published 1973.

22 contributors. 3 parts (20 chapters, with appended notes, references and French résumés): Introduction - General studies - Special studies. Chapter 14: 'The extent and intensity of the 1969-73 drought in Nigeria: a provisional analysis', p.114-26 (notes; 27 references: résumé). No index. A *Drought in Africa 3* would certainly now be timely. *Class No: 551.577.3*

Avalanches

[1795]

Avalanche atlas: illustrated international avalanche classification. International Commission on Snow and Ice of the International Association of Hydrological Sciences. Paris, Unesco, 1981. 265, [1]p. £24; $16.95. (*Natural hazard series*, 2.) ISBN: 9230016969.

Presents a systematic scheme of classification for avalanches and snow data, supported by a 'Photographic guide' (descriptive data, in English, French, Spanish, Russian and German, facing photographs). *Class No:* 551.578.48

Climate

Bibliographies

[1796]

RIGBY, M. Bibliography of climate textbooks and studies. Geneva, World Meteorological Organization (World Climate Programme), 1984. 170 + 6p.

Records 1,171 references to climate textbooks, atlases, reviews and handbooks, mostly post-1950 publications. Excludes periodical articles and the like, but includes some WMO *Technical notes* and conference reports. Numerous indexes: personal author, corporate author and title entry, subject and geographical name, as well as index of atlases, maps and charts, and index of handbooks, textbooks and training material. *Class No:* 551.58(01)

Encyclopaedias

[1797]

Encyclopedia of climate and weather. Schneider, S.H., *ed.* Oxford, University Press, 1996. 2v.(929p.) illus.,charts,maps. £165; $195. ISBN: 0195094859.

Contains more than 350 signed articles, Absolute humidity ... Zones, and some biographies of important meteorologists. Each article has a bibliography and there is also a lengthy glossary of terms, p.853-74. Subject index. Directory of contributors, p.875-83. Wider-ranging and more current than *Encyclopedia of climatology* (*q.v.*). For academic libraries. *Class No:* 551.58(031)

[1798]

The Encyclopedia of climatology. Oliver, J.E. *and* Fairbridge, R.W., *eds.* New York, Van Nostrand, 1986. 986p. $109.95; £80. (*Encyclopedia of earth sciences, 11.*) ISBN: 0879330090.

Over 200 documented articles, A-Z, mainly on developments in climatology during the past years. Many cross-references. Author, subjects and geographic indexes. Includes entry on recent issues such as acid rain. The coverage of palaeontology has been significantly extended, but an important topic such as ozone is given short shrift (*New technical books*, January/February 1988, item 286). Supplemental to R.W. Fairbridge's *Encyclopedia of atmospheric science and astrogeology* (*q.v.*). *Class No:* 551.58(031)

Handbooks & Manuals

[1799]

The Guinness book of weather facts and feats. 2nd ed., by I. Holford. Enfield, Middlesex, Guinness Superlatives, 1984. 253p. illus. (incl. col.), ports., diagrs., tables, maps. £8.95. ISBN: 0851122434.

First published 1977 (240p.).

20 sections (*e.g.* 1. The radiating sun; 2. The invention of thermometers; 4. The pressure and character of the atmosphere; 5. The nature of wind; 6. Weather charts; 13. Rain, flood and drought; 14. Snow and thaw flood; 18. Optical phenomena; 19. Microclimate; 20. Forecasting). Bibliography (by chapters), p.243-5; detailed index, p.247-55. The 2nd ed. updates records, with 'further examples of weather which overstep average conditions' (*Introduction*). *Class No:* 551.58(035)

[1800]

—ROTH, G.D. Collins' guide to the weather. London, Collins, 1981. 256p. illus. (incl. col.), maps. ISBN: 0002190109.

A basic introduction, translated from the German, *Wetterkunde für Alles* (1979). Chapters include 'All about weather maps', 'Typical European weather and conditions', 'More advanced meteorology', 'Weather observation' and 'Climatic statistics'. Glossary, p.245-9; detailed index, p.251-6. Small format. *Class No:* 551.58(035)

[1801]

SCHWARZBACH, M. Climates of the past: an introduction to paleoclimatology. Translated and edited by R.O. Muir. Princeton, N.J., etc., Van Nostrand, [1963] (reprinted 1977). xii, 328p. illus. diagrs., charts, tables, maps. $24. ISBN: 0404162150.

Translated from the 2nd completely revised and enlarged German ed.

The standard work on the subject. Supported by an extensive bibliography, p.265-300. *Class No:* 551.58(035)

Dictionaries

[1802]

MAUNDER, W.J. Dictionary of global climate change. London, UCL Press, 1992. 240p. ISBN: 1857280237.

Approximately 1,500 entries, including cross-references, covering not only scientific terms but also including details of organizations in main A-Z sequence. 'Greenhouse ...' and 'Ozone ...' entries are well covered. Abbreviations and acronyms are contained in a five-page section. *Class No:* 551.58(038)

Glossaries

[1803]

Glossary of weather and climate: with related oceanic and hydrologic terms. Boston, American Meteorological Society, 1996. 272p. $29.95.

Contains over 3,000 terms, aimed at a general audience. Includes related hydrologic and oceanographic terms. Produced under the Project ATMOSPHERE initiative. *Class No:* 551.58(038.1)

Maps & Atlases

[1804]

WALTER, H. *and* **LIETH, H. Klimadiagram Weltatlas.** Jena, Fischer, 1960-67. 3 Lfg. Loose-leaf.

33 main and 22 subsidiary maps, displaying statistics of 8,000 climate stations. Lfg.1 (1960) comprises 12 maps and 65 supplementary sheets, with 2,836 diagrams of climate stations of the world. Page size, 60 x 45cm. Aimed to solve in graphic form climatic analogues 'from the perhaps limited and rather specialised point of view of plant ecology' (*Geographical journal*, v.129, December 1963, p.562-3). *Class No:* 551.58(084.3)

[1805]

—Weltkarten zur Klimakunde. [World maps of climatology.] Rodenwald, E. *and* Jusatz, H.J., *eds.* 2. Aufl. Berlin & London, Springer-Verlag, 1965. 28p. diagrs., maps.

Edited under the sponsorship of the Heidelberger Akademie der Wissenschaften. As a collection of 5 world and climatic maps, it continues the maps in v.1-3 of the *World atlas of epidemic diseases* (*qv*), on the same projection and scale, *i.e.*, 1:45,000,000. Coverage: mean January and July sunshine (hours), annual total hours of sunshine, general isolines of global radiation, and seasonal climates of the earth. *Class No:* 551.58(084.3)

Histories

[1806]

LAMB, H.H. Climate: present, past and future. London, Methuen, 1972-77. 2v. illus., graphs, tables, maps. ISBN: 0416115306, v.1; 0416115403, v.2.

1. *Fundamentals and climate now.* 1972. xxxi, 613p. 2. *Climatic history and the future.* 1977. xxx, 835p.

Highlights physical and dynamic climatology. A feature is the provision of extensive bibliographies (chapter references: v.1, p.555-96; v.2, p.715-802). Each volume also carries geographical and analytical subject indexes. A major review of climate change. *Class No:* 551.58(091)

Worldwide

[1807]

Monthly climatic data for the world. Asheville, North Carolina, US National Climatic Data Center, 1948-. 12pa. $48. ISSN: 00270296.

Sponsored by the World Meteorological Organization, in co-operation with [The US] Weather Bureau.

Data: mean values (at the surface) of pressure, temperature, relative humidity and precipitation (with departures from normal of these three elements) are issued with comparatively little delay for *c.*1,500 stations. Mean values of upper-air temperature, dew point and wind are included for *c.*400 stations. A thoroughly comprehensive monthly data service. The subscription includes an annual summary. Available on microfiche. *Class No:* 551.58(100)

[1808]

PEARCE, E.A. *and* **SMITH, C.G. The Hutchinson world weather guide.** London, Helicon, 1998. 464p. tables. £16.99 ISBN: 1859862330.

Previously published as *World weather guide*.

A-Z arrangement of nations, providing hours of sunshine, temperature and rainfall figures etc., in over 500 tables. Aimed at travel and tourist industry. *Class No:* 551.58(100)

[1809]

PEARCE, E.A. *and* SMITH, C.G. **The World weather guide.** 3rd ed. Oxford, Helicon, 1993. 483p. graphs, tables, maps. £14.99. ISBN: 0091782414.

First published 1990.

Continent and country data schedules: Africa - North America - Central and South America - Asia - Australia - Caribbean islands - Europe - Oceanic islands, with Germany treated as a united country for the first time and with the CIS, Czech and Slovak republics added. (Australia, p.278-305, is divided into 5 climatic regions, with 12 weather stations listed. Data: temperature (highest recorded); average daily; lowest recorded); relative humidity; precipitation. Analytical index, p.477-83). Impressive, useful for both the actual and armchair traveller. *Class No:* 551.58(100)

[1810]

Tables of temperature, relative humidity, precipitation and sunshine for the world. London, HMSO, 1958-.

1. *North America and Greenland*, (including Hawaii and Bermuda). 1981. (Met. O. 856a). £23.

3. *Europe and the Azores.* 1973. (Met.O. 856c).

4. *Africa; the Atlantic Ocean south of 35 degrees north and the Indian Ocean.* 1983. (Met. O. 856d). £23.

V.2, 5 & 6 bear the older series title, - *Tables of temperature, relative humidity and precipitation of the world*.

2. *Central and South America, the West Indies and Bermuda.* 2nd ed. 1975. (Met. O. 617b). £1.50.

5. *Asia.* 2nd ed. 1966. (Met. O. 617c).

6. *Australasia and the south Pacific Ocean, the corresponding sectors of Antarctica.* 2nd ed. 1975.

Monthly data (average and extremes for about 1,000 carefully selected and well distributed stations throughout the world). *Class No:* 551.58(100)

[1811]

—World weather records, 1971-1980. Washington, National Climate Data Center, 1987-89. 2v.

V.1. *North America.* 1989; v.2. *Europe.* 1987.

Tabulates average readings of sea-level pressure, monthly and annual mean temperatures and precipitation. 'Lake and river levels and dates of freezing and thawing are noted for some locations' (*Reference services review*, v.13(3), Fall 1985, p.92).

Earlier records appear in the Smithsonian Institution's *Miscellaneous collection* publication no.79 (1929, covering pre-1921 data), no.90 (1934, covering 1921-30) and no.105 (1947, covering 1931-40). The US Weather Bureau issued *World weather records, 1941-50* (USGPO, 1959) and *World weather records, 1951-60* (1965-68), while Environmental Data and Information published *World weather records, 1961-70*, (v. 1-3, 6), 1979-. *Class No:* 551.58(100)

[1812]

The Weather handbook: a summary of climatic conditions and weather phenomena for selected cities in the United States and around the world. Conway, M. *and* Liston, L. L., *eds.* Rev. ed. Norcross, Ga., Conway Data, 1990. 548p. illus., maps. $39.95. ISBN: 0910436290.

Gives basic climatic information on 250 US cities and over 600 other cities throughout the world. *Class No:* 551.58(100)

[1813]

World survey of climatology. Landsberg, H.E., *ed.-in-chief.* New York, Elsevier, 1969-. ISBN: 0444422056, v.1A; 0444417761, v.3; 0444413367, v.6.

1A. *General climatology: heat balance climatology*, edited by H.E. Landsberg. 1985. $84.75.

2-3. *General climatology*, edited by H. Flohn, H.E. Landsberg. 1969-81. $164, v. 3.

4. *Climate of the free atmosphere*, edited by D.F. Rex. 1969.

5. *Northern and Western Europe*, edited by C.C. Wallén. 1970.

6. *Central and Southern Europe*, edited by C.C. Wallén, 1977. $146.25.

7. *Soviet Union*, edited by P.E. Lydolph. 1977.

8. *Northern and Eastern Asia*, edited by H. Arakawa. 1969.

9. *Southern and Western Asia*, edited by H. Arakawa and K. Takahashi. 1981.

10. *Africa*, edited by J.F. Griffiths. 1972.

11. *North America*, by R.A. Bryson and F.K. Hare. 1974.

12. *Central and South America*, by Schwerdtfegar. 1976.

13. *Australia and New Zealand*, by J. Gentilli. 1971.

14. *Polar regions*, edited by S. Orvig. 1970.

15. *Oceania*, by H. Van Loon. 1984.

Each volume consists of contributions by specialists, with appended bibliography of references, plus author and subject indexes. *Class No:* 551.58(100)

Europe

[1814]

Climatic atlas of Europe. [Atlas climatique de l'Europe.] Paris, UNESCO; Geneva, World Meteorological Organization, [1970]. Loose-leaf, maps. $164.

Two sets of 13 maps (scale: 1:5,000,000 and 1:10,000,000). Each set shows distribution, monthly and annual, of the mean atmospheric temperature and precipitation, plus a map representing annual temperature ranges. Based on data collected 1931-60 from several thousand stations. 'The first atlas to include annual as well as monthly temperature and precipitation maps for the entire European region' (*Stechert-Hafner book news*, v.26(1), September 1971, p.3). Page size: 60 x 42cm.

Companion atlases: *Climatic atlas of Asia* (1981. 28 maps); *Climatic atlas of North and Central America* (1979), and *Climate atlas of South America*, (v.1. 1975). *Class No:* 551.58(4)

Great Britain

[1815]

BRAZELL, J.H. **London weather.** London, HMSO, 1968. 249 + 21p. illus. (incl. pl.), diagrs., maps. (*Met. O. 783*.)

Revised and updated version of W.A.L. Marshall's *A Century of London weather* (1952), adding statistics of weather from earliest times in A.D.4 up to 1964. A systematic study of London's weather by the month, season, public holiday and type of weather, - fog, warm and cold spells, flood and drought. Bibliography, p.242-3. 23 plates. *Class No:* 551.58(410)

[1816]

Climates of the British Isles: present, past and future. Hulme, M. *and* Barrow, E., *eds.* London, Routledge, 1997. xxxi,454p. illus.,figs.,maps,tables. £65; £17.99 (pbk). ISBN: 0415130174.

28 contributors. Four parts (16 chapters): 1. The British Isles climate - 2. Reconstructing the past - 3. Monitoring the present (9. The changing temperature of central England) - 4. Forecasting the future (15. Global warming and the British Isles). Four appendices (*e.g.* 'Listings of climate datasets'). Glossary; Name index; Index of place names; General index. Many figures and black-and-white photographs. Each chapter has a list of notes appended. *Class No:* 551.58(410)

[1817]

PAGE, J. *and* LEBEN, S.R. **Climate in the United Kingdom:** a handbook of solar radiation, temperature and other data in the thirteen principal cities and towns. London, HMSO, 1986. x, 391p. tables, maps. £19.95. ISBN: 0114123012.

Produced under contract to the Energy Technology Support Unit of the UK Department of Energy.

5 sections: 1. Solar geometry and solar energy - 2. Other meteorological data - 3. Physical properties of materials - 4. Algorithms - 5. Appendices (including Glossary, p.373-9; 41 references). *Class No:* 551.58(410)

[1818]

—ATKINSON, D.W. Weather. Oxford, Pergamon Press, for the Royal Statistical Society and Social Research Council, 1985. p.1-105, diagrs., graphs, tables.

No.29 in the *Reviews of United Kingdom statistical sources* series, sharing the volume (xiii, 224p.) with no.30 (*Water*, by E.C. Penning-Russell and D.J. Parker). Surface data, upper air data and organizational data are supported by a bibliography of 163 references. *Class No:* 551.58(410)

[1819]

STIRLING, R. **The Weather of Britain.** London, Giles de la Mare, 1997. xii,306p. illus., diagrs., tables, maps. £19.99 ISBN: 1900357062.

First published 1982.

24 chapters: 1. The weather and the sea around us ... 10. Drought ... 16. Some notable snowfalls ... 22. City weather ... 24. Is our climate changing? Notes appended to each chapter. Further reading, p.290-1. Some suppliers of meteorological instruments, p.292. Index. Highly readable account, crammed with facts and figures. For anyone interested in British weather. *Class No:* 551.58(410)

[1820]

WHITE, E.J. *and* SMITH, R.I. **Climatological maps of Great Britain.** Penicuik, Midlothian, Institute of Terrestrial Ecology, 1982. 14p. + 23p. of maps. £2. ISBN: 0904282694.

Bibliography, p.6. 28 illus. (23 in colour). *Class No:* 551.58(410)

Asia—South & South East

[1821]

PANT, G.B. *and* RUPA KUMAR, K. **Climates of South Asia.** Chichester, John Wiley, 1997. xxiii,320p. figs.,tables,maps. £85. (*Belhaven studies in climatology*.) ISBN: 0471949485.

Two sections (nine chapters): 1. Meteorological background (1. South Asia: an introduction to the region ... 4. Other meteorological features and systems of south Asia) - 2. Climatic characteristics (5.

....(contd.)

Mean climatology of South Asia ... 9. The changing climate of South Asia: its environmental impact). Two appendices: 1. All-India monthly and seasonal rainfall (1871-1994) - 2. Climatological tables of some stations in South Asia. Bibliography, p.299-314, and index. For academic libraries. *Class No:* 551.58(54+59)

USA

[1822]

Weather America: the latest detailed climatological data for over 4,000 places - with rankings. Garwood, A.N., *ed.* Milpitas, Calif., Toucan Valley Publications, 1996. xvi,1,412p. maps,tables. $99.95. ISBN: 188492560x.

Arranged alphabetically by state. Contains data for 1965-94 from 4,158 weather stations. The 13 categories of information include: total precipitation; heating and cooling degree days; total snowfall; maximum, minimum, mean temperatures. National rankings are also given. 'This is the best source of US climatological information for the last 30 years ... highly recommended for all libraries' (*Choice*, January 1997, p.776). *Class No:* 551.58(73)

[1823]

WOOD, R.A. Weather almanac: a reference guide to weather, climate, and related issues in the United States and its key cities. 8th ed. Detroit, Mich., Gale, 1998. viv, 741p. illus.,tables, charts. £104; $135. ISBN: 0810355221.

5th ed., 1991.

Gives 864 detailed weather records in narrative and tabular form for 108 key US cities, plus a climatic overview of the country. The remainder of the book concerns areas such as air pollution, weather extremes, etc., plus a glossary and index. *Class No:* 551.58(73)

Antarctic

[1824]

KING, J.C. *and* **TURNER, J. Antarctic meteorology and climatology.** Cambridge, University Press, 1997. xii,410p. figs.,tables. £55. ISBN: 0521465605.

Seven chapters: 1. Introduction ... 3. Physical climatology ... 5. Synoptic-scale weather systems and fronts ... 7. Climate variability and change. Two appendices list weather stations in the Antarctic and on sub-Antarctic islands. References, p.386-404. Index. A comprehensive survey. For academic libraries. *Class No:* 551.58(99)

Research Projects

[1825]

BAKER, D.J. Planet earth: the view from space. Cambridge, Mass., Harvard University Press, 1990. 194p. illus. $26. ISBN: 0674670702.

A survey of international research projects to predict global climate changes. Focuses mainly on *Mission to Planet Earth*, the US long-range study of the planet as a whole. Glossary. References. 'Strongly recommended for all libraries whose collections encompass environmental issues' (*New technical books*, May/June 1991, item, 656). *Class No:* 551.58:061:061.62.005

Stratigraphy (Historical Geology)

[1826]

DOTT, R.H., *Jr* **and** **PROTHERO, D. Evolution of the earth.** 5th ed. New York, etc., McGraw-Hill, 1993. 704p. illus., facsims., diagrs., tables, maps. $62.50 ISBN: 0070745552.

First published 1971.

17 chapters (nearly double number in previous ed.) including: The numerical dating of the earth; Earliest Paleozoic history; Pleistocene glaciation and the advent of humans. Glossary. Index. Two appendices: 1. The classification and relationships of life - 2. English equivalents of metric measures. *Class No:* 551.7

[1827]

Geologic time scale 1989. Harland, W.B., *and others.* Cambridge, Cambridge University Press, 1990. xvi,263p. figs., tables. £25. ISBN: 0521383617.

Revised edition of *A geologic time scale 1982*.

7 sections: 1. Introduction - 2. The chronometric (numerical) scale - 3. The chronostratic scale - 4. Isotopic methods, dates, precision and database - 5. Chronometric calibration of stage boundaries - 6. The magnetostratigraphic time scale - 7. Geologic events and the time scale. 6 appendices, *e.g.* 2. Recommended three-character abbreviations for chronostratic names with alternative symbols. References and selected bibliography, p.223-46. General index, p.243-48. Stratigraphic index, p.249-63. *Class No:* 551.7

[1828]

International stratigraphic guide: a guide to stratigraphic classification, terminology and procedure. Hedberg, H.D., *ed.* New York, etc., Wiley, 1976. xvii, 200p. illus. $32.50. ISBN: 0471367435.

Prepared by the International Subcommission on Stratigraphic Classification of IUGS Commission on Stratigraphy.

8 chapters, - introduction; principles, definitions and procedures; stratotypes; lithostratigraphic units; biostratigraphic units; chronostratigraphic units; relation between different units. Bibliography. Standard work on stratigraphic nomenclature. *Class No:* 551.7

[1829]

Lexique stratigraphique international. Publié sur l'initiative de la Commission de Stratigraphie du Congrès Geologique International. Paris, Centre National de la Recherche Scientifique, 1956-77. 8v., each in fascicules (*c.*17,000p.). 'Nouvelle Serie', Pergamon Press, 1983- .

1. *Europe.*
2. *URSS.*
3. *Asie.*
4. *Afrique.*
5. *Amérique latine.*
6. *Océanie.*
7. *Amérique du nord.*
8. *Termes stratigraphiques majeurs.* 1963-77.

Contributions by *c.*100 specialists. Each country fascicule (*e.g.* v.4. fasc. 96: *Iran.* 1972. 376p.) has a detailed description of stratigraphic formations (A-Z), followed by a list of references, a stratigraphic index and folding maps. The dictionary of stratigraphic terms (v.8) is particularly helpful. A standard source of reference, now continued in a new series from 1983. No.1 (West Africa, geological introduction and stratigraphic terms, 396p) ' cannot be regarded as a second edition of the previous volume as it presents a complete summary of the geology of West Africa as up to date as possible' (*Preface*). *Class No:* 551.7

Quaternary

[1830]

CATT, J.A. Soils and Quaternary geology: a handbook for field scientists. Oxford, Clarendon Press, 1986. x, 267p. illus., diagrs., tables. £55. (*Monographs on soil and resource surveys, no.11.*) ISBN: 0198545681.

7 well-documented and illustrated sections (*e.g.* Climatic change during the Quaternary; Processes of erosion and disturbance during the Quaternary; Stratigraphic nomenclature and classification; Soil formation during the Quaternary; Effects of the Quaternary on soils & present land surfaces). Bibliography, p.233-61. Assumes some prior knowledge of soils, although is not an introduction to soil science but to Quaternary geology. *Class No:* 551.79

Petrology

[1831]

Dictionary of petrology. Tomkeieff, S.I., *and others.* New York, etc., Wiley, 1983. x, 680p. tables. $250. ISBN: 0471101591.

Definitions (Aa lava ... Zwiller rock) are followed by reference[s] to first or early use, as well as any change in meaning or usage; actual derivation; reference to synoptic table. Synoptic tables regroup the terms into different subject areas of petrology. Index to synoptic tables. *Class No:* 552

[1832]

The Encyclopedia of igneous and metamorphic petrology. Bowes, D.R., *ed.* New York, Van Nostrand Reinhold, 1989. xviii,666p. illus., figs., graphs. $125.95. (*Encyclopedia of earth sciences.*) ISBN: 0442206232.

Important alphabetically-arranged reference work aimed at petrologists working with igneous and metamorphic rocks. Rock nomenclature listed (e.g. granite ... granulite, etc), with extensive bibliographical and cross-references. Over 100 contributors from 18 countries. Many illustrations, graphs, and charts. Author and subject indexes. *Class No:* 552

[1833]

Zentralblatt für Mineralogie. Teil 2. Petrographie, Technische Mineralogie, Geochemie und Lagerstättenkunde. Stuttgart, E. Schweizerbart'sche Verlagsbuchhandlung, 1950-. 13pa. $349; DM6,050. ISSN: 05147123.

About 1,200 abstracts per issue, with profuse cross-references. Coverage: rocks, technical aspects of mineralogy, geochemical and mineral deposits. Closely classified entries. Annual author and subject-geographical index. *Class No:* 552

Rocks

Handbooks & Manuals

[1834]

DEER, W.A. Rock-forming minerals. 2nd ed. Harlow, Essex, Longman Group, 1978-. illus. (incl. col.), diagrs., graphs, tables.

First published 1963.

1A. *Orthosilicates.* 2nd ed. 1982. 936p. £85.

1B. *Disilicates and ring silicates.* 2nd ed. 1986. £91.

2A. *Chain silicates.* 1978. 668p. £34.

3. *Sheet silicates.*

4. *Framework silicates.*

5. *Non-silicates.* 1996. 383p.

V.2A: *Chain silicates* (2nd ed. 1978. [viii], 668p.) is well sectionalized and documented (*e.g.* Non-pyroxenes: 9 sections, Wollastonite ... Serondibite). Non-analytical index. Primary aim of the volumes: 'to provide a work of reference useful to advanced students and research workers in the geological sciences'. (*Preface to first edition*). *Class No: 552.1/.4(035)*

[1835]

The Macdonald encyclopedia of rocks and minerals. London & Sydney, Macdonald, 1983. 608p. illus. (incl. col.). £10.99. ISBN: 0356091473.

First published by Mondadori (Milan), 1977.

Part 1: Minerals (text facing col. illus. on right), nos.7-276 (*e.g.* silicates, nos.157-274) - Part 2: Rocks, nos.277-377 (*e.g.* Igneous rocks, nos.277-323). A lengthy introduction (p.7-83; p.43-39) precedes each part. Symbols indicate grade of rarity (very rare; rare; common; very common). Over 1,000 col. illus. Index of entries, p.594-604. Small format. A remarkably cheap compendium. *Class No: 552.1/.4(035)*

[1836]

POUGH, F.H. A Field guide to rocks and minerals. 5th ed. Boston, Mass., Houghton Mifflin, 1996. xv,396p. illus. (incl. col.), diagrs. (*Peterson field guide series, 7.*) ISBN: 0395240476.

First published 1953; 4th ed., 1976.

Part 1: An introduction to the study of rocks and minerals (collection; locations; physical properties of minerals; crystal classifications; chemical classification of minerals; texts; techniques and tips) - Part 2: Mineral descriptions. Uranium ores. Glossary. Annotated bibliography. Detailed index. A practical book, designed for the amateur. *Class No: 552.1/.4(035)*

Dictionaries

[1837]

The Collector's encyclopedia of rocks and minerals. Deeson, A.F.L., *ed.* Newton Abbot, David and Charles, 1973. 288p. illus., charts.

Well over 2,000 different types (AA or Aphrolith ... Zussmanite). Data include composition, physical properties, distinguishing characteristics, methods of identification, environment, variety. 1,000 small col. illus. 'Designed primarily to assist the amateur collector, whether he is a collector already or somewhere along the line' (*Introduction*). *Class No: 552.1/.4(038)*

[1838]

MITCHELL, R.S. Dictionary of rocks. New York, Van Nostrand Reinhold, 1985. xi, 228p. illus. (incl. col.). $43.95. ISBN: 0442263287.

Has *c.*5,000 definitions, categorized. Appended glossary, p.219-28. Recent igneous-rock definitions published by the International Union of Geological Sciences are included. Claims to be 'the first dictionary in the English language devoted exclusively to the names of rocks' (*Preface*). A fitting companion to the earlier book, *Mineral names: what do they mean?*, by R.S. Mitchell, with J.R. Henry (Van Nostrand Reinhold, 1979). *Class No: 552.1/.4(038)*

Reviews & Abstracts

[1839]

Geomechanics abstracts. Norwich, Elsevier Science, 1997-. 6pa. Dfl.1,730;$419. ISSN: 13651617.

Formerly published in *International journal of rock mechanics and mining sciences & geomechanics abstracts* (1964-97).

Over 2,000 abstracts pa. Sections: Geology - Hydrogeology - Properties of rocks and soils - *In situ* stress - Site investigation and field observation - Analysis techniques and design methods - Rock breakage and excavation - Rock and soil reinforcement and support - Surface structures - Underground excavations - Subjects peripheral to geomechanics (*e.g.* Snow and ice mechanics). Online since 1977 via QUESTEL-ORBIT. *Class No: 552.1/.4(048)*

Tables & Data Books

[1840]

CRC handbook of physical properties of rocks. Carmichael, R.S., *ed.* Boca Raton, Florida, CRC Press, 1982-84. 3v. (1089p.). tables, graphs. $129.95, v. 1; $119, v. 2; $110, v. 3. ISBN: 0849302269, v.1; 0849302277, v.2; 0849302285, v.3.

16 contributors. V.1: Mineral composition of rocks. Electrical and spectroscopic properties of rocks and minerals - V.2: Seismic velocities. Magnetic and engineering properties of rocks and minerals - V.3 Density of rocks and minerals. Elastic constants of minerals. Inelastic properties of rocks and minerals: strength and sheology. Radioactivity properties of minerals and rocks. Seismic attenuation. All chapters have appended bibliography. Each volume carries an index. 'The intent is to bridge the gap between individual reports with only specific limited data, and massive assemblies of data which are uncritically presented' (*Preface*).

An updated and abridged edition of this work appeared in 1989, *CRC practical handbook of physical properties of rocks and minerals* (741p. CRC Press). *Class No: 552.1/.4(083)*

[1841]

Physical properties of rocks and minerals. Touloukian, S., *and others.* New York, etc., McGraw-Hill, 1981 (reprinted New York, Hemisphere, 1989). xx, 548p. diagrs., graphs, tables. $112. (*CINDAS data series on material properties, Group 2, v.2/2.*) ISBN: 0891168834.

31 contributors. 13 chapters (most of them with bibliographies appended). Chapters 3-12, on the physical, mechanical, electrical, magnetic and thermophysical properties of rocks. Chapter 13: Heat flow in the earth's crust. Detailed table of contents rather than an index. Emphasis is on data useful to geothermal applications. *Class No: 552.1/.4(083)*

[1842]

Rock physics and phase relations: a handbook of physical constants. Ahrens, T.J., *ed.* Washington, D.C., American Geophysical Union, 1995. vii,236p. diagrs., charts. $50. (*AGU reference shelf, 3.*) ISBN: 0875908535.

V.3 of a series of three publications expanding and revising *Handbook of physical constants*, edited by S. Clark (Geological Society of America, 1966). Includes chapters and quantitative data on soils, sediments, and rheology. Many charts, diagrams, and an extensive index and bibliography. *Class No: 552.1/.4(083)*

Great Britain

[1843]

Igneous rocks of the British Isles. Sutherland, D.S., *ed.* New York, etc., Wiley, 1982. 645p. £78.60; $245; $160. ISBN: 0471278106.

37 contributors. 7 sections, reviewing the major occurrences of igneous rocks in Great Britain and Ireland. 'An obligatory purchase for any geological institution library, and will find itself constantly thumbed through by students, teachers and research workers' (*Geological magazine, v.120, July 1983, p.407*). *Class No: 552.1/.4(410)*

America—North

[1844]

The Audubon Society field guide to North American rocks and minerals. Chesterman, C.W. New York, Knopf, 1979. 850p. illus. (col. pl.), diagrs., tables. $17.95. ISBN: 0394502698.

A pocket-sized guide to 232 mineral species and 40 types of rocks, in 4 parts. Pt.1, Minerals and pt.2, Rocks, both include a guide to identification, a visual key, and colour plates 1-702 and 703-94 respectively. Pt.3, Mineral collecting; pt.4, Appendices (Glossary, p.785-97; Bibliography, p.799-801; Rock forming minerals; localities; etc.). Index, p.831-50. *Class No: 552.1/.4(71+73)*

Meteorites

[1845]

BRITISH MUSEUM (NATURAL HISTORY). The Catalogue of meteorites, with special reference to those represented in the collection of the British Museum (Natural History). 4th ed., edited by A.L. Graham, and others. London, British Museum (Natural History), with the Univ. of Arizona Press, Tucson, 1985. 464p. £20. ISBN: 0565009419.

3rd ed., 1966; Appendix, 1977. M.H. Hey was the compiler of the 3rd ed.

Data on each meteorite name; place where found (or place of impact), plus co-ordinates; chemical content (with citations to the original literature); weight; present owner; specimen number (if appropriate). The British Museum (Natural History)'s collection runs to *c.*2,784 meteorites (*Astronomy, v.14 , March 1986, p.72*). A standard work of reference, the definitive list of all well-documented meteorites known worldwide.

Next edition of the *Catalogue* is not until 1992. Meanwhile an updating set of floppy discs is available. *Class No: 552.6*

[1846]

—HUGHES, D.W. 'The History of meteors and meteor showers.' (In *Vistas in astronomy*, v.2, 1982, p.325-45).

Effectively starts with the work of Edward Halley (1686-). 14 chronology-sections extend to 1947. 81 references. *Class No: 552.6*

Economic Geology

[1847]

Bibliography of economic geology. Didcot, Geosystems, 1982-. 6pa. £85; $170. ISSN: 02644126.

Formerly *Geocom bulletin*, 1968-81.

Over 5,000 references pa. Classes 100000-900000, 'arranged by subject according to the economic geology subset of *Geosaurus: Geosystems thesaurus of geoscience,*' in 32 sections (General publications ... Geoscience information). Each issue has subject, locational, stratigraphical, geographical and author indexes. Available online via DIALOG, and on CD-ROM. *Class No: 553*

[1848]

World resources 1998-99. New York, Oxford, Oxford University Press, 1998. 382p. tables, maps. £35. ISBN: 0195214080.

'Eighth biennial issue of the most authoritative report on the global environment brings together ... the latest ideas on a broad spectrum of natural resource issues and suggests strategies for addressing them' (*Publisher's announcement*). Includes data from 157 countries. Also available on CD-ROM. *Class No: 553*

Minerals & Ores

Databases

[1849]

ATHENA: mineralogy. URL: http://un2sg4.unige.ch/athena/mineral/mineral.html

Mainly taken up with two databases - an alphabetically indexed list of minerals and their chemical formulas, plus a systematic list of minerals arranged according to chemical classes. Other pages include tables of synonyms and varietal names for the more common minerals. Good quality photographs, regular updating, and a good attempt at being comprehensive make this site one of the best in this area. *Class No: 553.2/.4(003.4)*

Encyclopaedias

[1850]

Concise encyclopedia of mineral resources. Carr, D.D. *and* Herz, N., *eds.* Oxford, Pergamon Press, 1989. xxiii,426p. diagrs., tables. £80; $145. (*Advances in materials science and engineering, v.8.*) ISBN: 0080347347, UK; 0262031558, US.

Mainly a compilation of articles from the *Encyclopedia of materials science and engineering* (Pergamon Press, 1986), arranged A-Z (Abrasives ... Zirconium and hafnium resources). Larger topics are subdivided, *e.g.* coal: geology; mining; world resources. Short bibliographies are appended to the articles. Subject index. *Class No: 553.2/.4(031)*

Handbooks & Manuals

[1851]

JENSEN, M.L. *and* **BATEMAN, A.M. Economic mineral deposits.** Revised printing of 3rd ed. New York, etc., Wiley, 1981. viii, 593p. illus., diagrs., graphs, maps. ISBN: 0471090433.

First published 1942.

3 parts (29 documented sections): 1. Principles - 2. Processes of formation of mineral deposits - 3. Metallic mineral deposits - 4. Nonmetallic mineral deposits. General references on economic geology, p.579-80. Analytical index, p.581-93. 'Instead of following a classification of mineral deposits, processes of mineral formation and concentration are emphasized' (*Preface*). *Class No: 553.2/.4(035)*

Tables & Data Books

[1852]

CRIDDLE, A.J. *and* **STANLEY, C.J. Quantitative data file for ore minerals.** 3rd ed. London, Chapman & Hall, 1993. lxiv, 635p. ISBN: 041246750x.

Contents: Introduction; Historical background ... keys for identification; bibliography (p.xxiii-xxiv); COM wavelength key. Data file, p.1-635 (Acanthite ... Zvyagintsevite), providing chemical formulae, chemical composition, X-ray data, etc. Major increase in size on the second ed., 1986. Produced under the auspices of the Commission on Ore Mineralogy of the International Mineralogical Association. *Class No: 553.2/.4(083)*

[1853]

Mineral physics and crystallography: a handbook of physical constants. Ahrens, T.J., *ed.* Washington, D.C., American Geophysical Union, 1995. vii,354p. diagrs, charts. $65. (*AGU reference shelf, 2.*) ISBN: 0875908527.

V.2 of a series of three publications expanding and revising *Handbook of physical constants*, edited by S. Clark (Geological Society of America, 1966). Contains topical chapters and quantitative data on crystal structure and properties of minerals. Many charts, diagrams, and an extensive index and bibliography. *Class No: 553.2/.4(083)*

[1854]

World mineral statistics, 1990-94. Taylor, L.E., *ed.* 18th ed. Nottingham, British Geological Survey, 1995. 305p., tables. £70. ISBN: 0852722680.

Now a single-volume work containing data, in tabular form, on 70 minerals. Includes figures for production and trade, exports and imports, for the period. Only estimated figures are given for many Eastern European countries. *Class No: 553.2/.4(083)*

Maps & Atlases

[1855]

DIXON, C.J. Atlas of economic mineral deposits. London, Chapman & Hall, 1979. 142p. diagrs., tables, maps. £89. ISBN: 0412143801.

5 sections: 1. Deposits in geological environments at the earth's surface - 2. Mineral deposits in sedimentary rocks - 3. Deposits associated with felsic magmatic environment - 4. Mineral deposits in basic and ultrabasic magmatic rocks - 5. The world distribution of mineral deposits. Glossary of mineral names; Units of measurement; Key to stratigraphic names. Index, p.141-2. A valuable aid for the teaching of economic geology. The author, senior lecturer in Mining Geology, Imperial College, London. *Class No: 553.2/.4(084.3)*

Worldwide

[1856]

Overseas geology and mineral resources. London, HMSO, 1950-.

New series in print: nos.41-63 (1973-86). Some of the original series (v.1 1950-71) were entitled *Colonial geology and mineral resources.* The range is now worldwide (*e.g.* no.49: *Outline of the geology and mineral deposits of the Democratic Republic of the Sudan and adjacent areas,* by J.R. Vail. 1978; no.58: *An annotated bibliography of Ecuadorian geology,* by C.R. Bristow. 1981).

The *Overseas memoirs* series (no.1-. 1976-) supplements the above as more specialised monographs (*e.g. The geology of Guadalcanal, Solomon Islands,* by B.D. Hackman. 1980). *Class No: 553.2/.4(100)*

[1857]

RENSBURG, W.C.J., van. Strategic minerals. Englewood Cliffs, N.J., Prentice-Hall, 1986. 2v. (xvi, [1], 552p. + xiii, 362p.). diagrs., graphs, tables. $149.80ea; £160.30ea. ISBN: 0138513872, v.1; 0138514119, v.2.

V.1: *Major mineral exporting regions of the world: issues and strategies* has 6 parts: Canada; Southern Africa; Australia; Latin America; China; The oil-crop economies. Bibliography (6 parts), p.527-42. Detailed index. V.2: *Major mineral consuming regions of the world* covers 4 parts: United States; Japan; Western Europe; USSR. Bibliography (4 parts), p.331-47. Detailed index. p.349-62. A major aim was to analyze 'the effects of government policies, laws and regulations on the availability, reliability, and cost of producing minerals' (*Preface*). *Class No: 553.2/.4(100)*

[1858]

RIDGE, J.D. Annotated bibliographies of mineral deposits in Africa, Asia (exclusive of the USSR) and Australasia. Oxford etc., Pergamon Press, 1976. viii, 546p. maps. $200. ISBN: 0080204597.

Similar treatment to the *Europe* volume. Main parts: Africa (Morocco ... Zambia), Asia (Burma ... Turkey), Australasia (Australia, New Zealand, Papua, New Guinea, New Caledonia, Fiji). Appendix 1: Classification of ore deposits. Index of authors; A-Z list of deposits; Index of deposits (according to metals and minerals produced; age of mineralization; modified Lindgren classification). 'I have tried to include as many references as possible to languages other than English' (*Abstract*). *Class No: 553.2/.4(100)*

[1859]

WOLFE, J.A. Mineral resources: a world review. London, Chapman and Hall, 1984. xv, 293p. ISBN: 0412251906.

Part 1 consists of short essays on various aspects of the mineral industries (*e.g.* exploration). Part 2 includes reports on 21 metals and 18 non-metals. Glossary; briefly annotated bibliography; index. 'This reference tool is designed for those interested in mineral resources and economy but with training in another field' (*New technical books,* November 1985, item 1185). *Class No: 553.2/.4(100)*

Marine Environment

[1860]
EARNEY, F.C.F. **Marine mineral resources.** London and New York,
Routledge, 1990. xxiv,387p. illus., graphs, tables, maps. £65. (*Ocean
management and policy series*.) ISBN: 041502255x.
2 parts: 1. Implications of Law of the Sea negotiations - 2.
Resources of continental shelves (petroleum, construction aggregates,
minerals, etc.). Extensive chapter references; 30p. bibliography.
Class No: 553.2/.4(26)

Europe

[1861]
Mineral deposits of Europe. Dunning, F.W., *and others, eds.* London,
the Institution of Mining and Metallurgy; the Mineralogical Society,
1978-1989. 5v. in 4. £30, v.1; £42, v.2; £65, v.3; £120, v.4/5. ISBN:
0900488441, v.1; 0900488638, v.2; 0900488905, v.3; 1870706072,
v.4/5.
V.1. *Northeast Europe.* 1978. 362p. V.2. *Southeast Europe.* 1982.
304p. V.3. *Central Europe.* 1986. 355p. V.4/5. *Southwest and eastern
Europe, with Iceland.* 1989. 454p.
V.4/5 arranged by country, *e.g.* Spain, Italy. Bibliographies
appended to each chapter. Name and subject indexes. 'Some national
chapters are landmarks, being the first comprehensive descriptions in
English (or any other language) of their ore deposits', (*Foreword*).
Class No: 553.2/.4(4)

[1862]
RIDGE, J.D. **Annotated bibliographies of mineral deposits in Europe.**
Oxford, etc., Pergamon Press, 1984-1989. ISBN: 0080302424, v.1;
0080302432, v.2; 0080240224, set.
Pt.1. *Northern Europe including examples from the USSR in both
Europe and Asia.* 1984. viii,778p. £125. Pt.2. *Western and south
central Europe.* 1989. viii,473p. £76.
Pt.1 covers Ireland; Great Britain; Norway; Sweden; Finland;
Poland; USSR. Pt.2 covers Portugal; Spain; France; Belgium-
Germany-Netherlands; Switzerland; Italy; Iran. References in Pt.1 are
mostly in English, while Pt.2 references are made up of the major
European languages. Pt.2 has only an author index, thus greatly
reducing its usefulness, while Pt.1 has an index to authors; A/Z index
of deposits; index of deposits (according to metals and minerals
produced; according to age of mineralization; according to the
modified Lindgren classification). *Class No:* 553.2/.4(4)

America

[1863]
RIDGE, J.D. **Annotated bibliographies of mineral deposits in the
Western Hemisphere.** Boulder, Colo., Geological Society of America,
1972. xiv, 681p. maps. Supplement, 1974. 8p. $160. (*Geological
Society of America. Memoir* no.131, - revision and expansion of
Memoir no.75, 1958.) ISBN: 083575491x. ISSN: 00107053.
Covers North and South America; arrangement, under country/US
state/Canadian province, is by deposit. For each deposit: minerals
mined; age and position in the Lindgren classification, plus
bibliography and notes. Indexes of authors and deposits (A-Z, by age,
by metals and minerals produced, by Lindgren classification).
Appendices provide a classification of ore deposits, and topics for
consideration. Aimed, like the other two volumes, at the economic
geologist in his study of specific deposits. *Class No:* 553.2/.4(7)

Inorganic Minerals

Salt

[1864]
LEFOND, S.J. **Handbook of world salt resources.** New York, Plenum
Press, 1969. xxiii, 384p. tables, charts, maps.
Concise country data under continents (North America, p.1-136 -
Central America - South America - Europe, p.173-260 - Africa - Asia -
Oceania) on rock salt deposits and solar salt production. Location of
salt mines; output statistics. 'Sources of information' and
'Bibliography' appended to each country entry. Subject index. 76
maps, 162 charts, tables. *Class No:* 553.631

Hydrocarbons

Coal

[1865]
Coal geology and coal technology. Ward, C.R., *ed.* Oxford, Blackwell
Scientific, 1984. [ix], 345p. illus., diagrs., graphs, tables. ISBN:
0867930969.
7 contributors. 9 chapters (1. Chemical analysis and classification of
coal - 3. Coal petrology and petrographic analysis - 4. Coal utilization
- 5. Geology of coal - 6. Coalfield exploration - 7. Coal-mining
geology - 8. Coal properties and marketing - 9. Coal and the

....(contd.)
environment). Appendix: List of national and international standards
for coal and coke analysis and testing. References (authors, A/Z),
p.319-34. Analytical index, p.335-45. *Class No:* 553.94

[1866]
TODD, A.H.J. **Lexicon of terms relating to the assessment and
classification of coal resources.** London, Graham & Trotman, 1982.
136p. tables. £42.95. ISBN: 0860104036.
A dictionary of terms used in 15 countries and in international
organizations. Terms, where necessary, are translated into English.
Appended list of sources. *Class No:* 553.94

Petroleum

[1867]
BEYDOUN, Z.R. **The Middle East regional geology and petroleum
resources.** Beaconsfield, Bucks., Scientific Press, 1988. 292p. diagrs.,
maps. ISBN: 090136021x.
'Geological evolution of the region, overview of main producing
regions and fields, national surveys of producing fields, unproducing
discoveries, and future reserves' (*Books in the earth sciences*, no.43,
April 1985, p.862). 7 folding maps, cross-sections.
Class No: 553.982

[1868]
EARNEY, F.C.F. **Petroleum and hard minerals from the sea.** V.H.
Winston & Sons, and L.E. Arnold, 1980. 291p. illus., diagrs., graphs,
tables, maps. ISBN: 0470270098.
Part 1: The continental margin - Part 2. The deep seabed. Chapter 3:
Offshore petroleum, p.33-61, with 6 maps, 3 graphs, 3 tables, 2
diagrs., 592 references, p.261-81. Analytical index, 283-91.
Worldwide coverage. *Class No:* 553.982

[1869]
Elsevier's oil and gas field dictionary in English/American, French,
Spanish, Italian, Dutch, German and Arabic. Chaballe, L.Y., *and
others.* Amsterdam, etc., Elsevier, 1980. xii, 672p. $200; £128.12.
ISBN: 0444418334.
4,843 English/American base-terms, their synonyms and variants,
with equivalents and indexes in French, Spanish, Italian, Dutch and
German. A supplementary section deals with Arabic terms.
Class No: 553.982

[1870]
—**Russian-English oil-field dictionary.** Stoharov, D.E., *ed.* Oxford, etc.,
Pergamon Press, 1983. 431p.
30,000 entries, terms being drawn from scientific literature
published in the 1970s. Usefully meets a deficiency in the language
coverage of the Elsevier dictionary. *Class No:* 553.982

[1871]
HOBSON, G.D. *and* TIRATSOO, E.N. **Introduction to petroleum
geology.** 2nd ed. Beaconsfield, Scientific Press, 1981. 352p. illus.,
diagrs., charts, tables, maps. £18. ISBN: 0901360120.
10 documented chapters: 1. The nature of petroleum - 2. The origin
of petroleum - 3. The migration of petroleum - 4. The nomenclature of
petroleum - 5. Surface exploration for petroleum - 6. Subsurface ... 7.
Formation evaluation - 11. Delineation of the reservoir - 9. Petroleum
in space and time (p.269-307; 120 references) - 10. Petroleum
production and units. Statistics, to 1979. 50 tables; nearly 100 figures.
Analytical index, p.343-52. *Class No:* 553.982

Hydrology

CD-ROM

[1872]
Water resources abstracts. Bethesda, Cambridge Scientific Abstracts,
1993-. 4pa. £917. ISSN: 0037136x.
Formerly in print format as *Selected water resources abstracts*,
1968-1992.
CD-ROM with 250,000 records covering reports on water research
from academic organizations, research institutes, government agencies,
and independent bodies. Available online via DIALOG and on the
Internet. *Class No:* 556(003.40)

Bibliographies

[1873]
WATER RESOURCES CENTER ARCHIVES. University of
California. **Dictionary catalog. [Water Resources Center Archives].**
Boston, Mass., G.K. Hall, 1970. 5v. (3373p.). Supplements, 1-.
1971-. $545, set; $285, supp. 6. ISBN: 0816108846, set;
0816102449, supp. (6th. 1978).
The main catalogue has 97,000 photolithographically reproduced
catalogue-card entries. Coverage embraces water quality, pollution and
reclamation, waste disposal, water as a natural source and its uses,
flood control, sediment transport and coastal engineering.
Class No: 556(01)

Handbooks & Manuals

[1874]

UNITED NATIONS. Educational, Scientific and Cultural Organization. **Ground-water studies: an international guide for research and practice.** Brown, R.H., *and others, eds.* Paris, UNESCO, 1972-. (*Studies and reports in hydrology, 7.*)

The original 8 chapters (now o.p.) have been added to by 4 supplements (to 1984; only supp. 3 (1979. $12) in print), including further chapters (9,10,14,15). *Class No:* 556(035)

Dictionaries

Polyglot

[1875]

Elsevier's dictionary of environmental hydrogeology. Pfannkuch, H.O., *comp.* Amsterdam, Elsevier, 1990. 332p. £85.93. ISBN: 0444872698.

Previously published, 1969, as *Elsevier's dictionary of hydrogeology in three languages.*

Defines 5,422 terms in English, with German and French equivalents and indexes. Coverage extends beyond ground water and includes interdisciplinary terms from hydro-meteorology, water resources planning, water quality control, etc.

Class No: 556(038)=00

[1876]

Hydrographic dictionary. 3rd ed. Monaco, International Hydrographic Bureau, 1974. 370p.

2nd ed. 1951(259p.).

About 1,000 terms in each of 12 languages. - English, French, Danish, Dutch, Portuguese, Spanish, Argentine, Uruguayan, Italian, Norwegian, Swedish, German. The left-hand page gives numbered keywords in English and French, with definitions; the right-hand page gives equivalents in the other 10 languages. 11 language indexes.

Class No: 556(038)=00

[1877]

TUIN, J.D. van der. Elsevier's dictionary of hydrology and water quality management. Amsterdam, Elsevier, 1991. xiv,528p. $214.50. ISBN: 0444886729.

5,928 terms in English dealing with the freshwater environment. Equivalents in French, Spanish, Dutch, and German.

Class No: 556(038)=00

[1878]

Vattenordlista. [Glossary of water.] Stockholm, Tekniska Nomenklaturcentralen, 1968-74. ISBN: 9171960414.

1. *Hybrobiologiska termer.* 1968. 84p. 2. *Geologiska, hydrologiska, meteorologiska termer.* 1970. 80p. 3. *Vattenordlistregister.* 1974. 132p.

1,410 Swedish terms and definitions, in all, with equivalent terms in English, French, German and Finnish. Notes often contain 'cross-references to cognate and/or contrasting terms listed elsewhere in the glossary' (*The Incorporated linguist,* v.10(3), July 1971, p.91, on v.1). *Class No:* 556(038)=00

[1879]

WORLD METEOROLOGICAL ORGANIZATION. International glossary of hydrology. 2nd ed. Paris, UNESCO, 1994. 422p. tables. £25. (*WMO/OMN/BMO no.385.*) ISBN: 9230027456.

First published 1974.

1,418 English-base terms, with Russian, French and Spanish equivalents (identified by serial numbers), plus UDC numbers. Subject scope: hydrology, surface water, hydrometeorology, soil moisture, hydraulics, water resources management. List of abbreviations of sources precedes. Appendix B: symbols and units.

Class No: 556(038)=00

English

[1880]

VEATCH, J.O. *and* **HUMPHREYS, C.R. Water and water use terminology.** Kaukauna, Wisconsin, Thomas Printing and Publishing, 1966. xvi, 375, [v]p. illus.

About 1,500 definitions in terms relating to lakes, surface water and wetlands, with references appended. Numerous cross-references. Good and plentiful illus. General bibliography of 7 items.

Class No: 556(038)=20

Scandinavian

[1881]

Nordic glossary of hydrology: English - Danish - Finnish - Icelandic - Norwegian - Swedish, with definitions in English. Johansson, I., *ed.* Stockholm, Almqvist, 1984. 224p. £22.50. ISBN: 9122006923.

Class No: 556(038)=395

Russian

[1882]

DEEV, G.N. *and* **LOSEV, K.S. Anglo-russkiĭ gidrologicheskiĭ slovar'.** Moscow, Izdat. 'Sovetskaya Entsiklopediya', 1966. 299p. illus., diagrs.

14,000 English hydrological terms, with Russian equivalents, Russian word index, p.267-99. *Class No:* 556(038)=82

Reviews & Abstracts

[1883]

Aqualine abstracts. Swindon, WRc plc, 1927-. Monthly. £620 pa.; £1,900 print form and CD-ROM. ISSN: 07482531.

Formerly *WRC information* (1974-84), incorporating *Water pollution abstracts,* 1949-73.

About 6,000 abstracts pa. 8 sections: 1. Water resources and supplies - 2. Water quality - 3. Monitoring and analysis of water and wastes - 4. Water treatment - 5. Underground services and water use - 6. Sewage - 7. Industrial effluents - 8. Effects of pollution (sewage; heated discharges; metals; pesticides; fossil fuels; radio-activity). Annual author, subject and KWOC indexes.

Available online via Questel/ORBIT and ESA-IRS and on CD-ROM quarterly. *Class No:* 556(048)

Tables & Data Books

[1884]

The Water encyclopedia. Leeden, F. van der, *and others, eds.* 2nd ed. Chelsea, Mich., Lewis Publishers, 1990. xii,808p. illus., tables, maps. $149.95. (*Geraghty and Miller groundwater series.*) ISBN: 0873711203.

First published 1970.

Substantially revised and expanded from previous ed. More than 700 tables, diagrams, and charts. 11 chapters (*e.g.* 'Climate'; 'Surface and ground water'; 'Water management'). Subject index. US-slanted.

Class No: 556(083)

Histories

[1885]

BISWAS, A.K. History of hydrology. Amsterdam, etc., North-Holland Publishing Co., 1970. xxi, 336p. ISBN: 0720480183.

Documented chapters (Hydrology prior to 600 BC ... Rain gauges in the 17th, 18th and 19th centuries). Subject index. The first comprehensive account up to the end of the 19th century, although more space could have been devoted to the period during the 19th century when the first countrywide instrument networks were being installed (*Nature,* v.228, 12 September 1970, p.1119).

Class No: 556(091)

Europe

[1886]

International hydrogeological map of Europe. Paris, UNESCO, with Bundesanstalt für Geowissenschaften und Rohstoffe, Hanover, 1970-. Maps.

49 sheets, in up to 55 colours, plus 1 general sheet. Legend in English, French and German, but notes in English only. Sheet size: 63 x 63cm. *Class No:* 556(4)

Great Britain

[1887]

Hydrological data United Kingdom: 1994 yearbook: an account of rainfall, river flows, groundwater levels and river quality, January to December 1994. Wallingford, Oxon., Institute of Hydrology, 1995. 176p. tables.

First published 1985. Contains data previously published in the discontinued *Surface water: United Kingdom* and *Groundwater: United Kingdom.*

Contains: scope and sources of information - hydrological review of 1994 - Chichester flood, January 1994 - river flow data - surface water quality data - groundwater level data. Directory of measuring authorities, p.172-4.

Every five years, a catalogue of river flow gauging stations and groundwater level recording sites together with statistical summaries, is published. *Class No:* 556(410)

Rivers & Lakes

Worldwide

[1888]

CZAYA, E. Rivers of the world. Translated from the German by S. Furness. Cambridge, University Press, 1983. 248p. illus. (incl. col.), diagrs., tables, maps. $22.95. ISBN: 0521258359.

8 chapters: 1. Arteries of the continents - 2. Rivers shape their

....(contd.)

valley - 3. Cataclysmic events in river history - 4. Waterfalls and rapids - 5. Pluvial lakes - 6. Inland drainage - 7. Lowland rivers and river mouths - 8. Rivers in harness. Bibliography, p.233-5 (authors, A-Z). Detailed, non-analytical index, p.236-48. 192 illus. A mass of factual information, clearly presented. *Class No:* 556.5(100)

[1889]

Discharge of selected rivers of the world. Paris, UNESCO, 1969-86. 3v. in 6. £3.75, v.3, pt.3; £8.25, v.3, pt.4. (*Studies and reports in hydrology, 5.*)

1. *General and regime characteristics of stations selected.* 1969. 70p. 2. *Monthly and annual discharges recorded at various selected stations [up to 1964].* 3. *Mean monthly and extreme discharges.* 4 pts. [covering 1965-79].

Title and text in English, French, Spanish and Russian. *Class No:* 556.5(100)

[1890]

GRESSWELL, R.K. *and* **HUXLEY, A. Standard encyclopedia of the world's rivers and lakes.** London, Weidenfeld & Nicolson, 1962. 384p. illus. (pl.), maps.

40 contributors. Main section consists of nearly 500 entries, each of *c.*200 words. Supported by 11 location maps, and extensive gazetteer (with data on rivers, etc., length, course, etc.) and an index. Well illustrated; 16 colour plates. 'The maps let the book down' (*Geographical journal,* v.12(3), September 1966, p.425): distance scales and projections are not given. *Class No:* 556.5(100)

[1891]

Rand McNally encyclopedia of world rivers. Chicago, Ill., Rand McNally, 1980. 352p. illus. (incl. col.), maps. ISBN: 0528810680.

Data on 1,750 rivers, continent by continent. Profiles state source, length, tributaries, natural features, dams, hydroelectric power stations, industrial activity, agriculture, fauna and flora, history, etc. Major rivers are treated in depth. No index or bibliographies. *Class No:* 556.5(100)

Great Britain

[1892]

British rivers. Lewin, J., *ed.* London, Allen & Unwin, 1981. [x], 216p. illus., diagrs., graphs, tables, maps. ISBN: 0045510474.

7 contributors. 6 chapters: 1. River systems and river regimes - 2. Contemporary erosion and sedimentation - 3. Mountain streams - 4. Channel forms and channel changes - 5. Water quality - 6. River management. References, p.196-211. Analytical index. 'This book is intended for a wide readership' (*Preface*). *Class No:* 556.5(410)

[1893]

—**MUIR, R.** *and* **MUIR, N. The National Trust rivers of Britain.** Exeter, Devon, Webb & Dower, in association with Michael Joseph, London. 1986. 225p. illus., (incl. col.). ISBN: 0863501109.

11 sections (3. Rivers of the wetlands ... 5. Rivers in service - 6. To get to the other side: bridges; fords and ferries ... 10. Rivers in danger - 11. River management - which way forward). Includes notes on flora and fauna, canals, boxed information on nature reserves, ports, villages, buildings, etc. Partly analytical index. No bibliography. *Class No:* 556.5(410)

America—North

[1894]

Rolling rivers: an encyclopedia of America's rivers. Bartlett, R.A., *ed.* New York, etc., McGraw-Hill, 1984. 398p. illus. $36.50. ISBN: 0070039100.

Signed, documented essays on 117 major North American rivers, with their tributaries and other rivers. Data head each essay: origin, length, geologic history, discovery and settlement, events in its history, dams, reservoirs, agricultural products and industries, etc. Essays fall into 6 geographical sections. The collection lacks maps and the index fails to include tributaries of most rivers, events, and the like 'There is no other work that covers American rivers at a comparable level of detail' (*RQ,* v.24(1), Fall 1984, p.109-110). *Class No:* 556.5(71+73)

56 Palaeontology (Fossils)

Palaeontology

Bibliographies

[1895]

LUM, A. 'Palaeontology'. in *Information sources in the earth sciences*, edited by D.N. Wood *and others*. 2nd ed. London, Bowker-Saur, 1989. p.236-273.

Readable and authoritative review of major works in the subject. Headings, after general historical survey, are: Taxonomy - Palaeontological texts (including techniques, and popular up to advanced textbooks) - Palaeoecology & palaeoclimatology - Evolution & the fossil record - Micropalaeontology - Palynology - Palaeobotany - Invertebrate palaeontology - Vertebrate palaeontology (including brief review of popular books on dinosaurs) - Abstracting & indexing services. Appendix lists 132 currently published palaeontological periodicals. The author is on the staff of the Palaeontology library at the British Museum (Natural History). *Class No: 560(01)*

Encyclopaedias

[1896]

ARDUINI, P. *and* TERUZZI, G. The Macdonald encyclopedia of fossils. London, Macdonald, 1986. 317, [3]p. col. illus., diagrs. £9.95. ISBN: 035612367x.

Has text and illus. on 260 fossils; Plants, entries 1-16; invertebrate fossils, 17-186; vertebrate fossils, 187-260. Text, including symbols for geological eras and habitats, faces text. Glossary, p.307-17. Index. A neat, small-format guide. *Class No: 560(031)*

[1897]

The Encyclopedia of palaeontology. Fairbridge, R.W. *and* Jablonski, D., *eds*. Stroudsburg, Pa., Dowden, Hutchinson and Ross, 1979. xii, [1], 886p. illus., tables, maps. (*Encyclopedia of earth sciences, v.7*). ISBN: 0879331852.

122 contributors. Most of the signed articles carry bibliographies. 'Vertebrate palaeontology' (p.843-51) has sections: 'Preservation of vertebrate fossils'; 'Fossil vertebrates and organic evolution'; 33 references; 19 cross-references. 'The entries are written at several conceptual levels, from the most basic and inclusive articles such as *Invertebrate Paleontology* and *Evolution*, to specialized, technical treatments such as *Morphology*, *Constructional* and *Taxonomy, Numerical*' (*Preface*). The index, partly analytical, has *c*.5,000 entries. According to *Bulletin des bibliothèques de France* (July 1981, entry 909), the *Encyclopedia* almost entirely ignores the work done in any language other than English. Thus, Lamarck is omitted in the 'History of palaeontology before Darwin' article. *Class No: 560(031)*

[1898]

STEEL, R. *and* HARVEY, A.P. The Encyclopedia of prehistoric life. London, Mitchell Beazley, 1979. 218p. illus., charts. ISBN: 0070609209.

Has 23 contributors (13 of them at the British Museum (Natural History)). The initialled articles - 'Academia Sinica' to 'Zone fossils' - include biographies but lack bibliographies, although a grouped bibliography appears on p.213. Glossary, p.214-5; index (in tiny print), p.216-8. Careful, captioned line-drawings (nearly 300). 14p. of coloured evolutionary charts (Invertebrates ... Primates). An attractively-produced, popular treatment. *Class No: 560(031)*

Handbooks & Manuals

[1899]

CROUCHER, R. *and* WOOLLEY, A.R. Fossils, minerals and rocks: collection and preservation. London, British Museum (Natural History), with Cambridge Univ. Press, 1982. 60p. illus., diagrs. £4.25. ISBN: 0521247365.

Devotes p.27-52 to fossil collection and preservation. The other short sections concern field equipment, information sources (guides and memoirs; journals: books; maps), minerals and rocks. Appended: 'Further reading and sources of reference'; 'Materials, manufacturers and suppliers'; 'Addresses'. Analytical index. *Class No: 560(035)*

[1900]

FORTEY, R. Fossils: the key to the past. 2nd ed. London, British Museum (Natural History), 1991. 187p. illus. (incl. col.). £12.95. ISBN: 0565011073.

First published 1982.

Provides a lively yet authoritative, fully-illustrated survey for the amateur palaeontologist. The 10 chapters include 'How to recognise fossils', 'Making a collection' (with notes on collecting, preserving and identifying), and a new chapter recounting the identification of a new dinosaur from recently-discovered fossil remains. 'In this book I have tried to show how fossils, far from being mere dry bones, can be used to reconstruct the history of the Earth' (*Preface*). *Class No: 560(035)*

[1901]

Fossils of the world: a comprehensive, practical guide to collecting and studying fossils. Turek, V., *and others*. London, Hamlyn, 1988. 495p. illus. (col.). ISBN: 0600550141.

Consists mainly (p.36-483) of colour illustrations of fossils, arranged into plant, protista, and animal, kingdoms. The last is sub-divided into porifera, archaeocyatha, coelenterata, bryozoa, brachiopoda, mollusca, annelida, arthropoda, echinodermata, hermichordata, and chordata. Nearly all the specimens are of central European origin, and the picture quality is excellent. The book's section on collecting fossils is perhaps less valuable (p.484-6) and there is a 1-page bibliography. *Class No: 560(035)*

[1902]

KUMMEL, B. *and* RAUP, D. Handbook of palaeontological techniques. Prepared under the auspices of the Palaeontological Society. San Francisco & London, W.H. Freeman, 1965. xiii, 852p.

80 contributors. 5 parts: 1. General procedures and techniques applicable to major fossil groups - 2. Description of specific techniques - 3. Techniques in palynology - 4. Bibliography on palaeontological techniques (collecting; labeling and storage; preservation ...) - 5. Compilation of bibliographies (p.768-832; 739 unannotated entries). *Class No: 560(035)*

[1903]

LAMBERT, D. *and* THE DIAGRAM GROUP. The Cambridge field guide to prehistoric life. Cambridge, University Press, 1985. 256p. illus., diagrs. £27.95.

'A concise key to prehistoric animals, plants and other organisms' (*Foreword*). 10 chapters: 1. Fossil clues to prehistoric life - 2. Fossil plants - 3. Fossil invertebrates - 4. Fossil fishes - 5. Fossil amphibians - 6. Fossil reptiles - 7. Fossil birds - 8. Fossil mammals - 9. Records in the rocks - 10. Fossil hunting. 'Further reading', by chapters, p.248; index, p.249-56. Marginal 'field guide' illus.; a neat production. Uses both popular and scientific terms and a balanced account aimed at the enquiring eleven-year old as well as the budding scientist. *Class No: 560(035)*

[1904]

MACFALL, R.D. *and* WOLLIN, J.C. Fossils for amateurs: a handbook for collectors. Rev. ed. New York, Van Nostrand Reinhold, 1983. 374p. illus., maps. $24.95; $19.95. ISBN: 0442263481.

First published 1972.

Expansion and updating of the 1972 ed. with a lengthy appended list of books and magazines, and an adequate index. Relates fossils to other aspects of geology. 'Should be in every fossil collector's library' (*Technical book review index*, v.50(6), June 1984. p.207). *Class No: 560(035)*

[1905]

NEAVERSON, E. Stratigraphical palaeontology: a study of ancient life-provinces. 2nd ed., rev. and enl. Oxford, Clarendon Press, 1955. xii, 806p. illus. (incl. pl.).

First published 1928.

The introduction notes some of the more important works, and the 18 chapters each have an evaluated reading list appended. 90 illus., apart from 18 plates. Palaeontological, stratigraphical and geographical indexes, p.741-806. A standard work. *Class No: 560(035)*

[1906]

NIELD, E.W. *and* TUCKER, V.C.T. Palaeontology: an introduction. Oxford, Pergamon Press, 1985. xx, 178p. illus., diagrs. £28. ISBN: 0080238548.

12 chapters surveying the field (*e.g.* 2. The origin of life and the earliest fossils ... 11. Vascular plants - 12. The meaning of fossils) with 'Suggested further reading', plus brief evaluative notes. Author, systematic and non-analytical subject indexes. Fine line-drawings, keyed/captioned, are a feature. Quarto-format. Designed for students embarking upon a study of palaeontology. *Class No: 560(035)*

[1907]

PIVETEAU, J. Traité de paléontologie; publié sous la direction de J. Piveteau. Paris, Masson, 1952-69. 7v. in 10, illus., diagrs., tables.

1. *Les stades inférieurs du règne animal. Généralités. Protistes. Spongiaires. Coelentérés. Bryozoaires.* 1952. 782p. FFr653.
2. *Problèmes d'adaptation et de phylogenèse. Brachiopodes. Chétognathes. Annélides. Mollusques.* 1952. 790p. FFr653.
3. *Les formes ultimes d'invertébrés: morphologie et évolution. Onychophores. Anthropodes. Échinodermes. Stomochordés.* 1953. 500p. FFr848.
4. *Agnathes. Placodermes, etc.* 1964-69. 3pts. (pts.1-2. FFr1,032).
5. *La sortie des eaux. Naissance de la tétrapodie, L'exubérance de la végétative. La conquête de l'air. Amphibiens. Reptiles. Oiseaux.* 1955. 114p. FFr830.
6. *L'originie des mammifères et les aspects fondamentaux de leur évolution. Mammifères (évolution).* 1958-61. 2v. FFr1,553.
7. *Vers la forme humaine. Le problème biologique de l'homme. Les époques de l'intelligence. Primates. Paléontologie humaine.* 1957.

Each chapter, by a specialist, covers systematic and biological aspects of fossil groups, their ecology and the evolution of species. Vertebrates, especially mammals and humans, are given particular attention. An important and comprehensive work of reference. *Class No:* 560(035)

[1908]

STEARN, C.W. *and* **CARROLL, R.L. Paleontology: the record of life.** New York, Wiley, 1989. 453p. illus. £52. ISBN: 0471845280.

Arranged into 3 parts: 1. Introduction - 2. The fossil record - 3. Lessons from the record. Well illustrated with photographs and line drawings, the book has a North American bias (the authors are Canadian) and 'the book is designed as a textbook for a first course in paleontology ... for a typical student who has a general science education up to college level but little knowledge of geology'. Suggested reading listed after each chapter, and an index, p.433-53. *Class No:* 560(035)

Reviews & Abstracts

[1909]

Geographical abstracts. Physical geography. Norwich, Elsevier; Geo Abstracts, 1989-. fl.1,239; $1,378. ISSN: 09540504.

Formerly *Geo abstracts. A. Landforms and the Quaternary,* 1966-85 and *Geographical abstracts. A. Landforms and the Quaternary,* 1986-88. Merged with other titles in the series - B. *Climatology and hydrology;* E. *Sedimentology;* G. *Remote sensing, photogrammetry and cartography.* Continues *Geological abstracts: palaeontology and stratigraphy.*

This journal, which abstracts 'over 1,000 leading geographical journals, plus books, conference proceedings, reports and theses' (*Editorial introduction*) includes in its subject coverage such relevant headings as Palaeogeography; Sedimentation and tectonics; Systematic palaeoecology; Quaternary. Mainly author abstracts listed, up to 300 words each. 12 issues pa., each with regional index, plus separately published index issue arranged by subject, authors, and geographical areas. Online GEOBASE (*q.v.*), via DIALOG, and on CD-ROM. *Class No:* 560(048)

[1910]

Zentralblatt für Geologie und Paläontologie. Teil 2: Paläontologie. Stuttgart, E. Schweizerbart'sche Verlagshandlung, 1950-. 7pa. Price varies. ISSN: 00444189.

Formerly *Zentralblatt für Geologie und Paläontologie. Teil 2: Historische Geologie und Paläontologie.*

Contains *c.*900 abstracts pa. 3 main sections: Allgemeine Paläontologie - Paläozoologie (Evertebrata; Vertebrata) - Paläobotanik. Each bimonthly issue carries one or more review articles and a subject index. Annual author index. *Class No:* 560(048)

[1911]

The Zoological record, being the record of zoological literature relating to the year... York, BIOSIS, UK, and London, Zoological Society, 1865 (covering 1864)-. v.1-. 27 annual parts. $3,250. ISSN: 01443607.

Includes palaeontology in its coverage, each of the annual parts carrying a palaeontological index.

Described as 'the most important life science database for palaeontology' (A. Lum, in D.N. Wood's *Information sources in the earth sciences* (2nd ed. 1989), p.269). Online via DIALOG (1978-) and on CD-ROM (1985-). *Class No:* 560(048)

Tables & Data Books

[1912]

The Fossil record 2. Benton, M.J., *ed.* London, Chapman and Hall, 1993. 845p. $149.95. ISBN: 0412393808.

Revised version of *The Fossil record: a symposium with documentation,* edited by W.B. Harlan *and others,* 1967.).

Covers every recognized family of organisms. 45 chapters, each giving data on a major group of organisms and organized

....(contd.)

taxonomically down to between order and superfamily, followed by family (arranged alphabetically within each higher taxon). Short bibliography appended to each chapter. For specialist and postgraduate reference. *Class No:* 560(083)

[1913]

Fossilium catalogus. Berlin, W. Junk, 1913/14-(with reprints). 2 series.
1. *Animalia.* Edited by F. Frech, and others. 1913-. (pt.127. 1983).
2. *Plantae.* Edited by W.J. Jongmans, and others. 1914-; from pt.81, 1988, published by Kugler Publications, Amsterdam. (pt.91. 1985).

Each of the two series comprises catalogues by specialists on individual fossil orders or genera (*e.g. Bryozoa (genera),* by R.S. Bassler, *Fossilium catalogus,* series 1, pt.67. 1934), with index and bibliography. Series 1. pt.72, 1938, *Catalogus bio-bibliographies* is a worldwide list of palaeontologists, past and present. 'By far the most comprehensive and most important index to published generic and specific names' (Lum, A. 'Palaeontology'; In Wood, D.N., and others, eds. *Information sources in the earth sciences,* 2nd ed. London, Bowker-Saur, 1989, p.236-73). *Class No:* 560(083)

Maps & Atlases

[1914]

HALLAM, A., *ed.* **Atlas of palaeobiogeography.** Amsterdam, Elsevier, 1973. xii, 531p. illus., maps. $154. ISBN: 0444409750.

47 contributions, by specialists, on distribution of a wide variety of fossil groups during the last 600 million years (*e.g.* Ondovician trilobites; articulate brachiopods; graptolites; corals; conodonts, p.13-58. Jurassic plants, p.329-38; Jurassic and cretaceous dinosaurs, p.339-52). Chapter bibliographies. Index of genera and references. Authoritative; assumes some geological and palaeontological knowledge. *Class No:* 560(084.3)

Histories

[1915]

EDWARDS, W.N. The Early history of palaeontology. London, British Museum (Natural History), 1967. vii, 58p. illus., facsims. £1.50. ISBN: 0565006584.

Based on *Guide to an Exhibition illustrating the early history of palaeontology* (British Museum (Natural History). 1931. Special guide no.8).

Succinct account up to the early 19th century, plus chapters on geological terminology, the rise of museums and the Department of Palaeontology, British Museum (Natural History). Illus. include 4 plates, mainly from early books. *Class No:* 560(091)

Biographies

[1916]

Directory of palaeontologists of the world. Doescher, R.A., *ed.* 5th ed. Washington, International Paleontological Association, 1990. vi,447p. $20. ISBN: 0962257702.

4th ed., 1984, *Directory of paleontologists.*

Arranged A-Z. Data: name; address; telephone number; subject specialties. Taxonomical index; geographic index. Includes China and Russia. *Class No:* 560(092)

[1917]

Palaeontologi. Catalogus bio-bibliographicus. In *Fossilium catalogus.* 1. Animalia. Pars 72. 1938. Lambrecht, K., *and others.* xxii,495p. $40.

Reprinted 1978 as *Paleontologi: a biographical and bibliographical register of paleontologists* (Salem, N.H. Ayer).

'Contains sentence-length biographical notes and references to biographies and memorials of over three thousand palaeontologists and geologists of all countries; it is an important reference work and the point of beginning for biographical searching for non-Americans and even for some Americans' (*Stechert-Hafner book news,* v.18(3), November 1963, p.30). A major source of information, not limited to palaeontologists; includes some geologists. *Class No:* 560(092)

Great Britain

[1918]

BRITISH MUSEUM (NATURAL HISTORY). British Caenozoic fossils (Tertiary and Quaternary). 5th ed. London, British Museum (Natural History), 1975. vi, 132p. illus. (pl.), map. £4.95. ISBN: 0565055402. *Class No:* 560(410)

[1919]

—**BRITISH MUSEUM (NATURAL HISTORY). British Mesozoic fossils.** 6th ed. London, British Museum (Natural History), 1983. xi, 207p. illus. (pl.), map. £4.95. ISBN: 0565008722. *Class No:* 560(410)

[1920]

—BRITISH MUSEUM (NATURAL HISTORY). British Palaeozoic fossils. 4th ed. London, British Museum (Natural History), 1975. vi, 203p. illus. (pl.), map. £4.95. ISBN: 0565056247.

Each volume includes explanatory notes on the plates, a coloured distribution-map, bibliography and index. Simply written, attractively produced and inexpensive booklets, 'to enable the young, or those without experience, to know about fossils they may expect to find and to identify for themselves those they have collected' (Preface to *British Mesozoic fossils*). *Class No:* 560(410)

[1921]

Directory of British fossiliferous localities. London, Palaeontographical Society, 1954. xiv, 268p.

Three sections: England; Wales; Scotland. Arrangement is A-Z by counties, then towns, in each section. A guide to some 2,000 sites. Each entry states exact location, 1-inch Geological Survey and Ordnance Survey (New popular ed.) map-references, and a brief summary of geological and palaeontological data. Appended is a list of section references. Now much dated for South, South East and Midland England, but still of value for remote areas.

Class No: 560(410)

America—North & Central

[1922]

THOMPSON, I. The Audubon Society field guide to North American fossils. New York, Knopf, 1982. 846p. illus. (incl. col.), diagrs., geol. maps. $17.95. ISBN: 0394524128.

Fossils found in the US have priority. Over 500 excellent colour plates. 'The geologic maps are less successful' and text descriptions are difficult for the casual collector to follow (*Library journal,* 1 March 1983, p.490). Appendices; index. Addressed to the serious amateur palaeontologist. *Class No:* 560(71/73)

Museums

[1923]

CLEEVELY, R.J. World palaeontological collections. London, British Museum (Natural History) and Mansell, 1983. 365p. £50. ISBN: 0565008501.

Main contents: Bibliography (p.17-23: the history of palaeontology and fossil collecting; Collections and collecting; Biographical and other reference sources) - Bibliography of published catalogues of cited material - Alphabetical list of collections (persons, museums, etc., p.38-328) - Index of museums and collection holdings (British Isles; Europe; N. America; Latin America; Australia and New Zealand; Africa; Asia (including Middle East)). A revision of C.D. Sherborn's *Where is the ... collection?* (1940). The Cleevely directory is, however, limited to fossil (and mineral) collections and excludes 'rock' collections (for which see *World directory of mineral collections* (2nd ed., 1977)). *Class No:* 560:061:069

[1924]

—BASSETT, M.G. 'Bibliography and index of catalogues of type, figured and cited fossils in museums in Britain' *Palaeontology,* v.18(4), 1975, p.753-73).

Lists 109 catalogues, with taxonomic, stratigraphic and museum indexes. Supplementary details of reference aids for the curator/researcher who is trying to locate old collections and specimens. Prepared as an aid to tracing type collections and individual specimens. *Class No:* 560:061:069

Palaeoclimatology

[1925]

CROWLEY, T.J. *and* NORTH, G.R. Paleoclimatology. Oxford, University Press, 1991. 339p. diagrs. £45. ISBN: 0195039637.

Aimed at graduate-level readers, this book summaries observational and modelling studies as aids to understanding climatic change. Includes detailed list of scientific references (p.277-322), but the authors work on the possibly controversial assumption that the Cretaceous period ended with the impact of an extra terrestrial body, such as a comet or meteor. 'Those who wish to anticipate future climatic change will be well served if they read *Paleoclimatology*' (*Science,* 16 August, 1991). *Class No:* 560:55

[1926]

SCHWARZBACH, M. Climates of the past: an introduction to paleoclimatology. Translated and edited by R.O. Muir. Princeton, N.J., etc., Van Nostrand, [1963] (reprinted 1977). xii, 328p. illus. diagrs., charts, tables, maps. $24. ISBN: 0404162150.

Translated from the 2nd completely revised and enlarged German ed.

The standard work on the subject. Supported by an extensive bibliography, p.265-300. *Class No:* 560:55

Palaeobiology

[1927]

BRIGGS, D.E.F. *and* CROWTHER, P.R. Palaeobiology: a synthesis. Oxford, Blackwell, 1990. 583p. illus. £89.50. ISBN: 0632025255.

Comprises 120 chapters by a large number of international experts on all aspects of the subject, arranged into following subdivisions - 1. Major events in the history of life - 2. Evolutionary process and the fossil record - 3. Taphonomy - 4. Palaeoecology - 5. Taxonomy, phylogeny, and biostratigraphy - 6. Infrastructure of palaeobiology. 'Each chapter stands on its own as a well-crafted analysis of a portion of science ... highly recommended for any undergraduate or university collection' (*Choice,* April, 1991, p.1336). *Class No:* 560:57

[1928]

The Palaeobiogeography of China. Hongfu, Y., *ed.* Oxford, Clarendon Press, 1994. xii, 370p. diagrs., graphs, tables, maps. ISBN: 0198536718.

18 contributors. 15 chapters, each with references, *e.g.* 11. Cretaceous; 15. Implications of palaeobiogeographical provincialization from the Mesozoic and Cenozoic palaeoclimate and palaeodrainage of China. Index of Chinese geographical localities. Detailed index, p.357-70. *Class No:* 560:57

Palaeoecology

[1929]

The Ecology of fossils: an illustrative guide. McKerrow, W.S., *ed.* London, Duckworth, 1978. 384p. illus., diagrs., maps. ISBN: 0715609440.

7 contributors. Following introduction and classification of organisms, chapters deal with geological periods (Precambrian ... Cretaceous - Cenozoic - present day). Glossary, p.365-9; references, p.370-6. Non-analytical index in tiny print. 125 illus. and diagrs. *Class No:* 560:574

[1930]

Treatise on marine ecology and paleoecology. Volume 2: Paleoecology. Ladd, H.S., *ed.* New York, Geological Society of America, 1957. x, 1077p. illus., maps. (*Memoir of the Geological Society of America.*)

Important for its 'Annotated bibliography of marine palaeoecology' (p.691-1032), with 54 divisions (*e.g.* 'Diatoms': introduction; 27 well-annotated references. 'Nautiloids': introduction, p.829-46; bibliography of 44 items). Index, p.1033-77. *Class No:* 560:574

Palaeopathology

[1931]

AUFDERHEIDE, A.C. *and* RODRIGUEZ-MARTIN, C. The Cambridge encyclopedia of human paleopathology. Cambridge, University Press, 1998. xvii,478p. illus. £75;$100 ISBN: 0521552036.

Fifteen parts: 1. History of paleopathology ... 4. Congenital anomalies ... 6. Joint diseases ... 14. Diseases of the dentition - 15. Miscellaneous conditions. References, p.425-61. Index. Information is clearly presented and is accompanied by over 300 black-and-white photographs. *Class No:* 560:616

Micropalaeontology

[1932]

Bibliography and index of micropaleontology. New York, Micropaleontology Press, American Museum of Natural History, 1972-. v.1-. Monthly. $75; $600 (corporate). ISSN: 03007227.

About 2,500 references pa., in 12 classes. (01. Algae ... 06. Foraminifera ... 09. Palynomorphs ... 11. Radiolarea - 12. Miscellaneous (including papers that mention more than one microfossil group)). Text in original language, with English translation. Entries record illus., sheet maps, tables and number of references. Author index per issue and annually. Highly relevant to petroleum exploration. Online, GEOREF. *Class No:* 560.086

[1933]

BRASIER, M.D. **Microfossils.** London, Allen & Unwin, 1980. xii, 193p. diagrs. £16.45. ISBN: 0045620024.

10 documented chapters on general aspects of micropalaeontology. Includes naming of parts; naming and classification of specimens; general history of groups; geological applications; preparatory methods. Bibliography, p.169-175. Appendix on reconnaissance methods, p.162-78. Systematic and general indexes. 'Invaluable and long-awaited textbook' (Nield, E.W. and Tucker, V.C.T. *Palaeontology: an introduction* (Pergamon Press, 1985, p.164)). *Class No: 560.086*

[1934]

POKORNÝ, V. **Principles of zoological micropalaeontology.**

Allen, K.A., *trans and* Neale, J.W., *ed..* Oxford, Pergamon Press, 1963-65. 2v.

Translated from the German, *Grundzüge der zoologischen Mikropaläontologie* (Berlin, VEB Deutsche Verlag der Wissenschaften, 1958. 2v.).

18 chapters on micropalaeontology, concentrating on a systematic approach (*e.g.* Foraminifera, v.1 p.91-471; Ostracoda. v.2, p.69-348). Chapter bibliographies at end of each volume, plus English - French - German - Russian glossary of terms. V.1 has fossil, subject and author indexes; v.2 has author and subject indexes only. 'Intended as a textbook and as a manual for practising micropalaeontologists' (*Foreword*). *Class No: 560.086*

Palaeobotany

[1935]

ANDREWS, H.N., *Jr.* **Index of generic names of fossil plants, 1820-1965.** Washington, US Geological Survey, 1970. 354p. (*US Geological Survey bulletin 1300.*)

Revises and updates *Andrews' Index ... 1820-1950.* 1955 (bulletin 1013).

Based on the US Geological Survey's working Compendium index of Paleobotany, now comprising over 200,000 cards. Gives full coverage of all known genera and species of fossil plants, but omits diations, spores and pollen. Other groups of microfossils are dealt with, but not completely. Full references for all citations. Not a critical study, but 'intended rather as an information source concerning the origin of the respective generic contents' (*Geographical abstracts,* 1971/4, abstract 71B (1978)).

Supplement, A.M. Blazer, *Index of generic names of fossil plants, 1966-1973* (US Government Printing Office, 1975. 54p.). *Class No: 561*

[1936]

BOUREAU, E. **Traité de paléobotanique.** Paris, Masson, 1964-. v.1-. illus., tables.

A comprehensive treatise, planned in 9v.:
1. *Introduction. Généralités Thallophyta.*
2. *Bryophyta. Psilophyta. Lycophyta.* 1967. 846p. FFr990.
3. *Sphénophyta, Noeggerathiophyta.* 1964. 544p. FFr700.
4(1). *Filicophyta.* 1970. 520p. FFr646.
4(2). *Pteridoyphylla.* 1975. 772p. FFr1,510.
5. *Périodospermophyta.*
6. *Glossopteriodophyta. Cycadophyta. Cordaitophyta. Ginkgophyta. Coniferophyta.*
7. *Chiamydospermophyta, Angiospermophyta.*
8. *Sporologie.*
9. *Paléophytogéographie. Conclusions générales du traité.*

V.4(1), ([iv], 519p.) has 378 figures, section bibliographies and a partly analytical index. A standard work. *Class No: 561*

[1937]

—BOUREAU, E. **Rapport sur la paléobotanique dans le monde,** 1950/1974. [World report on palaeobotany, 1950/1974.] Utrecht, Oosthoek's Uitg. B.V., 1956-73. 9v. (*Legnum vegetabile, 7, etc.*)

Edited by the International Organization of Palaeobotany and published by the International Bureau for Plant Taxonomy and Nomenclature. V.9 (1973) carries 1,647 references in 5 sections (1. Généralités, biographies, méthodes, techniques, travaux généraux... 5. Tertiaire (et Quaternaire)). No index, but does include a directory of c.1,148 palaeobotanists and their addresses. *Class No: 561*

[1938]

ERDTMAN, G. **Handbook of palynology:** morphology - taxonomy - ecology; with 'Appendix on groups other than spores and pollen', by W.A.S. Sarjeant. Riverside, N.J., Hafner, 1969. 486p. illus. $36.95. ISBN: 0028442504.

Bibliography, p.245-6. A comprehensive textbook and a corrective to those handbooks of palynology that 'very often prove to be concerned exclusively with pollen and spores' (Sarjeant, W.A.S. and Harvey, A.P. in Wood, D.N. *Use of earth sciences literature* (1973), p.269). *Class No: 561*

[1939]

HUNTLEY, B. *and* BIRKS, H.J.B. **An Atlas of past and present pollen maps for Europe 0-13000 years ago.** Cambridge Univ. Press, 1983. 667p. + 34 overlaps as a separate volume, maps.

Maps show relative percentage for 40-50 species of pollen at various intervals of time over the past 13,000 years. Included are 'maps of vegetational reconstruction and of refugial areas' (*Choice,* v.21(10), June 1984, p.1446). *Class No: 561*

[1940]

MEYEN, S.V. **Fundamentals of palaeobotany.** London, Chapman & Hall, 1987. xxii, 432p. diagrs. ISBN: 0412271109.

Translated from Russian under author's supervision.

8 chapters: Preservation types and techniques of study of fossil plants - Principles of typology and of nomenclature of fossil plants - Fossil plants systematics - Palaeopalynology - Epidermal-circular studies - Plant palaeoecology - Palaeofloristics - Relationship between palaeobotany and other fields of natural history. Good reference bibliography, p.383-414. Index covers illustrations as well as text. 'A useful basic text in any university college or public library' (*New technical books,* January/February 1988, item 2987). *Class No: 561*

[1941]

TRALAU, H. **Bibliography and index to palaeobotany and palynology, 1950-70.** Stockholm, the Author, Stockholm Museum of Natural History, 1974. 2v.

About 23,000 references under authors in v.1, v.2 being a KWIC index. A continuation covering 1971-75 (2v.) appeared in 1983. *Class No: 561*

Palaeosols

[1942]

RETALLACK, G.J. **A Colour guide to paleosols.** Chichester, Wiley, 1997. xi, 175p. tables. £50. ISBN: 0471967114.

5 chapters: 1. Recognition of paleosols (buried soils) - 2. Alteration of paleosols after burial - 3. Interpretation - 4. Colour photographs (144) - 5. Methods in paleopedology. References, p.129-146; glossary p.147-162; index p.163-175. Text illustrations and tables are used to supplement excellent colour section in this attractive approach to a specialized area of palaeontology. 'A much-needed and accessible text' (*Geological magazine,* v.135, March 1998, p.295). *Class No: 561.0*

Fossil Invertebrates

[1943]

CLARKSON, E.N.K. **Invertebrate palaeontology and evolution.** 3rd ed. London, Allen & Unwin, 1993. ix,434p. illus., diagrs., maps. £19.95. ISBN: 0412479907.

First published 1979.

Documented chapters; 2 parts. Part 1: General palaeontological concepts (chapters 1-3) - Part 2: Invertebrate phyla (chapters 4-12). Chapter 11: 'Arthropods', p.339-95. 27 figures; 5p. of bibliography. Detailed analytical index, p.425-34. Numerous carefully drawn examples. Systematic index, p.417-24. 'A course book for second and third year students reading Geology or Earth Science' (*Preface*). *Class No: 562*

[1944]

Treatise on invertebrate paleontology. Prepared under the guidance of the Joint Committee on Invertebrate Paleontology. Moore, R.C., *ed.* New York, Geological Society of America; Laurence, Kansas, Univ. of Kansas Press, 1953-.

Sponsored by the Geological Society of America, the Paleontographical Society, the Paleontological Society and the Society of Economic Paleontologists and Mineralogists.

1. A. *Introduction.* B-D *Protista* (C. pt.2, 1964; D. pt.3, 1954). E. *Archaeocyatha, porifera.* 1955. Rev. ed. 1972. F. *Coelenterata.* 1956. (Supplement 1. *Rugosa and tabulata.* 2v. 1981). G. *Bryozoa.* 1953. H. *Brachiopoda.* 1965. 2v. I-N. *Mollusca* (I. 1960; K. 1964; L. 1957; N. 1969-71. 3v.). O-R. *Arthropoda.* 1955-69. 5v. (v.4 *Superclass hexapoda.* 1992.). S-U. *Echinodermata* (S. 1967. 2v; U. 1966. 2v.). V. *Graptolithina.* 1955. 2nd ed. 1970. W. *Miscellanea.* 1962. Suppt. 1: *Trace fossils and problematica.* 2nd ed., 1975. Suppt. 2. 1981. X. *Addenda. Index.*

Aims 'to present the most comprehensive statement of knowledge concerning invertebrate fossil groups' up to 1950 (*Editorial preface*). Each volume contains detailed descriptions; section references; detailed index. A feature is the wealth of line-drawings and diagrams. Part F. *Coelenterata* (1956. xx, 498p.) has 358 diagrs. According to P.-M. Guelpa (Malclès, L.-M. *Les sources du travail bibliographique,* v.3, p.250), Moore is stronger on systematics than is Piveteau (*Traité de paléontologie*) (qv). The standard work on invertebrate

....(contd.)
palaeontology, written by the world's leading authorities (about 150 contributors).

The revised and enlarged editions of certain of the volumes (Boulder, Colo., Geological Society of America) began in 1970. *Class No: 562*

Foraminifera

[1945]

ELLIS, B.F. *and* **MESSINA, A.R. Catalogue of Foraminifera.** New York, American Museum of Natural History, 1940. 30v. (+ loose-leaf supplements, 1945-), illus.

Special publication (official report no.65-1-97-21 WP16) conducted under the auspices of the Work Progress Administration.

Systematic descriptions: genera, species and varieties arranged A-Z by genera, etc. Index to synonyms. V.30: 'Index to taxonomic changes and Bibliography'. A monumental work. 'Since foraminifera are the most economically important group of fossils, the literature is vast and bibliographic aids are especially needful' (W.A.S. Sarjeant and A.P. Harvey, in D.N. Wood's *Use of earth sciences literature* (1973, p.266)). *Class No: 563.12*

[1946]

—Catalogue of index Smaller Foraminifera. Ellis, B.F., *and others*. New York, American Museum of Natural History, 1968-69. 3v. illus. *Class No: 563.12*

[1947]

—ELLIS, B.F. and MESSINA, A.R. Catalogue of index Foraminifera. New York, American Museum of Natural History, 1965-67. 3v. illus. *Class No: 563.12*

[1948]

HAYNES, J.R. Foraminifera. London, Macmillan, 1981. x, 433p. illus., ports., maps. £50. ISBN: 0333286812.

About two-thirds of the book is devoted to descriptive morphology and classification. Extensive bibliography, p.340-89. Comprehensive, well illustrated, 'Despite its price, this book has no real competition, and it must be recommended very highly' (*New scientist*, 15 July 1982, p.166). *Class No: 563.12*

[1949]

Stratigraphical atlas of fossil foraminifera. Jenkins, D.G. *and* Murray, J.W., *eds.* 2nd ed. Chichester, Ellis Horwood Ltd; Halsted Press, 1989. 593p. illus., tables, maps. £69.95. (*British Micropalaeontological Society series*.) ISBN: 0745801536, Ellis Horwood; 0470212268, Halsted Press.

First published 1984.

25 contributors. Arrangement is by litho-stratigraphical systems in 13 documented chapters. In this edition, range charts have been added and there is new information for the Cambrian to Devonian, Triassic, Jurassic and for the Cretaceous and Cenozoic periods of the North Sea. Important foraminiferal taxa are illustrated with taxonomic and morphological data. General index and index of general and species. British in scope. *Class No: 563.12*

Fossil Vertebrates

[1950]

BENTON, M.J. Vertebrate palaeontology: biology and evolution. London, Chapman & Hall, 1997. xii, 452p. figs. ISBN: 0412738007.

11 chapters: 1. Vertebrate origins ... 4. The early tetrapods and amphibians ... 8. The age of dinosaurs ... 11. Human evolution. Appendix: classification of the vertebrates. Glossary. References, p.409-35. Index. Aimed at both the layperson and the specialist, this is an extensive revision of the first edition, and includes an added chapter on how to study fossil vetebrates. *Class No: 566*

[1951]

Bibliography of fossil vertebrates, exclusive of North America, 1509-1927. Romer, A.S., *and others*. New York, Geological Society of America, 1962. $160. (*Geological Society of America, Memoir 87*.) ISBN: 0835771830.

A comprehensive bibliography of published work, particularly periodical articles. Nearly 40,000 entries, under authors A-Z, then chronologically. No subject or locality index, - a severe handicap to non-specialists, at least. About 2,000 periodicals are cited (p.xiii, lxxxix). *Class No: 566*

[1952]

CAMP, C.L., *and others*. **Bibliography of fossil vertebrates, 1928/1933-.** New York, Geological Society of America, 1940-73. 9v. 5 yearly.

Preceded by O.P. Hay's *Bibliography and catalogue of the fossil vertebrates of North America* (Washington, Geological Survey, 1902. *Bulletin* no.179) and his *Second bibliography* (Washington, Carnegie Institution, 1929-30. Publication no.390).

Camp's *Bibliography of fossil vertebrates, 1969-72* (1973, xlvi, [i], 733p. Geological Society of America. *Memoirs*) is, like Romer's (*qv*), an author catalogue subarranged chronologically, with *c*.7,500 entries. Subject index (p.388-575) has detailed subdivision under countries and includes obituaries. Systematic index, p.577-733. Supplementary list of serials, p.xi-xxxix.

Continued in *Bibliography of fossil vertebrates, 1973-1977*, by M. Green and others (South Dakota School of Mines and Technology, 1979), and now annually by *Bibliography of fossil vertebrates, 1978-*, (1985 ed. Berkeley, Calif., Society of Vertebrate Paleontology. 624p.). *Class No: 566*

[1953]

Fossil vertebrates of Africa. Leakey, L.S.B., *ed.* Orlando, Florida, Academic Press, 1969-76. 4v. ISBN: 0124404014, v.1; 0124404022, v.2; 0124404030, v.3; 0124404049, v.4.

V.4 (1976. 402p. $81), edited by R.J.G. Savage and S. Coryndon, has 6 specialized chapters,- on aspects of elephant shrews (E. and S. Africa), rodents, primates from East Africa, pigs from Miocene African sites, etc. 'Although too detailed for the general reader, the volume will become an established reference work for those working in the field of African prehistory, vertebrate palaeontology and evolution' (*British book news*, October 1976, p.754). *Class No: 566*

[1954]

ROMER, A.S. Vertebrate palaeontology. 3rd ed. Chicago, Ill., Univ. of Chicago Press, 1966. viii, 468p. illus. $45. ISBN: 0226724883.

First published 1933.

Includes an outline classification (p.347-96) and an extensive bibliography (p.397-418). The standard one-volume work.

A companion volume is his *Notes and comments on vertebrate palaeontology* (Univ. of Chicago Press, 1968. viii, 304p.). *Class No: 566*

[1955]

Vertebrate paleontological techniques, Volume 1. Leiggi, P. *and* May, P., *eds.* Cambridge, University Press, 1994. xvii, 344p. illus. £45. ISBN: 0521443571.

34 contributors. 12 chapters: 1. Conservation of vertebrate paleontological collections ... 6. Laboratory preparation ... 9. Histological techniques ... 12. Methods and use of CT-scan and X-ray. Index, p.341-4. Manual covering subject from field collecting, through curatorial laboratory techniques, to skeleton-mounting for public viewing. V.2 'already in progress' (*Preface*). *Class No: 566*

Fish

[1956]

FRICKHINGER, K.A. Fossil atlas: fishes. [Fossilen Atlas: Fische.] Stillwater, Minn., Voyageur Press, 1996. 1088p. illus.(col.). $79.95; £70. ISBN: 1564651150.

Based on 60 leading palaeontology museums and 18 private collections. A colour photograph illustrates each entry while data include size, discovery and present museum locations, genus information, list of synonymous names, and a citation to a printed authority. Line-drawings show the reconstructed fish. Bibliography lists publications cited in the entries. Five indexes: name; order; formations; localities; recent relatives. A specialized, mammoth work but 'a significant paleontological reference' (*Reference books bulletin*, August 1996, p.1925) which is of interest to both the academic and the amateur. *Class No: 567*

[1957]

MOY-THOMAS, J.A. Palaeozoic fishes. 2nd ed., rev. by R.S. Miles. London, Chapman and Hall, 1971. xi, 259p. illus.

First published 1939.

Extensively revised and enlarged. Sections on the probable life-history patterns of the major groups of fishes dealt with are added. 'This work is of major importance and contains excellent bibliographies' (Sarjeant, W.A.S. and Harvey, A.P., in Wood, D.N., ed. *Use of earth sciences literature* (1973), p.279). *Class No: 567*

Reptiles & Amphibians

[1958]

SWINTON, W.E. Fossil amphibians and reptiles. 5th ed. London, British Museum (Natural History), 1973. ix, 133p. illus. (incl. pl.). £1.40. ISBN: 056500543x.

First published 1954.

A compact work, with 17 plates and 68 keyed line-drawings. Appended are a geological time scale, a classification, and a glossary

....(contd.)
(p.127-9). Detailed, non-analytical index. 'Asterisks after the names of fossils in the text indicate that specimens are on exhibition' (*Preface*).
Class No: 568.1

Dinosaurs

Bibliographies

[1959]
FLEURY, B.E. **Dinosaurs: a guide to research.** New York, Garland, 1992. 468p. illus. ISBN: 0824053443.

Annotated bibliography of 1,153 citations, arranged by broad subject categories, which are each preceded by a bibliographic essay. Limited to English language items. Author and subject indexes in addition to a topical index to curricular materials. Many cross-references. '...an excellent resource for developing courses and encouraging student research' (*Library journal*, August 1992, p.88), although its summaries of cited works are generally uncritical, and some fiction is included.
Class No: 568.19(01)

Encyclopaedias & Dictionaries

[1960]
Encyclopedia of dinosaurs. Currie, P.J. *and* Padian, K., *eds*. San Diego, Academic Press, 1997. xxx,870p. illus., figs.,tables. £70. ISBN: 0122268105.

A-Z arrangement of over 270 articles by over 200 contributors. Covers all aspects of dinosaurs *e.g.* evolution, behaviour. Many cross-references. Bibliographies include English and non-English language material. A-Z list of dinosaur genera. Chronology. Glossary. Many black-and-white illustrations. Less technical than Glut's *Dinosaurs: the encyclopedia* (*q.v.*). For public libraries. *Class No:* 568.19(03)

[1961]
GLUT, D.F. **Dinosaurs: the encyclopedia.** Jefferson, North Carolina, McFarland, 1997. 1088p. illus. £145. ISBN: 0899509177.

First published 1972 as *The Dinosaur dictionary* and in 1982 as *The New dinosaur dictionary*.

More technical than the 1982 publication. Five sections: Background; Dinosaurian systematics; Dinosaurian genera (Abelisaurus ... Zizhonosaurus); Nomina nuda; Excluded genera. The section on dinosaurian genera includes information on first publication in palaeontological literature. 1,439 photographs and illustrations. Glossary; index; bibliography. A definitive work; for academic libraries. *Class No:* 568.19(03)

[1962]
LAMBERT, D. *and* THE DIAGRAM GROUP. **Dinosaur data book:** the definitive, fully illustrated encyclopedia of dinosaurs and other prehistoric reptiles. New York, Facts on File with the British Museum (Natural History), 1990. 320p. figs., maps. £7.95. ISBN: 0816024316.

7 chapters: 1. The age of dinosaurs - 2. The A to Z of dinosaurs - 3. Dinosaurs classified - 4. Dinosaur life - 5. Dinosaurs worldwide - 6. Dinosaurologists - 7. Dinosaurs revived. Bibliography, p.306-10. Authoritative and lively text, with illustrations and maps on virtually every page.

The same author has also written *The Ultimate dinosaur book* (New York, Dorling Kindersley, 1993. 192p.) which does not take as thorough an approach as the *Dinosaur data book* but would be suitable for school and public libraries. *Class No:* 568.19(03)

[1963]
NORMAN, D. **The Illustrated encyclopedia of dinosaurs.** London, Salamander Books, 1985. 208p. illus. (mostly col.), ports., facsims., diagrs., maps. £14.95. ISBN: 0861012259.

35 sections, including 'Controversies', 'Geography of finds', 'Museums and displays'. Glossary, p.202-3. Index (over 2,000 entries, in tiny print), p.204-8. *Author's foreword* has notes on 6 'serious books of recent years'. A quarto volume, copiously illustrated, with 25 double-page spreads. Claims to provide 'one of the most detailed and comprehensive layman's guides to the dinosaurs yet published'. Author is a lecturer in zoology at Brasenose College, Oxford.
Class No: 568.19(03)

Handbooks & Manuals

[1964]
BENTON, M.J. **The Penguin historical atlas of dinosaurs.** London, Penguin, 1996. 144p. illus.(col.), maps. £9.99 ISBN: 0140513361.

An unusual approach to a 'saturated' subject, this book is attractively-illustrated but at the expense of much detail. Well-written text. One page bibliography and seven pages of index.
Class No: 568.19(035)

[1965]
LAMBERT, D. *and* THE DIAGRAM GROUP. **Collins' guide to dinosaurs.** London, Collins, 1985. 256p. illus. (two-colour), ports., diagrs., charts. £6.95. ISBN: 0001953877.

First published 1983.

6 chapters: 1. What were the dinosaurs? - 2. Dinosaurs in the making - 3. Dinosaurs identified - 4. Their changing world - 5. Discovering dinosaurs - 6. Dinosaurs displayed (listing over 70 museums with exhibits from the Age of Dinosaurs; Argentina ... USSR). Brief entries for over 300 kinds of dinosaurs, - 'all currently known dinosaur genera, one in five of which have been named since 1970' (*Foreword*). Further reading, by chapters, p.248; detailed, analytical index (dinosaur names no longer used are followed by current names). Illus. include 'field guide' silhouettes and family trees. 'This book can be recommended to the seriously interested beginner or amateur' (*Natural history book reviews*, v.7(3), 1984, p.149).
Class No: 568.19(035)

[1966]
—**Dinosaurs and their living relatives.** 2nd ed. London, British Museum (Natural History), with Cambridge Univ. Press, 1985. 72p. col. illus. £5.95. ISBN: 056506426x.

Explains dinosaurs and how they evolved into the crocodiles and birds alive today. Copiously illustrated. 'The work will probably appeal to those in their early teens' (*Children's books (British book news)*), June 1986, p.32). *Class No:* 568.19(035)

[1967]
—HALSTEAD, L.B. *and* HALSTEAD, J. **Dinosaurs.** Poole, Dorset, Blandford Press, 1981. 170p. illus. (incl. col.). ISBN: 0713710179.

10 short chapters, describing *c.*125 species.'The colour section [p.61-108] illustrates all the major types of dinosaurs, including many that have never previously figured in books' (*Preface*). Includes a chapter on the classification of 12 families. 'An entirely new approach, along the lines of a field identification manual' (*Natural history book reviews*, v.6(3/4), 1983, p.149-50). *Class No:* 568.19(035)

[1968]
The Macmillan illustrated encyclopedia of dinosaurs and prehistoric animals: a visual who's who of prehistoric life. Cox, B., *and others*. London, Macmillan, 1988. 312p. illus. (col.). ISBN: 0333486994.

7 sections, covering over 600 species: Fishes - Amphibians - Reptiles - Ruling reptiles - Birds - Mammal-like reptiles - Mammals. Data in each entry give name, period of existence, locality, size and general description. 2-page glossary. Classification of vertebrates, p.300-3. Brief bibliography, p.304. List of international museums, p.305. Well illustrated, with an extensive index.
Class No: 568.19(035)

[1969]
THULBORN, T. **Dinosaur tracks.** London, Chapman and Hall, 1990. 410p. illus. £37. ISBN: 0412328909.

A comprehensive summary of, and introduction to, dinosaur trace fossils, including chapters: 4. Dinosaur tracks in the field and laboratory - 5. Identify the track-maker ... 7. Problematical and anomalous tracks - 8. Estimating the size of the track-maker. 'Will appeal to a variety of palaeontologists, sedimentologists, and biologists. It should even prove attractive to amateur dinosaur fanatics ... a remarkably original book' (*Geological magazine*, v.128(1), 1991, p.84). *Class No:* 568.19(035)

Birds

[1970]
SWINTON, W.E. **Fossil birds.** 3rd rev. ed. London, British Museum (Natural History), 1975. v, 81p. illus. (incl. col. front.), chart. £1.50. ISBN: 0565053973.

First published 1958.

Companion volume to his *Fossil amphibians and reptiles (qv)*. Contents: Introduction - The history of flight - How birds fly - Jurassic birds - Cretaceous birds - Tertiary birds - Origin of ratites. Geological chart; Classification; Glossary (p.71-74). Analytical index. 27 line-drawings; col. front. Good value. *Class No:* 568.2

Mammals

[1971]
Evolution of tertiary mammals of North America. Janis, C.M., *and others*, *eds*. Cambridge, University Press, 1998. 691p. illus.,figs.,maps. £165; $260. ISBN: 0521355192.

V.1. *Terrestrial carnivores, ungulates, and ungulatelike mammals*.

Concentrates on fossils of carnivorous and large herbivorous mammals. Six sections (44 chapters): 1. Overview of context for the evolution of North American tertiary mammals; 2. Carnivorous mammals; 3. Archaic ungulates and ungulatelike mammals; 4. Artiodactyla; 5. Perissodactyla and proboscidea; 6. Eutheria incerta sedis. Includes coverage of taxonomy, phylogeny, evolutionary patterns, locality lists, etc. Bibliographies are also often included. Three appendices: 1. Tertiary mammal localities; 2. References for

....(contd.)
locality listings; 3. Museum acronyms. 'It will be a standard reference for paleontologists of the 21st century' (*Choice*, October 1998, p.344). *Class No: 569*

[1972]
HOPWOOD, A.T. *and* **HOLLYFIELD, J.P. An Annotated bibliography of the fossil mammals of Africa (1742-1950).** London, British Museum (Natural History), 1954. 194p. (*Fossil mammals of Africa, no.8.*)
About 1,000 entries, with annotations, especially taxonomic and stratigraphic. Geographic, systematic and nominal indexes. 'Designed for zoologists interested in the comparative anatomy, distribution and history of the mammalian faunas of Africa, rather than for geologists and archaeologists' (*Introduction*). *Class No: 569*

[1973]
KURTÉN, B. Pleistocene mammals of Europe. London, Weidenfeld & Nicolson 1968. viii, 367p. illus., maps. (*World naturalist.*)
'Has become a classic; it breaks new ground and remains a frequently quoted text' (*Nature*, v.290, 12 March 1981, p.168). *Class No: 569*

[1974]
KURTÉN, B. *and* **ANDERSON, E. Pleistocene mammals of North America.** New York, Columbia Univ. Press, 1980. 442p. tables. $82. ISBN: 0231037333.
Part 1 lists *c*.250 faunal sites, with notes on geology, geography, ecology and faunal composition. Part 2 is a critical and annotated list for the Blancan and Pleistocene mammal species in Canada, USA and Northern Mexico. 'It will be an invaluable reference source for those working not only on Pleistocene faunas, but on problems of evolution, extinction and biogeography' (*Nature*, v.290, 12 March 1981, p.168). *Class No: 569*

[1975]
Mesozoic mammals: the first two-thirds of mammalian history. Lillegraven, J.C., *and others, eds.* Berkeley, Calif., & London, University of California Press, 1979. 320p. illus. $65. ISBN: 0520055828.
Covers the period *c*.240 to 64 million years before the present. 'As such it will be of great value to those actively involved in research in this group, as well as of those generally interested in a technical account of early mammalian evolution' (*Library journal*, 1 November 1979, p.2360). *Class No: 569*

[1976]
SAVAGE, D.E. *and* **RUSSELL, D.E. Mammalian paleofaunas of the world.** Reading, Mass., & London, Addison-Wesley, 1983. 432p. ISBN: 0201064944.
Lists more than 3,000 genera and at least twice that number of species over a 200-million year time-span. 'A highly reliable work, an indispensible reference source and a monumental data base from which to test our theories, be they evolutionary, faunal or geographical' (*Nature*, v.304, 4 August 1983, p.471). *Class No: 569*

Man

[1977]
Catalogue of fossil hominids. Oakley, K.P., *and others, eds.* London, British Museum (Natural History), 1971-77. 3v. illus., (incl. pl.), maps. £70. ISBN: 0565006614; 0565007114; 056500767x.
1. *Africa.* 1977. xiv, 210p. £20. 2. *Europe.* 1971. xiv, 370p. £30. 3. *America, Asia & Australasia.* xiv, 228p. £20.
Each part is arranged by country/location. Data at place-name designate the fossil, describe site and geographical location, name of discoverer, geological deposit, burial (or not), stratigraphic age, archaeological context, palaeontological context, relative dating of bone, antler and dentine, absolute data, relationship of bones, first published report, anatomical description, most recent revision of the morphological evaluation, reference to best illustrated account, any other important publications, postal address of repository of fossil, and of moulds for casts. Index and location maps per volume. *Class No: 569.9*

[1978]
DAY, M.H. Guide to fossil man. 4th ed. London, Cassell; Chicago, University Press, 1986. xv, [i], 432p. illus., diagrs., tables, maps. ISBN: 0304312886; 0226138895, US ed.
First published 1965.
Three parts. 1: The anatomy of fossil man - 2. The fossil hominids (Europe, plus country division; Near East; Northwest Africa; East Africa; Southern Africa; The Far East; Oceania), p.16-401 - 3. Essays on fossil man (with references). Records new evidence from 34 sites featured in previous editions, plus details of 15 new sites. Appended 'Geologic and palaeomagnetic time scales'; Glossary. Partly analytical index. Author is Professor of Anatomy, United Medical and Dental Schools of Guy's and St. Thomas's Hospital, Univ. of London. *Class No: 569.9*

[1979]
Early hominids of Africa. Jolly, C.J., *ed.* London, Duckworth, 1978. x, 598p. illus., diagrs., graphs, tables. ISBN: 0715609289.
4 parts: 1. The sites - 2. Geological, fauna and archeological evidence - 3. Anatomical evidence - 4. The interpretation of hominid diversity. 24 contributions, - papers read at a New York conference in 1974. Coverage is Africa south of the Sahara, over a specific span of time: the Plio-Pleistocene. General and author indexes. *Class No: 569.9*

[1980]
KENNEDY, G.E. Paleoanthropology. New York, McGraw-Hill, 1980. xiii, [1], 479p. illus., tables. $39.95. ISBN: 0070340463.
10 chapters: 1. Evolutionary biology, taxonomy and paleoanthropology - 2. The order primates - 3. Early primates: Cretaceous to Oligocene - 4. Miocene hominoid radiation - 5. The family hominidae - 6. Hominids of the Plio-Pleistocene - 7. Plio-Pleistocene hominid localities - 8. Hominids of the Middle Pleistocene - 9. Hominids of the Early Pleistocene - 10. Summary. Each chapter has 'Summary' and 'Suggestions for further reading', Appendix: Dating techniques. Glossary, p.426-30; bibliography (authors, A-Z; p.431-67). Analytical index, p.469-79. 'Intended for students who have completed an introductory course in physical anthropology or biology' (*Preface*). The emphasis is on the fossil record itself. The author, - Assistant Professor of Anthropology, Univ. of California, Los Angeles. *Class No: 569.9*

[1981]
LAMBERT, D. Cambridge guide to prehistoric man. Cambridge Univ. Press, 1987. 256p. illus., (incl. col.), tables. £9.50. ISBN: 0521336449.
A companion to the popular *Cambridge Field guide to prehistoric life (q.v.).* Its brief non-technical text on prehistoric man's biological and cultural evolution is followed by copious line-drawings and tables. 'Further reading', p.248. Index. *Class No: 569.9*

[1982]
SMITH, F.H. *and* **SPENCER, F. The Origins of modern humans:** a world survey of the fossil evidence. New York, Wiley, 1985. $93.95. ISBN: 047183419x.
11 contributors, of which 9 concern skeletal remains found in Europe, Western Asia, East Asia and Australasia, China, and the Americas. While conceding that the text is refreshingly free from the Eurocentric bias, the review in *Nature* (v.314, 18 April 1985, p.649) quarrels with the maps and quality of photographs and drawings. Nevertheless, 'An invaluable source of reference for those already familiar with the fossil record, anatomy and population genetics'. *Class No: 569.9*

572 Anthropology

Anthropology

Databases

[1983]

Anthropology Internet resources. Department of Social Sciences, Western Connecticut State University. URL: http://www.wcsu.cstateu.edu/socialsci/antres.html.

A listing of many anthropological Internet sites, divided into subject categories, *e.g.* physical anthropology, culture. Examples of sites include *LC: Ethnographic studies resources*, journals, *Native American resources*. *Class No:* 572.0(003.4)

[1984]

BRADY, F. *and* **LAMBERT, M.** 'Alternative databases for anthropology searching'. In *Database*, v.7(1), February 1984, p.28-35. ISSN: 01624105.

The *Database* article cites PSYCINFO, SOCIAL RESEARCH, LLBA, BIOSIS and MEDLINE as relevant bibliographical databases. Droessler, J.B. and Wilke C. ('Physical anthropology literature: online access', *Reference Services Review*, v.12(2), Summer 1984, p.22-26) cite BIOSIS REVIEWS, LIFE SCIENCES COLLECTIONS, MEDLINE and EMBASE, there being no database specifically devoted to anthropological literature. *Class No:* 572.0(003.4)

Bibliographies of Bibliographies

[1985]

LIBRARY-ANTHROPOLOGY RESOURCE GROUP.
Anthropological bibliographies: a selected guide. Smith, M.L. *and* Damien, Y.M., *eds.* 2nd ed. South Salem, New York, Redgrave, 1981. 307p.

About 3,200 entries for material mainly published 1957-77. 7 chapters; 1-6: Geographical (Africa, America, Asia, Europe, Oceania, USSR); 7: Topical coverage includes filmographies, discographies, books, article-length bibliographies and 'hidden' bibliographies appended to articles and books. Some entries are annotated. Detailed index, insufficiently analytical. 'The work is definitely not as useful as it first appears' (*Reference services review*, v.11(3), Fall 1983, p.67), but 'Of first importance' (Webb, W.H., and associates. *Sources of information in the social sciences*, item F457). *Class No:* 572.0(009)

[1986]

—**CURRIER, M.** 'Problems in anthropological bibliography'. In *Annual review of anthropology*, no.5, 1976, p.15-34.

Surveys 100 years of trends in anthropological indexing and abstracting services, including the relevance of early general indexes. Sections embrace computer indexing and abstracting, and compilation and publishing of bibliographies. Limited attention to monographic bibliographies. Bibliography of 30 items. No index. *Class No:* 572.0(009)

Bibliographies

[1987]

Author and subject catalogues of the Tozzer Library. 2nd ed. Boston, G.K. Hall, 1988. Microfiche. ISBN: 0816117314.

Successor to the *Catalogue of the Library of the Peabody Museum of Archaeology and Ethnology.* Consists of 1,122 negative microfiches, accompanied by a printed fiche guide. Supplements appear annually. *Class No:* 572.0(01)

[1988]

—**HARVARD UNIVERSITY.** Peabody Museum of Archaeology and Ethnology. Library. Catalogue. [Peabody Museum of Archaeology and Ethnology, Library]. Authors, 1963. 27v. Supplements 1-4. 1970-79. 14v. Subjects. 1963. 27v. Supplements 1-4. 1970-79. 16v. Boston, Mass., G.K. Hall, 1963-. 54v. (29302p.) Supplements-. ISBN: 0816106479.

Over one million photolithographed catalogue cards in all. International in scope, the Peabody Museum Library has one of the most comprehensive collections of anthropological material. The *Catalogue* indexes periodicals, books and collections of essays, symposia, congresses and festschrifts. 'The best retrospective index to the anthropological literature' (*Reference services review*, v.12(4), Winter 1984, p.37). *Class No:* 572.0(01)

[1989]

—**HARVARD UNIVERSITY.** Peabody Museum of Archaeology and Ethnology. Library. Index to subject headings. [Peabody Museum of Archaeology and Ethnology, Library]. 2nd rev. ed. Boston, Mass., G.K. Hall, 1981. 177p. ISBN: 0816104080.

First published 1963 (117p.).

Comprises *c.*18,000 headings and cross-references. *Class No:* 572.0(01)

[1990]

Bibliographic guide to anthropology and archaeology 1987. Boston, G.K. Hall, 1988. 382p. ISBN: 081617069x.

The first annual supplement to the *Author and subject catalogues of the Tozzer Library,* on microfiche (G.K. Hall, 1988).

Lists material catalogued between June 1986 and August 1987 by Harvard University's Tozzer Library. Subject areas include linguistics, cultural anthropology, physical anthropology and archaeology. *Class No:* 572.0(01)

[1991]

Ecce homo: an annotated bibliographic history of physical anthropology. Spencer, F., *comp.* New York & London, Greenwood Press, 1986. xiii, [1], 459p. illus., facsims. £45; $95. (*Bibliographies and indexes in anthropology, no.2.*) ISBN: 0313240566.

2,340 annotated entries. 4 parts: 1. Ancient, medieval, Renaissance and early modern literature - 2. Eighteenth century - 3. Nineteenth century (945 entries) - 4. Twentieth century (1,168 entries: Human population biology; Primatology; Paleoprimatology; Paleo-anthropology - Old World; New World). Name and subject indexes. *Class No:* 572.0(01)

[1992]

Finding the source in sociology and anthropology: a thesaurus - index to the reference collection. Brown, S., *comp.* Newport, Conn., Greenwood Press, 1987. 269p. $49.95. (*Finding the source series.*) ISBN: 0313252637.

A subject bibliography of 578 titles - selected from Sheehy's *Guide to reference books* and C. White's *Sources of information in the social sciences* (2nd ed. 1973), with title and author indexes, - plus a 'thesaurus-index' of the relevant descriptors, synonyms, related and narrower terms. '*Finding the source* is useful for someone who lacks the intellectual context of reference genres and who is looking for specific information'. (*Wilson library bulletin*, v.61(10), June 1987, p.83). *Class No:* 572.0(01)

[1993]

GRAVEL, P.B. *and* **RIDINGER, R.B.M. Anthropological fieldwork:** an annotated bibliography. New York, Garland, 1988. 241p. $33. (*Garland reference library of social science, 419.*) ISBN: 0824066421.

700 entries to journal articles, monographs, book chapters, and collected essays in English, French and German. Arranged A-Z by author, with annotations of *c.*100 words. Geographical index. Very brief subject index (2p.). Not comprehensive but covers the most important aspects of anthropological fieldwork. *Class No:* 572.0(01)

[1994]

International bibliography of social and cultural anthropology. [Bibliographie internationale d'anthropologie sociale et culturelle.] London, Tavistock Publications, 1955-. v.1-. Annual. £125; $230. (*International bibliography of the social sciences.*)

Prepared by the International Committee for Social Science Information and Documentation.

Each issue contains *c.*1,700 entries. 10 sections: A. Anthropology: general studies; B. Materials and methods of anthropology; C. Morphological foundations; D. Ethnographic studies of people and communities; E. Social organisation and relationships; F. Religion, magic, witchcraft; G. Problems of knowledge, arts and science, folk traditions; H. Studies of culture and personality. 'National character'; I. Problems of acculturation and social change; contact situations; J. Applied anthropology. Author and analytical subject indexes. Available online via QL Systems. *Class No:* 572.0(01)

[1995]

MEXICO. Biblioteca National de Antropología e Historia, Mexico City. **Catalogo. [Biblioteca National de Antropología e Historia, Mexico City.** Boston, Mass., G.K. Hall, 1977. 10v. (7081p.). $960.

143,000 photolithographed catalogue cards, in one author, title, subject and added entry sequence, A-Z. *Class No:* 572.0(01)

[1996]

WESTERMAN, R. 'Anthropology'. In *Sources of information in the social sciences: a guide to the literature* (3rd ed, edited by W.H. Webb and associates. Chicago & London, American Library Association, 1986), p.332-402. ISBN: 083890405x.

Two main sections: Survey of the field (F1-F149) - Survey of the reference works (F420-F1072). The first section has 15 subsections each with an introduction and unannotated lists of items. The second section, also closely subdivided, has short introductions highlighting major material, plus annotated entries or running commentary. A revision and updating of chapter 6, Anthropology, in *Sources of information in the social sciences* (2nd ed., edited by C.M. White and associates. 1973). A basic bibliographical tool in this field.
Class No: 572.0(01)

Encyclopaedias & Dictionaries

[1997]

The Dictionary of anthropology. Barfield, T., *ed.* Oxford, Blackwell, 1997. 626p. £19.99; ISBN: 1577180577.

Entries range in length from a few sentences to several pages. More than 500 entries, including biographies. Does not include pronunciation. Many cross-references. For academic libraries.
Class No: 572.0(03)

[1998]

HUNTER, D.E. *and* WHITTEN, P., *eds.* **Encyclopedia of anthropology.** New York, Harper & Row, 1976. xi, 411p. illus., tables, maps. ISBN: 0060470941.

About 1,400 entries, by 87 contributors. 'Monotheistic religions': 2 columns; 4 references. Includes brief biographies (*e.g.* Levi-Strauss: nearly 1 column). Well illustrated, with *c.*200 photographs and line drawings. Cross-references, and subject index, less adequate. Some US slant. Aims to be a 'compact, comprehensive, accessible reference source' (*Preface*) and largely succeeds.

Fuller in coverage and more comprehensive than *Dictionary of anthropology*, edited by C. Winwick (New York, Philosophical Library, 1956. vii, 579p). *Class No:* 572.0(03)

[1999]

SEYMOUR-SMITH, C. **Macmillan dictionary of anthropology.** London, Macmillan Press, 1986. [vi], 305p. ISBN: 0333365909.

About 2,000 entries (*e.g.* 'Kinship terminology': nearly 2 columns). Includes short biographies (*e.g.* 'Mead, Margaret: nearly 2 columns). Ample cross-references. 'Selective bibliography and further reading' (authors, A/Z), p.293-305. Stresses social and cultural aspects, and conceptual issues. 'There are few fixed definitions in anthropology. Instead ours is a discipline which advances by constantly revising and interrogating current concepts and their use' (*Foreword*). Lacks the supporting illus. in Hunter-Whitten's *Encyclopedia (q.v.)*. Praised in *RQ* (v.27(1), Fall 1987, p.139) for the quality of its definitions.
Class No: 572.0(03)

[2000]

—DAVIES, D. A Dictionary of anthropology. London, F. Muller, 1972. 197p. illus. (incl. 37 plates). ISBN: 0584100647.

Gives several hundred definitions, plus comment. Includes very brief biographies. Bibliography (authors, A-Z), p.195-7. Written in simple language; amateurish line-drawings, in addition to the photographs. Stresses ethnological aspects. For the lay person. *Class No:* 572.0(03)

[2001]

STEVENSON, J.C. **Dictionary of concepts in physical anthropology.** Westport, Conn., Greenwood Press, 1991. 448p. $85. ISBN: 0313247560.

74 concepts are examined with coverage extending to current usage, development, bibliography, and additional sources of information. Name and subject indexes. Criticized in *Choice,* March 1992 for being an expensive under-graduate book and for not providing clearer definitions. *Class No:* 572.0(03)

Handbooks & Manuals

[2002]

Companion encyclopedia of anthropology. Ingold, T., *ed.* London, Routledge, 1994. 1127p. £85. ISBN: 0415021375.

A series of essays surveying current thinking on biological, social, and cultural anthropology. 37 contributors; editor is Professor of Social Anthropology at the University of Manchester. Index, p.1067-1127. 'Aimed primarily at the academic reader and does presuppose a certain familiarity with anthropological terminology and concepts ... the price is rather high but there is no truly comparable work' (*The Year in reference* 1994, 212). *Class No:* 572.0(035)

[2003]

Handbook of social and cultural anthropology. Honigmann, J.J., *ed.* Boston, Houghton Mifflin, 1973. viii, 1295p. tables. $67. ISBN: 0395306310.

33 contributors. 28 review articles on cognitive anthropology, symbolism, structuralism and semiotics (*e.g.* 1. History of cultural anthropology; 5. Ecological anthropology and anthropological ecology; 15. The structural anthropology of Claude Lévi-Strauss (references, p.704-16); 21. Cultural psychiatry). Chapter 'credits and acknowledgements', p.1251-5. Name index; analytical subject index.
Class No: 572.0(035)

[2004]

MARTIN, R. **Lehrbuch der Anthropologie in systematischer Darstellung,** mit besonderer Berücksichtigung der anthropologischen Methoden. 3. Aufl. hrsg., von K. Saller. Stuttgart, Fischer, 1957-62. 3v. (2416p.). illus., tables.

2nd ed., 1928 (1816p.).

A standard treatise, systematically arranged, with numerous section bibliographies. Profusely illustrated with *c.*1,000 illus. in all. V.3 included a 600-page bibliography, plus subject and author indexes.
Class No: 572.0(035)

Theses

[2005]

SOCIAL SCIENCE RESEARCH COUNCIL. Social Anthropology Committee. **Research in social anthropology, 1975 - 1980:** register of theses in social anthropology accepted for higher degrees at British universities. Webber, J., *comp.* London, Royal Anthropological Institute, 1983. xxxix, 404p. £14. ISBN: 090063233x.

425 entries, with abstracts and note of availability of theses at British Library Lending Division. Prelims. include: 'List of authors in this Register'; 'List of Univ. depts., presented ...'; university and county indexes; subject and culture, and subject indexes.
Class No: 572.0(043)

Reviews & Abstracts

[2006]

Abstracts in anthropology: archaeology/cultural & physical anthropology/linguistics. Amityville, N.Y., Baywood Publishing Co., 1970-. 8pa. $323 (US); $333.50 (non US). ISSN: 00013455.

V.25(2), 1992 (189p.) has 750 abstracts. Two sections: Archaeology - Physical anthropology (General; Fossil record and evolution; Living humans: population, genetics; calcified tissues; growth and development; body composition and adaptation, living non-human primates). Abstracts average 100 words in length; *c.*300 periodicals scanned. Twice annually includes a cumulative index, listing all periodicals abstracted within the volume. *Class No:* 572.0(048)

[2007]

Abstracts in German anthropology. Göttingen, Edition Re, 1980-. 2pa. DM96; $58. ISSN: 01732986.

About 250 abstracts in German per issue. Covers *c.*50 German periodicals on aspects of anthropology worldwide. Sections: General/theoretical/historical/studies - Regional studies (Africa, The Americas, Asia, Australia, Oceania, Europe). Includes theses in German. Author and subject indexes and list of periodicals seen, per issue.
Class No: 572.0(048)

[2008]

Anthropological index to current periodicals in the Museum of Mankind Library (incorporating the former Royal Anthropological Institute Library). London, Royal Anthropological Institute, 1963-. 4pa. £80; $132. ISSN: 00035467.

As *Index to current periodicals received in the Library of the Royal Anthropological Society*, 1963-67.

About 100,000 articles from over 2,500 journals and 20,000 books pa. are listed. Sections: 1. General - 2. Africa - 3. Americas - 4. Asia - 5. Australasia. Pacific - 6. Europe. Subdivisions (where appropriate): General; Physical anthropology; Archaeology; Cultural anthropology; Ethnography; Linguistics. The first issue of each volume lists additions and amendments to current periodicals, while a revised list of current periodicals, with abbreviations, is published separately. Annual author and subject indexes. Excellent for current awareness.

Available on CD-ROM as *Anthropological index online.*
Class No: 572.0(048)

[2009]

Anthropological literature: an index to periodical articles and essays; compiled by Tozzer Library. Cambridge, Mass., Tozzer Library, 1979-. 4pa. $225. ISSN: 01903373.

Each volume contains a minimum of 8,000 references; v.13, 1991, contains 8,575 entries taken from 988 journals and 92 edited works. 5 sections: Archaeology - Biological/physical - Cultural/social - Linguistics - Research in related fields and topics of general interest. 4 indexes per issue (author; subject; list of journals indexed; list of edited works), all of which cumulate in the fourth issue of each volume. Some overlap with *Anthropological index (q.v.)*, 'but each has

....(contd.)

material not in the other' (University of London Institute of Archaeology. *Bulletin* no.17, 1980, p.194) and this publication uses Library of Congress subject headings rather than geographic and broad topic headings.

Published in CD-ROM format as *Anthropological literature on disc* (1984-) and includes more than 90,000 records. *Class No:* 572.0(048)

[2010]

Excerpta medica. 1. Anatomy, anthropology, embryology and histology. Amsterdam, Elsevier Science, 1947-. 12pa. (2v.). $1,365. ISSN: 00144053.

Section 3, 'Anthropology', has nearly 150 abstracts pa. on physical aspects. Subsections: 1. Techniques and apparatus; 2. Paleoanthropology; 3. Evolution; 4. Variability; 5. Heredity of normal features; 6. Body build and body composition; 7. Ecologic factors and adaptations. Online in EMBASE, and also available on microfilm from University Microfilms International. Available on CD-ROM. *Class No:* 572.0(048)

Periodicals

[2011]

American anthropologist: journal of the American Anthropological Association. Arlington, Virginia, the Association, 1888-. 4pa. $105pa. ISSN: 00027294.

Sections: Applied anthropology - General/theoretical anthropology - Social/cultural anthropology - Biological anthropology - Linguistic anthropology - Archaeology - Film review. Annual title and author indexes. A major reviewing journal in its field. *Class No:* 572.0(051)

[2012]

The Journal of the Royal Anthropological Institute: incorporating *Man.* London, the Institute, 1995-. 4pa. £95; $147pa. ISSN: 13590987.

Formerly *Man: the journal of the Royal Anthropological Institute of Great Britain and Ireland,* 1966-1994.

V.1(4), December 1995 contains 7 documented papers, *e.g.* 'Hunter-gatherer structural transformations', p.679-702. Summaries of each article in French. This issue has 50 signed book reviews and a 'Books Received' section. A leading academic journal on social anthropology. Also available in microform and on CD-ROM. *Class No:* 572.0(051)

[2013]

LIBRARY-ANTHROPOLOGY RESOURCE GROUP. Serial publications in anthropology. Grollig, F.V. *and* Tax, S., *eds.* 2nd ed. South Salem, N.Y., Redgrave, 1982. 177p.

First published 1973 (Univ. of Chicago Press).

4,387 titles, A-Z, of periodicals and other serials that carry anthropological material. Cross-references. Subject index includes names of issuing bodies. *Class No:* 572.0(051)

[2014]

—WILLIAMS, J.T. Anthropology journals and serials: an analytical guide. Westport, Conn., Greenwood Press, 1986. 152p.

Has fewer than 4,387 titles listed in Grollig and Tax, but its arrangement is complementary. 4 of the 5 chapters concern archaeology, cultural anthropology, linguistics, physical anthropology. Chapter 5 covers appropriate indexes and abstracts. Title, subject and geographic indexes. *Class No:* 572.0(051)

Progress Reports

[2015]

Annual review of anthropology. Palo Alto, Calif., Annual Reviews, Inc., 1972-. Annual. $110 (US); $120 (non US). ISSN: 00846570.

V.27, 1998 has 28 contributors (560p.). 23 documented articles: Mission archaeology ... Modeling the genetic architecture of modern populations ... Wittgenstein and anthropology ... Coming to terms with human variation. Author and subject indexes. Cumulative index of contributing authors, v.20-27; cumulative index of chapter titles, v.20-27. For the specialist-researcher. *Class No:* 572.0(055)

[2016]

Research in economic anthropology: a research annual. Greenwich, Conn., Jai Press, 1978-. v.1-. Irregular. ISSN: 01901281.

V.6, 1984, has 5 parts (10 papers): 1. Hunter-gatherers - 2. Slavery, trade and production - 3. Property of the dead - 4. East Africa: Turkana and Gezera - 5. Marxism analysis. Bibliography appended to each paper. 'A state-of-the-art yearbook that should reflect what anthropologists specifically have to say about the economy' (*Preface*). Most recent volume in print is v.18, 1997 ($78.50). *Class No:* 572.0(055)

Teaching Materials

[2017]

ROYAL ANTHROPOLOGICAL INSTITUTE. Teachers' resource guide. 4th ed. London, Royal Anthropological Institute, 1990. 58p. ISBN: 0900632380.

First published 1973.

3 sections: A. Anthropology in education (1. School examinations in anthropology ... 6. Some libraries with anthropological content) - B. Anthropological resources (*e.g.* visual aids, museums) - C. Bibliography (1. General introductions ... 6. Family, marriage and gender ... 15. Teachers' guides and sourcebooks). No index. A helpful tool. *Class No:* 572.0(072)

Films

[2018]

HEIDER, K.G. *and* **HERMER, C. Films for anthropological teaching.** 8th ed. Arlington, Virginia, American Anthropological Association, 1995. vi, 326p. $10. (*Special publication of the AAA, no.29.*) ISBN: 0913167657.

Lists films (and videos) by geographical area, topic, and A-Z by title, with italicized annotations summarizing content. References to reviews. People index. List of distributors' codes. *Class No:* 572.0(084.122)

[2019]

The Royal Anthropological Institute Film Library catalogue. Woodburn, J., *ed.* London, the Institute, 1982. viii, 86p. £4.

A/Z title list of films, p.1-79. Data include type of film (in colour/ black-and-white), length, time/name of director, etc., annotation, and references to reviews. Analytical index, p.81-88. Insert: 'Hire charges'. *Class No:* 572.0(084.122)

Histories

[2020]

EVANS-PRITCHARD, E.E. A History of anthropological thought. London, Faber & Faber, 1981. xxxvi, 218p. £16.50. ISBN: 0571117620.

15 chapters: 1. Montesquieu (1689-1775) ... 15. Hertz (1882-1915), p.3-183. Appendix; Notes and comment on Max Miller (1823-1900) ... L.A. White (1900-1975). Bibliography, p.205-9. Detailed, analytical index, p.211-8. *Class No:* 572.0(091)

[2021]

The History of anthropology: a research bibliography. Kemper, R.V. *and* Phinney, J.F.S., *eds.* New York, Garland, 1977. xvi, 212p. (*Garland reference library of social science, v.3.*)

2,439 references. 4 sections: 1. General sources on the history of anthropology - 2. Background - 3. Modern anthropology (sections A-J, p.47-177) - 4. Related social sciences - 5. Bibliographical sources. Author index. Focuses on secondary and primary sources. A starting point for students of the subject. *Class No:* 572.0(091)

Biographies

[2022]

International dictionary of anthropologists. Winters, C., *ed.* New York, Garland, 1991. xl,823p. $75. (*Garland reference library of the social sciences, v.638.*) ISBN: 0824050940.

First published as *Biographical directory of anthropologists born before 1920* (Garland, 1988).

Includes only individuals born before 1920, thus excluding many important figures. *c.*725 contributions from over 50 countries. Each entry consists of a biographical essay of *c.*500 words, a list of the individual's publications and a short bibliography. Brief glossary and good name/subject index. *Class No:* 572.0(092)

[2023]

Fifth International directory of anthropologists. Spurr, H., *managing ed.* 5th ed. Chicago, Ill., Univ. of Chicago Press, 1976. x, 496p. $29.95. ISBN: 0226790770.

First published 1938.

Very brief biographical data on 4,373 anthropologists (name; date of birth; position and affiliation; sex; research interests; publications; languages). Geographical, chronological and subject/methodological indexes. The subject index has four sections: cultural anthropology; archaeology; physical anthropology; linguistics. *Class No:* 572.0(092)

[2024]

KENNA, M.E. *and* **KENNA, J.C. 'Published portraits of anthropologists and workers in allied fields'.** In *Current anthropology,* v.14, 1973, p.83-101; v.16, 1975, p.271-81.

Lists a total of *c.*1,250 individuals (names; dates of birth and death; references to published portraits in journal articles and monographs). *Class No:* 572.0(092)

[2025]

Women anthropologists: a biographical dictionary. Gacs, U., *and others*. Westport, Conn., Greenwood Press, 1988. 448p. $59.95. ISBN: 0313244146.

Biobibliographies of *c.*58 women anthropologists. The period covered encompasses approximately a hundred years. Entries are 3-7 pages in length, with a list of references by, or about, the individual. *Class No: 572.0(092)*

Somatology (Anatomy of Man)

[2026]

BROTHWELL, D.R. Digging up bones: the excavation, treatment and study of human skeletal remains. 3rd ed. London, British Museum (Natural History); Oxford University Press, 1981. 208p. illus. ISBN: 0198585047.

1. Notes for guidance in excavating and reporting on human remains - 2. Description and study of human bone - 3. Demographic aspects of selected biology - 4. Measurement and morphological analysis of human bones - 5. Injuries and marks on bone - 6. Ancient disease - 7. Concluding remarks. For the layperson as well as the specialist. Bibliography, p.179-99. Index, p.201-8. 17 plates. *Class No: 572.5*

[2027]

FRISANCHO, A.R. Anthropometric standards for the assessment of growth and nutritional status. Ann Arbor, University of Michigan Press, 1990. 189p. graphs, tables. $75. ISBN: 0472101463.

5 sections: 1. Necessity for new anthropometric standards - 2. Methods and materials - 3. Anthropometric classification - 4. Anthropometric standards (p.37-118) - 5. The standard in practice: examples. Literature cited, p.133-42. Appendices: A. Anthropometric tables for blacks - B. Anthropometric tables for whites. Subject index. *Class No: 572.5*

[2028]

History of physical anthropology: an encyclopedia. Spencer, F., *ed.* New York, Garland, 1997. 2v. (xviii, 1,195p. illus.,maps). £149; $195. (*Garland reference library of social science, v.677.*) ISBN: 0815304900.

Claims to be the the first encyclopedia in this subject. International in scope, there are specific and general articles, as well as biographies. Subject coverage includes genetics, demography, anthropometry, neuroanatomy, etc. Bibliographies appended to each entry give primary and secondary sources as well as the location of primary archives. Will be a standard work in its field. For academic libraries. *Class No: 572.5*

Ethnology (Races)

Bibliographies

[2029]

Demos: internationale ethnographische und folkhistorische Informationen. Chur, Gordon & Breach-Harwood Academic, 1960-. 4pa. $89. ISSN: 0011832x.

Annotated bibliography of books, periodical articles and pamphlets, cumulated 10-yearly. Texts in English, French and German. *Class No: 572.9(01)*

[2030]

Guide to information resources in ethnic museum, library and archival collections in the US. Buttlar, L. *and* Wynar, L.R., *comps.* Westport, Conn., Greenwood Press, 1996. xi,369p. (*Bibliographies and indexes in ethnic studies.*)

Covers collections in the US. *Class No: 572.9(01)*

Encyclopaedias

[2031]

Encyclopedia of world cultures. Riverside, N.J., G.K. Hall, 1991-. £80ea (£800, set); $109.95ea ($879.95, set).

V.1. *North America*, edited by T.J. O'Leary and D. Levinson. 1991. 424p. maps. V.2. *Oceania*, edited by T.E. Hays. 1991. 409p. maps. V.3. *South Asia*, edited by P. Hockings. 1992. V.4. *Central, Western and Southeastern Europe*, edited by L.A. Bennett. 1992. V.5. *Southeast and East Asia*, edited by P. Hockings. 1993. V.6. *Russia and Eurasia - China*, edited by P. Friedrich and N. Diamond. 1993. V.7. *South America*, edited by J. Wilbert. 1994. V.8. *Middle America and the Caribbean*, edited by J. Dow. 1995. V.9. *Africa and the Middle East*, edited by J. Middleton and A. Rassam. 1995. V.10. *Cumulated indexes, bibliographies and maps.* 1996.

Describes more than 1,500 cultural groups. Volume 1 contains 223 articles arranged alphabetically on cultures in the US, Canada and

....(contd.)

Greenland, varying in length from a few lines, *e.g.* 'Koyukon', to six pages, *e.g.* 'Apache'. Data in each entry include ethnonyms, history and cultural relations, linguistic and geographic orientation, economy, kinship, marriage and family, and religion. Short bibliographies of six or seven items are appended to each entry. Appendix lists extinct native American tribes. Glossary and ethnonym index. Filmography lists *c.*300 films and videos. No illustrations. 'When complete, the *Encyclopedia of world cultures* will be unique in its provision of concise summaries for almost all cultural groups' (*Booklist*, v.87(21), July 1991 p.2062). The reviewer in *Choice*, November, 1996, p.428 points out some inconsistencies in the index but concludes '*Encyclopedia of world cultures* remains the master work for current encyclopedia articles about living cultures for undergraduate and research libraries'. Sponsored by the Human Relations Area Files at Yale University.

Available on CD-ROM (Macmillan Library Reference USA, 1998. $650 single user), offering three means of searching: Cultures A-Z; Cultures by region; Research idea. *Class No: 572.9(031)*

[2032]

The Illustrated encyclopedia of mankind. Carlisle, R., *and others, eds.* 3rd ed. London, Marshall Cavendish, 1990. 22v. illus., maps. ISBN: 1854350323.

First published 1978, 2nd ed. 1984.

V.1, 2-15 contain A-Z treatment of racial, ethnic and cultural groups and nationalities. V.16-20 cover general themes (unchanged from the 1984 ed.), *e.g.* 'Costume'; 'Social organization'; 'Beliefs of the world'. There is a new *Origins of mankind* volume with its own index. V.22 contains general, thematic and geographic indexes; population charts; bibliography; glossary. Over 3,000 colour photographs. Recommended for public and school libraries which do not already possess the 1984 ed. Otherwise the 1984 ed. would suffice. *Class No: 572.9(031)*

[2033]

—**Family of man: people of the world, how and where they live.** Widdows, R., *ed.* London, Marshall Cavendish, 1974-76. 7v. (2748p.) illus. (incl. col.), maps.

Appeared in 98 weekly parts, arranged A-Z, with interposed articles (*e.g.* 'The future of mankind'). Part 98 consists of index and 5p. of 'Further reading'. Well illustrated. *Class No: 572.9(100)*

Handbooks & Manuals

[2034]

COLE, S. Races of man. 2nd ed. London, British Museum (Natural History), 1965. 131p. front., illus., diagrs., maps.

First published 1961.

Chapters: 1. Definitions of race - 2. Physical characters of race - 3. Genetics and evolution - 4. Blood groups and other biochemical characters - 5. Racial origins - 6. Caucasoids - 7. Australoids and Pacific islanders - 8. Mongoloids (including American Indians) - 9. Negroids. Chapter references, p.125-7; well illustrated with half-tones and line-drawings. A sound introduction for beginners. *Class No: 572.9(035)*

[2035]

LEVINSON, D. Ethnic groups worldwide: a ready reference handbook. Phoenix, Ariz., Oryx, 1998. 436p. $65. ISBN: 1573560197.

Four sections: Africa; Americas; Asia/Pacific; Europe. Arranged A-Z by country within each section. Profile for each ethnic group includes history, proportion of overall population, and social status. Bibliographies. 'Convenient source for hard-to-locate global ethnic information' (*Choice*, December 1998, p.670). *Class No: 572.9(035)*

Dictionaries

[2036]

Dictionnaire de l'ethnologie et de l'anthropologie. Bonte, P. *and* Izard, M., *eds.* Paris, Presses Universitaires de France, 1991. xii,755p. FFr496. ISBN: 2130433839.

Encyclopaedic format with entries ranging from *c.*200 words to several pages in length. Bibliography appended to each entry. 83 biographies. Cross-references could be improved and an effective index is absent. However, a useful reference tool. *Class No: 572.9(038)*

[2037]

WINTHROP, R. Dictionary of concepts in cultural anthropology. Westport, Conn., Greenwood, 1991. 347p. $65. (*Reference sources for the social sciences and humanities, 11.*) ISBN: 0313242801.

80 concepts are discussed, each beginning with a definition followed by a detailed examination of the use and history of the concept. Each entry has a list of further reading appended. Many cross-references. Name and subject indexes. *Class No: 572.9(038)*

Tables & Data Books

[2038]
MURDOCK, G.P. Atlas of world cultures. Pittsburgh, Univ. of Pittsburgh Press, 1981. 151p. $18.95. ISBN: 0822934329.
Revision of his *Ethnographic atlas* (1967).
Not an atlas but coded data on 563 cultures 'most fully described in the ethnographic literature', applying 76 factors. (The 1967 *Atlas* coded 862 cultures). 'Although the coded format requires skill to utilize, the mass of information presented makes the effort worthwhile' (*Library journal*, 1 June 1981, p.1210). *Class No: 572.9(083)*

[2039]
—**Outline of cultural materials.** Murdock, G.P., *and others*. 5th ed. New Haven, Conn., Human Relations Area Files Press, 1982. 247p. $25. ISBN: 0875366546.
Delineates the basic HRAF classification scheme placing data into 79 major and 619 major subject divisions, plus cross-references. *Class No: 572.9(083)*

[2040]
—**Outline of world cultures.** Murdock, G.P., *and others*. 6th ed. New Haven, Conn., Human Relations Area Files Press, 1983. xii, 359p. $25. ISBN: 0875366643.
The companion volume, takes a geographical/historical stance. 8 main regions: World; Asia; Europe; Africa; Middle East; North America; Oceania. Detailed index, p.195-259. Aims to provide 'an outline organization and classification of the known cultures of the world'. *Class No: 572.9(083)*

Maps & Atlases

[2041]
Atlas narodov mira. Moscow, Akademiya Nauk SSSR, 1964. 184p. maps, tables.
'Atlas of peoples of the world'. 112p. of coloured maps, (average scale: 1,10M.), with 72p. of text. Data on world population, races, languages, religion, ethnic groups, etc., as of 1961. Index of names of groups, in cyrillic and romanized. 'The finest collection of ethnographic maps of all areas of the globe' (Soviet Information Service. *Bulletin* no.2188, 10 August 1964, p.1). Page size: 34 x 24cm. *Class No: 572.9(084.3)*

[2042]
—**SPENCER, R.F.** *and* **JOHNSON, E. Atlas for anthropology.** 2nd ed. Dubuque, Iowa, W.C. Brown, 1968. [61]p. maps.
First published 1960.
Provides 15 distribution maps, - 1 general, 5 for N. America, S. America, Africa, Eurasia and Oceania respectively; 5 tribal and linguistic maps for those areas, and 4 for Old World and New World prehistory. *Class No: 572.9(084.3)*

[2043]
PRICE, D.H. Atlas of world cultures: a geographical guide to ethnographic literature. Newbury Park, Calif., Sage Publications, 1989. 155p. maps. $48; $17.95. ISBN: 0803932405.
Published in cooperation with the Human Relations Area Files.
'A geographical guide to ethnographic books, articles, reports, archival materials, maps and atlases, and other materials of use to anthropologists' (*Introduction*). Bibliographical and geographical information on over 3,500 cultural groups. Contains 41 maps. 1,237 references cited in the bibliography. Culture index, p.127-55, contains cross-references to listings of cultures in *Human Relations Area Files* and Murdock's *Atlas of world cultures (q.v.). Class No: 572.9(084.3)*

Worldwide

[2044]
Ethnologie régionale. Poirier, J., *ed.* Paris, Gallimard; New York, French & European, 1972-8. 2v. (xv, [1], 1608p.). illus., diagrs., tables, maps. $59.95, v.1; $92.60, v.2. (*Encyclopédie de la Pléiade, 33, 42.*) ISBN: 0686564413, v.1; 0686564421, v.2.
1. *Afrique-Océanie.* 1972. 2. *Asie-Amérique.* 1978.
Documented essays (*e.g.* Mozambique, p.922-65; 4p. of bibliography). Particularly rich in indexes: names of people; geographical; authors; subjects (p.1509-58); detailed contents list; list of maps and illus. An outstanding contribution to the Encyclopédie series. *Class No: 572.9(100)*

[2045]
Peoples of the world. Stacey, T., *editorial director.* New York, Dansbury Press: Grolier, 1972. 20v. (each 148p.). col. illus., maps. ISBN: 0854682759.
1. *Australia and Melanesia* (incl. New Guinea). 2. *Africa, from the Sahara to the Zambesi.* 3. *Europe.* 4. *Mexico and Central America.* 5. *Islands of the Atlantic, and the Caribbean.* 6. *Amazonia and pampas.* 7. *Andes.* 8. *The Pacific - Polynesia and Micronesia.* 9. *Southern Africa and Madagascar.* 10. *Indonesia, Philippines and Malaysia.* 11. *South-east Asia.* 12. *The Indian subcontinent* (incl. Ceylon). 13. *China* (incl. Tibet), *Japan and Korea.* 14. *USSR east of the Urals.* 15. *Western and Central Asia.* 16. *The Arctic.* 17. *The Arab world.* 18.

....(contd.)
North America. 19. *Man the craftsman.* 20. *The future of mankind. General index.*
20 well-illustrated, slim volumes. Numerous contributors. *Class No: 572.9(100)*

[2046]
Sixty cultures: a guide to the HRAF probability sample files. Lagacé, R.O., *ed.* New Haven, Conn., Human Relations Area Files. 1977-.
Part A (1977, 506p. Loose-leaf) comprises profiles of the 60 cultures (Amhara-Yangama) on which HRAF has files. Appendix ('Sample unit concordance') displays 4 types of listing: 1, by cultural units; 2, by G.P. Murdock's *Ethnographic atlas* codes; 3, by 'Outline of world cultures' codes; 4, by 'Standard cross-culture numbers'. 'Major subject index'. Part B promises to cover 60 more cultures (Webb, W.H. *Sources of information in the social sciences*, 3rd ed., 1986, p.391). *Class No: 572.9(100)*

[2047]
SWEET, L.E. *and* **O'LEARY, T.J.,** *eds.* **Circum-Mediterranean peasantry: introductory bibliographies.** New Haven, Conn., Human Relations Area Files, 1969. xxv[i], 106p. map. $15. (*Behavior science bibliographies.*) ISBN: 0875362346.
Short sections on the countries of North Africa, the Middle East and southern Europe that border on the Mediterranean (*e.g.* Albania, p.29-35, including 3p. of references). No index. An introduction 'for the student who is approaching this area' (*Preface*). *Class No: 572.9(100)*

Developing Countries

[2048]
KURIAN, G.T. Glossary of the Third World: words for understanding Third World peoples and cultures. New York, Facts on File, 1989. 300p. $35. ISBN: 0816018421.
About 10,000 words useful for cultural or anthropological research. Over 70 languages from 120 countries. Appended 'Language families of the world'. No bibliography. *Class No: 572.9(4/9-77)*

Europe

[2049]
East European peasantries: social relations. An annotated index of periodical articles. Sanders, I.T., *and others, comps.* Boston, Mass., G.K. Hall, 1976. vi, 179p. $18. ISBN: 0816178607.
Lists over 800 periodicals on East European peasantries during the 20th century. While the bibliography concentrates on social relations, the articles also concern the demographic, economic and cultural aspects of rural life in the area before and after World War II. Arrangement is by countries: Bulgaria, Czechoslovakia, Greece, Hungary, Poland, Rumania and Yugoslavia, - but not Albania. *Class No: 572.9(4)*

[2050]
KUTER, L. The Anthropology of Western Europe: a selected bibliography. Bloomington, West European Studies, Indiana Univ., 1978. 132p.
Comprises 1,112 numbered, unannotated entries in 2 sections. Section 1 lists apposite journals; section 2 groups by geographical area, with A-Z author subdivision. General author index. 'Strong in French and English sources' (Webb, W.H., and associates. *Sources of information in the social sciences,* item 864). *Class No: 572.9(4)*

[2051]
THEODORATUS, R.J. Europe: a selected ethnographic bibliography. New Haven, Conn., Human Relations Area Files Press, 1969. xi, 544p. $25. (*Behavior science bibliography.*) ISBN: 0875362397.
About 8,000 entries, arranged under major European ethnic groups. Cyprus, Iceland, the Azores, the Canaries, Cape Verde Islands and Tristan da Cunha appear because of their European cultural connections. Main emphasis is on 19th and 20th centuries. *Class No: 572.9(4)*

[2052]
'The Times' guide to the peoples of Europe. London, Times Books, 1994. 416p. maps £15.99 ISBN: 0723006245.
12 chapters (1. The maritime north - 2. The Atlantic arc ... 11. The Urals and Caucasus - 12. Dispersed peoples). Bibliography (by chapters), p.401-8. Detailed, analytical index. *Class No: 572.9(4)*

Russia

[2053]
AKINER, S. Islamic peoples of the Soviet Union: an historical and statistical handbook. 2nd ed. London, KPI, 1986. 462p. maps. £65. ISBN: 071030188x.
First published 1983.
5 sections: 1. Introduction - 2. General information - 3. European USSR and Siberia - 4. Transcaucasia and northern Caucasus - 5.

....(contd.)

Central Asia and Kazakhstan. Appendix on non-Muslim Turkic peoples of the Soviet Union. Gives details of history and origin, occupations, education and religious diversions. Chronological table. Bibliography, p.446-52. Of the previous ed., 'A helpful supplement to Zev Katz's *History of the major Soviet nationalities*' (*Choice*, v.21(7), March 1984, p.945). *Class No:* 572.9(47)

[2054]

BENNIGSEN, A. *and* WIMBUSH, S.E. **Muslims of the Soviet empire: a guide.** Bloomington, Indiana Univ. Press, 1986. 294p. tables, maps. $29.95. ISBN: 0253339588.

3 parts. Part 1 traces the historical roots of Islam. Part 2 examines Muslim groups by regions. Part 3 is a selected bibliography of sources. 88 statistical tables; 3 maps; extensive index. For students and general readers. Very favourable review in *Choice*, v.24(8), April 1987, p.1194. *Class No:* 572.9(47)

[2055]

Handbook of major Soviet inhabitants. Katz, Z., *ed.* New York, Free Press, 1975. 481p. *Class No:* 572.9(47)

[2056]

HORAK, S.M. **Guide to the study of the Soviet nationalities: non-Russian peoples of the USSR.** Littleton, Colo., Libraries Unlimited, 1982. 365p. $35. ISBN: 087287270x.

11 contributors. 1,345 numbered, annotated entries, averaging *c*.100 words apiece. Sections (with introductions): Balts; Belorussians; Ukrainians; Moldavians; Jews; Peoples of the Caucasus (non-Islamic); Islamic peoples (p.174-229); Germans; People of Siberia. Index of authors, compilers and editors, p.255-65. *Class No:* 572.9(47)

[2057]

TITOVA, Z.A. **Etnografiya. Bibliografiya russkikh bibliografii po etnografii narodov SSSR (1831-1969).** [Ethnography. Bibliography of Russian bibliographies on the ethnography of the peoples of the USSR.] Moscow, Kniga, 1970. 143p.

Annotated list of 734 titles, in historico-ethnographical sections. Index of ethnic appellations, names and titles, and geographical names. *Class No:* 572.9(47)

China

[2058]

OLSON, J.S. **An Ethnohistorical dictionary of China.** London, Aldwych Press, 1998. x,434p. £79.95. ISBN: 0861721071.

Details of 400 ethnic groups, with entries varying in length. Data include names of the group, social status, language, customs, religion, etc. Some bibliographical references. Appendices include a chronology of Chinese history and a general index. *Class No:* 572.9(510)

Asia—Middle & Near East

[2059]

The Central Middle East: a handbook of anthropology and published research on the Nile Valley, the Arab Levant, southern Mesopotamia, the Arabian Peninsula, and Israel. Sweet, L.E., *ed.* New Haven, Conn., HRAF Press, 1971. 323p. $9. ISBN: 0875361072.

First published 1968.

5 chapters, one on each area concerned. (*e.g.* The Arabian Peninsula, p.199-266). Each chapter has two parts: a narrative, and a selected, annotated bibliography (*e.g.* Israel; text - anthropology, religion and culture, p.267-303; bibliography, 46 items). Non-analytical index, p.313-23. *Class No:* 572.9(53+56)

[2060]

FIELD, H. **Bibliography on Southwestern Asia.** Coral Gables, Florida, Univ. of Miami Press, 1953-62. 7v. *Supplement* (8v. in 7), 1968-72.

31,254 of the 47,165 entries concern anthropology, drawing on material in about 40 languages. 'Southwestern Asia', in this context, ranges from Egypt to West Pakistan, Turkey and the Caucasus to the Arabian peninsula. Systematic arrangement (of the other entries, 11,505 deal with zoology, and 4,406 with botany). A monumental work.

The *Supplement* (Coconut Grove, Florida, Field Research Projects) is by H. Field and E.M. Laird. *Class No:* 572.9(53+56)

Asia—South & South East

[2061]

Ethnic groups of insular Southeast Asia. LeBar, F.M., *ed. and comp.* New Haven, Conn., Human Relations Area Files Press, 1964. 2v. $25, v.1; $25, v.2. ISBN: 0875364039, v.1; 0875364055, v.2.

1. *Indonesia, Andaman Islands, and Madagascar.* 226p. 2. *Philippines and Formosa.* 167p.

A series of descriptive ethnographic summaries. Thus, v.1, with 19 contributors, has 3 main regions. Short appended bibliographies under tribal groups. Bibliography (authors, A-Z), p.196-219. Index of ethnic names, p.221-6. 10 maps. A companion volume to *Ethnic groups of mainland Southeast Asia (q.v.).* *Class No:* 572.9(54+59)

[2062]

Ethnic groups of mainland Southeast Asia. LeBar, F.M., *and others.* New Haven, Conn., Human Relations Area Files, 1964. [xiii], 288p. maps. $75.

9 contributors, 4 parts: 1. Sino-Tibetan - 2. Austroasiatic - 3. Tai-Kandai - 4., Malayo-Polynesian. 151 tribal groups, each with appended references. Bibliography (general), p.267-79. Index of names. Country-name concordance. *Class No:* 572.9(54+59)

[2063]

FÜRER-HAIMENDORF, E., von. **An Anthropological bibliography of South Asia:** together with a directory of recent anthropological field work. Paris & The Hague, Mouton, 1958-70. 3v. $112, v.1; $78.75, v.2; $102, v.3. ISBN: 0686225317, v.1; 9027962065, v.2; 9027963029, v.3.

12,603 numbered references. V.1 (1958) covers the period up to 1954; v.2 (1964), 1955-59; v.3 (1970), 1960-64. 'South Asia' implies the Indian sub-continent. V.1 has 20 sections, 19 of them on particular areas (each section is subdivided: A. Select bibliography of works issued prior 1940; B. Bibliography of works issued 1940-45; C. Field research, 1940-1954. A & B include periodical articles and unpublished theses). Author index. Continued in:
Class No: 572.9(54+59)

[2064]

—An Anthropological bibliography of South Asia, ... together with a directory of anthropological field research. Kanitkar, H.A., *comp.* Paris & The Hague, Mouton, 1976-.

Continues Fürer-Haimendorf, but drops physical anthropology and prehistoric archaeology. V.1 (1976) covers a 5-year period, 1965-9. *Class No:* 572.9(54+59)

India

[2065]

NATIONAL LIBRARY. Calcutta. **Bibliography of Indology. v.1: Indian anthropology.** Kanitkar, J.M., *ed.* Rev. and enl. ed. by D.L. Banerjee and A.K. Obdedar. Calcutta, 1960. 290p.

2,067 entries, mostly annotated, in 10 geographical regions. Covers books and selected periodical articles. Author and subject indexes. *Bibliography of anthropology of India (including index to current literature)* (Calcutta, Anthropological Survey of India, 1976-) provides a more detailed continuation in its v.1: 1960-1964. *Class No:* 572.9(540)

Islamic World

[2066]

Muslim peoples: a world ethnographic survey. Weekes, R.V., *ed.* 2nd ed. Westport, Conn., Greenwood Press, 1984. 2v. maps. $95, v.1; $95, v.2; $135, set. ISBN: 0313246394, v.1; 0313246408, v.2.

First published 1978.

Extensively revised and expanded. 139 contributors. 110 documented groups, Acehnese ... Yoruk, (*e.g.* 'Bengalis', p.137-43, including 2p. of bibliography - books, articles, unpublished manuscripts). 3 appendices: 1. Muslim nationalities of the world; 2. Muslims and their ethnic groups (1983); 3. Major Muslim ethnic groups (1983). Index, p.931-53. 8 maps showing locations of Muslim groups. Of the 1978 ed., 'A timely reference work for both public and academic libraries' (*Library journal*, 15 April 1979, p.587). A scholarly reference tool. *Class No:* 572.9(5.297)

Africa

[2067]

COMITÉ INTERNATIONAL DU FILM ETHNOGRAPHIQUE ET SOCIOLOGIQUE. **Premier catalogue sélectif international de films ethnographiques sur l'Afrique noire.** Paris, UNESCO, 1967. 408p.

Catalogue of 467 films, with annotations and, occasionally, brief critiques. A country-by-country survey, following Africa in general. Indexes of films, subjects, ethnic groups, and film directors. 'This outstanding catalogue' (*Guide to research and reference works on sub-Saharan Africa* [1971], edited by P. Duignan, item 1110).
Class No: 572.9(6)

[2068]

GIBSON, G.D. **'A Bibliography of anthropological bibliographies: Africa'.** In *Current anthropology*, v.10(5), December 1969, p.527-66. map.

872 numbered and closely classified items, with annotations and cross-references. Section 2: General encyclopaedic - 2.04. European dependencies (former and present) - 2.1. North Africa, general ... 2.8. Malagasy Republic. Further subdivided by subjects. 43 library locations 'A research aid of exceptional importance' (Webb, W.H., and others. *Guide to sources of information in the social sciences.* 3rd ed., 1986, item F459). Updated, to 1975, in *African journal* (New York, Africana Publishing), v.8, 1977, p.232-42; v.9, 1978, p.293-206. *Class No:* 572.9(6)

[2069]

JONES, R., *comp*. **African bibliographies:** ethnography, sociology, linguistics and related subjects. London, International African Institute, 1958-61.

West Africa. 1958. v, 116p. *North-east Africa*. 1959. ii, 51p. *East Africa*. 1960. [1], iii, [3], 62p. *South-east Central Africa and Madagascar*. 1961. 53p. *West Central Africa*. 1963. 60p.

Sub-title of each volume: 'general, ethnography/sociology, linguistics'. Three regional bibliographies are based on the Institute's library card-index. The main source is the 'Bibliography of current publications' in each issue of *Africa* (quarterly), 1929-70, - now issued separately as *International African bibliography* (quarterly. 1971-). Aims to list all significant works rather than to produce an exhaustive bibliography. Stresses the cultures, languages and institutions of tropical Africa. *Class No:* 572.9(6)

[2070]

OLSON, J.S. **The Peoples of Africa:** an ethnohistorical dictionary. Westport, Conn., Greenwood, 1996. 681p. $99.50. ISBN: 0313279187.

Covers more than 1,800 ethnic groups, with data including population estimates and brief ethnographic description. Many cross-references to variant spellings and names. Includes an African chronology. Bibliography. 'It is hard to imagine a more complete dictionary' (*Choice*, December 1996, p.593). *Class No:* 572.9(6)

[2071]

WIESCHHOFF, H.A. **Anthropological bibliography of negro Africa.** New Haven, Conn., American Oriental Society, 1948. Reprinted, Millwood, N.Y., Kraus Reproduction. xi, 461p. $48. (*American Oriental series, v.23*.) ISBN: 0527026972.

A 'Tribal index' of *c*.18,000 entries, arranged under tribes, A-Z, further subdivided to accommodate travellers' accounts, history, geography, etc. Numerous cross-references for tribal names. Periodical article sources, drawn from over 200 scholarly journals, as well as books and pamphlets. *Class No:* 572.9(6)

Nigeria

[2072]

ITA, N.O. **Bibliography of Nigeria:** a survey of anthropological and linguistic writings, from the earliest times to 1966. London, Cass, 1971. xxxv, 273p. ISBN: 0714624586.

5,411 annotated entries. Part 1: Nigeria - general (4 sections) - Part 2: Ethnic divisions (A-Z), p.79-245, subdivided into 'General and ethnographic studies' and 'Linguistic studies' and further into Edo, Fulani, Hausa ... Author and ethnic indexes; index of Islamic studies. *Class No:* 572.9(669)

Africa—Southern

[2073]

The Bantu-speaking peoples of Southern Africa. Hammond-Tooke, W.D., *ed*. 2nd ed. London, Routledge & Kegan Paul, 1974. xxii, 525p. illus., maps.

First published 1937; edited by I. Schapera.

Contributions by specialists. Extensive bibliography, p.473-510. 22p. of plates. Index. *Class No:* 572.9(68)

[2074]

Bibliographie de l'Afrique sud-saharienne, sciences humaines et sociales. Tervuren (Belgium), Musée Royal de l'Afrique Centrale, 1978-. Biennial. BFr12.

Earlier (1925-59) as *Bibliographie ethnographique du Congo Belge* and *Bibliographie ethnographique de l'Afrique sud-saharienne* (1960-77).

About 1,500 annotated entries for books and articles pa. Authors A-Z, with subjects and tribes indexes. Locations in 4 Belgian libraries. *Class No:* 572.9(68)

[2075]

The Peoples of Southern Africa. Hammond-Tooke, W.D. *and* West, M., *eds*. Cape Town, Philip, 1978-.

A 14-volume series that began with *The peopling of Southern Africa*, by R. Inskeep in 1978. A second volume, *Peoples of South West Africa*, by W. Pendleton has been followed by others on Khoisan peoples; Xhosa-speaking peoples; Southern Sotho and Tewara peoples; Northern Sotho peoples; Venda, Tsonga and Ndebele peoples; Afrikaans-speaking white people; English-speaking white people; Coloured peoples; Indian peoples; Rural life and urban life. (Source: Musker, R. *Guide to South African reference books. Supplement 1970-1976* (1977), entry no.72). *Class No:* 572.9(68)

South Africa

[2076]

SCHAPERA, I., *comp*. **Select bibliography of South African native life and problems.** Compiled for the Inter-University Committee for African Studies. London, Oxford Univ. Press. 1941. xii, 249p. Supplements. Cape Town, 1956-74.

About 2,500 briefly but critically annotated items in 6 sections: Physical anthropology - Archaeology - Ethnography (p.36-109; 714 items) - Modern status and conditions (p.110-204) - Linguistics, includes periodical articles and government reports. Author index only. The 4 supplements cover 1939-70. *Class No:* 572.9(680)

America

[2077]

GIBSON, G.D. 'A Bibliography of anthropological bibliographies: the Americas'. In *Current anthropology*, v.1, January 1960, p.61-75.

Annotated bibliography of 200 items, with locations in 13 libraries, Geographical sections: 1. America, general - 1.1 North America - 1.2. Latin America ... 1.22. Antilles ... 1.23. Western South America ... 1.24. Eastern South America. Index of authors, subjects, journal titles. *Class No:* 572.9(7)

[2078]

PAN AMERICAN INSTITUTE OF GEOGRAPHY AND HISTORY. **Boletín bibliográfico de antropologia americana.** Tocubaya, Mexico. Instituto Panamericano de Geografia e Historia, 1937-72. Annual (irregular).

About 2,000 items pa. Apart from reviews of books and periodicals, covers physical, social and applied anthropology, archaeology, art and prehistory, ethnography, folklore, linguistics. Index volume covers 1937-67.

Continued in 'Revista de libros y revistas' (*Bibliografia anthropológica*, v.36(45)-. 1973-). *Class No:* 572.9(7)

America—North

[2079]

Harvard encyclopedia of American ethnic groups. Thernstrom, S., *and others, eds*. Cambridge, Mass., Belknap Press of Harvard Univ. Press, 1980. xxv, 1076p. tables, maps. $95. ISBN: 0674375122.

120 contributors; 106 signed articles (Acadians ... Zoroastrians); 29 thematic essays. The 'Acadians' article has sections: Acadia [East Canada] and diaspora; The Acadians in Louisiana; Social and family life; Group maintenance; Bibliography of 21½ lines. Cross-references. 2 appendices (1. 'Methods of estimating the size of groups'). 87 maps. Lacks an index. Nevertheless, 'a compact, authoritative encyclopedia' (*Choice*, v.15(5), January 1981, p.636). *Class No:* 572.9(71 + 73)

[2080]

MURDOCK, G.P. *and* O'LEARY, T.J. **Ethnographic bibliography of North America.** 4th ed. New Haven, Conn., Human Relations Area Files, 1975. 5v. $35, v.1; $74, v.2; $73.80, v.3; $35, v.4; $111.30, v.5. ISBN: 0875362052, v.1; 0835728021, v.2; 0317106155, v.3; 0875362117, v.4; 0317106163, v.5.

First published 1941; 3rd ed., 1960.

Supplement, 1973-87, by M.M. Martin and T.J. O'Leary, published 1990. 3v. (v.1 *Indexes*; v.2-3 *Citations*).

1. *General North America*. 2. *Arctic and Subarctic*. 3. *Far West and Pacific coast*. 4. *Eastern United States*. 5. *Plains and Southwest*.

About 40,000 entries, arranged by geographical areas, with ethnic group subdivisions. No index of authors or subject listings. 'Its value and long-term use are well worth its cost' (*Choice*, v.13(10), December 1976, p.1276). *Class No:* 572.9(71 + 73)

America—North & Central

[2081]

BERNAL, I. **Bibliografia de arqueologia y etnografia: Mesoamerica y norte de México, 1514-1960.** Mexico, Instituto Nacional de Antropologia e Historia, 1962. 634p. maps. (*Memoria, 7*.)

13,134 items (books and periodical articles), arranged by area. Described in *Handbook of Latin American studies* (v.25, 1963, p.6-7) as 'the most complete bibliography ... ever assembled on the pre-Hispanic culture of Mesoamerica and northern Mexico'. Includes references to reviews. Rather uneven; weak on southern Mesoamerican ethnography. *Class No:* 572.9(71/73)

Canada

[2082]

The Native peoples of Canada: an annotated bibliography of population biology, health and illness. Meiklejohn, C. *and* Rokala, D.A., *eds*. Ottawa, Canadian Museum of Civilization, 1988. 564p. $29.95. (*Archaeological Survey of Canada, no. 134*.) ISBN: 0660107740.

2,100 citations to books, articles and theses. Length of annotations ranges from one line to half a page. Scope is mostly English-language publications, with a few French and German. Entries arranged

....(contd.)
alphabetically by author. Subject coverage includes culture, medical history, demography, genetics, and environment. Author and subject indexes. *Class No: 572.9(71)*

[2083]
Review of ethnohistorical research on the native peoples of Quebec. Proulx, J.-R., *comp.* Quebec, Consulting Services on Social Sciences, Development and Cultural Change, Ministère des Affaires Culturelles du Québec.
1. *Assessment of research.* vp. 2. *Bibliography of ethnohistorical works, 1960-1983.* xvii, 163p. 3. *Bibliography of published works.* xiii, 172p.
V.2 covers Amerindians of Quebec (12 sections) and Inuit of Quebec. V.3 concerns primary and secondary sources on 12 tribes (Amerindians ... Inuit). *Class No: 572.9(71)*

USA
[2084]
ALLEN, J.P. *and* **TURNER, E.J. We the people: an atlas of America's ethnic diversity.** New York, Macmillan, 1988. 315p. tables, maps. (some col.). $105. ISBN: 0029014204.
Distribution of 67 ethnic groups is shown using 115 maps (111 in colour). 13 chapters, the first 3 of which discuss the methods and techniques used in compiling the data, while the remaining 10 look at geographical ancestry origin. Summary table for each group includes data on multiple ancestry; number of persons claiming single ancestry; the 5 US counties with the largest population of that group. Almost one third of the book is made up of appendices of county ethnic census data. Brief ethnic populations and places indexes. 'Outstanding reference source' (*Booklist*, 15 April 1988, p.1399). *Class No: 572.9(73)*

[2085]
—'Ethnics in American society'. In *Booklist*, July 1990, p.2109-12.
49 briefly annotated entries, covering references sources on ethnic minorities. Sections: General; African Americans; Asian Americans; Hispanic Americans. *Class No: 572.9(73)*

[2086]
JOSEY, E.J. *and* **DELOACH, M.L. Ethnic collections in libraries.** New York, Neal Schuman, [c.1983]. xvi, 361p. $39.50. ISBN: 0918212634.
18 original essays on non-European ethnic collections (i.e. Hispanic American, Afro-American, Asian-American and native American) in US academic and public libraries, with data on accessibility, special items, publications, etc. 'An excellent starting point' (*Reference books bulletin, 1983-1984*, p.87). *Class No: 572.9(73)*

[2087]
WASSERMAN, P. *and* **MORGAN, J. Ethnic information sources of the United States.** 2nd ed. Detroit, Mich., Gale, 1983. 2v. (1380p.). $175. ISBN: 0810303671.
First published 1976.
Covers more than 90 ethnic groups, A-Z, with data on each under 26 heads. Omits such major groups as blacks, American Indians and Eskimos, - adequately treated elsewhere. Indexes. *Class No: 572.9(73)*

Black Races
[2088]
Afro-American reference. Davis, N., *ed.* Westport, Conn., Greenwood Press, 1985. 288p. $55. (*Bibliographies and indexes in Afro-American studies, no.9.*) ISBN: 031324930x.
An annotated guide to 105 general reference works on black studies, plus topical chapters on 537 books covering slavery, sociology, family, etc. 'A boon to public and academic libraries' (*Wilson library bulletin*, April 1986, p.62). *Class No: 572.9(73)(=96)*

[2089]
Black Americans information directory: a guide to approximately 4,500 organizations, agencies, institutions, programs, and publications concerned with black American life and culture. Smith, D.L., *ed.* Detroit, Gale Research, 1990. 424p. ISBN: 0810374439. ISSN: 10458050.
1990-91 ed.: 17 sections: 1. National associations ... 4. Library collections (143 entries) - 5. Museums and other cultural organizations ... 14. Publications (newspapers, periodicals, newsletters and directories) ... 15. Videos. Master name and keyword index. *Class No: 572.9(73)(=96)*

[2090]
HOWARD UNIVERSITY LIBRARY. Washington, D.C. Dictionary catalog of the Jessie E. Moorland Collection of negro life and history. Boston, Mass., G.K. Hall, 1970. 9v. Supplement (3v.), 1976. $980. $400, supp. ISBN: 0816108714; 0816109443, supp.
150,000 photolithographed catalogue cards. Subject, title and author entries. Appended index to African and American periodicals. *Class No: 572.9(73)(=96)*

[2091]
Index to black periodicals. Thorndike, Maine, G.K. Hall, 1984-. Annual. $195. ISSN: 08996253.
Originally *Index to selected periodicals received in the Hallie Q. Brown Library. Decennial cumulation, 1950-1959* (1962); then as *Index to periodical articles by and about negroes. Cumulation, 1960-1970* (1971); then *Index to periodical articles by and about blacks* (1973-83).
Indexes *c.*3,000 articles pa. in 37 journals. Late in appearance, states *Magazines for libraries* (6th ed. 1989, p.23). *Class No: 572.9(73)(=96)*

[2092]
NEW YORK PUBLIC LIBRARY. Dictionary catalog of the Schomburg Collection of negro literature and history. Boston, Mass., G.K. Hall, 1962. 9v. (8474p.). Supplements, 1967-.
The Schomburg Collection, states the prospectus, is international in scope 'covering every phase of Negro activity wherever Negroes have lived in significant numbers'.
Available on CD-ROM is the *Cumulative catalog of the Schomburg Centre for Research in Black Culture*, entitled *Black studies on disc* (Annual). *Class No: 572.9(73)(=96)*

[2093]
—A Bibliography of the negro in Africa and America. Work, M.N., *comp.* New York, H.W. Wilson, 1928. xxi, [ii], 698p. Reprinted in New York, Octagon, 1965.
Lists more than 17,000 entries for books, pamphlets and articles in different languages issued before 1928. Pt.1: 'The negro in Africa'; (p.1-247); pt.2: 'The negro in America'. Systematic subdivision. In the author index, names of negro authors are asterisked.
Bibliographies in the quarterly *Journal of negro history* (Washington, Association for the Study of Negro Life, 1916-) update. *Class No: 572.9(73)(=96)*

[2094]
STEVENSON, R.M. Index to Afro-American reference resources. Westport, Conn., Greenwood Press, 1988. 315p. $39.95. (*Bibliographies and indexes in Afro-American and African Studies, no. 20.*) ISBN: 0313245800.
Covers 181 sources, mainly published in the US, but also including South America, Canada, and the Caribbean. Author and title indexes. *Class No: 572.9(73)(=96)*

America—South
[2095]
Handbook of Latin American studies: Social sciences. Austin, Texas, Univ. of Texas Press, v.27-, 1965- (previously published, 1935-). Two-yearly.
Carries a regular section on anthropology. Thus, v.55 (1997. $85), 'Anthropology' has five section: General - Archaeology (*e.g.* 'An ancient Zapotec calendrical cosmogram'; 'Tropical time capsule')- Ethnology - Anthrolinguistics - Human biology. The volume has subject and author indexes, plus a list of journals covered. The oldest continuous reference work in this field.
Now available in electronic format as *HLAS online* on CD-ROM, produced and annually updated by the Fundacion MAPRE América (Madrid, Spain), and on the Internet at http://lcweb2.loc.gov/hlas/. *Class No: 572.9(8)*

[2096]
O'LEARY, T.J. Ethnographic bibliography of South America. New Haven, Conn., Human Relations Area Files, 1963. xxiv, 387p. $27.50. (*Behavior science bibliographies.*)
24,000 entries, arranged into cultural areas, subdivided by tribal groups, A-Z. Significant works are asterisked. *Class No: 572.9(8)*

[2097]
OLIEN, M.D. Latin Americans: contemporary peoples and their cultural traditions. New York, Holt, Rinehart & Winston, 1973. vii, 408p. illus., tables, maps. ISBN: 0030862525.
Features an extensive bibliography, p.321-96, helpfully subdivided. 'Designed to give the student and general reader an understanding of the temporal, spiritual and cultural setting of the region' (*Handbook of Latin American Studies: Social sciences.* v.37, item no.518). *Class No: 572.9(8)*

Indonesia
[2098]
KENNEDY, R. Bibliography of Indonesian peoples and cultures. Rev. ed., edited by T.W. Maretzki and H. Th. Fischer. New Haven, Conn., Southeast Asia Studies, Yale Univ., by arrangement with Human Relations Area Files, 1955. 2v. (xxviii, 663p.). maps. (1962 ed. in 1v.). $57.30.
First published 1945.
About 12,000 unannotated entries. Area coverage: Indonesia, Sumatra, Bornea, Celebes, Java (and Madura), Lesser Sunda Islands, Moluccas. No indexes.

....(contd.)

Repertorium op de literatuur betreffende de Nederlandiche Kolonien is cited (v.1, p.1-3) as listing all publications issued between 1595 and 1932.

The 1962 ed. of Kennedy's *Bibliography* adds no new titles since 1951. Important items are asterisked. *Class No:* 572.9(910)

Melanesia

[2099]

ELKIN, A.P. Social anthropology in Melanesia: a review of research. London, Oxford Univ. Press, 1953 (reprinted Greenwood Press, 1976). xiii, 166p. maps.

Issued under the auspices of the South Pacific Commission.

3 parts: 1. Types of ethnographical record and research, up to 1950 (chapters 1-3) - 2. Survey of anthropological knowledge of the region, with suggestions for research projects (chapters 4-10; many references) - 3. Principles of a plan of anthropological research in Melanesia, related to native welfare and development. *Class No:* 572.9(932)

Papua—New Guinea

[2100]

AUSTRALIAN NATIONAL UNIVERSITY, Canberra. Department of Anthropology and Sociology. **An Ethnographic bibliography of New Guinea.** Canberra, Australian National Univ. Press, 1968. 3v.

V.1: Author index; v.2: District index; v.3: Proper names index. About 10,000 entries, ranging from mid-19th century publications to those of 1964. *Class No:* 572.9(954)

Polynesia

[2101]

BERNICE P. Bishop Museum, Honolulu. **Dictionary catalog of the Library of Bernice P. Bishop Museum.** Boston, Mass., G.K. Hall. 9v. (6443p.). First and second supplements, 1967-69. 676p. +239p. ISBN: 0816106797.

The main catalogue comprises 135,000 cards, photolithographically reproduced. Concentrates on Polynesia and the adjacent areas of Micronesia and Melanesia. 'Emphasis is on materials relating to the network of relationships in culture and nature throughout the island area'. *Class No:* 572.9(96)

[2102]

A Pacific bibliography: printed matter relating to the native peoples of Polynesia, Melanesia and Micronesia. Taylor, C.R.H., *comp.* 2nd ed. London, Oxford Univ. Press, 1965. xxx, 692p. map.

First published 1931.

More than 16,000 references (to periodical articles and books), classified into island groups and by subjects. Covers every island group of Polynesia, Melanesia and Micronesia, plus New Zealand. Over 13% of entries concern the Maori, over 5%, Hawaii, and 4%, the Fiji Islands (Ad Orientem. *Catalogue nine,* 1967, p.147). *Class No:* 572.9(96)

Gypsies

[2103]

FRASER, A. The Gypsies. Oxford, Blackwell, 1992. 359p. illus. ISBN: 0631159673.

Restricted mainly to Europe. 9 chapters: 1. Origins - 2. Early migrations - 7. Forces for change - 9. Modern times. Bibliography, p.319-39. 'The best general book on Gypsies available ... a valuable bibliographic tool for scholars' (*Choice*, May 1993, p.1508). *Class No:* 572.9(=914.9)

Amerindians, North

Bibliographies

[2104]

American Indians. Markowitz, H., *consulting ed.* Englewood Cliffs, N.J., Salem Press, 1995. 3v.(953p.) illus. maps. charts. $270.

1,129 articles varying in length from 200 to 3,000 words covering Indians from the US and Canada and some Mesoamerican groups. Many cross-references. 200 photographs, charts, and maps. *Class No:* 572.9(=97)(01)

[2105]

HOXIE, F.E. *and* **MARKOWITZ, H. Native Americans: an annotated bibliography.** Englewood Cliffs, N.J., Salem Press, 1991. 325p. $40. ISBN: 0893566705.

Over 1,000 annotated entries. 4 sections: 1. General studies and references - 2. History - 3. Culture areas - 4. Contemporary life. Annotations are non-evaluative. Updates and complements Hirschfelder's *Guide to research on North American Indians (qv)* (Chicago, ALA, 1983). Author index but no subject index. *Class No:* 572.9(=97)(01)

[2106]

Index to literature on the American Indian, 1970-. San Francisco, Indian Historian Press, 1972-. Annual.

Published for the American Indian Historical Society.

An author and subject index of monographs and periodical articles, initially from US and Canadian journals. *Class No:* 572.9(=97)(01)

[2107]

Indians of the United States and Canada: a bibliography. Smith, D.L., *ed.* Santa Monica, Calif., 1974-83. 2v. (*Clio bibliography series 3, 9.*) ISBN: 0874361494.

4,905 annotated entries in all, drawn from *America: history and life abstracting service*, 1954-78, on native North American history from pre-Columbian times to date. 4 period sections, divided by regions, then tribes. Subject and author indexes. *Class No:* 572.9(=97)(01)

[2108]

NEWBERRY LIBRARY CENTER FOR THE HISTORY OF THE AMERICAN INDIAN. Bibliographical series. [Newberry Library Center for the History of the American Indian]. Bloomington, Indiana Univ. Press, 1976-. v.1-. maps.

A series of critical bibliographies (more than 30 titles, to date). *The Yakimas: a critical bibliography,* by H.H. Schuster (1983. 158p.) includes a bibliographical essay, a basic reading list, suggested titles for a core library collection, and a discussion of Yakima tribal publications. ('An excellent introduction to the ethnicity of the Pacific Northwest population' *Choice,* v.20(2), October 1982, p.247). *Class No:* 572.9(=97)(01)

[2109]

SMITHSONIAN INSTITUTION. National Museum of Natural History. National Anthropological Archives. **Catalog to manuscripts at the National Anthropological Archives.** Boston, Mass., G.K. Hall, 1975. 4v. (2855p.). $435, set. ISBN: 0816111944.

22,800 photolithographed catalogue cards, on the languages, technology and history of North American Indians. About 5,000 main entries. Includes transcripts of oral history and music, drawings, manuscript maps, and maps with manuscript annotations. *Class No:* 572.9(=97)(01)

[2110]

WALSH, J. 'Native American reference sources'. In *Booklist*, 1/15 June 1993, p.1879-88.

Includes material dealing with native Americans as a group rather than individual tribes. Sections: Guides to the literature - Encyclopedias - Dictionaries - Directories - Biographical sources - Atlases - Maps - Travel books - Miscellaneous compendiums - Specialized bibliographies - Electronic sources. *Class No:* 572.9(=97)(01)

[2111]

WHITE, P.M. American Indian studies: a bibliographic guide. Englewood, Colo., Libraries Unlimited, 1995. xi, 163p. $29. ISBN: 1563082438.

Covers mainly North American Indians. Critically annotated list of almost 400 sources published from 1970 to 1993. Includes periodicals, directories, encyclopaedias, and electronic sources. Bibliographies are arranged by tribe. Author-title and subject indexes. Useful for its extensive bibliographies. *Class No:* 572.9(=97)(01)

[2112]

WOLF, C.E. *and* **CHIANG, N.S. Indians of North and South America:** a bibliography based on the collection at the Willard E. Yager Library-Museum, Hartwick College, Oneonta, N.Y. Supplement. Metuchen, N.J., Scarecrow Press, 1988. 654p. $59.50. ISBN: 0810821273.

Supplements the original bibliography (Scarecrow Press, 1978).

Contains 3,542 entries. Listed items may be borrowed from the library. Indexes to titles, series and subjects. Criticized in *Choice,* v.26(4), December 1988 for typographical errors, 'otherwise, it is an excellent volume of great value to research libraries.' *Class No:* 572.9(=97)(01)

[2113]

—**WOLF, C. Indians of North and South America, second supplement.** Lanham, Md., Scarecrow Press, 1997. 492p. £56.55. ISBN: 0810833018.

Five types of material are included: 1. Books primarily on Indians - 2. 135 collections of essays in which some or all of the essays discuss Indians - 3. Books on anthropology and archaeology dealing primarily with Indians - 4. Doctoral dissertations and master's theses - 5. Major collections in microform. Lists 3,495 unannotated items. Title, series and subject indexes, followed by separate lists of tribes, caves, mounds, reservations, and sites cited in the subject index. *Class No:* 572.9(=97)(01)

Encyclopaedias

[2114]

Encyclopedia of North American Indians. Hoxie, F.E., *ed*. Boston, Houghton Mifflin, 1996. x,756p. illus.,maps. £27.50; $45. ISBN: 0395669219.

Signed entries by 260 authors, plus many unsigned items. Articles include subjects such as religion, hunting, treaties, etc. Also covers contemporary subjects such as the status of women and urban Indians. Biographies are included and the longer articles have short bibliographies. Detailed index. For school and public libraries. *Class No:* 572.9(=97)(031)

[2115]

The Gale encyclopedia of Native American tribes. Malinowski, S., *and others*. New York, Gale, 1998. 4v. illus.,maps. £270; $349. ISBN: 0787610852.

Contains information on *c*.400 tribes, arranged by geographical region (v.1, the Northeast and Southeast; v.2, the Great Basin and Southwest; v.3, the Arctic, Subarctic, Plateau, and Great Plains; v.4, the Pacific Northwest and California). Data are presented clearly, *e.g. c*. 300 boxed biographical profiles, while entries are subdivided into history, religion, language, buildings, subsistence, clothing, healing practices, customs, oral literature, and current tribal issues. Over 600 black-and-white photographs. Includes bibliographies and a glossary, along with contents pages for each volume, plus a cumulative contents page for the complete set. More detailed and up-to-date than *Encyclopedia of native American tribes* (Facts on File, 1988) (*q.v.*). For public and academic libraries. *Class No:* 572.9(=97)(031)

[2116]

WALDMAN, C. Encyclopedia of native American tribes. New York; Oxford; Facts on File, 1988. xiii,293p. illus. (col.). ISBN: 0816014213.

Alphabetical list of tribes and peoples (Abnaki ... Zuni), p.1-263. Glossary, p.265-73. 4-page list of further reading. Index. Suitable for school and public libraries. *Class No:* 572.9(=97)(031)

Handbooks & Manuals

[2117]

Handbook of Middle American Indians. Wauchope, R., *ed*. Austin, Univ. of Texas Press, 1964-76. 16v. Supplements, 1981-.

1. *Natural environment and early cultures.* 1964. 2-3. *Archaeology of Southern Mesoamerica.* 1965. 4. *Archaeological frontiers and external connections.* 1966. 5. *Linguistics.* 1967. 6. *Social anthropology.* 1967. 7-8. *Ethnology.* 1969. 9. *Physical anthropology.* 1970. 10-11. *Archaeology of Northern Mesoamerica.* 1971. 12-15. *Guide to ethnohistorical science.* 1973-75. 16. *Sources cited and artifacts illustrated.* 1976.

Each volume consists of specialist contributions on the life, customs, culture, milieu, etc., plus an extensive bibliography and detailed index. Lacks any preface or formal introduction to the work as a whole. Covers the area South of F.W. Hodge's *Handbook of American Indians (qv)*, and updates J.H. Steward's *Handbook of South American Indians (qv)*. 'It would be hard to exaggerate the importance of this series' (*American anthropologist*, v.67, 1965, p.1333). Supplements are published irregularly. *Class No:* 572.9(=97)(035)

[2118]

Handbook of North American Indians. Sturtevant, W.C., *ed*. Washington, Smithsonian Institution, 1978-. illus., maps.

1. *Introduction.* 2. *Indians and Eskimos in contemporary society.* 3. *Environment, origin and population.* 4. *History of Indian-white relations.* 1991. 5. *Arctic;* edited by D. Damas, 1984. 6. *Subarctic;* edited by J. Helm. 1981. 7. *The Northwest coast;* edited by W.C. Sturtevant and W. Suttles. 1990. 8. *California;* edited by R.F. Heizer. 1978. 9/10. *Southwest;* edited by A. Ortiz, 1979-83. 11. *The Great Basin*; edited by W.L. D'Azevedo. 1989. 12. *The Plateau.* 1998. 13. *The Plains.* 14. *The Southeast;* edited by B.G. Tripper. 1990. 16. *Technology and the visual arts.* 17. *Native languages.* 18/19, *Biographical dictionary.* 20. *Consolidated index.*

Planned in 20v. V.7, *The Northwest coast*, (1990), comprises 58 chapters, made up of introductory chapters on human biology, language, history of research, early prehistory, followed by 24 chapters on particular peoples. Profusely, and well illustrated; well documented (v.7 has a 100-page bibliography) and indexed. Authoritative. 'The unrelenting excellence of these volumes marks an editorial achievement of the first rank' (Webb, W.H., and associates. *Sources of information in the social sciences* (3rd ed., 1986. item F989)). *Class No:* 572.9(=97)(035)

[2119]

JENNESS, D. The Indians of Canada. 7th ed. Toronto, Univ. of Toronto, with National Museum of Canada, 1977. 432p. illus., (incl. col. pl.), ports., maps. $118.10. (*National Museum bulletin, no.65. Anthropological series, no.15.*) ISBN: 0835781801; 0802022863.

Part 1 concerns social and cultural aspects; part 2, individual tribes. Well documented; general index. *Class No:* 572.9(=97)(035)

Tables & Data Books

[2120]

STUART, P. Nations within a nation: historical statistics of American Indians. Westport, Conn., Greenwood Press, 1987. x,251p. tables. $50. ISBN: 0313238138.

9 sections: 1. Introduction, scope and purpose ... 3. Population ... 8. Employment, earnings, and income - 9. Indian resources and economic development. Bibliography, p.233-41. A quick reference tool for historical statistics. *Class No:* 572.9(=97)(083)

Maps & Atlases

[2121]

WALDMAN, C. Atlas of North American Indians. New York, Facts on File, 1985. 276p. illus. (incl. col.), maps. $29.95; $16.95. ISBN: 0871968509.

Over 100 two-colour maps. Appendices include a chronology of North American Indian history, a list of US and Canadian tribes, with locations, reservations, a directory of Indian museums and archaeological sites, and a list of major Indian place-names in the US and Canada. *Class No:* 572.9(=97)(084.3)

Research Methods

[2122]

HAAS, M.L. Indians of North America: methods and sources for library research. Hamden, Conn., Shoestring Press, 1983. xii, 160p. $29.50. ISBN: 0208019804.

3 parts: 1. Library methodology and research library reference tools - 2. Annotated bibliography of books by topic - 3. A list of books on individual tribes. Adequate index. Well organized. 'A first-rate general guide to researching the Indians of North America' (*RQ*, v.24(1), Fall 1984, p.108). *Class No:* 572.9(=97):001.891

Research Projects

[2123]

Guide to research on North American Indians. Hirschfelder, A.B., *and others*. Chicago, Ill., American Library Association, 1983. 330p. $32.50. ISBN: 0838903533.

27 topical chapters, in 4 major areas: general studies; history; economic and social aspects; religion, arts and literature. About 1,100 annotated entries for books, periodical and government documents. Author-title and subject indexes. 'A good guide to basic tools published before 1980' (*Wilson library bulletin*, November 1983, p.225-6). *Class No:* 572.9(=97):061:061.62.005

Amerindians, South

[2124]

Handbook of South American Indians. Steward, J.H., *ed*. Washington, Smithsonian Institution, 1946-59. 7v. illus., maps.

1. *The marginal tribes.* 1946. 2. *The Andean civilizations.* 1946. 3. *The tropical forest tribes.* 1948. 4. *The circum-Caribbean tribes.* 1948. 5. *The comparative ethnology of South American Indians.* 1949. 6. *Physical anthropology, linguistics and cultural geography of South American Indians.* 1950. 7. *Index.* 1959.

A truly comprehensive study, with extensive chapter bibliographies. V.7, the general index, has *c*.20,000 entries. Some of the volumes have glossaries. *Class No:* 572.9(=98)

[2125]

SALZANO, F.M. and CALLEGARI-JACQUES, S.M. South American Indians: a case study in evolution. Oxford, Clarendon Press, 1988. xii,259p. tables, maps. ISBN: 0198576358.

Describes what is known about the origin and differentiation of the South American Indians. 10 chapters: 1. Origins and early differentiation ... 3. Population structure - 4. Ecology, nutrition and physiological adaptation ... 6. Morphology ... 9. Discontinuous genetic variability: multivariate analysis - 10. Synthesis. 3 indexes: author; population; subject. Bibliographies appended to each chapter in addition to an appendix listing *c*.400 items and 14 statistical tables. *Class No:* 572.9(=98)

Maoris

[2126]

BARLOW, C. Tikanga whakaaro: key concepts in Maori culture. Oxford, University Press, 1991. xvii,187p. illus. £13.50. ISBN: 0195582128.

Explanations in English and Maori of 70 terms which are important in Maori culture. Entries, which are arranged A-Z, vary in length from ½-page to several pages. Brief bibliography, p.187. *Class No:* 572.9(=992.32)

[2127]

METGE, J. **The Maoris of New Zealand: Rautatu.** Rev. ed. London, etc., Routledge & Kegan Paul, 1976. xx, 382p. illus., diagrs., tables. ISBN: 0710083521.

First published 1967.

18 chapters: 1/2. The Maoris before 1800 ... 6. The bases of daily living ... 14. Leadership and social control ... 17. Literature and art - 18. Maori and Pekeha. Appendix: Maori spelling and pronunciation. Glossary. Bibliography (grouped), p.351-67. Non-analytical index. 16 plates; 11 tables. *Class No:* 572.9(=992.32)

[2128]

TAYLOR, C.R.H. **A Bibliography of publications on the New Zealand Maori** and the Moriori of the Chatham Islands. Oxford, Clarendon Press, 1972. 152p. ISBN: 0198181566.

A revision of the New Zealand and Maori section of the author's *Pacific bibliography (q.v.).* 42 sections. Includes books and periodical articles. Index. *Class No:* 572.9(=992.32)

Aborigines

[2129]

COPPELL, W.G. **World catalogue of theses and dissertations about the Australian aborigines and Torres Strait islanders.** Sydney, University Press, 1977. x, 113p. ISBN: 0424000393.

An author list of *c.*700 entries. Subject index.

Class No: 572.9(=995)

[2130]

GREENWAY, J. **Bibliography of the Australian aborigines and native peoples of Torres Strait, to 1959.** Sydney, London, etc., Angus E. Robertson, 1963. xv, 420p. map.

10,283 numbered entries under authors A-Z. A list of abbreviated titles of *c.*1,000 periodicals precedes. The subject index (p.371-420) includes a list of tribes and a key map locating 554 tribles, but as a subject index it is poorly constructed. Under 'Language : Linguistic studies; General' there are *c.*700 undifferentiated references to entry numbers. The heading 'General works' features on p.398-420, and there are insufficient specific headings throughout.

Class No: 572.9(=995)

[2131]

—TINDALE, N.B. **Aboriginal tribes of Australia: their terrain, environmental controls, distribution, limits and proper names.** Berkeley, Calif., University of California Press, 1974. 2v. (Text; Maps). $150. ISBN: 0520020057.

Text (xii, 404p) has 4 parts: 1. The people and the land - 2. Catalogue of Australian aboriginal tribes (by states, then by tribes, A-Z, with references, p.161-262) - 3. Alternatives, variant spellings and invalid terms. Appendix: 'Tasmanian tribes'. Bibliography, p.389-401. Non-analytical index, p.389-401. Non-analytical index, p.389-401; Tasmanian tribe index, p.402-4. V.2 consists of 4 folding location maps. *Class No:* 572.9(=995)

[2132]

THAWLEY, J. *and* GAUCI, S. **Bibliographies on the Australian aborigine:** an annotated listing. 2nd ed. Bundoora, Vic., Borchardt Library, La Trobe University, 1987. 44p. (*La Trobe University Library publication no. 32.*) ISBN: 0858166623.

First published 1979.

163 entries, arranged alphabetically by author. Scope covers English language monographs, bibliographical articles in scholarly Australian journals, and some unpublished bibliographies available in Australian libraries. Appendix: 'List of useful Australian periodicals'. Subject and geographic index. *Class No:* 572.9(=995)

573 Biology

Biology

Abbreviations & Symbols

[2133]

DUPAYRAT, J. Dictionary of biomedical acronyms and abbreviations. 2nd ed. Chichester, John Wiley & Sons, 1990. 162p. £19.50. ISBN: 0471926493.

First published 1984.

About 7,000 definitions for the 4,000 most common biomedical acronyms. Increase in the number of basic acronyms is 30% up on the previous edition. Intended primarily for researchers, physicians and translators. *Class No:* 573.0(003)

Databases

[2134]

BIOSIS PREVIEWS. Philadelphia, Pa., BIOSIS, 1969-.

Contains almost 8,000,000 citations from *Biological abstracts, Biological abstracts/RRM,* and *Bio-research index.* The *Biological abstracts* records, 1976- have abstracts while most *BA/RRM* records do not contain abstracts; *BioResearch index* records have abstracts. Updated weekly, and available on CD-ROM from Silverplatter. *Class No:* 573.0(003.4)

[2135]

World databases in biosciences and pharmacology. Armstrong, C.J. and Fenton, R.R., *eds.* East Grinstead, Bowker, 1996. 1325p. £195. ISBN: 1857390687.

World databases, p.1-1080, arranged in eight subject areas, with three chapters on techniques, commercial aspects, and patents. Addresses p.1081-1112. Subject, producer, and database name indexes, p.1113-1325. Attempts 'to make sense of the myriad files in the marketplace' (*Introduction*). *Class No:* 573.0(003.4)

Bibliographies

[2136]

Biologie-Dokumentation: Bibliographie der deutschen biologischen Zeitschriftenliteratur, 1796-1965. Scheele, M. *and* Natalis, G. Munich, K.G. Saur, 1981-82. 24v. $2,200. ISBN: 3598302959.

274,752 author entries, A-Z, occupy v.1-19. Catchword index, v.20-22. Systematic index, v.23-24. Bibliographical data in entries include illus., tables, and language of original. *Class No:* 573.0(01)

[2137]

Coping with the biomedical literature: a primer for the scientist and the clinician. Warren, K.S., *ed.* New York, Praeger, 1981. xi, 233p. illus., diagrs., facsims., tables. $45. ISBN: 0275913554.

12 contributors. 4 parts (12 contributors): 1. The structure of the information system - 2. Producing biomedical information - 3. Utilizing biomedical information - 4. Sources of biomedical information (*e.g.* 'The National Library of Medicine'). Each contribution has appended references (*e.g.* 'Ecology of the biomedical literature', 21 references). Detailed analytical index. Stresses research techniques. *Class No:* 573.0(01)

[2138]

DAVIS, E.B. *and* **SCHMIDT, D. Using the biological literature: a practical guide.** 2nd ed. New York, Marcel Dekker, 1995. x,421p. (*Books in library and information science, 57..*) ISBN: 082479477x.

First ed. 1981.

13 sections: 1. Introduction to the biological literature - 2. Subject access to biological information ... 7. Genetics ... 10. Plant biology ... 13. Zoology. Each section is subdivided by type of material *e.g.* directories, nomenclature, handbooks, etc. New to this edition is information on electronic sources, such as CD-ROM, and Internet resources. No overall index, but helpful contents list at beginning of each chapter. 'Highly recommended for academic libraries' (*Choice,* June 1996, p.1613). *Class No:* 573.0(01)

[2139]

Information sources in the life sciences. Wyatt, H.V., *ed.* 4th ed. East Grinstead, Bowker, 1997. vii, 264p. £35. (*Guide to information sources.*) ISBN: 1857390709.

First published 1966, as *Use of biological literature:* edited by R.T. Bottle and H.V. Wyatt; 3rd ed. 1987.

Completely updated from the previous ed. of 1987. 25 chapters (*e.g.* 1. Reading for profit: current awareness ... 9. Statistics and software ... 25. Botany, plant ecology and the environment), 19 of them by H.V. Wyatt, the rest by eight other contributors, with new material on cell biology, biotechnology, and evaluation of services providing AIDS information. Previous lack of information on patents has been addressed, but the index is still no more than adequate. Internet and CD-ROM sources are included, although these are spread throughout the work rather than concentrated in one section or in a chapter of their subject coverage. Some bibliographic details or URLs are omitted. Still an important resource, but could be even more so with better organization and more attention to detail. *Class No:* 573.0(01)

[2140]

—**KIRK, T.G.,** *Jr.* Library research guide to biology: illustrated research strategy and sources. Ann Arbor, Mich., Pierian Press, 1978. 83p. facsims. $25. (*Library research guide series, no.2.*) ISBN: 087650098x.

Stresses methodology, with numerous examples. Appended lists of recent serials, guides to the literature, and 'Basic reference sources for biology courses', plus 'Using *Chemical abstracts*' and '*Zoological record*'. Brief index of titles. Addressed to students, teachers and librarians. *Class No:* 573.0(01)

[2141]

KRONICK, D.A. The Literature of the life sciences. Philadelphia, Pa., ISI Press, 1985. 219p. $29.95. ISBN: 0894950452.

Provides an overview of the literature, primary and secondary, rather than a detailed examination of titles (484 are listed) and subject areas. Methods of searching the literature, via bibliographies and other retrieval services (including online) are discussed. Index. Addressed mainly to librarians, students and scientists. *Class No:* 573.0(01)

[2142]

LEE, R. How to find information: medicine and biology. 2nd ed. London, British Library, 1996. iv, 20p. ISBN: 0712308377.

First published 1992 as *How to find information: a guide to searching in published sources* (this sub-title appears on 1996 cover only).

Handy little guide, encouraging independent searching. The new ed. 'covers the same subject area as the earlier book, but has been largely rewritten to account for recent innovations in information-searching techniques' (*Introduction*). *Class No:* 573.0(01)

[2143]

Smith's guide to the literature of the life sciences. Smith, R.C., *and others.* 9th ed. Minneapolis, Minnesota, Burgess Publishing Co., 1980. xi, 223p. ISBN: 0808755762.

First published 1943, as *Guide to the literature of the zoological sciences;* 8th ed. 1972.

About 2,000 annotated entries in 11 sections: 1. The scientist and research librarian - 2. The mechanics of the library and book classification - 3. Secondary literature: textbooks and reviews - 4. Bibliographic form; bibliographies and indexes of the life sciences - 5. Abstracts and abstracting journals - 6. Ready reference works - 7. Serials and primary research journals - 8. Literature of taxonomy - 9. Searching the literature (including databases) - 10. Preparations for writing theses and dissertations - 11. Preparation for scientific writing. Designed to help young scientist-aspirants to become familiar with the searching, reviewing, reporting, publishing and indexing systems in the life sciences. Primarily a library guide. *Class No:* 573.0(01)

Encyclopaedias

[2144]

Encyclopedia of biostatistics. Armitage, P. *and* Colton, T., *eds.* New York, John Wiley, 1998. 6v.(4,898p.) £1,595; $2,400. ISBN: 0471975761.

Over 800 contributors. 1,028 articles, arranged A-Z, covering statistical methods in the health sciences and medicine. Numerous cross-references which appear in bold type. Many bibliographies and lists of further reading, review articles, acronyms, and abbreviations. Each volume contains an alphabetical table of contents for the

....(contd.)

complete set. For academic libraries. 'A colossal work of immense importance' (*British medical journal, 20 February 1999*).
Class No: 573.0(031)

[2145]
Encyclopedia of environmental biology. Nierenberg, W.A., *ed.* San Diego, Academic Press, 1995. 3v. illus., tables, maps. $475. ISBN: 0122267303, set; 0122267311, v.1; 012226732x, v.2; 0122267338, v.3.
170 internationally-based contributors. Each of the 154 entries consists of an outline, glossary, cross-references, and a bibliography, usually very brief. V.3 includes a 10,000 entry subject index and an index of related titles. For academic libraries. *Class No:* 573.0(031)

[2146]
Encyclopedia of human biology. Dulbecco, R., *ed.-in-chief.* 2nd ed. San Diego, Academic Press, 1997. 9v. £1,200;$1,799. ISBN: 0122269705, set; 0122269713, v.1; 0122269721, v.2; 012226973x, v.3; 0122269748, v.4; 0122269756, v.5; 0122269764, v.6; 0122269772, v.7; 0122269780, v.8; 0122269705, v.9.
First published 1991.
75% of the previous ed. has been revised and updated. More than 670 articles in 37 different biological fields, including anthropology, biophysics, ecology, genetics, physiology, and toxicology. For medical, life science and biology libraries. Each entry consists of a glossary, text, and bibliography, and usually comprises a number of pages (*e.g.* 'Mood disorders'; 8p. 'Artificial kidney'; 16p.). Criticism of index in first edition has been largely met by devoting V.9 entirely to subject index (p.1-158) and 'index by subject area' (p.159-75). Many cross-references, although these could be more visually prominent. *Class No:* 573.0(031)

[2147]
SCOTT, T. Concise encyclopedia biology. Rev. ed. Berlin, Walter de Gruyter, 1996. v,1287p. illus.(some col.). £62; $99.95. ISBN: 3110106612.
Translation and revision of *ABC Biologie* (Brockhaus, 1986).
*c.*7,000 entries arranged A-Z and covering molecular biology, biochemistry, ethology, ecology, genetics, botany, zoology, physiology, and palaeontology. *c.*1,000 line-drawings plus 48 poor-quality colour and black-and-white photographs and drawings. Numerous cross-references but no index. 'It is the most comprehensive one-volume encyclopedic dictionary covering biology' (*Reference books bulletin*, August 1996, p.1921). *Class No:* 573.0(031)

Handbooks & Manuals

[2148]
The Cambridge encyclopedia of life sciences. Friday, A. *and* Ingram, D.S., *general eds.* Cambridge Univ. Press, 1985. 432p. illus. (incl. col.), diagrs., tables, maps. £25. ISBN: 0521256968.
Three major parts (15 chapters), each with further reading. 1. Processes and organization (1. The cell ... 5. The geology) - 2. Environments (6. Marine environments ... 10. Living organisms and environments) - 3. Evolution and the fossil record (11. The evolutionary process ... 15. Recent history of the fauna and flora). 31 contributors. Species index; subject index (in tiny print). The book's central theme is 'the adaptations of plants and animals to their environments and their relations with other organisms within those environments' (*Foreword*). Well integrated and well illustrated. *Choice*, (v.23(5), January 1986, p.724) finds coverage uneven, although the book - as much a textbook as an encyclopaedia - is 'highly recommended for undergraduate and public libraries'. *Class No:* 573.0(035)

[2149]
KEETON, W.T. *and* **GOULD, J.L. Biological science.** 5th ed. New York, W.W. Norton, 1993. xxiv, 1194p + 92p. illus., (incl. col.), diagrs. ISBN: 0393962237.
First published 1967.
6 sections (40 chapters): 1. The chemical and cellular basis of life - 2. The perpetuation of life - 3. Evolutionary biology - 4. The genesis and diversity of organisms - 5. Biology of organisms - 6. Ecology. More coloured illus. than in 4th ed. Appendix: A classification of living things, p.A1-A6. Glossary, p.A15-A34. Index, p.A35-A921. Also available in two paperback volumes. *Class No:* 573.0(035)

Dictionaries

Polyglot

[2150]
HAENSCH, G. *and* **HABERKAMP DE ANTON, G. Dictionary of biology** in English, German, French, Spanish. 2nd ed. Amsterdam, Elsevier, 1981. xii, 680p. £127; $169.25; DM128. ISBN: 0444419683.
First published 1976.
12,809 numbered English-base terms, with equivalents and indexes in German, French and Spanish. The aim is 'to obtain as proportionate

....(contd.)

a selection of terms as possible from all areas of biology' (*Preface*), although topics such as environment, ethology and ecology figure more prominently than in the 1976 ed. Genders are stated.
Class No: 573.0(038)=00

English

[2151]
BLINDERMAN, C. Biolexicon: a guide to the language of biology. Springfield, Ill., C.C. Thomas, 1990. 363p. $39.75. ISBN: 0398056714.
Lists several hundred Greek and Latin elements which form the base of terms in biology, medicine and science. Many illustrations. Index. *Class No:* 573.0(038)=20

[2152]
Cambridge illustrated thesaurus of biology. Gutteridge, A.C. Cambridge, University Press, 1983. 245, [12]p. col. illus., graphs, tables.
Over 2,500 definitions of terms, including other words related to the same topic. 38 broad headings/sections (*e.g.* cells; bacteria; plants (p.45-79); animals, nervous system), combining to some extent functions of dictionary and thesaurus. A/Z index of words. Much use of colour; keyed illus. Small format. *Class No:* 573.0(038)=20

[2153]
Chambers biology dictionary. Walker, P.M.B., *ed.* Cambridge, W.R. Chambers; University Press, 1989. xii,324p. diagrs. £17.50. ISBN: 185296152x.
Derived from *Chambers science and technology dictionary (q.v.).* Contains *c.*10,000 definitions, including *c.*3,000 in zoology, *c.*2,500 in botany, and *c.*1,200 in biochemistry, molecular biology and genetics. Definitions are concise, with some terms given fuller treatment in a series of over 100 special articles, *e.g.* genetic manipulation, poison. Synonyms and cross-references are indicated in italic and bold type. Largely a duplication of the same subject areas in the parent dictionary but has a good, clear layout and would be useful for the more specialized life sciences library.
Class No: 573.0(038)=20

[2154]
Collins dictionary of biology. Hale, W.G., *and others.* 5th ed. Glasgow, Harper Collins, 1995. 659p. diagrs. £8.99. ISBN: 0004708059.
Has more than 6,500 entries and includes brief biographies. 300 diagrams. Considerable revision and updating has taken place since the publication of the 4th ed. in 1988. The authors are all past and present members of staff at Liverpool John Moores University, Dept. of Biology. *Class No:* 573.0(038)=20

[2155]
Elsevier's dictionary of biology. Tirri, R., *and others.* Amsterdam, Elsevier, 1998. vii, 757p. £114.80. ISBN: 0444825258.
10,000 entries, including cross-references. Derivations are given, but no pronunciation guide or biographical entries. 4 appendices: 1. Symbols, units, and nomenclature in physics - 2. Chemical elements - 3. Systematics of organisms - 4. Geological timetable.
Class No: 573.0(038)=20

[2156]
The Facts-on-File dictionary of biology. Tootill, E., *ed.* Rev. ed. New York, Facts on File, 1988. 326p. illus. $24.95. ISBN: 0816018650.
Defines *c.*3,500 terms used in the life sciences. Covers developing fields such as genetics, biotechnology and AIDS research. Keyed line-drawings. For students of medicine/biology.
Class No: 573.0(038)=20

[2157]
GRAY, P. The Dictionary of the biological sciences. Melbourne, Fla., Krieger, 1982 (reprint of 1967 ed.). xx, 602p. $52.50. ISBN: 0898744414.
An outgrowth of *The Encyclopedia of the biological sciences (q.v.).* More than 40,000 very concise definitions in the field of organisms, their anatomy, function and mutual interactions. A drawback is the massing of words, derived from the same root (*e.g.* 'Metabolic' is under '-bolic'). 'Acquire, even if Henderson (which it complements) is available' (*Library journal*, v.93(8), 15 April 1968, p.1585). *Class No:* 573.0(038)=20

[2158]
HENDERSON, I.F. *and* **HENDERSON, W.D. Henderson's dictionary of biological terms.** 11th ed., by E. Lawrence. Harlow, Longman Scientific and Technical, 1995. xi,693p. £33.99; £8.50. ISBN: 0582227089.
First published 1920; as *A Directory of scientific terms.* (1st-8th eds.).
Over 23,000 headwords. Updates existing definitions and extends subject coverage into the areas of ecology and animal behaviour. Appendices (p.649-93) comprise structural formulae, outlines of plant and animal kingdoms, the fungi, the kingdom Protista, the

....*(contd.)*
prokaryotes, virus families, and etymological origins of some common word elements in biology. Intended for use by students and teachers. *Class No:* 573.0(038)=20

[2159]
International dictionary of medicine and biology. Landau, S.I., *ed.-in-chief.* New York, Wiley, 1986. 3v. (li, 3200p.). $395. ISBN: 047101849x.

Over 100 contributors; more than 150,000 entries, thanks to the inclusion of biology. Among the subjects most extensively covered are ecology, environmental health, infectious diseases, occupational medicine, toxicology. A concise guide to usage precedes. Highly recommended as 'indispensable for medical and science libraries' (*Library journal,* 15 June 1986, p.61). *Class No:* 573.0(038)=20

[2160]
JAEGER, E.C. A Source-book of biological names and terms. 3rd ed. Springfield, Ill., Thomas; Oxford, Blackwell, 1955 (reprinted 1978). xxxv, 317p. illus. $48.50. ISBN: 0398009163.

First published 1944; 2nd ed. 1950.

Lists nearly 15,000 elements from which scientific biological names and terms are made. 32p. supplement adds *c.*1,000 terms to those in the 2nd ed. Final section of 300 short biographies of 'persons commemorated in botanical and zoological generic names' (*Preface*). *Class No:* 573.0(038)=20

[2161]
McGraw-Hill dictionary of the life sciences. Lapedes, D.N., *editor-in-chief.* New York, etc. McGraw-Hill, 1976. 907, 38p. ISBN: 0070452628.

Over 20,000 concise entries, either drawn from *McGraw-Hill Dictionary of scientific and technical terms* (1974) or else specially prepared. Embraces agriculture, analytical chemisty, veterinary medicine, virology, zoology and other related fields of biology. Appendix (38p.) of measurement systems, antibiotics, clinical pathology, animal taxonomy, etc. 1,200 small marginal illus. 'Highly recommended' (*Library journal,* v.102(5), 1 March 1977, p.546). *Class No:* 573.0(038)=20

[2162]
The New Penguin dictionary of biology. Abercrombie, M., *and others.* 8th ed. London, Penguin Books, 1990. 599p. diagrs. £5.99. ISBN: 0140511776.

First published 1951 as *The Penguin dictionary of biology.*

Contains *c.*6,000 of the more common biological terms. Length of entries varies from a few words to more than a page, *e.g.* 'Species'. Abbreviations for categories indicate application to botany and/or zoology. Numerous cross-references. *Class No:* 573.0(038)=20

French

[2163]
VAILLANCOURT, J. Lexique anglais-français: termes techniques à l'usage des biologistes. Ottawa, Editions de l'Université d'Ottawa, 1978. xii, 427p.

Over 10,400 numbered English terms are given French equivalents. The index of French terms is keyed by number to the main section. English terms are categorized and French terms are given genders. Invaluable for the student and professional alike. *Class No:* 573.0(038)=40

Russian

[2164]
CARPOVICH, E.A. Russian-English biological and medical dictionary. 2nd ed. New York, Technical Dictionaries Co., 1960. 400p. $25. ISBN: 0911484019.

First published 1958.

32,650 entries, giving direct adjective-noun approach, - very acceptable to the inexperienced translator and occasional reader of Russian scientific papers. Particularly valuable on biological terms that frequently appear in the medical literature, - terms not found in other dictionaries. Applications of terms appear in parentheses. *Class No:* 573.0(038)=82

[2165]
English-Russian biological dictionary. Chibisova, O.I. *and* Koziar, L.A., *eds.* 4th ed. Oxford, etc., Pergamon Press, 1980. 732p. ISBN: 0080231632.

About 60,000 entries, including abbreviations and Latin names. 29 contributors. 'Nerve': 1½ columns. The dictionary is to be used with caution, since terms consisting of attribute and a key word will be found under the key word; for example, the term 'Chromosome complex' will be found under the key term 'complex'. Although described in the CIP details as 'revised and enlarged', the pagination and number of entries are identical with those in the 3rd ed. published two years earlier. *Class No:* 573.0(038)=82

Theses

[2166]
BILBOUL, R.R. *and* **KENT, F.L.,** *eds.* **Retrospective index to theses of Great Britain and Ireland, 1716-1950. Volume 3: Life sciences.** Oxford, European Bibliographic Center-Clio Press, 1977. [vii], xi, 327p. £66. ISBN: 0903450054.

About 10,000 entries on the biological and medical sciences. Subject index (Abdomen ... Zygorhynchus). Author index (Name - Title of thesis - Degree - Date - University). *Class No:* 573.0(043)

Reviews & Abstracts

[2167]
ALLAN, B. *and* **LIVESEY, B.** How to use *Biological abstracts, Chemical abstracts, Index chemicus.* 2nd ed. Aldershot, Gower, 1994. ix,103p. $51.95. ISBN: 0566075563.

First published 1987.

Cites results of sample searches from the three indexes, and explains how each index is organized. Subject index and index of examples. Spiral binding for easy use by librarians and information scientists; includes CD-ROM searching. *Class No:* 573.0(048)

[2168]
Biocontrol news and information: a quarterly journal of news items, review articles and abstracts from the CAB abstracts database, prepared by the Commonwealth Institute of Biological Control. Wallingford, Oxon., CAB International, 1980-. 4pa. £180; $315. ISSN: 01431404.

Contains *c.*2,800 abstracts pa, covering *c.*2,500 journal articles, in addition to reports, books, and conferences. Subject coverage includes crop pests; weeds; medical and veterinary pests; techniques; biology; taxonomy and catalogues; ecology. Mini-reviews of literature on topical subjects included in each issue which also contains author and subject indexes. Available online as part of the *CAB Abstracts (q.v.)* database, on the CD-ROM equivalents and, from 1991, on floppy disk. Also available on the Internet via PEST CABWeb at http://pest.cabweb.org. *Class No:* 573.0(048)

[2169]
Biological abstracts. Philadelphia, Pa., BioScience Information Service (BIOSIS), 1926-. Semi-monthly. $8,330 (USA); $9,160 (non US) pa. ISSN: 00063169.

The world's leading abstracting service in biology and biomedicine. Over 235,000 abstracts pa. from *c.*9,500 journals. Arranged in 84 sections, A-Z, including Aerospace and underwater biological effects; Cardiovascular system; Ecology (Environmental biology); Genetics and Cytogenetics; Immunology; Neoplasms and neoplastic agents; Nervous system; Pharmacology; Public health; Toxicology; Virology. Author index; Biosystematics index; Generic index; Subject index - per issue. Cumulative indexes, 2pa., and 5-yearly (on microfiche, *e.g.* 1975-79). Available on CD-ROM and on-line.

Reprints from *Biological abstracts* include *Abstracts of mycology* and *Abstracts of entomology.*

Biological abstracts/RRM (q.v.) is complementary to *Biological abstracts* in its coverage. Both services feed into *BIOSIS PREVIEWS* database (1969-). *Class No:* 573.0(048)

[2170]
Biological abstracts/RRM: reports, reviews, meetings. Philadelphia, Pa., BioScience Information Services (BIOSIS), 1980-. Fortnightly. $4,160 (US) and $4,520 (non US). ISSN: 01926985.

As *Bioresearch index,* v.1-17 (1965-79).

About 235,000 references pa. (No abstracts, despite the title, but keywords are appended to entries). Coverage: symposia, meetings, reviews, monographs, book chapters, etc., - thus complementary to the coverage of *Biological abstracts.* Author, biosystematic, generic and subject indexes. *BIOSIS PREVIEWS* database (1969-). Also available on CD-ROM. *Class No:* 573.0(048)

[2171]
Biological and agricultural index: a cumulative subject index to periodicals in the fields of biology, agriculture and related sciences. New York, H.W. Wilson, 1964/65-. 11pa. ISSN: 00063177.

Continues *Agricultural index,* 1919-64.

Covers 226 key English-language journals, selected by subscriber vote, with *c.*56,000 records added annually. Includes experimental station publications and book reviews. Entry under topic. US slanted, as compared with *Bibliography of agriculture* and *Agrindex.* About 40,000 entries pa. Available online (WILSONLINE) - database contains more than 540,000 records - and CD-ROM, in addition to magnetic tape and diskette format. *Class No:* 573.0(048)

[2172]
Biology digest. Medford, N.J., Plexus Publishing, Inc., 1974-. 9pa. $129. ISSN: 00952958.

About 4,000 abstracts pa. from *c.*200 periodicals (including *Nature* and *Scientific American*). Sections: Viruses, microflora and plants; Animal kingdom; The human organism; Infectious diseases; Population and health; Cell biology and biogenesis; Environmental quality; General topics. Occasionally carries a feature article; some book reviews. Author and keyword indexes per issue and annually. Available online via OCLC. *Class No:* 573.0(048)

[2173]
Current awareness in biological sciences (CABS). Amsterdam, Elsevier Science, 1983-. 24pa. fl.12,850; $7,385. ISSN: 07334443.

Formerly *International abstracts of biological sciences,* 1954-82.

About 15,000 references pa., with authors' addresses. Sections (closely subdivided): Biochemistry - Cell and developmental biology - Ecological sciences - Genetics and molecular biology - Microbiology - Plant science - Pharmacology and toxicology - Immunology - Physiology. Journal list, p.viii-xvi. Author index, but no subject index. Available online as *Elsevier BIOBASE* via Datastar, DIALOG, and DIMDI. Also available in microform. *Class No:* 573.0(048)

[2174]
Current contents: Agriculture, biology and environmental sciences. Philadelphia, Pa., Institute for Scientific Information, 1970-. Weekly. $730. ISSN: 00900508.

Previously (1970-72) subtitled 'Agriculture, food and veterinary sciences'.

Issue for 25 Mar 1996 contains title-pages of 124 journals. Sections include: Biology ... Environment/Ecology ... Plant sciences ... Entomology/Pest control ... Veterinary medicine/Animal health. Title word index; author index and address directory; publishers' address directory. Available on diskette, CD-ROM version, and online on the CURRENT CONTENTS SEARCH database. Internet access as *Current Contents Connect* at http://connect.isihost.com. *Class No:* 573.0(048)

[2175]
Current contents: Life sciences. Philadelphia, Pa., Institute of Scientific Information, 1958-. Weekly. $1,015. ISSN: 00113409.

Provides contents lists of *c.*250 journal titles per issue, 1,000 journals altogether. Subject coverage includes: multidisciplinary; chemistry ... neurosciences & behavior; animal & plant science. Author, title and address directory; Publishers address directory. Request-a-print service available. Available online, on CURRENT CONTENTS SEARCH, on diskette, and in a CD-ROM version. Internet access as *Current Contents Connect* at http://connect.isihost.com. *Class No:* 573.0(048)

Periodicals & Progress Reports

[2176]
The Author's guide to biomedical journals. 2nd ed. Larchmont, N.Y., Mary Ann Liebert, Inc., 1996. 800p. $184. ISBN: 0913113727.

First published 1993.

Contains manuscript submission instructions for 250 biomedical periodicals as well as a list of publishers, with addresses, phone and fax numbers, and e-mail addresses. *Class No:* 573.0(05)

[2177]
BIOSIS serial sources. Philadelphia, Pa., BioSciences Information Service, 1996-. Annual. $175.

Previously *Serial sources for the BIOSIS database* (1971-89) and *Serial sources for the BIOSIS previews database* (1989-96).

Records *c.*20,000 serials and books in over 40 languages from almost 7,000 publishers worldwide covered in *Biological abstracts* (*q.v.*) and *Biological abstracts/RRM* (*q.v.*). Prelims. note new serial titles and ceased/changed serial titles. Data: title, CODEN, frequency, publisher. Appended key to frequency codes and list of publishers. Also available on CD-ROM. *Class No:* 573.0(05)

Tables & Data Books

[2178]
ALTMAN, P.L. *and* **DITTMER, D.S. Biology data book.** 2nd ed. Bethesda, Md., Federation of American Societies for Experimental Biology, 1972-74. 3v. (2123p.) diagrs., tables.

First published 1964.

V.1 has tables on genetics, cytology, reproduction, development and growth, properties of biological substances; materials and growths. 5,941 references. - V.2, on biological regulations and toxins, environment and survival, parasitism, sensory and neuro-biology. 5,970 references. - V.3, on nutrition, digestion and excretion, metabolism, respiration, bood and other body fluids. Each volume has its own index. *Class No:* 573.0(083)

[2179]
FISHER, Sir R.A. *and* **YATES, F. Statistical tables for biological, agricultural and medical research.** 6th ed. Edinburgh, Oliver & Boyd, 1963. x, 146p. tables.

First published 1938; 5th ed. 1956.

50 tables (numbered 1-34, with interpolations). Main additions to the 6th ed. are: v, 'Fiducial limits for a variance component', and xvii, 'Balanced incomplete blocks-combinatorial solutions'. The valuable introduction give examples of the ways in which the tables can be used and includes 82 references to books, monographs and papers on statistic methods up to 1963. No index. A standard source. *Class No:* 573.0(083)

[2180]
PARKER, S.P., *ed.* **Synopsis and classification of living organisms.** New York, etc., McGraw-Hill, 1982. 2v. (1282p.) illus., diagrs. $295. ISBN: 0070790310.

8,200 articles by nearly 200 contributors. V.2 has a taxon and common name index. 'The compilation that covers both the characteristic and taxonomic position of all taxa down to and including families of viruses, bacteria, plants and animals in a single source' (*RQ,* v.21(4), Summer 1982, p.421-2). *Class No:* 573.0(083)

Nomenclatures

[2181]
JEFFREY, C. Biological nomenclature. 3rd ed. London, Edward Arnold, 1989. ix,86p. ISBN: 0713129832.

First published 1973.

8 sections (The systematic background - Names and codes - Scientific names ... Name changes and synonymy - Authorities and their citation - Special cases). Notes to the text. Bibliography, glossary/index. Of the 2nd ed. (1977), 'The author [Principal Scientific Officer. Royal Botanic Gardens, Kew] has made an excellent job of reducing them [the rules] to the level where they should be understandable by the teacher...' *The School science review*, v.10(208), March 1978, p.570). For all schools with a sixth-form library. *Class No:* 573.0(083.72)

[2182]
WOODS, R.S. The Naturalist's lexicon: a list of Classical Greek and Latin words used, or suitable for use, in biological nomenclature; with abridged English-Classical supplement. Pasadena, Calif., Abbey Press, 1944. xviii, 282p. Addendum, 1947. 47p.

A Greek and Latin-English lexicon, covering more than 15,000 terms. The English-Classical supplement (p.259-82) is classified, dealing in turn with nouns, adjectives, verbs and prefixes. *Class No:* 573.0(083.72)

Patents

[2183]
CRESPI, R.S. Patenting in the biological sciences. Chichester, Wiley, 1982. 211p. £50. ISBN: 0471101516.

An introduction to patenting procedures for research workers in biotechnology and the pharmaceutical and agrochemical industries. The laws of the UK, USA and other countries, as well as the European Patent Convention and other treaties, are discussed. *Class No:* 573.0(088.8)

Histories

[2184]
ALLEN, G.E. Life science in the twentieth century. Cambridge Univ. Press, 1979. xxv, 258p. illus. £20; £5.95. ISBN: 0471023361.

7 chapters (1. The influence of Darwinian thought on late nineteenth-century biology ... 7. The origin and development of molecular biology). Bibliography, with running commentary, by chapters, p.229-49. Index. 'The history of a few selected areas whose growth and development is characteristic of the vast field that has become general biology'. *Class No:* 573.0(091)

[2185]
DAWES, B. A Hundred years of biology. London, Duckworth, 1952. 429p. diagrs. (*Hundred years series.*)

19 chapters (including 15. Marine biology - 16. Parasites and parasitic diseases - 17. Antibiotics - 18. Agricultural history - 19. Some research institutes [very largely British] and their work). Chapter bibliographies, p.385-418. Index, p.419-29, lists *c.*2,000 names of biologists. *Class No:* 573.0(091)

[2186]
MAGNER, L.N. A History of the life sciences. New York & Basle, Dekker, 1979. xi, 489p. $49.75. ISBN: 082478071x.

14 chapters: 1. In the beginning - 2. The Greeks: natural philosophers and scientists ... 14. Genetics in the twentieth century: molecular biology, or all the world's a phage. Notes and references appended to chapters. Detailed, non-analytical index, p.457-89. Biographical sketches are a feature.

7th ed., 1994 (496p.). *Class No:* 573.0(091)

[2187]
NORDENSKIÖLD, E. **The History of biology.** Translated from the Swedish by L.B. Eyre. London, Kegan Paul, 1929; reprinted New York, Tudor, 1960. xii, 629, xvp. illus.

Based on a series of lectures, originally published in 3v. (Stockholm, 1920-29). Bibliography, p.617-29. 'Still the best one-volume reference history of biology' (*Stechner-Hafner book news,* v.20(3), November 1965, p.34). *Class No:* 573.0(091)

[2188]
OVERMIER, J.A. **The History of biology:** a selected, annotated bibliography. New York, Garland Publishing, 1989. xviii,157p. $21. (*Bibliographies of the history of science and technology, v.15.*) ISBN: 0824091183.

619 annotated entries covering biology from the 18th to the mid-20th century. Cited items published prior to 1985 and mostly English language. Aimed at students and those new in the field. Does not claim to be comprehensive. *Class No:* 573.0(091)

[2189]
SMIT, P. **History of the life sciences: an annotated bibliography.** London, A & C Black, 1974.; Forest Burgh, N.Y., Lubrecht & Cramer. xiv,1071p. $96.

About 5-6,000 annotated entries. Chapter 1: General reference tools - 2. Historiography of the life and medical sciences (A. Ancient and medieval period; B. Renaissance and later periods). Appended: 'Selected list of biographies, bibliographies, etc. of famous biologists, medical men, etc., including some modern reviews of their publications'. Index of personal names, p.1037-71. 'Originated as a plan to provide an extension of those parts of Sarton's *Guide to the history of science* that dealt with the life sciences' (*Introduction*). *Class No:* 573.0(091)

Biographies

[2190]
American men and women of science 1998-99: a biographical directory of today's leaders in physical, biological and related sciences. 20th ed. New Providence, N.J., Bowker, 1998. 8v. $900. ISSN: 00001287.

First published 1906, as *American men of science.*

Covers 190 fields in 10 major areas of study. 119,600 scientists and engineers are listed, with 4,300 profiled for the first time. Each entry comprises name, subject area, current position, previous posts held, personal data, degrees and honorary degrees, honours and awards, concurrent positions held, research interests, mailing address. Separate discipline index (A-Z by specialty). Updated every three years. Also available online via DIALOG and on CD-ROM. *Class No:* 573.0(092)

[2191]
Notable women in the life sciences: a biographical dictionary. Shearer, B.F. *and* Shearer, B.S., *eds.* Westport, Conn., Greenwood, 1996. 440p. illus. $49.95. ISBN: 0313293023.

Contains data from 63 contributors, on 97 women, with a bias towards 20th-century US scientists. Data is more personal than in larger and wider-scope dictionaries and each entry consists of 2-3 pages. Bibliographies and index, p.425-32. Two appendices: Scientists by field; Scientists by awards received.

A more library-orientated and formal work is *Women in the biological sciences: a biobibliographic sourcebook* by L.S. Grinstein and others (*q.v.*). The 59 contributors cover 65 subjects. Entries have lengthy bibliographies, *e.g.* Edith Quimby's entry has works about and by, p.417-23. Four appendices: Chronological list of biographies; List by place of birth; List by references in biographical dictionaries; Index of sources. *Class No:* 573.0(092)

[2192]
Women in the biological sciences: a biobliographical sourcebook. Grinstein, L.S., *and others.* Westport, Conn. Greenwood, 1997. 610p. £79.50. ISBN: 0313291802.

Profiles by 59 contributors, arranged A-Z, of 65 women. Three main sections in each profile: Biography; Work; Bibliography. Scope is international and includes deceased and those born 1930. Entries have lengthy bibliographies, *e.g.* Edith Quimby's entry has works about and by, p.417-23. Four appendices: Chronological list of biographies; List by place of birth; List by references in biographical dictionaries; Index of sources. Name and subject index. Most of those featured are included in other biographical dictionaries but in this work the entries go into greater depth and are lengthier. *Class No:* 573.0(092)

Libraries

[2193]
Life sciences libraries in and around London. Yeadon, J., *and others, eds.* 6th ed. London, Imperial College: King's College, 1986. 60p. ISBN: 0852871597.

5th ed., 1982.

4 sections: A. Library provision in the life sciences at Imperial College - B. Library provision in the life sciences at King's College (KQC) - C. Libraries in London of interest to life scientists - D.

....(contd.)
Libraries within reach of London of interest to life scientists. Data on each library include opening hours; admission and access; sizes and nature of stock; other services offered, *e.g.* photocopying. 'Library searching' (p.5-8) notes on computer based searches, current-awareness journals, abstracting and indexing journals, etc. Index lists 92 main libraries. *Class No:* 573.0:061:026/027

[2194]
World directory of biological and medical sciences libraries. Poland, U.H., *ed.* Munich, New York, etc., K.G. Saur, 1988. 203p. $30. ISBN: 3598217722.

Lists libraries from over 100 countries. Appendices cite union lists; computer service centres; national and international library directories; addresses for biological and medical library associations. *Class No:* 573.0:061:026/027

Institutions & Associations

[2195]
Life sciences organizations and agencies directory: a guide to approximately 8,000 organizations and agencies providing information in the agricultural and biological sciences. Darnay, B.T. *and* Young, M.L., *eds.* Detroit, Mich., Gale. 1988. xxi, 864p. $175. ISBN: 0810318261.

7,662 numbered entries. 18 chapters (*e.g.* 5. Computer information services: international; 6. Consulting firms; 10. Research centers: international; 16. US federal government research centers). Basic data on each organization include date of foundation and name of contact, research activities and fields. Master name and keyword index. US emphasis. *Class No:* 573.0:061:061.2

[2196]
—BIOLOGICAL COUNCIL. Handbook of UK biological societies. London, the Council, 1991. 48p. £1.50. ISSN: 09513884.

Has sections: Officers of the Council. Reports of Sub-committees, Panels and Representatives. Publications of the Council. Addresses of societies affiliated to the Biological Council (p.9-20). Provisional dates of meetings of biological societies, 1991-1993. International meetings to be held in the UK during 1991-1994. Universities in England, Wales, Scotland and Northern Ireland. Polytechnics in England and Wales. *Class No:* 573.0:061:061.2

Research Projects

[2197]
Current research in Britain. Biological sciences. London, Cartermill, in association with the British Library. Annual. £150.

Replaces *Research in British universities, polytechnics and colleges* (RBUPC). First published 1985.

One of a set covering 4 subject areas, registering research in every British university and polytechnic, many colleges and other institutions, with details of *c.*60,000 projects in all. *Biological sciences* (10th ed. 1995. 2v. £135) lists *c.*20,000 projects. 'Research in progress' (p.1-515) lists universities, colleges (other than univ. colleges), and other institutions (including government depts.) numerically. Data number, name, and dept., address, head of dept., researchers and title of project, dates, bequests, etc. Name, study area and keyword indexes. The standard British research tool in biological sciences. Available on CD-ROM. *Class No:* 573.0:061:061.62.005

[2198]
Research topics in the life sciences 1996. Sheffield, Sheffield Academic Press, 1995. 2v. (xi,1218p.). £25. ISBN: 1850757798.

Gives outlines of research topics offered as possible projects for graduate students in the UK. Over 130 institutions are listed. *Class No:* 573.0:061:061.62.005

Practical Work & Techniques

Collections

[2199]
World directory of collections of cultures of micro-organisms. McGowan, V.F. *and* Skerman, V.B.D., *eds.* 2nd ed. [Brisbane], World Data Centre, Queensland University, 1982.

First published 1972 (New York, Wiley-Interscience), compiled by S.M. Martin and others.

Lists 356 culture collections in 56 countries (1972 ed.: 349 collections).

Mycological Institute's *Directory of collections of micro-organisms* (CAB, 1979) is confined to locations in the UK. *Class No:* 573.082

Microscopy

[2200]

Dictionary of light microscopy. Bradbury, S., *and others, comps.* Oxford Univ. Press; Royal Microscopical Society, 1989. x,139p. diagrs., tables. £6.95 (pbk). (*Microscopy handbooks 15.*) ISBN: 0198564139, pbk.

Covers *c.*1250 terms: A (symbol for absorbance, etc.) ... Zoom. Entries range from 2 to *c.*15 lines. Non-preferred terms are indicated as such. Numerous cross-references. Appendices give equivalent terms in English, French and German. Compiled by the Nomenclature Committee of the Royal Microscopical Society. Well-produced. *Class No:* 573.086

[2201]

Electron microscopy abstracts. London, PRM Science & Technology Agency, Ltd., 1973-. 4pa. £45. ISSN: 03066869.

*c.*600 abstracts pa. Sections: Electron optics and instrumentation - Theory of image formation - Non-biological specimen preparation - Biological specimen preparation - Bacteriology - Biological micromolecules - Cells and tissues - Metals and alloys - Semiconductors - Non-metals - Petrology, mineralogy and geochemistry - Miscellaneous. Subject and author indexes per issue. *Class No:* 573.086

[2202]

GRAY, P., *ed*. The Encyclopedia of microscopy and microtechniques. New York, etc., Van Nostrand Reinhold, 1973 (reprinted 1982). xi, 638p. illus., diagrs., graphs, tables. $49.50. ISBN: 0898743354.

Nearly 200 contributors. Entries A-Z. The signed article 'X-ray microscopy' (p.603-11) has sections: Image formation - Microanglography - Technique - Historadiography - Conclusion - Commercial sources (8 illus., diagrs., graphs. 70 references). Many micrographs (*e.g.* 'Kidney', p.284-8; 6 micrographs. 29 references). *Class No:* 573.086

[2203]

LOCQUIN, H. *and* LANGERON, M. Handbook of microscopy. Translation edited by H. Hillman. [Manuel de microscopie.] London, etc., Butterworths, 1983. xii, 322p. illus., graphs, diagrs., tables, formulas. ISBN: 0408106794.

Original French as *Manuel de microscopie* (1978).

6 chapters (subdivided): 1. Instruments and techniques - 2. Methods of fixation, examination, cutting and mounting - 3. Stains - 4. Staining and impregnation - 5. Topological stains - 6. Non-specific cytological stains. Appendix 1: Physical constants. Bibliography, p.303-8. Detailed, analytical index, p.309-22. *Class No:* 573.086

Staining

[2204]

CLARK, G. *and* KASTEN, F.H. History of staining. 3rd ed. Baltimore, Williams & Wilkinson, 1983. x,304p. illus. ISBN: 0683017055.

2nd ed. published 1948.

24 chapters: 1. Ralph Dougall Lillie ... 5. Cochineal dyes ... 9. Aniline dyes in histology ... 15. The staining of blood and parasitic protozoa ... 22. Immunological staining ... 24. A history of protein and nucleic acid histochemistry. Bibliography, p.253-90. Index. 'Provides the most useful historical summary now available in English in the development of stain technology' (*Science*, v.223, 17 February 1984, p.694). *Class No:* 573.086.16

[2205]

H.J. Conn's biological stains: a handbook on the nature and uses of the dyes employed in the biological laboratory. Conn, H.J., *and others*. 9th ed., edited by R.D. Lillie, with others. Baltimore, Md., Williams & Wilkins, 1977. xi, 692p. diagrs., tables, chemical structures.

First published 1925; 8th ed., 1969 (xii, 498p.).

20 chapters (1. Use and standardization of dyes as biological stains - 2. General nature and classification of dyes ... 19. Tables 1-9 - 20. Methods for testing biological stains). Bibliography, with brief notes, p.613-56. Detailed index, p.657-92. *Class No:* 573.086.16

Tissue & Cell Cultures

[2206]

DONNELLY, D.J. *and* VIDAVER, W.E. Glossary of plant tissue culture. London, Belhaven Press, 1988. 141p. £40. ISBN: 1852930616.

Short definitions of *c.*1,500 terms (ABA ... Zygotic embryo). Many cross-references. 3-page list of sources. A few entries list individuals important in plant tissue culture science. Includes eponyms but excludes plant species names. *Class No:* 573.086.8

[2207]

GIBCO search: an information service to our customers in tissue culture laboratories. University of Sheffield. Biomedical Information Service. Paisley, GIBCO, Ltd., 1981-. 6pa.

Replaces *Tissue culture abstracts,* 1966-79.

About 200 references per issue. 10 sections (1. Books, reviews, symposia ... 3. Growth factors ... 6. Epithelial cells - 7. Carcinoma cells - 8. Nerve cells - 9. Muscle cells). A current awareness service. *Class No:* 573.086.8

Exobiology

[2208]

ANGELO, J.A. The Extraterrestrial encyclopedia: our search for life in outer space. 2nd ed. New York, Facts on File, 1991. 272p. illus. (some col.), tables. $40. ISBN: 0816022763.

First published 1985.

Explains major space technologies and developments in the search for extraterrestrial life. Articles, arranged A-Z, vary in length from a paragraph to several pages. Many tables and cross-references. Black-and-white drawings and photographs, some of which are in colour. An improvement on the previous edition is the inclusion of an index. For public, academic and special libraries. *Class No:* 573.5

[2209]

SABLE, M.H. Exobiology: a research guide. Brighton, Mich., Green Oak Press, 1978. xi, 324p.

The bibliography section has 3,633 references in 16 subsections (Astronomy and origin of life and of planets ... Life in individual planets ... Unidentified flying objects, including flying saucers). Directory section: Organizations; periodicals. Author and subject indexes; index to directory section. *Class No:* 573.5

Ecology

Abbreviations & Symbols

[2210]

WENNRICH, P., *comp*. Anglo-American and German abbreviations in environmental protection. Munich, K.G. Saur, 1980. vi, 618p. $35. ISBN: 3598100604.

About 30,000 German and Anglo-American abbreviations plus full forms, in one sequence. Coverage: environmental protection and areas with related problems: biology, chemistry, agriculture, medicine and physics. *Class No:* 574(003)

[2211]

—**DAWSON, E. Directory of environmental abbreviations.** London, Environment Council, 1988. 69p. ISBN: 0903158345.

Contains *c.*1,000 abbreviations. Each entry includes an expansion of the abbreviations and a line or two on its meaning or function. Short bibliography. *Class No:* 574(003)

Databases

[2212]

COX, J. Environment databases 1991. London, Aslib, 1991. 65p. (*Aslib online guide.*) ISBN: 0851422616.

58 databases listed, Acidoc ... Westlaw Multistate Environmental Law Database. Data include producer; telephone, fax and telex numbers; host; content and coverage; number of references; frequency of updating; type of database; language; user aids. 4-page index of hosts. Covers air, water, land, minerals, climatology, acid rain, ozone depletion, etc. *Class No:* 574(003.4)

[2213]

ECO directory of environmental databases in the United Kingdom 1992. Barlow, M., *eds*. Bristol, ECO Environmental Education Trust, 1992. 290p. £35. ISBN: 1874666008.

Lists *c.*300 databases. Data include main speciality, subject range, area and timespan, methods of access, and charges. 3 main sections: 1. Databases in non-profit-making organizations - 2. Databases from commercial organizations - 3. Services, projects, and useful information. Abbreviations, p.281-2. Bibliography. Indexes: database name; organization name; subject; area; organization categories; media; users. *Class No:* 574(003.4)

[2214]

SCHUPP, J.F. **Environmental guide to the Internet.** Rockville, Md., Government Institutes Inc., 1995. 252p. $49. ISBN: 0865874492.

Five sections: 1. Electronic mailing lists - 2. Usenet newsgroups - 3. Other sources accessible through e-mail - 4. Electronic journals and newspapers - 5. Bulletin board systems. Brief descriptions accompanied by instructions for access. Guides to Internet resources cannot be recommended for timeliness because of constant changes on the WWW, but this will provide a useful starting point. *Class No:* 574(003.4)

Bibliographies

[2215]

Beacham's guide to environmental issues and sources. New York, Beacham, 1993. 5v. (3335p.) $240. ISBN: 0933833318.

39 chapters, closely subdivided, covering food, climate, population, health, energy, pollution, waste disposal, wildlife and ecology, natural resources, perspectives on the environment, etc. Several thousand citations, most published since 1988. 'A major contribution to the environmental literature' (*Choice*, December 1993, p.579). *Class No:* 574(01)

[2216]

Encyclopedia of environmental information sources: a subject guide to about 34,000 print and other sources of information on all aspects of the environment. Balachandran, S., *ed*. Detroit, Gale Research, 1993. 1813p. ISBN: 0810385686.

Exclusively US in coverage. A-Z list of 1,100 areas of interest, p.1-1508, (*e.g.* municipal sewage, municipal wastes) showing sources of information available. 13 types of information source: abstracts/ indexing services; bibliographies; directories; encyclopaedias/ dictionaries; general works; handbooks/manuals; online databases; statistical sources; trade associations/professional societies. The sources cited are listed A-Z by title, p.1509-1813. *Class No:* 574(01)

[2217]

Environment impact assessment: a bibliography, with abstracts. Clark, B.D., *and others*. London, Mansell; New York, Bowker, 1980. vi, 516p. ISBN: 0720108993.

About 1,000 entries, some with lengthy annotations. 5 sections: 1. Aids to impact assess - 2. Critiques and reviews of environmental assessments - 3. Environmental income assessment and other aspects of planning - 4. Environmental impact assessment in selected countries (USA, Canada, Australia, Continental Europe, other countries), p.249/483 - 5. Information sources, p.487-94. Selected periodicals. Author and subject indexes. As this is a topic which is now generating more interest, this publication needs to be updated soon if it is to retain its value. *Class No:* 574(01)

[2218]

Environmental studies reviews. Douville, J.A., *comp*. Middletown, Ct., Association of College and Research Libraries, 1995. 164p. $38. ISBN: 0838978088.

About 900 book and electronic media reviews originally published in *Choice* between 1990 and 1994. Arranged by broad subject categories, with a substantial reference section. Author and title indexes. A handy collection. *Class No:* 574(01)

[2219]

NIBLEY, B. **'Environmental reference sources'.** In *Reference books bulletin*, 15 January 1995, p.949-54.

Sections: Directories and sourcebooks - Bibliographies - Dictionaries and encyclopedias - Atlases - Abstracts and indexes - Statistical sources - Guides, handbooks, almanacs - Miscellaneous - Electronic sources. US bias. Lists material published after 1989. *Class No:* 574(01)

[2220]

SARGENT, F., II., *comp*. **Human ecology: a guide to information sources.** Detroit, Mich., Gale, 1983. xi, 293p. $68. (*Health affairs information guide studies, v.10.*) ISBN: 0810315041.

An annotated guide to books and periodical articles. Each section (subdivided) has an introductory essay. Subject coverage, - 'nature and scope of human ecology, the setting (abiotic and biotic), human-environment manipulations, human-environment interactions, environmental quality, community health, and disease control' (*Reference books bulletin*, 1983-1984, p.104). Author, title and subject indexes. *Class No:* 574(01)

[2221]

—JONES, O.J. and JONES, E.A. **Index of human ecology.** London, Europa, 1974. ix, 169p. £5.50. ISBN: 0900362669.

Has 3 parts. 1. Principal secondary journals (28 subjects, Agriculture ... Theology) - Part 2. Secondary journals; ancillary services, (*i.e.*, abstracting journals; reviews) - Part 3. Consolidated index (*c*.7,000 terms, coded to pt. 1). *Class No:* 574(01)

[2222]

The Sourcebook of the environment: a guide to the literature. Hammond, K.A., *and others, eds*. Chicago, Ill., Chicago Univ. Press, for American Association of Geographers, 1978. 613p. $27.50. ISBN: 0226315223.

26 contributors on aspects of the environment literature. About 3,800 references. Critical introductions to the basic material, 'with directions for examination of more advanced and more specialized works' (*Preface*). 'Basic guide' (*A geographical bibliography for American libraries,* edited by C.D. Harris (1985), p.113)). *Class No:* 574(01)

Encyclopaedias

[2223]

ASHWORTH, W. **The Encyclopedia of environmental studies.** New York, Facts on File, 1991. viii,470p. diagrs., tables. ISBN: 0816015317.

Lists terms from biology, physics, chemistry, ecology, and geology encountered in environmental literature. Also includes in the alphabetical listing short biographies of environmental activists, *e.g.* John Muir; abbreviations and organizations, *e.g.* Friends of the Earth. Many cross-references. Bibliography, p.435-40. Detailed index. Has a US bias (includes information on US government and state agencies, and legislation) but would be useful in any library covering environmental issues. *Class No:* 574(031)

[2224]

The Encyclopedia of ecology and environmental management. Calow, P., *ed.-in-chief*. Oxford, Blackwell, 1998. xv,805p. illus.(some col.). £125. ISBN: 0865428387.

3,000 entries (Aapa fens ... Zooxanthellae). 210 contributors. Well cross-referenced. Bulky; library use only. *Class No:* 574(031)

[2225]

The Environment encyclopedia and directory. 2nd ed. London, Europa Publications, 1998. xvi,560p. maps. £210. ISBN: 185743028x.

First published 1994.

Five main sections: Maps; A-Z of the environment (*c*.1,000 definitions; many cross-references); Directory of environmental organizations (*c*.4,000 entries; international in scope); bibliography of environmental periodicals; Who's who of the environment (*c*.700 entries). Index of environmental organizations by field of activity. *Class No:* 574(031)

[2226]

FRANCK, I. **The Green encyclopedia.** Brownstone, D. Englewood Cliffs, N.J., Prentice Hall, 1992. 512p. illus. $20. ISBN: 0133656853.

Over 1,000 concise entries on environmental matters. Includes data on environmentalists, pesticides, national parks, etc. Many cross-references and illustrations. Lists of relevant organizations and their publications, endangered species, toxic chemicals, etc. For public and school libraries. *Class No:* 574(031)

[2227]

McGraw-Hill encyclopedia of environmental science and engineering. Parker, S.P. *and* Corbitt, R., *eds*. 3rd ed. New York, McGraw-Hill Book Company, 1993. 749p. illus., diagrs., graphs, tables. ISBN: 0070513961.

First published 1974. 2nd ed. as *McGraw-Hill encyclopedia of environmental science,* (1980).

250 signed articles, many of them new to this volume, arranged A—Z from 'Acid rain' to 'Zooplankton', and followed by short bibliographies. 390 contributors. 'Hazardous waste', p.281-6, has 2 tables, 6 refs. An overview of current environmental problems. *Class No:* 574(031)

[2228]

Natural resources. Coyne, M.S. *and* Allin, C.W., *eds*. Pasadena, Calif., Salem Press, 1998. 3v.(976p.) illus. tables, charts. $290. ISBN: 0893569127.

127 contributors and 438 articles, arranged A-Z, of between 250-4,000 words in length. Subject coverage includes biology, geology, environmentalism, energy resources, etc. Brief articles on organizations and historical events, alongwith 22 biographies. 200 black-and-white photographs; 135 charts and tables. Well-laid out, with articles being divided by sub-headings, and numerous cross-references. Glossary and bibliography of *c*.240 books. A useful overview, encompassing many subject areas. *Class No:* 574(031)

Handbooks & Manuals

[2229]

Ecological engineering: an introduction to ecotechnology. Mitsch, W.J. *and* Jorgensen, S.E., *eds*. New York, Wiley, 1989. xiv,472p. figs. $59.95. ISBN: 0471625590.

2 sections: 1. Basic principles (1. Introduction to ecological engineering ... 4. Principles of ecological modeling ... 7. Agriculture and ecotechnology) - 2. Case studies of ecological engineering (12

....(contd.)
chapters, *e.g.* 16. Ecotechnological approaches to the restoration of lakes). Chapter references. Index. For the academic library. *Class No:* 574(035)

[2230]
Grzimek's encyclopedia of ecology. Grzimek, B., *and others*, eds. English ed. New York, London, etc., Van Nostrand Reinhold, 1976. 705p. illus. ISBN: 0442229488.
Originally published Zurich, Kindler Verlag AG, 1971. A supplement to *Grzimek's animal life encyclopedia (qv)*.
42 contributors. Part 1: The environment of animals (1. Adaptations to the abiotic environment; 3. Habitats and their fauna; 4. Man as a factor in the environment of animals) - Part 2. The environment of man. Many coloured plates; excellent coloured maps. 'A worthy purchase' (*New technical books,* November 1977, entry 1564). *Class No:* 574(035)

[2231]
ODUM, E.P. Fundamentals of ecology. 3rd ed. Philadelphia, Pa., Saunders, 1971. 574p. $37. ISBN: 0721669417.
First published 1953.
Includes sections on applied and human ecology. A 40-page bibliography; detailed index. 'Perhaps the best all-round treatment of ecology' (Brewer, J.G. *The literature of geography.* 2nd ed., 1973, p.183). *Class No:* 574(035)

Dictionaries

Polyglot

[2232]
EUROPEAN PARLIAMENT. Ecological terminology. Luxembourg, European Parliament, 1982. 259p. $24.95. ISBN: 0828809437.
Based in part on *Terminology of the Environment* (European Parliament, 1974).
Entries in French; equivalents in English, German, Danish, Dutch and Italian. Indexes in the six languages, plus a bibliography. *Class No:* 574(038)=00

[2233]
PAENSON, I. Environment in key words: a multilingual handbook of the environment, English-French-German-Russian. Oxford, Pergamon Press, 1990. 2v. xxxiv,662p.,268p. figs., tables. £150. ISBN: 0080245242.
First published in 1972 as *Multilingual systematic glossary of environmental terms.*
3 chapters, each in 4 languages: 1. The ecological balance - 2. Disruption of the ecological balance - 3. Some measures for the re-establishment of the ecological balance. Words and phrases in bold type in the text appear in the index (v.2). The chapters are written in half-page column style so that the reader can see all 4 language equivalents spread over 2 pages and in context. 'The author considers each term in the context of a given discipline or even group of disciplines' (*Preface*). *Class No:* 574(038)=00

English

[2234]
ALLABY, M. Macmillan dictionary of the environment. 4th ed. London, Macmillan, 1994. 377p. ISBN: 0333616553.
First published 1977 ([v], 532p.).
About 6,700 interdisciplinary terms, including profuse cross-references, and straying into many fields, - botany, zoology, chemistry, physics, mathematics, economics (*e.g.* ½p. each on Ice Age, nuclear reactor, mangrove). Includes a few biographical entries, for Darwin, Malthus, Lamarck, etc., as well as environmental disasters, *e.g.* Chernobyl, Braer, etc., but not Exxon Valdez. *Class No:* 574(038)=20

[2235]
The Concise Oxford dictionary of ecology. Allaby, M., *ed.* Oxford, University Press, 1994. vii,415p. ISBN: 0192116894.
Nearly 5,000 entries, derived from Allaby's *Oxford dictionary of natural history* (1985) (*q.v.*). Subject areas include oceanography, climatology, animal physiology, pedology, etc. Also includes short biographies of those eminent in this field. Many cross-references. For the student and layperson. *Class No:* 574(038)=20

[2236]
Dictionary of ecology and environment. Collin, P.H., *and others.* 3rd ed. Teddington, Middx., Peter Collin Publishing, 1995. 253p.+15p. ISBN: 0948549742; 1579580750, US ed.
*c.*8,000 entries, some of them single-line definitions, and including some abbreviations, but no cross-references. Unusually, includes editorial comment on some definitions, and relevant quotes from recent publications (but without bibliographical details); *e.g.* 'diversification' is followed by a pronunciation guide, etymological definition, then editorial comment on types of farm diversification, with quotes from two British journals not greatly adding to the information already

....(contd.)
provided. Attractively produced, with a clear type-face.
US ed. published by Fitzroy Dearborn, 1998 ($35). *Class No:* 574(038)=20

[2237]
The Dictionary of ecology and environmental science. Art, H.W., *ed.* New York, Holt, 1993. 632p. diagrs. $60. ISBN: 0805020799.
More than 8,000 entries of no more than 100 words each. Many cross-references. A few good quality line-drawings. 30-page appendix includes periodic table, geologic time scale. For public and academic libraries. *Class No:* 574(038)=20

[2238]
A Dictionary of ecology, evolution and systematics. Lincoln, R.J., *and others.* 2nd ed. Cambridge, University Press, 1998. 361p. charts, tables, maps. £50; £17.95; $74.95. ISBN: 0521591392; 052143842x, pbk.
First published 1982.
More than 11,000 rather short working-definitions, with more emphasis placed on new techniques in climate change, developmental genetics, and molecular biology than in the previous ed. Produced by British Museum (Natural History) staff. 29 appendices, *e.g.* 'Quaternary Ice Age'; 'Plankton size categories'. 'Those in need of a first-rate biology dictionary would do well to acquire this one' (*Choice*, January 1999, p.858). *Class No:* 574(038)=20

[2239]
DOOLEY, D. *and* **KIRKPATRICK, N. Environmental glossary.** Leatherhead, Surrey, PIRA International, 1993. 181p. diagrs. ISBN: 1858020158.
*c.*1,200 definitions, including cross-references, from A-Weighting to Zinc and including relevant slang, *e.g.* NIMBY, NIMTO. 'Carefully thought out and thoroughly planned ... extremely useful as a quick-reference guide' (*The Year in reference* 1994, no.230). *Class No:* 574(038)=20

[2240]
The Green book. Pope, S., *and others.* London, Hodder & Stoughton, 1991. viii,337p. £12.95. ISBN: 034053298x.
Over 500 subjects, arranged A-Z (Acid rain ... Zoos). Length of entries ranges from a few lines to several pages (*e.g.* Chernobyl; 4p.). Many cross-references. Appendix of useful addresses, p.333-37. No bibliographies. Useful for school and public libraries. *Class No:* 574(038)=20

[2241]
—**CRUMP, A. Dictionary of environment and development:** people, places, ideas and organizations. London, Earthscan Publications, 1991. 272p. £15. ISBN: 185383078x.
Over 800 definitions, arranged A-Z (Aborigines ... Zinc). Definitions are more concise than *The Green book (qv)* (*e.g.* Chernobyl; ½-page) but the book covers a wider range of issues. Many cross-references. No bibliographies. Suitable for academic and public libraries. *Class No:* 574(038)=20

[2242]
Longman dictionary of environmental science. Lawrence, E., *and others.* Harlow, Essex, Longman, 1998. xii, 491p. £12.99. ISBN: 058225356x.
12,700 terms from A (alpha) to Zymogenous, including cross-references. Includes acronyms but no pronunciation guide or biographical entries. 11 appendices: 1. Chemical symbols ... 6. Outline of the fungi ... 10. Virus families. Unattractive print layout, but pocket volume likely to prove useful to workers in the field. *Class No:* 574(038)=20

Reviews & Abstracts

[2243]
Current advances in ecological and environmental sciences. Amsterdam, Elsevier Science, 1989-. 12pa. $1,820. ISSN: 09556648.
One of a series of 12 Pergamon *Current advances.* Formerly *Current advances in ecological sciences* (1975-88).
About 18,000 references pa. 58 sections, *e.g.* 4. Distribution; 6. Community ecology - 7. Population dynamics - 8. Animal behaviour - 9. Productivity and growth rates (plant, animal, microbiological systems); 17. Interactions with the physical environment; 23. Reproduction; 27. Nutrition; 29. Autoecology; 43. Pollution). Author index per issue. 'Designed by working scientists for the working scientist'. Also available on microfiche. Online in *Elsevier BIOBASE* database via Datastar, DIALOG, and DIMDI. *Class No:* 574(048)

[2244]

Current contents: Agriculture, biology and environmental sciences.
Philadelphia, Pa., Institute for Scientific Information, 1970-. Weekly.
$730. ISSN: 00900508.

Previously (1970-72) subtitled 'Agriculture, food and veterinary sciences'.

Issue for 25 Mar 1996 contains title-pages of 124 journals. Sections include: Biology ... Environment/Ecology ... Plant sciences ... Entomology/Pest control ... Veterinary medicine/Animal health. Title word index; author index and address directory; publishers' address directory. Available on diskette, on CD-ROM version, and online on the CURRENT CONTENTS SEARCH database. Internet access as *Current Contents Connect* at http://connect.isihost.com.
Class No: 574(048)

[2245]

Ecological abstracts. Norwich, Elsevier Geo Abstracts, Ltd., 1974-.
12pa. $1,587. ISSN: 0305196x.

1,500 abstracts per issue. Sections: Global and general ecology - Marine ecology - Tidal and estuarine ecology - Freshwater ecology - Terrestrial ecology (plants & animals) - Applied ecology - Evolution, palaeoecology and historical ecology - General theory, methods and techniques. Subject index per issue. Annual subject, author and regional indexes. List of journals. Online GEOBASE (1987), available on DIALOG (Search file 292) and ORBIT. Also available on microfilm and CD-ROM (1990-) as ECODISC. *Class No:* 574(048)

[2246]

Ecology abstracts. Bethesda, Md., Cambridge Scientific Abstracts, 1980-. 12pa. $945 (US) $1,085 (non US) pa. ISSN: 01433296.

Formerly *Applied ecology abstracts, 1975-79.*

25 sections: Contains *c.*11,000 abstracts pa. Sections include: Ecosystem studies - General; Arid zones; Microorganisms; Paleoecology; Human settlements; Recreation/Landscaping. Author and subject indexes per issue, plus cumulative annual subject and author indexes. Available online (LIFE SCIENCES COLLECTION) via DIALOG, on magnetic tape, and CD-ROM. There is also an Internet edition. *Class No:* 574(048)

Periodicals

[2247]

Environmental periodicals bibliography. Baltimore, Md., National Information Services Corporation, 1972- . Price varies.

Compiled by the Environmental Studies Institute of the International Academy of Santa Barbara. International in scope, covering scientific, technical and popular journals. Contains over 500,000 citations collected since 1972. Subject areas include human ecology, water and land resources, nutrition, air and energy. Available on CD-ROM and on-line. *Class No:* 574(051)

Progress Reports

[2248]

Advances in ecological research. San Diego, Academic Press, 1962-.
v.1-. Irreg. diagrs., graphs. ISSN: 00652504.

V.27, 1997 has nine contributors. The five well-documented papers include 'The ecology of root lifespan'p. 1-60; 'Nocturnal insect migration: effects of local winds', p.61-92. Analytical subject index. Cumulative list of titles, v.1-25 in V.26. *Class No:* 574(055)

Yearbooks & Directories

[2249]

DEZIRON, M. *and* **BAILEY, L. A Directory of European environmental organizations.** 2nd ed. Oxford, Blackwell, 1993.
237p. £40. ISBN: 0631191143.

First published 1991.

2 sections: 1. Governmental organizations - 2. Non-governmental organizations. Data for each entry cover name; address of headquarters; telephone/fax; director and principal staff; contact person; foundation date; purpose; organization; activities; publications; funding; members. Six-page list of abbreviations. Alphabetical and country indexes. Well laid out and easy to read. *Class No:* 574(058)

[2250]

Directory for the environment: organisations, campaigns and initiatives in the British Isles. Frisch, M., *ed.* 4th ed. London, Green Print, 1994. xxii, 294p. ISBN: 1854250833.

Previously published as *Directory for the environment*, 3rd ed. 1990.

Lists local and national organizations, campaigns and government bodies concerned with the human and natural environment. Coverage includes consultancies, charities, research institutes, campaigning groups, learned societies, and commercial enterprises throughout Britain and Ireland. *Class No:* 574(058)

[2251]

Directory for the environment: organisations, campaigns and initiatives in the British Isles. Frisch, M., *ed.* 4th ed. London, Green Print, 1994. xxii, 294p. ISBN: 1854250833.

Previously published as *Directory for the environment*, 3rd ed. 1990.

Lists local and national organizations, campaigns and government bodies concerned with the human and natural environment. Coverage includes consultancies, charities, research institutes, campaigning groups, learned societies, and commercial enterprises throughout Britain and Ireland. *Class No:* 574(058)

[2252]

Environmental consultants directory: 1997/98. London, Environmental Data Services, 1997. vi,322p. (includes 1 CD-ROM). ISBN: 0907673120.

First published 1988. Previous ed. (1995) published as *Directory of environmental consultants*.

Details of *c.*400 organizations in the UK, arranged A—Z. Data include address; telephone/telex/fax numbers; contact name; e-mail address; number of UK projects; qualified staff; skills; facilities; client groups; areas of interest. Appendices, including quick reference guide and late entrants. *Class No:* 574(058)

[2253]

The Environmental yearbook. Northampton, Taylor Marketing Services, 1989. 390p. £58. ISBN: 0946749019.

UK in scope. 2 sections: 1. Organizations involved with the environment - 2. Local government environmental personnel. Section 1 is arranged alphabetically by subject, *e.g.* 'Bird organizations'; 'Horticulture'. Data consists only of address and telephone number. Section 2 is arranged by council. Useful for its wide-ranging coverage but it should be regularly updated, and typographical errors corrected. *Class No:* 574(058)

[2254]

Gale environmental sourcebook: a guide to organizations, agencies, and publications. Hill, K. *and* Piccirelli, A., *eds.* Detroit, Gale Research, 1992. xvii,688p. ISBN: 0810384035. ISSN: 10590919.

Information on 8,634 environmental organizations, mainly derived from other Gale directories, with additional data added by editors. Six sections: US and international organizations; Government agencies and programs; Research facilities and educational programs; Publications and information services; Green consumerism; Scholarships and awards. US-slant. *Class No:* 574(058)

[2255]

MILNER, J.E. The Green index. 2nd ed. London, Cassell, 1994.
612p. ISBN: 0304324779.

First ed. published 1990.

A-Z list of environmental organizations (Abberdale Industrial Hamlet ... Zoological Society of Wales, p.24-441). Indexes, p.445-612, include numerical, scope, and alphabetical lists of codes used in the main entries, as well as category and keyword indexes of organizations and 'umbrella' groups. The information provided is minimal; includes telephone numbers but no contact names. *Class No:* 574(058)

[2256]

Répertoire des organisations non gouvernementales dans les pays membres de l'OCDE pour l'environnement et le developpement. [Directory of non-governmental environment and development organisations in OECD member countries.] Paris, OECD, 1992. 409p. FFr300. ISBN: 9264035362.

Gives information on 649 NGOs whose activities are linked to the environment. *Class No:* 574(058)

[2257]

WOOLLETT, S. Environmental grants: a guide to grants for the environment from government, companies and charitable trusts. 2nd ed. London, Directory of Social Change, 1993. 201p. £14.95. (*Directory of Social Change publication.*) ISBN: 0907164927.

1. Introduction. 2. Grants - government departments and agencies - 3. Grants - charitable trusts and foundations - 4. Donations and sponsorship - companies - 5. Grants - independent organizations - 6. Award schemes - 7. Support from local authorities - 8. Partnerships, brokerage, technical and financial services - 9. Useful publications and organizations. British in scope. Index, p.197-201. *Class No:* 574(058)

[2258]

World directory of environmental organizations a handbook of national and international organizations and programs - governmental and non-governmental - concerned with protecting the earth's resources. Trzyna, T.C., *and others, eds.* 5th ed. Sacramento, Calif., International Institute for the Environment and Public Policy; London, Earthscan Publications, 1996. 263p. £50. ISBN: 1880028077, US ed; 185383307x.

4th ed., 1992.

Describes more than 3,200 organizations in over 200 countries. Seven sections: 1. Introduction - 2. Who's doing what: problems, resources, and biomes - 3. The world regions: an overview - 4. The

....(contd.)

United Nations system - 5. Other intergovernmental organizations - 6. International non-governmental organizations - 7. Country and area listings. Index. *Class No:* 574(058)

Quotations

[2259]
RODES, B.K. *and* ODELL, R. **A Dictionary of environmental quotations.** New York, Simon & Schuster, 1992. 335p. $30. ISBN: 0132105764.

About 3,700 identified quotations in English or English translation. Alphabetical subject arrangement; chronological within categories. Indexes: author; subject. 'Highly recommended' (*Choice,* December 1992. p.600). *Class No:* 574(082.2)

Maps & Atlases

[2260]
LEAN, G. *and* HINRICHSEN, D. **Atlas of the environment.** 2nd ed. New York, HarperPerennial, 1994. 192p. illus.(col.),diagrs., tables, maps. $39. ISBN: 0062733141.

Previous ed. published 1992.

Topics include literacy rates, disasters, land issues, demographics, etc. Only includes data from the 1980s and 1990s. Over 200 full colour maps and diagrams. No index. A general overview; for school and public libraries. *Class No:* 574(084.3)

[2261]
MASON, R.J. *and* MATTSON, M.T. **Atlas of United States environmental issues.** New York, Macmillan, 1991. 252p. illus., diagrs., tables, maps. $90. ISBN: 0028972619.

Includes maps and information on agricultural land, forests, natural hazards, solid wastes and pollution. More than 130 maps, tables and diagrams. Glossary, bibliography, and index. Although sometimes lacking in detail, the information is well written and precise. Recommended for school, public and academic libraries. *Class No:* 574(084.3)

[2262]
MIDDLETON, N. **Atlas of environmental issues.** New York, Facts on File, 1989. 63p. illus., maps. $16.95. (*World contemporary issues.*) ISBN: 081602023x.

Consists of double-page spreads devoted to environmental themes, *e.g.* noise, soil erosion, irrigation. In addition to colourful charts and maps, a few paragraphs discuss the problem in general. Brief index. Aimed at young adults and suitable for school and public libraries. *Class No:* 574(084.3)

Worldwide

[2263]
Ecosystems of the world. Goodall, D.W., *ed.* Amsterdam, etc., Elsevier, 1977-. illus., diagrs., tables, maps.

1. *Wet coastal ecosystems*; edited by V.J. Chapman. 1977. 2. *Dry coastal ecosystems*; edited by E.V.D. Maarel. 1993. 3v. 4. *Mires: swamp, bog, fen and moor;* edited by A.J.P. Gore. 4A. *General studies*; 1983. 4B. *Regional studies*; 1983. 5. *Temperate deserts and semi-deserts*; edited by N.E. West. 1983. 7. *Temperate deciduous forests*; edited by E.Röhrig and B. Ulrich. 1991. 8A. *Natural grasslands*; edited by R.T. Coupland. 1995. 8B. *Natural grasslands*; edited by E. Röhrig and B. Ulrich. 1991. 9. *Heathlands and related shrublands*; edited by R.L. Specht. 2v. 1979-81. 10. *Temperate broad-leaved evergreen forests*; edited by J.D. Ovington. 1983. 11. *Mediterranean-type shrublands*; edited by F. Di Castri, etc. 1981. 12. *Hot deserts and arid shrublands*; edited by M. Evenari. 1985-6. 2v. 13. *Tropical savannas*; edited by F. Bourlière. 1983. 14A. *Tropical rain forest ecosystems*; edited by F.B. Golley. 1983. 14B. *Tropical rain forest ecosystems;* edited by H. Lieth and M.J.A. Werger. 1989. 15. *Forested wetlands*; edited by A. Lugo. 1989. 16. *Ecosystems of disturbed ground*; edited by L.R. Walker. 1999. 17A. *Managed grasslands: regional studies;* edited by A. Breymeyer. 1989. 17B. *Managed grasslands*; edited by R.W. Snaydon. 1987. 18. *Field-crop ecosystems;* edited by C.J. Pearson. 1991. 21. *Bioindustrial ecosystems*; edited by D.J.A. Cole and G.C. Brander. 1986. 22. *River and stream ecosystems*; edited by C.E. Cushing *and others.* 1995. 23. *Lakes and reservoirs*; edited by F.B. Taub. 1984. 24. *Intertidal and littoral ecosystems*; edited by A.C. Mathiespn and P.H. Nienhuis. 1993. 25. *Coral reefs*; edited by Z. Dubinsky. 1990. 26. *Estuaries and enclosed seas*; edited by B.H. Ketchum. 1983. 27. *Continental shelves*; edited by H. Postma and J.J. Zijlstra. 1987. 29. *Managed aquatic ecosystems;* edited by R.G. Michael. 1987.

Each volume is the work of a team of specialists. Extensive bibliographies.

Monumental compendium of information about processes and characteristics of ... ecosystems of the world ... 'The most thorough treatment of its kind to date' (*Geographical bibliography for American libraries;* edited by C.D. Harris (1985), p.76-77)). *Class No:* 574(100)

Marine Environment

[2264]
DAVIES, B.R. *and* WALKER, K.F. **The Ecology of river systems.** The Hague, W. Junk; Norwell, Mass., Kluwer, 1986. 793p. $232.

Concentrates on the ecology of 13 major rivers outside Europe: Africa (6), Americas (5), Australia (1). (*Nature* v.325, 26 February 1987, p.769) queries omission of the Indus, Ganges, Irrawaddy, Yangtze, Amur, Lene, Yenirei, Ob, plus the Mississipi and Orinoco). Attention is rightly directed towards draining basins and dams. *Class No:* 574(26)

[2265]
A Directory of wetlands of international importance: sites designated for the list of Wetlands of International Importance. 2nd ed. Gland, Switzerland, Cambridge, IUCN for the Ramsar Convention Bureau; Washington, D.C., Island, 1990. 782p.

First published 1987.

Covers 52 countries, Algeria ... Yugoslavia. The entry for the Volga delta, p.631-2, has data on location; area; degrees of protection; site description; international and national importance; changes in ecological character; management practices; scientific research and facilities; principal reference material. Introductory notes on each country precede data on individual wetlands. Italy, Austria and Denmark have the most entires. Lack of funds means that this edition is not a thorough revision, and the publishers accept that some inconsistencies will occur and information may be out of date. *Class No:* 574(26)

[2266]
HUGHES, R.H. *and* HUGHES, J.S. **A Directory of African wetlands.** Cambridge, World Conservation Union (IUCN), 1992. xxxiv,820p. maps. ISBN: 2880329493.

Six sections: North west - North east - West - Central - Southern Africa - Madagascar. Data include climate, flora and fauna, and vegetation, with much detailed information. Bibliography. *Class No:* 574(26)

[2267]
Marine ecology: a comprehensive integrated treatise on life in oceans and coastal waters. Kinne, O., *ed.* New York, etc., Wiley, 1970-84. 5v.

1. *Environmental factors.* 1970. 3pts. 2. *Physiological factors.* 1975. 2pts. 3. *Cultivation.* 1976. 3pts. 4. *Dynamics.* 1978. 5. *Ocean management.* 1984. 4pts.

Many specialist contributors. Emphasis on laboratory methods. Bibliographies. Author, taxonomic and subject indexes. 'Highly recommended' (*Nature*, v.272, 23 March 1978, p.380-1). *Class No:* 574(26)

[2268]
PATRICK, R. **Rivers of the United States.** New York, John Wiley, 1994-98. 5v. figs.,maps,tables. ISBN: 0471303453, v.1; 0471107522, v.2; 0471303461, v.3; 0471197416, v.4A; 0471197424, v.4B.

V.1. *Estuaries.* (807p. £155); v.2. *Chemical and physical characteristics.* (237p. £155); v.3. *The eastern and southeastern states.* (829p. £100); v.4A. *The Mississippi river and tributaries north of St. Louis.* (389p.); v.4B. v.4A. *The Mississippi river tributaries south of St. Louis.* (862p.)

A major work on the structure and functioning of ecosystems in US rivers. Extensive bibliographies accompany each chapter. *Class No:* 574(26)

[2269]
The Shore environment. Price, J.H., *and others, eds.* London, New York, Academic Press, for the Systematics Association, 1980. 2v. £76.50, v.1; £109, v.2. (*Systematics Association special volumes.*) ISBN: 0125647018, v.1; 0125647026, v.2.

1. *Methods.* xx, 321, xlip. 2. *Ecosystems.* xx, 622, cp. Papers from an international meeting. 44 contributors, The 27 papers include 'Field teaching methods in shore ecology', and 'Strategies of data collection and analysis of subtidal vegetation'. Both volumes carry a taxonomic index. Substantial subject index. Appended list of Systematics Association publications. *Class No:* 574(26)

[2270]
—BARNES, R.S.K. *and* MANN, K.H. **Fundamentals of aquatic ecology.** 2nd ed. Oxford, Blackwell, 1991. vii,270p. illus., diagrs., graphs, tables, maps. £39.50. ISBN: 0632029811.

2nd ed. of *Fundamentals of aquatic ecosystems* (1980).

9 contributors; 5 parts, with each of the 13 chapters followed by 'Further reading'. Pt.1. Introduction - 2. Aquatic ecosystems - 3. Aquatic individuals and communities - 4. Habitat types peculiar to aquatic systems - 5. Human effects. Detailed, analytical index. *Class No:* 574(26)

[2271]
—BAXTER, J.M. The Mitchell Beazley pocket guide to the seashores of Britain and Northern Europe. London, Mitchell Beazley, 1990. 144p. illus. (col.). £2.99. ISBN: 0855337699.

Intended as a companion and field guide for identification. Includes animals and plants of the shore, the more common coastal flowering plants, the birds of the shore and coastal waters, and some mammals. Habitat symbols are given for each entry. 400 illustrations. Brief glossary, index and bibliography. For public libraries.
Class No: 574(26)

Europe
[2272]
European environmental information sourcebook. Newman, O. *and* Fisher, A., *comps.* Andover, Gale Research International, 1994. xxiii,357p. £75. ISBN: 1873477201.

Contains listings of information sources - publications and organizations - in 12 environmental subject areas (Air Quality ... Miscellaneous), with telephone numbers, contact names, and prices, where appropriate. List of acronyms precedes text. English and French introductions. Geographical and alphabetical indexes, p.313-57.
Class No: 574(4)

[2273]
European environmental yearbook: nature conservation, protection of the environment, town and country planning in Belgium, Denmark, the Federal Republic of Germany, France, Greece, Ireland, Italy, Luxembourg, the Netherlands, Portugal, Spain and the United Kingdom, with special surveys on Australia, Japan, USA and USSR. 4th ed. London, Docter International, 1990. xxii,897p. charts, tables, maps. $150. ISBN: 0871796910.

At head of title page: 'DOCTER. Institute for Environmental Studies, Milan'. Prepared with the co-operation and financial assistance from the Commission of the European Communities, Brussels.

188 contributors. Part 1 deals with 22 topics in nature conservancy and town and country planning in the then 12 member countries of the European Economic Community. Bibliographical references. Part 2 comprises special surveys (*e.g.* 'Australia'). Part 3: Environmental institutes and associations. Legislation. Part 4, Documentation.
Class No: 574(4)

Great Britain
[2274]
GOUDIE, A.S. *and* BRUNSDEN, D. The Environment of the British Isles: an atlas. Oxford, Clarendon Press, 1994. 184p. ISBN: 0198741723.

Information on geomorphology, climate, hydrology, biogeography, human impact, etc., are represented on outlines maps of the British Isles, *e.g.* snowfall, p.72-5; 3 maps showing frequency, depth, and water equivalent of lying snow. References (headed 'Acknowledgments') p.183-4. *Class No:* 574(410)

India
[2275]
Ecology and biogeography in India. Mani, M.S., *ed.* The Hague, Junk, 1974. xix, 773p. illus., diagrs., graphs, tables, maps. (*Monographiae biologicae, v.23.*) ISBN: 9061930758.

24 documented chapters (1. Introduction - 2. Physical features - 3. Geology - 4. Weather and climate patterns ... 19. Biography of the Peninsula ... 23. Biogeography of the Indo-Gangetic plains - 24. Biogeographical evolution in India). Chapter 11, 'The tribal man in India: a study in the ecology of the primitive communities', p.281-321, has 56 references. Detailed index, p.725-73. Numerous tables and maps. *Class No:* 574(540)

Africa
[2276]
A Bibliography of African ecology: a geographically and topically classified list of books and articles. Rogers, D.J., *comp.* Westport, Conn., Greenwood Press, 1979. 499p. $85. (*African Bibliographic Center. Special bibliographic series, n.s.,6.*) ISBN: 0313205523.

About 8,000 references, in 5 geographical regions, each with 10 subject divisions (plants; animals; aquatic ecology; abiotic environment; palaeoecology; anthropology; human health; history and geography; conservation; general and miscellaneous). Two lists of relevant serials: those published in Africa; those published outside Africa. No author index. A well organized bibliography.
Class No: 574(6)

[2277]
JAMES, V.U. **Africa's ecology:** sustaining the biological and environmental diversity of a continent. Jefferson, N.C., McFarland, 1993. xxi,293p. ISBN: 0899508596.

Two parts: 1. The status of the African continent (8 chapters: 1. Africa's parks and reserves ... 8. Impact on water and soil resources); 2. International and domestic policies for developing Africa's resources (3 chapters: *e.g.* 10. Women's contribution to the preservation of Africa's resources). Bibliography, p.279-86. Brief index, p.287-93.
Class No: 574(6)

America—North
[2278]
BOLEN, E.G. Ecology of North America. New York, John Wiley, 1998. xv,448p. illus.,maps,tables. £65. ISBN: 0471131563.

Eleven chapters: 1. Introduction ... 4. Easter deciduous forests ... 7. Deserts ... 11. A selection of special environments. Appendix, p.413-28, lists scientific names of organisms mentioned in the text. Glossary, p.429-40. Index. The strength of this book is the extensive bibliographies - with brief annotations at many entries - appended to each chapter. For students and academic libraries.
Class No: 574(71+73)

Antarctic
[2279]
Antarctic ecology. Laws, R.M., *ed.* Orlando, Florida, & London, Academic Press, 1984. 2v. (368p. + 544p.). $112, v.1; $118, v.2. ISBN: 0124395015, v.1; 0124395023, v.2.

Updates M.W. Holdgate's *Antarctic ecology* (1930).

1. *Terrestrial environment and ecology.* 2. *Marine environment and ecology.* 13 contributors. 15 chapters in all (1. The terrestrial environment ... 4. Introduced mammals ... 15. Conservation and the Antarctic). Each chapter has an extensive bibliography, and each volume a composite 25-p. subject index. An authoritative survey.
Class No: 574(99)

[2280]
MAY, J. The Greenpeace book of Antarctica: a new view of the seventh continent. London, Dorling Kindersley, 1988. 192p. illus. (col.), figs., maps. £16.99. ISBN: 0863182836.

4 sections: 1. Terra incognita (14 chapters: 1. Antarctica evolving ... 7. Beneath the ice ... 12. Meteorites ... 14. Map of Antarctica) - 2. Life at the end of the world (9 chapters: 1. Land flora and fauna ... 4. Krill ... 9. Whales) - 3. The human presence (12 chapters: 1. Exploration ... 5. Protected sites ... 12. A scientist's view) - 4. Greenpeace perspectives. 2 appendices (*e.g.* 'Antarctic bases & refuges'). Bibliography. Brief list of abbreviations. Gazetteer; index. Many colour illustrations. For public libraries. *Class No:* 574(99)

Hydrobiology (Marine Biology)

Bibliographies
[2281]
FRESHWATER BIOLOGICAL ASSOCIATION, Cumbria. **Catalogues of the Library of the Freshwater Biological Association.** Boston, Mass., G.K. Hall, 1979. 6v. $725, set. ISBN: 0816102899.

About 126,000 author-catalogue cards, photolithographically reproduced. Coverage: biology, physics and chemistry of inland waters worldwide, with emphasis on freshwater algae, planktonic and benthic invertebrates, fishes and lake sediments. Represents one of the world's finest collections of limnological literature.
Class No: 574.5(01)

[2282]
MARINE BIOLOGICAL ASSOCIATION OF THE UNITED KINGDOM, Plymouth. **Catalogues of the Library.** [Marine Biological Association of the United Kingdom]. Boston, Mass., G.K. Hall, 1977. 16v. (12246p.). ISBN: 0816100764.

The Main catalogue is an A/Z author/name listing of *c.*13,000 books, 40,000v. of periodicals, 1,450 current periodicals and serials, and over 50,000 reprints and pamphlets. Analytical entries for relevant periodical articles, technical reports, conference proceedings, etc. are included since 1968. The Subject catalogue primarily lists books and monographs but also covers review-type papers. Marine and estuarine pollution material has been collected since 1970. *Class No:* 574.5(01)

[2283]
WOODS HOLE OCEANOGRAPHIC INSTITUTION. Catalog of the
Library of the Marine Biological Laboratory and the Woods Hole
Oceanographic Institution. Boston, Mass., G.K. Hall, 1971. 12v.
(9339p.). ISBN: 0816109370.

About 339,000 author-catalogue cards for books, reports of
expeditions, and articles, photolithographically reproduced. V.12,
Journal catalog (418p.), lists over 4,000 titles. Coverage includes
biology, zoology, botany, physiology, microbiology, medicine,
physics, chemistry, mathematics, geology, meteorology, fisheries and
oceanography. *Class No:* 574.5(01)

[2284]
—Oceanographic index. Cumulation 1946-1973: Marine organisms,
chiefly planktonic. Sears, M., *comp.* Boston, Nass., G.K. Hall,
[1974?]. 3v, (2307p.). $240, set. ISBN: 0816109338.

An outgrowth of the Woods Hole Oceanographic Institution's
Catalog. Subject cumulation. Class No: 574.5(01)

Encyclopaedias

[2285]
Encyclopedia of marine sciences. Baretta-Bekker, E.K., *and others,
eds.* Berlin, New York, Springer-Verlag, 1992. 311p. illus. maps.
ISBN: 0387545018.

1,850 brief entries covering marine biology, marine geology,
physical oceanography, and marine chemistry. Many cross-references,
plus 120 black-and-white illustrations. Bibliography, p.309-11.
Class No: 574.5(031)

Handbooks & Manuals

[2286]
Biological surveys of estuaries and coasts. Baker, J.M. *and*
Wolff, W.H.J., *eds.* Cambridge Univ. Press, 1987. xx, 449p. diagrs.,
graphs, tables, maps. ISBN: 0521324076.

18 contributors. 15 documented chapters (1. Planning biological
surveys ... 4. Flora and microfauna of intertidal sediments ... 10.
Bacteria and fungi ... 13. Birds ... 15. Safety). Appendices throughout
the work (*e.g.* Appendix 11.2: Estimation of a flushing time-scale for
an estuary). Mainly European material. *Class No:* 574.5(035)

[2287]
—MAITLAND, P.S. Biology of fresh waters. 2nd ed. Glasgow, Blackie;
New York, Chapman and Hall, 1990. xi,276p. illus. £37. ISBN:
0216929881.

First published 1978.

9 sections: 1. The aquatic environment - 2. Plants and animals of
fresh waters ... 5. Field studies: sampling in fresh waters ... 7.
Communities and energy flow - 8. Fresh water and humans - 9. A
global view. Bibliography, p.257-68. Index. Suitable for academic
libraries. *Class No:* 574.5(035)

[2288]
HORSMAN, P.V. The Seafarer's guide to marine life. London, etc.,
Croom Helm, 1985. xiv, 256p. illus. (incl. col.), diagrs., tables, maps.
ISBN: 0709937156.

13 chapters: 1. The ecology of the sea ... 4. The coelenterates ... 6.
The crustacea ... 8. The fish - 9. The reptiles - 10. The mammals - 11.
The Sargassum community - 12. The seashore and marine fouling -
13. The future of the marine world. Bibliography, p.246-7. Glossary,
p.248-52. Detailed, analytical index, p.253-6. 'Written mainly at sea
as a result of my observations and the data accumulated in ships'
logbooks' (*Introduction*). 160 small drawings; 80p. of distribution
maps. Well produced. *Class No:* 574.5(035)

[2289]
HUTCHINSON, G.E. A Treatise on limnology. New York, Wiley;
London, Chapman & Hall, 1957-93. 4v. illus., diagrs., graphs, tables.

1. *Geography, physics and chemistry.* 1957. xiv, 1015p. 2.
Introduction to lake biology and the limnoplankton. 1967. xi, 115p. 3.
Limnological botany. 1975. x, 660p. 4. *The zoobenthos.* 1993. xx,
944p (this vol. ed. by Y.H. Edmondson).

38 chapters in all. Each volume carries a bibliography and index of
authors; index of lakes and rivers (giving co-ordinates); index of
genera and species of organisms; general index. *Class No:* 574.5(035)

Dictionaries

[2290]
Lexique anglais-français du thesaurus ASFIS et index français-
anglais. [English-French dictionary of the ASFIS thesaurus with a
French-English index.] Banks, D., *and others.* Plouzane, Institut
Français de Recherche pour l'Exploitation de la Mer, 1994. i,208p.

Lists *c.*8,000 descriptors and terms concerned not only with
aquaculture, but also geology, environmental pollution, biology,
fishing, etc. Many cross-references and usage notes. For all involved
in marine biology. *Class No:* 574.5(038)

Reviews & Abstracts

[2291]
Aquatic sciences and fisheries abstracts. Bethesda, Md., Cambridge
Scientific Abstracts, 1978-. 12pa. 3pts. $ $1,045 (US); $1,195 (non
US), pt.1; $815; ($945), pt. 2, $350; ($385) pt. 3 (7pa.). ISSN:
01405373.

Replaces *Aquatic sciences and fisheries abstracts,* 1971-77 (an
amalgamation of *Aquatic biology abstracts* and *Current bibliography
for aquatic sciences and fisheries*).

Pt.1. *Biological sciences and living resources.* Pt.2. *Ocean
technology, policy and non-living resources, (qv).* Pt. 3. *Aquatic
pollution and environmental quality.*

Pt. 1 contains *c.*24,000 abstracts pa. Main parts: 1. General aspects;
6-7. Biology; 74-194. Ecology, ecosystems and pollution; 195-245.
Fisheries. Author and subject indexes per issue and annually. CD-
ROM and online via DIALOG and the Internet. Magnetic tape also
available. *Class No:* 574.5(048)

Progress Reports

[2292]
Oceanography and marine biology: an annual review. Aberdeen,
Aberdeen University Press, 1963-. Annual. Price varies. ISSN:
00783218.

V.34, 1996 has eight articles with extensive lists of references
appended. They include 'Beach clam fisheries' and 'Coastal fisheries
in the Pacific islands'. Author, systematic and analytical subject
indexes. *Class No:* 574.5(055)

Tables & Data Books

[2293]
Practical handbook of marine science. Kennish, M.J., *ed.* 2nd ed.
Boca Raton, Fla., CRC Press, 1994. 556p. graphs, tables. ISBN:
0849337127.

First published 1989 as *CRC practical handbook of marine science.*

5 sections: 1. Physical oceanography - 2. Marine chemistry - 3.
Marine geology - 4 Marine biology - 5. Marine pollution. Largely
reworked since first edition with 'updated information on open and
estuarine circulation, elemental cycling, seafloor spreading centres,
deep-sea hydrothermal vents, biological production, trophic
relationships (and) a new section on marine pollution' (*Preface*).
Bibliographies total about 1,000 entries. For marine scientists,
administrators and other professionals. *Class No:* 574.5(083)

Underwater

[2294]
Deep-sea biology. Rowe, G.T., *ed.* New York, etc., Wiley-Interscience,
1983. [x], 560p. illus., diagrs., graphs, tables, maps. (*The sea,* v.8.)
ISBN: 0471044024.

19 contributors. 12 chapters, well documented: 1. Problems of deep-
sea biology: an historical perspective (with 10½p. of references) ... 3.
Recent advances in instrumentation in deep-sea biological research
(3½p. of references) ... 7. Biochemical and physiological adaptations
of deep-sea animals (12p. of references) ... 12. Parasitism in the deep-
sea (over 11p. of references). Analytical index, p.553-60. Aims 'to
reflect the progress in broad general subjects made in the last few
years' (*Preface*). Authoritative. *Class No:* 574.5(204)

[2295]
The Encyclopedia of underwater life. Banister, K. *and*
Campbell, A.C., *eds.* London, Allen & Unwin, 1985. xxxii, 287p.
illus. (mostly col.), diagrs., maps. $25. (*Unwin Animal library.*) ISBN:
0045000352.

Contributions by 17 specialists, apart from the two editors. Equal
attention to fishes and aquatic invertebrates, but omitting aquatic
insects. Well-illustrated, medium-length articles. Short glossary and
bibliography. Detailed index, in tiny print. For the general reader.
Class No: 574.5(204)

Biogeography (Geographical Scatter of Organisms)

[2296]
BROWN, J.H. *and* GIBSON, A.C. Biogeography. St. Louis, Missouri,
C.V. Mosby, 1983. 653p. $39.95. ISBN: 0801608244.

Documented chapters on both historical and ecological biogeography
(*e.g.* the distribution of plant and animal taxa). Glossary. Over 1,800
bibliographical references in all. More than 600 illustrations and maps.
Detailed index. University student level. 'Praised in *Science* (v.222, 14
October 1983, p.157) for 'the wealth of information presented and its
accumulation into a coherent framework'. *Class No:* 574.9

[2297]

PEARS, N. Basic biogeography. 2nd ed. London, Longman, 1985. x, 358p. illus., diagrs., charts, tables. £13.99. ISBN: 0582301203.

First published 1977.

Two parts (10 documented chapters): 1. Basic considerations (*e.g.* Plant dynamics and the nature of vegetation. Ecosystems) - 2. Selected examples (*e.g.* The vegetation. The soils. The impact of man). General index, p.343-53; Species index. *Class No: 574.9*

[2298]

VINCENT, P. The Biogeography of the British Isles: an introduction. London, Routledge, 1990. xv,315p. figs., tables, maps. £40. ISBN: 0415034701.

10 chapters: 1. The history and scope of British biogeography - 2. The physical environment ... 6. Limitations of the environment - 7. Geographical relationships - 8. Environmental change ... 10. The consequences of urban and industrial growth. Glossary, p.271-77. Bibliography, p.278-91. Aimed at the layperson and academic. *Class No: 574.9*

Genetics

Dictionaries

[2299]

BIASS-DUCROUX, F. *and* **NAPP-ZINN, K.,** *comps.* **Glossary of genetics in English, French, Spanish, Italian, German, Russian.** Amsterdam, etc., Elsevier, 1970. xvi, 436p. $91. (*Glossaria interpretum, 16.*) ISBN: 044440712x.

2,938 entries in English, with French, Spanish, Italian and German equivalents. Russian numerical index; French, Spanish, Italian, German and Russian indexes. Avoids mere transposition of words from one language into the others. *Class No: 575(038)*

[2300]

Glossary of genetics: classical and molecular. Rieger, R.O., *and others.* 5th rev. ed. Berlin, etc., Springer Verlag, 1991. 553p. diagrs., tables. $39. ISBN: 0387520546.

First published 1954 as *Genetisches und cytogenetisches Wörterbuch.*

About 4,000 entries, stating first use of term (author; date). Bibliography. 100 diagrams, etc. Of the 4th ed. (1976), 'Remains the outstanding reference glossary of genetics' (*Heredity,* v.41(1), 1978, p.115-6). The *Glossary* has also been translated into Russian and Polish. *Class No: 575(038)*

[2301]

—OLIVER, S. *and* WARD, J.M. A Dictionary of genetic engineering. Cambridge Univ. Press, 1985. [v], 153p. diagrs., tables. £19.95. ISBN: 0521260809.

Defines several hundred technical terms and jargon, with 43 diagrs. 6 short appendices, on genetic maps, genotype nomenclature, etc. The terms are carefully selected, 'to avoid those found in ordinary dictionaries of genetics'. *Class No: 575(038)*

[2302]

KAHL, G. Dictionary of gene technology. Weinheim, VCH, 1995. xii,550p. illus., tables, graphs. $90. ISBN: 3527300058.

More than 4,000 entries from the areas of molecular genetics, bacteriology, biophysics, chemistry, etc. Many useful illustrations and tables. Many cross-references. Criticized for lack of references in *Choice,* September 1995. For students and researchers. *Class No: 575(038)*

[2303]

KING, R.C. A Dictionary of genetics. 5th ed. New York, Oxford University Press, 1997. vii, 439p. illus., diagrs., chemical structures. £45. ISBN: 0195094417.

First published 1968.

*c.*7,000 concise definitions. Four appendices: A. Classification - B. Domesticated species - C. Chronology; Index of scientists listed in the chronology; Bibliography - D. Periodicals cited in the literature; Multijournal publishers; Foreign words commonly found in scientific titles - E. Genetic databases. *Class No: 575(038)*

[2304]

MACLEAN, N. Macmillan dictionary of genetics & cell biology. London, Macmillan Press, 1987. xxi, 422p. diagrs., tables, chemical structures. £12.99. ISBN: 0333394631.

About 4,000 entries (*e.g.* 'Extraembryonic membranes': over 2 columns; & diagrs.). Many cross-references. 5 appendices precede (*e.g.* 2. Chromosome numbers in various species; 5. Classification of vicious organisms). For students and those working in the related fields of microbiology and biotechnology. *Class No: 575(038)*

[2305]

MIGLANI, G.S. Dictionary of plant genetics and molecular biology. New York, Food Products Press/Haworth Press, 1998. 348p. $49.95. ISBN: 1560228717.

Brief definitions of *c.*3,500 terms, arranged A-Z, covering areas such as cytogenetics, plant biotechnology, population genetics, etc. Lengthy bibliography. Excludes biographies and has no diagrams, but is a useful reference tool. *Class No: 575(038)*

Reviews & Abstracts

[2306]

Excerpta medica. 22: Human genetics. Amsterdam, Elsevier Science, 1963-. 24pa. $2,690. ISSN: 00144266.

About 200 abstracts (150-300 words) per issue. 39 sections (1. General sections ... 13. Heredity ... 17. Blood and hemopoietic system ... 19. Metabolism: inborn errors ... 30. Demography). Subject and author indexes per issue. Online in EMBASE, and available on microfilm and CD-ROM. *Class No: 575(048)*

[2307]

Genetics abstracts. Bethesda, Md., Cambridge Scientific Abstracts, 1968-. 12pa. $1,035 (US); $1,095 (non US). ISSN: 0016674x.

Each issue carries *c.*1,200 abstracts, monitoring some 5,000 primary and other journals. 21 sections (Molecular genetics ... Invertebrate genetics, Human genetics - Medical genetics). Book notices. Author and subject indexes. Online, LIFE SCIENCES COLLECTION. Also available on CD-ROM and magnetic tape. *Class No: 575(048)*

Progress Reports

[2308]

Advances in genetics. San Diego, Academic Press, 1947-. Irregular. illus., graphs, tables. $89.95. ISSN: 00652660.

V.38, 1998 (225p.) has eight contributors. The five documented articles include 'Body plan genes and human malformation'; 'Genetics of biological rhythms in drosophila'; 'DNA breakage and repair'. Each article has extensive lists of references. Analytical subject index. *Class No: 575(055)*

[2309]

Annual review of genetics. Palo Alto, Calif., Annual Reviews Inc., 1967-. v.1-. $120 (US); $130 (non US). ISSN: 00664197.

V.32, 1998 (720p.) has 46 contributors. The 23 documented papers include 'The genetics of breast cancer susceptibility'; 'The diverse and dynamic structure of bacterial genomes'; 'The critical role of chromosome translocations in human leukemias'. Analytical subject index. Cumulative indexes: Contributing authors, v.28-32; chapter titles, v.28-32. 'Some related articles in other *Annual reviews',* are given. Abstracts of papers available online 3 months before publication date at http://www.AnnualReviews.org. *Class No: 575(055)*

Evolution

[2310]

CHAPMAN, R.G. *and* **DUVAL, C.T. Charles Darwin, 1809-1882:** a centennial commemorative. Wellington, Nova Pacifica, 1982. vii, 376p. illus. (incl. col). ISBN: 090860310x.

Limited ed. of 750.

11 contributors. 4 sections, each subdivided: 1. Darwin biography - 2. Darwin and the 19th century - 3. Darwin and the sciences - 4. Darwin and the 20th century. Many illus., including 27 colour plates. Bibliography, p.355-67. *Class No: 575.8*

[2311]

—Biological journal of the Linnean Society, v.17(1), February 1982. Linnean Society of London. 135p.

A special issue devoted to Charles Darwin on the occasion of the centenary of his death. 9 documented contributions (*e.g.* 'Turning points in Darwin's life' (with 37 references); 'Darwin and the historian' (with 83 footnotes); 'Dogma and doubt' (27 references); 'Epilogue' (18 references)). Analytical index, p.127-35. *Class No: 575.8*

[2312]

Encyclopedia of human evolution and prehistory. Tattersall, I., *and others, eds.* New York, Garland, 1988. 900p. illus., diagrs., tables. $95. ISBN: 1558621172.

*c.*2,000 entries, arranged A-Z. Extensive coverage of all aspects of evolutionary theory, primatology, evolutionary and prehistoric hominid research, genetics, primate palaeontology and palaeontology. Many cross-references and references for further reading. Numerous clear illustrations. Useful for lay persons or undergraduates. 'An excellent reference tool, and the only one of its type' (*Science and technology libraries,* v.10(1), 1989, p.125). *Class No: 575.8*

[2313]

Keywords in evolutionary biology. Keller, E.F. *and* Lloyd, E.A., *eds.* Cambridge, Mass., Harvard University Press, 1992. xlii,414p. $45. ISBN: 0674503120.

Clarification of common terms which have multiple concurrent and historically varying meanings. 51 short essays by 47 biologists. 20-page name and subject index. Bibliography, p.343-93. *Class No:* 575.8

[2314]

MILNER, R. The Encyclopedia of evolution: humanity's search for its origins. New York, Facts on File, 1991. 481p. illus., figs., maps. $45. ISBN: 0816014728.

Contains more than 600 articles (500-1,000 words in length) covering topics which include adaptation, natural selection, theorists and animal models of evolution. Length of entries varies from a single paragraph to several pages. More than 200 drawings, photographs and charts. Maps are not of high quality. Good cross-references, brief bibliographies and detailed index. Aimed at a general audience but would also be suitable for academic libraries. *Class No:* 575.8

[2315]

SAVAGE, R.J.G. *and* **LONG, M.R. Mammal evolution:** an illustrated guide. London, British Museum (Natural History), 1986. vi, 259p. illus. (incl. col.), diagrs. £19.50. ISBN: 0565009427.

13 sections (*e.g.* 1. Bones into stones ... 5. Insectivores ... 5. Early roosters and browsers ... 13. Of men and monkeys). Systematic tables on endpapers. Bibliography, p.251-4. Colourful illus. Index, p.255-9. Takes a popular approach and 'contains a glossary to help reading for the novice'. *Class No:* 575.8

[2316]

—PATTERSON, C. Evolution. London, British Museum (Natural History), with Cornell Univ. Press, and others, 1978. vii, 197p. illus., ports.

1970 ed. as *A Handbook on evolution.*

15 chapters (1. Propositions; 2. Species; 3. Variations within species; 4. Heredity; 5. Genetics and variations; 6. Mutation; 7. Natural selection theory; 8. Selection in action; 9. The origin of species; 10. Speciation in the Galapagos Islands; 11. Evolution beyond the species level; 12. Proof and disproof; 13. The origin and early evolution of life; 14. Evolution and man; 15. Who's who (17 short biographies)). Further reading (21 titles); Glossary (88 terms). Aims to be 'simple enough to be comprehensible to those with little or no technical knowledge of biology' (*Foreword*), - and succeeds. An excellent introduction. *Class No:* 575.8

[2317]

SMITH, F.H. *and* **SPENCER, F. The Origins of modern humans:** a world survey of the fossil evidence. New York, Wiley, 1985. $93.95. ISBN: 047183419x.

11 contributors, of which 9 concern skeletal remains found in Europe, Western Asia, East Asia and Australasia, China, and the Americas. While conceding that the text is refreshingly free from the Eurocentric bias, the review in *Nature* (v.314, 18 April 1985, p.649) quarrels with the maps and quality of photographs and drawings. Nevertheless, 'An invaluable source of reference for those already familiar with the fossil record, anatomy and population genetics'. *Class No:* 575.8

Cells (Cytology)

[2318]

Annual review of cell and developmental biology. Palo Alto, Calif., Annual Reviews Inc., 1995-. v.1-. illus. $128 (US); $138 (non US). ISSN: 10810706.

Previously *Annual review of cell biology* (1985-94).

V.14 (1998) has 38 contributors. 17 documented reviews (*e.g.* 'Functions of lipid rafts in biological membranes'; 'Intracellular pathogens and the actin cytoskeleton'; 'Isoform sorting and the creation of intracellular compartments'). Subject index. Cumulative indexes of contributing authors and chapter titles, v.10-14. Commenting on v.1, *Nature* (v.320, 13 March 1986, p.117) noted pleasing use of illus. and readability of many of the articles. Abstracts of papers available online 3 months before publication date at http://www.AnnualReviews.org. *Class No:* 576

[2319]

DE ROBERTIS, E.D.P. *and* **DE ROBERTIS, E.M.F. Cellular and molecular biology.** 8th ed. Philadelphia, Pa., Lea & Febiger, 1987. xxix,734p. illus., diagrs., graphs, tables. ISBN: 0812110129.

24 sections, each with references and summary: 1. The cell-structural organization ... 4. Cell membrane and permeability ... 13. The interphase nucleus, chromatin, and the chromosome ... 19. The genetic code and genetic engineering ... 24. Cellular and molecular neurobiology. 'Literary sources in cell and molecular biology', p.25-

....(contd.)

26. Detailed analytical index, p.721-34. Well illustrated with micrographs, etc. A popular college textbook that has been translated into 7 languages. *Class No:* 576

[2320]

The Dictionary of cell biology. Lackie, J.M. *and* Dow, J.A.T., *eds.* 2nd ed. London, Academic Press, 1995. viii,390p. tables. £15. ISBN: 0124325637.

First published 1989.

1,000 new terms have been added to this new edition, making a total of 5,000. Obsolete terms have been dropped. 7 contributory authors. Includes areas such as cell chemistry, cytogenetics, and cell structure. Many cross-references. 30 tables. It is claimed that it is available on the Internet so that it can be updated regularly. For undergraduates and professionals. *Class No:* 576

[2321]

International review of cytology: a survey of cell biology. San Diego, Academic Press, 1952-. v.1-. Irregular. ISSN: 00747696.

V.164, 1996 (ix,336p.) has 9 contributors. The 6 documented articles include 'Some characteristics of neoplastic cell transformation in transgenic mice', p.37-90 (11p. of references); 'Developmental failure in preimplantation human conceptuses', p.139-188 (14p. of references). Detailed, analytical index. *Class No:* 576

Parasites (Parasitology)

[2322]

Advances in parasitology. San Diego, Academic Press, 1963-. v.1-. Irregular. ISSN: 0065308x.

V.40, 1998 has 12 papers by 19 contributors, (*e.g.* 'Antibody-based immunotherapy of cryptosporidiosis', p.121-49; 'Biology of microsporidian species infecting mammals', p.283-320). Analytical index. *Class No:* 576.8

[2323]

FOSTER, W.D. A History of parasitology. Edinburgh & London, Livingstone, 1965. vii, 202p. illus., ports.

Chapter 1 traces the general development of parasitology from ancient times to about 1850. Chapters 2-13 deal with certain parasites 'chosen because investigations related to them opened up new fields in parasitology' (*Preface*), *e.g.* 2. The Cestodes (tapeworm) ... 6. Hookworm. Chapter 14 'Parasitology established', covers the period 1860 to 1932. 284 references. Index to personal names. 15 plates, mostly portraits. Aims 'at a level comprehensive to the non-professional parasitologist' (*Preface*). *Class No:* 576.8

[2324]

Index-catalogue of medical and veterinary zoology. US Bureau of Animal Industry. Zoological Division. Authors A-Z. Washington, US Government Printing Office, 1932-52. 12v. Supplement 1-. 1953-.

Index to world literature 'on parasites and parasitisms of man, of domestic animals, and of wild animals whose parasites may be transmitted to man and domestic animals' (*Bulletin of the Medical Library Association, v.41, no.2, April 1953, p.110*). In the Author catalogue, each author's papers are arranged chronologically.

Supplements 1-6 (1953-56) covered backlog. Since then, supplements (authors, A-Z) are annual. Beginning with suppt.15, *Parasite subject catalogues* (containing indexes to the author references in the *Author catalogues* and including a catalogue of hosts) have been issued in addition. *Class No:* 576.8

Biochemistry

Encyclopaedias & Dictionaries

[2325]

GLICK, D.M. Glossary of biochemistry and molecular biology. 2nd ed. London, Portland Press, 1997. 214p. £16.50. ISBN: 1855780887.

First published 1990.

Brief definitions of over 2,800 terms - 1,000 more than in the previous ed. 'Should be of interest to students, new researchers, and to other professions having to interface with modern biochemistry or molecular biology' (*Preface*). Handy format. 2p. of refs., including Internet sources. *Class No:* 577.1(03)

[2326]

HOOD, W. A-Z of clinical chemistry. New York, Halsted: Wiley, 1980. vii, 386p. illus. ISBN: 0470270292.

Concise definitions of *c.*1,300 terms on techniques, tests, diagnostic methods, etc. Cross-references; additional references where considered appropriate, plus a short list of general textbooks. 'This volume is a welcome source for undergraduates and trainees starting any kind of course in clinical chemistry' (*Choice*, v.18(9), May 1981, p.1236).
Class No: 577.1(03)

[2327]

Oxford dictionary of biochemistry and molecular biology. Smith, A.D., *and others, eds.* Oxford, University Press, 1997. 740p. illus. £34.95; $60. ISBN: 0198547684.

*c.*17,000 headwords (most of which are in current use) in A-Z order, with cross-references. The brief entries include the essential features of *c.*2,000 enzymes and proteins. Covers 950 chemical structures. Appendices, p.697-740: A. Greek alphabet and characters ... D. The Internet ... H. Species names. 'The best conceived and produced specialized dictionary this reviewer has ever seen ... it is enthusiastically recommended to all libraries' (*Choice*, July/August 1998, p.1834). For academic and research libraries.
Class No: 577.1(03)

[2328]

SCOTT, T. *and* **MERCER, E.I. Concise encyclopedia biochemistry and molecular biology.** 3rd ed. Berlin, Walter de Gruyter, 1997. vii,737p. diagrs., tables, charts, formulas. $105. ISBN: 3110145359.

First ed. (1983) based on 2nd ed. of *Brockhaus ABC Biochimie* (1981).

Extensive revision. Entries, A-Z, vary in length from one paragraph to several pages. Each enzyme is given its Enzyme Commission number. Adequate cross-references. An excellent aide-mémoire.
Class No: 577.1(03)

[2329]

STENESH, J. Dictionary of biochemistry and molecular biology. 2nd ed,. New York, Wiley, 1989. vii,525p. $69. ISBN: 0471840890.

Originally *Dictionary of biochemistry*, published in 1975.

Approximately 16,000 entries 'representing an increase of about 30% over the first edition ... drawn from over 500 books and 1,000 articles' (*Preface*). Includes abbreviations, cross-references, names of specific compounds, and additional information inserted into definitions (average 40 words) where appropriate. Designed for scientists and students in the life sciences. 'Will prove a valuable addition to most research and academic collections' (*New technical books*, November/December 1990, item 1747). *Class No:* 577.1(03)

Handbooks & Manuals

[2330]

FLORKIN, M. *and* **STOTZ, E.H. Comprehensive biochemistry.** Amsterdam, etc. Elsevier, 1962-. illus., tables, formulas.

Sections: 1. (v.1-4): *Physico-chemical and organic aspects of biochemistry.* 2. (v.5-11): *Chemistry of biological compounds.* 3. (v.12-16): *Biochemical reaction mechanisms.* 4. (v.17-21): *Metabolism.* 5. (v.22-29): *Chemical biology.* 6. (v.30-32): *A history of biochemistry.*

V.35 (1983. xviii, 404p.): Selected topics in the history of biochemistry: Personal recollections. Pt. I, has 12 well-documented chapters (*e.g.* 5. Sir Frederick Gowland Hopkins, p.103-128). 24 references. Name index, p.390-404. *Class No:* 577.1(035)

[2331]

ISI atlas of science. Biochemistry and molecular biology, 1978/80, including mini-reviews of 102 research fund specialties. Philadelphia, Pa., Institute for Scientific Information, 1981. xvi, 540p, charts.

11 contributors. Cluster maps/charts are used to trace the historical development of an area of research and identify the papers that made the most important contributions to the subject. Each map is accompanied by a short essay or 'mini-review'. Journal, author, subject and specialty title word indexes. *Class No:* 577.1(035)

[2332]

Varley's practical clinical biochemistry. Gowenlock, A.H., *and others, eds.* 6th ed. London, Heinemann Medical Books, 1988. xv,1050p. illus. tables. £75. ISBN: 043338067.

First published 1954.

36 chapters: 1. Hazards in the clinical biochemistry laboratory ... 12. Quality control ... 14. Collection of specimens ... 22. Enzymes ... 30. Thyroid function tests ... 36. Drugs and poisons. Chapter references. Appendices, p.1017-24. Analytical index. For use as a 'bench book' by practising clinical biochemists. A standard text.
Class No: 577.1(035)

Periodicals & Progress Reports

[2333]

Annual review of biochemistry. Palo Alto, Calif., Annual Reviews, Inc., 1932-. v.1-. Annual. $136 (US); $148 (non US). ISSN: 00664154.

V.67, 1998 (900p.) contains 27 well-documented papers, including 'Sphingolipid functions in *Saccharomyces cerevisiae*: comparison to mammals'; 'How cells respond to interferons'; 'The green fluorescent problem'. Author, subject indexes. Cumulative list of contributing authors, v.63-67. Cumulative index of chapter titles, v.63-67. A list of some related articles in other *Annual reviews* is given. Abstracts of papers available online 3 months before publication date at http://www.AnnualReviews.org. *Class No:* 577.1(05)

[2334]

Scientific serials review: biomedicine. New York, Wiley/ASFRA, 1986-. 6pa. $148. ISSN: 08848319.

V.1, 1986 includes 'Trends in genetics'; 'Health libraries review'; as well as articles on vaccine, clinical nutrition, alternative medicine, etc. The aim is to evaluate each biomedical journal every 3 years. Entries are based on a matrix of 60 questions/data: previous titles; languages; inclusion of book reviews, abstracts; online availability; changes of subject coverage. Annual list of journals covered. 'Developed to provide libraries and scientists with time, up-dated reviews of both new and existing periodicals' (*Preface*). *Class No:* 577.1(05)

Tables & Data Books

[2335]

CRC handbook of biochemistry and molecular biology. Fasman, G.B. 3rd ed. Cleveland, Ohio, CRC Press, [1976-77]. 9v. tables.

First published 1968.

A. Proteins - amino acids, peptides, polypeptides, proteins. 3v. B. Nucleic acids - purines, pyrimidines, nucleotides, oligonucleotides ... 2v. C. Lipids, carbohydrates, steroids. D. Physical and chemical data, miscellaneous - ion exchange, chromatography, buffers, miscellaneous. 2v. Cumulative series index.

The cumulative index (1977. [x], 295p.) has subject entries, chemical substances entries, errata and addenda. A comprehensive source of data. *Class No:* 577.1(083)

[2336]

Data for biochemical research. Dawson, R.M.C., *and others.* 3rd ed. Oxford, Clarendon Press, 1986. 580p. tables, chemical structures. £37.50. ISBN: 0198553587.

Features 25 tables, arranging compounds in functional groups, *e.g.* amino acids, amines, amides, peptides and their derivatives, vitamins and co-enzymes. Within each table, compounds are arranged A-Z. Data cover synonyms, molecular formula and weight, melting point, solubility, plus reference to the relevant literature on methodology. 'Directed towards the scientist's laboratory, but should be a very handy reference source for chemistry & biology library collections' (*Science and technology libraries*, v.7(4), Summer 1987, p.118). *Class No:* 577.1(083)

Histories

[2337]

TEICH, M. *and* **NEEDHAM, D.M. A Documentary history of biochemistry 1770-1940.** Leicester, University Press, 1992. xxxvii,579p. figs., tables. £90. ISBN: 071851341x.

Contains a selected collection of reprints and covers the period beginning with the work of Priestley and Lavoisier and ending with the split from molecular biology in the 1940s. 7 sections: 1. Enzymes ... 3. Respiration - 4. Carbohydrates ... 6. Lipids - 7. Conceptual and disciplinary issues. Many footnotes. Select bibliography, p.571-79.
Class No: 577.1(091)

Biographies

[2338]

FRUTON, J.S. A Bio-bibliography for the history of the biochemical sciences since 1800. Philadelphia, Pa., American Philosophical Society, 1982. xii, 885p. $20. ISBN: 0871699834.

Nearly 10,000 entries (name; dates; references), *e.g.* 'Mendel, Gregor': 4 book references, 10 periodical references; 'Pasteur, Louis': 10 book references, 7 periodical references. Abbreviations for sources: reference works (*e.g.* Poggendorff), p.848-58; serial publications, p.859-85. 'This reference work is most valuable, primarily for the less well known biochemists' (*Choice*, v.20(11/12), July/August 1983, p.1574). *Class No:* 577.1(092)

Nucleic Acids

[2339]

Nucleic acids abstracts. Bethesda, Md., Cambridge Scientific Abstracts, 1994-. 12pa. $885 (US); $945 (non US). ISSN: 10702466.

Continues *Nucleic acid abstracts* (1970-79) and *Biochemistry abstracts. Part 2: Nucleic acids* (1980-93).

Contains *c.*11,000 abstracts pa. Sections: Reviews - Purines, pyrimidines & analogs - Nucleosides & analogs ... Transfer RNA - Protein biosynthesis - RNA - DNA - Enzymes - Immunological aspects - Protein-nucleic acid association - Book notices, author and subject indexes per issue and annually. Online, LIFE SCIENCES COLLECTION. Also available on magnetic tape and CD-ROM. *Class No:* 577.113

Lipids

[2340]

The Lipid handbook. Gunstone, F.D., *and others, eds.* 2nd ed. London, Chapman & Hall, 1994. xiii, 722p + 551p. ISBN: 0412433206.

First published 1986.

A major compendium on the occurrence, isolation, chemical identification and technical applications of fatty acids. 3 editors, 17 contributors. 12 sections, p.1-721: 1. Fatty acid structure - 2. Lipid structure - 6. Analytical methods - 11. Lipid metabolism - 12. Medical and agricultural aspects of lipids. Dictionary Section follows p.*1-432,* compound name index, p.*433-470,* formula index, p.*471-510,* CAS Registry Number index, p.*511-551* For more advanced students in chemistry, biochemistry, food science, etc. *Class No:* 577.115

Enzymes

[2341]

Enzyme handbook. Schomburg, D. *and* Salzmann, M., *eds.* New York, Springer-Verlag, 1990- . Price varies. ISBN: 0387525793, v.1; 0387525807, v.2.

First published 1969.

A multi-volume work, with each volume having multiple parts - most recently published part is V.17: First supplement, part 3 (xii, 339p. 1998). Enzymes are arranged according to the 1984 Enzyme Commission list of enzymes and subsequent supplements. Data for each enzyme is divided into 7 sections: 1. Nomenclature - 2. Reaction and specificity - 3. Enzyme structure - 4. Isolation and preparation - 5. Stability - 6. Cross-references to structure databanks - 7. Bibliography. Looseleaf format. *Class No:* 577.15

[2342]

Enzyme nomenclature 1992. London, Academic Press, 1992. xiii,862p. ISBN: 0122271645.

Previous ed. published 1984.

Based on the recommendations of the Nomenclature Committee of the International Union of Biochemistry and Molecular Biology on the nomenclature and classification of enzymes. Includes chapters on nickel proteins, flavoproteins, and molybdenum proteins. 5,715 references to the enzyme list. Bibliography, p.576-727. Unattractive typeface. *Class No:* 577.15

[2343]

The Enzymes. Boyer, P.D., *ed.* 3rd ed. New York & London, Academic Press, 1970-.

First published as *The enzymes: chemistry and mechanism of action,* edited by J.B. Sumner and K. Myrback (1950-52. 2v. in 42).

V.19 (1991), *Mechanisms of catalysis* (459p.), has 7 chapters: 1. Binding energy and catalysis ... 3. Steady-state kinetics ... 7. Stereochemistry of enzyme-catalyzed reactions at carbon. Chapter references. Author and subject indexes. An authoritative treatise. *Class No:* 577.15

Vitamins

[2344]

Handbook of vitamins: nutritional, biochemical and clinical aspects. Machlin, L.J., *ed.* 2nd ed. New York, Dekker, 1991. x,595p. diagrs., tables. $125. (*Food science and technology, v.40.*.) ISBN: 0824783514.

First published 1984.

16 chapters, reflecting research accomplished over the previous six years. Detailed data on all known vitamins, including chemistry, food content, metabolism, functions and deficiency symptoms. New to this ed. are state-of-the-art reviews of each vitamin. Over 230 diagrams and tables. An authoritative and comprehensive source of information. Of the first ed., 'For nutritionists, biochemists and even the interested lay person' (*Science & technology libraries,* v.5(4), Summer 1985, p.98). Recommended for professional and advanced students of food science and technology, nutrition, dietetics, pharmacology, and toxicology. *Class No:* 577.16

[2345]

The Vitamins: chemistry, physiology pathology, methods. Sebrell, W.H., *Jr and* Harris, R.S., *eds..* 2nd ed. New York & London, Academic Press, 1967-72. 7v. tables.

1-5, edited by W.H. Sebrell, Jr., and R.S. Harris. 6-7, edited by P. Gyorgy and W.H. Pearson.

V.1 (xiii, 570p.) musters 17 contributions; author and subject indexes. Chapter 2 of v.1, 'Ascorbic acid requirements of animals', has 70 references. v.3 (xv, 601p.) has 30 contributors. The standard treatise on vitamins. *Class No:* 577.16

Antibiotics

[2346]

Dictionary of antibiotics and related substances. Bycroft, B.W., *ed.* London, Chapman & Hall, 1988. 944p. figs. £475. ISBN: 0412254506.

Partially derived from the 5th ed. of *Dictionary of organic compounds* (Chapman & Hall, 1982) and its annual supplements, although each entry has been reviewed and updated. 7 sections: 1. Introduction - 2. Descriptions of main antibiotic types (*e.g.* 'Nucleoside antibiotics') - 3. Entries in alphabetical order, p.1-748 - 4. Name index - 5. Molecular formula index - 6. CAS Registry Number index - 7. Type of compound index. Short bibliographies are appended to each entry. *Class No:* 577.18

[2347]

GLASBY, J.S. Encyclopedia of antibiotics. 3rd ed. Chichester, etc., Wiley, 1992. 515p. chemical formulae. ISBN: 0471929220.

First published 1976.

About 2,300 entries for antibiotics, with data on formula, melting point, elaborating organism, method of preparation and purification, those organisms against which it is effective, and toxicity. 'Penicillic acid': 1 column, 8 references, formula, chemical structure. Antibiotics with similar substituents are grouped together, with substituents cross-referenced. References to major background papers in scientific and patent literature. Landscape format. *Class No:* 577.18

Molecules

[2348]

The Encyclopedia of molecular biology. Kendrew, J., *ed.* Oxford, Blackwell Science, 1994. xxvi,1195p. illus.(some col. pl.), diagrs. £99.50. ISBN: 0632021829.

300 contributors; 5,500 entries. Arranged A-Z, with occasional long entries amounting to mini-reviews of subjects. Numerous cross-references and diagrams, with black-and-white photographs and colour plates. 'A truly magnificent volume' (*Reference reviews,* v.9(2) 1995, p.24). *Class No:* 577.2

[2349]

Encyclopedia of molecular biology and molecular medicine. Meyers, R.A., *ed.* Weinheim, VCH, 1996-97. 6v. figs., tables £1,380; $1,650. ISBN: 3527284788, set.

A six-volume set consisting of *c.*300 articles. Emphasis is on human, rather than plant, genetics and molecular medicine. A detailed overview of the Human Genome Project is included. Bibliographies at the end of each article. *Glossary of basic terms* at the end of each volume. V.6 (1997. 460p. £190) has a detailed cumulative subject index, a complete list of articles, and a compilation of key words. The editorial board includes seven Nobel Prizewinners. 'Highly recommended' (*Choice,* January 1997, p.768). *Class No:* 577.2

[2350]

EVANS, A. Glossary of molecular biology. London, Butterworths, 1974. [iv], 55p. ISBN: 0408706406.

About 400 terms, A-Z, plus cross-references. The appended bibliography, p.510-55, consists of 139 references. *Class No:* 577.2

[2351]

SCOTT, T. and MERCER, E.I. Concise encyclopedia biochemistry and molecular biology. 3rd ed. Berlin, Walter de Gruyter, 1997. vii,737p. diagrs., tables, charts, formulas. $105. ISBN: 3110145359.

First ed. (1983) based on 2nd ed. of *Brockhaus ABC Biochimie* (1981).

Extensive revision. Entries, A-Z, vary in length from one paragraph to several pages. Each enzyme is given its Enzyme Commission number. Adequate cross-references. An excellent aide-mémoire. *Class No:* 577.2

Biophysics

[2352]

Annual review of biophysics and biomolecular structure. Palo Alto, Calif., Annual Reviews, Inc., 1992-. Annual $140 (US); $150 (non US). ISSN: 10568700.

Formerly *Annual review of biophysics and bioengineering* (1972-85) and *Annual review of biophysics and biophysical chemistry* (1986-91).

V.27, 1998 (550p.) contains 18 well-documented papers, including: 'Spatio-temporal resolution of exocytosis from individual cells';

....*(contd.)*

'Biosensors in chemical separations'; 'RNA recognition by RNP proteins during RNA processing'. Analytical subject index; cumulative index of contributing authors, v.23-27; cumulative index of chapter titles, v.23-27. 'Some related articles appearing in other *Annual reviews*' is also included. Abstracts of papers available online 3 months before publication date at http://www.AnnualReviews.org. *Class No:* 577.3

[2353]
Elsevier's dictionary of biometry. Rasch, D., *and others, eds.* Amsterdam, Elsevier, 1994. x,887p. £104.90; $225.75. ISBN: 0444814957.

A dictionary of biometrics in 7 languages (English, French, Spanish, Dutch, German, Italian, and Russian). 2,430 terms are listed. 44 contributors. Many entries are quite lengthy. *Class No:* 577.3

[2354]
McAINSH, T.F., *ed*. Physics in medicine & biology encyclopedia: medical physics, bioengineering and biophysics. New York, Pergamon Press, 1986. 2v. $420. ISBN: 0080264972.

More than 200 documented articles (1 to 7 pages in length), by experts. A bonus is a classified list of the articles into 25 broad topics. Adequate cross-references. A glossary of terms associated with anatomy, physiology and pathology is appended. The intended readership is described as 'hospital physicians, medical technicians and clinicians' (*Science & technology libraries*, v.7(4), Summer 1987, p.109). *Class No:* 577.3

Viruses (Virology)

[2355]
Encyclopedia of virology. Webster, R.G. *and* Granoff, A., *eds.* San Diego, Academic Press, 1994. 3v. illus. $475. ISBN: 0122269608, set.

Over 250 contributors, with entries covering animal, insect, plant, and bacterial viruses. V.1. covers Adenoviruses to Furoviruses; v.2, Geminiviruses to Parsnip yellow fleck virus group; v.3, Partitiviruses to Zoonoses. Appended bibliographies list reviews only. Complete lists of entries are included at the beginning of each volume. Expensive, but the only comprehensive work on virology recently published. For academic and medical libraries. Available in CD-ROM version as *Encyclopedia of virology plus* ($475).

A second edition is planned for 1999. *Class No:* 578

[2356]
MAHY, B.W.J. A Dictionary of virology. 2nd ed. San Diego, Academic Press, 1997. [vii], 348p., tables, formulas. ISBN: 0124653251.

First published 1981.

Extensive revision of the previous edition. Approximately 3,500 entries for viruses, using nomenclature approved by the International Committee for the Taxonomy of Viruses. Title of the book should be 'A dictionary of *vertebrate* viruses'. Includes cross-references for viral synonyms, non-scientific names, etc., and helpful references to 'key journal articles or reviews'. *Class No:* 578

[2357]
NICHOLAS, R. *and* NICHOLAS, D. Virology: an information profile. London, Mansell, 1983. viii, 236p. £30. ISBN: 0720110732.

3 parts. 1. Overview of virology and its literature (history and scope; organizations; conferences; the literature; searching the literature), p.1-168 - 2. Bibliography (392 unannotated entries), p.169-95 - 3. Directory of organizations, culture collections and libraries, p.197-223. Analytical index, p.227-36. Excludes biochemistry and genetics. Despite some omissions, it is a 'very good analytical critical work that fills a gap in the literature available' (*British book news*, March 1984, p.162). *Class No:* 578

[2358]
Virology and AIDS abstracts. Bethesda, Maryland, Cambridge Scientific Abstracts, 1988-. 12pa. $935 (US); $1,015 (non US). ISSN: 08965919.

Originally as *Virology abstracts* (1967-87).

c.9,000 abstracts pa. drawn from *c*.5,000 primary sources. Sections include: Acquired Immunodeficiency Syndrome - Virus taxonomy and classification ... Immunology - Antiviral agents ... Viral infections of man ... Viral infections of higher plants. Author and subject indexes per issue and annually. Online: DIALOG, ORBIT, etc. and on CD-ROM. *Class No:* 578

[2359]
Virology: directory and dictionary of animal, bacterial and plant viruses. Hull, R., *and others.* London, Macmillan, 1989. x,325p. figs. £39.50. ISBN: 0333390636.

Has data on all the viral species classified by the International Committee on the Taxonomy of Viruses. Includes equations, formulae, definitions of units, and references to recent reviews of particular topics. 6 appendices give lists of insects infected by certain viruses. Extensively cross-referenced. *Class No:* 578

Microbiology

Encyclopaedias

[2360]
Encyclopedia of microbiology. Lederberg, J., *ed.* San Diego, Academic Press, 1992. 4v. illus., figs., diagrs. £450; $595. ISBN: 0122268911, v.1; 012226892x, v.2; 0122268938, v.3; 0122268946, v.4.

204 articles written by 293 contributors. The articles vary in length from six to thirty pages, each with short bibliographies. Scope includes protozoa, bacteria, and viruses. 1,300 glossary entries; 300 tables and 750 figures. Subject and related title indexes. *Class No:* 579(031)

Handbooks & Manuals

[2361]
PELCZAR, J., *Jr and* CHEN, E.C.S. Microbiology. 5th ed. New York, etc. McGraw-Hill, 1986. x, 918p. illus., diagrs., tables. £48.36. ISBN: 0070492344.

8 sections, each with appended bibliography (1. Introduction - 2. Microorganisms - 3. Microbial physiology and genetics - 4. The world of bacteria - 5. Microorganisms; fungi - 6. Control of microorganisms - 7. Environmental and industrial microbiology - 8. Microorganisms and disease). Glossary. Name, organism and subject indexes. A student textbook. *Class No:* 579(035)

[2362]
Topley and Wilson's microbiology and microbial infections. Collier, L., *and others, eds.* 9th ed. New York, Oxford University Press, 1998. 6v. £795. ISBN: 0340614706, set.

First published 1929.

V.1. *Virology.* xxiv, 1086p.; v.2. *Systematic bacteriology.* xxxix, 1501p.; v.3. *Bacterial infection.* xxxv, 1163p.; v.4. *Medical mycology.* xxxii, 711p.; v.5. *Parasitology.* xxxiv, 701p.; v.6. *Cumulative index.* xxviii, 247p.

Comprises signed articles from 209 contributors in 47 chapters in 6 volumes. Also available on CD-ROM. An important reference work. *Class No:* 579(035)

[2363]
WISTREICH, G.A. *and* LECHTMAN, M.D. Microbiology. 5th ed. New York, Macmillan; London, Collier Macmillan, 1988. xx,989p. illus., diagrs., tables. ISBN: 0024289507.

8 chapters, each with short appended bibliography. 1. Introduction to microbiology ... 7. Practices of immunology ... 8. Microorganisms and infectious diseases. 6 appendices. Glossary. Guide to organism pronunciation. Index. *Class No:* 579(035)

Dictionaries

[2364]
COWAN, S.T. A Dictionary of microbial taxonomy. Hill, L,.R., *ed.* Cambridge Univ. Press, 1978. xxii, 285p. ISBN: 052121890x.

First published 1968.

4 preliminary chapters (*e.g.* 2. 'Source material for taxonomy') are followed by the dictionary, p.33-281 (*c*.2,500 entries). Some entries are short essays (*e.g.* 'Patronymic prefixes': over 5½p.). Includes brief biographies and organizations. Frequent references to International Code of nomenclature of bacteria and International Code of botanical nomenclature. References, p.269-85. 'An accurate guide to taxonomic practice' (*Choice*, v.16(1), June 1979, p.506). *Class No:* 579(038)

[2365]
SINGLETON, P. *and* SAINSBURY, D. Dictionary of microbiology and molecular biology. 2nd ed. Chichester, New York, Wiley, 1987. xii, 1019p. illus., diagrs., charts, tables, chemical structures. £87.50; $160. ISBN: 0471911143.

First published 1978 as *Dictionary of microbiology* (viii, 481p.).

About 10,000 terms; many cross-references. 'AIDS': 3 columns; 'Salmonella': over 2 columns; 'Electron microscope': over 4p. plus keyed diagrams. 5 appendices (*e.g.* Biosynthesis). Key to journal-title abbreviations. Key to book references (202 in all), p.1011-19. For undergraduates and postgraduates in this field, primarily. *Class No:* 579(038)

Reviews & Abstracts

[2366]

Microbiology abstracts. Bethesda, Md., Cambridge Scientific Abstracts, 1972-. 12pa. $975; (US); $1085 (non US), sect.A; $1045 ($1085), sect.B; $975 ($1085), sect.C. ISSN: 03012328.

A. *Industrial and applied microbiology.* B. *Bacteriology.* C. *Algology, mycology and protozoology.*

Section A. contains *c.*7,700 abstracts pa. Sections include 'Products of microorganisms'; 'Mineral microbiology'; 'Quality control'; 'Methodology'. Author and subject indexes per issue and annually.

Section B. *Bacteriology* carries *c.*13,200 abstracts pa. Sections are numbered (1-3. Methodology, media and culture apparatus ... 191-203. Ecology and destruction - 205. Miscellaneous topics). Books. Proceedings. Author and subject indexes per issue and annually.

Section C. *Algology* carries *c.*9,900 abstracts pa. in 17 sections (Taxonomy, structure and function ... Spoilage & biogeneration - Pollution - Miscellaneous topics). Book notices. Notification of proofs. Author and subject indexes per issue and annually.

All 3 sections are available online (LIFE SCIENCES COLLECTION), and on CD-ROM. *Class No:* 579(048)

Progress Reports

[2367]

Advances in applied microbiology. San Diego, Academic Press, 1956-. Irregular. ISSN: 00652164.

V.45, 1997 has 13 contributors. The seven documented papers include 'Formation of flavor compounds in cheese', p.17-85; 'Gene transfer among bacteria in natural environments', p.153-212. Index. *Class No:* 579(055)

[2368]

Annual review of microbiology. Palo Alto, Calif., Annual Reviews, Inc., 1947-. Annual. illus., diagrs., tables. $120 (US) and $130 (non US). ISSN: 00664227.

V.52, 1998 (820p.) contains 23 well-documented papers which include: 'Bacteria as modular organisms'; 'Metabolic changes of the malaria parasite during transition from the human to the mosquito host'; 'Cell polarity and morphogenesis in budding yeast'; 'Cooperative organization of bacterial colonies: from genotype to morphotype'. Subject index. Cumulative indexes to contributing authors and chapter titles, v.48-52. Abstracts of papers available online 3 months before publication date at http://www.AnnualReviews.org. *Class No:* 579(055)

[2369]

Methods in microbiology. San Diego, Academic Press, 1969-. Irregular. ISSN: 05809517.

V.27 (1998) has 15 documented papers by 28 contributors. (*e.g.* 'Detection of virulence genes expressed within infected cells', p.3-12; 'Interaction of bacteria and their products with tissues in organ culture', p.73-81). Detailed, analytical index. *Class No:* 579(055)

Tables & Data Books

[2370]

CRC handbook of microbiology. Laskin, A.I. *and* Lechevalier, H.A., *eds.* 2nd ed. Cleveland, Ohio, CRC Press, 1977-. tables.

First published 1973.

1. *Bacteria.* 1977. 2. *Fungi, algae, protozoa and viruses.* 1978. 3/4. *Microbial composition.* 1981-2. 5. *Microbial products.* 1984. 6. *Growth and metabolism.* 1984. 7. *Microbial transformation.* 1984. 8. *Genetics and immunology.* 1987. 9. Pt.A. *Antibiotics*; Pt.B. *Antimicrobial inhibitors.* 1988.

V.1 ([xi], 787p.) has 30 contributors. Bacteria are considered in 33 sections, each with tables and bibliography. Appended: 'General information' (including immunological and immunochemical classification of micro-organisms); Glossary, p.519-49; Important culture collections; Literature guide for microbiology, p.597-647. Taxonomic and topical indexes. *Class No:* 579(083)

Marine Environment

[2371]

RHEINHEIMER, G. Mikrobiologie der Gewässer. [Aquatic microbiology.] 4th ed. Jena, Gustav Fischer Verlag, 1991; Chichester, Wiley, 1992. viii,363p. illus. $79.50. ISBN: 0471926957.

First published 1971.

15 chapters: 1. Introduction ... 3. The microorganisms of waters ... 7. Pathogens in aquatic plants and animals and their control ... 11. Geomicrobiological processes in waters ... 14. The economic significance of aquatic microorganisms - 15. Outlook. References, p.313-50. Index of names of genera. Subject index. Aimed at undergraduates and professionals. *Class No:* 579(26)

Bacteria

[2372]

Bergey's manual of systematic bacteriology. 2nd ed. Baltimore, Md., Williams & Wilkins 1984-89. 4v. illus., tables. ISBN: 0683041088, v.1; 0683078933, v.2; 0683079085, v.3; 0683090615, v.4.

Replaces *Bergey's Manual of determinative bacteriology* (8th ed. 1974).

V.1 by N.R. King. 1984. xxvii, 964p. V.2 by H.A. Sneath, 1984. xviii, 634p. V.3 by J.T. Staley, 1989. xxviii, 714p. V.4 by S.T. Williams, 1989. xxii,420p.

205 contributors and 17 main sections in all. Each volume contains an extensive bibliography (*e.g.* v.1: p.837-942) and an index of scientific names of bacteria. V.1 covers the Gram-negative bacteria; v.2, the Gram-positive bacteria; v.3, the archaebacteria, cyanobacteria and remaining Gram-negatives; v.4, the actinomycetes. *Class No:* 579.8

[2373]

—**Index Bergeyana: an annotated alphabetical listing of names of the taxa of the bacteria.** 7th ed,. Edinburgh & London, Livingstone, 1966. xiv, 1472p.

A companion volume to Bergey's *Manual of determinative bacteriology* 'It represents an earnest effort to assess the significance of more than twenty thousand names of bacterial taxa that have been found in the literature' (*Preface*). Bibliography (A-Z authors), p.1211-1472. *Class No:* 579.8

[2374]

International code of nomenclature of bacteria. Sneath, P.H., *and others.* Rev. ed. Washington, American Society for Microbiology, 1992. 232p. $47. ISBN: 155581039x. *Class No:* 579.8

[2375]

Microbiology abstracts. Section B: Bacteriology. Bethesda, Md., Cambridge Scientific Abstracts, 1972-. 12pa. $1045 (US); $1085 (non US). ISSN: 03008398.

Formerly as Section B: *General microbiology and bacteriology,* 1966-71.

About 13,200 abstracts pa. 16 sections: Methodology, media and culture - Identification, taxonomy and typing - Cell structure and function - Genetics and evolution - Phage-host interactions - Antibiotics - Antibacterial agents - Immunology - Human, Animal, Invertebrate bacteriology - Plant diseases - Microbial symbioses, antibioses and predation - Ecology and distribution - Miscellaneous topics. Books. Proceedings, Author and subject indexes per issue and annually. Available online (LIFE SCIENCES COLLECTION), and CD-ROM. *Class No:* 579.8

[2376]

SAMSON, P. Glossary of bacteriological terms. London, Butterworths, 1975. 165p. diagrs.

Not strictly confined to bacteria; rather, a glossary of microbiological terms. 'A very useful book, not only for those first entering a medical microbiological field but as a quick reference for many workers in laboratories' (*British book news,* August 1975, p.570). *Class No:* 579.8

58/59 Natural History

Natural History

Bibliographies

[2377]

AMERICAN MUSEUM OF NATURAL HISTORY. **Research catalog of the Library. [American Museum of Natural History].** Boston, Mass., G.K. Hall, 1977-78. 13v. + 12v. $1320. ISBN: 0816100640; 0816102384.

Authors. 1977. 13v. (9180p.). *Classed catalog.* 1978. 12v. (8859p.).

The library houses one of the world's leading natural history collections. Its 325,000 volumes comprehensively cover a wide variety of subject areas, 'including anthropology, general natural history, entomology, geology, herpetology, mineralogy and peripheral biological sciences'. The *Authors* catalogue has entries for *c.*17,000 serial titles as well as for rare books, manuscripts, pamphlets, visuals, letters. *Class No:* 58/59(01)

[2378]

—ACADEMY OF NATURAL SCIENCES OF PHILADELPHIA. Catalog of the Library. [Academy of Natural Sciences of Philadelphia]. Boston, Mass., G.K. Hall, 1972. 16v. $1755. ISBN: 081610946x.

First published 1980.

Has about 258,000 dictionary-catalogue entries, photolithographically reproduced, in the main *Catalog.* The collection is strongest in systematics, palaeontology and stratigraphic geology, plus limnology, marine biology, ecology and animal behaviour. Many analytical entries. *Class No:* 58/59(01)

[2379]

—AMERICAN MUSEUM OF NATURAL HISTORY. **The New catalogue of the Library. [American Museum of Natural History].** Boston, Mass., G.K. Hall, 1983. 6v. ISBN: 0816102740.

Catalogues material acquired by the Library since the 1960s. More than 69,000 entries, typeset from computer type, it continues the 1977/78 volumes. *Class No:* 58/59(01)

[2380]

Archives of natural history. London, the Society for the Bibliography of Natural History, 1982-. 3pa. $150. ISSN: 02609541.

Formerly *Journal of the Society for the Bibliography of Natural History* (1936-81).

Carries original papers, reviews and bibliographical surveys (*e.g.* 'A check-list of natural history bibliographies and bibliographical scholarship', v.5(6), p.428-67, - a valuable unannotated list of *c.*900 items and supplemented in later issues). V.19(2), 1992 contains 42 signed book reviews, in addition to 12 documented papers. *Class No:* 58/59(01)

[2381]

BRITISH MUSEUM (NATURAL HISTORY). **Catalogue of the books, manuscripts, maps and drawings in the British Museum (Natural History).** London, the Trustees, 1903-15. 5v. (1903-15); Supplement, v.6-8 (1922-40).

Reprinted New York, Stechert-Hafner, 1964.

An author catalogue of the General Library and Departmental libraries (Zoology, Geology, Mineralogy, and Botany). V.1-5: 90,000v.; v.6-8: 30,000v. Four form divisions are used: atlases; dictionaries; encyclopaedias; gazetteers. Within each heading, order is chronological. Periodicals are entered under title or location of issuing society. Maps initially appear under name of country charted, Many cross-references from names to places, etc. V.6 (1922) has 48p. of addenda and corrigenda.

Lists of accessions to the Museum Library (1955-74. 6pa.) has 3 parts: (A) Books, pamphlets and special publications; (B) New periodicals; (C) Selected papers and monographs from periodicals received. *Class No:* 58/59(01)

[2382]

FREEMAN, R.B. **British natural history books, 1495-1900: a handlist.** Folkestone, Kent, Dawson, 1980. 437p. £5. ISBN: 0712909710.

Two parts: 1. Alphabetical list (4,206 numbered entries); 2. List of titles in date order from 1495-1800. Subject index, partly analytical, p.403-37. Numbers in italics indicate 'those works which, in the opinion of the author, are the most important contributions to the subject of the entry'. 'Something more than a short title list and something more than a bibliography' (*Introduction*). It reveals 'an unassailable completeness, scrupulous care over minor details, and a

....(contd.)

seemingly total freedom from printers' slips' (*British journal for the history of science,* v.14(2), no.46, March 1981, p.86-87). *Class No:* 58/59(01)

Encyclopaedias & Dictionaries

[2383]

The Cambridge illustrated dictionary of natural history. Lincoln, R.J. and Boxall, G.A. Cambridge, University Press, 1987. 413p. illus. £24.95. ISBN: 0521305519.

Provides *c.*10,000 concise definitions of terms, - 'adequate to explain the meaning or essential concept of a term or to briefly outline the characteristics of a group of organisms' (*Preface*). Entry is under scientific name, with cross-reference from common name. Ecological terms are included. 700 small but clear line-drawings. Both authors are at the British Museum (Natural History). *Class No:* 58/59(03)

[2384]

Marshall Cavendish international wildlife encyclopedia. Burton, M. and Burton, R., *eds.* Rev. ed. London, Marshall Cavendish, 1990. 25v. illus. £291.45; $449.95. ISBN: 086307734x.

Covers fish, reptiles and amphibians, birds, and mammals, with insects, crustaceans and invertebrates given more selective coverage. Articles arranged A-Z. Animals listed by common name. V.25 includes a 3-part index - animal; subject; list of animals classified by phylum. 13-page bibliography. Many illustrations. *Class No:* 58/59(03)

[2385]

The Oxford dictionary of natural history. Allaby, M., *ed.* Oxford University Press, 1985. xiv, 688p. £22.50. ISBN: 0192177206.

56 countributors and consultants. More than 12,000 entries, A-Z, listing taxa of animals and plants down to family level, including 'any lower taxa of particular interest' (*Preface*). Numerous cross-references, especially from common to scientific name. 'Felidae (cats)': 2/3 column; 'Dance language': ¾ column. A few brief biographies (*e.g.* Darwin: ½ column). Failure to give priority to common-name entry is criticized in *New scientist* (10 April, 1986, p.68). However, 'It's an essential book to have about the classroom, laboratory, library or study' (*British book news,* March 1986, p.165). *Class No:* 58/59(03)

[2386]

Philip's nature encyclopedia. Luck, S., *and others.* London, Philip, 1998. 376p. illus.(col.) £24.99. ISBN: 0540075205.

First published as *Family encyclopedia of nature,* 1992.

Arranged by theme: 1. Shaping the planet - 2. The power of the atmosphere - 3. Evolution and adaptation - 4. Reproducing to survive - 5. The search for food - 6. Movement and shelter - 7. Attack and defence - 8. Senses and communication - 9. The living environment - 10. Ready reference. Index, p.359-75. Popular, but detailed. *Class No:* 58/59(03)

Handbooks & Manuals

[2387]

PALMER, E.L. *and* FOWLER, H.S. **Fieldbook of natural history.** 2nd ed. New York, etc., McGraw-Hill, 1975. xviii, 779p. illus. $42.95. ISBN: 0070481962.

First published 1949 (x, [1], 664p.).

Five parts (astronomy; the earth; rocks and minerals; plant kingdom; animal kingdom), but concentrating on botany and zoology, - using a new classification. Fine line-drawings are a feature. A valuable popular compendium. 'It may be useful as a resource book for elementary-school teachers and others interested in a single volume covering natural history' (*Choice,* v.12(5/6). July/August 1175, p.664,. *Class No:* 58/59(035)

Reviews & Abstracts

[2388]

Wildlife review: an indexing and abstracting publication of wildlife literature. [Washington], US Dept. of the Interior, Fish and Wildlife Service, 1935-. no.1-. 6pa. $32pa. ISSN: 00435511.

About 12,000 references pa., covering over 1,300 periodicals. Sections: General conservation - Plants - Wildlife - Mammals - Birds - Amphibians and reptiles. Entries include names of organizations, etc., for contact purposes. Appended 'Book reviews and new journals'. Author, geographic and subject indexes per issue; annual cumulative index adds a taxonomic index. 'Serves to alert wildlife biologists of

....(contd.)

current worldwide literature on wildlife management and conservation.' Available on microfilm from UMI, and on CD-ROM from National Information Services Corporation. *Class No:* 58/59(048)

Periodicals

[2389]

BRITISH MUSEUM (NATURAL HISTORY). Serial publications in the British Museum (Natural History) on microfiche. London, the Museum, 1985-. ISSN: 02673347.

Supersedes *List of serial publications in the British Museum (Natural History) Library* (1975. 3v. (1275p.)). Microfiches are updated at six-monthly intervals.

24,000 entries for serial publications relating to the life and earth sciences. One of the most comprehensive collections in its field. *Class No:* 58/59(051)

Yearbooks & Directories

[2390]

MEENAN, A., *comp. and ed.* **Directory of natural history and related societies in Britain and Ireland.** London, British Museum (Natural History), 1983. vii, 407p. £16.50. ISBN: 0565008595.

Nearly 1,000 entries, Aslib Biological and Agricultural Sciences Group ... Zoological Society of Northern Ireland. Data on each society include aims, membership, meetings, publications, additional information (*e.g.* library). Arranged under English and Welsh counties, Scotland, Ulster, and Eire. Appended geographical and subject indexes. A much-needed comprehensive and up-to-date directory, superseding A. Lysaght's *Directory of natural history and other field study societies in Great Britain* (1959). *Class No:* 58/59(058)

[2391]

The Naturalists' directory and almanac (international). Cambridge, Mass., 1877-. Irregular. $32.50. ISSN: 0277609x.

Title and publisher vary.

47th ed., 1995. 458p. Two main sections: a directory of natural scientists worldwide, A-Z, (stating location and special interests), under continents and countries (largely USA); and a listing of natural history museums, societies, associations, etc. *Class No:* 58/59(058)

Illustrations

[2392]

CLEWIS, B. Index to illustrations of animals and plants. New York, Neal-Schumann, 1991. 217p. $49.95. ISBN: 1555700721.

3 sections: 1. How to use this book - 2. Key to abbreviations of sources - 3. Common-name index (161p.). Data for each entry include code citation, type of illustration and page number. Scientific-name index and 9-page bibliography. 'An outstanding reference for science collections and picture researchers' (*Booklist*, 1 May 1991, p.1740). *Class No:* 58/59(084.1)

[2393]

DESMOND, R. Wonders of creation: natural history drawings in the British Library. London, British Library, 1986. 248p. col. illus. (pl.), facsims. £25. ISBN: 0712300716.

10 chapters (2. The foundations of natural-history drawing - 3. Flowers in religious art - 4. Herbals - 5. The Renaissance - 6. The seventeenth century - 7. The golden age - 8. Voyages and explorations - 9. The Islamic world and Asia - 10. From Victorian times to the present). 40 colour plates, with captions facing, p.143-201. Select bibliography, p.240. Index of manuscripts, p.242. Detailed index. 'Drawings have been chosen to represent national and regional development, different aspects of natural history studies - plants, mammals, birds, fishes, insects, etc. - and examples of the work of some of the best artists' (*Preface*). A finely produced quarto. *Class No:* 58/59(084.1)

[2394]

MUNZ, L.T. and SLAUSON, N.G. Index to illustrations of living things outside North America: where to find pictures of flora and fauna. Hamden, Conn., Archon/Shoe String Press, 1981. 441p. $55. ISBN: 0208018573.

About 9,000 entries for plant and animal illus. Entry under common name, with reference to source of illus., - 206 books, mostly published since 1963. Index of scientific names. Complementary to J.W. Thompson's *Index to illustrations of the natural world: where to find pictures of the living things of North America* (qv). For school libraries. *Class No:* 58/59(084.1)

[2395]

THOMPSON, J.W., *comp.* **Index to illustrations of the natural world:** where to find pictures of the living things of North America. Slauson, N., *ed.* Syracuse, N.Y., Gaylord, 1977. (Reprinted Hamden, Conn., Shoe String Press, 1983). 265p. $47.50. ISBN: 0208020381.

About 6,000 entries for plant and animal illus. Entry states common name and letter-code reference to source of illus. Bibliography of sources (178 books published since 1960) under titles, A-Z. Index of scientific names. Follows on from *Natural history index-guide: an index to 3,365 books and periodicals in libraries*, compiled by B. Altsheler (2nd ed., rev. and enl. New York, H.W. Wilson, 1940. 583p.). For school libraries. *Class No:* 58/59(084.1)

Films

[2396]

AMERICAN MUSEUM OF NATURAL HISTORY. Department of Library Services. **Catalog of the American Museum of Natural History film archives.** Root, N.J., *ed.* New York, Garland, 1987. 410p. $71. (*Garland Reference library of the humanities, 723.*) ISBN: 0824084594.

Annotated list of 291 films in the archives, produced 1908-1981, on mainly ethnographic or zoological themes. Entries provide descriptive summary and technical data. Detailed indexes by date, genre, subject, personal or corporate name, geographic location, expedition or film title. (Based on annotation in *Choice*, v.25(1), September 1987, p.85). *Class No:* 58/59(084.122)

Maps & Atlases

[2397]

The Atlas of the living world. Whitfield, P., *and others.* London, Weidenfeld and Nicolson, 1989. 220p. illus. (col.), figs., maps. ISBN: 0297796429.

6 sections with a 2-page spread on each topic within the section: 1. Global patterns - 2. Habitat patterns - 3. Niche patterns - 4. Changing patterns - 5. The human impact - 6. A catalogue of life (*e.g.* 'Flowering plants'. 'Successful families: birds'; 'Endangered species: invertebrates'). Index. Charts. 1-page bibliography. For school and public libraries. *Class No:* 58/59(084.3)

Histories

[2398]

Annual bibliography of the history of natural history. London, British Museum (Natural History), v.1: Publications of 1982-. 1985-. Irregular. £12 per v.

V.6: 1987 (published 1993) has 2,831 author-title entries, A-Z. Sources: holdings of the British Museum (Natural History) libraries, Science Museum, Victoria & Albert Museum, and Wellcome Institute for the History of Medicine collections. Non-analytical subject index, p.84-102. Index of biographies and persons as subjects; index of institutions. Late in appearance. *Class No:* 58/59(091)

Biographies

[2399]

Biographical dictionary of American and Canadian naturalists and environmentalists. Sterling, K.B., *and others, eds.* Westport, Conn., Greenwood, 1997. 937p. £140; $175. ISBN: 0313230471.

134 contributors. Timespan is from the late 15th century to 1997. Entries, arranged A-Z, for 445 deceased naturalists and environmentalists. Data include birth and death dates and places, education, career summary, major contributions, short bibliography, etc. Appendix arranges names by fields of specialization. For academic and larger public libraries. *Class No:* 58/59(092)

[2400]

BRITISH MUSEUM. Department of Printed Books. **A Catalogue of the works of Linnaeus.** 2nd ed. London, Trustees of the British Museum, 1933. xi, 246, 68p. illus., facsims.

First published 1907.

Catalogues of the British Museum (Bloomsbury) and the British Museum (Natural History) (South Kensington). 20 sections (19: Bibliography). Appendices 1-8 (1: Societies, periodicals, gardens, islands, towns, squares, etc. named after Linnaeus). Index to his works, p.67-68. Followed by *An index to the authors (other than Linnaeus) mentioned in the catalogue ...* (2nd ed. London, Trustees of the British Museum, 1953. 59p.). *Class No:* 58/59(092)

[2401]

MIALL, L.C. The Early naturalists: their lives and work (1530-1789). London, Macmillan, 1912. xi, 396p.

An account of the naturalists who worked and wrote in the period between the Reformation and the French Revolution. Some 40 are dealt with in detail. Discusses not only their work but their characters and the intellectual climate in which they worked. Works are listed. Footnote references; analytical index. *Class No:* 58/59(092)

[2402]
PEATTIE, D.C. **Green laurels:** the lives and achievements of the great naturalists. London, Harrap, 1937. 384p. illus. (pl.), ports.

15 chapters, providing an historical survey from the Middle Ages to Jean-Henri Fabre. 'Sources and reference material' (by chapters), p.369-75. Most of the 21 plates are portraits. *Class No:* 58/59(092)

[2403]
PRAEGER, R.L. **Some Irish naturalists:** a biographical note-book. Dundalk, Tempest, 1949. 208p. ports.

Brief biographical notes on over 300 professional and amateur geologists, zoologists and botanists, from 12th to 20th centuries (p.38-182); also a section detailing societies, institutions and team-work surveys (p.183-200). *Class No:* 58/59(092)

[2404]
RAVEN, C.E. **English naturalists from Neckam to Ray:** a study of the making of the modern world. Cambridge, University Press, 1947. x, 379p.

A survey to about 1660. Brief notes on the naturalists and their writings. Many footnote references. Indexes of subjects, flora, fauna and persons (p.359-79). The Preface states that this work was a preliminary for 'A History of Natural History in Britain'. *Class No:* 58/59(092)

[2405]
—MARTIN, E.A. A Bibliography of Gilbert White, the naturalist and antiquarian of Selborne, with a bibliography and a descriptive account of the village of Selborne. 2nd ed., reprinted with additions. Folkestone, Kent, Dawson, 1970. viii, 193p. [7]p. illus.

Devotes chapters 1-5 to biography and chapters 6-14 to bibliography. Bibliographical descriptions of various editions of *The natural history of Selborne*, etc., are accompanied by 7 plates and 10 text illus. 'A full-scale revision, including biographical and critical works, not included by the original biographer', is called for (*British book news*, April 1971, p.269). *Class No:* 58/59(092)

Manuscripts & Incunabula

[2406]
Natural history manuscript resources in the British Isles. Bridson, G.D.R., *and others, comps.* London, Mansell, 1980. 812p. £105. ISBN: 0720115590.

A directory of *c.*800 manuscript collections of scientific material held in *c.*400 repositories in the British Isles and Eire. Main subject fields: botany, zoology, biology, ecology, conservation, geology, mineralogy, palaeontology, palaeoanthropology and oceanography. Pre-1600 manuscripts are excluded. Index to persons, places and species. Altogether the book is a remarkable 'achievement of British scholarship' (*British book news*, February 1981, p.78). *Class No:* 58/59(093)

[2407]
THACKRAY, J.C. **A Catalogue of manuscripts and drawings in the General Library of the Natural History Museum, London.** London, Mansell, 1995. xiii,126p. illus. £65. (*Historical studies in the life and earth sciences, no.4.*) ISBN: 0720122910.

The catalogue, p.1-103 - 131 entries consisting of a brief biography of the author/donor, followed by a list of material in the collection. An addendum lists photocopies in the General Library manuscripts. Index of personal, institutional and ship names, p.114-24. Index of places, p.125. *Class No:* 58/59(093)

Europe

[2408]
HARRIS, T. **The Natural history of the Mediterranean.** London, Pelham Books, 1982. 224p. ISBN: 0720713919.

Part 1 (50p.) surveys the diverse habitats of the region. Part 2 is a guide to representative flora and fauna (*e.g.* seaweeds, flowering plants, invertebrates, fish, amphibians, reptiles, birds and mammals): Bibliography, p.212-3. Index. Lavishly illustrated in colour. Not a field guide, but highly recommended for the novice or short-stay visitor (*British book news*, September 1982, p.552). *Class No:* 58/59(4)

[2409]
The Natural history of Britain and Northern Europe. London, Hodder and Stoughton; 1978-9. 5v., ea.224p. illus. (mostly col.), maps. ISBN: 0340226145; 0340231548; 0340226153; 0340231556; 034023153x.

1. *Mountains and moorlands,* by A. Darlington. 1978. 2. *Towns and gardens,* by D. Owen, 1978. 3. *Fields and lowlands,* by D. Boatman. 1979. 4. *Coasts and estuaries,* by R. Barnes. 1979. 5. *Rivers, lakes and marshes,* by B. Whitton. 1979.

The five volumes cover the whole of the northern half of Europe west of Russia and the Baltic states, and include Iceland. V.3 has 2 parts: 1. Ecological survey, with map of lowland vegetation of Northern Europe; 2. A field guide to a representative selection of plants and animals. Plates (p.74-213) of plants, invertebrates,

.... (contd.)
amphibians, reptiles, birds, mammals. Detailed index. Entry is under the vernacular names of plants and animals. Aimed at the traveller-naturalist. *Class No:* 58/59(4)

[2410]
Pocket guide: wildlife of Britain & Europe. Chinery, M., *ed.* London, Larousse, 1995. 256p. col. illus. £5.99. ISBN: 0752300199.

Previously published as *Field guide to the wildlife of Britain & Europe* (London, Kingfisher, 1987).

4 contributors. 5 chapters: 1. Mammals - 2. Birds - 3. Reptiles and amphibians - 4. Fishes - 5. Invertebrates. Index (small type), p.248-55, Useful addresses. Illustrates 800 species of fauna in Western Europe in a most attractive pocket format. *Class No:* 58/59(4)

Great Britain

[2411]
AUTOMOBILE ASSOCIATION. **Book of the British countryside.** London, Reader's Digest; A.A. Distribution, 1973 (reprinted 1988). 535, [1]p. illus., maps. ISBN: 0276420160.

35 contributors. Mainly an A-Z encyclopaedia, with 1,800 entries on the geomorphology, archaeology, flora and fauna of Britain. Extended articles on 49 topics (*e.g.* Beechwoods; Estuaries). Appendices include notes on Country Code; national parks; organizations. Glossary of natural history terms. Over 3,000 illus. in colour, - a leading feature. No index. Useful to both amateur and professional naturalists, although not always helpful for identifying animals and plants. 'To my mind, still the best illustrated natural history encyclopaedia relating to this country' (*British book news*, October 1980, p.585). Companion volume: *A.A. Wildlife in Britain, (qv). Class No:* 58/59(410)

[2412]
—The 'Country Life' book of the natural history of the British Isles. Morris, P., *consultant ed.* London, Country Life Books, 1979. 320p. col. illus., maps. ISBN: 0600315401.

7 sections: The sea - The coast - Woodlands - Lowland grasslands and heaths - The uplands - Wetlands and freshwater - Man-made habitats. Analytical index (tiny print), with *c.*3.500 entries. Over 1,600 well-captioned coloured illus. No bibliography. 'With its superb colour photography, masterly artwork and competent text, this is a book that any naturalist ... might treasure and use with profit' (*British book news*, March 1980, p.158). *Class No:* 58/59(410)

[2413]
—CRAWFORD, P. **The Living isles-Safari UK:** a natural history of Britain and Ireland. London, BBC, 1985. 320p. col. illus., maps. £14.95. ISBN: 0563203692.

Written as a companion to the BBC television series. Earlier chapters deal with the various habitats. A gazetteer of 450 nature reserves in 20 areas, open to the public occupies p.227-309. Bibliography, p.310. Detailed index, in tiny print, p.312-20. *Class No:* 58/59(410)

[2414]
—The Natural history of Britain and Ireland. Angel, H., *and others.* London, Michael Joseph, 1981. 256p. col. illus., maps. ISBN: 0718119894.

Essentially a pictorial record, taking six different habitats, - coastlands and islands; freshwater wetlands; lowland grasslands and heaths; upland; woodlands and hedgerows; towns and suburbs. 6 contributors to the text. 'Further reading', p.246. Detailed, analytical index (in tiny print). 200 col. illus. and maps. Quarto format. *Class No:* 58/59(410)

[2415]
The New naturalist library. London, Collins.

The series extended to 82v. by 1995, its Golden Jubilee year, dealing in detail with flora and fauna, localities, and conservation of the land and nature. 'The aim of this series is to interest the general reader in the wildlife of Britain by recapturing the enquiring spirit of the old naturalists' (publisher's announcement). V.83, *The Natural history of pollination,* by M. Proctor, *and others* (1997, 479p. illus. (some pl.). £35; £16.99), is an updated revision of *The Pollination of flowers,* published in 1973.

V.82, *The New naturalists,* by Peter Marren (1995. 304p. illus. (some col.). ISBN: 000219998x) is a history of the series, recording its origins, editorial history, bibliographical, and authorship details in a highly enjoyable narrative. *Class No:* 58/59(410)

[2416]
RACKHAM, O. **The History of the countryside.** London, Melbourne, Dent, 1986. xvi, 445p. illus., facsims, tables, maps. £9.95. ISBN: 0460125524.

17 chapters: 1. Regions - 2. Historical methods and use of evidence - 3. Conservation - 4. Animals and plants: extinctions and new arrivals - 5. Woodland ... 8. Fields ... 10. Trees of hedgerow and farmland ... 14. Moorland ... 17. Marshes, fens, rivers and the sea. Bibliography, p.396-7. 629 References, p.398-414. Glossary; detailed analytical index. Scholarly; well-documented. Author, lecturer in the Botany Dept. at Cambridge. *Class No:* 58/59(410)

Wales

[2417]

CONDRY, W. The Natural history of Wales. London, Collins, 1981. 287p. illus., maps. (*The New naturalist*.) ISBN: 0002395682.

9 chapters: 1. Corries, crags and summits - 2. Moorlands, mires and conifers - 3. Rivers, lakes and marshes - 4. The native woodlands - 5. The flora of the limestones - 6. Farmlands, villages and estates - 7. The industrial scene - 8/9. The coast. Appendix 1: Reserves and places of interest; 2. Glossary. Bibliography, p.272-6 (Background notes; Flora and fauna; Conservation). Index, detailed, partly analytical and in tiny print, p.277-87. 65 black-and-white photographs. A comprehensive survey that keeps to the popular themes. *Class No:* 58/59(429)

[2418]

—DAVIES, R.B. A Guide to the literature of Welsh natural history, including material relating to Wales or written in the Welsh language. London, Library Association, 1981.

Thesis submitted for Fellowship of the Library Association.

500 numbered entries. 'Historical survey of natural history writers in Wales' is followed by annotated list of the literature, closely subdivided: Natural history (items 1-308) - Botany (items 309-80) - Zoology (items 385-500). Index to authors and works [including periodicals] identified by title; index to locations; index by region and county with systematic subdivisions. A thorough piece of research. *Class No:* 58/59(429)

Russia

[2419]

KNYSTAUTAS, A. The Natural history of the USSR. London, etc., Century, 1987. 224p. illus (incl. col.), maps. ISBN: 071261401x.

9 chapters: 1. The shaping of a subcontinent - 2. Vegetation and animal distributions - 3. Conservation - 4. The icy north - 5. The largest forest in the world - 6. Mixed forests - 7. Mountains - 8. Steppes and deserts - 9. Wetlands. Appended tables (*e.g.* 'Typical birds of the wetlands of the USSR', p.218-9). Bibliography, p.220. 272 full-colour photographs; location maps. Index (in tiny print), p.221-4. Quarto format. A popular approach. *Class No:* 58/59(47)

China

[2420]

The Natural history of China. Zhao, Ji, *and others*. London, Collins, 1990. 224p. illus. (col.), maps. ISBN: 0002190435.

8 sections: 1. Introduction - 2. The geography of China - 3. Forests ... 6. Grasslands - 7. Deserts - 8. Conservation and nature protection. Pronunciation guide. Appendices (*e.g.* Typical mammals of the forests; Typical reptiles of the steppes). 220 colour plates and maps. No bibliography. 'A fine compendium for nature lovers' (*Booklist*, v.86(19), 1 June 1990, p.1859). *Class No:* 58/59(510)

India

[2421]

Encyclopedia of Indian natural history. Hawkins, R.E., *general ed.* Delhi, Oxford Univ. Press, on behalf of the Bombay Natural History Society, 1986. [xiii], 620p. illus. (incl. col.) diagrs., maps. $65. ISBN: 0195616235.

Over 550 signed articles, 'Accentors' ... 'Z.S.I., The Zoological Survey of India'. 'Palms': 7½ columns, 9 illus. Cross-references. Covers natural history of India, Pakistan, Bangladesh, Sri Lanka, Burma, Bhutan, Nepal. Detailed index and glossary, p.609-20. Authoritative; 96 distinguished contributors. *Class No:* 58/59(540)

America—North

[2422]

COLLINS, H.H. Harper & Row's complete field guide to North American wildlife. Eastern edition. New York, Harper & Row, 1981. 714p. illus. (incl. col.). ISBN: 0690019696.

Earlier ed. as *Complete field guide to American wildlife, central and north* (1959).

'Covering 1500 species of birds, mammals, reptiles, amphibians, food and game birds of both fresh and salt waters, mollusks, and the principal marine invertebrates occurring in North America east of the 100th meridian from the 55th parallel to Florida north of the Keys' (*Subtitle*). Data include appearance, behaviour, habitat. Index. *Class No:* 58/59(71+73)

[2423]

RANSOM, J.E. Harper & Row's complete field guide to North American wildlife. Western edition. New York, Harper & Row, 1981. 809p. illus. (incl. col.). ISBN: 0690019696.

'Covering 1800 species of birds, mammals, reptiles, amphibians, food and game fishes of both salt and fresh waters, mollusks, and the principal marine invertebrates occurring in North America West of the 100th meridian from the 55th parallel to the border of Mexico' (*Subtitle*). Data include appearance, behaviour, habitat. Index. *Class No:* 58/59(71+73)

[2424]

RICCIUTI, E. The Natural history of North America: in association with the American Museum of Natural History. New York, Facts on File, 1990. 224p. illus. (col.), maps. ISBN: 0831763140.

10 sections: 1. The evolution of a continent - 2. The high Arctic and tundra ... 5. Mountains - 6. Grasslands - 7. Deserts ... 9. Subtropical wetlands - 10. Conservation. 5 appendices, *e.g.* Canyons ... Bird migration ... Bibliography of field guides and field books. Index. Lavishly illustrated. Suitable for public libraries. *Class No:* 58/59(71+73)

USA

[2425]

MEISEL, M. A Bibliography of American natural history, the pioneer century, 1769-1865. Brooklyn, Premier Publishing Co., 1924-29. (Reprinted New York, Hafner, 1967). 3v.

V.1: 'Annotated bibliography of the publications relating to the history, biography and bibliography of American natural history and its institutions during colonial times and the pioneer century, which have been published up to 1924, with a classified subject and geographical index and a bibliography of biographies'. V.2-3 cover institutions. 1760-1844 and 1845-1865. *Class No:* 58/59(73)

Australia

[2426]

BREEDEN, S. *and* BREEDEN, K. A Natural history of Australia. London, Collins, 1970-77. 3v. illus. (incl. col), maps.

1. *Tropical Queensland*. 1970. 262p. 2. *Australia's South-east*. 1973. 256p. 3. *Australia's North*. 1977. 308p.

V.1 has 11 chapters: 1. North of Capricorn - 2/6. Tropical rain forest - 7. Streams - 8. Mangroves and paperbarks - 9. Lagoons - 10. Open woodland - 11. Conservation. Bibliography, p.255-6 (A-Z authors). Detailed, partly analytical index. A well-produced quarto, the fully captioned col. illus. being a feature. V.2 includes Tasmania. *Class No:* 58/59(94)

[2427]

—KEAST, A. Australia and the Pacific Islands. London, Hamish Hamilton; New York, Random House, 1966. [v], 298p. illus. (incl. col.), maps.

Covers the diverse natural history of Australia, New Zealand, New Guinea and Indonesia. 14 chapters (1. Gum trees, bowerbirds, and koalas ... 14. Fiords, glaciers and Antarctic beeches). Supplementary reading, p.293. Analytical index. Quarto format; strikingly large illus., with descriptive captions. *Class No:* 58/59(94)

Nature Study

[2428]

DARLINGTON, A. Natural history atlas. London, Warne, 1970. 112p. illus. (incl. col. plates), maps.

'The maps show various habitats in Great Britain (*e.g.* sand dunes, heathland, moorland). For each type of habitat the colour plates illustrate the animals and plants. General ecology of each habitat is discussed in the text and notes on field study methods are given' (*Geographical abstracts*, 1971(4), abstract no. 71B/1112). Prepared for young pupils and amateur naturalists. *Class No:* 58/59:502

[2429]

A Handbook for naturalists. Seaward, M.R.D., *ed.* London, Constable, 1981. 202p. illus., maps. ISBN: 0094623902.

First published 1968.

13 contributors. Contents: The Country Code, plus 11 contributions (1. Natural history in Britain ... 6. Natural history museums; 7. Zoos and wildlife parks; 8. Nature trails; 9. Wildlife and the law; 10. Natural history and wildlife conservation organizations; 11. Books and periodicals (p.167-90; grouped). Appendices: A. Vice-counties; B. Grid references. Partly analytical index. Offers 'practical help for those taking up natural history fieldwork for the first time' (*Preface*). Not aimed solely at the young naturalist. Does not entirely replace the 1968 ed. *Class No:* 58/59:502

Research Projects

[2430]

Keyword-index of wildlife research. Zurich, Swiss Wildlife Information Service, 1974-. v.1-. Annual (irregular). SFr70.

Text in English or German. Indexes international publications in wildlife biology and management.
Class No: 58/59:502:061:061.62.005

Museums

[2431]

DAVIS, P. *and* **BREWER, R.C. A Catalogue of natural science collections in North-East England,** with biographical notes on the collections. [Durham], North of England Museum Service, 1986. [iv], 333p. ISBN: 0951094507.

Main catalogue (*c.*1,500 entries, under authors, A-Z), p.7-165. Biographical notes on the collections, p.166-266. Taxonomic and geographical indexes. A quarto volume. *Class No:* 58/59:502:061:069

[2432]

STEARN, W.T. The Natural History Museum at South Kensington: a history of the British Museum (Natural History), 1735-1980. London, Heinemann, in association with the British Museum (Natural History), 1981. (Reprinted 1998, The Natural History Museum.) xxiii, 414p. illus., ports., graph. ISBN: 0434736007.

5 parts (22 chapters): 1. The Bloomsbury years, 1753-1880 - 2. The Museum at South Kensington - 3. The Natural History Museum, 1883-1949 - 4. The Museum Departments (Zoology; Entomology; Palaeontology (formerly Geology); Mineralogy; Botany; Library Services (p.317-30)) - 5. An era of change and independence, 1950 - 1980. Appendices: *A.* Principal Librarians and senior Natural History officials; *B.* Directors and senior officials; *C.* Trustees; *D.* Number of visitors to the Museum [graph]. Detailed analytical index. 88 plates. The definitive history, to 1980. *Class No:* 58/59:502:061:069

Nature Reserves

Worldwide

[2433]

International handbook of national parks and nature reserves. Allin, C.W., *ed.* Westport, Conn., Greenwood Press, 1990. 560p. tables, maps. $75. ISBN: 0313249024.

Describes and evaluates national parks and nature reserves in 25 nations and one regional cluster. Data include history of park preservation and administrative structures concerned with park protection. Bibliography appended to each chapter. Suitable for academic libraries. *Class No:* 58/59:502.4(100)

Tropics

[2434]

IUCN directory of neotropical protected areas. Dublin, Tycooly International Publishing, Ltd., for the International Union for the Conservation of Nature and Natural Resources, 1982. xx, 436p. maps.

Region surveyed: Central and South America, Caribbean, and Florida. Protected areas, under countries, Antigua ... Virgin Islands (US). Ecuador has 8 such areas, including Galápagos (21 headings, *e.g.* physical location, physical features, vegetation, noteworthy fauna, principal reference material, staff, budget). Outline maps. No index, but detailed contents. The first of ICUN's new series of protected-area directories, a contribution to the Global Environmental Monitoring System. *Class No:* 58/59:502.4(213)

Europe

[2435]

DUFFEY, E. National parks and reserves of Western Europe. London, Macdonald, 1982. 288p. col. illus., col. maps. ISBN: 0356085864.

18 contributors, for 18 countries; Norway and Iceland; Sweden; Finland; Denmark; West Germany; Austria; Switzerland; Netherlands; Belgium and Luxembourg; United Kingdom and Eire; France; Spain; Portugal; Italy; Yugoslavia; Greece. Glossary and map key. Index to plants and animals, p.273-83; General index, p.284-5. Addresses of conservation organizations. Bibliography, p.287 (general; by country chapters). Helpful marginal data. Excellent colour photographs and maps. A worthy quarto for any library. *Class No:* 58/59:502.4(4)

Great Britain

[2436]

Enjoying wildlife: a guide to RSPB nature reserves. Scott, B., *ed.* Sandy, Beds., Royal Society for the Protection of Birds, 1994. 297p. illus. (incl. col.), maps. £4.95. ISBN: 0903138735.

Succeeds *RSPB nature reserves*, 2nd. ed., 1984.

Guide to 130 reserves in England (p.24-181), Scotland (p.182-256), Wales (p.257-84), and Northern Ireland (p.285-94), and sub-arranged by area. Details of habitat, bird species, access, etc., with a simple map of each site. Accommodation advertisements.
Class No: 58/59:502.4(410)

[2437]

The Macmillan guide to British nature reserves. Hywell-Davies, J., *and others.* 2nd ed. London, Macmillan, 1989. xii,654p. col. illus., maps. ISBN: 0333467906.

First published 1984.

Arranged under English and Welsh counties, and Scottish regions. About 3,000 entries (some regrettably brief) for nature reserves and wildlife sites throughout the British Isles (excluding Eire). Data on each: location, type of reserve; features; visiting seasons; description. List of contributors. No bibliography. Well illustrated in colour. The most comprehensive of British nature reserve gazetteers, although bulky as a guide. *Class No:* 58/59:502.4(410)

[2438]

A Nature conservation review: the selection of biological sites of national importance to nature conservation in Britain. Ratcliffe, D., *ed.* Cambridge, University Press, 1977. 2v. (xvi, 401p; viii, 320p.); illus., tables, maps. £110 + £85. ISBN: 052121159x, v.1; 0521214033, v.2.

V.1 has 13 sections: 1. The ecological background to the site selection ... 4-10. Types of ecosystem sites (*e.g.* coastland, open waters, upland grassland and heaths). Bibliography, p.389-91. Site index; detailed subject index. V.2 (*Site accounts*) describes the 735 locations, both public and private. Data on location, size, geology, topography, soil, past and present land-use and notable species of plants and animals. Sites are arranged by region under type of ecosystem, as in v.1. Detailed index. Editor: Chief Scientist, Nature Conservancy Council 'Invaluable for general reference' (*Nature*, v.269(5625), 1977, p.271). *Class No:* 58/59:502.4(410)

[2439]

Protected areas of the world: a review of national systems. Gland, Switzerland; Cambridge, UK, International Union for Conservation of Nature and Natural Resources, 1992. 4v. maps. $150. ISBN: 2831700906, v.1; 2831700914, v.2; 2831700922, v.3; 2831700930, v.4.

1. *Indomalaya, Oceania, Australia and Antarctic.* xx,351p. 2. *Palaearctic.* xxviii,556p. 3. *Afrotropical.* xxii,360p. 4. *Nearctic and neotropical.* 400p.

Entry for each country includes area; population; economic indicators; policy and legislation; international activities; administration and management; systems reviews; addresses; references; summary of protected areas. *Class No:* 58/59:502.4(410)

[2440]

Protected landscapes: experience around the world. Gland, Switzerland; Cambridge, UK, International Union for Conservation of Nature and Natural Resources, 1987. x,404p.

Covers 26 countries and discusses over 140 individual sites. Data for each entry include geographical location; date and history of establishment; area; land tenure; altitude; climate; vegetation; fauna; local human population; scientific research and facilities; conservation management; budget; local administration; references.
Class No: 58/59:502.4(410)

South Africa

[2441]

A Scientific bibliography on the national parks of South Africa. Bryden, H.B., *and others. Koede,* Supplement, 1994. 133p. ISSN: 00756458.

5,032 references arranged in 14 sections, *e.g.* bibliographies and directories; techniques in botany; faunistic descriptions; veterinary ecology. Geographical and author indexes.
Class No: 58/59:502.4(680)

Australasia & Oceania

[2442]

PAINE, J.R. IUCN directory of protected areas in Oceania. Gland, IUCN, 1991. xxiii,447p. tables, maps. ISBN: 2831700698.

Gives data on 23 islands or groups of islands. Information includes area, population, parks and reserves, list of protected areas. Information on the last named includes name, biogeographical province, date established, location, fauna, vegetation, etc. Geographic and taxonomic indexes.

Also published is *IUCN directory of South Asian protected areas* by M.J.B. Green (IUCN, 1990. xxiv,294p.). *Class No:* 58/59:502.4(9)

Nature Conservation

Bibliographies

[2443]
DENVER PUBLIC LIBRARY. Catalog of the Conservation Library of the Denver Public Library. Boston, Mass., G.K. Hall, 1974. 6v. (3436p.). First supplement. 1978. 2v. (1154p.). $630. ISBN: 0816111138.

The Conservation Library in Denver, Colo. is considered 'one of the most comprehensive of its kind in the world'. (*RQ*, v.14(3), Spring 1975, p.255). The collection is particularly strong on fish and wildlife management, biology, pollution control, and economics, and international in scope. *Class No: 58/59:502.6(01)*

[2444]
World plant conservation bibliography. [London], Royal Botanic Gardens, Kew; World Conservation Monitoring Centre, 1990. xv,645p. £15. ISBN: 0947643249.

Designed to complement *Plants in danger; what do we know?* (World Conservation Monitoring Centre, 1986) (*qv*). Contains over 10,000 citations to published literature, ranging from specific to general, local to international. Includes data from the late 1970s onwards. Includes references on conservation of rare and threatened plants; erosion and conservation of plant genetic resources; extent and loss of habitats and vegetation; a selection of forestry papers; role and work of botanical institutions in plant conservation; conservation thinking and policy; protected areas. 3 indexes: 1. Plant names - 2. Plant families - 3. Geographical. Supplements and revisions are planned. *Class No: 58/59:502.6(01)*

Encyclopaedias

[2445]
Macmillan encyclopedia of the environment. Kellert, S.R., *ed*. New York, London, Macmillan, 1997. 6v.(150p. each) illus.,tables,maps. £225; $250. ISBN: 002897381x, set.

Arranged A-Z. Included are articles on ecology, desertification, and people who are important in the environment movement, *e.g.* John Muir. Many cross-references and sidebars which give additional information. Numerous illustrations. Subject and general indexes at the end of v.6. Further reading. Has a US bias with regard to environmental organizations and legislation. Suitable for school and public libraries. *Class No: 58/59:502.6(031)*

Handbooks & Manuals

[2446]
Conservation in progress. Goldsmith, F.B. *and* Warren, A., *eds*. 3rd ed. Chichester, Wiley, 1993. xiii, 364p. illus., diagrs., graphs, tables, maps. ISBN: 0471936413.

First ed. published as *Conservation in practice* (1974); 2nd ed. as *Conservation in perspective* (1984).

20 British contributors. Four parts (20 documented sections): 1. Concepts - 2. Species and habitats - 3. Approaches to conservation - 4. Organizations. *Class No: 58/59:502.6(035)*

Dictionaries

[2447]
ALLABY, M. Macmillan dictionary of the environment. 4th ed. London, Macmillan, 1994. 377p. ISBN: 0333616553.

First published 1977 ([v], 532p.).

About 6,700 interdisciplinary terms, including profuse cross-references, and straying into many fields, - botany, zoology, chemistry, physics, mathematics, economics (*e.g.* ½p. each on Ice Age, nuclear reactor, mangrove). Includes a few biographical entries, for Darwin, Malthus, Lamarck, etc., as well as environmental disasters, *e.g.* Chernobyl, Braer, etc., but not Exxon Valdez. *Class No: 58/59:502.6(038)*

[2448]
DUNSTER, J. *and* DUNSTER, K. Dictionary of natural resource management. Wallingford, CAB International, 1996. xv,363p. £49.95;$74.95. ISBN: 0851991483.

Includes over 6,000 terms from botany, forestry, soil science, and other areas not normally associated with natural resources, *e.g.* philosophy. Three appendices: Classification of organisms; Geological time scales; Conversion tables and other measurements. *Class No: 58/59:502.6(038)*

Films

[2449]
JOY, S., *ed*. Environmental film directory. 4th ed. London, CoEnCo, 1984. 63p.

Completely revised ed. of *A Directory of natural history and conservation films* (3rd ed. Council for Nature, 1978). *Class No: 58/59:502.6(084.122)*

Maps & Atlases

[2450]
The Atlas of endangered species. Burton, J.A., *ed*. London, Macmillan, 1991. 256p. illus., maps. £16.99. ISBN: 0028370810.

20 contributors. 7 biogeographic regions, each subdivided into sections: Habitats and plants - Wildlife - Species in focus. Many colour photographs and maps. 7 world maps show climatic and biogeographic regions, pollution, population, protected areas, natural disasters, and countries which have signed international environmental conventions. List of endangered animals. List of organizations. Brief bibliography. *Class No: 58/59:502.6(084.3)*

[2451]
The Last rain forests: a world conservation atlas. Collins, M., *ed*. London, Mitchell Beazley, in association with IUCN; the World Conservation Union, 1990. 200p. illus. (col.), maps. £17.99. ISBN: 0855337893.

7 sections: 1. What are rain forests? - 2. Why we need rain forests ... 4. How rain forests work ... 6. Atlas of the rain forests - 7. The challenge of conservation. Excellent photographs and maps, with a well-organized text. Glossary. Index. For all libraries covering this subject. *Class No: 58/59:502.6(084.3)*

Worldwide

[2452]
1997 IUCN red list of threatened plants. Walter, K.S. *and* Gillett, H.J., *eds*. Cambridge, UK; Gland, Switzerland, International Union for Conservation of Nature and Natural Resources, 1998. 862p. tables. £30.

First list of the 27,000 plants under threat worldwide. Data is more detailed than in other *Red list* compilations. Includes scientific and common names, along with distribution, BRU standard, local and global threat. All data is properly sourced. A comprehensive survey. *Class No: 58/59:502.6(100)*

[2453]
Plants in danger: what do we know? Davis, S.D., *and others*. Gland, Switzerland; Cambridge, UK, International Union for Conservation of Nature and Natural Resources, 1986. xlv,461p. $30. ISBN: 2880327075.

Aim is to show how to find information on threatened plants. Entries arranged alphabetically by country (Afghanistan ... Zimbabwe). Data include area; population; floristics; vegetation; checklists and floras; information on threatened plants; laws protecting plants; voluntary organizations; botanic gardens; useful addresses; additional references. 3 appendices: 1. General and regional references - 2. Index to bibliography - 3. The implementation of conservation conventions relevant to plants. Geographical index. *Class No: 58/59:502.6(100)*

Great Britain

[2454]
British red data books. Peterborough, English Nature, 1977-.

1. *Vascular plants.* 2nd ed., 1984. 128p. £5.50. 2. *Insects.* 1987. 448p. 3. *Invertebrates other than insects.* 253p. 1991. £8.

Vascular plants (1977 ed. [3], xxvi, 98p. maps) covers 321 species, - about 18% of the native flora, and it adopts IUCN categories (endangered; vulnerable; rare). *Class No: 58/59:502.6(410)*

[2455]
ENGLISH NATURE. Bibliography series. Peterborough, English Nature, 1979. ISSN: 01431722.

1. *Nature conservation and agriculture.* 1979. [12]p. £1. 2. *Wildlife in the city.* 1979. [16]p. £1. 3. *The New Forest.* 1979. 34p. £2. 4. *Natural environment of the Severn Estuary and British Channel areas.* 1981. 47p. £3. *Class No: 58/59:502.6(410)*

[2456]
EVANS, D. A History of nature conservation in Britain. 2nd ed. London, Routledge, 1997. xix,288p. illus., tables. £50; £16.99. ISBN: 0415144914; 0415144922, pbk.

First published 1992.

10 chapters: 1. The why and the wherefore ... 4. 1940s: national parks and nature reserves ... 9. 1990s: government inertia and global initiative - 10. Future: the mechanics and the mission. References and further reading. Species and general indexes. For public and academic libraries. *Class No: 58/59:502.6(410)*

[2457]

SHEAIL, J. **Nature conservation in Britain.** London, Stationery Office (for Institute of Terrestrial Ecology), 1998. xi, 282p., illus. £19.95. ISBN: 0117023086.

Story of 'official' conservation in the UK over 50 years, by detailing the histories of such organisations as the Nature Conservancy, NCC, ITE, etc. Readable and candid. References, p.267-76. Index, p.277-82. *Class No:* 58/59:502.6(410)

Asia

[2458]

The Conservation atlas of tropical forests: Asia and the Pacific. Collins, N.M., *ed.* London, Macmillan, 1991. 256p. illus. (col.), tables, maps. £65. ISBN: 0333539923.

2 parts: 1. The issues (*e.g.* 'Shifting cultivation'; 'Tropical timber trade') - 2. Country studies, p.84-249 (*e.g.* 'India', p.126-40). References appended to each chapter. Acronyms and glossary, p.250. Index of species. General index, p.253-56. Illustrations and maps are of excellent quality. More detailed, and perhaps, more technical than the same author's *The Last rain forests (q.v.).* Recommended for academic and special libraries supporting research in this area.

The second volume in the series, *Conservation atlas of tropical forests: Africa* (256p. $85), published 1992. *Class No:* 58/59:502.6(5)

America—North

[2459]

Conservation directory 1999: a guide to worldwide environmental organizations. Gordon, R.E. *and* Anderson, J.N., *eds.* Vienna, Virginia, National Wildlife Federation, 1956-. Annual. ISSN: 0069911x.

First published 1950.

44th ed. 1999 (xix,546p.) contains entries for more than 3,000 organizations. Main sections concern US government, state and provincial organizations and agencies (*e.g.* Maine; 23 entries), as well as Canadian and international bodies. Data include date founded, descriptions of functions, office-bearers, publications. Also includes *c.*18,000 conervation community members. Subject, name, and publications, indexes. Limited access to data is available on the Internet at: http://www.nwf.org/pubs/consdir/showlist.html. *Class No:* 58/59:502.6(71+73)

Wildlife Conservation

CD-ROM

[2460]

Beacham's international threatened, endangered, and extinct species. Washington, D.C., Beacham Publishing Corp, 1996. 1 CD-ROM. $465.

20-130p. articles covering 1,400 species worldwide. *c.*2,700 colour photographs. Indexes of common and scientific name, taxonomical group, and state or country. Glossary of 900 wildlife terms. 10,000 item bibliography. Available for Windows and Macintosh. *Class No:* 58/59:502.7(003.40)

Bibliographies

[2461]

BAKER, S. **Endangered vertebrates:** selected, annotated bibliography, 1981-1988. New York, Garland, 1990. xv,197p. $30. (*Garland reference library of social science, no.480.*) ISBN: 0824047966.

International in scope and includes a wider range of publications than *Official World Wildlife Fund guide to endangered species of North America, (q.v.).* Coverage includes books, symposia, journal articles, and dissertations. Appendix gives names and serial publications of appropriate organizations. Indexes allow access by common name, scientific name, author or geographic area. Has both academic and general appeal. *Class No:* 58/59:502.7(01)

Handbooks & Manuals

[2462]

SALVADORI, F.B. *and* FLORIO, P.L. **Wildlife in peril.** Newton Abbot, Devon, Westbridge Books: David & Charles, 1978. 208p. col. illus. ISBN: 0715376969.

Translated from the Italian (1977), has data on 84 mammals (p.14-129), 31 birds and 8 reptiles endangered: Latin name; class; order; family; French, Italian and German terms; description; geographic distribution; habitat; population. Bibliography, p.199-200; index (in small type), p.201-8. The fine coloured illus. are the main feature. *Class No:* 58/59:502.7(035)

[2463]

Save the birds. Diamond, A.W., *and others.* Cambridge, University Press, 1989. 384p. col. illus., maps. ISBN: 0521343674.

3 main sections: 1. Earth's great ecosystems (*e.g.* 'Coasts and estuaries'; 'Arid lands') - 2. Save the birds - we need them - 3. Saving Britain's wildlife. Lavishly illustrated. Suitable for school and public libraries. *Class No:* 58/59:502.7(035)

Tables & Data Books

[2464]

INTERNATIONAL UNION FOR CONSERVATION OF NATURE AND NATURAL RESOURCES. Red data book. 2nd ed. Morges, Switzerland, IUCN, 1978-. v.1-. Loose-leaf.

Prepared and published with the assistance of UNESCO, the UN Environment Programme (UNEP) and World Wildlife Fund International (WWF).

1. *Mammalia.* 2nd rev. ed., by J. Thornback. 1978. 2. *Aves.* 2nd rev. ed., by W.B. King, 1979. 3. *Amphibians and reptiles.* Rev. ed. by R.E. Honecker. 1979. 4. *Pisces.* 5. *Angiosperms.*

Data: Status and summary. Distribution. Population. Habitat and ecology. Threats to survival. Conservation measures taken. Conservation measures proposed. Remarks. References.

The series is continued by publications on specific topics, *e.g. Lemurs of Madagascar and the Comoros: the IUCN red data book.* 1990. 240p. illus. *Class No:* 58/59:502.7(083)

[2465]

—GROOMBRIDGE, B., *World Conservation Monitoring Centre.* World checklist of threatened amphibians and reptiles. 5th ed. Peterborough, Joint Nature Conservation Committee, 1993. vi,99p. ISBN: 1873701462.

7 sections: 1. Amphibia: Anura ... 4. Reptilia: Crocodylia ... 7. Reptilia: Serpentes. 22-page bibliography (738 items). Indexes of generic and common names, and specific names, with synonyms. *Class No:* 58/59:502.7(083)

[2466]

—WORLD CONSERVATION MONITORING CENTRE. World checklist of threatened mammals. Inskipp, T. *and* Barzdo, J., *comps.* 2nd ed. Peterborough, Joint Nature Conservation Committee, 1993. vi,150p. ISBN: 1873701446. *Class No:* 58/59:502.7(093)

[2467]

1996 IUCN red list of threatened animals. Bailie, J. *and* Groombridge, B., *eds.* Cambridge, UK; Gland, Switzerland, International Union for Conservation of Nature and Natural Resources, 1997. 368p. illus. £26.75. ISBN: 2831703352.

Covers mammals; birds; reptiles; amphibians; fishes; invertebrates (anthozoa-insecta). Lists over 5,000 taxa, with category indicating the degree of threat. The first global compilation to use the complete new *IUCN red list* category system. Additionally, all mammals have been assessed for the first time. Only mammals and birds have been comprehensively evaluated, while reptiles, fishes, and amphibians will be covered more completely in future editions. Available on the Internet at http://www.wcmc.org.uk/species/animals. *Class No:* 58/59:502.7(083)

Worldwide

[2468]

BALOUET, J.-C. *and* ALIBERT, E. **Extinct species of the world:** lessons for our future. Translated by K.J. Hollyman. London, Charles Letts in association with David Bateman, 1990. 192p. col. illus., maps. $19.95. ISBN: 1852381000.

Descriptions of *c.*300 extinct animals. A broad historical survey is followed by 11 chapters: The Indian Ocean - The North Pacific - The South Pacific - The Atlantic Ocean - The Mediterranean - Europe - Africa - Asia - Australia - North America - South America. Appended is a section on plants and animals that humans have made extinct. Detailed, analytical index. Lavishly illustrated. *Class No:* 58/59:502.7(100)

[2469]

Beacham's guide to international endangered species. Beacham, W. *and* Beetz, K.H., *eds.* New York, Beacham Publishing, 1998. 2v.(1085p.) illus. $195. ISBN: 0933833342.

V.1 & 2. *Mammals listed 1970 to July 1997.*

Derived from *Beacham's international threatened, endangered and extinct species* on CD-ROM (*q.v.*). 351 endangered species (183 in v.1; 168 in v.2) (excluding those in the US) arranged by taxonomic family. Data include description, habitat, distribution, conservation, recovery, etc. A colour photograph is used to illustrate each species. General and country indexes. Glossary of scientific terms. Bibliography of general, rather than scholarly, references at the end of each volume. For public and academic libraries. *Class No:* 58/59:502.7(100)

[2470]
Birds to watch 2: the world list of threatened birds: the official source for birds on the IUCN red list. Collar, N.J., *and others*. Cambridge, BirdLife International, 1995. 407p. £25; $25. (*BirdLife conservation series, 4.*) ISBN: 0946888302.

Five species accounts: Globally threatened species (1,111 species); Extinct species (16 species); Conservation dependent species (11 species); Data deficient species (66 species); Near-threatened species (875 species). Almost half of the book is made up of three appendices detailing the listed species by geopolitical area and listings of species in higher threat categories. References, p.348-71, although each chapter has its own notes and bibliography appended. Index, p.378-407. A major work. *Class No:* 58/59:502.7(100)

[2471]
Encyclopedia of endangered species. Emanoil, M., *ed.* Detroit, Gale, 1994. 1230p. illus., maps. $95. ISBN: 081038857x.

Covers 700 endangered species of plants and animals, with the emphasis on the latter (animals, p.1-1052; plants, p.1053-1180). A black-and-white photograph accompanies most entries. Data include common and scientific names, habitat, current distribution, and conservation measures. Some wildlife and conservation organizations are listed. The bibliography is arranged by major groups, *e.g.* mammals, birds. Indexes include a combined scientific and common-name species index with cross-references, and a geographical index. *Class No:* 58/59:502.7(100)

[2472]
Endangered wildlife of the world. New York, Marshall Cavendish, 1993. 11v. (1536p.), illus.(col.), maps. $399.95. ISBN: 1854354892.

Covers 1,200 species and subspecies. Arranged A-Z, entries are one to three pages in length. Over 700 photographs and 600 maps. Compiled from IUCN *Red data books* and US Fish and Wildlife Service. V.11 contains an animal kingdom chart, three indexes (geographic; scientific names; comprehensive), appendices (A: North American wildlife organizations and US government agencies; B: Addresses of US state offices and wildlife refuges in the US and Canada), and a bibliography (18p.). Full colour throughout. For school and public libraries, although the emphasis in the appendices on US organizations will limit that section's usefulness elsewhere. *Class No:* 58/59:502.7(100)

[2473]
MOUNTFORT, G. Rare birds of the world: a Collins/ICBP handbook. London, Collins, 1988. 256p. illus. (some col.), figs. £12.95. ISBN: 0002198355.

Based on ICBP/IUCN *Red data books*. 8 sections: 1. Birds and man ... 3. The Nearctic region ... 7. The Australasian region - 8. The Pacific islands. Concise entries for each species. 32 colour plates showing habitat and 50 black-and-white drawings. 2 appendices, in tabular form: 1. The world's threatened species - 2. Birds presumed to have become extinct since 1600. Small bibliography. Indexes of vernacular and scientific names. Author one of the founders of the WWF. *Class No:* 58/59:502.7(100)

[2474]
World Wildlife Fund guide to extinct species of modern times. Beacham, W., *ed.* New York, Beacham Publishing, 1997. 410p. illus.,maps. $39. ISBN: 0933833407.

Gives data on 211 species which have become extinct since the seventeenth century (mainly in Africa, the Atlantic and Pacific islands, New Zealand and Australia, the Caribbean and North America). Information includes description, habitat, behaviour, reason for extinction. Glossary. Common and scientific name index. No bibliographies. *Class No:* 58/59:502.7(100)

Europe

[2475]
Birds in Europe: their conservation status. Tucker, G.M., *and others*. Cambridge, Birdlife International, 1995. 600p. tables,maps. £32; $40. (*BirdLife conservation series, 3.*.) ISBN: 0946888299.

Compiled by more than 400 contributors and consisting mainly of species accounts. Data for each species include: population trends; distribution; ecology threats. Five appendices: Summary of conservation staus for all European species ... Species with particularly poorly monitored breeding populations in Europe ... Instructions given to national data compilers of the Dispersed Species Project. References, p.551-596. Index of species. A detailed and essential reference work. *Class No:* 58/59:502.7(4)

[2476]
GRIMMETT, R.F.A. and JONES, T.A., comps. Important bird areas in Europe. Cambridge, International Council for Bird Preservation, 1989. x,888p. tables, maps. £21.50. (*ICBP technical publication no.9.*) ISBN: 0946888175.

Inventories arranged A-Z by country, Albania ... Yugoslavia. Describes 2,444 sites and provides an indication of the extent to which they are unprotected or threatened. The chapter on each country is subdivided into sections on general information, ornithological

....(contd.)
importance, conservation infrastructure and protected-areas system, international resources relevant to the conservation of sites, overview of the inventory, glossary, inventory and main references. Maps showing the sites are also included. 6 appendices: 1. Numerical criteria used to select sites for migratory species ... 6. English names of species mentioned in the text. 'It is intended for international agencies, governmental and non-governmental nature conservationists, land-use planners and professional and amateur ornithologists' (*Introduction*). *Class No:* 58/59:502.7(4)

[2477]
SMIT, C.J. *and* **WIJNGAARDEN, J.N. Threatened mammals in Europe.** Wiesbaden, Akademische Verlagsgesellschaft, 1981. 259p. maps. ISBN: 3400004383.

Supplementary volume of *Handbuch der Säugetiere Europas* and written in English to attract a wider readership.

The Introduction states the case for conserving animals, summarising the threat to their survival. Detailed 'Data sheets on the threatened species' follow, accompanied by distribution maps. Favourably reviewed in *Natural history book reviews*, v.7(1/2), 1984, p.41. *Class No:* 58/59:502.7(4)

Great Britain

[2478]
Important bird areas in the United Kingdom including the Channel Islands and the Isle of Man. Pritchard, D.E., *and others, eds.* Sandy, Beds., RSPB, 1992. 540p. maps. £35. ISBN: 0903138468.

Lists 256 sites of international importance which qualify for protection under the EC's Directive on the conservation of wild birds. Site accounts (p.73-475) are arranged geographically, *e.g.* 'Scotland'. Maps show site location. 6 appendices (1. Bird species named in text). Index to sites. Companion volume to *Important bird areas in Europe (q.v.)*, 1989. *Class No:* 58/59:502.7(410)

[2479]
SITWELL, N. The Shell guide to Britain's threatened wildlife. London, Collins. 1984. 208p. col. illus. £8.95. ISBN: 0002190503.

Pictorial guide to 172 plants, birds, mammals, reptiles, amphibians, fish and invertebrates considered to be in danger of extinction. 'No similar collection [of natural history photographs] has ever been produced before' (*British book news*, October 1984, p.612). *Class No:* 58/59:502.7(410)

America—North

[2480]
Bird conservation 3. Jackson, J.A., *ed.* Madison, Wis., published for the International Council for Bird Preservation, United States Section by Wisconsin, 1989. 177p. $17.50. ISBN: 0299111202.

V.3 devoted to the single theme of North American forest ecosystems and their birds. Covers seven forest types. No subject index but contains index of bird species. No illustrations. *Class No:* 58/59:502.7(71+73)

[2481]
The Official World Wildlife Fund guide to endangered species of North America. Moseley, C. Washington, D.C., Beacham Publishing, 1990-92. 3v. illus. $280.

Describes more than 500 animals and plants. V.1 deals with mammals and plants; v.2 with birds, fishes, insects and other species; v.3 adds species federally listed from August 1989 to December 1991. Entries are 2 pages in length and include a map, black-and-white photograph and a table giving information on habitat, food, reproduction and threats to the species. Each entry concludes with a general essay plus a bibliography. Each volume has a glossary, an index of occurrence by state and an index of common and scientific names. No cumulative index. *Class No:* 58/59:502.7(71+73)

USA

[2482]
'Official state lists of endangered, threatened, or rare species'. In *Reference services review*, v.19(1), Spring 1991, p.23-38, 48. Gardner, R.L., *and others*.

Bibliography of lists produced by state government agencies, arranged alphabetically, Alabama ... Wyoming. Each entry gives a brief description of the publication and its arrangements. A 3-page list of responding agencies and their addresses is given. *Class No:* 58/59:502.7(73)

58 Botany

Botany

Bibliographies

[2483]

DAVIS, E.B. *and* **SCHMIDT, D. Guide to information sources in the botanical sciences.** 2nd ed. Englewood, Colo., Libraries Unlimited, 1996. xxi, 275p. $49.50. ISBN: 1563080753.

First edition, 1987.

11 chapters: 1. Bibliographical sources - 2. Abstracts, indexes, and databases - 3. Current awareness sources - 4. Dictionaries, encyclopedias - 5. Handbooks and methods - 6. Directories and groups - 7. Identification sources - 8. Taxonomy - 9. Bibliographical and historical material - 10. Textbooks and treatises - 11. Key publishers, etc. 934 annotated entries. Indexes, p.239-75. The main focus is on printed materials and computerized databases. A useful, much-enlarged, guide for students, librarians, avocational and professional botanists. American slant (of 46 botanical societies listed, only 17 are non-US), although an improvement on the first edition.

Class No: 580(01)

[2484]

HENREY, B. British botanical and horticultural literature before 1800: computing a history and bibliography of botanical and horticultural books printed in England, Scotland and Ireland from the earliest times until 1800. London, Oxford Univ. Press, 1975. 3v. facsims., port.

1. *The sixteenth and seventeenth centuries: history and bibliography.* xxvi, 290p. 2. *The eighteenth century: history.* xvi, 748p. 3. *The eighteenth century; bibliography.* xvii, 142p.

V.3 includes items 377-1524, with addenda of 15. Location in 65 libraries, including USA(5), Canada (1) and Paris (2). Also, a list of private libraries, booksellers, etc. A finely produced work.

Class No: 580(01)

[2485]

Huntia: a journal of botanical history. Pittsburgh, Pa., Hunt Institute for Biological Documentation, Carnegie Mellon University, 1964-. Irregular. $60 per vol. ISSN: 00734071.

Devoted, states the editor, to 'studies of the literature on systematic botany and horticulture, botanical voyages and exploration, early agriculture, medical botany, and related subjects of botanical biography, iconography and bibliography'. *Class No:* 580(01)

[2486]

KENT, D.H., *comp.* **Index to botanical monographs.** A guide to monographs and taxonomic papers relating to phanerogams and vascular cryptogams found growing wild in the British Isles. London, Academic Press, for the Botanical Society of the British Isles, 1967. xii, 163p.

Nearly 1,900 references to monographs, taxonomic and cytotaxonomic papers published since 1800. Abbreviations of titles of periodicals, etc. (c.350), p.1-24. Index to botanical monographs, systematically arranged, p.25-153; index to families and genera, etc. 'A very useful book for amateurs and students, especially those without easy access to a large botanical library' (*Aslib book list,* v.35(4), April 1968, entry no.185). *Class No:* 580(01)

[2487]

PRITZEL, G.A. Thesaurus litteratura botanicae omnium gentium. Ed. nov. reform. Leipzig, Brockhaus, 1872-[1877]; reprinted Milan, Görich, 1950, and Königstein, Koeltz, 1972. viii, 547p. $89. ISBN: 3874290352.

An author list of 10,871 books, followed by anonyma and periodica. Includes a valuable subject index of early floras, monographs, etc. The most important reference work for early botanical literature up to 1870; confined to separately published material. *Class No:* 580(01)

[2488]

—**JACKSON, B.D.** Guide to the literature of botany: being a classified selection of botanical works, including nearly 6,000 titles not given in Pritzel's *Thesaurus.* London, Longman, for the Index Society, 1881 (reprinted, Koeltz, 1974). xl, 626p. $39. ISBN: 3874290697.

Comprises *c.*9,000 short-title entries, with author index. Supplements Pritzel. *Class No:* 580(01)

[2489]

ROYAL BOTANIC GARDENS, Kew. Library. **Author and classified catalogues.** [Royal Botanic Gardens, Kew, Library]. Boston, Mass., G.K. Hall, 1973. 9v.

Author catalogue. 5v. (3347p. $545). *Classified catalogue.* 4v. (2372p. $455).

177,000 photolithographed catalogue cards in all. Particularly rich in early botanical books and in works on plant taxonomy and distribution.

Class No: 580(01)

[2490]

STAFLEU, F.A. *and* **COWAN, R.S. Taxonomic literature:** a selective guide to botanical publications and collections, with dates, commentaries and types. 2nd ed. Utrecht, Bohn, Scheltema and Holkema, 1976-88. 7v. 6250p. + Supplement I (1992) - Supplement V (1998). $1,360. (*Regnum vegetabile, 94, 98, 105, 110, 112, 115, 116, 125 (Supplement I), 130 (Supplement II), 132 (Supplement III), 134 (Supplement IV), 135-136 (Supplement V).*.) ISBN: 9031302244.

Arranged under authors, A-Z, with brief biographical notes. 16,614 items from 6,186 authors are contained in v.1-6. Also, information on composite works, herbaria with collections, sources of bibliographical and biographical notes, annotated list of authors, most important works, etc. Name and title indexes per volume. *Class No:* 580(01)

[2491]

—Index to European taxonomic literature. Utrecht, International Bureau for Plant Taxonomy.

Published annually in the *Regnum vegetabile* series.

Class No: 580(01)

[2492]

SWIFT, L.H. Botanical bibliographies: a guide to bibliographic materials applicable to botany. Minneapolis, Minn., Burgess, 1970. xxxix, 804p.

5 main sections: general bibliography; background literature (*e.g.* biological), botanical literature (general and reference works; taxonomic, ecological and physiological botanical works); literature of applied botany (plant cultivation, etc.); literature of auxiliary studies (style manuals; botanical illustration, etc.). 'Highly recommended for all reference libraries' (*Library journal,* v.96(11), 1 June 1971, p.1963-4). *Class No:* 580(01)

[2493]

UNITED STATES. Department of Agriculture. **Botany subject index.** Boston, Mass., G.K. Hall, 1958. 15v. (15050p.). ISBN: 0816105065.

315,000 photolithographically reproduced catalogue cards. Entries are arranged under subjects (subdivided, as necessary) and scientific names. Includes textbooks (arranged chronologically), voyages and travels, biographies and geographical botany. Worldwide in scope.

Class No: 580(01)

Encyclopaedias

[2494]

The Marshall Cavendish illustrated encyclopedia of plants and earth sciences. Moore, D.M., *ed.* London, Marshall Cavendish, 1988. 10v. ISBN: 0863079016.

V.1-2: *Dictionary of plants.* V.3-5: *Flowering plant families.* V.6-7: *Plant ecology.* V.8-9: *Earth sciences.* V.10 includes indexes, glossary and bibliography. International in scope though the majority of the 120 contributors are British or European. Numerous colour photographs and diagrams throughout. Many cross-references. For school and public libraries. *Class No:* 580(031)

Handbooks & Manuals

[2495]

CULLEN, J. The Identification of flowering plant families: including a key to those native and cultivated in north temperate regions. 4th ed. Cambridge, University Press, 1997. xii, 215p. £37.50. ISBN: 052158485x.

First published by Oliver & Boyd, 1965.

Introduction: Examining the plant (1. Duration and habit; 2. Underground plant parts; 3. Above-ground parts). Using the keys. Key, p.50-90. Arrangement and description of families, p.91-187. Bibliography, p.188-93. Glossary. Index, p.203-15. Aimed at undergraduate readers. Lacks illustrations. *Class No:* 580(035)

[2496]
The Guinness book of plant facts and feats. Duncalf, W.G. Enfield, Middlesex, Guinness Superlatives, Ltd., 1976. 204p. illus. (incl. col.), facsims., tables. ISBN: 0900424257.

Has 15 sections: 1. Evolution of plant life - 2. Plants in relation to man ... 5. Glossary ... 7. Trees (p.41-88) ... 9. Flowering plants ... 12. Vegetables and fruits - 13. Plants of death ... 15. Radiocarbon dating and dendrochronology. Bibliography, p.199-200. Index (in tiny print, p.201-4).

Also, *The Guinness guide to plants of the world* (1992. 256p. illus. £19.95). *Class No:* 580(035)

[2497]
Plant science: growth, development and utilization of cultivated plants. Hartmann, H.T., *and others.* 2nd ed. Englewood Cliffs, N.J., Prentice-Hall International, 1988. xii,674p. illus., diagrs., tables, maps. $51. ISBN: 0136810659.

First published 1981.

3 sections (31 documented chapters): 1. Plants: structure, classification, growth, reproduction and utilization (1-12) - 2. An overview of the fruit crops and ornamental plants (13-22) - 3. Major agronomic, vegetable and fruit crops (23-31). Appendix includes 'Nutritive values of the edible part of plants'. Glossary, p.649-66. Index. Intended as a textbook for university and college students. *Class No:* 580(035)

[2498]
STRASBURGER, E. Strasburger's textbook of botany. Denffer, D. von, *and others*. New English ed., translated from the 30th German ed., by P. Bell and D. Coombe. London, Longman, 1976. xvi, 877p. illus., diagrs., tables, maps.

First published 1894.

4 parts: 1. Morphology - 2. Physiology - 3. Systematics and evolution - 4. Plant geography. Chronology, p.xv-xvi. References (by parts and sections), p.798-816. Excellent analytical index, p.817-77. Claimed to be the most comprehensive and up-to-date textbook of plant science in a single volume. *Class No:* 580(035)

Dictionaries

[2499]
ARAB LEAGUE EDUCATIONAL, CULTURAL AND SCIENTIFIC ORGANIZATION. Lexicon of botany: English, French, Arabic. Rabat, 1971. 172, xxviip. *Class No:* 580(038)

[2500]
BAILLON, H. Dictionnaire de botanique. Paris, Hachette, 1876-92. 4v. (xii, 2660p.) illus.

Reputed to be 'the most complete dictionary of the plant kingdom' (Lawrence, G.H.M. *Taxonomy of vascular plants,* p.319). It is fully illustrated and particularly useful for its inclusion of biographies of the great botanists. *Class No:* 580(038)

[2501]
The Concise Oxford dictionary of botany. Allaby, M., *ed.* Oxford, University Press, 1992. vi,442p. ISBN: 0198661630.

Based on *The Oxford dictionary of natural history, (q.v.)* with many expanded entries. World-wide coverage of taxonomic groups, taking account of recent taxonomic revisions. Contains *c.*5,000 alphabetically arranged definitions, with selective cross-referencing. No derivations, illustrations, or pronunciations of terms. Aimed at students and amateur naturalists, although useful for biologists as it includes terms from, among others, genetics, ecology, and earth sciences. *Class No:* 580(038)

[2502]
Elsevier's dictionary of botany. Amsterdam, etc., Elsevier, 1979-82. 2v. ISBN: 0444417877, v.1; 0444419772, v.2.

1. *Plant names in English, French, German, Latin and Russian.* 1978. viii, 580p. $169.25. 2. *General terms in English, French, German and Russian.* 1982. vi, 744p.

V.1 has 6,131 English-base terms, with French, German and Russian equivalents and indexes. The Russian (cyrillic) index is separate. V.2 (9,967 terms) includes terms from closely related fields, *e.g.* biochemistry, agriculture, forestry, grassland research, medical properties of plants. *Class No:* 580(038)

[2503]
The Facts-on-File dictionary of botany. Tootill, E., *ed.* New York, Facts-on-File, 1984. 390p. illus. $24.95. ISBN: 0871968614.

Over, 3,000 entries on pure and applied botany, from taxonomy to ecology. Concise and readable definitions, often supported by illus. Extensive cross-references. Intended for students, naturalists, geographers and anyone else interested in plants. *Class No:* 580(038)

[2504]
HARRIS, J.G. Plant identification terminology: an illustrated glossary. Payson, Utah, Spring Lake Publishing, 1994. 197p. illus. $17.95. ISBN: 096402215x.

Lists more than 2,400 terms, many illustrated with small line drawings. The first section, p.3-118, is an alphabetical listing of terms which is followed by a section gathering terms together in categories. A useful ready-reference tool. *Class No:* 580(038)

[2505]
JACKSON, B.D. A Glossary of botanic terms, with their derivation and accent. 4th ed., rev. and enl. London, Duckworth, 1928. x, [ii], 481p.

First published 1900.

Latin equivalents accompany most of the 10,000 terms defined. Sub-entries are grouped under the generic term (*e.g.* the entry for 'Cryptanthous' occupies one column and has 23 sub-entries). Appendix D: Bibliography of botanical dictionaries (40 annotated items), p.478-81. The standard English-language botanical glossary. *Class No:* 580(038)

[2506]
Russian-English botanical dictionary. Macura, P., *ed.* Columbus, Ohio, Slavica Publishers, Inc.; Oxford, Holden Books, 1982. 678p. $49.95. ISBN: 0893570923. *Class No:* 580(038)

[2507]
USHER, G. A Dictionary of botany, including terms in biochemistry, soil sciences and statistics. London, Constable, 1966. v, 404p.

About 10,000 terms (all the phyla, classes, orders, orders and families) are briefly described in 1-100 terms; cross-references. 'Compiled to meet the needs of university students and grammar school pupils' (*Author's preface*). *Class No:* 580(038)

[2508]
VICKERY, R. A Dictionary of plant lore. Oxford, University Press, 1995. xx,437p. £14.99. ISBN: 0198661835.

Covers British and Irish plant lore. Includes plants used in games, religion, folk customs, etc. Lists common and Latin names in alphabetical order in addition to conditions treated. Bibliography and index of scientific names. 'Handy in size, attractively produced and very reasonably priced' (*Watsonia*, V.22(1) 1998, p.124/5.) *Class No:* 580(038)

Reviews & Abstracts

[2509]
Current advances in plant science (CAPS). Amsterdam, Elsevier Science, 1972-. 12pa. fl.2,725; $1,556. ISSN: 03064484.

About 25,000 references pa. 48 sections: 1. Photosynthesis ... 3. Cell organization ... 6. Plant molecular biology ... 12. Enzymes ... 17. Reproductive development of seed plants ... 21. Growth regulators ... 26. Taxonomy, systems and evolution ... 30. Environmental physiology - 31. Agronomy and horticulture ... 33. Crop protection - 34. Plant pathology - 35. Ecology... 45. Plants and medicine. Author index per issue. Included in *Elsevier BIOBASE* database via Datastar, DIALOG, and DIMDI. *Class No:* 580(048)

[2510]
—Botanisches Zentralblatt. Referierendes Organ für das Gesamtgebiet der Botanik In- und Auslandes. Kassel (later Jena, Dresden), Fischer, 1880-1945. v.1-179.

Was the international reporting service that preceded *Excerpta botanica*. *Class No:* 580(048)

[2511]
Excerpta botanica. Section B. Sociologica. Jena, Fischer, 1959-. Irregular. DM248; £128 abroad. ISSN: 00144045.

Carries bibliographies on specific topics and selected countries. About 2,000 references pa., systematically arranged, with author index. Edited in connection with the International Association for Plant Taxonomy, Utrecht. *Class No:* 580(048)

Periodicals & Progress Reports

[2512]
Advances in botanical research. San Diego, Academic Press, 1963-. Irregular. ISSN: 00652296.

V.29 (1998) has eight contributors. Five chapters, *e.g.* 'The calcicole-calcifuge problem revisited'; 'Signal transduction networks and the integration of responses to environmental stimuli'. Each chapter has a lengthy bibliography appended. Analytical subject index. *Class No:* 580(05)

[2513]

B-P-H: botanico-periodicum-Huntianum. Lawrence, G.H.M., *and others, eds.* Pittsburgh, Pa., Hunt Botanical Library, 1968. 1063p. $20. ISBN: 091319610x.

Cites *c.*12,000 titles of botanical periodicals. List of selected reference works, p.15; selected references used in *B-P-H*, p.21-23. 'A compendium of information on all periodical (serial) publications that regularly contain (or, in some period of their history, included) articles dealing with the plant sciences and botanical literature, and with the persons who have contributed to botany and to literature' (*Preface*).

A *Supplementum* was published by the Hunt Institute for Botanical Documentation in 1991 (edited by G.D.R. Bridson and E.R. Smith, 1068p. ISBN: 0913196541) which doubles the number of titles specified in total (25,000) up to the end of 1990. It is 'both a supplement to, and a partial revision of, the B-P-H' (*Introduction*). *Class No:* 580(05)

[2514]

Botanical review, interpreting botanical progress. New York, Botanical Garden, 1935-. v.1-. 4pa. illus. $82 (US); $89 (non-US) pa. ISSN: 00068101.

1-3 contributions per issue with extensive bibliographies. Annual list of articles. Available in microform from UMI, and on-line. 'The primary review journal in the field' (Katz, B., & L.S. *Magazines for libraries.* 6th ed., 1989, p.175). *Class No:* 580(05)

[2515]

ROYAL BOTANIC GARDENS, Kew. **List of periodical publications in the Library.** Kew, Royal Botanic Gardens, 1978. 94p. ISBN: 0112411495.

Although compiled over 20 years ago, this listing is still relevant as, being a national collection, titles are never discarded. *Class No:* 580(05)

Nomenclatures

[2516]

GLEDHILL, D. The Names of plants. 2nd ed. Cambridge, University Press, 1989. vi,202p. figs., tables. £22.50. ISBN: 0521366682.

First published 1985.

7 sections: The nature of the problem; The size of the problem; Towards a solution to the problem; The rules of botanical nomenclature; The International Code of Nomenclature for Cultivated Plants; Botanical terminology; The glossary. Does not deal with specific names of plants but with individual stems or words which combine to make up the complete name of a plant. Bibliography, p.199-202. *Class No:* 580(083.72)

[2517]

HOLMES, S. Outline of plant classification. London & New York, Longman, 1983. vii, 181p. ISBN: 0582446481.

10 chapters (1. The classification of plants - 2. The organization of the higher taxa - 3. Schizophyta - 4. Algae ... 9/10. Spermophyta). Glossary, p.157-69. References and further reading, p.171-2. Detailed non-analytical index, p.173-81. Aims 'to provide how and why names have been changed and to describe the characteristics of each taxonomic group' (*Preface*). 'A reference work that will be useful to many botanists and naturalists generally' (*Natural history book reviews*, v.7(3), 1984, p.124-5). *Class No:* 580(083.72)

[2518]

HUNT, T. Plant names of medieval England. Cambridge, D.S. Brewer, 1989. lvi,334p. £29.50. ISBN: 0859912736.

4 sections: 1. Introduction (The arrangement of the materials; The manuscripts; List of incipits; The principal sources of medieval botany; Synonymies; The plant names in the *synonyma herbarum;* Bibliographies) - 2. Text - 3. Index of vernacular names - 4. Index of botanical names. Includes over 1,800 vernacular names, covering over 600 plant species. Arranged A-Z (Aaron ... Zizannia), using Latin headwords. Many entries have references to works which include discussions or indicate relevant material. *Class No:* 580(083.72)

[2519]

HYAM, R. *and* **PANKHURST, R. Plants and their names: a concise dictionary.** Oxford, University Press, 1995. x,545p. £14.99; $29.95 ISBN: 0198661894.

16,000 entries, with 2,600 definitions of Greek and Latin terms. Common names are cross-referenced. Five-page glossary. No pronunciation guide. *Class No:* 580(083.72)

[2520]

International Code of Botanical Nomenclature, adopted by the 15th Botanical Congress, Berlin, July-August 1993. Greuter, W., *and others, eds.* Königstein, Koeltz, 1994. xiii,389p. (*Regnum vegetabile, v.131.*) ISBN: 387429367x.

Consists of authoritative rules for the codifying of plants, the main part of the volume, p.91-335, delineating plant families in detail. English language only. The quarterly *Taxon* reports changes in the Code. *Class No:* 580(083.72)

[2521]

RADCLIFFE-SMITH, A. Three-language list of botanical name components. Kew, Royal Botanic Garden, 1998. 143p. £11.50. ISBN: 1900347504.

Main list: Greek-Latin-English, Latin-English-Greek, English-Latin-Greek, (p.3-101). Plant-name supplement and numerical supplement. Excludes generic names. *Class No:* 580(083.72)

[2522]

STEARN, W.T. Botanical Latin: history, grammar, syntax, terminology and vocabulary. 4th ed. Newton Abbot, Devon, David & Charles, 1992. xiv, 546p. illus. ISBN: 0715300522.

First published 1966 (London, Nelson, xiv, 566p.).

Comprises: 1. Introduction (p.3-56, including 'How to use this book', p.3-6); 2. Grammar; 3. Syntax and other matters; 4. Vocabulary (*c.*7,000 terms) and bibliography (p.361-546). Intended primarily to help botanists to read the extensive literature of their subject, and to describe new species in language that is correct, lucid and unambiguous. *Class No:* 580(083.72)

Illustrations

[2523]

CLEWIS, B. Index to illustrations of animals and plants. New York, Neal-Schumann, 1991. 217p. $49.95. ISBN: 1555700721.

3 sections: 1. How to use this book - 2. Key to abbreviations of sources - 3. Common-name index (161p.). Data for each entry include code citation, type of illustration and page number. Scientific-name index and 9-page bibliography. 'An outstanding reference for science collections and picture researchers' (*Booklist*, 1 May 1991, p.1740). *Class No:* 580(084.1)

[2524]

NISSEN, C. Die Botanische Buchillustration: ihre Geschichte und Bibliographie. Stuttgart, Hierbemann, 1951. 2v. (vii, 264p. + v, 324p.). Supplement, 1966, viii, 97p.

Arranged by periods and countries (*e.g.* Germany, p.161-222). V.1: *Geschichte.* V.2: *Bibliographie* (2,207 numbered items, under authors, A-Z, p.1-204), with brief biographical notes; appended list of periodicals, anonymous works and titles in series. Indexes of artists, plants, countries and authors. *Class No:* 580(084.1)

[2525]

—Index Londiniensis to illustrations of flowering plants, ferns and fern allies, being an amended and enlarged edition, continued up to the end of the year 1920, of Pritzel's 'Alphabetical register of representation of flowering plants and ferns' ... prepared under the auspices of the Royal Horticultural Society of London at the Royal Botanic Gardens, Kew. Stapf, O. Oxford, Clarendon Press, 1929-31. 6v. Supplement for 1921-35. 1941. 3v.

An A/Z index, by genus and species. The illustration is listed under the name used in the particular book - a possible cause of error.

Updated in the asterisked entries (denoting illustrated) in *Index Kewensis* supplements (*q.v.*). *Class No:* 580(094.1)

Histories

[2526]

CURLE, R.H.P. The Ray Society: a bibliographical history. London, Quaritch, for the Ray Society, 1954. vi, 101p. ports. £5. ISBN: 0903874075.

The object of the Ray Society (founded 1844) was to publish monographs and memoirs on zoology and fauna, with special reference to British fauna and flora. This history, produced on the occasion of the Society's centenary, includes a list of the Ray Society's publications, 1844-1951 (p.95-101), plus a subject bibliography, with notes on each item, p.32-95. *Class No:* 580(091)

[2527]

Green planet: the story of plant life on earth. Moore, D.M., *ed.* Cambridge, University Press, 1982. 288p. illus. (mostly col.), ports., diagrs., maps. ISBN: 0521246105.

30 contributors. 7 chapters (1. Charting the green planet; 2. Tools of the trade (*e.g.* nomenclature); 3. Evolution of the green planet; 4. Environmental factors; 5. Vegetation today; 6. The realms of plants; 7. Man and the green planet). Biographies, p.274-7; Glossary, p.278-81. Analytical subject index. Index of plant names, p.286-8. Bibliography of 30 items, p.288. 445 illus. (300 col.). *Class No:* 580(091)

[2528]

GREENE, E.L. Landmarks of botanical history. Egerton, F.N., *ed.* Stanford, Calif., Stanford Univ. Press, 1983. 2v. (xi, 1139p.). $125. ISBN: 0804710759.

Part 1: Introduction to the philosophy of botanical history (The Rhizotomi ... Valerius Cordatus, 1515-1544). Appendices on pre-Grecian and medieval knowledge of plants - Part 2: Introduction to the Italian forefathers of the fifteenth century. Appendix: Biology in the seventeenth century. Each volume has *c.*50p. of notes appended. Bibliography, p.1039-1109. Combined analytical index, p.1116-39. *Class No:* 580(091)

[2529]

MORTON, A.G. History of botanical science: an account of the development of botany from ancient times to the present time. London, New York, etc., Academic Press, 1981. xii, 474p. illus., ports. $39.95. ISBN: 0125083823.

11 chapters (1. The beginnings of the knowledge of plants ... 11. Botany in the twentieth century), plus 4p. of chapter notes, including biographical data. The central theme: the evolution of botanical theory. Addressed to university students, the author being Emeritus Professor of Botany, London University. *Class No:* 580(091)

[2530]

ZOHARY, D. and HOPF, M. Domestication of plants in the Old World: the origin and spread of cultivated plants in West Asia, Europe, and the Nile Valley. 2nd ed. Oxford, Clarendon Press, 1993. [x], 278p. illus., charts, maps. ISBN: 0198547951.

First published 1988.

11 chapters: 1. Sources of evidence for the origin and spread of cultivated plants - 2. Cereals - 3. Pulses - 4. Oil and fibre crops- 5. Fruit trees and nuts - 6. Vegetables and tubers - 7. Condiments - 8. Dye crops - 9. Fruit collected from the wild - 10. Plant remains in representative archaeological sites - 11. Conclusions. References, p.245-71. Chronological chart. 25 site orientation maps. Analytical index. *Class No:* 580(091)

Biographies

[2531]

DESMOND, R. Dictionary of British and Irish botanists and horticulturists, including plant collectors, flower painters and garden designers. 4th ed. London, Taylor & Francis, 1994. xxxix, 825p. ISBN: 0850668433.

The *Dictionary* is the latest revision of *A biographical index of British and Irish botanists,* by J. Britten and G.E.S. Boulger (1893), revised by A.B. Rundle (1931). Last previously published, 3rd ed, 1977.

About 11,200 entries, A-Z, for deceased people, mainly those born in the British Isles, with the addition of 1,400 flower painters, 1,500 gardeners, and 1,800 nurserymen. Data: name, date and place of birth and death; education; qualifications; honours officeship in relevant societies; brief details of career; serial publications; editorship of periodical(s); biographical references in books and periodicals; location of plant collections, herbaria, manuscripts, drawings, portraits, state of collections, any plant commemorating the individual, and that person's name. Subject index classifies many of the entries under profession, plants on the country where the flora were collected and studied. 'There is no direct equivalent among the relevant biographical sources (but) the binding of the new ed. seems inadequate for the weight of the book and the expected heavy usage' (*The Year in reference,* 1994, no.216). *Class No:* 580(092)

[2532]

—NEW YORK BOTANICAL GARDEN. Library. Catalog of the manuscript and archival collections and index to the correspondence of John Torrey. Boston, Mass., G.K. Hall, 1973. 482p. ISBN: 0816110182.

Lists *c.*180,000 items from a major US botanical horticultural research library. Scope: events and developments in botany, horticulture and natural history from late 19th century to the present. *Class No:* 580(092)

[2533]

HUNT BOTANICAL LIBRARY. Biographical dictionary of botanists, represented in the Hunt Institute Portrait Collection, Hunt Botanical Library, Carnegie Mellon Univ., Pittsburgh, Pa. Boston, Mass., G.K. Hall, 1972. viii, 451p.

About 10,000 entries, stating name, dates, place of birth and death, and category (*e.g.* plant taxonomist). *Class No:* 580(092)

[2534]

NEW YORK BOTANICAL GARDEN. Library. Biographical notes upon botanists. Boston, Mass., G.K. Hall, 1974. 3v. (1658p.). $370. ISBN: 0816106959.

Notes on *c.*44,000 botanists, arranged A/Z. Details: dates, education, honours, professional positions and memberships, outstanding contributions and writings, as well as printed works referring to the botanists (*e.g.* in Pritzel and national biographical dictionaries). *Class No:* 580(092)

Libraries

[2535]

MATHEW, M.V. The History of the Royal Botanic Garden Library, Edinburgh. Edinburgh, HMSO, 1987. 134p. ISBN: 0114933421.

The history of what is now the United Kingdom's most comprehensive library (dating from 1670) on taxonomic botany, horticulture and related subjects outside London. *Class No:* 580:061:026/027

Botanical Gardens

[2536]

DESMOND, R. The History of the Royal Botanic Gardens, Kew. London, The Harvill Press, 1995 (paperback published in 1998). xvi,468p. illus.(some col.), maps. £24.75. ISBN: 1860465293, pbk.

20 chapters: 1. A queen's garden ... 8. Collectors and collecting ... 13. Overseas activities ... 18. Imperial Kew ... 20. Towards the future. 15 appendices: 1. Some botanic facts ... 4. Boundary walls ... 14. Brief biographies - 15. Printed and archival sources for the history of Kew. Bibliography, abbreviations, notes and sources, and index. Many illustrations. The author was formerly Chief Librarian and Archivist at the Royal Botanic Gardens, Kew. An authoritative work. *Class No:* 580:061:061.6

[2537]

International directory of botanical gardens V. Heywood, C.A., *and others.* 5th ed. Königstein, Koeltz, 1990. 1019p. $150. ISBN: 387429319x.

First published 1963.

1,400 entries, under countries A-Z. Data: status (*e.g.* governmental); date of foundation; co-ordinates; rainfall; taxa (number of species and varieties grown); herbarium; publications; greenhouses; hours open to the public; name of director and staff). 'USSR': p.849-938. The new computerized format makes the book needlessly bulky and there are no page headings for guidance. *Class No:* 580:061:061.6

[2538]

—HYAMS, E. Great botanical gardens of the world. London, Nelson, 1969. 288p. illus.

A sumptuous volume, with nearly 100 colour plates. Arranged by continents and countries. 41 gardens, their history, research activities, specialists, etc. (Kew, p.104-21). Index map of the world's botanical gardens (525 locations); index. *Class No:* 580:061:061.6

Practical Work

[2539]

BRITISH MUSEUM (NATURAL HISTORY). Instructions for collectors. No. 10. Plants. 6th ed. (reprinted, with minor amendments). London, Trustees of the British Museum (Natural History), 1965. 72p. illus.

5th ed., 1921.

Includes 'Notes on collecting special groups' (*e.g.* Algae), p.35-60. *Class No:* 580.08

Collections

[2540]

British and Irish herbaria: an index to the location of herbaria of British and Irish vascular plants. Kent, D.H. *and* Allen, D.E., *comps.* 2nd ed. London, Botanical Society of the British Isles, 1984. *c.*350p. £8. ISBN: 0901158089.

First published 1958.

8 sections, especially 2: 'Universities, museums and other institutions possessing herbaria': principal collections and contributions (over 630) institutions, under locations, A-Z). Section 3: Collectors. Privately owned herbaria are listed in a further section. Extensive bibliography, p.317-31. Classified index to locations of collections. *Class No:* 580.082

[2541]

—HANCOCK, E.G. *and* MORGAN, P.J. A Survey of zoological and botanical material in museums and other institutions of Great Britain. Secretary, Biology Curators Group, c/o City Museum, Sheffield, 1980. 32p. tables. ISBN: 0950709204.

2 sections: 1. Zoological holdings; 2. Botanical holdings. Mainly tables (*e.g.* Section 1, table 2: Zoological holding of national and university museums). Zoological appendix: numbers of zoological specimens of 32 phyla, class or order present in museums - Botanical appendix: numbers of botanical specimens present in museums and universities. Needs updating. *Class No:* 580.082

[2542]

Index herbariorum: a guide to the location and contents of the world's public herbaria. 8th ed. New York, New York Botanical Gardens for the International Association for Plant Taxonomy, 1990. 693p. $70. (*Regnum vegetabile, v.120.*) ISBN: 0893273589. ISSN: 00800694.

First published 1952.

Pt.1: *The Herbaria of the world.* 8th ed., by P.K. Holmgren and others. 1990.

Covers *c.*1,800 herbaria worldwide. Arranged A-Z by country (10 appearing for the first time), with sites arranged alphabetically within each country. Data: addresses, important collections, sponsoring organizations, geographical arrangment, herbarium abbreviations, name of director and staff. Indexes include important collections; staff; cities, p.615-93. Indispensable and well-organized. *Class No:* 580.082

[2543]

The National Plant Collections directory 1998, including 'The Pink Sheet' (a list of rare and endangered garden species). Woking, Surrey, National Council for the Conservation of Plants & Gardens, 1998. 148p. illus. (col. pl.). £4.95. ISBN: 0951862383.

Lists 600 National Plant Collections in the UK containing 400 genera and 50,000 plants. Data include information on size, location, directions, opening times, special open days, publications. Now also available as part of *The Plant finder reference library* CD-ROM 1998/9. *Class No:* 580.082

Plants (Flora)

Bibliographies

[2544]

Flora & fauna of localities: a bibliography of books and articles dealing with plants and animal life of specific countries and regions of the world. Huckin, D., *ed.* Caldicote, Biggleswade, Beds., Clover Publications, 1981. 2v. £12.50, set. ISBN: 0907755003, set.

1. *Great Britain and Europe.* [ix], 118p. 2. *Africa, America, Asia, Australia & USSR.* viii, 158p.

The bibliography excludes school texts, conference papers and symposium proceedings, as well as erudite material only likely to be of use to a specialist. *Class No:* 581.1(01)

[2545]

Key works to the fauna and flora of the British Isles and Northwestern Europe. Kerrich, G.J., *and others, eds.* London, Systematics Association, 1978. xii, 179p.

First published 1942.

About 2,500 entries, with occasional annotations, covering books and periodical articles. Systematic arrangement. Supersedes the Systematics Association's *Bibliography of key works for the identification of the British fauna and flora*, by J. Smart and G. Taylor (1953). No index. For more specialized scientific libraries. 'Graduate and professional levels' (*Choice*, v.16(1), March 1979, p.54,56). *Class No:* 581.1(01)

Illustrations

[2546]

MUNZ, L.T. *and* **SLAUSON, N.G. Index to illustrations of living things outside North America:** where to find pictures of flora and fauna. Hamden, Conn., Archon/Shoe String Press, 1981. 441p. $55. ISBN: 0208018573.

Companion to *Index to illustrations of the natural world: where to find pictures of the living things of North America; (q.v.)* compiled by J.W. Thompson (Syracuse, N.Y., Gaylord, 1977, 265p.).

Entries for over 9,000 species, drawn from illustrations in 206 books. The main index has entry under common name, plus scientific name and source, indicating type of illus. (coloured or black-and-white). Scientific name index follows. Bibliography, under titles. Wide-ranging, but highly selective (*Choice*, v.19(8), April 1982, p.1046). *Class No:* 581.1(084.1)

[2547]

NOVAK, F.A. The Pictorial encyclopedia of plants and flowers. Barton, J.G., *ed.* London, Hamlyn; New York, Crown, 1968. 589p. illus. (pl.).

Originally published by Artia (Czechoslovakia), 1965.

Consists of 1,120 photogravure illus. (48 in colour), with descriptive captions, p.9-559. The excellent illus. usually show plants in flower or fruit. Index of botanical and common names. Supplements the line-drawing approach to illustration of flora. *Class No:* 581.1(084.1)

[2548]

Plant, animal and anatomical illustration in art & sciences: a bibliographical guide from the 16th century to the present day. Bridson, G.D.R. *and* White, J.J., *comps.* Winchester, Herts., St. Paul's Bibliographies; Detroit, Omnigraphics, 1990. ix,450p. facsims. £75. ISBN: 0906795818.

7,670 entries arranged chronologically in each section and including articles as well as books. Sections: A. Bibliographies - B. Nature in general - C. Plants - D. Animals - E. The human body - F. Artist biographies - G. Periodicals. Appendices: Books on colour; Organizations. Title, subject, and name indexes. For research libraries. *Class No:* 581.1(084.1)

Histories

[2549]

COATS, A.M. The Quest for plants: a history of the horticultural explorers. London, Studio Vista, 1969. 400p. ISBN: 0289239852.

10 chapters, geographically arranged (The Mediterranean and Near East ... South America). Bibliography, p.379-85. Detailed, non-analytical index, p.386-400. 26 illus. 'This book is chiefly, although not exclusively, concerned with the exploits of professional gardeners who travelled abroad expressly for the purpose of collecting hardy horticultural plants'. (*Foreword*). *Class No:* 581.1(091)

Worldwide

[2550]

BLAKE, S.F. Geographical guide to floras of the world: an annotated list, with special reference to useful plants and common plant names. Washington, US Government Printing Office, 1942-61. (reprinted, Koeltz, 1974). (*US Dept. of Agriculture. Miscellaneous publication, no.401, 797.*) ISBN: 3874290689, v.1; 3874290603, v.2.

1. *Africa, Australia, North America, South America, and the islands of the Atlantic, Pacific and Indian Oceans.* 1942. $40. 2. *Western Europe: Finland, Sweden, Norway, Denmark, Iceland, Great Britain with Ireland, Netherlands, Belgium, Luxembourg, France, Spain, Portugal, Andorra, Monaco, Italy. San Marino and Switzerland.* 1961. $65.

Annotated bibliography based on US Dept. of Agriculture Library's subject card-catalogue of botany. Pt.1: *c.*2,597 main entries, 428 subsidiary; admits periodical articles but omits works of a popular nature and terms now only of historical value. Pt.2 (*c.*4,000 entries). *Class No:* 581.1(100)

[2551]

Flowering plants of the world. Heywood, V.H., *ed.* 2nd ed. Oxford, University Press, 1993. 336p. illus. (incl. col.), maps. $45; £19.99 (pbk). ISBN: 0195210379; 071347422x, pbk.

First published 1978.

A taxonomic review (44 contributors) of 250,000 species in 305 families of flowering plants; also data on orders. Each family is illustrated with a distribution map, diagnostic features, classification details, below family level, affinities to other families, and economic uses. *c.*200 specially commissioned illus. Short bibliography (headed 'Acknowledgments'). Pleasing layout. Of the first ed, 'Certainly a useful reference work for any library' (*New scientist*, v.80(1126), 28 October 1978, p.204). 'There is a good deal of information packed into this volume' (*Kew magazine*, v.3, November 1986, p.196). Few changes from the previous edition in this revised version. *Class No:* 581.1(100)

[2552]

—**TAKHTAJAN, A.** Floristic regions of the world. Translated from the Russian. Berkeley, Calif., Univ. of California, 1986. 522p. $75. ISBN: 0520040279.

Derived from the Russian text of 1978, uses such chorinomic categories as kingdom, regions, provinces, districts and intermediate areas. 'A remarkable compendium ... The book contains many individual insights into the origin and history of the regional floras' (*Nature*, v.328, 23 July 1987, p.304). *Class No:* 581.1(100)

[2553]

FRODIN, D.G. Guide to standard floras of the world: an annotated, geographically arranged systematic bibliography of the principal floras, enumerations, checklists and chronological atlases of different areas. Cambridge, University Press, 1984. xx, 619p. ISBN: 0521236886.

Combined a thorough analysis of floras and floristics with a geographically arranged guide to the most useful floras and checklists of vascular plants of the world (*Nature*, v.315, 2 May 1985, p.2). Systematic bibliography (999 entries) has 10 divisions (0. World floras; 1. North America; 6. Europe; 9. Melanesia and Oceania). Appendix A: Major general bibliographies; B. Abbreviations of serials cited. Geographical and author index. *Class No:* 581.1(100)

[2554]

International bibliography of vegetation maps. Küchler, A.W., *ed.* Lawrence, Univ. of Kansas Libraries, 1966-. 4v.

1. *Vegetation maps of North America.* 2nd ed. 1980. xi,324p. 2. *Vegetation maps of Europe.* 1966, vii, 584p. 3. *Vegetation maps of Union of Soviet Socialist Republics, Asia and Australia.* 1968. 359p. 4. *Africa, South America, and World maps.* 1970.

Each volume has *c.*1,500 entries for published vegetation maps. Data: date, title of map, colour, scale, legend; author of map, when and where published. *Class No:* 581.1(100)

[2555]
Vegetationsmonographien der einzelnen Grossräume. Walter, H., *ed.*
Stuttgart, Gustav-Fischer Verlag, 1965-. maps.
  1. *Vegetation von Nord und Mittelamerika;* edited by R. Knapp.
1965. 373p. 2. *Die Wälder Südamerikas;* edited K. Hueck. 1966.
122p. 2a. *Vegetationskarte von Südamerika;* edited by K. Hueck and
P. Siebert. 1972. 71p. DM48. 3. *Die Vegetation von Afrika.* edited by
R. Knapp. 1973. 626p. 4. *The Vegetation of Australia;* edited by
N.C.W. Beadle, 1980. 690p. 7. *Die Vegetation Osteuropas, Nord- und
Zentralasiens.* by H. Walter. 1974. 452p. 10. *Klimadiagramm-Karten
der einzelnen Kontinente und die ökologische Klimagliederung der Erde;*
edited by H. Walter, and others. 1975. 36p. DM98.
  Detailed survey of regional plant embryology and vegetation. V.4 is
in English. 'The most thorough, cohesive treatment of regional
vegetation available' (Harris, C.D., *ed. A geographical bibliography
for American libraries,* 1985. p.78). *Class No:* 581.1(100)

Tropics

[2556]
LÖTSCHERT, W. *and* **BEESE, G. Collins' guide to tropical plants:** a
descriptive guide to 323 ornamental and economic plants, with 274
colour photographs. King, C., *trans.* London, Collins, 1983. 256p.
col. illus. £12.95. ISBN: 0002191121.
  German original, *Pflanzen der Tropen* (BLV Verlagsgesellschaft,
1981).
  Sections: Introduction - Ornamental plants - Colour photographs
(p.81-176: 3 or more per page) - Economic plants. Glossary, p.249-
50. Index of scientific names; index of English common names. Small
format. *Class No:* 581.1(213)

Europe

[2557]
BLAMEY, M. *and* **GREY-WILSON, C. The Illustrated flora of
Britain and Northern Europe.** London, Hodder & Stoughton, 1989.
544p. illus. (incl. 446 col. pls.). £25. ISBN: 0340401702.
  A copiously illustrated handbook of *c.*2,500 flowering wild plants
from Britain and Northern Europe, comprising specially-commissioned
colour paintings to aid identification. (With up to 10 species shown per
page, a larger page-size might have been advisable, as the book is
already too bulky as a field guide). Detailed family descriptions,
preceded by helpful introduction (p.9-30)and glossary (p.31-38). Some
tree families included (p.41-59). Key to plant families (p.489-518) and
English and Latin indexes. An attractive flora aimed at the serious
amateur botanist. *Class No:* 581.1(4)

[2558]
The European garden flora: a manual for the identification of plants
cultivated in Europe, both out-of-doors and under glass. Cambridge,
University Press, 1984-. illus.,maps.
  v.1. *Pteridophyta, gymnospora, angiospermae-monocotyledons (Part
1).* (Reprinted 1990); v.2. *Monocotyledons (Part 2);* v.3-4.
Dicotyledons (Part I-II); v.5. *Dicotyledons (Part III)* (1997. £95;
$155).
  A major work sponsored by the Royal Botanic Garden, Edinburgh,
the Royal Horticultural Society and the Stanley Smith Horticultural
Trust, Cambridge. 'Attempts to provide a scientifically accurate and
up-to-date means for the identification of plants cultivated for amenity
in Europe, and to provide what are correctly thought to be their current
names' (*Introduction*). A sixth volume will complete the set. For all
libraries serving botanists and horticulturists. *Class No:* 581.1(4)

[2559]
**FITTER, A. New generation guide to the wild flowers of Britain and
Northern Europe.** Austin, Texas, Univ. of Texas Press, 1987. 320p.
col. illus., tables. $16.95. ISBN: 029275535x.
  New ed. of *The wild flowers of Britain and Northern Europe* (1974).
3 sections: 1. The evolution of flowering plants - 2. The directory of
species - 3. The natural history of wild flowers. Section 1 gives an
analysis of structure and anatomy. The directory has detailed
descriptions and over 1,000 coloured illus. of all but the rarest species
in the area, - over 1,400 wild flowers. Also details of status,
conditions, locations, habitat, times and methods of germination,
range, flowering, pollination and breeding. Final section, - on each
stage in the life of the wild flower. Appendix of scarce species. Index,
p.308-20. *Class No:* 581.1(4)

[2560]
Flora europaea. Tutin, T., *and others.* Cambridge, University Press,
1964-. 6v. illus., maps.
  1. *Psilotaceae to Platanaceae.* 1992. 2nd ed. 530p. £100. 2.
Rosaceae to Umbelliferae. 1968. xxvii, 454p. 3. *Dispensiceae to
Myoporaceae.* 1972. xxix, 370p. 4. *Plantaginaceae to Compositae
(and Rubiacead).* 1976. xxix, 505p. 5. *Alismataceae to Orchidaceae.*
1980, xxxviii, 452p., *Checklist and chromosome index.* 1982. 440p.
Consolidated index. 1982. 212p.
  The first complete flora of Europe. The project is sponsored by the
Linnean Society of London and is based on studies in herbaria and in

....(contd.)
the field. Systematic descriptions of all flowering plants and ferns in
Europe and intended primarily for professional botanists. Handsomely
produced. The 2nd ed. of v.1 revises the descriptions and updates the
first 79 families, incorporating many taxa new to Europe.
Class No: 581.1(4)

[2561]
—**POLUNIN, O. Flowers of Europe: a field guide.** London, etc. Oxford,
University Press, 1969. xii, 662p. illus. (incl. col. pl.).
  Describes 2,600 wild flowers growing in Europe. Description of
species, p.38-585, is followed by 192p. of coloured illus (1,926 in all).
Glossary, p.8-22, with marginal line-drawings, and keys to families
precede. Bibliography (p.586-91) of regional and country floras.
English and Latin indexes. Should appeal at several levels, although
bulky for the rucksack or pocket. *Class No:* 581.1(4)

[2562]
—**POLUNIN, O.** *and* **WALTERS, M. A Guide to the vegetation of
Britain and Europe.** Oxford, University Press, 1985. [ix], 238p. illus.
(incl. col.), maps. £25. ISBN: 0192177133.
  Has 3 parts: 1. General introduction; 2. Plant communities of
Europe; 3. The National Parks and nature reserves of Europe. Selected
bibliography, p.215-8, glossary of terms, p.219-23. Indexes of Latin
and English names of illustrated types; index to plant communities of
Europe. 170 col. plates of over 1,000 plants; 280 line-drawings.
Claims 'to be the first attempt to bring together all the information on
the subject at a layman's level' (*Preface*). The authors 'have struck the
right balance between the superficial and the overly learned' (*Nature,*
v.318, 14 November 1985, p.123). *Class No:* 581.1(4)

[2563]
POLUNIN, O. *and* **SMYTHIES, B.E. Flowers of South-west Europe:**
a field guide. Oxford, University Press, 1973. xv, 480p. £12.95.
ISBN: 0192881787.
  3 chapters: 1. Landform, climate and vegetation - 2. The plant-
hunting region (23, Algarve ... Camargue). National parks, nature
reserves and national walks - 3. The identification of species, p.167-
413. Bibliography, p.476-80 (7 groups). Index of popular names.
Index of place names. 64p. of colour plates. Index of plants. 21 terrain
colour plates; 12 maps. Indebtedness to *Flora Europaea* is
acknowledged. *Class No:* 581.1(4)

[2564]
SELL, P. *and* **MURRELL, G. Flora of Great Britain and Ireland.**
Cambridge, University Press, 1996. xxix,410p. figs.
  Projected set of five volumes, with v.5, *Butomaceae-orchidaceae*
(440p. 1996. £60) published first. 'The aim of our flora is to supply
full descriptions of all the species in Stace's *New flora of the British
Isles* (*q.v.*), to include all large apomictic genera and many infra-
specific variants, and to add more information about hybrids'
(*Introduction*). V.5 includes: New taxa and combinations; Glossary;
Index. When complete, this will be a major work. *Class No:* 581.1(4)

Great Britain

[2565]
Atlas of the British flora. Perring, F.H. *and* Walters, S.M., *eds.* 3rd
ed. [S.l.], Botanical Society of the British Isles, 1982 (reprinted 1990).
xxiii,444p. £23.50. ISBN: 0901158194.
  First published 1962.
  Distribution maps (4 per page): Pteridophyta; Gymnospermae;
Angiospermae (dicotyledones; monocotyledones), p.1-406. 3
appendices 1. List of aggregate and provisional maps; 2. Vice-county
records omitted from the maps. The introduction includes a history of
mapping of plant distribution. Bibliography, p.425. Index (tiny print),
p.435-42. *Class No:* 581.1(410)

[2566]
—**Critical supplement to the Atlas of the British flora.** Perring, F.H. *and*
Sell, P.D., *eds.* EP Publishing, Ltd., 1976. [viii], 159p.
  Has distribution maps of 500 flowering plants and ferns, plus
explanatory text. Appendix: Key to herbarium abbreviations.
Bibliography, p.154-5. Index (in tiny print), p.156-9.
Class No: 581.1(410)

[2567]
BENTHAM, G. Handbook of the British flora: a description of the
flowering plant and ferns indigenous to or naturalized in the British
Isles. Hooker, Sir J.D., *rev.* 7th ed., revised by A.B. Rendle.
Ashford, Kent, Reeve, 1924. 606p.
  A descriptive flora, with keys and distributional ranges. The
introduction includes explanations of growth, morphology of
structures, notes on classification, herbaria techniques, a glossary and
key to the families. Bentham's *Handbook,* replaced by Clapham, Tutin
and Warburg's *Flora of the British Isles* (qv), will nevertheless remain
for many years the familiar work for the amateur botanist.
Class No: 581.1(410)

[2568]

Bibliography of key works for the identification of the British fauna and flora. Kerrich, G.J., *and others, eds.* 3rd ed. London, Systematics Association, c/o British Museum (Natural History), 1967. vii, 186p. *Class No:* 581.1(410)

[2569]

—KENT, D.H. 'Floras great and small'. In *Natural history book reviews*, v.5(1/2), p.3-15.

Concerns regional and local floras in the British Isles (and Ireland), 1964-80. A valuable running commentary that pays tribute to *Flora europaea*. *Class No:* 581.1(410)

[2570]

British plant communities. Rodwell, J.S., *and others, eds.* Cambridge, University Press, 1991-. ISBN: 0521235588, v.1.

V.1. *Woodlands and scrub.* 1991. x,395p. £70;£27.95. V.2. *Mires and heaths.* 1991. £95;£29.95. V.3. *Grasslands and montane vegetation.* 1992. £105;£29.95. V.4. *Aquatic communities, swamps and tall-herb fens.* 1995. £24.95. V.5. *Maritime and weed communities and vegetation of open habitats.* Due to be published in 1999. £95.

A projected set of 5 volumes, which aims to describe over 250 plant communities in Great Britain (excluding Northern Ireland). V.1 contains an introduction, a key, and 25 community descriptions. Each community description contains data on synonymy, constant species, physiognomy, sub-communities, habitat, zonation and succession, distribution, affinities, floristic tables, and distribution maps. Index of synonyms to woodlands and scrubs, p.369-76. Index of species in woodlands and scrub, p.377-84. Bibliography, p.385-95. Culmination of 15 years' detailed survey and analysis of British vegetation by those involved in the National Vegetation Classification. *Class No:* 581.1(410)

[2571]

—TANSLEY, A.G. The British islands and their vegetation. Cambridge, University Press, 1939 (reprinted, with corrections, 1949). 2v. illus. (pl.), diagrs.

Parts: 1. The British Isles as environment of vegetation - 2. History and existing distribution of vegetation - 3. The nature of classification of vegetation - 4. The woodlands - 5. The grasslands - 6. Hydroseres - 7. Heath and moor - 8. Mountain vegetation - 9. Maritime and submarine vegetation. Each volume has 163 plates, 179 figures. Chapter-end references. Index in v.2. *Class No:* 581.1(410)

[2572]

Flora of the British Isles. Clapham, A.R., *and others.* 3rd ed. Cambridge, University Press, 1987. ISBN: 0521309859.

First published 1952; 2nd ed., 1962.

Main sections: Pteridophyta - Gymnospermae - Angiospermae (Dicotyledons. Monocotyledons). Data on habit; whether native/introduced; ecology; geographical distribution; evolutionary history; agricultural significance, etc. Bibliography, p.633. Notes on families and life forms. 'Likely to be the standard British flora well into the next century' (*Nature*, v.328, 27 August, p.772). *Class No:* 581.1(410)

[2573]

—Flora of the British Isles: illustrations. Drawings by S.I. Roles. Clapham, A.R., *and others.* Cambridge Univ. Press, 1957-65. 4v. illus. ea.£11.95.

Follows the sequence and nomenclature of the parent work. 1,910 black-and-white drawings. *Class No:* 581.1(410)

[2574]

GODWIN, Sir H. The History of the British flora: a factual basis for phytogeography. 2nd ed. Cambridge, University Press, 1975. x, 541p. illus., graphs, tables, maps.

First published 1956.

7 sections: 1. Introduction - 2. Collection and identification of plant remains - 3. The background scale of Pleistocene events - 4. Recorded sites - 5. The plant record - 6. Pattern of change in the British flora - 7. Conclusion. Bibliography, p.503-21 (A-Z authors). Analytical index. *Class No:* 581.1(410)

[2575]

MABEY, R. Flora Britannica. London, Sinclair-Stevenson, 1996. 480p. illus.(col.). £25. ISBN: 1856193772.

Covers 1,000 species by family. Examines the popular culture of plants, their history, and uses. 10 sections: Introduction - Churches and churchyards ... Spring festivals - Wild foods ... Urban commons - Plant medicine - Meadows. A list of Scottish vernacular plant names follows. Source notes, p.456-67. Index of places. General index. *c.*500 colour photographs. For public, academic, and personal libraries. *Class No:* 581.1(410)

[2576]

PERRING, F. *and* WALTERS, M. The Macmillan field guide to British wildflowers. London, Macmillan, 1989. xxx,226p. col. illus. £9.95. ISBN: 0333445228.

3 sections: 1. General identification keys - 2. Special identification keys - 3. Flower species, p.1-221. 750 coloured illustrations accompanied by textual information. Index. Although not claiming to be comprehensive - it omits trees, shrubs and the more rare wildflowers - this is a useful guide. A flexible hard-wearing cover would have added to its value. *Class No:* 581.1(410)

[2577]

—McCLINTOCK, D. *and* FITTER, R.S.R. The Pocket guide to wild flowers. London, Collins, 1956. xii, 340p. illus.

Main purpose is to enable anyone to name any wild flower, grass, sedge, tree or shrub that he or she is likely to see in the British Isles. 112 plates (64 in colour and arranged in colour sequence, blue ... yellow). Glossary. Indexes to English and Latin names 'One of the most successful attempts made in recent years to put down our Flora inside a single manageable volume'. (*Journal of the Royal Horticultural Society*, v.85(8), August 1960, p.375). *Class No:* 581.1(410)

[2578]

—McCLINTOCK, D. Supplement to 'The Pocket guide to wild flowers'. Platt, Kent, D. McClintock, [1959]. ix, 89p.

Describes 450 further species. The *Supplement* also adds a long list of hybrids not recorded in the parent work; a valuable list of albinos, a bibliography and a list of county floras and checklists. *Class No:* 581.1(410)

[2579]

ROSS-CRAIG, S. Drawings of British plants; being illustrations of species of flowering plants growing naturally in the British Isles. London, Bell, 1964-74. 31pts. and index (pts.1-9 in 3v.; pts.10-23).

Systematic arrangement (*e.g.* pts.8-9: Rosaceae; 15-18: Compositae), giving brief description of the plant and its common name. Partly replaces Fitch and Smith's *Illustrations of the British flora* and R.W. Butcher's *Further illustrations of British plants* (1930). The drawings (*c.*30 plates per part) of inflorescence, the plant's constituent parts and its general habit are of a high standard, and the reproductions are uniformly excellent. *Class No:* 581.1(410)

[2580]

SIMPSON, N.D. A Bibliographical index of the British flora, including floras, herbals, periodicals, societies and references relating to the identification, distribution and occurrences of phanerogams, vascular cryptogams and charophytes in the British Isles. Bournemouth, privately printed for the Author, 1960. xix, 429p.

More than 65,000 entries for books, articles and manuscripts relating to the British Isles (including Ireland), from the 15th century to date. Data are included on plant lore, local names, poisonous plants and weeds. A much needed bibliographical tool, even if its coverage is admittedly incomplete, its arrangement dispersive, and full pagination of periodical articles is not given. *Class No:* 581.1(410)

[2581]

STACE, C.A. New flora of the British Isles. 2nd ed. Cambridge, University Press, 1997. xxx, 1130p. illus. £28.95. ISBN: 0521589355.

First published 1991.

Contains around 3,200 keyed and number species, with 320 taxa added since the first edition. Designed to identify plants found in the wild in the British Isles. Preceding the main section are chapters designed to ensure maximum use of the book, *e.g.* 'Geographical scope'; 'Identification keys'. Many black-and-white photographs and line-drawings illustrate over half the taxa. 'Undoubtedly the standard flora for the British Isles for years to come' *Watsonia* v22(1), 1998, p.123/4.) *Class No:* 581.1(410)

Scotland

[2582]

BURNETT, J.H., *ed.* The Vegetation of Scotland. Edinburgh & London, Oliver & Boyd, 1964. xiii, 614p. illus., diagrs., tables, maps.

9 contributors. 3 pts: 1. The physical background - 2. The vegetation - 3. History and pattern of Scottish vegetation. Chapter bibliographies (*e.g.* 6. Grasslands of the forest and sub-alpine zones, p.168-215; references, p.209-15). Indexes of authors, place names and plant names; general index. Very readable, but no glossary for non-technical readers. Handsomely produced. *Class No:* 581.1(411)

Ireland

[2583]

WEBB, D.A. An Irish flora. 6th rev. ed. Dundalk, Dundalgan Press; Chester Springs, Penn., 1977. xxi, 277p. illus. $27. ISBN: 085221023x.

First published 1943.

Description of families, genera and species (p.1-233) follows the taxonomic scheme of *Flora europaea*. Prelims, including a bibliography (p.xvii-xviii) and general key to families. Glossary of technical terms. Index to Irish names; index to Latin and English names. Pocket sized; small type. *Class No:* 581.1(415)

Wales

[2584]

ELLIS, R.G. Flowering plants of Wales. Cardiff, National Museum of Wales, 1983. ix, 338p. ISBN: 0720002710.

Catalogue of Welsh flowering plants, p.41-193. Data: Latin name; Welsh name; English name; Status; Habitat; Months of flowering; Vice-county distribution; Frequency. Valuable introductory survey. Distribution maps, p.194-280. 3 appendices: 1. Key to the abbreviations of recorder's initials; 2. List of references (p.285-93); 3. World distribution of Welsh plants. Detailed and analytical index, p.296-338. An impressive production, on stout paper. Definitive. *Class No:* 581.1(429)

France

[2585]

BONNIER, G. Flore complète illustrée en couleurs de France, Suisse et Belgique. Paris, Librairie Général de l'Enseignement, n.d. 120 fascicules + Table générale. ea. fasc., FFr39; FFr62, table générale.

First published 1927.

Revised continuously since 1927. Each fascicule consists of 8 plates, with appropriate commentary. Indispensable reference tool for French libraries (Beaudiquez, M., and others. *Ouvrages de référence pour les bibliothèques publiques.* 3rd ed. 1986, item 566). *Class No:* 581.1(44)

Russia

[2586]

CZERPANOV, S.K. Vascular plants of Russia and adjacent states (the former USSR). 2nd ed. Cambridge, University Press, 1995. 516p. $100. ISBN: 0521450063.

First published as *Plantae vasculares URSS* (1981).

Nomenclature of 21,770 species and 500 subspecies in 1,945 genera and 216 families, resulting in over 50,000 epithets. 'This book is an attempt to compile a modern and to a certain extent critical list of the flora of the territory covered in *Flora URSS (q.v.)* (30v. 1934-64) as well as the results of subsequent studies, updating *Plantae vasculares URSS* (1981), this work's first edition' (*Introduction*). *Class No:* 581.1(47)

[2587]

Flora SSSR. Moscow & Leningrad, Akademiya Nauk SSSR, 1934-64. 30v. and index. illus. (pl.).

A monumental achievement: 22,000p. of text; 1,250p. of illus. Originally edited by V.L. Komarov and completed under Prof. E.G. Bobrov (*Nature,* v.205 (4,976), 13 March 1965, p.1046-49). 92 contributors.

The English translation by the Israel Program for Scientific Translations, under the sponsorship of the National Science Foundation and the Smithsonian Institution - *Flora of the USSR* - has 24v. 'A valuable source of reference for studies involving the flowering plants of the Northern Hemisphere, and especially of the Eurasian land mass' (*Aslib book list,* v.37(4), April 1972, entry 161). *Class No:* 581.1(47)

Asia

[2588]

FIELD, H. Bibliography on Southwestern Asia. Coral Gables, Florida, Univ. of Miami Press, 1953-62. Supplement, 1968-72. 8v. in 7.

V.1 ('A first compilation') - 7. ('A seventh compilation'), 1953-62, form a series of bibliographies: 47,165 titles (anthropology: 31,254; zoology: 11,505; botany: 4,406) in about 40 languages, covering some 2,500 journals as well as books. Author index. A monumental work. *Class No:* 581.1(5)

[2589]

MERRILL, E.D. and WALKER, E.H. A Bibliography of Eastern Asiatic botany. Jamaica Plain, Mass., Arnold Arboretum of Harvard Univ., 1938. xiii, 719p. Supplement 1, 1960. (Forestburgh, N.Y., Lubrecht & Cramer. $18.50). ISBN: 0934454116, supp.1.

Sponsored by the Smithsonian Institution. Arnold Arboretum, New York Botanical Garden and Harvard-Yenching Institute.

Annotated bibliography of over 21,000 items, covering the botanical literature of Japan, China, Formosa, Korea, Manchuria, Mongolia, Tibet, E. Siberia and the Far East (but not the East Indies or Pacific area). Author A-Z sequence, with subject and geographical indexes.

....(contd.)

Appended lists of Chinese and Japanese botanical works of historical interest and serials. The supplement, covering 1936-58, has 11,000 entries. *Class No:* 581.1(5)

Africa—Southern

[2590]

Flora of Southern Africa: the Republic of South Africa, Basutoland, Swaziland and South West Africa. Codd, L.E.W., *and others, eds.* Pretoria, Botanical Research Institute, 1963-.

To be completed in 50v. V.1,9,13,22 and 26 (1963-78) have at least been published (Musiker, R. *South Africa* (1979), entry 43), with v.18, pt.3, and v.33, pt.7, subsequently, in 1986 and 1983 . *Class No:* 581.1(68)

America—North

[2591]

The Audubon Society field guide to North American wildflowers. New York, Knopf, 1979.

Eastern region, by W.A. Niering and M.C. Olmstead. 863p. *Western region,* by R. Spellenberg. 1979. 862p.

Together cover North America. Both devote the first part to colour plates, arranged by colour; a detailed descriptive text forms the second part. Generic and English name indexes. *Class No:* 581.1(71+73)

[2592]

Flora of North America. Flora of North America Editorial Committee. New York, Oxford University Press, 1993-97. 3v.

V.1. *Introduction.* xxi,372p. V.2. *Pteridophytes and gymnosperms.* xiii,475p. V.3. *Magnoliophyta: Magnoliidae and hamamelidae.* 1997. xxiii,590p. illus.,maps.

V.1 has 22 contributors; v.2, 55. Essays outlining physical and biological factors affecting evolution and distribution of plant life in North America. V.1 has five sections: 2. Vegetation and climates of the past ... 5. Classifications and classification systems. V.3 has 15 sections: Magnoliales ... Ranunculales ... Juglandales ... Casuarinales. Each volume includes a lengthy 'Literature cited' section (p.542-70 in v.3) and an index. Many drawings, figures, and maps. 'Will rank as one of the great Floras of the world' (*Watsonia,* v22 (1) 1998, p.124/5). *Class No:* 581.1(71+73)

[2593]

SHETLER, S.G. and SKOG, L.E. A Provisional checklist of species for Flora North America. St. Louis, Missouri, Missouri Botanical Garden, for Man and Biosphere, Flora North America, 1978. xix, 199p. (*Monographs in systematic botany from the Missouri Botanical Garden, v.1.*)

Revision *Flora North America Report 64.*

Revised checklist of 16,274 species, 2,350 genera and 233 families, and a further step towards a Flora North America. Geographical coverage: USA, Canada and Greenland. In taxonomic order. Data include plant characteristics, geographical region of sources of species entry. *Class No:* 581.1(71+73)

USA

[2594]

RICKETT, H.W. Wild flowers of the United States. New York, McGraw-Hill, 1966-75. 6v. and index. illus. (pl.), maps. ISBN: 0893272744, v.1; 0893272779, v.2; 0893272809, v.4; 0893272841, v.5; 0893272876, v.6.

Publication of the New York Botanical Garden.

1. *The Northeastern states.* 1966. $65. 2pts. 2. *The Southeastern states.* 1967. $85. 2pts. 3. *Texas.* 1969. 2pts. 4. *The Southwestern states.* 1970. 2pts. $92. 5. *The Northwestern states.* 1972. $85. 6. *The Central mountains and plains.* 1973. $92. 3pts. *Complete index.* 1975.

V.1 (2pts. 559p.) has 180 plates, with concise systematic description, plus distribution, facing. End-paper maps. Each volume carries an index. *Class No:* 581.1(73)

[2595]

TORREY BOTANICAL CLUB. New York, *comp.* **Index to American botanical literature.** Boston, Mass., G.K. Hall, 1968. 4v. Supplements, 1977-.

The main *index* has entries for *c.*106,000 author catalogue cards, photolithographically reproduced. It covers the period 1886-1966. The first *supplement* (1977) covers 1967-76. Further supplements are planned to be ten-yearly. *Class No:* 581.1(73)

America—South

[2596]

'Bibliografia botanica para América Latina'. In *Boletín de la Sociedad Argentina Botanica,* v.17, 1976, p.368-83. *Class No:* 581.1(8)

New Zealand

[2597]

Flora of New Zealand. Wellington, Whenua Press, 1961-88. 4v. illus., maps. ISBN: 0477010563, v.1; 0477013538, v.2; 0477010415, v.3; 0477025293, v.4.

V.1 (liv, 1085p.) gives systematic descriptions of indigenous vascular plants (ferns and their allies, conifers and the dicotyledonous flowering plants), except monocotyledons. Glossary, p.977-97. Maori names of plants, p.998-1007. Bibliography, p.xiii-xxxiv. Maps and end-papers only. 'An indispensable tool' (*Nature*, v.192, 23 December 1961, p.1108). *Class No:* 581.1(931)

[2598]

WARDLE, D. Vegetation of New Zealand. Cambridge, University Press, 1991. 672p. illus., diagrs., graphs, tables, maps. £105. ISBN: 0521258731.

16 chapters: 1. The physical and biological environment ... 3. Plant form in relation to habitat ... 5. Description, nomenclature and classification of vegetation, environment and ecological processes ... 9. Grassland and heathfield ... 14. Biomass: growth, nutrition and tolerance ... 16. Disturbances, regeneration and trends in native forest. 2 appendices (2. Common names and Latin equivalents). References, p.615-36. Index of plant genera and species. General index. *Class No:* 581.1(931)

Australia

[2599]

BURBIDGE, N.T. Dictionary of Australian plant names: gymnosperms and angiosperms. Sydney, Angus & Robertson, 1963. xviii, [2], 345p. maps.

About 45,000 entries. Data under each accepted name: citation (author; place of publication), synonymy, family or families; phytogeographic details; bibliographical references. Many cross-references; italicized names are synonyms and homonyms. Genera, arranged under families, p.315-45. Genera asterisked in both gymnosperms and angiosperms are naturalized aliens. *Class No:* 581.1(94)

[2600]

Flora of Australia. Canberra, CSIRO/Australian Biological Resources Study, 1981-. Pagination varies, illus.(some col.). Price varies. ISBN: 0642066523.

V.1. *Introduction*. 1981. V.3. *Hamamelidales to Casuarinales*. 1989. V.4. *Phytolaccaceae to Chenopodiaceae*. 1984. V.8. *Lecythidales to Batales*. 1982. V.12. *Mimosaceae (excluding Acacia), Caesalpiniaceae*. 1998. V.16. *Elaeagnaceae, Protoeaceae 1*. 1995. V.17B. *Proteaceae 3: Hakea to Dryandra*. 1994. V.18. *Podostemaceae to Combretaceae*. 1990. V.19. *Myrtaceae-Eucalyptus, Angophora*. 1988. V.22. *Rhizopharales to Celastrales*. 1984. V.25. *Melianthaceae to Simaraoubaceae*. 1985. V.28. *Gentianales*. 1996. V.29. *Solanaceae*. 1982. V.35. *Brunoniaceae, Goodeniaceae*. 1992. V.45. *Hydatellaceae to Liliaceae*. 1987. V.46. *Iridaceae to Dioscoraceae*. 1986. V.48. *Ferns, gymnosperms and allied groups*. 1998. V.49. *Oceanic Island 1*. 1994. V.50 *Oceanic Islands 2*. 1993. V.54. *Lichens - Introduction, Lecanorales 1*. 1992. V.55. *Lichens - Lecanorales 2, Parmaeliaceae*. 1994.

Number of volumes to be published appears not yet finalized but it could be *c*.60v. when complete. Vol.1 comprises introduction to series, key to flowering plant families, and glossary. Vol.2-48 intend to cover 20,000 vascular plant species, 49-50 flora of a number of Australian islands, including sub-Antarctic areas, 51-53 bryophytes, 54-58 lichens. Includes keys for identification, detailed descriptions, notes, illustrations, distribution maps, and bibliographical references. 'Algae and fungi are expected to require another 20-30 volumes in this massive flora' (Davis, E.B. and Schmidt, D. *Guide to information sources in the botanical sciences*, 2nd edition, 1996, p.147).

Flora of Australia supplementary series, published irregularly by ABRS, is made up of bibliographic, monographic, nomenclatural and compendium works which have been the basic references for the research carried out for the main series. *Class No:* 581.1(94)

[2601]

HARRIS, T.Y. Wild flowers of Australia. 8th ed. London, Sydney, etc., Angus & Robertson, 1979. xiii, 207p. illus. (*Australian natural science library*.) ISBN: 0207136440.

First published 1938.

Part 1: Popular descriptions, with plates. Part 2: Key to the families of plants. Technical descriptions of plants, p.76-184. Glossary of botanical terms, p.185-94. Books of reference (24 titles). Names of authors and abbreviations. Analytical index, p.198-207. Descriptions face illus. A standard guide. *Class No:* 581.1(94)

Micronesia

[2602]

SACHET, M.H. *and* **FOSBERG, F.R. Island bibliographies: Micronesian botany.** Land environment and ecology of coral atolls. Vegetation of tropical Pacific islands. Compiled under the auspices of the Pacific Science Board. Washington, National Academy of Sciences, National Research Council, 1955. v, 577p. Supplement. 1971. 427p. *Class No:* 581.1(965)

Physiology

[2603]

Annual review of plant physiology and plant molecular biology. Palo Alto, Calif., Annual Reviews, Inc., 1950-. V.1-. Annual. $120 (US); $130 (non US). ISSN: 10402519.

Published as *Annual review of plant physiology*, 1950-1989.

V.49, 1998 (750p.) has 29 documented chapters (*e.g.* 'Genetic analysis of ovule development'; 'Meiotc chromosome organization and segregation in plants'; 'Genes and enzymes of carotenoid biosynthesis in plants'). Author and subject indexes. Cumulative index of contributing authors, v.41-49; Cumulative index of chapter titles, v.41-49. Prelims. include 'Related articles of interest to readers'. Abstracts of papers available online 3 months before publication date at http://www.AnnualReviews.org. *Class No:* 581.10

[2604]

Encyclopedia of plant physiology. Pirson, A. *and* Zimmermann, M., *eds*. New series. Cambridge, Heffer, 1975-93.

Continues old series, (*Handbuch der Pflanzenphysiologie* (in 3 pts: 1. General foundations (2v.) - 2. Metabolism (v.3-13) - 3. Growth, development, movements (v.14-18)).

The new monograph series is in English. 1-3. *Transport in plants*. 1975-76. 4. *Physiological plant pathology*. 1975. 5-6. *Photosynthesis*. [I-II]. 1977. 7. *Physiology of movements*. 1979. 8. *Secondary plant products*. 1980. 9/11. *Hormonal regulation of development*. 1980-85. 12. A-D. *Physiological plant ecology*. 1981-83. 13. A,B. *Plant carbohydrates*. 1981-82. 14. A,B *Nucleic acids*. 1982. 15.A. *Inorganic plant nutrition*. 1983. 16. A,B. *Photomorphogenesis*. 1983. 17. *Cellular interactions*. 1984. 18. *Higher plant cell respiration*. 1985. 19. *Photosynthesis*. III. 1986. 20. *General index*. 1993. *Class No:* 581.10

[2605]

SALISBURY, F.B. Units, symbols, and terminology for plant physiology: a reference for presentation of research results in the plant sciences. Oxford, University Press, 1996. x, 234p. £24.95. ISBN: 019509445x.

27 contributors. Four sections (18 chapters): 1. The basics - 2. Plant biophysics - 3. Plant biochemistry and molecular biology - 4. Plant growth and development. Three appendices on 'Presenting scientific data'. Index, p.217-34. 'Presents a handy guide to preferred terminology ... in the plant sciences' (*Introduction*). *Class No:* 581.10

Carnivorous Plants

[2606]

LECOUFLE, M. Comment choisir et cultiver vos plantes carnivores. [Carnivorous plants: care and cultivation.] London, Blandford, 1990. 144p. illus. (col.). £18.99; £8.95. ISBN: 0713721855.

3 sections: 1. General principles - 2. Traps and flowers - 3. Principal species in cultivation, p.50-142. Data for each species include etymology; habitat; description; reproduction; pests and diseases; related species; prey. Glossary. Brief bibliography. List of carnivorous plant societies. Many colour illustrations. *Class No:* 581.13

[2607]

TEMPLE, P. Carnivorous plants. 2nd ed. London, Cassell for the Royal Horticultural Society, 1993. 64p. illus. (col.). (*A Wisley handbook*.) ISBN: 0304320641.

Popular, well-illustrated, guide to the identification and cultivation of carnivorous plants, aimed at beginners. Concentrates on the more easily obtainable species, *e.g.* pitcher plants, Venus fly trap etc. *Class No:* 581.13

Diseases

[2608]

Annual review of phytopathology. Palo Alto, Calif., Annual Reviews, Inc., 1963-. v.1-. Annual. $124 (US); $134 (non US). ISSN: 00664286.

V.36, 1998 (500p.) contains 21 documented papers (*e.g.* 'Current concepts of active defense in plants'; 'Application of mating type gene technology to problems in fungal biology'; 'Satellite tobacco mosaic virus'). Subject index. Contributing authors, v.27-36; chapter titles, v.27-36. Prelims. include 'Some related articles in other *Annual reviews*'. Abstracts of papers available online 3 months before publication date at http://www.AnnualReviews.org. *Class No:* 581.2

[2609]

BUCZACKI, S.T. *and* **HARRIS, K.M. Collins' guide to the pests, diseases and disorders of garden plants.** London, Collins, 1981. 512p. illus., (incl. col.). ISBN: 0002191032.

General introduction - A/Z key to symptoms - 24 col. plates (captions facing) - Pests (eelworms ... mammals), p.132-264 - Diseases (rusts ... viruses), p.267-471. - Disorders (mineral nutrient; non-nutritional disorders (*e.g.* drought; pollution)). Data: symptoms; biology; treatment. Grouped bibliography, p.493-5. Glossary. Index, p.500-12. 'Highly practical, authoritative and free from waffle' (*Natural history book reviews*, v.6 (1/2), 1982, p.78).

Shorter guide to pests, diseases and disorders of garden plants (Collins, 1983. 320p. illus (incl. col.)) is by K.M. Harris, and others. *Class No:* 581.2

[2610]

Glossary of plant-pathological terms. Shurtleff, M.C. *and* Averre, C.W., *eds.* St. Paul, Minn., APS Press, 1997. iv,361p. $58. ISBN: 0890541760.

*c.*7,000 concise entries, although there are some longer discussions of topics. Cross-references. Excludes plant diseases. Clearly laid out and easy to use. For academic libraries. *Class No:* 581.2

[2611]

HOLLIDAY, P. A Dictionary of plant pathology. 2nd ed. Cambridge, University Press, 1998. xxiv,536p. £85. ISBN: 0521594537.

First published 1989 and reprinted with corrections in 1990.

Contains over 11,000 entries (3,000 more than in the previous ed.). Lists authoritative names of pathogens (including fungi from over 500 genera, 800 viruses, mollicutes, bacteria, nematodes and viroids) with brief descriptions and bibliographic references. Entries also include references and notes on plant pathologists, names of diseases (now also included under the relevant crop), crops and their pathology, terminology, names of disorders, taxonomic groups, fungicide names, vectors of viruses and toxins. Of the previous ed., 'An excellent dictionary with a wealth of bibliographic information' (*Science and technology libraries*, v.10(4) Summer 1990, p.120). *Class No:* 581.2

[2612]

PIRONE, P.P. Diseases and pests of ornamental plants. 5th ed. New York, etc., Wiley; Interscience, 1978. 566p. illus., diagrs. $55. ISBN: 0471072494.

First published 1943.

2 parts: 1. Diseases and pests in general, p.3-102, including selected bibliography. 2. Diseases and pests of particular hosts, arranged A-Z by botanical names of host plants. Involves nearly 500 genera of ornamental and commonly grown plants (*e.g.* Prunus persica: 2 columns on symptoms of disease and control by fungicides, pesticides, etc.). *Class No:* 581.2

Embryology

[2613]

DARLINGTON, C.D. *and* **WYLIE, A.D. Chromosome atlas of flowering plants.** 2nd ed., rev. and expanded. London, Allen & Unwin, 1955. xix, 519p.

First published 1945.

The 1st ed. dealt with cultivated plants only. The 2nd ed. includes other flowering plants and covers more than 15,000 species. For each species: the somatic number of the chromosomes; the authority who made the count; use made of the plant; and its distribution. Appended exhaustive bibliography, p.459-500. *Class No:* 581.3

[2614]

A History of embryology. The eighth symposium of the British Society for Developmental Biology, Nottingham, 1983. Horder, T.J., *and others.* Cambridge, University Press, 1986. xxiv, 477p. diagrs. ISBN: 0521259533.

15 documented papers, including 'Embryology and classical zoology in Great Britain'; 'Hans Spemann and the organiser'; 'Primary embryonic induction in retrospect'; 'Regeneration and holism in biology'. Chronological outline precedes, p.xviii-xxiv. Very useful 'References to resources relating to the history of embryology', p.435-62. Index, p.463-77. *Class No:* 581.3

Spores

[2615]

KREMP, G.O.W. Morphologic encyclopedia of palynology and illustrations of spore and pollen. Tucson, Univ. of Arizona Press, 1965. xiii, 186p. illus. (pl.).

1,280 terms relating to spores and pollen are explained; definitions are quoted from original sources and over 800 are illustrated. Very thorough, although it does not attempt to weed out incorrect definitions (*Nature*, v.209, 12 February 1966, p.651). *Class No:* 581.33

Anatomy

[2616]

Handbuch der Pflanzenanatomie. Begründet von K. Linsbauer. Fortgeführt von G. Tischler und A. Paschler. [Encyclopedia of plant anatomy.] 2. völlig neubearb. Aufl., hrsg von W. Zimmermann, P.G. Ozenda. Berlin, Borntraeger, 1934-. (v.14(1): *Leaf structure of a Venezuelan cloud forest in relation to the microclimate*. 1990. xi,244p. DM148). illus.

First published 1922- (not completed by 1943).

An extensively documented treatise on plant anatomy (*e.g.* v.2, *Allgemeine Pflanzenkaryologie. Erganzunsband* (1953-63. ix, 1227p.) has a massive list of references, p.776-1121). V.8(5), *Die primäre Bau der Angiospermenwurzel* (1968. viii, 472p.) has 372 text illus., bibliography (A-Z authors, p.410-39), and author subject indexes. Contributions are in English or German. *Class No:* 581.4

Seeds

[2617]

MARTIN, A.C. *and* **BARKLEY, W.D. Seed identification manual.** Berkeley & Los Angeles, Univ. of California Press, 1961. (reprinted 1973). [vii], 221p. illus.

824 seed photographs (farmlands; wetlands; woodlands), p.7-122, followed by 'Identification clues' (systematically arranged; 287 figures). Selected bibliography (largely US), p.207-9. Index, p.211-2. *Class No:* 581.48

[2618]

—**BARTON, L.V. Bibliography of seeds.** New York & London, Columbia Univ. Press, 1967. [v], 858p. $121.50. ISBN: 0231029373.

Comprises 20,163 references to published literature, under authors A/Z. Plant index, p.706-816; subject index, p.817-58 (usually analytical, but the entry at 'Viability' has *c.*700 unspecified references). Based on the file at the Boyce Thompson Institute for Plant Research, Yonkers, N.Y. *Class No:* 581.48

[2619]

Seed abstracts. Wallingford, Oxon., CAB International, 1978-. 12pa. £225; $395. ISSN: 01410180.

About 4,200 abstracts pa. Sections include: Seed morphology and anatomy; Seed chemistry; Germination; Seed production; Pests and diseases; Breeding and selection; Seed assessment and testing; Miscellaneous. Reports; Conferences; Books. Author and subject indexes per issue and annually. Cross-reference to other abstract journals published by CAB International. Online, CAB ABSTRACTS and available on CAB ABSTRACTS CD-ROM. Also available on the Internet via HORT CABWeb (http://hort.cabweb.org). *Class No:* 581.48

Ecology

[2620]

Comparative plant ecology: a functional approach to common British species. Grime, J.P., *and others.* London, Unwin Hyman, 1988. ix,742p. diagrs., graphs. £85. ISBN: 0045810281.

Provides standardized Antecological Accounts of the biology and ecology of common vascular plants of the British flora. Gives data sources; contents; interpretation and use. Antecological Accounts, p.53-615. Tables of attributes. Summary and conclusions. Appendix: Patterns of specialization (*e.g.* 'Statistical rationale'; 'Clustering policy'). References, p.670-98. Analytical subject, author and species (generic, binomial and vernacular) indexes. *Class No:* 581.5

Economic Aspects

[2621]

Applied botany abstracts. Lucknow, India, Economic Botany Information Service, National Botanical Research Institute, 1981-. 4pa. $150. ISSN: 09702377.

Formerly *Current literature in plant science.*

About 800 abstracts per issue. 8 sections: 1. Non-traditional/under-utilized plants - 2. Biomass/energy plants (*e.g.* fuel crops) - 3. Ornamental plants - 4. Plants and environmental pollution - 5. Traditional herbal drugs - 6. Ethnobotany - 7. Rare/endangered/threatened plants - 8. Other economic plants. New publications (books and periodicals). Key word index; author index. List of journals consulted (*c.*300). *Class No:* 581.6

[2622]

LEWINGTON, A. Plants for people. London, Natural History Museum, 1990. vii,232p. col. illus. £19.95. ISBN: 0565010948.

Gives an insight into the ways in which plants are used. 7 sections: 1. Starting the day ... 3. From first foods to fast foods ... 6. Getting around - plants that transport us - 7. Recreation - plants that entertain us. Index. No bibliography. A popular treatment, attractively presented, with many colour illustrations. For school and public libraries. *Class No:* 581.6

[2623]

MERINO-RODRIGUEZ, M. Plants and plant products of economic importance: vocabulary - Latinus, English, Français, Español. Deutsch. Rome, Food and Agriculture Organization, 1974. (*FAO Terminology bulletin 25.*) *Class No:* 581.6

[2624]

Phytochemical dictionary: a handbook of bioactive compounds from plants. Harborne, J.B., *and others, eds.* 2nd ed. London, Taylor and Francis, 1999. 976p. diagrams. £250. ISBN: 0748406204.
First published 1993.
3,000 natural substances from plants described in 60 chapters grouped in five parts: 1. Carbohydrates and lipids - 2. Nitrogen-containing compounds - 3. Alkaloids - 4. Phenolics - 5. Terpenoids. References precede group entries. Subject and species indexes, p.893-976. *Class No:* 581.6

[2625]

Plants for food and medicine: proceedings of the joint conference of the Society for Economic Botany and the International Society for Ethnopharmacology, London, 1-6 July 1996. Prendergast, H.D.V., *ed.* Kew, Royal Botanic Garden, 1998. ix, 438p., illus. £24. ISBN: 1900347555.
30 papers by divers hands in three un-numbered sections: 'Food, medicine and health', 'Cross-cultural plant exchange', 'Botany - what's in it for drylands development'. Index of plants, p.389-402. Subject index, p.403-38. For the subject specialist. *Class No:* 581.6

[2626]

TANAKA, T. Tanaka's cyclopedia of edible plants of the world. Nakao, S., *ed.* Tokyo, Keigaku Publishing Co., 1976. [ix], 924p.
Lists more than 10,000 edible plants, giving bibliographical source and date (*e.g.* 'Uphof 1968'). Bibliography (authors, A-Z, p.791-80). Detailed index, p.803-924. 'The real aim of the book is to save the peoples of the world' (*Preface*). *Class No:* 581.6

[2627]

UPHOF, J.C.T. The Dictionary of economic plants. 2nd ed. Lehre, Cramer, and New York, Stechert-Hafner, 1968. [viii], 591p. $49. ISBN: 3768200019.
First published 1959.
The 2nd. ed. adds over 3,000 species, bringing total different species of economic plants briefly described to 9,500. Entry is under Latin name, with reference from common name. Data on geographical distribution, products and principal uses. Bibliography, systematically arranged, p.453-91. Helpful group references (*e.g.* from 'Confectionery, Plants used in'). A valued reference tool. *Class No:* 581.6

[2628]

—HOWES, F.N. A Dictionary of useful and everyday plants and their common names. Cambridge Univ. Press, 1974. [x], 290p. ISBN: 0521085209.
Contains *c.*8,000 entries. 'Some useful reference works', p.289-86. No index. Based on material contained in J.C. Willis's *A dictionary of the flowering plants and ferns* (6th ed. 1931) (*q.v.*). *Class No:* 581.6

[2629]

—Popular encyclopedia of plants. Heywood, V.H. *and* Chant, S.R., *eds.* Cambridge, University Press, 1982. 368p. col. illus. ISBN: 0521246113.
Has a misleading title. It concerns plants and plant products useful to human beings. 2,200 entries, A-Z under Latin and common names, provide data on natural distribution, habit, usefulness, etc. Glossary of technical terms. 773 colour illus., adjacent to the pertinent text. *Class No:* 581.6

[2630]

—USHER, G. A Dictionary of plants used by man. London, Constable, 1974. 619p. ISBN: 0094579202.
Comparable in scope to Uphof. Main entries are under genera. While Usher is fuller than Uphof in providing cross-references from common names, Uphof is richer in local names and plants and their uses (*e.g.* by North American Indians). *Class No:* 581.6

[2631]

VAUGHAN, J.G. *and* GEISSLER, C. The New Oxford book of food plants. Oxford, Univiversity Press, 1997. xx,239p. illus.(col.), tables. £25. ISBN: 0198548257.
First published in 1969 as *The Oxford book of food plants*.
19 sections: Grain crops ... Fruits ... Herbs ... Seaweeds ... World food plants. Full-page colour illustration of each crop in its various forms accompanies the text. Two additional sections on nutrition and health and nutrition tables. Recommended reading, p.227-28. Index of plant names and subject index. For all those interested in the nutritional role of food plants. 'A much updated, expanded and reworked version ... an indispensible work' (*Watsonia*, v.22 (2), 1998, p.202.) *Class No:* 581.6

Systematic Botany (Categories of Plants)

Herbal & Medicinal Plants

[2632]

The Complete book of herbs. Bremness, L., *ed.* London, Dorling Kindersley, 1988. 288p. illus. (col.). £15.99. ISBN: 0863183131.
8 sections: Herbs in the garden - Herbal index - Using herbs (*e.g.* herbal decorations; herbs in the kitchen; herbs for the household) - Herbs for beauty - Essential oils - Herbs for health - Cultivating and harvesting herbs - A catalogue of herbs. Glossary. Useful addresses. Bibliography. Index. Many useful illustrations. *Class No:* 582:615.32

[2633]

The Encyclopedia of herbs and their uses. London, Dorling Kindersley, 1995. 424p. illus. £35. ISBN: 0789401843.
International in scope and covering more than 1,000 herbs, this work uses a broad definition of 'herb' to include shrubs, trees, fungi, etc. Full botanical descriptions are given and a herb dictionary lists historical uses, parts of the plant used, etc. Many colour photographs and cross-references. *Class No:* 582:615.32

[2634]

LAUNERT, E. The Hamlyn guide to edible and medicinal plants of Britain and Northern Europe. London, Hamlyn, 1981. 288p. col. illus. ISBN: 0600372162.
Published in paperback (Hamlyn, 1989; £6.99) as *Guide to edible and medicinal plants of Britain and Northern Europe*.
Colour illus. accompanied by brief descriptions and indication of habitat and distribution. Entries also state active ingredients, effect, parts used and application. Indicates differences between species that look alike. Short list of suppliers of medicinal herbs and plant-based preparations. Glossaries of botanical and medical terms, p.278-81. 4 appendices: 1. Notes on the most important ingredients of medicinal plants - 2. Table of edible plants, with their uses - 3. Recipes for edible plants - 4. List of common ailments and plant species recommended for their treatment. Bibliography, p.277. Index p.282-8. *Class No:* 582:615.32

[2635]

PDR for herbal medicines. Montvale, N.J., Medical Economics, 1998. 1,264p. illus. £42; $59.95. ISBN: 1563632926.
Based on the findings of the German Regulatory Authority, Commission E, this work gives details of 300 common botanicals. Additionally, data on 300 other herbs not covered by the Commission are also included. Arranged by Latin name, each herb has an entry which includes plant names, botanical description, pharmacology, adverse effects, dosage, and bibliography (mainly of articles in German). Glossary; directories of poison control and drug information centres in the US. Useful herb identification guide, with 350 colour pictures of common herbs. Many cross-references. *Class No:* 582:615.32

Flowerless Plants (Cryptogams)

[2636]

BOEDIJN, K.B. Plants of the world: the lower plants. London, Thames & Hudson, 1965. 312p. illus. (incl. pl.).
Published in the Netherlands under the title *Lagere Planten*. Translated by A.J. Pomerans.
Covers ferns, fungi, mosses and lichens. Botanical descriptions, copious illus. (157 in colour, 383 in black-and-white) No bibliographies. Analytical index, p.297-312. Complementary to H.C.D. De Wit's *Plants of the world, the higher plants (q.v.).* *Class No:* 582.2

[2637]

FARLOW REFERENCE LIBRARY OF CRYPTOGAMIC BOTANY, Harvard, University. Catalog. [Farlow Reference Library of Cryptogamic Botany]. Boston, Mass., G.K. Hall, 1979. 6v. $760. ISBN: 0816102791.
Lists *c.*60,000 books, periodical titles and reports in one author-title sequence. The library is particularly rich in pre-1850 cryptogamic material. *Class No:* 582.2

[2638]

The Oxford book of flowerless plants: ferns, fungi, mosses and liverworts, lichens and seaweeds. Brightman, F.H. *and* Nicholson, B.E., *illus.* 2nd ed. London, Peerage Books, 1979. viii, 208p. illus. (col.). ISBN: 090740846x.
Grouped ecologically: Seashore - Grasslands - Uplands - Wet places - Woodlands. 688 plants (including 250 fungi and 78 species of seaweed), drawn from actual specimens. Not to scale. 'Suggestions for further reading', p.201. Index, p.202-8. Text faces well-coloured illus. Primary aim: 'to help the beginner with identification'. *Class No:* 582.2

Algae, Seaweeds, etc.

[2639]

BRITISH MUSEUM (NATURAL HISTORY). Seaweeds of the British Isles. London, British Museum (Natural History)(later vols., HMSO), 1977-. diagrs., tables.

1. *Rhodophyta.* 1977- (pt.1 1977. £13.75; pt.2A. 1983. £13; pt.2B 1994. £30; pt.3A. 1993. £35.). 2. *Chlorophyta.* (1991-. £27). 3. *Fucophyceae* (Phaeophyceae) (pt.1. 1987. £30). 4. *Tribophyceae* (Xanthophyceae) (1987. £7.50).

The result of many years' research carried out by the British Museum (Natural History) and the British Phycological Society. Bibliographical references. The series is to cover all the British and the majority of northern Atlantic seaweeds. Description of each species incorporates notes on ecology and distribution, plus 1 or more illus. *Class No:* 582.26

[2640]

CHAPMAN, V.J. *and* **CHAPMAN, D.J. The Algae.** 2nd ed. London, Macmillan, 1973. xiv, 497p. illus., tables, maps. ISBN: 0333142705.

First published 1962.

22 documented chapters (1. Classification; 2. Cyanophyta; 3/5. Chlorphyta ... 7/8. Chrytophyta ... 13. Fossil algae (p.309-27, including 1p. of references) ... 18. Fresh water ecology (p.388-403, with 8 tables and ½p. of references) ... 22. Algal physiology). A neat production. 'Intended as a brief introductory text only' (*Preface* to the 2nd ed.). *Class No:* 582.26

[2641]

LÜNING, K. Seaweeds: their environment, biogeography, and ecophysiology. New York, Wiley, 1990. xiii,527p., illus., diagrs., graphs, tables. $89.95. ISBN: 0471624349.

First published 1985 as *Meeresbotanik* (Stuttgart, Thieme).

Pt.1: Distribution and structure of seaweed vegetation (chapters 1-5) - Pt.2: Ecophysiology of seaweeds (chapters 6-8). Bibliography, p.371-483 (A-Z author). Appended: 'Taxonomic overview of genera'. Detailed, analytical index, p.489-527. The German first edition 'was an immediate success, prompting the production of this translation, for which the text has been updated and expanded by about twenty per cent' (*Journal of the Marine Biological Association*, v.71(1), February 1991, p.246). *Class No:* 582.26

Fungi, Moulds

Encyclopaedias & Dictionaries

[2642]

AINSWORTH, G.C. Ainsworth & Bisby's dictionary of the fungi. 8th ed., by D.L. Hawksworth *and others*. Wallingford, Oxon., CAB International, 1995. xii,616p. illus., diagrs., tables. £30. ISBN: 0851988857.

First published 1943; 7th ed., 1983.

*c.*20,000 entries, 55 contributors. Covers more than the taxonomy of the fungi; morphology, structure, spore types and various aspects of physiology, metabolism and ecology are also treated. Lichens have been included, starting with the 6th ed., 1971. 'The *Dictionary* is the place to begin any enquiry concerning the fungi' (*Natural history book reviews*, v.7(3), 1984, p.169). *Class No:* 582.28(03)

[2643]

Index of fungi. Wallingford, Oxon., CAB International, 1948-. 2pa. £70; $125. ISSN: 00193895.

Formerly *Review of applied mycology: supplement* 1940-47.

Comprises a list of names (A-Z) of new genera, species, infraspecific taxa, new combinations and new names of fungi. About 1,500 entries per issue. Online, CAB ABSTRACTS. *Class No:* 582.28(03)

[2644]

Mykologisches Wörterbuch: 3,200 Begriffe in 8 Sprachen - Deutsch, Englisch, Französisch, Spanisch, Latein, Tschechisch, Polnisch, Russisch. Berger, K., *ed.* Stuttgart & New York, Fischer, 1980. 432p. illus., tables. ISBN: 0685059022.

10 collaborators. 3,190 numbered German terms with English, French, Spanish, Latin, Czech, Polish and Russian equivalents and indexes. Genders are shown. Bibliography, p.393-4. *Class No:* 582.28(03)

[2645]

SNELL, W.H. *and* **DICK, E.A. A Glossary of mycology.** 2nd rev. ed. Cambridge, Mass., Harvard Univ. Press; London, Oxford Univ. Press, 1971. $17. ISBN: 0674354516.

Expansion of W.H. Snell's *Three thousand mycological terms* (1936).

Over 7,000 terms on fungi research and its applications. Includes terms that cannot strictly be called mycological from their presence in mycological literature or generally of interest to mycologists. *Class No:* 582.28(03)

[2646]

WROBEL, M. *and* **CREBEL, G. Elsevier's dictionary of fungi and fungal plant diseases** in Latin, English, German, French and Italian. Amsterdam, Elsevier, 1998. 414p. £98; $158. ISBN: 0444827749.

Lists 5,156 terms covering the name of fungi and fungal plant diseases. Excludes general concepts, illustrations, prefix terms and historical notes. For academic libraries. *Class No:* 582.28(03)

Handbooks & Manuals

[2647]

BRESINSKY, A. *and* **BESL, H. A Colour atlas of poisonous fungi:** a handbook for pharmacists, doctors and biologists. London, Wolfe Publishing, 1990. xi,198p. illus. (col.), diagrs. £70. ISBN: 0723415765.

3 sections: 1. Poisoning by fungi - 2. The poisoning syndromes and the poisonous fungi - 3. Index to the identification of fungi (including identification keys). Glossary. Bibliography, p.269-88. Index. *Class No:* 582.28(035)

[2648]

The Fungi: an advanced treatise. Ainsworth, G.C. *and* Sussman, A.S., *eds.* New York & London, Academic Press, 1965-73. 4v. in 5.

1. *The fungal cell.* 1965. 748p. 2. *The fungal organism.* 1966. 805p. 3. *The fungal population. Ecology.* 1966. 738p. 4A. *A taxonomic review, with keys. Ascomycetes and fungi imperfecti.* 1973. 621p. 4B. *A taxonomic review with keys. Lower fungi and busiodimycetes.* 1973. 536p.

A well-documented treatise, the work of numerous specialist contributors. V.1, chapter 12. 'Carbohydrate metabolism' (p.302-47) has references, p.338-47. V.1 has author and subject indexes, index to fungi and actinomycetes. *Class No:* 582.28(035)

Reviews & Abstracts

[2649]

Abstracts of mycology, reporting worldwide research in mycology. Philadelphia, Pa., Biosciences Information Service (BIOSIS), 1967 - 12pa. $290pa. ISSN: 00013617.

About 5,000 abstracts and references pa. Each monthly issue contains entries from two consecutive issues of *Biological abstracts* and from two consecutive issues of *Biological abstracts/RRM (Reports, Reviews, Meetings)*. Covers: Fungi in biochemistry; cytology; genetics; microbiology - medical and industrial; pathology, plant and animal; systematics. Indexes: author, biosynthetic, generic, subject. *Class No:* 582.28(048)

[2650]

Bibliography of systematic mycology. Egham, Surrey, International Mycological Institute, 1947-. 2pa. £75; $125. ISSN: 00061573.

About 1,600 references pa. Lists papers and books on all aspects of the taxonomy of fungi. Systematically arranged, with author index. Also on CD-ROM. *Class No:* 582.28(048)

[2651]

Review of medical and veterinary mycology. Wallingford, Oxon., CAB International, 1943-. 4pa. £210; $370 overseas. ISSN: 00346624.

As *Annotated bibliography of medical mycology*, 1943-50.

About 3,500 records added pa. Covers mycoses of man and domestic, farm and wild animals, allergic disorders associated with fungi, and poisoning by fungi or mould-contaminated foods. Quarterly, annual author and subject indexes. Online, CAB ABSTRACTS and on CD-ROM. *Class No:* 582.28(048)

Yearbooks & Directories

[2652]

International mycological directory. Hall, G.S. *and* Minter, D.W., *eds.* 3rd ed. Wallingford, Oxon, CAB International, 1994. 163p. ISBN: 0851989470.

First published 1971.

Based on responses from 167 organizations (45 added since 2nd ed.). Individual entries arranged A-Z (Academia Sinica ... Yokohama Agricultural University). Data include status; organization type; scope; interests; portrait; culture collection; herbarium; publications; database; visual materials; awards; courses. Indexes, p.123-42, to collection holdings; databases; libraries; herbaria; interests; meetings; visual materials; publications. Sources of further information, p.154-59 (*e.g.* 'Patents or patent depositing authorities'). IMA Statutes, p.152-57. *Class No:* 582.28(058)

Histories

[2653]

AINSWORTH, G.C. Introduction to the history of mycology. Cambridge Univ. Press, 1976. xi, 359p,. illus., facsims., ports. ISBN: 0521210135.

11 chapters and epilogue. A documented outline, taking 'a number of the important themes and to trace each one from early times to the present day' (*Preface*). Notes on the text p.291-307. Chronology and bibliography. Name and subject indexes. *Class No:* 582.28(091)

[2654]

—**AINSWORTH, G.C.** Introduction to the history of medical and veterinary mycology. Cambridge, University Press, 1986. xi,228p. illus. £40. ISBN: 0521307155.

10 sections: 1. Introduction ... 3. Names: problems of nomenclature ... 5. Epidemiological problems - 6. Therapeutic problems ... 10. Regional developments. Notes on the text. Bibliography and chronology, p.181-214. Name and subject indexes.
Class No: 582.28(091)

[2655]

A Century of mycology. Sutton, B., *ed.* Cambridge, University Press, 1996. 398p. £55. ISBN: 0521570565.

Commemorates the centenary of the British Mycological Society and relates the British contribution to mycology in 11 chapters (*e.g.* 1. A century of British mycology'... 7. The flagellated fungal spore). References follow each chapter and there is an overall index (16p.).
Class No: 582.28(091)

Yeasts

[2656]

The Yeasts. Rose, A.H. *and* Harrison, J.S., *eds.* 2nd ed. London & New York, Academic Press, 1987-95. 4v. £48.50, v.1; £47.50, v.2; £59, v.3; £72.50, v.4; £75, v.5; £70, v.6. ISBN: 0125964110, v.1; 0125964129, v.2; 0125964137, v.3; 0125964145, v.4; 0125964153, v.5; 0125964161, v.6.

Previously published in 3v., 1969-71.

1. *Biology of yeasts.* 1987. xii,423p. 2. *Yeasts and the environment.* 1987. xvi,309p. 3. *Metabolism and physiology of yeasts.* 1989. xxiv,635p. 4. *Yeast organelles.* 1991. xxx,765p. 5. *Yeast technology.* 1993. xl,620p. 6. *Yeast genetics.* 1995. xlvi,660p.

33 contributors in v.6. Chapter 5: 'Yeast genome structure', p.179-222, includes references (p.213-22). Author and analytical subject indexes. A detailed, authoritative, treatise. *Class No:* 582.282

[2657]

Yeasts: characteristics and identification. Barnett, J.A., *and others.* 2nd ed. Cambridge, University Press, 1990. ix,1002p. illus. £135. ISBN: 0521350565.

First published 1983.

Describes 597 yeast species recognised by the Centraalbureau voor Schimmelcultures at the beginning of September 1991. 11 sections: 1. Introduction ... 4. Laboratory methods for identifying yeasts ... 6. Summary of specific characteristics ... 8. The keys - 9. Tables for identifying individual species - 10. Register of yeast names - 11. Register of specific epithets. Glossary. References, p.955-98. Subject index. 850 photomicrographs. A yeast identification program for microcomputers, for use with this book, is also available.
Class No: 582.282

Mushrooms & Toadstools

Encyclopaedias & Dictionaries

[2658]

BELS-KONING, H.C. *and* **KUIJK, W.M., van. Mushroom terms:** ... polyglot on research and cultivation of edible fungi. English-German-Dutch-Danish-French, Italian, Spanish & Latin. Wageningen, Centre for Agricultural Publishing and Documentation [PUDOC], 1980. xxii, [1], 312p. £23. ISBN: 9022006735.

Supersedes *Mushroom terms in five languages* (PUDOC, 1966).

1,169 English-base terms (plus synonyms), with equivalents and indexes in the other 7 languages. Genders are given. 'Literature', p.311-2. *Class No:* 582.287(03)

[2659]

Elsevier's dictionary of edible mushrooms: botanical and common names in various languages of the world. Chandra, A., *comp.* Amsterdam, Elsevier, 1989. xxxix,259p. £54.68. ISBN: 0444883886.

Latin names of 628 species of fungi listed in alphabetical order. Each entry gives as many common names as possible from Bulgarian; Chinese; Czech; Danish; Dutch; English; Filipino; Finnish; French; German; Hungarian; Indian languages; Italian; Japanese; Norwegian; Pakistani (Urdu); Polish; Romanian; Russian; Spanish; Swedish. Indexes to common names in each language. References given for each species. *Class No:* 582.287(03)

[2660]

HUANG, N. Edible fungi cyclopedia. Beijing, Agricultural Sci-tech Publishing House of China, 1993. 448p. illus.(some col. pl.), figs. ISBN: 7109026140.

11 sections: 1. History of the cultivation of edible fungi in China; relevant research institutes, societies, and scientific journals; edible fungi in Chinese culture ... 3. Chinese fungal resources ... 6. Edible fungus cultivation - 7. Pest and disease control ... 9. Storage and processing - 10. Research techniques - 11. Recipes. Section of 103 colour plates and many line drawings throughout the text.
Class No: 582.287(03)

[2661]

JORDAN, M. The Encyclopedia of fungi of Britain and Europe. Newton Abbot, David & Charles, 1995. 384p. illus.(col.). ISBN: 0715301292.

Four sections: The biology of higher fungi - How to use this book - Reference section ('Authors of fungal names'; 'BMS database'; 'Bibliography'; 'Glossary') - The encyclopedia. Entry for each fungus consists of a colour photograph with data including name, description, dimensions, fruiting body, spores, odour, taste, chemical tests, occurrence, and indications as to whether it is edible. Index, p.377-84. The illustrations are excellent in this up-to-date and authoritative work. *Class No:* 582.287(03)

Handbooks & Manuals

[2662]

BUCZACKI, S. Collins New Generation guide to the fungi of Britain and Europe. London, Collins, 1989. 320p. illus. (col.). £12.95; £8.95. (*Collins New Generation Guide.*)

3 sections: 1. What is a fungus? - 2. The directory of fungus species - 3. The natural history of fungi. Contains over 1,300 colour illustrations. Each entry includes information on appearance, size, colours and features necessary for identification, habitats and substrates. Glossary, p.307-11. Index, p.312-20, restricted to names of species. *Class No:* 582.287(035)

[2663]

COURTECUISSE, R. *and* **DUHEM, B. Field guide to mushrooms and toadstools of Britain and Europe.** Glasgow, HarperCollins, 1995. 500p. illus.(col.) £14.99.

Covers every species which can be identified in the field. Describes *c.*3,500 species, with data on identification, habitat, and geographic range. Detailed keys and *c.*1,750 colour illustrations. A major new guide. *Class No:* 582.287(035)

[2664]

LAESSøE, T. *and* **LINCOFF, G. Mushrooms.** New York, DK Publishing, 1998. 304p. illus. $17.95. ISBN: 0789432862.

16 separate sections according to type of fungi. Over 2,000 colour illustrations of 500 species. Data given ensure easy identification of most of the common species of northern temperate regions. 'A must for libraries' (*Choice*, December 1998, p.711).
Class No: 582.287(035)

[2665]

PEGLER, D. Larousse field guide to the mushrooms and toadstools of Britain and Europe. London, Larousse, 1997. 192p. illus. (col.). £12.99. ISBN: 0752300504.

Reprint of *Field guide to the mushrooms and toadstools of Britain and Europe* (Kingfisher Books, 1990).

Covers 450 species, illustrating 386 in colour and with accurate detail. Chapters are devoted to different groups and each species has a concise text dealing with appearance, habitat, frequency and season. 'Similar species' distinguishes fungi that are liable to be confused. Pages colour coded for ease of reference. Glossary, index, list of useful addresses + bibliography. 'A cheap, well illustrated and easily used guide' (*Reference reviews*, v.5(1) 1991, p.18). Author is Head of Mycology at the Royal Botanic Gardens, Kew.
Class No: 582.287(035)

[2666]

PHILLIPS, R. Mushrooms and other fungi of Great Britain and Europe. London, Ward Lock & Pan Books, 1981. 288p. illus. (col.). ISBN: 0330264419.

Contents: Introduction; Visual index; Glossary. Agarics - Gomphediaceae - Chanterelles - Bolates - Polypores - Ascomycetes. Bibliography, p.282. Full colour illus., with descriptive captions, identifying over 900 specimens, showing the various stages of growth. A handsome quarto that deserves a place in every public library at least. *Class No:* 582.287(035)

[2667]
RINALDI, A. *and* TYNDALO, V. The Complete book of mushrooms: over 1,000 species and varieties of American, European, and Asiatic mushrooms, with 460 illustrations in black and white and in color. Mancinelli, I. *and* Mancinelli, A., *tr.* New York, Crown, 1974. 331p. illus. (incl. col.). ISBN: 0517514931.

Arranged by genera and species. Includes sections on nutritional properties, toxicity, etc. Glossary. 300 colour plates. *Class No:* 582.287(035)

Lichens

[2668]
HAWKSWORTH, D.L. *and* SEAWARD, M.R.D. Lichenology in the British Isles, 1568-1978: an historical and bibliographical survey. Richmond, Surrey, Richmond Publishing Co., 1977. vii, 231p. £9.95. ISBN: 0855462000.

About 2,695 references, - a valuable, comprehensive bibliography, indexed under vice-county headings, plus a well-illustrated text. In many ways this is a volume for the specialist, but beginners should not be discouraged from using it (*British book news,* June 1978, p.451). *Class No:* 582.29

Mosses

[2669]
CROSBY, M.R. *and* MAGILL, R.E. A Directory of mosses: an alphabetical listing of genera, ... together with a systematic arrangement of the families of mosses and a catalogue of family names. St. Louis, Missouri, Missouri Botanical Garden, 1977. vii, 43p.

The first detailed guide to the familial composition of the genera of mosses published for more than 50 years (*Preface*). *Class No:* 582.34

[2670]
SMITH, A.J.E. The Moss flora of Britain and Ireland. Cambridge, University Press, 1978. 706p. illus. £30. ISBN: 052129973x.

A comprehensive treatise on nearly 700 species of moss. Well illustrated, with identification keys for all genera and species described. *Class No:* 582.34

[2671]
WATSON, E.V. British mosses and liverworts: an introductory work, with full descriptions and figures of over 200 species and keys for the identification of all except the very rare species. 3rd ed. Cambridge, University Press, 1981. xviii, 519p. illus. (incl. pl.). ISBN: 0521285364.

First published 1955.

Main sequence: Musci (p.124-401); Hepaticae (p.401-498). Introduction includes notes on works of reference. Appended habit lists, p.1-24. Detailed index, p.511-9. Well illustrated, with descriptive captions. A standard work. *Class No:* 582.34

Vascular Plants

[2672]
BSBI abstracts: abstracts from literature relating to the vascular plants of the British Isles. London, Botanical Society of the British Isles, c/o Dept. of Botany, British Museum (Natural History), 1971-. Annual. £18; £20 overseas. ISSN: 03072657.

Replaces 'Abstracts from literature', in *Proceedings of the Botanical Society of the British Isles,* 1954-69.

About 800 abstracts and references pa. Sections: Introduction - History - Herbaria - Biography - Floras, catalogues, etc. (Europe ... North America) - Chromosome surveys, etc. - Pteridophyta - Gymnospermae - Angiospermae - Miscellaneous. *Class No:* 582.35

[2673]
Gray Herbarium index. Harvard University. Boston, Mass., G.K. Hall, 1968. 10v. (8121p.). $945. ISBN: 0816107548.

An index of vascular plants of the Western hemisphere. 259,000 cards are reproduced. These cards note newly proposed names, stating genus, species and subordinate categories. Duplicates *Index Kewensis* (*qv*) for generic names and binomials, 'but it is invaluable to students of New World plants since 1873, irrespective of the category and irrespective of whether published in a New World or Old World publication' (Lawrence, G.H.M. *Taxonomy of vascular plants,* p.287). *Class No:* 582.35

[2674]
KENT, D.H. List of vascular plants of the British Isles. London, Botanical Society of the British Isles, 1992. xvi,384p. £11.50. ISBN: 0901158216.

Updates and revises J.E. Dandy's *List of British vascular plants* (1958).

Includes those plants which are, at the present time, native or have been introduced and established in the UK, Eire, the Isle of Man, and the Channel Islands. Also lists extinct native species. Entries contain information on nomenclature, synonyms, hybrids, species, and

....(contd.)
subspecies. 2-page bibliography. Will be the standard work and is essential for any library with a collection in this subject. *Class No:* 582.35

[2675]
Kew record of taxonomic literature relating to vascular plants. London, HMSO, 1971-. 4pa. £110. ISBN: 0112501079. ISSN: 03072835.

1995(3) issue, for material scanned during August-October 1995, contains 1,821 references. Sections include: General; Systematics; Floristics; Palynology; Personalia; Botanical institutions. Genus and author indexes. Periodical abbreviations. *Class No:* 582.35

[2676]
LAWRENCE, G.H.M. Taxonomy of vascular plants. New York, Macmillan, 1951. xiii, 823p. illus. $46.95. ISBN: 002368190x.

Includes a lengthy, well annotated and invaluable 'Literature of taxonomic botany', p.284-331. Entries are grouped: General taxonomic indexes - World floras and manuals (by areas) - Monographs and revisions - Bibliographies, catalogues and review serials - Periodicals - Glossaries and dictionaries - Cultivated and economic plants - References to miscellaneous topics (including maps and cartography, biographical references, and outstanding botanical libraries). The volume has an extensive index, p.777-823. *Class No:* 582.35

[2677]
PERRING, E.M. *and* FARRELL, Ll., *comps.* British red data books. 1. Vascular plants. 2nd rev. ed. Nettleham, Lincoln, Royal Society for Nature Conservation, 1984. 128p. £5.50. ISBN: 0902484044.

A third ed., edited by M.J. Wigginton and containing accounts and maps of over 300 species, is due to be published in 1999 (£30). *Class No:* 582.35

Ferns

[2678]
Index filicum supplementum septimum pro annis 1991-1995. Johns, R.J., *ed.* Kew, Royal Botanic Gardens, 1997. viii, 124p. £20. ISBN: 1900347261.

Continuation of C. Christensen's *Index filicum* (1906), and Supplements 1-3, 1906-33, republished 1973; 4 (1934-60), 1965; 5 (1961-75) 1985; 6 (1976-1990) 1996.

An index to the family, generic, infrageneric and specific names of ferns and their allies, published 1991-95. List of species, p.1-100, Catalogus literaturae, p.101-18, supplement to authors of scientific names, p.119-21. Contents list inappropriately follows preface and introduction. 'Is to ferns what *Index Kewensis* is to the taxonomy of flowering plants' (Davis, E.B. and Schmidt, D.: *Guide to information sources in the botanical sciences,* 2nd ed., 1996, p.175). *Class No:* 582.350

[2679]
JAHNS, H.M. *and* MASSFLINK, A.K. Collins' guide to the ferns, mosses and lichens of Britain and Northern and Central Europe. Launert, E., *and others, tr. and rev.* London, Collins, 1983. 272p. illus. (mostly col. pl.), diagrs., maps. £8.95. ISBN: 0002192543.

Original as *Ferne, Moose, Flichten ...* (Munich, 1980).

Sections: Ferns - Mosses and liverworts - Lichens - Keys. 679 numbered entries for plants (over 750 species described). Glossary. Further reading and societies. 650 col. photographs. Index of genera; index of common names. 'The result is a very useful handbook for the English-speaking naturalist on British and European criptogens' (*Natural history book reviews,* v.7(1/2), 1984, p.106). *Class No:* 582.350

[2680]
JERMY, C. *and* CAMUS, J. The Illustrated field guide to ferns and allied plants of the British Isles. London, Natural History Museum Publications, 1991. xiv,194p. figs. £7.95. ISBN: 0565011723.

Aimed at the amateur botanist. Silhouettes or drawings are supplemented by data on leaves; leaf-base; habitat; habit; distribution; conservation status; similar plants. Indexes to Latin and English names. Both authors are members of the Botany Department of the Natural History Museum, London. *Class No:* 582.350

[2681]
JONES, D.L. Encyclopaedia of ferns: an index to ferns, their structure, biology, economic importance, cultivation and propagation. London, British Museum (Natural History), 1987. xvii, 433p. illus. (incl. col.), diagrs. ISBN: 0565010190.

7 parts (1. Introduction; structure and botany of ferns - 2. The cultural requirements of ferns - 3. Pests, diseases and other ailments of ferns - 4. Propagation and hybridisation of ferns ... 6. Ferns to grow (p.202-385). 7 appendices (*e.g.* Ferns for wet soils)). Glossary. Bibliography, p.417-20. Fern societies and study groups. Detailed index, p.422-33. 400 illus. (250 in colour). Well produced; by a professional Australian horticulturalist. *Class No:* 582.350

[2682]

PAGE, C.N. The Ferns of Britain and Ireland. 2nd ed. Cambridge, University Press, 1996. xx,540p. illus.,figs., maps. £95; £40. ISBN: 0521583802; 0521586585, (pbk).

First published 1982.

Incorporates changes and additions to knowledge since publication of the previous ed. Three main sections: Ferns; Clubmosses and quillworts; Horestails. Many figures, maps, and photographs (although the quality of some of these could be better). Extensive bibliography, p.521-32. Index, p.533-40. For both beginners and professional botanists. *Class No:* 582.350

Flowering Plants (Seed Plants & Phanerogams)

[2683]

BELL, A.D. Plant form: an illustrated guide to flowering plant morphology. Oxford, New York, Oxford University Press, 1991. 341p. illus. (col.), diagrs. £25. ISBN: 0198542194.

2 parts: 1. Morphological description (*e.g.* 'Leaf morphology'; 'Vegetative multiplication') - 2. Constructional organization (*e.g.* 'Meristem position'; 'Plant branch construction'). Many coloured illustrations supplemented by clearly drawn diagrams. Bibliography, p.317-20. Index. Many cross-references. Aimed at students and amateur horticulturalists. *Class No:* 582.4

[2684]

DE WIT, H.C.D. Plants of the world: the higher plants. London, Thames & Hudson, 1963-65. 2v. (335p. + 340p.). illus. (incl. pl.).

Translated from the Danish, *Hogere planten* (1963-65).

V.1 concerns monocotyledons and part of the dicotyledons; v.2 completes the dicotyledons. A number of families are discussed in each order, with descriptions of the flower, reference to distribution and habitat, plus such added information as garden species, herbal use and evolution of common name. Magnificent and profuse illus. (in all, 362 in colour, 573 black and white). Each volume has an analytical index. Only 5 items 'For further reading' (v.2. p.317). *Class No:* 582.4

[2685]

Dictionary of generic names of seed plants. Wielgorskaya, T., *ed.* New York, Columbia University Press, 1995. xi,570p. £61.50; $80. ISBN: 0231078927.

Discusses *c.*16,000 genera found in modern botanical literature, with about 500 families treated separately. Generic name entries include family, geographical distribution, number of species, authority and year of publication. Each family name has data on order, distribution, number of genera and species plus notes on the sub-families. Includes synonyms. *Class No:* 582.4

[2686]

Flowering plant index of illustration and information. Isaacson, R.T., *comp.* Boston, Mass., G.K. Hall, 1979. 2v. $230, set; $260, supp. ISBN: 0816103011, set; 0816104034, supp.

50,000 catalogue cards, photolithographically reproduced, for coloured illustrations of flowering plants. The sources represent over 100 books, mostly published since 1930. Indexed by both common and botanical names.

A 2v. supplement was published in 1982. *Class No:* 582.4

[2687]

HUTCHINSON, J. The Families of flowering plants, arranged according to a new system based on their phylogeny. 3rd ed. Oxford, Clarendon Press, 1973. xviii, [1], 908p. illus., diagrs., tables, maps.

First published 1926.

Part 1: Dicotyledones (descriptions of orders and families of dicotyledons, with keys to genera of smaller families), p.153-634 - Part 2: Monocotyledones. Glossaries, p.126-8, p.906-7. 430 figures. Hutchinson (who died in 1972) rearranged the families of plants - under dicotyledones and monocotyledones - in ascending order. *Class No:* 582.4

[2688]

Index Kewensis plantarum phanerogamarum nomina et synonyma omnium generum et specierum a Linnaeo usque a annum MDCCCLXXXV complectens. Oxford, Clarendon Press, 1893-95. 2v. Supplementum, 1901-. (1991-95. 1996. 338p £76.)

Added title-page in English: 'Index Kewensis: an enumeration of the genera and species of flowering plants from the time of Linnaeus to the year 1885 inclusive ...' Includes authors' name, works in which first cited, native countries and synonyms. The present volumes list over 500,000 names, A/Z. *Index Kewensis* is the reference employed to determine the source of the original publication of a generic name or binomial of a seed plant. It does not account for names of terms nor of any plants in divisions subordinate to the Spermatophytes, nor for names of plants as placed in categories below that of species' (Lawrence, G.H.M. *Taxonomy of vascular plants*, p.286). Available on CD-ROM. *Class No:* 582.4

[2689]

MABBERLEY, D.J. The Plant-book: a portable dictionary of the vascular plants. Cambridge, University Press, 1997. xvi, 858p. £32.50. ISBN: 0521414210.

First published 1987 as *The Plant-book: a portable dictionary of the higher plants*.

Over 20,000 entries, including 2,500 new entries. Generic entries include data such as family to which the genus has been assigned, distribution, English names for species, and other botanical, medicinal, or agricultural details. Family entries include number and genera of species, classification and subdivision, and principal genera. Cross-references from English names to the generic entries. Reviewer in *Watsonia* (v.22, 1998, p.197-8) praised book's content but believed poor production values would limit its use as a pocket-book. *Class No:* 582.4

[2690]

WILLIS, J.C. A Dictionary of flowering plants and ferns. 8th ed., student ed., rev. by H.K.A. Shaw. Cambridge Univ. Press, 1985. xxii, 1245, lxvip. ISBN: 0321313953.

First published 1897.

Over 50,000 entries, giving for every genus an outline of its distribution, family and often some additional facts. 'It is good value and all serious students of botany should have a copy' (*Natural history book reviews*, v.8(2), 1986, p.115-6). *Class No:* 582.4

Monocotyledons

[2691]

METCALFE, C.R. Anatomy of the monocotyledons. Oxford, University Press, 1960-.

1. *Gramineae*, by C.R. Metcalfe. 1960. 2. *Palmae*, by P.B. Tomlinson. 1961. 3. *Commelinales - Zingiberales*, by P.B. Tomlinson, 1969. £32. 4. *Juncales*, by D.F. Cutler. 1969. £32. 5. *Cyperaceae*, by C.R. Metcalfe. 1971. £40. 6. *Dioscoreales*, by E.S. Ayensu. 1972. £40. 7. *Helobiae (Alismatidae)*, by P.B. Tomlinson. 1982. £70. 8. *Iridaceae*, by P. Rudall. 1995.

A companion work to his *Anatomy of the dicotyledons (qv)*. V.1 includes a valuable introduction, including the general morphology of the grass plant. Descripton of genera and species, in A/Z order, is in 2 groups: 1. Genera not in the Bambuseae (p.1-540); 2. Genera in the Bambuseae (p.540-89). Bibliography, p.630-50. Index, p.715-31. C.R. Metcalfe died in 1991, v.8 being edited by Cutler and Gregory. *Class No:* 582.52

Grasses

[2692]

CLAYTON, W.D. *and* **RENVOIZE, S.A. Genera graminum: grasses of the world.** London, HMSO, 1986. 389p. figs. £25. (*Kew bulletin additional series XIII.*) ISBN: 0112500064.

2 parts: 1. The grass plant - 2. Enumeration of genera (651 entries). Data for each entry include bibliographic references; description; anatomy; habitat; chromosomes; geographical distribution. Index to genera and names of higher rank, p.379-89. *Class No:* 582.542

[2693]

FITTER, R. *and* **FITTER, A. Collins' guide to the grasses, sedges, rushes and ferns of Britain and Northern Europe.** London, Collins, 1984. 256p. illus. (col.), maps. £10.95; £9.99. ISBN: 0002191288.

Data on 26 families of grasses, sedges, rushes, and ferns (20 species), preceded by keys. Colour illus. of over 420 plants. Glossary, p.220-3. 500 tiny distribution maps. Further reading, p.250. Indexes of English and scientific names. Apart from native grasses, etc., the text includes 'a number of widely established aliens' (*Introduction*). *Class No:* 582.542

[2694]

Grasses, ferns, mosses and lichens of Great Britain and Ireland. Phillips, R. *and* Grant, S., *eds.* London, Pan Books, 1980. 191p. £12.99. ISBN: 0330259598.

Contents: Grasses, p.12-79; Ferns, p.76-117; Mosses (including liverworts), p.118-63; Lichens, p.164-81. A glossary precedes. Analytical indexes of botanical and common names. Full-colour illus. (1-6 per page), with descriptive captions. 'Nearly 160 species out of the total British *bryophyta* flora, around 1,000, have been described' (*Introduction*). No bibliography. A good popular introduction. Quarto. *Class No:* 582.542

[2695]

HUBBARD, C.E. Grasses: a guide to their structure, identification, uses and distribution in the British Isles. 3rd ed., revised by J.C.E. Hubbard. Harmondsworth, Penguin Books, 1984. 476p. illus. ISBN: 0140222790.

2nd ed. 1968 (462p.).

Description and illus. of individual grass, p.59-372, with text facing illus. page. Introduction includes 'Key for naming wild and agricultural grasses'. Appendices include 'The uses of grass' and a classification. Bibliography, p.47-52. Indexes to common and botanical names. A standard work. *Class No:* 582.542

[2696]
Manual of grasses. Darke, R., *ed.* London, Macmillan, 1994. xlvi,169p. figs. £35. ISBN: 0333615352.

Introduction followed by descriptions of the genera which are in alphabetical order. Each genus has a general description and cultural information, with descriptions of species suitable for ornamental use. Contains a list of names no longer in use and an index of popular names. Based on *The New Royal Horticultural Society dictionary of gardening* (*q.v.*) but with some additional information. *Class No:* 582.542

[2697]
ROSE, F. Colour identification guide to the grasses, sedges, rushes and ferns of the British Isles and north-western Europe. London, Viking, 1989. 240p. illus. £35. ISBN: 0670806889.

420 species described in the text, with more than 350 illustrated by 62 colour plates. Descriptions of each are followed by distribution and ecological data. Useful feature is the use of keys to several plant groups. Many clear and accurate line drawings. Well presented. Useful for both the beginner and the professional botanist. *Class No:* 582.542

[2698]
SMITHSONIAN INSTITUTION. Index to grass species. Chase, A. *and* Niles, C.D. Boston, Mass., G.K. Hall, 1970. 3v. (1746p.). $330. ISBN: 081610445x.

62,400 cards reproduced. Entries give name, authority and complete bibliographic citation for each taxa. Lists the scientific names of all species, sub-species and varieties of grasses described since the time of Linnaeus (fl. 1737), claims the prospectus). *Class No:* 582.542

Orchids

[2699]
BUTLER, K.P. Steinbachs Naturführer: Orchideen. [Field guide to orchids of Britain and Europe: the species and subspecies growing wild in Europe, the Near East and North Africa.] Rev. English ed. Munich, Mosaik Verlag GmbH, 1986; Swindon, Wilts., The Crowood Press, 1991. 288p. illus. (col.), diagrs., maps. £9.99. ISBN: 1852235918.

Describes and illustrates, with 562 excellent colour photographs, every European species and subspecies of orchid. Gives descriptions of characteristics; habitat; synonyms; flowering period; distribution; key; variation. Bibliography, p.278-79. Indexes to English and scientific names. *Class No:* 582.594

[2700]
DAVIES, P., *and others*. Wild orchids of Britain and Europe. London, Chatto & Windus: Hogarth Press, 1983. 256p. col. pl. ISBN: 0701126436.

6 sections: 1. Orchid biology - 2. Orchid ecology - 3. Classification - 4. Species descriptions (p.49-184, with cross-references to col. plates) - 5. In search of orchids (Great Britain ... Israel) - 6. Photographing wild orchids. Bibliography, p.245-7 (books; journals). Analytical index, p.249-56. A neat production. Orchids are the second largest family of plants in the vegetable kingdom. *Class No:* 582.594

[2701]
The Illustrated encyclopedia of orchids. Pridgeon, A., *ed.* Portland, Timber Press, 1992. 304p. illus. (col. pl.). $39.95 ISBN: 0881922676.

Introduction is followed a list of orchids, arranged A-Z, written by 15 orchid experts. Data include descriptions, taxonomy, accepted names and synonyms, geographic distribution, etc. Many colour photographs to help with identification. Aimed at all those interested in orchids. Editor is based at Royal Botanic Gardens, Kew. *Class No:* 582.594

Dicotyledons

[2702]
METCALFE, C.R. *and* CHALK, L., *and others*. Anatomy of the dicotyledons. 2nd ed. Oxford, Clarendon Press, 1987-. illus. (pl.), diagrs., tables. ISBN: 0198542534, v.1; 0198545940, v.2; 0198545932, v.3.

First published 1950 (2v.).

1. *Systematic anatomy of the leaf and stem.* 1988. 286p. £27.50 2. *Wood structure and conclusion of the general introduction.* 1989. 297p. £30. 3. *Magnoliales, illiciales and laurales.* 1987. 234p. £60.

V.1-2 of this proposed multi-volume work, provide a general introduction to principles and data. V.1 (12 chapters) includes a brief history of systematic anatomy. Each chapter provides 'Suggestions for further reading'. Bibliography (A/Z authors). Name and analytical subject indexes. *Class No:* 582.6/9

Water Plants

[2703]
MÜHLBERG, H. The Complete guide to water plants: a reference book. Translated from the German. East Ardsley, Wakefield, W. Yorkshire, EP Publishing, Ltd., 1982. 392p. illus. (incl. col.). ISBN: 0715807897.

German ed., 1980.

Two parts: 1. The biology of water plants - 2. The families, genera and species of aquatic plants (Liverworts ... Cattails, p.92-376). Data on species: named by ...; distribution; cultivation and propagation. Appended: Explanation of specific epithets; List of authorities (p.381-5). Bibliography, p.386. Index of scientific names of the species, p.387-91. 221 black-and-white and col. illus. Sources of illus. *Class No:* 582.671

[2704]
PRESTON, C.D. *and* **CROFT, J.M. Aquatic plants in Britain and Ireland:** joint project of the Environment Agency, Institute for Terrestrial Ecology, and the Joint Nature Conservation Committee. Colchester, Harley, 1997. 365p. illus., maps. £25. ISBN: 0946589550.

Introduction. Sources of records. Systematic accounts (generic level, *e.g.* Rosaceae, p.93-5) p.19-326. Conservation designation of the rarer species, p.329-31. List of localities, p.332-6. References, p.337-61. Index to accounts of species, subspecies, and hybrids, p.362-5. 'A serious scientific work written for experienced botanists' (*Watsonia*, v.22, 1998, p.119), although the lack of advice on identification was criticized. *Class No:* 582.671

[2705]
Water plants of the world: a manual for the identification of the genera of freshwater macrophytes. Cook, C.D.K., *and others*. The Hague, W. Junk; Kinderhook, N.Y., IBD, 1974. viii, 561p. $175.

Aims at exhaustive coverage of water plants (aquatic macrophyta) down to genus level. The initial key is based largely on vegetative character. Glossary of technical terms, for the non-botanist. An authoritative guide. *Class No:* 582.671

59 Zoology

Zoology

Databases

[2706]

Zoological record online. Philadelphia, Pa., BIOSIS, 1978-.

Online version of *Zoological record (q.v.)*. Contains *c.*1,500,000 records giving worldwide coverage of zoological literature, scanning *c.*6,000 journals. Updated monthly. Available on CD-ROM (1985-. Updated quarterly). *Class No: 590(003.4)*

Bibliographies

[2707]

AMERICAN MUSEUM OF NATURAL HISTORY. Research catalog of the Library. [American Museum of Natural History]. Boston, Mass., G.K. Hall, 1977. 13v. $1320. ISBN: 0816100640.

Class No: 590(01)

[2708]

BELL, G.H. *and* **RHODES, D.B. A Guide to the zoological literature:** the animal kingdom. Englewood, Colo., Libraries Unlimited, 1994. xxiii, 504p. £91.95; $85. ISBN: 1563080826.

1,655 annotated entries with complete bibliographic information. Eight sections: General reference sources; Invertebrates; Arthropods; Vertebrates; Fishes; Amphibians and reptiles; Birds; Mammals. Each section is divided according to reference source, *e.g.* dictionaries, field guides, bibliographies, etc. Appendix of Internet sources. Author-title and subject indexes. 'There is no comparable guide to the literature', (*Booklist*, 1 December 1994, p.702). *Class No: 590(01)*

[2709]

BRITISH MUSEUM (NATURAL HISTORY). Animal identification: a reference guide. London, British Museum (Natural History); Chichester, Wiley, 1980. 3v. £79.50, the set. ISBN: 0471277657; 0471277665; 0471277673.

1. *Marine and brackish water animals;* edited by R.W. Sims, 1980. vi, 111p. £14.55. 2. *Land and freshwater animals,* (not insects); edited by R.W. Sims. 1980. x, 120p. £14.55 3. *Insects;* edited by D. Hollis. 1980. viii, 160p. £20.95.

Systematically arranged. V.3 (Insects, general) (Thysanura ... Hymenoptera), with regional grouping as necessary; *c.*4,500 references. 'This work should be of immense value to applied biologists, biologists working a poorly worked region of the world, expedition zoologists or amateur naturalist collecting on an overseas holiday' (*Natural history book reviews,* v.5(3/4), 1982, p.128-9). *Class No: 590(01)*

[2710]

ENGELMANN, W. Bibliotheca historico-naturalis. Verzeichnis der Bücher über Naturgeschichte, welche in Deutschland, Scandinavien, Holland, England, Frankreich, Italien und Spanien in den Jahren 1700-1846 erschienen sind. Leipzig, Engelmann, 1846. ix, 786p.

About 10,000 references to books and pamphlets on natural history, published 1700-1846 in Northern and Western European countries. Sections cover bibliographies, general works, comparative anatomy and physiology, zoology and palaeontologie. Author and subject indexes. Stresses local material. Continued in: *Class No: 590(01)*

[2711]

—Bibliotheca zoologica. Verzeichnis der Schriften über Zoologie welche in den periodischen Werken enthalten und vom Jahre 1846-1860 selbständig erschienen sind. Leipzig, Engelmann, 1861. 2v. (x, xxiv, 2144p.).

Similarly arranged. 40,000 entries, including periodical articles since 1700. *Class No: 590(01)*

[2712]

—Bibliotheca zoologica II. Verzeichnis... 1861-1880. Leipzig, Engelmann, 1886-1923. 8v. (6620p.).

Has *c.*160,000 entries. *Class No: 590(01)*

[2713]

HARVARD UNIVERSITY. Catalogue of the Library of the Museum of Comparative Zoology. Boston, Mass., G.K. Hall, 1970. 8v. First supplement 1976. 770p. $835; $140, supp. ISBN: 081610767x; 0816108110, supp.

169,100 catalogue cards in all, photolithographically reproduced. Main entries under author, or title, plus added entries for joint authors, editors, series, etc. All important monograph series are analysed. No subject entries, except for biographies, works about institutions, scientific institutions, and ships used in such expeditions. *Class No: 590(01)*

[2714]

McGILL UNIVERSITY. Montreal. **A Dictionary catalogue of the Blacker-Wood Library of Zoology and Ornithology.** Boston, Mass., G.K. Hall, 1970. 9v. $930. ISBN: 081610719x.

140,000 dictionary catalogue cards, photolithographically reproduced. The 60,000 volumes include *c.*2,000 periodical sets, of which only 500 are current. *Class No: 590(01)*

Encyclopaedias

[2715]

BURTON, M. *and* **BURTON, R. Marshall Cavendish international wildlife encyclopedia.** Rev. ed. London, Marshall Cavendish, 1990. 25v. illus. £291.45; $449.95. ISBN: 086307734x.

Covers fish, reptiles and amphibians, birds, and mammals, with insects, crustaceans and invertebrates given more selective coverage. Articles arranged A-Z. Animals listed by common name. V.25 includes a 3-part index - animal; subject; list of animals classified by phylum. 13-page bibliography. Many illustrations. *Class No: 590(031)*

[2716]

Illustrated encyclopedia of wildlife. Lakeville, Conn., Grey Castle Press, 1991. 15v. 3053p. $495. ISBN: 1559050527.

V.1-5. *Mammals.* 6-8. *Birds.* 9. *Reptiles and amphibians.* 10. *Fish.* 11-15. *Invertebrates.*

Arrangement is by class, sub-divided by families, each of which has a chapter devoted to it. The 1,400 colour drawings and 4,000 colour plates are of high quality and are this encyclopaedia's outstanding feature. Easier to see relationships among animals in a class in this set than in the Marshall Cavendish set, which is arranged alphabetically. V.15 has an index of scientific and common names. An excellent reference tool for school and public libraries. *Class No: 590(031)*

Handbooks & Manuals

[2717]

GRASSÉ, P.-P. Traité de zoologie: anatomie, systématique, biologie. Paris, Masson, 1948-. (v.16; fasc.7, 1982). 17v. (various fascicules).

v.1: *Phylogenie. Protozoâires* ... 8-10. *Insects.* 11: *Echinodermes. Stomocordés. Procordés.* 12: *Vertébrés.* 12. *Agnathes et poissons.* 14: *Reptiles.* 15: *Oiseaux.* 16-17: *Mammifères.*

Each volume/fasc. is fully illustrated with section bibliographies and partly analytical subject index. Shows a remarkable unity and uniformity of a high standard, although bibliographies are uneven. The only major treatise on zoology worthy of the name, according to M.-G. Madier (Malclès, L.-N. *Les sources du travail bibliographique,* v.3, p.327). *Class No: 590(035)*

[2718]

Handbuch der Zoologie. Eine Naturgeschichte der Stämme der Tierreiches. Kukenthal, W. 2. Aufl., hrsg. von J.G. Helmake [u.a.]. Berlin, de Gruyter, 1968-.

First published 1925.

An important, standard treatise on the families of the animal kingdom, comprehensive, with emphasis on systematic zoology. Latest part of 2nd ed: Bd.4(34), 1999, *Dictionary of insect morphology* (405p.). *Class No: 590(035)*

[2719]

—The Cambridge natural history. Harmer, S.F. *and* Shipley, A., eds. London, Macmillan, 1895-1909. Reprinted Weinheim, Engelmann, 1958. 10v. illus., maps.

Was, in its day, the standard British treatise on zoology. Systematically arranged (v.1: *Protozoa, Porifera, Coelenterata and Ctenophora, Echinodermata* ... v.10: *Mammalia.*). Well illustrated, with numerous footnote references. Each volume has an index. V.1 (21 chapters, by 4 specialists, contains 291 line-drawings; index, p.625-71). *Class No: 590(035)*

Dictionaries

[2720]
ARAB LEAGUE EDUCATIONAL, CULTURAL AND SCIENTIFIC ORGANIZATION. Lexique de zoologie. Rabat, Morocco, Bureau Permanent de Coordination de l'Arabisation, 1971. 124, xxiip.
English - French - Arabic. *Class No:* 590(038)

[2721]
BILLY, C. Glossaire de zoologie. Paris, Doin, 1985. 240p.
Class No: 590(038)

[2722]
The Concise Oxford dictionary of zoology. Allaby, M., *ed.* Oxford, University Press, 1991. viii,508p. ISBN: 0198661622.
Intended for the zoologist or zoology student, this reference work consists of *c.*8,000 entries, including cross-references. Definitions vary from 10-400 words, covering taxa (down to familial level for vertebrates, but with less complete coverage of other phyla); earth history; ecology; evolutionary concepts; genetics; physiology; taxonomic principles; zoogeography; as well as some biographical material on individuals distinguished in the science. Taxonomic names are given in Latin with common names cross-referenced. Comprehensive and workmanlike subject dictionary.
Class No: 590(038)

[2723]
HENDERSON, I.F. *and* HENDERSON, W.D. Henderson's dictionary of biological terms. 11th ed., by E. Lawrence. Harlow, Longman Scientific and Technical, 1995. xi,693p. ISBN: 0582227089.
First published 1920; as *A Directory of scientific terms.* (1st-8th eds.).
Over 23,000 headwords. Updates existing definitions and extends subject coverage into the areas of ecology and animal behaviour. Appendices (p.649-693) comprise structural formulae, outlines of plant and animal kingdoms, the fungi, the kingdom Protista, the Prokaryotes, virus families, and etymological origins of some common word elements in biology. Intended for use by students and teachers.
Class No: 590(038)

[2724]
KLEMM, M. Zoologisches Wörterbuch. Paläarktische Tiere. Deutsch/Lateinisch/Russisch, Russisch/Lateinische/Deutsch, mit Registern der wissenschaftlichen Namen. Berlin & Hamburg, Parey, 1973. xiv, 854p. $350. ISBN: 068656474x.
2 parts: 1. Vertebrates; 2. Invertebrates. Each part has *c.*30,000 entries. Index of scientific names follows the German/Latin/Russian and Russian/Latin/German sequences. Bibliography, p.398-833.
Class No: 590(038)

[2725]
LEFTWICH, A.W. A Dictionary of zoology. 3rd ed. London, Constable; New York [etc.], Van Nostrand, 1973. ix, 478p.
First published as *A Student's dictionary of zoology* (1963).
About 6,700 concise definitions (4-100 words). Cross-references. Part 2: 'English names'; Part 3: 'Principles of classification and nomenclature'. Excludes 'such medical and anatomical terms which are to be found in any medical dictionary and such elementary biological terms as are to be found in any school textbook' (*Preface*). Appended simplified classification of the animal kingdom, p.468-74. Bibliography, p.475-8. *Class No:* 590(038)

[2726]
PENNAK, R.W. Collegiate dictionary of zoology. Melbourne, Fla., Krieger, 1987. 594p. $26.50. ISBN: 0898749212.
About 20,000 definitions of terms in zoology and allied fields, - unlike Leftwich. Many cross-references; references from common names to Latin names. Appended: condensed taxonomic outline of the animal kingdom. *Class No:* 590(038)

Reviews & Abstracts

[2727]
The Zoological record, being the record of zoological literature relating to the year... York, BIOSIS, UK, and London, Zoological Society, 1865 (covering 1864)-. v.1-. Annual parts. $3,250pa. ISSN: 01443607.
V.1-6 as *Record of zoological literature;* v.43-52 (1906-15) formed Section N of the *International catalogue of scientific literature.* Since v.115 (covering 1978) published jointly by BIOSIS UK and the Society.
1. *Comprehensive zoology.* 2. *Protozoa* (1. Recent; 2. Fossil). 3. *Porifera.* 4. *Coelenterata.* 5. *Echinodermata.* 6. *Platyhelminthes, annelida, conodonta* (A,B,C). 7. *Brachiopoda.* 8. *Bryozoa* (Polyzoa). 9. *Mollusca.* 10. *Crustacea* (1. Recent; 2. Fossil). 11. *Trilobita.* 12. *Arachnida.* 13. *Insecta* (A,B,C,D,E,F). 14. *Protochordata.* 15. *Pisces* (1. Recent; 2. Fossil). 16. *Amphibia.* 17. *Reptilia.* 18. *Aves.* 19. *Mammalia.* 20. *List of new genera and subgenera.*
About 80,000 references pa. (27 parts). Each part consists of author list of papers and books, with subject, geographic, palaeontological and systematic indexes. The most important record for retrospective

....(contd.)
searching in systematic zoology (including palaeontology). Online database, 1978-, via DIALOG and Ovid Technologies. CD-ROM version also available. *Class No:* 590(048)

Nomenclatures

[2728]
GOZMANY, L. Vocabularium nominum animalium Europae system linguis redactum. Budapest, Akadémiae Kiadó, 1979. 2v. (lxiii, 1171p. + 1015p.).
1979 ed. published in the US and UK in 1990 as *Seven-language thesaurus of European animals* (Chapman & Hall. £135).
V.1 contains 12,000 numbered entries for terms in Latin, German, English, French, Hungarian, Spanish and Russian. V.2 is an index of vernacular names, linked by the numbers to the scientific names of European animals (including insects) in v.1. *Class No:* 590(083.72)

[2729]
International code of zoological nomenclature. 3rd ed. London, International Trust for Zoological Nomenclature, in association with British Museum (Natural History), etc., 1985. xx, 338p. £15. ISBN: 085301003x.
Adopted by the 20th General Assembly of the International Union of Biological Sciences. Previous ed., 1964.
The Code (in French and English facing) occupies 18 sections, p.3-179. Appendices A-F include A. Code of ethics; D. Recommendations on the formation of names. Glossary, p.251-97. Index of scientific names; English index. The new Code came into force on 1 January 1983. An important key. *Class No:* 590(083.72)

[2730]
Nomenclator zoologicus: a list of names of genera and subgenera in zoology, from the tenth edition of Linnaeus, 1758, to the end of 1945. Neave, S.A., *ed.* London, Zoological Society of London, 1939-75. v.1-7.
V.4 includes a short supplement (addenda and corrigenda). V.5: 1936-45 (1950) includes further addenda and corrigenda to v.1-4. V.6 (1960) covers 1945-55; v.7 (1975), 1956-65.
Entries consist of name; namer; data; source (journal reference, etc.); genus. About 270,000 entries, so far. *Class No:* 590(083.72)

[2731]
SHERBORN, C.D. Index animalium: sive, Index nominum quae ab A.D. MDCCLVII generibus et speciebus animalium imposita sunt ... Sectio prima a kalendis Ianuariis MDCCLVIII usque ad finem Decembris MDCCC. Cambridge Univ. Press, 1902. liv, 1195p. ISBN: 0565008030. *Class No:* 590(083.72)

[2732]
—SHERBORN, C.D. Sectio secunda a kalendis Ianuariis MDCCCCI usque ad finem Decembris MDCCCL. London, the Trustees of the British Museum (Natural History, 1922-33). 33pts. i.
This set, one of the basic reference works of taxonomic zoology, covering the period 1758-1850, contains 440,000 references, recorded over 43 years. It has been described as one of the most outstanding examples of patient, painstaking and self-sacrificing industry of all times. *Class No:* 590(083.72)

Illustrations

[2733]
MUNZ, L.T. *and* SLAUSON, N.G. Index to illustrations of living things outside North America: where to find pictures of flora and fauna. Hamden, Conn., Archon/Shoe String Press, 1981. 441p. $55. ISBN: 0208018573.
Companion to *Index to illustrations of the natural world: where to find pictures of the living things of North America; (q.v.)* compiled by J.W. Thompson (Syracuse, N.Y., Gaylord, 1977, 265p.).
Entries for over 9,000 species, drawn from illustrations in 206 books. The main index has entry under common name, plus scientific name and source, indicating type of illus. (coloured or black-and-white). Scientific name index follows. Bibliography, under titles. Wide-ranging, but highly selective (*Choice,* v.19(8), April 1982, p.1046). *Class No:* 590(084.1)

[2734]
NISSEN, C. Die Zoologische Buchillustration. Stuttgart, Hiersemann, 1969-78. 2v.
V.1 (*Bibliographie*) records 4,826 numbered items, with bibliographical notes. Detailed indexes, under titles of books, countries, subjects and authors. List of sources cited, p.5-7. V.2 (*Geschichte*) concerns the history of zoological illustration.
Class No: 590(084.1)

[2735]

—KNIGHT, D. Zoological illustration: an essay towards a history of printed zoological pictures. Folkestone, Kent, Dawson, 1977. 224p. illus. £14. ISBN: 0712907866.

Has 103 illus. of average quality. Each chapter carries a fairly lengthy bibliography. Thorough text; inadequate index (*Journal of natural history*, v.12(5), September/October 1978, p.591-2). *Class No*: 590(084.1)

Histories

[2736]

Turning points in zoological sciences: a Royal Society Discussion organized ... as part of the 150th anniversary celebrations of the Zoological Society of London, 30th September 1976. London, Royal Society, 1977. vi, 107p. ISBN: 085403093x.

First published in *Proceedings of the Royal Society of London*, series B, v.199, no.1138, p.335-443.

8 papers: 1. Concepts in morphongesis - 2. The physiology of wild animals - 3. Chemical communication - 4. Chromosomal changes in vertebrate evolution - 5. Genes and the structure of organisms - 6. Mechanics, fields, and statistical mechanics in development biology - 7. On integration and teleonomy - 8. Hormones and behaviour. Each paper has its own bibliography and was 'chosen to illustrate some of the advances that have taken place over a wide field during the past 150 years' (*Preface*). *Class No*: 590(091)

Libraries

[2737]

'Sci-tech libraries serving zoological gardens'. In *Science and technology libraries*, v.8(4), Summer 1988, p.1-60.

The introduction is followed by 7 documented contributions. Confined to US zoological libraries. Final contribution: 'American zoological park libraries: historical considerations and their archival status'. *Class No*: 590:061:026/027

Institutions & Associations

[2738]

CURLE, R.H.P. The Ray Society: a bibliographical history. London, Quaritch, for the Ray Society, 1954. vi, 101p. ports. £5. ISBN: 0903874075.

The object of the Ray Society (founded 1844) is to publish monographs and memoirs on zoology and botany, with special reference to British fauna and flora. This history, produced on the occasion of the Society's centenary, includes a list of the Ray Society's publications, 1844-1951, as well as a bibliography, arranged by subjects, with bibliographical notes on each item (p.32-95). *Class No*: 590:061:061.2

[2739]

ISIS world geographic and zoological institution directory: a listing of the world's zoos and aquariums, natural history museums of the United States and Canada, and world geopolitical divisions. Makey, D.G., *and others*. St. Paul, Minn., ISIS (International Species Inventory System), 1974. x, 342, xp. Loose-leaf.

Geographical arrangement (Continental Europe ... Oceania). Institution bibliography, p.339. *Class No*: 590:061:061.2

[2740]

ZUCKERMAN, S. The Zoological Society of London, 1826-1976 and beyond. Symposium of the Zoological Society of London. London, etc., Academic Press, for the Zoological Society, 1976. xviii, 353p. illus., graphs, plans, tables, maps. ISBN: 0126133409.

20 documented contributions (*e.g.* 'The Royal Society of London: evolution of a constitution'; 'The Library and scientific publications of the Zoological Society of London' ... 'The introduction of new species of animals for the purpose of domestication'). General index, p.337-53. *Class No*: 590:061:061.2

Zoos

[2741]

International zoo yearbook. London, Zoological Society of London, 1961-. Annual. Price varies. ISSN: 00749664.

V.36, 1998 (viii, 663p. 1998) has 3 sections by various hands: 1. Old world primates. p.11-142 - 2. The developing zoo world, p.143-258 - 3. Reference section, p.259-663 : (*e.g.* Species of fishes bred in captivity during 1995/6 and multiple generation births; Census of rare animals in captivity 1996/97). Appendix 1: Taxonomic authorities consulted in the *Yearbook*. Author and suject indexes, v.35-36. Articles are documented. *Class No*: 590:061.3

[2742]

The World of zoos: a survey and gazetteer. Kirchshofer, R., *ed*. 1st English language ed. Translated by H. Morris. London, Batsford, 1968. 327p. illus. (incl. col.).

Originally as *Zoologische Gärten der Welt* (Frankfurt-am-Main, Umschau Verlag). 1966.

Two main sections - apart from introduction and articles - are the illus. (p.33-145), plates, usually in colour, plus action photographs of animals etc., and a gazetteer. The latter (p.219-321) arranges the world's zoological gardens by countries A-Z. Abbreviations denote availability of conducted tours, demonstrations, facilities for filming and photography, research work, size, staff, opening hours, etc. *Class No*: 590:061.3

Practical Work (Techniques)

[2743]

MAHONEY, R. Laboratory techniques in zoology. 2nd ed. London, Butterworths, 1973. 516p. illus., diagrs., illus. ISBN: 0408704675.

First published 1966.

12 chapters (each with small bibliography): 1. Phylum technology - 2. Aquarium and vivarium management - 3. Histological technique - 4. Electron microscope technique (new) - 5. Embryological techniques - 6. Fluid preservation - 7. Injection and corrosion techniques - 8. Museum techniques - 9. Techniques for the preparation of vertebrate skeletons - 10. Physiological techniques - 11. Palaeontological techniques - 12. Useful data. The sections on electrophoresis and chromatography are deliberately kept short because of adequate coverage in other textbooks. Index, p.499-518. *Class No*: 590.08

Collections

[2744]

HANCOCK, E.G. *and* **MORGAN, P.J. A Survey of zoological and botanical material in museums and other institutions of Great Britain.** Secretary, Biology Curators Group, c/o City Museum, Sheffield, 1980. 32p. tables. ISBN: 0905709204.

2 sections: 1. Zoological holdings; 2. Botanical holdings. Mainly tables (*e.g.* Section 1, table 2: Zoological holdings of national and university museums). Zoological appendix: numbers of zoological specimens of 32 phyla, class or order present in museums - Botanical appendix: numbers of botanical specimens present in museums and universities. Needs updating. *Class No*: 590.082

Physical Zoology

[2745]

DAVIS, S.J.M. The Archaeology of animals. London, Batsford, 1987. 224p. illus., facsims., diagrs., tables, maps. £19.99. ISBN: 0713445718.

Part 1 (chapters 1-4): Methods and problems in zoo-archaeology - Part 2 (chapters 5-8): 5. Our hunting; 6. From hunter to herder: the origin of domestic animals; 7. Later domesticates and the secondary use of animals; 8. Britain: a zoo-archaeological case study. Over 150 drawings. References, p.197-208. Index, p.215-24 (most entries are for goat, pig and sheep). 'Intended primarily for students of archaeology and anyone with an interst in both natural history and the history of our own species' (*Introduction*). *Class No*: 591.04

Animals (Fauna)

Bibliographies

[2746]

QUINN, M.E. 'Animals: a selected list of reference tools'. In *Booklist*, v.88(20), 15 June 1992, p.1869-74.

21 annotated entries covering general works; birds; fish; insects; mammals; reptiles and amphibians. *Class No*: 591.1(01)

Encyclopaedias

[2747]

TREMAIN, R. The Animals who's who: celebrated animals in history, popular culture, literature and lore. London, Routledge & Kegan Paul, 1982. xv, 335p. illus., facsims. ISBN: 0710094493.

Features over 1,100 animals, 'Aardy' [Aardvak] ... 'Zsa Zsa' [a rabbit]. Inclusions: Balaam's ass; Mickey Mouse; The Cheshire cat; Winnie the Pooh; Black Beauty. Entries include information on the significance or derivation of the name or phrase. Selected biography,

....(contd.)
p.289-93; Picture credits, p.295-304. Detailed index of over 2,000 terms, listing titles, authors, individuals, names of nonbook sources, etc. *Class No:* 591.1(031)

Handbooks & Manuals

[2748]
BALOUET, J.-C. *and* ALIBERT, E. **Extinct species of the world:** lessons for our future. Translated by K.J. Hollyman. London, Charles Letts, 1990. 192p. illus. (col.), maps. $19.95. ISBN: 1852381000.

After an introductory section, 'The extinct species', there are 11 sections, arranged geographically, *e.g.* 'The Indian Ocean'; 'North America'. 'Plants and animals that humans have made extinct', p.182-88. Many colour drawings. Index. For school and public libraries. *Class No:* 591.1(035)

[2749]
Grzimek's animal life encyclopedia. Grzimek, B., *ed.* New York, London, etc., Van Nostrand Reinhold, 1972-74. 13v. illus., maps. ISBN: 0317388533.

Originally Kindler Verlag AG, Zurich, 1966-70.

About 150 contributors, mostly German. Coverage: v.1. Lower animals - v.2. Insects - 3. Mollusks - 4/5. Fishes. Amphibians - 6. Reptiles - 7/9. Birds - 10/13. Mammals. Each volume has an index and appendices (including a four-language dictionary in English, German, French and Russian; conversion tables; supplementary readings). Well illustrated. 'Emphasis is on what animals do, their habitats, behaviour, feeding and breeding biology ... Anatomy, physiology and ethnology take second place' (*TLS*, no.3669, 23 June 1972, p.729). 'The single most complete source on the animal kingdom' (*RQ*, v.25 (1), Fall 1985, p.146). *Class No:* 591.1(035)

[2750]
Longman illustrated animal encyclopedia. Whitfield, P., *consultant ed.* Harlow, Essex, Longman, 1984. 600p. ISBN: 0582556910.

US edition as *Macmillan illustrated animal encyclopedia.* Also republished in a 'compact edition', Longman, 1988 (600p.).

Covers c.2,000 species of living vertebrate animals: mammals (p.10-193); birds (p.194-401); reptiles; amphibians; fishes. Data: name, range, habitat, size, commentary. Two-page spreads, illus., facing text. Classification, p.584-7. Detailed analytical index. *Class No:* 591.1(035)

[2751]
—The New Larousse encyclopedia of animal life. Burton, M., *ed.* Rev. ed. London, Hamlyn, 1980. 640p. col. illus. ISBN: 0883321327.

1967 ed (also 640p.) as *Larousse encyclopedia of animal life.*

Chief feature: the generous-sized full-colour illustrations. Systematic order of text, from protozoa to mammalia. Glossary. Further reading list (revised and updated). Index. Good value. *Class No:* 591.1(035)

[2752]
Remarkable animals: a unique encyclopaedia of wildlife wonders. Sundén, U., *ed.* Enfield, Middx., Guinness Superlatives Ltd., 1987. 239p. illus. (col.). £12.95. ISBN: 085112867x.

Contents: Mammals (p.7-81) - Birds (p.82-129) - Fishes (p.130-65) - Amphibians and reptiles (p.166-205) - Insects and arachnids (p.206-35). Popular, almost sensationalistic, treatment of zoology, but well-produced and highly readable. *Class No:* 591.1(035)

Illustrations

[2753]
CLEWIS, B. **Index to illustrations of animals and plants.** New York, Neal-Schuman, 1991. 217p. $49.95. ISBN: 1555700721.

3 sections: 1. How to use this book - 2. Key to abbreviations of sources - 3. Common-name index (161p.). Data for each entry include code citation, type of illustration and page number. Scientific-name index and 9-page bibliography. 'An outstanding reference for science collections and picture researchers' (*Booklist*, 1 May 1991, p.1740). *Class No:* 591.1(084.1)

[2754]
Plant, animal and anatomical illustration in art & sciences: a bibliographical guide from the 16th century to the present day. Bridson, G.D.R. *and* White, J.J., *comps.* Winchester, Herts., St. Paul's Bibliographies; Detroit, Omnigraphics, 1990. ix,450p. facsims. £75. ISBN: 0906795818.

7,670 entries arranged chronologically in each section and including articles as well as books. Sections: A. Bibliographies - B. Nature in general - C. Plants - D. Animals - E. The human body - F. Artist biographies - G. Periodicals. Appendices: Books on colour; Organizations. Title, subject, and name indexes. For research libraries. *Class No:* 591.1(084.1)

Marine Environment

[2755]
BANISTER, K. *and* CAMPBELL, A. **The Encyclopedia of aquatic life.** New York, Facts on File, 1985. 367p. illus (mostly col.). $45. ISBN: 0816012571.

3 sections: Fishes - Invertebrates - Marine mammals. Data concentrate on classification, body structure, habits. A feature: 400 colour photographs and fine line-drawings. Glossary. Index (in tiny print). 'One of the best encyclopedias on this topic' (*Library journal*, 1 March 1986, p.87). *Class No:* 591.1(26)

[2756]
COLEMAN, N. **Encyclopedia of marine animals.** London, Blandford, 1991. 324p. illus. (col.), maps. £12.50. ISBN: 0713722894.

Sections: Sponges - Cnidarians - Flatworms - Segmented worms - Sea mosses - Crustaceans (p.79-109) - Molluscs - Echinoderms - Sea squirts - Fishes (p.189-285) - Reptiles - Mammals. Bibliography, p.306. Over 1,000 colour photographs (mostly small). Index of common names; index of scientific names; index of family names. The photographs are taken from the files of the Australasian Marine Photographic Index (AMPI). *Class No:* 591.1(26)

[2757]
ERWIN, D. *and* PICTON, B. **Guide to inshore marine life.** London, Immel Publishing, 1987. 120p. col. illus. £9.95. ISBN: 0907151345.

Covers 200 of the most common species found in European waters. Includes fish; cnidaria; mollusca; worms; algae. Brief bibliography and index. Colour illustration of each species. Aimed at the enthusiast and suitable for public libraries. *Class No:* 591.1(26)

[2758]
HALSTEAD, B.W. **Poisonous and venomous marine animals of the world.** 2nd ed. Princeton, N.J., Darwin Press, 1988. 1168+288p. illus. (incl. col.). $250. ISBN: 0878500502.

First published 1965-70.

Taxonomic order of well over 500 species; documented chapters. 288 pages of plates. Personal name index. Subject index. Numerous illus. *Class No:* 591.1(26)

[2759]
The Marine fauna of the British Isles and north-west Europe. Hayward, P.J. *and* Ryland, J.S., *eds.* Oxford, Clarendon Press, 1990. 2v. (996p.) figs. £95, v.1; £85, v.2. ISBN: 0198573561, v.1; 0198575157, v.2.

V.1. *Introduction and protozoans for arthropods.* V.2. *Molluscs to chordates.*

Provides dichotomous keys, illustrations, brief descriptions, and distribution notes for over 2,000 species. Cumulated index of technical terms and taxonomic index appear in each volume.

A concise edition, *Handbook of the marine fauna of north-west Europe*, was published in 1995 (OUP. 566p. £60; £29.50). *Class No:* 591.1(26)

[2760]
Multilingual illustrated dictionary of aquatic animals and plants. 2nd ed. Osney Mead, Oxford, Fishing News Books, 1998. 1, 548p. figs. ISBN: 0852382405.

First published 1993.

Contains details of more than 1,450 species of fish, crustaceans, molluscs, seaweeds, and other fishery products. Data for each entry include: reference number, scientific name, family name, and the name in 11 languages: English; French; German; Italian; Dutch; Danish; Spanish; Portuguese; Greek; Finnish; Swedish. Many illustrations. *Class No:* 591.1(26)

Diseases

[2761]
Zoo and wild animal medicine. Fowler, M.E., *ed.* 4th ed. Philadelphia, Pa., etc., W.B. Saunders Co., 1999. xxiii, 747p. illus., diagrs., tables. $89. ISBN: 0721686648.

Sponsored by Morris Animal Federation, Denver, Colorado. Previous ed. published 1993.

*c.*100 contributors. Four parts: 1. General topics - 2. Amphibians and reptiles - 3. Birds - 4. Mammals. Appendices include relevant legislation and useful addresses. Many illustrations. Detailed, analytical index. Cover and title-page carry sub-title 'Current therapy 4'. *Class No:* 591.2

Embryology

[2762]
A History of embryology. The eighth symposium of the British Society for Developmental Biology, Nottingham, 1983. Horder, T.J., *and others.* Cambridge, University Press, 1986. xxiv, 477p. diagrs. ISBN: 0521259533.

15 documented papers, including 'Embryology and classical zoology in Great Britain'; 'Hans Spemann and the organiser'; 'Primary embryonic induction in retrospect'; 'Regeneration and holism in

....(contd.)

biology'. Chronological outline precedes, p.xviii-xxiv. Very useful 'References to resources relating to the history of embryology', p.435-62. Index, p.463-77. *Class No: 591.3*

Behaviour

Encyclopaedias & Dictionaries

[2763]

BEAVER, B.V. The Veterinarian's encyclopedia of animal behavior. Ames, Iowa, Iowa State University Press, 1994. xi,307p. $29.95. ISBN: 0813821142.

Defines specialist terms, many of which are applicable to all domestic animals but with the main emphasis on cats and dogs. Arranged A-Z with definitions; cross-references to related topics. *Class No: 591.5(03)*

[2764]

Dictionary of farm animal behavior. Hurnik, J.F., *and others*. 2nd ed. Ames, Iowa State University Press, 1995. ix,200p. £19.95; $19.95. ISBN: 0813824648.

First published 1985.

*c.*4,000 terms covering all aspects of farm animal behaviour. Includes colloquialisms. The authors are respected academics in this subject area. *Class No: 591.5(03)*

[2765]

HEYMER, A. Ethological dictionary, German - English - French. New York & London, Garland, 1977. 238p. illus. ISBN: 0824070054.

Several hundred German base-terms, with English and French equivalents and indexes - 'Aggression': 4½ columns in the three languages. Bibliography, p.206-20. 138 illus. *Class No: 591.5(03)*

[2766]

IMMELMANN, K. *and* BEER, C. A Dictionary of ethology. Cambridge, Mass., Harvard University Press, 1989. xiii,336p. $35. ISBN: 0674205065.

Covers *c.*900 terms. Abnormal behavior ... Zoosemiotics. Entries vary in length - 'Companion': 1½ lines, 'Habituation': 1 page. Many cross-references. 3-page bibliography. 'An excellent companion to *The Oxford companion to animal behaviour* (1981) and to *Grzimek's encyclopedia of ethology*' (*Science and technology libraries*, v.11(1), Fall 1990, p.137). *Class No: 591.5(03)*

[2767]

The Oxford companion to animal behaviour. McFarland, B., *ed*. Oxford Univ. Press, 1981. (Re-issued, with new index, 1987). [xii], 657p. illus., diagrs., charts, maps. £25; £12.95.

69 contributors. Over 200 longish articles (*e.g.* 'Facial expression': 11p.; 'History of the study of animal behaviour' : 17p.; 'Migration': p.380-7, with 3 maps). Bibliography, p.609-10. Index of English names of animals; index of scientific names of animals. Carefully drawn illus. The first *Oxford companion* on a scientific subject, and 'an impressive addition to a distinguished series' (*Reference book bulletin, 1983-1984*, p.136). Aimed at the layperson. 'Cramped layout and tiny print' (*New scientist*, 20 August 1981, p.483). *Class No: 591.5(03)*

[2768]

PRESTON-MAFHAM, R. *and* PRESTON-MAFHAM, K. The Encyclopedia of land invertebrate behaviour. London, Blandford, 1993. 320p. illus. (some col.). £30. ISBN: 0713721960.

A series of essays describing in considerable detail as many types of behaviour as possible (sexual; egg-laying; parental care; feeding; defensive). 215 photographs and 41 line drawings. Bibliography, p.298-313. Index, p.313-20. Attractively presented. 'Good value for any student or enthusiast requiring a basic and readable introduction to this fascinating aspect of zoology' (*The Year in reference* 1994, no.228). *Class No: 591.5(03)*

Handbooks & Manuals

[2769]

The Audubon Society encyclopedia of animal life. Buettmer, G., *ed*. New York, Clarkson Potter (distributed by Crown), 1982. 606p. illus. (incl. col.).

6 major sections (Animals; Birds; Reptiles; Amphibians; Fishes; Invertebrates), subdivided mostly by families. Data on physical characteristics, social habits, range, habitat and reproductive behaviour. Over 1,000 illus., well captioned and cross-referenced from text. 'Even libraries that own the 13v. Grzimek (1972) will want this harmony of words and pictures' (*Wilson library bulletin*, January 1983, p.428). *Class No: 591.5(035)*

[2770]

Grzimek's encyclopedia of ethology. Grzimek, B., *ed*. English ed., edited by K. Immelmann. New York, London, etc., Van Nostrand Reinhold, 1977. xx, 708p. illus.

Originally published by Kindler Verlag AG, Zurich, 1973.

43 contributors. 43 chapters on animal behaviour (1. History of ethology ... 8. Behavioural functions of hearing ... 18. Predictable patterns in animal signals ... 26. Forms and the study of animals in captivity ... 43. Phytogenetic adaptations in human behaviour). Supplementary readings, p.681-4. Dictionary of ethological terms. Very good coloured illus; descriptive captions. Supplements *Grzimek's animal life encyclopedia. Class No: 591.5(035)*

Reviews & Abstracts

[2771]

Animal behavior abstracts. Bethesda, Md., Cambridge Scientific Abstracts, 1973-. 4pa. $615 (US); $655 (non US) pa. ISSN: 03018695.

Previously published by Information Retrieval, Ltd., London; initially as *Behavioural biology abstracts. Section A, Animal behaviour*.

About 1,200 abstracts per issue, drawn from *c.*5,000 primary and other journals. Subjects of papers range from neurophysiology to ecology, from genetics to social anthropology, and the biology of particular taxonomic groups. Appended: Book notices; Notices of proceedings. Author and analytical subject indexes per issue and annually. Online (LIFE SCIENCES COLLECTION) and also available on magnetic tape and CD-ROM. Also accessible as an Internet version. *Class No: 591.5(048)*

Maps & Atlases

[2772]

JARMAN, C. Atlas of animal migration. London, Heinemann, 1972. 124p. illus., diagrs., maps. ISBN: 0434371459.

6 chapters: 1. Why animals migrate - 2. Birds - 3. Mammals - 4. Fishes - 5. Reptiles and amphibians - 6. Insects. Also a list of migratory bird refuges in the US and bird migration watchpoints in Europe, - each accompanied by a map. World maps show routes used by various migratory bird species and by migratory land and sea animals. Index to text, illus. (or their captions), and map keys. Colourfully illustrated, with numerous maps and easy-to-read text. *Class No: 591.5(084.3)*

Sound Recordings & Tapes

[2773]

BRITISH BROADCASTING CORPORATION. Catalogue of natural history recordings. 4th ed. London, BBC Recorded Programme Library, 1969. 2v. [vi], 488p.

Previous issue, 1961.

V.1 covers species, with index of scientific names; v.2, habitat (atmosphere).

Wildlife Sound Recording Society, c/o BLOWS (British Library of Wildlife Sounds) has a National Sound Archive, London, that includes a collection of recordings of more than 5,000 species of bird calls and song (Wyatt, H.V., *ed. Information sources in the life sciences*. 3rd ed., 1987, p.158). *Class No: 591.5(086.7)*

Europe

[2774]

The 'Country Life' guide to animals of Britain and Europe: their tracks, trails and signs. London, Country Life Books, 1984. 320p. illus. (mostly col.). $64. ISBN: 0600388042.

Covers tracks and trails of most European mammals and many types of birds and invertebrates. Also a guide to feeding remains, pellets, droppings, etc. Glossary, p.311-2; selected bibliography, p.313. Analytical index, p.314-20. Illus. have descriptive captions. *Class No: 591.5(4)*

Histology

[2775]

KRSTIĆ, R.V. Illustrated encyclopedia of human histology. Berlin, Springer-Verlag, 1984. 450p. illus. ISBN: 3540131426.

Etymology and definitions of terms are supported by more than 1,500 illustrations (photographs, micrographs, line drawings), with adequate suggestions for further readings and cross-references. 'This excellent volume should be available for all students of biology, lower-division onwards' (*Choice*, v.22(9), May 1985, p.1306). *Class No: 591.8*

Geographic Distribution of Animals

[2776]

BARTHOLOMEW, J.G. **Atlas of zoogeography:** a series of maps illustrating the distribution of over seven hundred families, genera and species of existing animals. Under the patronage of the Royal Geographical Society. Edinburgh, Bartholomew, 1911. vi, 67, xip. + 36 double pl. of maps.

Formed v.5 of Bartholomew's *Physical atlas*.

About 220 (chiefly world) maps, illustrating distribution of 'the higher animals [mammals, birds, reptiles and amphibians, with selected fishes, molluscs and insects] over the surface of the earth' (*Preface*). Sections of text: 1. General principles - 2. Historical and geographical - 3. Zoological explanation of plates - 4. Bibliography, p.57-67 (*c*.1,000 items, arranged by regions and then by animals). General index. Size: 45 x 30cm. *Class No: 591.9*

[2777]

Flora & fauna of localities: a bibliography of books and articles dealing with plants and animal life of specific countries and regions of the world. Huckin, D., *ed.* Caldicote, Biggleswade, Beds., Clover Publications, 1981. 2v. £12.50, set. ISBN: 0907755003, set.

1. *Great Britain and Europe*. [ix], 118p. 2. *Africa, America, Asia, Australia & USSR*. viii, 158p.

The bibliography excludes school texts, conference papers and symposium proceedings, as well as erudite material only likely to be of use to a specialist. *Class No: 591.9*

[2778]

Key works to the fauna and flora of the British Isles and Northwestern Europe. Kerrich, G.J., *and others, eds.* London, Systematics Association, 1978. xii, 179p.

First published 1942.

About 2,500 entries, with occasional annotations, covering books and periodical articles. Systematic arrangement. Supersedes the Systematics Association's *Bibliography of key works for the identification of the British fauna and flora*, by J. Smart and G. Taylor (1953). No index. For more specialized scientific libraries. 'Graduate and professional levels' (*Choice*, v.16(1), March 1979, p.54,56). *Class No: 591.9*

[2779]

LEVER, C. **The Naturalized animals of the British Isles.** London, Hutchinson, 1977. 600p. illus., tables, maps. ISBN: 0091277906.

4 parts (59 sections): 1. Mammals - 2. Birds - 3. Amphibians and reptiles - 4. Fish. Section 29: 'Mandarin ducks', p.282-98 (with 2 illus., 1 location map). Chronological table of introduction of animals. Chapter bibliography, p.521-56; general bibliography, p.557-8. Indexes of people, species and places. End-paper maps. 'The first comprehensive account of the exotic vertebrates of the British Isles; (*Foreword*). 'A work of formidable scholarship' (*British book news*, January 1986, p.37). *Class No: 591.9*

Systematic Zoology (Categories of Animals)

Invertebrates

[2780]

GEORGE, J.D. *and* GEORGE, J.J. **Marine life:** an illustrated encyclopedia of invertebrates in the sea. London, Harrap, 1979. 288p. illus. (col. pl.).

Combines text and 128p. of colour plates (10 illus. per plate). The text includes biological, behavioural and ecological notes. Valuable bibliography (p.264-8), including identification guides. Glossary, p.269-70. Detailed index, p.273-88 (*c*.3,000 entries). *Class No: 592.0*

[2781]

HYMAN, L.H. **The Invertebrates.** New York, London, etc., McGraw-Hill, 1940-1967. 6v.

1. *Protozoa thru ctenophora*. 1940. 2. *Platyhelminthes and rhynochocoeia*. 1951. 3. *Acanthocephala: aschelminthes and entroproeta*. 1951. 4. *Echinodermata*. 1955. 5. *Smaller coelomate groups*. 1950. 6. *Mollusca, 1*. 1967.

A comprehensive treatise on the morphology, embryology, physiology, etc. of the invertebrates, concentrating on the group rather than on the species. Each volume-section has extensive references to the literature. Fully illustrated. *Class No: 592.0*

[2782]

Living invertebrates. Pearse, V., *and others.* Palo Alto, Calif., Blackwell Scientific Publications, 1987. xi, 848p. illus. (incl. col.), diagrs. ISBN: 0865423121.

31 chapters include Sponges; Nemerteans; Mollusc body plan; Crustaceans; Chelicerates; Myriapods; Insects; Echinoderms; Invertebrate chordates. 'For each taxon we give a proper name, common name if any, brief nontechnical characterization, notes on habits and habitats, and examples of common or representative genera'

....(contd.)

(*Preface*). Names chosen are those thought best to express relationships between the animals. Small-type notes supplement the text. Bibliography, p.821-9. Index, p.831-48. *Class No: 592.0*

[2783]

NICHOLS, D. *and* COOKE, J.A.C. **The Oxford book of invertebrates:** protozoa, sponges, coelemerates, worms, molluscs, echinoderms and arthropods (other than insects). London, Oxford Univ. Press, 1971. viii, 218p. illus. (col.).

Coloured illus. on recto (*c*.5 species per illus.), facing descriptions; arranged phylum by phylum. 'A classification of invertebrates', p.192-207; glossary, p.208-9. 'Sources of further information' includes societies and associations, p.210. Illus. are all drawn to the same scale, 'except where great differences in size have made this impossible' (*Introduction*). Good colour. *T.S.L.* (24 November 1971, p.1611) notes lack of simple, illustrated keys. Intended for the layman. *Class No: 592.0*

[2784]

RUPPERT, E.E. **Invertebrate zoology.** 6th ed. Fort Worth, Texas, Saunders College Publishing, 1994. xii, 1056p. illus., diagrs. ISBN: 0030266688.

First published 1963. 5th ed., 1987. Editions 1-5 by R.D. Barnes.

A textbook on major, minor and even some fossil invertebrate phyla. 6th edition contains new chapters on bilateral symmetric organisms, and protochordates. Authoritative, readable and finely illustrated by photographs and drawings (300 new to this edition). 'With attention to living invertebrates, this textbook emphasizes the correlations between structure and function and the development of conceptual themes' (*Booknews Inc*, October 1994). *Class No: 592.0*

Protozoa

[2785]

Protozoological abstracts. Wallingford, Oxon., CAB International, 1977-. 12pa. £425; $745. ISSN: 03091287.

About 4,000 abstracts and references pa. Sections: Hosts; General reviews; Associations; Taxonomy and nomenclature; Morphology and ultrastructure; Evolution and genetics; Immunity, serology and resistance; Pathology and pathogenicity; Biochemistry, physiology and behaviour; Epidemiology and epizootiology; Control; Technique; Life-history; Free-living forms; Unclassified. Reports; Conferences; Books. Author and subject indexes per issue and pa. Online, CAB ABSTRACTS. *Class No: 593.1*

Marine Plankton

[2786]

BOLTOVSKOY, E. **Diccionario de la terminologia de plancton marine** en cinco idiomas: inglés, español, alemán, francés y ruso. Buenos Aires, República Argentina, Secretaria de Marina, Servicio de Hidrografia Naval, 1963. xix, 107p.

3,773 numbered items in English, with equivalents in Spanish, German, French and Russian. Groups of organisms (*e.g.* foraminifera) are categorized. Spanish, German, French and Russian indexes. *Class No: 593.14*

[2787]

—WIMPENNY, R.S. **The Plankton of the sea.** London, Faber, 1966. 3-426p. illus. (incl. pl.), diagrs., tables.

Gives a detailed account of the distribution and behaviour of planktonic animals. Extensive bibliography, p.308-28. *Class No: 593.14*

Molluscs. Shellfish & Shells

[2788]

ABBOTT, R.T. *and* DANCE, S.P. **Compendium of seashells:** a colour guide to more than 4,200 of the world's marine shells. New York, Dutton, 1982 (reprinted 1986, Melbourne, Fl., American Malacologists; London, Letts, 1991). ix, 410p. col. illus. $49.95. ISBN: 0525932690.

Univalves (p.18-283) - Dentaliums and tusk shells - Bivalves - Nautilus and squids. Strange forms of shells and non-mullusks - Taxonomic classification of mollusca, with major bibliographic references, p.379-90. Includes data on 180 species of cowries, 334 cones, 132 volutes, 140 scallops, etc. Captioned col. illus. Index to popular names; index to scientific names. 'Offers a quick guide to those maritime species the amateur conchologist is most likely to encounter when doing fieldwork, exchanging or purchasing from commercial sources' (*Preface*). *Class No: 594*

[2789]
KERNEY, M.P. *and* CAMERON, R.A.D. **A Field guide to the land snails of Britain and north-west Europe.** London, Collins, 1979. 288p. col. illus., tables, maps.
Coverage: Great Britain and Ireland, Scandinavia, East and West Germany, France, Belgium and Holland. Text sections: The biology of slugs and snails; Finding, collecting and preserving slugs and snails; Mapping schemes. Glossary of shell terms. Systematic check-list of the land molluscs of N.W. Europe (26 families), p.39-212. Greenhouse aliens. Bibliography and societies, p.213-4. Index. 24 colour plates; 276 + 116 distribution maps. A compact compendium. *Class No: 594*

[2790]
The Macdonald encyclopedia of shells. London, Macdonald, 1982. 512p. col. illus., tables, maps. ISBN: 0356085759.
5 chapters: Soft surface mollusks (entries 1-133) - Firm surface mollusks (134-221) - Coral dwellers (222-302) - Other marine mollusks (303-35) - Land and fresh water mollusks (336-57). Classified table of the species mentioned in text. Glossary. Detailed index of entries, p.503-12. Data on appearance, size, geographical occurrence and ecological environment; symbols roughly indicate dimensions. Small format. 1,230 col. illus.; distribution maps. *Class No: 594*

[2791]
—ROGERS, J.E. **The Shell book:** a popular guide to a knowledge of the families of living mollusks, and an aid to the identification of shells, native and foreign. Boston, Mass., C.T. Branford, 1908. (Reprinted 1936). xxi, 503p. illus. (incl. col.).
Rev. ed. 1951 adds preface and appended 'List of modern names'.
5 parts: 1. How to know shells - 2. The univalves and chitons - 3. The tooth shells - 4. The bivalves - 5. The cephalopods. Analytical index, p.467-80. Illustration index, p.481. 104 illus. (8 in colour). *Class No: 594*

[2792]
SMITH, S.M. *and* HEPPELL, D. **Checklist of British marine mollusca.** Edinburgh, National Museums of Scotland, 1991. 114p. (*National Museums of Scotland information series, no.11.*) ISSN: 09527737.
Aims to present an up-to-date taxonomy of the species. Includes deep-water and pelagic species. Systematic list of higher taxa, p.4-8. Notes on the taxonomy and nomenclature, p.80-9. References, p.89-93. Index to genera and species, p.94-114. *Class No: 594*

[2793]
TEBBLE, N. **British bivalve seashells:** a handbook for identification. 2nd ed. London, HMSO, 1976, for the Royal Scottish Museum. v, 212p. illus. (incl. col.). ISBN: 011491401x.
First published 1966 (Trustees of the British Museum (Natural History, v, 212p.).
Descriptions of seashells (Nut-shells: Nuculacea ... Poromyas and cuspidarias: Potomyacea), p.23-206. Index to superfamily, family and specific names, p.207-12. Literature, p.6-7; glossary, p.7-11. 110 illus. *Class No: 594*

[2794]
Wagner and Abbott's standard catalog of shells. Wagner, R.J.L. *and* Abbott, R.T., *ed.* 3rd ed. Greenville, Delaware, American Malacologists, Inc., 1978-. vp. maps. Loose-leaf.
First published 1964 as *Van Nostrand's standard catalog of shells.*
A systematic account of the molluscs, with biological data on families and genera. Other sections note world size-records and values, shell collection catalogues, maps, glossary, bibliographies, collecting methods, expeditions, history, biography, newsletter, etc. Indexes. *Class No: 594*

[2795]
WYE, K.R. **The Illustrated encyclopaedia of shells.** London, Headline; New York, Facts on File, 1991. 288p. illus. (col.). £19.95. ISBN: 0747204683; 0816027021, US ed.
Published in the US as *The Encyclopedia of shells.*
Data on about 1,200 shells include common name; species name; locality; habitat depth; average size; general description; stylized shape. A colour illustration accompanies each entry. Glossary, indexes to Latin and common names, and brief bibliography. For serious shell-collectors although its coverage is not as extensive as Abbott and Dance's *Compendium of seashells (q.v.). Class No: 594*

Worms

[2796]
Helminthological abstracts. CAB Institute of Parasitology, St. Albans. Wallingford, Oxon., CAB International, 1932-. 12pa. £305; $550.
Continues *Helminthological abstracts. Series A. Animal and human helminthology.*
Contains *c.*5,000 abstracts pa. in 15 sections (Animal hosts - Associations - Morphology, taxonomy and nomenclature ... Cytology, genetics and evolution - Hirudinea - Unclassified). Reports.

....(contd.)
Conferences. Books. Author and subject indexes per issue and annually. Available online CAB ABSTRACTS, and on CD-ROM. *Class No: 595.1*

[2797]
POZNIAK, G.I., *comp.* **Russian-English dictionary of helminthology and plant nematology.** Farnham Royal, Slough, Commonwealth Agricultural Bureaux, 1979. 108,xp. £17.85. (*Commonwealth Institute of Helminthology, TC no.49.*) ISBN: 0851984479.
Defines and explains more than 6,000 terms from the fields of helminthology (animal and human) and nematology (plant and parasites and free-living forms). Intended for scientific translators and abstractors, professional linguists and scientists. *Class No: 595.1*

Spiders

[2798]
HAMMEN, L. van der, *ed.* **Glossaire de la terminologie acarologique.** [Glossary of acarological terminology.] The Hague, W. Junk, 1976-. v.1-.
1. *General.* 2. *Opilioacarida.* 3. *Holothyrida.* 4. *Gamasida.* 5. *Ixodida.* 6. *Actinedida.* 7. *Oribatida.* 8. *Tarsonemida.* 9. *Acaridida.*
V.1 has *c.*2,000 entries for terms in French, English and German. *Class No: 595.4*

[2799]
The Insect and spider collections of the world. Arnett, R.H., *and others.* 2nd ed. Gainsville, Fla., Sandhill Crane Press, 1993. vi,310p. $30. (*Flora and fauna handbook, no.11.*) ISBN: 1877743151.
First published 1986.
Data for each entry: number of specimens; curators; region covered; means of storage; loan policy. Taxonomic index. Name index to curators or private owners. Brief bibliography. *Class No: 595.4*

[2800]
JONES, D. **A Guide to spiders of Britain and northern Europe.** Rev. ed. London, Hamlyn, 1989. 320p. col. illus. £10.95. ISBN: 0600567109.
First published 1983 as *Country Life guide to spiders of Britain and northern Europe.*
Covers over 350 spiders and harvestmen. Each entry contains a description of male and female; habitat; size; season; distribution. Many coloured illustrations. Brief list of further reading and equipment suppliers and societies. Index in very small type. *Class No: 595.4*

[2801]
LOCKET, G.H. *and* MILLIDGE, A.F. **British spiders.** London, Ray Society, 1951-74. 3v. illus. £25, v.1-2; £15, v.3. ISBN: 0903874156, v.1-2; 0903874024, v.3.
A systematic description of the species. Each volume has bibliography and index. V.2 includes addenda to v.1, new species, and a check-list of British spiders. V.3 updates the information in v.1-2, providing descriptions of the additional species discovered in Britain, revising nomenclature and giving much more information on distribution. *Class No: 595.4*

[2802]
PRESTON-MAFHAM, R. *and* PRESTON-MAFHAM, K. **Spiders of the world.** Poole, Dorset, Blandford Press; New York, Facts on File, 1984. 191p. illus. (incl. col.). £14.99. ISBN: 0713713771.
8 chapters (2. Structure of spiders - 3. Classification of spiders - 4. Courtships and mating - 5. Life history of spiders - 6. Prey capture - 7. Spider defence mechanisms - 8. Spiders and man). Appendix: Spider families. Glossary. Guide to further reading. Index, p.187-91. 130 illus. (62 in colour). 'It should be very useful to the biologists and a reference for students at all levels' (*Choice*, v.22(3), November 1984, p.449). *Class No: 595.4*

[2803]
ROBERTS, M.J. **Collins field guide: spiders of Britain and northern Europe.** London, Harper Collins, 1995. 383p. illus. (inc. col.). £14.99. ISBN: 0002199815.
Well illustrated (32 col. pl., 1,300 drawings) field guide to 450 species of spider arranged by family (p.76-370), with introductory material on biology of spiders, collecting and preserving, identifying, etc. Glossary, p.371-3. List of associations, suppliers of equipment and books, bibliography, p.375-7. Index, p.377-83. *Class No: 595.4*

[2804]
ROBERTS, M.J. **The Spiders of Great Britain and Ireland.** Colchester, Essex, Harley Books, 1985-87. 3v. (2v. of text; v.3: Colour plates). £150, set. ISBN: 0946589054, v.1; 0946589062, v.2; 0946589070, v.3; 0946589186, set; 094658947x, appendix.
1. *Atypidae - Therdiosomatidae.* 1985. 250p. £50. 2. *Linyphiidae and check list.* 1987. 204p. £50. 3. *Colour plates.* 1985. 250p. £60.
V.1 includes a general introduction to arachnology, including morphology and behaviour, classification and nomenclature. V.1 and 2 are supplemented by 16p. appendix (1993) containing corrections and new species; indexed. V.3 has 237 colour plates illustrating 307 species (in some cases, both sexes). An authoritative textbook for

....*(contd.)*

identification, supplementing both J. Blackwall's pioneer work, *A History of the spiders of Great Britain and Ireland* (1861-64). and *British spiders*, by G.H. Locket and A.F. Millidge (*q.v.*).
Class No: 595.4

Insects

Databases

[2805]

Entomology index of Internet resources URL:http://www.ent.iastate.edu/List/
The Iowa State Entomology Index of Internet Resources is a Web-based directory of Internet insect-related resources. At time of writing, 26 categories (Beekeeping ... Usenet Newsgroups). May also be searched by keyword. Updated weekly and contains a wide breadth of information. *Class No:* 595.7(003.4)

Bibliographies

[2806]

Entomological literature 1800-1864. Gilbert, P., *ed.* Cambridge, Chadwyck-Healey, 1989-91. 49 double-frame, 105mm x 148mm positive monochrome and colour microfiche. £17,950 (complete collection with printed guide and cataloguing on tape/cards).
Approximately 1,800 monographs, in original published language, published between 1800 and 1864, based on Hager's *Bibliotheca entomologica* (Leipzig, 1862). Source of the documents is the British Museum (Natural History) and the editor is that organization's Entomology Librarian. Printed guide provides bibliographic access by author. *Class No:* 595.7(01)

[2807]

GILBERT, P. *and* **HAMILTON, C.J. Entomology: a guide to information sources.** 2nd ed. London, Mansell, 1990. [viii],259p. £40. ISBN: 0720120527.
First published 1983.
8 chapters: 1. Introduction - 2. Naming and identification of insects - 3. Specimens and collections - 4. The literature of entomology (p.72-147: primary journals; review journals; monograph series) - 5. Searching and locating the literature - 6. Keeping up with current events (newsletters, *c.*80 entries) - 7. Entomologists and their organizations - 8. Miscellaneous services (translation services and guides; apicultural information). 1,822 entries for books, periodical articles, journals and organizations. Detailed analytical index, p.243-59. Of the 1st ed., 'A most useful reference work, well ordered, judiciously annotated ...' (*Natural history book reviews*, v.7(3), 1984, p.156). *Class No:* 595.7(01)

[2808]

ROYAL ENTOMOLOGICAL SOCIETY OF LONDON. Catalogue of the Library. [Royal Entomological Society of London]. Boston, Mass., G.K. Hall, 1979. 5v. $565. ISBN: 0816103151.
An author card-catalouge, photolithographically reproduced. About 78,500 entries for 9,000 monographic works, 50,000 pamphlets and 600 journals, as well as manuscripts and drawings. No subject index. Important for earlier material.
Royal Entomological Society of London has also produced *Serial publications in the Library* (1983). *Class No:* 595.7(01)

Handbooks & Manuals

[2809]

BRIAN, M.V. Social insects: ecology and behavioural biology. London, Chapman & Hall; Forestburgh, N.Y., Lubrecht & Cramer, 1983. [x], 377p. illus., diagrs. £45; £22.95; $24.95. ISBN: 041222920x; 0934454450, US ed.
17 chapters (2. Food - 3. Foraging by individuals ... 6. Nests ... 8. Defence - 9. Food processing ... 12. Reproduction - 13. Evolution of insect societies ... 16. Communities - 17. Two themes (*e.g.* 2. Social organization). References, p.322-61. Author and subject indexes. Well produced. *Class No:* 595.7(035)

[2810]

DAVIES, R.G. Outlines of entomology. 7th ed. London, Chapman and Hall, 1988. 408p. diagrs. £44. ISBN: 0412266709.
9 sections: 1. Introduction - 2. Insect structure and function - 3. Development and metamorphosis - 4. Classification and biology ... 7. The biology of insect populations - 8. Biology and control of injurious insects - 9. Select classified bibliography (p.343-83). Index. More fully illustrated than earlier editions. Aimed at all serious students of entomology. *Class No:* 595.7(035)

[2811]

IMMS, A.D. Imms' general textbook of entomology. 10th ed, by O.W. Richards, and R.G. Davies. London, Chapman & Hall, 1977. 2v. (1354p.). £17.95, v.1; £38, v.2. ISBN: 041215210x, v.1; 0412152304, v.2.
9th ed. 1964 (London, Methuen).
1. *Structure, physiology and development.* 2. *Classification and biology.*
A comprehensive treatise, well documented (*e.g.* v.2. Order 26; Diptera, p.951-1071, has bibliography, p.1046-71). Detailed index to v.2 (p.1281-1304), including authors of articles. 'A workmanlike updating by two of the most experienced general entomologists of the day' (*Journal of natural history*, v.12(2), March/April 1978, p.233). *Class No:* 595.7(035)

[2812]

—**COGAN, B.H.** *and* **SMITH, K.G.V.** Insects: instructions for collectors. No.4A. 5th ed. London, British Museum (Natural History), 1974. vi, 169p. ISBN: 056500705x.
Has 37 illus. One of a popular series. *Class No:* 595.7(035)

[2813]

ROYAL ENTOMOLOGICAL SOCIETY OF LONDON. Handbooks for the identification of British insects. London, the Society, 1949-. 11v. illus.
1. 16pts. (General introduction. Thysanura ... Siphonaptera). 1949-57. 2. *Hemiptera*. 8pts. 1965-84. 3. *Lepidoptera*. 4/5. *Coleoptera*. 15pts. 1952-96. 6/8. *Hymenoptera*. 5pts. 1951-78 9/10. *Diptera*. 11pts. 1949-93. 11. *Check list of British insects*. 2nd ed. 5pts. 1964-78.
A detailed, invaluable series, with clear illus., systematic descriptions, and bibliographies. Indispensable for entomologists. *Class No:* 595.7(035)

[2814]

WOOTTON, A. Insects of the world. Poole, Dorset, Blandford Press, 1984. 224p. illus. (incl. col.). £14.99. ISBN: 0713713631.
16 chapters (1. What is an insect? ... 4. Anatomy and movement - 5. Senses and communication - 6. Feeding, digestion and excretion ... 8. Life histories - 9. Courtship and reproduction ... 13. Defences - 14. Migration - 15. Insects and man - 16. Nomenclature and classification). Glossary. 'Guide to further reading', p.241-5. Detailed index, p.216-24. *Class No:* 595.7(035)

Dictionaries

[2815]

KÉLER, S., von. Entomologisches Wörterbuch mit besonderer Berücktigung der morphologischen terminologie. 3. durchgesehene und erw. Aufl. Berlin, Akademie-Verlag, 1963. xvi, 788p. illus. (incl. pl.), tables.
First published 1956.
About 10,000 terms are defined and discussed, sometimes at length and well-documented (*e.g.* Hymenoptera: 7 columns, including 2 columns of bibliography). Different applications of terms are explained with references to sources. Profuse cross-references. A valuable chronological list of glossaries and handbooks precedes (p.1-24). 67p. of plates (drawings, with commentary facing). *Class No:* 595.7(038)

[2816]

SÉGUY, E. Dictionnaire des termes techniques d'entomologie elementaire. Paris, Lechevalier; New York, French & European, 1967. 465p. $175. (*Encyclopédie entomologique, no.41.*) ISBN: 2720504661.
Standard dictionary for French entomological terms.
Class No: 595.7(038)

[2817]

TORRE-BUENO, J.R. de la. The Torre-Bueno glossary of entomology. Nichol, S.W., *comp.* Rev. ed. *Supplement A*, by G.S. Tulloch. New York, New York Entomological Society, in co-operation with the American Museum of Natural History, 1989. xvii,840p. $24.95. ISBN: 0934454450.
First published 1937 (ix,336p.), 2nd ed. 1962.
Greatly expanded from previous eds. with definitions of *c.*16,000 terms. Extensive cross-referencing. Includes a bibliography and classification by orders. Illustrations now omitted. A standard source. *Class No:* 595.7(038)

Reviews & Abstracts

[2818]

Abstracts of entomology, incorporating worldwide research in entomology, pure and applied studies of insecta and arachnida, including chemical, physical, biological controls, economic entomology, physiology, pathology, morphology, systematics, medical entomology, ecology. Philadelphia, Pa., BioScience Information Service, 1970-. 12pa. $540. ISSN: 00013579.
Reprints entries from *Biological abstracts* (*q.v.*) and *Biological*

....(contd.)
abstracts/RRM(q.v.). Author index. Biosystematic index. General index. Subject list. Indexes are in very small type.
Class No: 595.7(048)

[2819]
—LEFTWICH, A.W. A Dictionary of entomology. London, Constable, 1976. [v], 360p.
Provides concise, non-technical definitions of over 4,000 terms, describing nearly 3,000 species of insect. Cross-references. Classification of insects, p.352-800. Bibliography, p.359-60. Aimed at amateur entomologists, naturalists and students of zoology with a special leaning towards entomology. See *Entomology: a guide to information sources*, by P Gilbert and C.J. Hamilton for many errors in the definitions given (*Entomology*, entry 220).
Class No: 595.7(038)

[2820]
Entomology abstracts. Bethesda, Md., Cambridge Scientific Abstracts, 1969-. Monthly. $985pa. ISSN: 00138924.
About 950 abstracts per issue. Sections: General. Bibliography - Systematics - Techniques - Morphology - Physiology, anatomy, histology & biochemistry - Reproduction & development - Behaviour, biology & ecology - Genetics - Evolution - Geography & present-day faunas - Fossil forms & faunas. Notification of proceedings. Book notices. Detailed author and subject indexes per issue. Reprinted from *Biological abstracts*, (q.v.) with its BIOSIS PREVIEWS database. Available on CD-ROM and on-line. *Class No: 595.7(048)*

[2821]
Review of agricultural entomology. Wallingford, Oxon., CAB International, 1989-. 12pa. £545; $955. ISSN: 09576762.
Formerly *Review of applied entomology. Series A: Agriculture,* (1913-1989).
About 1,000 abstracts per issue. 14 sections (Taxonomy - Anatomy, morphology - Reproduction and development - Physiology and biochemistry - Genetics and sterility - Ecology and behaviour - Geographical distribution, faunas ... Disorders - Protection against arthropods and use of arthropods for biological control - Chemicals, including toxicity tests and environmental effects). Books, reports, conferences. Author and subject indexes per issue and annually. Online, CAB ABSTRACTS. *Class No: 595.7(048)*

Progress Reports

[2822]
Advances in insect physiology. London, New York, etc., Academic Press, 1963-. v.1-. Annual. illus., diagrs., tables.
V.27, 1998 has 8 contributors. 4 documented papers (*e.g.* 'Chordontal organs of insects', p.1-228; 'Activity-dependent functional and developmental plasticity of Drosophila neurons', p.385-440. Index. *Class No: 595.7(055)*

[2823]
Annual review of entomology. Palo Alto, Calif., Annual Reviews, Inc., 1956-. v.1-. Annual. $120 (US); $130 (non US). ISSN: 00664170.
V.43, 1998 (750p.) has 30 documented papers (*e.g.* 'Fire and insects in northern and boreal forest ecosystems of North America'; 'Integrated pest management: historical perspectives and contemporary developments'; 'Parasites and pathogens of mites'; 'Spatial heterogeneity and insect adaptation to toxins'). Subject index. Cumulative index of contributing authors, v.34-43. Cumulative index of chapter titles, v.34-43. An important source on current entomological research. Abstracts of papers available online 3 months before publication date at http://www.AnnualReviews.org.
Class No: 595.7(055)

Yearbooks & Directories

[2824]
COLVIN, M. *and* **REAVEY, D.** A Directory for entomologists. 2nd ed. Feltham, Amateur Entomologists' Society, 1993. 62p. (*Amateur Entomologists' Society pamphlet, no.14.*) ISBN: 0900054573.
Contents include national and local societies and special interest groups, conservation, legislation, field courses, entomological reference libraries, periodicals, trade fairs, other directories, etc. For UK field entomologists. *Class No: 595.7(058)*

Biographies

[2825]
GILBERT, P. A Compendium of the biographical literature on deceased entomologists. London, British Museum (Natural History), 1977. vii, 455p. illus. (pl.). ISBN: 0565007866.
Class No: 595.7(092)

[2826]
—OSBORN, H. A Brief history of entomology, including time of Demosthenes and Aristotle to modern times, with over five hundred portraits. Columbus, Ohio, Spahr and Glenn, 1952. iii, 303p. ports.
A popular outline history, of particular value for its *c.*1,000 biographical sketches and the portraits. *Class No: 595.7(092)*

Manuscripts & Incunabula

[2827]
Catalogue of manuscripts in the Entomology Library of the Natural History Museum. Harvey, J.M.V., *and others*. London, Mansell, 1996. xv,251p. £65. (*Historical studies in the life sciences, no.5..*) ISBN: 0720122902.
The introduction gives a brief overview of the collection. The catalogue, p.1-229, contains 355 collections and dates from 1694. Data include brief biographical details of the collector/author and followed by a detailed list of the collection. Name and geographical indexes.
Class No: 595.7(093)

Europe

[2828]
CHINERY, M. A Field guide to the insects of Britain and northern Europe. 3rd ed. London, HarperCollins, 1997. 448p. illus. (mostly col.), £17.99.
First published 1962. Previous ed. 1976.
More than a key with chapters on biology and classification. Number of illustrations has doubled since the previous ed. with *c.*780 colour and *c.*1,000 black-and-white illustrations. A classic work.
Class No: 595.7(4)

[2829]
—GIBBONS, B. Field guide to the insects of Britain and Northern Europe. Marlborough, Wilts., Crowood, 1995. 320p., illus.(col.) £14.99. ISBN: 1852239379.
Covers 22 insect orders and aids identification of *c.*1,500 species. *c.*700 photographs. Well-produced - 'Excellent field guide' (*Choice*, June 1996, p.1667), although is largely identical to Chinery's established work, even in price. *Class No: 595.7(4)*

Museums

[2830]
The Insect and spider collections of the world. Arnett, R.H., *and others*. 2nd ed. Gainsville, Fla., Sandhill Crane Press, 1993. vi,310p. $30. (*Flora and fauna handbook, no.11.*) ISBN: 1877743151.
First published 1986.
Data for each entry: number of specimens; curators; region covered; means of storage; loan policy. Taxonomic index. Name index to curators or private owners. Brief bibliography.
Class No: 595.7:061:069

Butterflies & Moths

Worldwide

[2831]
D'ABRERA, B. Butterflies of the world. Faringdon, Oxon., & Melbourne, Lansdowne Editions, 1977-. 5v. illus., maps.
1. *Butterflies of the Australian region.* 3rd ed. 1990. 416p. (Melbourne, Hill House). 2. *Butterflies of the Afro-tropical region.* Rev. ed. 1997-. (Pt. 1 only; £195). 3. *Butterflies of the Neo-tropical region.* 1987-1995. 7pts. 4. *Butterflies of the Oriental region.* 1982-86. 3pts. 5. *Butterflies of the Holarctic region.* 1990-1993. 3pts.
V.1 includes New Zealand, Papua, New Guinea, Timor, Solomon Islands, and surrounding areas. Arranged in taxonomic sequence. Lavishly illustrated. Bibliography, p.397-4001. Index, p.403-15. No geographical index. Only 3 maps. Large format. An identification guide. The continued revision of other parts of the series make this a major work. *Class No: 595.78(100)*

Europe

[2832]
CARTER, D.J. *and* **HARGREAVES, B.** A Field guide to caterpillars of butterflies and moths in Britain and Europe. London, Collins, 1986. 296p. col. illus. tables. £10.95. ISBN: 000219080x.
A systematic guide to more than 500 species of caterpillars and their food. Bibliography, p.270-1. Foodplant lists, p.272-86. General index, p.286-92. Foodplant index, p.293-6. Over 300 coloured illus. The aim is 'to provide an identification guide to caterpillars that are likely to be encountered in gardens, parks and the countryside, and a useful reference work for students and ecologists interested in insect-plant relationships' (*Preface*). *Class No: 595.78(4)*

[2833]

CHINERY, M. **Butterflies and day-flying moths of Britain and Europe.** London, Collins, 1989. 320p. illus. (col.). £12.95; £8.95. ISBN: 0002197855.

Contains information on all 360 European butterflies and 260 day-flying moths. 3 sections: 1. The evolution of butterflies and moths - 2. The directory of species (p.26-199) - 3. From egg to adult (*e.g.* 'Feeding behaviour'; 'Finding a mate'). Over 1,500 colour paintings of every identified stage in the life-cycle, and distribution maps for every species. Glossary. Index. *Class No: 595.78(4)*

[2834]

—CHINERY, M. **Collins guide to butterflies: a photographic guide to the butterflies of Britain and Europe.** London, HarperCollins, 1998. 652p. illus.(col.),figs.,maps. £14.99. ISBN: 0002200597.

Three parts: 1. Colour plates (over 900 colour photographs of upper- and under-sides of butterflies) - 2. Family and species descriptions - 3. Appendices (Conservation of butterflies; Glossary; Picture credits; Index). A useful field guide. *Class No: 595.78(4)*

Great Britain

[2835]

EMMET, A.M. **The Scientific names of the British lepidoptera:** their history and meaning. Colchester, Essex, Harley Books, 1991. 288p. illus. £24.95. ISBN: 0946589283.

Gives the meanings of 2,494 specific names together with the names of genera, families and suborders to which they belong. 4 appendices: 1. People commemorated in the names of lepidoptera - 2. Geographical names - 3. Unresolved names - 4. Apparent errors in R.D. Macleod's *Key to the names of the British butterflies and moths.* Bibliography, p.245-49. 3 indexes: 1. Scientific names - 2. Special index to the Phycitinae - 3. List of monochrome plates. The author is one of Britain's leading lepidopterists. *Class No: 595.78(410)*

[2836]

The Moths and butterflies of Great Britain and Ireland. Heath, J. and others. Colchester, Essex, Harley Books, 1976-. illus. (incl. col.), maps.

V.1. *Micropterigidae to heliozelidae.* 1976. 343p. V.2. *Cossidae to heliodinidae.* 1985. 460p. V.3. *Yponomeutidae to Elachistidae.* 1996. 452p. V.7. Pt.1 *Hesperiidae to nymphalidae.* 1987. 370p. V.7. Pt.2. *Lasiocampidae to thyatiridae.* 1991. 400p. V.9. *Sphingidae to noctuidae.* 1983. 288p. V.10. *Noctuidae (Cuculliinae to hypeninae) and agaristidae.* 1983. 459p.

Projected in 11v. V.10: *Noctuidae (part 2) and Agaristidae* (1983) features 225 distribution maps (although lacking a situation map covering the whole area) and 13 superb colour plates, with 23 text figures. A check list of species is not included. 'Despite these criticisms, this volume *is* a definitive work and is far superior to anything currently available on the group' (*Natural history book reviews,* v.7(3), 1984, p.157-9). V.1,2,3,7,9 and 10 have so far appeared. Aims 'to provide a complete, fully illustrated, and up-to-date work of identification' (*Introduction*). A standard work. *Class No: 595.78(410)*

[2837]

PORTER, J. **The Colour identification guide to the caterpillars of the British Isles (Macrolepidptera).** London, Viking, 1997. xii, 275p. illus.(col.). £40. ISBN: 0670875090.

Illustrates over 850 larvae in 49 colour plates. Text description of species (p.1-154). Indexes of scientific and common names. Probably too large for field use, but well-reviewed - 'an authoritative reference work ... the colour illustrations are superb' (*Entomologist's gazette,* v.49, 1998, p.130). *Class No: 595.78(410)*

[2838]

SKINNER, B. **Colour identification guide to moths of the British Isles.** 2nd ed. London, Viking, 1998. xi, 276p. illus.(incl. col.), diagrs. £45. ISBN: 0670879789.

First published 1980.

Contains 43 colour plates of all species resident in the British Isles during the last 100 years. Includes recent changes in distribution, new resident species, and changes in nomenclature. Description of species, p.1-166. Cross-references. 'Further information', p.254 gives a brief list for further reading and the addresses of four relevant societies. Also includes glossary, abbreviations, a list of scientific names of food plants, and index. General book, for the nonspecialist. *Class No: 595.78(410)*

[2839]

THOMAS, J. *and* LEWINGTON, R. **The Butterflies of Britain and Ireland.** London, Dorling Kindersley, 1991. 224p. illus. (incl. col. pl.), maps. £16.99. ISBN: 0863185916.

Covers every species of butterfly regularly seen in Britain, plus some migrants. The fine illustrations display every stage of the life cycle, including local variations. Area bibliography and good index. Well written. *Class No: 595.78(410)*

America—North

[2840]

The Common names of North American butterflies. Miller, J.Y., *ed.* Washington, Smithsonian Institution Press, 1992. 177p. ISBN: 1560981229.

Arranged by family, subfamily, tribe, species, and subspecies, this book lists all recorded subspecies north of Mexico and includes Hawaii. All published common names are listed, with preferred names indicated. Geographical distribution is shown and, as well as a bibliography, there is also a 68-page index. For public and academic libraries. *Class No: 595.78(71+73)*

Australia

[2841]

COMMON, I.F.B. **Moths of Australia.** Carlton, Victoria, Melbourne University Press, 1993. vi,535p. illus. (some col.) $150. ISBN: 0522843263.

Begins with a summary of embryo development, anatomy, life history, growth cycle, population control, economic significance, ecology, evolution, and geographical distribution of moths in general. Many references to the literature. Over 400 pages devoted to the taxonomy of the Australian moth fauna. Many figures and 1,000 photographs (many in colour). Glossary; bibliography, p.495-511. 'The definitive reference work on Australian moths ... for many years to come' (*Choice*, May 1994, p.1458). *Class No: 595.78(94)*

Vertebrates

[2842]

BLACKWELDER, R.E. **Guide to the taxonomic literature of vertebrates.** Ames, Iowa, Iowa State Univ. Press, 1972. xviii, [1], 259p. $10.95. ISBN: 0813816300.

About 12,000 references. Sections: Animalia in general - Cephalochordata - Pisces - Amphibia - Reptiles - Aves - Mammalia - Addenda. Subdivisions for general works, bibliographies, persons and institutions, exploration and localities, taxonomic methods, nomenclature studies, regional studies (faunas; checklists; keys); special subject lists, etc.. No indexes. For beginners in taxonomy. *Class No: 596*

[2843]

COLBERT, E.H. **Evolution of the vertebrates:** a history of the backboned animals through time. 4th ed. New York, Wiley-Liss, 1991. xvii,478p. illus. $49.95. ISBN: 0471850748.

31 chapters (1. Introduction ... 6. Early vertebrate faunas ... 8. The advent of the reptiles ... 16. Years of the dinosaurs ... 19. Marsupials ... 31. The age of mammals), followed by appendix, 'A classification of the chordates'. Well illustrated. Bibliography, p.439-46. Index. *Class No: 596*

[2844]

WOOD, C.A. **An Introduction to the literature of vertebrate zoology,** based chiefly on the titles in the Blacker Library of Zoology, the Emma Shearer Wood Library of Ornithology, the Bibliotheca Osleriana, and other libraries of McGill University, Montreal. London, Oxford Univ. Press, 1931 (reprinted 1974, Lubrecht & Cramer). xiv, 643p. $95. ISBN: 3487053578.

Three main sections: (1) 19 chapters on the literature of vertebrate zoology; (2) a geographical index to items in section (1); and (3), 'a partially annotated catalogue of the titles on vertebrate zoology in the libraries of McGill University' (p.173-643). A valuable bibliographical tool. *Class No: 596*

[2845]

YOUNG, J.Z. **The Life of vertebrates.** 3rd ed. Oxford, University Press, 1981. xx, 645p. illus., diagrs., graphs. $25. ISBN: 0198571739.

First published 1950.

33 chapters. Includes the embryology, anatomy, physiology, biochemistry, palaeontology and ecology of all vertebrates. 'The whole book is organized around the theme that mechanisms of homeostasis have become increasingly more complex during vertebrate evolution, allowing life to continue under conditions not possible before' (*Preface to the third edition*). Chapter references, p.586-608. Author index; analytical subject index (p.613-43). *Class No: 596*

[2846]

—The **Oxford book of vertebrates:** cyclostomes, fish, amphibians, reptiles and mammals. Nixon, M. *and* Whitely, D. London, Oxford Univ. Press, 1972. 224p. illus., maps.

Describes and illustrates *c.*340 species, excluding birds. 'An unusual and useful book (especially for higher school level, with detailed biological information)' (*British book news,* February 1973, p.98). *Class No: 596*

Fishes

CD-ROM

[2847]

Fishbase 97: concepts, design and data sources. International Center for Living Aquatic Resources Management (ICLARM), Metro Manila, Philippines, 1997-. 2 discs; user manual (256p.). $95. ISBN: 9718709061.

Intended to be a comprehensive survey of all fishes, with over 200 specialist contributors, and due for completion in 2000. One disk contains 60 main tables, with nomenclature and common and formal names, fishery biology, ecology, fish morphology, species search lists, FAO catches, country fish reviews, etc. The second disk contains pictures only. The user manual is being translated from English to other languages to enable wider usage. Updated annually ($50). A major work. *Class No:* 597(003.40)

Bibliographies

[2848]

DEAN, B. A Bibliography of fishes. Eastman, C.R., *rev. and ed.* New York, American Museum of Natural History, 1916-23. 3v. Reprinted New York, Lubrecht & Cramer, 1973.

1. *Author lists, A-K.* 1916. 2. *Author lists, L-Z;* anonymous titles, nos.1-650. 3. *Anonymous titles,* nos.651-712; addend. to v.1-2, etc.

Includes *c.*50,000 titles. V.3 also lists pre-Linnean publications, general bibliographies that include references to fishes, voyages and expeditions, and periodicals relating to fish and fish culture. 3-section subject index. One of the most complete works of its kind. *Class No:* 597(01)

[2849]

—ATZ, J.W. Dean bibliography of fishes, 1968. New York, American Museum of Natural History, 1971. 512p.

Computer-produced, lists items in 5 parts: a systematic index, taxonomically arranged; a subject index; a geographic index; an author index; and the bibliography (in accession number order). The 1969 v., also by J.W. Atz (1973. [xiii], 853p.) brings total entries to 89,101. *Class No:* 597(01)

Encyclopaedias & Dictionaries

[2850]

Encyclopedia of fishes. Paxton, J.R. *and* Eschmeyer, W.N., *eds.* 2nd ed. San Diego, Academic Press, 1998. 240p. illus.(col.),maps. £24.95; $34.95. ISBN: 0125476655.

First published 1994.

45 contributors. Two parts: 1. The world of fishes; 2. Kinds of fishes. Data for *c.*24,000 species of fish include different orders, number of genera, habitat, and biological adaptations. Beautifully illustrated and written in an accessible style. For public libraries. *Class No:* 597(03)

[2851]

Piatiiazychnyi slovar nazvanii zhivotnykh. ryby: latiniskii, russkii, angliiskii, nemetskii, frantuzskii. [Dictionary of animal names in five languages: fishes: Latin, Russian, English, German, French.] Sokolov, V.E. Moscow, Russky Yazyk Publishers, 1989. 733p. ISBN: 5200002370.

Lists *c.*11,700 names, arranged in 5 sections: Leptocardii (lancelets) - Cephalapspidomorphi (lampreys) - Myxini (hagfishes) - Chrondrichthyes (cartilaginous fishes) - Osteichthyes (bony fishes). *Class No:* 597(03)

[2852]

WHEELER, A. The World encyclopedia of fishes. London, Macdonald, 1985. xiv, 368p. illus. (incl. col.). ISBN: 0356107159.

Previously published as *Fishes of the world* (New York, Macmillan, 1975).

Describes nearly 1,500 species individually (A-Z), with entry under scientific names. Data include size, distribution and colour. Glossary and plates (96p.) precede. These colour plates - 50 in all - are arranged in systematic order of families. Some 700 fine line-drawings in text. The author, Principal Scientific Officer at the British Museum (Natural History). *Class No:* 597(03)

Handbooks & Manuals

[2853]

Fishes of the north-eastern Atlantic and the Mediterranean. [Poissons de l'Atlantique du nord-est et de la Méditerranée.] Whitehead, P.J.P., *and others, eds.* Paris, Unesco, 1984-86. 3v. figs., maps. $180. ISBN: 9230022152, v.1; 9230023086, v.2; 9230023094, v.3.

A continuation of *Check-list of the fishes of the north-eastern Atlantic and of the Mediterranean* (Unesco, 1973). A fauna of saltwater fish of the palaearctic region. Data on 220 families and 1,250 species. Entries include line-drawings, diagnoses, keys, biological data, synonyms, distribution maps and literature. V.3 contains an

....(contd.)

additional bibliography to *Check-list of the fishes of the north-eastern Atlantic and the Mediterranean,* p.1415-26, as well as an alphabetical index of common names, p.1429-42, and an alphabetical index of scientific names, p.1443-73. *Class No:* 597(035)

Reviews & Abstracts

[2854]

Aquatic sciences and fisheries abstracts. Part 1: Biological sciences and living resources. Compiled by United Nations Dept. of International Economic and Social Affairs, FAO, and the Intergovernmental Oceanographic Commission, with the collaboration of the ASFI Input Partners. Bethesda, Md., Cambridge Scientific Abstracts, 1978-. 12pa. $1,045 (US); $1,115 (non US) pa. ISSN: 01405373.

Sub-title: 'An international journal for the science, technology and management of marine and freshwater environments'.

Contains *c.*24,000 abstracts pa. Main parts: General aspects - Biology - Ecology - Fisheries. 27 sections ('Ichthyology' is subdivided: General; Geographical distribution; Taxonomy and morphology; Reproduction and development; Genetics and evolution; Physiology, biochemistry, biophysics). Author, subject and taxonomic indexes. Available on magnetic tape, online, and CD-ROM. *Class No:* 597(048)

Maps & Atlases

[2855]

BERRA, T.M. An Atlas of distribution of the freshwater fish families of the world. Lincoln, Nebraska, Univ. of Nebraska Press, 1981. xxix, 197p. tables, maps. ISBN: 0803214111.

Includes a bibliography (p.181-91) and index. *Class No:* 597(084.3)

Worldwide

[2856]

LEVER, C. Naturalized fishes of the world. San Diego, Academic Press, 1996. xxiv,408p. illus.,tables. £75;$120. ISBN: 0124447457.

Describes when, where, why, how, and by whom alien inland freshwater fishes now living in a wild state throughout the world were introduced. Species accounts, p.1-338. Two appendices: 1. Fishes which are or may be naturalized in major African lakes - 2. Countries and island groups in which introduced fishes are, or may be, naturalized. Glossary. Extensive list of references, p.369-401. Index of animals and plants, p.402-8. *Class No:* 597(100)

[2857]

NELSON, J. Fishes of the world. 3rd ed. New York, Wiley, 1994. 600p. illus., maps. $72.50. ISBN: 0471547131.

First published 1976.

Systematic treatment of fishes; orders, sub-orders and families, and listing genera. Anatomical data; ecological status, distribution maps of classes/families worldwide. The clear drawings are well linked to the text. Includes the most recent systematic work. Readership: professional ichthyologists and those students intending to pursue the study of fishes. 'An indispensable reference' (*Choice,* November 1994, p.482). *Class No:* 597(100)

[2858]

STERBA, G. Freshwater fishes of the world. Rev. ed. Translated [from the German] and revised by D.W. Tucker. Reigate, Surrey, T.F.H. (Great Britain), Ltd., 1973. 2v. (879p. + 282p.) illus. (incl. pl.), tables.

Previous ed. 1962. as *Süsswasserfische aus aller Welt* (Leipzig, 1959).

Basic data, systematically arranged on identification and aquarium biology of *c.*1,300 species of freshwater fishes kept in aquaria in Central Europe. Annotated bibliography, v.1, p.850-9. The 1973 ed. adds 90p. of plates to the 192 in the 1962 ed. Author was at the time Director of the Zoological Institute, Univ. of Leipzig. A major reference source in its field. *Class No:* 597(100)

Europe

[2859]

WHEELER, A. The Fishes of the British Isles and North-west Europe. London, Macmillan, 1969. xvii, 613p. illus. maps.

Has 3 main sections: Marsipobranchii (lampreys and hagfish) - Selachii (sharks, rays and rabbit fishes) - Pisces (Osteichthyes) (bony fishes). Data: common and Latin names; French, Dutch, German, Danish and Swedish names; identification; biology; line-drawings. Small distribution maps. Bibliography (grouped), p.589-601. Index. *Class No:* 597(4)

Africa—Southern

[2860]

Smith's sea fishes. Smith, M.M. *and* Heemstra, P.C., *eds.* 6th ed. Berlin, Springer-Verlag, 1986. xx, 1047p. illus., diagrs. $162. ISBN: 0387168516.

Originally published by Trustees of the Sea Fishes of Southern Africa Book Fund, 1949 as J.L.B. Smith's *The sea fishes of Southern Africa.*. 5th ed., 1977.

Contents: Anatomy of fishes - Biology of fishes - Dangers of the sea - Scientific nomenclature and classification - Common names - Oceanography of the Southern African region - Ichthyology in South Africa - Key to classes - Class Agnatha - Class Chondrichthyes - Class Osteichthyes - Literature list - Numerical key for identification - Glossary - Special numbers list; old and new numbers. Index. Fully illustrated (*c.*1,800 figures). Authoritative for the region.

Class No: 597(68)

Reptiles & Amphibians

Encyclopaedias

[2861]

Encyclopedia of reptiles and amphibians. Cogger, H.G. *and* Zweifel, R.G., *eds.* 2nd ed. San Diego, Academic Press, 1998. 240p. illus.(col.),maps. £24.95; $34.95. ISBN: 0121785602.

First published 1986.

18 contributors. Begins with chapters on behaviour, ecology, physiology, etc., then looks at various groups of reptiles and amphibians, detailing food, enemies, life cycles, habitats, etc. Profusely and beautifully illustrated with *c.*200 colour photographs and paintings. A good, general work. *Class No:* 598.1(031)

Dictionaries

[2862]

PETERS, J.A. Dictionary of herpetology: a brief and meaningful definition of words and terms used in herpetology. New York, Hafner, 1964. 392p. illus. (pl.). ISBN: 0685020371.

About 3,000 terms defined. Different meanings stated; citation of sources, including references to articles in periodicals. Author: Associate Curator of Herpetology, US National Museum, Washington. *Class No:* 598.1(038)

Worldwide

[2863]

Amphibian species of the world: a taxonomic and geographical reference. Frost, D.R., *ed.* Lawrence, Kansas, Allen Press, and the Association of Systematics Collections, 1985. 732p. ISBN: 0942924118.

Data on 4,014 named species, with taxonomic index. 'Compiled for the Parties to the Convention on International Trade in Endangered Species of Wild Fauna and Flora to serve as a standard reference to amphibian nomenclature ...' *Class No:* 598.1(100)

Europe

[2864]

ARNOLD, E.N. *and* **BURTON, J.A. A Field guide to the reptiles and amphibians of Britain and Europe.** London, Collins, 1978. 272p. illus. (incl. col. pl.). £14.99. ISBN: 0002193183.

Coverage is Europe west of Moscow. 5 sections: Salamanders and newts; Frogs and toads; Tortoises, terrapins and sea turtles; Lizards and amphisbaenians (7 areas); Snakes. Glossary, p.243-7; Bibliography (grouped), p.248-52. 126 small distribution maps. 35 illus. (257 in colour). Concise, synoptic text, but remarkably readable. 'This book is a very real contribution to herpetology and will be of great value not only to the travelling naturalist but to all students of the subject' (*Journal of natural history*, v.19(1), January/February 1979, p.126). *Class No:* 598.1(4)

Great Britain

[2865]

ARNOLD, H.R. Atlas of amphibians and reptiles in Britain. Monk's Wood, Huntingdon, Institute of Terrestrial Ecology, 1995. 40p. £8.95. ISBN: 0117018244.

Despite its lack of illustrations, this is a good quick-reference work listing species, p.8-35, with 2 pages per species, giving a brief description, and showing distribution (past and present), protection status, habitat information. List of introduced species, p.36-37; references p.39-40. *Class No:* 598.1(410)

[2866]

FRAZER, D. Reptiles and amphibians in Britain. London, Collins, 1983. 256p. illus. £11. ISBN: 0002197068.

Rewrites and updates M. Smith's classic *British amphibians and reptiles* (1973). Appended is an annotated 'Taxonomy of British herpetology'. 'An essential book' (*Natural history book reviews*, v.7(3), 1984, p.151), although the reviewer detects 'a certain sloppiness'. *Class No:* 598.1(410)

America—North

[2867]

DITMARS, R.L. The Reptiles of North America: a review of the crocodilians, lizards, snakes, turtles and tortoises inhabiting the United States and Northern Mexico. New York, Doubleday, 1936. 476p. illus, (incl. col.). *Class No:* 598.1(71+73)

[2868]

ERNST, C.H. Venomous reptiles of North America Washington, Smithsonian Institution Press, 1992 236p. £27.25. ISBN: 1560981148.

Covers biology of 21 species in the US and Canada. Length of articles ranges from 3 to 19 pages. Data include scientific name, common name fossil record, distribution, habitat, behaviour, food and feeding, population. Distribution maps, line drawings, monochrome photographs, and 55 colour plates. Lengthy bibliography (50p.), containing *c.*1,000 entries, and a short glossary of 54 scientific terms. Index of subjects, and scientific and popular names. Valuable addition to academic libraries. *Class No:* 598.1(71+73)

Australia

[2869]

COGGER, H.G. Reptiles and amphibians of Australia. 5th ed. Cornell, Comstock Publishing, 1992. 775p. illus. £77.95. ISBN: 0801427398.

First published 1975.

Data on 942 species include: physical description; distribution; description of habitat. Entries accompanied by good quality colour photographs. Glossary of anatomical terms, taxonomic index. Lengthy bibliography. Essential for any library specializing in this area. *Class No:* 598.1(94)

[2870]

WORRELL, E. Reptiles of Australia: crocodiles, turtles, tortoises, lizards, snakes; describing all Australian species, their appearance, their haunts, their habits ... Sydney, Angus & Robertson, 1963. xv, 207p.

Over 330 illus., many in full colour. The check-list of Australian reptiles (p.161-98) is claimed to be the most complete ever compiled and published in Australia. Glossary, p.157-60. Index. *Class No:* 598.1(94)

Snakes

[2871]

FITZSIMONS, V.F.M. Snakes of southern Africa. London, Macdonald, 1962. 424p. illus., maps.

Taxonomic aspects are precisely and lucidly defined. Detailed record of localities, with keys and location maps. Valuable field notes. Bibliography of over 750 items, p.383-406. An excellent example of a regional study. 'Undoubtedly one of the great books on snakes' (*Tropical diseases bulletin*, v.60(7), July 1963. p.677-8). *Class No:* 598.12

[2872]

HARDING, K.A. *and* **WELCH, K.R.G. Venomous snakes of the world:** a checklist. Oxford, Pergamon Press, 1980. x, 188p. ISBN: 0080254950.

Published as Supplement no.1 (1980) in the journal, *Toxicon*.

2 sections: 1. Taxonomy (arranged by families, subfamilies and tribes, genera, and species, listed A-Z). 2. Geographical distribution, arranged by continent. Bibliography of 4p. Taxonomic references (7p.). Author and subject indexes. *Class No:* 598.12

[2873]

MATTISON, C. Snakes of the world. Poole, Dorset, Blandford Press, 1986. 190p. illus. (mostly col.), chart, maps. £9.99. ISBN: 0713723408.

9 chapters (2. Size, shape and function - 3. Colour and markings - 4. Reproduction - 5. Food and feeding ... 7. Ecology and behaviour ... 9. Snake families (p.124-79)). Bibliography, p.180-3 (5 sections, each with short introduction). Detailed analytical index to text and illus. Well balanced, with good quality illustrations. *Class No:* 598.12

[2874]

PARKER, H.W. Snakes - a natural history. 2nd ed., rev. and enlarged, by A.G.C. Grandison. London, British Museum (Natural History), with Ithaca, N.Y., Cornell Univ. Press, 1977. iv, 108p. illus. (incl. col. pl.). £6.95. ISBN: 0565010107.

Replaces his *Natural history of snakes* (1965).

Includes glossary and bibliography. 16p. of colour plates; 29 figures. 'The illustrations are quite outstanding' (*Journal of natural history*, v.11(8), November/December 1977, p.719).

Class No: 598.12

[2875]

PHELPS, T. Poisonous snakes. 2nd ed. Poole, Blandford, 1989. viii, 237p. illus. (some col.). £10.95. ISBN: 0713721146.

First published 1981.

10 chapters 1. Introduction - 2. Classification and distribution ... 4. The elapids ... 7. Venom and snakebite - 8. Snakes and Man - 9. Poisonous snakes in captivity - 10. In the field. 2 appendices. Index, p.226-37. *Class No:* 598.12

[2876]

Poisonous snakes of the world. United States. Department of the Navy. Bureau of Medicine and Surgery. Mineola, N.Y., Dover Publications, 1991. xiii,203p. illus. (some col. pl.), figs., maps. $14.95. ISBN: 048626629x.

Reprint of 1966 ed., published by the US Government Printing Office.

9 chapters: 1. General information - 2. Precautions to avoid snakebite ... 4. First aid ... 7. Distribution and identification of poisonous land snakes - 8. The sea snakes - 9. Antivenin sources; glossary; general references; index. Over 170 photographs and illustrations, with 54 in colour. Clearly presented. For the specialist and layman. *Class No:* 598.12

[2877]

WILLIAMS, K.L. *and* **WALLACH, V. Snakes of the world.** Melbourne, Fla., Kriefer, 1989-. $31.50, v.1. ISBN: 0894642154.

1. *Synopsis of snake generic names.* 1989.

Based on A.S. Romer's *Oestology of the reptiles,* although expanded and with cross-references added. Aims to provide a list of all snakes, both living and extinct. Arranged alphabetically with brief bibliographic record of the first article describing the genera. Includes invalid as well as valid names, with cross-referencing between each. *Class No:* 598.12

Birds

Bibliographies

[2878]

MILLER, M.A. Birds: a guide to the literature. New York & London, Garland Publishing, Inc., 1986. 912p. $86. ISBN: 0824087100.

1,942 entries, with notes on coverage, description, illus., additional features. 8 sections: 1. Guide to general works - 2. Guide to subjects - 3. Species and group studies - 4. Area studies - 5. Field studies - 6. Children's literature - 7. Biographies - 9. Fiction. Cross-references. Appendix (list of journals, periodicals and organization publications). Index of names (including anonymous works), p.845-87.

Class No: 598.2(01)

[2879]

—**STRONG, R.M. A Bibliography of birds, with special reference to anatomy, behavior, biochemistry, embryology, pathology, physiology, genetics, ecology, aviculture, economic ornithology, poultry culture, evolution and related subjects.** Chicago, Ill., Natural History Museum, 1939-59. 4pts.

Consists of pts.1-2: author catalog of *c.*25,000 entries in the *Zoological record* section 18, up to *c.*1938; pt.3: subject index; pt.4: finding index (supporting the author index). *Class No:* 598.2(01)

Encyclopaedias & Dictionaries

[2880]

CAMPBELL, B. *and* **LACK, E., eds. A Dictionary of birds.** Calton, England, T. & A.D. Poyser, for the British Ornithologists' Union, 1985. 670p. illus. £49.50. ISBN: 0856610399.

Contributed by *c.*280 specialists. Entries, A-Z, are under English names of birds chosen. Data: definition; general characteristics; mode of life, distribution; familial taxonomy, 'Cuckoo': p.123-6, with 6 references; 'Poetry, Birds in': p.475-8, with 15 references. Many cross-references. Over 500 photographs, drawings, etc. (*Nature,* v.317, 3 October 1985, p.392, finds the drawings disappointing, failing to complement the text.) The *Dictionary* is in line of succession from A. Newton and H. Gadow's *Dictionary of birds.* Intended as a greatly expanded updating of H.F. Witherby's *Handbook of British birds* (London, Witherby, 1938-41. 5v. illus., maps). The illus. are a definite improvement on Witherby's tiny quarter-page illus. 'Highly recommended for college, university and public libraries' (*Choice,* v.23(5), January 1986, p.724-5). *Class No:* 598.2(03)

[2881]

PERRINS, C.M. *and* **MIDDLETON, A.L.A. The Encyclopedia of birds.** London, Allen & Unwin; New York, Facts on File, 1985. £30; $45. (*Unwin Animal library.*) ISBN: 0045000328.

90 contributors. A series of articles in systematic order (3 parts: 1. Ostriches to Bulton quails - 2. Plovers to woodpeckers - 3. The passerines). Data on each family/group of families include physical adaptations, distribution, evolutionary history, classification, breeding, diet and feeding habits, spatial organization. 'Woodpecker', p.296-303: 12 col. illus., 5 line-drawings, distribution map. Bibliography, p.xvi-xvii. Glossary. Analytical index (tiny print), p.xx-xxi. Superb illus., mostly in colour - the book's strength. Like Campbell & Lack, Perrins & Middleton has much to offer. 'But, if forced to choose, I would regard the Encyclopaedia as desirable and the Dictionary as necessary' (*Nature,* v.317, 3 October 1985, p.392). *Class No:* 598.2(03)

[2882]

—**THOMSON, Sir A.L., ed. A New dictionary of birds.** London, Nelson, 1964. 928p. illus.

A centenary publication of the British Ornithologists' Union.

Entries, A-Z, describe bird habits, plumage, distribution and migration, and the relations between birds and man. Many articles are of encyclopaedic length (*e.g.* 'Heron': p.365-8; 10 items of bibliography). Shorter definitions for ornithological terms and British bird-names. Includes American and overseas usage. 48p. of colour and black-and-white plates. Index of generic names. Succeeds *Dictionary of British birds,* by A. Newton and H. Gadow (1896), which must still be retained for its excellent introductory history of ornithology, missing from Thomson. The latter, however, is admirably produced and remains an invaluable encyclopaedic dictionary. *Class No:* 598.2(03)

[2883]

PERRINS, C.M. The Illustrated encyclopaedia of birds: the definitive guide to birds of the world. London, Headline, 1990. 420p. illus. ISBN: 074720277x.

Lists 9,300 species, with 1,200 of them illustrated in colour and keyed to the colour plate. World checklist of species, p.366-411. Indexes of scientific and common names. No bibliography. 'A very good compromise between academic lists and the more popular treatments' (*Reference reviews,* v.5(1) 1991, p.19). *Class No:* 598.2(03)

[2884]

WEAVER, P. The Birdwatcher's dictionary. Calton, England, T. & A.D. Poyser, Ltd., 1981. 155p. illus., maps. £8.50. ISBN: 0856610283.

About 1,000 entries, Abdomen ... Zygodactyl. Includes names of organizations, but omits highly technical terms (*e.g.* anatomical). Cross-references. 4 appendices: A. Abbreviations; B. North American birds; C. Birdwatcher's Code of conduct; D. The British and Irish list of species in families and orders. British English equivalents are given for North American 'English names' of birds. *Class No:* 598.2(03)

Handbooks & Manuals

[2885]

The Cambridge encyclopedia of ornithology. Brooke, M. *and* Birkhead, T., eds. Cambridge, University Press, 1991. 362p. illus. (incl. col.), diagrs., graphs, tables. £24.95. ISBN: 0521362059.

39 contributors. 11 sections: 1. Introduction - 2. Anatomy and physiology - 3. Movement ... 5. The daily activities of birds ... 8. Bird populations ... 10. Behaviour - 11. People and birds. Ornithological organizations, p.327-30. Further reading, p.334-5. Index of scientific names; index of common names; index of subjects. Authoritative, well presented and clearly written. Its coverage of ecological and topical issues complements that of Perrins' *The Illustrated encyclopaedia of birds (qv).* 'Very good value ... thoroughly recommended' (*Reference reviews,* v.6(1), 1992, p.24). *Class No:* 598.2(035)

[2886]

FULLER, E. Extinct birds. London, Rainbird, 1987. 256p. illus. (some col.). ISBN: 0670817872.

Features those birds which have vanished since 1600. 18 sections: 1. Ratites ... 7. Diurnal raptors ... 11. Pigeons and doves ... 14. Owls ... 18. Hypothetical species and mystery birds. 59 colour, and 81 black-and-white, plates. Bibliography, p.245-51. Index, p.252-56. Does not claim to be comprehensive, but attractively presented. *Class No:* 598.2(035)

Reviews & Abstracts

[2887]

Recent ornithological literature: supplement to *The Emu, The Auk, Ibis.* [Washington & London], American Ornithological Union, British Ornithologists' Union, and Royal Australasian Ornithologists Union, 1983-. Quarterly.

About 750 references per issue. Sections: General biology (general; African; Australian; Nemotic; Neotropical; Oriental; Palearctic) -

....(contd.)

Taxonomy. 4th supp. each year includes list of journals received (over 900 journals). Over 150 volunteers co-operate in this project.
Class No: 598.2(048)

Yearbooks & Directories

[2888]

The Birdwatcher's yearbook and diary. Maids Moreton, Bucks., Buckingham Press, Buckinghamshire, 1981-. Annual. ISSN: 0144364x.

The 1999 *Yearbook* (1998. 320p. £16.50) has 9 parts: 1. County directory - 2. National directory - 3. International directory - 4. Quick reference - 5. Diary 2000 - 6. Log charts - 7. Features - 8. Books and articles - 9. Reserves and observatories. Index of reserves and observatories. Useful reference, primarily for British birdwatchers.
Class No: 598.2(058)

Tables & Data Books

[2889]

HOWARD, R. *and* **MOORE, A. A Complete checklist of the birds of the world.** 2nd ed. London, Academic Press, 1991. xxxiv,622p. £22.50. ISBN: 0123569109.

First published 1980.

Arranged by orders and families, Struthioniformes ... Passeriformes, p.1-542. References, by families, p.8-47. Indexes of Latin and English names, p.543-622. As a checklist, goes down to subspecies. Preceded by J.L. Peters' *Checklist of birds of the world* (1931-87. 16v.) which it, in part, updates, but lacks Peters' taxonomic notes, references and distribution notes. *Class No:* 598.2(083)

Nomenclatures

[2890]

JOBLING, J.A. A Dictionary of scientific bird names. Oxford, University Press, 1991. 272p. ISBN: 0198546343.

An A-Z, listing of over 10,000 bird species by their Latin names, with etymology and derivation fully explained, with reference to original sources. Many excellent line drawings but lacks an English-language index. Extensive bibliography. Highly recommended.
Class No: 598.2(083.72)

[2891]

LODGE, W. Birds: alternative names: a world checklist. London, Blandford, 1991. 208p. £10.95. ISBN: 0713722673.

List of birds which have one or more names in common usage. Excludes local or dialect names. Bibliography, p.195-97. Indexes of English and generic names. Not comprehensive but good value.
Class No: 598.2(083.72)

[2892]

Nomina anatomica avium: an annotated anatomical dictionary of birds. Prepared by the International Committee on Avian Anatomical Nomenclature, a committee of the World Association of Veterinary Anatomists. Baumel, J.J., *and others, eds.* London, Academic Press, 1979. xxv, 637p. illus. £56.50. ISBN: 0120831503.

Detailed annotations, giving homology, synonymy, structure and species variation. Chapters include Osteologia - Myologia - Systema respiratorium - Organa senoria. Taxonomic list gives scientific and common names. Bibliography, p.535-72. General index, p.573-637, embracing items in the list of terms, annotations, illus. or their legends. *Class No:* 598.2(083.72)

Illustrations

[2893]

LYSAGHT, A.W. The Book of birds: five centuries of bird illustration. London, Phaidon Press, 1975 (reprinted 1984). 208p. illus. (incl. col.).

40 of the 142 illus. are in colour. *Class No:* 598.2(084.1)

Biographies

[2894]

Who's who in ornithology. Pemberton, J.E., *ed.* Buckingham, Buckingham Press, 1997. 416p. £29.95. ISBN: 0951496581.

Biographies of those involved in ornithology in the UK, although there are a few entries for ornithologists now resident in Europe or Europeans who have had work published in the UK. Entries include name, date of birth, degrees, quotations, memberships, publications, other interests, address. *Class No:* 598.2(092)

Worldwide

[2895]

Handbook of the birds of Europe, the Middle East and North Africa: the birds of the Western Palearctic. Cramp, S. *and* Simmons, K.E.L., *and others, eds.* Oxford Univ. Press, 1977-94. col. illus., diagrs., tables, maps.

1. *Ostrich to ducks.* [ix], 722p. 1977. £85. 2. *Hawks to bustards.* 696p. 1980. £85. 3. *Waders to gulls.* 1000p. 1983. £85. 4. *Terns to woodpeckers.* 970p. 1985. £85. 5. *Tyrant flycatchers to thrushes.* 800p. 1987. £85. 6. *Warblers.* 736p. 1992. £75. 7. *Flycatchers to shrikes.* 577p. 1993. £75. 8. *Crows to finches.* 899p. 1994. £95. 9. *Buntings and New World warblers.* 488p. 1994. £85.

The Western Palearctic includes all Europe, plus the Middle East to Turkey, Iraq and Jordan, and North Africa down to 19°N. The 9v. describe all 795 species of birds, of which *c.*600 are breeding species. V.9 has 34 colour plates, numerous distribution maps, and sonagrams. The text consists mainly of accounts of species, listed under orders. 'Rock Bunting' (*Emberiza cia*) occupies p.182-94, with 2 distribution maps, 1 illus. and 8 sonagrams rendering song patterns diagrammatically. Field characteristics: Habitat, distribution, population, movement, social pattern and behaviour, voice, breeding, plumages, etc. Plates include illus. of eggs and nest down. References, p.375-418; glossary; errata p.419-41; indexes p.441-6. Also indexes v.1-9, p.447-88, including those for scientific names, and names in English, French, German, Italian, and Spanish. 'Against all the odds *The Birds of the Western Palearctic* is complete' (*Foreword*).

An abbreviated 2v. ed. (1,850p. £150), describing 936 species and containing 594 colour plates (19 more than in the original edition), (1,850p. £150) was published in 1997. A CD-ROM version is in preparation. The *Birds of the Western Palearctic journal* prevents the series from going out of date by including accounts of new species, etc. *Class No:* 598.2(100)

[2896]

Handbook of the birds of the world. Hoyo, J. del, *and others.* Jacksonville, Fla., American Lynx Editions, 1992-. ISBN: 8487334105, v.1; 8487334156, v.2.

v.1. *Ostrich to ducks.* 1992. 696p. illus.,maps. £110; v.2. *New World vultures to guinea fowl.* 1994. £110; v.3 *Hoatzin to auks.* 1996. £110; v.4. *Sandgrouse to cuckoos.* 1997. 679p. £110.

A projected 10-volume series (v.5 *Barn owls to hummingbirds* is due mid-1999). Each chapter covers a family and gives an introduction, with more detailed information on systematics, morphological aspects, general habits, etc. Species are then detailed, and data include description, common and scientific names, subspecies, distribution, habitat, etc. Both the family and species sections have bibliographies appended. Distribution maps are given, along with an indication as to population status, *e.g.*, endangered. High quality plates of the adult male of each species. Index in each volume. Folio format.
Class No: 598.2(100)

[2897]

LEVER, C. Naturalized birds of the world. Harlow, Essex, Longman, 1987. xx,615p. illus., tables, maps. ISBN: 0582460557.

Describes 133 species 'imported from its natural range to a new country or region either deliberately or accidentally by human agency' (*Preface*) and the effects on the native biota. Maps compare natural distribution with naturalized distribution. Bibliography, p.537-89. Geographical index. Index of vertebrate species. The author is the authority on naturalized animals. *Class No:* 598.2(100)

[2898]

SIBLEY, C.G. *and* **MONROE, B.L.,** *Jr.* **Distribution and taxonomy of birds of the world.** New Haven; London, Yale University Press, 1990. xxiv,1111p. maps. $125.

Taxonomic listing covering 9,672 living species of birds. Data in each species entry include scientific name; author of the name and year of description; standardized English name; coded world number; a brief description of preferred habitats; detailed description of species distribution; alternative common names. Also contains a world numbers cross-listing, 24 maps, gazetteer, p.875-906, bibliography, p.907-39 and an index which includes common and scientific names. Authoritative.

A *Supplement to distribution and taxonomy of birds of the world* by the same authors was published in 1993 (Yale University Press. 108p. £19.95).

A checklist based on the original book and the supplement is *A World checklist of birds* (Yale University Press, 1993. 393p. £35), also by Sibley and Monroe. *Class No:* 598.2(100)

Marine Environment

[2899]

HARRISON, P. Seabirds: an identification guide. Rev. ed. Beckenham, Kent, Croom Helm, 1985. 448p. illus. £24.99. ISBN: 0709937873.

A selection of 88 col. plates, with facing captions, is followed by a systematic section (Penguins ... Seaducks), p.200-409. Data on over 800 species include range, plumage, flight, habit, distribution and movement. Distribution maps, p.410-42; bibliography (cross-

....(contd.)
referenced to main text). p.443-5. 'This book will be a standard work for many years to come' (*Natural history book reviews,* v.8(3), 1986, p.219-20). *Class No:* 598.2(26)

Europe

[2900]
The Birdwatcher's handbook a guide to the natural history of the birds of Britain and Europe. Ehrlich, P.R., *and others.* Oxford, University Press, 1994. xxxix,660p. ISBN: 0198584075.

Includes details of 516 species, along with 170 short, natural history essays. Brief data on nesting, diet, conservation, breeding, etc. No illustrations. Bibliography of around 650 items. 3 indexes: English and scientific names; German, French, Dutch, Spanish, and Swedish bird names; subject index. 'Good value for money' (*Reference reviews,* v.8(7), 1994, p.23), although the same reviewer feels 'it would have been a much better book if it had been written by European ornithologists'. *Class No:* 598.2(4)

[2901]
EBCC atlas of European breeding birds: their distribution and abundance. Hagemeijer, W.J.M. *and* Blair, M.J., *eds.* London, T. & A.D. Poyser, 1997. 903p. illus. £55;$99. ISBN: 0856610917.

46 contributors, although the data has been gathered by over 10,000 field ornithologists. 513 species are covered. Two species accounts sections: 1. Mapped species (496 full species accounts; each account is 1-2 pages in length, explaining world and European distribution and population, breeding habitats, migration patterns, etc.); 2. Unmapped species (17 species lacking satisfactory data). All bird names are given in 14 European languages. Includes a list of national and regional bird atlases of Europe, a bibliography, and technical index. A major work, of interest to ecologists, conservationists, and ornithologists. *Class No:* 598.2(4)

[2902]
A Field guide to the birds of Britain and Europe. Peterson, R., *and others.* 4th ed. London, Collins, 1983. 384p. illus. (col. pl.). £14.99. ISBN: 0002190737.

First published 1954.

77 colour plates, with brief data facing, depict more than 1,100 birds of 505 species. Main sequence: Divers ... Buntings. p.36-210. Prelims. 'How to identify birds', 'European check-list', 'The ornithological societies'. 362 small distribution maps. Index, p.227-39. Small format. Excludes the former USSR. 'Basic stock item for all libraries and schools' (*Library world,* March 1966, p.279, on the 1965 ed.). *Class No:* 598.2(4)

[2903]
—Glossarium Europae avium. Jorgensen, H.J. *and* Blackburne, C.I. Copenhagen, Munksgaard, 1941. 192p.

A list of European birds arranged primarily by Latin names. Equivalents in 17 other languages, - Czech, Danish, German, English, Spanish, French, Icelandic, Italian, Hungarian, Dutch, Norwegian, Polish, Portuguese, Russian, Finnish, Swedish and Turkish. The number of species (bar one) tallies with that in R. Peterson's *A Field guide to the birds of Britain and Europe,* which also gives Dutch, French, German and Swedish names. *Class No:* 598.2(4)

[2904]
GOODERS, J. Larousse field guide to the birds of Britain and Europe. London, Larousse, 1995. 319p. illus. (mostly col.). ISBN: 1856970148.

Attractive pocket guide devoting half a page to each species and using colour coding to indicate bird distribution and generic type. Well illustrated. Introductory material, p.6-33; index, p.314-19. Author is one of Britain's best-known ornithologists. *Class No:* 598.2(4)

[2905]
PFORR, M. *and* LIMBRUNNER, A. The Breeding birds of Europe: a photographic handbook. London, Croom Helm, 1981-82. 2v. col. illus. £27.50, set. ISBN: 0709920482.

1. *Divers to auks.* 1981. 327, [6]p. 2. *Sandgrouse to crows,* 1982. 394p.

Over 700 high-quality colour photographs by German, Austrian and Danish wildlife photographers, depicting more than 250 species of birds. Data on habitat, food, breeding, biology and migration. Does not deal with identification. Index of photographers. Indexes of English and Latin names of birds. 'Very highly recommended' (*Natural history book reviews,* v.6(3/4), 1983, p.146-7). *Class No:* 598.2(4)

[2906]
—VOOUS, K.H. Nelson's atlas of European birds. London, Nelson, 1960. 284p. illus., maps.

Translated from the Dutch, *Atlas van de europese vogels* (1960).

Distribution maps show the world breeding-range of 419 species of birds breeding in Europe west of the Urals. Basic data on habitat, food and nesting requirements of each species, with notes on movements. The 335 excellent half-tone supporting plates are included not for identification purposes but to show birds in their characteristic habitat. *Class No:* 598.2(4)

[2907]
Tracks & signs of the birds of Britain and Europe: an identification guide. Brown, R., *and others.* London, Christopher Helm, 1992. 232p. illus. (some col.), figs. £14.99. ISBN: 0713635231.

Covers resident, visiting and vagrant birds of Europe. Includes their feeding and behavioural signs, droppings, pellets, feathers and skulls. Over 1,000 illustrations, including 47 colour plates. Brief bibliography and a list of European bird protection and study organizations. Useful for both the amateur and scientist. *Class No:* 598.2(4)

Great Britain

[2908]
BANNERMAN, D.A. The Birds of the British Isles. Edinburgh & London, Oliver & Boyd, 1952-63. 12v. illus. (pl.). maps.

Systematically arranged. Entry for each bird species includes notes on identification, occurrence in Britain, distribution, habits and migration, breeding and nesting habits. The accurately coloured plates are a feature, each volume containing about 30 such plates. Footnote references. V.12 includes a short comparative list of Celtic bird-names of the British Isles (p.405-23), and an index of scientific names in the 12v. A classic work. *Class No:* 598.2(410)

[2909]
—The Handbook of British birds. Witherby, H.F., *ed.* London, Witherby, 1938-41. 5v. illus., maps.

Arranged by families. For each species details concern habitat, characteristics, distribution (in Britain and abroad), and descriptions, plus a col. illus. 520 numbered entries. V.5 includes general indexes of English and scientific names in the 5v., and each volume has an index of English names and a glossary of terms. 'A standard work of reference for British and, indeed, European ornithologists' (*Nature,* v.196, 17 November 1962, p.610). *Class No:* 598.2(410)

[2910]
Checklist of the birds of Great Britain and Ireland. Knox, A.G., *comp.* 6th ed. Tring, Herts., British Ornithologists' Union, 1992. 50p. ISBN: 0907446159.

The standard list, referred to in other bird books; *i.e.,* birds are cited by their check-list number on this work. Systematic list, p.4-24. 2 appendices, *e.g.* 2. List of species. Indexes to scientific and English names. *Class No:* 598.2(410)

[2911]
LOCKWOOD, W.B. The Oxford dictionary of British bird names. Oxford, University Press, 1993. ix,175p. ISBN: 0198661967.

Rev. ed. Formerly *The Oxford book of British bird names* (1984).

Discusses the origin of more than 1,500 names, Aberdevine ... Yuckle, relating to 257 species. Includes standard and local names. Bibliography, p.17-20. *Class No:* 598.2(410)

[2912]
MULLENS, W.H. *and* SWANN, H.K. A Bibliography of British ornithology, from the earliest times to the end of 1912, including biographical accounts of the principal writers and bibliographies of their published works. London, Macmillan, 1916-17. xv, 691p. Supplement, by H.K. Swann, 1923. xvi, 42p.

Under authors A-Z, only those authors being included who have published separate works on ornithology. The biographies carry notes on published works. Also, lists of works cited, - bibliographies, biographical works, and periodicals. A valuable and informative bibliography. *Class No:* 598.2(410)

[2913]
The New atlas of breeding birds in Britain and Ireland: 1988-1991. Gibbons, D.W., *and others.* London, T and A D Poyser for the British Trust for Ornithology, the Scottish Ornithologists' Club and the Irish Wildbird Conservancy, 1993. xiv,520p. maps. ISBN: 0856610755.

Previous ed. published 1976.

Contains 221 species and maps, derived from more than 1.2 million records from 42,736 2km squares. Most species have a distribution map and a map showing changes since 1976. Bibliography, p.499-513. 'A treasure trove for the enquiring birdwatcher as well as the professional' (*Birds magazine,* Spring 1994, p.22). *Class No:* 598.2(410)

[2914]
SWANN, H.K. A Dictionary of English and folk-names of British birds, with their history, meaning and first usage; and their folk-lore legends, etc. relating to the more familiar species. London, Witherby, 1913. (Reprinted London, EP Publishing, Ltd., 1977). xii, 266p.

About 5,000 names of birds. Attempt to combine 'the English "book"-names from past authors, giving the history and first usage of the "accepted" names of the species, and also the provincial, local or dialect names in use now or formerly in the British Isles, indicating the locality and meaning where possible' (*Preface*). 'Raven': nearly 2p. Bibliography, p.ix-xii. *Class No: 598.2(410)*

Russia

[2915]
A Field guide to birds of the USSR, including Eastern Europe and Central Asia. Translated from the Russian by N. Bourso-Leland. Flint, V.E., *and others*. Princeton, N.J., Princeton Univ. Press, 1984. 353p. illus. (incl. col.), tables, maps. $85; $29.95. ISBN: 0691082448.

Originally published in the USSR, 1968; updated and revised.

48 colour plates, plus 71 line-drawings, illustrate 654 of the USSR 728 species. The sections for each species state field marks, habits, range and distribution. The maps are hard to read; only breeding ranges are shown. 'A landmark publication, opening the door to the vast avifauna heretofore unavailable to the Western World' (*Choice*, v.22(1), September 1984, p.62). *Class No: 598.2(47)*

Asia—Far East

[2916]
An Annotated checklist of the birds of the oriental region. Inskipp, T., *and others*. Sandy, Beds., Oriental Bird Club, 1996. 294p. £9.95. ISBN: 0952954508.

Doesn't claim to be comprehensive but summarizes the available data on birds in this area. Lists 2,586 species. References (814 items), p.215-31; index to English names, p.233-61; index to scientific names, p.263-94. All three are in very small type. A useful, up-to-date tool. *Class No: 598.2(51/52+57)*

Indian Subcontinent States

[2917]
Handbook of the birds of India and Pakistan: together with those of Bangladesh, Nepal, Bhutan, and Sri Lanka. Ali, Salim *and* Ripley, S.D., *eds*. 2nd ed. Delhi, Oxford Univ. Press, 1978-. illus. (incl. col.), maps.

1. *Divers to hawks*. 2nd ed. 1979. 440p. £42.50 2. *Megapodes to crab plover*. 2nd ed. 1980. 362p. £42.50. 3. *Stone curlews to owls*. 2nd ed. 1981. 344p. £42.50. 4. *Frogmouths to pittas*. 2nd ed. 1983. 284p. £42.50. 5. *Larks to the grey hypocolius*. 2nd ed. 1987. 278p. £37.50. 6. *Cuckoo-shrikes to babaxes*. 1997. £19.50. 7. *Laughing thrushes to the mangrove whistler*. 1996. 52p. £19.50. 8. *Warblers to redstarts*. 1997. 281p. £19.50. 9. *Robins to wagtails*. 324p. £19.50. 10. *Flowerpeckers to buntings*. 256p. £21.

Geographical coverage extends to Bangladesh, Nepal, Bhutan and Sri Lanka.

The one volume *Compact handbook* (2nd ed. 1987. $98) comprises v.1-4 of the 2nd ed. and v.5-10 of the 1st ed. Also, *Concise handbook of the birds of India and Pakistan* (Oxford, University Press, 1989. $39.95). *Class No: 598.2(54.)*

Africa

[2918]
BROWN, L.H. The Birds of Africa. Urban, E.K., *and others, eds*. London, New York, etc., Academic Press, 1982-. illus. (incl. col.), diagrs., maps. ISBN: 0121873016.

V.1. *Ostriches to falcons* (xii, [1], 521p.); v.2. *Gamebirds to pigeons* (1986. 552p.); v.3. *Parrots to woodpeckers* (1988. 611p.); v.4. *Broadbills to chats* (1992. 632p.); v.5. *Thrushes to puffback flycatchers* (1997. 669p.)

V.1. covers 10 orders of birds, Strutheoniformes ... Falconiformes. Data: range and status, description, field characteristics, voice, general behaviour, food, breeding, biology. Each species is fully illustrated in colour. Bibliography, p.479-507: 1. General and regional references; 2. References for each family; 3. Sources of sound recordings. Indexes of scientific names, English names, French names. Quarto format. *Class No: 598.2(6)*

Africa—Southern

[2919]
Illustrated guide to the birds of southern Africa. Sinclair, I., *and others*. London, New Holland, 1992. 426p. illus. (col.). ISBN: 0691044694, US ed; 1853682810, UK ed.

Published in the US in 1995 by Princeton University Press.

A guide to identification only, with brief information on distribution, plumage, and calls, this field guide presents 900 species of birds. Prelims. include 'Bird classification and nomenclature'; 'Bird habitats'; 'Aids to birding'. Variations in plumage depending on sex, age, and season are shown in the 200 colour plates. One of its strengths is the many 'in-flight' images which are shown. Data on southern Africa's ornithological clubs and organizations are given. *Class No: 598.2(68)*

[2920]
PROZESKY, O.P.M. A Field guide to the birds of Southern Africa. London, Collins, 1971. 350p. illus., maps. £9.95. ISBN: 0002120267.

Emphasis on bird song and bird calls as aids to identification; no information on breeding habits. Clear, concise and well-printed text. According to *TSL* (no.3600, 26 February 1971, p.254), the illustrations fall short of expectations, and the colours are not always true to the written description. *Class No: 598.2(68)*

America—North

[2921]
The Audubon Society encyclopedia of North American birds. Terres, J.K. New York, Knopf, 1980. 1109p. illus. (incl. col.). $75. ISBN: 0394466519.

A compendium on the 647 species of birds recorded in the USA and Canada. About 6,000 entries, A-Z, on the life histories of the bird species, biographical notes on American ornithologists, articles on avian biology (*e.g.* courtship, migration, song), definitions of terms, organizations. Full cross-references. Cites over 4,000 sources within the text, with full references in the bibliography. 'By far the most ambitious and extensive book of its kind' (*Reference books for small and medium-sized libraries* 4th ed. ALA, 1984, item 1064). *Class No: 598.2(71+73)*

[2922]
BAICICH, P.J. *and* HARRISON, C.J.O. A Guide to the nests, eggs and nestlings of North American birds. 2nd ed. San Diego, Academic Press, 1997. 347p. illus.(col. pl.), figs. £24.95. ISBN: 0120728311.

First published in 1978 as *A Field guide to the nests, eggs and nestlings of North American birds* by C. Harrison.

Describes 669 breeding species. Data include nest habitat, breeding season, nest construction, nestling period, and nestling. 48 colour plates show the eggs of 597 species; an additional 16 show a range of typical young. Bibliography, p.328-31. Index of common and scientific names, p.332-47. *Class No: 598.2(71+73)*

[2923]
PALMER, R.S. Handbook of North American birds. New Haven & London, Yale Univ. Press, 1962-88. 5v. illus. ISBN: 0300008147, v.1; 0300020783, v.2/3; 0300040598, v.4, pt.1; 0300040601, v.5, pt.2.

Sponsored by the American Ornithologists' Union.

1. *Loons through flamingoes*. 1962. 2/3. *Waterfowl*. 1976. (xi, 521p.); vii, 560p.). 4/5. *Condors & raptors*. 1988. (448p. $45; 400p. $45).

V.2-3 have 32 contributors. 'Atlantic Canadian goose' (v.2. p.190-2) has a distribution map and data on measurements, weight, breeds, nesting, migration, captive geese, introduction abroad, etc. V.3 contains index to v.2-3. Excellent colour plates and line-drawings. A standard work. *Class No: 598.2(71+73)*

[2924]
—GRUSON, E.S. Words for birds: a lexicon of North American birds, with biographical notes. New York, Quadrangle Books, 1972. 305p.

An ornithological, etymological, biographical and historical guide to 800 American birds. *Class No: 598.2(71/73)*

America—South

[2925]
The Birds of South America. Ridgely, R.S., *and others*. Oxford, University Press, 1989-94. ISBN: 0198572174, v.1; 0292770634, v.2. 1. *The oscine passerines*. 1989. $70. 2. *The suboscine passerines*. 1994. $85.

First two volumes in a projected four which will eventually include data on *c*.3,000 species. V.1 covers 750 birds in this group; V.2 adds 1,200. General chapters on habitat, biogeography, migration and conservation are followed by colour plates which group similar genera together. Text opposite the plates refer the reader to entries in the second part of the book which give details of identification, similar species, habitat and behaviour, range, and maps showing distribution. Bibliography. Indexes to English and scientific names. *Class No: 598.2(8)*

[2926]
BLAKE, E.R. Manual of neo-tropical birds. Chicago, Ill., Univ. of Chicago Press, 1977-. v.1-. illus., maps. ISBN: 0226056414.

Planned in 4v. 1. *Spheniscidae (Penguins) to Laridae (Gulls and allies)*. 640p. $100.

Aims to provide descriptions of all Central and South American subspecies of birds. Literature references. Favourably reviewed in *Library journal* (v.102(10), 1 June 1977, p.1265). *Class No: 598.2(8)*

Australasia & Oceania
[2927]
Handbook of Australian, New Zealand and Antarctic birds. Melbourne, Oxford University Press, 1990-. illus. (some col.), tables, maps. ISBN: 0195530683, v.1; 0195530691, v.2; 0195530705, v.3.

V.1: *Ratites to ducks* (2 pts.: A. *Ratites to petrels;* B. *Australian pelican to ducks*). 1400p. V.2: *Raptors to lapwings*. 984p. V.3: *Snipe to pigeons*. 1028p.

First three volumes in a projected series of five to be published under the auspices of the Royal Australasian Ornithologists Union. Species accounts give data on field identification; habitat; distribution; food; movements; population; social organization; social behaviour; breeding; voice; plumage; breeding. A bibliography is appended to each species account. Maps show the distribution of breeding birds. Appendices (*e.g.* 'Aboriginal names'). Indexes of scientific and English names. Excellent colour plates. Aimed at ornithologists at all levels. *Class No: 598.2(9)*

New Zealand
[2928]
HEATHER, B.D. and ROBERTSON, H.A. The Field guide to the birds of New Zealand. Oxford, University Press, 1997. 432p. illus.(col.),maps. £50. ISBN: 0198501463.

Two main sections: Identification guide (p.18-166); Handbook (p.167-424). Data in the identification section include common and Latin names, description, habitat, frequency of breeding. Colour plates show the birds on land and in flight. Data in the handbook section include size, distribution, population and behaviour - where possible, further reading is also given. Index, p.425-32. *Class No: 598.2(931)*

Australia
[2929]
Field guide to the birds of Australia: the most complete one-volume book of identification. Simpson, K. *and* Day, N., *eds*. 4th ed. London, Christopher Helm, 1994. 392p. illus. (incl. col.). ISBN: 071363930x.

Covers all Australian bird species in 2,000 illustrations on 128 coloured plates. Distribution map and diagrammatic illustration for individual species; p.16-275 form a useful key, with more generalised information in 'Handbook' section, p.276-378. Glossary, index, p.382-92. Light enough as a field guide. 'This is a true new edition of *The Birds of Australia, a book of identification* in both the physical and bibliographical senses'*(Preface)*. *Class No: 598.2(94)*

Wildfowl
[2930]
DELACOUR, J. The Waterfowl of the world. London, Country Life, 1954-64. 4v. illus. (incl. col. pl.), tables.

1. *The magpie goose, whistling ducks, swans and geese, sheldgeese and shelducks*. 1954. 2. *The dabbling ducks*. 1956. 3. *Elders, pochards, perching ducks, scotens, golden-eye and mergansers*. 1967. 4. *General habitats* ... 1964.

V.4 (364p.) has 5 contributors, rounding off v.1-3 with chapters of general interest (1. General habits; 2. The reproduction cycle (with 8p. of bibliography); 3. Ecology; 4. Distribution and special relationships; 5. Fowling; 6. Conservation and management; 7. Aviculture; 8. Domestic waterfowl; 9. The anatomy of the waterfowl; 10. Fossil anseriformes - 11. Corrections and additions). Index to chapters 1-9, p.355-64. A definitive work, with well-documented chapters. *Class No: 598.412*

[2931]
MADGE, S. and BURN, H. Wildfowl: an identification guide to the ducks, geese and swans of the world. London, Christopher Helm, 1988. 298p. col. illus., maps. £22.99. ISBN: 0747022011.

47 colour drawings, depicting over 700 individual birds, with range maps accompanying. Text referring to the bird is in a separate section. Data include field identification; voice; description; measurements; habitat; population. 'This is the first field guide to all 155 of the world's waterfowl in virtually every plumage' (*Library journal,* 15 April 1988, p.40). *Class No: 598.412*

[2932]
—SOOTHILL, E. *and* WHITEBREAD, P. Wildfowl of the world. Poole, Dorset, Blandford Press, 1978. iii, viii, 297p. (mainly col.), maps. £14.99. ISBN: 0713721103.

Descriptive data and distribution maps for 128 species of wildfowl. Bibliography, p.292-3; index of Latin and English names of wildfowl. A bonus is the directory of wildfowl collections worldwide. *Class No: 598.412*

Pigeons & Doves
[2933]
GOODWIN, D. Pigeons and doves of the world. 3rd ed. London, British Museum (Natural History), with Ithaca, New York, Cornell Univ. Press, 1983. 363p. illus. (incl. col. pl.), maps. £25. ISBN: 0565008471.

First published 1967 (vi, 446p).

10 chapters (1. Nomenclature, genera, species, sub-species, varieties and breeds ... 3. Coloration and plumage ... 5. Maintenance behaviour ... 7. Display and social behaviour). 24 sections, each with readings. Index of English names. Index of scientific names. *Class No: 598.65*

Eagles & Birds of Prey
[2934]
Birds of prey. Newton, I., *ed*. London, Merehurst Press, 1990. 240p. illus. (col.). £25. ISBN: 1853911313.

3 sections: Raptors of the world - Raptor biology - Relations with man. Checklist of living diurnal raptors, p.226-29. Lavishly illustrated. *Class No: 598.91*

[2935]
BROWN, L. and AMADON, D. Eagles, hawks and falcons of the world. London, Country Life Books, 1965. 2v. illus. (incl. col.), maps.

V.1 has 18 chapters on taxonomy, morphology, flight, hunting methods, migration, breeding, etc. V.2 has chapters 19-21, on the genera and species, nomenclature and taxonomy, with grouped supplementary bibliography and 94 maps. Index to v.1-2, p.933-45. 414 plates in all. *Class No: 598.91*

[2936]
BURTON, P. Birds of prey of the world. Limpsfield, Surrey, Dragon's World, 1989. 208p. illus. (col.). £18.95. ISBN: 1850280851.

Arranged in 5 sections: 1. New World vultures - 2. The osprey - 3. Kites, vultures, eagles and hawks - 4. The secretary bird - 5. Caracaras and falcons. Distribution maps, and systematic list and measurements, are apart from the text and illustration. Brief bibliography. Index. 256 excellent illustrations. *Class No: 598.91*

Mammals

CD-ROM
[2937]
Mammals: a multimedia encyclopedia. Washington, D.C., National Geographic Society, 1990. $99. ISBN: 0792218825.

Combines text, sound illustrations, and video. Data on more than 200 animals. Each article contains essays and fact boxes equivalent to *c.*600 pages of text. More than 700 colour photographs, 150 maps, 155 animal sounds, and 45 full-motion movie clips. Easy to use and reasonably priced. *Class No: 599(003.40)*

Encyclopaedias
[2938]
GOULD, E. *and* McKAY, G. Encyclopedia of mammals. 2nd ed. San Diego, Academic Press, 1998. 240p. illus. maps. £24.95: $39.95. ISBN: 0122936701.

First published as *The Encyclopedia of animals: mammals* (Merehurst, 1990).

19 contributors. Two sections: 1. World of mammals (chapters on classification, habitats, etc.) - 2. Kinds of mammals (marsupials, insectivorous, lagomorphs, etc.). Bibliography and index. Profusely illustrated in full colour. Distribution maps. Popular appeal but authoritative. *Class No: 599(031)*

[2939]
Grzimek's encyclopedia of mammals. Grzimek, B., *ed*. New York, McGraw-Hill Publishing Company, 1990. 5v. illus. maps. $500. ISBN: 0079095089, set.

Based on *Grzimek's animal life encyclopedia (q.v.)*.

More than 200 contributors. Entries in each volume are arranged by order and suborder. Each entry has an introductory section, with a map showing geographical distribution, followed by chapters discussing specific families or species. Standardized summary charts include data on scientific name; number of species and sub-species; size; life span; food; habitat; enemies. Outstanding feature is the 3,500 colour photographs which have been laser-scanned. Bibliography and

....(contd.)

index at the end of each volume, although there is no index for the complete set. Recommended for school, public and academic libraries.

Produced on CD-ROM as *The Multimedia encyclopedia of mammalian biology* (McGraw-Hill, 1992. $995), with additional articles, movies, and sound clips. The reviewer in *Reference books bulletin*, 1 March 1993 claims that, because of the complexity of the user interface, much practice is needed before making this an easy-to-use multimedia tool and is therefore more suited for academic libraries. *Class No:* 599(031)

Handbooks & Manuals

[2940]

The Encyclopedia of mammals. Macdonald, D., *ed*. 2nd ed. London, Unwin Hyman, 1989. 896p., col. illus.; col. diagrs. ISBN: 0044405413.

First published in 2v., 1984.

About 200 contributors in all. 1: The carnivores (7 families: the cat family ... the hyena family), sea mammals, primates, etc., herbivores, insectivores, bats and marsupials. Index, xxiv-xlvi (Roman page numbering at front and end of book). The entry 'Squirrel': p.612-27; 25 col. illus.; 2 col. diagrs. 1,200 col. illus., superbly presented. 'Its main market is likely to be naturalists, yet the technical detail should appeal to students and biologists' (*British book news*, February 1985, p.100, on v.2 of 1st ed). *Class No:* 599(035)

[2941]

YOUNG, J.Z. The Life of mammals: their anatomy and physiology. 2nd ed., with assistance of M.J. Hobbs. London, Oxford Univ. Press, 1975. xv, 528p. £25.50. ISBN: 0198571569.

First published 1957.

53 chapters (6. The framework of the body - 7. Muscles ... 11. The head of mammals ... 15. Respiration ... 21. The heart and circulation ... 30. The automatic nervous system ... 38. Receptor organs ... 48. The pituitary gland ... 53. The development of mammals). Bibliography (by chapters), p.494-507. Author and subject index. *Class No:* 599(035)

Tables & Data Books

[2942]

CORBET, G.B. *and* **HILL, J.E. A World list of mammalian species.** 3rd ed. Oxford, University Press; Natural History Museum Publications, 1991. viii,243p. figs. £30. ISBN: 0198540175.

First published 1980.

Systematic list of 4,327 species. Data: Latin name; common name; distribution. Bibliography (general works; geographical sources; taxonomic sources), p.213-31. Detailed index, p.232-43. *Class No:* 599(083)

[2943]

McKENNA, M.C. *and* **BELL, S.K. Classification of mammals:** above the species level. New York, Columbia University Press, 1997. 631p. $175. ISBN: 023111012x.

A revision of G.G. Simpson's *Principles of classification and a classification of mammals* (American Museum of Natural History, Bulletin v.85, 1945).

Eight contributors. Two parts: 1. History and theory of classification - 2. A classification of mammals, p.35-504. Four appendices, *e.g.* 'Some close mammalian outgroups'. Extensive bibliography. An authoritative work which assumes some previous knowledge. For academic and special libraries. *Class No:* 599(083)

[2944]

Mammal species of the world: a taxonomic and geographic reference. With the assistance and cooperation of the American Society of Mammalogists. Wilson, D.E. *and* Reeder, D.M., *eds*. 2nd ed. Washington, D.C., Smithsonian Institution Press, in association with the American Society of Mammalogists, 1993. xviii,1206p.

First ed. published 1981 and compiled for the Parties to the Convention on International Trade in Endangered Species of Wild Fauna and Flora.

Lists 4,629 species in taxonomic order and, at 1206p. in length, is almost double the previous edition. Data: scientific name and authority; type locality; geographical distribution; legal status of endangered species and controlled species. Bibliography of cited sources. Taxonomic index. A standard work. *Class No:* 599(083)

[2945]

—**BURTON, M.** Systematic dictionary of mammals of the world. 2nd ed. London, Museum Press, Ltd., 1965. 307p. illus.

First published 1962.

Provides data: general characteristics; habits; habitats; food; breeding; range; longevity; special comments; other statistics. Detailed analytical index, p.275-307. Careful drawings. *Class No:* 599(083)

Nomenclatures

[2946]

GOTCH, A.P. Mammals - their Latin names explained: a guide to animal classification. Poole, Dorset, Blandford Press, 1979. 271p. illus. charts. ISBN: 0713709391.

Part 1: The animal kingdom; part 2: The mammal orders. Bibliography, p.231. General index; index of English names; index of Latin ones. Selects over 1,000 of the *c.*4,300 known species of mammals. *Class No:* 599(083.72)

Worldwide

[2947]

BURTON, J.A. *and* **BURTON, V.G. Collins' guide to the rare mammals of the world.** London, Collins, 1987. 240p. col. illus. ISBN: 0002191725.

Sections: Monotremes - Marsupials - Bats - Primates ... Rodents - Carnivora - Seals and sea lions - Elephants - Perissodactyls - Sea cows - Artiodactyls - Cetaceans. Data: description; characteristics (habitat, feeding, breeding); distribution and population; reasons for scarcity; location and captive populations. Bibliography, p.232-3. Index, p.233-40. 98 col. plates illustrate more than 440 species. *Class No:* 599(100)

[2948]

LEVER, C. Naturalized mammals of the world. London, Longman, 1985. xvii, 487p. illus., tables, maps. ISBN: 0582460565.

Describes 66 species 'imported from its natural range to a new country either deliberately or accidentally by human agency' (*Preface*). 9 sections: 1. Marsupiala - 2. Edentata - 3. Insectivora - 4. Primates - 5. Carnivora - 6. Perissodactyla - 7. Artiodactyla - 8. Rodentia - 9. Lagomorpha. Bibliography, p.441-74. Index of vertebrata species, p.475-87. 26 appended country tables, p.413-40. 'Very thorough' (*New scientist*, 2 January 1986, p.44-45). *Class No:* 599(100)

[2949]

NOWAK, R.M. Walker's mammals of the world. 5th ed. Baltimore, Md., Johns Hopkins Press, 1991. 2v. (1629,lxiii), illus., charts, tables. $89.95. ISBN: 080183970x.

First published 1964.

V.1: Monotremata ... Rodentia; v.2: Rodentia ... Artiodactyla. V.2 includes a bibliography of literature cited, p.1501-1614 (A-Z authors), - a major contribution, and greatly expanded from the 4th ed. V.1 has an analytical index of orders, families and genera, with bold type for scientific names. Numerous black-and-white illus. (*c.*1 per page), substantial revision of a classic. Of the 4th ed., 'This monumental work is indispensable' (*Library journal*, 15 April 1984, p.784). A 6th ed. is due to be published in 1999. *Class No:* 599(100)

Tropics

[2950]

EMMONS, L.H. Neotropical rainforest mammals: a field guide. Chicago and London, University of Chicago Press, 1990. xiv,281p. illus. (some col.), figs., maps. £35.95; £15.95. ISBN: 0226207161.

Includes the lowland rainforest mammals found in Central and South America at elevations below 1,000 metres - *c.*500 species. These consist of opossums, anteaters, sloths and armadillos, bats, monkeys, carnivores, dolphins, tapirs, peccaries and deer, manatees, rodents and rabbits. Data for each species include means of identification, variation, similar species, sounds, natural history, geographic range, status, map showing distribution, and references. 6 appendices: A. Glossary ... D. Tracks of large mammals ... F. Checklist and index of scientific names. 29 colour plates. Index of genera and common names, p.275-81. *Class No:* 599(213)

[2951]

Mammals of the neotropics. Eisenberg, J.F. *and* Redford, K.A. Chicago and London, University of Chicago Press, 1989-92. 2v. illus., tables, maps. £67.95, v.1; £75.95, v.2. ISBN: 0226195406, v.1; 0226706818, v.2.

V.1. *The northern neotropics: Panama, Colombia, Venezuela, Guyana, Suriname, French Guiana.* x,449p. V.2. *The southern cone: Chile, Argentina, Uruguay, Paraguay.* 430p.

V.1 has 16 well-documented sections, v.2, 14. Data include physical description; summary of range; habitat. Colour and black-and-white plates. Each volume has an index of scientific and common names. A third volume covering Brazil, Bolivia, Peru and Ecuador is planned for 1999, as is v.4., covering Mexico. *Class No:* 599(213)

Marine Environment

[2952]

FOOD AND AGRICULTURE ORGANIZATION. Mammals in the seas. Rome, FAO, 1978-82. 4v.

1. *Report of the FAO ACMRR Working Party on Marine Animals.* 1978. xxv, 264p. 2. *Principal species summaries and report on sirenians.* 1979. xiii, 151p. 3. *General papers and large cetaceans.* 1981. x, 504p. 4. *Small cetaceans, seals, sirenians and otters.* 1982. x, 931p. $85.

....*(contd.)*

V.4 includes a paper 'The status of seals in the United Kingdom' (p.253-265), summaries in French and Spanish preceding. (Sections: Identification; distribution and movements; status of stocks; vital parameters; food habits and relations to fisheries; economic value; conservation legislation; conclusions. 33 references). A detailed study. *Class No:* 599(26)

[2953]

RIDGWAY, S.H. *and* HARRISON, R.J. **Handbook of marine mammals.** New York & London, Academic Press, 1981-94. 5v. illus., tables. ISBN: 0125885016, v.1; 0125885024, v.2; 0125885032, v.3; 0125885040, v.4; 0125885059, v.5.

1. *The walrus, sea lions, fur seals and sea otter.* 1981. xiv, 235p. 2. *Seals.* 1981. xv, 359p. 3. *The sirenians and baleen whales.* 1985. xviii, 362p. 4. *River dolphins and the larger toothed whales.* 1989. 442p. $105. 5. *The first book of dolphins.* 1994. 416p. £55.

Documented contributions by various hands, planned in 6v., highlighting life history, population dynamics, reproduction and diseases. 'The *Handbook* should appeal to all those seeking an introduction to these mammals and will also serve as a useful reference work for marine mammalogists' (*British book news,* February 1982, p.102). Well written. *Class No:* 599(26)

Europe

[2954]

CORBET, G. *and* OVENDEN, D. **The Mammals of Britain and Europe.** London, Collins, 1980. 253p. illus. ISBN: 000219774x.

'Includes all species of mammals that occur in a wild state in Europe West of the USSR, including Spitzbergen and Iceland, and in the northeastern Atlantic north of 35 degrees north' (*Preface*). Excludes extinct species of the region. Colour plates and drawings of 190 species are followed by 15 sections: 1. Tracks and signs - 2. Skulls and teeth - 3. Antlers and horns - 4. Marsupials - 5. Insectivores - 6. Lagomorpha - 7. Rodents - 8. Primates - 9. Carnivores - 10. Pinnipedes - 11. Odd-toed ungulates - 12. Even-toed ungulates - 13. Cetaceans - 14. Checklist of European mammals - 15. Mammals in Britain and Ireland (plus distribution maps of British and Irish species). *Class No:* 599(4)

Great Britain

[2955]

CORBET, G.B. *and* HARRIS, S. **The Handbook of British mammals.** 3rd ed. Oxford, Blackwell Scientific Publications for the Mammal Society, 1991. xiv,588p. illus., maps. £49.50; £28.50. ISBN: 0632016914.

First published 1964 (edited by H.N. Southern).

An extensive revision of the previous edition. A systematic account of the 98 species known to be feral in the British Isles and surrounding seas. Data include: recognition; sign; description; relationships; measurements; variation; distribution; habitat; feeding; population. 3 appendices: 1. Extinct species - 2. Ephemeral introductions and escapes - 3. Sound recordings. Items in the bibliographies appended to each chapter total 3,186. Glossary, list of abbreviations and index. 'It will definitely be the standard work for the next two decades' (*Reference reviews,* v.5(2), 1991, p.24). *Class No:* 599(410)

[2956]

MATTHEWS, L.H. **Mammals in the British Isles.** London, Collins, 1982. 208p. (*New naturalist library, no.68.*) ISBN: 0002197383.

Devotes the first third of the text on geological, climate and human influence, shaping the range of British mammal habitat. Ecology and behaviour are then considered. 'It is an excellent introduction to the natural history of British mammals for anyone, amateur or professional' (*Nature,* v.300, 9-15 December 1982, p.556). *Class No:* 599(410)

Africa

[2957]

HALTENORTH, T. *and* DILLER, H. **A Field guide to the mammals of Africa, including Madagascar.** Hayman, R.W., *trans.* London, Collins, 1980. 400p. col. illus. maps. £14.99. ISBN: 0002197782.

Translated from *Säugetiere Afrikas und Madagaskars.*

Describes *c.*324 species, including the largest and middle-sized, but omitting small-sized species (*e.g.* bats). Introduction outlines geological and climatological history of Africa, plus the history of mammalian fauna of Africa and Madagascar. Appended section on introduced fauna. Bibliography, p.1-2.

Superior illus. 'Should become a basic reference for any professional or amateur interested in the wildlife of Africa' (*Natural history book reviews,* v.5(3/4), 1982, p.142-3). *Class No:* 599(6)

Africa—Southern

[2958]

SMITHERS, R.H.N. **The Mammals of the Southern African subregion.** 2nd ed. University of Pretoria, 1990. xxxii,769p. illus., tables, maps. ISBN: 0869798022.

First published 1983.

340 species of mammals, including sea mammals (whales and seals) are described. Data: colloquial name; taxonomic notes, description, distribution, habitat, habits, food, reproduction, skull. Coverage: South Africa, Namibia, Botswana, Zimbabwe south of the river Zambezi, and adjacent oceans. Of the previous ed., 'A mammoth undertaking' (*Nature,* v.312, 13 December 1985, p.677). *Class No:* 599(68)

America—North & Central

[2959]

HALL, E.R. **The Mammals of North America.** 2nd ed. New York, Wiley, 1981. 2v. (xv, 690p. + 679p.). illus., diagrs., maps. ISBN: 0471054437; 0471054445.

First published 1959.

Details of 3,607 subspecies and monotypic species of native mammals of the post-Columbian period (1492-1977), in Greenland, Canada, USA, central America (down to and including Panama), the Greater and Lesser Antilles south to, and including, Grenada. Data on each: measurements, description, comparison with other members of the species, citations to original descriptions, distribution, etc. Each volume contains the same 80p. index to technical names and 10p. index to vernacular names. *Class No:* 599(71/73)

America—Central

[2960]

REID, F.A. **A Field guide to the mammals of Central America and southeast Mexico.** Oxford, University Press, 1997. 334p. illus.(col.) £45;$55. ISBN: 0195064003.

52 colour plates of 118 species of bats and 63 rodents drawn from life. Sketches of tracks of most larger species. Data include species accounts, measurements, description, distribution, where to see them, and range maps. 'A first-rate contribution to mammalogy and an essential addition to the mammalian library' (*Choice,* November 1998 p.548). *Class No:* 599(728)

Australia

[2961]

The Complete book of Australian mammals. Strahan, R., *ed.* London, Angus & Robertson, 1984. 529p. col. illus. £37.50. ISBN: 0207144540.

107 specialist contributors. A feature: colour photographs of 251 of the 273 species included with illus. of almost all the 129 placental mammals. Bibliographical references for each species. 'Sets a standard, although it does not cover critical identification requiring internal characteristics' (*Nature,* v.312, 13 December 1984, p.677). *Class No:* 599(94)

Whales, etc.

[2962]

WATSON, L. **Whales of the world.** 2nd ed. London, etc., Hutchinson, 1985. 302p. illus. (col.), charts, maps. £12.99. ISBN: 0091597110.

First ed. published as *Sea guide to whales of the world,* 1982.

7 chapters: 1. Cetology and cetologists - 2. The origin and evolution of whales - 3. Description - 4. Stranded cetaceans - 5. Natural history - 6. Status [population] - 7. Distribution. 3 appendices (3. Biography, p.285-6: 100 selected 2-4 line notes). Bibliography, 287-97 (A/Z; including many periodical articles). 76 species are listed, p.10-11; 96 species illus., 167 col. diagrs., 82 distribution maps (for dolphins and purpoises, as well as whales). Non-analytical index, p.298-302. 'An outstanding work' (*Library journal,* 1 February 1982, p.249). *Class No:* 599.5

[2963]

—FRASER, F.C. **British whales, dolphins and porpoises: a guide to the identification and reporting of standard whales, dolphins and porpoises on the British coasts.** 5th ed. London, British Museum (Natural History), 1976. xi, 34p. illus. £1.50. ISBN: 0565055496.

First published 1950.

Has notes on 6 whalebone whales and 18 toothed whales, one per page. Data on each: length, colour, form, teeth, general remarks, plus illus. 31 illus. in all. *Class No:* 599.5

[2964]
The World's whales: the complete illustrated guide. Minasian, S.M., *and others*. Washington, Smithsonian Books, 1984. 224p. col. illus. ISBN: 0895990148.

Covers all 70 recognized cetacean species, - whales, dolphins and porpoises. Arranged by suborder, then family, genus and species. Data include name and date of first description and year of discovery. Introductory chapter offers basic facts about cetacean biology. Glossary. List of selected readings. A feature: 'nearly 160 colour photographs of most of the species swimming in the open seas' (*Science & technology libraries*, 1985/6, v.8(1/2), p.177-8).
Class No: 599.5

[2965]
—Whales and dolphins. Martin, A.R., *and others*. London, Salamander Books, 1990. 192p. illus. (col.), maps. £6.95. ISBN: 086101488x.

Covers 76 species of whales, dophins and porpoises. The first section gives a general overview while the second looks at each species. Information includes indication of size; distribution maps; classification; description; habitat; food and feeding; behaviour; life history; world population; man's influence. At least one colour illustration of each species. Suitable for school and public libraries.
Class No: 599.5

Ungulates

[2966]
MOCHI, U. *and* CARTER, T.D. Hoofed mammals of the world. New York, Scribner, 1971. xxi, 268p. illus., maps. ISBN: 0684123827.
First published 1953.

Describes 300 species and subspecies of ungulates. Bibliography, p.257-8 (A-Z authors). Index of animals illustrated. Line drawings are mostly silhouettes. A few small distribution maps. *Class No:* 599.6

Horses

[2967]
HENDRICKS, B.L. International encyclopedia of horse breeds. Norman, University of Oklahama, 1995. xx,486p. illus. $65. ISBN: 0806127538.

Arranged A-Z and describes more than 390 breeds using 500 black-and-white and 32 colour photographs. Data include average height, origin of the breed, population status and aptitudes. 3 appendices: A. Countries of origin; B. Horse and pony breeds not included in this volume; C. Directory of organisations. Brief bibliography and glossary. *Class No:* 599.723

Deer

[2968]
WHITEHEAD, G.K. Deer of the world. London, Constable, 1972. xii, 194p. illus. (incl. pl.), maps.

Concentrates on taxonomy and the worldwide distribution of the family. 32 plates. *Class No:* 599.735

[2969]
—CHAPLIN, R.E. Deer. Poole, Dorset, Blandford Press, 1977. 218p. illus.

Supplementary to Whitehead. 'An excellent introduction to the general biology of ruminants' (*Journal of natural history*, v.12(2), March/April 1978, p.235). *Class No:* 599.735

Carnivores

[2970]
EWER, R.F. The Carnivores. London, Weidenfeld & Nicolson, 1973. xv, 494p. illus., tables. (*World naturalist series*.)

10 chapters (2. The skeleton; 3. Anatomy of the soft parts; 4. The special senses; 5. Food and food finding; 6. Signals and social organization; 7. Social organization and living space; 8. Reproduction; 9. Fossil relatives; 10. Classification and distribution of the living spaces). References (A-Z authors), p.416-53. Author index; species and analytical subject index. *Class No:* 599.74

Seals

[2971]
KING, J.E. Seals of the world. 2nd ed. Oxford Univ. Press, and London, British Museum (Natural History), 1983. 240p. illus. (incl. col.), diagrs., maps. £9.95. ISBN: 0565008684.
First published 1964.

Introduction; Section 1: The diversity of pinnipeds (including fossils); Section 2: Pinniped biology. Section 3: Appendices (Origin of scientific names. Geographical index. References, p.217-35; further reading, p.236). Detailed analytical index, p.237-40. 38 colour plates illustrate nearly every species. 'A completely new, much enlarged and greatly improved book, and like its predecessor it is destined to

....(contd.)
become a successful standard text for all marine mammalogists' (*Natural history book reviews*, v.7(3), 1984, p.141-2).
Class No: 599.745

Primates

[2972]
Current primate references. Seattle, Univ. of Washington, Primate Information Center, 1973-. 12pa. $50 (individual); $60 (organizations). ISSN: 05904102.

Contains *c*.150 references per issue. 37 sections: Bacterial infections ... Viral infections. References include names and addresses of authors, for contacting. Book reviews. Primate index. Author index. *Class No:* 599.8

[2973]
International directory of primatology. Madison, Wis., Wisconsin Regional Primate Research Center Library, 1992. Price varies. ISSN: 10643286.

Contains information on 182 organizations, arranged geographically, dealing with primates. Data include research personnel; training opportunities; principal research programmes. Serials list, with addresses and contacts. Subject, species, training programme, and personal name indexes. *Class No:* 599.8

[2974]
NAPIER, J.R. *and* NAPIER, P.H. A Handbook of living primates. London & New York, Academic Press, 1967. xiv, 456p. illus. (pl.), tables.

Three parts: 1. Functional morphology of primates - 2. Profiles of primate genera - 3. Supplementary and comparative data (*e.g.* taxonomy and nomenclature; habitats of primates; limbs and locomotion). References (A/Z authors; *c*.900 items), p.417-46. 113 plates. Index to illus. and plates, p.447-56. 'A work of great scholarship' (*Science journal*, v.4(3), March 1969, p.92). *Class No:* 599.8

[2975]
—NAPIER, J.R. *and* NAPIER, P.H. The Natural history of the primates. London, British Museum (Natural History), 1985. 200p. illus., (incl. col.), charts, maps. £15. ISBN: 0565008706.

By comparison with the *Handbook*, lavishly illustrated in a larger format and clearly written. 6 chapters (1. What are primates? ... 5. Profiles of primates - 6. Human evolution). Glossary, p.187-9; Further reading, p.190; References, p.191-5 (A-Z authors). Analytical index, p.196-200. But some definitions are open to questions and citation of sources could be more numerous. 'A book which will better serve the keen amateur rather than the student or professional' (*Nature*, v.316, 18 July 1985, p.323). *Class No:* 599.8

[2976]
WOLFHEIM, J.W. Primates of the world: distribution, abundance and conservation. Seattle, Washington, Univ. of Washington Press, 1983. 832p. illus. $57.50. ISBN: 0295958995.

Assesses the status in the wild of about 150 primate species and discusses the future in terms of their habitats, distributions and, ultimately their population. Over 1,000 references to the literature. 'A well-designed framework ... An excellent job' (*Nature*, v.312, 13 December 1984, p.676). *Class No:* 599.8

Apes & Monkeys

[2977]
KAVANAGH, M. A Complete guide to monkeys, apes and other primates. New York, Viking Press, 1984. 224p. col. illus., maps. ISBN: 0670435430.

7 sections: 1. Primates in perspective; 2. The prosimians; 3. The "almost monkeys"; 3. The odd ones and the dry-nosed prosimians; 4. The monkeys of the New World; 5. The monkeys of the Old World; 6. The tailless primates: apes and man; 7. Prospects for the primates. Outstanding colour illus. Distribution maps. Appended classification of the order primates; glossary; short bibliography; subject index. Claims to have a set of photographs covering every living genus of primates. *Class No:* 599.82

[2978]
TUTTLE, R.H. Apes of the world: their social behavior, communication, mentality and ecology. Park Ridge, N.J., Noyes, 1987. 421p. illus, tables. $55. ISBN: 0815511043.

Data provide readable, succinct accounts of the taxonomy, locomotion, feeding, nesting, tool use, cognition and communication, sociobiology. Extensive bibliography. 'Tuttle has written a scholarly work that could serve as a standard reference for many years'. (*Nature*, v.328, August 1987, p.678). *Class No:* 599.82

6 Technology

Biotechnology

Databases

[2979]

Chemical engineering and biotechnology abstracts. [Deutsche gesellschaft für chemisches Apparatewesen] Cambridge, Royal Society of Chemistry.

Produced jointly by The Royal Society of Chemistry, the DECHEMA, FIZ CHEMIE and IChemE.

Covers industrial practice and theoretical chemical engineering. Includes processes, substances, operations, transport, equipment, safety. About 180,000 records, updated monthly. Available via DIALOG, DataStar, FIZ Technik, Orbit, STN International; on CD-ROM (Dialog OnDisc, updated quarterly); and on the Internet from ChemWeb (URL: http://www.chemWeb.com).

Class No: 6:573(003.4)

CD-ROM

[2980]

Biotechnology citation index. Philadelphia, Pa., Institute for Scientific Information, 1991-. 6 disks pa. $1950.

Citation index, with abstracts. About 50,000 records from 2,800 publications. Also available online as part of Scisearch from various hosts. *Class No:* 6:573(003.40)

Bibliographies

[2981]

Biotechnology information sources: North and South America. Rapp, B.A., *ed.* Medford, NJ, Learned Information, 1994. 144p. $32.50. ISBN: 0938734814.

8 chapters, each devoted to a particular source of information, *e.g.* primary research databases, journals and newsletters, patents, the Internet, etc. Appended lists of online service providers, CD-ROMs and publishers. Bibliography; detailed, analytical index.

Class No: 6:573(01)

[2982]

CRAFTS-LIGHTY, A. Information sources in biotechnology. 2nd ed. London, Macmillan; New York, Stockton Press, 1986. [xii], 403p. tables. ISBN: 0333392806.

First published 1983.

13 sections: 1. What is technology? The science and the business - 2. Information sciences in biotechnology (p.24-32) - 3. Monographs, book series and textbooks (p.33-93) ... 7. Abstracting and secondary sources - 8. Computer databases - 9. Patents and patenting - 10. Market surveys. 16 appendices (*e.g.* 1. Bibliographies in technology). Author is Managing director, Biocommerce Data, Ltd.

Class No: 6:573(01)

[2983]

EUESDEN, M., *ed.* **Introduction to biotechnology information.** London, British Library, Science Reference and Information Service, 1991. 90p. £19.75. ISBN: 0712307621.

5 sections: 1. Scientific information - 2. Biotechnology - patents - 3. Online databases - 4. British official publications - 5. Business information in biotechnology. 9 appendices, A-I (I: Further reading). Detailed, analytical index, p.83-88. *Class No:* 6:573(01)

Handbooks & Manuals

[2984]

ATKINSON, B. and MAVITUNA, F. Biochemical engineering and biotechnology handbook. 2nd ed. Basingstoke, Macmillan, 1991. 1271p. diagrs., graphs, tables. £148.50. ISBN: 0333424041.

First published 1983.

20 chapters, closely subdivided, with reference and 'further reading'. Covers properties of micro-organisms, production processes, economics, measurement and instrumentation, nomenclature. Numerous tables. Detailed, analytical index. '... wealth of detail and breadth of coverage' (*Reference reviews*, v.6(6), 1992, p.25).

Class No: 6:573(035)

[2985]

BAJAY, Y.P.S., *and others.* **Biotechnology in agriculture and forestry.** Berlin, etc., Springer Verlag, 1986-. illus., micrographs, tables. ISBN: 0387518096.

An important, comprehensive work. So far (1986-91) 16v. have appeared. Trees (1986-91. 3v.); Crops (1986-88. 2v.); Potato (1987); Medical and cosmetic plants (1988-91. 3v.); Plant, protophasts and genetic engineering (1989. 3v.); Legumes and oilseed crops (1990-); Somaclonal variation in crop improvement (1990-); Wheat (1990); Rice (1990). Full sub-section references. Each volume carries a subject index. *Class No:* 6:573(035)

[2986]

Biotechnology: a multi-volume comprehensive treatise. Rehm, H.-J. *and* Reed, G., *eds.* 2nd ed. Weinheim, New York, VCH, 1991-. V.1-. illus., graphs, tables. £208 each. ISBN: 3527283110, V.1.

First published 1981-89.

V. 1. *Biological fundamentals* (1993. 641p.).

V. 2. *Genetic fundamentals and genetic engineering* (1993. 880p.).

V. 3. *Bioprocessing* (1993. 816p.).

V. 4. *Measuring, modelling and control* (1991. 658p.).

V. 5. *Genetically engineered proteins and monoclonal antibodies* (1997).

V. 6. *Products of primary metabolism* (1995).

V. 7. *Products of secondary metabolism* (1996).

V. 8. *Biotransformations* (1996).

V. 9. *Enzymes, biomass, food, and feed* (1995).

V. 10. *Special processes* (1997).

V. 11. *Environmental processes* (1997).

V. 12. *Modern biotechnology: legal, economic and social dimensions* (1995. 600p.).

Over 350 contributors overall. V.3 has 4 parts: I. Nature and issues of bioprocessing - II. Product formation (upstream processing) - III. Product recovery and purification - IV. Process validation, regulatory issues. Volume index. *Class No:* 6:573(035)

[2987]

BRITISH LIBRARY. Science Reference Library. **Health and safety in biotechnology.** London, SRL [1986]. [1], [1], 80, [1]p. *Gratis.*

7 sections: 1. Biotechnology, general (national and international surveys and proposals) - 2. Recombinant DNA - 3. Laboratory safety - 4. Industrial applications - 5. Environmental considerations - 6. General information sources (journals and newspapers; abstract journals; online databases) - 7. Organizations. Keyword index (p.47-80). *Class No:* 6:573(035)

[2988]

Comprehensive biotechnology: the principles, applications and regulation of biotechnology in industry, agriculture and medicine. Moo-Young, M., *ed.* Oxford, etc., Pergamon Press, 1985. 4v. illus., diagrs., graphs, tables. £695.

1. *The principles of biotechnology: scientific fundamentals.* A.T. Bull and H. Dalton, volume editors. 1985. xxv, 688p.

2. *The principles of biotechnology: engineering considerations.* C.L. Clooney and A.E. Humphrey, volume editors, 1985. xxv, 633p.

3. *The principles of biotechnology: current commodity products.* H.W. Blanch, and others, volume editors. 1985. xxv, 1136p.

4. *The practice of biotechnology: speciality products and service activities.* C.W. Robinson and J.A. Howell, volume editors. 1985. xxix, 308p.

V.4 has 3 sections (67 subsections): 1. Specialized activities and potential applications - 2. Governmental regulations and concerns - 3. Waste: management and pollution control. Appended: Glossary of terms; Nomenclature. Cumulated subject index to the 4v., p.1165-1308. Nearly 100 contributors. Subsection 18: 'Assay of industrial waste enzymes', p.329-60; 4½p. of references. 'A notable success ... *Comprehensive biotechnology* will be an essential purchase for all departments and institutions, academic or industrial, that claim an interest in any aspect of ... biotechnology' (*Nature*, v.321, 5 June 1986, p.571-2).

A supplementary volume, *Annual biotechnology,* ed. by L.A. Babiuk appeared in 1989. *Class No:* 6:573(035)

[2989]
HIGGINS, I.J., *and others, eds*. **Biotechnology: principles and applications.** 22nd ed. Oxford, Blackwell Scientific Press, 1993. 500p. illus., diagrs., graphs, tables, chemical structures. £39.50; £19.50. ISBN: 0632027258.

First published 1985.

Expanded edition, with new chapters on biotechnology and analysis, plus data on biosensors, genetic finger-printing and AIDS technology. *Class No:* 6:573(035)

[2990]
The UK biotechnology handbook '98/99. Crafts-Lighty, A. *and* Williams, R., *eds*. 9th ed. London, BioCommerce Data Ltd., 1998. [xiv], 739p. £195; $320. ISBN: 1871393094.

First published 1988.

Part 1 includes a discussion of various issues, *e.g.* risk, resource and regulaton, gene therapy; transgenic crops, etc). Part 2 is a directory of companies and organizations in 5 sections: 1. Manufacturers and suppliers - 2. Service providers - 3. Financial services - 4. Academic institutions - 5. Government agencies. Indexes: organizations; products and services; areas of interest. *Class No:* 6:573(035)

Dictionaries

[2991]
BAINS, W. **Biotechnology from A to Z.** 2nd ed. Oxford Univ. Press, 1998. [x], 411p. diagrs. ISBN: 0199636931.

First published 1993.

About 380 terms explained, some at length (*e.g.* 'DNA probes', *c*.2p.). Lively and readable. The *New Scientist* commented on the first ed.: 'Any dictionary that lists the phrase "yuk factor" has to be worth buying ... a wonderfully lucid guide'. *Class No:* 6:573(038)

[2992]
COOMBS, J. **Dictionary of biotechnology.** 2nd ed. London, Macmillan, 1992. 364p. £45; £12.99.

First published 1986.

Over 3,000 definitions, plus numerous cross-references. Defines biotechnology as 'the application of organisms, biological systems or biological processes to manufacturing and service industries'. Contains terms not found elsewhere. 'Fills a void in this rapidly developing field' (*Science & technology libraries*, v.8(1), Fall 1987, p.170, on the 1st ed.). *Class No:* 6:573(038)

[2993]
Dictionary of biotechnology: English, German. Babel, W., *and others, eds*. Amsterdam, Elsevier, 1989. 113p. ISBN: 0444989005.

About 7300 English-base terms with German or 'Germanized' (*Preface*) equivalents. Genders given. *Class No:* 6:573(038)

[2994]
WALKER, J.M. *and* COX, M. **The Language of biotechnology:** a dictionary of terms. 2nd ed. Washington, D.C., American Chemical Society, 1995. 296p. $29.95. (*ACS Professional reference books*.) ISBN: 0841229821.

First published 1988.

Several hundred new terms have been added to this edition. Emphasis is on technology rather than biology. 'Deserves a place in all biology, chemistry, and general science collections. (*Choice*, January 1996, p.768). *Class No:* 6:573(038)

Glossaries

[2995]
Biotechnology glossary. EEC Translation Service, *ed*. Amsterdam, Elsevier, 1990. vi,1074p. £85. ISBN: 1851665692.

About 700 terms with equivalents in each of the nine EC languages. Intended for translators dealing with technical works. *Class No:* 6:573(038.1)

Reviews & Abstracts

[2996]
Abstracts in biocommerce. Slough, Berks., Biocommerce Data, Ltd., 1982-. 26 pa. £459; $878 pa. ISSN: 02636778.

200 abstracts per issue. Coverage: 'Commercial news in biotechnology, including genetic engineering, monoclonal antibodies, enzymes' (*Inventory of abstracting and indexing services produced in the UK*. Compiled by J. Stephens. 2nd ed., 1986, item 3). Available on CD-ROM and floppy disk. *Class No:* 6:573(048)

[2997]
Biodeterioration abstracts: a world abstract journal covering the fields of materials, biodeterioration and biodegradation of wastes. Prepared from the CAB ABSTRACTS database by the CAB International Mycological Institute. Wallingford, Oxon., CAB International, 1987-. 4 pa. + index. ISSN: 09510621.

About 4,000 abstracts pa. 2 main groups: Biodeterioration; Biodegradation. Appended: Reports; Conferences; Books. Author and subject indexes per issue; the annual index includes a list of source journals. *Class No:* 6:573(048)

[2998]
Biotechnology research abstracts. Bethesda, Md., Cambridge Scientific Abstracts, 1984-. 6pa. $585 pa. ISSN: 07335709.

About 4,200 abstracts pa., monitoring *c*.5,000 primary journals and other sources. Sections: General topics and reviews ... Patents ... Genetic engineering - Immobilization - Cell culture - Products of biotechnology - Applications - Fermentation and process engineering - Proceedings - Books. Author and subject indexes per issue. Online as LIFE SCIENCES COLLECTION (DIALOG and other hosts; CD-ROM). *Class No:* 6:573(048)

[2999]
Current biotechnology. Cambridge, Royal Society of Chemistry, 1983-. Monthly. £661; $1117. ISSN: 02643391.

A subset of *Chemical engineering and biotechnology abstracts*. About 5000 abstracts pa. 4 parts (15 sections): Technocommunications (*e.g.* 2. Legal issues and safety) - Techniques (*e.g.* Fermentation technology) - Industrial areas (8. Pharmaceutics; 9. Energy production; 10. Agriculture; 11. Chemical industry; 12. Food) - Information (14. Forthcoming events; 15. Books, reviews, etc.). Subject, substance, and company indexes per issue and annually. No author index. Available online via DataStar and DIALOG. *Class No:* 6:573(048)

[3000]
Derwent biotechnology abstracts. London, Derwent Pubrs., Ltd., 1982-. 26pa. ISSN: 02625318.

About 600 abstracts per issue. Classes A-M: A. Microbiology; D. Pharmaceuticals; E. Agriculture; H. Other chemicals; M. Waste disposal. Indexes (per issue and cumulated pa.): Author; Corporate Affiliate; Patentee; Subject. 'Covers all aspects of biotechnology from manipulation through biomedical engineering and fermentation to downstream processing' (*Notes*). About 30% of the records cover patents.

Available online via DIALOG, file 357 and other hosts. Over 200,000 records. Also available on CD-ROM (SilverPlatter) and on the Internet. *Class No:* 6:573(048)

Periodicals

[3001]
DOWNS, L.J. **The Biotechnology marketing sourcebook.** London, British Library, Science Reference and Information Service, Biotechnology Information Service, 1990. [iv],137p. £30.

Introduction - Record structure - Alphabetical list of journals (p.1-120; 251 titles) - Publishers' addresses - Keyword index. The first of a new series. Worldwide listing of 251 English-language periodicals, newsletters and abstracts for workers in 'biotechnology, the life sciences, health care, biochemistry and related fields' (*Introduction*). Details include advertising contact/scope/readership. For marketing managers, science, technology and medical publishers, conference organizers and information officers. *Class No:* 6:573(051)

Progress Reports

[3002]
Biotechnology and genetic engineering reviews. Russell, G.E., *ed*. Newcastle upon Tyne, Intercept, 1984-. Annual. ea. £95.

Each annual volume encompasses the entire field, from pest control and wastewater treatment to energy production and the genetics of human disease. 'Aims to avoid the two traps into which annual reviews often fall - either surveying particular fields frequently and exhaustively, even when there is nothing useful to say, or pulling together batches of *ad hoc* reviews with no organic coherence' (*British book news*, July 1987, p.392). *Class No:* 6:573(055)

Yearbooks & Directories

[3003]
The Biotechnology directory, 1999. Hackwood, S., *ed*. 20th ed. Basingstoke, Hants., Macmillan, 1998. 640p. £179. ISBN: 0333687892.

First published 1980.

Data on more than 9,000 organizations and academic institutions. Covers Europe, North America, South America, Australasia and Japan. 5 parts: Activity index - Profiles (sorted by country and commercial activity) - Products, equipment and services - Sources of information - Indexes. Includes list of French and German equivalents for about 600 terms. J. Coombs and Y.R. Alston, responsible for a

....*(contd.)*
number of earlier editions, acted as consulting editors. Also available on the World Wide Web: URL: http://www.biotech.nature.com. *Class No:* 6:573(058)

[3004]
The European biotechnology directory '98. Johnson, E., *and others, eds*. London, Biocommerce Data, Ltd, 1998. [xii], 739p. £195; $320. ISBN: 1871393086.
Profiles of about 750 organizations in 18 countries; includes universities, trade associations and venture capital providers. Product and subject indexes. Data include contact details, products and services, and interest areas. *Class No:* 6:573(058)

Great Britain
[3005]
DUNNILL, P. *and* **RUDD, M. British biotechnology and British industry.** Swindon, Wilts., Biotechnology Directorate of the Science and Engineering Research Council. 89p. ISBN: 0901660574.
A report, in 12 sections (e.g., The food processing study; Energy supply or saving; Inter-industry linkage). 22 references. *Class No:* 6:573(410)

Russia
[3006]
RIMMINGTON, A. *and* **GREENSHIELDS, R. Technology and transition:** a directory of biotechnology in the post-coup USSR. London, Pinter, 1992. 224p. £75. ISBN: 1855670380.
Includes books and likely developments. *Class No:* 6:573(47)

Japan
[3007]
Biotechnology guide Japan, 1990-91: company directory and comprehensive analysis. Nikkei Biotechnology, *eds*. New York, Stockton Press; Basingstoke, Macmillan, 1990. xv,591p. £95. ISBN: 0935859667, US; 0333518055, UK.
Data on about 800 Japanese companies: operations, finance, R & D projects, major patents. Subject index, p.568-91. *Class No:* 6:573(52)

USA
[3008]
DIBNER, M.D. Biotechnology guide U.S.A.: companies, data, analysis. 3rd ed. Triangle Park, NC, Institute for Biotechnology Information, 1995. 692p. $249. ISBN: 1886041024.
First published 1988; 2nd ed. 1991.
Data on over 1,000 companies working with the technologies of genetic engineering. 7. Sections: 1. Introduction - 2. Directory of companies ... 5. Company areas of interest (*e.g.* bioseparations, vaccines, fungi, etc.) - 6. Partnerships - 7. Analysis of the industry. 5 appendices (c. 'Dead companies'). Index of companies. *Class No:* 6:573(73)

[3009]
UNITED STATES. Congress. Office of Technology. **Commercial biotechnology:** an international analysis. Washington, US Government Printing Office, 1984. [vi], 612p. illus., diagr., tables, chemical structures. $20. (*OTA-BA-218*.)
Parts 1-3 (chapters 3-10): 1. The technologies - 2. Firms commercializing biotechnology 3. Applications of biotechnology in specific industries (*e.g.* pharmaceuticals; agriculture; specialty chemicals and food additives; environmental applications; commodity chemicals and energy production; bioelectronics). Chapters 11-21: Analysis of US competitiveness in biotechnology. Glossary. Appendices A-K. Detailed, analytical index, p.605-12. *Class No:* 6:573(73)

Information Services
[3010]
BRITISH LIBRARY. Science Reference Library. **Guide to research information sources in biotechnology.** London, SRL, [1986]. [iii], 10, [1]p. *Gratis*.
3 parts: 1. International directories - 2. European directories (A. Europe and the EEC; B. National directories of the EEC countries: Belgium, Britain, Denmark, Eire, France, Italy, the Netherlands, West Germany) - 3. Databases. *Class No:* 6:573:061:025.5

Technology

Abbreviations & Symbols
[3011]
Abkürzungen in der technik. [Abbreviations and acronyms in technology.] Leipzig, Fachbuchverlag Leipzig, 1991. 372p. ISBN: 3343007315.
About 10,000 entries, with English definitions for about half of them. Bibliography, p.372. *Class No:* 60(003)

[3012]
Pugh's dictionary of acronyms and abbreviations: abbreviations in management, technology and information science. Pugh, E., *comp*. 5th ed. London, Library Association Publishing, 1987. £60 (£48 to L.A. members). ISBN: 0853655375.
First published 1968.
More than 34,000 entries, stating country of origin or organization, as considered necessary. Unlike the wide-ranging *Acronyms, initialisms and abbreviations dictionary* with its 500,000 odd terms, plus *International acronyms, initialisms and abbreviations dictionary* (2nd ed. Gale, 1987), for terms of foreign origin, Pugh concentrates largely on management, technology and information science. *Class No:* 60(003)

[3013]
VLIESTRA, J. Dictionary of acronyms and technical abbreviations for IT, industrial, and scientific applications. London, Springer Verlag, 1997. 692p. ISBN: 3540761527.
About 32,000 items, A-Z. No explanatory material, so the work does nothing but identify a number of possibilities for each acronym (*e.g.* over 20 for 'MR'). *Class No:* 60(003)

Databases
[3014]
NTIS [National Technical Information Service]. Springfield, Va., US Department of Commerce.
A wide range of disciplines: management, agriculture, building, business, chemistry, engineering, energy, materials science, medicine, transportation, etc. Lists unclassified US reports and these of other countries. A wealth of information. Over 1,900,000 records; updated twice a month. Available on DIALOG, file 6 and from other hosts. On CD-ROM (DIALOG onDisc; SilverPlatter) and the Internet. *Class No:* 60(003.4)

CD-ROM
[3015]
Applied science and technology abstracts . New York, H.W. Wilson. CD-ROM. Updates vary, depending on the subscription. ISSN: 00036986.
An electronic version of *Applied science and technology index*, with abstracts. A subject guide to *c*.410 English-language journals, mostly US, with indexing coverage back to October 1983 and abstracting to March 1993. Also available on magnetic tape and the World Wide Web (URL: http://www.hwwilson.com). *Class No:* 60(003.40)

Bibliographies
[3016]
Bibliographic guide to technology. Boston, Mass., G.K. Hall, 1976-. Annual. ISSN: 03602761.
Records not only the relevant publications catalogued by the New York Public Library's Research Libraries but also additions to the Library of Congress MARC tapes and to the New York Engineering Society Library. *Class No:* 60(01)

[3017]
Führer durch die technische Literatur: Katalog technischer Werke für Studium und Praxis. Hannover, F. Weidemanns Buchhandlung. Annual. ISBN: 3878910118.
First published 1906/07.
About 15,000 entries pa. in 8 classes: 1. Basic sciences (mathematics, astronomy, physics); 2. Architecture, building; 3. Mechanical engineering, mining, energy; 4. Electricity & electronics ... 6. Chemisty & chemical engineering; 7. Management, dictionaries, patents, technical literature as a whole, standards; 8. Technical periodicals. Subject and author indexes. List of publishers cited. *Class No:* 60(01)

[3018]
RINK, E. **Technical Americana:** a checklist of technical publications printed before 1831. Millwood, N.Y., Kraus International, 1981. xxviii, 776p. ISBN: 0527754471.

Sponsored by the Eleutherian Mills Memorial Library.

6,065 numbered entries for separately published works. 12 sections (each with chronological arrangement): 1. General works - 2. Technology - 3. Agriculture - 4. Crafts and trades - 5. Medical technology - 6. Military technology - 7. Civil engineering - 8. Mechanical engineering - 9. Manufacturing - 10. Mining and mineral production - 11. Sea transportation - 12. Inland transportation. Bibliographic references, p.xvi-xvii. Key to locations (*c.*170). Detailed, analytical index. 'This is a valuable bibliography, carefully compiled and very thorough in its coverage' (*College & research libraries*, v.43, July 1982, p.339). *Class No:* 60(01)

[3019]
SUBRAMANYAM, K. 'Technical literature'. In *Encyclopedia of library and information science* (New York, Dekker), v.30 (1980), p.144-209. facsim., diagrs., table.

Introduction - Technical reports - Standards and specifications - Trade catalogs. 79 references. Bibliography (p.200-9): Information needs of engineers and technologists; Technical reports; Standards and specifications - Trade catalogs - House journals (13 titles). *Class No:* 60(01)

[3020]
TECHNISCHE INFORMATIONSBIBLIOTHEK. Hannover. **Katalog der Technischen Informationsbibliothek (TIB),** Hannover. Microfiche ed. Mainz-Kastel, N. Gärtner, 1983. (Distributor, K.G. Saur). £1,500. ISBN: 3598304455.

1,254,960 entries on 664 fiches. Includes title entries for monographs, periodicals, all German dissertations and, in particular, published and unpublished research reports. Records the holdings of a leading scientific and technical library. *Class No:* 60(01)

[3021]
UNITED NATIONS. Industrial Development Organization. **Guides to information sources.** New York, United Nations, 1972-. ea. $4. (*UNIDO/LIB/SE.D/1-.*)

1. *Information sources on the meat-processing industry.* Rev. ed. 1976. xii, 88p. 2. *Information sources on the cement and concrete industry.* Rev. ed. 1977. xii, 70p. 3. *Information sources on the leather and leather goods industry.* 1979. xiii, 85p. 4. *Information sources on the furniture and joinery industry.* 1977. xii, 89p. Rev ed. 5. *Information sources on the foundry industry.* 2nd ed. 1977. xii, 87p. 6. *Information sources on industrial quality control.* Rev. ed. 1980. xii, 71p. 7. *Information sources on the vegetable and processing industry.* 1977. xii, 109p. 8. *Information sources on agricultural implements and machinery industry. 1973. xii, 108p. 9. Information sources on building boards* ... 1974. 94p. 10. *Information sources on the pesticides industry.* Rev. ed. 1982. xii, 77p. $3. 11. *Information sources on the pulp and paper industry.* 1974. xii, 92p. 12. *Information sources on the clothing industry.* 1974. xii, 116p. 13. *Information sources on the animal feed industry.* 1975. xii, 62p. 14. *Information sources on the printing and graphics industry.* 1975. xii, 65p. 15. *Information sources on the non-alcoholic beverage indust*

*Each guide has c.*12 sections: 1. Professional, trade and research organizations, learned societies and special information services - 2. Directories - 3. Sources of statistics, marketing and other economic data - 4. Basic handbooks, textbooks and manuals - 5. Monograph series - 6. Current periodicals - 7. Current abstracting and indexing periodicals - 8. Proceedings, papers and reports - 9. Specialized dictionaries and encyclopaedias - 10. Bibliographies - 11. Films and film catalogues - 12. Other potential sources of information (*e.g.* conferences; patents and licences; translation sources). A few of the sections are annotated. Appended (in most cases): 'Bibliographical sources used in compiling the present guide'. A helpful series, if somewhat dated, for researchers. *Class No:* 60(01)

Indexes

[3022]
Applied science and technology index. New York, H.W. Wilson, 1913-. 11pa.; quarterly, annual cumulations. $255 (minimum subscription). ISSN: 00036986.

As *Industrial arts index*, 1913-57.

Subject index to *c.*410 English-language journals, mostly US. Closely subdivided (*e.g.* 'Electronics industry', October 1995: 13 subject and country subheadings, plus cross-references). Appended 'Book reviews'. Selection of periodicals for indexing is determined by subscriber vote. Time-lag about 4 months. Also available online from a number of hosts; CD-ROM; magnetic tape; and the World Wide Web (URL: http://www.hwwilson.com). *Class No:* 60(014)

[3023]
Clover index. Caldecote, Biggleswade, Beds., Clover Publications, 1975-. 4pa. £37 pa.

Title varies.

About 3,000 entries in each issue, A-Z. Draws upon 90 popular science magazines such as *Amateur gardening, Flight, New Scientist, Wireless World* and *Your model railway.* Titles of articles are occasionally given brief explanatory notes. Cheaply produced from typescript. To some extent supplements *Abstracts in new technologies and engineering* for public libraries. Annual cumulation. Available on CD-ROM and on the World Wide Web: URL: http://www.cloverweb.co.uk. *Class No:* 60(014)

Encyclopaedias

[3024]
Encyclopedia of physical science and technology. Meyers, R.A.M., *ed.* 2nd ed. San Diego, Ca., Academic Press, 1992. 18v. illus., diagrs., graphs, tables. £1500. ISBN: 0122269306.

First published 1987.

Over 750 contributors. 705 documented articles covering aeronautics; space technology; earth sciences; physical sciences; computer science and telecommunication; electronics; mathematics; nuclear technology. Available on CD-ROM as *Academic Press encyclopedia of physical science and technology* (Knight-Ridder OnDisc; $3000). *Class No:* 60(031)

[3025]
LUEGER, O. **Lexikon der Technik.** Hrsg. von A. Ehrhardt und Hermann Franke. 4. vollst. neubearb. und erw. Aufl. Stuttgart, Deutsche Verlags-Anstalt, 1960-72. 17v. illus., diagrs., tables.

First published 1894.

1. *Grundlagen des Maschinenbaues.* 1960.
2. *Lexikon der Elektrotechnik und Kerntechnik.* 1960.
3. *Lexikon der Werkstoffe und Werkstoffprüfung.* 1961.
4. *Lexikon der Bergbaues.* 1962.
5. *Lexikon der Huttentechnik.* 1963.
6-7. *Energietechnik und Kraftmaschinen.* 1965.
8-9. *Fertigungstechnik und Arbeitsmaschinen.* 1967-68.
10-11. *Bautechnik.* 1966.
12. *Fahrzeugtechnik.* 1967.
13-14. *Feinwerktechnik.* 1969.
15. *Fabrikorganisation, Fördertechnik.* 1970.
16. *Verfahrenstechnik Nahrungsmitteltechnik, Haushaltechnik.* 1971.
17. *Registerband.* 1972.

A series of specialized technological dictionaries, each in A-Z entry order. Chemical engineering is excluded (on which see *Ullmann's Encyclopädie*, at 66.0(031). V.5 (xii, 824p.; 3,000 entries; 232 illus. and diagrs.; 334 tables) has 22 contributors. All articles are signed, and many carry references. Technical terms mentioned in articles are italicized and appear as entries. Clear, keyed diagrams. Numerous cross-references. V.17, the general index, has *c.*60,000 entries. *Class No:* 60(031)

[3026]
Magill's survey of science: applied science series. Magill, F.N., *ed.* Englewood Cliffs, N.J., Salem Press, 1993. 6v. (2917p.). $475. ISBN: 0893567051.

More than 380 signed articles, averaging seven pages in length, alphabetically arranged by topic, and also including many emerging disciplines, such as hazardous wastes and biotechnology. 190 contributors. Each entry has appended a glossary, cross-references, and annotated bibliography. V.6 contains a general index. For public and academic libraries. Supplement V.7 was published in 1998 ($90; ISBN: 0895369348). The series is also available on CD-ROM ($750; ISBN: 0893562718). *Class No:* 60(031)

[3027]
Technology in action: science applied to everyday life. Engelbert, P., *ed.* UXL, 1998. 3v. (523p.). $79.95. ISBN: 0787628093.

Includes 64 articles grouped into eight chapters: Communication - Electronics and computers - Energy - Food and agriculture - Health and medicine - Civil engineering - Manufacturing and materials - Transportation. Chronology, 33p. 'An excellent resource for public and school libraries' ('Reference book bulletin', *Booklist*, Feb. 15, 1999, p. 1094). *Class No:* 60(031)

Handbooks & Manuals

[3028]
The Technology management handbook. Dorf, R.C., *ed.* Boca Raton, Fl., CRC Press, 1999. v.p. illus., diagrs., graphs, tables. $95. ISBN: 0849835776.

Published in association with the IEEE Press.

About 200 contributors and 200 articles covering technology management in a wide range of areas and from several perspectives,

....*(contd.)*
including industry, government and education. Extensive references. 'Recommended' (*Choice*, March 1999, p.1294). Also available on CD-ROM ($129. ISBN: 0849397545). *Class No:* 60(035)

Dictionaries

Polyglot
[3029]

Elsevier's dictionary of industrial technology in English, German and Portuguese. Phillippsborn, H.E., *comp.* Amsterdam, Elsevier, 1994. v, 943p. £207. ISBN: 0444894454.
14,529 English-base terms. German and Portuguese equivalents and indexes. *Class No:* 60(038)=00

[3030]

Gale five-langauge technology dictionary; English/French/German/Italian/Spanish. Detroit, Mi., London, Gale, 1993. 447p. ISBN: 1873477953.
About 20,000 headwords, chiefly nouns, in all; 80,000 translations. Single sequence of words. *Class No:* 60(038)=00

[3031]

SCHLOMANN, A., *ed.* **Illustrated technical dictionaries in six languages.** London, Constable, 1906-32. (Also published Munich, Oldenbourg; New York, McGraw-Hill). 17v. illus., diagrs. (*Schlomann - Oldenbourg series*.)
1. *Elements of machinery and tools.* (1,632 diagrs.). 2. *Electrical engineering, including telegraphy and telephony.* 3. *Steam boilers and steam engines.* 4. *Internal combustion engines.* 5. *Railway construction and operation.* 6. *Railway rolling stock.* 7. *Hoisting and conveying machinery.* 8. *Reinforced concrete.* 9. *Machine tools.* 10. *Motor vehicles.* 11. *Metallurgy of iron.* 12. *Pneumatics.* 13. *Structural engineering.* 14. *Raw materials of the textile industry.* 15. *Spinning.* 16. *Weaving and woven fabrics.* 17. *Aeronautics.* (omits Spanish and Russian terms).
A monumental, much dated series. Compilation has been most thorough, and even the most recondite terms (*e.g.* in railway engineering; weaving) appear. The pattern of classified sections, keyed parts of diagrams, and equivalents in the six languages (English, German, French, Russian, Italian, Spanish supported by language indexes) has proved acceptable for later technical dictionaries. V.2, 14, 17 have been reprinted (Munich, Oldenbourg). *Class No:* 60(038)=00

German
[3032]

Fachwörterbuch technik und angewandte wissenschaften: Deutsch/Englisch. [Dictionary of technology and applied sciences: German/English.] 5th ed. Berlin, Paris, Hatier, 1993. 1177p. £93.10. ISBN: 3861178435.
About 100,000 headwords in all. German into English only. *Class No:* 60(038)=30

[3033]

FREEMAN, H.G. Wörterbuch technischer Begriffe mit 4,300 Definitonen nach DIN, Deutsch und Englischer. Berlin, Beuth-Verlag, 1983. 702p. ISBN: 3416108041.
German definitions are given of the 4,300 German headwords, plus English equivalent of the headword and English-German index. *Class No:* 60(038)=30

[3034]

Routledge German technical dictionary. [Universal-Wörterbuch der technik Englisch.] London, Routledge, 1995. 2 vols. (850p.; 750p.). £90 (vol.). ISBN: 0415093929.
Vol. 1: German-English; vol. 2: English-German.
About 100,000 entries per language in 63 technical subject areas (*e.g.* acoustics, electricity, opticsmechanics, quality assurance, textiles, etc.). Appended list of over 3,000 abbreviations; details of inflexion; cross references. A major dictionary. An electronic version is available on CD-ROM (£199) and computer diskette. *Class No:* 60(038)=30

French
[3035]

JOLY, H, *ed.* **Dictionnaire des industries:** 36,000 définitions. Index anglais-français. Paris, Conseil International de la Langue Française [CILF], 1986. xvi, 1082p. £136.
French terms are explained; English equivalents of terms. English-French index, p.633-1082. Quarto. Also available on CD-ROM. *Class No:* 60(038)=40

[3036]

Routledge French technical dictionary. [Routledge Dictionnaire technique anglais.] London, Routledge, 1994. 2 vols. (xxiv, 777p.; xxxiv, 841p.) £92.50 (vol.). ISBN: 0415056705.
Vol. 1: French-English; vol. 2: English-French.
34 contributors. About 100,000 entries per language in 70 technical subject areas (*e.g.* acoustics, mechanics, quality assurance, recycling, etc.). Appended list of abbreviations, chemical elements, conversion tables. A major dictionary. An electronic version is available on CD-ROM and computer diskette. *Class No:* 60(038)=40

Italian
[3037]

MAROLLI, G. Dizionario tecnico, inglese-italiano, italiano-inglese. [Technical dictionary, English-Italian, Italian-English.] 13th ed. Milan, Ulrico Hoepli Editore, 1996. xxi, 1848p.
12th ed. 1991.
About 130,000 entries for each language. Includes a number of plates (*e.g.* a boring machine) with parts clearly labelled in each language. A CD-ROM version is available. *Class No:* 60(038)=50

Spanish
[3038]

Elsevier's dictionary of technology: English-Spanish; Spanish-English. Thomann, A.E. Amsterdam, Elsevier, 1990-93. 4v. (c.3000p.). £159; £185.
About 80,000 entries and sub-entries in each part. Near-print — hardly legible. *Class No:* 60(038)=60

[3039]

Routledge Spanish technical dictionary. [Routledge diccionario técnico inglés.] London, Routledge, 1997. 2v. (xxx, 846p.; xxx, 848p.). £180. ISBN: 0415112745.
Vol.1: Spanish-English; vol.2: English-Spanish.
About 100,000 entries per language, drawn from traditional areas of technology including mechanical engineering, electrical engineering and electronics, and construction, as well as newer fields such as fuelless energy sources, safety engineering and quality assurance. Includes terms from Spain and Latin America. 40 contributors. A major dictionary. Also available on CD-ROM (ISBN: 415139732; £199). *Class No:* 60(038)=60

Russian
[3040]

CALLAHAM, L.I., *and others.* **Callaham's Russian-English dictionary of science and technology.** 4th ed. New York, etc., Wiley, 1996. xxxiv, 814p. $125. ISBN: 0471611395.
First published 1947; 3rd ed., 1975. The 4th ed. was completed by P.E. Newman and J.R. Callaham; L.I. Callaham died in 1990.
Over 120,000 scientific and technical terms and about 5,000 frequently used, non-technical ones. Terms are categorised, genders given; abbreviations, prefixes and common Russian word-endings included. Good typography for cyrillic. Particularly helpful in the fields of pure and applied chemistry.
This new ed. incorporates the life sciences, including medicine, physiology, botany and ornithology. Numerous computing terms and those relating to nuclear power and weapons have also been added. *Class No:* 60(038)=82

Czech
[3041]

Česko-anglický technický slovník. [Czech-English technical dictionary.] 5th ed. Prague, SNTL, 1992. 2v. (944p.; 1026p.). £18.25; £19.55. ISBN: 8003004438.
About 55,000 entries for each language; arranged in some 40 categories. *Class No:* 60(038)=850

Japanese
[3042]

TUNG, L.W. Japanese/English, English/Japanese glossary of scientific and technical terms. New York, John Wiley, 1993. xxi,1146p. £90. ISBN: 0471574635.
Includes 120 subject areas, with c.3,000 chemical terms, 1,600 mathematical terms, 900 computer and logic terms, 3,200 engineering terms, and 3,700 biological terms. *Class No:* 60(038)=956

Theses

[3043]
BILBOUL, R.R., *ed*. **Retrospective index to theses of Great Britain and Ireland, 1716-1950. Volume 2: Applied sciences and technology.** Oxford, ABC-Clio, 1976. [8], xi, 159p. facsim.

About 1,500 entries under subjects (Acetaldehyde ... Zirconium), p.1-90. Subject cross-references. 'Metal alloys': nearly 4 columns. Author index, p.91-159. *Class No:* 60(043)

Reports Literature

[3044]
Corporate author authority list. Karl, A.V., *ed*. 2nd ed. Detroit, Mich., Gale., in cooperation with National Technical Information Service. 2v. (xiv, 2,103p.). $180, the set. ISSN: 07413270.

A 40,000 entry authority list of main entries for US government-sponsored research, development and engineering reports - as well as foreign technical reports and other analyses prepared by national and local government agencies, their contractors/grantees.
Class No: 60(047)

[3045]
Report series codes dictionary: a guide to more than 20,000 alphanumeric codes used to identify technical reports. Aranson, E.J., *ed*. 3rd ed. Detroit, Mich., Gale, 1986. x, 647p. $175. ISBN: 0810321475.

Rev. ed. of *Dictionary of report series codes* (2nd ed. Special Libraries Association, 1973; first published 1962).

Includes over 20,000 codes found in a database produced jointly by the US Departments of Commerce and Energy, NASA and the Department of Defense. 2 major sections: report series codes, A-Z; corporate author or issuing agencies, A-Z. *Class No:* 60(047)

Reviews & Abstracts

[3046]
Abstracts in new technologies and engineering. London, Bowker-Saur, 1998-. 6pa., with annual cumulation. £850; $1550 pa. ISSN: 13679899.

Formerly *British technology index*, 1962-80; *Current technology index*, 1980-1997. Published by the Library Association until 1990.

Abbreviated *ANTE*. About 12,500 items pa., with abstracts. 25 sections (1. General ... 8. Energy ... 11. Communication ... 22. Leather, paper, textiles and wood). A feature is the use of chain subject headings (*e.g.* 'Petroleum, Pipelines, Repair, Freezing, Carbon dioxide' - virtually a highly compressed descriptive annotation). Coverage: general technology, applied sciences, engineering, chemical technology, manufactures and technical services. *ANTE* is available on CD-ROM, Dialog (File 238) and Datastar. *Class No:* 60(048)

[3047]
Current contents: Engineering, computing & technology. Philadelphia, Pa., Institute for Scientific Information, 1975-. Weekly. $315 pa. ISSN: 00957917.

Preceded by *Current contents: Engineering & technology*. (1970-74); *Current contents: Engineering, technology & applied sciences*.

Reproduces contents pages of *c.*100 journal issues each week, covering some 700 journals during the year. 13 disciplines (*e.g.* management, aerospace, chemistry, metallurgy, nuclear power, optics and acoustics). Prelim. pages note journal coverage changes, book announcements, etc. Title index; author index, plus address dictionary; publishers address directory. Available online and CD-ROM.
Class No: 60(048)

[3048]
Japanese technical abstracts. Ann Arbor, Mich., Japanese Technical Information Service, University Microfilms International, 1986-. Quarterly. ISSN: 08825246.

Draws on *c.*700 Japanese journals on technology, applied sciences, engineering and business management. 80% in Japanese, according to *RQ*, v.26(1), Fall 1986, p.114,116. *Class No:* 60(048)

[3049]
New technical books: a selective list with descriptive annotations. New York Public Library, Science & Technology Research Center, 1915-. 6pa. £25. ISSN: 00286869.

Each issue contains *c.*500 annotated entries for noteworthy books, mostly in English. Entries, in broad Dewey Decimal Classes feature two paragraphs: 'Content' and 'Note', the latter indicating readership, level and standing. Parts of continuing multi-volume works (*e.g.* Kirk-Othmer) and annual review series (*e.g. Advances in ...*) receive attention. The annual author and catchword indexes occupy middle pages of the December issue each year. A valuable selection tool, although somewhat late in appearance. *Class No:* 60(048)

Periodicals

[3050]
BALACHANDRAN, S., *ed*. **Directory of publishing societies:** the researcher's guide to journals in engineering and technology. New York, etc., Wiley, 1982. ISBN: 0471092002.

Lists 224 journals, A-Z. Bibliographical data: aims and scope; manuscript submission procedures; style guide; refereeing procedures; acceptance rate and time between submission and publication. Page-charge information. 'For science library schools' (*New technical books*, v.68(1), January 1983, item 1). *Class No:* 60(051)

Progress Reports

[3051]
New technologies and development. Johnston, A. *and* Sasson, A., *eds*. Paris, Unesco, 1986. 281p. diagrs., tables. (*Notebooks on world problems, 1*.) ISBN: 923102454x.

6 sections. 1. Introduction; society, technology and industry - 2. Information technologies and telecommunication - 3. Biotechnologies - 4. Health and technologies - 5. New energy technologies - 6. Technological advances and environmental change. Selective, grouped bibliography, p.274-81. *Class No:* 60(055)

Yearbooks & Directories

[3052]
Directories held by the Science Reference and Information Service. 2nd ed., compiled by the Business Information Service. London, SRIS, 1986. [iii], 101p. £7. ISBN: 0712307419.

Lists more than 2,000 directories held by SRIS. Arranged under titles, A-Z. Class-marks and availability of earlier issues shown. *Trade directories subject index* (7th ed., 10p., on blue tinted paper) may also be consulted, as part of the SRIS's Business Information Service. *Class No:* 60(058)

[3053]
—Leading consultants in technology. 2nd ed. Detroit, Mich., Gale Research Co., 1989. 2v. (xxii, 1,996p.). ISBN: 089235089x.

A directory of *c.*18,000 scientific and technical consultants active in the USA. V.1 provides who's who data on the specialities in 6 broad categories: electronics, mechanical technology, chemistry, civil engineering/energy technology/earth sciences, physics and biotechnology. V.2: 'Expertise index' (1,500 subject headings) and index of names. Selected from *Who's who in technology*.
Class No: 60(058)

Standards

[3054]
BRITISH STANDARDS INSTITUTION. **BSI Standards Catalogue, 1998-99.** London, BSI, 1998. Annual. 1067p. ISBN: 0580289826. ISSN: 09530339.

First published 1984; continues *British Standards yearbook*, 1937-83.

British Standards and related publications. General series, p.26-453 - Automobile series - Aerospace series - Marine series - Codes of practice - Electronic components of assessed quality ... BS ISO and BS EN ISO publications ... Detailed, analytical index, p.860-1061. *Class No:* 60(083.74)

[3055]
DIN [Deutsche Industrie Normen]. **Katalog für technische regeln.** Berlin, Beuth Verlag, Annual. 2v.

Gives details of standards in both German and English. Over 4000 DIN standards have been translated in full into English. Updated monthly (new standards and information on drafts and revisions in *DIN Mittelungen Electronom* (Berlin, Beuth Verlag)).

Available online as DITR database (about 115,000 records); hosts include DataStar DIALOG. CD-ROM from the Deutsches Institut für Normung. *Class No:* 60(083.74)

[3056]
INTERNATIONAL ORGANIZATION FOR STANDARDIZATION. **Catalogue 1994 [ISO].** Geneva, ISO, 1994. 888p. ISBN: 926710196x. ISSN: 03033309.

Classified list of standards, p.39-338. Withdrawals, p.349-56. Alphabetical index, p.437-888. Includes information for ordering. *Class No:* 60(083.74)

[3057]
KWIK index of international standards. Geneva, International Organization for Standardization, 1993. 758p. ISBN: 926710182x.

Standards, A-Z; small type. *Class No:* 60(083.74)

[3058]

Standards and specifications database. Bethesda, Md., National Standards Association, Inc.

US government and industry standards and specifications. Data: issuing organization, Federal Supply Classification code, adoption, ANSI designation. Suppliers of products conforming to standards included. About 125,000 records; updated monthly. Available on DIALOG, file 113 and on CD-ROM from the publisher. *Class No:* 60(083.74)

Chronologies

[3059]

BUNCH, B. *and* **HELLEMANS, A. The Timetables of technology:** a chronology of the most important people and events in the history of technology. New York, Simon & Schuster, 1993. vi, 490p. $35; £20. ISBN: 0671769189.

Covers general technology, architecture and construction, communication, energy, materials, medical technology, tools and devices, transportation. 7 sections: Stone ages - Metal ages - Age of water and wind - Industrial revolution - Electric age - Electronic age - Information age. Indexes: name; subject *Class No:* 60(090)

[3060]

—**HARDUP, P.,** *ed*. The Timetable of technology. New York, Harvest Books, 1982. 240p. $29.50. ISBN: 0878512098.

Compares scientific events for 1900-82 and beyond, in a series of two-page spreads per year. 6 broad topics: Communications and information; Transport; Warfare and space exploration; Energy and industry; Medicine and food production; Fringe benefits (inventions). British emphasis. *Class No:* 60(090)

Histories

[3061]

DAUMAS, A., *ed*. **A History of technology and invention:** progress through the ages. Translated from the French. London, J. Murray, 1980. 3v. illus., diagrs.

1. *The origins of technological civilization, to 1450* vi, 596p. 2. *The first stage of mechanization, 1450-1725.* [x], 794p. 3. *The expansion of mechanization, 1725-1870.* ix, 768p.

Original French ed. as *Histoire générale des techniques* (Paris, Presses Universitaires de France, 1962-68), - the work of 20 contributors, with collaboration of Centre de Documentation Historique des Techniques. M. Daumas: Conservateur du Musée du Conservatoire National des Arts et Métiers. 'It would be a good thing if this work were to find its way into the libraries of our schools' (*The Times*, 16 May 1980, p.9). *Class No:* 60(091)

[3062]

GILLE, B. Histoire des techniques: techniques et civilisations; techniques et sciences. Tours, Gallimard, 1978. xx, 165p. illus., table. (*Encyclopédie de la Pléiade, v.41.*)

5 specialist contributors. Broad subject grouping: Prolégomènes à une histoire - Techniques et civilisations (Ancient world; Greeks, Romans; Middle Ages; Industrial Revolution; Modern) - Techniques et sciences (economics; geography; language; science, politics; etc). Subsections have bibliographies appended. Chronological table. Name index (3,000 persons, with brief designations). Title and subject indexes. *Class No:* 60(091)

[3063]

History of technology. Hollister-Short, G. *and* James, F., *eds*. London & New York, Mansell, 1976-. illus. diagrs. ISSN: 03075451.

V.17 (1996. xi, 235p.) has 9 papers including 'Archimedes the engineer' (185 references) and 'Space, time and innovation characteristics: the contribution of diffusion process theory to the history of technology' (66 references). 'Contents of former volumes', p.229-35. *Class No:* 60(091)

[3064]

McNEILL, I., *ed*. **An Encyclopedia of the history of technology.** London, Routlege, 1990. 1085p. illus., diagrs., charts. £80. ISBN: 0415013062.

22 contributions, each with further reading, by an international team of specialists. Theme: important inventions and their development, from Stone Age to Space Age. Subject and name indexes. 150 black-and-white illus. Editor was formerly Executive Secretary of the Newcomen Society for the Study of the History of Science and Technology. Published in paperback, 1996 (ISBN: 04151471921; £35). *Class No:* 60(091)

[3065]

SINGER, C., *and others, eds*. **A History of technology.** Oxford, Clarendon Press, 1954-84. 8v. illus. (incl. pl.), tables, maps. v.1-7, ea. £50; v.8, £27.50. ISBN: 019858105x.

1. *From early times to the fall of the ancient empires.* 1954, iv, 627p.

2. *The Mediterranean civilizations and the Middle Ages, c.700 BC to c.1500.* 1956. ix, 802p.

3. *From the Renaissance to the Industrial Revolution, c.1600-c.1750.* 1957. 804p.

4. *The Industrial Revolution, c.1750-c.1850.* 1958. xxxiii, 728p.

5. *The late nineteenth century, c.1850-c.1900.* 1958. xxxviii, 888p.

6-7. *The twentieth century (c.1900-c.1950)*, edited by T.I. Williams. 1978. 2v.

8. *Consolidated indexes.* 1984. 232p.

Intended as a comprehensive history of the 'methods and skills by which man has attained a gradual easing of his earthly lot through mastery of his natural environment' (*Preface*). Technology as an aspect of history, especially social history, and as an influence on the development of civilization. Each chapter is by a specialist, and each volume is well equipped with illus. (incl. plates), tables, maps and bibliographies. V.8 comprises 4 parts: 1. List of contents for v.1-7; 2. Index of names; 3. Index of place-names; 4. Index of subjects (p.127-232). 'An interesting authoritative account of inestimable value' (*Aslib book list,* May 1979, item 199). *Class No:* 60(091)

[3066]

—**DERRY, T.K.** *and* **WILLIAMS, T.I.** A Short history of technology, from the earliest times to AD 1900. London, Oxford Univ. Press, 1960. xviii, 782p. illus., chron., tables. ISBN: 0198581238.

Owes a good deal to Singer, although it is no abridgement. Whereas Singer is for the specialist student, Derry and Williams is for the general reader. Geographically it is largely confined to the ancient Near East, Western Europe and North America. 353 line-drawings, mainly taken from Singer. Select bibliography (p.750-8), plus chapter bibliographies. Index of subjects; index of persons and place names.

Reprinted London, Constable, 1993 (ISBN: 0486274721; £16.95). *Class No:* 60(091)

[3067]

—**WILLIAMS, T.I.** A Short history of twentieth-century technology. London, Oxford Univ. Press, 1982. xix, 414p. £15. ISBN: 0198581159.

Designed for the general reader, providing a broad conspectus of technological development and 'a glimpse of the social, economic and political factors that influenced the development' (*Nature*, v.302, 3 March 1983, p.90). 30 chapters. Well-written, with many well chosen illus., and excellent bibliographies. The author is one of the general editors of *A history of technology. Class No:* 60(091)

Bibliographies

[3068]

FERGUSON, E.S. Bibliography of the history of technology. Published jointly by the Society for the History of Technology and the M.I.T. Press. Cambridge, Mass. & London, Massachusetts Inst. of Technology Press, 1968. xx, 347p.

About 1,500 annotated entries, in 14 main groups (1. General works - 2. General bibliographies and library lists - 3. Directories of technical, academic and business organizations - 4. Early source books and monographs - 5. Encyclopaedias, compendia and dictionaries of technology - 6. Biography - 7. Government publications and records - 8. Manuscripts - 9. Illustrations - 10. Travel and descriptions - 11. Periodicals and serial publications - 12. Technical societies, education and exhibitions - 13. Technology and culture - 14. Subject fields. Detailed analytical index, p.307-47. Aims 'to provide a reasonably comprehensive introduction to primary and secondary sources' (*Preface*). A valuable bibliography in its field. Updated by annual 'Current bibliography in the history of technology' in *Technology and culture. Class No:* 60(091)(01)

[3069]

Guide to the history of technology in Europe 1996. Angliss, S., *and others, comps*. 3rd ed. London, Science Museum, 1996. xii, 235p. ISBN: 0901805866.

First published 1992; 2nd ed. 1994. Published with the support of the European Commission Directorate General XII.

Covers a range of research interests: general; approaches; policy studies; motive power and energy sources; materials and processes; mechanical; civil engineering; transport; electrical and communications; medical and biological. 4 sections: Researchers (by interest) - Journals (by interest) - Institutions (by country, city) - Indexes. *Class No:* 60(091)(01)

[3070]

JOHN CRERAR LIBRARY. A List of books on the history of industry and industrial arts. Josephson, A.G.S., *comp.* Chicago, Ill., John Crerar Library, 1915 (reprinted 1976). [ix], 486p. (*Bibliographical publications, no.11.*)

Companion volume to *A list of books on the history of science.*

Lists the Library's resources, - *c.*3,300 titles - on the subjects concerned, in classified order. Includes history of commerce and banking, but not of economics. Gives bibliographical descriptions, contents of symposia and similar works, annotating as necessary. Includes bibliographies and periodicals with some titles in French, German and Italian. *Class No:* 60(091)(01)

Periodicals

[3071]

Technology and culture: an international quarterly of the Society for the History of Technology. Chicago, Ill., Univ. of Chicago Press, 1960-. v.1(1).

The April issue each year includes an annual 'Current bibliography in the history of technology', with *c.*1,000 briefly annotated entries. Author and subject indexes. *Class No:* 60(091)(051)

[3072]

—History of technology index, 1991: journal articles in the Science Museum Library. London, Science Museum, 1992. *c.*100p. £16.95. ISBN: 0901805505.

Complements the 'Current bibliography' published annually in *Technology and culture. Class No:* 60(091)(051)

20th Century

[3073]

HERRING, S.D. From the Titanic to the Challenger: an annotated bibliography on technological failures of the twentieth century. New York, Garland, 1989. 486p. $54. ISBN: 0824030435.

Evaluative annotations; indicates inclusions of photographs/ drawings. 'Has no comparable equivalent' (*RQ,* v.29(3), Spring 1990, p.440). *Class No:* 60(091)"19"

Biographies

[3074]

Australian men and women of science, engineering and technology. 12th ed. Melbourne, Reed Reference Australia, 1995. xxvi, 661p. £102. ISBN: 1875589643.

Published in association with the Australian Academy of Science and the Australian Academy of Technological Sciences and Engineering.

Brief biographical details of about 3,500 scientists. Indexes: areas of specialisation; location. Also available on CD-ROM. *Class No:* 60(092)

[3075]

Biographical dictionary of the history of technology. Day, L. *and* McNeill, I., *eds.* London, Routledge, 1996. 844p. £110. ISBN: 0415060427.

About 1,300 brief biographies, most with short bibliographies. Emphasis is on figures from the 18th century to the present, British and contintental rather than American. Indexes: subject areas (aerospace to weapons and armour); topics; names. 'This work is unlikely to be bettered in the foreseeable future' (*Reference reviews,* 10, 1 (1996), p.27). *Class No:* 60(092)

[3076]

Who's who in industry. Margetts, J., *ed.* London, Fulcrum, 1991. vii,964p. ISBN: 1870452038. ISSN: 09604642.

About 10,000 entries, A-Z. Usual 'Who's Who' biographical information. Indexes: Company; Sector; Regional. A brief check reveals surprisingly little overlap with *Who's Who.* Publishers plan annual volumes, which so far have seemed not to appear. *Class No:* 60(092)

[3077]

Who's who in technology. Unterburger, A., *ed.* 6th ed. Detroit, MI, Gale, 1989. 2v. (2742p.). $380 (set). ISBN: 0810349507 (set).

First published 1979 as *Who's who in technology today* by Technology Recognition Corp.

V.1. *Biographies.* 1830p.

V.2. *Indexes.* 912p.

About 38,000 biographies, giving data on employment, education, special interests, expertise, publications, addresses. 4 indexes: Expertise; Geographic; Employer. Emphasis on US. *Class No:* 60(092)

Worldwide

[3078]

World technology policies. Cunningham, P. *and* Parker, P., *eds.* Harlow, Essex, Longman, 1994. xiv, 940p. tables. £145. (*Longman guide to world science and technology.*) ISBN: 0582057302.

17 contributors; 2 parts: 1. Editorial surveys (*e.g.* Environmental policies) - 2. Regional profiles (1. Africa and the Middle East - 2. The Amazons - 3. Asia, Australia and Antarctica - 4. Europe). 'A valuable and timely book' (*Science & technology libraries,* 14(4), Summer 1994, p.129). *Class No:* 60(100)

Ancient Greece & Rome

[3079]

OLESON, J.P. Bronze age, Greek and Roman technology: a select, annotated bibliography. New York, Garland, 1986. xvi,515p. (*Bibliographies of the history of science and technology, v.7. Garland reference library of the humanities, v.646.*) ISBN: 0824086775.

2030 items in 11 chapters (subdivided by topic): 1. Sources (ancient authors; bibliographies, etc.) - 2. General surveys ... 6. Construction and civil engineering - 7. Manufacturing and trade (handtools; metalworking; ceramics, etc.) - 8. Transportation ... 10. Military technology. Each section begins with a brief introduction indicating coverage. Includes record keeping and cultural attitudes to technology as well as traditional subject matter. Entries include a descriptive, occasionally evaluative annotation, and a number of citations. Index of modern authors (p.485-515); no subject index. *Class No:* 60(37/38)

[3080]

WHITE, K.D. Greek and Roman technology. London, Thames & Hudson, 1984. 272p. illus., maps. £20. (*Aspects of Greek and Roman life.*) ISBN: 050040044x.

Part 1 concerns methods of investigation, transmission of technical processes and technical resources of the Classical world. Part 2 analyses technological developments in building, civil engineering, mining and metallurgy, food and agriculture, land and sea transport, and hydraulic engineering. 177 illus. closely complement the text. Extensive appendices. Author is Professor Emeritus in Ancient History, Univ. of Reading. *Class No:* 60(37/38)

Developing Countries

[3081]

Applied technology index: an indexing service to the literature of appropriate technology and related fields (ATI). Brighton, Noyce, 1980-. (Temporary mailing address, 1986-: J. Noyce, Burwood, Sydney). Quarterly. £60pa.

About 1,200 references pa. Classified order of entries AA. General; AB. Appropriate technology; AT. Transfer of technology; BA. Agriculture, general ... EA. Biofuels ... MA. Health, general ... XF. Water pumps; Z. Miscellaneous. A current-awareness service. 4th issue pa is an author index. *Class No:* 60(4/9-77)

[3082]

DARROW, K. *and* **SACEMIAN, M. Appropriate technology sourcebook.** London, Intermediate Technology Publications, 1993. 800p. illus. £19.95. ISBN: 0917704177.

Covers small water-supply systems, renewable energy equipment agricultural implements, crop preservation, sanitation, housing, health care, forestry, small business management and transportation. About 1,100 entries, each with bibliographic information, price and evaluative abstract; many entries are illustrated. Glossary. A valuable feature is the index to a microfiche library from which many items may be obtained. 'Extremely good value for money' (*Reference reviews,* 1995, 9(3), p.25). *Class No:* 60(4/9-77)

[3083]

GHOSH, P.K. and MORRISON, D.E., *eds.* **Appropriate technology in Third World development.** Westport, Conn., Greenwood Press, 1984. xxiv, 494p. (*International development resource books, 14.*)

Part 1: Current issues, trends, analytical methods, strategies and policies, country studies - Part 2: Statistical information and sources - Part 3: Resources bibliography (annotated) of items published after 1965 - Part 4: Directory of information sources. Aims to investigate trends in 'appropriate technology' that might contribute to Third World economic development, and to provide information and data related to appropriate technology policies. Emphasises policy-making for development rather than advocacy or technical feasibility. *Class No:* 60(4/9-77)

[3084]

HEAWOOD, R. *and* **LARKE, C. The Directory of appropriate technology.** London, Routledge, 1989. xi,[i],317p. ISBN: 0415627016.

Originated in the Work of the Alternate Technology Information Group (1976-).

Sections include: General/multi-disciplinary organizations; Ecology/ environment; Education. Appended lists cite reference material, serial publications, audiovisual aids, etc. Intended for people - young and old - who want to explore options. *Class No:* 60(4/9-77)

[3085]

PACEY, A. Technology in world civilization. a thousand-year history. Cambridge, Mass., MIT Press, 1990. 238p. $19.95. ISBN: 0262161186.

Includes the transfer of technology to less-common areas — China, Islamic India, and the hunters and farmers of South America, Africa and Asia. The thousand-year period runs from 700AD to 1970. Pacey is a leader in the appropriate technology movement. *Class No: 60(4/9-77)*

Europe

[3086]

FREEMAN, C., *and others*. Technology and the future of Europe: global competition and the environment. London, Pinter, 1991. 450p. £45. ISBN: 0861870751.

5 parts: 1. The background of European industry and technology - 2. Information and communication in technology - 3. Other industries and technologies (*e.g.* chemical industry) - 4. Energy, environment and regulation - 5. The international context and policy agenda. References (authors A-Z), p.397-414. Detailed, analytical index. *Class No: 60(4)*

Japan

[3087]

Japan technology Washington, D.C., Scan 2C2, Inc., 1985-.

English-language citations, with abstracts, of articles from major Japanese business and technical jorunals and research reports. Some patents and standards. About 170,000 records, updated monthly. Available online via Data-Star DIALOG and ESA-IRS.

Class No: 60(52)

[3088]

TALBOT, D.E. Japan's high technology: an annotated guide to English-language information sources. Phoenix, Az., Oryx, 1991. 171p. $45; £32. ISBN: 0897745280.

About 500 entries for English-language materials. 13 chapters covering guides, conference reports, abstracting and indexing services, bibliographies, subject dictionaries, directories and handbooks, yearbooks, newsletters and magazines, industry reports, newspapers, online databases, patents and translations. Descriptive annotations, with prices and directory data included in citations. 4 appendices: Booksellers - Libraries - Other sources of information (noncommercial organizations) - Online vendors. 'Highly recommended' (*Choice,* May 1991, p.1468). *Class No: 60(52)*

Islamic World

[3089]

AL-HASSAN, A.Y. *and* HILL, D.R. Islamic technology: an illustrated history. Cambridge Univ. Press, 1986. xiv, 304p. illus., facsims. £25.

11 chapters: 1. Introduction - 2. Mechanical engineering - 3. Civil engineering - 4. Military technology - 5. Ships and navigation - 6. Chemical technology - 7. Textiles, paper and leather - 8. Agriculture and food technology - 9. Mining and metallurgy - 10. Engineers and artisans - 11. Epilogue. Selected bibliography, p.287-95. Index. Fully illustrated (163 half-tones and line-drawings). A readable introduction to a hitherto largely neglected field. *Class No: 60(5.297)*

Writing & Lecturing

[3090]

SIDES, C.H. How to write and present technical information. 3rd ed. Phoenix, Az., Oryx Press, 1998. 224p. $24.95. ISBN: 1573561339.

Previous ed. 1991.

Covers audiences, papers and reports, proposals, memos, production descriptions, writing and designing electronic media including multimedia applications, and editing. A practical treatment. *Class No: 60:001.81*

Thesauri

[3091]

BRITISH STANDARDS INSTITUTION. ROOT thesaurus. 3rd ed. London, BSI, 1988. 2v. ISBN: 058016991x.

1. *Subject display.* xxxi,588p. 2. *Alphabetical list.* iii,632p.

V.1 comprises an introduction (including symbol notation for descriptions), a subject display contents list, and the subject display schedules. V.2 gives the supporting alphabetical list (*c.*1,600 entries and cross-references) plus a chemical formula index. Schedules mainly concern technology and science. 'ROOT's presentation in the form of a subject display with a complementing alphabetical list ensures that experienced and new users alike are able to achieve a new standard of consistency' (*Foreword*, v.1). *Class No: 60:025.43*

[3092]

International technical thesaurus: Noriane/Isonet/databases on standards. English version. Paris, Afnor, 1981. 471p. ISBN: 2121602119.

An 'enriched' edition of the International Organization for Standardization (ISO) thesaurus of 1976. The English version provides 1,500 preferred terms and synonyms. Part 1: a structured A/Z list of terms, with French equivalents; Part 2, a permuted list; part 3, a structured subject list. *Class No: 60:025.43*

[3093]

Thesaurus of scientific, technical, and engineering terms. Science Information Resource Center. Cambridge, Mass., etc., Hemisphere Publishing, 1988. xix, 841, 376p. $125. ISBN: 0891167943.

Based primarily on the NASA *Thesaurus* and the *DOD Thesaurus of scientific and engineering terms.* 2 v. (in one). V. 1. *Hierarchical listing* contains subject terms and USE cross references; V. 2. *Access vocabulary* lists permuted terms, embedded terms, postable and nonpostable terms and other word entries. *Class No: 60:025.43*

Information Services

[3094]

European technical consultancies. Harlow, Essex, Longman, 1988. 342p. £95. ISBN: 0582931877.

A directory of more than 700 technical consultancies throughout Europe. Data: names of senior executives, type of consultancy work undertaken and categories of industry concerned. *Class No: 60:061:025.5*

[3095]

REYNARD, K.W. Data activities: a guide to scientific and technical data collection in the United Kingdom. London, Aslib, 1993. ix, 89p. ISBN: 0851422942.

A directory of over 300 organizations, A-Z; appended list of acronyms. Data on each body: name and address; phone/fax numbers; acronyms; type of organization; subject; printed publications; contact. Subject index, p.83-89. Considered 'a very useful directory' by *Reference reviews* (1994, 8(1), p.24) despite some reservations, especially over virtual duplication of some entries. *Class No: 60:061:025.5*

[3096]

Technical services in the United Kingdom. Harlow, Essex, Longman, 1989. 964p. £295. ISBN: 0582056640.

A directory of nearly 2,000 commercially available services offering technical support and information in the UK. Subject, industrial application and name of establishment indexes. *Class No: 60:061:025.5*

Government Organizations

[3097]

Government research directory: a guide to approximately 3,000 US government research and development centers. Piccirelli, A., *ed.* Detroit, Mich., Gale, 1996. 1038p. £375. ISBN: 0810349418.

First published 1980.

Arranged under sponsoring government agencies. Data on each centre include description of research, special facilities, publications and information services. Indexes: master name, keyword and agency; geographic; subject. *Class No: 60:061:061.1*

Institutions & Associations

[3098]

GRAYSON, L. Science parks: an experiment in high technology transfer. London, British Library, Science Reference and Information Service, 1992. 143p. tables. £50. ISBN: 0712307885.

5 parts: 1. The science park in context - 2. Development and management of science parks - 3. The overseas science park experience - 4. Do science parks work? - 5. Science parks: a view from UKSPA. Personal author index; subject and organization index. *Class No: 60:061:061.2*

Research Establishments

Great Britain

[3099]

Industrial research in the United Kingdom: a guide to organizations and programmes. 16th ed. London, Cartermill, 1995. 592p. £240.

First published 1946 as *Industrial research in Britain.* 15th ed. 1993.

Details of 4,250 laboratories active in agricultural and environmental sciences, chemical and materials sciences, earth and astronomical sciences, electronics and computer sciences, pharmaceutical, biomedical and biological sciences, and engineering and transportation. 6 Sections: 1. Industrial firms - 2. Research associations and consultancies - 3. Government departments, and their laboratories - 4.

....(contd.)

Universities and polytechnics - 5. Trade and development associations - 6. Learned and professional societies. Indexes: personal name; title of establishments; subject; establishments by subject. Data is a subset of *World research database*, available online via ESA-IRS and on CD-ROM. *Class No:* 60:061:061.62(410)

Russia

[3100]

Research and development in Russia. London, SilverPlatter. CD-ROM.

Lists about 4,500 research establishments in the former Soveity Union and describes their activities using some 7,500 specific categories. Includes abstracts of bibliographies and reports published. About 18,000 records, updated semi-annually

Class No: 60:061:061.62(47)

USA

[3101]

Directory of American research and technology: 1998. 32nd ed. New York, Bowker, Annual. 822p. £300. ISSN: 08860076.

Formerly published as *Industrial research laboratories of the United States.*

Lists over 13,000 US and Canadian organizations, of which about 8,000 are parent companies. Geographical, personnel and R&D indexes; subject guide to R&D activities.

Class No: 60:061:061.62(73)

Research Projects

[3102]

Technology assessment. Karlsruhe, Institute for Technology Assessment, 1975-.

Online database covering worldwide projects and publications on the potential economic, environmental and social impacts of the introduction of new or modified technologies. Sources include journals, surveys, books, reports and nonconventional literature. Data include bibliographic information, abstracts, institution names and locations, research staff and project contents. About 8,000 records, updated periodically. *Class No:* 60:061:061.62.005

Technical Drawing

[3103]

FRENCH, T.E., *and others.* **Engineering drawing and graphic technology.** 13th ed. New York, etc, McGraw-Hill, 1986. 752p. illus. ISBN: 0070221638.

4 parts: 1. Basic graphs - 2. Elements of space geometry - 3. Applied graphics and design - 4. Special topics (*e.g.* maps and technology). Appendices. 1,210 illus. *Class No:* 60:744.42

[3104]

GIESECKE, F.E., *and others.* **Technical drawing.** 8th ed. New York, Inc.; London, Collier-Macmillan, 1991. *c.*900p. illus., diagrs., tables. £37.50. ISBN: 0023426505.

Numerous chapters (*e.g.* Instrumental drawing; geometric construction; sectional views; perspective; graphs). Covers computer applications. Analytical index. Intended as a class text and reference book in technical drawing. *Class No:* 60:744.42

Women

[3105]

BINDOCCI, C.G. Women and technology: an annotated bibliography. New York, Garland, 1993. 229p. $39. (*Garland reference library of the social sciences, 517.*) ISBN: 0824057899.

Covers the role of women and technology over the last 20 years. Annotated listing of books, articles, dissertations and conference proceedings in 16 categories. Author and subject index. Often brief but informative annotations. *Class No:* 60-0055.2

[3106]

STANLEY, A. Mothers and daughters of invention: notes for a revised history of technology. Metuchen, NJ, Scarecrow Press, 1993. xlviii, 1116p. $97.50. ISBN: 0810825864.

5 sections: Agriculture and food - Health and medicine - Reproduction - Machines - Computers (*e.g.* 'Augusta, Ada, Lady Lovelace', p.630-34). Full index, p.1043-16. 26 appendices. Major bibliography, p.919-1041. 'A pioneering work' (*Choice,* January 1994, p.810). *Class No:* 60-0055.2

Patents & Inventions

Handbooks & Manuals

[3107]

BAINBRIDGE, D. Intellectual property. 2nd ed. London, Pitman, 1994. xxxi, 510p. ISBN: 0273604228.

First published 1990.

21 sections in 6 parts: 1. Preliminary - 2. Copyright - 3. Law of breach of confidence - 4. Patent law - 5. Design law - 6. Business goodwill and reputation. 4 appendices (2. Trade mark classification for goods and services). Bibliography, p.501-3; detailed, analytical index, p.504-10. *Class No:* 608(035)

[3108]

Butterworths intellectual property law handbook. Phillips, J., *ed.* 2nd ed. London, Butterworth, 1994. ix, 990p. £35.95. ISBN: 0406504717.

First published 1990.

Covers primarily UK legislation on patents, copyrights, registered/unregistered designs, trade marks, plant varieties, intellectual property, professional status and practice. Detailed, analytical index, p.973-90. *Class No:* 608(035)

[3109]

CRAWFORD, N.K. *and* **MORGAN, E.J. The Innovators handbook: 1988/89:** a guide for firms seeking external help with innovation, technology transfer, and successful product development. Harlow, Essex, Longman, 1988. v.p. ISBN: 0582025648.

4 parts, 17 chapters: 1. Developing technology - 2. Financing technological development - 3. Purchasing and selling technology - 4. Protecting technological development. Includes brief case studies. Directory of 425 organizations (contact, phone, service, etc.). Index of organizations. *Class No:* 608(035)

[3110]

FOLTZ, R.D. *and* **PENN, T.A. Protecting scientific ideas and inventions.** 2nd ed. Boca Raton, Fl., CRC Press; Cleveland, Oh., Penn Institute, 1990. vi,377p. ISBN: 0944606067.

First published 1987.

Covers patents, trademarks, product warranties, copyright. Emphasis is on US legislation. An essentially practical treatment, written for the layperson. The first edition was 'recommended' by *Choice* (April 1988, p.1222). *Class No:* 608(035)

[3111]

Intellectual property world desk reference: a guide to practice by country, state and province. Deventer, Kluwer, 1992-. loose leaf. tables.

25 country reports (Argentina ... Italy / Canadian provinces / US states and possessions). 5 appendices (*e.g.* agreements; conventions). *Class No:* 608(035)

[3112]

JACOB, R. *and* **ALEXANDER, D. A Guidebook to intellectual property:** patents, trade marks, copyright and designs. 4th ed. London, Sweet & Maxwell, 1993. xvii, 213p. tables. ISBN: 0421487305.

Tables of cases. 26 chapters in 4 parts (4. Copyright). For lay persons. *Class No:* 608(035)

[3113]

McCARTHY, J.T. McCarthy's desk encyclopedia of intellectual property. Washington, D.C., BNA Books, 1991. 385p. $57. ISBN: 0871796821.

About 600 terms, clearly defined, most with references. 5 appendices (*e.g.* 'Registers of copyright, 1897-1985'). 'A mine of information ... highly recommended' (*Choice,* March 1992, p.1052). *Class No:* 608(035)

[3114]

SHAW, L. The Practical guide to patents, trademarks, copyright, designs. Rev. ed. Birmingham, Bilgrey Sampson Ltd, 1996. x, 224p. Looseleaf. ISBN: 0950855928.

First published 1982; 2nd ed. 1990.

Provides a basic introduction to current UK intellectual property law, with 'how-to' tips. Covers plant varieties and breeders' rights. Supplements are planned. For the lay person. *Class No:* 608(035)

Trade Names, Trade Marks, Brand Names

Databases

[3115]

Trademarks international. Paris, Institut National de la Propriété.

Includes references to registrations, renewals and modifications to the international register of marks filed with the World Intellectual Property Organisation and published in *Les Marques internationales.*

....*(contd.)*

Available online from a number of hosts (*e.g.* DIALOG, Questel SA, etc.) in a variety of national sub-files. Many of these are entitled *Trademarkscan. Class No:* 608(088.7)(003.4)

Internet

[3116]

Brands and their companies. Detroit, Mi., Gale Research. URL: http:// www.gale.com/gale/galenet/btc.html.

Formerly *Trade names database*

About 375,000 consumer brand names and and 80,000 companies. Data include brand name, Standard Industrial Classification Code, Patent Trademark Office code, copany name and contact details. Updated and expanded annually. *Class No:* 608(088.7)(003.41)

Bibliographies

[3117]

KASE, F.J. Trade marks: a guide to official trademark literature. Dobbs Ferry, N.Y., Oceana; Leiden, Sijthoff, 1974. viii, 420p. ISBN: 0379002299; 9028602143.

Entries A-Z by country (65 countries). Each entry gives: name and address of office in charge of trademark registrations; official trademark journal and any other official publications relating to trademarks; duration of protection. Description of contents of journal, with explanation of heading data, etc. Facsimiles of title pages and representative page provided. International trademark treaties in appendix. Bibliography. Index. *Class No:* 608(088.7)(01)

[3118]

NEWTON, D.C. Trade names: an introductory guide and bibliography. London, British Library, 1991. [ii],202p. £30. ISBN: 0712307532.

Substantially based on *Trade marks - a guide to the literature and directory of lists of trade names* by B.M. Rimmer (British Library, 1976).

Part 1 (p.7-59): 8 chapters on legal aspects and international agreements; 6 appendices (6: Periodicals); Index. Part 2: Introduction; Directory of lists of trade marks; Index. Includes some guidance on databases. Sources are based on the Science Reference and Information Service (SRIS) collection of the British Library.

Class No: 608(088.7)(01)

Dictionaries

[3119]

ROOM, A. Dictionary of trade name origins. London, Routledge & Kegan Paul, 1982. 217p. £8.95. ISBN: 0710201745.

Reprinted, with corrections, 1982, 1983.

Famous brand names are listed A-Z, with a description giving the identity of the product, the name of the manufacturer, and the history of the trade name. A new edition was due in 1992.

Class No: 608(088.7)(038)

[3120]

UEXKÜLL, J.D. F. von *and* REICH, H.J. Wörterbuch der patent - und markenpraxis. [Dictionary of patent and trademarks.] 5th ed. Koln, Carl Heymanns Verlag, 1998. xxxi, 354p. £52.95. ISBN: 3452193225.

A German-English, English-German dictionary of patent terms and abbreviations and trademarks. *Class No:* 608(088.7)(038)

Laws

[3121]

BLANCO WHITE, T.A. *and* JACOB, R. Kerly's law of trade marks and trade names. 12th ed. London, Sweet and Maxwell, 1986. lxxv, 873p. £65. ISBN: 0421350601.

An authoritative text on UK law now including commentary on service marks. Appendices give texts of laws, rules and conventions. *Class No:* 608(088.7)(094.1)

[3122]

—**REID, B.C. A Practical introduction to trademarks.** London, Waterlow, 1984. viii, 184p. £14.95.

Includes chapters on procedure in the UK Trade Marks Registry, following a historical introduction. Legal remedies are discussed, and there are two chapters on international aspects. *Class No:* 608(088.7)(094.1)

[3123]

—**TRADE MARK REGISTRY. Work manual.** London, Patent Office, 1984-. Loose-leaf.

Issued in chapters. States the working procedures used by the British Trade Mark Registry in the processing of applications. *Class No:* 608(088.7)(094.1)

[3124]

GYNGELL, J. *and* POULTER, A. A User's guide to trade marks: the new law. London, Butterworth, 1994. xxvi, 399. £37.50. ISBN: 040600577x.

Covers the UK Trade Marks Act 1994. Topics include registrable trade marks; the registration process; oppositions and observations; rights; infringement; dealings; certification and collective marks, etc. An appendix comprises the text of the new Act and a comparison between the 1938 and 1994 Acts. Subject index. *Class No:* 608(088.7)(094.1)

[3125]

MEINHARDT, P. *and* HAVELOCK, K.R. Concise trade mark law and practice. Aldershot, Gower, 1983. xv, 206p. £21. ISBN: 0566023695.

A survey of law and practice in the UK, of EEC rules and of continental practice relevant to British exporters. *Class No:* 608(088.7)(094.1)

Worldwide

[3126]

ARRIGUCCI, M. Trademarks: a comparative guide. Florence, Morgana Edizioni, 1992. 367p.

Provides brief summary of trademark information for 159 countries, A-Z (Afghanistan - Zimbabwe). United Arab Emirates are entry 160. Data include duration, classification, licensing, etc. Information in English, French, German, Spanish, Italian. *Class No:* 608(088.7)(100)

[3127]

JACOBS, A.J. Trade marks throughout the world. 3rd ed. New York, Trade Activities, 1982-. Loose-leaf. ISBN: 0876321260.

Updated three times pa.

Brief details are provided of the trade mark procedures in about 200 countries. Appendices list the international and national classification schemes, international conventions and give at-a-glance tables by country of various features. *Class No:* 608(088.7)(100)

[3128]

Marques internationales. Geneva, World Intellectual Property Organization, 1893-. ea. SF30. ISSN: 00253936.

Contains registrations, renewals etc. of trade marks on the international register maintained by WIPO under the Madrid Agreement. Available online as part of *Trademarks international*. *Class No:* 608(088.7)(100)

[3129]

—**Répertoire alphabétique et phonétique des marques internationales.** Mortsel, Compu-Mark, 1949/69. 1956/76. 1977-.

Indexes registrations and renewals published in *Marques internationales (qv)*. 42 classes, in 5 groups, kept up-to-date by quarterly supplements that supersede the previous supplement and cumulate annually. *Class No:* 608(088.7)(100)

EU

[3130]

A-Z of European brands. London, Euromonitor Pubs., 1991. 400p. £95. ISBN: 0863384004.

Over 5000 brands, considered by country, product sector and owner. Leading brands sold in the European market, both US and European. *Class No:* 608(088.7)(40)

Great Britain

[3131]

The Trade mark journal. London, Patent Office, 1976-. Weekly. ea. £4.50.

Contains official notices, applications for trade marks advertised before registration, marks registered, renewals and other proceedings. Trade mark applications are arranged in classified order. *Class No:* 608(088.7)(410)

[3132]

UK trade names including imported items 1990-1991. 11th ed. East Grinstead, Kompass Publishers, 1990. 343,201p. ISBN: 0862682061.

A list of 60,000 trade names in alphabetical order; a list of 14,000 companies using those names (on pink pages); a list of foreign companies with UK agents. Lapsed trade names and those for food, drink, tobacco and pharmaceuticals are excluded. Imported items are marked with an asterisk. *Class No:* 608(088.7)(410)

[3133]

United Kingdom trade mark handbook. Chartered Institute of Patent Agents *and* Institute of Trade Mark Agents, *eds*. London, Longman, 1991-. 2v.; looseleaf. ISBN: 0851218512.

V.1 has 27 chapters of background and introductory material (*e.g.* 21. 'Court procedures for trade mark cases'). V.2 includes source materials (Statutes; SIs; European and international provisions). *Class No:* 608(088.7)(410)

Canada

[3134]

Canadian trademarks Ottawa, STM Systems Corporation.

Descriptions of Canadian trademarks, including owner, agent, type of trademark, licensing, etc. Produced in cooperation with the Consumer and Corporate Affairs Canada, Register of Trademrks. About 300,000 records, updated weekly. Available online via STM Systems Corporation. *Class No:* 608(088.7)(71)

USA

[3135]

DIAMOND, S.A. Trade mark problems and how to avoid them. 2nd ed. Chicago, Crain Books, 1981. xii, 276p. £19. ISBN: 087251059x.

A practical book on US trade mark practice for the non-technical reader. The text includes choosing, clearing and protecting trade marks, slogans, acronyms, characters, nicknames, use in advertising, and licensing and is liberally illustrated with case studies. *Class No:* 608(088.7)(73)

[3136]

HILL, C.R. Trade marks and brand management: selected annotations. New York, United States Trademark Association, 1976. 188p.

An annotated bibliogoraphy, with sections on journals and periodicals and on books subdivided by subject. An appendix lists other sources of information. *Class No:* 608(088.7)(73)

[3137]

Official gazette of the United States Patent and Trademark Office: Trademarks. Washington, US Patent and Trademark Office, 1872-. Weekly.

Since February 1971 published separately from Patents section. Weekly issues include offical notices; trademarks published for opposition; trademark registrations issued; details of renewals and cancellations; index of registrants.

Annual index of registrants published separately from *Annual index of patents* since 1927. *Class No:* 608(088.7)(73)

[3138]

WOOD, D., ed. Trade names dictionary. Detroit, Mich., Gale, 1974-. 2v. ISSN: 02728818.

7th ed. 1989. 1,952p. $320.

A-Z list of about 206,000 US consumer-oriented trade names, brand names, etc., with names and addresses of 44,000 manufacturers and suppliers. Companion vol. *Trade names dictionary: company index* (7th ed. 1989. $320). *New trade names* is a supplement to both. *Class No:* 608(088.7)(73)

[3139]

—Trade marks register of the United States. Washington, Trademarks Registry, 1961-. Annual. ISSN: 00825786.

Lists active trademarks, arranged in classified order. Information now available online from the US Patent and Trademark Office. *Class No:* 608(088.7)(73)

[3140]

—WOOD, D., ed. Trade names dictionary: company index. 7th ed. Detroit, Mich., Gale, 1989. 2v. $320.

First published 1979.

An A-Z list of US companies, with addresses and their trade names. *Class No:* 608(088.7)(73)

Worldwide

[3141]

International treaties on intellectual property. Leaffer, M.A., *ed.* Washington, DC, Bureau of National Affairs, 1990. 630p. tables. $58. ISBN: 0871796597.

Lists treaties in force. Text of treaties, preceded by summary. 7 parts: 1. Intellectual property - 2. Patents - 3. Trademarks - 4. Copyright and neighbouring rights - 5. Industrial design - 6. Classification - 7. Organizations. Detailed, analytical index, p.623-36. *Class No:* 608(100)

Inventions

Encyclopaedias

[3142]

The Inventions that changed the world. London, Reader's Digest Association, 1982. 368p. illus., diagrs.

Details of significant inventions arranged alphabetically according to subject-matter. There are shorter lists of great inventors, a chronology of inventions and a comprehensive index. *Class No:* 608.1(031)

Handbooks & Manuals

[3143]

BAKER, R. New and improved: inventors and inventions that have changed the modern world. London, British Museum Publications, 1976. 168p. illus., facsims. £4.50.

The introduction gives a short history of the patents system and the main body of the work provides references to patents, with their numbers, of well-known inventions (mostly British) under 363 headings. Historical notes on later developments, and in all 800 to 900 patents are cited. Drawings from patent specifications. Chronological, inventor and subject indexes. Suggestions for further reading, p.27-29. *Class No:* 608.1(035)

[3144]

EISENSCHITZ, T.S. *and* **PHILLIPS, J. The Inventors' information guide.** 2nd ed. London, Queen Mary College, University of London, 1985. 100p. £6.50. ISBN: 0951066404.

Aimed at the individual inventor with few resources, it contains details of information sources, acquiring a patent, developing an invention, professional services, finance, marketing, design, addresses, publications etc. *Class No:* 608.1(035)

[3145]

GISCARD D'ESTAING, V-A., ed. The Book of inventions and discoveries. London, Queen Anne Press, 1990. 291,[i]p. col. illus., facsims., tables. £9.95. ISBN: 0356188353.

Based on *Le livre mondial des inventions*.

Transport - Warfare - Science - Space - Medicine - Information technology - Ecology and the environment - Power and industry - Everyday life - Games, toys, sport - The bizarre - Media and Communications - The arts. Index of inventors and of inventions. Dates are given throughout; boxed information. Excellent for quick reference, teenagers and browsers. *Class No:* 608.1(035)

Yearbooks & Directories

[3146]

Directory of associations of inventors. Geneva, World Intellectual Property Organization, 1994. viii, 94p. (*WIPO publication no. (622 EF)*.)

A loose-leaf publication listing the inventors' organizations in 68 countries. *Class No:* 608.1(058)

Chronologies

[3147]

The Harwin chronology of inventions, innovations, discoveries from pre-history to the present day. London, Constable, 1987. vp. £10.95. ISBN: 0094661502.

A chronological list of technological achievements from flint-knapping of three million years ago to the variable-geometry vertical-axis wind turbine of 1986. Entries generally give the year of invention, its title, inventors and their place of origin and a brief note. Contains an extensive 35p. index to subject matter and a short bibliography. *Class No:* 608.1(090)

Histories

[3148]

PETROSKI, H. The Evolution of useful things. New York, Knopf, 1992. 256p. $25. ISBN: 0679412263.

Brief accounts of the origin and evolution of a range of everyday items, *e.g.* safety pins, paper clips, sand paper 'post-it' notes, etc. Index. 'Penetrating' and 'anecdotal' (*Booklist,* December 1, 1992, p.609). *Class No:* 608.1(091)

[3149]

WILLIAMS, T.I. Science: invention and discovery in the twentieth century. London, Harrap, 1990. 256p. illus. (mostly col.), facsims., ports., diagrs., graphs. £15.95. ISBN: 0245600248.

4 consultant editors. 6 periods: 1900/1914 ... 1973/1989. Appended: Biographies, p.228-49 (*c.*200 major Scientists and technologists); Glossary; Further reading, p.250. Detailed, analytical index. Text includes 12 'special features' (*e.g.* 'The structure of the nucleus', p.120-37). Covers physical sciences, biological and medical sciences and technology. About 350 illus., many in colour. For the lay person. *Class No:* 608.1(091)

Patents

Databases

[3150]

Claims/US Patent abstracts. Alexandria, Va., IFI/Plenum Data Corporation.

The online version of the patents listed in the general, chemical, electrical and mechanical sections of the *Official gazette* of the US patent office, as well as US design patents. Over 2,800,000 records; updated weekly or monthly. Available on DIALOG, files 23 (1950-

....*(contd.)*
1970), 24 (1971-1981), 25 (1982-present), 340 (1950-present), Questel/ORBIT and STN International. Numerous database subsets are available. *Class No:* 608.3(003.4)

[3151]
Derwent world patents index. London, Derwent Publications, Ltd.
Covers 40 patent issuing authorities. Coverage and dates: Pharmaceuticals (from 1963) - Agricultural and veterinary medicine (from 1965) - Plastics and polymers (from 1966) - Chemistry (from 1970) - Electronics, electrical and mechanical engineering (from 1974) - Technology (from 1974). The online version of *World patents abstracts journal.* Over 8,100,000 records; updated weekly. Available on DIALOG, ORBIT, Questel SA and STN International.
Class No: 608.3(003.4)

[3152]
Inpadoc/Family and legal status. Vienna, European Patent Office.
Lists patents in all areas of technology issued in 56 countries. Corresponds to the COM microfiche publication *INPADOC Patent gazette.* Over 26,400,000 records. Updated weekly. Available on DIALOG, file 345, Questel/ORBIT, STN International and from the Eurpean Patent Office. *Class No:* 608.3(003.4)

[3153]
SIBLEY, J.F. Online patents trademarks and service marks databases: 1992. [4th ed.] London, Aslib, 1992. [vi], 70p. £29.95 ISBN: 0851422896.
First published 1983 as *Patents databases.* 2nd ed. 1987. 3rd ed. 1988 as *Online patents and trademarks databases.*
Describes 69 patents and trademark databases, including updating, producer, host, costs, conditions, search aids, language. Directory of hosts, producers and CD-ROM products. Useful but inevitably dated. *Class No:* 608.3(003.4)

[3154]
SIMMONS, E.S. 'Patents'. *Manual of online search strategies.* Editors, C.J. Armstrong and J.A. Large, pp.51-127. 2nd ed. Aldershot, Ashgate, 1992. ISBN: 1857420071.
Useful introduction to the range of patent databases available, their coverage and host systems. Includes information on formulating searchers for effective retrieval. *Class No:* 608.3(003.4)

[3155]
World databases in patents. Armstrong, C.J., *ed.* London, Bowker-Saur, 1995. [xii], 324p. £125. (*World database series.*) ISBN: 1857391063.
The series 'aims to become the de facto authority on electronically published databases' (*Introduction*). Lists about 300 databases. Entries include a brief description of contents and coverage, online hosts, CD-ROM and internet availability, etc. Database 'families' and subsets identified. Indexes: addresses; database name; subject. *Class No:* 608.3(003.4)

Bibliographies

[3156]
Information sources in patents. Auger, C.P., *ed.* New Providence, NJ, Bowker Saur, 1992. c.300p. $70. ISBN: 0862919061.
Covers all forms of patent literature, including online and CD-ROM sources. Includes life sciences and the engineering, chemical and pharmaceutical industries. International in scope. *Class No:* 608.3(01)

[3157]
International guide to official industrial property publications. Van Dulken, S., *ed.* 3rd ed. London, British Library, Science, Technology and Industry, 1992. v.p. facsims. £45. (*Key resource series.*) ISBN: 0712307925.
First published 1985, ed. by B. Rimmer; 2nd ed. 1988, updating supplement 1990.
15 sections: 2-13. Countries (in geographical groupings) - 14. International conventions - 15. Computer-based searches. Detailed, analytical index. An 'indispensable volume' (*Reference reviews,* V.7(1), 1993, p.26). *Class No:* 608.3(01)

[3158]
Introduction to patents information. Van Dulken, S., *ed.* 2nd ed. London, British Library Science Reference and Information Service, 1992. 126p. facsims. £25. (*Information in focus.*) ISBN: 0712307907.
Chapters on value of patents, layout, granting procedure, publications, classification and electronic retrieval. 4 countries (UK, US, Germany, Japan) are covered closely. Glossary, country code listing, 'indispensable' (*Reference reviews,* V.7(1), 1993, p.26) bibliography, detailed, analytical index. *Class No:* 608.3(01)

[3159]
NAGANAGOUDAR, I.R., *and others.* **World literature on patents (1900-1981).** [New Delhi]: Council of Scientific and Industrial Research, 1981. 204p.
Prepared for the National Seminar on Patent Systems held at Hyderabad in 1981.
A bibliography of 1,828 books, conference papers and journal articles covering invention, history and development of the patent system, patenting procedure, patent law, patent information and patent surveys. Entries are arranged according to date of publication in ten-year periods, and indexed by author and subject. *Class No:* 608.3(01)

Handbooks & Manuals

[3160]
CARR, F.K. Patents handbook: a guide for inventors and researchers to searching patent documents and preparing and making an application. Jefferson, N.C., McFarland, 1995. xiv, 221p. £34.20. ISBN: 0786400269.
An introductory work, intended for 'persons involved in research, prior art searching, and inventing' (*Preface*). Emphasis is on US, but European (esp. Swedish) and Japanese patents are also covered. 17 chapters (4. The patent application . . . 11. Patents as information tools); sample US patent; brief index. A practical treatment. *Class No:* 608.3(035)

[3161]
LEVY, R.C. Inventing and patenting sourcebook: how to sell and protect your ideas. Piccirelli, A., *ed.* 2nd ed. New York, Gale, 1992. xxv, 1024p. $105. ISBN: 0810376164.
First published 1990.
Supplies a wealth of directory-type information from a US angle. *Class No:* 608.3(035)

Dictionaries

Polyglot

[3162]
KASE, F.J. Dictionary of industrial property. Legal and related terms. English, Spanish, French and German. Alphen aan den Rijn, Sijthoff and Noordhoff, 1980. xii, 216p. £76. ISBN: 902860619x.
2,416 terms in English, A-Z, with Spanish, French and German indexes. *Class No:* 608.3(038)=00

[3163]
SZENDY, G.L. Wörterbuch des Patentwesens in fünf Sprachen. 2nd ed. Düsseldorft, VDI-Verlag, 1985. xxxvii, 1088p. ISBN: 3184005917.
A multilingual dictionary of German, English, French, Spanish and Russian terms covering patent terminology as well as industrial property in the broader sense. German-base terms, with equivalents and indexes in the other four languages. *Class No:* 608.3(038)=00

[3164]
UEKI, E. Six-languages dictionary of industrial properties. Tokyo, Patent Data Center, 1979. Y58,000.
4,000 industrial property and copyright terms are listed in each of the six sections: Japanese, English, French, German, Russian, Spanish. Against each term are the translations in each of the other five languages. *Class No:* 608.3(038)=00

[3165]
—Industrial property glossary. Geneva, World Intellelectual Property Organization, 1980-81. 4v. (WIPO publications 817-8 824-5).
Gives translations of about 300 terms, in Russian, English and French; Portuguese, French and English; Chinese, English and French; German, English and French, respectively.
Class No: 608.3(038)=00

[3166]
—MIATELLO, A. Trilingual glossary on industrial property. Turin, A. Meynier, 1985. 93p.
Covers 500 terms and phrases. Three parts: French - Italian, English - Italian, and Italian - French - English. Most of the terms are followed by references to provisions of relevant texts in which the terms are used. *Class No:* 608.3(038)=00

German

[3167]
UEXKÜLL, J.D. F. von *and* **REICH, H.J. Wörterbuch der patent - und markenpraxis.** [Dictionary of patent and trademarks.] 5th ed. Koln, Carl Heymanns Verlag, 1998. xxxi, 354p. £52.95. ISBN: 3452193225.
A German-English, English-German dictionary of patent terms and abbreviations and trademarks. *Class No:* 608.3(038)=30

[3168]

WITTMANN, A. *and* **KLOS, J. Dictionary of patent terms:** English/ German, German/English. 5th ed. Munich, Wila Verlag, 1986. 520p. ISBN: 3870191507.

Rev. and enlgd. ed. of the work established by B. Klaftan (1971). Appended to each part is a supplement of special terms used in patent drawings and in text processing. *Class No:* 608.3(038)=30

Japanese

[3169]

RUSSELL, R.W. Patents and trademarks in Japan. 3rd ed. Tokyo, Russell, 1974. [5], 401p.

Over 700 Japanese terms are transliterated and arranged in alphabetical order of English meaning, with a full explanation of their significance in Japanese law. *Class No:* 608.3(038)=956

Reviews & Abstracts

[3170]

Abstracts and abridgements of patent specifications. London, Patent Office, 1883-. Weekly. Annual volume. illus.

Abstracts of British patent specifications published under the Patents Act, 1977, plus abridgements published (decreasingly) under the Patents Act, 1979. About 400 items per issue. Subject and name indexes weekly, cumulated. *Class No:* 608.3(048)

[3171]

Auszüge aus den Europäischen Patentanmeldungen. Munich, Wila Verlag, 1980-. Weekly.

Abstracts in English, French or German of applications for European Patents. Published in thee parts: Chemistry; Electricity and physics; and General, with abstracts arranged according to the International Patent Classification. Earlier abstracts were published by the European Patent Office in a different format.
Class No: 608.3(048)

[3172]

—**European patent bulletin.** Munich, European Patent Office, 1978-. Weekly. ea. DM 20.

Contains bibliographical details of patent applications published and patents granted. Details are given of other stages reached by each European patent application. Annual name indexes to granted patents and to published applications are published separately.
Class No: 608.3(048)

[3173]

Gewerblicher Rechtsschutz und Urheberrecht (GRUR). Internationaler Teil. Weinheim, VCH Verlagsgessellschaft, 1967-. Monthly. ISSN: 04358600.

Abstracts in German but international in scope. Classified coverage of periodical articles, textbooks and case law on various aspects of protection of industrial property and copyright. Sections on decisions in industrial property cases. Includes book reviews. Some items, but not the abstracts, appear in English translation in the quarterly *International Review of Industrial Property and Copyright Law* (IIC) by the same publisher (ISSN 00189855). *Class No:* 608.3(048)

[3174]

World patents abstracts journal. London, Derwent Publications, Ltd., 1975-. Weekly.

Currently divided into four subject-based sections giving abstracts of general and mechanical patents.

Individual country coverage by Derwent abstract journals: *German patents gazette* (1968-), *German patents abstracts* (1953-), *Soviet inventions illustrated* (1961-), *United States patents abstracts* (1971-), *Belgian patents abstracts* (1955-), *British patents abstracts* (1951-), *French patents abstracts* (1961-), *Japanese patents report* (1962-), *Japanese patents gazette* (1975-), *Netherlands patents report* (1964-), *European Patents Report* (1978-), *PCT Patents Report* (1978-). *Chemical Patents Index* (1951-) is a weekly abstracting service dealing with chemical patents and *Electrical Patents Index* (1980-), is the corresponding service covering patents on electrical technology.
Class No: 608.3(048)

[3175]

World patents index gazette. London, Derwent Publications Ltd., 1974-. Weekly.

Four sections: Chemical, General, Mechanical, Electrical. Currently each section has four indexes: Patentee, IPC, Accession number, Patent number. Separate priority concordance index covering all four sections. Cumulations for all indexes on microfiche. Covers about 30 patenting authorities. *Class No:* 608.3(048)

Periodicals

Bibliographies

[3176]

BARTON, H.M. Industrial property literature: a directory of journals. London, British Library, Science Reference Library, 1981. 60p. £5. ISBN: 0902914588.

Gives details of the contents of the official patent, trade mark and design gazettes and the unofficial periodicals from 80 countries as well as series with multinational coverage. *Class No:* 608.3(051)(01)

Worldwide

[3177]

Industrial property. Geneva, World Intellectual Property Organization, 1961-. Monthly. ISSN: 00198625.

Source of information on developments to international treaties, at the international bureau of WIPO and within member countries. Contains calendar of events, book reviews, removable sections on new industrial property laws and annual statistics.
Class No: 608.3(051)(100)

[3178]

PCT [Patent Cooperation Treaty] gazette. Geneva, World Intellectual Property Organization, 1978-. fortnightly. ea. SF18. ISSN: 02507757.

In four sections: 1. Published international applications, giving bibliographic details and an abstract - 2. Notices relating to Applications - 3. Indexes - 4. General information. Annual name and subject-matter indexes. *Class No:* 608.3(051)(100)

[3179]

World patent information. Oxford, Pergamon, Published for the Commission of the European Communities and the World Intellectual Property Organization, 1979-. Quarterly. DM290 pa. ISSN: 01722190.

Covers patent documentation, classification and statistics and contains articles, short communications, details of meetings, and literature reviews. *Class No:* 608.3(051)(100)

Europe

[3180]

Official journal of the European Patent Office. Munich, European Patent Office, 1978-. Monthly. ea. £5.50. ISSN: 01709291.

Contains reports of the EPO Boards of Appeal, general information from the EPO and from the contracting states, lists of professional representatives and a calendar of events. *Class No:* 608.3(051)(4)

Great Britain

[3181]

Official journal (patents). London, Patent Office, 1854-. Weekly. ea. £4.30.

Contents: official notes; details of applications for patents; applications published; granted patents (including European patents designating the UK); details of designs registered and renewed; progress of patents and legal proceedings; receipts of foreign patents in the Science Reference and Information Service. Appended list of additions to the Science Reference Library (Holborn). Annual cumulated name index, annual cumulated subject-matter indexes in each volume of abstracts of patent applications.
Class No: 608.3(051)(410)

USA

[3182]

Official gazette of the United States Patent and Trademark Office: Patents. Washington, US Patent and Trademark Office, 1872-. Weekly.

Includes offical notices, abstracts of rexamination, reissue, utility, plant and design patents; abstracts of statutory invention registrations.

Annual index published separately. Part I: cumulated lists of applicants for patents, reexaminations, etc. Part II: index to subjects of invention - separate classified listings of patents, design patents, etc., and summary of publication statistics.

Available online as *Claims/US Patent abstracts,* DIALOG, files 23, 24, 25, 340. *Class No:* 608.3(051)(73)

Tables & Data Books

[3183]

100 years of industrial property statistics. Geneva, World Intellectual Property Organization, 1983. 245p. (*WIPO publication no. 876.*) ISBN: 9280501046.

A compilation of statistics from the periodical *Industrial property* (*qv*) and other WIPO publications. Contains synoptic tables on patents, trademarks, designs, utility models and plant varieties.
Class No: 608.3(083)

[3184]

BOSWORTH, D.L. **Intellectual property rights.** Oxford, Pergamon Press, 1986. xiii, 288p. (£33. Reviews of United Kingdom statistical sources. V.19. Review 32.). ISBN: 0080339026.

A review of publicly available sources of statistical information on patents, designs, plant protection and royalties. Contains factual information about statistical series in the form of a Quick Reference List, extensive appendices and a subject index. *Class No:* 608.3(083)

Europe

CD-ROM

[3185]

ESPACE-EP. Munich, European Patent Office, 1982-.

Complete collection of full European patent applications. 13 searchable fields, including IPC codes, applicant names, title words in English, German, French. Availalbe in two subsets: EP A Documents for patent applications (About 90 CD-ROMs pa.; £2,000); EP B Documents for granted patents (about 50 CD-ROMs pa.; £1,920). *Class No:* 608.3(4)(003.40)

USA

CD-ROM

[3186]

Patent View: US patent information on CD-ROM. Woodbridge, CT., Reading, Berks., Research Publications International. £5000 pa.

Full-image US Utility Patents on CD-ROM. Searchable on 23 bibliographic fields. About 104 CD-ROMs pa. *Class No:* 608.3(73)(003.40)

Information Management

[3187]

Global patent services. London, Derwent Information Ltd., 1995. v.p. £25.

3 parts: 1. Introduction (to patents, their treatment and documentation) - 2. Source documents (36 countries, Australia to United States) - 3. 'Putting it together' (explanation of Derwent services). Useful as an introduction and summary of patent information. *Class No:* 608.3:025.4

Information Services

[3188]

EISENSCHITZ, T.S. **Patents, trade marks and designs in information work.** London, Croom Helm, 1987. 236p. £40. ISBN: 0709909586.

Introductory section on the concepts behind industrial property followed by sections on patents, industrial copyright and designs, trade marks and EEC competition law. The book is intended as a source book for information workers, with details of the documentation particularly of the UK and US. *Class No:* 608.3:061:025.5

[3189]

EUROPEAN COMMUNITIES COMMISSION. **Patent information and documentation in Western Europe.** 3rd ed. Munich, K.G. Saur, 1988. 219p.

Lists patent literature in 18 Western European countries, with additional sections on Japan, Soviet Union, USA, the World Intellectual Property Organization and the Patent Cooperation Treaty, - plus international standards for patent literature, abstracting services, and databases. *Class No:* 608.3:061:025.5

[3190]

Patent information and documentation handbook. Geneva, World Intellectual Property Organization, 1981-.

An English/French, multivolume, loose-leaf work updated periodically with replacement sheets. Sections are devoted to standards for patent documentation, the international patent classification, Patent Cooperation Treaty, kinds of patent publications, microforms, and access to patent documentation. *Class No:* 608.3:061:025.5

[3191]

World directory of sources of patent information. Geneva, World Intellectual Property Organization, 1985. Loose-leaf. (*WIPO publication no. 209 (E).*) ISBN: 9280501097.

Lists detailed holdings of Patent Office libraries and other major patent libraries. Listing is by information centre with indexes to classified collections, numerical collections, official gazettes and abstracts by office of publication. *Class No:* 608.3:061:025.5

Institutions & Associations

[3192]

Directory of national and regional industrial property offices. Geneva, World Intellectual Property Organization, 1986. (*WIPO publication no. 601.*) ISBN: 9280500988.

A loose-leaf publication updated at least once a year containing the addresses, telephone numbers etc., of patent offices. *Class No:* 608.3:061:061.2

Patent Law

Worldwide

[3193]

FYSH, M. *and* THOMAS, R.W. **Industrial property citator.** London, European Law Centre, 1982. xiv, 321p. £65. ISBN: 0907451047.

Updated by a supplement published in 1985.

Comprises a list of cases in alphabetical order of the name of the plaintiff with subject indexes for UK and Ireland and for overseas cases. Coverage is reported court cases on patents, trade marks, designs, plant varieties, copyright and neighbouring rights. *Class No:* 608.3:347.77(100)

[3194]

JACOBS, A.J., *ed.* **Patents throughout the world.** 4th ed. New York, Trade Activities, 1989-. loose-leaf. ISBN: 0876321252.

Updated three times a year.

Brief details are provided of the patent procedures of over 150 countries. Separate tables enable features such as taxes to be compared at a glance for all countries and there is an extensive section on international conventions. *Class No:* 608.3:347.77(100)

[3195]

Manual for the handling of applications for patents, designs and trade marks throughout the world. 2nd ed. Amsterdam, Manual Industrial Property B.V., 1936-. loose-leaf, in 4 v. ISBN: 9071888010.

Updated by supplements about once a year.

For each of over 180 countries details are given of the patent, design and trade mark laws and procedures. There are also sections on international conventions and agreements. This title is commonly referred to as the 'Dutch Manual'. *Class No:* 608.3:347.77(100)

[3196]

MELVILLE, L.W. **Forms and agreements on intellectual property and international licensing.** 3rd ed. London, Sweet and Maxwell; New York, Clark Boardman, 1984. 2v. £160. ISBN: 0421053002.

Loose-leaf, updated anually.

Details of the UK, US and European Community Law on intellectual property: patents, know-how, trade secrets, copyright, and plant variety rights. Model clauses or 'precedents' for use in licensing agreements, tables of statutes, regulations, and agreements are given. *Class No:* 608.3:347.77(100)

[3197]

REVERDIN, A. *and* SCHLAEPFER, F., *eds.* **Katzarov's manual on industrial property.** 9th ed. Geneva, Katzarov S.A., 1981. Loose-leaf, in two binders.

Kept up-to-date with annual or more frequent supplements.

After extensive sections on international agreements there are separate sections for each country giving basic national information and details of patent, trade mark and other industrial property law and procedures. For each country there are lists of publications and industrial property offices, societies and agents. *Class No:* 608.3:347.77(100)

Europe

[3198]

CHARTERED INSTITUTE OF PATENT AGENTS. **European patents handbook.** 2nd ed. London, Longman Professional, 1988-. Loose-leaf.

First published 1978.

100 sections; updated with 'Releases'. For patent practitioners contains introductory material, commentary, source material, decisions, legal advice and a noter-up as part of the updating service. It is concerned with the European Patent Convention and the Community Patent Convention. *Class No:* 608.3:347.77(4)

[3199]

—**Guidelines for examination in the European Patent Office.** Munich, European Patent Office, 1979-. Loose-leaf, updated periodically by replacement pages. £20.

Written for the staff of the EPO, but useful as a guide on practice and procedures for patent practitioners. *Class No:* 608.3:347.77(4)

[3200]
HEARN, P. The Business of industrial licensing: a practical guide to patents, trade marks and industrial design. 2nd ed. Aldershot, Gower, 1986. xii, 252p. £25. ISBN: 0566025876.

Written for business executives, the book describes licensing law and practice in the UK and European Community. The final section sets out sample heads of agreement and is referenced to corresponding portions of text. *Class No:* 608.3:347.77(4)

[3201]
—**CAWTHRA, B.** Patent licensing in Europe. 2nd ed. London, Butterworths, 1986. xxi, 249p. £40. ISBN: 0406148414.

Traces developments in the patent licensing laws in the European Community, citing significant decisions of the European Court. A commentary on clauses in licensing agreements is given, and recent developments in Community patent licensing law are discussed. *Class No:* 608.3:347.77(4)

[3202]
PATERSON, G. The European patent system. London, Sweet & Maxwell, 1992. 600p. £70. ISBN: 0421430508.

Commentary on case law developed by the Board of Appeal following introduction of the European Patent Convention. *Class No:* 608.3:347.77(4)

[3203]
WALTON, A.M., *and others*. Patent law of Europe and the United Kingdom. London, Butterworths, 1981-82. £120. ISBN: 040641503x. Loose-leaf, updated to 1982 by substitute pages. 2v.

A commentary on the UK 1949 and 1977 Patents Acts, the European Patent Convention, Community Patent Convention and Patent Cooperation Treaty. Various statutes are reproduced and other sections contain information on forms, practice and precedents. *Class No:* 608.3:347.77(4)

Great Britain

[3204]
BLANCO WHITE, T.A. Patents for invention. 5th ed. London, Stevens, 1983. xxxv, 304p. £41. ISBN: 0420463100.

A text for practitioners on the earlier UK patent law. *Class No:* 608.3:347.77(410)

[3205]
CHARTERED INSTITUTE OF PATENT AGENTS. CIPA Guide to the Patents Acts: text, commentary and notes on practice. 4th ed. London, Sweet and Maxwell, 1995. cxix, 1465p. £125. ISBN: 0421493402.

Updated by supplements.

Reproduces the UK Act of 1977, Patent Rules 1995, and sections 274-295 of the Copyright, Designs and Patents Act 1988, with commentary. Appendices provide text and commentary on the 1949 Patents Act and relevant rules and other statutes, including those of the European Community. *Class No:* 608.3:347.77(410)

[3206]
CORNISH, W.R. Intellectual property: patents, copyright, trade marks and allied rights. London, Sweet and Maxwell, 1989. xlvi,528p. £30. ISBN: 0421379707, ; 0421379804, Pbk.

A detailed text on British law in the context of the EEC written for the relative novice to intellectual property. Two chapters are given on the common ground including enforcement of rights and the remaining fifteen chapters are divided into sections on patents, confidence, copyright and trade marks. There are appendices on control of monopolies & restrictive practices, 'old' patents, joint interests in mark and protection of plant varieties. *Class No:* 608.3:347.77(410)

[3207]
—Intellectual property rights and innovation. London, H.M. Stationery Office, 1986. iv, 78p. £6.70. (*Cmnd. 9712.*)

The UK Government's White Paper containing proposals for reform of patents, designs and copyright, following the Green Papers *Intellectual property rights and innovation* (Cmnd. 9117), *Copyright and design law* (Cmnd. 6732), *Reform of the law relating to copyright, designs and performer's protection* (Cmnd. 8302), and *The recording and rental of audio and video copyright material* (Cmnd. 9445). *Class No:* 608.3:347.77(410)

[3208]
GRALLAFENT, R.J., *and others*. Intellectual property law and taxation. 3rd ed. London, Longman, 1989. xxvi, 338p. ISBN: 0851213227.

2nd ed. 1984.

In three parts: intellectual property law by type; the taxation of intellectual property rights; and practical examples in the form of four case studies. Appendices list model agreements, statutes, and relevant tax publications. *Class No:* 608.3:347.77(410)

[3209]
MERKIN, R. Richards Butler on copyright, designs and patents: the new law. London, Longman, 1989. xl,693p. £55. ISBN: 0851215653.

A commentary on the current British patent law followed by the full text of the 1988 Act. Detailed, analytical index, p.677-93. *Class No:* 608.3:347.77(410)

[3210]
REID, B.C. A Practical guide to patent law. 2nd ed. London, Sweet and Maxwell, 1994. xxi, 359p. £29.95. ISBN: 042145220x.

Written for the student, lawyer or business reader this book provides a guide to UK patent practice with reference to international conventions. Lists of statutes, appendices and a glossary are given. *Class No:* 608.3:347.77(410)

[3211]
YOUNG, D., *and others*. Terrell on the law of patents. 14th ed. London, Sweet and Maxwell, 1994. lxxi, 1040p. £95. ISBN: 0421408901.

First published 1884; 13th ed. 1982.

After a short history and discussion of the nature of patentable inventions, the 1977 and the surviving parts of the 1949 UK Patents Acts are analysed in detail. The effect of the European Patent Convention (EPC) is considered and appendices give the texts of the EPC, Patent Cooperation Treaty, rules of the Supreme Court, articles from the Treaty of Rome, as well as the 1977 and 1949 UK Patents Acts. Covers the law as at the end of May 1994. *Class No:* 608.3:347.77(410)

Korea

[3212]
DRAZIL, J.V. Guide to Japanese and Korean patents and utility models. London, British Library, Science Reference Library, 1976. 135p. £5. ISBN: 0902914219.

A historical survey of the protection of industrial property in the two countries with extensive details of the gazettes and specifications published. *Class No:* 608.3:347.77(519)

Japan

[3213]
Japanese laws relating to industrial property. Revised and reprinted 1975. Tokyo, Japanese Group of AIPPI, 1966-. 2 vol. loose-leaf.

Translated by the Japanese Patent Office.

English language translations of the Japanese law and regulations on patents, utility models, designs and trade marks. *Class No:* 608.3:347.77(52)

USA

[3214]
LIPSCOMB, E.B. Walker on patents. 3rd ed. Rochester, N.Y. Lawyers Cooperative Publishing; San Francisco, Bancroft-Whitney, 1984-. 11 vol.

The third edition of 'Walker' is being issued in volumes as they are prepared. Aimed at the US bench and bar, it provides a detailed commentary on US patent law and procedure. *Class No:* 608.3:347.77(73)

[3215]
ROSENBERG, P.D. Patent law fundamentals. 2nd ed. New York, Clark Boardman, 1986-. Loose-leaf. $155. ISBN: 0876320981.

Two vols. updated by supplements.

The work is an extensive text on US patents, trade secrets, trade marks and copyright with a final part devoted to international patent conventions and comparative foreign patent law. Appendices give samples of forms and documentation, related laws and rules. *Class No:* 608.3:347.77(73)

Industrial Designs & Models

[3216]
FRENCH, M.J. Invention and evolution: design in nature and engineering. 2nd ed. Cambridge, Univ. Press, 1994. xx, 367p. illus., diagrs. £50. ISBN: 0521465036.

Covers numerous examples of design for function. 11 chapters, closely subdivided (*e.g.* 2. Energy - 3. Materials ... 5. Structures (beams; feathers, etc.) ... 8. Economy, form and beauty ... 10. Designing and inventing - 11. Some case studies). Detailed, analytical index. *Class No:* 608.4

[3217]

FYSH, M. Russell-Clark on copyright in industrial design. 5th ed. London, Sweet and Maxwell, 1974. xxiii, 314p. £40. ISBN: 0421176008.

Though this book does not include recent court decisions on the subject, it remains a definitive commentary on British law for the practitioner. This edition also contains a chapter on EEC legislation as well as tables of cases and statutes. *Class No:* 608.4

[3218]

GREENE, A.M., *ed*. Designs and utility models throughout the world. Updated by A.J. Jacobs. New York, Trade Activities, 1983-. Loose-leaf. ISBN: 0876323786.

Updated periodically.

Brief details are provided of the design and petty patent or utility model procedures of over 200 countries. Appendices provide details of international conventions, national and international classification schemes and at-a-glance comparative tables of available protection, type of examination, renewal terms, etc. *Class No:* 608.4

[3219]

KASE, F.J. Designs: a guide to official literature on design protection. Dobbs Ferry, N.Y., Oceana; Leyden, Sijthoff, 1975. 411p. ISBN: 0379003686; 9028603956.

Introduction to official literature on the protection of industrial designs and utility models. Entries are arranged by country (89). Each gives name and address of industrial property office and then information on: kinds of protection and definitions; Official journal and other publications; other official publications relating to designs; duration of protection. Includes facsimile reproductions of official journals. Appendix; international classification for industrial designs. Bibliography. Index. *Class No:* 608.4

[3220]

—MYRANTS, G. Protection of industrial designs. London, McGraw-Hill, 1977. xx, 211p. illus. £6.95. ISBN: 007084495x.

A practical reference tool on the procedures involved and advice in selling protection of industrial designs in the UK and abroad. Artistic copyright and design copyright are covered in one chapter. Index. *Class No:* 608.4

61 Medicine

Abbreviations & Symbols

[3221]
DUPAYRAT, J. Dictionary of biomedical acronyms and abbreviations. 2nd ed. Chichester, John Wiley and Sons, 1990. 162p. £19.50. ISBN: 0471926493.

First published 1984.

About 7,000 definitions for the 4,000 most common biomedical acronyms. Increase in the number of basic acronyms is 30% up on the previous edition. Intended primarily for researchers, physicians and translators. *Class No:* 610(003)

[3222]
HABER, K. Common abbreviations in clinical medicine. New York, Raven Press, 1988. xii,227p. $17.50. ISBN: 0881673390.

Compilation of abbreviations found in patients' records and on medical charts. 2 parts: 1. Abbreviations, their meanings, and specialties most likely to use these abbreviations - 2. Abbreviations according to the usage of various medical subspecialties (Anesthesiology ... Urology). *Class No:* 610(003)

[3223]
HEISTAR, R. Dictionary of abbreviations in medical sciences: with a list of the most important medical and scientific journals and their traditional abbreviations. London, Springer-Verlag, 1989. viii,287p. $39. ISBN: 0387504877.

Contains *c.*15,000 abbreviations, including some in Latin, French, German, Italian and Spanish. 13-page appendix lists 460 journal title abbreviations. *Class No:* 610(003)

[3224]
JABLONSKI, S. Dictionary of medical acronyms and abbreviations. 2nd ed. Philadelphia, Pa., Hanley & Belfus; St. Louis, etc., C.V. Mosby, Co., 1993. 330p. ISBN: 1560530529.

First published 1987.

Has *c.*20,000 entries, 2,000 added since last ed. Handy small format. *Class No:* 610(003)

[3225]
LOGAN, C.M. *and* **RICE, M.K. Logan's medical and scientific abbreviations.** Philadelphia, Pa., J.B. Lippincott Co., 1987. xix, 673p. $29.95. ISBN: 0397545894.

Compiled from over 60 sources. 6 sections: 1. Abbreviations - 2. Symbols - 3. Chemotherapy regimes - 4. Latin terms: charting and prescriptions - 5. Cancer staging abbreviations - 6. Elements. Extensive coverage, *e.g.* the single letter A has 53 terms. Useful bibliography, p.671-3. *Class No:* 610(003)

[3226]
MASA: medical acronyms, symbols and abbreviations. Hamilton, B. *and* Guidos, B., *eds.* 2nd ed. New York, Neal-Schuman, 1988. 277p. $55. ISBN: 1555700128.

First published 1984.

Over 32,000 entries, 12,000 added since the previous edition. Terms found in older literature and medical records are included in addition to current abbreviations. Numerous cross-references. *Class No:* 610(003)

[3227]
MELLONI, B.J. *and* **MELLONI, J.L. Melloni's illustrated dictionary of medical abbreviations.** New York, Parthenon, 1998. 485p. illus. £18.50; $26.95. ISBN: 1850707081.

15,000 abbreviations from A (a-band) to Zz (Ginger), but with no explanatory information beyond a brief entry. *c.*150 illustrations. Aimed at doctors, nurses, and paramedics. US-slanted. *Class No:* 610(003)

[3228]
SLOANE, S.B. Medical abbreviations and eponyms. 2nd ed. Philadelphia, W.B. Saunders Company, 1997. x,905p. £26.50. ISBN: 0721670881.

First published 1985.

Two main sections: Medical abbreviations, p.1-683; Medical eponyms, p.684-885. Five appendices (*e.g.* Symbols; Positions of fetus). This edition contains over 10,000 new abbreviations, over 1,000 new eponyms and a new appendix listing over 400 anti-cancer drug combinations. *Class No:* 610(003)

[3229]
Stedman's abbreviations, acronyms & symbols. Baltimore, Md., Williams & Wilkins, 1992. ix,664p. $24. ISBN: 0683079263.

About 20,000 entries arranged clearly in 2 columns per page. Derived from the literature studied to enhance the coverage in *Stedman's medical dictionary (q.v.).* 2 sections: 1. A-Z abbreviations & acronyms, p.1-655 - 2. Symbols (*e.g.* 'Arrows'; 'Numbers'; 'Primes, checks, dots and miscellany'). A useful quick-reference tool. *Class No:* 610(003)

[3230]
STEEN, E.B. Baillière's abbreviations in medicine. 5th ed. London, Baillière Tindall, 1984. 256p. $10. ISBN: 0702010367.

First published 1960.

Lists more than 7,500 common medical and related abbreviations ('CD': 16 different meanings), p.1-248. Appended abbreviations of titles of the principal medical journals. 'Some useful sources', p.254-5; Symbols. Still covers most needs. *Class No:* 610(003)

[3231]
Units, symbols, and abbreviations: a guide for biological and medical editors and authors. Baron, D.N., *ed.* 4th ed. London, Royal Society of Medicine Services, 1988. 64p. £5. ISBN: 0905958780.

First published 1971.

Sections: 1. Metrication and SI units - 2. Symbols and nomenclature (p.21-51; 23 references) - 3. Layout of references - 4. Proof correction. 'Many journals quote this booklet as a guide in their Instructions to Authors', *(Introduction). Class No:* 610(003)

Databases

[3232]
EMBASE. Amsterdam, Excerpta Medica/EMBASE Publishing Group, 1974-.

International in coverage and contains nearly 7 million citations, many with abstracts, from more than 4,000 journals from more than 70 countries. All medical subject areas included. Updated weekly, with *c.*415,000 records added each year. Corresponds mainly to the *Excerpta medica* series but *c.*25 percent of the citations added to the database each year do not appear in the corresponding hard copy journals. Available on CD-ROM, diskette, magnetic tape.

A *List of journals abstracted* is published annually. *Class No:* 610(003.4)

[3233]
LYON, E. Online medical databases 1991. 5th ed. London, Aslib, 1991. 96p. (*Aslib online guide.*) ISBN: 0851422748.

First published 1983.

A list of 135 bibliography or full-text databases, all commercially available online. Data include content; producer; text; costs. The addresses of hosts, producers and suppliers are listed. Bibliography and index. Now in need of updating and revision. *Class No:* 610(003.4)

[3234]
MEDLINE [Medical Analysis and Retrieval Service On-Line]. Washington, National Library of Medicine, 1971-.

Database, with full coverage of *Index medicus* by 1974, with monthly update of *c.*25,000 entries. Covers *c.*3,500 journals published in 70 countries. Search aids: MESH [Medical Subject Headings], an annual thesaurus of headings used in *Index medicus,* and Permuted Mesh headings. The UK contribution to MEDLINE is provided by the British Library, Boston Spa. Available on CD-ROM and also free on the Internet, with limited searching, at various sites, *e.g.* http://www.healthgate.com/medline/search-medline.shtml. *Class No:* 610(003.4)

[3235]
OMNI (Organising Medical Networked Information) URL: http://www.omni.ac.uk

Internet site, based at the University of Nottingham, providing access to good quality medical sites on the Internet. Subject areas covered include education, medical history, and medical information. *Class No:* 610(003.4)

[3236]

Online databases in the medical and life sciences. New York, Cuadra/ Elsevier, 1987. xxi, 170p. $29.95. ISBN: 0444012729.

Descriptions of 795 online databases, p.1-128. Data on each: type; subject; producer; online service; content; language; coverage; countries; time span; updating. Addresses of online services and gateways, p.129-36. Subject index; online service/gateway index; master index. *Class No:* 610(003.4)

[3237]

World databases in medicine. Armstrong, C.J., *ed.* London, Bowker-Saur, 1993. 2v. (1646p.) £170; $165. ISBN: 0862916135.

A detailed, evaluative guide to databases currently available in medicine and the biosciences. The 19 topics covered include dentistry, ethics, genetics, toxicology, veterinary medicine, and nursing. Within each section, the databases are arranged alphabetically and further subdivided by types of media, *e.g.* CD-ROM; diskette; tape; etc. Data for each database include database type, number of journals covered, start year, number of records, keywords, and description. Index allows access by hosts, media, producers, and database types. A useful tool for librarians and researchers. *Class No:* 610(003.4)

Bibliographies of Bibliographies

[3238]

BESTERMAN, T. **Medicine: a bibliography of bibliographies.** Totowa, N.J., Rowman and Littlefield, 1971. 409p. (*The Besterman World bibliographies.*)

Entries are extracted from Besterman's *A world bibliography of bibliographies* (4th ed. 1965-66. 4v.). Arrangement is under subjects A-Z (*e.g., Anatomy*) and also specific topics. Extensive language coverage. *Class No:* 610(009)

Bibliographies

[3239]

BELMONTE, F.R. **Women and health:** an annotated bibliography. Lanham, Md., Scarecrow Press, 1997. 203p. £33.25; ISBN: 0810833859.

Covers academic and popular works from 1970s to mid-1990s. Six sections: Descriptions of women ... Care by women ... Costs and benefits - Addictions. Author, title, and subject indexes. For public and academic libraries. *Class No:* 610(01)

[3240]

BIBEL, B. 'Medical reference sources': In *Reference books bulletin*, 1 February 1997, p.956-60. Chicago, American Library Association.

Sections include general sources, electronic resources, encyclopedias and handbooks, cancer, nutrition, etc. Brief annotations are given. *Class No:* 610(01)

[3241]

BRANDON, A.N. *and* HILL, D.R. 'Selected list of books and journals for the small medical library'. In *Bulletin of the Medical Library Association*, v.79(2), April 1991, p.195-222.

A revision of the list in *Bulletin of the Medical Library Association,* v.77(2), April 1989, p.139-69.

Book list contains 607 unannotated entries, AIDS ... Urology. 'Dictionaries, directories and encyclopedias', nos. 109-119. Author/ editor index. Intended as a selection guide for the small or medium-sized library in a hospital or other medical facility or as a core collection for a group of small hospital libraries. US slanted, but regularly updated. *Class No:* 610(01)

[3242]

COLE LIBRARY OF EARLY MEDICINE AND ZOOLOGY. **Catalogue of books and pamphlets. [Cole Library of Early Medicine and Zoology].** Eales, N.B. [Oxford], Aldine Press, for the Library, Univ. of Reading, 1969-75. 2pts. ISBN: 070490148x, Pt. 2.

1. *1477 to 1800.* xiv, 425p. 2. *Catalogue of books, monographs and principal papers, 1800 to the present day,* (£7) and *Supplement to part 1.* xvii, 428p.

Part 1 records *c.*2,000 items, arranged chronologically. *Class No:* 610(01)

[3243]

Consumer health information source book. Rees, A.M., *ed.* 5th ed. London, Oryx Press, 1998. 226p. $59.50. ISBN: 1573560472.

First published 1981.

Annotated entries covering information available from professional literature, 136 Internet sites, 600 books, hotlines, newsletters, electronic databases, etc. Nine sections: 1. Medical consumers in the age of managed care - 2. The best sources of consumer ehalth information ... 4. Consumer health magazines and newsletters ... 6. Consumer health on the Internet - 7. Supportive professional literature - 8. Consumer health books - 9. Pamphlets. Author, title, and subject indexes. For public and medical libraries. *Class No:* 610(01)

[3244]

Coping with the biomedical literature: a primer for the scientist and the clinician. Warren, K.S., *ed.* New York, Praeger, 1981. xi, 233p. facsims., graphs, tables. $45. ISBN: 0275913554.

12 contributors. 4 parts (12 chapters, mostly documented): 1. The structure of the information system (*e.g.* 'Selective aspects of the biomedical literature') - 2. Producing biomedical information (*e.g.* 'Reviewing reviews') - 3. Utilizing biomedical information - 4. Sources of biomedical information ('The National Library of Medicine'; 'The Institute for Scientific Information'; 'Libraries and how to use them'). Partly analytical index. Addressed, authoritatively, to a specialized readership. Thus, chapter 9, 'Evaluation: requirements for clinical application', 'has been summarized for those clinicians who are behind in their clinical reading'. *Class No:* 610(01)

[3245]

Core collection of medical books and journals. Hague, H. *and* Jackson, M., *comps.* Manchester, Medical Information Working Party, Haigh and Hochland, 1992. 64p. £2.50. ISBN: 1869888065.

List of over 800 books, arranged under 47 subject headings, and over 200 journals. Unannotated entries but useful for inexperienced medical librarians and aimed at postgraduate medical libraries.

2nd ed. published 1994 as *Core collection of medical books 1994/95* (69p.). *Class No:* 610(01)

[3246]

Current bibliographies in medicine. Washington, D.C., US Government Printing Office, 1991-. $3ea; $52 (20-issue series).

Replaces *Literature search.*

Compiled by the National Library of Medicine. Each issue varies in length from 14 to 50 pages and contains lists of books, periodicals and audio-visual materials on topics of current popular interest. Recent titles include: 'Medical waste disposal'; 'Laboratory animal welfare'; 'Nutrition and AIDS'. *Class No:* 610(01)

[3247]

Encyclopedia of health information sources: a bibliographic guide to over 13,000 citations for publications, organizations and databases on health-related subjects. Rees, A.M., *ed.* 2nd ed. Detroit, Mich., Gale, 1993. xxi,521p. ISBN: 0810369095.

First published 1986.

Offers health information (literature and organizations) on over 450 medical subjects, with ample cross-references. *Class No:* 610(01)

[3248]

FRANCIS A. Countway Library of Medicine (Harvard Medical Library). **Author-title catalog ... for imprints through 1959.** [Francis A. Countway Library of Medicine]. Boston, Mass., G.K. Hall, 1973. 10v. (8104p.). $1,755. ISBN: 0816110247.

Author-title catalogue of *c.*263,000 photolithographed cards - the merged catalogue of Harvard and Boston medical libraries. The collection is rich in medical Hebraica and Judaica, manuscripts, histories of medicine, and clinical medicine. *Class No:* 610(01)

[3249]

GANN, R. **The Health information handbook:** resources for self-care. Aldershot, Hants, Gower, 1986. xii, 251p. £35. ISBN: 0566035499.

5 chapters, each with references: 1. Responsibility for health - 2. The informed patient - 3. Health information in the UK (p.114-26) - 4. Health information in other countries (p.169-179) - 5. Getting started: collecting and organising health information (books, booklets/leaflets, periodicals. Subject range: 'The aged' ... 'Women's health', p.204-25. Thesaurus of subject headings, p.229-42). Detailed, non-analytical index. A practical guide for librarians and other providers of basic medical information. Some UK slant. *Class No:* 610(01)

[3250]

Health science books, 1876-1982. New York, Bowker, 1982. 4v. (4601p.). $225. ISBN: 0835214478.

Subject index. 3v. (A-Z). *Author index. Title index.*

A comprehensive bibliography of over 132,000 books published in the United States and catalogued by Library of Congress during the last 107 years. 'Subjects covered include all major health disciplines as well as biomedical and related sciences' (*Preface*). V.4 (p.3989-4601) includes 'Guide to MeSH/LC equivalents in health science books' and 'Guide to LC/MeSH equivalents'. *Class No:* 610(01)

[3251]

'Health sciences supplement'. In *Choice*, May 1999. Middletown, Conn., Association of College and Research Libraries. 32p.

Reviews of *c.*140 recently published books, divided into 12 subject categories, *e.g.* history of medicine, nutrition and fitness. Items are graded 1-5 stars. *Class No:* 610(01)

[3252]
Information sources in the medical sciences. Morton, L.T. *and* Godbolt, S., *eds*. 4th ed. London, Bowker-Saur, 1992. xvi,608p. £50. (*Guides to information sources*.) ISBN: 0862915961.

First published 1974 as *Use of medical literature*.

27 contributors. 24 chapters: 1. Medical libraries and their use - 2. Primary sources of information ... 5. Online and CD-ROM sources - 6. Audio-visual materials ... 9. Public health ... 12. Pathology, clinical and experimental ... 16. Diagnostic radiology ... 21. Dentistry ... 24. Historical, biographical and bibliographical sources. Index to subjects and some titles but not to authors. *Class No:* 610(01)

[3253]
Introduction to reference sources in the health sciences. Roper, F.W. *and* Boorkman, J.A., *eds*. 3rd ed. Metuchen, N.J., Medical Library Association and the Scarecrow Press, 1995. 301p. £35; $35. ISBN: 0810828898.

First published 1980.

Three sections: Reference collection; Bibliographic sources; Information sources. Chapters on such areas as indexing and abstracting sources; audiovisual material; conferences, reviews and translations. Computerized databases, and history sources, are backed by further readings. Mainly US emphasis. A well-organized tool, aimed primarily at library school students, librarians, and library users in the medical field. *Class No:* 610(01)

[3254]
—CHEN, C.-C. **Health sciences information sources.** Cambridge, Mass., and London, MIT Press, 1981. xxxviii, [1], 767p. $80; £71.95. ISBN: 0262030748.

Arranges *c*.3,500 annotated entries by type of material (1. Selection tools - 2. Guides to the literature - 3. Bibliographies - 4. Encyclopedias - 5. Dictionaries ... 22. Nonprint materials - 23. Professional societies and their publications - 24. Databases (chart), p.1-632). 'Reference literature' (periodical article references). Title and author indexes; author index to 'Reference literature'. Each class is divided by subject fields, A-Z. Absence of a subject index detracts considerably from the usefulness of this tool, - intended for library schools, with priority for the structure of the literature rather than its contents. *Class No:* 610(01)

[3255]
—Finding the source of medical information: a thesaurus index to the reference collections. Shearer, B.S. *and* Bush, G.L., *comps*. Westport, Conn., Greenwood Press, 1985. 275p. $42.95; £36.95. ISBN: 0313240949.

Lists 447 reference books and textbooks, by titles, as medical sources. Alternate title and author indexes follow. The main part of the work is the thesaurus subject index, p.43-275, A-Z, with cross-references from specific to more inclusive subjects. Useful as a quick-reference source-key. *Class No:* 610(01)

[3256]
—STRICKLAND-HODGE, B. *and* ALLAN, B. **Medical information: a profile.** London, Mansell, 1986. ix, 145p.

Also intended mainly for library-school students. Six chapters stress printed reference sources, on-line searching, the role of organizations and people as contacts, and the search strategy, with six case-studies, plus an index. 'The book would have been improved by involving someone experienced in the practice of answering medical enquiries in a clinical setting' (*British book news*, July 1986, p.410-11). *Class No:* 610(01)

[3257]
Keyguide to information sources in paramedical sciences. Hewlett, J., *ed*. London, New York, Mansell, 1990. xii,270p. £45. ISBN: 0720120578.

3 sections: 1. Overview of paramedical sciences and their literature (1. Information and the paramedical professions ... 9. Radiography, diagnostic and therapeutic) - 2. Bibliographical listing of sources of information, p.105-206 (1,012 items) - 3. List of selected organizations (1. International associations and societies ... 8. Audio-visual and non-book material producers). Index of subjects, titles and authors, p.239-70. Written by, and for, practitioners in the UK. 'It is, however, an exemplary model for anyone who perceives the need for producing a similar book directed toward an American readership' (*Choice*, v.28(9), May 1991, p.1460). *Class No:* 610(01)

[3258]
KURIAN, G. T. **Global guide to medical information.** New York, Elsevier, 1988. 808p. $101.75. ISBN: 0444013008.

International in scope, listing over 13,000 publications and organizations. Largest section lists periodicals. Medical publishers listed according to country. Names and addresses for national, regional, and international associations are given for each medical subject area. Not comprehensive but a good starting point for those looking for international information. *Class No:* 610(01)

[3259]
LEE, R. **How to find information: medicine and biology.** 2nd ed. London, British Library, 1996. iv, 20p. ISBN: 0712308377.

First published 1992 as 'How to find information: a guide to searching in published sources'(this sub-title appears on 1996 cover only).

Handy little guide, encouraging independent searching. The new ed. 'covers the same subject area as the earlier book, but has been largely rewritten to account for recent innovations in information-searching techniques' (*Introduction*). *Class No:* 610(01)

[3260]
LONDON SCHOOL OF HYGIENE AND TROPICAL MEDICINE. University of London. **Dictionary catalogue. [London School of Hygiene and Tropical Medicine].** Boston, Mass., G.K. Hall, 1965. 6v. Serials catalogue, 286p. First supplement. 1971. 441p.

A photo-offset reproduction of the 90,000 cards, - author and subject entries for *c*.40,000 monographs, pamphlets and non-serial reports in the library, with additional sequences for periodical titles and serial reports.

The *Serials catalogue* comprises 6,000 cards. The *First supplement*, *c*.20,300 cards. *Class No:* 610(01)

[3261]
Medical and health care books and serials in print: an index to literature in the health sciences. New Providence (N.J.), etc, Bowker, 1985-. Annual. 2v. ISBN: 0835239926.

Originally as *Bowker's medical books in print* (1972-77); editions 1-6, then as *Medical books and serials in print* (1978-84).

1. *Subjects. Authors*. 2. *Titles. Serials. Publishers*.

The 1998 annual lists '91,753 entries in 133,478 appearances under 7,906 headings'. Subject (Library of Congress headings), author and title indexes. Also available online through DIALOG Information Services. Available on *SciTech reference plus* CD-ROM. *Class No:* 610(01)

[3262]
Medical reference works, 1679-1966: a selected bibliography. Blake, J.B. *and* Roos, C., *eds*. Chicago, Ill., Medical Library Association, 1967. viii, 343p. Supplements 1-3, 1970-75. $4.35, supp. 2; $3, supp. 3. ISBN: 081082440x, supp.2; 0810824418, supp.3.

2,703 numbered entries, concisely annotated, in the main volume. Nos.1-413: Medicine, general (indexes and abstracts; reviews; bibliographies; translations; theses; congresses; dictionaries; periodicals; directories; encyclopedias. - Nos.414-832: History of medicine - Nos.833-2073: Special subjects, A-Z (Aerospace and submarine medicine ... Zoology)). Excludes bibliographies of individuals, etc. Basic reference works for the smaller medical library are asterisked. A primary selection tool in its day.

Supplements 1-3 carry 1,059 items. Further supplements are due from National Library of Medicine computer bases. *Class No:* 610(01)

[3263]
MORTON, L.T. *and* WRIGHT, D.J. **How to use a medical library.** 7th ed. London, Library Association Publishing, 1990. v,88p. £14.95. ISBN: 0851574661.

First published 1934.

10 sections: 1. Introduction - 2. Finding your way around the library - 3. Periodicals - 4. Indexes and abstracts - 5. Searching the literature - 6. Basic reference works - 7. Aids for writers and speakers - 8. Historical and biographical sources - 9. Audio-visual aids - 10. Biomedical library facilities in Britain. References, p.78-82. Analytical index, p.83-88. Written as a guide for medical practitioners, research workers and those who are training for a career in medical librarianship. *Class No:* 610(01)

[3264]
NEW YORK ACADEMY OF MEDICINE. Library. **Author catalog. [New York Academy of Medicine Library].** Boston, Mass., G.K. Hall, 1969. 43v. (38339p.). 1st supplement. 1974. 4v. (3474p.). $4,290 + $545. ISBN: 0816108293; 081610851x.

The catalogue and its supplement comprise 877,900 photolithographically reproduced cards. At the end of 1967 the Library included 365,000 bound volumes and 165,000 pamphlets. *Class No:* 610(01)

[3265]
—NEW YORK ACADEMY OF MEDICINE. Library. **Subject catalog. [New York Academy of Medicine Library].** Boston, Mass., G.K. Hall, 1969. 34v. 1st Supplement. 1974. 4v. $3,550, set; $545, supp. 1. ISBN: 0816101841, supp. 1; 0816108269, set. *Class No:* 610(01)

[3266]
UNITED STATES. National Library of Medicine. **A Catalog of sixteenth century printed books in the National Library of Medicine.** Dorling, R.J., *comp.* Bethesda, Md., US Dept. of Health, Education and Welfare, Public Health Service, National Library of Medicine, 1967. xii, 698p.

4,808 numbered items, p.1-618. Lengthy titles, concise bibliographical notes. Bibliographical references, p.vii-xii. Indexes of printers and publishers (geographical index; name index). Concordance of *Short-title catalogue* items and serial numbers in this catalogue. Index of vernacular imprints. *Class No:* 610(01)

[3267]
UNITED STATES. National Library of Medicine. **National Library of Medicine current catalog.** Bethesda, Md., US Dept. of Health, Education and Welfare, 1966-. 4pa. (previously 24pa., then 12pa), with annual and 5-yearly cumulation.

Preceded by the *Armed Forces Medical Library catalog ..., 1950-1954* (1955. 6v.) and *National Library of Medicine catalog, 1955-1959* (1960. 6v.) and 1960-1965 (1960. 6v.).

Annual cumulation 1989 (2v. 3211p. $58) has 4 sections: Monographs: name and title section - Serials - Serials, subject section - Medical reference works. *Class No:* 610(01)

[3268]
UNITED STATES. War Department. Surgeon-General's Office. **Index-catalog of the Library of the Surgeon General's Office, United States Army.** Washington, Government Printing Office, 1880-1955. 58v.

Series 1, 1880-95. 16v.; series 2, 1896-1916. 21v.; series 3, 1918-1932, 10v.; series 4, v.1-11 (A-MN), 1936-55.

A dictionary catalogue of 485,334 entries, listing contents of one of the world's largest medical libraries, covering book and periodical articles. Includes many biographical entries. Invaluable as a bibliographical tool in this field.

Concluded in US Dept. of Health, Education and Welfare, Public Health Service's *Index-catalog of the Library of the Surgeon General's Office, National Library of Medicine.* 5th series (Washington, G.P.O., 1959-61. 3v.). 'Entries are for items which are monographic in nature and they are for 1950 or earlier imprints' (*Preface*). V.1 covers Authors; v.2-3, Subjects. *Class No:* 610(01)

[3269]
WALTERS, B. 'Medical reference tools for the layperson'. In *Reference books bulletin*, 1988/89, p.1-5.

38 annotated entries. Includes dictionaries; directories; drug handbooks; manuals and handbooks; statistics; medical education; physician and medical facility evaluations; indexes. 'This list selectively identifies key reference materials on diseases, drugs, physicians, health facilities and other personal health concerns' (*Introduction*). *Class No:* 610(01)

[3270]
WELCH, J. *and* **KING, T.A. Searching the medical literature:** a guide to printed and online sources. With a chapter on drug information services, by D.E. Hands. London & New York, Chapman & Hall, 1985. x, 154p. facsims., diagrs., tables, map. ISBN: 041225610x.

8 chapters: 1. Introduction: the new information environment - 2/3. Searching the periodical literature (print resources; online (*e.g.* MEDLARS)) - 4. Drug information services - 5. Sources of statistical information - 6. The reference collection - 7. Background reading (primary and secondary sources; bibliographies and review articles; book reviews; library networks) - 8. Source of advice for medical communications. Each chapter carries further reading or references. Detailed index, p.147-54. A well organized guide. *Class No:* 610(01)

[3271]
WELLCOME HISTORICAL MEDICAL LIBRARY. A Catalogue of printed books in the Wellcome Historical Medical Library. London, the Library, 1962-.

1. *Books printed before 1641.* 1962. xv, 407p. 2. *Books printed from 1641 to 1850.* A-E. 1966. 3. *Books printed from 1641 to 1850.* F-L. 1976. 565p.

Author catalogues. V.1, compiled by F.N.L. Poynter, records 7,000 items in 'perhaps the greatest collection of medico-historical works in the world' (*British book news*, no.270, February 1963, p.91-92). Brief references to items listed in *Catalogue of incunabula* (1951). (*qv*). Indexes follow, to places of publication, and to printer and publishers; concordance with STC numbers for English books.

V.2 lists *c.*18,000 items, some with biographical notes. If an item is not listed in Wing's STC, this is stated. Cross-references. Well-produced. *Class No:* 610(01)

[3272]
WORLD HEALTH ORGANIZATION. Publications catalogue, 1948-1989. [World Health Organization]. Geneva, WHO, 1990. *Gratis.*

5 sections: 1. Publications grouped by subject - 2. Nonserial publications - 3. Series - 4. Periodicals - 5. Official publications - 6. Regional publications - 7. Publications of the International Agency for Research on Cancer - 8. Publications of the Council for International Organizations of Medical Sciences.

WHO have also published *Publications catalogue: new books, 1986-90* and *Publications catalogue: new books, 1991. Class No:* 610(01)

Russia

[3273]
PERKINS, L. A Bibliography of Soviet sources of medicine and public health in the USSR: a publication of Geographic Health Studies by the John E. Fogarty International Center for Advanced Study in the Health Service. [Bethesda, Md.], US Dept. of Health, Education and Welfare, Public Health Service, National Institutes of Health, 1975. xiv, 235p.

About 10,000 entries. Sections 1-23 (1. Allergy ... 22. Urology and kidney disease - 23. Miscellaneous). Sections 24-31 (24. Biomedical research ... 31. Medicine and society). Entries are in tiny print. *Class No:* 610(01)(47)

Encyclopaedias

[3274]
Black's medical dictionary. 38th ed. London, A. & C. Black, 1995. 581p. ISBN: 0713640197.

First published 1906.

For the general public, with notes on causes, symptoms and treatment, and written in simple English. The 38th ed. has 30 contributors, and contains *c*5,000 terms (inc. cross-references) in A-Z sequence, p.1-564. Appendices: basic first aid, addresses, travel and health, medical tests, vitamins, measurements. A new ed. is due in 1999. *Class No:* 610(031)

[3275]
Blakiston's Gould medical dictionary: a modern comprehensive dictionary of the terms used in all branches of medicine and allied sciences. 4th ed. New York, etc., McGraw-Hill, 1979. xxi, 1632p. illus. (pl.), tables. $36. ISBN: 0070057001.

First published 1949 as *Blakiston's New Gould medical dictionary.*

A defining dictionary, with over 80,000 entries, giving syllabification and etymolgy. 34 contributors. 26 keyed anatomical plates (between letters N and O). Appendix tables (p.1499-1632) include 'Chemical constituents of blood', 'Thermoelectric equivalents', 'Weights and measures'.

Also, *Blakiston's Gould pocket medical dictionary* (4th ed. 1979. 992p. $28.50). *Class No:* 610(031)

[3276]
Butterworth's medical dictionary. 2nd ed. Editor-in-chief, M. Critchley. London, Butterworths, 1978. xxxii, 1942p. £29.50. ISBN: 040700193x.

First published as *The British medical dictionary,* edited by Sir A.S. McNally (1961; rev. ed., 1965).

About 58,000 entries, revised by a team of 50 consultants. 'Paralysis': 5½ columns; 'Spasm': 2 columns. Very brief biographical data under eponyms. Pronunciation of entry-words; chemical structures. Appendix: 'Anatomical nomenclature', tabulated. Regarded as a landmark in British medical lexicography. '99.9% of the time this lexicon does exactly what one would expect of it' (*The Lancet,* no.8063, 11 March 1978, p.536). *Class No:* 610(031)

[3277]
Dictionnaire français de médecine et de biologie. Manuila, A., *and others.* Paris, Masson; New York, French and European, 1970-73. 4v. $175, v.1; $175, v.2; $195, v.3; $195, v.4. ISBN: 0686570324, v.1; 0686570332, v.2; 0686570340, v.3; 082885856x, v.4.

About 150,000 entries, including lengthy entries as well as definitions. Bibliographical references are provided for descriptions of illnesses and relatively rare syndromes. V.4 is intended as a guide to users of the *Dictionnaire.* Definitions are excellent and clear. A basic work for French and for French special libraries. It also provided the *International dictionary of medicine and biology* (*q.v.*) with a valuable starting point to build an 'exhaustive list of English terms' (*Acknowledgements,* v.1). *Class No:* 610(031)

[3278]
—**Reallexikon der Medizin und ihrer Grenzgebiete.** Munich, Urban & Schwartzenberg, 1966-77. 6v.

The German equivalent of the *Dictionnaire. Class No:* 610(031)

[3279]

Dorland's illustrated medical dictionary. 28th ed. Philadelphia, Pa., W.B. Saunders, 1994. xxxiv, 1940p. illus., tables. ISBN: 0721628591.

1st-23rd eds. as *The American illustrated medical dictionary*.

39 consultants. Over 80,000 entries, including abbreviations. 'Cell' (with subentries for types of cell in bold): 15 columns and 2 plates. Claims to establish 'certain standards of etymological propriety' by including 'Fundamentals of medical etymology', p.xii-xxxiv. Occasional small line-drawings in addition to the more detailed 55 plates (not full colour). Generally considered to be reliable. *Class No:* 610(031)

[3280]

—Dorland's medical dictionary: shorter edition. Philadelphia, Pa., W.B. Saunders, 1980. 768p. illus. (col.). ISBN: 0721631428.

Has *c*.45,000 entries on medicine and health care, and is addressed to the general public. Includes anatomical illus. in colour and various tables. For the small library unable to afford the full dictionary. *Class No:* 610(031)

[3281]

—Dorland's pocket dictionary. 24th ed. Philadelphia, Pa., W.B. Saunders, 1989. 688p. illus (col. pl.), charts, tables. $21. ISBN: 072162202x.

First published 1898.

Also gives pronunciation. Preliminary note on 'Combining forms in medical etymology', p.xiii-xxi. *Class No:* 610(031)

[3282]

Gale encyclopedia of medicine. New York, Gale, 1998. 5v. illus.,figs.,tables. $499. ISBN: 0787618683.

Covers more than 1,500 topics. The signed entries are arranged A-Z, varying in length from one to three pages, with a bibliography appended to each. Details are given of 905 disorders and diseases, 235 tests and procedures, and 325 treatments and therapies. Also lists contact data for organizations and URLs for Internet sites. The style of the encyclopaedia is non-technical and this makes the articles easy to understand. For large public libraries. *Class No:* 610(031)

[3283]

Melloni's illustrated medical dictionary. Dox, I., *and others*. 3rd ed. Pearl River, N.Y., Parthenon, 1993. lii,535p. illus.(col.). £24.95. ISBN: 1850704791.

First published 1979 (2nd ed. 1985).

Defines *c*.26,000 terms in non-technical language. Includes lengthy contributions, sometimes 20 pages in length. A distinguishing feature - the supporting 2,500 illus., usually occupying the top half of each page. Useful as a reference for students of the health services. Well produced. *Class No:* 610(031)

[3284]

—RIGAL, W.A. The Inverted medical dictionary: a method of finding medical terms quickly. Westport, Conn., Technomic Pub. Co., Inc., 1976. v, 261p.

Groups all aspects of a part of the body, etc, for rapid identification (*e.g.* 'face' - enlargement, fissure, pains, spasms. etc.), followed by the correct medical term, plus a brief definition. 'To be used as a supplement' (*Choice*, v.4(9), November 1977, p.1194).

Also, Stanaszek, M.J., *The Inverted medical dictionary* (Lancaster, Pa., Technomic, 1991. $75). *Class No:* 610(031)

[3285]

MILLER, B.F. *and* **KEANE, C.B. Encyclopedia and dictionary of medicine, nursing and allied health.** 6th ed. Philadelphia, Penn., W.B. Saunders, 1997. xxxii, 1960p. illus. (incl. col.), diagrs., tables. £20.95. ISBN: 0721662781.

First published 1972, as *Encyclopedia and dictionary of medicine* (1089p.). 5th ed., 1992.

47 contributors. Over 30,000 entries ('Vocabulary', with anatomical tables and col. plates), p.1-1765. Preceded by 'Combining forms in medical terminology'. Table of muscles. Many cross-references. 45 appendices (2. MetLife height and weight tables; 13. The cranial nerves). Thumb-indexed. 'Medical speller' supplied on disk enclosed in wallet. Title-page headed 'Miller-Keane'. *Class No:* 610(031)

[3286]

Mosby's medical, nursing, and allied health dictionary. 5th ed. St. Louis, Mo., C.V. Mosby Company, 1998. xxvi,2042p. illus. (col.), diagrs., graphs, tables. ISBN: 0815148003.

First published 1983.

119 consulting contributors. Over 30,000 entries, 5,000 new to this edition. Length of entries varies from a few words to several columns, *e.g.* 'Burn therapy': method; intervention; outcome criteria; 2 columns. 44-page colour atlas of human anatomy. 23 appendices, p.1753-2042 (*e.g.* 1. Units of measurement ...7. Assessment guides ...11. Nutrition ... 22 Omaha classification system ... 23. UK appendix with British spellings). Pronunciation and stress of terms is given. Cross-references. 2,000 colour illustrations. Well produced; thumb ed. *Class No:* 610(031)

[3287]

The Oxford medical companion. Walton, J., *and others, eds*. Oxford, University Press, 1995. 1038p. illus. $50. ISBN: 0192623559.

Previous edition published in two volumes as *The Oxford companion to medicine* (1986).

192 contributors. More than 8,000 entries arranged A-Z, with each article having a list of references for further reading. Length of entries range from one-sentence definitions to longer essay-type articles (there are 182 of these). Includes data on medical tests; associations; diseases; drugs; biographies, etc. Two appendices list major medical qualifications and medical abbreviations. Many cross-references, charts, photographs, and tables. Gives quick information on the development and state of modern medicine and is useful for both reference and browsing. *Class No:* 610(031)

[3288]

—The Faber medical dictionary. Wakeley, Sir C., *ed.* 2nd ed. by J.G. Bate. London, Faber & Faber, 1975. [iv], 483p.

First published 1925, with *Supplement*, 1965.

Carries *c*.30,000 concise entries, including eponyms. Etymology and pronunciation are given. Supplements Dorland in providing anglicized spelling of medical terms. *Class No:* 610(031)

[3289]

SLOANE, S.B. The Medical word book: a spelling and vocabulary guide to medical transcription. 3rd ed. Philadelphia, Pa., W.B. Saunders, 1991. xi,1097p. illus., tables. $27.95. ISBN: 0721632432.

First published 1973.

Has 3 parts: 1. General terms; 2. Systems and specialities (15 heads); 3. Guides to terminology (*e.g.* abbreviations). Small format. *Class No:* 610(031)

[3290]

Stedman's medical dictionary. 26th ed. Baltimore, Md., Williams & Wilkins, 1995. xli,2030p. illus. (col.). ISBN: 0683079220.

First published 1911 as *A Practical medical dictionary*.

Compiled and reviewed by 40 consultants. About 110,000 entries, with 12,000 and 1,000 new colour illustrations, photographs, and tables added since the previous ed. New specialties are biotechnology, nursing, statistics/epidemiology, neurosurgery, and neuropathology. Syllabification and stress are shown. Short entries for well-known medical persons, plus cross-reference to eponym. Lengthy prelims. include 'Wordfinder', listing multiple-term entries. 125 high profile terms have expanded definitions. The most common Greek and Latin word parts are indicated. The 13 appendices include 'Blood groups' and 'CDC universal precautions'. Like *Blakiston's Gould*, a defining medical dictionary omitting notes on treatment. Vocabulary is more technical than in *Dorland* or *Blakiston's Gould*. Thumb ed. In 1996, *Stedman's electronic medical dictionary: version 3.0*, was published ($79.95).

A spin off from this work is *The American Heritage Stedman's medical dictionary*, edited by M.S. Berube (Houghton, 1995. 923p. $24.95). Aimed at a more general audience, it contains *c*.45,000 entries and 100 drawings and diagrams. *Class No:* 610(031)

[3291]

—STEDMAN, T.L. Illustrated Stedman's medical dictionary. 5th unabridged Lawyer's ed. Cincinnati, Ohio, Anderson, 1982. vp. illus.

Includes a 67-p. "Lawyers' section". *Class No:* 610(031)

[3292]

Taber's cyclopedic medical dictionary. Thomas, C.L., *and others, eds*. 18th ed. Philadelphia, Pa., F.A. Davis Co., 1997. 2,439p. illus. (incl. col.), tables. + 2 3.5in diskettes. $32.95. ISBN: 080360193x.

First published 1940, 17th ed. 1993.

c.70,000 definitions, varying in length, with etymology and pronunciation shown. Over 200 illustrations and 75 tables. 21 appendices (*e.g.* 7. Symbols; 19. Nursing organizations). Written primarily for the North American market and strong on nursing concepts. A useful reference which is best used in conjunction with other medical dictionaries. *Class No:* 610(031)

[3293]

WINGATE, P. *and* **WINGATE, R. The Penguin medical encyclopedia.** 3rd ed. London, Penguin, 1988. viii,519p. diagrs £5.95. ISBN: 0140512209.

First published 1972.

Entries range from a few words to several pages (*e.g.* 'Immunity': 7 pages, covering general principles, natural and adaptive immunity, immunopathology, hypersensitivity, antoimmunity, immunity and therapeutic). Short biographical non-technical language. Many cross-references. Aimed at patients and those caring for them. *Class No:* 610(031)

Handbooks & Manuals

[3294]
The American Medical Association encyclopedia of medicine. Clayman, C.B., *ed.* New York, Random House, 1989. 1184p. illus., figs. $44.45. ISBN: 0394565282.

A-Z guide to over 5,000 terms, including symptoms, treatments and drugs. Contains more than 2,200 drawings and pictures showing medical techniques, anatomy and disease processes. Entries vary from one paragraph to over a page in length. Informative. 'Reasonably priced and highly recommended for all libraries' (*Choice,* v.27, no.2, 1989 p.278). *Class No:* 610(035)

[3295]
BEVAN, J. Your family doctor: the home medical encyclopaedia. London, Mitchell Beazley, 1980. 2v. (viii, 1030p.). illus. (incl. col.), diagrs., graphs, charts. ISBN: 0855332956.

1. *Reference volume: guide to current medical practice.* 502p. 2. *Practical volume.* p.503-1030p.

V.1 operates on the question-and-answer principle, with numerous cross-references. V.2 covers first aid; treating minor injuries and disorders; What could be wrong?; Family safety; What you should have on hand; Care of the sick at home; Professional care for the sick; Pregnancy and childbirth; The healthy child; the growing child; Age-by-age chart (p.808-933); Taking care of your own body; Physical fitness and exercises; Mental fitness. Detailed analytical index, p.1010-30.

US ed. as *Home medical encyclopedia* (Chicago, Ill., World Book-Childcraft International, 1980. 4v. (1029p.)). *Class No:* 610(035)

[3296]
—**Medical update, 1982-: the 'World Book' family medical annual.** Chicago, Ill., World Book, [1981]. illus., (incl. col.). ISSN: 07320183.

Supplements Bevan. The 1983 annual ([4], 268p.) has 33 contributors. Apart from 13 signed articles, it carries a 'Medical file' section, reporting current research on aging, alcoholism, birth control, weight control, etc. For schools, public libraries and home use. *Class No:* 610(035)

[3297]
Cambridge textbook of accident and emergency medicine. Skinner, D., *and others, eds.* Cambridge, University Press, 1997. xii,1271p. illus.,tables. £155; $250. ISBN: 0521433797.

110 contributors, three parts: 1. General principles (1. The accident and emergency department ... 16. Deaths) - 2. Trauma (17. Concepts of trauma management ... 43. Envenomation) - 3. Medical, surgical and obstetrics emergencies (44. Adult respiratory emergencies ... 63. The febrile patient). References at the end of each chapter. Index. Definitive textbook giving theory behind the practice. *Class No:* 610(035)

[3298]
Oxford textbook of medicine. Weatherall, D.J., *ed.* 3rd ed. Oxford, University Press, 1996. 3v. 4376 + 510p. illus. (incl. col.), diagrs., tables. £175. ISBN: 0192621408.

First published 1983.

1: Sections 1-10. 2: Sections 11-17. 3: Sections 18-33. Each volume contains overall index, 170p.

About 450 contributors. 33 documented sections (7: Infections. p.263-1034). New sections on medical ethics, clinical trials, evidence-based medicine, and forensic medicine. 'As in previous editions, we have attempted to provide a global view of internal medicine rather than describe it as it is seen in day-to-day practice in the richer industrial countries' (*Preface*). The leading British postgraduate textbook.

Also available as *Oxford textbook of medicine on CD-ROM,* (OUP, 1987-. £305). *Class No:* 610(035)

[3299]
ROYAL SOCIETY OF MEDICINE. Family medical guide. Harlow, Essex, Longman, 1980 (reprinted 1988). 720p. £16.95.

30 chapters, concentrating on parts of the body (*e.g.* 18: Ear, nose and throat, p.418-41, with outstandingly good drawings, carefully keyed. Encyclopedia of medical terms, p.616-86; glossary, p.687-9.). Analytical index, p.690-719. A well-balanced, well-produced quarto. *Class No:* 610(035)

[3300]
WORLD HEALTH ORGANIZATION. International classification of procedures in medicine. Geneva, WHO, 1978. 2v. *Class No:* 610(035)

Dictionaries

Polyglot

[3301]
Eight-language dictionary of medical technology, comprising approximately 8000 technical terms, English, German, French, Russian, Spanish, Polish, Hungarian, Slovak. Albert, R. *and* Hahnewald, H., *eds.* Oxford, etc., Pergamon Press; Berlin VEB

....(contd.)
Verlag Technik, 1978. [vii], 594p. ISBN: 0080237630.

English-base terms, with equivalents (across the double page) and indexes in the other 7 languages. Strictly medical terminology. 'In addition to the quoted sources, catalogues, company brochures and other publications of the medical, technical industry, articles in medical and medical-technical journals have formed the basis of this dictionary' (*Preface*). *Class No:* 610(038)=00

[3302]
—**Lexicon medicum: Anglicum, Russicum, Gallicum, Germanicum, Polonicum.** Zlotnickiego, B., *pod red.* Warsaw, Panstwowy Zaklad Wydawnictw Lekatskich, 1971. xii, 1603p.

About 15,000 English-based entry-words, with Russian, French, German, Latin and Polish equivalents and indexes. Horizontal arrangement of entries. *Class No:* 610(038)=00

[3303]
Elsevier's encyclopaedic dictionary of medicine. Dorian, A.F., *ed.* Amsterdam, etc., Elsevier, 1987-90. ISBN: 0444872930, Pt.C; 0444428267, Pt.D; 0444428232, Pt.A; 0444428240, Pt.B.

A. *General medicine.* 1987. ix, 1175p. £171.87 B. *Anatomy.* 1987. ix, 601p. £121.56 C. *Biology, genetics and biochemistry.* 1989. xii,708p. £123.43 D. *Therapeutic substances.* 1990. x,492p. £93.75.

In 5 languages: English, French, German, Italian and Spanish. About 17,000 terms in v.A-B. Concise English definitions, with equivalents in the other 4 languages. 'Based on the English equivalents of the Nomina Anatomica as set forth by the sixth International Congress of Anatomists in Paris in 1955' (*Preface*). *Class No:* 610(038)=00

[3304]
Europäisches medizinisches Wörterbuch: Deutsch, English, Spanisch, Französisch, Italienisch. Stuttgart, Schattauer, 1991, [vi],1022p. illus.

Nearly 10,000 German-based entries (including abbreviations), with English, Spanish, French, and Italian equivalents and indexes. *Class No:* 610(038)=00

[3305]
NOBEL, A. Dictionary of medical objects. / Medizinisches Sachwörterbuch/Dictionnaire d'objets médicaux. 7th ed. Berlin, Springer-Verlag, 1983. x, 1344p. DM348. ISBN: 0387121382.

A trilingual dictionary of medical terms, with a Latin supplement. 19,114 English-base terms, with German and French equivalents (or explanations) and indexes. Usage of English creaks somewhat and entry-words must be sought with caution. (Why, for example, entry 'Factors, diabetic' and none for 'Diabetic factors'?). *Class No:* 610(038)=00

[3306]
Questionarium medicum. Meyboom, F., *comp.* Amsterdam, Elsevier, 1961. viii, 213p. (*Glossaria interpretum.*)

About 400 terms in 17 languages, - English, French, Italian, Spanish, Portuguese, German, Dutch, Norwegian, Swedish, Finnish, Polish, Russian, Greek, Chinese, Japanese, Malay and Esperanto. Reverse language keys. Intended primarily for physicians who have to deal with foreign patients. Now out of print. *Class No:* 610(038)=00

[3307]
Radcliffe European medical dictionary. Oxford, Radcliffe Medical Press, 1991. 1022p. £49.95. ISBN: 1870905652.

Almost 4,000 key medical words and phrases are translated into 5 languages; English; French; German; Italian; Spanish. There is a list of abbreviations at the end of each language's section. Many words relating to new and emerging medical disciplines are included. Pocket reference version also available (208p. £8.50). *Class No:* 610(038)=00

[3308]
SLIOSBERG, A. Elsevier's medical dictionary in five languages: English/American, French, Italian, Spanish and German. 2nd rev. ed. Amsterdam, etc., Elsevier, 1975. [xi], 1452p. £175.62. ISBN: 0444411038.

First published 1964.

Over 20,000 English/American base entries (numbered 1-18,341, with interpolations, - the same total as in the 1st ed.). French, Italian, Spanish and German equivalents and indexes. Index of English synonyms. Bibliography, p.[x] - [xi]. Omission of Russian continues to be a drawback. *Class No:* 610(038)=00

[3309]
SPILKER, B. Medical dictionary in six languages. New York, Raven Press, 1995. xxi,665p. ISBN: 0781701821.

Contains over 7,500 terms. English terms are listed alphabetically in the first section, while the remaining five sections list French, Italian, German, Spanish, and, what makes this dictionary unusual, Japanese equivalents. Instructions for cross-referencing are given. Differences between UK and American spellings are indicated. *Class No:* 610(038)=00

[3310]

VEILLON, E. **Medical dictionary** / Medizinisches Wörterbuch/ Dictionnaire médical. 5. vollstandig neubearb. und erw. Aufl. von A. Nobel. Berne, etc., Huber, 1969 (6th ed., 1977. 1329p.). xxii, 1320p. Erganzungsband. 1974. iv, 464p.

First published 1950.

A bilingual medical dictionary in 3 sections. English-French-German (40,944 numbered English entries); French-German-English, German-English-French. German and French genders given. The supplement adds c.10,000 entries. Popular for quick-reference and favourably reviewed in *Lebende Sprachen,* v.20(2), March/April 1974, p.60-61. *Class No:* 610(038)=00

[3311]

—GARRIDO JUAN, A. Diccionario médico-suplemento español. Berlin & New York, Springer, 1970. [xi], 536p.

Adds a fourth language to the Veillon trilingual dictionary (1968), - Spanish. *Class No:* 610(038)=00

English

[3312]

Churchill's illustrated medical dictionary. New York, Edinburgh, Churchill Livingstone, 1989. xxx,2128p. illus. $33.95. ISBN: 0443086915.

Contains c.100,000 entries covering 65 subject areas in clinical medicine and related sciences. 32,000 pronunciations are given and specially commissioned line-drawings are included. Good coverage of international usage. Thumb-indexed. *Class No:* 610(038)=20

[3313]

Concise medical dictionary. 5th ed. Oxford, University Press, 1998. 717p. illus. ISBN: 0192629166.

First published 1980.

4th ed. reprinted as *Concise colour medical dictionary* (OUP, 1996. £9.99), with terms given in blue print.

Brief definitions. Many cross-references and examples. Line drawings are given where necessary. Tends to omit more obscure and outmoded terms in its aim to be of value to both medical and lay persons. This ed. includes many new entries in the fields of accident and emergency medicine, recently developed drugs, and infertility treatments. *Class No:* 610(038)=20

[3314]

DAVIES, P.M. **Medical terminology:** a guide to current usage. 4th ed. London, Heinemann Medical Books, 1985. 365p. ISBN: 0433071842.

First published 1969 as *Medical terminology in hospital practice.*

5 parts: 1. Introduction - 2. Medical terms referring to certain general pathological processes - 3. Medical terms referring to certain infectious diseases (5 sections) - 4. Medical terms referring to diseases of the various systems of the body and obstetric terms (17 sections, p.63-305) - 5. Certain other types of diseases (*e.g.* tropical diseases). Appendix: Standard works and journals consulted by the author, p.321-5. Glossary. Some important abbreviations. Detailed index, p.335-65. Good use of bold type. *Class No:* 610(038)=20

[3315]

—COHEN, B.J. Medical terminology: an illustrated guide. 3rd ed. Philadelphia, Lippincott Williams and Wilkins Publishers, 1998. 572p. $32. ISBN: 0781714117.

An introduction for those without easy access to a library and who need to learn medical terminology. Practical exercises are given, alongwith case studies. An instructor's manual is also available. Useful for students. *Class No:* 610(038)=20

[3316]

The Dictionary of modern medicine. Segen, J.C., *comp. and ed.* Carnforth, Lancs.; Park Ridge, N.J., Parthenon Publishing Group, 1992. 800p. illus. $75. ISBN: 1850703213.

Lists more than 10,000 terms, many of recent vintage, used in everyday medical life. Does not include terms from classicial anatomy, eponyms and pronunciation guidelines but aims to complement the traditional medical dictionary. *Class No:* 610(038)=20

[3317]

International dictionary of medicine and biology. Landau, S.I., *ed.-in-chief.* New York, Wiley, 1986. 3v. (li, 3200p.). $395. ISBN: 047101849x.

Over 100 contributors; more than 150,000 entries, thanks to the inclusion of biology. Among the subjects most extensively covered are ecology, environmental health, infectious diseases, occupational medicine, toxicology. A concise guide to usage precedes. Highly recommended as 'indispensable for medical and science libraries' (*Library journal,* 15 June 1986, p.61). *Class No:* 610(038)=20

[3318]

Medical phrase index: a one-step reference to the terminology of medicine. Lorenzini, J.A., *comp. and ed.* 2nd ed. Oradell, N.J., Medical Economics Books. 1989. xi,948p. $45. ISBN: 0874895391.

Over 100,000 entries, A-Z. 'Bone(s)': 6 columns of compound words of which 'bone' is the qualifying adjective (*e.g.* bone-marrow); from 'b., absorption' to 'b., zygomatic'.

3rd ed., 1994 (1261p.) published by LA Practice Management Information Corporation. *Class No:* 610(038)=20

[3319]

Medical speciality terminology. Young, C.G., *and others.* St. Louis, C.N. Mosby Co., 1971-1972. 2v. illus., tables.

1. *Pathology, clinical cytology and clinical pathology.* 1971. vii, [1], 251p. 2. *X-ray and nuclear medicine.* 1972. ix, 124p.

V.1 has 3 main sections, 20 subsections, each of which carries references and a subject index. *Class No:* 610(038)=20

[3320]

Merriam-Webster's medical desk dictionary. Springfield, Mass., Merriam-Webster, 1993. 816p. $24.95. ISBN: 0877791252.

An update of *Webster's medical desk dictionary* (1986).

Format is little changed from the 1986 version although the publisher claims there are more than 5,000 new words, with 6,000 definitions having been revised. Biographies of c.1,000 individuals are included. The definitions are concise but useful for those who only need to check the spelling of a term. For the layperson.

New edition published in 1995 as *Merriam-Webster's medical dictionary* (798p. 08077799148). *Class No:* 610(038)=20

[3321]

—AMERICAN MEDICAL ASSOCIATION. CMIT / Current medical information and terminology. 5th ed. Chicago, Ill., the Association, 1981. 801p.

First published 1963 as *Current medical terminology.*

3,262 'preferred terms and definitions' ... 'for the naming and description of diseases and conditions in practice and in areas related to medicine' (*cover sub-title*). Includes a section of cross-references from French, German and Spanish names of diseases. *Class No:* 610(038)=20

[3322]

ROBERTS, F. **Medical terms, their origin and construction.** 6th ed., revised by B. Lennox. London, Heinemann Medical, 1980. x, 132p. ISBN: 0433191511.

First published 1954.

5 parts: 1. Our classical roots - 2. Word construction - 3. Exemplary word lists, p.45-88 (49 subheadings, including 'Words not to be confused') - 4. Non-Classical origins (including acronyms and eponyms), p.89-102 - 5. Miscellany (notes). Detailed index, p.119-32. 'One of the best guides available to the meaning and derivation of medical terms for that vast majority of medical students who know 'small Latin and less Greek' (*Times literary supplement,* no.2,990, 19 June 1959, p.374, on the 3rd ed). *Class No:* 610(038)=20

[3323]

SKINNER, H.A. **The Origin of medical terms.** 2nd ed. Baltimore, Md., Williams & Wilkins, 1961. x, 438p. illus. (Reprinted London, Collier-Macmillan, 1970).

First published 1949.

Lists c.4,000 commonly used terms of chemical, anatomical and clinical practice, plus detailed explanation of origin and significance. 'On anatomical nomenclature and the basic sciences there is little to fault, but in clinical and historical matters the work is less satisfactory' (*The Lancet,* 17 March 1962, p.57). *Class No:* 610(038)=20

[3324]

—HAUBRICH, W.S. Medical meanings: a glossary of word origins. San Diego, Harcourt Brace Jovanovich, 1984. 285p. ISBN: 0151585199.

Covers c.1,500 medical terms, giving etymolgies and concise definitions, plus historical background. Aims to update Skinner's *The origin of medical terms,* adding new meanings and new words. Groups, phobias, colours, etc. *Class No:* 610(038)=20

[3325]

SLOANE, S.B. **The Medical word book:** a spelling and vocabulary guide to medical transcription. 3rd ed. Philadelphia, Pa., W.B. Saunders Company, 1991. xi,1097p. illus. $27.95. ISBN: 0721632432.

First published 1973.

18,000 more entries than previous ed. and a new section on immunology. 3 parts: 1. General terms - 2. Systems and specialties (*e.g.* 'Gastroenterology') - 3. Guide to terminology (*e.g.* 'Abbreviations and symbols'). *Class No:* 610(038)=20

German

[3326]

BUNJES, W.E. Wörterbuch der Medizin und Pharmazeutik, Deutsch-Englisch. 3. neubearb. Aufl. Stuttgart, Thieme, 1981. xxvii, 574p. £67.15; DM152. ISBN: 3133705032.

First published 1951 (author: F. Lejeune): 2nd ed. (1968-69).

About 50,000 entries. 'Lungen' (pulmonary): 3 columns of subentries. Prelims. include a bibliography of medical reference books (p.x), abbreviations and conversion tables. About 80 categories are applied to terms. Stress of German words is indicated. *Class No:* 610(038)=30

[3327]

—**BUNJES, W.E.** Medical and pharmaceutical dictionary: English-German. 4th ed. Stuttgart, etc., Thieme, 1981. xxviii, 556 + 140p. tables. DM152.

Has *c.*85,000 entries, of which the 140-p. supplement includes 17,000 new to the 3rd ed of 1974. Subentries appear in bold type. About 80 categories are applied. Prelims. include 'Bibliography of medical reference books' (p.xiii), conversion tables, list of Latin and Greek prefixes. *Class No:* 610(038)=30

[3328]

Medical dictionary, English-German, German-English. [Medizinisches Wörterbuch, Englisch-Deutsch, Deutsch-Englisch.] Eichhorst, C., *ed.* 2nd ed. Berlin, Eschenbach Verlag, 1989. 703p. DM68. ISBN: 3980144801.

This ed. contains *c.*80,000 terms, more than double the previous ed. Covers all branches of medicine. *Class No:* 610(038)=30

[3329]

NÖHRING, J. Routledge dictionary of medicine, Volume 1. German-English. London, Routledge, 1997. 1117p. £70. ISBN: 041517130x.

Based on 2nd edition of *Langenscheidt's dictionary of medicine.*

About 92,000 German terms, 16,000 new to this edition, covering all branches of medicine, with English equivalents. *Class No:* 610(038)=30

[3330]

—German-English medical dictionary. Schoenewald, T.S., *comp.* London, H.K. Lewis, 1952. viii, 241p. £8.

About 15,000 main entries. Still valued for its citing of words in context. 'A phrase dictionary illustrating the various shades of meaning of a word or expression by giving suitable examples of it' (*Introduction*). *Class No:* 610(038)=30

[3331]

NÖHRING, J. Routledge dictionary of medicine, Volume 2. English-German. 3rd ed. London, Routledge, 1997. 904p. £70. ISBN: 041517337x.

Based on 2nd edition of *Langenscheidt's dictionary of medicine.*

Translates *c.*67,000 English terms, 13,000 new to this edition, covering all branches of medicine. *Class No:* 610(038)=30

[3332]

UNSELD, D.W. Medizinisches Wörterbuch der deutschen und englischen Sprache. [Medical dictionary of the English and German languages.] 9th ed., rev. and enl. Stuttgart, Wissenschaftliche Verlagsgesellschaft GmbH, 1988. 695p. tables. DM68. ISBN: 3804709923.

First published 1946 (authors: M. Goertz and D.W. Unseld): 8th ed., 1982.

Englisch-Deutsch, p.3-349; Deutsch-Englisch, p.353-691. About 25,000 entries in each half. American and British English spelling are differentiated. German genders given. Eponyms are included. Appendix of weights, measures and temperatures. Small format. A handy dictionary for translators.

10th ed., 1991 (701p.). *Class No:* 610(038)=30

Dutch

[3333]

MOSTERT, F.J.A. Medisch woordenboek, engels/nederlands, nederlands/engels. 3rd ed. Utrecht, Bohn, Scheltema & Holkema, 1990. 206p. ISBN: 9031305669.

First published 1971.

Lists *c.*5,000 terms. Bibliography, p.201-6.
Class No: 610(038)=393

French

[3334]

DELAMARE, J. and DELAMARE-RICHE, T. Dictionnaire français-anglais des termes de médecine. [English-French dictionary of medical terms.] 3. éd., rev. et augm. Paris, Maloine, 1992. 510 + 542p. £67.20; FFr432. ISBN: 2224011202.

First published 1970. 2nd ed., 1986.

About 35,000 entries in each half, obsolete terms being indicated. Numerous eponyms and cross-references. Grouped headings (*e.g.* Fever: 4½p. of types). Better balanced halves than in Lépine (*q.v.*).

3rd ed., 1992 (916p. £67.20). *Class No:* 610(038)=40

[3335]

—**LÉPINE, P.** Dictionnaire français-anglais, anglais-français des termes médicaux et biologiques. Paris, Flammarion Médicines-Sciences, 1984. 878p. FFr350.

First published 1974.

Has 25,000 French terms, and is primarily intended for French users. *Class No:* 610(038)=40

[3336]

Dictionnaire de médecine Flammarion. 6. éd. Paris, Flammarion Médecine-Sciences, 1998. xiv,1030p. £21.95.

First published 1975.

A French-French medical dictionary, with *c.*20,000 entries, with 600 new entries for this ed. Included is an English-French vocabulary, a list of English and French abbreviations, a list of leading journals, table of biological constants, etc. *Class No:* 610(038)=40

[3337]

French glossary of medical terms: French-English, English-French. London, Impact Books, 1995. 185p. diagrs. £6.95. ISBN: 1874687455.

Lists over 4,000 words in each language. Appendices include anatomical diagrams, hospital documents, and useful phrases. A quick, basic reference guide for anyone needing to use French in a medical context. *Class No:* 610(038)=40

[3338]

GARNIER, M. and DELAMARE, J. Dictionnaire des termes techniques de médecine. 25. éd. Paris, Maloine, 1998. xxxiv,973p. £23.90.

Has *c.*30,000 headwords, with numerous subentries. Includes abbreviations and symbols. Standard French-French medical dictionary. *Class No:* 610(038)=40

[3339]

GLADSTONE, W.J. and ROCHE, P. Dictionnaire anglais-français des sciences médicales et paramédicales. [English-French dictionary of medical and paramedical sciences.] 4. éd. Saint-Hyacinthe, Québec, Edisem; Paris, Maloine, 1996. vi, 1282p. £75. ISBN: 2891301277.

First published 1978. 3. ed., 1990.

Contains *c.*90,000 entries in over 70 specialized areas. This edition includes terms from biotechnology; genetics; immunology; molecular biology; AIDS. A definitive and comprehensive reference work of medical terms and expressions plus, as necessary, contextual information, explanatory notes and categorization of terms. Of the 1978 ed., a model of 'how translators would like a dictionary prepared' (*The incorporated linguist*, v.17(3), p.58, 68). *Class No:* 610(038)=40

Italian

[3340]

LUCCHESI, M. Dizionario medico, inglese/italiano, italiano/inglese. Milan, Rafaello Cortina Editore, 1987. 1456p. ISBN: 8870780376.

English-Italian section, p.1-1179. Italian-English section which follows, p.1185-1456, is a list of Italian words with English equivalents. Abbreviations are included, and homeopathic terms are new to this edition. *Class No:* 610(038)=50

Spanish

[3341]

McELROY, O.H. and GRABB, L.L. Spanish-English, English-Spanish medical dictionary. [Diccionario médico, español-inglés, inglés-español.] Boston, Little, Brown and Company, 1992. xliii,506p. ISBN: 0316555614.

Contains more than 20,000 entries. List of medical abbreviations; sections on English and Spanish grammar; tips on pronunciation. 3 appendices, *e.g.* 'Signs and symptoms in most common disorders and diseases'. *Class No:* 610(038)=60

[3342]

NASR, I. and CORDERO, M. Medical Spanish: an instant translator. Philadelphia, W.B. Saunders, 1996. xiii, 386p. £14. ISBN: 0721660525.

Pocket dictionary. Three sections: 1. Introduction - 2. Adult chief complaints - 3. Pediatric chief complaints. Sections 2 and 3 arranged by body area (*e.g.* head and neck). Quotations in Spanish are repeated phonetically. *Class No:* 610(038)=60

[3343]

Ruiz Torres diccionario de términos médicos. 6th ed. Madrid, Editorial Alhambra, 1989. 880p.

First published 1957; 3rd ed. 1965 (714p.).

About 35,000 entries in the English-Spanish half (p.1-581), including abbreviations. Many compounds (*e.g.* 'Ligament': over 2 columns). Spanish-English: p.585-880. *Class No:* 610(038)=60

[3344]
—GARRIDO JUAN, A. Diccionario inglés-español para medicos y estudiantes de medicina. 3rd ed. Barcelona, Editorial Pediátrica, 1987. 772p. ISBN: 8471930862.

First published 1972.

Simple list of English medical terms with Spanish equivalents. Small, chunky format makes it useful as a vade mecum.

Class No: 610(038)=60

Classical Languages

[3345]
ANDERSON, D. *and* BUXTON, R. **A Pocket etymology of medical terms:** an introduction to the Greek and Latin roots of medical terminology. Bristol, Bristol Classical Press, 1981. iii, 47p. ISBN: 0862920159.

450 terms. Introduction includes Greek alphabet and its transliteration, common changes in word-forms, stems, common prefixes and suffixes. Will help readers to work out the meaning of other words which, for brevity's sake, we have omitted' (*Preface*). Aimed primarily at medical students. *Class No:* 610(038)=7

Russian

[3346]
Anglo-russkiĭ meditsinskiĭ slovar'. Akzhigtov, G.N., *ed.* Moscow, Russky Yazyk, 1988. 604p.

70,000 English terms, with Russian equivalents. Appendix of abbreviations and symbols. Companion volume:

Class No: 610(038)=82

[3347]
—Russko-angliĭskiĭ meditsinskiĭ slovar'. Moscow, Izdat. Ruskiĭ Yazyk, 1975. 647p.

Has *c.*50,000 entries and sub-entries. The Russian terminology is based on the 2nd ed. of *Bol'shaya meditsinskaya entsiklopediya* (1965) and 2nd ed. *Malaya meditsinskaya entsiklopediya* (1970), among other sources. English equivalents have American spelling.

Class No: 610(038)=82

[3348]
CARPOVICH, E.A. **Russian-English biological and medical dictionary.** 2nd ed. New York, Technical Dictionaries Co., 1960. 400p. $25. ISBN: 0911484019.

First published 1958 (398p.).

32,650 entries, giving direct adjective-noun approach, - very acceptable to the inexperienced translator and occasional reader of Russian scientific papers. (See *Science reference notes,* v.6(1), January 1959, p.19-21, for comparison with S. Jablonski's dictionary). Particularly valuable on biological terms that frequently appear in the medical literature, - terms not found in other dictionaries. Applications of terms appear in parentheses. *Class No:* 610(038)=82

[3349]
JABLONSKI, S. **Russian-English medical dictionary.**
Levine, B.S., *ed.* New York & London, Academic Press, 1958. xi, 423p.

About 29,000 entries, giving genders and parts of speech for Russian words. Jablonski barely gives common usage of terms; Carpovich does. Jablonski, however, lists frequently used Russian medical abbreviations, including discipline concerned. Carpovich does in general categorize terms. Jablonski is particularly good on drug terminology. The two dictionaries complement each other well.

Class No: 610(038)=82

[3350]
PETROV, V.I. *and* CHUPIATOVA, S.I. **Russko-angliĭskiĭ meditsinkiĭ slovar'-razgovornik.** [Russian-English medical dictionary phrasebook.] Izd. 2-e, ispr. i dop. Moscow, Rus. iaz, 1987. 595p. illus. (some col.).

First published 1983. *Class No:* 610(038)=82

Polish

[3351]
JEDRASZKO, S. **Slownik lekarski, angielsko-polski i polski-anglielski.** Wyd. 3. Warsaw, Panstwowe Zaklad Wydawnictw Lekarskich, 1969. 683, [1]p.

English-Polish, p.19-520 (*c.*40,000 entries, with pronunciation of English words, but no genders of Polish nouns. 'Zapalenie' (Inflammation): 31/3p. of sub-entries. Abbreviations. Latin words and conversion tables, p.521-2. *Class No:* 610(038)=84

Chinese

[3352]
Han Ying i hsueh ta tzu tien. [The Chinese-English medical dictionary.] Peiching Shih, Jen min wei sheng chu pan she; Hsin hua shu tien Peiching fa hsing so fa hsing, 1987. xxviii,1837p. ISBN: 7117004746.

2 sections, each arranged A-Z: Section 1 covers anatomy, physiology, diseases, chemicals, medical equipment - Section 2 includes acupuncture, natural remedies, symptoms, homeopathy. *Class No:* 610(038)=951

Negro-African

[3353]
A Short English-Swahili medical dictionary. White, T.H. *and* Sorsbie, C.E., *eds.* Expanded and edited by C.E. Sorsbie, with others. Edinburgh, etc., Churchill Livingstone, 1978. 105p. £2.50. ISBN: 0443016720.

About 2,500 entries for terms and expressions. 'A short bibliography' (A-Z authors), p.103-5. *Class No:* 610(038)=96

Reviews & Abstracts

[3354]
Bibliography of medical reviews. Washington, National Library of Medicine, 1955-67. Annual. 12v.

Lists review articles - as opposed to single book reviews - has subsequently appeared in monthly *Index medicus* and annual *Cumulated index medicus. Class No:* 610(048)

[3355]
Excerpta medica. Amsterdam, Elsevier Science, 1947-. 41 sections, 6-32pa. $43,522, complete series (includes a semi-annual cumulation on CD-ROM); price varies for individual series.

The most comprehensive medical abstracting service. The 41 sections contain 250,000 abstracts pa. in English from *c.*3,500 medical journals. Monthly and annual author and subject indexes. Computerized indexing since 1969.

38. *Adverse reaction titles.* 1966-. 12pa. $9,269. 54. *AIDS* (ceased 1991). 1. *Anatomy, anthropology, embryology and histology.* 1947-. 12pa. $1,365. 24. *Anesthesiology.* 1966-. 10pa. $1,157. 31. *Arthritis and rheumatism.* 1965-. 8pa. $876. 27. *Biophysics, bio-engineering and medical instrumentation.* 1967-. 16pa. $1,858. 16. *Cancer.* 1953-. 32pa. $2,769. 18. *Cardiovascular diseases and cardiovascular surgery.* 1957-. 24pa. $2,162. 15. *Chest diseases, thoracic surgery and tuberculosis.* 1948-. 16pa. $1,419. 29. *Clinical and experimental biochemistry.* 1948-. 40pa. $3,256. 30. *Clinical and experimental pharmacology.* 1948-. 32pa. $3,909. 13. *Dermatology and venereology,* 1947-. 12pa. $1,584. 21. *Developmental biology and teratology.* 1961-. 12pa. $1,657. 40. *Drug dependence, alcohol abuse, and alcoholism.* 1973-. 6pa. $909. 3. *Endocrinology.* 1947-. 24pa. $2,051. 46. *Environmental health and pollution control.* 1971-. 16pa. $2,109. 50. *Epilepsy abstracts.* 1969-. 6pa. $911. 49. *Forensic science abstracts.* 1975-. 6pa. $911. 48. *Gastroenterology.* 1971-. 16pa. $1,464. 5. *General pathology and pathological anatomy.* 1948-. 30pa. $3,167. 20. *Gerontology and geriatrics.* 1958-. 8pa. $967. 36. *Health policy, economics and management.* 1971-. 24pa. $1,117. 25. *Hematology.* 1967-. 24pa. $2,068. 22. *Human genetics.* 1963-. 24pa. $2,690. 26. *Immunology, serology and transplantation.* 1967-. 32pa. $2,571. 6. *Internal medicine.* 1947-. 24pa. $2,033. 4. *Microbiology, bacteriology, mycology, parasitology and virology.* 1948-. 40pa. $4,140. 8. *Neurology and neurosurgery.* 1948-. 32pa. $2,985. 23. *Nuclear medicine.* 1964-. 10pa. $1,325. 10. *Obstetrics and gynecology.* 1948-. 10pa. $1,980. 35. *Occupational health and industrial medicine.* 1971-. 12pa. $1,543. 12. *Ophthalmology.* 1947-. 12pa. $1,442. 33. *Orthopedic surgery.* 1956-. 12pa.

Also issued are monthly current bibliographies, and two indexing services: *Adverse reaction titles* and *Drug literature index.* Online, EMBASE and available on CD-ROM. *Class No:* 610(048)

[3356]
Index medicus. Bethesda, National Library of Medicine, 1960-. 12pa. $509. ISSN: 00193879.

Covers *c.*3,000 journals. Each issue has subject and author sections, plus - since 1967 - 'Bibliography of medical reviews' (articles are all well documented surveys of the recent biomedical literature). A comprehensive index to the world's medical literature. Annual cumulation as *Cumulated index medicus.* The computerized information retrieval service, MEDLINE (*q.v.*), is associated with *Index medicus.* Available on CD-ROM. Indispensable in its field. *Class No:* 610(048)

[3357]

—Cumulated index medicus. Bethesda, Md., National Library of Medicine, 1961-. Annual. ISSN: 00901423.

Compiled in 16v. *Medical subject headings (MeSH)*, - the primary listing of subject descriptions that appear in *Index medicus* (January issues) and here reprinted (1963-). V.2: *Journals indexed*. Bibliography of medical reviews; Author index, A-Bs, V.3-7: Author index, Bu-Z. V.8-16: Subject index. Available on microfiche and microfilm. *Class No:* 610(048)

[3358]

STRICKLAND-HODGE, B. How to use *Index Medicus, Psychological Abstracts, Excerpta Medica*. 2nd ed. Aldershot, Gower, 1994. xiii,114p. ISBN: 0566075555.

First published 1986.

'This manual aims to improve searching techniques in the most widely used indexing and abstracting services in the medical sciences' (*Introduction*). Spiral binding for easy use by librarians and information scientists; includes CD-ROM searching.

Class No: 610(048)

Periodicals & Progress Reports

[3359]

Annual review of medicine: selected topics in the clinical sciences. Palo Alto, Calif., Annual Reviews, Inc., 1950-. $120 (US); $130 (non US). ISSN: 00664219.

The well-documented papers of v.49, 1998 (520p.) include: 'Pathophysiology of atrial flutter'; 'New approaches to supporting the failing liver'; 'Surgical implications of obesity'; 'Endovascular treatment c. abdominal aortic aneurysms'. Analytical subject index; cumulative index of contributing authors, v.45-49; cumulative index of chapter titles, v.45-49. 'Some selected articles in other *Annual reviews*' precedes. Abstracts of papers available online 3 months before publication date at http://www.AnnualReviews.org. *Class No:* 610(05)

[3360]

The Author's guide to biomedical journals. 2nd ed. Larchmont, N.Y., Mary Ann Liebert, Inc., 1996. 800p. $184. ISBN: 0913113727.

First published 1993.

Contains manuscript submission instructions for 250 biomedical periodicals as well as a list of publishers, with addresses, phone and fax numbers, and e-mail addresses. *Class No:* 610(05)

[3361]

'List of journals indexed', in the January issue of *Index medicus* each year (1963-), is reprinted in annual *Cumulated index medicus*, and also available separately. About 2,500 titles, listed (1) by abbreviations, (2), by full titles. *Class No:* 610(05)

[3362]

—Vital notes on medical periodicals. Chicago, Ill., Medical Library Association, 1952-82. v.1-30. 3pa.

Listed new, change-of-title, deceased, etc., medical periodicals. 'Vital' refers to birth and death dates. Place of publication and frequency are given. Latterly (v.7-30) *Vital notes* had a section on congresses and list of directories. Since contributed by a variety of libraries, this provided a union list of sorts. *Class No:* 610(05)

[3363]

—World medical periodicals. 3rd ed. New York, World Medical Association, 1961. xli, 407p. *Supplement*. 1968. 68p.

First published 1953 (Paris, WHO and UNESCO); 2nd ed. 1957.

Adds nearly 1,000 titles to the 4,841 of the 2nd ed. Ceased items are asterisked. International, with cross-references and including abstracting journals, plus veterinary medicine. Prefaces and subject and country indexes in English, French, Spanish and German. *Class No:* 610(05)

Yearbooks & Directories

[3364]

COUNCIL FOR PROFESSIONS SUPPLEMENTARY TO MEDICINE. Professions Supplementary to Medicine Act, 1960, section 2 (d). London, the Council. Annual. 7v.

The chiropodists register. The dieticians register. The medical laboratory scientific officers register. The occupational therapists register. The orthoptists register. The physiotherapists register. The radiographers register.

The 25th ed. of the *Medical laboratory scientific officers register*, 1987/88, states qualifications required for inclusion, lists names of the Council members, and records names and addresses of those on the Register (p.19-411). *Class No:* 610(058)

[3365]

Directory of physicians in the US. Chicago, Ill., American Medical Association, 1906-. (36th ed. 1998. $695). 4v.

1. *Alphabetical index;* 2-4. *Geographical register.*

'Directory of physicians in the United States, Puerto Rico, Virgin Islands, certain Pacific Islands and the US physicians temporarily located in foreign countries' (*subtitle*). More than 790,000 listings. Brief who's who data on physicians. Also lists leading medical societies, hospitals and medical journals. Also available on CD-ROM. *Class No:* 610(058)

[3366]

Health care buyers guide, 1996. 21st annual ed. Tonbridge, Miller Freeman Ltd., 1996. 320p. ISBN: 086382269x. ISSN: 09673881.

Formerly *Sell's health service buyers guide*.

Alphabetical list of equipment/services, p.43-140; exhibition diary; key health care organisations; index to the buyers' guide; brands and trade names; company data section (p.163-305); associations and organizations; index to display advertisements. *Class No:* 610(058)

[3367]

The Medical annual: the year book of general practice. Bristol, Clinical Press, 1884-.

The 1993/94 ed. (xv, 376p.) has 47 well-documented essays. Papers include 'Recent events in primary care in Canada'; 'Teamwork in general practice'; 'Recent advances in obstetrics and gynaecology'. *Class No:* 610(058)

[3368]

The Medical directory, 1998. 154th ed. London, FT Healthcare, 1998. 2v. (xix + xxiii, 4498 + 407p.) £175. ISBN: 186067285x. ISSN: 03053342.

First published 1845.

The main sequence (v.1: A-L, v.2: M-Z) covers medical practitioners registered to practise in the UK. Data include qualifications, appointments (past and present) and publications. V.2 has appended: NHS Executive regions; Health boards in Scotland; Health and social services boards in Northern Ireland; Hospitals in the Channel Islands; Hospitals in the Isle of Man; Ministry of Defence and special hospitals; Independent hospitals. For most purposes, the *Directory* is preferred to the *Medical register*, because of its inclusion of Eire, and fuller information on individual doctors.

Available on CD-ROM. *Class No:* 610(058)

[3369]

The Medical register, 1998 ... comprising the principal list of the Register of Medical Practitioners on 1st January 1998, with other information concerning medical registration. London, General Medical Council, in pursuance of the Medical Act, 1983, 1998. Annual. 4v. (xxxi, 5599p.). tables.

First published 1859.

The official list of medical men and women, - c.100,000 brief entries (name, date of birth, address, medical qialifications, type of registration) in volumes arranged A-E, F-L, M-R, S-Z. Prelims. in v.1 state registrable qualifications, including recognized overseas qualifications. *Class No:* 610(058)

[3370]

The Official ABMS directory of board certified medical specialists. 28th ed. Chicago, Ill., Marquis Who's Who, for the American Board of Medical Specialties, 1996. 4v. $439.95. ISBN: 0837905397.

First published 1940. Combines *Directory of medical specialists* and *ABMS compendium of certified medical specialists*.

Has more than 465,000 entries in all, listed by speciality and then geographically. Brief curriculum vitae and official address in each case, - more detailed than in *American medical directory (q.v.)*. Outlines requirements for certification in the case of each speciality. *Class No:* 610(058)

Teaching Materials

[3371]

Health education index: incorporating guide to voluntary and other support organizations and self-help groups concerned with healthcare: 1987/88. Webb, D., *comp.* 9th ed. London, Edsall, 1987. ISBN: 0902623508.

Lists over 2,000 aids to health education, - booklets and pamphlets, books, films, film strips and slides, audiovisual and nonprint material; organizations - voluntary and professional. Subject index; sources of supply index; initials and abbreviations.

Health education index (1980-), revised 2-3 yearly, is aimed at schoolteachers. Definitive reference of health education resources available in the UK. *Class No:* 610(072)

Quotations

[3372]

Medical quotes: a thematic dictionary. Daintith, J. *and* Isaacs, A., *eds*. Oxford, New York, Facts on File, 1989. 260p. £13.95. ISBN: 0816020949.

Published in paperback as *Dictionary of medical quotations* (Collins. 1989).

About 1,600 quotations, arranged A-Z by theme (Abortion ... Youth), ranging from old favourites through to film, television and radio broadcasts. Cross-references given to related topics. 2 indexes: keyword-key phrase and author. 'Every waiting room should have one' (*Library Association record,* January 1990, p.68). *Class No:* 610(082.2)

[3373]

STRAUSS, M.B. Familiar medical quotations. London, Churchill, 1968 (reprinted, Little, Brown, 1985). xix,968p. £42. ISBN: 0316819158.

About 7,500 quotations, under subjects A-Z. Index of authors, p.679-705 (entries for authors with more than 50 quotations are asterisked and page numbers omitted). Index of keywords, p.709-968. Fills a gap. *Class No:* 610(082.2)

Tables & Data Books

[3374]

FISHER, Sir R.A. *and* YATES, F. Statistical tables for biological, agricultural and medical research. 6th rev. ed. Edinburgh, Oliver & Boyd, 1963. x, 146p. tables.

First published 1938; 5th ed. 1956.

50 tables. The valuable introduction gives examples of the ways in which the tables can be used and includes 82 references, covering books, monographs and papers on statistical methods, up to 1963. No index. *Class No:* 610(083)

[3375]

Geigy scientific tables. 8th rev. and enl. ed., edited by C. Lentner. West Caldwell, N.J., Ciba-Geigy Corpn., 1981-. ISBN: 0914168509, v.1; 0914168517, v.2; 0914168525, v.3; 0914168533, v.4; 0914168541, v.5.

7th ed., edited by K. Diem and C. Lentner.

1. *Units of measurement; body fluids; composition of the body; nutrition.* 1981. 295p. 2. *Introduction to statistics; statistical tables; mathematical formulae.* 1982 240p. 3. *Physical chemistry; composition of blood; hematology; somatometric data.* 1984. 359p. 4. *Biochemistry; metabolism of xenobiotics; inborn errors of metabolism; pharmacogenetics and ecogenetics.* 1986. 330p. 5. *Heart and circulation.* 1990. 280p.

Further volumes are in preparation. Ready reference source of basic data in biomedicine. *Class No:* 610(083)

[3376]

Health statistics: an annotated bibliographic guide to information sources. Weise, F.O., *ed.* 2nd ed. Lanham, Md., Medical Library Association and Scarecrow Press, 1997. 178p. £39.90. ISBN: 0810830566.

First published 1980 as *Health statistics: a guide to information sources.*

Lists sources of information for US health statistics. Eight sections: 1. General references - 2. Compilations of health statisticss ... 5. Health resources ... 8. Population characteristics. Four appendices: A. Newsletters and journals - B. Government agencies - C. Associations and foundations - D. Regional depository libraries. Glossary and index. *Class No:* 610(083)

[3377]

World health statistics annual. Geneva, World Health Organization, 1965-. Annual. tables, maps. $135. ISSN: 02503794.

Formerly *Annual epidemiological and vital statistics* (1951-65).

The 1996 v. (xxvi, 856p. 1998) covers 84 countries, 20 included for the first time. Three sections: Health and demographic area - Detailed mortality statistics - Causes of death and life expectancy. Annexes include: Users' guide to standardized transcripts on electronic storage media. Now also available on microfiche. *Class No:* 610(083)

[3378]

—'Medical statistics' In *Aslib proceedings,* v.38 (5), May 1986, p.131-75. diagrs., tables.

Consists of 4 documented papers presented at the Aslib Biological and Agricultural Group seminar, London, 29 November 1985 (*e.g.* 'Handling statistical enquiries in the medical library: some practical examples'). *Class No:* 610(083)

Illustrations

[3379]

THORNTON, J.L. *and* REEVES, C. Medical book illustration: a short history. Cambridge & New York, Oleander Press, 1983. 142p. illus. £15; $35. ISBN: 0906672074.

8 Chapters. 1. Materials, methods and general sources - 2. Ancient medical illustration - 3. Mediaeval manuscripts - 4. The invention of printing and the sixteenth century - 5. The seventeenth century - 6. The eighteenth century - 7. The nineteenth - 8. The twentieth century. Bibliography, p.128-35 (authors, A-Z). Detailed index, p.136-42. Helps to fill a gap in the history of medicine. *Class No:* 610(084.1)

Portraits

[3380]

NEW YORK ACADEMY OF MEDICINE. Portrait catalog of the New York Academy of Medicine. [New York Academy of Medicine]. Boston, Mass, G.K. Hall. 1971. 5v. $360. ISBN: 0816102333, set.

Includes 10,784 separate portraits, plus 151,792 entries of portraits appearing in books and journals. If biographical data or an obituary accompanies a portrait, the entry is asterisked or obelisked. 3 supps., ($120ea.), 1965-76. The set covers holdings 1959-75. *Class No:* 610(084.10)

[3381]

—NEW YORK ACADEMY OF MEDICINE. Illustration catalog of the Library. 3rd ed. Boston, Mass., G.K. Hall, 1976. 264p. $40. ISBN: 0816100381.

Contains *c.*5.500 card references to some 20,000 illus. in histories and journals, and also in early volumes in the Rare Book Dept. A library tool, and as such neither complete nor perfected. *Class No:* 610(084.10)

[3382]

ROYAL COLLEGE OF PHYSICIANS OF LONDON. Portraits. Piper, B. *and* Wolstenholme, G., *eds.* London, Churchill, 1964. 468p. illus.

Each portrait is illustrated and accompanied by biographical notes; references to other portraits; notes on provenance and sources of information. Details of over 200 portraits (in oils/chalk/pencil, busts, miniatures, etc.). Coloured frontispiece of College Arms. *Class No:* 610(084.10)

[3383]

—RIEDMAN, S.R. *and* GUSTAFSON, E.T. Portraits of Nobel Laureates in medicine and physiology. London, Abelard-Schuman, 1964. 343p. *Class No:* 610(084.10)

[3384]

—ROYAL COLLEGE OF PHYSICIANS OF LONDON. Catalogue of engraved portraits of the Library. [Royal College of Physicians of London]. Driver, A.H. London, the College, 1952.

Records over 4,500 portraits, principally of British physicians. But surgeons are also represented by eminent medical men of other nations. 'The index of portraits in books', maintained in the College, is available on microfilm. *Class No:* 610(084.10)

[3385]

—WELLCOME INSTITUTE FOR THE HISTORY OF MEDICINE. Portraits of doctors and scientists in the Wellcome Institute: a catalogue. Burgess, R., *ed.* London, the Institute, 1973. xxiv, 459p. illus. £19. *Class No:* 610(084.10)

Films

[3386]

Catalogue of films and videos in the British Medical Association library. London, Library Association Publishing, 1993. 330p. £35. ISBN: 1856040828.

Detailed annotated list of films and videos in the BMA library as of 31 December 1992. Entries include filmographic details, synopses, target audience, reviewers' comments and distributors' information. Alphabetical listing, followed by classified sequence using MESH. Index. *Class No:* 610(084.122)

Audio-Visual Materials

[3387]

Health media review index: a guide to reviews and descriptions of commercially-available nonprint material for the medical, mental, allied health, human service and related counseling professions. Provan, J.E. *and* Hunter, J.W., *eds.* Metuchen, N.J., Scarecrow Press, 1985. 862p. $59.50. ISBN: 081081739x.

'Indexes more than 4,000 health-related audiovisual items, as reviewed and described in 139 journals, 1980-83, Uses MeSH (National Library of Medicine Subject Headings). Sources of items comprise over 1,000 organizations and individuals. 'Its value is in bringing together nonprint reviews for the broad field of health'.

....*(contd.)*

(*Library journal*, August 1985, p.83).

Ed. covering 1984-86 (D.J. McAlpin and others, *eds.* xx,751p. $52.50) was published 1988. *Class No:* 610(086)

[3388]

JONES, M.C. International guide to locating audio-visual materials in the health services. Aldershot, Hants., Gower, 1986. ix. 54p. £25. ISBN: 0566035529.

4 parts 4: 1. Aids to locating health sciences audio-visual materials within the UK (A. Printed research aids; B. Computers and manual search services; C. Current awareness. 64 references) - 2. Aids to locating health sciences audio-visual materials in the USA and Canada. - 3. Aids to locating health sciences audio-visual materials in countries other than the UK, USA and Canada. - 4. Aids to the selection of health services audio-visual materials (includes D: Published reviews). 4 appendices: 3. Guides to assessing audio-visual materials; 4. Glossary of acronyms. Name, country and general indexes. Covers films, videocasettes, slides, overhead projection transparencies, flipcharts and educational computer software. Excludes microfilms. Particularly helpful on selecting materials. *Class No:* 610(086)

[3389]

—STEWART, M.C. 'Audio-visual materials': In *Information sources in the medical sciences*, edited by L.T. Morton and S. Godbolt (4th ed., 1992), p.109-34.

A survey, backed by over 5p. of references. 3 appendices: 1. Addresses of organizations; 2. Directories listing producers/distributors of audio-visual aids; 3. A select list of journals concerned with audio-visual aids in medicine (those asterisked carry reviews of new materials). *Class No:* 610(086)

Chronologies

[3390]

MORTON, L.T. and MOORE, R.J. A Chronology of medicine and related sciences. Aldershot, Scolar, 1997. 784p. £75. ISBN: 1859282156.

Arranged from 3000 BC to AD1996, listing Nobel Prizes, announcements of discoveries (with reference where appropriate), then one line entries for deaths of eminent medical researchers, all for a particular year. Personal and subject indexes, p.669-769. Dry, unattractive format, but undoubtedly useful for medical historians. *Class No:* 610(090)

Histories

Bibliographies

[3391]

Bibliography of the history of medicine, US Dept. of Health, Education and Welfare, Public Health Service, National Institute of Health, National Library of Medicine. Washington, Superintendent of Documents, US Govt. Printing Office, 1965-. Quinquennial. (No. 28, 1990-93. $55). ISSN: 00677280.

Each v. has 3 main sections: list of biographies, subject index; author index. Prepared from HISTLINE since 1970. Considerable overlap with *Current work in the history of medicine* (4pa) and tardy in appearance. *Class No:* 610(091)(01)

[3392]

—Bibliotheca Osleriana: a catalogue of books illustrating the history of medicine and science, collected, arranged and annotated by Sir William Osler, Bt. and bequeathed to McGill University. Oxford, Clarendon Press, 1929. xxxvi, 786p.

Reprinted Montreal, McGill-Queen's Univ. Press, 1969.

Lists *c.*7,600 bound volumes, representing major contributions to medicine and allied sciences. Entry arrangement renders reference a little difficult, but this is facilitated by the index. Annotations are of special interest, being typically Oslerian. Contains a wealth of bibliographical knowledge and remains readable.

The 1969 reprint (xliii, 792p.) includes a new prologue, addenda and corrigenda. 'A vast resource of accurate bibliographic and historical information' (*TLS, no.3566*, 2 July 1970, p.732). *Class No:* 610(091)(01)

[3393]

CORSI, P. and WEINDLING, P. Information sources in the history of science and medicine. London, Butterworth Scientific, 1983. xvi, 531p. facsims., diagrs. £43. (*Butterworths guides to information sources.*) ISBN: 0408107642.

Relevant chapters: 2. The historiography of medicine; 19. Medicine since 1500; 20-23. Science and medicine in America, Islam, India and China, respectively. *Class No:* 610(091)(01)

[3394]

Current work in the history of medicine: an international bibliography of references received ... London, Wellcome Institute for the History of Medicine, 1954 - 4pa. £21pa (individuals), £31.35pa (institutions). ISSN: 00113999.

Issue no.168, October 1995 contains 1,806 entries. Appended: Address of authors; Subject index; Author index; New books (p.610-29). 'Latest issue can be accessed online via JANET (Joint Academic Network) (uk.ac.ucl.wihm) or the Internet (wihm.ucl.ac.uk)'. *Class No:* 610(091)(01)

[3395]

MORTON, L.T. Morton's medical bibliography: an annotated checklist of texts illustrating the history of medicine (Garrison and Morton). 5th ed., by J.M. Norman. Aldershot, Scolar Press, 1991. 1267p. £85. ISBN: 0859678970.

First published 1943.

8,927 main entries (1,051 of them new), arranged by subject, *e.g.* biology, epidemiology, leprosy, obstetrics, then chronologically. Includes translations and reprints. Sections on medical biography, medical bibliography and medical lexicography. Indexes of personal names and subjects. Unrivalled. *Class No:* 610(091)(01)

[3396]

Thornton's medical books, libraries and collectors: a study of bibliography and the book trade in relation to the medical sciences. Besson, A., *ed.* 3rd ed. Aldershot, Hants., Gower, 1990. xxi,417p. facsims. £55. ISBN: 0566054817.

First published 1949.

10 contributors, 10 chapters: 1. Medical books before the invention of printing - 2. Medical incunabula ... 7. The growth of medical periodical literature ... 9. Private medical libraries - 10. Medical libraries of today. Extensive bibliography, p.342-57. Detailed, analytical index, p.358-417. A survey in depth. *Class No:* 610(091)(01)

[3397]

WELLCOME INSTITUTE FOR THE HISTORY OF MEDICINE. Subject catalogue of the history of medicine and related sciences. Munich, Kraus International Pubns., 1980. 18v.

1-9. *Subject section.* 10-13. *Topographical section.* 14-18. *Biographical section.*

Coverage is from 1954 to 1977; acts as an authority list for *Current work in the history of medicine* (*q.v.*) for the period concerned. 'Not an index to the entire collection, but is probably one of the most comprehensive guides in existence to the modern secondary literature of the history of medicine and allied sciences' (*Preface*). *Class No:* 610(091)(01)

[3398]

—The Truman G. Blocker, Jr., History of medicine collections: books and manuscripts. Wygant, L.J., *ed.* Galveston, Univ. of Texas Medical Branch, 1986. 432p. facsims. $50. ISBN: 0292780931.

Records 13,000 books and manuscripts in the Univ. of Texas's Moody Medical Library on the subject. Included is a brief but helpful bibliography. 'The collection is the largest resource in the Southwest' (*New technical books*, November 1986, item (259)). Well-produced. *Class No:* 610(091)(01)

Encyclopaedias

[3399]

Companion encyclopedia of the history of medicine. Bynum, W.F. and Porter, R., *eds.* London, Routledge, 1993. 2v.(xxvi,1,806p.) £190;$305 ISBN: 0415092426, v.1; 0415092434, v.2; 0415047714, set.

Covers all aspects of medical history. V.1 has four parts: 1. The place of medicine - 2. Body systems - 3. Theories of life, health and disease - 4. Understanding disease. V.2 continues with - 5. Clinical medicine - 6. Medicine in society - 7. Medicine, ideas and culture. Each chapter has a list of further reading. Index, p.1713-1806. *Class No:* 610(091)(031)

[3400]

McGREW, R.E. and McGREW, M.P. Encyclopedia of medical history. New York, etc., McGraw-Hill, 1985. xiv, [i], 400p. $41.25. ISBN: 0333288025.

103 lengthy entries, 'Abortion' ... 'Yellow Jack', each with 'Additional readings' (*e.g.* 'Quackery/Charlatanism': 8 columns; 21 lines of readings 'Drug abuse': 10½ columns; 2/3p. of readings, 1 cross-reference.) Includes entries for Chinese, Indian, etc. medicine. Analytical index - a bonus - carries over 4,000 entries, p.365-400. No biographies. A highly readable text, written for lay persons rather than practitioners. *Class No:* 610(091)(031)

Handbooks & Manuals

[3401]
ACKERKNECHT, C.H. A Short history of medicine. Bethesda, Md., Johns Hopkins University, 1982. 263p. $11.95.

Original German as *Geschichte der Medizin* (4th ed. Stuttgart, Enke, 1979. viii, 236p.).

A well-packed survey, from prehistoric medicine to present times. 'Every chapter has at least one statement that causes one to admire the men and women who preceded us. An extensive bibliography and index included. All in all, a thought-provoking 240 pages!' (*Delaware medical journal*, v.54, December 1982, p.705). *Class No:* 610(091)(035)

[3402]
—**CASTIGLIONI, A.** A History of medicine. Translated from the Italian and edited by E. B. Krumbhaar. 2nd ed. New York, Knopf, 1947. 1192, xlip. illus. New York, J. Aronson, 1978. 1216p.

Original Italian, 1936.

Of special value for the early history of medicine, particularly Greek and Roman, supplementing Garrison (*qv*). Extensive bibliographies. *Class No:* 610(091)(035)

[3403]
The Cambridge illustrated history of medicine. Porter, R., *ed.* Cambridge, University Press, 1996. 400p. illus.(some col.) £24.95; $39.95. ISBN: 0521442117.

10 chapters: 1. The history of disease ... 4. Primary care ... 8. Mental illness ... 10. Looking to the future. A reference guide contains sections: Chronology; Major human diseases; Notes; Further reading; Index of medical personalities; General index, p.394-400. An overview suitable for public libraries. *Class No:* 610(091)(035)

[3404]
GARRISON, F.H. An Introduction to the history of medicine, with medical chronology, suggestions for study, and bibliographic data. 4th ed., rev. and enl. Philadelphia, Pa., Saunders, 1929. 996p. ports. $32.75. ISBN: 0721640303.

Reprinted 1960 as *History of medicine*.

Chiefly of bibliographical interest. Numerous portraits. Details of bibliographies of medicine. Appendices include a chronology of medicine and public hygiene (p.809-72) and bibliographic notes for collateral reading (p.884-922). Recognized as a standard history of medicine. *Class No:* 610(091)(035)

[3405]
SIGERIST, H.E. A History of medicine. New York, Oxford Univ. Press, 1951-61 (reprinted 1987). 2v. illus. (pl.). $39.95ea. (*Department of the History of Medicine, Yale Univ. Publication nos.27, 38.*) ISBN: 0195001028, v.1; 0195001036, v.2.

1. *Primitive and archaic medicine.* xxi, 564p. 2. *Early Greek, Hindu and Persian medicine.* xvi, 352p.

Each volume has chapter references. In v.1 appendices cover bibliographies of histories of medicine, museums of medical history, and literature on palaeogeography since 1930. Originally conceived as a definitive history in 8v. The author's death in March 1957 brought this design to a premature end. V.2 was drafted but not completed, and has been edited by L. Edelstein. *Class No:* 610(091)(035)

[3406]
—**RHODES, P.** An Outline history of medicine. London, Butterworths, 1985. 236p. illus., diagrs., maps. £17.50; £11.50. ISBN: 0407004106.

Updates Singer by giving generous coverage to 20th-century changes and stressing such innovations as the use of the stethoscope and the emergence of bacteriology. General social attitudes are also traced. Appended chronology, bibliography and index. 'A lively up-to-date survey of medicine from earliest times to today' (*British book news*, August 1985, p.481). *Class No:* 610(091)(035)

[3407]
SINGER, C. and UNDERWOOD, E.A. A Short history of medicine. 2nd ed. Oxford, Clarendon Press, 1962. xvi, 854p. illus. pl.

First published 1928.

Over 70% of the 2nd ed. is on the 19th and 20th centuries, and this part has been rewritten and expanded, whereas the earlier part shows only modest changes. Substantial bibliography, p.761-95. The standard general history of medicine, now somewhat dated. *Class No:* 610(091)(035)

[3408]
Western medicine: an illustrated history. Loudon, I., *ed.* Oxford, University Press, 1997. 347p. illus. (some col.) £19.99; $49.95. ISBN: 0198205090.

Two sections (19 chapters): From the Hippocratic corpus to twentieth-century medicine (2. Medicine in the classical world ... 8. Medicine in the second half of the twentieth century); Medicine in context (9. The growth of medical education and the medical profession ... 19. The patient's view). Further reading, p.307-15; Chronology, p.316-23; Glossary, p.324-28; Illustration sources, p.329-30; Index. No previous knowledge is assumed so this would be suitable for public libraries. *Class No:* 610(091)(035)

Biographies

[3409]
BENDINER, J. *and* **BENDINER, E. Biographical dictionary of medicine.** New York, Facts on File, 1990. 284p. $40. ISBN: 0816018642.

International in scope, with entries varying in length from one paragraph to two pages. Written for the lay person. Cross-references and a brief bibliography. Quick-reference guide which may be useful for school and public libraries. *Class No:* 610(092)

[3410]
Dictionary of American medical biography. Kaufman, M., *and others.* Westport, Conn., Greenwood Press, 1984. 2v. (1027p.). $175. ISBN: 031321378x.

Continues H.A. Kelly and W.L Bussage's *Dictionary of American medical biography* (1928).

Records more than 1,000 medical personalities of the 17th-20th centuries who died before 31 December 1976. Includes references to other sources (*e.g., Dictionary of American biography*). Nearly 100p of appendices, listing biographees by date and place of birth, by state where prominent, by speciality/occupation, by medical school attended. Extensive index. *Class No:* 610(092)

[3411]
ELLIS, H. Bailey and Bishop's notable names in medicine and surgery. 4th ed. London, H.K. Lewis & Co., 1983. xv,272p. illus. ports. £18.95. ISBN: 0718604660.

3rd ed., 1959, as *Notable names in medicine and surgery: short biographies of some whose discoveries (not necessarily the greatest medical discoveries) have become eponymous in the medical and allied professions.*

69 biographical sketches of eponymous medical men, arranged A-Z (Addison ... Winslow). List of biographies for further reading, p.256-62. Index. *Class No:* 610(092)

[3412]
FIRKIN, B.G. *and* **WHITWORTH, J.A. Dictionary of medical eponyms.** Carnforth, Lancs., Parthenon Publishing Gp., 1987. vii, 591, [1]p. ports. £28. ISBN: 1850701385.

About 1,500 entries. Length varies from single line to 2 pages (*e.g.* 'Down syndrome': ¾p; 'Listeria monocytogenes': 2p.). 'Reference Books that we particularly relied upon ...', p.vii. 'This book is an endeavour to list eponyms used in the practice of internal medicine in Australia and probably in most of the English-speaking countries in the world' (*Introduction*). Well produced.

A 2nd ed. is due to be published in 1995. *Class No:* 610(092)

[3413]
—**LOURIE, J.** Medical eponyms: who was Coudé? London, Pitman Medical, 1982. 220p. £4.95. ISBN: 0272226433.

Has *c.*900 eponymous entries, with brief biographical details, thus supplementing Bailey and Bishop. *Class No:* 610(092)

[3414]
HAVARD, C. Medical eponyms. Chichester, Barry Rose Law Publishers, 1998. viii,252p. £35; £26 (pbk). ISBN: 1872328695; 1872328881, pbk.

Three sections: Diseases - Syndromes - Signs. Gives no biographical details but gives a brief listing of major symptoms. Glossary, p.225-37. Index, p.241-52. Designed to be a quick reference tool. *Class No:* 610(092)

[3415]
HIRSCH, A. Biographisches Lexikon der hervorragenden Ärzte aller Zeiten und Völker. 2. Aufl. durchgesehen und ergänzt von F. Hübotter und H. Vierordt. Berlin, Urban, 1929-35. 5v. and Supplement. ports. (Reprinted 1962).

First published 1884-88.

A unique universal biographical dictionary of physicians who attained prominence in their profession before 1880. Entries include lists of their writings and sources of additional information. The supplement includes corrigenda and addenda. *Class No:* 610(092)

[3416]
Medical sciences international who's who. 6th ed. Harlow, Essex, Longman Group, 1994. x,1235p. £365. (*Reference on research.*) ISBN: 058225664x.

First published 1980. 2nd ed. as *International medical who's who.*

Biographical details of more than 10,000 senior medical and biomedical scientists from over 90 countries. 2 parts: 1. Biographical profiles (A to Z, p.1-1207) - 2. Country and subject index. Data also available on the CD-ROMs *Current research in medicine worldwide* and *Current research worldwide*. *Class No:* 610(092)

[3417]
—**The International who's who in medicine.** Law, N.S., *and others, eds.* Cambridge, International Biographical Centre, 1995. 554p. illus. ISBN: 0948875917.

Includes *c.*5,000 biographies of professionals in medical and related fields. *Class No:* 610(092)

[3418]
MORTON, L.T. *and* MOORE, R.J. A Bibliography of medical and biomedical biography. 2nd ed. Aldershot, Hants., Scolar Press, 1994. 333p. $99.95. ISBN: 0859679810.

First ed., 1989 was originally intended as 3rd ed. of J.L. Thornton's *Select bibliography of medical biography*, (2nd ed. Library Association, 1970).

2,368 individuals listed (Abano-Zuntz), compared with 1,600 in the previous ed. This is mainly due to the inclusion of references to Western European language sources. Each entry contains birth and death dates, nationality, and a brief description of the person's contribution to the field. Up to seven biographical references are given. Locations of archival material are also listed. Appendices include collective biographies; a short list of books on the history of medicine and related subjects; a discipline index of biographees. *Class No: 610(092)*

[3419]
The Roll of the Royal College of Physicians of London; comprising biographical sketches of all the eminent physicians whose names are recorded in the annals ... 2nd ed., rev. and enl. London, the Royal College, 1878-. (v.8. 1989). £22ea, v.1-7; £55, v.8.

V. 1-3 (1878) cover the period 1518-1825 and constitute the most authentic source of biographical information for many physicians. V.4 (1955): 1826-1925, records Fellows elected up to 1925 who died before 1 January 1954. V.5 (1968) covers 1954-65; v.6-8 continue the record up to 1988. *Class No: 610(092)*

[3420]
ROYAL COLLEGE OF PHYSICIANS OF LONDON. William Harvey, 1578-1657: an exhibition of books and pamphlets illustrating his life and work. London, The Royal College, 1957. 25p. port.

39 annotated entries, plus notes on the portraits and genealogy of William Harvey, 'In this tercentenary exhibition the chief emphasis has been placed on the life of Wm. Harvey and in particular on his association with the College' (*Foreword*). *Class No: 610(092)*

[3421]
SOURKES, T. Nobel Prize Winners in medicine and physiology, 1901-65. New and rev. ed. New York, London, etc., Abelard-Schuman, 1966. xii, 464p. ports.

First published 1953 (covering 1901-50), by L.G. Stevenson.

About 100 biographical sketches (chronologically arranged) each with small portrait, description of the prize-winning work and its consequences in theory and practice, plus references. Classification of the awards, by topic. Index, p.451-60. *Class No: 610(092)*

[3422]
—Nobel Laureates in medicine or physiology. Fox, D.M., *and others, eds.* New York, Garland, 1990. 595p. $95. (*Garland reference library of the humanities, v.552.*) ISBN: 0824078926.

Articles arranged A-Z by name and covers 1901-89. Index of prizewinners and scientists mentioned in text or bibliographies. No subject index. *Class No: 610(092)*

[3423]
TALBOT, C.H. *and* HAMMOND, E.A. The Medical practitioners in medieval England: a biographical register. London, Wellcome Historical Medical Library, 1965. x, 503p.

Arranged A-Z, each with references. 'List of books consulted and abbreviations' p.427-49. Analytical general index, p.451-503. Aims 'to bring together in convenient form all the discoverable biographical information on the medical profession in medieval Britain' (*Introduction*). *Class No: 610(092)*

[3424]
Women in medicine: a bibliography of the literature on women physicians. Chaff, S.L., *and others.* Metuchen, N.J., Scarecrow Press, 1977. 1136p.

Annotated bibliography of 4,000 items written by and about women, 1750 onwards. Sectionalized, - biography, history, psychosocial aspects of female doctors, their wartime activities, and even citations of references in fiction. Includes foreign-language material, 'An excellent reference book for large medical collections and for public and high school libraries which are heavily used for research' (*Library journal*, v.103(4), 15 February 1978, p.451). *Class No: 610(092)*

Manuscripts & Incunabula

[3425]
ISKANDAR, A.Z. A Catalogue of Arabic manuscripts on medicine and science in the Wellcome Historical Medical Library. London, the Library, 1967. xvi, 255, [1]p. front., facsims. £22.

Valuable introductory comments on some of the most important MSS, p.1-72; catalogue, p.73-228 (A-Z titles). Bibliographical references; p.xv-xvi. Index to introduction; indexes of manuscripts, authors, scribes, former owners, and places. Facsims. of *c.*150-200 items. *Class No: 610(093)*

[3426]
KLEBS, A.C. Incunabula scientifica et medica: short-title list. Bruges, St. Catherine Press, 1938 (reprinted, Hildesheim, George Olms, 1963). 359p.

First published as v.4(1) of *Osiris.*

Registers more than 850 editions of medical books published in the 15th century. Under authors A-Z, with editions in chronological order. *Class No: 610(093)*

[3427]
—OSLER, Sir W. Incunabula medica: a study of the earliest printed medical books, 1467-1480. Oxford Univ. Press, for the Bibliographical Society, 1921. 140p.

Contains 217 entries. *Class No: 610(093)*

[3428]
—POYNTER, F.N. A Catalogue of incunabula in the Wellcome Historical Medical Library. London, Oxford Univ. Press, 1954. 160p. illus (pl.).

Contains 610 main short-title entries, many of which represent unique items. An invaluable illustrated guide to the finest collection of medical incunabula in Britain. *Class No: 610(093)*

[3429]
WELLCOME HISTORICAL MEDICAL LIBRARY. Catalogue of Western manuscripts on medicine and science in the Wellcome Historical Medical Library. Moorat, S.A.J. London, the Library, 1962-73. 2v. in 3.

1. *MSS written before 1650 A.D.* 1962. 2. *MSS written after 1650 A.D.* 1973. 2pts. (768 + 720p.).

V.1 contains detailed bibliographical descriptions of *c.*1,500 individual works, with 11 indexes, - chronological, linguistic, scribes, bindings, owners, book-plates, subjects, etc. *Class No: 610(093)*

Laws

[3430]
WORLD HEALTH ORGANIZATION. International digest of health legislation. Geneva, WHO, 1948-. v.1(1)-. 4pa. $184. ISSN: 00206563.

Scope includes new or amended health legislation. V.50(1), 1999 summarizes health laws and regulations, citing appropriate clauses, under countries, Austria ... Venezuela. The chronological index also includes a section on international texts. 22 section: 1. General provisions ... 12. Death and related issues ... 2. Health information and statistics. Also includes 'News and views'; 'Book reviews'; 'In the literature'. Subject index published after the publication of the last issue of each volume. Microfiche ed., v.1-25, covering 1948-1974. 1980-1995 available on diskette. *Class No: 610(094.1)*

Underwater

[3431]
SHILLING, C.W. *and* WERTS, M.F. Underwater medicine and related sciences; a guide to the literature; an annotated bibliography, keyword index and microthesaurus. New York, IFI/Plenum, 1973-75. 2v.

Updates *An annotated bibliography on diving and submarine medicine* (New York, Gordon and Breach, 1971).

Sponsored by the Bureau of Medicine and Surgery, and the Office of Naval Research.

Each volume carries *c.*1,800 annotated entries. Permuted subject index, author index, and microthesaurus. *Class No: 610(204)*

[3432]
—The Underwater handbook: a guide to physiology and performance for the engineer. Shilling, C.W., *and others, eds.* New York, etc., Wiley, 1977. 912p.

Practical and wide-ranging - 'as shown when it covers underwater blast, electric shock, safety precautions in pressure chambers, the design and use of underwater breathing equipment and tools, and the selection and training of divers' (*British medical journal*, 10th September 1976, p.696). *Class No: 610(204)*

Tropics

[3433]
Tropical and geographical medicine. Warren, K.S. *and* Mahmoud, A.A.F., *eds.* 2nd ed. New York, etc., McGraw-Hill, 1990. 1159p. $125. ISBN: 007068328x.

7 parts, by 154 specialists. 1. Clinical, biological and epidemiological considerations in the approach to tropical medicine - 2. Protozoan diseases - 3. Metazoan diseases (including anthropods and venomous animals) - 4. Viral and chlamydial diseases - 5. Bacterial, spirocheral and rickettsial diseases - 6. Fungal diseases - 7. Nutritional diseases. 4 appendices and index, p.1115-59. Of the first ed., 'This is the most comprehensive reference on tropical diseases which embodies an ecological perspective' (Harris, C.D., ed. *Geographical bibliography for American libraries* (1985), item 2760). *Class No: 610(213)*

Ancient Egypt

[3434]

NUNN, J.F. **Ancient Egyptian medicine.** London, British Museum Press, 1996. 240p. ISBN: 0714109819.

10 chapters: 1. The land of the Nile - 2. The medical papyri ... 4. The pattern of disease ... 7. Drug therapy ... 9. Specialised branches of medicine - 10. Epilogue. Four appendices: A. Chronological table - B. Concordance of tabulations of known doctors - C. Pharmacological properties of some Egyptian herbal remedies - D. Egyptian words appearing in the text. Bibliography, p.227-33. Index of citations and translations of medical texts, p.234-5; general index. For public and academic libraries. *Class No:* 610(32)

Great Britain

[3435]

HAM, C. *and* MERRY, P. **NHS handbook:** 1997/98. 12th ed. Tunbridge Wells, JMH Publishing, 1997. ISBN: 0952074451.

First published 1980.

Covers NHS today, management, funding, current trends, etc. Index. Provides an up-to-date overview. *Class No:* 610(410)

[3436]

NHS yearbook 1995/6. London, Highgrove Publishing, 1995. 600p. ISBN: 1899401636.

Contains data on NHS Trusts, GP fundholders, health commissions and boards, independent hospitals, local authorities etc., for each of 11 areas in the UK. Index, p.583-600. Lists 60,000 individuals working in the NHS, but only by employer; an additional name index would greatly improve this publication. *Class No:* 610(410)

Scotland

[3437]

COMRIE, J.D. **History of Scottish medicine.** 2nd ed. London, Baillière, Tindall & Cox, for Wellcome Historical Medical Museum, 1932. 2v. illus., maps.

First published 1927.

A marked improvement on the 1-volume ed. of 1927. Noteworthy for its illustrations and biographical information. *Class No:* 610(411)

India

[3438]

JAGGI, O.P. **History of science and technology in India.** Delhi, Atma Ram & Sons, 1969-80. 15v. illus.

8 of the 15v. relate to Indian medicine. 3. *Folk medicine.* 1973. 3. *Indian system of medicine.* 1973. 5. *Yogic and Tantric medicine.* 1973. 8. *Medicine in medieval India.* 1977. 12-15. *Western medicine in India.* 1979-80.

V.3 (xxxii, 228p.) has 2 parts: 1. Tribal medicine (section 3: 'Causation of diseases', p.37-66, with 42 references) - 2. Village medicine. Each part has appended select bibliography. General index (non-analytical), p.221-8. *Class No:* 610(540)

Islamic World

[3439]

AGHA, Z.M. **Bibliography of Islamic medicine and pharmacy.** [Bibliographie der Islamischen Medizin und Pharmacie.] London, E.J. Brill, 1983. 108p.

698 entries, often briefly annotated, under authors; A-Z. British Library locations are shown. *Class No:* 610(5.297)

[3440]

—EBIED, R.Y. **Bibliography of mediaeval Arabic and Jewish medicine and allied sciences.** London, Wellcome Institute of the History of Medicine, 1971. 150p. £12.50. (*Occasional series,* 2.) ISBN: 0822432251.

Is, unlike Agha's *Bibliography,* restricted to the Middle Ages. It also includes reference material not strictly relevant. *Class No:* 610(5.297)

[3441]

ULLMANN, M. **Islamic medicine.** Edinburgh Univ. Press, 1978 (reprinted in paperback, 1997). xiv, 138p. illus., facsims. (*Islamic surveys,* 11.) ISBN: 0748609075, pbk.

'An account of a medical system which was introduced into Arab countries in the 9th century A.D. and was practised throughout the Middle Ages and right up to modern times' (*Introduction*). Survey of previous books on the subject, p.xii-xiii. Source, p.115-6; notes, p.117-30. Excludes such topics as surgery, hospital institutions, medical teaching, the doctor's social standing and relations with patients. *Class No:* 610(5.297)

America—North

[3442]

Bibliography of the history of medicine of the United States and Canada, 1939-1960. Miller, G., *ed.* 2nd ed. Baltimore, Md., Johns Hopkins Press, 1965. xv, 425p. $34.50.

Arranged by broad topics, with author index. A re-issue, in consolidated form, of the annual bibliography published in the *Bulletin of the history of medicine* since 1940.

Continued by 4v. set covering the years 1964-1984 (v.1. 1964-1969, v.2. 1970-1974, v.3. 1975-1979, v.4. 1980-1984; Bethesda, Md., DHEW, 1972-85). *Class No:* 610(71+73)

Writing & Lecturing

[3443]

'BRITISH MEDICAL JOURNAL'. **How to do it. Volume 1.** 2nd ed. London, British Medical Association 1985. xiii, 266p. illus., tables. ISBN: 0727901869.

First published 1979.

Reprints 47 articles from *British medical journal* on a wide variety of practical challenges, - organizing an international medical meeting, writing the MD thesis, becoming a medical journalist/editor, editing a specialist journal, reviewing a book. Some of the contributions carry references. *Class No:* 610:001.81

[3444]

DUDLEY, H. **The Presentation of original work in medicine and biology.** Edinburgh, Churchill Livingstone, 1977. vii, 99p. diagrs., graphs. ISBN: 044301583x.

5 chapters, each with references. 1. Deciding to communicate - 2. Structure of scientific thought in relation to spoken and written communication - 3. Matters of detail (*e.g.* referees) - 4. English, particularly but not exclusively for written communication - 5. Aspects of speaking at scientific meetings, 15. 'textual acknowledgements'. Appendices: 1. General references and scientific writing (17 items, with brief-evaluative annotations); 2. Reference conventions; 3. Abstracts for the Surgical Research Society; 4. Statistic sources useful to the medical biologist. Author, then Professor of Surgery, Univ. of London. *Class No:* 610:001.81

Research Methods

[3445]

BENNINGTON, J.L. **Saunders dictionary & encyclopedia of laboratory medicine and technology.** Philadelphia, Pa., W.B. Saunders, 1984. xx, 1674p. illus., diagrs., tables. $79.95. ISBN: 072161714x.

46 contributors. Vocabulary (p.1-1621) of *c.*30,000 entries, a mixture of definitions and explanations. 'Enzymes': nearly 3p. Adequate cross references. Eponyms included. 3 appendices: A. Cancer chemotherapy drugs; B. Bacteriologic specimen collection; C. Reference ranges and laboratory values of clinical importance. For 'laboratorians, clinicians, nurses, allied health and public health personnel, basic scientists, and students preparing for courses in health care fields' (*Preface*). 'A rich source for the physician whose primary interest is patient care and teaching' (*Journal of the American Geriatrics Society,* v.33, August 1985, p.572). *Class No:* 610:001.891

[3446]

Dictionary of medical laboratory sciences. Farr, A.D., *ed.* Oxford, Blackwell Scientific Pubns., 1988. viii, 318p. £17.99. ISBN: 0632017627.

About 3,500 entries, Ab ... Zymosan. Includes acronyms (*e.g.* ACB: Association of Clinical Biochemists); trade names (*e.g.* OKT serum) and a few important names in medical history (*e.g.* Edward Jenner). Bold type for entries and cross-references. *Class No:* 610:001.891

[3447]

Introduction to medical laboratory technology. Baker, F.J., *and others.* 6th ed. London, Butterworths, 1984, x, 408p. illus., diagrs., tables. £24.50. ISBN: 0407732527.

First published 1954.

6 sections (44 subsections): 1. General (*e.g.* Health and safety in the laboratory) - 2. Clinical chemistry - 3. Cellular pathology - 4. Microbiology - 5. Haematology - 6. Blood transfusion technique. Systematic treatment, stressing methods and techniques. 'Recommended for further reading' (5 headings), p.383. Appendix 1: Manufacturers' names and addresses; Useful information (*e.g.* Saturated solutions). Analytical index, p.393-408. Standard textbook. *Class No:* 610:001.891

[3448]
—WORLD HEALTH ORGANIZATION. Manual of basic techniques for a health laboratory. Geneva, WHO, 1980. [v], 487p.

A revised version of *Basic techniques for a medical laboratory*, by E. Lévy-Lambeth (1974). 3 main parts: 1. General laboratory procedures - 2. A. Parasitology; B. Bacteriology; C. Serology; D. Mycology - 3: A. Examination of urine; B. Examination of cerebrospinal fluid; C. Haematology: D. Blood chemistry; E. Blood transfusion. Reagents and their preparation, p.479-87. Detailed analytical index, p.479-87. *Class No: 610:001.891*

Information Management

[3449]
Handbook of medical library practice. Darling, L., *ed.* 4th ed. Chicago, Ill., Medical Library Association, 1982-1988. 3v. $70, set; $19.40, v.1; $23.80, v.2; $30.80, v.3. ISBN: 0912176113, v.1; 0912176121, v.2; 0912176210, v.3.

First published 1943; 2nd ed. 1970.

1. *Public services in health science libraries.* 1982. 2. *Technical services in health science libraries.* 1983. 3. *Health science librarianship and administration.* 1988.

Notably updates the 3rd ed. by including in v.1, chapters on databases and computerized methods. For 'beginning and experienced medical librarians as well as teachers and students in library schools' (*Library journal*, 15 January 1983, p.114). *Class No: 610:025.4*

[3450]
LIVESEY, B. *and* STRICKLAND-HODGE, B. How to search the medical sources. Aldershot, Hants., Gower, 1989. viii,119p. figs. £25. ISBN: 0566035332.

6 sections: 1. Searching the medical sources - 2. Recording information - 3. Sources: background information - 4. Periodicals and periodical articles - 5. Other sources - 6. Organizing and presenting information. 91 figures reproduce extracts from the publications under discussion. List of references, p.113-16. For the library student and medical library staff. *Class No: 610:025.4*

[3451]
Medical librarianship. Carmel, M., *ed.* London, Library Association Publishing, 1981. xi, 359p. £26.50; £14.95. (*Handbooks on library practice.*) ISBN: 0853655022.

23 contributors. 21 chapters (1/3: The professions - 4/5: Information: serials, books, AV ... 11/14: Enquiry service ... 18: Some recent developments in health science libraries in North America - 19. Third World medical libraries - 20. Library and information research in health care - 21. Keeping in touch. Chapter references. Analytical index, p.351-9. Aimed at 'practising medical and health care librarians and seriously interested students' (*Library Association record*, v.84(3), March 1982, p.113). *Class No: 610:025.4*

Libraries

[3452]
Directory of health information resources in Scotland. Edinburgh, Association of Scottish Health Sciences Librarians, 1993. 52p. ISBN: 0900649860.

Previous ed. published as *Directory of health library resources in Scotland*.

A comprehensive list of c.110 entries. Data on each: location; telephone; accessibility; subject specializations; hardware/software used; classification systems; staff. *Class No: 610:061:026/027*

[3453]
Directory of medical and health care libraries in the United Kingdom and Republic of Ireland 1997-8. Forrester, W.H., *comp.* 10th ed. London, Library Association Publishing, 1997. 273p. £35. ISBN: 1856042197.

First published 1957. Editions 1-4 as *Directory of medical libraries in the British Isles.* 9th ed., 1994.

Lists in geographical order 851 libraries concerned with medicine, nursing, occupational therapy, and pharmacology. Data include availability; stock policy; special collections; classification, hours of opening. Indexes: personal names, hospitals, towns. *Class No: 610:061:026/027*

[3454]
Guide to libraries and information sources in medicine and health care. Dale, P., *ed.* 2nd ed. London, Science Reference and Information Service, 1997. 185p. £39. (*Key resource series.*) ISBN: 0712308393.

First published 1995.

Arranged A-Z by name. Details of 727 libraries and information sources which are willing to provide information to researchers. Includes professional and voluntary organizations. Subject, acronym, and organization indexes. Appendix: 'Medical resources and the Internet'. *Class No: 610:061:026/027*

[3455]
World directory of biological and medical sciences libraries. Poland, U.H., *ed.* Munich, New York, K.G. Saur, 1988. 203p. $30. ISBN: 3598217722.

Libraries from over 100 countries are listed. Data include addresses; subject areas; holdings; availability of materials. Appendices list national and international library directories; union lists; cooperative service centres; addresses of biological and medical library associations. *Class No: 610:061:026/027*

Institutions & Associations

[3456]
Directory of European societies and associations: medicine 1992. London, AG Publishing, 1992. 130p. ISBN: 1874305005.

Lists 200 medical societies and associations in 27 countries, A-Z by name. Data include full address, telephone/fax numbers, contact name, publications, conferences. Indexes: subject; mailing list; 1992/93 conference; country; society. *Class No: 610:061:061.2*

[3457]
Directory of international and national medical and related societies. Zeitak, G. *and* Berman, F., *eds.* 2nd ed. Rehovot, Israel, PBZ Informatics, and Oxford, Pergamon Press, 1990. 340p. ISBN: 0080374956.

4 parts: 1. Introduction - 2. Listing of societies (international; national, Afghanistan ... Zimbabwe, p.51-262) - 3. Indexes: Countries list with reference numbers; Alphabetical list of society names; Thesaurus of subject headings; Key to subject codes; Societies listed by subject - 4. Questionnaire used. About 4,500 well-indexed entries. *Class No: 610:061:061.2*

[3458]
Encyclopedia of medical organizations and agencies. 8th ed. Detroit, Mich., Gale, 1998. 1205p. $249: £190. ISBN: 0787627194.

First published 1983.

69 subject chapters, covering the programs of more than 14,000 of the leading US organizations in medicine and health, concerned with information, funding, research, education, etc. Detailed subject cross index; master name and keyword index. *Class No: 610:061:061.2*

[3459]
Medical and health information directory. Boyden, K., *ed.* 10th ed. Detroit, Mich., Gale, 1999. 3v. $590; £450, set. ISBN: 0787627208, set.

First published 1977.

1. *Organizations, agencies and institutions.* 1999. 2. *Publications, libraries, and other information services.* 1999. 3. *Health services including clinics, treatment centers, care programs and counselling/diagnostic services.* 1999.

For US medical and health professionals, government officials, librarians, consumers, and others. Covers nearly 60,000 organizations. Each volume is self-contained. *Class No: 610:061:061.2*

Conferences

[3460]
Calendar of congresses of medical sciences. [Calendrier des congrès des sciences médicales.] Geneva, Council for International Organizations of Medical Sciences. 1949- . Annual. ISSN: 03012891.

No. 58, 1997 lists congresses planned for 1997-2002. Data for each entry includes date; place; title of congress; contact name and address. Indexes of subjects and countries. *Class No: 610:061:061.3*

[3461]
World meetings: Medicine. New York, Macmillan, 1978-. 4pa., cumulated. $175. ISSN: 01612875.

Previously part of *World meetings: United States and Canada* (1963-. 4pa.) and *World meetings outside USA and Canada* (1968-. 4pa.), covering scientific, engineering and medical meetings.

Details of more than 1,000 medical meetings pa. *Class No: 610:061:061.3*

[3462]
—BISHOP, W.J. Bibliography of international congresses of medical sciences. Prepared ... under the auspices of the Council for International Organizations of Medical Sciences [CIOMS], with the financial assistance of UNESCO. Oxford, Blackwell, 1958. xxii, 238p.

Lists 363 congresses chronologically under subjects A-Z, and provides bibliographical data on published proceedings. *Class No: 610:061:061.3*

Research Establishments

[3463]

Medical research centres: a world directory of organizations and programmes. 12th ed. London, Cartermill, 1997. £325. (*Reference on research*.)

Succeeds *Medical research index* (5th ed. Hodgson, 1979); *Medical research centres* (8th ed. Longman, 1988).

Arranged A-Z by country, Albania ... Zimbabwe. A guide to over 9,500 organizations and laboratories (1,000 more than previous ed.) which conduct or finance medical or biological research and development in 130 countries. Data: name and address; telephone, telex and fax numbers; names of key personnel; finance; activities; publications; clients. Indexes of establishments and subject. Data also available on the CD-ROMs *Current research worldwide* and *Current research in medicine worldwide*. *Class No:* 610:061:061.62

[3464]

MEDICAL RESEARCH COUNCIL. Handbook 1998/99. [Medical Research Council]. London, the Council, 1998. 300p.

Includes information on: Research of MRC establishments and staff; Research supported by grants; Health services research; Research and development contracts; Outside support; International collaboration; Clinical research professorships and senior fellowships; Fellowships and scholarships; Publications. Personal names index; analytical subject index. *Class No:* 610:061:061.62

Research Projects

[3465]

GREAT BRITAIN. Department of Health. Department of Health listings of research and development 1991. London, HMSO, 1991. x,132p.

Formerly *Research and development report and handbook* and (to 1990) *DH Yearbook of research and development*.

4 sections: 1. Health and personal social services research: DH-funded units - 2. Health and personal social services research: programmes and projects (incl. AIDS p.42-6) - 3. NHS information technology research - 4. Medical devices directorate research. Indexes by name; research agency; subject. *Class No:* 610:061:061.62.005

Museums

[3466]

WEIR, S. Weir's guide to medical museums in Britain. 2nd ed. London, Royal Society of Medicine Press, 1996. xvi,241p. maps. £11. ISBN: 1853153044.

First published 1993.

Includes details of 170 museums containing medical artefacts. County maps, and subject and museum indexes. Omits medical and pathological museums in the medical schools and universities. A useful listing. *Class No:* 610:061:069

Medical Schools

[3467]

The Directory of schools of medicine and nursing: British qualifications and training in medicine, dentistry, nursing and related professions. 2nd ed. London, Kogan Page, on behalf of International Hospital Group, 1984. x, 752p. ISBN: 0850387884.

First published 1983.

9 parts: 1. Introduction - 2. Medicine - 3. Dentistry - 4. Nursing, midwifery and health visiting - 5. Professions supplementary to medicine - 6. Professions relating to medicine (*e.g.* clinical psychology; pharmacy - 7. Alternative medicine - 8. Health-care technology - 9. Further information (list of useful addresses; further reading). Index of qualifications and abbreviations. Detailed general index (in small type, p.742-54). Part 2-5 each have subsection: 'Directory of qualifications and training by institutions'. A comprehensive guide. *Class No:* 610:061:378

[3468]

—Directory of British postgraduate medical qualifications. Higson, N. London, Chapman & Hall Medical, 1987. xix, 299p. maps. £35. ISBN: 0412291002.

Arranged under organizing bodies. 1 entry per page. Two indexes precede: Index by type of qualification and subject (certificates; diplomas; master degrees; other degrees and awards) - Index by organizing body. Outline location maps. *Class No:* 610:061:378

[3469]

—Directory of postgraduate medical centres, 1986. [London], Council for Postgraduate Medical Education in England and Wales, and National Association of Clinicals, [1986]. 87p.

Has data on 381 postgraduate medical centres, including those in psychiatric hospitals and in teaching hospitals: England (14 regions; p.4-70), Wales, Northern Ireland, Scotland. Appendices. Index. *Class No:* 610:061:378

[3470]

World directory of medical schools. 6th ed. Geneva, WHO, 1988. 311p. £14.

First published 1953.

Lists institutions of undergraduate medical education in 127 countries and areas, Afghanistan ... Zimbabwe. Data: administration; conditions of admission; curriculum; examinations; number of hospital beds; statistics for academic year; licence to practise; type of degree. Annex: number of medical schools in 1955, 1960, 1970, 1975, and 1985, by country or area.

Regularly updated in *WHO chronicle* (monthly). *Class No:* 610:061:378

Ethics

[3471]

Bibliography of bioethics. Washington, Kennedy Insitute of Ethics; London, Collier-Macmillan, 1975-. Annual. $60 (US); $70 (non US). ISSN: 03630161.

Carries *c.*3,600 subject entries pa. Topics include abortion, AIDS, euthanasia, genome mapping, organ transplantation, and surrogate motherhood. Descriptions are appended to entries, some of which contain annotations. Bioethics thesaurus. Title and author indexes. One of the ongoing research projects of the Kennedy Institute of Ethics. Also available on a National Library of Medicine database, BIOETHICSLINE, and on CD-ROM as BIOETHICSLINE Plus. *Class No:* 610.17

[3472]

BRITISH MEDICAL ASSOCIATION. The Handbook of medical ethics. 2nd rev. ed. London, the Association, 1984. 111p. £5. ISBN: 0727901117.

First published 1981.

6 sections: The history of medical ethics - Relationships between doctors and individuals - Relationships between doctors and groups - Etiquette, professional discipline and the law - Ethical dilemmas - Ethical codes and statements (p.69-87) - Resolutions of BMA Annual Representative Meetings. Bibliography (8 sections), p.95-98. Analytical index, p.99-111. A well-received concise survey. *Class No:* 610.17

[3473]

Dictionary of medical ethics. Duncan, A.S., *and others, eds.* 2nd ed. London, Darton, Longman and Todd, 1981. xxxi, 459p. diagrs., tables. ISBN: 0232514925.

First published 1977.

About 150 contributors. All articles are signed, with references (*e.g.* 'Mental illness, Certification of': 2½ columns, 12 references; 'Psychiatry, Misuse of': 4p. 17 references). 'The work is of high standard and includes questions of social as well as purely medical importance ... Can be unreservedly recommended' (*British book news*, March 1978, p.196-7). 'This much needed and valuable book' (*British medical journal*, 5 November 1977, p.1218-9), on the 1st ed. *Class No:* 610.17

[3474]

Encyclopedia of bioethics. Reich, W.T., *ed*. Revised ed. New York, Macmillan, 1995. 5v. 2950p. $425. ISBN: 0028973550, set.

First edition published 1978.

The number of volumes has increased from four to five with this edition. Covers issues which are topical and includes subjects which have grown in prominence since the publication of the previous edition, *e.g.* female circumcision. 437 contributing authors from throughout the world. 464 new and updated signed and well-documented articles, with ample cross-references. Arranged alphabetically, with many topics subdivided into sub-topics. The extensive bibliographies have been completely revised and contain material from 1994. Useful section is 'Additional resources in bioethics' which contains listings of relevant organizations and journals arranged by country. V.5 includes a detailed 100-page index. 'This valuable addition to any library is highly recommended' (*Library journal*, July 1995).

A smaller edition, *Bioethics: sex, genetics, and human reproduction* (Macmillan, 1998. 1,152p. $125. ISBN: 0028649192), is also available.

Available on CD-ROM ($525), where it is linked to *BIOETHICSLINE (q.v.)*, giving the user access to articles published since 1974. *Class No:* 610.17

[3475]

International directory of bioethics organizations. Nolen, A.L. *and* Coutts, M.C., *eds.* Washington, DC, National Reference Center for Bioethics Literature, Kennedy Institute of Ethics, Georgetown University, 1993. 371p. $35. ISBN: 188391311x.

International in scope, listing almost 350 organizations from more than 40 countries, although there is a US bias, with more than half the organizations listed based in that country. Data include address; director; staff; educational programs; publications, etc. The

....(contd.)
alphabetical index is supplemented by indexes of organizations awarding academic degrees, provide consultancy services, or have an international remit. *Class No:* 610.17

[3476]
National Reference Center for Bioethics Literature. URL: http://adminweb.georgetown.edu/nrcbl/
Lists books, periodicals, newspaper articles, legal materials, and US government publications. Includes a link to *BIOETHICSLINE* (*q.v.*) and a thesaurus. Updated every two months. A useful starting point for anyone looking for bioethics material. *Class No:* 610.17

[3477]
Source book in bioethics. Jonsen, A.R., *and others, eds.* Washington, D.C., Georgetown University Press, 1998. 510p. £59.30; $95. ISBN: 0878406832.
Five parts: 1. The ethics of research with human subjects; 2. The ethics of death and dying ... 5. Ethical issues in the changing health care system. Each section includes a short history of the ethical issue, as well as bibliographic references and further reading suggestions. The public policy documents and legal decisions are from the US, although this will reflect areas of concern in other countries. For all those interested in bioethical issues in the US. *Class No:* 610.17

Anatomy

Handbooks & Manuals

[3478]
Gray's anatomy: the anatomical basis of medicine and surgery. Williams, P.L. 38th ed. New York, Edinburgh, Churchill Livingstone, 1995. xx, 2092p. illus. (incl. col.), tables. ISBN: 0443045607.
First published 1858.
120 contributors. 16 subject sections: 1. Introduction to human anatomy - 3. Embryology and development - 7. Muscle. - 12. Alimentary system - 16. Surface anatomy. Bibliography (authors, A/Z), p.1937-2044. Analytical index, p.2045-92. Many new diagrams, plates, and radiological images. The classic textbook on anatomy. *Class No:* 611(035)

[3479]
—DIAGRAM GROUP. The Human body on file. Swan, R., *ed.* New York, Facts on File, 1983. v.p. illus. Loose-leaf. $145. ISBN: 0871967065.
Consists of black-and-white outline drawings of the various systems/parts of the human body, from nervous system to endocrine system. Each section has a one-page introductory text. Three major uses are claimed: 'as an atlas of anatomy, as a reference source of images for photocopying, and as a basis for examination paper illustration' (*Foreword*). Although a good source for anyone studying or teaching anatomy at a basic level, it lacks adequate text matter. *Class No:* 611(035)

Dictionaries

[3480]
DONÁTH, T. **Anatomical dictionary,** with nomenclatures and explanatory notes. English ed., edited by G.N.C. Crawford. Oxford, etc., Pergamon Press, 1969. 634p.
Original ed. in Hungarian (1959).
A comparison of the nomenclature of Basle, Jena and Paris (10 sections), with additional terms, p.15-315. Explanatory dictionary, p.317-517. About 5,000 definitions, with a selection of biographical data on 500 prominent anatomists, p.519-47. Index, p.537-634. Of academic rather than general interest (*RQ*, v.10(1), Fall 1970, p.70). *Class No:* 611(038)

[3481]
—FIELD, E.J. *and* HARRISON, R.J. Anatomical terms: their origin and derivation. 3rd ed., rev. and enl. Cambridge, Heffer, 1968. xvii, 312p.
2nd ed. published in 1957.
Nearly 2,000 entries, including biographical notes. *Class No:* 611(038)

[3482]
MELLONI, B.J. **Melloni's illustrated dictionary of the musculoskeletal system.** New York, Parthenon Publishing Group, 1998. 308p. $29.95 ISBN: 1850706670.
Contains *c*.5,000 terms, with good quality illustrations keyed to their text entries by colour codes. Gives quick and easy access. Useful for students and academic libraries. *Class No:* 611(038)

[3483]
Stedman's anatomy & physiology words. Baltimore, Md., Williams & Wilkins, 1992. v,450p. $28. ISBN: 0683079417.
Basically a listing of *c*.44,000 words used in anatomy and physiology. Presented in context as one would hear or write them, with preceding words or adjectives. Does not give definitions. A quick-reference tool for 'anyone who transcribes, records, copy edits, or reads medical records, reports, and other material generated by health care professionals' (*Explanatory notes*). *Class No:* 611(038)

Reviews & Abstracts

[3484]
Excerpta medica. 1. Anatomy, anthropology, embryology and histology. Amsterdam, Elsevier Science, 1947-. 12pa. (2v.) $1,365. ISSN: 00144053.
About 4,000 abstracts pa. 9 sections: 1. General aspects - 2. Anatomy (systematic; functional and experimental; typographic)- 3. Anthropology; 4. Histology (methods; all, tissue and organ culture; general cytology; general histology); 5. Microscopic structure of vertebrates; 6. Microscopic structure of invertebrates; 7. Embryology; 8. Transplantation and regeneration; 9. Breeding of experimental animals. Annual subject and author indexes. Online in EMBASE, and available on CD-ROM. Available on microfilm. *Class No:* 611(048)

Tables & Data Books

[3485]
INTERNATIONAL COMMISSION ON RADIOLOGICAL PROTECTION. **Report of the Task Group on Reference Man.** Oxford, etc., Pergamon Press, 1975. xix, 480p. (*ICRP publication no.23.*) ISBN: 0080170242.
3 main sections: (1). Anatomical values for Reference Man - (2). Gross and elemental content of Reference Man - (3). Physiological data for Reference Man. Supporting each section: addendum, summary, and references. 'Produced for the purpose of simplifying radiological damages from radionuclides used in medicine ... A particularly useful compilation of quantitative data on the human body' (Welch, J., and King T.A. *Searching the medical literature* (1985), p.125). *Class No:* 611(083)

Nomenclatures

[3486]
Nomina anatomica. 6th ed. Edinburgh, Churchill Livingstone, 1989. 211p. ISBN: 0443040850.
Prepared by the International Anatomical Nomenclature Committee and is systematically arranged, setting the standard for anatomical nomenclature. *Class No:* 611(083.72)

Illustrations

[3487]
Atlas of human cross-sectional anatomy: with CT and MR images. Cahill, D.R., *and others.* 3rd ed. New York, Wiley-Liss, 1995. xii,312p. illus. ISBN: 0471591653.
High quality photographic images. Each illustration is accompanied by an orientation diagram to show location from which slice was taken. 3rd ed. includes new sections on the major joints and head. Highly recommended. *Class No:* 611(084.1)

[3488]
A Colour atlas of human anatomy. McMinn, R.M.H., *and others.* 3rd ed. London, Wolfe Medical Publications, Ltd., 1993. 359p. col. illus. ISBN: 0723419180.
First published 1977 (532p.). 2nd ed. 1988.
Has 750 coloured and keyed natural-sized photographs of bones and dissections of the human body. Appended lists of vessels and nerves. Intended for the undergraduate medical or dental student, nurse, physiotherapist, or paramedic. *Class No:* 611(084.1)

[3489]
Plant, animal and anatomical illustration in art & sciences: a bibliographical guide from the 16th century to the present day. Bridson, G.D.R. *and* White, J.J., *comps.* Winchester, Herts., St. Paul's Bibliographies; Detroit, Omnigraphics, 1990. ix,450p. facsims. £75. ISBN: 0906795818.
7,670 entries arranged chronologically in each section and including articles as well as books. Sections: A. Bibliographies - B. Nature in general - C. Plants - D. Animals - E. The human body - F. Artist biographies - G. Periodicals. Appendices: Books on colour; Organizations. Title, subject, and name indexes. For research libraries. *Class No:* 611(084.1)

Histories

[3490]
COLE, F.J. **History of comparative anatomy:** from Aristotle to the eighteenth century. London, Constable; New York, 1975. viii, 524p. $13.25. *Class No:* 611(091)

Physiology

[3491]
Handbook of physiology: a critical comprehensive presentation of physiological knowledge and concepts. Rev. ed. Baltimore, Md., Williams & Wilkins, for the American Physiological Society, 1977-. illus. $50-$395 per v.

First published 1959-83 (10 sections). Rev.

1. *The nervous system.* 5v. (8pts.). 1977-87. 2. *The cardiovascular system.* 4v. (6pts.). 1979-84. 3. *The respiratory system.* 4v. 1985-88. 4. *Environmental physics.* 1996. 6. *The gastrointestinal system.* 4v. 1989-90. 7. *The endocrine system,* (v.1. *Cellular endocrinology).* 1998. 8. *Renal physiology.* 2v. 1991. 9. *Reactions to environmental agents.* 1977. 10. *Skeletal muscle.* 1983. 11. *Aging.* 1995.

The revised ed. was started in 1977 before completion of the earlier ed. The latter's intention was 'to cover the physiological sciences in their entirety and in about 10 years, and to repeat the process periodically thereafter' (*Foreword,* v.1, Section 1). Well documented multivolume treatise. *Class No:* 612

[3492]
O'CONNOR, W.J. **Founders of British physiology:** a biographical dictionary, 1820-1885. Manchester Univ. Press, 1988. ix, 278p. £45. ISBN: 0719025370.

Arranged chronologically. 3 parts: 1. Physiologists, 1820-35 - 2. Physiologists, 1835-70 - 3. Experimental physiologists, 1870-85. About 100 short biographies, based primarily on obituaries. Contain brief descriptions of institutions involved with physiology during that period. Touches on botanists and zoologists (*e.g.* Balfour; Vines). Short bibliographies appended to each chapter. *Class No:* 612

[3493]
—O'CONNOR, W.J. **British physiologists 1885-1914:** a biographical dictionary. Manchester, University Press, 1991. xvii,582p. £55. ISBN: 0719032822.

Continues *Founders of British physiology: a biographical dictionary, 1820-1885,* by W.J. O'Connor (Manchester, University Press, 1988) (*q.v.*).

13 sections: 1. Physiologists and physiology 1885-1914 - 2. Physiologists in Cambridge 1805-1914 ... 5. London teaching hospitals ... 7. Physiology in Scotland 1885-1914. In addition to a general index, there is an index of physiological topics. *Class No:* 612

[3494]
Textbook of physiology (BDS). Emslie-Smith, D., *and others.* 11th ed. Edinburgh, Churchill Livingstone, 1988. xii,548p. illus., diagrs., tables. ISBN: 0443034125.

First published 1950 as *Textbook of physiology and biochemistry.*

Has 21 contributors. 41 chapters (The blood ... Energy balance and exercise ... Thermoregulation). Numerous half-tones, line-drawings, and tables. Standard text, with many chapters completely rewritten, and with the medical student mainly in mind. Some references follow each chapter. Index p.535-548. 'BDS' is the book's 'affectionate nickname' (*Preface* to 11th ed.) and comprises the initials of the first editors' surnames. *Class No:* 612

Bioengineering

[3495]
Bioengineering abstracts. Bethesda, Maryland, Cambridge Scientific Abstracts, 1993-. Monthly. $665 (US); $785 (non US). ISSN: 10685693.

Drawn from *Engineering index monthly.* Formerly *Bioengineering and biotechnology abstracts* (1974-92).

About 2,500 abstracts pa. on engineering disciplines applied to medicines. Follows the A-Z subject arrangement used in *Engineering index monthly* (*q.v.*), with full cross-references. Each issue covers 25 core journals. Author and subject indexes per issue, cumulated annually. List of acronyms, initials and abbreviations of organizations precedes. Online COMPENDEX (the machine-readable version of *Engineering index*) and on CD-ROM. *Class No:* 612.08

[3496]
Dictionary of medical equipment. Brown, M., *and others.* London, Chapman & Hall, 1986. viii, 288p. £28. ISBN: 0412282909.

Briefly describes equipment (*e.g.* artificial kidney) as used in the Institute of Medical and Dental Bioengineering, Royal Liverpool Hospital. Entries A-Scanner ... X-Y recorder. 3 appendices: 1. List of abbreviations; 2. Grouped minor entries (Anaesthesia ... Medical ultrasound); 3. Reference list, p.288. No illus. *Class No:* 612.08

[3497]
Encyclopedia of medical devices and instrumentation. Webster, J.G., *ed.* New York, Wiley, 1988. 4v. 3022p. illus., tables, graphs. $525. ISBN: 0471829366, set; 0471629685, v.1; 0471629693, v.2; 0471629707, v.3; 0471611352, v.4.

Over 250 documented articles describing every aspect of medical devices and instrumentation. Articles are several pages in length and are well-illustrated, *e.g.* 'Blood rheology': 7p.; 10 graphs; 60 refs. Over 2,000 illustrations and 200 tables in the set. V.4 has a detailed, analytical index, p.2945-3022. For any person with a scientific background and an interest in technology. *Class No:* 612.08

[3498]
Medical equipment: a guide to selected literature and sources of information. Anthony, K., *comp.* London, Science Reference and Information Service, 1986. [ii], 40p. illus. (facsims.). £5. ISBN: 0712307397.

9 sections: Books; Journals; Directories; Market research reports; Statistics; Company information; Abstracting and indexing journals (with SRL locations); Patents; Further sources of information. Briefly annotated entries. Index, p.38-40. *Class No:* 612.08

[3499]
SKALAK, R. *and* CHIEN, S. **Handbook of bioengineering.** New York, etc., McGraw-Hill, 1987. 932p. illus. $107.50. ISBN: 0070577835.

Numerous sections (Mechanics of soft tissue - Properties of bone ... Theory and design of implantable pacemakers - Circulatory assist devices - The artificial kidney - Bioengineering of total joint replacement - Biomechanics of the human spine and trunk). 393 illus. *Class No:* 612.08

Digestive System

Nutrition

Dictionaries

[3500]
Dictionary of food and nutrition. Adrian, J., *and others.* Chichester, Ellis Horwood; Weinheim, VCH Verlagsgesellschaft mbH, 1988. v,233p. illus., diagrs., tables. ISBN: 0895734044.

Translation of *Dictionnaire de biochemie alimentaire et de nutrition* (Paris, Tecnique et Documentation, 1981) and revised and updated.

Brief explanations of terms relating to human food science, nutrition, and mineral feedstuffs. Includes tables, chemical formulae, and illustrations. Appendices give composition details of selected foodstuffs and animal feeds. Well presented and easy to use.
Class No: 612.39(038)

Progress Reports

[3501]
Annual review of nutrition. Palo Alto, Calif., Annual Reviews, Inc., 1981-. v.1-. Annual. $120 (US); $130 (non US). ISSN: 01999885.

V.18, 1998 (500p.) has 37 contributors, 19 documented papers (*e.g.* 'Dietary oxidative stress and the potentiation of viral infection'; 'Nitrogen cycling in the gut'; 'Diet, nutrition and prostate cancer'). Subject index. Cumulative index of contributing authors, v.14-18; Cumulative index of chapter titles, v.14-18. 'Some related articles in other *Annual reviews*' is also given. Abstracts of papers available online 3 months before publication date at http://www.AnnualReviews.org. *Class No:* 612.39(055)

Vitamins

[3502]
Handbook of vitamins: nutritional, biochemical and clinical aspects. Machlin, L.J., *ed.* 2nd ed. New York, Dekker, 1991. x,595p. diagrs.,tables. $125; £91.45. (*Food science and technology, v.40.*) ISBN: 0824783514.

First published 1984.

16 chapters, reflecting research accomplished over the previous six years. Detailed data on all known vitamins, including chemistry, food content, metabolism, functions and deficiency symptoms. New to this ed. are state-of-the-art reviews of each vitamin. Over 230 diagrams and tables. An authoritative and comprehensive source of information. Of the first ed., 'For nutritionists, biochemists and even the interested lay person' (*Science & technology libraries,* v.5(4), Summer 1985, p.98). Recommended for professional and advanced students of food science and technology, nutrition, dietetics, pharmacology, and toxicology. *Class No:* 612.392.5

[3503]
MERVYN, L. **The Dictionary of vitamins:** the complete guide for vitamins and vitamin therapy. Wellingborough, Northants., Thorsons, and West Byfleet, Surrey, Turner Pubns., 1984. 208p. tables. ISBN: 0722509065.

About 1,000 entries, A ... Yogurt. 'Losses in food processing', p.125-34 (15 tables). Includes very brief biographical notes. Cross-references. Bibliography (books; periodicals), p.207-8. Clearly written text; for lay persons. *Class No:* 612.392.5

[3504]
MERVYN, L. **Thorson's complete guide to vitamins and minerals.** 2nd ed. Wellingborough, Northants., Thorson's, 1989. 384p. graphs. £5.99. ISBN: 0722521472.

First published 1986.

Arranged A-Z (A ... Zirconium). Gives general information on each mineral and vitamin, in addition to details of supplementation regimes and the use of vitamins and minerals in conjunction with drugs prescribed by the doctor. Author is Technical Director of Booker Nutritional Products. *Class No:* 612.392.5

Reproduction & Growth

[3505]
BUCKLER, J.M.H. **A Reference manual of growth and development.** 2nd ed. Oxford, Blackwell, 1997. vii, 116p. £19.95. ISBN: 0865426805.

First published 1979.

17 chapters: 1. Identification of the normal ... 2. Units of measurement ... 5. Head circumference ... 10. Puberty ... 13. Dental development ... 17. Blood pressure and electrocardiography. Appendix on equipment and supplies. References and index (1 page each). 'Normal' data on children are presented in a handy, quick reference, format; suitable for GPs as well as child specialists. Does not deal with abnormal growth conditions. *Class No:* 612.6

[3506]
The Cambridge encyclopedia of human growth and development. Ulijasek, S.J., *and others, eds.* Cambridge, University Press, 1998. xii, 497p. illus.,diagrs.,tables. £65; $95. ISBN: 0521560462.

127 authors contributing to 104 chapters arranged in 13 sections: 1. Measurement and assessment ... 4.Fetal growth ... 9.The ecology of post-natal growth ... 13. The future. Many photographs. Three appendices include short biographies of 25 researchers, a glossary, and a bibligraphy. Well-designed reference tool which will become a standard work. *Class No:* 612.6

[3507]
Encyclopedia of reproduction. Knobil, E. *and* Neill, J.D., *eds.-in-chief.* San Diego, Academic Press, 1998. 4v. (xxxvi,4000p.), figs.,tables. £260; $599.95. ISBN: 0122270207.

Covers all aspects of reproduction in the animal kingdom, including humans. Prelims. include 'Guide to the encyclopedia'. Articles, with a bibliography appended to each, are relatively brief, *e.g.* 'Amphibian ovarian cycles'; 'Median eminence'; 'Parasites and reproduction'. Over 550 separate articles, 1,350 figures, 300 tables, and 3,000 glossary entries. Many cross-references to other relevant articles. *Class No:* 612.6

[3508]
Human reproduction update: incorporating *Bibliography of reproduction* and *Oxford reviews of reproductive biology.* Oxford, Published for the European Society of Human Reproduction and Embryology by Oxford University Press, 1995-. 6pa. with CD-ROM. £387; $710. ISSN: 13554786.

V.1(6) November 1995 issue has three sections: Oxford reviews; Keeping in touch; Diagnostic methods. Author and subject indexes. The CD-ROM contains videos on fertilization, early embryology, and surgery; Tributes; Database; Dictionary ('Dictionary of terms used in reproductive medicine'); Human reproductive bibliography (covers October 15 1994 - November 10 1995). *Class No:* 612.6

[3509]
Reproductive medicine: from A to Z. Reiss, H.E., *ed.* Oxford, University Press, 1998. 152p. figs. £24.50. ISBN: 0192629018.

Defines over 800 terms, with many cross-references. Two appendices: 1. Abbreviations - 2. Drugs. *Class No:* 612.6

Death

[3510]
Encyclopedia of death. Kastenbaum, R. *and* Kastenbaum, B., *eds.* Phoenix, Ariz., Oryx, 1989. 320p. $74.50; £59.95. ISBN: 089774263x.

60 contributors, and 131 articles arranged alphabetically by topic. Coverage includes historical, medical, literary, practical, and psychological aspects related to death. A thorough examination of the issues raised. Highly recommended. *Class No:* 612.67

[3511]
SIMPSON, M.A. **Dying, death and grief:** a critically annotated bibliography and source book of thanatology and terminal care. 2nd ed. Pittsburgh, University of Pittsburgh Press, 1987. xv,259p. $29.95. ISBN: 0822935619.

Annotated entries for material published 1979-87. Coverage extends to key journals, films, audio-visual material available in Great Britain teaching material, kits, etc., and to European literature on the topics concerned. Subject and author indexes. *Class No:* 612.67

[3512]
—The Oxford book of death. Enright, D.J., *ed.* Oxford Univ. Press, 1983. xiii, 351p. £6.99. ISBN: 0192141295.

A wide-ranging book of quotations, with index. *Class No:* 612.67

[3513]
Sourcebook on death and dying. Fruehling, J.A., *ed.* Chicago, Ill., Marquis Who's Who, 1982. 788p. illus. ISBN: 0837958016.

Part 1, 'Current issues', reprints in their entirety periodical articles on euthanasia, wills, bereavement, counselling and hospices. Part 2 provides vital statistics, survivor benefits and legal tax information for the US and Canada. A directory of institutions precedes a substantial bibliography (include audiovisual items). Scant coverage of such topics as children, and autopsies. *Class No:* 612.67

Health & Hygiene

Encyclopaedias

[3514]
AMMER, C. **The New A-Z of women's health:** a concise encyclopedia. Rev. and expanded ed. San Bernardino, Calif., Borgo Press, 1994. xiii,472p. illus., tables.

First published 1989.

c.1,000 entries arranged alphabetically. Many cross-references. Length of entries varies fron one paragraph to several pages. Two appendices (Subject index and a list of resources). Easy to use. No bibliographies. *Class No:* 613(031)

[3515]
Complete family health encyclopedia. Smith, T., *ed.* London, Dorling Kindersley, 1990. 1184p. illus. (inc. col.). £25. ISBN: 0863184383.

Previous ed. (1980) as *Family health encyclopedia* (720p.).

c.5,000 entries and 2,000 illus. 2 sections: 1. The A-Z of health and medicines, p.49-1094 - 2. Drugs glossary, p.1095-1114. Detailed, analytical index, p.1115-54. Boxed information and well-captioned illustrations. Aims to be a sound, up-to-date medical reference source for use in the home. A handsome quarto, well produced. *Class No:* 613(031)

[3516]
STOPPARD, M. **Everywoman's medical handbook.** London, Dorling Kindersley, 1988. 384p. illus., diagrs., tables. £14.95; $19.95. ISBN: 0863182755.

Covers over 2,000 diseases, disorders and conditions. 3 main parts: The healthy female body, (p.9-69) - the A-Z of conditions, diseases, procedures and symptoms (p.71-345; 1-2p. per topic) - Women and medicine (*e.g.* Drugs index; Glossary, p.366-75; Health directory (grouped); Index (p.378-83)). Boxed information on symptoms throughout. *Class No:* 613(031)

Handbooks & Manuals

[3517]
CARROLL, S. **The Which? guide to men's health.** London, Which? Books, 1995. 252p. diagrs.,tables. £9.99. ISBN: 0852025734.

Six chapters: 1. Understanding the male body. - 2. How to stay physically healthy ... 6. Common health problems in men. Glossary, p.231-39. Addresses, p.240-44. Brief bibliography. Index, p.246-52. Well-written and and easy to understand. For public libraries. *Class No:* 613(035)

[3518]
JOLLY, H. **Book of child care:** complete guide for today's parents. 4th ed. London, Allen & Unwin, 1985. [xv], 569p. illus. £14.95; £8.99. ISBN: 0046490345.

First published 1978.

Part 1: The healthy child (1. Pregnancy and birth ... 7. Looking after your new baby ... 9. Effects of the new baby on family life ... 12. How children grow and develop ... 17. Discipline and punishment ... 18. Play ... 23. The one-parent family - 24. Travel, holidays and living in the tropics). Part 2: The sick child (26. The sick child at home ... 31. Coughs and colds ... 41. Measles and other infectious diseases ... 47. The mentally handicapped child ... 49. Accidents - 50. When a child dies). Useful addresses, p.559-62. Detailed analytical index, p.563-9. Well produced; fully illustrated. Translated into several foreign languages as a basic text. *Class No:* 613(035)

[3519]
The Macmillan guide to child health. Hull, D., *ed.* London, Macmillan, 1985. 382p. illus., diagrs., charts. ISBN: 0333392507.

46 contributors. 4 parts: 1. Care of the child - 2. Care of sick child - 3. Problems, diseases and disorders (p.120-310) - 4. Appendices: resources (support groups and publications, etc.). Emergency actions, p.330-41. Index of syndromes, p.342-3. Analytical index, p.344-52. Over 500 two-colour illus. A guide that spans the child's life from conception to adolescence. For public library and home use. Analytical index. *Class No:* 613(035)

[3520]
The New 'Our bodies, ourselves': a book by and for women, by the Boston Women's Health Book Collective. Rev. ed. New York, Simon & Schuster, 1992. 751p. illus. $17.95. ISBN: 0671791761.

Formerly *Our bodies, ourselves* (1976. 352p.).

A compendium on women's physical and health issues (*e.g.* birth control, menopause, estrogen replacement therapy and surgery, growing old). One section details 40 symptoms, with step-by-step diagrams for each symptom and its treatment. Bibliography and index. Of the previous ed., 'Essential for consultation' (*Choice*, v.22(10), June 1985, p.1478). *Class No:* 613(035)

[3521]
SHEPHERD, B.D. and SHEPHERD, C.A. **The Complete guide to women's health.** 2nd ed. New York, Penguin Books, 1990. xxiv,502p. illus., diagrs., tables. $15.95. ISBN: 0452264391.

Ten sections on health strategies, choosing a doctor, birth control, pregnancy planning, pregnancy and childbirth, sexual issues, menopause, and nutrition and physical fitness for a healthy life. A final section, 'What your symptoms mean', has step-by-step diagrams. Appended glossary, further reading, and how to carry out a breast self-examination. Bibliography, p.477-79. Index. 'Comprehensive reference work on diagnoses and treatments' (*RQ*, v.22(4), Summer 1983, p.419). *Class No:* 613(035)

[3522]
SMITH, T. **The New Macmillan guide to family health.** 2nd ed. London, Macmillan, 1987. 848p. illus. (incl. col.), charts, tables. £24.95. ISBN: 0333455258.

29 contributors. 4 parts: 1. The healthy body - 2. Symptoms and self-diagnosis - 3. Diseases, disorders and other problems - 4. Caring for the sick. Boxed information, a feature. Appended: Helpful organizations, p.762-3; drug index, p.792-801. Glossary. 'Accidents and emergencies', p.815-32. Detailed, analytical index, p.833-46. Designed for use in both sickness and health. *Class No:* 613(035)

[3523]
Travellers' health: how to stay healthy abroad. Dawood, R., *ed.* 3rd ed. Oxford, University Press, 1992. xxiv,472p. £7.99. ISBN: 0192622471.

About 40 contributors. 14 sections. 1. Staying healthy abroad - 2. Diseases spread mainly by food, drink and poor hygiene ... 5. Diseases spread by insects - 6. Animal bites; rabies; venomous bites and stings - 7. Air and sea travel - 8. Environmental and recreational hazards (*e.g.* skiing) - 9. Some common troubles (*e.g.* skin and blisters) - 10. Sex and contraception abroad (*e.g.* AIDS) - 11. Travellers with special needs (*e.g.* the disabled traveller) - 12. Becoming an expatriate - 13. Preparation for travel - 14. A special achievement. 9 appendices (6: Medical kit check-list). Further reading, p.446-50. Glossary. Index, p.455-72. 'An anthology of invited, *specialist* opinion on a wide range of problems of concern to travellers' (*Preface*). Eminently practical. *Class No:* 613(035)

Reviews & Abstracts

[3524]
Abstracts on hygiene and communicable diseases. Wallingford, CAB International, 1926-. 12pa. £315; $551. ISSN: 02605511.

Incorporates *Bulletin of hygiene*.

Contains abstracts of 100-600 words, some of them signed, and preceded by full bibliographical information. March 1996 issue has 'Public health news', followed by 'Environmental health' - 'Community health' - 'Diseases and their control'. Book reviews. Author, geographical, and subject indexes. Forthcoming meetings. Available online via DIMDI and in microform. *Class No:* 613(048)

Yearbooks & Directories

[3525]
The Health directory. Macdonald, F., *comp.* 2nd ed. London, Bedford Square Press, 1990. 121p. £6.95. ISBN: 0719912563.

First published 1979.

Lists nearly 1,000 national bodies, advice services, and informal self-help groups in the UK. Subject index. Aimed at the non-specialist but also a useful reference tool for the professional. *Class No:* 613(058)

Tables & Data Books

[3526]
World health statistics annual. Geneva, World Health Organization, 1965-. Annual. tables, maps. $135. ISSN: 02503794.

Formerly *Annual epidemiological and vital statistics* (1951-65).

The 1996 v. (xxvi, 856p. 1998) covers 84 countries, 20 included for the first time. Three sections: Health and demographic area - Detailed mortality statistics - Causes of death and life expectancy. Annexes include: Users' guide to standardized transcripts on electronic storage media. Now also available on microfiche. *Class No:* 613(083)

Food

CD-ROM

[3527]
Human nutrition. London, SilverPlatter, 1993-. 4pa. CD-ROM. $2,195.

A compilation of information from the National Library of Medicine, Cambridge Scientific Abstracts, the International Food Information Service, and CAB International. Coverage is from 1982. Contains over 500,000 records, with 40,000 records added annually. Subjects covered includes the agricultural and food industries, food additives, food allergies, nutritional evaluation, etc. *Class No:* 613.2(003.40)

Bibliographies

[3528]
PRYTHERCH, R. *and* STANLEY, S. **Food, cookery and diet:** an information guide. Aldershot, Gower, 1989. ix,109p. £15. ISBN: 0566035685.

Lists the standard, basic sources. 6 sections: 1. Basic reference sources - 2. The scientific background - 3. Professional catering - 4. Training, education and careers - 5. Home cooking - 6. Healthy eating and special diets. Index. *Class No:* 613.2(01)

Encyclopaedias

[3529]
Encyclopedia of human nutrition. Sadler, M., *and others, eds.* San Diego, Academic Press, 1998. 3v.(2,200p.) tables £570; $925. ISBN: 0122266943.

More than 270 articles arranged A-Z (Adaptive responses to malnutrition ... Zinc). Many cross-references, bibliographies appended to articles, appendices. Incorporates many changes in nutritional science since the early 1990s. Assumes previous knowledge of the subject. For academic libraries. Buyers of the printed work have access to the online version. *Class No:* 613.2(031)

[3530]
RONZIO, R.A. **The Encyclopedia of nutrition and good health.** New York, Facts on File, 1997. ix,486p. ISBN: 0816037558.

Contains over 2,500 concise entries on subjects including food ingredients, diet therapy, additives, safety and food processing, diet-related diseases, etc. Many cross-references. Detailed index. *Class No:* 613.2(031)

[3531]
TVER, D.F. *and* RUSSELL, P. **The Nutrition and health encyclopedia.** 2nd ed. Princeton, N.J., Van Nostrand Reinhold, 1989. vii,639p. illus., diagrs., charts, tables. $44.95. ISBN: 0442233973.

First published 1981.

A-Z definitions and longer articles (150 revised definitions; 86 new terms), the latter on carbohydrates, toxins, drugs, bodily functions, etc. Tabular data on food, caloric and vitamin values have been expanded and updated for this ed. 'An important encyclopedic source of nutritional information' (*New technical books*, v.75(2), March/April, 1990, no.572). 13 appendices, *e.g.* 3. Table of international atomic weights. *Class No:* 613.2(031)

Handbooks & Manuals

[3532]
ROGERS, J. **The Encyclopedia of food and nutrition.** London, Merehurst, 1990. 480p. illus. (col.), tables. £25. ISBN: 1853911690.

29 sections, *e.g.* 'Fruits'; 'Pulses'; 'Fast foods'. Most entries include a coloured illustration and data cover major nutrients; nutritional information; description; origin and history; buying and storage; preparation and use; processing; varieties. Tables, p.468-73, give figures for recommended daily intake of minerals, vitamins, etc. Index but no bibliography. Attractively presented. Suitable for the layperson, public libraries, and quick reference. *Class No:* 613.2(035)

Dictionaries

[3533]

BENDER, A.E. Dictionary of nutrition and food technology. 6th ed. London, Butterworths, 1990. [vi], 336p. tables. £29.50. ISBN: 0408037539.

First published 1960.

About 4,000 entries and cross-references, p.1-309. Entries for abbreviations and trade names. Includes 300 new terms; 300 entries revised. Bibliography (now separated from entries), p.310-24 (Additives and ingredients ... Toxicology). Tables, p.327-36. Aims 'to assist the specialist from one field to understand the technical terms used by the variety of specialists in the food fields' (*Preface* to 5th ed.). Author was Professor of Nutrition, Queen Elizabeth College, Univ. of London.

An excellent cheaper alternative is *A Dictionary of food and nutrition* by A.E. and D.A. Bender (Oxford University Press, 1995. 413p. £7.99), containing *c*.6,000 brief entries (Abalone ... Zymotachygraph), and 10 appendices. Includes colloquial names for some foods, and some trade names. *Class No:* 613.2(038)

[3534]

—The A-Z of nutritional health: a guide to the relation between diet and health. Mayes, A., *comp.* Wellingborough, Northants., Thorsons, 1991. 303p. tables. £7.99. ISBN: 0722524765.

Has *c*.2,000 entries, usually concise, A-Z. 'Fibre, dietary': 3p.; 'Proteins': 3p. Final table: 'Dietary restrictions practised by religious and ethnic groups', p.295. Bibliography, p.301-3. Clearly written; good layout. *Class No:* 613.2(038)

[3535]

—The Penguin encyclopedia of nutrition. Yudkin, J. Harmondsworth, Middlesex & New York, Penguin; Viking, 1985. 431p. ISBN: 0713916621.

Has entries 'Absorption ... Zinc'. 'Food additives': 2½p. Includes biographies. Numerous cross-references. Detailed, analytical index, p.393-431. Author was Professor of Nutrition and Dietetics at University College, London, 1954-71.

The Nutrition bible, by J. Anderson and B. Deskins (Morrow, 1995. 476p. $30) defines 2,500 terms and is useful for the many charts giving nutrient content of foods and comparing different varieties of the same food, *e.g.* 14 different types of milk are listed.

Class No: 613.2(038)

[3536]

LEITZMANN, C. and DAUER, U. Dictionary of nutrition. Stuttgart, Verlag Eugen Ulmer GmbH, 1996. 516p. ISBN: 3800121484.

c.3,000 English terms with English definitions and German, French, Italian, and Spanish equivalents. Many cross-references.

Class No: 613.2(038)

[3537]

RUSSELL, P.J. and WILLIAMS, A. The Nutrition and health dictionary. New York, Chapman and Hall, 1995. v,525p. graphs.,tables. £42.50. ISBN: 0412989816.

Contains terms covering not just human nutrition, but also those from medicine, economics, biochemistry, etc. which are linked to that subject area. Many cross-references, graphs, and tables. Subject index. For nutrition professionals and students. *Class No:* 613.2(038)

Reviews & Abstracts

[3538]

Nutrition abstracts and reviews. Series A. Human and experimental. Wallingford, Oxon., CAB International, 1931-. 12pa. £680; $1,190. ISSN: 03091295.

About 8,5000 abstracts pa. Main sections: Techniques - Foods - Physiology and biochemistry - Human health and nutrition - Disease and therapeutic nutrition. Cross-references. Abstracts not signed. Review article precedes abstracts. Author and subject (analytical) indexes per issue and annually. Online, CAB ABSTRACTS. Available on CABCD. *Class No:* 613.2(048)

Progress Reports

[3539]

Advances in food and nutrition research. San Diego, Academic Press, v.33- 1989-. Annual. ISSN: 10434526.

Previously *Advances in food research* 1948-88.

V.42 (1998. ix, 278p. ISBN 0120164426) has seven documented articles (*e.g.* 'Design of emulsification peptides', p.93-130. 6p. of references). A major source of reviews for nutritionists.

Class No: 613.2(055)

[3540]

World review of nutrition and dietetics. Basle & London, Karger; Wiley, 1959-. v.1-. Irregular. Price varies. ISSN: 00842230.

Each volume has documented contributions on a particular theme (*e.g.* v.49 (1986): 'Nutrition and the quality of life'), with an adequate index. Intended to provide a forum for critical reviews such as cannot be published in the ordinary journals, nor in textbooks. 'Reviews are necessarily coloured by the views of the authors, but most of them, though not all, succeed in providing a critical survey of the field. They also serve as valuable platforms to promulgate ideas' (*Chemistry & industry,* 6 August 1977, p.659). Highly priced (v.55(1988). 266p.: £96.25). *Class No:* 613.2(055)

Tables & Data Books

[3541]

BENDER, A.E. and BENDER, D.A. Nutrition: a reference handbook. Oxford, University Press, 1997. xxxvii, 573p. tables. £49.50. ISBN: 0192623680.

Arrangement is by topic. 29 chapters. 1. Historical development of nutritional concepts ... 7. Carbohydrates ... 15. Vitamin E and Selenium ... 21. Folate and Vitamin B12 ... 29. Miscellaneous tables. References p.515-43. Index, p.544-73. Mainly tabular in format, aimed at workers in fields of diet, health, food or nutrition sciences. 'We hope that we have managed to include the information to answer any nutrition-related questions that any reader may ask' (*Introduction*). *Class No:* 613.2(083)

[3542]

CARPER, J. Food - your miracle medicine: how food can prevent and treat over 100 symptoms and problems. London, Simon and Schuster, 1994. xiv,511p. £9.99 ISBN: 0671713361.

Arranged by medical condition - cardiovascular system, digestive system, cancer (p.189-252, subdivided into general information and six types of cancer), with foods suggested to prevent or alleviate problems, and those likely to worsen it. Index, p.485-511. Intended for the general reader. *Class No:* 613.2(083)

[3543]

Food composition and nutrition tables. Compiled by H. Scherz, and others, on behalf of the Bundesministerium für Ernährung Landwirtschaft und Forsten, Bonn. 5th ed. Stuttgart, Medpharm; Boca Raton, CRC Press, 1994. xxviii, 1091p. tables. $225. ISBN: 3887630270; 0849375509.

3rd ed., 1986.

An extensive revision covering: Milk and milk products; Fats and oil/margarine; Meat; Fish and molluscs; Cereals; Vegetables, fruits. Glossary of the food constituents. Data columns: protein, fat, carbohydrates, constituents. New tables, *e.g.* Soy milk. Tables are mainly in English, with captions in English, French, and German, and have been revised for improved legibility. Subject and author indexes. For all nutritional experts. *Class No:* 613.2(083)

[3544]

McCANCE, R.A. and WIDDOWSON, E.M. The Composition of foods. 5th rev. and extended ed. London, Royal Society of Chemistry; Ministry of Agriculture, Fisheries and Food, 1991. xiii,462p. tables. £35. ISBN: 0851863914.

3 sections: 1. Introduction - 2. Tables, p.21-388 (*e.g.* Milk and milk products; Herbs and spices; Nuts; Beverages) - 3. Appendices (*e.g.* Organic aids; Recipes; References; Index). Supplements published from 1992. A standard work.

1st supp., *Fruit and nuts.* (1992. 144p. £24.50); 2nd supp., *Vegetable dishes.* (1992. 200p. £24.50); 3rd supp. to the 4th ed., *Cereals and cereal products.* (1988. 147p.); 4th supp., *Miscellaneous foods.* (1994. 193p.); 5th supp., *Meat, poultry and game.* (1995. 161p.). 6th supp., *Meat products and dishes.* (1996. 162p. £25.95); 7th supp., *Fatty acids.* (1998. 200p. £32.50).

The nutrient composition data are also available on floppy disk in ASCII format. *Class No:* 613.2(083)

[3545]

—BRIGGS, D. and WAHLQVIST, M. Food facts: the complete no-fads plain facts guide to healthy eating. Harmondsworth, Middlesex, Penguin Books, 1984. [vii], 256p. illus., diagrs., tables, charts. ISBN: 0140465421.

First published by Penguin Books Australia.

Features 50 detailed food charts, p.45-222. Lists of further reading and organizations. Detailed analytical index, p.254-6. A bargain. *Class No:* 613.2(083)

[3546]

—BRITISH MEDICAL ASSOCIATION. Diet, nutrition and health: report of the Board of Science and Education, March 1986. London, the Association, [1986]. 69p.

Has 6 sections: 1. General introduction - 2. Food trends - 3. Factors affecting food consumption - 4. Food and health - 5. Dietary objectives for the nation - 6. Implementing dietary objectives. 72 references, p.65-69. No index. Aims at providing guidance on what constitutes a healthy diet. *Class No:* 613.2(083)

[3547]
Manual of nutrition. 10th ed. London, HMSO, 1995. [ix], 166p. £5.95. ISBN: 0112429912.
First published 1945.
2 parts (13 sections). 1. Nutrients and their utilization (*e.g.* carbohydrates, fats, energy needs and food consumption, digestion and absorption of major nutrients, minerals, vitamins; dietary reference value for nutrients) - 2. Nutritional value of food and diets. 9. Appendices (7. Food additives; 9. Books for further reading (29 items)). *Class No: 613.2(083)*

[3548]
PENNINGTON, J.A.T. Bowes and Church's food values of portions commonly used. 16th ed. Philadelphia, Pa., Lippincott, 1993. 328p. tables. $29.95. ISBN: 0399550871.
Lists both generic and brand names. Includes values for proteins, cholesterol, fats, and vitamins. Tables for biotins, amino acids, caffeine, salicylates, etc. Bibliography of additional sources for food composition data. Good index. 'This is the source for information on food composition' ('Reference book bulletin', *Booklist*, January 1, 1994, p.846). *Class No: 613.2(083)*

[3549]
SKYPALA, I. What are you eating?: the food fact file. London, Michael O'Mara Books, 1998. 336p. tables. £17.99. ISBN: 1854792733.
Four sections: 1. What should we eat? - 2. Food in sickness and in health - 3. The balance of good health - 4. Ready-made meals and eating out. Section 3, p.59-304, consists of tables listing nutrients present in individual foods and meals. Index, p.332-6. A useful quick reference. *Class No: 613.2(083)*

Histories

[3550]
DRUMMOND, J.C. *and* **WILBRAHAM, A. The Englishman's food:** a history of five centuries of English diet. New and rev. ed. London, Cape, 1957 (reprinted 1991. London, Pimlico). 482p. illus., tables. £10.
First published 1939. 1991 reprint as *The Englishman's food: five centuries of English diet*.
5 parts (24 chapters): 1. Medieval and Tudor England - 2. The seventeenth century - 3. The eighteenth century - 4. The nineteenth century - 5. The twentieth century. 3 appendices, on diets and nutritional value tables. Many footnote references. Analytical index, p.471-82. A mine of information, dealing with such topics as scurvy, dental caries, prison diets, and English cooking of cabbages. *Class No: 613.2(091)*

[3551]
TOUSSAINT-SAMAT, M. A History of food. Blackwell, Oxford, 1992. 801p. £25. ISBN: 0631177418.
Nine chapters: 1. Collecting, gathering, hunting - 2. Stock-breeding, arable farming, meat, milk, cereals ... 9. Science and conscience in the diet. 14-page index. *Class No: 613.2(091)*

Vegetarianism

[3552]
DYER, J.C. Vegetarianism: an annotated bibliography. Metuchen, N.J., Scarecrow Press, 1982. xi, 280p. $22.50. ISBN: 081081532x.
1,412 entries. Part 1: Early works (pre-20th century, through 1899; 1900-1959); Part 2: Recent works, 1960-1980 (in 33 subject categories, *e.g.* 'Medical aspects of vegetarian diets'). Brief helpful annotations. Appendix lists 200 vegetarian cookbooks. Author and detailed subject index. 'Because of the wide range of material covered, this will be a useful source in both public and academic libraries' (*Reference books bulletin, 1983-1984*, p.102). *Class No: 613.261*

Industrial Health

Aerospace Medicine

[3553]
Aerospace medicine and biology: a continuing bibliography. Washington, National Aeronautics and Space Administration, Scientific and Technical Information Branch, 1952-. 12pa. $16.50.
Formerly *Aerospace references in medicine and biology*.
About 110 abstracts per issue. 5 categories: 51. Life sciences (general) - 52. Aerospace medicine - 53. Behavioral sciences - 54. Man/system technology and life support - 55. Planetary biology. 7 indexes: subject; personal author; corporate source; foreign technology; contract number; report number; accession number. Annual cumulative index. A selection of annotated references to unclassified reports and journal articles announced in the previous month's *Scientific and technical aerospace reports* (STAR) and *International aerospace abstracts* (IAA). *Class No: 613.69*

Physical Welfare

[3554]
WISEMAN, J. SAS survival guide. Glasgow, Harper Collins, 1993. 384p. illus. (incl. col.). £3.99. ISBN: 0004701674.
Previous ed. published as *The SAS survival handbook*, 1986.
Pocket sized guide (three inches high) listing essentials for outdoor survival (equipment, water supply), climate and terrain, food, camp craft, reading the signs (*e.g.* weather prediction), survival at sea (*e.g.* dangerous fish), rescue (*e.g.* signals and codes), health, disaster strategies. Fully illustrated (*e.g.* 'Arctic shelters', p.168-71, has nine small line-drawings). Boxed information. No index. The author served 26 years in the Special Air Service (SAS). *Class No: 613.7*

Sports Medicine

[3555]
Encyclopaedia of sports medicine. Oxford, Blackwell Scientific Publications, 1988-. ISBN: 0632019638, v.1; 0632030356, v.2; 0632030313, v.3; 0632033312, v.4; 0632037857, v.5; 0865429049, v.6.
V.1. *The Olympic book of sports medicine*, 1988, ed. by A. Dirix and others. xii,692p. 2. *Endurance in sport*, 1992, ed. by R.J. Shephard and P.-O. Astrand. xvi,638p. 3. *Strength and power in sport*, 1992, ed. by P.V. Komi. xii,404p. 4. *Sports injuries: basic principles of prevention and care*, 1993, ed. by P.A.F.H. Renstrom. xviii,482p. 5. *Clinical practice of sports injury prevention and care*, 1994, ed. by P.A.F.H. Renstrom. xviii,727p. 6. *The Child and adolescent athlete*, 1995, by O. Bar-Or. 720p. £67.50.
Produced by the International Olympic Committee's Medical Commission and the International Federation of Sports Medicine. V.2 has 66 contributing authors and 7 sections: 1. Definitions ... 3. Measurements of endurance ... 4. Principles of endurance preparation ... 7. Specific issues in individual sports. A bibliography is appended to each chapter. Abundant figures and graphs, with easy to read text. *Class No: 613.70*

[3556]
The Oxford dictionary of sports science and medicine. Kent, M., *ed.* 2nd ed. Oxford, University Press, 1998. xiv,568p. figs. £19.95. ISBN: 0192628453.
First published 1994.
Contains over 7,500 entries (A-band ... Zygomatic bone) with brief definitions. Four appendices: 1. Banned substances ... 4. Units of measurements and conversions. A useful quick reference tool. *Class No: 613.70*

[3557]
Oxford textbook of sports medicine. Harries, M., *and others.* 2nd ed. Oxford, University Press, 1998. xv,957p. illus.(some col.). £99. ISBN: 0192627171.
First published 1994.
93 contributors present signed chapters arranged in 7 sections: 1. Sports science (physiology, nutrition) - 2. Sport and the environment - 3. Medical aspects - 4. Acute sports injuries - 5. Chronic and overuse sports injuries - 6. Considerations for unique groups - 7. Special considerations. Index, p.925-57. *Class No: 613.70*

[3558]
PETERSON, L. *and* **RENSTRÖM, P. Sports injuries: their prevention and treatment.** London, Martin Dunitz, 1986. 488p. illus. (mostly col.). £19.95. ISBN: 0906348919.
Originally published in Sweden, 1983.
9 sections (6. Sports injuries by specific area, p.174-389; 'Tennis elbow'; 42/3p.; 3 col. illus., 1 black-and-white). Final sections: 8. Risks to children and adolescents; 9. Training of different parts of the body. Bibliography, p.463-5 (authors, A-Z). Glossary, p.466-77. Detailed analytical index, p.478-88. Attractively produced. *Class No: 613.70*

[3559]
POTPARIC, O. *and* **GIBSON, J. A Dictionary of sports injuries and disorders.** New York, Parthenon Publishing Group, 1996. 155p. £24. ISBN: 1850706867.
Definitions of *c.*400 terms, arranged A-Z (Abductor digiti (minimi) nerve entrapment ... Zygomatic fracture). Many cross-references. Alternative terms are also given. *Class No: 613.70*

[3560]
Textbook of science and medicine in sport. Bloomfield, J.E., *and others, eds.* Melbourne, Blackwell, with support of the Australian Sports Commission, 1992. xv,591p. illus. (col.), diagrs., graphs, tables. £34.50. ISBN: 0867937612.
5 parts (527 sections): 1. The anatomy and biomechanics of sports performance ... 4. Sports medicine, p.139-419 - 5. Special considerations in sports medicine. Detailed, analytical index. *Class No: 613.70*

[3561]
TVER, D.F. *and* **HUNT, H.F. Encyclopedic dictionary of sports medicine.** London, Chapman & Hall, 1986. 232p. illus. $32.50. ISBN: 0412013614.

Over 600 entries, A/Z, with a separate glossary (that should have been incorporated). 'Although it cannot compare in scope to the classic *Encyclopedia of sports sciences and medicine* (1971), it fills a need for a quick-reference tool defining illness and injuries related to sports and physical activities' (*Choice*, v.24(4), December 1986, p.611). For example, it includes entries on athlete's foot, altitude sickness, etc. *Class No:* 613.70

[3562]
The Year book of sports medicine. St Louis, MO., Mosby Year Book Inc. 1979-. Annual. $71.95 ISSN: 01620908.

A literature review from over 900 leading journals. The 1994 ed. (619p. illus. $68.95) includes sections: 'A discussion of the issue of football helmet removal in suspected cervical spine injuries'; 'The diagnosis and treatment of anterior instability in the throwing athlete'. Articles would be of interest to medical practitioners, teachers, sports scientists and physical educationalists. *Class No:* 613.70

Physical Education

[3563]
DIAGRAM GROUP. The Complete encyclopedia of exercises. New York & London, Paddington Press, 1979. 335p. diagrs.

More than 350 exercises of all types. Includes official national fitness programmes of the UK, USA and People's Republic of China. Crudely-drawn diagrams. Brief bibliography and index. *Class No:* 613.72

[3564]
—Trends and developments in physical education. Proceedings of the VII Commonwealth and International Conference on Sport, Physical Education, Dance, Recreation and Health, Glasgow, 18-23 July 1986. London & New York, Spon, 1986. xiii, 493p. diagrs., tables. ISBN: 0419139109.

Comprises 66 papers in 3 sections: 1. Keynote and supporting papers - 2. Theme related presentations (*e.g.* 'Sport within the Chinese educational system'. 18 references) - 3. Allied contributions. Brief index. *Class No:* 613.72

[3565]
Landmarks in the history of physical education. McIntosh, P.C., *and others*. 3rd ed. London, Routledge & Kegan Paul, 1981. x, 262p. illus. £9.99. ISBN: 0710007965.

Has 9 documented chapters (*e.g.* 'Landmarks in the history of physical education since World War II' with 54 references, plus 9 book items). Detailed, analytical index, p.251-62. Based on lectures given in the University of Birmingham. *Class No:* 613.72

[3566]
Sports documentation monthly bulletin. Birmingham, Centre for Sports Science and History, Univ. of Birmingham, 1971-. 12pa. £48(individuals), £60 (institutions). ISSN: 01421794.

About 3,500 abstracts pa. Two main parts. *General* (25 headings: Administration... Women, including Physical education and Sports injuries). *Individual sports and activities* (8 grouped headings: Association football, Australian Rules football ... Triathlon, Volleyball, Weightlifting, Wrestling). Author and subject indexes per issue, cumulated annually. *Class No:* 613.72

[3567]
Sportsearch: the contents of current journals/Titres d'articles courants. Gloucester, Ontario, Sports Information Resource Centre, 1985-. 12pa. $240. ISSN: 0882550x.

Monitors nearly 250 periodicals in sport and physical education over the world, most of them being published in English. 5 sections: 1. Specific sports - 2. Sport medicine and science - 3. Professional - 4. Abstracts - 5. Forthcoming conferences. Appended list of journal publishers and addresses. Available online via BRS, Data-Star and DIALOG; on *Sport Discus* CD-ROM (SilverPlatter). *Class No:* 613.72

[3568]
VAN DALEN, D.B. *and* **BENNETT, B.L. A World history of physical education,** cultural, philosophical, comparative. 2nd ed. Englewood Cliffs, N.J., Prentice Hall, 1971. x, 694p. ISBN: 0139679197.

First published 1953.

5 parts (28 chapters): 1. Physical education in ancient societies - 2. Physical education in the Middle Ages and early modern times - 3. Physical education in modern Europe (GDR, Swedish, Danish, French, English, Soviet, etc. nationalism) - 4. Physical education in the US (p.365-550). Final chapter 28: Physical education in education for internationalism. Well-footnoted. Bibliography, p.649-78 (by chapter). Name and analytical subject indexes. 'Will continue to be standard work in the field' (*Choice*, v.8(5/6), September 1971, p.702). *Class No:* 613.72

Sleep

[3569]
Sleep research. Los Angeles, Univ. of California, Brain Information Service, Brain Research Institute, 1972-. Annual. $92. ISSN: 00930407.

2 main sections: 'Ongoing research' (including abstracts; 290p.); 'A record of published research', - a 'sleep bibliography'. 20 subject categories are applied in the 'Sleep bibliography', *e.g.* 1. Books, reviews and theoretical discussions; 2. Neurophysiology - general; 16a. Pathology and disorders associated with sleep; 20. Biological rhythms and altered environments. KWIC index; author index. *Class No:* 613.79

[3570]
THORPY, M.J. *and* **YAGER, J. The Encyclopedia of sleep and sleep disorders.** New York, Facts on File, 1990. 356p. $45. ISBN: 0816018707.

880 terms, arranged A ... Z, varying in length from one sentence to several pages. Entries include cross-references and short bibliographies. Some of the information on the diagnostic classification and history of sleep disorders would be difficult to find elsewhere. Appendices include organizations providing information on sleep disorders and a list of sleep laboratories and centres. Intended for the layperson and the professional. *Class No:* 613.79

Alcoholism

[3571]
Alcohol and the public health: a study by a working party of the Faculty of Public Health Medicine and the Royal Colleges of Physicians on the prevention of harm related to the use of alcohol and other drugs. London, Macmillan in association with the Faculty of Public Health Medicine, Royal Colleges of Physicians, 1991. viii,218p. graphs. £30; £8.99. ISBN: 0333547780.

12 documented sections: 1. How much do we drink? - 2. Medical and psychiatric problems related to acohol use - 3. Alcohol and harm to the community ... 8. Provision of adequate and early help ... 11. Educating doctors - 12. Recommendations for actions. Useful addresses, p.204-6. Index. *Class No:* 613.81

[3572]
Lexicon to alcohol and drug terms. Geneva, World Health Organization, 1994. 65p. SFr17. ISBN: 9241544686.

A-Z list of definitions from 'Absolute alcohol' to 'Zoopsia'. Can be used with 10th revision of *International classification of diseases* (ICD10). *Class No:* 613.81

[3573]
MADDEN, J.S. A Guide to alcohol and drug dependence. 2nd ed. Bristol, Wright, 1984. xii, 288p. ISBN: 0723607559.

First published 1979, tables.

9 documented chapters (1. Terminology, prevalence, causation ... 3. Disabilities and social features in drug dependence, p.62-114, with 7½p. of references ... 8. Treatment of drug misuse and dependence - 9. Prevention). Analytical index, p.279-88. Author: Consultant-in-charge, Mersey Regional and Drug Dependence Unit. *Class No:* 613.81

[3574]
O'BRIEN, R. *and* **CHAFETZ, M. The Encyclopedia of alcoholism.** 2nd ed. New York, Facts on File, 1991. 346p. tables. $45. ISBN: 081601955x.

First published 1982.

Over 500 entries, A-Z, covering a wide variety of aspects of alcohol and alcoholism: production, consumption by ethnic groups, regulations and customs worldwide, medical aspects, psychological theories, treatment of alcoholism, organizations, and slang. Many statistical tables; 24p. of bibliographies. Subject index. Of the first ed., 'Clear, concise style; useful to both the layperson and the professional' (*Library journal*, 1 April 1983, p.733). US-slanted. *Class No:* 613.81

Drugs (Narcotics)

[3575]
ABEL, E.L. A Dictionary of drug abuse terms and terminology. Westport, Conn., Greenwood Press, 1984. xi, 187p. $49.95. ISBN: 0313240957.

Over 1,000 words and expressions on the use of drugs likely to be abused. Includes slang terms as well as common and technical words. Bibliography, p.185-7. Extensive, 'but by no means exhaustive' (*Science & technology libraries*, v.6(3), Spring 1986, p.132).

Updates Abel's *Marihuana dictionary: words, terms, events and persons relating to cannabis* (Greenwood Press, 1982. 136p. $39.95). *Class No:* 613.83

[3576]
ANDREWS, T. **A Bibliography of drug abuse, including alcohol and tobacco.** Littleton, Colo., Libraries Unlimited, 1977. Supplement, 1977-1980. 306p. + 312p. ISBN: 0872872521.

The main volume has 752 annotated entries. Items, mostly in English, are post-1960 publications. Part 1: general reference sources, including journal titles. Part 2: classed list of subject areas (*e.g.* psychology, education, the law, medical aspects, hallucinogens, marihuana, stimulants). Alcohol and tobacco products: 30p. Author/ title and subject indexes. The *Supplement, 1977-1981*, ($27.50) similarly arranged, covers 341 items. *Class No:* 613.83

[3577]
The Encyclopedia of drug abuse. Evans, G., *and others.* 2nd ed. New York, Facts on File, 1991. 370p. tables. $45. ISBN: 0816019568.

First published 1984.

Over 500 entries, ranging in length from several lines to several paragraphs. Covers political and legal aspects of drug abuse as well as medical and psychological issues. 4 appendices, including lists of drug slang, statistical tables, and a directory of relevant agencies. Extensive bibliography; index. Designed as a companion to *The Encyclopedia of alcoholism*, by R. O'Brien and M. Chafetz (1991) (*q.v.*). Of the first ed., 'No library should be without this comprehensive and timely resource on drug abuse' (*Choice*, v.22(3), November 1984, p.405-6). *Class No:* 613.83

[3578]
Encyclopedia of drugs and alcohol. Jaffe, J.H., *ed.* New York, Simon and Schuster/Macmillan, 1995. 4v. illus., tables., charts. $340. ISBN: 002897185x, set.

Contains 725 signed articles,*e.g.* 'Women and substance abuse' and 'Drunk driving', some as long as 60 pages, aimed at the student and researcher. V.1-3 are arranged A-Z, with a bibliography appended to each article. Many of the references are from the 1990s, and some have 1995 as the date of publication. The final volume contains five appendices relating to drug control in the US, *e.g.* directories of poison control centres by state. An index to the complete set is also included. The entries are longer than those in *Encyclopedia of alcoholism (q.v.)* and *Encyclopedia of drug abuse (q.v.)* (Facts on File, 1991) which also do not cover tobacco. *Class No:* 613.83

[3579]
Encyclopedia of psychoactive drugs. Leader, M., *ed.* London, Burke, 1985-.

Amphetamines, by S.E. Lukas. 1985. 101p. *LSD,* by M.E. Trulson. 1988. 121p. *Marijuana,* by M. Cohen. 1985. 109p. *Nicotine,* by J.E. Henningfield. 1985. *Alcohol: customs and rituals,* by T. Babor. 1988. 121p. *Alcohol and alcoholism,* by R. Fishman. 1988. 106p. *Inhalants,* by G.R. Glowa. 1988. 98p. *Barbiturates,* by J.E. Henningfield. 1988. 82p. *Cocaine,* by C.-E. Johanson. 1988. 97p. *Alcohol: teenage drinking,* by A.R. Lang. 1988. 133p. *Escape from anxiety and stress,* by T. McLellan. 1988. 82p. *Over-the-counter drugs,* by P. Sanberg and R.M.T. Krema. 1988. 118p. *Tranquillizers,* by G. Winger. 1988. 113p. *Heroin,* by F. Zackon. 1988. 129p. *Drugs and civilization,* by S. Freeman. 1988. 111p. *Methaqualone: the quest for oblivion,* by M. Carroll and G. Gallo. 1988. 148p. *Flowering plants,* by P.M. Richardson. 1988. 112p. *Mushrooms psychedelic fungi,* by P.E. Furst. 1988. 114p. *Getting help: treatments for drug abuse,* by S.H. Schnoll. 1989. 87p. *Treating mental illness,* by R. Byck. 1988. 83p. *Teenage depression and drugs,* by J. Chiles. 1988. 148p. *Caffeine,* by R.J. Gilbert. 1988. 135p.

A series of monographs, to be completed in 25v., - 3 on alcohol, 5 on hallucinogens, 3 on narcotics, 1 on non-prescription drugs, 4 on sedative hypnotics (including inhalants), 4 on stimulants, and 5 on understanding drugs (*British book news,* January 1986, p.11). *Class No:* 613.83

[3580]
Excerpta medica. 40. Drug dependence, alcohol abuse and alcoholism. Amsterdam, Elsevier Science, 1972-. 6pa. $909. ISSN: 09255958.

About 1,800 abstracts pa. 12 sections: 1. General aspects - 2. Drugs - 3. Individual response - 4. Diagnosis - 5. Medical treatment - 6. Rehabilitation - 7. Epidemiology - 8. Social aspects - 9. Prevention - 10. Human behavior - 11. Brain metabolism - 12. Drug related diseases. Subject and author indexes per issue and annually. Online, EMBASE and available on CD-ROM. *Class No:* 613.83

[3581]
Multilingual dictionary of narcotic drugs and psychotropic substances. London, HMSO, 1984. 876p. £37. ISBN: 0119080907.

Part 1 consists of monographs on the substances under international control. Data: structure, molecular weight, molecular formula, structural formula. Part 2 is a comprehensive A-Z cross-index of all the names cited in the monographs, in English, French and Russian, with Arabic and Chinese translations of the substances' names. Also *Addendum, 1* (x,65p. £11.50). *Class No:* 613.83

Smoking

[3582]
Bibliography on smoking and health. US Dept. of Health and Human Services, Public Health Service, Office on Smoking and Health; WHO collaborative Centre for Reference on Smoking and Health, 1967-. Annual. *Gratis.* ISSN: 00677361.

Supersedes *Smoking and health bulletin,* from 1989, listing articles on the prevention and cessation of tobacco use and protection of the non-smoker. *Class No:* 613.84

[3583]
Fourth report of the Independent Scientific Commmittee on Smoking and Health. Froggatt, P., *Sir, chairman.* London, HMSO, 1988. 68p. £5.70. ISBN: 0113211317.

5 sections: 1. The Product Modification programme - 2. Smoking related diseases and the reduction in sales weighted average tar yields ... 5. Additives to tobacco and cigarette papers. 7 appendices, *e.g.* 'Summary of research programmes supported through the Tobacco Products Research Trust'. The bibliography cites 97 papers. *Class No:* 613.84

[3584]
ROYAL COLLEGE OF PHYSICIANS OF LONDON. **Smoking or health:** the third report from the Royal College of Physicians of London. London, Pitman Medical, 1977. 128p. £5. ISBN: 0272794126.

First published 1962.

10 sections: 1. Tobacco consumption, promotion and control in Britain ... 3. Pharmacology and toxicology ... 4. Smoking and cancer ... 6. Smoking, bronchitis and other conditions ... 9. The smoking habit - 10. Prevention of disease due to smoking. Appended: 'Summary of recommendations for action'. 3p. of references, p.125-7. *Class No:* 613.84

Sex

[3585]
NEWMAN, J. *and* TILKE, A. **Sex education:** a guide to evaluation of materials. 2nd ed. Birmingham, Youth Libraries Group of the Library Association, 1989. 74p. £7.50. ISBN: 0946581096.

First published 1978.

7 sections: 1. Introduction - 2. Books for younger children ... 5. AIDS ... 7. Materials for parents, carers and teachers. Appendix: List of addresses, p.69-70. Author and subject indexes. *Class No:* 613.88

[3586]
Sex research: bibliographies from the Institute of Sex Research [Indiana University]. Scherer-Brewer, J. *and* Wright, R.W., *comps.* Tucson, Arizona, Oryx Press, 1979. x, 212p. $71.50. ISBN: 0720108330.

A list of 4,267 references on all aspects of human sexuality, stressing current rather than historical material. 11 major categories (*e.g.* Sex behaviour, sex variations, sex and society). Citations cover books, book chapters, periodical articles, conference papers and non-print items. Author and subject indexes. Well-organized. *Class No:* 613.88

Public Health

[3587]
Elsevier's dictionary of public health in six languages: English, French, Spanish, Italian, Dutch and German. Deblock, N.J.L., *comp.* Amsterdam, etc., Elsevier, 1976. [xii], 196p. £54.06; $82. ISBN: 0444413952.

2,363 English-base terms, (13,000 entries), with French, Spanish, Italian, Dutch and German equivalents and indexes. *Class No:* 614

[3588]
Excerpta medica. 17. Public health, social medicine and hygiene. Amsterdam, Elsevier Science, 1955-. 24pa. $2,617. ISSN: 09245723.

About 6,000 abstracts pa. 15 sections: 1. General aspects - 2. Statistics - 3. Communicable diseases - 4. Social hygiene - 5. Industrial medicine and work - 6. Dental hygiene - 7. Sanitation - 8. Military medicine - 9. Atomic warfare - 10. Nutrition - 11. Veterinary medicine - 12. Medical zoology - 13. Developing countries - 14. Ethnography - 15. Alternative medicine methods. Subject and author indexes per issue and annually. Online, EMBASE. Available on CD-ROM. *Class No:* 614

[3589]
Glossary of health care terminology. Hogarth, J., *comp.* Copenhagen, WHO Regional Office for Europe, 1975. 476p.

An English glossary of *c.*350 headwords with index entries for numerous other terms. Coverage: health care and services; resources; finance; manpower; building; drugs; management; planning; statistics. *Class No:* 614

[3590]

On the state of the public health: the annual report of the Chief Medical Officer of the Department of Health. London, Stationery Office, 1921-. Annual. Price varies. ISSN: 00726087.

10 sections: 1. Vital statistics - 2. The nation's health - 3. The strategy for health - 4. Health in the workplace - 5. Health care - 6. Communicable diseases - 7. Environmental health and toxicology - 8. Medical education, training and staffing - 9. Other events of interest in [year] - 10. International health. Appendix (tables). *Class No:* 614

[3591]

Oxford textbook of public health. Holland, W.W., *and others, eds.* 3rd ed. Oxford, University Press, 1997. 3v. diagrs., graphs, tables. £200, set; £70, ea. (*Oxford medical publications.*) ISBN: 0192625500, v.1; 0192625519, v.2; 0192625527, v.3; 0192625535, set.

First published 1984-85 as a revision of W. Hobson's *The theory and practice of public health* (1961).

1. *Influences of public health.* 2. *Methods of public health.* 3. *Applications in public health.*

Over 100 contributors. Extensive coverage, relating to developed countries. Includes sections on public health policies and strategies, provision of public health services, epidemiological approaches, health service planning and evaluation and needs of special client groups. Bibliographies are appended to each chapter and each volume has an index covering the set. *Class No:* 614

Pollution Control

Air Pollution

[3592]

GREAT BRITAIN. Department of the Environment. Air Pollution Monitoring Management Group. **Glossary of air pollution terms.** London, HMSO, 1979. ii, 47p. £2. (*Pollution report no.5.*) ISBN: 0117514322.

Defines about 500 terms in 1-7 lines. Appendix: 'List of specialist and more definitive glossaries, p.47. *Class No:* 614.71

[3593]

Handbook of air pollution analysis. Harrison, R.M. *and* Perry, R., *eds.* 2nd ed. London, Chapman & Hall, 1986. xxii, 634p.

12 contributors; 15 sections: 1. General sampling techniques - 2. Air pollution meteorology ... 5. Metal analysis ... 9. Halogen compounds ... 12. Analysis of precipitation ... 15. Quality assurance in air pollution monitoring. Index, p.628-34. *Class No:* 614.71

[3594]

TEKNISKA NOMENKLATURCENTRALEN. Luftbehandlingsordlista. [Glossary of air treatment.] Stockholm, the Centre, 1978. 204p. (*TNC 69.*)

742 numbered Swedish base terms, plus explanations, with equivalents and indexes in English, French, German and Finnish. *Class No:* 614.71

[3595]

WORLD HEALTH ORGANIZATION. Regional Office for Europe. **Glossary of air pollution.** Copenhagen, the Office, 1980. 114p. (*WHO Regional publications, European series, no.9.*) ISBN: 9290201096.

Defines *c.*1,000 terms, with cross-references. 'Spectroscopy', 'Hydrocarbons', - each ½p. *Class No:* 614.71

Radioactivity

[3596]

CRC handbook of management of radiation protection programs. Miller, K.L. *and* Weidner, W.A., *eds.* Boca Raton, Florida, CRC Press, 1988. 498p. tables. $139.95.

Includes substantial appendices on transport and packaging of radioactive materials. 2nd ed. (464p.) published 1992. *Class No:* 614.73

[3597]

Sources and effects of ionizing radiation. United Nations Scientific Committee on the effects of atomic radiation: UNSCEAR 1993 report to the General Assembly, with scientific annexes. New York, United Nations, 1993. 922p. graphs, tables. ISBN: 9211422000.

Consists of a brief report (p.1-30) of the committee, followed by nine appendices, p.31-922; A - Exposure from natural sources of radiation - B - Exposure from sources of man-made radiation ... E - Mechanisms of radiation oncogenesis ... I - Late deterministic effects in children. *Class No:* 614.73

[3598]

SUBE, R. Dictionary of radiation protection, radiobiology and nuclear medicine. Amsterdam, etc., Elsevier, 1986. 474p. $195; £95.31. ISBN: 0444995498.

An enlargement of R. Sube's *Dictionary of nuclear engineering in English, German, French, Russian* (1965).

About 12,000 English-base terms, with equivalents and indexes in German, French and Russian. *Class No:* 614.73

Public Safety

[3599]

COLEMAN, R.J. *and* **WILLIAMS, K.H. Hazardous materials dictionary.** Lancaster, Pa., Technomic Publishing Co., Inc., 1988. vi, 176p. tables. $39. ISBN: 0877625395.

About 2,500 brief entries. Includes acronyms and abbreviations. 'Hazardous material categories', p.69-70. Aims to 'help document and standardize the nomenclature of hazardous material' (*Introduction*). 2nd ed. (209p.) published 1994. *Class No:* 614.8

[3600]

The Health and safety directory, 1991/92. Kingston-upon-Thames, Kluwer, 1991. 950p. ISBN: 1870080432.

6 parts (25 sections): A. Regulatory authorities and national bodies - B. Regional and local public services - C. Organizations world-wide - D. Health & safety in industry - E. Professional bodies, safety organizations and training - F. Miscellaneous (section 19: Research; 21. Bibliography and sources of information; 22: Acronyms, synonyms and abbreviations)). Index of individuals; index of committees; detailed general index, p.863-910; classified section. *Class No:* 614.8

[3601]

Health and safety science abstracts. Bethesda, Md., Cambridge Scientific Abstracts, in conjunction with the Institute of Safety and Systems Management, Univ. of Southern California, 1987-. 4pa. $775pa (US); $835 (non US), including annual index. ISSN: 08929351.

Previously (1973-86) as *Safety science abstracts journal.*

Contains *c.*6,400 abstracts pa. 6 main sections: SGO: Monographs, conferences & bibliographies - SI: Industrial and occupational safety - ST: Transportation safety - SA: Aviation and aerospace safety - SM: Medical safety. Analytical subject and author indexes per issue and annually. Available on magnetic tape, online, and on CD-ROM. *Class No:* 614.8

[3602]

Information sources in environmental protection. Eagle, S. *and* Deschamps, J., *eds.* London, Bowker Saur, 1997. xiv,280p. £40 (*Guides to information sources.*) ISBN: 1857390628.

20 contributors. Four sections (17 chapters): 1. The official and unofficial - 2. Effects and the affected - 3. Practicalities (10. Land use) - 4. Controls and public awareness (13. Environmental law ... 16. The public library and the environment). Each chapter has a list of references appended. Appendix: Organizations and associations. Index. Doesn't aim to be comprehensive but provides evaluations of selected material. *Class No:* 614.8

Industrial & Occupational Safety

Databases

[3603]

HSELINE. Sheffield, Health and Safety Executive, 1981-.

A database and major source of bibliographical references to published documents on health and safety at work. About 148,000 references by December 1992, adding *c.*1,000 entries monthly. Coverage emphasizes mining, nuclear technology, explosions, explosives, hazardous chemicals, occupational hygiene, industrial pollution, occupational safety and agricultural safety. Online access, ESA-IRS, Pergamon INFOLINE. Available on CD-ROM. *Class No:* 614.8-027(003.4)

Bibliographies

[3604]

Health and safety at work. Winship, I., *comp.* Newcastle-upon-Tyne, Information North, 1989. 18p. £5. ISBN: 0906433053.

2 sections: Books (*e.g.* 'Legislation'; 'Construction'; 'Industrial diseases') - Other sources of information (*e.g.* 'Specialist information'; 'Computerized sources'; 'Organizations'). Most of the references are from the 1980s. *Class No:* 614.8-027(01)

Encyclopaedias

[3605]

Encyclopaedia of occupational health and safety. 4th ed. Geneva, International Labour Organization, 1998. 4v. (4018p.) illus. (incl. col. pl.), diagrs., plans, tables. $495. ISBN: 9221098141.

First published 1930; 3rd ed., 1983.

Extensive review of previous ed., reflecting recent trends and research. Gives a broad overview of available information, while still providing in-depth discussion on the majority of topics. Areas covered include occupational disease and its prevention, legal issues, and accident control measures. Descriptions of *c.*2,000 chemicals and their effects. V.4 contains indexes and cross-references. For all libraries involved in this area. *Class No:* 614.8-027(031)

Handbooks & Manuals

[3606]
Environmental and occupational medicine. Rom, W.N., *ed.* 2nd ed. Boston, Little, Brown & Co., 1992. xxv,1493p. illus., diagrs., graphs, tables. $106. ISBN: 0316755605.
Over 150 contributors. 125 documented sections. 3 parts: Diseases (1-53) - Exposures (56-100) - Control of environmental and occupational diseases and exposures (111-125). Detailed, analytical index, p.1449-93. An important contribution. *Class No:* 614.8-027(035)

[3607]
HARRINGTON, J.M. *and* **GILL, F.S. Occupational health.** 3rd ed. Oxford, Blackwell Scientific Publications, 1992. v,350p. £16.95. ISBN: 0632031891.
First published 1983.
13 sections: 1. Introduction - 2. Health services ... 5. Chemical agents - 6. Physical agents ... 9. Control of airborne contaminants ... 11. Some legal background to occupational health - 12. Education - 13. Sources of information. Index. This ed. incorporates the latest European legislative changes and has improved coverage of epidemiology and the evaluation of workplace exposure. *Class No:* 614.8-027(035)

[3608]
HUNTER, D. The Diseases of occupations. 6th ed. London, Hodder & Stoughton, 1978. xxii, 1257p., illus., graphs.
First published 1955.
15 chapters: 1. Man and his work - 2. The Industrial Revolution, 1760-1830 - 3. Social reforms in the 19th century - 4. Health of the worker in the twentieth century - 5. The ancient metals - 6. The other metals - 7. The newer metals - 8. The aromatic carbon compounds - 9. The aliphatic carbon compounds ... 12. Occupational diseases of the skin and occupational cancer - 13. Diseases due to physical agents - 14. The pneumoconioses - 15. Accidents. Detailed analytical index, p.1171-1257. *Class No:* 614.8-027(035)

[3609]
Safety at work. With 24 specialist contributors. In association with the Institution of Occupational Safety and Health. Ridley, J.R., *ed.* 4th ed. Oxford, Butterworth-Heinemann, 1994. 794p. illus., facsims., diagrs. ISBN: 0750607467.
First published 1983.
4 parts: 1. Law (8 chapters, *e.g.* 'Consumer protection') - 2. The management of risk (7 chapters, *e.g.* 'Records and statistics') - 3. Occupational health and hygiene (8 chapters, *e.g.* 'Radiation'). 4. General science (8 chapters, *e.g.* 'Safe use of chemicals'). 6 appendices (4. List of abbreviations). Bibliography appended to each chapter. Analytical index, p.782-94. *Class No:* 614.8-027(035)

Dictionaries

[3610]
CONFER, R.G. *and* **CONFER, T.R. Occupational health and safety: terms, definitions, and abbreviations.** Boca Raton, Fla., Lewis Publishers, 1994. 213p. $55. ISBN: 1566700779.
Quick reference tool listing *c.*5,000 terms, some of them a one-line explanation of acronyms. Coverage from many areas includes epidemiology, radiation, toxicology, biology, etc. For academic and public libraries. *Class No:* 614.8-027(038)

Reviews & Abstracts

[3611]
Excerpta medica. 35. Occupational health and industrial medicine. Amsterdam, Elsevier Science, 1971- . 12pa. $1,543. ISSN: 00144398.
About 2,500 abstracts pa. 22 sections: 1. General aspects - 2. Legislation. Social security - 3. Medical examination - 4. Labor, sex and age - 5. Working time, leisure activities - 6. Ergonomics - 7. Physical and mental activity: workload - 8. Micro environmental - 9. Physical environment - 10. Chemical environment ... 20. Accidents - Disablement. Rehabilitation - 22. Medical treatment. Subject and author indexes per issue and annually. Online, EMBASE and available on CD-ROM. *Class No:* 614.8-027(048)

Fires & Fire Prevention

[3612]
BRITISH STANDARDS INSTITUTION. Glossary of terms associated with fire. London, the Institution, 1975-90. 9pts. (*BS 4422.*)
1. *General terms and phenomena of fire.* 1987. 8p. £20. 2. *Structural fire protection.* 1990. 4p. £20. 3. *Fire detection and alarm.* 1990. 12p. £26. 4. *Fire extinguishing equipment.* 1994. 16p. £36. 5. *Smoke control.* 1989. 4p. £20. 6. *Evacuation and means of escape.* 1988. 4p. £20. 7. *Explosion detection and suppression means.* 1988. 4p. £20. 9. *Marine terms.* 1990. 4p. £20. *Class No:* 614.84

[3613]
BURKLIN, R.W. *and* **FURINGTON, R.Q. Fire terms: a guide to their meaning and use.** Boston, Mass., National Fire Prevention Association, 1980. vii, 212p. illus. $18.50. ISBN: 087765185x.
Has 'over 4,000 words and phrases in daily use in the United States, plus a selection of terms in current British use' (*Introduction*). 100 small illus. of equipment and procedures. Appendices list government agencies and private organizations. *Class No:* 614.84

[3614]
Dictionary of fire technology. 3rd ed. Leicester, Institution of Fire Engineers, 1979. 170p. £4. ISBN: 090334503x.
Defines *c.*3,500 terms, mostly technical, with cross-references. Entries average 2 lines. Refers, where relevant, to British Standards. 'It is believed that this book contains virtually every word and term a Fire Service Officer or Fire Engineer is likely to encounter' (*Preface*). *Class No:* 614.84

[3615]
—**Fire sciences dictionary.** Kuvshinoff, B.W., *and others.* New York, etc., Wiley; Interscience, 1977. viii, 439p. diagrs. ISBN: 0471511137.
Definitions, some with commentary, of *c.*10,000 terms in firemanship (*e.g.* 'Smoke': nearly 1 column). Draws on British and Canadian as well as US sources. Includes abbreviations. Some 150 diagrams. *Class No:* 614.84

[3616]
Fire-CD. London, SilverPlatter, 1995-. 4pa. CD-ROM. $1,077.
This CD-ROM gives full text coverage to many aspects of fire and fire prevention, including fire safety, legislation, Government regulations, etc. Documents included are relevant European Union directives, UK legislation, training manuals, UK White Papers, standards, reports, journals, and research. *Class No:* 614.84

[3617]
Fire directory, 1996. Hargreaves, V., *ed.* Redhill, Surrey, FMJ Publications, 1995. 512p. £75.80.
Pocket size directory listing government departments and agencies, public fire brigades in the UK (A-Z, p.21-52), industrial brigades, training centres, testing stations, etc. Buyer's guide section (also available on computer disk) p.179-430. Who's who in fire prevention p.431-510. Index to advertisers. *Class No:* 614.84

[3618]
Manual of firemanship. New series. London, HMSO, 1974-. Books 1-12, illus. (incl. pl.).
1. *Elements of combustion and extinction.* 1974. 128p. £4.95. 2. *Fire service equipment.* 2nd ed. 1992. 116p. 3. *Hand pumps, extinguishers and foam equipment.* 2nd ed. 1988. xiii,102p. £5.50. 4. *Incidents involving aircraft, shipping and railways.* 1985. xxvii, 266p. £7.50. 5. *Ladders and appliances.* 1984. 204p. £6.50. 6. *Breathing apparatus and resuscitation.* 2nd ed. 1989. xiii,123p. £5.95. 7. *Hydraulics, pumps and pump operation.* 2nd ed. 1986. xvi,208p. £6.50. 8. *Building construction and structural fire protection.* 2nd ed. 1992. 162p. 9. *Fire protection of buildings.* 2nd ed. 1990. xii,208p. £6.50. 10. *Fire brigade communications and mobilizing.* 2nd ed. 1991. xvi,149p. £5.95. 11. *Practical firemanship. 1.* 1981. 192p. £5.50. 12. *Practical firemanship. 2.* 1983. 276p. £7.95.
Covers both theory and practice. Book 9 has 3 parts: Fire extinguishing systems; Fire alarm systems; Fire-venting systems. 21 chapters. Glossary and terminology. Further reading, p.181-3. 47 plates. Includes concise practical instructions. *Class No:* 614.84

Hazardous Chemicals

Bibliographies

[3619]
LEES, N. Hazardous materials: sources of information on their transportation. London, the British Library, Science Reference and Information Service, 1990. [v],70p. (*British Library bibliography.*) ISBN: 0712307737.
7 sections: 1. Introduction ... 4. Landbased transport - 5. Water: sea and inland waterways - 7. Transfrontier movement of hazardous waste. 2 appendices: A. Useful addresses - B. Further information (*e.g.* 'List of abbreviations'). Author and subject indexes. Entries have annotations and state availability of items. Covers the period 1979 to January 1990. *Class No:* 614.878(01)

Handbooks & Manuals

[3620]
CARSON, P.A. *and* **MUMFORD, C.J. Hazardous chemicals handbook.** Oxford, Butterworth-Heinemann, 1994. 378p. ISBN: 0750602783.
Intended for use by emergency services personnel, environmental health officers etc., and written by two subject experts, but its value is diminished by a poor index - only 500 entries to cover all the chemicals mentioned in the book. *Class No:* 614.878(035)

[3621]
CRC handbook of laboratory safety. Furr, A.K., *ed.* 4th ed. Boca Raton, CRC Press, 1995. xxiii 783p. diagrs., tables. £99.50. ISBN: 0849325188.

First published 1967.

18 contributors. 6 chapters, with documented subsections: 1. Introduction - 2. Emergencies - 3. Laboratory facilities - design and equipment - 4. Laboratory operations - 5. Nonchemical laboratories - 6. Personal protective equipment. Appendix: Laboratory checklist. Index, p.759-83. *Class No:* 614.878(035)

[3622]
Genium's handbook of health, safety, and environmental data. New York, Genium Publishing Company, 1998. 2v.(4,000p.) illus. $295. ISBN: 0070245770.

10,000 illus. and covering more than 4,500 of the most common hazardous materials. Each entry includes data on toxicity, fire, synonyms, exposure limits, regulations, and analytical methods. Six indexes, including an index to chemicals by 87,500 material names. Also available on CD-ROM. *Class No:* 614.878(035)

[3623]
Handbook of reactive chemical hazards. 3rd ed. London, Butterworths, 1985. xxvi, 22, 1852p. chemical structures. ISBN: 0406013885.

First published 1975.

1. 'Special chemical section': about 4,900 elements and compounds in formula order, p.1-1414. 2. 'Class, group and topic section' follows, A-Z. 5 appendices: 1. Source title abbreviations used in references; 3. Glossary of abbreviations and technical terms used in the text; 4. Index of chemical names used in section 1; 5. Index of class, group and topic titles used in section 2. 'For research students, practising chemists, safety officers and others concerned with the safe handling of reactive chemicals' (*Introduction*). *Class No:* 614.878(035)

[3624]
Hazards in the chemical laboratory. Bretherick, L., *ed.* 4th ed. London, Royal Society of Chemistry, 1986. xiii, 604p. graphs, tables. £29.50. ISBN: 0851864899.

First published 1971; edited by G.D. Muir.

10 documented chapters. Introduction - Health and Safety at Work Act, 1974 - Safety planning and management - Fire protection - Reactive chemical hazards - Chemical hazards and toxicology - Health care and first aid - Hazardous chemicals - Precautions against radiation - An American view (legislation and safety measures in the US). Authoritative and practical. 5th ed. was due to be published late 1992/early 1993 (700p. £45). *Class No:* 614.878(035)

[3625]
MARSHALL, V.C. Major chemical hazards. Chichester, E. Horwood, Ltd; New York, etc., Wiley, 1987. [xiii], 587p. illus., diagrs., tables, plans, maps. £82. ISBN: 085312969x.

26 chapters (*e.g.* 4. The nature of hazards and risks; 9. The handling and storage of liquids and gases; 15. Case histories of toxic releases; 17. Methods of control of major chemical hazards; 24. Research and consultancy; 26. Summary and conclusions)). 4 appendices: 1. Glossary of terms - 2. Abbreviations - 3. Access to databases on chemical accidents - 4. Notes on the TNT equivalence of organic products. References (authors, A/Z), p.540-75. Non-analytical index. p.576-87. *Class No:* 614.878(035)

[3626]
Safe practices in chemical laboratories. London, Royal Society of Chemistry, 1989. [iv],50p. £10. ISBN: 0851863094.

Sections include: 'Organization for safety'; 'Design'; 'Operation'; 'Legislation and bibliography'. Appendix 1: The reporting of injurious diseases and dangerous occurrences regulations 1985. *Class No:* 614.878(035)

[3627]
SITTIG, M. Handbook of toxic and hazardous chemicals and carcinogens. 3rd ed. Park Ridge, N.J., Noyes Publications, 1991. 2v. xi,1685p. illus. ISBN: 0815512864.

Previously as *Handbook of toxic and hazardous chemicals.* (2nd ed. 1985).

Each chemical is classified as a carcinogen, hazardous substance, hazardous potential and/or priority toxic pollutants. An excellent source of economic information. *Class No:* 614.878(035)

Reviews & Abstracts

[3628]
Chemical hazards in industry. Cambridge, Royal Society of Chemistry, 1984-. Monthly. £482pa.; $811 (overseas). ISSN: 02655721.

200 abstracts per issue. A current-awareness monthly on health and safety, chemical and biological hazards, plant safety, legislation, protective equipment and storage related to the chemical and allied industries. Online via Data-Star and on CD-ROM. *Class No:* 614.878(048)

Tables & Data Books

[3629]
Hazardous chemical data book. Weiss, G., *ed.* 2nd ed. Park Ridge, N.J., Noyes Data, 1986. 1069p. $98. ISBN: 0815510721.

Information on 1,015 hazardous chemicals (1 per page): their physical and chemical properties, chemical reactivity, hazard classification, labelling, shipping data, fire, exposure and water pollution, health hazards and toxicity. *Class No:* 614.878(083)

[3630]
LEWIS, R.J., Sr. Hazardous chemicals desk reference. 4th ed. New York, John Wiley, 1997. xxii,1644p. $139. ISBN: 0471287792.

First published 1987.

Entries for more than 6,000 hazardous chemicals (400 added since previous ed.) presenting poisonous, irritant, corrosive, explosive and carcinogenic properties; 1-to-3 hazard ratings, synonyms, CAS, NIOSH & DOT number identifiers, standards for explosive limits & general physical properties. Also includes consensus reports from WHO and other major bodies. *Class No:* 614.878(083)

[3631]
LEWIS, R.J., Sr. Sax's dangerous properties of industrial materials. 9th ed. New York, Van Nostrand Reinhold, 1996. 3v. $500. ISBN: 0442020252, set; 0442022557, v.1; 0442022565, v.2; 0442022573, v.3.

7th ed. (1989), *Dangerous properties of industrial materials.*

V.1 contains 3 sections: 1. CAS Registry cross-index - 2. Synonym cross-index (contains French, German, Italian, Dutch, Japanese and Polish synonyms, in addition to English) - 3. References. V.2 and v.3 contain chemical data and hazard potential for over 20,000 substances (with 2,000 completely new chemicals, drugs, and biological agents) including 14,000 updated entries. 100,000 US and international synonyms. Available on CD-ROM ($495). *Class No:* 614.878(083)

[3632]
NORBACK, C.T. and NORBACK, J.C., eds. Hazardous chemicals on file. New York, Facts on File, 1988. Annual update. 3v. loose-leaf. $250, set. ISBN: 0816013535.

327 main entries for common toxic chemical substances. Data include exposure limit; leak and spill procedures; health hazards. More limited in coverage than Sax and Lewis but a quick reference tool for the general reader. US-slant. *Class No:* 614.878(083)

[3633]
PLUNKETT, E.R. Handbook of industrial toxicology. 3rd rev. ed. London, Edward Arnold, 1987. 605p. £92. ISBN: 071313626x.

2nd ed., 1976 [iii], 552p.

Intended as a quick reference guide; substances A-Z. Concise data on each: synonyms; description; occupational exposure threshold limit value; toxicity; preventive measures; references (if any). Appendices. Bibliography. Index. *Class No:* 614.878(083)

First Aid

[3634]
First aid manual: the authorised manual of St. John Ambulance, St. Andrew's Ambulance Association, and the British Red Cross. Webb, M., *and others.* 7th ed. London, Dorling Kindersley, 1997. 288p. illus.(col.). £9.99. ISBN: 0751303992.

Previous ed. published 1992.

19 sections: 1. What is first aid? ... 4. Resuscitation ... 7. Wounds and bleeding ... 10. Burns and scalds ... 14. Bites and stings ... 19. Emergency first aid. Index, p.281-87. Step-by-step instructions which are well illustrated. *Class No:* 614.88

[3635]
KIRBY, N.G. and MATHER, S.J. Baillière's handbook of first aid. 7th ed. London, Baillière Tindall, 1985. vii, 360p. illus. £7.95. ISBN: 0702010979.

First published 1941.

3 parts (36 sections): 1. Assessment of the casualty and casualty report - 2. Structure and function - 3. Clinical practice (15. Asphyxia and respiratory disorders ... 36. Transport by stretcher (p.331-52. 27 line-drawings)). Detailed, analytical index, p.353-60. Improved line-drawings. 'This book is intended for instructors and for those who will practise advanced first aid' (*Preface*). *Class No:* 614.88

[3636]
ROYAL LIFE SAVING SOCIETY. National Technical Committee. [Handbook, Royal Life Saving Society]. 4th ed. 8 booklets, in binder. illus. (incl. col.), charts.

First published 1963.

1. *Life saving and water safety.* iii, 31p. 2. *Water rescue skills.* 54p. 2nd ed., 1982. 40p. 3. *Teaching water safety.* 58p. £1.80. 4. *Life saving teachers guide.* 23p. £1.50. 5. *Resuscitation and first aid.* [viii], 38p. £2.50. 6. *The award scheme.* [v], 47p. 7. *Lifeguard manual.* 84p. £3.75. 8. *Examiners' guide and the award scheme.*

Sections 1, 2, 6, and 8 are available in one vol. (1990. £6.50). *Class No:* 614.88

Pharmacology

Databases

[3637]
World databases in biosciences and pharmacology. Armstrong, C.J. and Fenton, R.R., eds. East Grinstead, Bowker, 1996. 1325p. £195. ISBN: 1857390687.

World databases, p.1-1080, arranged in eight subject areas, with three chapters on techniques, commercial aspects, and patents. Addresses p.1081-1112. Subject, producer, and database name indexes, p.1113-1325. Attempts 'to make sense of the myriad files in the marketplace' (*Introduction*). *Class No:* 615(003.4)

Bibliographies

[3638]
ANDREWS, T. Guide to the literature of pharmacy and the pharmaceutical sciences. Littleton, Colo., Libraries Unlimited, 1986. viii, 383p. tables. ISBN: 0872574206.

958 numbered entries. 10 sections: 1. Guides to the literature and bibliographies - 2. Abstracting and indexing services - 3. Reviews, surveys and yearbooks - 4. Pharmacopoeias and standards - 5. Comprehensive works - 6. Pharmacy - 7. Historical works - 8. Dictionaries and encyclopedias - 9. Databases and catalogs - 10. Handbooks, manuals and guides. 'The primary intended audience ... is librarians, especially those in pharmaceutical, medical, health science and related libraries'. (*Preface*). *Class No:* 615(01)

[3639]
Information sources in pharmaceuticals. Pickering, W.R., ed. London, Bowker-Saur, 1990. xvii,566p. tables. £55. ISBN: 0408025182.

International in scope; 28 contributors; not an annotated bibliography. 3 parts (20 documented chapters): Part 1 details information needed at all stages of drug development; Part 2 emphasizes information produced by the medical community and the pharmaceutical industry; Part 3 considers information needs and availability. General appendix to Part 3 contains sections on literature sources; online databases; centres of excellence; health statistics. Index, p.554-66. Editor is in charge of the Wellcome Foundation's central R & D information function. *Class No:* 615(01)

[3640]
Side effects of drugs annual: a yearly critical survey of the world's literature on adverse reactions to drugs. Amsterdam, Elsevier Science, 1977-. v.1-. Irregular. ISSN: 03786080.

Succeeds *Side effects of drugs: adverse reactions as reported in the medical literature of the world,* (sub-title:1955/56-76) and sub-title *a worldwide yearly survey of new data and trends,* (1996-).

Annual 21 (1998. 590p.) has 75 contributors, 49 documented papers. Articles include, 'Drugs acting on the immune system'; 'Radiological contrast agents'; 'Insulin, glucagon and oral hypoglycemic drugs'. Address list of national centres participating in the WHO drug monitoring scheme. Indexes of drugs, and side effects. Available online via DATA-STAR and Ovid Technologies, and on CD-ROM. *Class No:* 615(01)

[3641]
STRICKLAND-HODGE, B. *and* **JEPSON, M.H. Keyguide to information sources in pharmacy.** London, Mansell, 1989. x,178p. £30. ISBN: 0720119669.

Part 1: Survey of pharmacy and its information sources (4 sections, *e.g.* 3. Finding out about pharmacy; 4. Keeping up to date with the subject) - Part 2: Bibliography (615 annotated entries, under type of literature: directories ... online database directories) - Part 3: Directory of organizations (selected list of national pharmaceutical associations, arranged alphabetically by country). 716 numbered entries in all. Index, combining authors, titles and type of publication, p.163-78. Aimed at the information worker and researcher. *Class No:* 615(01)

Encyclopaedias

[3642]
Encyclopedia of pharmaceutical technology. Swarbrick, J. *and* Boylan, J.C., eds. New York, Marcel Dekker, 1988-1998. 18v. $195 per v. (subscription); $230 per individual v.

V.1. *Absorption of drugs to bioavailability of drugs and Bioequivalence.* V.2. *Biodegradable polyester polymers as drug carriers to Clinical pharmacokinetics and pharmacodynamics.* V.3. *Clinical supplies to Dermal diffusion and delivery principles.* V.4. *Design of drugs to Drying and driers.* V.5 *Economic characteristics of the R & D-intensive pharmaceutical industry to Fermentation processes.* V.9. *Liposomes as pharmaceutical dosage forms to Microencapsulation.* V.10. *Microsphere technology and applications to Nuclear magnetic resonance in pharmaceutical technology.* V.11. *Nuclear medicine and pharmacy to Permeation enhancement through*

....(contd.)
skin. V.12. *Pharmaceutical packaging to Prescribing of drugs.* V.13. *Preservation of pharmaceutical products to Salt forms of drugs.* V.14. *Self-medication to Technology transfer consideration for pharmaceuticals.* 1996. V.15. *Thermal analysis of drugs and drug products to Unit processes in pharmacy: fundamentals.* 1996. V.16. *Unit processes in pharmacy: the operations to Zeta potential.* 1997. V.17. *Index for volumes 1-16.* 1997. V.18. *Supplement 1.* 1998.

Multi-volume set which, at the time of writing, is nearing completion. Includes illustrations (some coloured), bibliographies, and indexes. *Class No:* 615(031)

Dictionaries

[3643]
BOWMAN, W.C. *and* **BOWMAN, A. Dictionary of pharmacology.** Oxford, Blackwell Scientific Publications, 1986. vii, 234p. diagrs. £12.50. ISBN: 0632011319.

About 1,000 terms, including cross-references (*e.g.* 'Abstinence syndrome' *See* 'Withdrawal syndrome'). Many entries contain references to relevant literature. Drug names are generally excluded, although drug classes and prototype drugs have entries. Terms are in large, bold, easily readable type. 'More an encyclopedia than a dictionary in the depth of information given for most entries' (*British book news,* September 1986, p.536). *Class No:* 615(038)

[3644]
—**Thesaurus of subject terms and cross-references to 'International pharmaceutical abstracts'.** 4th ed. Bethesda, Md., American Society of Hospital Pharmacists, 1987. 195p. ISBN: 0930530772.

Also known as *IPA thesaurus and frequency list.*
Class No: 615(038)

[3645]
DRAKE, E. *and* **DRAKE, R. Saunders pharmaceutical word book.** Philadelphia, W.B. Saunders Company, 1999. 707p. £21.50. ISBN: 072167268x.

26,282 entries, giving brief definitions. Six appendices: A. Sound-alikes - B. Investigational code names - C. Street drug slang - D. Abbreviations used with medications and dosages - E. Therapeutic drug levels - F. The most prescribed drugs. Appears to now be revised annually. *Class No:* 615(038)

[3646]
Pharmacological and chemical synonyms: a collection of names of drugs, pesticides and other compounds drawn from the medical literature of the world. Marler, E.E.J., comp. 10th ed. Amsterdam, Elsevier, 1994. viii,593p. $285. ISBN: 0444820817.

First published 1956.

Entry is under international accepted name, with cross-references from alternate, proprietary or chemical names. 'Intended as a guide to the identification of substances which appear under a bewildering variety of names' (*Preface to 3rd ed.*). *Class No:* 615(038)

[3647]
SLIOSBERG, A. Dictionary of pharmaceutical science and techniques, in five languages, English-French-Italian-Spanish-German. Amsterdam, etc., Elsevier, 1968-80. 2v. (xii, 686p. + 552p.). $255.50, set. ISBN: 0444405445, v.1; 0444416641, v.2; 0686859251, set.

1. *Pharmaceutical technology.* 1968 (2nd reprint, 1980). 2. *Materia medica.*

V.1 has 7,507 numbered English terms, with French, Italian, Spanish and German equivalents and indexes. Lacks chemical formulas; inadequate cross-references. V.2 has 4,688 entries for English, French, Italian Spanish, German and Latin equivalents and indexes. *Class No:* 615(038)

[3648]
WINSLADE, J. Dictionary of drug development. 2nd ed. Aldershot, Hants., Acix Scientific Publications, 1997. iv,212p. £15.75. ISBN: 1901635007.

First published 1996.

Brief definitions. 'Covers all aspects of the drug development process from discovery to the marketing of the new drug' (*Editorial comment*). Three sections: Common abbreviations, p.1-48; Definitions of common terms, p.49-202; Understanding medical terms. Appendix: Declaration of Helsinki. Many cross-references. *Class No:* 615(038)

Reviews & Abstracts

[3649]
Excerpta medica. 30. Clinical and experimental pharmacology. Amsterdam, etc., Elsevier Science, 1992-. 32pa. $3,909. ISSN: 09272798.

Formerly *Excerpta medica. 30. Pharmacology*, 1948-91.

About 8,000 abstracts pa. 37 sections: 1. General aspects - 2. Automotive nervous system - 3. Motor system ... 6. Psychotropic and neurotropic agents ... 11. Cardiovascular system ... 16. Respiratory systems ... 18. Endocrine system ... 20. Anti-infective agents ... 24.

....(contd.)
Antineoplastic agents and carcinogens ... 27. Immunologic agents ... 31. Vehicles and additives - 32. Toxic substances and antagonists - 33. Drug addiction ... 37. Drugs used in opthalmology. Online, EMBASE and available on CD-ROM. *Class No:* 615(048)

[3650]
International pharmaceutical abstracts: key to the world's literature of pharmacy. Bethesda, Md., American Society of Health System Pharmacists, 1964-. 24pa. $425. ISSN: 00208264.
*c.*15,000 abstracts are added annually. 26 sections (Pharmaceutical technology ... Adverse drug reactions ... Pharmaceutics ... Pharmaceutical chemistry ... Environmental toxicology ... Sociology, economics and ethics - Pharmacy practise). Subject index per issue; semi-annual author and subject indexes. Available online and CD-ROM (1970-). *Class No:* 615(048)

Yearbooks & Directories

[3651]
Annual register of pharmaceutical chemists. London, Pharmaceutical Society of Great Britain. Annual. £110. ISSN: 0260955x.
The 1995 *Register* (1089p. ISBN: 0953693153) comprises names and addresses of all registered pharmacists, bodies operating retail pharmacy businesses and names of their superintendents, and business titles/addresses of all the registered retail pharmacies in country, county (pre-1929 county names), and town order. *Class No:* 615(058)

[3652]
SITTIG, M. *and* KOWALSKI, J.S. **Drug companies and products world guide.** Kingston, N.J., Sittig and Noyes, 1988. 596p. $60. ISBN: 0800242394.
Entries, arranged A-Z, are drawn from *Pharmaceutical manufacturing encyclopedia* (Sittig and Noyes). Coverage extends to over 2,000 US and 2,000 non-US companies. *Class No:* 615(058)

Histories

[3653]
COWER, D.L. *and* HELFAND, W.H. **Pharmacy: an illustrated history.** New York, Abrams, 1990. 272p. illus. $75. ISBN: 0810914980.
Traces the evolution of pharmacology from ancient civilizations to modern genetic engineering. Contains 308 high-quality illustrations, including 151 colour plates of sculptures, paintings, documents, manuscripts and institutions. *Class No:* 615(091)

[3654]
KREMERS, E. *and* URDANG, G. **Kremers and Urdang's history of pharmacy.** 4th ed., revised by G. Sonnedecker. Philadelphia, Pa., Lippincott, 1976. xv,571p. illus., ports.
First published 1940.
In 4 sections (18 chapters): 1. Pharmacy's early antecedents - 2. The rise of professional pharmacy in representative countries of Europe - 3. Pharmacy in the United States - 4. Discoveries and other contributions to society by pharmacists. 7 appendices, *e.g.* 1. Representative drugs of the American Indians. Notes and references, p.495-556. Index. *Class No:* 615(091)

Homeopathy

[3655]
CASTRO, M. **The Complete homeopathy handbook:** a guide to everyday health. London, Macmillan, 1990. 257p. figs. ISBN: 0333428889; 0330349260, pbk.
4 sections: 1. History, principles and prescribing - 2. The Materia Medicas and Repertories - 3. Prescribing guidelines and follow-through (Stress as a cause of disease ... Repertorising chart - Sample cases) - 4. The appendices (Glossary - First-aid kits, pharmacies and courses - Homeopaths and homeopathic organizations - Useful reading and bookshops).
Paperback ed. published in 1996. (Pan Books. xiv,568p. figs. £8.99). *Class No:* 615.015.32

[3656]
SMITH, T. **An Encyclopaedia of homoeopathy:** a comprehensive reference book and survey of the subject from its beginnings to the present day. Worthing, Sussex, Insight Editions, 1983. [viii], 283p. £9.95. ISBN: 0946670013.
About 1,000 entries, A-Z. Highlights history, philosophies, major personalities, remedies and illnesses. Cites major works by homeopathic practitioners. *Class No:* 615.015.32

Pharmacopoeias

Yearbooks & Directories

[3657]
Chemist & druggist directory. Tonbridge, Kent, Miller Freeman Information Services, 1868-. Annual. illus., tables. £107; £132 (overseas). ISSN: 02625881.
1996 ed. (490p. £97) has 11 sections including manufacturers and trade pharmaceutical supplies; brands and trade names; associations and organizations; tablet and capsule identification guide. *Class No:* 615.11(058)

Worldwide

[3658]
The International pharmacopeia. 3rd ed. Geneva, World Health Organization, 1979-. (v.1-4, 1979-94). $27.50, v.1; $41.95, v.2; $65, v.3; $76.50, v.4. ISBN: 9241541512.
To be in 5v. V.1 describes 42 general methods of analysis. V.2-3 consist of monographs: 'Quality specifications'. V.4. *Tests, methods, and general requirements; quality specifications for pharmaceutical substances, excipients, and dosage forms* (xv, 343p. 1994). V.2 (1981, 342p.) has specifications for 126 individual drugs widely used in health care. Although published by WHO, the series, produced by an international group of experts, does not have legal force in itself. *Class No:* 615.11(100)

Great Britain

[3659]
British national formulary London, Royal Pharmaceutical Society of Great Britain, 1981-. 2pa. £16.95. ISSN: 0260535x.
Pocket-sized for easy reference for those involved in prescribing and dispensing, arranged by physiological area of treatment. 1. Gastro-intestinal system ... 3. Respiratory system ... 5. Infections ... 9. Nutrition and blood ... 15. Anaesthesia. Appendices, index of manufacturers, general index. *Class No:* 615.11(410)

[3660]
British pharmacopoeia 1998. Published on the recommendation of the Medicines Commission pursuant to the Medicines Act 1968, and notified in draft to the European Commission in accordance with Directive 83/189/EEC (as amended). 16th ed. London, Stationery Office, 1998. 2v. 2,166p.+ appendices. £595. ISBN: 0113221002. ISSN: 13546643.
Published with *British pharmacopoeia (Veterinary) since 1994*.
Contains over 2,740 monographs on items and substances used in medicine. V.1 features medicinal and pharmaceutical substances. V.2 contains the formulary, blood products, immunological products, radiopharmaceutical preparations, surgical materials, and infra-red spectra. Formulary extensively revised. 24 appendices, *e.g.* 6. Qualitative sections and tests; 18. Methods of sterilisation. V.2 has index (395p.) to both volumes. Updated by an annual addendum, (1996 addendum; £80); all addenda are semi-cumulative and should be retained. Available on CD-ROM. *Class No:* 615.11(410)

[3661]
MARTINDALE, W. **The Extra pharmacopoeia.** Parfitt, K., *ed*. 32nd ed. London, The Pharmaceutical Press, 1999. 2500p. £235.
First published 1883.
An extensive revision of the previous edition. Prepared by 14 experts who have scanned over 30,000 references before giving their evaluations. 3 sections: 1. Monographs on drugs and ancillary substances (*c.*4,500 substances) - 2. Supplementary drugs and other substances (more than 800 drugs are covered) - 3. Preparations (*c.*70,000 preparations from 17 countries). Directory of manufacturers has 6,000 entries containing full names and addresses. Includes herbal medicines (200 monographs, 5,000 preparations). General index contains *c.*130,000 terms. Available online and on CD-ROM. *Class No:* 615.11(410)

USA

[3662]
Physicians' desk reference / PDR. Montvale, N.J., Medical Economics. Annual. $69.95. ISSN: 00934461.
First published 1947.
The 49th ed. 1995 covers 2,800 pharmaceuticals, A-Z. Data: indicates usage, dosage, description, clinical pharmacology, supply, warnings, contraindicators, adverse reactions, overdose and precautions. Appendices: Conversion tables ... Guide to management of drug overdose. Comprehensive. Prepared by drug manufacturers and their consultants. For the American practitioner.
Available on CD-ROM as *PDR library on CD-ROM: physicians' desk reference library* and also as part of EuroPharm CD-ROM. Also online. *Class No:* 615.11(73)

[3663]
—Complete drug reference: United States Pharmacopeia. 1999 ed. Washington, Consumer Reports Books, 1998. v.p. $39.95. ISBN: 0890439079.

Covers over-the-counter and prescription drugs in the US. Entries include details on proper use, side effects, precautions, and dosage. More comprehensive than *Physicians' desk reference* (*q.v.*) but written in clear and direct language for general readers, rather than those in the medical professions. *Class No:* 615.11(73)

[3664]
—Physicians' desk reference for nonprescription drugs. Montvale, N.J., Medical Economics, 1980-. Annual. $43.95. ISSN: 10441395.

A companion volume to *Physicians' desk reference,* for nonprescriptive drugs. Product identification and data, plus list of useful addresses. 16th ed., 1995, comprises 888p., including 100p. full-colour section illustrating proprietary pharmaceuticals and their packaging. *Class No:* 615.11(73)

[3665]
—Physicians GenRx. St. Louis, Mosby, 1995. 2700p. tables. Annual, with two updates. $67.75.

Covers generic drugs, arranged A-Z by generic name, with numerous cross-references. Data include chemical description; precautions; adverse reactions; usage; prices; suppliers; brand names. Keyword index. For the physician, pharmacist, and medical, public, and university libraries. Available on diskettes and as a CD-ROM edition which is updated quarterly. *Class No:* 615.11(73)

[3666]
The United States pharmacopeia (23rd revision, official from January 1, 1995) [and] *The National formulary* (18th ed., official from January 1, 1995). Rockville, Md., US Pharmacopeial Convention, 1994. 5-yearly. $450. ISSN: 01957996.

Combines and updates *The Pharmacopoeia of the United States of America* (1820-1975) and *The National formulary* (1888-1975).

The United States pharmacopoeia part covers official monographs of USPXXIII (drug substances and dosages, A-Z), Reagents. Tables. *The National formulary* part covers official monographs of NFXVII (pharmaceutical ingredients). Combined analytical index. Three supplements were published in 1995 and a new ed. is due to be published mid-1999. Available on CD-ROM. *Class No:* 615.11(73)

Medications & Drugs

[3667]
ABPI compendium of patient information leaflets. London, Datapharm, 1994. 744p. ISBN: 0907102115.

Contains leaflets for the information of patients produced by the Association of the British Pharmaceutical Industry. Arranged A-Z by name of issuing company. 'This first edition ... brings together examples of leaflets which will increasingly be found in packs of medicines. It is intended that the compendium will be regularly updated' (*Introduction*). *Class No:* 615.2

[3668]
The British Medical Association new guide to medicines and drugs. Henry, J., *ed.* 3rd ed. London, Dorling Kindersley, 1994. 472p. illus., diagrs. £12.99. ISBN: 0863186122.

Previously *The British Medical Association guide to medicines and drugs,* 2nd ed. 1991.

Structured information (general; quick reference; information for users; special precautions; possible adverse effects) on 235 of the most widely used drugs. 5 parts: 1. Understanding and using drugs - 2. Drug finder index - 3. Major drug groups - 4. A-Z of drugs - 5. Glossary and index. Appended drug poisoning emergency guide. *Class No:* 615.2

[3669]
Dictionary of drugs; chemical data, structures and bibliographies. Elks, J. and Ganellin, C.R., *eds.* London, Chapman and Hall, 1990. 2v. £815. ISBN: 0412273004.

Spin-off of the *Dictionary of organic compounds* (1982) and its annual supplements, plus additional data and references. Entries in v.1 include CAS registry numbers and literature references. V.2 contains name index; molecular formulae; CAS registry number index; type of compound index; structure index. Serves 'as a definitive source of concise data about significant drugs' (*Science & technology libraries,* v.11(2), 1991, p.219). Available online via HEILBRON database. *Class No:* 615.2

[3670]
Drugs handbook, 1995-96. Turner, P., *and others.* 15th ed. Basingstoke, Macmillan, 1995. xix,184p. ISBN: 0333630785. ISSN: 02653931.

First published 1978. Now annual.

Definitions of drug group names and medical terms. Part 1: Approved names (c.1,500, A-Z), p.1-102. - 2. Trade names (with cross-references to appropriate approved names), p.103-76. Data: mechanism of action; therapeutic indications; chief unwanted effects.

....(contd.)

Appendix: Common slang names for misused drugs. Paul Turner (deceased 1994) was Professor of Clinical Pharmacology, St. Bartholomew's Hospital, London. *Class No:* 615.2

[3671]
MIMS: monthly index of medical specialities. London, Haymarket Publishing, Ltd. 12pa. £72; £155 (overseas). ISSN: 09579095.

Lists prescriptive products. The March, 1996 issue has five sections: New this month - New products - Cumulative list - Prescription products, p.18-333 (covers over 3,500 products) - Tables. Manufacturers' and alphabetical indexes. For use only by registered medical practitioners in the UK, to whom it is distributed free. *Class No:* 615.2

[3672]
PARISH, P. Medical treatments: the benefits and risks. London, Penguin, 1991. xii,1310p. tables. £9.99. ISBN: 0140098992.

89 sections: 1. The benefits and risks of drug treatments ... 20. Angina ... 29. Migraine ... 49. Penicillins ... 75. Skin diseases ... 89. Risks of one drug reacting with another drug. 2 appendices (1. Generic prescription drugs and their brand names - 2. Update). Index. Packed with information and written for both the layperson and professional. Good value. *Class No:* 615.2

[3673]
PARISH, P. Medicines: a guide for everybody. 8th ed. Harmondsworth, Middx., Penguin Books, 1997. £12.99. ISBN: 0140513582.

First published 1976.

Layman's guide to the prescription and use of drugs for all types of disorders, *e.g.,* common cold, bronchial asthma, blood pressure, thyroid disorders, cancer, etc. Includes A-Z of all prescription medicines describing use, adverse effects and precautions. Of the 6th ed., 'The standard popular pharmacopoeia' (*Reference reviews,* v.3(1), March 1989, p.25). *Class No:* 615.2

[3674]
PEARCE, M.E. Medicines and poisons guide. 4th ed. London, Pharmaceutical Press, 1984. 220p. diagrs., tables. ISBN: 0853691738.

First published 1978.

Prepared in Law Dept. of the Pharmaceutical Society of Great Britain.

4 sections: 1. Medicines for human use - 2. Veterinary drugs, p.119-76 - 3. Non-medicinal poisons - 4. Prescribed dangerous substances, p.196-205. The guide is intended primarily as a practical guide to the legal classification of medicinal products and non-medical poisons for the purpose of retail sale or supply. *Class No:* 615.2

Origins of Medicines & Therapy

Plant Medicines

Bibliographies

[3675]
A Bibliography on herbs, herbal medicine, 'natural' foods, and unconventional medical treatment. Andrews, T., *and others.* Littleton, Colo., Libraries Unlimited, 1982. 339p.

749 entries, with comparative annotations, for both scientific and popular works. 21 chapters, in 2 parts: 4 chapters on reference items; 17 chapters, on subject areas (*e.g.* herb cookery; folk medicine). Appended directory of organizations, associations and groups. Author/ title and subject indexes. 'This exhaustive bibliography' (*Choice,* v.20(3), November 1982, p.405). *Class No:* 615.32(01)

[3676]
Herbs: an indexed bibliography, 1971-1980: the scientific literature on selected herbs, and aromatic and medicinal plants of the temperate zone. Simon, J.T., *and others.* Hamden, CT, Archon Books, 1984. xviii, 770p.

7,900 citations, covering 64 commercially significant herbs. Ten broad subject categories. Data on each herb: botanical, cultural and chemical uses. A short section includes books on herbs, reports, conferences and symposia, and general references. *Class No:* 615.32(01)

Handbooks & Manuals

[3677]
British herbal pharmacopoeia, 1990. Bournemouth, British Herbal Medicine Association. V1. 107p. ISBN: 0903032082.

First published 1971. Consolidated ed. 1983, ISBN 0903032074.

84 monographs arranged A-Z from Aloes to Yarrow. Data: characteristics, identification, quantitature, action. Methods of analysis p.93-97; reagents p.98-102; index 103-7. V.2 was announced in preparation in 1990, with a unified volume 'to follow'. The 1990 ed. does not supersede the 1983 ed. *Class No:* 615.32(035)

[3678]

CRC handbook of medicinal herbs. Duke, J.A. Boca Raton, Florida, CRC Press, 1985. [xi], 677p. illus, tables. $275. ISBN: 0849336309.

Catalogue of herbs, p. 1-516, with details of 365 medicinal species (uses, folk medicinal applications, chemistry and toxicity). 5 tables, p.517-98 (*e.g.* 1. Medicinal herbs, toxicity ranking and price list). References, p.585-594. *Class No:* 615.32(035)

[3679]

DARWIN, T. The Scots herbal: the plant lore of Scotland. Edinburgh, Mercat Press, 1996. xiv,198p. illus. £12.99. ISBN: 1873644604.

Two parts: 1. The role of wild plants - 2. The plant families. Data include Scots name, local name, Gaelic name. Descriptive information, habitat, and uses are given. Bibliography, index of plants, and general index. Some small black-and-white drawings. *Class No:* 615.32(035)

[3680]

GRIEVE, M. A Modern herbal: the medicinal, culinary, cosmetic and economic properties, cultivation, folklore of herbs, grasses, fungi, shrubs and trees, with all their modern scientific uses... [2nd ed.] edited by Mrs. C.F. Leyel. London, Cape, 1974. 1032p. illus.

First published 1931, in 2v.

Herbs are arranged A-Z under common names, followed by Latin names and orders; synonyms. Index of country names of plants covered. Many line-drawings. The work, an exhaustive compilation, is marred by its lack of reference to the sources of information. *Class No:* 615.32(035)

[3681]

HOFFMAN, D. New holistic herbal. 3rd ed. Shaftesbury, Element Books, 1990. 284p. £9.99. ISBN: 1852301937.

Describes the most effective herbs for treating the different body systems (digestive, respiratory, etc.). A very good herbal.

Thorson's guide to medical herbalism: a comprehensive and practical introduction by the same author (3rd ed. Thorson's 1991. £7.99) is more medical and technical. It 'would be excellent for any doctor wishing to use herbal remedies' (*British book news,* February 1992, p.78). *Class No:* 615.32(035)

[3682]

LAUNERT, E. The Hamlyn guide to edible and medicinal plants of Britain and Northern Europe. London, Hamlyn, 1981. 288p. col. illus. ISBN: 0600372162.

Published in paperback (Hamlyn, 1989; £6.99) as *Guide to edible and medicinal plants of Britain and Northern Europe.*

Colour illus. accompanied by brief descriptions and indication of habitat and distribution. Entries also state active ingredients, effect, parts used and application. Indicates differences between species that look alike. Short list of suppliers of medicinal herbs and plant-based preparations. Glossaries of botanical and medical terms, p.278-81. 4 appendices: 1. Notes on the most important ingredients of medicinal plants - 2. Table of edible plants, with their uses - 3. Recipes for edible plants - 4. List of common ailments and plant species recommended for their treatment. Bibliography, p.277. Index p.282-8. *Class No:* 615.32(035)

[3683]

MILLS, S.Y. The A-Z of modern herbalism: a comprehensive guide to practical herbal therapy. Wellingborough, Thorson's, 1989. 222p. £6.99. ISBN: 072251882x.

Previously published as *Dictionary of modern herbalism* (1985).

Arrangement is A-Z (Abortifacient ... Zingiber officinale). Data for herbs include synonyms; habitat; constituents; actions; applications; dosage. Brief list of useful addresses. Author is Joint Director of the Centre for Complementary Health Studies at the University of Exeter. *Class No:* 615.32(035)

[3684]

ROSS, I.A. Medicinal plants of the world: chemical constituents, traditional and modern medicinal uses. Totowa, N.J., Humana Press, 1999. xi,415p. illus. £72.50; $99.50. ISBN: 0896035425.

The title is something of a misnomer as only 26 plants are discussed. Data include, common name, botanical desciption, distribution, uses (includes a bibliographical reference), chemical constituents, pharmacological effects. Numerous colour illustrations; glossary; common name index; bibliography (67p., 1,600 items). 'No other single volume brings such depth and intense research to the systematic understanding of the uses and effects of the plants discussed' (*Reference books bulletin,* 15 February, 1999). For academic and research libraries covering this subject, but could also be useful in large public reference collections. *Class No:* 615.32(035)

Dictionaries

[3685]

Heilpflanzenlexikon: Wirkungen, Verordnung, Selbstmedikation. [Dictionary of medicinal plants: medicinal properties, prescription and self-medication.] Braun, H., *ed.* 6th ed. Stuttgart, Gustav Fischer Verlag, 1994. xii,692p. DM58. ISBN: 3437115510.

Introduction describes preparation, availability, and registration of herbal drugs. Describes *c.*300 medicinal plants. Data in each plant

....(*contd.*)

monograph include Latin and common names, plant family, origin and plant habitat, medicinal properties, active substances, and references on relevant pharmacological studies. Index of registered drug names in addition to an index listing medicinal plant names, active substances, and traditional herbal drug names. *Class No:* 615.32(038)

Therapeutic Treatments

Databases

[3686]

Complementary medicine index. London, British Library, 1986-. 3.5in. diskette. 12pa. £170. ISSN: 09506667.

Contains *c.*3,000 mainly English-language citations pa. *Class No:* 615.8(003.4)

Bibliographies

[3687]

ALLAN, B. Guide to information sources in alternative therapy. Aldershot, Gower, 1988. viii,216p. £27.50. ISBN: 0566056119.

3 parts: 1. Information sources in alternative therapy (1. Introduction ... 4. Searching for information) - 2. The information sources: a bibliography (5. General information sources ... 8. Specialized sources: rebirthing to yoga) - 3. People, organizations and activities. Index (includes authors, subjects and titles) p.193-216. Not comprehensive but aims to be a starting point for finding required information. *Class No:* 615.8(01)

[3688]

WEST, R.W. *and* **TREVELYAN, J.E. Alternative medicine: a bibliography of books in English.** London, Mansell, 1985. xiii, 210p. £35. ISBN: 0720117216.

2,189 entries with one-line annotations. 8 sections: Homoepathy - Herbal medicine - Naturopathy - Clinical nutrition - Osteopathy - Chiropractice - Chinese medicine - Acupuncture. Non-analytical index. Aims to 'provide a good balanced 'first' that is of use to all who have an interest in alternative medicine' (*Introduction*). *Class No:* 615.8(01)

Encyclopaedias

[3689]

The Encyclopedia of complementary medicine. Endacott, M., *ed.* [s.l.], Carlton, 1996. 320p. illus.(col). £17.99. ISBN: 1858681898.

30 contributors, seven parts: 1. Natural healing - 2. The power of plants ... 6. Massage and touch - 7. Eastern therapies. Glossary of terms, p.288-91. Bibliography, p.292-96. Useful addresses, p.297-309. Index, p.310-18. Numerous colour photographs and coloured information panels. For public libraries. *Class No:* 615.8(031)

[3690]

Reader's Digest family guide to alternative medicine. London, Reader's Digest Association, 1991. 399p. figs., illus. £25.95. ISBN: 0276420101.

Arranged A-Z (About healing ... Zone therapy) and lists alternative methods of treating more than 200 ailments. Entries vary in length, *e.g.* 'Dysentery', 1 column; 'Immune system', 4 pages. Also gives orthodox views of alternative treatments. Bibliography and index. *Class No:* 615.8(031)

[3691]

SMYTH, A. The Complete encyclopedia of natural health. London, Thorson's, 1997. xiv,428p. figs. £9.99. ISBN: 0722534558.

First published in 1994 as *Gentle medicine.*

Main section is 'Ailments A-Z', p.14-404. Data for each ailment can include a description, prevention, and treatment (practical advice; dietary; aromatherapy; herbal; homoeopathy; Chinese medicine; acupressure; reflexology; exercise; orthodox treatment). Four appendices: 1. Therapies - associations; 2. Ailment support groups and information; 3. Distributors and suppliers; 4. Further reading *Class No:* 615.8(031)

[3692]

STANWAY, A. Alternative medicine: a guide to natural therapies. Rev. ed. Harmondsworth, Penguin Books, 1986. 319p. diagrs. ISBN: 0140085610.

Information on 32 therapies, arranged A-Z (*e.g.* Acupuncture; Biofeedback; Naturopathy, Yoga). Each entry carries a definition, background, how it's done, how it works, why does it work, what's it used for, does it work etc. Useful bibliography, p.50-63. Index. *Class No:* 615.8(031)

[3693]

STILLERMAN, E. **The Encyclopedia of bodywork:** from acupuncture to zone therapy. New York, Facts on File, 1996. xiv,320p. figs. £28. ISBN: 0816031878.

Provides information on more than 200 alternative therapies. A US bias is reflected in the resource and Boards of Massage lists but the numerous notes, further reading, and bibliography will have universal value. *Class No:* 615.8(031)

[3694]

WILDWOOD, C. **The Bloomsbury encyclopedia of aromatherapy.** London, Bloomsbury, 1996. xiii, 302p. illus. £11.99; £9.99. ISBN: 0747520852; 1856278549.

Paperback bears imprint 'Grange Books'.

Seven parts. 1. Basic principles (Brief history ... Essential oil safety ... Creative therapeutic blending) - 2. Aromatherapeutics - 3. Body, mind, and soul - 4. Massage - 5. Aesthetic aromatherapy - 6. Home and garden - 7. Aromatic profiles. Glossary, bibliography (2p.), index, p.296-302. Uncomplicated introduction to the subject; includes erotic aspects. *Class No:* 615.8(031)

Dictionaries

[3695]

SEGEN, J.C. **Dictionary of alternative medicine.** Stamford, Conn., Appleton and Lange, 1998. 407p. illus.,tables. £18;$29.95. ISBN: 0838516203.

Descriptive entries for all types of alternative medicine. Synonyms are listed and there are numerous cross-references. Many entries list further reading. An extensive bibliography lists the sources used in compiling the dictionary. *Class No:* 615.8(038)

Great Britain

[3696]

Alternative medicine in Britain. Saks, M., *ed.* Oxford, Clarendon Press, 1992. x,271p. £35; £9.95. ISBN: 0198272782.

18 contributors. 4 parts (18 documented chapters): 1. Health care in Britain before the mid-nineteenth century - 2. The rise of medical orthodoxy and the development of alternative medicine - 3. Alternative medicine in modern Britain - 4. Alternative medicine: the future. Detailed, analytical index. *Class No:* 615.8(410)

Acupuncture

[3697]

CAMPBELL, A. **Acupuncture: the modern scientific approach.** London, etc., Faber and Faber, 1987. xi, [2], 151p. $4.95. ISBN: 057114652x.

10 documented chapters: 1. Traditional Chinese medicine -2. Scientific acupuncture - 3. Learning acupuncture - 4. Acupuncture tools and their use - 5. General principles - 6. The treatment of musculoskeletal disorders - 7. Other disorders - 8. Electro-acupuncture and other specialised techniques - 9. Transcutaneous electrical nerve stimulation - 10. Clinical research in acupuncture. Annotated bibliography, p.143-5. Detailed, non-analytical index. Author is consultant physician, Royal London Homoeopathic Hospital. *Class No:* 615.814

Hydrotherapy & Spas

[3698]

DENBIGH, K. **A Hundred British spas.** London, Spa Publications, 1981. xxi, 287p. illus, maps, plans. ISBN: 0150757403.

8 sections: 1. Early spas of noble patronage - 2. London's old spas - 3. A ring of spas - 4. Spas patronised by George III - 5. Regency and early Victorian spas - 6. Early hydropathic spas - 7. Rural and provincial spas - 8. Spas of the north (*e.g.* Harrogate). Pharmaceutical notes (saline, chalybrate and sulphur waters). Bibliography, p.281-2. Detailed analytical index. 87 illus., 42 location maps and plans. *Class No:* 615.838

[3699]

JOSEPH, J. **Spa-finders guide to spa vacations at home and abroad.** New York, John Wiley, 1990. xi,286p. $12.95. ISBN: 0471515558.

Provides complete descriptions for 120 spas throughout the world, although most are in the US. Covers seven major types of spas: Fitness and beauty spas; Luxury spas; Weight-loss spas; New Age retreats; Mineral spas; Spas abroad. Spa almanac, p.273-9, groups spas according to their strengths, *e.g.* 'Spas for women only'; 'Vegetarian spas'. *Class No:* 615.838

Radiology

[3700]

ETTER, L.E. **Glossary of words and phrases used in radiology, nuclear medicine, and ultrasound.** 2nd ed. Springfield, Ill., C.C. Thomas, 1970. xxv, 355p. illus., diagrs., tables. $45. ISBN: 0398005265.

First published 1960 as *Glossary of words and phrases used in radiology and nuclear medicine.*

Definitions of *c.*7,000 words and phrases. Footnote references. Prelims. include list of eponyms, and index of radiological and ultrasonic reports (p.52-96). Appendix of keyed figures, p.349-55. 'Prepared from various sources for medical secretaries, x-ray technicians, medical students and residents in radiology ... ' (*Title-page*). *Class No:* 615.849

[3701]

Excerpta medica. 14. Radiology. Amsterdam, Elsevier Science, 1947-. 20pa. $2,035. ISSN: 00144185.

About 8,000 abstracts pa. 6 sections: 1. General aspects - 2. Physics and techniques - 3. Hazards and protection - 4. Radiology - 5. Radiodiagnosis - 6. Radiotherapy. Analytical subject and author indexes per issue and annually. Online, EMBASE; CD-ROM. *Class No:* 615.849

[3702]

Excerpta medica. 23. Nuclear medicine. Amsterdam, Elsevier Science, 1964-. 10pa. $1,325. ISSN: 00144274.

About 5,000 abstracts pa. 8 sections: 1. General aspects - 2. Nuclear physics in biology and medicine - 3. Radiochemistry - 4. Radiation hygiene - 5. Radiology - 6. Tracer techniques - 7. Diagnostics - 8. Therapy. Subject and author indexes per issue and annually. Online, EMBASE; CD-ROM. *Class No:* 615.849

[3703]

ITURRALDIE, M.P. **Dictionary and handbook of nuclear medicine and clinical imaging.** Boston, Mass., CRC, 1990. 520p. $125. ISBN: 0849332338.

Contains over 500 terms, some of them unique, in Part 1. Part 2 comprises tables, *e.g.* Chemical properties of substances used in imaging; measurements and calculations. *Class No:* 615.849

[3704]

MYERS, P.A. *and* MARTIN, T.A. **Glossary for radiologic technologists.** New York, Praeger, 1981. ix, [i], 194p. illus., diagrs., graphs. $35. ISBN: 0275913511.

About 1,500 concise, 1-4 line entries. Appended (p.165-92) terminology of procedures; electrical symbols; x-ray circuit; weights and measures. References, p.193-4. *Class No:* 615.849

[3705]

—BRITISH STANDARDS INSTITUTION. Glossary of electrotechnical, power, telecommunication, electronics, lighting and colour terms. Terms particular to electromedical equipemnt. Radiology and radiological physics terminology. London, BSI, 1985. 58p. £80. (*BS 4727: Pt.5: Group 01:1985.*)

Supersedes BS 2597:1955.

About 400 terms. Sections include: General terms; Ionizing radiations; Radiological apparatus; Dosimetry; Radiation protection. Appendix: A. Values of fundamental physical constants. Index. *Class No:* 615.849

Psychotherapy

[3706]

WALROND-SKINNER, S. **A Dictionary of psychotherapy.** London, Routledge & Kegan Paul/Methuen, 1986. [xi], 379p. £40. ISBN: 0710099789.

About 850 documented entries (*e.g.* 'Cartesian': 1½ columns; 6 references, 2 cross-references; 'Leadership': 1½ columns, 6 references, 3 cross-references) Brief biographies (*e.g.* Jung). Embraces classical concepts as well as new psychotherapies. The author is currently Associate Director of Ordinands and Tutor in Pastoral Studies for the Diocese of Bristol. 'This new dictionary definitely fills a gap in the field' (*Choice*, v.24(2), October 1986, p.288). *Class No:* 615.851

Toxicology (Poisons)

Databases

[3707]

TOXLINE Bethesda, National Library of Medicine, 1966-.

Contains over 1 million records (50,000 records added annually) with abstracts of published and research material. Topics covered include occupational hazards, adverse drug reactions, air pollution, food contamination, etc. Also available on CD-ROM. *Class No:* 615.9(003.4)

Bibliographies

[3708]

HARGREAVES, J.M. Literature sources in toxicology: a survey. London, British Library, 1980. [v],70p. £8. ISBN: 0905984595.

British Library. Research & Development report, no.5542.

Includes such information sources as databases; databanks; manual sources; centres and research organizations in UK, USA, etc. Also, related programmes in progress of national and international organizations. Appendices: Addresses of on-line service suppliers; Sources of information used in the compiling of this survey; Selected references, p.69-70. 'Covers only those aspects of toxicology which relate to man and his environment' (*Introduction*).

Class No: 615.9(01)

[3709]

WEXLER, P. Information resources in toxicology. 2nd ed. New York, Elsevier, 1988. xxiv,510p. £67.81. ISBN: 0444012141.

First published 1982.

2 sections: 1. United States resources (16 chapters, *e.g.* 'History'; 'Journals'; 'Audiovisuals'; 'Poison control centres') - 2. International organizations (20 chapters, *e.g.* 'International Union of Toxicology'; 'China'; 'Italy'; 'Sweden'). Entries on books, journals, etc. are annotated. Concentrates on health effects. Topics not stressed include management of hazardous wastes, aspects of pollution control, drug, alcohol and tobacco abuse. Heavy US slant. *Class No:* 615.9(01)

Encyclopaedias & Dictionaries

[3710]

COLEMAN, R.J. and **WILLIAMS, K.H. Hazardous materials dictionary.** Lancaster, Pa., Technomic Publishing Co., Inc., 1988. vi, 176p. tables.

About 2,500 brief entries. Includes acronyms and abbreviations. 'Hazardous material categories', p.69-70. Aims 'to help document and standardize the nomenclature of hazardous material' (*Introduction*). 2nd ed. (209p.) published 1994. *Class No:* 615.9(03)

[3711]

Dictionary of plant toxins. Harborne, J.B. *and* Baxter, H., *eds.* Chichester, John Wiley, 1996. xv,523p. £140. ISBN: 0471951072.

*c.*1,500 substances known to have adverse effects on any animal life are listed. Data include structural formulae, the plants in which they occur, and reference to the primary literature. subject, plant species, molecular formulae, and common plant name indexes.

Class No: 615.9(03)

[3712]

Dictionary of toxicology. Hodgson, E., *and others.* 2nd ed. Basinstoke, Macmillan Reference, 1998. 504p. £75. ISBN: 1561592161.

First published 1988.

4,000 brief descriptions (800 new) rather than detailed definitions. Subject areas include chemicals, drugs, physiology. For the non-specialist scientist who is likely to encounter toxicological terms in the course of a study. Tends to have a US bias with regard to organizations and regulatory listings of chemicals, but some UK and European information is included. For academic and public reference collections. *Class No:* 615.9(03)

[3713]

LEWIS, R.A. Lewis' dictionary of toxicology. Boca Raton, Fla., Lewis Publishers, 1998. 1,127p. £64; $84.95. ISBN: 1566702232.

International in scope (includes local and scientific names) and covering all aspects of toxicology, *e.g.* ecotoxicology, nutritional toxicology. Many cross-references. 'This is a unique reference work' (*Choice*, September 1998, p.96). For toxicologists and academic libraries. *Class No:* 615.9(03)

[3714]

PEARCE, M.E. Medicines and poisons guide. 4th ed. London, Pharmaceutical Press, 1984. 220p. diagrs., tables. ISBN: 0853691738.

First published 1978.

Prepared in Law Dept. of the Pharmaceutical Society of Great Britain.

4 sections: 1. Medicines for human use - 2. Veterinary drugs, p.119-76 - 3. Non-medicinal poisons - 4. Prescribed dangerous substances, p.196-205. The guide is intended primarily as a practical guide to the legal classification of medicinal products and non-medical poisons for the purpose of retail sale or supply. *Class No:* 615.9(03)

[3715]

PLUNKETT, E.R. Handbook of industrial toxicology. 3rd rev. ed. London, Edward Arnold, 1987. 605p. £92. ISBN: 071313626x.

2nd ed., 1976 [iii], 552p.

Intended as a quick reference guide; substances A-Z. Concise data on each: synonyms; description; occupational exposure threshold limit value; toxicity; preventive measures; references (if any). Appendices. Bibliography. Index. *Class No:* 615.9(03)

Handbooks & Manuals

[3716]

Casarett and Doull's toxicology: the basic science of poisons. Amdur, M.O., *and others, eds.* 5th ed. New York, McGraw-Hill, 1996. xv,1111p. figs. $75. ISBN: 0071054766.

First published 1975, *Toxicology: the basic science of poisons*, L.J. Casarett and J. Doull, eds.

Five sections: 1. General principles of toxicology - 2. System toxicology - 3. Toxic agents - 4. Environmental toxicology - 5. Applications of toxicology. Index. Designed primarily to be used as a textbook for courses in toxicology although research scientists in toxicology will find some sections useful, as will those concerned with community health, food technology, agriculture, pharmacy, and veterinary medicine.

A *Companion handbook*, aimed at those without access to the main text and who need quick, concise information, has also been published (896p. 1998. $32). *Class No:* 615.9(035)

[3717]

General and applied toxicology. Ballantyne, B., *and others.* New York, Stockton Press; Basingstoke, Macmillan, 1993. 2v. (1456p.). ISBN: 1561591076; 0333498011.

Comprehensive account of toxicology and its applications, aimed at the undergraduate and new practitioner, in 67 chapters. 84 contributors. Analytical index (37p.) for both volumes, included in each. 'Abridged ed.' (57 chapters in 1v.) published in 1995 by Macmillan (ISBN: 0333631668). *Class No:* 615.9(035)

[3718]

SITTIG, M. Handbook of toxic and hazardous chemicals and carcinogens. 3rd ed. Park Ridge, N.J., Noyes Publications, 1991. 2v. xi,1685p. illus. ISBN: 0815512864.

Previously as *Handbook of toxic and hazardous chemicals.* (2nd ed. 1985).

Each chemical is classified as a carcinogen, hazardous substance, hazardous potential and/or priority toxic pollutants. An excellent source of economic information. *Class No:* 615.9(035)

[3719]

Toxicology desk reference: the toxic exposure and medical monitoring index. Ryan, R.P. *and* Terry, C.E., *eds.* 4th ed., 1997-98. Washington, Taylor and Francis, 1997. 3v.(xv,2414p.) £325; £395 (includes CD-ROM). ISBN: 1560326158.

Comprises A-Z of toxic substances, arranged under 'TDR Profiles', p57-2326. (*e.g.* Arsenic, p.261-98; discussed under general toxicology, chemical manifestations, lab. tests and interpretation, (US) Federal and state requirements, case reports and references (97), and OSHA standard details). Postal update service. *Class No:* 615.9(035)

Yearbooks & Directories

[3720]

REGULATORY ASSISTANCE CORPORATION. Directory of toxicological and related testing laboratories. New York, Hemisphere Publishing Corporation, 1991. xvi,102p. $99.95. ISBN: 0891169040.

Directory of US toxicology, ecotoxicology, environmental, analytical, and support service laboratories. 2 parts: 1. Listing of toxicology laboratories (data include: name and address; services offered; tests performed; special expertise; equipment available; key personnel; FDA approval) - 2. Appendices (A. Summary list of laboratory contacts - B. List of studies conducted and/or services provided - C. Types of chemicals tested). *Class No:* 615.9(058)

[3721]

Tackling toxics in everyday products: a directory of organizations. Lilienthal, N., *and others.* New York, INFORM, 1992. ix,179p. $19.95. ISBN: 091878056x.

Data on 253 international organizations (207 in the US). Includes academic institutions, government agencies, professional institutions, etc. *Class No:* 615.9(058)

Tables & Data Books

[3722]

LEWIS, R.J., *Sr.* **Hazardous chemicals desk reference.** 4th ed. New York, John Wiley, 1997. xxii,1644p. $139. ISBN: 0471287792.

First published 1987.

Entries for more than 6,000 hazardous chemicals (400 added since previous ed.) presenting poisonous, irritant, corrosive, explosive and carcinogenic properties; 1-to-3 hazard ratings, synonyms, CAS, NIOSH & DOT number identifiers, standards for explosive limits & general physical properties. Also includes consensus reports from WHO and other major bodies. *Class No:* 615.9(083)

[3723]

LEWIS, R.J., *Sr.* Sax's dangerous properties of industrial materials.
9th ed. New York, Van Nostrand Reinhold, 1996. 3v. $500. ISBN:
0442020252, set; 0442022557, v.1; 0442022565, v.2; 0442022573,
v.3.

7th ed. (1989), *Dangerous properties of industrial materials.*

V.1 contains 3 sections: 1. CAS Registry cross-index - 2. Synonym
cross-index (contains French, German, Italian, Dutch, Japanese and
Polish synonyms, in addition to English) - 3. References. V.2 and v.3
contain chemical data and hazard potential for over 20,000 substances
(with 2,000 completely new chemicals, drugs, and biological agents)
including 14,000 updated entries. 100,000 US and international
synonyms. Available on CD-ROM ($495). *Class No:* 615.9(083)

Europe

[3724]

FROHNE, D. *and* PLANDER, H.J. A Colour atlas of poisonous
plants: a handbook for pharmacists, doctors, toxicologists, and
biologists. London, Wolfe Publishing, 1984. 291p. illus (incl. col.),
diagrs., tables, chemical structures. £55. ISBN: 0723408394.

Translated from the 2nd German ed., by N.G. Bisset.

5 sections, of which 3, 'The most important plants with alleged or
actual toxic properties (Amaryllidacea ... Verbenaceae)' occupies p.31-
231. 'Taxus baccata (yew)', p.223-5, has 1 col. illus., 2 micrographs,
1 diagr., 1 table of boxed data. Bibliography; extensive index. Limited
to plants indigenous to/naturalised in Central and Western Europe, plus
commonly met decorative plants and house plants. *Class No:* 615.9(4)

Great Britain

[3725]

COOPER, M.R. Poisonous plants and fungi in Britain: animal and
human poisoning. London, Stationery Office, 1998. xviii, 398p. illus.
(incl. col.). £55. ISBN: 0112429815.

Revision of MAFF Bulletin 161, *British poisonous plants.* (last
reprinted 1979) and previously published in 1984 as *Poisonous plants
in Britain and their effects on animals and man.*

Over half of the book concerns the families of poisonous plants,
ranging form Alliaceae to Umbelliferae, but is more concerned with
their poisonous effects. Details involve, in each case, poisonous
principles, poisoning in animals, human poisoning and treatment, etc.
Complements Frohne and Plander's *A Colour atlas of poisonous plants*
(1984) (*q.v.*), being well-documented but deficient in illus. For
farmers, vets, and doctors. *Class No:* 615.9(410)

[3726]

Poisonous plants in Britain and Ireland: an identification system on
CD-ROM. London, HMSO, 1995. CD-ROM. £89.00.

Produced by the Royal Botanic Gardens, Kew and the National
Poisons Unit. System of visual identification for several thousand
species of toxic plants. Severity and type of toxicity is indicated and
advice on emergency aid is given. *Class No:* 615.9(410)

Clinical Medicine

[3727]

Current contents: Clinical medicine. Philadelphia, Pa., Institute for
Scientific Information, 1974-. Weekly. $730. ISSN: 08913358.

Formerly *Current contents. Clinical practice.*

Each issue reproduces contents-pages of *c.*200 issues of journals as
'Discipline guide', (General medicine ... Dermatology). Title-word
index author index; and address directory; publishers address
directory. Available online as CURRENT CONTENTS SEARCH, on
CD-ROM, and on diskette. Internet access as *Current Contents
Connect* at http://connect.isihost.com. *Class No:* 616

Types of Disorders

Inflammations

[3728]

Excerpta medica. 15. Chest diseases. Thoracic surgery and
tuberculosis. Amsterdam, Elsevier Science, 1948-. 16pa. $1,419.
ISSN: 00144193.

About 5,000 abstracts pa. 38 sections, *e.g.* 1. General aspects; 2.
Tuberculosis; 3. Pneumonia and other respiratory infections; 7.
Allergy and bronchial asthma; 8. Neoplastic diseases of the lung; 19.
Cardiovascular diseases related. Detailed analytical subject index and
author index per issue and annually. Online, EMBASE; CD-ROM.
Class No: 616.002

Tumours. Cancer

[3729]

Encyclopedia of cancer. Bertino, J.R., *ed.-in-chief.* San Diego,
Academic Press, 1996. 3v. 2134p. illus., tables. £385. ISBN:
012093230x, set; 0120932318, v.1(A-F); 0120932326, v.2(G-Q);
0120932334, v.3(R-Z).

Contains 163 articles by 297 scientists on various aspects of the
disease of cancer, including its epidemiology, treatment, and its
molecular and genetic processes. The text is arranged into articles
bearing specific titles (*.e.g.,* three articles on prostate cancer), although
there is no syndetic system among titles (*e.g.,* prostate cancer is also
listed under the 'Epidemiology' heading). However, the index, which
contains *c.*10,000 entries, appears to be comprehensive and brings
together prostate references which are not included in the three main
chapters. 'Glossary of key terms', p.2015-56. '*The Encyclopedia of
cancer* is an essential source for biological and health sciences
collections' (*Reference books bulletin,* 1/15 January 1997, p.892).
Class No: 616.006

[3730]

Excerpta medica. 16. Cancer. Amsterdam, Elsevier Science, 1953-.
32pa. $2,769. ISSN: 00144207.

About 10,000 abstracts pa. 3 sections, closely subdivided: 1.
General aspects - 2. Experimental cancer research - 3. Clinical aspects.
Detailed analytical subject index and author index per issue and
annually. Online, EMBASE; CD-ROM. *Class No:* 616.006

[3731]

International directory of cancer institutes and organizations. 5th ed.
Geneva, UICC, 1990.

Published under the auspices of the Committee on International
Collaborative Activities (CICA). Previously published as *International
directory of specialized cancer research and treatment establishments.*

Countries, Argentina ... Yugoslavia, and their international cancer
establishments, *e.g.* Australia, 14 entries; Taiwan, 2. Data: director:
major depts.; cancer-related personnel; projected expenditure; annual
cancer-patient statistics; fields of activity; annual report; cancer
registry ... Index of establishments; index of establishment directors
and departmental heads; member organizations of the UICC. Also
available on the Internet at: http://www.uicc.org/directory/.
Class No: 616.006

[3732]

The New cancer sourcebook: basic information about major forms and
stages of cancer. Cook, A.R., *ed.* Detroit, Mich., Omnigraphics,
1996. 1313p. $75. (*Health reference series, 12.*) ISBN: 0780800419.

Composed of 64 publications produced by US health agencies. Four
sections covering information on detection of cancer, therapy, coping
with cancer, and a glossary of common medical terms. Cancers which
predominantly afflict women are excluded. Well written.
Class No: 616.006

[3733]

—The Cancer reference book: direct and clear answers to everyone's
questions. Levitt, P.M., *and others.* Rev. ed. New York, Facts on
File, 1983. 287p. $24.95. ISBN: 0871966840.

First published 1979.

Topical chapters in question and answer form (*e.g.* 'What evidence
is there that cigarettes cause cancer?') on the nature of cancer, proven
and unproven methods of treatment, terminal care, current research
and theories on prevention. A lengthy chapter discusses how mortality
rates differ among various forms of cancer. Appended brief glossary, a
list of cancer centres worldwide, a list of British and American titles,
and a detailed index. 'Suitable for public libraries' (*Reference books
bulletin, 1983-84,* p.60). *Class No:* 616.006

[3734]

WORLD HEALTH ORGANIZATION. International Agency for
Research on Cancer (IARC). Directory of on-going research in
cancer epidemiology, 1992. Coleman, M.P., *and others, eds.* Lyons,
etc, IARC Publications, 1992. xxii,773p. £42. ISBN: 9283221176.

List of projects, Algeria ... Zimbabwe, 7 indexes: investigators;
topics; sites; types of study; chemicals; occupations; countries. List of
cancer registries. List of biological materials banks. Indexes on
diskette. *Class No:* 616.006

Deformities

[3735]

Excerpta medica. 21. Developmental biology and teratology.
Amsterdam, Elsevier Science, 1961-. 12pa. $1,657. ISSN: 00144258.

About 5,000 abstracts pa. 9 sections: 1. Books, reviews, congresses
- 2. Demography, epidemiology and geographic pathology - 3.
General biology of development - 4. Gonads, gametogenesis and
development - 5. Maternal-foetal relations - 6. Pathology and
teratology - 7. Experimental developmental biology - 8. Cell, tissue
and organ cultures - 9. Techniques. Subject and author indexes per
issue and annually. Online, EMBASE. Available on CD-ROM.
Class No: 616.007

[3736]

WYNBRANDT, J. *and* **LUDMAN, M.D. The Encyclopedia of genetic disorders and birth defects.** New York, Facts on File, 1991. 426p. tables. $45. ISBN: 0816019266.

Arranged A-Z (Aarskog syndrome ... Zygodactyly). Length of entries varies from a few paragraphs to more than three pages. Data include prenatal diagnosis, discovery and name, prognosis and incidence in the population. Names and addresses of relevant organizations are given. Cross-references and brief bibliography. Index enables user to locate entries by subject and by racial or ethnic group affected. No illustrations. US/Canada-slanted. *Class No:* 616.007

Diseases (Pathology)

Handbooks & Manuals

[3737]

Disease data book. Fry, J., *and others.* Lancaster etc., MTP Press, 1986. viii, 405p illus., diagr., graphs, tables. £33.75. ISBN: 0852009224.

Takes 22 important medical conditions, using an economic synoptic style. It follows throughout a sequence of questions and answers for each condition, - 'What is it? Who gets it when? What happens? What to do?' The sections range from 1: High blood pressure to 22: Cancers. Detailed analytical index, p.397-405. For rapid reference as an aide-mémoire on procedure for the medical trainee and others in the profession. *Class No:* 616.01(035)

[3738]

Human health and disease. Altman, P.L. *and* Katz, D.D., *comps. and eds.* Bethesda, Md., Federation of American Societies for Experimental Biology, 1977. xxi, [i], 435p. diagrs., graphs, tables. (*Biological handbooks,* 2.) ISBN: 0913822116.

More than 300 contributors. 7 parts (186 sections): 1. Infectious diseases - 2. Immunological factors - 3. Metabolic disorders - 4. Organ system diseases -5. Neurologic diseases - 6. Endocrinology and endocrinopathies - 7. Radiation. Numerous tables and references ('Adrenal hormones', p. 328-32; 40 references). Detailed, analytical index (p.375-435) includes entries for diagrams, footnote and headnote items). A mine of information; for specialists. *Class No:* 616.01(035)

Reviews & Abstracts

[3739]

Excerpta medica. 5. General pathology. Amsterdam, Elsevier Science, 1948-. 30pa. $3,167. ISSN: 00144096.

About 7,5000 abstracts pa. 4 main sections, closely subdivided: 1. General aspects of pathology - 2. General pathology - 3. Organ pathology - 4. Techniques and laboratory methods. Subject and author indexes per issue and annually. Online, EMBASE and available on CD-ROM. *Class No:* 616.01(048)

Nomenclatures

[3740]

International nomenclature of diseases. Geneva, Council for International Organizations of Medical Sciences; World Health Organization, 1979-. 4v.

V.2. *Infectious diseases.* 208p. 1987. V.3. *Diseases of the lower respiratory tract.* 1979. V.4. *Diseases of the digestive system.* 269p. 1991. V.5. *Cardiac and vascular diseases.* 113p. 1991.

'The principal objective of IND is to provide, for every morbid entity, a single recommended name' (*Introduction*).
Class No: 616.01(083.72)

[3741]

ROYAL COLLEGE OF PHYSICIANS OF LONDON. Joint Committee. **The Nomenclature of disease.** 8th ed. (subject of decennial revision). London, HMSO, 1960. xi, 398p.

15 sections: 1. Etiological classification - 2. Deseases of the body as a whole ... 14. Disease of the ear - 15. List of eponyms (p.229-48). Detailed analytical index, p.249-398. *Class No:* 616.01(083.72)

Maps & Atlases

[3742]

CLIFF, A.D. *and* **HAGGETT, P. Atlas of disease distributions:** analytic approaches to epidemiological data. Oxford, Blackwell, 1988. 300p. £100; £25. ISBN: 0631131493.

International in scope. Primarily describes charting, statistical and mapping techniques but will be of interest to practitioners and students of epidemiology. Bibliographies appended to each chapter as well as a lengthy list of data sources, references and atlases at the end of the

....(contd.)

volume. 'Recommended for both the mapmaker and the user of epidemiological data' (*Choice*, v.27, no.2, 1989, p.282). *Class No:* 616.01(084.3)

[3743]

—Atlas of diseases. May, J.M., *ed.* New York, American Geographical Society, 1950-5. 17pl.

Coloured maps on 17 sheets, 64 x 97 cm. Each plate forms a unit, complete with text and list of sources on the verso. Aimed to map world distribution of some 25 diseases. 'An extension of the idea behind the Seucher Atlas', - a wartime German production showing epidemic diseases in the areas for which military operations were planned (*Geographical magazine*, April 1960. p.558). Now somewhat dated. *Class No:* 616.01(084.3)

[3744]

—The Welt-Seuchen Atlas. [World atlas of epidemic disease.] Hamburg, Falk-Verlag, 1952-61. 3v.

Hrsg. in Auftrage der Heidelberger Akademie der Wissenschaften von E. Rodenwaldt unter Mitarbeit von H.J. Jusatz.

An enlargement of the World War II *Seuchen Atlas*. It contains *c.*120 maps. Text in German and English; European slant. An outstanding, detailed atlas. *Class No:* 616.01(084.3)

[3745]

HOWE, G.M. National atlas of disease mortality in the United Kingdom. Rev. and enl. ed., on behalf of the Royal Geographical Society. London, Nelson, 1970. [viii], 197p. tables, maps.

First published 1963.

Part 1 includes 56 maps (27 x 22 cm.) of the 1st ed., covering 1954-58; part 2 has 29 new maps, and covers 1959-63. Maps, all on a 1:3 million scale, show geographical distribution of the Standard Mortality Ratio, 1954-58, in England, Wales, Scotland and Ireland for each sex separately for 14 groups of causes of death and for all causes of death. Maps and text, p.17-159. Transparencies can be superimposed, to reveal place names and administrative units. Helpful historical introduction. 'Intended for geographers and epidemiologists, and workers in public health and social services as well' (*British medical journal*, no.5714, 11 July 1970, p.94). Somewhat critically reviewed in *The Lancet*, 26 March 1970, p.658. *Class No:* 616.01(084.3)

Histories

[3746]

The Cambridge world history of human disease. Kiple, K.F., *ed.* Cambridge, University Press, 1993. xxiv,1176p. maps. $150. ISBN: 0521332869.

Eight sections, subdivided into chapters, with the first four section giving background information, the following three discussing disease in various parts of the world at different periods. The final part of the book covers individual diseases, from AIDS to Yellow fever. Extensive bibliographies with each chapter. Name (with short biographical details of the more prominent scientists) and subject indexes. *Class No:* 616.01(091)

Worldwide

[3747]

A World geography of human diseases. Howe, G.M., *ed.* London, New York, etc., Academic Press, 1977. xxviii, [2], 621p., diagrs., tables, maps. £102.50. ISBN: 0123571502.

22 contributors, nearly all British. States 'what is known about a selected range of important diseases in terms of pattern, distribution and trend' (*Foreword*). 20 sections (1. Schistosomiasis ... 20. Deficiency diseases), with appended references. Some of the maps are adapted from American Geographical Society's *Atlas of diseases*, 'It is a book which will become not only a standard work of reference, but also provoke debate on the major issues of world health and the provision of health services in the future' (*International affairs*, v.54(3), July 1978, p.475-6). 'Should be available to all students of medicine' (*British medical journal*, no.6114, 18 March 1978, p.708). *Class No:* 616.01(100)

Classifications

[3748]

Manual of the international statistical classification of diseases, injuries and causes of death. Based on the Recommendations of the Ninth Revision Conference, 1975, and adopted by the 25th World Health Assembly, 1977-78. Geneva, WHO, 1977-78. 2v. (xxxvii, 773p.; 670p.). tables.

8th revision, 1967-69. 2v.

V.1 tabulates 17 categories of diseases (1. Infectious and parasitic diseases ... 17. Injury and poisoning. Supplementary classification of external causes of injury and poisoning and of factors affecting health status and contact with health services. Also, medical participation and rules for classification (p.697-741). V.2, *Alphabetical index* to v.1. *Class No:* 616.01:001.33

[3749]
—International classification of impairments, disabilities and handicaps: a manual of classification relating to the consequences of disease. Geneva, WHO, 1980. 207p. tables. £7.25. ISBN: 9241541261.

Supplements the International classification of diseases. 4 sections, all subdivided: 1. The consequences of disease - 2. Classification of impairments - 3. Classification of disabilities - 4. Classification of handicaps. Only section 1 has any bibliographic references, and only section 2 has an index. *Class No:* 616.01:001.33

[3750]
—ROYAL COLLEGE OF GENERAL PRACTITIONERS. Classification of diseases, problems and disorders. London, the College, 1984. 70p. £4.75. ISBN: 0850840945.

Provides a summary version of the International classification. *Class No:* 616.01:001.33

Tropical Diseases

[3751]
Hunter's tropical medicine. Strickland, G.T. 7th ed. Philadelphia, Pa., W.B. Saunders, 1991. xxix,1153p. illus., micrographs, diagrs., graphs, tables, maps. $150. ISBN: 0721629709.

First published as *A Manual of tropical medicine* (1945). 6th ed., 1984.

116 contributors. 10 parts (1. Clinical practice in the tropics ... 10. Tropical diseases in a temperate climate). Many subdivisions. Extensive sections on parasitic diseases, nutritional deficiencies, and tuberculoses. Sectional and subsectional bibliographies. Detailed, analytical index, p.1097-1153). The most detailed and comprehensive clinical medicine textbook.

A new edition is planned for 1999. *Class No:* 616.01-036.21

[3752]
Manson's tropical diseases. Cook, G.C., *ed.* 20th ed. London, Saunders, 1996. xvi, 1797p. illus., diagrs., tables, maps.

First published 1898.

A well-established classic, overhauled for this ed. 5 sections totalling 83 chapters: 1. History of disease and warm climates. 2A. Symptoms and signs. 2B. System-oriented disease. 3. Related specialties in the Tropics. 4. Environmental/genetic disorders. 5. Infections (*e.g.* chapter 58. Leprosy, p.1016-46). 93 contributors. Index. p.1755-79. *Class No:* 616.01-036.21

[3753]
Tropical diseases bulletin. Wallingford, Bureau of Hygiene and Tropical Diseases, CAB International, 1912-. 12pa. £220; $585. ISSN: 00413240.

V.93(4), April 1996 issue contains 299 abstracts. Sections: Environmental health - Community health - Diseases and their control - Medical entomolgy. Adequate cross-references. Author and subject indexes per issue and annually. Earlier subtitle: 'selective and critical abstracts and reviews of world literature in all aspects of health and disease in tropical and sub-tropical regions'. Available online via DIMDI. *Class No:* 616.01-036.21

Epidemics

[3754]
A Dictionary of epidemiology. Last, J.M., *and others.* 3rd ed. New York, Oxford Univ. Press; International Epidemiology Association, 1995. xvii,180p. ISBN: 0195096673.

*c.*1,400 entries, including cross-references, 300 new to this edition. 78 contributors. Appended list of sources, p.177-80. For undergraduates and clinicians. *Class No:* 616.01-036.22

[3755]
Encyclopedia of plague and pestilence. Kohn, G.C., *ed.* New York, Facts on File, 1995. viii, 408p. £21.95. ISBN: 0816027587.

Does not claim to be comprehensive but lists major and unusual epidemics throughout the world from ancient times to the present. Arranged A-Z (Afghan influenza epidemic of 1918 ... Zanzibar cholera epidemic of 1869) with each entry listing a few items of further reading. Timetable of plague and pestilence, p.360-72. Bibliography, p.373-91. Geographical appendix, p.393-400. Useful index, p.401-8. *Class No:* 616.01-036.22

Patient types

Paediatrics

[3756]
Excerpta medica. 7. Pediatrics and pediatric surgery. Amsterdam, Elsevier Science, 1947-. 18pa. $2,104. ISSN: 03736512.

Formerly *Pediatrics,* 1947-72.

About 8,000 abstracts pa. 41 sections: 1. General aspects ... 5.

....(contd.)
Newborn, infant and fetus ... 10. Handicapped child ... 12. Preventive and social pediatrics ... 19. Cardiovascular system ... 21. Respiratory system ... 2. Nervous system ... 25. Metabolism ... 31. Locomotor system ... 35. Accidents ... 40. Children in hospital - 41. Cancer. Subject and author indexes per issue and annually. Online, EMBASE and on CD-ROM. *Class No:* 616.01-053.2

Geriatrics

Databases

[3757]
AGELINE. Washington, DC, American Association of Retired Persons, 1978-.

Database containing over 39,000 references with abstracts of material (English language only) published since 1978 (selective coverage of pre-1978 items). *c.*3,000 references are added annually. Based on the collection of AARP's National Gerontology Research Center and covers about 500 journals in addition to books, conference papers, government documents etc. Subject coverage includes psychological, political, social and economic aspects of aging. US-slanted. Available through BRS and DIALOG, and on CD-ROM. *Class No:* 616.01-053.9(003.4)

CD-ROM

[3758]
AgeInfo. London, Library and Information Service, Centre for Policy on Ageing, 1999. 1 CD-ROM.

Contains over 30,000 books, articles, and reports from the specialist collection on social gerontology held at the Centre. Data on 3,500 organizations worldwide. Also has an international 'Calendar of events' listing conferences, training sessions, and meetings. *Class No:* 616.01-053.9(003.40)

Bibliographies

[3759]
ETHEL PERCY ANDRUS GERONTOLOGY CENTER. Library. **Catalogs of the Ethel Percy Andrus Gerontology Center,** University of Southern California. Boston, Mass., G.K. Hall, 1976. 2v. (1193p.). 1. *Author-title catalog.* 2. *Subject catalog.*

22,500 photolithographed catalogue cards. The collection comprises *c.*5,500 book titles, conference proceedings, federal documents, hearings and legislation, city and state reports, journals, annual reviews. The library is the most comprehensive in the US on life-span development and aging. *Class No:* 616.01-053.9(01)

[3760]
Health care of the elderly: an information sourcebook. Petersen, M.D. *and* White, D.L., *eds.* Newbury Park, Calif., Sage, 1989. 576p. £49.95. ISBN: 0803933355.

Critcally reviews the research literature on selected aspects of health care for the elderly. Topics include: nursing homes; special support services; case management. Most of the references cited are from the 1980s. *Class No:* 616.01-053.9(01)

Encyclopaedias

[3761]
The Encyclopedia of aging: a comprehensive resource in gerontology and geriatrics. Maddox, G.L., *editor-in-chief.* 2nd ed. New York, Springer Publishing Co., 1995. 1216p. tables. £99; $159. ISBN: 0826148417.

First ed. published 1987.

554 entries, arranged A-Z and 2-4 pages in length, with *c.*70 per cent of the material new or revised. Subject and contributor indexes. Bibliography of more than 200 pages. A broad introduction. *Class No:* 616.01-053.9(031)

[3762]
Encyclopedia of gerontology: age, aging, and the aged. Birren, J.E., *ed.* San Diego, Academic Press, 1996. 2v. 1403p. £225. ISBN: 0122268601, set; 012286861x, v.1; 0122868628, v.2.

A non-technical approach, with chapters such as 'Abuse and neglect of elders'; 'Accidents: falls'... 'Achievement'. Articles are 10-15 pages long. Short bibliographies after each chapter. Many cross-references. Subject index, p.653-710. Has greater depth than *The Encyclopedia of aging and the elderly* (Facts on File, 1992) although some of its articles are not as accessible for the layperson. For students and research professionals. *Class No:* 616.01-053.9(031)

Handbooks & Manuals

[3763]

CRC handbook of physiology in aging. Masoro, E.J., *ed.* Boca Raton, Florida, CRC, 1981. 502p. tables. $139.95. ISBN: 0849331439.

A compendium of lists, tables, etc. summarizing data, with full references. 'It deserves a place on the desks of all those who practice geriatric medicine as well as those who teach or study the physiologic processing of aging' (*Journal of the American Geriatric Society,* v.30, March 1982, p.225). *Class No:* 616.01-053.9(035)

[3764]

Oxford textbook of geriatric medicine. Evans, J.G. *and* Williams, T.F., *eds.* Oxford, University Press, 1992. xvii,756p. illus., graphs, tables. £85. ISBN: 0192615904.

26 documented sections: 1. The ageing of populations and communities ... 3. Infections ... 8. Gastroenterology ... 13. Joints and connective tissue ... 17. Skin disease ... 22. Symptom management and palliative care ... 26. Reference values for biological data in older persons. Index, p.729-56. Designed as companion to *Oxford textbook of medicine* and intended for specialists, trainees and other health professionals involved with elderly people. *Class No:* 616.01-053.9(035)

Reviews & Abstracts

[3765]

Excerpta medica. 20. Gerontology and geriatrics. Amsterdam, Elsevier Science, 1958-. 8pa. $937. ISSN: 0014424x.

About 2,000 abstracts pa. 25 sections: 1. General aspects - 2. General medical treatment - 3. Surgery - 4. Infectious diseases - 5. Cardiovascular system - 6. Respiratory organs - 7. Alimentary tract - 8. Urinary system ... 15. Endocrine system - 16. Nervous system ... 24. Hospitalization, nursing - 25. Social welfare (housing). Subject and author indexes per issue and annually. Online, EMBASE; CD-ROM. *Class No:* 616.01-053.9(048)

Research Projects

[3766]

Old age: a register of social research 1985-1990. Crosby, G., *ed.* London, Centre for Policy on Ageing, 1991. iv,188p. £18. ISBN: 0904139786.

Lists UK research projects, both current and those completed between 1985 and 1990, being undertaken in universities, central and local government, research institutes, and voluntary bodies. Data include address, contact, abstract, aims, methodology, research methods, funding, public availability of research, publications. Indexes to subjects, funding bodies, authors, and institutions. *Class No:* 616.01-053.9:061:061.62.005

Allergies

[3767]

WINTER, R. The People's handbook of allergies and allergens. Chicago, Contemporary Books, 1984. 168p. ISBN: 0809253917.

Dictionary of concise but thorough definitions. Appendices include questions and guidelines to assist identification of allergens, the causes of allergic contact dermatitis, pollen alerts by region and month, food allergies by family, and sources for further information. 'A useful and needed source for data on allergens and terms related to allergies' (*Library journal*, 1 January 1985, p.88). *Class No:* 616.01-056.4

Syndromes

[3768]

Dictionary of medical syndromes. Magalini, S.I., *and others.* 3rd ed. Philadelphia, Pa., J.B. Lippincott, 1990. xiii,1042p. ISBN: 0397508824.

First published 1971.

Entries for *c.*3,000 syndromes. 'Riley-Day': synonyms; symptoms; signs; etiology; pathology; diagnostic procedures; therapy; prognosis; bibliography (3 references). Detailed analytical index, p.957-1042. *Class No:* 616.01-06

[3769]

JABLONSKI, S. Jablonski's dictionary of syndromes and eponymic diseases. 2nd ed. Malabar, Fla., Krieger, 1991. ix,665p. illus. $99.50.

1st ed. as *Illustrated dictionary of eponymic syndromes and diseases, and their eponyms* (1969).

Greatly expanded from previous ed. About 3,000 entries, with a wealth of cross-references. 'Alagille syndrome': ½ column, 2 references; 'Aortic arch syndrome': nearly 1 column, 3 references, 14 synonyms; 'Balingall disease': ½ column, 1 reference. Aims 'to gather together in one volume the profusion of eponymous and noneponymous syndromes and eponymous diseases' (*Introduction*). *Class No:* 616.01-06

Symptoms & Diagnosis

[3770]

French's index of differential diagnosis. Bouchier, I.A.D., *and others, eds.* 13th ed. Oxford, Butterworth Heinemann, 1996. xv, 812p. illus. (incl. col.) tables. £42.50. ISBN: 0750628049.

First published 1912.

Completely revised. Symptoms listed alphabetically. 236 colour plates and 34 libe-drawings. The detailed, analytical index is a quick-reference bonus. A classic encyclopaedic dictionary of diagnosis. *Class No:* 616.01-07

[3771]

GRIFFITH, H.W. Complete guide to symptoms, illness and surgery. Tucson, Ariz., Body Press; HP Books, 1985. 896p. charts. $14.95. ISBN: 039951709x.

3 sections: (1) symptoms, possible problems and recommended action; (2) disorders, A-Z; what to expect and when to see G.P.; (3) surgery, recommendations re. postoperative care. Information is 'An excellent reference book for today's patient' (*American reference book annual,* v.17 1986, p.640).

By the same author, *Complete guide to symptoms, illness and surgery for people over 50* (Body Press, 1992. 896p. $29.95). *Class No:* 616.01-07

[3772]

The Merck manual of diagnosis and therapy. Berkow, R., *and others.* 16th ed. Rahway, N.J., Merck & Co., 1992. 2v. illus., tables. ISBN: 0911910174.

First published 1899.

1. *General medicine.* 2. *Specialties: gynecology, obstetrics, pediatrics, psychiatry, pharmacology, other specialties.* Claims to be 'probably the most widely-used medical text in the world' (*Foreword*). Designed for easy carrying in a medical bag. Also available as a CD-ROM which is updated quarterly. *Class No:* 616.01-07

[3773]

SHREEVE, C.M. The Alternative dictionary of symptoms and cures: a comprehensive guide to disorders and their orthodox and alternative remedies. London, etc., Century, 1986. viii, 504p. £12.99. ISBN: 0712612920.

Three parts. 1. A-Z of symptoms and conditions - 2. Disorders - 3. Therapies of the body (*e.g.* herbal medicine), of the mind (*e.g.* psychotherapy), of the soul (*e.g.* spiritual healing), p.427-98. Many cross-references. Bibliographical references to parts 1-2, 3. Keyed illus. *Class No:* 616.01-07

Treatment

[3774]

STANWAY, A. A Dictionary of operations. London, Paladin; Grafton Books, 1981. 436p.

3 parts: 1. Having an operation - 2. An A-Z of operations - 3. Procedures and investigations. Amniocentesis ... X-ray computed tomographs. 'Some self-help organizations of interest to surgical patients', p.427-31. Analytical subject index. Aims to make a stay in hospital more understandable and less stressful. *Class No:* 616.01-08

[3775]

TREVELYAN, J. *and* DOWSON, D. Thorsons guide to medical tests: the complete handbook of diagnostic and preventive tests. Wellingborough, Thorsons, 1989. 256p. illus., diagrs. £7.99. ISBN: 0722515030.

A consumer guide which gives the patient information about medical tests. 9 sections: 1. Introduction - 2. Diagnostic tests - 3. The role of preventative and occupational tests - 4. Major diseases, infections and conditions ... 8. Mental health - 9. Conclusions. For each area information is provided on: What tests are available; What can be asked for and where; What each test entails; How safe are the tests:

....(contd.)

Are the tests necessary. Index, p.250-56. Some black-and-white illustrations of medical equipment. Useful for public libraries. *Class No:* 616.01-08

Nursing

Bibliographies

[3776]
CLAMP, C.G.L. Resources for nursing research: an annotated bibliography. 2nd ed. London, Library Association Publishing, 1994. 480p. £45. ISBN: 1856041174.

First published 1991.

Covers English-language material, with more than half coming from the US. Has almost doubled in size from the previous edition with 2,150 entries compared to 1,300. Three sections: Sources of literature; Methods of inquiry; Background to research. *Class No:* 616.01-083(01)

[3777]
Core collection in nursing and the allied health sciences: books, journals, media. Peretz, A.A., *and others, eds.* Longman, Oryx Press, 1990. 256p. ISBN: 0897744640.

Lists *c.*1,000 books, periodicals and nonprint materials. Divided into broad subject headings, *e.g.* AIDS; Computers. Contains media source list and a publishers', distributors', and producers', directory. Author, title and subject indexes. Aimed at both the consumer and the professional. *Class No:* 616.01-083(01)

[3778]
ROYAL COLLEGE OF NURSING. A Bibliography of nursing literature. London, Library Association for the Royal College of Nursing, 1968-. ISBN: 0853654700; 085365316x; 0853656231; 0853657467.

1. *1859-1960, with an historical introduction.* Edited and compiled by A.M.C. Thompson. 1968. xx, 132p. £3. 2. *1961-1970.* Edited and compiled by A.M.C. Thompson. 1974. xiii, 223p. £36.50. 3. *1971-1975.* Edited and compiled by F. Walsh. 1985. xix, 256p. £68. 4. *1976-1980.* Edited and compiled by F. Walsh. 1986. xxii, [i], 405p. £68.

About 45,000 unannotated entries in all. Subject arrangement. The 1976-1980v. has *c.*20,000 entries in 14 classes (Nursing as a profession ... Nurse and patient - Education and research - Health services and hospitals - Child health ... Medicine and therapeutics - Surgery, accidents and emergencies. Occupational health - Psychiatry - Diseases and treatment). Author index, p.355-405. *Class No:* 616.01-083(01)

[3779]
STRAUCH, K.P. *and* **BRUNDAGE, D.-J. Guide to library resources for nursing.** New York, Appleton-Century-Crofts, 1980. 309p. illus. ISBN: 0838535283.

Section 1, - an annotated bibliography of the most important books, periodicals, etc. Arranged under specializations, *e.g.* women's health, nursing education, nursing research, psychology. Section 2 is an excellent aid to the use of a library and its bibliographical research tools. Author, title and subject indexes. 'The most important volume on a nurse's bookshelf'. (*Choice,* v.18(5), January 1980, p.641).

A 2nd, shorter ed. was published by Oryx Press in 1992 (224p. $45). *Class No:* 616.01-083(01)

Encyclopaedias & Dictionaries

[3780]
Baillière's encyclopaedic dictionary of nursing and health care. Weller, B.F., *ed.* London, Baillère Tindall, 1989. xxvi,1042p. figs. £12.95. ISBN: 0702011967.

Aimed at the UK-trained and practising nurse and compiled by 45 specialists. Over 32,000 main and sub-entries (A ... Zymosis). Definitions vary in length, *e.g.* Balm, 1 line; Intracranial, 3 columns, and include pronunciation. 3 appendices: 1. Degrees, organizations and abbreviations - 2. Units of measurement and table of chemical elements - 3. Useful addresses. *Class No:* 616.01-083(03)

[3781]
Encyclopedia of nursing research. Fitzpatrick, J.J., *ed.* New York, Springer Publishing, 1998. xxxiv, 701p. $100. ISBN: 082611170x.

US-biased, but containing well-written entries on relevant topics, *e.g.* the Internet. Includes useful lists of organizations, acronyms, etc. Many cross-references. Bibliography, p.609-71. For all nurses. *Class No:* 616.01-083(03)

[3782]
McGraw-Hill nursing dictionary. New York, etc. McGraw-Hill, 1979. xxvii, [1], 1008 + 30p. graphs, tables. $23.95. ISBN: 0070450196.

39 contributors. About 50,000 entries, rarely more than 100 words in length, but showing pronunciation, stress and syllabification. Anatomical, conversion and dietary appendix tables. A spin-off from the database of *Blakiston's Gould medical dictionary* (4th ed., 1979), plus terms of particular importance in nursing education and practice, plus a 'Language interpreter for nurses'. For students, practitioners and teachers of nursing. *Class No:* 616.01-083(03)

[3783]
MILLER, B.F. *and* **KEANE, C.B. Encyclopedia and dictionary of medicine, nursing and allied health.** 6th ed. Philadelphia, Penn., W.B. Saunders, 1997. xxxii, 1960p. illus. (incl. col.), diagrs., tables. £20.95. ISBN: 0721662781.

First published 1972, as *Encyclopedia and dictionary of medicine* (1089p.). 5th ed., 1992.

47 contributors. Over 30,000 entries ('Vocabulary', with anatomical tables and col. plates), p.1-1765. Preceded by 'Combining forms in medical terminology'. Table of muscles. Many cross-references. 45 appendices (2. MetLife height and weight tables; 13. The cranial nerves). Thumb-indexed. 'Medical speller' supplied on disk enclosed in wallet. Title-page headed 'Miller-Keane'. *Class No:* 616.01-083(03)

[3784]
Mosby's medical, nursing, and allied health dictionary. 5th ed. St. Louis, Mo., C.V. Mosby Company, 1998. xxvi,2042p. illus. (col.), diagrs., graphs, tables. ISBN: 0815148003.

First published 1983.

119 consulting contributors. Over 30,000 entries, 5,000 new to this edition. Length of entries varies from a few words to several columns, *e.g.* 'Burn therapy': method; intervention; outcome criteria; 2 columns. 44-page colour atlas of human anatomy. 23 appendices, p.1753-2042 (*e.g.* 1. Units of measurement ...7. Assessment guides ...11. Nutrition ... 22 Omaha classification system ... 23. UK appendix with British spellings). Pronunciation and stress of terms is given. Cross-references. 2,000 colour illustrations. Well produced; thumb ed. *Class No:* 616.01-083(03)

[3785]
Pearce's medical and nursing dictionary and encyclopaedia. 15th ed. London, Faber & Faber, 1983. 413p. £7.99. ISBN: 0571180809.

First published 1933, as *A short encyclopaedia for nurses.*

About 3,000 entries, both 1-2-line definitions and 1-column description (*e.g.* 'Poliomyelites, acute (infantile paralysis: symptoms; nursing and treatment; prophylaxis)). Historical appendix (including 'Old entries'), p.423-38. Select bibliography, p.441-440. Select list of organizations, p.438, 442-3. Cross-references. 'Where treatment is mentioned, it is only to place it in its context in the ward or clinic, it is *not* to be used as providing sufficient information for *undertaking* treatment' (*Preface*). *Class No:* 616.01-083(03)

Handbooks & Manuals

[3786]
The Handbook of nursing. Howe, J., *and others, eds.* New York, Wiley, 1984. 1756p. diagrs., charts, tables. ISBN: 0471895245.

Contribution with short annotated bibliographies, by nurses for practising nurses, focusing on the management of care. Parts of the text were previously published in *McGraw-Hill handbook of clinical nursing* (1979). Chief themes: maternity, pediatrics, medical-surgical, aging, psychiatric and behavioural problems, and emergency care. 7 appendices of tables and charts. 17-p. of subject index. *Class No:* 616.01-083(035)

Dictionaries

[3787]
HINCHLIFF, S. Churchill Livingstone's dictionary of nursing. 17th ed. New York, Churchill Livingstone, 1996. xxvi,457p. figs.,tables. £5.95. ISBN: 0443055343.

*c.*6,000 entries with brief definitions. Some longer entries are set off in boxes. 14 appendices: 1. SI units and the metric system ... 7. Drugs and the law ... 9. Useful addresses ... 14. RCN Association of Nursing students. Practical, hardwearing, washable cover. *Class No:* 616.01-083(038)

[3788]
WELLER, B.F. Baillière's nurses' dictionary. 22nd ed. London, Baillère Tindall, 1997. 545p. illus. £1.30. ISBN: 0702020222.

First published 1912.

Entries vary from a few words to more than a column. Pronunciation guide is given. Many cross-references and illustrations. The 15 appendices are a useful feature (*e.g.* 'Drugs and their control'; 'The Patient's Charter'). Pocket-sized format. Good value. *Class No:* 616.01-083(038)

Theses

[3789]

Steinberg collection of nursing research: catalogue. London, Royal College of Nursing, 1989. 57p.

Lists 513 dissertations and theses by nurses, or about nursing, submitted for higher degrees in the UK. *Class No:* 616.01-083(043)

Reviews & Abstracts

[3790]

International nursing index. New York, Nurses' Association (Lippincott-Raven), 1966-. 4pa.; annual cumulation. $324 (US); $354 (non US). ISSN: 00208124.

Published in co-operation with National Library of Medicine.

Indexes over 270 nursing journals published worldwide, as well as nursing articles in the 2,600 biomedical titles indexed in *Index medicus*. A list of current books published by and for nurses is appended to each issue and the cumulation. Online access is available through MEDLINE. 'This is the master index to nursing literature' (*Reference service review*, v.9(4), October/December 1981, p.22). Available on CD-ROM. *Class No:* 616.01-083(048)

[3791]

—Cumulative index to nursing and allied health literature. Glendale, Calif., Glendale Adventist Medical Center, 1984-. v.22-. 6pa., with annual cumulation. $315.

Continues annual *Cumulative index to nursing*, 1961-76. v.1-21, with wider scope and more acceptable frequency. Covers the major English language and popular nursing journals, as well as selective indexing of medical periodicals. Appended to each issue is a list of audiovisual items and of book reviews. 'CINAHL would be my first choice for any hospital or school of nursing' (*Magazines for libraries* (5th ed., 1986), p.22). Available online and on CD-ROM. *Class No:* 616.01-083(048)

[3792]

Nursing bibliography: a monthly list of current publications on nursing and allied subjects. London, Royal College of Nursing, 1972-. Monthly. £75pa; £88 (overseas). ISSN: 03009947.

8-9,000 references pa. under subjects, Abortion ... Wounds. Selectively indexes more than 200 English-language periodicals. Coverage: books, reports, articles, pamphlets and theses. Each issue carries an author index. The separate list of subject headings and of journals indexed is revised annually. Also on CD-ROM. *Class No:* 616.01-083(048)

Histories

[3793]

Nursing: a historical bibliography. Bullough, B., *and others*. New York, Garland, 1981. xxiv, 408p. (*Garland reference library of social sciences, v.66.*) ISBN: 0824095111.

5,203 numbered, unannotated entries for books and articles. 20 sections, *e.g.* 1. Indexes, bibliographies and abstracts; 2. History of nursing; 7. Biographies and autobiographies; 9. Nursing specialties; 10. Education; 17. Sociology; 20. Nurses and nursing in literature. Author index. Updated through Wellcome Medical Historical Museum and National Library of Medicine bibliographies. *Class No:* 616.01-083(091)

Biographies

[3794]

A Bio-bibliography of Florence Nightingale; completed by S. Goldie. Bishop, W.J., *comp.* London, Dawsons of Pall Mall, for the International Council of Nurses, with which is associated the Florence Nightingale International Foundation, 1962. 160p. port.

10 chapters. 1 Nursing - 2. The army - 3. Indian and colonial welfare - 4. Hospital - 5. Statistics - 6. Sociology - 7. Memoirs and tributes - 8. Religion and philosophy - 9. Miscellaneous work - 10. Selected writings about Florence Nightingale and her times. Appendix: Chronological list of Florence Nightingale's writing. 150 numbered and annotated items. Index. *Class No:* 616.01-083(092)

Education Courses

[3795]

WELL, J. The Directory of continuing education for nurses, midwives and health visitors. London, Newpoint Publishing Company, 1990. 239p. £4.95. ISBN: 0862631297.

14 sections: 1. Introduction - 2. Statutory control of nursing education ... 8. Courses for midwives ... 22. Higher education courses - 12. Teacher preparation courses - 13. Management courses - 14. Open and distance learning. 5 appendices (*e.g.* 'Alphabetical list of courses'; 'Useful addresses'). *Class No:* 616.01-083:377.3

Pathological Anatomy

Histopathology

[3796]

LAW, J.W. *and* **OLIVER, H.J. Glossary of histopathological terms.** London, Butterworth, 1973. [v], 138p. diagrs., chemical structures.

Concise definitions of *c.*700 terms likely to be encountered in normal laboratory practice. Includes short biographies. *Class No:* 616.01-091.8

Immunology

Bibliographies

[3797]

NICHOLAS, R. *and* **NICHOLAS, D. Immunology: an information profile.** London, Mansell, 1985. vii, 216p. ISBN: 0720117240.

3 parts. 1: Overview of immunology and its literature (5 sections, including 3. Organisations in immunology; 4. Immunology: its conferences; 5. Immunology: its literature (journals, reviews and monographic series, books, dissertations, patents, reference works, audiovisual aids, library classification schemes as applied to immunology)) - 2. Bibliography, p.133-61 - 3. Directory of organizations and database hosts. Index, p.204-16. 854 numbered entries. Aims 'to provide for the everyday information needs of immunologists'. Mainly restricted to English language sources. *Class No:* 616.01-097(01)

Encyclopaedias & Dictionaries

[3798]

Dictionary of immunology. Rosen, F.S., *and others*. London, Macmillan Reference Books, 1989. 223p. £25; £15.95. ISBN: 0333347420.

*c.*1,200 definitions, some encyclopedic in length and detail, *e.g.* 'Interleukin': 2p. Many cross-references. Covers terms from molecular biology, cell biology and genetics as well as from immunology. Does not contain as many abbreviations and assumes more clinical knowledge than *Dictionary of immunology* (3rd ed. Oxford, Blackwell Scientific Publications, 1985) (*q.v.*). 'This is the best immunology dictionary that is currently available', (*Science & technology libraries*, v.10(4), 1990, p.119). *Class No:* 616.01-097(03)

[3799]

Dictionary of immunology. Herbert, W.J., *and others, eds.* 4th ed. London, Academic Press, 1995. 171p. diagrs.,tables. £30. ISBN: 0127520252.

First published 1971.

A third of the entries have been rewritten for this edition, while the others have been revised. Focuses on the basics of immunology, while generally omitting those terms dealing with laboratory methods and practical aspects. Extensive cross-references. There are 30 diagrams and seven tables in the text, while there is a list of standard abbreviations, single letter symbols for amino acids, and a Greek alphabet at the end. For experts, students, and lay persons. *Class No:* 616.01-097(03)

[3800]

Encyclopedia of immunology. Delves, P.J. *and* Roitt, I.M., *eds.* 2nd ed. London, Academic Press, 1998. 4v.(3072p.), illus.(some col.), tables. £570; $799. ISBN: 0122267656, set.

First published 1992.

This new ed. has expanded from three volumes to four and covers 31 subject areas. *c.*630 articles from 700 contributors, with more than 60 new articles added since the previous ed. and most other articles updated and revised. Many cross-references. A section of colour plates has been included in each volume. List of further reading. Complete list of entries given at the beginning of each volume and each volume contains the index for the set, while a glossary has also been added. Those purchasing the printed work will be eligible to register for access to the online version which will be free until December 1999, after which time access will be on a subscription basis. Of the previous ed., 'The encyclopedia will continue to be a major reference in immunology' (*Choice*, December 1992, p.601). *Class No:* 616.01-097(03)

Handbooks & Manuals

[3801]

WEIR, D.M. *and* STEWART, J. **Immunology.** 7th ed. Edinburgh, Churchill Livingstone, 1993. 372p. figs., tables. £11.95. ISBN: 0443046603.

First published 1970.

2 sections (10 documented chapters): 1. Basic immunology - 2. Immunology in action. Theory and application of immunological principles for under- and postgraduate students. *Class No:* 616.01-097(035)

Reviews & Abstracts

[3802]

Excerpta medica. 26. Immunology, serology and transplantation. Amsterdam, Elsevier Science, 1967-. 32pa. $2,571. ISSN: 00144304.

About 9,000 abstracts pa. 15 sections: 1. General aspects - 2. Laboratory methods and techniques - 3. Treatment ... 7. Antibodies - 8. Cell-mediated immune responses - 9. Modulation of immune responses ... 15. Transplantation immunology. Subject and author indexes per issue and annually. Online, EMBASE. Available on CD-ROM. *Class No:* 616.01-097(048)

Histories

[3803]

SILVERSTEIN, A.M. **A History of immunology.** San Diego, Academic Press, 1989. xxi,422p. $44.95. ISBN: 012643770x.

12 chapters, with appended bibliographies: 1. Theories of acquired immunity - 2. The royal experiment on immunity, 1721-1722 ... 5. The concept of immunological specificity ... 10. Anti-antibodies and anti-idiotype immunoregulation, 1899-1904 ... 12. Magic bullets and poisoned arrows: the uses of antibody. 3 appendices: A. The calendar of immunological progress (includes 'Important books in immunology, 1892-1968'), p.327-40 - B. Nobel Prize highlights in immunology, p.341-50 - C. Biographical dictionary (Akroyd ... Zinsser). Glossary, name and subject indexes. *Class No:* 616.01-097(091)

Biographies

[3804]

LEFANU, W. **A Bibliography of Edward Jenner.** 2nd ed. Winchester, St. Paul's Bibliographies, 1985. xv, 160p. illus. £30. ISBN: 0906745192.

First published 1951 as *A bio-bibliography of Edward Jenner.*

8 chapters (1. Experiments and observations ... 5. Posthumous works ... 8. Biographies, dedications and portraits). 150 entries, with very detailed notes on each, including collation, contents, and copy used. Notes (p.145-50) include bibliographic references. Index, p.151-60. *Class No:* 616.01-097(092)

Special Pathology

Cardiovascular Diseases

[3805]

Excerpta medica. 18. Cardiovascular diseases and cardiovascular surgery. Amsterdam, Elsevier Science, 1966-. 24pa. $2,162. ISSN: 00144223.

Formerly *Cardiovascular diseases,* 1957-65.

About 7,000 abstracts pa. 18 sections: 1. General aspects ... 3. Diagnostic procedures ... 6. Coronary heart disease ... 11. Heart rate and rhythm ... 13. Hypertension - 14. Thrombosis and embolism ... 17. Treatment - 18. Prevention and rehabilitation. Subject and author indexes per issue and annually. Online, EMBASE; CD-ROM. *Class No:* 616.1

Haematology

[3806]

BRACONI, L.R. **Hematology:** a glossary of terms in English/ American, French, Spanish, Italian, German, Russian. Amsterdam, etc., Elsevier, 1964. [vii], 306p. (*Glossaria interpretum, G9.*)

2,210 English/American base terms, with French, Spanish, Italian, German and Russian equivalents and indexes. *Class No:* 616.15

[3807]

Excerpta medica. 25. Hematology. Amsterdam, Elsevier Science, 1967-. 24pa. $2,068. ISSN: 00144290.

About 8,000 abstracts pa. 20 sections: 1. General aspects ... 4. Anemia ... 6. Leukocytes and related cells ... 10. Blood clotting, fibrosolysis ... 15. Blood groups ... 17. Transfusion ... 24. Laboratory techniques. Subject and author indexes per issue and annually. Online, EMBASE. Available on CD-ROM and microfilm. *Class No:* 616.15

Ear, Nose & Throat

[3808]

Excerpta medica. 11. Oto-, rhino-, laryngology. Amsterdam, Elsevier Science, 1948-. 12pa. $1,442. ISSN: 00144150.

Contains *c.*4,000 abstracts pa. 35 sections: 1. Skull - 2. Face and lips ... 5. Salivary glands ... 9. Larynx and esophagus ... 14. Nasal cavity ... 19. Middle ear ... 26. Hearing - 27. Speech disorders ... 35. General aspects. Author and subject indexes per issue and annually. Online, EMBASE. Available on CD-ROM and microfilm. *Class No:* 616.21

[3809]

LARRAURI, A. **Dictionnaire d'oto-rhino-laryngologie,** en cinq langues: français-anglais-espagnol-allemand-italien. Paris, Librairie Maloine; New York, French & European, 1971. 5v. $95. ISBN: 0686569989.

About 3,000 ear, nose and larynx terms in 5 sequences: French - English - Spanish - German - Italian ... Italian - French - English - Spanish - German. *Class No:* 616.21

Hearing (Otology)

[3810]

GALLAUDET COLLEGE. Washington, D.C. **Dictionary catalog on deafness and the deaf.** Boston, Mass., G.K. Hall, 1971. 2v. (1683p.). ISBN: 0816108773.

39,300 catalogue cards, photolithographically reproduced. Entries include dissertations, reports and microfilms. Author, title, series and subject entries. *Class No:* 616.28

[3811]

Gallaudet encyclopedia of deaf people and deafness. Van Cleve, J.V. New York, etc., McGraw-Hill, 1987. 3v. (1400p.). $330. ISBN: 0070792291, set.

Sponsored by Gallaudet College, Washington, D.C.

271 articles, most of them documented, on sign language, audiology, auditory disorders organizations, deaf community publications, rehabilitation, demographics, biographies of distinguished deaf individuals, educational programmes, conditions and status of the deaf community in most major countries, etc. 250 illus. 8,000-entry index. 'Likely to become the standard work in its field' (*Choice,* v.24(8), April 1987, p.1198). *Class No:* 616.28

[3812]

Terminology of communication disorders: speech - language - hearing. Nicolosi, L., *and others.* 4th ed. Baltimore, Md., Williams and Wilkins, 1996. xx,373p. diagrs.,tables. £29.50. ISBN: 068306505x.

First published 1978.

Aims to 'provide a comprehensive dictionary/source book containing definitions of terminology in the fields of speech, language, and hearing professions' (*Preface*). Short definitions, sometimes accompanied by a figure or table. 15 appendices: 1. Developmental sequences of language behavior: overview ... 9. Langiage tests and procedures ... 15. Diagnostic differences. *Class No:* 616.28

[3813]

TURKINGTON, C. *and* SUSSMAN, A. **Encyclopedia of deafness and hearing disorders.** New York, Facts on File, 1992. 320p. illus. $45. ISBN: 0816022674.

Over 500 entries, by specialists, A-Z. Includes clinical terms, parts of the ear, noted hearing specialists, and deaf personalities, *e.g.* Beethoven. Suggested reading. 13 appendices, including lists of organizations and support agencies. *Class No:* 616.28

Dentistry

Bibliographies

[3814]

CLENNETT, M.A. **Keyguide to information sources in dentistry.** London, Mansell, 1985. 287p. facsim. £40. (*Keyguide series.*) ISBN: 072011747x.

Part 1: Survey of dentistry and its libraries (8 sections, *e.g.* 5. Finding out about the literature; 7. Sources of special information: patents, audiovisual material, etc., 8. Language problem) - Part 2: Bibliography (666 annotated entries, under subjects: anaesthesia ... radiography; miscellaneous subjects) - Part 3: Directory of organizations (selected list of dental libraries; national dental associations; dental associations and societies; schools and university depts.; publications). 1,445 numbered entries in all. Detailed and analytical index, p.273-87. Well researched. Intended for the information worker or non-dental researcher. *Class No:* 616.314(01)

Dictionaries

Polyglot

[3815]

FÉDÉRATION DENTAIRE INTERNATIONALE. A Lexikon of English dental terms, with their equivalents in español, Deutsch, français, italiano. The Hague, Sijthoff, 1966 (reprinted 1974). 424p.

Over 7,000 English-base terms, with Spanish, German, French and Italian equivalents and indexes. The multilingual vocabulary is based on WHO terminology and its 'Application of the Internal classification of diseases to dentistry and stomatology', etc. *Class No:* 616.314(038)=00

English

[3816]

FAIRPO, J.E.H. *and* FAIRPO, C.G. **Heinemann dental dictionary.** 3rd ed. London, Butterworth-Heinemann, 1987. xiv, 311p. tables. £12.95. ISBN: 0750600985.

First published 1962 as *Heinemann Modern dictionary for dental students.*

About 5,000 terms ('Cavity': 1 column). Includes eponyms. Lists of abbreviations and signs precede. 4 appended tables on arteries, muscles, nerves and veins of the head and neck. 'Dental periodicals', p.287-311. *Class No:* 616.314(038)=20

[3817]

HARTY, F.J. **Concise illustrated dental dictionary.** Oxford, J. Wright, 1994. ix, 289p. illus. ISBN: 0723610142.

About 4,700 entries ('Crown': 2 columns, with 2 illus.). 12 appendices (*e.g.* radiographic technique and anatomy). *Class No:* 616.314(038)=20

[3818]

JABLONSKI, S. **Illustrated dictionary of dentistry.** Philadelphia, Pa., W.B. Saunders, 1982 (reprinted Krieger, 1990). xviii, 919p. illus., tables. $79.50. ISBN: 0894644777.

Attempts to standardize North American usage of dental terminology. 1.3 million words. Entries provide background to definitions as well as indicating pronunciation, synonyms, etymology, etc. 'An authoritative reference' (*British dental journal,* v.153, 16 November 1982, p.356). *Class No:* 616.314(038)=20

Reviews & Abstracts

[3819]

Dental abstracts. St Louis, Mo., Mosby Yearbook Inc. for the American Dental Association, 1956-. 24pa. $82.50pa (US) and $97.50 (non US). ISSN: 00118486.

About 750 longish abstracts pa. More than 100 dental and medical journals are scanned. 5 illustrated sections: Hands-on (diagnosis ... temporomandibular joint) - The front office (staff relations; practice management; academics (undergraduate study)) - Inquiry (anatomy ... research methodology) - The big picture (health; history; perspective). Annual author and subject indexes. *Class No:* 616.314(048)

[3820]

Index to dental literature, 1939-. Chicago, Ill., American Dental Association, 1943-. 4pa. $250 (US) and $264.90 (non US). ISSN: 00193992.

Initially (1939-61) as *Index to dental literature in the English language.*

About 10,000 references pa. Contents: Dental books published; Dissertations and theses; Serials indexed; Dental descriptors; Cross-references; Qualifiers; Bibliography of dental reviews (subject and name sections); Index to dental literature (subject and name sections). Annual cumulation. Available online on MEDLINE database and on CD-ROM. *Class No:* 616.314(048)

Yearbooks & Directories

[3821]

American dental directory. Chicago, Ill., American Dental Association, 1947-. Annual. $187.50 (US) and $215.63 (non US). ISSN: 00658073.

Primarily a local list, with entries under state and city, with an A-Z name index. Data include specialization and date of dental graduation. *Class No:* 616.314(058)

[3822]

The Dentists register, 1994, comprising the names and addresses of dental practitioners registered at 31 January 1994, together with the local list of names so registered, and the list of bodies corporate carrying on the business of dentistry. London, General Dental Council, 1994. 56p. + 538p. tables.

First published 1879.

The register is preceded by text of the Dentists Act 1984, plus table of registrable qualifications. Monthly amendments are issued. *Class No:* 616.314(058)

Histories

[3823]

RING, M.E. **Dentistry: an illustrated history.** New York, Abrams, 1985. 320p. illus. $75. ISBN: 0810911000.

A well-written and finely illustrated account that 'will become the most up-to-date resource on the history of dentistry in the English language' (*Journal of American Dental Association,* v.112, January 1986, p.84). *Class No:* 616.314(091)

Stomach (Gastric Disorders)

[3824]

Excerpta medica. 48. Gastroenterology. Amsterdam, Elsevier Science, 1971-. 16pa. $1,464. ISSN: 00313580.

About 5,000 abstracts pa. 9 sections: 1. General aspects - 2, Morphology - 3. Physiology - 4. Diagnostic procedures - 5. Gastrointestinal diseases - 6. Gastrointestinal infections - 7. Liver and biliary system - 8. Pancreas - 9. Peritoneum, mesentery and omentum. Analytical subject and author index per issue and annually. Online, EMBASE and available on CD-ROM. *Class No:* 616.33

Endocrinology

[3825]

Excerpta medica. 3. Endocrinology. Amsterdam, Elsevier Science, 1947-. 24pa. $2,051. ISSN: 0014407x.

About 7,000 abstracts pa. 9 sections: 1. General aspects - 2. Diagnosis, diagnostic procedures and techniques - 3. Treatment - 4. Growth, development and aging ... 6. Endocrine glands ... 8. Reproductive system - 9. Hormone-related metabolism. Subject and author indexes per issue and annually. Online, EMBASE. Available on CD-ROM and microfilm. *Class No:* 616.4

[3826]

MARTIN, C.R. **Dictionary of endocrinology and related biomedical sciences.** New York, Oxford, Oxford University Press, 1995. 785p. £56.50; $75. ISBN: 0195060334.

Workmanlike listing of *c*12,500 definitions, from one line in length to more than a page, including abbreviations, acronyms, and some cross-references. Chemical structures are illustrated diagrammatically. Recommended for medical and research libraries. *Class No:* 616.4

Skin (Dermatology)

[3827]

FRY, L. **Illustrated encyclopedia of dermatology.** 2nd ed. Lancaster, MTP Press, 1985. viii, 575p. illus., tables. ISBN: 0852008678.

58 sections (1. Acanthosis nigricans ... 11. Eczema ... 25. Lupus erythematosus ... 58. Viral infections and AIDS). Emphasis is on the clinical aspects and skin diseases. The treatment sections of all the chapters have been revised. No bibliography. Inadequate index. *Class No:* 616.5

[3828]

LEIBER, M. *and* ROSENBLUM, M.A. **A Dictionary of dermatological words, terms and phrases.** New York, etc., McGraw-Hill, 1968. xviii, 440p.

Entries for about 1,500 terms and expressions. Some contributions are lengthy, *e.g.* 'Eczema': 2/3p., with a further 2p. on types of eczema. Pronunciation is indicated. Readable. No illus. *Class No:* 616.5

Arthritis

[3829]

Excerpta medica. 31. Arthritis and rheumatism. Amsterdam, Elsevier Science, 1965-. 8pa. $876. ISSN: 00144355.

About 3,000 abstracts pa. 22 sections, *e.g.* 1. General surveys and diagnostic procedures; 2. Anatomy and morbid anatomy; 3. Biochemistry, pharmacology and physiology; 6. Rheumatoid arthritis; 17. Diseases of the spinal and peripheral joint. Subject and author indexes per issue and annually. Online, EMBASE. *Class No:* 616.72

Neurology

[3830]

Current advances in neuroscience. Amsterdam, Elsevier Science, 1984-. 12pa. fl.2,545; $1,463. ISSN: 07411677.

About 1,600 abstracts per issue. 28 sections: 1. Neurochemistry; 8. Physiology of the peripheral nervous system; 11. Central nervous system; 12. Pharmacology of the central nervous system; 17. Neurotransmitters, their receptors, agonists and antagonists; 19. Sensory systems; 25. Invertebrate neurophysiology; 29. General concepts, reviews and symposia. Author index and journals list per issue. Included on *Elsevier BIOBASE* database via Datastar, DIALOG, and DIMDI, and on CD-ROM. *Class No:* 616.8

[3831]
Desk reference for neuroscience. 2nd ed. Berlin, Springer-Verlag, 1992. 306p. figs. $69. ISBN: 0387976299.

A revision of Lockard's *Desk reference for neuroanatomy* (1977).

Brief definitions of *c.*4,500 terms related to neuropathology, neurophysiology and neuropharmacology. 53 line drawings. Bibliography of *c.*100 items. For academic libraries, as a quick-reference tool. *Class No:* 616.8

[3832]
Elsevier's encyclopedia of neuroscience. Adelman, G. *and* Smith, B.H., *eds.* New York, Elsevier, 1997. 1 CD-ROM. $169.95. ISBN: 0444826149.

Previously published in paper format as *Encyclopedia of neuroscience* (Springer Verlag, 1987).

Uses Netscape and there is easy access to the encyclopedia's Web site from the CD-ROM. Four indexes: Alphabetical table of contents; Theme index; Keyword index; Full-text keyword search. Review in *Choice*, December 1998, p.667 is critical of the manual and the omission of telephone technical support but adds 'extremely useful for undergraduates in biology and psychology'. *Class No:* 616.8

[3833]
Excerpta medica. 8. Neurology and neurosurgery. Amsterdam, Elsevier Science, 1948-. 32pa. $2,985. ISSN: 00144126.

About 10,000 abstracts pa. v. 46 sections: 1. General aspects. History - 2. Neuroanatomy - 3. Neurophysiology - 4. Neuropathology ... 36. Neurological aspects of mental disease ... 44. Developmental and genetic disorders - 45. Diagnostic processes - 46. Treatment. Author and subject indexes per issue and annually. Online, EMBASE and available on CD-ROM and microfilm. *Class No:* 616.8

[3834]
GARRISON, F.H. Garrison's history of neurology; rev. and enl., with a bibliography of classical, original and standard work in neurology. McHenry, L.C. Springfield, Ill., Thomas, 1969. xiii, [1], 552p. $77.50. ISBN: 039801261x.

Chapters 1-8. From ancient times to the 19th century - 9. Clinical neurology - 10. The neurological examination - 11. Neurological diseases. 411 references; bibliography, p.471-527 (authors, A-Z). *Class No:* 616.8

Epilepsy

[3835]
Dictionary of epilepsy. Part 1: Definitions. Gastaut, H., *and others*. Geneva, World Health Organization, 1973. 76p. $8. ISBN: 9241540273.

More than 1,500 entries, chiefly on clinical aspects. Includes eponyms and syndromes. 'If a term is followed by a definition, this indicates that it is the recommended term for that concept ...' All terms not followed by definitions are 'obsolete, inaccurate or not recommended for some other reason'. *Class No:* 616.853

[3836]
Excerpta medica. 50. Epilepsy abstracts. Amsterdam, Elsevier Science, 1969-. 6pa. $911. ISSN: 00310743.

About 1,500 abstracts pa. 9 sections: 1. General aspects - 2. Basic sciences - 3. Seizures - 4. Etiology - 5. Genetics - 6. Systematic changes related to seizures - 7. Diagnostic aids - 8. Psychology, sociology and epidemiology - 9. Treatment. Subject and author indexes per issue and annually. Online, EMBASE and available on CD-ROM, and microfilm. *Class No:* 616.853

Psychiatry

Bibliographies

[3837]
GREENBERG, B. How to find out in psychiatry: a guide to sources of mental health information. Oxford, etc., Pergamon Press, 1978. xii, [1], 112, [1]p. facsims., tables.

12 chapters (2. Guides to libraries & the psychiatric literature - 3. Primary sources of information: periodicals and books - 4. Secondary sources of information: bibliographies, indexes, abstracts & reviews - 5. Dictionaries, glossaries, encyclopedias and handbooks - 6. Directories - 7. Nomenclature and classification - 8. Education - 9. Mental health statistics - 10. Drugs & drug therapy - 11. Tests and measurements - 12. Nonprint material). References, p.83. Appendix A: Classics in psychiatric literature, p.82-97. Index of titles, authors, 'Highly recommended' (*Choice,* v.16(5/6), July/August 1979, p.648). *Class No:* 616.89(01)

[3838]
GUHA, M. 'Psychiatry'. In *Information sources in the medical sciences*, edited by L.T. Morton and S. Godbolt, Chapter 17 (4th ed. 1992), p.387-412.

Sections on periodicals; abstracts, indexes, bibliographies; dictionaries; reviews; conferences, monographs, books; reference works, and biography and history of psychiatry. 1½p. of bibliography. *Class No:* 616.89(01)

[3839]
MENNINGER FOUNDATION, Topeka, Kansas. **Catalog of the Menninger Clinic Library.** Boston, Mass., G.K. Hall, 1972. 4v. (1704p.). First supplement, 1978. 2v. (914p.). $435, set. ISBN: 0816109613.

56,700 cards reproduced in the main catalogue; 19,100 cards in the *First supplement* Author-title and subject catalogue parts. Includes serial holdings under titles of journals. The Menninger Foundation is the centre for treatment, research and professional education in psychiatry. *Class No:* 616.89(01)

Encyclopaedias

[3840]
BRUNO, F.J. The Family mental health encyclopedia. New York, Wiley, 1989. 422p. ISBN: 0471635731.

*c.*500 clearly-written definitions of theories, disorders, people, drugs, and therapies. Designed for the layperson in dealing with mental health professionals. *Class No:* 616.89(031)

[3841]
CAMPBELL, R.J. Psychiatric dictionary. 7th ed. New York, Oxford University Press, 1996. 799p. £49.50. ISBN: 0195102592.

First published 1940.

Encyclopaedic dictionary of *c.*12,300 terms and cross-references, covering relevant definitions in both technical language (using DSM-IV nomenclature) and lay person's terms. Very brief biographical entries. Preceded by 'Key to pronunciation', book references (1p.) and abbreviations (9p.). The standard dictionary in its field. *Class No:* 616.89(031)

[3842]
Encyclopedia of mental health. Friedman, H.S., *ed.* San Diego, Academic Press, 1998. 3v.(2,398p. illus.,figs.,tables) £310; $425. ISBN: 0122266757.

More than 250 contributors. *c.*200 detailed articles, *e.g.* 'Defense mechanism'; 'Exercise and mental health'; 'Self-esteem', giving an overview of genetic, neurological, social, and psychological factors relating to mental health. Each article contains an outline, glossary, cross-references, and bibliography (*c.*1,000 items). Index of *c.*7,500 entries. *Class No:* 616.89(031)

[3843]
International encyclopedia of psychiatry, psychology, psychoanalysis & neurology. Wolman, B.B., *ed.* New York & London, Van Nostrand Reinhold, for Aesculapius Publishers, Inc., 1977. 12v. (5627p.). diagrs. $675, set. ISBN: 0918228018, set.

1,500 authors, some 300 editors and consultants. Nearly 2,000 survey articles, each documented. 305 biographies (*e.g.* 'Adler': v.1, p.235-40; ½ column of bibliography). 1,605 articles on concepts and issues (*e.g.* 'Aggression in children', v.1, p.348-53; 1½ columns of bibliography). V.12 (410p.) comprises author and subject indexes, although the subject index is non-analytical (*c.*200 unspecififed entries under 'Transference'). 'This eminently readable and impressive encyclopedia' (*Library journal*, 15 April 1978, p.817).

Progress volume 1 (1983. xxxiv, 509p. $89. ISBN 091822828x) continues the tradition of the 12-v. set. 136 signed articles, by 125 specialists. *Class No:* 616.89(031)

Handbooks & Manuals

[3844]
American handbook of psychiatry. Arieti, S., *editor-in-chief.* 2nd ed. New York, Basic Books, Inc., 1974-86. 8v.

First published in 3v., 1959-60.

1. *The foundation of psychiatry.* 2. *Child and adolescent psychiatry.* 3. *Adult psychiatry.* 4. *Organic disorders and psychosomatic medicine.* 5. *Treatment.* 6. *New psychiatric frontiers.* 7. *Advances and new directions.* 8. *Biological psychiatry.*

A much expanded, updated 2nd ed. V.6 has 5 parts, 44 documented chapters (*e.g.* chapter 26. 'Human sexuality research and treatment frontiers, p.665-91, has 137 references; chapter 36. 'Computer applications in psychiatry', p.811-40, 109 references). Each volume carries name and detailed, analytical subject indexes. *Class No:* 616.89(035)

[3845]
Companion to psychiatric studies. Johnstone, E., *and others, eds.* 6th ed. Edinburgh, Churchill Livingstone, 1998. viii, 919p. diagrs., graphs, tables. ISBN: 0443057826.
First published 1973; 5th ed. 1993.
Covers current psychiatric thought and practice. For this ed., completely new chapter on ethical and legal aspects of psychiatry. Detailed analytical index. 'Intended as a general textbook for all postgraduate students of psychiatry' (*Preface*). *Class No:* 616.89(035)

[3846]
Handbook of psychiatry. Shepherd, M., *ed.* Cambridge Univ. Press, 1982-85. 5v.
1. *General psychopathology.* 1983. xi, 307p. 2. *Mental disorders and somatic illness.* 1983. 337p. 3. *Psychoses of uncertain etiology.* 1982. xiv, 313p. 4. *The neuroses and personality disorders.* 1983. xviii, 500p. 5. *The scientific foundations of psychiatry.* 1985. xiv, 359p.
Each volume carries an extensive bibliography (*e.g.* v.3, *c*.1,300 references). Chapters include such topics as 'The historical background'; 'Neurological disorders'; 'Affective psychoses'; 'Philosophy and psychiatry'. Cross-references between the volumes. Author and subject indexes. *Class No:* 616.89(035)

[3847]
Oxford textbook of psychiatry. Gelder, M., *and others.* 3rd ed. Oxford, University Press, 1996. xi,944p. tables. £29.50. ISBN: 0192625004.
First published 1983.
22 chapters, each with 'Further reading' appended: 1. Signs and symptoms of mental disorder ... 4. Aetiology ... 12. Psychiatry and medicine ... 22. Forensic psychiatry. References, p.788-878. Appendix: 'The law in England and Wales'. Author and detailed analytical indexes. 'An introductory textbook for trainee psychiatrists, and also ... an advanced textbook for clinical medical students' (*Preface*). *Class No:* 616.89(035)

Dictionaries

Polyglot

[3848]
PETERS, U.H. Wörterbuch der Psychiatrie und medizinischer Psychologie. 3rd ed. Munich, Baltimore, Urban & Schwarzenberg, 1984. 716p. $65. ISBN: 3541049634.
Several thousand German base-terms, with definitions, plus English-German and French-German indexes. Bibliography, p.715-6.
Class No: 616.89(038)=00

English

[3849]
AMERICAN PSYCHIATRIC ASSOCIATION. Joint Commission on Public Affairs. **A Psychiatric glossary.** 6th ed. Washington, D.C., American Psychiatric Association, 1989. ix, 142p. tables. $39.60. ISBN: 0880480270.
First published 1957.
Defines *c*.1,500 terms, plus brief notes on 'prominent names' and schools of psychiatry. Nearly all the terms derive from 'dynamic psychiatry'. 7 extensive tables on drugs, psychological tests, research terms, etc. Full cross-references. Aimed at personnel in the mental health field, whereas *Chambers' dictionary of psychiatry,* by J.A. Bressel and G. La Fond Cantzlaar (1967. xiv, 234p.), with *c*.2,000 terms, is intended primarily for the general public.
Class No: 616.89(038)=20

[3850]
Dictionary of psychiatry. Walton, H., *ed.* Oxford, Blackwell Scientific Pubns., 1985. 170p. £16.50. ISBN: 0632009721.
Has 13 contributors. Entries include brief biographies (*e.g.* Nietzsche: ½p. 'Migraine': 1/3p.; 'Psychoanalytical theory'; 2/3p.). Cross-references, but no bibliography. 'Embodies a response to the expressed need for an authoritative, accessible and compact set of definitions and terms used in psychiatry and cognate subjects' (*Foreword*). Editor is Professor of Psychiatry, University of Edinburgh. *Class No:* 616.89(038)=20

[3851]
LANCASTER HEALTH AUTHORITY. Glossary of terms, tests and drugs used in psychiatric practice. 4th ed. Lancaster, the Authority, 1984. [i], 91p.
First published 1962 as *A guide to psychiatric and psychological terminology.*
5 sections: 1. Terminology - 2. List of common phobias - 3. List of psychological tests - 4. Drugs in use for the treatment of psychiatric disorders - 5. The Mental Health Acts. 'Produced to satisfy a demand for this type of literature not only in Psychiatric Hospitals but many other areas concerned with Mental Health Services' (*Preface*).
Class No: 616.89(038)=20

[3852]
—THAKURDAS, H. *and* THAKURDAS, L. Dictionary of psychiatry. Revised by B. Thakurdas. Lancaster, MTP, 1979. vii, 111p. diagrs. £9.75; £5.50. ISBN: 0852002351.
Defines *c*.900 terms. 8 useful appendices: A. International Standard Classification of Mental Disorders - B. List of abbreviations - C. A guide to prefixes and suffixes - D. Common phobias - H. Essentials of the Mental Health Act, 1969. Designed as a ready reference for doctors, medical students, psychiatric nurses, social workers 'or anybody involved with psychiatric patients' (*Introductory note*).
Class No: 616.89(038)=20

[3853]
Lexicon of psychiatric and mental health terms. 2nd ed. Geneva, World Health Organization, 1994. vii,108p. SFr25. ISBN: 924154466x.
Designed for use with the 10th Revision of the *International Classification of Diseases, (ICD-10).*
Contains definitions of over 700 terms in ICD-10. Companion to *Lexicon to alcohol and drug terms. Class No:* 616.89(038)=20

[3854]
WORLD HEALTH ORGANIZATION. Mental disorders: a glossary and guide to their classification in accordance with the Ninth Revision of the International Classification of Diseases. Geneva, WHO, 1978. 95p. £6. ISBN: 924154377.
Offprint of chapter 5 'Mental disorders' of the *International Classification of Diseases* (9th ed. 1977-78), and successor to WHO *Glossary of mental disorders and guide to their classification* (1974).
Quick reference lists 1-3, p.58-60. 3 annexes. Detailed, analytical index, p.83-95. *Class No:* 616.89(038)=20

German

[3855]
HAAS, R. Dictionary of psychology and psychiatry: English/German. Toronto, C.J. Hogrefe, 1980-88. 2v. $78, v.1; $98, v.2. ISBN: 0889370001, v.1; 0889370133, v.2.
Published under the auspices of the Centre for Psychological Information and Documentation at the University of Trier, West Germany.
V.1. *English/German* 1980. 453p. V.2. *German/English.* 1988. 440p.
V.1 contains more than 30,000 English terms, with German equivalents, covering such subjects as neurophysiology, cybernetics, sexology. *Class No:* 616.89(038)=30

Reviews & Abstracts

[3856]
Excerpta medica. 32. Psychiatry. Amsterdam, Elsevier Science, 1948-. 20pa. $1,942. ISSN: 00144363.
About 6,000 abstracts pa. 36 sections: 1. History and general aspects - 2. Medical psychology - 3. Mental tests - 4. Psychophysiology ... 10. Mental deficiency ... 12. Psychosis - 15. Sexology ... 21. Group therapy ... 23. Psychopharmacology ... 28. Social psychiatry - 29. Child psychiatry ... 32. Suicide - 33. Forensic psychiatry - 34. Military psychiatry - 35. Preventive mental hygiene - 36. Education and training. Annual subject and author indexes. Online, EMBASE; CD-ROM. *Class No:* 616.89(048)

Progress Reports

[3857]
Psychiatry: the state of the art. Proceedings of the 7th World Congress of Psychiatry, July 11-16, 1983. Pichot, P., *and others, eds.* New York & London, Plenum Press, 1985. 8v. graphs, charts, tables. ISBN: 0306416018, v.1; 0306416026, v.2; 0306416034, v.3; 0306416042, v.4; 0306416050, v.5; 0306416069, v.6; 0306416077, v.7; 0306416085, v.8.
1. *Clinical psychopathology, nomenclature and classification.* 2. *Biological psychiatry, higher nervous activity.* 3. *Pharmacopsychiatry.* 4. *Psychiatry and psychosomatic medicine.* 5. *Child and adolescent psychiatry, mental retardation and geriatric psychiatry.* 6. *Drug dependence and alcoholism, forensic psychiatry, military psychiatry.* 7. *Epidemiology and community psychiatry.* 8. *History of psychiatry, national schools, education and transcultural psychiatry.*
More than 100 contributors. V.7 (xxi, 693p.) contains 103 documented papers in 15 sections, plus addendum. The paper 'Psychiatric epidemiology since three years after retirement', p.541-9, carries 22 references. Another, 'On the history of American psychiatry', p.179-81, has 40 references. International in scope.
Class No: 616.89(055)

[3858]
Year book of psychiatry and applied mental health. Chicago, Ill., Mosby Year Book, 1970-. Annual. illus., diagrs., graphs, tables. ISSN: 00843970.

Continues *Yearbook of neurology, psychiatry and neurosurgery*.

The *1998 Year book* (550p. illus. $73) is a review of material taken from more than 500 journals. Tables and illustrations form the original articles are also included to enhance the abstracts. Subject coverage includes genetics and mental health, biological psychiatry, community psychiatry, etc. Aims 'to highlight the emerging trends and directions'. Subject and author indexes. Also on-line. *Class No:* 616.89(055)

Histories

[3859]
ALEXANDER, F.G. *and* **SELESNICK, S.T. The History of psychiatry:** an evaluation of psychiatric thought and practice, from prehistoric times to the present. London, Allen and Unwin, 1967. xvi, 471, [1]p. illus.

4 parts (25 chapters): 1. The age of psychiatry - 2. From the ancients through the modern era - 3. The Freudian age - 4. Recent developments. Appendices A-C (C. The organization of psychoanalytic and psychiatric teaching, practice and research). Chapter notes, p.415-30. Bibliography (general; 25 chapters), p.431-51. Partly analytical index. *Class No:* 616.89(091)

[3860]
HUNTER, R. *and* **MACALPINE, I. Three hundred years of psychiatry, 1535-1860:** a history present in selected English texts. Hartsdale, N.Y., Carlisle Publishing, Inc., 1982. xxvi, [1], 1107p. facsims. $95. ISBN: 0910177007.

This is a reprint of 1963 ed.

About 300 extracts from original sources, each with a short introduction. Chronological arrangement: Barthomaeus Anglicus, 1535 ... Thomas Laycock, 1860. Lengthy general introduction precedes. Index of names; index of subjects (partly analytical).

Class No: 616.89(091)

Biographies

[3861]
AMERICAN PSYCHIATRIC ASSOCIATION. Biographical directory of fellows & members of the American Psychiatric Association. New York & London, Bowker; Jaques Cattell Press, 1989. 1956p. $137.50; $93.50. ISBN: 0890421862.

Lists *c.*30,000 American and some foreign psychiatrists, with data on career, specialization and publications. Geographical index.

Class No: 616.89(092)

Research Methods

[3862]
Research methods in psychiatry: a beginner's guide. Freeman, C. *and* Tyrer, P., *eds.* 2nd ed. London, Royal College of Psychiatrists, 1992. 318p. £15. ISBN: 0902241486.

First published 1990.

Aimed at all researchers in social and medical science.

Class No: 616.89:001.891

Communicable Infections & Fevers

[3863]
Abstracts on hygiene and communicable diseases. Wallingford, CAB International, 1926-. 12pa. £315; $551. ISSN: 02605511.

Contains abstracts of 100-600 words, some of them signed, and preceded by full bibliographical information. March 1996 issue has 'Public health news', followed by 'Environmental health' - 'Community health' - 'Diseases and their control'. Book reviews. Author, geographical, and subject indexes. Forthcoming meetings. Available online via DIMDI and in microform. *Class No:* 616.9

[3864]
Infectious diseases in Europe: a fresh look. Velimirovic, B., *and others.* Copenhagen, WHO Regional Office for Europe, 1984. x, 330p. tables, maps. £4. ISBN: 9289010150.

8 review-chapters: 1. Does Europe have a communicable disease problem? ... 3. Figures and trends for selected infectious diseases in Europe, 1950-1980 ... 8. Changes in outlook: communicable as opposed to infectious diseases. 10 annexes (*e.g.* on the increase of AIDS in Europe). Many statistical tables and graphs. Bibliographies appended to chapters. No index. *Class No:* 616.9

[3865]
MAHY, B.W.J. A Dictionary of virology. 2nd ed. San Diego, Academic Press, 1997. [vii], 348p., tables, formulas. ISBN: 0124653251.

First published 1981.

Extensive revision of the previous edition. Approximately 3,500 entries for viruses, using nomenclature approved by the International Committee for the Taxonomy of Viruses. Title of the book should be 'A dictionary of *vertebrate* viruses'. Includes cross-references for viral synonyms, non-scientific names, etc., and helpful references to 'key journal articles or reviews'. *Class No:* 616.9

[3866]
Mandell, Douglas and Bennett's principles and practice of infectious diseases. Mandell, G.L., *and others, eds.* 4th ed. New York, etc., Churchill Livingstone, 1995. 2v., (xxxi, 2804p.) illus., diagrs., graphs, tables, chemical structures, maps. £216. ISBN: 0443089353.

First published 1979 as *Principles and practice of infectious diseases*. 3rd ed., 1990.

Over 250 contributors. 4 parts (302 documented chapters): 1. Basic principles in the diagnosis and management of infectious diseases - 2. Major clinical syndromes - 3. Infectious diseases and their etiologic agents - 4. Special problems. Chapter 148: 'Poliovirus', p.1613-19, with 104 references. Detailed 113-page index. 'This 4th edition reflects the rapid pace of developments in the broad field of infectious diseases'(*Preface*). Pocket-sized handbook entitled *Principles and practice of infectious diseases: antimicrobial therapy, 1993-4*, came from the same editor and publishers in 1993. *Class No:* 616.9

[3867]
TURKINGTON, C. *and* **ASHBY, B. Encyclopedia of infectious diseases.** New York, Facts on File, 1998. 370p. £30.95; $50. ISBN: 0816035121.

Length of entries varies from one sentence to five pages. Covers history, aetiology, symptoms, diagnosis, treatment, complications and prevention. Appendices include information on organizations dealing with infectious diseases, Web sites, and disease hotlines. Lists drugs used in the treatment of diseases. Many cross-references. Glossary. Detailed bibliography. 'An excellent source for ready reference and overview information' (*Reference books bulletin*, 15 December, 1998, p.763). For public and academic libraries. *Class No:* 616.9

AIDS

[3868]
AIDS abstracts. Oncology Information Service, University of Leeds/ Carfax Publishing Co., 1993-. 12pa. £238; £428 (overseas). ISSN: 09531580.

Formerly *AIDS information: world literature on human retroviruses and acquired immuno-deficiency systems*, 1985-1992.

Contains *c.*1,800 abstracts and references pa. 11 sections (*e.g.* Transmission; Treatment; Immunology; Assay methods and virology; 7-cell leukaemia viruses; Public policy, ethical and legal statistics; [worldwide]; Future conferences). Keyword index. Culled from 1,300 international biomedical journals. A current-awareness service; online. *Class No:* 616.98

[3869]
The AIDS directory: an essential guide to the 1500 leaders in research, services, policy, advocacy, and funding. Horsham, Penn., LRP Publications. Annual. $250. ISSN: 10656162.

Descriptions of 1,500 US national, regional, and international organizations. Arranged A-Z by name, data include contact person, type of organization, finance, staff names, addresses and telephone numbers, publications, etc. Numerous cross-references. 10 indexes, *e.g.* location, services offered. For academic and large public libraries. *Class No:* 616.98

[3870]
AIDSLINE. Bethesda, Md., National Library of Medicine, 1980-.

Online equivalent of *AIDS bibliography* (1988-. 12pa.). Contains more than 99,000 citations, with abstracts, to international, primarily English-language, literature. *c.*13,000 records added each year. Also available on CD-ROM. *Class No:* 616.98

[3871]
Virology and AIDS abstracts. Bethesda, Maryland, Cambridge Scientific Abstracts, 1988-. 12pa. $935 (US); $1,015 (non US). ISSN: 08965919.

Originally as *Virology abstracts* (1967-87).

*c.*9,000 abstracts drawn pa. from *c.*5,000 primary sources. Sections include: Acquired Immunodeficiency Syndrome - Virus taxonomy and classification ... Immunology - Antiviral agents ... Viral infections of man ... Viral infections of higher plants. Author and subject indexes per issue and annually. Online: DIALOG, ORBIT, etc. and on CD-ROM. *Class No:* 616.98

[3872]
WATSTEIN, S.B. *and* CHANDLER, K. The AIDS dictionary. New York, Facts on File, 1998. ix,340p. £27.70; $45. ISBN: 081603754x.

More than 3,000 entries, covering all aspects - including social - of HIV/AIDS. Three appendices: 1. Frequently used abbreviations - 2. The global epidemic at a glance - 3. Selected resources for practitioners, researchers, and persons with HIV/AIDS. This last section is basically a list of US resources but it also includes some useful Internet sites. Bibliography and index. Aimed at the non-specialist. For public libraries. *Class No:* 616.98

Surgery

Reviews & Abstracts

[3873]
Excerpta medica. 9. Surgery. Amsterdam, Elsevier Science, 1947-. 20pa. $2,251. ISSN: 00144134.

About 7,000 abstracts pa. 26 sections: 1. General aspects ... 5. Nervous system - 6. Head ... 13. Alimentary tract ... 19. Kidney... 21. Circulatory system: vascular disorders ... 24. Instrumentation - 25. Experimental surgery - 26. Surgical development. Subject and author indexes per issue and annually. Online, EMBASE and available on CD-ROM. *Class No:* 617(048)

Progress Reports

[3874]
Recent advances in surgery. Edinburgh, etc., Churchill Livingstone, 1998. illus., diagrs., graphs, tables. ISSN: 01438395.

First published 1928.

V.22, 1998 (260p.) includes documented articles: 'Surgical principles in the management of soft tissue sarcomas'; 'Intestinal stomas'; 'What's new in general surgery - a review of the journals'. Analytical subject index. *Class No:* 617(055)

Portraits

[3875]
ROYAL COLLEGE OF SURGEONS OF ENGLAND. A Catalogue of the portraits and other paintings and sculpture in the Royal College of Surgeons of England. LeFanu, W. Edinburgh & London, Livingstone, 1960. xii, 119p. illus. (incl. col.).

245 painted or carved portraits of surgeons are recorded, plus a descriptive phrase to indicate their association, if any, with the College. Provenance and sources of information are indicated. Nearly half the entries are illustrated. *Class No:* 617(084.10)

Biographies

[3876]
PLARR, V.G. Plarr's lives of the Fellows of the Royal College of Surgeons of England. Power, Sir D'A., *and others*. Bristol, Royal College; London, Simpkin, Marshall, 1930. 2v.

Records lives of the Fellows from 1843 to those who died before 1930, with citations of their significant publications. Continuation volumes bring the roll of Fellows up to the end of 1973: for 1930-1951, by Sir D'Arcy Power and W.R. LeFanu (1953); for 1952-1964, by R.H.O.B. Robinson and W.R. LeFanu (1970); and for 1965-1973, by J.P. Ross and W.R. LeFanu (1981). *Class No:* 617(092)

[3877]
POWER, Sir D'A. Lives of the Fellows of the Royal College of Surgeons of England, 1930-1951. LeFanu, W.R. London, Royal College of Surgeons of England, 1953. xii, 889p.

Continues Plarr. 'An account of all the Fellows whose death was reported between the beginning of 1930 and the end of 1951'. Entries are detailed and authoritative; information was checked with relatives and the source stated. The biographee's publications are listed and reference made to other published obituaries. Includes lives of some Fellows who died before 1930, omitted from Plarr. *Class No:* 617(092)

[3878]
ROBINSON, R.H.O.B. *and* LEFANU, W.R. Lives of the Fellows of the Royal College of Surgeons of England, 1952-1964. Edinburgh & London, Churchill Livingstone, 1970. [vii], 470p. £3.50. ISBN: 0043006814.

Continues Plarr and Power.

About 800 entries, - brief, accurate and informative, biographical sketches. 'Victor Bonney': c.2p., with 12 lines of bibliographical notes. 'Contributions do not always include a succinct account of each individual's contribution to medicine' (*British medical journal,* no.5698, 21 March 1970, p.742). *Class No:* 617(092)

[3879]
ROSS, J.P., *Sir and* LEFANU, W.R. Lives of the Fellows of the Royal College of Surgeons of England, 1965-1973. London, Pitman, 1981. 405p. £10. ISBN: 0272796107.

Continues Plarr, Power and Robinson.

'Contains biographical details of surgeons who have died between 1965 and 1973'. Perhaps of more topical interest than the previous volumes as it includes details of senior colleagues and teachers of surgeons currently in practice. *Class No:* 617(092)

Techniques

Anaesthesia

[3880]
Excerpta medica. 24. Anesthesiology. Amsterdam, Elsevier Science, 1966-. 10pa. $1,157. ISSN: 00144282.

About 2,500 abstracts pa. 6 sections: 1. General aspects (1.21: Resuscitation and intensive care) - 2 General anesthesia 3. Local anesthesia (3.2: Spinal anesthesia) - 4. Special anesthesia - 5. Physiology - 6. Pharmacology. Subject and author indexes per issue and annually. Online, EMBASE and available on CD-ROM. *Class No:* 617-089.5

[3881]
International practice of anaesthesia. Prys-Roberts, C. *and* Brown, B.R., *eds*. London, Butterworth-Heinemann, 1996. 2v.(xviii,2542p.) figs. tables. £195. ISBN: 0750602406.

Successor to *General anaesthesia* (5th ed. London, Butterworths, 1989), edited by J.F. Nunn, *and others*.

More than 200 contributors. Six sections (167 chapters): 1. Anaesthesia and analgesia ... 3. Obstetrics and pediatrics ... 6. Montioring and anaesthesia equipment. Each chapter has a list of references. Both volumes contain the cumulative index and contents pages. *Class No:* 617-089.5

[3882]
A Short history of anaesthesia: the first 150 years. Rushman, G.B., *and others*. Oxford, Butterworth-Heinemann, 1996. viii,218p. illus. £14.99. ISBN: 0750630663.

20 chapters: 1. The background to anaesthesia ... 6. Premedication ... 12. Cardiothoracic anaesthesia ... 16. Monitoring ... 20. Calendar of interesting and important events in the history of medicine and anaesthesia. Each chapter has a list of references, *e.g.* 'Intravenous drugs in anaesthesia' has 108 references. three appendices: 1. The organization of the speciality - 2. Early publications on anaesthesia - 3. Books on the history of anaesthesia. index, p.207-18. Clear overview of the subject. *Class No:* 617-089.5

Orthopaedics

[3883]
BLAUVELT, C. *and* NELSON, F.R.T. A Manual of orthopaedic terminology. 6th ed. St. Louis, Mosby, 1998. xvi,463p. illus.,figs.,tables. £25. ISBN: 0815127871.

First published 1978.

13 chapters: 1. Classifications of fractures, dislocations, and sports-related injuries ... 5. Laboratory evaluations ... 9. The spine ... 13. Musculoskeletal research. Each chapter begins with an introduction, followed by brief definitions of terminology according to speciality. Four appendices, *e.g.* 'Etymology of orthopaedics'. Bibliography and index. *Class No:* 617.3

[3884]
Excerpta medica. 33. Orthopedic surgery. Amsterdam, etc., Elsevier Science, 1956-. 12pa. $1,404. ISSN: 00144371.

About 7,000 abstracts pa. 10 sections: 1. General aspects - 2. Experimental orthopedics - 3. Diagnoses, diagnostic procedures and techniques - 4. Treatment - 5. Growth and development - 6. Injury - 7. Infections - 8. Neoplasms - 9. General orthopedics - 10. Orthopedic aspects of systematic disorders. Subject and author indexes per issue and annually. Online, EMBASE; CD-ROM. *Class No:* 617.3

Ophthalmology

Bibliographies

[3885]
BRITISH OPTICAL ASSOCIATION. Library catalogue. London, the Association, 1932, 1935, 1957. 3v.

Consists of author catalogues, with annotated entries. Subject index provides broad groupings. V.3 has c.3,000 entries. *Class No:* 617.7(01)

Encyclopaedias & Dictionaries

[3886]

Dictionary of visual science. Cline, D., *and others*. 3rd ed. Radnor, Pa., Chilton Book Co., 1980. xviii, 711p. illus., diagrs., charts.

2nd ed., 1968, edited by M. Schapero, and others.

68 contributors. About 20,000 entries, some of them lengthy (*e.g.* 'Lens': p.346-65). Coverage spans ocular anatomy, ocular physiology, ocular pathology, ocular embryology, illumination and physical optics. Entries include eponyms, organizations and abbreviations.

4th ed., 1989. (xxi,820p. $55). *Class No:* 617.7(03)

[3887]

MILLODOT, M. Dictionary of optometry. 3rd ed. London, Butterworth, 1993. xii 196p. £19.95. ISBN: 0750608471.

About 3,400 terms used in optometric practice (400 added since 2nd ed. 1990), with definitions, synonyms, abbreviations, examples, and cross-references. Intended for students and practitioners. *Class No:* 617.7(03)

[3888]

SARDEGNA, J. *and* **PAUL, T.O. The Encyclopedia of blindness and vision impairment.** New York, Facts on File, 1991. vii, 329p. $45. ISBN: 0816021538.

Over 500 entries, arranged A-Z. Entries, many of which have bibliographies, vary from a few lines to articles of 1 or 2 pages. Appended list of agencies, institutions, schools, national organizations, rehabilitation centres, disability databases, etc. Extensive bibliography. Name and subject index. For the layperson. *Class No:* 617.7(03)

[3889]

THORNTON, S.P. Ophthalmic eponyms: an encyclopedia of named signs, syndromes and diseases in ophthalmology. Birmingham, Alabama, Aesculapius Publishing Co., 1967. 324p.

Entries, A-Z in each of 2 sections: 1. Signs, symptoms and diseases in medical, pediatric, and neuro-ophthalmology - 2. Eponyms in ophthalmic surgery. Sources are often cited. *Class No:* 617.7(03)

Reviews & Abstracts

[3890]

Ophthalmic literature. Oxford, Elsevier Science, 1947-. 4pa. fl.730; $419. ISSN: 00303720.

More than 4,000 abstracts specially-commissioned pa. V.48(4), December 1995 contains 534 abstracts, divided into 18 sections: 1. Globe and sclera ...6. Lens ... 15. Visual function ... 17. Veterinary - 18. Miscellaneous. Subject and author index. *Class No:* 617.7(048)

Yearbooks & Directories

[3891]

The Opticians register, 1996; comprising the following registers and lists kept by the General Optical Council: The Register of ophthalmic opticians who both test sight and fit and supply optical appliances: The Register of ophthalmic opticians who test sight but do *not* fit and supply optical appliances, and The Register of dispensing opticians; together with the list of bodies corporate carrying on business as ophthalmic opticians, and the list of bodies corporate carrying on business as dispensing opticians, containing registrations and enrolments up to 31st December 1995. London, General Optical Council. lxv,478p.

The lists of opticians are followed by the 'Local list' (p.335-478), in 7 areas, - London postal region, Greater London, England, Wales, Scotland, N. Ireland and outside the UK, broken down into postal districts. *Class No:* 617.7(058)

[3892]

—International optical year book and diary. Sutton, Surrey, Consumer Industries Press. Annual. ISBN: 0617010102.

89th ed., 1993. (376p. + diary). Contents include 'Professional organisations addresses and activities' p.9-63; 'Who's who', p.99-174, 'Trade names', p.193-234, and 'Product information', p.237-94. Index to articles in *The Optician*, p.175-82. *Class No:* 617.7(058)

Biographies

[3893]

OVIO, G. Storia dell'oculista. Genoa, Tipografia Ghibaudo, 1950-52. 2v. (131p.; 1020p.). ports.

1. *Delle origine al 1850.* 2. *Dal 1850 al 1900.*

Biographical data on oculists. Each volume carries an extensive bibliography (v.1: 2,031 references; v.2: 7,795 references) and subject index. *Class No:* 617.7(092)

Gynaecology

[3894]

O'DOWD, M.J. *and* **PHILIPP, E.E. The History of obstetrics and gynaecology.** Carnforth, Lancs., Parthenon Publishing Group, 1994. x,710p. illus. $125. ISBN: 1850702241.

Chapters cover a wide range of subjects related to gynaecology and obstetrics, *e.g.* Infertility; Laparoscopy. A bibliography and chronology are appended to most chapters. Short biographies of prominent historical figures are listed in the final section. Name and subject indexes. *Class No:* 618.1

Obstetrics

[3895]

ANDERSON, M. An A-Z of gynaecology, with comments on aspects of management and nursing. London, Faber & Faber, 1986. 125p. illus. £3.50. ISBN: 0571139663.

Five sections: 1. Anatomy and physiology - 2. Benign disorders - 3. Malignant diseases - 4. Surgical procedures - 5. Hormones and related drugs. Some entries have brief notes on nursing and general management. Further readings, p.117-8: Useful organisations, p.119. Detailed analytical index, p.121-5. *Class No:* 618.2

[3896]

How to find out: information sources in midwifery. Bristol, Midwives Information and Resource Service, 1991. 64p. £2.95. (*MIDIRS fact pack, no.* 2.) ISBN: 0951424106.

14 chapters: 1. Planning your search ... 5. Libraries and information services ... 9. Indexes, abstracting and current awareness services - 10. Computer databases ... 13. Voluntary and self-help organizations - 14. Further reading. *Class No:* 618.2

[3897]

The National Childbirth Trust book of pregnancy, birth, and parenthood. Tucker, G., *ed.* 2nd ed. Oxford, University Press, 1996. viii,487p. illus.,figs. £10.99. ISBN: 0192861875.

First published 1992.

Three sections (32 chapters): 1. Pregnancy (1. Beginning a pregnancy ... 7. Pregnancy discomforts ... 12. Getting ready for the birth) - 2. Birth (13. Anatomy and physiology of labour ... 21. Stillbirth) - 3. Parenthood (22. Early days ... 32. Returning to work). Also includes a glossary of terms, further reading, useful addresses, and index. A useful overview of early pregnancy through to the baby's first year. *Class No:* 618.2

[3898]

Obstetric-gynecologic terminology, with section on neonatology. Hughes, E.C., *ed.* Philadelphia, Pa., F.A. Davis Co., 1972. xxi, 731p. ISBN: 0803647255.

9 sections, each with an A-Z sequence of entries. 1. Anatomy - 2. Anatomy of generative organs - 3. Diseases and conditions of generative organs - 4. Benign and malignant neoplasmas - 5. Selected gynecologic topics (*e.g.* menopause) - 6. Physiology of reproduction - 7. Obstetrics - 8. Neonatology - 9. Glossary of congenital anomalies. Sources, p.645-6. Abbreviation index. Detailed, analytical index, p.651-731. Well organized. *Class No:* 618.2

[3899]

Obstétrique et gynécologie: glossaire des termes obstétricaux et gynécologiques en français, latin, anglais, russe, allemand, espagnol, italien, grec. Louros, N.C., *and others.* Amsterdam, etc., Elsevier, 1964. [vii], 444p. (*Glossaria interpretum, G8.*)

2,576 French-base terms, with Latin, English, Russian, German, Spanish, Italian and Greek equivalents and indexes. Genders not shown. *Class No:* 618.2

[3900]

PEEL, J. The Lives of the Fellows of the Royal College of Obstetricians and Gynaecologists, 1929-1969. London, Heinemann Medical, 1976. xviii, 390p.

An account of the most important activitites of 318 Fellows, as far as it has been possible to collect the necessary details. A list of honorary Fellows precedes. *Class No:* 618.2

62 Engineering

Engineering

Abbreviations & Symbols

[3901]

Dictionary of engineering acronyms and abbreviations. Keller, H. *and* Erb, U. 2nd ed. New York, Neal-Schuman, 1994. [viii], 878p. $125.. ISBN: 0155701290.

First published 1989.

About 70,000 entries. 2 parts: A. Acronyms and abbreviations in science and engineering - B. Periodical title abbreviations and acronyms in science and engineering. Well-produced with bold type for entry terms. *Class No:* 620(003)

[3902]

POLON, D.D., *ed.* **EESS/Encyclopaedia of engineering signs and symbols.** New York, Odyssey Press, 1965. xviii, 412p. diagrs., tables.

5,000 graphic symbols in standard use by engineers, draughtsmen and other technicians. Sections: Electrical-electronics graphic symbols - Material graphic symbols - Aircraft and spacecraft mechanical graphic symbols - Architectural and structural graphic symbols ... Engineering drawings - Color codes - Designations. Index to graphic symbols, p.403-12. *Class No:* 620(003)

Databases

[3903]

Compendex*Plus. New York, Engineering Information Inc., 1988-.

Compendex*Plus comprises the databases *Compendex* and *Ei Engineering meetings*. The files were merged in 1988 and duplicate records removed. International coverage of all aspects of engineering. About 3,000,000 records. Numerous hosts including DIALOG, ESA-IRS, Bath Information and Data Services (BIDS), Questel/ORBIT, etc. Also available on CD—ROM (Dialog; SilverPlatter) and magnetic tape.

Several subsets of the database are offered, both as online databases and CD-ROMs. SilverPlatter offers *EI Tech index* with 285,000 records suitable for smaller technical and academic libraries. *Class No:* 620(003.4)

[3904]

—Ei Compendex. New York, Engineering Information Inc., 1970-.

Compendex is the machine-readable database for *Engineering index monthly*. About 2,500,000 records. Among its hosts are STN International.

SHE subject headings in engineering supplies the terms used in *Engineering index* and its associated COMPENDEX databases. *Class No:* 620(003.4)

[3905]

HANSON, T.A. 'Electronic sources of engineering information'. *Information sources in engineering.* Eds. K.W. Mildren and P.J. Hicks (3rd ed., 1996), p.107-20.$c£80. London, Bowker-Saur, 1996. ISBN: 1857390571.

Lists a wide range of bioliographic databases with their coverage and online hosts. Also covers information sources and services, both formal and informal, on the Internet. *Class No:* 620(003.4)

[3906]

MOON, M. 'Engineering'. *Manual of online search strategies.* Editors, C.J. Armstrong and J. A. Large, pp.288-308. 2nd ed. Aldershot, Ashgate, 1992. ISBN: 1857420071.

Lists 52 engineering databases, with their focus of interest and host systems. *Class No:* 620(003.4)

Bibliographies

[3907]

Key guide to electronic resources: engineering. McBurney, M., *ed.* Medford, N.J. Information Today, 1995. 196p. $39.95. ISBN: 1573870080.

Lists and describes online databases, CD-ROMs, locally loaded databases, OPACs, bulletin boards and electronic journals. Some evaluations are included. Indexes: companies; subjects; titles. *Class No:* 620(003.4)(01)

Internet

[3908]

EEVL. Edinburgh, Heriot-Watt University Library. URL: http://www.eevl.ac.uk.

The web site provides a gateway to networked engineering information, including library catalogues, indexes to printed literature, electronic journals, product reviews, buyer's guides, recruitment agencies, newsgroups, etc. EEVL is an e-lib project, managed by the (UK) Joint Information Systems Committee; the partners include Heriot-Watt, Edinburgh, Napier and Cambridge Universities, the Imperial College of Science, Technology and Medicine and the Institution of Electrical Engineers. *Class No:* 620(003.41)

[3909]

Ei Village. New York, Engineering Index, 1998-. URL: http://www.ei.org.

The web site offers access to a range of information sources, including technical jounrals and abstracts, business information, industrial research and projects, education and training, meetings and conferences, etc. A subscription is charged. *Class No:* 620(003.41)

[3910]

HE, J. Internet resources for engineers. Oxford, Butterworth-Heinemann, 1998. pp. vi, 298. illus. £25. ISBN: 0750689498.

Covers search tools and engines, directories, library access, online databases and catalogues, education and courses, and engineering communities. A beginner's guide; useful, but will obviously date quickly. *Class No:* 620(003.41)

[3911]

THOMAS, B.J. The World wide web for scientists and engineers: a complete reference for navigating, researching, and publishing online. Bellingham, Wa., The International Society for Optical Engineering, 1998. xv, 357p. illus. ISBN: 0768001862.

Co-published by the Institute of Electrical and Electronics Engineers, American Society of Mechanical Engineers, Society of Automotive Engineers and the Institution of Electrical Engineers.

In 3 parts: 1. Essential tools and applications - 2. Web authoring and publishing - 3. Searching and researcing. Includes list of web-based resources, divided by discipline (*e.g.* chemistry; computer science). A useful survey, but will obviously date quickly. 'An excellent World Wide Web ready reference survey' (*Choice,* September 1998, p.168). *Class No:* 620(003.41)

Software

[3912]

Engineering and industrial software directory. New York, Engineering Information Inc.

Details on about 5,000 computer programs from 1,000 software producers. Data: product name; vendor; description; hardware requirements; etc. Updated semi-annually. Available online via ESA-IRS and on magnetic tape from the publisher. *Class No:* 620(003.42)

Bibliographies

[3913]

ENGINEERING SOCIETIES LIBRARY, New York. **Classed subject catalog, Engineering Societies Library.** Boston, Mass., G.K. Hall, 1963. 12 v.; Index (1963. 956p.). Supplements, 1964-74. 10 v. ISBN: 0816146533.

The main subject catalogue (215,000 cards) is classified by UDC (modified). It covers all the separate books, pamphlets, reports and bulletins in the Library. Continued in *Bibliographic guide to technology* (*qv*). *Class No:* 620(01)

[3914]

Information sources in engineering. Mildren, K.W. *and* Hicks, P.J., *eds.* 3rd ed. London, Bowker-Saur, 1996. xix, 772p. £80. (*Guides to information sources.*) ISBN: 1857390571.

First published 1976 as *The use of engineering literature;* 2nd ed. 1985.

40 contributors; 36 chapters. 4 main sections: Introduction - Primary infomation sources (Reports ... Product information) - Secondary information sources (Abstracting and indexing services, bibliographies and reviews ... standard reference sources) - Specialized subject fields (chapters 10-36; 10. Stress analysis ... 36. Concurrent engineering). Index covers subjects, information sources and services, and organizations, p.661-772. A useful volume, but lacks detail in some contributions (*e.g.* publications data; contacts; URLs) which would

....*(contd.)*

improve its value. Chapter 8, however, provides a comprehensive coverage of electronic information sources including those based on the World Wide Web. *Class No:* 620(01)

[3915]
MACKERLE, J. **Finite element methods:** a guide to information sources. Amsterdam, Elsevier, 1991. xii,371p.

Over 800 entries, with extensive annotations. 7 chapters: 1. Books - 2. Conference proceedings ... 5. Journals ... 7. Databases. 7 appendices (*e.g.* A. 'List of publishers with addresses', p.295-99). Indexes: author/editor; subject. *Class No:* 620(01)

[3916]
TECHNISCHE INFORMATIONSBIBLIOTHEK. Hannover. **Katalog der Technischen Informationsbibliothek (TIB),** Hannover. Microfiche ed. Mainz-Kastel, N. Gärtner, 1983. (Distribtuion, K.G. Saur). £1,500. ISBN: 3598304455.

1,254,960 entries on 664 fiches. Includes title entries for monographs, periodicals, all German dissertations and, in particular, published and unpublished research reports. Records the holdings of a leading scientific and technical library. *Class No:* 620(01)

Encyclopaedias

[3917]
McGraw-Hill encyclopedia of engineering. Parker, S.P., *ed.* 2nd ed. New York, etc., McGraw-Hill, 1992. [x], 1412p. illus., diagrs., graphs. £82.95. ISBN: 0070513929.

First published 1982

700 documented articles by specialists, taken from the *McGraw-Hill Encyclopedia of science and technology* (7th ed., 1992), without abridgement. 9 major branches of engineering are covered: design, electrical, industrial, mechanical, metallurgical, mining, nuclear, petroleum, and production. List of contributors; detailed, analytical index. Well-illustrated. *Class No:* 620(031)

Handbooks & Manuals

[3918]
BIRD, J.O. *and* CHIVERS, P.J. **Newnes engineering and physical science pocket book.** Oxford, Butterworth-Heinemann, 1996. 624p. illus., diagrs., graphs, tables. £16.99. ISBN: 0750628979.

Basic formulas and theorems. 4 sections: General engineering - Electrical engineering - Mechanical engineering and physical sciences - Chemistry. Detailed, analytical index. A handy compendium. *Class No:* 620(035)

[3919]
The Engineering handbook. Dorf, R.C., *ed.* Boca Raton, Fl., CRC Press; New York, IEEE Press, 1996. xlix, 2298p. illus., diagrs., graphs, tables. formulas. $99.95 ISBN: 0849383447.

'A ready reference for the practicing engineer in industry, government, and academia' (*Preface*). About 250 contributors. 211 chapters, closely subdivided, in 30 sections: 1. Statics - 2. Mechanics of materials ... 5. Structures ... 15. Water resources engineering ... 19. Digital systems ... 27. Safety ... 30. Mathematics. 3 indexes: author; key equations; subject. 'This excellent reference work' (*Choice*, June 1996, p.1674). Also available on CD-ROM ($129. ISBN: 0849385768). *Class No:* 620(035)

[3920]
Eshbach's handbook of engineering fundamentals. Tapley, B.D., *ed.* 4th ed. New York, Wiley, 1990. [2368p.] diagrs., charts, tables. $74.95. ISBN: 0471890847.

3rd ed. 1975.

Some 78 contributors. 16 documented sections (*e.g.* 12. Electronics: 174p. 50 references). Many formulas. Detailed, analytical index. Covers mechanical, electrical, chemical and civil engineering. Significantly revised, with an added chapter on computer science, and a much expanded chapter on automatic control. Equations, definitions and explanations are a feature. Bibliographies, although updated, rarely list post-1980 publications. *Class No:* 620(035)

[3921]
Handbook of reliability engineering and management. Ireson, W.G. *and* Coombs, C.F., Jr., *eds.* New York, McGraw-Hill, 1988. v.p. diagrs., graphs, tables. $59.50. ISBN: 007032039x.

17 contributors. 19 chapters in 4 parts: 1. Introduction to reliability - 2. Management of reliability - 3. Engineering for reliability - 4. Mathematics of reliability. Appendices of tables and charts. Detailed, analytical index, 10p. *Class No:* 620(035)

[3922]
HEISLER, S. **The Wiley engineer's desk reference.** 2nd ed. New York, Wiley, 1998. xix, 690p. illus., diagrs., graphs, tables, formulas. £48. ISBN: 0471168270.

First published 1984.

12 chapters, closely subdivided: 1. Mathematics - 2. Mechanics/materials - 3. Structures - 4. Fluid mechanics - 5. Thermodynamics/heat transfer - 6. Electricity and electronics - 7. Controls - 8. Economics/statistics - 9. Energy sources - 10. The design process - 11. Engineering operations - 12. Tables (69 in all). A wealth of data. *Class No:* 620(035)

[3923]
Maynard's industrial engineering handbook. Hodson, W.K., *ed.* 4th ed. New York, McGraw-Hill, 1992. 1872p. illus., diagrs., graphs, tables. £86.95. ISBN: 0070410860.

Data on methods of improvement, work measurement, planning and control of manufacturing systems, quality control, facilities and material flow. 800 illus. Detailed, analytical index. *Class No:* 620(035)

[3924]
SALVENDY, G. **Handbook of industrial engineering.** 2nd ed. New York, Wiley, 1992. xxvii,2780p. illus., diagrs., graphs, tables. £115. ISBN: 0471502766.

Published in association with the Institute of Industrial Engineers. First ed. 1982.

Over 150 contributors. 5 parts (108 subsections, with references): 1. Industrial engineering function - 2. Technology - 3. Human dimensions - 4. Planning, design and control - 5. Quantitative methods for decision making. Detailed, analytical index, p.2705-80. *Class No:* 620(035)

Adolescents

[3925]
MACAULEY, D. *and* ARDLEY, N. **The Way things work.** London, Guild Publishing, 1988. 384p. illus (col.). £15.99. ISBN: 0863183239.

4 parts: 1. The mechanics of movement - 2. Harnessing the elements - 3. Working with waves - 4. Electricity and automation (including 'Robots': 2p. spread). Appended: 'Eureka! The invention of machines', p.358-73. Technical terms, p.374-9; index p.380-4. Suitable for school libraries. *Class No:* 620(035)-0053.7

Dictionaries

English

[3926]
Industrial engineering terminology: a revision of ANSI Z94.0-1982: an American national standard, approved July 10, 1989. Norcross, Ga., Industrial Engineering and Management Press, Institute of Industrial Engineers, 1990. 535p. $72.95. ISBN: 0898061059.

About 15,000 technical terms, acronyms and abbreviations. 17 sections, each with bibliography: Biomechanics ... Manufacturing systems. Detailed, analytical index, p.489-535. 'Highly recommended' (*Choice,* April 1991, p.1290).

Also published by McGraw-Hill (1992; £70; 0070317305). *Class No:* 620(038)=20

[3927]
McGraw-Hill dictionary of engineering. Parker, S.P., *ed.* New York, etc., McGraw-Hill, 1997. xiii, 582p. $17.95; £12.99. ISBN: 0070524351.

Nearly 17,000 entries, drawn from the *McGraw-Hill Dictionary of scientific and technical terms* (5th ed., 1994). One of 13 categories or 'fields' of engineering is applied to each term. No illus. *Class No:* 620(038)=20

[3928]
McKENNA, T. *and* OLIVERSON, R. **Glossary of reliability and maintenance terms.** Houston, Tx, Gulf, 1997. 256p. $30; £20. ISBN: 0884153606.

About 1,000 general engineering terms briefly defined. *Class No:* 620(038)=20

[3929]
SCHARF, B. **Engineering and its language.** London, Muller 1971. viii, [1], 398p. illus., tables.

21 subject chapters (1. Engineering materials - 2. Iron and steel ... 6. Plastics ... 10. Machine tools and cutters ... 15. Engines ... 20. Electricity and magnetism - 21. Process instrumentation). Bold type for terms; uses and types described (*e.g.* 'Switches': p. 278-80). 343 line-drawings. Appended conversion tables; revision questions. Index (*c.*4,000 entries). The vocabulary of engineering (shown in context) for translators and authors. *Class No:* 620(038)=20

German

[3930]

Wörterbuch der industriellen Teknik. [Dictionary of engineering and technology.] 5. Aufl. Wiesbaden, Brandstetter, 1985-89. 2v. £79.95ea.

First published 1948.

1. *Deutsch-Englisch.* 5. Aufl. 1989. 1258p. 2. *Englisch-Deutsch.* 5. Aufl. 1985. 1422p.

V.1 has *c.*157,000 entries. V.2 has an introduction on 'The nature of technical English'. Regarded as the standard work in the field. Also available on CD-ROM. *Class No:* 620(038)=30

French

[3931]

FORBES, J.R. Dictionnaire des techniques et technologies modernes: anglais-francais. [Dictionary of engineering and modern technology: English-French.] 3rd ed. Paris, Lavoisier, 1997. 2v. £61 each.

First published 1990; 2nd ed. 1993..

About 40,000 entries in each vol. Headwords in bold type. *Class No:* 620(038)=40

[3932]

KETTRIDGE, J.O. French-English and English-French dictionary of technical terms and phrases used in civil, mechanical, electrical and mining engineering, and allied sciences and industries; with a method of telegraphic coding. Rev. ed., with suppt. by Y.R. Arden. London, Routledge & Kegan Paul, 1980. (reprinted 1989). 2v. £60, set; £35, ea. ISBN: 0415043093, v.1; 0415027683, v.2.

First published 1959.

1. *French-English.* 640p. 2. *English-French.* 672p.

About 100,000 entries for terms and phrases, covering both volumes. Each volume has a supplement and an appendix of abbreviations, symbols and conversion tables. *Class No:* 620(038)=40

Reviews & Abstracts

[3933]

The Engineering index monthly: the index to the world's engineering developments. New York, Engineering Index, Inc., (now Engineering Information), 1884-. 12 pa. with annual cumulation. $2,450 pa. ISSN: 07421974.

Until September 1962 as *Engineering index.*

Now produces *c.*200,000 abstracts pa. Coverage includes some conference proceedings. About 75% of articles are English-language material. Author and subject indexes per issue. *The Engineering index annual* (with 4-year cumulations) includes author, author affiliation and cumulative subject indexes, as well as the abstracts themselves. The *Index* is available online as COMPENDEX [COMPuterized ENgineering InDEX], 1970-. A major abstracting service. On CD-ROM. *Class No:* 620(048)

Periodicals

[3934]

'The Engineer' index, 1856-1959: names and subjects. Proctor, C.E., *comp.* London, Morgan, 1964. [vi], 212p.

Index of illustrated articles, plus articles over a ½ column long, excluding editorials, letters, book reviews and other features. Two sequences: 'Names' (p. 1-159) and 'Subjects'. 'Names': names of authors, personal and place names written about, pseudonyms, firms, names of ships, etc. The 'Subjects' index (p. 161-213) is inadequate, - generic rather than specific, and non-analytical. References are to volume and page numbers only. But a representative world-list of 77 libraries holding complete or near-complete sets of *The engineer* is given. Of value to historical researchers in this field. *Class No:* 620(051)

[3935]

The Innovative engineer: 125 years of 'The Engineer'. London, Morgan-Grampian, 1981. 232p. illus., diagrs. £8.50.

13 articles to celebrate 125 years of the journal, and of engineering progress (and occasionally disaster). Topics include the London underground, telephones, electric light, the Tay Bridge, Tower Bridge, motor cars and the submarine. Numerous original illustrations are reproduced. *Class No:* 620(051)

Yearbooks & Directories

[3936]

ASSOCIATION OF CONSULTING ENGINEERS. The ACE directory, 1998/9. London, Emap Consulting Directories, 1998. 222p. ISBN: 13513672.

First published 1946.

Authorized list of members. 6 sections: 1. Guide - 2. Alphabetical listing - 3. Profiles - 4. Classification tables - 5. Alphabetical listing of qualified principals - 6. Indexes (geographical; alphabetical). *Class No:* 620(058)

[3937]

—International directory of consulting engineers, 1995-96. London, Rhys Jones, 1995. 299p. tables. ISBN: 0950845663.

Produced by the International Federation of Consulting Engineers.

Includes entries for *c.*200 firm-consultants (1 per page) in about 25 countries, Australia ... USA. Data on each include international experience, personnel, services offered, fields of specialization, and typical projects. Also lists consultants from developing countries, Bangladesh ... Zimbabwe. Index of fields of specialization and experience; index of international offices. *Class No:* 620(058)

[3938]

Consultant engineers 500. 8th ed. London, Anchorage Press, 1998. 320p. ISBN: 0951662783.

Lists about 500 consultancies in the UK and Europe recommended by the Engineering Council. Also describes UK and European professional organizations. *Class No:* 620(058)

[3939]

'The Engineer' buyers guide, 1999. Tonbridge, Kent, Miller Freeman, 1999. xii, 988p. £80. ISBN: 0863823955. ISSN: 01431455.

Sections: Index to products and services - Buyers' guide - Brands and trade names - Company data - Overseas companies and UK agents - Associations, institutions and societies. *Class No:* 620(058)

Tables & Data Books

[3940]

COOK, J.L. Conversion factors. Oxford Univ. Press, 1992. 160p. tables. $12.95. ISBN: 0198563523.

More than 3,500 conversion factors, arranged by areas of application. SI units. 'Well formatted ... reasonably priced ... a valuable addition to a reference collection' (*Choice,* September 1992, p.74). *Class No:* 620(083)

[3941]

GANIC, E.N. *and* **HICKS, T.G. McGraw-Hill handbook of essential engineering information and data.** New York, McGraw-Hill, 1991. 1072p. illus. $89.50. ISBN: 0070227640.

A collection of basic engineering information, data and principles for day-to-day problem solving. Drawn from various McGraw-Hill engineering handbooks, supplemented by explanatory comments. About 20 sections. 760 illus. 'Highly recommended' (*Choice,* March 1991, p.1102). *Class No:* 620(083)

[3942]

GIECK, K. *and* **GIECK, R. Engineering formulas.** 7th ed. New York, McGraw-Hill, 1996. v.p. diagrs., tables. $29.95. ISBN: 007024572x.

English ed. first published 1967, as *A collection of technical formulae.* 6th. ed. 1990. Original German work as *Technische Formelsammlung* (26. Aufl. 1979).

A classic collection of *c.*2,000 technical and mathematical formulas. Small format. A CD-ROM version was published, New York, McGraw-Hill, 1996; it provides interactive access to 500 formulas and 400 graphic images. *Class No:* 620(083)

[3943]

—BARNETT, S. *and* CRONIN, T.M. Mathematical formulas for engineering and science students. 4th ed. London, Butterworth, 1986. 77p. $9.95. ISBN: 0582447585.

Covers most of the commonly used mathematical formulas at University and college level. Omits logarithmic tables and other functions, here replaced by some frequently used statistical tables. 'Best for personal purchase' (*New technical books,* January 1987, p.12). *Class No:* 620(083)

[3944]

HICKS, T.G. *and* **HICKS, S.D.,** *eds.* **Standard handbook of engineering calculations.** 3rd ed. New York, etc., McGraw-Hill, 1995. xviii, v.p.. illus., graphs, tables. ISBN: 0070288127.

First published 1972; 2nd ed. 1985.

The 3rd ed. reflects particularly recent developments in environmental engineering, energy conservation and the use of personal computers for calculation. Over 5,000 direct and related calculation procedures. Types of engineering dealt with: civil, architectural, mechanical, electrical, elctronics, chemical control, aeronautical and astronautical, marine, nuclear, process plant, environmental and sanitary. Also, engineering economics. Detailed analytical index *Class No:* 620(083)

[3945]

Kempe's engineer's year-book for 1998. 103rd ed. Tonbridge, Kent, Miller Freeman, 1998. v.p., illus., diagrs., graphs, tables. ISSN: 00755400.

About 60 contributors. 13 sections, A-M: A. Fundamentals - B. Materials - C. Manufacturing - D. Measurement and testing - E. Prime movers - F. Computers and electronics - G. Environmental engineering - H. Electrical engineering - I. Communications - J. Mechanical engineering ... L. Energy - M. Emissions. With the 1997 ed. certain

....*(contd.)*

'non-core' subjects (*e.g.* Risk management) are not published in every edition, but 'once over a cycle of three or four years' (p.x). A major engineering reference tool. *Class No:* 620(083)

[3946]
MATTHEWS, C. Engineers' data book. London, Professional Engineering Publishing, 1998. xiv, 178p. diagrs., tables. £9.95. ISBN: 1860581757.

Covers regulations, units, design, mechanics, quality, catalogues and data sources. Small, handy format. *Class No:* 620(083)

[3947]
Reference data for engineers: radio, electronics, computer, and communication. 8th ed. Carmel, In., Sams, 1993. v.p. diagrs., graphs, charts, tables, circuits. £90. ISBN: 0672227533.

First published in UK 1942. Previous ed. 1985.

40 chapters by 84 contributors, with much emphasis on satellite and network communication. 40p. index. A wealth of data in a standard work. *Class No:* 620(083)

[3948]
TUMA, J.J. Engineering mathematics handbook. 4th ed. New York, etc., McGraw-Hill, 1998. 566p. illus., tables. $79.95. ISBN: 0070655294.

First published 1970; 3rd ed. 1987.

22 chapters. Main parts: Algebra; geometry; trigonometry; plane analytical geometry; space analytical geometry; elementary functions. Differential calculus; sequences of series; integral calculus; vector analysis; functions of a complex variable; Fourier series; ordinary differential equations; partial differential equations; Laplace transforms. Numerical methods; probability and statistics. Tables of indefinite integrals; tables of definite integrals; plane curves and areas; space curves and surfaces. Aims to serve as a desk-top reference book for engineers, scientists and architects. 'A gold mine of information' (*Choice*, September 1998, p.163). *Class No:* 620(083)

Standards

[3949]
KVERNELAND, K.O. World metric standards for engineering. New York, Industrial Press, 1978. xi, [735p.] diagrs., tables. ISBN: 0831111135.

Aimed to assist engineers, manufacturers, designers, and draughtsmen in North American and other countries where transition to the metric system is taking place; this work provides comparisons of the standards in 8 of the largest industrial countries of the world and is thus of value even in areas where SI units are already in use. 16 of its 20 sections cover components, systems, materials and practices of general engineering interest, but 6 in particular concern mechanical engineering: 8. Seven threads - 9. Fasteners ... 12. Bearings - 13. Mechanical power transmission systems - 14. Fluid power systems and components ... 17. Metal cutting tools. Text, tables and illustrations are adequate for their intended purpose and impressive in coverage. *Class No:* 620(083.74)

Models

[3950]
JACKSON, A. and DAY, D. The Model maker's handbook. Driver, E., *ed.* London, Pelham Books, 1981. 352p. illus. (incl. col.), charts, tables.

Cover subtitle: an illustrated manual of over 1,000 techniques for making all types of models, miniatures and diagrams. Sections concern basic techniques (tool kit, materials, etc.); painting and finishing; figures; dioramas and landscapes; railways; motors and engines; radio control; aeroplanes; boats; cars. Useful addresses; glossary. Detailed analytical index, p.344-50. Step-by-step instructions. Hundreds of illus., with descriptive captions. *Class No:* 620(086.48)

Histories

[3951]
ARMYTAGE, W.H.G. A Social history of engineering. [4th ed]. London, Faber & Faber, 1976. 381p. illus. (pl.), ports., tables.

First published 1961.

27 readable chapters, from prehistory onwards, with an amount of biographical data. Appendix A: Chapter bibliographies (p. 337-55); B: List of professional institutions. Index of subjects and plates; index of persons. Three aims: 'to chart technological developments with special reference to Britain, to indicate how they affected and seem affected by social life at certain stages and to offer some clues as to the origin of innovations and institutions' (*Preface*). *Class No:* 620(091)

[3952]
CHANNEL, D.F. The History of engineering science: an annotated bibliography. New York, Garland, 1989. *c.*300p. $42. (*Reference library of the humanities, 1150.*) ISBN: 0824066367.

Includes books, articles and dissertations in English, French and German. 'Well-researched ... recommended' (*Library Journal*, January 1990, p.100). *Class No:* 620(091)

[3953]
GARRISON, E. A History of engineering and technology: artful methods. Boca Raton, Fl., CRC Press, 1991. 176p. illus., diagrs. $39.95. ISBN: 0849388368.

Engineering advances and their industrial and social significance from antiquity to the present day. Well-illustrated with a useful bibliography. *Class No:* 620(091)

[3954]
HILL, D. A History of engineering in classical and medieval times. London, Croom Helm, 1984. [xiv], 263p. illus. (incl. pl.). ISBN: 0709912099.

Describes the important engineering achievements in Europe and western Asia, 600BC-AD1450. 3 parts (12 chapters): 1. Civil engineering - 2. Mechanical engineering - 3. Fine technology (instruments; automata; clocks). Chapter notes (*e.g.* 5. Roads: p.76-82. 29 references). Bibliography, p.248-55. Detailed analytical index. Pays considerable attention to descriptions of techniques and machines. *Class No:* 620(091)

[3955]
NEWCOMEN SOCIETY FOR THE STUDY OF THE HISTORY OF ENGINEERING. Transactions, 1920/21-. [Newcomen Society]. London, Newcomen Society, 1922-. v. 1-. illus. (incl. pl.), diagrs., tables.

In addition to historical papers, most volumes carry 'Analytical bibliography of the history of engineering and applied science', arranged under subjects. V.38, for 1965-6 (1968), includes 'Sir Robert Smirke; a pioneer of concrete construction' (p.5-22) and 'Origin of the canning industry' (p.145-52; 28 footnote references). *General index* to v.1-32, 1920-60 (Cambridge, Heffer, 1963) is a name and subject index; items are asterisked if they contain illus. The longest running British journal for the history of engineering and technology. *Class No:* 620(091)

Biographies

[3956]
TURNER, R. and GOULDON, S.L., eds. Great engineers and pioneers in technology. New York, St. Martin's Press, 1982-. v.1-. illus.

1. *From antiquity through the Industrial Revolution.* 1981. 488p.

6 contributors. 373 profiles, in 5 sections: 1. Engineering in the ancient world (prior to 600AD) - 2. Medieval engineering: Islam and Europe - 3. Engineering in the Far East - 4. Engineering in the Renaissance - 5. The Industrial Revolution. Each section comprises an introdutory essay, biography and 'further reading'. Chronology, to 1850. Bibliographical essay, p.461-5. List of illus. Index of names and subjects, p.475-88. Well produced. 'No other comparable work' (*RQ*, Winter 1982, p.201). *Class No:* 620(092)

[3957]
—The Biographical dictionary of scientists: engineers and inventors. Abbott, D., *ed.* London: Blond Educational, 1985. [vi], 189p. diagrs. £12.95. ISBN: 0584700040.

Provides basic facts on about 200 engineers and inventors, p.7-163 (*e.g.* Edison; Brunel - each 2½ columns). Glossary and index follow. Diagram, but no portraits. Aims to fill the gap, at an economic price, between too long and costly or too short and insufficiently informative works of this sort. Criteria for selection of names is queried in *Choice* (v. 24(2), September 1986, p.78). *Class No:* 620(092)

[3958]
—CARVILL, J. Famous names in engineering. London, Butterworth, 1981. [x], 93p. illus., ports., table. £8.95. ISBN: 0408005394.

Aims to provide 'brief and ... interesting and informative biographies of 83 famous people whose laws, theories, and inventions form the basis of any advanced course in Engineering' (*Preface*). Names, A-Z. Each biographical note occupies about one page, plus portrait drawing and relevant formula or illus. Index of subjects groups the names. Chronological table, Pythagoras ... Ernst Nussett (died 1957). Bibliography gives further reading on each person. *Class No:* 620(092)

[3959]
Who's who in science and engineering, 1998-99. 4th ed. New Providence, N.J., Marquis Who's Who, 1997. xxxiv, 1638p. $259.95 ISBN: 0837957567.
First published 1992.
Over 31,000 living scientists from 125 countries (80% US). Data: current address, birth date and place, family members, education, career history. Indexes: geographic; professional area; awards. Also available on *The Complete Marquis who's who on CD-ROM*.
Class No: 620(092)

Great Britain
[3960]
WALKER, D. *and* PAPADAKIS, A., *eds*. Great engineers: a survey of British engineers, 1837-1987. London; Academic Editions/St. Martin's Press, in association with the Royal College of Art, 1987. 288p., illus. (incl. col.). £29.95. ISBN: 0856709174.
22 essays by leading engineers, historians and industrialists. Covers the period from the Industrial Revolution to the present day, including both major 19th century engineers such as Brunel and the Stephensons, as well as 20th-century exponents (*e.g.* Ove Arup and Partners, Felix Samuely and Büro Happold). Added section of biographies of over 60 engineers, a list of great British inventions, an extensive bibliography, and index. More than 400 illus. (200 in colour). Quarto format.
Class No: 620(092)(410)

[3961]
—BELL, S.P., *comp.* A Biographical index of British engineers in the 19th century. New York & London, Garland Publishing, 1975. x, 246p. $22.
A key to biographical information (*e.g.* obituary notices) on *c.*3,000 engineers, appearing in 24 periodicals, 1823-1900. 1-2 references each, on average, per entry (Sir Henry Bessemer: 10).
Class No: 620(092)(410)

USA
[3962]
Who's who in engineering. Davis, G., *ed.* 8th ed. New York, American Assocation of Engineering Societies, 1994. xx, 1026p. ISBN: 0876150164.
First published 1970 as *Engineers of distinction, including scientists in related fields* (New York, Engineers Joint Council).
About 15,000 entries, A-Z, for North American (mostly US) engineers of distinction. Data include employment, education, achievements, addresses. Engineering societies, p.3-85. Appended indexes by state/province and specialization. *Class No:* 620(092)(73)

[3963]
—ROYSDEN, C. *and* KHARTI, L.A. American engineers of the nineteenth century: a biographical index. New York & London, Garland Publishing, 1978. xx, 247p.
Concentrates - like its companion volume, S.P. Bell's *A biographical index of British engineers in the 19th century* (*qv*) - on obituary notices in journals, transactions and proceedings of professional societies, plus references to such general sources as *Dictionary of American biography*. A quick-reference source. 'Also the obituaries quoted will give some idea of the importance of the person and provide the basic leads for a more detailed investigation' (*Library review*, v. 28, Autumn 1979, p. 189). *Class No:* 620(092)(73)

[3964]
—Who's who in engineering: a biographical dictionary of the engineering profession, 1922/1923-64. New York, Lewis Historical Publishing Co., 1922-64.
The 9th and last ed. (2198p.) appeared in 1964, with 20,000 entries for US engineers and foreign engineers who had undertaken important work in the USA. Preceded by list of US organizations; abbreviations and addenda. Geographical cross-index of persons.
Class No: 620(092)(73)

Writing & Lecturing
[3965]
HASLAM, J.M. Writing engineering specifications. London, Spon, 1988. xvi,172p. diagrs., tables. ISBN: 0419137505; 0419137602, Pbk.
7 chapters, closely subdivided: 1. Context - 2. Presenting - 3. Effect - 4. Writing - 5. Grammar - 6. Models and layout - 7. Claims. Appendix: 'Word processing management'. Index (8p.). Emphasis is practical and commercial, rather than academic. A basic manual.
Class No: 620:001.81

[3966]
MICHAELSON, H.B. How to write and publish engineering papers and reports. 3rd ed. Phoenix, Az., Oryx Press, 1990. xvi,221p. illus., diagrs., tables. £17.95. ISBN: 0897746503.
Covers writing techniques, parts of the paper (abstracts; tables; citations, etc.), submission to a publisher and technical developments (DTP; networking, etc.). References, p.205-11. Detailed, analytical indedx, p.213-21. *Class No:* 620:001.81

[3967]
PARADIS, J.G. *and* ZIMMERMAN, M.L. The MIT guide to science and engineering communication. Cambridge, MA., MIT Press, 1997. x, 290. ISBN: 0262161427.
The handbook covers four kinds of communication - written, oral, graphic, electronic - and the techniques necessary, both individually and collectively. Numerous practical examples. *Class No:* 620:001.81

[3968]
VAN EMDEN, J. A Handbook of writing for engineers. London, Macmillan, 1990. 96p. £4.99. ISBN: 0333469429.
Practical guide to writing style for a range of documents in engineering: letters, reports, technical notes, instructions.
Class No: 620:001.81

Equipment & Instruments
[3969]
WALL, R.A., *ed.* Engineers' guide to product information: sources and use. London, Aslib, 1992. xv, 253p. £25. ISBN: 0851422918.
10 chapters in 4 parts: 1. Information needs - 2. Sources of product information - 3. Product information services - 4. Advisory and consultancy services. Index. *Class No:* 620:002.50

Thesauri
[3970]
SHE: subject headings for engineering. New York, Engineering Information Inc., 1987. xviii,218p. ISBN: 0873940190.
First published 1972; supplement, 1977. Previous ed. 1983.
Thesaurus of terms for use with various Engineering Information services, from *Engineering index monthly* to *Energy abstracts* to *Compendex*. Arranged by main headings, followed by subheadings. Numerous 'see' and 'see also' references to preferred indexing terms.
Class No: 620:025.43

Research Establishments
[3971]
Engineering research centres: a world directory of organizations and programmes incorporating *Electronics research centres*. 4th ed. Harlow, Essex, Cartermill, 1995. x, 845p. £299. ISBN: 1860670164.
1st ed. 1984; 3rd ed. 1993.
Data on more than 6,000 laboratories, industrial companies and educational establishments active in engineering and electronics research. By country, then body, A-Z. Entries include name of organization, address, phone, fax, status, senior personnel, facilities, graduate research staff, annual expenditure, activities, clients, publications. Index of establishments; subjects.
Class No: 620:061:061.62

Education Institutions
[3972]
UNITED NATIONS. Educational, Scientific and Cultural Organization. Directory of engineering education institutions: Africa, Arab States, Asia, Latin America and the Caribbean. 3rd ed. Paris, Unesco, 1986. xiv, 303p. ISBN: 9230023930.
First published 1962.
Information on 781 degree-awarding institutions in 61 countries.
Class No: 620:061:37

Engineering Design
[3973]
BRITISH LIBRARY. Science Reference Library. Useful books of reference for designers (1926-1983) held by the Science Reference Library. Palyza, M.M., *ed.* London, SRL, 1984. 3v. ea.£5.
1. *Metrication; physical units; databooks for various materials; use of computers in engineering; Hand- and databooks for designers in civil engineering*. [iv], 163p.
2. *Hand- and databooks for designers in electrical and electronic engineering*. [iii], 71p.
3. *Hand- and databooks for designers in mechanical engineering*. [iii], 121p.
Each of the 3 parts carries *c.*1,000 references. Subject index precedes. *Class No:* 620.001.6

[3974]

CULLUM, R.D. **Handbook of engineering design.** London, Butterworths, 1988. [vii], 303p. illus., diagrs. graphs. £59.50. ISBN: 0408005580.

19 contributors. Part 1 (chapters 1-11, each with bibliography: 1. Stages in design; 2. Engineering materials; 3. Stress analysis; 4. Bearings; 5. Fastenings; 7. Design aspects of production processes) - Part 2 (chapters 12-16; *e.g.* 13. Structure and organization in design offices). Directory; addresses. Detailed analytical index, p.301-3. Well illustrated. *Class No:* 620.001.6

[3975]

FRENCH, M.J. **Invention and evolution:** design in nature and engineering. 2nd ed. Cambridge, Univ. Press, 1994. xx, 367p. illus., diagrs. £50. ISBN: 0521465036.

Covers numerous examples of design for function. 11 chapters, closely subdivided (*e.g.* 2. Energy - 3. Materials ... 5. Structures (beams; feathers, etc.) ... 8. Economy, form and beauty ... 10. Designing and inventing - 11. Some case studies). Detailed, analytical index. *Class No:* 620.001.6

[3976]

Handbook of solid modeling. LaCourse, D.E., *ed.* New York, McGraw-Hill, 1995. v.p. illus. (some col.), diagrs. $89.50. ISBN: 0070357889.

Numerous contributors. Covers design, evaluation, implementation and operation. Case studies; glossary; detailed, analytical index. 'Well presented' (*Choice*, February 1996, p. 979). *Class No:* 620.001.6

[3977]

HICKS, P.J. **'Design and ergonomics'.** *Information sources in engineering.* K.W. Mildren and P.J. Hicks, eds. (3rd ed., 1996), p.329-51. 3rd ed. London, Bowker Saur, 1996. £80. ISBN: 1857390571.

Covers creativity, management, CAD, industrial design. Information sources include journals, standards and guides, computer sources, databases, abstracts, conferences and exhibitions, and organizations. Extensive list of references, p.341-51. *Class No:* 620.001.6

[3978]

INSTITUTION OF ENGINEERING DESIGNERS. **Official reference book and buyers' guide.** London, Sterling Publications, 1991. 248p. illus. £30.

19 brief articles (*e.g.* 'Designing for quality' (p.46-52)). Classified buyers' guide: Engineering design tools and computers - Materials ... Coatings and finishes - Power transmission ... Production and manufacturing technology - Test measurement and instrumentation - Professional services. *Class No:* 620.001.6

[3979]

MUCCI, P. **Handbook for engineering design using standard materials and components.** 3rd ed. Southampton, P.E.R. Mucci, 1990. vi,240p. illus., tables. ISBN: 0951155520.

First published 1986; 2nd ed. 1987.

10 chapters (*e.g.* 2. Materials ... 5. Bearings ... 9. Mechanical components (seales; springs), most including names and address of manufacturers and suppliers. 7 appendices (D. Fits and tolerances for holes, p.220-21). Index, p.236-40. Much tabular information. *Class No:* 620.001.6

Materials Science

Databases

[3980]

Engineered materials abstracts. Metals Park, Oh., ASM International; London, Institute of Metals.

Corresponds to the print publication of the same name. Covers the science of polymers, ceramics and composite materials and the practices of materials science and engineering. Over 100,000 records; updated monthly. Avaialable online, on CD-ROM and on the World Wide Web from Cambridge Scientific Abstracts (URL: http://www.csa.com). *Class No:* 620.02(003.4)

CD-ROM

[3981]

Advanced materials CD-ROM. Shrewsbury, Rapra Technology, Ltd., Columbus, Oh., ASM International, 1997. £2460; $3450.

Bibliographic citations covering polymers, ceramics and composite materials intended for use in the design, construction and operation of structures, equipment and systems. About 9,000 records, from 1985 to present. Updated quarterly. *Class No:* 620.02(003.40)

[3982]

Materials science citation index. Philadelphia, Pa., Institute for Scientific Information, 1991-. 6 disks pa. $1950.

Citation index, with abstracts. About 90,000 records from 1,700 publications. Also available online as part of Scisearch from various hosts. *Class No:* 620.02(003.40)

Bibliographies

[3983]

SARGENT, P. **'Materials information sources for engineers'.** *Information sources in engineering.* K.W. Mildren and P.J. Hicks, eds. (3rd ed., 1996), p.301-14. 3rd ed. London, Bowker Saur, 1996. £80. ISBN: 1857390571.

Covers standards, organizations, databases, handbooks and databooks, textbooks, conferences, journals, abstracts and indexes, data transfer methods, CALS, expert systems. *Class No:* 620.02(01)

Encyclopaedias

[3984]

BEVER, M.B., *ed.* **Encyclopedia of materials science and engineering.** Oxford, etc. Pergamon Press, 1986. 8v. (6105p.). illus., diagrs.

More than 1,400 contributors. 1,580 signed, documented articles on 45 broad subject areas (*e.g.* metals, ceramics, polymers, magnetic materials, welding). Some articles, designated 'An overview', introduce and survey a subject, furnish systematic and comprehensive bibliographic references to the entire subject, and are extensively cross-referenced (*e.g.* 'Advanced ceramics: an overview', v.1, p.98-105: 4 sections, 3 diagrs., 9 illus., 16 references). V.8, *Index*, includes systematic outline of the *Encyclopedia*, list of contributors, citation index, subject index (*c.*50,000 entries), materials information sources (p.527-42, supplementing article references), and list of acronyms. Aims to produce a comprehensive work to 'serve the needs of education and industry' (*Introduction*). Supplementary v.3 (1993) carried 120 articles (*e.g.* 'Laser coating of surfaces', p.1726-34, with a bibliography of 20 items).

A number of *Concise encyclopedias* on specific aspects of materials science have been produced using articles from the full *Encyclopedia* and revised, updated material. Consult the index for those included in this edition of *Walford*. *Class No:* 620.02(031)

[3985]

—Concise encyclopedia of composite materials. Kelly, A., *and others, eds.* Rev. ed. Oxford, Pergamon, 1994. xxix, 349p. illus., diagrams, tables. $57.50. (*Advances in materials science and engineering.*) ISBN: 0080423000.

First published 1989.

67 articles, each with extensive bibliobraphy, some drawn from the *Encyclopedia of materials science and engineering* and others newly commissioned. A useful, up-to-date supplement to the full *Encyclopedia. Class No:* 620.02(031)

[3986]

—Encyclopedia of advanced materials. Bloor, D., *and others, eds.* Oxford, Pergamon Press, 1994. 4v. (3152p.) illus., diagrs., graphs, tables. $1600. ISBN: 0080406068.

Over 500 well-documented articles on the specialized subject of advanced materials. To an extent develops and updates topics appearing in the *Encyclopedia of materials science and engineering,* although it is by no means one of the 'Concise' spinoffs. *Class No:* 620.02(031)

[3987]

Encyclopedia of materials characterization. Brundle, C., *and others, eds.* Oxford, Butterworth Heinemann, 1992. v.p. illus., diagrs., tables. £75. ISBN: 0750691689.

Covers techniques (description, data obtained, use, future trends) used in modern materials analysis. *Class No:* 620.02(031)

[3988]

GRAYSON, M., *ed.* **Encyclopedia of composite materials and components.** New York, etc., Wiley, 1983. xxviii, 1161p. illus., diagrs., graphs, tables.

Reprints of more than 50 articles from Kirk and Othmer's *Encyclopedia of chemical technology.* Ablative materials ... Sealants. Many data tables, standards, specifications and literature references. Detailed analytical index, p.1109-61. Designed as a definite and comprehensive guide to the properties, manufacturing methods and components. *Class No:* 620.02(031)

[3989]

International encyclopedia of composites. Lee, S.M., *ed.* New York, etc., VCH, 1990-91. 6v. £180 each; £315 set. ISBN: 0895732904, set.

Includes more than 300 contributors. Lengthy, documented articles ('Aramid fiber composites', p.37-56, 120 references), with cross-references. Each volume includes a list of 'main entries'. Topics covered fall into 4 groups: Special types, *e.g.* engineering materials; Behaviour under varying conditions; Those with special properties; Design aspects. Of value to practising scientists and engineers and advanced-level students. A major work. *Class No:* 620.02(031)

Handbooks & Manuals

[3990]

ASM Engineered materials reference book. Bauccio, M., *ed.* 2nd ed. Materials Park, Oh., ASM International, 1994. v, 580p. diagrs., graphs, tables. ISBN: 0871705028.

4 sections: 1. Composites - 2. Ceramics - 3. Plastics - 4. Electronic materials. Glossary of terms, p.1-59. 6 appendices. Numerous tables. *Class No:* 620.02(035)

[3991]

BOLTON, W. Newnes engineering materials pocket book. 2nd ed. Oxford, Butterworth-Heinemann, 1996. 256p. diagrs., tables. £14.99. ISBN: 0750628863.

First published 1989.

Contents: terminology; test methods; ferrous alloys; aluminium alloys; cop magnesium; nickek; titanium; polymeric materials; ceramics; composites; comparative properties; semiconductors; selection of materials. Index. Small format. Intended for students with project work and practising engineers. *Class No:* 620.02(035)

[3992]

Elsevier materials selector. Waterman, N.A. and Ashby, M.F., *eds.* London, Elsevier Applied Science, 1991. 3v. (2228p.), diagrs., graphs, tables. ISBN: 1851666052, set, UK; 0849377900, set, US.

Includes information on (1) Selection and specification of materials and manufacturing routes for a new product and (2) Evaluation of alternative materials and manufacturing routes for an existing product. Covers a variety of materials (*e.g.* steels, aluminium alloys, ceramics, coatings, nylons, PVC) and testing procedures. *Class No:* 620.02(035)

[3993]

—Advanced materials sourcebook: 1994-95. Binner, J., *and others, eds.* 2nd ed. Oxford, Elsevier Advanced Technology, 1994. 590p. £175. ISBN: 1856172384.

Material collected from Elsevier Advanced Technology newsletters, with editorial comment. 4 chapters: 1. Ceramics - 2. Plastics - 3. Composites - 4. Addresses (over 1,000 organizations). A useful compilation. *Class No:* 620.02(035)

[3994]

Engineered materials handbook: prepared under direction of the ASM International Handbook Committee. Metals Park, Oh., ASM International, 1987-. v.1-. illus. ISBN: 0871702797, v.1.

V. 1. *Composites.*

V. 2. *Engineering plastics.*

V. 3. *Adhesives and solvents.*

Comprehensive, with charts and graphs. Each volume has its own subject index and glossary. *Class No:* 620.02(035)

[3995]

Handbook of industrial materials 2nd ed. Oxford, Elsevier, 1992. ix, 803p. illus., tables. £95. ISBN: 0946395837.

10 sections: 1. Ferrous metals ... 4. Thermoplastics ... 7. Materials for specific applications (*eg*, abrasives) ... 10. Engineering data. Extensive tables; index, p.789-803. *Class No:* 620.02(035)

[3996]

LUBIN, C., *ed.* **Handbook of composites.** New York, etc., Van Nostrand Reinhold, 1982. x, [1], 786p. illus., graphs, tables, chemical formulas. ISBN: 0442248976.

Sponsored by the Society of Plastic Engineers.

4 sections (28 documented chapters): 1. Raw materials - 2. Processing methods - 3. Design - 4. Applications. Chapter 24, 'Testing of reinforced concretes', has 17 references and 1p. of bibliography. Glossary, p.753-78. 3 Appendices (A. Typical properties of reinforced composites). Non-analytical index, p.779-86. *Class No:* 620.02(035)

[3997]

MALLICK, P.K. and **NEWMAN, S.,** *eds.* **Composite materials technology:** process and properties. Oxford Univ. Press, 1990. 480p. illus., diagrs., tables, graphs. $98. ISBN: 0195208471.

13 contributors. 10 documented chapters covering sheet, compression, reaction injection molding, resin transfer molding, filament winding pultrusion, injection molding and quality systems. 'A good reference' (*Choice*, September 1991). *Class No:* 620.02(035)

[3998]

Materials and technology: a systematic encyclopaedia of the material used in industry and commerce, including foodstuffs and fuels. London, Longmans; Amsterdam, de Bussy, 1968-76. 8v. illus. (incl. pl.), diagrs., tables.

Based on J.F. Van Oss's *Warenkennis en Technologie* (5th ed. 1948-50). Updated and rewritten.

U.S. title as *Chemical technology: an encyclopedic treatment* (New York, Barnes & Noble, 1968-76. 8v.).

1. *Air, water, inorganic chemicals and nucleonics.* 1968.

2. *Non-metallic ores, silicate industries and solid mineral fuels.* 1971.

3. *Metals and ores.* 1970.

4. *Petroleum, organic chemicals and plastics.* 1972.

5. *Natural organic products and related mineral fuels.* 1972.

6. *Wood, paper, textiles, plastics and photographic materials.* 1973.

7. *Vegetable food products and luxuries.* 1975.

8. *Edible oils and fats, and animal food products.* 1975.

V.1 (xxiv, 703p.) mentions *c.*300 compounds, for some 30 of these the processes selected for extensive treatment. Chapter 6 of v.2 'Glass' (p.331-412) has 41 figures, 20 tables and 8 references. 'May be viewed as an introduction to chemical technology' (*Aslib book list,* v.34(3), March 1969, entry no.154). *Class No:* 620.02(035)

[3999]

Materials handbook: an encyclopedia for managers, technical professionals, purchasing and production managers, technicians, and supervisors. Clauser, H. *and* Vaccari, J.A., *eds.* 14th ed. New York, etc., McGraw-Hill, 1997. viii, 1136p. ISBN: 0070070849.

First published 1929; 13th ed. 1991.

More than 13,000 entries, A-Z. Materials covered include chalk, detergents, glass jewelry alloys, peppermint, stainless steel and zinc. Data: full description; definition; use; relationships to other materials. Index, 95p. *Class No:* 620.02(035)

[4000]

Materials science and technology: a comprehensive treatment. Cahn, R.W., *and others, eds.* New York, VCH, 1991-. V1-. £176 each. ISBN: 3527268146, V.1.

To be complete in 19 v. V. 17, *Processing of ceramics* (1995. 800p.), includes chapters on die pressing and isostatic pressing, tape casting, vitrification, flaw origins, etc., each closely sub-divided, with extensive references. Vol. indexes. *Class No:* 620.02(035)

[4001]

SCHWARTZ, M.M. Composite materials handbook. 2nd ed. New York, etc., McGraw-Hill, 1992. v.p. $79.50. ISBN: 0070558191.

First published 1983.

Covers component materials, composite systems, fabrication methods, joining and quality control. *Choice* (November 1992, p.500) identifies a lack of 'state-of-the-art techniques for the mechanical analysis of composites' as a shortcoming, but recommends the work as an 'excellent addition'. *Class No:* 620.02(035)

[4002]

SMITH, C.O. The Science of engineering materials. 3rd ed. Englewood Cliffs, N.J., Prentice-Hall, 1986. xii, 579p. illus., diagrs., graphs, tables. £49.20. ISBN: 0137948840.

First published 1969. 2nd ed. 1977.

10 chapters on design and selection, bonding, behaviour, applications development and failure, analysis of materials. Most chapters end with a number of 'questions and problems' for solution and discussion. 5 appendices of data tables. Bibliography. Subject index. Covers the basic materials science needs in a first course for engineering students. *Class No:* 620.02(035)

[4003]

Treatise on materials science and technology. Herman, H., *ed.* Orlando, Florida, London, etc., Academic Press, 1972-. (v.1-28. 1972-93). illus., graphs, charts, tables. ISBN: 0123418011.

V. 10, pt. B: *Properties of solid polymeric materials* contains a paper 'Electronic properties of polymers', p.637-76, with 17 charts and graphs, 3 tables and 3p. of references. 4v. (v.12, 17, 22, 26) have so far been devoted to glass. V.28 (600p.): *Characterization of materials* (1993); each article carries a list of symbols. *Class No:* 620.02(035)

Dictionaries

Polyglot

[4004]

HOLMSTROM, J., *and others.* **Trilingual dictionary for materials and structures.** Oxford, etc., Pergamon Press, 1971. xxxvi, 947p.

Published with the assistance of Unesco. At head of title-page: 'RILEM. International Union of Testing and Research Laboratories for Materials and Structures'.

8,063 numbered terms (English terms, equivalents and indexes in French and German, and definitions in all three languages). Grouped: A. General aspects - B. Metals - C. Cement and concrete - D.

....(contd.)
Siliceous, calcareous, agrilaceous materials - E. Soils - F. Wood - G. Other organic materials. - H. Water. Bibliography of sources, p.821-4.
Class No: 620.02(038)=00

English

[4005]
ASM materials engineering dictionary. Davis, J.R., *ed.* Metals Park, Oh., ASM International, 1992. *c.*500p. illus., diagrs., tables. ISBN: 0871704471.
About 7,500 terms, some defined at length. 64 'Technical briefs' provide overviews of selected materials. Brief bibliography (mostly of ASM publications). *Class No:* 620.02(038)=20

[4006]
Chambers materials science and technology dictionary. Walker, P.M.B., *and others, eds.* Edinburgh, Chambers, 1993. vi, 346p. illus., diagrs., tables. £20. ISBN: 0530132486.
About 6,500 terms. Panels throughout provide additional information (*e.g.* 'high-performance fibres', 2p.). Good value. *Class No:* 620.02(038)=20

[4007]
CUBBERLY, W.H. Dictionary of materials and testing. Warrendale, Pa., Society of Automotive Engineers, Inc., 1993. [v], 402p. £85. ISBN: 1560913614.
About 11,000 terms, briefly defined, including nearly 3,000 related to PC hardware and software. Expensive. *Class No:* 620.02(038)=20

[4008]
Macmillan dictionary of materials and manufacturing. John, V., *ed.* London, Macmillan, 1990. vi,431p. diagrs., formulas. £35. ISBN: 0333455584.
6 contributors; *c.*3,500 terms, A-Z. Definitions range from 2 lines to 1 column. Cross-references. Covers metallic, ceramic, polymeric and composite materials; includes processes and manufacturing systems, where appropriate. *Class No:* 620.02(038)=20

German

[4009]
GOEDECKE, W. Wörterbuch der werkstoffprüfung. [Dictionary of materials testing.] Düsseldorf, VDI-Verlag, 1992. ix, 705p. £99.95. ISBN: 3184011593.
12,049 numbered entries in German, with indexes in English and French. *Class No:* 620.02(038)=30

French

[4010]
CHEMIN, L. Terminologie des matériaux complexe. Paris, La Maison du Dictionnaire, 1992. 308p. £23.75.
About 5,000 entries, English/French, French/English.
Class No: 620.02(038)=40

Reviews & Abstracts

[4011]
Engineered materials abstracts. London, Institute of Metals and Metals Park, Ohio, ASM International, 1986-. 12pa. $1,340; £880, full price (discount for members). ISSN: 09519998.
Covers polymers, ceramics and composite materials for use in the design, construction and operation of structures, equipment and systems. 7 sections: 1. Fundamental characteristics - 2. Laboratory techniques and quality control - 3. Properties - 4. Raw materials - 5. Fabricating and finishing - 6. Engineering design and application - 7. Other coverage. 5 indexes per issue: subject; trade names; materials; author; corporate author. Avaialable online, on CD-ROM and on the World Wide Web from Cambridge Scientific Abstracts (URL: http://www.csa.com). *Class No:* 620.02(048)

[4012]
Key abstracts: advanced materials. London, Institution of Electrical Engineers, 1987-. Monthly. ISSN: 09504753.
About 3,500 abstracts pa. Covers methods of preparation, surface treatments, and materials testing in 3 major sections: 1.0 Composite materials - 2.0 Ceramics, refractories and glasses - 3.0 Polymers and plastics. Subject index per issue. *Class No:* 620.02(048)

Progress Reports

[4013]
Annual review of materials science. Palo Alto, Ca., Annual Reviews Inc., 1970-. Annual. illus., graphs, tables. ISSN: 00846600.
V.26 (1996. 730p.) includes papers on polymers. Cumulative indexes for contributing authors and chapter titles.
Class No: 620.02(055)

Tables & Data Books

[4014]
CRC materials science and engineering handbook. Shackleford, J.F., *and others, eds.* 2nd ed. Boca Raton, Fl., CRC Press, 1994. v.p. tables. $99.50. ISBN: 0849342503.
Covers organic and inorganic materials, as well as metals, glasses, semiconductors and polymers. Mostly tabular data. 2 sections: properties of materials; selecting properties. Index, 65p. Available on CD-ROM (MathSoft; £149). A new edition was due in February 1999. *Class No:* 620.02(083)

[4015]
—**CRC practical handbook of materials selection.** Shackleford, J.F., *and others, eds.* Boca Raton, Fl., CRC Press, 1995. xii, 625p. tables. $69.95. ISBN: 0849337097.
Serves as a companion volume to *CRC materials science and engineering handbook* (2nd ed.). Contents: Professional societies - ABET accredited educational programs - Education and employment trends - Selecting metals - Selecting ceramics - Selecting polymers - Index. A wealth of data. *Class No:* 620.02(083)

[4016]
—**Practical handbook of materials science.** Lynch, C.T., *ed.* Boca Raton, Florida, CRC Press, 1989. [viii],636p. tables. £33.50. ISBN: 084933702x.
Data largely taken from *CRC Handbook of materials science (1974-80. 4v.)*, and updated where necessary. Sources identified. 13 sections: 1. The elements - 2. Elemental properties - 3. Physical properties of compounds - 4. Conversion tables - 5. Miscellaneous materials properties - 6. Ceramics - 7. Composites - 8. Electronic - 9. Graphite - 10. Metallic - 11. Nuclear - 12. Polymeric - 13. Material information. Detailed, analytical index, p.619-36. *Class No:* 620.02(083)

[4017]
HOULDCROFT, P.T., *ed.* Materials data sources. Compiled for the Materials Group, the Institution of Mechanical Engineers, and sponsored by the Institute of Metals. London, Mechanical Engineering Pubns., for the Institution of Mechanical Engineers, 1987. vi, 111p. tables. £10. ISBN: 085298636x.
6 sections: 1. Metals and alloys - 2. Refractories, ceramics, glasses and hardmetals - 3. Polymers and composites - 4 Timber - 5. Databases and materials selectors - 6. Educational establishments. Appendices: A. Addresses of standards organizations; B. Joining and adhesive bonding consumables. Small format. For quick-reference. *Class No:* 620.02(083)

[4018]
MORRELL, R. Handbook of properties of technical and engineering ceramics. National Physical Laboratory. London, H.M. Stationery Office, 1985-. pt.1-. illus. ISBN: 0114800529; 0114800537.
Part 1 (1985. 360p. £33) initiates a multi-part handbook by providing a broad comparison of the different types of ceramic. Part 2, *Data reviews,* section 1: *High alumina ceramics* (1987. 270p. £29.50) deals with the properties of a group of widely used types of materials. *Class No:* 620.02(083)

India

[4019]
The Wealth of India: a dictionary of Indian raw materials and industrial products. New Delhi, Council of Scientific & Industrial Research, 1948-76. 20v. illus.
Raw materials. Industrial products.
Industrial products, v.7: Plastics - shuttles (1971. xvi, [1] 5, 367, 12p.) has 29 lengthy articles and an index. Bibliography, p.xi-xiv. Well illustrated. *Class No:* 620.02(540)

Information Services

[4020]
REYNARD, K.W. UK materials information sources. 2nd ed. London, The Design Council, 1992. *c.*200p. ISBN: 0850722357.
First published 1989.
About 650 entries, A-Z, covering government departments and research laboratories, trade and professional organizations, commercial companies, publishers, higher education and consultants. Includes name, address, telephone, fax, contact and in some, but certainly not all, cases brief note of areas of interest and publications. Index of subjects, acronyms, trade and individual names, published titles. No criteria given for selection of entries. Handy, but much of what is here is available in the *Aslib directory.* *Class No:* 620.02:061:025.5

Research Establishments

[4021]

Materials research centres: a world directory of organizations and programs in materials science. 6th ed. Harlow, Essex, Cartermill, 1995. 798p. £295. ISBN: 1860670202.

First published 1983.

Data on over 5,000 research units in more than 80 countries. Coverage: industrial chemistry and chemical process engineering, hydrocarbon processing, refined technology, metallurgy, synthetic materials and fibres, composite materials, wood technology and fine chemicals. Subject and title of establishments indexes. *Class No: 620.02:061:061.62*

Materials Testing

[4022]

AMERICAN SOCIETY FOR TESTING AND MATERIALS. Annual book of ASTM standards. Philadelphia, Pa., the Society, 1939-. Annual. 66v. diagrs.

16 sections: 1. *Iron and steel products.* 6v. 2. *Nonferrous metal products.* 6v. 3. *Metals test methods and analytical procedures.* 6v. 4. *Construction.* 9v. 5. *Petroleum products, lubricants and fossil fuels.* 5v. 6. *Paints, related coatings, and aromatics.* 3v. 7. *Textiles.* 2v. 8. *Plastics.* 4v. 9. *Rubber.* 2v. 10. *Electrical insulation and electronics.* 5v. 11. *Water and environmental technology.* 4v. 12. *Nuclear, solar and geothermal energy.* 2v. 13. *Medical devices.* 1v. 14. *General methods and instrumentation.* 2v. 15. *General products, chemical specialities and end use products.* 9v. 16. *Index.* 1v.

Annual series that includes 'all current formally approved ASTM standards and tentative test methods, definitions, recommended practices, classifications, and specifications, and other related material, such as proposed methods' (*Introduction*). Each part has its own index, v.16 being the general index. Internationally recognized for quality and up-to-dateness of its standards (some lengthy). Supplemented by monthly *ASTM standardization news. Class No: 620.1*

[4023]

AMERICAN SOCIETY FOR TESTING AND MATERIALS. Compilation of ASTM standard definitions. Sponsored by ASTM Committee E-8 on Nomenclature and Definitions. 3rd ed. Philadelphia, Pa., the Society, 1976. vii, 731p. diagrs.

Formerly as *Glossary of ASTM definitions.*

A compilation of all terms listed under the heading 'Definitions' in the 1973 ed. of the *Annual book of ASTM standards.* Numerous cross-references. Excludes symbols and abbreviations. Entries consist of concise definition plus designation of the ASTM standard containing them. *Class No: 620.1*

[4024]

AMERICAN SOCIETY FOR TESTING AND MATERIALS. Directory of testing laboratories, 1990-91. Philadelphia, Pa., ASTM, 1989. 274p. $50. ISBN: 0803112211.

Covers US, Canada, other countries. A-Z index and subject indexes. *Class No: 620.1*

[4025]

NATLAS year book. National Testing Laboratories Accreditation Scheme year book, 84/85. 3rd ed. Teddington, Middx., NATLAS Executive, National Physical Laboratory, 1984. 206p.

11 sections: 1. The UK National Testing Laboratory Accreditation Scheme ... 4. Other national schemes ... 11. List of NATLAS Accreditation laboratories. Data: name; address; telephone; telex; registration number. Advertisers index. *Class No: 620.1*

[4026]

NDE Handbook: non-destructive examination methods for condition monitoring. Böving, K.G., *ed.* London, Butterworths, 1989. 417p. illus., diagrs., graphs. £70. ISBN: 040804392x.

Covers 36 tests, each with NDE principle, development method, areas of applications, practical examples, training desired or required and references. Detailed, analytical index, p.413-17. A practical approach. *Class No: 620.1*

[4027]

Nondestructive testing database. Didcot, Oxon., UK Atomic Energy Authority.

Bibliographic database covering all aspects of nondestructive testing and evaluation. Over 53,000 records. Available online via ESA-IRS. *Class No: 620.1*

Strength

[4028]

TEKNISKA NOMENKLATURCENTRALEN. Hallfasthetsoralista: svenska-engelsk-fransk-tysk-dansk. Stockholm, the Centre, 1977. 230p. ISBN: 9171960686.

850 Swedish terms concerning strength of materials, with equivalents and indexes in English, French, German and Danish. *Class No: 620.17*

Stress, Vibration etc.

[4029]

BRITISH STANDARDS INSTITUTION. Glossary of terms relating to mechanical vibration and shock. London, BSI, 1991. 59p. (*BS 3015: 1991.*)

Defines terms used in studying and testing the effect of mechanical vibration and shock on human beings and on equipment. *Class No: 620.178.3*

[4030]

ROARK, R.J. Roark's formulas for stress and strain. Young, W.C., *ed.* 6th ed. New York etc., McGraw-Hill, 1989. 763p. illus., tables. $36.25. ISBN: 0070725411.

First published 1938. 5th ed. 1976.

3 sections: 1. Definitions - 2. Facts, principles and methods - 3. Formulas and examples. Extensive chapter bibliographies. Appendix lists factors of stress. A classic in the field. *Class No: 620.178.3*

[4031]

The Shock and vibration digest. Willowbrook, Il., Vibration Institute, 1969-. 6 pa. $250. ISSN: 05831024.

Published by Shock and Vibration Information Center, Naval Research Laboratory, 1969-1986.

About 2,000 abstracts pa. 13 sections: Machines - Structures ... Mechanical components ... Computational techniques ... Design. Prelims. include feature article, review article, book reviews, notes of short courses, reviews of meetings. Appended list of periodicals scanned. Annual indexes of feature articles, review aricles, book reviews, author and subject indexes. *Class No: 620.178.3*

[4032]

STANLEY, P. and SMART, J. 'Stress analysis'. *Information sources in engineering.* K.W. Mildren and P.J. Hicks, eds. (3rd ed., 1996), p.133-149. 3rd ed. London, Bowker Saur, 1996. £80. ISBN: 1857390571.

Sections: Introduction - Stress analysis techniques (experimental; numeric) - Professional organizations (UK) - Other professional organizations - Handbooks and data sources - Journals - Conferences - Reference texts and suppliers. *Class No: 620.178.3*

Non-Destructive

[4033]

BRITISH STANDARDS INSTITUTION. Glossary of terms used in non-destructive testing. London, BSI, 1984/85. 4 pts. (*BS 3683: 1984/85.*)

1. *Penetrant flaw detection.* 1985. 8p.
2. *Magnetic particle flaw.* 1985. 14p.
4. *Ultrasonic flaw detection.* 1985. 18p.
5. *Eddy current flaw detection.* 1985. 14p.

Makes particular reference to the terms likely to be mentioned in technical reports. Part 3 has been withdrawn. *Class No: 620.179*

[4034]

The NDT year book: the official year book of the British Institute of Non-Destructive Testing, '96. Northampton, The Institute, 1996. 189p. tables. ISSN: 09522395.

7 sections: 1. The British Institute of Non-Destructive Testing - 2. NTD methods and capabilities - 3. Guide to the market place - 4. Buyers' guide to equipment and services - 5. Standards and literature - 6. NDT operator certification - 7. Members of the Institute. *Class No: 620.179*

Metallography

[4035]

SMITH, C.S. A History of metallography: the development of ideas on the structures of metals before 1890. Chicago, Ill., Univ. of Chicago Press, 1960. xxi, 291p. illus.

5 sections: 1. The background of metallography in works of art - 2. The philosophic background - 3. Observations of structure before Sorby - 4. The work of Henry Clifton Sorby (1863-87) - 5. The period of active observation. 110 good illus. ('Kris': p. 35-39, with 8 illus.). Chapter references, p.261-80. 'Highly recommended' (*Nature*, v.192 (4805), 2 December 1961, p.543-4). *Class No: 620.18*

Defects & Deterioration

Corrosion

Bibliographies

[4036]

GABE, D.R. 'Corrosion, corrosion-resistance and protection'. *Information sources in metallic materials.* Editor, M.N. Pattern, p.253-63. London, Bowker-Saur, 1989. (*Guides to information sources.*) ISBN: 0408014911.

Sections: Introduction - Learned societies - Dictionaries and

....(contd.)

glossaries - Standards organizations - Data sources (handbooks; trade associations, etc.) - Books (63 items) - Current research (abstracts; journals; reviews; conferences). *Class No:* 620.193(01)

Handbooks & Manuals

[4037]

Corrosion. Shrier, L.L., *and others, eds.* 3rd ed. Oxford, Butterworth-Heinemann, 1994. 2v. (v.p.) diagrs., charts, tables. £185. ISBN: 0750610778.

First published 1963; 2nd ed. 1976.

V.1. *Metal/environment reactions.*

V.2. *Corrosion control.*

Over 160 contributors. 21 sections, subdivided (*e.g.* 21.1 Tables; 21.2 Glossary of terms; 21.3 Symbols and abbreviations; 21.4 Calculations illustrating the economics of corrosion). Bibliographies appended to parts of sections (*e.g.* 12.1 'Electroplating' has 163 references). V.2 carries an index to both volumes. Good layout and typography. A standard work.

Also available on CD-ROM as *Engineering materials selector,* either singly (£199) or in conjunction with *Smithell's metals reference book* and/or *Tribology handbook. Class No:* 620.193(035)

[4038]

Corrosion handbook: corrosive agents and their interaction with materials. Behrens, D., *ed.* Weinheim, VCH for DECHEMA, 1987-1993. 12 vols. + supplement, index. £1824 (set). ISBN: 3527266526, V.1.

V.12 (1993. ix, 351p.) covers chlorinated hydrocarbons, chloroethanes and phosphoric acid. Includes a key to materials compositions, p.322-35. Detailed analytical index, p.336-51. A cumulative index to v.1-12 was published in 1993; a supplement, *Concordance of U.S. and German designations for metallic materials,* in 1992. *Class No:* 620.193(035)

[4039]

Handbook of corrosion data. Craig, B.D. *and* Anderson, D.S., *eds.* 2nd ed. Metals Park, Oh., ASM International, 1995. 998p. graphs, tables. ISBN: 0871705184.

First published 1989.

In 2 parts: 1. Corrosion of metals and alloys - 2. Corrosion media. Data are arranged by chemical compound. No index, but a list of 'expanded contents'. *Class No:* 620.193(035)

[4040]

KUHN, A.T., *ed.* **Techniques in electrochemistry, corrosion and metal finishing:** a handbook. Chichester, Wiley, 1987. xviii,567p. illus., tables. ISBN: 047191407x.

8 contributors. In 3 parts: A. Introduction to experimental methods - B. Specialized techniques (Section I: Methods based on light; Section II: Spectroscopic methods; Section III: Other methods (*e.g.* physiochemical; radio-chemical; acoustic emission; dyes, etc.) - C. The literature (37p. bibliography of post-1960 monographs, most from the British Library Science Reference and Information Service). 28 chapters, most with extensive references (*e.g.* 'Raman spectroscopy', p.237-49, includes 166). Subject index. Dedicated - gracefully - to the 'Library' and its 'staff'. *Class No:* 620.193(035)

Dictionaries

[4041]

GROSS, H. Wörterbuch korrosion und korrosionsschutz: Englisch-Deutsch/Deutsch-Englisch. [Dictionary corrosion and corrosion control: English-German/German-English.] 2nd ed. Berlin, Verlag Technick GmbH, 1991. c.400p. £48.50. ISBN: 3341009574.

About 13,500 entries in each part. *Class No:* 620.193(038)

[4042]

TEKNISKA NOMENKLATURCENTRALEN. Korrosions-ordlista. Norkiska termer... [Glossary of corrosion terms in Scandinavian languages, with equivalents in English, French, German.] Stockholm, the Centre, 1968. 130p. (*TNC 40.*)

Glossary of 326 Swedish terms, with equivalents in Danish, Finnish, Norwegian, German, English and French, and definitions in Scandinavian languages and English. Indexes are in Danish, Finnish, Norwegian, German, English and French. 'Appears to be rather deficient in terms relating to relevant chemical compounds as well as in methods and materials used for the protection of metals and alloys against corrosion' (*The Incorporated linguist,* v.9 (2), April 1970, p.51). *Class No:* 620.193(038)

Reviews & Abstracts

[4043]

Corrosion abstracts. Houston, Texas, NACE International 1951-. 6pa. $215 - $270 pa. ISSN: 00109339.

About 4,000 abstracts pa. No subject arrangement. Subject and author indexes per issue. Aslo available on CD-ROM. *Class No:* 620.193(048)

Progress Reports

[4044]

Progress in the understanding and prevention of corrosion. Costa, J.M. *and* Mercer, A.D., *eds.* London, Institute of Metals, 1993. 2v. (1701p.). illus., diagrs., graphs, tables. ISBN: 0901763675.

About 300 papers on atmospheric, marine, microbial, etc. corrosion. *Class No:* 620.193(055)

Tables & Data Books

[4045]

SCHWEITZER, P.A. Corrosion resistance tables: metals, nonmetals, coatings, mortars, plastics, elastomers and linings, and fabrics. 5th ed. New York & Basle, Dekker, 1995. 3v. (xix, 3160p.). tables. ISBN: 0824795911.

3rd ed. 1991.

Substances: Acetaldihyde ... Zinc sulfate. Data are tabulated under 12 heads. Temperature range: 15 deg. C. to 228 deg. C. Online as *Corrosion,* available on Questel/ORBIT. *Class No:* 620.193(083)

Protection

[4046]

GREAT BRITAIN. Department of Trade and Industry. **Wear resistant surfaces in engineering:** a guide to their production, properties and selection. London, H.M. Stationery Office, 1986. vi. 171p. illus., diagrs. graphs, tables. £18.95. ISBN: 0115138269.

11 documented sections: 1. Types of wear - 2. Comparison of surface treatment processes - 3. Applications - 4. Thermal hardening - 5. Thermochemical treatment - 6. Electrochemical treatment - 7. Chemical treatment - 8. Chemical vapour deposition - 9. Physical vapour treatment - 10. Spraying processes - 11. Weld hardfacing. 3 appendices (1. Wear test methods). Detailed analytical index, p. 168-71. *Class No:* 620.197

Energy (Sources)

Databases

[4047]

Energy science and technology. Washington, D.C., US Department of Energy.

Formerly *DOE Energy database.*

Energy topics included: nuclear, wind, fossil, geothermal, tidal, solar. Also covers the environment, energy policy and conservation. Over 2,500,000 records; updated biweekly. Available on DIALOG and CD-ROM. *Class No:* 620.9(003.4)

[4048]

Energyline. New York, Bowker, 1971-93.

The online version of *Energy information abstracts.* About 80,000 records. Available on DIALOG, file 69, as a closed file. *Class No:* 620.9(003.4)

[4049]

EUROPEAN COMMUNITIES COMMISSION. Directory of energy databases. Luxembourg, the Commission, 1985. (*Eur 9097.*)

Lists more than 100 databases available through European hosts. *Class No:* 620.9(003.4)

[4050]

LUEDTKE, J.R. 'Energy and the environment' *Manual of online search strategies.* Editors, C.J. Armstrong and J.A. Large, pp.236-87. 2nd ed. Aldershot, Ashgate, 1992. ISBN: 1857420071.

Extensive list of databases, both online and CD-ROM, which cover energy and the environment. Hosts and disc suppliers identifed. *Class No:* 620.9(003.4)

CD-ROM

[4051]

World energy CD-ROM. Harlow, Essex, Longman, 1992. £1750.

Covers oil and gas, mining and chemical companies. 30,000 biographical entries, accounts, financial data, major activites, etc. IBM PC. *Class No:* 620.9(003.40)

Bibliographies

[4052]

ANTHONY, L.J., *ed.* **Information sources in energy technology.** London, etc., Butterworths, 1988. xii, 324p. £35. (*Butterworths Guides to information sources.*) ISBN: 040803050x.

11 contributors. 3 parts (16 documented chapters): 1. Energy in general - 2. Fuel technology - 3. Specific energy sources (solid, liquid and gaseous fuels; nuclear energy; solar and geothermal energy;

....*(contd.)*
alternative energy sources). Detailed, analytical 'Index to subjects, information services and organizations'. Well up to the Butterworths' series standards. *Class No:* 620.9(01)

[4053]
BERKOVITCH, I. Energy sources and policy: an overview and guide to the literature. London, The British Library Science Reference and Information Service, 1996. ii, 180p. £33. ISBN: 0712308059.
Covers the main energy sources - coal, petroleum, gas, nuclear and renewables - with brief histories and an examination of the technical, economic and green issues associated with each. 'Organizations connected with energy', p.151-64. *Class No:* 620.9(01)

[4054]
Energy bibliography & index. Houston, Texas, Gulf Publishing Co., 1978-83. 6v. in 7.
Lists material on energy - including synthetic fuel - consisting of documents captured from the Germans in World War II, and available in translation, in the collection of Texas A & M University. V.6 (2pts.) comprises the index. *Class No:* 620.9(01)

[4055]
McMULLAN, J.T. 'Energy technology'. *Information sources in engineering.* K.W. Mildren and P.J. Hicks, eds. (3rd ed., 1996), p.223-57. 3rd ed. London, Bowker Saur, 1996. £80. ISBN: 1857390571.
Covers international agencies, national organizations, abstracting and indexing services, online databases, information sources by energy area (*e.g.* gas; coal, etc.). Comprehensive and a valuable update to *Information sources in energy technology* (ed. L.J. Anthony). *Class No:* 620.9(01)

[4056]
RUDOLPH, J.R. Energy. Metuchen, NJ, Scarecrow/Salem Press, 1995. 177p. $29.50. ISBN: 0810830116.
A bibliography of books in 6 sections: The human condition - Resources - Economics - Politics - The environment - Future. Omits journals articles, government resources and nonprint material. *Class No:* 620.9(01)

[4057]
WEBER, R.D. Energy information guide. Santa Barbara, Calif., & Oxford, ABC-Clio, 1982-91. 3v. (xvi, xix, xxi, 1355 [1]p). ea. $39.95.
1. *General and alternative energy sources.* 2. *Nuclear and nuclear power.* 3. *Fossil fuels.*
3,082 annotated entries in all for English language reference works on production, distribution, storage and/or consumption of energy. The chapters in v.1 are subdivided by form. Online databases are cited. Four indexes: author, title, subject and government document index. V.3 carries a cumulative index. US slanted. 'Fills a serious gap in the literature' (*RQ*, Winter 1982, p.200-1). *Class No:* 620.9(01)

[4058]
—WEBER, R.D. Energy update: a guide to current reference literature. San Carlos, Calif., Energy Information Press, 1991. 455p. $42.50. ISBN: 096285185x.
Supplements the author's *Energy Information Guide*. Concentrates on readily available reference literature. 6 categories: 1. Dictionaries and encyclopedias - 2. Handbooks and manuals - 3. Directories - 4. Statistical sources - 5. Indexes, abstracts and bibliographies - 6. Online databases (75). 4 indexes: author; title; subject; document number. Updates are planned every four years. 'Well-researched and carefully planned' (*Choice*, November 1991, p.424). *Class No:* 620.9(01)

Encyclopaedias

[4059]
Encyclopedia of energy technology and the environment. Bisio, A. *and* Boots, S., *eds.* New York, Wiley, 1995. 4v. (2964p.) illus., diagrs. graphs, tables. $900; £595. (*Wiley encyclopedia series in environmental science.*) ISBN: 0471544582.
200 contributors. About 175 signed articles, most with extensive bibliographies. Topics covered include acid rain, air pollution, building systems, coal combustion, environmental law, geothermal energy, oil spills, risk assessment, etc. Cross references; detailed, analytical index. 'Highly recommended' (*Choice*, September 1995, p.80). *Class No:* 620.9(031)

[4060]
—BOOTS, S., . *eds.* Encyclopedia of energy and the environmnet. Bisio, A. Chichester, Wiley, 1996. 2v. (1578p.) illus., diagrs., graphs, tables. £170. ISBN: 047114827x.
Articles, A-Z, are largely derived from the same editors' *Encyclopedia of energy technology and the environment.* Covers technology and legal policy issues. Suitable for non-specialists. *Class No:* 620.9(031)

[4061]
McGraw-Hill encyclopedia of energy, by the staff of the 'McGraw-Hill Encyclopedia of science and technology'. Parker, S.P., *ed.* 2nd ed. New York, etc., McGraw-Hill, 1980. [ix], 838p. ISBN: 0070452687.
First published 1976.
About 300 contributors. 'Energy perspectives', consisting of 6 articles (*e.g.* 'Outlook for full reserves'), precedes 'Energy technology', p.65-791, an A-Z sequence of signed and documented articles (*e.g.* 'Internal Combustion engine', p.336-49, with 8 references, 21 figures). 3 appendices (3: Energy-related publications). Analytical index, p.823-38. Many of the articles appear in the 1977 edition of *McGraw-Hill Encyclopedia of science and technology*. *Class No:* 620.9(031)

[4062]
—GLASSTONE, S. Energy desk book. New York, etc., Van Nostrand Reinhold, 1983. xii, 453p. illus. diagrs.
400 entries A/Z, a combined glossary, encyclopedia. Covers all energy sources, with emphasis on general principles rather than technology. Length of entries ranges from 15 lines ('Benfield process')— to 40p. (on solar energy, including its collection, application, conversion). Cross-references. Intended for scientists, engineers, administrators, government officials. *Class No:* 620.9(031)

Handbooks & Manuals

[4063]
CASSEDY, E. *and* **GROSSMAN, P.Z. Introduction to energy:** resources, technology and society. Cambridge Univ. Press, 1990. 338p. illus., diagrs., tables. £30; $66. ISBN: 0521350913.
Fossil fuels (coal, oil, natural gas) and nuclear fission; economic, health and safety criteria, and decision-making. Diagrs., tables and photos. Chapter notes and references. *Class No:* 620.9(035)

[4064]
DRYDEN, I.G.C. The Efficient use of energy. 2nd ed. Sevenoaks, Kent, Butterworth Scientific, in collaboration with the Institute of Energy, on behalf of the UK Dept. of Energy, 1982. xiii, 602p. illus., diagrs. graphs, tables. ISBN: 0408012501.
First published 1973 (xiii, 602p.), - an update of the Ministry of Power's *Efficient use of energy* (HMSO, 1958).
More than 60 contributors. 6 sections (20 chapters): Production of heat - Use of heat - Production of mechanical and electrical energy - Total energy systems and heat salvage - Materials and control - Environmental aspects. Chapter references. Appendices A-F (A. Natural fuels and their chief marketable products; E. World energy resources and demands). Analytical index, p.593-602. A major textbook that reflects the Brirtish viewpoint, with stress on conservation. *Class No:* 620.9(035)

[4065]
HUNT, V.D. Handbook of energy technology; trends and perspectives. New York, etc., Van Nostrand Reinhold, 1982. [viii], 1018p. illus., diagrs., tables, maps. ISBN: 0442225555.
7 parts: 1. Energy technology overview - 2. Fossil energy - 3. Solar, geothermal, electric and storage systems - 4. Fusion energy - 5. Nuclear waste management - 6. Magnetic fusion energy - 7. Reference information, p.965-92 (*e.g.* glossary; abbreviations and acronyms; references - a bibliography, in 9 sections). Detailed, analytical index, p.993-1018. US slanted. *Class No:* 620.9(035)

[4066]
STOUT, B.A. Handbook of energy for world agriculture. London and New York, Elsevier, 1990. xiii,504p.
9 chapters (each with summary): 1. Overview - 2. Energy use - 3. Energy flow - 4. Energy arrangement - 5. Energy from biomass (p.197-307) - 6. Solar energy - 7. Wind energy - 8. Hydropower - 9. Alternatives. Appendix 1: Sources of further information (organizations); 2: Conversion of units. Detailed, analytical index. Bibliography (A-Z author), p.466-94. *Class No:* 620.9(035)

[4067]
WILBUR, L.S., ed. Handbook of energy systems engineering: production and utilization. New York, etc., Wiley, 1985. xiii, 1775p. illus., diagrs., graphs, tables. ISBN: 0471866334.
98 contributors. 16 chapters (most of them with references and bibliographies) cover a wide spectrum of energy applications. These include demographics, coal, nuclear, petroleum and gas technologies, hydroelectric and solar power, electricity, advanced energy systems and engineering mathematics. A massive volume. Intended for professionals as a 'mini primer' for decision-making (*Preface*). *Class No:* 620.9(035)

Dictionaries

Polyglot

[4068]
WORLD ENERGY COUNCIL. Energy dictionary. Paris, Conseil Mondial de l'Energie, 1992. xix, 633p.

In English, French, German, Spanish. For each language about 2000 terms are defined. Arranged in 20 broad subject areas (*e.g.* general; energy balances; energy uses; electricity; wind energy, etc.). Versions in other languages (*e.g.* Portuguese; Arabic) are planned. *Class No: 620.9(038)=00*

[4069]
—**TEKNISKA NOMENKLATURCENTRALEN.** Energiordlista. [Glossary of energy.] Stockholm, the Centre, 1984. 112p. (*TNC 81.*)

Includes *c.*700 Swedish-base terms (with definitions), plus equivalents and indexes in English, French, German, Danish and Norwegian. *Class No: 620.9(038)=00*

English

[4070]
CRABBE, D. *and* **McBRIDE, R.,** *eds.* **The World energy book:** an A-Z, atlas and statistical source book. London, Kogan Page, 1978. 259p. diagrs., graphs, tables, maps. ISBN: 0850380812.

6 contributors. A-Z dictionary of *c.*1,000 terms and definitions, p.9-194 ('Fusion reactor': 3 columns, 1 diagr., 1 graph). Cross references. 24 energy resources maps. 4 Statistical appendices (1: Figures, to 1976; 4.2: Natural and manufactured hydrocarbons derived from petroleum). 'Intended as a comprehensive reference guide to energy sources, energy related technology, economics and all factors related to the search for, extraction of, and utilization of the major alternative sources of energy' (*Introduction*). *Class No: 620.9(038)=20*

[4071]
KUT, R. Dictionary of applied energy conservation. London, Kogan Page; New York, Nichols, 1982. 214p. illus. ISBN: 0850385776.

About 2,000 entries, with numerous cross-references. 'Solar chimney': 1¼ columns; 'Induction heating': 1½ columns. 120 fine line-drawings are a feature. 3 appendices of conversion factors, units and symbols. The author is a consultant engineer. *Class No: 620.9(038)=20*

[4072]
SLESSER, M., *ed.* **Dictionary of energy.** 2nd ed. London, Macmillan, 1988. 318p. diagrs., tables. £29.95; £10.95. ISBN: 0333454618; 0333454626, Pbk.

First published 1982.

About 2000 terms, some defined at length. Includes organization, laboratories and acronyms. Numerous cross-references. Good coverage of economic terms as they apply to energy. *Class No: 620.9(038)=20*

[4073]
—**BRACKLEY, P.** Energy and environmental terms: a glossary. Aldershot, Hants., Gower, 1988. 200p. diagrs., tables. £18.95. ISBN: 056605759x.

Provides a layman's guide to hundreds of words, acronyms, agreements, organizations, chemical names, etc. *Class No: 620.9(038)=20*

[4074]
—**COUNIHAN, M.** A Dictionary of energy. London, Routledge & Kegan Paul, 1981. x, 157p. diagrs., graphs, tables. ISBN: 0710008473.

Nearly 1,000 entries, 'Absolute zero' ... 'Zincaloy'. 'Geothermal energy': 3p., including 2 graphs. Appendix: 'International energy statistics', p.150-5. Bibliography (A-Z authors), p.156-7. For the student, general reader and professional. *Class No: 620.9(038)=20*

[4075]
—**GILPIN, A.** *and* **WILLIAMS, A.** Dictionary of energy technology. Guildford, Surrey, Butterworth Scientific, 1982. [viii], 392p. diagrs., tables, maps.

First published as *Dictionary of fuel technology,* 1970.

Its 2,500 entries depict energy in its contemporary setting. Includes formulas and adequate cross-references. 2 appendices of conversion factors and a bibliography, p.387-92. For professionals. *Class No: 620.9(038)=20*

[4076]
—**HUNT, V.D.** Energy dictionary. New York, etc., Van Nostrand Reinhold, 1979. vii, [1], 518p. illus., diagrs., graphs, charts, tables. ISBN: 0442273959.

Contains more than 4,000 concise entries, 'Abatement' ... 'Zone refining'. Has the advantage of a bibliography (9 sections), p.509-18 and is well furnished with diagrams, etc. Appended conversion factors and glossary of acronyms. US slanted. *Class No: 620.9(038)=20*

Reviews & Abstracts

[4077]
Energy research abstracts. Oak Ridge, Conn., U.S. Department of Energy, Technical Information Centrer, 1977-. Monthly. $171 (domestic); $213.75 (foreign). ISSN: 0106360x.

Began as *ERDA reports abstracts* (1975), changed to *ERDA research abstracts* (1975-76), then *ERDA energy research abstracts* (1976-77).

About 60,000 abstracts pa., covering 'all scientific and technical reports, journal articles, conference papers and proceedings, books, patents, theses and monographs originated by the US Dept. of Energy, its laboratories, energy centers and contractors'. Sections: Coal and coal products - Petroleum - Natural gas - Oil shales and tar sands - Nuclear fuels ... Solar energy - Geothermal energy - Wind energy ... Energy management and policy ... Materials ... Biomedical sciences, applied studies ... Physics research. Corporate, author, subject, contract number, report number indexes per issue; semi-annual index. Available online as part of *Energy science and technology* (*qv*). *Class No: 620.9(048)*

[4078]
The Engineering index. Energy abstracts: a monthly review of energy technology. New York, Engineering Information, Inc., 1974-. 2pa. ISSN: 00938404.

About 12,000 abstracts pa., drawn from *Engineering index monthly* (*qv*). Main sections: 01. Coal and coal products - 02. Petroleum - 03. Natural gas ... 14. Solar energy ... 20. Electric power engineering - 21. Nuclear power plants ... 39. Energy, conservation, consumption, and utilization ... 53. Environmental-social aspects of energy technologies ... 70. Controlled thermonuclear research. Author, author affiliation and subject indexes per issue. Covers both conventional and alternative energy sources. *Class No: 620.9(048)*

[4079]
Fuel and energy abstracts: a bimonthly summary of world literature on all technical, scientific, commercial and environmental aspects of fuel and energy. Guildford, Butterworth Scientific, on behalf of the Institute of Energy, 1978-. 6pa. £580 pa. ISSN: 01406701.

Formerly *Fuel abstracts and current titles*/FACTS (1960-), succeeding monthly *Fuel abstracts* (1945-58).

About 8,000 abstracts pa. Classified sections: 01. Solid fuels - 02. Liquid fuels - 03. Gaseous fuels ... 06. Electric power operation and utilization ... 15. Environment - 16. Fuel science and technology ... 18. Energy conversion and recycling. Subject and author indexes per issue and pa. Coverage: 'World literature on scientific, technical, commercial and environmental aspects of fuel and energy'. Highly regarded. *Class No: 620.9(048)*

Periodicals

[4080]
VIOLA, J., *and others.* **Energy research guide:** journals, indexes and abstracts. Cambridge, Mass., Ballinger Publishing Co., 1983. xi, 284, [1]p. ISBN: 0884100979.

Master list of over 500 English-language periodicals, indexes and abstracting journals, followed by 7 subject lists (energy use and conservation; renewable and alternative energy services; oil and gas; coal; selective power, including nuclear; environment; world energy). Descriptions of periodicals, indexes and abstracts, A-Z, p.57-284 (data: frequency, scope, price, address and telephone number). *Class No: 620.9(051)*

[4081]
—**GREAT BRITAIN.** Department of Energy Library. Periodicals list. London, the Dept. Library, 1986. [45]p.

Lists about 800 titles currently held, noting frequency and holdings. 3 sections: Dept. of Energy Library, Thames House South, London; Offshore Suppliers Office Library, Glasgow; Gas and Oil Measurement Branch, Leicester. Entries for abstracting/indexing services are asterisked. Cross-references. *Class No: 620.9(051)*

Progress Reports

[4082]
Annual review of energy and the environment. Palo Alto Ca., Annual Reviews, Inc. 1976-. ISSN: 10563466.

Previously as *Annual review of energy*.

V.19 (1994. 543p. $76) has articles by a range of contributors, *e.g.* 'New technologies for air conditioning and refrigeration'; 'The Economics of sustainable development'; 'Nuclear power operations: a cross-cultural perspective', etc. Subject index. Cumulative indexes of contributing authors; chapter titles. *Class No: 620.9(055)*

Yearbooks & Directories

[4083]

Energy world yearbook 1995. 11th ed. Harrietsham, Kent, Howland, for the Institute of Energy, 1995. 212p. illus. £50. ISSN: 02674939.

Lists information sources (*e.g.* online databases, CD-ROMs, energy management software), then UK, European and worldwide energy organizations, suppliers, products, etc. *Class No:* 620.9(058)

[4084]

The World directory of renewable energy suppliers and services 1998. Cross, B., *ed.* London, James & James, 1998. 488p. illus., diagrs. ISBN: 1873936796. ISSN: 13617524.

Contents: General articles - Finance - Biomass - Energy in buildings - Geothermal - Hydro and wave - Software/resources - Photovatics - Solar thermal - Wind - Conferences and bibliography - Classified listing - Organization listing - A-Z company listing. The directory is also available, free of charge to users, on the World Wide Web; URL: http://www.jxj.com. *Class No:* 620.9(058)

Tables & Data Books

[4085]

International energy statistics sourcebook. Tulsa, Ok., PennWell, 1991. 643p. mainly tables, maps. ISSN: 10582843.

Also available on diskette ($1200 for entire sourcebook).

Main sections: Primary energy - Exploration drilling and production - Petroleum and natural gas processing - Petroleum product demand - Prices - Statistics by individual country (p.133-614). 4 appendices: chronology; glossary; OPEC; conversion factors. *Class No:* 620.9(083)

[4086]

LOFTNESS, R.L. Energy handbook. 2nd ed. New York, etc., Van Nostrand Reinhold, 1984. 703p. illus., diagrs., graphs, tables. ISBN: 0442259921.

First published 1978.

A sourcebook of tabular data, supported by 16 chapters of text on energy resources, consumption patterns, fossil fuel, energy conversion, efficiency and transport, environment, energy costs, futures. No bibliography as such, but footnote references, as required. The author is Director of the Washington Office of the Electric Power Research Institute. *Class No:* 620.9(083)

[4087]

—DORF, R.C. The Energy factbook. New York, etc., McGraw-Hill, 1980. vii, [1], 226p. illus., diagrs., graphs, tables. ISBN: 007017623x.

21 short chapters, replete with captioned illus., graphs and statistics (up to 1978). Chapters include: 6. Petroleum; 12. Nuclear fission power and fusion research; 16. Energy storage systems and alternate technologies; 17. Conservation of energy; 21. Energy policy. 'The book is intended for anyone who needs to make decisions that in part require information about energy supplies and uses' (*Preface*). *Class No:* 620.9(083)

[4088]

—OSBORN, P.D. Handbook of energy data and calculations, including directory of products and services. Sevenoaks, Kent, Butterworths, 1985. 287p. graphs, charts, tables. ISBN: 0408013273.

Includes data charts and tables, as well as calculation and analysis procedures. Appended bibliography and sources. *Class No:* 620.9(083)

Worldwide

[4089]

INTERNATIONAL ENERGY AGENCY. Energy statistics and main series from 1960. [Statitstiques de l'energie, 1970-1985.] Paris, Organization for Economic Co-operation and Development, 1987. 2v. (xl, 513p. + xv, 624p.).

V.1. OECD; IEA; North America; Pacific; OECD Europe; EEC; Australia ... Iceland. V.2, Ireland ... Yugoslavia. The tables include all 'commercial' sources of energy, both primary and secondary (coal products, manufactured gases, petroleum products and electricity). 'Other solid fuels' covers peat, wood and waste (*General notes*). *Class No:* 620.9(083)(100)

[4090]

—BP Statistical review of world energy. London, BP, 1987. [i], 38p. illus., diagrs., tables. *gratis*.

Covers, in turn, oil, natural gas, nuclear energy, hydro-electricity and primary energy. Appended conversion factors and definitions. A handy pictorial quick-reference source. *Class No:* 620.9(083)(100)

[4091]

UNITED NATIONS. Energy statistics yearbook. diagrs., graphs, tables. ISBN: 9210611020.

Formerly *World energy supplies, 1952-1978*; *Yearbook of world energy statistics, 1979-1981*; *Energy statistics yearbook*, 1982-.

Sections: Commercial energy - Production, trade and consumption - Solid fuels - Liquid fuels - Gaseous fuels - Electrical energy - Nuclear fuels, energy resources and prices. Numerous tables. Bibliography, countries, A-Z. *Class No:* 620.9(083)(100)

Europe

[4092]

Energy statistical yearbook. Luxembourg, Eurostat. ISBN: 9282568733.

The *Yearbook* provides statistics on coal, oil, gas and electricity for Community countries. Main parts: Energy economics: characteristic features - Energy indicators - Balance sheet: energy supplies - Tables by energy sources. *Class No:* 620.9(083)(4)

Great Britain

[4093]

GREAT BRITAIN. Department of Trade and Industry. Digest of United Kingdom energy statistics, 1998. London, The Stationery Office, 1998. 276p. diagrs., charts, tables, maps. £32.95. ISBN: 0115154477. ISSN: 03070603.

Commenced with Ministry of Power *Statistical digest for the years 1948 and 1949* (1950).

10 sections: Energy - Coal and other solid fuels - Oil and gas resources - Petroleum - Gas - Electricity - Combined heat and power - Prices and values - Foreign trade - Renewable sources of energy. Explanatory notes on tables, plus footnotes. 5 appendices (A: 'Energy and the environment'). A publication proposing changes to the *Digest* was published in 1998. *Class No:* 620.9(083)(410)

Biographies

[4094]

Energy and nuclear sciences international who's who. 5th ed. Harlow, Essex, Longman Group, 1994. 340p. £225. (*Longman Reference on research series*.) ISBN: 0582256631.

Previously as *International who's who in energy and nuclear sciences* (1983).

Part 1 contains professional biographical profiles of about 4,100 scientists and engineers from 74 countries. Part 2 is a country index, subdivided by subject specialists. *Class No:* 620.9(092)

Information Management

[4095]

Croner's energy management. Ffloyd, T., *ed.* Kingston upon Thames, Croner, 1998. Looseleaf (v.p.). ISBN: 1855244608.

'A guide for organizations wishing to reduce their energy costs in a structured and sustainable way' (*Preface*). 5 sections: 1. Legislation and guidance - 2. Energy management - 3. Practical energy efficiency - 4. Information systems - 5. Further information. Updates are produced. *Class No:* 620.9:025.4

Information Services

[4096]

World directory of energy information. Compiled by Cambridge Information and Research Services, Ltd. Farnborough, Hants., Gower, 1981-84. 3v. ISBN: 0566021956; 0566023741; 0566023873.

1. *Western Europe*. 1981. [x], 323, [2]p.
2. *Middle East, Africa and Asia/Pacific*. 1982. xii, 418p.
3. *The Americas, including the Caribbean*. 1984. x, 360p.

A guide to organizations and publications worldwide concerning energy development and management. Each volume has 4 parts, - the energy framework; country reviews; energy organizations; energy publications (with indexes for titles, subjects and countries, and publishers). Statistics need to be updated, as available in the United Nations, *Energy statistics yearbook* (qv). *Class No:* 620.9:061:025.5

Institutions & Associations

[4097]

World energy and nuclear directory: organizations and research activities in atomic and non-atomic energy. 3rd ed. Harlow, Essex, Cartermill, 1995. x, 480p. £255. ISBN: 1860670199.

First ed. 1990; combines former *World energy directory* (2nd ed. 1985) and *World nuclear directory* (7th ed. 1985).

Data on 3,000 laboratories and industrial companies involved in energy research on coal technology, electricity, gas technology, nuclear power, radiation, solar power, renewable energy and water power, energy conservation and waste handling. Arranged A-Z by

....(contd.)

country, then organization (contact details, senior staff, budgets, summaries of research interests). Establishment and subject indexes. *Class No:* 620.9:061:061.2

Conferences

[4098]

Conferences in energy, physics and mathematics. Karlsruhe, Fachinformationszentrum Karlsruhe.

Database of conferences, past, present and future. Data include title, sponsoring organization, location and dates, notes on related publications, etc. 100,000 records; updated weekly. Available online via STN International and on the internet. *Class No:* 620.9:061:061.3

[4099]

Energy and the environment in the 21st century. Tester, J.W., *and others*. Cambridge, Mass., MIT Press, 1991. xix,1006p. $50. ISBN: 0262200783.

Proceedings of the conference held at the Massachusetts Institute of Technology. The 2 plenary sessions comprise sections A-F: A. Transport systems - B. Industrial processes - C. Building systems - D. Electric power for the developing countries - E. Economics and policy - F. Advanced energy supply technologies. Numerous tables and charts. Detailed, analytical index. 'A valuable contribution to all academic library collections' (*Choice,* March 1992, p.1099). *Class No:* 620.9:061:061.3

Energy Conservation & Exploitation

Bibliographies

[4100]

SPURGEON, K. Renewable energy and its environmental impact: an information pack. London, Institution of Electrical Engineers, Technical Information Unit, 1991. c.90p. £33. ISBN: 0852964935.

Abstracts of technical papers from INSPEC database. Sections: Geothermal - Tidal - Ocean thermal energy conversion (OTEC) - Hydroelectric - Solar - Biomass - Wind. Further chapters on books, equipment suppliers, professional and trade association. *Class No:* 620.92(01)

Handbooks & Manuals

[4101]

TWIDELL, J.W. *and* **WEIR, A.D. Renewable energy resources.** London, Spon, 1986. xx, 439p. illus., diagrs., graphs, tables. £24.99. ISBN: 0419120009.

16 documented chapters: 1. Principles of renewable energy ... 3. Heat transfer ... 5. Solar water heating ... 8. Hydro-power - 9. Power from the wind ... 11. Biofuels ... 13. Tidal power - 14. Ocean thermal energy conservation - 15. Geothermal energy - 16. Energy storage and distribution. Appendices of units, data and formulas. Detailed analytical index, p.425-39. 'Primarily intended to support courses for undergraduates in physical science and engineering beyond first year level' (*Preface*). *Class No:* 620.92(035)

Dictionaries

[4102]

EUROPEAN PARLIAMENT. Terminology Office. **Terminology of new and renewable sources of energy.** Luxembourg, the Office. 1990. 99p.

Previous ed. 1982.

English-base terms, with French, Italian, German, Dutch, Danish, and now Greek indexes. A list of organizations in the energy field, units of measurement, plus abbreviations, precede. Appended bibliography. *Class No:* 620.92(038)

Reviews & Abstracts

[4103]

Renewable energy bulletin. Brentwood, Essex, Multi-Science Publishing Co., 1980-. 6 pa. ISSN: 0306364x.

About 1,500 abstracts pa. Covers solar energy, distillation, wind, ocean energy, methane, waste heat and recycling. Annual author and subject indexes. *Class No:* 620.92(048)

Tables & Data Books

[4104]

INTERNATIONAL ENERGY AGENCY. Renewable sources of energy. Paris, Organization for Economic Development and Cooperation (OECD), March 1987. 334p. illus., diagrs., tables.

55 statistical tables - a feature - with figures up to December 1985. 6 preliminary chapters. Annex 1: Nature, status and outlook of renewable energy sources and conversion technologies (p.79-293): solar, wind, biomass, geothermal and ocean energies. Annex 2: Economics of renewable energy technologies. No index. *Class No:* 620.92(083)

Maps & Atlases

[4105]

MUSTOE, J.E.H. An Atlas of renewable energy resources in the United Kingdom and North America. New York, Wiley, 1984. [v], 202p. diagrs., graphs, tables, maps. ISBN: 0471102938.

10 chapters (2. Solar energy - 3. Wind energy - 4. Wave energy - 5. Ocean thermal energy - 6. River energy - 7. Biofuels - 8. Geothermal energy - 9. Tidal energy - 10. Conclusion). 8 appendices (2. Thermal value of fuels). References, p.189-94; bibliography, p.195. Analytical index, p.197-202. 17 tables; 16 maps. *Class No:* 620.92(084.3)

Developing Countries

[4106]

KRISTOFERSON, L.A. *and* **BOKALDERS, V. Renewable energy technologies:** their applications in developing countries: a study of the Beiger Institute, the Royal Swedish Academy of Sciences. Oxford, etc., Pergamon, 1986. xviii, 319p. illus. $60.

An investigation of the potential of renewable energy sources (*e.g.* solar, tidal, wind) for the economic development of Third World countries. *Class No:* 620.92(4/9-77)

Government Organizations

[4107]

GREAT BRITAIN. Department of Energy. **New and renewable sources of energy:** a directory of UK expertise. 32p.

Compiled for the United Nations Conference on New and Renewable Sources of Energy, Kenya, 1981, by the Information Office Energy Technology Support Unit, Atomic Energy Research Establishment, Harwell, Oxon., Feb. 1981.

A directory of 75 bodies, boards and institutes. Sections: A. General - B. Fuels from biomass - C. Fuelwood. Charcoal - D. Solar technology - E. Hydropower - F. Wind - G. Geothermal - H. Ocean. A-Z index to organizations. *Class No:* 620.92:061:061.1

Research Establishments

[4108]

International directory of new and renewable energy information sources and research centres. 3rd ed. Paris, Unesco, 1993. 593p. $135. ISBN: 1873936206.

First published 1981; 2nd ed. 1988.

Lists research centres (A-Z by country) with descriptions and contact information. Information on resources, organizations, institutions and publications (journals, directories and databases) covering new and renewable energies. *Class No:* 620.92:061:061.62

Solar Energy

[4109]

ASSET: abstracts of selected solar energy technology New Delhi, Tata Energy Research Institute for the United Nations University, 1979-. 4pa. $80. ISSN: 0379573x.

About 400 abstracts pa. 6 sections, subdivided: General - Solar energy - Bio-conversion energy - Wind energy - Energy storage - Socio-economic and environmental aspects. Most issues include a well-documented review article. *Class No:* 620.92:523.9

[4110]

DICKINSON, W. *and* **CHEREMISINOFF, P.N., eds.** **Solar energy technology handbook.** New York, Dekker; London, Butterworths, 1980. 2v. illus., diagrs., graphs, tables. (*Energy, power and environment, 6.*) ISBN: 0824768728; 0824769279.

A: *Engineering fundamentals.* xiii, 882p.

B: *Applications, systems design, and economics.* xii, 805p.

Pt. A has 58 contributors. 6 units (26 documented chapters): 1. The solar resource - 2. Solar thermal collectors - 3. Photovoltaics - 4. Bioconversion - 5. Wind energy - 6. Solar energy storage system. Chapter 22, 'Characteristics and uses of wind machines' (p.665-717) has 53 references and a bibliography of 6 items. Pt. B, sponsored by the American Section of International Solar Energy, concerns unit 7, 'Applications of solar technology' and unit 8, 'Nontechnical issues' (*e.g.* environmental, health and safety issues). *Class No:* 620.92:523.9

[4111]

EGGERS-LURA, A. **Solar energy in developing countries:** an overview and buyers' guide for solar scientists and engineers. Oxford, etc., Pergamon, 1979. vii, 205p. (*The Pergamon European heliostudies, 1.*) ISBN: 0080232531.

7 chapters (2. General information on solar energy activities of interest for developing countries - 3. State of the art - 4. Solar R & D activities in developing countries - 5. Sources of literature and information ... 7. Bibliography (annotated), p.89-97). Detailed, analytical index, p.199-205. *Class No: 620.92:523.9*

[4112]

LEWIS, O. **The European passive solar handbook.** London, Batsford, 1992. 304p. illus. £40. ISBN: 0713469188.

Design information on passive solar architecture. Review of the EC solar programme. *Class No: 620.92:523.9*

Hydrogen Energy

[4113]

Hydrogen energy quarterly literature review. Albuquerque, New Mexico, Global Resources and Associates, 1983-. Quarterly.

Previously as *Hydrogen energy : a bibliography with abstracts* (Albuquerque, Technical Application Centre, Univ. of New Mexico).

About 1,000 abstracts pa. 6 sections on hydrogen energy: general references; production; utilization; storage, transmission and distribution; safety; materials. Annual author, title and keyword indexes. *Class No: 620.93*

Biomass Energy

[4114]

Biomass handbook. Kilani, P. *and* Wexall, C., *eds.* New York, Gordon & Breach, 1989. 963p. $349. ISBN: 0881242693.

Sections: Biomass production - Biomass conversion - Biomass utilization - Biotechnology for biomass - Biomass statistics and properties. Index. A comprehensive source with numerous literature references. *Class No: 620.95*

[4115]

LOWENSTEIN, M.Z., *ed.* **Energy applications of biomass.** New York, Elsevier, 1985. ix, 325p. illus.

Papers from the National Meeting on Biomass R & D for Energy Applications, 1-3 October 1984 at Arlington, Virginia. 3 sections: 1. Issues of importance to biomass energy research - 2. Research interests of biomass sponsors - 3. Biomass energy research projects. *Class No: 620.95*

[4116]

MILNE, T.A., *and others.* **Source book of methods of analysis for biomass and biomass conversion processes.** Amsterdam, Elsevier, 1990. 438p. tables. £56; $104. ISBN: 1851665277.

Identifies international references to standard testing methods. *Class No: 620.95*

Alternative Sources

[4117]

BRITISH LIBRARY. Science Reference and Information Service. **Sources of information on alternative energy technology held at the Science Reference and Information Service.** Dunning, P.H., *comp.* London, British Library, Science Reference and Information Service, 1986. 52p. £7. ISBN: 071230732x.

A briefly annotated guide to the holdings of the Science Reference Library during the last ten years. Coverage: biomass energy, energy recycling, geothermal energy, solar energy, wave and wind energy. Arrangement is by form of material (*e.g.* books, directories, business reports). Shelf-marks are given. Index to list of organizations with an interest in alternative energy technologies. 'A most useful guide in its field' (*Aslib information,* v.14(10), October 1986, p.235). *Class No: 620.97*

[4118]

CLARE, R., *ed.* **Tidal power:** trends and developments. London, Thames Telford, 1992. 334p. £35. ISBN: 072771905x.

Covers both national and international works and studies on tidal power. *Class No: 620.97*

[4119]

GRAYSON, L., *ed.* **Recycling: energy from community waste:** a guide to sources. 2nd ed. London, British Library, Science Reference and Information Service, 1991. iv,143p. £25. ISBN: 0712307613.

International survey in 4 sections: 1. Legislative background - 2. Energy recovery options - 3. Bio-conversion - 4. Thermo-chemical conversion (p.68-126). Indexes of personal authors, corporate bodies, subjects. 576 numbered references under sub-sections. *Class No: 620.97*

[4120]

UNITED NATIONS. Industrial Development Organization. **Information sources on non-conventional sources of energy.** New York, United Nations, 1978. xii, 110p. (*Guides to information sources, no.30.*)

669 numbered entries. 11 sections: 1. Professional, trade and research organizations, learned societies and special information services - 2. Directories - 3. Sources of statistics, marketing and other economic data - 4. Basic handbooks, textbooks and manuals - 5. Monograph series - 6. Current periodicals - 7. Current abstracting and indexing periodicals - 8. Proceedings, papers and reports - 9. Other potential sources of information (*e.g.* A: Consulting and engineering services ... G. Packaging - H. Patents and licences). 'Bibliographical sources used in compiling the present guide'. Sections 2-3, 6-7, 9-11 have annotated entries. *Class No: 620.97*

[4121]

VEZIROGLU, T.N., *ed.* **Alternative energy sources. VII.** Washington, Hemisphere, 1987. 6v., illus.

1. *Solar energy.*
2. *Solar Applications.*
3. *Indirect solar/nuclear.*
4. *Bioconversion/hydrogen.*
5. *Hydrocarbons/energy transfer.*
6. *Energy economics and planning.*

Proceedings of the 7th Miami International Conference on Alternative Energy Sources, 9-11 December 1985. Includes bibliography and index. *Class No: 620.97*

Mechanical Engineering

Abbreviations & Symbols

[4122]

POLON, D.D. **Dictionary of mechanical engineering abbreviations, signs and symbols.** New York, Odyssey Press, 1967. xviii, 725p. diagrs.

The purpose is to collect, verify and report those abbreviations ... in standard use. Sections: Abbreviations for use in text - Associations and societies - Unions - Degrees - Letter symbols - Use on drawings - Graphic symbols. Still the standard work. *Class No: 621(003)*

Databases

[4123]

ISMEC: Mechanical engineering abstracts. Bethesda, Md., Cambridge Scientific Abstracts.

Covers 1967 to date. A bibliographic database providing references, with abstracts from 1982, to the literature of mechanical and production engineering and related fields, including engineering management. File size: *c.*210,000 citations. Various hosts including DIALOG and STN International. Also on CD-ROM (SilverPlatter) and on the Internet (http://www.csa.com). *Class No: 621(003.4)*

Bibliographies

[4124]

AMERICAN SOCIETY OF MECHANICAL ENGINEERS. **Seventy-seven year index: technical papers, 1880-1956.** New York, the Society, 1957. [viii], 382p. $20.

Continuation author and subject indexes have been published by Nichigai Associates Inc., Tokyo, covering 1957-70 and 1971-75 (1976. ix, 542p., XXIIIp.). The latter also includes a paper number index. *Class No: 621(01)*

[4125]

AUGER, C.P. **Engineering eponyms:** an annotated bibliography of some named elements, principles and machines in mechanical engineering. 2nd rev. ed. London, Library Association, 1975. viii, 122p. £7 (£5.60 to members). ISBN: 0853654379.

First published 1965. Originally a thesis approved for L.A. Fellowship.

Entries for *c.*650 eponyms (Abbott Profiolometer ... Zoelly Turbine). Gives name and dates of inventor; type of invention, machine, etc. (patents sometimes cited); *c.*2 references per entry. Cross-references. List of principal works consulted, p.108-11. Subject index groups entries by types. *Class No: 621(01)*

[4126]
BRITISH LIBRARY. Science Reference Library. **Useful books of reference for designers (1926-1983) held by the Science Reference Library. Part 3: Mechanical engineering.** Dalyza, M.M., *sel.* London, the Library, 1984. i, 121p. £5. ISBN: 0712307141.

A bibliography of about 700 works arranged under *c*.400 headings by the Library's unique classification system. There is a Contents list to indicate the broad groupings and an index of subjects which leads easily to specific groups of relevant publications. The scope is far wider than the conventional interpretation of mechanical engineering, extending to aerodynamics, aircraft, automobile, traffic, marine and sanitary engineering. Clearly set out in reproduced typescript, the entries include an occasional annotation - more would greatly enhance the value of this compilation. Most of the standard works are listed but there are few recent publications and one or two over 50 years old. *Class No:* 621(01)

[4127]
INSTITUTION OF MECHANICAL ENGINEERS. Brief subject and author index of papers published in the *Proceedings,* **1847-1950.** London, the Institution, 1951. 235p.
1937-1960. 252p.
1. 1951-64. 335p. £12. ISBN: 0852982062.
2. 1960-69. 1971. 491p. £15. ISBN: 0852982070.
3. 1968-72. 1974. 412p. £20. ISBN: 0852982488.
4. 1973-76. 1979. 154p. £30. ISBN: 0852984235.

Continuation volumes of the index appear at about five-yearly intervals and overlap, considerably in the earlier years. They are now numbered in a series and published by Mechanical Engineering Publications, the Institution's publishing arm. From v.4 the subject headings are based on the EJC *Thesaurus of engineering and scientific terms (TEST)* (Engineers Joint Council, 1969). *Class No:* 621(01)

Handbooks & Manuals

[4128]
The CRC handbook of mechanical engineering. Kreith, F., *ed.* Boca Raton, Fa., CRC Press, 1998. v.p. (*c*.2600p.). illus., diagrs., graphs, tables. ISBN: 084939418x.

The purpose of the handbook is to provide 'a ready reference for the practising engineer' (*Preface*). Covers manufacturing and design, robotics, computer engineering, environmental engineering, economics and project management, patent law, bioengineering, and communication and information systems. In 20 sections, closely subdivided; over 50 contributors. The review in *Choice* (September 1998, p.162) criticised the lack of discussion on new and emerging topics and the quality of the index. Also available on CD-ROM ($129. ISBN: 0849397510). *Class No:* 621(035)

[4129]
Dubbel Handbook of mechanical engineering. Beitz, W. *and* Küttner, K.-H., *eds.* Berlin, Springer-Verlag, 1994. v.p. diagrs., graphs, tables. ISBN: 3540198687.

First published 1914; last revision 1990. English ed. edited by B.J. Davies; translated by M.J. Shields.

Sections A-L, closely subdivided (*e.g.* A. Mechanics: 7 parts; F. Mechanical machine components: 10 parts). 1,258 figures. Detailed, analytical index, 17p. The first English language edition of a standard German reference. *Class No:* 621(035)

[4130]
KUTZ, M., *ed.* **Mechanical engineer's handbook.** 2nd ed. New York, etc., Wiley, 1998. xxiii, 2352p. illus., diagrs., graphs, tables. ISBN: 0471130079.

First published 1986.

The 2nd ed. comprises 26 new chapters, 33 revised ones, and the remaining 19 unchanged — about 70% new material. 95 contributors. 5 parts: Materials and mechanical design - 2. Systems and controls - 3. Manufacturing engineering - 4. Energy, power, and pollution control technology - 5. Management, finance, quality, law, and research. Includes a useful discussion of information sources available on the Internet. *Class No:* 621(035)

[4131]
Mechanical engineer's reference book. Smith, E.H., *ed.* 12th ed. Warrendale, Pa., Society of Automotive Engineers, Inc.; Oxford, Butterworth-Heinemann, 1994. v.p., illus. diagrams, tables. $155; £95. ISBN: 1560914505, (SAE); 0750611952, (B-H).
11th ed., 1973.

This revised ed. includes tribology , nuclear and offshore engineering and health and safety for the first time; expands coverage of computer applications in engineering. About 50 contributors. 19 sections, closely subdivided: 1. Mechanical engineering principles ... 6. Design standards ... 15. Plant engineering ... 17 . Engineering mathematics. Similar to *Mark's Standard handbook* (*qv*), but with more emphasis on explanation than data tables. 'An excellent resource' (*Choice*, January 1995, p.820). *Class No:* 621(035)

[4132]
TIMINGS, R. Newnes mechanical engineers' pocket book. 2nd ed. Oxford, Butterworth-Heinemann, 1997. xxii, 850p. diagrs., graphs, tables. £16.99. ISBN: 0750632623.

First published 1990.

The 2nd ed. has been 'expanded to incorporate additional material requested by its readers' (*Preface*) and to take account of changes in manufacturing and standards (BSI and others). 5 sections, closely subdivided: 1. Engineering mathematics and science - 2. Engineering design data - 3. Engineering materials - 4. Computer aided engineering - 5. Cutting tools. 3 appendices (3. Contributing companies). Index. *Class No:* 621(035)

Dictionaries

Polyglot

[4133]
SCHVARTS, V.V. Illustrated dictionary of mechanical engineering: English - German - French - Dutch - Russian. The Hague, Lancaster, Nijhoff, 1984. 416, [6]p. diagrs., tables. $49.50. ISBN: 9020116681.

Based on author's *Kratkii illystrirovannyii russko-angliiskii slovar' po mashinostroeniyu* (*qv*).

Over 3,600 terms, uniquely numbered and arranged systematically under 14 conventional subheadings of mechanical engineering (1. Engineering mechanics - 2. Strength of materials ... 4. Machine elements ... 9. Welding ... 11. Machining ...). Key language English. Most entries clearly illustrated. Indexes in all six languages. '... designed for people who have just started studying mechanical engineering terms in a foreign language, particuarly for those who have little or no knowledge of either the terms or their meaning ...' (*Foreword*). *Class No:* 621(038)=00

English

[4134]
NAYLER, G.H.F. Dictionary of mechanical engineering. 4th ed. Oxford, Butterworth-Heinemann; Warrendale, Pa., Society of Automotive Engineers, Inc., 1996. viii, 454p. diagrs. £27.50. ISBN: 0750630094.

First published 1967; 3rd ed, 1985.

About 4,500 terms, briefly defined. This new edition includes micromachining and nano-technology, and places more emphasis on North American terms. *Class No:* 621(038)=20

Russian

[4135]
SHVARTS, V.V. Kratkiĭ illystrirovannyĭ russko-angliiskiĭ slovar' po mashinostroeniya: 3795 terminov. [The Concise illustrated Russian-English dictionary of mechanical engineering: 3795 terms.] Moscow, Russian Language Publishers, 1980. 224p. illus.

'This dictionary ... supplements almost all terms with ... internationally accepted symbols, formulae, diagrams, engineering drawings, sketches, etc.' [*Preface*]. Intended, therefore, to be especially helpful to users with limited technological experience. Russian terms are arranged in 15 groups (*e.g.* Machine elements, Welding), subdivided into sections (*e.g.* Arc welding, Gas welding), numbered sequentially, with English equivalents. Index of Russian terms leads to numbered items. Used as foundation for same author's *Illustrated dictionary of mechanical engineering* (*qv*). *Class No:* 621(038)=82

Reviews & Abstracts

[4136]
Applied mechanics reviews. New York, American Society of Mechanical Engineers, 1948-. Monthly. $642. ISSN: 00036900.

Each issue contains one or more review articles; book reviews; and a review of the journal literature, containing upwards of 1,000 author or indicative abstracts. (Before 1984 many informative abstracts supplemented the indicative abstracts - all signed - and author summaries were not used.) The abstracts are in one of 9 groups (*e.g.* Mechanics of solids, Heat transfer, Automatic control), each of which is subdivided (*e.g.* Robotics). Annual author and subject indexes - latter index matches the classification scheme used to group the abstracts and is merely the latest in a series of different methods practised. Specific subject retrieval has not been easy for many years. About 475 core journals are scanned. Available on CD-ROM. *Class No:* 621(048)

[4137]

Mechanical engineering abstracts. Bethesda, Md., Cambridge Scientific Abstracts, 1973-. v.1(1)-. Monthly. ISSN: 10637311.

Originally published by the Institute of Mechanical Engineering as an index to current literature. Published monthly. 2 vols. per year before 1979. Subsequently published by Data Courier Inc., the present publishers took over in 1981 and, in 1982, v.15, began to publish abstracts. Groups contents into 9 sections, (*e.g.* 1000. Management and production; 3000. Mechanics, materials and devices; 4000. Production processes, tools and equipment) with sub-sections (*e.g.* 3600. Tribology) also sub-divided (*e.g.* 3610. Bearings). Each issue has author and subject indexes. Cumulative annual indexes. Scope: 250 journals, theoretical and applied, plus many conferences and books. Each entry has unique identifier and full citation. Abstracts of variable quality and efficiency - often verbose. Annual content has been diminishing from 15,000 in 1982 to 11,000 in 1995. Also available as a computerized database, ISMEC, online via DIALOG and STN International. On CD-ROM (SilverPlatter) and on the Internet (URL: http://www.csa.com). *Class No:* 621(048)

[4138]

Referativnyĭ zhurnal. 14. Tekhnologiya mashinostroeniya. Moscow, VINITI, 1963-. Monthly. diagrs. R.224.40. ISSN: 00342599.

About 25,000 signed indicative and informative abstracts pa. 4 sections covering: Metal cutting, machine tools and tools - Technology and equipment for machine tools - Technology and equipment for forging - Technology and equipment for foundry work. Abstracts illustrated with diagrams. English contents list for Part A.

Class No: 621(048)

Yearbooks & Directories

[4139]

Engineering components and materials index. Bracknell, Berks., Technical Indexes, Ltd., 2pa. £40pa. ISBN: 0860413349. ISSN: 03088383.

This data book is the index to the associated microform file of the catalogues of manufacturers and suppliers of a wide variety of mechanical, electrical, hydraulic and pneumatic engineering components, materials and products. Covers iron and steel and non-ferrous metals and alloys; plastics, rubber, ceramics and glass processing and treatment. Includes transducers, transformers, switches, relays, electrical connectors and cables, and clutches, brakes, bearings, gears, belts, plus pumps, compressors, valves, seals.

Class No: 621(058)

[4140]

Machinery buyers guide. Horton Kirby, Kent, Findlay Publications, 1998. 2v., boxed. illus., tables. ISSN: 01420658.

First published 1926. Publisher varies.

'Annual directory of engineering products and services' (*Cover subtitle*). Alphabetical by product, tool, service, etc., followed by addresses section (A-Z list of *c.*6,000 firms). Includes trade names and agencies list and miscellaneous tabulated reference material, Many advertisements. Also available on CD-ROM. *Class No:* 621(058)

[4141]

Manufacturing and materials handling index. Bracknell, Berks., Technical Indexes, Ltd., 2pa. £30 pa. ISSN: 02688093.

Previously entitled *Materials handling index.*

This data book is the index to the associated microform file of the catalogues of manufacturers and suppliers of engineering products, tools, machines and equipment for materials handling, packaging and maintenance work, available on separate subscription. 10 sections (A: Buildings and associated fixtures ... E: Production machines and tools ... G: Materials handling equipment ... Z: Services).

Class No: 621(058)

Tables & Data Books

[4142]

AMERICAN SOCIETY OF MECHANICAL ENGINEERS. Metal Engineering Board. **ASME handbook.** New York, etc., McGraw-Hill, 1956-1964. 4v. (*Handbook series.*)

Engineering tables. 2nd ed. 1956. 695p., $89. ISBN 0070015163.
Metals engineering: design. 2nd ed. 1965. 619p. $79.50. ISBN 00701518x.
Metals engineering: processes. 1958. 928p. ISBN 0070015147.
Metals properties. 1954. 440p. ISBN 0070015139.

Engineering tables covers, in 15 sections, bearings, gears, keys, bolts, screws, nuts, springs, tubes, gaskets, etc. Has bibliography of sources. *Metals engineering: design* is much enlarged, has over 100 contributors, and arranges its 59 sections in 5 parts, with references, many tables and detailed index. *Metals engineering: processes* has 49 contributors, 40 sections grouped under 9 heads (*e.g.* 1: Heat treatment of steel; 7: Machining; 9: Electro-forming). Many illus., diagrams, tables. Concise index. *Metal properties* gives data on individual metals, such as chemical composition, characteristics,

.... (contd.)

technological, physical and mechanical properties, thermal conductivity, coefficient of thermal expansion. The *Handbook* was reprinted in 1987. *Class No:* 621(083)

[4143]

CARVILL, J. Mechanical engineer's data handbook. Oxford, Butterworth-Heinemann, 1993. x, 342p., illus., tables. £40. ISBN: 075061014x.

8 sections: 1. Strength of materials - 2. Applied mechanics - 3. Thermodynamics and heat transfer - 4. Fluid mechanics - 5. Manufacturing technology - 6. Engineering materials - 7. Engineering measurements - 8. General data. Extensive use of illus. and tables. Glossary, p.311-29; detailed, analytical index, p.330-42.

Class No: 621(083)

[4144]

Handbook of mechanical engineering calculations. Hicks, T.G., *ed.* New York, etc., McGraw-Hill, 1998. v.p. diagrs., graphs, tables, formulas. ISBN: 0070288135.

21 contributors. About 5,000 worked-out calculations procedures covering the major areas of mechanical engineering. Calculations take account of non-engineering 'pressures': the environment and the environmental lobby; the economy; regulatory agencies (US). 25 sections in 4 parts: 1. Power generation - 2. Plant and facilities engineering - 3. Environmental control - 4. Design engineering. There is some overlap with the editor's *Standard handbook of engineering calculations*, 3rd ed. *Class No:* 621(083)

[4145]

Machinery's handbook: a reference book for the mechanical engineer, draftsman, toolmaker and machinist. Green, R.E. *and* McCauley, C.J., *eds.* 25th ed. New York, Industrial Press, 1997. viii, 2547p. diagrs., graphs, tables. ISBN: 0831125756.

First published 1914. Previous edition 1992.

A comprehensive data book. Main sections: Mathematics - Mechanics - Strength of materials - Properties, treatment and testing of materials - Plastics - Dimensions, gaging and measuring - Tooling and toolmaking - Machining operations - Manufacturing processes - Fasteners - Threads and threading - Gears, splines and cams - Machine elements - Measuring units. Covers American and British practice. Detailed, analytical index, p.2485-2543. A standard work that remains indispensable *Class No:* 621(083)

[4146]

—**Machinery's handbook guide to the use of tables and formulas.** Green, R.E., *ed.* 25th ed. companion. New York, Industrial Press, 1996. xi, 249p. diagrs. £10. ISBN: 0831125993.

Previously entitled *The use of 'Handbook' tables and formulas.* First published 1931.

Designed for use in conjunction with the 24th ed. of *Machinery's handbook*, with hundreds of examples, solutions, test questions and typical applications to enable *Handbook* users to get to know it thoroughly and to use it effectively and speedily. *Class No:* 621(083)

[4147]

Marks' Standard handbook for mechanical engineers. Avallone, E.A. *and* Baumeister, T., *eds.* 10th ed. New York, etc., McGraw-Hill, 1996. v.p. diagrs., graphs, tables. $125. ISBN: 0070049971.

First published 1916; 9th ed. 1987.

170 contributors. Framework of 19 main sections unchanged, covering conventional physical science and engineering topics, plus transportation, electrical and electronic engineering and building construction and equipment (*e.g.* 3. Mechanics of solids and fluids - 4. Heat ... 6. Materials of engineering (205p.) ... 8. Machine elements (216p.) ... 14. Fans, pumps and compressors ... 17. Industrial engineering). Dual system of units used. Extensive index (158p.). About 3,000 illus. and 900 tables. 'Highly recommended' (*Science and technology libraries*, 17(1) 1997, p.99). A CD-ROM version is available (1998; $149.95; ISBN: 007134411x). *Class No:* 621(083)

[4148]

Spon's mechanical and electrical services price book, 1999. 30th ed. London, Spon, 1998. Annual. xviii, 543p. graphs, tables. £77. ISBN: 041924140x. ISSN: 03054543.

First published 1968.

4 parts: 1. Approximate estimating - 2. Rates of wages and working rules - 3. Material costs/measured work prices - 4. Daywork. Annual editions are generally published in September. *Class No:* 621(083)

Standards

[4149]

Mechanical standards: basic standards; complete to 31 August 1983. 1st English ed. Berlin, DIN (Deutsches Institut für Normunge.V.)/Beuth Verlag, 1984. 408p. diagrs., tables. DM128. (*DIN Handbook 1.*) ISBN: 3410116451. ISSN: 07227337.

English-language translations of 50 basic standards in mehcanical engineering, including ISO threads, metrology, dimensioning, drawings, tolerances, surfaces, fasteners and gearing. Arranged in DIN number order, with alphabetical subject index and a separate classified

....(contd.)

contents list. Based on the 20th ed. of the *DIN Handbook 1* (*TAB 1*) and closely related to and overlapping with *DIN Handbook 3* (*i.e., TAB 3*): 'Mechanical engineering standards for study and practice'. This overlap will be removed in future editions of *TAB 3*. New editions of the Handbooks normally appear every 3 years. *Class No:* 621(083.74)

Histories

[4150]

BURSTALL, A.F. A History of mechanical engineering. London, Faber & Faber, 1963. 456p. illus. £3; £1.40. (*Technology today and tomorrow.*)

9 chapters, each with bibliographies and references, cover successive periods of history from 4,500 BC to the 1960s. In each chapter significant advances are helpfully pinpointed under 5 standard headings. Author has leaned heavily on Singer and Holmyard's *History of technology* and the *Proceedings* of the Institution of Mechanical Engineers, with obvious benefit. *Class No:* 621(091)

[4151]

STRANDH, S. Machines: an illustrated history, translated by A. Henning. London, Artists House/Mitchell Beazley, 1979. 240p. illus., (incl. col.) diagrs. £14.95. ISBN: 0861340124.

Originally published by A.B. Nordbok (Gothenburg, 1979).

Adopts a wide definition of 'machines' to include all forms of tool, instrument and utensil and covers their origin and use in 9 chapters with different themes, *e.g.* 2. Machine elements and elementary machines - 3. From hand tool to industrial robot ... 8. Computers. Chapters 1 and 9 cover earliest times and the present day respectively. Chapters 4-6 discuss the classes of prime mover. Bibliography, p.234. Good index. Liberal provision of excellent drawings, many coloured. Author is Director, Museum of Science and Technology, Stockholm. *Class No:* 621(091)

[4152]

—VINCE, J. Power before steam. London, Murray, 1985. 160p. illus. £8.95. ISBN: 0719541751.

A brief account of 'the manner in which man has used his own muscle power, and power derived from animals, water, wind and gravity' (*Introduction*). Much emphasis on water and wind mills. Text in author's own calligraphy adorned by his line-drawings. List of places to visit, p.154-5. Bibliography and index. *Class No:* 621(091)

Biographies

[4153]

AMERICAN SOCIETY OF MECHANICAL ENGINEERS. Mechanical engineers in America, born prior to 1861: a biographical dictionary. New York, American Society of Mechanical Engineers, 1980. xix, 330p. ports. $20.

Comprises, first, a list, with dates, of 1,688 people - the great majority male - born before 1861 (a) in the US and active there or abroad, or, (b) born elsewhere and active in America, in areas nowadays recognized as mechanical engineering, from the late 18th to the early 20th century. Biographical sketches are provided in the second part of the work for 500 of these regarded as prominent in their own time or since. There are portraits of 50. Sources of information are listed. *Class No:* 621(092)

Turbines

[4154]

Referativnyĭ zhurnal. 49. Turbostroenie. Akademiya Nauk SSSR. Moscow, VINITI, 1963-. Monthly. R.27.40. ISSN: 00342629.

About 2,400 signed indicative and informative abstracts pa. on turbine engineering. 3 main sections: Steam and gas turbines; Hydraulic turbines; Wind turbines. UDC numbers. Annual subject index. English contents summary. *Class No:* 621-135

Precision Engineering

[4155]

BOLTON, W. Newnes instrumentation and measurement pocket book. Oxford, Butterworth-Heinemann, 1996. 320p. illus., diagrs., graphs. £14.99 ISBN: 0750628855.

Systems and instruments for the measurement of quantities encountered in engineering, such as temperature, radiation, stress and strains, and chemical composition. Includes microprocessor based instruments. Samll, handy format. *Class No:* 621-187

[4156]

DAVIDSON, A., ed. Handbook of precision engineering. London, Macmillan, 1970-74. 12v. illus.

Original Dutch ed. (Eindhoven, Philips), 1966-70. 1. *Fundamentals.* 2. *Materials.* 3. *Fabrication of non-metals.* 4. *Physical and chemical fabrication techniques.* 5. *Joining techniques.* 6. *Mechanical design applications.* 7. *Electrical design applications.* 8. *Surface treatment.* 9. *Machining processes.* 10. *Forming processes.* 11. *Production engineering.* 12. *Precision measurement.*

This set aims to cover the design and manufacture of fine mechanisms and to relate these explicitly to precision engineered products and parts. V. 3-5 cover production techniques; v. 6, 7, 11, 12, with practical design and the equipment and compounds needed. All chapters are by experts. A review of v.10 in *Production engineering* (v.53(12), Dec. 1974, p.522) commends it as clearly written, amply illustrated, and with an extensive index. *Class No:* 621-187

[4157]

FARAGO, F.T. Handbook of dimensional measurement. 2nd ed. New York, Industrial Press, 1982. xv, 524p. illus., diagrs., tables. £49.50. ISBN: 0831111364.

First published 1968.

Principles and practices of measurements, including instruments such as gauges, microscopes and other optical devices. Separate chapters cover measurement of angles, straightness, flatness, roundness, surfaces, etc. New chapters in this edition deal with screw threads, gears, process control and automated methods. 80 tables with illustrations and synopses are particulary useful in facilitating speedy and efficient consultation. Many instruments are illustrated in half-tones.

'It must be emphasized that this book is American and aimed primarily at the American reader. The concept of the book and its format ... is (!) very good. Unfortunately, the author does not cover the British or ISO standard ... In general, this is a thoroughly practical and useful book' (*International journal of machine tool design & research*, v.23 (2/3), 1983, p.169). *Class No:* 621-187

Springs

[4158]

CARLSON, H. Spring designer's handbook. New York, Dekker, 1978. xv, 350p. illus., diagrs., graphs, tables. £16.95. (*Mechanical engineering series, 1.*) ISBN: 0824766237.

A compact reference work containing sufficient descriptive, factual information and data to serve as an adequate working guide for engineers concerned with the practical problems of spring design. The 20 chapters cover materials (1-10); design (11-14); manufacture (15-18); plus a glossary and miscellaneous tables. There are 219 illustrations, diagrams, curves and data tabulations. Imperial and SI units are both used. *Class No:* 621-272

[4159]

—CARLSON, H. Spring manufacturing handbook. New York, Dekker, 1982. 362p. illus., tables. $69.00. (*Mechanical engineering series, 15.*) ISBN: 0824716787.

Companion volume to the same author's *Spring designer's handbook* (*qv*). Covers all aspects of manufacturing springs of all types and of many materials, supported by numerous illustrations and tables of data and specifications. A third book by Carlson entitled *Springs: troubleshooting and failure analysis* deals with problems of design, materials and manufacturing processes. *Class No:* 621-272

Maintenance Engineering

[4160]

BRITISH STANDARDS INSTITUTION. Glossary of maintenance management terms in terotechnology. 3rd ed. London, BSI, 1993. 53p. (*BS3811: 1993.*)

First published 1974.

Technical terms in installation and maintenance of equipment. 6 sections (*e.g.* 3: Operational terms). Examples of use often provided. Index. *Class No:* 621-7

[4161]

Maintenance engineering handbook. Higgins, L.R., *and others, eds.* 5th ed. New York, etc., McGraw-Hill, 1995. v.p. illus., diagrs., charts, tables. $79.50. ISBN: 0070288119.

1st and 2nd eds. (1957, 1965), edited by L.C. Morrow. 4th ed. 1987.

55 contributors. The 5th ed. claims new ways of using computers to manage maintenance procedures and new material on lubrication, instruments and vibration, and chemical corrosion control and cleaning. *Class No:* 621-7

[4162]

Standard handbook of plant engineering. Rosaler, R.C., *ed.* 2nd ed. New York etc., McGraw-Hill, 1995. v.p. diagrs., graphs, tables. $104.50. ISBN: 0070521646.

The first ed. (1983) superseded *Facilities and plant engineering handbook* (1973), edited by B.T. Lewis and J.P. Marron.

Numerous contributors. 4 parts, 20 sections. A. The basic plant facility: construction, equipment and maintenance - B. Plant operation equipment: selection and maintenance - C. The maintenance function: basic equipment and supplies - D. Supplementary technical data. Appendices contain brief guide to mainly non-published US sources of information and metric conversion tables. Brief glossary and good index. Almost 900 diagrs., graphs, tables, etc. 'An excellent handbook' (*Choice*, April 1995, p.1334). *Class No:* 621-7

Protection of Machinery

Fluid Sealing

[4163]

BROWN, M. Seals and sealing handbook. 4th ed. Oxford, Elsevier, 1995. viii, 621p. illus., diagrs., graphs, tables. £70. ISBN: 1856172325.

First published 1981.

Combines a survey of the technology and processes with a buyers' guide. Brief glossary, p.579-86. *Class No:* 621-762

[4164]

Fluid sealing abstracts. Cranfield, Beds., British Hydromechanics Research Association, 1966-. v.1-. Quarterly. £84pa. ISSN: 00154660.

About 600 informative abstracts pa. of items drawn from over 1,000 journals, plus reports, books, standards and conference proceedings. Selected British patents are included. Main sections: Seals in general - Static seals - Dynamic seals - Reciprocating seals - Rotary seals - Seal materials. Issue and cumulative annual indexes of personal and corporate authors and of subjects. *Class No:* 621-762

[4165]

Seal users handbook. Austin, R.M. *and* Nau, B.S. 2nd ed. Cranfield, B.H.R.A. Fluid Engineering, 1979. 220p. illus., diagrs., graphs, tables. $73. ISBN: 0900983728.

Previous edition 1974.

Technical section (Chapters 1-6, covering selection, economics, materials, standards - British, German, Japanese, Swedish, American - servicing, failures) followed by trade directory - list of manufacturers and product index with specifications chart. List of tradenames, a glossary and a bibliography complete this compact handbook-cum-directory. *Class No:* 621-762

Nuclear & Atomic Engineering

Databases

[4166]

ENSDF (Evaluated Nuclear Structure Data File). Upton, N.Y., Brookhaven National Laboratory National Nuclear Data Center.

Covers 1930 to date. A numeric data bank providing data on nuclear structure and radioactive decay for all known isotopes. Critcally evaluated data is obtained from 11 cooperating countries, including US, UK, Germany, Netherlands and the CIS. Available via FIZ Karlsruhe. Printed version: *Nuclear data sheets*. *Class No:* 621.039(003.4)

[4167]

INIS (International Nuclear Information System). Vienna, International Atomic Energy Agency.

Covers 1970 to date. A bibliographic database, providing references, with abstracts, to the literature of nuclear physics and nuclear engineering and related topics (*e.g.* isotopes, radiation protection, safety, the legal social, environmental, economic, medical aspects). File size: 1,700,000 references. Updated fortnightly or monthly (varies with host). 90,000 additions pa. Hosts include IAEA, ESA-IRS, STN International and others. Available on magnetic tape and CD-ROM. Publications: *Thesaurus*. Printed versions: *INIS atomindex*. In English. *Class No:* 621.039(003.4)

[4168]

RTD-Publications [Research and Technical Developments Publications]. Luxembourg, Commission of the European Communities.

Formerly *EABS*.

Covers Euratom records 1962 to date. A bibliographic database, providing references, with abstracts (since 1984), to research reports and EEC, ECSC and Euratom conference papers. Covers nuclear science and technology, coal and steel, new energy sources, the environment, radiation protection, etc. File size: 58,000 citations.

....(contd.)

Updated monthly. Host: ECHO Service. Printed versions: *Euro-abstracts* (Section I covers Euratom research). In English, French and German. *Class No:* 621.039(003.4)

Bibliographies

[4169]

CHESTER, K., *comp.* **Nuclear energy and the nuclear industry:** a guide to selected literature and sources of information. 2nd ed. London, Science Reference and Information Service, 1986. 44p. £9. ISBN: 0712307427.

Previous ed. 1982.

A valuable guide, with annotations, to over 100 publications in the subject field: 30 abstracting/indexing services; almost 60 periodicals; 12 directories and yearbooks; 4 publications with data on nuclear reactors; 4 bibliographies series. Also contains list of 35 organizations and 19 suppliers, companies and consultants, plus 12 publications giving market research and survey information. Notes about books, reports, conference and patents are included, but no entries. No index. *Class No:* 621.039(01)

[4170]

HARRIS, J. 'Nuclear engineering'. *Information sources in engineering.* K.W. Mildren and P.J. Hicks, eds. (3rd ed., 1996), p.259-67. 3rd ed. London, Bowker Saur, 1996. £80. ISBN: 1857390571.

Sections: Introduction - Main reactor types - Principal UK companies - Organizations - Regulatory authorities - Learned Societies - Textbooks - Public reports - Journals - Abstracting and indexing journals - Handbooks, databooks, directories. Primarily a listing; little description or analysis of titles. *Class No:* 621.039(01)

[4171]

INTERNATIONAL ATOMIC ENERGY AGENCY. Catalogue: International Atomic Energy publications. Vienna, IAEA, 1958-.

A cumulation listing all sales publications of the IAEA issued from 1958 to date which are still available, plus some which are now out of print. Irregular supplements. Part 1 lists all publications by subject, under 7 major headings (1. Life sciences - 2. Nuclear safety and environmental protection - 3. Physics - 4. Chemistry, geology and raw materials - 5. Reactors and nuclear power - 6. Industrial applications - 7. Miscellaneous) with subdivisions for each. Bibliographical details, price and description for each publication. Part 2 comprises indexes of the various series and an alphabetical index of titles and keywords. *Class No:* 621.039(01)

[4172]

—**INTERNATIONAL ATOMIC ENERGY AGENCY. Bibliographical series.** Vienna, IAEA, 1960-80. nos. 1-43.

Each bibliography covered a particular aspect of the peaceful utilization of atomic energy. No. 43, *Peaceful uses of nuclear explosions* (1980, 443p.), was the second of this title. The first (no. 38, 1970, 466p.) recorded 1,759 references. The second listed 1,335 references to the literature published 1969-79, with abstracts in English. Arranged by subject, with author and specific subject indexes. *Class No:* 621.039(01)

[4173]

JEDRUCH, J. Nuclear engineering databases, standards and numerical analysis. New York, Van Nostrand Reinhold, 1985. xix, 295p. illus., diagrs., graphs, tables. £64.35. ISBN: 0442245742.

A guide to sources of information, data projects and collections, computerized databases, regulations, standards, computer-aided design methods, property and performance data centres and bases, government bodies and engineering societies and their publications, concerned with nuclear reactor engineering. Heavily orientated to the US. Many useful lists and tabulations. Classified bibliography (p.267-81). Extensive references. 'Nuclear engineers, public utilities personnel and government regulatory officials will find this guide to the software of nuclear engineering an indispensable on-the-job tool' (*Mechanical engineering*, v.107, August 1985, p.72). *Class No:* 621.039(01)

[4174]

SCHLACHTER, G.A., *ed.,.* **Nuclear America:** a historical bibliography. Santa Barbara, Calif., ABC-Clio Information Services; Oxford, Clio Press, 1984. xiii, 184p. £21.85. (*ABC-Clio Research guides.*) ISBN: 0874363608.

More than 800 abstracts of publications selected from 2,000 periodicals published in 90 countries, 1973 - 1982, concerned with peaceful and (predominantly) military uses of nuclear energy and restricted to items directly concerned with US. Subject and author indexes. '... anyone involved explicitly in the nuclear debate may find it useful in exploring the American Scene' (*Nuclear energy*, v.23(4), August 1984, p.209). *Class No:* 621.039(01)

[4175]

UNITED KINGDOM. Atomic Energy Authority. **UKAEA list of publications available to the public.** Harwell, Atomic Energy Research Establishment, 1955-. Monthly. Annual cumulation. *Gratis.* ISSN: 00417289.

Periodical articles, books, pamphlets, reports and patents by UKAEA staff, grouped under these categories. Annual cumulation is classified into 21 categories with subdivision into articles, books and pamphlets, and reports. Patents and non-UKAEA reports are separately listed. Cumulation no. 31: January - December 1986 (1987. 90p. £7.25. ISBN 0705811263) lists 1,147 numbered items under headings such as: Nuclear physics; Fuel processing and reprocessing; Health and Safety; Accelerators; Transport and handling of materials; Waste management. Author and report number indexes.
Class No: 621.039(01)

[4176]

UNITED STATES. Nuclear Regulatory Commission. **Title list of documents made publicly available.** Washington, the Commission, 1979-. v.1-. Monthly. (*1. NUREG-0540.*)

Successor to *Power reactor docket information,* issued by the U.S. Department of Energy until 1979.

Covers documents received or published by the Nuclear Regulatory Commission, categorized as docketed (relating to civilian nuclear power plant and other uses of radioactive material) and non-docketed (material received by or issued by the Commission as a regulatory agency). Documents include all kinds of reports, correspondence, licences, etc. Items are arranged in categories, under docket number where given one, with one-line annotations. Indexes of personal authors and corporate sources and of report numbers.
Class No: 621.039(01)

Handbooks & Manuals

[4177]

Nuclear power: policy and prospects. Jones, P.M.S., *ed.* New York, Wiley, 1987. 416p. $154. ISBN: 0471907324.

16 contributors. 4 sections: 1. Introduction - 2. Areas of controversy - 3. National experience of nuclear power (US, France, Canada, UK, FRG, Japan, India; the former USSR and other planned economies are largely omitted) - 4. Policy and prospects. Chapter references; detailed, analytical index. 'An excellent resource' (*Choice,* May 1988, p.1424). *Class No:* 621.039(035)

[4178]

RAHN, F.J., *and others.* **A Guide to nuclear power technology:** a resource for decision making. New York, etc., Wiley, 1984. xi, 985p. illus., diagrs., graphs, tables. £77.50. ISBN: 0471889148.

Aims at comprehensive coverage of the technology associated with nuclear power, 'tuned to the person who has some technical background but is not a specialist in the field' (*Preface*). In addition to reactors and nuclear power plant operation there are chapters on fuel, materials, radioactivitiy and waste disposal, health, safety, regulations, economics and proliferation factors. 10 pages of statistics. 3 glossaries of acronyms. Very useful chapter bibliographies. Index (29 pages). *Class No:* 621.039(035)

Dictionaries

Polyglot

[4179]

CLASON, W.E., *comp.* **Elsevier's dictionary of nuclear science and technology in six languages:** English, American, French, Spanish, Italian, Dutch and German. 2nd rev. ed. Amsterdam, etc., Elsevier, 1970, reprinted 1993. [ix], 787p. £177.65. ISBN: 044440810x.

First published 1958. Russian supplement 1961.

7,806 English/American terms and phrases, with equivalents in the other 5 languages. Each entry consecutively numbered. Indexes in each other language.

Reactor technology (Pt. B, v.1(4), February 1961, p.238) questions the validity of a 'neat row of five foreign equivalents' and hints that some of the equivalents may have been concocted.
Class No: 621.039(038)=00

[4180]

International nuclear information system multilingual dictionary. 2nd ed. Vienna, International Atomic Energy Agency, 1995. 5v., *c.*550p. each. *c.*£60 each.

V.1 in English with equivalents in French, German, Spanish and Russian. V.2 French; V.3 German; V.4 Russian; V.4 Spanish — each with equivalents in the other languages. *Class No:* 621.039(038)=00

[4181]

SUBE, R., *ed.* **Wörterbuch Kerntechnik:** Englisch - Deutsch - Französisch - Russisch. [Dictionary of nuclear engineering: English - German - French - Russian.] Essen, Girardet; Berlin, VEB Verlag Tehnik; Oxford, Elsevier, 1985. 1199p. £169. ISBN: 3773651252; 0444995935.

18,500 terms in English, with unique alphanumeric codes for each and equivalents in German, French and Russian, in columns. Indexes in German, French and Russian, utilizing codes for referral. Although atomic and nuclear physics are included, emphasis is on nuclear engineering (installations, materials, power, generation and reactors), radiation and weapons. Very thorough coverage. Numerous cross-references. Larger and much-improved version of author's 1961 *Dictionary of nuclear physics and technology.*
Class No: 621.039(038)=00

English

[4182]

BRITISH STANDARDS INSTITUTION. Glossary of terms used in nuclear science and technology. 2nd ed. London, BSI, 1973. 52p. (*BS 3455:1973.*) ISBN: 0580078558.

First published as *Glossary of terms used in nuclear science* (1962).

Scope and size have been reduced to concentrate on the technology and engineering terminology. About 750 terms and cross-references.
Class No: 621.039(038)=20

[4183]

—**HANCHETT, J.G.** *and* **HASSELBERG, F.W.,** *comps.* Glossary of terms: nuclear power and radiation. Singh, M.H., *ed.* Washington, U.S. Nuclear Regulatory Commission, 1981. 52p. $3.75. (*NUREG-0770.*)

300 terms defined to be understandable to the layman.
Class No: 621.039(038)=20

[4184]

Chambers nuclear energy and radiation dictionary. Walker, P.M.B., *ed.* Edinburgh, Chambers, 1992. viii,260p. diagrs., tables. £20; $40. ISBN: 0550132465.

About 2,500 terms, briefly defined (*e.g.* 'alpha particle': 5 lines). Cross-references. Preceded by 11 chapters on historical development and themes of nuclear energy (*e.g.* 3. Energy from nuclear fission ... 5. Nuclear safety ... 8. Radiation detection ... 11. Biological effects). 'An invaluable reference work, highly recommended' (*Choice,* May 1993, p.1436). *Class No:* 621.039(038)=20

French

[4185]

FRANCE. Commisariat a L'Énergie Atomique. **Dictionnaire des sciences et techniques nucléaires.** 3rd ed. Paris, Eyrolles, 1975. 488p. graphs, tables. F175.

First published 1964. Previous ed. 1966.

Present ed. has weeded obsolete terms and added new ones to give a total of 3,400, each defined in French in Part 1, with English equivalents. Part 2. lists the latter and gives French equivalents. Part 3 (Annexes) contains 7 tables (Fundamental particles; SI units; radioactive elements; Periodic table, etc).
Class No: 621.039(038)=40

Reports Literature

[4186]

UNITED STATES. Nuclear Regulatory Commission. **Regulatory and technical reports:** abstracts index journal. Washington, the Commission, 1976-. v.1-. Quarterly. (*NUREG-0304.*)

Bibliographic data and informative abstracts for the regulatory and technical reports issued by the US Nuclear Regulatory Commission (successor to the Atomic Energy Commission) and its contractors, in NUREG report number order. Issue and cumulated annual indexes of personal authors, subjects, originating organizations, contractors and licencsed facilities. *Class No:* 621.039(047)

Reviews & Abstracts

[4187]

INIS Atomindex. Vienna, International Nuclear Information System, International Atomic Energy Agency, 1920-. v.1(1)-. 24pa. Sch., 5,100pa. ISSN: 00047139.

Successor to *Nuclear science abstracts* (ceased 30 June 1976). V.1-20 as *List of bibliographies on nuclear energy.*

About 90,000 indicative and informative abstracts pa. Classified order: A00. Physical sciences - B00. Chemistry, materials and earth sciences - C00. Life sciences - D00. Isotopes, isotope and radiation applications - E00. Engineering and technology - F00. Other aspects of nuclear energy. Each section subdivided in detail, *e.g.* E10.00 Engineering - 16.00 Accelerators - E16.30. Components and auxiliaries - E16.31. Ion sources. Each abstract lists subject headings used in indexes. Each issue has personal author, corporate entry,

....*(contd.)*

subject, conference date, conference place and report, standard and patent number indexes. (*N.B.,* No index of conference *names*.) Semi-annual indexes cumulative annually. English abstracts and translations of foreign-language titles. Covers reports, conference papers, patents, journal articles and books (in that order for each section). Also available on magnetic tape (from which the printed version is prepared), and online via DIALOG, ESA-IRS, and other hosts, and on CD-ROM. First issue in each volume (1st January) contains list of over 4,300 journals scanned regularly. *Class No:* 621.039(048)

[4188]

Nuclear science abstracts. A semi-monthly publication of the United States Atomic Energy Commission (1975-1976: Energy Research and Development Association). Washington, U.S. Government Printing Office, 1948- June 1976. V.1-33, no.12.

First issued 1947 as *Abstracts of declassified documents.*

Covered journal articles, books, patents and reports issued by the US Atomic Energy Commission and other US government agencies and by universities and industrial and research bodies worldwide. 2 vols. pa. 1973-1976. V. 31-32, 1975, contained 66,208 indicative and informative abstracts in 21 alphabetically arranged sections (Chemistry ... Engineering ... Particle accelerators ... Physics (Nuclear) ... Reactor technology and radiation - General and miscellaneous) with subdivisions. Personal and corporate author indexes, subject index and report number index, plus five-year cumulations. With 940,000 abstracts, this remains a unique and invaluable guide to the unclassified literature of the first 30 years of the nuclear age. Succeeded by *INIS Automindex (qv).*

Available online (944,236 records) as a closed file on DIALOG and on CD-ROM. *Class No:* 621.039(048)

[4189]

Physics abstracts. Science abstracts. Section A. Stevenage, Herts, Institution of Electrical Engineers, 1898-. v.1-. Twice monthly. £2430. ISSN: 00368091.

This section of *Science abstracts* includes nuclear physics, nuclear engineeering, radioactivity, nuclear power, atomic and molecular physics, spectra and properties, and thus constitutes a major souce of abstracts derived from the INSPEC database of more than 4,000 journals, plus books, reports, conferences, etc. A significant proportion of the 180,000 abstracts pa. relate to these subjects. Half-yearly and 4-yearly cumulative indexes of authors, subjects, etc., enhance the value. Available online from a number of hosts. CD-ROM. *Class No:* 621.039(048)

[4190]

—**Euro abstracts. Section 1: Euratom and EEC R & D and demonstration projects. Scientific and technical publications and patents.** Luxembourg, Commission of the European Communities; Oxford, Learned Information, 1963-. V.1(1)-. Monthly. £54.40pa. ISSN: 00142352.

About 1,200-1,400 informative abstracts pa. 10 sections, subdivided (General and miscellaneous ... Nuclear technology - Physics). Indexes of authors and inventors (of patents cited). In English. Available online *gratis* through ECHO (European Commission Host Organization). *Class No:* 621.039(048)

Progress Reports

[4191]

Advances in atomic, molecular and optical physics. San Diego, Ca., Academic Press, 1965-. Annual. ISSN: 1049250x.

V.38 (1997. 400p.) has extensively documented review articles. Index. *Class No:* 621.039(055)

[4192]

Advances in nuclear physics. New York, Plenum Press, 1968-. v.1-. ISSN: 00652970.

V.23 (1996. 315p.) has review articles with extensive references. Contents of earlier volumes. *Class No:* 621.039(055)

[4193]

Advances in nuclear science and technology. New York, Plenum Press, 1962-. v. 1-. ISSN: 00652989.

Reviews of selected fields with greater interest for nuclear engineers. Some vols. have special theme (*e.g.* v.17, 1986: Simulators for nuclear power; V.18 contained 5 papers on aspects of nuclear power plant - 3 concerned light water reactors). Occasional Festschrift vols. (*e.g.* v.19 1987. 490p. $85) in honour of Eugene Wigner). V.25 (1997. 302p.). *Class No:* 621.039(055)

[4194]

Annual review of nuclear and particle science. Palo Alto, Ca., Annual Reviews Inc., 1978-. v. 28-. ISSN: 01638998.

Formerly (1952-77) as *Annual review of nuclear science.*

V.46 (1996. 658p.) includes review articles with extensive references. Indexes. *Class No:* 621.039(055)

[4195]

Progress in nuclear energy. Oxford, etc., Elsevier. 4 pa. £350; $557. ISSN: 01491970.

Two series of this title have been published. One presents conventional reviews in different parts of the subject field, sometimes more than once yearly (*e.g.* vols. 12-14 were published in 1985). The other (the 'New series' published a number of reviews in 12 specific series fields (*e.g.* II. Reactors; IX. Analytical chemistry). Additionally a 12v. set (desribed as 'Old series') was published in 1976 to disseminate the proceedings of a European Conference with the title *Nuclear energy maturity*. It is also published as a more conventional 'international review journal covering all aspects of nuclear science and engineering' (*Aims and scope*) intended, from 1987, to give rapid publication by direct reproduction from authors' typescripts. Special issues and supplements appear regularly. *Class No:* 621.039(055)

Yearbooks & Directories

[4196]

Nuclear power plants worldwide. Dresser, P.D., *ed.* Detroit, Mi., Gale, 1993. 556p. maps. $129. ISBN: 0810388804.

741 entries by country, A-Z. Data include address, phone, fax; plant size; construction details; equipment suppliers; plant performance; political issues; future plans. Appendices: technical problems worldwide; US Nuclear Regulatory Commission 'report cards' on domestic plant performance. Glossary. 'An excellent source of sought-after information' ('Reference books bulletin', *Booklist*, November 1, 1993, p.568). *Class No:* 621.039(058)

[4197]

World nuclear industry handbook, 1998. Sutton, Surrey, Nuclear Engineering International, 1998. 244p. graphs, tables. ISSN: 00295507.

Sections: Diary of events - Power reactors (country-by-country summary; data for individual units; contact details) - Research and test reactors (countries, A-Z) - Fuel cycle (facilities and operator addresses) - National and international organizations - Buyer's guide. *Class No:* 621.039(058)

Almanacs

[4198]

GREENHALGH, G. *and* **JEFFS, E.,** *eds.* **Nuclear industry almanac.** V.1. Western Europe. Great Missenden, Bucks., Nuclear Energy Intelligence, 1982. tables. £35. ISBN: 0907643000.

Energy profiles of 18 West European countries (UK, p. 153-68, covering nuclear plant construction and operation, licensing procedures, radiation protection, research activities, uranium supplies, enrichment, reprocessing, spent fuel, waste management). Surveys of nuclear industries of 11 countries, with details of firms. Directory of almost 400 companies and organizations. *Class No:* 621.039(059)

Tables & Data Books

[4199]

Atomic data and nuclear data tables. Orlando, Fl., Academic Press, 1973-, v.12-. 6pa. (3 v. of 2 issues each). diagrs., tables. $497 pa. ISSN: 0092640x.

Formerly *Atomic data* (vs.1-5, 1969-73) and *Nuclear data*, Section A (1965-70) and *Nuclear data tables* (vs.1-11, 1965-73). Replaces *NBS Circular 499: Nuclear data*.

Experimental and theoretical data in various areas of atomic and nuclear-structure physics. About 120 categories, from absorption coefficients to x-rays. Some issues contain a single paper, others five or six. Cumulative indexes of authors and subjects covering 1965-87, all vols. to v.37, appeared in v.37(ii), November 1987.

Available online from the publisher's International Digital Electronic Access Library (IDEAL). *Class No:* 621.039(083)

[4200]

BASHKIN, S. *and* **STONER, J.O.,** *Jr.* **Atomic energy level and Grotrian diagrams.** Amsterdam, North-Holland, 1976-82 (v. 1-4).

1. *Hydrogen I - Phosphorus XV.* 1976. xx, 616p. $137.75. ISBN 072043227. Addendum v. 1978. viii, 176p. ISBN 0444852360.

2. *Sulphur I - Titanium XXII.* 1978. xviii, 650p. $137.75. ISBN 0444851496.

3. *Vanadium I - Chromium XXIV.* 1981. xvi, 550p. $137.75. ISBN 0444860061.

4. *Manganese I - Manganese XXV.* 1982. xiv, 354p. $97.75. ISBN 0444864636.

Pictorial representation of energy levels and electron transitions. Special and structural data for atoms and molecules. Extensive bibliographies. 'These two volumes [v. 1-2] are extremely useful to atomic spectroscopists and are highly recommended' (*Applied spectroscopy*, v.33(4), 1979, p. 422-3). *Class No:* 621.039(083)

[4201]

CINDA. Vienna, International Atomic Energy Agency, 1979-.

A worldwide bibliography of the literature on microscopic neutron data, published on behalf of the US National Nuclear Data Centre, the USSR Nuclear Data Centre, the NEA Data Bank and the IAEA Nuclear Data Section. Contains well over 200,000 entries, with data on microscopic cross sections, angular distributions, energy spectra and resonance parameters, arranged by element and isotope. 2 archival volumes plus supplements: CINDA - A. 2 vols. 1979. 1,929p. Sch.1,050 (Entries for literature 1935-1976). CINDA - B. 1984. 771p. Sch.700 (Entries for literature 1977-81).

Annual cumulated updates began with CINDA 84. Also available online from the Brookhaven National Laboratory, National Nuclear Data Center, Upton, New York). *Class No:* 621.039(083)

[4202]

ERDTMANN, G. Neutron activation tables. Verlag Chemie International, 1976. 146p. $45.90. (*Topical presentations in nuclear chemistry, v.6.*) ISBN: 3527256938.

Includes cross section values of thermal, epithermal and fast reactor neutrons, decay rates of the activation products and data tables on radionuclides and natural isotopes.

'The presentation of the data is clear and practical ... A valuable and useful data tabulation for all those who use the activation with reactor and 14-MeV generator neutrons as an analytical tool or for the production of isotopes' (*Nuclear science & engineering*, v. 63, August 1977, p. 514). *Class No:* 621.039(083)

[4203]

Neutron cross sections. New York, London, etc., Academic Press, 1981-1984. 2v. graphs, tables. ISBN: 0125097018.

V.1 *Neutron resonance parameters and thermal cross sections* by S.F. Mughabghab, M. Divadeenam and N.E. Holden. 2 Parts. 1981-1984. $65.00 Part A. Z = 1-60. Part B. Z = 61-100.

The 4th ed. of a work previously known as BNL-325, *Neutron cross sections*, v.1, *Resonance Parameters* (3rd ed. 1973). Originally by D.J. Hughes and J.A. Harvey. Also referred to as the 'Barn Book'.

Presents recommended thermal cross sections, resonance properties and resonance parameters for masses Z = 1 to 100. V.1 contains a survey of the physics of thermal and resonance neutrons. V.2 gives data for neutron cross section curves. *Class No:* 621.039(083)

[4204]

Nuclear fact book. Platt, A.M., *and others, eds.* 2nd ed. Chur, Switzerland; London, etc., Harwood, 1985. xv, 176p., graphs, tables. ISSN: 87553376.

Sponsored by the US Department of Energy.

Intended as 'an annual desk-reference ... on energy production, consumptions and costs'. Miscellaneous data, facts, statements, summaries of legislation drawn from many sources (cited). Covers development and use of nuclear power, waste, reprocessing, disposal, proliferation, radiation, environmental and sociopolitical facts, in relation to the US. Glossaries of acronyms and radiation terms. *Class No:* 621.039(083)

Standards

[4205]

BRITISH STANDARDS INSTITUTION. Nuclear energy. Milton Keynes, BSI, 1985. 2p. £1. (*SL 36.*)

One of the Sectional List series, giving the number, title and price group of 62 British Standards - specifications, glossaries, etc. - covering nuclear energy and its applications and other relevant standards. No index. (Full details are to be found in the annual catalogue (*qv*)). *Class No:* 621.039(083.74)

[4206]

EUROPEAN COMMUNITIES COMMISSION. Directorate - General Research, Science and Education. Nuclear Plant Safety Division. **Nuclear standards:** catalogue and classification. Fichtner, N., *and others, comps.* 3rd ed. Berlin, Cologne, Beuth Verlag, 1981. 230p. (*EUR 7135.*) ISBN: 3410580026.

Compiled under study contract granted to DIN (Deutsches Institut für Normung e.V.). First published 1975 as *Catalogue and classification of technical safety rules for light-water reactors and reprocessing plants* by M. Bloser, N. Fichtner and R. Neider (EUR 5362). Previous ed. 1977 with slightly modified title and compiled by present authors (EUR 5849). Title, issuing body, standard number, date and status (Amendment, Draft, Published, etc.) for 2,500 documents issued by 35 countries and international bodies. 4,000 entries in 19 main categories (*e.g.* Radiation protection; Containment; Material standards) and subdivisions (*e.g.* Radiological shielding; leakage). Section 1.1 provides a useful bibliography of glossaries of terminology and symbols (*c.*60 items). *Class No:* 621.039(083.74)

Histories

[4207]

LONGSTAFF, M. Unlocking the atom: a hundred years of nuclear energy. London, Muller, 1980. 175p. illus., diagrs., tables. £7.95. ISBN: 058410457x.

A brief account, by an enthusiast from within the industry. Chapters on early experimental work and wartime developments precede the main body of the work which outlines nuclear power's growth, with emphasis on the UK. All kinds of reactor are described and there is discussion of fuels, wastes and safety factors. Bibliography p. 171. *Class No:* 621.039(091)

Biographies

[4208]

Energy and nuclear sciences international who's who. 5th ed. Harlow, Essex, Longman Group, 1994. 340p. £225. (*Longman Reference on research series.*) ISBN: 0582256631.

Previously as *International who's who in energy and nuclear sciences* (1983).

Part 1 contains professional biographical profiles of about 4,100 scientists and engineers from 74 countries. Part 2 is a country index, subdivided by subject specialists. *Class No:* 621.039(092)

Thesauri

[4209]

INIS: Thesaurus. Vienna, International Atomic Energy Agency, 1987. (*INIS reference series.*) ISBN: 9201781873.

First published 1970 and based on the 1969 ed. of *EURATOM Thesaurus*.

Contains 17,243 accepted terms (descriptors) and 5,803 forbidden terms (non-descriptors) from the fields of nuclear physics and reactor technology and related topics. Identifies deleted and added terms (since previous ed.) in separate lists, and arrows in main alphabetical sequence also identify added terms. Scope notes for many terms. Appendix gives full listings of narrower terms in certain cases. *Class No:* 621.039:025.43

Conferences

[4210]

Meetings on atomic energy. Vienna, International Atomic Energy Agency, 1969-. Quarterly. Sch.480 pa. ISSN: 00476641.

Details of conferences, exhibitions and training courses. Conferences section has KWIC index of titles and place/date index. International training courses are arranged by date and national courses alphabetically by country. Final section gives detailed information on IAEA meetings, past and planned. *Class No:* 621.039:061:061.3

Reactors

[4211]

ELECNUC. Paris, Commissariat à l'Energie Atomique (CEA).

Coverage: mid-1950s to date. A textual/numeric databank of information on more than 980 nuclear power stations and nuclear reactors worldwide. Detailed information for each on planning, design, dates, component and plant manufacturers, technical and operational data (power input and output, cooling, reactor type, etc). Updated monthly. Available, with CEA permission, via CISI. *Class No:* 621.039.4

[4212]

GLASSTONE, S. and SESONSKE, A. Nuclear reactor engineering. 4th ed. New York, Chapman & Hall, 1994. 2v. 848p.). illus., diagrs., graphs, tables. £94. ISBN: 0412055112.

First published 1963; 3rd ed, 1981..

V.1: *Reactor design basics.* V.2: *Reactor systems engineering.*

Covers 'the fundamental scientific and engineering principles of nuclear reactor systems, especially those used for the generation of electric power' (*Preface*). Emphasis is on nuclear fission and reactor design. Has chapters on reactor analysis, kinetics and control, materials, fuels, radiation protection, shielding and safety and types of power reactor. Chapter references. *Class No:* 621.039.4

[4213]

INTERNATIONAL ATOMIC ENERGY AGENCY. Nuclear research reactors in the world. Vienna, IAEA, 1986. 105p. graphs, tables. Sch.100. (*Reference data series, no. 3.*) ISBN: 9201592868.

First ed. of a publication which replaces the Agency's previous two guides: *Power and research reactors in member states* and *Research reactors in member states*. Intended to be issued periodically.

17 tables showing research reactors in 55 countries with details of category (test, training, etc.), operating experience, current status (operating, under construction, planned, etc.), types (heavy water, graphite, etc), thermal power, general information and technical data for each. Includes shut-down facilities and covers 1957-85. *Class No:* 621.039.4

[4214]

MARSHALL, W., *ed.* **Nuclear power technology.** Oxford, Clarendon Press, 1983. 3v. illus., diagrs. £150. (*Oxford science publications.*)

    1. *Reactor technology.* xv, 503p. £50. ISBN 0198519486.

    2. *Fuel cycle.* xv, 456p. £50. ISBN 0198519583.

    3. *Nuclear radiation.* xv, 363p. £50. ISBN 0198519591.

    32 contributors in 24 chapters cover all aspects of nuclear power from 'How reactors work', through various types of fission reactor (with one chapter on fusion), fuel (design, reprocessing, etc.), waste, with a separate vol. on radiation, its risks and its applications in medicine and dating. Chapter references, suggestions for further reading and glossaries are valuable adjuncts. Separate volume indexes.

    Various reviews from within the industry pay tribute to content, style, range, clarity, with isolated criticisms about the book's treatment of waste and costings, but an independent authority should be cited: 'A noble effort, which has produced a fine work of science' (*Nature*, v. 309, June 7, 1984, p. 565). *Class No:* 621.039.4

[4215]

POCOCK, R.F. **Nuclear power:** its development in the United Kingdom. London, Institution of Nuclear Engineers/Unwin, 1977. x, 272p. illus., diagrs., graphs. £12.80; £5.10. ISBN: 0905418158, hardback; 0905418166, paperback.

    An account by an engineer employed within the industry relying on public domain sources - government papers, reports, periodicals, newspapers and books.

    [The author] 'is to be congratulated on having achieved an extremely readable volume of little more than 250 pages ... It is quite clear that the author recognized the difficulty of covering such a wide canvas in a small book and if one accepts this limitation, the book provides the reader with a good picture of how people have looked on nuclear power, its difficulties and its organizational problems year by year' (*Nuclear energy*, v.17(2), April 1978, p.75-6). *Class No:* 621.039.4

[4216]

Referativnyĭ zhurnal. **50. Yadernye reaktory.** Moscow, VINITI, 1964-. Monthly. diagrs. R25. ISSN: 00342653.

    About 3,000 signed abstracts pa. on nuclear reactors. 2 main sections: nuclear reactors and thermonuclear reactors, subdivided into 18 and 4 subsections respectively, *e.g.* design, calculation, fuel elements, control, materials. Illustrated with diagrams. UDC numbers. Annual subject index. English contents summary.

Class No: 621.039.4

Radioactive Elements

[4217]

BADASH, L. **Radioactivity in America:** growth and decay of a science. Baltimore, Md., Johns Hopkins Univ. Press 1979. xviii, 327p. illus., diagrs. $18.95. ISBN: 0801821878.

    Outlines the development of work on the chemical and physical aspects of the science connected with radioactivity, emphasizing the work done in America bween 1900 and 1920, and with particular attention to chemists Bertram Boltwood and Herbert McCoy. Full notes and index. Apart from quibbles about 'America' and 'decay' in the title and criticism of the 'tedious' presentation of the 40-odd naturally occuring radioactive isotopes, this book is warmly welcomed and labelled 'excellent' by a distinguished reviewer in *Physics today* (v.33 (7), July 1980, p.45). *Class No:* 621.039.5

[4218]

Handbook of radioactivity analysis. L'Annunziata, M.F., *ed.* San Diego, Ca., Academic Press, 1998. 771p. diagrs., graphs, tables. $115; £79.95. ISBN: 0124362559.

    Covers a wide rang of topics including radioisotope decay, radiation detectors, statistical techniques in nuclear counting, methods for the detection and counting of emissions, liquid scintillation analysis, environmental sampling, radio analytical methods, and robotics and automation. Detailed, analytical index. *Class No:* 621.039.5

[4219]

HOLMES-SIEDLE, A. *and* ADAMS, L. **Handbook of radiation effects.** Oxford Univ. Press, 1993. xxii, 479p. illus., graphs, tables. £45, $75. ISBN: 0198563477.

    Intended 'for designers of equipment and scientific instruments where they are required to ensure the survival of the equipment in radiation environments' (*Introduction*). 14 chapters (14. 'Conclusions'). Appendices (chiefly test data), p.421-53. Subject, author indexes. An engineering rather than a medical approach. *Class No:* 621.039.5

[4220]

MILLER, E.W. *and* MILLER, R.M. **Environmental hazards: radioactive materials and wastes:** a reference handbook. Santa Barbara, Calif., ABC-Clio, 1990. 298p. $39. ISBN: 0874362342.

    Various chapters with a range of information (*e.g.* nature and characteristics of radioactive materials; directory of organizations that deal with waste; annotated bibliography of books; listing of journal articles and government documents; select list of journal titles; bibliography of a-v materials). Glossary; index. 'An excellent addition to any reference collection' (*Choice,* April 1991, p.1292). *Class No:* 621.039.5

Isotopes

[4221]

BROWNE, E. *and* FIRESTONE, R.B. **Table of radioactive isotopes.** New York, etc., Wiley, 1986. v.p. illus., tables. ISBN: 047184909x.

    The isotopes are tabled in progressive atomic number order. Included: some 262 drawings of the mass-chain decay scheme. 'This massive and highly detailed work should satisfy the demand for *adopted* properties of *all* radiations emitted by nuclei' (*Science & Technology libraries*, v.8 (1), Fall 1987, p.183). *Class No:* 621.039.8

[4222]

ROYAL SOCIETY OF CHEMISTRY. **Isotopes: essential chemistry and applications.** London, the Society, 1980. 412p. £17. (*Special publication no.35.*) ISBN: 0851868304.

    Covers, in detail, the chemistry of isotopes and their industrial applications. V.2 appeared in 1988 (262p.; £44; Special publication no.68; ISBN: 0851867464). *Class No:* 621.039.8

Steam Power

Handbooks & Manuals

[4223]

GOODALL, P.M., *ed.* **The Efficient use of steam.** Guildford, Surrey, IPC Science and Technology Press, 1980. 469p. illus., diagrs., graphs, tables. £22. ISBN: 0861030184.

    Previously published 1947, written by Sir O. Lyle.

    23 contributors. Aims to assist industrial steam engineers or designers in safe and cost-effective use of steam. Covers theory, practice and equipment, *e.g.* 1: Properties of water and steam; 4: Shell boilers; 11: Turbines and engines; 12: Heat transfer; 13: Steam heating; 19: Steam costing. Lists relevant British standards. Appendix contains shortened steam tables (0.01 to 374.15 deg. C; 0.01 to 221 bar). References and index. *Class No:* 621.1(035)

Dictionaries

[4224]

Wörterbuch der dampferzeugungs technik: Deutsch - Englisch - Spanisch - Französisch. [Dictionary of steam generator engineering: German - English - Spanish - French, with emphasis on nuclear energy.] 2nd ed. Essen, Vulkan, 1993. 768p. £78.60. ISBN: 3802725042.

    9,407 headwords in German; indexes in the other languages. Particular emphasis on nuclear steam generation.

Class No: 621.1(038)

Tables & Data Books

[4225]

HAAR, L., *and others.* **NBS/NRC steam tables:** thermodynamic and transport properties and computer programs for vapor and liquid states of water in SI units. Washington, Hemisphere Publishing Corp., New York, McGraw-Hill, 1984. xii, 320p. tables, $34.50. ISBN: 0891163549.

    Thermodynamic property values for the specific volume, density, specific internal energy, specific enthalpy, and specific entropy of water and steam for the range 0 - 2000 deg. C and 0 - 30,000 bar. Tables for transport and other thermophysical property values are also given (*e.g.* viscosity, Prondtl number, dielectric constant). Appendices provide details of the Helmholz function used for derivation of values and of the computer programs used, and the relevant equations. 'These tables have been reviewed and approved by the Office of Standard Reference Data of the [US] National Bureau of Standards ...' (*Foreword*). 70 references. *Class No:* 621.1(083)

[4226]

—RIVKON, S.L., *and others*. Thermodynamic derivatives for water and steam. Translated by J. Kestin. New York, etc., Wiley, 1978. v, 264p. graphs, tables. $25. ISBN: 0470263636.

These tables of derivative values are based on the IFC 1968 Formulation for Scientific and General Use, and cover specific volume, enthalpy, entropy and isobaric specific heat as functions of pressure and temperature, - deemed to be more useful in engineering applications. Entries cover pressure range 0.1 to 50 MPa, and temperature range 0 to 600 deg. C. *Class No:* 621.1(083)

[4227]

IRVINE, T.F. *and* LILEY, P.E. **Steam and gas tables**, with computer equations. Orlando, Florida, Academic Press, 1984. xiv, 185p. graphs, tables. $29.50. ISBN: 0123740800.

Tables cover saturation and superheat properties of steam and properties of air and 12 other gases. Relevant equations are given, which were used in microcomputer programs published by the authors. Appendices contain tabulated conversion factors and list of references. SI Units used. *Class No:* 621.1(083)

[4228]

KEENAN, J.H., *and others*. **Steam tables:** thermodynamic properties of water, including vapor, liquid and solid phases. 2nd ed. New York, Wiley - Interscience, 1978. xxiii, 156p. diagrs., charts, tables. $20.95. ISBN: 0471042102.

Previous ed. 1969.

The Keenan and Keyes Tables were first published in 1936. The present tables appeared in 1969 and extended their range to 1300 deg. C and 100 MPa in pressure, with independent correlation of all new data. This 2nd ed. now provides full conformity with SI units. Values for specific volume, internal energy, enthalpy and entropy are tabulated for pressure and temperature parameters. Mollier and temperature-entropy charts are included. *Introduction to the steam tables* is repeated in French, German, Italian, Japanese, Russian and Spanish. *Class No:* 621.1(083)

[4229]

SCHMIDT, E. **Properties of water and steam, in SI units.** [Thermodynamische Eigenschaften von Wasser und Wasserdampt: 0 - 800 deg. C, 0 - 1,000 bar.] 2nd rev. and updated printing. New York, Berlin, etc., Springer-Verlag, 1979. 190p. tables. $40.20. ISBN: 0387096019.

Previously published 1969.

Parallel texts in English and German. Main tables (on equilibrium properties of water and steam), based on 1967 IFC Formulation for Industrial Use, are repeated, and there are revised tables for transport properties - dynamic viscosity, thermal conductivity, Prandtl number and surface tension. New Skeleton Tables and relevant equations are provided and there is a bibliography of 265 items.
Class No: 621.1(083)

[4230]

—POTTER, J.H. Steam charts. New York, American Society of Mechanical Engineers, 1976. xiv, 128p. $25. (*ASME SI-10*.)

'Thermodynamic properties of steam, h-v, in graphical form for the superheated, vapor and liquid conditions in both SI (Metric) and US customary units' (*Sub-title*). Enthalpy - volume charts are provided first in SI, then in US Customary Units. *Class No:* 621.1(083)

Histories

[4231]

BRIGGS, A. **The Power of steam:** an illustrated history of the world's steam age. London, Joseph, 1982. 208p. illus. (some col.). £10.50. ISBN: 0718120760.

A non-technical account of the uses of steam power from the earliest days to the present time when nostalgia has nurtured a strong revival of interest, manifesting itself in a steam preservation movement. All applications are described and illustrated (more than 200 photographs and drawings). A list of places (mostly in the UK) where steam engines may be seen is included.

'An illuminating and infuriating book ... It's a coffee-table book with references - although in most instances the illustrations add to, rather than detract from the text' (*New Scientist*, v.93, 11 Mar. 1982, p. 664). *Class No:* 621.1(091)

[4232]

HILLS, R.L. **Power from steam: a history of the stationary steam engine.** Cambridge, Univ. Press, 1989. xv,338p. illus., diagrs., tables. £45. ISBN: 0521343569.

Traces 'the technical development of the steam engine as applied in industry and centred on the cotton textile industry in the Lancashire region' (*Preface*). 15 chapters: 1. The noblest machine ... 10. The internal operation of the machine ... 15 The most economical mode of power. Extensive chapter notes and bibliography, p.292-326. Detailed, analytical index, p.327-38. A scholarly treatment.
Class No: 621.1(091)

Electrical Engineering

Abbreviations & Symbols

[4233]

BRITISH STANDARDS INSTITUTION. **Guide to graphical symbols for electrical equipment.** London, BSI, 1981. 240p. £166. (*BS 6217:1981(1989)*.)

Replaces BS 3939, which has been withdrawn.

Establishes uniform graphical symbols, including form, meaning and application. Covers symbols placed on equipment to provide instructions in use and handling. *Class No:* 621.3(003)

[4234]

Index of acronyms and abbreviations in electrical and electronic engineering. Weinheim, etc., VCH, 1989. [vii],538p. £75. ISBN: 0895738120.

About 45,000 entries. More comprehensive than Keller (*qv*), but little to choose between them. *Class No:* 621.3(003)

[4235]

INSTITUTE OF ELECTRICAL AND ELECTRONICS ENGINEERS. **Electrical and electronics graphic symbols and reference designations.** 2nd ed. New York, IEEE, 1987. v.p. diagrs. ISBN: 0471634565.

Includes all IEEE and ANSI standards. Covers logic functions, parts and equipment, diagrams and electrical wiring. *Class No:* 621.3(003)

[4236]

INTERNATIONAL ELECTROTECHNICAL COMMISSION. **Letter symbols, including conventions and signs for electrical technology:** a handbook for everyday use. Geneva, I.E.C., 1983. vi, 114p. illus. S Fr.45. ISBN: 2287300053.

'This handbook contains ... the principles governing conventions for electric and magnetic circuits ... and the standardization of letter symbols, together with a list of letter symbols in general use ... The terms used are those of the latest edition of the IEV (International Electrotechnical Vocabulary) ...' (*Introduction*). Letter symbols and graphic symbols for quantities are linked to SI units. All text and entries in English and French. Index in each language.
Class No: 621.3(003)

[4237]

WENNRICH, P. **International dictionary of abbreviations and acronyms of electronics, electrical engineering, computer technology, and information processing.** München, Saur, 1992. 2v. (502; 458p.). ISBN: 3598109776.

Over 90,000 abbreviations, most of English-language derivation.
Class No: 621.3(003)

Databases

[4238]

INSPEC. Stevenage, Herts., Institution of Electrical Engineers, 1969-. Updated weekly.

INSPEC database provides online access to *Physics abstracts, Electrical and electronic abstracts, Computer and control abstracts* and *Information technology*. Over 6,000,000 records. D.T. Hawkins notes both bibliographic (INSPEC, PHYS, SPIN, Atomicindex and Nuclear science) and numeric (Superindex, PHYSCOMP, OECD Nuclear Energy Agency database, and GAPHYOR) databases covering physics (*Database*, v.8(1), February 1985, p.15-16, with a comparison table and references, p.17-18). Available online via DataStar, DIALOG, EINS, FIZ-TECHNIK, OCLC, Ovid, Orbit, STIC and STN International and on CD-ROM. *Class No:* 621.3(003.4)

[4239]

Merlin-Tech. Grenoble, Merlin-Gerin Documentation.

Covers 1973 to date. A bibliographic database providing references, with abstracts, to world literature on electrical engineering, electronics and telecommunications in periodical articles and books. File size: 33,000 citations. Updated monthly, *c*.2,500 additions pa. Host: ESA-IRS. In French. *Class No:* 621.3(003.4)

[4240]

ZDE (Zentralstelle Dokumentation Elektrotechnik). Frankfurt-am-Main, FDR, FIZ Technik.

Covers 1968 to date. A bibliographic data base, providing references, with abstracts, to world literature of electrical engineering, electronics, communications, computers and control engineering, and including semiconductor physics, plasma physics, superconductivity and other aspects of electronic and magnetic materials. File size: 1,300,000 citations. Updated monthly. 60,000 additions pa. Available via FIZ Technik. In English and German. *Class No:* 621.3(003.4)

Bibliographies

[4241]

ARDIS, S.B. A Guide to the literature of electrical and electronics engineering. Poland, J.M., *ed.* Littleton, Colorado, Libraries Unlimited Inc., 1987. xx, 190p. £29.95. (*Reference sources in science and technology series.*) ISBN: 0872874745.

The first English-language, wide-ranging and substantial guide to the field since Burkett and Plumb's *How to find out in electrical engineering* (1967), and therefore very welcome. Its subject range extends to communications and computing engineering and includes microwaves, radar, materials science and satellite technology. Excluded are robotics, electrical wiring and construction and applications of electronic devices in music, biomedicine and avionics. Coverage is restricted to English-language reference material published post-1978. Arrangement is by type of material (bibliographies, abstracts, data bases, patents, standards, etc.). 8 parts, 25 chapters, with annotated entries for almost 700 publications and information sources.

British users will note omission, over-brief treatments, mis-spelling of some British sources of information, and will be disadvantaged by the American publisher and price data given, but will still find this a valuable guide overall, especially its strong coverage of the many handbooks in this subject area. *Class No: 621.3(01)*

[4242]

BRITISH LIBRARY. Science Reference Library. Useful books of reference for designers (1926-1983) held by the Science Reference Library. Part.2: Electrical and electronic engineering. Palyza, M.M., *sel.* London, the Library, 1984. i, 71p. £5. ISBN: 0712307133.

A bibliography of almost 500 works arranged under *c.*200 headings by the Library's unique classification system. There is a Contents list to indicate the 12 broad groupings and an index of subjects which leads easily to specific groups of relevant publications (despite many surprising omissions, *e.g.* no entries for microelectronics or microprocessors). Strong on circuits and electronic data sources. Clearly set out in reproduced typescript, the entries include an occasional annotation - more would greatly enhance the value of this compilation. *Class No: 621.3(01)*

[4243]

Index to IEEE publications. New York, IEEE Press, 1951-. Annual.

Lists all articles in the Institute's journals, transactions and magazines; published papers presented at IEEE-sponsored conferences; summaries of standards, books, conference records, special issues, etc. *Class No: 621.3(01)*

Encyclopaedias

[4244]

Wiley encyclopedia of electrical and electronics engineering. Webster, J.G., *ed.* Chichester, Wiley, 1999. 22v. (*c.*19,000p.). illus., diagrs., graphs, tables. £4925. ISBN: 0471139467.

About 1,300 reviewed articles, A-Z. Covers a very wide range of topics including aerospace and electronic systems, automatic control, communications, consumer electronics, energy conversion, engineering management, industry applications, knowledge and data engineering, lightwave technology, multimedia, packaging and manufacturing technology, photonics technology, power delivery and systems, reliability, solid state circuits, VLSI systems, etc. Articles have bibliographies and cross references. Detailed, analytical index. Annual supplements are planned and a World Wide Web version will be available shortly after publication. *Class No: 621.3(031)*

Handbooks & Manuals

[4245]

CHANG, S.S.L., *ed.* **Fundamentals handbook of electrical and computer engineering.** New York, Wiley, 1982-3. 3v. diagrs., graphs, charts, circuits, tables. £50. ISBN: 0471862150, v.1; 0471862134, v.2; 0471862142, v.3.

1. *Circuits, fields and electronics.* xi, 707p.
2. *Communication, control, devices, and systems.* xi, 737p.
3. *Computer hardware, software, and applications.* xi, 507p.

Aims to provide details of current research and development across a wide range of topics. Claims that the set will enable non-specialists to enter and carry out design work in an unfamiliar research area seem exaggerated. The work is strong, however, on basic principles and theory in all the subjects it treats. Chapter references, bibliographies and glossaries are provided. (Citations later than 1979 are hard to find). Review in *IEEE Spectrum* complains that 'treatment of subjects is often too brief - and sometimes erroneous or out-of-date' (v.20, August 1983, p.14). *Class No: 621.3(035)*

[4246]

The Electrical engineering handbook. Dorf, R.C., *ed.* 2nd ed., published in cooperation with IEEE Press. Boca Raton, Fl., CRC Press, 1998. 2660p. illus., diagrs. graphs, tables. $115.. ISBN: 0780334671.

First published 1993.

'A ready reference for the practicing engineer' (*Preface*). About 250 contributors. 12 sections: 1. Circuits - 2. Signal processing - 3. Electronics 4. Electromagnetics - 5. Electrical effects and devices - 6. Energy - 7. Communications - 8. Digital devices - 9. Computer engineering - 10. Systems - 11. Biomedical - 12. Mathematics, symbols, and physical constants. 5 indexes: author; key tables; key figures; key equations; subject. Also available on CD-ROM ($129. ISBN: 08493975002). *Class No: 621.3(035)*

[4247]

Electrical engineer's reference book. Jones, G.R., *and others, eds.* 15th ed. Oxford, Butterworth-Heinemann, 1993. v.p. illus., diagrs., graphs, tables. £100. ISBN: 0750612029.

First published 1945; 14th ed. 1985.

83 contributors. 53 chapters, closely subdivided, in 6 sections: General principles - Materials - Power generation - Transmission and distribution - Power systems - Electricity utilization. Detailed subject index. A new ed. of a major work; Professor Say, who had been an original editor, died shortly before this one was completed. New or extensively updated topics include digital and programmable electronic systems, reliability analysis, EMC, optical fibres and aeronautic transportation. *Class No: 621.3(035)*

Dictionaries

Polyglot

[4248]

COMMISSION ÉLECTROTECHNIQUE INTERNATIONALE. Electricity, electronics and telecommunications multilingual dictionary. 2nd ed. Amsterdam, Elsevier, 1992. 5v. ISBN: 0444895116.

Previous ed. 1983 as *IEC multilingual dictionary of electricity.*

V.1/2 contain entries and definitions in English with translations in French, Russian, German, Spanish, Italian, Dutch, Polish, Swedish. Yellow pages in each volume indicate topics covered. V.3: German, Dutch and Swedish indexes. V.4: Spanish and Italian indexes. V.5: Russian and Polish indexes. This 2nd ed. is based on about 70 International Electrotechnical Vocabulary chapters and includes 18,000 terms and symbols.

'This Dictionary is not intended to replace the IEV [*International electrotechnical vocabulary,* (*qv*)] in which terms remain classified by specialized fields, but supplements it by giving in alphabetical order all the terms arranged under key words ...' (*Foreword*). *Class No: 621.3(038)=00*

[4249]

INTERNATIONAL ELECTROTECHNICAL COMMISSION. International electrotechnical vocabulary. 3rd ed. Geneva, the Commission, 1973-. In progress.

First published 1938. Previous ed. 1954-70.

A standard multilingual (8 or 9 languages) dictionary previously issued in 22 subject parts (*e.g.* Machines and transformers; Electric traction; Lighting), with terms arranged in classified lists and including definitions in English, supplemented by indexes in all languages. *Class No: 621.3(038)=00*

[4250]

ISHIBASHI, S. Dictionary of electronics and electrical engineering: English - Japanese - German - Russian. 3rd ed. New York, Plenum, 1987. v.p. £143.40. ISBN: 0306427494.

First published 1964.

About 42,000 entry words in English, with translations and indexes in the other languages. Includes abbreviations and units common in the four languages. *Class No: 621.3(038)=00*

[4251]

LUGINSKY, Y.N., *and others.* **Dictionary of electrical engineering:** English-German-French-Dutch-Russian. Deventer, Netherlands, Kluwer; Moscow, Russky Yazyk Publishers, 1985. 480p. £58.75. ISBN: 9020119109.

About 8,000 terms, uniquely identified by initial letter and index number, are given in English, with equivalents in other four languages (with genders and - where necessary - plurals). Indexes in other four languages enable translations between any combinations of languages. Emphasis is on basic electrical engineering subjects: circuit theory; measurements; power generation, transmission and distribution; electric machines, etc. *Class No: 621.3(038)=00*

English

[4252]
Electrical engineering dictionary: CRC netBase 1999. Laplante, P., *ed*. Boca Raton, Fl., CRC Press, 1998. 1 CD-ROM. $129. ISBN: 0849397650.

About 8,000 terms with 120 tables and figures and about 6,500 hypertext links. Areas covered include applied electrical engineering, microwaves, control and power engineering, digital systems and device electronics. *Class No:* 621.3(038)=20

[4253]
INSTITUTE OF ELECTRICAL AND ELECTRONICS ENGINEERS. The New IEEE standard dictionary of electrical and electronic terms: [including abstracts of all current standards]. Kurpis, G.P. *and* Booth, C.J., *eds*. 6th ed. New York, IEEE, 1997. 1300p. illus. $95. *(IEEE Std 100-1996.)* ISBN: 1559378336.

First published 1972; 5th ed. 1993

Definitions of over 30,000 technical terms, many with explanatory notes. Includes list of acronyms and abbreviations. All definitions are derived from IEEE or other standards (about 450 sources) and are thus authoritative. Abstracts and sources. Highly recommended. An enhanced version with about 33,000 terms is available on CD-ROM. *Class No:* 621.3(038)=20

[4254]
JACKSON, K.G. *and* **FEINBERG, R. Dictionary of electrical engineering.** 2nd ed. London, Butterworths, 1981. [8], 350p. illus. £15. *(Butterworths technical dictionaries.)* ISBN: 0408004509.

First published 1965, with reprints.

Upwards of 3,000 terms 'in general use among engineers' *(Preface)*, including electronics terms where applications are relevant in electrical engineering areas. 2nd ed. contains 200 new entries and substantial revision of many others. Appendices include SI units, decimal prefixes and common abbreviations. Many clear line drawings. *Class No:* 621.3(038)=20

German

[4255]
BUDIG, P.K., *ed*. **Wörterbuch elektrotechnik und electronik.** [Routledge German dictionary of electrical engineering and electronics.] London, Routledge, 1997-98. 2v. (1600p.). £65 each. ISBN: 0415171318.

V.1: *German-English* (5th ed.).
V.2: *English-German* (6th ed.).

Each volume contains around 67,000 terms from all fields of electrical engineering, electronics, telecommunications, with special attention to modern developments in, for example, lasers, superconductivity, microelectronics, opto-electronics, computing. Layman's terms and those formed by hyphenation are, for the most part, excluded. Also available on CD-ROM. *Class No:* 621.3(038)=30

[4256]
—**HABERLE, G.D.** *and* **HARBERLE, H.D.** Kurzlexikon der Elektrotechnik: elektrotechnische Begriffe und Ihre Erklärung. Frankfurt-a-m, Frankfurter Fachverlag, 1979. 104p. DM15. ISBN: 3872340549.

1,300 entries, including cross-references (few) and abbreviations, briefly defined for a wide range of topics within electrical engineering and electronics, concentrating thereby on more frequently encountered terms. In German. *Class No:* 621.3(038)=30

[4257]
Dictionary of power engineering: German/English with definitions and English index. Amsterdam, Elsevier, 1993. 320p. £114. ISBN: 0444899847.

4,102 numbered entries, German/English. Produced by Bharat Heavy Electricals Ltd, Hyderatad, India. *Class No:* 621.3(038)=30

[4258]
Fachwörterbuch industrielle elektrotechnik, energie- und automatisierungs-technik. [Dictionary of electrical engineering, power engineering and automation.] Bezner, H., *ed*. 4th ed. Munich, Publicis MCD, 1998. 2v. [viii], 607p.; [x], 532p. £45 each. ISBN: 3895780774.

Previously published as *Dictionary of power engineering and automation;* 3rd ed. 1993.

V.1: *Deutsch/Englisch*.
V.2: *English/German*.

V.1 includes about 67,000 entries, V.2, 54,000; 2,500 are new to each volume. Emphasis is on German abbreviations and standards. Also available on CD-ROM (£95; ISBN: 3895780839).

'... a thoroughly scholarly work and well worth the effort to master its intricacies' *(Physical science, measurement and instrumentation, management and education, reviews (IEEE Proceedings A),* v.134(4), April 1987, p.342, on the 2nd ed.). *Class No:* 621.3(038)=30

[4259]
SCHWENKHAGEN, H.F. *and* **MEINHOLD, H. Wörterbuch elektrotechnik und elektronik:** Deutsch-Englisch/Englisch-Deutsch. [Dictionary of electrical and electronic engineering, German-English, English-German.] 5th ed. Düsseldorf, Cornelson Girardet, 1989. 868p. £93.50. ISBN: 3464494004.

First published 1959 as *Fachwörterbuch Elektrotechnik*, by H.F. Schwenkhagen.

About 40,000 entries in each half. Entry terms clearly set out in bold face with equivalents in roman. Noun/adjectival compounds and phrases *(e.g. to put a transmitter on the air)* indicated below entry word *(put)*. Covers electrical, electronic and control engineering with terminology of related fields. Context of many terms is indicated by UDC numbers. Genders and verb functions not given. A welcome new edition of a standard work. *Class No:* 621.3(038)=30

[4260]
WENNRICH, P. Encyclopedic dictionary of electronics, electrical engineering and information processing: English-German, German-English. [Enzyklopädisches Wörterbuch der elektrotechnik, elektronik und informations verarbeitung.] Munich, K.G. Saur, 1990-95. 8v. £110 each. ISBN: 3598106815, (V.1); 3598106807, (8 volume set).

V.1: A-C (English-German). xv,431p.

8v. (English-German, v.1-4; German-English, v.5-8). 200,000 English entries; 600,000 German equivalents. Includes alternative uses, further explanations and differentiates American and British English. A definitive work. *Class No:* 621.3(038)=30

[4261]
—**WENNRICH, P.** Encyclopedic dictionary of electronics, electrical engineering and information processing. Munich, K.G. Saur, 1990. 2v., each with 400p. £65. each. ISBN: 3595108807, set.

V.1: Englisch-Deutsch.
V.2: Deutsch-Englisch.

A shortened version of his 8v. set. 100 specialised categories are applied. Entries (c.50,000 per volume) mostly consist of headwords and equivalents. *Class No:* 621.38(038)=30

French

[4262]
PIRAUX, H. Dictionnaire français-anglais des termes relatifs à l'électronique, l'électrotechnique, l'informatique et aux applications connexes. New ed., rev. and corrected by J. Milsant. Paris, Eyrolles, 1981. 208p.

Over 10,000 terms with c.20,000 equivalent English terms, covering electrical engineering, electronics, telecommunications and related subjects in physics. A companion vol. to the author's *Dictionnaire anglais-français relatifs à l'électronique, et électrotechnique* (13th ed. 1980).

Noted: 10th ed. 1984 of the French-English dictionary and 16th ed. 1989 of the English-French dictionary. *Class No:* 621.3(038)=40

Spanish

[4263]
IBEAS, F.F. Diccionario technologico inglés-español de electricdad, electronica, telecomunicacion y materias afines con la fisica, la optica y la quimica. Madrid, Alhambra, 1974. xi, 441p. diagrs., graphs, tables. E950. ISBN: 8420504920.

Spanish equivalents for about 38,000 terms and abbreviations in electricity, electronics and telecommunictions, supported by several thousand terms from physics, chemistry, optics and nuclear energy. Separate section for about 1,700 English abbreviations and initialisms. 36 tables of units, conversions and miscellaneous data. 2,000 illus. *Class No:* 621.3(038)=60

[4264]
KAPLAN, S.M. Electrical and computer engineering dictionary: English - Spanish, Spanish - English. [Diccionario de ingenieria eléctrica y de computadoras: Inglés - Español, Español - Inglés.] New York, Wiley, 1996. viii, 792p. £45. ISBN: 0471010375.

About 50,000 entry terms in each half, with equivalents (usually one word or phrase) in the other language. *Class No:* 621.3(038)=60

Russian

[4265]
MACURA, P. Russian-English dictionary of electrotechnology and allied sciences. With supplement. Malabar, Florida, Krieger, 1986. x, 707p. + 234p. (Supplement). ISBN: 0898748692.

First published 1971.

This reprint, with supplementary material, contains about 60,000 entries, ranging beyond its title scope into related fields, *e.g.* computing, physics, acoustics, control, astronomy. It also includes many non-technical words and proper nouns and names. Grammatical forms and noun genders are given. The bound-in Supplement adds a further 10,000 entries to photoset typescript. *Class No:* 621.3(038)=82

Chinese

[4266]

English-Chinese glossary of electronic and electrical engineering. New York, French and European, 1980. 636p. $29.95. ISBN: 068697364x.

Few English-Chinese dictionaries are currently available. This example is reputed to be 'especially strong in electrical and power teminology' (Ardis, S.B. *Guide to the literature of electrical and electronic engineering.* 1987). *Class No:* 621.3(038)=951

Glossaries

[4267]

BRITISH STANDARDS INSTITUTION. Glossary of electrotechnical, power, telecommunication, electronics, lighting and colour terms. London, BSI, 1971-97. 5 parts. (*BS 4727: 1971-97.*)

Supersedes BS 204, BS 205, BS 233 and BS 1611. Pt. 1: *Terms common to power, telecommunications and electronics.* Groups 01-13. 1971-1992. Pt. 2: *Terms particular to power engineering.* Groups 01-19. 1971-1997. Pt. 3: *Terms particular to telecommunications and electronics,* Groups 01-17. 1971-1995. Pt. 5: *Terms particular to electromedical equipment,* Group 01. 1985.

'Titles to any further groups will be added in due course' (*Guide to the glossary,* p.4). *Class No:* 621.3(038.1)

Reviews & Abstracts

[4268]

Current papers in electrical and electronics engineering. London, Institution of Electrical Engineers. 1964-. no. 1-. Monthly. £295. ISSN: 00113778.

Originally as *Current papers for the professional electrical and electronics engineer,* then as *Current papers in electrotechnology.* Present title 1969-. An INSPEC alerting service produced jointly by the IEE and the Institute of Electrical and Electronics Engineers Inc., in association with the Institution of Electronic and Radio Engineers.

About 75,000 items pa. giving bibliographical citations only, covering everything published in *Electrical and electronics abstracts* (*qv*), arranged by the same classification, and including periodical articles, reports, books, theses and conference papers. No indexes. Nowadays published virtually simultaneously with the abstracts journal and therefore loses its 'current awareness' value.

Class No: 621.3(048)

[4269]

Electrical and electronics abstracts. Science abstracts. Section B. London, INSPEC/Institution of Electrical Engineers, in association with the Institute of Electrical and Electronics Engineers, Inc., New York, 1898-. v.1-. Monthly. £1910. ISSN: 00368105.

Currently more than 105,000 abstracts pa. and still growing! Classifed into 8 major categories (*e.g.* 1000: Circuit theory and circuits - 2000: Components, electronic devices and materials; ... 8000: Power systems and applications), subdivided (*e.g.* 1200: Electronic circuits; 1270: Filters; 1270F: Digital filters). Each issue has 6 indexes (subjects, authors, bibliographies, books, conferences, corporate authors). Half-yearly indexes, plus cumulative 4-5 year indexes. The major abstacting service in its field. Available on-line as part of the INSPEC data base. Also INSPEC magnetic tapes are available twice monthly. CD-ROM. *Class No:* 621.3(048)

[4270]

Key abstracts. Hitchin, Herts., INSPEC/Institution of Electrical Engineers, 1975-. 22 pts. Monthly. £135, per part; £2235 all sections.

Advanced materials. Preparation, structure, properties, testing.

Antennas and propagation. Includes radiowave propagation, radar, radio navigation.

Artificial intelligence. Includes expert systems and knowledge engineering.

Business automation.

Computer communications and storage. Multiprocessor systems, discs, interfaces, networks.

Computing in electronics and power. Computer applications in electronics, communications, etc.

Electronic circuits. Power electronics, amplifiers, pulse circuits, filters, etc.

Electronic instrumentation. Includes measurement systems, transducers, display devices.

Factory automation.

High-temperature superconductors.

Human-computer interaction.

Machine vision.

Measurements in physics In mechanics, heat, optics, fluid dynamics, radiation.

Microelectronics and printed circuits.

Microwave technology.

Neural networks.

Optoelectronics. Fibre optics, lasers, holography, etc.

Power systems and applications. Networks, apparatus, electric machines, industrial applications.

Robotics and control. Includes applications in industry, production,

....(contd.)

transport.

Semiconductor devices Includes integrated circuits.

Software engineering Includes programming languages, operating systems, data base management.

Telecommunications. Includes information theory, switching, optical communications.

Selections from the INSPEC data base of about 250 key papers which deliberately restrict the subject coverage to match more aptly the interests of researchers and practical engineers. Originally in 8 parts, extended to 11 and now expanded to 22. The parts are groupd into 5 subject areas: computing and control; communications and optics; automation and control; electronics and power; materials and measurement. A current awareness service. *Class No:* 621.3(048)

[4271]

PASCAL folio. F21: Électrotechnique. Paris, Centre National de la Recherche Scientifique, 1985-. 10 pa. F570.

First published (1940-) as *Bulletin signalétique. 4. Physique. II. Électricité.*

As *Bulletin signalétique,* Part 140, (1961-84) contained about 5,500 entries, many with informative or indicative abstracts, systematically arranged in 11 main groups, with sections and sub-sections for each, *e.g.* Matériaux - 09. Electrotechnique - 10. Électroénergetique - 11. Applications ... Items drawn from 13,000 journals, conference papers, reports and theses. Subject and author indexes per issue and annually. Available on paper or in microform. Also available on-line as part of PASCAL file, through ESA-IRS or Questel. *Class No:* 621.3(048)

[4272]

Referativnyĭ zhurnal. 21. Elektrotekhnika. Moscow VINITI, 1982-. Monthly. R.206.

Formerly *Referativnyĭ zhurnal Elektrotekhnika i elektroenergetika* (1980-81). Originally *Referativnyĭ zhurnal Elektrotekhnika i energetika* (1961-1979).

Since the hiving off in 1982 of the *Energetika* (power) portion, now contains about 27,000 indicative and informative signed abstracts pa. with UDC numbers, some illustrations and graphs. 11 sections: General problems - Electrotechnical materials, capacitors, wires and cables - Electrical machines and transformers - Electrical switchgear - Power conversion techniques - Electrical drives and industrial automation - Electrotechnology - Electrical equipment in transport - Electrification and automation in agriculture - Domestic electrification - Lighting and infra-red techniques. Annual author and subject indexes. *Class No:* 621.3(048)

Periodicals

[4273]

List of journals and other serial sources, INSPEC. London, INSPEC/ Institution of Electrical Engineers, 1983-. Annual. ISSN: 02647508.

Continues *List of journals* (*INSPEC*).

Lists about 4,000 titles of serial publications (including monograph series, annual reviews, report series) which are currently scanned for the INSPEC data base. Additionally, publications, which have ceased or which are no longer scanned and cross references (for changed titles) are included. Bibliographical details for each include ISSN, CODEN and British Library Document Supply Centre shelfmark. There are indexes of abbreviated titles, CODENs, ISSNs, and journals abstracted completely, plus an arrangement of titles under country of publication. *Class No:* 621.3(051)

Yearbooks & Directories

[4274]

Electrical and electronics trades directory: 1998. 116th ed. Stevenage, Herts., Peregrinus, 1997. Annual. *c.*650p. ISBN: 0863413196.

First published 1883.

Lists *c.*4,000 organizations. Covers manufacturers, suppliers, servicing companies, representatives, wholesale distributors, and associations and institutions. A classified list of products and materials comprises half the content. Indexes of products and materials. Also available on CD-ROM. Emphasis is British. *Class No:* 621.3(058)

Tables & Data Books

[4275]

CROFT, T. *and* **SUMMERS, W.I.,** *eds.* **American electricians' handbook.** 13th ed. New York, etc., McGraw-Hill, 1996. v.p. illus., diagrs., tables. $79.95. ISBN: 0070139369.

First published 1913. Previous ed. 1992.

Long-established compendium. Conforms to the 1996 ed. of the National Electrical Code. Aims to give complete guidance on selection, installation, maintenance and operation of all types of electrical equipment and wiring. Extensively revised to incorporate developments in energy saving, new conductor and cable types, surge protection devices, etc. Numerous tables. There are over 1,500 illus.,

.... (contd.)

clear and apposite. A standard reference for electricians; referred to as 'The Electrician's Bible'. 'Highly recommended' (*American reference book annual*, 1998, p.650). *Class No:* 621.3(083)

[4276]

Electrical engineering handbook. Berlin, Siemens / London, Heyden, 1976. Reprinted 1981. xii, 750p. diagrs., graphs, tables. £28.35. ISBN: 0855012315.

English translation of *Handbuch der Elektrotechnik*, first published 1969.

63 contributors. 16 chapters. 4 main parts: 1. Electrical engineering fundamentals - 2. Electrical power engineering - 3. Power engineering applications - 4. Control engineering and automation. An abundance of data and factual information. 361 tables.

1982 ed. published by Wiley Heyden (ISBN: 0471260207). *Class No:* 621.3(083)

[4277]

FINK, D.G. *and* **BEATY, H.W.,** *eds*. **Standard handbook for electrical engineers.** 13th ed. New York, etc., McGraw-Hill, 1993. v.p. illus., diagrs., graphs, circuits, tables. ISBN: 0070209847.

First published 1907; 12th ed., 1987.

A companion to Christiansen's *Electronic engineers' handbook*. 105 contributors. 28 sections. Scope: generation, transmission, distribution, control, conservation and application of electrical power, with relevant supporting material. Major sections: 2. Electric and magnetic circuits - 3. Measurements and instruments - 4. Properties of materials - 5. Generation ... 10. Power system components ... 14. Transmission systems ... 18. Power distribution ... 20. Motors and drives ... 22. Electronics - 23. Power quality. Considerable revision and much new material. Complete chapter on standards, with full list of US standards in alphabetical subject order. Almost all sections have reference lists and bibliographies, but relatively few are recent; most of the pre-World War II citations have been removed! The contents of each section are better displayed but identification of topics by paragraph number makes location more difficult. Worse: the index practice is inconsistent in referring - conventionally - to pages. *Class No:* 621.3(083)

[4278]

Newnes electrical pocket book. Reeves, E.A., *ed*. 22nd ed. Oxford, Butterworth-Heinemann, 1995. 544p. illus., diagrs. £14.99. ISBN: 075062566x.

First published 1937.

Contains chapters of theoretical background, followed by practical applications in: generators; transformers and tap changers; switchgear; fuses and protection relays; wires and cables; motors and drives; power electronics; batteries and fuel cells; electroheat; power systems; batteries and fuel cells; and electroheat. Adequate index; numerous line drawings and half-tones. *Class No:* 621.3(083)

Standards

[4279]

INTERNATIONAL ELECTROTECHNICAL COMMISSION. Catalogue of publications, complete to 1st January 1996: world standards for electrical and electronic engineering. Geneva, IEC, 1960-. Annual.

Lists all IEC standards valid as of 1st January 1996, in order by standard number, giving title, date, pagination and edition, and identifying the Technical Committee responsible, with annotation varying from a few words to a detailed summary. A page subject index aids consultation.

A bi-monthly *IEC Bulletin* includes lists of newly issued standards in its regular contents. *Class No:* 621.3(083.74)

[4280]

—**BRITISH STANDARDS INSTITUTION.** Electrical engineering: power, electronics, telecommunications, acoustics, illuminations, domestic appliances. Milton Keynes, BSI, 1985. 45p. £2. (*SL 26*.)

Gives the number, title and price group of about 1,300 BSI publications - standards, codes of practice, published documents (PD) and drafts for developments (DD) - covering the whole field of electrical and electronic engineering, arranged alphabetically under 50 subject headings. Full details and summaries are to be found in the annual *Catalogue* (*qv*). No index. *Class No:* 621.3(083.74)

[4281]

—**INTERNATIONAL ELECTROTECHNICAL COMMISSION.** Yearbook. [International Electrotechnical Commission]. Geneva, etc., IEC, Annual. *c*.600p.

Describes work and progress of all Technical Committees, supplemented by complete list of all final drafts of standards about to be published and those recently published. *Class No:* 621.3(083.74)

[4282]

—Quick reference to IEEE standards. New York, IEEE, 1980. [vi], 568p.

A complete index of all terms in IEEE standards and ANSI standards published by IEEE. The index section (p.418) lists the terms which appear in the detailed Document Contents section and identifies the standard numbers containing the selected term. The full tables of contents are given for all standards in the second section. Computer-generated, the index throws up many terms which are unlikely to be sought (*e.g.* Even, Event, Evidence, Example).

Also noted: a series of 8 IEEE catalogues known by their colours and covering different areas of interest, *e.g. IEEE Brown book: Recommended practice for power system analysis*. 1980. *Class No:* 621.3(083.74)

[4283]

WILLIAMS, D., *ed*. **Electrical standards in world trade.** Morden, Surrey, IPC Middle East Publishing Co. / IEC, 1982. 109p. illus., diagrs. Sw.Frs.70. ISBN: 0946325006.

Details of main standards and approval marks of 43 member countries of the IEC, with reviews of the standards scene in the countries and regions of the world which constitute the major markets for electrical and electronic equipment. Based on a series of articles published in *Middle East electricity*. Chapters 2-6 provide valuable succinct explanations of the various international standards bodies and their activities, including CMEA (the Council for Mutual Economic Assistance) covering the Eastern Bloc countries, the EEC and PASC (the Pacific Area Standards Congress). 9 chapters give details for the main exporting countries. *Class No:* 621.3(083.74)

Patents

[4284]

Electrical patents index: (EPI). London, Derwent Publications, 1980-. Weekly.

One of the 4 major services of the Derwent patents organization. Based on two weekly bulletins which each contain *c*.4,300 abstracts spread over 6 sections of the Derwent classification (S. Measuring; Testing - T. Computing and control - U. Semi-conductors and electronic circuitry - V. Electronic components - W. Communications - X. Electric power engineering). *EPI Bulletin (Country order)* groups the entries under country, arranged by patent number, with abstracts and diagrams. *EPI Bulletin (Classified)* contains essentially the same information, but arranged by EPI class within the 6 sections. Cumulative indexes are also available (on microfiche). *Monthly Profile booklets* cover 50 separate subject classes, enabling scanning of narrower areas (*e.g.* U13. Integrated circuits). The whole system is available online as an integral part of the *World Patents Index* database. *Class No:* 621.3(088.8)

Chronologies

[4285]

DAVIS, H.B.O. Electrical and electronic technologies: a chronology of events and inventors, to 1900. Metuchen, N.J., Scarecrow Press, 1981. viii, 213p. £17.50. ISBN: 0810814641.

Potted history from *c*.640 BC to 1900 AD in six chapters. Chapters 1 and 2 cover the centuries before 1500 and the remaining centuries to 1900 have one chapter each. Arrangement in each is strictly by date and each entry is devoted to a particular activity, discovery, publication or event in the life of individual scientists; thus each can receive several entries. Biographical material is given at the birth-year entry for many of them. Bibliography of sources: pp 176-81. Index of persons, subjects and places (31p). *Class No:* 621.3(090)

[4286]

—**DAVIS, H.B.O.** Electrical and electronic technologies: a chronology of events and inventors from 1900 to 1940. Metuchen, N.J., Scarecrow Press, 1983. xi, 208p. £17.50. ISBN: 0810815907.

Continues the 1981 work. It covers the first four decades of the 20th century in 4 chapters, with longer introductions and many entries under subjects (*e.g.* TV standards) and devices (*e.g.* Radio range beacons). Two appendices index vacuum tubes and radio stations. 32p. index of persons, subjects, organizations. Similar format to the 1981 vol., but biographical entries are omitted. *Class No:* 621.3(090)

[4287]

—**DAVIS, H.B.O.** Electrical and electronic technologies: a chronology of events and inventors, 1940-1980. Metuchen, N.J., Scarecrow Press, 1985. 313p. £25. ISBN: 0810817268.

Continues the foregoing, bringing the story up to the previous decade. *Class No:* 621.3(090)

Histories

[4288]

ATHERTON, W.A. From compass to computer: a history of electrical and electronics engineering. London, Macmillan; San Franciso, San Francisco Press, 1983. xiv, 337p. illus., diagrs., graphs, tables. £26; £11.95. ISBN: 0333352661, Macmillan Hardback; 0333352688, Paperback.

The development of electrical engineering and the other technologies it has spawned, from the early investigations of electricity and magnetism to microelectronics and computers. Describes the work of the pioneers - workers and companies - in chapters covering discrete topics, *e.g.* electric lighting, telecommunications, radio. Chapter references. Name and subject indexes. *Class No:* 621.3(091)

[4289]

History of technology. Hollister-Short, G. *and* James, F., *eds*. London, Mansel, 1976-. illus., diagrs. ISSN: 03075451.

V. 17 (1996. xi, 235p.) has 9 papers including 'Archimedes the engineer' (185 references) and 'Space, time and innovation characteristics: the contribution of diffusion process theory to the history of technology' (66 references). 'Contents of former volumes', p.229-35. *Class No:* 621.3(091)

[4290]

RYDER, J.D. *and* FINK, D.G. Engineers and electrons: a century of electrical progress. New York, IEEE Press, 1984. xix, 251p. illus., diagrs. $29.95. ISBN: 087942172x.

A popularized history of the developments in electrical engineering over two centuries culminating in microelectronics and computing, with emphasis on American contributions and the role of the Institute of Electrical and Electronics Engineers and its predecessors. Chapter bibliographies.

'Delightful reading and sometimes thought-provoking ... Highly recommended'. (*IEEE Proceedings,* v.73, Jan. 1985, p. 169).
Class No: 621.3(091)

Bibliographies

[4291]

FINN, B. The History of electrical technology: an annotated bibliography. New York, Garland, 1991. 342p. $48. (*Garland reference library of science and technology, 18.*) ISBN: 0824091205.

About 1500 entries to secondary sources, largely in English, published through 1986. 4 main sections: 1. Historical works - 2. Communications - 3. Power - 4. Miscellaneous (*e.g.* computers, lasers, music). Author and subject indexes. Author is curator of the Electricity and Modern Physics Division, National Museum of American History. *Class No:* 621.3(091)(01)

Biographies

[4292]

IEEE membership directory. New York, Institute of Electrical and Electronics Engineers, 1998. Annual. 2v.

In addition to standard information, gives short biographies of IEEE Fellows. *Class No:* 621.3(092)

[4293]

INSTITUTION OF ELECTRICAL ENGINEERS. Yearbook and list of members: 1998. London, IEE. Annual. *c.*800p. ISBN: 0852963556.

Provides standard biographical information about members. *Class No:* 621.3(092)

Thesauri

[4294]

Thesaurus 1999. London, Institution of Electrical Engineers, 1999. 752, 95p. ISBN: 085296966x.

Formerly published as INSPEC Thesuarus; 1st ed. 1973.

The thesaurus remains the subject key to the INSPEC database. Contains about 16,000 terms, of which 8,300 are preferred and 7,700 lead-ins. In two sections: alphabetical display; hierarchical display. *Class No:* 621.3:025.43

Classification Systems

[4295]

Classification 1995: a classification scheme for the INSPEC database. London, Institution of Electrical Engineers, 1995. ix, 136p. + index, 36p. ISBN: 0852969651.

A new version of the scheme designed for use with the INSPEC 2 version of the database. Includes classification codes (in order, A ... to D ...) and textual headings. Invaluable for a careful, structured search of the database or the printed indexes. *Class No:* 621.3:025.44

Institutions & Associations

[4296]

READER, W.J. A History of the Institution of Electrical Engineers, 1871-1971. London, Peregrinus, for Institution of Electrical Engineers 1987. x, 327p, illus., (1 col), tables, map. £15. ISBN: 0863411037.

Extends R. Appleyard's *History of the Institution of Electrical Engineers* (1939), which covered the period 1871-1931, to a centenary history, which also contains a chapter giving a brief glance at events since 1971. 17 chapters grouped into 3 parts illustrate the 3 phases of development: telegraph engineers; power engineers; electronics engineers. Appendices contain valuable reference material: Brief chronology; text of Royal Charter and Bylaws; complete list of Presidents and Secretaries to 1986, with portraits and biographical notes for 1939-1986; membership and financial statistics; list of sources. Index of names and subjects. *Class No:* 621.3:061:061.2

Circuits

Encyclopaedias

[4297]

GIBILISCO, S. International encyclopedia of integrated circuits. 2nd ed. Blue Ridge Summit, Pa., TAB, 1992. 1086p. illus., diagrs., graphs, tables. $84.95. ISBN: 0830630260.

First published 1989.

Lists over 800 ICs from 10 manufacturers in the US and Canada, arranged by application and manufacturer. Data include electrical and thermal ratings, static and dynamic characteristics, electrical characteristics, applications, recommended operating conditions. Cross-references. Detailed, analytical index. *Class No:* 621.3.04(031)

Handbooks & Manuals

[4298]

BUCHSBAUM, W.H. Encyclopedia of integrated circuits: a practical handbook of essential reference data. Englewood Cliffs, N.J., Prentice-Hall, 1981. xxii, 420p. diagrs. $24.95. ISBN: 013275875x.

Covers over 200 IC'S four categories: Analog, Consumer, Interface, Digital, giving for each a brief description, functional block or logic diagram, key parameters and applications. Six appendices contain dimensional outlines, brief list of US manufacturers, operating and circuit characteristics of selected IC's and a brief glossary. Index. *Class No:* 621.3.04(035)

[4299]

SEIDMAN, A.H., *ed*. Integrated circuits applications handbook. New York, etc., Wiley 1983. xxv, 673p. illus., diagrs., graphs, circuits, tables. (*Wiley electrical and elctronics technology handbook series.*) ISBN: 0471077658.

Comprehensive coverage of all aspects and applications of IC's, arranged in 3 parts, 20 chapters, each contributed by an expert. Part 1 (chapters 1-8) covers digital IC's (TTL, MOS and CMOS logic, semiconductor memories, microprocessors and microcomputers, etc); Part 2 (chapters 9-17) deals with linear IC's (*e.g.* operational amplifiers, active filters, data conversion, IC's in communications, etc); Part 3 (chapters 18-20), is concerned with fabrication (thick and thin film technologies, etc). 200 examples, numerous tables, circuits and flowcharts make this a practice-oriented handbook, well supported by chapter references and index. *Class No:* 621.3.04(035)

[4300]

—**PARR, E.A. Logic designer's handbook.** London, Granada, 1984. xvi, 456p. illus., diagrs. £18. ISBN: 0246118881.

14 chapters of theoretical and practical information for designers of digital circuits. Coverage: theory, logic families and application circuits (*e.g.* timers, counters, shift registers). Emphasis is on TTL and CMOS. While the book has been praised as a practical, up-to-date and highly readable survey of current logic engineering, the review in *IEE Proceedings* (v.132(3), May 1985, p.185) points to lack of references, occasionally misleading simplicity and inaccuracies. *Class No:* 621.3.04(035)

[4301]

WILLIAMS, A.B., *ed*. Designer's handbook of integrated circuits. New York, etc., McGraw-Hill, 1984. xxvi, 805p. diagrs., graphs, charts, tables. £75. ISBN: 007070435x.

22 contributors provide a large collection of popular and frequently used IC's. Aim is to assist selection of devices and circuits, by providing comparison charts, discussions and design examples. Each chapter concentrates on a family of IC's, *e.g,* operational amplifiers, active filters, telecommunications, timing circuits, analogue (digital and digital/analogue) conversion, logic circuits, microprocessors, optoelectronics. Chapter references and glossaries provide valuable support.

'A very useful compendium of electronic techniques and circuits' (*Electronics & Power,* v.31, Jan. 1985, p.85).
Class No: 621.3.04(035)

Tables & Data Books

[4302]

IC Master, 1987. New York, Hearst Business Communications, 1987. 2v. [vp]. £85.

Directory and source of data and application notes for integrated circuits, microcomputer boards, microprocessors, linear and memory devices and interfaces available from US manufacturers. Various indexes permit different approaches and facilitate product selection - companies; functions; part numbers. There are also sections covering different product categories - military parts; digital devices; microprocessors; microcomputer boards - an equivalents index and a directory of manufacturers and distributors. *Class No:* 621.3.04(083)

Power Supply

Databases

[4303]

EDF-DOC Clamart, France, Electricité de France, 1972-.

Citations, with abstracts to the technical, economic, commercial and social aspects of electric power generation, transportation and sale. Includes journal literature, reports and internal papers. International coverage. About 436,000 records, updated monthly. Available online via ESA-IRS and Questel SA. *Class No:* 621.311(003.4)

[4304]

Electric power database. Palo Alto, Ca., Electric Power Research Institute.

Corresponds to the print work *Digest of research in the electric utility industry.* Covers US and Canadian research in hydroelectric power, fossil fuels, nuclear power, transmission, economics, advanced power systems and environmental assessment. Over 36,000 records; updated monthly. Available on DIALOG, file 241.
Class No: 621.311(003.4)

Bibliographies

[4305]

METZ, K.S. Information sources in power engineering: a guide to energy science and technology. Westport, Conn., Greenwood Press, 1975. xiii, 114p. £8.50. ISBN: 0837185386.

Annotated entries in 9 sections: Journals, newsletters, translations - Conferences and published proceedings - Abstracting and indexing services - Organizations - US government organizations - Information centers, services and libraries - Textbooks - Bibliographies - Reference sources (*e.g.* handbooks; directories; thesauri and dictionaries) - Keeping informed (journals). Annotated bibliography, p. 107-9.
Class No: 621.311(01)

[4306]

—BARBOUR, M., *comp.* Uninterruptible power supplies: a select bibliography. London, Institution of Electrical Engineers, 1986. 77p. ISBN: 0852963343.

193 English-language items from the INSPEC database, 1979-1985, with indicative and informative abstracts, grouped under 9 headings (*e.g,* Systems - Rectifiers - Switches - Batteries). Author and subject indexes. *Class No:* 621.311(01)

[4307]

PARKER, A.M. 'Electrical power systems and machines'. *Information sources in engineering.* K.W. Mildren and P.J. Hicks, eds. (3rd ed., 1996), p.425-39. 3rd ed. London, Bowker Saur, 1996. £80. ISBN: 1857390571.

Covers electrical power engineering, power systems, generation, transmission and distribution, system analysis, machine drives, electric motors and power electronics for drives. *Class No:* 621.311(01)

Handbooks & Manuals

[4308]

HICKS, T.G. Power generation: calculations reference guide. New York, McGraw-Hill, 1987. 366p. illus. $36.50. ISBN: 0070288003.

Calculations for power generation compiled from *Standard book of engineering calculations. Class No:* 621.311(035)

[4309]

Modern power station practice. British Electricity International, London. 3rd ed., incorporating *Modern power system practice.* Oxford, etc., Pergamon Press, 1991. 12v. illus., diagrs. £80 each. ISBN: 0080164366.

First published 1963-64. 5v. 2nd ed. 1971. 8v.
A. *Station planning and design.*
B. *Boilers and ancillary plant.*
C. *Turbines, generators and associated plant.*
D. *Electrical systems and equipment.*
E. *Chemistry and metallurgy.*
F. *Control and instrumentation.*
G. *Station operation and maintenace.*
H. *Station commissioning.*
J. *Nuclear power generation.*

....(contd.)
K. *EHV transmission.*
L. *System operation.*
M. *Index.*

A revised and expanded series of textbooks (in the broadest sense of the word) with exercises, covering all aspects of power station practice. The impact of privatisation appears as a running theme. Volume indexes, as well as a consolidated index (V.M.) enhance the value of this authoritative work. *Class No:* 621.311(035)

Histories

[4310]

BOWERS, B. A History of electric light and power. London, Peregrinus, 1982. vii, 278p., illus., diagrs. (*IEE history of technology series, v. 3.*) ISBN: 0906048710.

The first section deals with early developments in the understanding and use of electricity. The remaining three quarters considers applications, with emphasis on lighting, describing the methods of generation and creating illumination. There are chapters on public supply and power stations; legislation; local vs. national supply (all with particular reference to Britain). Modern developments and practices in lighting, electric heating and traction conclude the history. Generous use of photographs and quotations from contemporary catalogues and reports. *Class No:* 621.311(091)

Great Britain

[4311]

ELECTRICITY COUNCIL. Electricity supply in Great Briatin: a chronology - from the beginnings of the industry to 31 December 1976. 2nd ed. London, Electricity Council, 1977. [iii], 99p. ISBN: 0851880533.

First published 1973.

Covers 1831-1976. Includes brief descriptions of Acts, Bills, White Papers. Overseas developments are indicated by asterisk. References, p.84-85. Detailed analytical index. *Class No:* 621.311(410)

[4312]

ELECTRICITY COUNCIL. Handbook of electricity supply statistics. London, Electricity Council. Annual. tables, graphs. ISSN: 04401905.

The statistics are predominantly for England and Wales, with separate sections for Scotland and Northern Ireland, for the UK as a whole and for member countries of the EU. Tables cover generation, transmission, sales, consumption, finance, prices and tariffs.
Class No: 621.311(410)

[4313]

Electricity supply handbook, 1999. 52nd ed. Sutton, Surrey, Reed Business Publishing, 1998. Annual. 298p. illus. £98. ISBN: 0617012660.

First published 1948.

Sections: ESI structure and information - Generation - Transmission - Distribution and supply - Government and regulation organizations - Research, trade and professional bodies - Engineering consultants - Gazetteer. No index, so difficult to use. *Class No:* 621.311(410)

[4314]

HANNAH, L. Engineers, managers and politicians: the first fifteen years of nationalized electricity supply in Britain. London, Macmillan, 1982. xiii, 336p. diagrs., tables. £33. ISBN: 0333220870.

Covers the period 1947-62. Commissioned by the Electricity Council but independent in views expressed. Based on free access to documents and interviews with politicians, civil servants and staff within the industry at all levels. Document citations, liberal notes and references, statistical appendices and a good index help to make this a valuable source. *Class No:* 621.311(410)

[4315]

—HANNAH, L. Electricity before nationalization: a study of the development of the electricity supply industry in Britain to 1948. London, Macmillan, 1979. xiii, 467p. £33. ISBN: 0333220862.

The same author was originally commissioned to write an authoritative history of the industry to cover the period from 1880. Benefitting from access to official documents, he emphasizes the period from 1918 and concentrates on national rather than local developments. Full notes and references. *Class No:* 621.311(410)

Hydroelectric Power

[4316]

BROWN, J.G., ed. Hydro-electric engineering practices. 2nd ed. London, Blackie, 1958-70. 3v. illus., diagrs., tables.

1. *Civil engineering.* 2nd ed. 1964. xxviii, 1233p. £11.50.
2. *Mechanical and electrical engineering.* 2nd ed. 1970. xxvi, 861p. £20.
3. *Economics, operation and maintenance.* 1958. xxv, 473p. £19.95.

....(contd.)
25 specialist contributors. Chapter bibliographies. Volume indexes. Still the only encyclopaedic coverage of its subject. *Class No:* 621.311.21

[4317]

GULLIVER, J.S. *and* ARNDT, R.E.A., *eds.* **Hydropower engineering handbook.** New York, McGraw-Hill, 1991. illus., diagrs., graphs, tables. v.p. $85. ISBN: 0070251932.
Emphasises design aspects and cost estimates, with some attention to the environmental effects of hydropower plant. Case studies and examples feature. Chapters carry references. Index. *Class No:* 621.311.21

Wind Power

[4318]

GIPE, P. **Wind energy comes of age.** New York, Wiley, 1995. 536p. ilus., diagrs., tables. $64.95. ISBN: 047110924x.
A comprehensive review of wind energy, with particular emphasis on the solution of technical problems which have plagued development. Extensive bibliographies. 'Recommended' (*Choice*, October 1995, p.324). *Class No:* 621.311.24

[4319]

GOLDING, E.W. **The Generation of electricity by wind power:** with an additional chapter by R.I. Harris. London, Spon; New York, Halstead Press (Wiley), 1955; reprinted 1976. xviii, 332p. illus., diagrs., graphs, tables. £6.
Widely regarded as a classic text in its field, this work was reprinted in the wake of the 'energy crisis' of the mid-1970s, with an Appendix to update the account of research and technical developments. 19 chapters cover 3 broad areas: wind behaviour and its determination; wind-driven machines; economic use of wind power under different conditions. The first section, especially chapters 3-10, contains a large amount of data, presented in tabulated and graphical form. In addition to chapter bibliographies, there is a selected bibliography of surface wind data, classified geographically, and a short French-English-German glossary. The Subject index relates to the main text and not to the content of the updating Appendix. 'Includes work done on wind surveying in the 1950's ... still thought to be the definitive statement on wind characteristics in the UK' (*Engineer*, v. 243, Sept. 30 1976, p. 243). *Class No:* 621.311.24

[4320]

HUNT, V.D. **Windpower:** a handbook on wind energy conversion systems. New York, Van Nostrand Reinhold, 1981. xvii, 610p. illus., diagrs., graphs, tables. $39.50. ISBN: 0442273894.
14 chapters (1. Introduction - 2. Historical development - 3. Wind characteristics and their impact ... 6. Towers and systems installation ... 8. Wind energy conversion systems - 9. Applications ... 11. Commercialization (small-scale and large-scale conversion systems) - 12. Environmental, institutional and legal barriers ... 14. The future of wind power). Chapter references. Bibliography (p. 513-20). Glossary (p. 521-7). Points of contact (people and organizations). Reference information (*i.e.,* 50 pages of tabulated information and useful data, *e.g.* units, symbols, conversion factors, average windpower data for North American locations). Index. *Class No:* 621.311.24

[4321]

—ELDRIDGE, F.R. Wind machines. 2nd ed. New York, Van Nostrand Reinhold, 1980. xiii, 214p. illus., diagrs., graphs, tables, maps. (*MITRE energy resources and environment series.*) ISBN: 0442261349.
First published 1975 and then sponsored by the US National Science Foundation.
This rev. ed. gives great emphasis on small and wind machines, although large-scale systems remain dominant. 9 chapters: 1. Viability ... 3. Taxonomy ... 5. Applications - 6. Siting - 7. Performance - 8. System design - 9. Future utilization. Appendix contains short glossary; list of US suppliers; references and selected, classified bibliography (p. 199-209). Liberally illustrated and attractively produced. 'An excellent source for the professional engineer' (Park, J. *The wind power book* (1980), p.237). *Class No:* 621.311.24

[4322]

—PARK, J. The Wind power book. Palo Alto, Calif., Cheshire Books, 1981. 240p. illus., diagrs., graphs, tables, maps. $21.95; $14.95. ISBN: 091735203x.
An expanded, rewritten version of Park's *Simplified wind power systems for experimenters* (2nd ed. Sylmar, Calif., Helion, Inc., 1975). This book remains an essentially practical manual for non-professional designers and users of wind machines. 7 chapters: 1. Introduction - 2. Wind power systems - 3. Wind energy resources - 4. Wind machine fundamentals - 5. Wind power design - 6. Building a wind power system ... Appendix (p. 156-236) of numerical, climatic and design data (including wind-power tables and maps, and degree-day tables, - all for the North American continent - water consumption and electrical load tables, for domestic requirements, etc). Bibliography, p. 237-40. *Class No:* 621.311.24

[4323]

WALKER, J.F. *and* JENKINS, N. **Wind energy technology.** Chichester, Wiley, 1997. 178p. illus., diagrs. £24.95. ISBN: 0471960446.
Provides information on theory and practical applications. 2 sections: Basic principles and their influence on the design of modern turbines - Project development and engineering. *Class No:* 621.311.24

[4324]

Wind energy and the environment. Swift-Hook, D.T., *ed.* London, Peregrinus, 1989. xiii,170p. diagrs., graphs, tables. $68. ISBN: 0863411762.
Covers environmental and legal aspects of wind-generated energy from a European point-of-view. 31 contributors. 17 chapters, subdivided, most with references. Index, p.168-70. 'A valuable resource for public officials and environmental groups' (*Choice,* February 1990, p.969). *Class No:* 621.311.24

[4325]

Wind engineering abstracts. Brentwood, Multi-Science Publishing Co., 1982-, v.1-. Quarterly. £107. ISSN: 02630915.
Upwards of 250 informative abstracts pa. for relevant articles in the major journals in physics, engineering, the environment, energy and architecture, with coverage also of conference proceedings, reports, occasional books and patents. 9 sections: Meteorology, geography, topography - Aerodynamics, rotors, and blades ... Installations and applications ... Power generation and transmission; Energy conversion and storage ... Economic, environmental and legal aspects - Reviews and miscellaneous. Annual author and subject indexes. *Class No:* 621.311.24

Machines

[4326]

BEZNER, H. **Electrical machines dictionary.** [Elektromaschinen Wörterbuch: German-English, English-German.] Wiesbaden, Brandstetter, 1978. [x], 275, 257p. £43.80. ISBN: 3870970871.
About 18,000 entries covering all kinds, parts, construction, operation and testing of electrical machines. Standard and most-frequently used equivalents are given first. Clear layout. Grammatical forms and genders indicated. *Class No:* 621.313

[4327]

Electrical motor handbook. Chalmers, B.J., *ed.* London, Butterworths, 1988. [x],546p. illus., diagrs., graphs, tables. £65. ISBN: 0408007079.
Covers rotating machines above 10kw output. 15 contributors. 11 chapters, closely subdivided, with references: 1. Characteristics - 2. Environment - 3. Selection - 4. Variable-speed drives and motor control - 5. Materials and motor components - 6. Insulation - 7. Ancillary equipment - 8. Works and acceptance testing - 9. Installation, site testing and commissioning - 10. Maintenance and failures - 11. Units, dimensions and conversion factors. Detailed, analytical index, p.529-46. Intended 'to stand alongside the *J & P Transformer book* and the *J & P Switchgear book.*' (*Preface*). *Class No:* 621.313

[4328]

LAITHWAITE, E.R. **A History of linear electric motors.** Basingstoke, Hants., Macmillan, 1987. ix, 389p. illus., diagrs., tables. £33. ISBN: 0333399285.
A highly personalized account of the development of linear induction motors and their applications by an engineer whose work over many years will ensure that his name remains associated with them. Chapters 1-3 deal largely with the 19th century. The remainder of the book is concerned with electromagnetic levitation and applications in high-speed transport systems. Chapter 10 gives a potted history of the decade after 1975. A bibliography of 1,000 items (p. 234-84), classified in 5 groups and arranged chronologically in each, covers 1902-75.
'A conducted tour of the author's personal memory bank, plus some very interesting historical material ... It is all very untidy, but much more interesting than it would have been had the editor tried to order the contents' (*New scientist*, no. 1554, 2 April 1987, p. 53). *Class No:* 621.313

[4329]

LITMAN, T. **Efficient electric motor systems handbook.** Lilburn, Ga., Fairmont Press; London, Prentice-Hall, 1995. xi, 320p. illus., diagrs., tables. $72. ISBN: 0133781348.
13 chapters covering motor system characteristics, energy efficiency, motor controls, maintenance and repair, cost analysis, safety, etc. 9 appendices including resources (publications, software packages), regulations and standards, trade associations, professional societies, etc. 'A useful book' (*Choice*, January 1996, p.822). *Class No:* 621.313

[4330]
SMEATON, R.W., *ed*. **Motor application and maintenance handbook**. 2nd ed. New York, etc., McGraw-Hill, 1986. xi [676]p. illus., diagrs., graphs, tables. £59.95. ISBN: 0070584486.

First published 1969.

33 contributors, 20 sections. Sections 1-3 cover basic information - load requirements, power supply, motor types - to aid selection for particular applications. Types of motor are dealt with in considerable detail in Sections 4-10, treating motors for special applications in Sections 9 and 10. Sections 11-20 cover components, installation, maintenance, repair and specific problems - *e.g*, insulation, bearings, lubrication, noise. Liberal illustration, graphical and tabulated presentation of data relating to design, characteristics, performance, supplemented by extensive reference to American standards make this a very useful reference work. Supported by chapter references and an effective index. Units for dimensions and ratings are 'US Customary', *i.e., not* metric. *Class No:* 621.313

Transformers

[4331]
FRANKLIN, A.C. *and* FRANKLIN, D.P. **J & P transformer book**. 11th ed. Oxford, Butterworth-Heinemann, 1983. 815p. illus., diagrs. £110. ISBN: 0750617918.

First published 1925, by Johnson & Phillips, Ltd. Previous ed. 1973.

Oustanding reference book for design, installation and maintenance of power transformers. Aimed at users, suppliers, students, rather than at specialists, and presents infomation clearly. Takes account of changes in design, materials and standards.

'This 11th ed. lives up to its high reputation ... while the book contains much that is useful it is sometimes scattered over a number of chapters. Some sections are rather wordy and these two factors make searching for details a longer operation than it would have been if a more thorough revision had been undertaken' (*Electronics and power*, v.30, August 1984, p. 641). *Class No:* 621.314

[4332]
SCOLES, G.J. **Handbook of rectifier circuits**. Chichester, E. Horwood, 1980. 238p. diagrs., circuits. £22. (*Ellis Horwood series in electrical and electronic engineering*.) ISBN: 0853121265.

Presents about 230 circuits with diagrams and brief descriptions, indicating combinations for special applications. 'It should be emphasized ... that the very comprehensive listing of such a huge variety of circuits has necessitated a rather superficial treatment of any one particular type ... A stimulating source of ideas for anyone who is responsible for the design of DC power supplies' (*Electronic circuits and systems (IEE Proceedings G)*, v.129(1), February 1982, p.28). Index. *Class No:* 621.314

Transmission

Cables

[4333]
Electric cables handbook. Bungay, E.W.G. *and* McAllister, D., *eds*. 2nd ed. Oxford, BSP Professional Books, 1990. xiv, 977p. illus., diagrs., graphs, tables. ISBN: 063202299x.

First published 1982.

28 contributors, almost all from BICC. 5 parts: 1. Theory, materials, design - 2. Wiring cables - 3. Supply distribution cables - 4. Transmission cables - 5. Submarine cables. Appendices (p. 707-941) contain tables of data on all commonly used cable types. Classified bibliography (25p.), index and chapter references.

'... gives a comprehensive and authoritative account of the state of the art ... [and] ... has the merit of presenting much good explanatory material rather than merely giving factual information...' (*Electrical review* of the first ed.). *Class No:* 621.315.2

[4334]
KURTZ, E.B. *and* SHOEMAKER, T.M. **Lineman's and cableman's handbook**. 9th ed. New York etc., McGraw-Hill, 1997. xi, v.p. illus., diagrs., circuits, tables. $89.95. ISBN: 0070360111.

First published 1928; previous ed. 1992.

A complete, self-contained guide to theory and practice, intended for home study but usable 'on the job' as a reference source. Covers electricity and its applications, construction and maintenance of overhead and underground distribution and transmission lines, and specific safety issues. Self-test questions; index relates to American practice, National Electrical Code and standards. Illus, on almost every page.

'The definitive work on the elements of an electrical transmission system' (*Public Works*, v. 113, April 1982, p.20, on the 6th ed.). *Class No:* 621.315.2

[4335]
RICHLING, C. *and* DREWITZ, I. **Wörterbuch der kabeltechnik**, Deutsch-Englisch-Französisch. Wiesbaden, Brandstetter, 1976. 616p. DM60. ISBN: 3870970723.

About 5,500 main entries, with equivalents. Three sequences: German-English-French; English-German-French; French-German-English. Parts of speech are stated. *Class No:* 621.315.2

Wires

[4336]
BLACK, R.M. **The History of electric wires and cables**. London, P. Peregrinus, 1983. [xiii], 290p. illus. £24. (*IEE history of technology series, v. 4*.) ISBN: 0863410014.

Outlines the development of the principal types of electric wires and cables from the 18th century to the present day use of optical fibre telecommunication links. Electric lighting, submarine telephone and power cables and the specialized needs of collieries, ships and aircraft are covered in separate chapters, and recent advances are dealt with in a final chapter. Chapter references and bibliographies.

'The serious historian will find it less than totally satisfactory because it does not go sufficiently deeply into many details and often does not suggest a line of research to fill the gaps ... If one asks whether this book adds to knowledge, whether it makes available previously inaccessible information, then it clearly succeeds'. (*Physical science, measurement and instrumentation, management and education, and Reviews (IEE Proceedings A)*, v. 132, no. 1, Jan 1985, p. 75).

'Well illustrated, and the contents are well set out to facilitate locating any particular aspect ...' (*Electronics and power*, v. 30, Feb. 1984, p. 158). *Class No:* 621.315.3

[4337]
RICHTER, H.P. *and* SCHWAN, W.C. **Practical electrical wiring:** residential, farm and industrial. 15th ed. New York, McGraw-Hill, 1990. 645p. illus., diagrs. $33. ISBN: 0070523032.

Updated to meet requirements of the 1990 National Electrical Code (NEC). Explores new topics, *e.g.* fluorescent lamps, incendiary circuits for hazardous locations. Less technical and detailed than *American electricians' handbook* (McGraw-Hill, 1987). A substantial index; short bibliography; glossary. For novices and professionals; a handy DIY home reference. *Class No:* 621.315.3

Insulation

[4338]
CONFERENCE ON ELECTRICAL INSULATION AND DIELECTRIC PHENOMENA. Committee on Digest of Literature, and National Research Council. Committee on Dielectrics. **Digest of literature on dielectrics**. Washington, National Academy of Sciences. 1937-79, v.1-42. tables. ISBN: 0309029341.

A valuable review series with extensive surveys in the different areas of its subject field, covering the publications of the previous calendar year. Occasionally (as in v. 42, 1979) reproduced tables of data reported in the literature covered. V. 42, 1979, contains 14 reviews (1. Tables of permittivity, dipole moment, and dielectric relaxation time ... 3. Dielectric breakdown of solids ... 5. Electrical breakdown in gases ... 10. Piezoelectricity .... 13. Cryogenics - 14. Applications). The bibliographies for these reviews list an astonishing 3,687 references.

Continued in *IEE Transactions on electric insulations*. 1984-. *Class No:* 621.315.6

[4339]
SHUGG, W.T. **Handbook of electrical and electronic insulating materials**. New York, Van Nostrand Reinhold, 1986. xv, 598p. diagrs., tables. £53. ISBN: 0442281226.

A tightly organized reference work which groups dielectric materials into product groups (*e.g.*Thermoplastic moulding compounds; thermosetting moulding compounds; magnetic wire enamels; dielectric films; tapes and coated fabrics; mica products; ceramic and glass insulations) and for each insulating material sets out the chemistry, grades, processing methods, properties and end uses. Properties and ranking data are clearly tabulated. Detailed references to American (notably ASTM and Military) standards. Excellent index structured to lead directly to all infomation about each material. *Class No:* 621.315.6

Distribution & Control

[4340]
INSTITUTE OF ELECTRICAL AND ELECTRONICS ENGINEERS. **National electrical safety code handbook**. 4th ed. New York, IEEE Press, 1998. 504p. diagrs., tables. $89. (*American National Standards*.) ISBN: 1559377240.

'Basic provisions for safeguarding of persons from hazards arising from the installation, operation, or maintenance of conductors ... equipment in electric-supply stations and ... electric-supply and communication lines ... [and] ... work rules for ... construction, maintenance and operation ...' An authorized American National

....(contd.)
Standard, containing definitions and grounding rules. Covers supply stations, overhead lines, underground lines and work rules. Index. *Class No:* 621.316

[4341]

—McGraw-Hill National Electrical Code handbook. McPartland, J.F. *and* McPartland, B., *eds*. 23rd ed. New York, etc., McGraw-Hill, 1998. v.p. illus., diagrs. $65. ISBN: 0070472343.
First published 1932.
Follows the order of articles in the *Code*, but does not include the text or any tabulated data. Claims 'greater analysis and interpretation' (*Preface*) than other handbooks. Extensively illustrated. Also available on CD-ROM. *Class No:* 621.316

[4342]

INSTITUTION OF ELECTRICAL ENGINEERS. Requirements for electrical installations BS 7671: 1992. 16th ed. Hitchin, Herts., IEE, 1981. viii, 266p., diagrs., graphs, tables. ISBN: 0852965109.
First published 1882. 15th ed. 1991.
Arrangement accords with IEC Publication 364 '*Electrical installations of buildings*'. 24 chapters in 7 parts: 1. Scope, object and fundamental requirements for safety - 2. Definitions - 3. Assessment of general characteristics - 4. Protection for safety - 5. Selection and erection of equipment - 6. Special installations or locations - 7. Inspection and testing. Invaluable.
Republished with the first (1994) and second (1997) amendments (1997; £55; ISBN: 085296 9287). Also available on CD-ROM. *Class No:* 621.316

[4343]

—COOK, P. Commentary on BS 7671: 1992 requirements for electrical installations. Stevenage, Herts., IEE, 1998. 409p. diagrs., graphs, tables. £35. ISBN: 0863413188.
A comprehensive guide to the IEE Wiring Regulations (including amendment 2). Provides design guidance including data and worked examples. *Class No:* 621.316

[4344]

—WHITFIELD, J.F. The Electrician's guide to the 16th edition of the IEE wiring regulations, BS7671. Wendens Ambo, Essex, EPA Press, 1997. *c*.200p. diagrs., graphs, tables. ISBN: 0951736264.
Guide and explanation of most of the wiring regulations aimed to help electricians and technicians understand and apply them in practical situations. Clear text and numerous simple diagrams assist. *Class No:* 621.316

[4345]

LAWRENCE, S. The 'Which?' book of wiring and lighting. Rev. ed. London, Which Ltd., 1997. 159p. col. illus., diagrs., tables. ISBN: 0852026749.
First published 1993.
Sections: Problem checklist - Wiring basics - Wiring techniques - Wiring jobs - Rewiring a house. Glossary; useful addresses; index. Clearly presented material. *Class No:* 621.316

[4346]

SEIP, G.G., *ed*. Electrical installations handbook; translated by K.G. King. 2nd rev. and enl. ed. Berlin, etc., Siemens AG, Chichester, Wiley, 1987. 3v. (1522p). illus., diagrs., graphs, tables. £100. ISBN: 047191343x, Wiley; 3800914670, Siemens.
First German ed. 1971.
59 contributors. 6 major sections, 29 sub-sections, with many more subdivisions: 1. Electrical installation engineering for power supply and distribution 2. Electrical installations engineering for space heating, air conditioning and ventilation - 3. Lift installations - 4. Electrical installations engineering in large buildings and outdoors - 5. Electrical installations engineering for special installations and systems - 6. Installation specifications and safety measures. Section 1. Electrical installation ... for power supply and distribution (p.17-569). Subdivisions: 1-1. Definition of terms (p. 17-101); ... 1-4. System protection - 1.4.5. Protective devices for high-voltage systems - 1.4.5.5. Protection of ring feeders ... 1-12 Earthing systems. Clearly displayed text, illus. and tables, with helpful use of colour and marginal bold face subheadings. Subsection 28 contains references to VDE standards and relationship to CENELEC. *Class No:* 621.316

Switchgear

[4347]

SMEATON, R.W. *and* UBERT, W.H., *eds*. Switchgear and control handbook. 3rd ed. New York, etc., McGraw-Hill, 1998. v.p. illus., diagrs., graphs, tables. ISBN: 0070584516.
First published 1976; 2nd ed. 1987.
Over 50 contributors; 30 new to this ed. 32 chapters in 4 parts: 1. Electrical systems - 2. Switchgear and distribution equipment and accessories - 3. Motor and industrial systems - 4. Solid state electronic, programmable, and microprocessor-based controls, controllers and logic systems. Part 4 is new to this ed. Glossary of electrical and electronic terms, 12p. *Class No:* 621.316.3

Measurement

[4348]

Concise encyclopedia of measurement and instrumentation. Finkelstein, L. *and* Grattan, K.T.V., *eds*. Oxford, Pergamon Press, 1994. xvii, 434p. diagrs., graphs, tables. £135. (*Advances in systems control and information engineering*.) ISBN: 0080362125.
65 contributors; 86 articles, A-Z. Detailed, analytical index, p.409-34. Intended 'as a complementary companion' to *Systems and control encyclopedia* (*qv*) (*Introduction*), but 'comprising almost entirely new material specially commissioned' (*Preface*). 'As excellent and thorough a resource as can be found on the subject' (*Choice*, September 1994, p.66). *Class No:* 621.317

[4349]

JUNGE, H.D. Wörterbuch messtechnik und einheiten: Deutsch/ Englisch. [Dictionary of measurement engineering and units: English/ German.] Weinheim, VCH, 1991. 593p. £62. (*Parat.*) ISBN: 3527264221.
About 10,000 entries in each part of the dictionary. Tinted pages list all essential old and new English and German units, together with their conversion factors. *Class No:* 621.317

[4350]

NOLTINGK, B.E., *and others*. Instrumentation reference book. 2nd ed. Oxford, Butterworth-Heinemann, 1995. v.p. illus., diagrs., graphs, tables. £105. ISBN: 0750620560.
First published 1988.
39 chapters in 5 parts: 1. Mechanical measurement - 2. Measurement of temperature and chemical composition - 3. Electrical and radiation measurement - 4. Instrumentation systems - 5. Further scientific and technical information. 4 appendices (*e.g.* B. 'Professional societies and associations'). Index. About 35 main contributors with chapters by various hands. Well produced. *Class No:* 621.317

[4351]

O'DELL, T.H. Circuits for electronic instrumentation. Cambridge Univ. Press, 1991. 218p. illus., diagrs. $69.50; £35. ISBN: 0521404282.
Covers a wide range of circuits (*e.g.* comparators, wideband direct couple feedback amplifiers, phased locked loops, voltage controlled oscillators, etc.) at an advanced level. Extensive chapter bibliographies. *Class No:* 621.317

Magnetic Materials

[4352]

EVETTA, J.E. Concise encyclopedia of magnetic and superconducting materials. Oxford, Pergamon Press, 1992. xviii,703p. illus., diagrs. £140. (*Advances in materials science and engineering, 7.*) ISBN: 0080347223.
Incorporates relevant material from the *Encyclopedia of materials science and engineering* (1986) and newly commissioned articles. *Class No:* 621.318

[4353]

WOHLFARTH, E.P., *ed*. Ferromagnetic materials: a handbook on the properties of magnetically ordered substances. Amsterdam, etc., North-Holland, 1980-. V.1- illus., diagrs., graphs, tables. $382. ISBN: 0444853138, set.
A 5v. set intended to replace the monumental *Ferromagnetism* by R.M. Bozorth (Princeton, Van Nostrand, 1951). V.1 contains 7 and v.2 contains 8 lengthy reviews on different materials.
With v.6 (1991) the title continued and changed to *Handbook of magnetic materials*. V.9 (1995) has 5 lengthy reviews, each well-documented (*e.g.* 'Magnetic materials studies by muon spin rotation spectroscopy ' has 37 cols. of references). *Class No:* 621.318

[4354]

—DEMAW, M.F. Ferromagnetic-core design and application handbook. Englewood Cliffs, N.J., Prentice-Hall, 1981. x, 256p., illus., diagrs., graphs, tables. £16.45. ISBN: 0133140881.
Applications chapters cover : rods, bars and slugs; toroids; beads, sleeves and pot cores. Separate chapter on permanent magnets. Practical circuit examples for narrow-band and broadband transformers and inductors; ferrite loop antennas, RF chokes, etc. Appendices of design data. Glossaries, Bibliography. Index. *Class No:* 621.318

Batteries

[4355]

APPLEBY, A.J. *and* FOULKES, F.R. Fuel cell handbook. New York, Van Nostrand Reinhold, 1989. xxvi,762p. illus., diagrs., graphs, tables. £67.50. ISBN: 0442319266.
Covers both technology and economics. 5 parts; 19 chapters, closely sub-divided: 1. General aspects of fuel cells - 2. Fuel cell programs, concepts, and areas of application - 3. Design considerations for practical fuel cell systems - 4. State of the art - 5. References (2802 items). Detailed, analytical index, p.749-62. A specialised treatment for the expert; well-produced. *Class No:* 621.355

[4356]
CROMPTON, T.R. **Battery reference book.** 2nd ed. Oxford, Butterworth-Heinemann, 1995. 592p. illus., diagrs., graphs, tables. £55. ISBN: 0750625678.
First published 1990.
Contents: Introduction - Battery characteristics - Theory and design - Performance evaluation - Applications - Charging - Suppliers - Glossary - Standards - Journals, trade organizations and conferences. Bibliography; detailed, analytical index. 'Fills a gap' (*Choice*, November 1990, p.513, on the 1st ed.). *Class No:* 621.355

[4357]
LINDEN, D., *ed*. **Handbook of batteries.** 2nd ed. New York, etc., McGraw-Hill, 1995. v.p. illus., diagrs., graphs, tables. $125. ISBN: 0070379211.
First published 1984 as *Handbook of batteries and fuel cells.*
Some 50 contributors. Covers: principles of operation; primary batteries; secondary batteries; reserve batteries. For each type gives general characteristics, chemistry, construction, charging and performance characteristics, applications. Appendices contain definitions, properties of materials, symbols, conversion factors, bibliography, manufacturers. Excellent index, many clear diagrams and tabulations. 'Can be expected to be the authoritative reference on batteries for years to come' (*Choice*, December 1995, p.644).
Class No: 621.355

Electroplating

[4358]
DURNEY, L.J., *ed*. **Electroplating engineering handbook.** 4th ed. New York, etc., Van Nostrand Reinhold, 1984. x, 790p. illus., graphs, tables. $69.50. ISBN: 0442220022.
First published 1954. Previous ed. 1971 by A.K. Graham.
51 contributors. Coverage includes surface preparation, pre-and post-treatments, engineering data to aid materials selection and choice of equipment. New techniques such as pulse plating and high-speed plating are included.
Part 1. General processing data - Part 2. Engineering fundamentals and practice. Most parts of this work have been completely or substantially re-written. Aim is 'a useable handbook', with 'frequent references to other sources ... The present goal is proper guidance and the provision of the most frequently required facts, not everything that is available' (*Preface*). 'The new handbook is a worthwhile addition to the finisher's library...' (*Metal finishing*, v.83, Jan. 1985, p.110).
Class No: 621.357

[4359]
Tables and operating data for electroplaters. Redhill, Surrey, Portcullis Press, 1975. xiv, 414p. graphs, tables. £17.65. ISBN: 0901994707.
Based on a translation of *Tabellen und Betriebsdaten für die Galvanotechnic,* 4th ed. 1971 (Leuze Verlag, Saulgau, Germany), revised by C.R. Draper. The 4 German eds. were by E. Luther, H. Benninghoff and O.P. Krämer.
Contains data on constants, acids, bases, surface area, electro-deposition, properties, standards, tests, commonly used chemicals, abrasives and troubleshooting. *Class No:* 621.357

Electric Heating

[4360]
HOBSON, L. **Electroheat references.** London, British National Committee for Electroheat, 1986. iv, 74p.
Supersedes *Electroheat teaching references* (BNCE, 1980).
More than 300 references, with abstracts, derived from a computer-based literature search. Arranged in 13 categories (1. General electroheat references ... 3. Dielectric heating ... 7. Induction heating ... 10. Microwave heating ... 13. Heat pumps), each subdivided into: Design and construction; operation; theory and calculations; power supplies; applications. *Class No:* 621.36

[4361]
—BRITISH STANDARDS INSTITUTION. Glossary of electrotechnical, power, telecommunication, electronics, lighting and colour terms. Part 2. Terms particular to power engineering. Group 10. Industrial electroheating terminology. London, BSI, 1985. 36p. (*(BS 4727: Part 2: Group 10: 1985.)*
Supercedes BS 2759:1956.
About 500 terms defined in systematic order. Alphabetical index. *Class No:* 621.36

Waves & Oscillations
Microwaves

[4362]
Handbook of microwave and optical components. Chang, K., *ed*. New York, Wiley, 1989-91. 4v. illus., diagrs., graphs, tables. £45 each v.
1. *Microwave passive and antenna components.* xiv,907p. ISBN: 0471613665.
2. *Microwave solid-state components.* xiv,635p. ISBN: 0471843652.
3. *Optical components.* xiii,616p. ISBN: 0471613673.
4. *Fiber and electro-optical components.* xi,484p. ISBN: 0471613657.
V.3 has 14 contributors, 9 chapters ('gas lasers', p.451-596, carries 298 references). Volume indexes. *Class No:* 621.37.029

[4363]
HOFFMANN, R.K. **Handbook of microwave integrated circuits;** translated by G.A. Edis and N.J. Keen. Norwood, Mass., Artech House, 1987. illus., diagrs., graphs, tables. (*Artech House microwave library.*) ISBN: 0890061637.
Originally published in German as *Integrierte Mikrowellenschaltungen* (Springer, 1983).
'This book provides the fundamental information for the design of MICs, with emphasis on the electrical properties of the various forms of strip transmission lines ... [and] ... an introduction to the technology of these circuits and a treatment of the spurious electrical effects ... such as field distortions ... (*Preface*). A comprehensive text with a noteworthy bibliography of 1,256 references. *Class No:* 621.37.029

[4364]
LAVERGHETTA, T.S. **Handbook of microwave testing.** Dedham, Mass., Artech House, 1981. [xviii], 518p. illus., diagrs., tables. £54. ISBN: 0890060703.
Companion volume to same author's *Microwave measurements and techniques* (1976). Covers the major areas of test equipment for power levels, noise measurements, frequency, etc. 12 appendices contain much useful information. Concentrates on US equipment and excludes all European and Japanese instruments. Bibliography p.511-5. Brief index.
'... A practical microwave engineer working for a firm that is well equipped with modern US microwave test equipment will find this book very valuable' (*Microwaves, optics and antennas (IEEE H)* v.129 (4), August 1982, p.160). But 'omission of such matters as testing mixers, microwave transistors and ... microwave semiconductor devices generally, and of problems involved in testing microcircuits is regrettable. Nevertheless, technicians new to the microwave techniques and wishing to familiarise themselves with equipment and methods still in use will find the book useful if they can come to terms with the garrulous, direct approach. The presentation of text is very good' (*Electronics and power*, v.28, June 1982, p.465).
Class No: 621.37.029

[4365]
The Microwave engineering handbook. Smith, B.L. *and* Carpentier, M.-H., *eds*. London, Chapman & Hall, 1992-93. 3v. (*c.*1400p.) illus., diagrs., graphs, tables. £60 each. ISBN: 0412456702.
V.1: *Microwave components.* 448p.
V.2: *Microwave circuits, antennas and propagation.* 436p.
V.3: *Microwave systems and applications.* 558p.
V.3 has 8 chapters, closely sub-divided, with references. Volume indexes. *Class No:* 621.37.029

[4366]
Microwave handbook. Dixon, M.W., *ed*. Potters Bar, Radio Society of Great Britain, 1989-92. 3v. illus., diagrs., graphs, tables.
V.1. *Components and operating techniques.* 1989.
V.2. *Construction and testing.* 1991.
V.3. *Bands and equipment.* 1992.
V.1 has 5 contributors; 6 chapters. Apart from much referenced information, it is a timely collection of practical diagrams, hints and tips. 2-page index. *Class No:* 621.37.029

[4367]
POZAR, D.M. **Microwave engineering.** Reading, Mass., Addison-Wesley, 1990. xvii, [i], 726p. illus., forumlas, graphs. £56.95. (*Addison-Wesley series in computer engineering.*) ISBN: 0201504189.
12 documented chapters: Electromagnetic theory ... Lines and waveguides - Network analysis ... Resonators ... Filters ... Circuits - Systems. 10 appendices (C. 'Bessel functions'). Detailed, analytical index, p.719-26. A textbook for advanced undergraduates; problems. *Class No:* 621.37.029

[4368]

THUÉRY, J. Microwaves: industrial, scientific, and medical applications. Grant, E.H., *ed*. Boston, Ma., London, Artech House, 1992. xviii, 670p. $88; £66. ISBN: 0890064482.

Translated from the French.

4 sections: 1. Microwaves - 2. Industrial applications (drying, treatment of elastomers, etc.) - 3. Applications in the food industry - 4. Biological effects and medical applications. More than 4000 references, most from English-language sources. List of industries, organizations and universities active in the field. 'Highly recommended' (*Choice*, October 1992, p.334). *Class No: 621.37.029*

Filters

[4369]

DICKENSON, T.C. Filters and filtration handbook. 4th ed. Amsterdam, Elsevier, 1997. xiii, 1079p. illus., graphs, tables. ISBN: 1856173224.

9 sections, subdivided (*e.g.* 9. Filter selection). Buyers' guide; editorial index. *Class No: 621.372*

Waveguides

[4370]

MARCUVITZ, N. Waveguide handbook. London, P. Peregriuus, 1986. xviii, 428p. diagrs., graphs, tables. (*IEE Electromagnetic waves series, no.21*.) ISBN: 0863410588.

First published 1951.

This edition reprints the original with correction of known typographical and other errors. Chapters 1-3 summarize field and network theory. Chapters 4-8 provide equivalent circuit parameters for a variety of microwave structures, supported by numerous graphs. 'The book is for those requiring a fairly fundamental approach to their waveguide problems. It does not explicitly deal with the more practicable problems and as such the title "Handbook" is a little misleading ... For all that, the work does form a useful reference book for the shelf' (*Electronics and power*, v.33(2), Feb. 1987, p.142). *Class No: 621.372.8*

Pulses

[4371]

BRITISH STANDARDS INSTITUTION. Guide to pulse techniques and apparatus. London, BSI, 1989. 2 parts. graphs. (*BS 5698: 1989*.)

1. *Pulse terms and definitions*. 28p.

2. *Pulse measurement and anlysis, general considerations*. 20p.

About 150 terms defined in systematic order, with formulae as appropriate. Alphabetical index. *Class No: 621.374*

Amplifiers

Lasers

Bibliographies

[4372]

GOMERSALL, A. Lasers in materials processing: a bibliography of a developing technology. Kempston, Beds., IFS (Publications), 1986. vii, 167p. illus. £35. ISBN: 0948507241, UK edition.

Aims to cover all the major applications in addition to publications on the physics and metallurgy of laser systems. Emphasis is (intentionally) on laser processes (welding, cutting, drilling, machining), surface modification (coating, cladding, heat treatment, etching) and alloying. Includes US, European and Japanese sources. Almost 900 items arranged under 5 main heads with 30-odd subdivisions. Author index but no subject index. Includes conference papers. Informative abstracts. *Class No: 621.375.826(01)*

[4373]

High-power lasers: improvements and applications: a literature study. Sigmond, J. *and* Terpstra, M., *eds*. London, Elsevier Applied Sciences, 1988. ix,226p. illus. £50. ISBN: 1851662340.

A review US, Japanese, French, West German, UK, European (Munich) and international (PCT, Geneva) patents, patent applications, technical and scientific literature published between 1980 and 1985. Over 200 references. 'List of patentees', p.209-24. *Class No: 621.375.826(01)*

Handbooks & Manuals

[4374]

ANDREWS, D.L. Lasers in chemistry. 2nd ed. Berlin, Springer-Verlag, 1990. xii,188p. diagrs., graphs, tables. ISBN: 0387517774.

First published 1986.

5 main chapters: 1. Principles of laser operations - 2. Laser sources - 3. Laser instrumentation in chemistry - 4. Chemical spectroscopy

....(contd.)

with lasers - 5. Liquid-inducted chemistry. Each chapter has applied questions, with references. 113 figures. 4 appendices (3. Selected bibliography). *Class No: 621.375.826(035)*

[4375]

HECHT, J. The Laser guidebook. 2nd ed. New York, etc., McGraw-Hill, 1992. xiv, 498p. illus., diagrs., tables. £35.95. ISBN: 0070277370.

First published 1986.

Concentrates on the 'functional characteristics of lasers' (*Preface*). 29 chapters: 1-6 (introductory explanation); 7-29 (types of lasers, *e.g.* 7. Helium neon ... 10 Carbon dioxide ... 17. Dye ... 29. X-ray). Appendix: types of lasers by wavelength. Detailed, analytical index, p.489-98. Earlier, shorter versions of much of the material first appeared in the journal *Lasers & optronics*. *Class No: 621.375.826(035)*

[4376]

Laser handbook. Amsterdam, etc., North-Holland, 1972-90. 6v. diagrs., graphs, tables.

1-2., edited by F.T. Arecchi and E.O. Schulz-Dubois. 1972. xxvii, 1947p. £181.25. ISBN 0720402131.

3., edited by M.L. Stitch. 1979. v, 878p. £129.69. ISBN 0444852719.

4., edited by M. Bass and M.L. Stitch. 1985. x, 594p. £90.63. IBSN 0444869271.

5., edited by M. Bass and M.L. Stitch. 1985. ix, 692p. £102.13. ISBN 0444869344.

6., edited by W.B. Colson and C. Pellegrini. 1990, 580p. £107.90. ISBN 0444869530.

A series of 'expository monographs' (*Preface*) on laser technology and applications by specialists, no longer (since v.3) limited by length of article. V.3 has 11 articles; v.5 has 5. 'With the increasing use of lasers in such a wide variety of scientific applications, this book [v.3] will be a valuable reference for advanced students and practising scientists in physics, chemistry and engineering' (*Philosophical magazine*, part B, v.41(6), 1980, p.706). A review in *Physics today* (Dec. 1980, p.59-60) draws attention to inevitable omissions of recent information in v.3. but commends the series, and ends: 'Every research group in quantum mechanics should have access to this set of references'. *Class No: 621.375.826(035)*

[4377]

MALLOW, A. *and* **CHABOT, L. Laser safety handbook.** New York, etc., Van Nostrand Reinhold, 1978. xiii, 353p. illus., diagrs., graphs. $24.50. ISBN: 0442250924.

Brings together diverse information otherwise scattered in the literature. 15 chapters. Chapters 1-5 introduce lasers (theory, properties, etc.) and the hazards associated with them. Chapter 6 covers protective standards and deals with factors affecting maximum permissible exposure (MPE). Chapter 7 and 8 are concerned with laser beam evaluation and classification, control of beam and other laser hazards. US Federal legislation is extensively described in Chapter 10. Safety programmes and medical surveillance, protective eyewear and atmospheric effects in outdoor use are covered in the remaining chapters. The 3 appendices contain a glossary (p.277-301) and American standard guidance codes. *Class No: 621.375.826(035)*

[4378]

MILONNI, P.W. *and* **EBERLY, J.H. Lasers.** Chichester, Wiley, 1988. 731p. $50. ISBN: 0471627313.

18 chapters. 1-9 cover basic principles and 10-18 provide details of laser operations and applications. End-of-chapter problems. 'Outstanding ... highly recommended' (*Choice*, May 1988). *Class No: 621.375.826(035)*

Reviews & Abstracts

[4379]

Journal of current laser abstracts. Littleton, Mass., PennWell Publishing Co/Laser Focus Publications, 1967-. v.4(1)-. Monthly. $455 pa. ISSN: 00220264.

First published as *Laser/maser international* (v.1-3. 1964-66).

About 5,000 indicative abstracts pa. Entries are in 4 main groups, each subdivided: General laser publications (including textbooks, conference proceedings and bibliographies) - Theoretical aspects of lasers - Experimental laser research - Applications of lasers. Issue indexes of personal and corporate authors and patents. Annual personal and corporate author indexes. *Class No: 621.375.826(048)*

Yearbooks & Directories

[4380]

Industrial laser annual handbook. Belforte, D. *and* Levitt, M., *eds*. Tulsa, Oklahoma, PennWell Books, 1986. 250p. $110.

4 sections: Laser materials processing data and guidelines - Review of laser processing - Company and product directory - Related products and services. 'In their preface the editors state that it is intended that future editions ... will build upon the present one. It is

....*(contd.)*

hoped that they do; this could become a very valuable database' (*Optics and laser technology, v.18, Dec. 1986, p.324*). *Noted*: 1987 ed. 350p. $125. ISBN 0878143203. *Class No: 621.375.826(058)*

Tables & Data Books

[4381]
BENNETT, W.R. Atomic gas laser transition data: a critical evaluation. New York, Plenum Press, 1979. 293p. diagrs., tables. $75. (*IFI database library.*) ISBN: 0306651874.

159p. of tables and 120p. of annotated references (432 citations). The tables contain only critically evaluated data (oscillation criteria, laser wavelength measurements, ion species and transition identification). Other useful data, not evaluated, are contained in the descriptive summaries in the bibliography. No index of authors.

'... a carefully compiled set of tables arranged in alphabetical order for the 51 elements which have been used to create atomic gas lasers ... This is a useful volume ... Which will, one hopes, sound the death-knell on other less carefully prepared sets of tables' (*Microwaves, optics and antennas (IEE Proceedings H*), v.127(2), April 1980, p.106). *Class No: 621.375.826(083)*

[4382]
—DONALDSON,, R.W. *and* EDWARDS, J.G. Concise databook of optical materials: a selection of optical and physical data for the laser and optics laboratory. Teddington, Middx., National Physical Laboratory, 1983. [1], 65p. graphs, tables. ISBN: 0946754004.

Data for 20 optical materials useful for laser research and the laser industry. Materials include gallium arsenide, lithium niobate, neodymium YAG, yttrium aluminium garnet (YAG) and potassium chloride. Data for up to 22 properties, including Young's modulus, melting point, specific heat, temperature coefficients of refractive index and optical path, laser damage threshold, electrostriction. Refractive index and transmission data are presented in graphs. 179 literature references listed. Conversion tables facilitate interpretation in units other than SI. *Class No: 621.375.826(083)*

[4383]
CRC handbook of laser science and technology. Weber, M.J., *ed.* Boca Raton, Florida, CRC Press, 1982-87. 5v. diagrs., graphs, tables. (*CRC Handbook series of laser science and technology.*)

Update and expansion of *CRC Handbook of lasers, with selected data on optical technology* (1971).

1. *Lasers and masers.* 1982 552p. $133. ISBN 0849335019.
2. *Gas lasers.* 1982. 584p. $133. ISBN 0849335027.
3. *Optical materials. Part 1. Nonlinear optical properties/radiation damage.* 1986. 480p. $125. ISBN 0849335035.
4. *Optical materials. Part 2. Properties. Fundamental properties.* 1986. 496p. $135. ISBN 0849335045.
5. *Optical materials. Part 3 Applications, coatings and fabrication .* 1987. 544p. $126.50. ISBN 0849335051.

Suppt.1. *Lasers.* 1991. 560p. £151. ISBN 084933506x.
Suppt.2. *Optical materials.* 1993. 750p. £156 ISBN 0849335078.

Extensive tables of experimental data on all types of primary lasers with bibliographical citations to original sources and work are contained in v.1-2. Later volumes cover physical properties of laser optical materials and fabrication techniques.
Class No: 621.375.826(083)

Electronics

Abbreviations & Symbols

[4384]
BROWN, P. Electronics and computer acronyms. 2nd ed. London, etc., Butterworths, 1988. [vii], 272p. diagrs. £24. ISBN: 0408023988.

First published 1985 as *Dictionary of electrical electronics and computer abbreviations*.

Nearly 400 new entries, bringing the total to almost 2,500, shift the emphasis heavily to the title subjects, although telecommunications, microprocessors, lasers, fibre optics, radio, television, audio and general electrical engineering terms are also included. Definitions and explanations range from one line to fifteen, are often illustrated and are clear and concise. Unexpected entries include whole words, *e.g.* jack, tweeter, X-ray, whilst the Appendix (p.270-2) oddly concentrates entirely on battery choice and use. *Class No: 621.38(003)*

[4385]
—Electronic abbreviations, symbols and terms. 2nd ed. Basingstoke, Hants., Macmillan Educational Ltd., 1985. vi, 79p. £1.95. ISBN: 0333391675.

Previous ed. 1984.

Identifies *c.*200 common abbreviations, *c.*120 circuit and component symbols and *c.*70 logic symbols (showing British and US variants). Defines *c.*70 terms. Highly selective and brief, but simple and satisfactory for limited amateur use. *Class No: 621.38(003)*

[4386]
Index of acronyms and abbreviations in electrical and electronic engineering. Weinheim, etc., VCH, 1989. [vii],538p. £75. ISBN: 0895738120.

About 45,000 entries. More comprehensive than Keller (*qv*), but little to choose between them. *Class No: 621.38(003)*

[4387]
INSTITUTE OF ELECTRICAL AND ELECTRONICS ENGINEERS. Electrical and electronics graphic symbols and reference designations. 2nd ed. New York, IEEE, 1987. v.p. diagrs. ISBN: 0471634565.

Includes all IEEE and ANSI standards. Covers logic functions, parts and equipment, diagrams and electrical wiring. *Class No: 621.38(003)*

[4388]
WENNRICH, P. International dictionary of abbreviations and acronyms of electronics, electrical engineering, computer technology, and information processing. München, Saur, 1992. 2v. (502; 458p.). ISBN: 3598109776.

Over 90,000 abbreviations, most of English-language derivation. *Class No: 621.38(003)*

Databases

[4389]
ELCOM. Bethesda, Md., Cambridge Scientific Abstracts.

Covers 1980 to date. A bibliographic database providing references, with abstracts, to world literature on electronics, computing and communications, including research, commercial and marketing information. Sources include journal articles, government reports, conference papers, theses, patents. File size: 129,000 citations. Updated monthly; *c.*10,000 additions pa. Host: STN International. Available on the internet (http://www.csa.com). Printed versions: *Electronics and communications abstracts journal* and *Computer and informative systems abstracts journal*. 'ELCOM ... might be the best choice for the undergraduate student or computer hobbyist who is not interested in exotic foreign language materials ... Elcom covers newspapers and trade literature that may not be considered scholarly enough [for INSPEC and COMPENDEX]' (*Database*, v.4(2), June 1981, p.13-29). *Class No: 621.38(003.4)*

[4390]
—VIDEOLOG. Santa Clara, Calif., Videolog Communications, 1985-.

Textual and numeric databank. Contains 10 files relating to the electronics industry. Product data, covering the contents of the Harris Directory: *Who's who in electronics, D.A.T.A. Books*, and product specifications from many manufacturers. Covers 650,000 semiconductors, integrated circuits and microcomputer systems. Trade directory (14,000 companies); 18,000 product categories. Semiconductor prices. Specifications of military devices. US-based. Daily updates. Available through TELENET and TYMNET. *Class No: 621.38(003.4)*

Bibliographies

[4391]
DELL, J. 'Electronics'. *Information sources in engineering.* K.W. Mildren and P.J. Hicks, eds. (3rd ed., 1996), p.411-24. 3rd ed. London, Bowker Saur, 1996. £80. ISBN: 1857390571.

Three main sections: Professional organizations - Primary sources (journals; conferences; product data; standards and specifications) - Secondary sources. *Class No: 621.38(01)*

[4392]
UNITED NATIONS. Industrial Development Organization. Information sources on the electronics industry. New York, United Nations, 1979. xii, 103p. (*UNIDO Guides to information sources, no.32.*)

822 numbered entries. Standard UNIDO Guide format of 11 sections: 1. Professional, trade and research organizations, learned societies and special information services (regional listing) - 2. Directories (regional and subject listing) - 3. Sources of statistics, marketing and other economic data (regional listing) - 4. Basic handbooks, textbooks and manuals - 5. Monograph series - 6. Current periodicals - 7. Current abstracting and indexing periodicals - 8. Proceedings, papers and reports - 9. Specialized dictionaries and encyclopaedias - 10. Bibliographies - 11. Other potential sources of information (A. Consulting and engineering services - H. Standards and specifications - J. Translation services). Bibliography of sources used. Strengths: Organizations - 268 entries; Periodicals - 227 entries. *Class No: 621.38(01)*

Encyclopaedias

[4393]

DOUGLAS-YOUNG, J. Portable electronics data book. Englewood Cliffs, N.J., Prentice Hall, 1989. vii,360p. diagrs., graphs, tables. £36. ISBN: 0136858279.

Entries, A-Z ('Alternating current' - 'Waveguides and cavities'). Cross-references. Numerous tables. Several entries contain computer programmes for calculations (*e.g.* 'Energy stored in a capacitor'). Handy format. *Class No:* 621.38(031)

[4394]

GIBILISCO, S. *and* **SLATER, N.,** *eds.* **Encyclopedia of electronics.** 2nd ed. Blue Ridge Summit, Pa., TAB Books, 1990. 960p. illus., diagrs., graphs, circuits, tables. $69.50. ISBN: 0830633898.

First published 1985.

A collection of over 3,000 short articles, A-Z, presenting clear definitions and explanations, with appropriate illustrations (nearly 2 per page), from the whole field of electronics and related subjects. The entries are also listed under 17 categories which alphabetically display the scope (Antennas and feed lines - Audio electronics - Broadcasting and communications ... Computers and digital electronics - Electricity and magnetism ... Switching and control ... Wiring and construction). A specific subject index of 5,500 entries facilitates reference to relevant articles for terms not found in the main encyclopaedia section. 'A good book for public, high school and college libraries' (*Choice,* v.28(6), December 1990. p.607). *Class No:* 621.38(031)

[4395]

McGraw-Hill encyclopedia of electronics and computers. Parker, S.P., *ed.* 2nd ed. New York, London, etc. McGraw-Hill, 1988. [x], 964p. illus., diagrs., graphs, tables. £59.50. ISBN: 007045499x.

First published 1984.

'Much of the material ... has been published previously in the *McGraw-Hill Encyclopedia of science and technology,* 6th edition [1987]' (t.p. verso.). Contains 520 articles, 120 of them 'completely revised' (*Preface*), by 328 contributors, alphabetically arranged by topic. Conveniently collects articles from three main areas: principles of electronics; science and technology of electronic devices; applications of devices, with emphasis on computing. Extensive analytical index facilities retrieval. Useful article bibliographies. 1250 illus. *Class No:* 621.38(031)

[4396]

TRAISTER, J.E. *and* **TRAISTER, R.J. Encyclopedic dictionary of electronic terms.** Englewood Cliffs, N.J., Prentice-Hall, 1984. [iv], 604p. illus., diagrs., circuits, tables. £45.65. ISBN: 0132767780.

Fewer than 1,500 descriptive entries, frequently lengthy, well illustrated with excellent line drawings, cast in simple language understandable by the novice. Avoids the temptation to bulk the work by the inclusion of computer terminology. *Class No:* 621.38(031)

[4397]

Wiley encyclopedia of electrical and electronics engineering. Webster, J.G., *ed.* Chichester, Wiley, 1999. 22v. (*c.*19,000p.). illus., diagrs., graphs, tables. £4925. ISBN: 0471139467.

About 1,300 reviewed articles, A-Z. Covers a very wide range of topics including aerospace and electronic systems, automatic control, communications, consumer electronics, energy conversion, engineering management, industry applications, knowledge and data engineering, lightwave technology, multimedia, packaging and manufacturing technology, photonics technology, power delivery and systems, reliability, solid state circuits, VLSI systems, etc. Articles have bibliographies and cross references. Detailed, analytical index. Annual supplements are planned and a World Wide Web version will be available shortly after publication. *Class No:* 621.38(031)

Handbooks & Manuals

[4398]

BELOVE, C., *ed.* **Handbook of modern electronics and electrical engineering.** New York, etc., Wiley, 1986. xxviii, 2401p. illus., diagrs., graphs, circuits, tables. £112. ISBN: 0471097543.

105 US and 1 Canadian contributors. 69 chapters grouped in 13 parts (1-3 cover mathematics, materials and components; 4-7 deal with circuits, systems engineering and automobile control; 8-13 contain chapters on medical applications, sound and video recording, communications, navigation and radar, computers and energy engineering). Emphasis is heavy on electronics. Each chapter starts with basics, provides overview of its subject, design information and bibliography.

'A handy source of practical, state-of-the-art information on the design, development and manufacture of electronic circuits and systems ... The Handbook's coverage of telecommunications is unprecedented' (*IEEE Power Engineering review,* PER-6, Dec. 1986, p.27). *Class No:* 621.38(035)

[4399]

CHRISTIANSEN, D., *ed.* **Electronics engineers' handbook.** 4th ed. New York, etc., McGraw-Hill, 1997. v.p. illus., diagrs., graphs, circuits, tables. $110.50. (*McGraw-Hill handbooks.*) ISBN: 0070218625.

First published 1975. 3rd ed. 1989.

'New edition now covers the entire range of electronics' (*Preface*). 180 contributors; 31 chapters, closely subdivided, in 4 parts: 1. Principles and techniques - 2. Materials and hardware - 3. Circuits and functions - 4. Systems and applications. New sections cover light-emitting diodes, semiconductor lasers and digital filters. Chapter 31 identities informations resources including computer packages and web sites. Detailed, analytical index. Contains over 1,600 illustrations and over 2,500 references. A CD-ROM version is available (1998; $149.95; ISBN 0071343784). *Class No:* 621.38(035)

[4400]

COLLINS, T.H. Analog electronics handbook. New York, Prentice-Hall, 1989. xxiv, 460p. diagrs., graphs, tables. ISBN: 0130331198.

28 chapters, each in numbered sections. Chapters 1-6 cover background theory and mathematics; 7-28 cover applications (*e.g.* 7. Passive components; 15. Active filters; 23. Modulation; 27. Microwaves and radar principles). Worked examples and over 500 diagrs., etc. Includes glossary of symbols (letter and graphic); Tables (*e.g.* Laplace transforms); analytical index. No bibliography or 'further reading'. 'A useful and well-written book' (*Choice,* May 1989, p.1548). *Class No:* 621.38(035)

[4401]

Electronic materials and process handbook Harper, C.A. *and* Sampson, R.N., *eds.* 2nd ed. New York, McGraw-Hill, 1994. v.p. illus., diagrs., graphs, tables. £71.95. ISBN: 0070542996.

First published 1970.

14 contributors. 11 chapters, closely sub-divided, in 3 parts: Materials - Processes - Advanced packaging. Detailed, analytical index, 10p. *Class No:* 621.38(035)

[4402]

Handbook for electronics engineering technicians. Kaufman, M. *and* Seidman, A.S., *eds.* 2nd ed. New York, etc., McGraw-Hill, 1984. xxxiv, [715]p. tables. £32.95. ISBN: 0070334080.

24 chapters, by 8 contributors, cover resistors, capacitors, coils, transformers, meters and measurements, semiconductor devices, integrated circuits, operation amplifiers, power supplies, batteries and (new to this edition): microprocessors, microwaves, fibre optics, active filters and oscilloscopes. Each chapter contains definitions, types and characteristics of components, problems and solutions, data tables and nomographs. 13 appendix tables provide miscellaneous data (some of doubtful value in the age of pocket calculators). Good index.

Condensed soft-cover version as *Electronics sourcebook for technicians and engineers* (New York, etc., McGraw-Hill, 1988. 592p. £19.95. ISBN 0070335591). *Class No:* 621.38(035)

[4403]

Handbook of electronic package design. Pecht, M., *ed.* New York, Marcel Dekker, 1991. xiii,871p. illus., diagrs., graphs, tables. £115. (*Mechanical engineering, 76.*) ISBN: 0824779215.

12 contributors. 12 documented chapters (2. Electronic components ... 4. Electronic assemblies ... 6. Layout ... 9. Design for vibration and shock ... 12. Electronic materials and properties). Chapter 7, 'Thermal design analysis': 91p., 9 sections, 3 exercises, 207 references. Appendices, A-E (A: 'Acronyms used in electronics'). Detailed, analytical index, p.861-71. Well-produced. *Class No:* 621.38(035)

[4404]

Handbook of electronics calculations: for engineers and technicians. Kaufman, M. *and* Seidman, A.H. 2nd ed. New York, McGraw-Hill, 1988. v.p. illus., diagrs., graphs, tables. ISBN: 0070335281.

First published 1979.

Several hundred worked-out problems covering a range of topics from analog and digital circuits. Practical rather than theoretical. 25 chapters, closely subdivided, each with brief bibliography. Appendices, A-R (*e.g.* K: 'Exponentials'). Detailed, analytical index. *Class No:* 621.38(035)

[4405]

HARPER, C.A., *ed.* **Handbook of electronic systems design.** New York, etc., McGraw-Hill, 1980. 849p. illus., diagrs., graphs, circuits, tables. £59.95. ISBN: 0070266832.

29 contributors. Covers computers, communications networks and systems, radar measurement and digital systems, with relevant factual information and technical data in appropriate form (graphs, tables, etc.) Glossaries and references, supplemented by detailed index, assist consultation and understanding. *Class No:* 621.38(035)

[4406]

MANDL, M. Electronics handbook. Reston, Va., Reston Publishing Co., 1983. xiv, 360p. diagrs., graphs, circuits, tables. $34.95. ISBN: 0835916030.

'... contains a broad coverage of electronic topics ranging from basic concepts to radio, television, communications and digital circuitry. It is intended as a reference text ...' (*Preface*). Provides description, definition, explanation, circuits, data, symbols and other information for many aspects of electronics and communications, supported by glossary and index. *Class No:* 621.38(035)

[4407]

MATISOFF, B.S. Handbook of electronics packaging design and engineering. New York, Van Nostrand Reinhold, 1990. x, 656p. illus., diagrs., tables. ISBN: 0442265026.

A determinedly practical guide covering all factors in the design and fabrication of electronic components, including project planning, ergonomics, materials selection, thermal control, environmental protection and safety. Contains chapter of reference data and a glossary of terminology. Supported by numerous diagrams and tables and a succinct index. *Class No:* 621.38(035)

[4408]

MAZDA, F., *ed.* **Electronic engineer's reference book.** 6th ed. London, etc., Butterworth, 1989. v.p. illus., diagrs., graphs, circuits, tables. ISBN: 0408054301.

First published 1958 by Haywood Books. 5th ed. 1983.

85 contributors. Follows the five-part arrangement of the 5th ed.: 1. Mathematical and electrical techniques - 2. Physical phenomena - 3. Materials and components - 4. Electronic circuit design and instrumentation - 5. Applications (including communication satellites, networks, computers, videotape). 6 added chapters on newer topics, *e.g.* application specific integrated circuits, computer aided design techniques, digital system analysis, software engineering, local area networks, integrated services digital network (ISDN). Clear text; attractively laid out; simple diagrams; excellent analytical index; useful reference and 'further reading' lists. *Class No:* 621.38(035)

[4409]

MAZDA, F. Power electronics handbook: components, circuits and applications. 3rd ed. Oxford, Butterworth-Heinemann, 1997. 480p. illus., diagrs. £35. ISBN: 0750629266.

Contents include eletromagnetic compatibility; power semiconductor circuits; static switches; A.C. line control converters; forced commutation techniques; D.C. to D.C. converters; smart power, etc. The 1990 ed. was recommended 'for the wealth and diversity of useful material summarized in a single volume' (*Choice*, November 1990, p.518). *Class No:* 621.38(035)

[4410]

SCROGGIE, M.G. *and* **JOHNSTONE, G.G. Radio and electronic laboratory handbook.** 9th ed. London, etc., Newnes-Butterworths, 1980. xiv, 592p. illus., diagrs., graphs, circuits, tables. £17.95. ISBN: 0408003731.

First published 1938. Previous ed. 1971.

A highly regarded 'classic' in its field. Aimed, as always, to provide guidance for experiments 'without unlimited funds and space ... or substantial qualifications and experience' (*Preface*). The guidance is essentially practical and contained in 13 chapters: 1. The ends and the means - 2. Premises and layout - 3. Fundamental principles of measurement - 4. Sources of power and signals ... 8. Choice and care of equipment - 9. Measurement of circuit parameters - 10. Signal measurements ... 12. Dealing with results - 13. For reference (units, symbols, laws, concepts, data). A commendatory review in *Wireless world* (v.86,(3), March 1980, p.70) referred to 'lavish provision of references in the text'. *Class No:* 621.38(035)

Dictionaries

Polyglot

[4411]

MIRIMANOV, R.G., *and others.* **Dictionary of electronics:** English - German - French - Dutch - Russian. Deventer, Netherlands, Kluwer, 1985. 544p. £49.95. ISBN: 9020117882.

9,000 entries in English, with foreign-language equivalents, cross-referenced from other language indexes by alphanumeric code for each term. A version with Spanish rather than Dutch was published in 1988 (£47.95). *Class No:* 621.38(038)=00

English

[4412]

AMOS, S.W. *and* **AMOS, R.S.,** *eds.* **Dictionary of electronics.** 3rd ed. Oxford, Newnes, 1996, reprinted 1997. iv, 363p. diagrs., graphs, circuits. ISBN: 0750624051.

First published 1981; 2nd ed. 1987.

3rd ed. includes about 2,700 entries, 400 of them new. 'Many of the

....(contd.)

existing definitions have been extended to reflect recent developments or re-worded to improve clarity' ('Preface to third edition', p.10). *Class No:* 621.38(038)=20

[4413]

GRAF, R.F. Modern dictionary of electronics. 6th ed., revised and updated Boston, Ma., Oxford, Newnes, 1997. 1152p. diagrs., graphs, circuits. ISBN: 0750698705.

First published 1962. Previous ed. 1977; 6th ed. first published 1984.

Definitions for about 25,000 terms (5,000 more than in 5th ed.). Liberal illus. with identifying captions. Clear definitions, as simple as possible. Metric equivalents for cutomary US measurement units. Good presentation, arrangement and cross-reference. *Class No:* 621.38(038)=20

[4414]

The Illustrated dictionary of electronics. Gibilisco, S., *ed.* 7th ed. New York, etc., McGraw-Hill, 1997. 788p. illus. $39.95. ISBN: 0070241864.

First published 1980; 6th ed. 1994.

Over 22,000 terms and abbreviations briefly defined (*c*.5 to 6 lines). Numerous cross references and extensively illustrated. Appendices: schematic symbols; tables and data; electronics abbreviations. Good value. *Class No:* 621.38(038)=20

[4415]

—**YOUNG, C. The Penguin dictionary of electronics.** 2nd ed. Harmondsworth, Penguin, 1988. [viii], 671p. diagrs., circuits. £7.99. ISBN: 0140511873.

First published 1979 as *New Penguin dictionary of electronics*.

About 3,500 terms defined, some at length (*e.g.* 'loudspeaker': 2p.) Cross-references. 15 tables appended (2. colour Codes). *Class No:* 621.38(038)=20

[4416]

SCLATER, N. *and* **MARKUS, J. McGraw-Hill electronics dictionary.** 5th ed. New York, etc. McGraw-Hill, 1997. ix, 596p. illus. $55. ISBN: 0070404348.

First published 1945; 5th ed. 1994.

About 14,000 entries, most defined briefly (*e.g.* 'high-definition television', 6 lines). A comprehensive, yet accessible dictionary. J. Markus is still identified as an author although he died in 1982. 'An excellent, general-purpose dictionary' (*American reference books annual*, 1998, p.652). *Class No:* 621.38(038)=20

[4417]

SINCLAIR, I.R. The HarperCollins dictionary of electronics. London, Collins, 1991. 362p. diagrs., graphs, tables. £12.95; $25. ISBN: 0062715283.

Over 2,000 terms, briefly defined (*e.g.* 'logic gate': 11 lines). Covers theoretical and practical applications. 4 appendices: D. graphical symbols. References, p.vi. *Class No:* 621.38(038)=20

[4418]

WILSON, F.A. A Reference guide to practical electronic terms. London, Bernard Babani, 1992. [vi], 433p. diagrs. £5.95. ISBN: 0859342328.

About 1200 terms, some defined at length (*e.g.* 'Impatt diode': *c*.1p., with diagram). Cross references. *Class No:* 621.38(038)=20

German

[4419]

FERRETTI, V. Dictionary of electronics, computing and telecommunication: English-German, German-English. [Wörterbuch der elektronik, datentechnik und der telekommunikation.] Berlin, Springer Verlag, 1992. 2v. (xxviii, 609p. + xxviii, 636p.) £58.50 each. ISBN: 3540541101, (G/E); 3540542027, (E/G).

About 60,000 entries in each half. Prelims. include 'Applied morphology of subject fields'. Bibliography, 5p. Also available on CD-ROM. *Class No:* 621.38(038)=30

[4420]

OPPERMANN, A. Wörterbuch der Elektronik: Englisch-Deutsch. [Dictionary of electronics: English-German.] Munich, etc., Saur, 1984, 1987. 2v. ISBN: 068698305x.

1. *Englisch-deutsch.* 2nd ed. 1987. *c*.800p. £77.95. ISBN: 3980122735.

2. *Deutsch-englisch.* 1984. *c*.794p. £65. ISBN 3980122700.

German equivalents of *c*.100,000 terms covering electronics and related areas such as computing, radar, nuclear physics. *Class No:* 621.38(038)=30

French

[4421]

FLEUTRY, M. **Dictionnaire encyclopédique d'électronique:** English-French. [Encyclopedic dictionary of electronics: English-French.] Paris, La Maison du Dictionnaire, 1991. 1072p. FF1200; £127.90. ISBN: 285608043x.

40,000 entries; 20,000 definitions. Ample cross-references. '... a must for any serious technical translator working either into or from French' (*The Linguist*, v.31(5), 1992, p.164). *Class No:* 621.38(038)=40

[4422]

KING, G.G. **Elsevier's dictionary of electronics:** English/French; French/English. Amsterdam, etc., Elsevier, 1986-88. 2v. (619 + 625p.) £169.85 each. ISBN: 0444426426.

About 30,000 terms in each volume. *Class No:* 621.38(038)=40

Spanish

[4423]

MATAIX, M. **Diccionario de electrónica y energía nuclear, inglés-español.** Barcelona, Danae, 1969. 772p. 620pstas.

10,000 English-language terms, ranging over electronics, computing and nuclear energy, with Spanish equivalent and brief Spanish definitions. Index of Spanish terms. Severely limited by age and subject spread. *Class No:* 621.38(038)=60

Russian

[4424]

KALUGIN, I.K., *and others*. **Modern English-Russian dictionary of radioelectronics.** [Anglo-russkiĭ slovar' po sovremennoĭ radioelektronike.] 2nd ed. Moscow, 'Soviet Encyclopaedia' Publishing House, 1972. 448p. diagrs.

Russian equivalents of *c.*20,000 terms drawn from the electronics field, not radio, as its title would seem to suggest. (Although radio, televison and telecommunications are included, there are many surprising omissions). Includes lists of abbreviations and symbols. Indexes Russian terms by page and line number references. *Class No:* 621.38(038)=82

Reviews & Abstracts

[4425]

Electronics and communications abstracts journal. Bethesda, Md., Cambridge Scientific Abstracts; Engineering Information, Inc., 1972/3-. Monthly. $975pa. ISSN: 03613313.

Formerly *Electronics abstracts journal,* (v.1-3, 1966-1971/2).

About 11,000 indicative and informative abstracts, unsigned, pa. 5 main sections, subdivided: Civil engineering - Mining engineering - Mechanical engineering - Electrical engineering - Chemical engineering. Sources: periodical articles, reports, conference papers, books, theses, patents. Issue indexes of authors and subject. Annual subject and author indexes. Available online as ELCOM (*qv*), via STN International and on the Internet (URL: http://www.csa.com). *Class No:* 621.38(048)

[4426]

PASCAL Explore. Part F20. **Électronique et Télécommunications.** Paris, Centre National de la Recherche Scientifique. 1985-. 10pa. F850.pa.

First published (1940-) as *Bulletin signalétique. 4. Physique. II. Electricité.*

As *Bulletin signalétqiue,* Part 145 (1961-84) contained about 7,500 indicative and informative abstracts pa. (v.42, 1981, had 11,019 abstracts) systematically arranged in 10 main groups, with sections and sub-sections for each, *e.g.* 03. Dispositifs à l'étatsolide ... 05. Circuits ... 07. Télécommunications. Items drawn from 13,000 journals, conference papers, theses and reports. Subject and author indexes per issue and annually. Available on paper or microform. Also available online as part of PASCAL file, through ESA-IRS or QUESTEL. *Class No:* 621.38(048)

[4427]

Referativnyĭ zhurnal. 23 Elektronika. Academiya Nauk, SSSR. Moscow, VINITI, 1980-. Monthly. R148. ISSN: 04862287.

Formerly: *Referativnyĭ zhurnal elektronika i ee primenenie* (1963-1979).

More than 20,000 indicative and informative, signed abstracts pa. 4 sections: Electronic tubes and devices - Semiconductor devices - Optoelectronic devices - Electronic materials. Half of the content is in the semiconductors section. Issue author and patent indexes and scanned journals list. Annual author and subject indexes. English contents summary. UDC nos. *Class No:* 621.38(048)

Yearbooks & Directories

[4428]

DATA digests. San Diego, Calif., D.A.T.A., Business Publishing, 1978-. (UK distributor: H.T.I. Ltd., Romford, Essex). diagrs., tables. £85-£125 pa.

The largest collection of device data. Currently published in 19 books (annually with quarterly or semi-annual updates). Separately available. 4 groups: Integrated circuits (5 books, *e.g. Digital ICs*, plus *IC Alternate Source digest*); Discretes (5 books, *e.g. Diodes*, plus *Discrete Alternate source digest*); Special applications (3 books, *i.e., High reliability electronic components*; *International semiconductor directory; Application notes*); Materials (4 books, *e.g. Adhesives*). The publishing pattern undergoes continuing revision and a major change is taking place in 1988 with the reduction of titles from over 30 to 19, the change of name to *Digest* (from *Book*) and the abandonment of a separate set of books listing discontinued devices. The series aims to provide manufacturer information and technical data and the identification of replacements and alternatives. Magnetic tape versions are also available. *Class No:* 621.38(058)

[4429]

The **Electronics buyers' guide** 1997. Tonbridge, Kent, Miller Freeman, 1996. vii, 1128p. £68. ISBN: 0863823165. ISSN: 13606999.

Contents: World's 20 leading electronics companies - Index to products and services - Buyers' guide - Brnads and trade names - Distributors - Company data. *Class No:* 621.38(058)

[4430]

European electronics directory 1994: systems and applications: a classified directory of manufacturers, representatives and sales offices. Wedgewood, C.G., *ed.* Oxford, Elsevier, 1994. iv, 623p. ISBN: 1856172295.

Previously published as *European electronics component distributors directory.*

8 Sections: 1 Manufacturers, country by country - 2. Agents and representatives, country by country - 3. Sales Subsidiaries - 4. Company index - 5. Products and services - 6. Index - 7. Glossary of German and French technical terms - 8. List of product numbers. *Class No:* 621.38(058)

[4431]

INTEL CORPORATION. **Handbooks.** Santa Clara, Calif., the Corporation, 1985. 10v. diagrs., tables. $120 (set).

Comprising: *Quality/reliability handbook. CHMOS handbook. Memory components handbook. Telecommunication products handbook. Microcontroller handbook. Microsystem components handbook. Development systems handbook. OEM Systems handbook. Software handbook. Military handbook. Class No:* 621.38(058)

[4432]

MULLARD, LTD. **Mullard technical handbooks.** London, Mullard, Ltd. Annual. diagrs., graphs, circuits.

Comprises 4 sets of books, each consisting of several parts.

1. *Semiconductor devices.* 7 parts, plus sub-parts (*e.g.* Part 4a. Power diodes. Part 4b. Thyristors and triacs).

2. *Electronic tubes.* 4 parts, plus sub-parts (*e.g.* Part 16. Cathode ray tubes).

3. *Components, materials and assemblies.* 7 parts, plus sub-parts (*e.g.* Part 1c. Fixed resistors. Part 6. Loudspeakers).

4. *Integrated circuits.* 10 parts, plus sub-parts (*e.g.* Part 3. ICs for telephony).

Information includes general and functional description, electrical and other data, performance characteristics and ratings. Also: *Quick reference guide* (Annual). Lists alphanumerically and briefly describes all Mullard products.

Many of the large manufacturers of electronic components and devices publish detailed series of handbooks covering all their products, with diagrams, specifications, description, applications notes and tabulated data of characteristics, performance, etc., with aim of assisting designers in the selection and use of their products; equivalents and alternatives are also often listed. Two typical examples are here shown. Similar handbooks are available from other companies, *e.g.* Mostek Corporation, Motorola Semiconductor Products, RCA, Ltd., Signetics Corporation, Texas Instruments, Ltd. *Class No:* 621.38(058)

Tables & Data Books

[4433]

BRAND, J.R. **Handbook of electronics formulas, symbols and definitions.** 2nd ed. New York, Van Nostrand Reinhold, 1992. 400p. diagrs., tables. £22. ISBN: 0442003021.

First published 1979.

A pocket book intended to provide the majority of formulas and definitions needed for calculations in passive and active circuit technology. About 100p. of new material, with an additional section on operational amplifiers. *Class No:* 621.38(083)

[4434]
CLIFFORD, M. **Master handbook of electronic tables and formulas.**
5th ed. Blue Ridge Summit, Pa., TAB Books, 1990. xx,553p. diagrs.,
tables. $22.95 (Pbk). ISBN: 083062192x; 0830621911, pbk.
4th ed. 1984.
Aims to provide solutions to problems in electronics and
communications by copious provision of tables giving data for the
many hundreds of relevant formulas, obviating the need for
calculations. 25 chapters cover basic concepts (resistance, inductance,
power, etc.), applications (recording, video, antennas, etc.),
computers, constants, conversions numbers. One chapter lists all
formulas. Extensive tables. Detailed, analytical index, p.541-53.
Class No: 621.38(083)

[4435]
Electronic databook. Graf, R.F., *ed*. 3rd ed. Blue Ridge Summit, Pa.,
TAB Books, 1983. viii, 407p. diagrs., graphs, tables, nomograms.
$24.95; $19.95. ISBN: 0830601384; 0830615385, pbk.
First published 1971 as *Electronic design databook*. Previous ed.
1974.
A very wide-ranging and useful compilation of information and
calculation aids, clearly presented. Organized in 6 sections (1:
Frequency data - 2: Communication - 3: Passive components and
circuits - 4: Active components and circuits - 5: Mathematical data,
formulas, symbols - 6: Physical data). Includes a glossary (p.192-205)
of integrated circuits and microelectronics terms. Marred only by
incorrect index page number references to section 6.
4th ed. 1988. 528p. £19.75. ISBN: 0830629580.
Class No: 621.38(083)

[4436]
—BRINDLEY, K. Newnes radio and electronic engineer's pocket book.
18th ed. Oxford, Heinemann Newnes, 1992. 341p. illus., diagrs.,
tables. £9.95. ISBN: 0434901873.
First published 1940. Previous ed. 1987.
This new edition remains a handy source of a wide range of
fundamental facts and data, supported by an effective index, but
occasionally needing a magnifying glass to extract the required
information from the tiny page. *Class No:* 621.38(083)

[4437]
Electronic engineering index. Bracknell, Berks., Technical Indexes
Ltd., 1978-. 3pa. illus. £60pa. ISSN: 03088375.
This data book is the index to the associated microform file of the
catalogues of manufacturers and suppliers of electronic components,
devices and equipment, which is available on separate subscription.
Includes products and trade names; distributors and selector charts;
professional and trade organizations; addresses.
Class No: 621.38(083)

[4438]
HUGHES, F.W. **Illustrated guidebook to electronic devices and
circuits.** Englewood Cliffs, N.J., Prentice-Hall, 1983. xvi, 431p.
diagrs., graphs, circuits, tables. ISBN: 0134513282.
The title well reflects the scope of this book, which identifies the
basic theory, components and function of each circuit and system and
gives advice on testing and troubleshooting methods. 14 chapters
cover: components; solid-state devices; optoelectronic devices; vacuum
tubes; power supplies; amplifiers; oscillators; audio circuits; radio
circuits; television circuits; integrated circuits; operational amplifiers;
digital circuits; microcomputers. Excellent text and illustrations but
access is impeded by lack of index. *Class No:* 621.38(083)

[4439]
PASAHOW, E. **Electronic ready reference manual.** New York, etc.,
McGraw-Hill, 1984. xv, 569p. diagrs., tables. $28.95. ISBN:
0070487235.
A pocket book (14 x 10cm) which aims 'to provide a single source
of current electronics information' for users at all levels. Presents
formulas, equations, tables, diagrams, data and circuits for basic
concepts, passive and active components, linear circuits, filters, power
supplies, measurement, communications, digital circuits,
microprocessors and computers in 10 sections. Final 6 sections cover
mathematics, symbols, conversion formulas, properties of materials
and safety. Contents page shows range of each section (except microprocessors) but index is too brief. Absence of many page numbers
hampers access to required information. *Class No:* 621.38(083)

Standards

[4440]
**Annual book of ASTM standards. Section 10. Electrical insulation
and electronics. Vols. 10.04 and 10.05 . Electronics.** Philadelphia,
Pa., American Society for Testing and Materials, 1992. 2v. £64 each.
ISSN: 01922998.
These 2v. of section 10 of the *Annual book of ASTM standards*
contain the texts of over 260 standards in alphanumeric sequence of
their designation codes, grouped under 13 headings (*e.g.* Electro-

....(contd.)
optics; Microelectronic packaging; Silicon, electrical properties;
Silicon, mechanical properties; Photolithography). Subject indexes.
Class No: 621.38(083.74)

Histories

[4441]
DUMMER, G.W.A. **Electronic inventions and discoveries:** electronics
from its earliest beginnings to the present day. 4th ed. Bristol, Institute
of Physics, 1997. 284p. illus. £68 (Hbk); £21 (Pbk). ISBN:
075030376x, (Hbk); 0750304936, (Pbk).
First published in 1977 as *Electronic inventions 1745-1946*. 3rd ed.
1983.
Some 500 events described in chronolgical order from 1745-1996.
The descriptions are taken from the text of the source in the literature.
Indexes of subjects, inventors and bibliographies are appended. Brief
chapters with concise histories of branches of electronics (e.g. radar,
television) with illustrative charts. Lists inventions by subject,
chronologically for each. Bibliography. *Class No:* 621.38(091)

[4442]
—SHIERS, G. Bibliography of the history of electronics. Metuchen,
N.J., Scarecrow Press, 1972. xiii, 423p. $8.50. ISBN: 0810804999.
Annotated bibliography of 1,820 periodical articles, books and
reports on the history of electronics and communications from 1850.
Grouped by subjects. *Class No:* 621.38(091)

Worldwide

[4443]
TODD, D. **The World electronics industry.** London, Routledge, 1990.
[xiv],335p. figs., graphs, maps, tables. £35. ISBN: 0415024978.
8 chapters, closely subdivided: 1. Introduction - 2. Pivotal global
players - 3. Structural factors - 4. Defense electronics - 5. Innovation
and enterprise - 6. Japanese powerhouse - 7. NIC [Newly-
industrialising countries] challenge - 8. Conclusions. Extensive notes
and references (*e.g.* chapter 4 has 79). Glossary ('AAM' - 'Wafer'),
p.307-14; non-analytical index, p.327-35. A scholarly treatment,
marred by poor quality camera-ready copy. *Class No:* 621.38(100)

Equipment & Instruments

[4444]
COOMBS, C.F., Jr., *ed*. **Electronic instrument handbook.** 2nd ed.
New York, McGraw-Hill, 1995. v.p. illus., diagrs., graphs, tables.
£68.95. ISBN: 007012616x.
First published 1972.
33 contributors. 44 chapters, closely subdivided, in 12 parts (*e.g.* 3.
Current and voltage measurement; 6. Lightwave test; 8. Digital
domain; 12. Software in insturments and virtual instruments). Detailed,
analytical index, 14p. *Class No:* 621.38:002.50

Components

[4445]
BRINDLEY, K. **Newnes electronics assembly pocket book.** Oxford,
Newnes, 1991. vi,298p. illus., diagrs., graphs. £10.95. ISBN:
0750602228.
Covers a wide range of areas in assembly and wiring (*e.g.* safe
working practice; specifications; component identification; cables; thin
film modules, etc.). Nearly 1000 illus. Small, handy format.
Class No: 621.38.032

[4446]
CODUS. Sheffield, Codus, Ltd.
A data bank (textual-numeric) for quality assured electronic
components, providing comprehensive technical information on all
components approved to CECC BS 9000 and (UK) IECQ
Specifications. Covers 1967 onwards. File size: 71,000 entries (July
1986). Updated daily. Host. Codus Ltd: Costs: £200 pa., plus £55 per
connect hour. Available to subscribers only. *Class No:* 621.38.032

[4447]
ECDB: (Electronic Components Data Bank). Frascati, Italy, European
Space Agency.
A data bank containing full descriptions and physical and operational
characteristics of electronic components currently available in Europe.
Includes passive (*e.g.* resistors) and active (*e.g.* thyristors) components
and integrated circuits. Data include manufacturers and distributors.
File size: 130,000 items (1981). Updated monthly. 30,000 additions
pa. Host: ESA.
Printed equivalent: *Passive components reference book.* (*NB. Active
components are excluded*). Not available commercially.
Class No: 621.38.032

[4448]

Electronics reliability data: a guide to selected components. London, INSPEC/Institution of Electrical Engineers, 1981. tables.

Presents reliability data sheets to show failure rates for over 100 different components (resistors, capacitors, diodes, rectifiers, transistors, thyristors, microcircuits), derived from data in the Systems Reliability Service (SRS) of the National Centre for Systems Reliability. In addition provides a collection of about 720 relevant abstracts, reprinted from the INSPEC data base, classified by type of component, as above. Bibliography, p.151. *Class No:* 621.38.032

[4449]

GINSBERG, G.L. **A User's guide to selecting electronic components.** New York, Wiley, 1981. xii, 249p., illus., diagrs., tables. £21.80. ISBN: 0471083089.

Intended as an aid for design engineers in the selection of suitable components. Provides information about types, advantages and disadvantages, behaviour, construction, effect on circuits, failure and applications. 6 Parts: Resistors - Capacitors - Electromagnetic components (transformers, etc) - Power sources (including batteries) - Special-function components (oscillators, filters, etc) - Solid-state devices (*e.g.* diodes, rectifiers, transistors, optoelectronic devices). 130 references. Index. *Class No:* 621.38.032

Circuits

Encyclopaedias

[4450]

GRAF, R.F. *and* SHEETS, W. **Encyclopedia of electronic circuits.** New York, etc., McGraw-Hill, 1996. V.6. illus., tables. $60 ISBN: 0070112754.

Previously published in 5v. (1985-).

V.6 includes all circuits published in earlier vols. as well as new ones. Circuits presented in alphabetically arranged sections (Alarms ... Metal detectors ... Zero crossing detectors). Brief descriptive notes for most circuits and sources (books, periodicals, trade literature) given for each. Specific index leads directly to required circuits. Fully illustrated. The review in *American reference books annual* (1997, p.595) criticized the index but found the work 'an invaluable storehouse'. Also available on CD-ROM (1999. $149.95. ISBN: 007135008x). *Class No:* 621.38.04(031)

[4451]

LENK, J.D. **McGraw-Hill circuit encyclopedia and trouble shooting guide.** New York, etc. McGraw-Hill, 1993-96. 3v. (xiii, 630p.; xlii, 691p.; 706p.). illus., graphs, tables. $59.50 each. ISBN: 0070376034, v.1; 0070376107, v.2.

About 700 circuits in each vol. grouped by function (*e.g.* 'comparator'). Includes operation and testing information for each group, as well as titles, descriptions and drawings. 'A valluable work' (*Choice*, December 1996, p.643 on v.3). *Class No:* 621.38.04(031)

Handbooks & Manuals

[4452]

DI GIACOMO, J., *ed.* **VLSI handbook:** silicon, gallium arsenide, and superconductor circuits. New York, etc., McGraw-Hill, 1989. xiv,v.p. illus., diagrs., graphs. ISBN: 0070169039.

32 contributors, most from US industry. 'A practical manual ... to describe and explain the VLSI design methodology process from the customer's point of view' (*Preface*). 11 parts (32 chaps.): 1. Design - 2. Test - 3. Fabrication ... 7. Packaging - 8. Economics ... 10. Analog circuits - 11. Special topics. Appendices (7) cover definitions, acronyms, constants, scaling factors, etc. Detailed analytical index. *Class No:* 621.38.04(035)

[4453]

MARSTON, R.M. **Newnes electronic circuits pocket book.** Oxford, Butterworth Heinemann, 1991. [viii],336p. diagrs., tables. ISBN: 0750601329.

625 diagrams; 22 chapters (*e.g.*6. 'Norton op-amp circuits', p.76-87). A practical approach in a handy format (for use if not for library shelves). *Class No:* 621.38.04(035)

[4454]

O'DELL, T.H. **Circuits for electronic instrumentation.** Cambridge Univ. Press, 1991. 218p. illus., diagrs. $69.50; £35. ISBN: 0521404282.

Covers a wide range of circuits (*e.g.* comparators, wideband direct couple feedback amplifiers, phased locked loops, voltage controlled oscillators, etc.) at an advanced level. Extensive chapter bibliographies. *Class No:* 621.38.04(035)

[4455]

VLSI Electronics: microstructure science. Einspruch, N.G., *ed.* New York, etc., Academic Press, 1981-. v.1-. illus., diagrs., graphs, tables.

A multi-volume treatise on Very Large Scale Integration, each volume independent, which aims to provide 'a comprehensive exposition that describes the state of this science and technology and that assesses trends for the future of VLSI electronics and the scientific base that supports its development ... Includes subjects ... from microscopic aspects of materials behaviour and device performance ... through ... fabrication of VLSI circuits ... to ... VLSI in systems applications'. (*Editor's Preface*).

'The books ... contain a very impressive and well-presented multi-disciplinary cross-section of today's state-of-the-art in microelectronics and should certainly be part of the library of anyone who is seriously interested in the subject' (Review of v.1-6, *Microelectronics J.* v.15(1), Jan. 1984, p.60). *Class No:* 621.38.04(035)

[4456]

VLSI Handbook. Einspruch, N.G., *ed.* Orlando, Florida, Academic Press, 1985. xxvi, 902p. diagrs., graphs, tables. £93. (*Handbooks in science and technology.*) ISBN: 0122341007.

74 contributors. Aims to be 'a comprehensive compilation to provide data, performance application information, and guidelines for the entire range of VLSI [Very Large Scale Integration] technology' - circuits, fabrication and applications (*Preface*). 52 chapters cover circuit design, manufacturing processes, applications in microprocessors, RAM, ROM, computers, electronic warfare, radar, medicine, communications, image and speech processing, automobiles. Chapter references, bibliographies and glossaries vary in provision. Certain chapters contain large numbers of tables and figures. Excellent index. *Class No:* 621.38.04(035)

[4457]

WILLIAMS, T. **The Circuit designer's companion.** Oxford, Butterworth Heinemann, 1991. vi,302p. illus., diagrs., graphs, tables. $75. ISBN: 0750611421.

9 chapters, with emphasis on reliability in analog circuit design: 1. Grounding and wiring - 2. Printed circuits ... 5. Laser integrated circuits ... 9. General product design. Appended: British & related IEC standards. Bibliography; index, p.295-305. 'Highly recommended' (*Choice*, January 1992, p.772). *Class No:* 621.38.04(035)

Dictionaries

Polyglot

[4458]

NAGY, P. *and* TARJÁN, G. **Elsevier's dictionary of microelectronics:** in English, German, French, Spanish and Japanese. Amsterdam, etc., Elsevier, 1988. £171. ISBN: 0444426590.

8,521 English-base terms, with translations into other languages; Romanicized Japanese. Indexes: English (in place of cross references in the main list; 12,293 items); German (12,866); French (11,491); Spanish (10,956); Japanese (11,697). *Class No:* 621.38.04(038)=00

English

[4459]

DOUGLAS-YOUNG, J. **Illustrated encyclopedic dictionary of electronic circuits.** Englewood Cliffs, N.J., Prentice-Hall, 1983. 444p. diagrs., circuits, tables. $27.95. ISBN: 0134507347.

Aims to give guidance on choice, design building, testing and fault identification of several hundred basic electronic circuits. Alphabetical arrangement, with descriptions, schematic diagrams, parts lists and cross references. Appendices of useful data. Index of limited utility. *Class No:* 621.38.04(038)=20

[4460]

HOLLAND, R.C. **Illustrated dictionary of microelectronics and microcomputers.** Oxford, etc., Pergamon Press, 1985. v, 162p. diagrs., tables. £28; £11.75. ISBN: 0080316344, Hardback; 0080316352, Flexicover.

About 850 terms, including cross-references, with definitions and explanations ranging from a few words to several hundred, supported by diagrams. Clear and simple. Includes a number of manufacturing terms from the trade literature. 'For those bewildered by the new language of microelectronics it is a very useful dictionary [which explains] often-used words, phrases and abbreviations' (*Aslib book list*, v.50(9), Sept. 1985, item 441). *Class No:* 621.38.04(038)=20

[4461]

—PLANT, M. Microelectronics, A to Z. Harlow, Essex, Longman, 1985. xiv, 209p. £2.95. ISBN: 0582892856.

Upwards of 2,000 entries, including cross-references, with terms defined and, in many cases, explained in simple language. *Class No:* 621.38.04(038)=20

German

[4462]
BINDMANN, W. Fachwörterbuch mikroelektronik: Englisch-Deutsch, Deutsch-Englisch. [Dictionary of microelectronics: English-German, German-English.] 4th ed. Berlin, Paris, Hatier, 1992. 686p. £89.95. ISBN: 3861170299.
First published 1984.
Equivalents of *c.*29,000 terms in each half in the fields of microelectronics, solid state physics, microlithography, integrated circuits, microcomputers, software and peripherals. Includes abbreviations. No distinction between British and American English *Class No:* 621.38.04(038)=30

[4463]
—**ATTIYATE, Y.H.** *and* **SHAH, R.R.** Wörterbuch der Mikroelektronik und Mikroechnertechnick. [Dictionary of microelectronics and microcomputer technology: Deutsch-Englisch, Englisch-Deutsch.] Düsseldorf, VDI Verlag, 1984. vi, 469p.
Gives equivalents for *c.*7,500, with definitions and explanations for *c.*2,000 key terms, - intended to be 'easily understood and yet precise' (*Preface*). This objective has been met. Wide scope, including data processing and application in automation and production. American spellings (*e.g.* fiber optics). *Class No:* 621.38.04(038)=30

[4464]
—Wörterbuch der Mikroelektronik. [Dictionary of microelectronics: English-German, German-English.] Vaterstetten, IWT Verlag; Düsseldorf, VDI Verlag, 1980. 218p. $39.95. ISBN: 3883220019, IWT; 3184190692, VDI.
Records *c.*7,000 terms in current use, with emphasis on industrial needs. Includes entries under abbreviations. A supplementary volume for new technology is planned. *Class No:* 621.38.04(038)=30

Tables & Data Books

[4465]
MARKUS, J., *comp.* **Digital circuits ready-reference.** New York, etc., McGraw-Hill, 1982. xx, 162p. £21.95. (*Ready-reference series.*) ISBN: 0070404577.
A collection of circuits for clock signals, converters, data transmission, memories, microprocessors, etc., drawn from journals, books and trade literature. Component values, brief description and bibliographical citation for source are given for each. Author and subject indexes. Others in series: *Electronics projects ready-reference* (1982. 181p.) *e.g.* burglar alarms, battery chargers, remote control; *Popular circuits ready-reference* (1982. 216p.) *e.g.* amplifiers, converters, oscillators; *Special circuits ready-reference* (1982. 234p.) *e.g.* audio-control, fibre optics, optoelectronics; *Communications circuits ready-reference* (1982. xvii, 216p.)
Author and McGraw-Hill have published 4 earlier, large collections: *Sourcebook of electronic circuits* (1968. viii, 888p), 3,000 circuits; *Electronic circuits manual* (1971. ix, 988p), 3,180 circuits; *Guidebook of electronic circuits* (1974. 1067p), 3,600 circuits; *Modern electronic circuits reference manual* (1980. 1238p), 2,700 circuits. These 9v. together contain over 14,000 circuits and, it is claimed, virtually no duplication. *Class No:* 621.38.04(083)

[4466]
—**MARKUS, J.** *and* **WESTON, C.** Essential circuit reference guide. New York, McGraw-Hill, 1988. 531p. diagrs. $59.50. ISBN: 0070402623.
Selection of 'classic' circuits culled from 3 of Markus's earlier works. Diagrams and schematics of available, still-in-use circuits for industrial and hobby applications. 62 sections, arranged by type of circuit. Author and subject indexes. List of sources. *Class No:* 621.38.04(083)

Printed Circuits

[4467]
BÖHSS, G., *comp.* **Dictionary of printed circuit technology;** English-German/German-English. Oxford, etc., Elsevier, 1985. 185p. £45.30. ISBN: 0444995552.
About 7,000 terms, including phrases, with equivalents. Genders given. Clear presentation, sans serif typeface used (bold for entry terms). *Class No:* 621.38.049.75

[4468]
COOMBS, C.F., Jr., *ed.* **Printed circuits handbook.** 3rd ed. New York, etc., McGraw-Hill, 1988. xxxvi, [884]p. illus., diagrs., graphs, tables. $59.50. ISBN: 0070126097.
First published 1967; previous ed. 1979.
27 contributors. Aims to provide in one volume the information needed to design, manufacture, test and repair printed wiring boards and assemblies (*Preface*). 8 parts, 35 chapters (1. Introduction to printed wiring - 2. Engineering - 3. Fabrication (the largest part; 8 chapters, 241p.) - 4. Assembly and test - 5. Soldering - 6. Quality and reliability - 7 Multilayer circuits - 8 Flexible circuits). The newest techniques, *e.g.* surface mount technology (SMT), are generously covered. Numerous tables, chapter references and a glossary are

....(contd.)
valuable adjuncts to a clear, logically-presented, essentially practical text. Good index. Emphasis is heavy on US sources. *Class No:* 621.38.049.75

[4469]
HINCH, S.W. Handbook of surface mount technology. New York, Wiley; Harlow, Longman, 1988. xvi,481p. illus., diagrs., graphs, tables. ISBN: 0582005175, UK; 047021094x, US.
15 chapters in 4 parts: I. Overview - II. Components - III. Design - IV. Manufacturing technology. 2 appendices (Acceptance criteria for visual inspection; glossary); index (9p.). Surface mount technology (SMT) has made 'dramatic changes' in the manufacture of electronic assemblies; Hinch (of Hewlett-Packard) has attempted a 'thorough, balanced treatment ... from a single source' of the skimpy and fragmented literature (*Preface,* p.v). For practising engineers. One of the first works in a new field, this is 'highly recommended for technical libraries' (*Choice,* April 1989, p.1360). *Class No:* 621.38.049.75

[4470]
SCARLETT, J.A., *ed.* **The Multilayer printed circuit board handbook.** Ayr, Electrochemical Publications, 1985. xxiii, 590p. illus., diagrs., tables. £59. ISBN: 0901150150.
24 chapters by 17 UK expert contributors cover the entire field of multilayer PCBs. The editor is responsible for over one third of the text, including a wide-ranging Introduction (60p.). Boards made by printing, etching, bonding and plating processes are covered and there are chapters on quality and inspection, design, repair, presses and machining, with a final chapter on the Multiwire process. Emphasis throughout is on manufacture. Effective subject index but no glossary.
'... is an essential reference source for designers and provides comprehensive, authoritative guidance on the design, manufacture and use of expensive and complex types of PCBs' (*Microelectronics journal,* v.16(14), July 1985, p.35).
'This is undoubtedly the most authoritative and comprehensive book yet written on multilayer circuit boards and should be on the shelf of every multilayer circuit board manufacturer and user' (*Microelectronics and reliability,* v.25(6), 1985, p.1157). *Class No:* 621.38.049.75

[4471]
ZARROW, P. *and* **KOPP, D. Surfact mount technology: terms and concepts.** Oxford, Butterworth-Heinemann, 1995. 166p. £17.99 ISBN: 0750693142.
About 1,000 terms defined briefly, each followed by a short explanation of the meaning and how it fits into the surface mount industry. *Class No:* 621.38.049.75

Connectors

[4472]
CLAYTON, P.A., *ed.* **Handbook of electronic connectors.** Ayr, Scotland, Electrochemical Publications, 1982. xix, 297p. illus., diagrs., graphs, tables. £47. ISBN: 0901150118.
14 contributors. 6 chapters on the main groups of connectors (RF interconnection, multiway connectors, printed circuit board connectors, hermetic and underwater connectors, flat cable systems); 2 chapters on fibre optics connectors; 1 each on plating finishes and quality control. *Class No:* 621.38.06

[4473]
HARPER, C.A., *ed.* **Electronic packaging and interconnection handbook.** New York, McGraw-Hill, 1991. v.p. illus., diagrs., graphs, tables. $79.50. ISBN: 0070266840.
3 sections: 1. Fundamental technologies - 2. Interconnection technologies - 3. System packaging technologies. References to industry and military standards and specifications. Detailed, analytical index. *Class No:* 621.38.06

[4474]
—**HARPER, C.A.** *and* **MILLER, M.B.** Electronic packaging, microelectronics, and interconnection dictionary. New York, etc., McGraw-Hill, 1993. vii, 235p. ISBN: 0070266883.
About 6,000 terms, briefly defined. Acronyms, symbols and abbreviations appended. *Class No:* 621.38.06

Semi-conductors

Abbreviations & Symbols

[4475]
BRITISH STANDARDS INSTITUTION. Specification for letter symbols for semiconductor devices and integrated microcircuits. London, BSI, 1980. 36p. (*BS 3363: 1980.*)
Supplement 1: 1981. 20p. Supplement 2: 1981. 16p. Confirmed 1988. Lists international symbols for the description of semiconductors and integrated microcircuits. *Class No:* 621.382(003)

Databases

[4476]

SCPR: (Semiconductor Parameter Retrieval). Englewood, Colorado, Information Handling Services.

An alpha-numeric data bank containing technical descriptive data for over 160,000 semiconductor devices available from 150 manufacturers and distributors, with references to location of the maker's data sheet in IHS's Visual Search Microfilm Service (VSMF) and company information. Updated 3 times pa. *Class No:* 621.382(003.4)

Indexes

[4477]

Semicon international indexes. London, Semicon Indexes, 1998. 3v. looseleaf. tables

V.1: *International transistor index.* 24th ed. ISBN: 0904944964.

V.2: *Diodes and thrysitors.* 17th ed. ISBN: 0904944905.

V.3: *Integrated circuits.* 16th ed. ISBN: 090494493x.

Provides basic information for the identification and testing of a large range of semiconductor devices. Data include maximum ratings, characteristics and suppliers. Update packs are available.
Class No: 621.382(014)

Encyclopaedias

[4478]

GRAYSON, M., *ed.* **Encyclopedia of semiconductor technology.** New York, etc., Wiley, 1984. xxviii, 940p. illus., diagrs. £94.95. (*Encyclopedia reprint series.*) ISBN: 0471881023.

34 lengthy articles, alphabetically arranged under subject, all reprinted from the 3rd ed. of the Kirk-Othmer *Encyclopedia of chemical technology.* They cover methods of manufacture, properties and uses of semiconductors and elements from which they are derived. A comprehensive index with heavy emphasis on chemical compounds facilitates reference. It must be remembered that many of the articles (from the early part of the alphabet) appeared in Kirk-Othmer as far back as 1980. *Class No:* 621.382(031)

[4479]

MAHAJAN, S. *and* **KIMERLING, L.C. Concise encyclopedia of semiconducting materials and related technologies.** Oxford, Pergamon Press, 1992. xxiii,582p. illus., diagrs. £130. (*Advances in materials science and engineering, 8.*) ISBN: 008034724x.

Incorporates relevant material from the *Encyclopedia of materials science and engineering* (1986) and newly commissioned articles. Topics include growth of bulk crystals, metallization, passivation. *Class No:* 621.382(031)

Handbooks & Manuals

[4480]

Digital systems reference book. Holdsworth, B. *and* Martin, G.R. Oxford, Butterworth Heinemann, 1991. v.p. illus., diagrs. $250; £120. ISBN: 0750610085.

Covers mathematical techniques, integrated circuit technologies and software design to applications. Criticized in *Choice* for the inconsistent use of British, American and international standards, but nevertheless 'an important reference tool' (*Choice,* April 1992, p.1205). *Class No:* 621.382(035)

[4481]

Handbook for digital signal processing. Mitra, S.K. *and* Kaiser, J.F., *eds.* New York, Wiley, 1993. xxxi, 1268p. illus., graphs, tables. £80. ISBN: 0471619957.

Aim is a 'distillation ... of the central ideas ... and primary methods of DSP' (*Preface*). 16 chapters, well-documented and closely subdivided (*e.g.* 4. 'Finite impulse response filter design' has 13 sections, 6p. of references). Detailed, analytical index, p.1243-68. 'A handy reference ... highly recommended' (*Choice,* December 1993, p.634). *Class No:* 621.382(035)

[4482]

MOSS, T.S., *ed.* **Handbook on semiconductors.** Rev. and enlarged ed. Amsterdam, etc., Elsevier, 1992-94. 4v. diagrs., graphs, tables. ISBN: 0444893881, set.

1. *Basic properties of semiconductors.* 1992. xiv, 1204p. £219.

2. *Optical properties of semiconductors.* 1994. xv, 857p. £194.

3. *Materials, properties and preparation.* 1994. xv, 2388p. £439.

4. *Device physics.* 1993. xiv, 1230p. £94.

V.4 contains 13 chapters by 24 expert contributors. Extensive references; volume author and subject indexes.
Class No: 621.382(035)

Dictionaries

[4483]

WRIGHT, H.C. Semiconductor reference book: from acceptor impurities to zeher breakdown. Bromley, Kent, Chartwell-Bratt, 1991. 78p. diagrs. £8.95. ISBN: 9144349017.

Brief entries (1 to 3 per page) with definitions, mathematical formulae, diagrams, 'further reading'. School level and upwards. 'A very useful book' (*Reference reviews,* V.6(2) 1992, p.27), particularly at the price. *Class No:* 621.382(038)

Tables & Data Books

[4484]

BEADLE, W.J., *and others, ed.* **Quick reference manual for silicon integrated circuit technology.** New York, etc., Wiley, 1985. 736p. diagrs., graphs, tables. £75. ISBN: 0471815888.

15 sections covering fundamental constants, processing data, evaluation of processes, device properties. Presented in many hundreds of tables, curves, graphs, measurements, and drawn from numerous cited sources. Supported by 1,200-item index.

'It is particularly useful to have a concise description of measurement techniques and theory alongside data ... The data which are presented has [sic] been carefully assessed and sifted ... [The volume's] generally high quality and ease of use [justify] the publisher's price' (*Solid-state and electron devices (IEEE Proceedings I*), v. 133(1), Feb. 1986, p.28). *Class No:* 621.382(083)

[4485]

—**Semiconductor general-purpose replacements.** Indianapolis, Indiana, H.W. Sams, 1978. 1116p. $14.95. ISBN: 0672215764.

Lists 180,000 replacement devices by reference number, covering 10 US manufacturers and ranging over transistors, diodes, rectifiers and integrated circuits. *Class No:* 621.382(083)

Electron Photocells

[4486]

NENTWIG, K., *comp.* **Elsevier's dictionary of opto-electronics and electro-optics:** in four languages: English/German/French/Spanish. Amsterdam, etc., Elsevier, 1986. [vii], 295p. £136. ISBN: 0444426175.

3,500 English-base terms, with German, French and Spanish equivalents, followed by indexes in each language referring to numbered entry in Basic table. No definitions and no genders given. *Class No:* 621.383

[4487]

TEXAS INSTRUMENTS. Optoelectronics data book: infrared, imaging and visible products. Berrill, D.J., *ed.* 6th ed. Bedford, Texas Instruments, 1984. [443]p. diagrs., tables. £5. ISBN: 0904047369.

First published 1974.

A collection of data sheets, application reports, etc., for more than 250 standard devices arranged in product groups (*e.g.* Infrared-emitting devices, Photodetectors, Light-emitting diodes), with sections on quality and reliability and applications. An interchangeability index links over 600 devices produced by other manufacturers with TI equivalents. *Class No:* 621.383

Telecommunications

Abbreviations & Symbols

[4488]

TAVAGLIONE, D. Acronyms and abbreviations of computer technology and telecommunication. New York, Dekker, 1993. xi, 291p. ISBN: 0824787471.

About 7,000 entries, A-Z. Use and derivation occasionally given. 2 appendices: sources; recommended references (some very dated). *Class No:* 621.39(003)

[4489]

Telecommunications acronyms and organisations. Manchester, NCC; Oxford, Blackwell, 1991. [vi], 116p. £16.95. ISBN: 1855540681.

Compiled by Logica Cambridge Ltd.

About 900 acronyms. 5 sections: 1. Acronyms and abbreviations - 2. Structure and function of international organisations - 3. European telecommunications organisations - 4. Standardisation organisations - 5. Users' organisations. Small format. *Class No:* 621.39(003)

Databases

[4490]

Telecommunications. New York, EIC/Intelligence, Inc.

Formerly TELECOM. Covers Oct. 1984 to date. A bibliographic data base providing references, with abstracts, to world literature on telecommunications, including commercial and economic aspects. Derived from journal articles, conference papers, reports, patents, etc. File size: over 4,000 items. Updated monthly. Hosts: DIALOG, ESA-IRS. Printed version: *Telecommunications abstracts*. *Class No:* 621.39(003.4)

[4491]

TELEDOC. Issy les Moulineaux, Centre National d'Études des Télécommunications.

Covers 1972 to date. A bibliographic data base providing references, with abstracts, to world literature on telecommunications, electronics and related subjects, including acoustics, optics, computing. File size: 105,000 items. Updated monthly. About 8,000 additions pa. Available via QUESTEL. Printed version: *Bulletin signalétique des télécommunications*. In English and French. *Class No:* 621.39(003.4)

CD-ROM

[4492]

Computing and communications. London, SilverPlatter, 1999. CD-ROM. 2pa.

About 30,000 bibliographic records from 6 databases. Covers popular computing, telecommunications, interactive and information science services. Emphasis in on Australian and New Zealand material and includes references to journal and newspaper articles, theses, research reports and conference proceedings. *Class No:* 621.39(003.40)

Bibliographies

[4493]

BREWSTER, R.L. 'Communications engineering'. *Information sources in engineering*. K.W. Mildren and P.J. Hicks, eds. (3rd ed., 1996), p.441-50. 3rd ed. London, Bowker Saur, 1996. £80. ISBN: 1857390571.

Covers general communications theory, the IEE communications telecommunications series ('the most comprehensive collection of books covering the complete range of telecommunications topics', p.443), networks, mobile communications, satellite and radio systems, optical communications, journals, standards, conferences and databases. *Class No:* 621.39(01)

Encyclopaedias

[4494]

The Froelich/Kent encyclopedia of telecommunications. Froelich, F.E. *and* Kent, A., *eds.* New York, Dekker, 1991-. V.1-. illus., diagrs., graphs, tables.

The encyclopedia is being published in alphabetical sequence. V.11 (1996. vii, 531p.) has 20 contributors to 15 articles ('Microwave communication' to 'Modern optical character recognition'). No volume indexes. *Class No:* 621.39(031)

[4495]

GARDNER, R. *and* **SHORTELLE, D. From talking drums to the Internet:** an encyclopedia of communications technology. Santa Barbara, Ca., ABC-CLIO, 1997. 355p. illus., diagrs. $65. ISBN: 0874368324.

Entries (A-Z) cover people, organizations, techniques, concepts, terms, historical events, social change and technology. *Class No:* 621.39(031)

Handbooks & Manuals

[4496]

The Digital signal processing handbook. Madisetti, V.K. *and* Williams, D.B., *eds.* Boca Raton, Fa., CRC Press, 1998. v.p. illus., diagrs. graphs, tables. $130. ISBN: 0849385725.

Published in association with the IEEE.

138 contributors; 14 major sections covering basic signals and systems, signal processing, filtering digital audio communications, speech processing, and image processing and hardware. Also available on CD-ROM ($129). *Class No:* 621.39(035)

[4497]

Electronic communications handbook. Inglis, A.F., *ed.* New York, McGraw-Hill, 1988. v.p. illus., diagrs., graphs, tables. £59.50. ISBN: 0070317119.

22 chapters, closely subdivided, in 2 parts: 1. Transmission and switching technologies - 2. Electronic communications systems. 29 contributors, most from industry. 12p. detailed, analytical index. 'A compendium of reference data' (*Preface*). *Class No:* 621.39(035)

[4498]

NATIONAL COMPUTING CENTRE. Handbook of data communications. 2nd ed. Oxford, NCC, Blackwell, 1993. x, 491p. diagrs. £25. ISBN: 1855540029.

First published 1975; slightly revised 1982.

'To be used as a reference to help in the understanding of a wide range of data communication topics' (*Preface*). 14 chapters by various hands in 5 parts: Transmission theory - Coherent data transmission - Distributed connection services - Network management - The future. 3 appendices (1. Glossary, p.453-58). Detailed, analytical index, p.463-91. Well-produced; good value. *Class No:* 621.39(035)

[4499]

PETERSEN, D. Audio, video and data telecommunications. New York, McGraw-Hill, 1992. 344p. illus. £17.95. ISBN: 0077074270.

The basic theories of telecommunications, with modern applications. Practical examples and case studies. *Class No:* 621.39(035)

[4500]

Telecommunications engineer's reference book. Mazda, F., *ed.* 2nd ed. Oxford, Butterworth-Heinemann, 1998. 1120p. diagrs., graphs, tables. £110. ISBN: 0240514912.

About 70 contributors. 62 chapters in 4 sections: 1. Mathematical techniques - 2. Physical phenomena - 3. Communications fundamentals - 4. Communications applications. Topics covered include network management, standards, switching, voice processing, fibre optics, etc. Glossary; index. *Class No:* 621.39(035)

[4501]

TOOLEY, M. Data communications pocket book. 2nd ed. Oxford, Butterworth-Heinemann, 1992. 176p. diagrs., tables. £10.95. ISBN: 0750604271.

First published 1989.

Covers ISDN, LAN software, network operating systems, fault-finding on RS-232 systems, optical fibre technology and IEEE interface standards. Samll, handy format; part of the 'Newnes' series. *Class No:* 621.39(035)

Dictionaries

Polyglot

[4502]

BETTEX, J. Lexique telecom lexicon: Français-Deutsch-Anglais Crossier; Lausanne, Datelec, 1994. [x], 206p. ISBN: 2970006502.

About 500 terms defined in French and German. English index. *Class No:* 621.39(038)=00

[4503]

CLASON, W.E., *comp.* **Elsevier's telecommunication dictionary in six languages:** English/American, French, Spanish, Italian, Dutch and German. 2nd rev. ed. Amsterdam, etc., Elsevier, 1976. [ix], 604p. £22.12.

First ed. (compiled by A. Visser) 1955, with Danish as the basic language. 7,095 numbered terms, A-Z, in English/American main section, with equivalents in other languages. Alphabetical indexes in other languages refer to numbered entries in main section. Genders are given. Subject area indicated for 35 categories. *Class No:* 621.39(038)=00

[4504]

Elsevier's dictionary of communications in English, German, French and Russian. Delijska, B. *and* Manilova, P., *comps.* Amsterdam, Elsevier, 1997. [viii], 1043p. £131.90. ISBN: 0444824391.

Covers fields relating to technical communications, including theory, computer and satellite, broadcasting, information systems, data conversion, security and cryptography. About 13,000 entries in English, with equivalents and indexes in the other languages. *Class No:* 621.39(038)=00

[4505]

Wörterbuch der telekommunikations- technik. [Dictionary of telecommunication technology.] 3rd ed. Berlin, Springer, 1997. 428p. £57. ISBN: 3540620680.

First published 1989; 2nd ed. 1991.

Covers German, French and English, with about 5000 entry words for each language. Produced by German Telecom. *Class No:* 621.39(038)=00

English

[4506]

ARIES, S.J. Dictionary of telecommunications. London, Butterworths, 1981. [iv], 329p. diagrs., tables. £15. ISBN: 0408003286.

About 3,200 entries, including cross-references. Definitions, many supplemented by extensive explanatory material and some illustrated by diagrams, cover the entire field of telecommunications (defined here as 'the transmission of information from one point to another by wire, radio, optical or other electromagnetic systems').

Deliberate and coordinated overlap with S.W. Amos' *Dictionary of electronics* and R.S. Roberts' *Dictionary of audio, radio and video*

....(contd.)

(qv). Aims to include North American terminology where this differs. Appendix (p.317-324) identifies almost 500 abbreviations and acronyms. *Class No:* 621.39(038)=20

[4507]
CLAYTON, J. McGraw-Hill illustrated telecom dictionary. New York, etc., McGraw-Hill, 1998. 501p. illus., diagrs. $29.95. ISBN: 0070120633.

About 2,000 terms briefly defined. A section on numbers from 0 to 965TD precedes the terms. 6 appendixes (international calling codes; cable colour codes, etc.). 'The best reference work in the field' ('Reference books bulletin', *Booklist*, December 15, 1998, p.700). *Class No:* 621.39(038)=20

[4508]
GRAHAM, J. and LOWE, S. The Facts on File dictionary of telecommunications. 2nd ed. New York, Facts on File, 1991. 240p. diagrs., tables. $24.95. ISBN: 0816020299.

First published 1983.

Covers acronyms, abbreviations, computer-related terms and a few commercial products. Major concepts have extended definitions. 'Highly recommended for academic and technical libraries' (*Library Journal*, 1 July 1991, p.86,88). *Class No:* 621.39(038)=20

[4509]
HELD, G. Dictionary of communications technology: terms, definitions and abbreviations. 2nd ed. Chichester, etc., Wiley, 1995. x, 692p. illus., tables. £80. ISBN: 0471975168.

About 18,000 terms, briefly defined. Includes information on trade names. Definitions of numbers (*e.g.* 2B1Q) appear at the end. Comprehensive; compiled with the assistance of commercial communications organizations. *Class No:* 621.39(038)=20

[4510]
LANGLEY, G. Telephony's dictionary. 2nd ed. Chicago, Ill., Telephony Publishing Corp./London, Pitman, 1986. xi, 402p. . £24.95. ISBN: 0273026690.

Cover title (as published in UK): 'International dictionary of telecommunications'. First published 1982.

16,000 terms covering the entire field of telecommunications, with many terms from computing and data processing, defined or explained, briefly or at considerable length (from a few words to 200). Appendices: acronyms and abbreviations; SI units and the electromagnetic spectrum terminology. *Class No:* 621.39(038)=20

[4511]
ROBERTS, R.S. Dictionary of audio, radio and video. London, Butterworths, 1981. 256p. diagrs., graphs, circuits. £15. ISBN: 0408001356.

Definition and explanation of *c*.1700 terms aimed at general readers. Well cross-referenced. Deliberate and coordinated overlap with S.W. Amos' *Dictionary of electronics* and S.V. Aries' *Dictionary of telecommunications* (qv). Aims to include North American terminology where this differs. *Class No:* 621.39(038)=20

[4512]
WEIK, M.H. Communications standard dictionary. 2nd ed. New York, Van Nostrand Reinhold, 1989. xii, 1219p. illus., diagrs., tables. ISBN: 0442205562.

First published 1983.

Intended as 'a comprehensive compilation of terms and definitions used in the field of communications' - which is widely defined. Over 12,000 entries, abbreviations and cross-references, with definitions based wherever possible on standards. Definitions generally range from 3 to 12 lines. New topics for this edition include communication services, encryption, local-area networks, surveillance, etc. *Class No:* 621.39(038)=20

German

[4513]
FERRETTI, V. Dictionary of electronics, computing and telecommunication: English-German, German-English. [Wörterbuch der elektronik, datentechnik und der telekommunikation.] Berlin, Springer Verlag, 1992. 2v. (xxviii, 609p. + xxviii, 636p.) £58.50 each. ISBN: 3540541101, (G/E); 3540542027, (E/G).

About 60,000 entries in each half. Prelims. include 'Applied morphology of subject fields'. Bibliography, 5p. Also available on CD-ROM. *Class No:* 621.39(038)=30

French

[4514]
LUCCA, J. de. Dictionnaire des télécommunications et de l'internet, avec une list d'acronymes sur CD-ROM. [Dictionary of telecommunications and the Internet. with a list of acronyms on CD-ROM.] 2nd ed. Paris, Masson, 1997. 493p. £34.95.

Previous ed. 1988 as *Dictionnaire des télécommunications*.

Over 35,000 entry terms in English, with equivalents in French. *Class No:* 621.39(038)=40

[4515]
WITTERING, S. French dictionary of telecommunications: French-English, English-French. [Dictionnaire anglais des télécommunications: français-anglais, anglais-français.] London, Routledge, 1997. xxviii, 440p. £85. ISBN: 0415133483.

About 30,000 terms in each language. Subjects covered include television and video, radio, telephony and telegraphy, data transmission, signalling, switching, applications and service, terminal and peripheral apparatus, parts and materials, computing, control technology, testing procedures and power systems. *Class No:* 621.39(038)=40

Spanish

[4516]
FREEMAN, R.L. English-Spanish, Spanish-English dictionary of communications and electronic terms. Cambridge Univ. Press, 1972. xii, 206p. £7.50. ISBN: 0521080800.

Contains, 8,000 English terms with Spanish equivalents and 9,000 Spanish terms with English equivalents. Coverage extends to data processing, reliability, video and space communications. Additional features: lists of abbreviations and initialisms with equivalents in each language; words and abbreviations deriving from 'decibel'. *Class No:* 621.39(038)=60

[4517]
Routledge Spanish dictionary of telecommunications: Spanish-English, English-Spanish. London, Routledge, 1998. 550p. £85. ISBN: 0415152666.

About 30,000 terms in both languages. Covers applications and services, climate control, components and materials, computing, control technology, power systems, radio-based technologies, signalling, switching, television and video, and transmission. *Class No:* 621.39(038)=60

Reviews & Abstracts

[4518]
Referativnyǐ zhurnal. 64. Elektrosviaz. Moscow, VINITI, 1968-. Monthly. R64. ISSN: 01347772.

Previously as *Referativnyǐ zhurnal Radiotechnika i electosviaz* (1963-66).

About 9,000 indicative and informative signed abstracts pa. Covers all aspects of telecommunications in 12 sections (*e.g.* Communication theory - Telecommunication equipment ... Telegraphy - Data transmission - Telephony - Facsimile transmission ... Power supply). Issue indexes of authors, periodicals abstracted and patents. Annual author and subject indexes. *Class No:* 621.39(048)

Progress Reports

[4519]
HORROCKS, J. Future trends in telecommunications. New York, Wiley, 1993. 496p. illus. £39.95. (*Wiley series in communications and distributed systems*.) ISBN: 047193724x.

Covers 4 main areas: fibre optics; coding; radio; OSL. *Class No:* 621.39(055)

Yearbooks & Directories

[4520]
Communications: the most comprehensive guide to the UK telecommunications industry. Egan, M., *ed.* London, Macmillan, 1986. vii, 290p. £65. ISBN: 0333386906.

Directory of 2,000 companies, A-Z, with usual information plus brief descriptions of their activities and products, complemented by classified section listing these firms under one more of 80 category headings, *e.g.* Answering machines, Message switching systems, Viewdata. Also brief listings of trade associations, consultancies, etc., and reviews of major organizations, particularly British Telecom. '... an essential reference source for telecommunications managers, telecommunications and computer companies ... (*Telecommunications journal*, v.54(8), 1987, p.541). *Class No:* 621.39(058)

[4521]
Telecommunications directory 1996-97: an international guide to organizations, systems, and services concerned with the interactive electronic transmission of voice, image, and data. Krol, J., *ed.* New York, Gale, 1996. 1209p. ISSN: 10558454.

First published 1983.

About 2,500 entries from 80 countries, A-Z. Data include name, contact details, general description; specific applications; means of access; geographic areas served, etc. Brief glossary. Indexes: function/ service; geographic; personal name; master name/keyword. *Class No:* 621.39(058)

Tables & Data Books

[4522]

FREEMAN, R.L. Reference manual for telecommunications engineering. 2nd ed. New York, etc., Wiley 1994. 2308p., illus., diagrs., graphs, charts, tables, nomograms. $195; £125. ISBN: 0471579602.

First published 1985.

Aims 'to provide a central source of basic information' for designers and users of all kinds of telecommunications systems. Content is assembled in 31 chapters (*e.g.* Signaling, Fiber optics transmission, Radio transmission, Electromagnetic interference), each type with introductory material, essential information, references and, often, a bibliography. Most of the material is drawn from authoritative sources, which are identified. Index of more than 3,500 entries. 'A necessary reference tool for any library' (*Choice*, May 1994, p.1412).
Class No: 621.39(083)

[4523]

MARKUS, J. Communications circuits ready-reference. New York, etc., McGraw-Hill, 1982. xvii, 216p. diagrs. (*Ready reference series.*) ISBN: 0070404607.

A collection of about 400 circuits grouped in 15 alphabetically arranged chapters (*e.g.* Antennas, Frequency modulation, Receivers, Telephones, Teleprinters, Televisions, Transmitters). Circuit diagrams, component values, brief descriptions and bibliographical citation for sources are given for each. Author and subject indexes. For details of other four vols. in the 'Ready reference series' see entry at 621.38.04(083). *Class No:* 621.39(083)

Standards

[4524]

HORROCKS, J. European guide to telecommunications standards. Pirbright, Surrey, Horrocks Technology, 1995. 2v. looseleaf. ISBN: 1900015021.

V.1 is in 4 parts: 1. The European standards scene - 2. European organizations - 3. International organizations - 4. Subject areas (*e.g.* quality, broadband ISDN, etc.). V.2 includes lists of standards. Updates are planned. A wealth of data and information in this rapidly evolving field. *Class No:* 621.39(083.74)

[4525]

MACPHERSON, A. International telecommunication standards organizations. Boston, Mass., London, Artech House, 1990. xiii,317p. diagrs., tables. ISBN: 0890063656.

13 chapters. Focuses on international organizations and the main North American, Asian-Pacific and European standards bodies. Glossary of acronyms, p.309-17. *Class No:* 621.39(083.74)

Histories

[4526]

LEBOW, I. Information highways and byways: from the telegraph to the 21st century. New York, Institute of Electrical and Electronics Engineers, 1995. 307p. illus. $29.95. ISBN: 078031073x.

A social as well as a technical history of communications. 'Recommended' (*Choice*, February 1996, p.984).
Class No: 621.39(091)

Institutions & Associations

[4527]

International directory of telecommunications: market trends, companies, statistics and personnel. Robert, S. *and* Hay, T., *eds.* 4th ed. Harlow, Essex, Longman Group, 1990. xiv,386p. tables. £140. ISBN: 0582647382.

Profiles of *c.*800 telecommunications services companies, equipment manufacturers and broadcasting concerns. Data: company structure; address; phone and fax number; activities; turnover; product areas; operating territory. Arranged geographically. Indexes of organizations, products and key personnel. *Class No:* 621.39:061:061.2

Wave Signals

[4528]

ADAMS, M.S. *and* **HENNINGS, I.D. Optical fibres and sources for communications.** New York, Plenum, 1990. 180p. £35. (*Updates in applied physics and electrical technology.*) ISBN: 0306437112.

Includes abstracts of about 300 papers. Contents: Introduction - Propagation in multimode fibres - Propagation in monomodel fibres - Semiconductor luminescence - Light-emitting diodes - Semiconductor lasers - Selected abstracts. *Class No:* 621.391.6

[4529]

BODSON, D. *and* **BOTEZ, D., eds. Electro-optical communications dictionary.** Rochelle Park, N.J., Hayden, 1983. [viii], 168p. £22.50. ISBN: 0810409615.

Contains about 2,500 entries and cross-references covering fibre optic and lightwave communication systems 'consistent with international, federal, industry, and technical society standards' (*Preface*). Definitions are therefore full and are often annotated. An appendix contains almost 200 acronyms and abbreviations.
Class No: 621.391.6

[4530]

CHRISTMAS, P. EDI implementation and security. Oxford, Elsevier, 1994. 114p. (looseleaf) diagrs. £175. ISBN: 1856171833.

6 sections: 1. A guide to EDI - 2. EDI The way forward - 3. EDI standards - 4. X400/EDI and the law - 5. EDI security - 6. EDI in finance. 3 appendices: glossary of terms; glossary of acronyms; products and suppliers. *Class No:* 621.391.6

[4531]

CLARRICOATS, P.J.B., ed. Progress in optical communications. London, P. Peregrinus, 1980-82. 2v. (*IEE Reprint series, v.3-4.*)
    1. 1980. 247p. £14.30. ISBN: 090604832x.
    2. 1982. 328p. £25. ISBN: 0906048842.

Collections of letters (brief communications) to *Electronics letters*, 1978/79 and 1980/81 respectively. Each has groupings covering: fibre theory and measurement; fibre properties, design and manufacture; components and splices; systems and instruments. V.2 additionally has a section on sources and detectors. Because *Electronics letters* has played a major role in disseminating research results in this field and practises strict refereeing of submitted letters, these volumes constitute a valuable source of information. Subject and author indexes. Reviews in *Electronics and power* (v.26(12), 1982, p.905; v.30(4), 1984, p.325) commend them for beginners in the subject.
Class No: 621.391.6

[4532]

GEISLER, J., *and others*. Optical fibres. Oxford, etc., Pergamon, 1986. xiv, 635p. illus., diagrs. (*EPO Applied technology series, v. 5.*) ISBN: 0080305776.

Aims to explain the technology 'from a practical point of view by making use of the latest information described in patent and other literature from all over the world' (*Foreword*) based on the files of the European Patent Office by three of its examinees. They present a well-structured literature survey of around 1,100 national and international patents (including about 300 US, 300 Japanese, 100 British, 100 French and 75 German) in simple language, supported by ample illustration. 3 parts: Making optical fibres; Connectors, terminals, branches; Optical fibre transmission. Indexes of patent numbers, patentees and specific subjects. *Class No:* 621.391.6

[4533]

LAN Buyers' guide. Bath, Elan Business Publishing, 1995. 448p. ISBN: 0951909681.

Sections: File servers and work stations - Bridges and routers - Hubs - LAN adaptors - Other hardware (gateways, etc.) - LAN software - Services - Company profiles (*c.*500 organizations).
Class No: 621.391.6

[4534]

WEIK, M.H. Fiber optics standard dictionary. 3rd ed. New York, Chapman & Hall, 1997. xxiii, 1218p. £85. ISBN: 0412122413.

2nd ed. 1989

The 3rd ed. is much expanded to 16,000 entries. An extended preface and introduction establish the encyclopedic scope of the dictionary. Particular emphasis on fiber optic and lightwave communications systems. 12 pages of bibliography. An essential dictionary in its specific field. *Class No:* 621.391.6

[4535]

YEH, C. Handbook of fiber optics: theory and applications. San Diego, Calif., Academic Press, 1990. 384p. $89.95. ISBN: 0127104558.

Practical or theoretical basis for the study of optical fibres and how they contact light waves along their length. Index.
Class No: 621.391.6

Radio & Television Apparatus

Dictionaries

German

[4536]

ARD [Arbeitsgemeinschaft der öffentlich rechlichen Rundfunkanstalten der Bundesrepublik Deutschland], *comp.* **Dictionary of radio and television terms, English-German, German-English;** compiled and edited by ARD ... in collaboration with the BBC ... and the ZDF. 2nd ed. London, New York, etc. Heyden, 1975. xxi, 199p. ISBN: 085501251x.

First published 1972 by Pitman.

'Comprises about 12,000 items in the German-English part and

....(contd.)

about 17,000 items in the English-German part' (*Foreword*). Based on a German-French dictionary published in 1970. Includes a brief joint list of abbreviations (p.xiii-xxi). Genders given for German nouns. *Class No:* 621.396/.397(038)=30

Radio

Encyclopaedias

[4537]

GIBILISCO, S. **Amateur radio encyclopedia.** Blue Ridge Summit, Pa., TAB, 1994. 593p. illus., diagrs., graphs, tables. $50; $29.95. ISBN: 0830640959, (Hb); 0830640967, (Pb).

About 1,000 entries, A-Z, most 2-3 paragraphs in length. Numerous cross references. 4 appendices: CW abbraviations; 'ham radio lingo'; physical conversions; schematic symbols. Detailed, analytical index. *Class No:* 621.396(031)

Handbooks & Manuals

[4538]

The ARRL handbook for the radio amateur. Hutchinson, C.L., *ed.* 62nd ed. Newington, Conn., American Radio Relay League, 1984-. Annual. illus., diagrs., graphs, circuits, tables. US $22.50; elsewhere $24. (*Radio amateur's library, publications no. 6.*) ISBN: 087259162x, cloth; 0872590623, paper.

First published as *Radio amateur's handbook* and with this title until 61st ed. 1983.

60th ed. [640p]. had 23 chapters (1. Amateur radio - 2. Electrical laws and circuits ... 4. Solid-state fundamentals ... 6. HF transmitting - 7. VHF and UHF transmitting - 8 Receiving systems ... 14. Specialized communication systems ... 16. Test equipment and measurements ... 23. Vacuum tubes and semiconductors). Glossary (chapter 3, p.17-20); data tables (drill sizes, wire gauges, etc., chapter 17); base and case diagrams for vacuum tubes and semiconductors and operating data for transmitting valves (chapter 23). Index (11p.).

'Any amateur radio enthusiast would be ill-advised to pursue his hobby without it' (Review of 1980 ed. in *Wireless world*, v.8-6(4), April 1980, p.82). *Class No:* 621.396(035)

[4539]

ORR, W.I. **Radio handbook.** 23rd ed. Oxford, Butterworth-Heinemann, 1987. 672p. illus., diagrs., circuits, tables. £25.. ISBN: 0750699477.

First published 1967. Previous ed. 1982.

A standard handbook. Chapters cover all theoretical aspects of radio, transmitting and receiving, including components and devices, design, interference, power supplies, mobile equipment, propagation, and construction practices. Index lacks some expected terms. Little attention to audio and output stages. *Class No:* 621.396(035)

[4540]

RADIO SOCIETY OF GREAT BRITAIN. **Radio communication handbook.** 6th ed. London, the Society, 1994. 763p. illus., diagrs, graphs, circuits, tables. £9.88. ISBN: 1872309240.

First published 1938; 5th ed. 1976-77, in 2v.

Aims to cover everything the active radio amateur needs to know, from first principles and simple components to satellite and image communication. Comprehensive. *Class No:* 621.396(035)

[4541]

SAVESKIE, P.N. **Radio propagation handbook.** Blue Ridge Summit, Pa., TAB Books, 1980. 499p. diagrs., graphs, tables, maps. $17.95. ISBN: 083069949x.

Presents much information and guidance in a popular style. Covers ground wave, ionospheric, microwave, VHF, UHF and millimetre wave propagation in 8 chapters with hundreds of tables, graphs and maps. The second half of the book contains 33 appendices, including noise maps for different locations and seasons, refractivity and K-factor data for 61 worldwide locations, rain attentuation data for 29 locations. Brief index. *Class No:* 621.396(035)

Reviews & Abstracts

[4542]

Referativnyĭ zhurnal. 24. Radiotekhnika. Akademiya Nauk SSSR. Moscow, VINITI, 1967-. Monthly. illus. R280. ISSN: 0034267x.

Formerly: *Referativnyĭ zhurnal radiotekhnika i elektrosviaz* (1963-1966).

35,000 indicative and informative, signed, occasionally illustrated abstracts pa., on radio engineering, widely interpreted to include television, radar and quantum electronics. 7 sections: General and theoretical radio engineering - Aerials - Broadcasting - Radiolocation, radionavigation, radio control, television - Radio transmitters and receivers - Quantum electronics - Manufacture of radio equipment and parts. UDC numbers. English contents summary. List of journals scanned in issue no. 1 of each vol. Annual author and subject indexes. *Class No:* 621.396(048)

VHF

[4543]

JESSOP, G.R., *ed.* **VHF/UHF manual.** 4th ed. London, Radio Society of Great Britain, 1983. [viii], [528]p. illus., diagrs., graphs, circuits, tables. £8.50. ISBN: 0900612630.

First published 1969. Previous ed. 1976.

Covers the spectrum above 30 MHz. 11 chapters, *e.g.* 2. Propagation ... 4. Receivers - 5. Transmitters ... 8. Antennas - 9. Microwaves - 10. Space communications. Extensively illustrated.

'Previous editions ... gained worldwide acceptance as the standard handbook for amateur radio on v.h.f. and u.h.f. and microwaves. This fully revised and greatly expanded fourth edition provides a wealth of design and constructional information for a wide variety of equipments ...' (*Radio and electronic engineer*, v.54(5), May 1984, p.214). *Class No:* 621.396.029

Apparatus & Circuits

[4544]

Antenna engineering handbook. Johnson, R.C., *ed.* 3rd ed. New York, etc., McGraw-Hill, 1993. v.p. illus., diagrs., graphs, tables. £103.95. ISBN: 007032381x.

First published 1961, 2nd ed. 1984.

64 contributors. 46 chapters, reviewed and updated, grouped into 4 sections (Introduction and fundamentals; Types and design methods; Applications; Associated topics). Bibliographies and 11-page index. A definitive work. *Class No:* 621.396.6

[4545]

PHILLIPS, V.J. **Early radio wave detectors.** London, P. Peregrinus, 1980. xv, 222p., illus., diagrs. £16. (*IEE History of technology series, v. 2.*) ISBN: 0906048249.

Covers the period from the experiments of Heinrich Hertz in the late 1860s to the coming of the crystal detector and thermionic valve in the early 1900s with the work of J.A. Fleming and Lee De Forest. Chapter references. *Class No:* 621.396.6

Stations

[4546]

DRAKE, C.F. *and* ATTFIELD, J.B., *eds.* **Amateur radio call book.** 1984 ed. Potters Bar, Herts., Radio Society of Great Britain, 1984. 297p. ISBN: 0900612657.

More than 50,000 amateur radio call signs, with holders' names and addresses, compiled from Department of Trade and Industry records and covering England, Isle of Man, Northern Ireland, Jersey, Scotland, Guernsey, Wales and Eire in separate sequences. *Class No:* 621.396.7

[4547]

GREAT BRITAIN. Department of Trade and Industry. **United Kingdom table of radio frequency allocations.** London, H.M. Stationery Office, 1985. vi, 308p. tables, map. £12. ISBN: 0115138196.

Sets out the internationally agreed frequency allocations and their uses and gives the UK allocations in parallel, with footnote annotations to explain subdivisions or limitations. Annexes provide greater detail for the UK of the subdivisions of certain bands. Glossary, p.5-20. *Class No:* 621.396.7

[4548]

Guide to broadcasting stations. Darrington, P., *ed.* 20th ed. Newnes, Heinemann, 1989. 236p. figs., tables. £10.95. ISBN: 0434903094.

International in scope, listing radio stations broadcasting in the long, medium, and short wave bands. Arranged by frequency, geographical location, and alphabetical order. *Class No:* 621.396.7

Space Radiocommunication

Satellites

[4549]

International satellite directory, 1995: the complete guide to the satellite communication industry. 10th ed. Sonoma, Ca., Design Publishers, 1995. v.p. illus., maps. $240. ISBN: 0936361204. ISSN: 10414541.

About 25,000 companies in 15 classified groups. Covers government and international agencies, satellite operators, uplink locations, equipment manufacturers, launch vehicles, viedo and teleconferencing centres, research centres, licensing agents, etc. 'The Bible of the industry' (*American reference books annual*, 1996, p.748). *Class No:* 621.396.94.04

[4550]
MORGAN, W.L. *and* GORDON, G.D. **Communications satellite handbook.** New York, Wiley, 1989. 900p. illus. $69.95. ISBN: 0471316032.

5 main parts covering: teletraffic; communications; satellite systems; multiple access techniques; space craft technology; satellite orbits. Extensive chapter references. Lists of symbols, constants and acronyms. *Class No:* 621.396.94.04

[4551]
WILLIAMSON, M. **The Communications satellite.** New York, A. Hilger, 1990. 420p. $70. ISBN: 0852741928.

Includes a case study of direct broadcasting by satellite (DBS). Excludes electronic control systems design and transmission and coding methods. *Class No:* 621.396.94.04

[4552]
The World satellite almanac, 1995. Kenny, M.L., *and others, eds.* 7th ed. Potomac, Md., Phillips Publishing, 1995. 550. illus., diagrs., maps. $247. ISBN: 1881537285.

Information on satellite operators, transponder frequency brokers and resellers, and telecommunications policy and regulatory organizations. Data include technical information, maps of transmission ranges, contact and focus information. Incorporates *Satellite systems handbook* and *The World satellite annual*, previously published separately. *Class No:* 621.396.94.04

Radar

[4553]
BARTON, D.K., *ed*. **Radars.** Dedham, Mass., Artech House Inc., 1974-1983. 6v. illus., diagrs., graphs. £21 per v. (*Artech Radar Library*.)

Collections of papers, largely American, reprinted from scattered journals and reports, on aspects of radar. 1. *Monopulse radar*. 1974. ISBN 0890060304. 2. *The radar equation*. 1974. ISBN 0890060312. 3. *Pulse compression*. 1975. ISBN 0890060320. 4. *Radar resolution and multipath effects*. 1975. ISBN 0890060339. 5. *Radar clutter*. 1975, rep. 1977. ISBN 0890060347. 6. *Frequency agility and diversity*. 1977. ISBN 0890060673. Annotated bibliographies. *Class No:* 621.396.96

[4554]
LEONOV, S.A. *and* BARTON, W.F. **Russian-English and English-Russian dictionary of radar and electronics.** Boston, Ma., Artech House, 1993. 161p. £39. ISBN: 0890067058.

About 5,000 entries in each half. Transliteration table. *Class No:* 621.396.96

[4555]
MORCHIN, W.C. **Radar engineer's sourcebook.** London, Artech, 1992. xv, 472p. diagrs. £66. ISBN: 0890065594.

A distillation of technical material from publications and conferences over the last 5 years. Includes a number of design specifications for common radar engineering problems. *Class No:* 621.396.96

[4556]
SWORDS, S.S. **Technical history of the beginnings of radar.** London, P. Peregrinus, 1986. xiv, 325p. illus., diagrs. £30. (*IEE History of technology series, v.6.*) ISBN: 086341043x.

Traces developments from the beginning of the 20th century to the Second World War, with separate accounts for the UK, Germany, USA, France, Italy, Japan, Russia, Holland and Hungary, with valuable annotated bibliographies for the first seven. A more comprehensive treatment of work in the UK is given in chapter 5 (p.174-257). Appendices reproduce several historical memoranda, provide maps and mathematical analysis.

'I found little to criticise in this book ... Probably the best single volume on the subject ever published' (*IEEE Spectrum*, v.23, Sept. 1986, p.17). *Class No:* 621.396.96

Television

[4557]
BENSON, K.B. *and* WHITAKER, J.G., *eds*. **Television and audio handbook for technicians.** New York, etc., McGraw-Hill, 1990. v.p. illus., diagrs. $90. ISBN: 0070047871.

Much of the text and many illus. derived from *Television engineering handbook* and *Audio engineering handbook*. Limited chapter references; subject index. Suitable for public libraries and technical colleges. *Class No:* 621.397

[4558]
BENSON, K.B. **Television engineering handbook.** New York, etc., McGraw-Hill, 1985. 1478p. illus., diagrs. $89.50. ISBN: 0070047790.

Data for all aspects of design and operation, including signal generation, processing, transmission and reproduction.

'A reference source for engineers involved in the design, development, maintenance and operation of television equipment and systems ... Enhanced by 1,091 illustrations' (*SMPTE journal*, v.95, March 1986, p.340).

A new ed., with accompanying CD-ROM, was due for publication April 1999 (Mcgraw-Hill; $125; ISBN: 0070696276). *Class No:* 621.397

[4559]
BURNS, R.W. **British television: the formative years.** London, P. Peregrinus/Science Museum, 1986. xv, 488p. illus., diagrs., tables. £48. (*History of technology series, No. 7.*) ISBN: 0863410790.

An account of the beginnings and experimental work of Baird and others; early developments, tests and public transmissions; the emergence of competition from EMI Ltd; the establishment, work and findings of the 1934 joint BBC/GPO Television Committee; and the eventual launch of a public high-definition television service by the BBC in 1936. Ends with the closure of the service on the outbreak of war in September 1939. Based very soundly on primary source material and supported by 4 appendices and numerous contemporary illustrations. *Class No:* 621.397

[4560]
CLASON, W.E., *comp*. **Elsevier's dictionary of television and video-recording in six languages:** English/American-French-Spanish-Italian-Dutch-German. Amsterdam, etc., Elsevier, 1975. [viii], 608p. £156.90. ISBN: 0444412247.

Based on *Elsevier's Dictionary of television, radar and antennas* (1955), this polyglot version excludes terms on radar and antennas (other than for television); these will be found in *Elsevier's Telecommunications dictionary* (*qv*).

5,300 terms and phases are listed, numbered and defined in English, with equivalents in French, Spanish, Italian, Dutch and German. For each foreign language there is an A-Z index referring to the English section via the reference numbers. *Class No:* 621.397

[4561]
JACKSON, K.G. *and* TOWNSEND, B. **Television and video engineer's reference book.** London, Butterworth Heinemann, 1991. 772p. illus., diagrs. £125. ISBN: 0750610212.

Comprehensive, including television transmitters, transformers, sound editing, audio recording, mixers and special effects, studio lighting, lighting control, receiving antennae, semiconductors and microelectronics. *Class No:* 621.397

[4562]
TRUNDLE, E. **Newnes guide to TV and video technology.** 2nd ed. Oxford, Butterworth-Heinemann, 1996. vii, 382p. illus., diagrs. £14.99. ISBN: 0750623748.

First published 1988.

26 chapters: 1. Basic television ... 4. PAL system ... 14 Cable TV ... 17. Video tape: tracks and transport ... 25. Care, operation and maintenance of VTRs. Comprehensive and practical. *Class No:* 621.397

Apparatus

[4563]
STEPHENSON, D.J. **Newnes guide to satellite TV:** installation, reception and repair. 4th ed. Oxford, Butterworth-Heinemann, 1997. 350p. diagrs., graphs, tables. £19.99. ISBN: 0750634758.

Chapters cover antennae, satellite receivers, installations, and repair of satellite equipment. Appendices. A practical treatment. *Class No:* 621.397.6

Heat Engineering

[4564]
GUYER, E.C., *ed*. **Handbook of applied thermal design.** New York, etc., McGraw-Hill, 1989. xv, v.p. illus., diagrs., graphs, tables. £56.95. ISBN: 0070253536.

67 contributors. Intended to provide 'a general perpsective' (*Preface*) on heat transfer analysis, materials performance, heating and cooling technology and instrumentation and controls. 13 parts, each with a number of chapters: 1. Fundamentals of thermal design and analysis ... 4. Structural materials in thermal design - 5. Heat transfer fluids ... 9. Refrigeration ... 12. Thermal sensors - 13. Automatic temperature controls. Appendix: 'Classified unit conversions'. Detailed subject index (12p.). 'Recommended for libraries serving a technical clientele' (*Choice*, Feb. 1989, p.968). *Class No:* 621.4

[4565]

HEWITT, G.F., *ed*. **Hemisphere handbook of heat exchanger design.** New York, etc., Hemisphere, 1990. xxxviii, v.p., illus., diagrs., graphs, tables. £203. ISBN: 0891168664.

Incorporates the 5 volume *Heat exchanger design handbook* and all supplements, 1983.

73 contributors, most of them practising engineers. 5 parts: 1. Heat exchanger theory - 2. Fluid mechanics and heat transfer - 3. Thermal and hydraulic design - 4. Mechanical design - 5. Physical properties. Analytical subject index (48p.). A wealth of data but a rather unwieldy volume. *Class No:* 621.4

[4566]

Standard handbook of powerplant engineering. Elliott, T.C., *and others, eds*. 2nd ed. New York, etc., McGraw-Hill, 1998. v.p. illus., diagrs., graphs, tables. ISBN: 0070194351.

First published 1989.

60 chapters in 10 sections: 1. Energy resources for power generation - 2. Steam powerplants - 3. Prime movers - 4. Plant electric systems - 5. Instrumentation and control - 6. Nuclear plant systems - 7. Hydroelectric power stations - 8. Alternative energy plants—emerging technologies - 9. Environmental controls - 10. Appendixes. 55 contributors from industry. A practical approach. *Class No:* 621.4

Internal Combustion Engines

[4567]

BRITISH STANDARDS INSTITUTION. **Vocabulary for reciprocating internal combusion engines.** London, BSI, 1979. Addendum, 1983. 28p. (*BS 5676: 1979.*)

130 terms defined in English, French and Russian, in systematic order with indexes in each language. Addendum 1. Symbols. 1983. 6p. *Class No:* 621.43

[4568]

FIRTH, C., *ed*. **World engine digest.** 5th ed. London, PRS Business Publications, 1985. [xiv], 264p. graphs, charts, tables, maps. £164.05. ISBN: 0906237351.

Provides production and market data for petrol and diesel engines; profile of 31 leading manufacturers, A-Z; selective directory of manufacturers worldwide, arranged under project/country/name. Based on a computerized engine data bank developed by the publishers. *Class No:* 621.43

[4569]

Referativnyĭ zhurnal. 39. Dvigateli vnutrennogo sgoraniya. Akademiya Nauk SSSR. Moscow, VINITI, 1963-. Monthly. R48.60. ISSN: 04862279.

About 5,500 indicative and informative, signed abstracts pa., on all aspects and types of internal combustion engines, classified in sections (*e.g.* Construction and calculation ... Diesel engines ...). Annual subject index. English contents summary. UDC numbers. *Class No:* 621.43

Diesel Engines

[4570]

Diesel engines of the world, 1984. Cannon, S., *ed*. London, John Martin, 1984. ii, 195p. tables. [£75?]. (*PRS yearbooks.*) ISBN: 0906237335.

'... The first comprehensive directory of the world's diesel engines' (*Introduction*). Lists *c*.8,000 engines with specifications (including no. of cylinders, configuration, RPM, HP, capacity, piston data and dimensions) drawn from a computerized data base held by the publishers. Covers *c*.200 engine builders and provides alphabetical and geographical listings. Production statistics for 1982, definitions and standards information complete the work. *Class No:* 621.436.1

[4571]

LILLY, L.C.R., *ed*. **Diesel engine reference book.** London, Butterworths, 1984. [707]p. illus., diagrs., graphs. £95. ISBN: 0408004436.

Successor to *Diesel engine principles and practice*, by C.C. Pounder, first published 1955. Previous ed. (2nd) 1962.

32 contributors and chapters, grouped into: Theory; Engine design practice; Lubrication; Environmental pollution; Crankcase explosions; Engine types; Engine testing; Maintenance. Chapter references. Index (*c*.1,700 entries). Lists of engine types and manufacturers, institutions, and fuel injection equipment manufacturers.

'A comprehensive work on the design, operation and maintenance of all types of diesel engines ... Ranges through subjects which will be of long-term use to engine designers, installation engineers and ... enormous number of users ...' (*Automotive-engineering*, v.92, Dec. 1984, p.102). *Class No:* 621.436.1

[4572]

MAHON, L.L.J. **Diesel generator handbook.** Oxford, Butterworth Heinemann, 1992. viii,646p. illus., diagrs., graphs, tables. £75. ISBN: 0750611472.

15 chapters, closely subdivided: 1. Reciprocating internal combustion engines ... 3. A.C. generators - general ... 6. Engine governing ... 9. Switchgear and control gear ... 12. Fuels and lubricating oils ... 15. Operation and maintenance. 4 appendices (*e.g.* B: Batteries). Detailed, analytical index. *Class No:* 621.436.1

Gas Turbines

[4573]

BOYCE, M.P. **Gas turbine engineering handbook.** Houston, Texas, Gulf Publishing Co., 1982. ix, 603p. illus., diagrs., graphs, tables. $79. ISBN: 0872018784.

Information on design, components (compressors and turbine types), materials, fuels, lubrication, operation and maintenance of gas turbines, supported by chapter references and tabulated data. *Class No:* 621.438

Pneumatic Energy Machines

[4574]

BARBER, A. **Pneumatic handbook.** 7th ed. Morden, Surrey, Trade & Technical Pr., 1989. 640p., xv. illus., diagrs., tables. £64. ISBN: 0854611374.

First published 1965. Previous ed. 1982.

Standard reference work for pneumatic and compressed air engineering. 12 sections cover principles, compressors, air lines, valves, actuators, circuits, tools, techniques, devices and machines, miscellaneous data, lists of standards and symbols and buyers' guide, glossary and index. Copious illustrations and many tables. Interspersed advertisements. *Class No:* 621.5

Vacuum Technology

[4575]

BRITISH STANDARDS INSTITUTION. **Vacuum technology - graphical symbols.** London, BSI, 1978. 20p. diagrs. (*BS 5543: 1978.*)

50 symbols defined and illustrated. *Class No:* 621.52

[4576]

WEBER, F., *comp*. **Elsevier's dictionary of high vacuum science and technology in six languages:** German, English, French, Spanish, Italian, Russian. Amsterdam, etc., Elsevier, 1968. [xiv], 539p. £136.90.

3,692 numbered entries, German-based, with English, French, Spanish, Italian, Russian equivalents and occasional explanatory notes. English, French, Spanish and Italian indexes. Russian numerical and alphabetical indexes. *Class No:* 621.52

[4577]

WEISSLER, G.L. and CARLSON, R.W., *eds*. **Vacuum physics and technology.** New York, Academic Press, 1979. 616p. diagrs., graphs, tables. $55. (*Methods of experimental physics, v.14.*) ISBN: 0124759147.

15 contributors to 16 chapters which cover theory, production and measurement of vacua, design of systems protective devices, operation and maintenance of vacuum systems and properties of materials used in vacuum technology. This work 'presents fundamental vacuum-design criteria and practice in a clear manner. On balance it will be a valuable addition to modernize a vacuum laboratory library'. (*Physics Today*, v.33(5), May 1980, p.58. *Class No:* 621.52

Compressed Air Equipment

[4578]

GREENE, R.W., *ed*. **'Chemical engineering' guide to compressors.** New York, etc., McGraw-Hill, 1984. vii, 264p. $37.50. (*Chemical engineering books.*) ISBN: 0070243123.

29 articles reprinted from *Chemical Engineering*, 1973-1983, aimed to present information on all aspects of compressors. 8 sections (1. Selection - 2. Calculations and evaluations - 3. Surge control - 4. Operation and maintenance - 5. Seals and packings - 6. Prime movers - 7. Adjustable speed drives - 8. Fans and blowers). Index. *Class No:* 621.54

Wind Power & Windmills

[4579]

REYNOLDS, J. **Windmills and watermills.** London, Evelyn, 1970. 196p. illus. (incl. col.), diagrs. £4.20. (*Excursions into architecture.*) ISBN: 0238789438.

An authoritative survey of the origins, development and applications of the various kinds of windmill and watermill used in many parts of the world. Chapters on the machinery, its principles, components and materials. Illustrated on every page by photographs and the author's isometric drawings, and supplemented by extensive glossary (p.183-191) and selected bibliography. Index of names. *Class No:* 621.548

[4580]

SHILLINGFORD, A.E.P. **England's vanishing windmills.** London, Godfrey Cave Associates, 1979. 157p. illus. (mostly col.), diagrs. £7.95. ISBN: 0906223156.

This copiously illustrated book contains a brief history of windmills in England, and sections describing the several types and their structure and machinery. A gazetteer section lists and describes windmills of London and 21 counties. Photographs of 'lost and decayed' windmills. Appendix, listing windmills open to visitors. Bibliography, p.150. Glossary of 130 terms, with index. *Class No:* 621.548

[4581]

—WAILES, R. **The English windmill.** London, Routledge & Kegan Paul, 1954. xxii, 264p. illus., diagrs., maps.

3 parts (22 chapters): 1. The mills - 2. The machinery - 3. The men. 4 appendices. Glossary. Bibliography. Index. 32 plates, 64 diagrs. Mentions over 300 mills in the text (37 in Lincolnshire, 46 in Norfolk, and 47 in Suffolk). *Class No:* 621.54

Refrigeration

Handbooks & Manuals

[4582]

AIR-CONDITIONING AND REFRIGERATION INSTITUTE. **Refrigeration and air-conditioning.** Englewood Cliffs, N.J., Prentice-Hall, 1979. xii, 863p. illus., diagrs., graphs, tables. ISBN: 0137701640.

A comprehensive text presented informally at technician/d.i.y. level, which has some value as a reference work because of the large number of tables, graphs, charts containing relevant data. *NB.* Equipment information and environmental factors relate to North America. Includes glossary, problems/answers and good index.

2nd rev. ed. 1987. (779p. £34.25. ISBN 0137701810).

Class No: 621.56(035)

[4583]

BOAST, M. **Newnes refrigeration pocket book.** Oxford, Butterworth Heinemann, 1991. viii,450p. illus., diagrs., graphs, tables. £14.95. ISBN: 0750600799.

14 chapters (2. Evaporators and coolers ... 4. Refrigerants ... 9. Cold room capacities ... 12. Glossary (p.379-93)). Index, p.445-50. A wealth of information in a handy format. *Class No:* 621.56(035)

[4584]

WANG, S.K. **Handbook of air conditioning and refrigeration.** New York, McGraw-Hill, 1993. v.p. illus., diagrs. graphs. $96.50. ISBN: 0070681384.

32 chapters, closely sub-divided, with references. Includes numerous case studies from a range of situations. Detailed, analytical index, 13p. A comprehensive treatment. 'A work that should be in every library' (*Choice*, October 1994, p.317). *Class No:* 621.56(035)

Dictionaries

[4585]

BOOTH, K.M., *comp.* **Dictionary of refrigeration and air conditioning.** Amsterdam, etc., Elsevier, 1970. viii, 315p. . £21. ISBN: 044420069x.

More than 2,600 terms from both sides of the Atlantic are defined in entries ranging from a few words to more than 200. Copious cross-references. Author's Preface insists 'The book is a dictionary and not an encyclopedia'. Because of the impending changeover to use of SI units at the time of publication, metric equivalents to Imperial units are frequently given. Inevitably lacks terms relating to important recent developments (*e.g.* new refrigerants, use of computer and microprocessor control methods) but sound, descriptive definitions of fundamental material make this a brief dictionary of continuing importance in its field. *Class No:* 621.56(038)

[4586]

BRITISH STANDARDS INSTITUTION. **Glossary of refrigeration, heating, ventilating and air-conditioning terms.** London, BSI, 1984. 88p. £38. (*BS 5643: 1984.*)

Supersedes BS 1584 and BS 5643: 1979.

Contains around 2,300 terms, of which more than one third are cross-references, many to noun/adjective forms from the alternative (*e.g.* dark smoke *see* smoke, dark), apparently assuming that the reader will overlook the clear explanation of policy in the Foreword! Concise definitions. *Class No:* 621.56(038)

[4587]

INTERNATIONAL INSTITUTE OF REFRIGERATION. **New international dictionary of refrigeration.** Oxford, etc., Pergamon, 1975. xxxvii, 560p. £35.

About 3,500 terms in English with definitions in English and French, followed by equivalents in Russian, German, Spanish, Italian and Norwegian. Classified arrangement. 14 sections (A. Basic data and instrumentation ... Q. International applications - Miscellaneous). A-Z index for each language. *Class No:* 621.56(038)

[4588]

ROZENBERG, M.B. **English-Russian dictionary of refrigeration and low-temperature technology.** 2nd ed., rev. and enl. Oxford, etc., Pergamon, 1979. 467p. tables. £25. ISBN: 0080247377.

Identical publication with variant title: *English-Russian dictionary of refrigerating and cryogenic engineering/Anglo-russkii slovar' po kholodil'noi tekhnike* (Moscow, Russian Language Publishers, 1978).

About 20,000 terms with Russian equivalents and indication of acceptable synonyms and with explanations in Russian of certain translations. Covers refrigeration equipment, manufacture and use, heat transfer equipment, insulating materials, air conditioning and cryogenics. Includes abbreviations list and 18 conversion tables. *Class No:* 621.56(038)

Progress Reports

[4589]

Advances in cryogenic engineering. New York, Plenum Press, 1960-. v.1-. illus., diagrs.

A review series generated by joint biennial conferences. V.42 (1997. 2v.) contains about 200 papers from the 11th conference, 1995, focusing on superconductors and structural materials. *Class No:* 621.56(055)

Yearbooks & Directories

[4590]

The Refrigeration and air conditioning year book. Croydon, EMAP, 1999. Annual. 300p. illus. £36. ISSN: 14657406.

Published since 1975 as part of subscription to *Refrigeration and air conditioning and heat recovery*; also available separately.

10 sections: 1. A-Z of companies - 2. Product guide - 3. Suppliers: regional - 4./5. Specialist services - 6. Industry contacts - 7. Training providers - 8. Recruitment consultants - 9. Trade names - 10. UK sources for overseas suppliers. *Class No:* 621.56(058)

Tables & Data Books

[4591]

SCHWARTZBERG, F. **Cryogenic materials data handbook.** Wright-Patterson Air Force Base, Ohio, Air Force Materials Laboratory 1970. 2v. (vi, 750p.). graphs. (*Report AFML-TOR-64-280.*)

1. Sections A-C. 2. Sections D-I, plus References, Testing bibliography and Materials guide.

Mechanical and physical property data and information on 88 metallic and non-metallic materials, arranged in 11 sections, with materials, properties and cumulative indexes and complete list of references. *Class No:* 621.56(083)

Histories

[4592]

THÉVENOT, R. **A History of refrigeration throughout the world;** translated by J.C. Fidler. Paris, International Institute of Refrigeration, 1979. 476p.

The author modestly claims only 'to present a preliminary sketch', but he ranges comprehensively over the whole field of the production and use of artificial cold from 1755 onwards, identifying the contributions of around 1,000 scientists and engineers to the development of the technologies associated with refrigeration. The descriptive survey in Part 1 is divided into 4 epochs (1755-1875; 1875-1914; 1919-1939; 1945-). Part 2 presents chronologies of inventions, advances, applications under 10 headings (*e.g.* Refrigerated transport, Air conditioning, Cryology). Part 3 contains brief biographical sketches of 65 important men in the history of the subject. *Class No:* 621.56(091)

Research Projects

[4593]

Directory of low temperature research in Europe. McDonald, P., *ed.* London, Adam Hilger, 1992. 408p. illus. £47.50. ISBN: 0750301767.

A survey of research and development. Data: institution, research team members, description of project, specialist equipment. *Class No:* 621.56:061:061.62.005

Heat Pumps

[4594]

DYAKOWSKI, T. *and* **BRODOWICZ, K. Heat pumps.** Oxford, Butterworth-Heinemann, 1993. 240p. £40. ISBN: 0750606118.

Systematic treatment of the design and operation of both compression and absorption heat pumps. Over 190 illus. *Class No:* 621.577

[4595]

HOLLAND, F.A., *and others*. **Thermodynamic design data for heat pump systems.** Oxford, etc., Pergamon, 1982. vii, 347p. graphs, tables. £75. ISBN: 0080287271.

Intended as 'A comprehensive database and design manual' (*subtitle*), the book presents design data (graphical and tabular) for 21 working fluids for heat pump systems, each designated by its R code number based on the International Numbering System detailed in BS 4580: 1970. Two introductory chapters cover theory and derivation of the data and its use.

'This handbook can be a reference and a guide to the process design engineer involved in the conservation, recovery and re-cycling of heat energy in a wide range of industries' (*Heating/Piping/Air conditioning,* v.54, August 1982, p.172). *Class No:* 621.577

[4596]

LOYD, S. The Heat pump: an annotated bibliography with a survey of suppliers. 2nd ed. Bracknell, Berks., Building Services Research and Information Association, 1981. iv, 106p. £9. (*Bibliography LB 103/81*.) ISBN: 0860220990.

First published 1975.

505 numbered items, with citations and indicative or informative abstracts, drawn largely from English-language and German sources - periodicals (mainly), books, reports and standards. 21 sections (General Surveys ... Air source - Water source - Earth source ... Testing ... Heat recovery ... District heating). Appendix lists suppliers and their products, trade names and importers. *Class No:* 621.577

Fluids Handling Engineering

Databases

[4597]

FLUIDEX. BHRA Fluid engineering abstracts. Cranfield, Beds., British Hydromechanics Research Association.

Covers 1973 onwards. References, with abstracts, to literature of fluids, including aerodynamics, fluid flow, fluid engineering, offshore technology and rheology. About 250,000 records updated monthly. Available on DIALOG, file 96 and Data-Star. Available on CD-ROM and on the World Wide Web. Publications: *BHRA Fluid Engineering thesaurus; Guide to the Fluidex database, Fluidex Notes, Fluidex Newsline. Class No:* 621.6(003.4)

[4598]

—Fluid abstracts: process engineering. Oxford, Elsevier, 1991-. Monthly. £500; $795. ISSN: 09627162.

Formed by the merger of *Fluid power abstracts; Fluid sealing abstracts; Solid-liquid flow abstracts; Pumps and other fluids machinery abstracts; Fluid flow measurement abstracts; pipelines abstracts; Computer-aided process control abstracts* and *Mixing and separation technology abstracts.* About 6,500 abstracts pa. Available online as part of FLUIDEX. *Class No:* 621.6(003.4)

Bibliographies

[4599]

WATTON, J. 'Fluid mechanics and fluid power systems'. *Information sources in engineering.* K.W. Mildren and P.J. Hicks, eds. (3rd ed., 1996), p.301-14. 3rd ed. London, Bowker Saur, 1996. £80. ISBN: 1857390571.

Sections: Introduction - Textbooks and handbooks - Fluid properties ... Transmission line dynamics ... Computer simulation (CAD) - Further reading - Fundamental fluid mechanics studies. *Class No:* 621.6(01)

Dictionaries

[4600]

TROSKOLANSKI, A.T. Dictionary of hydraulic machinery: in English, German, Spanish, French, Italian and Russian. Amsterdam, etc., Elsevier, 1985. xxiii, 737p. illus., diagrs., graphs, tables. £155. ISBN: 0444997288.

Revised and enlarged translation from Polish original *Magzynyi urzgdzenia hydrauliczne - Projecia podstawave* (1974).

Contains about 4,300 entries classified in 14 sections (1-4. Concepts - 5-14. Hydraulic machinery types, problems and applications). Base language is English. Concise definitions for most terms, with foreign-language equivalents. Indexes in each language lead to main entries by means of number codes. *Class No:* 621.6(038)

Periodicals

[4601]

List of periodicals scanned and abstracted for inclusion in the FLUIDEX DATABASE. Cranfield, Beds., BHRA Fluid Engineering, 1981. 18p.

Lists *c*.700 periodicals covering a wide field. Gives abbreviated titles and Codens. *Class No:* 621.6(051)

Standards

[4602]

NATIONAL FLUID POWER ASSOCIATION. Fluid power standards. 7th ed. Milwaukee, Wisconsin, the Association, 1986. 10v. $380.

Covers pumps, motors, power units and reservoirs, filtration and contamination, cylinders, accumulators, fluids, lubricants and sealing devices, hose, tubes, and fittings, valves and testing procedures. Contains bibliographies, glosssary and graphical symbols list. 'The most complete reference work available on design and performance standards for hydraulic and pneumatic fluid power products' (*Mechanical engineering,* v.109, March 1987, p.80). *Class No:* 621.6(083.74)

Thesauri

[4603]

Thesaurus for fluid engineering. Guy, N.G., *ed.* Cranfield, Beds., BHRA, 1981. xiii, 128p. £15. ISBN: 0906085578.

Two aims: (a) to give guidance to the vocabulary used in the fluid engineering literature; (b) to guide searchers using the BHRA FLUIDEX computerized database. Derived from actual use in that database, the scope is wide and includes some general terms (*e.g.* Introduction; Study). Direct entry is used, with each term (word or phrase) followed by a conventional set of broader, narrower, related, preferred terms. Upwards of 9,000 terms. *Class No:* 621.6:025.43

Fans

[4604]

DALY, B.B. Woods practical guide to fan engineering. 3rd rev. ed. Colchester, Woods of Colchester, Ltd., 1978. xxxi, 376p. diagrs., graphs, charts, tables. £9. ISBN: 0950294128.

First published 1952. Previous ed. 1960.

Aimed at users and engineers responsible for selection and installation, not at specialists or designers of fans. Nevertheless it is an invaluable assembly of information and data, covering its subject widely in 14 chapters (1. The air and human well-being - 2. General ventilation - 3. Air distribution and circulation ... 7. Fans and fan performance - 8. Fan drives and fan control ... 10. Noise, vibration and fatigue - 11. Fan testing and performance prediction ... 13. Ventilation of tunnels and mines - 14. Useful data (p.312-365)). Over 80 tables and charts, identified easily by alphabetical list (e.g., Beaufort wind scale; Relative humidities). Over 160 diagrams and graphs are similarly identified (*e.g.* Psychrometric chart). Data section includes conversion factors and tables, properties of air, water, etc., climatic data, weights and measures. Bibliography, p.366. *Class No:* 621.63

[4605]

JORGENSEN, R., *ed.* **Fan engineering:** an engineer's handbook on fans and their applications. 8th ed. Buffalo N.Y., Buffalo Forge Co., 1983. xvi, [1030]p. diagrs., graphs, charts, tables. $40.

First published. 1914. Previous ed. 1970.

Pocket-size format. 4 parts. Part 1, Fundamentals, contains 8 chapters. Part 2, Fans, has 11 chapters, covering terminology, fan types, laws, testing, control, noise, motors and drives, and selection. Part 3 deals with applications in 10 chapters (*e.g.* ventilation, drying, air cleaning). Part 4 contains 8 appendices (*e.g.* units, nomenclature, miscellaneous data, selected bibliography). Author and subject indexes. 'Will be a very useful reference tool for any engineer involved with the design and operation of fan systems' (*Chemical engineering,* v.91, Dec. 10, 1984, p.197). *Class No:* 621.63

Pipes & Pipelines

Abbreviations & Symbols

[4606]
BRITISH STANDARDS INSTITUTION. **Specification for graphical symbols for general engineering. Part 1. Piping systems and plant.** London, BSI, 1977. 36p. diagrs. (*BS 1553: Part 1: 1977.*)

Supersedes BS 974 and BS 1553, Part 4, 1956.

Specifies symbols for use in flow and piping diagrams for process plant and heating and ventilating installations. *Class No:* 621.643(003)

[4607]
—BRITISH STANDARDS INSTITUTION. Glossary of terms and symbols for measurement of fluid flow in closed conduits. London, BSI, 1991. 51p. (*BS EN 24006; ISO 4006: 1991.*)

Formerly BS 5875: 1991.

Covers general and special areas, *e.g.* differential pressure devices, critical flow measurement, velocity area methods, tracer methods, flow meters, etc. Over 200 terms defined in systematic order with alphabetical index. *Class No:* 621.643(003)

Bibliographies

[4608]
GUY, N.G., *ed.* **Pipe protection bibliography.** London, Elsevier/BHRA Fluid Engineering Centre, 1987. viii, 285p. unpriced. ISBN: 1851660771.

A classified bibliography, with abstracts, of 620 items published 1975-1985 ('a period of considerable activity' (*Introduction*) in developments in pipe protection) derived from the FLUIDEX computerized database. Periodical articles and conference papers in almost equal proportions. Covers pipeline transportation of oil, water, gas, sewage, solids and power and process plant pipework. Contents spread over 38 sections in six main subject categories which cover corrosion, coatings, cathodic protection and applications. Author and corporate source indexes, but no subject index. 18 other bibliographies cited. *Class No:* 621.643(01)

Handbooks & Manuals

[4609]
MILLER, R.W. **Flow measurement engineering handbook.** 3rd ed. New York, etc., McGraw-Hill, 1996. v.p. illus., diagrs., graphs, tables. ISBN: 0070423660.

First pub. 1983; 2nd ed. 1989.

A comprehensive guide to the selection, design, specification and installation of flowmeters to measure liquid, gas and steam flows. 15 chapters, extensively illustrated (*e.g.* 2: 'Fluid properties': 118p.; 23 figures; 29 tables; 62 references; numerous formulas). 9 appendices (*e.g.* H. 'Viscosities of gases'). *Class No:* 621.643(035)

Dictionaries

[4610]
SCHMITZ, H.P. **Wörterbuch der druckbehälter- und vohrleitungstechnik.** [Dictionary of pressure vessel and piping technology.] 2nd ed. Essen, Vulkan, 1991. ix, 683 + 125p. illus. £134.15. ISBN: 380272299x.

First published 1986-87 in 2v.

About 12,000 terms in each half, English and German. 2 appendices: illlustrations; bibliography. *Class No:* 621.643(038)

Reviews & Abstracts

[4611]
Pipe joints: a state of the art review. London, Institution of Mechanical Engineers, 1984-86. 3v. illus., diagrs., graphs, tables.

1. *Gaskets.* 1984. x,47p.
2. *Non-metallic pipe joints.* 1985. xv,93p.
3. *Metallic pipe joints.* 1986. xiii,98p.

Part 1 covers types of gaskets, selection of materials, bolting leads and effect of surface finishes. Part 2, in 9 sections, covers materials (plastics, rubbers, glass), design, joints and linings; Part 3, in 8 sections, covers materials, preparation, welding, joints and reliability. Both 2 and 3 list relevant BSI Standard numbers and corrosion data. No index, but detailed contents pages help overcome this. Intended to provide 'a practical summary' of 'current knowledge and experience' (*Foreword,* p.ii). For practising engineers. Small, handy format. *Class No:* 621.643(048)

[4612]
Referativnyi zhurnal. 45. Truboprovodnyi transport. Moscow, VINITI, 1963-. Monthly. illus. R30. ISSN: 00342610.

About 2,500 signed abstracts on pipelines and pipeline transportation. 12 sections (General problems ... Construction of pipelines ... Operation of gas pipelines ... Oil storage - Gas storage ... Corrosion and anticorrosive protection. Annual subject index. UDC numbers. English contents summary. Some illustrations. *Class No:* 621.643(048)

Tables & Data Books

[4613]
KENTISH, D.N.W. **Pipework design data.** New York, etc., McGraw Hill, 1982. viii, 239p. diagrs., tables. £44.95. ISBN: 0070845581.

Companion volume to the author's *Industrial pipework*, which wa concerned with design and selection of tubes, fittings, valves and othe pipework equipment and with basic pipework techniques. This wor has 6 chapters on matters related to pipework in plant: plant layout platforms, stairs and personnel access; pumping design and layout structural steelwork; estimating; specification writing. Chapter 7 (p.75 215) consists of designer's tables (A. Abbreviations (over 500 ar listed) - B. British Standards (about 350 standards, Codes of practic and Handbooks are included) - C. Conversions - D. Dimensions ... F Flange tables ... N. Nomograms ... P. Properties of tube and pipe .. V. Velocities ... Y. Young's Modulus values - Z. Z values). Glossar (p.217-234 - over 500 terms). Clearly and attractively presented wit illustrations reflecting superb draughtsmanship. *Class No:* 621.643(083)

[4614]
WALLINGFORD, H.R. *and* BARR, D.I.H. **Tables for the hydrauli design of pipes, sewers and channels.** 7th ed. London, Thoma Telford, 1998. 2v. (x, 291p.; xii, 292p.) tables. £70. ISBN 0727726374, v.1; 0727726382, v.2.

First published 1963; 6th ed. 1994.

Presents Colebrook-White resistance solutions for 65 differen diameters of pipes. *Class No:* 621.643(083)

Valves & Taps

[4615]
BARBER, M.J., *and others, eds.* **Handbook of power cylinders valves and controls.** Morden, Surrey, Trade and Technical Press 1986. ix, 364p. illus., diagrs., graphs, charts, tables. £46. ISBN 0854611002.

Aims to provide 'essential information on the principles and contro of hydraulics and pneumatics, together with detailed coverage of al types of hydraulic and pneumatic cylinders, valves and their electroni controls'. 8 sections of text with information on theory, construction operation, performance, selection, including relvant tables and graphs followed by data section listing standards and symbols. Concise, bu adequate index (8p.). *Class No:* 621.646

[4616]
LYONS, J.L. **Valve designer's handbook.** New York, Van Nostranc Reinhold, 1982. xiii, 882p. illus., diagrs., graphs, tables. £70.95 ISBN: 0442244632.

A compilation of 100 articles, papers, data tables and charts by many contributors, some reprinted, others original material, designec to 'alleviate the burden of searching for information that is generally widespread throughout the industry' (*Preface*). 21 sections (*e.g.* Valve engineering and design data - Cavitation - Screw threads and fasteners - Materials - Valve test methods). The many data tables are particularly valuable. Contains a bibliography of books, articles, standards, etc. and an index of variable quality. *Class No:* 621.646

[4617]
—BRITISH VALVE MANUFACTURERS ASSOCIATION. Valve users manual: a technical reference book on industrial valves for the control of fluids. Kempley, J., *ed.* London, Mechanical Engineering Publications, 1980. 103p. illus., diagrs., charts, tables. £8. ISBN: 0852984286.

Supersedes 3 eds. of *Technical reference book on valves for the control of fluids.* Authoritative definition, description and illustration o all commonly used valve types and variants. 18 sections, from the simple ball and butterfly valves to pressure control, automatic action and special purpose valves. Also covers construction materials, corrosion resistance (tabulated), selection, installation, maintenance (with tables of flow data), steam, SI units. Index. *Class No:* 621.646

[4618]
SKOUSEN, P. **Valve handbook.** New York, etc., McGarw-Hill, 1998. xv, 726p. illus., diagrs., tables.

Concentrates on the basic designs and principles which underpin the valve industry. Covers the common valves: manual, check, relief, control and smart. Glossary, p. 667-708. A highly practical approach. *Class No:* 621.646

Pumps

Handbooks & Manuals

[4619]
KARASSIK, I.J., *and others eds.* **Pump handbook.** 2nd ed. New York, etc., McGraw-Hill, 1986. xxii, [1351]p. illus., diagrs., graphs, tables. £95. ISBN: 0070333025.

First published 1976.

72 contributors. Contents assembled in 13 sections. Major sections: 2. Centrifugal pumps (330p.) - 3. Displacement pumps - all types (127p.) - 6. Pump drivers (178p.) - 8. Pumping systems (118p.) - 9.

....(contd.)

Pump services, *i.e.*, applications and areas of use (317p). Other sections cover: materials; controls; intakes; selection and purchase; installation, operation and maintenance; testing. Extensive appendix of general technical data supplements hundreds of specialized tables in the text. Excellent index provides good access to well-organized and clearly presented contents. SI and US Customary units are used and bibliographial references are provided. 'Readers may be overwhelmed by the magnitude of the material. It is truly a matter of having access to more information on pumps than most people care to know or are able to absorb. But that is really the mark of a good reference text ... The editors have done an excellent job of providing an authoritative guide ...' (*Chemical engineering*, v.93, Nov. 10, 1986, p.140).
Class No: 621.65(035)

[4620]
Pumping manual. Dickenson, C. 9th ed. Oxford, Elsevier, 1995. x, 1129p. illus., diagrs., graphs, tables. £95. ISBN: 1856172155.
First published 1964. Previous ed. 1988.
Aims to provide a comprehensive compendium of practical information and data on the selection, installation, operation and maintenance of industrial pumps. 8 sections: 1. Introduction - 2. Pump performance and characteristics - 3. Types of pumps - 4. Pump materials and construction - 5. Pump ancillaries - 6. Pump operation - 7. Pump applications - 8. Reference (buyers' guide; indexes).
Class No: 621.65(035)

[4621]
—McNAUGHTON, K., *ed.* 'Chemical engineering' guide to pumps. New York, etc., McGraw-Hill, 1984. vii, 325p. illus., diagrs., tables, graphs. £39.95. (*Chemical engineering trade books*.) ISBN: 007024314x.
43 articles reprinted from *Chemical Engineering* 1973-1983, aimed to provide an overview for money-conscious designers and users. 5 sections (1. Selection, design and costing - 2. Centrifugal pumps - 3. Positive displacement pumps - 4. Special applications - 5. Drives, seals, packing and piping). Index. *Class No:* 621.65(035)

[4622]
WARRING, R.H., *ed.* **Pumps: selection systems and applications.** 2nd ed. Morden, Surrey, Trade & Technical Press, 1984. [iv], 271p. illus., diagrs., graphs, tables. £17. ISBN: 0854610960.
15 chapters covering theory and practice of pumping fluids (1. Types of fluids ... 3. Fundamentals of pump performance), kinds of pumps (4. Centrifugal pumps ... 7. Hand pumps), products handled, materials, pipework calculations, pumping systems design, testing and selection of appropriate pumps, followed by a data section (p.254-263) and efficient index.
'This compact, well-devised and very practical work is completed with a comprehensive index, and should prove of particular value to those involved with pumping problems in mining/mineral processing' (*Mining magazine*, v.151, August 1984, p.145).
Class No: 621.65(035)

Dictionaries

[4623]
Europump terminology. 2nd ed. Morden, Surrey, Trade & Technical Press, 1978-82. 3v. illus.
First published 1968.
1. *Pump appllications.* 1978. 700p. £107.35.
2. *Pump names.* 1982. xx, 158p. £83.15.
3. *Pump component names.* Rev. ed. 1992. xxi, 612p. £179.90
The work of the European Committee of Pump Manufacturers, these dictionaries list terms, with definitions, numbers and brief explanations in German, with equivalents and explanations in English, French, Spanish and Italian. Indexes in other languages lead to entries in main section. *Class No:* 621.65(038)

Reviews & Abstracts

[4624]
Pumps and other fluids machinery abstracts. Cranfield, Beds., British Hydromechanics Research Association, 1971-. v.1-. 6 pa. £90pa. ISSN: 03022870.
Over 1,100 abstracts pa., of items drawn from 1,000 journals, plus reports, books, conference papers and selected British patents. Main sections: Fluids machinery - Fans, blowers, compressors - Jet ejectors and pumps (all kinds) - Marine craft propulsion - Hydraulic turbines - Instrumentation and experimental techniques. Issue and cumulative annual indexes of personal and corporate authors and of subjects. Accessible on-line via FLUIDEX (*qv*). *Class No:* 621.65(048)

[4625]
Referativnyĭ zhurnal. 61. Nasosotroenie i Kompressorostroenie Kholodil'noe mashinostroenie. Akademiya Nauk SSSR, Moscow, VINITI, 1970-. Monthly. diagrs. R36.
Formerly *Referativnyĭ zhurnal nasosostroenie i Kompressorostroenie* (1964-69).
About 4,000 signed abstracts pa. on pumps, compressors, refrigeration and air conditioning. Annual subject index.
Class No: 621.65(048)

Production Engineering

Databases

[4626]
CAD/CAM online. New York, EIC/Intelligence Inc.
Covers 1983 to date. A bibliographic database providing references, with abstracts, to world literature on computer-integrated manufacturing, covering computer-aided design and and manufacture (CAD/CAM) and commercial and economic aspects. Sources include periodical articles, conference papers, research reports, government reports, patents and books. File size: more than 20,000 items. Updated monthly. 1,500 additions pa. Hosts: DIALOG; ESA-IRS. Printed version: *CAD/CAM abstracts. Class No:* 621.7/.9(003.4)

Bibliographies

[4627]
COX, J., *and others.* **Keyguide to information sources in CAD/CAM.** London, Mansell; Lawrence, KS, Ergosyst Associates, 1988. xxi,257p. ISBN: 072011974x, UK; 0916313158, US.
3 parts. I. Survey of CAD/CAM and its information sources (7 documented chapters, p.3-110). II. Bibliography (514 items). III. Directory of organizations (217 research centres, online hosts; international in scope). Detailed, analytical index, p.245-57. Glossary (AGV-Workstation), p.xv-xxi. An authoritative survey.
Class No: 621.7/.9(01)

[4628]
HORNICK-LOCKARD, B. 'Computer-aided design: a selected bibliography for community college libraries'. *Choice,* V.30(1), September 1992, p.57-62.
About 50 annotated entries in 10 sections, with running commentary. Material suitable for community college and further education libraries. *Class No:* 621.7/.9(01)

Laws

[4629]
DEVINE, J. *and* **WATTS, A.,** *comps.* **Information pack on product liability.** London, Information and Library Service, Institution of Mechanical Engineers, 1987. vii,80p. £14.50. (*Information pack, 6.*) ISBN: 0852986505.
3 parts: 1. Product liability information (abstracts and indexes - text books), p.1-41; 2. Recent liability coverage (26 items), p.42-48; Product liability references (122 items; aeronautical engineering - welding), p.49-73. Author and subject indexes. A useful series.
Class No: 621.7/.9(01)(094.1)

Handbooks & Manuals

[4630]
BENEDICT, G.F. Nontraditional manufacturing processes. New York, Dekker, 1987. xiii, 381p. illus., diagrs., graphs, tables. $95. (*Manufacturing engineering and materials processing, no. 19.*) ISBN: 0824773527.
21 chapters cover the use of energy in new ways or the application of forms of energy preivously not used in manufacturing processes concerned with machining (removal processes), joining and forming. Each chapter deals with a different process in the same format: principles and equipment; capabilities and parameters; application; summary (succinct pros and cons); references. There are 8 chapters each for mechanical and thermal processes. 2 Appendices list US equipment manufacturers and acronyms. Each chapter has a list of references. Excellent illustrations.
'For those seeking a single volume of information, defining the principles and capabilities, together with advantages to be gained and pitfalls to be avoided, this book is to be recommended' (*Production engineer* v.66(7), July/August 1987, p.11). *Class No:* 621.7/.9(035)

[4631]
BRALLA, J.G., *ed*. **Handbook of product design for manufacturing:** a practical guide to low-cost production. New York, etc., McGraw-Hill, 1986. xiii, [1120]p. illus., diagrs., tables. £95. ISBN: 0070071306.

The aim of this handbook is easy and economical production. Emphasis is on products, not processes or functional design, which are fully covered in related handbooks. 55 contributors present information and recommendations in 74 chapters grouped into 8 sections (Introduction - Raw materials - Formed metal components - Machined components - Castings - Nonmetallic parts - Assemblies - Finishes). Each chapter is tightly organized: processes are summarized; applications outlined; economical production quantities, suitable materials, design recommendations, dimensional factors and tolerances are indicated. Adequately supported by illustrations and relevant data and 43-page index. Vast majority of material has appeared elsewhere in other forms, but this is a highly convenient compilation of it, enhanced by important new material. There is a very useful quick-reference chapter. *Class No:* 621.7/.9(035)

[4632]
DROZDA, T.J., *ed*. **Tool and manufacturing engineers handbook.** 4th ed. Dearborn, Mich., Society of Manufacturing Engineers, 1983-86. 5v. illus., diagrs., graphs, tables. $99 per v.

First published as *Tool engineers handbook* in 1949. Previous ed. 1976.
1. *Machining.* 1983. [1484]p. ISBN 0872630854.
2. *Forming.* 1984. [900]p. ISBN 0872631354.
3. *Materials and finishing.* 1985. [864]p. ISBN 0872631761.
4. *Quality control and assembly.* 1986. [750]p. ISBN 087263177x.
5. *Manufacturing management.* 1988. [551]p. ISBN 0872633063. 6 sections, subdivided: 1. Operations and strategic planning - 2. Managerial leadership and its foundations - 3. Human resources - 4. Manufacturing/engineering interface - 5. Resource utilization - 6. Quality. Detailed, analytical index, 9p. *Class No:* 621.7/.9(035)

[4633]
Flexible manufacturing systems handbook; prepared by the staff of the Automation Management Systems Division of the Charles Stark Draper Laboratory, Cambridge, Mass. Park Ridge, N.J., Noyes Publications, 1984. xviii, 392p. diagrs., charts, tables. $ 48. ISBN: 0815509839.

Based on a 5-volume set of publications produced under contract to the US Army. (v.5 of the original set, containing user's manuals for software packages, not included.)

Defines, describes and illustrates FMS technology. Provides practical design and operational guidance. Glossary of terms. Bibliography. No index. *Class No:* 621.7/.9(035)

[4634]
HEINZOLD, G. **Handbook of geometrical tolerancing:** design, manufacturing and inspection. New York, Wiley, 1995. 413p. illus., diagrs., graphs, tables. ISBN: 0471948160.

Includes detailes coverage of ISO standards with how they differ from American (ANSI), British (BS) and German (DIN) standards. Extensive examples; well illustrated. Detailed, analytical index. 'A very helpful reference' (*Choice,* January 1996, p.821). *Class No:* 621.7/.9(035)

[4635]
Manufacturing engineer's reference book. Kershal, D., *ed*. Oxford, Butterworth-Heinemann, 1993. v.p. illus., diagrs., graphs, tables. £95. ISBN: 0750611545.

20 contributors. 19 sections, closely sub-divided (1. Materials, properties and selections ... 19. Ergonomics). Detailed, analytical index, 20p. *Class No:* 621.7/.9(035)

[4636]
WALSH, R.A. **McGraw-Hill machining and metalworking handbook.** New York, McGraw-Hill, 1994. xvii, 1518p. illus. diagrs., graphs, tables. £55. ISBN: 0070679584.

23 chapters, closely sub-divided (*e.g.* 13. Springs, 52p., 17 sections). 900 illus.; 480 tables. Detailed, analytical index, p.1489-1518. A practical approach. *Class No:* 621.7/.9(035)

Dictionaries

[4637]
Dictionary of CAD. Clarke, J. *and* Mayer, T., *eds*. Oxford, Butterworth Heinemann, 1991. 484p. illus. £40. ISBN: 0750612398.
About 2,500 terms, most defined briefly. *Class No:* 621.7/.9(038)

[4638]
Dictionary of flexible manufacturing systems and robotics: English, German, French, Dutch, Russian. Voskoboynikov, B.S., *and others, eds*. Dordrecht, Kluwer, 1991. 392p. £40.99. ISBN: 204018810x.
356 English-base terms. Indexes in other languages.
Class No: 621.7/.9(038)

[4639]
HUNT, V.D. **Dictionary of advanced manufacturing technology.** Amsterdam, etc., Elsevier, 1987. xi, 431p. illus., diagrs. £34.53. ISBN: 0444012087.

Over 5,800 terms, acronyms and abbreviations defined and illustrated, from the fields associated with the application to manufacturing of computers, robots, artificial intelligence and automatic control. Preceded by a chapter giving an overview of advanced manufacturing technology. Brief directory of organizations and companies, a list of abbreviations and acronyms and a short bibliography complete the work. *Class No:* 621.7/.9(038)

[4640]
INTERNATIONAL INSTITUTE FOR PRODUCTION ENGINEERING RESEARCH (CIRP). **Wörterbuch der Fertigungstechnik.** [Dictionary of production engineering.] Pahlitzsch, G., *ed*. Essen, Girardet, 1962-1984. 9v. illus. DM350 per set. ISBN: 3773656904.

1. *Forging and deep forging.* 1962. 108p. 2. *Grinding - surface roughness.* 1963. 139p. 3. *Sheet metal forming.* 1965. 136p. 4. *Fundamental terms of cutting.* 1969. 123p. 5. *Cold extrusion and upsetting.* 1969. 157p. 6. *Planing, slotting, broaching, turning.* 1972. 194p. 7. *Drilling, countersinking, counterboring, reaming, thread production.* 1977. 220p. 8. *Milling, sawing, gear manufacturing.* 1979. 359p. 9. *Electrochemical, electrodischarge, electron beam, photonen beam (laser) and chemical machining.* 1984. 170p.

A German-English-French dictionary edited by expert committees of CIRP (Collège International Recherche Production). V.1 has entries for *c*.400 German-base terms with English and French indexes and nearly 100 illus. V.1 has 2 other versions: V.1N (covering Danish, Norwegian, Swedish, Finnish) and V.1R (German, Spanish, Italian, Portugese).

Work began on the 2nd ed. in 1997. V.1 and 2 cover terms on metal forming in German, with indexes in English and French.
Class No: 621.7/.9(038)

[4641]
TVER, D.F. *and* BOLZ, R.W. **Encyclopedic dictionary of industrial technology:** materials, processes and equipment. New York, London, Chapman and Hall, 1984. [vi] 353p. diagrs., tables. £39. ISBN: 0412005018.

Wide-ranging coverage of materials, machine tools, computers, robots, manufacturing processes and treatments, and equipment, handling, inspection and testing. Definition and description of *c*.1,800 terms vary from one line to fifty. Cross-references. Select bibliography p.349-53. *Class No:* 621.7/.9(038)

Tables & Data Books

[4642]
CHEREMISINOFF, P.N. *and* CHEREMISINOFF, N.P. **Process engineering data book.** New York, Techomic, 1995. 349p. illus., diagrs., tables. $45. ISBN: 1566762243.

Covers unit operations on pumps, gas propulsion, separation, mixing, filters, heat exhangers, evaporators, distillation, etc. Appendices contain tables of physical properties and unit definitions and relationships. Material included is brief and concise, but accessible. 'An excellent practical handbook' (*Choice,* September 1995, p.163). *Class No:* 621.7/.9(083)

Workshop Practice

[4643]
AVITZUR, B. **Handbook of metal-forming processes.** New York, etc., Wiley, 1983. xxxi, 1020p. illus., diagrs., graphs, tables. £100. ISBN: 0471034746.

A descriptive but analytical approach to the wide variety of metal-forming processes now available. For each process discussed the relevant principles and concepts are introduced to enable the engineer to gain complete understanding. Problems are appended to assist in this. 18 chapters (*e.g.* 1. Basic concepts - 2. Forging ... 6. Impact extrusion - 7. Hydrostatic extrusion ... 10. Deep drawing ... 13. Rolling ... 17. Soft tooling - 18. Replacing brute force). Copious references and illustrations. *Class No:* 621.7

[4644]
Handbook of metal forming. Lange, K., *ed*. Dearborn, Mi., SME, 1995. 1176p. illus., diagrs., tables. ISBN: 0872634574.

Emphasis is on the metal forming process as a system. Covers metallurgy, tribology, material properties and process data.
Class No: 621.7

[4645]

ROSS, R.B. **Handbook of metal treatments and testing.** 2nd ed. London, Chapman and Hall, 1988. xix,568p. Tables. £35. ISBN: 0412313901.

A-Z listing of processes, treatments and testing methods with brief definition and, either, a cross-reference to one of 8 major sections for fuller treatment, or extended explanation with sub-sections. The major sections are: blasting; electroplating; hardness testing; heat treatment; mechanical testing; non-destructive testing; painting; welding. 'List of processes covered', p.xi-xix. 9 appendices of miscellaneous data. *Class No: 621.7*

Dies & Patterns

[4646]

STREET, A., *ed*. **The Diecasting book.** 2nd ed. Redhill, Surrey, Portcullis Press, 1986. [xi],774p. illus., diagr., tables. ISBN: 0861082354.

First published 1977.

A comprehensive handbook on all aspects of the technology of diecastings covering processes, the various alloys and ferrous metals used, management and related topics. *Class No: 621.7.07*

Forge Work

[4647]

BYRER, T.G., *ed*. **Forging handbook.** Cleveland, OH, Forging Industry Association, and Metals Park, OH, ASM, 1985. ix,296p. illus., diagrs., graphs, tables. ISBN: 0871701944.

Numerous contributors. 4 sections, each with a number of parts: 1. Introduction and applications - 2. Forging design - 3. Material characteristics - 4. Manufacture of forgings. Extensively illustrated. Glossary, p.275-87; analytical subject index, p.289-96. A very practical treatment for the 'expert and newcomer' (*Preface,* p.v.). *Class No: 621.73*

[4648]

OPEN DIE FORGING INSTITUTE. Metallurgical and Research Committee. **Open die forging manual.** 3rd ed. Cleveland, Ohio, Forging Industry Association, 1982. viii, 200p. illus., diagrs., tables.

A 'reference book of basic technical information on open die forging metallurgy, equipment, testing, quality assurance, design and purchasing considerations' (*Preface*). Includes chapters on manufacturing methods, materials, service life factors. Glossary of about 300 terms, 3 appendices and index supplement the text. There are charts of heat and temper colours. *Class No: 621.73*

Foundry Work

Bibliographies

[4649]

UNITED NATIONS. Industrial Development Organization. **Information sources on the foundry industry.** New York, United Nations, 1973. xix, 95p. (*UNIDO Guides to information sources, no. 5.*)

565 numbered items. 13 sections. 1. Professional, trade and research organizations, learned societies and special information services - 2. Directories - 3. Sources of statistics and economic data - 4. Basic handbooks, textbooks and manuals - 5. Mono-encyclopedias - 6. Monograph series - 7. Specialized dictionaries and encyclopaedias - 8. Bibliographies - 9. Current periodicals - 10. Current abstracting and indexing periodicals - 11. Proceedings, papers and reports - 12. Films on foundry practice - 13. Other potential sources of information (*e.g.* patents, standards). Worldwide coverage of organizations and publications. Bibliography of sources used. *Class No: 621.74(01)*

Dictionaries

[4650]

BRUNHUBER, E. **Giesserei fachwörterbuch.** [Foundry dictionary.] 4th ed. Berlin, Schiele and Schön, 1988. 14, 1157p. £108.90.

4 parts (German, English, French, Italian). Each part has about 8,500 headwords with equivalents in the other 3 languages. Genders given; US usage indicated. *Class No: 621.74(038)*

[4651]

SIMONS, E.N. **Dictionary of foundry work.** London, Crosby Lockwood, 1972. viii, 227p. illus., tables. £2.95. ISBN: 0258968516.

About 900 entries and cross-references. Definitions are explanatory, clear and understandable, ranging from one line to two pages ('sands'); most occupy a few lines. 35 clear line-drawings. *Class No: 621.74(038)*

[4652]

STÖLZEL, K., *ed*. **Dictionary of metallurgy and foundry technology.** Amsterdam, etc., Elsevier, 1984-87. 2v.

1. *English-German.* 1984. 418p. £79.58. ISBN 0444996125.

2. *German-English.* 1987. 464p. £75.08. ISBN 0444995145.

Wide-ranging scope. Brief entries, with equivalents and occasional definition or explanation.

Review of v.1: 'It will be of particular value to linguists, documentation experts and scientists as well as teachers and students ...' (*Iron and steelmaker*, v.14, August 1987, p.65). *Class No: 621.74(038)*

Reviews & Abstracts

[4653]

BCIRA **abstracts of international literature on metal castings production.** Birmingham, British Cast Iron Research Association, 1986-. v.34-. 6pa. £110 pa. ISSN: 02683393.

First published 1923 as *BCIRA bulletin and foundry abstracts.* Subsequently part of *BCIRA journal* (to 1968). Then *BCIRA abstracts of foundry literature* (1969-77) and latterly *BCIRA abstracts of international foundry literature* (1978-85).

About 1,000 indicative and informative abstracts pa., covering books, patents and articles from *c.*50 journals published in 30-odd countries. Classified arrangement: 11 sections (Raw materials and energy - Melting and casting - Moulding and coremaking - Quality control ... Management and organization ... Environmental pollution and protection - General). Annual author and subject indexes, but none in issues. *Class No: 621.74(048)*

Yearbooks & Directories

[4654]

European Foundry directory and register of forges. 17th ed. Worcester Park, Surrey, Metal Bulletin Books, 1993. xx, 340p. £49. ISBN: 0947671692. ISSN: 00718130.

First published 1959 as Foundry directory and register of forges: Uk and Western Europe.

Foundries and forges by country, A-Z (Austria - UK). Data include company information, contact details, casting methods, dimensions, products, etc. Buyers' guide to castings and forgings, p.171-268; suppliers of equipment and services, p.269-337. International and national associations, p.338-39. *Class No: 621.74(058)*

[4655]

Foundry yearbook and casting buyer's directory, 1999. Redhill, Surrey, Foundry Trade Journal, 1999. Annual. 239p. £129. ISSN: 02645319.

2 main sections: 1. Trade directory (UK foundry industry; organizations in the UK and oversea; UK and Eire foundries and forges) - 2. Buyers' guide. *Class No: 621.74(058)*

Tables & Data Books

[4656]

Foseco Foundryman's handbook. Brown, J.R. 10th ed. Oxford, Butterworth-Heinemann, 1994. xi, 380p. illus., diagrs., graphs, tables. £35. ISBN: 0750619392.

Previous ed. 1986.

Practical guidance and recommendations on making castings by all common casting methods. 12 sections: 1. Tables and general data - 2. Sands and sand bonding systems ... 4. Light alloys casting ... 6. Iron castings ... 8. Steel castings ... 12. Principal FOSECO products (including publications). SI Units. Many tables. Good index. *Class No: 621.74(083)*

Smelting

[4657]

World survey of non ferrous smelters. Taylor, J.C. *and* Traulsen, H.R., *eds*. Warrendale, Pa., Metallurgical Society, 1987. ix,398p. diagrs., tables. ISBN: 0873390261.

Covers copper, nickel, lead and zinc. Gives company names, addresses and operating data. *Class No: 621.745*

Casting

[4658]

CAMPBELL, J. **Castings.** 2nd ed. Oxford, Butterworth-Heinemann, 1993. 288p. illus., diagrs. £22.50. ISBN: 0750616962.

Covers casting from melt to finished product. Contents: melt ractions; fluid dynamics; mould dynamics; solidification; linear contraction; accuracy; structure, defects and properties. *Class No: 621.746*

[4659]

WIESER, P.F., *ed*. **Steel castings handbook.** 5th ed. Rocky River, Ohio, Steel Founders' Society of America, 1980. [525]p. illus., diagrs., graphs, tables. $35. ISBN: 0960467408.

First published 1941, edited by C.W. Briggs. Revised every decade.

Intended primarily for designers, materials engineers and purchasers of steel castings. 6 parts: (1. General information - 2. Designing castings - 3. Manufacture - 4. Material selections (A. Mechanical and chemical properties. B. Processing properties. C. Physical properties). - 5. Specifying - 6. Buying castings). Emphasis is on mechanical and chemical properties, especially of structural carbon and low alloy steels. Abundant tables, graphs and illustrations, supplemented by extensive glossary (*c*.1,350 terms). *Class No:* 621.746

Powder Metallurgy

Bibliographies

[4660]

COLEMAN, D.S. 'Powder metallurgy'. *Information sources in metallic materials.* Editor, M.N. Patten, p.217-31. London, Bowker-Saur, 1989. (*Guides to information sources.*) ISBN: 0408014911.

Sections: Introduction (process; advantages; production statistics; products - 16 references) - Information sources (*e.g.* reference journals (20 references); books (31 references); conferences; associations; standards (40). *Class No:* 621.762(01)

Handbooks & Manuals

[4661]

FAYED, M.E. *and* OTTEN, L., *eds*. **Handbook of powder science and technology.** New York, etc., Van Nostrand Reinhold, 1984. xiv, 850p. illus., diagrs., graphs, tables. $79.50. ISBN: 0442226107.

26 contributors from 7 countries. 19 chapters cover particle size analysis and measurement, fundamental properties of powders and their behaviour, size enlargement and reduction, mixing, storage, fluidization technology, pipeline transport, sedimentation, filtration, cyclones, wet scrubbers, etc. Chapter references.

'I definitely can recommend this handbook to all chemical engineers who are involved with the storage, handling and processing of particulate solids and powders' (*Chemical engineering*, v.92, Jan. 7, 1985, p.113). *Class No:* 621.762(035)

[4662]

HAUSNER, H.H. *and* MAL, M.K. **Handbook of powder metallurgy.** 2nd ed. Chemical Publishing Co., 1982. 608p. $85. ISBN: 0820603015.

21 chapters. Principles of powder metallurgy and characteristics of powders and processes, Chapters 1-11. Remainder cover currently-produced materials. An appendix covers statistics, applications, physical and chemical data, and terminology.

'... the authors have compiled a concentrated handbook consisting of graphs and tables, practically without text, useful not only for practicing (!) powder metallurgists but all materials engineers and scientists. ... this handbook should be in the hands of everyone interested ... in metal powders and powder metallurgy' (*International journal of powder metallurgy*, v.19(3), July 1983, p.233-4). *Class No:* 621.762(035)

[4663]

Metals handbook; v.7. Powder metallurgy: prepared under the direction of the ASM Handbook Committee. Klar, E., *ed*. 9th ed. Metals Park, Ohio, American Society for Metals, 1984. xviii, 897p. illus., diagrs., graphs, tables. $92. ISBN: 0871700131.

The first completely new volume in the 9th ed., rather than a revision of an 8th ed. volume. About 300 contributors/reviewers. Four major sections: Production of metal powders - Characterization and testing of metal powders - Consolidation of metal powders - Powder systems and applications. Detail much greater than elsewhere in the literature 'such that the book serves as an introduction ... for the technically trained individual and as a reference book for the experienced engineer' (*Preface*). Includes glossary (p.1-13) and brief history. Analytical index (p.852-97).

'It is an excellent and stimulating book of current technology and a standard work for many years' (H.H. Hausner. *International Journal of powder metallurgy and powder technology*, v.20(4), Oct. 1984, p.362). *Class No:* 621.762(035)

[4664]

—**Metals handbook; v.9. Metallography and microstructures.** Metals Park, Ohio, American Society for Metals, 1985. $104. ISBN: 0871700158.

Contains much information of importance to the powder metallurgist, including metallographic preparation techniques and many high quality micrographs relating to powder metallurgy microstructures. '... this is a high-quality volume which will be of genuine assistance to anyone involved in P/M. Together, vols. 7 and 9 [of *Metals Handbook*] constitute a complete treatise on modern powder

....(contd.)

metallurgy technology' (*International journal of powder metallurgy and powder technology*, v.22(2), April 1986, p.128). *Class No:* 621.762(035)

Dictionaries

[4665]

BRITISH STANDARDS INSTITUTION. **Glossary of terms relating to particle technology.** London, BSI, 1993. 35p. diagrs. (*BS 2955: 1993.*)

Replaces *Glossary of terms relating to powders* (1958).

11 sections: 1. General - 2. Types of powder - 3. Powder properties ... 7. Particle shape - 8. Pore size ... 11. Test methods. Index; list of references. *Class No:* 621.762(038)

[4666]

—BRITISH STANDARDS INSTITUTION. Powder metallurgical materials and products. Part 1, Section 1.2. Glossary of terms. London, BSI, 1981. 14p. (*BS 5600: 1981.*)

About 150 terms defined in systematic order with A-Z index. *Class No:* 621.762(038)

Reviews & Abstracts

[4667]

Metal powder report: the monthly journal for the PM industry. Oxford, Elsevier, 1946-. 12 pa. £121. ISSN: 00260657.

Issues contain short 'Literature review' with citations and informative abstracts of recent periodical and conference papers, arranged under subjects and patents. *Class No:* 621.762(048)

Progress Reports

[4668]

Modern developments in powder technology. Princeton, N.J., Metal Powder Industries Federation/American Powder Metallurgy Institute 1973-. v.6-. (v.1-5, 1966-71 published by Plenum Press). illus., diagrs., graphs. ISSN: 00972223.

The proceedings of International Powder Metallurgy Conferences have been published under this title since the second conference, 1965, whose papers appeared in v.1-3 of the series. Proceedings of these International Conferences also comprise certain vols. in the *Progress in powder metallurgy* series (*qv*). V.36 comprises proceedings of the 6th International Conference, Washington, 1980. *Class No:* 621.762(055)

[4669]

Progress in powder metallurgy. Princeton, N.J., Metal Powder Industries Federation, 1947-. v.1-. illus., diagrs., graphs. ISSN: 00796719.

The Proceedings of the Annual Powder Metallurgy Conference are published under this title. Proceedings of the International Powder Metallurgy Conferences held every few years are also published as vols. in this series. *Class No:* 621.762(055)

Maps & Atlases

[4670]

HUPPMANN, W.J. *and* DALAL, K. **Metallographic atlas of powder metallurgy.** Freiburg, West Germany, Verlag Schmid GmbH, 1986. 190p. illus., diagrs. $100.

A short, comprehensive and illustrated overview of processes and methods is followed by over 460 micrographs illustrating powder particles, microstructure of selected powder metallurgy materials (*e.g.* various steels, non-ferrous metals and alloys) and microstructural features of components (*e.g.* surface roughness) and defects in materials and their effects. Classified arrangement. No index.

'The quality of the micrographs ... is excellent. The atlas is highly recommended to those involved in production, testing, quality control, research and development, in the field of powder metallurgy (*International journal of powder metallurgy and powder technology*, v.22(4), Oct. 1986, p.282-3). *Class No:* 621.762(084.3)

Boiler Making

[4671]

BEDNAR, H.H. **Pressure vessel design handbook.** 2nd ed. New York, Van Nostrand Reinhold, 1986. xi, 431p. diagrs., graphs, charts, tables. £46.50. ISBN: 0442213859.

First published 1981.

Aimed as a practical aid to design in conformity with section 8 of the ASME Boiler and Pressure Vessel Code, there are chapters on loads and stresses; design for tall and short vertical vessels and supports for horizontal vessels; welds; materials; numerical methods for stress analysis. 10 Appendices include 172 bibliographical references, a list of relevant US standards and a glossary. Imperial units used.

'Should be a valuable resource not only to junior mechanical and vessel design engineers but also to practicing professionals who wish to

....(contd.)

expand their knowledge of the subject. Bednar has done a fine job in organizing and condensing much widely scattered information ...' (_Chemical engineering_, v.93, Oct. 13 1986, p.95). _Class No:_ 621.772

[4672]
CHUSE, R. _and_ **EBER, S.M. Pressure vessels:** the ASME Code simplified. 6th ed. New York, etc., McGraw-Hill, 1984. x, 267p. illus., diagrs., tables. £29.95. ISBN: 0070108749.

First published 1954. Previous ed. 1977.

Concentrates on the requirements of Section 8 of the 1980 ed. of the ASME Boiler and Pressure Vessel Code, which deals with pressure vessels, and aims to assist the designer, fabricator or inspector who may use the Code infrequently. Provides various charts and tables to enable such users to apply and interpret the Code's requirements. 6 appendices of fundamental data relating to wall thicknesses, dimensions, volumes, corrosion. Two new chapters cover power boilers and nuclear vessels.

'Brings many frequently overlooked items to the reader's attention and suggests methods for better design, fabrication and inspection control that will lead to more efficient and economical operations and better quality control systems' (_Mechanical engineering_, v.106, Nov. 1984, p.106). _Class No:_ 621.772

[4673]
MEGYESY, E.F. Pressure vessel handbook. 7th ed. Pressure Vessel Handbook Publishing, 1986. 480p. illus., diagrs., tables, maps. $38. ISBN: 0914458124.

First published 1972. Previous ed. 1983.

An invaluable assembly of formulas, data, guidance on design and construction for engineers concerned with pressure vessels. Relates to the provisions of section 8 of the ASME Boiler and Pressure Vessel Code, 1983 ed. In parts: 1. Design and construction - 2. Geometry and layout - 3. Measures and weights - 4. Design of steel structures - 5. Miscellaneous (_i.e.,_ Abbreviations; Codes and standards; Laws; Literature; Definitions; Index). Hundreds of tables.

'Serves as an important and needed reference for those involved in the practical aspects of pressure vessels' (_National safety news_, v.129, Feb. 1984, p.62, - Review of previous ed.). _Class No:_ 621.772

[4674]
Referativnyĭ zhurnal. 42. Kotlostroenie. Moscow, VINITI, 1963-. Monthly. diagrs. R18pa. ISSN: 00342424.

About 1,200 signed indicative and informative abstracts pa. on all aspects of boilers. 8 sections, covering general questions, boiler theory, design and calculations, control, plant and special materials. Illustrated with diagrams. UDC numbers. Annual subject index. English contents summary. _Class No:_ 621.772

Tube Making

[4675]
Tube industry yearbook, 1998. Leamington Spa, Warwickshire, Intras, 1998. 400p. illus.

Product category list; Product and equipment directory. Indexes in English, German, French, Spanish, Italian, Russian, Japanese. ITA committees and membership. Covers tube and pipe materials, machinery and equipment. _Class No:_ 621.774

Wire Drawing & Working

[4676]
CLAYTON, P.A., _ed._ **The Encyclopaedia of wire.** Oxted, Surrey, Magnum Publications, 1979. 168p. illus., diagrs. £7.25.

A _Wire industry_ publication. More than 1,500 terms relating to the manufacture and uses of all types of wire defined, sometimes briefly, but frequently at considerable length with descriptions of processes, etc. _Class No:_ 621.778

[4677]
Wire industry yearbook, 1999. 39th ed. Hatfield, Herts., Mack-Books, 1999. 472p. £74. ISSN: 00840424.

World coverage. 900 product groups, each listed in 5 languages (English, German, French, Spanish, Italian), under 7 headings (Ferrous wire - Non-ferrous wire - Machinery for wire manufacture - Machinery and plant for making wire products - Machinery and plant for cable and rope manufacture - Dies, tools, etc. - Lubricants, raw materials & services). Subject list of wire products, with manufacturing companies and suppliers. _Class No:_ 621.778

Welding

Databases

[4678]
WELDASEARCH. Abington, Cambridge, The Welding Institute.

Covers 1967 to date. A bibliographical data base providing references, with abstracts, to the literature of all aspects of welding: design, metallurgy, fabrication, performance of welds, soldering, brazing, thermal cutting, joining of metals and plastics. Derived from

....(contd.)

journal articles, research reports, books, standards, patents, theses, business news. File size: 145000 records. Updated monthly. Available online and on the World Wide Web from Cambridge Scientific Abstracts (URL: http://www.csa.com). Corresponds to the printed _Welding abstracts_ and _Weldasearch industry news_. _Class No:_ 621.791(003.4)

Bibliographies

[4679]
DUMPER, L. _and_ **LOADER, J. 'Welding, brazing and soldering'.** _Information sources in metallic materials._ Editor, M.N. Patten, p.278-315. London, Bowker-Saur, 1989. (_Guides to information sources._) ISBN: 0408014911.

Sections: Information sources - Types of literature (_e.g._ bibliographic services; journals (53 titles); standards; reports) - Subject literature (_e.g._ processes; metallurgy; markets; consumables; health and safety; nondestructive testing; design) - Education and training. _Class No:_ 621.791(01)

[4680]
FISCHER, K. 'Welding: a core list for community college libraries'. _Choice,_ V.28(10), June 1991, p.1599-1608.

Running commentary in 10 sections. Annotated entries; for community college and further education libraries. _Class No:_ 621.791(01)

Encyclopaedias

[4681]
Jefferson's welding encyclopedia. O'Brien, R.G., _ed._ 18th ed. Miami, Fl., American Welding Society, 1997. 758p. illus., diagrs., tables. $120. ISBN: 0871715066.

First ed. 1921.

Brief entries, well illustrated, with ample cross references. Appendices comprise about 20% of the work and cover history, product directories, standards, etc. US emphasis. _Class No:_ 621.791(031)

Handbooks & Manuals

[4682]
AMERICAN WELDING SOCIETY. Welding handbook.

Kearns, W.H., _ed._ 7th/8th eds. Miami, Florida, American Welding Society/London, Macmillan, 1975-. 5v. illus., diagrs., graphs, tables.

1. _Welding technology._ 8th ed. 1987. 638p. £150.

2. _Welding processes - arc and gas welding and cutting, brazing, and soldering._ 8th ed. 1991. 900p. £150.

3. _Resistance and solid-state welding and other joining processes._ 7th ed. 1980. 459p. £29.

4. _Metals and their weldability._ 1983. 582p. £39. ISBN 0333293428.

5. _Engineering, costs, quality and safety._ 1985. 456p. £68. ISBN 0333293436.

The major work of reference, with contributions by specialists from many countries. Revised volume by volume. Whole set currently in 7th ed. Extensively provided with bibliographical references. Generously illustrated. Separate indexes.

Publication of the 8th ed. began in 1987. _Class No:_ 621.791(035)

[4683]
Metals handbook; v.6. Welding, brazing and soldering: prepared under the direction of the ASM Handbook Committee. Nippes, E.F., _ed._ 9th ed. Metals Park, Ohio, American Society for Metals, 1983. xvii, 1152p. $92. ISBN: 0871700077.

Recent developments, a widening of scope and a high proportion of new sections have led to a 50 per cent increase in size of this volume since the previous (8th) ed. of 1971. The work of _c._200 contributors is presented under 13 main headings, of which 2 are introductory, 8 relate to welding, 1 to brazing and 1 to soldering. Welding accounts for over 50 of the articles, brazing has 14 and soldering 1. A glossary (p.1-20), index (p.1113-52), list of abbreviations and symbols and many references effectively enhance this work.

The 10th ed. was published in 1993. _Class No:_ 621.791(035)

[4684]
—**STEWART, J.P. The Welder's handbook.** Reston, Va., Reston Publishing Co., 1981. ix, 534p. $21.95. ISBN: 0835986055.

A practical guide to processes and essential information and data for welders, designers, engineers and managers. 20 chapters (_e.g._ 1. Basic welding consumables ... 6. TIG welding ... 11. Welding special alloys - 12. Brazing guide ... 19. Comparative welding costs - 20. Pipe welding). Appendix ('Useful information'), p.491-527. Index (inconsistent in construction). Numerous tables and illus.

'Gives operating data for many welding processes, helpful to welders; solutions to shop problems, which supervisors often need;

....(contd.)
cost data ... useful for estimators and designers; and technical data ... required by metallurgists and welding engineers' (*Welding design and fabrication* v.54, Oct. 1981, p.174). *Class No:* 621.791(035)

Dictionaries

[4685]
BRITISH STANDARDS INSTITUTION. Welding terms and symbols.
London, BSI, 1980-91. diagrs., charts. £72.20. (*BS 499: 1980-1991*.)
Pt.1: *Glossary for welding, brazing and thermal cutting.* 1991. 113p.
Pt.2: *Specification for symbols for welding.* 1980 (1989). 20p. AMD 7439, Nov. 1982.
Pt.2c: *Welding symbols.* (Chart). 1980. 1p.
The *Glossary* defines over 850 terms, arranged in systematic order and supported by A-Z index. *Class No:* 621.791(038)

Reviews & Abstracts

[4686]
Referativnyĭ zhurnal. 63. Svarka. Moscow, VINITI, 1968-. Monthly. R72.60. ISSN: 01313525.
About 9,000 signed indicative and informative abstracts pa. on welding. 14 sections (General problems ... Arc welding and cutting ... Beam welding ... Gas welding and cutting ... Soldering; brazing ... Welded metal constructions). Annual author and subject indexes. UDC numbers. English contents summary. *Class No:* 621.791(048)

[4687]
Welding abstracts. Cambridge, The Welding Institute, 1988-. Monthly. £390pa. ISSN: 09520287.
About 500 abstracts per issue. Sections: Processes - Production - Equipment and materials - Properties and testing - Manufacturing and construction - General. Author and subject indexes per issue. Includes patents and standards. Available online as *Weldasearch*.
Class No: 621.791(048)

Yearbooks & Directories

[4688]
The Welding and metal fabrication buyers' guide 1998. Redhill, Surrey, DMG Business Media, 1998. [iv], 640p. £60. ISBN: 0861089448.
Contents: Manufacturers of equipment and materials - Suppliers of contract services - Welding distributors - Index.
Class No: 621.791(058)

Standards

[4689]
BRITISH STANDARDS INSTITUTION. Welding. Milton, Keynes, BSI, 1986. 3p. £1. (*SL 7.*)
One of the Sectional List series, giving the number, title and price group of 63 British Standards specifications, published documents (PD) and drafts for development (DD), covering all types of welding and brazing and including relevant standards from other fields. No index. (Full details are to be found in the annual *Catalogue* (*qv*)).
Class No: 621.791(083.74)

[4690]
International standards index: welding and related processes.
Abington, Woodhead, 1991. 646p. £300. ISBN: 1855730219.
Loose-leaf. Bi-annual supplements planned.
Lists nearly 5000 standards on welding and allied techniques from 16 countries. Includes European and international standards.
Class No: 621.791(083.74)

Thesauri

[4691]
INTERNATIONAL INSTITUTE OF WELDING. The International welding thesaurus. 3rd ed. Abington, Cambridge, Welding Institute, 1989. 195p. £45.
First published 1974, based on 2nd ed. of *A thesaurus for welding and allied processes* (Welding Institute, 1971). Prepared by a joint British-French-German study group. Contains about 1,500 descriptors and synonyms, broader, narrower and related terms, in English, with trilingual lists of descriptors in each language. Tables show the 'families' of descriptors (*e.g.* Properties; Phenomena). Preface and introduction in English and French. *Class No:* 621.791:025.43

Metal Finishing

CD-ROM

[4692]
Surface finishing CD. Cambridge, The Welding Institute. £499; $765.
About 30,000 citations with abstracts on surface treatment and metal finishing. Updated quarterly. *Class No:* 621.793(003.40)

Bibliographies

[4693]
RUDZKI, G.J. Surface finishing systems: metal and non-metal finishing handbook guide. Metals Park, Ohio, American Society for Metals / Teddington, Middx., Finishing Publications, 1983. 421p. charts, tables. £35. ISBN: 090447707x.
The third part of this book - half of it - comprises a cumulative index to *Metal finishing abstracts*, 1960-82, in which entries are arranged alphabetically under chemical element, Actinium - Zirconium, with subdivision for processes, *e.g.* Spray coatings.
'This section will prove invaluable to researchers and information scientists undertaking literature searches. There are, however, two limitations. The first that ... the references are limited to new techniques or conditions which are not generally known. The second ... is that ... it is not complete. The references were ... carefully chosen.' *Class No:* 621.793(01)

[4694]
Surface treatment plant and processes; incorporating *Metal finishing plant and processes*. Teddington, Middx., Finishing Publications, Ltd., May/June 1986-. v. 22(3)-. 6 pa. £67. ISSN: 09505202.
As *Metal finishing plant and processes*, (v.1-22, 1965-86). 900 brief descriptions of new products and processes pa., in 21 sections (Cleaning and degreasing ... Electroplating ... Vacuum and gas coatings ... Waste treatment and recovery ... General and miscellaneous). Index to company names with annual cumulative indexes of company names, trade names and subjects.
Class No: 621.793(01)

Handbooks & Manuals

[4695]
Advanced surface coatings: a handbook of surface engineering. Rickerby, D.S. *and* Matthews, A., *eds.* Glasgow, Blackie, 1991. xiii,368p. illus., diagrs., graphs. £75. ISBN: 0216928990.
16 contributors. 13 chapters, closely subdivided: 2. Use of plastics in deposition technologies ... 4. Evaporation - 5. Spatter disposition (129 references) ... 9. Thermal spraying ... 12. Evaluation of coatings - 13. Market perspective and future trends. Detailed, analytical index, p.365-68. *Class No:* 621.793(035)

[4696]
The Canning handbook: surface finishing technology. 23rd ed. Birmingham, W. Canning / London, Spon, 1982. xiv, 1094p. illus., diagr., tables. ISBN: 0419129006.
First published 1889 as *Practical instructions for gold, silver, nickel, brass and copper, plating and polishing*. Previously published (1st ed. 1901; 22nd ed. 1978) as *Handbook on electroplating*.
35 chapters: 1-5. Polishing; 6-32. Electroplating; 33-34. Lacquering and bronzing; 35. Safety precautions. Index: p.1068-94. A standard handbook produced by a company with a 200-year history in the field whose recent diversification is matched by the widening of scope of this edition. *Class No:* 621.793(035)

[4697]
KUHN, A.T., *ed.* Techniques in electrochemistry, corrosion and metal finishing: a handbook. Chichester, Wiley, 1987. xviii,567p. illus., tables. ISBN: 047191407x.
8 contributors. In 3 parts: A. Introduction to experimental methods - B. Specialized techniques (Section I: Methods based on light; Section II: Spectroscopic methods; Section III: Other methods (*e.g.* physiochemical; radio-chemical; acoustic emission; dyes, etc.) - C. The literature (37p. bibliography of post-1960 monographs, most from the British Library Science Reference and Information Service). 28 chapters, most with extensive references (*e.g.* 'Raman spectroscopy', p.237-49, includes 166). Subject index. Dedicated - gracefully - to the 'Library' and its 'staff'. *Class No:* 621.793(035)

Reviews & Abstracts

[4698]
Surface treatment technology abstracts; incorporating *Metal finishing abstracts* and *Printed circuits abstracts*. Stevenage, Herts., Finishing Publications, Ltd., 1986-. v. 28(1)-. 6 pa. £395; $840 pa. ISSN: 09505199.
As *Metal finishing abstracts*, v. 1-27, 1959-85. Previously appeared in *Electroplating and metal spraying* (1947-1959).
Over 7,000 indicative and informative abstracts and citations pa. covering surface treatment, in 21 classes (Cleaning and degreasing ... Electroplating ... Metal spraying and hard facing ... Corrosion and

....(contd.)
electrochemistry ... General and miscellaneous). Covers journal articles, books, standards, reports and patents - full coverage for UK, European and US patents. Also available on CD-ROM
Class No: 621.793(048)

Yearbooks & Directories
[4699]

'Metal finishing': 64th guidebook and directory issue. New York, Elsevier, 1996. Annual. 912p. illus., diagrs., graphs and tables. $48 pa., including the monthly journal. ISSN: 00260576.

Published each January as the 13th issue of the volume. Comprises a comprehensive handbook of finishing, plating and treatments processes and a brief directory of the industry. Technical section has 8 sections: (Mechanical surface preparation ... Electroplating solutions ... Surface treatments - Organic finishing ... Finishing plant engineering - Tables and data sheets). Directory contains classified buyers' guide for equipment, material and processes, alphabetical list of manufacturers, regional list of US distributors, and trade names index. Subject index. Many tables. *Class No:* 621.793(058)

[4700]

Product finishing handbook and directory. Redhill, Surrey, DMG Business Media, 1998. 383p. £81. ISBN: 0861089839. ISSN: 13623680.

'Encyclopaedia of finishes' (p.1-115) precedes 5 chapters on finishing techniques. Directory: Trade finishers' services; Trade and brand names; Names and addresses; Associations and technical organizations. *Class No:* 621.793(058)

[4701]

—The Anti-Corrosion handbook and directory. Bean, J.E., *ed.* 2nd ed. London, Sawell Publications, [1989]. 195p. illus., tables.

12 chapters on corrosion in various industries and of particular materials. 'Encyclopaedia', p.6-20; 'Reference tables', p.115-21. Directory of associations and buyers' guide. Handy format.
Class No: 621.793(058)

Tables & Data Books
[4702]

ASH, M. *and* **ASH, I.,** *comps.* **Handbook of industrial surfactants:** an international guide to more than 21,000 products by trade name, composition, application, and manufacturer. 2nd ed. Aldershot, Hants., Gower, 1997. 2v. (xvi, 2403p.). ISBN: 0566078929.

First published 1993.

Covers emsulfiers, wetting agents, detergents, dispersants, stabilizers; plus detergent raw materials, defoamers and anti-foaming agents. 4 parts: I. Trade name reference - II. Chemical dictionary cross reference III. Application cross reference - IV. Manufacturers directory. 6 appendices (CAS numbers, etc.). Available on CD-ROM (Gower). *Class No:* 621.793(083)

[4703]

BENNINGHOFF, H. Index of chemicals used for the treatment of metal surfaces. [Chemikalien-Index für die Oberflächentechnik der Metalle.] Amsterdam, etc., Elsevier, 1974. xxiv, 1260 columns. diagrs., tables. ISBN: 0444410759.

1,034 chemicals and chemical products, named in accordance with IUPAC recommendations in German, English and French, with empirical and structural formulae, characteristics, solubility in water and acids, reactions and hazard classification and data. Indexes of chemicals in each language, including popular names, and of formulae.
Class No: 621.793(083)

Packaging

Databases
[4704]

PIRA Abstracts. Leatherhead, Surrey, PIRA, the Research Association for the Paper and Board, Printing and Packaging Industries.

Covers 1975 to date. A bibliographic database providing references, with abstracts, to the literature of paper and pulp manufacture, printing and packaging. Packaging materials, operations and equipment, products, markets and companies are covered. Sources: over 700 periodicals, books, reports, standards and conference papers. File size: 422,000 items. Updated biweekly. Available via DIALOG, Questel/ ORBIT and STN International; CD-ROM (DIALOG OnDisc); and on the World Wide Web (URL: http://www.pira.co.uk).
Class No: 621.798(003.4)

[4705]

PSTA. Frankfurt-a-M., FRG, International Food Information Service.

Covers 1982 to date. A bibliographic database providing references, with abstracts, to the literature of all aspects of packaging, with emphasis on foodstuffs. Includes aerosols, coatings, filling, handling, storage, transport, labelling, law, materials, marketing, waste. Sources: periodical articles, books, conference papers, standards, reports, trade literature. About 38,000 records; updated 5 times a year. Available online via DIALOG, file 252, and several other hosts. Also available on magnetic tape. *Class No:* 621.798(003.4)

Bibliographies
[4706]

UNITED NATIONS. Industrial Development Organization. **Information sources on the packaging industry.** New York, United Nations, 1977. xii, 110p. $4. (*UNIDO guides to information sources, no. 27.*)

858 entries. 12 sections: 1. Professional, trade and research organizations, learned societies and special information services - 2. Directories (88 listed) - 3. Sources of statistics, marketing and other economic data - 4. Basic handbooks, textbooks and manuals - 5. Monograph series - 6. Current periodicals (119 listed) - 7. Current abstracting and indexing periodicals - 8. Proceedings, papers and reports - 9. Specialized dictionaries and encyclopedias - 10. Bibliographies - 11. Films and film catalogues - 12. Other potential sources of information (*e.g.* G. Meetings and conferences; I. Standards and specifications). Bibliography of sources used.
Class No: 621.798(01)

Encyclopaedias
[4707]

The Wiley encyclopedia of packaging technology. Brody, A.L. *and* March, K.S., *eds.* 2nd ed. New York, Wiley, 1997. xii, 1023p. illus., diagrs. $225. ISBN: 0471063975.

First published 1987.

About 250 entries, A-Z; most have brief bibliographies and general references. Appendix B is a glossary, p.985-1001. Detailed, analytical index, p.1003-23. Covers relevant US legislation. Comprehensive.
Class No: 621.798(031)

Handbooks & Manuals
[4708]

HANLON, J.F. Handbook of packaging engineering. 2nd ed. New York, etc., McGraw-Hill, 1984. viii, [536]p. illus., diagrs., graphs, tables. $74. ISBN: 0070259941.

First published 1971.

Aims 'to contain in a single volume all the pertinent data on packaging that is likely to be needed' (*Preface*). New packaging materials - *e.g.* stretch and metallized films - and developments in established practices - *e.g.* aerosol use, labelling and marking systems, etc. - have been included. 20 chapters (1. Elements of packaging - 2. Paper and paperboard - 3. Films and foils ... 8. Plastics ... 13. Closures, applicators, fasteners, and adhesives ... 19. Quality control - 20. Laws and regulations). Detailed coverage of films and plastics - Chapters 3 and 8 account for over a quarter of the book. Numerous illustrations and tables of data. 20-page index is thorough, but access if often indirect - *i.e.,* 'propellants' are traced via 'Aerosols'; 'polyethyene' is found via 'films' or 'plastics'.
Class No: 621.798(035)

[4709]

HARPER, C.A., *ed.* **Electronic packaging and interconnection handbook.** New York, McGraw-Hill, 1991. v.p. illus., diagrs., graphs, tables. $79.50. ISBN: 0070266840.

3 sections: 1. Fundamental technologies - 2. Interconnection technologies - 3. System packaging technologies. References to industry and military standards and specifications. Detailed, analytical index. *Class No:* 621.798(035)

[4710]

—HARPER, C.A. *and* MILLER, M.B. Electronic packaging, microelectronics, and interconnection dictionary. New York, etc., McGraw-Hill, 1993. vii, 235p. ISBN: 0070266883.

About 6,000 terms, briefly defined. Acronyms, symbols and abbreviations appended. *Class No:* 621.798(035)

Dictionaries
[4711]

BRITISH STANDARDS INSTITUTION. Glossary of packaging terms. London, BSI, 1974-94. 5 pts. diagrs. (*BS 3130: 1973-1994.*)
pt. 1: *General.* 1989. 16p.
pt. 2: *Paper and board packaging.* 1990. 20p.
pt. 4: *Metal containers and aerosols.* 1976. 28p.
pt. 5: *Plastics and flexible packaging* (excluding paper). 1994. 12p.
pt. 6: *Wooden packaging.* 1981. 10p.

....(contd.)

Over 1,000 terms are defined and illustrated in systematic order with alphabetical indexes. Parts 3, 7 and 8 have been withdrawn. *Class No:* 621.798(038)

[4712]
HOFFMANN, J.P.A. Fachwörterbuch verpacking. [Dictionary of packaging] 2nd ed. Heidelberg, Hüthig, 1990. 1093p. £171.90. ISBN: 3778517724.

Rev. by E. Klämer.

4,580 German terms, with equivalents in English, French, Italian, Spanish and Russian across the double page. Indexes in non-German languages. *Class No:* 621.798(038)

Reviews & Abstracts

[4713]
International packaging abstracts. Leatherhead, Surrey, Pira, 1981-. Monthly. £725. ISSN: 02607409.

Compiled by the Information Section of Pira (the Research Association for the Paper & Board, Printing & Packaging Industries). More than 5,000 informative abstracts pa., derived from over 250 periodicals, and from books, reports, standards, conference proceedings and newspapers. 8 sections (1. Packaging in general - 2. Materials - 3. Components - 4. Retail unit packages - 5. Transit packs - 6. Packaging for specific products - 7. Packaging operations and machinery - 8. Distribution), each subdivided (*e.g.* 3.1 Labels; 6.13 Beverages). Author and subject indexes in each issue. Mean delay time for abstracts less than 3 months. Also available online as part of the *Pira* database from a range of hosts. *Class No:* 621.798(048)

[4714]
Packaging Science and Technology Abstracts. [Referatedienst Verpackung.] Frankfurt-am-Main, International Food Information Service, in cooperation with Fraunhofer-Institut für Lebensmittel technologie und Verpackung. 1982-. v.1-. 6pa. DM 500 pa. ISSN: 07223218.

About 3,200 informative abstracts pa., in English, for non-German originals, and in English and German for German originals. Covers scientific, technical, marketing and management aspects of packaging. Derived from worldwide literature: 400 periodicals, books, pamphlets, standards, specifications, patents, conference papers, research reports and trade literature. Each abstract liberally indexed with descriptors which are 'rotated' to provide multi-access subject indexes in each issue, in English and in German. Author index in each issue. Cumulated annual subject and author indexes. Classified in 25 sections covering 10 subject groups (Packaging economy - Packaging material ... Packaging machines ... Transport, storage). Available on magnetic tape. Online version: PSTA (*qv*). *Class No:* 621.798(048)

Yearbooks & Directories

[4715]
Packaging industry directory, 1997. 21st ed. Tonbridge, Kent, Benn, 1995. Annual. viii, 468p. £87. ISSN: 02699834.

Previously entitled '*Packaging review' buyers' guide.*

Lists almost 2,300 manufacturers and suppliers. Classified buyers' guide; brand names index; company data; who's who in the industry. Includes UK agents, consultants, trade organizations and institutes. *Class No:* 621.798(058)

Information Management

[4716]
FARRELL, S. International packaging information sources 2nd ed. Leatherhead, Surrey, 1990. [vi], 428p. ISBN: 0902799304.

Sources include associations and research organizations, membership lists, statistics, exhibitions, standards and test methods, libraries, etc. Indexes: country; organizations; publications; subject. A valuable source. *Class No:* 621.798:025.4

Containerization

[4717]
'Containerisation international' year book, 1997. London, Emap Response, 1997. 768p. £195. ISSN: 03057402.

A world directory in a fast-growing service area. Sections: Ports and terminals by continent - Services - Equipment - Leasing and repair - Register of vessels - Shipbrokers. 7 appendices (7. Bibliography). Indexes: ships; companies; advertisers. Editorial review precedes. *Class No:* 621.798.12

Machine Elements

[4718]
ANTONI, T. Wörterbuch antriebstechnic. [Dictionary of drives.] Munich, Publicis MCD, 1996. 788p.

About 40,000 entry words, with 87,00 translations into English. Main fields covered include electrical machines, AC and DC converters, closed-loop controls, control engineering and automation, industrial systems and field busses. Also available on floppy disk. *Class No:* 621.8

[4719]
BÖGELSACK, G., *and others.* **'Terminology for the theory of machines and mechanisms'.** In *Mechanism and machine theory,* v.18(16), 1983. p.379-408.

A draft produced by Commission A of the International Federation for the Theory of Machines and Mechanisms as the first step to the publication of a standard terminology. Over 800 terms are defined and presented in a classified arrangement - 4 major sections with 17 sub-sections: Structure of machines and mechanisms; Kinematics; Dynamics; Machine control and measurements. A-Z index facilitates quick access to any definition. *Class No:* 621.8

[4720]
Handbook of mechanical power drives. 3rd ed. Morden, Surrey, Trade & Technical Press, 1980. vi, 680p. illus., diagrs., graphs, charts, tables. £52. ISBN: 0854610855.

Previous ed. 1977. Five sections: 1. Systems and fundamentals - 2. Power transmission equipment (*e.g.* belts, bearings, drives, clutches, brakes, gears) - 3. Related mechanisms and systems (*e.g.* pulleys, springs, speed reducers, seals) - 4. List of relevant British Standards - 5. Buyers' guide (25p.). Index. Well illustrated and supported by data tables. *Class No:* 621.8

[4721]
Handbook of rotordynamics. Ehrich, F.F. New York, McGraw-Hill, 1992. v.p. illus., diagrs., graphs, tables. $59.95. ISBN: 0070193304.

4 chapters, closely subdivided, with references: 1. Vibration - 2. Analytical prediction of response - 3. Rotor balancing - 4. Performance verification. Useful practical examples. Well up to the standard of other McGraw-Hill *Handbooks. Class No:* 621.8

[4722]
LINGAIAH, K. Machine design data handbook. New York, McGraw-Hill, 1994. v.p. diagrs. graphs, tables. $136.50; £80.95. ISBN: 0070379335.

Covers a wide range of machine elements, *e.g.* cams, pipes, disks, joints, clutches, brakes, etc. Largely tables. Detailed, analytical index, 14p. 'The most comprehensive English language book of its kind in print' (*Choice,* March 1995, p.1154). *Class No:* 621.8

[4723]
PARMLEY, R.O., *ed.* **Mechanical components handbook.** New York, etc., McGraw-Hill, 1985. xii, [757]p. illus., diagrs., tables. £59.95. ISBN: 0070485143.

Many contributors. 14 chapters covering all types of component, *e.g.* gears, chains, belts, bearings, clutches, springs, fasteners and retaining and locking devices. Supported by hundreds of diagrams and tables of data. *Class No:* 621.8

[4724]
ROTHBART, H.A., *ed.* **Mechanical design handbook.** 3rd ed. New York, etc., McGraw-Hill, 1996. v.p. illus., diagrs., graphs, charts, tables. $115.50. ISBN: 0070540381.

First published 1964; 2nd ed. 1985 as *Mechanical design and systems handbook.*

'The new title reflects a reduction of the emphasis on systems' (*Preface*) and concentrates on the principles and data that optimize mechanical or machine design. 30 sections covering topics such as reliability, composites, seals, belts, chains, etc. *Class No:* 621.8

[4725]
Standard handbook of machine design. Shigley, J.E. *and* Mischke, C.R., *eds.* New York, etc., McGraw-Hill, 1995. 1700p. diagrs., graphs, charts, tables. ISBN: 0070569584.

Contributors cover the entire field of machine design. Initial sections deal with specific machine elements (springs, clutches, cams, etc.) and design techniques (*e.g.* load cycle analysis); the remaining 13 cover factors such as wear, stress, etc., or measurement, numerical methods, etc. Almost 1,000 illustrations of various kinds, numerous tables, formulae and data. Detailed, analytical index. *Class No:* 621.8

Bearings & Shafts

[4726]
BRITISH STANDARDS INSTITUTION. Metrical spherical plain bearings. Part 6. Glossary of terms. London, BSI, 1983. 16p. (*BS 5983: 1983.*)

About 60 terms defined and illustrated with A-Z index. *Class No:* 621.833.2

Gears & Clutches

[4727]

BRITISH STANDARDS INSTITUTION. **Glossary for gears.** London, BSI, 1976. 2 parts. diagrs. (*BS 2519: 1976; ISO 701.*)

pt. 1: *Geometrical definitions.* 1976. 40p. pt. 2: *Notation.* 1976. 8p.

Over 300 terms defined and illustrated in systematic order. 85 symbols listed and identified. *Class No:* 621.833.3

[4728]

DRAGO, R.J. **Fundamentals of gear design.** Boston, Mass., etc., Butterworth, 1988. xiii,560p. illus., diagrs., graphs, tables. ISBN: 040990127x.

Intended as a 'general design reference guide' for the 'beginning or occasional' gear designer (*Preface*, p.xi). 11 chapters (with references and sometimes bibliography) in 4 parts: I. Introduction (history; types of gears; theory) - II. Fabrication and inspection - III. Failure and load capacity evaluation - IV. Lubrication. 3 appendices (gear geometry; nomenclature; quality designations); index (15p.). Author is a practising and consulting engineer. Well-produced; extensively illustrated. 'An excellent general reference to the basics of gear design' (*Choice*, Feb. 1989, p.968). *Class No:* 621.833.3

[4729]

Dudley's gear handbook. Townsend, D.R., *ed.* New York, etc., McGraw-Hill, 1991. v.p. illus., diagrs., charts, tables. $75. ISBN: 0070179034.

First published 1962 as *Gear handbook*, ed. by D.W. Dudley.

Most chapters have been completely rewritten for this ed. New chapters on gear vibration and gear noise have been included. A practical handbook on gear elements and formulae, gear teeth design, gear calculations, loading and rating, gear cutting and forming, finishing and grinding, gear efficiency and lubrication. Data tables. For practising engineers. *Class No:* 621.833.3

[4730]

ORTHWEIN, W.C. **Clutches and brakes:** design and selection. New York Dekker, 1986. xii, 358p. illus., diagrs., graphs, tables. $55. (*Mechanical engineering series, no. 50.*) ISBN: 0824773934.

13 chapters cover various types of brake and clutch, friction materials, vibration and heat dissipation factors. Chapter 11 lists SAE standards, reproducing the text of 15. Aim is to derive relevant formulas, display examples of use and offer access to appropriate flow charts and computer programs.

'This reference work contains the formulas for the design and selection of a variety of brakes and clutches ... simplifies the design selection process by deriving lengthy formulas and accelerating iteration procedures' (*Mechanical engineering*, v.109, Oct. 1986, p.81). *Class No:* 621.833.3

[4731]

SOUTH, D.W. *and* EWERT, R.H. **Encyclopedic dictionary of gears and gearing.** New York, McGraw-Hill, 1995. xviii, 414p. diagrs., tables. $54.50; £46. ISBN: 0070597960.

Several thousand terms defined and explained. In a number of cases fields of coverage are indicated. Useful illustrations.
Class No: 621.833.3

[4732]

STOKES, A. **Gear handbook:** design and calculations. Oxford, Butterworth-Heinemann, 1992. 290p. illus., diagrs., tables. £40; $95. ISBN: 0750611499.

Covers spur gears, helical gears, straight, spiral, zerol and hypoid gears and worm gears in a practical approach. 'A valuable reference book' (*Choice*, December 1992, p.651). *Class No:* 621.833.3

Materials Handling

[4733]

BRITISH STANDARDS INSTITUTION. **Glossary of terms used in materials handling.** London, BSI, 1964-75. 9v. diagrs. (*BS 3810: 1964-1975.*)

pt. 1: *Terms used in connection with pallets, stillages, hand and powered trucks.* 1964. 36p.

pt. 2: *Terms used in connection with conveyors and elevators (excluding pneumatic and hydraulic handling).* 1965. 28p.

pt. 3: *Terms used in connection with pneumatic and hydraulic handling.* 1967. 28p.

pt. 4: *Terms used in connection with cranes.* 1968. 28p.

pt. 5: *Terms used in connection with lifting tackle.* 1971. 36p.

pt. 6: *Terms used in connection with pulley blocks.* 1973. 24p.

pt. 7: *Terms used in connection with aerial ropeways and cableways.* 1973. 24p.

pt. 8: *Terms used in connection with lifts, lifting platforms and inclined haulage.* 1975. 16p.

pt. 9: *Terms used in connection with rail transport.* 1975. 16p.

600 items defined and illustrated. *Class No:* 621.86

[4734]

Materials handling handbook. Kulwiec, R.A., *ed.* 2nd ed. New York, etc., Wiley, 1984. xviii, 1,458p. illus., diagrs., graphs, tables. £81.25. ISBN: 0471097829.

First published 1958.

83 contributors. Sponsored by the American Society of Mechanical Engineers and the International Material Management Society. The development of computer-controlled automatic plant and warehouses has made this new edition imperative. The objective of the Joint Committee of the Societies was 'a useful ... working tool for users and designers of materials handling systems and equipment' (*Foreword*) with emphasis 'on presenting data that the working engineer can use to select, size or apply equipment and systems' (*Preface*). 5 Parts, 36 Chapters and 2 Appendices: 1. Introduction - 2. Unit materials handling - 3. Bulk materials handling - 4. Transportation interface - 5. Safety, environment and human factors. Appendix B lists sources of information. Index (p.1,437-58).

'Offers a good deal of problem-solving guidance ... It will prove to be a very useful reference source for engineers involved in unit-handling and/or bulk-handling operations' (*Chemical engineering*, v.93, March 3, 1986, p.134). *Class No:* 621.86

Fasteners

[4735]

Industrial fasteners handbook. 3rd ed. Morden, Surrey, Trade & Technical Press, 1985. vi, 650p. illus., diagrs., tables. £57.50. ISBN: 0854610979.

Complete revision and updating of earlier editions to take account of new manufacturing techniques and new types of fasteners and materials. Attempts to provide detailed description and data for all known types, arranged logically in sections. 1. Review of mechanical fasteners (including design, performance, materials, manufacture) - 2. Bolts and machine screws - 3. Special duty fasteners (*e.g.* vibration-resistant, fasteners for plastics, furniture, buildings) - 4. Special purpose fasteners (*e.g.* rivets, plugs, pins, clips, staples) - 5. Tools used for fastening - 6. Data, standards, trade associations - 7. Buyers' guide (including trade names, classifed index, manufacturers' addresses). Well illustrated, copious data tabulations and effective index. Advertisements. *Class No:* 621.88

[4736]

—PARMLEY, R.O., *ed.* **Standard handbook of fastening and joining.** 2nd ed. New York, etc., McGraw-Hill, 1989. [672]p. illus., tables. £55. ISBN: 0070485224.

First published 1977.

15 sections: Threaded fasteners - description and standards - Standard pins ... Rope splicing and tying - Metrics and general data. The 2nd ed. contains over 50% new or revised material. For engineers, machinists and technicians in all fields. 880 illus.
Class No: 621.88

[4737]

SIDDERS, P.A., *ed.* **Guide to world screw threads.** 1st American ed. New York, Industrial Press, 1969. 318p. diagrs., tables. $19.50. ISBN: 0831110929.

Previously published in England under the title: *Machinery's screw thread book* (20th ed. 1969. Machinery Publishing).

American ed. contains additional data, largely of US concern. 12 sections covering all types of screw threads - British Whitworth and non-Whitworth; Unified and American; American pipe threads; Continental series; Horological screws; Inspection; Nut, bolt and screw dimensions; Tapping sizes. Details of ISO metric screw threads where available. (Work on metrication was proceeding when book was published.) 235 tables of relevant data and dimensions. Brief glossary (English-French-German). *Class No:* 621.88

[4738]

—BRITISH STANDARDS INSTITUTION. **Glossary of terms for cylindrical screw threads.** London, BSI, 1984. 14p. diagrs. (*BS 6528: 1984.*)

34 fundamental terms and definitions in English and French, with appendices listing Russian, German and Italian equivalents.
Class No: 621.88

Lubrication

Databases

[4739]

TRIBO (Tribology Index). Berlin, BAM (*i.e.,* Bundestanstalt für Materialprüfung).

Covers 1972 to date. A bibliographic database, providing references to the literature of all aspects of tribology - friction, wear and lubrication of moving parts. Includes stressing conditions, materials, machine parts, biomechanics. Derived from journal articles, conference papers, standards, books, reports, theses. Citations in English (some titles in vernacular). About 92,500 records. Updated

....*(contd.)*

every 2 months. Hosts include FIZ Karlsruhe (formerly INKA), STN International. Citations prior to 1985 correspond to *Documentation Tribology: Wear, friction and lubrication. Class No:* 621.89(003.4)

[4740]

—Documentationtribology: wear, friction and lubrication. Berlin, BAM (*i.e.*, Bundestantalt für Materialprüfung). $150.

Previously *Dokumentation Versch Leiss, Reibung und Schmierung.*

Printed version, TRIBO database. Classified arrangement - Sections, sub-sections, alphabetical by author. Indexes of personal, corporate authors, report numbers, standards numbers, subjects and conference titles. *Class No:* 621.89(003.4)

Bibliographies

[4741]

FOX, M.F., *and others, comps*. **Bibliography on engine lubricating oil.** Aldershot, Hants., Gower Technical Press, 1987. xv, 223p. £45. ISBN: 0291397069.

More than 3,000 citations, without abstracts, to the literature of 20 countries, drawing on over 200 periodicals, on conference papers, research reports, books and standards, in 16 subject sections (A. Composition and consumption of lubricating oil ... D. Degradation of lubricating oils ... G. Lubricating oils for diesel engines ... P. Alternative bearings and dry lubricants) plus Q. Future trends and S. Standards (almost 300 from 9 countries are listed). Items arranged chronologically by year and A-Z by author, uniquely numbered. Language is indicated. Scope notes introduce each section. Cross-references are given. Journals list, with abbreviations (but not always consistent with those used in entries). Author index. Sadly, no subject index. *Class No:* 621.89(01)

Encyclopaedias

[4742]

KAJDAS, C., *and others, eds*. **Encyclopedia of tribology.** Amsterdam, Elsevier, 1990. viii,478p. £100. (*Tribology, v.15.*) ISBN: 0444884017.

About 1500 terms (Abrasion - Zirconium ...) are briefly described (*e.g.* 'detergent', *c.*1p.). Most entries carry references, 1,750 in all. *Class No:* 621.89(031)

Handbooks & Manuals

[4743]

CRC handbook of lubrication and tribology. Booser, E.R., *ed*. Boca Raton, Florida, CRC Press, 1984-94. 3v. illus., diagrs., graphs. $253. ISBN: 0849339014, v.1; 0849339022, v.2; 0849339030, v.3.

1. *Application and maintenance*. 1984. [xiv], 600p. 2. *Theory and design*. 1984. [xiv], 689p. 3. *Monitoring, materials, synthetic lubricants, and applications*. 1994. [xiv], 619p.

Sponsored by the American Society of Lubrication Engineers as successor to McGraw-Hill *Standard handbook of lubrication engineering* (1968).

80 contributors. V.1. gives approximately equal treatment to: applications in automobiles, aircraft and machine tools; other industries; maintenance. V.2. is similarly divided between: friction, wear and lubrication theory; lubricants and their properties and uses; design principles. Chapter bibliographies. *Class No:* 621.89(035)

[4744]

CROOK, S., *and* MORTIER, R.M., *eds*. **Chemistry and technology of lubricants.** Glasgow, Blackie Academic, 1991. 320p. illus. ISBN: 0216929210.

Designed for chemists and chemical engineers working with lubricants and as an information source for research and academic institutions. *Class No:* 621.89(035)

[4745]

KRAGELSKY, I.V. *and* ALISIN, V.V., *eds*. **Friction wear, lubrication, tribology handbook;** translated by F. Palkin and V. Palkin. Moscow, Mir Publishers; Oxford, Pergamon, 1981. 3v. diagrs., graphs, tables. ISBN: 0080275915.

Published originally as *Trenie, iznashivanie i smazka* (Moscow, Mashinostroenie Publishers, 1978).

This, the first tribology handbook to be published in the USSR, is a compilation of contributions by more than 50 experts, 'conceived as an aid to design engineers in choosing materials and lubricants', and 'summarizes the results of ... research on the friction and wear of machine parts and gives data on lubricants and lube additives' (*Preface*). 'Excellent translation. ... a good appreciation of the present-day status of the subject within the USSR' (Barwell, F.T. 'A semi-centennial perspective of lubrication'. Paper C251/87 in *Tribology - friction, lubrication and wear: fifty years on*. London, Inst. Mech. E., 1987. v.1, p.13). *Class No:* 621.89(035)

[4746]

NEALE, M.J., *ed*. **The Tribology handbook.** 2nd ed. Oxford, Butterworth-Heinemann, 1995. v.p. illus. diagrs., graphs, tables. ISBN: 0750611987.

First published 1973.

Over 100 contributors. Topics: bearings; rotary and linear drives; seals; lubricants; environmental effects; failures; maintenance; repair; basic information sources; design reference. Index. Helpful presentation, with much of the information in graphical or tabular form.

Also available on CD-ROM as *Engineering materials selector*, either singly (£199) or in conjunction with *Smithell's metals reference book* and/or *Tribology handbook. Class No:* 621.89(035)

[4747]

PETERSON, M.B. *and* WINER, W.O., *eds*. **Wear control handbook.** New York, American Society of Mechanical Engineers, 1980. 1358p. illus., diagrs., graphs, tables. $75.

34 contributors. This handbook, with its pioneering attempt to collect all wear data for machinery design and maintenance, was sponsored by the ASME's Research Committee on Lubrication. The content is presented in 36 chapters under 6 headings: 1. Introduction - 2. Wear fundamentals - 3. Materials - 4. Designing for wear - 5. Component wear - 6. Appendices. Section 5, Component wear, has 16 sections (*e.g.* Bushings; Rolling bearings; Gear wear; Cutting tool wear). Emphasis throughout is on wear, rather than lubrication and lubricants. Appendices contain useful 8-language glossary prepared for the OECD and covering 650 terms. Index (p.1323-58). *Class No:* 621.89(035)

Yearbooks & Directories

[4748]

Lubricants Europe: the directory of lubricants and lubricant additive suppliers in Europe. 2nd ed. Deal, Kent, Leaf Coppin, 1995. [x], 316p. ISBN: 0951342673.

About 800 companies; sections: Companies (A-Z by country) - Product details (A-Z by country) - Indexes (company name; brand name; products). *Class No:* 621.89(058)

Histories

[4749]

DOWSON, D. **History of tribology.** 2nd ed. London, Professional Engineering Publishing, 1998. xxiv, 768p. ilius., diagrs. ISBN: 186058070x.

First published 1979.

A comprehensive history of studies, concepts and devices associated with friction, lubrication, wear and bearings from prehistoric times to the present when the subject has acquired a specific term to isolate it: tribology. The treatment is chronological; chapters 1-8 cover the period before the Industrial Revolution; chapters 9-12 deal with the period since. Chapter 12 illustrates major developments of recent years and supplements the original text. Each chapter is subdivided by topics (*e.g.* Bearings), facilitating concentration on particular aspects of the subject. An appendix provides biographical sketches of scientists important for their contributions, from Leonardo da Vinci onwards, including 10 twentieth-century tribologists. Bibliography and references, p.703-47. Subject and name indexes. The standard work. *Class No:* 621.89(091)

Machine Tools

Abbreviations & Symbols

[4750]

BRITISH STANDARDS INSTITUTION. **Symbols for machine tools.** London, BSI, 1971-83. 3 pts. (*BS 3641: 1971-83.*)

pt. 1: *General symbols*. 1971 (confirmed 1990). 36p.

pt. 2: *Specification for numerical control symbols*. 1980 (confirmed 1987). 20p.

pt. 3: *Additional general symbols*. 1983 (confirmed 1990). 36p.

Supplement: *Guide to application of additional symbols (and index) for machine tools*. 1980 (confirmed 1987). 16p. *Class No:* 621.9(003)

Bibliographies

[4751]

UNITED NATIONS. Industrial Development Organization. **Information sources on the machine tool industry.** New York, United Nations, 1976. xii, 71p. £2.60. (*UNIDO Guides to information sources, no. 22.*)

486 items. 11 sections (some annotated): 1: Professional, trade and research organizations, learned societies and special information services - 2: Directories - 3: Sources of statistics, marketing and other economic data - 4: Basic handbooks, textbooks and manuals - 5: Current periodicals - 6: Current abstracting and indexing periodicals - 7: Proceedings, papers and reports - 8: Specialized dictionaries and

....(contd.)

encyclopaedias - 9: Bibliographies - 10: Films, transparencies and film catalogues - 11: Other potential sources of information (*e.g.* meetings and conferences, patents, standards, translation services). Worldwide coverage of organizations and publications. Bibliography of sources used. *Class No:* 621.9(01)

Handbooks & Manuals

[4752]

ASM specialty handbook: tool materials. Davis, J.R., *ed.* Metals Park, OH., ASM International, 1995. 501p. illus., diagrs. $159. ISBN: 0871705451.

Largely derived from the *ASM Handbook* (10th ed., 1990-), with some new material. Covers the selection of materials for specific applications, heat treatment, microstructural analysis and failure analysis. Chapters have extensive bibliographies; index. A useful compilation. *Class No:* 621.9(035)

[4753]

JACKSON, A. and DAY, D. The Complete book of tools. London, M. Joseph, 1978. 352p. illus. ISBN: 0718117579.

Describes and illustrates over 600 different hand and power tools. Carefully drawn (often two-colour) illus.; well-captioned. 'Saws': p. 74-117; 'planes': p. 134-49. Glossary, p. 343-4. Detailed analytical index, p. 345-52. *Class No:* 621.9(035)

[4754]

WECK, H. Handbook of machine tools; translated by H. Bibring. New York, etc., Wiley, 1984. 4v. illus., diagrs., graphs. £97.50. ISBN: 0471262269 set.

1. *Types of machines, forms of construction and applications.* xx, 285p.
2. *Construction and mathematical analysis.* xx, 296p.
3. *Automation and controls.* xx, 451p.
4. *Metrological analysis and performance tests.* xvi, 145p.

Originally published in German; derived from lectures at the Technical University in Aachen. Comprehensive treatment of all types of machine tools and processes, including developments in automation and control technology.

Lists of references in each volume, all predominantly German. *Class No:* 621.9(035)

Dictionaries

[4755]

CLASON, W.E. Elsevier's dictionary of tools and ironware, in English/American, French, Spanish, Italian, Dutch and German. Amsterdam, etc., Elsevier, 1982. viii, 298p. £116. ISBN: 0444420851.

2,578 English-base terms, with equivalents and indexes in the other 5 languages. Terms are categorized. *Class No:* 621.9(038)

[4756]

GUTIÉRREZ, M.F., *comp.* Elsevier's dictionary of machine tools and elements: in three languages, English, German and Spanish. Amsterdam, Elsevier, 1990. [viii],298p. £105.90. ISBN: 0444886974.

About 5,500 English-base terms with equivalents and indexes in the other languages. Genders given. *Class No:* 621.9(038)

[4757]

HEILER, T. Technisches Bildwörterbuch für spanende Werkzeuge zur 'Metallbearbeitung': Französisch, englisch, deutsch, italienisch, spanisch und einem Anhang in russisch, von Paul Hüter. 2. überarb. Aufl. Munich, Hanser, 1970. [xi], 580p. illus., diagrs.

First published 1965.

1,800 terms in French, with English, German, Italian, Spanish equivalents and brief descriptions, p. 1-409 (and Russian supplement, p. 475-580). Systematically arranged (A. Chisels - A1. General terms - A2. Types of chisels ... M. Grinding wheels). About 1,500 illus., and very helpful diagrs. of tools. Also cites the appropriate standard, *e.g.* BS or DIN. *Class No:* 621.9(038)

[4758]

JUNGE, H.D. Dictionary of machine tools and mechanical engineering: Englisch/Deutsch, Deutsch/Englische. Weinheim, VCH, 1991. 551p. £54. (*Parat.*)

About 10,000 entries in each half. German genders given. *Class No:* 621.9(038)

Yearbooks & Directories

[4759]

Toolroom directory 1998. Redhill, Surrey, DMG Business Media, 1997. 264p. £90. ISSN: 13557580.

Produced by *Precision toolmaker*.

Directory of suppliers, products and services in toolmaking. Also covers associations, institutions, government bodies, standards and trade names. *Class No:* 621.9(058)

Tables & Data Books

[4760]

MACHINABILITY DATA CENTER. Machining data handbook. 3rd ed. Cincinnati, Ohio, Metcut Research Associates, 1980. 2v. $150. ISBN: 0936974001 Set.

First published 1966.

Aims to provide starting recommendations for the important material-removing operations for each of 61 work materials, including certain non-metals, in both SI and 'English' (!) Units. Sections 1-8 cover conventional operations (*e.g.* turning, milling, drilling, tapping, planing, sawing); Sections 9-13 deal with non-traditional processes (mechanical, electrical, thermal, chemical). Other sections (in v.2) cover tool materials, tool geometry, cutting fluids, power requirements, etc.

Data for each specific task are easily located step-by-step to determine feed, speed, tool material and geometry, cutting fluid and power required for each process for each material for specified conditions. *Class No:* 621.9(083)

Standards

[4761]

BRITISH STANDARDS INSTITUTION. Machine tools: engineers' tools and cutting tools. Milton Keynes, BSI, 1985. 6p. £1. (*SL 20.*)

One of the Sectional List series, giving number, title and price group of 135 British standards, specifications, glossaries and published documents (PD) covering all types of tools and related topics, in 17 sections. (For full details and summaries, see the BSI annual *Catalogue* (*qv*)). *Class No:* 621.9(083.74)

Histories

[4762]

ROLT, L.T.C. Tools for the job: a history of machine tools to 1950. Rev. ed. London, H.M. Stationery Office, 1986. 274p. illus., facsims., ports. £9.95. ISBN: 0112964335.

First published 1985. At head of title-page: 'Science Museum'.

11 sections: 1. Machines in the craftman's workshop - 2. Industrial machine-tools of the eighteenth century ... 5. Clement, Fox, Roberts, Nasmyth and Whitworth ... 8. American machine tools and their makers ... 10. Metal-cutting becomes a science - 11. Into the twentieth century. Bibliography, p.256-9. Detailed, analytical index, p.260-74. *Class No:* 621.9(091)

Numerical Control

[4763]

AMKREUTZ, J.J. Wörterbuch numerische Steuerung und Werkzeugmaschinen. [Dictionary of numeric control and machine tools. [Dictionnaire de commande numérique et machines-outils].] Cologne, Datakontext-Verlag, 1985. 254p; 251p; 251p. DM120. ISBN: 3921899397.

Three separately-paged vocabularies bound together: German-English-French; English-German-French; French-German-English. Each contains *c.*10,000 words with equivalents in other languages, without definitions. Produced by word-processing programs. *Class No:* 621.9-52

Cutting Tools

[4764]

BROOKES, J.K.A. World directory and handbook of hard metals. 5th ed. East Barnet, Herts., International Carbide Data, 1992. v.p. illus., diagrs., graphs, tables. ISBN: 0950493120.

First published 1975; 4th ed. 1987.

Part 1: *Handbook* comprising 13 chapters and an index (1. Historical; 2. Manufacture of sintered hard metals; 4. Properties of sintered carbides; 10. Hard metals in the machine shop). A good lavishly illustrated guide to the technology. Part 2: *Directory* provides company and product information and technical data for a claimed 95% of the world's suppliers of carbide tools and other hard metal products. Chapter 16 has unique tabulations of applications data for the various grades manufactured. Indexes of companies, trade names and hard metal grades. *Class No:* 621.9.02

[4765]

HIGGINBOTHAM, R., *ed.* Jet cutting and cleaning bibliography. London, etc., Elsevier, 1988. ix, 258p. £58. ISBN: 185166226x.

About 600 items, all from the FLUIDEX (*qv*) database, covering the literature of water jetting from 1980-87. In 11 sections: 1. Fluid mechanics of jets ... 3. Equipment ... 7. Mining and tunnelling ... 10. Safety - 11. Bibliography. Most references are to periodical articles and conference papers. Personal and corporate author indexes. Effective editing of downloaded records with good use of bold type, but at this price an expensive alternative to online searching. *Class No:* 621.9.02

[4766]
STEKHOVEN, G.S. *and* VALK, W.B., *comps*. **Elsevier's dictionary of metal-cutting tools** in seven languages: English/American - German - Dutch - French - Spanish - Italian - Russian. Amsterdam, etc., Elsevier, 1970. [viii], 458p. diagrs. £125. ISBN: 0444408568.

More than 1,900 terms listed, numbered and defined in English (some definitions extensive), with equivalents in other languages. Separate indexes in these languages keyed by numbers to English section. Brief bibliography and 12p. of figures to illustrate selected terms. *Chartered mechanical engineer* (v.18(6), June 1971, p.232) queries selection and notes inaccuracies and criticizes use of 'outdated British and metric units'. *Class No: 621.9.02*

Industrial Diamonds

[4767]
Industrial diamond review. Ascot, Berks., IDRL, 1965-. v.25-. 4 pa. £49 pa. ISSN: 00198145.

Formerly *Bibliography of diamond tools and related subjects* (1944-57); *Industrial diamond abstracts* (1958-1964). Part of trade journal.

About 1,000 indicative and informative abstracts and references to journal articles, plus book notices, patents lists, lists of other publications, films and videos. Sections (36. Properties of diamonds - 38. Properties of ceramics - 47. Truing and dressing - 52. Gem working - 55. Non-traditional machining processes ...). *Class No: 621.9.025.7*

[4768]
SMITH, N.R. **Users' guide to industrial diamonds.** London, Hutchinson, Benham, 1974. 352p. illus., diagrs., graphs, tables. £4.50. ISBN: 0091170508.

11 chapters covering the nature of diamonds (varieties, structure and characteristics), methods of working, range of products and tool making. 8 chapters cover applications in the transport, electrical and electronics industries, glass, stone, building and civil engineering fields, mineral development, jewellery, and watchmaking. Citations of appropriate standards and patents, with useful chapter bibliographies. Data tabulations and index (p. 334-52).

'... Contains a wealth of up-to-date and explicit information in a compact form ... It is well balanced, clear, very readable and ... something of a model for a book of its type' (*Production engineer* v.54(12), Dec. 1975, p.648). *Class No: 621.9.025.7*

Drills

[4769]
MOUREAU, M. *and* BRACE, G. **Dictionnaire du forage et des puits:** anglais/français; français/anglais. [Dictionary of drilling and boreholes: English/French; French/English.] Paris, Éditions Technip, 1990. [xii], 403p. £60.10. ISBN: 2710805825.

About 4,000 entries, including abbreviations, in each half. *Class No: 621.95*

Sheet Metal Working

[4770]
Sheet metal industries year book, 1995.. Redhill, Surrey, Sheet Metal Industries, 1995. Annual. 332p. £28. ISBN: 0861089529. ISSN: 03057798.

4 chapters: 1. Standards - 2. Buyers guides (services; stockholders, etc.) - 3. Metals, alloys, processes and machines (largely tables) - 4. General information (addresses; memberships of relevant trade associations, etc). Index of advertisers. *Class No: 621.98*

Mining

Databases

[4771]
MinSys. Didcot, Oxon, Geosystems, 1980-. Updated weekly.

Online database covering both practical and economic aspects of mining. About 10,000 items added pa.

Stark, M.M. 'Databases', in his *Mining and mineral industries*, has no less than 48 annotated entries for online services, p.28-45. Of these 6 or 7 concern British systems - Coal database; GEOARCHIVE; Geomechanics Abstracts; HSELINE; IMMAGE and Minsys. *Class No: 622(003.4)*

Bibliographies

[4772]
SHAW, C.T. 'Mining'. *Information sources in engineering.* K.W. Mildren and P.J. Hicks, eds. (3rd ed., 1996), p.607-21. 3rd ed. London, Bowker Saur, 1996. £80. ISBN: 1857390571.

Information sources include organizations, journals, statistics, conferences, abstracts and indexes, and books. Covers as specialized topics surface and underground mining, rock mechanics, and ventilation. References, p.617-21. *Class No: 622(01)*

[4773]
STARK, M.M. **Mining and mineral industries:** an information sourcebook. Phoenix, Arizona, Oryx Press, 1988. [ix], 124p. $35.50. (*Oryx sourcebook series in business and management*.) ISBN: 0097742958.

558 numbered entries, in 12 form sections: Core library collection (general; journals) - Dictionaries and encyclopedias - Handbooks and manuals- Directories - Bibliographies and literature reviews - Indexes and abstracts - Databases (items 221-68) - Industry surveys - Conferences and symposia - Texts and treatises - Journals - Maps and Atlases. 'Associations and research centers'. Sources. Section title and subject indexes. 'The literature selected varies from introductory to extremely technical and scholarly' *(Introduction)*. *Class No: 622(01)*

Handbooks & Manuals

[4774]
SME mining engineering handbook. Hartman, H.L., *and others, eds.* 2nd ed. Littleton, Co., Society for Mining, Metallurgy, and Exploration, Inc., 1992. 2v. (2260p.) illus., diagrs., graphs, tables. ISBN: 087351002x.

First published 1973. Supercedes R. Peele and J.A. Church's *Mining engineers' handbook* (3rd ed. New York, Wiley, 1941, reprinted 1970), not only updating on traditional underground and surface-mining practices, but introducing such subjects as surface mining, solution mining, Arctic mining, nuclear applications, as well as rock mechanics, fragmentation techniques, systems engineering, and the use of computers *(Foreword)*.

A welcome updating of a classic text on mining engineering. The aim of the editorial board was 'a comprehensive reference work ... [whose] ... primary function is to provide professional practitioners with an authoritative reference and design source' *(Preface)*. About 250 contributors. 24 sections, most with closely subdivided chapters (*e.g.* Section 14, 'Surface mine development', has 6 chapters, including 'In-pit crushing and conveying', with *c*.60 references). 10 tables appended (I. 'Ship measures'). Detailed, analytical index, 26p. A model of its kind. *Class No: 622(035)*

Dictionaries

Polyglot

[4775]
AMSTUTZ, G.C., *with others*. **Glossary of mining geology:** in English, Spanish, French and German. Stuttgart, Enke, 1971. xii, 196. illus., tables.

About 900 English-base terms and definitions, with Spanish, French and German translation of terms and definitions. Keyed illus. Cites authorities. 4 language indexes. 10 appendices (*e.g.* 4. Major part of a (coal) mine; 5. Geologic and mine map symbols). 50 figures. *Class No: 622(038)=00*

[4776]
DORIAN, A.F. **Elsevier's dictionary of mining and mineralogy:** in English, Franch, German and Italian. Amsterdam, Elsevier, 1993. [x], 300p. £127. ISBN: 0444890394.

3,585 English-base terms, briefly defined. Indexes in other languages. *Class No: 622(038)=00*

[4777]
ETNER, F.F., *and others*. **Russo-anglo-nemetsko-frantsazki gorny slovar'.** [Russian-English-German-French mining dictionary.] Moscow, Ruskii Iazyk, 1987. 420p.

About 3000 Russian-based terms, with eqivalents and indexes in English, German and French. *Class No: 622(038)=00*

[4778]
WYLLIE, R.J.M., *and* ARGALL, G.O., *eds*. **World mining: glossary of mining, processing and geological terms.** English/Svenska/Deutsch/français/español. Translated by R. Lambert. Rev. ed. San Francisco, Calif., Miller Freeman Pubns., 1975. 432p. ISBN: 0879300310.

First published 1968 (G.O. Argall, ed.).

11,406 numbered entries. Glossary of English terms, p.9-270. Swedish, German, French and Spanish equivalents and indexes. No genders given. Index to advertisers. Covers 'terms mostly commonly used for geology, hydrography, exploration, underground and open pit mining, minerals benification, hydrometallurgy, smelting and refining' (*sub-title*). *Class No: 622(038)=00*

English

[4779]

NELSON, A. **Dictionary of mining.** London, Newnes, 1964. [vii], 523p. illus.

About 5,000 entries, some lengthy (*e.g.* 'Rockhurst': 9½p.). Includes eponyms; cross-references. Covers terms in applied geophysics, mechanics, and automation. 'Prepared for the convenience of mining men - the student, the official and the miner' (*Preface*). *Class No:* 622(038)=20

[4780]

THRUSH, P.W., *ed.* **A Dictionary of mining, minerals, and related terms.** Washington, US Dept. of the Interior, 1968. vii, [1], 1269p.

About 55,000 terms (including abbreviations), with *c.*150,000 definitions. Quotes sources (listed on p.1259-68). Cross-references. Compared with A.H. Fay's *A glossary of the mining and mineral industry* (Washington, USGPO, 1920. 745p.), which Thrush revises and enlarges. Fay (*c.*20,000 terms) should be retained for its several thousand Spanish American mining terms. *Class No:* 622(038)=20

German

[4781]

LENK, G. *and* BÖRNER, H. **Technisches Fachwörterbuch der Grundstoff - Industrien.** 2. Aufl. Göttingen, Vandenhoeck & Ruprecht, 1958-62. 2v. tables.

First published 1949-54. 1. *Englisch-Deutsch.* 1958. 638p. 2. *Deutsch-Englisch.* 1962. 732p.

Sub-title: 'Mining, non-metallic mineral industry; dressing; metallurgy; metal-working industry; building materials in industry'. Each volume has *c.*30,000 main entries, with compounds subsumed. V.2 carries a lengthy supplement, p.579-682, also available separately. Abbreviations are appended. US terminology is differentiated from British. Symbols, a feature. A strictly technical dictionary, giving the context of each term instead of - as in De Vries - a string of equivalents. *Class No:* 622(038)=30

French

[4782]

AUGER, P. *and* ROUSSEKU, L.J. **Lexique anglais-français de l'industrie minière.** Quebec, Office de la Langue Française, Government de Quebec, 1981. 89p. + 81, [1]p.

Two parts: 1. L'Exploration; 2. La minéralogie. Part 1 features 7,355 terms, English-French, with index of French terms. Part 2 has 1,066 terms, English French, with index of French terms. Each part has an appended 2-p. bibliography. *Class No:* 622(038)=40

Russian

[4783]

KOSMINSKII, B.M., *and others, comps.* **Anglo-russkii govnotekhnicheskii slovar'.** Moscow, Ugletekhizdat, 1958. 478p.

An English-Russian mining-technology dictionary with *c.*30,000 terms. Abbreviations, p.462-78; bibliography, p.6-7. More strictly technical than *Anglo-russkii gornii slovar',* by Baron, L.I. and Erishov, M.N. (1958). *Class No:* 622(038)=82

Glossaries

[4784]

BRITISH STANDARDS INSTITUTION. **Glossary of mining terms.** London, BSI, 1969-74. 11 sections. (*BS 3618.*)

1. *Planning and surveying.* Rev. ed. 1969. 14p.
2. *Ventilation.* Rev. ed. 1971. 18p.
3. *Boring and ventilation.* 1971. 16p.
4. *Drainage.* 1971. 14p.
5. *Geology.* 1971. 20p.
6. *Drilling and blasting.* 1972. 24p.
7. *Electrical engineering and lighting.* 1973. 12p.
8. *Winning and working.* 1974. 30p.
9. *Shifts and associated equipment.* 1974. 16p.
10. *Transport.* 1967. 20p.
11. *Strata control.* 1967. 16p.

Primarily concerned with coal mining, although account has been taken of other forms of mining and quarrying in Britain. All sections reconfirmed in 1987. *Class No:* 622(038.1)

Reviews & Abstracts

[4785]

IMM abstracts: a survey of world literature on economic geology, mining, mineral dressing, extraction metallurgy [and] allied subjects. London, Institution of Mining and Metallurgy, 1950-. 6pa. £215 pa. ISSN: 00190020.

About 3,000 abstracts pa. 13 sections: Generalities - Minerals industry - Economic geology - Mining - Mineral processing - Metallurgy - Non-metals extraction - Health and safety - Environment -

....(contd.)

Mathematical methods and computing - General engineering - Civil engineering - Analysis and instrumentation. Annual index. Online through IMM. *Class No:* 622(048)

Yearbooks & Directories

[4786]

'Financial Times' energy yearbook mining 1999. London, FT Energy, 1998. Annual. xliii, 442p. tables. £195. ISBN: 1840830557.

Previously as *Walter Skinner's Mining international year book* (founded 1887 as *Mining Year book*) and *Financial Times Mining international year book.*

Companies, A-Z (entries 1-578); data: business; properties and operations; latest ore reserves; financial summary) - Associations (579-671). Geographical, product, company indexes. International professional sources. Suppliers' directory and business guide. Advertisers' index. Directory of over 650 companies worldwide. *Class No:* 622(058)

[4787]

Mining annual review, 1994. London, Mining Journal, 1994. 556p. illus., tables, maps. ISBN: 0900117680.

Main sections: Technical articles (mineral exploration; mineral and coal processing; surface mining; underground mining) - Countries (*c.*150, A-Z). Appended: Professional directory; Buyers guide; Index to mines and companies; Index to advertisers. *Class No:* 622(058)

[4788]

The Mining directory 1999: mines and mine-equipment companies worldwide. 10th ed. London, Don Nelson, 1999. 777p. ISBN: 0946004153. ISSN: 02627965.

Main portion: A-Z listing of mines and mine-equipment companies (*c.*3,000). Appended buyers' guide lists companies by subject. Geographical index. Brief glossary. *Class No:* 622(058)

Histories

[4789]

GREGORY, C.E. **A Concise history of mining.** Oxford, etc., Pergamon Press, 1980. xviii, 259p. illus., maps. ISBN: 0080238823.

5 parts: 1. What is mining? - 2. The eight ages of man (Paleolithic ... The uranium age, from 1950) - 3. Chronological development of particular aspects of mining (Mine drainage ... Working conditions) - 4. Traditions, customs and folklore of mines - 5. Epilogue (*e.g.* The impact of mineral production on national economies). Appendix: Significant dates in mining history. Glossary of mining terms. Bibliography (A-Z authors), p.245-50. Non-analytical index, p.251-8. A popular account, with 43 illus. *Class No:* 622(091)

Great Britain

[4790]

Directory of mines and quarries. London, British Geological Survey.

Records all known operational mineral workings in the UK. Data include name, location, map reference, commodity, company operating and basic statistics. *Class No:* 622(410)

Africa

[4791]

African mining, '91. London, New York, Elsevier, 1991. 346p. ISBN: 1851666540.

Many contributors; 11 sections, including mining, metallurgy, geology. Near-print. *Class No:* 622(6)

Australasia & Oceania

[4792]

Johnson's mining year book, 1995/96. Sydney, Dun & Bradstreet, 1995. xi, 910p. illus., tables, maps. ISSN: 00753777.

Directory-type information for mining in Australasia. *Class No:* 622(9)

Thesauri

[4793]

INSTITUTION OF MINING AND METALLURGY. IMMAGE Thesaurus. London, The Institution, 1984. [178]p.

Terms for use with *IMM abstracts,* both print and online. *Class No:* 622:025.43

Methods

Oil extraction

[4794]

HYNE, N.J. Dictionary of petroleum exploration, drilling and production. Tulsa, Oklahoma, Penn Well Books, 1990. [v],623p. illus. ISBN: 0878143521.

About 20,000 terms. Definitions range from a single word to one column (*e.g.* 'Sucker-rod pump'). Well-produced. *Class No:* 622.276

[4795]

Petroleum engineering handbook. Bradley, H.B., *and others, eds.* Richardson, Tx., Society of Petroleum Engineers, 1987, second printing 1989. xxiv,v.p. illus., diagrs., graphs, tables. ISBN: 1555630103.

First published 1962 as *Petroleum production handbook*.

59 chapters, closely subdivided, in 3 sections: 1. Mathematics (basic tables; calculation procedures - 1 chapter) - 2. Production engineering (materials; methods; tools - 18 chapters) - 3. Reservoir engineering (properties; recovery data and methods; reserves; formation evaluation; etc. - 40 chapters). Author index (14p.); detailed, analytical index (59p.). Numerous tables and illustrative material; extensive chapter references. Comprehensive and invaluable. *Class No:* 622.276

Offshore

[4796]

CHRYSSOSTOMIDIS, M. Offshore petroleum engineering: a bibliographic guide to publications and information sources. New York, Nichols Publishing Co.; London, Kogan Page, 1978. 367p. maps. ISBN: 089397045x.

About 2,500 references. Class A-X (*e.g.* E. Offshore/Ocean engineering; F. Oceanography and ocean environment description; G. Offshore structure engineering; J. Offshore petroleum engineering and development; Q. Diving, underwater and deep ocean operations; T. Oil spills; W. Maps). Appendices include 'Supplementary sources & suggestions for keeping up to date'; 'Sources consulted'. Directory of publishers and other organizations. Permuted topic, author and titles indexes. *Class No:* 622.276.04

[4797]

—**MACLACHLAN, M.** An Introduction to marine drilling. Ledbury, Herefordshire, Oilfield Publications, 1987. 346p.

Includes an insert 'The North Sea: oil and gas activity and concession map'. *Class No:* 622.276.04

[4798]

—**TAYLOR, G.E.** 'Offshore engineering'. *Information sources in engineering* (2nd ed. Editor L.J. Anthony. 1985), p.474-90. 2nd ed. London, Butterworths, 1985.

Includes 'Primary sources of documentary information' (p.480-6) and 'Secondary sources of information' (p.486-90: abstracting and indexing services; directories; books). Offshore engineering as a distinct topic was not featured in the 3rd ed. of *Information sources in engineering* (1996). *Class No:* 622.276.04

[4799]

Register of offshore units, submersibles & diving systems, 1995-96. London, Lloyd's Registry of Shipping, 1995. Annual. v.p. tables. ISBN: 0900528958.

Sections: Mobile drilling rigs - Submersibles - Underwater systems - Work units (*e.g.* pipe handling) - Owners and managers of offshore equipment - Owners and managers of offshore support ships. Closely tabulated data. No index. *Class No:* 622.276.04

[4800]

WHITEHEAD, H. An A-Z of offshore oil & gas: an illustrated glossary and reference guide to the offshore oil & gas industries and their technology. 2nd ed. London, Kogan Page, 1983. 438p. illus., diagrs., tables, chemical structures. £27.50. ISBN: 0850386276.

First published 1976.

About 4,000 terms and abbreviations defined, plus cross-references. 30 appendices, p.315-426 (*e.g.* 1. Offshore oil and gas regions of the world; 29. Bibliography, p.433-4; 30. Abbreviations commonly used in relation to offshore oil and gas. Well illustrated (200 line-drawings, 20 full-page maps); keyed diagrams. 'An indispensable reference for engineers, economists and geoscientists concerned with petroleum resources' (*Choice*, v.21, October 1983, p.258). *Class No:* 622.276.04

Types of Mine

Oilfields

[4801]

Elsevier's oil and gas field dictionary, in English/American, French, Spanish, Italian, Dutch, German and Arabic. Chaballe, L.Y., *and others*. Amsterdam, etc., Elsevier, 1980. xii, 672p. $200; £128.12. ISBN: 0444418334.

....(contd.)

4,843 English/American base-terms, with French, Spanish, Italian, Dutch and German equivalents and indexes. Arabic supplement. *Class No:* 622.323

[4802]

RÅDET FOR TEKNISK TERMINOLOGI. Norwegian-English-French dictionary of petroleum production: boring and production, geophysics and geology. Oslo, R.T.T., 1976. 170p.

Classified arrangement of *c*.1,550 terms in all, with Norwegian, English and French indexes. *Class No:* 622.323

[4803]

SOCIETY OF PROFESSIONAL WELL LOG ANALYSTS. Glossary of terms and expressions used in well logging. 2nd ed. Houston, Texas, the Society, 1984. 116p. illus., diagrs., graphs.

About 500 terms, p.7-104. 'Introduction log': 1 column. Sources, p.5-6. Appended: Nomenclature for well-logging services used by service organizations. *Class No:* 622.323

[4804]

STOHAROV, D.E., *ed.* **Russian-English oil-field dictionary.** Oxford, etc., Pergamon Press, 1983. 431p.

30,000 entries, terms being drawn from scientific literature published in the 1970s. Usefully meets a deficiency in the language coverage of the Elsevier dictionary. *Class No:* 622.323

[4805]

TIRATSOO, E.N. Oilfields of the world. 3rd ed., rev. Beaconsfield, Berks., Scientific Press, 1986. xvi, [416]p. illus., maps, tables. ISBN: 090136018x.

First published 1973; 3rd ed., 1983 (xvi, 392p.).

Extensive data on the geology, history and economic geography of *c*.2,500 oilfields in some 90 countries. The 3rd ed., rev., includes a 24p. *Supplement* which incorporates new developments and updated statistical information. Appendices cover properties of crude oil and world oil reserves. Chapter references. 183 tables, 83 line-drawings, 4 plates and 8p. of maps. *Class No:* 622.323

Coal Mines

[4806]

BRITISH STANDARDS INSTITUTION. Glossary of coal preparation terms. London, BSI, 1994. 29p. £40. (*BS 3552: 1994.*) ISBN: 0580130878.

Previously as *Glossary of terms used in coal preparation*. (BS 3552: 1962).

About 400 terms defined in 11 sections (*e.g.* 4. sizing; 5. cleaning; 11. automatic control). Appended: 'Bibliography of international standards defining terms for automatic control'. *Class No:* 622.33

[4807]

Guide to the coalfields, 1994. Redhill, Surrey, FJM International, 1994. 108p. £88.60. ISSN: 00728713.

Contents: British Coal Corporation - UK independent coal production - Associated UK coal industry organisation - International guide to coal producers - Buyers' guide. The extent of the *Guide* has shrunk significantly in recent years, perhaps reflecting the state of the British coal industry. *Class No:* 622.33

[4808]

INTERNATIONAL ENERGY AGENCY. Concise guide to world coalfields. Compiled by World Coal Resources and Reserves, IEA Coal Research. London, the Agency. Loose-leaf. graphs, maps. ISBN: 9290290889.

4 sections: 1. Contents and introduction - 2. Major coal-bearing countries (A-Z) - 3. Indexes, classifications and remaining coal-bearing country descriptions - 4. Glossary of terms. Appendix. *Class No:* 622.33

[4809]

International guide to the coalfields '98/99. East Markham, Notts., Trade Link, 1999. 169p. illus. £100. ISSN: 13647512.

Directory information (contact details; mining methods; output capacity, etc.) in sections: International guide to coal producers - International ports - Consumers of coal worldwide - International traders - Equipment suppliers - Products and services. *Class No:* 622.33

Gold & Silver Mines

[4810]

Silver: exploration, mining and treatment. Institution of Mining and Metallurgy. London, Institute of Mining and Metallurgy, 1988. x,344p. illus., maps, tables. £46.80. ISBN: 1870706048.

31 papers presented at the international conference on 'Silver-exploration, mining and treatment' organized by the IMM, in association with the Cámara Minera de México and The Silver Institute, and held in Mexico City, 21-24 November 1988. Sections: Geology and mineralogy - Case histories - Silver in complex sulphide minerals - Flotation - Extraction and refining. *Class No:* 622.342

Quarries

[4811]

INSTITUTION OF MINING AND METALLURGY. Surface mining and quarrying. London, the Institution, 1983. [vii], 449p. illus., diagrs., graphs, tables. ISBN: 0900438662.

38 documented papers presented at the 2nd International Surface Mining and Quarrying symposium organized by IMM in association with the Institute of Quarrying, held in Bristol, 4-6 October 1983. 'Developments in remote sensing for mineral exploration' has 17 references. *Class No: 622.35*

[4812]

SHEPPARD, R.P. A Dictionary of quarrying terms. Nottingham, Institute of Quarrying, 1992. 192p. illus.

Some 1,500 terms, briefly defined, mainly from the aggregate-producing sector of the industry. *Class No: 622.35*

Drainage

[4813]

Mine drainage bibliography, 1910-1976. Gleason, V.E. *and* Russell, H.H., *comps.* Washington, United States Environmental Protection Agency; Pennsylvania Dept. of Environmental Resources, 1976. vii, 288p.

About 1,200 indicative and informative abstracts, arranged chronologically. Author and analytical subject index, p.238-88. *Class No: 622.5*

Safety

[4814]

RLSD bibliography. Sheffield, Health and Safety Executive, Library and Information Services, 1986-. Annual.

Continues *SMRE* [Safety in Mines Research Establishment] *bibliography* (3rd ed. 1968), *SMRE/HSL* bibliography, 1969-78, and HSL bibliographies, 1979, 1980, 1981/82, 1983, 1984, 1985.

1986 annual contains *c.*70 abstracts, headed 'List of papers arranged alphabetically by name of author'. Cross-references from joint authors. No subject index.'RLSD': Research and Laboratory Services Division of the Health and Safety Executive.

HSELINE online database (1981-) indexes *RLSD bibliography* and all other Health and Safety Executive publications, updating monthly with 1000 items. Hosts: ESA-IRS. *Class No: 622.8*

Military & Naval Engineering

Abbreviations & Symbols

[4815]

MORINGO, F.P. Aerospace and defense acronyms. 2nd ed. Washington, D.C., American Institute of Aeronautics and Astronautics, 1992. 207p. ISBN: 0930403630.

About 25,000 entries. Covers June 1982- July 1992. List of 'Reference codes' precedes. *Class No: 623(003)*

[4816]

PRETZ, B. Dictionary of military and technological abbreviations and acronyms. London, Routledge & Kegan Paul, 1983. [iv], 496p. £60. ISBN: 0710092741.

Records *c.*50,000 acronyms and abbreviations used by the British, American, German and Soviet military. Bibliography, p.495-6. *Class No: 623(003)*

Bibliographies

[4817]

Jane's index of indices, 1991-92. 2nd ed. Coulsdon, Surrey, 1992. *c.*300p. £135. ISBN: 0710610343.

Covers 21 1991-92 Jane's yearbooks. Entries A-Z, equipment and manufacturers. Indexes: country; *Jane's Defence Weekly; Jane's Intelligence Review.* An index to many of the Jane's publications. *Class No: 623(01)*

[4818]

UNITED STATES. Military Academy. West Point, N.Y. Library. **Subject catalog of the military art and science collection,** with selected author and added entries, including a preliminary guide to the manuscript collection. Westport, Conn., Greenwood Press, 1970. 4v.

A dictionary catalogue with *c.*66,000 photolithographed cards. 'Catalog of one of the most comprehensive collections on military engineering' (Chen, C-C. *Scientific and technical information sources.* 1977, p.8). *Class No: 623(01)*

Handbooks & Manuals

[4819]

CHANT, C. A Compendium of armaments and military hardware. London, Routledge & Kegan Paul, 1987. 568p. £45. ISBN: 0710207204.

4 Sections: 1. Land weapons - 2. Warships - 3. Aircraft - 4. Missiles. Data: type, dimensions, weight, propulsion, performance. No illus. *Class No: 623(035)*

Dictionaries

Polyglot

[4820]

Brassey's multilingual military dictionary. London, etc., Brassey's Defence Publishers, 1987. xvii, 815p. £48. ISBN: 0080270328.

6,960 entries in American English (with British English index), plus equivalents and indexes in French, Spanish, German, Russian and Arabic. 6 appendices: A. Ranks; B. Units/formations; C. Numerals/notation; D. Colors; E. Points of the compass; F. Tools, etc. Cross references. Fills a need. *Class No: 623(038)=00*

English

[4821]

Jane's defence glossary. Kay, I. *and* Walker, M., *comps.* Coulsdon, Surrey, Janes Information Group, 1993. x, 295p. £30. ISBN: 0710611188.

Includes 11,000 acronyms and their expanded descriptions. 16 appendices (*e.g.* JEDS coding system). Available as part of Jane's CD-ROM. *Class No: 623(038)=20*

[4822]

UNITED STATES. Joint Chiefs of Staff. Department of Defense Dictionary of military and associated terms, incorporating the NATO and IADB dictionaries. Washington, Government Printing Office, 1984. 403p.

Initially as US Department of Defense. *A dictionary of military terms* (1963).

Defines *c*5,000 standardized military terms, including abbreviations. *Class No: 623(038)=20*

German

[4823]

KROLLMAN, F. Langenscheidt's Fachwörterbuch Wehrwesen: Englisch-Deutsch; Deutsch-Englisch. Berlin-Schönberg, Langenscheidt; London, Methuen, 1957. 769p.

More than 46,000 military terms and equivalents, with skilful use of symbols and abbreviations. Extensive section of 1,500 British and US abbreviations. Terms on structure and equipment of modern armed forces are well represented. Appendices include table of interrelation of units of measurement. The editor worked in the German Ministry of Defence's Language Section. More useful for purely military (as opposed to colloquial) terms than Eitzen, K.H. *German-English, English-German military dictionary* (1957. 549p.). *Class No: 623(038)=30*

French

[4824]

CHABALLE, J.H. *and* DAVIAUT, P. Military dictionary, English-French, French-English. Ottawa, Cloutier, 1943. xix, 1016p.

Prepared under the direction of the Chief of General Staff, Department of National Defence, Canada.

Includes many aeronautical, radar and other terms. Appendices: Abbreviations (p.951-68) - Army trades - Grammar - Conversion tables, etc. Bibliography, p.xvii. *Class No: 623(038)=40*

[4825]

DOBENIK, R.H. *and* HARTLINE, G.W. Dictionnaire technique de la marine: Anglais/Français et Français/Anglais. [Naval technical dictionary: English/French and French/English.] Paris, La Maison du Dictionnaire, 1989. [xxii],646,[19]p. illus. £51.70. ISBN: 2856080316.

About 35,000 entries in each half. Includes nautical, military, technical terms. Brief bibliography (28 items). *Class No: 623(038)=40*

Spanish

[4826]

WELLS, R.A. English-Spanish, Spanish-English modern dictionary of military technology. Fairfax, Va., Lexicon Press, 1977. viii, 323p.

Entries emphasize technology. *Class No: 623(038)=60*

Russian

[4827]

JOINT TECHNICAL LANGUAGE SERVICE. Cheltenham. **Russian-English, English-Russian military dictionary.** London H.M. Stationery Office, 1983. x, [1], 688p. ISBN: 0112300189.

About 30,000 entries in each half. About 200 categories are applied to terms. Many compounds. Appended list of abbreviations. The dictionary contains vocabulary encountered in a wide variety of modern Russian texts covering military, technical and general subjects. *Class No:* 623(038)=82

[4828]

SUDZILOVSKII, G.A., *and others.* **Anglo-russkiĭ voennyĭ slovar'.** [English-Russian military dictionary.] Izd.2.,perer. i dop. Moscow, Voennoe Izdat, Ministerstva Oborony SSSR, 1968. 1060, [3]p.

First published 1960.

About 59,000 entry-words ('Gun': 4 columns; 'Launching': 1¼ columns). Abbreviations (mostly American), p.917 - 1004. Terms are categorized. *Class No:* 623(038)=82

[4829]

—**NADYSEV, M.A.** Russko-angliiskiĭ voehnotekhicheskiĭ slovar' [Russian-English military and technical dictionary.] Moscow, Voenore Izdat, 1975. 622p.

Over 30,000 terms, abbreviations and symbols. *Class No:* 623(038)=82

Arabic

[4830]

KAY, E. Arabic military dictionary: English-Arabic, Arabic-English. London, Routledge & Kegan Paul, 1986. 320p. £30. ISBN: 0710204582.

About 10,000 terms, abbreviations and symbols. *Class No:* 623(038)=927

Japanese

[4831]

CRESWELL, H.T., *and others.* **A Dictionary of military terms, English-Japanese, Japanese-English.** Tokyo, Kaitakusha, [1973]. iv, 1226p.

American edition: Univ. of Chicago Press, [1973].

Japanese-English part (p.513-1226) has c.17,500 entries and sub-entries. Headwords are romanized, followed by Japanese characters. Many compounds and idioms. *Class No:* 623(038)=956

Reviews & Abstracts

[4832]

Air University Library index to military periodicals. Alabama, Maxwell Air Force Base, Air University Library, 1949-. Quarterly. With annual cumulative issues. ISSN: 00022586.

Originally as *Air University periodical index.*

About 15,000 entries pa. under subjects A-Z, with cross-references. It forms 'a subject index to significant articles, news items and editorials appearing in 78 English language military and aeronautical periodicals' (*Preface*). Available on CD-ROM. *Class No:* 623(048)

[4833]

Current military and political literature. Oxford, The Military Press, 1983-. 6pa. $324pa. ISSN: 02041674.

Section J, *Technology* has headings: Missiles & rockets; Armoured vehicles; Artillery; Infantry; Engineer; Electronics, computers; Logistic; Ammunition, mines & explosives; Surveillance, intelligence, optronics; Nuclear, biological & chemical (NBC) warfare; Power, fuels & engines; Naval; Aviation; Navigation; Internal Security; Air defence; Directed enemy weapons; Space; Environment. About 3,000 abstracts pa. in this section. *Class No:* 623(048)

[4834]

Military science index. Shrivenham, Wilts., Royal Military College of Science, 1962-. 12pa., with annual cumulation.

1985: c.2,700 references to periodical articles, with brief notes on article titles where considered necessary. Arranged under topics, alphabetically, from 'Aerodynamics' to 'Weather'. Periodicals are chiefly British and American.

Defence news, a daily newspaper current-awareness service, reproducing cuttings, is circulated by the library as back-up. *Class No:* 623(048)

Periodicals

[4835]

IMPERIAL WAR MUSEUM. Department of Printed Books. **List of current journals, corrected to August 1980.** London, the Museum, 1981. [ii], 49p. £1.

About 400 titles, A-Z, noting subtitles, publishers, addresses and frequency. Appended 8 subject groups: 1. General and military history, politics and international affairs - 2. Army and joint service publications - 3. Naval - 4. Aviation - 5. Ex-servioce - 6. Heraldry and collecting - 7. Weaponry and modelling - 8. Museum and professional. *Class No:* 623(051)

Museums

[4836]

UNITED STATES. Department of the Army. Center of Military History. **Guide to US army museums and historic sites.** Cary, N.M., *Jr.* Washington, US Government Printing Office, 1975. vii, 116p. illus., maps.

7 parts: 1. US army and army national guard museums - 2. Other Dept. of Defense museums - 3. Federal museums and historic areas with military connections (*e.g.* Smithsonian Institution) - 4. Private, state and municipal military museums - 5. Historic sites on US army property - 6. Sources of information on military history - 7. Bibliography. 2 appendices (2. US army museum locations). Local maps. 'This volume is concerned with artifacts and landmarks' (*Foreword*). *Class No:* 623:061:069

[4837]

WISE, T. A Guide to military museums. 6th ed. Town Moor, Doncaster, S.Yorks., Athena Books, 1988. [80]p. £1.95, illus.

First published 1969.

Over 200 entries, under place-names, Abingdon ... York, Aberdeen ... Stirling, Brecon ... Tenby, Armagh ... Enniskellen, Gorey ... St. Peter's (Jersey), plus 'Other places of interest'. Data: description; admission; hours; facilities; approaches. Index of regiments & their museums; index of special museums (name, subject). Small illus. of regimental insignia. *Class No:* 623:061:069

Forts

[4838]

HOGG, I.V. Fortress: a history of military defence. London, Macdonald and Jane's, 1975. 160p. illus., facsims., plans, maps. ISBN: 0356081223.

7 chapters: 1. Ramparts and palisades - 2. The great leveller - 3. The entry of the masters (*e.g.* Vauban) - 4. The drawing board approach - 5. The years of plenty (17th-18th centuries) - 6. The testing time (19th century) - 7. The ferro-concrete revival (*e.g.* Maginot Line). Glossary, p.155-8. Index, p.159-60. No bibliography. Very fully illustrated quarto. *Class No:* 623.1

[4839]

ROBERTS, R.B. Encyclopedia of historic forts; the military, pioneer and trading posts of the United States. London, Macmillan, 1987. 894p. $95. ISBN: 002926880x.

Entries A-Z by state and then by post name within each state. Limited to military posts, omitting Navy and Air Force establishments (with some exceptions). Data include dates and construction details, history and fate. Prelims. include a glossary of fortification terms. 'This is the first comprehensive effort to treat this subject for the entire country' (*Choice,* v.25(7), March 1988, p.1070). *Class No:* 623.1

Weapons & Arms

Encyclopaedias

[4840]

CHANT, C. World encyclopedia of modern air weapons. Wellingborough, P. Stephens, 1989. 312p. illus. £19.95; $29.95. ISBN: 1852600284.

A companion to his *World encyclopedia of modern aircraft armament* (1988). Includes a section on 'variants and applications'. Covers air-to-air surface, bombs, guns, etc., with technical data. Good captions and good black-and-white illus. Inferior to Gunston's *Illustrated encyclopedia of aircraft armament* in this respect, but superior in its background information. The full index gives official and common names, weapons by manufacturer. *Class No:* 623.4(031)

[4841]

HOGG, I.V. The Encyclopedia of weaponry. London, Quarto, 1992. 224p. illus. (col.). £19.95. ISBN: 0851125212.

Also known as *The Guinness Encyclopedia of weaponry.*

8 chapters, closely subdivided: 1. The first weapons - 2. Medieval developments - 3. The age of gunpower - 4. Mobile warfare - 5. The age of invention - 6. The First World War - 7. The Second World War - 8. Today and tomorrow. Detailed, analytical index, p.216-22. Lavishly illustrated; a popular treatment. *Class No:* 623.4(031)

[4842]

MACKSEY, K. **The Penguin encyclopedia of weapons and military technology:** prehistory to present day. London, Viking, 1993. xxii, 392p. illus., maps. £20. ISBN: 067084411x.

Aim is to present 'the essential and vital elements creating the interaction of technology and weapons upon the evolution of warfare' (*Introduction*, p.ix). Covers inventors, scientists, manufacturers, materials, products, techniques and battles. Entries A-Z ('grenades', 1 col.); chronology (4000 BC to 1991), p.xi-xxi; detailed, analytical index, p.377-92. Brief bibliography. Useful illustrations.
Class No: 623.4(031)

[4843]

TARASSUK, L. *and* BALAIR, C., *eds*. **The Complete encyclopedia of arms and weapons.** 1st UK ed., translated from the Italian by S. Mulcahy and others. London, Batsford, 1982. 544p. illus. (incl. col.). £29.95. ISBN: 0713415959.

Originally Mondadori (Milan), 1979, as *Enciclopedia ragionata delle armi.*

9 contributions, from 6 countries. 'The guiding principle behind this encyclopedia has been to provide extensive information on offensive and defensive weapons and armour over a wide period of history and a vast range of countries' (*Preface*). Entries A-Z. That on bayonets (p.78-79) describes 19 types of bayonet, with keyed line-drawings. Cross-references. 'Select bibliography' (grouped) p.534-44. The 1,250 illus. include 90 colour plates. 'Incomparable' (*Wilson library bulletin,* March 1983, p.606). *Class No:* 623.4(031)

Handbooks & Manuals

[4844]

FRIEDMAN, R.S. **An Illustrated examination of advanced technology warfare:** detailed study of the latest weapons and techniques for warfare today and into the 21st century. London, Salamander Books, Ltd., 1985. 208p. col. illus., maps. ISBN: 0861012550.

6 British and American contributors. 7 sections: 1. Electronic warfare - 2. Straegic warfare -3. Space warfare - 4. Air warfare - 5. Land warfare - 6. Naval warfare - 7. Conventional warfare (*e.g.* anti-terrorism weapons). Index (in tiny print), p.206-8. Quarto sized.
Class No: 623.4(035)

[4845]

HARTCUP, G. **The Silent revolution:** development of conventional weapons, 1945-1985. London, Brassey's Publications Ltd., 1992. 192p. £26. ISBN: 008036702x.

Surveys weapons against the background of rational strategic priorities. Includes personal accounts and views of officers, scientists and officials. *Class No:* 623.4(035)

[4846]

Jane's land-based air defence, 1999-2000. Coulsdon, Surrey, Jane's Information Group, 1999. *c.*300p. illus. £245; $395. ISBN: 071061909x.

Over 350 systems from 100 manufacturers. Covers SAMs and anti-aircraft guns, as well as installation. Data: development history, description, variants, specification, manufacturer details. Entries illustrated. Available online and on CD-ROM. *Class No:* 623.4(035)

[4847]

RHEINMETALL. **Handbook on weaponry.** 1st English ed. Dusseldorf, Rheinmetall GmbH, 1982. xxxv, 752p. illus., diagrs., graphs, tables.

Translation of *Waffentechnisches Taschenbuch* (5th ed., 1980).

15 sections by various hands. 1. Explosives - 2/4. Ballistics - 5. The application of probability theory - 6. Sighting and aiming - 7. Automatic weapons - 8. Guns (p.215-412) - 9. Gun mechanics - 10. Gun and gun turret test rigs - 11. Ammunition - 12. Rockets - 13. Fuzes and propelling charge igniters - 14. Ballistics and weapon testing methods - 15. Tables (24). Detailed, analytical subject index, p.731-52. Small format and illus. *Class No:* 623.4(035)

Dictionaries

[4848]

BRASSEUR, B. *and* DOBENIK, R.H. **Dictionnaire technique de l'armament:** anglais/français et français/anglais. [Dictionary of weapon engineering and weapon systems: English/French and French/English.] Paris, La Maison du Dictionnaire, 1992. xiv, 864p. £67.75. ISBN: 2856080464.

About 30,000 entries in all (categories indicated). Bibliography, p.xiii-xiv. *Class No:* 623.4(038)

[4849]

QUICK, J. **Dictionary of weapons and military terms.** New York, etc., McGraw-Hill, 1973. xii, 515p.

About 15,000 terms are briefly defined in 10-100 words, with many cross-references. 'Cover': 6 meanings. Includes abbreviations, acronyms, code words and slang. Tables list weapon types. Over 1,000 illus. US slanted. *Class No:* 623.4(038)

Histories

[4850]

DIAGRAM GROUP. **Weapons: an international encyclopedia, from 5000 BC to 2000 AD.** Harding, D., *ed*. Rev. ed. London, Macmillan, 1990. 336p. illus., facsims., diagrs. £12.95. ISBN: 0333540069.

First published 1980.

Progressive survey in 7 sections. 1. Arming the hand (clubs, daggers, swords, bayonets, etc.) - 2. Hand-thrown missiles - 3. Hand held missile throwers - 4. Mounted missile throwers - 5. Positioned weapons - 6. Bombs and self-propelled missiles - 7. Chemical, nuclear and biological weapons. New developments in weaponry. Regional and historical indexes. Famous names; grouped bibliography; analytical index. Over 2,500 scaled drawings, well captioned.
Class No: 623.4(091)

Underwater

[4851]

Jane's underwater warfare systems, 1999-2000. Coulsdon, Surrey, Jane's Information Group, 1999. 480p. tables. £245; $395. ISBN: 0710619200.

Includes over 600 systems. Contents: submarines; anti-submarine warfare; underwater weapons; mine warfare; mine countermeasures vessels; inventories; systems analysis. Available online and on CD-ROM (£475). *Class No:* 623.4(204)

Scotland

[4852]

CALDWELL, D.H. **Scottish weapons and fortifications.** Edinburgh, D. Donald Publishers, Ltd., 1981. x, 452p. illus., facsims., ports. ISBN: 0859760472.

14 contributors. 17 chapters (3. 'Late medieval defences in Scotland', p.21-54; 7. 'The early basket-hilt in Britain', p.153-252, with 167 references and notes; 9. 'The birth of the Scottish pistol', p.315-38; 11. The word *claymore*, p.378-87, with 27 references and notes. Detailed analytical index, p.442-52. 236 illus. in all. Not 'confined to matters primarily relating to Scotland' (*Preface*).
Class No: 623.4(411)

Russia

[4853]

BONDS, R., *ed*. **The Illustrated directory of modern Soviet weapons.** London, Salamander Books, Ltd., 1986. 480p. illus. (incl. col.), maps. ISBN: 0861012526.

3 sections: 1. Land weapons and equipment (p.6-159) - 2. Naval weapons and equipment (p.161-319) - 3. Air weapons and equipment (p.321-480). No bibliography or index, but contents list is detailed.
Class No: 623.4(47)

Equipment & Instruments

[4854]

British Army Equipment Exhibition, 22-27 June 1986, Aldershot. London, Defence Export Services Organisation, [1986]. cx, 272p. illus.

Catalogue of exhibitors' entries (1 per page), 'Aardvark Clear Mines, Ltd. ...' 'Zengrange, Ltd.'. Exhibitors index; Product index (in English, French, Spanish, Chinese Arabic, p.ix-cx). Well illustrated.

British Defence Equipment catalouge, 1987, 1988 (17th ed. 1987). comprises 3v. V.1/2 contain descriptions of the products and services offered by all participants, in 59 sections. V.3, Products and series index consists of company directory, trade names directory and abbreviations index. *Class No:* 623.4:002.50

Artillery & Rockets

[4855]

DASTRUP, B.L. **The Field artillery:** history and sourcebook. Westwood, Ct., Greenwood, 1994. 220p. $65. ISBN: 0313272646.

A survey of the history and bibliography of artillery from 1350 to 1991. Covers technology, tactics, operations. Includes brief biographies, a chronology, lists of artillery pieces of specific eras and a short glossary. Index. 'Recommended' (*Choice*, January 1995, p.746). *Class No:* 623.41

[4856]

HOGG, I.V. **The Illustrated encyclopedia of artillery:** an A-Z guide to artillery techniques and equipment throughout the world. London, Stanley Paul, 1987. 256p. illus. (incl. col.), tables. ISBN: 0091726549.

'A short history of artillery from 1326 to the present' precedes an A-Z guide to artillery, with tabulated or boxed information. 14 nationalities: American/US, Austrian, Belgian, British, Chinese, Czech, French, German, Israeli, Italian, Japanese, Russian, South African, Swiss. *Class No:* 623.41

[4857]
Jane's armour and artillery, 1998-99. Coulsdon, Surrey, Jane's Information Group, 1998. Annual. *c.*730p. illus., diagrs., tables. £270; $410. ISBN: 0710617909.

Technical data on: MBTS - Reconnaissance vehicles - Armoured personnel carriers - Armoured fighting vehicle families. Tank destroyers - Self propelled guns and howitzers - Self-propelled anti-aircraft guns and surface-to-surface missiles - Towed anti-tank guns - Towed guns - Multiple rocket launchers - Coastal artillery guns and missiles. Addenda. Armour and artillery in service. Index; 1-3 illus. per page. Available on online and CD-ROM.

The series (1979-1993) is also available on microfiche.
Class No: 623.41

[4858]
—**Jane's armour and artillery upgrades,** 1998-99. Coulsdon, Surrey, Jane's Information Group, 1998. 650p. illus., diagrs., tables. £235; $350. ISBN: 0710617917.

Reviews over 900 packages intended to update obsolete weapons. Covers ammunition, AFV engines, mobility, weapon control, meterological sensors, etc. Available online and on CD-ROM.
Class No: 623.41

Armoured Vehicles

[4859]
GELBERT, M. Tanks: main battle and light tanks. London, Brassey, 1996. 160p. illus. £15.95. Brassey's military equipment ISBN: 185753168x.

Entries are by country, A-Z, and listed chronologically. Data include level of protection, firepower, mobility, design, fighting qualities, etc. *Class No:* 623.42

[4860]
Jane's military vehicles and logistics, 1999-2000. Coulsdon, Surrey, Jane's Information Group, 1999. *c.*750p. illus. £250; $405. ISBN: 071061912x.

Formerly *Jane's Military vehicles and ground support equipment* (8th ed., 1987).

About 2,000 items of logistical equipment. Sections: Armoured engineer vehicles - Recovery vehicles and equipment - Bridging systems - Mine warfare equipment - Transport equipment - Miscellaneous equipment (*e.g.* Rapid runway repair equipment/portable runways). Fully illustrated; technical data, a feature. Glossary precedes. Index. Available online and on CD-ROM. *Class No:* 623.42

[4861]
—**VANDERVEEN, B.** World directory of modern military vehicles: unarmoured vehicles from 1970. London, Warne, 1983. 256p. illus. ISBN: 0723231656.

Covers such types as motorcyles and three-wheelers, cars and light transports, personnel carriers and buses, trucks, tractors and wreckers, amphibians and tracked vehicles, handling and construction equipment. Over 1,000 plates, many of them small. Non-analytical index, p.254-6. *Class No:* 623.42

[4862]
SENGER und Etterlin, F.M., von. **Taschenbuch der Panzer.** [Tanks of the World.] 6th ed. Munich, Bernard & Graefe Verlag, 1983. 827p. illus., diagrs., tables.

First published 1960.

Part 1: Type data sheets (19 countries, p.25-715); Part 2: Tables. Appendices A-M (A. Soviet exports; H. Distribution of armoured carriers). Data in Part 1 include development and production; distinguishing features; role; assessment. 'There is no comparable source in English' (Luttwak, E. *A dictionary of modern war* (1971). p.11). Fully illustrated. Small format. *Class No:* 623.42

Small Arms

[4863]
EZELL, E.C. and **PEGG, T.M. Small arms of the world:** a basic manual of small arms. 12th ed. London, Arms and Armour Press, 1983. 894p. illus., diagrs, tables. £25.

First published 1943 as *Basic manual of military small arms*. A completely new and revised version of the classic work by W.H.B. Smith.

Part 1. Small arms development since 1945 (Rifles and carbine development; Machine gun development; Submarine gun development; Handgun developments; Special purpose weapons development (*e.g.* Grenade launches). Part 2: Description of small arms by nations (44) and a basic manual of recent weapons: Argentina ... Yugoslavia, p.194-843. Characteristic of each given. Appended: Small arms for outdoor sports. Small arms ammunition. Selected bibliography, p.883-5. Detailed, analytical index, p.889-94. 2,000 illus. *Class No:* 623.44

[4864]
GREAT BRITAIN. Department of Trade and Industry. Translation Service. **Small arms glossary, English-French-German.** London, the Department, 1986. [*c.*130]p. £6.

Revised version of the 'Small arms glossary' produced for the 1984 Small Arms Conference.

3 sequences, each with *c.*500 entries: English/German/French (on white paper) - French/English/German (on green paper) - German/French/English (on yellow paper). Terms on which decision was not definitive are asterisked. Oblong format. *Class No:* 623.44

[4865]
HOGG, I.V. and **WEEKS, J. Military small arms of the 20th century:** a comprehensive illustrated encyclopedia of the world's small calibre firearms. 5th ed. London, Arms & Armour Press, 1985. 303p. illus., tables. ISBN: 0853687080.

First published 1973.

Coverage: handguns; submachine guns; bolt-action rifle; automatic rifles; machineguns; anti-tank rifles; ammunition. 40 countries involved. Technical descriptions. About 700 illus. *Class No:* 623.44

[4866]
Jane's infantry weapons, 1999-2000. Coulsdon, Surrey, Jane's Information Group, 1999. *c.*500p. illus., diagrs., tables. £250; $405. ISBN: 0710619251.

Over 2,000 weapons and accessories from 240 manufacturers in 70 countries. Technical data on: personal weapons; crew-served weapons; ammunition; ancillary equipment. Available online and on CD-ROM. *Class No:* 623.44

[4867]
MARCHINGTON, J. Handguns and sub-machine guns: semi-automatic pistols and revolers. London, Brassey, 1997. 128p. illus. £15.95. Brassey's modern military equipment ISBN: 1857531639.

Covers modern weapons as well as some older designs which might be found in the hands of terrorists. *Class No:* 623.44

Pistols

[4868]
HOGG, I.V. and **WEEKS, J. Pistols of the world:** the definitive illustrated guide to the world's pistols and revolvers. London, Arms and Armour Press, 1992. 352p. illus. ISBN: 1854090364.

Covers about 2,000 pistols. 3 parts: 1. Introduction (including glossary and bibliography) - 2. Directory (pistols by manufacturer, A-Z (*e.g.* Colt, about 96 models)) - 3. Appendices (Databank, pistol names A-Z; Ammunition). Well-designed with excellent illustrations. *Class No:* 623.443

[4869]
SMITH, W.H.B. Book of pistols and revolvers; completely updated by J.E. Smith. Secaucus, N.J., Castle Books, 1979. xvi, 816p. illus., diagrs.

First published 1946. 1968 ed. (Harrisburg, Pa., Stackpoole Books) reprinted 1979.

Part 1.: Handguns, to include World War II (13 chapters, p.1-590; 7 appendices: 3. Glossary of pistol and revolver terms) - Part 2: Pistol and revolver trends, 1945-1968 (countries, A-Z). Index. Covers handguns worldwide, their identification, calibre and operation, illustration, description and history, construction, ammunition, dismounting and assembling. The standard reference work on handguns of the world. *Class No:* 623.443

Swords & Knives

[4870]
MARCHINGTON, J. Knives: military edged tools and weapons. London, Brassey, 1997. 160p. illus. £15.95. (*Brassey's modern military equipment*.) ISBN: 1857531876.

Provides details of blades used worldwide for combat, general field use and survival. Lavishly illustrated. *Class No:* 623.444

Ammunition

[4871]
HOGG, I.V. The Illustrated encyclopedia of ammunition. London, Apple Press, 1985. 256p. illus. (incl. col.), facsims. ISBN: 1850760438.

Sections: A history of ammunition, p.8-64; A/Z of ammunition; Small arms; Mortars and grenades; Artillery; New developments (*e.g.* Laser guidance), General index, p.[254]; Index to headwords, p.255. Fully illustrated. *Class No:* 623.45

[4872]
Jane's ammunition handbook, 1998-99. 7th ed. Coulsdon, Surrey, Jane's Information Group, 1998. 624p. illus., diagrs. £235; $350. ISBN: 0710617895.

Covers: small arms; cannon; air defence; tank and artillery; mortar; grenades; pyrotechnics. Data include: description; history; specifications; equivalent projectiles by country; list of equipment. *Class No:* 623.45

Atomic Weapons

[4873]
COCHRAN, T.B., *and others*. **Nuclear weapons databook.** National Resources Defense Council, Inc. Cambridge, Mass., Ballinger, 1984-. V.1-. illus., maps. ISBN: 088410172x, v.1.

1. *U.S. nuclear forces and capabilities.* 1984. xix, 340p.
2. *U.S. nuclear warhead production.* 1987. xv, 223p.
3. *U.S. nuclear warhead facility profiles.* 1987. xv, 132p.
4. *Soviet nuclear weapons.* Harper & Row, 1989. 433p.
5. *British, French, and Chinese nuclear weapons.* Westview Press, 1994. 437p.

The first of a series of 8v. V.1-3 concentrate on US weapons; v.4 on Soviet weapons; v.5-8 to be on the environment, command and control of nuclear weapons and strategy, arms control in general, and a history of nuclear weapons. V.1 has 9 chapters (1. The nuclear weapons system: an overview ... 9. Army nuclear weapons. 75p. of statistics. Glossary. Index, p.329-40. 150 photographs); v.5 has 7 chapters. *Class No:* 623.454.8

[4874]
FOWLER, W. *and* **NORRIS, J.A. NBC: nuclear, biological and chemical warfare on the modern battlefield.** London, Brassey, 1997. 160p. illus. £15.95 (*Brassey's modern military equipment..*) ISBN: 1857531825.

Covers the agents themselves, delivery systems and equipment available for military and civil defence. *Class No:* 623.454.8

Missiles

[4875]
Guided weapons. Lee, R.G., *and others, eds*. London, Brassey, 1997. 286p. £29.95. ISBN: 1857531523.

Covers the technology and development of guided weapons and their use on the battlefield. Contents: Introduction - Propulson - Electrical power - Supplies - Airframes - Guidance - Control - Electronic warfare - Payload - Anti-tank guided weapons - surface-to-surface guided weapons. Brief glossary. *Class No:* 623.46

Field Engineering

Communications

[4876]
Jane's military communications, 1999-2000. Coulsdon, Surrey, Jane's Information Group, 1999. c.800p. illus., diagrs. £250; $405. ISBN: 0710619111.

First published 1979 (for 1979/80).

Includes 4,000 equipment entries. Contents: Radio communications - Line communications. Overview of each country's systems. Includes tactical and satellite communications, encryption. Abundant technical data. Available online and on CD-ROM. *Class No:* 623.61

Radar Countermeasures

[4877]
HALL, P.S., *and others*. **Radar.** London, Brassey's, 1991. xiii,170p. £22.50. (*New battlefield weapons systems and technology*, 9.) ISBN: 0080377106.

Specific function and operation of radar equipment in a military setting. Includes electronic warfare. *Class No:* 623.62

[4878]
The International countermeasures handbook. Wiseman, C.H., *ed*. 11th ed. Palo Alto, Calif., E.W. Communications, Inc., 1986. Annual. 444p. ISBN: 0918994128.

First published 1975.

5 main parts: Electronic warfare budgets - [Electronic] systems of the West - Guided missiles of the world - Soviet weapons and electronics, p.197-282 - Analysis and technology (17 sections, including 'Electric warfare bibliography', p.393-412). Indexes and references, p.437-43. *Class No:* 623.62

[4879]
Jane's radar and electronic warfare systems, 1998-99. 10th ed. Coulsdon, Surrey, Jane's Information Group, 1998. 624p. illus. ISBN: 0710618077.

Includes over 2,000 systems currently in service or under development. Contents: radar systems; electronic warfare systems; simulation and training systems. *Class No:* 623.62

[4880]
WALDMAN, H. The Dictionary of SDI [Strategic Defense Initiative]. Wilmington, Delaware, SR Books, 1988. 173p. illus., diagrs., tables. ISBN: 0842022813.

Over 1,000 entries on Strategic Defense Initiative, including persons, laboratories. 'Antisatellite' (ASAT) weapon: over 1p., illus. Appended: 'Text of Treaty between the United States of America and the Union of Soviet Socialist Republics on the limitation of anti-ballistic missile systems, 1972'. Aims 'to classify and simplify SDI's complex terrain, lay out the technology involved, and identify those areas of debate'. *Class No:* 623.62

Aircraft

Encyclopaedias

[4881]
ANGELUCCI, E., *ed*. **The Rand McNally encyclopedia of military aircraft, 1914-1980.** Translated by S.M. Harris. Chicago, Ill., Rand McNally, 1981. 546p. col. illus., diagrs., charts. ISBN: 0528815474.

Original as *Atlantec encilopedico degli aerei militari del mondo* (Milan, Mondadori, 1980).

A splendidly illustrated record of 800 types of military craft flown between 1914 and 1980. 4 chapters: 'The First World War'; 'Military aviation between the two World Wars'; 'The Second World War'; and 'Military aviation from 1945 to the present day'. Subdivision by types. Country index; general index. Colour illus. of over 1,700 individual aircraft; 772 line-drawings (usually three-view); charts of national markings. Appended 3p. bibliography. Omits helicopters. Supplements *Jane's all the world's aircraft* by giving historical treatment. 'Indisepensable for aviation history and military science collections' (*Wilson library bulletin*, March 1982, p.545-6). *Class No:* 623.7(031)

[4882]
CHANT, C. Encyclopaedia of modern aircraft armaments. Wellingborough, P. Stephens, 1988. 304p. £19.95. ISBN: 0850598621.

Includes helicopter armament. *Class No:* 623.7(031)

[4883]
The encyclopedia of world air power. Gunston, B., *ed*. 2nd ed. Twickenham, Middx., Temple Press, 1986. 319p. illus. (incl. col.). £17.50. ISBN: 0600351653.

First published 1980.

The world's air forces (Western Europe ... South America), p.7-66. The world's military aircraft, A-Z, p.67-301. Data on each type: description; specification; illus. - cutaway drawings and silhouettes. The world's air-launched missiles, p.302-15. Detailed index, p.316-9. *Class No:* 623.7(031)

Handbooks & Manuals

[4884]
GUNSTON, B. An Illustrated guide to modern fighters. London, Salamander, 1984. 159p. col. illus., diagrs. ISBN: 0861010858.

Details of 57 fighter aircraft, Aeritalia G81 ... Yakovlev. Data: origin; type; engines; dimensions; weight; performance; armament; history; users; development. Col. illus.; 3-way view line-drawings. *Class No:* 623.7(035)

[4885]
Jane's avionics, 1998-99. Coulsdon, Surrey, Jane's Information Group, 1998. c.600p. illus., diagrs. £235; $350. ISBN: 0710617925.

Over 2,700 avionics products and systems. Sections: Sensors - Data processing and displays - Radio communications. Directory of manufacturers. 1200 illus. Available online and on CD-ROM. *Class No:* 623.7(035)

Yearbooks & Directories

[4886]
Brassey's world aircraft and systems directory 1999-2000. Taylor, M., *ed*. 2nd ed. London, Brassey's, 1999. 797p. illus. tables. £95. ISBN: 1857532457.

First published 1996.

Covers combat, reconnaissance, airliners, helicopters, general and recreational aviation, missiles, airships, spaceflight, airborne raiders and airport runway bearing strengths. Data include manufacturer, history, technical detals, performance. *Class No:* 623.7(058)

Worldwide

[4887]

FRAWLEY, G. *and* **THORN, J. The International directory of military aircraft 1996-97.** Shrewsbury, Airlife, 1996. 189p. illus. £16.95. ISBN: 1853107638.

About 280 aircraft types, A-Z, with technical and production data, country of origin, history, and colour illustration for each. A companion v. to the authors' *The International directory of civil aircraft 1995-96. Class No:* 623.7(100)

[4888]

Globemac: the global military aircraft census. Brindley, J.F., *ed.* Geneva, Globemac, 1993. 760p. tables. £600.

Surveys strengths, dispositions, organization and procurement plans for about 140 air forces. 2 main sections: Country (politics, defence policy, military manpower, etc.) - Aircraft (manufacturer, type, number in service, country, etc.). Numerous tables.

Three up-dating supplements pa. also available, £200. *Class No:* 623.7(100)

[4889]

Jane's helicopter markets and systems. Coulsdon, Surrey, Jane's Information Group, 1996. 400p., looseleaf binder. illus., diagrs. tables. £495. ISBN: 0710613636.

Over 150 main models, civil and military. Data: manufacturer; structure; programme details; variants; compressor; turbines; gearbox; fuel system and consumption. Available online and on CD-ROM (£595). Updates are issued. *Class No:* 623.7(100)

Great Britain

[4890]

EVERETT-HEATH, J. British military helicopters. London, Arms and Armour Press, 1986. 224p. illus. £14.95.

A survey of military helicopter types, from Cierva helicopters and Bristol helicopters to Westland 30 and EH-101. 4 appendices (*e.g.* helicopter projects and designs). List of abbreviations. Glossary. Bibliography, p.220. Over 200 photographs. Detailed, non-analytical index. *Class No:* 623.7(410)

Russia

[4891]

GUNSTON, B. Aircraft of the Soviet Union: the encyclopedia of Soviet aircraft since 1917. Baldry, D., *ed.* London, Osprey, 1983. 414, [2]p. illus., ports, diagrs. ISBN: 085045445x.

Includes biographies. Entries: 'Alexandrov-Kalinin ... Zlokazov'. Prelims include 'Soviet aircraft designations', 'Air weapons', 'Materials', 'Engines', 'Soviet organizations', 'Miscellaneous data'. Appended list of grouped light aircraft, p.408-14. Cross-sections, a feature. *Class No:* 623.7(47)

USA

[4892]

WATERS, A.W. All the US Air Force airplanes, 1907-1983. New York, Hippocrene Books, [c.1983]. [vii], 413p. ISBN: 0882548825.

'Historical index section' and 'Historical aircraft section' precede the main part, on US aircraft, 1944 to the present, p.59-311, plus 'Space vehicles, 1974 to the present'. 7 appendices include Bibliography (p.316-7); Air Force bases. Detailed index, p.399-413. *Class No:* 623.7(73)

Navies

Abbreviations & Symbols

[4893]

WEDERTZ, B. Dictionary of naval abbreviations. 3rd ed. Annapolis, Md., Naval Institute Press, 1984. 330p.

First published 1970; 2nd ed. 1977 (360p).

Explains *c.*45,000 abbreviations 'commonly used by the naval establishment and ... unavailable in standard dictionaries' (*Preface*). Pruned of entries in the 2nd ed. not related to strictly naval matters. *Class No:* 623.8(003)

Bibliographies

[4894]

SMITH, M.J. Battleships and battle-cruisers, 1884-1984: a bibliography and chronology. New York, Garland Publishing Co., 1985. 691p. (*Garland reference library of social science, 203.*) ISBN: 0814089022.

5,500 references to books, periodical articles, scholarly papers, government publications, etc. Chapter and section introductions. The chronology has appended index of ship names, major battles,

....(contd.)

conferences and treaties. 'This outstanding bibliography, the most extensive compilation to date' (Choice, v.23(5), January 1986, p.730). *Class No:* 623.8(01)

Handbooks & Manuals

[4895]

FRIEDMAN, N. The Naval Institute guide to world naval weapons systems. Anapolis, MD, Naval Institute Press, 1989. 511p. photos, diagrs. $89.95. ISBN: 0870212953.

Arranged by type of system. Sections: Surveillance and control - Strategic strike systems - Strikes - Surface warfare - Anti-aircraft warfare - Anti-submarine warfare - Mine warfare. Index. *Class No:* 623.8(035)

[4896]

The Naval Institute guide to combat fleets of the world, 1998-1999: their ships, aircraft, and systems. Baker, A.D., *ed.* Annapolis, Md., Naval Institute Press, 1998. 1224p. illus., diagrs. $150. ISBN: 1557501114.

The content of this ed. reflects current trends, including an expanded section on the Russian Navy, the gradual shrinking of the world's fleets and the distribution of retired naval units to other countries. 3,500 illus. Also available on CD-ROM. *Class No:* 623.8(035)

Dictionaries

[4897]

PALMER, J., *comp.* **Jane's dictionary of naval terms.** London, Macdonald & Jane's. 1975. [iv], 342p.

Over 6,000 entries for naval military terms as well as those in general seamanship, plus some purely mercantile terms. Different meanings are numbered. Many cross-references. Sources (p.2) include Royal Navy, US Navy and NATO manuals. *Class No:* 623.8(038)

[4898]

—**NOEL, J.V. Naval terms dictionary.** 5th ed. Annapolis, Md., Naval Institute Press, 1986. 352p.

First published 1952; 4th ed. 1978.

About 6,000 entry-words, - US Navy colloquialisms, slang and technical terminology, including abbreviations. 5 appendices (*e.g.* ship, aircraft and missile designation systems; electronic nomenclature). *Class No:* 623.8(038)

[4899]

UNITED STATES. Naval Institute. **Naval phraseology:** English-French-Spanish-Italian-German-Portuguese. 2nd ed. Annapolis, Md., the Institute, 1953. [ix], 326p.

First published 1944 (v, 326p.).

4 parts: 1. Naval terms (*c.*1,800) in sections A-H (Administration ... War), with indexes of English terms - 2. Colloquies (*i.e.,* dialogues) in English, with translations in French, Spanish, Italian, German and Portuguese - 3. Correspondence - 4. Tables of ranks, with sleeve markings. *Class No:* 623.8(038)

Anthologies

[4900]

Warship 1998-1999. Preston, A., *ed.* London, Conway Maritime, 1999. Annual. 224p. illus. £30. ISBN: 0851777244.

Reprints of original articles; 238 illus. Emphasis is on design of ships. Appended: Naval events of the year. *Class No:* 623.8(082.21)

Histories

[4901]

Conway's all the world's fighting ships. London, Conway Maritime Press, 1979-95. 4v. illus., diagrs. ISBN: 0870219235.

Conway's All the World's fighting ships, 1860-1905. 1979. [vii], 440p.

Conway's Fighting Ships, 1906-1921. 1983. [viii], 439p.

Conway's All the World's fighting ships, 1922-1946. 1980. [viii], 456p.

Conway's All the World's fighting ships, 1947-1995.

The 1947-1995 (1995; 675p.; £75; ISBN: 0851776051) covers the break-up of the Soviet Union and includes technical information from the Eastern Bloc that was previously inaccessible. The set provides an historical survey (beginning with the introduction of ironclad ships), complementing *Jane's Fighting ships*, as well as correcting data in the latter's volumes. Each of the Conway volumes provides technical data on types of ships, photographs and line drawings, plus a detailed index. 'Conway's is an invaluable addition to naval reference collections of any size' (*Reference books bulletin, 1984-1985* (1986). p.42). *Class No:* 623.8(091)

[4902]

—FRIEDMAN, N. Navies in the nuclear age: warships since 1945. London, Conway Maritime Press, 1993. 224p. illus. (*Conway's history of the ship.*)

Emphasises broader themes (*e.g.* anit-submarine warfare, modern electronics). 260 illus. *Class No:* 623.8(091)

[4903]

GEORGE, J.L. The History of warships: from ancient times to the twenty-first century. London, Constable, 1999. *c.*250p. illus. £25. ISBN: 0094797005.

Covers warships from Greek triremes to the proposed Sea Shadow stealth for the US Navy. Includes design, construction, weapons and defence systems. *Class No:* 623.8(091)

[4904]

GOODWIN, P. The Construction and fitting of the English sailing men of war, 1650 - 1850. London, Conway Maritime Press, 1987. xi, 276p. illus., diagrs., tables. ISBN: 0851773265.

10 chapters (1. The construction of a ship of War in frame ... 10. Hull protection). 8 appendices (2. The quantities of timber used in ship construction; 4e. The 1745 Establishment list). Bibliography, p.267. Detailed, analytical index, p.269-76. Fully illustrated; meticulously drawn diagrams, to scale. *Class No:* 623.8(091)

[4905]

—LAVERY, B. The Arming and fitting of English ships of war 1600-1815. London, Conway Maritime Press, 1987. 319p. illus., diagrs., tables. ISBN: 0851774512.

11 parts (47 chapters): 1. Steering ... 5. Guns ... 9. Internal fittings. 11 appendices, each linked to a part (2. Anchors, capstans). Extensive chapter references to contemporary documents. Intended 'in the tradition' of Peter Goodwin (*Preface*) (*qv*). *Class No:* 623.8(091)

[4906]

LAVERY, B. The Ship of the line. London, Conway Maritime Press, 1983-84. 2v. illus., diagrs., tables. ea. £20. ISBN: 0851772528.

1. *The development of the battleship, 1650-1850.* 1983.

2. *Design, construction and fittings, 1650-1850.* 1984.

V.1 (224p.) covers the general historical background, and includes extensive tables listing all ships of 50 guns and above, divided by period, rate, class and design, with full technical data. 130 plates, 65 line-drawings. V.2 concerns technical developments in hull design, construction, rigging, armament and fittings. *Class No:* 623.8(091)

[4907]

—LAMBERT, A. Battleships in transition: the creation of the steam battlefleet, 1815-1860. London, Conway Maritime Press, 1984. 168p. illus. £11.95. ISBN: 085117315x.

Bridges the gap between B. Lavery's *The ship of the line*, 1650-1850 and Conway's *All the World's fighting ships*, 1860-1982. 95 illus. *Class No:* 623.8(091)

Worldwide

[4908]

BISHOP, C., *ed*. The Encyclopedia of world sea power. Lonsdon, Temple Press, 1988. 319p. illus. (incl. col.). £17.50. ISBN: 0600332748.

Sections: Missile submarines - Nuclear attack sumbarines - Diesel submarines - Aircraft carriers - Cruisers - Destroyers - Western frigates - Frigates - Patrol craft - Amphibious assault ships - Military hovercraft - Mine warfare vessels - Anti-ship missiles - Naval artillery - Naval surface-to-surface missiles - Naval anti-aircraft weapons - Underwater weapon systems - Underwater weapons. World navies, (p.291-319), Albania ... Zaire. Detailed captions. Fully illustrated. *Class No:* 623.8(100)

[4909]

Jane's fighting ships, 1999-2000. Sharpe, R., *ed.* Coulsdon, Surrey, Jane's Information Group, 1999. Annual. 912p. illus., diagrs., tables. £280; $445. ISBN: 0710619057.

Founded in 1879 by F.T. Jane.

Covers over 8,000 warships from 150 nations. Sections: foreword on worldwide naval affairs; flags and ensigns; ranks and insignia; pennant list of major surface ships; ship reference (A-z by country). Data include: main machinery, speed, missiles, countermeasures, combat data systems, radars, modernisation, sales. 3,000 illus. The leading authority on current navies worldwide. Available online and on CD-ROM.

The series (1897-1993) is available on microfiche. *Class No:* 623.8(100)

[4910]

—Weyers Flottentaschenbuch. Munich, Lehman, Biennial.

First published 1900 as *Taschenbuch der deutschen Kriegsflotte.* The German counterpart of 'Jane'. *Class No:* 623.8(100)

[4911]

Warships of the world: an illustrated encyclopedia. Gallipini, G. New York, Times Books, 1986. 320p. col.illus. $70. ISBN: 0812911296.

Each section covers one class of ships; includes submarines. Technical data. Indexes: Country; name of ship. *Class No:* 623.8(100)

Russia

[4912]

POLMAR, N. Guide to the Soviet navy. 4th ed. London, Arms & Armour Press, 1986. xiv, 536p. £35. ISBN: 0853685214.

3rd ed. 1983 ([xv], 465p.).

Detailed analysis of the Soviet navy of the late 1980s, the ships, their weaponry and electronic systems. 425 illus., including many photographs previously unpublished. Detailed drawings of new ships. Index. *Class No:* 623.8(47)

[4913]

—MOORE, J. Warships of the Soviet Navy. London, etc., Jane's Publishing Co., 1981. 192p. illus. ISBN: 0710601034.

Describes 33 types of vessel (nuclear-powered, ballistic missile submarines ... Tugs/floating docks). Data include: name; displacement; aircraft; missiles, guns; propulsion; range; complement; radar. Glossary of abbreviations used. Class index. General (detailed) index. *Class No:* 623.8(47)

USA

[4914]

Dictionary of American naval fighting ships. Mooney, J.L., *ed.* Washington, Government Printing Office, for the U.S. Naval History Division. 8v. $142, the set.

Descriptions and histories of *c.*10,000 US fighting ships since 1775; entries under ships names, A-Z, through the 8 volumes. Appendices scattered throughout, list the ships by type and class. No general index. Well illustrated. Revision of the historical sketches of ships in the earlier volumes is in hand. *Class No:* 623.8(73)

20th Century

[4915]

All the world's battleships: 1906 to the present. Sturton, I. London, Conway. 1996. 192p. illus., diagrs. ISBN: 0851776914.

Covers technical data, design background and careers of the world's battleships and battlecruisers. Lavishly illus. *Class No:* 623.8"19"

Submarines

[4916]

HERVEY, J.D. Submarines. London, Brassey, 1994. xxviii, 289p. illus., diagrs., tables. (*Brassey's sea power, v.7.*)

A general survey in 16 chapters, closely subdivided: 2. Roles ... 6. Masts ... 8. Sonar ... 16. Future trends. Author spent 13 years in the Submarine Branch of the Royal Navy. *Class No:* 623.827

[4917]

MILLER, D. Submarines of the world. London, Salamander, 1991. 189p. illus. £18.95. ISBN: 0861015622.

A technical directory of the major submarines from 1888 to the present. *Class No:* 623.827

[4918]

'The Submarine'. In *Navy International*, May 1988, p.224-75.

Includes data on international submarine forces; design; combat information; sonar; periscopes; electronic warfare; machinery; weapons. *Class No:* 623.827

Naval Defence

[4919]

Jane's naval weapon systems. Coulsdon, Surrey, Jane's Information Group, 1992-. 300p. Looseleaf binder + updates (3pa.). £425; $685. ISBN: 0710608934.

Data on 300 weapons and systems, 110 manufacturers. Contents: handling systems; equipment (missiles, guns, launchers, etc.); display systems. Supplements published April, August, December. Available online and on CD-ROM. *Class No:* 623.9

[4920]

KIELY, D.G. Naval electronic warfare. London, Brassey's, 1988. xiii, 122p. £9.95. (*Brassey's Sea power: naval weapons, weapon systems and technology series, no. 5.*)

A survey of naval electronic warfare systems. *Class No:* 623.9

Civil Engineering

Databases

[4921]

ICONDA Stuttgart, Fraunhofer-Gesellschaft.

International bibliographic database, with abstracts, covering construction, civil engineering, urban and regional planning and architecture. 350,000 records from 1976. Subjects: structural engineering; construction equipment and materials; building maintenance, restoration and conservation; engineering geology; financial planning and project management. Online from CISTI, Questel SA, Questel/ORBIT, STN International. Also available on CD-ROM (SilverPlatter) and on the Internet. *Class No:* 624(003.4)

[4922]

RSWB. Stuttgart, Fraunhofer-Gesellschaft.

Bibliographic database of German and international publications on building and construction, including civil engineering. 550,000 records of which about 60% have abstracts in German. Available on STN International (updated monthly) and on CD-ROM (SilverPlatter, updated quarterly). *Class No:* 624(003.4)

CD-ROM

[4923]

KR OnDisc; Ei Civil Disc: ASCE members edition, 1974-March 1996. New York, Engineering Information; Knight Ridder, 1997. 2 discs. $175.

About 500,000 entries containing bibliographic information and abstracts related to civil engineering. *Class No:* 624(003.40)

Bibliographies

[4924]

SKEMPTON, A.W. British civil engineering literature, 1640-1840: a bibliography of contemporary printed reports, plans and books. London, Mansell, 1987. xvii, 302p. illus., facsims, maps. £45. ISBN: 0720112461.

1,914 numbered entries. Topics covered: fen drainage, river navigation, canals, docks and harbours, bridges, roads, railways and water supply, 'with a selection of related pamphlets, and works on mechanism, strength of materials and hydraulics' (*Preface*). 'Guide to the literature' (running commentary), p.ix-xiv. Bibliography, p.1-275; under authors, A-Z, with annotations and locations; addenda. Subject index: Aqueduct ... Water supply, p.287-302. *Class No:* 624(01)

Handbooks & Manuals

[4925]

BELL, F.G. Ground engineer's reference book. London, Butterworth, 1987. 1264p. illus., tables. £99.50. ISBN: 0408011734.

About 70 contributors. 5 parts (59 chapters): 1. Properties and behaviour of the ground - 2. Investigation in ground engineering - 3. Treatment of the ground - 4. Construction in ground engineering - 5. Numerical methods and modelling in ground engineering. Chapter 11: 'Stability of soil slopes' (16p. 19 references; 2 items of further reading; 10 figures). 1,028 illus. in all. For practising civil engineers. *Class No:* 624(035)

[4926]

BLAKE, L.S., *ed.* **Civil engineer's reference book.** 4th ed. London, Butterworth, 1990. v.p. illus., diagrs., graphs, tables. £90. ISBN: 0408012080.

First published 1951 as *Civil engineering reference book;* 3rd ed. 1975.

52 contributors. 45 documented sections (2. Strength of materials - 3. Theory of structures ... 11. Site investigation ... 18. Dams ... 24. Airports ... 32. Tunnelling ... 44. Offshore construction). Section 5, 'Hydraulics': 28p., 62 line drawings, 15 tables, 44 references, brief bibliography. Detailed, analytical index, 19p.

A paperback of the 4th ed. was published in 1994 (£40; ISBN: 0750619643). *Class No:* 624(035)

[4927]

The Civil engineering handbook. Chen, W.F., *ed.* Boca Raton, Fl., CRC Press, 1995. xxvi, 2609p. illus., diagrs., graphs, tables, formulas. ISBN: 0849389534.

About 70 contributors. 64 chapters, closely subdivided and with extensive references. 8 sections: 1. Construction - 2. Environmental engineering - 3. Geotechnical engineering - 4. Huydraulic engineering - 5. Materials engineering - 6. Structural engineering - 7. Surveying engineering - 8. Transportation. Much emphasis on CAD/CAE. Detailed, analytical index, p.2569-2609. Selected by *Choice* as an outstanding academic book for 1995. *Class No:* 624(035)

[4928]

Construction materials reference book. Doran, D.K., *ed.* Oxford, Butterworth-Heinemann, 1992. v.p. illus., diagrs., tables. £95; $205. ISBN: 0750610042.

2 parts: 1. Metals - 2. Non-metals. Topics include cement, concrete, ceramics, timber, stone, aluminium, steel, etc. Chapters identify relevant British standards. Several hundred literature references. 'Recommended' (*Choice,* November 1992, p.500). *Class No:* 624(035)

[4929]

Field engineer's manual. Parmley, R.O., *ed.* 2nd ed. New York, McGraw-Hill, 1996. 611p. diagrs., tables. ISBN: 0070485798.

First published 1981.

Covers construction materials, surveying, mechanical systems, electrical construction, drainage and hydraulics. Basic engineering data to assist in preliminary surveys, field problems and supplement technical materials. *Class No:* 624(035)

[4930]

The Handbook of groundwater engineering. Delleur, J.W., *ed.* Boca Raton, Fl., CRC Press, 1999. v.p. illus., diagrs., graphs, tables. $99.85. ISBN: 0849326982.

44 contributors; 27 chapters in 5 parts: Introduction - Basic equations and analyses of seepage and infiltration - Well and aquifer hydraulics - Contaminent transport and modelling - Environmental engineering and legal aspects. Chapter references; glossary. Detailed, analytical index. Also available on CD-ROM. *Class No:* 624(035)

[4931]

Standard handbook for civil engineers. Merritt, F.S., *and others, eds.* 4th ed. New York, etc., McGraw-Hill, 1996. v.p. illus., diagrs., graphs, tables, formulas. £104.95. ISBN: 0070415978.

First published 1968; 3rd ed. 1983.

26 contributors; 23 sections (Systems design ... Specifications ... Construction materials ... Structural steel design and construction ... Wood design and construction ... Earthwork ... Building engineering - Highway engineering - Bridge engineering - Airport engineering ... Tunnel engineering - Water resources engineering - Environmental engineering - Coastal and harbour engineering). Section references. Detailed, analytical index of 52p. Also available on CD-ROM (1998; $149.95; ISBN: 0071344195). *Class No:* 624(035)

[4932]

—**MERRITT, F.S.** *and* **KURTZ, M.,** *eds.* Civil engineering reference guide. New York, etc., McGraw-Hill, 1986. [608]p. illus. $49.50. ISBN: 0070415226.

A condensation of F.S. Merritt's *Standard handbook for civil engineers.* 11 contributors. 9 sections: 1. Structural theory - 2. Structural steel design - 3. Concrete design and construction - 4. Wood design and construction - 5. Bridge engineering - 6. Geotechnical engineering - 7. Water engineering - 8. Environmental engineering - 9. Surveying. Analytical index (24p.). *Class No:* 624(035)

[4933]

Structural engineering handbook. Gaylord, E.H., Jr. *and* Gaylord, C.N., *eds.* 3rd ed. New York, McGraw-Hill, 1990. v.p. diagrs., graphs, tables. $49.50. ISBN: 0070231885.

This ed. has been substantially revised and updated (*e.g.* on fatigue), with a new section on curved steel I-girder bridges. 46 contributors. 30 sections, each with a lengthy bibliography. 763 illus. An authoritative reference work, for engineers, architects and students in these fields. Analytical index (over 2,000 entries). *Class No:* 624(035)

Dictionaries

Polyglot

[4934]

Elsevier's dictionary of civil engineering in four languages: English, German, Spanish and French. Gutiérrez, M.F. Amsterdam, Elsevier, 1991. [x], 392p. £101. ISBN: 0444889876.

Over 6,000 terms. Bibliography. *Class No:* 624(038)=00

[4935]

GROS, E. *and* **SINGER, L.,** *comps.* **Russian-English-French-German constructional engineering dictionary.** London, Scientific Information Consultants, Ltd., 1965. ii, 194p.

About 1,500 terms 'from structural mechanics and related fields most frequently used in building, bridge construction and civil engineering, with particular emphasis on steel structures' (back of title-page). Russian entry-words, with English, French and German equivalents, but no indexes. Genders not stated. *Class No:* 624(038)=00

[4936]

TEKNISKA NOMENKLATURCENTRALEN. **Kommunaltekniska ordlista.** [Glossary of municipal engineering.] Stockholm, the Centre, 1976. 214p. (*TNC 61.*) ISBN: 9171960627.

472 Nordic language terms, with definitions in Swedish and equivalents in English, French and German. Indexes in English, Danish, Finnish, French, German, Norwegian and Swedish.
Class No: 624(038)=00

English

[4937]

SCOTT, J.S. **Dictionary of civil engineering.** 4th ed. Harmondsworth, Penguin, 1991. 608p., illus. £8.99. ISBN: 0140512462.

3rd ed. 1981.

About 5,000 terms are concisely defined. Includes a wide range of terms in soil mechanics, heavy construction and mining. 'Retaining wall': 1p. with illus. US usage is covered. For the layman and non-specialist engineer. *Class No:* 624(038)=20

[4938]

WEBSTER, L.F. **The Contractors' dictionary of equipment, tools and techniques** for civil engineering, construction, forestry, open-pit mining, and public parks. New York, etc., Wiley, 1995. xi, 666p. ISBN: 0471115231.

About 15,000 terms briefly defined (2-3 lines). North American emphasis. Reprinted in 1997 and issued as *The Wiley dictionary of civil engineering and construction* (ISBN: 0471181153). Librarians beware.
Class No: 624(038)=20

German

[4939]

BUCKSCH, H. **Wörterbuch für Bautechnik und Baumaschinen.** [Dictionary of civil engineering and construction machinery and equipment.] 8. Aufl. Wiesbaden, Bauverlag GmbH, 1982-87. 2v.

First published 1955.

V. 1: German-English; V. 2: English-German. About 65,000 entry-words in each volume. British and US usage differentiated. Entries are grouped *e.g.* 'Tunnel and Stollenbau' (construction of tunnels and galleries), v.1, with separate lines for subentries. Many compounds. German genders shown. Appended conversion tables.
Class No: 624(038)=30

[4940]

JUNGE, H.D. *and* LUKHAUP, D. **Special-purpose dictionary of civil engineering and architecture:** English-German. [Terminus: bauwessen und architektur] 2nd ed. Berlin, Ernst & Sohn, 1991. [iv], 467p. £57. ISBN: 3433028265.

First published 1987 in 2 v.

About 20,000 entries in each half. *Class No:* 624(038)=30

[4941]

SOUSA FERREIRA, K. de. **Terminologie des Hoch- und Brückenbaues.** Englisch-deutsch, deutsch-englisch. [Glossary of building and bridge construction.] Berlin, Ernst, 1969. viii, 216p. ISBN: 3433001235.

About 3,000 terms, each shown in context. 10 chapters: 1. Strength of materials - 2. Structures - 3. Building materials - 4. Timber construction - 5. Stone, brick and concrete construction - 6. Steel construction - 7. Composite construction in steel and concrete - 8. Structural elements of building construction - 9. Bridges - 10. Foundations, mechanics of soil. Bibliography. German and English indexes. *Class No:* 624(038)=30

Swedish

[4942]

TEKNISKA NOMENKLATURCENTRALEN. **Byggordsamling.** [Construction vocabulary: Swedish-English, English-Swedish.] Stockholm, the Centre. 1979. 351p. (*TNC 72.*)

About 9,000 terms, Swedish and English. 'Contains many terms from other TNC glossaries on house-painting, concrete, industrial engineering, planning and building, geotechnics, timber construction and municipal engineering' (*Incorporated linguist,* Summer 1977, p.75). *Class No:* 624(038)=397

French

[4943]

BUCKSCH, H. **Dictionnaire pour les travaux publics.** [Dictionary of civil engineering and construction machinery and equipment.] 9th ed. Paris, Eyrolles, 1982. 2v.

French-English. 547p. *English-French.* 420p.

Each volume has *c.*30,000 entry-words. There are German-French and German-Spanish volumes, apart from the German-English volumes.

.... (contd.)

The 10th ed. appeared in 1996. The English/French v. (ISBN: 2212010907) has 420p. and about 30,000 entry words.
Class No: 624(038)=40

[4944]

MONTAGUE, D. **Dictionary of building and civil engineering.** [Dictionnaire du bâtiment et du génie civil] London, Spon, 1996. xvii, 450p. £40 ISBN: 0419199101.

English and French; over 20,000 entries in each language. Appendix A lists 'False friends or faux amis'— words in one language that look like the same word in another, but that have other, related or completely different meanings in the second language.
Class No: 624(038)=40

Spanish

[4945]

KENNEDY, F. **The Wiley dictionary of civil engineering** English-Spanish/Spanish-English New York, etc., Wiley, 1996. xiii, 532p. £50. ISBN: 0471122467.

About 50,000 terms in each half. Covers architecture, engineering, surveying, building, heavy construction and municipal engineering.
Class No: 624(038)=60

Russian

[4946]

BHATNAGAR, K.P. **Elsevier's dictionary of civil engineering:** Russian-English. Bhattacharya, S.K., *ed.* Amsterdam, etc., Elsevier, 1988. x, 694p. £141. ISBN: 0444429611.

About 36,000 Russian entry-words, covering civil and structural engineering. Includes eponyms and trade names. 'Reference works', p.vii-x. *Class No:* 624(038)=82

Arabic

[4947]

KAY, E. **Arabic dictionary of civil engineering:** English-Arabic, Arabic-English. London, Routledge & Kegan Paul, 1986. 272p. £30. ISBN: 0710204299.

About 1,500 terms, covering civil engineering and the construction industry, from theory and planning through on-site requirements to office practices. *Class No:* 624(038)=927

Glossaries

[4948]

BRITISH STANDARDS INSTITUTION. **Glossary of building and civil engineering terms.** Oxford, Blackwell Scientific, 1993. xv, 624p. £45. ISBN: 0632028513.

Brings together some 9,000 buidling and civil engineering terms comprising BS6100. *Class No:* 624(038.1)

Reviews & Abstracts

[4949]

ASCE publications information. New York, American Society of Civil Engineers, 1966-. 6pa. ISSN: 07341962.

Contents of 21 issues of 16 ASCE journals. 'Special publications and manuals & reports' follows, plus *c.*200 abstracts of these items. Subject and author indexes. Annual combined index.
Class No: 624(048)

[4950]

International civil engineering abstracts. Dublin, New York, CITIS, Ltd., 1982-. 10pa. $700. ISSN: 03324095.

Formerly *ICE abstracts,* 1974-81.

About 4,000 abstracts pa. 9 sections: Structural engineering - Bridges - Buildings; materials; construction - Foundations; soil mechanics - Miscellaneous - Hydroelectric; power stations; dams - Coastal engineering; ports; waterways - Public health engineering; water supply; irrigation; hydrology - Highways and traffic engineering; transportation; airports. Available on CD-ROM. *Class No:* 624(048)

Periodicals

[4951]

INSTITUTION OF CIVIL ENGINEERS. LIBRARY AND INFORMATION SERVICES. **Catalogue of periodical publications 1665-1994.** Lawless, V., *comp.* London, Institution of Civil Engineers, 1995. [iv], 347p.

'The first comprehensive catalogue of the Library's serials holdings to be published since 1895' (*Introduction*). Titles are listed, A-Z, with holdings and location. *Class No:* 624(051)

Yearbooks & Directories

[4952]

Ground engineering yearbook, 1997/98. London, Thomas Telford, 1997. v.p. illus. £65

Contents: 1. Materials, equipment, plant, products and services - 2. Consulting engineers and services - 3. Contractors and services - 4. Brand and trade names - 5. Company data - 6. Associations and institutions - 7. Ground information. *Class No:* 624(058)

Tables & Data Books

[4953]

Construction and civil engineering index. Bracknell, Berks., Technical Indexes, Ltd.

Comprises a data book, the index to the associated microfile of manufacturers' catalogue. Sections: Products and trade names - Selector charts - Foreign Trade offices - What's new - Addresses - Professional and trade organizations. *Class No:* 624(083)

[4954]

HICKS, T.G. Civil engineering calculations reference guide. New York, etc., McGraw-Hill, 1987. xii, 291, [1]p. diagrs., graphs, tables. £35. ISBN: 0070287988.

A condensation of Hick's *Standard handbook of engineering calculations* (2nd ed. 1985).

18 sections, closely subdivided (*e.g.* Principles of statics; Geometric properties of areas; Analysis of stress and strain; Steel beams and girders; Timber engineering; Reinforced concrete, Prestressed concrete; Fluid mechanics; Soil mechanics). Coverage includes surveying and photogrammetry. References, p.286. Index, p.287-91. Calculations are in dual units. *Class No:* 624(083)

[4955]

Spon's civil engineering and highway works price book, 1999. London, Spon, 1998. 656p. £97.50. ISBN: 0419241205. ISSN: 0957171x.

First published 1984.

13 parts: 1. General - 2. Preliminaries and general terms - 3. Resources - 4. Unit costs (civil engineering works) - 5. Unit costs (highway works) - 6. Oncosts and profits - 7. Costs and tender prices indices - 8. Daywork - 9. Professional fees - 10. Approximate estimates - 11. Outputs - 12. Tables and memoranda - 13. Updates. Detailed, analytical index. *Class No:* 624(083)

Histories

[4956]

NORRIE, C.M. Bridging the years: a short history of British civil engineering. London, E. Arnold, 1956. [xii], 212p. illus.

A general survey from 1760 to 1914 (160p.) is followed by description of some notable tunnels, harbours and bridges, river works, canals and dams. Included: a list (up to 1950) of professional engineers who were Fellows of the Royal Society, and a list of founder members of the Federation of Civil Engineering Contractors. *Class No:* 624(091)

[4957]

STAPLETON, D.H. The History of civil engineering since 1600: an annotated bibliography. New York, Garland, 1984. xxxiii, 232p. (Bibliographies of the history of science and technology, 14.). ISBN: 0824089480.

1,283 entries, most with brief, primarily descriptive annotations. Arranged in chronological sections, subdivided by topics (*e.g.* government agencies ... Dams and river control - Waterways and canals ... City planning - Highways - Bridges, etc.). Emphasis is on American and European scholarly material; literature for the 'amateur or buff' is avoided (*Introduction*, p.xiv). Bibliographic essay, p.xix-xxxiii. Author-name index; no subject index. *Class No:* 624(091)

[4958]

STRAUB, H. A History of civil engineering an outline from ancient to modern times. English translation by E. Rockwell. London, Hill, 1952. Reprinted Cambridge, Mass. & London, MIT Press, 1964. xviii, 256p. illus.

German original: *Die Geschichte der Bauingerieurkunst* (Basle, Verlage Birkhauser, 1949).

The English translation introduces some amendments, and corrections. 78 illus. A chronological table (p.242-7) precedes a selected bibliography, p.248-50. Biographical details are given of the principal engineers whose theories are described. *Class No:* 624(091)

Ireland

[4959]

Civil engineering heritage: Ireland. Cox, R.C. *and* Gould, M.H., *eds*. London, Telford, 1998. 304p. illus., maps. £12.50. ISBN: 0727726277.

Organized by the Panel for Historical Engineering Work of the Institution of Civil Engineers.

Covers all Ireland in 7 chapters, each dealing with a geographical area. Chapter bibliographies; detailed index. Intended for civil engineers and general readers. *Class No:* 624(415)

England

[4960]

Civil engineering heritage: Eastern and Central England. Labrum, E.A., *ed.* London, Telford, 1993. 304p. illus., maps. £12.50. ISBN: 072771970x.

Organized by the Panel for Historical Engineering Work of the Institution of Civil Engineers.

Covers the region from the Humber to the Thames, and from East Anglia to central England, but excludes the industrial areas around Birmingham. Chapter bibliographies; detailed index. Intended for civil engineers and general readers. *Class No:* 624(420)

[4961]

Civil engineering heritage: Northern England. Rennison, R.W., *ed.* 2nd ed. London, Telford, 1996. 300p. illus., maps. £12.50. ISBN: 0727725181.

Organized by the Panel for Historical Engineering Works of the Institution of Civil Engineers. First published 1981.

Covers the region of Northern England from South Yorkshire and Merseyside up to the border beween England and Scotland. Includes Isle of Man. Chapter bibliographies; detailed index. Index of additional sites. Intended for civil engineers and general readers. *Class No:* 624(420)

[4962]

Civil engineering heritage: Southern England. Otter, R.A., *ed.* London, Telford, 1993. 246p. illus., maps. £12.50. ISBN: 0727719718.

Organized by the Panel for Historical Engineering Work of the Institution of Civil Engineers.

Covers the area of southern England, including Cornwall, Somerset, the south coast, Wiltshire, Surrey and Kent. Chapter bibliographies; detailed index. Intended for civil engineers and general readers. *Class No:* 624(420)

Wales

[4963]

Civil engineering heritage: Wales & Western England. Cragg, R., *ed.* 2nd ed. London, Telford, 1997. 304p. £12.99. ISBN: 0727725769.

Organized by the Panel for Historical Engineering Work of the Institution of Civil Engineers. First published 1986.

Covers the civil engineering heritage in Wales and Western England to just south of Bristol. Chapter bibliographies; detailed index. Intended for civil engineers and general readers. *Class No:* 624(429)

USA

[4964]

SCHODEK, D.L. Landmarks in American civil engineering. Cambridge, Mass., MIT, 1987. 383p. illus. $50. ISBN: 026219256x.

A survey of nearly 100 projects. Sections: canals, roads, railroads, bridges, tunnels, water supply and control, environmental engineering, dams, buildings, urban planning, power systems, surveying and mapping, coastal facilities, airports. 250 illus. Index. 'Recommended' (*Choice*, January 1988, p.792). *Class No:* 624(73)

Information Services

[4965]

CONSTRUCTION INDUSTRY RESEARCH AND INFORMATION ASSOCIATION. The CIRIA UK construction information guide. Richardson, B. London, E. & F.N. Spon, 1989. xi,361p. £37.50. ISBN: 0419148906.

First published 1979.

Part 1: Alphabetical list of UK local authorities (but not identifying the relevant specific departments); part 2: Alphabetical list of UK construction information sources (p.39-283). No references to HMSO publications (including The Building Regulations); no mention of BRIX, etc. databases. Subject and acronym keys. Dated but still valuable. *Class No:* 624:061:025.5

Measurements

[4966]

INSTITUTION OF CIVIL ENGINEERS. **CESMM3.** 3rd ed. London, Telford, 1991. 110p. tables. £20. ISBN: 0727715615.

First published 1976; 2nd ed, 1985.

The standard for the preparation of bills of quantities in civil engineering work. Includes amendments to come into line with the ICE condition of contract (6th ed.) and with changes in British Standards. *Class No: 624-18*

[4967]

—BARNES, M. CESMM3 handbook. London, Telford, 1992. 256p. £23.50. ISBN: 0727716581.

Provides practical guidance, along with examples, for use with the Institution of Civil Engineers' *CESMM3*. *Class No: 624-18*

Safety Devices

[4968]

KING, R.W. **Construction hazard: safety handbook.** London, Butterworth, 1983.

Focuses on on-site safety in building, civil engineering, chemical and process plant construction and offshore engineering. Sufficiently detailed to cover hazards of individual trades. Based on British examples and experience. *Class No: 624-7*

Structures

[4969]

ADDIS, W. *and* BUSSELL, M. 'Structural engineering'. *Information sources in engineering.* K.W. Mildren and P.J. Hicks, eds. (3rd ed., 1996), p.547-68. 3rd ed. London, Bowker Saur, 1996. £80. ISBN: 1857390571.

Covers existing structures and specific design guidance, loadings, fire, materials, building elements, building types (*e.g.* bridges; towers and masts, etc.). *Class No: 624.01*

[4970]

BARLOW, L.H. **The reference guide to famous engineering landmarks of the world:** bridges, tunnels, dams, roads and other structures. Phoenix, Az., Oryx, 1997. 250p. illus., diagrs. $60. ISBN: 0897749669.

About 600 structures, A-Z. Entries include location, date of construction, size, distinctive features. Appendices cover designs, biographies and chronology. Geographical and subject indexes; list of Internet sites. 'A wonderful reference work ... of interest in public and academic libraries' ('Reference books bulletin', *Booklist*, April 1, 1998, p.1349). *Class No: 624.01*

[4971]

HOLMSTROM, J., *and others.* **Trilingual dictionary for materials and structures.** Oxford, etc., Pergamon Press, 1971. xxxvi, 947p.

Published with the assistance of Unesco. At head of title-page: 'RILEM. International Union for Testing and Research Laboratories for Materials and Structures'.

8,063 numbered entries, English-French-German. Classified arrangement; English, French and German indexes. Classes A-H: A. General aspects - B. Metals - C. Cement and concrete - D. Siliceous, Calcareous and argillaceous material - E. Soils - F. Wood - G. Other organic materials - H. Water. Each class has set subdivisions: 1. Materials; 2. Manufacture; 3. Properties and phenomena; 4. Measurements; 5. Constructional use. Bibliography of sources, p.821-4. *Class No: 624.01*

[4972]

JACKSON, N, *ed.* **Civil engineering materials.** 3rd ed. New York, Scholium, 1984. 429p. illus., diagrs., graphs, tables. $39.50. ISBN: 0333347919.

7 contributors. 5 parts (26 chapters): 1. Metals - 2. Timber - 3. Concrete - 4. Bituminous materials - 5. Soils (with 23 references). Some chapters (*e.g.* 11. Types of timber) carry further reading as well as references. Detailed, analytical index. Addressed to students of civil engineering, emphasizing the factors that affect the engineering decisions. *Class No: 624.01*

[4973]

LIU, H. **Wind engineering:** a handbook for structural engineers. Englewood Cliffs, N.J., Prentice-Hall, 1991. 209p. illus., diagrs., graphs, tables. $45.20. ISBN: 0139602798.

Covers general characteristics of wind, wind pressures, scale mode/ testing, current building codes and standards (US). *Class No: 624.01*

[4974]

PILKEY, W. **Formulas for stress, strain, and structural matrices.** York, Wiley, 1994. 1458p., formulas. $74.95. ISBN: 0471527467.

Formulas on a range of topics: experimental stress analysis, fracture mechanics, contact stresses, beams, columns and frames, dynamic loading, curved bars, plates and shells. Appended: fundamental mathematics. 'Extremely valuable' (*Choice*, January 1995, p.821). *Class No: 624.01*

Concrete

[4975]

Concrete structures reference guide. Gaylord, E.H., Jr. *and* Gaylord, C.N., *eds.* New York, McGraw-Hill, 1988. v.p. illus., diagrs., graphs, tables. £25.95. ISBN: 0070230676.

Material taken from the editors' *Structural engineering handbook* (1979).

8 contributors; 6 sections, closely subdivided: 1. Design of reinforced concrete structural members - 2. Design of prestressed concrete structural members - 3. Concrete construction methods - 4. Masonry construction - 5. Thin-shell concrete structures - 6. Reinforced concrete bunkers and silos. Detailed, analytical index. *Class No: 624.012.3*

[4976]

FINTEL, M.J., *ed.* **Handbook of concrete engineering.** 2nd ed. New York, Van Nostrand Reinhold, 1985. xiv [1], 892p. illus., diagrs., graphs, tables. £99.50. ISBN: 0442226233.

First published 1974.

25 contributors. 27 mostly documented sections (6. Properties of materials for reinforced concrete; 8. Prestressed concrete (58 references); 11. Tabular structures for tall buildings; 16. Silos and bunkers (36 references); 19. Concrete pipes; 26. Computer applications; 27. Structural plain concrete). Detailed analytical index, p.575-92. *Class No: 624.012.3*

[4977]

KONG, F.K., *and others, eds.* **Handbook of structural concrete.** London, Pitman, 1983. v.p. illus., diagrs., graphs, tables, formulas. ISBN: 0273085557.

6 parts (41 documented chapters): 1. Introduction - 2. Material - 3. Design and analysis - 4. Construction - 5. Structures - 6. Practical construction. Chapter 15, 'Earthquake: resistant structures' has 78p. and includes 84 references and a glossary; chapter 41, 'Structural design: practical guidance and information sources', 44p., 85 references. *Class No: 624.012.3*

[4978]

REYNOLDS, C.E. *and* STEEDMAN, J.C. **Reinforced concrete designer's handbook.** 10th ed. London, Spon, 1988. xii,436p. diagrs., graphs, tables. £29.99 ISBN: 0419145400.

First published 1932; 9th ed. 1981.

In 2 parts. Part I includes general and descriptive material (*e.g.* structural analysis; materials and stresses (p.36-48); electronic computational aids). Part II gives tables, data, worked examples for specific structures (*e.g.* continuous beams (p.150-72); columns (p.340-76)). 3 appendices: A. Mathematical formulae and data; B: Metric/ imperial length conversions; C: Metric/imperial equivalents for common units. Analytical index, p.433-6. *Class No: 624.012.3*

[4979]

WANG, Chu-Kia *and* SALMON, C.G. **Reinforced concrete design.** 4th ed. New York, Harper & Row, 1985. x, 947p. illus., diagrs., graphs, tables, formulas. ISBN: 0066468963.

22 sections (with 'Selected references'), *e.g.* 1. Introduction, materials and properties; 5. Shear strength and shear reinforcement; 6. Development of reinforcement; 16. Members in compression and bending; 15. Length effects on columns; 19. Torsion; 21 Introduction to prestressed concrete; 22. Composite construction.

Reflects changes in design rules arising from publication of the 1983 American Concrete Institute *Building code and commentary*. *Class No: 624.012.3*

Metal

[4980]

HAYWARD, A. *and* WEARE, F. **Steel detailers' manual.** Oxford, etc., BSP Professional Books, 1989. xii,203p. diagrs., illus., graphs, tables. ISBN: 0632018453.

6 sections (1. Use of structural steel - 2. Detailing practice - 3. Design guidance - 4. Detailing data - 5. Typical connection details - 6. Examples of structures). 'Further reading', 'Bibliography', Index. Frequent reference to British Standards and Codes of Practice. Of value to practising draughtsmen, engineers, students. Highly detailed. *Class No: 624.014*

[4981]

The Sections book. Redcar, Cleveland, British Steel Corporation, 1982. 10pts. (Loose-leaf). diagrs., graphs, tables.

Published jointly by BSC Sections and Commercial Steels and the British Constructional Steelwork Association (BCSA).

The 10 parts comprise sections A-V (A: Explanatory notes; H: Safe load tables for grade 42 steels (78p.); U: Cranes; V: Other steel products). Detailed, analytical index. Collections of relevant standards and technical data for the structural steelwork designer. *Class No: 624.014*

[4982]

Steel designers' manual. 5th ed. Oxford, Blackwell Scientific, 1992. 1000p. illus. £69.50. ISBN: 0632024887.

First published 1955 (Crosby, Lockwood).

Based on limit state design and UK code of practice, BS 5950. Covers single and multi-storey buildings, industrial steelwork and bridges. *Class No:* 624.014

Plant

[4983]

Plant engineer's reference book. Snow, D.A., *ed.* Oxford, Butterworth-Heinemann, 1991. v.p. illus., diagrs., graphs, tables. £100. ISBN: 0750610158.

38 contributors, most from UK industry. 38 chapters, ranging from site location, building design and specification, energy conservation, insurance cover, health and safety and education and training. Detailed, analytical index of 15p. *Class No:* 624.05

Rock Engineering

[4984]

TEKNISKA NOMENKLATURCENTRALEN. Bergteknisk ordlista. [Glossary of rock engineering.] Stockholm, the Centre, 1979. 306p. (*TNC 73.*) ISBN: 9171960732.

791 Swedish base-terms, with explanations, followed by equivalents and indexes in 7 other languages: English, French, Spanish, German Danish, Norwegian and Finnish. *Class No:* 624.12

Soil Engineering

Encyclopaedias

[4985]

VOLLMER, E. Encyclopaedia of hydraulics, soil and foundation engineering. Amsterdam, etc., Elsevier, 1967 (Reprinted 1983). [viii], 398p. illus., tables. Dfl.225. ISBN: 0444406158.

About 4,500 brief entries, definitions ranging from 2 to *c.*100 words. Subjects: hydraulic engineering; hydromechanics; river training weirs and dams; water resources; soil mechanics; soil extraction; soil deposition; slope protection; foundation engineering; soil mechanics; foundation excavation in dry soil; foundation materials behaviour in soil. 4 appendices (symbols, abbreviations and conversion factors). Bibliography, p.[viii]. 48 line drawings. 16 tables. *Class No:* 624.13(031)

Handbooks & Manuals

[4986]

BELL, F.G. Fundamentals of engineering geology. London, Butterworths, 1983. [viii], 648p. illus., graphs tables, maps. ISBN: 0408011696.

14 documented chapters (*e.g.* 'Mechanical properties of soils', p.488-527, with 2½p. of references). Detailed non-analytical index, p.342-8. Written as a companion to the author's *Engineering geology and geotechnics* (1980). Primarily written for engineering geologists, civil engineers and mining engineers, plus students of engineering geology (*Preface*). *Class No:* 624.13(035)

[4987]

CARTER, M. Geotechnical engineering handbook. London, Pentech Press, 1983. [xx], 226p. illus., diagrs., tables. ISBN: 0727307029; 0412003414, US.

14 Chapters on site investigation procedure and geo-technical design practice (1. Soil description and classification ... 3. Laboratory testing - 4. Field testing ... 11. Retaining Walls ... 14. Flexible pavements). Includes a number of design charts in the form of data tables, extensively illustrated, each covering a specific topic (*e.g.* Data sheet 11-4: Construction for active wedges). Subject index. Intended for practising engineers, postgraduates and final year undergraduate students. *Class No:* 624.13(035)

[4988]

LEGGET, R.F. *and* KARROW, P.F. Handbook of geology in civil engineering. New York, etc., McGraw-Hill, 1982. [1184]p. illus., diagrs. ISBN: 0070370613.

5 parts (50 chapters): 1. Geological background - 2. Preliminary studies - 3. Civil engineering works (chapters 18-36) - 4. Special problems - 5. Geology and the environment. 'Dam foundations' (chapter 25) has 3p. of references, plus 'Suggestions for further reading'. Appendices: A. Glossary of geological terms; B. Geological Surveys of the world; C. Geological societies of the world; D. Some useful journals; E. Illustration credits. Subject index; name index.

Geology and engineering, by R. Legget and A.W. Hatheway (1988. 832p.), plus *Solutions manual,* is based on the *Handbook.* *Class No:* 624.13(035)

Dictionaries

[4989]

SOMERVILLE, S.M. *and* PAUL, M.A. Dictionary of geotechnics. London Butterworths, 1983. [ix], 283p. illus., diagrs., graphs, tables. £32.50. ISBN: 0408004371.

About 3,000 terms defined. Accommodates abbreviations, eponyms and formulas. Sources are cited. 20 appended tables (*e.g.* 10. 'Restivities of rocks and soils'). 100 illus. Scores over J.A. Barker's *Dictionary of soil mechanics* because of its fuller definitions and inclusion of illus. 'The definitions are geared for students and practitioners and may well be beyond the general reader's grasp' (*Choice,* v.21(1). September 1983, p.68). *Class No:* 624.13(038)

[4990]

—**JENKINS, J.D. *and* SMITH, A.M.,** *comps.* Thesaurus of rock and soil mechanics terms. Oxford, etc. Pergamon Press, 1984. 62p. £9.25. ISBN: 0018031038.

Provides a structured list of 'controlled terms' for keywords used to index material in *Geomechanics abstracts* database (at Imperial College of Science and Technology, London). Terms are arranged A-Z, with preferred terms in bold type. *Class No:* 624.13(038)

[4991]

TEKNISKA NOMENKLATURCENTRALEN. Geoteknisk ordlista. [Glossary of geotechnics.] Stockholm, the Centre, 1975. 176p. (*TNC 59.*)

503 Swedish base-terms, with explanations, plus equivalents and indexes in Finnish, German, French, English and Russian. Classified list of terms precedes the glossary. *Class No:* 624.13(038)

Reviews & Abstracts

[4992]

Geotechnical abstracts. Sonoma, Ca., Geodex Retrieval Systems, 1970-. 3 pa.

1,500 abstracts pa., covering more than 500 international journals, series and conference proceedings. Sections: A. General - B. Geological and environmental aspects - C. Site investigations - D. Soil properties - E. Analysis of soil-engineering problems - F. Rock properties - G. Analysis of rock-engineering problems - H. Design, construction and behaviour of engineering works - K. Construction methods and equipment - S. Snow and ice mechanics and engineering. An index-card service, incorporated into GEODEX SYSTEM/G. *Class No:* 624.13(048)

Soil Mechanics

[4993]

ALVIN, R.G. *and* SMOOTS, V.A. Construction guide for soils and foundations. New York, Wiley, 1988. xxi,276p. illus., diagrs., tables. $50. ISBN: 047180486x.

30 chapters in 2 parts: 1. Concepts (soil behaviour, etc.) - 2. Applications (subsurface exploration; excavations; foundations; linings and membranes, etc.). Chapters 6 and 7 cover information sources. Detailed, analytical index, p.267-76. A practical treatment. *Class No:* 624.131

[4994]

BARKER, J.A. Dictionary of soil mechanics and foundation engineering. London, Construction Press, 1981. [v], 210p. ISBN: 086095885x.

Defines over 2,500 terms, with commentary. US terms and acronyms are included. Numerous cross-references, but lacks diagrams. Aimed at a wide audience. Has clearer, if more concise definitions than Somerville and Paul's *Dictionary of geotechnics (qv).* *Class No:* 624.131

[4995]

Developments in soil mechanics: the second Ten Rankine lectures. London, Institution of Civil Engineers, 1983. [vii], 566p. illus., ports., diagrs., charts, graphs, tables. ISBN: 0727701800.

10 documented lectures (*e.g.* 'Friction of rocks and stability of rock slopes', with 3p. of references; 'Considerations in the earthquake-resistant design of earth and rockfill dams', with 2p. of references'). No index.

The first Ten Rankine lectures, entitled *Milestones in soil mechanics* (ICE, 1970) were published annually in June issues of *Géotechnique.* *Class No:* 624.131

[4996]

Geomechanics abstracts. Compiled by Rock Mechanics Information Service, Imperial College of Science and Technology, London. In *International journal of rock mechanics.* Oxford, etc., Pergamon Press, 1970-. 6pa.

Formerley *Rock mechanics abstracts.*

3-400 abstracts per bi-monthly issue of *International journal of soil mechanics.* Coverage: rock and soil mechanics, engineering geology, mining, tunnelling, foundation engineering, site investigation, analysis techniques, and design methods. Online database. *Class No:* 624.131

Excavation

[4997]

CHURCH, H.K. Excavation handbook. New York, etc. McGraw-Hill, 1981. xvi, [962]p. illus., diagrs., tables, maps. ISBN: 0070108404.

18 chapters, with each section summarized, covering the 'methods, machinery, and costs for excavating the earth's mantle' (*Preface*, p.xv). Excludes underground excavation, *e.g.* mining and tunnelling, except where supplementary to surface excavation. Glossary; bibliography; index. Intended for students, practising engineers and equipment suppliers. *Class No:* 624.133

Foundations

[4998]

PILOT, G., *ed.* **Foundation engineering.** Paris, Presses Ponts et Chausées, 1985-, v.1-. illus. ISBN: 2859780394.

1. *Soil properties. Foundation design and construction.*

V.1 (358p.) covers soil properties and site investigation, shallow and deep foundations. V.2 is to deal with retaining structures, improvement of soil properties, techniques and earthworks. Emphasizes French practice. *Class No:* 624.15

[4999]

WINTERKORN, H.F. *and* **FANG, H.-Y.,** *eds.* **Foundation engineering handbook.** 2nd ed. New York, etc., Chapman & Hall, 1995. 843p. illus., charts, tables. £105. ISBN: 0412988917.

First published 1975

Numerous contributors. 25 sections (1. Subsurface explorations and sampling ... 25. Earthquake effects on soil-formation systems). Extensive bibliography; detailed analytical index. *Class No:* 624.15

Earthquake Engineering

[5000]

Abstract journal in earthquake engineering. Berkeley, Calif., Earthquake Engineering Research Center, Univ. of California, 1971-. Annual. $100. ISSN: 03635732.

About 800 abstracts per issue. 9 sections: 1. General topics of conference proceedings - 2. Selected topics in seismology - 3. Engineering seismology - 4. Strong motion seisometry - 5. Dynamics of soils, rocks and foundations - 6. Dynamics of structures - 7. Earthquake-resistant construction and hazard reduction - 8. Earthquake effects - 9. Earthquakes and natural disasters. Title, author and analytical subject indexes. Abstracts cover technical papers, research reports, books, codes and conference proceedings. *Class No:* 624.159.1

[5001]

Soil dynamics and earthquake engineering: proceedings of the 2nd International Conference, on board the liner, the Queen Elizabeth 2, New York to Southampton, June/July 1985. Brebbin, C.A., *and others, eds.* Berlin, etc., Springer-Verlag, 1985. [xiv, 633]p. illus., diagrs. (Computational mechanics publication). ISBN: 0905451341.

Includes 54 papers on the 'State of the Art' and the sessions covered at the conference: 1. Seismicity, ground motion and site response - 2. Soil behaviour under dynamic loads: analytical and experimental procedures - 3. Liquefacation of soils - 4. Soil structure interaction - 5. Earth dams and stability of slopes under dynamic loads - 6. Dynamic earth pressures and earth retaining structure.

Computational Mechanics Publications (Ashurst Lodge, Ashurst, Southampton SO4 2AA) aslo produce a quarterly journal, *Soil dynamics and earthquake engineering. Class No:* 624.159.1

Tunnels

[5002]

GRAYSON, L. Channel Tunnel: the link to Europe: an overview and guide to the literature. London, British Library, Science Reference and Information Serivce, 1995. xiii, 202p. £39. ISBN: 0712308164.

Also available in a French language version.

8 sections (8. Regional impact). Preceded by 'Sources of information', p.iv-xiii. 3 indexes: authors; corporate bodies; subjects. *Class No:* 624.19

[5003]

SANDSTRÖM, G.E. The History of tunnelling: underground workings through the ages. London, Barrie & Jackson, 1963. xii, 427p. illus., diagrs., maps.

19 chapters, with separate chapters on the St. Gothard, Lotschberg and Simplon tunnel operations, and ending with the Mont Blanc tunnel. Glossary, p.411-4. Bibliography, p.415-7. Analytical index, p.419-27; end-papers maps. Lavishly illustrated (151 illus.). *Class No:* 624.19

[5004]

Tunnel engineering handbook. Bickel, J.O., *and others, eds.* 2nd ed. New York, Chapman & Hall, 1996. 544p. illus., diagrs., graphs. $119.95. ISBN: 0412992914.

First published 1982.

The 2nd ed. includes 8 new chapters covering rehabilitation and repair, stabilization and lining, difficult ground, deep shafts, water conveyance tunnels, small-diameter tunnels, fire line safety and construction contracting. No index, but an annotated table of contents and extensive cross references. 'Recommended' (*Science and technology libraries*, 17(1) 1997, p.98). *Class No:* 624.19

[5005]

—**HOWIE, W.** *and* **CHRINES, M.,** *eds.* **Thames Tunnel to Channel Tunnel:** 150 years of civil engineers. Selected pages from the *Journal of the Institution of Civil Engineers*, published to celebrate its 150th anniversary. London, Telford, 1987. 294p. illus., diagrs., tables, plans. £15. ISBN: 072770396x.

Reprints 13 papers, some of them facsimiles (*e.g.* Sydney Harbour Bridge, p.180-239). Chronology, 1916-79, plus 'Retrospects'. *Class No:* 624.19

[5006]

Tunnelling 91. Institution of Mining and Metallurgy. Oxford, etc., Elsevier, 1991. 523p. illus. £85. ISBN: 1851668249.

Proceedings of the 6th International Symposium, organized by the IMM, London, 14-16 April 1991. Rail and sewer tunnel work. International aspects. 465 illus. *Class No:* 624.19

Bridges

[5007]

JERVOISE, E. The Ancient bridges [of England and Wales]. London, Architectural Press, 1932-36. 4v, illus.

The ancient bridges of the south of England. 1930. xvi, 138p.
The ancient bridges of the north of England. 1931. xii, 146p.
The ancient bridges of mid and eastern England. 1932. xi, 164p.
The ancient bridges of Wales and western England. 1936. xii, 180p.

Written on behalf of the Society for the Preservation of Ancient Buildings. Many brief descriptions, with dates. Each volume has 78-90 illus. No bibliographies. Detailed indexes. *Class No:* 624.2

[5008]

LEONHARDT, F. Brücken: Ästhetik and Gestallung. [Bridges: aesthetics and design.] London, Architectural Press, 1982; Stuttgart, Deutsche Verlags-Anstall GmbH. 308p. illus. (incl. col.), diagrs. ISBN: 0851397646.

German and English text.

13 chapters (4. Guidelines for the aesthetic design of bridges; 5. Influence of alignment; 6. Influence of building materials; 7. Old stone bridges; 8. Pedestrian bridges; 10. Elevated bridges; 11. Large beam bridges; 12. Large arch and frame bridges; 13. Suspension bridges). Bibliography (952 items). Detailed, analytical index, p.299-308. Excellent illus. *Class No:* 624.2

[5009]

RICHARDS, J.M. The National Trust book of bridges. London, Cape, 1984. x, 214p. illus. (incl. col.). £12.50. ISBN: 0224021060.

10 chapters: 1. The Middle Ages - 2. The improved highway: seventeenth to nineteenth centuries - 3. Private and ornamental bridges; 4. Early iron bridges - 5. Canal bridges and aqueducts - 6. Railway bridges and viaducts - 7. Suspension bridges - 8. Footbridges - 9. New styles, techniques and purposes: the last hundred years - 10. Bridges never built. Glossary. Bibliography, p.203-4. Analytical index, p.207-14. For the general reader. Well produced. *Class No:* 624.2

[5010]

WITTFOHT, H. Building bridges: history, technology, construction. Düsseldorf, Beton-Verlag 1984. 327p. illus. $99. ISBN: 3764001703.

Translated and revised ed. of *Triumph der Spannweiter*.

Sections: Use of timber - Reinforced concrete - Launching the entire bridge - Prestressed concrete's limits - Lightweight concrete - Bridges of tomorrow. About 500 photographs. Portrays 'a level of professionalism and scholarship which makes it ideal not only for the most technical collections but also for a large readership who are non-specialists but just plain bridge lovers' (*New technical books,* v.71(3), March 1986, entry 464). *Class No:* 624.2

Railway Engineering

Handbooks & Manuals

[5011]

BAKER, R.F., *ed.* **Handbook of railway engineering.** Malabar, Florida, R.F. Krieger, 1982. x, 894p. illus., diagrs., tables. ISBN: 0818744822.

4 parts (22 sections): Policies, administration & planning - Traffic

....(contd.)

control, design & construction - Bridges, tunnels, lighting - Cost, maintenance. Detailed, analytical index. 51 contributors. US slanted. Quarto. *Class No:* 625.1(035)

[5012]

HAY, W.W. Railroad engineering. 2nd ed. New York, Chichester, etc., Wiley, 1982. xvi, 758p. illus., diagrs., tables. ISBN: 0471364002.

First published 1953.

The 2nd ed. again covers 'fundamentals' of 'location, construction and maintenance of a modern railroad' from the 1st ed. (*Preface to the first edition*, p.xi), as well as up-to-date developments including track-train dynamics and economic problems. Name and subject indexes. Intended for students and the railroad industry. *Class No:* 625.1(035)

Dictionaries

[5013]

JACKSON, A.A. The Railway dictionary: an A-Z of railway terminology. 2nd ed. Stroud, Glouces., Alan Sutton, 1996. x, 325p. illus., diagrs. ISBN: 0750911379.

First published 1992.

Over 6,000 terms and abbreviations (including acronyms and companies). Includes new terms which have emerged from privatization schemes arising from the Railways Act of 1993, the channel tunnel, and the new national rail systems in Eastern Europe. International in scope. *Class No:* 625.1(038)

[5014]

UNION INTERNATIONALE DES CHEMINS DE FER. RailLexic: railway dictionary, thesaurus and information databese on CD-ROM. Paris, The Union, 1996. 1 CD-ROM. £250.

About 16,000 terms, with translations, in Danish, Dutch, English French, German, Hungarian, Italian, Polish, Portuguese, Romanian, Slovak, Spanish, Swedish and Esperanto. Replaces *Lexique général des termes ferrovaires* (4th ed. 1988). *Class No:* 625.1(038)

[5015]

—Dictionnaire technique des chemins de fer. Berlin, VEB Verlag Technik, 1984. 399p.

Covers English, French, German and Russian terms. *Class No:* 625.1(038)

[5016]

—HERBERT, J., *comp.* Glossary of railway terms, English-French-German-Italian-Spanish-Swedish. Amsterdam, etc., Elsevier, 1960. [v], 413p. (Glossaria interpretum).

Covers 1,995 terms, including American English vocabulary. Main sequence is French-based, with equivalents and indexes in the other languages. Whereas the *Lexique des termes ferroviaires* was intended primarily for use in railway offices, this handy *Glossary* - now dated - is most suited for translation of railway terms at international meetings. *Class No:* 625.1(038)

[5017]

—UNION INTERNATIONALE DES CHEMINS DE FER. Lexique général des termes ferroviaires. 4. éd. Paris, The Union, 1988. 1250p.

First published 1957; 3rd ed. 1975.

About 10,200 French-based railway terms, with German, English, Italian, Spanish and Dutch equivalents and indexes. *Class No:* 625.1(038)

Glossaries

[5018]

COOPER, B.K. Railway terminology. Hersham, Surrey, Ian Allan, 1994. 96p. illus. ISBN: 1994.

A narrative treatment with terms highlighted. Sections: steam power; laws of traction, diesel power; electrification; electric traction; traction control, braking systems; permanent way; bogies and suspension; signalling; freight services; passenger stock; rail in the environment; light rail systems. Index. *Class No:* 625.1(038.1)

Reviews & Abstracts

[5019]

Fachinformation Bahn. Dokumentation der Fachliteratur. Mainz, Deutscher Bahn AG., 1993-. Monthly. ISSN: 00235695.

Formerly *Kurzauszuge aus dem Schrifttum für des Eisenbahnwesen*, 1956-76; *Information Eisenbahn. Dokumentation der Fachschrifttums*, 1976-1992.

About 3,500 abstracts. 9 sections, with supplement of patents, translations, etc. *Class No:* 625.1(048)

Yearbooks & Directories

[5020]

Railway directory: a *Railway gazette* year book, 1999. Sutton, Surrey, Reed Business Publishing , Ltd., 1999. Annual. 532p. illus., maps. ISSN: 00799513.

A comprehensive guide to the world railway industry. Sections: Government - Railways A-Z - City railways ... Rolling stock ... Diesel engines ... Electrification ... Track ... Professional services. Indexes: general; personnel; advertisers. Also available on CD-ROM. *Class No:* 625.1(058)

Tables & Data Books

[5021]

FRANKLIN & ANDREWS, International Property and Construction Consultants. **Spon's railways construction price book.** London, Spon, 1999. 496p. tables. £125. ISBN: 0419242104.

Contents: railway contruction measured rates; signalling; electrification; permanent way; telecommunications; property; level crossings; bridges; tunnels, etc. *Class No:* 625.1(083)

[5022]

WESTWOOD, J.N. The Railway data book. Cambridge, P. Stephens, 1985. 224p. diagrs., tables, maps. £8.95. ISBN: 0850596297.

23 chapters (2. Railway ownership and control; 4. Track and its terminology; 8. Signals; 11. Steam locomotive trends and trend-setters; 12. Electrification; 14. The diesel loco; 26. The passenger train; 23. A note on stations). 3 appendices (1. Preserved steam railways - 2. Major railway museums - 3. Railway enthusiast societies (British, French, German, US and Canadian)). Further reading (magazines, books, timetables). Non-analytical index. Concentrates on Western Europe (especially Britain) and North America. For the railway enthusiast. *Class No:* 625.1(083)

Histories

[5023]

BURMAN, P. *and* **STRATTON, M. Conserving the railway heritage.** London, Spon, 1996. 244p. illus. £32.50. ISBN: 0419212809.

Defines the nature of railway heritage, from signalboxes, viaducts, tunnels and locomotive depots, and considers priorities and best practice. *Class No:* 625.1(091)

[5024]

GARRATT, C. Hamlyn history of trains. London, Reed Consumer Books, 1998. 191p. illus. £18.99. ISBN: 0600592332.

Includes evolution, builders, aerodynamics, haulage, diesel, electric, the industrial revolution, wartime, disasters, preservation, light rail and the future. Glossary; index. Lavishly illustrated. A popular treatment. *Class No:* 625.1(091)

[5025]

Railway history sources: a handlist of the principal sources of original material. Clinker, C.R., *comp.* Bristol, Avon-Anglia, 1976. 20p.

Contents: Summary of sources (p.5-10); Notes and information (p.10-19). Includes discussion of timetables, maps, diagrams, newspapers, official records, etc. *Class No:* 625.1(091)

[5026]

A Tentative check-list of early European railway literature, 1831-1848. Haskell, D.C., *comp.* Cambridge, Ma., Baker Library, Harvard Graduate School of Business Administration, 1955. 192p.

Documents the extensive collection of railway literature in the library, much of it a result of association with the Railway and Locomotive Historical Society. Also includes material from other collections, including the New York Public Library, Library of Congress, Hopkins Railway Library at Stanford University, Transportation Library at the University of Michigan and the Library of the Bureau of Railway Economics. Arranged chronologically by year of publication, then A-Z by authors. Cross references; index of names and anonymous titles. *Class No:* 625.1(091)

Biographies

[5027]

MARSHALL, J. A Biographical dictionary of railway engineers. Newton Abbot, Devon, David & Charles, 1978. 247, [2]p. ISBN: 0715374875.

Concise data on more than 600 railway engineers of the past (Stephenson, George: 2 columns; 8 references. Brunel: 1½p.; 5 references). Important North American and European railway engineers are included. 2-p. non-analytical index. Intended as a work of reference for the railway historian. *Class No:* 625.1(092)

Worldwide

[5028]

FONTGALLAND, B. The World railway system. Cambridge Univ. Press, 1984. xiv, 209p. diagrs., maps. ISBN: 0521245419.

Originally published as *Le Système ferroviaire dans le monde* (Paris, CELSE, 1980).

A theoretical discussion of railways in terms of systems analysis and cybernetics. 7 chapters: 1. Principles - 2. Technology - 3. Production [of a transport system] - 4. Sales - 5. Management - 6. Macrosystems - 7. International Organizations. The author was Honorary Secretary General of the International Union of Railways. Brief bibliography; no index. *Class No:* 625.1(100)

[5029]

Jane's world railways 1998-99. Coulsdon, Surrey, Jane's Information Group, 1998. *c.*800p. illus., diagrs., tables. £220; $425. ISBN: 0710618131.

Manufacturers - Private freight wagon leasing companies - International rail services - International associations - Consultancy services - Railway systems, country-by-country. Available online and on CD-ROM.

The series (1950-1993) is available on microfiche.

Class No: 625.1(100)

Europe

[5030]

BALL, M.G. European railway atlas. London, Ian Allan, 1993-. 5v. illus. £10.99 each.

Scandinavia and Eastern Europe. (1993. 80p. ISBN: 07110211724).

France, Netherlands, Belguim, Luxembourg. (2nd ed. 64p. ISBN: 0711020116).

British Isles. (2nd ed. 55p. ISBN: 0711024073).

Denmark, Germany, Austria, Switzerland. (64p. ISBN: 07712328x).

Spain, Portugal, Italy, Greece. (64p. ISBN: 0711020876).

Class No: 625.1(4)

Great Britain

[5031]

AWDRY, W. *and* **COOK, C. A Guide to the steam railways of Great Britain.** London, Pelham Books, 1978. 240p. illus., maps.

1. The South-west - 2. London and the Home Counties - 3. East Anglia - 4. The Midlands - 5. Wales - 6. Lancashire and the North-west - 7. Yorkshire and the North-east - 8. Scotland. Gazetteer (p.221-38) and list of minor railway sites in Britain and Ireland. Description and history. Index, p.239-40. Well illustrated, popular treatment.

Class No: 625.1(410)

[5032]

—NOCK, O.S. O.S. Nock's Pocket encyclopaedia of British steam railways and locomotives. Poole, Dorset, Blandford Press, 1983. 195 + 192p. col. illus., maps. ISBN: 0713713127.

Combines the two volumes, *The pocket encyclopaedia of steam railways of Britain in colour* (1967) and *The pocket book of British steam locomotives in colour* (1964).

Each part has historical introduction, descriptions, coloured illus. and index. Good use of colour. A popular account.

Class No: 625.1(410)

[5033]

BAKER, S.K., *comp.* **Rail atlas of Britain and Ireland.** 8th ed. Oxford Publishing Co., 1996. 123p. maps. ISBN: 0860935345.

First published 1977.

104 pages of maps, preceded by key map. Colours, symbols, etc. indicate surface, tunnels, depots, etc. Index (gazetteer) (nearly 2,800 entries), p.105-23. *Class No:* 625.1(410)

[5034]

JOHNSON, J. *and* **LONG, R.A. British railways engineering, 1948-80.** Bond, R.C., *ed.* London, Mechanical Engineering Publications, Ltd., 1981. 636p. ISBN: 0852984464.

15 chapters (1. End of an era, 1923 to 1947; 2. Nationalization; 5. The final years of steam traction; 6. Diesel traction; 6. Civil engineering; 11. The contribution of technological research and development; 15. Past, present and future). Appendix: Headquarters and Regional Chief Engineers, 1948-80. Bibliography, p.604-6. Index of engineers. Detailed, analytical index, p.623-36. Records the achievements of the engineering and research departments of British Railways during the first thirty years of nationalization since January 1, 1948. *Class No:* 625.1(410)

[5035]

—JAMES, L. A Chronology of the construction of Britain's railways, 1778-1855. London, Ian Allan, 1983. 120p. illus., maps. £10.95. ISBN: 0711012776.

Begins with the earliest tramway, the Froghall Railway in Staffordshire, and ends with the mid-19th century railway boom. A series of maps plots the growth of track in England, Wales and Scotland. The author was Principal of the British Railways School of Transport, Derby, 1968-1976. Index. *Class No:* 625.1(410)

[5036]

JONES, E. The Penguin guide to the railways of Britain. London, Allen Lane, 1981. x, 377p. illus., maps. ISBN: 0713911379.

12 sections: 1. The coming of railways - 2. The path of technical development - 3. The railways of London - 4. The Great Western ... 7. The Midland ... 11. Scotland - 12. Conclusions: the new age of railways. 3 appendices: 1. Steam, Diesel and electric wheel arrangement; 2. Railway company liveries; 3. Railway museums. Glossary of architectural terms. Guide to further reading (running commentary), p.363-5. Detailed index, p.361-77. 41 plates; 24 maps. A comprehensive historical survey of the 9 regional mainland networks; dated, but provides an accessible overview.

Class No: 625.1(410)

[5037]

WIGNALL, C.J. Complete British railway maps and gazetteers, 1825-1985. Fully rev. ed. Poole, Dorset, Oxford Publishing Co., 1985. [iv], 71 + 79p. maps. ISBN: 086093294x.

First published 1983.

Detailed maps (p.2-71), indicating by colour distinction 6 types of lines (*e.g.* lines open/closed to passenger; lines underground at this point). 79p. gazetteer of stations. Coverage includes Isle of Man but not Northern Ireland. A well-constructed atlas. *Class No:* 625.1(410)

Encyclopaedias

[5038]

AWDRY, C. Encyclopedia of British railway companies. Yeovil, Patrick Stephens, 1990. 288p. illus. £20. ISBN: 1852600497.

At their peak, railways in Britain covered 20,000 miles and involved 1,000 separate companies. By 1918 these were reduced to *c.*150, and in 1923 were grouped into GWR, LMS, LNER and SR; nationalization occurred in 1948; privatization in 1996. "Family trees" for railway companies are shown diagramatically. Brief entries (*c.* 20-30 lines) are organized by the four post-1923 groupings, with a fifth section covering independent lines and the London Passenger Transport Board contituents. Brief bibliography. *Class No:* 625.1(410)(031)

Yearbooks & Directories

[5039]

ASSOCIATION OF TRACK OPERATING COMPANIES. Railguide, 1997-98. London, ATOC; Railtrack, 1997, Annual-. 81p.

Contents: Train operating companies (with maps of their operating areas; personnel summary; contact details) - Railtrack zones - Freight companies - Other organizations (ATOC; Office of Passenger Rail Franchising; Office of Rail Regulator; RUCC; Department of Transport; BR Board; BR Property Board; British Transport Police; Heathrow Express) - Rolling stock leasing companies - Services (projects; research; College of Railway Technology; quality and safety services, etc.) - Infrastructure services - Track renewal companies.

Class No: 625.1(410)(058)

Maps & Atlases

[5040]

JOWETT, A. Jowett's railway atlas of Great Britain and Ireland from pre-grouping to the present day. Wellingborough, Patrick Stephens, 1989. 321p. maps. £30. ISBN: 1852600861.

Excellent, hand-drawn maps compiled from original documents. indes (32p.); brief bibliography. *Class No:* 625.1(410)(084.3)

[5041]

—JOWETT, A. Jowett's atlas of railway centres of Great Britain showing their development from the earliest times up to and including the 1990s. Yeovil, Patrick Stephens, 1993-. V. 1-. 240p. maps. £30. ISBN: 1852604204.

Focuses on 20 major centres (Barnsley, Birmingham, Bradford ... Tiverton, Yarmouth). Brief bibliography. "It is hoped to be the first of a series" (*Introduction*). *Class No:* 625.1(410)(084.3)

Chronologies

[5042]

MORRISON, G. Britain's railways 1948-1993: a personal view of 50 years of change. Hersham, Surrey, Ian Allan, 1999. 256p. illus. £34.99. ISBN: 0711026297.

A chronological survey, year-by-year. Lavishly illustrated.

Class No: 625.1(410)(090)

Histories

[5043]

OTTLEY, G. A Bibliography of British railway history. 2nd ed. London, H.M. Stationery Office, 1983. 683p. ISBN: 0112903347.

First published 1965 (683p.). 2nd ed., - a reprint. At head of title-page 'Science Museum/National Railway Museum'.

7,950 numbered entries, many annotated briefly, with locations in 16 contributing libraries (notably the British Museum) and private collections. Excludes children's books (usually) and highly technical specialized books, but includes spotter's books and others not specifically railway books yet containing useful railway material. Detailed classification. Main classes A-T (B. Railway transport at particular periods; C. Railway transport in particular areas; R. Research and study of railways and railway history; T. General directories, gazetteers, atlases, guide books, lists of stations, distance tables, time-tables). Entries state number of illus. Appended lists and 'genealogies' of railway companies. Extensive author-title and subject index (p.477-683). A model of its kind. *Class No:* 625.1(410)(091)

[5044]

—**OTTLEY, G. A Bibliography of British railway history. Supplement.** London, HMSO, 1988. 544p. ISBN: 0112903649.

Includes records numbered 7951-12956. Covers parts of books, pamphlets and academic theses on the history and description of public rail transport in the British Isles published up to the end of 1980, with an addenda to entries in the original work. *Class No:* 625.1(410)(091)

[5045]

—**OTTLEY, G. Ottley's bibliography of British railway history. Second supplement 12957-19605.** Boyes, G., *and others, comps.* York, National Railway Museum in association with the Railway and Canal Historical Society, 1998. 647p. £49.50. ISBN: 1872826105.

Preface by G. Ottley. Covers mainly 1981-1995, but with some earlier works, new editions for existing entries, etc. Now includes more government and official publications and British contributions to work overseas. Updates appear in the *Journal* of the Railway and Canal Historical Socoiety. *Class No:* 625.1(410)(091)

[5046]

The Oxford companion to British railway history from 1603 to the 1990s. Simmons, J. *and* Biddle, G., *eds.* Oxford Univ. Press, 1997. xv, 591p. illus., maps. £45. ISBN: 0192116975.

80 contributors. About 600 entries, A-Z, covering technical, historical, social, economic, political and artistic aspects. Many entries have short bibliographies and cross references. Clear, 2-column layout. A popular treament for the enthusiast. *Class No:* 625.1(410)(091)

England & Wales

[5047]

HAWKINGS, D.T. Railway ancestors: a guide to the staff records of the railway companies of England and Wales 1822-1947. Stroud, Alan Sutton, 1995. xviii, 509. illus., tables. £25. ISBN: 0750908831.

Published in association with the Public Record Office.

Covers the sources of information and access to them. Chapters: Staff registers and staff histories - Paybills and voucher books - Sickness and accidents - Boards of directors meetings - Committee and sub-committee meetings - Miscellaneous records - Trade Union appeals and disputes - Railway magazines and newspapers. Appendices include A-Z listing of railway companies to 1947, county lists pre-1923, railway staff records, etc. Bibliography, p.485-89 (*c.*150 items); index of persons. *Class No:* 625.1(42)

America—North

[5048]

TABER, T.T. Guide to railroad historical sources in the United States and Canada. Muncy, Pa., T.T. Taber III, 1993. 4 vols. ISBN: 0960339868.

V.1 (271p.) identifies resource locations by abbreviations and by state/province. Includes detailed descriptions of collections, listing periodicals and proceedings, books and biographies, as well as predecessor companies, technical societies and the disposition of former printed and corporate collections and archives. Numerous cross references. Vols. 2-4 (*c.* 500p. each) are indexes. Massive and meticulous. *Class No:* 625.1(71+73)

USA

[5049]

FREY, R.L. Railroads in the nineteenth century. New York, Facts on File, 1988. 491p. illus., maps. $75. (*Encyclopedia of American business history and biography,* 2.) ISBN: 0816020124.

48 contributors; 126 articles, most fairly lengthy (3,000 to 5,000 words). Emphasis is biographical, but also covers brakes, coupling, locomotives, etc. Bibliographies follow most articles and locate archival material. Extensively illustrated. 'A must' for scholars and railway enthusiasts (*Choice,* April 1989, p.1312). *Class No:* 625.1(73)

[5050]

HUBBARD, F. Encyclopedia of North American railroading: 150 years of railroading - the United States and Canada. New York, etc., McGraw-Hill, 1981. vi, 376, [1]p. illus., ports., maps. ISBN: 0070308284.

A-Z arrangement of entries (mostly documented: Air conditioning ... Zulu cars. Traces US and Canadian railway history from the 1830s onwards. Includes biographies and railway companies. Cross-references. Detailed, analytical index. Dramatizes 'the interesting instead of sticking too closely to the nuts and bolts' (*What this book is all about*). *Class No:* 625.1(73)

Museums

[5051]

Guide to tourist railroads and musuems. Drury, G.H., *comp.* 4th ed. Waukesha, Wi., Kalmbach, 1995. 320p. illus. $18.95. ISBN: 0890242461.

About 350 tourist railroads and railroad museums in the US and Canada. A-Z by state, then city; Canada is in a separate section. Data include features and attractions, equipment, opening hours, etc. *Class No:* 625.1:061:069

Model Railways

[5052]

CAIN, T. The Model engineer's handbook. 3rd ed. Hemel Hempstead, Nexus Special Interests, 1996. 200p. illus., diagrs. ISBN: 1854861344.

First published 1980.

13 sections covering metrology, standards, screw threads, workshop practice, metal joining, properties of materials, steam and steam engines, gases, boilers, pistons and electrical matters. A delightful book. *Class No:* 625.1-181.4

[5053]

SIMMONS, N. Railway modeling. 8th ed. Yeovil, Somerset, Patrick Stephens, 1998. 320p. illus. £19.99; $39.95. ISBN: 1852605960.

Includes detailed descriptions on designing and building model railways. Covers track design and construction, wiring, locomotives, rolling stock, etc. *Class No:* 625.1-181.4

Track & Permanent Way

[5054]

WHITEHOUSE, P.B. *and* **SNELL, J.B. Narrow gauge railways of the British Isles.** Newton Abbot, Devon, David & Charles, 1984. 160p. illus., facsims., maps. £10.95. ISBN: 0715385232.

Describes narrow-gauge railways with gauges of 15in.-3 feet, now mainly used as tourist routes. Despite the title, this volume includes Ireland, where 3ft. was the norm for this type of railway. Bibliography, p.158. Index. Quarto format. *Class No:* 625.14

Underground Railways

[5055]

HOWSON, N.F. London's Underground. London, Ian Allan, 1999. *c.*180p. illus., maps. ISBN: 0711018995.

Covers the historic railways (Metropolitan; Inner Circle); the first tube railways; growth and expansion; new railways (Victoria and Jubilee lines; and the long awaited extension to the Jubilee. Management and organization of the Underground are also considered. Appendices: Chronology of principal events in London's underground railways (1863-1997); 2. List of underground lines and routes. Lavishly illustrated. *Class No:* 625.42

Tramways

[5056]

DUCKLEY, R.J. History of tramways from horse to rapid transit. Newton Abbot, Devon, David & Charles, 1987. 184p. ISBN: 0713306416.

8 chapters, international in scope. 1. Horse tramways - 2. Mechanical traction - 3. The early electrical tram - 4. The standard era (American, British and European) - 5. Beyond the city boundary - 6. Modernization - 7. The rapid tramway. Bibliography, p.178-9. Detailed index (countries; subjects). *Class No:* 625.46

Cable Railways & Ropeways

[5057]

Internationale Seilbahn-Rundschau. [International air/lift review.] Vienna, Bohmann, 1990-. 8pa. 1136 Schillings. ISSN: 02533715.

Text is in French and German. *Class No:* 625.5

[5058]

Internationale Seilbahnterminologie. [International ropeway terminology.] Vienna & Heidelburg, Bohmann, 1965. 8pts. illus.

German-based terms, with English, French and Italian equivalents. 8 parts: 1. Ropeway systems - 2. General data - 3. Ropes - 4. Stations - 5. Line equipment - 6. Rolling stock - 7. Operating equipment - 8. Operations. No index. *Class No: 625.5*

Roads

Databases

[5059]

IRRD/International Road Research Documentation. Paris, OECD.

A database produced by the Organization for Economic Cooperation and Development/OECD, Paris. Available through hosts ESA-IRS and DATA-STAR.

Compendex*Plus also covers road engineering and has a number of hosts, including both ESA-IRS and DATA-STAR.
Class No: 625.7(003.4)

Bibliographies

[5060]

STYLES, B.R. 'Highway, transport and constructional engineering'. In *Information sources in engineering* (2nd ed. Editor, L.J. Anthony. 1985), p.409-28. London, Butterworth, 1985.

Organizational sources of information - Highway and transport engineering - Documentary sources of information (abstracting and indexing services; journals, conferences, monographs and textbooks). Highway engineering as a distinct topic was not featured in the 3rd ed. of *Information sources in engineering* (1996). *Class No: 625.7(01)*

Handbooks & Manuals

[5061]

MONTGOMERIE, G., ed. The Transport engineer's handbook. 2nd ed. London, Kogan Page, 1984. 231p. illus. ISBN: 0850387930.

Covers road transport only. Topics include UK legislation and its effects on commercial road haulage, vehicle design, construction and road testing., technical developments, commercial driving techniques. Directory of manufacturers, distributors and trade associations (p.195-227). Index. *Class No: 625.7(035)*

[5062]

OGLESBY, C.H. and HICKS, R.G. Highway engineering. 4th ed. New York, London, etc., Wiley, 1982. xiii, [1], 844p. illus., charts, tables. £74; £21.95. ISBN: 047102936x, HB; 0471871451, PB.

First published 1954; 3rd ed. 1975.

The new edition gives 'added attention' (*Preface*, p.vi) to rehabilitation and maintenance, efficient management, public transport, energy shortages and costs, safety, new materials and problems of developing nations. 21 chapters, each with problems: 3. Highway and urban transporation planning ... 8. Driver, vehicle, traffic and road characteristics - 9. Highway design ... 15. Constructing the road bed ... 19. Bituminous pavements ... 21. Highway maintenance and rehabilitation. Index, p.809-44. For practising engineers and administrators, for junior, senior and fifth-year college students, and as a starting point for advanced courses and individual study. A neat production. *Class No: 625.7(035)*

[5063]

SALTER, R.J. Highway design and construction. 2nd ed. London, Macmillan Education, 1984. x, 288p. illus., diagrs., graphs, tables. ISBN: 0333459289.

First published 1979.

8 documented chapters. 1. Highway pavement materials - 2. The production and testing of bituminous mnaterials - 3. Flexible pavement - 4. Concrete pavement - 5. Dressings - 6. Earthworks - 7. Permanent construction - 8. Pavement maintenance (p.220-83. 31 references). Detailed, analytical index. The author is at the University of Bradford. *Class No: 625.7(035)*

Dictionaries

[5064]

BRITISH STANDARDS INSTITUTION. Glossary of building and civil engineering terms. Part 2. Civil engineering. Subsection 2.4.1 Highway engineering. London, BSI, 1992. 44p. (*BS 6100: Subsection 2.4.1:1992(1998)*.)

Supercedes BS 892: 1967.

Terms defined in systematic order. Alphabetical index. *Class No: 625.7(038)*

[5065]

INTERNATIONAL ROAD RESEARCH DOCUMENTATION. Thesaurus 1975: English alphabetical list: English-French-German. Paris, IRRD: OECD, [1975?]. [v], 105, 7p.

About 3,00 English-base terms, with selected equivalents in French and German. Coverage: Highway engineering and administration - Design of roads and related structures - Materials - Soils and rocks - Construction and supervision of construction - Maintenance - Traffic - Accident studies - Vehicles. *Class No: 625.7(038)*

[5066]

—Ordbok for veg- og traffikk teknikk. Norsk-dansk-engelsk-fransk-svensk-tysk. Oslo, Universitetsforlaget, 1973. 137p. illus. (*Radet for teknisk terminololgi RTT31.*)

Records *c.*1,000 Norwegian-based terms on road and traffic engineering, with Danish, English, French, Swedish and German equivalents and indexes. *Class No: 625.7(038)*

Reviews & Abstracts

[5067]

Documentation strasse. Cologne, Farschungsgesellschaft für Strassen und Verkehrswesen, 1961-. Monthly.

About 100 abstracts per issue, covering administration, legal aspects, planning, materials, trial methods, road building in developing countries, road bridges and tunnels. Indexes per issue. *Class No: 625.7(048)*

[5068]

HRIS abstracts. Washington, Highway Research Information Service, National Research Council, 1968-. Quarterly. ISSN: 00176222.

About 1,800 abstracts per issue, covering research reports, technical papers in conference proceedings, and journal articles. Classified order (*e.g.* 11. Administration; 17. Energy and environmental; 32. Cement and concrete; 51. Safety; 54. Operations of traffic control; 62. Foundations (soil); 90. Highway research, general). Source, author and retrieval term indexes.

TRIS (Transportation Research Information Service) is the online service, hosted by DIALOG, and available to US and Canadian users. *Class No: 625.7(048)*

Yearbooks & Directories

[5069]

Road construction and traffic directory 1994. Lomas, C., ed. 3rd ed. London, Thomas Telford Directories, 1993. 448p. £30. ISBN: 0727719602.

Directory-type information in two subject areas: highways and bridges; traffic and parking. Indexes: personnel; subject; trade names. *Class No: 625.7(058)*

Histories

[5070]

SCHREIBER, H. The History of roads, from amber route to motorway. Translated by S. Thomson. London, Barrie & Rockliff, 1961. vii, 311p. illus., map.

Chronological treatment, in 17 chapters. Chapters 1-9 deal with ancient and Roman roads. Bibliography, p.293-5. Analytical index. *Class No: 625.7(091)*

Great Britain

[5071]

BALLAN, D. Bibliography of road making and roads in the United Kingdom. London, King, 1914. xviii, 281p.

Lists 4,000 items, covering the period 1535 to the beginning of the 20th century, - an enlargement of a bibliography prepared in 1906 by Beatrice and Sidney Webb. Sections: General works - Great Britain - England and Wales - London - Wales - Scotland - Ireland - Construction and repair of roads - Traffic. Author and subject indexes. Full bibliographical details, plus British Museum shelf numbers and locations in the British Library of Political and Economic Science, or, failing that, elsewhere. *Class No: 625.7(410)*

Research

[5072]

INTERNATIONAL ROAD FEDERATION. IRF research and development. Washington, International Road Federation (IRF). Annual.

1980 ed. as *World survey of current research and development on roads and road transport.*

Sponsored by the US Federal Highway Administration, OECD, and the Transportation Research Board.

An inventory of ongoing road research in 77 countries. Criticized by B.R. Styles (in *Information sources in engineering.* 2nd ed, 1985,

....(contd.)

p.417) for loose editing, an inadequate index and 'an awkward-to use subject arrangement', despite its invaluable coverage. *Class No:* 625.7.001.5

Hydraulic Engineering

Databases

[5073]
FLUIDEX. BHRA Fluid engineering abstracts. Cranfield, Beds., British Hydromechanics Research Association.

Covers 1973 onwards. References, with abstracts, to literature of fluids, including aerodynamics, fluid flow, fluid engineering, offshore technology and rheology. About 250,000 records updated monthly. Available on DIALOG, file 96 and Data-Star. Available on CD-ROM and on the World Wide Web. Publications: *BHRA Fluid Engineering thesaurus*; *Guide to the Fluidex database, Fluidex Notes, Fluidex Newsline. Class No:* 626(003.4)

Bibliographies

[5074]
KUO, C. 'Marine technology'. *Information sources in engineering.* K.W. Mildren and P.J. Hicks, eds. (3rd ed., 1996), p.467-83. 3rd ed. London, Bowker Saur, 1996. £80. ISBN: 1857390571.

Covers both technical aspects of the ship (*e.g.* naval architecture) and offshore engineering. Topics include construction, design, legislation, hydrodynamics, materials, operations, safety, structures, surfaces and forms, etc. A comprehensive treatment of the information sources. *Class No:* 626(01)

[5075]
Petroleum and marine technology information guide: a bibliographic sourcebook and directory of services. Myers, A., *and others, eds.* 4th ed. London, Spon, 1993. x, 405p. ISBN: 0419182101.

First published 1981; 3rd ed. 1988 as *Offshore information guide*.

In 4 sections: A. Bibliography with offshore and petroleum literature classification - B. Organizations providing information services - C. Online databases and CD-ROMs - D. Directory (addresses relevant to petroleum and marine technology). Comprehensive, but in need of updating to include Internet and web-based information sources. *Class No:* 626(01)

Encyclopaedias

[5076]
VOLLMER, E. Encyclopaedia of hydraulics, soil and foundation engineering. Amsterdam, etc., Elsevier, 1967 (Reprinted 1983). [viii], 398p. illus., tables. Dfl.225. ISBN: 0444406158.

About 4,500 brief entries, definitions ranging from 2 to *c.*100 words. Subjects: hydraulic engineering; hydromechanics; river training weirs and dams; water resources; soil mechanics; soil extraction; soil deposition; slope protection; foundation engineering; soil mechanics; foundation excavation in dry soil; foundation materials behaviour in soil. 4 appendices (symbols, abbreviations and conversion factors). Bibliography, p.[viii]. 48 line drawings. 16 tables. *Class No:* 626(031)

Handbooks & Manuals

[5077]
BRATER, E.G., *and others.* **Handbook of hydraulics** for the solution of hydraulic engineering problems. 7th ed. New York, etc., McGraw-Hill, 1996. v.p. diagrs. graphs, tables, formulas. ISBN: 0070072477.

First published 1918; well known as *King's handbook of hydraulics*.

14 sections: 1. Fluid properties and hydraulic units - 2. Hysrostatics ... 5. Weirs - 6. Pipes ... 12. Measurement of flowing water ... 14. Computer programs in hydraulics. Small, handy format. *Class No:* 626(035)

[5078]
HUNT, T. *and* **VAUGHAN, N. The Hydraulic handbook.** 9th ed. Oxford, Elsevier, 1996. viii, 742p. illus., diagrs., graphs, tables. ISBN: 1856172503.

First published 1958; 8th ed. 1983, published by Trade and Technical Press.

8 sections covering fluids, pumps, valves, accumulators, mechanics and much more. This revised ed. reflects the greater dependence on microprocessor control within the industry (as nearly everywhere else!), as well as the requirement for smaller, quieter units of higher power. The standard handbook, reflecting current developments in oil hydraulic engineering. *Class No:* 626(035)

[5079]
PARMLEY, R.O., *ed.* **Hydraulics field manual.** New York, McGraw-Hill, 1992. xxii, 334p. illus. diagrs., graphs, tables. £36.95. ISBN: 0070485569.

10 sections: 1. Hydrology ... 3. Groundwater - 4. Pumps ... 6. Flow in pipes - 7. Culverts and storm water ... 10. Supplemental data. Numerous tables; a practical approach. *Class No:* 626(035)

[5080]
PINCHES, M.J. *and* **ASHBY, J.G. Power hydraulics.** Englewood Cliffs, N.J., Prentice Hall, 1989. 400p. diagrs. $54.67. ISBN: 0136874436.

Covers pumps, hydraulic valves, actuators, fluids, hydraulic system design, maintenance and control systems. Detailed, analytical index. Appendix includes exercises and answers. 'An excellent practical reference' (*Choice,* May 1989, p.1548). *Class No:* 626(035)

[5081]
ZIPPARRO, V. *and* **HASEN, H. Davis' handbook of applied hydraulics.** 4th ed. New York, etc., McGraw-Hill, 1993. v.p. illus. £77.95. ISBN: 0070730024.

First published 1952; erd ed. 1969.

Coverage: Hydrology and basic hydraulics - Water conveyance - Dams - Water use, control and disposal. 28 documented sections. Over 900 illus. US slant. *Class No:* 626(035)

Dictionaries

Polyglot

[5082]
ACADEMY OF THE HEBREW LANGUAGE. Dictionary of hydraulics: Hebrew - English - French - German. Jerusalem & Haifa, Academy of the Hebrew Language & Technion - Israel Institute of Technology, 1961. 175, 15, 14, 15p.

About 450 terms. English, French, German and Hebrew sequences, plus number key to classified list (Hebrew, with English, French and German equivalents). *Class No:* 626(038)=00

[5083]
Fachwörterbuch für Bewässerung und Entwässerung: Englisch, Deutsch, Französisch, Spanisch. [Multilingual technical dictionary on irrigation and drainage: English, French, German, Spanish.] 2., erw. Aufl. Bonn, Der Verband, 1983. 1009p. illus. £25.35.

First published 1971.

Contains *c.*12,000 terms in one sequence. Over 300 line drawings. English, French, German, and Spanish indexes.

Supplementary volumes in French, Spanish, Arabic, Indian, Japanese, Persian and Portuguese. *Class No:* 626(038)=00

[5084]
TROSKOLANSKI, A.T. Dictionary of hydraulic machinery: in English, German, Spanish, French, Italian and Russian. Amsterdam, etc., Elsevier, 1985. xxiii, 737p. illus., diagrs., graphs, tables. £155. ISBN: 0444997288.

Revised and enlarged translation from Polish original *Magzynyi urzgdzenia hydrauliczne - Projecia podstawave* (1974).

Contains about 4,300 entries classified in 14 sections (1-4. Concepts - 5-14. Hydraulic machinery types, problems and applications). Base language is English. Concise definitions for most terms, with foreign-language equivalents. Indexes in each language lead to main entries by means of number codes. *Class No:* 626(038)=00

English

[5085]
TAYLOR, P.A. Dictionary of marine technology. Oxford, Butterworth, 1989. 244p. $105.

Defines terms in marine and offshore engineering, naval architecture, shipbuilding, shipping and ship operations. Intended to displace the *Dictionary of marine engineering and nautical terms* (Newnes, 1965), emphasizing marine technology terms. 'See' references; some illus. *Class No:* 626(038)=20

German

[5086]
VOLLMER, E. Wasserwesen, Erd- und Grundbau; Deutsch-Englisch. 2.Aufl. Stuttgart, Fischer, 1973. 415p. illus., tables. ISBN: 3437201182.

First published 1967 (415p.).

German-English, dictionary of hydraulics, soil and foundation engineering. About 5,000 German terms are given concise definitions. English index, p.332-413. Bibliography, p.414-5.; conversion tables. 52 illus. *Class No:* 626(038)=30

French

[5087]

DOBENIK, R.H. *and* HARTLINE, G.W. **Dictionnaire technique de la marine:** Anglais/Français et Français/Anglais. [Naval technical dictionary: English/French and French/English.] Paris, La Maison du Dictionnaire, 1989. [xxii],646,[19]p. illus. £51.70. ISBN: 2856080316.

About 35,000 entries in each half. Includes nautical, military, technical terms. Brief bibliography (28 items).
Class No: 626(038)=40

Reviews & Abstracts

[5088]

Fluid abstracts: civil engineering. Oxford, Elsevier, 1990-. Monthly. $795; £500 pa. ISSN: 09627170.

About 6,500 abstracts pa. Sections: Fluid mechanics - The atmosphere - Experimental techniques - Hydraulics - Coastal engineering - Offshore engineering - Operations and utilities - Ports and harbours. Subject index per issue; annual cumulated subject and author indexes. Online as FLUIDEX. *Class No:* 626(048)

[5089]

Fluid abstracts: process engineering. Oxford, Elsevier, 1991-. Monthly. £500; $795. ISSN: 09627162.

Formed by the merger of *Fluid power abstracts; Fluid sealing abstracts; Solid-liquid flow abstracts; Pumps and other fluids machinery abstracts; Fluid flow measurement abstracts; pipelines abstracts; Computer-aided process control abstracts* and *Mixing and separation technology abstracts.* About 6,500 abstracts pa. Available online as part of FLUIDEX. *Class No:* 626(048)

Periodicals

[5090]

BARNETT, J.B. **Marine science journals and serials:** an analytical guide. London, etc., Greenwood Press, 1986. 171p. (*Annotated bibliography of serials: a subject approach, 7.*) ISBN: 030324717x.

Lists 327 items under titles, A-Z. International in scope (*c.*30 countries). Excludes titles concerning maritime commerce and transport, seafood preservation, and fish marketing. Geographical index; index of publishers; subject index; index of variant titles. *Class No:* 626(051)

Progress Reports

[5091]

Developments in hydraulic engineering. Novak, P., *ed.* Amsterdam, etc., Elsevier, 1983 - Annual. illus.

V.5 (1988. 234p. £75). The volumes in the series each concentrate on an aspect of hydraulic engineering, including rivers, coasts, lakes, tidal power generation, groundwater, etc. *Class No:* 626(055)

Yearbooks & Directories

[5092]

Lloyd's international marine equipment guide. London, Lloyd's, 1992. 372p. £75. ISBN: 1850444889.

Section 1: Product categories with suppliers, A-Z by area. Section 2: *c.*7,000 suppliers. *Class No:* 626(058)

Tables & Data Books

[5093]

MORGAN, N., *ed.* **Marine technology reference book.** Boston, Mass., Butterworth, 1990. v.p. tables. $195. ISBN: 0408027143.

13 sections, with 'references and further reading': 1. Ocean environments - 2. Offshore structures ... 12. Electronic navigation and radar - 13. Maritime law. Well-produced. 17p. index. 109 photos; 750 line-drawings. 19 contributors. 'Designed to serve as a first point of reference' (*Preface*). *Class No:* 626(083)

Histories

[5094]

GARBRECHT, G., *ed.* **Hydraulics and hydraulic research:** a historical review. Rotterdam & Boston, Mass., Balkema, 1987. ix, 362p. illus., ports., facsims., graphs, tables. ISBN: 9061316216.

At head of title-page: 'International Association for Hydraulic Research, 1935-1985'. Jubilee volume.

35 contributors. Papers include 'Birth of hydraulics during the Renaissance period', p.55-79 (16 references); 'Great names in the development of hydraulic machinery', p.251-60 (28 references). No index. *Class No:* 626(091)

Libraries

[5095]

Directory of library and information facilities. Moulder, D.S., *comp.* 2nd ed. Plymouth, Marine Biological and Information Services, 1986. 37p.

Provides information on libraries. Subheadings include hours: of opening; affiliation; availability; loan services; catalogue; stock; Institute publications; Library publications.
Class No: 626:061:026/027

Underwater Work

[5096]

GREAT BRITAIN. Ministry of Defence. Director of Naval Warfare. **Diving manual.** London, the Ministry, 1972 (reprinted 1976, incorporating changes). v.p. illus., diagrs., tables. Loose-leaf. (BR.2806).

Supersedes BR.155, *Diving manual* (1964) and *Diving regulations* (1965).

7 chapters: 1. Theory of diving - 2. Regulations - 3. Conduct of diving operations - 4. Breathing apparatus: drill and operation - 5. Decompressor - 6. Divers' illness and injuries - 7. Civilian and expedition diving. Bibliography (8 items). 5-p. index.
Class No: 626.02

[5097]

HAUX, G.F.K. **Subsea manned engineering.** London, Bailliere, Tindall, 1982. x, 538p. illus., diagrs. ISBN: 0702007498.

12 sections (1. Hyperbaric diving simulators and test facilities; 3. Deep diving systems; 7. Submersibles; 8. Submarines; 11. Underwater welding, repair and construction habitats; 12. Animal experiment and equipment test chambers). 4 appendices: Research centres, institutes, government agencies and training schools; Selected diving contractors; Equipment manufacturers; Scientific and technical journals, newsletters and trade magazines. Bibliography, p.527-8. Analytical index, p.531-8. Well illustrated. An authoritative survey by the director, Haux-life-support GmbH, Waldbronn, West Germany. *Class No:* 626.02

[5098]

Jane's underwater technology, 1999-2000. Coulsdon, Surrey, Jane's Information Group, 1999. *c.*500p. illus., diagrs. £245; $395. ISBN: 0710619413.

Covers equipment for underwater engineering. Contents: Platforms/vehicles - Acoustic systems - Imaging systems - Oceanographic instruments - Navigation and positioning systems - Communication systems - Vehicle and robotic manipulators - Vehicle-handling systems - Diver chambers - Vehicle operators and survey companies - Manufacturers. Available online and on CD-ROM. *Class No:* 626.02

[5099]

LARN, R. *and* WHEELER, R. **Commercial diving manual.** Newton Abbot, Devon, David & Charles, 1984. vp. illus., diagrs., tables. £20. ISBN: 0715381447.

2 parts (24 chapters): 1. Basic diving practice - 2. Surface and underwater skills (chapter 24: Conversion factors and tables). Index of 7p. *Class No:* 626.02

[5100]

MILNE, P. H. **Underwater engineering surveys.** London, Spon, 1980. ix, 366p. illus., diagrs., graphs, tables. ISBN: 041911310x.

10 documented chapters (*e.g.* 3. Underwater navigation systems; 4. Hydraulic surveying (with 3p. of references); 7. Underwater photography and television; 8. Underwater work systems; 10. Underwater inspection and maintenance). Partly analytical index, p.332-6. Quotes examples, with good illus. 'May be recommended as a pioneer work for both students and practitioners' (*British Book news,* June 1981, p.353). *Class No:* 626.02

[5101]

SOCIETY FOR UNDERWATER TECHNOLOGY. **Advances in underwater technology, ocean science and offshore engineering.** Dordrecht, etc., Kluwer, 1985-. illus., diagrs., tables.

25v. to date.

Volumes consider the entire field of offshore technology. V.25, *Safety in offshore drilling: the role of shallow gas surveys* (ed. D.A. Ardus and C.D. Green. 1990. viii,293p. £54.50. ISBN: 0792308991) has 13 chapters in 5 parts (Introduction - Acquisition - Processing, analysis and interpretation - Application of geophysical data - Procedures, regulations and guidelines). *Class No:* 626.02

Canals

[5102]

CALVERT, R. **Inland waterways of Europe.** London, Allen & Unwin, 1963. 259p. illus, maps.

13 chapters (1. The Rhine; 3. The Danube; 4/6. France; 6. Benelux; 7. Germany; 8. Russia; 9. Scandinavia; 10. Finland and the Baltic states; 11. Central Europe; 12. Southern Europe; 13. Conclusion). Appendices: 1. Maps and level profiles; 2. Passenger services. Bibliography, p.248-50. Author index. 48 illus. *Class No:* 626.1

[5103]
McKNIGHT, H. **The Shell book of inland waterways.** 2nd ed. Newton Abbot, Devon, David & Charles, 1981. 493p. illus. (incl. col.), maps. £12.95. ISBN: 071538233x.

First published 1975.

18 chapters (*e.g.* 3. Water supply; 4. Locks and lifts; 5. Bridges; 6. Aqueducts; 7. Towns; 8. Railways and design; 11. Operation and maintenance; 12. Working boats; 13. Commercial carriers; 14. Pleasure cruising; 15. Boatyards and marinas; 17. Waterway museums; 18. Associations and boat clubs). Selected bibliography, p.208. Gazetteer (Note on derelict waterways; England and Wales; Scotland; Ireland), p.212-484. Detailed, non-analytical index. Well illustrated. *Class No:* 626.1

[5104]
PAGET-TOMLINSON, E. **The Illustrated history of canal and river navigation.** Rev. ed. Sheffield, Sheffield Academic Press, 1993. xiv, 399p. illus. (incl. colour), ports., maps. £19.95. ISBN: 1850752761.

First published 1978.

6 chapters (1. Some events in waterway history ... 6. Carrying, carriers and crew). Appendices: A. Carriers (a selection); B. Engineers and personalities. Glossary; annotated bibliography (grouped), p.371-80; index of ships and boats. Detailed index, p.384-99. *Class No:* 626.1

Docks & Harbours

[5105]
BRUUN, P. **Port engineering.** 4th ed. Houston, Texas, Gulf Publishing Co., 1988. 2v. illus., diagrs., charts, tables. $350, set.

First published 1973. 3rd ed. 1981.

V. 1. *Harbour planning, breakwaters, and marine terminals.*

V. 2. *Harbour transportation, fishing ports, sediment transport, geomorphology, inlets, and dredging.*.

A comprehensive reference work. V. 2 carries an index. *Class No:* 627.2/.3

Cargo Handling

[5106]
BRODIE, P.R. **Illustrated dictionary of cargo handling.** London, Lloyds of London Press, 1991. xvi, 175p. illus., diagrs. £39.50. ISBN: 1850443408.

About 1,200 terms diefined and briefly explained (*e.g.* 'hog (to)': 6 lines). *Class No:* 627.35

[5107]
INTERNATIONAL CARGO HANDLING COORDINATION ASSOCIATION. **A Multilingual glossary of cargo handling terms.** 3rd ed. London, the Association, 1987. 205p. illus. ISBN: 0906297974.

First published 1982; 2nd ed. 1984.

462 terms in 6 sections: 1. Transport vehicles - 2. Handling and securing equipment - 3. Goods and unit loads -4. Infrastructure and terminals - 5. Cargo Administration - 6. Abbreviations. English terms with Dutch, Finnish, French, German, Italian, Portuguese, Spanish and Swedish translations. Each entry has a brief definition in English. Language indexes. *Class No:* 627.35

[5108]
International Logistics abstracts. Cranford, Beds., National Materials Handling Centre, 1971-. 6pa. £110 pa. ISSN: 01419501.

From 1976-91 *International distribution and handling review.*

About 700 abstracts pa. Coverage: distribution systems, freight transport, storage and warehousing, packaging safety, and training of workers. *Class No:* 627.35

Floods & Flood Control

[5109]
HANDMER, J., *ed*. **Flood hazard management:** British and continental perspectives. Norwich, Geo Books, 1987. viii, 297p. ISBN: 0860942082.

6 sections (with subsection references): 1. Introduction: the British urban flood hazard - 2. Flood related institutions and policy in Britain - 3. Implementation of land use policy: local and international experience - 4. Hazard response - 5. Project appraisal and risk assessment - 6. Conclusion. The product of research and policy development activity at the Middlesex Polytechnic Flood Hazard Research Centre. *Class No:* 627.51

[5110]
NATURAL ENVIRONMENT RESEARCH COUNCIL. **Flood studies report.** London, the Council, 1975. 5v. charts, graphs, tables, maps.

1. *Hydrological studies.* 2. *Meteorological studies.* 3. *Flood routeing studies.* 4. *Hydrological data.* 5. *Maps.*

V.5 ([viii], 541p.) describes the collection, appraisal and processing of hydrological data used in the investigation and presents the basic data. Apart from flood record statistics, it provides a master list of gauging stations, catchment characteristics and flood statistics. The 24 maps in v.5 illustrate v.1-2. The work of hydrologists at the Institute of Hydrology. Confined to Great Britain and Ireland. *Class No:* 627.51

[5111]
UNITED NATIONS. Educational, Scientific and Cultural Organization. **World catalogue of very large floods.** Paris, Unesco, 1976. 424p. (*Studies and reports in hydrology.*)

This overview of flood situations throughout the world includes information enabling more elaborate methods to be used for treatment of data. English, French, Spanish and Russian versions available. *Class No:* 627.51

Navigation Aids

Lighthouses

[5112]
HAGUE, D.B. *and* CHRISTIE, R. **Lighthouses:** their architecture, history and archaeology. London, Gower, 1975. xiv, [i], 307p. illus., maps.

The setting is mainly Great Britain and Ireland. 8 chapters: 1. History - 2. British lighthouse administration - 3. General design and construction - 4. Rock towers - 5. Illumination and fog signals - 6. Light vessels and floating aids - 7. Unit beams, daymarks or seamarks - 8. Lighthouse builders. Glossary. Appendix (*e.g.* Light dues; building estimates). Bibliography (grouped, including Acts of Parliament, manuscript sources). Analytical index. 29 plates; 47 line-drawings. *Class No:* 627.715

[5113]
—STEVENSON, D.A. **The World's lighthouses before 1820.** London, Oxford Univ. Press, 1959. xxiv, 310p. illus., diagrs., tables, maps.

Records the history of development of seamarks 'from wood fires of antiquity to the reflector lights of 1819'. *Class No:* 627.715

Dams

[5114]
GOLZE, A.R., *ed*. **Handbook of dam engineering.** New York, etc., Van Nostrand Reinhold, 1977. [xiii], 793p. illus., diagrs., charts.

14 sections, by various hands, with references or bibliographies. 1. Planning and environmental studies - 2. Hydrological studies - 3. Materials suitable for construction ... 7. Design of rockfill dams ... 14. Public safety controls for dams and reservoirs. Reflects current American practice. Recommended 'unreservedly for students, graduates and practising engineers' (*New Scientist*, 27 April 1978, p. xviii). *Class No:* 627.8

[5115]
INTERNATIONAL COMMISSION ON LARGE DAMS. **Technical dictionary on dams.** 2nd ed. Moscow, the Commission, 1962. 380p.

Prepared for publication by the Committee for the USSR Participapation in International Power Conferences.

About 4,500 terms in Russian, French, English, German, Spanish, Italian, Portugese, Rumanian, Czech, French. 4 Subject sections: 1. General; 2. Dams; 3. Appurtenant works; 4. Construction works. Languages index.

Norwegian edition - *Onbok for dambygging* (2nd ed. Oslo, RTT, 1968. [ix], 270p. illus.), similarly arranged, has *c.*4,500 Norwegian terms, with French, English, German, Spanish, Italian, Portugese equivalents. 7 language indexes. *Class No:* 627.8

[5116]
World register of dams. [Registre mondial des barrages.] Paris, International Commission on Large Dams, 1984. 752p. illus., tables.

Earlier ed. 1964; supplement 1966.

List of dams (member countries, Corée ... Zimbabwe) p.147-728. List of dams (non-member countries). p.729-51. Data on each include location: high and crest length of dam; volume; gross capacity of reservoir; owner; engineering by; construction by. Bibliography, p.652. Classified and statistical tables precede lists. 25 illus. A 'large dam' is defined as one of at least 15 metres (50 ft.) high, from lowest general foundations to crest. *Class No:* 627.8

Public Health Engineering

Abbreviations & Symbols

[5117]
WENNRICH, P. **Anglo-American and German abbreviations in environmental protection.** Munich, Verlag Documentation, 1980. vi, 618p. $35. ISBN: 3598100604.

A supplement to Wennrich's one A-Z sequence *Anglo-American and German abbreviations in science and techology* (1976-77. 3v.).
Class No: 628(003)

Databases

[5118]
ENVIROLINE. Bethesda, Md., Congressional Information Service.

ENVIROLINE is the database corresponding to *Environment abstracts*. About 200,000 records; updated monthly. Available online via DIALOG, ESA-IRS, Questel/ORBIT; EDA-IRS and other hosts.
Class No: 628(003.4)

[5119]
Environment online: the greening of databases. Wilton, Ct., Eight Bit Books, 1992. vii, 76p. illus. $19.95. ISBN: 0910965056.

Reprinted from the 'Environmental series' in *Database* magazine, August 1991, October 1991 and August 1992, with 'Additions and changes' for updating. Includes 6 'Cited columns' from *Databese* and *Online* (*e.g.* 'TOXLINE search tips'). No index and poor quality 'perfect' binding. *Class No:* 628(003.4)

[5120]
RITTNER, D. **Ecolinking:** everyone's guide to online environmental information. Berkeley, Ca., Peachpit Press, 1992. xi, 352p. illus. $18.95; £17.99. ISBN: 0938151355.

Chiefly concerned with internet sources, *e.g.* electronic bulletin boards and commercial online services (CompuServe; America Online, etc.). Also lists research databases and CD-ROM sources. 5 appendices (A. Selected communications software; B. Internet mailing lists). Index. Useful for those who are not information specialists.
Class No: 628(003.4)

CD-ROM

[5121]
The OCLC environment library. London, SilverPlatter. Annual. CD-ROM.

Nearly 825,000 bibliographic records drawn from the OCLC Online Union Catalog. Updated annually. *Class No:* 628(003.40)

Internet

[5122]
Environmental engineering abstracts. Bethesda, Md., Cambridge Scientific Abstracts. URL: http://www.csa.com.

Jointly published with Engineering Information.

Covers the technological and engineering aspects of air and water quality, environmental safety and alternate energy sources. About 12,000 abstracts pa, updated monthly, with backfiles to 1990. Only available on the Internet and on magnetic tape. *Class No:* 628(003.41)

[5123]
Environmental RouteNet. Bethseda, Md., Cambridge Scientific Abstracts. URL: http://www.csa.com/routenet/.

The web site provides access to a wide range of environmental sources including 11 databases, patents, site-specific information on hazards and accidents, grants and funding sources, education and training, news, thesauri, dictionaries, etc. *Class No:* 628(003.41)

Bibliographies

[5124]
ANDERSON, G.K. *and* ELLIOTT, D.J. 'Environmental control engineering'. *Information sources in engineering.* K.W. Mildren and P.J. Hicks, eds. (3rd ed., 1996), p.486-94. 3rd ed. London, Bowker Saur, 1996. £80. ISBN: 1857390571.

Topics covered include examination and standards, water pollution and treatment, solid and hazardous wastes, air pollution, odour, noise and environmental impact assessment. *Class No:* 628(01)

[5125]
Beacham's guide to environmental issues and sources. New York, Beacham, 1993. 5v. (3335p.) $240. ISBN: 0933833318.

39 chapters, closely subdivided, covering food, climate, population, health, energy, pollution, waste disposal, wildlife and ecology, natural resources, perspectives on the environment, etc. Several thousand citations, most published since 1988. 'A major contribution to the environmental literature' (*Choice*, December 1993, p.579).
Class No: 628(01)

[5126]
Encyclopedia of environmental information sources: a subject guide to about 34,000 print and other sources of information on all aspects of the environment. Balachandran, S., *ed.* Detroit, Gale Research, 1993. 1813p. ISBN: 0810385686.

Exclusively US in coverage. A-Z list of 1,100 areas of interest, p.1-1508, (*e.g.* municipal sewage, municipal wastes) showing sources of information available. 13 types of information source: abstracts/indexing services; bibliographies; directories; encyclopaedias/dictionaries; general works; handbooks/manuals; online databases; statistical sources; trade associations/professional societies. The sources cited are listed A-Z by title, p.1509-1813. *Class No:* 628(01)

[5127]
Information sources in environmental protection. Eagle, S. *and* Deschamps, J., *eds.* London, Bowker-Saur, 1997. xviii, 280p. £58. (*Guides to information sources.*) ISBN: 1857390628.

20 contributors; 17 documented chapters in 4 parts: I. The official and the unofficial - II. Effects and the effected - III. Practicalities - IV. Controls and public awareness. Provides 'a narrative introduction to the principal sources of information on the subject of environmental protection' (*Introduction*, p.xv). Some, but not all, chapters include references to web sites. *Class No:* 628(01)

[5128]
—GOODIER, J. 'Environmental technology and technology and the environment'. *Information sources in environmental protection.* Eds., S. Eagle and J. Deschamps, p.173-82. London, Bowker-Saur, 1997. ISBN: 1857390628.

Covers current industrial technology and the protection and remediation of the environment, including land use, transportation systems, mines, etc. Specific information sources, including archives, are identified. *Class No:* 628(01)

[5129]
The Island Press bibliography of environmental literature. Miller, J.A., *and others, comps.* Washington, D.C., Island Press, 1993. xviii, 396p. $48. ISBN: 1559631899.

Produced in association with the Yale School of Forestry and Environmental Studies.

3,084 annotated entries. 14 sections, each with introduction, in 2 parts: 1. Natural environments - 2. Human environment. Author-title index, p.295-352; subject index, p.353-96. Well produced.
Class No: 628(01)

[5130]
LEES, N. *and* WOOLSTON, H. **Environmental information:** a guide to sources. 2nd ed. London, British Library, Science Reference and Information Service, 1997. viii, 271p. £25. ISBN: 0712308253.

First published 1992.

14 sections, with annotated entries: 1. General environmental information ... 3. Environmental law (UK; EU; international) ... 5. Water pollution ... 9. Energy ... 11. Recycling ... 14. Agriculture and food. 3 appendices: databases; printed sources; organizations. Detailed, analytical index, p.247-67. The 2nd ed. is much expanded, reflecting the increasing interest in the environment.
Class No: 628(01)

Encyclopaedias

[5131]
ASHWORTH, W. **The Encyclopedia of environmental studies.** New York, Facts on File, 1991. viii,470p. diagrs., tables. ISBN: 0816015317.

Lists terms from biology, physics, chemistry, ecology, and geology encountered in environmental literature. Also includes in the alphabetical listing short biographies of environmental activists, *e.g.* John Muir; abbreviations and organizations, *e.g.* Friends of the Earth. Many cross-references. Bibliography, p.435-40. Detailed index. Has a US bias (includes information on US government and state agencies, and legislation) but would be useful in any library covering environmental issues. *Class No:* 628(031)

[5132]
Encyclopedia of energy technology and the environment. Bisio, A. *and* Boots, S., *eds*. New York, Wiley, 1995. 4v. (2964p.) illus., diagrs. graphs, tables. $900; £595. (*Wiley encyclopedia series in environmental science.*) ISBN: 0471544582.

200 contributors. About 175 signed articles, most with extensive bibliographies. Topics covered include acid rain, air pollution, building systems, coal combustion, environmental law, geothermal energy, oil spills, risk assessment, etc. Cross references; detailed, analytical index. 'Highly recommended' (*Choice*, September 1995, p.80). *Class No:* 628(031)

[5133]
Encyclopedia of environmental control technology. Cheremisinoff, P.N., *ed*. Houston, Texas, Gulf Publishing Co., 1989-. V.1-. diagrs., charts, tables.

V.1. *Thermal treatment of hazardous wastes.* 1989. 828p. $155.
V.2. *Air pollution control.* 1989. 1066p. $155.
V.3. *Wastewater treatment technology.* 1989. 684p. $155.
V.4. *Hazardous waste containment and treatment.* 1990. 776p. $155.
V.7. *High-hazard pollutants.* 1995. 663p. $155.
V.8. *Work area hazards.* 1995. 804p. $155.
V.9. *Geotechnical applications, leak detection, treatment options.* 1996. 1137p. $155.

Each volume has chapter references and an index. V.1 covers current treatment methods in the field and projects future trends in research and technologies. *Class No:* 628(031)

[5134]
Encyclopedia of environmental health: law and practice. Hawke, N., *ed*. London, Sweet & Maxwell, 1968-. 4v. loose-leaf. (*The Local government library.*)

A comprehensive catalogue of statute law, instruments and government (UK) circulars. Regular updates issued. *Class No:* 628(031)

[5135]
Environmental analysis and remediation. Meyers, R.A., *ed*. Chichester, Wiley, 1998. 8v. (5488p.) illus., diagrs., graphs, tables. £1650. (*Encyclopedia series in environmental science.*) ISBN: 0471117080.

About 350 articles, A-Z, from numerous contributors. Covers distribution and transport, sampling methods, instruments and analytical techniques, remediation methodologies, pollution control and risk assessments, regulatory and management issues. Pollutants discussed include heavy metals, dioxin, nuclear waste, chemical warfare agents and weapons grade plutonium. A major work. *Class No:* 628(031)

[5136]
Environmental encyclopedia. Cunningham, W.P., *and others, eds*. Detroit, Mi., Gale, 1994. xxi, 981p. illus., diagrs. $195. ISBN: 0810349868. ISSN: 10725083.

Brief articles, A-Z, some with 'Further reading' (*e.g.* 'Acid rain': 2p.; map; 5 readings). Historical chronology, p.935-38; environmental legislation in the US, p.939-44; general index, p.945-81. A popular treatment. *Class No:* 628(031)

[5137]
McGraw-Hill encyclopedia of environmental science. 3rd ed. New York, etc., McGraw-Hill, 1992. 749p. illus., diagrs., graphs, tables, maps. $84.50. ISBN: 0070513961.

First published 1974; 2nd ed. 1980.
Articles mainly drawn from the *McGraw-Hill Encyclopedia of science and technology*. Added section of feature articles on broad topics of special importance. *Class No:* 628(031)

[5138]
—TUDGE, C., *ed*. The Encyclopedia of the environment. London, Croom Helm, 1988. 248, [8]p. illus. (col.), ports, diagrs., maps.

Has 6 contributors. 9 sections: 1. Observation and explanation - 2. Animal abilities - 3. Animal behaviour - 4. Ecology and ecosystems - 5. The rise of humanity - 6. Support from the law - 7. Support from the water (*e.g.* fish-farming) - 8. Destruction and pollution - 9. Conservation. Further reading and credits. Glossary of terms. Detailed analytical index of 5p. The main feature: the many and striking col. illus. Main theme: conservation of the natural world. *Class No:* 628(031)

Handbooks & Manuals

[5139]
Clay's handbook of environmental health. Bassett, W.H., *ed*. 18th ed. London, Spon, 1999. 928p. illus., tables. £99. ISBN: 0419229604.

First published 1933; 17th ed. 1996.
In 7 parts: 1. The organization of environmental health - 2. Environmental health law and administration - 3. Epidemiology - 4. Housing and development control - 5. Occupational health and safety -

....(contd.)
6. Food safety and hygiene - 7. Environmental protection. Most chapters have 'Further reading'. Index. Cites Acts in full. A basic handbook. *Class No:* 628(035)

[5140]
Environmental management in practice. Nath, B., *and others, eds*. London, Routledge, 1999. 3v. (544p.; 352p.; 320p.). illus., diagrs. graphs. £200. ISBN: 0415191645.

V.1. *Instruments for environmental management.*
V.2. *Compartments, stresses and sectors.*
V.3. *Managing the ecosystem.*
About 60 contributors; covers research and practical applications. V.2 deals with environmental problems in air, water and soil, as well as the socio-ecomomic impact of industry, traffic and energy. *Class No:* 628(035)

[5141]
JACKSON, M.H., *and others*. Environmental health reference book. London, Butterworths, 1988. *c.*600p. illus. £70. ISBN: 0408026006.

15 sections: Introduction - Food poisoning and hygiene - Food control - Pathology of food animals - Housing administration - Building science and technology - Health and safety - Atmospheric pollution - Water quality and water supply - Sewerage and waste water disposal - Solid waste management - Noise control - Radiation - Pestology - Communicable diseases. Well illustrated. Emphasis is on the technical aspects rather than on legislation. *Class No:* 628(035)

[5142]
Standard handbook of environmental engineering. Corbitt, R.A., *ed*. New York, McGraw-Hill, 1990. v.p. illus., diagrs., graphs, tables. $89.50. ISBN: 0070131589.

Comprehensive, covering technical aspects of air and water quality control standards and treatment, wastewater and solid waste disposal, and hazardous waste management. Separate legislation/regulations section. Over 900 tables, charts and diagrams. Extensive chapter references; lengthy subject index. US slanted.

A new ed. was published in 1998 ($125; 0070131600). *Class No:* 628(035)

Dictionaries

Polyglot

[5143]
Dictionary of environmental technology: English/French/German/ Russian. Amsterdam, Elsevier, 1988. 527p.

4-column page; compressed layout. 'This appears to be an excellent dictionary' (*Language monthly*, May 1988, p.22). *Class No:* 628(038)=00

[5144]
TEKNISKA NOMENKLATURCENTRALEN. Miljöordlista. svensk-engelsk-fransk-tysk. [Glossary of environmental terms. Swedish-English-French-German.] Stockholm, the centre, 1972. vi, 86p.

772 terms relating to human environments. In Swedish, with English, French, and German equivalents and indexes. *Class No:* 628(038)=00

English

[5145]
CRUMP, A. Dictionary of environment and development: people, places, ideas and organizations. London, Earthscan, 1991. 272p. £15. ISBN: 185383078x.

Entries range from brief definitions to short articles. Includes current and retrospective statistics. 'Recommended' (*Choice*, March 1992, p.1042). *Class No:* 628(038)=20

[5146]
GILPIN, A. Dictionary of environment and sustainable development. Chichester, Wiley, 1996. 262p. £45 (Hbk); £16.99 (Pbk). ISBN: 0471962198, (Hbk); 0471962201, (Pbk).

About 2,000 entries covering environmental planning, management, conservation and sustainable development. Includes sectional bibliographies, acronyms and examples of usage. *Class No:* 628(038)=20

[5147]
KEMP, D. The Environmental dictionary. London, Routledge, 1998. 480p. illus., diagrs., maps. £55. ISBN: 0415127521.

About 1,600 terms, some with brief bibliographies, covering the physical elements of the environment, and well as socio-economic, cultural, historical and political issues. Boxed entries highlight issues of particular importance or topicality. *Class No:* 628(038)=20

[5148]

LEE, C.C. Environmental engineering dictionary. 2nd ed. Washington, D.C., Government Institutes, 1992. 462p. $88. ISBN: 0865873283.

First published 1989.

Several thousand entries covering air, drinking water, industrial effluents, landfill, radioactive, solid, medical wastes, etc. Includes list of acronyms and explanations of all environmental requirements in the *Code of Federal Regulations* [US]. *Class No:* 628(038)=20

[5149]

PORTEOUS, A. Dictionary of environmental science and technology. 2nd ed. Chichester, Wiley, 1996. xvi, 635p. illus., diagrs., graphs, tables. £13.99 ISBN: 0471935441.

First published 1991 by Open University Press.

'This book is written in the hope that it may contribute to environmental literacy' ('Introduction', p.ix). Entries, A-Z defined, sometimes at length (*e.g.* 'Nuclear reactor waste': *c.*4p.). Cross references. 4 appendices (1. 'Pollution and the environment: organizations'). Author is professor of environmental engineering at the Open University. *Class No:* 628(038)=20

[5150]

STEVENSON, H. *and* **WYMAN, B. The Facts on File dictionary of environmental science.** New York, Facts on File, 1991. 294p. $25; £18.50. ISBN: 0816023174.

A popular treatment, with about 3,000 current terms and some acronyms (*e.g.* 'Not-in-my-backyard syndrome: NIMBY'). 'Useful in undergraduate libraries' (*Choice*, March 1992, p.1056), but not detailed enough for the specialist. *Class No:* 628(038)=20

German

[5151]

Routledge German dictionary of environmental technology: German-English, English-German. London, Routledge, 1997. 272p. £85. ISBN: 0415112435.

About 25,000 terms in ech language, covering energy sources, pollution, law, water supplies, waste treatment, methodology and safety. Also available on CD-ROM. *Class No:* 628(038)=30

Spanish

[5152]

Dictionary of environmental science and engineering. [Diccionario de ciencia e ingeniería ambiental] Headworth, H. *and* Staines, S., *eds*. Chichester, Wiley, 1998. xii, 312p. £18; $39.95.. ISBN: 0471962732.

English and Spanish; about 15,000 terms in each language.Covers 21 subject areas with the emphasis on civil, water and environmental engineering. *Class No:* 628(038)=60

[5153]

Routledge Spanish dictionary of environmental technology: Spanish-English, English-Spanish. London, Routledge, 1998. 261p. £85. ISBN: 0415152658.

About 25,000 terms in ech language, covering energy sources, pollution, law, water supplies, waste treatment, methodology and safety. Also available on CD-ROM. *Class No:* 628(038)=60

[5154]

VILLATE, J.T. Dictionary of environmental engineering and related science. [Diccionario de ingenieria ambiental y ciencias afines. English-Spanish, Spanish-English.] Miami, Florida, Ediciones Universal, 1979. xvi, 445p. tables. £26.90. ISBN: 089729209x.

Each half has *c.*1,500 headwords. English-Spanish, p. 1-216 (plus tables of measures; prefixes). Spanish-English, p. 217-445. Includes phrases eponyms. 'References consulted', p. 445.
Class No: 628(038)=60

Russian

[5155]

MILOVANOV, E.V. *and* **WEIZMAN, E.A. English-Russian dictionary of environmental control.** Moscow, Russian language Publishers, 1980. 367p.

About 14,000 English terms, A-Z, with Russian equivalents. Appended: List of international organizations (p. 326-56); Regulations and legislation; International treaties and conventions.
Class No: 628(038)=82

Reviews & Abstracts

[5156]

Environment abstracts. Bethseda, Md., Cambridge Scientific Abstracts, 1971-. Monthly. $1070. ISSN: 00933287.

About 20,000 abstracts pa. Sections (01. Air pollution ... 03. Energy ... 05. Environmental design and urban ecology... 09. Land use and pollution... 14. Radiological contamination ... 15/16. Renewable resources (terrestrial; water) ... 19. Water pollution ... 21.

....(contd.)

Wildlife. Conferences. Subject, industry and author indexes, cumulated in annual *Environmental abstracts annual*. The leading abstracting service in the environment field. ENVIROLINE database on DIALOG and other hosts; also available on CD-ROM.
Class No: 628(048)

[5157]

Environmental studies reviews. Douville, J.A., *comp.* Middletown, Ct., Association of College and Research Libraries, 1995. 164p. $38. ISBN: 0838978088.

About 900 book and electronic media reviews originally published in *Choice* between 1990 and 1994. Arranged by broad subject categories, with a substantial reference section. Author and title indexes. A handy collection. *Class No:* 628(048)

[5158]

Excerpta medica. 46: Environmental health and pollution control. Amsterdam, etc., Elsevier, 1971-. 10 pa. ISSN: 03005194.

About 3,000 abstracts pa. 16 sections: 1. General aspects - 2. Types and sources of pollutants - 3. Effects of pollution - 4. Measurement of pollution - 5. Meteorological aspects of pollution - 6. Dangerous goods - 7. Legal and administrative aspects - 8. Criteria, and standards of pollution - 9. Treatments, prevention and control of pollution - 10. Socioeconomic aspects of pollution - 11. Noise and vibration - 12. Pesticides and herbicides - 13. Radiation - 14. Thermal pollution - 15. Biometeorological research - 16. Disaster control. Subject and author indexes per issue, and annually. *Class No:* 628(048)

[5159]

Green engineering: a current awareness bulletin. London, Information and Library Service, Institution of Mechanical Engineers, 1991-. 12pa. £99pa.; $193 pa. ISSN: 09608796.

Briefly annotated entries arranged by type of publication (*e.g.* 'articles', 'news', etc.), then alphabetically by subject (*e.g.* 'aerosols' - 'waste management'). About 70 entries per issue. Annual author index. Likely to have a broad appeal. *Class No:* 628(048)

Yearbooks & Directories

[5160]

Environment industry yearbook, 1996. 4th ed. London, Macmillan, 1995. v.p. tables. ISBN: 0333658116. ISSN: 09683046.

11 sections: A. Industry information and contacts - B. Information services - C. Training and recruitment - D. Laboratory analysis services - E. Computer services and software - F. Legal advisors - G. Environmental consultants - H. Waste management - I. Recycling and paper - J. Water and waste water treatment - K. Equipment and suppliers guide. A comprehensive survy of services, etc. in the UK.
Class No: 628(058)

[5161]

Who's who in the environment: England. Aldous, K., *and others, eds*. Rev. ed. London, The Environment Council, 1995. x, 404p. ISBN: 0903158523.

First published 1990; 2nd ed. 1992.

Covers organizations at regional and national level, A-Z. Information includes name, address, telephone, contact, scope, number of staff and volunteers, membership, local branches. List of organizations which provide speakers, training, funding and photographic libraries. Subject index, p.370-98. *Class No:* 628(058)

[5162]

Who's who in the environment: Scotland. 2nd ed. Perth, Scottish National Heritage, 1993. viii, 116p. ISBN: 1853970190.

First published 1988.

Covers organizations at regional and national level, A-Z. Information includes name, address, telephone, contact, scope, number of staff and volunteers, membership, local branches. List of organizations which provide speakers, training, funding and photographic libraries. Subject index, p.91-106. *Class No:* 628(058)

[5163]

World directory of environmental testing, monitoring and treatment 1997/98. Cross, B., *ed*. London, James & James, 1997. 312p. illus., diagrs. ISBN: 187393677x.

Several editorial features (*e.g.* Air; Consultancy; Software) precede classified and A-Z listings of organizations and companies offering services. The directory is also available, free of charge to users, on the World Wide Web; URL: http://www.jxj.com. *Class No:* 628(058)

Quotations

[5164]

RODES, B.K. *and* **ODELL, R. A Dictionary of environmental quotations.** New York, Simon & Schuster, 1992. 335p. $30. ISBN: 0132105764.

About 3,700 identified quotations in English or English translation. Alphabetical subject arrangement; chronological within categories. Indexes: author; subject. 'Highly recommended' (*Choice*, December 1992. p.600). *Class No:* 628(082.2)

Tables & Data Books

[5165]

BITTON, G. **Formula handbook for environmental engineers and scientists.** Chichester, Wiley, 1997. 310p. £34.95. (*Environmental science and technology*.) ISBN: 047113905x.

About 200 formulas for solving problems dealing with biological or biochemical processes in natural and engineered systems. Conversion tables. *Class No:* 628(083)

[5166]

CRC handbook of environmental control. Bond, R.G. *and* Straub, C.P., *eds.* Cleveland, Ohio, CRC Press, 1972-78. 5v. diagrs., graphs, tables. ISBN: 0878192700.
1. *Air pollution.* 1972. xii, 876p.
2. *Solid waste.* 1973. ix, 880p.
3. *Water supply and disposal.* 1973. [x], 835p.
4. *Waste water treatment* 1974. [xi], 905p.
5. *Hospital and health care facilities.* 1975. 440p.
Cumulative series index for volumes 1-5. 1978. xii, 101p.

V.1 has 4 sections: 1. The atmosphere and air pollutants - 2. Effects of air pollution - 3. Emission sources - 4. Air pollution and control measures. Volumes consist largely of tables, with cross-references. Each volume has an analytical subject index. The *Cumulative series index* numbering system is, however, faulty; entry numbers do not necessarily correspond to volume numbers. *Class No:* 628(083)

[5167]

—Practical handbook of environmental control. Straub, C.P., *ed.* Boca Raton, Fl., CRC Press, 1989. 537p. tables. $45. ISBN: 0879337070.

Based on data in the *CRC Handbook of environmental control* (5v.). Many tables; numerous references. Substantial subject index. For professionals and students in the field of environmental control. *Class No:* 628(083)

[5168]

GREAT BRITAIN. Department of the Environment. **Digest of environmental protection and water statistics.** London, H.M. Stationery Office, 1979-. Annual.

Covers trends, air and water quality, radio-activity, noise, lead concentrations, solid waste, water supply, landscape and nature conservation, public attitude, and environmental monitoring. Appended: Statistical bulletins; Discontinued tables; DOE pollution papers and reports. *Class No:* 628(083)

[5169]

UNITED NATIONS. Department of International Economic and Social Affairs. **Directory of environment statistics.** v, 305p. £30. (*ST/ESA/STAT/Ser M/75*.)

Part 1: National publications (p. 6-283): Albania ... Zaire. Part 2: Subjects. Includes environmental statistical publications published by other international organizations. Data collected by 150 member states. 2 annexes (1. Environmental areas and parameters). *Class No:* 628(083)

Maps & Atlases

[5170]

LEAN, G. *and* HINRICHSEN, D. **Atlas of the environment.** 2nd ed. New York, HarperPerennial, 1994. 192p. illus.(col.),diagrs., tables, maps. $39. ISBN: 0062733141.

Previous ed. published 1992.

Topics include literacy rates, disasters, land issues, demographics, etc. Only includes data from the 1980s and 1990s. Over 200 full colour maps and diagrams. No index. A general overview; for school and public libraries. *Class No:* 628(084.3)

America—North

[5171]

World environmental directory: North America. Gough, B.E., *ed.* 5th ed. Silver Spring, Md., Business Publishers, Inc., 1989. v.p. ISBN: 0916742059.

15 sections covering a range of areas: products; professional services; government and independent agencies; environmental databases; education institutions; grants. Separate section covers Canada. *Class No:* 628(71+73)

Information Management

[5172]

GOODAY, L. *and* DEVINE, J., *comps.* **Sourcebook on green business.** London, Institution of Mechanical Engineers, Information and Library Serivce, 1993. v, 177p. £29.50 (*Sourcebook 7*.) ISBN: 0852988915.

2 broad sections. 'Green business information' covers abstracts and indexes, conferences, directories, grants, standards and legislation, etc. 'Green business references' lists 288 bibliographic references, with annotations. Indexes: author; subject. Emphasis is on the UK. *Class No:* 628:025.4

Information Services

[5173]

ENDOC directory: environmental information and documentation centres of the European Communities. Hitchin, Herts., P. Peregrinus, for the Commission of the European Communities, 1981. vi,600p.

Pilot ed. 1978.

519 centres, in Belgium, Denmark, Federal Republic of Germany, France, Ireland, Netherlands, UK. Data on each: name and address, contact, 'phone-number;' nature (*e.g.* governmental); aims; environmental subject areas; information activities. Subject indexes (in six languages). Online on ECHO. *Class No:* 628:061:025.5

Research Projects

[5174]

FARRELL, S. **World environmental research directory.** Leatherhead, Surrey, Pira International, 1992. viii,299p. ISBN: 0902799959.

Organizations, by country A-Z, in broad subject groupings: Manufacture and process control - Energy - Environmental management - Air pollution - Water and effluent - Hazardous waste management - Solid waste management and recycling - Contaminated land - Noise pollution - Agriculture - Nature conservation - Aquatic environment - Flora conservation - Wildlife conservation. Data: name; research project titles; research personnel; length of project; funding; published papers. Indexes: project leaders; subject; organizations. *Class No:* 628:061:061.62.005

Water Supply

Databases

[5175]

Water resources abstracts. Reston, Va., US Department of the Interior, Geological Survey.

Covers water planning (demand, economics, cost allocations), water cycle (precipitation, snow, groundwater, lakes, erosion) and water quality (pollution, waste treatment). About 3000,000 records; updated monthly. Available on DIALOG, file 117 and on CD-ROM (SilverPlatter). Also available on the World Wide Web from Cambridge Scientific Abstracts (URL: http://www.csa.com). *Class No:* 628.1(003.4)

[5176]

—Waternet. Denver, Co., American Water Works Association.

Covers drinking water, treatment, water quality, groundwater, surface water, development, reuse, regulations, pollution, wastewater disposal and treatment. About 23,000 records; updated bimonthly. Available on DIALOG, file 245. *Class No:* 628.1(003.4)

Bibliographies

[5177]

WATER RESOURCES CENTER ARCHIVES. University of California. **Dictionary catalog. [Water Resources Center Archives].** Boston, Mass., G.K. Hall, 1970-. 5v. (3373p.). Supplements, 1-. 1971-. $545; set; $285, supp. 6. ISBN: 0816108846; set; 0816102449, supp. (6th, 1978).

The main volumes comprise 97,000 photolithographed catalogue cards. The Water Resources Center Archives is a research library on engineering, economic, social and legal aspects of water. It largely concentrates on US report material, government publications (federal, state, regional, municipal), publications of water-related bodies, conferences and symposia; photographs and maps. *Class No:* 628.1(01)

Handbooks & Manuals

[5178]

DE ZUANE, J. **Handbook of drinking water quality:** standards and control. New York, Van Nostrand Reinhold, 1990. 523p. illus., diagrs., tables. $69.95. ISBN: 0442239092.

Chapters cover basic physical and chemical parameters of water, potential contaminants, standards for water analysis and treatment. Includes US federal and state acronyms and table of conversions. 'An especially handy book' (*Choice*, May 1991, p.1508). US slanted. *Class No:* 628.1(035)

[5179]

FRESENIUS, W., *and others, eds.* **Water analysis:** a practical guide to physico-chemical, chemical and microbiological water examination and quality assurance. Berlin, etc., Springer-Verlag, 1988. xxv, 804p. illus., tables. ISBN: 354017723x; 038717723x US.

Highly detailed survey, including the physics and chemistry of water, methods for analysis in laboratories with simple equipment or in the field (*e.g.* for third world countries), theoretical investigation and evaluation of analysis techniques. Sections: 1. Sampling, local testing - 2. Methods of water analysis - 3. Inorganic parameters - 4. Organic parameters - 5. Biological analysis - 6. Evaluation of data analysis. Detailed index; brief bibliography. *Class No:* 628.1(035)

[5180]
LINSLEY, R.K. *and* FRANZINI, J.B. **Water resources engineering.** 4th ed. New York, etc., McGraw-Hill, 1992. 768p. tables. £22.99. ISBN: 0071126899.
First published 1964; 3rd ed., 1979.
Chapters: Descriptive hydrology ... Groundwater - Reservoirs - Dams, spillways, gates, and outlet works ... Hydraulic machinery ... Irrigation - Water supply systems - Hydroelectric power - River navigation - Drainage - Sewerage and wastewater treatment - Flood damage mitigation - Planning for water resources development. Appendix: 'useful tables'. Name and subject indexes. Comprehensive and wide-ranging. *Class No:* 628.1(035)

[5181]
MILLER, E.W. *and* MILLER, R.M. **Water quality and availability:** a reference handbook. Santa Barbara, Ca., ABC-Clio, 1992. 430p. graphs, maps. $39.50. (*Contemporary world issues.*) ISBN: 087436647x.
6 parts: 1. History of water use and contamination - 2. Chronology of water use - 3. Laws and regulations - 4. National and international water organizations - 5. Annotated bibliography - 6. Annotated mediagraphy. Glossary; index (mostly authors and titles listed in the bibliography). Emphasis is on the US water supply and its preservation. *Class No:* 628.1(035)

Dictionaries

Polyglot

[5182]
JOVULOT, W. **Lexique trilingue de l'eau.** Paris, Johenet, 1989. 230p.
Terms in French, English, German. *Class No:* 628.1(038)=00

[5183]
MEINCK, F. *and* MÖHLE, H. **Dictionary of water and sewage engineering;** in German, English, French and Italian. 3rd ed. Munich, R. Oldenburg, 1993. 937p. £82.20. ISBN: 3486853546.
About 18,000 German-base terms, with English, French and Italian equivalents and indexes. Genders are stated. Appended weights and measures tables. *Class No:* 628.1(038)=00

[5184]
RÅDET FOR TEKNISK TERMINOLOGI. **Andbok for vann og avlop.** [Dictionary of water and waste water.] [Oslo], Universitetsforlaget, 1973. 274p. (*RTT 38.*)
About 2,500 Norwegian-base terms and definitions, with English, French and German equivalents and indexes.
Class No: 628.1(038)=00

[5185]
—TEKNISKA NOMENKLATURCENTRALEN. **Va-teknisk ord lista.** [Glossary of water supply and sewerage.] Stockholm, the Centre, 1977. 236p. diagrs. (*TNC 65.*)
A revision of TNC 51 (1973).
Lists 791 Swedish-base terms, with equivalents in Danish, English, Finnish and French, plus indexes in the five languages.
Class No: 628.1(038)=00

[5186]
VAN DER TUIN, J.D. **Elsevier's dictionary of water and hydraulic engineering,** in five languages: English, French, Spanish, Dutch, German. Amsterdam, etc. Elsevier, 1987. xiv, [2], 449p. £141. ISBN: 0444427686.
5,117 English-base terms, with French, Spanish, Dutch and German equivalents and indexes. Coverage: Water, hydraulic engineering, water management, experimental aspects. *Class No:* 628.1(038)=00

[5187]
—AMMON, F. von. **Wörterbuch der Wasserchemie.** [Dictionary of water chemistry. Dictionnaire de la chimie de l'eau.] Deerfield Beach, Florida, VCH Verlagsgesellschaft, 1985. 203p. $58. ISBN: 0895734966.
A German-English-French dictionary, promoted by the German Chemical Society's Water Chemistry Section. Main coverage: Water composition and quality, water purification, and all aspects of water chemistry. US terms are cross-referenced to British.
Class No: 628.1(038)=00

English

[5188]
NELSON, A. *and* NELSON, K.D. **Dictionary of water and water engineering.** London, Butterworths, 1973. vi, 271p. illus. £17.50. ISBN: 0408000902.
About 3,000 brief definitions, with many cross-references. 'Levee': *c.*100 words. Includes terms in hydraulics, hydrology, hydrogeology and meteorology. Appendix: Organizations, p.267-71. Both SI and imperial units are used. *Class No:* 628.1(038)=20

[5189]
SCOTT, J.S. *and* SMITH, P.G. **Dictionary of waste and water treatment.** London, etc., Butterworths, 1981. vi, 359p. illus. ISBN: 0408004959.
About 2,500 terms, with definitions ranging from 1 line to *c.*½p. Appendix lists conversion factors and maximum contaminants in drinking water by various authorities. *Class No:* 628.1(038)=20

French

[5190]
Dictionnaire de l'eau. Quebec, Assocation québécoise des techniques de l'eau, Office de la langue francaise, 1981. xxiv, 544p. tables. (*Cahiers de l'office de la langue francaise.*) ISBN: 2551042291.
3,694 numbered French terms, with English equivalents and French explanations. Index of English terms, p. 471-534. Appendix of weights and measures. *Class No:* 628.1(038)=40

Reviews & Abstracts

[5191]
Aqualine abstracts. Swindon, WRc plc, 1927-. Monthly. £600 pa. ISSN: 02635534.
Formerly *WRC information* (1974-84), incorporating *Water pollution abstracts*, 1949-73.
About 6,000 abstracts pa. 8 sections: 1. Water resources and supplies - 2. Water quality - 3. Monitoring and analysis of water and wastes - 4. Water treatment - 5. Underground services and water use - 6. Sewage - 7. Industrial effluents - 8. Effects of pollution (sewage; heated discharges; metals; pesticides; fossil fuels; radio-activity). Annual author, subject and KWOC indexes.
Available online via Questel/ORBIT and ESA-IRS and on CD-ROM. *Class No:* 628.1(048)

Yearbooks & Directories

[5192]
INTERNATIONAL WATER SUPPLY ASSOCIATION. **IWSA yearbook** 1998. London, IWSA/AISE, 1998. xviii, 396p. £43.
Provides data on the committee work of the IWSA and lists members of the national committees by country. *Class No:* 628.1(058)

[5193]
Water and wastes. Stirling, Environmental Data Research Ltd, 1996. 312p. illus., tables.
A directory of products, technologies and services for those involved in the design and implementation of water and wastes-related projects. Includes information required for the measurement, monitoring, treatment, disposal and reuse of water, effluents, solid and gaseous wastes. *Class No:* 628.1(058)

[5194]
The Water directory 1998. London, Telford, 1998. 150p. £55. ISBN: 0870308068.
Sections cover materials, products and services, contracting and consulting engineers, trade names and company data, and plant and equipment. Water reference section includes UK water holding companies and authorities, government organizations and forthcoming events. *Class No:* 628.1(058)

[5195]
Who's who in the water industry, 1998. Rickmansworth, Herts., Turret Group, Plc., for the Water Services Association. 199p. maps.
Contents: 1. Water service companies - 2. Water supply companies - 3. UK water industry - 4. Regulators - 5. Water organizations - 6. Other related organizations - 7. International water interests - 8. European trade associations - 9. Biographies - 10. Suppliers A-Z - 11. Buyers' guide *Class No:* 628.1(058)

Tables & Data Books

[5196]
ASH, M. *and* ASH, I., *comps.* **Handbook of water treatment chemicals:** an international guide to more than 3,400 products by trade name, chemical, function, and manufacturer. Aldershot, Gower, 1996. xvii, 642p. ISBN: 0566078015.
Data for entries include chemical description, uses, properties, toxicology, precautions, storage, regulations, hazardous decomposition products. Brief glossary. *Class No:* 628.1(083)

[5197]
PARKER, D.J. **Water.** (Review of the United Kingdom statistical sources. Review no. 30). Oxford, Pergamon Press, for the Royal Statistical Society and Science Research Council. p. 107-226.

7 sections: 1. Introduction - 2. Data sources - 4. Water supply statistics - 4. Water pollution and related statistics - 5. Water recreation and amenity statistics - 6. Flood allevation - 7. Evaluation. Quick-reference list, p.183-201; bibliography (49 references), p.203-4. Appendices. Subject index (non-analytical), p.223-6.
Class No: 628.1(083)

Histories

[5198]
ROBINS, F.W. **The Story of water supply.** London, Oxford Univ. Press, 1946. 207p. illus. (incl pl.).

A survey, in non-technical language, of the means employed by peoples in many parts of the world, to obtain supplies of water for drinking, irrigation and sanitation. 45 illus. (including plates). Index to subjects and plates; topographical index. Footnotes and text references.
Class No: 628.1(091)

Thesauri

[5199]
Aqualine thesaurus 2. Smith, J.G. *and* Jennings, P.G., *comps.* 2nd ed. Chichester, Ellis Horwood Ltd., for the Water Research Centre, 1987. 994p. . £75. ISBN: 085312938x.

First published 1980.

43,000 index terms (13,000 preferred; 30,000 non-preferred) for searching both the WRC AQUALINE database and *Aqualine abstracts.* In three parts: general subject terms; trade names; taxonomic names. Intended for librarians/information officers and subject specialist end users; probably essential for efficient searching of the database.
Class No: 628.1:025.43

Treatment

[5200]
LORCH, W., *ed.* **Handbook of water purification.** 2nd ed. Chichester, E. Horwood, 1987. 777p. illus., diagrs., tables. ISBN: 0853129916.
First published 1981.

19 editors and contributors. 3 parts (22 documented chapters): 1. Background to water purification - 2. Purification processes (membrane; distillation; disinfection) - 3. Purified water practice. Chapter 18: 'Sterile and apyrogenic water', p.640-92; 124 references. Detailed index, p.773-7. *Class No:* 628.16

[5201]
Water treatment handbook. 5th English ed., translated from French, by Language Consultants. New York, Halsted: Wiley, 1979. xxx, 1,186p. ISBN: 0470267106.

Previously published in Paris (Degrémont), 1973. First French ed., 1950.

Sections: 1. General aspects of water and water treatment - 2. Treatment plant and processes - 3. Treatment methods according to the nature and final use of the water - 4. General information - 5. Formulae - Legislation (including 'Useful addresses': France; other countries). Bibliographic data: p. 1,151-58. Index. Well designed.
Class No: 628.16

Pollution

[5202]
INSTITUTE OF WATER POLLUTION CONTROL. **Glossary of terms used in water pollution control.** Maidstone, Kent, the Institute, 1975. 153p.

Nearly 2,000 terms defined, p.9-150. Appended list of acronyms, p.151-2. Publications consulted, p.6. One of a series of manuals on British practice in water pollution control published by the Institute.
Class No: 628.19

[5203]
[Water pollution]: literature review. *In Journal of Water Pollution Control Federation*, v.56(6), June 1984, p.491-806.

Literature review of water pollution in the US. Sections (each with several papers, plus references and tables, highlighting various aspects): administration; chemical analysis of water and wastewater; wastewater treatment; industrial wastes; fate and effects of pollutants.
Class No: 628.19

Sewerage

[5204]
Handbook of UK wastewater practice glossary. 2nd ed. London, The Institution of Water and Environmental Management, 1993. [iv], 119p. ISBN: 1870752139.

First published 1975.

About 1,200 terms briefly defined and explained. Intended as a companion volume to the series *Handbooks of UK wastewater practice.* Includes entries for manufacturing processes.
Class No: 628.2/.3

[5205]
METCALF & EDDY, Inc. **Wastewater engineering:** treatment, disposal, refuse. New Delhi, Tata; McGraw-Hill 1979. xviii, 929p. illus., diagrs., tables.

14 sections (*e.g.* 1. Wastewater engineering: an overview; 5. Fundamentals of process analysis; 10. Design of facilities for the biological treatment of wastewater; 13. Land-treatment systems; 14. Effluent disposal and reuse). Discussion topics and problems. References (21). Appended conversion tables, etc. Name and analytical indexes. *Class No:* 628.2/.3

[5206]
STANBRIDGE, H.H. **History of sewage treatment in Britain.** Maidstone, Kent, Institute of Water Pollution Control, 1976-77. 3v. (16 pts). illus., diagrs.

pts. 1-5: *Introduction of the water-carriage system.* 1976.
pt. 6: *Biological filtration.* 1976.
pts. 7-16: *Activated sludge process.*1977.

A well-documented, mimeographed survey. Part 12, 'Utilization and disposal of sewage sludge' (86p.) has 186 references, 11 illus. Part indexes. *Class No:* 628.2/.3

Marine Pollution

[5207]
CHAMP, M.A. *and* PARK, P.K. **Global marine pollution bibliography:** ocean dumping of municipal and industrial wastes. New York, etc. IFI/Plenum, 1982. xiv, 399p. $69.50. ISBN: 0306652056.

Lists 1,742 entries, some with abstracts, most dating from the 1970s. Arranged A-Z by author, with a broad subject index (*e.g.* c.270 undifferentiated items under 'municipal wastes - sewage sludge') and an author index. Topics covered include municipal and industrial wastes, legislation, international conventions, ocean dumping criteria, dump sites, waste management strategies. A new edition 'in three years' indicated in the *Preface* appears not to have been published.
Class No: 628.394

[5208]
Marine pollution research titles. Plymouth, Marine Pollution Information Centre, Marine Biological Association of the United Kingdom, 1974-. Monthly. £105; $224 pa. ISSN: 02048051.

About 5,000 abstracts pa. on marine and estuarine pollution. 8 sections: 1. General - 2. Petroleum hydrocarbons - 3. Metals - 4. Radioactivity - 5. Other chemicals - 6. Biological wastes - 7. Heat - 8. Solids. No indexes. A current awareness service. *Class No:* 628.394

[5209]
Wastes in the ocean. New York Wiley, 1983. 6v.

1. *Industrial and sewage wastes in the ocean;* edited by I.W. Duedall and others. 1983. xviii, 431p.

2. *Dredged material disposal in the ocean;* edited by K.P. Parr and others. 1983. xxii, 522p.

3. *Radioactive wastes in the ocean;* edited by K.P. Parr. 1983. xxii, 522p.

4. *Energy wastes in the ocean;* edited by I.W. Duedall. 1985. 818p.

5. *Deep-sea waste disposal,* edited by by D.H. Kester. 1985. 346p.

6. *Near-shore waste disposal,* edited by B.H. Ketchum and others. 1985. 534p. *Class No:* 628.394

Waste Disposal

Bibliographies

[5210]
MASLIN, D. **'Wastes management'.** *Information sources in environmental protection.* S Eagle and J. Deschamps, eds. (1997), p.107-119. London, Bowker-Saur, 1997. £58. ISBN: 1857390628.

Covers directories, updating services and year books, dictionaries, monographs and reports, serials, conference procedings, official publications and statistics, databases and information services, and organizations. 68 references, some (irritatingly) incorrectly numbered.
Class No: 628.4(01)

[5211]
Waste and environment today: bibliographic journal. Abingdon, Oxon., AEA Technology, 1992-. 12pa. £216pa. ISSN: 09654496.

Formerly *Waste Management today,* 1988-91.

Covers disposal, recycling/recovery, environmental hazards, legislative and policy aspects, business opportunities, etc. About 200 entries per issue in 9 broad areas (*e.g.* waste recycling and recovery; environmental hazards, etc.). Non-analytical subject index per issue.

Available on CD-ROM as *WasteInfo* (SilverPlatter).
Class No: 628.4(01)

Handbooks & Manuals

[5212]
Biotechnology of waste treatment and exploitation. Sidwick, J.M. *and* Holdon, R.S., *eds*. Chichester, Ellis Horwood, New York, Halsted Press, 1987. 332p. diagrs., graphs, tables. £55. ISBN: 0853129177, UK; 0470210311, US.

18 contributors. 13 chapters, closely subdivided and extensively documented (*e.g.* chapter 3, 'Immobilized whole-cell biocatalysts', p.32-80, includes 248 references). Detailed, analytical index, p.326-32. *Class No:* 628.4(035)

[5213]
CRC handbook of incineration of hazardous wastes. Rickman, W.S., *ed*. Boca Raton, Fl., 1991. [viii],593p. illus., diagrs., tables. £176. ISBN: 0849305578.

Covers incinerator technology, regulatory requirements, siting issues and includes case histories. 19 contributors; 9 chapters, some extensively documented (*e.g.* 'Regulatory requirements and the permitting process': 116p.; 344 references). Index, 16p.
Class No: 628.4(035)

[5214]
Croner's hazardous waste disposal guide. Kingston upon Thames, Surrey, Croner Publications, 1988. [viii],368p. £30. ISBN: 0900319623. ISSN: 09542922.

Information for the United Kingdon in 3 parts: 1. Commentary (legal aspects; waste management; disposal contractors, etc.) - 2. Disposal information (charts; index) - 3. Directory.
Class No: 628.4(035)

[5215]
Croner's waste management. London, Croner, 1991-. v.p. looseleaf. ISBN: 185524117x.

The purpose of the work is to provide a 'first point of reference for all those responsible for dealing with waste' (*Preface*). 5 parts: 1. Legal aspects of waste management - 2. Practical waste management - 3. Waste Charts - 4. Directory - 5. Further information and index (*e.g.* statutes; standards, etc.). Updated regularly by amendment sheets.
Class No: 628.4(035)

[5216]
Environmental science and technology handbook. Ayers, K.W., *and others, eds*. Washington, D.C., Government Institutes, 1994. 389p. $75. ISBN: 0865873623.

Emphasis is on the control, stoarage, treatment and disposal of contaminants in air, water and soil. 11 chapters, by various hands, most with extensive list of recent references. 'An excellent introductory reference source' (*Choice,* May 1994, p.1456).
Class No: 628.4(035)

[5217]
Hazardous waste management. LaGrega, M., *and others, eds*. New York, etc. McGraw-Hill, 1994. 1025p. illus., diagrs., maps, tables. $46.95; £27.99. ISBN: 0070195536.

In 4 parts: Fundamentals - Current management practices - Treatment and disposal methods - Site remediation. Topics covered include the regulatory process; toxicology; transport; environmental audits; physico-chemical processes; biological methods; quantitative risk assessment; containment; land disposal, etc. Detailed, analytical index. *Class No:* 628.4(035)

Glossaries

[5218]
ISAAC, P.C.G. A Glossary of sanitation engineering terms. Newcastle-upon-Tyne, University of Durham, 1955. iv. 72p. tables. (*Univ. of Durham, King's College, Dept. of Civil Engineering. Bulletin no. 4.*)

Concise definiton of *c.*3,000 terms. Appendix on hardness factors; also conversion tables and abbreviations. *Class No:* 628.4(038.1)

[5219]
—BRITISH STANDARDS INSTITUTION. Glossary of building and civil engineering terms. Part 2. Civil engineering. Section 2.7 Public health. Environmental engineering. London, BSI, 1992. 26p. (*BS 6100: Section 2.7:1992(1998).*)

Supercedes BS 6100: Section 2.7:1988.

Defines 289 terms in systematic order, Solid waste ... Disposal ... Processing ... Pollution and odour. Alphabetical index.
Class No: 628.4(038.1)

Yearbooks & Directories

[5220]
Waste, recycling and environmental directory: 1993. London, Thomas Telford, 1992. 536p. ISBN: 0727718452. ISSN: 09678905.

68 sections in 3 parts: Waste disposal - Recycling - Environmental management. UK company information includes name, address, phone, fax, services, branches. Indexes: trade names; company and personnel; subject; advertisers. *Class No:* 628.4(058)

[5221]
Water and wastes. Stirling, Environmental Data Research Ltd, 1996. 312p. illus., tables.

A directory of products, technologies and services for those involved in the design and implementation of water and wastes-related projects. Includes information required for the measurement, monitoring, treatment, disposal and reuse of water, effluents, solid and gaseous wastes. *Class No:* 628.4(058)

Radioactive Waste

[5222]
CROMER, D.E. *and* **THOMAS, D.R.** 'Radioactive waste management and disposal information sources'. *Science and technology libraries,* v.11(3), Spring 1991, p.119-38.

15 sections, including 'Statistical information', 'Encyclopedias', 'Conference proceedings', 'Journals', 'Technical reports', 'Indexes (online and printed)', 'Social and political perspectives'. 6 references.
Class No: 628.4.047

[5223]
LAMBERT, C.M., *comp*. **Radioactive waste:** a select list of material. London, Departments of the Environment and Transport, 1982. 61p. £1.90. (*Bibliography series, no.190E.*) ISBN: 0718402057.

230 items, published since 1978, frequently with indicative or informative abstracts, arranged in 7 sections: 1. Official publications - 2. Administrative and environmental - 3. Technological and scientific - 4. General and background material ... Plus sections for series; annual reports and surveys; further sources of information (bibliographies, abstracting and indexing journals, periodicals). Excludes press and Parliamentary coverage and DOE-sponsored research reports.
Class No: 628.4.047

[5224]
MILLER, E.W. *and* **MILLER, R.M. Environmental hazards: radioactive materials and wastes:** a reference handbook. Santa Barbara, Calif., ABC-Clio, 1990. 298p. $39. ISBN: 0874362342.

Various chapters with a range of information (*e.g.* nature and characteristics of radioactive materials; directory of organizations that deal with waste; annotated bibliography of books; listing of journal articles and government documents; select list of journal titles; bibliography of a-v materials). Glossary; index. 'An excellent addition to any reference collection' (*Choice,* April 1991, p.1292).
Class No: 628.4.047

[5225]
Waste management research abstracts: information on radioactive waste programmes in progress. Vienna, International Atomic Energy Agency, 1970-. Annual. *Gratis,* on request.

Consists of research data sheets sent by governments of member states. 6 sections: 1. Studies related to the treatment of radioactive wastes and effluent - 2. Studies concerning the storage and disposal of radioactive wastes ... 4. Safety and environment studies ... 6. Miscellaneous. Alphabetical descriptor index; author index.
Class No: 628.4.047

Environmental Pollution Measures

Databases

[5226]
LUEDTKE, J.R. 'Energy and the environment'. *Manual of online search strategies.* Editors, C.J. Armstrong and J.A. Large, pp.236-87. 2nd ed. Aldershot, Ashgate, 1992. ISBN: 1857420071.

Extensive list of databases, both online and CD-ROM, which cover energy and the environment. Hosts and disc suppliers identifed.
Class No: 628.5(003.4)

Encyclopaedias
[5227]
FRANCK, I. **The Green encyclopedia.** Brownstone, D. Englewood Cliffs, N.J., Prentice Hall, 1992. 512p. illus. $20. ISBN: 0133656853.

Over 1,000 concise entries on environmental matters. Includes data on environmentalists, pesticides, national parks, etc. Many cross-references and illustrations. Lists of relevant organizations and their publications, endangered species, toxic chemicals, etc. For public and school libraries. *Class No:* 628.5(031)

Handbooks & Manuals
[5228]
BENARDE, M.A. **Global warning ... global warming.** New York, Wiley, 1992. [xiii],317p. illus., graphs, maps. $29.95. ISBN: 0471519237.

5 parts (1. Reasons for seasons ... 5. Approaches to energy information), well-documented. Helpful introduction, p.1-13, with 11 references. Glossary; appendix; index. *Class No:* 628.5(035)

[5229]
Industrial pollution prevention handbook. Freeman, H.M., *ed.* New York, McGraw-Hill, 1995. 935p. illus., diagrs., tables. $94.50. ISBN: 0070221480.

78 contributors. 53 chapters (1. Ounce of prevention ... 53. Information sources) covering processes and technologies from design to implementation. Numerous case studies of specific industries. Distinguishes legal requirements and voluntary programmes. Detailed, analytical index. 'This essential guide' (*Choice*, Febraury 1996, p.979). *Class No:* 628.5(035)

[5230]
KIMBALL, D. **Recycling in America:** a reference handbook. 2nd ed. Santa Barbara, Ca. ABC-Clio, 1997. 330p. $39.50. ISBN: 0874368898.

First published 1992.

A broad, non-technical treatment covering history and chhronology, biography and facts and figures for a range of materials (e.g. glass, paper, aluminium, plastic, etc.). Brief glossary; bibliography. Very little change from the 1st ed., according to the review in *Choice* (July/August 1998, p.1834). *Class No:* 628.5(035)

[5231]
The McGraw-Hill recycling handbook. Lund, H.F., *ed.* New York, McGraw-Hill, 1993. v.p. illus., diagrs., graphs, tables. $84.50; £74. ISBN: 0070390967.

35 chapters by specialists on types of recyclable materials, processing, training, quality control monitoring, case histories, etc. Appendices list US organizations, data tables, glossary. Detailed, analytical index. A practical treatment for professionals. 'A valuable addition to the ... literature' ('Reference books bulletin', *Booklist*, April 1, 1993, p.1457). 'Still the most thorough and informative reference in the field' (*Choice*, July/August 1998. p.1834). *Class No:* 628.5(035)

[5232]
NATIONAL SOCIETY FOR CLEAN AIR. NSCA reference book. Dunmore, J., *ed.* Brighton, Sussex, the Society, 1985. viii, 294p. ISBN: 090347428x.

First published 1978.

4 sections: 1. Air pollution - 2. Noise - 3. Water pollution - 4. Wastes. Each section features an outline of the law; British Standards are appended. Annex 1: Community environmental measures. References, p.27-84. Detailed analytical index (in small type), p.285-90. *Class No:* 628.5(035)

Dictionaries
[5233]
JOHNSON, C. **Green dictionary.** London, Optima, 1991. 320p. £9.99. ISBN: 0356195688.

Simple explanations of over 400 terms, issues and ideas connected with the environmental debate. *Class No:* 628.5(038)

[5234]
JONES, G., *and others.* **Collins dictionary of environmental science.** Glasgow, Harper Collins, 1990. vi,473p. illus., graphs, maps, tables. £6.99. ISBN: 0004343484.

Published in the US as *The Harper Collins dictionary of environmental science* (New York, Harper Perennial, 1992. 453p. ISBN: 006271533x ($25); ISBN: 0064610403 ($13)).

Over 1800 terms, briefly defined (*e.g.* 'epeirogenesis': 9 lines). Covers topics from the biological, physical and social sciences. Cross-references. *Class No:* 628.5(038)

[5235]
KING, J.J., *comp.* **The Environmental dictionary: and regulatory cross-reference.** 3rd ed. New York, Wiley, 1995. xviii, 1295p. £90. ISBN: 0471119954.

A specialized dictionary with definitions taken from the *Code of Federal Regulations, Title 40, Protection of the Environment* (1987) and the *Federal Register* (updates to June 1994). Summary of *Title 40*, p.729-1216. *Class No:* 628.5(038)

[5236]
NATIONAL SOCIETY FOR CLEAN AIR. NSCA environmental glossary. Dunmore, J., *ed.* Brighton, the Society, 1985. 89p. ISBN: 0903474298.

About 1,000 terms, concisely defined. Sections: Air pollution terms; Noise terms; Waste terms; Radiation terms. 'Additional references', p.89. Covers vocabulary of technical articles and lectures. *Class No:* 628.5(038)

Reviews & Abstracts
[5237]
Pollution abstracts. Bethesda, Md., Cambridge Scientific Abstracts, 1970-. Monthly. $435. ISSN: 00323624.

About 12,000 abstracts pa.; 1,500 abstracts per issue. Sections: Air pollution - Marine pollution - Freshwater pollution - Sewage and wastewater treatment - Waste management - Land pollution - Toxicology and health - Noise - Radiation - Environmental action. Analytical subject and author indexes per issue, cumulated annually. Available online via DIALOG, file 41, and other major hosts; About 200,000 records, updated monthly. Also available on the World Wide Web; URL: http://www.csa.com. *Class No:* 628.5(048)

Progress Reports
[5238]
Global warming: the Greenpeace report. Leggatt, J., *ed.* Oxford Univ. Press, 1990. xi,554p.

19 Sections: 1-4: Science - 5-7: Impacts - 8-19: Policy responses. 20 contributors. Notes and chapter references, p.481-544. Detailed, non-analytical index. *Class No:* 628.5(055)

Yearbooks & Directories
[5239]
The Environment encyclopedia and directory. 2nd ed. London, Europa Publications, 1998. xvi, 560p. maps. £210. ISBN: 185743028x.

First published 1994.

Almost 1,000 brief non-technical definitions are followed by a directory of *c.*4,000 environmental organizations, by country, A-Z. Bibliography of over 1,000 journals, and short biographical details of almost 700 environmentalists. Other sections include lists of abbreviations and maps showing environmental issues. Brings together in one volume a lot of useful information, but libraries will be able to purchase several texts cumulating the same information for a fraction of the price. *Class No:* 628.5(058)

Tables & Data Books
[5240]
Statistical record of the environment. Darney, A.J., *ed.* 3rd ed. Detroit, Mi., Gale, 1995. 1118. graphs, tables, maps. £84. ISBN: 0810364328.

About 900 statistical tables in sections, closely subdivided. Includes data gathered between 1987 and 1994, largely from US government sources. Appendices include list of sources, abbreviations and acronyms. Keyword index. *Class No:* 628.5(083)

Worldwide
[5241]
World guide to environmental issues and organizations. Harlow, Essex, Longman, 1990. xxviii,386p. ISBN: 0582002705.

21 contributors. 4 parts: 1. Issues (*e.g.* nuclear power and the environment; vehicle emissions) - 2. Politics - 3. Conventions, reports, directives and agencies - 4. Organizations. Further reading and references, p.357-65. Detailed, analytical index, p.366-86. *Class No:* 628.5(100)

Industrial Pollution
[5242]
Acid rain abstracts annual. New York, Bowker A & I Publishing, 1989-. $149.

Focuses on the sources, causes and effects of acid deposition, and the economic, political, health and natural resource issues. Now published as part of *Environment abstracts*. Available online and on CD-ROM. *Class No:* 628.51

[5243]

Acid rain and the environment 1988-1991: a select bibliography. Grayson, L., *Comp*. London, British Library Science Reference and Information Service; Letchworth, Technical Communications, 1991. iv,217p. ISBN: 0946655421.

Acid rain and the environment 1980-84: a select bibliography. P. Farmer, ed.

Acid rain on the environment 1984-88: a select bibliography. L. Grayson, ed.

Over 900 entries in 6 sections: 1. The issue - 2. The causes - 3. Research - 4. Surveys - 5. The effects - 6. Mitigation strategies. Descriptive annotations. Indexes: authors and editors; corporate bodies. *Class No:* 628.51

[5244]

Air pollution. Stern, A.C. 3rd ed. New York, Academic Press, 1976-77. 5v. (*Environmental sciences*.)

V. 1. *Air pollutants, their transformation and transport.*

V. 2. *The effects of air pollution.*

V. 3. *Measuring, monitoring, and surveillance of air pollution.*

V. 4. *Air quality management.*

V. 4 (xxii,946p.) is the work of 29 contributors. 21 chapters, with references, in 3 parts: A. Control concepts - B. Control devices - C. Process emissions and their control. Detailed, analytical index, p.931-46.

3 supplementary volumes were published, 1986-88. *Class No:* 628.51

[5245]

Air pollution control handbook. Alley, E.R., *and others, eds*. New York, etc., McGraw-Hill, 1998. 1008p. illus., diagrs., graphs, tables. £82.99 ISBN: 0070014116.

Covers the available technologies for air pollution control, testing and regulations. Contents: Introduction - Definitions - Setting air pollution control policy ... Management programme ... Training and communication ... Federal regulations and pollution control ... Atmospheric diffusion models ... Emission identification. US emphasis. *Class No:* 628.51

[5246]

STOPP, G.H., Jr. **Acid rain:** a bibliography of research, annotated for easy access. Metuchen, N.J., Scarecrow, 1985. xiv, 174p. ISBN: 0810818221.

886 annotated entries, under authors A-Z. Items - books, periodical articles, conference proceedings and reports - are all in English. Annotations indicate technical level of item. US and Canadian references predominate. The partly analytical index is 'seriously flawed', states *Reference books bulletin 1985-1986*, p. 22. *Class No:* 628.51

Noise Abatement

Bibliographies

[5247]

BRAGDON, C.R. Noise pollution: a guide to information sources. Detroit, Mich., Gale, 1979. xvi, 524p. ISBN: 0810313456.

Annotated entries for more than 4,000 periodicals, reports, books, etc. 9 chapters: 1. Physiological effects - 2. Behavioral effects - 3/4. Abatement - 5. Community noise - 6. Environmental impact - 7. Acoustics - 8. Noise legislation - 9. References (primary periodicals; secondary periodicals; Indexes). Addendum p.443-66. Author, title, and subject indexes. US slanted. *Class No:* 628.517(01)

[5248]

FLINDELL, I. 'Noise as a pollutant'. *Information sources in environmental protection*. Eds., S. Eagle and J. Deschamps, p.121-29. London, Bowker-Saur, 1997. £58. ISBN: 1857390628.

Covers instrumentation and loudspeakers, engineering and architectural acoustics, transportation noise, standards and regulations, and sources of practical advice (*e.g.* the public library and the local authority environmental health officer). No references. *Class No:* 628.517(01)

[5249]

VULKAN, G. *and* **GOMERSALL, A. Traffic noise:** a review and bibliography on surface transportation noise. Kempston, Beds., I.F.S. Publications Ltd., 1979. [216]p. ISBN: 0903608103.

1,561 annotated entries for the period 1964-78. Sections A-L (*e.g.* A. General information on surface transportation noise - B. Traffic noise and its abatement - C. Railway noise and its abatement - D. Vehicle design for noise reduction G. Social and economic impact of traffic noise ... J. Legislation regulations and general standards for surface transportation noise control - K. Literature reviews and bibliographies on surface transportation noise - L. Reports). Bibliographic sources. Author index. *Class No:* 628.517(01)

Handbooks & Manuals

[5250]

Handbook of noise and vibration control. Barber, A., *ed*. 6th ed. Oxford, Elsevier, 1992. viii, 479p. illus., charts, tables. £95. ISBN: 1856170799.

5th ed., 1983.

'The sixth edition ... has been completely revised' (*Preface*). 10 sections covering basic accoustics; hearing conservation, protection, health and safety; vibration; types of noise (fan, factory, aircraft, etc.); sound insulation and absorption. 2 indexes: editorial; advertisers. Fewer advertisements than previous editions. *Class No:* 628.517(035)

[5251]

NELSON, P.M., *ed*. **Transportation noise reference book.** London, Butterworths, 1987. [492]p. illus., diagrs., graphs, tables. £90. ISBN: 0408014466.

27 contributions. Main parts (24 documented sections): Introduction and physical assessment - The effects of transportation noise on man - Train noise - Aircraft noise - Decision making methods for transport noise control. 4 appendices (3. standards relating to traffic noise and its control; 4. list of addresses). Index. 405 illus., including 20 halftones. 'Highly recommended' (*Choice,* March 1988, p.1126). *Class No:* 628.517(035)

[5252]

SÁENZ, A.L. *and* **STEPHENS, R.W.B.,** *eds*. **Noise pollution:** effects and controls. New York, etc., Wiley, published on behalf of the Scientific Committee on Problems of the Environment (SCOPE) of the International Council of Scientific Unions (ICSU), 1986. xix, 446p. illus., graphs, tables, formulas. (*SCOPE 24*.) ISBN: 0471903256.

3 parts (18 documented chapters): 1. Fundamentals of noise and hearing - 2. Effects of noise on man - 3. Sources of noise and control. (Chapter 10: 'Noise pollution during the night', p. 265-82, including 3½ p. of references.) Author index. Detailed, analytical subject index. *Class No:* 628.517(035)

Reviews & Abstracts

[5253]

NVI/Noise and vibration in industry: an international quarterly digest. Brentwood, Essex, Multi-Science Publishing, 1986-. 4pa. £78. ISSN: 09508163.

About 50 fairly lengthy abstracts per issue. 8 sections (Measuring and recording instrumentation and analysis ... Audiology and audio - Standards, legislation and regulations - Contested cases). No index. Current awareness bulletin for factory managers, occupational health and safety officers, etc. *Class No:* 628.517(048)

Periodicals

[5254]

NVB (Noise & vibration bulletin). Brentwood, Essex, Multi-Science Publishing, 1970-. Monthly. ISSN: 00290041.

Issues include about 20 'abridgements', plus 'News and comment'. Coverage: industrial; aircraft; road and other transport; general; meetings; products and information. Each issue carries a review article. *Class No:* 628.517(051)

Tables & Data Books

[5255]

Handbook of acoustical measurements and noise control. Harris, C.A., *ed*. 3rd ed. New York, McGraw-Hill, 1991. v.p. illus., diagrs., graphs, tables. $89.50. ISBN: 0070268681.

First published 1957 as *Handbook of noise control*.

6 chapters by experts. Extensive technical information presented in graphs, charts and tables. Detailed, analytical index, 34p. *Class No:* 628.517(083)

Industrial Effluents & Wastes

[5256]

KENWORTHY, L. *and* **SCHAEFFER, E. A Citizens guide to promoting toxic waste reduction.** New York, INFORM, 1990. 122p. $15. ISBN: 0918780543.

Aimed at environmental groups, not individuals, seeking to develop strategies to reduce waste from industrial plants. Based heavily on *Toxics Release Inventory* produced by the US Environmental Protection Agency. Appendices include state government contacts, health effects, right-to-know entitlements, glossary. An obvious US slant, should be of value to similar groups in other countries. *Class No:* 628.54

[5257]
PATRICK, P.K., *comp*. **Glossary of solid waste.** Copenhagen, World Health Organization, Regional Office for Europe, 1980. v, 92p. £4.80. ISBN: 9290201991.

About 700 definitions ('Incinerator: 2/3p). Cross-references. Interdisciplinary. For use professionally or otherwise. *Class No:* 628.54

[5258]
ROBINSON, W.D., *ed*. **The Solid waste handbook:** a practical guide. New York, Chichester, etc., Wiley, 1986. xxvii, 811p., illus., diagrs., maps, tables. £89. ISBN: 0471877115.

Concerned with solid waste management rather than engineering design. The emphasis is on public issues, legislation, regulation, finance, economics, waste recovery, and on the situation in the US. 21 chapters in 3 parts: 1. Public issues - 2. Implementation issues: systems, hardware, operations - 3. Hazardous solid wastes. 42 contributors. Index. Intended for use at all levels of government, national to local. *Class No:* 628.54

Lighting Engineering

Bibliographies

[5259]
BARNETT, D.A. **The Literature of lighting:** an annotated bibliography of the literature of illuminating engineering up to 1965. University Microfilms Ltd., 1968. 173p.

Thesis accepted for Fellowship of the Library Association.

A selective listing, mainly for 1945-1965. Covers periodical titles, but not periodical articles. Historical introduction, followed by 10 sections: 1. Abstracts and indexing services ... 3. Handbooks and sources of data - 4. Books (68p.; *c*.150 titles) ... 6. Conferences, preprints of papers ... 8. Standards, codes of practice, government publications, and patents - 9. Education and research in illuminating engineering; theses - 10. Historical supplement: books published before 1945. Index of authors and titles. *Class No:* 628.9(01)

Handbooks & Manuals

[5260]
CAYLESS, M.A. *and* MARSDEN, A.M., *ed*. **Lamps and lighting:** a manual of lamps and lighting prepared by members of staff of Thorn EMI lighting, Ltd. 3rd ed. London, E. Arnold, 1983. 522p. ISBN: 0713134879.

First published 1966.

5 parts (29 sections, each with further reading): 1. Fundamentals - 2. Lamps - 3. Luminaries and circuits - 4. Interior lighting - 5. Exterior lighting (*e.g.* roads; navigation). 2 appendices: 1. Lamp data; 2. Glossary. References (A-Z authors), p.489-99. Author and subject indexes. 'Written as a reference source for building service engineers, architects and specialists in the lighting industry, as well as others ...' (*Preface*). 'A delightfully practical book' (*Lighting research and technology* v.17(4), 1985, p.194). *Class No:* 628.9(035)

[5261]
LAWRENCE, S. **The 'Which?' book of wiring and lighting.** Rev. ed. London, Which Ltd., 1997. 159p. col. illus., diagrs., tables. ISBN: 0852026749.

First published 1993.

Sections: Problem checklist - Wiring basics - Wiring techniques - Wiring jobs - Rewiring a house. Glossary; useful addresses; index. Clearly presented material. *Class No:* 628.9(035)

[5262]
MURDOCH, J.B. **Illumination engineering** - from Edison's lamp to the laser. New York, Macmillan Publishing Co.; London, Collier Macmillan, 1985. xiv, [i], 541p. diagrs., graphs, tables. ISBN: 0029485800.

11 documented chapers, *e.g.* 2. Lighting calculations and measurements; 5. Vision and color; 6. Lamps; 7. Interior lighting design: average illuminance; 9. Daylighting; 10. Optics and control of light; 11. Exterior lighting (11 references). Problems, p.491-526, with answers to selected problems, p.527-9. Detailed, analytical index, p.533-41. 'A scientific and technical treatment of lighting, rather than an architectural and design treatment' (*Preface*). *Class No:* 628.9(035)

Dictionaries

[5263]
ZIMMERMANN, R., *comp*. **Dictionary of lighting engineering in four languages:** English, German, French, Russian. [Wörterbuch lichtechnik.] Amsterdam, etc., Elsevier, 1990. 426p. £111. ISBN: 0444988505.

Intended to replace 8-language dictionary by the same author

....(contd.)
published in 1977. Approximately 11,000 entries with equivalents. German, French and Russian indexes. Cross references. Genders given. *Class No:* 628.9(038)

Reviews & Abstracts

[5264]
Lighting research and technology. London, Chartered Institution of Building Services Engineers, 1969-. 4pa. £40. ISSN: 00243426.

Formerly *Illuminating Engineering Society Transactions*.

Includes abstracts and occasional reviews. About 150 abstracts pa. *Class No:* 628.9(048)

Histories

[5265]
BOWERS, B. **Lengthening the day:** a history of lighting technology. Oxford Univ. Press, 1998. 240p. diagrs. 24.99. ISBN: 0198565488.

Traces the evelopments in artificial light sources from the oil lamps of antiquity to present day electric lights and their effects on domestic and business life. The author is Curator of Lighting at The Science Museum, London. *Class No:* 628.9(091)

629 Transport Vehicles

Transport Vehicles

Models

[5266]

WILLIAMS, G.R. The World of model[s]. London, A. Deutsch, in association with Rainbow Reference Books, 1970-76. 4v. illus., (incl. col). ea. £9.95.
The world of model aircraft. 1973. 224p.
The world of model cars. 1976. 256p. (See entry at 629.114.6(086.48)).
The world of model ships and boats. 1971. 256p.
The world of model trains. 1970. 256p.
Each volume has 32 pages of colour plates and over 200 black-and-white illus. *Class No:* 629.0(086.48)

Carriages & Carts

[5267]

BERKEBILE, D.H. Carriage terminology: an historical dictionary. Washington, Smithsonian Institution Press, and Liberty Corp. Books, 1978. 487p. illus.
Carriage types, p.13-305; Carriage nomenclature, p.307-409; Harness nomenclature, p.411-66; William Fulton's 1796 glossary, p.467-82. Selected bibliography, p.483-7. Profusely illustrated. Well produced. *Class No:* 629.11

Motor Vehicle Engineering

Internet

[5268]

Virtual automotive information centre. Nuneaton, Warwickshire, Motor Industry Research Association, 1998-. URL: http://www.mira.co.uk.
Offers access to the association's key databases, including profiles of automotive companies, reviews of industry areas, production and registration statistics, events diary, summaries of technical articles and major industry news items. Subscription. *Class No:* 629.113(003.41)

Bibliographies

[5269]

Cumulative index of SAE Technical papers (1906-1991). Warrendale, Pa., Society of Automotive Engineers, 1992. 4v. 3722p. £271.
A set comprising the 11th ed. (1965-1991) and the historical ed. (1906-1964).
About 40,000 SAE technical papers in 1800 subject areas. Papers listed by subject and author. *Class No:* 629.113(01)

[5270]

SHIELD, M.J. *and* **ROBINSON, M.S.** 'Automotive engineering'. *Information sources in engineering.* Editor, L.J. Anthony (2nd ed., 1985), p.270-93. London, Butterworth, 1985.
Sections: Legislation - Standards - Organizational sources of information (learned societies and institutions; research institutes; cooperative organizations) - Documentary sources of information (abstracting and indexing services; directories and buyers' guides; commercial information; journals). Automotive engineering as a distinct topic was not featured in the 3rd ed. of *Information sources in engineering* (1996). *Class No:* 629.113(01)

Handbooks & Manuals

[5271]

Automotive handbook. Aldrich, U., *and others, eds.* 3rd ed. Düsseldorf, Robert Bosch, GmbH, 1993. 852p. diagrs., graphs, tables. $31.95 ISBN: 0837603307.
Previous ed. 1986. Trans. by Peter Girling and others.
By a team of contributors. 40 sections revised for this edition, with 11 new subject areas, including sensors, actuators, navigation systems and mobile telephones. International in scope and covering passenger cars and commercial vehicles. Detailed contents section and index. 'A unique reference book with few, if any, comparable sources' ('Reference books bulletin', *Booklist*, July 1994, p.1972).
Class No: 629.113(035)

[5272]

NEWTON, K. *and* **STEEDS, W. The Motor vehicle;** for students, draughtsmen and owner-drivers. 11th ed. Oxford, Butterworth-Heinemann, 1991. 888p. illus., diagrs., graphs. £35. ISBN: 0750604077.
First published 1929. 10th ed. 1983.
Sections: 1. Fundamentals - 2. The engine - 3. Transmission - 4. The carriage units. Covers both petrol and diesel engines. Carefully drawn illus. *Class No:* 629.113(035)

[5273]

WASHINO, S. Automobile electronics. New York, Gordon and Breach, 1989. xvi,127p. diagrs., graphs, tables. $49. (*Japanese technology review.*)
Valuable for the English-language coverage of Japanese research (*New technical books,* v.75(2), March/April 1990, p.501).
Class No: 629.113(035)

Dictionaries

Polyglot

[5274]

BLOK, C. *and* **JEZEWSKI, W. Illustrated automobile dictionary in six languages:** Nederlands/Ruskii/English/Français/Deutsch/Italiano. Deventer, Holland, Kluwer Technische Bocken, and Warsaw, Wydawnictwa Komunikacj i Lacznosci, 1978. 502p. illus. ISBN: 9020110705.
About 3,000 terms in each language across the page, with line-drawings facing. 8 sections: Vehicles; Drive line (US), Transmission (GB); Chassis; Body; Electrical equipment; Appendix; Service terms. Alphabetical index. *Class No:* 629.113(038)=00

[5275]

—**BLOK, C.** *and* **JEZEWSKI, W.** Six-language illustrated dictionary of the motor car: Polish/Russian/English/French/German/Italian. Warsaw, 1976. 867p. illus.
Includes *c.*7,000 Polish terms, with equivalents and indexes in other languages. *Class No:* 629.113(038)=00

[5276]

DE COSTER, J. Dictionary for automotive engineering: English-French-German. 3rd ed. Munich, K.G. Saur, 1990. 620p. £96.40 ISBN: 3598108818.
2nd ed. 1986.
About 2,000 English-base terms, with French and German definitions. Cross-references. Index of French and German terms. Brief bibliography. *Class No:* 629.113(038)=00

[5277]

KONDO, K., *comp.* **Elsevier's dictionary of automotive engineering in five languages:** English, German, French, Italian and Spanish. Amsterdam, etc., Elsevier, 1977. [vii], 639p. illus. Dfl.360. ISBN: 0444415904.
Previous ed. (1960) as *Elsevier's Automobile dictionary in eight languages* (qv). The 8 languages included Russian, Japanese and Portugese.
6,425 English-base terms, with German, French, Italian and Spanish equivalents and indexes. Illustrations, p.540-639, nos.1-91 (keyed parts, *e.g.* 26: Diesel engine, injection system: 25 parts). 'An unusual, excellent and one-of-a-kind reference book' (*Choice*, v.15(1), March 1978, p.44).
A new ed. (English, German French, Dutch, Polish) appeared in 1998. *Class No:* 629.113(038)=00

[5278]

—**STEKHOVEN, G.S.** Elsevier's automobile dictionary; in English/American (with some definitions), French, Italian, Spanish, Portuguese, German, Russian, Japanese. Amsterdam, etc., Elsevier, 1960 (2nd reprint 1983). viii, 946p. Dfl.375. ISBN: 0444405178.
Covers 5,225 terms, with equivalents and indexes. Differs from the Kondo dictionary in concentrating on the motor car, its parts and upkeep, as well as its extended language cover.
Class No: 629.113(038)=00

English

[5279]

Dictionary of automobile engineering. Teddington, Middlesex, 1996. [vi], 286p. diagrs. ISBN: 0948549661.

Based on the English text of PONS Fachwörterbuch der Kfz-Technik (englisch-deutsch), Ernst Klett Verlag, 1996.

About 7,500 words, briefly defined; some have short comments or descriptions appended. Supplement has detailed diagrams, with labels, of car parts. *Class No:* 629.113(038)=20

[5280]

GOODSELL, D. Dictionary of automotive engineering. 2nd ed. Warrendale, Pa. Society of Automotive engineers; Oxford, Butterworth-Heinemann, 1995. 280p. illus. $49; £19.99. ISBN: 1560916834, (SAE); 0750627956, (B-H).

First published 1989.

Some 3,000 technical terms, including some slang. Distinguishes US and UK terminology and usage. The 2nd ed. expands coverage of fuels and lubricants, materials, tyres, construction, off-road vehicles, testing and electronics. *Class No:* 629.113(038)=20

[5281]

SAE glossary of automotive terms. 2nd ed. Warrendale, Pa., Society of Automotive Enginers, 1992. 460p. £61. ISBN: 1560911980.

Nearly 800 terms, extracted from new and revised technical reports between 1986 and 1992. Emphasis is on materials, components and systems used in land and sea vehicles. *Class No:* 629.113(038)=20

[5282]

SOUTH, D.W. *and* **DWIGGINS, B.H. Delmar's automotive dictionary.** Albany, NY., Delmar, 1997. 281p. $22.95. ISBN: 0827374054.

Terms are briefly defined and cover automobile parts, repairs, trucking and slang words. Appendixes: decimal and metric equivalents; common abbreviations. A popular treatment. *Class No:* 629.113(038)=20

German

[5283]

BOSCH, R. Technical dictionary for automotive engineering. Brookfield, Vermont, Renouf USA, 1976-77. 2v.

1. *German-English.* 1976. 354p. 2. *English-German* 1977. 369p.

Each volume has *c.*15,000 strictly technical entries. Cross-references for variant spelling. *Class No:* 629.113(038)=30

[5284]

JUNGE, H.D. *and* **LUKHAUP, D. Wörterbuch kraftfahrzeugtechnik:** Englisch/Deutsch; Deutsch/Englisch. [Dictionary of automotive engineering: English/German; German/English.] Weinheim, VCH, 1991. [viii],388p. £42. (*Parat.*) ISBN: 3527281711. ISSN: 09306862.

About 10,000 entries in each half. Genders given. American spelling preferred. *Class No:* 629.113(038)=30

Reviews & Abstracts

[5285]

Automobile abstracts: a monthly survey of worldwide technical literature. Nuneaton, Warwickshire, Motor Industry Research Association, 1955-. Monthly. £250pa. ISSN: 03090817.

Originally as *Monthly summary of automobile engineering literature*, 1955-67; as *MIRA abstracts* 1972-74.

About 2,700 abstracts pa., in sections: Motor industry - Vehicles: design and performance - Components - Fluids - Materials (metals, plastics, etc.) - Production - Testing - Road tests. Author and subject indexes; diary of events. Available online via Data-Star (File: MIRA). *Class No:* 629.113(048)

[5286]

—Automotive business news. Nuneaton, Warwickshire, Motor Industry Research Association, 1978-. 24 pa. looseleaf. £320.

Former title: *Business news index*.

Covers company, national and international news, financial results, investment plans, appointments, production and sales information, industry reviews and statistics. Updated indexes in each issue. A current-awareness source. *Class No:* 629.113(048)

[5287]

Bulletin mensuel de documentation UTAC. Paris, Union Technique de l'Automobile, du Motocycle et du Cycle, 1947-. Monthly. ea. FFr.35. ISSN: 0041705x.

Parts: 1. 'Documentation analytiqué (8 sections; *c.*2,700 abstracts pa.) - 2. Patents (US, German, French, British) - 3. Translations - 4. Bibliography - 5. Standards (Bureau des Normes de l'Automobile, BNA) - 6. News items. *Class No:* 629.113(048)

[5288]

SOCIETY OF AUTOMOTIVE ENGINEERS. Technical literature abstracts. Warrendale, Pa., the Society, 1975-. Quarterly.

The abstracts are of papers presented at SAE conferences. Subjects cover aircraft, diesel engines, fuels and lubricants, transportation systems, trucks and buses. *Class No:* 629.113(048)

Yearbooks & Directories

[5289]

Automotive consultants directory, 1992. Warrendale, Pa., Society of Automotive Engineers, 1992. 141p. £19. ISBN: 1560912693.

Listings for 198 consulting engineers, support personnel and test facilities. International. *Class No:* 629.113(058)

Tables & Data Books

[5290]

Automotive technical data book: tune-up data for petrol-engined cars and light commercial vehicles from 1983 to 1992. McGeoch, J., *comp.* Sparkford Nr. Yeovil, Somerset, Haynes, 1992. v.p. diagrs., tables. £30. ISBN: 1850108005.

About 60 makes of vehicle. Data include engine capacity, cooling system, fuel system, ignition system, brakes, tyres, suspension, torque wrench settings, capacities. *Class No:* 629.113(083)

[5291]

Gale's auto sourcebook, 1991: a guide to information on 1987-91 cars and light trucks. Hill, K. *and* Palmisano, J.M., *eds.* Detroit, Mich., Gale, 1991. 469p. $89.50. ISBN: 0810383128.

Data include model descriptions, features, dimensions, general specifications, evaluations, recalls, safety and repair reports, repair manuals. *Class No:* 629.113(083)

[5292]

SAE handbook. Warrendale, Pa., Society of Automotive Engineers, 1924-. Annual. ISSN: 03628205.

1. *Materials, fuels, emissions, and noise.* 2. *Parts & components.* 3. *On-highway vehicles & off-highway machinery. Index.*

Originally in 1v., now runs to 3v.; 44 sections. Includes over 2,000 specifications and more than 1,000 standards, plus recommended practices and information reports on ferrous and nonferrous metals, nonmetallic metals, threads, etc. *Class No:* 629.113(083)

Histories

[5293]

DETROIT PUBLIC LIBRARY. The Automotive history collection of Detroit Public Library: a simplified guide to its holdings. Boston, Mass., G.K. Hall, 1966. 2v.

22,900 photolithographed catalogue cards reproduced in page form. Pt. 1: Dictionary catalog of books - pt. 2: Periodical shelf-list - pt. 3: Check-list of automobile catalogs - pt. 4: Descriptions of special collections. This collection is the largest of its kind in the US. *Class No:* 629.113(091)

Great Britain

[5294]

SOCIETY OF MOTOR MANUFACTURERS AND TRADERS. Motor industry of Great Britain 1995: world automotive statistics. London, Statistical Dept., SMMT, 1995. Annual. 328p., tables. £105 (non-members).

4 chapters: 1. Production - 2. Registrations: new registrations; vehicles in use - 3. Overseas trade - 4. Miscellaneous (*e.g.* International registration letters). The SMMT constitution and organization. Short list of SMMT publications. Organizations connected with the motor industry: 1. UK; 2. Overseas. Tables of statistics. An essential source in its field.

SMMT Buyers guide to the motor industry is issued annually. *Class No:* 629.113(410)

Thesauri

[5295]

ASLIB. Motor Industry Information Group. **Automotive engineering terms: a thesaurus.** [London, Aslib, the Group], 1974. [ii], 38p.

For indexing managerial, scientific and technical information applied to the motor industry as a whole. Indicates what term to use, and not to use. *Class No:* 629.113:025.43

Museums

[5296]

NICHOLSON, T.R. **The World's motor museums.** London, Dent, 1970. 143p. illus. ISBN: 0460039296.

Arranged under 26 countries, Argentina ... USA. Great Britain, p.76-94, with 21 illus.; USA, p.114-43. Includes brief description of the collection, with a list of outstanding specimens, and dates and times of opening. Good half-tone illus. (8 in colour).
Class No: 629.113:061:069

Lorries & Vans

[5297]

GEORGANO, N. **World truck handbook.** 2nd ed. London, Jane's Publishing Co., 1986. [vi], 328p. £7.95. ISBN: 0710602154.

6 sections (p.11-331): Two-axle trucks - Three-axle trucks - Four-axle trucks - Articulated trucks - Dump trucks - Road tractors. Glossary. Bibliography. Index. 1 illus., per page. Oblong format.
Class No: 629.114.4

[5298]

MILLER, D., *with others.* **The illustrated encyclopedia of trucks and buses.** London, Hamlyn. ISBN: 0600388204.

15 historical chapters, tracing developments, 1769-. A-Z sequence of trucks and buses follows, p.65-308, describing over 4,000 individual marques. Glossary. More than 1,000 illus., usually small.
Class No: 629.114.4

Buses & Coaches

[5299]

JENKINSON, K.A. **Preserved buses.** 2nd rev. ed. London, Ian Allan, 1978. 304p. ISBN: 0711008329.

Bodywork - Abbreviations of ownership - Types of buses (p.16-301), listing over 1,530 preserved passenger vehicles of *c.*270 different models. Data: original and current owners; year of manufacture; make and type of bodywork; etc. 1 photograph per page. Small format. *Class No:* 629.114.53

[5300]

—HIBBS, J. 'The History of the motor bus industry: a bibliographical survey'. *Journal of transport history,* v.2, February 1973, p. 41-55. 270 references.

Supplements his *The history of British bus services* (Newton Abbot, Devon, David & Charles, 1968. 280p. illus). *Class No:* 629.114.53

Private Cars

Encyclopaedias

[5301]

The Encyclopedia of cars. New York, Chelsea House, 1998. 7v. illus. $200.

Provides an overview of about 200 international car companies and models. Includes company histories, design developments, events and evolution of names. Vol. indexes, but no cumulative index. A popular treatment *Class No:* 629.114.6(031)

[5302]

GEORGANO, N. **The New encyclopedia of motorcars,** 1885 to the present. New York, Dutton, 1983. 688p., illus. $45.

First published 1968 as *The complete encyclopedia of motorcars 1885 to the present.* 2nd ed. 1973 (751p).

Includes profiles of about 4,300 makes of cars built over the last century worldwide. One illustration per make, as far as possible. Data on each make: nationality; date(s); principal place of manufacture; history; technical information (selective). 'An excellent contribution to existing automotive historical materials' (*Antique Automobile* v.47, November/December 1982, p.17). *Class No:* 629.114.6(031)

Handbooks & Manuals

[5303]

AUTOMOBILE ASSOCIATION. **Know your car.** Basingstoke, Hants. 319p. illus., diagrs.

Explains the modern motor car, how to service it, and how to diagnose faults and put them right. Some 16 sections: Engine - Transmission - Cooling - Electrics - Suspension - Steering - Brakes - Tyres - Bodywork - Heating and ventilation - The MOT test - Second-hand buying - Accessories - Music on the move - Curing faults - Weekend workshop. Index, p.316-9. Keyed and captioned illus.
Class No: 629.114.6(035)

[5304]

BALDWIN, N., *and others.* **The World guide to automobile manufacturers.** New York, Facts on File, 1987. 584p. illus. (incl. col). $50. ISBN: 0816018448.

Restricted to 1,000 makes. About one-third of the *c.* 950 illus., are in colour, captions state make, model and year. More selective than Georgano's *Encyclopedia of motorcars,* concentrating on the manufacturers. 'A reference book for a broad audience' (*Wilson library bulletin,* April 1988, p.104). *Class No:* 629.114.6(035)

[5305]

CURTIS, A. **The Penguin book of the car.** Harmondsworth, Middx., Penguin Books, 1985. 336p. illus., graphs. ISBN: 0140463119.

14 chapters: 1. The basic elements - 2. The conventional petrol engine - 3. More about the petrol engine ... 7. The electrical system ... 10. Tyres, handling and suspension - 11. The brakes - 12. Styling, structure and safety - 13. The practical side - 14. Legal and insurance. Index, p.325-36. Keyed illus. *Class No:* 629.114.6(035)

Dictionaries

[5306]

SAE glossary of automotive terms. 2nd ed. Warrendale, Pa., Society of Automotive Enginers, 1992. 460p. £61. ISBN: 1560911980.

Nearly 800 terms, extracted from new and revised technical reports between 1986 and 1992. Emphasis is on materials, components and systems used in land and sea vehicles. *Class No:* 629.114.6(038)

Tables & Data Books

[5307]

The Guinness world car record. Berg, I. London, Guinness Publishing, 1992. 768p. illus. £14.99. ISBN: 0851125298.

Performance and technical data of cars offered for sale since 1885. Entries under various headings; cross-references to makers and models. *Class No:* 629.114.6(083)

[5308]

World motor vehicle data. Detroit, Mich., Motor Vehicle Manufacturers Association of the United States, 1964-. Annual. tables.

Tabulated data; international coverage. Details concern models, fuel types, weight, cylinder, and age of vehicle in use. Retrospective statistics on production, sales, registrations, imports and exports. *Class No:* 629.114.6(083)

Models

[5309]

WILLIAMS, G.R. **The World of model cars.** London, A. Deutsch, in association with Rainbow Reference Books 1976. 256p. illus. (incl col.). £9.95. ISBN: 0233962875.

11 chapters (*e.g.* 1. The world of model cars and other road vehicles; 5. Die-cast model cars; 7. The age of plastics; 11. Radio-controlled model cars). Glossary and abbreviations. 'For further reading', p.199-200. Index. 32 col. pl.; over 200 black-and-white illus. *Class No:* 629.114.6(086.48)

Chronologies

[5310]

McSHANE, C. **The Automobile:** a chronology of its antecedents, development and impact. Westport, Ct., Greenwood, 1997. 216p. illus. $69.50. ISBN: 0313303088.

Covers the period *c.*8000 BC (the domestication of animals) to 1994. Topics include inventions, manufacturing, production and the social impact of the car. 2 appendices: 1. car data (*e.g.* prices); 2. North American car museums. *Class No:* 629.114.6(090)

Histories

[5311]

FLOWER, R. *and* JONES, M.W. **One hundred years of motoring:** an RAC social history of the car. Croydon, Royal Automobile Club, in association with McGraw-Hill, 1981. [iv], 224p. illus., (incl. col). ISBN: 0862110181.

Sections: The first spark, 1885-1905 - The challenge of the years, 1900-1914 - Middle class motoring, 1914-1935 - Town and countryside, 1922-1945 - The triumph of technology, 1945-1960 - Countries fit for cars, 1960-1980. Traces the impact of motoring on the British way of life since 1885. Fully illustrated. Partly analytical index, p.221-4. *Class No:* 629.114.6(091)

[5312]

RUIZ, M. One hundred years of the motor car, 1882-1986. London, Collins: Willow, 1987. 280p. illus. (incl. col.). £30. ISBN: 0002181940.

Translated from the Italian (Mondadori) by M. Piòtrowska.

2 main parts: One hundred years of progress; One hundred years of different marques (Alfa Romero … Volvo, plus other countries, A-Z. Porsche: 2p., 8 illus). Includes history of rallying and motor racing. A handsome quarto. *Class No: 629.114.6(091)*

Worldwide

[5313]

World cars, 1985. Lösch, A., *ed.* New York, Herald Books: Pelham, [1985]. Annual. 439p. illus. (incl. col). tables. ISBN: 0910714177.

Published and edited annually by l'Editrice dell' Automobile LEA, publishing company of the Automobile Club of Italy.

Motor racing - Special bodies - World automobile production (p.42-409: Europe … Australia). Data: engine; transmission; performance; steering; electrical equipment; dimensions and weight; optionals. Indexes: Name of car; Maximum speed; Makes, models and prices. *Class No: 629.114.6(100)*

Great Britain

[5314]

CULSHAW, D. *and* **HORROBIN, P. The Complete catalogue of British cars.** New York, W. Morrow, 1974. 511p. illus., diagrs., tables.

Lists all production models by nearly 700 manufacturers, 1895-1974. Excludes racing cars, commercial vehicles and special cars. Tabulated technical data. 9 appendices on electric cars, names and addresses of manufacturers, motoring clubs and organizations, etc. Detailed, non-analytical index. Profusely illustrated (*c.*1,100 illus). *Class No: 629.114.6(410)*

[5315]

NICHOLSON, T.R. The Birth of the British motor car. London, Macmillan, 1982. 3v. (506p.). illus. (pl). ISBN: 0333327179.

1. *A new machine, 1769-1842.* 2. *Revival and defeat, 1842-93.* 3. *The last battle, 1894-97.*

Each volume has notes and an index. V. 3 also carries a select bibliography p. 499-506, in 3 sections. Well researched. A work of 'tremendous scope and unquestionable thoroughness' (*Antique automobile,* v.47, May/June 1983, p.3). *Class No: 629.114.6(410)*

Japan

[5316]

CUSUMANO, M.A. The Japanese automobile industry: technology and management at Nissan and Toyota. Cambridge, Mass., Council on East Asian Studies, Harvard Univ., 1985. xxi, 487p. graphs, charts, tables. ISBN: 0674472551.

6 chapters (1. Company origins and truck technology transfer … 6. Quality control: manufacturing and design). Appendices, p.385-401. Chapter notes, p.403-33. Bibliography, p.434-52. Detailed, analytical index, p.453-87. *Class No: 629.114.6(52)*

USA

[5317]

GUNNEL, J.A., *ed.* **Standard catalog of American cars, 1946-1975.** 2nd ed. Motor Book International, 1987. 800p. illus. $24.95. ISBN: 0873410459.

First published 1982.

A companion volume, edited by J. Flammang, covering the period 1976-86, appeared in 1988. *Class No: 629.114.6(73)*

Sports Cars

[5318]

COTTON, M. Directory of world sportscars. Bourne End, Bucks., Aston Pubns., 1988. 216p. illus. £11.95. ISBN: 094662738x.

Over 70 distinct car makes and models appearing since 1982 in world championships. 165 illus. *Class No: 629.114.62*

[5319]

HOUGH, R. A History of the world's sports cars. London, Allen & Unwin, 1961. 223p. illus. (incl col).

Part 1: The world's sports cars: an outline history. p.13-96. Appended: Specifications of the world's sports cars, p.97-140. Part 2: Sports car racing (trophies; races), p.141-218. Index includes references to illus. *Class No: 629.114.62*

[5320]

—**BATCHELOR, D.** *and* **ROBSON, G. The Great book of sports cars.** Yeovil, Somerset, Foulis, 1988. 420p. illus. £29.95. ISBN: 0854296948.

Mainly concerned with post-World War II period, dovetailing into Hough's *History*. Includes more than 200 profiles of personalities. *Class No: 629.114.62*

[5321]

—**LAWRENCE, M.** A-Z of sport's cars since 1946 Brideford, Devon, Bay Tree Books, 1991. 336p. illus. £24.95. ISBN: 1870979230.

Some 850 makers, A-Z. Indexes: models; personalities. Lavishly illus. *Class No: 629.114.62*

Motor Cycles

[5322]

AYTON, C., *ed.* **World motorcycles.** Yeovil, Somerset, Foulis, 1983. 238, [6]p., illus.

Covers 16 countries, Austria … USSR (Italy, p.52-104). Technical data: manufacturer; engine; transmission; suspension; brakes; dimensions, etc. Appended 'Model finding index' (6p.): *c.*500 models. 1-2 illus. per page. *Class No: 629.118*

[5323]

CHRISTENSEN, R.D. Motorcycles in magazines, 1895-1983. Metuchen, N.J., Scarecrow Press, 1985. [viii], 342p. illus. ISBN: 081081756x.

2,503 numbered entries, usually with brief annotations. 3 parts: 1. General interest and popular technical magazines, 1895-1983 - 2. Automotive magazines, 1950-1983 - 3. *Cycle* magazines, 1978-83. Indexes: A. Motorcycle tests, impressions, descriptions and model announcements; B. Competition reports; C. General, p.333-42. *Class No: 629.118*

[5324]

COLLINS, P. British motorcycles since 1900. Heersham, Surrey, Ian Allan, 1998. 128p. illus. £16.99. ISBN: 071102572x.

A-Z coverage of British motorcycle manufacturers. Data include name, dates, marques, design features, etc. *Class No: 629.118*

[5325]

FRANCIS, G. *and* **PROST, P. The Penguin book of the motorcycle:** a guide to maintenance and problem solving. Harmondsworth, Middx., Penguin Books, 1985. 302p. illus. ISBN: 0140465898.

7 sections: 1. Engines: the basic difference - 2. Maintenance and servicing - 3. Solving engine problems - 4. Engine failure problems - 5. Engine performance problems - 6. Electrical problems - 7. Tips and tricks. Glossary of motorcycling terms, p.273-85. Useful addresses. Your bike's specifications. Analytical index, p.299-302. Designed for all motorcycle riders, regardless of mechanical knowledge or motorcycling experience. *Class No: 629.118*

[5326]

—**COUNTER, C.F.** Motorcycles: a historical survey, as illustrated by the collection of motorcycles in the Science Museum. 2nd ed. London, H.M. Stationery Office, 1970. xiii, 117p. illus.

First published 1956.

10 chapters (1. The pioneers, 1869-1894 … 10. Accessories and ancillaries, from 1956). Bibliography, p.109. *Class No: 629.118*

[5327]

SAE motorcycle safety and environmental terminology. Warrendale, Pa., Society of Automotive Engineers, 1977. v, 179p.

About 1,500 terms defined (*e.g.* 'Ignition system': ½p). Entries make references to SAE standards. The latter are listed in Appendix 1, p.169-77. Appendix 2: 'Use and example of permuted-term index'. US vocabulary. *Class No: 629.118*

[5328]

WILSON, H. The Encyclopedia of the motorcycle. London, Dorling Kindersley, 1995. 320p. illus. (mostly col). £25. ISBN: 0751303208.

Sections: A-Z of motorcycles (p.9-210) - Directory of motorcycles (marques, A-Z, by country of origin; p.209-308). Appended: glossary; useful addresses; bibliography. Index, p.313-19. Beautifully produced and lavishly illus. 'An important addition to the history of transportation' (*Choice*, January 1996, p.770). *Class No: 629.118*

Bicycles

[5329]

COLES, C.W. *and* **GLENN, H.T. Glenn's complete bicycle manual:** selection, maintenance, repair. New York, Crown, 1973. 339p. illus.

Each chapter deals with a part of the bicycle (*e.g.* sprocket cluster; brake). 'The owner or servicer of American, European or Japanese bicycles will find this a useful manual to determine bicycle repairs needed and how to do them. Fully illustrated, with step by step instructions' (*Library journal*, 15 April 1974, p.1100). No index. *Class No: 629.118.3*

[5330]

WATSON, R. *and* **GRAY, M. The Penguin book of the bicycle.** London, Allen Lane, 1978. 333p. illus. ISBN: 0713910992.

7 chapters: 1. The bicycle in fashion again - 2. The bicycle today; naming the parts - 3. The aesthetics of it all - 4. Some more history, technical and social - 5. A visit to the industry - 6. Cycle sport - 7. The bicycle in fashion again: another look. Books consulted and further reading, p.313-8. Useful addresses. Well illustrated. Detailed, analytical index, p.325-33. *Class No:* 629.118.3

Shipbuilding

Bibliographies

[5331]

KUO, C. 'Marine technology'. *Information sources in engineering.* K.W. Mildren and P.J. Hicks, eds. (3rd ed., 1996), p.467-83. 3rd ed. London, Bowker Saur, 1996. £80. ISBN: 1857390571.

Covers both technical aspects of the ship (*e.g.* naval architecture) and offshore engineering. Topics include construction, design, legislation, hydrodynamics, materials, operations, safety, structures, surfaces and forms, etc. A comprehensive treatment of the information sources. *Class No:* 629.12(01)

Encyclopaedias

[5332]

BLACKBURN, G. The Illustrated encyclopedia of ships, boats, vessels and other water-borne craft: comprising an alphabetical directory of all types of craft past and present, containing much discussion of the development of hulls and rigging, together with mention of some of the most outstanding warships and commercial vessels. Supplemented by a glossary, bibliography and index. London, Murray, 1978. 447p. illus.

Over 700 types of craft, A-Z, p.19-392. Glossary p.395-441. Bibliography of relevant books (13 items, with brief evaluative annotations). Index of names of vessels in text, p.445-7. Includes hovercraft and hydrofoils. An essentially personal approach, being reproduced from longhand script, with over 600 elegant line-drawings by the author. Although 'ideal for college and public libraries in general ... [it] does not fill the need for an authoritative nautical dictionary' (*Choice*, v.16(4), June 1979, p.505). *Class No:* 629.12(031)

[5333]

DUDSZUS, A. *and* **HENRIOT, E. Dictionary of ship types:** ships, boats and rafts, under oar and sail. Translated from the German ed., *Das Schiffstypen Lexikon* (1983), by K. Thomas. London, Conway Maritime Press, 1986. 252p. illus. (incl. col.), facsims, tables. ISBN: 0851773605.

Dictionary of ship types, A-Z, p.38-239, describing 1,300 vessels. Chronology (to 1964), p.8-14. Bibliography (A-Z, authors), p.241-5. 6 appendices (*e.g.* Wind strength; 4. Sail area and displacement of significant sailing ship types). Splendidly illustrated, with 800 photographs and line drawings. The *Dictionary* retains strong emphasis on German and Dutch craft. *Class No:* 629.12(031)

[5334]

The Oxford companion to ships and the sea. London, Oxford Univ. Press, 1976. (reissued 1988). £14.95 (paperback). ISBN: 0192820842.

3,700 articles on nautical terms, famous ships, seamen, navigators, ports, explorers. etc. 'Diving' (unassisted, assisted and free diving), p.250-5; 5 illus., references to Bathyscope, Bathysphere. Biographical sketches (*e.g.* 'Tasman', 'Von Spee', 'Conrad'). Also, Maritime museums, naval instuments. Generally omits material on oceanography and small-boat pleasure sailing. 5 appendices (1. Equivalent ranks; 3. Rules of the road). 226 half tones; 187 line-drawings. 'Highly recommended' (*Library journal*, 15 January 1977, p.188). *The Economist* (23 October 1976, p.142) finds that 'Modern technology has largely been sacrificed for the sake of history'. *Class No:* 629.12(031)

Handbooks & Manuals

[5335]

The Guinness book of ships and shipping facts and feats. Hartman, T. Enfield, Middx., Guinness Superlatives, 1983. 265p. illus. (incl. col.), facsims., ports., tables, maps. ISBN: 0851122698.

Sections: Experiment and exploration - Warships and warfare - Trade and transport - Distress and disaster - Odd facts. Appendices: Types of vessel. Glossary of nautical terms, p.242-54. Bibliography, p.255. Index of ships' names; Index of proper names. *Class No:* 629.12(035)

[5336]

Ship construction sketches and notes. Eyres, D.J., *ed.* 2nd ed. Oxford, Butterworth-Heinemann, 1997. 160p. illus., diagrs. £14.99. (*Kemp and Young.*) ISBN: 0750637560.

Contents include shipyard practices, design, construction methods and overall arrangement of different types of merchant and passenger vessels. *Class No:* 629.12(035)

[5337]

TAGGART, R., *ed.* **Ship design and construction:** written by a group of authorities. New Society, Society of Naval Architects and Marine Engineers, 1980. xiv, 734p. illus., diagrs., tables.

Evolved from the *Design and construction of steel merchant ships* (1955), and a 1969 revision.

18 sectionalised chapters (1. Mission analysis and basic design ... 4. Load-line assignments ... 8. Hull materials and welding ... 16. Ship construction - 17. Launching - 18. Trials and preparation for delivery). Glossary, p.717-28. Detailed analytical index. 'Concerned with the practical aspects of ship design as they relate to the requirements of the owner and operator, and as they relate to the characteristic of the mission that the ship is to perform' (*Introduction*). *Class No:* 629.12(035)

[5338]

TUPPER, E. Introduction to naval architecture. 3rd ed. Oxford, Butterworth-Heinemann, 1996. 416p. illus., diagrs., £27.50. ISBN: 0750625295.

First published 1975 as *Naval architecture for marine engineers*, by W. Muckle.

Contents: Definitions, dimensions and form coefficients - Classification societies and governmental bodies - Ship form calculations - Buoyancy, stability and trim - The sea and ship motions - Structural strength - Resistance - Propulsion - Manoeuvering - Vibration - Ship design. *Class No:* 629.12(035)

Dictionaries

Polyglot

[5339]

PAASCH, H. From keel to truck: dictionary of naval terms; English-French-German-Spanish-Italian. Based upon the original dictionary by Captain Paasch, by L. Bataille and M. Burnet. 5th ed., rev. and enl. London, Philip, 1937. [c.1000]p. pl.

First published 1885.

About 17,500 English entry-words and definitions, arranged by subjects, with translations and equivalents in the other 4 languages; 5 language indexes. Plates are on verso pages; that on the schooner shows 50 keyed parts. Many compounds (*e.g.* 'Ballast-donkey-valve-rod stuffing-box-gland', p.820). A classic dictionary, unrivalled for its definitions in all 5 languages covered and for its many plates (103 in all) showing plans and detailed parts of ships. *Class No:* 629.12(038)=00

[5340]

Schiffahrts-Wörterbuch: deutsch-englisch-französisch-spanisch-italienisch. Hamburg, Horst Kamm-Verlags-und Handelsgesellschaft GmbH, 1987. 837p.

About 8,000 German base-terms, with equivalents in English, French, Spanish and Italian, across the double page. Appended section: 'Ships papers', in German, Portugese, Danish, Norwegian, Swedish and Dutch. Abbreviations, p.791-837. *Class No:* 629.12(038)=00

[5341]

—**BERSCH, E.,** *ed.* **Shipbuilding, seafaring technical dictionary;** in Russian, English and German. East Berlin, Verlag Technik, 1980. 880p.

Includes several indexes. *Class No:* 629.12(038)=00

[5342]

VANDENBERGHE, J.P. *and* **JOHNEN, M. Elsevier's nautical dictionary:** English/American, French, Spanish, Dutch and German. 3rd ed. Amsterdam, etc., Elsevier, 1994. 828p. $257; £160. ISBN: 044489604x.

First published 1965-66 (3v.) by P.E. Segditsas; 2nd ed. 1978.

13,462 entries in English with indexes in the other languages. Coverage: 'shipbuilding, types of sea-going vessels, equipment aboard, seamanship, navigational aids and their use on board, sea-going staff and port-personnel, active or passive beaconing, new shipping techniques, goods handling, insurance and trading, commercial and financial documents, international law of the sea, yachting and racing, port terminology' (*Preface*). *Class No:* 629.12(038)=00

English

[5343]

INSTITUTE OF MARINE ENGINEERS. Glossary of marine technology terms. London, Heinemann, in association with the Institute of Marine Engineers. 434p. ISBN: 0434908401.

Defines *c.*1,500 terms ('Ignition': 2/3p.; 'Propellor': 1p). Involves seamanship, ship construction, marine engineering, electricity and electronics. Amusing explanation of why a ship is called 'she' (quoting *Annual report*, RINA, 1976, v.118, p.liv).
Class No: 629.12(038)=20

[5344]

LAYTON, C.W.T. Dictionary of nautical words and terms: 8,000 definitions in navigation, seamanship, rigging, meterology, astronomy, naval architecture, average, ship economics, hydrography, cargo, stowage, marine engineering, ice terminology, buoyage, yachting, etc. Rev. 3rd ed. Glasgow, Brown, Son, & Ferguson, 1987. 397p. £22. ISBN: 0851745369.

First published 1955.

8,000 definitions in navigation, seamanship, rigging, metrology, astronomy, naval architecture, ship economics, hydrography, cargo stowage, marine engineering, ice terminology, buoyage, yachting, etc. (*e.g.* 'Lloyd's Register of Shipping': 11 lines). Includes acronyms, organizations. Appended list of abbreviations.
Class No: 629.12(038)=20

[5345]

NOEL, J.V. The VNR dictionary of ships and the sea. New York, etc., Van Nostrand Reinhold, 1987. vi, 393p. illus. ISBN: 0442256310.

About 6,000 entries, including abbreviations and acronyms, briefly defined (*e.g.* 'Gulf stream system': 9 lines; 'Beaufort scale': ½p). Cross-references. International code flags and pennants, on end papers. *Class No:* 629.12(038)=20

German

[5346]

DLUHY, R., *comp*. **Schifftechnisches Wörterbuch.** 4 erw. Aufl. Hannover-Wülfel, Industrie und Handelsverlag GmbH, 1974-75. 2v. (xxxi, 1,709p.; xxxix, 1,631p.).

First published 1956 (Bremen, Dorn). 1. *Deutsch-Englisch*. 2. *Englisch-Deutsch*.

A maritime dictionary. Each v. has *c.*70,000 entry-words, categorized, and including abbreviations. Coverage: shipbuilding, shipping, marine engineering and related fields (*e.g.* oceanography, maritime law). Many compounds (*e.g.* 'ventil', (valve): 9½ columns). Idioms and technical expressions. German genders stated. Each v. carries lists of weights and measures. Authoritative.

A shorter, updated version, with similar title, appeared in 1981 (Hannover, Vincentz-verlag. 741p.). *Class No:* 629.12(038)=30

Norwegian

[5347]

ASKIM, P. Engelsk-norsk maritim-teknisk ordbok. 2. opplag. Oslo, Grondahl, 1959. 137p.

English-Norwegian dictionary, with *c.*10,000 entry-words covering shipping and shipbuilding. Appended specification- survey for general overhaul of diesel machinery on a ship, in English and Norwegian.

This and its companion Norwegian-English dictionary form an established pair of technical dictionaries, with reprints.
Class No: 629.12(038)=396

[5348]

ASKIM, P. Norsk-engelsk maritim-teknisk ordbok. 7. opplag. Oslo, Grondahl, 1962. 219p.

First published 1936.

Norwegian-English dictionary, with *c.*15,000 entry-words covering shipping and shipbuilding. Appended specification for a ship's survey and sundries report in both Norwegian and English (p.213-9).
Class No: 629.12(038)=396

French

[5349]

Dictionnaire anglais-français et français-anglais des termes et locutions martitimes. 2nd éd., rev. et augm. Paris, Éditions Maritimes et d'Outre-Mer, 1971. 319p.

About 5,000 entry-words in each part. Based on H. Paasch's multilingual *From keel to truck: dictionary of naval terms, English-French-German-Spanish-Italian* (*qv*). *Class No:* 629.12(038)=40

Spanish

[5350]

ALFARA PEREZ, T. Diccionario marítimo y de construcción naval (inglés-español y español-inglés). [Dictionary of maritime amd shipbuilding terms (English-Spanish, Spanish-English).] Barcelona, Carriga, [1976]. 479p.

About 10-12,000 headwords in each part: English-Spanish, p. 17-263; Spanish-English, p.267-460. 'Helm': nearly 1 column. Many categories of terms. Pronunciation guide to English words only. Appendices of geographical names, weights and measures.
Class No: 629.12(038)=60

Russian

[5351]

ANASHKIN, I.A., *and others*. **Morskoĭ slovar'.** Moscow, Voennoe Izdat. Ministerstvo Oborony SSSR, 1959. 2v. (892p.). illus., diagrs.

'Maritime dictionary'. About 12,000 entry-words. Gives English translations of Russian terms and idioms, as well as Russian definitions. *Class No:* 629.12(038)=82

Reviews & Abstracts

[5352]

BMT [British maritime technology] abstracts. Wallsend, Tyne & Wear, BMT Ltd., Wallsend Research Station, 1946-. Monthly. ISSN: 02689650.

Previously as *Journal of abstracts of the British Ship Research Association* (1962-67), and originally as *Journal of the British Shipbuilding Research Association* (1946-62).

About 3,000 abstracts pa. 6 sections: Design and construction - Operation - Fluid mechanics - Structures and materials - Naval vessels and defence technology - Miscellaneous. Indexes: author; ship and structure; keyword. Online through BSRA database at Wallsend, which also covers the output of *Ship abstracts* (published by a consortium headed by the Norwegian Ship Research Institute). Also on CD-ROM.
Class No: 629.12(048)

[5353]

Maritime information review: a combination of *Marna News* and *The Ship abstract journal*. Delft, Maritime Information Centre/Delft University of Technology Library. ISSN: 09201610.

Sections 01-90 (*e.g.* 01. Ships; 02. Shipping; 03. Shipbuilding; 04. Ports and waterways; 05. Fishing industry; 06. Offshore oil and gas; 07. Ocean mining; 08. Inland shipping; 09. Marine pollution; 10. Energy generating and floating plants; 11. Driving; 12. Navy; 13. Sailing ships, yachts; 14. Ice, icing, icebreaking; 80. Laws, recommendations, regulations and rules; 90. Reference books.

Databases: MARNA (updated weekly); SHIPDES (ship descriptions, updated fortnightly); available on ESA/IRS. *Class No:* 629.12(048)

Yearbooks & Directories

[5354]

European Community shipping directory: 1992. Colchester, Lloyd's of London Press, 1992. 176p. maps. £55. ISBN: 1850444838. ISSN: 09616764.

Alphabetically by country (Belgium ... United Kingdom). Data include classification societies, liner services by agent, ports, ship suppliers and brokers, towage, salvage and offshore services. Table of airlines and EC airports. *Class No:* 629.12(058)

[5355]

Fairplay world shipping directory. London, Fairplay Publications. Annual. ISSN: 09593101.

Previously (1976-77) as *'Financial times' World shipping year book*. Lists over 26,000 addresses, *c.*5,000 operators with details of more than 30,000 ships. Sections include ship operators, ship managers, ship builders and repairers, marine insurance, maritime organisations, consultants and surveyors, port authorities, etc. Company, personnel, vessel, and advertisers' index.

World shipping statistics, 1989-, is a geographical analysis of the marine industry worldwide. *Class No:* 629.12(058)

[5356]

Lloyd's maritime directory: 1998. Colchester, Essex, Lloyd's of London Press, 1998. 2v. ISSN: 0268327x.

Contents: The year in shipping - Index to vessels - Towage, salvage and offshore services - Ship earth station directory - Ship management services - Shipbuilders/ship repairers - Marine equipment builders/repairers - Banking/finance - Insurance/P & I Club - Marine solicitors/lawyers - Marine consultants - Classification societies - General maritime organizations. Index to vessels and index to owners, managers, agents precedes. Appended index of advertisers.
Class No: 629.12(058)

Published Series
[5357]

NATIONAL MARITIME MUSEUM. The Ship series.
Greenhill, B., *ed.* Greenwich, the Museum, 1980-81. 10v. illus.

1. *Rafts, boats and ships from prehistoric times to the medieval era*, by S. McGioul. 1981. 88p.

2. *Long boats and round ships: warfare and trade in the Mediterranean, 3000 BC - 500 AD*, by J. Morrison. 60p.

3. *Tiller and whipstaff: the development of the sailing ship, 1400-1700*, by A. McGowan. 1984. 60p.

4. *The century before steam, 1700-1820*, by A. McGowan. 1980. 60p.

5. *Steam tramps and cargo lines, 1850-1970*, by R. Craig. 1980. 60p.

6. *Channel packets and ocean liners, 1850-1970*, by J. Maber. 1980. 60p.

7. *The life and death of the merchant sailing ship*, by B. Greenhill. 1980. 60p.

8. *Steam, steel and torpedoes: the warship in the 19th century*, by D. Lyon. 1980. 60p.

9. *Dreadnought to nuclear submarine*, by A. Preston. 1980. 60p.

10. *The revolution in merchant shipping, 1950-1980*, by E. Corlett. 1981. 60p.

10 illustrated hardbacks that trace the development of fighting and trading ships from 3000 BC to the present day. Authoritative, dispelling old myths and replacing them with hard facts. *Class No:* 629.12(082.1)

Tables & Data Books
[5358]

Register of ships. London, Lloyd's Register of Shipping, Annual. 3v. (2041p.). ISSN: 01414909.

3v., arranged by ships names, A-G, H-O, P-Z. V.3 has appendices: Ships' names; Former names of ships; Compound names of ships; Ship-borne barges; Mooring barges; Miscellaneous pontoons; Air cushion vessels; Docking installations. *Class No:* 629.12(083)

Illustrations
[5359]

The Maritime compendium: an encyclopedia of designs and motifs. Cordingly, D., *ed.* London, Conway, 1997. 192p. chiefly illus. £33. ISBN: 0851777147.

Over 16,000 maritime and related illustrations from antiquity onwards. *Class No:* 629.12(084.1)

Histories
[5360]

BARNABY, K.C. The Institution of Naval Architects, 1860-1960: an historical survey of the Institution's 'Transactions' and activities over 100 years. London, the Institution, in association with Allen & Unwin, 1960. 645p. illus. (pl.), diagrs.

Constitutes a detailed survey of the progress of shipbuilding. Includes lists of contents of the *Transactions*, 1860-1959 in an appendix (incorrectly listed in 'Contents' as 1910-1959). Indexes of personal and ships' names. *Class No:* 629.12(091)

[5361]

BROUWER, N.J. International register of historic ships. Oswestry, Shropshire, A. Nelson, in association with the World Ship Trust, 1985. xii, 321p. illus. £10.95. ISBN: 0904614115.

Data on more than 700 ships; 43 countries (Argentina ... Yugoslavia). 'To be included ships have to survive as virtually complete hulls' (*Introduction*) Details on each include: year built; builders; original and present owner; type of engines; superstructure; displacement; condition; alterations; bibliography; history and significance. Appended list of ships by type. Detailed index, p.319-21. 1-4 illus., per type. *Class No:* 629.12(091)

[5362]

HAWS, D. *and* **HURST, A.A. The Maritime history of the world:** a chronological survey of maritime events from 5000 BC until the present day, supplemented by commentaries. Brighton, Sussex, Teredo Books, Ltd., 1985. xxv, 494p. illus. (incl. col.), maps. ISBN: 0903662108.

V.1: 3000 BC - AD 1816 (xxv, 494p.), with bibliography p.xviii - xxv. V.2: 1816 - 1984 (vii, 419p.). with 'Epilogue' and 'Addenda'. Detailed, analytical index, p.318-419, covering both volumes ('France': 2 columns). 203 illus., (62 in colour), 31 maps. Scope: wars, battles, trade exploration, chartered companies, slavery, piracy, jurisprudence, navigational developments, ship design, etc. Quarto format. *Class No:* 629.12(091)

[5363]

LANDSTROM, B. The Ship: a survey of the history of the ship, from the primitive raft to the nuclear-powered submarine, with reconstructions in words and pictures. London, Allen & Unwin, 1961. 309, [9]p. illus. (incl. col.).

Translated from Skeppet (Stockholm, Bokforlaget Forum AB, 1961), by M. Phillips.

A notable feature: the 807 carefully-drawn illus., about 2 per type of ship described. Appended list of sources. Non-analytical index. A definitive work on the history of ships. *Class No:* 629.12(091)

[5364]

PAINE, L.P. Ships of the world: an historical encyclopedia. New York, Houghton-Mifflin, 1997. 680p. illus. $50; £35. ISBN: 0395715563.

Also published by Conway (ISBN: 0851777392).

Covers over 1,000 individual ships, including some in literature (*e.g.* the Flying Dutchman and the Beatles' Yellow Submarine). Data include a basic specification and brief, readable articles about each vessel. Maps, chronology, glossary; index lists names of ships, persons, places, wars, etc. Selective rather than exhaustive, according to the *Preface*. But fascinating. *Class No:* 629.12(091)

[5365]

WOODMAN, R. The History of the ship: the comprehensive story of seafaring from the earliest times to the present day. London, Conway, 1997. 352p. illus. £30. ISBN: 085177721x.

Covers the early dugouts and rafts, the development of the galley, sailing ships, steam-propelled ships, ocean liners and battleships. Lavishly illustrated. *Class No:* 629.12(091)

Bibliographies
[5366]

ADAMS, T.R. *and* **WATERS, D.W.,** *comps.* **English maritime books printed before 1901:** relating to ships, their construction and their operation at sea, including articles in the *Philosopical transactions of the Royal Society* and the *Transactions of the American Philosophical Society*. Providence, R.I., The John Carter Brown Library; Greenwich, The National Maritime Museum, 1995. xxxi, 602p. ISBN: 0916617432.

About 3,800 works, A-Z. In 2 parts. Part I lists the works; Part II is a 'topical arrangement' ('Aids to navigation' - 'Weather'). *Class No:* 629.12(091)(01)

Archives
[5367]

The Shipbuilding industry: a guide to historical records. Ritchie, L.A., *ed.* Manchester Univ. Press, 1992. 206p. £45. (*Studies in British business archives*.) ISBN: 0719038057.

Gives present location of shipbuilding archives. Brief histories of *c.*200 businesses. 3 indexes: geographic; subject; name. *Class No:* 629.12(093.20)

Information Services
[5368]

Maritime information : a guide to libraries and sources of information in the United Kingdom. Bryon, R.V. *and* Bryon, T.N., *eds.* 3rd ed. London, Witherby for the Maritime Information Association, 1993. vi, 222p. ISBN: 1856090698.

First published 1973; 2nd ed. 1983.

500 UK libraries, record offices, museums, institutions and associations (A-Z) which hold maritime information or collections of materials. Entries include subject coverage, special collections, publications. Detailed, analytical index, p. 209-22. *Class No:* 629.12:061:025.5

Museums
[5369]

AYMAR, B. A Pictorial treasury of the marine museums of the world: a guide to the maritime collections, restorations, replicas, and marine museums in twenty-three countries. New York, Crown Publications, 1967. viii, 248p. illus., facsims., ports.

Part 1: Marine museums and maritime collections, United States (p.2-77), Argentina ... Yugoslavia - 2. Restorations and replicas (5 countries) - 3. Special. Non-analytical index. *Class No:* 629.12:061:069

[5370]

STAMMERS, M.K. Discovering maritime museums and historic ships. Princes Risborough, Bucks., Shire Publications Ltd., 1978. 84p. illus. £0.70.

Arranged under counties of England, Isle of Man, Northern Ireland, Scotland and Wales, subdivided by towns. Short glossary; 'Useful books and periodicals' (p.82), 'Useful addresses'. Index. 236 black-and-white illus. *Class No:* 629.12:061:069

Sailing Ships

[5371]
WHITLOCK, P.C., *and others.* **The 'Country Life' book of nautical terms under sail.** Feltham, Middlesex, 'Country life' books, 1978. [352]p. illus., facsims., maps.

Brief definitions of words associated with sailing and sailing ships. *Class No:* 629.123.1

Passenger Ships

[5372]
BAYNARD, F.O. *and* **MILLER, W.H. Fifty famous liners.** Willingborough, P. Stephens, 1982-87. 3v. illus., diagrs., tables.

Each volume deals with 50 famous passenger ships (*e.g. Titanic:* v.1, p.59-62. 4 illus., 4 cross-sections), each given descriptive text and technical data. Each volume has an index. A combined index is called for. *Class No:* 629.123.3

[5373]
DAWSON, P. Cruise ships: an evolution in design. London, Conway, 1998. 256p. illus., diagrs. £40. ISBN: 0851776604.

Covers cruise liners from the 1930s to the present day with analysis of design influences. Lavishly illustrated. *Class No:* 629.123.3

[5374]
KLUDAS, A. Great passenger ships of the world. Cambridge, P. Stephens, 1975-77. 5v. illus.

First published as *Die grossen Passagierschiffe der Welt.* (Oldenbourg, 1972). V. 1: 1858-1912(1975); V. 2: 1913-1923(1976); V. 3: 1924-1935; V. 4: 1936-1950(1977); V. 5: 1951-1970(1977).

Deals with ships either in classes (*e.g.* Elder Dempster liners) or individually (*e.g.* 'Queen Elizabeth'). Covers passenger vessels of 10,000 gross tons or more. General data: chronology; yard number; launching and commissioning dates; handed over to ...; retired; rebuilt. Technical data: dimensions; propulsion; power; speed; passengers; crew. Historical data: owners; builders; completion; routes. V.5 (226p). carries a bibliography, p.212-3. Index of ships' names. Well illustrated, - about 1 per page. *Class No:* 629.123.3

Cargo Ships

[5375]
GILMAN, S., *and others.* **The Shipping revolution:** the merchant ship, 1960-the present. Couper, A. *and* Greenhill, B., *eds.* London, Conway Maritime, 1992. 192p. illus., maps. £28. (*Conway's History of the Ship.*) ISBN: 0851775691.

Focuses on the rapid advances in maritime technology, as well as the political, economic and social reasons for these. Over 200 illus. *Class No:* 629.123.4

[5376]
GREENWAY, A. Soviet merchant ships. 4th ed. Havant, Hants., Mason, 1982. 226 p. illus.

First published 1969.

A concise recognition manual of merchant ships, fish-factory vessels and research fleet of the USSR. Vessels, for inclusion, must exceed 1,000 deadweight tons. Data include builders, tonnage, main engines and hull dimensions of each ship listed. *Class No:* 629.123.4

[5377]
Jane's merchant ships, 1998-99. Coulsdon, Surrey, Jane's Information Group, 1998. 800p. illus., diagrs., tables. £270; $410 ISBN: 071061800x.

Over 6,000 ship classes identified using the Talbot-Booth system. Ship drawings section (drawn to a common scale and grouped by similarity of shape) is followed by 'Ship directory and data section'. Glossary. Available online and on CD-ROM. *Class No:* 629.123.4

[5378]
MacGREGOR, D.R. Merchant sailing ships. London, Conway Maritime Press, 1984-85. 3v. illus., facsims., ports, plans. ea. £15. ISBN: 0851772301; 0851172943; 0851773165.

1. *Merchant sailing ships, 1775-1815: sovereignty of sail.* 2nd ed. 1985.

2. *Merchant sailing ships, 1815-1850: supremacy of sail.* 1984.

3. *Merchant sailing ships, 1850-1875: heyday of sail.* 1984.

Covers barques, brigs and schooners, as well as the more spectacular vessels of the merchant navy. A feature: the many reconstructed and redrafted plans of ships, - poorly documented craft until now. The second volume (192p). has 110 photographs and 100 line-drawings. Each volume carries a bibliography. *Class No:* 629.123.4

Tankers

[5379]
The Tanker register: tankers and combined carriers of all countries. New York, Int. Publications Service, Annual.

Contents: Glossary - Tropical and winter deadweight and draught diagrams - Comparative tables of specific gravities - Statistical tables. In sections including: Names of tankers in size and age groups; Particulars of tankers, including special purpose types; List of owners and/or managers. *Class No:* 629.123.56

Small Craft

Hovercraft

[5380]
Jane's high-speed marine technology, 1999-2000. Coulsdon, Surrey, Jane's Information Group, 1999. *c.*520p. illus., tables. £265; $425. ISBN: 0710619065.

Formerly *Jane's high-speed marine craft.*

Includes vehicles over 20 metres in length with a speed in excess of 30 knots. Contents: Builders - Civil operators - Principal engineering components - Services - Bibliography. Also available online and on CD-ROM. *Class No:* 629.125.8

Rail Vehicle Engineering

[5381]
HOLLINGSWORTH, B. An Illustrated guide to modern trains. London, Salamander, 1985. 235p. illus. (incl. col.). ISBN: 0861012208.

Concentrates on 80 powerful locomotives since 1945, tracing the cycle from steam to diesel, diesel electric and electric, then back to steam. Most of the illustrations are in colour. 'Very appropriate for public libraries and special collections on railroading' (*Science and technology libraries,* v.8(1), Fall 1987, p.172). *Class No:* 629.4

[5382]
UNION INTERNATIONALE DES CHEMINS DE FER. Recueil des termes concernant l'emploi et l'échange de matériel roulant. Warsaw, Ministry of Communications, 1958-65. 2v. illus.

V.1 is a rolling-stock glossary of 4,981 numbered terms in English, French, German, Italian, Polish and Russian. V. 2, *Nomenclature illustrée,* has a glossary of 4 sections: A. Coaches and wagons - B. Parts of coaches and wagons - C. Equipment for universal transport and its essential parts - D. Various accessories and tools for trailer stock. A-Z indexes: French, German, English, Italian, Polish and Russian. 2,982 illus. *Class No:* 629.4

Locomotives

[5383]
Guide to North American steam locomotives. Drury, G.H., *comp.* Waukesha, Wi., Kalmbach, 1993. 448p. illus. ISBN: 0890242062.

About 125 brief chapters covering the history and development of steam locomotives in North America. Lavishly illustrated. *Class No:* 629.42

[5384]
HOLLINGSWORTH, B. *and* **COOK, A. The Great book of trains.** London, Salmander, 1987; reprinted 1998. 413p. illus. £15.99. ISBN: 0862881587.

2 sections: Steam passenger locomotives - Modern locomotives. About 300 locomotives described and illustrated. Data include axle load, steam pressure, etc. Brief glossary, p.8-15; index. *Class No:* 629.42

[5385]
NOCK, O.S. British locomotives of the 20th century. Cambridge, P. Stephens, 1983-85. 3v. illus., diagrs., charts, tables. ISBN: 0850595959.

1. *1900-1930.* 1983.

2. *1930-1960.* 1985.

3. *1960-to present day.* 1985.

V.1 (255p) has 17 chapters. Illustrations (396) include cross-sections and are plentiful and well captioned. Bibliography, p.252. Detailed, analytical index. *Class No:* 629.42

Steam Trains

[5386]
JONES, K.P. Steam locomotive development: an analytical guide to the literature on British steam locomotive development, 1923-1962. London, Library Association, 1969. [xii], 413p.

Based on a thesis accepted for the Fellowship of the Library Association in 1968.

About 4,000 items (books, periodical articles, reports, etc.), many

....(contd.)

with brief annotations. Sections (Great Western Railway ... Locomotives manufacturers' products) and sub-sections have introduction. Name index; index of locomotive classes. Bibliography, p.12-13. General reference works, p.14-21. 'A most comprehensive work' (*British book news*, November 1969, p.830-1). *Class No: 629.422*

[5387]

NOCK, O.S. British steam locomotive, 1928-1965. London, I. Allan, 1988. 276p. illus., diagrs., maps. £12.95. ISBN: 0711001251.

First published 1969; new impression, 1988.

Reprint of the author's classic study of the development of the British steam locomotive in its heyday. *Class No: 629.422*

Aircraft Engineering

Bibliographies

[5388]

CLAXTON, M. *and* **HALLAM, L.,** *comps.* **Information pack on fly-by-wire:** reference to fly-by-light, fly-by-speech and power-by-wire aerospace technology. London, Information and Library science, Institution of Mechanical Engineers, 1987. iv,69p. £12.50. (*Information pack, 5.*) ISBN: 0852986491.

Fly-by-wire is an advanced flight control system. 2 parts: 1. Fly-by-wire information (abbreviations - patents), p.1-36; 2. Fly-by-wire references (126 items) with abstracts, p.37-62. Indexes: author, subject/aircraft. *Class No: 629.7(01)*

[5389]

HANNIBALL, A. Aircraft, engines and airmen: a selective review of the periodical literature, 1930-1969. Metuchen, N.J., Scarecrow Press, 1972. xxiv, 825p.

5 parts: 1. Aircraft (3,157 numbered references) - 2. Aircraft engines - 3. Biography - 4. Air Forces (history and organization; equipment; air bases; unit histories) - 5. Miscellany. Indexes: aircraft names; aircraft manufacturers; aircraft symbols; engine names; engine's symbols. 'An outstanding work of reference' (MacAdam, E.J., in *Information sources in engineering* (2nd ed., 1985), p.323). *Class No: 629.7(01)*

Encyclopaedias

[5390]

Concise encyclopedia of aeronautics and space systems. Pélegrin, M. *and* Hollister, W., *eds.* Oxford, Pergamon Press, 1993. xiii, 478p. illus., diagrs., graphs, tables. £135. (*Advances in systems, control and information engineering.*) ISBN: 0080370497.

Topics covered include communication, simulation, remote sensing, satellites, etc.; emphasis is on automatic control in civil aviation. About 25 contributors; 100 articles. Intended 'as a complementary companion' to *Systems and control encyclopedia* (*qv*) (*Introduction*), but 'comprising almost entirely new material specially commissioned' (*Preface*). *Class No: 629.7(031)*

[5391]

GARRISON, P. The Illustrated encyclopedia of general aviation. 2nd ed. Blue Ridge Summit, Pa., TAB Books, 1990. 402p. illus. $24.95. ISBN: 0830633182.

Lists aviation organizations, manufacturers, publications, etc. Does not include specifications strictly for military or commercial aviation. 'Suitable for all libraries' (*New technical books*, May/June 1991, item 797). *Class No: 629.7(031)*

[5392]

Jane's encyclopedia of aviation. London, Jane's Publishing Co. 5v. (1078p.). illus. (incl. col.), ports., diagrs. ISBN: 0710607105.

Aircraft, AAMSA ... Zlin, with data on about 5,000 different aeroplanes, including spacecraft and gliders. V.1 includes glossary, a world directory of airlines, world directory of air forces, aerospace world records, and the first part of the A-Z sequence of aircraft - AAMSA ... Antonov. Includes biographies. Index (tiny print) in v.5, p.1065-78. About 3,000 illus. in all. Online via DIALOG. *Class No: 629.7(031)*

[5393]

ROBINSON, A. Dictionary of aviation: eighty years of powered flight. London, Orbis, 1984. 304p. illus. (incl. col.), ports. ISBN: 085613533x.

3 sections: 1. Pilots and personalities - 2. Aerial warfare (*e.g.* Pacific War, 1941-45) - 3. Aircraft manufacturers. A-Z entries in each section. Fully illustrated (2 or more illus. per page) and captioned. No general index. *Class No: 629.7(031)*

Handbooks & Manuals

[5394]

RENDALL, D. Jane's aircraft recognition guide. Glasgow, HarperCollins, 1996. 505p. illus., diagrs.

First published 1979 as *jane's world aircraft recognition handbook*.

3-view silhouette, photograph and brief description of over 500 types of military and civil aircraft. Civil aircraft registrations; glossary of recognition terms. *Class No: 629.7(035)*

Dictionaries

Polyglot

[5395]

AÉROSPATIALE. Dictionnaire aérospatiale: français, anglais, allemand, espagnol. Paris, Gauthier-Villars, 1984. 4v.

4.v. expansion of *Dictionnaire des techniques aéronautiques et spatiales, français-anglais-allemand aerospatiale* (1978). 114p. illus. 2.éd. (1984. 152p.), with Spanish added.

The 4v. comprise: French, English (*Aerospace dictionary*), German (*Wörterbuch der Luft-und Raumfahrt*) and Spanish (*Diccionario aéroespacial*) dictionaries, each covering the four languages concerned. 36,000 entry-words in all. *Class No: 629.7(038)=00*

[5396]

Complete multilingual dictionary of aviation and aeronautical terminology: English, French, Spanish. Demaison, H., *ed.* Chicago, Il., Passport books, 1984. xvi,671p. £34.95.

13,000 English-base terms, with French and Spanish equivalents and indexes. Appendices A-L (F: 'Abbreviations of common usage'). *Class No: 629.7(038)=00*

[5397]

FRENOT, G.H. *and* **HOLLOWAY, A.H.,** *eds.* **AGARD aeronautical multilingual dictionary.** London, Pergamon Press, 1960. Supplement 1, 1963. 1072p. Loose-leaf. DFl.295.

A NATO Advisory Group on Aeronautical Research and Development publication.

1,574 numbered English entry-words, plus definitions, equivalents and indexes in French, German, Spanish, Italian, Dutch, Turkish and Russian. (Supplement 1 adds 1,287 entries and a ninth language, Greek). 15 sections (1. Aeronautics (General) ... 14. Radiocommunication and radiolocation - 15. Meteorology). Russian terms are lacking in sections 13-14. Criticized in *Interavia* (v.16(2), February 1961, p.242) for containing only basic words and expressions in the sections. 'If enlarged the dictionary could form the basis for a comprehensive standard work. Despite uneveness, it is a classic for accuracy, up-to-dateness and clear presentation of complex data' (*Library journal*, v.89(6), 15 March 1964, p.1226-7). *Class No: 629.7(038)=00*

[5398]

—**DORIAN, A.F.** *and* **OSENTON, J.** Elsevier's dictionary of aeronautics in six languages: English/American, French, Spanish, Italian, Portuguese and German. Amsterdam, etc., Elsevier, 1964. [vii], 842p. DFl.295. ISBN: 0444401776.

5,919 numbered English/American entry-words, with definitions; equivalents and indexes in the other languages. Genders given. Primarily concerned with civil aviation. Covers terms used in radio communication, meteorology, electronics, practical mechanics, etc., as well as jargon. *Interavia* (v.30(8), August 1965, p.300) notes some clumsy expressions and inaccurate translations. *Class No: 629.7(038)=00*

French

[5399]

WINGROVE, R.G. *and* **JAMMES, J.R.J. The Aviator's English and French dictionary.** [Dictionnaire français et anglais des aviateurs.] Aldershot, Hants., Ashgate, 1995. [viii], 263p. £19.95. ISBN: 0291398235.

Includes terms dealing with all aspects of aircraft operation. About 1,100 terms in each half. *Class No: 629.7(038)=40*

Russian

[5400]

KONARSKI, M.M. Russian-English dictionary of modern terms in aeronautics and rocketry. Oxford, etc., Pergamon Press, 1962. xi, 515p.

Over 14,500 numbered Russian terms used in Soviet aeronautics and allied fields, - radio, electronics, meteorology and aerial photography. English equivalents and index, making the dictionary virtually two-way. Includes a list of Russian abbreviations and mathematical signs, etc. *Spaceflight* (v.5(1), January 1961, p. 34-35) praises the work as being meticulously accurate, complaining only of the excessive inclusion of ordinary words. *Class No: 629.7(038)=82*

[5401]
MURASHKEVICH, A.M. Anglo-russkiĭ aviatsionnyĭ slovar'. Moscow, Izdat. 'Sovetskaya Entsiklopediya', 1964. 687p.
English-Russian aviation dictionary. 42,000 entry-words, covering all aspects of aviation; abbreviations, p.663-87.
Class No: 629.7(038)=82

Reports Literature
[5402]
NORTH ATLANTIC TREATY ORGANIZATION. Advisory Group for Aeronautical Research and Development (AGARD). **AGARD index of publications, 1952/1970-.** Neuilly-sur-Seine, AGARD, 1972-.
Lists by form (*e.g.* reports, Agardographs, etc.) of all unclassified publications issued by AGARD. Analytical entries for collections. The 1952/70 set had 4 parts: abstract section, subject index, author index, and addendum. The *Index* has subsequently covered 3-year periods.
Class No: 629.7(047)

Reviews & Abstracts
[5403]
CIVIL AVIATION AUTHORITY. CAA Central Library. **Library bulletin: a monthly review of books, reports, periodical articles and other items of interest available in CAA libraries.** London, CAA Central Library, 1978-. Monthly. ISSN: 01410498.
More than 150 entries per issue, for books and technical reports (annotated entries), book reviews (references), periodical articles (annotated entries). 'Coming events in aviation' include conferences (date; organizer; subject; location). 9 library locations.
Class No: 629.7(048)

Periodicals
[5404]
UNITED STATES. Library of Congress. Science and Technology Division. **Aeronautical and space serial publications: a world list.** Washington, the Library 1962. 255p.
4,551 serial publications, under countries A-Z (especially USA, Germany, Great Britain, France and Russia). Covers periodicals, reports, annuals. Library of Congress call numbers given.
A select annotated list of 25 leading current aeronautical periodicals appears in *Information sources in engineering* (2nd ed., 1985), p.314-20. *Class No: 629.7(051)*

Progress Reports
[5405]
Progress in aerospace: an international review journal. Oxford, etc., Pergamon Press, 1964-. illus., diagrs., graphs. $410; £275. ISSN: 03760421.
V.32 (2/3), 1996, carries 3 documented articles including 'Application of modern aluminum alloys to aircraft' (p.1312-72; 81 references). *Class No: 629.7(055)*

Yearbooks & Directories
[5406]
'Flight International' Directory, part 1: United Kingdom and Ireland Directory, 1995-96, incorporating Who's who in British aviation. Potter's Bar, Flight International Directories, 1995. 522p. £48. ISBN: 0951418580.
Coverage: civil and military aviation; airports; airlines; smaller operators (*e.g.* air taxis); flying and gliding clubs; museums; the press; manufacturers and suppliers. *Who's who* includes officials, industrial personnel, journalists, aviation artists, etc. Indexes.
Class No: 629.7(058)

[5407]
'Flight International' Directory, part 2: Mainland Europe and Ireland, 1994/95. Potters Bar, Herts., Flight International Directories, 1994. 623p. map. £45. ISBN: 0951418572.
International section, Albania ... Ukraine, 27 countries. Data include name of director, business; affiliation. 'Who's who'. Detailed index. Advertisers' index. 'European time zones'. *Class No: 629.7(058)*

[5408]
FRAWLEY, G. *and* THORN, J. **The International directory of civil aircraft 1995-96.** Weston Creek, Australia, Aerospace Publications, 1995. 207p. illus. £16.95. ISBN: 1875671099.
Aim is to include all aircraft still in service. About 350 aircraft types, A-Z, with technical and production data, history, colour illustration for each. Appendix: world airlines. *Class No: 629.7(058)*

[5409]
Interavia ABC aerospace directory, 1992. 41st ed. Coulsdon, Surrey, Jane's Information Group, 1992. *c.*1850p. tables, maps. £200. ISBN: 0710609574.
Covers authorities/organizations/institutions; air carriers; manufacturers; airport services; airport structures and equipment; aviation services. A-Z index of people listed. Comprehensive (195 countries). *Class No: 629.7(058)*

Tables & Data Books
[5410]
ROBERTSON, B. **Aviation enthusiasts' data book.** Cambridge, P. Stephens, 1982. 153p. illus., diagrs. ISBN: 0850595002.
19 chapters (1. The world scene and aeronautics; 4. World aircraft industries; 16. Aero engines; 19. Airships). 12 appendices (1. Works of reference; 2. Aeronautical periodicals; 12. Schneider Trophy winners). Detailed, non-analytical index. Well-captioned illus. International in scope. *Class No: 629.7(083)*

Chronologies
[5411]
BAKER, D. **Flight and flying:** a chronology. New York, Facts on File, 1994. ix, 549p. £39.95; $65. ISBN: 0816018545.
About 5,000 entries covering aircraft design, military, civil and commercial aviation and political and industrial events. Two indexes: subject; aircraft type. Glossary; list of abbreviations. 'An excellent work' (*Reference reviews*, 9 (2), 1995, p.27.); 'a highly recommended reference source for all libraries' ('Reference books bulletin', *Booklist*, February 15, 1994, p.1108). *Class No: 629.7(090)*

[5412]
GUNSTON, B. **Chronicle of aviation.** London, Chronicle Communications, 1992. 984p. £29.95. ISBN: 1872043135.
Coverage of developments in flight from earliest times to mide-1992. Appendices include aircraft engines and directory of current world airlines. Lavishly illus. Indexes: subject; aircraft manufacturers and types. *Class No: 629.7(090)*

Histories
[5413]
GIBBS-SMITH, C.H. **Aviation: an historical survey;** from its origin to the end of World War II. 2nd ed. London, HM Stationery Office, 1985. xiv, 320p. illus., tables. £10.95. ISBN: 0112904211.
First published 1970. At head of title: 'Science Museum'
18 chapters. 'Quotations on flying', p.221-229. Folding table on powered flight. 'A chronology of aviation from antiquity to 1945', p.239-52. Glossary. Bibliography, p.273-80. Conversion tables, etc. Addenda, p.289-92. Detailed, analytical index, p.293-320. Well illustrated (22 plates of small photographs; 128 line-drawings). A classic in the literature of aviation history. *Class No: 629.7(091)*

Biographies
[5414]
LONGYARD, W.H. **Who's who in aviation history:** 500 biographies. Shrewsbury, Airlife, 1994. 203p. illus. £19.95 ISBN: 1853102725.
Includes pioneers, inventors, designers, fighter pilots, record breakers, etc., A-Z. Sparsely illus. An 'interesting and useful work' (*Reference reviews*, 8, 7 (1994), p.28). *Class No: 629.7(092)*

Women
[5415]
WELCH, R. **Encyclopedia of women in aviation and space.** Santa Barbara, Ca., ABC-CLIO, 1998. 286p. ilus. $65. ISBN: 0874369584.
About 200 entries ranging from a few paragraphs to 2 pages; some have extensive bibliographies. Detailed, analytical index.
Class No: 629.7(092)-0055.2

Worldwide
[5416]
Jane's all the world's aircraft, 1998-99. Coulsdon, Surrey, Jane's Information Group, 1998. *c.*800p. illus. £270; $410. ISBN: 0710617887.
Contents: Military, airline, business and general aircraft from 48 countries - Fixed wing aircraft, helicopters and airships - Programme history - Customers - Design features - Systems - Landing gear - Power plant - Avionics - Armament - Dimensions - Weights and loadings - Operations noise levels - Profiles of 500 manufacturers. Also available online and on CD-ROM.
The series (1903-1993) is available on microfiche.
Class No: 629.7(100)

Museums

[5417]

ALLEN, J.L. **Aviation and space museums of America.** New York, Asco, 1975. 257p. illus.

Details of 57 aviation and space museums, including 3 in Canada. Two or more illus. of items in each collection. Appended list of aviation organizations and publications. *Class No: 629.7:061:069*

[5418]

OGDEN, B. **Aviation museums.** (worldwide, including USA). Hounslow, Middx., Airline Publications & Sales, Ltd. 1979. 144p. illus., tables, maps. ISBN: 090511362x.

Museums in 54 countries, Albania ... Zimbabwe-Rhodesia. Data: Address; admission days; situation; exhibits (in detail). No bibliography or index. For the traveller and historian. *Class No: 629.7:061:069*

Aircraft Engines

[5419]

GUNSTON, B. **World encyclopedia of aero engines.** 2nd ed. Wellingborough, P. Stephens, 1989. 192p. illus. £19.95. ISBN: 085059717x.

First published 1987.

Entries, ABC (United Kingdom) ... Wright (USA). Glossary. Detailed, analytical index. Fully illustrated with 1 or 2 illus., well captioned, per page. Fills a gap in aeronautical history. *Class No: 629.7.02*

Aircraft

[5420]

BOWER, P.M. **Unconventional aircraft.** 2nd ed. Blue Ridge Summit, Pa., TAB Books, 1990. 323p. illus. (col.). $19.95. ISBN: 0830024503.

Brief descriptions of over 200 unconventional planes (Tandem-wing aircraft ... Flying automobiles) that have existed since Orville and Wilbur Wright flew. *Class No: 629.73*

[5421]

Brassey's world aircraft and systems directory 1999-2000. Taylor, M., *ed.* 2nd ed. London, Brassey's, 1999. 797p. illus. tables. £95. ISBN: 1857532457.

First published 1996.

Covers combat, reconnaissance, airliners, helicopters, general and recreational aviation, missiles, airships, spaceflight, airborne raiders and airport runway bearing strengths. Data include manufacturer, history, technical details, performance. *Class No: 629.73*

[5422]

Guinness aircraft facts and figures. Taylor, M. *and* Mondey, D. Enfield, Middx., Guinness Superlatives, 1984. 256p. illus., (inc. col.)., tables. £9.95. ISBN: 0851124162.

First published 1970.

8 sections: Lighter than air - Pioneers of flying - At last: flight - First World War - Between the World Wars - Post-War aviation - Modern aviation - Rocketry and space flight. Index (tiny print), p.243-56. *Class No: 629.73*

[5423]

HAMILL, T. **'Commercial aircraft of the world'.** *Flight International,* 4/10 September 1991, p.35-90. illus., tables.

Covers the range of types available to the air-transport operator, Airbus Industrie ... SAIC. Appended comparative data tables. This survey appears annually, usually in a September or October issue. *Class No: 629.73*

Great Britain

[5424]

JACKSON, A.J. **British civil aircraft, 1919-1972.** London, Putnam, Conway Maritime Press, 1959-.

First published 1959 (2v.).

1. ABC ... Chilton. 1959 (New ed. 1973). 567p.
2. Chrislea ... Hawker Siddeley. 1960. 560p.
3. Hawker Siddeley ... Zlin. 1960. 636p.

Detailed description, illustration and listing of all transport aircraft, light aeroplanes, home-built, civil registered planes, plus military types and helicopters built in Britain, or imported for British operators, 1919-72. V.3 deals with *c.*150 aeroplanes. 7 appendices (A. Other British-built civil aircraft, p.248-337). Each volume has detailed, analytical index. Data accompanying illus. have congested layout. *Class No: 629.73(410)*

Russia

[5425]

GUNSTON, B. **Aircraft of the Soviet Union:** the encyclopedia of Soviet aircraft since 1917. Baldry, D., *ed.* London, Osprey, 1983. 414, [2]p. illus., ports, diagrs. ISBN: 085045445x.

Includes biographies. Entries: 'Alexandrov-Kalinin ... Zlokazov'. Prelims include 'Soviet aircraft designations', 'Air weapons', 'Materials', 'Engines', 'Soviet organizations', 'Miscellaneous data'. Appended list of grouped light aircraft, p.408-14. Cross-sections, a feature. *Class No: 629.73(47)*

Museums

[5426]

ELLIS, K. *and* BUTLER, P., *comps.* **British museum aircraft:** 39 museums and the histories of their exhibits. Liverpool Airport, Merseyside, Merseyside Aviation Society, Ltd., 1977. 160p. illus., map. ISBN: 0902420151.

39 museums (plus 2 late additions), A-Z under names. Bibliography, p.158-60. Aircraft index, p.164-5. 24 pages of illus. Location map. *Class No: 629.73:061:069*

[5427]

MARCH, P.R. **Preserved aircraft.** Shepperton, Ian Allan, 1980. 160p. illus.

Chronological list of preserved original aircraft, 1909-1973. One or two illus., per page. Appendix: The British Aircraft Preservation Council. Aircraft museums and collections, p.154-6. Bibliography, p.156-7. Detailed analytical index, p.158-60. *Class No: 629.73:061:069*

Aircraft Markings

[5428]

MARCH, P.R. **Military aircraft markings, 1991.** London, I. Allen, 1991. 176p. illus. £4.95. ISBN: 0711019681.

Annual listing of all military aircraft based in Britain (British and American) and a selection of military aircraft based in Western Europe. *Class No: 629.73.088*

[5429]

WRIGHT, A.J. **Civil aircraft markings, 1992.** London, I. Allen, 1992. 320p. illus. £4.95. ISBN: 0711020272.

16 sections, plus Addenda. 'British civil registrations' (in-sequence), p.11-143; 'British civil registrations' (out-of-sequence), p.144-87; Overseas airlines registrations; Radio frequencies; BAPC register. Small format. A bargain. *Class No: 629.73.088*

Balloons

[5430]

CAMERON, D. **Ballooning handbook.** London, Pelham Books, 1980. 174p. illus., diagrs., tables, maps. ISBN: 0720712203.

8 chapters: 1. Fundamentals of ballooning - 2. Flying techniques - 3. Advanced flying techniques - 4. Hot-air technology - 5. Navigation - 6. Meteorology - 7. Ballooning law - 8. Organizations for ballooning. 10 appendices (1. Requirements for pilots' licences (UK), p.155-6 ... 9. Bibliography - 10. Useful addresses). 'I have tried to write this book in international terms' (*Preface*). *Class No: 629.733.3*

Airships

[5431]

BEAUBOIS, H. **Airships: an illustrated history,** Translated and adapted by M. and A. Kelly. London, Macdonald and Jane's, 1974. 235p. illus. (incl. col.). ISBN: 0856081036.

The period: 1780-1972. 8 chapters. The USS Akron 1931 (p.204-5) is described with data on aircraft suspension equipment, power unit and forward nacelle, plus 6 illus., including a cross-section. Bibliography, p.235. Well illustrated (82 drawings in colour, 125 black-and-white photographs; descriptive captions). Index of airship names. *Class No: 629.733.5*

Gliders & Sailplanes

[5432]

COATES, A. **Jane's world sailplanes and motor gliders.** 2nd ed. London, Jane's Publishing Co. 1980. 207p. illus., diagrs. ISBN: 0710600176.

First published 1980.

Covers 20 countries, Australia ... Yugoslavia. Technical data under 17 heads. Appendix: International gliding championships, 1937-1978. FAI world gliding championships, 1937-1978. Index by country. Index of aircraft types, p.203-7. *Class No: 629.734*

[5433]

REAY, D.A. **The History of man-powered flight.** Oxford, etc., Pergamon Press, 1977. 355p. illus., diagrs., graphs, tables. ISBN: 0080217389.

17 chapters (1. Mythology or fact: flight in early civilizations; 12. The first man-powered simulator - one of several Canadian projects; 17. Future prospect). 6 appendices (1. Patents; 4. Bibliography, p.328-32 (chronological); 6. Definitions). Detailed, analytical index. Well-presented. *Class No:* 629.734

Parachutes and Parachuting

[5434]

POYNTER, P. **The Parachute manual:** a technical treatise on the parachute. 2nd. ed., completely revised. Santa Barbara, Calif., Parachuting Publications, 1977. 497p. illus., diagrs. ISBN: 0915516068.

First published 1972.

9 chapters: 1. Regulations ... 4. Parachute materials ... 6. Parachute component parts - Maintenance, alteration and manufacturing procedures. Fully illustrated and captioned. Combined glossary and index, p.480-97. US slant. *Class No:* 629.734.7

Helicopters

[5435]

EVERETT-HEATH, J. **British military helicopters.** London, Arms and Armour Press, 1986. 224p. illus. £14.95.

A survey of military helicopter types, from Cierva helicopters and Bristol helicopters to Westland 30 and EH-101. 4 appendices (*e.g.* helicopter projects and designs). List of abbreviations. Glossary. Bibliography, p.220. Over 200 photographs. Detailed, non-analytical index. *Class No:* 629.735.4

[5436]

Jane's helicopter markets and systems. Coulsdon, Surrey, Jane's Information Group, 1996. 400p., looseleaf binder. illus., diagrs. tables. £495. ISBN: 0710613636.

Over 150 main models, civil and military. Data: manufacturer; structure; programme details; variants; compressor; turbines; gearbox; fuel system and consumption. Available online and on CD-ROM (£595). Updates are issued. *Class No:* 629.735.4

Rockets & Missiles

[5437]

ROSENBERG, A., *comp.* **Russian-English glossary of guided missile, rocket and satellite terms.** Washington, Library of Congress, 1958. vi, 351p.

More than 4,000 Russian terms, with English equivalents, taken from Soviet monographs and periodicals, 1955-58. The English equivalents are based mainly on Soviet translations of US and British Publications (*Introduction*). *Class No:* 629.76

[5438]

—MURASHKEVICH, A.M., *and others, comps.* English-Russian guided missiles and space flight dictionary. Moscow, Military Publishing House, 1966. 920p.

Russian terms, with English equivalents. *Class No:* 629.76

[5439]

WINTER, F.H. **Rockets into space.** Cambridge, Ma., Harvard Univ. Press, 1990. xii,165p. illus. $22.50. (*Frontiers of space.*) ISBN: 0674776607.

7 chapters: 1. The founders of spaceflight theory - 2. The experimenters - 3. The V-2 rocket - 4. Rockets enter the space age - 5. Modern rockets - 6. Space shuttles - 7. The future of rocketry. Extensive source notes, p.149-56. Detailed, analytical index, p.159-65. *Class No:* 629.76

Astronautics (Space Craft)

Abbreviations & Symbols

[5440]

MORINGO, F.P. **Aerospace and defense acronyms.** 2nd ed. Washington, D.C., American Institute of Aeronautics and Astronautics, 1992. 207p. ISBN: 0930403630.

About 25,000 entries. Covers June 1982- July 1992. List of 'Reference codes' precedes. *Class No:* 629.78(003)

Bibliographies

[5441]

MacADAM, E.J. 'Aerospace engineering'. In *Information sources in engineering*. 2nd ed., Editor, L.J. Anthony. p.294-324. chart. London, etc., Butterworths, 1985.

Contents: International organizations - Official sources of information (USA ... Israel) - Periodicals - Abstracting and indexing services - General reference material (directories and guides; bibliographies; monographs and textbooks). Particularly useful on official reports. Aerospace engineering as a distinct topic was not featured in the 3rd ed. of *Information sources in engineering* (1996). *Class No:* 629.78(01)

Encyclopaedias

[5442]

BOOTH, N. **The Encyclopedia of space.** London, Brian Todd, 1990. 200p. illus. (col.). £17.95. ISBN: 1853611166.

6 sections: 1. Developments in space (11 articles: 'Pioneers'; 'Moon race'; 'Space shuttle', etc.) - 2. Manned missions - 3. Solar system exploration - 4. Earth satellites - 5. Future solar exploration - 6. Milestones (chronological list). Indexes: general; astronauts; vehicles and equipment. A glossy production, suitable for school libraries. *Class No:* 629.78(031)

[5443]

The Cambridge encyclopedia of space. Rycroft, M., *ed.* Cambridge Univ. Press, 1990. 386p. col. illus., tables. ISBN: 0521364264.

Originally published 1987 as *Le Grand atlas de l'espace*.

In 4 parts (From dream to reality - Going into space - Exploring the universe - Living with space) each with numerous chapters by various hands. A popular treatment. *Class No:* 629.78(031)

[5444]

FURNISS, T. **Space flight:** the records. Enfield, Middx, Guiness Superlatives, 1985. 168p. illus., ports., tables. ISBN: 0851124518.

5 sections: 1. Manned space flight diary [12 April 1961 - 29 April 1985] - 2. Firsts in manned space flight - 3. Manned space machines - 4. An A to Z of space travellers (p.69-107) - 5. Manned space flight, tables (Manned space flight duration tables ... Space shuttle schedule). Postscript (latest flight 1985). Glossary. Detailed index, p.162-8. *Class No:* 629.78(031)

[5445]

The Illustrated encyclopedia of space technology. Gatland, K.W., *ed.* 2nd ed. London, New York, Salamander Books, 1989. 306p. illus., diagrs., maps. £16.95. ISBN: 0861014499.

First published 1981.

A popular history including weather patrols, manned flights, military systems, space cities, lunar and planetary probes. 'Space diary' (p.252-97) covers events from 360 BC to 1989. Glossary of terms; subject index. Lavishly illustrated, many in colour. *Class No:* 629.78(031)

[5446]

USA in space. Magill, F.N. *and* Tobias, R.T., *eds.* Pasadena, Ca., Salem Press, 1996. 3v. illus. $210. ISBN: 0893569240.

197 articles on manned and unmanned speace missions, space centres, launch sites and issues of importance to the US space programme. 160 of the articles were originally published in *Magill's survey of science: space exploration series*, now out of print. Extensive list of World Wide Web pages. 'A fine reference set' (*American reference books annual*, 1997, p.594). *Class No:* 629.78(031)

[5447]

—CURTIS, A.R. Space almanac: facts, figures, names, dates, places, lists, charts, tables, maps covering space from Earth to the edge of the universe. Woodsboro, Md., Arcsoft Publishers, 1990. 955p. illus., tables, charts, maps. $19.95. ISBN: 0866680659.

8 major sections: Astronauts - Space stations - Shuttles - Rockets - Satellites - Solar system - Deep space - Calendar of events. 33-page index. Many photographs, drawings and illustrations, although these are of variable quality. However, full of useful information, and a handy reference tool. A smaller 2nd ed. (746p.) was published in 1992 (Houston, Gulf Publishing). *Class No:* 629.78(031)

[5448]

—Space year 1991: the complete record of the year's space events. MacKnight, N., *ed.* Oscelola, Wi., Motorbooks International, 1990. 176p. illus. $19.95; £11.95. ISBN: 0879384824.

Covers space missions (manned, unmanned, planetary between 1 July 1989 and 30 June 1990. 'Into orbit' (p.157-71) lists every spacecraft launch (type of craft, purpose, launch time and site, etc.) for the period. Index, p.173-76. 'Accessible and informative' ('Reference books bulletin, *Booklist*, February 1, 1991, p.1155). *Class No:* 629.78(031)

Dictionaries

Polyglot

[5449]

Aerospace dictionary: English, French, German, Spanish. Paris, Gauthier-Villars, 1984. [vi], 828p. col. illus. ISBN: 2040119523.

Earlier ed. (1978) as *Dictionnaire des techniques aéronautique et spatiale* (French-English-German).

About 36,000 English entry-words, with equivalents in the other three languages. 45 categories applied.

3 companion volumes give priority to each of the other languages, *i.e.*, *Dictionnaire aérospatial* (French-English-German-Spanish); *Wörterbuch der Luft-und Raumfahrt* (German-English-French-Spanish); *Diccionario aéroespacial* (Spanish-French-English-German). *Class No:* 629.78(038)=00

[5450]

KLECZEK, J. *and* **KLECZKOVÁ, H. Space sciences dictionary;** English, French, German, Spanish, Portuguese, Russian. Amsterdam, Elsevier, 1990-92. 4 vols. ISBN: 0444988726.

V.1: *Radiation; matter.*
V.2: *Motion; space flight; data.*
V.3: *Space technology; space research.*
V.4: *Earth sciences; solar system; deep space.*

English terms, numbered, are grouped by subject (*e.g.* 'spectrum'; 'molecules') with equivalents in the other lnaguages spread across the double page. Indexes for each language. *Class No:* 629.78(038)=00

[5451]

KOTIK, M.G., *comp.* **Dictionary of aerospace engineering in Russian, English and German.** Amsterdam, Elsevier, 1986. 879p. £71. ISBN: 0444995064.

Co-edited with VEB Verlag Technik, Berlin.

About 35,000 specialized Russian terms, with equivalents and indexes in English and German. *Class No:* 629.78(038)=00

[5452]

TEKNISKA NOMENKLATURCENTRALEN. Rymdorlista: svensk-engelsk-fransk-tysk-rysk. Stockholm, the Centre, 1973. xxiii, 171p. (*TNC 53.*) ISBN: 9171960538.

'Glossary of astronautics'. 510 Swedish technical terms dealing with outer space, plus equivalents and indexes in English, French, German and Russian. *Class No:* 629.78(038)=00

English

[5453]

The Aviation space dictionary. Reithmaier, L.W., *ed.* 7th ed. Los Angeles, Ca., Aero, 1990. 461p. illus. $32.95. ISBN: 0830680926.

Previous ed. 1980.

About 6,000 concise entries, drawing heavily on the NASA *Dictionary of technical terms for aerospace use.* 16 appendices, including essays. *Class No:* 629.78(038)=20

[5454]

Chambers air and space dictionary. Walker, P.M.B. Edinburgh, Chambers, 1990. viii,216p. illus., diagrs. £17.95; £8.95. ISBN: 0550132422; 0550132430, Pbk.

Published in the US as *Cambridge air and space dictionary.*

About 6,000 terms derived from *Chambers science and technology dictionary.* Most definitions are brief (*e.g.* 'luminance': 3 lines), but includes 50 'special articles' in separate panels (*e.g.* 'Quasars' 1p.). Good use of bold and italic type. *Class No:* 629.78(038)=20

[5455]

Jane's aerospace dictionary. Gunston, B., *ed.* 3rd ed. Coulsdon, Surrey, 1988. *c.*600p. £30. ISBN: 0710605803.

First published 1980.

About 28,000 entries, ranging in length from 3 to 100 words. Many acronyms and abbreviations as entries. Different meanings of terms are numbered. Headwords are categorized. *Class No:* 629.78(038)=20

[5456]

SAE dictionary of aerospace engineering. Tomsic, J.L., *ed.* 2nd ed. Warrendale, Pa., Society of Automotive Engineers, 1998. x, 748p. ISBN: 0768002451.

First published 1992.

Over 20,000 terms, derived from SAE Aerospace standards and reports and the *NASA Thesaurus.* Numerous computer terms related to data processing and PC technology. *Class No:* 629.78(038)=20

[5457]

WILLIAMSON, M. Dictionary of space technology. Bristol; New York, Adam Hilger, 1990. xi,401p. illus., diagrs. £25; $50. ISBN: 0852743394.

Over 1,600 entries ('Solar energy': *c.*½p.). Over 100 photos and diagrs. Final 3 sections: Physics and astronomy - Space Centres and organizations - Miscellaneous. Classified list of dictionary entries under 12 headings. Cross-references (plentiful). Good use of bold type and uncongested layout. *Class No:* 629.78(038)=20

German

[5458]

CESCOTTI, R. Aerospace-Wörterbuch: Deutsch-Englisch/Englisch-Deutsch. [Aerospace dictionary: German-English/English-German.] Stuttgart, Motorbuch-Verlag, 1994. ix, 382p. ISBN: 3613015366.

About 50,000 words in each half. Appended: abbreviations in English. Foreword and explanations in German only. *Class No:* 629.78(038)=30

[5459]

HYMAN, C.J. German-English, English-German astronautics dictionary. New York, Consultants Bureau, 1968. viii, 237p.

About 9,000 entry-words in each part (p.1-122; 125-237). Includes vocabulary of allied subjects such as automation, cosmic rays, aviation fuel, guiding devices, propulsion, radio engineering and telecommunications. *Class No:* 629.78(038)=30

French

[5460]

EUROPEAN SPACE AGENCY. Recueil de terminologie spatiale. [A Glossary of space terms.] Taillefer, Y., *comp.* Paris, the Agency, 1982. [iii], 432p. diagrs. ISSN: 03796566.

About 4,000 French entry-words, with English explanations. Also available online via ESA-IRS with German terms as well. *Class No:* 629.78(038)=40

Russian

[5461]

KONARSKI, M.M. Russian-English space technology dictionary. Oxford, etc., Pergamon Press, 1970. x, [i], 416p. illus., diagrs.

Over 10,000 selected terms in satellite and other spacecraft operations, spaceflight guidance and control, and space exploration. Part 1: Russian-English dictionary of categorized terms plus 'Index of English cross-reference terms' (p.237-370); short glossary of aerospace biomedical terms; Russian abbreviations. Part 2: 12 data tables; list of personal names of scientists (*i.e.,* Russian forms of surnames of scientists in space technology, with English forms). An essential complement to Konarski's *Russian-English dictionary of modern terms in aeronautics and rocketry* (1962). *Class No:* 629.78(038)=82

Reports Literature

[5462]

Scientific and technical aerospace reports (STAR): an abstract journal. Washington, DC., Scientific and Technical Information Office, National Aeronautics and Space Administration (NASA), 1963-. Monthly. $1700pa. ISSN: 00368741.

Also available on microfiche.

About 30,000 abstracts pa. Main divisions (01-99): Aeronautics - Astronautics - Chemistry and materials - Engineering - Geosciences - Life sciences - Mathematical and computer sciences - Physics - Social sciences - Space sciences. Indexes: subject; personal author; corporate source; contact number; report/accession number index per issue, quarterly, semi-annual and annual. A companion service to *International aerospace abstracts*, and equally indispensable to the researcher.

Available online in the *Aerospace database* (DIALOG, file 108). CD-ROM (KR Information Ondisc). *Class No:* 629.78(047)

Reviews & Abstracts

[5463]

International aerospace abstracts. New York, American Institute of Aeronautics and Astronautics Technical Information Service, for NASA, Scientific and Technical Information Branch, 1961-. Monthly. $1625pa. (US), $2240 (other countries). ISSN: 00205842.

Replaces abstracts in *Aero/Space engineering* (formerly *Aeronautical engineering review*), 1942-60.

About 50,000 abstracts pa. Sections: Aeronautics - Astronautics - Chemistry and materials - Engineering - Geosciences - Life sciences - Mathematics and computer sciences - Physics - Social sciences - Space sciences - General. Coverage: periodicals (including government-sponsored), books, meetings, papers, conference proceedings, translations of journals, and journal articles. Indexes of subjects, personal authors, contract numbers, meetings papers and report numbers, accession number. A basic abstracting service. (Abstracts and indexes of report literature are the province of *Scientific and technical aerospace reports* (STAR)).

Available online in the *Aerospace database* (DIALOG, file 108). CD-ROM (KR Information OnDisc). *Class No:* 629.78(048)

Yearbooks & Directories

[5464]

Jane's international ABC aerospace directory 1998. Durham, S., *ed.*
48th ed. Coulsdon, Surrey, Jane's Information Group, 1998. cxxiv,
1716p. illus., diagrs., tables. £355; $575. ISBN: 0710617623.

Sections: Quick reference - Contact reference - Product/service
index - Product/supplier link - Who is where - Electronic address link.
Available online and on CD-ROM. *Class No: 629.78(058)*

[5465]

Jane's space directory, 1998-99. 14th ed. Coulsdon, Surrey, Jane's
Information Group, 1998. 560p. illus., diagrs., tables. ISBN:
0710618107.

Contents: satellites; launch vehicles; world space centres;
government and NGO space programmes; space industry; contractors;
space logs. Covers military and civil satellites. *Class No: 629.78(058)*

[5466]

United States space directory. 1995-96 ed. Betheseda, Md., Space
Publications, 1995. 213p. $79.99 ISBN: 1887022023.

Directory-type information on organizations contributing to the US
space industry. 5 major sections: companies; government; universities
and nonprofit research institutions; education; miscellaneous. Indexes.
Class No: 629.78(058)

Tables & Data Books

[5467]

Interavia space directory, 1992-1993. Wilson, A., *ed.*   3rd ed.
Coulson, Surrey, Jane's Information Group, 1992. 630p. illus.,
diagrs., tables. £135. ISBN: 0710610017.

Previously *Jane's Spaceflight directory.*

Main contents: National space programmes - International space
programmes - Military space - Launchers - Communications - Satcom
ground segments and contractory - Earth observation (space) - Earth
observation (ground) - Microgravity - World space centres - The solar
system - Space industry. Detailed index. An up-to-date compendium.
Class No: 629.78(083)

[5468]

TODD, D. World aerospace: a statistical handbook. London, Croom
Helm, 1987. 226p. tables.

Aerospace activity in Soviet bloc, Europe [& other regions].
Changes in materials and avionics. Space technology forecast.
Statistical appendices. For all reference collections in aerospace
activities (*New technical books,* March/April 1987, item 614).
Class No: 629.78(083)

Chronologies

[5469]

BAKER, D. Spaceflight and rocketry: a chronology. New York, Facts
on File, 1996. 528p. illus. $65. ISBN: 0816018537.

About 7,000 entries covering human rocket construction and the
exploration of space. Ranges from rockets fired at Alexander the Great
to the US space programme. The index was criticized in the review in
American reference books annual (1997, p.593), but the chronology
itself 'is fascinating'. *Class No: 629.78(090)*

Histories

[5470]

DICKSON, K.M. History of aeronautics and astronautics: a
preliminary bibliography. Washington, National Aeronautics and Space
Administration (NASA), 1968.

A selected, annotated guide to 921 publications on the history of
space exploration from earliest times to 1967. *Class No: 629.78(091)*

[5471]

LAUNIUS, R.D. Frontiers of space exploration. Westport, CT.,
Greenwood, 1998. 204p. illus. $39.95. ISBN: 0313299684.

Contents include a historical overiew, the race to the moon,
scientific exploration, and the attempt at a permanent, manned
presence in space. Biographical sketches; facsimiles of primary
documents; bibliography; appendix (US space flights between 1961
and 1997); index. *Class No: 629.78(091)*

Biographies

[5472]

CASSUTT, M. Who's who in space. Rev. ed. New York, Macmillan,
1993. 450p. illus. $75. ISBN: 0028970926.

First published 1987.

11 sections, by nationality and space programme. Biographies, A-Z
within a section, include dates and brief description of space activities.
Numerous appendices, *e.g.* manned spaceflights, shuttle approach and
landing tests; manned time-in-space log, 1961-92, etc. Index.
Class No: 629.78(092)

[5473]

UNITED STATES. House of Representatives. Committee on Science
and Technology. **Astronauts and cosmonauts:** biographical and
statistical data. Washington, US Government Printing Office, 1976.
180p. ports.

'The astronauts whose biographical sketches and portraits are
included in this directory were involved variously with NASA, the X-
15 program, Air Force - NASA X-20 Dyna-Sore program and DOD
Manned Orbiting Lab Program. Soviet cosmonauts are also described'
(*RSR,* v.5(4), October/December 1977, p.40). The statistical data
covers Soviet - US space flights. *Class No: 629.78(092)*

Great Britain

[5474]

MASSEY, Sir H. *and* **ROBINS, M.O. History of British space
science.** Cambridge Univ. Press, 1986. xxii, 514p. illus., diagrs.,
graphs, formulas, tables. £45. ISBN: 052130783X.

16 chapters (3. The initiation of the Skylark rocket programme - 4.
Post-IQY developments - 5. The Ariel programme - 6. The European
Space Research Organization - 7. Commonwealth cooperation in space
research ... 13/14. Scientific studies by British space scientists).
Appendices A-G (F. Details of the principal UK space science groups,
1982). Glossary of abbreviations, p.xiii-xv. Index.
Class No: 629.78(410)

Russia

[5475]

BATTELLE MEMORIAL INSTITUTE, Columbus, Ohio. Columbus
Laboratories. **Handbook of Soviet space-science research.**
Wikelic, G.E., *ed.* New York, Gordon & Breach, 1969. xx, 506p.
illus.

20 documented chapters, with author and subject indexes. Aims to
be a comprehensive and authoritative English-language summary of the
first 10 years of Soviet space-science research. *Class No: 629.78(47)*

[5476]

BEARD, R. Soviet cosmonautics, 1957-1969: a bibliography of articles
published in British periodicals and foreign books. Swindon, Wilts.,
the Author, 1970. 43p. Mimeographed.

Part 1: *c.*300 items, listing all books published since October 1957
throughout the world on Soviet space-flight; A-Z, authors. Part 2:
*c.*700 items, listing all articles in periodicals published in Britain, 1
October 1957 to 30 June 1969; A-Z, periodicals.
Class No: 629.78(47)

Institutions & Associations

[5477]

Aerospace technology centres: a world directory of organizations and
programmes. 2nd ed. Harlow, Essex, Longman, 1991. 250p. £250.
ISBN: 0582082757.

Over 80 countries, arranged by country, then organizations A-Z.
Data include recent activities, estimate of annual expenditure and list of
organizations' publications. Subject index; index of organizations by
titles. *Class No: 629.78:061:061.2*

[5478]

Space industry international: markets, companies, statistics and
personnel. Harlow, Essex, Longman Group, 1987. xx, 353p.

12 regional chapters describe for each country its national and
international space activities, governmental space policies and
programs, and the role of private industry in the space market.
Directory-type entries cover private firms, associations and institutes.
There is also an introduction on relevant international organizations.
Glossary. Bibliography. Indexes of companies and organizations,
products, and personnel. *Class No: 629.78:061:061.2*

[5479]

—**BRITISH NATIONAL SPACE CENTRE.** Directory of UK space
capabilities. London, HM Stationery Office, 1987. *c.*250p. ISBN:
0115139818.

Has as subtitle: 'A guide to the space-related expertise of UK
manufacturers, agencies and universities and their capabilities'.
Class No: 629.78:061:061.2

Research Projects

[5480]

Aerospace research index: a guide to world research in aeronautics,
meteorology, astronomy and space science. Willmore, A.P. *and*
Willmore, S.R., *eds.* Harlow, Essex, Longman Group, 1981. 597p.

World directory, detailing information on aerospace research
conducted in *c.*70 countries by government laboratories, public
companies, industrial firms, research associations, universities and
technical colleges. Coverage extends to astronomy, meteorology and
aeronautics. Omits USSR. Title and keyword index; subject index.
Early revision is clearly called for. *Class No: 629.78:061:061.62.005*

UFOs

[5481]

CATOE, L.E., *comp.* **UFOs and related subjects: an annotated bibliography.** Prepared by the Library of Congress Science and Technology Division for the Air Force Office of Scientific Research. Supplemented by 'Unidentified flying objects: a selected bibliography', compiled by K. Rodgers. Washington, Library of Congress, 1976. Republished by Gale Research Co., Detroit, 1978. xviii, 411p.

A reprint of the bibliography published in 1969, plus updating supplement.

A guide to more than 1,600 books, journal articles, pamphlets, conference proceedings, tapes, original manuscripts, and other material. Subject classes; author index. Includes an appendix on mirages. For the general reader. *Class No:* 629.78.001

[5482]

—**RASMUSSEN, R.M.** The UFO literature: a comprehensive annotated bibliography. Jefferson, N.C., McFarland, 1985. 271p. $29.95.

Lists, under author, more than 1,100 titles of English-language books, booklets and special-issue magazines. Subject and title index. *Class No:* 629.78.001

[5483]

CLARK, J. **The UFO encyclopedia.** 2nd ed. Detroit, Mi., Omnigraphics, 1998. 2v. (1180p.). illus. $140.. ISBN: 0780800877.

First published 1990-96 in 3v.

Includes 273 entries, A-Z, covering a range of topics (*e.g.* organizations, crashes, abduction) with recent documentation. Content attempts to be factual and balanced. *Class No:* 629.78.001

[5484]

The UFO encyclopedia. Spencer, J., *ed.* London, Headline, 1991. 448p. £5.99. ISBN: 0747224949.

Comprehensive reference book for both converts and sceptics. *Class No:* 629.78.001

Spacecraft

[5485]

WILSON, A. **Solar system log.** London, Jane's, 1987. 128p. illus., diagrs., tables. £7.95. ISBN: 0710604440.

Chronological listing of solar missions between 1958 and 1985. Data include launch date, vehicle, spacecraft mass, destination, mission, payload, etc., as well as a brief discussion (*c.*1p.) of noteworthy features or results. *Class No:* 629.782

[5486]

YENNE, B. **The Encyclopedia of US spacecraft.** London, Hamlyn, 1986. 192p. illus. (mostly col.), diagrs. £8.95.

Largely a pictorial record. Data on satellites include launches, launch date, weight, size and shape, and purpose of launching. 3 appendices list space stations, launchers, and seronyms. While providing a fairly comprehensive picture of NASA and commercial spacecraft, Yenne gives a much less complete sample of satellites originating with other agencies. *New scientist* reviewer (16 January 1986, p.53) notes errors and the fact 'that dozens of satellites are omitted'. 'The US has been responsible for less than 20 per cent of the space launches in the past 20 years', he adds. *Class No:* 629.782

Satellites

[5487]

The RAE table of earth satellites, 1957-1986; compiled at the Royal Aircraft Establishment, Farnborough, by D.G. King-Hele, and others. 3rd ed. London, Macmillan Publishers, 1987. xviii, 936p. £65. ISBN: 0333353749.

First published 1981, covering 1957-1980.

Lists over 13,000 satellites including fragments. Data: name and international designations of earth satellite and its associated rocket(s), plus date of launch, lifetime (actual or estimated), mass, shape, dimensions and at least one set of orbital parameters. Listed (without details): other fragments associated with a launch space vehicle that escape from the earth's influence. Index (name; description; page). *Class No:* 629.783

[5488]

Space satellite handbook. Curtis, A.R., *ed.* 3rd ed. Houston, Tx., Gulf, 1994. vi, 346p. £32. ISBN: 0884151921.

Over 22,000 satellites. 10 sections (*e.g.* communication; weather; navigation; science and technology; manned, etc.). Glossary, p.170-89. 'Master list of all satellites', p.191-331. *Class No:* 629.783

63 Agriculture & Livestock

Agriculture

Abbreviations & Symbols

[5489]
FOOD AND AGRICULTURE ORGANIZATION. **Abbreviations used by FAO** for international organizations, congresses, commissions, committees, etc. 4th revision. Rome, FAO, 1988. 205p. £11.25. (*FAO terminology bulletin 27/rev. 4.*) ISBN: 9250026595.
   Previous ed. 1976 (60p.).
   Abbreviations in English, French and Spanish. *Class No:* 63.0(003)

Databases

[5490]
AGDEX. Edinburgh, Agdex Information Services (SAC), 1973-.
   Database of *c.*70,000 records on articles covering UK agriculture which appear in the 'popular' agricultural press, thus complementing *CAB ABSTRACTS (q.v.)*. Most of the records have abstracts. Paper products from the database include monthly bulletins, student index, and occasional bibliographies of subjects of topical interest, *e.g.* Chernobyl. *Class No:* 63.0(003.4)

[5491]
AGRICOLA. Beltsville, Md., US National Agricultural Library, 1970-.
   Citations to journals, serials, monographs, government reports, patents, theses, etc. which have been acquired by NAL. Contains *c.*3 million records. Updates of *c.*9,000 records a month. Online equivalent of *Bibliography of agriculture (q.v.).* Available on CD-ROM. Available on the Internet at http://www.nal.usda.gov/ag98/ag98.html. This site is free to anyone with Internet access, but some features provided by commercial publishers are unavailable. In addition, there is no full-text searching but some of the indexes can be browsed. *Class No:* 63.0(003.4)

[5492]
AgriGator: agricultural and related information. URL: http://www.ifas.ufl.edu/www/agator/htm.
   Site is maintained by the Institute of Food and Agricultural Science (IFAS), University of Florida. A collection of worldwide agricultural resources, regularly maintained. *Class No:* 63.0(003.4)

[5493]
AGRIS. Rome, Food and Agriculture Organization, 1975-.
   Contains more than 2 million citations (10 percent with abstracts) to international agricultural literature. Titles in original languages and 1986- index terms in English, French, and Spanish. *c.*10,000 records are added each month. Online equivalent of *Agrindex (q.v.).* Available on CD-ROM. *Class No:* 63.0(003.4)

[5494]
CAB ABSTRACTS. Wallingford, Oxon. CAB International, 1973-.
   Contains over 3.5 million records and covers 47 abstracting journals published by CAB International. 11,000 journals are scanned as well as books, reports, theses, conference proceedings, etc. About 160,000 items are indexed each year. Updated monthly. Available on CD-ROM as CABCD, while specialist areas are covered by AgECONCD, TREECD, PlantGene CD, HORTCD, VETCD, PlantPATHCD, NutritionCD, BEASTCD, SOILCD, CABPestCD, and CROPCD. *Class No:* 63.0(003.4)

[5495]
Key guide to electronic resources: agriculture. Drew, W., *ed.* Medford, N.J., Learned Information, Inc., 1995. 123p. $35. ISBN: 1573870005.
   Five sections: Databases - CD-ROM - Locally mounted databases - Libraries - Networked services (Internet). Data vary depending on the section, but usually included is a brief description, producer, vendor, reviewer's comments, price, required equipment, etc. A useful guide, although the editor admits to not having seen some of the sources listed and, as with most guides to electronic resources, it can never be completely up-to-date. *Class No:* 63.0(003.4)

[5496]
World databases in agriculture. Armstrong, C.J., *ed.* London, Bowker Saur, 1996. xii,1130p. £150. ISBN: 1857390431.
   Gives details of more than 1,000 electronic sources on the Internet, online, on CD-ROM, realtime, on diskette, and on tape. Each entry includes name, type, years of coverage, number of records, geographical coverage, language, full description, search software, search aids and manuals, references to evaluative literature. Addresses, p.713-37. Database name and subject indexes. Criticized in *Choice* (April 1996, p.1294) for too much general information obscuring the specialized material and for an unwieldy 375-page index.
   Class No: 63.0(003.4)

CD-ROM

[5497]
Agrisearch. London, SilverPlatter, 1975-. Annual. CD-ROM.
   Incorporates five databases covering research in agriculture, food, and nutrition: CRIS from USDA detailing research from US agencies; ICAR from the Canadian Agricultural Research Council covering research projects in Canada; ARRIP from the Australian Standing Committee on Agriculture containing research projects on soil science, food, and horticulture; SIS from the Special Program for African Agricultural Research covering research on the sustainable use of renewable natural resources in Africa; AGREP from Commission of the European Communities listing European agricultural research. Database holds some 80,000 records, with *c.*5,000 added pa. Also available on CD-ROM (1992-). *Class No:* 63.0(003.40)

Bibliographies

[5498]
ACCIS guide to United Nations information sources on food and agriculture. Advisory Committee for the Co-ordination of Information Systems, *comp.* Rome, FAO, 1987. vii, 124p.
   10 sections (*e.g.* 2. Plant production and protection information sources; 5. Land and water development and natural resources information sources; 10. Statistics information sources). 3 annexes (2. Addresses of database hosts). Subject, names, publications and systems indexes. *Class No:* 63.0(01)

[5499]
FOOD AND AGRICULTURE ORGANIZATION. **FAO books in print.** Rome, FAO. Annual. *Gratis.*
   10 sections: 0. Agriculture - 1. Plant production and protection - 2. Animal production and health - 3. Forestry - 4. Fisheries - 5. Land and water development - 6. Economic and social development - 7. Statistics - 8. Food and nutrition - 9. General. Alphabetical titles index and prices. Author index. List of FAO sales agents and booksellers. *Class No:* 63.0(01)

[5500]
Guide to sources for agricultural and biological research. Sponsored by the United States National Agricultural Library, United States Department of Agriculture. Blanchard, J.R. *and* Farrell, L., *eds.* 2nd ed. Berkeley, etc., Univ. of California Press, 1981. xi, 735p. $60. ISBN: 0520032268.
   First published 1958 as *Literature of agriculture research*, by J.R. Blanchard and H. Ostvold, and known as the 'hayseed Winchell'.
   12 contributors. 5,779 annotated, evaluative entries in 9 classes (subdivided, with introductions: A. Agriculture and biology: general - B. Plant sciences - C. Crop protection - D. Animal sciences - E. Physical sciences - F. Food and nutrition - G. Environmental science - H. Social sciences - I. Computerized databases for bibliographic research). Appendix: Acronyms and abbreviations. The general introduction has helpful pages on 'Depositories of information in libraries and documentation centres' and 'Information networks for agriculture and biology'. Author, analytical subject (p.667-735) and title indexes. 'Fills a need that has existed for years' (*RQ,* v.21(4), Summer 1982, p.418). *Class No:* 63.0(01)

[5501]

—BUSH, E.A.R. Agriculture: a bibliographical guide. London, Macdonald, 1974. 2v. (xxxi, iv, 1561p.). (*Macdonald bibliographical guides*.)

Has 9,404 entries (in 172 sections) for books and periodical articles, 1958-71. Annotations state number of items in bibliographies and period covered. Omits items on preserved foods, vegetable oils, etc. Author index includesjoint authors, subject index, p.1369-1561. List of cited periodicals, p.xv-xxxi. A massive basic bibliography, awarded the LA Besterman Medal for 1974. Now somewhat dated.
Class No: 63.0(01)

[5502]

Information sources in agriculture and food science. Lilley, G.P., *ed.* London, etc., Butterworths, 1981. xiv, 603p. (*Guides to information sources*.) ISBN: 0408106123.

18 contributors. 2 parts: 1. General (chapters 1-7) - 2. Specialized areas (8. Soils and fertilizers; 9. Agricultural engineering; 10. Weed biology, weed control and herbicides; 12. Field crops and grasslands; 13. Temperate horticulture; 14. Tropical agriculture; 15. Animal production; 16. Veterinary science; 17. Forestry; 18. Food science; 19. Agricultural economics; 20. Agrarian and food history). Appendix: List of abbreviations used. Index (subjects, organizations, journal titles), p.591-603. Thin on coverage of fish and fisheries; omits beekeeping.

Now of chiefly historical interest; planned new edition has been abandoned. *Class No:* 63.0(01)

[5503]

ROTHAMSTED EXPERIMENTAL STATION. Library. **Catalogue of printed books and pamphlets on agriculture published between 1471 and 1840.** 2nd ed. Harpenden, Herts., 1940. 293p.

First published 1926.

An author catalogue, with indexes of authors, translations, and an historical and geographical list of foreign authors and translations.
Supplement (1949. ii, 15p.) lists additions since 1940.
Class No: 63.0(01)

[5504]

—UNITED STATES. National Agricultural Library. Historic books and manuscripts concerning general agriculture in the collection of the National Agricultural Library. Washington, the Library, 1967. [iv], 94p.

Has *c.*700 entries, with full titles and brief biographical notes. An author catalogue of 16th-18th-century material. NAL shelf-marks.
Class No: 63.0(01)

[5505]

—WYE COLLEGE LIBRARY. A Catalogue of agricultural & horticultural books, 1543-1918, in Wye College Library. Ashford, Kent, the Library, 1977. iv, 100p. £1.50. ISBN: 090185963x.

An author list of *c.*1,000 items. Includes locations in 12 libraries' catalogues (*e.g.* British Museum, *STC*, Wing). *Class No:* 63.0(01)

[5506]

UNITED STATES. National Agricultural Library. **Dictionary catalog of the National Agricultural Library, 1862-1965.** New York, Rowman & Littlefield, Inc., 1967-70. 73v.

Over 1,700,000 catalogue cards, photolithographically reproduced. V.1-72: A-Z sequence of authors, titles and subjects for monographs, serials and analytics, as catalogued for the NAL main collection, for its Bee Culture Branch, and for the former Beltsville Branch. V.73: Translations of periodical articles (authors, A-Z). The most comprehensive catalogue of its kind. Entries are not always legible.

Continued as *National Agricultural Library catalog,*
Class No: 63.0(01)

Encyclopaedias

[5507]

Encyclopedia of agricultural science. Arntzen, C.J. *and* Ritter, E., *eds.* San Diego, Academic Press, 1994. 4v. illus., maps, tables. $595. ISBN: 0122266706, set.

210 articles, *e.g.* 'World Hunger and Food Security'; 'Food Irradiation', on average each ten pages in length and covering all aspects of agriculture, arranged A-Z. A complete contents table is found at the beginning of each of the four volumes. Each article contains an outline, cross-references, a glossary, and a bibliography. 650 black-and-white photographs and 450 tables. Volume four contains a list of contributors, a 138-page subject index, and an index grouping together related entries. The two appendices list US colleges and universities offering academic courses in agriculture, and UN agriculture and related organizations. *Class No:* 63.0(031)

[5508]

McGraw-Hill encyclopedia of food, agriculture and nutrition. Lapedes, D.N., *editor-in-chief.* New York, etc., McGraw-Hill, 1977. vii, 732p. illus., tables, maps. ISBN: 0070452636.

Nearly 300 contributors. 5 leading articles (p.1-47) precede the main sequence ('Milk', p.395-403; sectionalized; 7 illus., 1 table; 11 references). Analytical index, p.709-32. 'Designed to inform the student, librarian, scientist, teacher, engineer and layperson about all aspects of agriculture, the cultivation, harvesting and processing of food crops, food manufacturing; and health and nutrition - from the economic and political to the technological' (*Preface*). Some articles derive from the *McGraw-Hill encyclopedia of science and technology* (4th ed. 1977). Well produced. *Class No:* 63.0(031)

[5509]

Sel'skokhozyaistvennyi entsiklopedicheskii slovar'. [Encyclopaedia of agriculture.] Mesyats, V.R., *ed.* Moscow, Izdatel'stvo 'Sovetskaya Entsiklopediya', 1989. 656p. illus. (some col.), figs., maps.

Contains *c.*4,000 entries, A-Z, many with bibliographies and cross-references. Numerous line-drawings and some full-page colour illustrations. Useful maps of the USSR showing agriculture and agroclimatic regions and soil types. Detailed, subject index.
Class No: 63.0(031)

Handbooks & Manuals

[5510]

FREAM, W. **Fream's principles of food and agriculture.**
Spedding, C.R.W., *ed.* 17th ed. Oxford, Blackwell Scientific Publications, 1992. xxvii,308p. tables, graphs. £25. ISBN: 0632029781.

First published 1892 as *Fream's elements of agriculture,* 16th ed. (1983), *Fream's agriculture.*

10 sections: 1. The food and agricultural industry - 2. Meeting human needs - 3. World agriculture ... 7. The inputs to agriculture - 8. The principles of processing of products ... 10. Feeding the world in the future. References, p.xi-xii. Glossary, p.xv-xxiv. Fewer than half the number of pages of the previous ed. and has only 10 contributors compared with 42. This edition 'builds on the principles of agriculture ... and relates these to a more international view of agriculture, and its past, present and future roles in society' (*Preface*).
Class No: 63.0(035)

[5511]

McCONNELL, P. **Primrose McConnell's 'The agricultural notebook'.** Soffe, R.J., *ed.* 19th ed. Oxford, Blackwell Science, 1995. xviii, 646p. illus., diagrs., tables. ISBN: 0632036435.

First published 1883.

Four sections (25 chapters): Farm management (includes chapters on agricultural law, alternative enterprises, etc.) - Crop production (includes chapters on soil management, crop health, etc.) - Animal production (includes chapters on animal welfare, livestock feeds and feeding, etc.) - Farm equipment (includes chapters on farm buildings). Facts and figures for farmers, students and all engaged or interested in farming. *Class No:* 63.0(035)

[5512]

SEYMOUR, J. **The Complete book of self-sufficiency.** London, Faber, 1976 (reprinted Dorling Kindersley, 1997). 256p. illus., (incl. col.), diagrs. £14.99. ISBN: 0571110959.

Six ways in which to cultivate self-sufficiency; Food from the fields - Food from animals - Food from the garden - Food from the wild - Natural energy (p.210-8: saving energy; power from water; heat from the sun; power from the wind; fuel from waste. 20 illus. and diagrams), Crafts and skills. Analytical index. An encyclopaedia of practical advice, illustrated step-by-step. *Class No:* 63.0(035)

Dictionaries

Polyglot

[5513]

FOOD AND AGRICULTURE ORGANIZATION. Terminology and Reference Section. Publications Division. **Dictionaries and vocabularies** in the Terminology Reference Library, 1982-85. [Dictionnaires et vocabulaires à la bibliothèque de terminologie et références.] Rome, FAO, 1987. vi,66p. $12. ISBN: 9250024142.

First published 1968.

Lists several hundred dictionaries and vocabularies in 3 parts: 1. Dictionaries arranged by subjects - 2. Language dictionaries in Arabic, Chinese, English, French, Spanish, German, Italian, Russian and Latin. 3. Subject, author and language indexes.
Class No: 63.0(038)=00

[5514]
HAENSCH, G. *and* HABERKAMP DE ANTON, G. **Dictionary of agriculture in six languages:** German, English, French, Spanish, Italian, Russian. 5th completely rev. and enld. ed. Amsterdam, etc., Elsevier, 1986. xxix, 1264p. £165.62. ISBN: 0444995129.

First published 1959; 4th ed., 1975 (xxiv, 1000p.).

11,163 numbered German-base entries, with equivalents in the other five languages. Subject sections A-Q (*e.g.* A. Food and agriculture: general terms; D. Economics and sociology of agriculture; E. Processing of animal produce; J. Plant cultivation: special part; N-O. Animal breeding; P. Farm buildings; Q. Agricultural machinery). Genders given. German, English, French, Spanish, Italian, Russian and Latin indexes. *Class No:* 63.0(038)=00

[5515]
Landwirtschaftliches Wörterbuch in acht Sprachen: russisch, bulgarisch, tschechisch, polvisch, ungarisch, romanisch, deutsch, englisch. Kratochvil, Y. *and* Urbanova, S., *eds.* Berlin, Landwirtschaftsverlag. 1970. 2v. (1045p.; 670p.).

An eight-language agricultural dictionary. 25,780 Russian-base entries, with Bulgarian, Czech, Polish, Hungarian, Rumanian, German and English equivalents. V.2 contains language indexes. If a term is frequently used and well-known, the Latin term is included, with a separate Latin index in v.2. *Class No:* 63.0(038)=00

[5516]
LOGIE, G. **Glossary of land resources,** in English, French, Italian, Dutch, German, Swedish. Amsterdam, Elsevier, 1984. xxvii, 303p. (*International planning glossaries, 4.*) ISBN: 0444422811.

2,117 Engish-base terms (plus explanations in context), with equivalents in the other 5 languages. Sections: Land resources - Land property - Land form - Climate - Agriculture - Forestry - Recreation - Urbanization - Pollution. Introductions to sections. A/Z index of terms in each of the six languages. Bibliography, p.299-303. *Class No:* 63.0(038)=00

[5517]
Norsk landbruksordbok. Utgitt av Nemnda for Norsk Landbruksordbok. Rommetveit, N., *ed.* Oslo, Det Norske Samlaget, 1979. 2v. (581p. + 402p.). ISBN: 8282107923, v.1; 8282108709, v.2.

'Norwegian dictionary of agriculture'. V.1: Norwegian-Norwegian. V.2: Lappish - Swedish - Danish - English - German - Icelandic - Finnish: index of equivalents. The English index has *c.*20 entries. *Class No:* 63.0(038)=00

English

[5518]
The Agricultural handbook. Whitby, M., *and others*. Oxford, BSP Professional Books, 1988. viii,236p. £12.99. ISBN: 0632018216.

Terms arranged A-Z (Abattoir ... Zygote). Includes acronyms and cross-references. An introductory reference source. Suitable for undergraduates, and public libraries.

The *Dictionary of agriculture: from abaca to zoonosis* by K.L. Lipton (Lynn Rienner, 1995. 345p.$75.) gives short definitions of more than 3,000 terms, with the emphasis on agricultural policy and economics, and North American terms. *Class No:* 63.0(038)=20

[5519]
Agricultural terms, as used in the Bibliography of Agriculture, from data provided by the National Agricultural Library, US Department of Agriculture. 2nd ed. Phoenix, Arizona, Oryx Press, 1978. 122p. $35. ISBN: 0912700459.

First published 1976.

About 37,000 terms. Word variants are grouped together, with synonymous terms (*c.*12,000) in parentheses, italicized, following the key term. 2,000 cross-references. *Class No:* 63.0(038)=20

[5520]
DALAL-CLAYTON, D.B. **Black's agricultural dictionary.** 2nd ed. London, A. & C. Black, 1985. xiii, 432p. illus., diagrs., tables. ISBN: 0713626798.

First published 1981.

About 4,000 entries (*e.g.* 'Plough': nearly 1p., including keyed line-drawing; 'Chart of common sheep names', p.338). Ample cross-references. Appendix of abbreviations, acronyms and initials. Concerned essentially with agriculture in the UK. *Class No:* 63.0(038)=20

[5521]
A Dictionary of agricultural and allied terminology. Winburne, J.N., *ed.* East Lansing, Mich., Michigan State Univ. Press, 1962 (reprinted 1974). viii, 905p. $24.95. ISBN: 0870130676.

About 18,000 terms, drawn from *c.*250 books, magazines and catalogues. Definitions, free from highly technical words, follow a pattern; (a) entry word, (b) scientific name (if any), (c) general description, (d) agricultural implications, (e) synonyms, (f) cross-references. Locations of plants in USA. Appendix A (p.897-903) lists terms under subjects. *Class No:* 63.0(038)=20

[5522]
Dictionary of agriculture. Stephens, A., *ed.* 2nd ed. Teddington, Peter Collin, 1996. 277p. £9.95. ISBN: 0948549785.

First published 1991.

*c.*6,500 terms from agriculture, veterinary science, and horticulture are briefly defined. International in scope. For public and academic libraries. *Class No:* 63.0(038)=20

[5523]
—LIPTON, K.L. Dictionary of agriculture: from abaca to zoonosis. Boulder, Colo., Lynne Rienner, 1995. xi,345p. ISBN: 1555875238.

Defines more than 3,000 terms used in US agriculture. Many cross-references. Appendices include a list of terms under broad subject headings; commonly used acronyms; major US legislation concerning trade and agriculture. Complements *Black's agricultural dictionary, (q.v.)*. *Class No:* 63.0(038)=20

French

[5524]
BOURKE, D. O'D. **French-English agricultural dictionary** with English-French index. Wallingford, Oxon., CAB International, 1992. x,293p. £29.50; $56. ISBN: 0851986269.

Contains over 20,000 terms. Coverage includes agriculture in its widest sense; there are terms from statistics, agricultural engineering, soil science, etc. A companion to the author's *French-English horticultural dictionary with English-French index (q.v.)*. *Class No:* 63.0(038)=40

[5525]
Dictionnaire d'agriculture et des sciences annexes; index anglais et espagnol. Paris, La Maison Rustique, in collaboration with International Council of the French language [CILF], 1977. x, 219p. illus., tables.

About 3,000 French terms, with definitions, plus equivalents in English and Spanish. About 40 categories applied. 3p. of keyed parts of the horse; table of chief valuable crops cultivated. *Class No:* 63.0(038)=40

Italian

[5526]
FAVATI, F. **Dizionario di agricoltura: inglese-italiano, italiano-inglese.** [Dictionary of agriculture: English-Italian, Italian-English.] Ed. 2. Bologna, Edizioni Agricole, 1990. xii,1018p. illus.,tables. ISBN: 8820630540.

Covers plants, animals, and machinery. Includes 334 detailed drawings indicating terms in both languages. Indicates whether an English term is unique to the USA or UK. Tables at end show metric conversions. *Class No:* 63.0(038)=50

Spanish

[5527]
RICE, R.P. **Spanish-English/English-Spanish illustrated agricultural dictionary.** Fresno, Calif., Thomson Publications, 1993. 160p. illus. $27.95.

Also includes botanical and horticultural terms. Designed for use on a day-to day basis. *Class No:* 63.0(038)=60

[5528]
SANCHEZ MONGE Y PARELLADA, E. **Diccionario de agronomia:** español-inglés nombres cientificos. [Dictionary of agronomy: Spanish-English scientific names.] Madrid, Editorial Agricola Española, 1995. 701p. ISBN: 8485441346.

Covers all aspects of agronomy, with Latin American variations. Terms are given in Spanish, alongwith Spanish synonyms, English equivalents and scientific equivalents where necessary. English and scientific name indexes. *Class No:* 63.0(038)=60

Russian

[5529]
RAKIPOV, N.G. *and* GEYER, B. **Elsevier's dictionary of agriculture and food production: Russian-English.** Amsterdam, Elsevier, 1994. x,900p. Dfl400. ISBN: 0444899294.

Contains *c.*80,000 Russian terms with English definitions; includes American equivalents and Latin names of plants, organisms, etc. Covers a wide range of agricultural areas and is useful as a quick reference tool. *Class No:* 63.0(038)=82

[5530]
USOVSKII, B.N. *and* **LINNARD, W. Comprehensive Russian-English agricultural dictionary.** 2nd ed., rev and enl. Oxford, etc., Pergamon Press, 1967. xii, 470p.

Considerably revised and enlarged ed. of *Russko-angliiskii sel'kokhozyaistvennyi slovar'* (Moscow, Fizmatgiz, 1960, xii, 470p).

About 45,000 entries (1960 ed.: over 30,000). Includes botanical and zoological entries, with Latin names, chemical formulas. Shows Russian stress and gender. Appendix of abbreviations in Russian agricultural and biological lierature. *Class No:* 63.0(038)=82

[5531]
—**English-Russian dictionary of agriculture.** Adamenko, P.A., *and others, eds.* Oxford, etc., Pergamon Press, 1984. 700p.
Class No: 63.0(038)=82

[5532]
—**USOVSKII, B.N.** Anglo-russkii sel'skokhozyaistvennyi slovar'. 3. perer izd. Moscow, Gos. Izd. Tekhniko - Teoreticheskii Literatury, 1956. 532p. illus.

Is the companion dictionary. A feature is the section of 85 illus. (p.493-532), with specified parts. *Class No:* 63.0(038)=82

Czech

[5533]
Anglicko-Český zemedelsky slovnik. [English-Czech agricultural dictionary.] Prague, Ustav Vedeckotechnickych Informaci pro Zemedelstvi, 1992. 170p.

Lists 2,492 numbered English words dealing with animals and plants, with the Czech equivalents listed alphabetically, thus giving an English-Czech dictionary in addition. An appendix gives Czech and English equivalents for common everyday terms, *e.g.* colours, months. *Class No:* 63.0(038)=850

Chinese

[5534]
Dictionary of Chinese Communist agricultural technology. Wong, S., *comp.* Kowloon, Hong Kong, Union Research Institute, 1968. [vi], 557 + 17p. illus.

About 20,000 Chinese agricultural terms explained in English, with *c.*200 illus. Chinese characters are arranged by phonetic sounds (romanized spelling), following Mathews's *Chinese-English dictionary* system. *Class No:* 63.0(038)=951

Reviews & Abstracts

[5535]
Agrindex. AGRIS International Information System for the Agricultural Sciences and Technology. Rome, Food and Agriculture Organization, 1975-. 12pa. $500.

About 135,000 references pa. Provides complete bibliographic data on all items listed, with availability information. Classes A-U (closely subdivided): A. Agriculture in general - B. Agricultural economics, development and rural sociology ... F. Plant science and production ... K. Forestry - L. Animal science, production and protection ... P. Natural resources and environment ... R. Processing of agricultural products - S. Human nutrition - T. Pollution - U. Methodology. Descriptors appended to entries. Includes films and standards. Bulky. Personal author, corporate entry, report and patent number, and subject indexes. *Agrindex* is available in English, French and Spanish. Available online as AGRIS, via DIMDI, DIALOG, ESA. CD-ROM edition also available. *Class No:* 63.0(048)

[5536]
Bibliography of agriculture: data provided by National Agricultural Library, US Department of Agriculture. Phoenix, Arizona, Oryx Press, 1942-. 12pa. $795pa. ISSN: 00061530.

Contains *c.*8,000 items per issue. Some 96 subject areas, further subdivided, record proceedings, annual and special reports, pamphlets and government publications, as well as periodical articles. Corporate author, personal author and analytical subject (based on title catchword) indexes per issue (*c.*20,000 subject index references), cumulated annually. 'The most indispensable single source in the field' (*Library trends*, v.15(4), April 1967, p.882). Available on microfiche. Online database: AGRICOLA (*q.v.*), and available on CD-ROM. *Class No:* 63.0(048)

[5537]
Biological and agricultural index: a cumulative subject index to periodicals in the fields of biology, agriculture and related sciences. New York, H.W. Wilson, 1964/65-. 11pa. ISSN: 00063177.

Continues *Agricultural index*, 1919-64.

Covers *c.*200 English-language journals, selected by subscriber vote, with*c.*56,000 records added annually. Includes experimental station publications and book reviews. Entry under topic. US slanted, as compared with *Bibliography of agriculture* and *Agrindex*. About

....(contd.)
40,000 entries pa. Available online (WILSONLINE) - database contains *c.*540,000 records - and CD-ROM, in addition to magnetic tape and diskette format. *Class No:* 63.0(048)

[5538]
Current contents: Agriculture, biology and environmental sciences. Philadelphia, Pa., Institute for Scientific Information, 1970-. Weekly. $730. ISSN: 00900508.

Previously (1970-72) subtitled 'Agriculture, food and veterinary sciences'.

Displays contents-pages of *c.*900 current issues of journals. (issue for 25 Mar 1996 contained contents pages from 124 journals). Sections: 'Features' (*e.g.* Current book contents); 'Discipline guide', grouping contents-pages by areas of interest (*e.g.* Multidisciplinary; Biology; ... Animal sciences; Veterinary medicine; Animal health). Weekly title word index. Author and address directory. Publishers' address directory. Available on diskette, in CD-ROM version, and online on the CURRENT CONTENTS SEARCH database. Internet access as *Current Contents Connect* at http://connect.isihost.com. *Class No:* 63.0(048)

[5539]
—**FAO documentation: current bibliography.** Rome, Food and Agriculture Organization, 1972-. 6pa. *Gratis.* ISSN: 0304582x.

Began life as *FAO documentation current index* (1967-71).

It now carries *c.*4,500 references pa., with author, subject and geographic indexes per issue. *Class No:* 63.0(048)

[5540]
Landwirtschaftliches Zentralblatt. Hrsg. von der Deutschen Akademie der Landwirtschaftswissenschaften zu Berlin. Institut für landwirtschaftliche Information und Dokumentation. Berlin, Akademie-Verlag, 1955-. 4 Abt., each monthly.

Agroselekt. Reihe 1. *Landtechnik.* 1955-. DM320. 2. *Pflanzenlicheproduktion.* 1956-. DM453. 3. *Tierproduktion.* 1956-. DM453. 4. *Veterinärmedizin.* 1956-. DM453.

The 4 parts deal respectively with agronomy, crops, animal husbandry and fishing, and veterinary medicine. Part 1, *Landtechnik*, carries *c.*5,000 abstracts pa., with monthly author index and annual subject and author indexes. *Class No:* 63.0(048)

Periodicals & Progress Reports

[5541]
Advances in agronomy. Prepared in cooperation with the American Society of Agronomy. San Diego, Academic Press, 1949-. v.1-. Annual. diagrs., tables, graphs. ISSN: 00652113.

V.66, 1999 (304p.) has 12 contributors. The five papers include 'The rhizosphere and its management to improve plant growth'; 'Transfer of phosphorus from agricultural soils', with each paper having a lengthy bibliography appended. Analytical index. *Class No:* 63.0(05)

[5542]
Agricultural and animal sciences journals and serials: an analytical guide. Jensen, R.D. *and* Smith, M.M., *comps.* Westport, Conn., Greenwood Press, 1986. 211p. $49.95. (*Annotated bibliographies of serials: a subject approach, no.4.*) ISBN: 031324331x.

Covers 374 English-language journals, of which only 46 are British. Appended directories of online databases and of microform and reprint companies. Geographical, publisher, subject and title indexes. *Class No:* 63.0(05)

[5543]
Agricultural journal titles and abbreviations. 2nd ed. Tucson, Arizona, Oryx Press, 1984. 136p. $45. ISBN: 0897740718.

First published 1982.

Lists all the titles (*c.*15,000) indexed in the *Bibliography of agriculture* (January 1979-March 1981), with their abbreviations, ISSNs, and the number of times each is cited in the *BOA* over the period. *Class No:* 63.0(05)

[5544]
Index to periodicals on agriculture held by the Science Reference Library. Jackson, G., *comp.* London, Science Reference Library, 1981-84. ISBN: 0902914650, set.

pt.1. *Agricultural research and industry.* 1981. [11], v, 143, [5]p.

pt.2. *Agronomy and other aspects of plant science.* 1984. x, 206p.

Title entry. V.1 carries *c.*1,850 titles. V.2 *c.*2,500 titles. Annuals are included. Data: country, holding, class-mark. *Class No:* 63.0(05)

[5545]
International union list of agricultural serials. Wallingford, CAB International, 1990. xiii,767p. £99.50; $189. ISBN: 0851986617.

Lists serials indexed in AGRICOLA, AGRIS, and CAB ABSTRACTS. Gives details of 11,567 publications from 129 countries, with titles in 53 languages. Subject and country indexes. Available in CD-ROM version as *World list of agricultural serials* which contains over 64,000 records (Silverplatter. £358 (subscribers to databases);£551 (non-susbcribers). *Class No:* 63.0(05)

[5546]
Quarterly bulletin of the International Association of Agricultural Librarians and Documentalists. 1956-. 4pa. £45.
Carries articles (with abstracts in English, French and Spanish). Occasional bibliographies of 'Professional literature' (6th appearance in v.31(4), 1986, p.179-91), as well as news items.
Class No: 63.0(05)

Yearbooks & Directories

[5547]
Directory of research workers in agricultural and allied sciences. Vernon, R., *ed.* Wallingford, Oxon., CAB International, 1989. ix, 490p. ISBN: 0851986234.
Previous ed. 1982 as *List of research workers, 1981, in the agricultural sciences in the Commonwealth.*
4 sections: 1. Organisations and research workers, by country - 2. Subject index - 3. Index of persons - 4. Index of institutions. Data on approximately 29,000 research workers include name, educational qualifications, and studies. Now in need of revision.
Class No: 63.0(058)

[5548]
UNITED STATES. Department of Agriculture. **The Yearbook of agriculture.** Washington, Government Printing Office, 1895-. Annual. illus., tables. ISSN: 00843628.
As from 1936 the *Yearbook* has dealt compendiously with particular themes (*e.g. Landscape for living.* 1972). During the 1970s scope widened to embrace consumer objectives (*e.g. Shoppers guide,* 1974). The 1993 issue is entitled *Nutrition: eating for good health.*
Class No: 63.0(058)

Tables & Data Books

[5549]
FAO production yearbook. Rome, FAO, 1947-. Annual (v.51: 1997. 1998.). tables.
Statistical data on all important aspects of food and agriculture, including land population, index numbers of agricultural production, food supplies, wages and freight rates. V.51 (xxxvii, 239p.) has 106 tables.
FAO quarterly bulletin of statistics (1988-) updates.
Class No: 63.0(083)

[5550]
FISHER, Sir R.A. *and* **YATES, F. Statistical tables for biological, agricultural and medical research.** 6th ed. Edinburgh, Oliver & Boyd, 1963. x, 146p. tables.
First published 1938; 5th ed. 1956.
50 tables in all (numbered 1-34, with interpolations). The main addition to the 6th ed. are v, Fiducial limits for a variance component, and xvii, Balanced incomplete blocks with 11-15 replicates. The valuable introduction gives examples of the ways in which the tables can be used and includes 82 references, covering books, monographs and papers on statistical methods, up to 1963. No index.
Class No: 63.0(083)

[5551]
FOOD AND AGRICULTURE ORGANIZATION. Technical conversion factors for agricultural commodities. Rome, FAO, 1960. vi, 346p. tables.
Arranged by countries, A/Z. Includes tables for converting measures of capacity into weight. Typical factors under countries: average fat content of cow's milk (Germany): boneless meat yield of bone-in-meat (New Zealand); extraction rate of oil from olives (Syria); average clean yield of greasy wool (India). Principally for those concerned with agricultural statistics. *Class No:* 63.0(083)

[5552]
Practical handbook of agricultural science. Hanson, A.A., *ed.* Boca Raton, CRC Press, 1990. 534p. tables. $59.95. ISBN: 0849337062.
'A "quick reference" to a variety of topics pertaining to soils and the production and use of plants and animals' (*Preface*). Sections include soil, plants, tillage and rotations, cereal grains, forage, animals, environmental control of livestock, common statistical terms, glossary. Index, p.487-534. US-slanted. *Class No:* 63.0(083)

Maps & Atlases

[5553]
MORGAN, B.A. 'Maps and atlases as sources of agricultural information'. In *Information sources in agriculture and food science,* edited by G.P. Lilley. London, Butterworths, 1981. p.128-141.
Sections: Introduction - Types of maps relevant to agriculture (topographical, natural features, land capability and land classification, 'interference' or 'modification' maps) - Representations of agriculture (*e.g.* land utilization) - Agricultural atlases - Sources of information. 8 references. *Class No:* 63.0(084.3)

[5554]
World atlas of agriculture: under the aegis of the International Association of Agricultural Economists. Novara, Istituto Geografico de Agostini, 1969-76. maps. loose-leaf.
Land utilization maps and relief maps prepared by the Committee for the 'World atlas of agriculture.' Maps (main scale: 1:5,000,000) - double-page spread, backed by key map, list of sources, and relief map. 4 text vols. accompany: Europe, USSR, Asia minor; South and east Asia, Oceania; the Americas; Africa. Unique, but now dated.
Class No: 63.0(084.3)

Histories

[5555]
The Agricultural history review. Exeter, British Agricultural History Society, 1953-. 2pa. £30. ISSN: 00021490.
V.43(1), 1995 features 'Annual list and brief review of articles on agrarian history, 1993', p.73-89. Also, 24 book reviews, six articles, and one review article, 'City and countryside in medieval England'. Available on microfilm from UMI. *Class No:* 63.0(091)

[5556]
HURT, R.D. *and* **HURT, M.E. The History of agricultural science and technology:** an international annotated bibliography. New York, Garland, 1994. 485p. $75. (*Bibliographies on the history of science and technology, 20.*) ISBN: 0824071824.
International in scope, listing 1,380 citations, mainly from the last 20 years, and chiefly from scientific rather than historical sources. A useful introduction. A keyword index would have been helpful.
Class No: 63.0(091)

Biographies

[5557]
Agricultural and veterinary sciences international who's who: a biographical guide in the agricultural and veterinary sciences. 5th ed. London, Cartermill Publishing, 1994. vii,1157p. £385. (*Reference on research.*) ISBN: 0582041007.
First published 1979 (F. Hodgson).
Professional biographical profiles of more than 10,000 senior research and advisory scientists in agricultural and veterinary sciences from over 132 countries. Two sections: 1. Biographies - 2. Country (subdivided by subject). Country and subject index. Available on *Current research worldwide* CD-ROM. *Class No:* 63.0(092)

Worldwide

[5558]
GRIGG, D.B. The Agricultural systems of the world: an evolutionary approach. Cambridge Univ. Press, 1974. 358p. tables. £17.50. ISBN: 0521098432.
Part 1 concerns the history, diffusion, and evolution of modern agriculture. Part 2, a detailed analysis of individual systems. Notes, p.289-307. Extensive bibliography, p.308-43. Analytical index. 'Aims to describe the chief characteristics of the major agricultural regions of the world and to attempt some explanations of how they come into being' (*Introduction,* chapter 1). *Class No:* 63.0(100)

[5559]
—Farming systems of the world. Duckham, A.N., *and others.* London, Chatto & Windus, 1970. xviii, 542p. illus. (pl.), tables.
Has 3 parts: 1. Analysis of location factors (7 chapters) - 2. Farming systems (by areas; 14 chapters; Canada and USA, p.109-69) - 3. Conclusions; Chapter references and further reading. Glossary and non-analytical subject index. 'Intended for students and research workers in agriculture and its related disciplines, and for teachers of agriculture and geographers in all parts of the world' (*Authors' Introduction*). *Class No:* 63.0(100)

Tropics

Bibliographies

[5560]
IMPERIAL COLLEGE OF TROPICAL AGRICULTURE. Catalogue. [Imperial College of Tropical Agriculture] University of the West Indies (Trinidad). Boston, Mass., G.K. Hall, 1975. 8v.
130,000 photolithographed catalogue cards for international literature on tropical and sub-tropical agriculture and related sciences.
Class No: 63.0(213)(01)

[5561]
WORTLEY, P.J. 'Tropical agriculture'. In *Information sources in agriculture and food science* (Editor, G.P. Lilley). London, Butterworths, 1981. p.357-406.
A well-organized survey that includes sections: 'Computer-based bibliographic services'; 'Guides to institutes, organizations and societies'. 5 references. *Class No:* 63.0(213)(01)

Handbooks & Manuals

[5562]
Agriculture in the tropics. Webster, C.C. *and* Wilson, P.N., *eds*. 3rd ed. Oxford, Blackwell, Science, 1998. x, 539p. illus, tables. £69.50. ISBN: 0632040548.

First published 1966. 2nd ed., 1980.

18 chapters : 1. Socio-economic background: the world food problem ... 4. Soil and water conservation ... 11. Production of animal feed ... 18. Livestock improvement through breeding. Authoritative, all-embracing 'account of the basic factors affecting agriculture in the tropics' but 'does not set out to give a comprehensive treatment of any given crop or farm animal' (*Preface*). *Class No:* 63.0(213)(035)

[5563]
Farming systems in the tropics. Ruthenberg, H., *and others*. 3rd ed. Oxford, Clarendon Press, 1980. xxii, 424p. illus., graphs, tables, maps. ISBN: 019839481x.

First published 1971.

11 chapters (2. Some characteristics of farming in a tropical environment; 6. Systems with permanent upland cultivation; 8. Grazing systems). Appendix notes. Bibliography, p.391-414. Non-analytical index, p.415-24. *Class No:* 63.0(213)(035)

[5564]
Tropical agriculture series. Wrigley, G., *general ed.* London, etc., Longman Scientific & Technical, 1953-. Volumes in print:

Agriculture in the tropics, by C.C. Webster and P.N. Wilson. 2nd ed. 1980. £32. *Bananas*, by N.W. Simmonds. 3rd ed., 1987. £61. *The camel*, by R.T. Wilson. 1984. £41. *Cattle production in the tropics*. v.1, by W.J.A. Payne. 1970. *Climate, water and agriculture in the tropics*, by I.J. Jackson, 2nd ed., 1989. £14.99. *Cocoa*, by G.A.R. Wood and R.A. Lass. 4th ed., 1985. £68.*Coffee*, by G. Wrigley. 1988. £68. *Cotton*, by J.M. Monroe. 2nd ed., 1987. £50. *An introduction to animal husbandry in the tropics*, by W.J.A. Payne. 4th ed. 1990. £55. *East African crops*, by J.D. Acland. 1972. £9.35. *Introduction to tropical agriculture*, by A. Youdeouwei, and others. 1986. £13.50. *The oil palm*, by C.W.S. Hartley. 3rd ed. 1989. £66. *Oilseed crops*, by E.A. Weiss. 1983. £64. *Rice*, by D.H. Grist, 6th ed., 1986. £74. *Rubber*, by C.C. Webster and W.J. Baulkwill. 1989. £60. *Sheep production in the tropics and sub-tropics*, by R.M. Gatenby. 1986. *Sorghum*, by H. Doggett. 2nd ed. 1988. £60. *Spices*, by J.W. Purseglove, and others. 1981. 2v. £42. *Sugar cane*, by F. Blackburn. 1984. £66. *Tobacco*, by B.C. Akehurst. 2nd ed. 1981. £88. *Tropical crops* (v.1 Monocotyledons; v.2 Dicotyledons), by J.W. Purseglove. 1975. £25. *Tropical forest and its environment*, by K.A. Longman. 2nd ed. 1987. £26. *Tropical fruits*, by J.A. Samson. 2nd ed. 1986. £40. *Tropical grassland husbandry*, by L.V. Crowder and H.R. Chheda. 1982. £57. *Tropical oilseed crops*, by E.A. Weiss. 1983.

D.H. Grist's *Rice* (6th ed. 1986. xx, 599p. illus. (pl.) ISBN 058240402), was first published 1953. Its four parts (22 chapters) cover rice, the plant; genetics and breeding of rice; paddy and production; rice, the product. 4 appendices, including 1. 'Standardization of rice terminology; 4. Species of rice. Bibliography, p.543-76. Detailed, analytical index. 49 plates. A definitive contribution. *Class No:* 63.0(213)(035)

[5565]
Tropical and subtropical agriculture. Ochse, J.J., *and others*. New York, Macmillan Co.; London, Collier-Macmillan, 1961. 2v. (xxii, 1446p.). illus., tables.

2 parts: 1. General; 2. Crops. 14 documented chapters ('Bananas and citrus', p.371-522; 11p. of references). Section on 'Oil palm' (p.1047-66) has sub-sections: world production; botany; varieties; pollination; breeding and selection; climate and soil requirements; culture; harvesting and processing; products and users; diseases and insect pests. Glossary. Author and subject index per volume, index of plant names. 144 tables in all. A valuable but dated compendium. *Class No:* 63.0(213)(035)

Reviews & Abstracts

[5566]
Agriculture and environment for developing countries. Amsterdam, Koninklijk Instituut voor de Troper KIT/Royal Tropical Institute, 1996-. 12pa. DFl525. ISSN: 03045951.

Formerly *Tropical abstracts* (1953-74) and *Abstracts on tropical agriculture* (1975-1995).

About 4,500 abstracts pa. Classes A-Q (*e.g.* A. Farming systems research and development; F. Cereal crops; H. Grain legume crops; P. Miscellaneous crops and forestry; Q. Miscellaneous subjects). Geographic, subject, plant taxonomic name and author index per issue; annual subject and plant taxonomic names index. Coverage is worldwide. Includes review articles. Database: TROPAG (1975-). Available on CD-ROM as *Tropag & Rural* (Silverplatter). *Class No:* 63.0(213)(048)

Periodicals

[5567]
TROPICAL DEVELOPMENT AND RESEARCH INSTITUTE LIBRARY. List of current periodicals. London, the Institute Library, 1986. ii, 82p.

About 1,600 periodical titles. Currently received. A-Z, excluding irregular serials. Details: title; first year taken; location (central and 5 sub-libraries). Includes many non-tropical agriculture titles. *Class No:* 63.0(213)(051)

Tables & Data Books

[5568]
ILACO BV., Arnhem. **Agricultural compendium for rural development in the tropics and subtropics.** 3rd ed. Amsterdam, Elsevier, 1989. xxxviii,740p. illus., graphs, tables, maps. £40.93.

First published 1981. Commissioned by the Ministry of Agriculture and Fisheries, The Hague.

11 chapters (some documented): 1. Climate - 2. Soil and classification ... 4. Water control - 5. Land improvement - 6. Agriculture (4½p. of references) - 7. Animal production and fisheries ... 9. Economic and financial appraisal of progress - 10. Sociology - 11. Tables and supporting data. *Class No:* 63.0(213)(083)

Ancient Rome

[5569]
WHITE, K.D. A Bibliography of Roman agriculture. Reading, Berks., Univ. of Reading, 1970. xxviii, 63p. £0.85. (*Institute of Agricultural History. Bibliographies in agricultural history, no.1.*) ISBN: 090072403x.

915 entries, with evaluative annotations. Many periodical articles. Sections: Contemporary literature - Archaeological sources ... Practical agriculture and farm management ... Agricultural labour ... Food-processing industries - Transport and communications. *Class No:* 63.0(38)

Europe

[5570]
The Cambridge economic history of Europe from the decline of the Roman Empire. Clapham, J.H. *and* Power, E., *eds*. 2nd ed. Cambridge Univ. Press, 1966. xvi, 871p. tables, maps. £95. ISBN: 0521045053.

1. *Agrarian life of the Middle Ages;* edited by M.M. Postan. (first published 1942).

A scholarly, detailed study, well documented. Chapter bibliographies. Analytical index. *Class No:* 63.0(4)

[5571]
COMMISSION OF THE EUROPEAN COMMUNITIES. The Agricultural situation in the Community. 1996 report. Brussels & Luxembourg, the Commission. Annual. 308p. diagrs., tables. ISBN: 928279007x.

Seven sections: 1. The agricultural year ... 3. Agricultural markets ... 5. Financing of the CAP in 1996 ... 7. Agricultural development: Statistical information. *Class No:* 63.0(4)

[5572]
FUSSELL, G.E. Agricultural history in Great Britain and Western Europe before 1914: a discursive bibliography. London, The Pindar Press, 1983. 157p. £50. ISBN: 0907132049.

9 chapters on 'the history of the evolution of writing on agricultural history'. Chapter 1: The nativity of agricultural history in England; 4: The medievalists; 6. The Germans and other Europeans, to 1914; 7. France. Index of titles; index of authors. *Class No:* 63.0(4)

Great Britain

Bibliographies

[5573]
GREAT BRITAIN. HM Stationery Office. Agriculture catalogue 1996. London, HMSO, 1996. 64p. *Gratis*.

Four sections: Agriculture (includes sections on crops, fertilisers, statistics)- Fisheries - Food - Forestry. Index to book titles, p.61-4. *Class No:* 63.0(410)(01)

[5574]
McDONALD, D. Agricultural writers, from Sir Walter of Henley to Arthur Young, 1200-1800: reproductions in facsimile and extracts from their actual writings; enlarged and revised from articles which have appeared in The Field from 1903-1907. To which is added an exhaustive bibliography. London, Cox, 1908. v, 228p.

'The literature and bibliography of British agriculture, 1200 to 1800', *c.*650 items, chronologically arranged. Author index. *Class No:* 63.0(410)(01)

[5575]
SOUTHAMPTON UNIVERSITY. Library. **Catalogue of the Walter Frank Perkins Agricultural Library.** Southampton Univ. Library, 1961. xii, 291p.

Author catalogue of 2,009 numbered items. Appended: Books printed in England and Scotland up to 1700 ; Periodicals; Board of Agriculture County Reports - England, Scotland, Wales, Islands; Dublin Society. Statistical surveys of Irish counties. Supplementary notes. List of 15 authorities (*e.g.* Wing, *STC*), p.xi. Earliest imprint: 1600. The collection is perhaps richest in 18th-century material. The catalogue of a valuable library specializing in British agricultural history. *Class No:* 63.0(410)(01)

Yearbooks & Directories

[5576]
POWELL, E.M. *and* TAYLOR, D. **Directory of rural organisations.** Ipswich, Farming Press, 1997. viii,311p. £24.95. ISBN: 0852363494.

Contains details of over 1,800 UK organizations. Dealing primarily with rural bodies, much of the directory includes organizations involved in agriculture, livestock, animal health and welfare, and livestock breeds. Acronym and subject indexes. An excellent reference tool. *Class No:* 63.0(410)(058)

Tables & Data Books

[5577]
The Digest of agricultural census statistics: United Kingdom 1997. London, Stationery Office, 1998. vp. tables, maps. £24. ISBN: 0112430465. ISSN: 00654590.

Previously *Agricultural statistics, United Kingdom*.

Gives aggregate figures for each year in the period 1987 to 1997, based on the main results of the annual UK agricultural and horticultural censuses. Chapters include data on land use and crops, pigs, sheep, cattle, poultry, labour force, maps of selected main items, frequency distributions of main holdings by size. *Class No:* 63.0(410)(083)

[5578]
Reviews of United Kingdom statistical sources. V.23: Agriculture. Edited by M.F. Maunden, with M.C. Fleming. Peters, G.H. *and* Clark, K.R. London & New York, Chapman & Hall, for the Royal Statistical Society and the Economic and Social Research Council, 1988. xiii, 209p. tables. ISBN: 0412316706.

12 sections (7. Farm income and management; 12. An overall assessment of agricultural statistics). Quick-reference lists, p.147-88. Data, to 1984. Bibliography, p.189-92 (71 references). Detailed subject index, p.201-9. An impressive piece of research. *Class No:* 63.0(410)(083)

Histories

[5579]
ORWIN, C.S. *and* WHETHAM, E.H. **History of British agriculture, 1846-1914.** 2nd ed. London, Longmans, 1971. xx, 411p. tables.

First published 1964 (xx, 411p.).

Combined product of an historian and an agricultural economist. Bibliographical footnotes; authors quoted are named in the index. A standard work. *Class No:* 63.0(410)(091)

[5580]
—British and Irish writers on agriculture. Perkins, W.F., *comp.* 3rd ed. Lymington, C.T. King, 1939. 226p.

A list of *c.*1,300 writers, A-Z, 'from the earliest printed books until, and including, the year 1900'. *Class No:* 63.0(410)(091)

[5581]
—RUSSELL, Sir E.J. A History of agricultural science in Great Britain, 1620-1954. London, Allen & Unwin, 1966. 493p. illus., port., tables.

Includes biographical data. The author was a former Director of Rothamsted Experimental Station. *Class No:* 63.0(410)(091)

Scotland

[5582]
COPPOCK, J.T. **An Agricultural atlas of Scotland.** Edinburgh, John Donald, 1976. 260p. maps, graphs, tables.

Over 100 black-and-white maps, based on Department of Agriculture [and Fisheries], Scotland, with supporting text. The maps mainly relate to 1965. Scales 1:1M and 1:6M. 'It should find a place on the shelves of all geographical, agricultural and planning libraries' (*Geographical journal*, v.143(2), p.291). *Class No:* 63.0(411)

England & Wales

[5583]
COPPOCK, J.T. **An Agricultural atlas of England and Wales.** New and rev. ed. London, Faber & Faber, 1976. 267p. tables, maps.

First published 1964.

9 chapters on the agriculture of England and Wales (4. Tillage crops - 5. Grassland - 6. Horticulture - 7. Livestock - 8. Enterprises and prospects). 233 small black-and-white chloropath maps (square dot pattern) in text. Bibliography (general and by chapters), p.256-61. Index. *Class No:* 63.0(42)

[5584]
HARVEY, N. **The Industrial archaeology of farming in England and Wales.** London, Batsford, 1980. 232p. illus. ISBN: 0713418451.

9 chapters: 1. The winning of the waste - 2. Fields and field systems - 3. Water supply and irrigation schemes - 4. Sources of fertility - 5. Field draining - 6. Historical crop varieties - 7. Historical breeds of livestock - 8. Tools, implements and machines - 9. Farm buildings. Well documented: References, p.180-223; Sources of information (museums; journals); Selective book list (grouped), p.225-7. Detailed, analytical index, p.228-32. *Class No:* 63.0(42)

Information Services

[5585]
At the farmer's service. London, MAFF Publications, 1993. v.p. *Gratis*.

A compilation of ten booklets, bound in a plastic folder, giving information on MAFF's role in UK agriculture: 1. The agriculture departments - 2. Farm management - 3. Farm woodlands and forestry - 4. Conservation and environmental protection - 5. Pesticides and pest control - 6. Health and welfare of livestock - 7. Production, marketing and export - 8. Education and training - 9. Government publications - 10. Appendices containing addresses of relevant organisations. *Class No:* 63.0(42):061:025.5

England

[5586]
The Agrarian history of England and Wales. Thirsk, J., *general ed.* Cambridge, University Press, 1967-. illus., diagrs., plans, tables.

1 (1): *Prehistory;* edited by S. Piggott. 1981. £65. (2): *A.D.43-1042;* edited by H.P.R. Finberg. 1972. £50. 2: *1042-1348;* edited by H.E. Hallam. 1988. £110. 3: *1350-1500;* edited by E. Miller. 1991. £85. 4: *1500-1640;* edited by J. Thirsk. 1967. £60. 5(1): *1640-1750: Regional farming systems.* 1984. £60. (2): *Agrarian change.* 1985. £95; both parts edited by J. Thirsk. 6: *1750-1850.* 1985. £105. 7: *1850-1914.* 8: *1914-1939;* edited by C.H. Whetham. 1978. £35.

V.5(2), xxx, 952p. has 21 footnoted chapters, with 3 appendices. (1. Agricultural weights and measures; 2. Land measures; 3. Statutes), a select bibliography, p.903-21 (authors, A-Z) and a detailed analytical index to v.5(1) and (2). A scholarly series, still in progress. *Class No:* 63.0(420)

[5587]
—SEEBOHM, M.E. The Evolution of the English farm. 2nd rev. ed. London, Allen & Unwin, 1952. 365p. illus. (Facsim. ed. E.P., 1976).

Covers the development of English farms and farming from Neolithic times to the present century. Many footnote references; chapter bibliographies, p.344-50. *Class No:* 63.0(420)

[5588]
FUSSELL, G.E. **Old English farming books, 1523-1793:** Fitzherbert to the Board of Agriculture. Colliston, Aberdeen Rare Books, 1978. [7], 141p.; 186p. illus., facsims., ports. £12.50. ISBN: 0950660701, v.1; 0907132030, v.3; 0907132197, v.4; 0907132243, v.5.

Continues, with additions, his *The old English farming books, from Fitzherbert to Tull, 1523 to 1750* (London, Crosby Lockwood, 1947) and *More old English farming books from Tull to the Board of Agriculture, 1731 to 1793*. 1950). The work is updated by v.3, covering 1793-1839 (London, Pindar Press, 1983. 304p. £75); v.4, covering 1840-1860 (London, Pindar Press, 1984. 115p. £50); and v.5, covering 1861-1900 (London, Pindar Press, 1991. 145p. £95).

Written in narrative form. Author and title indexes. The 1950 work has an appendix of editions of Arthur Young's work, with locations. An authoritative work. *Class No:* 63.0(420)

[5589]
READING UNIVERSITY. Library. **Historical farm records:** a summary guide to manuscripts and other material in the University Library collected by the Institute of Agricultural History and the Museum of English Rural Life. Reading, Berks., the University Library, 1973. xiii, 320p.

Under English countries, A-Z, p.1-290. Indexes to individual farms (under country and place), and place-names, etc. 'The catalogue should be a useful guide to the relatively few records of practical farming which have survived' (*Aslib proceedings*, v.26(3), March 1974, p.133). *Class No:* 63.0(420)

Russia

[5590]

Atlas sel'kogokhozyaistvo SSSR. Tulupnikov, A.L. *and* Nikishov, M.I., *eds*. Moscow, Glavnoye Upravleniye Geodezii i Okrani Nyedr SSSR, 1960. vii, 309p.

378 individual maps on agriculture in the USSR (scales, 1:1.5M to 1:4). Rich in detail. 9 sections, on different aspects, - climate, rainfall, soils, topographical relief, population densities, and distribution of principal crops and livestock herds. *Class No:* 63.0(47)

Asia

[5591]

Guide to agricultural information sources in Asia and Oceania. Levick, G.R.T., *ed.* The Hague. Fédération Internationale de Documentation (FID), 1980. v, 72p. (*FID publication 592.*)

172 briefly annotated entries. Part 1: International. Part 2: Country-by-country. 3 types of sources: bibliographical; organizational; research programmes. *Class No:* 63.0(5)

China

[5592]

The Agriculture of China. Xu Guohua *and* Peel, L.J., *eds.* Oxford, University Press, 1991. xviii,300p. tables, maps. £45. ISBN: 0198592086.

8 sections: 1. Natural environment - 2. The historical and social background - 3. The components of agriculture - 4. The ten agricultural regions of China - 5. Infrastructure and agriculture inputs - 6. The rural economy - 7. Agricultural education, research, and extension - 8. Summary and conclusions: the characteristics and problems of Chinese agriculture and prospects for the future. Bibliographies appended to each section. 4 appendices, *e.g.* 2. Economic terms. A general overview. *Class No:* 63.0(510)

[5593]

ZHANG, Q.Q. Directory of Chinese agricultural and related organizations. Wallingford, Oxon., CAB International, 1994. viii,350p. £49.50. ISBN: 0851987893.

980 entries covering agriculture in its broadest sense so that organizations dealing with biological sciences, hydrology, meteorology, health sciences, environmental sciences, etc. are included. Data for each entry include address, fax, telex and telephone numbers, name of head, number of professional staff, contact name, subject coverage, publications, etc. *Class No:* 63.0(510)

Asia—South & South East

[5594]

Agriasia: a current bibliography of Southeast Asian agricultural literature. Laguana, Philippines, Agricultural Information Bank of Asia, Southeast Asian College, 1970-. 4pa.

About 5,000 abstracts pa. Classes A-U (*e.g.* F. Plant genetics and breeding; H. Pests of plants; L. Animal husbandry; P. Natural resources and environment; Q. Processing of agricultural products). Author and keyword indexes per issue. AIBA database. *Class No:* 63.0(54+59)

India

[5595]

KAMATH, M.G. A Dictionary of Indian agriculture. New Delhi, Allied Publishers Private Ltd., 1992. vi,607p. Rs150.

Contains terms, idioms, and phrases from all aspects of Indian agriculture and includes subject areas such as agricultural economics, food processing, and veterinary medicine. *Class No:* 63.0(540)

[5596]

SINGH, J. An Agricultural atlas of India: a geographical analysis. Kurukshera, Haryana, Vishal Publications, 1974. xxvi, 356p.

147 maps, with a 10-chapter commentary. Accompanying booklet: *The Green revolution in India* (1974. 48p.). 'The atlas is very well presented, straightforward and unpretentious' (*Geographical journal*, v.142(1), March 1974, p.169). *Class No:* 63.0(540)

USA

[5597]

Bibliography of books and pamphlets on the history of agriculture in the United States, 1607-1967. Schlebecker, J.T., *ed.* Santa Barbara, Calif., ABC-Clio, Inc., 1969. vii, 183p.

2,042 numbered entries, under authors, A-Z. Occasional annotations. Presence of illus., maps, bibliographies, etc. is noted. Includes fiction. 274 entries on slavery. The subject index (p.103-89) is non-analytical, having *c.*135 undifferentiated entries under 'Agrarian discontent'. 'Well printed and readable bibliography' (*RQ*, v.10(2), Winter 1970, p.166). *Class No:* 63.0(73)

[5598]

SCHAPSMEIER, E.L. *and* **SCHAPSMEIER, F.H. Encyclopedia of American agricultural history.** Westport, Conn. & London, Greenwood Press, 1976. 480p. $55. ISBN: 0837179580.

Has entries A-Z and a subject index. Many entries have further references. Considered best at coverage of US legislation, agricultural agencies and organizations, as well as frontier and rural life (*Library journal*, 15 September 1976, p.1844-5). *Class No:* 63.0(73)

[5599]

U.S. agricultural groups: institutional profiles. Browne, W.P. *and* Cigler, A.J., *eds.* Westport, Conn., Greenwood, 1990. 274p. $55. ISBN: 031325088x.

Lists 103 private US organizations, with data including address, list of publications, summary of purpose, origins, funding and organizational structure. An appendix of related groups is included. Index of corporate and personal names. *Class No:* 63.0(73)

Information Management

[5600]

Directory of training specialists in agricultural information. Johnson, J., *and others, eds.* Wageningen, Technical Centre for Agricultural and Rural Cooperation, 1993. xii,188p. ISBN: 9290810866.

Identifies experts in agricultural information training. Arranged alphabetically by country of residence of the trainer. Indexes for names, subjects, geographical areas of experience. *Class No:* 63.0:025.4

Thesauri

[5601]

Agrovoc: multilingual agricultural thesaurus. 2nd ed. Rome, Apimondia in association with FAO, 1992. xvi,798p. $120, monolingual ed.; $580, 5-language v.

First published 1982.

Lists 14,714 indexing terms used by *AGRIS (q.v.)* and CARIS. Available in 5 languages: English; French; Spanish; German; Italian. The English, French, and Spanish versions each have a trilingual index. *Class No:* 63.0:025.43

[5602]

CAB thesaurus. 1990 ed. Wallingford, Oxon., CAB International, 1990. 2v. £99.50. ISBN: 0851986870.

First published 1983.

Contains *c.*57,000 entries, including cross-references. Each preferred term is displayed with its complete hierarchy of broader, narrower and related terms. Contains all the indexing terms for the AGRICOLA database of the National Agricultural Library (NAL) of the US in addition to those used in the CAB abstracting journals and database. New features for this edition are 'History notes', distinction between American and British spelling variants, and the adoption of the group names approved by the International Committee on Taxonomy of Viruses. A new edition is due to be published in 1999. *Class No:* 63.0:025.43

Libraries

[5603]

Agricultural information resource centers: a world directory 1990. Johnson, J.S., *and others.* Twin Falls, Idaho, International Association of Agricultural Librarians and Documentalists, 1995. 600p. $140. ISBN: 0962405213.

Contains over 3,500 entries for libraries and documentation centres from 250 countries, arranged A-Z by country. Coverage includes universities, research institutes, and government libraries. Data include staff, main subjects, e-mail address, loan policy, photocopy policy, etc. Subject and institution indexes. *Class No:* 63.0:061:026/027

Institutions & Associations

[5604]

COMMISSION OF THE EUROPEAN COMMUNITIES. AGREP: Permanent inventory of agricultural research projects in the European Communities. Luxembourg, CEC, 1992. 2v.

1. *Main list: research projects.* 2. *Indexes.*

V.1 has data on *c.*20,000 research projects. Classified index. V.2 provides subject and country (Belgium ... The Netherlands) indexes. List of research organizations. List of scientists. AGREP functions as an online database on AGRISEARCH (*q.v.*); *c.*5,000 records are added pa. *Class No:* 63.0:061:061.2

[5605]
COMMISSION OF THE EUROPEAN COMMUNITIES. Directory of non-governmental agricultural organizations. Rev. ed. Munich, etc., K.G. Saur, 1989. 320p. £55. ISBN: 359810801x.

About 150 organizations. Sections A-G (A. Agricultural producers; B. Agricultural and food products processing industries; C. Agricultural and food trading D. - Agricultural cooperatives - E. Agricultural and food industry - E. Consumers - G. Miscellaneous (*e.g.* Eurogroup for Animal Welfare)). *Class No:* 63.0:061:061.2

[5606]
COMMISSION OF THE EUROPEAN COMMUNITIES. Economic and Social Committee. Directory of European agricultural organizations. London, Kogan Page, for Office for Official Publications of the European Communities, Luxembourg, 1984. 718p. £39. ISBN: 0850389291.

5 parts. 1. General overview and basic data - 2. Agriculture in member states of the European Community and national agricultural organizations. (10 countries, Federal Republic of Germany ... Greece) - 3. Agriculture and agricultural organizations in other countries of Western Europe (7, including Spain and Portugal) - 4. Organizations of farmers in Europe (by countries) - 5. The institutions of the European Community and agriculture. *Class No:* 63.0:061:061.2

Research Establishments

[5607]
Agricultural research centres: a world directory of organizations and programmes. 12th ed. London, Cartermill Publishing, 1995. x,679p. £299. (*Reference on research.*) ISBN: 1860670067.

9th ed. 1988. Previously as *Agricultural research index* (F. Hodgson).

Arranged alphabetically by country, Albania ... Zimbabwe. Lists over 8,000 organizations that conduct or finance agricultural research. Covers 155 countries, including those of the Third World. Food, environmental and biological sciences are included in the subject coverage. Data include affiliation, status, senior staff, annual expenditure and publications. Index of names of establishments. Non-analytical subject index. Apart from the organizational headings, in very small type. Accessible on *Current research worldwide* CD-ROM. *Class No:* 63.0:061:061.62

Research Projects

[5608]
Agricultural research, 1931-1981: a history of the Agricultural Research Council, and a review of developments in agricultural science in the last fifty years. Cooke, G.W., *ed.* London, the Council, 1981. ix, 367p. illus., facsims., ports., diagrs., tables. £6.50. ISBN: 0708401805.

Has 13 contributions. Topics range from plant breeding to milk and milk products. 7 appendices. Detailed, non-analytical index. *Class No:* 63.0:061:061.62.005

Education Courses

[5609]
Directory of courses in land-based industries 1999-2000. Bond, Nicholas, *ed.* Ipswich, Farming Press, 1998. 270p. £14.95. ISBN: 0852365217.

Published annually. Contains details of full-, part-time, and sandwich courses in the UK. 70 institutions are included, initially listed under subject heading, while a second section lists them alphabetically. Many cros-references. *Class No:* 63.0:377.3

Agricultural Economics

[5610]
COMMISSION OF THE EUROPEAN COMMUNITIES. Directorate-General for Research, Science & Education. Agricultural economics and rural sociology - multilingual thesaurus. Munich, K.G. Saur, 1979. 5v. (4v. & index), plus 16 microfiche. (English language volume. 104p.).

English, French, German and Italian language volumes, plus index. Coverage: Agricultural and rural law - Agricultural economics - Countries - Livestock, crops and products - Methodology - Research development and education - Rural sociology. *Class No:* 63.003

[5611]
GIANNINI FOUNDATION OF AGRICULTURAL ECONOMICS LIBRARY. Dictionary catalog. [Giannini Foundation of Agricultural Economics Library]. Boston, Mass., G.K. Hall, 1971. 12v. $1,305. ISBN: 0816109087.

377,000 photolithographically reproduced catalogue cards. Most of the collection is in English, with emphasis on the US, Western European countries, Spanish America and English-language-speaking countries. *Class No:* 63.003

[5612]
OLSEN, W.C. Agricultural economics and rural sociology: the contemporary core literature. Ithaca, London, Cornell Press, 1991. xi,346p. tables. (*The literature of the agricultural sciences.*) ISBN: 0801426774.

10 chapters: 1. Trends and development of agricultural economics and rural sociology in the United States ... 4. Citation analysis ... 6. Current primary journals and serials - 7. Core lists of primary monographs (p.92-267) ... 10. Reference update. Appendices: A. Languages in AGRICOLA/CABI databases; B. American Agricultural Economics Association classic book list. Index. The other projected 6 volumes in the series are: *Agricultural engineering; Animal science and health; Soil science; Crop improvement and protection; Food science and human nutrition; Forestry and silviculture.* *Class No:* 63.003

[5613]
World agricultural economics and rural sociology abstracts. Wallingford, Oxon., CAB International, 1958-. 12pa. £472; $995. ISSN: 00438219.

About 8,000 abstracts pa. Sections include: Agricultural economics; Agricultural policy and development; Agrarian reform; Employment and income; Supply, demand and prices; Food policy; Marketing and distribution; International trade; Finance and credit; Farm economics; Cooperatives; Rural sociology. Author and subject indexes per issue and annually. Annual geographical index. Online through CAB ABSTRACTS database and available on CD-ROM. *Class No:* 63.003

Co-operative Enterprises

[5614]
Directory of agricultural co-operatives and other farm-controlled businesses in the United Kingdom. Oxford, Plunkett Foundation for Co-operative Studies, 1992-. Annual.

Formerly *Directory of agricultural co-operatives in the United Kingdom.*

Sections: Digest of statistics - Central organizations - Agricultural marketing boards - FAC in Europe - Representatives on COGECA and EEC committees - Federal organizations - Directory of agricultural co-operatives, (England, Northern Ireland, Scotland, Wales) - Fishery co-operatives - Cottage industries - Country index. *Class No:* 63.009.11

[5615]
The World of co-operative enterprise. Oxford, Plunkett Foundation for Co-operative Studies, 1996. £16.95.

Formerly *Yearbook of co-operative enterprise.*

Focuses on four subject areas: 1. Co-operation between co-operatives - 2. Health and care co-operatives - 3. New ways of financing co-operatives - 4. Annual review of co-operation in the United Kingdom. *Class No:* 63.009.11

Forestry

Bibliographies

[5616]
International bibliography of dictionaries, glossaries and terminological publications in forestry and related sciences. Vienna, IUFRO Secretariat, 1997. v,50p. (*IUFRO occasional paper, no.8.*)

Lists 374 items, covering 10 subject areas. More than 40 languages are represented although most are English-language. Author and language indexes. *Class No:* 630(01)

[5617]
The Literature of forestry and agroforestry. McDonald, P. *and* Lassioe, J., *eds.* Ithaca, Cornell University Press, 1996. 445p. $79.95. (*Literature of the agricultural sciences.*) ISBN: 0801431816.

14 chapters: 1. Trends and development in modern forestry ... 4. Agro-forestry directions and literature trends ... 9. Forestry education in the United States ... 14. Primary historical literature of U.S. forestry. 'for all forestry libraries ... an excellent work'(*Choice,* November 1996, p.483). *Class No:* 630(01)

[5618]
REHDER, A. The Bradley bibliography: a guide to the literature of the woody plants of the world published before the beginning of the twentieth century. Compiled at the Arnold Arboretum of Harvard University. Cambridge, Mass., Riverside Press, 1911-18 (reprinted Champaign, Ill., Koeltz Science Books, 1976). 5v.

1. *Dendrology,* pt.1. 1911. 2. *Dendrology,* pt.2: 'Gymnospermae'. 1912. 3. *Arboriculture, economic properties of woody plants,* 1915. 4. *Forestry,* 1914. 5. *Index of authors and titles* (p.1-943); Index of Greek authors and titles. Index of Russian and Serbian authors and titles; Subject index to v.1-4.

A classic bibliography. V.1, pt.1 records *c.*20,000 items, with bibliographical notes, on more general aspects and allied studies, and has a subject index. *Class No:* 630(01)

[5619]

YALE UNIVERSITY. Yale Forestry Library. Dictionary catalogue of the Yale Forestry Library, Henry S. Graves Memorial Library. Boston, Mass., G.K. Hall, 1962. 12v. $1,305. ISBN: 0816106312.

The catalogue (217,000 cards) of one of the largest libraries of its kind. Strongest on all aspects of the history of forestry, especially that of American forestry. Records 90,000v.; also periodical articles, indexed from leading forestry magazines and lumber journals, thus conveniently preceding *Forestry abstracts* (1939-) *(q.v.).*
Class No: 630(01)

Encyclopaedias

[5620]

Lesnaya entsiklopediya. [Forest encyclopaedia.] Vorob'ev, G.I., *ed.* Moscow, Sovetskaya Entsiklopediya, 1985-.

V.1. *Abelia-Lemon.* 1985. 563p.

Projected set of 2v., which, when completed, will contain 3,600 articles, with particular emphasis on the utilization of timber and other forest resources. *Class No: 630(031)*

Handbooks & Manuals

[5621]

Forestry handbook. Wenger, K.F., *ed.* 2nd ed., edited for the Society of American Foresters. New York, etc., Wiley, 1984. xix, 1335p. graphs, tables, maps. $75. ISBN: 0471062278.

First published 1958.

25 chapters on forest ecology, geology and soils, meteorology and climatology, insect and disease management, timber measurements, silviculture, logging, safety, remote sensing, mathematics and statistics. 'Further reading'. Detailed subject index.
Class No: 630(035)

[5622]

JAMES, N.D.G. The Forester's companion. 4th ed. Oxford, Basil Blackwell, 1989. xii, 310p. tables. £14.95. ISBN: 0631167242.

First published 1955.

33 chapters (1. Forest trees grown in Britain ... 8. Forest management ... 12. Diseases and pests ... 16. Utilization ... 27. Societies, organizations, establishments, and trusts concerned with forestry work). 1. Appendix: Abbreviations. Index, p.302-10. Small format. *Class No: 630(035)*

Dictionaries

[5623]

CHARLOT, G. Vocabulaire technique en arboriculture: lexique anglais/français, français/anglais [Technical vocabulary of arboriculture: English-French/French-English dictionary.] Paris, Centre Technique Interprofessionnel des Fruits et Légumes, 1993. 74p. FFr150. ISBN: 2879110351.

Contains lists of French to English and English to French terms. Subjects include soils, propagation, plant protection, mechanization, etc. Samples of the terms in context are given. *Class No: 630(038)*

[5624]

Dictionary of forestry, in five languages: German, English, French, Spanish, Russian. Weck, J., *and others, comps.* Amsterdam, etc., Elsevier, 1966 (reprinted 1979). xxvi, 573p. tables. £93.43.

About 10,000 German-base terms, with English, French, Spanish and Russian equivalents and indexes. Appendices list species of trees and plants, plus animals, under scientific names, with equivalents in the five languages concerned. *Class No: 630(038)*

[5625]

Lexicon forestale / Metsäsan akirja / Skogsardbok / Forest dictionary / Forstwörterbuch / Lesnoï slovar'. Ahlsved, K.-J., *and others.* Porvoo, Finland, Werner Söderstrum, 1979. xix, 594p.

9,582 numbered Finnish terms, with Swedish, English, German and Russian equivalents and indexes. A dictionary of forestry, timber and paper words. Areas covered: tree species, vascular plants, mosses and liverworts, fungi and bacteria, vertebrates, weights and measures, institutes, organizations and associations. Many cross-references. Genders stated. *Class No: 630(038)*

[5626]

RUOKONEN, M. Forestry and forest products vocabulary. Slough, Bucks., Commonwealth Agricultural Bureaux, 1984. xv, 459p. £26. ISBN: 0851985483.

About 14,000 terms are defined, with coded reference to sources. 'Key to sources', p.ix-xiv. Includes acronyms and abbreviations, dialect/geographical limitations. Ample cross-references. Both British and American spelling given. Supplements the list of terms provided annually in *Forestry abstracts* and *Forestry products abstracts.*
Class No: 630(038)

[5627]

Skoglista. [Glossary of forestry.] 2nd rev. and enlgd. ed. Stockholm, Tekniska Nomenklaturcentralen, 1978. 676p. illus. (*TNC 71.*)

First published 1969.

A classified dictionary, Swedish-English, with Swedish definitions and index to terms in both languages. About 5,000 Swedish entries.
Class No: 630(038)

[5628]

Terminologie Forsteinrichtung/Waldinventur mit deutsch-russischem und russisch-deutschem Fachwörterbuch. [Terminology of forest management/forest inventory, with a German-Russian and Russian-German technical dictionary.] Bick, U., *and others.* Hamburg, Bundesforschungsanstalt für Forst- und Holzwirtschaft, 1994. 117p. (*Mitteilungen der Bundesforschungen für Forst- und Holzwirtschaft. 1994, no.177.*)

Three sections: Section 1 consists of 400 German terms arranged A-Z with German definitions; Section 2 is a Russian-German vocabulary; Section 3, a German-Russian vocabulary. *Class No: 630(038)*

[5629]

Terminology of forest science, technology, practice and products: English language version. Ford-Robertson, F.C. *and* Winters, R.K., *eds.* Rev. ed. Washington, Society of American Foresters, 1983. xxi, 370p. illus. $10. (*Multilingual forestry terminology series, no.1.*) ISBN: 0939970163.

First of a series of multilingual forestry terminologies authorized by the joint FAO/IUFRO Committee on Forestry Bibliography and Terminology. This ed. is a reprinting of the 1971 ed. + an addendum.

*c.*7,000 entries, differentiating US usage. Includes abbreviations. Many cross-references. 6 appendices (*e.g.* 1. Key to published sources drawn on; 4. Deprecated key and secondary terms with their preferred synonyms). *Class No: 630(038)*

Reviews & Abstracts

[5630]

Forestry abstracts. Prepared by the CAB International Forestry Bureau. Wallingford, Oxon., CAB International, 1939-. 12pa. £405; $735. ISSN: 00157538.

9,500 abstracts pa. 16 sections: General publications and general techniques - General aspects of forestry - Silviculture - Forest mensuration and management - Physical environment - Fire - Plant biology - Mycology and pathology - Insects and other invertebrates ... Catchment management. Soil conservation - Other land use. Nature conservation - Arboriculture - Dendrochronology and dendroclimatology. Author and subject indexes per issue and annually. The major source.

Online through CAB ABSTRACTS database (covering the 19 major CAB abstract journals). Available on the CAB ABSTRACTS CD-ROM and TREECD, also produced by CAB International.
Class No: 630(048)

Periodicals

[5631]

COMMONWEALTH FORESTRY INSTITUTE. Forestry Library list of serials. 4th rev. ed. Oxford, the Institute, 1984. 264p.
Class No: 630(051)

[5632]

HAUGEN, C. *and* **DURST, P.B. Directory of selected tropical forestry journals and newsletters.** 2nd ed. Bangkok, FAO Regional Office for Asia and the Pacific (RAP), 1997. x,130p.

First published 1987.

Listed alphabetically, information includes editors' and publishers' names, address, telephone number, language, frequency, date of first publication, and subscription price. *Class No: 630(051)*

Yearbooks & Directories

[5633]

Directory of forestry research organizations. Rome, Food and Agriculture Organization/International Union of Forestry Research Organizations, 1993. vii,167p. (*FAO forestry paper, no.109.*) ISBN: 9251033617.

Arranged by country, *c.*650 organizations are listed with dettails of address, graduate staff, main research areas, head of organization, and establishment date. *Class No: 630(058)*

Maps & Atlases

[5634]

Weltsforstatlas. Reinbeck, Bundenanstalt für Forst und Holzwirtschaft, in collaboration with FAO Berlin-Grünewald, Haller, 1951-.

Commissioned by the FAO Forestry Division.

Each map (in 5-10 colours) covers one country or area, showing distribution of forest types and wood species, location of woodworking industries, and the like. Legends in English, Spanish, German and

....(contd.)

French. Lieferung 21 (6 maps) was received in 1981. Page size, c.59 x 72cm. Of value to foresters and forest students, economists, geographers, botanists and regional planners. *Class No:* 630(084.3)

China

[5635]
China forest yearbook 1949-1986. Beijing, China Forestry Publishing House, 1987. xix,718p. illus. (col. pl.).

24 chapters covering forestry in China, including forest products industries and recent history. Detailed glossary of 125 terms (112 with English equivalents). Chinese subject index. *Class No:* 630(510)

USA

[5636]
Encyclopedia of American forest and conservation history. Davis, R.B., *ed.* New York, Macmillan, 1983. 2v, (871p.), illus., maps. $200. ISBN: 0029075302.

203 contributors. 413 articles (some lengthy), with references for further reading and cross-references. Scope covers US forest industries, national parks, personalities, legislation, and topical issues. Appendices concern national forests and parks, officials, etc., and carry an atlas. Black-and-white illus. only. 'An excellent set which belongs in any library serving those interested in American forestry, conservation and ecology'. (*Reference books bulletin, 1984-1985*, p.53). *Class No:* 630(73)

Forest Products

[5637]
BOLZA, E. German-English glossary of forest products terms. South Melbourne, CSIRO, Division of Forest Products, 1959. 169p. Supplement. 1962. 87, [5]p.

'The alphabetical glossary also contains many silvicultural and forest-utilization terms' (*Forestry abstracts*, v.21(2), April 1980, p.289). *Class No:* 630:8

[5638]
FOOD AND AGRICULTURE ORGANIZATION. Yearbook of forest products, 1989. Rome, FAO, 1991. 392p. $30. ISBN: 9250030304.

Statistics and data on production, trade and consumption in roundwood, sawnwood, sleepers, plywood, wood pulp, varied types of paper, paper-board and fibre-board. Sources from more than 100 countries. *Class No:* 630:8

[5639]
Forest products abstracts. Wallingford, Oxon., CAB International, 1978-. 6pa. £210; $375. ISSN: 01404784.

Coverage includes: c.2,600 abstracts pa. Coverage includes: General publications and general techniques; General aspects of forest products and industry; Wood properties; Timber extraction, conversion and measurement; Damage to timber and timber protection; Utilization of wood; Veneers; Composite boards, laminated wood, panels, improved wood, glues; Pulping; Marketing and trade. Economics. Author and subject indexes. Occasional review articles precede abstracts (*e.g.* 'Forest products thesis summaries', April 1987, p.137-41).

Online through CAB ABSTRACTS database, CAB ABSTRACTS CD-ROM and TREECD. Hosts include DIALOG, ESA-IRS. *Class No:* 630:8

Trees (Silviculture)

Encyclopaedias

[5640]
DAVIS, B. The Gardener's illustrated encyclopedia of trees and shrubs: a guide to more than 2000 varieties. Harmondsworth, Middx., Penguin Books; Viking, 1987. 256p. illus. (incl col.) £19.99. ISBN: 0670812374.

Dictionary of trees, p.10-71; dictionary of shrubs, p.72-221. Data under 11 heads in both sequences: origin; description; hardiness; shade aspect ... average height and spread. Advice on planting and pruning. Practical glossary; botanical glossary. Choosing the right trees and shrubs. Pronunciation glossary. Index of common names; Index of Latin names. *Class No:* 630.2(031)

[5641]
The Hillier colour dictionary of trees and shrubs. Newton Abbot, Devon, David & Charles, 1993. 323p. col. illus. £17.99. ISBN: 0715300911.

Has c.three-line descriptions of 3,500 trees and shrubs selected for their garden value. The colour dictionary has 3 sections: trees and shrubs; climbers; conifers (p.35-319), preceded by cultural, etc. notes. Contains c.600 illustrations. Glossary of botanical terms, p.320-3. Notes on many of the plants are based on conditions in the British Isles. *Class No:* 630.2(031)

[5642]
The Hillier manual of trees and shrubs. 6th ed. Newton Abbot, Devon, David & Charles, 1991. 704p. £25; £14.99. ISBN: 071539942x.

First published 1971, as a nurseryman's catalogue.

Very brief descriptions of over 9,000 plants, including more than 1,000 new entries. 4 main sections: Trees and shrubs; Climbers; Conifers; Bamboos. Appended sections on botanical names; trees and shrubs for selected soils, sites and ornamental effect; flowering trees and shrubs for every month. A standard guide.

Based on this title and published in the US in 1997 by Reader's Digest, *The Hillier gardener's guide to trees and shrubs*(ISBN: 0895779730; 640p., illus.; $50) which is also available as part of *The Plant finder reference library* CD-ROM 1998/9. *Class No:* 630.2(031)

[5643]
JOHNSON, H. Hugh Johnson's encyclopaedia of trees. Rev. and updated ed. Editor, D. Taylor. London, Mitchell Beazley, 1984. 336p. col. illus., diagrs., charts, maps. ISBN: 0855335467.

First published as *The international book of trees* (1973).

Guide to the world's trees, p.66-246 (the conifers; the broad leaves). A new feature, 'Reference section', - an illustrated A-Z index of tree species, p.247-31). This section includes; A twelve month succession of ornamental flowers, fruit and foliage; rates of tree growth; a guide to choosing trees; the meaning of botanical names. Illustrations (more than 1,000 covering over 600 species) are well captioned. Index. *Class No:* 630.2(031)

[5644]
KRÜSSMANN, G. Manual of cultivated broad-leaved trees & shrubs. London, Batsford, 1984-86. 3v. (1519p.), illus., maps. £70ea. ISBN: 0713446013; 0713453486; 0713454083.

Translation of *Handbuch der Laubgehölze* (1976-.).

The 3v. (A-D, E-PRO, PRU-Z) record data on over 5,000 species and c.6,000 cultivars of trees, shrubs, subshrubs and vines. Entries are under Latin names of genera. V.1 includes an A/Z guide to botanical terms in English, Latin, German, French and Dutch, and 'List of abbreviations to other reference works'. Over 300 black-and-white illus. per volume. Hardiness zone maps. *Class No:* 630.2(031)

[5645]
The Oxford encyclopedia of trees of the world. Hora, B., *consultant ed.* Oxford Univ. Press, 1981. 288p. col. illus., tables. ISBN: 0192177125.

39 contributors. Devotes the main section to 149 wild and cultivated genera. Data: structure; distribution; history; ecology; cultivation; economic use. A further section concerns native trees of Asia, Africa and America. Appended keys to families, a general bibliography (p.277); glossary. Indexes to common and Latin names. 365 illus., well captioned. 'An excellent choice' (*RQ*, v.21(4), Summer 1982, p.420). *Class No:* 630.2(031)

Handbooks & Manuals

[5646]
Diseases of trees and shrubs. Sinclair, W.A., *and others.* Ithaca, N.Y., & London, Comstock Pubg. Associates, Cornell Univ. Press, 1987. 547p. col. illus. £52.50; $52.50. ISBN: 0801415179.

Descriptive data, facing 247 colour-plates. Glossary, p.509-11. A feature is the extensive bibliography, p.512-46: over 2,200 references, under authors, A-Z. Detailed analytical index, p.547-74. Large quarto format. *Class No:* 630.2(035)

[5647]
PHILLIPS, D.H. and BURDEKIN, D.A. Diseases of forest and ornamental trees. London, Macmillan, 1982. xv, 435p. illus. (incl. col.). £60. ISBN: 0333323572.

19 well-documented chapters (*e.g.* 'Diseases of willow', p.301-25, including 2½p. of references). Glossary, p.410-411. Detailed, analytical index, p.412-35. Concentrates on diseases found in Britain on forest and ornamental trees. 64 plates. Where possible, information is given on 'symptoms, factors affecting disease expression, host-range and resistance, and brief descriptions of causal organisms' (*Preface*). 2nd ed. promised 1992/93 (£75). *Class No:* 630.2(035)

Dictionaries

[5648]
VAUCHER, H. Elsevier's dictionary of trees and shrubs, in Latin, English, French, German and Italian. Amsterdam, etc., Elsevier, 1986. xiv, 414p. £110; $164. ISBN: 0444425691.

2,500 Latin names of trees and shrubs (stating genera and species, with popular name equivalents in English, French, German and Italian). The trees and shrubs are mostly those found in the northern and southern hemispheres. Appended list of reference book sources, p.413. *Class No:* 630.2(038)

Nomenclatures

[5649]

WELCH, H. *and* **HADDOW, G. The World checklist of conifers.**
Bromyard, Herefordshire, published by Landsman's Bookshop Ltd. on
behalf of the World Conifer Data Pool, 1993. viii,427p. ISBN:
0900513098.

Contains *c*.10,000 names of conifers. Each entry lists botanical and
horticultural names and also gives 'illegitimate, obsolete,
undocumented and 'other' names' (*Introduction*). The date of the first
valid publication, height, and broad indication of country/area of
origin are also listed. Many synonyms and cross-references.
Class No: 630.2(083.72)

Worldwide

[5650]

PHILLIPS, R. Trees in Britain, Europe and North America. London,
Ward Lock, 1978. 234p. illus. £12.99. ISBN: 0330254804.

Illustrates well over 500 trees (A-Z, Latin names, p.60-215) in full
colour, showing leaf, fruit, inflorescence, bark, silhouette. Unusual
leaf index. Helpful colour supplement to Bean (*qv*), which has only
black-and-white photographs and line drawings. Quarto format.
Class No: 630.2(100)

Europe

[5651]

**MITCHELL, A. A Field guide to the trees of Britain and Northern
Europe.** 2nd ed. London, Collins, 1978. 416p. illus. (incl. col.).
£14.99. ISBN: 0002192136.

Describes 800 trees (49 families), p.48-390. Data: common and
Latin names; habit; use; size; bark; crown; foliage; flowers (and
cone); similar species. Appended glossary. 'Collections of trees open
to the public'. Index to English names; index to scientific names. 40
col. plates; 640 clear line-drawings. 'Designed to describe in
systematic detail every tree species and cultivar (variety) found in
parks, gardens, large and small, towns and countryside, and to provide
guides and keys with which to identify them' (*Preface*). An excellent
compendium. *Class No:* 630.2(4)

Great Britain

[5652]

BEAN, W.J. Trees and shrubs hardy in the British Isles. 8th ed. Chief
editor, D.L. Clarke. London, Murray, 1970-80. 4v. illus. Supplement.
432p. 1988. £60ea; £50, supp. ISBN: 0719524285, set; 0719517907,
supp.

First published 1914-33.

Entries, A-C, D-M, N-Rh, Ri-Z, under Latin names. V.1 (Abelia-
Cytisus. xx, 848p.) contains a glossary (p.112-20) and select
bibliography, the descriptive list of genera and species (p.137-831),
with 77 plates and 112 botanical drawings, and an index. Data: full
description (corrected or updated) of species and varieties (but no keys
to identification), common name, synonyms, distribution, date of
introduction, features, merits and cultivation, plus 'references for
illustrations'. V.4 (xv, 808p.) covers 115 genera, with 111 black-and-
white photographs, and index, p.785-808. *Class No:* 630.2(410)

USA

[5653]

The Audubon Society field guide to North American trees. Little, E.C.
New York, Knopf, 1980-2. 2v. (1353p.). col. illus. ISBN:
0394507606; 0394507614.

1. *Eastern region.* 1980., 714p. 2. *Western region.* 1982. 639p.

V.1 records 368 species; v.2. 314 species. The main feature - as of
others in the Audubon Society Field guide series - is pictorial
presentation (v.2 has 855 illus., mostly in colour), grouped by
similarities of leaf or needle shape, fruit, etc. The second part of each
volume is descriptive text, with characteristics of each tree.
Geographic range of v.1 extends to the eastern base of the Rockies,
then south to Texas. Portable format. Ideal 'for someone needing a
quick and painless tree identification' (*RSR*, v.12(3), Fall 1984, p.38).
Class No: 630.2(73)

Agricultural Trade

[5654]

FAO trade yearbook. Rome, FAO, 1947-. Annual.

V.50 (1996. 398p.) has 196 tables. Three sections: 1. Trade in
agricultural products (p.3-318) - 2. Trade in means of agricultural
production (*e.g.* tractors; pesticides) - 3. Value of agricultural, fishery
and forestry trade by countries (p.331-398). Years covered: 1994,
1995, 1996. Flimsy paper; small print. *Class No:* 631.003.1

Farms

Organic Farming

[5655]

LAMPKIN, N. Organic farming. Ipswich, Farming Press, 1990.
xiii,701p. illus. (some col.), tables. £19.95. ISBN: 0852361912.

15 chapters: 1. Organic farming-agriculture with a future - 2. The
living soil ... 4. Management of manures, slurry and organic residues -
5. Rotation designs for organic systems ... 8. Livestock husbandry ...
12. Marketing and processing ... 14. Converting to organic farming -
15. The wider issues. 6 appendices (1. Standards for organic
agriculture ... 4. Addresses ... 6. Some metric conversion factors).
Sections on animal husbandry particularly useful. Bibliographies
appended to each chapter. Author is lecturer in agricultural economics
at the University College of Wales, Aberystwyth and Development
Director of the Aberystwyth Centre for Organic Husbandry and
Agroecology. Good value. *Class No:* 631.147

[5656]

Organic agriculture worldwide: directory of the member organizations
and associates of IFOAM, 1996/97. Tholey-Theley, International
Federation of Organic Movements, 1997. 54p.

Lists 527 organizations from 92 countries. Data include address,
contact person, postal and e-mail address, and areas of activity.
Class No: 631.147

Management

[5657]

NIX, J. *and* **HILL, P. Farm management pocketbook.** 29th ed.
Ashford, Kent, Wye College Press, 1998. vii, 232p. tables. £9.75.
ISBN: 0862660599.

First published 1966.

Seven sections: 1. General ... 3. Labour ... 6. Capital, taxation and
grants - 7. Miscellaneous data. Index. Virtually annual update. J. Nix
is National Westminster Bank Professor. *Class No:* 631.15

Buildings

[5658]

**BRUNSKILL, R.W. Traditional farm buildings of Britain and their
conservation.** 3rd ed. London, Gollancz, 1998. 208p. illus. £35.
ISBN: 0575066342.

First published 1982.

10 chapters: 1. Farming history and the standard farmstead - 2.
Barns and the processing of grain crops - 3. Accommodation for
animals - 4. Accommodation for birds - 5. Farmsteads - 6. Farmsteads -
7. Materials and construction - 8. Later developments - 9.
Conservation and re-use of farm buildings - 10. Regional variations.
Notes and references; Bibliography; Index. *Class No:* 631.22

[5659]

HARVEY, N. A History of farm buildings in England and Wales.
New ed. Newton Abbot, Devon, David & Charles, 1984. 279p. illus.
£17.50. ISBN: 0715383833.

First published 1970.

12 chapters (with appended notes): 1. Prologue: to AD1000 ... 4.
The agrarian revolution: the agrarian phase, 1750-1820 ... 10. Post-
war farmsteads: some examples. Appendix: 'Dating pre-industrial farm
buildings'; 'A note on sources', p.267-72. Analytical index, p.275-9.
Class No: 631.22

[5660]

—**NOTON, N.H.** Farm buildings. Reading, College of Estate
Management, 1982. [xii], 359p. illus., diagrs., plans. ISBN:
0902132733.

Has 18 sections: 1. Principles of construction ... 3. Foundations ...
6. Waste and drainage ... 9. Design considerations ... 12. Pigs ... 17.
Dairy buildings ... 20. Domestic building design. Further reading,
p.347. Detailed, analytical index, p.349-59. Comprehensive, with
numerous photographs, 'but rarely giving more than a general view'.
(*Farm buildings digest*, v.18(3), 1983, p.16). *Class No:* 631.22

Agricultural Machinery

Bibliographies

[5661]

The Literature of agricultural engineering. Hall, C.W. *and*
Olsen, W.C., *eds.* Ithaca, N.Y., Cornell University Press, 1992.
viii,416p. illus. (*Literature of the agricultural sciences.*) ISBN:
0801428122.

One of a series of books which looks at the various types of
information sources in agricultural subject areas. Includes databases,
bibliographies, encyclopaedias, dictionaries, periodicals, etc.
Class No: 631.3(01)

[5662]
MORGAN, B. **Keyguide to information sources in agricultural engineering.** London & New York, Mansell, 1985. vi, 209p. tables. £40. (*Keyguide to information sources series*.) ISBN: 0720117208.

3 parts: 1. Survey of agricultural engineering and its literature (6 documented chapters, p.3-92) - 2. Annotated bibliography of sources of information (p.95-162: entries 1-436, with brief annotations, except for list of journals) - 3. Organizational sources of information (p.165-92; includes organizations concerned with audio-visual materials; international scope). Detailed, analytical index. An authoritative survey of types of sources. *Class No: 631.3(01)*

Handbooks & Manuals

[5663]
Agricultural engineer's handbook. Richey, C.B., *and others, eds*. New York, etc., McGraw-Hill, 1961. 880p. diagrs., graphs, tables. ISBN: 0070526176.

4 sections (with documented chapters): 1. Crop-production equipment - 2. Soil and water conservation - 3. Farmstead structures and equipment - 4. Basic agricultural data. Index. Despite its age and US slant, 'it remains the only work of its kind in the field' (B.A. Morgan, in *Information sources in agriculture and food science*. (1981), p.222). *Class No: 631.3(035)*

[5664]
CULPIN, C. **Farm machinery.** 12th ed. Oxford, Blackwell, 1992. x,444p. illus. £24.99. ISBN: 063203159x.

First published 1938.

23 documented chapters: 2. Tractors: constructional operations ... 4. Ploughs: components and features ... 7. Equipment for sowing and planting ... 10. Pumps and irrigation equipment ... 15. Root harvesting machinery - 16. Horticultural machinery ... 19. Equipment for livestock husbandry - 20. Equipment for milk production ... 22. Machinery for land drainage, reclamation and estate maintenance - 23. Environmental control in crop and stock buildings. 6 appendices (*e.g.* 5. Electricity on the farm). Index. Well illustrated and captioned. A standard textbook, written for farmers and those who advise them. *Class No: 631.3(035)*

Dictionaries

[5665]
BRITISH STANDARDS INSTITUTION. **Glossary of terms relating to agricultural machinery and implements.** AMD 1395. 1983. London, BSI, 1963. 94p. illus. £94. (*BS 2468: 1963; AMD 4395: 1983.*)

About 1,000 terms defined. Sections: General definitions - Class O: Agricultural power units - 1. Equipment for sowing, planting and distributing manure - 3. Equipment for crop protection - 4. Harvesting machinery - 5. Equipment for preparing and storing produce on farms. *Class No: 631.3(038)*

[5666]
Dictionary of agricultural machinery and agricultural engineering: English-Japanese, Japanese-English. Kaburaki, H., *ed*. Tokyo, Shin-Norin Sha Co. Ltd., 1994. 998p. ISBN: 4880280399.

Coverage includes agricultural machinery and engineering, biotechnology, horticultural machinery, and general Japanese agricultural terms. *Class No: 631.3(038)*

[5667]
Dictionnaire technique de la mécanisation agricole. Paris, Centre National d'Études et d'Experimentation du Machinisme Agricole Tropical; New York, French & European, 1968-71. 3v. (xxxvi, 957p.). $59.95. ISBN: 0828853940, US ed.

V.1-2 consist of a classified arrangement. Languages: French, English, German, Spanish and Italian. V.3 comprises the alphabetical index to each language. Wide-ranging subject field. *Class No: 631.3(038)*

[5668]
English-Chinese dictionary of agricultural machinery. Peking, Mechanical Engineering Publishing House, 1974. 440p. illus.

About 30,000 English-Chinese entries, with a 20-page Chinese-English section and 42p. of illus. captioned in both English and Chinese. *Class No: 631.3(038)*

[5669]
Machinisme et équipements agricoles. Français, anglais, allemand, espagnol, italien, portugais. 3 ème éd. Paris, La maison du dictionnaire, 1990. 1295p. FFr700. (*Dictionnaire technologique, v.8.*)

19 subject areas: General terms ... Farm machinery ... Tractors and cultivators ... Crop protection equipment ... Harvesting machinery ... Processing equipment ... Soil conservation and forestry equipment. *Class No: 631.3(038)*

[5670]
STEINMETZ, H. **Agricultural engineering:** multilingual illustrated dictionary. 5th ed. Weikersheim, Verlag Josef Margraf, 1987. 502p. illus., figs. $35; £20.50. ISBN: 382361116x.

First published 1960.

About 6,000 terms in English, German, French, Spanish and Chinese. Coverage includes energy in agriculture, engines/tractors, aircraft, soil cultivation, plant protection, harvesting and earth moving. 1,730 line drawings. *Class No: 631.3(038)*

Reviews & Abstracts

[5671]
Agricultural engineering abstracts. Wallingford, Oxon., CAB International, 1976-. 12pa. £300; $670. ISSN: 03088863.

*c.*3,500 abstracts pa. Coverage includes: Mechanical power; Land improvement; Crop production; Protected cultivation; Crop harvesting and threshing; Handling and transport; Crop processing and storage; Animal housing, farm buildings and equipment; Aquaculture. Appended: Reports; Conferences; Books. Author and subject indexes per issue and annually. Online, CAB ABSTRACTS, and available on CAB ABSTRACTS CD-ROM. *Class No: 631.3(048)*

Yearbooks & Directories

[5672]
The Green book. Birmingham, Guardian Communications, 1951-. Annual. ISSN: 0965867x.

First published 1951 as *British tractors and farm machinery: the Green book series*.

Now incorporated into *The Institution of Agricultural engineers members' handbook and buyers'guide*.

1993/94 edition (76p.) has four sections: 1. Alphabetical index to manufacturers and suppliers - 2. Index to classifications - 3. Classified section - 4. Product analysis section; index to tables. *Class No: 631.3(058)*

Farm Tools

[5673]
BROWN, J. **Farm tools and techniques** a pictorial history. London, Batsford, 1993. 111p. illus. £14.99. ISBN: 0713474998.

Collection of photographs, mainly from the collection of the Rural History Centre, University of Reading, with each section accompanied by brief introductory text. For public and school libraries.

Also useful is *Farm tools through the ages*, by M. Partridge (London, Osprey Publishing, 1973. 240p.). *Class No: 631.31*

[5674]
FUSSELL, G.E. **The Farmer's tools:** the history of British farm implements, tools and machinery, AD1500-1900. London, Orbis Pubn., 1981. 246p. illus. (pl.). ISBN: 0856133590.

First published 1952.

7 chapters: 1. Field drainage - 2. Preparing the seed bed - 3. Sowing the seed - 4. Harvesting the crops - 5. Threshing the grain - 6. Barn and miscellaneous machinery - 7. Brief retrospect. Notes, p.201-17. Chronological list of tools (1523-1904). Glossary. Bibliography, p.226-30. Detailed analytical index, p.231-46. 111 plates. *Class No: 631.31*

Soil Science

[5675]
AVERY, B.W. **Soils of the British Isles.** Wallingford, CAB International, 1990. xi,463p. illus. (some col.), figs., tables. £67.50. ISBN: 0851986498.

9 chapters: 1. Soil and its variability - 2. Soil surveys and soil classification in the British Isles ... 5. Brown soils - 6. Podzols ... 9. Peat soils. References, p.429-49. Index. Author is former deputy head of the Soil Survey of England and Wales. *Class No: 631.4*

[5676]
BRIDGES, E.M. **World soils.** 3rd ed. Cambridge, University Press, 1997. vi, 170p. £19.95. ISBN: 0521497779.

First published 1970. 2nd edition, 1978.

14 chapters: 1. Introduction - 2. Composition of soils ... 5. Soil classification ... 11. Soil development in arid regions ... 14. Using soil information. References after each chapter. Index, p.166-70. Aimed at undergraduates in geology and environmental sciences. *Class No: 631.4*

[5677]
The Encyclopedia of soil science. Fairbridge, R.W. *and* Finkl, C.W., *Jr., eds.* Stroudsbourg, Pa., Dowden, Hutchinson & Ross, 1979. Part 1. xxi, 646p. illus., diagrs., graphs, tables, chemical structures. (*Encyclopedia of earth sciences, v.12.*) ISBN: 0897331763.
Part 1: *Physics, chemistry, biology, fertility and technology.* Entries: Acidity ... zero tillage. Documented articles (*e.g.* 'Humus': 1½ columns of references; 'Soil structure' (5½p.): 2 columns of references; 4 illus., 1 table). Cross-references to other volumes in the series. Subject (non-analytical) and author indexes.
Part 2, to cover soil morphology, genesis, classification and geography, is still in preparation. *Class No:* 631.4

[5678]
The Literature of soil science. McDonald, P., *ed.* Ithaca, N.Y., Cornell University Press, 1994. vi,448p. illus. $67.50 (*Literature of the agricultural sciences.*.) ISBN: 0801429218.
Looks in detail at the historical developments, characteristics, and present state of soil science literature. For all agricultural research libraries. *Class No:* 631.4

[5679]
LOZET, J. *and* MATHIEU, C. Dictionnaire de science du sol. 2nd ed. Paris, Technique et Documentation - Lavoisier, 1990. 384p. illus. (pl.), figs., tables.
Lists more than 2,800 terms from soil science, micromorphology, mineralogy, petrography and geology. English equivalents are given and appendices list the American, French, German, and FAO-UNESCO soil classification schemes. 52 plates and numerous tables and figures. French-English index. *Class No:* 631.4

[5680]
PLAISANCE, G. *and* CAILLEUX, A. Dictionary of soils, French-English. New Delhi, etc., Amerind Publishing Co., 1981. xii, 1109p. tables.
Translation of *Dictionnaire des sols* (Paris, La Maison Rustique), 1958.
Over 10,000 French terms, with etymology, definition, example of usage, etc. 'Humus' (p.521-7) includes use of the word in context, history and various types of humus, 'Granulométrie': 2½p., plus a chart. 3 appendices: 1. Symbols and measures; 2. British and American units; 3. Common abbreviations. *Class No:* 631.4

[5681]
Soils and fertilizers. Wallingford, Oxon., CAB International, 1938-. 12pa. £590; $1,065. ISSN: 00380792.
About 17,000 abstracts pa. Coverage includes: Soil chemistry; Soil physics; Soil biology; Soil fertility; Soil management; Soil classification; Soil formation; Soil conservation; Land reclamation; Irrigation and drainage; Fertilizer technology; Fertilizer use; Plant nutrition; Environmental aspects. Author and subject indexes per issue and annually. Online, CAB ABSTRACTS database, and CAB ABSTRACTS CD-ROM.
Rothamsted Experimental Station's *Soil maps* (scales, 1:25,000, 1:63,360 and 1:1,000,000) are based on the Ordnance Survey sets; the accompanying *Memoirs* ceased publication in 1977. The Soil Survey of Scotland's *Memoirs* are published by the Macaulay Land Use Research Institute. *Class No:* 631.4

[5682]
—Bibliography of soil science, fertilizers and general agronomy, 1931-62. Prepared by the Imperial Bureau of Soil Science (subsequently Commonwealth Bureau of Soils, Harpenden, Herts.). Farnham Royal, Bucks., Commonwealth Agricultural Bureaux, 1953-63. 10v.
Has a subject sequence in each volume. V.10 has 9 classes: 1. Soil pedology - 2. Cultivation; fertilizers; plant disesases and protection; land reclamation; agricultural systems - 3. Agricultural crops - 4. Orchards, fruit. Forestry, forests - 5. Vegetables - 6. Floriculture - 7. Physical geography. Meteorology. Geology - 8. Botany - 9. Miscellaneous. V.10 has *c.*13,000 entries, lists *c.*2,000 periodicals referred to, and author and subject indexes. Cross-references to abstracts in *Soils and fertilizers. Class No:* 631.4

Soil Surveys

[5683]
FOOD AND AGRICULTURE ORGANIZATION. Soil map of the world. Paris, UNESCO, with Rome, FAO, 1971-81. 10v. tables, maps.
Group 1. *General legend.* 1974. 69p. 1 sheet. 2. *North America.* 1976. xiv, 210p. 2 sheets. 3. *Mexico and Central America.* 1976, xiv, 96p. 1 sheet. 4. *South America.* 1971. xiv, 193p. 2 sheets. 5. *Europe.* 1981. 201p. 2 sheets. 6. *Africa.* 1977. xiv, 209p. 3 sheets. 7. *South Asia.* 1977. 117p. sheets 1 & 3. 8. *North and Central Asia.* 1978. 165p. 3 sheets. 9. *South-east Asia.* 1979. xiv, 149p. 1 sheet. 10. *Australasia.* 1978. xii, 221p. 2 sheets.
Sheet maps, 115 x 82cm, scale 1:5,000,000, have a 22-colour base, plotting 101 major soil groups. The accompanying texts include numerous tables and describe various soil characteristics and types. 'Valuable aid for economic development programs and agricultural

....(contd.)
planning' (Harris, C.D. ed. *Geographical bibliography for American libraries* (1985), item 620).
Also, *Soil map of the European Communities 1:1,000,000* (Luxembourg, Office for Official Publications of the EC, 1985. vii,124p. £60). *Class No:* 631.47

Plant Cultivation

[5684]
Plant growth regulator abstracts. Wallingford, Oxon., CAB International, 1975-. 6pa. £216; $485. ISSN: 03059154.
Over 2,500 abstracts pa. Sections include: Growth stimulators; Gibberellins; Growth retardants; Metabolic inhibitors and plant poisons. Reports. Conferences. Books. Author and subject indexes per issue and annually. Online, CAB ABSTRACTS and available on CAB ABSTRACTS CD-ROM. *Class No:* 631.5

Propagation

Seeds

[5685]
Encyclopedia of seed production of world crops. Kelly, A.F. *and* George, R.A.T., *eds.* Chichester, Wiley, 1998. x,404p. figs.,tables. £100. ISBN: 0471982024.
Covers production, usage, and storage of all the world's major crops. Clearly laid out; comprehensive index. 'A must for anybody connected with the seed industry, its science and agronomy' (*Aslib book guide*, November 1998, entry 1208). *Class No:* 631.531

[5686]
Seed abstracts. Wallingford, Oxon., CAB International, 1978-. 12pa. £225; $395. ISSN: 01410180.
About 4,200 abstracts pa. Sections include: Seed morphology and anatomy; Seed chemistry; Germination; Seed production; Pests and diseases; Breeding and selection; Seed assessment and testing; Miscellaneous. Reports; Conferences; Books. Author and subject indexes per issue and annually. Cross-reference to other abstract journals published by CAB International. Online, CAB ABSTRACTS and available on CAB ABSTRACTS CD-ROM. Also available on the Internet via HORT CABWeb (http://hort.cabweb.org).
Class No: 631.531

Tending & Care

Greenhouses

[5687]
The Complete book of the greenhouse: a complete guide to the construction and maintenance of greenhouses, to the modern aids available in running them and to the care and culture of greenhouse plants. Walls, Ian G., *and others.* 4th ed. London, Ward Lock, 1988. 304p. illus. (some col. pl.), figs., tables. £20. ISBN: 0706370171.
First published 1973.
Part 1: On the design and running of greenhouses (chapters 1-17). Part 2: On the growing of plants in greenhouses (chapters 18-31). Many clearly laid out tables. An appendix of useful addresses, p.295-98. No bibliography. Analytical index. *Class No:* 631.544

Agricultural Products

[5688]
Food focus. London, Food from Britain, 1989. 2v. tables. £9.99ea. ISBN: 0902373072, v.1; 0902373080, v.2; 0902373099, set.
V.1 *A Handbook of agricultural and horticultural produce from the United Kingdom.* xii,376p. V.2. *A Guide to sources of fresh, lightly processed and speciality foods in the United Kingdom.* v,266p.
In v.1, produce is arranged A-Z (Apples-Yogurt). Data include consumption, source of supply, tonnage, value, cultivation, history, freezing, varieties. Information sources, p.368-76. V.2 lists companies and has 9 sections: 1. Meat ... 4. Dairy ... 6. Fruit, vegetables and herbs - 7. Prepared foods ... 9. Beverages. Lists of regional organizations, marketing boards, and associations. Company, geographic, and product indexes. *Class No:* 631.57

[5689]
PILLSBURY, R. *and* FLORIN, J. Atlas of American agriculture: the American cornucopia. New York, Macmillan Library Reference USA/ Simon & Schuster/Prentice Hall International, 1996. 278p. illus.(col.), tables,maps. $100. ISBN: 002897333x.
Based on data from the 1992 Census of Agriculture, the work is divided into two main sections presenting data by agricultural region and by product. Contains a useful historical analysis and over 300 colour photographs, although these are uneven in quality. Bibliography, p.265-8; general index, p.269-73; geographical index, p.275-8. For academic libraries. *Class No:* 631.57

[5690]
UNITED NATIONS. Industrial Development Organization. **Information sources on bioconversion of agricultural wastes.** New York, United Nations, 1980. 84p. £4. ISBN: 0119060930.

689 numbered entries. 11 sections (1. Professional, trade and research organizations, learned societies and special information services. 2. Directories - 3. Sources of statistics, marketing and other economic data - 4. Basic handbooks, textbooks and manuals - 5. Monograph series - 6. Current periodicals - 7. Current abstracting and indexing periodicals - 8. Proceedings, papers and reports - 9. Specialized dictionaries and encyclopaedias - 10. Bibliographies - 11. Other potential sources of information (E. Meetings and conferences; F. Patents and licences; 1. Translation services)). Bibliographical sources used ..., p.82-84. *Class No:* 631.57

Irrigation

[5691]
CRC handbook of irrigation technology. Finkel, H.J., *ed.* Boca Raton, Florida, CRC Press, 1983. 2v. ([vii], 369p. + [vii], 223p.). diagrs., graphs, tables. $119.95, v.1; $95, v.2. ISBN: 0849332311, v.1; 0849332338, v.2.

V.1 has 12 documented sections on soil-water and plant-water relationships, and on types of irrigation, *e.g.* sprinkler, dip, pumps and pumping. V.2 has 13 documented sections on economics of irrigation and types of crops of irrigation, *e.g.* sugar, oil, cereal and citrus crops. Each volume carries a detailed, analytical index. *Class No:* 631.67

[5692]
Fachwörterbuch für Bewässerung und Entwässerung: Englisch, Deutsch, Französisch, Spanisch. [Multilingual technical dictionary on irrigation and drainage: English, French, German, Spanish.] 2., erw. Aufl. Bonn, Der Verband, 1983. 1009p. illus.

First published 1971.

Contains *c.*12,000 terms in one sequence. Over 300 line drawings. English, French, German, and Spanish indexes.

Supplementary volumes in French, Spanish, Arabic, Indian, Japanese, Persian and Portuguese. *Class No:* 631.67

[5693]
Irricab: current annotated bibliography of irrigation. Bet Dagan, Israel, International Irrigation Information Centre (IIIC) 1976-. 4pa. $95pa. ISSN: 03165083.

Cites *c.*4,000 publications pa. 9 subject sections (Irrigation water quality ... Irrigation policy, planning and development). Appended; Books and conferences. Miscellaneous. Author, subject and geographic indexes per issue and annually. *Class No:* 631.67

[5694]
—INTERNATIONAL COMMISSION ON DRAINAGE AND FLOOD CONTROL. Bibliography on irrigation, drainage, river training and flood control. New Delhi, ICID, 1956-. Annual. $10 per issue. ISSN: 0523302x.

Carries entries usually annotated, classified by UDC. Author index. *Class No:* 631.67

[5695]
Irrigation and drainage abstracts. Wallingford, Oxon., CAB International, 1975-. 4pa. £195; $350. ISSN: 03067327.

About 4,000 abstracts pa. 11 sections (Water-management - Irrigation - Irrigation of crop plants ... Plant-water relations - Salinity and toxicology problems ... Other topics (*e.g.* aquatic weeds). Reports. Conferences. Books. Author and subject indexes per issue and annually. Online CAB ABSTRACTS database and available on CAB ABSTRACTS CD-ROM. *Class No:* 631.67

Fertilizers

[5696]
Fertilizer dictionary: [English-French-Spanish-Arabic]. London, British Sulphur Corporation; Arab Federation of Chemical Fertilizer Producers, 1982. 132p.

Terms are arranged alphabetically within general topics, *e.g.* 'Raw materials'; 'Plant operation'; 'Fertilizer handling'. 9 appendices, *e.g.* 'Fertilizer minerals'; 'Nutrient factors'; 'Abbreviations'. *Class No:* 631.8

[5697]
Soils and fertilizers. Wallingford, Oxon., CAB International, 1938-. 12pa. £590; $1,065. ISSN: 00380792.

About 17,000 abstracts pa. Classes: 0. Documentation - 1. Soil science - 2. Fertilizers. Soil management ... 6. Other agricultural topics ... 8. Botany. Ecology - 9. Other topics. Author and subject indexes per issue and annually. Online CAB ABSTRACTS database and CD-ROM. *Class No:* 631.8

[5698]
World directory of fertilizer manufacturers. 10th edition. London, British Sulphur Publishing, 1999. Irregular. 104p. £260. ISBN: 1873387385.

Section 1. Manufacturers p.13-94 arranged by country (Afghanistan - Zimbabwe). Each entry gives contact details, personnel, manufacturing facility details etc. 2. Fertilizer associations, A-Z by country. Company index. *Class No:* 631.8

Pests & Diseases

Bibliographies

[5699]
Bibliography of plant viruses and index to research. Beale, H.P., *comp. and ed.* New York, Columbia Univ. Press, 1976. xiii, 1495p. $163.50. ISBN: 0231037635.

More than 29,000 references, under authors, A-Z, then chronologically. Periodical articles, p.1892-1970. Two extensive subject indexes (one, by virus genus and host; the other, by individual virus, - with over 2,700 entries for 'Tobacco mosaic virus' alone), p.1453-95. For specialists in plant virology. *Class No:* 632(01)

[5700]
Pest management: a directory of information sources. Volume 1: Crop protection. Hamilton, C.J., *ed.* Wallingford, Oxon., CAB International, 1991. 331p. £29.50. ISBN: 0851986757.

First volume in a projected 3: v.2 will cover animal husbandry, v.3, public health. Sections: Books - Primary literature - Secondary sources - Computerized information retrieval - Libraries and information centres (arranged by country, Angola ... Zimbabwe) - Suppliers - Regulatory bodies. Adequate reference to older, classic texts. Aimed at everyone involved in crop pest management. Good value. *Class No:* 632(01)

Handbooks & Manuals

[5701]
European handbook of plant diseases. Smith, I.M., *and others, eds.* Oxford, Blackwell Scientific Publications, 1988. 583p. £65. ISBN: 0632012226.

Emphasizes diseases affecting crops which are economically important though includes garden plants which are commercially grown. Omits wild plants. Arranged by pathogen which are presented alphabetically within each chapter. Chapters cover viruses, rickettsia, bacteria, oomycetes, ascomycetes, chytridiomycetes and basiomycetes. Each entry contains a description of the pathogenic organism, host plants and diseases, epidemiology, geographic distribution, economic impact, and methods of control. Two indexes: host and pathogen. *Class No:* 632(035)

[5702]
NYVALL, R.F. **Field crop diseases handbook.** 2nd ed. New York, Van Nostrand Reinhold, 1989. 912p. $104.95. ISBN: 0442267223.

Covers *c.*1,200 diseases of 25 field crops grown throughout the world. Looks at causes, distribution, symptoms and control of major crop diseases. *Class No:* 632(035)

[5703]
SCOPES, N. **Pest and disease control handbook.** Stables, L., *ed.* 3rd ed. Thornton Heath, British Crop Protection Council, 1989. xiii, 732p. ISBN: 0948404280.

First published 1979.

16 chapters, by various hands. Chapters 5-15 concern pests and diseases of different types of crop plants (*e.g.* chapter 10, - vegetables, p.261-321; 31 references). Chapter 16: 'Insect, mite and fungal pests of stored cereals and oilseed crops'. Detailed, analytical index. A mine of authoritative information. *Class No:* 632(035)

[5704]
Vegetable crop pests. McKinlay, R.G., *ed.* Basingstoke, Macmillan, 1992. xv,406p. illus. ISBN: 0333455991.

15 contributors. Covers main invertebrate pests which harm economically important vegetable crops in temperate regions. Nine sections: 1. Introduction ... 4. Pests of cruciferous crops ... 9. Pests of umbelliferous crops. Data for each pest gives geographical distribution, life cycle, description, plant damage and control. Includes biological control methods. Bibliography at the end of each section. *Class No:* 632(035)

Dictionaries

[5705]
COOMBS, J. *and* HALL, K.E. **Dictionary of biological control and integrated pest management.** 2nd ed. Newbury, CPL Press, 1998. 196p. £40. ISBN: 1872691765.

First published 1993.

Contains over 5,500 descriptions and definitions for Latin and

....(contd.)
commonnames of beneficial and pest organisms, diseases, fungi, insects, mites, pheromones, nematodes, microorganisms, bacteria, viruses, and biological pesticides. *Class No:* 632(038)

[5706]
Elsevier's dictionary of pests and diseases in useful plants in English, French, Spanish, Italian, German, Dutch and Latin. Eylenbosch, E., *ed.* Amsterdam, Elsevier, 1995. ix,487p. DFl375;$234.50. ISBN: 0444880666.
Lists diseases and causal agents affecting agricultural and horticultural plants. The first section, which contains common and scientific names in English, is followed by separate alphabetical indexes for the other languages. *Class No:* 632(038)

[5707]
HOLLIDAY, P. A Dictionary of plant pathology. 2nd ed. Cambridge, University Press, 1998. xxiv,536p. £85. ISBN: 0521594537.
First published 1989 and reprinted with corrections in 1990.
Contains over 11,000 entries (3,000 more than in the previous ed.). Lists authoritative names of pathogens (including fungi from over 500 genera, 800 viruses, mollicutes, bacteria, nematodes and viroids) with brief descriptions and bibliographic references. Entries also include references and notes on plant pathologists, names of diseases (now also included under the relevant crop), crops and their pathology, terminology, names of disorders, taxonomic groups, fungicide names, vectors of viruses and toxins. Of the previous ed., 'An excellent dictionary with a wealth of bibliographic information' (*Science and technology libraries,* v.10(4) Summer 1990, p.120). *Class No:* 632(038)

Reviews & Abstracts

[5708]
Biocontrol news and information: a quarterly journal of news items, review articles and abstracts from the CAB abstracts database, prepared by the Commonwealth Institute of Biological Control. Wallingford, Oxon., CAB International, 1980-. 4pa. £180; $315. ISSN: 01431404.
Contains *c.*2,800 abstracts pa, covering *c.*2,500 journal articles, in addition to reports, books, and conferences. Subject coverage includes crop pests; weeds; medical and veterinary pests; techniques; biology; taxonomy and catalogues; ecology. Mini-reviews of literature on topical subjects included in each issue which also contains author and subject indexes. Available online as part of the *CAB Abstracts (q.v.)* database, on the CD-ROM equivalents and, from 1991, on floppy disk. Also available on the Internet via PEST CABWeb at http://pest.cabweb.org. *Class No:* 632(048)

[5709]
Review of plant pathology. Wallingford, Oxon., CAB International, 1970-. 12pa. £380; $680. ISSN: 00346438.
Formerly *Review of applied mycology,* 1922-1969.
About 8,000 abstracts pa; preceded by review article. Covers journal articles, reports, conferences and books on subjects such as diseases of crop plants; non-parasitic diseases; mycorrhizas; and includes aspects of taxonomy; morphology; genetics; control; fungicides and antibiotics; physiology; molecular biology. Author and subject indexes per issue and annually. Online CAB ABSTRACTS and available on CAB ABSTRACTS CD-ROM. *Class No:* 632(048)

Thesauri

[5710]
Thesaurus of agricultural organisms: pests, weeds and diseases. Derwent Publications, *ed.* London, Chapman and Hall, 1990. 2v. £225. ISBN: 0412372908.
V.1. *A to M.* 802p. V.2. *N to Z; Index of inverted species names.* 728p.
Contains main entries for *c.*17,000 organisms, with 80,000 synonyms or common names. In addition to weeds, pests and disease microorganisms, there is also extensive coverage of crop species. Each main entry includes higher taxa, Latin synonyms and the most frequently used common names in English, French and German. *Class No:* 632:025.43

Weeds

[5711]
Diccionario español-inglés de malherbologia. [Spanish-English dictionary of weed science.] Zaragoza, C., *and others.* Valencia, Phytoma España, 1993. 80p. ISBN: 8460483452.
400 terms used in weed science are defined in Spanish; alternative terms in use in Argentina and Mexico are given. English equivalents are listed. *Class No:* 632.51

[5712]
Elsevier's dictionary of weeds of Western Europe, their common names and importance, in Latin, Danish, German, English, Spanish, Finnish, French, Icelandic, Italian, Dutch, Norwegian, Portuguese and Swedish. Williams, G., *comp.* Amsterdam, etc., Elsevier, 1982. [ix], 320p. £101.87. ISBN: 0444419780.
1,043 numbered entries in Latin, with equivalents and indexes in the other 12 languages. 25 contributors. *Class No:* 632.51

[5713]
Interdisciplinary dictionary of weed science. Williams, G.H. *and* Zweep, W. van der, *eds.* Wageningen, Centre for Agricultural Publishing and Documentation (PUDOC), 1990. 546p.
Contains *c.*3,000 technical and scientific forms in English, Danish, German, Spanish, French, Italian, Dutch and Portuguese. Prepared under the auspices of the European Weed Research Society. *Class No:* 632.51

[5714]
World weeds: natural histories and distribution. Holm, L., *ed.* New York etc., Wiley, 1997. xv, 1129p., illus. maps. £145. ISBN: 0471047015.
104 chapters, examining around 200 species of weeds affecting crops in more than 100 countries, with 90% accuracy aimed for in its (black-and-white) distribution maps. Each chapter consists of a black-and-white illustration, distribution map, then textual description, biology and habitat, agricultural importance, common names. Bibliography of 3,300 references. Index p.1115-29. *Class No:* 632.51

Poisonous Plants

[5715]
COOPER, M.R. Poisonous plants and fungi in Britain: animal and human poisoning. London, Stationery Office, 1998. xviii, 398p. illus. (incl. col.). £55. ISBN: 0112429815.
Revision of MAFF Bulletin 161, *British poisonous plants.* (last reprinted 1979) and previously published in 1984 as *Poisonous plants in Britain and their effects on animals and man.*
Over half of the book concerns the families of poisonous plants, ranging form Alliaceae to Umbelliferae, but is more concerned with their poisonous effects. Details involve, in each case, poisonous principles, poisoning in animals, human poisoning and treatment, etc. Complements Frohne and Plander's *A Colour atlas of poisonous plants* (1984) (*q.v.*), being well-documented but deficient in illus. For farmers, vets, and doctors. *Class No:* 632.52

[5716]
Poisonous plants in Britain and Ireland: an identification system on CD-ROM. London, HMSO, 1995. CD-ROM. £89.
Produced by the Royal Botanic Gardens, Kew and the National Poisons Unit. System of visual identification for several thousand species of toxic plants. Severity and type of toxicity is indicated and advice on emergency aid is given. *Class No:* 632.52

Insects (Pests)

[5717]
Crop pests in the UK collected edition of MAFF leaflets. Gratwick, M., *ed.* London, Chapman and Hall, 1992. xii, 490p., illus.(col.) ISBN: 0412562605, (UK); 0442316445, (US).
Cumulated volume of 91 advisory leaflets published by MAFF/ADAS. 9 sections: Aphids and other bugs (Hemiptera) ... Molluscs (Mollusca). 2 appendices: A. Leaflet titles listed alphabetically; B. Leaflet titles listed alphabetically under major host crops. Index of plants; index of plant diseases and pathogens. Numerous illustrations. *Class No:* 632.7

[5718]
Review of agricultural entomology. Wallingford, Oxon., CAB International, 1989-. 12pa. £545; $955. ISSN: 09576762.
Formerly *Review of applied entomology. Series A: Agriculture,* (1913-1989).
About 1,000 abstracts per issue. 14 sections (Taxonomy - Anatomy, morphology - Reproduction and development - Physiology and biochemistry - Genetics and sterility - Ecology and behaviour - Geographical distribution, faunas ... Disorders - Protection against arthropods and use of arthropods for biological control - Chemicals, including toxicity tests and environmental effects). Books, reports, conferences. Author and subject indexes per issue and annually. Online, CAB ABSTRACTS. *Class No:* 632.7

Pesticides

[5719]

Crop protection reference. 15th ed. New York, Chemical and Pharmaceutical Press, 1999. Annual. loose-leaf. $150. ISBN: 0471532827.

First published 1985 as *Crop protection chemicals reference.*

Contains information on crop protection substances in use in the US with full-text label information. Products can be found using brand or company names. Includes hazardous chemical inventory and list of US regulatory agencies and officials. Symbols are used to indicate products which have a restricted use. New for this ed. is an adjuvant reference. An updating service is provided on the Internet at http://greenbook.net. *Class No: 632.95*

[5720]

European directory of agrochemical products. (EDAP). Kidd, H. *and* James, D., *eds.* 4th ed. London, Royal Society of Chemistry, 1991. 4v. £285, set; £96ea. ISBN: 0851869335, v.1; 0851869432, v.2; 085186953x, v.3; 0851869637, v.4; 0851869734, set.

First published 1984.

1. *Fungicides.* 700p. 2. *Herbicides.* 700p. 3. *Insecticides and acaricides.* 700p. 4. *Plant growth regulators, etc.* 400p.

EDAP lists over 26,000 products from 25 European countries. Data include registered users, toxicity, limitations to use, active ingredient proportions, preharvest intervals. Appended directory of European companies that market pesticides, a products index, and an active ingredients index. Online via DATA-STAR and DIALOG. *Class No: 632.95*

[5721]

FIALA, I. *and* **FEVRE, F. Dictionnaire des agents pathogenes des plantes cultivées.** [Dictionary of crop plant pathogens.] Paris, INRA, 1992. 136p. ISBN: 2738003354.

Lists 300 viruses, 300 fungi, and 84 bacteria in Latin, French, and English. *Class No: 632.95*

[5722]

HILL, D.S. Agricultural insect pests of temperate regions and their control. Cambridge Univ. Press, 1987. [viii], 659p. illus., tables, maps. £75. ISBN: 0521240131.

10 chapters: 2. Pest ecology - 3. Principles of pest control - 4. Methods of pest control - 5. Pest damage to crop plants - 6. Biological control of crop pests - 7. Pesticide applications - 8. Pesticides in current use - 9. Major temperate crop pests - 10. Major temperate crops and their test spectra. General bibliography, p.597-610. 4 appendices (B. Glossary of terms used in applied entomology and crop protection.). Detailed, analytical index, p.625-59.

Agricultural insect pests of the tropics and their control, by D.S. Hill (2nd ed. CUP, 1983. £55) is the companion volume. *Class No: 632.95*

[5723]

The Pesticide manual: a world compendium. Tomlin, C., *ed.* 11th ed. Bracknell, Berks., BCPC Publications, 1997. 1,606p. tables, chemical structures. £110. ISBN: 1901396118.

First published 1968. Now incorporating *The Agrochemicals handbook.*

Details 759 chemical compounds or microbial agents used as active ingredients of pesticides. Part 1: Compounds in use: main entries (pesticides, A-Z; data include: nomenclature; development; properties; formulations; uses; toxicology; analysis; manufacturing companies). Part 2: Superseded compounds (1,342 listed). 6 appendices, including: Abbreviations and codes; Glossary of species; Directory of companies; Bibliography. 6 indexes: *Chemical abstracts* Service Registry Numbers; Molecular formulae; Code numbers; General names; Chemical names; Classes. Now available on CD-ROM as *The Electronic pesticide manual* (£250 + VAT). *Class No: 632.95*

[5724]

UNITED NATIONS. Industrial Development Organization. **Information sources on the pesticides industry.** Rev. ed. New York, United Nations, 1982. 90p. £4. (*UNIDO guides to information sources, no.10.*)

First published 1974.

Contains *c.*700 entries. 12 sections (1. Professional, trade and research organizations, learned societies and special information services ... 7. Current abstracting and indexing periodicals ... 9. Specialized dictionaries and encyclopaedias ... 11. Films - 12. Other potential sources of information (A. Counselling and engineering services; G. Safety and health measures; H. Standards and specifications). 'Bibliographical sources used ...' Entries in some sections are annotated. *Class No: 632.95*

[5725]

World directory of pesticide control organisations. Ekstrom, G., *ed.* 3rd ed. London, Royal Society of Chemistry, 1996. 520p. £49.50. ISBN: 085404437x.

Revised edition of *Control of pesticide applications and residues in food,* by B. Hofsten and G. Ekstroöm (Swedish Science Press, 1986). First ed. of this title published 1989. Counting its Swedish antecedent, this is actually the 7th ed. and the 3rd published by the Royal Society of Chemistry.

Includes data from 180 countries. Contents: Intergovernmental forum on chemical safety; International activities on persistent organic pollutants; Bilateral pesticide-related training facilities; The GIFAP safe-use project; Appropriate technology for pesticide analysis in developing countries; International organisations and programmes; Directory of national pesticide control organisations; Information sources on nationally approved/registered and other pesticides. Data for each country include: main authority responsible for registration and use of pesticides; main authority responsible for establishing maximum pesticide residue limits; Codex contact point; national association of pesticide manufacturers. An index to the organizations would make this publication more useful. *Class No: 632.95*

Weedkillers

[5726]

Weed control handbook. Hance, R.J. *and* Holly, K.K. 8th ed. Oxford, etc., Blackwell Scientific Publications, 1978-90. 2v. illus., tables.

1. *Principles.* 8th ed., 1990. viii,582p. £59.50 2. *Recommendations, including plant growth regulators.* 8th ed., 1978. [xv], 332p.

V.2 has 14 chapters (*e.g.* 1. The control of annual weeds in cereal crops; 3. The control of weeds in perennial crops, flowers and greenhouses; 10. The control of aquatic weeds). 5 appendices. (1. Glossary of technical terms; 4. The definition of soil types). Extensive, detailed and analytical index, p.444-532. *Class No: 632.954*

Field Crops

Bibliographies

[5727]

The Literature of crop science. Olsen, W.C., *ed.* Ithaca, N.Y., Cornell University Press, 1996. x,511p. illus.,tables. $79.95. (*Literature of the agricultural sciences.*) ISBN: 0801431387.

11 chapters covering crop improvement, plant pathology, and plant protection. Chapters 8 and 9 list 1,663 monographs and 79 journals, while chapter 10 details important reference sources. Chapter 11 consists of more than 100 pages on the primary US historical lierature from 1850 to 1949. Index, p.501-11. The sixth volume in the series *Literature of the agricultural sciences.* For all agricultural research libraries. *Class No: 633(01)*

Handbooks & Manuals

[5728]

FACCIOLA, S. Cornucopia: a source book of edible plants. Vista, Calif., Kampong Publications, 1990. 677p. $37.75. ISBN: 0962808709.

Identifies 3,000 food plants. 3 sections: Section 1 lists species by plant family, gives the plant product, its uses, distribution, bibliographic citations and source; Section 2 lists cultivars and includes data on days to maturity, important features, bibliographic citations and source; Section 3 includes the names and addresses of 1,350 firms who can supply these plants. Bibliography and indexes to vernacular names, usage, species, families and genera. US-slanted.

Also available on diskette (1994. $70). *Class No: 633(035)*

[5729]

LANGER, R.H.M. *and* **HILL, G.D. Agricultural plants.** 2nd ed. Cambridge, University Press, 1991. xiii,387p. diagrs., tables. £45; £17.95. ISBN: 0521224500.

First published 1982.

17 documented chapters (1. World population and crop production - 2. Plant structure - 3. Liliaceae (with 5 references) ... 15. Papaveraceae ... 17. Physiological basis of yield). Numerous line-drawings. Index. 'Aims to provide a description of important crop and pasture plants, illustrated wherever possible as a basis for a foundation course in agricultural botany or plant science' (*Preface* to 1st ed.). *Class No: 633(035)*

[5730]

ROUGEMONT, G.M. de. A Field guide to the crops of Britain and Europe. London, Collins, 1989. 367p. illus., figs., tables, maps. £14.95. ISBN: 0002197138.

Arranged by family and covering the economic plants of Britain and Europe. Data include a brief introduction to each family; description; names, including Latin synonyms and the vernacular names in some European languages; uses; origin, distribution and cultivation; similar plants. Husbandry is not included except where it is an aid to identification. 42 colour plates and many small maps showing plant

....*(contd.)*

distribution. Glossary, meanings of some Latin specific epithets common in cultivated plants and indexes of English and scientific names. *Class No:* 633(035)

Dictionaries

[5731]

Glossary of crop science terms. Barnes, R.F. *and* Beard, J.B., *eds*. Madison, Wis., Crop Science Society of America, 1992. 88p. ISBN: 0891185356.

3 sections, covering general terminology, cell biology and molecular genetics, and crop terminology (divided into a list of field crops by common name, scientific name, and an explanation of the use of scientific names). Brief bibliography. For all libraries supporting agricultural courses. *Class No:* 633(038)

[5732]

REHM, S. Multilingual dictionary of agronomic plants. Dordrecht, Kluwer, 1994. ix,286p. Dfl200; £80. ISBN: 0792329708.

2,454 entries listed alphabetically by Latin name with equivalents in English, French, German, Portuguese, and Spanish. Includes weeds but excludes purely ornamental plants. Index to common plant names. Based on the databank of the Institute of Tropical Agronomy and Animal Health at the University of Göttingen. *Class No:* 633(038)

Reviews & Abstracts

[5733]

Crop physiology abstracts. Wallingford, Oxon., CAB International, 1975-. 6pa. £380; $845. ISSN: 03067556.

About 5,000 abstracts pa. Coverage includes: Seed germination; Growth; Reproductive development; Metabolism; Water relations; Photosynthesis; Respiration; Nutrition; Postharvest physiology. Author and subject indexes per issue and annually. Online CAB ABSTRACTS database and available on CAB ABSTRACTS CD-ROM. *Class No:* 633(048)

[5734]

Field crop abstracts. Wallingford, Oxon., CAB International, 1948-. 12pa. £592; $1,330. ISSN: 0015069x.

9,500 abstracts pa. Sections: Cereals - Legumes - Root crops - Fibre plants - Oil plants - Miscellaneous crops - Green manures - Field crops, general - Crop botany - Weeds - Pests and diseases - Surveys and land use - Farming systems - Soil and water conservation - Agricultural meteorology - Miscellaneous. Appended: Reports. Conferences. Books. Author and subject indexes per issue and annually. Online CAB ABSTRACTS database and CD-ROM. *Class No:* 633(048)

[5735]

Plant breeding abstracts. Wallingford, Oxon., CAB International, 1930-. 12pa. £684; $1,495. ISSN: 00320803.

About 1,000 abstracts per issue. Coverage includes: Breeding; Genetic resources; Varietal trials and new varieties; Cytology and ploidy; Reproductive behaviour; Evolution and taxonomy; Stress tolerance; Quality and yield components. Occasional review articles. Author, subject and significant varieties indexes per issue and annually. Online, CAB ABSTRACTS database, and also available on CAB ABSTRACTS CD-ROM. *Class No:* 633(048)

Tropics

[5736]

LÖTSCHERT, W. *and* **BEESE, G. Collins' guide to tropical plants:** a descriptive guide to 323 ornamental and economic plants, with 274 colour photographs. London, Collins, 1983. 256p. illus. (incl. col.), tables, maps. ISBN: 0002191121.

German original, *Pflanzen der Tropen* (BLV Verlagsgesellchaft, 1981).

Introduction - Ornamental plants - Economic plants - Colour plates (p.81-176). 'Some recommended botanic gardens and parks in the tropics', p.247. Glossary. Index of scientific names; index of English common names. 325 plants described; 274 col. illus. (*e.g.* 'Oil palm': 1p., 2 col. illus.). Deals mainly with decorative and economic plants common in all regions of the tropics. *Class No:* 633(213)

Cereals & Grain

[5737]

Advances in cereal science and technology. St. Paul, Minn., American Association of Cereal Chemists, Inc., 1980-. Annual. ISBN: 091325066x.

V.10, 1990 (xiii, 557p. 89) has eight documented sections including 'Structural studies of cereal prolamins, including wheat gluten', 'Phytic acid cereal technology', and 'Wheat hardness: its genetic, structure and significance. Detailed, analytical index. *Class No:* 633.1

Maize

[5738]

Maize abstracts. Wallingford, Oxon., CAB International, in association with International Maize and Wheat Improvement Center, 1985-. 6pa. £316; $720. ISSN: 02672987.

c.3,200 abstracts pa. Coverage includes: Plant breeding and genetics; Plant physiology; Soil science; Pests and diseases; Crop science, Seeds and grains; Nutrition and quality. Author and subject indexes per issue and annually. Online, CAB ABSTRACTS database, and available on CAB ABSTRACTS CD-ROM. *Class No:* 633.15

Rice

[5739]

Rice abstracts. Wallingford, Oxon., CAB International, in association with the International Rice Research Institute, 1978-. 4pa. £200; $440.

c.3,000 abstracts pa. Coverage includes: Breeding, genetics and genetic resources; Crop husbandry and farming systems; Ecology of rice fields; Crop protection and the biology of important pests and diseases; Physiology, biochemistry and the effects of environmental factors; Harvesting and storage;... Economics of production, storage, processing, consumption and marketing; Rural development. Appended: Reports. Conferences. Books. Author and subject indexes per issue. Online, CAB ABSTRACTS database, and available on CAB ABSTRACTS CD-ROM. *Class No:* 633.18

[5740]

Rice almanac. Second ed. Los Banos, Philippines, International Rice Research Institute, 1997. 181p. figs., tables. maps. ISBN: 9712200922.

First ed. published 1993.

Brings together general information on rice, including production and geographical data. Six chapters: 1.Introduction ... 4. Rice environments - 5. Rice around the world - 6. International research. Additional sections include rice-related databases and rice facts. A collaborative effort amongst IRRI, Centro Internacional de Agricultura Tropical and the West Africa Rice Development Association. Available on the Internet at: http://www.riceweb.org where the *Almanac* will be regularly updated. The Internet site also includes links to many information sources and databases. *Class No:* 633.18

Forage Grasses

[5741]

Grasslands and forage abstracts. Wallingford, Oxon., CAB International, 1994-. 12pa. £352; $780. ISSN: 00180602.

Formerly *Herbage abstracts*, 1931-1993.

About 4,000 abstracts pa. Coverage includes: Land use and farming systems including sustainability; Forage conservation; Toxic plants; Plant physiology and forage composition; Descriptions of species and cultivars. Reports. Conferences. Books. Author and subject indexes per issue and annually.

Online, CAB ABSTRACTS database, and available on CAB ABSTRACTS CD-ROM. *Class No:* 633.2

[5742]

Manual of grasses. Darke, R., *ed.* London, Macmillan, 1994. xlvi,169p. figs. £35. ISBN: 0333615352.

Introduction followed by descriptions of the genera which are in alphabetical order. Each genus has a general description and cultural information, with descriptions of species suitable for ornamental use. Contains a list of names no longer in use and an index of popular names. Based on *The New Royal Horticultural Society dictionary of gardening (q.v.)* but with some additional information. *Class No:* 633.2

Legumes

Soyabeans

[5743]

Soyabean abstracts. Wallingford, Oxon., CAB International, 1978-. 4pa. £176; $385. ISSN: 01410172.

About 2,000 abstracts pa. Coverage includes: Agronomy; Growth and physiology; Nitrogen fixation; Effects of climate and environment; Pests and their control; Harvesting and storage; Genetics; Breeding and cultivars; Processing technology; Uses in human and animal nutrition; Effects on health; Non-food uses; Production economics and marketing of soyabeans and soyabean products. Author and subject indexes per issue and annually.

Online, CAB ABSTRACTS database, and available on CAB ABSTRACTS CD-ROM. *Class No:* 633.34

Root Crops

Potatoes

[5744]

Potato abstracts. Wallingford, Oxon., CAB International, 1976-. 4pa. £180; $395. ISSN: 03087344.

About 1,800 abstracts pa. Coverage includes: Breeding, genetics and genetic resources; Crop husbandry and farming systems; Crop protection and the biology of important pests and diseases; Physiology, biochemistry and the effects of environmental factors ... Economics of production, storage, processing, consumption and marketing. Author and subject indexes per issue and annually.

Online CAB ABSTRACTS database and CD-ROM.

Class No: 633.491

[5745]

Potato terms: trilingual dictionary of the potato. Loon, C.D. van *and* Heij, D.G. van der, *eds.* Wageningen, Pudoc, Centre for Agricultural Publishing and Documentation, 1989. xv,402p. ISBN: 9022009629.

Rev. ed. of *Dictionary of technical terms relating to the potato* (1969).

Contains *c.*3,500 terms in the official languages of the European Association for Potato Research - English, German, and French. Latin index, p.398-402. Clearly arranged and presented. *Class No:* 633.491

Textile Plants

Cotton

[5746]

Cotton and tropical fibres: annotated bibliography. Wallingford, Oxon., CAB International. Annual. £27.50; $51.

Over 1,000 abstracts pa. Coverage includes: Tropical fibres; Cotton; Sisal; Jute; Kenaf; and roselle; Other fibres.

Online, CAB ABSTRACTS database, and CD-ROM.

Class No: 633.51

Sugar

[5747]

WITTE, G. 'Glossary of technical terms for the sugar industry'. In *Zuckerindustrie,* v.16(5), 1991. p.433-43.

About 250 German terms, in current use, are listed in 7 groups (general; beet; juice; sugar; by products; auxiliaries; effluents). Alphabetical list, with definitions, follows. Final section lists 79 non-preferred terms, with corresponding preferred terms. *Class No:* 633.6

Oil-Yielding Plants

[5748]

Tropical oil seeds: annotated bibliography. Wallingford, Oxon., CAB International. Annual. £26.50; $49. ISSN: 03082962.

About 1,000 abstracts pa. Coverage includes: Tropical oil seeds; Groundnuts; Safflowers; Coconuts; Oil palms; Castor; Sesame; Other oilseed crops and byproducts; Seed oils. Online, CAB ABSTRACTS database, and CD-ROM. *Class No:* 633.85

Horticulture

Handbooks & Manuals

[5749]

The Horticulturalist's handbook. London, Duncan Publishing, 1982-. 2 binders. Loose-leaf.

7 sections: 1. Management and finance - 2. Labour - 3. The land in relation to horticulture - 4. Buildings and equipment - 5. Marketing - 6. Crop production - 7. Research, development and advice. Index. Periodic instalments. *Class No:* 634(035)

[5750]

ROYAL HORTICULTURAL SOCIETY. The Royal Horticultural Society colour chart. London, the Society, [1966]. 28p.

Replaces the 1938-42 *Horticultural colour chart.* The primary aim is to provide a standard reference source for the colour specification of flowers, fruit and leaves, for matching purposes (especially in the case of flowers). 808 colour patches. *Class No:* 634(035)

Dictionaries

[5751]

BOURKE, D. O'D. French-English horticultural dictionary with English-French index. 2nd ed. Wallingford, CAB International, 1989. viii,240p. £28. ISBN: 085198626x.

First published 1974.

Contains *c.*19,000 terms from a wide range of horticultural literature. This ed. takes into account new developments in horticulture and includes terms from areas such as pollution, marketing, tissue culture, and greenhouse construction. *Class No:* 634(038)

[5752]

Elsevier's dictionary of horticulture in English, French, Dutch, German, Danish, Swedish, Spanish, Italian, Latin. Compiled under the auspices of the Ministry of Agriculture and Fisheries at The Hague, Netherlands. Amsterdam, etc., Elsevier, 1970-. xvi, 561p. $161.75. ISBN: 0444408126.

First published as *Woordenlijst voor der tuinbouw in seven talen ...,* by the Dutch Ministry of Agriculture, Horticultural Division, 1955.

4,240 English-base terms, with equivalents and indexes in the other 5 languages, for general horticultural vocabulary. *Library journal,* (v.95(15), 1 September 1970, p.2787) notes arbitrary selection of entries and inadequate cross-references, while querying reliability of translations into languages other than Dutch and German.

Also, *Elsevier's dictionary of horticultural and agricultural plant production* (1990. 818p. $205.25), which covers the same languages as those in *Elsevier's dictionary of horticulture* with the addition of Portuguese. *Class No:* 634(038)

[5753]

SOULE, J. Glossary for horticultural crops. Sponsored by the American Society for Horticultural Science. New York, etc., Wiley, 1985. xxvi, [1], 898p. $58.50. ISBN: 0471884995.

About 8,000 terms are defined. 6 broad categories (subdivided): 1. Horticultural crops - 2. Morphology and anatomy - 3. Horticultural taxonomy and plant breeding - 4. Horticultural physiology and crop ecology - 5. Propagation and nursery handling - 6. Post-harvest handling and marketing. Selected references, p.679-92 (authors, A-Z). Index of terms; index of crops. Over 300 line-drawings. Well constructed, but typography makes for reading difficulties.

Class No: 634(038)

[5754]

STEINMETZ, H., *ed.* **Gartenbautechnik.** Mehrsprechenbild-wörterbuch. [Horticultural techniques and implements: multilingual illustrated dictionary ...] Betzdorf/Sieg, Steinmetz Verlag, 1978. 568p. illus.

4,300 German-base terms, with English, French, Spanish, Italian and Dutch equivalents, and indexes in 6 languages. Sectionalized, covering glasshouses, machinery, tools and techniques. 1,330 line-drawings. *Class No:* 634(038)

Reviews & Abstracts

[5755]

Horticultural abstracts. Wallingford, Oxon., CAB International, 1931-. 12pa. £575; $1,040. ISSN: 00185280.

About 12,500 abstracts pa. 8 main sections: General aspects of research and its application - Temperate tree fruits and nuts - Small fruits - Viticulture - Vegetables; temperate, tropical and greenhouse - Ornamental plants - Minor industrial crops - Subtropical and tropical fruit and plantation crops. Author and subject indexes per issue and annually. Online, CAB ABSTRACTS database, and CD-ROM.

Class No: 634(048)

[5756]

Ornamental horticulture. Wallingford, Oxon., CAB International, 1975-. 6pa. £160; $285.

About 2,400 abstracts pa. Coverage includes: Orchids; Conifers; Roses; Trees and shrubs; Bulbs and tubers; Lawns and sports turf; Aquatic plants; Foliage and succulent plants. Reports; Conferences; Books. Author and subject indexes per issue and annually. Online, CAB ABSTRACTS database, and CAB ABSTRACTS CD-ROM.

Class No: 634(048)

Yearbooks & Directories

[5757]

The RHS plant finder. Philip, C., *comp.* 10th ed. Ashbourne, Moorland Publishing Co., Ltd., 1996. xxx,910p. maps. £12.99. ISBN: 095121618x.

First published 1987.

Lists more than 65,000 plants available from over 650 nurseries. Plant directory, p.27-712. Code, nursery index; Nursery code index. Additional nursery index; Seed suppliers; Cacti and succulent suppliers; Orchid suppliers. Reverse synonyms. Plant deletions. HPS search list. NCCPG collections. Bibliography, p.895-910. Display advertisements. Now also available as part of *The Plant finder reference library* CD-ROM 1998/9. *Class No:* 634(058)

America—North

[5758]

Hortus third: a concise dictionary of plants cultivated in the United States and Canada. Compiled by the staff of the Library Hyde Bailey Hortorium. New York, Macmillan Co., 1974. $150. ISBN: 0025054708.

Originally planned as a revision of *Hortus second,* compiled by L.H. and E.Z. Bailey (1941).

Entries for almost 300 families, 3,000 genera and 20,000 species

....(contd.)

under botanical names, stating sources of names and noting cultivation and use. Most family descriptions have drawings. General articles on important crops. Glossary of botanical names. Index of 10,408 common plant names, and list of botanists cited.
Class No: 634(71+73)

[5759]

North American horticulture: a reference guide. Barrett, T.M., *ed.* First published 1992. New York, Macmillan, 1992. xvii, 427p. illus. ISBN: 0028970012.

A directory of organizations, government programs, nomenclature authorities, garden and reference information, in chapter form. Within most chapters arrangement is under states, A-Z (less full on Canada). Indexed by subject, organization and botanical name. Of the previous ed., 'The most complete directory of North American horticultural organizations and programs currently available in one volume' (*RQ*, v.22(3), Spring 1983, p.309). *Class No:* 634(71+73)

USA

[5760]

EVERETT, T.H. The New York Botanical Garden illustrated encyclopedia of horticulture. New York & London, Garland, 1980-82. 10v. (*c.*4,000p.). illus. (incl. col.). $1,070. ISBN: 0824072227.

Detailed descriptions of more than 3,600 genera and over 26,000 species. Entry is under botanical name, with cross-references from common name. Longer articles concern such matters as fertilisers, propagation, pests and diseases. Well illustrated, mostly in black-and-white photographs. The standard US work. For English gardens, prefer *Marshall Cavendish Illustrated encyclopedia of gardening* (*q.v.*). *Class No:* 634(73)

Australia

[5761]

WRIGLEY, J.W. Australian native plants: a manual for their propagation, cultivation and use in landscaping. Sydney, Angus and Robertson (Australia), 1990. 623p. illus. (some col.). £46.95; $90. ISBN: 0002164167.

First published 1983.

16 chapters (3. Propagation; 7. Pests and diseases; 8. Ground cover; 10. Water features; 11. Shrubs; 12. Trees; 13. Climbers; 14. Container plants (with glasshouse plants); 15. Annual and bedding plants; 16. Plants for special purposes (*e.g.* windbreaks)). Glossary. Brief bibliography. Index. *Class No:* 634(94)

Institutions & Associations

[5762]

Horticultural research international: directory of horticultural research institutes and their activities in 74 countries. Borg, H.H. van der *and* Koning van der Veen, M., *eds.* 5th ed. Wageningen, International Society for Horticultural Science, 1993. 1000p. maps. ISBN: 9066051957.

First published 1966.

Entries for 1,800 research institutes, with 20,000 names of individual research workers. Arranged by country (Argentina ... Zimbabwe), p.1-804. Details mention senior staff by name and outline specializations, projects and programmes. Indexes for international organisations, names of places, names of research workers. Unlike the previous edition, this one includes Eastern European countries and has more input from Asia (13 countries). *Class No:* 634:061:061.2

Fruit & Vegetables

[5763]

Food from your garden: all you need to know to grow, cook and preserve your own fruit and vegetables. London, etc., Reader's Digest, 1977 (reprinted with amendment, 1987). [v], 380p. illus. £19.95. ISBN: 0274001702.

20 contributors and advisers. Sections: A basic guide to the kitchen - Growing and cooking - Pests and diseases - Home preserving - Food from the countryside - Making your own wine - Keeping poultry and bees. Index, p.375-80. Landscape format. A well-illustrated step-by-step guide. *Class No:* 634.1/635.1

[5764]

—Encyclopedia of vegetable gardening: the complete growing and freezing guide to vegetables, herbs & fruit. Biggs, A.G., *and others.* London, Octopus Books, Ltd., 1977. 255p. illus. (incl. col.) tables.

Has 3 main sections: Growing your own vegetables, by A.G. Biggs - Fruit in your garden, by A.G. Healey. - In the kitchen: freezing, preserving and cooking [50 recipes], by S. Allworthy and C. Ellwood. Introduction includes notes on tools and equipment. General index, p.248-52; Index to cooking. 375 col. illus., tending to swamp the text. Quarto. *Class No:* 634.1/635.1

[5765]

JOHNS, L. *and* **STEVENSON, V. The Complete book of fruit.** London, etc., Angus & Robertson, 1979. [vi], 309p. illus. (incl. col.), chart. ISBN: 0207143374.

4 sections: 1. Cultivation and harvest home (including world climate chart) - 2. The good cook's compendium - 3. The fruits of the earth (p.46-280: Akebia ... Wineberry) - 4. Less common fruit (*e.g.* capote). Glossary, p.293-6. Bibliography, p.297-301 (general; official bulletins and leaflets). Detailed index, p.303-9. International in scope. *Class No:* 634.1/635.1

[5766]

Mehrsprächiges Verzeichnis der Gemüsenamen. [Multilingual list of vegetable names.] Sahrmuller, R., *and others.* Grossberren, Institut für Gemüseproduktion Grossberren der Akademie der Landwirtschaftswissenschaften der DDR, 1990. 205p.

Lists more than 13,000 vegetable names in more than 60 languages, alongwith their scientific names in Latin. Includes plants used as vegetables throughout the world as well as those which are consumed locally, and plants which are considered worth cultivating. *Class No:* 634.1/635.1

[5767]

RUBATZKY, V.E. *and* **YAMAGUCHI, M. World vegetables: principles, production, and nutritive values.** 2nd ed. New York, Chapman & Hall, 1997. 843p., illus. £62.75. ISBN: 0412112213.

First published 1983.

Three parts (28 chapters): I. Introduction (chapters, 1-5) - II. Vegetable-growing principles (chapters, 6-7) - III. World vegetables - A. Roots, tubers and fruits (chapters, 8-16) (*e.g.* sweetcorn, p.235-53, including two pages of references) - B. Succulent roots, bulbs, leaves and fruit (chapters, 17-28)). Four appendices, *e.g.* C. Approximate nutrient composition of various vegetables. Glossary, p.823-30. Index p.831-43. *Class No:* 634.1/635.1

[5768]

SAMPSON, J.A. Tropical fruits. 2nd ed. Harlow, Essex, Longman, 1986. ix, [i], 336p. illus., diagrs., graphs, tables. £37.50. (*Tropical agriculture series.*) ISBN: 0582404096.

First published 1980.

11 chapters (3. Botany of tropical fruits - 4. Crop husbandry - 5. Citrus (p.78-138; 4½p. of references) - 6. Bananas and plantains - 7. Pineapple - 8. Mango - 9. Avocado - 10. Papaya - 11. The minor tropical fruits). Systematic treatment of chapters 5-9. Stressing cultivation. 3 appendices (1. List of families and genera of fruit crops; 2. Common names of fruit crops and their botanical equivalents). Crop index. Geographical index. General index (1p.). *Class No:* 634.1/635.1

[5769]

SIMMONS, A.F. Simmons' manual of fruit: tree, bush, cane and other varieties. Newton Abbot, Devon, David & Charles. 1978. 237p. ISBN: 0715376071.

Tree fruits (apples ... quinces), p.11-461 - Bush fruits (blueberries ... Worcesterberry) - cane fruits (brambleberries ... wineberry) - Vine gruits (grape) - Small plant fruits (*e.g.* cranberry) and miscellaneous (*e.g.* garden huckleberry). Data: period; shape; flower... health; cropping; historical notes). No index or references. *Class No:* 634.1/635.1

[5770]

SPLITTSTOESSER, W.E. Vegetable growing handbook: organic and traditional methods. 3rd ed. New York, Van Nostrand Reinhold, 1990. xii, illus., figs., tables. $46.95. ISBN: 0442239718.

9 documented chapters: 1. Planning the garden - 2. Plant growth - 3. Soil and plant nutrition - 4. Pest control - 5. Harvest and storage of vegetables - 6. Nutritional value of vegetables - 7. Growing common vegetables - 8. Growing special-use vegetables - 9. Growing and preserving herbs. Chapters 7-9 give detailed information on growing over 90 different vegetables, as well as many herbs. Detailed, analytical index, p.347-62. *Class No:* 634.1/635.1

Apples

[5771]

MORGAN, J. *and* **RICHARDS, A. The Book of apples.** London, Ebury/Brogdale Horticultural Trust, 1994. 304p. illus. £22.50; $29.95. ISBN: 0091777593.

2 main sections, with the first dealing with history, origins, uses, and economic, social, and scientific aspects of apples. The second section contains brief summaries of more than 2,000 cultivars in the Brogdale Horticultural Trust/Ministry of Agriculture collection in the UK. Colour plates and many black-and-white illustrations. Appendices contain recipes and a list of collections, organizations, and nurseries. Some information about US and French apple production but this is chiefly a book about UK apples. *Class No:* 634.11

Vines & Vineyards

[5772]

STEINMETZ, H. **Viticultural technique:** multilingual illustrated dictionary: D-E-F-S-I. Betzdorf, Verlag H. Steinmetz; New York, French & European, 1983. 314p. illus. $75. ISBN: 0828800715.

About 3,950 German-base terms, with English, French, Spanish and Italian equivalents and indexes. 600 line-drawings. *Class No:* 634.8

[5773]

VITIS: **Viticulture and enology abstracts.** International Food Information Service (IFISO). Geilweiherhof, Bundesforschungsanstalt für Rebenzüchtung, 1984-. 4pa. DM70. ISSN: 01758292.

About 180 abstracts per issue on grapes and grapevine science and technology. Classes A-M: A. General aspects - B. Morphology - C. Physiology - D. Biochemistry - E. Viticulture - F. Soils - G. Breeding - H. Plant pathology - J. Technology, engineering - K. Economics - L. Enology - M. Microbiology of wine. Annual author and subject indexes. Available online via DIMDI, ESA, DIALOG, ORBIT. *Class No:* 634.8

Gardening

Bibliographies

[5774]

ISAACSON, R.T. **Gardening: a guide to the literature.** New York, Garland Pubg. Co., 1985. xiii, 198p. ISBN: 0824090195.

784 annotated entries, in 7 sections (further subdivided): Reference - Landscape design - Ornamental garden plants - Methods of growing and using plants - Garden practices and plant problems - Miscellaneous gardening topics - Periodicals and catalogs ... List of libraries with extensive gardening collections. Name, title and subject indexes. 'Specially useful both to the serious gardener and to the librarian who wants to build a collection to support this subject' (*Reference books bulletin, 1985-86,* p.67). US-slanted. *Class No:* 635(01)

Encyclopaedias

[5775]

Encyclopaedia of alpines. Beckett, K., *ed.* Pershore, Worcs., AGS Publications, 1993-94. 1411p. ISBN: 0900048638.

2v (A-K), (L-Z).

Covers 1,000 genera. Data include family name; size of genus; subspecies; varieties; cultivar names, etc. Five-page glossary. 543 colour photographs and many line drawings. Arranged alphabetically, although the absence of an English language index is disappointing in an otherwise authoritative and attractive work of reference. *Class No:* 635(031)

[5776]

HERITAU, J. *and* CATHEY, H.M. **The National Arboretum book of outstanding garden plants:** the authoritative guide to selecting and growing the most beautiful, durable and care-free garden plants in north America. Engelwood Cliffs, N.J., Simon & Schuster; Stonesong Press, 1990. 292p. illus. $39.95. ISBN: 9671669575.

Lists 1,700 flowers, herbs, trees, shrubs, ground cover plants, vines, ornamental grasses and aquatics. Data given include appearance, growth rate, and light, soil and moisture needs. 'An essential guide for serious gardeners' (*Booklist,* 1 June 1990, p.1863). *Class No:* 635(031)

[5777]

The Marshall Cavendish illustrated encyclopedia of gardening. Hunt, P., *ed.* New York, Marshall Cavendish Corporation, 1968-70. 20v. (iv, 2799p.). col. illus., diagrs., maps.

V.1-17: Aaron's beard ... Zygopetalum, including entries on gardening operations, pests and diseases, as well as featuring plants and flowers. V.17 has appended 'Great gardens of the world', p.2362-80. V.18-20: Garden calendar. Index (in v.20), p.2717-79. Numerous cross-references. Quality, number and generous size of coloured illus. are outstanding ('Dahlia', v.4, p.426-37, has 51 illus.). Quarto. *Class No:* 635(031)

[5778]

The New Royal Horticultural Society dictionary of gardening. Huxley, A., *ed.* London, New York, Macmillan, 1992. 4v. figs., diagrs., maps. £400; $795. ISBN: 1561590010, US ed; 0333474945, UK ed.

Preceding the *Dictionary* are: List of biographies - List of general entries - List of plates - Maps: climatic zones, Europe and the US - Abbreviations - Botanical glossary - Glossary of plant taxonomy. Main section arranged A-Z (*e.g.* 'Apples'; 5p.; 3 cross-references; cultivation; training; maintenance; pruning; thinning and harvesting; pests; diseases). Illus. are line-drawings opposite the text. V.4 has sections: Pests, diseases and disorders - Horticultural glossary - Glossary of common botanic epithets - Index of authors cited - Bibliography (p.837-53) - Index of popular names. A *tour de force* and, like its predecessor, *Dictionary of gardening* (1951), will be the standard work for years to come. A paperback edition is to be published in 1999. *Class No:* 635(031)

[5779]

—POLLOCK, M. *and* GRIFFITHS, M. **Royal Horticultural Society shorter dictionary of gardening.** London, Macmillan, 1998. viii, 837p., illus. (some col.) £40. ISBN: 0333654404.

A-Z format with entries p.1-804 (*e.g.* Hydrangea = 6 columns plus small line drawing), pests and diagnostic chart, p.805-9, glossary of plant forms, p.810-20, indexes of common names and synonyms, p.821-36. 'Gathers in one volume all of the core horticultural matter to be found in the *New RHS dictionary* together with entries for over 1,900 genera of ornamental and culinary plants' (*Foreword*). Excellent single volume work. *Class No:* 635(031)

[5780]

Reader's Digest new encyclopedia of garden plants and flowers. London, Reader's Digest Association, 1997. 864p. illus. (col.), tables. £29.95. ISBN: 0276421914.

Formerly published as *Reader's Digest encyclopedia of garden plants and flowers* (1987).

'A-Z guide to garden plants', p.10-718, is followed by four sections: Food from the garden - What plant is that? - How to grow and increase plants - Trouble-shooting in the garden. Glossary. Throughout the book, there are 'special features' on specific topics, *e.g.* 'Rock plants'. Numerous colour illustrations. *Class No:* 635(031)

[5781]

The Royal Horticultural Society A-Z encyclopedia of garden plants. Brickell, C., *ed.-in-chief.* London, Dorling Kindersley, 1996. 1080p. illus.(col.) £50. ISBN: 0751303038.

A-Z plant directory, p.55-1071, covers over 15,000 ornamental garden plants. More than 6,000 colour photographs. Over 40 contributors. Additional sections include: Botany for the gardener; Cultivation; Ornamental plant groups. glossary, p.1072-78. For public libraries and anyone interested in gardening.

The US equivalent is *American Horticultural Society A-Z encyclopedia of garden plants* (New York, Dorling Kindersley, 1997. ISBN: 0789419432. $79.95), edited by C. Brickell and J.D. Zuk. 'As a one-volume encyclopedia, this resource has no competition'(*Reference books bulletin,* 1/15 January 1998, p.848). *Class No:* 635(031)

[5782]

The Royal Horticultural Society gardeners' encyclopedia of plants and flowers. Brickell, C., *ed.* London, Dorling Kindersley, 1989. 608p. illus. (col.). £27.50. ISBN: 0863183867.

Sections: How to use this book - Plant origins and names - Creating a garden - The planter's guide - The plant catalogue (p.38-400) - The plant dictionary (p.401-594, listing *c.*8,000 plants with their characteristics and cultivation). Glossary of terms. Index of common names. Lavishly illustrated, with *c.*4,000 colour photographs. *Class No:* 635(031)

Handbooks & Manuals

[5783]

Reader's Digest 1001 hints and tips for the garden. London, Reader's Digest Association, 1996. 416p. illus.(col.). £24.95. ISBN: 0276422317.

Four sections: The gardener's alphabet - Guide to plant disorders - The gardener's year - A guide to gardening terms. 18 special features, *e.g.*, 'Britain's changing climate', 'Solving the shade problem'. Many colour illustrations. Well laid out, with some topics set in coloured boxes to give emphasis. *Class No:* 635(035)

[5784]

The Royal Horticultural Society encyclopedia of gardening: the definitive guide to gardening techniques, planning and maintenance, and to growing flowering plants, fruits and vegetables. Brickell, C., *ed.* London, Dorling Kindersley, 1992. 648p. illus (col) £29.95. ISBN: 0863189792.

2 sections (24 chapters): 1. Creating the garden (2. Ornamental trees ... 8. The rock garden ... 12. The lawn ... 16. The indoor garden) - 2. Maintaining the garden (1. Tools and equipment ... 5. Soils and fertilizers ... 8. Basic botany). Seasonal reminders, p.581-4. Glossary. Index, p.590-647. Over 3,000 illustrations in colour, and many step-by-step guides. For amateur and professional gardeners. *Class No:* 635(035)

[5785]

—'Which?' **kind of garden.** Boyd, L., *ed.* London, Consumers' Association, and Hodder & Stoughton, 1983. 240p. illus. (mostly col.). £12.95. ISBN: 0340259353.

Has sections: Inheriting a garden - Analysis of a garden (*e.g.* seaside, riverside) - Which kind of garden (*e.g.* labour-saving) - Allotment - Garden upkeep - Popular garden plants. The ornamental garden - The kitchen garden. Detailed, analytical index, p.234-40. Fully illustrated. *Class No:* 635(035)

Dictionaries

[5786]

SMITH, A.W. **A Gardener's dictionary of plant names:** a handbook on the origin and meaning of some plant names. London, Cassell, 1972. xii, 391p. *Class No:* 635(038)

Nomenclatures

[5787]

Index of garden plants. Griffiths, M., *ed.* London, Macmillan Press, 1994. lxi, 1234p. ISBN: 0333591496.

Derived from *The New Royal Horticultural Society dictionary of gardening* (1992).

Researched by 250 botanists, this is a checklist of garden plants in Europe, North America, Australia, and South Africa. Lists 'currently accepted botanical names, synonyms and popular names for 60,000 plants in cultivation'. Also contains 22,000 botanical names which are no longer officially in use, and 10,000 popular names. Botanical glossary (p.xxii-lxi) explains all the terms. *Class No:* 635(083.72)

Organic Gardening

[5788]

COLEMAN, E. **The New organic grower:** a master's manual of tools and techniques for the home and the market gardener. London, Cassell, 1990. xv, 269p. figs. £10.95. ISBN: 0304340138.

22 chapters: 1. Agricultural craftsmanship ... 3. Scale and capital ... 9. Tillage ... 13. Soil blocks ... 15. Weeds ... 18. Marketing ... 22. L'Envoi. Annotated bibliography, p.225-36. 3 appendices (*e.g.* 'Tools'; 'From asparagus to zucchini: the major vegetable crops'). Index, p.261-9. Well presented, readable, and recommended for public and academic libraries. *Class No:* 635.0

[5789]

The Complete manual of organic gardening. Caplan, B., *ed.* London, Headline Book Publishing, 1992. xi, 406p. illus.(col.), tables. ISBN: 0747205159.

17 contributors. 23 sections: 1. Climate and weather ... 4. Mulches ... 19. Disease prevention ... 23. Tools. Many colour illustrations. Short lists of further reading, associations, and suppliers (UK). For public libraries. *Class No:* 635.0

[5790]

Encyclopedia of organic gardening, by the staff of *Organic gardening* magazine. New rev. ed. Aylesbury, Bucks., J.J. Rodale, 1979. x, [2], 1236p. illus., tables.

First published 1959; Rodale, T.I., and others, eds.

Over 1,500 entries, 'Abelia ... Zygopetalum'. Data include identification, cultivation and use of specific fruits, grains, nuts, vegetables and ornamentals. 'Mulch': 5p. 'Pruning': nearly 5p. 'Insect control', p.569-604. Notes on 'storage requirements for fresh produce'. Cross references. 375 illus. (73 col.). Standard text on avoidance of artificial fertilisers and pesticides in the growing of crops. A bulky but readable volume. *Class No:* 635.0

[5791]

The UK green growers guide. Lisansky, S., *and others, eds.* Newbury, Berks., CPL Press, 1991. 420p. £11.95. ISBN: 1872691102.

2 sections: 1. The green scene (1. Why do we need green products ... 8. The growers' needs ... 13. Green laws ... 15. Insects to control other insects ... 19. Green products for animal feed - 20. Silage additives and inoculants) - 2. The products and where to get them (A. Insect control - B. Disease control ... F. Fertilisers - G. Other products - H. Chemical products accepted by some green growers). Indexes of products by use and manufacturers and suppliers. Aimed at professional growers and individual gardeners. *Class No:* 635.0

[5792]

The Worldwide directory of agrobiologicals 1997/98. Newbury, Berks., CPL Press, 1997. 1 CD-ROM. £125; $225.

Formerly *Green growers guide 1990/91: the worldwide directory of agrobiologicals*.

*c.*2,200 product listings and *c.*400 companies. Products include fungal and disease control, silage inoculants, weed control, and products for animals. Details can be expanded in this CD-ROM version and a glossary is also included. *Class No:* 635.0

Shrubs & Trees

[5793]

DAVIS, B. **The Gardener's illustrated encyclopedia of trees and shrubs:** a guide to more than 2000 varieties. Harmondsworth, Middlesex, Penguin Books; Viking, 1987. 256p. illus. (incl. col.). £19.99. ISBN: 0670812374.

Dictionary of trees, p.10-71; dictionary of shrubs, p.72-221. Data: origin; description; hardiness; soil requirements; sun/shade aspect; pruning; propagation and nursery production; problems; varieties of interest; average height and spread. Appended: Practical glossary.

....(contd.)

Botanical glossary. Choosing the right trees and shrubs. Pronunciation glossary (p.237-42). Indexes of common names and Latin names. *Class No:* 635.054

[5794]

The Hillier colour dictionary of trees and shrubs. Newton Abbot, Devon, David & Charles, 1993. 323p. col. illus. £17.99. ISBN: 0715300911.

Has *c.*three-line descriptions of 3,500 trees and shrubs selected for their garden value. The colour dictionary has 3 sections: trees and shrubs; climbers; conifers (p.35-319), preceded by cultural, etc. notes. Contains *c.*600 illustrations. Glossary of botanical terms, p.320-3. Notes on many of the plants are based on conditions in the British Isles. *Class No:* 635.054

[5795]

The Hillier manual of trees and shrubs. 6th ed. Newton Abbot, Devon, David & Charles, 1991. 704p. £25; £14.99. ISBN: 071539942x.

First published 1971, as a nurseryman's catalogue.

Very brief descriptions of over 9,000 plants, including more than 1,000 new entries. 4 main sections: Trees and shrubs; Climbers; Conifers; Bamboos. Appended sections on botanical names; trees and shrubs for selected soils, sites and ornamental effect; flowering trees and shrubs for every month. A standard guide.

Based on this title and published in the US in 1997 by Reader's Digest, *The Hillier gardener's guide to trees and shrubs*(ISBN: 0895779730; 640p., illus.; $50) which is also available as part of *The Plant finder reference library* CD-ROM 1998/9. *Class No:* 635.054

[5796]

JAMES, N.D.G. **The Arboriculturalist's companion:** a guide to the care of trees. 2nd ed. Oxford, Basil Blackwell, 1990. xii, 244p. figs. £45; £12.95. ISBN: 0631167749.

First published 1972.

Concerned with the growing and maintenance of trees from the point of view of ornament and amenity. 24 chapters: 1. Introduction to arboriculture ... 3. Transplanting large trees ... 6. Tree surgery ... 10. Trees and urban development ... 14. Avenues, parks and amenity woods ... 20. Arboricultural education, training and research ... 23. Books, manuals and periodicals (p.22-32) - 24. Trees for urban areas. Appendix: Grants for tree planting. Index. Essential for any library supporting a horticultural course. *Class No:* 635.054

Bulbs

[5797]

BRYAN, J.E. **Bulbs.** London, Christopher Helm; Portland, Or., Timber Press, 1989. 2v. illus. (col. pl.), figs. £99; $120. ISBN: 0747002312.

V.1 has 9 chapters (1. Overview ... 5. Cultivation ... 8. Pests and diseases - 9. Introduction to the genera), followed by 'Alphabetical listing of the genera: Achimenes to Hypoxis'. V.2 completes the alphabetical listing with 'Ipheion to Zygadenus', followed by 10 appendices (A. Families of bulbous plants ... E. Flowering times ... G. Growing in containers ... J. Fragrance). Glossary, p.391-3. Bibliography, p.394-6. 300 colour plates. An authoritative work. *Class No:* 635.073

[5798]

GENDERS, R. **Bulbs:** a complete handbook of bulbs, corms and tubers. London, Hale, 1973. [xvi], 622p. illus., (incl. col.). £8.95. ISBN: 0709131569.

1. History, culture and characteristics, p.1-15 - 2. Alphabetical guide, p.153-541. Appendices A-G (A. Planting depths: outdoors; B. Bulbs and their habitat). Detailed, analytical index, p.601-22. *Class No:* 635.073

Indoor Plants

[5799]

BECKETT, K.A., in association with the Royal Horticultural Society. **The RHS encyclopaedia of house plants,** including conservatory plants. London, Century, 1987. 494p. illus. £19.95. ISBN: 0712614028.

House plants, A-Z (scientific names), p.44-485. Lengthy prelims. include 'A brief history of house plants', 'Cultivation', 'Maintenance and propagation', 'Pests and diseases'. Glossary, p.486-8. Index of common names, p.489-92. About 1,000 illus. Well-produced. *Class No:* 635.91

[5800]
GRAF, A.B. Exotica 4 international: pictorial encyclopedia of exotic plants from tropical and near-tropical regions. 11th ed. East Rutherford, N.J., Roehrs Co., 1982. 2v. (2560p.). illus., maps. $187. ISBN: 0911266178.

Exotica 1 (1957); *Exotica 3* (1970).

Part 1 (1280, [3]p.) comprises introduction and *c*.12,000 half-tone illus. (3-5 per page), most black-and-white. Part 2 describes the plants illustrated, their family, common names, etc., (p.2151-2479). Bibliography, p.2538-9. Index of common names, p.2540-60. Covers more than 8500 species and cultivars. *Class No:* 635.91

[5801]
—GRAF, A.B. Tropica: color cyclopedia of exotic plants and trees from the tropics and subtropics, in cool climate, the summer garden or sheltered indoors. 3rd ed., rev. and enl. East Rutherford, N.J., Roehrs Co., 1986. 1152p. col. illus., map. ISBN: 0911266232.

Companion to *Exotica*. First published 1978, it has over 7,000 colour photographs of *c*.1,600 species. Families, A-Z. Bibliography p.1117-8; references. Indexes of common and scientific names. *Class No:* 635.91

[5802]
Rodale's encyclopedia of indoor gardening. Halpin, A.M., *ed*. Emmaus, Pa., Rodale Press, 1980. vii, 902p. illus. (mostly col.). ISBN: 0878573194.

Six parts. 1. Understanding plant growth - 2. Tools and techniques for indoor gardening - 3. Growing different kinds of plants (p.168-513) - 4. Special environments and how to use them (*e.g.* chapter 29: Greenhouse gardening) - 5. A house plant encyclopedia (p.730-867). 6 appendices (*e.g.* Plant societies and publishers: US, Canada, UK); Some sources of greenhouse plants. Glossary. Select bibliography, p.875-6. Index of common plant names. Detailed, analytical general index, p.885-902. *Class No:* 635.91

Roses

[5803]
BEALES, P. Classic roses: an illustrated encyclopaedia and grower's manual of old roses, shrub roses and climbers. London, Collins Harvill, 1985. 432p. col.illus.,maps. ISBN: 0002727080.

Four sections: 1. The history and evolution of the rose - 2. Roses in the landscape - 3. The cultivation of roses - 4. The dictionary (lists over 1,000 roses, with maps showing geographical distribution). Three appendices, *e.g.* A. Rose gardens of Great Britain. Bibliography; index of roses; general index. *c*.550 colour photographs. A clear and beautifully produced guide. For public and botanical libraries.

Companion volume by the same author is *Twentieth-century roses: an illustrated encyclopaedia and grower's manual of classic roses from the twentieth century* (Collins Harvill, 1988. 320p. col.illus., map). *Class No:* 635.92:582.7

[5804]
STOCK, K.L. Rose books: a bibliography of books and important articles in journals on the genus Rosa, in English, French, German and Latin, 1550-1975. The Author, 1984. x, 533p. ISBN: 0980905607.

3,279 numbered entries, under authors A-Z. References (sources), p.vi-vii, Libraries and locations, p.viii-ix. *Class No:* 635.92:582.7

Cacti

[5805]
CULLMANN, W.S. The Encyclopedia of cacti. Thomas, K.M., *trans*. Sherborne, Dorset, Alphabooks, 1986. 340p. illus. (incl. col.). £35. ISBN: 0906670373.

German original as *Kakteen* (1963, 1964).

Structure, mode of living and classification of cacti - Cactus culture - Building up and accommodating a cactus collection - Special culture problems - The general and species of cacti, A-Z, p.124-316. Appendices include glossary, bibliography (p.322), associations and publications, plant suppliers. General index; index of Latin names. Many col. illus. A rewritten, expanded and re-illustrated ed. The revised text, which includes identification keys for all genera, now covers 750 species. *Class No:* 635.92:582.85

[5806]
LAMB, E. and LAMB, B. The Illustrated reference on cacti and other succulents. London, Blandford Press, 1955-78. 5v. illus.

Describes over 1,000 species (195 genera), with one page of brief descriptions per species. Note on culture could be fuller, especially on watering. The coloured plates provide excellent identification. V.4 has 280 illus. (94 in colour); v.5: 280 illus. (100 in colour).

Pocket encyclopaedia of cacti in colour (Rev. ed. London, Blandford Press, 1981, 218p. 326 col. illus. £7.99) was first published in 1970. *Class No:* 635.92:582.85

[5807]
—JACOBSEN, H. Lexicon of succulent plants: short descriptions, habitats and synonymy of succulent plants other than cactaceae. 2nd ed. London, Blandford Press, 1977. 682p. illus. (pl.). ISBN: 0713708263.

English ed., rev. and enl., of *Das Sukkulenten Lexikon* (Jena, 1970) - has 200 plates. Pt.1: A-Z; pt.2: Family Mesembryanthemaceae. Bibliography, p.585-90; 'Invalid designations', p.591-664. *Class No:* 635.92:582.85

Rhododendrons

[5808]
DAVIDIAN, H.H. The Rhododendron species. London, Batsford, 1982-92. 3v. illus. (some col. pl.), figs., maps. £70ea. ISBN: 0713416394, v.1; 0713416408, v.2; 0713437472, v.3.

V.1. *Lepidotes*. 1982. 431p. V.2. *Elepidote species: series Arboreum-Lacteum*. 1989. 344p. V.3. *Elepidotes: series Neriiflorum-Thomsonii, Azaleastrum and Camtschaticum*. 1992. 381p.

Lists 43 groups or 'Series'. Detailed descriptions of each species, alongwith many colour photographs and well-presented line-drawings. Included are unplaced species, glossary, list of synonyms, key to the series and subseries, etc. An authoritative work but the quality of the colour photographs is variable. *Class No:* 635.92:582.915

[5809]
—COX, P.A. and COX, K.N.E. The Encyclopedia of rhododendron species. Glencarse, Perthshire, Glendoick Publishing, 1997. xviii,396p. illus. (some col.) £75. ISBN: 095305330x.

Detailed descriptions of all non-vireya species in cultivation. Over 1,500 photographs of examples in the wild and in gardens. Bibliography, p.391. *Class No:* 635.92:582.915

Livestock & Animal Husbandry

[5810]
Animal behavior abstracts. Bethesda, Md., Cambridge Scientific Abstracts, 1973-. 4pa. $615 (US); $655 (non US). ISSN: 03018695.

Previously published by Information Retrieval, Ltd., London; initially as *Behavioural biology abstracts. Section A, Animal behaviour.*

About 1,200 abstracts per issue, drawn from *c*.5,000 primary and other journals. Subjects of papers range from neurophysiology to ecology, from genetics to social anthropology, and the biology of particular taxonomic groups. Appended: Book notices; Notices of proceedings. Author and analytical subject indexes per issue and annually. Online (LIFE SCIENCES COLLECTION) and also available on magnetic tape and CD-ROM. Also accessible as an Internet version. *Class No:* 636

[5811]
Dictionary of farm animal behavior. Hurnik, J.F., *and others*. 2nd ed. Ames, Iowa State University Press, 1995. ix,200p. £19.95; $19.95. ISBN: 0813824648.

First published 1985.

c.4,000 terms covering all aspects of farm animal behaviour. Includes colloquialisms. The authors are respected academics in this subject area. *Class No:* 636

[5812]
Tierproduktion. Mehrsprachen-Bildwörterbuch. [Animal production. Multilingual illustrated dictionary.] Tawfik, E.S., *and others, eds*. 6th ed. Weikersheim, Margraf Verlag, 1993. xxvi,833p. illus. DM56. ISBN: 3823612271.

First published 1962, edited by H. Steinmetz.

Contains 5,212 terms in German, English, French, Spanish, Italian, and Dutch relating to feeding, housing, and breeding of livestock, including fish and poultry. Full alphabetical indexes in each language. Small black-and-white drawings. *Class No:* 636

Laboratory Animals (Research)

[5813]
Alternatives to laboratory animals. Nottingham, FRAME/Fund for the Replacement of Animals in Medical Experiments, 1973-. 4pa. £65; $130. ISSN: 02611929.

Originally (v.1, 1973) as *Abstracts of alternatives to laboratory animals.*

Each issue contains *c*.150 abstracts under the heading 'Selected titles'. 11 book reviews precede. Intended to cover all aspects of the development, validation, introduction and use of alternatives to laboratory animals in biomedical research and toxicity testing. *Class No:* 636.028

[5814]

Laboratory animals: an annotated bibliography of informational resources covering medicine - science (including husbandry) - technology. Cass, J.S., *ed.* New York, Hafner, 1971. 3pts. (viii, vi, 136p.; vi, 250p.; [vi], 60p.). $23.95. ISBN: 0028426401.

Part 2: *Animals in research. Class No: 636.028*

[5815]

UFAW handbook on the care and management of laboratory animals. Poole, T.B. 6th ed. Edinburgh, Churchill Livingstone, 1987. x, 933p. diagrs., tables. £78. ISBN: 058240911x.

First published 1947.

59 contributors. 3 parts. 1. The laboratory animal - 2. Animal units - 3. Species kept in the laboratory (a) mammals; (b) birds; (c) reptiles; (d) amphibians; (e) fish. 56 chapters, each with 'Further reading'. References, p.848-918. Detailed, analytical index. *Class No: 636.028*

Breeds & Breeding

[5816]

Animal breeding abstracts. Wallingford, Oxon., CAB International, 1933-. 12pa. £440; $995. ISSN: 00033499.

7,500 abstracts pa. Sections: Livestock - Horses - Cattle - Buffalo - Sheep - Goats - Pigs - Fur bearers - Laboratory mammals - Other mammals - Poultry and other birds - General and theoretical genetics - Reproduction, general - Fish and invertebrates in aquaculture. News and notes. Reports. Conferences. Books. Occasional review articles. Author and subject indexes per issue and annually. Online, CAB ABSTRACTS database. Available on CAB ABSTRACTS CD-ROM and CAB International's BEASTCD. *Class No: 636.082*

[5817]

SAMBRAUS, H. A Colour atlas of livestock breeds: 220 breeds in words and pictures. London, Wolfe Publishing, 1992. 272p. illus. £15. ISBN: 0723418918.

Pictorial guide to the commercially and economically important breeds of cattle, horses, donkeys and mules, sheep, pigs, goats, rabbits and poultry. Data for each breed entry includes characteristics; world distribution; uses; breed history. A photograph of the breed is also included. A useful handbook. *Class No: 636.082*

Animal Feeds

[5818]

Nutrition abstracts and reviews. Series B. Livestock feeds and feeding. Wallingford, Oxon., CAB International, 1977-. 12pa. £392; $845. ISSN: 0309135x.

About 6,000 abstracts pa. Coverage includes: Analysis; Technology; Feedstuffs and feeds; Physiology; Biochemistry; Feeding of animals; Diet in aetiology of disease. Author and title indexes per issue and annually.

Online, CAB ABSTRACTS. Available on CAB ABSTRACTS CD-ROM, BEASTCD, and NutritionCD. Also available on the Internet via Nutrition CABWeb (http://nutrition.cabweb.org). *Class No: 636.084*

Veterinary Medicine

Bibliographies

[5819]

DINGLEY, P. Historic books on veterinary science and animal husbandry: the Comben Collection in the Science Museum Library. London, HMSO, 1992. 184p. illus. £35. ISBN: 0112905110.

Lists the 704 books and pamphlets plus 155 reference works dating from 1514 and the mid-19th century in the collection. Data on each include date of publication, pagination, and notes. 50 beautiful illustrations. *Class No: 636.09(01)*

[5820]

GIBB, M. Keyguide to information sources in veterinary medicine. London, Mansell, 1990. xiii,459p. £45. ISBN: 0720120187.

Contain 2,530 entries, some unannotated. 3 sections: 1. Survey of veterinary medicine and its literature (1. The history and scope of veterinary medicine ... 4. Keeping up to date with current information ... 8. Language problems) - 2. Bibliography (9. General works ... 11. Small animals - 12. Specialties) - 3. Directory of organizations. Lack of bibliographic information in the 'Other Journals' sections whose entries are not included in the index. *Class No: 636.09(01)*

[5821]

Index-catalogue of medical and veterinary zoology. US Bureau of Animal Industry. Zoological Division. Authors A-Z. Washington, US Government Printing Office, 1932-52. 12v. Supplement 1-. 1953-.

Index to world literature 'on parasites and parasitisms of man, of domestic animals, and of wild animals whose parasites may be transmitted to man and domestic animals' (*Bulletin of the Medical Library Association, v.41, no.2, April 1953, p.110*). In the Author catalogue, each author's papers are arranged chronologically.

Supplements 1-6 (1953-56) covered backlog. Since then, supplements (authors, A-Z) are annual. Beginning with suppt.15, *Parasite subject catalogues* (containing indexes to the author references in the *Author catalogues* and including a catalogue of hosts) have been issued in addition. *Class No: 636.09(01)*

[5822]

KERKER, A.E. *and* **MURPHY, H.T. Comparative & veterinary medicine:** a guide to the resource literature. [Madison], University of Wisconsin Press, 1973. xvi, 308p. $84.30. ISBN: 0835767892.

4,600 usually unannotated entries. 4 parts: 1. Materials of general interest (reference works, p.58-70) - 2. Specific disciplines (anatomy ... radiology and radiation biology) - 3. Veterinary medicine (animal management ... wild life and zoo animals) - 4. Laboratory animals. List of congresses and other meetings. Author index; subject index key; analytical subject index, p.268-308. *Class No: 636.09(01)*

[5823]

Pest management: a directory of information sources. Volume 2: Animal health. Hamilton, C.J., *ed.* Wallingford, Oxon., CAB International, 1995. 290p. £35; $60. ISBN: 0851987435.

Second volume in a projected 3: v.3 will cover public health. Lists books and reviews taken from the CAB ABSTRACTS database dealing with animal diseases and their control. Also contains lists of animal health journals plus addresses of animal health libraries and information centres. *Class No: 636.09(01)*

Encyclopaedias & Dictionaries

[5824]

Black's veterinary dictionary. Boden, E., *ed.* 19th ed. London, A. & C. Black, 1998. 595p. illus., diagrs., graphs, tables, maps. £25. ISBN: 0713644001.

First published 1928.

Several hundred undocumented entries (*e.g.* 'Hernia'; parts and types; signs; treatment). Fewer pages than the previous edition, with a few terms added and older material deleted. Coverage is patchy but useful as a quick reference tool for farmers, students, and animal owners. *Class No: 636.09(03)*

[5825]

BLOOD, D.C. *and* **STUDDERT, V.P. Saunders comprehensive veterinary dictionary.** 2nd ed. London, etc., W.B. Saunders, 1998. xxvi,1380p. tables. £34.95. ISBN: 0702024422.

Formerly *Bailliere's comprehensive veterinary dictionary* (1988).

20 consultants (19 of them based in Australia). The dictionary (p.1-1243) has *c.*65,000 entries, an increase of 10,000 on first edition. 'Rabbit': 18 entries; 'Manx': 23 lines. Anatomical tables. Appendix comprises 18 tables (*e.g.* Laboratory services; Important venomous snakes). 'Based on a survey of more than one hundred veterinary textbooks' (*Preface*), and aimed at veterinary student readership. *Class No: 636.09(03)*

[5826]

COLLIN, B. Petit dictionnaire de la médecine du gibier. [Small dictionary of game animal medicine.] Alleur-Liege, Editions du Perron, 1992. 521p. ISBN: 287114088x.

Arranged as an encyclopaedia and covering all aspects of European game animals and birds. *Class No: 636.09(03)*

[5827]

COMMONWEALTH BUREAU OF ANIMAL HEALTH. Controlled vocabulary for subject indexing in Veterinary bulletin, Index veterinarius, Animal disease occurrence, and Small animal abstracts. Weybridge, Surrey, the Bureau, 1985. [iv], 110p.

Columns: Description (non-descriptors, indented); date first used; remarks. Where no date is given, footnote states that the descriptor has been in use for at least 20 years, probably since the 1950's. Standard vocabulary for cataloguers and indexers in this field. *Class No: 636.09(03)*

[5828]

FENNER, W.R. Quick reference to veterinary medicine. Philadelphia, Pa., Lippincott, 1991. xiii,669p. tables. $44.95. ISBN: 0397508956.

Has 44 contributors, 3 parts: 1. Clinical signs and client complaints - 2. Laboratory abnormalities and principles of fluid management - 3. Physical and chemical injuries and intoxicants. Summary. Suggested readings to sections. Basic diagnostic approach (*i.e.*, based on signs and symptoms), complementing standard veterinary textbooks. *Class No: 636.09(03)*

[5829]
LEADER, R.W. *and* LEADER, I. **Dictionary of comparative pathology and experimental biology.** Philadelphia, Pa., W.B. Saunders, 1971. vi, [1], [1], 238p. illus., tables.

About 4,500 terms, omitting those already dealt with in standard medical dictionaries. Includes information on husbandry, breeds, genetic characteristics, and diseases of common laboratory animals, with special emphasis on rats, mice and rabbits. Particular attention to genetics in relation to disease. Bibliography (65 items) p.235-8. Addenda: Table of animal models. Table of zoonoses by type of etiologic agent. *Class No:* 636.09(03)

[5830]
MACK, R. **Dictionary for veterinary science and biosciences** German-English/English-German. Berlin, Paul Parey, 1988. 321p.

Contains *c.*10,000 terms, compiled over a period of 30 years from biomedical and veterinary literature. Trilingual Latin indexes of botanical, anatomical, and zoological names. *Class No:* 636.09(03)

[5831]
MACK, R. **Russo-English veterinary dictionary.** [Russsko-angliĭskiĭ veterinaryĭ slovar'.] Farnham Royal, Commonwealth Agricultural Bureaux, 1972. viii, 104p. £10. ISBN: 0851982557.

Equivalents of *c.*6,000 Russian veterinary terms, including relevant biological vocabulary. Bibliography, p.vii-viii. *Class No:* 636.09(03)

[5832]
Wörterbuch der Veterinärmedizin. [Dictionary of veterinary medicine.] Wiesner, E. *and* Ribbeck, R., *eds.* 3rd ed. Jena, Gustav Fischer Verlag, 1991. 1662p.

First published 1978; 2nd ed. 1983.

73 contributors. Contains *c.*50,000 entries. Many new terms have been added since the previous ed. *Class No:* 636.09(03)

Handbooks & Manuals

[5833]
Animal anatomy on file. Diagram Group. New York, Facts on File, 1990. loose-leaf. $145. ISBN: 0816022445.

Contains more than 200 exceptionally clear anatomical drawings depicting the anatomy of animal species from sponges to humans. Subdivided by major divisions in the animal world, each plate shows a specific anatomical structure, *e.g.* muscle system. Anatomical parts on each plate are numbered, with an accompanying key appearing below. Useful for school libraries. *Class No:* 636.09(035)

[5834]
Veterinary medicine: a textbook of the diseases of cattle, sheep, pigs, goats and horses. Blood, D.C., *and others.* 8th ed. London, etc., Baillière Tindall, 1994. xxiv, 1763p. illus. tables. ISBN: 070201592x.

First published 1960.

2 sections: 1. General medicine. 2. Special medicine. 35 chapters in all: 1. Clinical examination and making a diagnosis ... 8. Diseases of the cardiovascular system ... 12. Diseases of the nervous system ... 23. Diseases caused by rickettsia ... 25. Diseases caused by protozoa ... 28. Metabolic diseases ... 33. Diseases caused by allergy ... 35. Specific diseases of uncertain etiology. Conversion tables, p.1724-5. Reference laboratory values, p.1726-7. Index, p.1728-62. 95 tables. New diseases covered include bovine spongiform encephalopathy (BSE). Numerous bibliographies throughout. Standard text. *Class No:* 636.09(035)

[5835]
—GREAT BRITAIN. Ministry of Agriculture, Fisheries and Food. Tolworth Library. **Thesaurus** (for animal health, vertebrate pest biology and control). Surbiton, Surrey, the Library, 1975. 98p. *Class No:* 636.09(035)

[5836]
Zoo and wild animal medicine. Fowler, M.E., *ed.* 4th ed. Philadelphia, Pa., etc., W.B. Saunders Co., 1999. xxiii, 747p. illus., diagrs., tables. ISBN: 0721686648.

Sponsored by Morris Animal Federation, Denver, Colorado. Previous ed. published 1993.

*c.*100 contributors. Four parts: 1. General topics - 2. Amphibians and reptiles - 3. Birds - 4. Mammals. Appendices include relevant legislation and useful addresses. Many illustrations. Detailed, analytical index. Cover and title-page carry sub-title 'Current therapy 4'. *Class No:* 636.09(035)

Reviews & Abstracts

[5837]
Index veterinarius. Wallingford, Oxon., CAB International, 1933-. 12pa. £684; $1450. ISSN: 00194123.

Lists *c.*21,000 references pa., under subjects, A-Z. Supported by author index. 'Titles are selected from some 1,200 serial publications regularly scanned by the staff of the Bureau, and from books, annual reports, monographs, theses and other serial publications'. A list of the serials appears irregularly in the *Veterinary bulletin (qv).* CAB

....(contd.)
ABSTRACTS database, CD-ROM, BEASTCD, and available on the Internet via VET CABWeb (http://vet.cabweb.org). *Class No:* 636.09(048)

[5838]
Veterinary bulletin. Wallingford, Oxon., CAB International, 1931-. 12pa. £552; $1195.

About 8,500 abstracts pa. Covers the core literature of animal health. Animals included are: Cattle; Horses; Sheep; Goats; Pigs; Poultry; Cats; Dogs; Rabbits; Cagebirds; Other small animals; Laboratory animals; Wildlife; Zoo animals; Fish; Other domestic animals. Occasional review articles. Author and analytical subject indexes per issue and annually. CAB ABSTRACTS database. Also available on CAB ABSTRACTS CD-ROM, BEASTCD and available on the Internet via VET CABWeb (http://vet.cabweb.org) *Class No:* 636.09(048)

[5839]
—**Vetdoc abstract journal.** London, Derwent Publications, Ltd., 1968-. Fortnightly. $11,660pa.

Carries *c.*4,800 abstracts pa. relevant to manufacturers of veterinary products (*e.g.* veterinary drugs, vaccines, growth promotants, hormonal control of breeding). Online as *Derwent veterinary drug file* via Data-Star, Orbit, STN. *Class No:* 636.09(048)

Progress Reports

[5840]
Advances in veterinary science. Orlando, Fla., etc., Academic Press, 1953-. illus., diagrs., graphs, tables.

Formerly published as *Advances in veterinary science and comparative medicine.*

V.41, 1999 (815p.) has over 30 contributors. The documented articles include 'Genetic effects on vaccination' and 'The equine influenza surveillance program'. Each paper has a lengthy bibliography appended. Analytical index. Some volumes concentrate on particular themes (*e.g.* v.28: 'Research on nonhuman primates'). *Class No:* 636.09(055)

Yearbooks & Directories

[5841]
The Directory of practices. London, the Royal College of Veterinary Surgeons, 1991- . Annual.

Explanation of symbols and abbreviations is followed by: Gazetteer; Geographical list of practices; Alphabetical list of practices; Alphabetical list of members. Indicates main areas of practice, *e.g.* small animals. Not comprehensive as members are not obliged to give information for inclusion in the *Directory. Class No:* 636.09(058)

[5842]
ROYAL COLLEGE OF VETERINARY SURGEONS. **Registers and directory,** 1995/96. London, the Royal College, 1995. xiv,304p.

Three sections: 1. General list of members, p.9-210 - 2. Members resident overseas - 3. Members holding appointments in the United Kingdom and the Republic of Ireland other than in private practice (includes university veterinary schools, animal welfare societies, etc.). Index. *Class No:* 636.09(058)

[5843]
The Veterinary annual. 34th issue. Sevenoaks, Kent, Butterworth, 1994. Annual. xiii,257p. illus., diagrs., tables.

First published 1959-. (Bristol, Wright).

38 contributors. Sections: Cattle (5 articles) - Deer (1) - Sheep (1) - Swine (2) - Fowl (1) - Horses (5) - Small animals (11). Articles are documented (*e.g.* 'Sheep and melatonin' (2p. of references); 'Electromyographic examination in the horse' (1p. of references). Analytical subject index. *Class No:* 636.09(058)

Tables & Data Books

[5844]
Animal health yearbook. Food and Agriculture Organization, World Health Organization, and International Office of Epizootics (FAO-WHO-OIE). Rome, FAO, 1957-. Annual. tables, maps. ISSN: 00661872.

Contains tabular statistics of world livestock diseases, grouped under countries in 6 areas: Africa; America; Asia; Europe; Oceania, USSR. 10 appendices (*e.g.* number of livestock and human population). Arabic, Chinese, Russian and German glossaries. A-Z list of countries and areas, and of diseases and causal agents. *Class No:* 636.09(083)

[5845]

British pharmacopoeia (veterinary) 1998. Published on the recommendation of the Medicines Commission pursuant to the Medicines Act 1968 and notified in draft to the European Commission in accordance with directive 83/189/EEC (as amended). London, Stationery Office, 1998. xxii, 204p. ISBN: 0113221169.

The first part consists of monographs (*e.g.* 'Medicinal and pharmaceutical substances'). 16 appendices (*e.g.* 'Biological assays and tests'). Detailed analytical index. Well produced. This pharmacopoeia provides standards for the quality of substances, preparations and immunological products used in veterinary medicine, plus information on action, use, dose, solubility, storage and labelling. Available on CD-ROM. *Class No:* 636.09(083)

[5846]

The Henston large animal veterinary vade mecum 1996-1997. 8th ed. High Wycombe, Bucks., Henston, 1996. 464p. tables. £46.50. ISSN: 02684268.

Formerly *The Henston veterinary vademecum (large animals)*.

3 parts: 1. Diagnosis and disease (cattle; sheep and goats; pigs; horses) - 2. Therapeutic products ('Tables by therapeutic class') - 3. Useful information (*e.g.* 'Poisons'; 'Government departments'). Directory of products and services. Advertisers' index.

Also available on the *Henston vade mecum* CD-ROM.
Class No: 636.09(083)

[5847]

The Henston small animal veterinary vade mecum 1995-1996. Henderson, A., *ed.* High Wycombe, Bucks., Henston, 1995. iv,378p. tables. £30. ISBN: 1850541027. ISSN: 02684268.

Formerly *The Henston veterinary vademecum (small animals)*.

Six parts: 1. Tables by therapeutic class - 2. Diseases, conditions and signs - 3. Nutrition - 4. Contributed articles - 5. Useful information - 6. Directory. Index. Advertisers' index. Also available on the *Henston vade mecum* CD-ROM. *Class No:* 636.09(083)

[5848]

The Merck veterinary manual: a handbook of diagnosis, therapy, and disease prevention and control for the veterinarian. 8th ed. Whitehouse Station, N.J., Merck & Co., Inc., 1998. xxxv, 2305p. illus. ISBN: 0911910298.

First published 1955; 6th ed. (xxvii,1677p.), 1986.

Concerned with diagnosis, treatment, and prevention of animal diseases. About 500 contributors. 22 sections, with 14 based on body systems and eaight on special topics such as pharmacology and toxicology. Detailed, analytical index. Available on diskette. *Class No:* 636.09(083)

[5849]

TENNANT, B. Small animal formulary. 2nd ed. London, Manson for the British Small Animal Veterinary Association, 1997. 275p. £18.50. ISBN: 0905214447.

Includes 58 new drugs compared with previous ed. and the appendices have been extensively revised. Three main sections: How to use the formulary; Drug monographs; Appendices (*e.g.* Percentage solutions'; 'Normal vital signs'. Three indexes: Sorted by therapeutic class; Drugs new to the 2nd edition; Sorted alphabetically (generic/brand names). Third ed. due in 1999. *Class No:* 636.09(083)

[5850]

The Veterinary formulary: handbook of medicines used in veterinary practice. Bishop, Y., *ed.* 4th ed. London, Pharmaceutical Press, 1998. xvi,638p. £59.95. ISBN: 0853694125.

First published 1991.

Includes a section 'Additions to fourth edition'. Sections: Guidance on prescribing - Classified notes on drugs and preparations (18 sections: 1. Drugs used in the treatment of bacterial, fungal, viral, and protozoal infections ... 6. Drugs acting on the nervous system ... 14. Drugs acting on the skin ... 18. Herbal medicines). Appendices and indexes: 1. Drug interactions ... 4. Weights of animals; Index of manufacturers and organisations. Index, p.603-38.
Class No: 636.09(083)

Nomenclatures

[5851]

Illustrated veterinary anatomical nomenclature. Schaller, O., *ed.* Stuttgart, Ferdinand Enke Verlag, 1992. vi,614p. figs. ISBN: 3432995911.

Arranged so that verso pages contain numbered terms as in the *Nominal anatomica veterinaria,* with each term followed by a brief definition. Respective, clearly drawn, illustrations, labelled by numbers corresponding to those of the terms on the opposite page. Alphabetical index of terms. Includes changes approved for the 4th ed. of NAV. 280 plates, including 1,316 illustrations. *Class No:* 636.09(083.72)

Histories

[5852]

Animal health: a centenary, 1865-1965: a century of endeavour to control diseases of animals. London, HMSO, 1965. xviii, 396p. illus., maps.

3 parts. 1. The evolution of the Animal Health Divison - 2. The animal health responsibilities - 3. Aspects of disease control. Some footnote references. 13 illus., 2 maps. General index; index of acts, rules and regulations. *Class No:* 636.09(091)

[5853]

SMITH, Sir F.E. The Early history of veterinary literature and its development. London J.A. Allen, 1976. 4v. ports.

1. *From the earliest period to A.D.1700*. iv, 373p. 2. *The eighteenth century*. viii, 244p. 3. *The nineteenth century, 1800-1823*. viii, 244p. 4. *The nineteenth century, 1823-1900*. 161p.

V.1 was reprinted from *Journal of comparative pathology and therapeutics*, 1912-1918; v.2-3, from *The Veterinary journal*, 1923-24, 1929-30. V.1 has an index of names only; v.2-4 have author and 'works' indexes. Numerous footnotes. A classic account.
Class No: 636.09(091)

Information Management

[5854]

FOOD AND AGRICULTURE ORGANIZATION. Manual for small veterinary libraries. Alexandria, FAO Near East Animal Health Institutes, Coordinating Units, United Nations Development Programme, 1972. [iv], 65p.

5 chapters: 1. Consideration of some problems in the administration of small veterinary libraries - 2. Selection and acquisition - 3. Periodicals and serials - 4. Cataloguing and classification - 5. Reference and bibliographic service. Select list of reference aids for small veterinary medical libraries (p.28-65), - 187 briefly annotated entries, under subjects, A-Z. *Class No:* 636.09:025.4

Thesauri

[5855]

Veterinary multilingual thesaurus in English, French, Italian and German. Munich, K.G. Saur, 1979. 5v. (4v. and index). Microfiche also available. $270 (English language vol. 264p.). ISBN: 3598101090.

Full thesaurus, p.1-194. Microthesaurus (18 subject sections, Biology ... Zootechny, p.195-244). 4,922 descriptors in each language; 4,190 non-descriptors in English. Quadralingual index and microfiches in rear-pocket. *Class No:* 636.09:025.43

Diseases

[5856]

Animal disease occurrence. [Incidenza delle malatie degli animale. Commonwealth Bureau of Animal Health, Weybridge, Surrey.] Wallingford, Oxon., CAB International, in association with the Commission of the European Communities, 1980-. tables. Annual. $60. ISSN: 01443879.

About 1,000 abstracts per issue. *Section A:* General veterinary medicine; Animal diseases in general; Horse diseases; Cattle diseases; Sheep and goat diseases; Swine diseases; Dog and cat diseases; Poultry diseases; Fish diseases; Bee diseases; Diseases of other animals; Miscellaneous - *Section B:* Tables (12, including list of pathogens and parasites). Author and subject indexes per issue, cumulated annually. CAB ABSTRACTS database. *Class No:* 636.09:616

[5857]

World animal health in 1997. Paris, Office International des Epizooties, 1998. 2v.(755p.) ISBN: 9290444541.

Part 1: *Reports*; Part 2: *Tables*.

Compilation of data giving an overview of animal disease throughout the world from 200 countries. Part 1 gives an account of the most important animal health happenings in 1997, while Part 2 lists the impact of animal diseases in each country *Class No:* 636.09:616

Livestock

Bibliographies

[5858]

The Literature of animal science and health. Ithaca, Cornell University Press, 1993. 404p. £59.50. (*Literature of the animal sciences.*) ISBN: 0801428866.

Eight chapters: 1. Development of animal science in the United States ... 4. Statistics and databases in animal science ... 7. Reference updates (98p.) - 8. Primary historical literature 1860-1949. For all agricultural research libraries. *Class No:* 636.1/.5(01)

[5859]

MAGEL, C.R. Keyguide to information sources in animal rights.
London, Mansell; Jefferson, N.C., McFarland & Company, 1989.
iv,267p. £40. ISBN: 0720119847, UK ed; 0899504051, US ed.

Bibliographic essay with references keyed to the annotated
bibliography (335 items) and the unannotated list of literature cited
(c.1,000 items), plus a directory of relevant organizations (220
entries). 5 appendices (A. The rights of animals: a declaration against
speciesism ... D. Magazines and journals). Index of authors, titles,
subjects, persons, countries and organizations. 'An outstanding
resource' (*RQ*, v.29(3), Spring 1990, p.445-6). *Class No:* 636.1/
.5(01)

Encyclopaedias

[5860]

Encyclopedia of animal rights and animal welfare. Bekoff, M. *and*
Meaney, C.A., *eds*. Westport, Conn., Greenwood, 1998. 446p. £45;
$59.95. ISBN: 0313299773.

Essays arranged alphabetically, covering topics such as genetic
engineering, feral animals, and utilitarianism, and also including
biographies and entries for organizations. Each essay has a short
bibliography appended. Many cross-references. Includes a chronology
of significant events. Appendix: 'Resources on animal welfare and
humane education'. Index. For academic libraries. *Class No:* 636.1/
.5(031)

Handbooks & Manuals

[5861]

BLAKELY, J. *and* BADE, D.H. The Science of animal husbandry.
5th ed. Reston, Va., Reston Pubg. Co., 1989. 736p. illus., diagrs.,
tables. $43. ISBN: 0685447146.

40 chapters (with study questions): 2. The beef industry ... 9.
Diseases of cattle - 10. The dairy industry ... 15. Reproduction,
feeding and management of sheep ... 22. The swine industry ... 29.
Poultry: a general view ... 35. The horse industry ... 40. The rabbit
industry. 2 appendices. Detailed, analytical index. Written for the
student. *Class No:* 636.1/.5(035)

[5862]

BRIGGS, H.M. *and* BRIGGS, D.M. Modern breeds of livestock. 4th
ed. New York, Macmillan; London, Collier-Macmillan, 1980. xiv,
802p. illus., charts, tables. ISBN: 002314730x.

58 chapters. 4 sections: 1. The breeds of cattle - 2. The breeds of
swine - 3. The breeds of sheep and goats - 4. The breeds of horses.
Introduced on individual classes and groups. Detailed index, p.777-
802. US slanted. *Class No:* 636.1/.5(035)

[5863]

Handbook of animal science. Putnam, P.A., *ed*. San Diego, Academic
Press, 1991. xi,401p. graphs, tables. $69. ISBN: 0125683006.

Sections: History and background - Breeds and genetics - Statistics -
Health - Production - Product/UItilization - Future. Includes small
animals as well as the large, domestic animals. References appended to
each chapter. Many tables and graphs. A handy and convenient
reference source. *Class No:* 636.1/.5(035)

Dictionaries

[5864]

EUROPEAN ASSOCIATION FOR ANIMAL PRODUCTION, Rome.
Dictionary of animal production terminology, in English, French,
Spanish, German and Latin. 2nd ed. Amsterdam, etc., Elsevier, 1993.
xxvi, 656p. illus. £160. (*EAAP publication, No.60.*) ISBN:
0444880720.

First ed. published 1986.

Nearly 9,000 English-base terms with equivalents in the other four
languages. Includes terms from related disciplines such as
biochemistry, nutrition, genetics, etc. Classes A-Z (A. Anatomy - B.
Physiology - C. Genetics - D. Breeding - E. Feeding stuffs ... K.
Hygiene and therapy - L. Animal products - M. Forestry - N. Equine
production - O. Cattle production ... Z. General terms). Indexes in all
5 languages. *Class No:* 636.1/.5(038)

[5865]

**MASON, I.L. A World dictionary of livestock breeds, types and
varieties.** 4th ed. Wallingford, CAB International, 1996. xx,273p.
£40. ISBN: 0851991024.

First published 1951.

Includes c.9,000 entries (5,000 main entries, 4,000 cross-
references). c.2,300 entries have been amended and there is an 18%
increase in main entries. More information on Chinese breeds. 7
sections: Ass - Buffalo - Cattle - Goat - Horse - Pig - Sheep. Types and
varieties are arranged A-Z within each group. Bold type for important
and recognized breeds (*e.g.* Holstein). Incorrect forms, misspellings or
definite misnomers are included. Bibliography, p.267-73. An

....(contd.)

invaluable source of information on breeds and the correct or
recommended spelling of breed names in English. *Class No:* 636.1/
.5(038)

Histories

[5866]

DAVIS, S.J.M. The Archaeology of animals. London, Batsford, 1987.
224p. illus., facsims., diagrs., tables, maps. £19.99. ISBN:
0713445718.

Part 1 (chapters 1-4): Methods and problems in zoo-archaeology -
Part 2 (chapters 5-8): 5. Our hunting; 6. From hunter to herder: the
origin of domestic animals; 7. Later domesticates and the secondary
use of animals; 8. Britain: a zoo-archaeological case study. Over 150
drawings. References, p.197-208. Index, p.215-24 (most entries are
for goat, pig and sheep). 'Intended primarily for students of
archaeology and anyone with an interst in both natural history and the
history of our own species' (*Introduction*). *Class No:* 636.1/.5(091)

[5867]

**HALL, S.J.G. *and* CLUTTON-BROCK, J. Two hundred years of
British farm livestock.** London, British Museum (Natural History),
1989. 272p. illus. (some col.). £21.95. ISBN: 0565010778.

19 sections: 1. Introduction - 2. Western and northern cattle ... 7.
Channel Island cattle ... 14. Upland sheep ... 16. Goats ... 18. Heavy
draught horses - 19. Light horses, ponies and donkeys. Bibliography,
p.256-62. Attractively presented, with many colour illustrations of the
breeds. For public and academic libraries. *Class No:* 636.1/.5(091)

[5868]

ZEUNER, F.E. A History of domesticated animals. London,
Hutchinson, 1962. 560p. illus., diagrs., tables.

Part 1: The origins and evolution of domestication - Part 2.
Domesticated animals (pre-agricultural phase; agricultural phase;
subsequent domestication primarily for transport and labour; the pest-
destroyers; various other mammals; birds, fishes and insects).
Bibliography, p.509-37 (authors, A-Z). Index (very brief entries)
p.539-60. *Geographical review* (v. 54(1), January 1964) notes the
many and often unusual illus., but cites examples of extreme brevity of
treatment. 'When it is good, it is very, very good, and when it is bad,
it is horrid'. *Class No:* 636.1/.5(091)

[5869]

—**ANGRESS, S. *and* REED, C.A. 'An Annotated bibliography on the
origin and descent of domestic animals, 1900-1955'. In *Fieldiana
anthropology*, v.54(1). Chicago, Natural History Museum, 1962.
143p.

Systematically arranged, with concrete but apposite annotations.
Class No: 636.1/.5(091)

[5870]

—**CLUTTON-BROCK, J. The Natural history of domesticated mammals.**
London, British Museum (Natural History), 1987. 192p. illus. (incl.
col.). £9.95. ISBN: 0565010506.

Previously as hardback *Domesticated animals from early times*
(1981).

A popular account of how our familiar domestic breeds of mammals
were developed from their wild ancestors. *Class No:* 636.1/.5(091)

Great Britain

[5871]

TROW-SMITH, R. A History of British livestock husbandry to 1700.
London, Routledge & Kegan Paul, 1957. x, 286p. *Class No:* 636.1/
.5(410)

[5872]

—**A History of British livestock husbandry, 1700-1900.** London,
Routledge & Kegan Paul, 1959. x, [1], 351p.

The first work to deal specifically with the evolution of British
breeds of farm animal and the technique of animal husbandry. The
earlier volume has a list of principal sources (p.259-71) and an
analytical index (p.273-86). The later volume also has a bibliography
(p.327-39), but the index (p.341-51) could be fuller. *Class No:* 636.1/
.5(410)

Horses & Ponies

Bibliographies

[5873]

**GRIMSHAW, A. The Horse: a bibliography of British books, 1851-
1976,** with a narrative commentary on the role of the horse in British
social history, as revealed by the contemporary literature. London,
Library Association, 1983. xxxiv, 474p. illus., facsims. £29.95. ISBN:
0853655332.

Initially a limited ed., 1982.

3,226 entries, arranged chronologically in six periods. Limited to
books and pamphlets published in Britain, 1851-1976, but including

....(contd.)
American reprints and translations. 'Great riding schools of the world' has 1½ columns of annotation. Sources, p.x. Title and author indexes. 'The book meets a long-felt need and does it very well' (*Natural history book reviews*, v.7(3), 1984, p.29). *Class No:* 636.1(01)

Encyclopaedias & Dictionaries

[5874]
BONGIANNI, M. **The Macdonald encyclopedia of horses.** Milan, Arnoldo Mondadori Editore; London, Macdonald, 1988. 255p. illus. (col.), figs. £8.95. ISBN: 0356153193.
173 entries, each with a colour photograph. Data include breed name, place of origin, aptitudes, qualities, temperament, conformation. 3 sections: Light draft, pack and saddle breeds - Heavy draft breeds - Ponies. Introduction, p.10-41, includes sections on coats, head markings, stance. Brief bibliography, and index. For public libraries. *Class No:* 636.1(03)

[5875]
HOPE, C.E.G. *and* JACKSON, G.N., *eds*. **The Encyclopedia of the horse.** London, Ebury Press/ Pelham Books, 1973. 336p. illus., maps.
121 contributors. Entries (signed), A-Z (broad headings), cover all aspects, including show jumping, associations, breeds, biographies, and the horse in prehistoric art. Occasional references appended to articles. Over 300 black-and-white illus. and 32 unusually fine colour plates; clear diagrams. A handsome quarto. 'An exceptionally good book', comments *British book news* (December 1973, p.817), while objecting to the double columns of small print. *Class No:* 636.1(03)

[5876]
Illustrated dictionary of equine terms. Loveland, Colo., Alpine Publications, 1998. iv,298p. illus. $29.95. ISBN: 1577790146.
Clear, concise definitions covering training, behavioural, veterinary, nutritional, equipment, and anatomical terms. Pronunciation is given. 'Libraries that plan to buy only one equine dictionary should get this one' (*Choice*, December 1998, p.667). *Class No:* 636.1(03)

[5877]
ROSSDALE, P.D. *and* WREFORD, S.M. **The Horse's health, from A to Z.** Newton Abbot, Devon, David & Charles, 1974 (reprinted 1989). 433p. illus., tables. £18. ISBN: 0715392662.
An encyclopaedic dictionary (*e.g.* tables of muscles, p.265-77; drug manufacturers (British, Irish, US), p.429-32). Notes relevant associations and cites regulations re quarantine, etc. Includes abbreviations, cross-references. Etymology, p.12-13. References and further reading, p.433. *Class No:* 636.1(03)

Handbooks & Manuals

[5878]
EDWARDS, E.H., *general ed*. **A Standard guide to horse and pony breeds.** London, Macmillan, 1980. 352p. illus. (incl. col.). ISBN: 0333266498.
Main sequence (p.69-336) describes 150 horse and pony breeds in 5 geographical areas: Europe (p.69-258), South America, Australia, Soviet Union (p.275-326), Middle East and Asia. 'Breed description' includes height, colour, type, action and temperament. 'The Arab horse and extinct breeds are considered separately. 'The World's principal horse organizations', p.344-6. Detailed, non-analytical index. 350 photographs (100 in colour). *Class No:* 636.1(035)

[5879]
HAYES, M.H. **Veterinary notes for horse owners:** a manual of horse medicine and surgery. Rossdale, P.D., *ed*. 17th ed. London, Stanley Paul, 1987. viii,740p. illus. £30; £18.99. ISBN: 009173701x.
First published in 1877.
54 chapters (7. The skin and its diseases). 3 appendices, *e.g.* 1. Proprietary medicines. Detailed analytical index, p.712-40. 108 illus. *Class No:* 636.1(035)

Cattle

[5880]
FELIUS, M. **Cattle breeds: an encyclopedia.** Doetinchem, C. Misset bv, 1995. 799p. illus. (col.),maps. ISBN: 9054390174.
Describes over 700 breeds. Breeds are arranged geographically into 16 groups, *e.g.* six European groups, four Asian groups. The excellent illustrations (some of which are paintings) placed throughout the text and distribution maps increase the value of this attractively produced book. *Class No:* 636.2

[5881]
PORTER, V. **Cattle: a handbook to the breeds of the world.** London, Christopher Helm, 1991. 400p. illus. (col. pl.), maps. £39.95. ISBN: 0713680008.
7 sections: The cattle of Europe - Tropical cattle - The cattle of Africa - The cattle of Asia - The buffaloes - The cattle of America - The cattle of Australia and New Zealand. 6 appendices (1. Metrication table ... 3. Cattle breeds and their synonyms ... 6. Useful addresses). Bibliography. Index, p.392-400. Data for each breed include development, physical characteristics, historical and current role, special characteristics and, for the major breeds, a detailed history. Beautifully illustrated. Good value. *Class No:* 636.2

Sheep and Goats

[5882]
BERGER, P. **Goats: a bibliography.** Tiverton, L.R. Enterprise, 1998. iv,146p. £12.50. ISBN: 0953049809.
Lists books, booklets, pamphlets, and leaflets which are not only solely about goats but which also include goat sections. Some entries have brief annotations. *Class No:* 636.3

[5883]
Directory of current research on sheep and goats. King, J.W.B., *ed*. Wallingford, Oxon., CAB International, 1988. 271p. £13.95. ISBN: 0851986110.
International in scope, arranged A-Z by country, Argentina ... Zimbabwe. Data include address of organization, names of research workers, main sheep projects, main goat projects, and list of publications. Indexes of research works, goat projects and sheep projects. *Class No:* 636.3

[5884]
PORTER, V. **Goats of the world.** Ipswich, Farming Press, 1996. 179p. illus. (col.), maps. £24.95. ISBN: 0852363478.
Contains 'Wild goats and domestication, p.1-8, followed by a geographical arrangement: Britain, p.9-29, Scandinavia, p.30-4, etc. Distribution maps and colour plates (not photographs). Bibliography and index. Light, accessible, writing style. *Class No:* 636.3

[5885]
RYDER, M.L. **Sheep and man.** London, Duckworth, 1983. ix, [1], 846p. illus., diagrs., tables. £55. ISBN: 0715616552.
3 parts (14 chapters, each with contents and summary): 1. Ancient times - 2. The Middle Ages to recent times - 3. The association of man with sheep. Epilogue: 'Has the sheep come to the end of the world?' Appendix: 7 columns of data, p.785-801. References (A-Z authors), p.802-29. Very detailed, partly analytical index, p.830-46 ('Wool': 1 column, solid). *Class No:* 636.3

[5886]
Sheep and goat production. Coop, J.E., *ed*. Amsterdam, etc., Elsevier, 1982. xiii, 492p. diagrs., tables. $164. (*World animal series, C1.*) ISBN: 0444419896.
25 documented chapters (1. Ecology and distribution - 2. Breeding ... 7. Nutrition and diseases ... 12. Wool grading and marketing ... 15. Milk production in sheep and goats ... 16. Systems [of grazing] ... 25. Village and smallholding systems). 27 contributors; biographical notes, p.481-4. Subject index, p.485-92. Quarto. *Class No:* 636.3

Pigs

[5887]
Index of current research on pigs. Wallingford, Oxon., CAB International, 1960-. Annual. £48; $110. ISSN: 05652800.
No. 45, 1999 has *c.*5,000 references, arranged geographically. 49 countries are covered, with data including contact names, postal and e-mail addresses, etc. Author and subject indexes. *Class No:* 636.4

[5888]
PORTER, V. **Pigs: a handbook to the breeds of the world.** Mountfield, Helm; Ithaca, N.Y., Comstock Publishing Associates, 1993. 256p. illus. maps. $35. ISBN: 080142920x.
Data on over 190 breeds and species worldwide. 24 colour plates. Appendices contain synonyms, and information on breeding companies and extinct breeds. Distribution maps for Asia, Southeast Asia, the Americas, and Europe. Index is in very small type. *Class No:* 636.4

[5889]
WISEMAN, J. **A History of the British pig.** London, Duckworth, 1986. ix, 118p. illus., facsims., diagrs., tables. ISBN: 071561987x.
8 chapters: 1. The Anglo-Saxon and medieval pig ... 8. The proliferation of breeds ... 8. Recent developments and the role of minority breeds. Bibliography, p.113-6. Detailed, analytical index, p.117-8. Charmingly illustrated with old engravings and new photographs, but too short and lacking detail (*TLS*, 20 June 1986, p.685). *Class No:* 636.4

Poultry

[5890]

British poultry standards: complete specifications and judging points of all standardized breeds and varieties of poultry as compiled by the specialist Breed Clubs and recognized by the Poultry Club of Great Britain. Roberts, V., *ed.* 5th ed. Oxford, Poultry Club of Great Britain and Blackwell Science, 1997. viii, 368p. illus.(most col.). £39.50. ISBN: 0632040521.

First published in 1954.

This fifth edition carries colour photographs for the first time. *Class No:* 636.5

[5891]

Multi-lingual poultry dictionary, English-French-German-Spanish. Forscey, L.A., *comp.* Bologna, European Federation of Branches of the World's Poultry Science Association, 1969. [x], 356p.

About 3,000 terms, English base terms, p.2-69; French, German and Spanish equivalents and indexes. Monolingual English, French, German and Spanish glossaries follow. Genders are stated. *Class No:* 636.5

[5892]

Poultry abstracts. Wallingford, Oxon., CAB International, 1975-. 12pa. £252; $560. ISSN: 03661382.

About 3,000 abstracts pa. Coverage includes: Nutrition; Breeding and genetics; Egg production; Housing and equipment; Anatomy, physiology and biochemistry; Parasitic diseases; Nutritional and metabolic disorders; Pharmacology and therapeutics; Welfare and behaviour. Reports. Conferences. Books. Author and subject indexes per issue and annually.

Online, CAB ABSTRACTS. Available on CAB ABSTRACTS CD-ROM and BEASTCD. *Class No:* 636.5

Pets

[5893]

DIAGRAM GROUP. Pets: every owner's encyclopedia. London & New York, Paddington Press, 1978. 431p. illus.

7 sections: 1. Dogs; cats; mustelids (ferrets, skunks); rabbits; rodents; horses, ponies, donkeys; artiodactyls (goats, sheep, etc.) Wild mammals - 2. Fish (p.176-223) - 3. Invertebrates - 4. Amphibians (*e.g.* frogs) - 5. Reptiles - 6. Birds - 7. Conservation. Reference (including classification). Further reading (p.422-3). Index, p.424-31. Comprehensive, covering selection, handling, care, food and feeding, housing and equipment, illness, breeding and showing. *Class No:* 636.596/.9

[5894]

Small animals. Wallingford, Oxon., CAB International. Annual. £55; $93 (1995 ed.).

Formerly published as *Small animal abstracts: annotated bibliography.*

Contains *c.*2,000 abstracts pa. Covers the research literature on diseases, physiology, reproduction, nutrition and behaviour of dogs, cats, and other pets. Online, CAB ABSTRACTS. Available on CAB ABSTRACTS CD-ROM and BEASTCD. *Class No:* 636.596/.9

Doves & Pigeons

[5895]

GOODWIN, D. Pigeons and doves of the world. 3rd ed. London, British Museum (Natural History), with Ithaca, New York, Cornell Univ. Press, 1983. 363p. illus. (incl. col. pl.), maps. £25. ISBN: 0565008471.

First published 1967 (vi, 446p).

10 chapters (1. Nomenclature, genera, species, sub-species, varieties and breeds ... 3. Coloration and plumage ... 5. Maintenance behaviour ... 7. Display and social behaviour). 24 sections, each with readings. Index of English names. Index of scientific names. *Class No:* 636.596

Cage & Aviary Birds

[5896]

Encyclopedia of aviculture. Translated from the Dutch. Rutgers, A. *and* Norris, K.A., *eds.* Poole, Dorset, Blandford Press, 1970-77. 3v. £40ea. ISBN: 071370800x, v.1; 0713708018, v.2; 0713708026, v.3.

V.1 (414p.) deals mainly with aquatic species, birds of prey, pheasants, pigeons and doves. V.2 (290p.), with parrots, budgerigars, cuckoos, nightjars, humming birds and owls. The *Passeriformes* order occupies most of v.3 (241p.), with numerous varieties of canaries and finches. The *Encyclopedia* concludes with a bibliography of 160 items, and indexes of English and Latin names. It provides a wealth of information on captive birds, their adaptability and care of them. 44 col. illus. depict *c.*260 species (based on review in *Library review,* v.28, Spring 1979, p.53-54). *Class No:* 636.68

[5897]

The Handbook of cage and aviary birds. Alderton, D., *ed.* Revised ed. London, Blandford, 1996. iv,364p. £9.99. ISBN: 0713726547.

First published 1993.

Main text (p.49-356) describes species: Quail, partridges and pheasants - Pigeons and doves - Waterfowl - Parrots - Finches, toucans and related species. Preceding sections look at aviary accommodation, aviary furnishings, food and diet, stock, breeding, and health. Indexes of common and Latin names. 259 colour photographs *Class No:* 636.68

[5898]

MARTIN, R.M. The Dictionary of aviculture: keeping and breeding birds. London, Batsford, 1983. xi, 227, [1]p. illus., tables, maps. ISBN: 0713441569.

Entries 'Acclimatization ... Zygodactyol'. 'Starling': nearly 2p., with 5 identification drawings. Many cross-references. 93 illus. Appended: 'Books mentioned in the text'. Chiefly concerned with the study and breeding in captivity of wild bird species (*i.e.* it excludes pigeons, commercial domesticated forms, etc.). *Class No:* 636.68

[5899]

WOOLHAM, F. The Handbook of aviculture. Poole, Dorset, Blandford Press, 1987. 368p. col. illus. ISBN: 071371428x.

Devotes part 1 to 'general care' (diets; housing; breeding; disease and medicine; the law and ethics). Part 2. 'The birds', p.67-359: Rheinformes ... Passeriformes, provides data on range, status, etc. Appendix: Principal authorities responsible for licensing (Argentina ... USA). Bibliography, p.362. Indexes of scientific and common names. *Class No:* 636.68

Dogs

[5900]

AMERICAN KENNEL CLUB. The Complete dog book: the photograph, history and official standard of every breed admitted to AKC registration, and the selection, training, breeding, care and feeding of pure-bred dogs. 17th ed. New York, Howell Book House, 1985. 768p. illus. (incl. col.). ISBN: 0876054629.

First published 1929, 16th ed. 1980 (768p.).

Groups: 1. Sporting dogs - 2. Hounds - 3. Working dogs - 4. Terriers - 5. Toys - 6. Non-sporting dogs. Subdivided by breeds, with colour displays for each group. 'Caring for your dog', p.643-740. Glossary, p.741-64. Index.

18th ed., 1992. 832p. $27.50. *Class No:* 636.7

[5901]

JONES, E.G. A Bibliography of the dog: books published in the English language, 1570-1965. London, Library Association, 1971. 431p.

Based on a thesis accepted for Library Association Fellowship.

3,986 references, wth locations of titles in 4 libraries (including British Museum and Kennel Club). 19 classes: A. General works - B. Natural history - C. Domestication ... J. The dog at work ... R. The dog in literature - 5. The dog in children's literature ... W. Breeds. Full sub-titles are given. Index of names and titles; index of subjects. Chronological list, 1570-1850. *Class No:* 636.7

[5902]

MARDER, A. *and* **HORWITZ, D. Collins complete dog owner's manual.** London, HarperCollins, 1997. 224p. illus.(col.) £16.99. ISBN: 0004133188.

Six sections: You and your dog; Health care; Training your dog; Breeding and showing; A guide to breeds (details of the 100 most popular breeds of dog; Further information (contains a glossary, index, and brief infromation directory). For public libraries. *Class No:* 636.7

[5903]

SCANZIANI, P. The British encyclopedia of dogs. London, Orbis, 1985. 304p. illus. ISBN: 0856135755.

Illustrated guide to dog breeds - Classification of dogs and breeds - A/Z of breeds, p.43-199 - Dogs: their psychology and uses - Training, p.221-96. Boxed information on offical classification, country of origin, weight, coat, etc. Further reading, p.297-8. Detailed, analytical index. 270 well-coloured illus. *Class No:* 636.7

[5904]

WILCOX, B. *and* **WALKOWICZ, C. Atlas of dog breeds of the world.** Neptune City, NJ, TFH Publications, 1989. 912p. illus. ISBN: 0866229302.

First section contains essays on different types of dogs, *e.g.* scenthounds, mastiffs, terriers, gun dogs. The second part consists of alphabetically arranged entries for 400 breeds of dogs worldwide. Affenpinscher ... Yugoslavian Hounds. Entries consist of country of origin, size, description of coat and colour, groups with which it can be registered, and the larger category to which it belongs. Glossary, extensive bibliography and index. More than 1,000 excellent photographs illustrating each breed. It is more comprehensive than *The Complete dog book* (Howell Book House, 1989) (*q.v.*). *Class No:* 636.7

Cats

[5905]

BI-Lexikon Rassekatzen. [Dictionary of pedigree cats.] Muller-Girard, C., *and others*. Leipzig, VEB Bibliographisches Institut, 1988. 495p. illus. (some col.), figs.

Illustrated descriptions of many cat breeds. Also includes information on genetics, diseases, management, reproduction, physiology, and behaviour. 49 colour photographs. Extensive bibliography. For cat breeders and fanciers. *Class No:* 636.8

[5906]

EDNEY, A. RSPCA complete cat care manual. London, Dorling Kindersley, 1992. 192p. col.illus. ISBN: 0863188567.

10 chapters: 1. Introducing the cat - 2. Basic care - 3. Feeding ... 7. Nursing ... 10. Nursing. Index, p.188-9. Many colour illustrations. A clearly presented practical guide. For public libraries. *Class No:* 636.8

[5907]

MORRIS, D. Cat world: a feline encyclopedia. London, Ebury Press, 1996. 496p. illus.(col.) £30. ISBN: 0091820308.

A detailed overview which includes items on history, folklore, breeds, famous cats, etc. Health matters are deliberately excluded. Many bibliographies, including the author's selection of 'The 100 best cat books', and colour photographs. *Class No:* 636.8

[5908]

—FOGLE, B. The Encyclopedia of the cat. London, Dorling Kindersley, 1997. 240p. illus.,figs. £20; $34.95. ISBN: 078941970x.

Includes chapters on behaviour, breeds, and care. Index. Glossary. Brief bibliography. Many illustrations. For public libraries. *Class No:* 636.8

[5909]

NECKER, C. Four centuries of cat books, 1570-1970. Metuchen, N.J., Scarecrow Press, 1972. 511p.

Briefly annotated entries, with extensive cross-references. 'A detailed and comprehensive bibliography of books on cats in English. Limited to the domestic cat, with a few books on the cat family' (*Library journal,* 13 December 1972, p.3980-1). *Class No:* 636.8

[5910]

A Standard guide to cat breeds. Pond, G. *and* Raleigh, I., *eds.* London, Macmillan, 1979. 318p. illus. (incl. col.). £12.95. ISBN: 0333240420.

5 contributors. A general section concerns feline genetics, coat colours and patterns, eye colours. Glossary. Shorthair cats, p.38-177. Longhair cats, p.179-231. Appendices include such matters as show preparation, show rules, breeding, medicine and behaviour. Detailed, non-analytical index. Well illustrated. *Class No:* 636.8

Dairy Farming

[5911]

RUSSELL, K. The Principles of dairy farming. 11th ed., revised by K. Slater. Ipswich, Farming Press, 1991. v,359p. illus., tables. £13.95. ISBN: 0852362161.

First published 1953.

17 chapters: (1. The milk industry ... 3. Buildings and equipment ... 13. Breeding better cows ... 15. Disease in dairy herds ... 17. Profitability in milk production). 5 appendices (1. Breed comparison according to milk yield, butterfat and protein levels). Detailed, analytical index. Fully illustrated. No bibliography. A basic textbook. *Class No:* 637

Dairy Produce

[5912]

Dairy science abstracts. Wallingford, Oxon., CAB International, 1939-. 12pa. £440; $995. ISSN: 00115681.

7,500 abstracts pa. Subject areas covered include: Husbandry; Milk production; Technology; Physiology; Biochemistry; Nutrition; Immunology; Microbiology; Chemistry; Physics; Economics; Legislation and standards; Milk and public health; Dairy research; Education. Reports; Conferences; Books. Author and subject index per issue and annually. Online, CAB ABSTRACTS. Available on CAB ABSTRACTS CD-ROM and BEASTCD. *Class No:* 637.1

[5913]

Dairy vocabulary / Dictionnaire laitier/Milchwirtschaftliches Wörterbuch. Edited under the auspices of the International Dairy Federation. Munich, VV-GmbH Volkswirtschaftlicher Verlag, 1988. 596p.

First published 1963 as *Dairy dictionary.*

Over 6,000 entry-words in 3 sequences: English-French-German, French-German-English, German-French-English. Genders of French and German nouns stated. Editors and other contributors are either agriculturists or dairy science specialists. *Class No:* 637.1

[5914]

Dictionary of dairy terminology, in English, French, German and Spanish. 2nd ed. Amsterdam, Elsevier, 1996. 376p. ISBN: 0444896449.

First published 1983.

*c.*4,000 English-based terms (with explanations, as considered necessary), with equivalents and indexes in French, German and Spanish. An important tool. *Class No:* 637.1

[5915]

—Milk and milk products. Rome, FAO, 1979. 95p. ISBN: 925007582.

In three languages - French, English and Spanish. Bibliography, p.93-5. *Class No:* 637.1

[5916]

RENNER, E. Grosse Molkerei Lexikon. [Encyclopaedia of milk.] Munich, Volkswirtschaftlicher Verlag, 1988. 418p. tables.

New edition of *Grosse Molkerei-Lexikon* (Schulz & Voss, 1965).

3,530 entries, arranged A-Z, and 40 tables. Has a wider coverage of dairy science than the previous edition. Bibliography contains 104 references. Revised English ed. published 1991 as *Dictionary of milk and dairying* (Munich, VV-GmbH Volkswirtschaftlicher Verlag. 384p.). *Class No:* 637.1

Cheese

[5917]

ANDROUET, P. Guide to world cheeses. Githens, J., *tr.* English ed., revised. Henley-on-Thames, Oxon., Aidan Ellis, 1983. [v],561p. ISBN: 0856291794.

First published 1973. French title as *Guide du fromage.*

12 chapters (*e.g.* 4. Selecting cheeses by flavour and season; 8. Dictionary of cheese, p.159-471; 9. Special cheeses and non-French cheeses; 12. Some cheeses to try outside France). 'New cheeses', p.549-61. Glossary, p.519-41. Descriptions of *c.*500 varieties, highlighting French cheeses.

2nd ed. published as *Cheese guide* in 1988. (551p. £15). *Class No:* 637.3

[5918]

DAVIS, J.G. Cheese. London, J. & A. Churchill, 1965-76. 4v.

1. *Basic technology,* 1965. viii, 463p. 2. *Annotated bibliography, with subject index.* [viii], 275p. 3. *Manufacturing methods.* 1976. [iv], p.465-1012. 4. *Scientific aspects, with supplementary annotated bibliography.* 264p.

V.1 (19 chapters, with references) has 4 parts: 1. Introductory - 2. Milk - 3. Materials and equipment in cheesemaking - 4. After-treatment of cheese. V.2: 6,803 items; very briefly annotated, with analytical subject index. V.3 is a well-illustrated international survey of some 800 varieties of cheese. V.4 supplements v.2. The standard treatise on cheese, but now somewhat dated. *Class No:* 637.3

[5919]

EEKHOF-STORK, N. The World atlas of cheese. London, Paddington Press, 1976. 240p. illus., maps. ISBN: 0844701332.

Offers a tour of cheese-making regions of the world, plus a history and contemporary survey of cheeses and their manufacture. 50 international recipes; hints on purchase, storage and serving of cheese. 600 full-colour photos accompany the 240p. Atlas. *Class No:* 637.3

[5920]

FOX, P.F. Cheese: chemistry, physics and microbiology. First published 1987. London, Chapman and Hall, 1993. 2v. £330(set);£159ea. ISBN: 0412535009, v.1; 0412535106, v.2; 0412582309, set.

V.1. *General aspects.* xii,601p. V.2. *Major cheese groups.* xiii,577p.

Many revisions and updates from the previous ed. An authoritative technical study, aimed at the cheese-manufacturer, or agricultural/nutritional student, rather than the gourmet. *Class No:* 637.3

Beekeeping

[5921]
Apicultural abstracts: a journal of the International Bee Research Association. Cardiff, the Association, 1950-. Quarterly. £140; $245. ISSN: 0003648x.

About 360 abstracts per issue. UDC classification. Sections. Chemical aspects ... Various entomolygical aspects ... Apoidea, except *Apis-Apis*. Honeybee species ... Bee forage ... Rearing and rearing honeybees, including queens ... Honeybee diseases ... Honey - Beeswax - Honeybees as pollinators - Rearing bees, except honeybees. Annual author and subject indexes. *Index, 1950-72* (2v. 1976.). Online CAB ABSTRACTS. *Class No:* 638.1

[5922]
—CRANE, E. Bibliographical tools in apiculture. London, International Bee Research Association, 1984. 20p. ISBN: 0860981355. *Class No:* 638.1

[5923]
—CRANE, E. Bibliography of tropical apiculture. London, International Bee Research Association, 1978. 38 parts, maps. ISBN: 0860980760, v.2; 0860980308, v.1.

Also available in 2v. V.1 (1978. £30) contains pts.1-24; v.2 (1980. £25), pts.25-38.

Covers regions and topics (*e.g.* 2. *Beekeeping in Africa South of the Sahara*, with 346 references; 22. *Bees for pollination in the tropics*). *Class No:* 638.1

[5924]
British bee books: a bibliography, 1500-1976. London, International Bee Research Association, 1979. 270p. illus., facsims. £20. ISBN: 0860980774.

Records *c.*836 printed books and 12 manuscripts. 5 sections; the first lists libraries and beekeeping collections, and 'Publications with useful bibliographical information'. Other sections: Manuscripts before 1500; Chronological list of books (6 periods, 1500/1599 - 1900/1926); Another bibliography for the last fifty years, 1927 to 1976; Metaphorical titles; Books on special categories (*e.g.* in verse). Indexes of short titles, authors, special subjects. *Class No:* 638.1

[5925]
CRANE, E. Bees and beekeeping: science, practice and world resources. Oxford, Heinemann Newnes, 1990. xii,614p. illus., figs., tables. £95. ISBN: 0434902713.

6 sections: 1. The bees used in beekeeping, and background information - 2. Beekeeping with movable-frame hives - 3. Beekeeping with simpler and cheaper hives - 4. Maintaining honeybee health - 5. Honeybees' plant resources, and products from the hive - 6. Beekeepers. 2 appendices: 1. Important world honey sources and their geographical distribution - 2. Beekeeping gazetteer of individual countries. Bibliography, p.539-93. Plant, geographical name, and subject indexes. The author is a former Director of the International Bee Research Association and one of the foremost authorities on beekeeping and honey. With its readable text and clear illustrations, this book is essential for any library covering this area. *Class No:* 638.1

[5926]
Dictionary of beekeeping terms, with allied scientific terms. Crane, E., *ed.* Cardiff, International Bee Research Association. ISBN: 0860981940.

A series of English-base foreign-language dictionaries by the editor, on beekeeping terms. V.11 (1993. iv,193p.) gives translations of 1,036 terms from and into English, Hindi, Chinese, with Latin index. *Class No:* 638.1

[5927]
HUANG, W.C. Honey bee science. Beijing, Chinese Academy of Agricultural Sciences, 1993. 428p. illus. ISBN: 7109024911.

Entries are in Chinese with an English heading in brackets. Bibliography; list of scientific names in English, with Chinese equivalents. Chinese and English indexes. Many illustrations. *Class No:* 638.1

[5928]
MORSE, R.A. *and* HOOPER, T. The Illustrated encyclopedia of beekeeping. Poole, Dorset, Blandford Press, 1985. 432p. illus., ports., diagrs., tables, maps. ISBN: 071371624x.

46 contributors. Entries, A-Z, include some 30 biographies. The article 'Honey, food and drink products' (p.191-2) has references in text; 'Swarm behaviour and movement', p.370-2. Annotated glossary of anatomical terms. References from text to col. illus. Analytical index, p.427-32. Outstanding illus. Comprehensive and up-to-date. *Class No:* 638.1

Fish & Fisheries

Bibliographies

[5929]
Current references in fish research. Chippewa Falls, Wisc., Current References in Fish Research, 1976-. Annual. $20. ISSN: 0739540x.

Lists *c.*4,000 references pa. from more than 100 scientific titles. No particular order of entry. First author, second author, and keyword indexes. *Class No:* 639.2(01)

[5930]
Guide to reference works on marine science and fisheries. Shaw, M.J., *comp.* Lowestoft, Directorate of Fisheries Research, 1981. 78p.

Earlier as *Some books on fisheries and marine science*. K.G. Handley and M. Shaw, editors. 1980. 33p. (Library Information leaflet no.22).

122 annotated entries. 6 sections: Indexes abstracts and contents lists - Bibliographies - Catalogues of the publications of, or taken by, specific organizations - Review publications - Directories - Dictionaries, encyclopedias, glossaries, handbooks, name lists, etc. Author or editor index. Title index. *Class No:* 639.2(01)

[5931]
TURNBULL, D. Keyguide to information sources in aquaculture. London, Mansell, 1989. xvi,137p. £35. ISBN: 0720118530.

International in scope. 3 sections: 1. Survey of aquaculture and its literature - 2. Bibliography (p.11-78; 472 references, most with annotations) - 3. Directory of organizations. Index, p.119-37, lists books, periodicals, databases, and organizations. As most of the publications listed are from 1980 onwards, this is a good guide to current literature in the subject. *Class No:* 639.2(01)

Handbooks & Manuals

[5932]
CRC handbook of mariculture. McVey, J.P., *ed.* Boca Raton, Fla., CRC Press, 1991-93. 2v. $195, v.1; $159.95, v.2. (*CRC series in marine science.*) ISBN: 0849302552, v.1; 0849302196, v.2.

V.1 *Crustacean aquaculture.* 1993. 2nd ed. V.2. *Finfish aquaculture.* 1991. 256p.

V.1 has 4 sections: 1. Larval foods for crustaceans - 2. Maturation, spawning hatchery and grow-out techniques for crustaceans - 3. Pathology and disease treatments for crustaceans - 4. Crustacean nutrition. V.2 covers marine finfish culture in Europe, Japan, Taiwan and the US. Each chapter in the set has a bibliography appended. *Class No:* 639.2(035)

[5933]
CRESSWELL, R.L. Aquaculture desk reference. New York, Van Nostrand Reinhold, 1993. 206p. illus. ISBN: 0442010818.

Highly technical reference work 'which will alleviate the need for an extensive personal library to access basic information useful for practicing aquaculturalists' (*Preface*). Easy access to information for planning aquaculture projects and for day-to-day operation of aquaculture facilities, *e.g.* Table 4.37: 'Concentrations of some drugs used to tranquilize fish for transport'. Bibliography, p.183-206. *Class No:* 639.2(035)

Dictionaries

[5934]
FRIMODT, C. Multilingual illustrated guide to the world's commercial coldwater fish. Oxford, Fishing News Books, 1995. xix,244p. illus.,maps. £39.95. ISBN: 0852382138. *Class No:* 639.2(038)

[5935]
—FRIMODT, C. Multilingual illustrated guide to the world's commercial warmwater fish. Oxford, Fishing News Books, 1995. xix,240p. illus.,maps. £39.95. ISBN: 0852382146.

These two volumes cover over 300 species of finfish worldwide. Highlights of every species description are given in Danish, German, Spanish, French, and Italian. Data include names (in up to 18 languages), local names, maps, and nutrition information. Colour illustration of each fish. Bibliography and index. *Class No:* 639.2(038)

[5936]

Multilingual dictionary of fish and fish products / ... Danish, Dutch, English, Finnish, French, German, Greek, Icelandic, Italian, Japanese, Norwegian, Polish, Portuguese, Russian, Serbo-Croatian, Spanish, Swedish, and Turkish. [Dictionnaire multilingue des poissons et produits de la pêche.] 4th ed. Oxford, Fishing News Books Ltd., 1995. xv,352p. £29.50. ISBN: 0852382162.

First published 1968 (xv, 427p.).

Over 1,200 entries, giving scientific names, with equivalents and indexes in the other 16 languages. Brief notes included (*e.g.* Latin name; where found; family; marketing form of product; fresh, dried, frozen, smoked, etc.- in English, and French). Separate indices for scientific names. *Class No:* 639.2(038)

[5937]

—EUROPEAN PARLIAMENT. Terminology Office. **Terminologie du secteur de la pêche.** 3. éd. Luxembourg, the Parliament, 1977. [160]p.

First published 1967.

Comprises 291 French-base terms (with sub-entries) and equivalents in Italian, English, German, Dutch and Danish, - covering the then 6 official languages of the European Communities. Appended list of fish, crustaceans and molluscs. *Class No:* 639.2(038)

[5938]

RICKER, W.E. **Russian-English dictionary for students of fisheries & aquatic biology.** Ottawa, Department of the Environment, Fisheries Research Board, 1973. xi, 428p. (*Bulletin no.163.*)
Class No: 639.2(038)

[5939]

Selected terms in fish culture, English-French-Spanish-Arabic (with Latin for names of fish and fish diseases). [Choix de termes de pisciculture.] Rome, FAO, 1981. vii,151p. $20. (*FAO Terminology bulletin 22.*) ISBN: 9250009100.

First published 1972.

Basic list, with language equivalents. Bibliography, p.148-9.
Class No: 639.2(038)

Glossaries

[5940]

Aqualex: a glossary of aquaculture terms. Eleftheriou, M., *and others.* Chichester, Wiley, 1997. xiii, 397p. £75. ISBN: 0471978019.

2,742 definitions (from 'Abalone' to 'Zygote') of interest to fish farmers and aquatic biologists, and arranged in English, French, German, and Greek. Indexes (p.344-97) in these four languages; English index appears duplicatory. Landscape format; library or office use only. *Class No:* 639.2(038.1)

Reviews & Abstracts

[5941]

Aquatic sciences and fisheries abstracts. Part 1: Biological sciences and living resources. Bethesda, Md., Cambridge Scientific Abstracts, 1978-. 12pa. $1,045 (US); $1,115 (non US) pa. ISSN: 01405373.

Formerly part of *Aquatic sciences and fisheries abstracts, 1971-77.*

About 24,000 abstracts pa. Classes: 1. General aspects ... 21. Biology: general. 65. Entomology ... 79. Ichthyology ... 92. Ontology ... 98. Mammology - 99. Ecology, ecosystems and pollution ... 199. Fisheries ... 252. Marketing and economics of aquatic products. Author and subject indexes per issue. Draws upon *c.*5,000 primary and other journals. Available on magnetic tape, online and CD-ROM. *Class No:* 639.2(048)

Yearbooks & Directories

[5942]

European directory of research centers in the fisheries sector. Commission of the European Communities, *ed.* 2nd ed. Dordrecht, Kluwer Academic Publishers for the Commission of the European Communities, 1994. viii,616p. ISBN: 0792326911.

Includes non-EC countries such as Finland. Each country's entry begins with a summary on the current 'State of research' followed by a list of that country's institutes. Each entry includes name, address, head, type of institute, research activities, facilities, staff, research budget, description. Research centre index, p.603-16.
Class No: 639.2(058)

Tables & Data Books

[5943]

A Selective annotated bibliography of fishery statistical publications. Food and Agriculture Organization *and* Flood, R.C., *comp.* Rev ed. Rome, Food and Agriculture Organization, 1991. vi, 271p. (*FAO fisheries circular no.813 (Revision 1)..*)

First published 1988.

52 entries added since previous edition. National publications (Algeria ... Zimbabwe), p.1-218. Publications of international bodies, p.219-36. National fishery censuses, surveys, statistical systems,

....(contd.)
p.237-71. Data include: Title, issuing body, place and date of publication, pagination, frequency, notes, FAO call number, summary of contents. *Class No:* 639.2(083)

[5944]

Yearbook of fishery statistics. Rome, FAO, 1948-. tables. Annual (2 parts). tables, maps.

v.71: *Catches and landings, 1993.* 1995. v.72: *Fishery commodities, 1993.* 1995.

V.71 provides data on quantities of fish, crustacea, molluscs, caught and landed (arranged under country, itemised and according to main fishing areas, inland or marine). V.72 concerns disposition of catches, protection and international trade (arranged under county and major types of fishery commodity. Quantity and value statistics for imports and exports. Tables cover 1990/93. *Class No:* 639.2(083)

Freshwater Fishing

[5945]

Aquaculture: the farming and husbandry of freshwater and marine organisms. Bardach, J.E., *and others.* New York, etc., Wiley; Interscience, 1972. xii, [i], 888p. illus., diagrs., graphs, tables. $45. ISBN: 0471648259.

43 documented chapters (1. General principles and economics; 2. Culture of the common carp ... 6. Catfish culture in the United States ... 17. Milkfish culture ... 26. Commercial culture of freshwater salmonids ... 32. Shrimp culture ... 36. Oyster culture (with 2p. of references) ... 42. Culture of seaweeds - 43. Culture of edible freshwater plants). Index of names of animals and plants. Index of persons, places and institutions. Non-analytical subject index.
Class No: 639.2.052.2

[5946]

BERRA, T.M. **An Atlas of distribution of the freshwater fish families of the world.** Lincoln, Nebraska, Univ. of Nebraska Press, 1981. xxx, 197p. illus., maps. ISBN: 0803214111.

Includes a bibliography (p.181-91) and index.
Class No: 639.2.052.2

[5947]

Freshwater and aquaculture contents tables. Rome, Food and Agriculture Organization, 1978-. 12pa.

List contents pages of relevant journals. Appended schedule of future freshwater sciences and aquaculture meetings, conferences, etc. List of journals covered throughout the year (57), plus publishers' addresses. *Class No:* 639.2.052.2

Fishing Gear

[5948]

BRANDT, A., von. **Fish catching methods of the world.** 3rd ed. Farnham, Surrey, Fishing News Books, Ltd., 1984. xiv, 418p. illus., diagrs. £35. ISBN: 0852381255.

First published 1964.

31 detailed chapters (1. Introduction ... 31. Fishing systems and harvesting machines). Includes fishing gear and methods used by small-scale and subsistence-level fishermen. Appended: 'Classification of catching methods'. Bibliography of 690 entries, p.394-406 (A-Z, authors). Detailed, non-analytical subject index; Species and product index; Geographical index. The author was for many years head of Hamburg's Institute for Fishing Technology. *Class No:* 639.2.081

[5949]

Glossary of United Kingdom fishing gear terms. Bridger, J.P., *and others.* Farnham, Surrey, Fishing News Books, Ltd., 1981. xi, 115p. illus. £17.95. ISBN: 0852381190.

Lists more than 1,500 fishing gear terms 'known to be used currently by fishermen and their suppliers in England, Wales, Scotland and Northern Ireland' (*Introduction*). Headings: Term; Locality; Gear type; Definition; Figure. Identifies preferred terms and largely excludes obsolete terms. Appended line-drawings, p.82-114.
Class No: 639.2.081

Deep-Sea Fishing

Handbooks & Manuals

[5950]

Fishermen's handbook. Branson, C.R.P.C., *ed.* 2nd ed. Farnham, Surrey, Fishing News Books, Ltd., 1987. 319p. illus. (some col. pl.). £17.96. ISBN: 0852381433.

6 sections: 1. Management - 2. Navigation - 3. Watchkeeping, shiphandling - 4. Fishing operations - 5. Safety and survival at sea - 6. Anchors and cables-cordage and its uses. 5 appendices (*e.g.* 1. Finding the distance of objects at sea). Useful publications, p.304. Detailed, analytical index. *Class No:* 639.22(035)

[5951]
—Guide to fishing vessels. 1990-91. Ledbury, Herefordshire, Dayton's Publishing, Ltd., 1990. 450p. illus. £65. ISBN: 187104104x.
A compendium, with over 1,000 illus. *Class No:* 639.22(035)

Tables & Data Books

[5952]
UK sea fisheries statistics. London, HMSO, 1919-. tables. ISBN: 011243035x. ISSN: 00726702.
Formerly *Sea fisheries statistical tables*.
The 1996 ed. (viii,154p. £23) has tables covering catches and landings, imports/exports of fish, stock exploitation, world catch figures, etc. Three appendices: 1. Glossary - 2. Development of the UK fishing fleet, 1991 to 1996 3. Time series for select fisheries statistics. *Class No:* 639.22(083)

Maps & Atlases

[5953]
Atlas of the living resources of the seas. 4th ed. Rome, FAO, 1981. 23p. + 60 col. maps (some folded). $115. ISBN: 9250010001.
First published 1971. In English, French and Spanish editions.
Text: Introduction - Productivity of the seas - Exploitation and utilization of resources - Movements and migrations - Topography and nomenclature - Size and distribution of resources - Value of estimates. Alphabetical index of fish names (p.14-23). The maps illustrate geographical and vertical distribution, migration and existing state of exploitation. Oblong. 'A splendid example of the effectiveness of simplicity in compilation' (*Geographical journal*, v.140(1), February 1974, p.161, on 3rd ed., 1972). *Class No:* 639.22(084.3)

Histories

[5954]
SAHRHAGE, D. *and* **LUNDBECK, J. A History of fishing.** Berlin, New York, Springer-Verlag, 1992. viii,348p. illus. ISBN: 3540553320.
Describes origins and general trends in the development of fishing from earliest times. Covers techniques, and economic and social problems. Contains an evaluation of the use of existing stocks of fish worldwide. Bibliography, p.297-332. *Class No:* 639.22(091)

Worldwide

[5955]
Fishes of the north-eastern Atlantic and the Mediterranean. [Poissons de l'Atlantique du nord-est et de la Méditerranée.] Whitehead, P.J.P., *and others, eds.* Paris, Unesco, 1984-86. 3v. figs., maps. $180. ISBN: 9230022152, v.1; 9230023086, v.2; 9230023094, v.3.
A continuation of *Check-list of the fishes of the north-eastern Atlantic and of the Mediterranean* (Unesco, 1973). A fauna of saltwater fish of the palaearctic region. Data on 220 families and 1,250 species. Entries include line-drawings, diagnoses, keys, biological data, synonyms, distribution maps and literature. V.3 contains an additional bibliography to *Check-list of the fishes of the north-eastern Atlantic and the Mediterranean*, p.1415-26, as well as an alphabetical index of common names, p.1429-42, and an alphabetical index of scientific names, p.1443-73. *Class No:* 639.22(100)

Africa—Southern

[5956]
Smith's sea fishes. Smith, M.M. *and* Heemstra, P.C., *eds.* 6th ed. Berlin, Springer-Verlag, 1986. xx,1047p. illus., (incl. col. pl.). $162. ISBN: 0387168516.
First published 1949, as J.L.B. Smith's *The sea fishes of Southern Africa*.
Describes *c.*2,200 species found in the seas around Southern Africa, - about 15% of the total marine fauna of the world. Almost all of the species described are supported by line-drawings. Fin-formula key; index to scientific and common names. Glossary. Extensive bibliography. 'A monumental work of exceptional quality and scholarship' (*Choice*, v.24(10), June 1987, p.1539). *Class No:* 639.22(68)

Whaling

[5957]
TONNESSEN, J.N. *and* **JOHNSEN, A.O. The History of modern whaling.** Translated from Norwegian. Christopherson, R.I., *tr.* London, C. Hurst & Co; Canberra, Australian National Univ. Press. 1982. x, 798p. illus., maps.
A much-shortened version of *Den moderne hvalfangsts historie*.
3 parts (37 chapters): 1. Whaling off the coast of Finnmark - 2. Global whaling - 3. Pelagic whaling. Statistical appendix (to 1978).

....(contd.)
Bibliography (bibliographical literature); periodicals; books and articles. Index, 777-98: Persons; Vessels and companies; Geographical (including whaling stations); subject. *Class No:* 639.245

Aquaria

[5958]
AXELROD, H.R. *and* **SCHULTZ, L.P. Handbook of tropical aquarium fishes.** Rev. ed. Neptune City, N.J., T.F.H. Publications, 1983. xii, 718p. illus. (incl. col.). ISBN: 0876664915.
First published 1955.
Ichthyology. (p.1-58) - The aquarium and its management (p.59-98) - Plants in the home aquarium (p.99-122) - Diseases of fishes and their cure (p.123-53) - Catalog of fishes (p.155-675). Glossary, p.677-87. Selected references. Detailed analytical index, 691-728.
Class No: 639.33/.34

[5959]
Dr. Burgess's atlas of marine aquarium fishes. Burgess, W.E., *and others.* Portsmouth, TFH Publications, 1988. 736p. illus. £50. ISBN: 0866228969.
Primarily an identification guide to saltwater fish, with *c.*4,000 photographs and 560 colour plates. 'Systematic list of the families of fishes of the world' explains the arrangement of the *Atlas*. Lists of scientific names and their equivalents. Index. *Class No:* 639.33/.34

[5960]
Exotic tropical fishes. Axelrod, H.R., *and others.* 2nd rev. and expanded ed. Neptune City, N.J., T.F.H. Publications, 1983. 1300p.
First published 1962.
Principles of aquarium management; Aquarium plants and their cultivation; Exotic tropical fishes (A-Z; p.257-1216); Raising tropical fishes commercially, p.1217-48. Detailed index, p.1251-1300.
Class No: 639.33/.34

[5961]
—**AXELROD, H.R.** Dr Axelrod's mini-atlas of freshwater aquarium fishes. Mini-ed. Neptune City., N.J., T.F.H. Publications, 1987. 992p. ISBN: 0866323951.
Mainly an album of colour illus., p.33-672. Appended: Aquaria maintenance, plants and fish, p.693-924. Index of scientific names; index of common names, p.929-92. *Class No:* 639.33/.34

[5962]
—**AXELROD, H.R.** *and* VORDERWINKLER, W. Handbook of tropical fishes, with special emphasis on techniques of breeding. 27th ed. Jersey City, N.J., T.F.H. Publications, 1983. 631p. illus.
First published in 1957. *Class No:* 639.33/.34

[5963]
HOEDEMAN, J.J. Naturalists' guide to fresh-water aquarium fish. New York, Sterling, 1974. 1152p. illus. (mostly col.).
Translated from the Dutch.
Part 1: evolution, distribution, anatomy and life processes of fish, plus relationship of fish to science and to man. Part 2: a finely illustrated catalogue of hundreds of the best known aquarium fish. Bibliography of reference works; glossary; index. 'Those with less specialized interests will find Axelrod & Vorderwinkler's *Encyclopedia of tropical fishes* & Innes' *Exotic aquarium fishes* ... a better buy' (*Wilson library bulletin*, October 1976, p.185-6). *Class No:* 639.33/.34

[5964]
MILLS, D. *and* **VEVERS, G. The Practical encyclopedia of freshwater tropical aquarium fishes.** 2nd ed. London, Salamander Books, 1989. 208p. illus. (col.). £12.99. ISBN: 0861014901.
First published 1982.
2 sections: 1. Practical section (Selecting a tank ... Aquatic plants ... Basic fish anatomy ... Expanding the interest) - 2. Species guide (a survey of over 200 tropical freshwater fishes). Further reading; glossary; index. Many colour illustrations. Mills is a fishkeeping expert, while Vevers is a former Curator of the Aquarium at London Zoo. *Class No:* 639.33/.34

[5965]
—The Complete aquarium encyclopedia of tropical freshwater fish. Ramshorst, J.D. van, *ed.* Amsterdam, Elsevier; Oxford, Phaidon, 1978. 391p. col. illus. ISBN: 0729000095.
8 contributors. 3 main parts: Compendium (The aquarium ... Breeding) - Plants (a selective, systematic list), p.82-113 - Fishes (a selective, systematic list), p.115-384. Data: family; genus; English name (if any); origin; size; habitat. Index of fishes, p.388-90 (tiny print). Grouped bibliography, p.390-1. 900 good illus. (500 in colour). Quarto. *Class No:* 639.33/.34

[5966]

STERBA, G. The Aquarium encyclopedia. Mills, D., *English ed and* Simpson, S., *tr..* Cambridge, Mass., MIT Press, 1983. 605p. illus. (incl. col.), diagrs.

Translation of *Lexikon der Aquaristik und Ichthyologie (1978). English ed. as The aquarist's* encyclopedia (Poole, Dorset, Blandford Press).

Entries, A-Z, for fish genera and species, plants, diseases, etc. with numerous cross-references from common names to scientific names. Bibliography, p.[606]. 1,183 illus. in all. Intended as 'a reference on freshwater and sea water aquarium keeping', with basic data on 'general and specialist ichthyology, hydrology, fish economy, the biology of freshwater animals and marine biology' (*Foreword*). Sterba, - professor of zoology and animal physiology at Karl Marx University, Leipzig. Emphasis is thus on scientific aspects. *Class No:* 639.33/.34

64 Household Management

Household Management

Catering Establishments

Bibliographies

[5967]

HCIMA quarterly current awareness bulletin for hospitality management. London, Hotel & Catering International Management Association, 1980-. 4pa. £70; £80 (overseas).

Formerly *HCIMA bibliography of hotel and catering management* and *Current awareness bulletin for hospitality management.*

Covers over 60 periodicals and is subdivided into more than 150 subject headings, *e.g.* v.17(1), 1996 contains headings such as: Careers (Hospitality/Tourism); Healthy eating; Store catering; Vegetarian catering. Includes list of periodicals scanned. The *Current awareness bulletin* database from 1985 is also included on the WHATT (Worldwide Hospitality and Tourism Trends) CD-ROM. *Class No:* 640.02(01)

[5968]

A Literature guide to the hospitality industry. Sawin, P., *and others, comps.* Westport, Conn., Greenwood, 1990. 99p. $35. (*Bibliographies and indexes in economics and economic history.*) ISBN: 0313267219.

Contains *c.*600 entries giving full bibliographic data. Chapter headings are by format, *e.g.* 'Directories', 'Handbooks', 'Databases'. The chapter on statistics is particularly useful. *Class No:* 640.02(01)

[5969]

NIXON, J.M. Hotel and restaurant industries an information sourcebook. Phoenix, Ariz., Oryx, 1988. 240p. $43.50. (*Oryx sourcebook series in business and management, 7.*) ISBN: 0897743768.

More than 1,000 annotated entries up to 1987. Includes US and UK trade journals and books but omits nonprint material. Lists state, national and international associations as well as educational establishments. Author, title, and subject indexes. Essential for libraries covering this subject. *Class No:* 640.02(01)

Handbooks & Manuals

[5970]

CRACKNELL, H.L. *and* NOBIS, G. The New catering repertoire. London, Macmillan, 1989-90. 2v. illus., tables, maps. £100, set; £12.99ea., pbk. ISBN: 0333391659, v.1; 0333391667, v.2.

V.1. *Aide-mémoire du chef.* xiii,810p. 1989. V.2. *Aide-mémoire du restaurateur et sommelier.* xix,492p. 1990.

V.2 has 2 main sections: 1. The waiting staff handbook (1. Service procedures ... 4. Menus ... 9. Restaurant personnel ... 11. Eating habits of nations) - 2. The wine waiting and bar staff manual (12. Wine production and wine-making countries ... 15. Cocktails and mixed drinks ... 17. Cigars). 19 appendices (A. Glossary of restaurant terms for the service of wine ... E. Styles of folding table napkins ... I. The law and the restaurateur ... S. Stills for making wines and spirits). Many black-and-white drawings. No index. *Class No:* 640.02(035)

[5971]

Practical professional catering. Cracknell, H.L., *and others.* London, Macmillan, 1983. xiii, 469p. £11.99. ISBN: 0533360753.

14 chapters (1. The catering industry ... 5. Interpretation of demand - 6/7. Emergence of facilities - 8/9. Provisioning - 10/12. Production and distribution - 13. Control of costs and revenues - 14. Maintaining of consumer satisfaction). 5 appendices: A. Education and training: opportunities and career prospects. E. Select bibliography (grouped), p.456-60. Detailed, analytical index, p.461-9. 67 figures. *Class No:* 640.02(035)

Dictionaries

[5972]

COLLIN, P.H. Dictionary of hotels, tourism and catering management. Teddington, Middlesex, Peter Collin Publishing, 1994. 300p. tables. ISBN: 0948549408.

Contains over 5,000 headwords with over 20,000 entries. Covers all aspects of the catering, tourism, and hotel trades. Includes informative comments to expand entries, *e.g.* information on the difference in measurement between British and American pints. Examples of words

....(contd.)

in context. Tables in supplement include airport codes, international and public holidays. For undergraduates and professionals. *Class No:* 640.02(038)

[5973]

COMBES, S. Dictionary of cuisine: French for hoteliers, restaurauteurs and catering students. London, Barrie & Rockliff, 1962. xii, 145p. ISBN: 0091442419, US ed.

Published in US as *Dictionary of cuisine French* (1989. $70).

French-English, English-French dictionary. Aims 'to provide an extensive vocabulary of commodities, equipment, processes, manipulations, etc., and especially, a more comprehensive French-English coverage of the flora and fauna used in French cookery than the author has so far been able to find in any works of this kind' (*Author's preface*). *Class No:* 640.02(038)

[5974]

Dictionnaire technique de l'hôtellerie/ Hotel-Fachwörterbuch/ Dictionary of hotel technical terms. Halkin, P., *and others.* Brussels, Le Livre d'Enseignement; Paris, Dunod, [1975?]. 190p.

About 2,500 French-base terms, with German and English equivalents. The dictionary is in two parts: 1. Food; 2. Hotel. French, German and English indexes. *Class No:* 640.02(038)

Yearbooks & Directories

[5975]

CONNELL, J. Hospitality marketing: an information sourcebook. Glasgow, Search Publications, 1994. 37p. ISBN: 0952111829.

Includes information on computerized search services, textbooks, dictionaries, specialist library services, journals, and product, market and industry information sources. *Class No:* 640.02(058)

[5976]

Hotel, restaurant and catering supplies, 1991. 27th ed. Epsom, Surrey, Sell's Publications, Ltd. xxiv,422p. £40. ISBN: 0854996788.

Exhibitions. Products & services classified, p.1-286; Alphabetical list of companies, p.287-408. Trade names and brands directory. Advertisers index. A buyer's guide of equipment and services for the hotel and catering industry. Quarto. *Class No:* 640.02(058)

Hotels & Restaurants

Worldwide

[5977]

'Financial Times' world hotel directory 1999. London, Financial Times Management, 1999. 896p. ISBN: 0273637347.

Covers over 3,500 hotels in more than 200 countries, with data on hotel reservation system; style (*e.g.* traditional); location; manager; rooms and charges; services and facilities; conferences; period when hotel closed. Hotel groups and representatives. 1-5 star gradings. Prelims. include conference centres; incentive schemes for business travellers. Geographical index and hotel by group index. For the business executive. *Class No:* 640.024.1/.3(100)

[5978]

Hotel and travel index: the worldwide hotel directory. Secaucus, N.J., Reed Elsevier Group. 1939-. 4pa. illus. maps. $65 (US); $205 (non US).

Formerly *ABC worldwide hotel guide.*

V.58(1), Spring 1997 issue contains worldwide hotel listings, with *c.*64,500 updates since the previous edition. Sections include: Europe/ Middle East - Africa - Asia - Pacific - USA - Canada - Caribbean - Mexico, Central & South America. About 65 symbols indicate facilities. Covers hotel selection and reservation in over 170 countries, wth conference and business venues particularly in mind. Other data include world time zones; air travel times; hotel programs and companies. 325 city, airport, and city centre maps. Geographical index. *Class No:* 640.024.1/.3(100)

[5979]

OAG agents gazetteer. Dunstable, Reed Travel Group, 1995-. Annual. £235.

Formerly *ABC agents gazetteer* (1968-94).

1. *Mediterranean hotels.* 1999. 812p. 2. *European cities.* 1999. 506p. 3. *North America.* 1999. 309p. 4. *Ski, lakes and mountains.* 1999. 210p. 5. *Mediterranean apartments.* 1999. 494p.

V.1 concerns European countries arranged A-Z (Bulgaria ... Turkey). All the volumes have town plans. Price ranges given and the

....(contd.)

hotel description includes category, rooms, map ref., location, grounds, opinion, etc. Aims 'to provide travel agents and those engaged in the sale of travel with first hand unbiased reports on the location and amenities of all hotels'. At pains to be evaluative. *Class No:* 640.024.1/.3(100)

Europe

[5980]

The 1995 Good hotel guide to Britain and Europe. Rubenstein, H., *ed.* London, Vermilion, 1994. xxxv,826p. maps. ISBN: 0091785456.

Recommends hotels chosen for excellence and value in all price brackets based on first-hand reports. Part 1: Great Britain and Ireland, p.3-338. Part 2: The continent: Austria ... Switzerland (15 countries). Alphabetical list of hotels, p.763-78. 20 location maps. Appended hotel report form. *Class No:* 640.024.1/.3(4)

[5981]

Les Guides rouges. Paris, Michelin. Annual. maps.

Benelux. Deutschland. España. Europe. France. Great Britain and Ireland. Italia. Portugal. Suisse.

'Red guides', providing details of hotels, restaurants and garages in the countries concerned, under towns A-Z. About 70 symbols are applied; tariff ranges indicated. Keyed colour town plans are a feature. *France, 1999* (1999. 911p.) includes many coloured maps and an index of localities listed by departments. *Class No:* 640.024.1/.3(4)

[5982]

RAC hotels in Europe 1996. Croydon, RAC Publishing Ltd., 1995. 368p. col.illus.,maps. £14.99; £8.99. ISBN: 086211344x.

Data on more than 2,000 RAC appointed and recommended hotels in Western Europe and the North Mediterranean. Very brief description of locale and data on period open, facilities and tariff. 'Motels and hotels on or near motorways'. Road maps. *Class No:* 640.024.1/.3(4)

Great Britain

[5983]

AA hotel guide 1999. Basingstoke, Hants., Automobile Association, 1998. 1072p. col. illus., maps. £14.99. ISBN: 0749519312.

Six sections in the hotel directory: England - Channel Islands - Isle of Man - Scoltand - Wales -Ireland. Prelims. include 'Britain's best hotels', central reservation telephone numbers, etc. 1-5 star ratings for hotels, based on reports by AA hotel inspectors. Available on the Internet at http://www.theaa.co.uk/hotels/ and on CD-ROM as part of *AA guide to hotels and restaurants in Britain and Ireland.*
Class No: 640.024.1/.3(410)

[5984]

HARRISON, L. *and* **JOHNSON, K. UK hotel groups directory 1992/93.** 4th ed. London, Cassell, 1992. 293p. tables. ISBN: 0304325414.

Gives data on hotel groups and consortia in the UK. Information includes name, address, fax/telex numbers, star ratings, key personnel, location of each UK hotel, number of bedrooms in each hotel, etc. Gives an overview of the industry as a whole. *Class No:* 640.024.1/.3(410)

[5985]

Inspected hotels: Great Britain and Ireland 1999. Croydon, RAC Publishing, 1998. 650p. illus., tables, maps. £13.99. ISBN: 1900327201.

First published 1904.

Directory of hotels (England, Scotland, Wales, Channel Islands; Northern Ireland; Republic of Ireland). Prelims. include RAC hotel awards. 19p. map section. Includes many town plans. Covers nearly 6,000 establishments. Aimed primarily at the tourist. *Class No:* 640.024.1/.3(410)

France

[5986]

FÉDÉRATION NATIONALE DES LOGIS ET AUBERGES DE FRANCE. Logis de France: guide to hotels and restaurants: 1997. Paris, the Fédération, 1997. Annual. 809p. maps. £11.90. ISBN: 2903021198.

About 4,000 brief 2-3 line entries for inexpensive hotels and accommodation in France and Corsica. 1-3 star gradings. Appended list of places under départements. Atlas of coloured maps, with insets. *Class No:* 640.024.1/.3(44)

[5987]

Michelin France, 1999. 90th ed. Paris, Michelin, 1999. 1473p. col. maps. £14.75. ISBN: 2069649997.

A highly compressed guide to *c.*11,000 hotels and restaurants in France, arranged under towns, A-Z. Much use made of symbols to categorize facilities. Many good colour maps of towns, locating hotels, etc. Helpful preliminary text and atlas of France. The fullest and best-known of the eight Michelin 'Red guides': France, Benelux, Germany, Spain, Portugal, Great Britain and Ireland, Italy and Europe. *Class No:* 640.024.1/.3(44)

America—North & Central

[5988]

Hotel and motel red book. New York, American Hotel and Motel Association, 1886-. Annual. illus., maps. ISSN: 00733490.

Official directory of the Association's members, covering hotels, motels and resorts. Mainly for USA, Canada and Caribbean, with a brief international section. *Class No:* 640.024.1/.3(71/73)

Farms & Guest Houses

Great Britain

[5989]

Accessible holidays in the British Isles 1999: a guide for disabled people. Stanford, J., *ed.* London, Royal Association for Disability and Rehabilitation (RADAR), 1999. 672p. map. £7.50. ISBN: 0900270063.

1,600 accommodation sites, 10% of them new to this edition, are covered in 18 regions of England, London, Scotland, Wales, Channel Islands, Isle of Man, Northern Ireland, Republic of Ireland. Classifications: Holiday accommodation except self-catering - Self-catering accommodation - Accommodation with care - Accommodation for children and young people - Accommodation for groups. Includes activity holidays, transport, useful publications. Lacks contents page. *Class No:* 640.024.2(410)

[5990]

Bed and breakfast: Great Britain and Ireland 1997. South Croydon, RAC Publishing, 1996. 330p. illus.(col.), maps. £7.99. ISBN: 0862113601.

Prelims. include 'How to use this book', 'An entry explained'. 22 symbols used throughout to describe facilities. Sections: England-Scotland - Wales - Northern Irealnd - Republic of Ireland - Channel Islands - Isle of Man. 19 maps. *Class No:* 640.024.2(410)

[5991]

Stay on a farm. Norwich: Jarrold, 1999. 396p. illus., maps. £7.95. ISBN: 1852384409.

Arranged by area: Scotland - England - Wales - Northern Ireland. Also includes Europe. Nearly all described properties are illustrated. *Class No:* 640.024.2(410)

Scotland

[5992]

Where to stay: hotels and guest houses, '99. Edinburgh, Scottish Tourist Board, 1998. 442p. col. illus., maps. £8.99. ISBN: 0854195300.

*c.*1,400 graded entries for hotels, guest houses and university accommodation. About 50 symbols applied. Gradings range from 'Listed' to 5 crowns. *Class No:* 640.024.2(411)

[5993]

—Where to stay: bed & breakfast, '99. Edinburgh, Scottish Tourist Board, 1998. 544p. col. illus. maps. £5.99. ISBN: 0854195319.

Over 1,700 graded entries. About 50 symbols applied. *Class No:* 640.024.2(411)

[5994]

—Where to stay: self-catering holidays, '99. Edinburgh, Scottish Tourist Board, 1998. 351p. col. illus., tables, maps. £5.99. ISBN: 0854195335.

Has over 1,100 entries, applying *c.*50 symbols. *Class No:* 640.024.2(411)

Northern Ireland

[5995]

Where to stay in Northern Ireland 1996. Belfast, Northern Ireland Tourist Board, 1996. 250p. col. illus., tables. maps. £3.99. ISBN: 0946871841.

Includes details of over 1,000 hotels, guesthouses, farmhouses, bed & breakfast, self-catering accommodation, youth hostels, camping and caravan parks. 37 symbols applied; grading system. Index. *Class No:* 640.024.2(416)

Eire

[5996]

Ireland accommodation guide '92. Dublin, Irish Tourist Board. 226p. illus., tables, maps.

4 sections: 1. Hotels, guesthouses and Irish homes - 2. Holiday centres, holiday hostels and youth hostels - 3. Caravan and camping parks - 4. Specialist accommodation. 42 symbols indicate facilities. Appended data include youth hostels, services, excursions. Index to locations, p.217-19. *Class No:* 640.024.2(417)

England

[5997]

Where to stay England '99: bed & breakfast, including farmhouses, inns & hostels. London, English Tourist Board, 1998. 424p. illus.(some col.), maps. £8.99. ISBN: 086143207x.

12 regions: London; Cumbria; Northumbria ... Yorkshire ... East of England ... South east England. 6 rankings: 'Listed' to 5 crowns. Appended prices & 'Useful information'. 7 maps. London index; town index. Index to advertisers. *Class No:* 640.024.2(420)

Wales

[5998]

Wales 1995: hotels, guest houses & farmhouses. Cardiff, Welsh Tourist Board, 1995. 116p. illus. (incl. col.), maps. £2.95. ISBN: 1850130639.

Lists accommodation checked and graded by the Welsh Tourist Board. Information on tourist attractions and events. Full-colour detailed maps. *Class No:* 640.024.2(429)

Germany

[5999]

Deutscher Hotelführer: '99. Stuttgart, Hugo Matthaes Druckerei und Verlag GmbH. Annual. DM34.80. ISBN: 3875164296.

The edition for 1999 lists *c.*10,000 hotels in *c.*3,000 locations in Germany. 30 symbols applied. Easier to use than the Michelin Deutschland, but devoid of town maps. Accompanied by a CD-ROM version. *Class No:* 640.024.2(430)

Restaurants

[6000]

Britain: quality and value food accommodation 1995. London, Kuperard, 1994. 400p. £10.99. ISBN: 1857331419.

Formerly *Les Routiers guide to Britain.*

Lists more than 1,800 British pubs, restaurants, hotels and guest houses recommended for good food or good accommodation. *Class No:* 640.024.3

[6001]

Egon Ronay's Visa guide 1997: hotels and restaurants. London, Bookman Projects Ltd., 1996. 1056p.,tables, maps. £14.99. ISBN: 1898718881.

Six sections (London ... Northern Ireland), p.49-802. Awards for excellence; restaurants, 1-3 stars. Percentage ratings given for hotels. Quick reference lists. Prelims. include awards, *e.g.*'Hotel of the year';'Cellar of the year'. Concise, evaluative comments. Available on the Internet as *Egon Ronay alert* at http://www.egonronay.richbell.com *Class No:* 640.024.3

[6002]

The Good food guide 1996. Ainsworth, J., *ed.* London, Which? Books, 1995. 732p. maps. £14.99. ISBN: 0852025858.

Covers over 1,300 establishments, based on reports, by readers, of 10,000 meals. Divided into eight regional sections. 27 maps. Aimed at the individual but would be a suitable addition to general library collections. *Class No:* 640.024.3

[6003]

—Just a bite: eating out on a budget in the UK and Ireland. London, Pan Macmillan, 1994. 416p. maps. £9.99. (*Egon Ronay's Britvic guide 1994.*) ISBN: 0333610008.

Lists *c.*900 establishments in London, England, Scotland, Wales, Channel Islands and Isle of Man, in turn, and includes the Republic of Ireland for the first time. Quick-reference lists include Sunday eating, outdoor eating, vegetarian, etc. 15 maps in addition to London and Ireland maps. *Class No:* 640.024.3

[6004]

—The Vegetarian good food guide. Whittet, A., *ed.* London, Consumers' Association and Hodder and Stoughton, 1990. 480p. maps. ISBN: 0340514426.

Features nearly 900 cafés, pubs, hotels and restaurants in the UK. The editor's top ten restaurants, p.12, is followed by 5 sections: London - England - Scotland - Wales - Isle of Man. 5 appendices: Alphabetical list of entries - Restaurants awarded a star - Restaurants serving only vegetarian food - Maps (14) - Report forms. *Class No:* 640.024.3

[6005]

Les Routiers France 1997: a guide to quality and good value accommodation, restaurants, cafes and bistros. London, Routiers Ltd., 1997. 256p. maps. £7.99. ISBN: 1857331559.

Lists cafés, restaurants and hotels in France that provide cheap and good meals for motorists. Under regional sections, subdivided by towns, A-Z. 9 symbols provide data. 9p. of maps. *Class No:* 640.024.3

Inns & Public Houses

[6006]

The Good beer guide, 1999. Preece, J., *ed.* 26th ed. St. Albans, Campaign for Real Ale [CAMRA], 1998. 576p. maps. £10.99. ISBN: 1852491493.

Has brief information (applying 17 symbols) on *c.*5,000 British pubs serving *e.g.*2,000 traditional 'real' ales and beers, p.34-430, arranged under counties of England, Wales, Scotland, Isle of Man, Channel Islands, and Northern Ireland. 'Independent breweries' (p.432-533), follows, along with 'New breweries' and 'Pub groups', and an index of beers (p.553-70). Includes a 'Beer festival calendar'. Not to be confused with the *Good pub guide* (*q.v.*), providing fuller information on public houses. *Class No:* 640.024.4

[6007]

The Good pub guide 1997. Aird, A., *ed.* 14th ed. London, Vermilion, 1996. 1008p. maps. ISBN: 0091820146.

Independent evaluative guide to over 5,000 pubs in England (arranged by counties Berkshire-Yorkshire), Scotland, Wales, and Channel Islands, using reports from up to 8,000 contributors. Each geographical area opens with specifically recommended pubs, followed by a less-detailed 'lucky-dip' section for that area. Opening hours, food & drink specialists, entertainments, etc, are listed, with emphasis on value for money. Overseas 'lucky dip' appendix. *Class No:* 640.024.4

[6008]

PITT, H. The Complete innkeeper: the A-Z of running a pub. London, Robert Hale, 1991. 187p. £15.95. ISBN: 070904397x.

Misleading title as there are 13 chapters: 1. Having what it takes ... 4. Finance ... 8. The police ... 10. Staff ... 13. Expansion. Useful addresses. Further reading. Brief index. *Class No:* 640.024.4

Clubs & Hostels

[6009]

[Guide to budget accommodation] 1999. Welwyn, Herts., International Youth Hostel Federation, 1998. Annual. 2v. col. illus., town plans, maps.

Formerly *Youth hostel handbook.*

1. *Europe.* 2. *Americas, Africa, Asia and the Pacific.*

1999 ed. extensively revised. Both volumes now include a 32-page, four-colour introductory section giving essential information on the youth hostel movement. The introductions to each country have been re-styled. V.1 extends to North Africa and Middle Eastern countries bordering on the Mediterranean (Austria ... Turkey (includes Russia, Croatia)). About 40 signs and symbols give explanations on essential hostel services. Expanded profiles of selected, major hostels. General information, on tinted paper, is in English, French, German and Spanish. Outline location map; small town plans. *Class No:* 640.024.6

[6010]

YHA accommodation guide 1994 (England and Wales). St. Albans, Herts., Youth Hostels Association (England and Wales), 1994. Annual. 192p. town plans, maps.

Hostel entries in 28 areas (Northumberland and Roman Wall ... Northern Ireland), p.20-164. About 35 signs and symbols applied. Prelims. include notes on YHA activities, hostel information, membership, world travel, other services. Small town plans; map of England and Wales and Northern Ireland. Advertisers' index. General index. Hostel index.

Scotland (Stirling) and Eire (Dublin) each have a YHA, issuing an annual guide. *Class No:* 640.024.6

Camps & Caravan Sites

[6011]

Camping and caravanning: Great Britain & Ireland 1998. Croydon, RAC Publishing, 1997. 252p. tables, maps. £8.99. ISBN: 1900327163.

Over 2,000 sites (England; Scotland; Wales; Isle of Man; Channel Islands; Northern Ireland; Republic of Ireland), p.1-252. Preliminaries include caravans, trailers and the law, caravan security, and useful addresses. Index of sites by county. 19p. of maps. *Class No:* 640.028

[6012]

Camping, caravanning in France. Paris, Pneu Michelin. Annual. table, maps. ISBN: 2060061393.

The 1993 guide (436p. £7.25) gives particulars of more than 3,500 camping sites, A-Z, preceded by a table of localities, under *départements.* About 80 symbols applied. 22 pages of coloured maps, with numerous maps in text. Prelims. in French, English, German and Dutch. *Class No:* 640.028

[6013]

Europa camping + caravaning / Internationalen Führer/Guide international, 1999. 46. Ausg. Stuttgart, Drei Brunnen Verlag, GmbH, 1999. 959p. illus. (mostly col.), maps. DM29.80. ISBN: 3795602602.

Guide to more than 5,000 camping sites, - Europe (including Russia, Hungary, Bulgaria, Roumania); Near East; North Africa. Heavy use of symbols to include information. Coloured maps. Many advertisements. *Class No:* 640.028

[6014]

RAC camping and caravanning in Europe 1996. Croydon, RAC Publishing, 1995. 512p. tables, maps. £7.99. ISBN: 0862113318.

10 symbols applied; descriptive text on each country. Prelim. notes on Eastern European countries; Major tunnels; Mountain passes (tables). Index of places. Black-and-white maps. *Class No:* 640.028

[6015]

Where to stay in Britain '96: Camping and caravanning parks. London, BTA, 1996. Annual. 180p. maps. £3.99. ISBN: 0709563787.

Lists camping and caravan parks, with data on location; area, season, terms and facilities. 44 symbols used. Headings in English, French, German, Dutch. Appended: 'Useful addresses', 'Standards for camping and caravan parks ...' *Class No:* 640.028

Consumers & Shopping

Bibliographies

[6016]

FOREMAN, S. **Consumer monitor 2:** an annotated bibliography of British government and other official publications relating to consumer issues. Aldershot, Hants., Ashgate, 1996. x,407p. £45. ISBN: 185742302x.

First published 1987.

16 chapters: 1. General ... 7. Transport - 8. Fuel and water ... 13. Safety ... 16. Arts, leisure and sport. Annual reports, p.381-84. Publications sources, p.385-87. Index, p.388-407. Entries are arranged by section and, within each section, under sub-headings, then alphabetically by title. *Class No:* 640.03(01)

[6017]

Shopping in the eighties: a guide to sources of information. Kirby, D.A., *comp.* London, British Library, 1988. [v], 58p. £22.50. ISBN: 0712307559.

About 500 references. 18 sections, each with introduction, - Consumer behaviour - Hypermarkets and superstores - Retail (6 sections) - Shopping centres (3) - Teleshopping and new technology - Town centres - Trading hours - Traffic and transport. References are mostly to periodical articles. *Class No:* 640.03(01)

Encyclopaedias

[6018]

BROBECK, S. **Encyclopedia of the consumer movement.** Santa Barbara, Calif., ABC-Clio, 1997. 659p. £59.95; $99.50. ISBN: 0874369878.

Arranged A-Z, 198 entries, of varying lengths, covering the development of the consumer movement from its beginnings in the US to its current international status. Many cross-references and an extensive index. US-bias but 'this encyclopedia brings together a great deal of information never before gathered in one place' (*Reference books bulletin,* 1 April 1998, p.1344). *Class No:* 640.03(031)

Handbooks & Manuals

[6019]

REES, A.M. **A Consumer handbook.** Oxford, Blackwell Scientific, 1990. 160p. illus. £9.99. ISBN: 0632006927.

Guide for consumers to legislation, technical changes, and bodies supplying advice and information with regard to provision of goods and services. Covers safety, design and standards, advertising, consumer redress. *Class No:* 640.03(035)

Reviews & Abstracts

[6020]

Consumers index to product evaluations and information sources. Ann Arbor, Mich., Pierian Press, 1973-. 4pa., with annual cumulation. $139 (US); $265 (non US). ISSN: 00940534.

15 subject groups, with subdivisions: 1. Consumerism ... 3. Money and the law ... 5. Food and beverages - 6. Clothing ... 8. Sports, recreations and hobbies ... 10. Transportation ... 12. Computers - 13. The office and business management ... 15. Miscellaneous. Cross-references. For the general and special American consumer. Also online and on CD-ROM. *Class No:* 640.03(048)

[6021]

'Which?' cumulative index, 1957-1982. London, Consumers' Association, [1983]. 61p.

Covers a period of 25 years, coinciding with the ending of *Handyman Which?, Money Which?* and *Motoring Which?* supplements to *Which? Gardening from Which?* is not covered, since it only started publication in September 1982 and it carries its own index. Analytical index. About 350 entries. *Class No:* 640.03(048)

Periodicals

[6022]

Which? London, Consumers' Association, 1957-. 12pa. £59. ISSN: 00434841.

Each issue contains advice for consumers and evaluative reports on products. Issue for September 1995 has nine sections: 1. Regulars - 2. Food and health (Food poisoning; Medical insurance) - 3. Motoring (Fast-fit centres; Super-unleaded fuel) - 4. Travel and leisure (Weekend breaks) - 5. Public interest (Moving house; Charters) - 6. On test (CD-ROM drives; Video tapes) - 7. Money - 8. Home and DIY - 9. Update. Companion publications include *Holiday Which?, Gardening Which?, Which?* wine monthly and *Which? way to health.*

Equivalent consumer reports worldwide include: *Consumer reports* (USA; available online and on CD-ROM); *Que choisir?* (France); *Test* (Germany); *Rad & ron* (Sweden); *Consumer currents* and *IOCU newsletter* (International Organization of Consumers Unions). *Class No:* 640.03(051)

Yearbooks & Directories

[6023]

Directory of consumer information sources. London, Consumers' Association. 2v. loose-leaf.

Lists organizations in the UK. Includes government and voluntary bodies. Updated twice-yearly. *Class No:* 640.03(058)

[6024]

IGLESIA, M.E. de la. **International catalogue of catalogues.** New York, Harper & Row, 1982. 224p. illus. ISBN: 006014985x.

Describes the products offered by more than 1,500 mail-order firms worldwide; aimed at the affluent and others. *Class No:* 640.03(058)

Tables & Data Books

[6025]

The United States mail order industry. Homewood, Ill., Business One Irwin, 1991. 225p. tables. $55. ISBN: 1556234864.

Provides statistics on mail-order sales in the US. Direct mail in Europe is discussed in one brief chapter. Business profiles of 25 consumer mail-order companies and 25 business-to-business marketers include data on ownership, company history, quantity of catalogues mailed, markets, etc. *Class No:* 640.03(083)

Laws

[6026]

Encyclopedia of consumer law. Thomas, W.H., *general ed and* Ervine, C., *Scottish ed..* London, Sweet & Maxwell/W. Green & Son, 1980-. Loose-leaf v. Updates issued twice-yearly.

5 parts: 1. Statutes (all relevant statutes, including Consumer Protection Act, 1987) - 2. Statutory instruments - 3. Cases (competition; contract; credit; criminal; sale of goods; Scottish; services) - 4. Circulars and notices - 5. European Economic Community material (Treaty of Rome, and relevant secondary legislation). Index. *Class No:* 640.03(094.1)

[6027]
—STANESBY, A. Consumer rights handbook. London, Pluto Press, 1986. [vii], 236p. £7.50. ISBN: 0745301622.

Has 4 parts: 1. Buying goods - 2. Buying services - 3. Buying credit - 4. Dealing with problems. Appendices: Index of statutory instruments; Case index; Statutes index. Written by a solicitor 'for private consumers and not for people who are in business' (*Note*). *Class No:* 640.03(094.1)

[6028]
A Handbook of consumer law. 3rd ed. London, Consumers' Association, and Hodder & Stoughton, 1989. 252p. tables. £5.95. ISBN: 0340488778.

First published 1982.

15 chapters: 1. Consumer law - 2. Sensible buying and pursuing complaints - 3. Shops and shopping - 4. Prices - 5. Consumer safety - 6. Food - 7. Contracts, liabilities and exclusion clauses - 8. Misrepresentation - 9. Trade descriptions and labelling - 10. Defective goods - 11. Defective services - 12. Insurance - 13. Financial and professional services - 14. Consumer credit - 15. Fair trading. Appendices: 1. Useful addresses; 2. Suggestions for further reading, p.238 (5 evaluative annotated entries). Index, p.241-52. *Class No:* 640.03(094.1)

Great Britain

[6029]
DAVIS, D. A History of shopping. London, Routledge & Kegan Paul, 1966. xii, 322p. illus. (pl.). (*Studies in social history*.)

Four parts (13 chapters): The late Middle Ages - Queen Elizabeth to Queen Anne - The eighteenth century - Modern times [to the 1960s], from fairs, markets and travelling tallymen to the modern supermarket. Select bibliography, p.303-10. Detailed analytical index, Glossary, p.xi-xii. 16 plates. *Class No:* 640.03(410)

[6030]
Directory of shopping centres in Great Britain and the Republic of Ireland. Northern, R.I. *and* Leonard, J.E., *eds.* Reading, British Council of Shopping Centres, 1993. xxv,955p. tables. ISBN: 1897958053.

Covers over 950 retail developments. Prelims. include 'General information'; 'Index of shopping centres by name'. Centre fact sheets, p.3-955. Data for each entry include address, architects, catering, trading hours, facilities, features, etc. 'Shopping centres with food courts', p.xxii-xxiii; 'Shopping centres and markets', p.xxiv-xxv. *Class No:* 640.03(410)

[6031]
MONTAGUE, J. The A to Z of shopping by post. 2nd ed. Watford, Exley Publications, 1979. 252p. illus. ISBN: 0905521269.

35 chapters (1. Large department stores & mail-order houses; 2. Animal & pets; 3. Art ... 6. Books ... 18. Gardening equipment ... 29. Office supplies ... 33. Soft furnishings and fabrics ... 35. Toys & games). Index of *c*.1,000 firms. Product index. Data on catalogues available, terms of business. *Class No:* 640.03(410)

[6032]
WALSH, N. The Good mail order guide: everything you need to know about ordering top-quality goods from the comfort of your living room. London, Macmillan, 1996. ix, 550p. £9.99. ISBN: 033365238x.

Formerly *The Virgin home shopping handbook*.

Gives details of more than 1,200 companies. *Class No:* 640.03(410)

[6033]
Yesterday's shopping: the Army & Navy Stores catalogue, 1907. London, David & Charles, 1969. lxiii, 1282p. illus., tables, plans.

A facsimile of the Army & Navy Society's 1907 issue of 'Rules of the Society and price list of articles sold at the Store'. 15 departments involved. 'Export, shipping and passenger and baggage department', p.1229-82. Meticulous details and pricing. *Class No:* 640.03(410)

Thesauri

[6034]
Thesaurus of consumer terms. Askew, C., *comp.* London, Consumers' Association; The Hague, International Organization of Consumers' Unions, 1979-82. 2v. ISBN: 085202153x.

1. *Classified display*, 1979, li, 314p. 2. *Alphabetically structured display*. 1982. xxix, 289p.

About 7,000 terms involved. Pt.1 comprises 'Introduction and instructions for use' (p.iv-li), alphabetical index (p.3-116, on yellow-tinted paper), and classified display, p.117-314. *Class No:* 640.03:025.43

Libraries

[6035]
IOCU guide on consumer libraries. 2nd ed. The Hague, International Organization of Consumers' Unions, 1982. 53, [1]p. ISBN: 9070241064.

Directory of 49 libraries (1 per page) in 26 countries, Australia ... USA. Data on each note type of holdings (special holdings, classification, working language(s), library publications, information services provided, opening hours, library staff. Appended: 'Thirty recommended books on consumerism'. *Class No:* 640.03:061:026/027

Institutions & Associations

[6036]
Consumer sourcebook. 11th ed. Detroit, Mich., Gale, 1998. lxxxix, 1137p. ISBN: 0787620874.

First published 1974.

A compendium, under subject headings (*e.g.* child services; energy/ environment, financial services, food and drug safety, handicapped), of *c*.15,000 programs and advisory services available to the American consumer at little or no cost. Sources extend from federal and state agencies, associations and organizations, to information centres and clearing houses. Selected annotated bibliography. Master name and keyword index. *Class No:* 640.03:061:061.2

[6037]
International consumer directory. Harlow, Longman, 1989.

Formerly *Consumer directory*.

Coverage: of over 300 consumer organizations, arranged A-Z within each country. Data include details of staff and finance, description of organization, specific areas of work, regular publications. *Class No:* 640.03:061:061.2

Food & Drink

Food Preservation

[6038]
Home preservation of fruit and vegetables. 14th ed. London, HMSO, 1989. 215p. illus., tables. £4.95.

First published 1929.

19 sections: Principles of preservation - Preserving methods ... Jams ... Bottled fruit ... Freezing ... Chutneys ... Drying and salting - Storing fruit and vegetables - Some common faults and their likely causes. Numerous recipes. Detailed recipe and general indexes. *Class No:* 641.4

Cookery

Bibliographies

[6039]
Bibliography of cookery books, 1875-1914. Driver, E., *ed.* London, New York, Prospect Books/Mansell, 1989. 748p. illus. £50. ISBN: 0907325416.

Lists *c*.1,200 individual works. Gives locations in many libraries in the UK, US, Australia, Canada, and South Africa. Some biographical details of authors are given. 3 indexes: date; title; subject. *Class No:* 641.5(01)

[6040]
BULSON, C. Current cookbooks. Middletown, Conn., Choice, 1990. $12. ISBN: 091449208x.

Annotated list of 250 books, mostly published since 1970. Arranged alphabetically by cuisine, Armenian ... Vietnamese, cooking techniques, courses, foods and audience. *Class No:* 641.5(01)

[6041]
BULSON, C. 'Reference sources on food and cooking'. In *Reference books bulletin*, 1 January 1994, p.844-46.

35 sources are listed, including encyclopaedias, dictionaries, indexes, and bibliographies. *Class No:* 641.5(01)

[6042]
Cook's index: an index of cookbooks and periodicals from 1975-1987. Evanston, Ill., John Gordon Burke Publisher, 1989. Triennial. 536p. $55. ISBN: 0934272093.

Indexes, by author and subject, English-language cookbooks and periodicals from 1975-1987. *Class No:* 641.5(01)

[6043]

FERET, B.L. **Gastronomical and culinary literature:** a survey and analysis of historically-orientated collections in the US. Metuchen, N.J., Scarecrow Press, 1979. iii, 124p. $16.50. ISBN: 0810812045.

Part 1: The literature (Introduction; 11 sections, each with short introduction: Before printing; Italy, 15th and 16th centuries ... England and France, 19th and 20th centuries; United States, 18th, 19th and 20th centuries) - Part 2: The collections (by state, annotated entries, p.54-90; index precedes). Appendix: A. Culinary bibliographies and bibliographic commentaries; B. Secondary historical texts and references. Non-analytical index, p.111-24.
Class No: 641.5(01)

[6044]

Gastronomic bibliography. Bitting, K.G., *ed.* San Francisco, privately printed, 1939 (reprinted 1981. London, Holland Press). 718p. illus. ISBN: 0875567231.

6,000 entries, fully annotated, in 2 parts: authors; anonymous works. Short-title index, with a rough, incomplete subject index. The only bibliography that adequately covers both historical and more modern books on gastronomy. *Class No:* 641.5(01)

[6045]

—MACLEAN, V. A Short-title catalogue of household and cookery books published in the English tongue, 1701-1800. London, Prospect, 1981. xxiv, 1970p. facsims. ISBN: 0907325068.

With index. *Class No:* 641.5(01)

[6046]

—SIMON, A.L. Bibliotheca gastronomica: a catalogue of books and documents on gastronomy. London, Wine and Food Society, 1953. 196p. illus., facsims.

Carries 1,644 annotated entries. An author list, with short-title and subject indexes. Includes facsimiles of rare early books.
Class No: 641.5(01)

[6047]

—VICAIRE, G. Bibliographie gastronomique: a bibliography of books appertaining to food and drink and related subjects, from the beginning of printing to 1890. London, Versthoyle, 1954; Holland Press, 1978. xviiip., 974 cols.

A facsimile of the 1890 bibliography. An author list, with bibliographical notes. Records French, Latin, English, German and Spanish titles from 15th century up to 1889, with values. A collector's piece, like the Simon. *Class No:* 641.5(01)

[6048]

OSTROFF, H. *and* NICHOLS, T. Specialty cookbooks: a subject guide, v.1. New York, Garland, 1992. 659p. (*Garland reference library of the humanities, 1297.*) ISBN: 0824069471.

An unannotated list of 4,500 cookbooks, mostly published 1980-90. 4 sections: Specific ingredients; Specific dishes and courses; Specific meals; Special techniques. Full bibliographic citations are given and there are author and title indexes. A subject index would have been useful. Recommended for special and public libraries.
Class No: 641.5(01)

[6049]

PATTEN, M. Books for cooks: a handbook of cookery. London & New York, Bowker, 1975. viii, [1], 526p. ISBN: 0859350053.

1,660 numbered items, under authors A-Z, with 1-8 line annotations; 'Late entries', p.457-72. Emphasis on books published in Britain, with some foreign titles. Prices are given and some Braille books included. The very necessary subject index is detailed but only partly analytical (p.472-95); title index. *Class No:* 641.5(01)

[6050]

PRYTHERCH, R. *and* STANLEY, S. Food, cookery and diet: an information guide. Aldershot, Gower, 1989. ix, 109p. £15. ISBN: 0566035685.

Lists the standard, basic sources. 6 sections: 1. Basic reference sources - 2. The scientific background - 3. Professional catering - 4. Training, education and careers - 5. Home cooking - 6. Healthy eating and special diets. Index. *Class No:* 641.5(01)

[6051]

WEISS, H.U. Gastronomia: eine Bibliographie der deutschsprachigen Gastronomie 1485-1914: ein Handbuch für Sammler und Antiquare. Zurich, Bibliotheca Gastronomica, Buchantiauariat, 1996. xxii, 674p. illus. ISBN: 3952125504.

Contains 4,364 entries - many with brief annotations - on cookery books in the German language (p.1-605). Author, title, subject and geographical indexes. *Class No:* 641.5(01)

Encyclopaedias

[6052]

Cooking A to Z. Horn, J., *and others.* San Ramon, Calif., Ortho Books, 1988. 640p. illus. $32.95. ISBN: 0897211472.

Arrangement is A to Z, with over 600 recipes and nearly 500 entries, either defining cooking terms, describing and illustrating cooking techniques or offering information about specific ingredients. Well indexed and beautifully illustrated. *Class No:* 641.5(031)

[6053]

New Larousse gastronomique; the world's greatest cookery reference book. London, Hamlyn, 1977. [viii], 1064p. illus., maps. ISBN: 0828801576, US ed.

Original French ed. 1938, as *Larousse gastronomique.* As *Nouveau Larousse gastronomique,* 1968. Published in US, New York, French and European, 1984. (1152p. $150).

Entries 'Abaisse' ... 'Zweiback'. ('Fritter', p.394-8, records nearly 100 recipes, with brief cooking instructions; 'Hors d'oeuvres', p.457-88). 'International cookery', p.501-12, is a very brief survey of national specialities. 'Many of the recipes in this encyclopedia cater for large numbers of people and it would be merely pedantic to try to standardise quantities' (*Introduction* to 1961 ed.). Small type and illus., some lush whole-page colour plates. Detailed analytical index, p.1008-64. For the skilled cook. *Class No:* 641.5(031)

[6054]

STOBART, T. The Cook's encyclopedia. Owen, M., *ed.* New York, Harper & Row, 1981. 547p. ISBN: 0060141271.

An A-Z encyclopaedia of ingredients and processes, with cross-references. Not another compilation of recipes. Simon, A.L., and Howe, R. *Dictionary of gastronomy* (McGraw-Hill, 1970. 400p.) describes more concoctions and ingredients; Stobart concentrates rather on explaining processes. Well organized. *Class No:* 641.5(031)

Handbooks & Manuals

[6055]

BEETON, I.M. Mrs. Beeton's cookery and household management. London, Ward Lock, 1992. 1408p. illus. (incl. col.), diagrs., tables. £25. ISBN: 0706371011.

First published 1861 (reprinted Cape, 1968. 1112p.); previously in monthly parts, November 1859 - October 1961. The 1960 ed. is the first completely modern ed., 'although it contains not one recipe from the original "Mrs. Beeton"' (*The Observer,* 19 April 1964, p.33).

'Household management section' plays a secondary role to the 'Cookery section'. The latter ranges from 'Glossary of cookery terms and techniques', 'Seasonings and flavours' to 'Convenience foods', 'Regional British cookery', 'Foreign cookery', 'Menus' and 'Party food'. Detailed, analytical index. *Class No:* 641.5(035)

[6056]

CRACKNELL, H.L. *and* KAUFMANN, R.J. Practical professional cookery. 3rd ed. Basingstoke, Macmillan, 1992. vii, 908p. £14.99. ISBN: 0333559258.

First published 1972.

20 sections: 1. Introduction - 2. The methods and general principles of cookery ... 8. Eggs ... 10. Fish ... 13. Poultry, p.402-70 ... 16. Salads and salad dressings .... 20. Pastry and sweet dishes. Number of recipes has increased by 50 percent to over 2,000 and now includes a wide range of international and ethnic dishes. Glossary. Select bibliography, p.881-2. Index. Companion volume to *Practical professional catering (q.v.).* *Class No:* 641.5(035)

[6057]

ESCOFFIER, A. The Complete guide to the art of modern cookery. Cracknell, H.L. *and* Kaufmann, R.J., *tr.* London, Butterworth-Heinemann, 1991. xxvi, 646p. £30. ISBN: 0750602880.

Supersedes *A Guide to modern cookery* (2nd ed. 1957). Originally as *Le guide culinaire* (1902).

5,011 recipes. 17 chapters (1. Sauces ... 3. Soups ... 6. Fish ... 12. Roasts ... 16. Sweets, puddings and desserts ... 17. Poached fruits (compotes), jams and drinks). Both imperial and metric measures given. Glossary, p.589-92. Specimen menus, p.593-609 (Christmas menu, 1906: 31 items). Detailed index. *Class No:* 641.5(035)

[6058]

FITZGIBBON, T. The Food of the western world: an encyclopedia of food from Europe and North America. London, Hutchinson, 1976. xxx, 529p. illus., tables. ISBN: 0812904273.

About 6,000 entries for ingredients, dishes, methods of preparation, recipes (Soufflé, varieties: 3 columns, 1 illus.; Pizza: varieties: 1p., 1 illus.) and culinary terms from 34 countries. 2,500 brief recipes. Bibliography, p.xxix-xxx. Tables show cuts of meat for beef, veal, pork, lamb and mutton for America, England and France. Entry-words are insufficiently distinctive. 'A fine complement to the classic Larousse gastronomique' (*Choice,* v.13(8), October 1976, p.957).
Class No: 641.5(035)

[6059]
'Good Housekeeping' microwave cookbook. London, Ebury Press, 1989. 400p. illus. (col.). £14.99. ISBN: 0852237391.
3 parts: 1. Basic techniques, p.10-22 (includes boiling; frying, preserving; sweet making) - 2. Recipes, p.23-385 - 3. Charts, glossary and index. *Class No:* 641.5(035)

[6060]
'Good Housekeeping' new step-by-step cook book. London, Ebury Press, 1998. 448p. illus.(col.), tables. £19.99. ISBN: 0091864941.
First published 1993.
Sections include: Stocks and sauces - Soups ... Fish ... Eggs and cheese ... Pasta ... Pies, flans and pizza - Desserts ... Preserves - Food safety - Glossary - Index. A photographic reference index for every recipe included in the book precedes the recipes. Many colour photographs. *Class No:* 641.5(035)

[6061]
McGEE, H. On food and cooking: the science and lore of the kitchen. 3rd ed. London, Allen & Unwin, 1986. xix, 684p. illus., tables. £12.95. ISBN: 004306003x.
3 parts (14 chapters): 1. Foods (1. Milk and dairy products ... 10. Food additives) - 2. Food and the body - 3. The principles of cooking: a summary. Appendix: A chemistry primer - atoms, molecules, energy. Bibliography, p.648-52. *Class No:* 641.5(035)

Dictionaries

English

[6062]
ALLISON, S. The Cassell food dictionary. London, Cassell, 1990. xxxv,480p. figs. £19.95. ISBN: 0304318752.
More than 6,000 entries, à la ... Zwiebelrostbraten, in the dictionary section, p.1-452. Layout is 2 columns per page, with length of definition varying from a few lines to half a column. Occasional black-and-white drawings devoted to a particular subject, *e.g.* 'Puddings and deserts'. A thematic index, p.xiii-xxxv, arranges items of food according to type or country. Index of cross-references, p.453-80. No bibliography. Unexciting design and layout but contains useful information. *Class No:* 641.5(038)=20

[6063]
ANDERSON, K.N. *and* ANDERSON, L.E. The International dictionary of food and nutrition. New York, John Wiley, 1993. vi,330p. figs. ISBN: 0471559571.
Contains *c.*7,500 short definitions of food ingredients, garnishes, sauces, entrées, and appetizers. Each entry gives an indication of the source of the word or phrase, *e.g.* cuisset de porc (Fr); fonduta (It). For the cook rather than the nutritionist. *Class No:* 641.5(038)=20

[6064]
ANTHONY, P. Patrick Anthony's international menu dictionary. Luton, Lennard Publishing, 1988. 167p. ISBN: 1852910550.
4 sections: 1. At a glance translator (À la Grèque ... Zwiebel) (*c.*1,400 entries) - 2. The menu dictionary (Abalone ... Zwieback) - 3. Key translator of main foods: English-French-Spanish-German-Italian - 4. The history of beverages, p.160-66. Short bibliography. A handy pocket-size guide, international in scope, covering, among other things, food from Europe, India, the Caribbean and the Far East. *Class No:* 641.5(038)=20

[6065]
HERBST, S.T. The New food lover's companion: comprehensive definitions of over 3,000 food, wine and culinary terms. Hauppauge, Barron's, 1995. xvi,715p. illus., tables. £7.99. ISBN: 0812015207.
First published in 1990 as *The Food lover's companion*.
Length of definitions varies from a sentence to two pages. Covers foods, dishes and sauces, kitchen equipment, cooking techniques, names of drinks, menu terms and brand names. Pronunciation for foreign terms is given in addition to numerous cross-references. Appendix includes an additives directory, a detailed spice and herb chart and meat cut illustrations. Bibliography, p.702-10. Of the first ed., 'Comprehensive, accurate, interesting, well written and inexpensive' (*Booklist,* 1 June 1990, p.1923). Available online through Epicurious food http://food.epicurious.com.
Class No: 641.5(038)=20

[6066]
HERING, R. Hering's dictionary of classical and modern cookery, and practical reference manual for the hotel, restaurant and catering trade. 11th rev. ed. Translated by W. Giessen. Giessen (Germany), Pfanneberg, 1958; London, Mills & Boon, 1960 (and reprints). [iv], 852p.
First published as *Lexikon der Küche,* 1907.
A many-section dictionary (Hors d'oeuvre to Sweets), p.1-745. Vocabulary, English-French-German-Italian-Spanish, p.823-52. Claims to contain over 15,000 recipes, but average entry per recipe runs to only 2½ lines, - no more than a statement of ingredients. Includes

....(contd.)
regional dishes. A practical reference manual for hotel restaurant and catering rather than a cookery book in the accepted sense.
Class No: 641.5(038)=20

[6067]
International dictionary of food and cooking. Sinclair, C.G., *ed.* Oxford, Fitzroy Dearborn, 1998. 594p. £25; $55. ISBN: 1579580572.
More than 24,000 culinary terms from *c.*35 countries covering areas such as cooking processes, nutrition, and equipment. Over 1,500 entries concerning E numbers. Definitions are brief and the country of origin of the term is indicated by an abbreviation.
Class No: 641.5(038)=20

[6068]
Webster's new world dictionary of culinary arts. Labensky, S., *and others.* Upper Saddle River, N.J., Prentice Hall, 1997. v,447p. illus.,charts. £20.95; $25.95. ISBN: 0134757327.
Brief definitions of more than 15,000 terms covering cookery worldwide. Cross-references. Appendices list metric and temperature equivalents, and stages of cooked sugar. A few line-drawings, mainly of kitchen equipment. *Class No:* 641.5(038)=20

German

[6069]
NEIGER, E. Gastronomisches Wörterbuch zur Übersetzung and Erklärung der Speisekarten. [Gastronomic dictionary for the translation and explanation of menus.] 2. verbesserte und erw. Aufl. Munich, Gerber, 1971.
First published 1962.
German-French-English-Italian. About 2,000 terms defined in 20 sections (Saucen ... Gemüse ... Kartoffeln ... Frühstück). 3 appendices. *Class No:* 641.5(038)=30

French

[6070]
'Bon appétit': a French-English gastronomic dictionary. White, J.A., *comp.* Ely, Cambs., Peppercorn Books, 1990. 111p. £4.80. ISBN: 0951641301.
Small, handy guide containing over 3,500 definitions, including many regional and specialized dishes. *Class No:* 641.5(038)=40

Japanese

[6071]
HOSKING, R. A Dictionary of Japanese food: ingredients and culture. Totnes, Prospect Books, 1996. 239p. illus. £12.99. ISBN: 0907325742.
Arranged in three parts: Japanese-English, English-Japanese, and appendices (1. Chopsticks ... 6. Miso ... 13. The tea ceremony ... 17. Wasanbon sugar). Recommended reading, p.2-238. Each entry in the first section includes the Japanese term in Roman script, in kana or kanji, a Latin name where appropriate and, for most entries, a brief annotation. *Class No:* 641.5(038)=956

Tables & Data Books

[6072]
SCHMIDT, A. Chef's book of formulas, yields and size. New York, Van Nostrand Reinhold, 1990. 338p. $39.95. ISBN: 0442318359.
Arranged alphabetically, Abalone ... Yucca root. Data include the forms in which foods are available (*e.g.* canned, fresh, frozen), suggested serving sizes, number of servings from the most common packet sizes, and new meat cuts. Cross-references and index. Author is affiliated to the Culinary Institute of America. *Class No:* 641.5(083)

Great Britain

[6073]
British cookery: based on research undertaken for the British Food Information Service of Food from Britain and the British Tourist Authority by the University of Strathclyde. Boyd, L., *ed.* 2nd ed. London, Christopher Helm, 1988. 651p. £7.95. ISBN: 0747002231.
About 2,000 native English, Scots, Irish and Welsh recipes, ranging from yeast cookery to preserves and chutneys. New ed. 'includes changes and additions to the range of foodstuffs that are available' (*Foreword*). Of the previous ed., 'Bids fair to become a standard reference work' (*Daily telegraph,* 2 December 1976, p.13). Excellent value. *Class No:* 641.5(410)

[6074]
KAPOOR, S. Modern British food. London, Penguin, 1995. 342p. £13. ISBN: 014023814x.
Recipes arranged month by month to reflect seasonal food preferences and availability. Prelude to each recipe gives information on the history of either the ingredients or the dish. Select bibliography, p.332-3. Index. *Class No:* 641.5(410)

France

[6075]

La Cuisine: the complete book of French cooking. Translated from French. Létoile, V.-A., *and others.* London, Orbis, 1985. 552p. col. illus. £17.50. ISBN: 0356150836.

15 sections: Equipment - The value of food - Wine - French cheeses - Buffets - Basic cooking techniques ... Sauces ... First courses ... Meal - Vegetables ... Desserts, cakes and pastries. Recipes for *c.*2,000 dishes state French and English names, heating time, measures (American/Imperial, metric), ingredients, industrial. Glossary of French cookery terms, p.324-9. French and English indexes. Fully illustrated in colour. *Class No:* 641.5(44)

Spain

[6076]

CASADO, M.A. Spanish cuisine: the gourmet's companion. New York, John Wiley, 1997. 150p. £13.99;$16.95. ISBN: 0471137227.

Introduction looks at the cuisine of specific areas of Spain, *e.g.*, Castile, Galicia. Two parts: 1. Spanish and Portuguese dishes, by course (Tapas ... Arroz ... Bebidas y refrescos); English translations and definitions are given; 2. Spanish food and beverage vocabulary (Abadejo ... Zurrucutana). Author is an associate professor at the Northern Arizona University School of Hotel and Restaurant Management. *Class No:* 641.5(460)

Asia

[6077]

PASSMORE, J. The Letts companion to Asian food & cookery. London, Letts, 1991. 320p. figs. £16.95. ISBN: 1852381515.

Entries arranged A-Z (Aamchur ... Zoni), using names in English and anglicized Asian. Asian names are used as cross-references, of which there are more than 1,000. Pronunciation guides for all main entries and cross-references. Entries include information on cooking methods, country of origin, preparation techniques. Recipes appear throughout, and a recipe index is included. Brief bibliography. Packed with information. *Class No:* 641.5(5)

China

[6078]

HOM, K. Ken Hom's Chinese cookery. London, BBC, 1984. 260p. illus., diagrs., tables. £7.99. ISBN: 0563210532.

Introduction - Ingredients - Equipment - Techniques - Menus and how to eat Chinese food. - Soups - Meat - Chicken, duck and game - Fish and shellfish - Vegetables - Rice, noodles and dough. Snacks and sweets. Mail order list. Detailed, analytical index. Well illustrated. *Class No:* 641.5(510)

Recipe Books

[6079]

The International cookery index. Kleiman, R.H. *and* Kleiman, A.M., *comps.* New York, Neal-Schumann, 1987. 230p. $65. ISBN: 0918212871.

An index to 25,000 recipes, cited from 52 "classic" or well-known cookery books. 'Embraces most major ethnic and regional cultures' (*Library journal,* August 1987, p.116). *Class No:* 641.55

[6080]

—TORGESON, K.W. *and* WEINSTEIN, S.J. The Garland recipe index. New York, Garland Publishing Co., 1984. 372p. (*Garland reference library of the humanities, 414.*) ISBN: 0824091248.

Indexes 48 popular cookery books, both classics and specialized. Entries appear under name of recipe, stating principal food ingredients and method of cooking. Well cross-referenced. *Class No:* 641.55

[6081]

—Traditional recipes of the British Isles. Heaton, N., *comp.* London, Faber, 1951. 215p.

Has sections: Special days and their customs - Food and table manners - Northern counties and the Isle of Man - Southern counties - Eastern counties - Midlands - Western counties, Wales and Northern Ireland - Scotland and the Isles. Detailed index. *Class No:* 641.55

Vegetarian Cookery

[6082]

DYER, J.C. Vegetarianism: an annotated bibliography. Metuchen, N.J., Scarecrow Press, 1982. xi,280p. $22.50. ISBN: 081081532x.

Contains 1,412 entries covering all aspects of vegetarianism. Appendix lists 200 vegetarian cookbooks. *Class No:* 641.564

[6083]

ELLIOT, R. Rose Elliot's complete vegetarian cookbook. London, Collins, 1985. 361p. £10.95. ISBN: 0004120094.

Contains over 1,000 recipes. 14 sections: 1. Soups - hot and chilled ... 6. Main course vegetable and nut dishes ... 10. Savoury flans and pies ... 14. Bread and yeast cookery, including pizza. Detailed index, p.347-61. *Class No:* 641.564

[6084]

LOVELOCK, Y. The Vegetable book: an unnatural history. London, Allen & Unwin, 1972. 382p. illus.

3 main parts: 1. Leaves, stems, roots and fruit (Aku ... Yams, p.25-258) - 2. Miscellaneous nuts, grains and pastas (Acorns and beechnuts ... Wheat), p.261-312 - 3. Various herbs, spices and condiments. Gives geographical locale, history and use, and names of vegetables in various languages. 19 decorative illus. Indexes of Latin and common names. Aims 'to treat all the important foods and staples of the world, avoiding as far as possible a narrow Western viewpoint' (*Introduction*). *Class No:* 641.564

Drinks

[6085]

HALLEY, N. The Wordsworth dictionary of drink: an A-Z of alcoholic beverages. Ware, Wordsworth Editions, 1996. 512p. £2.99. ISBN: 1853263818.

Does not claim to be comprehensive but is international in scope and provides translations of terms, without being too technical. Arranged A-Z (Aalborg ... Zytnia), definitions are brief and simple. Useful, quick reference tool. *Class No:* 641.87

Condiments, Garnishes & Pickles

[6086]

MULHERIN, J. Spices and natural flavourings a complete guide to the identification and uses of common and exotic spices and natural flavourings. London, Ward Lock, 1988. illus. (col.). ISBN: 0025878500.

Review of more than 60 spices and flavourings. Entries include a brief identification with historical notes and information on the country of origin, culinary uses, methods of preparation, storage, and a recipe. List of suppliers and useful addresses. Index. *Class No:* 641.88

[6087]

NORMAN, J. The Complete book of spices. London, Dorling Kindersley, 1990. 160p. illus. (col.), maps. £14.99. ISBN: 0863184871.

5 main sections: The spice trade past and present - Spice index (arranged by botanical name) - Spice mixtures (*e.g.* 'Sambal'; 'Berbere') - Cooking with spices, p.110-45 - Spices in the home. Index. Bibliography (85 items). Data for each spice include distribution; appearance and growth; aroma and taste; culinary, medicinal and cosmetic uses. Clearly and colourfully presented. *Class No:* 641.88

[6088]

RINZLER, C.A. The Complete book of herbs, spices and condiments. New York, Facts on File, 1990. 199p. $19.95. ISBN: 0816020086.

Entries vary from one to three pages in length. Data include botanical name, common name, native habitat, medicinal properties, alternative uses, nutritional profile, effect on the body and how it may be grown. Index and bibliography. *Class No:* 641.88

[6089]

SKELLY, C.J. Dictionary of herbs, spices, seasonings, and natural flavorings. New York, Garland Publishing Inc., 1994. xiii,484p. $75. (*Garland reference library of social science, v.918.*) ISBN: 0815314655.

Lists A-Z herb and spice plants used in North America. Data include common, Latin, family, and vernacular names, plant part used, toxic properties etc. Two appendices: 1. Families (alphabetical list of plants in family order); 2. Genera (alphabetical list of plants by Latin name). Six-page bibliography. *Class No:* 641.88

[6090]

STOBART, T. Herbs, spices and flavorings. Woodstock, N.J., Overlook Press, 1986. 320p. illus. $22.50. ISBN: 0879511486.

A readable guide to some 400 herbs/spices, A-Z ('Mustard': 9p.). Common names and synonyms feature in 5 languages. *Class No:* 641.88

The Home

Bibliographies

[6091]

ATTAR, D. A Bibliography of household books published in Britain, 1840-1914. London, Passport Books, 1987. 438p. ISBN: 0907325351.

737 entries, p.63-388. Sections: Domestic economy - Servants - Domestic medicine and childcare - Etiquette - Selective notes on secondary works. British and US library locations. Subject index. Chronological list of short titles. Short-title index.
Class No: 643/645(01)

Encyclopaedias

[6092]

How to do just about anything. London, New York, Reader's Digest Association, 1988. 543p. illus. (col.). £22.95. ISBN: 0276419936.

16 contributors. Arranged A-Z (Abacus ... Zodiac) with about 2,000 entries, and including topics such as mending punctures, needlework, gardening and general home maintenance. Many colour illustrations. Index. Bibliography (in very small type). *Class No:* 643/645(031)

[6093]

The 'Which?' encyclopedia of the home. London, Consumers' Association, and Hodder & Stoughton, 1984. 671p. illus., tables. £14.95. ISBN: 0340351055.

68 sections, - Accidents and first aid ... Windows. Wide range of topics, *e.g.* Buying and selling a home; children; cookery (p.133-67); health; painting and decorating; pets; plumbing and drainage; sewing; taxation; vegetable growing. Bibliography (building and maintenance; health and fitness; household management; money, law and consumer issues). Addresses, p.658-62. Detailed analytical index, p.663-71. Well produced and excellent value. *Class No:* 643/645(031)

Handbooks & Manuals

[6094]

BREMNER, M. Enquire within upon everything. 2nd ed. London, Century, 1990. viii,756p. figs. £17.99. ISBN: 0091745535.

First published 1988.

16 sections: 1. Social behaviour - 2. Food ... 4. Domestic matters ... 9. Things mechanical - 10. Law - 11. Money - 12. In sickness ... 15. Organizations (Consumer bodies ... Medical - Police ... Travel and transport) - 16. Facts and figures. Bibliography. Index. 'It is a first source which will give the basics and provide pointers to where to find out anything else you want to know' (*Preface*).
Class No: 643/645(035)

[6095]

—Good Housekeeping household hints: the essential home facts. London, Ebury Press, 1989. 146p. ISBN: 0852237286.

9 sections: 1. Safety first ... 4. Pests and infestations ... 7. Flora and fauna ... 9. Emergency action. List of useful addresses. Index. For a small public library. *Class No:* 643/645

[6096]

Henley's formulas for home and workshop; containing ten thousand selected household, workshop and scientific formulas, trade secrets, food and chemical recipes, processes for money saving ideas. Hiscox, G.D., *ed.* New York, Avenue Books, 1979 (reprinted 1991, Outlet Book Company). $9.99. xxviii, 9-809p. illus. ISBN: 0517293072.

First published 1907.

Entries, 'Acid-proofing' ... 'Yeast tests'. Preceded by a section, 'Useful workshop and laboratory methods'. Small line-drawings.
Class No: 643/645(035)

Histories

[6097]

DU VALL, N. Domestic technology a chronology of developments. Boston, Mass., G.K. Hall, 1988. 535p. $40. ISBN: 0816189137.

2 sections: Part 1 consists of chapters on food, clothing, waste disposal cleaning, tools, lighting, heating and housing and health; Part 2 is a continuous chronology from 500,000 BC to 1987. Criticized in *Choice*, May 1989, for an inadequate index but still useful for academic and public libraries. *Class No:* 643/645(091)

[6098]

'Good Housekeeping' every home should have one. London, Ebury Press, 1997. 144p. illus. £16.99. ISBN: 0091852803.

Provides a general overview of how housework and life in the home have changed over a period of 75 years. Eight sections: each dealing with a specific decade: The 1920s: drudgery flies out at the window ... The 1950s: boom time ... The 1970s: freezers and feminism ... The 1990s: back to the future. Index. The many reproductions of contemporary articles and advertisements add considerably to the value of what is rather light text. *Class No:* 643/645 (091)

[6099]

HARDYMENT, C. From mangle to microwave: the mechanizaton of household work. Cambridge, Polity Press, 1988. xii,220p. illus. £10.95. ISBN: 0745602061.

10 Chapters: 1. Homes without machines - 2. Of pig-iron and parlourmaids ... 5. House-cleaning ... 8. Essential kitchen technology ... 10. The domestic mystique. Bibliography, p.203-11. Index. A good overview. *Class No:* 643/645(091)

[6100]

—YARWOOD, D. Five hundred years of technology in the home. London, Batsford, 1983. 184p. illus., ports. ISBN: 0713435062.

9 chapters: 1. Science and society - 2. Fuels and sources of power - 3. Food - 4/6. The home: The materials in use; Exterior and structure; The interior - 7. Textiles - 8. Communication and entertainment - 9. Modern technology: the way ahead (the microelectronic revolution). Select bibliography, p.176-7. Detailed, analytical index. 263 illus. Written primarily for students of social and economic history, as well as for home economics at O-level standard. *Class No:* 643/645(091)

Maintenance

[6101]

A Consumer's guide to home improvement, renovation, and repair. Santucci, R., *and others.* New York, John Wiley & Sons, 1990. xiv,270p. illus., tables. $34.95. ISBN: 0471519227.

Basic aim is to show the reader how to cut costs in home repair and improvement, while still maintaining safety standards. 2 sections: 1. Methods and materials (15 chapters: 1. Walls and ceilings ... 9. Carpentry ... 15. Outside work and foundations) - 2. Money-saving strategies (4 chapters: 16. Planning and design ... 18. Working with design professionals and contractors - 19. Saving money on tools and materials). Index. US-slanted, but contains ideas which would be applicable anywhere. *Class No:* 643.0045

[6102]

The Homeowner's complete manual of repair & improvement. Bragdon, A.D., *ed.* New York, Arco, [*c*.1983]. 576p. illus. $14.95. ISBN: 0668057378.

Originally as *Peterson's Home repair & maintenance guide.*

6 sections (subdivided into chapters): Interior repairs & decoration - Windows - Doors - Security & insulation - Furniture care & refinishing - Electrical fixtures, wiring and appliances - Plumbing and heating - Exterior maintenance & improvements. Excellent illus. and step-by-step instructions. Brief index. Given high marks for simplicity, completeness, accuracy and readability in *Reference books bulletin, 1983-1984*, p.102. *Class No:* 643.0045

[6103]

Mend it! A complete guide to repairers and restorers. Ball, R., *comp.* London, Orbis, 1985. 240p. ISBN: 0856135100.

Books and paper - Building and sculpture ... Carpets, canvas and other textiles ... Clocks, watches and barometers ... Furniture and woodwork - Glass ... Musical instruments and equipment ... Silver and other metals - Transport. Useful addresses (grouped). Bibliography, p.229-31. Detailed, analytical index. (*c*.1,000 entries).
Class No: 643.0045

[6104]

Reader's Digest new D-I-Y manual. London, Reader's Digest Association, 1987. 504p. illus. (col.), figs., diagrs. Loose-leaf. £32.95. ISBN: 0276404564.

2 sections: 1. Items for the home (*e.g.* Kitchens ... Bedrooms ... Outside the house) - 2. Techniques, tools and materials (*e.g.* Painting, wallpapering and tiling ... Home security ... Central heating ... DIY in the garden). Index, p.1-5. A step-by-step guide with numerous illustrations. A standard DIY title. *Class No:* 643.0045

[6105]

—Reader's Digest fix-it-yourself manual. London, Reader's Digest Association, Ltd., 1977. 480p. illus., diagrs.

Complementary to *Reader's Digest new D-I-Y manual.* It concentrates on several dozen types of devices and tools such as plumbing fixtures, locks, bicycles, lamps, typewriters and garden tools. Clear instructions, well illustrated. Detailed table of contents and index. *Class No:* 643.0045

[6106]

The 'Which?' book of do-it-yourself. London, Consumers' Association, and Hodder & Stoughton, 1992. 320p. illus., tables. £19.95. ISBN: 0340568682.

20 contributors. 12 chapters: 1. Decorating - 2. Electricity - 3. Woodworking - 4. Fixings - 5. Building - 6. Floors - 7. Roofs - 8. Doors and windows - 9. Security - 10. Metalworking - 11. Plumbing - 12. Damp, rot and woodworm. Useful names and addresses, p. 313. Index, p.315-20. Fully illustrated. Well captioned and produced. *Class No:* 643.0045

[6107]

The 'Which?' book of home improvements and extensions. London, Consumers' Association, and Hodder & Stoughton, 1983. 319p. illus., diagrs., tables.

18 contributors. 3 parts (12 chapters): 1. What's involved - 2. Improvements room by room - 3. Extensions and conversions (*e.g.* chapter 10: 'Loft conversions', p.278-95). Useful addresses. Index, p.315-9. Good illus.; well captioned. Attractively produced. Over 1,000 illus. *Class No:* 643.0045

Furnishings

[6108]

Laura Ashley complete guide to home decoration. Dickson, E., *and others*. London, Weidenfeld & Nicolson, 1989. 224p. illus. (mostly col.), diagrs. ISBN: 0706421552.

6 sections: Structure and style - Decorating - Window dressing - Soft furnishings - Beds & bedlinen - Accessories. Appendix includes 'Sewing techniques'; 'Measuring up'; 'Laura Ashley shops'. Index. *Class No:* 645

[6109]

WORMLEIGHTON, A. The Encyclopedia of home furnishing techniques. London, Headline, 1997. 192p. illus.(col.). £19.99. ISBN: 0747219982.

10 chapters: Decorative techniques ... Bed linen ... Cushions and seating. Glossary; index. Explains techniques used to complete soft-furnishings projects. Many colour photographs. *Class No:* 645

Clothing

Sewing & Needlework

[6110]

CLABBURN, P. The Needleworker's dictionary. London, Macmillan, 1976. 296p. illus. (incl. col.), diagrs.

Nearly 2,000 entries, A-Z, including short biographies. Cross-references. Appended select list of museums and collections exhibiting textiles. Bibliography, p.288-92. 350 photographs, 300 line-drawings. 'Mainly for students of needlework, amateur and professional embroiderers, art and costume historians, and the fashion world... An invaluable work of reference' (*British book news*, April 1977, p.313). *Class No:* 646.2

[6111]

LADBURY, A. The Dressmaker's dictionary. London, Batsford, 1982. 358p. illus., patterns. ISBN: 0713418230.

Entries, A-Z, include the 'traditional terms of stitches, processes and equipment in common use in dressmaking as well as new ideas and new aids' (*Preface*). Over 900 illus., captioned line-drawings. *Class No:* 646.2

[6112]

Reader's Digest complete guide to sewing. London, New York, etc., Reader's Digest Association, Ltd., 1978. 528p. illus., (incl. col.), diagrs. £18.95. ISBN: 0276001826.

Detailed, step-by-step approach. Sections: Sewing essentials - Patterns, fabrics and linings - Making clothes that fit - Designing your own patterns - Preparing to sew - Basic stitches - Seams - Darts and tucks - Pleats - Gathering, shirting, smocking and ruffles - Pockets - Hems and other edge finishes - Zip fasteners - Buttons and other fasteners - Tailoring - Sewing for the family - Sewing for the home (*e.g.* bedspreads). Sewing projects (p.440-516; *e.g.* dresses, dungarees). Over 2,000 two-colour illus. ('Collars', p.228-44; *c.*150 illus). Many patterns. Index, p.517-20. *Class No:* 646.2

Cleaning

[6113]

PHILLIPS, B. How to clean absolutely everything. Rev ed. London, Piatkus, 1992. 154p. £7.99. ISBN: 0749910925.

First published 1990 as *The Complete book of cleaning* which was a concise update of the author's *Wonder worker's complete book of cleaning (q.v.)* (1979).

Where appropriate, this book offers 3 methods of cleaning: 'right'; 'lazy'; 'green'. 15 chapters: 1. Laundering ... 6. Guidelines for housework ... 10. Cleaning windows and plate glass ... 13. A-Z of cleaning metals ... 15. A-Z of household products. Addresses, p.149-51. Index. *Class No:* 648.5

[6114]

PHILLIPS, B. Wonder worker's complete book of cleaning. London, Sidgwick & Jackson, 1980. 255p. illus. ISBN: 0283985461.

12 chapters: 1. A good wash [laundering] - 2. A to Z of fabrics and fibres - 3. Dry-cleaning - 4. Stain removing at home - 5. Dyeing - 6. Body care - 7. The lazy person's guide to housework - 8. Outdoor cleaning - 9. A to Z of household materials and how to clean them - 10. Choosing cleansing equipment - 11. Glossary and guide (p.222-41) - 12. Information sources (Consumer protection ... Specialist cleaners). Detailed, analytical index, p.245-58. *Class No:* 648.5

[6115]

—**MOORE, A.C.** How to clean everything: an encyclopedia of what to use and how to use it. Rev. ed. London, T. Stacey, 1972 (reprinted 1978, David and Charles). 232p. illus.

First published in 1952 (New York, Simon & Schuster).

Sections: 1. How to clean and what to use - 2. How to remove stains and marks - 3. Control of household pests - 4. Cleaning agents and their uses. 'This book is for women who dislike homework but like nice houses' (*Introduction*). Enlivened by humorous drawings. 'Highly recommended'. (*RQ*, v.8(4) 1969, p.288). *Class No:* 648.5

Pest Control

[6116]

BATEMAN, P.L.G. Household pests: a guide to the identification and control of insect, rodent, damp and fungoid problems. Poole, Dorset, Blandford Press, 1979. 174p. illus. (incl. col.). ISBN: 0713709154.

3 parts: 1. Background to pests and problems - 2. Insect and rodent pests, rots and moulds - 3. The broader viewpoint (*e.g.* Sources of further information). Bibliography (11 items), p.172. Some common insecticide chemicals. Non-analytical index, p.175-6. *Class No:* 648.7

Child Care

[6117]

JOLLY, H. Book of child care: complete guide for today's parents. 4th ed. London, Allen & Unwin, 1985. [xv],569p. illus. £14.95; £8.99. ISBN: 0046490345.

2 parts (each of 26 chapters): 1. The healthy child - 2. The sick child. Part 1 involves such topics as 1. Pregnancy and birth ... 25. The one-parent family; 26. Travel, holiday and living in the tropics. Part 2, - 27. Child, parents and their doctor ... 51. Accidents; 52. When a child dies. *Class No:* 649.1

[6118]

The Macmillan guide to child health. Hull, D., *ed.* London, Macmillan, 1985. 382p. illus., diagrs., charts. ISBN: 0333392507.

46 contributors. 4 parts: 1. Care of the child - 2. Care of sick child - 3. Problems, diseases and disorders (p.120-310) - 4. Appendices: resources (support groups and publications, etc.). Emergency actions, p.330-41. Index of syndromes, p.342-3. Analytical index, p.344-52. Over 500 two-colour illus. A guide that spans the child's life from conception to adolescence. For public library and home use. Analytical index. *Class No:* 649.1

Invalid Care

[6119]

Helping to care: a handbook for carers at home and in hospital. Kershaw, B., *and others*. London, Baillière Tindall, 1989. 189p. figs. £4.50. ISBN: 0702013374.

18 chapters: 1. The management of care ... 4. Mobilising ... 8. Meeting hygiene needs - 9. Waking and dressing ... 15. Caring for the sick child ... 17. Working with people with a mental handicap - 18. Where next? Further reading, p.176-7. Useful addresses, p.178-81. Index. *Class No:* 649.8

654/656 Communication

Telecommunication Services

[6120]
International directory of telecommunications: market trends, companies, statistics and personnel. Robert, S. *and* Hay, T., *eds*. 4th ed. Harlow, Essex, Longman, 1990. xiv,386p. tables. £140. ISBN: 0582047382.

First published 1984.

Profiles of *c*.800 manufacturers, telecommunication administrations and regulatory bodies in over 100 countries. Arranged in 12 geographical areas. Indexes of companies, products, services, registered trade names and key personnel. *Class No:* 654

[6121]
International encyclopedia of communications. Barnouw, E., *and others, eds*. New York, Oxford, University Press, 1989. 4v. illus., figs., maps. £250. ISBN: 019505802x, v.1; 0195058038, v.2; 0195058046, v.3; 0195058054, v.4; 0195049942, set.

A highly interdisciplinary work, covering communications in its widest sense, embracing topics in the humanities, arts, and sciences. 569 subjects covered include mass media; theatre; language; literature; cinematography. Documented articles, arranged A-Z, written by over 450 specialist contributors. Over 1,100 black-and-white photographs, in addition to many line drawings. Some articles would be considered too specialized for the lay person. However, 'this fine work is recommended for academic and large public libraries' (*Reference books bulletin*, 1988/1989, p.29-30). *Class No:* 654

[6122]
Marconi's international register. Larchmont, N.J., Telegraphic Cable & Radio Registrations, Inc. ISBN: 0916446174.

The 1991 *Register* (1336p. $150) includes fax, mail, telephone, and cable subscribers. International in scope, with prominent companies listed A-Z, and an international trade classification following. Index of cable addresses. *Class No:* 654

[6123]
WATSON, J. *and* **HILL, A.** **A Dictionary of communication and media studies.** 3rd ed. London, Edward Arnold, 1993. x,205p. figs.,diagrs. ISBN: 0340574259.

First published 1984.

Contains *c*.1,500 terms, with over 100 new definitions added since the previous edition. For students and teachers. *Class No:* 654

[6124]
WEIK, M.H. **Communications standard dictionary.** 2nd ed. New York, Van Nostrand Reinhold, 1989. 1219p. illus., diagrs., graphs. $69.95. ISBN: 0442205562.

About 13,600 entries and cross-references concerning the science and technology of communications ('A-and-not-B gate' ... 'Zoom lens'). Claims to cover 64 fields. *Class No:* 654

Telex

[6125]
International telex, 1990/91. Darmstadt, Telex International; J+International Telex.

Formerly *Jaeger + Waldmann Telex + teletex international.*

International guide for the hotel and tourist trade. 1-4. *Alphabetical section.* Countries: A-F, G-I, J-S, T-Z. 4v. 5-7. *Numerical* (Answerback code section). v.5-7: 1-3, 4-7; 8-9/A-Z. 8. *Products:* 0-34. 9. *Services:* 35-41.

'*Jaeger and Waldmann* constitutes probably the most extensive world-wide directory available' (*Printed reference material*. 2nd ed., edited by G.L. Higgins (1984), p.171). The Answerback section is particularly handy. *Class No:* 654.145

Fax

[6126]
J + W international telefax. 10th ed. Darmstadt, Telex-Verlag Jaeger + Waldmann GmbH, 1994. 8v.

Arranged alphabetically by country. Each entry gives full company name and address, in addition to the fax number. *Class No:* 654.146

[6127]
The Official United States fax directory. Johnson, Y.A., *ed*. 7th ed. Detroit, Gale Research, 1996. xxxi,2203p. ISBN: 0787608157.

Lists *c*.180,000 major businesses, agencies, and organizations in the US. Each entry includes name, address, fax and telephone numbers, address. Arranged both alphabetically by name and also by subject. *Class No:* 654.146

Telephone Services

[6128]
The Good code guide. Old Isleworth, Harp Publications, 1996. ix,188p. £14.99. ISBN: 1898308101.

A listing of telephone codes. Five sections: National codes alphabetically - National codes numerically - International codes alphabetically - International codes numerically. Also lists mobile 'phone codes although these may have altered since publication. *Class No:* 654.15

[6129]
PhoneNetUK. British Telecom. URL: http://www/phonenetuk/.

Searchable database by name (people/businesses and location) for telephone numbers in the UK. *Class No:* 654.15

[6130]
Telecom users handbook. London, Telecommunications Press, 1982-.

Has 20 sections (2. Telephone instruments and aids; 8. Data transmission; 14. The electronic office; 20. British Telecommunications price schedule). Glossary of terms. Index of advertisers. A practical guide to business communications. *Class No:* 654.15

Broadcasting Services

[6131]
The Blue book of British broadcasting 1999. Mann, R., *ed*. 25th ed. London, Tellex Monitors, 1999. 533p. ISBN: 0952975440.

Seven sections: 1. Regulation and standards ... 5. Satellite and cable channels ... 7. Digital broadcasting. Four indexes: 1. Broadcasters and broadcasting organisations - 2. Contracts - 3. Radio programmes - 4. Television programmes. Basically a list of contact names in British broadcasting. *Class No:* 654.19

[6132]
CRISELL, A. **An introductory history of British broadcasting.** London, Routledge, 1997. xvi,280p. £40. ISBN: 0415128021.

Three parts (11 chapters): 1. The phenomenon of broadcasting (1. The birth of radio ... 6. Pilkington and after ... 9. A growth of sights and sounds) - 2. The rise of the active audience (10. Cables, dishes and deregulation) - 11. And now the nineties) - 3. From broadcasting to multimedia. Bibliography, p.263-70. A useful overview of the subject. *Class No:* 654.19

[6133]
MacDONALD, B. **Broadcasting in the United Kingdom:** a guide to information sources. 2nd rev. ed. London, Mansell, 1994. xvii,316p. tables. ISBN: 0720120861.

First published 1988; 2nd ed. 1993.

Six sections: 1. Chronology of broadcasting in the United Kingdom - 2. Structure and organizations - 3. Primary sources of information and documentation - 4. Printed and electronic reference sources - 5. Researching into broadcasting: notes of guidance - 6. Directory of institutional sources of information. A wide-ranging and useful guide. *Class No:* 654.19

[6134]
Public broadcasting for the 21st century. Raboy, M., *ed*. Luton, John Libbey Media, 1996. xiv,303p. £25. (*Academia research monograph, 17*.) ISBN: 1860200060.

18 contributors. Aims 'to provide a general portrait of the situation of public broadcasting in different parts of the world' (*Preface*). The 16 chapters include overviews of broadcsating in Britain, Sweden, Canada, Japan, India, Cambodia, and Latin america. Each chapter has a list of references appended. No index, but a useful starting point. *Class No:* 654.19

[6135]
World radio TV handbook 1999: the directory of international broadcasting. [n.l], Watson-Guptill Publications, 1998. 608p. illus., tables, maps.

A guide to radio and television broadcasting stations throughout the world (including domestic and international radio listings), with data on frequencies, radiated power, exact location, operating hours, frequency schedules, languages broadcast, news bulletins, etc. Separate sections for radio and television, each arranged by continent and then alphabetically by country. Separate list medium wave stations. Information about international organizations. Miscellaneous data: world time; solar activity; reception conditions; receivers owned in each country; suitable megahertz bands, etc. User's guide. Equipment test reports. Advertisements. *Class No:* 654.19

Television Broadcasting

[6136]
The European television directory 1994/95. Henley-on-Thames, Oxon., NTC Publications, 1994. 235p. ISBN: 1870562593.

Prelims. include 'Contents by channel'; 'Contents by country'. 2 pages used per station. One page descriptive text and commentary. Details of legislation affecting channels also given. The second page gives channel ownership, delivery system, funding, viewing share, etc. *Class No:* 654.197

[6137]
HOLLINS, T. Beyond broadcasting into the cable age. London, BFI Publishing for the Broadcasting Research Unit, 1984. x, 385p. £5.95. ISBN: 0851701485.

Follows the BRU's *Report of the Working Party on new technologies.* (1984).

5 parts: 1. The cable debate - 2. Cable in Britain: the historical and political background - 3. The Canadian experience - 4. The United States (p.113-272) - 5. British plans and prospects. Conclusion: Into the Cable age. Appendices. Index. *Class No:* 654.197

The Book

Handbooks & Manuals

[6138]
GASKELL, P. A New introduction to bibliography. Oxford, Clarendon Press, 1972. xxii, [1], 438p. illus. £30. ISBN: 0198181507.

Intended as a successor to R.A. McKerrow's classic *Introduction to bibliography* (1927).

Contents: Introduction - Book production: the hand-press period, 1500-1800 - Book production, the machine-press period, 1800-1950 - Bibliographical application (*e.g.* bibliographical descriptions; textual bibliography). Reference bibliography, p.392-412 (running commentary; includes periodicals) - Detailed index. Well produced. Very favourably reviewed in *College & research libraries,* v.34(4), July 1973, p.295. *Class No:* 655.0(035)

[6139]
JENNETT, S. The Making of books. 5th ed. London, Faber, 1973. 554p. illus. (incl. col.), facsims.

First published 1951.

2 parts (24 chapters): 1. Printing and binding (chapters 1-12) - 2. The design of books (13-24). This ed. includes new techniques and technologies. List of 'further reading and reference', p.517-23. 'A polyglot glossary of technical terms' (English, French, German, Italian), p.524-39. Detailed, non-analytical index. 200 illus. A standard work for students of bibliography, typography and printing. *Class No:* 655.0(035)

[6140]
PEACOCK, J. Book production. 2nd ed. First published 1989. London, Blueprint Publishing, 1995. 512p. illus. £50. ISBN: 1857130081.

14 sections: 1. Choosing the format - 2. Preparing the text ... 8. Proofing the cover or jacket ... - 13. Binding styles - 14. Organising packing, despatch and distribution. 3 appendices: 1. Technical data - 2. Further information sources - 3. Dictionary. Index. A standard text for all those involved in book production. *Class No:* 655.0(035)

Dictionaries

[6141]
GLAISTER, G.A. Glaister's glossary of the book: terms used in papermaking, printing, bookbinding and publishing, with notes on illuminated manuscripts and private presses. 2nd ed. London, Allen & Unwin, 1979. [xv], 551p. illus. (incl. col.), facsims. £35. ISBN: 0040100065.

First published 1960.

3,932 entries, including biographies (*e.g.* Gutenberg: nearly 2p.; 2

....(contd.)
facsims.). Updated to include such entries as 'Computer assisted typesetting' (1½ columns; 7 cross-references). Covers all book-making processes, with a natural emphasis on the historical (*e.g.* 'Islamic bookbinding: 2p.). Appendixes A-D (A. Some type specimens; D. A short reading list, p.547-51, grouped). 238 illus. 'Apart from specialist libraries, any general reference collection of any size must have a copy' (*Library Association record,* v.82(8), August 1980, p.370). *Class No:* 655.0(038)

[6142]
PETERS, J. The Bookman's glossary. 6th ed., rev. and enl. New York, etc., Bowker, 1983. ix, 223p. $39.95; £35. ISBN: 0855216861.

Defines *c.*2,000 terms used in the antiquarian book trade, bookmaking, computerized typesetting, printing, publishing and bookselling. 'Lithography': ½p.; 'Caxton': 1p. Cross-references. Selected reading list (grouped), p.216-21. *Class No:* 655.0(038)

[6143]
Russko-angliiskii slovar' knigovedcheskikh terminov. Elizarenkova, T.P., *comp.* Moscow, Izdat 'Sovetskaya Entsiklopediya', 1969. 264p.

9,300 terms, including abbreviations, covering book science, bibliography, librarianship, publishing, printing and the book trade. English abbreviations. *Class No:* 655.0(038)

Histories

[6144]
Annual bibliography of the history of the printed book and libraries. The Hague, Nijhoff (now Dordrecht, Kluwer Academic Publishers), 1973-. v.1-. Annual.

Compiled by the National Committees of 25 countries, v.26 (1998, 464p.) has over 3,000 entries for items published in 1996, plus additions from the previous years. List of periodicals (*c.*2,000). Sections A-M (E. Book illustration; G. Book trade, publishing; J. Libraries, librarianship, scholarship; L. Newspapers, journalism). Indexes: Authors' names and anonyms; Geographical and personal names. 'A basic item for any bibliographical reference shelf' (*TLS,* no.3951, 15 December 1977, p.1484), although the reviewer in *Reference reviews,* v.8,no.3, 1994 feels that it would find a wider market if the arrangement was more user-friendly. *Class No:* 655.0(091)

[6145]
FEATHER, J. A Dictionary of book history. London, Croom Helm, 1986. 288p. ISBN: 0709910436.

Published in paperback by Routledge, 1991. £50.

About 650 entries, varying in length from short definitions to lengthy articles. Covers history of printing, publishing and bookselling, bookbinding, paper, bibliographies, etc. Includes some biography. *Class No:* 655.0(091)

[6146]
ROSENBLUM, J. A Bibliographic history of the book: an annotated guide to the literature. Metuchen, N.J., Scarecrow/Salem Press, 1995. 425p. $55. ISBN: 0810830094.

Lists books and articles on all aspects of book production, *e.g.* paper, ink, binding, bookselling, etc., complete with annotations. Author and subject indexes. *Class No:* 655.0(091)

[6147]
WINCKLER, P.A. History of books and printing: a guide to information sources. Detroit, Mich., Gale, 1979. xiv, 209p. (*Books, publishing and libraries information guide series.*) ISBN: 0810314088.

776 annotated entries. 9 sections: 1. General bibliographies - 2. General information sources - 3. Materials and techniques used in graphic communication - 4. The history of books and printing - 5. Non-print media/filmstrips, slides, etc. - 6. Periodicals and annuals - 7. Associations, societies and clubs (UK, USA, chiefly; Canada and W. Germany, - 1 each) - 8. Libraries, special collections, and museum sources - 9. Book dealers. Author, title and subject indexes.

By the same author, *Reader in the history of books and printing* (Westport, Conn., Greenwood, 1983. 406p. $35). *Class No:* 655.0(091)

Printing Industry

Bibliographies

[6148]
Information sources on the printing and graphics industry. New York, United Nations, 1975. xii, 65p. £4. (*UNIDO guides to information sources, no.14.*) ISBN: 0119039850.

504 entries. 11 sections: 1. Professional, trade and research organizations, learned societies and special information sources - 2. Directories - 3. Sources of statistics - 4. Basic handbooks, textbooks

....(contd.)
and manuals - 5. Current periodicals - 6. Current abstracting and indexing periodicals - 7. Proceedings, papers and reports - 8. Specialized dictionaries and encyclopaedias - 9. Bibliographies - 10. Films - 11. Other potential sources of information (*e.g.* Translation services). List of bibliographical sources used. *Class No:* 655.1(01)

[6149]
—Book printing in Britain and America: a guide to the literature and a directory of printers. Brenni, V.J., *comp.* Westport, Conn., Greenwood Press, 1983. xiv, 163, [1]p. $38.95; £31.75. ISBN: 0313239886.
Has 1,021 references, in 21 chapters. 4 appendices (*e.g.* 'List of printers, typographers, calligraphers, and book designers'). Author and analytical indexes. *Class No:* 655.1(01)

Handbooks & Manuals
[6150]
The Print and production manual. Barnard, M., *and others, eds.* 8th ed. London, BPIF, 1998. vp. Loose-leaf. £150; $250. ISBN: 1858022385.
First published 1986.
Complete revision, now including information on all current prodcution technology, including the Internet and CD-ROM production. Updated annually, with *c.*25% contents revised each year. A comprehensive guide. *Class No:* 655.1(035)

Dictionaries
[6151]
BARKER, D. **An English-Chinese glossary of printmaking terms.** Belfast, University of Ulster, 1995. vii,344p. ISBN: 185923013x.
Lists *c.*3,000 terms in large, bold print. No definitions, only translations. *Class No:* 655.1(038)

[6152]
Dictionary of printing and publishing: English-German. Collin, P.H., *and others.* Teddington, Peter Collin Publishing, 1991. 380p. £25; £6.95. ISBN: 094854919x.
Contains *c.*5,000 words and phrases. Explanations are in English with some entries supplemented by additional explanatory comments. A glossary lists the translated German terms A-Z, with English equivalents. Appendices include dates of international book fairs, alphabets, and technical information for a periodical.
Class No: 655.1(038)

[6153]
Dictionary of the printing and allied industries, in English, French, German, Dutch, Spanish and Italian. Wijnekus, F.J.M. *and* Wijnekus, E.F.P.H., *eds.* 2nd rev. ed. Amsterdam, etc., Elsevier, 1983. xxxvi, 1026p. £150.93. ISBN: 0444422498.
First published 1967.
14,968 English-base terms, with equivalents and indexes in the other five languages. Spanish and Italian are added in this edition.
Class No: 655.1(038)

[6154]
—The Multilingual dictionary of printing and publishing. Isaacs, A., *ed.* London, F. Muller, 1981. 289p. ISBN: 0582555523.
1,600 entry-words in one A-Z sequence of English, German, French, Italian, Spanish and Portuguese terms, with equivalents in the other languages. Genders stated. When British and American English differ, both terms are given. *Class No:* 655.1(038)

[6155]
KENNEISON, W.C. *and* SPILMAN, A.J.B. **Dictionary of printing, papermaking and bookbinding.** London, Newnes, 1963. vii, 213p. illus., diagrs.
More than 2,000 entries, ranging in length from one line to 30 (*e.g.* 'Linotype'). Includes some biographical sketches. 9 appendices of abbreviations, symbols, sizes, proof-correction marks, etc. Concise and clear definitions. *Class No:* 655.1(038)

[6156]
PEACOCK, J. **Multilingual dictionary of printing and publishing terms:** English-French-Spanish-Italian-German-Dutch-Swedish. London, Blueprint, 1991. 242p. £45. ISBN: 0948905352.
Instant translation of over 2,000 common printing and publishing terms. Section A contains English-all language versions. Section B, French-English, Spanish-English, etc. *Class No:* 655.1(038)

Reviews & Abstracts
[6157]
Printing abstracts. Leatherhead, Surrey, PIRA international, 1945-. Monthly. £750; $1,200. ISSN: 0031109x.
Compiled by the Information Section of PIRA (Paper and Board, Printing and Packaging Industries Research Association).
April, 1996 issue contains 377 abstracts. 5 sections: 1. General - 2. Prepress and DTP (*e.g.* photography) - 3. Printing processes - 4. Post press (*e.g.* bookbinding) - 5. Products (*e.g.* newspapers, books and periodicals; business forms and stationery). Author and subject indexes per issue only. New diskette version enclosed with this issue. Also online through ORBIT, DATA-STAR. Available on the *Printbase Plus CD-ROM. Class No:* 655.1(048)

Progress Reports
[6158]
Advances in printing science and technology. Oxford, Pergamon, 1961-. illus., diagrs., graphs, tables. ISBN: 0471971588.
V.23, 1997 comprises the Proceedings of the 23rd Research Conference of the International Association of Research Institutes for the Graphic Arts Industry, Paris, France, September 1995. The 23 papers, each with abstract and summary of discussion, and occasionally documented include 'Improved color for the Worldwide Web'; 'A test model for proofing systems'; 'Water absorption and dimensional changes of newsprint during offset printing'.
Class No: 655.1(055)

Yearbooks & Directories
[6159]
Print buyers directory 1999/2000. London, British Printing Industries Federation, 1999. 392p.
A-Z arrangement within geographical location of *c.*3,000 print and print service companies throughout the UK. Data include full addresses, alongwith e-mail, contact name, etc. Lists companies, not individuals. *Class No:* 655.1(058)

[6160]
Printing trades directory. Tonbridge, Kent, M-G Information Services, Ltd., 1960-. Annual. £124; £132 (overseas). ISSN: 00795372.
The 1995 ed. (706p.) has two main sections: A. Printers and trade services - B. Manufacturers and suppliers. Additional sections include 'Print buyers'; 'Printing and allied trade organisations'; 'Colleges and schools of printing and graphic arts'. *Class No:* 655.1(058)

Histories
[6161]
The Art and history of book printing: a topical bibliography. Brenni, V.J., *comp.* Westport, Conn., Greenwood Press, 1984. xi, 147p. $42.95. ISBN: 0313243069.
1,199 references. 14 chapters, plus 2 classified checklists of selected titles, on writing and calligraphy, and on typography. Author and analytical subject indexes. 'The work will be especially helpful for students' (*Reference books bulletin, 1984-1985,* p.123).
Class No: 655.1(091)

[6162]
The Invention of printing: a bibliography. Prepared as an activity of the Work Project Administration (Illinois), Chicago Public Library Omnibus Project (OP no.65-1-54-273(3)). Section on Printed Bibliography, co-sponsored by the Chicago Club of Printing House Craftsmen. McMurtrie, D.C. *and* Adamson, J., *eds.* Chicago, Ill., 1942 (reprinted B. Franklin, 1970). xxiv, 413p. Mimeographed.
3,228 titles; some items have brief annotations. Locations in *c.*120 libraries (*c.*80 in USA). 8 sections: 1. Antecedents - 2. Invention - 3. Technique of the Gutenberg School - 4. Fust and Schoeffer - 5. Technique of the Dutch School - 6. Gutenberg - 7. Commemorative writing - 8. Bibliographies. *Class No:* 655.1(091)

[6163]
NEWBERRY LIBRARY. Chicago. **Dictionary catalogue of the history of printing,** from the John M. Wing Foundation, the Newberry Library. Boston, Mass., G.K. Hall, 1962. 6v. (6000p.). Supplements, 1970-. $655, set; $365, supp.1 (3v.). ISBN: 0816105871, set; 0816108099, supp. 1.
Offset-litho reproduction of 127,000 catalogue cards in the main 6v. The first part of the catalogue has entries for 20,000v. on the history of printing. The second part covers 'finely printed or historically significant books', including *c.*2,000 incunabula.
Class No: 655.1(091)

Great Britain

[6164]

[Dictionary of printers and booksellers in England, Scotland and Ireland]. London, Bibliographical Society, 1905-32. 3v.

Duff, E.G. *A century of the English book trade, 1457-1557.* 1905. McKerrow, R.B. *A dictionary of printers and booksellers ... 1557-1640.* 1910. Plomer, H.R. *A dictionary of the printers and booksellers ... 1641-1667.* 1907. Plomer, H.R. *A dictionary of the printers and booksellers ... 1668-1725.* 1922. Plomer, H.R. and others. *A dictionary of the printers and booksellers. 1726-1775.* 1932.

The only comprehensive source on the life and career of any British printers or booksellers, and not superseded. Each volume has an index of places, and biographies carry bibliographies.

Morrison, P.G. *Index of printers, publishers and booksellers ... 'A short-title catalogue', (1950), and Index of printers, publishers and booksellers in Donald Wing's 'Short-title catalogue'* (1950) are further sources, - both published by Bibliographical Society of the University of Carolina, Charlottesville, Va.

Supplemented by 'Scottish printers and booksellers, 1668-1775', by R.H. Carnie and R.P. Doig (*Studies in bibliography,* v.12, 1959; v.14, 1961, p.81-96; v.15, 1962, p.105-20). Index of places included. *Class No:* 655.1(410)

[6165]

Reviews of United Kingdom statistical sources. V.22: Printing and publishing. McLelland, W.D. Oxford, etc., Pergamon Press, for the Royal Statistical Society, and Economic and Social Research Council, 1987. xiii, 210p. tables. ISBN: 0080347819.

Comprises 2 statistical reviews. Review 39: *Printing and publishing newspapers and periodicals* (15 chapters; Quick reference lists; Table of contents; Bibliography; Subject index). Review 40: *General printing and publishing* (13 chapters). Bibliography + Postscript bibliography; subject index. *Class No:* 655.1(410)

England

[6166]

BLACK, M.H. Cambridge University Press, 1584-1984. Cambridge, University Press, 1984. xviii, 343p. illus., facsims., ports. ISBN: 0521264731.

A detailed account in 17 documented chapters, well stocked with quotations and anecdotes. 4 appendices (3. University printers, 1583-1984). Detailed, analytical index, p.335-43. *Class No:* 655.1(420)

[6167]

—McKITTERICK, D. History of Cambridge University Press. V.1. Printing and the book trade in Cambridge, 1534-1698. Cambridge, University Press, 1992. £65. *Class No:* 655.1(420)

[6168]

CARTER, H. A History of the Oxford University Press. v.1. To 1780. Oxford, Clarendon Press, 1975. xxxi, 640p. illus., facsims., ports. ISBN: 0199510326.

1. *To the year 1780, with an appendix listing the titles of books printed there, 1690-1780,.*

4 parts to v.1: 1. Introductory; 2. The Augustan Age, 1690-1713; 3. The bad time, 1713-1755; 4. The era of Blackstone, 1755-1780. Appendix. No further volumes yet announced. *Class No:* 655.1(420)

[6169]

—SUTCLIFFE, P. The Oxford University Press: an informal history. Oxford, University Press, 1978. xxviii, 303p. illus. (pl.), maps. ISBN: 0199510849.

Concentrates on the post-1800 period. *Class No:* 655.1(420)

Wales

[6170]

JONES, J.I. A History of printing and printers in Wales [and Monmouthshire] to 1810, and of successive and related printers to 1923. Cardiff, W. Lewis, 1925. x, 367p.

A strictly factual survey, - the basis on which more specialized bibliographical studies must be founded. *Class No:* 655.1(429)

Italy

[6171]

Biographical and bibliographical dictionary of the Italian printers, and of foreign printers in Italy, from the introduction of the art of printing into Italy to 1800. Cosenza, M.E., *comp.* Boston, Mass., G.K. Hall, 1970. $110. ISBN: 0816107661.

13,500 photolithographed cards. Does not aim to provide a complete bibliography for each printer, 'but to establish precisely in what town a given book was published by a given printer by listing one publication for each year that the printer exercised his art' (*Prospectus*). *Class No:* 655.1(450)

Private Presses

[6172]

CAVE, R. The Private press. 2nd ed., rev. and enl. New York, etc., Bowker, 1983. xvi, 389p. illus., facsims. $64.95. ISBN: 0835216950. First published 1971.

2 parts (27 chapters). 1. The private presses (chapter 3: The scholarly press; 14. Fine printing on the continent; 21, The United States today) - 2. Private press type faces (24. Early presses and their types; 27. The contemporary scene). Bibliography (by chapters), p.349-62. Detailed, analytical index. *Class No:* 655.15

[6173]

—ANDERSON, T.J. Private presswork: a bibliographic approach to printing as an avocation. South Brunswick & New York, A.S. Barnes; London, T. Yoseloff, 1977. 165p. facsims. ISBN: 0495018768.

16 chapters (1. Printing instruction manuals; 2. Selecting a press; 4. Type and typography; 8. Bookbinding; 11. Paper and papermaking; 12. Libraries and museums; 15. Directory of book dealers; 16. Basic book list (10 items)). Detailed, analytical index. *Class No:* 655.15

Processes & Printing Surfaces

Types

[6174]

The Encyclopaedia of type faces. Jaspert, W.P., *and others.* 4th ed. London, Blandford Press, 1970. xiii, [2], 420p. illus.

First published 1953, by W.T. Berry, and others. Paperback ed. published 1990.

About 2,000 alphabets, p.1-405 (in descending order of size, Roman - Lineales - Scripts). Appended literature on type and type founding. Typefounders, addresses. Index to designers. Index to type faces. Typewriter faces are excluded; historical examples are still generally lacking (*TLS,* no.3604, 26 March 1971, p.355). *Class No:* 655.24

[6175]

Modern encyclopedia of typefaces 1960-90. Wallis, L.W., *comp. and ed.* London, Lund Humphries, 1990. 192p. illus. ISBN: 0853315671.

Includes new typefaces available to a major composition system for continuous setting from 1960. 3 sections: Type samples (p.19-162); Supplement to type samples; Designer profiles. Select bibliography, p.180-81. Chronological index; index of designers; index of manufacturers and design agencies; index of alternative typeface names. *Class No:* 655.24

[6176]

PERFECT, C. and ROOKLEDGE, G. Rookledge's international type finder. Revised by P. Baines. 2nd ed. London, Sarema Press, 1990. 279p. illus., tables. £30; £20. ISBN: 187075803x.

First published 1983.

Part 1: Text typefaces (8 types, 1. Sloping e-Bar (Venetian serif) ... 8. Sans serif) - Part 2: Decorative (non-continuous text) typefaces (Flowering scripts ... Modified outrageous). 2 appendices: 1. Typefinder classification system/British Standards Classification - 2. Biographical notes on leading type designers - the latter being new to this edition. Bibliography/Further reading. Index. 'The first edition contained 700 typefaces, this new edition updates these, with the addition of selected faces released since that date' (*Introduction*). For designers, copywriters, editors, typesetters, printers and students to identify typefaces seen and used in their everyday work. *Class No:* 655.24

[6177]

SUTTON, J. and BARTRAM, A. Typefaces for books. London, British Library, 1990. 288p. illus. £40; £20. ISBN: 0712301900.

Over 100 monotype and linotype digitized typefaces in double-page specimen settings, in different sizes and spacings, plus display sizes, bold, roman, italian sloped roman, small caps. and figures. Also, the development of typefaces, and typographic problems and their solutions. 60 black-and-white illus. Caters admirably for the requirements of all those involved in specifying type for books. *Class No:* 655.24

Copy Presentation

[6178]

BUTCHER, J. Copy-editing: the Cambridge handbook for editors, authors and publishers. 3rd ed. Cambridge, University Press, 1992. xii,471p. illus., tables. £19.95. ISBN: 0521400740.

New and revised features include copyright law; how to deal with author-supplied disks and camera-ready copy. 15 sections (2. Estimates and specimen pages; 6. House style; 10. Bibliographical references; 13. Science and mathematics books; 15. Reprints and new editions). 13 appendices (1. Checklist of copy-editing; 4. Phonetic symbols; 13. Proof correction symbols). Glossary, p.425-42. Select bibliography. Detailed, analytical index. *Class No:* 655.25

[6179]
The Chicago manual of style; for authors, editors and copy writers. 14th ed. Chicago, Ill., & London, Univ. of Chicago Press, 1993. 936p. $40. ISBN: 0226103897.
First published 1906.
This edition reflects the changes which have taken place in publishing since the publication of the 13th ed. in 1982, with instructions, for example, on how to cite references taken from the Internet, and paper-durabilty statements. Almost 200 pages longer than the previous edition. A thorough revision of a standard tool.
Class No: 655.25

[6180]
HART, H. Hart's rules for compositors and readers at the University Press, Oxford. 39th rev. and updated ed. Oxford, University Press, 1983. 192p. £9.99. ISBN: 019212983x.
First published 1893.
States Oxford University Press practice on spelling, pluralizing, syllabification, capitalizing, punctuation, abbreviation, etc. Includes a guide to the setting of Welsh, Dutch, Afrikaans, and a new section on Machine Reader Codes. All words are brought into line with the *Oxford dictionary for writers and editors* (1981) *(q.v.)*.
Class No: 655.25

[6181]
HOWELL, J.B. Style manuals of the English-speaking world: a guide. Phoenix, Arizona, Oryx Press, 1983. 138p. $21. ISBN: 0897740890.
Surveys more than 200 English-language style manuals, both general and specific subject guides, and mostly post-1970. Some of the manuals consist of short pamphlets prepared by publishing houses for their authors. Author, title and subject indexes. *Class No:* 655.25

[6182]
Oxford dictionary for writers and editors. Compiled by the Oxford English Dictionary staff. Oxford, Clarendon Press, 1981. xiv, 448p. £8.95. ISBN: 0192129709.
Successor to 11th ed. of *Authors and printers dictionary*, by F.H. Collins, and others (1978), first published 1905.
About 12,000 terms are defined or briefly discussed. Covers abbreviations, foreign idioms, stress, pluralizing and abbreviating, spelling, capitalizing, hyphenating, as well as correct form of place-names, proper names, etc. Adopted by *The Times* and *The Sunday times* as their official style book. *Class No:* 655.25

Word Processing

[6183]
DANDO, S. Word processing dictionary. New York, etc., McGraw-Hill, 1987. 88p. ISBN: 0070849935.
A basic glossary of terms, free from jargon. A quick-reference for students following the elementary word-processing syllabuses of the RSA, Pitman, B/TEC, GCSE and LCCI. *Class No:* 655.254.4

[6184]
LANGMAN, L. An Illustrated dictionary of word processing. Phoenix, Arizona, Oryx, 1986. xiii, 289p. illus. $34.50. ISBN: 0897742869.
Covers more than 500 word-processing terms and functions. Extensive cross-references. Appendices. 'Primarily of assistance to beginners' *(Choice,* v.24 (2), October 1986, p.282), as well as to the prospective purchasers of word-processing software.
Class No: 655.254.4

[6185]
VOLLNHALS, O. Elsevier's dictionary of word processing, in English (with definitions), French and German. Amsterdam, etc., Elsevier, 1986. x, 304p. £91.87; $136. ISBN: 044442608x.
4,394 English based terms, plus definitions. Equivalents and indexes in French and German. Covers hardware, software applications (*e.g.* office automation) and allied areas, such as telematics and videotex.
Class No: 655.254.4

Typography

Encyclopaedias & Dictionaries

[6186]
Dictionary of the graphic arts industry, in English, German, French, Russian, Spanish, Polish, Hungarian and Slovak. Muller, W., *ed.* Amsterdam, etc., Elsevier, 1981. 1026p. $156.50; £100. ISBN: 0444997458.
About 14,000 English-base terms, with equivalents and indexes in the other 7 languages. Coverage: composition, platemaking, relief-printing; flat-bed printing, rotogravure printing, diestamping printing, collotype printing, machines, equipment, reproduction technology, bookbinding, measuring, storage and control technology, materials, etc. *Class No:* 655.26(03)

[6187]
FAUDOUAS, J.C. Dictionnaire technique des industries graphiques, anglais-français, français-anglais. Paris, Maison dictionnaire, 1989. 302+7p. FFr350. ISBN: 2856030388.
About 5,000 entries in all. 'Screen': 1 column. 5 appendix tables.
Class No: 655.26(03)

[6188]
GARLAND, K. Graphics, design and printing terms: an international dictionary. London, Lund Humphries, 1989. 248p. illus., facsims., diagrs. £18.95. ISBN: 0853315234.
Defines *c.*2,000 terms, A-Z with many cross-references. Includes many computing terms, abbreviations and illustrations. A useful quick-reference tool. *Class No:* 655.26(03)

[6189]
MINTZ, P.B. Dictionary of graphic arts terms: a communication tool for people who buy type and printing. New York, etc., Van Nostrand Reinhold, 1981. vii, [1], 318p. illus., diagrs. ISBN: 0442267118.
About 3,000 terms are defined (Phototype setting': 2p.; tables). Appendices: 1. Articles of the Code of Fair Practice; 7. Bibliography, grouped: p.312-8. US-slanted. *Class No:* 655.26(03)

[6190]
RODRÍGUEZ, C. Bilingual dictionary of the graphic arts ... English/ Spanish, Spanish/English. New ed. rev. and enl. by G.A. Humphrey. New York, G.A. Humphrey, 1966. 446p.
About 15,000 terms, with equivalents. Some 90 categories applied.
Class No: 655.26(03)

[6191]
STEVENSON, G.A. Graphic arts encyclopedia. 2nd ed. New York, etc., McGraw-Hill, 1979. x, 483p. illus., diagrs., tables. ISBN: 0070612889.
First published 1968 (xiv, [1], 492p.).
3,000 terms, A-Z with many cross-references, p.1-420. 'Deals with (1) the products and tools with which the image is formed, (2) the kind of image, and (3) the surface or material upon which the image is produced' *(Preface)*. Bibliography, p.421-2. Associations and societies (all in USA), p.423. Trade journals (US and British), p.426-8. Product, manufacturers; and general indexes. Clear, accurate and easy to use, with US slant.
3rd ed., 1992. 624p. $57.50. *Class No:* 655.26(03)

Handbooks & Manuals

[6192]
McLEAN, R. The Thames and Hudson manual of typography. London, Thames & Hudson, 1980. 216p. illus., facsims. ISBN: 0500670226.
12 sections (1. Historical outline; 4. Lettering and calligraphy; 6. Methods of composition; 9. Book design; 11. The parts of a book; 10. Jobbing typography; 12. Newspaper and magazine typography). Notes. 2 appendices (1. List of suppliers). Glossary of filmsetting terms. Further reading (by chapters), p.210-4. Brief index. 188 illus.
Class No: 655.26(035)

Reviews & Abstracts

[6193]
Abstracts (Graphic Arts Technical Foundation). Pittsburgh, Pa., Graphic Arts Technical Foundation, 1989-. 12pa. $90.
Formerly *Lithographic abstracts,* 1947-64 and *Graphic arts abstracts,* 1976-88.
Nearly 100 abstracts per issue. 32 sections (Advertising and marketing ... Typsetting and typography), plus 'Book reviews'. Includes abstracts on computer applications, electronic publishing. Annual index, with list of periodicals abstracted. A digest of scientific, technical and education information for the graphic communication industries. *Class No:* 655.26(048)

[6194]
Institute of Paper Science and Technology graphic arts bulletin. Atlanta, Ga., Institute of Paper Science and Technology, 1995-. 12pa. $400 per v. ISSN: 10649638.
Formerly *Graphic arts progress,* 1854-1972 and *Graphic arts literature abstracts (GALA),* 1973-1994.
About 2,000 abstracts pa. and covers *c.*160 titles. 9 sections: Business and financial - Marketing and sales - Printed products - Graphic design and copy preparation - Manufacturing operations - Materials management and handling - Science and technology - Research - Education and training. Author and keyword indexes per issue, plus 'Periodicals abstracted in this issue'.
Class No: 655.26(048)

Histories

[6195]

MEGGS, P.B. **A History of graphic design.** 2nd ed. New York, Van Nostrand Reinhold, 1992. xv,508p. illus. £35. ISBN: 0442318952.

First published 1983.

5 sections (25 chapters): 1. The prologue to graphic design - 2. A graphic renaissance - 3. The industrial revolution - 4. The modernist era - 5. The information age. Selected bibliography, p.475-94. Detailed, analytical index, p.499-508. Well produced, with numerous black-and-white illustrations. *Class No: 655.26(091)*

Typesetting & Composing

Electronic Publishing

[6196]

CARD, M. *and* FELDMAN, T. **Blueprint electronic publishing glossary.** London, Blueprint, 1992. 152p. figs. ISBN: 0948905603.

Contains *c.*1,500 concise definitions covering online information services, videotext, optical discs, audiotext, computer software, desktop publishing, graphic reproduction, handheld reference systems, etc. *Class No: 655.285*

[6197]

GURNSEY, J. 'Electronic publishing'. In *Printed reference material,* edited by P.W. Lea and A. Day (3rd ed., 1990), p.383-99.

On the dissemination of information in electronic form, surveying online databases as well as videotext. 28 references, 3 tables. *Class No: 655.285*

[6198]

SHIPCOTT, G. **Typography for desktop publishers.** London, Batsford, 1994. 96p. illus.(col.)

Eight sections: Introduction ... Nomenclature, typestyles and characteristics ... Choosing a typeface ... Further reading. Index.

Also useful is *Collier's rules for desktop design and typography* by D. Collier (Wokingham, Addison-Wesley, 1991. vi, 135p.) which is full of tips on how to produce computer-generated publications. *Class No: 655.285*

Techniques

[6199]

HUTCHINGS, E.A.D. **A Survey of printing processes.** 2nd ed. London, Heinemann, 1978. x, 246p. illus., tables.

First published 1970.

14 chapters: 1. Type production - 2. Camera work and process engraving - 3. Letterpress relief plates - 4. Letterpress printing - 5. Offset lithographic plates - 6. Offset lithographic printing - 7. Reprography - 8. The photogravure process - 9. Screen process printing - 10. Flexographic printing - 11. Collotype printing - 12. Finishing processes, binding machines and methods of binding - 13. Comparison of printing processes - 14. Modern technical developments. V.13-14 are new. Glossary. Reading list, p.241. Index. Covers 'the technical subjects which form the syllabus for examinations in General Printing Knowledge' (*Preface*). *Class No: 655.3*

[6200]

KOLLECKER, E. *and* MATUSCHKE, W. **Der Moderne Druck:** Handbuch der graphischen Techniken. 2. Aufl. Hamburg, Hammerich & Lesser, 1956. 696p. illus. (incl. col.).

Over 40 distinguished contributors. Covers printing in all its aspects, from historical to metal foil processes. Detailed descriptions of processes, with numerous black-and-white and colour illus. Particularly strong on colour printing, with machinery well described and depicted. A fine example of book production, in keeping with its subject, quality printing processes. Dated now, but still contains much useful information. *Class No: 655.3*

Lithography

[6201]

BRITISH STANDARDS INSTITUTION. **Glossary of terms used in offset lithographic printing.** London, the Institution, 1968. 48p. £80. (*BS 4277: 1968 (1991)*.)

Defines *c.*300 terms. 6 sections: 1. General terms - 2. Copy preparation - 3. Photographic and associated operations, including colour separation - 4. Plate and plate making - 5. Printing - 6. Machines and equipment. Index. *Class No: 655.342*

[6202]

The Lithographers manual. Destree, T., *ed.* 9th ed. Pittsburgh, Pa., Graphic Arts Technical Federation, Inc., 1994. v.p. illus. (incl. col.), diagrs., graphs, tables. $65. ISBN: 088362169x.

16 chapters (1. The history of lithography ... 4. The preparation of type and art ... 6. Colour separation photography ... 10. The platemaking department - 12. Lithographic presswork ... 15. Various supplementary processes). Lithographic terms. Bibliography (2p.; authors, A-Z). Appended: GATF Technical series reports. 5-p. index (tiny print). Authoritative *Class No: 655.342*

Book Trade

Dictionaries

[6203]

ORNE, J. **The Language of the foreign book trade:** abbreviations, terms, phrases. 3rd ed. Chicago, Ill., American Library Association, 1976. x, 333p. $10. ISBN: 038902197.

First published 1949.

26,000 entries in 14 non-English-language sections (each with English equivalent terms): Czech, Dano-Norwegian, Dutch, Finnish, French, German, Hungarian, Italian, Polish, Portuguese, Rumanian, Russian, Spanish, Swedish. German-English, the largest section, has *c.*2,800 entries. Not every term is limited to the book trade. Aims 'to provide a needed working tool in the major foreign languages for librarians' (*Preface*). *Class No: 655.4(038)*

Worldwide

[6204]

The Book trade of the world. Taubert, S. *and* Weidhaas, P., *eds.* Munich, K.G. Saur, 1972-84. 4v. $80ea. ISBN: 359810183x, v.1; 3598101848, v.2; 3598101856, v.3; 3598101869, v.4.

1. *Europe and international section.* 1972. 543p. £26. 2. *The Americas, Australia, New Zealand.* 1976. 377p. £26. 3. *Asia.* 1981. 284p. £26. 4. *Africa. With index to v.1-4.* 1984. 391p. £37.

The European section of v.1 (p.77-534) covers 35 countries, A-Z. Each country entry has data on 35 topics, including: retail prices; trade press; copyright; national bibliography; book production; book design; wholesale trade; book imports; book exports; literary prizes; reviewing journals; graphic arts. *Library journal* (v.97(19)), 1 April 1972, p.3556 finds the v.1 compendium invaluable for the bookseller, publisher and librarian, but it 'suffers a little from over organization'. An updating is certainly called for. *Class No: 655.4(100)*

[6205]

International bibliography of the book trade and librarianship, 1976-1979. 12th ed., edited by H. Lengenfelder and G. Hausen. Munich, K.G. Saur, 1981. xxix, 692p. $70. ISBN: 3598205153.

11th ed., 1973-1975. 1976.

The 12th ed. lists *c.*9,000 titles of books, brochures, research reports, standards, bulletins, guides, acquisition lists of libraries, etc. from 116 countries. Arranged by regions, then countries and finally by subject. Preponderance of European and US regions, - 433p. and 94p. respectively. Author and editor index, p.611-75; subject index, p.679-92. No annotations. *Class No: 655.4(100)*

[6206]

International literary market place: the directory of the international book publishing industry. New Providence, N.J., Bowker. Annual. ISSN: 00746827.

First published 1965.

The directory for 1999 (1,400p. £165) gives data on more than 18,000 book publishers and book-trade organizations in more than 180 countries, other than the US and Canada. Arranged alphabetically by country, sections include publishing; book trade information; library resources; literary associations. Industry Yellow Pages acts as an index to the directory. Companion to *Literary market place (q.v.).*

Available on CD-ROM as *International literary market place online* (Annual. £175). *Class No: 655.4(100)*

England

[6207]

BENNETT, H.S. **English books & readers.** Cambridge Univ. Press, 1952-70. 3v. £50, set (pbk).

1475-1557: being a study in the history of the book trade, from Caxton to the incorporation of the Stationers Company. 1952. 2nd rev. ed. 1969 (reprinted 1989) £65; £17.95. xiv,338p. *1558-1603: being a study of the book trade in the reign of Elizabeth I.* 1965, xviii, 320p. £70. *1603-1640: being a study of the book trade in the reigns of James I and Charles I.* 1970. xiv, 254p.

The 1558-1603 volume has chapters on patronage, regulation of the book trade, translations and translators, the variety of books, and

....(contd.)

printers and booksellers. Many footnotes (*e.g.* citing short-title catalogue entries). Bibliography, p.301-5. Analytical index. A scholarly series. *Class No:* 655.4(420)

[6208]

PLANT, M. The English book trade: an economic history of the making and sale of books. 3rd ed. London, Allen & Unwin, 1974. 520p. illus., facsims., ports. ISBN: 0046550127.

First published 1939.

2 parts (21 chapters): 1. The age of hand printing (chapters 1-12) - 2. The application of mechanical power. References, p.470-500. Detailed, analytical index, 501-20. A scholarly survey by the then deputy-librarian, British Library of Political and Economic Science. *Class No:* 655.4(420)

Asia—Middle & Near East

[6209]

A Book world directory of the Arab countries, Turkey and Iran. Rudkin, A. *and* Butcher, I., *comps.* London, Mansell; Detroit, Mich., Gale, 1981. xiv, [1], 143p. $110. ISBN: 0720108306, UK ed.

Directory of libraries, booksellers, publishers, international publishers, newspapers and periodicals in 20 countries of the Middle East. 1,400 numbered entries, with systematic data. 'General information on countries covered by the Directory' precedes. 13 appendices (1. Libraries classified by subject area; 8. Publishers classified by nature of literature; 11. Periodicals classified by content and scope). Fills a gap. *Class No:* 655.4(53+56)

Africa

[6210]

The African book world & press: a directory. Zell, H.M., *ed.* 4th ed. London, Munich, etc., Hans Zell Publishers, 1989. £75. ISBN: 0905450507.

First published 1977.

More than 4,400 entries for publishers, libraries, booksellers, research institutions, printing industries, publishing programmes, magazines, periodicals and major newspapers throughout Africa. Arrangement is A-Z by country, Algeria ... Zimbabwe. *Class No:* 655.4(6)

America—North

[6211]

American book trade directory. New York, Bowker, 1915-. Annual. ISSN: 0065759x.

The 1999-2000 directory, the 45th ed. (1998. 1,800p. $275), lists more than 30,000 bookstores, jobbers, wholesalers and distributors in the US and Canada, noting subject specialities. arranged geographically by state and city. Four indexes: Dealers in foreign language books, arranged by language; Types of stores, arranged by subject category; Wholesale remainder dealers, paperback distributors, exporters and importers; Retailers and wholesalers. *Class No:* 655.4(71+73)

[6212]

Literary market place: the directory of the American book publishing industry. New Providence, N.J., Bowker. Annual. ISSN: 00001155.

First published 1940.

The 1999 ed. (2,100p. 1998. £165) contains data on over 13,000 US and Canadian publishers (867 for the first time). Sections include editorial services and agents; advertising, marketing and publicity; book manufacturing; sales and distribution organizations; services and suppliers, associations, events, courses and awards; books and magazines for the trade. Industry Yellow Pages lists all organizations and personnel with addresses and telephone numbers (38,247 entries). Companion to *International literary market place (q.v.).*

Available on CD-ROM as *Literary market place online* (Annual. £175). Also available on the Internet at: http://lmp.bookwire.com/ and includes links to other Web sites. Updates are ongoing, making it more up-to-date than the printed version. *Class No:* 655.4(71+73)

Publishing

Databases

[6213]

Publishers' catalogues home pages. URL: http://www.lights.com/ publisher.

Based in Saskatoon, this Internet site lists publishers' Web sites from 53 countries (Albania ... Yugoslavia). Other links listed include book fairs. *Class No:* 655.41(003.4)

Encyclopaedias

[6214]

International book publishing: an encyclopedia. Altbach, P.G. *and* Hoshino, E.S., *eds.* London, Fitzroy Dearborn Publishers, 1995. xxvi,736p. tables. ISBN: 1884964168.

A series of 65 documented essays by 66 expert contributors (short biographies are given). 30 of the essays are geographically based but also included are topics of international interest, *e.g.* 'International copyright'; 'Reference publishing'; 'Feminist publishing'. Appendix and tables show statistics for titles in various languages. Detailed index. *Class No:* 655.41(031)

Dictionaries

[6215]

JACOB, H. A Pocket dictionary of publishing terms, including explanations and definitions of words and phrases commonly used in the production and distribution of books. London, Macdonald and Jane's, 1976. [x], 70p.

About 700 entry-words. 'The entries cover terms which publishers have made their own' (*Preface*). Short bibliography of 12 items. *Class No:* 655.41(038)

[6216]

Multilingual dictionary of publishing, printing and bookselling. Isaacs, A., *and others, eds.* London, Cassell, 1992. 439p. £50. ISBN: 0304325127.

Over 2,000 keywords and phrases in seven languages: English (British and American); French; German; Italian; Portuguese; Spanish; Swedish. Aimed at all those involved in the book or periodical trade. *Class No:* 655.41(038)

[6217]

Publisher's practical dictionary in 20 languages. Móra, I., *comp.* 3rd rev. ed. Munich, K.G. Saur; New York, French and European, 1983. ix, 418p. £81.30; $125. ISBN: 3598104499; 0828801908, US ed.

First published 1974 (German-base terms).

About 1,000 English-base terms, with equivalents and indexes in other 19 languages, - German, French, Russian, Spanish, Bulgarian, Danish, Finnish, Dutch, Italian, Croat, Norwegian, Polish, Portuguese, Rumanian, Swedish, Serb, Slovak, Czech and Hungarian. 'Very easy to use' (*RQ,* v.10(1), Fall 1974, p.67-68). *Class No:* 655.41(038)

[6218]

SCHUWER, P. Dictionnaire bilingue de l'édition: français-anglais; English-French. [Bilingual dictionary of book publishing.] 2nd ed. Paris, Editions du Cercle de la Librairie, 1993. 451p. £33; FFr240. ISBN: 276540500x.

First published in 1977 as *Dictionnaire de l'édition: art, technique, industrie et commerce du livre.*

Gives translations of *c.*6,500 terms concerning the book trade, agreements, book production, distribution, promtion, foreign rights, etc. *Class No:* 655.41(038)

[6219]

STIEHL, U. Satzwörterbuch des Buch- und Verlagswesen, Deutsch-Englisch. [Dictionary of book publishing, with 12,000 sample sentences and phrases, German-English.] Munich, Verlag-Dokumentation; New York, French and European, 1977. xx, 538p. £80.50; $250. ISBN: 0828833966.

German terms (explained, if considered necessary), with English equivalents and examples of English usage. Covers the book trade, publishing, editing and copyright, marketing and library science. *Class No:* 655.41(038)

Reviews & Abstracts

[6220]

World publishing monitor. Leatherhead, Surrey, PIRA International, 1983-. 12pa. £598; $957pa. ISSN: 0960653x.

Incorporates *Electronic publishing abstracts* and compiled by the Information Section of PIRA (Paper Industry Research Association).

Contain *c.*300 abstracts per issue on subjects including management; company information; agreements and contracts; health and safety; communications; graphic reproduction; storage media; television; marketing; storage and warehousing. Available online via DATA-STAR and on the *Printbase Plus* CD-ROM. Author and subject indexes. *Class No:* 655.41(048)

Tables & Data Books

[6221]

By the numbers: publishing: a statistical guide to the publishing industry. Lazich, R.S., *ed.* New York, Gale, 1998. 510p. tables. £65; $79. ISBN: 0787618608.

Compiled from a US perspective. Data mainly in chart form and includes information on the publishing industry, overseas markets, companies, non-book publishing, etc. Full of useful information. *Class No:* 655.41(083)

Worldwide

[6222]

5001 hard-to-find publishers and their addresses. 4th ed. London, Dawson, 1990. 147p. £30. ISBN: 0946291217.

First published 1981.

Includes details of over 8,000 publishers. Concentrates on Western Europe, the Commonwealth and USA. Arranged A-Z by publishers. Designed to complement such directories as Bowker's *Literary market place (q.v.)*. Considerably extended since the previous ed., its strength lies in listing specialized and small publishers. Now in need of revision. *Class No: 655.41(100)*

[6223]

Directory of publishing 1999. 24th ed. London, Cassell, 1999. 528p. ISBN: 0304704121.

The *UK, Commonwealth, and overseas* volume contains details of more than 1,400 publishers from 19 countries and over 500 associated organizations. Seven sections: 1. Introduction - 2. Publishers - 3. Packagers - 4. Authors' agents - 5. Trade and allied associations - 6. Trade and allied services - 7. Appendices (9), *e.g.* 2. Ownership of UK publishers; 6. Index of ISBN prefixes. *Class No: 655.41(100)*

[6224]

The International directory of little magazines and small presses 1998-99. Fulton, L., *ed.* 34th ed. Paradise, Calif., Dustbooks, 1998. 946p. $55; $34.95, pbk. ISBN: 0916685705; 0916685667, pbk.

International in scope, with over 6,000 entries. The main sequence is listed p.1-666, with magazine titles in upper case, and presses in lower. Each entry includes name, editor, address, founding year, type of material used, payment arrangements, etc. Regional and subject indexes, the former containing British listings under 'UK, Great Britain, England' etc., without cross-referring. *Class No: 655.41(100)*

[6225]

Publishers' international ISBN directory. Munich, etc., Bowker Saur. Annual.

The 26th ed., 1999-2000, (3v. 5,500p. 1998. £400) contains more than 450,000 entries from 210 countries. Three sections: Alphabetical (v.3); Geographical (v.1); ISBN (v.2). Includes microfilm, video and computer software publishers, complete with ISBN. Supplements *British books in print*, etc.

Available on CD-ROM as *Publishers' international ISBN directory plus* (Annual). *Class No: 655.41(100)*

Great Britain

[6226]

Book publishing in Britain. London, Bookseller Publications, 1995. xxii,490p. tables. ISBN: 0850212529.

15 sections, *e.g.* 'The costs facing publishers'; 'Consumer publishing'; 'Electronic publishing'. Short, evaluative summaries of the performance of major UK publishers plus a summary of their activities. A wide-ranging review with much statistical information. *Class No: 655.41(410)*

[6227]

FEATHER, J. A History of British publishing. London, Croom Helm, 1988. x, 292p. £40; £12.99. ISBN: 0709910673.

Introduction: 'The book trade before printing'. 4 parts (19 chapters): 1. The press in chains - 2. Licence and liberty - 3. The first of the mass media (19th century) - 4. The trade in the twentieth century. Notes. Bibliography, p.263-81. Index. Author is Senior Lecturer. Dept. of Library and Information Studies, Loughborough University. *Class No: 655.41(410)*

[6228]

MUMBY, F.A. Mumby's publishing and bookselling in the twentieth century. 6th ed. London, Bell & Hyman, 1982. 253p. ISBN: 0713515411.

First published 1930; 5th ed. (Cape), 1974.

An historical survey, in 3 parts: 1900-1939; 1939-1950; 1950-1980, plus 'Epilogue'. 6 appendices (1. Total number of books published; 2. Subject areas of titles published; 3. UK book sales, home and export). Bibliography, p.229-32. Abbreviations, p.233-4. Detailed analytical index, p.235-53. This 6th ed. supplements the scholarly 5th ed. (685p.) which covers the history from earliest times to 1970. *Class No: 655.41(410)*

France

[6229]

Histoire de l'édition française. Martin, H.-J. *and* Chartier, R., *eds.* Paris, Promodis, avec le concours du Centre National des Lettres, 1982-86. 4v. illus, facsims. (incl. col.), ports., maps. ISBN: 2903181063, v.1; 2903181314, v.2; 2903181446, v.3; 2903181543, v.4.

1. *Le livre conquérant: du Moyen-Age au milieu du XVII siècle.* 1982. FFr820. 2. *Le livre triomphant, 1660-1830.* 1982. FFr880. 3. *Le temps des éditeurs: du Romantisme à la Belle Epoque.* 4. *Le livre*

....(contd.)

concurrencé, 1900-1950. 1986. FFr970.

An elaborate, well-produced survey of book-publishing in France. Each volume has a bibliography and index. *Class No: 655.41(44)*

Africa

[6230]

ZELL, H.M. *and* **LOMER, C. Publishing and book development in sub-Saharan Africa:** an annotated bibliography. London, H. Zell/ African Publishers' Network, 1996. 409p. £48; $100. ISBN: 1873836465.

An expanded and improved second edition of *Publishing and book development in Africa: a bibliography* (Paris, Unesco, 1984).

Four sections: Serials, reference, biography, handbooks, and teaching guides - General, comparative, and regional studies - 44 countries - Studies by topic/subject. Coverage is from the early 1960s to end of 1995, and includes books, reports, journal articles, official publications, theses, and ephemera. Author, country, region, and subject indexes. Directory of African book trade associations. *Class No: 655.41(6)*

USA

[6231]

Books in print, 1999-2000. v.9: Publishers. New York, Bowker, 1999. Annual.

First published 1986.

Lists *c.*63,000 publishers and distributors whose titles are included in the main author and title indexes (v.1-8). 7 indexes; including geographical index to wholesalers and distributors; new publishers; inactive and out-of-business publishers. Available online and on CD-ROM. *Class No: 655.41(73)*

[6232]

Publishers directory, 1999: a guide to approximately 20,000 new and established commercial and nonprofit, private and alternative, corporate and association, government and institution publishing programs and their distribution. 20th ed. Detroit, Mich., Gale, 1998. 2v. £275; $357. ISBN: 0787624039. ISSN: 07420501.

Detailed information on US and Canadian publishers. Approx. 500 new entries. Includes producers of books, classroom materials, prints, reports, and electronic material. Now includes e-mail addresses and alternate formats (*e.g.* audio, braille, etc.). Indexes: publishers, imprints, and distributors; subjects; geographical location. *Class No: 655.41(73)*

[6233]

Publishers, distributors & wholesalers of the United States, 1999-2000. New York, Bowker, 1999. 2v.(4,000p.). $200. ISBN: 0835234261.

Contains data on more than 90,000 publishers, associations, distributors and wholesalers, museums and software producers. V.1 contains the name index and a list of imprints, divisions, and subsidiaries. V.2 contains 7 indexes, with lists of fax numbers, ISBNs, publishers by fields of activity, etc. Available online and on the *Publishing market place reference plus* CD-ROM. *Class No: 655.41(73)*

[6234]

TEBBEL, J. History of book publishing in the United States. New York, Bowker, 1972-81. 4v. (c.3,000p.). ISBN: 0835204898.

1. *The creation of an industry, 1630-1865.* 1972. 1646p. 2. *The expansion of an industry, 1865-1919.* 1973. 1813p. 3. *The golden age between two World Wars, 1920-1940.* 1978. 774p. 4. *1940 to the present.* 1981.

More than 2,600 pages of texts and notes, each volume having its own notes and index. Almost 270p. of indexes in all. A monumental achievement, although 'a weakness of the entire set is the scant attention paid to copyright' (*The journal of library history*, v.17(4), Fall 1982, p.503). *Class No: 655.41(73)*

[6235]

—**TEBBEL, J. Between covers:** the rise and transformation of book publishing in America. New York, Oxford Univ. Press, 1987. 528p. $35. ISBN: 0195041895.

Based on the author's four-volume work. A comprehensive single-volume history of the American publishing industry. *Class No: 655.41(73)*

Bookselling

[6236]

BOOKSELLERS ASSOCIATION. Directory: Booksellers Association members 1998. London, Booksellers Association, 1997. xvi,379p. Annual. ISBN: 0907972233.

Arranged A-Z (Abbots Bromley ... York) by location, then alphabetically by business name. Data include telephone number,

....(contd.)

address, stock range, BA group membership, services provided, etc. List of useful addresses. Head office and member indexes.
Class No: 655.42

[6237]
Bookshops of Greater London. Thomas, R.J., *ed.* 6th ed. Brentford, Middx., Roger Lascelles, 1990. 334p. £5.95. ISBN: 0903909820.
First published 1981 as *The Bookshops of London.*
This ed. expanded to cover the entire county of Greater London. Data on nearly 800 bookshops, grouped by postal district, include subjects; hours of opening; services; address; telephone number. Shop index, p.299-309. Subject index, p.310-34 (excludes general and major bookshops). *Class No:* 655.42

[6238]
Outlets for specialist new books in the UK: a subject classified, descriptive directory. London, Peter Marcan Publications, 1995. x,108p. ISBN: 1871811112.
Previous editions published as *Directory of specialist bookdealers in the UK handling mainly new books.*
Gives detailed information on 827 specialized booksellers in the UK. Arranged by subject. Data include address; subjects; catalogues; publications. Index of business names, p.101-8. *Class No:* 655.42

[6239]
Specialty booksellers directory. Kremer, J., *and others.* Fairfield, Iowa, Ad-Lib Publications, 1987. $19.95. ISBN: 0912411163.
Lists more than 2,100 specializing book dealers in North America. 48 broad subject categories. Entries are under store names. 4 indexes: subject interest; type of book (*e.g.* paperback; out-of-print); sideline merchandise sold; state/province. *Class No:* 655.42

Antiquarian & Second-hand Books

[6240]
Cole's register of British antiquarian & secondhand bookdealers, 1995. 12th ed. York, The Clique, 1995. vi,378p. ISBN: 187077356x.
Contains 2,778 addresses. Four parts: 1. Alphabetical listing (*c.*2,000 entries, p.1-160; data: name and address of booksellers; telephone; size of stock; specialization; catalogues) - 2. Specialist index and catalogue booksellers - 3. Geographical listing (London ... Yorkshire, west; Northern Ireland; Scotland; Wales) - 4. Supplementary index (names of booksellers). *Class No:* 655.425

[6241]
Sheppard's book dealers in Europe: a directory of antiquarian and secondhand book dealers on the continent of Europe. Farnham, Surrey, Sheppard's Directories. Biennial. 1999 ed. (320p.). £27; $48. ISSN: 09630171.
Bookdealers in *c.*30 countries are listed. Includes periodicals and current reference books. Alphabetical index; speciality index; list of advertisers. *Class No:* 655.425

[6242]
Sheppard's book dealers in North America: a directory of antiquarian and secondhand book dealers in the USA and Canada. Farnham, Surrey, Sheppard's Directories. Biennial. 1999 ed. (644p.). £30; $60. ISSN: 02691469; 09500715.
First published 1954.
Sections (as in *Sheppard's book dealers in the British Isles*): Miscellaneous information - Geographical directory of dealers - Alphabetical index - Speciality index - Index of advertisers. Includes e-mail addresses and Web sites. *Class No:* 655.425

[6243]
Sheppard's book dealers in the British Isles: a directory of antiquarian and secondhand book dealers in the United Kingdom, the Channel Islands, the Isle of Man and the Republic of Ireland. Farnham, Surrey, Sheppard's Directories, 1951-. Annual. 1998 ed. (590p.). £27; $54. ISBN: 187269957x. ISSN: 09500715.
Geographical directory of book dealers, (English counties; Wales, Scotland; Isle of Man; Northern Ireland; Republic of Ireland; Channel Islands). 'Miscellaneous information' precedes. Alphabetical index (including dealers' addresses, 'phone numbers, e-mail and Web sites). Speciality index lists dealers by subject, Academic/Scholarly ... Zoology. Dealers are also listed by business and name of proprietor. Index of advertisers. *Class No:* 655.425

[6244]
Skoob directory of secondhand bookshops in the British Isles. 6th ed. London, Skoob Books Publishing, 1996. 302p. maps. £6.99. ISBN: 1871438136.
Lists over 1,100 bookshops. 4 preceding essays, *e.g.* 'Nobel Prizewinners in Literature, 1901-95' (but arranged retrospectively). Directory of bookshops in the British Isles, p.1-202. Index of shops; subject index; index of towns. Good value. *Class No:* 655.425

Transport Services

Databases

[6245]
TRANSDOC. European Conference of Ministers of Transport. London, Departments of the Environment and Transport, 1970-.
Concerns the economic and social aspects of transport. Contains *c.*30,000 citations to material mainly published in Europe but also from other countries, *e.g.* USA. Coverage includes periodicals, books, reports, summaries of current research projects, theses, and conference papers. About 750 items added quarterly. Host: ESA. Available as part of the TRANSPORT CD-ROM issued by SilverPlatter.
Class No: 656(003.4)

[6246]
TRANSPORTATION RESEARCH BOARD. Washington. TRIS / Transportation Research Information Service. Washington, D.C., US Department of Transportation and Transportation Research Board NAS/NRC, 1968-.
Provides research information on air, road, rail and maritime transport. Subjects covered include energy, regulations and legislation, traffic control, communications, and environmental and maintenance technology. Organizations contributing to *TRIS* include the Highway Research Information Service (HRIS); the Maritime Research Information Service (MRIS); International Road Research Documentation (IRRD); the Air Transportation Research Information Service (ATRIS); the Railroad Research Information Service (RRIS).
IRRD (International Road Research Documentation) also runs a database, TRICS, hosted through ESA, in which 20 countries participate. Available as part of the TRANSPORT CD-ROM issued by SilverPlatter. *Class No:* 656(003.4)

CD-ROM

[6247]
TRANSPORT. London, SilverPlatter, 1994-. 4pa. CD-ROM $1,795.
Available in formats 1968 to present (*c.*500,000 records) or 1988 to present. *c.*12,000 records are added annually. Combines databases of three leading transport research organizations: OECD's International Road Research Documentation (IRRD); ECMT TRANSDOC database; and the TRB Transportation Research Information Services (TRIS) database. Mainly English language articles are covered but there is also coverage of French, Spanish, and German articles. Special emphasis on road transport and transport economics. Also available on the Internet. *Class No:* 656(003.40)

Bibliographies

[6248]
An Annotated bibliography on rural transport. Sieber, N., *ed.* London, International Forum for Rural Transport and Development, 1997. 128p. £9.95 ISBN: 1853394181.
Lists over 100 sources of information on rural transport in developing countries. 11 chapters: 1. Rural transport infrastructure ... 6. Financial and institutional issues ... 8. Gender and transport ... 11. How to get hold of the documents. Author, title, and keyword indexes. *Class No:* 656(01)

[6249]
Annual list of publications 1991 and 1992: a combined list of documents published by the Department of the Environment and the Department of Transport (excluding the publications of research establishments). London, Department of the Environment; Department of Transport, 1993. 91p. ISBN: 1851122060.
Arranged A-Z by subject (Air pollution ... Water). Entries give title, publisher, date of publication, ISBN, price, frequency, availability. Author and subject indexes.
List of publications available on the Internet at http://www.detr.gov.uk/pubs/index.htm. Updated monthly.
Class No: 656(01)

[6250]
CHARTERED INSTITUTE OF TRANSPORT. Library. **Transport technology.** London, the Institute, 1974. 71p. Mimeographed. (*Transport bibliography 16.*)
About 1,000 briefly annotated entries (Books; Pamphlets, reports, (p.12-69); Statutes; Bibliographies; Dictionaries; Annuals, statistics, etc.). Government department, ICAO, GLC, UN, US, etc. technical reports from the main feature. Book prices are given. No index.
Transport bibliography 16A: *Selected periodical articles* (1975. 51p. Mimeographed) is a contents-list of periodicals, A-Z by titles *Aeronautical journal ... World ports.*
These bibliographies are now replaced by a series of reading lists, one for each of the Chartered Institute of Transport's examination papers. *Class No:* 656(01)

[6251]

Information sources in transportation, material management, and physical distribution: an annotated bibliography and guide. Davis, B.J., *comp. and ed.* Westport, Conn., Greenwood Press, 1976. [xv], 715p. $67.95. ISBN: 0837183790.

About 10,000 entries in 67 sections, each of which accommodates A. Books and pamphlets; B. Periodicals; C. Organizations; D. Education; E. Miscellaneous (*e.g.* atlases and maps). Brief annotations. Author, title, subject index, p.635-715.

Class No: 656(01)

[6252]

NORTHWESTERN UNIVERSITY, Evanston, Ill. Transportation Center Library. **Catalog. [Northwestern University, Transportation Center Library].** Boston, Mass., G.K. Hall, 1972. 12v. (7697p.).

Author/title catalog. 3v. (1774p.) $1,305. *Subject catalog.* 9v. (5293p.) $980.

171,000 photolithographed catalogue cards, in all. Main emphasis on transportation management, operations, planning, economics, regulation and impact. International in scope.

Updated in monthly *Current literature in traffic and transportation* (Transportation Centre Library, 1960-.), arranged under subjects, A-Z. *Class No:* 656(01)

[6253]

STYLES, B.R. 'Highway, transport and constructional engineering'. In *Information sources in engineering.* 2nd ed. Editor, L.J. Anthony (1985), p.409-28.

Sections: Organizational sources of information - Documentary sources of information (abstracts and indexing services; journals; monographs and textbooks). *Class No:* 656(01)

Encyclopaedias & Dictionaries

[6254]

BEIN, G. Wörterbuch des internationales Verkehrs: Deutsch-Englisch. Leipzig, VEB Verlag Enzyklopädie; New York, State Mutual Book and Periodical Service Ltd., 1968. 232, [1]p. $15. ISBN: 0569051177, US ed.

About 11,500 entries, covering domestic and international road, rail and air transport and traffic, inland and maritime navigation, plus foreign trade. Appendix of translations of names of charters and Acts, mostly on shipping and maritime transport. 'A model publication of its kind' (*Incorporated linguist,* v.10(3), July 1971, p.91). *Class No:* 656(03)

[6255]

COMMISSION OF THE EUROPEAN COMMUNITIES. Terminology Office. **Glossaire nouvelles techniques de transport.** Luxembourg, CEC, 1975.

A six-language transport glossary, - in Danish, English, French, Italian, Dutch and German. Covers the means and modes of modern and future transport. 'There is still no good transport dictionary but if you must have something I should recommend *Glossaire nouvelles techniques de transport'* (*The incorporated linguist,* v.19(4), Autumn 1980, p.141). *Class No:* 656(03)

[6256]

Concise encyclopedia of traffic and transportation systems. Papageorgiou, M., *ed.* Oxford, Pergamon Press, 1991. xviii,658p. figs., illus. £205. (*Advances in systems, control and information engineering.*) ISBN: 0080362036.

118 articles arranged A-Z (Air traffic control: an overview ... Visual and instrument flying rules), written by 135 contributors. Each article has a bibliography appended. Cross-references. Aimed at academics, managers, operators, managers, engineers and graduate students. Contains some updated and revised articles from *Systems and control encyclopedia (q.v.)* (1987). *Class No:* 656(03)

[6257]

—The Illustrated encyclopaedia of transportation. Crow, G., *ed.* London & New York, Reference International, 1977. 261p.

10 contributors. Concise A-Z entries, on land, sea and air transport, both historical and technological. 'Pipelines' (operation; design and construction; freight pipelines): 2p., 3 illus. Includes biographies. Over 400 illus., including keyed line-drawings and cutaway diagrams. 16p. of colour plates. Non-analytical index. *Class No:* 656(03)

[6258]

UNION INTERNATIONALE DES TRANSPORTS PUBLICS. Dictionary of public transport / **Wörterbuch Nahverkehr** / Dictionnaire des transports publics. Elms, C.P., *and others, eds.* Dusseldorf, Alba Buchverlag; New York, French and European, 1981. 312p. $45. ISBN: 3870947637.

About 5,000 English-base terms, plus definitions, with equivalent terms and indexes in German and French. *Class No:* 656(03)

[6259]

—LOGIE, G. Glossary of transport, in English, French, Italian, Dutch, German and Swedish. Amsterdam, etc., Elsevier, 1980. xxviii, 206p. £64.06; $97.50. (*International planning glossaries,* 2.) ISBN: 0444418881.

Has 1,108 English-base terms, grouped into main and subsidiary headings, with equivalents in the other 5 languages. Indexes cover all 6 languages. Criticized in *The Incorporated linguist* (v.19(4), Autumn 1980, p.140) for inaccuracies. 'The majority of terms in this dictionary would undoubtedly be found in a good general bilingual dictionary'. Also, costly. *Class No:* 656(03)

Handbooks & Manuals

[6260]

Transportation and traffic engineering handbook. Homburger, W.S., *and others, eds.* 2nd ed. Englewood Cliffs, N.J., Prentice Hall, Inc., 1982. 883p. illus., graphs, tables. ISBN: 0139330626.

First published 1976, edited by J.E. Baerwald.

28 well-documented sections, stressing traffic engineering rather than mass transportation. Geographical and detailed subject indexes. *Class No:* 656(035)

Reviews & Abstracts

[6261]

TR news. Washington, Transportation Research Board, National Research Council, National Academy of Sciences, 1983-. 6pa. $25.

Formerly *Transportation research news.*

Features articles on timely subjects, abstracts of current transport literature, and announcements of TRB publications and meetings. Discusses activities of the Board, government, and industry. US-slanted. *Class No:* 656(048)

Histories

[6262]

The Journal of transport history. 3rd series. Manchester, Univ. Press, 1971-. 2pa. £75; $135. ISSN: 00225266.

First series, 1953- (Leicester University Press).

V.19(2), September 1998, has five documented articles (*e.g.* 'The nationalisation of the bus industry: the Transport Act, 1947, its underlying philosophy and intital progress', p.122-37; 53 references). 32 book reviews. *Class No:* 656(091)

Europe

[6263]

European transport trends and infrastructural needs. Paris, European Conference of Ministers of Transport, 1995. 312p. diagrs.,tables,graphs,maps.

Three main sections: 1. Overview - 2. The inadequacy of current responses: national approaches, sectoral forecasts and emerging concepts - 3. Possible strategies towards meeting the requirements of international traffic. Four annexes: 1. Breakdown of traffic data by trip purpose ... 4. Statistics derived from the COMEXT Database (Foreign trade flows). *Class No:* 656(4)

[6264]

UNITED NATIONS. Economic Commission for Europe. **Annual bulletin of transport statistics for Europe and North America.** New York, United Nations. Annual. ISBN: 9210163389. ISSN: 02509911.

Formerly *Annual bulletin of transport statistics for Europe.*

V.48, 1998 ($60) contains sections: General statistics - Railways - Roads - Inland waterways - International rivers - Sea ports - Combined transport - Oil pipelines - Others. 3 annexes (1. Definitions; 2. Sources of information and coverage of statistics. 3. List of publications from which monthly and/or quarterly transport statistics can be obtained). Notes appended to tables. In English, French, and Russian. *Class No:* 656(4)

Great Britain

Tables & Data Books

[6265]

MUNBY, D.L. Inland transport statistics, Great Britain, 1900-1970. Watson, A.H., *ed.* Oxford, Clarendon Press, 1978. xii, 693p. tables. £60. ISBN: 0198284098.

1. *Railways, public road passenger transport. London's transport.*

3 main sections: A. Railways - B. Public road passenger transport - C. London's transport. 3 annexes (1. General note on sources of labour statistics). Index, p.677-93. An impressive array of statistical data, with valuable commentaries. 'No self-respecting library can afford to be without this volume, despite its expense' (*History,*

....*(contd.)*
v.65(213), February 1980, p.175).
A second volume is to cover roads, private haulage and, presumably, inland waterways. *Class No:* 656(410)(083)

[6266]
Reviews of United Kingdom statistical sources. Oxford, etc., Pergamon Press, for the Royal Statistical Society and the Social Science Research Council, 1978-.
V.7. Review 12: *Road passenger transport,* by D.L. Munby. 13: *Road goods transport,* by A.N. Watson. 1978. xii, 138p. 127p. v.10. Review 17: *Ports and inland waterways,* by R.E. Baxter. 18: *Civil aviation,* by C.M. Phillips. 1978. xii, 302p. v.14. Review 24: *Rail transport,* by D.H. Aldcroft. 1981. 280p. £40. 25: *Sea transport,* by D. Mort. 1981. xii, 268p.
The aim of the series is 'to act as a work of reference to the sources of statistical material of all kinds, both official and unofficial' (*Introduction,* v.7). V.17, Review 18: *Civil aviation* (p.111-302) has 4 chapters, with appended quick-reference list; bibliography; coverage of publications; useful libraries and books; appendix of forms, and a subject index. Statistics are analysed in this *Review* up to September 1977. *Class No:* 656(410)(083)

[6267]
[Sources of transport statistics]. In *Aslib proceedings,* v.40 (11/12), November/December 1988, p.321-332.
3 papers presented at a seminar held on 8 June 1988: 'Use and abuse of statistics', by S. Hoyle; 'Statistics available from the Department of Transport', by J. Akinbolu; 'Sources of non-government transport statistics'; by E. Godward.
J. Akinbolu's paper briefly examines the types of publications produced by the Department of Transport, as well as the source guides on transport statistics. Includes major HMSO publications, non-HMSO publications and occasional publications. Statistic collection is also described. *Class No:* 656(410)(083)

[6268]
Transport statistics: Great Britain 1995. London, HMSO, 1995. xi, 241p. tables. £30. ISBN: 0115510788.
Prelims. include articles, *e.g.* 'Measuring traffic speeds'. Tables (each with commentary, notes and definitions, plus footnoted sources): 1. Transport: an overall view - 2. Energy and environment - 3. Vehicles, drivers and roads - 4. road traffic, freight and accidents, motor vehicle offences - 5. Public transport - 6. Water transport - 7. Air transport - 8. International comparisons - 9. Selected international series. Glossary, p.201-12. Data revised and updated quarterly in *Quarterly transport statistics. Class No:* 656(410)(083)

Histories

[6269]
BAGWELL, P.S. The Transport revolution. 2nd ed. London, Routledge, 1988. xiv,474p. illus., figs., tables, maps. £52.50. ISBN: 041500876x.
First published 1974.
Covers the development of transport in Great Britain from 1770 to 1985. 11 chapters: 1. Inland navigation in Britain ... 3. Coastal shipping ... 5. The economic and social effects of railways ... 8. The development of motor transport 1885-1939 - 9. British transport policy 1914-39 ... 11. Public transport in decline 1972-85. Notes, p.417-53. Bibliography, p.454-62. Index. A detailed work.
Class No: 656(410)(091)

[6270]
DYOS, H.L. *and* **ALDCROFT, D.H. British transport:** an economic survey, from the seventeenth century to the twentieth. Leicester, Univ. Press, 1969. 473p. tables, maps. £32.50. ISBN: 071851081x.
Paperback ed. 1974 (Harmondsworth, Middx., Penguin Books. 511p.).
13 chapters (1. The transport system of pre-industrial Britain ... 12. The development of motorised transport - 13. The birth of civil aviation). Chapter bibliographies, with running commentary (p.401-38) and author index. Non-analytical general index, p.445-73. An attempt at 'a full length general survey of the development of transport in Britain in modern times ... Careful attention has been given to the bibliography' (*Preface*). Well produced. *Class No:* 656(410)(091)

Institutions & Associations

[6271]
Transport organisations in the United Kingdom. King, D., *comp.* 2nd ed. London, Department of the Environment; Department of Transport, 1986. [1], [1], 42p. (*UB/INF/14A.*) ISBN: 1851120076.
Earlier ed. (1976) as *UK transport organizations.*
About 200 entries, with emphasis on Government departments and other official bodies, research institutes, professional organizations, trade associations, pressure groups. Generally omitted: enthusiasts' societies, employers' organizations and trade unions. Data on each body include date of founding, status and aim, publications.
Class No: 656(410):061:061.2

Asia—South East

[6272]
South-east Asian transport. Leinbach, T.R., *and others.* Singapore, Oxford University Press, 1989. xix,265p. tables, maps. £27.50. ISBN: 0195888952.
Covers the history and future development in this area. 9 chapters: 1. The role of transport in development ... 4. Road and rail transport systems ... 7. ASEAN air transport - 8. Urban transport - 9. Transport progress, problems, and policies in south-east Asia: a synthesis. 4 appendices give statistics on road transport, rail, merchant fleets, and air transport. Bibliography, p.248-60. Author and subject indexes. *Class No:* 656(59)

Libraries

[6273]
SPECIAL LIBRARIES ASSOCIATION. New York. Transportation Division. **Transportation libraries in the United States and Canada:** an SLA directory. 3rd ed. New York, the Association, 1978. 220p.
Data on 205 collections. Subject, geographic and personal name indexes. Needs updating. *Class No:* 656:061:026/027

Museums

[6274]
GARVEY, J. A Guide to the transport museums of Great Britain. London, Pelham Books, 1982. 238p. illus. (incl. col.), maps. ISBN: 0720714044.
Descriptions of 52 museums, plus list of a further 54 awaiting treatment. 10 areas: London; The South ... The Midlands; Wales ... Northern Ireland. Gazetteer follows. Data on each museum include access, exhibits, opening hours and facilities. Symbols indicate parking, refreshment, shop. Index. Attractively produced, but could now do with revision. *Class No:* 656:061:069

Routes & Services

[6275]
The guide to National Express coach services. Birmingham, National Express, Ltd. 2pa. tables, maps. £5.90.
Formerly *National Express guide.*
Guide No. 40, 24 May-26 September 1999 includes: Fares information, symbols, etc; Network maps; Index to places served; Interchange tables; Timetables and fares; Adult and discount fare category calculators. *Class No:* 656.02

Urban Transport

[6276]
BANISTER, D. *and* **PICKUP, L. Urban transport and planning:** a bibliography with abstracts. London, New York, Mansell, 1989. iv,354p. £40. ISBN: 0720116279.
Contains *c.*500 abstracts, covering English language material published since 1980. 8 sections: 1. The context - 2. Policy and planning in transport - 3. Social issues - 4. Travel modes - 5. Methods and evaluation - 6. Area studies - 7. Bibliographies and research registers - 8. Additional entries. Subject and author indexes. A companion volume to *Rural transport and planning: a bibliography with abstracts* (Mansell, 1985). *Class No:* 656.022.9

[6277]
Jane's urban transport systems, 1998-99. Bushell, C., *ed.* 17th ed. Coulsdon, Jane's Information Group, 1996. 642p. illus., tables. £235. ISBN: 0710618123.
Alphabetical profiles, city by city (Aachen ... Zurich) - Manufacturers (11 sections of suppliers, services, systems) - Consultancy and contracting services. Index. Available on *Jane's* CD-ROM (£475). *Class No:* 656.022.9

[6278]
Roads and traffic in urban areas. London, HMSO, 1987. xxiv, 418p. illus. (incl. col.), diagrs., tables, maps. £25. ISBN: 011550818x.
Replaces *Urban traffic engineering techniques* (1968) and *Roads in urban areas* (1966).
Reflects the enormous changes in car ownership, lorry weights, parking facilities, and many other recent trends. 'An important new standard reference work for traffic engineers and road designers ...' (*British book news,* July 1988, p.577). *Class No:* 656.022.9

Administration

Goods & Freight

[6279]
ABC freight guide. Bromsgrove, Ascent Publishing (Centaur Communications), 1973-. Annual. £49.99 ISSN: 03089304.
1997-98 ed. (49th ed. 264p.) is a directory of all types of freight service: Business and professional services ... General road haulage

....(contd.)

(regions, A-Z) - Storage and distribution - Breakdown and recovery - Vehicle, trailer hire - International services - Heavy haulage - Tanker wagons - Bulk tipping - Industrial removals - Light freight and express service - Temperature controlled distribution - Tachograph calibration centres - Rail, air and sea freight. General index and index of advertisers. *Class No:* 656.073

[6280]

FTA Yearbook of road transport law. Tunbridge Wells, Kent, Freight Transport Association. Annual. 352p. diagrs.,tables. £27. ISSN: 03001523.

Eight sections: Freight Transport Association - The law governing road transport operations - Insurance - Industrial relations and health and safety - The law governing overseas operations - The law governing specific vehicles. Addresses; Useful references; Index. *Class No:* 656.073

Road Transport

[6281]

The 1995 IRF motorway data bank for Europe. Geneva, International Road Federation, 1995. 300p. tables,graphs.,maps.(some col.). SFr3,590.

Gives data on 31 European countries. Tables include existing and future motorway links, traffic volumes, road ownership, motorway safety. 70 maps (30 in full colour). Diskettes accompany the hardback copy to allow users to make personalized queries of the tables. Also available as a Geographical Information System. *Class No:* 656.1

Handbooks & Manuals

[6282]

FAULKS, R.W. Bus and coach operation. 5th ed. London, Butterworth, 1987. 272p. illus. ISBN: 0408028106.

Sections: Introduction - Historical background - The infrastructure - Vehicle design - Organization and management - Statutory controls - The planning process - Commercial practices - Schedule compilation - Fare collection - Operational control - Finance - The future. 107 illus. For managers and aspiring managers in the road passenger industry, and especially for those taking the Chartered Institute of Transport Membership and Association Membership exams. *Class No:* 656.1(035)

[6283]

LOWE, D. The Transport manager's & operator's handbook 1999. 29th ed. London, Kogan Page, 1998. 624p. figs. £35. ISBN: 0749429119.

First published 1969. Formerly published as *The Transport manager's handbook.*

Sections include: Goods vehicle operator licensing ... Vehicle excise duty ... Road traffic law ... Maintenance records ... Services. Ten appendices: 1. The traffic area network ... 6. Tachograph manufacturers and approved centres ... 10. Training facilities for dangerous goods. New coverage in this edition includes: LGV tests and driving licences, EU plans for road tolling. Index. A standard text. *Class No:* 656.1(035)

Dictionaries

[6284]

Dictionary of road transport terminology in four languages, English, French, German and Spanish. Amsterdam, etc., Elsevier; New York, French and European, 1988. xxviii, 351p. $250; £111.56. ISBN: 0828823758, US ed; 0444428194.

4,387 English-based terms, with French, German and Spanish equivalents and indexes. 'Usual abbreviations', p.xi-xxviii. No genders given. *Class No:* 656.1(038)

Reviews & Abstracts

[6285]

Road documentation for developing countries. Crowthorne, Berks., Overseas Unit, Transport and Road Research Laboratory, 1974-. Annual. *Gratis.* ISBN: 0854296948.

500 abstracts per issue on road design, materials, construction and maintenance, traffic and transport, accident studies, vehicles, economics, administration. Online IRRD (International Road Research Documentation) database. *Class No:* 656.1(048)

Histories

[6286]

Explorations in motoring history: proceedings of the First United Kingdom History of Motoring Conference. Brown, B.J.H., *ed.* Oxford, Oxbow Books, 1996. 128p. illus. £18. (*Oxbow monograph, 87.*) ISBN: 1900188481.

Nine papers: Imaging of motoring ... The development of the petrol filling station, 1895-1939 ... The development of the high-performance engine: a revisionist history. References are appended to each paper. No index. *Class No:* 656.1(091)

Worldwide

[6287]

World road statistics, 1985-1989. Geneva, International Road Federation, 1990. 200p. diagrs., tables.

11 sections: 1. Road network - 2. Production and export of motor vehicles - 3. First registration and imports of motor vehicles - 4. Vehicles in use - 5. Road traffic - 6. Motor fuels - 7. Road accidents - 8. Rates and basis of assessment of road user taxes - 9. Examples of average annual taxation - 10. Annual receipts from road-user taxation - 11. Road expenditure. Headings in English, French, German. *Class No:* 656.1(100)

Europe

[6288]

The Little red book 1998/99: road passenger transport directory for the British Isles and Western Europe. Hersham, Surrey, Ian Allan Publishing, 1998. 236p. £29.99. ISBN: 071102572x.

Six sections: 1. Trade directory - 2. United Kingdom operators, p.62-171 - 3. PTAs and PTEs, traffic commissioners (Department of Transport) etc. - 4. Organisations and societies - 5. European operators - 6. Index (British Isles operators). A well laid-out guide. *Class No:* 656.1(4)

[6289]

Manuel du transport routier international. [Handbook of international road transport.] 10th ed. Geneva, International Road Union, 1988. 494p. tables, forms. Loose-leaf.

Countries, Austria ... Yugoslavia. Appendices: Customs Convention, on the international transport of goods under cover of TIR channels - Community transit systems - List of the principal juridical texts on international road transport - Table showing maximum size and weight permissible for road vehicles in Europe. *Class No:* 656.1(4)

Great Britain

[6290]

Basic road statistics, 1994. London, British Road Federation, [1994]. 40p. tables, graphs. £22

11 sections, 54 tables: 1. Motor vehicles - 2. Road network - 3. Road traffic - 4. Demand for transport - 5. Energy and transport - 6. Public expenditure on transport - 7. Taxation - 8. Road accidents - 9. Regional statistics - 10. County statistics - 11. International comparisons. Map: The strategic trunk road network. 3 appendices (3. List of sources). 'Quick comparisons'. *Class No:* 656.1(410)

[6291]

CHARLESWORTH, G. A History of British motorways. London, T. Telford, 1984. xii, 284p. illus., tables, maps. £21. ISBN: 0727701592.

12 documented chapters (2. Road policies between the wars; 4. 1950-60: motorway construction; 7. Trunk road motorways in England (39 references); 8. Trunk road motorways in Wales and in Scotland (19 references); 10. Planning, design and maintenance (60 references); 12. Some economic and social aspects). Detailed, analytical index. Well organized. Author was one-time Assistant Director at the Transport and Road Research Establishment. *Class No:* 656.1(410)

[6292]

The Highway code. Rev. ed. London, Stationery Office, 1999. 85p. illus. £1.49. ISBN: 0115519777.

First published 1946.

An advisory code of practice. Expanded to include new rules and details of recent changes in the law. More emphasis on safe driving, and special sections on vulnerable road users such as horse riders, the elderly, and cyclists. Index. *Class No:* 656.1(410)

[6293]

The Official driving manual. London, Stationery Office, 1999. vi,341p. illus. (col.). £12.99. ISBN: 0115521917.

Formerly published as *The Driving manual.*

Includes latest advice and legislation on good driving. areas covered include bends, towing, European information. Useful addresses. Index. Illustrations get the message across. Aimed at both the learner and experienced driver. *Class No:* 656.1(410)

Thesauri

[6294]

INTERNATIONAL ROAD RESEARCH DOCUMENTATION. **Thesaurus, 1985. [International Road Research Documentation].** English ed. Paris, OECD/IRRD. 2v. diagrs., tables. ISBN: 9264126287.

1. *Numerical list and English arrowed diagrams.* 2. *English alphabetical list.*

French and German versions of the *Thesaurus* are also available. *Class No:* 656.1:025.43

Traffic Signs

[6295]

EUROPEAN CONFERENCE OF MINISTERS OF TRANSPORT. **European rules concerning road traffic signs and signals.** London, Dept. of Transport, 1974. 178p. illus. (incl. col.), diagrs.

Part 1: Road traffic rules, and annexes - Part 2: Road signs and signals, and annexes. 18 countries were involved, plus associated countries (Australia, Japan) and observers (Canada, USA). *Class No:* 656.1.05

[6296]

Know your traffic signs. 4th ed. London, HMSO, 1995. 100p. col. illus. £2.50. ISBN: 0115516123.

Concerns the history, types and locations of UK road signs. Includes 770 signs, 300 of them new or redesigned. An authoritative explanation of the British traffic sign system. *Class No:* 656.1.05

Railway Transport

Dictionaries

[6297]

UNION INTERNATIONALE DES CHEMINS DE FER. **Lexique général des termes ferroviaires.** 4. éd. Paris, The Union, 1988. 1250p. £76.95.

First published 1957; 3rd ed. 1975.

About 10,200 French-based railway terms, with German, English, Italian, Spanish and Dutch equivalents and indexes. The standard dictionary in its field. An electronic version is *RailLexic: railway dictionary, thesaurus and information database* CD-ROM (1996. £250), containing *c*.16,000 terms. *Class No:* 656.2(038)

Worldwide

[6298]

Fodor's railways of the world. Whitaker, R.E.M. *and* Fisher, R.C., *eds.* London, Hodder and Stoughton, 1977. 374p. illus., maps.

Facts at your fingertips, p.12-34. 9 regional sections (North America; Western Europe; Eastern Europe; The Middle East; South and Southeast Asia; East Asia; The Pacific; Africa; South America). Index, p.371-4. Aimed at tourists. Notes on: classes of accommodation; train services; comparative distances and times; timetables, fares and reservations; catering; hotels and accommodation at stations; railway museums and reserved railways; photography. Somewhat dated. *Class No:* 656.2(100)

[6299]

MARSHALL, J. **The Guinness railway fact book.** Enfield, Guinness Publishing, 1994. 192p. £9.99. ISBN: 0851127649.

International in scope and giving information in a condensed form. Illustrations are variable and the index is not comprehensive. As it assumes previous knowledge, this book is suited to the enthusiast. *Class No:* 656.2(100)

[6300]

NOCK, O.S. **Railways of the world.** London, A. & C. Black, 1971-1979. 6v. illus. (some col.), maps. ISBN: 0713611065; 0713611901; 0713616865; 0713618558; 0713620064.

V.1: *Railways of Southern Africa.* 1971. 243p. V.2: *Railways of Australia.* 1971. 284p. V.3: *Railways of Canada.* 1973. 343p. V.4: *Railways of Western Europe.* 1977. xvi, 264p. V.5: *Railways of Asia and the Far East.* 1978. xvii, 226p. V.6: *Railways of the USA.* 1979. xvi, 317p.

Each v. covers the history, technology and routes, past and present, of the area in a chatty, informal style. Volume indexes. 'Recommended ... for transport historians and all those with a mature interest in trains' (*British book news,* January 1978, p.4 on v.4). Nock is a retired engineer and a prolific author of railway books. *Class No:* 656.2(100)

[6301]

Railway directory: a *Railway Gazette* yearbook. Sutton, Surrey, Reed Business Information. Annual. ISBN: 0617012679. ISSN: 00799513.

First published 1894. Formerly *Railway directory & year book.*

The 1999 ed. (532p. maps. £100) contains 21 chapters: Government - Railways ... Associations ... Diesel engines ... Station equipment ... Professional services. General, personnel, and advertisers' indexes. Numerous maps, all in colour. Also available on CD-ROM. *Class No:* 656.2(100)

Great Britain

Maps & Atlases

[6302]

WIGNALL, C.J. **Complete British railways maps and gazetteers, 1825-1985.** Rev. ed. Oxford, Oxford Publishing Co., 1983. iv, 71, 79p. ISBN: 086093294x.

First published 1983.

Atlas of 2-colour maps (71p.) distinguishes between 6 types of railway, *e.g.* Lines closed to passengers; Preserved lines open to passengers; Lines underground at this point. Gazetteer to maps (76p.) notes stations open or closed to passengers and HQ of preserved railways, plus preservation centres. Lists of mainland railway companies, p.77-79. A well-produced quarto. *Class No:* 656.2(410)(084.3)

[6303]

—British railways pre-grouping atlas and gazetteer. 5th ed. London, Ian Allan, 1972. 84p. maps. ISBN: 0711003203.

Maps show the railway system of Britain as it existed in the years prior to 1923. Includes every railway company at work at that time. Also shows junctions, the more important viaducts, tunnels, locomotive shed locations, and railway workshops. Gazetteer, p.47-83, includes list of company abbreviations, indexes of tunnels, water troughs, principal summits and viaducts, and stations. Smaller format than Wignall and a useful vade mecum for the enthusiast. *Class No:* 656.2(410)(084.3)

Histories

[6304]

AWDRY, C. **Encyclopaedia of British railway companies.** Yeovil, Patrick Stephens, 1990. 288p. illus. £20. ISBN: 1852600497.

A-Z list of railway companies, with dates of incorporation and major developments, arranged into the 4 major groups (GWR, SR, LMS, LNER) into which all Britain's railways were grouped 1923-48 before nationalization. Independent and London Transport undertakings are also listed, and there are 'family tree' charts of constituent companies, p.244-78. Authoritative and attractively presented. Good value. *Class No:* 656.2(410)(091)

[6305]

A **Bibliography of British railway history.** Ottley, G., *and others, comps.* London, Allen & Unwin, 1965. 683p.

1983 reprint (termed '2nd edition') by the Science Museum (HMSO. £25. ISBN 0112903347).

7,950 entries, many annotated, with 1 location in 16 British libraries (particularly the British Museum) and private collections. Excludes children's books (usually) and highly technical specialized books, but includes spotters books and others that contain useful railway history. Main classes, A-T (B. Railway transport at particular periods - C. Railway transport in particular areas ... T. General directories, gazetteers, atlases, guide books, lists of stations, distance tables, timetables). Entries state number of illus. Appended lists and 'genealogies' of railway companies. Extensive author-title and subject index, p.477-683. Comprehensive, and a model of its kind. *Class No:* 656.2(410)(091)

[6306]

—A Bibliography of British railway history. Supplement. Ottley, G., *comp.* London, HMSO, 1988. 544p. £35. ISBN: 0112903649.

2 parts: 1. Addenda and corrigenda to the main work; 2. Classification scheme (classes A-T). Bibliography, p.61-383 (entries no.7951-12956) of books and pamphlets published 1964-80, plus some pre-1963 publications recently discovered. One index, of authors, titles and subjects at head of title page: 'Science Museum/National Railway Museum'. *Class No:* 656.2(410)(091)

[6307]

—Ottley's bibliography of British railway history. Second supplement 12957-19605. Boyes, G., *and others*. York, National Railway Museum. 1998. 647p. ISBN: 1872826105.

Supplements already issued in 1965 and 1988.

Two parts: 1. Corrigenda and addenda to previous vols. - 2.Bibliography, p.61-436. Index p.445-647. Continues high standard of previous vols., mainly featuring railways of England and Wales. Excellent index. *Class No:* 656.2(410)(091)

[6308]

CLINKER, C.R. **Railway history sources.** Rev. and exp. ed. Bristol, Avon-Anglia Publications, 1976. 20p. £1. (*Reference aid series, no. 1.*)

First published as *Railway history: a handlist of principal sources of original material* (1969).

11 sections, including local records, newspapers, periodicals, timetables and maps. Appendix: 'Articles in the Journal of transport history, p.15-16'. *Class No: 656.2(410)(091)*

[6309]

ELLIS, C.H. **British railway history:** an outline, from the accession of William IV to the nationalisation of railways. London, Allen & Unwin, 1954-59. 2v. illus.

1. *1830-1876.* 443p. 2. *1877-1947.* 416p.

The first general, popular history of the British railway companies (excluding those of Ireland). It carries copious references to the individuals concerned, and includes mechanical and electric traction developments. Well illustrated. *Class No: 656.2(410)(091)*

[6310]

GOURVISH, T.R. **British railways, 1948-73:** a business history. Cambridge, University Press, 1986. xxvii, 781p. £75. ISBN: 0521264804.

3 parts (13 chapters): 1. The British Transport Commission and the Railway Executive, 1948-53 - 2. The British Transport Commission, 1953-62 - 3. The British Railways Board, 1963-73. Appendices A-J (J. Passenger service rationalisation, 1961-73). Notes, p.644-755. Bibliography ('a personal choice'), p.756-63. 'This is a commissioned but not an official history' (*Preface*). *Class No: 656.2(410)(091)*

[6311]

OTTLEY, G. **Railway history:** a guide to sixty-one collections in libraries and archives in Great Britain. London, Library Association, 1973. 80p. (*Subject guides to library resources, no.1.*)
Class No: 656.2(410)(091)

[6312]

The Oxford companion to British railway history from 1603 to the 1990s. Simmons, J. and Biddle, G., eds. Oxford, University Press, 1997. xv,591p. figs.,tables,maps. £45. ISBN: 0192116975.

Arranged A-Z (Abandonment of railways ... York Newcastle & Berwick railway). Includes entries on civil engineering, sociology, business, geography, etc. Short biographies are included. Numerous cross-references and many of the entries include several items for further reading. Sectional maps show ownership of the railways in 1922. *Class No: 656.2(410)(091)*

[6313]

A Regional history of the railways of Great Britain. Thomas, D. St. J. and Patmore, J.A., eds. Nairn, D. St. J. Thomas, 1960-. 15v. illus., maps.

1. *The West country,* by D. St. J. Thomas. 6th rev. ed. 1988. £12.95. 2. *Southern England,* by H.P. White. 5th ed. 1992. £19.95. 3. *Greater London.* 3rd ed. by H.P. White. 1987. £12.95. 4. *The North-east* by K. Hoole. 3rd rev. ed. 1986. £12.95. 5. *Eastern counties,* by D.I. Gordon. 3rd ed. 1990. £15.95. 6. *Scotland: the Lowlands and the Borders.* 2nd ed., by J. Thomas. 1984. £12.95. 7. *The West Midlands.* 3rd ed., by R. Christiansen. 1992. £19.95. 8. *South and West Yorkshire.* 2nd ed. by D.A.W. Joy. 1984. £12.95. 9. *The East Midlands,* New ed., by R. Leleux. 1984. £12.95. 10. *The North west.* 2nd ed., by G.O. Holt. 1986. £19.95. 11. *North and Mid Wales,* by P.F. Baughan. 2nd ed., 1992. £19.95. 12. *South Wales,* by D.S. Barrie. 1980. 13. *Thames and Severn,* by R. Christiansen. 1981. £14.95. 14. *The Lake counties,* 2nd ed., by D. Joy. 1990. £15.95. 15. *The North of Scotland,* by J. Thomas and D. Turnock. 2nd ed. 1993. £14.95.

Each volume is self-contained and well-illustrated. V.4 has 44 good-quality half-tone plates, 9 text illus., 8 regional maps, 1 folding map, plus a partly analytical index. A volume for Ireland was due to be published in 1996. *Class No: 656.2(410)(091)*

England & Wales

[6314]

SIMMONS, J. **The Railway in England and Wales, 1830-1914.** Leicester Univ. Press, 1978.

To be in 4v. 1. *The system and its working.* 1978. 196p.

Considers smaller and less successful railway companies as well as the most profitable and better-known ones. Supported by research at both the Public Record Office and local record offices. 'A major study' (*Annual bulletin of historical literature.* v.64: 1978 (1980), p.92). *Class No: 656.2(42)*

America—North & Central

[6315]

Railroad maps of North America: the first hundred years. Modelski, A.M., comp. Washington, Library of Congress, 1984. 186p. illus., maps. $28. ISBN: 0844403962.

Reproduces 92 of the 5,000 railroad maps in the Library of Congress's Geography amd Map Division. Coverage: USA, Canada, Mexico, The maps, arranged by type, have descriptive text and bibliographical notes. An introductory essay traces the history of railroad mapping in North America. 'This excellent atlas' (*Geographical bibliography for American libraries;* edited by C.D. Harris (1985), item 1627). *Class No: 656.2(71/73)*

Timetables

[6316]

Great Britain passenger railway timetable. London, Railtrack. 2pa. tables, maps.

Established 1853. Formerly British Rail passenger timetable.

The 30th May - September 25th 1999 (£9. 1952p.) issue 'contains rail services operated over the National Railtrack network, together with rail and shipping connections with Ireland, Isle of Man, the Isle of Wight, the Channel Islands and certain continental services to France, Belgium, etc'. Timetables 1-406, p.85-1941. Station index precedes. Includes list of service operators, sleeper services, private railway systems, and Eurostar services (including those not yet implemented). Local and suburban services are included. Unlike *OAG rail guide,* includes connections. *Class No: 656.222*

[6317]

OAG rail guide. Dunstable, Beds., OAG Worldwide (Reed Elsevier). 1853-. Monthly. tables, maps. £6.95 per issue; £79.50pa. ISSN: 13656112.

Formerly *ABC rail guide.*

June, 1999 issue contains an A-Z list of places in Great Britain served by rail, with information on fares and train times to and from London only, p.42-250; complete timetable for services in London and SE England, p.251-750; provincial Intercity section, p.751-801, arranged partly A-Z by 72 'major' cities and towns, partly tabular; ferry tables, p.23-24; Eurostar (London - Paris/Brussels), p.20-22. More up-to-date than the Railtrack timetable but not so easy to use for services outside southern England. *Class No: 656.222*

[6318]

Thomas Cook European timetable: railway and shipping services throughout Europe. Peterborough, Thomas Cook. 1873-. Monthly. tables, maps. £117.60; £159.60 (overseas). ISSN: 0952620x.

July 1999 issue (528p. £8.99) contains tables arranged into 'International' p.49-96, then within 36 countries. Information includes explanation of signs; city plans; car sleepers; airport links; holiday trains; public holidays; shipping services; books, guides and maps. The index now includes places which do not have a rail service. *Class No: 656.222*

[6319]

—Thomas Cook overseas timetable: railway, road and shipping services throughout America, Africa, Asia, Australasia. Peterborough, Thomas Cook Publishing. 1981-. 6pa. tables, maps. £58.80; £79.80 (overseas). ISSN: 01447475.

July-August 1999 issue (£8.99) contains basic travel facts (*e.g.* city maps and climatic information), p.2-41, followed by timetables for rail, bus, and internal waterborne services in America (Canada to South America), Africa, Asia, Australasia, as well as international shipping. Index to places served. *Class No: 656.222*

Signals

[6320]

ALLEN, D. and WOOLSTENHOLMES, C.J. **A Pictorial survey of railway signalling.** Yeovil, Haynes Publishing Group, 1991. 144p. illus. £14.99.

Restricted to UK in coverage and principally of interest to the rail enthusiast, this is a detailed treatment of railway signalling, both semaphore and electrical. No continuous text, the book comprises 244 plates with 2 captions each, brought together by good indexes (locations, locomotives and multiple units; signalling). Complements Nock's work on the same subject but does not supersede it. *Class No: 656.252*

[6321]

Railway control systems. Leach, M., ed. London, A & C Black, 1991. 291p. diagrs. £29.99. ISBN: 0713634200.

Compiled by a Project Group of the Institution of Railway Signal Engineers as a sequel to O.S. Nock's *Railway signalling* (1980).

11 chapters (*e.g.* 1. Recent changes in signalling philosophy ... 4. Immunisation and earthing of signalling systems ... 6. Level crossings ... 10 Automatic train protection). This is a highly-authoritative technical treatise. Lacks an overall index. *Class No: 656.252*

[6322]

Railway signalling: a treatise on the recent practice of British Railways. Nock, O.S., *ed.* London, A. & C. Black, 1980. viii, 312p. diagrs., charts. ISBN: 0713620676.

Prepared under the direction of a committee of the Institution of Railway Signal Engineers.

11 chapters (*e.g.* 2. Layout of signals and track circuits; 4. Equipment: relays, signals and point machines; 7. Track circuit principles and equipment; 8. Remote control systems; 10. The British Railways' automatic wiring system; 11. The future). Chapter-by-chapter index, p.311-2. *Class No:* 656.252

Marine Transport

Abbreviations & Symbols

[6323]

The Fairplay book of shipping abbreviations. Kapoor, P., *comp.* London, Fairplay Publications, 1980. 89p. ISBN: 0905045181.

Shipping abbreviations, A-Z, p.1-70. Code names, p.71-76. Abbreviations of company names; International code of signals; International Morse code; Operational yearbook and abbreviations; Astronomical yearbook; Greek alphabet; Roman numerals. *Class No:* 656.6(003)

Bibliographies

[6324]

Adventurers afloat: a nautical bibliography. A comprehensive guide to books in English recounting the adventures of amateur sailors upon the waters of the world in yachts, boats, and other devices and including works on the arts and sciences of cruising, racing, seamanship, navigation, design, building, etc. from the earliest writings through 1986. Toy, E.W., *Jr.* Metuchen, N.J., London, Scarecrow Press, 1988. 2v. $89.50. ISBN: 0810821893.

5,594 entries, most of which are annotated. 4 main sections: 1. The story of yachting and boating - 2. The arts, techniques, and information necessary for yachting and boating - 3. Pleasure craft: their ancestry, development, design, construction, equipment, and care - 4. Other aspects of yachting and boating. 2 appendices: 1. Chronological guide to sail racing rules - 2. Amateur Yacht Research Society publications. Indexes: author-title; ship and boat. *Class No:* 656.6(01)

[6325]

CRUISING ASSOCIATION, London. **The Cruising Association Library catalogue:** a collection of books for seamen and students of nautical literature, atlases and charts. Hanson, H.J. [2nd ed.]. London, the Association, 1939. Supplement, 1954-80. 1980. 349p. illus. (pl.).

The main catalogue, under author A-Z, with subject index, has *c.*5,000 entries. Includes list of periodicals and other serials, plus a note of 12 other nautical libraries, mostly in London. Well illustrated. *Class No:* 656.6(01)

[6326]

Guide to the manuscripts in the National Maritime Museum. Knight, R.J.B., *ed.* London, Mansell, 1977-80. 2v. 259p.; 250p. £35ea. ISBN: 0720107148, v.1; 0720115914, v.2.

V.1. *The Personal collections.* V.2. *Public records, business records, and artificial collections.*

Records the holdings of the NMM at the end of the 1970s. V.1: *The personal collections;* v.2: *Public records, business records, and artificial collections.* 'Artificial collections' refers to volume of manuscripts and other documents acquired singly. V.2 has a general index included to both volumes. *Class No:* 656.6(01)

[6327]

MARINERS MUSEUM, Newport, Va. **Dictionary catalog of the Library.** [Mariners Museum]. Boston, Mass., G.K. Hall, 1970. 9v. $980. ISBN: 0816106746.

About 118,820 photolithographed catalogue cards, covering over 43,400 volumes on shipbuilding, navigation, voyages and exploration, naval history, merchant shipping, etc. Library of Congress classification used, with separate card file of books arranged chronologically, 1518-1825.

Also: *Catalog of marine photographs* (1970. 5v. 78,000 cards. $545); *Catalog of marine prints and paintings* (1970. 3v. 50,000 cards. $330); *Catalog of maps, ships, papers and logistics* (1970. 1v. 10,000 cards. $110). *Class No:* 656.6(01)

[6328]

NATIONAL MARITIME MUSEUM. Catalogue of the Library. [National Maritime Museum]. London, HMSO, 1968-.

1. *Voyages & travel.* 1968. xi, 403p. 2. *Biography.* 1969. 2v. (501p.; 475p.). 3. *Atlases and cartography.* 1971. 2v. (xi, lx, 1166p.). 4. *Piracy & pioneering.* 1972. ix, 175, (8)p. 5. *Naval history.* pt.1: *The Middle Ages, to 1815.* 1976, [xi], 209p.

V.1 has 1,240 numbered entries, usually with annotations or bibliographical notes. V.5, pt.1: *The Middle Ages, to 1815,* lists 2,318 items. 5 parts: 1. Mediaeval; 2. The sixteenth century; 3. The seventeenth century; 4. The eighteenth century (to 1815); 5. General works. It includes periodical articles and all library accessions up to the end of June 1974. Brief notes on some items. Detailed, non-analytical index. The sequel (v.5, pt.2), aimed to continue the history to modern times, has not been published. *Class No:* 656.6(01)

[6329]

OBIN, A. Bibliography of nautical books, 1998: in print, forthcoming and recently out of print. 13th ed. Warsash (Southampton, UK), Warsash Nautical Bookshop, 1998. 826p. tables. £85. ISBN: 0948646136. ISSN: 13608487.

First published 1985.

11 sections: 1-3: Books - 4. Hydrographic Office (Admiralty) - 5. International Maritime Organization - 6. Statutory Instruments/Stationery Office - 7. M Notices (Department of Transport) - 8. British Standards - 9. Journals and periodicals - 10. Video cassettes - 11. Publishers and suppliers (addresses and telephone numbers). Lists English-language books only and a few selected books published in the US but not distributed in the UK. Claims to be 'the only single source of information on British nautical titles' (*Preface*). *Class No:* 656.6(01)

Encyclopaedias

[6330]

The Oxford companion to ships and the sea. Kemp, P., *ed.* Oxford Univ. Press, 1976 (reissued 1988). £14.95 (paperback). ISBN: 0192820842.

3,700 articles on nautical terms, famous ships, seamen, navigators, ports, explorers, etc. 'Diving' (unassisted, assisted and free diving), p. 250-5; 5 illus., references to Bathyscaphe, Bathysphere. Biographical sketches (*e.g.* 'Tasman', 'Von Spee', 'Conrad'). Also, Maritime museums, naval instruments. Generally omits material on oceanography and small-boat pleasure sailing. 5 appendices (1. Equivalent ranks; 3. Rules of the road). 226 half-tones; 187 line-drawings. 'Highly recommended' (*Library journal,* 15 January 1977, p.188). *The Economist* (23 October 1976, p.142) finds that 'Modern technology has largely been sacrificed for the sake of history'. *Class No:* 656.6(031)

[6331]

—**KEMP, P.** Encyclopedia of ships and seafaring. London, Stamford Maritime; New York, Crown, 1980. 256p. illus.

Has 9 topical chapters, followed by 3 A-Z sequences: 'Famous ships in history', 'Ship and boat types', and 'Great men of the sea'. Cross-references. Detailed index. Some overlap with *Oxford companion to ships and the sea,* but aimed at a more general public. *Class No:* 656.6(031)

Handbooks & Manuals

[6332]

BRANCH, A.E. Economics of shipping practice and management. 2nd ed. London, Chapman & Hall, 1988. xii, [2],360p. illus., diagrs., tables. £16.50. ISBN: 0412231309.

First published 1982.

18 chapters. 1. Services rendered by sea transport to international trade ... 5. Economics of containerization ... 7. Economics of ship operation ... 16. Role of British and international shipping organizations ... 17. Role of other national and international organizations - 18. Political factors. 3 appendices: A. Further recommended textbook reading - B. Addresses of organizations and institutions engaged in the field of shipping and international trade. - C. Ship diagrams. Index. *Class No:* 656.6(035)

Dictionaries

Polyglot

[6333]

DE KERCHOVE, R. International maritime dictionary: an encyclopedic dictionary of useful maritime terms and phrases, together with equivalents in French and German. 2nd ed. Princeton, N.J., Van Nostrand, [1961] (reprinted 1983, New York, French and European). [v], 1018p. $75. ISBN: 082804929x.

First published 1948.

About 12,000 terms in ship construction (including local and native craft), maritime law, shipping and marine insurance; many

....(contd.)

abbreviations have entries. Some terms carry bibliographical references. Diagrams are distinctly old fashioned. French and German indexes. *Class No:* 656.6(038)=00

[6334]

Multi-lingual dictionary of commercial international trade and shipping terms. Branch, A.E., *and others.* London, Witherby, 1990. 255p. £19.95. ISBN: 0948691905.

Intended for 'exporters, importers, travel agents, ship-brokers' etc., this is a handy little guide to some 2,200 terms (*e.g.* Discount rate ... Indivisible load), arranged English-French, p.13-94, English-Spanish, p.95-174, and English-German, p.175-255. No cross-translations into English. *Class No:* 656.6(038)=00

[6335]

VANDENBERGHE, J-P. *and* **JOHNEN, M. Elsevier's nautical dictionary.** 3rd ed. Amsterdam, Elsevier, 1994. 828p. £160; $257.25. ISBN: 044489604x.

Previous ed. published 1978.

Lists 13,462 terms in English/American, French, Spanish, Dutch, and German. Definitions are not included, nor are fishing and naval architecture. Bibliography of sources is given.

Class No: 656.6(038)=00

English

[6336]

BES, J. Chartering and shipping terms. 9th ed., brought up to date by including the revised York, Antwerp Rules. 1974. v.1. London, Barker & Howard, 1975. 506, [12]p. illus. £25. ISBN: 0900133082.

First published 1951.

V.1: 'Practical guide to steamship companies, masters, ship's officers, shipbrokers, forwarding agents, exporters, importers, insurance brokers and banks'. 14 chapters, each with terms A-Z (1. Charterings ... 4. Conditions of carriage ... 7. Shipping terms ... 13. Marine insurance - 14. Trade terms). New chapters on operations of tramp ships, of ships in line and tramp trade, and of container ships. 18 appendices (*e.g.* pro formas estimates for voyages, interpretation of charter party terms). Index. 10 illus. *Class No:* 656.6(038)=20

[6337]

BRANCH, A.E. Dictionary of shipping, international trade terms and abbreviations. 3rd ed. London, Witherby, 1987. xii, 587p. illus. £14.50. ISBN: 0948691204.

First published 1976; 2nd ed. 1982.

More than 9,000 terms (2nd ed.: 4,000), p.1-532. Appendices A-G (A. Further recommended textbook reading; B. Major ports of the world and their location; D. Addresses and roles of shipping organisations and institutes; G. Diagrams (1-14, *e.g.* Liquified natural gas carrier)). Author, chief examiner in Shipping and Export Practice. *Class No:* 656.6(038)=20

[6338]

BRODIE, P.R. Dictionary of shipping terms. 3rd ed. London, LLP, 1997. vii,219p. ISBN: 1859781195.

First published 1985.

Focuses on commercial aspects of shipping. Over 2,000 concise definitions (A/a ... York-Antwerp Rules) of words, terms, phrases, and abbreviations. This edition incorporates recent developments in cargo handling. Many cross-references. *Class No:* 656.6(038)=20

[6339]

Dictionary of nautical words and terms: 8,000 definitions in navigation, seamanship, rigging, meteorology, astronomy, naval architecture, average, ship economics, hydrography, cargo, stowage, marine engineering, ice terminology, buoyage, yachting, etc. Layton, C.W.T. Rev. 3rd ed. Glasgow, Brown, Son, and Ferguson, 1987. 397p. £22. ISBN: 0851745369.

The 8,000 entries range from 6 to *c.*100 words (*e.g.* 'Trinity House'). Words now obsolete or obsolescent are asterisked.

Class No: 656.6(038)=20

[6340]

—BLACKBURN, G. The Illustrated dictionary of nautical terms. Newton Abbot, Devon, David & Charles, 1982. 359p. illus., diagrs. ISBN: 0715382969.

Has *c.*3,000 entries, usually 2-15 lines in length (but 'Boom': 16½ lines, plus 4 illus). Where British and American spelling diverge, the former appears in brackets after the American. Keyed illus. are a feature. Adequate cross-references. *Class No:* 656.6(038)=20

[6341]

—The 'Country Life' book of nautical terms under sail. Whitlock, P.C., *and others.* Feltham, Country Life Books, 1978. 352p. illus. (incl. col.), facsims., diagrs., maps.

Defines *c.*4,000 terms. 20 sections: 1. The ship: basic terms - 2. General terms - 3. Building a ship, keel to bulwarks - 4. Masts, spars, sails and rigging ... 12. Sailing and seamanship ... 18. Pilotage charts - 19. Navigational instruments - 20. Inshore and ashore. 2p. of section bibliographies. 15p. index. Illus. are a feature.

Class No: 656.6(038)=20

[6342]

LENFESTEY, T. The Facts on File dictionary of nautical terms. New York, Facts on File, 1994. x,541p. diagrs. $35. ISBN: 0816020876.

Describes *c.*8,500 terms in common usage. Parts of speech are indicated. Many cross-references. Abbreviations, p.531-8. Bibliographhy, p.539-41. Has greater breadth than *Oxford companion to ships and the sea (1976) (q.v.)* and *Dictionary of nautical words and terms (1987) (q.v.).* *Class No:* 656.6(038)=20

[6343]

ROUSMANIERE, J. The Illustrated dictionary of boating terms: 2,000 essential terms for sailors and powerboaters. New York, W.W. Norton, 1998. 168p. illus. £13.95; $23. ISBN: 0393046494.

First published in 1976 as *A Glossary of modern sailing terms* (rev. 1989).

With 2,000 terms (Abaft ... Zulu), this ed. contains 800 more terms than the previous edition. Useful illustrations.

Class No: 656.6(038)=20

[6344]

SULLIVAN, E. The Marine encyclopaedic dictionary. 3rd ed. London, Lloyd's of London Press, 1992. vii, 497p. £45. ISBN: 1850443718.

About 20,000, entries, many for abbreviations. Some longer entries, *e.g.* 'International shipping organizations': 5½ columns; 'Coastguard': 3 columns' 'SOLAS (Safety of life at sea)': 7p.; 'Lloyd's Register of shipping': 6 columns. Covers all the terminology in use in the marine transport and shipping industry. Well-produced.

Class No: 656.6(038)=20

German

[6345]

DIETEL, W. Seefahrts-Wörterbuch: deutsch-englisch, englisch-deutsch. 2. Aufl. Munich, Lehmans Verlag, 1964. 1024p.

First published 1954.

A German-English, English-German maritime dictionary. About 35,000 terms in all, covering military and civil seafaring. Includes colloquialisms and slang, in quotation marks. 'Quite shamelessly padded' (*The Incorporated linguist,* v.9(2), April, 1970, p.51-52).

Class No: 656.6(038)=30

French

[6346]

BRODIE, P.R. Dictionary of shipping and shipbroking terms, French/English, English/French. London, Lloyd's of London, 1980. 216p. £15. ISBN: 0904093824. *Class No:* 656.6(038)=40

Italian

[6347]

BERNABO SILORATA, M. *and* **PICCHI, F. Grande dizionario di marina, italiano-inglese, inglese-italiano.** Salerno, Di Maura Editore; New York, French and European, 1970. 963p. illus. (incl. pl.), tables. $125. ISBN: 0686925513. *Class No:* 656.6(038)=50

Spanish

[6348]

SUÁREZ GIL, L. Diccionario tecnico maritimo, inglés-español-inglés. 2nd ed. Madrid, Editorial Alhambra; New York, French and European, 1983. vii, 704p. $110. ISBN: 0828804257, US ed; 8420509396.

First published 1981.

English-Spanish, p.1-292; Spanish-English, p.293-569. About 4,000 entries in each half. Terms and phrases are categorized. 'Arquitectura naval', p.644-704 (illus. plus keys). 8 appendices (*e.g.* abbreviations; naval expressions). *Class No:* 656.6(038)=60

Greek

[6349]

Dictionary of shipping: Greek/English, English Greek. Vlassopulos, B.P., *ed.* London, Lloyd's of London Press, 1988. 200p. £29. (*Foreign language dictionaries.*) ISBN: 1850441731.

A few thousand terms, each way, in modern commercial usage.

Class No: 656.6(038)=77

Russian

[6350]
IVANOV, A.O. **Dictionary of shipping terms: Russian-English and English-Russian.** London, LLP, 1997. xx,229p. £36. ISBN: 1859780733.
More than 4,000 terms. Coverage includes ports, vessel types, ship finance, cargo gear, navigation, common abbreviations.
Class No: 656.6(038)=82

Arabic

[6351]
BAKR, M. **Elsevier's maritime dictionary** in three languages, English, French, Arabic. Amsterdam, etc., Elsevier, 1987. [vii], 664p. £159.95. ISBN: 0444427376.
12,024 English-based terms, with French and Arabic equivalents and indexes. Thumb-indexed. *Class No:* 656.6(038)=927

Yearbooks & Directories

[6352]
Fairplay world shipping directory. Coulsdon, Surrey, Fairplay Publications. Annual. £145; $247 (overseas). ISSN: 09593101.
Previously (1976-77) as *'Financial times' World shipping year book*.
The 1998-99 *Directory* (xx,1758p.) is the ninth edition and contains 36% more data than the eighth. Sections include ship operators, ship managers, ship builders and repairers, marine insurance, maritime organisations, consultants and surveyors, port authorities, etc. Company, personnel, vessel, and advertisers' index.
World shipping statistics, 1989-, is a geographical analysis of the marine industry worldwide. *Class No:* 656.6(058)

[6353]
Lloyd's nautical year book. Hughes, D., *ed.* London, LLP Reference Publishing, 1979-. Annual. illus. $90. ISSN: 09525394.
Originally as *Lloyd's Calendar*, established 1899.
A compendium mixing editorial features (*e.g.* 'Tanker market overview') under 9 headings, with reference information under country information (Afghanistan-Zimbabwe) and general data (*e.g.* maritime organisations and services). Subject index. *Class No:* 656.6(058)

Histories

[6354]
ALBION, R.G. **Naval & maritime history:** an annotated bibliography. 4th ed., rev. and expanded. Mystic, Conn., Munson Institute of American Maritime History, the Maritime Historical Association, Inc., 1972. ix, 370p. $14.95. ISBN: 0913372056.
First published 1951; 3rd ed. 1963 (viii, 230p.).
Lists *c.*5,000 books in English, plus PhD. theses. Some entries are briefly annotated items considered to be 'the most substantial and useful' asterisked. 7 sections: 1. Reference works - 2. Merchantmen and warships - 3. Captains and crews - 4. Maritime science, exploration and expansion - 5. Commerce and shipping (p.103-9: divided by regions) - 6. Navies (p.229-302, by periods) - 7. Special topics (*e.g.* Auxiliary services; Main American maritime museums). Author and brief subject indexes. 'An indispensable companion to any writer on maritime history' (*Journal of the Institute of Navigation*, v.17(2), April 1964, p.211). US slant. *Class No:* 656.6(091)

[6355]
—Bibliography of periodical articles published in ... Mystic, Conn., Maritime Historical Association, 1970-.
Continues Albion's bibliography. *Class No:* 656.6(091)

[6356]
Five hundred years of nautical science, 1400-1900: conference proceedings. Howse, D., *ed.* London, National Maritime Museum, 1982. 418p. illus. £11. ISBN: 0955555554. *Class No:* 656.6(091)

[6357]
HARLAND, J. **Seamanship in the age of sail:** an account of the shiphandling of the sailing man-of-war, 1600-1860, based on contemporary sources. London, Conway Maritime Press, 1984. 320p. illus. £30. ISBN: 0851771793.
A comprehensive survey of how ships were handled, even down to the smallest detail of shipboard routine. Bibliography, p.313-5. Author is an active member of the Society for Nautical Research.
Class No: 656.6(091)

[6358]
HOPE, R. **A New history of British shipping.** London, John Murray, 1990. xviii,533p. illus., tables, maps. £35. ISBN: 0719547997.
3 sections: 1. The beginnings of British shipping 3000BC - 1400AD - 2. The rise of British shipping 1400-1890 - 3. The decline of British shipping 1890-1988. Epilogue: the great debate, p.471-87. Bibliography, p.488-504. Index. References and notes are appended to each chapter. *Class No:* 656.6(091)

Archives

[6359]
MATHIAS, P. *and* PEARSALL, A.W.H. **Shipping:** a survey of historical records. Newton Abbot, Devon, David & Charles, 1971. 162p. tables.
2 sections: 1. Shipping companies (42; A-Z, p.17-97), giving nature and details of records held; access - 2. Shipping records in country and other offices (50; A-Z, p.101-42), tabulating type of document, ship's name, period covered, voyage(s) made. Index of persons and firms; index of places and principal trades; index of ships' names.
Class No: 656.6(093.20)

Worldwide

[6360]
OAG cruise and ferry guide. Dunstable, Beds., OAG Worldwide (Reed Travel Group). 4pa. $125. ISSN: 13571214.
Formerly published as *ABC passenger shipping guide: worldwide guide to services and cruises* and *ABC cruise and ferry guide*.
Issue for March-May 1999 (412p.) has five main sections: Operators' addresses, telephone and telefax - Cruise ships - Cruises - Cargo passenger services - Ferries. Prelims. include international climate chart, and abbreviations. Indexes, p.370-412.
Class No: 656.6(100)

Libraries

[6361]
Marine transport: a guide to libraries and sources of information in Great Britain. Bolton, R.V. *and* Bryan, F.J., *eds.* 2nd ed. London, Library Association, Reference, Special and Information Section, and the Marine Librarians' Association, 1983. 76p.
First published 1974 (Allum, D.N. and others).
103 numbered entries. Part 1: Directory of marine libraries, 'Admiralty Marine Technology Establishment' ... 'Wirral Public Libraries'. Data include stock and periodical statistics, subject coverage, terms of admission, opening times, services, publications, indexes, special collections. Part 2: Other organizations (1-91). Name and subject (non-analytical) indexes. Appendix: 'List of the principal records of the Registry of Shipping and Seamen'. A good example of a guide to libraries in a specified field. *Class No:* 656.6:061:026/027

Museums

[6362]
HOWE, H.E. **North America's maritime museums:** an annotated guide. New York, BDD Promo Book Co., 1987. 371p. $19.98. ISBN: 0792445724. *Class No:* 656.6:061:069

[6363]
WHEATLEY, K. **National Maritime Museum guide to maritime Britain.** Exeter, Devon, Webb & Bower, 1990. 208p. illus. (some col.). ISBN: 0863502687.
10 chapters, arranged by region: Highlands and Islands ... The West Country ... Ulster. Each chapter contains an introduction followed by a gazetteer where, in addition to place names, museums and galleries of maritime interest are listed. *Class No:* 656.6:061:069

Ships' Flags

[6364]
WILSON, T. **Flags at sea:** a guide to the flags flown at sea by British and some foreign ships from the 16th century to the present day, illustrated from the collections of the National Maritime Museum. London, HMSO, 1986. 127p. illus. (incl. col.), charts. £7.95. ISBN: 0112903894.
Concentrates on the sea flags of Britain, Spain, the Netherlands, France and the United States. Special chapters on flag signalling and the manufacturing of sea flags. *Class No:* 656.6:929.925

[6365]
—Brown's flags and funnels of British and foreign steamship companies. Wedge, C.P., *comp.* 6th ed. Glasgow, Brown, Son & Ferguson, 1958. [iii], 381., 20p. col. illus.
Founded in 1926 by Captain F.J.N. Wedge.
Small coloured reproductions of *c.*1,000 flags and funnels. Flags with predominant colours tend to be grouped by colour. Index of companies (names and addresses), with flags and plate numbers.
Class No: 656.6:929.925

Maritime Navigation

Handbooks & Manuals

[6366]

Admiralty manual of navigation. London, HMSO. 5v. illus., diagrs., tables, maps. (*BR 45*.)

V.1 (Rev. ed. 1987. xviii, 697p.): *General navigation, coastal navigation and pilotage,* supersedes the edition of 1964. V.2 (1973, 348p.) is the text book of ocean navigation and nautical astronomy. V.3 includes chapters on radio aids, navigational instruments, logs and echo sounders, gyros and magnetic compasses, automated navigation and radar plotting systems. V.4 (classified) has data and information on navigation, fleetwork and shiphandling. V.5 (6 bound parts) provides exercises on the use of tables (*e.g.* astronomical, Great Circle, tidal and tidal streams, time and chronometer, relative velocity questions).

V.1 has 19 chapters, with 7 appendices (*e.g.* 4: Projections). Bibliography, p.675-7. Detailed, analytical index. Well produced. Written primarily for naval officers, but with a wider appeal.

The Admiralty issues updates and amendments for mariners in its weekly publication, *Admiralty notices to mariners,* now also available in electronic and CD-ROM/floppy disk forms. *Class No:* 656.61(035)

[6367]

Admiralty manual of seamanship. London, Stationery Office, 1995-. vii, 798p. illus., diagrs., graphs, tables, maps. £80. ISBN: 0117726966.

First amendment, *Change 1,* published 1996 (170p. £20).

For all those concerned with seamanship in the Royal Navy, giving detailed information. An international edtion was published in 1995 (vii, 900p. £25). *Class No:* 656.61(035)

[6368]

—Seaway code: a guide for small boat users. [4th] rev. ed. London, HMSO, 1983. 48p. col. illus. ISBN: 0115136568.

Revised at intervals, had a 3rd ed. in 1981.

'Small boat' includes yachts, canoes and dinghies. Chapters concern weather forecasts, emergency drills, first aids, insurance, buoys, as well as 'rules of the road'. Bibliography, p.44. *Class No:* 656.61(035)

[6369]

The Complete sailing handbook. Denk, D., *and others.* 2nd rev. ed. London, Dunitz, 1981. 344p. illus. (incl. colour), diagrs., tables, maps. ISBN: 0906348293.

First published 1979. Translation of *Das grosse Handbuch des Segelns.* Reprinted 1990. (London, Tiger Books International. £8.99).

About boats - Marlinspike seamanship & maintenance - The boat engine - Sailing theory and sail turning - Sailing practice - Multihulls - Windsurfing - Safety - Racing - Navigation - Weather - Navigation rules. Appended glossary; International code of signals. Grouped bibliography, p.338-9. Index. *Class No:* 656.61(035)

[6370]

The Macmillan nautical almanac. Incorporating *Reed's nautical almanac.* London, Pan, 1980-. Annual. illus., graphs, tables, maps.

1999 ed. (980p. £26.95). Claims to be 'the first comprehensive almanac designed specifically in North-West Europe'. Includes: rules of the road; coastal navigation; waypoints; international codes and flags; chartlet of harbours in UK, Belgium, France, Ireland, and Germany. Attractively produced, with over 800 charts and diagrams. Detailed index. Updated between editions by two free supplements. *Class No:* 656.61(035)

[6371]

The Mariners' handbook; containing information on Admiralty charts and navigational publications, general navigation, general meteorology and ice. 5th ed. Taunton, Hydrographer of the Navy, 1979. viii, 163p. illus., diagrs., maps. (*NP100.*)

Contents: Charts and books - Terms, symbols annd orthography (in general navigation, physical features, ports, harbours and water movements) - The use of charts and other navigational aids - Navigational hazards - Natural conditions - Ice (*e.g.* formation and movements of sea-ice, icebergs, ice navigation, icebreaker signals, ice accumulation on ships). *Class No:* 656.61(035)

[6372]

TATE, W.H. Handbook of the nautical rules of the road. Annapolis, Md., Naval Institute Press, 1991. xiv, 244p. illus. $29.95. ISBN: 1557505047.

First published 1974. Formerly published as *A Mariner's guide to the rules of the road,* 2nd ed., 1982.

Explains the rules and regulations (including amendments since 1986) governing the control and movement of vessels both on the high seas and on US inland waterways. Of the previous ed., 'Absolutely essential to professional mariners and serious marine hobbyists' (*Library journal,* 1 December 1982, p.2249). *Class No:* 656.61(035)

Dictionaries

[6373]

UNITED STATES. Naval Oceanographic Office. **Navigation dictionary.** 2nd ed. Washington, US Government Printing Office, 1969. iv, 292p.

First published 1956 (US Hydrographic Office).

Covers all types of craft. US-slanted and now somewhat dated. *Class No:* 656.61(038)

Maps & Atlases

[6374]

Catalogue of Admiralty charts and other hydrographic publications. Taunton, Hydrographer of the Navy. Annual. tables, maps.

Contains three main sections: Navigational charts - Other charts and diagrams - Publications. Keyed charts occupy right-hand pages, with lists of charts, stating scale and date, facing. Numerical index, with prices. The outsize oblong catalogue measures 41.25 x 37.5cm. *Class No:* 656.61(084.3)

Histories

[6375]

FANNING, A.E. Steady as she goes: a history of the Compass Department of the Admiralty. National Maritime Museum. London, HMSO, 1986. xlv, 462p. illus., ports. £27.50. ISBN: 0112904234.

13 documented chapters (*e.g.* 12: SINS, Polaris and the last naval director, 1961-71, 32 references). 12 appendices. Bibliography, p.445-6. Detailed, analytical index. Plates, p.381-418. *Class No:* 656.61(091)

Worldwide

[6376]

GREAT BRITAIN. Hydrographic Department. **Ocean passages for the world.** 3rd ed. [London], Hydrographer of the Navy, 1973. Supplement, no.1. 1277. viii, 288p. maps. (*NP 136.*)

2nd ed. 1950.

Routes for steam and sailing ships, with special reference to winds and currents. Part 1: Power vessel routes (1. Planning a passage; 2. North Atlantic Ocean ... 7. Pacific Ocean ...) - Part 2: Sailing vessel routes. General index. 25 diagrs. of routes. Insert of charts (world climate; routes; currents). *Class No:* 656.61(100)

[6377]

Sailing directions (Pilots). London, Hydrographic Department. Various editions; Supplements.

1-3. *African pilot.* 12th-13th eds. 1973-82. 4. *South-east Alaska pilot.* 5th ed. 1972. 5-7A. *South American pilot.* 2nd-15th eds. 1968-83. 8. *Pacific coasts of Central America and US pilot.* 8th ed. 1975. 9. *Antarctic pilot.* 4th ed. 1974. 10-12. *Arctic pilot.* 6th-7th ed. 1959-76. 13-17. *Australian pilot.* 6th ed. 1972-82. 18-20. *Baltic pilot.* 6th-10th. 1974-78. 21. *Bay of Bengal pilot.* 10th ed. 1978. 22. *Bay of Biscay pilot.* 5th ed. 1970. 23. *Bering Sea and Strait pilot.* 5th ed. 1980. 24. *Black Sea pilot.* 11th ed. 1969. 25-26. *British Columbian pilot.* 6th-9th ed. 1976-79. 27. *Channel pilot.* 2nd ed. 1977. (revised 1984). 28. *Dover Strait pilot.* 2nd ed. 1981. 30-32. *China Sea pilot.* 4th ed. 1975-82. 33-36. *Philippine Islands, Indonesia pilots.* 1975-80. 37. *West coast of England and Wales pilot.* 11th ed. 1974. 38. *West coast of India pilot.* 11th ed. 1975. 39. *Indian Ocean, south, pilot.* 8th ed. 1971. 505.00/01$a40. *Irish coast pilot.* 12th ed. 1985. 41-42. *Japan pilot.* 7th ed. 1979-82. 43. *Korea, south and east coasts, etc., pilots.* 6th ed. 1983. 44. *Malacca Strait pilot.* 5th ed. 1971. 45-49. *Mediterranean pilot.* 6th-10th eds. 1968-78. 50. *Newfoundland pilot.* 10th ed. 1978. 51. *New Zealand pilot.* 13th ed. 1971. 52. *North coast of Scotland pilot.* 1975. 54-55. *North sea pilot.* 1973-75. 56-58B. *Norway pilot.* 6th-8th ed. 1979-82. 59. *Nova Scotia, South-east coast, etc.* 11th ed. 1971. 60-62. *Pacific Islands pilot.* 9th-10th ed. 1970-84. 63. *Persian Gulf pilot.* 12th ed. 1982. 64. *Red Sea and Gulf of Mexico, East coasts pilot.* 12th ed. 1980. 65. *St. Lawrence pilot.* 12th ed. 1969. 66. *Scotland, West coast, pilot.* 11th ed. 1974. 67. *Spain and Portugal, west coast, pilot.* 5th ed. 1972 (revised 1983). 68-69. *United States, east coast, pilot.* 7th ed. 1975-78. 69A. *Central America and Gulf of Mexico pilot.* 1970. 70-71. *West Indies pilot.* 1st-11th ed. 1969-71. 72. *White Sea pilot.* 3rd ed. 1973.

Many of the major countries (*e.g.* USA, USSR, Japan) publish coastal guides for their own coasts. The Admiralty 'Pilots' provide a selective translation of these. *Class No:* 656.61(100)

Institutions & Associations

[6378]

Guide to the marine stations of the North Atlantic and European waters. Compiled on behalf of the Royal Society's Naples Zoological Station Committee, by J.E. Webb. London, Royal Society, 1974-77. 3v. maps. ISBN: 0854030689, v.1; 0854030794, v.2; 0854030905, v.3.

1. *Northern Europe and the East Atlantic coast.* £2.70. 2.

....(contd.)

Mediterranean Basin. £3.50. 3. Iceland, the West Atlantic coast and the Caribbean Sea ..., £4.85, with supplements to pts.1 and 2.

Countries A-Z in each part. Data include 'major accessible habitats, collecting and hydrogaphic facilities, laboratory services, living accommodation for visitors, publications' (British Council. *British scientific and technical reference books* (1975), p.20). *Class No:* 656.61:061:061.2

Signals

[6379]

The Admiralty list of radio signals. London, Hydrographic Office, 1985-86. 6v. (*NP 275(1)-(6)*.)

1. *Coast radio stations.* 1986 ed. 2. *Radio navigational aids.* 1986 ed. 3. *Radio weather messages. Meteorological codes.* 1985 ed. Diagrams. 4. *Lists of meteorological observation stations.* 5. *Radio time signals. Radio navigation warnings and position fixing systems.* 1986 ed. Diagrams. 6. *Port operations. Pilot services and traffic surveillance.* 1985 ed.

Updated by corrections in section 6 of the weekly edition of *Admiralty notices to mariners* until suspended. *Class No:* 656.61.054

[6380]

International code of signals, 1969. London, HMSO, 1969. xv, 149p. £9. ISBN: 011551015x.

Reprinted 1991, incorporating amendments 1, 2 and 3. *Class No:* 656.61.054

Lights & Beacons

[6381]

Admiralty list of lights and fog signals. Taunton, Hydrographer of the Navy. 1985-86 ed. 12v. tables, maps.

A. *British Isles and north coast of France.* 1986 ed. (NP 74). 2. B. *Southern and eastern sides of the North Sea.* 1986 ed. (NP 75). C. *Baltic Sea.* 1986 ed. (NP 76). D. *Eastern side of Atlantic Ocean.* (NP 77). E. *Mediterranean, Black Sea and Red Seas.* 1986 ed. (NP 78). F. *Arabian Sea, Bay of Bengal and North Pacific Ocean.* 1986 ed. (NP 79). G. *Western side of South Atlantic Ocean and East Pacific Ocean.* 1986 ed. (NP 80). M. *Northern and eastern coasts of Canada.* 1985 ed. (NP 81). J. *Western side of North Atlantic Ocean.* 1985 ed. (NP 82). K. *Indian and Pacific Oceans, south of the Equator.* 1985 ed. (NP 83). L. *Norwegian and Greenland Seas.* 1985 ed. (NP 84). M. *Arctic Ocean.* 1985 ed. (NP 85).

Mostly tables stating number, name and position, latitude and longitude, characteristics and intensity, elevation, range, structure, remarks. *Class No:* 656.61.057

Ports & Harbours

[6382]

BIRD, J. The Major seaports of the United Kingdom. London, Hutchinson, 1963. 454p. illus., charts.

18 chapters (*e.g.* 7: Bristol, the Avon and Avonmouth; 47 references, plus 8 further British references; 18: The ports in perspective; 27 references, with 'Selected further references published since 1953'). Copious explanatory notes. A detailed, fully documented survey submitted as evidence for the Rochdale Committee. 'A major contribution to port geography' (*Economic geography*, v.40(2), April 1964, p.182). 'Clearly destined to become a standard work of reference on this neglected subject for some time to come' (*Dock & harbour authority*, v.44(511), May 1963, p.15). Useful historical work. *Class No:* 656.615

[6383]

—JACKSON, G. The History and archaeology of ports. Kingswood, Tadworth, Surrey, World's Work, Ltd., 1983. 176p. illus. (incl. col.), facsims. ISBN: 0437075397.

6 chapters: 1. The rise of ports c.1450-1660 - 2. Harbour developments and port improvements, 1660-1860 - 3. The emergence of dock systems, 1690-1940 - 4. Expansion: new docks and new ports, 1640-1870 - 5. The height of prosperity, 1870-1914 - 6. Stagnation and decay, 1919-1980. Footnotes, p.168-70. Bibliography, p.171-2. Index. Details the various phases of development of all the major ports, and many minor ones of Britain. *Class No:* 656.615

[6384]

Lloyd's maritime atlas. 19th ed. London, Lloyd's of London Press, 1997. 156p. tables, col. maps. £66. ISBN: 1859781683.

First published as *Lloyd's maritime atlas*, 1951. Previously as *Lloyd's book of ports and shipping places* and *Lloyd's maritime atlas of world ports and shipping places*.

Three sections of maps: World maps; Ocean maps; Port maps. Begins with a chart showing distances and voyage times between 44 major ports worldwide. The maritime atlas section shows over 3,000 ports (130 of them new to this ed.) and shipping places. New to this ed. are maps of European canals. The quality of the maps is excellent,

....(contd.)

with much detail. 11 symbols indicate types of port. Geographic and alphabetic indexes. Designed for use with *Lloyd's ports of the world* (*q.v.*). *Class No:* 656.615

[6385]

Lloyd's ports of the world 1997. Pinchin, B.A., *ed.* 15th ed. Colchester, Lloyd's of London Press, 1997. iv,896p. maps (64p.) ISBN: 1859780520.

Directory of *c.*2,900 ports worldwide, specifying anchorage and berthing details, possible hazardous approaches, loading facilities etc. Divided into Africa, North America, Central America & West Indies, South America, Asia, Australia and Pacific Islands, Europe, European Union, Free Trade Zones, with ports and port-owning companies intermixed in A-Z sequence. Results in apparent filing anomalies ('Fosdyke' appears to follow 'Methil' - actually 'Forth Ports'), which better typography could have clarified. Indexes. *Class No:* 656.615

[6386]

Port statistics 1996. London, The Stationery Office, 1997. viii,107p. figs.,tables. £25. ISBN: 0115519742.

Four sections: 1. All ports of the United Kingdom: foreign and domestic traffic - 2. Unitised traffic - 3. Other port statistics (*e.g.* 'Ship arrivals') - 4. Historic port traffic statistics. Four appendices, *e.g.* C. List of port authorities and undertakings submitting port traffic returns. Index. *Class No:* 656.615

Canal & River Transport

Bibliographies

[6387]

Inland waterways. London, Library Association, 1975. 27p. (*Readers' guide no.7.*)

Checklist of *c.*250 unannotated entries. Sections: Inland waterways of Britain (general & regional histories) - Canals (English, Welsh, Scottish, Irish) - Boats and boatmen - Canal engineering and architecture - British reports - Leisure use and guides - Maps - Accounts of cruises on British inland waterways - East Anglican Broads - British rivers - Continental inland waterways (p.230-24) - North American inland waterways - Reference books - Periodicals - Organizations. No Index. *Class No:* 656.62(01)

Dictionaries

[6388]

Glossary for inland transport. New York, United Nations, 1970. [1], 44p. 116p. (*ME/TRANS/70/D/D40.*)

600 terms. Index precedes. 'No more than informative descriptions of an entirely general nature and cannot be taken as true definitions in the strict and precise sense of the term' (*Introductory note*).

A French version - ME/71/68/D.5 - helps to provide a two-way dictionary. *Class No:* 656.62(038)

Europe

[6389]

Inland waterways series. Huntingdon, Imray, Laurie, Norie & Wilson, 1950-. illus., maps, plans.

Inland waterways of Great Britain and Ireland; compiled by L.A. Edwards. 6th ed. 1985. 480p. £17.50. *Inland waterways of France,* by D. Edwards-May. 6th ed. 1992. viii,334p. £25. *Inland waterways of the Netherlands,* by E.E. Benest. 3v. 1966-72. *Inland waterways of Belgium,* by E.E. Benest. 1960.

The 6th ed. of *Inland waterways of France* (1992. viii,334p.) features particulars of the waterways, with distance tables, p.31-318. Numerous plans; short glossary (French-English, English-French). Index.

Inland waterways of Germany and Denmark, by B. Sheffield is due to be published in 1996. *Class No:* 656.62(4)

Great Britain

[6390]

BOUGHEY, Joseph. Hadfield's British canals. Hadfield, C. 8th ed. Stroud, Gloucs., Alan Sutton Publishing Limited, 1994. 343p. illus., facsims., maps. £17.99. ISBN: 0750900172.

First published 1950. Previous title: *British canals: an illustrated history*.

Paperback edition published as *British canals: inland waterways of Britain and Ireland* (Sutton Publishing, 1998. £12.99).

14 chapters: 1. The old days ... 8. The rivers during the canal age ... 14. In transformation. Further reading, p.321-27. Index to *The Canals of Britain* series. Detailed, analytical index. Well illustrated; 18 maps. This edition contains increased coverage of developments in the twentieth century. *Class No:* 656.62(410)

[6391]
HADFIELD, C. **The Canals of the British Isles.** Newton Abbot, Devon, David & Charles, 1950-.

1. *British canals: an illustrated history* by C. Hadfield. 7th ed. 1984. 2. *The canals of south and south-east England.* 1969. 3. *The canals of south-west England.* 2nd ed. 1985. 206p. £13.50. 4. *The canals of south Wales and the Border.* 2nd ed. 1967. £12.95. 5. *The canals of the West Midlands.* 3rd ed. 1985. 352p. 6. *The canals of the East Midlands* (including part of London). 2nd ed. 1970. £12.95. 7. *The canals of eastern England,* by J. Boyes and R. Russell. 1977. 8/9. *The canals of north-west England.* 1970. 2v. 10/11. *The canals of Yorkshire and north-east England.* 1970. 2v. £12.95ea. 12. *The canals of Scotland,* by J. Lindsay. 1968. 13. *The canals of the north of Ireland,* by A. McCutcheon. 1965. 14. *The canals of the south of Ireland,* by T.H. and D.R. Delaney. 1973.

V.10/11, on Yorkshire canals, covers the periods, up to 1970, and 1970-72. V.11 (254p. has 16 plates, 22 text illus. and maps, plus combined analytical index). Appendices: 1. Summary of facts about the canals and navigation of the North-east. 2. Principal engineering works.

C. Hadfield, author of v.1-6, 8-11 in the series, provides a combined index to v.2-14. *Class No: 656.62(410)*

[6392]
Ordnance Survey guide to the waterways. Perrott, D., *ed.* 5th ed. London, Nicholson, 1991. 3v. illus., maps. ISBN: 0702812595, v.1; 0702812609, v.2; 0702812641, v.3.

First published 1983.

1. *South.* 208p. 1991. £8.99. 2. *Central.* 176p. 1991. £8.99. 3. *North.* 192p. 1991. £8.99.

Detailed guide to inland navigation. V.3 charts navigation between Nottingham, Lincoln, Sheffield, Leeds, Manchester and Liverpool, on 2-inch scale maps. Gives general cruising information in addition to locations of tunnels, bridges, pubs, restaurants, boatyards and other facilities. Index. *Class No: 656.62(410)*

England

[6393]
McKNIGHT, H. **The Shell book of inland waterways.** 2nd ed. Newton Abbot, Devon, David & Charles, 1981. 493p. illus. (incl. col.), maps. £12.95. ISBN: 071538239x.

First published 1975.

18 chapters, covering such topics as locks and lifts, bridges, aqueducts, tunnels, building and design, boatyards and marinas, animal and plant life, waterway museums, associations and boat clubs. Selected bibliograpy, p.208-9. Descriptive gazetteer, p.212-484. Attractively produced. *Class No: 656.62(420)*

Air Transport

[6394]
Aerospace Europe: the directory of European aviation, 1999. 51st ed. Tonbridge, Kent, Miller Freeman Information Services, 1998. 376p. illus. £87. ISBN: 0863823858.

Alphabetical list of companies (over 7,000 established and operating within Europe). Classified products and services (index precedes) - Brands and trade names - Company data - Who's who - Associations and organisations. Advertisers' index. *Class No: 656.7*

[6395]
INTERNATIONAL CIVIL AVIATION ORGANIZATION. **Lexicon in English-French-Spanish-Russian.** Montreal, ICAO, 1974. 2v.

Previous ed. (1971) covered only English, French and Spanish.

1. *Vocabulary.* xii, 326p. 2. *Definitions.* 139p.

About 3,000 English-based terms, with French, Spanish and Russian equivalents and indexes. Terms defined in v.2 are asterisked. Some categorization of terms. *Class No: 656.7*

[6396]
OCRAN, E.B. **Dictionary of air transport and traffic control.** London, Granada, 1984. ix, 243p. ISBN: 0246123605.

Part 1: Definitions, p.1-205. Part 2: Grouped index (*c.*3,000 entries, in 18 sections: Accidents and safety ... Navigation. Includes abbreviations, organizations). Author is head of Bibliographical Services, Civil Aviation Authority Library, London. Intended for a wide audience. *Class No: 656.7*

[6397]
WOOD, K. *and* McDONALD, G. **The Round the world air guide** 1992. 6th ed. London, Fontana, 1992. 896p. £12.99. ISBN: 0006377777.

First published 1987.

Intended for those embarking on long-haul flights and gives data on the world's 52 most frequently visited cities - this edition includes Moscow and Mexico City for the first time. 3 sections: 1. Air travel round the world (*e.g.* 'Buying your ticket' ... 'Red tape' ... 'When you get there') - 2. Stop off destinations - 3. Appendix ('Airline two-letter codes' - 'Principal airports around the world' - 'Foreign tourist offices, embassies, etc'). Index. *Class No: 656.7*

[6398]
World air transport statistics. Montreal, International Air Transport Association, 1955-. Annual. $165. ISSN: 00841366.

Reviews air transport development and provides many statistical tables. *Class No: 656.7*

Airports & Airfields

[6399]
Jane's airports, equipment and services, 1998-99. Rider, D., *ed.* 17th ed. Coulsdon, Jane's Information Group, 1998. 686p. £235; $350. ISBN: 0710617879; 0710615728, CD-ROM.

Review of 1,500 airport suppliers and their products, e.g. cargo handling, aircraft recovery equipment, etc. Features a directory of more than 1,600 airports. New sections for this ed. include environmental monitoring and control and major international trade organisations. Also available on CD-ROM (£650; $1,075). *Class No: 656.71*

[6400]
Pooley's flight guide: United Kingdom 1998. Pooley, R. *and* Patel, R. Elstree, Herts., Pooley's Flight Guides Ltd., 1998. xviii,595p. tables, plans, maps. ISBN: 090203748x.

Although not an official publication, is compiled 'with the assistance of the Civil Aviation Authority'. Includes plans of airports and airstrips. *Class No: 656.71*

Airlines

[6401]
The Aerospace international directory of world airlines. Ginsberg, M., *ed.* Potters Bar, Herts., Aviation Directories (in association with the Royal Aeronautical Society), 1998. 356p. £36. ISBN: 190043802x.

Airlines listed A-Z, also by country, and by 2- and 3-letter codes; airports are similarly arranged. Handy small-format guide, attractively presented. *Class No: 656.73.01*

[6402]
The Airline bibliography: the Salem College guide to sources on commercial aviation. West Cornwall, Locust Hill Press, 1986-88. 2v. ISBN: 0933951000, v.1; 0933951124, v.2.

V.1 *US air transport.* 1986. 239p. $45. V.2 *Airliners and foreign air transport.* 1988. xxxii,464p. $75.

V.2 contains over 13,000 citations (V.1, *c.*6,000) from 690 journals. Coverage includes historic, operational and economic aspects of air transport organizations outside the US. Airliners and airlines sections contain short descriptive and historical reviews. Extensive author and subject indexes. *Class No: 656.73.01*

[6403]
BÁTOR, J.W. **International airline phrase book in six languages, English, French, German, Italian, Portuguese and Spanish.** New York, Dover, 1968. xiv, 204p. £4.45. ISBN: 0486220176.

700 numbered sentences and phrases, English-based, with French, German, Italian, Portuguese and Spanish translations or idiomatic equivalents. Arranged by topic (reservations; departure; boarding; flight; arrival; miscellaneous). English index only. *Class No: 656.73.01*

[6404]
DAVIES, R.E.G. **A History of the world's airlines.** London, Oxford Univ. Press, 1964. xxx, 591p. tables, maps.

A detailed study, with maps, tables of airlines and their fleets, photographs of 209 aircraft. Select bibliography, p.xxvii-xxx. *Class No: 656.73.01*

[6405]
Jane's world airlines. Pratt, D., *ed.* Coulsdon, Jane's Information Group, 1998. 2v. loose-leaf. £595. ISBN: 0710605919.

First published 1989.

Covers over 500 airlines. Arranged A-Z. Data include contact, type of operation, company structure (*e.g.* 'Major subsidiaries'; 'Scheduled destinations'; 'Traffic'; 'Business review'). Four updates are issued pa. Also available in electronic format to import into local databases. *Class No: 656.73.01*

Airways

[6406]
INTERNATIONAL AIR TRANSPORT ASSOCIATION *and* INTERNATIONAL AERADIO, LTD. **Air distances manual.** 9th ed. effective 1st April 1982. Southall, Middx., 1982. 36 + 285p. illus., tables.

4 sections: 1. Conversion tables - 2. Wind components - 3. G.M.T. of sunrise and sunset - 4. Distances (285p.): Aalborg ... Zurich. Data: nautical miles; standard mile, kilometre, route. *Class No: 656.73.02*

Timetables

[6407]

OAG flight planner: Europe, Middle East and Africa. Dunstable, Beds., Reed Travel Group. 12pa. tables. £120. ISSN: 13554980.

Formerly *ABC air Europe, Middle East and Africa* and *ABC executive flight planner.*

Timetables cover worldwide direct flights to, from and within the region, plus transfer connections, details of fares. Includes information on aircraft types, seating maps, airport diagrams, etc. *Class No:* 656.73.022

[6408]

OAG world airways guide: the complete guide to air travel in alphabetical From/To sequence. Dunstable, Beds., OAG Worldwide (Reed Elsevier). 12pa. 2v. tables. £430. ISSN: 14647958.

First published 1948 as *ABC world airways guide.*

Details of over 450,000 schedules, flights, and connections worldwide. April 1999 issue consists mainly of city-to-city schedules (v.1, A-M; v.2, N-Z). Prelims. include airlines of the world, minimum connecting times, aircraft seating plans, etc. Also available on CD-ROM 'Air travel disc'. *Class No:* 656.73.022

Postal Services

[6409]

DAUNTON, M.J. Royal Mail: the Post Office since 1840. London, The Athlone Press, 1985. xviii, 388p. illus., facsims., tables. £32. ISBN: 0485112809.

5 parts (10 chapters): 2. Carrying the mail - 3. Working for the Post Office - 4. Officials and politicians - 5. Epilogue: the post-war period. Chapter notes, p.357-78. Detailed, analytical index, p.379-88. The narrative ends at 1984. Daunton is Reader in History, University College, London. *Class No:* 656.8

[6410]

Directory of place names and associated postcodes. Buckingham, PC Services, 1986. 250p. £25.

A-Z directory covering the 120 postcode areas in the UK. *Class No:* 656.8

[6411]

Mail guide. Issued by HM Postmaster General. Bristol, Royal Mail, 1992.

Formerly *Post Office guide.*

Gives details of services provided by the Royal Mail. *Class No:* 656.8

[6412]

Postcode atlas of Great Britain and Northern Ireland. London, Bartholomew, 1995. ix,191p. maps. ISBN: 0702829374.

127 maps show boundaries and codes of all postcode areas and districts in Great Britain and Northern Ireland on a scale of four miles to the inch (nine miles to the inch for Northern Ireland); Central London on a scale of three inches to one mile. *Class No:* 656.8

[6413]

Postcodes: the new geography. Raper, J.F., *and others.* Harlow, Essex, Longman, 1992. xiv,322p. illus. (col. pl.), figs., maps. £25. ISBN: 0582092701.

4 sections: 1. The nature of postcodes and their role in postal services - 2. Handling postcoded data - 3. Non-postal applications of postcodes (*e.g.* 'Applications of postcodes in marketing') - 4. The future. 7 appendices (*e.g.* 'Glossary of abbreviations and terms'; 'The British National Grid system'). Index, p.316-22. *Class No:* 656.8

[6414]

UNION POSTALE UNIVERSELLE, Berne. **Nomenclature internationale des bureaux de poste.** Liste complète des bureaux de poste des pays et territoires compris dans le ressort de l'Union Postale Universelle. Berne, UPU, 1977. vp.

Lists *c.*300,000 post offices, A-Z by name, with postal code, name of country and territorial subdivision (*e.g.* département, canton, province, state). In French, with preface also in English. *Class No:* 656.8

[6415]

UNION POSTALE UNIVERSELLE. Bureau International. **Vocabulaire polyglotte du service postal international.** 3. éd. Berne, UPU, 1973 (reprinted 1986, Harper & Row). 323p. Loose-leaf.

First published 1954.

More than 1,000 terms defined, with equivalents in French, German, English, Spanish, Russian, Arabic and Chinese. *Class No:* 656.8

Postage Stamps

Bibliographies

[6416]

Catalogue of the Crawford Library of philatelic literature at the British Library. Rev. ed. London, The Printer's Stone Ltd., in association with the British Library, 1991.

Rev. ed. of: *A Bibliography of the writings general, special, and periodical forming the literature of philately.* 1911; *Catalogue of the philatelic library of the Earl of Crawford, K.T.,* its *supplement,* and *addenda.* 1911-1938. Also published as v.7 of *Bibliotheca Lindesiana,* with title *A bibliography of philately.*

This collection is now in the British Library, Reference Division. 'This edition includes the British Library shelfmarks for the books thus allowing easier access and better remote identification' (*Preface*). Lists monographs to 1908 and periodicals to 1906. An appendix records all the periodicals in chronological order. One of the most complete bibliographies of any subject, not confined to books actually in the Library. *Class No:* 656.835(01)

[6417]

COLLECTORS CLUB LIBRARY, New York City. **Philately:** a catalog of the Collectors Club Library. Boston, Mass., G.K. Hall, 1974. 682p. $130. ISBN: 0816110476.

21,800 photolithographed catalogue cards - 4 sequences: author, subject, title and periodical catalogues. One of the world's largest collections of books and periodicals on stamp collecting and postal history (handbooks; priced auction catalogues; exhibition brochures, annual catalogues, philatelic membership lists, US governmental reports, etc.). *Class No:* 656.835(01)

Handbooks & Manuals

[6418]

CABEEN, R.McP. Standard handbook of stamp collecting. New rev. ed. New York, Crowell, 1979. 630p. illus., tables. $9.95. ISBN: 0690017731.

First published 1957.

5 main sections: 1. Introduction to stamp collecting - 2. Postal history and cover collecting - 3. Miscellaneous subjects - 4. Technical matters - 5. Classification and identification. Glossary; comprehensive bibliography. Scope has both breadth and depth; moderately priced. Rivalled only by *Fundamentals of philately* (*qv*). *Class No:* 656.835(035)

[6419]

WILLIAMS, L.N. *and* **WILLIAMS, M. Fundamentals of philately.** State College, Pa., American Philatelic Society, 1971. 629, xxxp. illus.

A standard manual, with bibliographical references and index. Very favourably referred to in *Choice,* v.15(12), February 1980, p.1616. *Class No:* 656.835(035)

[6420]

—MACKAY, J. The Guinness book of stamps facts and feats. 2nd ed. Enfield, Middx., Guinness Publishing Ltd., 1988. 224p. illus. (incl. col.). £12.99.

First published 1982.

7 chapters: 1. The postal services - 2. Postmarks - 3. Adhesive stamps - 4. Kinds of stamps - 5. The technology of stamps - 6. Postal stationery and ancillary labels - 7. Philately. Index. By the Philatelic Curator at the British Museum. *Class No:* 656.835(035)

Dictionaries

[6421]

MACKAY, J. Philatelic terms illustrated. 3rd ed. London, Stanley Gibbons, 1987. 188p. illus. (incl. col. pl.). £2.50. ISBN: 0852591578.

First published in 1973 (192p.), having previously appeared serially in *Stamp monthly.*

Terms, Abnormal - Zip code, describe papers, errors, varieties, watermarks, perforations, etc., with cross-references to plates. *c.*1,500 stamps in all are shown, some in colour. Analytical index. For both beginner and experienced collector. *Class No:* 656.835(038)

[6422]

PATRICK, D. *and* **PATRICK, M. The Hodder stamp dictionary.** UK ed. London, Hodder & Stoughton, 1973. [vii], 277p. illus., facsims.

About 7,000 entries for technical terms. English-based (with French and German equivalents), abbreviations and acronyms. Some biographical sketches (*e.g.* Sperati, the stamp forger; Wells, Fargo). Also entries under countries. Non-Latin alphabets, p.273-7. Illus. of stamps. *Class No:* 656.835(038)

Yearbooks & Directories

[6423]

The British Philatelic Federation yearbook and philatelic societies' directory. London, British Philatelic Federation. Annual. £7.50. ISSN: 02601265.

1992 ed. (173p. £8) has 3 sections: 1. Yearbook (*e.g.* 'British exhibitions 1992'; 'Stamps for all seasons from Royal Mail') - 2. Directory of philatelic societies, p.54-148 - 3. General information (*e.g.* 'British philatelic magazines'; 'Philatelic bureaux worldwide'). *Class No:* 656.835(058)

Illustrations

[6424]

Scott standard postage stamp catalogue. New York, Scott Publishing, 1864-. Annual (1997 ed. 949p.). 4v. illus. ISBN: 0894871471, v.1; 089487148x, v.2; 0894871498, v.3; 0894871501, v.4.

V.1 covers the US and affiliated territories, the United Nations, Canada, Great Britain, and the British Commonwealth. V. 2-4 cover the rest of the world in an alphabetical listing of countries. Under each country, stamps are listed in chronological order, with special sections for airmail stamps, postage-due stamps, semi-postal stamps, and other special categories. Each volume has a cumulative index to the set. Supplements appear in *Scott's monthly journal*. The standard American general catalogue of stamps. *Class No:* 656.835(084.1)

[6425]

—Scott specialized catalogue of United States stamps. New York, Scott Publishing Co., 1923-. Annual.

Contains data on dates of issue, designers, printers and printing methods, perforations, watermarks, papers, gums, grills, printing flaws, errors transfers and colour varieties. Indexes and useful glossary of technical terms. 22p. identifier of definitive issues. 'This is an indispensable volume for the study of US philately' (*Reference services review,* v.17, no. 3, 1989, p.55). *Class No:* 656.835(084.1)

[6426]

Stanley Gibbons Great Britain specialised stamp catalogue. London, Stanley Gibbons Publications, Ltd. 5v.

First published 1963.

1. *Queen Victoria.* 11th ed. 1997. 464p. £22.95. 2. *King Edward VII to King George VI.* 10th ed. 1996. 448p. £18.95. 3. *Queen Elizabeth II. Pre-decimal issues.* 9th ed. 1993. 441p. £15.95. 4. *Queen Elizabeth II. Decimal definitive issues.* 7th ed. 1994. 688p. £19.95. 5. *Decimal special issues.* 1991. 392p. £16.95.

Each volume has introductory notes, appendices, and further reading. Thus, v.2 has sections M, N, P, Q for the four reigns, plus R: Postage due stamps; 6 appendices (E. Perforations) and 'Further reading' (Postal history ... Postmarks). *Class No:* 656.835(084.1)

[6427]

Stanley Gibbons simplified catalogue of stamps of the world. 1999 ed. London, Stanley Gibbons Publications, Ltd. 3v. illus. ISBN: 0852594488, v.1; 0852594496, v.2; 0852594518, v.3.

1. *Foreign countries, A-J.* 1312p. £27.50. 2. *Countries, K-Z.* 1280p. £27.50. 3. *Commonwealth countries.* 800p. £24.95. 1998 ed.

'An illustrated and priced three-volume reference to the postage stamps of the whole world, excluding changes of paper, perforation, shade and watermarks' (*subtitle*). Each volume has an index. *Class No:* 656.835(084.1)

[6428]

—MACKAY, J.A. The Dictionary of stamps in colour. London, Michael Joseph, 1973. 296p. illus. (col. pl.), tables).

Illustrates *c.*5,000 stamps in colour, on 120 plates - Examples from 130 countries. Plate 30, 'Russia': 25 stamps displayed, with descriptive notes p.172-3. Appended: World currency tables; The stamp printers; Cyrillic inscriptors. Index, p.292-6. End-paper map. Highly selective use of colour is the main feature. *Class No:* 656.835(084.1)

[6429]

Stanley Gibbons stamp catalogue. London, Stanley Gibbons.

1. Pt.1 *British Commonwealth, v.1. Great Britain and countries, A-I, 1999.* 1998. 928p. £28.95. 1. Pt.2. *British Commonwealth. Countries, J-Z, 1999.* 1998. 896p. £28.95. 2. *Austria & Hungary.* 5th ed. 1994. 312p. £14.95. 3. *Balkans.* 4th ed. 1998. 720p. £24.95. 4. *Benelux.* 3rd ed. 1988. x, 261p. £10.95. 5. *Czechoslovakia and Poland.* 5th ed. 1994. 264p. £15.95. 6. *France.* 3rd ed. 1987. x, 336p. £9.95. 7. *Germany.* 4th ed. 1992. 344p. £15. 8. *Italy & Switzerland.* 5th ed. 1997. 416p. £10.95. 9. *Portugal and Spain.* 4th ed. 1996. 456p. £14.50.

10. *Russia.* 4th ed. 1991. 400p. £16.50. 11. *Scandinavia.* 4th ed. 1994. 296p. £14.95. 12/14. *Africa since independence.* 2nd ed. 1981-83. 3v. (v.12. £9.95; v.13, £8.50; v.14, £10.50). 15. *Central America.* 2nd ed. 1984. x, 526p. £11.50. 16. *Central Asia.* 2nd ed. 1983. x, 212p. £8.95. 17. *China.* 5th ed. 1995. 288p. £16.95. 18. *Japan & Korea.* 4th ed. 1997. 432p. £22.50. 19. *Middle East.* 5th ed. 1996. 688p. £22.95. 20. *South America.* 3rd ed. 1989. 736p. £22. 21. *South-east Asia.* 3rd ed. 1995. 488p. £19.95. 22. *U.S.A.* 3rd ed. 1990.

....(contd.)
x, 213p. £9.95.

V.1, now in 2 parts, includes post-independence issues of Ireland, Pakistan and South Africa. Index precedes main sequence (Great Britain ... Zululand). Appended: Addenda and corrigenda; Stamps added; Catalogue numbers altered; General philatelic information. *Class No:* 656.835(084.1)

66 Chemical Industry

[6442]

RIEGEL, E.R. Riegel's handbook of industrial chemistry.
Kent, J.A., *ed*. 9th ed. New York, Van Nostrand Reinhold, 1992.
1280p. illus., charts tables. $83.50.
First published 1928 as *Industrial chemistry*. 8th ed. 1983.
Documented chapters, by specialists, on various sectors of the
chemical process industry, *e.g.* plastics, rubber, man-made textiles,
dyes and pigments. Index. Comprehensive; data gathered from
numerous sources. *Class No:* 66(035)

[6443]

STOCCHI, E. Industrial chemistry. New York, E. Harwood, 1990.
V.1-. illus., diagrs., graphs, tables. ISBN: 0134573188.
Originally published as *Chemica industriale*, v.1-. (Turin). Trans by
K. Holt and E.L. Short.
V.1 (712p.) has 15 chapters (*e.g.* 15. Bitumens, tars and their
derivatives). 9 appendices of tables and formulas. Detailed index,
p.703-12. Well illustrated. No bibliographies. 'Highly recommended'
(*Choice*, April 1991, p.1339). *Class No:* 66(035)

Dictionaries

Polyglot

[6444]

Dictionary of chemistry and chemical technology. Huimin, C. *and*
Wenchu, B., *eds.* Beijing, Chemical Industry Press; Amsterdam,
Elsevier, 1989. 1716p. £151.
Terms in English, Chinese, Japanese. *Class No:* 66(038)=00

[6445]

DORIAN, A.F. Elsevier's dictionary of industrial chemistry, in
English/American (with definitions), French, Spanish, Italian, Dutch
and German. Amsterdam, etc., Elsevier, 1964. 2v.(xii, 1220p.). $215.
ISBN: 0444407537.
8,426 numbered English/American base terms, with equivalents and
indexes in the other five languages. Coverage: apparatus, materials,
machinery, equipment and processes. V.1: A-O; v.2: P-Z and thumb-
indexed indexes. Some overlap with *Elsevier's Dictionary of chemical
engineering*, by W.E. Clason (2v. 1968). *Class No:* 66(038)=00

[6446]

SOBECKA, Z. and CHOINSKI, W., *eds.* **Dictionary of chemistry and
chemical technology in six languages:** English, German, Spanish,
French, Polish, Russian. Oxford, etc., Pergamon Press; Warsaw,
Wydawnictwa Naukowo-Techniczne, 1966. vii, 1325p. £125. ISBN:
0080116000.
First published 1962.
11,987 numbered entries in English, with German, Spanish, French,
Polish and Russian equivalents across the double page, and German,
etc., indexes, on tinted paper. Categorizes terms, notes differences in
meaning and gives genders of nouns. It omits current English terms
that have no corresponding expressions in one or other of the foreign
languages. No abbreviations. 'An excellent work of reference for any
European chemist' (*Chemistry & industry*, 3 December 1966, p.2035).
Class No: 66(038)=00

English

[6447]

ASHFORD, R.D. Ashford's dictionary of industrial chemicals:
properties, production, uses. London, Wavelength, 1994. viii, 1005p.
chemical formulas. ISBN: 0952267403.
About 6,800 entries. Data include structure, description, alternative
names, production, derivatives and uses. *Class No:* 66(038)=20

[6448]

NOETHER, D. *and* **NOETHER, H. Encyclopedic dictionary of
chemical technology.** New York, VCH, 1993. [v], 297p. $59.50;
£40. ISBN: 1560813296.
Brief A-Z entries, preceded by 'Abbreviations for compounds/
groups in formulas'; acronyms for organizations; WHO chemical
emergency numbers. *Class No:* 66(038)=20

Russian

[6449]

**CALLAHAM, L.I., *and* others. Callaham's Russian-English
dictionary of science and technology.** 4th ed. New York, etc., Wiley,
1996. xxxiv, 814p. $125. ISBN: 0471611395.
First published 1947; 3rd ed., 1975. The 4th ed. was completed by
P.E. Newman and J.R. Callaham; L.I. Callaham died in 1990.
Over 120,000 scientific and technical terms and about 5,000
frequently used, non-technical ones. Terms are categorised, genders
given; abbreviations, prefixes and common Russian word-endings
included. Good typography for cyrillic. Particularly helpful in the
fields of pure and applied chemistry.
This new ed. incorporates the life sciences, including medicine,

....(contd.)
physiology, botany and ornithology. Numerous computing terms and
those relating to nuclear power and weapons have also been added.
Class No: 66(038)=82

[6450]

DYMSHITS, L.B. Anglo-russkiĭ khimiko teknologicheskiĭ Slovar'. 5.
izd. sterotipnoe. Moscow, Izdat. Sovetskaya Entsiklopediya, 1966.
736p.
Gives equivalents of *c.*10,000 English terms. Chemical formulas
figure. Abbreviations, p.727-36. *Class No:* 66(038)=82

Reviews & Abstracts

[6451]

Chemical industry notes. Columbus, Ohio, Chemical Abstracts Service,
1973-. Weekly. $1000pa. ISSN: 0045639x.
About 12,000 entries p.a. 8 sections: A. Production -B. Pricing - C.
Sales - D. Facilities - E. Products and processes - F. Corporate
activities - G. Government activities - H. People. Keyword and
corporate named indexes per issue and annually. Carries 'business
oriented articles of value to the chemical industry'. Online (about
1,200,000 records; updated weekly) via STN International and other
hosts. *Class No:* 66(048)

Yearbooks & Directories

[6452]

Chemcats [Chemical catalogs online]. Columbus, Ohio, American
chemical Society, Chemical Abstracts Service.
Database providing information on commercially available chemicals
and their suppliers worldwide. About 350,000 entries derived from
about 300 different suppliers. Available on STN International.
Class No: 66(058)

[6453]

Chemical industry directory and who's who. Tonbridge, Kent, Benn,
1987. v.p. £10. ISBN: 086382059x.
Originally '*Chemical age' year book* (1923-58), thereafter '*Chemical
age' directory and who's who* (1959-63).
4 Sections. *A.* ABC to chemical manufacturers and traders. Buyers
guide to chemicals - *B.* ABC to plant & laboratory equipment
manufacturers ... Buyers' guide ... Trade names. European chemical
& oil storage; services for chemical storage - *C.* Who owns whom in
the British chemical and plant industries ... Independent consultants -
D. Who's who in the chemical industry. Index to advertisers.
Class No: 66(058)

[6454]

Chemical industry Europe '98. Tonbridge, Kent, Miller Freeman,
1998. xvi, 1452p. £96. ISBN: 0863823742. ISSN: 09602992.
Incorporates *Laboratory equipment buyers' guide.*
Data on about 10,000 companies. Sections: European chemical
companies (ranking tables) - Chemicals - Plant, equipment and services
- Brands and trade names - Company data - Country index -
Associations and organizations. *Class No:* 66(058)

[6455]

Industrial companies: chemicals. Harlow, Essex, Longman, 1992.
480p. illus. £130. (*Financial Times international year books.*) ISBN:
0582092728.
Corporate and financial profiles of 500 international companies.
Data: personnel, contact details, operations, sales figures.
Class No: 66(058)

[6456]

**WHITESIDE, R. Major chemical and petrochemical companies of
Europe, 1991-1992.** 5th ed. London, Graham & Trotman, 1991.
272p. £145. ISBN: 1859336203.
Nearly 1000 entries, with usual directory-type information.
Class No: 66(058)

CD-ROM

[6457]

ROYAL SOCIETY OF CHEMISTRY. Chemicals and companies:
chemicals, formulated products and their company sources.
Cambridge, Royal Society of Chemistry, 1998. CD-ROM. £910.
Contents: contact details for about 30,000 companies; basic physical
data and hazard information; chemical structure diagrams; CAS
registry and EINECS numbers; details of chemical constitutents of
formulated products. Searchable by product, company and location.
Updated quarterly. *Class No:* 66(058)(003.40)

Tables & Data Books

[6458]

BENNETT, H., *ed*. **The Chemical formulary:** a selection of valuable, timely, practical, commercial formulae and recipes for making thousands of products in many fields of industry. New York, Chemical Publishing Co., Inc; London Chapman & Hall (now Godwin), 1933-. (v.28. 1989).

Lists recipes for amateur or professional chemist. V.31 (1993. 219p.) gives recipes for adhesives, beverages and food, cosmetics, detergents and disinfectants, polishes, abrasives, etc. Appendix includes a list of trademark chemicals and their suppliers, information on federal food, drug and cosmetic laws, a list of incompatible chemicals and emergency first aid for chemical injuries.

Chemical formulary: cumulative index for volumes 1 through 25 (New York, Chemical Publishing Co., 1987. 474p. $75. ISBN 0820603193) provides many useful cross-references.
Class No: 66(083)

[6459]

DAUBERT, T.E. *and* DANNER, R.P. **Physical and thermodynamic properties of pure chemicals:** data compilation. New York, Hemisphere, 1989-97. 5v. (loose-leaf). $275; £196. ISBN: 0891169482.

A compilation of tables of recommended physical, thermodynamic and transport properties used in chemical processes and equipment design. Includes over 1,500 compounds. The 'awkward' format was criticized by *Choice* (February 1990, p.973) which nonetheless found the set 'a reliable source of documented data'. *Class No:* 66(083)

[6460]

Gardner's chemical synonyms and trade names. Ash, M. *and* Ash, I., *eds*. 10th ed. Aldershot, Hants., Gower, 1994. [xvi],1293p. Chemical formulas. £150. ISBN: 0566074915.

First published 1924; 9th ed. 1988.

2 parts: 1. Chemical and trade names - 2. Manufacturers directory. List of abbreviations (8p.) precedes. 4 appendices (including CAS number-to-chemical cross reference). A 1996 version is available on disk. *Class No:* 66(083)

Standards

[6461]

Official and standardized methods of analysis. Watson, C.A., *ed*. 3rd ed. Cambridge, Royal Society of Chemistry, 1994. xxiv, 778p. diagrs., tables. £110. ISBN: 0851864414.

2nd ed. 1973.

Compiled for the Analytical Methods Coommittee of The Royal Society of Chemistry.

Approved methods for analysis and testing of a variety of products: animal feeding stuffs; cosmetics; fertilisers; human foods (milk, meat, etc.); water; brewing materials. EC food methods, p.691-713; British Standards, p.714-55. Detailed, analytical index, p.759-78.
Class No: 66(083.74)

Trade Names, Trade Marks, Brand Names

[6462]

POHANISH, R.P. **Rapid guide to trade names and synonyms of environmentally regulated chemicals.** New York, Van Nostrand Reinhold, 1998. xiii, 850p. ISBN: 0442025947.

About 30,000 names and CAS registry numbers for hazardous chemicals regulated under US environmental laws. Includes translations. *Class No:* 66(088.7)

Histories

[6463]

HABER, L.F. **The Chemical industries, 1900-1930:** international growth and technological change. Oxford, Clarendon Press, 1971. xi, 452p.

Continues the volume on the 19th century. An international survey, dwelling particularly on Germany, Great Britain and USA. Emphasis is on economic rather than technological aspects. *Economic journal* (v.81(324), December 1971, p.968) notes the author's 'admirable factual clarity and historical insight'. *Class No:* 66(091)

[6464]

HABER, L.F. **The Chemical industry during the nineteenth century:** a study of the economic aspect of applied chemistry in Europe and North America. Oxford, Clarendon Press, 1958. x, 292p. diagrs., tables. £20.

An international survey. The nineteenth-century volume deals with the origins of the chemical industry. *Class No:* 66(091)

[6465]

MULTHAUF, R.P. **The History of chemical technology:** an annotated bibliography. New York, Garland, 1984. xx,299p. illus. (*Bibliographies of the history of science and technology, v.5. Garland reference library of the humanities, v.348.*) ISBN: 0824092554.

1528 items in 3 parts: 1. Histories (largely by country) - 2. 'Traditional' technology (ceramics, glass, paper, etc.) - 3. 'Modern' technology (artificial fibres, gases, petroleum, pharmaceuticals, etc.). Most citations very brief (2-3 lines). Author index (p.253-83); 'title' (key-word) index (p.284-99). Based largely on the collections of the Library of Congress and the Smithsonian Institute. *Class No:* 66(091)

Great Britain

[6466]

CLOW, A. *and* CLOW, N.L. **The Chemical revolution:** a contribution to social technology. London, Batchworth Press, 1952. xvi, 680p. illus. (*Industrial archaeology series.*)

Special emphasis on chemical industry of Scotland and north of England. Period covered: *c*.1750-1830. Individual industries have separate chapters, with many references in text. 'Glossary of dead chemical language', p.618-22. A chemical chronology to 1856. Extensive bibliography, p.633-61.

Reprinted June 1992 by Gordon & Breach (£32; ISBN: 2881245498) as part of their series *Classics in the history and philosophy of science*. *Class No:* 66(410)

[6467]

READER, W.J. **Imperial Chemical Industry:** a history. Oxford Univ. Press, 1970-. diagrs., charts, tables, maps.

1. *The forerunners, 1870-1926.* 1970. xvi, 563p.

2. *The first quarter century, 1926-1952.* 1975. 588p.
Class No: 66(410)

Russia

[6468]

SAGERS, M.J. *and* SHABAD, T. **The Chemical industry in the USSR:** an economic geography. Washington, American Chemical Society, 1990. 550p. diagrs., tables, maps. $89.95. ISBN: 0841217602.

Topics include chemical development, location factors, trends, changes, raw materials, technology and prospects, including foreign trends in chemicals and chemical equipment suppliers. A reference for graduate students and researchers. *Class No:* 66(47)

USA

[6469]

HAYNES, W. **American chemical industry:** a history. New York, Van Nostrand, 1945-54. 6v.

1. *Background and beginning, 1604-1911.* 1954.

2.3. *The World War I period, 1912-1922.* 1945.

4. *The merger period, 1923-29.* 1945.

5. *Decade of new products, 1930-1939.* 1954.

6. *The chemical companies.* 1949.

A comprehensive history of US industrial chemists, individual companies, processes and products. Industries may be grouped, *e.g.* coal-tar, chemicals, the alkalis, the acids. V.6 has data on companies, A-Z (p.1-491). Each volume carries name and product indexes.
Class No: 66(73)

Chemical Engineering

Databases

[6470]

Chemical engineering and biotechnology abstracts. [Deutsche gesellschaft für chemisches Apparatewesen] Cambridge, Royal Society of Chemistry.

Produced jointly by The Royal Society of Chemistry, the DECHEMA, FIZ CHEMIE and IChemE.

Covers industrial practice and theoretical chemical engineering. Includes processes, substances, operations, transport, equipment, safety. About 180,000 records, updated monthly. Available via DIALOG, DataStar, FIZ Technik, Orbit, STN International; on CD-ROM (Dialog OnDisc, updated quarterly); and on the Internet from ChemWeb (URL: http://www.chemWeb.com). *Class No:* 66.0(003.4)

Bibliographies

[6471]

PITT, M.J. 'Chemical engineering'. *Information sources in engineering*. K.W. Mildren and P.J. Hicks, eds. (3rd ed., 1996), p.269-83. 3rd ed. London, Bowker Saur, 1996. £80. ISBN: 1857390571.

Sections: Institutions - Basic references - Data compilations - Unit operations and general design - Chemical reactors - Physical chemistry - Fluid mechanics - Heat exchangers, heat pumps and refrigeration - Particle technology - Biochemical engineering - Control ... Software - Journals - Abstracts. An extensive treatment. *Class No:* 66.0(01)

[6472]

RAY, M.S. **Chemical engineering bibliography, 1967-1988.** Park Ridge, N.J., Noyes, 1990. xvii, 887p. ISBN: 0815512414.

About 20,000 references from 40 journals. 27 sections (*e.g.* energy conservation; biotechnology; mixing; reactors; distillation, etc). No annotations. Key word index *Class No:* 66.0(01)

[6473]

—RAY, M.S. Chemical engineering bibliography, 1989-1990. Perth, Western Australia, Curlin University of Technology, 1991. xiii, 305p. ISBN: 0949101079.

Supplements the main work with 8,000 references.
Class No: 66.0(01)

Handbooks & Manuals

[6474]

COULSON, J.M. and RICHARDSON, J.F. **Chemical engineering.** Oxford, Butterworth-Heinemann, 1991-. V.1-. illus., diagrs., graphs, tables.

First ed. (2v.) 1954-55.

V;1. *Fluid flow, heat transfer and mass transfer.* (5th ed. 1996. £29.99. ISBN: 0750625570.)

V.2. *Particle technology and separation processes.* (4th ed. 1992. £29.99. ISBN: 0750629428.)

V.3. *Chemical and biochemical reactors and process control.* (3rd ed. 1994. £29.99. ISBN: 0080410030.)

V.4. *Solutions to the problems in V.1.* (2nd ed. 1994. £19.99. ISBN: 0080420834.)

V.5. *Solutions to the problems in V.2.* (2nd ed. 1997. £19.99. ISBN: 0750626127.)

V.6. *Design.* (2nd ed. 1996. £29.99. ISBN: 0750625589.)

There is some overlap in the publication of editions. A standard work. *Class No:* 66.0(035)

[6475]

Handbook of chemical engineering calculations. Chopey, N.P., *ed.* 2nd ed. New York, McGraw-Hill, 1994. v.p. diagrs., graphs, tables. ISBN: 0070110212.

17 contributors; 16 sections, closely sub-divided. Index, 11p. Some chapters taken from *Standard handbook of engineering calculations* (*qv*). *Class No:* 66.0(035)

[6476]

PERRY, R.H. and GREEN, D.W. **Perry's chemical engineers' handbook.** 7th ed. New York, etc., McGraw-Hill, 1997. v.p. illus., diagrs., graphs, tables. $125. ISBN: 0070498415.

First published 1934; 5th ed., 1984.

About 140 contributors. 30 sections, each with contents page and references. Topics range from transport and storage of fluids and heat transfer equipment to process control and biochemical engineering. New sections for this ed. cover process safety and chemical reactions; those extensively revised include physical and chemical data, mathematics, mass transfer, reaction kinetics and process control. Detailed, analytical index. This compendium is known as the chemical engineer's 'Bible'. 'An outstanding reference work' (*American reference books annual 1998*, p.648). Also available on CD-ROM (1998; $149.95; ISBN: 0071344128). *Class No:* 66.0(035)

Dictionaries

[6477]

LYDERSEN, A.L. and DAHLO, J. **Dictionary of chemical engineering:** English, German, Spanish, French. New York, Wiley, 1992. 300p. £32.50. ISBN: 0471933929.

'An expansion and up-to-date revision of a corresponding Norwegian dictionary by the same authors in 1988' (*Preface*).

About 1,200 English-base terms, with equivalents and indexes in the other languages. Includes word use in the manufacturing industries and skilled trades within chemical engineering. *Class No:* 66.0(038)

Reviews & Abstracts

[6478]

'Applied chemistry and chemical engineering', *Chemical abstracts*, sections 47-64. Easton, Pa., American Chemical Society, 1907-. Alternate weekly.

One of the three groups constituting sections 47-80 of *Chemical abstracts*. The 15 sections comprise 47. Apparatus and plant equipment ... 64. Pharmaceutical analysis. *Class No:* 66.0(048)

Progress Reports

[6479]

Advances in chemical engineering. San Diego, Ca., Academic Press, 1956-. Irregular. diagrs., graphs, tables.

V.24 (1998, xi, 416p. ISBN: 0120085240) covers combustion synthesis, computation fluid dynamics and the use of risk analysis in pollution prevention. *Class No:* 66.0(055)

Yearbooks & Directories

[6480]

Chemical engineering and construction directory 1996/97. Sutton, Surrey, Reed Business, 1996. 260p. £135. ISBN: 0617005834.

In 2 parts: chemical engineering contractors and their activities; process technologies for license. Indexes: services; market sectors; regions. *Class No:* 66.0(058)

Tables & Data Books

[6481]

Rules of thumb for chemical engineers: a manual of quick, accurate solutions to everyday process engineering problems. Branan, C.R., *ed.* 2nd ed. Houston, Tx., Gulf, 1998. 418p. tables, formulas. $79. ISBN: 0884157881.

First published 1994.

25 chapters in 4 sections: 1. Equipment design - 2. Process design - 3. Plant design - 4. Operations. Covers a range of topics including unit operations, special processes, safety, controls, troubleshooting, startup, energy conservation, etc. For practicing engineers.
Class No: 66.0(083)

[6482]

SHUGAR, G.J., *and others, eds.* **Chemical technicians' ready reference handbook.** 4th ed. New York, etc., McGraw-Hill, 1997. *c.*900p. illus., diagrs., tables. $85. ISBN: 0070571864.

First published 1973 (463p.). 3rd ed. 1990.

Emphasis on step-by-step procedures. Explains frequently-used laboratory and spectroscopy techniques with concern for laboratory safety. *Class No:* 66.0(083)

Histories

[6483]

FURTER, W.F., *ed.* **History of chemical engineering:** papers from a symposium, Honolulu, April 1979. Washington, American Chemical Society, 1980. xii, 436p. illus. (*Advances in chemistry series, 190.*)

22 contributions (all but one written by chemical engineers). Includes essays on the individuals and institutions that contributed most significantly to the expression of chemical industry during the 20th century. Other papers deal with national aspects of the subject.
Class No: 66.0(091)

Research Methods

[6484]

THOMAS, C.L.P. and SCHOFIELD, H. **Sampling source book:** an indexed bibliography of the literature of sampling. Oxford, Butter-Heinemann, 1996. 299p. £75. ISBN: 0750619473.

Bibliographic references to journal articles, patents, conference proceedings, books, technical reports and standards. Contents: Equipment list - Index of suppliers - Consultants and contacts for finding further information - Index of contacts - Categorised bibliography - Index - Glossary/definitions. *Class No:* 66.0:001.891

Processes

Encyclopaedias

[6485]

McKETTA, J.J. and CUNNINGHAM, W.A., *eds.* **Encyclopedia of chemical processing and design.** New York, Dekker, 1976-. v.1-. (v.28. 1987). illus., diagrs., graphs, tables. ISBN: 0824724372.

A multi-volume encyclopedia, more restricted in scope than Kirk-Othmer. Each volume has 20-30 contributors, most recruited from industry. V.56 appeared in 1996 (508p.; $175). Many articles are reprinted from *Chemical engineering* and other journals.

....*(contd.)*

A selection of the articles here have been published as *Chemical processing handbook*, ed. J. McKetta (New York, Dekker, 1993. xv, 972p. ISBN: 0824787013). *Class No:* 66.02(031)

Handbooks & Manuals

[6486]

MEYERS, R.A. **Handbook of chemical production processes.** New York, etc., McGraw-Hill, 1986. v.p. illus., diagrs., graphs, tables. $75. ISBN: 0070417662.

Contributions from 19 firms located in the UK, the Federal Republic of Germany, Japan, Netherlands and the US. 3 parts (40 chapters): 1. Organic chemicals - 2. Polymers - 3. Inorganic chemicals. Abbreviations and acronyms. 10-p. index. Good layout. *Class No:* 66.02(035)

[6487]

SCHWEITZER, P.A., *ed*. **Handbook of separation techniques for chemical engineers.** 2nd ed. New York, etc. McGraw-Hill, 1988. v.p. illus., diagrs., graphs, tables. £69.95. ISBN: 0070558086.

Covers all major separation techniques used industrially. 45 contributors. 6 parts, closely subdivided into sections: 1. Liquid-liquid mixtures - 2 Liquids with dissolved solids - 3. Gas (vapor) mixtures - 4. Solid-liquid mixtures - 5. Solid mixtures - 6. Gas-solid mixtures. Some sections have extensive references (*e.g.* 2.1 Membrane filtration, 120 references). Detailed, analytical index. A wealth of accessible information for professional engineers. *Class No:* 66.02(035)

Dictionaries

Polyglot

[6488]

HARTMAN, K., *and others*. **Dictionary of process technology in four languages:** English, German, French, Russian. Amsterdam, etc., Elsevier, 1989. 319p. £107. ISBN: 0444988882.

Over 8,000 English-base terms, with German, French and Russian equivalents and indexes. *Class No:* 66.02(038)=00

English

[6489]

COMYNS, A.E. **Dictionary of named processes in chemical technology.** Oxford Univ. Press, 1993. xv, 338p. £45. ISBN: 0198553854.

About 5,000 terms defined and occasionally explained. Some carry references to journal articles and patent numbers. Appendix: 'Key to products', p.309-38. 'Highly recommended' (*Science and Technology Libraries*, 17(1) 1997, p.95). *Class No:* 66.02(038)=20

German

[6490]

Dictionary. Chemical processes and products. [Wörterbuch. Chemische Prozesse und Produkten. English/German, Deutsch/Englisch.] Widnau, Switzerland, Schnellmann Verlag. 1979. 117p. (*CHP. 0.3.*)

About 2,500 entries in each half, with equivalents in the other language. German genders given. *Class No:* 66.02(038)=30

French

[6491]

Dictionary. Chemical processes and products. [Dictionnaire. Procédés et produits chimiques. English/French, Français/Anglais.] Widnau, Switzerland, Schnellmann Verlag, 1987. 119p. (*CHP. 2.3.*) ISBN: 3907971256.

About 2,500 entries in each half, with equivalents in the other language. French genders given. Appendix of units. *Class No:* 66.02(038)=40

Italian

[6492]

Dictionary. Chemical processes and products. [Dizionario. Processi e prodotti chimici. English/Italian, Italiano/Inglese.] Widnau, Switzerland, Schnellmann Verlag, 1985. 119p. (*CHP. 1.3.*) ISBN: 3907971221.

About 2,500 entries in each half, with equivalents in the other language. Appendix of units. *Class No:* 66.02(038)=50

Heat Transfer Materials

[6493]

HALLA, C.W. **Dictionary of drying.** New York, Dekker, 1979. iv, [1], 350p. diagrs., graphs, tables. ISBN: 0824766820.

Entries A to WVTR (Water vapour transfer rate). Cross-references. 'Milk drying': nearly 2p. Much on applications. Includes a survey of recommendations on types of dryers and procedure for drying. References, p.349-50. *Class No:* 66.04

[6494]

Handbook of industrial drying. Mujundar, A.S., *ed*. 2nd ed. New York, Dekker, 1995. 2v. (xvii; 1423p.) illus., diagrs., tables. $295. ISBN: 0824789962.

First published 1987.

43 chapters in 4 parts: 1. Fundamental aspects - 2. Dryer types (*e.g.* rotary; freeze, etc.) - 3 Drying in various industrial sectors (*e.g.* fruits and vegetables; peat and biofuels; polymers, etc.) - 4. Miscellaneous topics in industrial drying (*e.g.* energy aspects; control systems, etc.). Comprehensive. *Class No:* 66.04

[6495]

KAKAC, D., *and others, eds*. **Handbook of single-phase convective heat transfer.** New York, Wiley, 1987. v.p. illus., diagrs., tables. $75. ISBN: 0471817023.

25 contributors; 22 chapters. Topics include convection in liquid metals; effects of electric and magnetic fields; natural convection in enclosures; non-Newtonian transfer. Numerous tables; detailed, analytical index. *Class No:* 66.04

Distillation

[6496]

UNDERWOOD, A.J.V. **Six-language vocabulary of distillation terms:** English/français/español/russkii/italiano/deutsch. Prepared by the Working Party on Distillation of the European Federation of Chemical Engineering. London, Institution of Chemical Engineers, for the European Federation, 1967. xii, 62p.

307 numbered English-based entries, with French, Spanish, Russian, Italian and German equivalents. Entries are grouped (with no headings). English, French etc., indexes. *Class No:* 66.048

Liquids

[6497]

BECHER, P., *ed*. **Encyclopedia of emulsion technology.** New York, Marcel Dekker, 1983-. 3v. diagrs., graphs, tables. ea. $115. ISBN: 0824718763.

V.1 (xiv, 725p.) covers basic theory. 9 chapters by various hands: 1. Liquid/liquid interfaces - 2. Formation - 3. Stability - 4. Microemulsions - 5. Phase properties - 6. Droplet size data - 7. Rheological properties - 8. Optical properties - 9. Dieletric properties. V.2 (472p. 1985.) covers applications of emulsions. 8 chapters by various hands: 1. Demulsification - 2. Research techniques - 3. Medical applications - 4/5 Applications in the food industry - 6. Applications in the cosmetic industry - 7. Applications in agriculture - 8. HLB - an update. V.3 (xi,437p. 1988.) Covers measurement applications. 4 parts (8 chapters); 1. Basic theory - 2. Measurement of properties - 3. Applications - 4. Appendix (HLB: a further update). V.4, 1996. Separate indexes for each volume. *Class No:* 66.06

[6498]

MURALIDHARA, H.S., *ed*. **Advances in solid-liquid separation.** Columbus, Ohio, Battelle Press, 1986. viii,485p. illus., diagrs., graphs, tables. £69.50. ISBN: 0851863639.

Published in conjunction with the International Conference on Recent Advances in Solid-liquid Separation, Ohio, 1986, but not conference proceedings as such. 27 contributors. 16 chapters (subdivided), each with extensive references. Among topics covered are thickening, filtration, equipment, dewatering (various techniques). Analytical index. *Class No:* 66.06

Solvents

[6499]

ASH, M. *and* ASH, I., *comps*. **The Index of solvents.** Aldershot, Gower, 1996. xviii, 589p. ISBN: 0566078848.

Lists about 1,700 products by trade name, chemical, application and manufacturer. International in scope. Data include CAS registry number, chemical formula, properties, uses, toxicology, precautions and regulations. *Class No:* 66.061

[6500]

COMMISSION OF THE EUROPEAN COMMUNITIES. **Solvents in common use:** health risks to workers. London, Royal Society of Chemistry, 1988. [vi],308p. £60. ISBN: 0851860885.

In-depth data on 10 most commonly used solvents: acetone, carbon disulphide, diethyl ether, 1,4-dioxane, ethylacetate, methanol, nitrobenzene, pyridine, toluene, xylene. Data: physical, chemical and spectroscopic properties; toxicology; storage, handling and use precautions; fire hazards; hazardous reactions; emergency action; first aid. Glossary and extensive references. 'An indispensable reference book wherever these solvents are used' (*Science and technology libraries,* v.11(1), Fall 1990, p.40). *Class No:* 66.061

[6501]

Industrial solvents handbook. Flick, E.W., *ed.* 3rd ed. Park Ridge, N.J. Noyes Data, 1985. 648p. diagrs., tables. £85.

First two editions (1970, 1977) by I. Mellan.

About 1,000 tables of basic data (citing sources) of physical properties of most solvents and on solubilities of a variety of the materials in these solvents. Sections on halogenated hydrocarbons, polyhydric alcohols, ethers, acids, esters. *Class No:* 66.061

[6502]

LO, TEH, C., *and others.* **Handbook of solvent extraction.** New York, etc., Wiley: Interscience, 1983. 980p. illus., diagrs., graphs, tables. ISBN: 0471041045.

80 contributors, an international team. 31 chapters, each with references and suggested readings. 4 parts: 1. General principles - 2. Industrial extraction equipment - 3. Industrial processors, organic and inorganic - 4. Cost and equipment. Detailed, analytical index. *Class No:* 66.061

Chemical Products

Databases

[6503]

Fine chemicals database. San Antonio, Texas, Chemron, Inc.

Data on chemical products available from over 50 manufacturers and distributors in North America and Europe. Data: catalogue number, product name, company name, address, etc. Over 207,000 records; semi annual reloads. Available on CD-ROM from the publisher ($495 pa). *Class No:* 661(003.4)

CD-ROM

[6504]

EUROPEAN COMMUNITY Office for Official Publications. **EINECS-Plus.** London, SilverPlatter, 1999. CD-ROM. Annual.

About 800,000 records covering over 100,000 substances. Includes the European Inventory of Existing Commercial Chemical Substances (EINECS), the European List of Notified Chemical Substances (ELINCS), list of dangerous substances whose classification and labeling is prescribed by EC legislation, European Customs Inventory of Chemical Substances, European Cosmetics Inventory, corrections list, and a consolidation of relevant legislation. Also available on the World Wide Web. *Class No:* 661(003.40)

Encyclopaedias

[6505]

The Merck index: an encyclopedia of chemicals, drugs and biologicals. 12th ed. Whitehouse Station, N.J., Merck & Co., 1996. 2561p. tables. $45. ISBN: 0911910123.

First published 1889.

Monographs of over 10,300 chemicals, drugs and biologicals, with notes on preparation, boiling point, toxicity, uses, etc., plus chemical structure and references. Appended: organic name reactions; miscellaneous tables, Chemical Abstracts Service names and Registry names; Therapeutic category and biological activity index; Formula index; Cross-index of names (plus titles of deleted 10th and 11th ed. monographs), etc. Index of 315p. (*c.*70,000 entries).

Online via Dialog, file 304, and STN International; semiannual reloads. Also available on CD-ROM. *Class No:* 661(031)

Handbooks & Manuals

[6506]

ASH, M. *and* ASH, I. **What every chemical technologist wants to know.** London, E. Arnold, 1988-90. 5v.
Emulsifier and welding agents. 1988 400p. £65.
Dispersants, solvents and solutions. 1988. 480p. £65.
Plasticizers, stabilizers and thickeners. 1989. 424p. £65.
Conditioners, emollients and lubricants. 1990. 412p. £65.
Resins. 1990. 400p. £65.

....(contd.)

Each volume includes trade name products, generic chemical symbols and trade name product manufacturers. Indexes by trade names, formulas, synonyms, etc. *Class No:* 661(035)

[6507]

Materials and technology: a systematic encyclopaedia of the material used in industry and commerce, including foodstuffs and fuels. London, Longmans; Amsterdam, de Bussy, 1968-76. 8v. illus. (incl. pl.), diagrs., tables.

Based on J.F. Van Oss's *Warenkennis en Technologie* (5th ed. 1948-50). Updated and rewritten.

U.S. title as *Chemical technology: an encyclopedic treatment* (New York, Barnes & Noble, 1968-76. 8v.).

1. *Air, water, inorganic chemicals and nucleonics.* 1968.
2. *Non-metallic ores, silicate industries and solid mineral fuels.* 1971.
3. *Metals and ores.* 1970.
4. *Petroleum, organic chemicals and plastics.* 1972.
5. *Natural organic products and related mineral fuels.* 1972.
6. *Wood, paper, textiles, plastics and photographic materials.* 1973.
7. *Vegetable food products and luxuries.* 1975.
8. *Edible oils and fats, and animal food products.* 1975.

V.1 (xxiv, 703p.) mentions *c.*300 compounds, for some 30 of these the processes selected for extensive treatment. Chapter 6 of v.2 'Glass' (p.331-412) has 41 figures, 20 tables and 8 references. 'May be viewed as an introduction to chemical technology' (*Aslib book list,* v.34(3), March 1969, entry no.154). *Class No:* 661(035)

[6508]

Specialty chemicals: innovations in industrial synthesis and applications. Pearson, B., *ed.* Amsterdam, Elsevier, 1991. xx,613p. diagrs., tables, chemical structures. ISBN: 185166646x.

About 60 contributors. Documented entries: Halogens ... Sodium, lithium and cesium. Final sections: Oxidations and reductions - New resources and catalyses - Biomassformations - Application innovations. *Class No:* 661(035)

[6509]

UNITED NATIONS. Department of International Economic and Social Affairs. **Consolidated list of products whose consumption and/or sale has been banned, withdrawn, severely restricted or not approved by governments.** 4th ed. New York, United Nations, 1991. xxxvii, 769p. ISBN: 9211301459.

Prepared in accordance with General Assembly regulations 37/137, 38/149, 39/229 and 44/228.

Pt.1: Regulating information (3 indexes); pt.2: Commercial information (2 indexes). 3 appendices. *Class No:* 661(035)

Reviews & Abstracts

[6510]

Natural products updates. London, Royal Society of Chemistry, 1987-. Monthly. £391; $645. ISSN: 09501711.

200 items per issue on isolation studies, structure determinations, new properties, total and biosyntheses. Includes chemical structures, molecular formulas, spectra data. 5 indexes: authors; sources; taxonomic names: trivial names; compound class. *Class No:* 661(048)

Yearbooks & Directories

Europe

[6511]

Directory of chemical producers: Western Europe. Menlo Park, Calif., SRI International, 1995. 2v.

1. *Companies.* 2. *Products. Regions.*

4 main sections. Company index (over 6,000 companies) - Companies (under countries) - Products (13,000 chemicals) - Regions (5,000 separate plant sites). Data on companies include ownership; subsidiary and affiliated companies; activities; plants and products. *Class No:* 661(058)(4)

Great Britain

[6512]

CHEMICAL INDUSTRIES ASSOCIATION. **Directory of products and buyers' guide:** 1992. 2nd ed. West Wratting, Cambridgeshire, 1992. xxii,582p. £105. ISBN: 0951600931.

Sections: Products - Tradenames - Companies - Contract processing services - EINECS index - CAS index - Chemical formula index - CIA code of conduct - Affiliated associations. 'Comprehensive ... an excellent catalogue' (*Reference reviews,* V.6(3) 1992, p.27). *Class No:* 661(058)(410)

[6513]
Chemist & druggist directory, and tablet & capsule identification guide. Tonbridge, Kent, Miller Freeman Information Services, 1972-. Annual. illus., tables. ISSN: 0954853x.

1999 ed. (ix, 480p. £112) has 11 sections including manufacturers and trade pharmaceutical supplies; brands and trade names; associations and organizations; tablet and capsule identification guide. *Class No:* 661(058)(410)

Japan

[6514]
Japan chemical directory, 1996. Tokyo, Chemical Daily Co., Ltd., 1996. 45 + 813p.

Manufacturers, A-Z (p.3-456) - Equipment - Traders - Other chemical and allied companies - Associations - Other organizations. Appended: Asian chemical firms (Australia; China; Hong Kong; Korea; Singapore; Tawain). Data include contact details, chief personnel, products, foreign partnerships. *Class No:* 661(058)(52)

USA

[6515]
Chem sources - USA. Clemson, South Carolina, Directories Publishing Co, 1958-. Annual.

First published 1958.

Contents: Chemical section (over 50,000 chemicals and chemical products) - Trade name section (yellow pages) - Company directory and index (blue pages). *Class No:* 661(058)(73)

[6516]
Directory of chemical producers: United States of America. Menlo Park, Calif., SRI International, 1995. vi, 1124p.

First published 1986.

3 main sections: Companies (1,500, A-Z; cross-references from former names) - Products (c.10,000 chemicals) - Regions (all 50 states). *Class No:* 661(058)(73)

Tables & Data Books

[6517]
Handbook of existing and new chemical substances. Chemical Products Safety Division [Japan], *ed.* 5th ed. Tokyo, The Chemical Daily Co., Ltd., 1992. [iv], 833p.

Lists about 20,000 substances registered for import and manufacture in Japan. Includes an English translation of the 'Law, Enforcement Order, Ministerial orders and notifications which we hope will be helpful to business' ('Recommendation', p.(1)). *Class No:* 661(083)

[6518]
LEUNG, A.Y. *and* **FOSTER, S. Encyclopedia of common natural ingredients used in food, drugs and cosmetics.** 2nd ed. New York, Wiley, 1996. xxxv, 649p. ISBN: 0471508268.

First published 1980.

About 300 of these common, natural ingredients described, specifying chemical composition, pharmacological/biological activities, uses and regulatory status. References are given for each substance. A number of Chinese natural products have been added to this edition. 2 indexes: general (p.565-622); chemical (p.623-49). *Class No:* 661(083)

Nomenclatures

[6519]
BRITISH STANDARDS INSTITUTION. Recommendations for names of chemicals used in industry. London, BSI, 1993. 40p. Chemical structures. (*BS 2474: 1993.*)

Names for industrial chemicals and for commercial descriptions of chemicals - Principles of nomenclature used. Appendices list the radicals cited and give guidance on computerized indexing of chemical names. *Class No:* 661(083.72)

Trade Names, Trade Marks, Brand Names

[6520]
ASH, M. *and* **ASH, I.,** *comps.* **Concise encyclopaedia of industrial chemical additives.** London, E. Arnold, 1991. xi,859p. £110. ISBN: 0304556226.

In four sections: Chemical trade names dictionary (p.1-611) - Chemical compound cross-references (p.612-709) - Functional classification of trade names - Chemical manufacturers directory (international). Over 18,000 entries for chemical trade name products currently used throughout the world. *Class No:* 661(088.7)

[6521]
Chemical manufacturers directory of trade name products 1997-1998. Ash, M. *and* Ash, I., *comps.* New York, Synapse Information Resources, 1997. 1023p. $195. ISBN: 1890595039.

About 57,000 chemical products listed in 2 parts: international chemical manufacturers with their trade name products; trade name products cross referenced to manufacturer. Available on CD-ROM ($195). Valuable for industry and manufacturing. *Class No:* 661(088.7)

Thesauri

[6522]
ASH, M. *and* **ASH, I.,** *eds.* **The Thesaurus of chemical products.** 2nd ed. London, E. Arnold, 1992. 2v. (c.1200p.). £175. ISBN: 0340583029.

First published 1986.

1. *Generic-to-tradename.* 2. *Tradename-to-generic.*

Over 40,000 up-to-date national and international tradename entries. Each volume has appendix of chemical manufacturers (c.950) and of their addresses; also 'Books for consultation'. *Class No:* 661:025.43

[6523]
—**SYNTHETIC ORGANIC CHEMICAL MANUFACTURERS ASSOCIATION. SCOMA handbook: Commercial organic chemical names.** Washington, D.C., American Chemical Society, Chemical Abstracts Service, 1965. 666p.

A thesaurus of c.20,000 chemical names, covering 6,800 commercially traded organic compounds. *Class No:* 661:025.43

Powders

[6524]
RHODES, M.J., *ed.* **Principles of powder technology.** Chichester, Wiley, 1990. xi[i],439p. illus., diagrs., graphs, tables. £36.50. ISBN: 0471924229.

11 chapters; 14 chapters with references. Covers characterization, mixing, storage, size reduction, hazards and separation techniques from an industrial point of view. Includes problems and worked examples. *Class No:* 661-492

Surface-active Agents

[6525]
CARRIÉRE, G. Dictionary of surface-active agents, cosmetics and toiletries, in English, French, German, Spanish, Italian, Dutch and Polish. Amsterdam, etc., Elsevier, 1978. 198p. £78.90. ISBN: 0444998098.

686 English-base terms, with equivalents and indexes in French, German, Spanish, Italian, Dutch and Polish. Covers the principal languages used in the industry. *Class No:* 661.185

[6526]
KARSA, D.R., *and others, eds.* **Surfactants applications directory.** Glasgow, Blackie, 1991. [xiv],399p. £55. ISBN: 0216926904.

2 parts: 1. Alphabetical (by tradename) listing of surfactants by industry sector - 2. Index of surfactant properties listed by industry sector. Data include tradename, supplier, property, chemical type, form, activity, comments. Appendix of company names, addresses. *Class No:* 661.185

[6527]
PORTER, M.R. Handbook of surfactants. 2nd ed. London, Blackie, 1994. p.324. ISBN: 0751401706.

First published 1991.

11 chapters (3. Information sources, p.14-25). 2 appendices. Detailed, analytical index, p.318-24. *Class No:* 661.185

[6528]
SANTHOLZER, R.W. *and* **SANTHOLZER, C. Five language dictionary of surface coatings, plating, products, finishing, corrosion, plastics and rubber:** English/American, Czech, Russian, German, French. Oxford, etc., Pergamon Press, 1969. v, 580p. tables.

4,000 Czech-base terms, with Russian, German, English and French equivalents and indexes. Extends the coverage of R. Santholzer and J. Korinsky's *Four-language dictionary of paints, lacquers and varnishes, surface treatment, corrosion* (Prague, 1959. 436p.). *Class No:* 661.185

[6529]
Surface treatment technology abstracts; incorporating *Metal finishing abstracts* and *Printed circuits abstracts.* Stevenage, Herts., Finishing Publications, Ltd., 1986-. v. 28(1)-. 6 pa. £395; $840 pa. ISSN: 09505199.

As *Metal finishing abstracts*, v. 1-27, 1959-85. Previously appeared in *Electroplating and metal spraying* (1947-1959).

Over 7,000 indicative and informative abstracts and citations pa. covering surface treatment, in 21 classes (Cleaning and degreasing ... Electroplating ... Metal spraying and hard facing ... Corrosion and electrochemistry ... General and miscellaneous). Covers journal

....(contd.)

articles, books, standards, reports and patents - full coverage for UK, European and US patents. Also available on CD-ROM. *Class No:* 661.185

[6530]

World surface coating abstracts. Compiled by Paint Research Assoiciation, Teddington, Middx. Oxford, etc., Pergamon Press, 1928-. Monthly. £350. ISSN: 75578409.

About 10,000 abstracts pa. 90 sections (01/02. Pigments, extenders, dyestuffs and phosphors; 23/24. Polymers containing silicon and other elements; 35/36. Water-borne paints and their components; 53/54. Weathering corrosion; 73/74. Industrial and other hazards; 87. Legislation and other official publications; 88. Standards and specifications. Books). Annual author and subject indexes. Online (170,000 records; updated monthly) via Questel/ORBIT. *Class No:* 661.185

Detergents

[6531]

CARRIÉRE, G. Lexicon of detergents, cosmetics and toiletries. Amsterdam, etc., Elsevier, 1966. ii, 204p. DFl.140. (*Elsevier lexica,* 8.) ISBN: 0444400990.

Part 1, *Detergents* (257 numbered entries), is a revision of G. Carriéres *Detergents* (1960). English-base terms, with French, Spanish, Italian, Portuguese, German, Dutch, Swedish, Danish, Norwegian, Russian, Polish, Finnish, Czech, Hungarian, Rumanian, Greek, Turkish and Japanese equivalents and indexes. Part 2, *Cosmetics and toiletries* (entries 258-523), also English-base has French, Spanish, Italian, Portuguese, German, Dutch and Swedish equivalents and indexes. *Class No:* 661.185.6

[6532]

JAKOBI, G. and LÖHR, A. Dictionary of washing: English/German/ French/Italian. [Wörterbuch Waschen: Englisch/Deutsch/Französisch/ Italianisch.] Weinheim, VCH, 1993. [ix], 353p. £31. ISBN: 3527269835.

About 7,000 English base entries, with indexes. Covers detergents, textiles, washing machines. *Class No:* 661.185.6

Soap Industry

[6533]

UNITED NATIONS. Industrial Development Organization. Information sources on the soap and detergent industry. New York, United Nations, 1977. 81p. $4. (*UNIDO guides to sources of information, no.24.*)

585 items. 12 sections: 1. Professional, trade and research organizations, learned societies and special information sources - 2. Directories - 3. Sources of statistics, marketing and other economic data - 4. Basic handbooks, textbooks and manuals - 5. Monograph series - 6. Current periodicals - 7. Current abstracting and indexing periodicals - 8. Proceedings, papers and reports - 9. Specialized dictionaries and encyclopaedias - 10. Bibliographies - 11. Films - 12. Other potential sources of information (*e.g.* Meetings and conferences). 'Bibliographical sources used'. *Class No:* 661.187

Sulphur

[6534]

PATAI, S.J. The Chemistry of sulphuric acids, esters and their derivatives. New York, Wiley, 1990. xvi,738p.

30 contributors. 23 documented chapters: 1. Sulphuric acid and carboxylic acid - a comparison ... 23. Biological activity of sulphuric acid derivatives. Author and sulphur indexes, p.677-738. *Class No:* 661.2

[6535]

World sulphur and sulphuric acid plant list and atlas. London, British Sulphur Publishing, 1995. 195p. maps. ISBN: 1873387172.

3 sections: Company data (capacity, etc.), A-Z by region, country, name of company (Africa ... North America) - Company addresses - Maps. Data derived from questionnaires. Indexes: country; advertisers. *Class No:* 661.2

Salt

[6536]

LEFOND, S.J. Handbook of world salt resources. New York, Plenum Press, 1969. xxiii, 384p. charts, maps, tables.

Covers both rock salt resources and solar salt operations. 'Country-by-country survey, with data on location and production of mines, plus relevant stratigraphical and other geographical information' (*Aslib book list,* v.35(1), January 1970, entry no.39). *Class No:* 661.422

Rare Earth Elements

[6537]

JEZOWSKA-TRZEBIATOWSKA, B., and others. The Rare elements: occurrence and technology. Amsterdam, Elsevier; Warszawa, PWN-Polish Scientific Publishers, 1990. x,536p. diagrs., graphs, tables. £131.25. (*Topics in inorganic and general chemistry,* 23.) ISBN: 0444988777.

Rev. and enlarged translation of the 1976 Polish original.

7 chapters, each with appended bibliography (6: The technology of rare elements, p.238-496 (copper ... uranium; each element, with references)). Indexes (subject; name), p.523-36. *Class No:* 661.865

Gases

Encyclopaedias

[6538]

Encyclopédie des gas. [Gas encyclopaedia.] Amsterdam, Elsevier, for L'Air Liquide, 1976. viii, 1150p. graphs, tables. ISBN: 0444414924.

5 chapters on physical properties and flammability of gases, their safe handling, general metrology, symbols and units. Over 100 monographs (p.61-1150), each with bibliography appended. 'Ammonia' (p.951-72; 26 references) has data under 6 heads: physical properties; flammability; biological properties; precautions in handling and storage; materials of construction; uses. *Class No:* 661.9(031)

Handbooks & Manuals

[6539]

AGA gas handbook. Ahlberg, K., *ed.* Lidingö, Sweden AB, 1985. x, 582p. illus., diagrs., tables. ISBN: 9197006114.

5 main sections: 1. Current information about gases - 2. Handling and storage of gases - 3. Choice of materials in gas systems - 4. Gases: physical data - 5. Gas information, p.86-540 (Acetylene ... Sulfur dioxide). Appendices include glossary; references, p.564-71. Addresses. Subject index. *Class No:* 661.9(035)

[6540]

TIRATSOO, E.N. Natural gas: a study. 3rd ed. Beaconsfield, Bucks., 1979. *c.*400p. illus., diagrs., graphs, tables.

First published 1966; 2nd ed. 1972.

21 chapters, with footnotes. 1. 'Natural' and other gases - 2. The non-hydrocarbon gases - 3. Methane and crude oil - 4. The production of gas and oil ... 8. The uses and applications of natural gas - 9. Liquefied natural gas ... 12. Natural gas in Britain ... 16. North America ... 18. The Middle East and East Asia - 19. Africa and Australia - 20. Reserves and resources - 21. Some economic factors. Index. *Class No:* 661.9(035)

Dictionaries

[6541]

BRITISH STANDARDS INSTITUTION. Glossary of terms used in the gas industry. 2nd revision. London, BSI, 1967. 133p. tables. (*BS 1179: 1967 (1989).*)

First published 1944.

About 1.000 definitions. 2 parts (16 sections): 1. Production - 2. Utilization. 2 appendices (A. Standard nomenclature of appliance parts not included in the 'Glossary', p.106-8). Index, p.110-33. Partially replaced by BS1179: Part 6: 1980, *Combustion and utilization including installation at consumers' premises.* *Class No:* 661.9(038)

[6542]

INTERNATIONAL GAS UNION. Dictionary of the gas industry: English, German, French, Russian. 2nd completely rev. and enl. ed. Essen, Vulkan-Verlag, 1982-85. 2v.

1. *English, German, French, Russian.*

2. *Arabic, Italian, Portuguese, Spain.*

7,300 entries, English-based, in v.1, with German, French and Russian equivalents and indexes. 11 appendices. Abbreviations. Bibliography, p.635-9. V.2 bibliography, p.591-3. Favourably reviewed in The *Incorporated linguist,* v.22(3), Summer 1983, p.163, 166. *Class No:* 661.9(038)

[6543]

—**INTERNATIONAL GAS UNION. International dictionary of the gas industry.** English version. Berlin, Kammer der Technik, 1978. 254p.

*c.*12,000 entries in sections A-G, with definitions. Alphabetical index. *Class No:* 661.9(038)

Reviews & Abstracts

[6544]

Gas abstracts. Chicago, Ill., Institute of Gas Technology, 1945-. Monthly. ISSN: 00164844.

About 2,500 abstracts pa. 8 sections: 1. Planning, policy, and supply - 2. Production and processing - 3. Transmission - 4. Storage and peaksharing - 5. Distribution - 6. Utilization - 7. Instrumentation and analytical methods - 8. Safety and environment. Author index per issue. Annual index volume. *Class No:* 661.9(048)

[6545]

Médagaz: bulletin bibliographique mensuel. Paris, Association Technique de l'Industrie du Gaz en France, 1982-. Monthly.

4 parts: Documents originaux - Traductions - Ouvrages - Reports. About 200 abstracts per issue. Classes: O. Arts, sciences et techniques; A. Production et traitement du gaz ... L. Classement géographique. *Class No:* 661.9(048)

Hydrogen

[6546]

COX, E.K. *and* **WILLIAMS, K.D. Hydrogen:** its technology and implications. Cleveland, Ohio, CRC Press, 1965-77. 5v. graphs, tables.

1. *Hydrogen production technology.* 1977.
2. *Transmission and storage.* 1977.
3. *Hydrogen properties.* 1975.
4. *Utilization of hydrogen.* 1976.
5. *Implications of hydrogen energy.* 1977.

V.3 (xii, 321p.) has 5 chapters: 1. Introduction - 2. Discussion of the properties - 3. Data graphs (for parahydrogen, unless otherwise stated) - 4. Data tables - 5. Unit conversions, physical constants and symbols. 287 references, in all, p.310-5. Index. Primarily graphs and tables. *Class No:* 661.96

Explosives

[6547]

PARTINGTON, J.R. A History of Greek fire and gunpowder. Cambridge, Heffer, 1960. xvi, 381p. illus.

7 chapters. 1. Incendiaries in warfare ... 3. The legend of Black Berthold - 4. Miscellaneous treaties, non-military arts - 5. Gunpowder and firearms in Muslim lands - 6. Pyrotechnics and firearms in China - 7. Saltpetre. Numerous chapter references (*e.g.* Chapter 3. 341 references). Indexes of names, places and nationalities. Non-analytical subject index, p.362-80. Index of Greek words. 22 illus., plus frontispiece. *Class No:* 662

[6548]

URBANSKI, T. Chemistry and technology of explosives. [14th] ed. Authorized translation by I. Jeczalikowa and S. Laverton. Oxford, etc., Pergamon Press; Warsaw, PWN, 1964-84. 4v. £480, the set. ISBN: 0680362521.

First published 1953-54.

'The chemical, physical and physico-chemical properties of explosives are dealt with, and processes of manufacture are described whenever the substance in question is of practical importance' (*Preface*). V.1 contains 20 well-documented chapters (*e.g.* 8. 'Nitro-derivatives of toluene'; (71 references). Author (of references) and such indexes to each volume. Well produced. *Class No:* 662

Fireworks

[6549]

PHILIP, C. A Bibliography of firework books: works on recreative fireworks from the sixteenth to the twentieth century. Winchester, C. Philip, in association with St. Paul's Bibliographies, 1985. xxix, 168p. illus. £23.60. ISBN: 0906795311.

Over 600 entries for books, of which more than 50% are not recorded in the *National union catalog,* and nearly 60% are not in the *British Library General catalogue.* 20 black-and-white illus., col. front. *Class No:* 662.1

Fuel Technology

[6550]

BECHTOLD, R.L. Alternative fuels guidebook: properties, storage, dispensing, and vehicle facility modifications. Warrendale, Pa., Society of Automotive Engineers, 1997. 204p. $39. ISBN: 0768000521.

Reviews the properties of alternative fuels, such as methanol, ethanol, CNG (compressed natural gas), LNG (liquefied natural gas), LPG (liquid petroleum gas) and hydrogen. Covers production techniques, emissions and changes in vehicle operation. Extensive chapters references; glossary; index. *Class No:* 662.6

[6551]

CLARK, G.H. Industrial and marine fuels reference book. London, etc., Butterworths, 1988. 528p. illus., diagrs. £95. ISBN: 0408014881.

26 sections (The choice of fuels - The chemistry of petroleum - Crude oil refining - Laboratory tests on fuels - Natural gas and LPG ... General operating problems of large diesel engines - Deposit formation and corrosion in steam boilers - Chimney stack emissions). Appendix. 239 illus. For mechanical, marine and plant engineers, plus shipowners, engine-builders and designers. *Class No:* 662.6

[6552]

Fuel and energy abstracts: a bimonthly summary of world literature on all technical, scientific, commercial and environmental aspects of fuel and energy. Guildford, Butterworth Scientific, on behalf of the Institute of Energy, 1978-. 6pa. £580 pa. ISSN: 01406701.

Formerly *Fuel abstracts and current titles*/FACTS (1960-), succeeding monthly *Fuel abstracts* (1945-58).

About 8,000 abstracts pa. Classified sections: 01. Solid fuels - 02. Liquid fuels - 03. Gaseous fuels ... 06. Electric power operation and utilization ... 15. Environment - 16. Fuel science and technology ... 18. Energy conversion and recycling. Subject and author indexes per issue and pa. Coverage: 'World literature on scientific, technical, commercial and environmental aspects of fuel and energy'. Highly regarded. *Class No:* 662.6

[6553]

ROSE, J.W. *and* **COOPER, J.R. Technical data on fuel.** 7th ed., completely revised in SI units. Edinburgh, Scottish Academic Press, for British National Committee, World Energy Conference, London, 1977. xi, 343p. diagrs., graphs, tables. ISBN: 0707301297.

First published 1928; 6th ed. 1961.

7 parts: 1. Quantitites, units and conversion factors - 2. Selected principles and methods of technical calculations - 3. Selected information on measurements and measuring techniques - 4. Properties of substances - 5. Fuels (flammability, gaseous fuels, liquid fuels, including petroleum products, solid fuels) - 6. Atomic energy and nuclear fuels - 7. Electroheat. Subsection references. 160 tables. Analytical index, p.333-43. Well produced; authoritative; practical. 'This 7th ed. omits certain earlier entries, and the 6th ed. is worth retaining' (*Fuel,* October 1977, p.463). *Class No:* 662.6

Peat

[6554]

FUCHSMAN, C.H. Peat: industrial chemistry and technology. New York, Academic Press, 1980. xviii, 279p. illus., diagrs., tables, chemical structures. ISBN: 0122646509.

16 chapters (*e.g.* 2. Chemical characterization of peat; 6. Peat carbohydrates; 16. Chemical methods of peat analysis). References, p.248-65. Detailed, analytical index, p.265-79. *Class No:* 662.641

[6555]

Peat abstracts. [Aithgiorrachtaí móna.] Droichead Nua, Co. Kildare, Eire, Mord na Mona Experimental Station, 1955-. 3pa.

About 100 abstracts and references per issue. 5 sections: 1. Classification, chemistry and physics of peat - 2. Production - 3. Utilization - 4. Reclamation of peatland - 5. General. Includes patents. No indexes. Computer printout from Commonwealth Agricultural Bureau, Farnham Royal. International in scope. *Class No:* 662.641

Coal

Bibliographies

[6556]

BLOCH, C.C. Coal information sources and databases. Park Ridge, N.J., Noyes, 1981. xvi, 128p. $24. ISBN: 0815508304.

Sections: General sources - Libraries - Publications and information - Coal policy, budget and procurement information - Coal related legislative committees and advisory committees - legal aid regulatory data - coal research and technology ... Principal state coal organizations. Detailed index. Confined to US sources. *Class No:* 662.66(01)

[6557]

COX, A.W. 'Solid fuels'. *Information sources in energy technology* (Editor, L.J. Anthony, 1988), p.173-99. London, Butterworth, 1988.

Introduction - Organizational sources - Documentary sources (journals; statistical sources; conferences; abstracting and indexing services; bibliographies; reference books, monographs and reports) - Specialized topics (open-cast mining; combustion of coal; coal gasification; liquefaction of coal) - International coal trade. 2½p. of references. *Class No:* 662.66(01)

Handbooks & Manuals

[6558]

MEYERS, R.A., *ed.* **Coal handbook.** New York, Dekker, 1981. xii, [1], 854p. ISBN: 0824712706.
20 contributors. 11 chapters on coal science and technology (1. Coal structure … 4. Surface mining of coal … 7. Coal utilization - 8. Underground mining … 10. Coal gasification - 11. Liquid fuels from coal (83 references). Glossary, p.817-37. Detailed, analytical index. Intended for a wide clientele. US slanted (20 contributors: 19 US; 1 Canadian). *Class No:* 662.66(035)

[6559]

SCHOBERT, H.H. Coal, the energy source of the past and future. Washington, American Chemical Society, 1987. 298p. $19.95. ISBN: 0841211728.
Sections: How coal was formed - Coal in the world - Chemistry and physics of coal - Heat and power from coal - Carbonizing coal - Chemicals from coal - A look at the future. Index. 'Mainly for public libraries and personal purchase' (*New technical books,* March/April, 1988, p.988). *Class No:* 662.66(035)

[6560]

SPEIGHT, J.G. The Chemistry and technology of coal. 2nd ed. New York, Dekker, 1994. xi, 642p. illus., diagrs., graphs, tables. ISBN: 0824792009.
First published 1984.
21 chapters, each with extensive references, in 2 parts: I. Classification, origin and properties - II. Utilization. Glossary, p.621-32; index, p.635-42. *Class No:* 662.66(035)

[6561]

VAN KREVELEN, D.W. Coal: typology, chemistry, constitution. 3rd ed. Amsterdam, Elsevier, 1993. 979p. illus., diagrs., tables. $397. ISBN: 0444895868.
First published 1961; 2nd ed. 1981.
A comprehensive work in 5 parts: 1. The use of coal - 2. Physical structure - 3. Chemistry and chemical processes of coal - 4. Physical and chemical characteristics; history of coal research - 5. Tables (physical and chemical factors; components; solvents). Extensive chapter references; detailed, analytical index. A standard work, for many years, on coal. *Class No:* 662.66(035)

[6562]

VOLBORTH, A., *ed.* **Coal science and technology.** Amsterdam, etc., Elsevier, 1986. 490p. DFl.250. ISBN: 0444427023.
Part 1: 7 review articles (*e.g.* 'Basic and applied aspects of the magnetic susceptibility of coal'). Subject index,. - Part 2: 12 reprint articles, documented, on environmental aspects of coal fly ash; the depolymerization of coal; new approaches to the characterization of lignites; etc. *Class No:* 662.66(035)

Dictionaries

[6563]

Fachwörterbuch: Carbochemie. Petrochemie: Englisch/Deutsch/Französisch/Russisch. [Dictionary of coal chemistry and petrochemistry: English/German/French/Russian.] Leipnitz, W., *ed.* Berlin, Paris, Alexandre Hatier, 1992. 304p. ISBN: 3861170396.
8000 English-based entries, with equivalent indexes.
Class No: 662.66(038)

[6564]

MERRITT, R.D., *comp. and ed.* **Dictionary of coal science and technology.** Park Ridge, N.J. Noyes, 1987. 384p. illus., tables. $46.90. ISBN: 0815511248.
About 3,000 entries (up to c.12 lines in length), citing sources. References (A-Z authors), p.378-88. Comprehensive, covering all aspects of coal, including geology, development, mining and reclamation. *Class No:* 662.66(038)

Reviews & Abstracts

[6565]

Coal highlights. London, IEA [International Energy Agency] Coal Research, 1995-. 4 pa. ISSN: 13567497.
Formerly *Coal abstracts,* 1977-1994.
About 800 abstracts per issue. A selection of the world's literature on coal science and technology. Available online as *Coal database* and on CD-ROM. *Class No:* 662.66(048)

[6566]

Euro abstracts. Section 2: Coal and steel. Research programmes and agreements. Scientific and technical publications and patents in German, English and French. Luxembourg, Commission of the European Communities, 1975-. Monthly. ISSN: 03783472.
Formerly part of Euro abstracts: scientific and technical publications and patents, 1970-74.
Fairly lengthy abstracts covering research programmes, research agreements, scientific and technical publications, patents, training courses and seminars, forthcoming conferences and symposia. Annual index. *Class No:* 662.66(048)

Worldwide

[6567]

Coal statistics international: monthly inventory of global coal production, price and market problems. Compiled by the editors of *Coal week international.* New York, etc. McGraw-Hill, 1981-. Monthly. tables.
56 tables: United States - Canada - Australia - European Community - South Africa - Japan - Columbia - Western Germany.
Class No: 662.66(100)

[6568]

International Conference on coal science. Proceedings, 10-15 September, Oviedo, Spain. IEA Coal Research, *eds.* Oxford, Elsevier, 1995. c.1000p. diagrs., graphs, formulas. £327.60
Sponsored by member countries of the International Energy Agency.
About 225 documented papers. Author index.
Class No: 662.66(100)

[6569]

INTERNATIONAL ENERGY AGENCY. Coal information, 1995. Paris, the Agency, 1995. Annual. c.500p. tables. £91.
First published 1985.
Part 1: Summary of world coal developments - Part 2: OECD coal data and projections. Data on the current world market; production figures; trends and prospects; trade; demand; prices; transport; coal-fired power stations. *Class No:* 662.66(100)

[6570]

INTERNATIONAL ENERGY AGENCY. Concise guide to world coalfields. Compiled by World Coal Resources and Reserves, IEA Coal Research. London, the Agency. Loose-leaf. graphs, maps. ISBN: 9290290889.
4 sections: 1. Contents and introduction - 2. Major coal-bearing countries (A-Z) - 3. Indexes, classifications and remaining coal-bearing country descriptions - 4. Glossary of terms. Appendix.
Class No: 662.66(100)

[6571]

International guide to the coalfields '98/99. East Markham, Notts., Trade Link, 1999. 169p. illus. £100. ISSN: 13647512.
Directory information (contact details; mining methods; output capacity, etc.) in sections: International guide to coal producers - International ports - Consumers of coal worldwide - International traders - Equipment suppliers - Products and services.
Class No: 662.66(100)

[6572]

JAMES, P. The Future of coal. 2nd ed. London, Macmillan, 1984. xxiv, 275p. diagrs., tables, maps. ISBN: 0333365674.
First published 1982.
9 chapters: 1. Coal: origins and exploitation - 2. Coal use: technology and markets - 3. Coal: environment and health - 4. The USA: Saudi Arabia of coal - 5. Red coal (E. Europe) - 6. The world coal trade - 7. Western Europe - 8. The Third World - 9. The future of coal. Postscript. Chapter notes and references, p.248-68. Many maps and tables. Statistics have been updated. *Class No:* 662.66(100)

Europe

[6573]

Annual bulletin of coal statistics for Europe. New York, Economic Commission for Europe, 1968-. Annual. tables.
Tables of coal statistics analysed into 'Primary energy' (hard coal; brown coal and lignite; other primary solid fuels) and 'Derivative energy' (patent fuel; coke). Footnoted sources. Appended 'Definitions and general notes'. 'Europe' includes Russia, plus USA and Canada. In English, French and Russian. *Class No:* 662.66(4)

Great Britain

[6574]

BENSON, J. *and* **NEVILLE, R.G. Bibliography of the British coal industry:** secondary literature, parliamentary and departmental papers. Oxford Univ. Press, for the National Coal Board, 1981. vii, 760p. £45. ISBN: 019920128x.
6,185 entries, occasionally annotated. 4 parts: 1. Secondary sources - 2. Parliamentary and departmental papers - 3. Mineral maps and plans. Guide to primary source collections (by regions). Combined author-subject index. *Class No:* 662.66(410)

[6575]

Guide to the coalfields, 1994. Redhill, Surrey, FJM International, 1994. 108p. £88.60. ISSN: 00728713.
Contents: British Coal Corporation - UK independent coal production - Associated UK coal industry organisation - International guide to coal producers - Buyers' guide. The extent of the *Guide* has shrunk significantly in recent years, perhaps reflecting the state of the British coal industry. *Class No:* 662.66(410)

[6576]

The History of the British coal industry,. Mathias, P., *ed.* Oxford Univ. Press, 1984-93. 5v. illus., diagrs., graphs, maps. (*Commissioned by the National Coal Board.*)

1. *Before 1700,* by J. Hatcher. 1993. 826p. £60.

2. *1700-1830. The Industrial Revolution,* by M.W. Flinn and D. Stoker. 1984. 528p. £40.

3. *1830-1913. Victorian pre-eminence,* by R. Church, and others, 1986.

4. *1913-1946: The political economy of decline,* by B. Supple. 1987. 700p. £80.

5. *1946-1982. The nationalized industry,* by W. Ashworth, 1986. 732p. £45.

A detailed, documented survey, written in the light of industrial and government records, but in no sense narrow official history. *Class No:* 662.66(410)

[6577]

MAUNDER, W., *ed.* **Reviews of United Kingdom statistical sources. V.11: Coal, gas, electricity.** Oxford, etc., Pergamon Press, on behalf of the Royal Statistical Society and the Social Science Research Council, 1980. xii, 297p. tables. ISBN: 008022461x.

Coal, by D.J. Harris, p.19-98. *Gas,* by H. Nabb, p.99-199. *Electricity,* by D. Nuttall.

The *Coal* Review has 12 sections (*e.g.* 5. Statistics on output; 6. Coal sales and consumption). Appended: Quick reference list. Bibliography (60 references). 'Energy: a prologue' (p.1-18; 13 references) precedes the Reviews. Both official and unofficial British statistical sources - up to the 1970s - are analysed. *Class No:* 662.66(410)

USA

[6578]

LOCKARD, D. Coal: a memoir and critique. Charlottesville, Va., Virginia U.P., 1998. 225p. $29.95. ISBN: 0813917840.

Provides a critical overview of the politics, economics, history and technology of the coal mining undustry in the US. Extensive chapter references; detailed, analytical index.. *Class No:* 662.66(73)

Thesauri

[6579]

Coal thesaurus. London, IEA Coal, 1985. 188p. ISBN: 9290291176.

'Simply a structured collection of the terms actually used to index the Coal Database up to April 1985. Only one level up and/or down in the hierarchy is displayed in a world block' (*Introduction*). Quarto format. *Class No:* 662.66:025.43

Coke

[6580]

LOISON, K. Coke: quality and production. London, Butterworth, 1989. 555p. ISBN: 040802870x.

2nd ed. of a French text on coke manufacture; intended primarily for technical personnel at coking plants. *Class No:* 662.741

Coal Tar

[6581]

Bitumen: background and applications. London, 1991. 49p.

Sections: Bitumen - Bitumen uses - Bitumen manufacturers - Bitumen test procedures - Health and safety aspects of bitumen - Optimizing bitumen performances - Bitumen developments: past, present and future. Glossary. Appended: 'Some typical applications'. *Class No:* 662.749

[6582]

HOIBERG, A.J., *ed.* **Bituminous materials:** asphalts, tars and pitches. Huntington, N.Y., R.E. Krieger Pubg. Co., 1979. 3v.

Originally published 1964-66. 1. *General aspects.* 446p. 2. *Asphalts.* 716p. 3. *Coal tars and pitches.* 603p. *Class No:* 662.749

Alcohol Fuel

[6583]

CHEREMISINOFF, N.P. and **CHEREMISINOFF, P.N. Gasohol sourcebook:** literature survey and abstracts. Ann Arbor, Mich., Ann Arbor Science Pubns. 1981. vii, 221p.

About 1,500 annotated entries on alcohol fuels. 5 sections: 1. Biotechnology and bio-conversion technology literature - 2. Ethanol and methanol - 3. Automotive and other fuel users - 4. Production of chemical feedstocks - 5. The economics of alcohol production. Author index. *Class No:* 662.754

Gas

[6584]

Annual bulletin of gas statistics for Europe. New York, Economic Commission for Europe, 1968-. Annual.

Tables of gas statistics analysed into 'Primary energy' (natural gas; IPG produced at crude petroleum and natural gas sources) and 'Derivative energy' (gasworks gas; coke-oven; blast furnace gas; substitute natural gas; LPG , excluding that produced at crude petroleum and natural gas sources). Footnoted sources. Appended 'Definitions and general notes'. 'Europe' includes Russia, plus USA and Canada. In English, French and Russian. *Class No:* 662.76

[6585]

Gas industry directory, 1999. 102nd ed. Tonbridge, Kent, Miller Freeman, 1998. 252p. tables, maps. £102. ISSN: 0954853x.

Incorporating *Gas journal directory,* and *Who's who in the gas industry.*

Main sections: key information contacts; buyers' guide; company data; who's who in the gas industry; UK gas suppliers; associations and organizations. *Class No:* 662.76

[6586]

WILLIAMS, T.I. A History of British gas industry. Oxford Univ. Press, 1981. xvii, [1], 304p. illus., tables, maps. ISBN: 0198581572.

5 parts (21 documented chapters): 1. The beginnings - 2. Development of the industry, up to the First World War - 3. The inter-war years - 4. The Second World Age and moves towards nationalization - 5 (chapters 13-21). Nationalization and its aftermath: the modern industry. Chapter 15, 'Natural gas', p. 139-55, has 18 references, plus 17 items of bibliography. General bibliography (23 items). Detailed, analytical index. *Class No:* 662.76

Acetylene

[6587]

MILLER, S.A. Acetylene: its properties, manufacture and uses. London, Benn, 1965-66. 2v. illus., tables.

V.1 (xxxii, 800p.) covers history of the industry, physical properties of acetylene, calcium carbide, decomposition and handling, combustion, fuel uses, etc. Fully documented. Thus, chapter 5, section 4, on partial combustion, has 104 major footnotes. V.2 (xvii, 406p.) has 6 sections (1. Hydrogenation and halogenation ... 6. Other vinylation). Each volume has 3 indexes: names, *i.e.,* authors of references); companies; subjects. *Class No:* 662.766

Furnace & Combustion Engineering

[6588]

LAWN, C.J., *ed.* **Principles of combustion engineering for boilers.** London, Academic Press, 1987. xii,628p. illus. (some col.), diagrs., graphs, tables. (*Combustion treatise.*) ISBN: 0124390358.

'Scope ... is the design of combustion equipment for the burning of heavy oil and coal in large boilers' (*Preface,* p.viii). 14 contributors. 6 chapters (subdivided), each with extensive references. Analytical index. *Class No:* 662.9

[6589]

OWEN, K *and* **COLEY, T. Automotive fuels reference book.** 2nd ed. Warrendale, Pa., Soceity of Automotive Engineers, 1995. xii, 963p. diagrs., graphs, tables. £110. ISBN: 1560915897.

First published 1990 as *Automotive fuels handbook.*

The emphasis is on gasoline (petrol) and diesel, although alternatives (*e.g.* LPG, ethanol) are also considered. International perspective, with a worldwide survey (*c.*50p.) of emissions legislation as Appendix 3. Detailed, analytical index, p. 895-963. A comprehensive treatment. *Class No:* 662.9

Industrial Microbiology & Mycology

[6590]

Microbiology abstracts. Section A: Industrial & applied microbiology. Bethesda, Md., Cambridge Scientific Abstracts, 1965-. Monthly. ISSN: 0300838x.

Formerly subtitled 'Section A: Industrial microbiology', 1967-71.

About 7,700 abstracts pa. Sections: Products of microorganisms - Fermentation & related processes. Food microbiology ... Plant diseases ... Mineral microbiology ... Microbial resistance ... Antibiotics - Vaccines - Environmental pollution - Methodology - Miscellaneous. Book notices. Notification of conferences. Author and subject indexes per issue and annually. Available online and on the World Wide Web (URL: http://www.csa.com.). *Class No:* 663.0

Beverages

[6591]

GREEN, S. 'Beverages'. *Food science and technology*. London, Mansell, 1985. p.163-7.

Items 330-381, briefly annotated. Form headings: Bibliographies - Abstracts - Dictionaries and encyclopaedias - Directories - Statistics. *Class No: 663.1*

Wines

Encyclopaedias

[6592]

Larousse encyclopedia of wine. Foulkes, C., *ed*. Paris, Larousse, 1994. 607p. col. illus. maps. $40. ISBN: 2035070228.

About 100 contributors. 3 sections: 1. Wine information (choosing, storing, etc.) - 2. Wine-growing regions, worldwide - 3. Reference (labelling laws, vintage charts, etc.). A basic treatment, less comprehensive than *The Oxford companion to wine* (*qv*). *Class No: 663.2/.3(031)*

[6593]

The Oxford companion to wine. Robinson, J., *ed*. Oxford Univ. Press, 1994. xvi, 1088p. illus. (some col.), maps. £30; $45. ISBN: 0198661592.

A magnificent achievement. Over 3,000 entries, A-Z, on all aspects of wine and wine-making (*e.g.* grape varieties, major appellations, viticulture, the literature and history of wine, glasses for wine, etc.). Some articles have one or two bibliographic references; cross-references where necessary, but no index. About 80 contributors, although over half the articles have been written by the distinguished editor herself (in the UK, the 'Wine Writer's Wine Writer'). Widely reviewed, to great acclaim. 'The best general book on grapes and wine ... erudite and beautiful ... a joy to read' (*Choice*, April 1995, p.1278).

A new ed. is planned for October 1999. *Class No: 663.2/.3(031)*

[6594]

RENOUIL, Y. *and* TRAVERSAY, P. de. **Dictionnaire du vin**. Éd. refondu et augm. Bordeaux, Féret, 1962. 1374p. illus., tables, maps.

Previous ed. as *Dictionnaire-manuel du négociant en vins et spiritueux et du maître de chai d'Édouard Féret.*

11 contributors. The article on Morocco (p.668-71) has subheadings for area planted, legislation, consumption, number of people employed in the wine industry and régione, production and export. Many tables and cross-references. List of works consulted, p.1149-52; bibliographies and references, p.1353-68. 800 illus., 6 coloured maps. A comprehensive encyclopedic dictionary. *Class No: 663.2/.3(031)*

[6595]

—BESPALOFF, A. **The New encyclopedia of wine**. London, Century, 1990. 572p. illus., maps. £10.99. ISBN: 0712639403.

A revised and expanded ed. of *The Encyclopedia of wine* by Frank Schoonmaker, first published 1964.

Lists entries A-Z, giving pronunciation of foreign terms. 2 appendices: wine and food; statistical charts (production; consumption, etc.). No bibliography or index. 'Excellent value for money' (*Reference reviews*, 5(1), 1991, p.23). *Class No: 663.2/.3(031)*

[6596]

STEVENSON, T. **The New Sotheby's wine encyclopedia**: a comprehensive guide to the wines of the world. Rev. ed. London, Dorling Kindersley, 1997. 600p. illus., diagrs., maps. $50. ISBN: 0789420791.

First published 1988 as *Sotheby's world wine encyclopedia.*

Identifies about 4,000 appellations or wine-growing districts and 2,000 producers, with some assessment and evaluation of the wine. Main articles arranged by country, then region. Introductory essays cover collecting and storing wine, tasting and assessing, and the technology of wine making. Beautifully illustrated. *Class No: 663.2/.3(031)*

Handbooks & Manuals

[6597]

ATKINS, S. *and* WOODS, S. **The 'Which?' wine guide** 1998. London, Which? Ltd., 1997. 496p. £13.99. ISBN: 0852026706.

4 main sections: 1. Features - 2. A-Z of wine-producing countries - 3. Where to buy - 4. Find out more about wine (courses, clubs, etc.). Special features in this edition include buying mail-order wine, wine 'leviathans' (large corporations taking over independent companies), food and wine. Index, but no bibliography. *Class No: 663.2/.3(035)*

[6598]

COATES, C. **The Wines of France**. London, Century, 1990. 416p. illus., facsims. (labels), tables, maps.

Preliminary articles (*e.g.* The French laws of wine); 10 chapters; 5 appendices (3. 1986 harvest breakdown; 5. Vins du pays (name/description)). Detailed index. 'Indeed almost every grower or merchant I have met in the last twenty-five years or more have contributed in some way' (*Preface*). *Class No: 663.2/.3(035)*

[6599]

LICHINE, A. **Alexis Lichine's New encyclopedia of wines & spirits**; in collaboration with W. Fifield. 7th ed. London, Cassell, 1987. xii, 771p. charts, tables, maps. £40. ISBN: 030432163x.

First published 1967.

10 chapters: 1. History of wine - 2. History of spirits and distillation - 3. Wine and food - 4. Serving wine - 5. Value and wine (with vintage listings) - 6. Starting a cellar - 7. Wine and health - 8. The vine - 9. Wine: what it is, how it is made - 10. Spirit making. Alphabetical entries, 'Abboccato' ... 'Yugoslavia', p.59-619. Appendices include 'Comparative table of spirit strengths' and a vintage chart. Select bibliography, p.721-4. Extensive index, p.731-77. 60 maps. A fine production. *Class No: 663.2/.3(035)*

Dictionaries

[6600]

PRICE, V. **Dictionary of wines and spirits**. London, Northwood Press, 1980. 394p. diagrs., tables, maps. ISBN: 0719827442.

Entries 'Aberfeldy' - 'Zwicker', including biographies. 'Armagnac': 2/3p.; 'Champagne': 1½p. Entries for wine-growing regions' (*e.g.* Rhine: 3p.). Map of Scottish whisky distilleries, p.347. 'Appropriate strength of principal drinks' (table). Bibliography, p.382-94. Effective use of bold type for cross-references. *Class No: 663.2/.3(038)*

[6601]

RUBASH, J. **Master dictionary of food and wines**. New York, Van Nostrand Reinhold, 1990. 972p. illus. $27.95. ISBN: 0444223468.

Sections: Food terms - Wine terms - Bibliography. Short definitions of food products and dishes worldwide. For food and wine gourmets and amateur cooks. *Class No: 663.2/.3(038)*

Yearbooks & Directories

[6602]

Harper's wine and spirit directory 1998. London, Harper Trade Journals, 1998. 380p. illus. £75.

8 sections: 1. Review - 2. Industry perspectives - 3. Wine report; spirits report; beers report - 4. Directory of the wine and spirit trade in the UK - 5. Overseas trade directory - 6. Index of brands - 7. Index of third party services and products - 8. Summary of trade agencies. *Class No: 663.2/.3(058)*

Maps & Atlases

[6603]

JOHNSON, H. **The World atlas of wine**. 4th ed. London, Mitchell Beazley, 1994. 320p. illus., maps. £30. ISBN: 1857322681.

First published 1971; 3rd ed. 1985.

Descriptions and maps of the world's chief wine producing areas. Sections: 1. Introduction - 2. France - 3. Germany - 4. Southern and Eastern Europe and the Mediterranean - 5. The new world (includes England and Wales). *Class No: 663.2/.3(084.3)*

Beers

Bibliographies

[6604]

UNITED NATIONS. Industrial Development Organization. **Information sources in the beer and wine industry**. New York, United Nations, 1977. 96p. $4. (*UNIDO Information sources, no.25.*)

634 numbered entries. 11 sections: 1. Professional, trade and research organizations, learned societies and special information services - 2. Directories - 3. Sources of statistics, marketing and other economic data - 4. Basic handbooks, textbooks and manuals - 5. Current periodicals - 6. Current abstracting and indexing periodicals - 7. Proceedings, papers and reports - 8. Specialized dictionaries and encyclopaedias - 9. Bibliographies - 10. Films, audio-visual materials and film catalogues - 11. Other potential sources of information (*e.g.* K. Training). 'Bibliographical sources used ... '. Items in sections 2, 3, 5, 6, 10, 11 are annotated. *Class No: 663.4(01)*

Encyclopaedias

[6605]
The Encyclopedia of beer. Rhodes, C.P., *and others, eds.* New York, Henry Holt, 1995. 509p. illus. $35. ISBN: 0805037993.
About 900 entries, A-Z, covering beer styles, brewing terminology, festivals, history, etc. Appendixes: organizations; collectors' clubs; mail-order (US); importers; publications. *Class No:* 663.4(031)

[6606]
GLOVER, B. The World encyclopedia of beer. London, Lorenz, 1997. 256p. col. illus. £16.95. ISBN: 1859674593.
'Hoppy Drop' covers history, ingredients, brewing and beer drinking. Main part of the work is a country-by-country survey of world beer brewing and drinking. A popular treatment, lavishly illustrated; the author was editor of publications for CAMRA (Campaign for Real Ale). *Class No:* 663.4(031)

Handbooks & Manuals

[6607]
Handbook of brewing. Hardwick, W.A., *ed.* New York, Dekker, 1995. ix, 712p. diagrs., tables. ISBN: 0824789083.
20 contributors; 21 chapters (*e.g.* 19. 'The properties of beer', with 3p. of references). Index, p.707-14. Well organized. *Class No:* 663.4(035)

Dictionaries

[6608]
EUROPEAN BREWERY CONVENTION. Elsevier's dictionary of brewing in English, French, German and Dutch. 2nd ed. Amsterdan, etc., Elsevier, 1983. viii, 264p. £102.35. ISBN: 0444421319.
First published 1961 as *Elsevier's Dictionary of barley, malting and brewing,* compiled by B.D. Hartong.
3,762 English-base terms (1961 ed.: 3,917 terms), with French, German and Dutch equivalents and indexes. Coverage of Danish, Italian and Spanish has been dropped in this 2nd ed. *Class No:* 663.4(038)

[6609]
GLOVER, B. CAMRA dictionary of beer. Harlow, Essex, Longman Group, 1983. 146p. ISBN: 0582892619.
Entries, 'Abbaye' ... 'Zymurgy' (the art and science of brewing). Claims to list every British brewery and all the beers they currently produce. Also included is a sample of well-known or distinctive foreign beers and breweries. Alcohol percentages given. Small format. *Class No:* 663.4(038)

Yearbooks & Directories

[6610]
The Brewery manual and who's who in British brewing and Scotch whisky distilling. Hampton, Middlesex, Hampton, 1998. 324, 32p. illus., tables. £69. ISBN: 0951710273.
Includes directory-type information on large, corporate brewers and smaller ones, beer imports, pub chains, wines and spirits. Buyers' guide. *Class No:* 663.4(058)

[6611]
ROBERTSON, J.D. The Beer-taster's log: a world guide to more than 6,000 beers. Pownal, Vt., Storey Communications, 1996. 599p. illus., maps. $24.95. ISBN: 0882669397.
Arranged by region. Includes a detailed description of each beer, including history, malt types, hop varieties, original gravitiy, alcoholic strength and tasting notes. Indexes: beers; brewers. *Class No:* 663.4(058)

Histories

[6612]
CORRAN, H.S. A History of brewing. Newton Abbot, Devon, David & Charles, 1975. 303p. illus. (incl. pl.), facsims., diagrs. ISBN: 0715367358.
19 chapters: 2. Medieval brewing - technical and social - 3. The early history of German brewing and introduction of hops ... 7. Brewing techniques in eighteenth-century England ... 9. The brewing industry, 1750-1800 ... 13. Porter, ale and competition ... 19. The development of brewing technology outside Britain. Appended: The strength of beer. Glossary. References and bibliography, p.286-94 (174 items). Index, p.297-303. *Class No:* 663.4(091)

Spirits

[6613]
JACKSON, M. The World guide to whisky. London, Dorling Kindersley, 1987. 223p. col. illus., diagrs., maps. £14.95. ISBN: 0863183372.
Sections: The water of life - Scotland (p.16-97) - Ireland - Canada - The United States - Japan. Index, p.218-223. *Class No:* 663.5

[6614]
MURRAY, J. The Complete guide to whisky: selecting, comparing and drinking the world's great whiskies. London, Carlton, 1998. 256p. £9.99. ISBN: 1858684501.
6 parts: 1. Art of making whisky - 2. Scottish malt whisky - 3. Irish whisky - 4. Bourbon - 5. Rye Whiskey - 6. Canadian whiskey. Brief glossary and index. Small format. Author has been 3 times 'Whisky writer of the year' (the Glenfiddich Award); a delightful read. *Class No:* 663.5

Non-Alcoholic Drinks

[6615]
UNITED NATIONS. Industrial Development Organization. Information sources on the non-alcoholic beverages industry. New York, United Nations, 1975. xii, 72p. $ 4. (*UNIDO Guides to information sources, no. 15.*)
507 numbered entries. 12 sections (1. Professional, trade and research organizations, learned societies and special information services - 2. Directories ... 6. Current periodicals ... 10. Bibliographies ... 12. Other potential sources of information (*e.g.* Legislation. Patents and licences)). Appended: 'Bibliographical sources used in compiling this guide'. *Class No:* 663.6/.8

Coffee, Cocoa & Tea

[6616]
Coffee international directory. Redhill, Surrey, DMG Business Media, 1998. 232p. graphs, tables. £116; $224. ISBN: 0861084381. ISSN: 02645378.
Includes a review of 1997, with statistics. Covers coffee boards and trade associations, roasters, exporters and importers, brokers, plant and machinery manufacturers, shipping and warehousing, food service and catering packers, and brand names. *Class No:* 663.9

[6617]
ICO Library monthly entries - COFFEELINE. London, International Coffee Organization (ICO), 1973-. monthly.
200 entries per issue, on farming, production, processing, marketing, consumption, physiological effects, etc. of coffee. Online: COFFEELINE. Host: DIALOG. *Class No:* 663.9

[6618]
SIVETZ, M. and DESROSIER, N.W. Coffee technology. Westport, Conn., AVI Publishing Co, 1979. 716p. illus., diagrs., tables, maps. ISBN: 0870552694.
5 parts (17 chapters, some documented): 1. History of coffee- 2. Green coffee technology - 3. Roast coffee technology - 4. Instant coffee technology - 5. Coffee and its influence on consumers. Useful tables, p.697-703. Detailed, analytical index, p.709-16. *Class No:* 663.9

[6619]
UNITED NATIONS. Industrial Development Organization. Information sources on the coffee, cocoa, tea and spices industry. New York, United Nations, 1978. xii, 74p. $4. (*UNIDO Information sources, no. 28.*)
619 numbered items. 11 sections: 1. Professional, trade and research organizations, learned societies and special information services - 2. Directories - 3. Sources of statistics, marketing and other economic data - 4. Basic handbooks, textbooks and manuals - 5. Current periodicals - 6. Current abstracting and indexing periodicals - 7. Proceedings, papers and reports - 8. Specialized dictionaries and encyclopaedias - 9. Bibliographies - 10. Films and film catalogues - 11. Other potential sources of information (H. Packaging; J. Standards and specifications). 'Bibliographical sources used ...'. Items in sections 2, 3, 5, 6, 10, 11 are annotated. *Class No:* 663.9

[6620]
WILLSON, K.C. and CLIFFORD, M.N. Tea: cultivation to consumption. London, Chapman & Hall, 1992. xviii,[2],769p. illus., diagrs., graphs, tables, chemical structures. £75. ISBN: 0412338505.
22 chapters, each with references/bibliography (*e.g.* 3. Selection and breeding of tea ... 7/8. Field operations ... 14. Production of black tea ... 19. The world trade in tea). Glossary. Detailed, analytical index, p.751-69. Authoritative and comprehensive. *Class No:* 663.9

[6621]
World cocoa directory 1996/97. London, International Cocoa Organization, 1996. v.p. Looseleaf. ISBN: 1856700046.
In English, French and Spanish. 3 sections: A. Cocoa associations and organizations - B. Research organizations - C. Company information. *Class No:* 663.9

Tobacco & Narcotics

[6622]

AKEHURST, B.C. **Tobacco.** 2nd ed. London, Longman, 1981. xii, 764p. illus., diagrs., tables. (*Tropical agriculture series*.) ISBN: 0582468175.

First published 1968.

3 parts (18 chapters): 1. The plant and its uses - 2. Culture and processing - 3. Chemical and technological matters. 8 appendices (1. Tobacco production by specified countries). Extensive bibliography, p.687-736. Detailed, analytical index, p.757-64. *Class No:* 663.97

[6623]

Tobacco abstracts: world literature on nicotiana. Raleigh, N. C., Tobacco Literature Sources, 1957-. 6pa. $35pa. ISSN: 00408298.

About 1,600 abstracts and citations pa. Sections: Botany - Chemical and physical properties - Cultural practices - Diseases (7 sections) - Economics, marketing, production and policy - Genetics and varieties - Insects - Molecular biology - Physiology and biochemistry - Seedling production. Subject and author indexes per issue and annually. A-Z order of sections tends to separate related material. *Class No:* 663.97

[6624]

VOGES, E., *comp. and ed*. **Tobacco encyclopedia.** Mainz, Tobacco Journal International, 1984. 468p. col. illus. ISBN: 8920615077.

Part 1: Entries, A-Z, p.13-360. Part 2: Articles (history; leaf type; sheet tobacco): Cultivation; Curing; Processing; Manufacture; Taxation; Science. 25 contributors. Chronological table (AD 1493-1983). Bibliography, p.466. List of advertisers. *Class No:* 663.97

[6625]

World tobacco directory. 46th ed. Redhill, Surrey, DMG Business Media, 1997. Annual. 380p. £108. ISSN: 00842273.

3 parts: 1. Tobacco directory of the world (countries, A-Z) - 2. International brand index - 3. Allied industries (machinery; manufacturing; supplies). *Class No:* 663.97

Food Industry

Databases

[6626]

Foods adlibra. Minneapolis, Mn., Foods Adlibra Publications.

Covers food products, packaging nutrition, toxicology, manufacturers, equipment supliers. Over 300,000 records; updated monthly. Available on DIALOG, file 79. *Class No:* 664(003.4)

[6627]

SZE, M.C. **'Computer-based information retrieval for the food industry'.** *Food technology.* v.34(6), 1980, p.64-70.

Assesses coverage and availability of the leading food database services (*e.g.* FSTA, based on *Food science and technology abstracts,* Foods ADLIBRA, and FROSTI (Leatherhead Food Research Association)). *Class No:* 664(003.4)

Bibliographies

[6628]

DANKBARS, A. **Source book guide to food industry information.** London, London Business School Information Service, 1992. 84p. £25. ISBN: 0951440187.

Lists 149 sources, including journals, reports, associations, statistics and databases, arranged by food category. Details of suppliers. 4 indexes; titles; producers and publishers; subjects; associations. A-5 format. 'Well-produced, an excellent buy' (*Reference reviews,* V. 6,(5) 1992, p.32). *Class No:* 664(01)

[6629]

Food and nutrition bibliography. Compiled from data provided by the National Agricultural Library. US Dept. of Agriculture. 11th ed. Phoenix, Arizona Oryx, 1984. viii, 557p. ISSN: 02782499.

An 'annotated index' of items drawn from the National Agricultural Library's database AGRICOLA. Covers print and audiovisual material on food, human nutrition, and food service management. Sectionalized. No less than 6 indexes, - for personal authors, corporate author, titles, subjects, intellectual level (graded), and media. Tardy in appearing. *Class No:* 664(01)

[6630]

GREEN, S. **Keyguide to information sources in food science & technology.** London, Mansell, 1985. viii, 231p. £25. (*Keyguide to information sources*.) ISBN: 0720117488.

Part 1: Food science and technology and their literature, - a survey of the field in 7 narrative chapters, each with appended references. Chapter 5, 'The literature of food science and technology', p.71-95 discusses forms of material (*e.g.* reports, dictionaries) - *Part 2:* Bibliography, consists of 715 briefly annotated entries (General aspects; Beverages ... Sugar sweetness, confectionary) - *Part 3:* Directory of selected organizations (by continent). Detailed index. Aimed at special librarians, lecturers and workers in the food industries, 'especially those involved in research and development' (*Preface*). *Class No:* 664(01)

[6631]

—GREEN, S. 'Food science'. *Information sources in agriculture and food science.* Lilley, G.P., *ed.* London, etc., Butterworth, 1981. p.477-99.

Short sections: Directories, dictionaries - Food chemistry and biochemistry ... Unconventional proteins - Congresses, conferences, symposia, etc. - Patents - Review series - Abstracting journals - Journals (listed). *Class No:* 664(01)

Encyclopaedias

[6632]

CONSIDINE, D.M. *and* CONSIDINE, G.D., *eds*. **Food and food production encyclopedia.** Princeton, N.J., Van Nostrand Reinhold, 1982. xvi, 2305p. £192. ISBN: 0442216122.

An impressive tome: *c.*1,200 articles, 1.9 million words, nearly 3,000 cross-references, 1,000 illus., 578 tables and a 6,200 entry-word index. Longer articles carry bibliographies. The editors identify three stages in food production: growth, nurture, processing. One of the appendices to the A-Z sequence tabulates data on additives (78p.). 'Because of its authority, currency and comprehensive scope, it promises to be of continuing value for some time to come' (*Reference books bulletin, 1983-1984.* p.92). *Class No:* 664(031)

[6633]

Encyclopaedia of food science, food technology and nutrition. Macrae, R., *and others, eds.* London, Academic Press, 1993. 8v. (6114p.). illus., diagrs., graphs, tables. £1100; $1795. ISBN: 0122268504.

About 1,000 signed articles, 5-20 pages each, on all aspects of food; 1,500 contributors. V.8 is a detailed, analytical index with about 50,000 entries. Cross references. British emphasis and thereby complementary to the American focus of Hui (*qv*). 'An important addition to collections on food science and nutrition (*Choice,* December 1993, p.584). *Class No:* 664(031)

[6634]

Encyclopedia of food science and technology. Hui, Y.H., *ed.* New York, Wiley, 1992. 4v. (2972p.) illus., diagrs., graphs, tables, chemical structures. £385; $495. ISBN: 0471505242.

Nearly 600 contributors; 380 articles. V.4: Q-Z; index, p.2911-72. Well-documented entries, covering three areas: 1. Basic and applied science - 2. Processing technology and engineering - 3. Food laws and legislation. 'An essential title for all industry, research and academic libraries' (*Choice,* September 1992, p.76). *Class No:* 664(031)

[6635]

Food and nutrition encyclopedia. Ensminger, A.H., *and others*. 2nd ed. Boca Raton, Fl., CRC Press, 1994. 2v., illus., tables. £258. ISBN: 084938981x.

First published 1983.

Data on over 2,500 food items; 189-page food compendium table. 1,600 illus. *Class No:* 664(031)

[6636]

ROGERS, J. **The Encyclopedia of food and nutrition.** London, Merehurst, 1990. 480p. illus. (col.), tables. £25. ISBN: 1853911690.

300 contributors. Sections: Vegetables ... Canned and packaged foods - Drinks. Appended tables. Index. Systematic treatment (*e.g.* 'Sago': Latin name; major nutrient; nutritional information; description, origin and history; buying and storage; preparation and use; varieties). 'Designed to help consumers in their choices for healthy and pleasant eating' (*Foreword*). *Class No:* 664(031)

Handbooks & Manuals

[6637]

Handbook of food engineering. Heldman, D.R. *and* Lund, D.B., *eds*. New York, Marcel Dekker, 1992. viii,756p. illus., diagrs., graphs, tables. ISBN: 0824784634.

19 contributors; 14 documented chapters (*e.g.* 'Reaction kinetics in food systems' (p.39-144) carries 12p. of references). Detailed, analytical index, p.741-56. *Class No:* 664(035)

[6638]

JONES, J.M. **Food safety.** Saint Paul, Mn., Eagan, 1992. 453p. tables. $42. ISBN: 0962440736.

14 chapters, well-documented, covering agencies responsible for regulation, consumer concerns, natural toxicants, molds and mycotoxins, environmental and incidental contaminants, and additives. Glossary; numerous tables. Detailed, analytical index.
Class No: 664(035)

[6639]

McGEE, H. **On food and cooking:** the science and lore of the kitchen. 3rd ed. London, Allen & Unwin, 1984. xix, 684p. illus., tables. £12.95. ISBN: 004306003x.

3 parts (14 chapters): 1. Foods (1. Milk and dairy products; 2. Eggs; 3. Meat ... 6. Bread, doughs and batters; 7. Sauces; 8. Sugar, chocolate and confectionary; 9. Wine, beer and distilled liquors; 10. Food additives) - 2. Food and the body (11. Nutrition; 12. Digestion and sensation) - 3. The principles of cooking: a summary. Appendix: A chemistry primer, - atoms, molecules, energy. Bibliography (by chapters), p.648-52. Detailed analytical index, p.653-84. Over 200 illus., included photographs taken through the electron microscope.
Class No: 664(035)

[6640]

POTTER, N.N. *and* HOTCHKISS, J.H. **Food science.** 5th ed. New York, Chapman and Hall, 1995. xiii, 608p. illus., tables. £39. ISBN: 0412064510.

First published 1971; 4th ed. 1986.

Covers food ingredients, processing, packaging, distribution and storage. 25 documented chapters (*e.g.* 2. Characteristics of the food industry; 10. Food dehydration and concentration (27 references); 18. Vegetables and fruit). Detailed, analytical index, p.593-608.
Class No: 664(035)

[6641]

RANKIN, M.D., *ed.* **Food industries manual.** 23rd ed. London, Blackie, 1993. Published with the authority of the Leatherhead Food Research Association. viii, 596p. diagrs., tables. ISBN: 0751400157.

22nd ed. 1988.

19 contributors. 17 chapters: 1. Meat and meat products - 2. Fish and fish products - 3. Dairy products - 4. Fruit and vegetable products ... 11. Snack foods - 14. Food preservation processes ... 17. Food issues. Index, p.582-96. Well organized. A standard compendium on food, processing and manufacturing techniques. *Class No:* 664(035)

Dictionaries

Bibliographies

[6642]

LÜCK, E.C. **Bibliography of dictionaries and vocabularies on food, nutrition and cookery.** Frankfurt am Main, IFIS, 1985. 139p. DM60. ISBN: 3922901046.

436 annotated entries. Author and subject indexes.
Class No: 664(038)(01)

English

[6643]

ADRIAN, J., *and others.* **Dictionary of food and nutrition.** Translated by B. Weitz. Weinheim, VCH, and Chichester, Ellis, Howood, 1988. [viii], 231p. facsims., graphs, tables, chemical structures. £29.45. ISBN: 0895734044.

Based on the orginal French ed., *Dictionnaire du biochimie alimentaire et de nutrition.* (Paris, Technique et Documentation, 1981). At head of title-page: 'Parat'.

Defines over 2,000 terms relating to biochemical aspects of food, nutrition and food compositions 'Abomasim' ... 'Zinc'. 'Oxalic acid': 1p. (table). Appendices: Composition of food (10 tables); Formulas.
Class No: 664(038)=20

[6644]

ALLISON, S. **The Cassell food dictionary.** London, Cassell, 1990. xxxv,480p. figs. £19.95. ISBN: 0304318752.

About 6,000 entries on food, ingredients and culinary techniques. Cross-references appear in an index. Thematic index. 'Excellent' (*Reference reviews*, V. 5(2) 1991, p.25). *Class No:* 664(038)=20

[6645]

BENDER, A.E. **Dictionary of nutrition and food technology.** 6th ed. London, Butterworths, 1990. [vi],336p. tables. £29.50. ISBN: 0408037539.

First published 1960; 5th ed. 1982.

About 4,000 entries, with some 300 revisions and 300 new terms for this edition. Appended grouped bibliography of more than 300 standard works. A well-known and valuable food dictionary.
Class No: 664(038)=20

[6646]

BODENHAM, D. **The Food dictionary.** Bristol, Redcliffe Press, 1993. viii, 264p. £15. ISBN: 1872971180.

About 2,700 terms explained (*e.g.* irradiation: 1/2 col.). Covers ingredients, preservatives and food safety (*e.g.* BSE). Definitions are clear and unambiguous. *Class No:* 664(038)=20

German

[6647]

LÜCK, E.C. **The Compact dictionary of food technology,** English-German, Deutsch-English. Hamburg, Behr's Verlag, 1985. 443, [1]p. £45.95.

Earlier ed. of the English-German part (Wiesbaden, Brandstetter) appeared in 1963.

English-German part (p.1-213) contains *c.*4,000 entries, plus appendix of weights and conversion tables. German-English part (p.217-443, [1]p.) also carries an appendix. *Class No:* 664(038)=30

French

[6648]

Dictionnaire agro-alimentaire: français/anglais, anglais/français. [Dictionary of food science and industry: French/English, English/French.] Adrian, J., *and others.* Paris, Technique et Documentation, 1996. xiv, 400p. £60. ISBN: 2743000929.

About 6,000 entries in each half. Mostly equivalents. French genders given. *Class No:* 664(038)=40

Glossaries

[6649]

French glossary of food industry terms: French-English, English-French. London, Impact, 1996. [vi], 185p. diagrs. £6.95. (*Eurolexus.*) ISBN: 187468751x.

About 4,000 terms in each language. Appendices include lists of food additives and labelled diagrams of widely used food processing equipment. *Class No:* 664(038.1)

Reviews & Abstracts

[6650]

Food science and technology abstracts. Wallingford, Oxon., CAB International: International Food Information Service (IFIS), 1969-. Monthly. $1520; £825. ISSN: 00156574.

Over 2,000 abstracts per issue. Over 1,200 journals searched. Sections A-T (A. Basic food science ... T. Additives, spices and condiments). Author and subject indexes per issue and annually. The main food science and technology abstracting service since 1969. Available online from various hosts, on CD-ROM (Silver Platter) and on the Internet. *Class No:* 664(048)

[6651]

Science and technology abstracts. Leatherhead, Surrey, Leatherhead Food RA. 12 pa. ISSN: 09501789.

Formerly British Food Manufacturing Industries Research Association *Leatherhead Research Association abstracts.*

About 6,000 abstracts pa. 23 sections (*e.g.* Analytical - Biochemical and chemical - Microbiological ... Food processing and biotechnology ... Packaging - Plant and equipment - Storage and transport - Legal). Appended cross-references. Available on computer disk and the Internet (URL: http://www.ifra.co.uk) as *International food abstracts.*
Class No: 664(048)

Progress Reports

[6652]

Advances in food and nutrition research. Orlando, Florida, Academic Press,. 1948- v.1-, Annual. illus., diagrs., tables.

Previous title *Advances in food research.*

V.43 (1999; 275p.; £59; ISBN: 0120164434) has documented articles on the role of flavouring substances in food allergy and intolerance, amino acid secquence alignments in genetically modified food, and sequence databases for assessing the allergenticity of proteins. A major source of reviews for food scientists and technologists. *Class No:* 664(055)

[6653]

World review of nutrition and dietetics. Basle & London, Karger; Wiley, 1959-. v.1-. Irregular.

Each volume carries 4-6 documented articles. Usually devoted to particular themes (*e.g.* v.82: *Nutrition and fitness.* 1997. 266p.), with subject index and list of contents of previous few volumes. 'Reviews are necessarily coloured by the views of the authors, but most of them, though not all, succeed in providing a critical survey of the field. They also serve as valuable platforms to promulgate ideas' (*Chemistry &*

....(contd.)

industry, 6 August 1977, p.659). Aims to provide a forum for critical reviews such as cannot be published in the ordinary journals, nor in textbooks. Highly priced (*e.g.* v.52: £101.25). *Class No:* 664(055)

Yearbooks & Directories

[6654]

Feast directory 1998. Leatherhead, Surrey, Leatherhead Food Research Association, 1998. [ii], 139p.

Lists names and addresses of suppliers of equipment, packaging, ingredients and commodities to the food industry. *Class No:* 664(058)

[6655]

Food trades directory of the UK and Europe 1999. 41st year; 28th ed. London, Newman Books, Ltd., 1998. 2v. (iv, 1203; xviii, 759p.). ISSN: 03090264.

V.1: UK; V.2: Contintental Europe.

V.1 covers food suppliers (A-Z, with products, contact details, turnover); outlets; services; and the food industry (machinery, packaging, distribution, etc.). Over 300p. of indexes. V.2 provides similar information, A-Z by country. *Class No:* 664(058)

Tables & Data Books

[6656]

Data sourcebook for food scientists and technologists. Hui, Y.H., *ed.* New York, VCH, 1991. xxxvii, 976p. tables. £85. ISBN: 1560810092.

10 chapters, closely subdivided, in 3 sections: A. Chemical and biological data - B. Product categories data - C. Safety, laws, and regulations [emphasis on US]. Detailed, analytical index, p. 879-976. Largely tables; a wealth of information. *Class No:* 664(083)

[6657]

PENNINGTON, J.A.T. Bowes and Church's food values of portions commonly used. 16th ed. Philadelphia, Pa., Lippincott, 1993. 328p. tables. $29.95. ISBN: 0397550871.

Lists both generic and brand names. Includes values for proteins, cholesterol, fats, and vitamins. Tables for biotins, amino acids, caffeine, salicylates, etc. Bibliography of additional sources for food composition data. Good index. 'This is *the* source for information on food composition' ('Reference book bulletin', *Booklist,* January 1, 1994, p.846). *Class No:* 664(083)

Histories

[6658]

DARBY, W.J., *and others*. Food: the gift of Osiris. Orlando, Florida, Academic Press, 1977. 2v. (452p.+425p.), illus.

'Deals with the use of food and the acceptance or rejection of its varieties for cultural or religious reasons, over a very long period in the Near East, mainly in Egypt' *(British medical journal,* 7 May 1977, p.1210). Lavishly illustrated. *Class No:* 664(091)

[6659]

TOUSSANT-SAMAT, M. A History of food. Oxford, Blackwell, 1992. xix, 801p. illus., tables. £25. ISBN: 0631177418.

First published, Paris, Bordas, 1987; trans. by Anthea Bell.

26 chapters in 9 parts. Arranged thematically so 'honey' rests with game in the section on 'Collecting, gathering, hunting'. Covers all aspects of food: cultivation; discovery (the 15th century explorers); the community of eating. Extensive chapter notes; detailed, analytical index, p.787-801. 'An excellent work of reference' *(Reference reviews,* 8, 4 (1994), p.32). *Class No:* 664(091)

USA

[6660]

MARIANI, J.F. The Dictionary of American food & drink. New York, Ticknor & Fields (distributed by Houghton), 1983. 475p. $11.95. ISBN: 0899193595.

A compendium that lays emphasis on the history and development of various foods, some of the entries being miniature essays. Word derivations are traced. Well documented. Index. 'Anecdotal as well as authoritative' *(Library journal,* 15 April 1984, p.782). *Class No:* 664(73)

Thesauri

[6661]

The Companion thesaurus to *Food science and technology abstracts*. Merryweather, L., *comp.* 3rd ed. Reading, Berks., International Food Information Service, 1992. xvii, 204p. ISBN: 0860141667.

First published 1970; 2nd ed. 1981.

Lists 7,375 terms of which 1,142 are non-descriptors (*i.e.* non-preferred). Hierarchical display. Intended to be used in connection

....(contd.)

with the CD-ROM and database versions of *Food science and technology abstracts* (*qv*), both, since 1993, indexed using the Thesaurus. *Class No:* 664:025.43

[6662]

EUROPEAN COMMUNITIES COMMISSION. Food multilingual thesaurus. Munich, etc., K.G. Saur, 1979. 5v. DM390, the set.

1. *Deutsche Ausgabe.* xx, 129p.
2. *English edition.* xx, 145p.
3. *Version française.* xx, 144p.
4. *Edizioni italiana.* xx, 132p.
5. *Quadrilingual index and microfiches.* viii, 168p. 24 microfiches.

The English edition (DM154. ISBN 3598101058) has alphabetically arranged sections: Compositions - Countries - Food science - Food technology - Food, including sciences and by-products - Health and environment - Industries, economics, agriculture-Methodology - Microorganisms - Properties and quality. *Class No:* 664:025.43

Information Services

[6663]

Directory of food and nutrition information services and resources. Frank, R.C., *ed.* Phoenix, Arizona, Oryx Press, 1985. vi, 288p. tables. $74.50. ISBN: 0897740785.

A directory of 627 organizations, 61 databases, 102 microcomputer software programmes, over 180 journals and newsletters, 19 abstracting indexing and curent-awareness services, more than 400 publishers of books, audio visual material and microcomputer software, and over 140 key reference books. Subject, organization and geographical indexes. 'For food and nutrition educators and health professionals, ... as well as a valuable reference for organizations, institutions and libraries' *(Food technology,* v.39, July 1985, p.100). *Class No:* 664:061:025.5

[6664]

INTERNATIONAL FOOD INFORMATION SERVICE. Proceedings of the 2nd International Conference on Food Science and Technology Information. Schützsack, U., *ed.* Berlin, May 13-22, 1987. 283p. facsims., tables.

31 papers, some with appended references (*e.g.* 'Processed food: the need for information', p.109-16. 13 references). 'BIOSIS: its coverage of the food sciences literature', p.49-[61], has 6 tables. List of authors. List of participants. *Class No:* 664:061:025.5

Food Engineering

Encyclopaedias

[6665]

HALL, C.W., *and others*. Encyclopedia of food engineering. 2nd ed. Westpoint, Conn., AVI Pubg. Co., 1986. x, [1], 882p. illus., diagrs., graphs, tables. ISBN: 0870551574.

First published 1971.

About 75 contributors. Entries (Absolute pressure controller ... Zinc) can be lengthy, *e.g.* 'Energy conservation in food processing', p.293-320, with 29 references. This volume, first of a 3v. set, emphasizes equipment and facilities used in food handling and transportation. *Class No:* 664.0(031)

Handbooks & Manuals

[6666]

BENDER, A.E. Food processing and nutrition. London, etc., Academic Press, 1978. [v], 243p. ISBN: 0120864509.

5 sections: A. Principles - B. Effects on nutrients - C. Effects of processes - D. Commodities - E. Addition of nutrients. 937 references, plus cross-references. Partly analytical index. *Class No:* 664.0(035)

[6667]

EGAN, H., *and others*. Pearson's chemical analysis of foods. 9th ed. Harlow, Essex, Longman, 1991. 624p. illus. £49. ISBN: 0582409101.

Extensive chapter references in this standard work. Appendices on UK food regulations. Profiles EC legislation for principal foods, the international codex, standards, developments in NIR spectroscopy, etc. *Class No:* 664.0(035)

[6668]

Engineering and Food. Speiss, W.E.L. *and* Schubert, H., *eds.* London, Elsevier. 3v. c.2,700p. illus., tables. £283 (set). ISBN: 1851664475, Set.

V.1. *Physical properties and process control.*
V.2. *Preservation processes and related techniques.*
V.3. *Advanced processes.*

About 100 papers from the 5th International Congress on Engineering and Food, Cologne, 28 May - 3 June 1989. 147 tables. Subject index. *Class No:* 664.0(035)

[6669]

FRAZIER, W.C. *and* **WESTHOFF, D. Food microbiology.** 4th ed. New York, etc., McGraw-Hill, 1988. 576p.

3rd ed., 1978.

7 sections: Food and microorganisms - Principal of food preservation - Contamination, preservation and spoilage of different kinds of foods - Foods and enzymes produced by microorganisms - Foods in relation to disease - Food sanitation - Control and inspection. Index. A classic text. *Class No:* 664.0(035)

[6670]

Handbook of cereal science and technology. Lorenz, K.J. *and* Kulp, K., *eds.* New York, Dekker, 1991. viii,882p. illus., diagrs., graphs, tables. $185. ISBN: 0824783581.

30 contributors. 24 documented chapters (1. Wheat ... 24. Ethanol production from cereal grains). Detailed, analytical index. For the specialist. *Class No:* 664.0(035)

[6671]

POMERANZ, Y. Functional properties of food components. 2nd ed. San Diego, Ca., Academic Press, 1991. ix,569p. illus., diagrs., graphs, tables. £60. (*Food science and technology.*) ISBN: 0125612828.

First published 1985.

12 chapters, each with extensive references, in 3 parts: 1. Components (water; carbohydrates; proteins, etc.) - 2. Engineering foods (additives; new and novel foods, etc.) - 3. Information and documentation. Bibliography, p.533-60. Detailed, analytical index, p.561-69. *Class No:* 664.0(035)

[6672]

Principles and practices for the safe processing of food. Shapton, D.A. *and* Shapton, N.F., *eds.* Oxford, Butterworth Heinemann, 1991. xiv,457p. illus., diagrs., graphs, tables. ISBN: 0750611219.

Based on procedures used in the processing plants of H.J. Heinz. 15 chapters covering such areas as buildings, sanitation, personnel, microrganisms, spoilage. Extensive data tables cover a range of processed foods. Detailed, analytical index. *Class No:* 664.0(035)

Dictionaries

[6673]

GOULD, W.A. Glossary for the food industries. 2nd ed. Baltimore, Md., CTI Publications, 1995. ix, 190p. ISBN: 093002723x.

First published 1990.

About 1,000 terms, briefly defined (*e.g.* 'Farina': 2 lines). Abbreviations/acronyms, p.1-19. 26 tables (16: 'Standard screen sizes'). *Class No:* 664.0(038)

Tables & Data Books

[6674]

McCANCE, R.A. *and* **WIDDOWSON, E.M. The Composition of foods.** 5th rev. and extended ed. London, Royal Society of Chemistry; Ministry of Agriculture, Fisheries and Food, 1991, reprinted 1997. xiii,462p. tables. £39.95. ISBN: 0851863914.

3 sections: 1. Introduction - 2. Tables, p.21-388 (*e.g.* Milk and milk products; Herbs and spices; Nuts; Beverages) - 3. Appendices (*e.g.* Organic aids; Recipes; References; Index). A standard work.

Supplements (some to the 4th ed.): *Vegetables, herbs and spices* (1991); *Fruit and nuts* (1992); *Vegetable dishes* (1992); *Fish and fish products* (1992); *Cereals and cereal products* (1988); *Milk products and eggs* (1989); *Food number index)* (1993); *Miscellaneous foods* (1994); *Meat, poultry and game* (1995); *Meat products and dishes* (1996); *Fatty acids* (1998).

The nutrient composition data are also available on floppy disk in ASCII format. *Class No:* 664.0(083)

[6675]

—**Food labelling data for manufacturers:** based on McCance and Widdowson's *The Composition of foods.* Welch, L.A., *and others, comps.* London, Royal Society of Chemistry and Ministry of Agriculture, Fisheries and Food, 1992. [vi],214p. tables. £27.50. ISBN: 0851869939.

Data for food labels, following requirements of EC Directive (1990). *Class No:* 664.0(083)

Sugar Industry

[6676]

CHABALLE, L.Y. Elsevier's sugar dictionary, in English/American, French, Spanish, Dutch, German. Amsterdam, etc., Elsevier, 1984. xiv, 322p.

2,741 English/American-based terms with French, Spanish, Dutch, and German equivalents and indexes. *Class No:* 664.1

[6677]

MARIE, S. *and* **PIGGOTT, J.R.,** *eds.* **Handbook of sweeteners.** Glasgow and London, Blackie, 1991. xiv,302p. diagrs., graphs, tables. £65. ISBN: 0216928362.

18 contributors. 11 well-documented chapters. Full contents list. Index, p.295-302. *Class No:* 664.1

[6678]

SCHALIT, M., *comp.* **Guide to the literature of the sugar industry:** an annotated bibligraphical guide to the literature on sugar and its manufacture from beet and cane. Amsterdam, etc., Elsevier, 1970. [xi], 172p.

About 1,000 annotated entries. 11 chapters: 1. Bibliographies, abstracts and reviews, indexes and patents - 2. Government publications - 3. Dictionaries, directories and yearbooks ... 8. Publications on technology and sugar chemistry - 9. Handbooks and tables - 10. Translations. 3 appendices (1. Bibliography of American doctoral dissertations on sucrose, sugarbeet and sugarcane since 1938; 3. Bibliography of papers presented at annual technical conferences of British Sugar Ltd., 1948-1966). Names and title indexes. *Class No:* 664.1

[6679]

Sugar industry abstracts. Wallingford, Oxon., 1948-. 6 pa. + index. ISSN: 09575022.

Published in association with Tate & Lyle; formerly *Tate & Lyle's Sugar industry abstracts,* 1981-89.

About 1,800 abstracts pa. 14 sections: 1. Cane sugar manufacture - 2. Beet sugar manufacture - 3. Sugar refining ... 7. By-products - 8. Properties and uses of sugar - 9. Nutrition and health aspects - 10. Economics ... 14. Books. Forthcoming conferences on sugar and related topics. Author and subject indexes per issue; annual index includes list of source journals. *Class No:* 664.1

[6680]

Sugar year book. London, International Sugar Organization, 1947-. Annual. tables.

Statistical tables covering 126 countries, A-Z, are followed by world tables (production, imports, exports, consumption, prices; stocks in selected countries; equivalent weights). Statistics (usually for 7 year span) relate to centrifugal sugar only. Small format. *Class No:* 664.1

[6681]

—**F.O.** Licht's Internationales zuckerwirtschaftliches Jahr- und Adressbuch... Weltzucker statistik. Ratzeburg, F.O. Licht. Annual.

The standard yearbook for the world's sugar economy, both sugar-beet and sugar-cane. It covers organization, production, imports, exports, plants and refineries, gives statistics, lists sources and includes an English-German glossary, plus an atlas of sugar factories. *Class No:* 664.1

Sweets

[6682]

CAOBISCO. Fünfsprachiges Süsswaren-Fachwörtesbuch. [Six language dictionary of the confectionery industry.] Hamburg, Benecke, 1984. 699p. £91.20

About 2,000 German-based terms, with equivalents and indexes in English, French, Italian, Dutch and Spanish. *Class No:* 664.14

Starch

[6683]

WHISTLER, R.L. Starch: chemistry and technology. 2nd ed., edited by H.L. Wilcke, and others. Orlando, Florida, Academic Press, 1984. xxiii, 718p. illus., diagrs., tables, chemical structures. ISBN: 0127462708.

First published 1965-67 (2v. xviii, 579p; xviii, 733p.).

24 contributors (mostly American). 23 chapters, well documented (*e.g.* 6. Molecular structure of starch, p.153-83, 201 references). Covers both fundamental and industrial aspects. Detailed, analytical index, p.691-718. *Class No:* 664.2

Baking & Flours

[6684]

DANIEL, A.R., *comp.* **The Baker's dictionary.** 2nd ed. Amsterdam, etc., Elsevier, 1971. [vi], 264p.

First published 1949 (London, McLaren).

About 5,000 entries and cross-references. 'Over': *c.*80 lines. Some chemical formulas. Bibliography, p.253 (no dates or publishers' names). *Class No:* 664.6

[6685]

MATZ, S.A. **The Chemistry and technology of cereals as food and feed.** 2nd ed. New York, Van Nostrand Reinhold, 1991. xix,751p. illus., diagrs., tables. £72. ISBN: 0442308302.

First published 1959.

21 chapters, closely subdivided, each with extensive bibliography. Covers the basic grains (*e.g.* wheat, corn, oats, barley, rye, rice) and the milling, processing and products (including 'popcorn' under snack foods). Detailed, analytical index, p.743-51. *Class No: 664.6*

[6686]

POMERANZ, Y. **Modern cereal science and technology.** New York, VCH Publications, 1987. 486p. $89.975.

Sections: Physical properties and structure - Wheat flour components in bread making ... Oats, sorghum and millets, and rye-extrusion products - Industrial uses of cereals. Index. 'For students, researchers, novices and experts in the area' (*New technical books*, May/June 1988, item 1375). *Class No: 664.6*

[6687]

SCHNEEWEISS, R. **Dictionary of cereal processing and cereal chemistry,** in English, German, French, Latin and Russian. Amsterdam, etc., Elsevier, 1982. xii, 520p. DFl.315. ISBN: 0444420485.

6,932 English-base terms, with German, French, Latin and Russian equivalents and indexes. Symbols indicate out-of-date, little used terms or terms often used in a sense that is not recommended. *Class No: 664.6*

Milling

Flour Mills

[6688]

Flour Milling and Baking Research Association abstracts. Chorleywood, Rickmansworth, Herts., the Association, 1967-. 6pa.

Formerly *Baking abstracts*, 1948-66.

About 1,500 abstracts pa. Sections: cereals and cereal products; bakery raw materials; bakery processes and products; laboratory techniques; nutrition; microbiology; plant; equipment; buildings; packaging; administration; legislation. Annual author and subject indexes. International. Online database. *Class No: 664.71*

Preservation & Treatments

[6689]

BRENNAN, J.G. **Food dehydration:** a dictionary and guide. Oxford: Butterworth-Heinemann, 1994. [vii], 189p. diagrs., graphs. ISBN: 0750611308.

In 4 parts: 1. Historical background and general principles - 2. Dictionary of food dehydration (p.17-135) - 3. A guide to dehydrated foods (Abattoir by-products - yeast) - 4. Bibliography. *Class No: 664.8/.9*

[6690]

CAMPBELL-PLATT, G. **Fermented foods of the world:** a dictionary and guide. Sevenoaks Kent, Butterworth, 1987. xxiii, 91p. map. ISBN: 0407063134.

Entries: Acidophilus milk ... Yoghurt. Foods by region; foods by class. 'Yoghurt' has sections: consumption; types; production; microbiology and biochemistry; composition and nutritive value. 4 references, 6 cross-references. Includes wine. Profuse cross-references. The introduction (xxiip.) includes 1½ pages of references. Well organized. Fills a gap. *Class No: 664.8/.9*

Additives

[6691]

ASH, M. *and* ASH, I., *comps.* **Handbook of food additives:** an international guide to more than 7,000 products by tradename, chemical, function and manufacturer. Aldershot, Hants., Gower, 1995. xiv, 1025p. £125. ISBN: 056607592x.

4 parts: 1. Tradename reference - 2. Chemical dictionary/Cross reference - 3. Functional cross reference (about 30 sections, *e.g.* fermentation aids; plasticizers) - 4, Manufacturers' directory. Appendices include tables of food regulations for US and EU. 'This is an excellent work by two of the best in the chemical products business' (*Information sources in science and technology*, 3rd ed, 1998, p.258). There is a companion *Food additives electronic handbook* (1995). *Class No: 664.8.022*

[6692]

CRC handbook of food additives. Furia, T.E., *ed.* 2nd ed. Cleveland, Ohio, CRC Press, 1972-. 998p.

First published 1968.

Part 1: 15 documented sections, p.1-789 (1. Enzymes - 2. Vitamins and amino acids - 3. Antimicrobial foods additives ... 8. Starch in the food industry ... 14. Color additives in food - 15. Phosphates in food processing). 1,005 references - Part 2: Regulatory status of direct food additives. Analytical index. US-slanted.

V.2 (1980. 412p.) updates both text and bibliographies in V.1. 'The most important guide to food additives' (Green, S. *Food science and technology*, p.184). *Class No: 664.8.022*

[6693]

—HANSSEN, M. *and* MARSDEN, J. The New E is for additives: the complete 'E' number guide. Wellingborough, Northants, Thorsons, 1987. 384p. £3.50. ISBN: 0722515626.

First published 1984.

Elucidates the categories of 'E' numbers: E100-E180: Permitted colours; E200-E290: Permitted preservatives; E300-E321: Permitted anti-oxidants; E222-494: Emulsified, stabilized and other; E905-907: Minerals, hydrocarbons. Data: Source; function; effects; A.D.I. (Acceptable Daily Intake); typical products. Appended A-Z list of additives and their 'E' numbers. Glossary of additive terms, p.347-57. *Class No: 664.8.022*

[6694]

FENAROLI, G. **Fenaroli's handbook of flavor ingredients.** Burdock, G.A., *ed.* 3rd ed. Boca Raton, Fl., CRC Press, 1995. 2v. (990p.). diagrs., graphs, tables, chemical structures. ISBN: 0849327105, (vol.1); 0849327113, (vol.2).

First published 1971.

V.1, pt.1: *General considerations.* pt.2: *Natural flavour.* V.2, pt.3: *Synthetic flavors.* pt.4: *Use of flavour ingredients.*

V.1, pt.2 has a list of *c.*250 natural flavour ingredients. V.2, pt.3 lists *c.*1,800 synthetic flavour ingredients. Each part has an extensive bibliography of references and a detailed index. Still the major source on flavours. *Class No: 664.8.022*

[6695]

—IGOE, R.S. Dictionary of food ingredients. 2nd ed. New York, Van Nostrand Reinhold, [1989]. [vi], 225p. tables. ISBN: 0442319274.

First published 1983.

In four sections: (1) a dictionary of *c.*1,000 food ingredients, their functional properties and applications; (2) classification by categories; (3) substances for use in foods; (4) bibliography of *c.*200 sources consulted, almost all pre-1984. Omits important ingredients such as lanolin and talc. *Class No: 664.8.022*

[6696]

LEWIS, R.L. **Food additives handbook.** New York, Van Nostrand Reinhold, 1989. xxxi,592p. ISBN: 0442205082.

An extensive list of additives alphabetically by chemical name. Data for each include identifiers (*e.g.* name, CAS, DOT, Molecular formula, etc.), properties, food specific information, occupational restrictions and toxicological data. Indexes: Purposes served in foods; Food type; CAS number; synonym. *Class No: 664.8.022*

[6697]

—SMITH, J., *ed.* Food additive user's handbook. Glasgow, Blackie; New York, Van Nostrand Reinhold, 1991. xv,286p. tables. £65. ISBN: 0216929113.

16 contributors. 15 chapters on types of additives (1. Antioxidents - 2. Sweeteners - 3. Flavourings - 4. Colours ... 8. Emulsifiers ... 11. Hydrocolloids ... 13. Flour improvers and raising agents ... 15. Chelating agents). No safety information; the user is referred to Lewis, *Food additives handbook. Class No: 664.8.022*

[6698]

Source book of flavors. Reineccius, G., *ed.* 2nd ed. New York, London, Chapman & Hall, 1994. xvi, 928 p. diagrs., tables. £135. ISBN: 0442003765.

1st ed. 1981 by Henry Heath.

9 contributors; 23 documented chapters (*e.g.* 3. Flavor chemistry, 9p. of references). Includes international legislation on flavourings. Will supplement but not replace Fenorali's *Handbook* (*qv*). *Class No: 664.8.022*

Canning

[6699]

UNITED NATIONS. Industrial Development Organization. **Information sources on the canning industry.** New York, United Nations, 1975. xii, 83p. (*UNIDO guide in sources of information, no. 19.*)

649 items in 12 sections: 1. Professional, trade and research organizations, learned societies and special information services - 2. Directories - 3. Sources of statistics, marketing and other economic data - 4. Basic handbooks, textbooks and manuals - 5. Monograph series - 6. Current periodicals - 7. Current abstracting and indexing journals - 8. Proceedings, papers and reports - 9. Specialized dictionaries and encyclopaedias - 10. Bibliographies - 11. Films and

....*(contd.)*
catalogues - 12. Other potential sources of information (E. Legislation; H. Packaging). 'Bibliographical sources used ...'.
Class No: 664.8.036.5

Freezing

[6700]
DESROSIER, N.W. *and* **TRESSLER, D.K. Fundamentals of food freezing.** Westport, Conn., AVI Publishing Co., 1977. vii, [2], 629p. illus., graphs, tables.
39 contributors. 16 chapters (3. Freezing vegetables ... 7. Freezing fish ... 10. Freezing of egg products ... 13. Microbiology of frozen foods - 14. The nutritive value of frozen foods ... 16. Warehousing and food cabinets). Each chapter has 'Additional reading'. Index, p.616-29. US slanted. *Class No:* 664.8.037

[6701]
Frozen and chilled foods year book 1998-99. Redhill, Surrey, DMG Business Media, 1998. 303p. £128; $224.
Suppliers of fish and fish products ... Suppliers of dairy produce - Processors - Packers - Agents and their products - Brand names - Frozen Food Federation members - Producers - Organizations - Wholesalers - Public cold stores: geographical guide - Contractors - Plant - Packaging - Machinery and equipment. Frozen food centres. *Class No:* 664.8.037

Meat

[6702]
KINSMAN, D.M., *ed.* **International meat science dictionary.** Storrs, Conn., University of Connecticut, 1978. 282p.
862 specialised, English/American-based terms, with equivalents and indexes in German, French, Spanish and Russian. Appended list of meat-research institutions in 32 countries. *Class No:* 664.91

[6703]
LEVIE, A. Meat handbook. 4th ed. Westport, Conn., AVI Publishing Co., 1979. [xi], 338p. illus., diagrs., graphs, tables. ISBN: 0870553151.
First published 1963.
18 chapters: 1. Livestock - 2. Slaughter and inspection ... 5. Refrigeration ... 12. Beef hindquarters ... 14. Veal - 15. Lamb ... 17. Processed, smoked and variety meats - 18. Cooking palatability. Detailed, analytical index. The 4th ed. includes revised grading standards and new roasting techniques. *Class No:* 664.91

[6704]
UNITED NATIONS. Industrial Development Organization. **Information sources on the meat-processing industry.** Rev. ed. New York, United Nations, 1976. xii, 86p. (*UNIDO Guides to information sources, no.1.*)
760 items. 11 sections: 1. Professional, trade and research organizations, learned societies and special information services - 2. Directories- 3. Sources of statistics, marketing and other economic data - 4. Basic handbooks, textbooks and manuals - 5. Current periodicals - 6. Current abstracting and indexing periodicals - 7. Proceedings, papers and reports - 8. Specialized dictionaries and encyclopaedias - 9. Bibliographies - 10. Films and film catalogues - 11. Other potential sources of information (*e.g.* consulting and engineering services) 'Bibliographical sources used ...'. *Class No:* 664.91

Fish

[6705]
AITKEN, A., *and others eds.* **Fish handling and processing.** 2nd ed. Edinburgh, HM Stationery Office, 1982. v, 192p. illus., diagrs., tables. ISBN: 0114917418.
First published 1965.
15 contributors. 16 chapters (*e.g.* 2. Basic facts about fish; 4. Handling wet fish at sea; 10. Smoking; 11. Canning; 12. Shellfish; 13. Other fish products (*e.g.* fish paste, salted fish); 16. Quality assessment and quality control). Detailed, analytical index. *Class No:* 664.95

Oils, Fats & Waxes

Bibliographies

[6706]
UNITED NATIONS. Industrial Development Organization. **Information sources on the vegetable oil processing industry.** New York, United Nations, 1973. xii, 90p. (*UNIDO guides to information sources, no. 7.*)
494 entries 11 sections: 1. Addresses of professional, trade and research organizations, learned societies and special information services - 2. Directories - 3. Sources of statistical and economic data -

....*(contd.)*
4. Basic handbooks, textbooks, and manuals - 5. Current periodicals - 6. Current abstracting and indexing periodicals - 7. Proceedings, papers and reports - 8. Specialized dictionaries and encyclopaedias - 9. Bibliographies - 10. Films -11. Other potential sources of information. (*e.g.* meetings and conferences). Appended list of bibliographical sources used. *Class No:* 665(01)

Handbooks & Manuals

[6707]
Essential oils and waxes. Linskins, M.F. *and* Jackson, J.E., *eds.* Berlin, Springer, 1991. xviii,337p. diagrs. (*Modern methods of plant analysis. New series, v.12.*) ISBN: 3540189157.
27 contributors. 17 papers, with references. 102 diagrs. *Class No:* 665(035)

Dictionaries

[6708]
SOLOMON, B. Dictionnaire de la technologie des corps gras en cinq langues: français, anglais, allemand, espagnol, italien. Paris, Institut des Corps Gras, 1971. iii, 62p.
660 French-base terms concerning fats, with equivalents and indexes in English, German, Spanish and Italian. *Class No:* 665(038)

Periodicals

[6709]
Journal of the American Oil Chemists Society. Chicago, Ill., the Society, 1939-. v.1(1)-. Monthly.
'Abstracts' section, monthly; *c.*2,000 abstracts pa. Coverage: biochemistry and nutrition; edible proteins; drying oils and paints; fats and oils. *Class No:* 665(051)

Progress Reports

[6710]
HAMILTON, R.J. *and* **BHATTI, A. Recent advances in chemistry and technology of fats and oils.** London & New York, Elsevier, 1987. xii, 188p. illus., graphs, tables.
8 contributors; 8 contributions (*e.g.* 'Physical properties of fats and oils' (15 references); 'The analysis of lipids with special reference to milk fat' (115 references)). Author and subject indexes. *Class No:* 665(055)

Tables & Data Books

[6711]
INTERNATIONAL UNION OF PURE AND APPLIED CHEMISTRY. Standard methods of the analysis of oils, fats and derivatives. 6th ed. Oxford, etc., Pergamon Press, 1979. Part 1 (sections 1&3). xxiv, 170p. graphs, tables. (*First published 1930.*)
1. *Oleaginous seeds and fruits.* 2. *Oils and fats.*
First supplement published 1992. *Class No:* 665(083)

Cosmetics & Perfumery

Bibliographies

[6712]
UNITED NATIONS. Industrial Development Organization. **Information sources on essential oils.** New York, UNIDO 1981. 94P. $4. (*UNIDO guides to sources of information no.38.*)
Lists entries covering oils used in the cosmetics and perfume industries. *Class No:* 665.57/.58(01)

Handbooks & Manuals

[6713]
Harry's cosmeticology. Wilkinson, J.B. *and* Moore, R.J., *eds.* London, G. Goodwin, 1987. xv, [1], 934p. illus., diagrs., tables, chemical structures. ISBN: 0711456798.
First published 1940.
4 parts, with documented chapters: 1. The skin and skin products - 2. The nails and nail products - 3. The hair and hair products - 4. The teeth and dental products. Chapter 15: 'Sunscreen, suntan and antisunburn products' (p.222-60. 81 references). Appendix: Proprietary materials cited, p.899-913. Index p.913-34. Well-researched. *Class No:* 665.57/.58(035)

[6714]

MÜLLER, P.M. *and* LAMPARSKY, D. **Perfumes:** art, science and technology. London, Elsevier, 1991. viii,658p. illus., tables, chemical formulas. £95. ISBN: 1851665730.

31 contributors. 20 chapters in 3 parts, covering trapping and classification of odours, composition, production, research, etc. Extensive references for some chapters (*e.g.* 3. 'Semiochemicals' carried 236). Detailed index includes chemical and trade names. *Class No:* 665.57/.58(035)

[6715]

POUCHER, W.A. **Perfumes, cosmetics and soaps.** Jouhar, A.J., *ed.* 9th ed. London, Chapman & Hall, 1991-. V.1 illus., tables.

First published 1923; 8th ed. 1974-5.

V.1 (vii,349p. ISBN: 0412272403) is part of 'A dictionary of the raw materials of perfumery and some cosmetics and toiletry products'. Entries (ABIR ... YLANG-YLANG oils) provide data on sources, appearances, odour; physical; uses. Appendix: 'Materials with IFRA guidelines, but not listed in Poucher's'. *Class No:* 665.57/.58(035)

Dictionaries

[6716]

CARRIÉRE, G. **Dictionary of surface-active agents, cosmetics and toiletries,** in English, French, German, Spanish. Italian, Dutch and Polish. Amsterdam, etc., Elsevier, 1978. 198p. £78.90. ISBN: 0444998098.

686 English-base terms, with equivalents and indexes in French, German, Spanish, Italian, Dutch and Polish. Covers the principal languages used in the industry. *Class No:* 665.57/.58(038)

[6717]

—CARRIÉRE, G. Lexicon of detergents, cosmetics and toiletries. Amsterdam, etc., Elsevier, 1966. ii, 204p. DFl.140. (*Elsevier lexica,* 8.) ISBN: 0444400990.

Part 1, *Detergents* (257 numbered entries), is a revision of G. Carriéres *Detergents* (1960). English-base terms, with French, Spanish, Italian, Portuguese, German, Dutch, Swedish, Danish, Norwegian, Russian, Polish, Finnish, Czech, Hungarian, Rumanian, Greek, Turkish and Japanese equivalents and indexes. Part 2, *Cosmetics and toiletries* (entries 258-523), also English-base has French, Spanish, Italian, Portuguese, German, Dutch and Swedish equivalents and indexes. *Class No:* 665.57/.58(038)

Reviews & Abstracts

[6718]

The Fritzsche - D & O Library bulletin: a monthly checklist of current literature covering research on perfume and flavour raw materials, essential oils, aromatic chemicals and their application in industry, with a special section on sensory problems and procedure. New York, Fritzsche, Dodge & Olcott, Inc., 1958-. Monthly. Free to qualified personnel.

Formerly *Fritzsche Library bulletin,* 1957-68. Originally included in *Perfumery and essential oil record.*

About 1,500 references pa., in 5 sections. No indexes. *Class No:* 665.57/.58(048)

Tables & Data Books

[6719]

ASH, M. *and* ASH, I. **Handbook of cosmetic and personal care additives:** an international guide to more than 15,000 products by trade name, function, composition and manufacturer. Aldershot, Hants., Gower, 1994. xx, 960p. ISBN: 0566074702.

About 15,000 trade name ingredients. 4 parts: Trade name reference - 2. Trade name/function cross reference - 3. Chemical component cross reference - 4. Manufacturers directory. 6 appendices, *e.g.* CAS Registry number-to-chemical cross reference. Available on CD-ROM from the publisher (£195). *Class No:* 665.57/.58(083)

[6720]

FLICK, E.W. **Cosmetics additives:** an industrial guide. Park Ridge, N.J., Noyes, 1991. xxx,886p. ISBN: 0851512554.

About 4,000 cosmetics additives, A-Z by manufacturer. Data include tradename, typical chemical properties, applications. No index, but detailed contents list. *Class No:* 665.57/.58(083)

Histories

[6721]

KENNETT, F. History of perfume. London, Harrap, 1975. 208p. illus., tables.

Chapters: The Far East - The land of the Nile - The Fertile Crescent - The Classical World - The World of Byzantium and Islam - Medieval England - Renaissance expansion - Perfumes from Paris - The fragrance industry. Further reading. Appended table of the most important natural ingredients used in perfumery today. Detailed, analytical index. Quotations - a feature. *Class No:* 665.57/.58(091)

Petroleum Industry

Abbreviations & Symbols

[6722]

D&D **oil standard abbreviator.** Association of Desk and Derrick Clubs, *comps.* 4th ed. Tulsa, Ok., PennWell Books, 1994. *c.*200p. ISBN: 0878144226.

First published 1973

About 11,500 abbreviations and definitions. 7 appendices (7. 'Common oilfield spellings'). Small format; a wealth of information. *Class No:* 665.6(003)

Databases

[6723]

APILIT. New York, API EnCompass.

Worldwide coverage of nonpatent literature pertaining to the petroleum and petrochemical industry since 1964. Over 500,000 records; updated weekly. Available on DIALOG, files 354, 954, Questel/ORBIT, STN International.

67 annotated entries on petroleum databases feature in the *Guide to the petroleum reference literature* (1987), p.65-129. *Class No:* 665.6(003.4)

[6724]

—APIPAT. New York, API EnCompass.

Covers patents in the petroleum and petrochemical industry. Over 250,000 records; updated monthly. Available on DIALOG, files 353, 953, and STN International. *Class No:* 665.6(003.4)

Bibliographies

[6725]

LESTER, D.E. 'Liquid fuels'. *Information sources in energy technology* (Editor, L.J. Anthony. 1988), p.200-24. London, Butterworth, 1988.

Melvin, A, 'Gaseous fuels', *op.cit.,* p.225-45, similarly structured, has 41 references.

Introduction - Books, monographs, reviews - Journals - Patents - Conference proceedings - Reports - Encyclopedias, handbooks, directories, standards - Trade literature - Statistics and databooks - Abstracting and indexing services - Bibliographies - Organizational sources. *Class No:* 665.6(01)

[6726]

PEARSON, B.C. *and* ELLWOOD, K.B. **Guide to the petroleum reference literature.** Littleton, Colo., Libraries Unlimited, 1987. xi, 193p. ISBN: 0872874737.

11 sections: 1. Guides to the literature and bibliographies - 2. Indexing and abstracting services - 3. Dictionaries - 4. Encyclopedias and yearbooks - 5. Handbooks, manuals and basic texts - 6. Directories - 7. Statistical sources - 8. Databases - 9. Periodicals - 10 Professional and trade associations - 11. Publishers. Sections 1-9 comprise 420 numbered entries. Author/title and subject index. 'For library school students new to the field' (*Marine and petroleum geology,* v.5(3), August 1988). *Class No:* 665.6(01)

[6727]

Petroleum and marine technology information guide: a bibliographic sourcebook and directory of services. Myers, A., *and others, eds.* 4th ed. London, Spon, 1993. x, 405p. ISBN: 0419182101.

First published 1981; 3rd ed. 1988 as *Offshore information guide.*

In 4 sections: A. Bibliography with offshore and petroleum literature classification - B. Organizations providing information services - C. Online databases and CD-ROMs - D. Directory (addresses relevant to petroleum and marine technology). Comprehensive, but in need of updating to include Internet and web-based information sources. *Class No:* 665.6(01)

Handbooks & Manuals

[6728]

CAMPBELL, C.J. **The Golden century of oil, 1950-2050:** the depletion of resource. Dordrecht, Kluwer, 1991. xv,348p. diagrs., graphs, tables. £64. ISBN: 0792314425.

3 parts: 1. World assessment - 2. Regional assessment - 3. Production by country and giant oil fields. 'Units of measurement and conversion factors' precedes. *Class No:* 665.6(035)

[6729]

International petroleum encyclopedia. Tulsa, Oklahoma, PennWell, 1995. 359p. col. illus., diagrs., graphs, tables, maps. ISBN: 0878144439.

Areas: North America; Latin America; Asia-Pacific; Middle East; Africa; Europe. Sections on worldwide production, prices, refining, refinery catalysis, pipelines. Advertisers index. *Class No:* 665.6(035)

[6730]
JENKINS, G. **Oil economists' handbook.** 5th ed. London and New York, Elsevier, 1989. 2v. ISBN: 1851683452, set.
V.1. Statistics [to 1987]. xvi,467p. £110. 29 sections (1. Crude oil prices ... 29. Oil quality data and conversion factors).
V.2. vii,396p. £90. Dictionary: an encyclopedic glossary; Chronology of significant events (to January 1989); Directory of organizations, under countries. V.2 includes a bibliography, p.375-6. *Class No:* 665.6(035)

[6731]
RIVA, J.P. **World petroleum resources and reserves.** Boulder, Colo., Westview Press, 1983. xxiii, 355p. illus., diagrs., tables. ISBN: 0865314462.
11 documented chapters (1. The occurrence of petroleum - 2. Exploration and production (27 references) ... 5. Reserves, resources and reserve/production ratios ... 7. The petroleum prospects of the United States (83 references) ... 11. Worldwide petroleum). Detailed, non-analytical index. About 150 tables. *Class No:* 665.6(035)

Dictionaries

Polyglot

[6732]
English - Azerbaijan - Russian dictionary on oil field industry. Kuliev, A.S., *ed.* 2nd ed. Baku, Aziz, 1995. 772p. £55. ISBN: 5824000069.
First published 1958.
About 17,700 English-base terms, with equivalents. No indexes; no guides to pronunciation. A poor quality publication, but few dictionaries cover Azerbaijan and the oil industry is developing rapidly there. *Class No:* 665.6(038)=00

[6733]
EUROPEAN COMMUNITIES COMMISSION. **Onshore/offshore oil & gas multilingual glossary:** a glossary of terms concerning the exploration and exploitation of oil and gas resources, in Danish, German, English, Spanish, Italian and Dutch. London, Graham & Trotman, for the Commission, 1979. 490p. ISBN: 0860101843.
573 sentences in the 6 languages. Sentences 1-381 are based on the original English texts, and sentences 382-573, on original French texts. *Class No:* 665.6(038)=00

[6734]
Fachwörterbuch: Carbochemie. Petrochemie: Englisch/Deutsch/Französisch/Russisch. [Dictionary of coal chemistry and petrochemistry: English/German/French/Russian.] Leipnitz, W., *ed.* Berlin, Paris, Alexandre Hatier, 1992. 304p. ISBN: 3861170396.
8000 English-based entries, with equivalent indexes. *Class No:* 665.6(038)=00

[6735]
KETCHIAN, S., *and others.* **Dictionnaire pétrolier des techniques de diagraphie, forage et production,** russe-français-anglais-allemand... [Technical petroleum dictionary of well-logging, drilling and production terms.] Paris Éditions Technip, 1965. xxxi, 334p. illus. (pl.).
7,770 numbered Russian terms, with French, English and German equivalents and indexes. Genders are stated. Bibliography, p.xvi-xxxi. 25 plates (*e.g.* drawing of a complete diesel-mechanical drilling-rig layout, with keyed parts). *Class No:* 665.6(038)=00

[6736]
—LEIPNITZ, W. **Erdölverarbeitung und Petrochemie:** Englisch/Deutsch/Französisch/ Russisch. Wiesbaden, Brandstetter, 1976. 268p. tables. ISBN: 3870979731.
About 6,000 English-based terms in petroleum processing and petrochemistry, with German, French and Russian equivalents and indexes. *Class No:* 665.6(038)=00

English

[6737]
HYNE, N.J. **Dictionary of petroleum exploration, drilling and production.** Tulsa, Oklahoma, Penn Well Books, 1990. [v],623p. illus. ISBN: 0878143521.
About 20,000 terms. Definitions range from a single word to one column (*e.g.* 'Sucker-rod pump'). Well-produced. *Class No:* 665.6(038)=20

[6738]
LANGENKAMP, R.D., *ed.* **The Illustrated petroleum reference dictionary.** 4th ed. Tulsa, Ok., PennWell Books, 1994. vii, 903p. illus. ISBN: 0878144234.
3rd ed. 1985.
Combines a dictionary of *c.*5,000 terms (apparently based on the editor's *Handbook of oil industry terms and phrases* (4th ed. 1994)) with other features, - D&D (Desk and Derrick Club) standard oil abbreviations, p.527-666; and 'Universal conversion factors', p.667-903. Very small illus. *Class No:* 665.6(038)=20

[6739]
STEVENS, P., *ed.* **Oil and gas dictionary.** London, Macmillan, 1988. 270p. graphs, tables. £45. ISBN: 033337844x.
About 2,000 entries, A-Z, some at length (*e.g.* 'Crude oil prices', p.39-46). Includes financial, business and general economic terms. Cross-references; abbreviations. Chronology, 1859-1986, p.221-37. Appended 'Energy data conversion tables' (*e.g.* 'Metric ton oil equivalents of gaseous fuels and electricity'). 'Highly recommended' (*Choice,* May 1989, p.1500). *Class No:* 665.6(038)=20

[6740]
TVER, D.F. *and* BERRY, R.W. **The Petroleum dictionary.** New York, etc., Yan Nostrand Reinhold, 1980. [xii], 374p. illus., diagrs., tables. ISBN: 0448240465.
About 4,000 entries (1-20 lines each). Claims to be first combined dictionary-handbook 'that covers virtually all aspects of the petroleum industry' (*Preface*). Stresses geological aspects. *Class No:* 665.6(038)=20

German

[6741]
PERSCH, F., *ed.* **Wörterbuch deutsch-englisch, englisch-deutsch: Erdöl und Erdgas,** mit besonderer Berüchsichtigung der Lagerstättenkunde und Gewinnung. Goslar, Hübener, 1970. 671p.
'Petroleum and natural gas dictionary, with special reference to exploration and exploitation, including offshore operations'.
About 12,000 entry-words in each part (English-German, p.9-325; German-English, p.329-671). Separate lines for sub-entries. German genders are stated. *Class No:* 665.6(038)=30

French

[6742]
MOUREAU, M. *and* BRACE, G. **Dictionnaire des sciences et techniques du pétrole:** anglais-français, français-anglais. [Dictionary of petroleum technology: English-French, French English.] 3rd ed. Paris, Technip, 1993. xxi, 990p. £130. ISBN: 2710806487.
First published in 1963 as *Dictionnaire technique des termes untilisés dans l'industrie du pétrole;* 2nd ed. 1977.
Nearly 70,000 terms, some with explanations (*e.g.* 'chemical': 1 1/3 columns). Includes abbreviations, technical names and colloquialisms. In between the two sequences, a list of symbols and conversion tables on tinted paper. *Class No:* 665.6(038)=40

[6743]
—AMOUD, M. *and* ZUBINI, F. **Les termes pétroliers:** dictionnaire anglais-français. Paris, Dunot, 1981. xii, 267p.
Includes *c.*6,000 entries, including abbreviations. Sources, p.ix-xii. Essentially practical. *Class No:* 665.6(038)=40

Reviews & Abstracts

[6744]
International petroleum abstracts incorporating offshore abstracts. London, Wiley Ltd, on behalf of the Institute of Petroleum, London, 1921-. Quarterly. ISSN: 03094944.
About 2,000 abstracts pa. Sections: Onshore oil and gas exploration - onshore oil and gas production - onshore oil and gas technology - Refining and related processes - Products - Offshore oil and gas exploration - Offfshore oil and gas production - Offshore oil and gas technology - Computer applications - Economics and marketing - Education and training - Pollution. Author index per issue; author and subject indexes annually. Available online. *Class No:* 665.6(048)

[6745]
Petroleum abstracts. Tulsa, Oklahoma, University of Tulsa, 1961-. Weekly. ISSN: 00316423.
About 10,000 abstracts pa., on petroleum exploration and production of crude oil and gas. Includes patents. Online as 'Petroleum exploration and production', a restricted file on DIALOG. A leading current-awareness source of petroleum exploration and production. Also available on CD-ROM (Dialog; updated 3 times pa.). *Class No:* 665.6(048)

[6746]
Petroleum/energy business news index. New York, American Petroleum Institute, 1975-. Monthly.
About 1,500 items per issue. About 120 journals are monitored over the year, plus news items reported in *API abstracts/Literature* and *API abstracts/Oilfield chemicals.* Arranged under subjects, 'Abandonment' ... 'Zinc'. Very small type. Available for online search, P/E NEWS. *Class No:* 665.6(048)

Periodicals

[6747]

Petroleum economist: the international energy journal. London, Petroleum Economist, 1934-. Monthly. tables, maps. £230pa. ISSN: 0306395x.

Up-to-date statistics and international spread are a feature. Editions in English and Japanese. Also available online. *Class No:* 665.6(051)

Yearbooks & Directories

[6748]

ANEP 98 European Petroleum year book. Hamburg, Urban-Verlag, 1998. v.p. maps, tables. ISSN: 03426947.

European industry data in 4 sections: 1. Fields, refineries, pipelines - 2. Statistics - 3. Companies' directory - 4. Suppliers' directory and buyers' guide. *Class No:* 665.6(058)

[6749]

'Financial Times' energy yearbook oil and gas 1999. London, FT Energy, 1998. Annual. xli, 462p. tables. £195. ISBN: 184083059x.

Companies : upstream (entries 1-330) - Companies: downstream (entries 331-563) - Brokers and traders (entries 564-613) - Associations (entries 614-694). Geographical and company indexes. 4 tables (*e.g.* World oil consumption). *Class No:* 665.6(058)

Standards

[6750]

INSTITUTE OF PETROLEUM. Standard methods for analysis and testing of petroleum and its products, and British Standard 2000 parts, 1998.. Chichester, Wiley, 1998. 2v., v.p. diagrs., tables. CD-ROM. £325. ISBN: 0471981982.

V.1 *Methods IP1-280.*

V.2 *Methods IP281-402.*

Provides standards and tentative methods of analysis and testing, plus methods jointly established by the Institute of Petroleum and the American Society for Testing and Materials (ASTM). An essential reference source for chemists and engineers in this field. A CD-ROM with complete text and artwork is included in the purchase price. *Class No:* 665.6(083.74)

Biographies

[6751]

'Financial Times' who's who in world oil and gas. London, FT Energy, 1979-. Annual. ISSN: 01413236.

The 1998 vol. has about 3,500 entries for key personnel from commercial, academic and government fields. Data include status, qualifications and a contact address. Index of organizations. *Class No:* 665.6(092)

Worldwide

[6752]

OPEC, its member states and world energy market. Brown, G., *ed.* 2nd ed. Harlow, Essex, Longman Group, 1991. xxiv, 680p. charts, tables, maps. £95. ISBN: 0582085276.

4 major sections: an overview of world oil and gas; OPEC and other international organizations; individual OPEC country surveys (Algeria ... Venezuela); chronology, 1960-90. *Class No:* 665.6(100)

[6753]

ORGANIZATION FOR ECONOMIC COOPERATION AND DEVELOPMENT. Annual oil and gas statistics, and main historical series. [Statistics Annuelles ...] Paris, International Energy Agency. Annual. diagrs., graphs, tables.

Numerous tables. 4 main sections: 1. Summary tables (areas and countries) - 2. Supply of products - 3. Finished products - 4. Imports and exports.

BP statistical review of world energy (London, British Petroleum Co., Ltd.) is annual. *Class No:* 665.6(100)

Europe

[6754]

Annual bulletin of liquid fuel statistics for Europe. New York, Economic Commission for Europe, 1968-. Annual.

Tables of liquid fuel statistics appear under 'Primary energy' (crude petroleum; other inputs to petroleum) and 'Derivative energy' - light products (aviation and motor gasoline; jet fuel; kerosene; naphthas) and heavy products (gas/diesel) oil; residual fuel oil; other petroleum products. Footnoted sources. Appended 'Definitions and general notes'. 'Europe' includes Russia, plus USA and Canada. In English, French and Russian. *Class No:* 665.6(4)

Great Britain

[6755]

BRITISH PETROLEUM. Our petroleum industry: a handbook dealing with the organization and functions of an integrated international oil company, with particular reference to the British Petroleum Company, Ltd. 5th ed. London, BP, 1977. 600p. illus., tables, maps.

First published 1947 as *Our Industry.*

58 contributors. 24 chapters (1. The structure of the industry ... 5. Petroleum exploration and development - 6. Drilling for oil and gas - 7. Production - 8. New oil and gas provinces: North Sea and Alaska ... 11. Transport of oil by tanker ... 13. Petroleum refinery products and petroleum refining processes ... 15. Proteins from petroleum - 16. International marketing ... 18. Natural gas and gas liquids - 19. Petroleum chemicals and polymers (plastics, rubbers and films) - 20. Research - 21. Computers and computer applications. - 22. Producing countries of the world - 23. Consuming areas of the world - 24. A brief history of BP. Glossary. 28 statistical tables. A mine of information. *Class No:* 665.6(410)

[6756]

—SHELL, Ltd. Petroleum handbook. 6th rev. ed. Amsterdam, Elsevier, 1983. xvii, 770p. illus., diagrs.

Roughly comparable to BP's *Our petroleum industry.* 257 illus.; 42 diagrs. *Class No:* 665.6(410)

[6757]

FERRIER, R.W. The History of the British Petroleum Company. Cambridge Univ. Press, 1982-. illus., facsims., ports., tables, maps.

V.1. *The developing years, 1901-1931.* 1982. xxx, 801p. £55.

V.2 *The Anglo-Iranian years, 1928-54.* 1994. *c.*600p.

V.1 has 13 chapters (1. The acquisition of the D'Arcy Concession, 1901 ... 13. The importance of the Persian dimension, 1926-32). Conclusion. Biographical details of important personalities p.688-97. Notes, p.698-775. Detailed, analytical index, p.776-804. Much emphasis has been placed on the primary archival material.

A full bibliography is promised in the final volume.

Class No: 665.6(410)

[6758]

GREAT BRITAIN. Department of Trade and Industry. The Energy report: oil and gas resources of the United Kingdom. London, H.M. Stationery Office. Annual. tables, maps. £40. ISBN: 0115154051.

Formerly *The Development of the oil and gas resources of the United Kingdom.*

The 1996 annual report (196p. £40) has 8 sections: 1. Historical overview - 2. Economic impact - 3. Regulatory regime - 4. Exploration, appraisal and licensing - 5. Reserves - 6. Development - 7. Production and disposal activities - 8. Review of fields. 14 appendices (*e.g.* 7. Gross gas production); 12 colour maps showing UK oil and gas activity. Known as the 'Brown' Book.

Class No: 665.6(410)

USA

[6759]

AMERICAN PETROLEUM INSTITUTE. Basic petroleum data book: petroleum industry statistics. Washington, The Institute, 1981-. 2pa. $250.

Includes worldwide statistical data on energy, reserves, exploration and drilling, finance, prices, demand, refining, imports, exports, offshore transportation, natural gas, Organization of Petroleum Exporting countries, and the environment. Includes a glossary and contact details for references. Available online. *Class No:* 665.6(73)

Thesauri

[6760]

AMERICAN PETROLEUM INSTITUTE. Thesaurus. [American Petroleum Institute]. Washington, The Institute, 1999. 380p. $225.

A-Z sequence of *c.*6,500 valid terms, plus cross references, for searching the APILIT and APIPAT databases. Also available on computer diskette. *Class No:* 665.6:025.43

Research Projects

[6761]

International petroleum research directory, 1994. 2nd ed. Harlow, Essex, Longman, 1994. vi, 740p. £125. ISBN: 0582238269.

First published 1992; published in association with The Petroleum Science and Technology Institute.

Over 2,700 projects listed by technical field (*e.g.* drilling; geochemistry; production equipment and systems, etc.). Data include researcher, institution, technical field, key words, duration, funding, etc. Research institutions, p.575-706. 2 indexes: researcher; key word. *Class No:* 665.6:061:061.62.005

Pipelines

[6762]
Lexique des pipelines à terre et en mer, anglais-français, français-anglais. [Glossary of onshore and offshore pipelines, English-French, French-English.] Paris, Editions Technip, 1979. xii, [1], 303p. £60.10.

English-French, p.1-133; Abbreviations; French-English, p.147-303. 'Pump' 1½ columns. 57 categories applied. List of sources.
Class No: 665.6.026

[6763]
Pipe line rules of thumb handbook: a manual of quick, accurate solutions to everyday pipe line engineering problems. McAllister, E.W., *ed.* 4th ed. Houston,Tx., Gulf, 1998. 604p. diagrs., graphs, tables. $79; £64. ISBN: 0884156710.

First published 1978; 3rd ed. 1993.
About 20 sections, closely subdivided (*e.g.* 'Corrosion/coatings' has 36 parts, including case histories). Extensive tables.
Class No: 665.6.026

Offshore Oil

Bibliographies

[6764]
CHRYSSOSTOMIDIS, M. **Offshore petroleum engineering:** a bibliographic guide to publications and information sources. New York, Nichols Publishing Co.; London, Kogan Page, 1978. 367p. ISBN: 089397045x.

Records *c.*2,500 books, conference proceedings and reports on offshore petroleum and related topics. Sections A-X (*e.g.* F. Oceanography and ocean environment description; G. Offshore structures engineering; J. Offshore petroleum engineering and development; T. Oil spills; V. Ocean law and management). 'Supplementary sources and suggestions for keeping up to date'. Sources consulted. Directory of publishers and other organizations. Permuted title, author and title indexes. *Class No:* 665.60(01)

[6765]
TAYLOR, G.E. **'Offshore engineering'.** *Information sources in engineering* (2nd ed. Editor L.J. Anthony. 1985), p.474-90. London, Butterworth, 1985.

Sections: Organizational sources - Legal aspects of offshore engineering - Primary sources of documentary information (journals; conferences; reports; patents; evaluated data) - Secondary sources of information (abstracting and indexing services; directories; books). Offshore engineering as a distinct topic was not featured in the 3rd ed. of *Information sources in engineering* (1996). *Class No:* 665.60(01)

Dictionaries

[6766]
RÅDET FOR TEKNISK TERMINOLOGI. **Ordbok for petroleumsvirksomhet,** norsk-engelsk-fransk. Oslo, Universitetsforlaget, 1976. 176p. charts. (*RTT 35.*) ISBN: 8200257290.

Dictionary of offshore oil operations. About 1,800 Norwegian-based terms, with definitions; English and French equivalents and indexes. Three sections: Boring production; Geophysics; Geology.
Class No: 665.60(038)

[6767]
WHITEHEAD, H. **An A-Z of offshore oil & gas:** an illustrated glossary and reference guide to the offshore oil & gas industries and their technology. 2nd ed. London, Kogan Page, 1983. 438p. illus., diagrs., tables, chemical structures. £27.50. ISBN: 0850386276.

First published 1976.
About 4,000 terms and abbreviations defined, plus cross-references. 30 appendices, p.315-426 (*e.g.* 1. Offshore oil and gas regions of the world; 29. Bibliography, p.433-4; 30. Abbreviations commonly used in relation to offshore oil and gas). Well illustrated (200 line-drawings, 20 full-page maps); keyed diagrams. 'An indispensable reference for engineers, economists and geoscientists concerned with petroleum resources' (*Choice*, v.21, October 1983, p.258).
Class No: 665.60(038)

Great Britain

[6768]
LOVEGROVE, M. **Lovegrove's guide to Britain's North Sea oil and gas.** 2nd ed. Cambridge, Energy Publications (Cambridge), 1983. xii, [i], 237+5p. diagrs., tables. £30. ISBN: 0905332296.

3 parts. 1. Government policies (*e.g.* licensing; taxation) - 2. Industry activities (*e.g.* exploration and appraisal; government revenues and company cash flow) - 3. Future. 7 appendices (1. UKCS Field broad sheets; 2. Company broad sheets; 3/4. Main UKCS gas and oil pipelines; 5. Main UKCS terminals; 6. UK crude oil refinery capacity statistics; 7. Conversion factors and miscellaneous information). 46 tables. *Class No:* 665.60(410)

[6769]
Offshore oil and gas directory 1998/99. Tonbridge, Kent, Miller Freeman, 1998. 1536p. £93. ISSN: 02655039.

Former title: *North seal oil and gas directory.*
Contents: Index to companies - Exploration and production companies - Drilling contractors - Offshore engineering, fabrication and project management companies - Manufacturers, suppliers and service contracting companies - Who's who in the industry - Index to products and services - Products and services buyers' guide - Official organizations - Conferences, exhibitions and courses. Available on CD-ROM. *Class No:* 665.60(410)

Information Services

[6770]
Information offshore. Glasgow, United Kingdom Offshore Supplies Office. Regularly updated. Gratis.

Lists information sources on offshore matters available from government departments and agencies. Also listed are government laboratories and organizations with interests in the UK offshore market. 'One of the most useful directories in this field' (*Information sources in engineering.* 2nd ed. Editor, L.J. Anthony. 1985, p.487).
Class No: 665.60:061:025.5

Refining

[6771]
MEYERS, R.A. **Handbook of petroleum refining processes.** New York, etc., McGraw Hill, 1986. [480]p. illus., diagrs., graphs, tables. £70. ISBN: 0070417636.

22 contributors. 11 parts (some with brief bibliographies appended): 1. Alkylation and polymerization - 2. Cracking ... 5. Isomerization ... 8. Separation processes ... 11. Gasification. Glossary. Abbreviations and acronyms. Detailed, analytical index (10p.). *Class No:* 665.66

Petrochemicals

Bibliographies

[6772]
UNITED NATIONS. Industrial Development Organization. **Information sources on the petrochemical industry.** New York, United Nations, 1978. $4. (*UNIDO guides to information sources, no.29.*) ISBN: 9211061644.

12 sections: 1. Professional, trade and research organizations, learned societies and special information services -2. Directories - 3. Sources of statistics, marketing and other economic data - 4. Basic handbooks, textbooks and manuals - 5. Monograph series - 6. Current periodicals - 7. Current abstracting and indexing periodicals - 8. Proceedings, papers and reports - 9. Specialized dictionaries and encyclopedias - 10. Bibliographies - 11. Films, tapes and film catalogues - 12. Other potential sources of information (A. Consulting and engineering services). Bibliographical sources used. Sections 2-3, 6-7, 10-12 have annotated entries. *Class No:* 665.7(01)

Handbooks & Manuals

[6773]
CHAPMAN, K. **The International petrochemical industry:** evolution and location. Oxford, Blackwell, 1991. xiv[i],322p. diagrs., graphs, maps. £45. ISBN: 0631160981.

12 chapters. References, p.294-312 (A-Z, authors). Detailed index. Emphasis is placed on the 'spatial evolution of the industry, both within individual countries and at the global scale' (*Introduction*).
Class No: 665.7(035)

[6774]
CLARK, G.H. **Industrial and marine fuels reference book.** London, etc., Butterworths, 1988. 528p. illus., diagrs. £95. ISBN: 0408014881.

26 sections (The choice of fuels - The chemistry of petroleum - Crude oil refining - Laboratory tests on fuels - Natural gas and LPG ... General operating problems of large diesel engines - Deposit formation and corrosion in steam boilers - Chimney stack emissions). Appendix. 239 illus. For mechanical, marine and plant engineers, plus shipowners, engine-builders and designers. *Class No:* 665.7(035)

Yearbooks & Directories

[6775]
Worldwide petrochemical directory. Tulsa, Ok., PennWell Publishing Co., 1962-. Annual. ISSN: 00842583.

Broad geographical regions: U.S.; Canada; Latin America; Europe; Africa; Middle East; Asia; Pacific. Each company entry includes list of key personnel, services, products. Company and geographical indexes; advertisers' index. Claims to identify all companies that manufacture petrochemicals. *Class No:* 665.7(058)

Tables & Data Books

[6776]
WELLS, G.M. Handbook of petrochemicals and processes. Aldershot, Hants., Gower, 1991. 400p. diagrs., chemical structures. £72. ISBN: 0566027755.

Data on *c.*100 petrochemicals, A-Z (*e.g.* 'Xylene': synonyms; processes; reaction; properties; yield; international classifications; applications; health and handling; major plants). 121 diagrs. Appendices include 'Transportation'; 'Health and safety'; 'Other organizations'. Licensor index; subject index. *Class No: 665.7(083)*

Glues & Adhesives

[6777]
Adhesives directory. Rickmansworth, Herts., Turret-Wheatland, Ltd. 232p. ISSN: 03053199.

8 sections, covering 'raw materials and additives for the adhesives-making industry, and of adhesives, mastics and related products used in all sectors and branches of industry'. Appended: Products, services directory. Advertisers index. Small format. *Class No: 665.93*

[6778]
HARRIS, L. Adhesives and adhesion: a guide to selected literature and sources of information. London, British Library, Science Reference and Information Service, 1986. 28p. £5. ISBN: 0712307303.

More than 100 briefly annotated entries. 6 sections: 1 Books (1.1: Adhesion and adhesives - general; 1.2: Particular types of adhesive; 1.3: Adhesives for specific application) - 2. Journals - 3. Abstracting and indexing journals - 4. Conference proceedings (published 1970-84) - 5. Business literature - 6. Patent publications. Science Reference Library Shelf marks are given. No index. *Class No: 665.93*

[6779]
KINLOCH, A.J. Adhesion and adhesives: science and technology. London, Chapman & Hall, 1987. xii,440p. illus., diagrs., graphs, tables. £35. ISBN: 041227440x.

8 chapters, closely subdivided, with extensive references: 1. Introduction - 2. Interfaced contract - 3. Mechanism of adhesion - 4. Surface pretreatments (17 sections; 227 references) - 5. Hardening of the adhesive - 6. Mechanical behaviour of adhesive joints - 7. Fracture mechanics of adhesive joints - 8. The service life of adhesive joints. Author and subject indexes. *Class No: 665.93*

[6780]
Klebstoff wörterbuch: German / English / French / Italian / Spanish / Dutch. [Adhesives dictionary: German / English / French / Italian / Spanish / Dutch.] Munich, Ad Liasion Bucherie, 1988. v.p. ISBN: 3574239025.

893 German-base terms. Coloured language indexes. *Class No: 665.93*

[6781]
SHIELDS, J. Adhesive handbook. 3rd ed. London, etc., Butterworth, 1984. [xii], 360p. ISBN: 0408013567.

First published 1970.

13 sections; *e.g.* 3. Adhesive selection; 4. Adhesive materials and properties (p. 30-86, including 6½p. of references); 5. Surface properties; 6. The bonding process; 7. Physical testing of adhesives; 8. Adhesive selection data; 9. Adhesive products directory (p.175-297); 10. Adhesives and trade services; 11. Glossary of adhesives technology terms; 12. Bibliography (books, reviews, journals), p. 342-52; 13. Useful addresses. No index. Well produced. *Class No: 665.93*

[6782]
SKEIST, I., ed. Handbook of adhesives. 3rd ed. New York, Van Nostrand Reinhold, 1990. $95. ISBN: 0342280130.

47 chapters on the physics, chemistry and applications of adhesives. Many diagrs., charts, tables. Chapter bibliographies (some plus 'further readings'). Lists of standards and commercial producers of materials. 'Recommended' (*Science and technology libraries*, V.11(4), Winter 1991, p.212). *Class No: 665.93*

Resins & Gums

[6783]
ASH, M. and ASH, I., comps. Handbook of plastic compounds, elastomers, and resins: an international guide by category, tradename, composition, and supplier. New York, VCH, 1992. xiv,872p. £132. ISBN: 1560815531.

Data on 15,000 tradename products. 4 parts: I. Tradename by category reference - II. Tradename cross reference - III. Chemical component cross reference - IV. Chemical manufacturer's directory. *Class No: 665.94*

[6784]
ASH, M. and ASH, I., comps. Resins. London, Edward Arnold, 1990. ix,381p. £69. (*What every chemical technologist wants to know about,* V.) ISBN: 0713136758.

4 parts: 1. Data on resins, A-Z (synonyms; tradename equivalents; category; processing; applications; properties; toxicity; storage). - 2. Tradename products and generic equivalents - 3. Generic chemical synonyms and cross references - 4. Tradename product manufacturers. *Class No: 665.94*

Glass Industry

Databases

[6785]
Glassfile Venice, International Commission on Glass.

Bibliographic and textual information; international coverage. About 63,000 records, updated bi-monthly. Available on ESA-IRS. *Class No: 666.1(003.4)*

Bibliographies

[6786]
UNITED NATIONS. Industrial Development Organization. Information sources on the glass industry. New York, United Nations, 1975. xii, 64p. $4. (*UNIDO guides to information sources, no.16.*)

11 sections: Professional, trade and research organizations, learned societies and special information sources - 2. Directories - 3. Sources of statistics, marketing and other economic data - 4. Basic handbooks, textbooks and manuals - 5. Current periodicals - 6. Current abstracting and indexing journals - 7. Proceedings, papers and reports - 8. Specialized dictionaries and encyclopaedias - 9. Bibliographies - 10. Film and film catalogues - 11. Other potential sources of information. 'Bibliographical sources used ...'. *Class No: 666.1(01)*

Encyclopaedias

[6787]
GRAYSON, M., ed. Encyclopedia of glass, ceramics and cement. New York., etc., Wiley: Interscience, 1985. xxviii, 925p. illus., diagrs, tables. (*Encyclopedia reprint series.*) ISBN: 047181931x.

'One in the series of carefully selected reprints from the world-renowned Kirk-Othmer *Encyclopedia of Chemical Technology*'.

57 contributors. Entries: Aluminum compounds (188 references) ... Silicon compounds, synthetic inorganic silicates. Section 'Clays (surveys)', p.320-36, has 99 references. Conversion tables, abbreviations and symbols precede. Detailed, analytical index, p.885-925. *Class No: 666.1(031)*

[6788]
NEWMAN, H. An Illustrated dictionary of glass: 2,442 entries, including definitions of wares, materials, processes, forms and decorative styles, from antiquity to the present. With an introductory survey of the history of glass making, by R.J. Charleston. London, Thames & Hudson, 1977. 351p. illlus. (incl. col.).

A companion to *Illustrated dictionary of ceramics*, by G. Savage and H. Newman (1974).

Includes histories of major factories and production centres. Some entries carry references. Cross-references. A finely illustrated volume, with 625 illus., 117 in colour. 'Intended primarily to define terms relating to glass and glassware ... and styles in various regions and periods, and also to describe some pieces that bear recognized names' (*Preface*). 'A necessary reference' (*Choice*, September 1978, p.843). *Class No: 666.1(031)*

[6789]
—**PHILLIPS, P., ed. The Encyclopedia of glass.** New York, 1981. 320p. illus. (incl. col.).

Covers both historical and regional aspects of glassmaking as well as techniques. It is complementary to Newman for its narrative approach and its 800 illus. Includes a glossary, a list of museums, and a grouped bibliography (p.298-314). *Class No: 666.1(031)*

Handbooks & Manuals

[6790]
BANSAL, N.P. and DOREMUS, R.H. Handbook of glass properties. Orlando, Florida, etc., Academic Press, 1986. viii, [1], 680p. graphs, tables. £121.50. ISBN: 0120781409.

5 parts (19 documented chapters): 1. Ornamental - 2. Thermodynamic and thermal properties - 3. Mechanical properties - 4. Electrical and transport properties - 5. Other properties. Appendices A-D (A. Glossary of symbols for data tables). Systems - property index.

....*(contd.)*
Subject index.
Available on CD-ROM as *Interglad* (Dai Nippon Printing Company Ltd), along with other reference sources. *Class No:* 666.1(035)

[6791]
Handbook of glass data. Mazurin, O.V., *and others, eds.* Amsterdam, Elsevier, 1983-. graphs, tables. ISBN: 0444416897.
Part A. *Silica glass and binary silicate glasses.*
Part B. *Single-component and binary non-silicant oxide glasses.*
Part C. *Ternary silicate glasses.*
Part D. *Ternary non-silicate oxide glasses.*
Part E. *Single-component, binary, and ternary oxide glasses.*
Part A (xv,669p.) includes much tabular data. References, p.597-642. Indexes: author, subject, formula.
Available on CD-ROM as *Interglad* (Dai Nippon Printing Company Ltd), which includes other glass sources as well.
Class No: 666.1(035)

[6792]
INTERNATIONAL COMMISSION ON GLASS. Electrical properties of glasses, glass-ceramics and amorphous solids: a bibliography covering the period 1967-1976. Charleroi, Belgium, the Commission, 1967-76. 2v.
V.1 (237p.) is devoted to chronological reference and author indexes; V. (267p.), to the subject index. 8,834 numbered entries. *Class No:* 666.1(035)

[6793]
McLELLAN, G.W. *and* **SHAND, E.B.**, *eds.* **Glass engineering handbook.** 3rd ed. New York, etc., McGraw-Hill, 1984. v.p. illus, graphs, tables. ISBN: 007044823x.
4 sections (23 documented chapters): 1. Glass technology - 2. Glass manufacture - 3. Applications - 4. Fibreglass (completely rewritten). 'Continuous-filament glass fiber applications' (38p.; 2p. of references). Appendixes: A. Specifications and standards of glass; B. Glossary; C. SI units. Detailed, analytical index (17p.). *Class No:* 666.1(035)

[6794]
SCHOLZE, H. Glass: nature, structure and properties. New York, Springer Verlag, 1991. *c.*425p. illus., graphs, tables, chemical structures. £70.50. ISBN: 0387973966.
First German ed. 1964. This ed. sponsored by the Institute of Glass Science and Engineering, New York State College of Ceramics; trans. by M.J. Lakin.
3 parts. 1. Introduction - 2. Nature and structure of glass - 3. Properties of glass. Bibliography, p.363-415 (1160 references). Author, subject indexes. *Class No:* 666.1(035)

[6795]
UHLMANN, D.R. *and* **KREIDL, N.J.**, *eds.* **Glass science and technology.** Orlando, Florida, Academic Press, 1980-. illus., tables. ISBN: 0127067051.
1. *Glass-forming systems.* 1983. 465p.
2. *Processing.* 1984. 360p. £73.50.
3. *Viscosity and relaxation.* 1986. 412p.
4A. *Structure, microstructure and properties.* 1990. 360p. £88.50.
4B. *Advances in structural analysis.* 1990. 400p. £88.50.
5. *Elasticity and strength in glasses.* 1980. 282p. £47.50.
V.3 has 7 documented chapters (Viscoelasticity of glass -Mechanical relaxation in inorganic glasses - Rheology and relaxation in metal glasses - Technological aspects of viscosity - Annealing of glass - Rheology of polymeric fluids - Physical aging of polymer glasses). Index. 'For more broad-based physical science collections in academe and industry' (*Science & technical libraries*, v.8(2), Winter 1987/88, p.138). *Class No:* 666.1(035)

Dictionaries

Polyglot

[6796]
INTERNATIONAL COMMISSION ON GLASS. Dictionary of glass-making. Amsterdam, etc., Elsevier, 1983. xxii 402p.
First published 1965.
A trilingual list of 4,428 numbered terms (in English, French and German), with A-Z lists in each of the 3 languages.
Supplements to the 1965 ed. are available in nine other languages: Czech, Dutch, Italian, Japanese, Polish, Portuguese, Russian, Spanish, and Swedish. *Class No:* 666.1(038)=00

English

[6797]
ZEITLYN, M.Z., *comp.* **Dictionary of glass names.** St. Helens, Lancs., Pilkington Bros., 1970. 120p.
More than 2,200 entries on glass products from 42 countries, but primarily on Pilkington products (*e.g.* safety glass, insulating glass, optical and opthalmic glass). 2 sections: an A-Z list of glass names,

....*(contd.)*
stating maker, brief description of glass type, and classified section of types (*e.g.* 'laminated', 'ophthalmic', 'patterned'). *Class No:* 666.1(038)=20

German

[6798]
ELMER, T.H. German-English dictionary of glass, ceramics, and allied sciences. New York, etc., Interscience: Wiley, 1963. viii, 304p.
About 12,000 German words encountered in books, periodicals and patent literature. Includes many abbreviations and some common general words. Mostly equivalents; no German genders. Terms are categorized. Clear layout. *Class No:* 666.1(038)=30

Glossaries

[6799]
BRITISH STANDARDS INSTITUTION. Glossary of terms used in the glass industry. London, BSI, 1962. AMD 1963. 56p. (*BS 3447: 1962 (1997).*)
About 500 terms are defined. 8 sections, *e.g.* Types and properties of glass; raw materials; melting, forming and finishing processes; forms of glass and glassware; imperfections in glass: occupational terms. *Class No:* 666.1(038.1)

Reviews & Abstracts

[6800]
Boron in glass: quarterly bulletin of abstracts. London, Borax, Ltd., 1950-. Quarterly. gratis.
50 abstracts per issue on the use of boron in vitreous systems. Index per issue. *Class No:* 666.1(048)

[6801]
BRITISH GLASS MANUFACTURERS CONFEDERATION. Digest of information and patent review. Sheffield, the Confederation, [1980?]-. 4 pa. ISSN: 0962032x.
About 100 brief abstracts per issue. 9 classes: Container glass - Domestic - Enamels - Flat glass - Glass manufacture general - Glass ceramics - Glass fibre - Refractories - Special glasses. Patents (11 classes). Annual subject and author indexes. *Class No:* 666.1(048)

[6802]
Glass technology (Section A: *Journal of the Society of Glass Technology***).** Sheffield, Society of Glass Technology, 1960-. 6pa.
About 1200 abstracts pa. Coverage: Raw materials and batch preparation - Fuels, furnaces and instrumentation - Refractories - Processses - Auxiliary processes and equipment ... Glass fibres - Composites and polymers - Industrial, historical, economics and biography - Environmental aspects. Annual author and subject indexes.
Section B: *Journal of the Society of Glass Technology, - Physics and Chemistry of glasses. Class No:* 666.1(048)

Yearbooks & Directories

[6803]
European glass directory & buyers guide, 1997. Redhill, Surrey Fuels & Metallurgical Journals, 1997. 208p.
sections, include: Glass industry index - Products of the glass industry - Suppliers to the glass industry - Trade marks - Country by country trends - European trade associations. Advertisers' index. *Class No:* 666.1(058)

[6804]
Glass-fibre directory and databook. Starr, T.F., *comp.* 2nd ed. London, Chapman & Hall, 1997. xiv, 326p. tables. ISBN: 0412783703.
First published 1992.
Usual directory-type information on glass fibre reinforcements available worldwide, with specifications, manufacturer and agent. *Class No:* 666.1(058)

Enamels

[6805]
BRANDT, J., *and others.* **Emails, enamels, émaux, smalti: a dictionary in four languages.** Leverkusen, Farbenfabriken Bayer AG, 1960. 181p.
About 1,200 terms, with equivalents. 4 sequences: German-English-French-Italian; English-French-Italian-German; French-Italian-German-English; Italian-German-English-French. Genders are given. Some terms are categorized. *Class No:* 666.29

Ceramics

Bibliographies

[6806]

MURFIN, D. 'Ceramics'. *Information sources in metallic materials.* Editor, M.N. Patten, p.232-52. London, Bowker-Saur, 1989. (*Guides to information sources.*) ISBN: 0408014911.

Sections: Dictionaries and glossaries - Textbooks and monographs - Conference proceedings - Primary journal literature (83 titles) - Reports - Patents - Standards - Property data - Business statistics and company information - Directories and trade literature - Market research reports - Abstracts and other secondary sources - Online services. *Class No: 666.3/.7(01)*

[6807]

UNITED NATIONS. Industrial Development Organization. **Information sources on the ceramics industry.** New York, United Nations, 1976. xii, 68p. $4. (*UNIDO guides to information sources, no. 17.*)

493 entries. 11 sections: 1. Professional, trade and research organizations, learned societies and special information services - 2. Directories ... 4. Basic handbooks, textworks and manuals - 5. Current periodicals - 6. Current abstracting and indexing periodicals ... 9. Bibliographies ... 11. Other potential sources of information (*e.g.* D. Marketing, exporting and purchasing). 'Bibliographical sources issued ...'. *Class No: 666.3/.7(01)*

Encyclopaedias

[6808]

BROOK, R.J., *ed.* **Concise encyclopedia of advanced ceramic materials.** Oxford, etc., Pergamon Press, 1991. xvi,588p. illus., diagrs., graphs, tables, chemical structures. £100. (*Advances in materials science and engineering.*) ISBN: 0080347207.

137 articles, with references, A-Z, on chemical systems, steps in processing ceramics and particular applications and phenomena (*e.g.* 'Magnesium and alkaline - earth oxides', p.283-86: 5 sections, 2 tables, 7 references). Detailed, analytical index, 49p. Some material taken from *Encyclopedia of materials science and engineering (qv)* and the supplementary vols.; other material is newly commissioned, but will appear in the supplements as well. Although convenient in the form, not essential for libraries holding the *Encyclopedia* and supplements. *Class No: 666.3/.7(031)*

Handbooks & Manuals

[6809]

HAMER, F. *and* HAMER, J. **The Potter's dictionary of materials and techniques.** 3rd ed. London, A. & C. Black, 1991. 384p. illus., diagrs. £35. ISBN: 0812231120.

Covers materials, processes, equipment, chemical and physical properties, glazes, terminology and historical developments. Extensively illustrated. A standard; the major changes in the 3rd ed. include additional tables and extensive revisions of the articles on 'Raku' and 'Salt glazes'. *Class No: 666.3/.7(035)*

[6810]

Handbook of ceramics and composites. Cheremisinoff, N.D., *ed.* New York, Marcel Dekker, 1990-. v.1-.

V.1. *Synthesis and properties.*

V.2. *Mechanical properties and specialty applications.* 1992. 510p. ISBN: 0824780031.

V.2 has 20 contributors; 12 documented chapters. Detailed, analytical index. Other volumes to follow. *Class No: 666.3/.7(035)*

[6811]

Handbook of structural ceramics. Schwartz, M.M., *ed.* New York, McGraw-Hill, 1992. v.p. illus., diagrs., graphs, tables. $62.50. ISBN: 0070557195.

Numerous contributors. 9 chapters: 1. Introduction to ceramic materials ... 9. The future. Topics include processing techniques, mechanical property data, manufacturing, fabrication, assembly processes. Detailed, analytical index. 'A very important source book ... excellent' (*Choice*, November 1992, p.500). *Class No: 666.3/.7(035)*

[6812]

MORRELL, R. **Handbook of properties of technical and engineering ceramics.** National Physical Laboratory. London, H.M. Stationery Office, 1985-. pt.1-. illus. ISBN: 0114800529; 0114800537.

Part 1 (1985. 360p. £33) initiates a multi-part handbook by providing a broad comparison of the different types of ceramic. Part 2, *Data reviews*, section 1: *High alumina ceramics* (1987. 270p. £29.50) deals with the properties of a group of widely used types of materials. *Class No: 666.3/.7(035)*

[6813]

NEWMAN, A.C.D., *ed.* **The Chemistry of clays and clay minerals.** London, Longman. 1987. 480p. £63. (*Mineralogical Society monograph, no. 6.*) ISBN: 0582301149.

Covers not only the chemical constitution of the silicate clays, with associated iron, aluminium and manganese oxides and hydroxides, but also the properties of those materials most useful to man, - particularly industrially. 'A major contribution to clay science' (*Nature*, v.328, 13 August 1987, p.588). *Class No: 666.3/.7(035)*

Dictionaries

English

[6814]

DODD, A. **Dictionary of ceramics.** 3rd ed. Revised and updated by D. Murfin. London, Institute of Materials, 1994. [viii] 371p. diagrs., tables. ISBN: 0901716561.

About 3,500 terms, with some 2,000 new ones. This ed. takes account of new developments in engineering ceramics, new processes in whitewares, developments in machinery and test methods, and the impact of environmental legislation. *Class No: 666.3/.7(038)=20*

[6815]

McCOLM, I.J. **Dictionary of ceramic science and engineering.** 2nd ed. New York, Plenum Press, 1994. x, 384p. tables. $90. ISBN: 0306445425.

Some 13,000 entries — 4,000 new to this edition — defined and described (*e.g.* 'Kyanite': 15 lines). 18 tables in an appendix (17. 'Ceramic colours'). *Class No: 666.3/.7(038)=20*

German

[6816]

BAUR, J. **Dictionary of ceramics and earths:** English/German, German/English. [Wörterbuch Keramik und erden.] Weinheim, VCH, 1993. [xii], 555p. (*Parat.*) ISBN: 3527284095.

About 12,000 terms in each half covering ceramic processes in the chemical, physical and mechanical fields. Ceramics for the arts are included. *Class No: 666.3/.7(038)=30*

Italian

[6817]

Glossario ceramico, italiano/inglese, inglese/italiano. Faenza, Faenza Editrice S.p.A., 1983. 323p.

About 3,000 terms in each half. Ranges from brickware to ovenware, tiles to refractories, and from sanitary-ware to artistic ceramics. Pocket-sized dictionary. *Class No: 666.3/.7(038)=50*

Reviews & Abstracts

[6818]

Ceramic abstracts. American Ceramic Society, *comp.* Colombus, Ohio, American Ceramic Society, 1918-. 6pa. $310. ISSN: 00959960.

Originally published in *Journal of the American Ceramic Society*.

About 10,000 abstracts pa. 18 sections: 1. Abrasives ... 3. Cements, limes and plasters ... 5. Glass ... 9. Electronics ... 15. Engineering materials - 16. Chemistry and physics - 17. General - 18. Books. Keyword index per issue. Annual author and subject indexes.

Available online (about 157,000 records) via DIALOG (file 335), Questel/ORBIT and STN International; CD-ROM. *Class No: 666.3/.7(048)*

[6819]

World ceramics abstracts. Stoke-on-Trent, Staffs., Ceram Research ltd, 1989-. Monthly. ISSN: 09578897.

Formerly *British ceramic abstracts* (1942-1988); originally British Ceramic Society. *Abstracts* (1930-1941).

About 6,000 abstracts pa. 16 sections (*e.g.* Intermediate and semi-finished products; Processing and treatment (including machines)). Subject index per issue and annually. Online via Questel/ORBIT. *Class No: 666.3/.7(048)*

Refractories

[6820]

BRITISH STANDARDS INSTITUTION. **Glossary of terms relating to refractory materials.** London, BSI, 1990. 3 parts, diagrs. (*BS 3446: 1990(1996).*)

1. *General and manufacturing.* 68p.

2. *Applications in the coke, glass, cement and other non-metallurgical industries.* 52p.

....*(contd.)*

3. *Applications in the metallurgical industries.* 40p.

Part 1 has over 700 terms in a systematic order. Alphabetical index. *Class No: 666.7*

[6821]
FÉDÉRATION EUROPÉENNE DES FABRICANTS DES PRODUITS RÉFRACTAIRES. Vocabulaire: les produits réfractaires et leurs applications (sidérurgie, verrerie, cimenterie, etc.). 2. éd. Zurich, the Federation (PRE), 1973. 342p.

First published 1964.

2,214 French-base terms, with German, English and Italian equivalents. Applications of refractory products (steel, glass, cement industries, etc.). Reverse index in one A-Z sequence. *Class No: 666.7*

Gypsum

[6822]
VOLKART, K. Gips-Wörterbuch. Dictionnaire du gypse et du plâtre. [Gypsum and plaster dictionary.] Paris, Eyrolles; Wiesbaden, Bauverlag GmbH, 1971. xv, 176p.

Part 1: German-English-French. 1,452 numbered items. Genders are stated. Parts 2-3: French and English indexes. *Class No: 666.91*

Cement Industry

Bibliographies

[6823]
UNITED NATIONS. Industrial Development Organization. Information services on the cement and concrete industry. 2nd rev. ed. New York, United Nations, 1977. xii, 90p. $4. (*UNIDO guides to information sources, no.2. Rev.ed.*)

First published 1972.

690 entries. 12 sections: 1. Professional, trade and research organizations, learned societies and special information services - 2. Directories - 3. Sources of statistics, marketing and other economic data - 4. Basic handbooks, textbooks and manuals. -5. Monograph series - 6. Current periodicals - 7. Current abstracting and indexing periodicals - 8. Proceedings, papers and reports - 9. Specialized dictionaries and encyclopaedias - 10. Bibliographies - 11. Films and film catalogues - 12. Other potential sources of information (*e.g.* Patents and licences. Translation services). 'Bibliographical sources used ...'. *Class No: 666.94/.98(01)*

Handbooks & Manuals

[6824]
LABAHN, O. and KONKOLHAUS, B. Cement engineers' handbook. Translated by C. Amerongen from the 6th German edition. 4th English ed. Wiesbaden, Bauverlag GmbH, 1982. 794p. illus., tables. $90. ISBN: 3762509751.

Original as *Zement-Ingenieure*.

Sections: Raw materials - Cement chemistry; cement quality - Manufacture of cement - Handling and feeding systems; continous conveyors - Maintenance and wear - Lubricants, storage and consumption. Subject index. Subject coverage includes testing and design of laboratory facilites. Standard text, for specialists. *Class No: 666.94/.98(035)*

[6825]
Lea's chemistry of cement and concrete. Hewlett, P.C., *ed.* 4th ed. London, Arnold; New York, Wiley, 1998. xxi, 1053p. illus., diagrs., graphs, tables. ISBN: 0340565896.

First published 1935; 3rd ed. 1970.

19 contributors, 16 chapters covering all aspects of cement and concrete: history; components; manufacture; additives, etc. Most chapters have extensive references and notes(*e.g.* ch.10: 502 references). Author and subject indexes. For specialists. *Class No: 666.94/.98(035)*

Dictionaries

[6826]
AMERONGEN C., van. Zement-Wörterbuch. Herstellung und Technologie. Deutsch/Englisch, Englisch/Deutsch. [Dictionary of cement, manufacture and technology.] 2. Aufl. Wiesbaden, Bauverlage GmbH, 1986. 332p. £55.45.

First published 1967.

German-English and English-German dictionary of cement manufacture and technology. Each half has *c.*12,000 entry-words. German genders are given. *Class No: 666.94/.98(038)*

[6827]
ONISI, T.R., *comp*. Elsevier's dictionary of the cement industry, in five languages, English, French, German, Spanish and Japanese. Amsterdam, etc., Elsevier, 1987. xii, 520p. £150. ISBN: 0444426299.

5,488 English-based terms (categorized) with equivalents and indexes in French, German, Spanish and Japanese. Bibliography, p.xi-xii. 11 appendices in the 5 languages (*e.g.* 9. Weights and measures). Genders given. Some inclusion of words extraneous or in common usage. *Class No: 666.94/.98(038)*

Yearbooks & Directories

[6828]
World cement directory. Paris, Cembureau, 1958-. xii, 295p. tables, maps.

Covers over 100 countries, under regions: Africa; North America; Central America; South America; Middle East; Asia; Europe; Eastern Europe. Tabular data on companies, cement mills, fuel usage and coal mills, cement kilns. *Class No: 666.94/.98(058)*

Concrete

Databases

[6829]
Cement and concrete technical information/CACTI. Slough, Berks., Cement and Concrete Assocaiation, 1976-.

Online database, updated 6pa. with 250 items, on the use and performance of concrete. Host: DATASOLVE. *Class No: 666.97(003.4)*

Handbooks & Manuals

[6830]
DEWAR, J.D. and ANDERSON, R. Manual of ready-mixed concrete. 2nd ed. Glasgow, Blackie, 1992. x,245p. illus., graphs, tables. ISBN: 0751400793.

First published 1988.

11 chapters in 2 parts: 1. Technology (*e.g.* materials; properties; mix design; quality control) - 2. Practice (*e.g.* production; specification and supervision; ready-mixed concrete on site; organizations). References. Detailed, analytical index, p.241-45. *Class No: 666.97(035)*

[6831]
GAMBHIR, M.L. Concrete technology. New York, etc., McGraw-Hill, 1987. 304p. illus. £4.95. ISBN: 0074516442.

12 sections on manufacture and production of structural concrete. Concrete-making materials (2 sections) - Properties of fresh concrete - Properties of hardened concrete - Statistical quality control of concrete - Proportioning of concrete mixes - Production of concrete - Extreme weather concreting - Special concrete and concreting techniques - Form work - Inspection and testing - Repair technology for concrete structures. 78 illus. *Class No: 666.97(035)*

Dictionaries

[6832]
FÉDÉRATION INTERNATIONALE DE LA PRÉCONTRAINTE. Multilingual dictionary of concrete, in English, French, German, Spanish, Dutch and Russian. Amsterdam, etc., Elsevier, 1978. viii, 202p.

1,416 English-based terms, with equivalents and indexes in French, German, Spanish, Dutch and Russian. 'Recommended for technical and engineering libraries' (*Choice*, v.14(12), February 1978, p.1626). *Class No: 666.97(038)*

[6833]
TEKNISKA NOMENKLATURCENTRALEN. Betongteknisk ordlista, svensk, engelsk, fransk, tysk, dansk, finsk, norsk. Stockholm, The Centre, 1971. 366p. (*TNC 46.*) ISBN: 9171960465.

1,310 Swedish-based concrete terms; classified arrangement. English, French, German, Danish, Finnish and Norwegian equivalents, Indexes in all 7 languages. References, p.362-4. *Class No: 666.97(038)*

Yearbooks & Directories

[6834]
The Concrete year book, 1998. London, Thomas Telford Directories, 1997. Annual. v.p. £66. ISSN: 00698288.

General information on concrete and construction. Sections: 1. Consulting engineers - 2. Contractors - 3. Materials, products and services - 4. Plant and equipment - 5. Brand and trade names. - 6. Company data - 7. Associations and institutions - 8. Concrete editorial features. *Class No: 666.97(058)*

Colour

[6835]

DANGER, L.E.P. The Colour handbook: how to use colour in commerce and industry. Aldershot, Hants, Gower Technical Press, 1987. xxi, 687p. £50.

Three parts: 1. Principles of light and colour - 2. Principles of colour selection - 3. Colour catalogue (character, attributes, applications); colour groups. Bibliography, p.678-87. Primarily for marketing managers, but also of interest to advertising agents, designers, interior-decoration retailers. One notable drawback: the lack of an index. *Class No:* 667

Dyes & Dyeing

[6836]

PONTING, K.G. A Dictionary of dyes and dying. London, Mills & Boon, Ltd., 1980. [v], 207p. illus. ISBN: 0263063984.

Several hundred entries, some lengthy (*e.g.* 'Dyeing, history': p.53-58; 'Indigo': p.103-17). Bibliography (A-Z authors), p.189-207. 30 illus. The natural dyes are described in some detail. Sources include The Textile Institute and the Society of Dyers and Colourists. *Class No:* 667.2

[6837]

Sigma-Aldrich handbook of stains, dyes and indicators. Green, F.J. Milwaukee, WI, Aldrich Chemical Co., 1990. 776p. $70. ISBN: 0941633225.

Guide to 325 compounds used as stains, dyes and indicators, A-Z by common name. Full data, plus reference to other sources and spectra when easily available. *Class No:* 667.2

Printing Inks

[6838]

Printing ink manual. Leach, R.H., *and others, eds.* 5th ed. London, Blueprint, 1993. xxi, 993p. illus., diagrs., tables. £79. ISBN: 0948905816.

First published 1961. 4th ed. 1988.

17 chapters (*e.g.* 2. Printing processes - 3. Colour and colour matching - 4. Raw materials ... 6. Lithographic inks ... 10. Screen inks ... 13. Manufacture of inks and varnishes ... 17. Health, safety and the environment). Glossary of abbreviations. Extensive references. Detailed, analytical index. *Class No:* 667.5

Paints & Varnishes

Databases

[6839]

World surface coatings abstracts. Teddington, Middlesex, Paint Research Association, 1976-.

Online, bibliographic database, with abstracts, to research literature on paints and other surface coatings. Covers pigments, dyestuffs, resins, solvents, plasticisers, fire retardants, corrosion resistant finishes, industrial hazards, pollution, marketing, regulations and statistics. About 200,000 records, updated monthly. *Class No:* 667.6(003.4)

Bibliographies

[6840]

UNITED NATIONS. Industrial Development Organization. Information sources on the paint and varnish industry. New York, United Nations, 1975. xii, 76p. $5. (*UNIDO guides to information sources, no,. 18.*) ISBN: 9211061458.

585 numbered items. 12 sections: 1. Professional, trade and research organizations, learned societies and special information services - 2. Directories - 3. Sources of statistics, marketing and other economic data - 4. Basic handbooks, textbooks and manuals - 5. Monograph series - 6. Current periodicals - 7. Current abstracting and indexing periodicals - 8. Proceedings, papers and reports - 9. Specialized dictionaries and encyclopaedias - 10. Bibliographies - 11. Films - 12. Other potential sources of information (*e.g.* meetings and conferences; patents and licences). List of bibliographical sources used. Some sections are annotated. *Class No:* 667.6(01)

Dictionaries

[6841]

DOORGEEST, T., *and others.* **Elsevier's paint dictionary in four languages:** English, French, German and Dutch. Amsterdam, Elsevier, 1990. [xiv],292p. ISBN: 0444880682.

4,081 English base terms, with equivalents. French, German, Dutch indexes. *Class No:* 667.6(038)

[6842]

RAAFF, J.J. Index vocabulorum quadrilinguis: Verf en verris; Peintures et vernis; Paint and varnish; Farbe und Lack. [2nd ed.]. The Hague, Van Goor Zonen den Haag, 1965. 1129p.

First published 1958.

About 10,000 terms, in 4 languages. 4 sequences: Dutch-French-English-German; German-English-French-Dutch; English-German-Dutch-French; German-Dutch-French-English. *Class No:* 667.6(038)

[6843]

TEKNISKA NOMENKLATURCENTRALEN. Farg-och lackteknisk ordlista: svensk-engelsk-fransk-tysk-finsk. [Glossary of paint terms: Swedish-English-French-German-Finnish.] Stockholm, the Centre. 1967. 243p.

Includes lists of abbreviations of polymers and plasticisers, and of selected elements, and a list of Danish and Norwegian words that deviate appreciably from their Swedish counterparts. *Class No:* 667.6(038)

Reviews & Abstracts

[6844]

Paint titles. Paint Research Association Services, Teddington. Oxford, etc., Pergamon, for Paint Research Association, [1971]-. Weekly. ISSN: 01444425.

About 250 references per issue: 19 classes (1. Pigments, extenders & dyestuffs ... 19. Adhesives. Sealants. Patent supplement.

The Paint Research Association's *World surface coatings abstracts* is online. *Class No:* 667.6(048)

Periodicals

[6845]

European paint and resin news. London, Information Research, Ltd., 1984-. Monthly. ISSN: 02667800.

Formerly *Continental paint and resin news,* 1977-83.

Issues cover a range of items, including changes in the industry, marketing news and statistics, financial results and comparisons, recent technology developments, forthcoming symposia and exhihitions, and a European patents review. No index. *Class No:* 667.6(051)

Tables & Data Books

[6846]

ASH, M. *and* **ASH, I.,** *comps.* **Handbook of paint and coating raw materials.** Aldershot, Gower, 1996. 2v. (xvi, 1000; xvi, 589p.). ISBN: 0566077876.

V.1: *Trade name products.*

V.2: *Chemical products with trade name cross reference.*

Describes about 11,000 trade name and generic chemical ingredients used in the formulation of paint and coating products for industry and commerce. Data include chemical description, uses, properties. *Class No:* 667.6(083)

Metallurgy

Databases

[6847]

METADEX. Materials Park, Oh., ASM International; London, The Institute of Metals, 1966-.

METADEX is the major database for metals and metallurgy. About 950,000 records; updated monthly. The online version of *Metals abstracts.* Available from DIALOG, STN International, ERINS and other hosts. Also available on the World Wide Web from Cambridge Scientific Abstracts (URL: http://www.csa.com). *Class No:* 669(003.4)

CD-ROM

[6848]

Metals infodisk: the database of metal grades, standards and manufacturers. Ascot, Berks., Index House, 1999. 1 CD-ROM. £495.

Four components: Materials (designation; controlled vocabulary description; chemical composition; mechanical properties; heat treatment provisions, etc.) - Standards (bibliographic details of about 5,000 worldwide standards for metallic materials) - Manufacturers (contact details, etc.) - Facilities for in-house record creation and notes. *Class No:* 669(003.40)

Bibliographies

[6849]
PATTEN, M.N., *ed.* **Information sources in metallic materials.** London, etc., Butterworths, 1989. xvi,415p. tables. £40. (*Guides to information sources.*) ISBN: 0408014911.

17 contributors; 18 chapters, sub-divided. 2 parts: I. Materials (1. General sources - 2. Extraction metallurgy - 3. Iron and steel ... 7. Lead ... 9. Zinc ...); II. Applications (11. Powder metallurgy ... 14. Design ... 18. Materials for the packaging industry). Appendices: abbreviations and addresses of organizations. Index, 8p. Forms of literature (*e.g.* reports, patents) are treated in their relation to a particular metal or application; *e.g.* chapter 13, 'Corrosion', p.253-63, covers learned societies, dictionaries, standards organizations, handbooks, data banks, marketing companies, trade associations, books, abstracts, journals, reviews. A valuable contribution to an important series, formerly *Butterworths guides to information sources.* *Class No:* 669(01)

[6850]
SMITH, M.R. **'Mineral process engineering'.** *Information sources in engineering.* K.W. Mildren and P.J. Hicks, eds. (3rd ed., 1996), p.589-606. 3rd ed. London, Bowker Saur, 1996. £80. ISBN: 1857390571.

Information sources include organizations, research centres, journals, books, conference proceedings, reviews and directories, abstracts and indexes, and online databases. *Class No:* 669(01)

Encyclopaedias

[6851]
TOTTLE, C.R. An Encyclopaedia of metallurgy and materials. London, Metals Society: Macdonald and Evans, 1984. ci, 380p. illus., tables, chemical structures. £65. ISBN: 0712105769.

Rev. and enl. ed, of Merriman, A.D. *Dictionary of metallurgy* (1958) and *A concise encyclopaedia of metallurgy* (1965).

An encyclopaedic dictionary, combining brief definitions with longer entries (*e.g.* 'Aluminium': 2 columns; 'Oxygen steelmaking': 2½ columns). 11 tables (p.xi-ci) precede the A-Z sequence. 210 figures, 66 tables. Aimed at a wide variety of users, technical and non-technical, engineers and also users in developing countries. *Class No:* 669(031)

Handbooks & Manuals

[6852]
ASM handbook. 10th ed. Metals Park, OH, American Society for Metals, 1990-. illus., diagrs., graphs, tables.

First published 1948; 9th ed. (17v.) 1978-1989.

Formerly *Metals handbook.*

1. *Properties and selection: irons, steels, and high-performance alloys.* 1990. 1063p.

2. *Properties and selection: nonferrous alloys and special purpose metals.* 1990. 1328p.

3. *Alloy phase diagrams.* 1992. v.p.

4. *Heat treating.* 1991. c.1200p.

5. *Surface cleaning, finishing and coating.* 1994. v.p.

6. *Welding, brazing and soldering.* 1993. v.p.

18. *Friction, lubrication and wear technology.* 1992. v.p.

V.2 is the work of over 400 authors, reviewers and contributors. 5 major sections (62 articles): 1. Specific metals and alloys - 2. Special-purpose materials - 3. Superconducting materials - 4. Pure metals - 5. Special engineering topics. Appended: Metric conversion guide; Abbreviations, symbols and trade names. Analytical index, p.1279-1328. Micrographs. Numerous tables. Written primarily for the industrial user of metals and alloys. A *Comprehensive index* (1994) includes vols. from earlier editions; Also available on CD-ROM (Dialog; £2500). *Class No:* 669(035)

[6853]
—**Metals handbook.** Boyer, H.E. *and* Gull, T.L., *ed.* Desk ed. Metals Park, Ohio, American Society for Metals, 1985. v.p.(*c.*1200p.). illus., diagrs., tables. ISBN: 087170188x.

4 parts (37 chapters): 1. General information (glossary; engineering tables, etc.) - 2. Properties and selection (chapters 4-20; *e.g.* 4. Carbon and alloy steels; 20. Materials for special application) - 3. Processing - 4. Testing and inspection (*e.g.* 37. Quality control). Some chapters have references appended. 61p. index. Aims 'to provide a single authoritative first-reference to all of metals technology' (*Preface*). *Class No:* 669(035)

[6854]
HARGREAVES, D. *and* **FROMSON, S. World index of strategic minerals:** production, exploitation and risk. New York, Facts on File, 1983. xiii, 300p.

4 parts: 1. Strategic risk assessment - 2. 37 minerals and mineral groups - 3. 34 countries, giving production; mining industry; investment and development; country risk factor - 4. 63 individual companies. Data up to 1982. 'Should be very useful in technical and business libraries' (*Reference books bulletin, 1983/1984,* p.175). *Class No:* 669(035)

[6855]
ROSS, R.B. Metallic materials specification handbook. 4th ed. London, Chapman & Hall, 1992. xiii[i],830p. £99.95. ISBN: 0412369400.

First published 1968 as *Metallic materials.* 3rd ed. 1980.

56 metals, with alloys, A-Z (Aluminium - Zirconium). Data include physical properties, specifications and tradenames, mechanical and other properties, symbols. Appended: suppliers, conversation tables. Index, p.635-830. *Class No:* 669(035)

[6856]
SIMONS, E.N. Guide to uncommon metals. London, F. Muller, 1967. 244, [1]p.

Data on 47 metals, Antimony ... Zirconium. Excludes alloy metal. Appended: 'Books for reference' (10 items). Facts and figures for the metallurgist, student, engineer and scientist. *Class No:* 669(035)

Dictionaries

Polyglot

[6857]
CAGNACCI-SCHWICKER, A., *comp.* **International dictionary of metallurgy, mineralogy, geology, mining, and oil industry.** Milan, Technoprint International Milano, in association with New York, etc., McGraw-Hill, 1968. [xv], 1530p.

20,372 numbered English-base terms, with French, German and Italian equivalents and indexes. Terms in the 3 main fields - metallurgy, geology, oil industry - are differentiated by means of symbols. *Class No:* 669(038)=00

[6858]
CLASON, W.E. Elsevier's dictionary of metallurgy and metal working, in six languages: English/American, French, Spanish, Italian, Dutch and German. Amsterdam, etc., Elsevier, 1978. [viii], 848p. DFl 375. ISBN: 0444416951.

First published 1966.

8,406 English/American terms, with equivalents and indexes in French, Spanish, Italian, Dutch and German. *Class No:* 669(038)=00

English

[6859]
BROWN, C.D. Dictionary of metallurgy. Chichester, Wiley, 1998. viii, 308p. diagrs., graphs. ISBN: 0471961558.

About 4,000 terms, briefly defined (*e.g.* Red brass: 9 lines). *Class No:* 669(038)=20

German

[6860]
STÖLZEL, K., *ed.* **Dictionary of metallurgy and foundry technology.** Amsterdam, etc., Elsevier, 1984-87. 2v.

1. *English-German.* 1984. 418p. £79.58. ISBN 0444996125.

2. *German-English.* 1987. 464p. £75.08. ISBN 0444995145.

Wide-ranging scope. Brief entries, with equivalents and occasional definition or explanation.

Review of v.1: 'It will be of particular value to linguists, documentation experts and scientists as well as teachers and students ...' (*Iron and steelmaker,* v.14, August 1987, p.65). *Class No:* 669(038)=30

[6861]
WANDERER, J.A. Metallurgisches Wörterbuch: teil 1: Englisch-Deutsch; teil 2: Deutsch-Englisch. [Metallurgical dictionary: part 1: English-German; part 2: German-English.] Heere, Wanderer Verlag, 1989. 608p. £25.55. ISBN: 3927726001.

Includes chemical compounds and abbreviations. *Class No:* 669(038)=30

Portuguese

[6862]

TAYLOR, J.L. **Dicionário metalúrgico:** inglês-português, português-inglês. [Dictionary of metallurgy: English-Portuguese, Portuguese-English.] São Paulo, Associação Brasileirà de Metais, 1976. [viii], 619, [2]p. £39.95. ISBN: 0916362006.

Rev. ed. of the 1963 English-Portuguese metallurgical dictionary. The Portuguese-English part is new.

About 30,000 entries in each half. Many phrases. Reprinted 1996. *Class No:* 669(038)=690

Russian

[6863]

MacANDREW, A.R., *ed*. **A Glossary of Russian technical terms used in metallurgy.** New York, Varangian Press, 1953. v, 127p.

Compiled at Columbia Univ., New York under contract with National Science Foundation.

About 6,000 Russian terms with English equivalents. Intended to supplement L.I Callaham's *Russian-English technical and chemical dictionary* (1947) and therefore excludes metallurgical terms in Callaham (*qv.*) Indicates stress in Russian pronunciation. Neiswender, R. (*Guide to Russian reference and language aids*, p.29) considers MacAndrew superior to Howeston, P.W. and Akhonin, A. *Russian-English glossary of metallurgical and metal-working terms* (Cambridge, Mass., Center for International Studies, MIT, 1955. iii, 175p.). *Class No:* 669(038)=82

Reviews & Abstracts

[6864]

IMM abstracts: a survey of world literature on economic geology, mining, mineral dressing, extraction metallurgy [and] allied subjects. London, Institution of Mining and Metallurgy, 1950-. 6pa. £215 pa. ISSN: 00190020.

About 3,000 abstracts pa. 13 sections: Generalities - Minerals industry - Economic geology - Mining - Mineral processing - Metallurgy - Non-metals extraction - Health and safety - Environment - Mathematical methods and computing - General engineering - Civil engineering - Analysis and instrumentation. Annual index. Online through IMM. *Class No:* 669(048)

[6865]

Metals abstracts. London, Metals Information: Institute of Metals, and Materials Park, Oh., ASM International, 12pa. $2115; £1345 pa. ISSN: 00260924.

About 4,000 abstracts and references pa. 72 sections (*e.g.* 11. Construction - 12. Crystal properties ... 21. Metallography ... 31 Mechanical properties ... 41 Ores and raw materials ... 51. Foundry ... 61. Engineering components and structures ... 71 General and non-classified - 72. Special publications. Author index per issue. Online as METADEX; CD-ROM. Also available on the World Wide Web (URL: http://www.csa.com). *Class No:* 669(048)

[6866]

Mineralogical abstracts. London, Mineralogical Society of Great Britain, and the Mineralogical Society of America, 1920-. 4pa. £165; $200. ISSN: 37915002.

Earlier (1920-58) published in *The mineralogical magazine*.

About 5,000 abstracts pa. 17 sections, A-V: Age determination - Apparatuses and techniques - Book notices ... Economic minerals and ore deposits ... Experimental mineralogy ... Geochemistry ... Meteorites and tektites - Mineral data ... Petrology. Author index per issue; annual author and subject indexes. Also available on CD-ROM. *Class No:* 669(048)

Periodicals

[6867]

AMERICAN SOCIETY FOR METALS. **Source journals in metals and materials.** 3rd ed. Metals Park, Ohio, the Society, 1985. 76p. $40.

Lists 1,000 scientific, engineering and trade journals, covering metallurgy in engineered materials. *Class No:* 669(051)

Yearbooks & Directories

[6868]

Industrial minerals directory: a world guide to producers of non-metallic, non-fossil minerals. 3rd ed. rev. Worcester Park, Surrey, Metal Bulletin Books, Ltd., 1995. 553p. £131. ISSN: 02691701.

A directory of producers, under countries, Argentina ... Zimbabwe. Buyers' guide, in a mineral-by-mineral guide to producers. Professional services directory. Index to advertisers. *Class No:* 669(058)

[6869]

'Metal bulletin's' prices & data 1998. Cooke, H. *and* Moreno, A., *eds*. Worcester Park, Surrey, Metal Bulletin Books, Ltd., 1968-. Annual. tables. ISSN: 02626454.

Until 1986 as *'Metal bulletin' handbook*.

The 1998 annual (431p.) has main parts: Non-ferrous prices subdivided by country - Iron and steel prices - Iron and steel scrap prices - iron ore prices - Statistics (non-ferrous; iron & steel)-Memoranda. Advertisers index. *Class No:* 669(058)

[6870]

Metal traders of the world. 6th ed. Worcester Park, Surrey, Metal Bulletin Books, Ltd., 1997. lv, 705p. ISSN: 01437607.

3 main sections: companies; buyers' guide; index to personnel. Data: address; phone and fax numbers; management; ownership; capital; subsidiaries; trade names; raw materials, etc. *Class No:* 669(058)

[6871]

Ryland's: the directory of the engineering industry, 1993. London, Guardian Communications, 1993. 504p. £125. ISSN: 0080505x.

Alphabetical section (countries, A-Z). Classified section: 1. Iron, steel, and ferro-alloys - 2. Rolled iron and steel sections - 3. Steel stockholders - 4. Non-ferrous metals - 5. Non-ferrous metal stockholders - 6. Engineering, engineers' products and services. Geographical index. Brand names & trade marks. Employers' and trade associations & trade unions. Index to advertisers. *Class No:* 669(058)

Tables & Data Books

[6872]

AMERICAN SOCIETY FOR METALS. **Guide to materials engineering data and information.** Metals Park, Ohio, ASM International, 1986. v.p. illus., tables.

10 sections 1. The ASM resource - 2. Physical data on the elements and alloys - 3. General engineering data - 4. Organizations and engineering data sources - 5. Standards: issuing organizations - 6. Directory of materials manufacturers - 7. Materials reference books and engineering journals (59p.) - 8. Style manual - 9. Milestones in the history of physical metallurgy - 10. Glossary of materials engineering terminology (108p., including small illus.). Over 4,000 entries. A 'compendium of fundamental engineering data - a one-stop reference to metals, metalworking, composites and engineering materials' (*Preface.*). *Class No:* 669(083)

[6873]

ASM metals reference book. Bauccio, M., *ed*. 3rd ed. Metals Park, Ohio, ASM International, 1993. 614p. $106. 500 2nd ed. 1983. ISBN: 0871704781.

Glossary of metallurgical and metalworking terms. Sections: Cast irons - Plain carbon and alloy steels - Tool materials - Wrought stainless steels - Heat- and corrosion-resistant alloys - Aluminum and aluminum alloys - Copper and copper alloys - Lead, tin, zinc, magnesium and magnesium-base alloys - Titanium and titanium alloys. 15 chapters in all. Numerous data tables. 'An excellent acquisition' (*Choice*, May 1994, p.1464). *Class No:* 669(083)

[6874]

Minerals handbook, 1996-97: statistics and analysis of the world's minerals industry. Crowson, P., *ed*. New York, Macmillan, 1996. Biennial. 350p. tables. £99. ISBN: 0333640845.

Statistical tables covering minerals (Aluminium, bauxite, and alumina ... Zirconium). 'Cobalt' (subdivided by country) has tabulated data: world reserves; world mine and metal production; production capacity; consumption; substitutes; prices; marketing (graph); supply and demand. Sources and notes. *Class No:* 669(083)

[6875]

NAYAR, A. **The Metal databook.** New York, McGraw-Hill, 1997. v.p. tables. ISBN: 0070460884.

Provides metallurgical information on grades of cast irons, steels, aluminium, copper, zinc and sintered materials. Data cover chemical composition, mechanical and physical proterties, applications, heat treatments, temperatures, etc. Largely tables. *Class No:* 669(083)

[6876]

ROBB, C. **Metals databook.** London, The Institute of Metals, 1987. [xvi],500p. diagrs., tables. £90. ISBN: 0904357694.

Data, largely in tabular form, on the chemical, physical and mechanical properties of commercially available metallic materials. Much of the data is specific to British Standards. Covers welding, heat treatment, test house and laboratory data. 4 appendices: 1. S.I. units - 2. Hardness testing - 3. Material specifications - 4. Equilibrium diagrams. No index, but detailed contents list. Small, handy format, but very expensive. *Class No:* 669(083)

[6877]
Roskill's directory of sources for metals and mineral data. London, Roskill Information Services, Ltd., 1976-. Biennial.

The 1997 ed. (248p. £210) lists statistical sources in 3 parts: 1. International - 2. Metals and minerals (Aluminium ... Zirconium) - 3. Country sections (Algeria ... Zambia). Data on each source include bibliographical details, publisher/distributor, number of years covered by statistics, frequency, and outline of contents relevant to metals and minerals. *Class No:* 669(083)

[6878]
SMITHELLS, C.J. Smithells metals reference book. Brandes, E.A. *and* Brook, G., *eds.* 7th ed. London, etc., Butterworth Heinemann, 1992. xvi,[1664]p. illus., graphs, tables. £150. ISBN: 0750610204.

First published 1949; 6th ed., 1983 (xiv,1600p.).

Includes data on isotopes, crystallography, gas-metal systems, electron emission, magnetic properties, heat treatment, corrosion control and superplasticity. A standard source of data on metals and alloys. The 7th ed. was published in paperback in 1997 (ISBN: 0750636246; £60).

Also available on CD-ROM as *Engineering materials selector*, either singly (£199) or in conjunction with *Smithell's metals reference book* and/or *Tribology handbook*. *Class No:* 669(083)

[6879]
—Smithells light metals handbook. Brandes, E.A. *and* Brook, G., *eds.* Oxford, Butterworth-Heinemann, 1998, vii, 194p. graphs, tables. £35. ISBN: 0750636254.

Covers common and popular metals including aluminium, magnesium and titanium. Data on properties, standards and international materials specifications. *Class No:* 669(083)

Nomenclatures

[6880]
EMBERY, P.G. *and* FULLER, J.P., *eds*. A Manual of new mineral names, 1892-1978. London, British Museum (Natural History) and Oxford Univ. Press, 1980. x, 467p. £32. ISBN: 0198585012.

A compilation from 30 lists published in the *Mineralogical magazines*, 1897-1976. About 5,500 'new' mineral names, A-Z, followed by an author list. Complements J.D. Dana's *System of mineralogy (qv)*. *Class No:* 669(083.72)

Histories

[6881]
AITCHISON, L. A History of metals. London, Macdonald & Evans, 1960. 2v. illus., diagrs., tables.

V.1 deals with the history of gold, copper, lead, zinc, tin, iron and mercury up to the end of the Dark Ages (c.1000 A.D.). V.2 (p.305-647), from that point onwards. Chapter bibliographies. A scholarly work, admirably illustrated and documented; fully indexed. Of value to those interested in social history as well as to the metallurgist. *Class No:* 669(091)

[6882]
TYLECOTE, R.F. The Early history of metallurgy. London, Longman, 1987. xxv, [1], 391p. illus., diagrs., graphs, tables, maps. (*Longman archaelogy series*.)

10 chapters (4. The origin of smelting and the design of smelting; 6. Fabrication techniques; 9. The coming of cast iron of Europe). Bibliography (A-Z authors), p.355-79. Detailed, analytical index. Well illustrated and produced. *Class No:* 669(091)

[6883]
—TYLECOTE, R.F. A History of metallurgy. London, Metals Society, 1976. viii, 182p. illus., charts, tables.

Devotes one-third of the text to early history. 'Strongly recommended as the most informative and complete work in the field' (*British book news*, May 1977, p.391). *Class No:* 669(091)

Worldwide

[6884]
The Minerals yearbook. US Bureau of Mines. Washington, US Governmment Printing Office, 1932/33-. Annual. 3v. ISSN: 00768952.

1. *Metals and minerals.*
2. *Area reports domestic.*
3. *Area reports international.*

V.1 provides data on individual metallic and non-metallic minerals (*e.g.* fuels), A-Z. V.2-3 consist mainly of statistical tables, with background notes. V.2 comprises area reports for the United States; V.3 has chapters on individual countries.

Updated by the US Bureau of Mines. *Mineral trade notes: a monthly inventory. Class No:* 669(100)

[6885]
World mineral statistics, 1990-94. Taylor, L.E., *ed.* 18th ed. Nottingham, British Geological Survey, 1995. 305p., tables. £70. ISBN: 0852722680.

Now a single-volume work containing data, in tabular form, on 70 minerals. Includes figures for production and trade, exports and imports, for the period. Only estimated figures are given for many Eastern European countries. *Class No:* 669(100)

USA

[6886]
Metal statistics. New York, American Metal Market, 1908-. Annual. diagrs., graphs, tables.

First published 1908.

Includes profiles of more than key metals (producers; end users; trends, etc.). *Class No:* 669(73)

Information Management

[6887]
JONES, L. *and* VAUGHAN, J. Scientific and technical information on the metals industry: report of the Metals Information Review Committee. London, British Library, 1982. vii, 110, [8]p. (*British Library. Research & Development report no. 5717*.)

The Committee's terms of reference were to study all aspects of the formation, transfer, storage, retrieval and use of metals information. The list of 11 recommendations concerned primary and secondary publications, databases, information for management, etc. Bibliography, p.48-56. *Class No:* 669:025.4

Thesauri

[6888]
CANADA. Centre for Minerals and Energy Technology. **Thesaurus of mineral processing and extractive metallurgy terms.** 2nd ed. Ottawa, Ministry of Supply and Services, Canada, Technology Information Division, 1985. xiii, [1], 345p.

About 1,700 terms in English and French. Appended list of descriptors. *Class No:* 669:025.43

[6889]
Thesaurus of metallurgical terms. 11th ed. Materials Park, Oh., ASM International; London, Institute of Metals, 1996. vi, 264p.

First published 1968; 10th ed. 1992.

About 6,500 main terms and nearly 35,000 cross-reference terms (narrower, broader, related and synonymous). Includes date of first use of term for indexing purposes. *Class No:* 669:025.43

Physical Metallurgy

[6890]
DENNIS, W.H. A Hundred years of metallurgy. London, Duckworth, 1963. ix, 342p. diagrs., tables. (*The hundred years series*.)

Covers 1850-1950. Concentrates on physical metallurgy, with chapters on developments in particular areas (*e.g.* ore dressing, pyrometallurgy, steelmaking, non-ferrous and precious metals, metal working, metallopgraphy, etc.). Brief chapter bibliographies, listing items on which much of the text is based. Short glossary. 'A book of general interest at a high technical level' (*Aslib book list*, v.29(3), March 1964, entry no. 172). *Class No:* 669.017

[6891]
TYRKIEL, E.F. Dictionary of physical metallurgy, in English, German, French, Polish and Russian. Amsterdam, etc., Elsevier, 1977. viii, 402p. £110.50. ISBN: 0444998101.

About 2,300 English-based terms and concise definitions in 17 groups (*e.g.* 05. Chemical elements; 85. Material defects). Equivalents and indexes in German, English, French, Polish and Russian. *Class No:* 669.017

[6892]
—FREIWILLIG, R.K., *and others*. Dictionary of physical metallurgy, in English, German, French, Russian and Spanish. Amsterdam, etc., Elsevier, 1986. c.220p. £101.95 ISBN: 0444995277.

Comprises 1,672 terms, subject-grouped in 5 languages. English, German, French, Russian and Spanish indexes. Not to be confused with E.R. Tyrkiel's dictionary of the same title, with its wider scope. *Class No:* 669.017

Alloys

[6893]

Alloys index. London, Institute of Metals, Materials Park, Ohio, ASM International, 1974-. 12 pa. $425; £280. ISSN: 00948233.

About 2,500 references per issue. Sections: Alloy steels ... Zirconium base alloys. Descriptions appended to entries. An index to specific alloys, metallurgical systems and intermetallic compounds cited in *Metals abstracts*. Online METADEX database.
Class No: 669.018

[6894]

Fatigue data book: light structural alloys. Henry, S.D., *and others, eds*. Materials Park, Oh., ASM International, 1995. 397p. tables. $110. ISBN: 0871705079.

3 sections: aluminium, magnesium and titanium. Data sets for each cover current knowledge, metallurgy, fatigue and fracture porperties, and applications, with further references. 'Well-edited and organized' (*American reference books annual*, 1997, p.597). *Class No: 669.018*

[6895]

Ferro-alloy directory and databook. 4th ed. Worcester Park, Surrey, Metal Bulletin Books, Ltd., 1996. xli, 362p. ISSN: 0953721x.

Data on about 1,000 companies, producing and trading in ferro-alloys. Buyers' guide. Memoranda (p.347-60) give details on association, production and trade by country. *Class No: 669.018*

[6896]

SIMONS, E.N. A Dictionary of alloys. London, F.Muller, 1969. 191p. diagrs., graphs, tables.

Alloys, AC 41 ... Zisium alloy. Preceded by numbered alloys. Appended British Standards. Includes 'a few obsolete or obsolescent terms because they still occur in enquiries or in commerce and export' (*Preface*). *Class No: 669.018*

[6897]

SMITH, W.F. Structure and properties of engineering alloys. New York, etc., McGraw-Hill, 1980. 512p. illus., diagrs., graphs, tables. (*Materials science and energy series*.)

11 documented chapters, with micrographs and appended 'Problems'. 'Nickel and cobalt alloys', p.458-501, has 21 references. 'Intended as refresher text and reference for practicing engineers who have become specialized or who have left the mainstream of technical work' (*Preface*). *Class No: 669.018*

[6898]

Woldman's Engineering alloys. Frick, J.P., *ed*. 8th ed. Materials Park, Oh., ASM International, 1994. [xii], 1374p. tables. $149. ISBN: 0871705443.

First published 1936. 1st-5th eds. as *Engineering alloys*. 7th ed. 1990.

The 8th ed. lists over 40,000 alloys. Data note trade name, composition, properties, uses. Manufacturers A-Z. 33 tables (*e.g.* 21. Compositions of standard stainless steels). *Class No: 669.018*

Furnaces

[6899]

SIMONS, E.N. A Dictionary of metal heat treatment. London, F. Muller, 1976. 248p. diagrs., graphs, tables. ISBN: 0584100795.

About 2,000 terms defined, Absolute scale ... White layer.
Class No: 669.04

[6900]

TYRKIEL, E.F., ed. Multilingual glossary of heat treatment terminology. London, Institute of Metals, 1986. 207p. . £55. ISBN: 0934357701.

Covers English, French, German and Russian in four language sequences. *Class No: 669.04*

Metal Fabrications

[6901]

Surface engineering. Datt, P. *and* Gray, J., *eds*. Cambridge, Royal Society of Chemistry, 1993. 3v. £52.50 each.

V.1. *Fundamentals of engineering* (384p.; ISBN: 0851866654).

V.2. *Engineering applications* (274p.; ISBN: 0851866751).

V.3. *Process technology* (274p. ISBN: 0851866859).

Covers the principles of coating and substrata design in high temperature and aqueous environments, including performance and development. *Class No: 669.056*

[6902]

Surface treatment technology abstracts; incorporating *Metal finishing abstracts* and *Printed circuits abstracts*. Stevenage, Herts., Finishing Publications, Ltd., 1986-. v. 28(1)-. 6 pa. £395; $840 pa. ISSN: 09505199.

As *Metal finishing abstracts*, v. 1-27, 1959-85. Previously appeared in *Electroplating and metal spraying* (1947-1959).

Over 7,000 indicative and informative abstracts and citations pa. covering surface treatment, in 21 classes (Cleaning and degreasing ... Electroplating ... Metal spraying and hard facing ... Corrosion and

....(contd.)
electrochemistry ... General and miscellaneous). Covers journal articles, books, standards, reports and patents - full coverage for UK, European and US patents. Also available on CD-ROM.
Class No: 669.056

Iron & Steel Industry

Bibliographies

[6903]

LAWRANCE, P.R. 'Iron and steel'. *Information sources in metallic materials*. Editor, M.N. Patten, p.59-85. London, Bowker-Saur, 1989. (*Guides to information sources.*) ISBN: 0408014911.

Sections: Reference sources - Periodicals - Abstract journals & conference proceedings - Conferences - Standards - Specialized databases and services - Company sources - Translation dictionaries - Statistics. *Class No: 669.1(01)*

[6904]

UNITED NATIONS. Industrial Development Organization. **Information sources on the iron and steel industry.** New York, United Nations, 1977. xii, 403p. $4. (*UNIDO guides to information sources, no. 26.*)

788 items, 12 sections: 1. Professional, trade and research organizations, learned societies and special information sources - 2. Directories - 3. Sources of statistics, marketing and other economic data - 4. Basic handbooks, textbooks and manuals - 5. Monograph series - 6. Current periodicals - 7. Current abstracting and indexing periodicals - 8. Proceedings, papers and reports - 9. Specialized dictionaries and encyclopaedias - 10. Bibliographies - 11. Films and film catalogues - 12. Other sources of information (H. Patents and licences). 'Bibliographical sources used'. *Class No: 669.1(01)*

Dictionaries

English

[6905]

GALE, W.K.V. The Iron and steel industry: a dictionary of terms. New ed. Newton Abbot, Devon, David & Charles, 1973. 238p.

First published 1971 (238p.).

About 3,500 brief entries. Many of the terms listed are now obsolete (marked '(obs)'). Local terms are also differentiated. Numerous cross-references. Appended: A. Birmingham gauge - B. British (Imperial) standard and wire gauge. - C. Tinplate denominations and size.
Class No: 669.1(038)=20

[6906]

SIMONS, E.N. Dictionary of ferrous metals. London, Muller, 1970. x, 244p. diagrs., tables.

About 2,500 entries, A-Z, preceded by a number sequence. 'Simple, brief but factual information of the terms chosen' (*Preface*). 'Nickel steels': 24p. Adequate cross-references. Companion volume to the author's *A dictionary of alloys* (*qv*). *Class No: 669.1(038)=20*

German

[6907]

BRITISH STEEL CORPORATION. Vocabulary of iron and steel terms: German/English, English/German. London, the Corporation, 1975. 104p. tables.

About 1,800 terms in each half of this pocket-sized dictionary. Conversion tables. *Class No: 669.1(038)=30*

[6908]

FREEMAN, H.G. Taschenwörterbuch Eisen und Stahl. Munich, Hueber, 1966-67. 2v.

1. *Deutsch-englisch.* 1966. 311p.

2. *Englisch-deutsch.* 1967. 289p.

Each volume has *c.*13,000 entry-words; categories and genders are shown. V.1 includes conversion tables (p.21-43) and a list of sources (p.44-46). *Class No: 669.1(038)=30*

French

[6909]

BRITISH STEEL CORPORATION. Vocabulary of iron and steel terms: French/English, English/French. London, the Corporation, 1974. 105p.

About 1,800 terms in each half of this pocket-sized dictionary. Conversion tables. *Class No: 669.1(038)=40*

Italian

[6910]

BRITISH STEEL CORPORATION. Vocabulary of iron and steel terms: Italian/English, English/Italian. London, the Corporation, 1974. 117p.

About 1,800 terms in each half of this pocket-sized dictionary. Conversion tables. *Class No: 669.1(038)=50*

Yearbooks & Directories

[6911]

Directory of iron and steel plants. Sukits, D., *ed.* Pittsburgh, Pa., Association of Iron and Steel Engineers, 1989. 584p. $40.

Covers North America and selected overseas nations. 5 sections and geographical indexes. Advertising index; company index. *Class No: 669.1(058)*

[6912]

Handbook of the European iron and steel works. 10th ed. Frankfurt, Montan- und Wirtschaftlsverlag, 1997. 728p. ISSN: 04402014.

About 900 firms, listed by country. Data include name, contact details, capital, plant, production programme. Index of persons products, but not companies; list of European steel associations. *Class No: 669.1(058)*

[6913]

Iron and manganese ore databook. ISBN: 0947671625. ISSN: 09677925.

4 parts: Index to countries (producers/traders, A-Z); Iron ore; Manganese ore; Traders and representatives. Appended 'memoranda' (*e.g.* principal loading and discharging ports; prices; glossary of ore trade terms). *Class No: 669.1(058)*

[6914]

Iron and steel works of the world. 12th ed. Worcester Park, Surrey, Metal Bulletin Books, Ltd., 1997. lxxiv, 726p. ISSN: 00750875.

Lists *c.*2,000 companies in some 100 countries, Albania ... Zimbabwe. Data include year of establishment, products, brands, sales office, agents. Company index precedes. Buyers' guide of products and index. Index to advertisers. *Class No: 669.1(058)*

Standards

[6915]

Worldwide guide to equivalent irons and steels. American Society for Metals. 3rd ed. Metals Park, Oh., The Materials Information Society, 1992. *c.*500p. £143. ISBN: 0871704544.

First published 1978.

Alloys organized by type of iron or steel, *e.g.* cast iron; cast stainless steel; steel castings; carbon steel; tool steel, etc. Data for each alloy specification: country of origin; standards organization; specification; designation; description; tensile strength; yield strenth; elongation. Indexes: specification; designation; standards organizations. *Class No: 669.1(083.74)*

Great Britain

[6916]

IRON AND STEEL STATISTICS BUREAU. Iron and steel industry: annual statistics for the United Kingdom. Croydon, Surrey, the Bureau. Annual. tables.

Contents include definitions; general summary; home and imported iron and manganese ores; sinter; energy; other materials; blast furnaces; crude steel; finished steel; iron castings; manpower; prices; general industrial tables; imports and exports. Statistics are usually for 6-year spans. Numerous tables. *Class No: 669.1(410)*

Cast Iron

[6917]

CONCAST AG, Zurich. **Concast dictionary:** English/French/Spanish/ Italian/ Russian/German/Japanese. 3rd ed. New York, Concast AG Zurich, 1975.

First published 1986.

About 3,000 English-based terms, with French, Spanish, Italian Russian, German and Japanese equivalents and indexes. *Class No: 669.13*

Steel

Bibliographies

[6918]

TUPHOLME, S. 'Stainless steels'. *Information sources in metallic materials.* Editor, M.N. Patten, p.86-102. London, Bowker-Saur, 1989. (*Guides to information sources.*) ISBN: 0408014911.

Sections: Key works of reference (36 items) - Periodicals -

....(contd.)

Abstracting services - Databases and datafiles - Standard specifications and codes of practice - Conferences - Advisory bodies, trade and research associations - Commercial aspects. *Class No: 669.14(01)*

Handbooks & Manuals

[6919]

Steel: a handbook for materials research and engineering. Verein Deutscher Eisenhüttenleute, *ed.* Berlin, Springer-Verlag, 1992. 2v. (xx, 736p.; xxiii; 839p.). illus., diagrs., graphs, tables. ISBN: 0387529683, V.1; 038754075x, V.2.

V.1: *Fundamentals.*
V.2: *Applications.*

Intended to replace an earlier publication *Manual of special steels* by E. Houdrement.

52 chapters in 4 parts: A. Microstructure of steels - B. Properties of steel - C. Characterizing properties for specific applications - D. Influence of production processes on proterties. V.1 has 41p. of references; V.2, 49p. *Class No: 669.14(035)*

Dictionaries

[6920]

EUROPEAN COMMUNITIES COMMISSION. Terminology Office. Glossaire des normes de l'acier. Brussels, the Bureau, 1972. 510p.

Glossary of more than 5,000 terms - definitions plus examples of usage - in French, German, Italian and Dutch. Based on *c.*100 European standards (1955-71). *Class No: 669.14(038)*

Reviews & Abstracts

[6921]

Euro abstracts. Section 2: Coal and steel. Research programmes and agreements. Scientific and technical publications and patents in German, English and French. Luxembourg, Commission of the European Communities, 1975-. Monthly. ISSN: 03783472.

Formerly part of Euro abstracts: scientific and technical publications and patents, 1970-74.

Fairly lengthy abstracts covering research programmes, research agreements, scientific and technical publications, patents, training courses and seminars, forthcoming conferences and symposia. Annual index. *Class No: 669.14(048)*

[6922]

Steels' alert. London, The Institute of Metals; Materials Park, Oh., ASM International, 1983-. 12 pa. £165. ISSN: 10480307.

Formerly *Steels supplement to metals abstracts,* 1953-82.

Covers fuel energy usage, raw materials and recycling; steel plants; economics, statistics, resources; world steel news; company information. Additional information on steel production, fabrication and use, and development. A news digest. Available on the World Wide Web from Cambridge Scientific Abstracts (URL: http://www.csa.com). *Class No: 669.14(048)*

Yearbooks & Directories

[6923]

Steel traders of the world. 7th ed. Worcester Park, Surrey, Metal Bulletin Books, Ltd., 1997. xlix, 920, [3]p. ISSN: 03088006.

Well over 2,000 firms in some 100 countries (Algeria - Zimbabwe). A-Z index to companies. Buyers' guide. *Class No: 669.14(058)*

Tables & Data Books

[6924]

Stainless steel databook. 3rd ed. Worcester Park, Surrey, Metal Bulletin Books, Ltd., 1995. xliii, 514p. ISSN: 09537228.

Data on about 1,500 companies producing or trading in stainless steel. Buyers' guide. Memoranda (p.443-514) give details on trade associations, production, consumption, etc. *Class No: 669.14(083)*

Standards

[6925]

EUROPEAN COMMUNITIES COMMISSION. Terminology Office. Steel standards glossary. Luxembourg, the Commission, 1979. xxxi, 689p. ISBN: 9282508331.

Explanations of *c.*2,500 terms in French, English, German, Italian, Dutch and Danish, p.1-354. Alphabetical indexes in the six languages, on tinted paper (that in English, on purple paper, is virtually indecipherable). Bibliographical references (to sources), p.638-84. *Class No: 669.14(083.74)*

Europe

[6926]

ECONOMIC COMMISSION FOR EUROPE. **Annual bulletin of steel statistics for Europe,** 1973-. New York, United Nations, 1974-. Annual. tables.

Basic tabular data on development of steel production and trade, consumption and trade of raw materials, movement of scrap, consumption of energy in the steel industry and steel deliveries to consuming industries in European countries, plus Canada, USA and Japan.

Quarterly bulletin of steel statistics for Europe (New York, U.N., 1950-. v.1(1)-) updates. *Class No:* 669.14(4)

Non-Ferrous Metals

[6927]

Non-ferrous metal data. Secaucus, N.J. American Bureau of Metal Statistics, Inc. Annual. tables.

Tables of data on non-ferrous metals, A-U; includes world production figures. *Class No:* 669.2

[6928]

Non-ferrous metal works of the world. 7th ed. Worcester Park, Surrey, Metal Bulletin Books, 1995. lxx, 662p. tables. ISBN: 094767182x. ISSN: 00780987.

First published 1967.

Indexes to countries and companies precede the company section, p.1-536. Index to buyers' guide; buyer's guide. Index to advertisers. Some 1,860 metal producers in 104 countries. *Class No:* 669.2

Gold

[6929]

BOYLE, R.W. **Gold: history and genesis of deposits.** New York, Van Nostrand Reinhold, 1987. 676p. $49.50. ISBN: 0442211627.

18 documented chapters, 51 contributors. An historical introduction is supported by a chapter on the geochemistry of gold and the type of auriferous deposits. Then follows reprints of some classic papers on gold. Name and subject indexes. 'Digests in one compact volume much of the vast scattered literature on the geology and geochemistry of gold' (*New technical books,* January/February 1988, item 284). *Class No:* 669.21

[6930]

Handbook of precious metals. Savitskii, E.M., *ed.* New York, Hemisphere, 1989. xix,600p. £96. ISBN: 0891167099.

Includes numerous tables and over 900 references, many to Russian journals. *Class No:* 669.21

[6931]

KETTELL, B. **Gold.** London, Graham & Trotman, 1982. xiv, [1], 283p. illus., graphs, tables. ISBN: 0860102572.

8 chapters: 1. Gold: importance, scientific properties and methods of extraction - 2. Early history - 3. The gold standard - 4. Gold: the major factors affecting its supply demand and price. Appendix: minted gold coins. Grouped bibliography, p.269-73. Index. 81 tables and figures. *Class No:* 669.21

[6932]

KUDRYK, V., *and others.* **Precious metals:** mining, extraction and processing. Wassendale, Pa., Metallurgical Society of AIME, 1984. xi, 621p. illus., diagrs., charts, tables, maps. ISBN: 089520469x.

45 papers, usually with references, read at an International Symposium of Precious Metals, by contributors from 12 countries. Sections: General overview - Sampling and ore evaluation - Chemistry of leaching and recovery - Electrolytic recovery - Ore processing - Recycling and byproduct recovery - Physical metallurgy. Example: 'Recovery of gold from arsenical ores '(41 references). Subject and author indexes. *Class No:* 669.21

[6933]

Precious metal databook. Serjeanston, R., *ed.* Worcester Park, Metal Bulletin Books, 1989. xxxiv,254p. £58. ISBN: 0947671242. ISSN: 09556532.

In two main sections (Companies; Buyers' guide) each subdivided into producers and traders. Appended: statistics by country (production; consumption; imports; exports). Indexes: countries; companies; advertisers. *Class No:* 669.21

Silver

[6934]

BUTTS, A. and COXE, C.D., *eds.* **Silver: economics, metallurgy and use.** Sponsored by Hardy and Harman in commemoration of their 100th anniversary. Princeton, N.J. etc., Van Nostrand, 1967. 488p. illus., charts, tables.

35 contributors. 34 chapters on history, sources, extracting, refining, properties, application, etc. 'Literature of silver', p.467-8. Name and subject indexes. Well illustrated. *Class No:* 669.22

[6935]

Silver: exploration, mining and treatment. Institution of Mining and Metallurgy. London, Institute of Mining and Metallurgy, 1988. x,344p. illus., maps, tables. £46.80. ISBN: 1870706048.

31 papers presented at the international conference on 'Silver-exploration, mining and treatment' organized by the IMM, in association with the Cámara Minera de México and The Silver Institute, and held in Mexico City, 21-24 November 1988. Sections: Geology and mineralogy - Case histories - Silver in complex sulphide minerals - Flotation - Extraction and refining. *Class No:* 669.22

Platinum

[6936]

MACDONALD, D. *and* HUNT, L.B. **A History of platinum and its allied metals.** London, Johnson Matthey, 1982. 462p. illus. (incl. col.), facsims., ports. ISBN: 0905118839.

24 documented chapters (*e.g.* 3. Early scientific enquiries into the properties and nature of platinum; 13. The discovery and early history of catalysis (37 references); 21. The growth of industrial catalysis with the platinum metals). Name index; detailed, analytical index. Well produced. *Class No:* 669.231

Nickel

[6937]

BETTERIDGE, W. **Nickel and its alloys.** Chichester, Ellis Horwood; New York, Halsted Press: Wiley, 1984. 216p. £30. (*Ellis Horwood series in industrial metals.*) ISBN: 0853127298.

9 documented chapters: 1. Introduction and physical properties - 2. Occurrence and extraction of nickel - 3. Consruction of nickel alloy systems - 4. Nickel in industrial alloys - 5. Metallography - 6. Production of semi-fabricated forms - 7. Processes applied in final manufacture - 8. Applications - 9. Economics. 2 appendices (*e.g.* Conversion factors). Detailed analytical index. *Class No:* 669.24

[6938]

BOLDT, J.R. **The Winning of nickel:** its geology, mining and extractive metallurgy. London, Methuen, 1967. xiv, 487p. illus., maps.

4 sections: 1. The geology of nickel - 2. Mining for nickel - 3. Extractive metallurgy of sulfide ores - 4. Extractive metallurgy of oxide ores. References, p.457-64. Analytical index, Micrographs. *Class No:* 669.24

Cobalt

[6939]

YOUNG, R.S., *ed.* **Cobalt: its chemistry, metallurgy and uses.** New York, Reinhold, 1960. vii, 424p. (*American Chemical Society Monograph series no.149, replacing no.108.*)

13 chapters, mustering nearly 1,500 references. Well presented data, but deficient in illustrations and flowsheets. *Class No:* 669.25

Chromium

[6940]

SULLY, A.H. *and* BRANDES, E.A. **Chromium.** 2nd ed. London, Butterworth, 1967. xiii, 373p. illus., diagrs., tables. (*Metallurgy of the rarer metals.*)

First published 1954.

8 chapters. 1. History and occurrence - 2. Production of chromium ferro-alloys and pure chromium - 3. Physical properties of pure chromium ... 6. Electroplating - 7. Chromizing - 8. Constitution and properties of chromium alloys (p.301-68; 173 references). Appendex: List of properties of chromium. Subject index. *Class No:* 669.26

Tungsten

[6941]

YIH, S.W.H. *and* WANG, C.T. **Tungsten: sources, metallurgy, properties and applications.** New York & London, Plenum Press, 1979. xvi, 500p. illus., diagrs., graphs, tables. ISBN: 0306311445.

11 chapters: 1. Occurrence, geology, mining and benefication of tungsten - 2. Extractive metallurgy ... 5. Fabrication. 7. Chemical properties of tungsten and tungsten compounds ... 10. Applications - 11. Industry and future outlook of tungsten. 2 appendices (2. Analytical chemistry of tungsten). Bibliography (by chapters and appendices), p.463-91. *Class No:* 669.27

Niobium & Tantalum

[6942]

MILLER, G.L. **Tantalum and niobium.** London, Butterworth, 1959. xxii, 767. illus., tables. (*Metallurgy of the rarer metals, no.6.*)

Data on occurrence; extraction; physical, chemical and mechanical properties, applications, etc. Companion to the same author's *Zirconium (qv). Class No:* 669.293/.294

Titanium

[6943]

DONACHIE, M.J., *Jr.* **Titanium: a technical guide.** Metals Park, Ohio, ASM International, 1988. xv, 469p. diagrs., graphs., tables. $65. ISBN: 0871703092.

13 chapters (13. Recent and future advances). Appendices A-J: A. Selected references (120) for additional reading; B. Glossary; G. General corrosion rate; H. List of manufacturers, suppliers, services; I. Standards and specifications; J. Designations, applications, purposes. Analytical index, p.453-69. 'Highly recommended' (*New technical books,* Sept./Oct. 1988, item 2318). *Class No:* 669.295

[6944]

FROES, F.H., *and others.* **Titanium technology:** present status and future trends. Dayton, Ohio, Titanium Development Association, 1985. 191p. illus., diagrs., graphs, tables. $19.95.

Based on articles, reprinted with permission, from the *Journal of metals.*

20 contributors. 17 documented papers (*e.g.* 'Advances in titanium extraction metallurgy', with 59 references). 'About the authors', p177-9. Detailed analytical subject and author indexes.

Titanium abstract bulletin (Wilton, Birmingham, ICI. 1955-. 6pa.) ceased publication in 1962. *Class No:* 669.295

Zirconium

[6945]

MILLER, G.L. **Zirconium.** 2nd ed. London, Butterworths, 1957. xxi, 548p. illus., tables. (*Metallurgy of the rarer metals, no. 2.*)

First published 1954.

Comprehensive survey of the metal, from its history and natural occurrence, extraction, physical, chemical and mechanical properties to alloys and applications. Chapter bibliographies. Subject index. *Class No:* 669.296

Copper

[6946]

BLACK, W.T., *and others.* **Thesaurus of terms in copper technology.** 7th ed. New York, Copper Development Association, 1981. vi, 401p. $40.

Assembles more than 8,700 metallurgical and engineering terms, with numerous cross-references. Of wide application; much of the information is common to all metals. *Class No:* 669.3

[6947]

BRITISH STANDARDS INSTITUTION. **Glossary of terms for copper and copper alloys.** London, BSI, 1988. 20p. (*BS 6931: 1988.*)

Supersedes BS 1420: 1965.

Defines terms used in the UK for raw materials, castings, wrought products and processes. *Class No:* 669.3

[6948]

CALLCUTT, V.A. 'Copper and copper alloys'. *Information sources in metallic materials.* Editor, M.N. Patten, p.120-37. London, Bowker-Saur, 1989. (*Guides to information sources.*) ISBN: 0408014911.

Sections: Introduction - Historical - Structure of the industry - *International Copper Information Bulletin* - Statistics and economics - Standards and specifications - Terminology - Technology - Analysis - Alloying relationships - Corrosion - Addresses (*c.*60). 75 references. *Class No:* 669.3

[6949]

WEST, E.G. **Copper and its alloys.** Chichester, Ellis Horwood; New York, Halsted Press: Wiley, 1982. 241p. illus. (incl. photomicrographs), diagrs., graphs. £34. (*Ellis Horwood series in industrial metals.*) ISBN: 0853125058.

9 chapters, each with 'Further reading': 1. Introduction and basic properties of copper - 2. Occurrence and extraction of copper ... 4. Copper alloy systems - 5. Properties of copper alloys ... 7. Manufacturing processes ... 9. Applications. 2 appendices (1. Metallography of copper and copper alloys). Detailed, analytical index. 'It is an excellent source of reference data' (*New technical books,* July 1983, item 869). *Class No:* 669.3

[6950]

World copper databook. 3rd ed. Worcester Park, Surrey, Metal Bulletin Books, 1996. 484p. £120 ISBN: 1900663007. ISSN: 09052267.

Two major sections: Producers, by country A-Z; Traders, by country A-Z. Data include contact details, plant, products, services, etc. Appendices (associations, statistics, etc.). *Class No:* 669.3

Lead

[6951]

BLASKETT, D.R. *and* BOXALL, D. **Lead and its alloys.** New York, E. Horwood, 1990. 161p. illus., diagrs., graphs, tables. $60. ISBN: 0135286964.

11 chapters, closely subdivided, with numerous references. Emphasis is on smelting and refining with consideration of health aspects. Recommended by *Choice* (May 1991, p.1514) as 'valuable' for industry, commerce and research. *Class No:* 669.4

[6952]

CONWAY, M.J. 'Lead'. *Information sources in metallic materials.* Editor, M.N. Patten, p.138-50. London, Bowker-Saur, 1989. (*Guides to information sources.*) ISBN: 0408014911.

Sections: Introduction - General information (books; reports; proceedings; periodicals) - Information sources arranged by major area of interest or uses (analysis; batteries; building; cables; chemicals; coatings; corrosion; electrochemistry; environment; joining; metal working; phase diagrams and thermodynamics; pigments; printing materials; statistics) - Organizations. *Class No:* 669.4

Zinc

[6953]

CONWAY, M.J. 'Zinc'. *Information sources in metallic materials.* Editor, M.N. Patten, p.171-89. London, Bowker-Saur, 1989. (*Guides to information sources.*) ISBN: 0408014911.

Sections: Introduction - General information (books; reports; etc.) - Information sources by major area of interest or uses (*e.g.* analysis; batteries; corrosion; diecasting; hot dip galvanizing; rubber and plastics) - Information centres (11). *Class No:* 669.5

[6954]

PORTER, F. **Zinc handbook:** properties, processing, and use in design. New York, Dekker, 1991. xiv,629p. illus., graphs, tables. (*Mechanical engineering.*) ISBN: 0824783409.

32 chapters, closely subdivided, with 'references and further reading'. Largely concerned with applications for zinc including coating and galvanizing. Detailed, analytical index, p.619-29. *Class No:* 669.5

Tin

[6955]

BARRY, B.T.K. *and* THWAITES, C.J. **Tin and its alloys and compounds.** Chichester, Ellis Horwood; New York, Halsted Press: Wiley, 1983. 268p. illus., diagrs., tables. (*Ellis Horwood series in industrial metals.*) ISBN: 0853126496.

12 chapters, each with 'Further reading': 1. Physical and chemical properties - 2. Occurrence and production - 3. Tin alloy systems - 4-11. Tin and tin alloy applications - 12. Economic factors. 114 illus; 36 tables. Detailed analytical index. *Class No:* 669.6

[6956]

DAVIES, R.L. 'Tin and tinplate'. *Information sources in metallic materials.* Editor, M.N. Patten, p.151-70. London, Bowker-Saur, 1989. (*Guides to information sources.*) ISBN: 0408014911.

Sections: Introduction - Information sources (*e.g.* reference books and handbooks; journals (43 titles); patents; standards, etc.) - Conferences ... Meetings. About 100 references. *Class No:* 669.6

Aluminium

Bibliographies

[6957]

KEEVIL, D. 'Aluminium'. *Information sources in metallic materials.* Editor, M.N. Patten, p.103-19. London, Bowker-Saur, 1989. (*Guides to information sources.*) ISBN: 0408014911.

Sections: Introduction - Abstracting services - Journals - Handbooks - Standards - Conferences - Standard texts - Aluminium in human health - Associations. 26 references. *Class No:* 669.71(01)

Handbooks & Manuals

[6958]

HATCH, J.E., *ed.* **Aluminum: properties and physical metallurgy.** Metals Park, Ohio, American Society for Metals, 1984. [ix], 424p. illus., diagrs., graphs, tables. ISBN: 0871701766.

Succeeds v.1 of the 3.v. series, *Aluminum* (1967).

53 contributors. 10 chapers: (1. Properties of pure aluminum & constitution of alloys ... 5. Metallurgy of heat treatment and general principles of precipitation hardening ... 7. Corrosion behavior ... 10. Aluminum powder and powder metallurgy products (52 references)). Detailed, analytical index. Micrographs. *Class No:* 669.71(035)

[6959]

KING, F. **Aluminum and its alloys.** New York, Halstead Press, 1987. 313p. illus., tables. $96.95. ISBN: 047024849x.

8 sections (Basic properties - Occurrences and extraction - Refining - Aluminum-alloy system - Properties of aluminum alloys - Production of semi-fabricated forms - Manufacturing processes - Economic factors). References. *Class No:* 669.71(035)

Reviews & Abstracts

[6960]

Aluminium industry abstracts. London, Institute of Materials; Metals Park, Oh., ASM International, 1992-. Monthly.

Sponsored by the European Aluminium Association and The Aluminum Association. Previously as *World aluminum abstracts (1969-91)*, *Aluminum abstracts* (1963-69); originally as *Light metals bulletin* (1949-62).

About 8,000 abstracts pa. 5 sections: Business - Environmental issues - Production - Research - Indexes (subject; alloy; author). Available online through DIALOG and ERINS. *Class No:* 669.71(048)

Yearbooks & Directories

[6961]

World aluminium: a Metal Bulletin databook. 3rd ed. Worcester Park, Surrey, Metal Bulletin Books, Ltd., 1996. lvi, 462p. ISSN: 02691698.

Lists some 850 producers and 575 traders of aluminium, bauxite and alumina worldwide. Companies (A-Z by country); buyers' guide. Memoranda include statistics and associations. *Class No:* 669.71(058)

Beryllium

[6962]

HAUSNER, H.H., *ed.* **Beryllium: its metallurgy and properties.** Berkeley & Los Angeles, Calif., Univ. of California Press, 1965. [vii], 322p. illus., diagrs., tables.

17 contributors. 12 chapters (4. The fabrication of beryllium, p.13-177 - 5. Beryllium alloys, p.179-90 (20 references) ... 11. Future trends in beryllium research - 12. Health hazards in handling beryllium). 2 appendices. Favourably reviewed in *Nature*, v.212, 19 November 1966, p.775-6. *Class No:* 669.725

Cadmium

[6963]

Cadscan. London, Cadmium Association, 1989-. 4pa. £50. ISSN: 09501576.

Formerly *Cadmium abstracts*, 1977-1988.

About 300 abstracts pa. Mainsections: Products and processes - Environment - Properties of materials - Refining and production - Recycling. Author, subject indexes. *Class No:* 669.73

[6964]

Minor metals survey. London, Metal Bulletin, Ltd., 1977. 162p. illus., tables.

Metals concerned: antimony, arsenic, bismuth, cadmium, cerium, chromium, cobalt, indium, manganese, mercury, shenium, selenium and tellurium, tantalum, zirconium. Data for indium: properties; production; price trends; uses, present and future. Occasionally appended 'Selected references'. *Class No:* 669.73

Uranium

[6965]

GITTUS, J.H. **Uranium.** London, Butterworth, 1963. xiii, 623p. illus., diagrs., tables. (*Metallurgy of the rarer metals, 8.*)

Chapters 1-5, on occurrence, exploitation and concentrates, and on separation of the metal, its fabrication. Chapters 6-12: properties (physical, mechanical, chemical, including effects of pile irradiation and corrosion). Chapter 13: 'Alloys of uranium', with 124 references. Final chapter, on metallographic examination. 5 Appendices on reactors, nuclear cross-sections, etc. Standard compendium, in its day. *Class No:* 669.822

[6966]

Uranium: resources, production and demand. OECD Nuclear Energy Agency, and International Atomic Energy Agency. 11th ed. Paris, OECD, 1986. 413p. graphs, charts, tables, map.

First published 1965; 10th ed. 1983.

Two main sections. The first summarizes data on resources, exploration, production, demand, supply and demand. The second (p.83-363) covers 57 countries in turn (excluding Eastern Bloc countries and China), with data submitted officially in response to questionnaires. '... the most authoritative source of information for WOCA (World Outside Centrally Planned Economies Area) countries, and this edition is the largest, most complete version yet ... This is the

.... (contd.)
last of the fully comprehensive Red Books to be published for several years ... [and] ought to be viewed as a must for any uranium industry library' (*Atom*, no. 363, January 1987, p.23). *Class No:* 669.822

Plutonium

[6967]

WICK, O.J., *ed.* **Plutonium handbook:** a guide to the technology. New York, Gordon & Breach, 1967-68. 2v. (x, 520p.; 448p.) illus., diagrs., tables.

Prepared under the auspices of the US Atomic Energy Commission. V.1 has main sections: Physics - Metallurgy - Chemistry. V.2: Chemical processing - Fabrication and utilization of plutonium and alloys - Analysis and inspection methods - Health and safety. Bibliographies. *Class No:* 669.824

Rare Earth Metals

[6968]

GSCHNEIDNER, K.A., *Jr and* EYRING, Le R., *eds..* **Handbook of the physics and chemistry of rare earths.** Amsterdam, etc., North-Holland Co., 1978-. graphs, tables.

1. *Metals.* 1978, xxv, 894p.

2. *Alloys and intermetallics.* 1979. xiii, 628p. £110.

3./4. *Non-metallic compounds.* 1979. xiii, 604p; xiii, 602p. £115; £105.

5. *Rare earth alloys and compounds.* 1982. x, 701p. £132.

10. *High energy spectroscopy.* 1987. 611p. £113.

11. *Two hundred year impact of rare earth on science.* 1988. xiv, 594p. £113.

13. *Rare earth elements.* 1990. xii,473p.

19. *Lanthanides/Actinides: Physics-II.* 1994. xvii, 700p.

Each volume carries documented chapters by specialists. V.19 includes chapters 130 to 134, by various hands, each with extensive bibliography. 'Indispensible for academic libraries and chemistry collections' (*New technical books*, June 1980, item 273). *Class No:* 669.85/.86

[6969]

Rare earth bulletin: an interdisciplinary abstracts journal. London, Multi-Science Publishing Co., 1972-. 6 pa. £165pa. ISSN: 03078531.

Includes *c.*700 abstracts pa. Sections: Extraction; Chemical properties; Crystallography; Nuclear properties; Solid state; Mechanical and accoustic properties; Applications. Subject index. *Class No:* 669.85/.86

Sodium

[6970]

SITTIG, M. **Sodium: its manufacture, properties and uses** ..., with a chapter on the physical and thermodynamic properties of sodium ... New York, Reinhold, 1956. viii, 529p. diagrs., tables.

9 well-documented chapters: 1. Introduction - 2. The manufacture of metallic sodium - 3. Solubility and alloy formation - 4. Handling metallic sodium (101 references) - 5. Uses of metallic sodium - 6. The inorganic reactions of sodium - 7. The use of sodium in organic reactions (679 references). - 8. The analytical chemistry of sodium - 9. Physical end thermodynamic properties of sodium. *Class No:* 669.883

67/68 Manufactures

[6971]
CORBETT, J. 'Manufacturing techniques'. *Information sources in engineering.* K.W. Mildren and P.J. Hicks, eds. (3rd ed., 1996), p.353-75. 3rd ed. London, Bowker Saur, 1996. £80. ISBN: 1857390571.

Covers abstracts and indexes, journals, conference proceedings, books, CAD/CAM/CIM/FMS (Flexible manufatuing systems), management, quality, standards, reference books, organizations. A narrative treatment, with some critical analysis. *Class No:* 67/68

[6972]
Manufacturing worldwide: industry analyses, statistics, products, and leading companies and countries. Darnay, A.J., *ed.* Detroit, Mi., Gale, 1995. 792p. tables. $105. ISBN: 0810396815.

In 2 parts: general statistics in chapters arranged according to the International Standard Industrial Code; world average tables and profiles for 119 countries. Data are drawn chiefly from UN Statistical Division publications. Detailed, analytical index. *Class No:* 67/68

Jewellery

[6973]
BLAKEMORE, K. **The Retail jeweller's guide.** 5th ed. London, Butterworth, 1988, reprinted 1994. 432p. illus. £35.

First published 1969,- designed to replace Selwyn, A. *The retail jeweller's handbook and merchandise manual for sales personnel* (7th ed. London, Heywood, 1962).

4th ed. 1983.

Sections: The metals - The gems - Antique silverwear - Boxes of the 18th and 19th centuries - How silverwares are made - Hallmarks on gold, silver and platinum - Jewellery of the past - The making of jewellery - The history of watches and clocks - Mechanical watches and clocks today - Electrical and electronic watches and clocks. Glossaries. Appendices. Both textbook and reference tool.
Class No: 671.12

[6974]
FORGET, C., *comp.* **Elsevier's dictionary of jewellery and watchmaking** in five languages: English, French, German Italian and Spanish. Amsterdam, etc., Elsevier, 1986. [vii], 507p. £127. ISBN: 044442279x.

5,673 English-base terms, with equivalents and indexes in French, German, Italian and Spanish. Misnomers are indicated.
Class No: 671.12

[6975]
Jeweler's resource: a reference of gems, metals, formulas, and terminology for jewelers. Eastlake, Co., Jewelers Press, 1994. *c.*125p. illus., diagrs., tables. $15.95

Numerous tables, e.g. gem characteristics; birthstones; international ring sizes, etc. Glossary; bibliography; index. *Class No:* 671.12

[6976]
MASON, A. *and* PACKER, D. **An Illustrated dictonary of jewellery.** Reading, Berks., Osprey Publishing Co.; New York, Harper & Row, 1973. 390p. illus. £5.95.

Over 3,000 definitions, many of them brief. Details with gemstones and their identification, the techniques of jewellery manufacture, the history of jewellery, etc. Adequate cross-references. Bibliography, p.388-90. 200 line-drawings. Intended as a reference tool for both those involved in the jewellery trade and those with a less specialized interest. 'Sure to become a standard reference' (*Library journal,* 1 May 1974, p.1290). *Class No:* 671.12

[6977]
UNTRACHT, O. **Jewellery: concepts and technology.** London, Hale, 1982. xxiv, 840p. illus. (incl. col.), diagrs., tables. £39.95. ISBN: 0709196164.

19 sections (*e.g.* 3. Metal, the jewel's raw material - 4. Basic techniques - 5. Sheet metal - 6. Wire - 7. Tubing - 8. Surface ornament, without heat - 9. Surface ornament, with heat - 10. Fabrication - 11. Casing - 12. Natural materials in jewellery - 13. Stones and their setting - 14. Metal finishing - 15. Metallic coating techniques - 16. Metallic build up - 17. Colouring - 18. Standard weights, measures and tables - 19. Glossaries (p.757-90)). Bibliography (grouped), p.791-8. Sources of tools, supplies and services (US, UK). Museums (p.vii). Analytical index (tiny print),

....(contd.)
p.808-40. Over 900 illus. in all, few in colour. A weighty, impressive volume, dealing with the work of 300 jewellers in 26 countries.
Class No: 671.12

Precious Stones

[6978]
BRUTON, E. **Diamonds.** 2nd ed. London, N.A.G. Press, Ltd., 1978, reprinted 1993. xiv, 532p. illus., graphs, tables. ISBN: 0719800714.

First published 1970.

21 chapters (*e.g.* 1. Diamonds in history - 2. Where diamonds are found - 3. The big mining companies - 4. Mining and recovery methods ... 12/14. Grading polished diamonds ... 18. Physical properties of diamonds ... 20. Famous diamonds - 21. Identification of diamonds. Glossary of terms, p.495-503. 6 appendices (*e.g.* 2.The world's largest polished gem diamonds). Analytical index, p.519-32.
Class No: 671.15

[6979]
COPELAND, L.L., *and others.* **The Diamond dictionary.** Los Angeles, Calif., Gemological Institute of America, 1960. viii, [1], 311p. illus., diagrs.

About 3,000 definitions, including notes on famous diamonds, biographies and abbreviations. Pronunciation given. Selected bibliography, p.314-5. Many illus., including reproductions of approximately actual size. 7 appendices, including 'United States and British ring-size equivalents'. *Class No:* 671.15

[6980]
Properties and growth of diamonds. Davies, G., *ed.* London: Inspec, 1994. xv, 437p. illus., diagrs., graphs, tables. ISBN: 0852968752.

12 documented chapters. Detailed, analytical index.
Class No: 671.15

[6981]
TABURLAUK, J. **Pearls: their origin, treatment and identification.** Translated from French by D. Ceriog-Hughes. Radnor, Pa., Chilton Book Co., 1985. 247p. maps.

4 well-documented parts: Natural pearls - Pearl shellfish and the formation of pearls - Cultivated pearls - Pearl working and setting. Glossary of important technical terms. Maps of the world's identified pearling beds. International standards of trade and sale. Classified index. (Based on *New technical books,* v.71(7), July 1986, item 971).
Class No: 671.15

[6982]
WILKS, J. *and* WILKS, E. **Properties and applications of diamonds.** 3rd ed. Oxford, Butterworth-Heinemann, 1991. 525p. diagrs., graphs, micrographs, tables. £90. ISBN: 0750610670.

17 documented chapters. 3 parts: 1. The structure of diamonds - 2. Mechanical properties - 3. Applications and wear of diamonds. 2 appendices: 1. Some numerical values; 2. Units and common factors. Detailed, analytical index. *Class No:* 671.15

Iron & Steel Goods

Cutlery

[6983]
PYBUS, S., *and others, comps.* **Cutlery: a bibliography.** 2nd ed. Sheffield City Libraries, 1982. [iv], 70p. £2.50. ISBN: 0900660848.

First published 1960.

About 1,000 entries for books and articles, often annotated. 14 sections: 1. History - 2. Individual products - 3. Design - 4. Manufacturing processes - 5. Standards - 6. Marketing and statistics - 7. Import controls - 8. Trade marks and patents - 9. Auxiliary tables - 10. Consumer guides - 11. Collections - 12. Illustrations - 13. Associations - 14. Bibliographies and periodicals. *Class No:* 672.7

Fasteners, Pins etc.

[6984]

PARMLEY, R.O., *ed.* **Standard handbook of fastening and joining.**
2nd ed. New York, etc., McGraw-Hill, 1989. [672]p. illus., tables.
£55. ISBN: 0070485224.
First published 1977.
15 sections: Threaded fasteners-description and standards - Standard
pins ... Rope splicing and tying - Metrics and general data. Index. The
2nd ed. contains over 50% new or revised material. For engineers,
machinists and technicians in all fields. 880 illus. *Class No: 672.8*

Non-Ferrous Metal Goods

Tin-Ware

[6985]

UNITED NATIONS. Industrial Development Organization. **Information
sources on the canning industry.** New York, United Nations, 1975.
xii, 83p. (*UNIDO guide in sources of information, no. 19.*)
649 items in 12 sections: 1. Professional, trade and research
organizations, learned societies and special information services - 2.
Directories - 3. Sources of statistics, marketing and other economic
data - 4. Basic handbooks, textbooks and manuals - 5. Monograph
series - 6. Current periodicals - 7. Current abstracting and indexing
journals - 8. Proceedings, papers and reports - 9. Specialized
dictionaries and encyclopaedias - 10. Bibliographies - 11. Films and
catalogues - 12. Other potential sources of information (E. Legislation;
H. Packaging). 'Bibliographical sources used ...'. *Class No: 673.8*

Timber

Encyclopaedias

[6986]

BOUTELJE, E.B. Encyclopedia of world timbers: names and technical
literature. Stockholm, Swedish Forest Products Laboratory, 1980.
338p. ISBN: 9186018000.
3 sections: Scientfic names in alphabetical sequences - Commercial
and local names (*c.*8,000, A-Z), p.99-311 - Key to the technical
literature (376 items, with locations at the Laboratory), p.313-38.
Quarto. *Class No: 674(031)*

[6987]

Concise encyclopaedia of wood and wood-based materials.
Schniewind, A.P., *ed.* Oxford, Pergamon, 1989. 354p. illus., diagrs.,
tables. $125; £70. (*Advances in materials science and engineering.*)
ISBN: 0080347266.
73 documented chapters (A-Z) by leading authorities in the field.
Subject index. An updated supplement to *Encyclopedia of materials
science and engineering*, edited by M.B. Beyer. *Class No: 674(031)*

Handbooks & Manuals

[6988]

DESCH, H.E. Timber: its structure, properties and utilization. 7th
ed., revised by J.M. Dinwoodie. London, Macmillan, 1996. xii, 410p.
illus., diagrs., graphs.
First published 1938.
4 parts (19 chapters): 1. The structure of wood - 2. The gross
features of wood (incl. chapter 6: 'Description of some of the more
important commercial harwoods, Abura ... Walnut (European)',
p.114-52 - 3. The properties of wood - 4. Considerations influencing
the utilization of wood. 2 appendices; 1. List of botanical equivalents
of common or trade names used in the text. Selective Bibliography, by
chapters, p.394-401. Detailed, analytical index, p.402-10.
Class No: 674(035)

[6989]

**Handbook of wood and wood-based materials for engineers,
architects and builders.** United States. Department of Agriculture.
Forest Service. Forest Products Laboratory. Rev. ed. New York,
Hemisphere, 1989. v.p. illus., diagrs., graphs, tables. $77. ISBN:
0891161244.
First published 1935 as *Wood handbook;* previous ed. 1974.
23 chapters of the properties, applications and treatments of wood.
Numerous tables. Glossary, p. G1-G11. 12p. detailed, analytical
index. Emphasis is on US. *Class No: 674(035)*

Dictionaries

Polyglot

[6990]

BOERHAVE-BEEKMAN, W., *comp.* **Elsevier's wood dictionary in
seven languages:** English/American, French, Spanish, Italian,
Swedish, Dutch and German. Amsterdam, etc., Elsevier, 1964-67. 3v.
illus. £122 each.
1. *Commercial and botanical nomenclature.* 1964. xviii, 479p.
2. *Production, transport, trade.* 1966. 642p.
3. *Research, manufacture, utilization.* 1968. 460p.
V.1 has 3,778 numbered entries; v.2, 5,658 entries; v.3, 3,728. In
v.1 the English/American terms are followed by botanical number,
sources of supply (areas), and equivalents in French, Spanish, Italian,
Swedish, Dutch and German. *Class No: 674(038)=00*

[6991]

TEKNISKA NOMENKLATURCENTRALEN. Träbyggnardsordlista.
[Glossary of timber construction.] Stockholm, the Centre, 1975. 224p.
illus. (*TNC 60.*)
725 Swedish entry-words and definitions; English, French and
German equivalents. Classified arrangement; German, French, English
and Swedish indexes. Swedish references p.10-11. Small line-
drawings. A neat production. *Class No: 674(038)=00*

English

[6992]

CORKHILL, T., *comp.* **A Glossary of wood:** 10,000 terms relating to
timber & its uses, explained and classified. London, Stobart, 1979.
viii, 656p. illus. £12.50. ISBN: 085442010x.
First published 1948 (London, Nema Press. viii. 656 p.).
Of the 10,000 terms mostly concisely defined, 1,000 are illustrated
in clear line-drawings, some measured. Lengthier notes on major types
of wood, *e.g.* mahogany. 'Veneers': 1p., with 6 illus. All aspects of
timber, from tree to finished product, especially the many uses and
fabrication of wood. Abbreviations are included in the A-Z sequence.
Keyed line-drawings (*e.g.* roof trusses). A standard dictionary on
wood. *Class No: 674(038)=20*

German

[6993]

BUCKSCH, H. Holz-Wörterbuch. [Dictionary of wood and
woodworking practice.] Wiesbaden & Berlin, Bauverlag GmbH. ISBN:
3762624114.
1. *Deutsch-Englisch.* 2. Aufl. 1978 (reprinted 1986). 461p.
2. *Englisch-Deutch.* 1966. 536p.
Each volume has *c.*20,000 entry-words, some with definitions and
notes on coverage, in addition to equivalents. German genders given.
Appended conversion tables. *Class No: 674(038)=30*

[6994]

MÜHLE, P. Dictionary of wood science and technology: English-
German, German-English. [Wörterbuch der Holzwirtschaft: Englisch-
Deutsch, Deutsch-Englisch.] Wiesbaden, Oscar Brandstetler, 1992.
[x],228,238p. £60.35. ISBN: 3870971576.
About 10,000 words, with equivalents in each half. Covers wood
anatomy, woodworking machinery, timber harvesting and conversion,
pulp and paper manufacturing. *Class No: 674(038)=30*

Reviews & Abstracts

[6995]

Forest products abstracts. Wallingford, Oxon., CAB International,
1978-. 6pa. £210; $375. ISSN: 01404784.
Coverage includes: *c.*2,600 abstracts pa. Coverage includes: General
publications and general techniques; General aspects of forest products
and industry; Wood properties; Timber extraction, conversion and
measurement; Damage to timber and timber protection; Utilization of
wood; Veneers; Composite boards, laminated wood, panels, improved
wood, glues; Pulping; Marketing and trade. Economics. Author and
subject indexes. Occasional review articles precede abstracts (*e.g.*
'Forest products thesis summaries', April 1987, p.137-41).
Online through CAB ABSTRACTS database, CAB ABSTRACTS
CD-ROM and TREECD. Hosts include DIALOG, ESA-IRS.
Class No: 674(048)

Periodicals

[6996]

**TIMBER RESEARCH AND DEVELOPMENT ASSOCIATION
(TRADA). List of current timber journals received by the TRADA
library.** Revised at intervals. High Wycombe, Bucks., TRADA, 1987.
[i], 9p. gratis. (*TLB 138. 1987.*)
Lists *c.*60 journals (title; country; address). Country index (giving
journals' frequency) precedes. *Class No: 674(051)*

Yearbooks & Directories

[6997]
Directory of the wood products industry, 1996. San Francisco, Ca., Miller Freeman, 1995. 760p.
Main sections: Head and division offices - Primary forest products producers - Wood treating - Wholesalers - Secondary wood products and manufacturers - Cross references - Directory of agencies and organizations - Buyers' guide. Covers US and Canada.
Class No: 674(058)

[6998]
Timber trades address book, 1999. Tonbridge, Kent, Miller Freeman, 1998. Annual. [viii], 696p. £72. ISSN: 09678093.
Contents: Buyers' guide - Company data - Who's who - Who owns whom. *Class No:* 674(058)

Tables & Data Books

[6999]
RIJSDIJK, J.F. *and* **LAMING, P.B. Physical and related properties of 145 timbers.** Dordrecht, Kluwer, 1994. vii, 381p. graphs, chemical formulas, tables. ISBN: 0792328752.
Properties: shrinkage/swelling - dimensional changes - ratios and differences - remarks. 2 graphs and data given for each type of timber. *Class No:* 674(083)

Nomenclatures

[7000]
BRITISH STANDARDS INSTITUTION. Nomenclature of commercial timbers, including sources of supply. London, BSI, 1991. 128p. tables. (*BS 7359: 1991.*)
Covers both hardwoods and softwoods in tabular form, with index of standard and other names. *Class No:* 674(083.72)

Standards

[7001]
TIMBER RESEARCH AND DEVELOPMENT ASSOCIATION (TRADA). List of British Standards relating to timber. High Wycombe, Bucks., TRADA, 1987. [i], [i], 12p. £3.75 (to non-members). (*TLB 232. 1987.*)
Listed under subjects (General; Adhesives ... Woodworking; Miscellaneous). *Class No:* 674(083.74)

Maps & Atlases

[7002]
ILIC, J. CSIRO atlas of hardwoods. Berlin, Springer Verlag, 1991. [v],525p. illus. £135. ISBN: 3540532420.
Macro atlas, p.4-69 (with anatomical and other features). Micro atlas, p.70-472. Worldwide. References, p.475. Species index, p.477-525. CSIRO: Commonwealth of Scientific and Industrial Research Organizations. *Class No:* 674(084.3)

Worldwide

[7003]
LINCOLN, W.A. World woods in colour. London, Stobart, 1986. 320p. col. illus., tables. ISBN: 0854420282.
World woods, Abura ... Zebrano. Data on each: botanical and commercial names; distribution; general description; mechanical properties; seasoning; working properties; durability; uses. Selected wood grains, p.288-91. Appended: Table of uses. Sources of further information. Bibliography (grouped), p.301-5. Coloured illus. are reproduced actual size. Index of standard names. Index of vernacular, trade and other names. Index of botanical names. *Class No:* 674(100)

[7004]
PATTERSON, D. Commercial timbers of the world. 5th ed. Aldershot, Gower Technical Press, 1988. x,339p. illus. £45. ISBN: 0291397182.
First published 1948, by F.H. Titmuss.
An encyclopedia of over 350 species. 4 sections: 1. Structure and properties - 2. Wood: its preparation for use - 3. Hardwoods (Abura - Zebrawood) - 4. Softwoods (Alerce - Yew). Bibliography, p.322-25. Index of wood species. *Class No:* 674(100)

[7005]
RENDLE, B.J., *comp.* **World timbers.** London, Benn, 1969-70. 3v. illus.
1. *Europe and Africa.* 1969. 191p.
2. *North and South America.* 1969. 148p.
3. *Asia, and Australia and New Zealand.* 1970. 176p.
About 200 colour plates of wood specimens, with brief descriptions of distribution, availability, characteristics and use. Most of the plates appeared in the periodical *Wood*, 1946-60. Short bibliography (40 classified items). 'Unlikely to be superseded for many years' (*British Book news*, February 1971, p.136). *Class No:* 674(100)

[7006]
TIMBER RESEARCH AND DEVELOPMENT ASSOCIATION (TRADA). Timbers of the world. Brook, W.H. Lancaster, TRADA, 1979-80. 2v. maps. ea. £30. ISBN: 0860958361; 086095837x.
Originally in 9v. 1978.
V.1: Africa; South America; Southern Asia; South-east Asia (1979. [x], 463p.). V.2: Philippines and Japan; Europe; North America; Australasia; Central America and the Caribbean (1980. [viii], 449p.). Data: description of the tree, strength and durability of the timber, its working qualities and uses. Each volume carries a bibliography. *Class No:* 674(100)

Scandinavia

[7007]
Handbook of the Northern wood industries, 1986/87. [Handbok for nordisk träindustri.] Stockholm, AB Svensk Trävaru-Tidning. 880p. ISBN: 9185464015.
Main countries: Sweden; Norway; Denmark; Finland (associations, etc.; timber industry sector; wood pulp and paper sectors; timber wood pulp and paper firms). Other countries (Argentina ... Yugoslavia), p.511-723. Indexes of shipbrokers, etc. General index. Index to advertisers. Appended list of Swedish and French names of some places in Finland. *Class No:* 674(48)

Woodworking

[7008]
MARTENSSON, A. The Woodworker's Bible. London, Pitman House, 1980 reprinted 1990. 288p. illus. £13.99. ISBN: 0273009222.
7 sections: The workshop - Portable power tools - Woodworking machines - Woodworking joints - Furniture construction - Wood as a material - Finishing. 'Dictionary of hand tools and devices', p.6-25. Step-by-step instructions. Addenda, p.288. Well captioned illus. (some in two-colour). Detailed analytical index, p.284-7. Good layout. *Class No:* 674.02

[7009]
TAYLOR, V. The Woodworker's dictionary. Pownal, VT, Storey Communications, 1991. *c*.264p. illus. $24.94 (HB); $12.95 (PB). ISBN: 0882666460; 0882666452, Pbk.
About 3,600 woodworking terms. Covers carpentry, cabinetmaking, joinery, furniture construction, upholstery, species of wood and finishes. Largely based on a series in the British magazine *Woodworker,* revised and expanded. Distinguishes between US and British terms. Brief appendices on major furniture designers, crafts people and styles. 'Recommended' (*Library journal,* January 1991, p.98). *Class No:* 674.02

[7010]
UNITED NATIONS. Industrial Development Organization. Information sources on woodworking machinery. New York, United Nations, 1978. xii, 99p. $4. (*UNIDO guides to information sources, no.31.*)
745 numbered entries. 12 sections: 1. Professional trade, and research organizations, learned societies and special information services - 2. Directories - 3. Sources of statistics, marketing and other economic data - 4. Basic handbooks, textbooks and manuals - 5. Monographic series - 6. Current periodicals - 7. Current abstracting and indexing periodicals - 8. Proceedings, papers and reports - 9. Specialized dictionaries and encyclopaedias - 10. Bibliographies - 11. Films and film catalogues - 12. Other potential sources of information *e.g.* K. Training). 'Bibliographical sources used in compiling the present guide.' Sections 2-3, 6-7, 9-11 have annotations. *Class No:* 674.02

Timbers & Woods

[7011]
BUILDING RESEARCH ESTABLISHMENT. Handbook of hardwoods. Farmer, R.H. 2nd ed. London HM Stationery Office, 1972. v, 243p. tables. £28. ISBN: 0114705410.
First published 1956.
Introductory sections (*e.g.* Working properties; Veneer and plywood; Uses). 'The timbers', p.11-213, Abura ... Willow (Data: other names; the tree; the timber, - properties, processing, durability and preservation uses). Appendices: 1. Properties of hardwoods; 2. Types of saws; 3. Kiln schedules. Index of botanical names; Index of trade and local names. *Class No:* 674.03

[7012]
BUILDING RESEARCH ESTABLISHMENT. A Handbook of softwoods. 2nd ed. London, HM Stationery Office, for the Department of Environment, 1972. 63p. £8. ISBN: 0114705631.
First published 1957 (Forest Products Research Laboratory).
Detailed descriptions of 49 British and imported softwoods, with brief notes on a further 6. Data on properties and use of each, giving specific reference to the wood-using industries of the UK. *Class No:* 674.03

Preservation

[7013]

BRITISH STANDARDS INSTITUTION. **Glossary of terms relating to timber preservation.** London, BSI, 1985. 24p. (*BS 4261: 1985 (1997).*)

Defines 484 terms, in 6 sections: 1. General - 2. Attack by fungi - 3. Attack by insects and marine borers - 4. Preservative processes - 5. Terms associated with preservative treatments - 6. Miscellaneous. Index. *Class No:* 674.04

Tools & Machinery

[7014]

GOODMAN, W.L. **The History of woodworking tools.** London, Bell, 1964. 208p. illus.

8 chapters: The axe and the adze - The plane - The saw - Boring tools - The carpenter's bench - The rule - Chisels and gouges - Miscellaneous tools (*e.g.* levels, the carpenter's bag or tool containers, set square, dividers, gouges, mallet, hammer, spokeshave). Bibliography. List of British museums with displays of such tools. 'The first comprehensive account of such tools in the Western hemisphere' (*Nature*, v.204, no.4956, 24 October 1964, p.314). *Class No:* 674.05

[7015]

HORTEN, H.E. **Woodworking machines in 4 languages.** London, C.R. Books, 1968. xiii, 353p. illus. (pl.), diagrs., tables.

Over 3,500 technical terms appear in 4 sequences: English, German, French, Spanish; German, English, French, Spanish; French, English, German, Spanish; Spanish, English, French, German. Pages 1-99 provide photographs of commonly-used machines. Conversion tables. *Class No:* 674.05

[7016]

SALAMAN, R.A., *ed.* **Dictionary of woodworking tools.** 2nd ed. London, Unwin Hyman, 1989. 544p. illus. £40. ISBN: 0044402562.

First published 1975.

A-Z sequence of tools, entries including much material from manufacturers' catalogues. A feature: clear line-drawings and illus., many of them keyed (*e.g.* violin maker's tools: 14 parts; wooden wagon: 42 parts). Profuse cross-references. A list of *c.*70 trades, from boiler maker to woodwind maker, precedes. Bibliography and references. 'Useful not only to historians, but to collectors and craftsmen; indispensable for museums collecting such artifacts' (*Library journal*, 1 December 1976. p.2471, of the 1975 ed.). Salaman's collection of tradesman's tools is exhibited in St. Albans City Museum. *Class No:* 674.05

[7017]

SIMS, W.L. **Two hundred years of history and evolution of woodworking machinery.** Melton Mowbray, Leics., Walders Press, 1985. illus., facsims. £8.

Traces the history from the advent of rotating cutters and saws to the present day. Profusely illustrated, including reproductions from manufacturers' catalogues. 'This comprehensive, fascinating and obviously meticulously research history' (*CME/Chartered mechanical engineer*, v.33, February 1986, p.54). *Class No:* 674.05

Carpentry & Joinery

[7018]

HEWETT, C.A. **English historic carpentry.** London & Chichester, Phillimore, 1980. xiv, 338p. illus. (incl. pl.). ISBN: 0850333547.

8 periods: 1. The Anglo-Saxon period (AD 449 to 1066) ... 8. The Renaissance and after (1581 to 1890). 6. appendices (*e.g.* 3. Joints used for framing of floors). Glossary, p.vii-xii. Bibliography, p.xii-xiv. 350 illus. and line-drawings. Index. *Class No:* 674.1/.2

Plywood

[7019]

WOOD, A.D. **Plywoods of the world:** their development, manufacture and application. 3rd rev. ed. Edinburgh, Johnston & Bacon, 1963. xiv, 489p. illus.

First published as *Plywoods* (1942).

10 Chapters. 1. Development - 2. Physical properties of wood - 3. The manufacture of multiply - 4. Laminboards, blackboards, composite boards, etc. - 5. Grading, testing, packing and storing - 6. Plywood-producing countries of the world (p.187-280) - 7. Commercial plywoods, etc. - 8. The plywood trade in the United Kingdom - 9. The development of wall panelling - 10. Applications. Appended terms and definitions, grading rules, plywood associations, publications consulted or recommended (p.323-5), trade journals and periodicals. 241 illus, incl. 19 plates. Comprehensive. *Class No:* 674.812

Leather

Bibliographies

[7020]

UNITED NATIONS. Industrial Development Organization. **Information sources on the leather and leather goods industry.** New York, United Nations, 1972. xix, 80p. (*UNIDO Guides to information sources, no.3.*)

497 items, in 10 sections: 1. Addresses of professional, trade and research organizations, learned and special information centres - 2. Directories - 3. Sources of statistics and other economic data - 4. Basic handbooks, textbooks and manuals - 5. Current periodicals - 6. Current abstracting and indexing services - 7. Special documents: proceedings, papers and reports - 8. Monographs - 9. Bibliographies - 10. Other potential sources of information (*e.g.* Information on standards and specifications). 'Bibliographical sources utilized', appended. *Class No:* 675(01)

Dictionaries

Polyglot

[7021]

INTERNATIONAL COUNCIL OF TANNERS and others. **International glossary of leather terms.** 2nd ed., rev. and enlarged. London, the Council, 1975. 320p. £59.75.

First published 1968.

About 300 terms in each of 5 languages, - English, French, German, Spanish and Italian. 5 sequences, each on differently coloured papers. Reprinted with addenda incorporated in 1997. *Class No:* 675(038)=00

[7022]

UNION INTERNATIONALE DES SOCIÉTÉS DE CHIMISTES DES INDUSTRIES DU CUIR. **Leather technical glossary in six languages.** Darmstadt, E. Roethe Verlag, 1976. 720p. ISBN: 3792900090.

5,429 numbered English-base terms, with explanations, and equivalents and indexes in French, German, Italian, Russian and Spanish. Genders given. *Class No:* 675(038)=00

English

[7023]

BRITISH STANDARDS INSTITUTION. **Glossary of leather terms.** London, BSI, 1983. 24p. diagrs. (*BS 2780: 1983(1995).*)

Previously as BS 2780: 1956.

277 terms are briefly defined in one A-Z sequence. Cross-references. 6 diagrams of parts of hides. *Class No:* 675(038)=20

[7024]

INDIAN STANDARDS INSTITUTION. **Indian Standard glossary of terms relating to hides, skins and leather.** New Delhi, the Institution, 1961. 110p. illus., diagrs. (*I.S. 1640: 1960.*)

Descriptive entries for *c.*1,500 terms, especially on types of tanning material. English entry-words are sometimes followed by the Sanskrit equivalent. Sources, p.2-3. Illus., p.103-10. *Class No:* 675(038)=20

Reviews & Abstracts

[7025]

Leather science abstracts. Adyar, India, Central Leather Research Institute, 1988-. Monthly.

Formerly *Current leather literature, 1968-1988.*

About 1,200 abstracts pa., drawing on *c.*250 journals. Sections: Leather science and industry - Footwear and leather goods - Wood technology ... Textile technology ... Biochemistry - Botany. Subject indexes per issue and annually. *Class No:* 675(048)

Yearbooks & Directories

[7026]

International leather guide, 1998. Tonbridge, Kent, Miller Freeman, 1997. xii, 596p. £110. ISSN: 09555080.

Sections: Master buyers' guide - Hides and skin suppliers - Merchants - Tanners - Chemical suppliers - Machinery manufacturers - Trade organizations and consultants - Master index to companies and organizations - Index to advertisers. *Class No:* 675(058)

Equipment & Instruments

[7027]
SALAMAN, R.A. **Dictionary of leather-working tools, 1700-1950,** and the tools of allied trades. London, Allen & Unwin, 1986. xxi, 377p. illus. ISBN: 004621030x.

13 chapters (1. Bookbinder; 2. Boot and shoe maker; 9. Harness maker and saddler; 10. Hat maker; 11. Leather manufacture (1. Tanner's tools; 2. Currie's tools); 13. Miscellaneous trades and tools (*e.g.* parchment and vellum maker; taxidermist)). References and bibliography, p.340-8. General index, p.346-77 ('Knife': 3 columns). List of museums and institutions. Fully illustrated.
Class No: 675:002.50

Furs

[7028]
BACHRACH, M. **Fur: a practical treatise.** 3rd ed. New York, Prentice-Hall, 1953. (Reprinted New York, Gordon Press, 1977). xii, 600p. illus., diagrs.

12 sections, dealing with the different types of fur-bearing animal. Appendix includes nomenclature of fur peltries, a fur-products name guide, and a subject bibliography, p.639-67. Detailed index. A standard work, covering geographical features, ranching, marketing and buying, plus technical aspects. *Class No:* 675.6

Paper

Databases

[7029]
Paperchem. Atlanta, Ga., Institute of Paper Science and Technology.

Covers patent and journal literature (1000 titles scanned). Corresponds to the print *Abstract bulletin of The Institute of Paper Science and Technology.* About 435,000 records; updated weekly. Available on DIALOG, file 240, and STN International.
Class No: 676(003.4)

[7030]
PIRA Abstracts. Leatherhead, Surrey, PIRA, the Research Association for the Paper and Board, Printing and Packaging Industries.

Covers 1975 to date. A bibliographic database providing references, with abstracts, to the literature of paper and pulp manufacture, printing and packaging. Packaging materials, operations and equipment, products, markets and companies are covered. Sources: over 700 periodicals, books, reports, standards and conference papers. File size: 422,000 items. Updated biweekly. Available via DIALOG, Questel/ORBIT and STN International; CD-ROM (DIALOG OnDisc); and on the World Wide Web (URL: http://www.pira.co.uk).
Class No: 676(003.4)

Bibliographies

[7031]
UNITED NATIONS. Industrial Development Organization. **Information sources on the pulp and paper industry.** New York, United Nations, 1974. xii, 91p. $4. (*UNIDO Guide to information sources, no.11.*)

629 entries, in 12 sections: 1. Addresses of professional trade and research organizations, learned societies and special information sources - 3. Directories ... 6. Current periodicals ... 9. Special dictionaries and encyclopedias - 10. Bibliographies ... 12. Other sources of reference (*e.g.* Standards and specifications). 'Bibliographical sources used', appended. *Class No:* 676(01)

Encyclopaedias

[7032]
LABARRE, E.J. **Dictionary and encyclopaedia of paper and paper-making,** with equivalents of the technical terms in French, German, Dutch, Italian, Spanish and Swedish. 2nd ed., rev. and enl. London, Oxford Univ. Press, 1952. xxiv 488p. illus.

First published 1937, as *A dictionary of paper and paper-making terms* (Amsterdam, Swets & Zweitlinger).

About 3,000 entries, including lengthy articles (*e.g.* 'Sizes', p.246-72; 'Wrapping papers', p.368-74). List of sources (5 sections), p.xi-xx. Indexes in 7 languages. *Class No:* 676(031)

[7033]
—LOCKER, E.J. Dictionary and encyclopaedia of paper and paper-making, Amsterdam, Swets & Zeitlinger, 1967. x, 104p.

A supplement to Labarre (*qv*) adds *c.*1,000 terms in English, with equivalents and indexes in the other 6 languages. *Class No:* 676(031)

Handbooks & Manuals

[7034]
BRISTOW, J.A. *and* KOLSETH, P. **Paper structure and properties.** New York, Dekker, 1986. x, [i], 390p. illus., diagrs., graphs, tables. ISBN: 0824775608.

17 contributors; 17 documented chapters. 1. The fiber - 2. Paper structure ... 17. The layered structure of paper (13 references). 3 appendices. Mechanical models of paper. Detailed, analytical index. 'Presents paper as a material with a structure which can be described at different levels' (*Preface*). For the professional. *Class No:* 676(035)

[7035]
HUNTER, D. **Paper-making:** the history and techniques of an ancient craft. 2nd ed., rev. and enl. London, Pleiades, 1957. xxix, 611, xxxviip. diagrs.

First published 1943.

Covers materials and methods, with a lengthy chronology, p.463-584, of paper-making, paper, and the uses of paper. Bibliography of 200 items (p.583-602): 1. Oriental - 2. Occidental - 3. Watermarking - 4. Paper colours and surface decoration. Chapter notes. Analytical index. 317 diagrs. in text. *Class No:* 676(035)

Dictionaries

[7036]
AMERICAN PAPER AND PULP ASSOCIATION. **The Dictionary of paper,** including pulp, paperboard, paper properties, and related papermaking terms. 3rd ed. New York, the Association, 1965. xii, 500p.

First published 1940.

About 2,567 terms (1,463 revised; 710 deleted; 329 new). Entries are lengthy at times (*e.g.* 'Pulps': p.5-30). Numerous cross-references. *Class No:* 676(038)

[7037]
BRITISH STANDARDS INSTITUTION. **Glossary of paper, board, pulp and related terms.** London, BSI, 1979 (1995). 28p. (*BS 3203: 1979(1995).*)

About 300 terms defined. 7 sections: 1. Pulp: general terms - 2. Pulp manufacture - 3. Types of pulp - 4. Paper and board: general terms - 5. Paper making - 6. Types of paper or border-converted products - 7. Properties of pulp, paper or board. Index of *c.*700 terms. *Class No:* 676(038)

[7038]
Fachwörterbuch papier: Deutsch/Englisch, Englisch/Deutsch. Gerssbach, Europäscher Wirtschaftsdisent, 1990. 243p. ISBN: 3886400433.

About 5000 entries in each half. *Class No:* 676(038)

[7039]
LAVIGNE, J.R. **Pulp and paper dictionary.** 2nd ed. San Francisco, Ca., Miller Freeman Publications, 1993. xxvi, 435p. diagrs. $75. ISBN: 0879303034.

First published 1986.

Nearly 6,000 entries, defined in 2-4 lines, usually; cross-references. Appendix A: References (including 'Magazines and trade journals', 'Standards and data sheets'); B. Conversion tables. Brief history and process of papermaking precede. *Class No:* 676(038)

[7040]
SVATON, M. **Dictionary of the pulp and paper industry in five languages:** English, German, French, Spanish, Russian. Amsterdam, Elsevier, 1993. [vi], 517p. £129. ISBN: 0444987894.

About 5,500 English base terms, with equivalents and indexes in the other languages. *Class No:* 676(038)

[7041]
TEKNISKA NOMENKLATURCENTRALEN. **Pappersordlista.** Stockholm, the Centre, 1980. 416p. illus. (*TNC 74.*) ISBN: 0171620826.

1,284 Swedish paper industry terms and definitions, with equivalents and indexes in English, French, German, Norwegian and Finnish. *Class No:* 676(038)

Reviews & Abstracts

[7042]
Abstract bulletin of the Institute of Paper Science and Technology. Atlanta, Ga., Institute of Paper Science and Technology, 1934-. Monthly. $2050. ISSN: 00203033.

About 15,000 abstracts pa. 2 sections: periodical abstracts; patent abstracts. Subject, author and patent indexes per issue. Separately published annual index, $75. Available online as *Paperchem.* *Class No:* 676(048)

[7043]

Paperbase abstracts Leatherhead, Surrey, Pira International, 1968-. Monthly. £550pa. ISSN: 13595156.

Formerly *Paper and board abstracts*

About 6,000 abstracts pa. Some 20 sections (*e.g.* Paper and board industry in general; Company information; Non-fibrous raw material; Paper and board making; Instrumentation and control; Properties and testing of paper and board; Paper and board grades and specialities; Synethetic paper and nonwovens). Available online as a subfile of Pira database on DIALOG, Data-Star, FIZ Technik, etc.; also on CD-ROM and the World Wide Web (URL: http://www.pira.co.uk).

Class No: 676(048)

Yearbooks & Directories

[7044]

International pulp and paper directory, 1992-93. San Francisco, Ca., Miller Freeman, 1991. xxx,916p.

7 sections: Pulp and paper mills (by continent, then country) - Mill grades (pulp; paper) - Market pulp (grades; producers) - Paper merchants (European; North American) - Industry information sources - Trade shows and conferences - Buyers' guide. *Class No:* 676(058)

[7045]

Phillips International Paper directory, 1990. 87th ed. Tonbridge, Kent, Benn, 1990. xiv,594p. £80. ISBN: 0863820417.

Contents: Mills of the world (countries, A-Z); Classified list of products - Merchants - Agents (paper; pulp) - Waste paper merchants and processors - Exporters and importers - Suppliers (machinery; equipment; materials) - Converters (packaging and other products) - Brand names and watermarks - Trade associations - Index to advertisers. *Class No:* 676(058)

Histories

[7046]

LEIF, I.P. An International sourcebook of paper history. Hamden, Conn., Archon; Folkeston, Dawson, 1978. viii, 160p. ISBN: 0713908277.

2,185 numbered references. 5 sections: 1. General histories of paper and watermarks - 2/4. The history of paper and papermaking in Asia and Australia, Europe and the Soviet Union, North and South America - 5. The study of paper history. Sections 2/4 are each subdvided by countries A-Z (items 817-1444). Author and analytical subject indexes. *Class No:* 676(091)

Thesauri

[7047]

Thesaurus of pulp and paper terminology. 3rd ed. Atlanta, Ga., Institute of Paper Science and Technology, 1991. xvi,557p. ISBN: 0870100009.

First ed. 1965; 2nd ed. 1971.

Includes over 22,000 main entries (11,000 'key' terms and 11,000 cross-references). Terms include chemical, biological, industrial nomenclature. Alphabetical display of terms (540p.) is followed by a 'Microthesaurus' of well-known proper names (countries, professional societies, etc.). *Class No:* 676:025.43

Information Services

[7048]

International pulp and paper sourcebook. 3rd ed. Leatherhead, Surrey, Pira International, 1997. vii, 293p. ISBN: 1858021642.

First published 1988 as *International pulp and paper information sources*; 2nd ed. 1991.

A range of information sources (*e.g.* published materials; training; exhibitions; markets) on all aspects of paper. About 50 countries. Indexes: Country; Organizations; Publications; Subject. A wealth of information. *Class No:* 676:061:025.5

Watermarks

[7049]

BRIQUET, C.M. Les filigranes. Dictionnaire historique des marques du papier, des leur apparition vers 1282 jusqu'en 1600. Avec 39 figures dans le texte et 16, 112 fac-similés de filigranes. 2nd éd. Leipzig, Hiensemann, 1923. 4v. (Reprinted New York, Hacker Art Books, 1966). 4v. (A-Ch, Ci-K, L-O, P-Z).

First published 1907 (Paris, Picard).

The 16,112 facsimiles of watermarks are arranged by subject of devices (*e.g.* 'Tête de boeuf'). Each volume carries a section of descriptive notes. References to sources precede the numbered illus. *Class No:* 676.026.4

[7050]

—**CHURCHILL, W.A.** Watermarks in paper in Holland, England, France, etc., in the 17th and 18th centuries, and their interconnection. Amsterdam, Hertzberger, 1935. 94 + 432p. illus. (pl.), tables.

Provides 578 examples of watermarks, 94p. of text, 432p. of plates. Includes chronological lists of Dutch and French papermakers. *Class No:* 676.026.4

Textiles

Databases

[7051]

Textile technology digest. Charlottesville, Va., Institute of Textile Technology.

Covers dyeing, laundering, mill operation, natural and man-made fibres, preservation, apparel design, marketing and statistics. Corresponds to the print *Textile technology digest.* Over 188,000 records; updated monthly. Available on DIALOG, file 119. *Class No:* 677(003.4)

[7052]

World textiles. Oxford, Elsevier, 1970-.

The database for *World textile abstracts.* Over 210,000 records; updated monthly. Available on DIALOG, file 67, on CD-ROM and on the Internet. *Class No:* 677(003.4)

Bibliographies

[7053]

DOIDGE, R.I. A Survey of textile industry information. London, City University, Centre for Information Science, 1982. v, 119 + 18l. facsims., tables.

Thesis accepted for MSc.

More than 1,000 annotated and evaluated entries. 9 sections: 1. General information sources - 2. Information retrieval methods and abstracting service - 3. Health and safety in the textile industry - 4. Textile trade - 5. Market research and statistical sources - 6. Energy use in the textile industry - 7. Care labelling and flammability of textiles - 8. Textile history and conservation - 9. Information on textile industry research. Includes 'Databases', 1.38-40. Well organized, although lacking an index. *Class No:* 677(01)

[7054]

VOGEL, J.T. and LOWRY, B.W. The Textile industry: an information sourcebook. Phoenix, Az., Oryx, 1989. 246p. $49.50. (*Oryx sourcebook series in business and management, 19.*) ISBN: 0897743547.

Gives priority to English-language sources and works published since 1980. Emphasis is on business rather than technology, and includes a 'Core library collection' as the final chapter. Author, title and subject indexes. *Class No:* 677(01)

Encyclopaedias

[7055]

Encyclopedia of textiles. 3rd ed., by the editors of *American fabrics and fashions magazine.* Englewood Cliffs, N.J., Prentice Hall, Inc., 1980. xvi, 636p. illus., facsims. ISBN: 0132765164.

First published 1960.

7 major sections (subdivided): The textile fibres - History & origins - Textiles in the Americas - The manufacturing processes - Fabric finishing - Specialty uses of textiles - Textile definitions, p.512-601. Detailed, analytical index, p.604-36. Fully illustrated. *Class No:* 677(031)

[7056]

GRAYSON, M., ed. Encyclopedia of textiles, fibres and nonwoven fibres. New York, etc., Wiley, 1984. xxvi, 581p. (*Encyclopedia reprint series.*)

One in the series of carefully selected reprints from the world-renowned Kirk-Othmer *Encyclopedia of Chemical Technology.* *Class No:* 677(031)

[7057]

JERDE, J. The Encyclopedia of textiles. New York, Facts on File, 1992. 260p. illus., diagrs., tables. $45. ISBN: 0816021058.

Entries cover types of textiles, history, manufacturing processes, A-Z. About 250 illus., 42 in colour. Bibliography. *Class No:* 677(031)

Handbooks & Manuals

[7058]
TEXTILE INSTITUTE. The Identification of textile materials. 7th rev. ed. Manchester, the Institute, 1985. v, 262p. illus., diagrs., tables. ISBN: 0900739770.

3rd ed. 1951.

Introduction - The properties of textile fibres: natural fibres, man-made fibres - Scheme of analysis - Note on reagents and methods of test - Photomicrographs (167). Index. The terms used are, whenever published, those listed in *Textile terms and definitions* (*qv*).
Class No: 677(035)

Dictionaries

Polyglot

[7059]
COMMISSION ON TEXTILE DOCUMENTATION OF THE EUROPEAN GROUP FOR THE EXCHANGE OF EXPERIENCE ON THE DIRECTION OF TEXTILE RESEARCH. Multilingual glossary of textile terminology, with translations into Danish, Dutch, English, Finnish, French, German, Japanese, Norwegian, Spanish and Swedish. Cambridge, Mass., Fibres and Polymers Laboratories, Massachusetts Institute of Technology, 1972. 9v.

Each volume gives priority to one particular language. The English-entry volume ([i], viii, 395, 73p.) has *c.*10,000 terms, translated into the other 8 languages, plus a separate English-Japanese (native characters) section. Omits Russian. *Class No:* 677(038)=00

[7060]
—TEKNISKA NOMENKLATURCENTRALEN. Textilordlista. [Glossary of textiles.] Stockholm, the Centre, 1981. 272p.

Defines *c.*770 terms in Swedish, with equivalents in English, French, German, Dutch, Norwegian and Finnish.
Class No: 677(038)=00

[7061]
COURTAULDS, Ltd. Courtaulds' vocabulary of textile terms. 2nd ed. London, Courtaulds, Ltd., 1972. 234p. tables. £10.

English-based terms in classified groups, with French, Spanish, German and Russian equivalents, and indexes in all five languages. Covers fibres (especially man-made), yarns and fabrics, their properties and processing. Appended conversion tables. Well produced. *Class No:* 677(038)=00

[7062]
ITS textile dictionary: English, Deutsch, Français, Italiano, Español, Portugês. New ed. Amsterdam, Elsevier; Zurich, International Textile Service, Ltd., 1989. viii,1537p.

29,300 entries. One A-Z sequence in all six languages.
Class No: 677(038)=00

[7063]
The Kendale glossary of basic textile terms. Huddersfield, Kendale Publications Ltd., 1990. 282p.

About 4,500 terms in English, with equivalents in German, Spanish, French and Italian. Indexes. *Class No:* 677(038)=00

[7064]
Textile dictionary: English/American - German - French - Spanish - Italllian. [Textiltechnisches Wörterbuch: Englisch/Amerikanisch - Deutsch - Französisch - Spanisch - Italienisch.] 2nd ed. Düsseldorf, VDI-Verlag, GmbH, 1991. [x], 885p. £110. ISBN: 3184008762.

First published 1979.

About 9,500 English head words, with equivalents in other languages. *Class No:* 677(038)=00

[7065]
VINCENTI, R. Elsevier's textile dictionary in five languages: English, German, French, Italian and Spanish. Amsterdam, Elsevier, 1993. 619p. £154.90. ISBN: 0444887091.

About 7,800 English-base terms, with equivalents and indexes.
Class No: 677(038)=00

English

[7066]
TEXTILE INSTITUTE. Textile terms and definitions.
Beech, S.R., *ed.* 10th ed. Manchester, the Institute, 1994. *c.*300p. illus., diagrs. £50; £90. ISBN: 0900739819.

First published 1954.

Defines *c.*3,900 textile terms, including 1,000 new and revised ones. Cross-references. Appendices include conversion tables and a classification of textile fibres. Aimed at lay users, students and specialists. Authoritative. *Class No:* 677(038)=20

[7067]
TORTORA, P.B. Fairchild's dictionary of textiles. 7th ed. New York, Fairchild, 1996. 662p. illus. ISBN: 0870057073.

First published 1915; 6th ed. 1979..

About 16,000 entries, including trade associations and ionstitutes. Covers textile technology, electronic equipment, dyeing, printing, finishing. A standard work; 'recommended' (*Information sources in science and technology*, 3rd ed., 1998, p.205).
Class No: 677(038)=20

German

[7068]
HOHENADEL, P. *and* **RELTON, J. A Modern textile dictionary,** English-German, German-English. 2nd ed. Wiesbaden, Brandstetter, 1991-96. 2v. (446; 437p.). £48.95 each.

First published 1977-79.

V.1: English-German has *c.*12,500 entry-words; v.2: German-English, *c.*10,500 entry-words. Massed subentries.
Class No: 677(038)=30

French

[7069]
HIRSCH, P. Lexique textile, français-anglais. 4th ed. Paris, Éditions Olifant, 1994. 205p. £23.70.

About 5,000 French entry-words. Abbreviations are listed separately. Appended list of weights and measures, as applied to textiles. The 2nd ed. of the English-French volume appeared in 1989 (223p. £30). *Class No:* 677(038)=40

Glossaries

[7070]
The Anstey Weston guide to textile terms. Weston, 1997. *c.*100p. ISBN: 0953013006.

About 900 terms, briefly explained, and arranged by subject: fibres, yarns, fabrics, dyeing, printing, finishing. Index.
Class No: 677(038.1)

Reviews & Abstracts

[7071]
Textile technology digest. Charlottesville, Va., Institute of Textile Technology, 1944-. Monthly. ISSN: 00405191.

About 750 entries per issue. 9 sectons (A. Fibers ... C. Fiber production ... E. End product fabrication ... G. Company practices ... I. Miscellaneous (conferences; education; etc.)). Author index per issue. *Class No:* 677(048)

[7072]
World textile abstracts. Oxford, Elsevier, 1969-. Monthly. £460, $686pa. ISSN: 00439118.

About 400 abstracts per issue. 10 sections: 1/3. Fibres, yarns, fabrics: manufacture and properties - 4. Chemical and finishing processes - 5. Products: manufacture, properties, aftercare - 6. Plant services and environment - 7. Management - 8. Analysis, testing, quality control - 9. Polymer science - 10. Generalities. Author, patent and subject indexes per issue, cumulated annually.

World textile abstracts: register of keywords (Shirley Institute, 1983. 2v. 91p., 28p.) consists of *Keyword list* and *Auxiliary lists*.

Available online as *World textiles* (DIALOG, file 67).
Class No: 677(048)

Yearbooks & Directories

[7073]
The Kendale textile industry directory. Huddersfield, Kendale Publications, Ltd., 1987. 432p.

List of textile industry companies, A-Z, p.18-224. Data on each include activities, names and directors and bankers. Buyers guide. Appended list of trade names. Index of advertisers.
Class No: 677(058)

Histories

[7074]
FLEMMING, E. Encyclopaedia of textiles: decorative fabrics, from antiquity to the beginning of the 19th century, including the Far East and Peru. Rev. ed. London, Zwemmer, 1958. illus. (incl. pl.).

First published 1927.

History of textiles, p.vii-xxvi. Concentrates on Europe, but includes China, Japan, Persia and Peru. 'The grouping within the individual areas has been made according to the weaving techniques employed, subdivided according to the available historical evidence' (*Preface*). Illus. include 304 plates (16 in colour). *Class No:* 677(091)

[7075]

The Illustrated history of textiles. Ginsburg, M., *ed.* London, Studio Editions, 1991. 224p. illus. £19.95. ISBN: 1851704469.

Development in textile production and design, from the Middle Ages to the present, and covering early woven cottons and silk to recent acrylics. Includes essays on the different categories of textiles, including lace and tapestry. *Class No:* 677(091)

Worldwide

[7076]

ECONOMIST INTELLIGENCE UNIT. World textile trade and production trends. Anson, R. *and* Simpson, P. London, the Unit, June 1988. 343p. graphs, tables. (*Special report no. 1108.*) ISBN: 0850582075.

3 parts (16 chapters): 1. General trends in production - 2. International trade in textiles and clothing - 3. Textile prospects and clothing prospects, by country (p.161-342). Appendix: Exchange rates. Statistics usually for 1980, 1985/87. Numerous tables. *Class No:* 677(100)

Thesauri

[7077]

BACKER, N. *and* **VALKO, E.I.,** *eds.* **Thesaurus of textile terms,** covering fibrous materials and processes. 2nd ed. Cambridge, Mass., and London, MIT Press, 1969. xv, 448p.

First published 1966.

8,000 keywords; 72,000 relationships (p.1-263). References used in preparing the *Thesaurus* (62 references), p.332-8. Appendices A-C (A. 'Problems of textile information retrieval'). 7-p. bibliography. 'Highly recommended, particulary for research oriented individuals' (*Choice,* v.6(8), October 1969, p.996). *Class No:* 677:025.43

Museums

[7078]

LUBELL, C., *ed.* **Textile collections of the world.** London, Studio Vista, 1976-77. 3v. illus. (incl. col. pl.).

1. *The United States and Canada.* 1976. 320p.
2. *United Kingdom and Ireland.* 1976. 224p.
3. *France,* 1977. 240p.

Illustrated guides, arranged under cities. V.1-2 contain 905 illus. (118 in colour), with introductory essays on national textile design and data on individual collections. Favourably reviewed in annual *Textile history,* v.8, 1977, p.194. *Class No:* 677:061:069

Production Processes

[7079]

BURNHAM, D.K. A Textile terminology, warp and weft. London, Routledge & Kegan Paul, 1980. xiv, 216p. illus., diagrs.

Expanded and adapted from H. Burnham's *The vocabulary of textile terms* (1964).

Defines more than 550 woven textile terms, usually with equivalents in French, German, Italian, Spanish, Portuguese and Swedish. Bibliography of citations, p.209-16. Well illustrated. 'Although of more obvious value in certain academic or school libraires, it would not be out of place in the reference section of a public library' (*Library review,* v.31, Winter 1982, p.300). *Class No:* 677.02

[7080]

FISCHER-BOBSIEN, C.H., *ed.* **International encyclopedia of textile finishing.** 3rd advance volume. Dalmen (W. Germany), Laumenn Verlag, 1985. DM260. illus.

Nearly 6,000 entries, mostly with photographs. Comprises the important terms, products, processes and materials associated with textile finishing. *Class No:* 677.02

Weaving

[7081]

PRITCHARD, M.E. A Short dictionary of weaving, including some spinning, dyeing and textile terms, and a beginner's guide to weaving and dyeing. London, Allen & Unwin, 1954. 196p. illus., diagrs.

Several hundred concise definitions, p.13-109, with clear line-drawings. 3 appendices: 1. Specimen loom, showing principal parts; types of loom - 2. Quick-reference sections (including calculating qualities; knots used in weaving; warping guide) - 3. The pattern in weaving. Bibliography, p.195-6. *Class No:* 677.024

Products

Carpets

[7082]

BRITISH CARPET MANUFACTURER'S ASSOCIATION LIMITED. Index of quality names. London, The Assocation. Annual, with quarterly supplements. v.p.

Names, A-Z, with type of carpet, finish, pile content and manufacturer. *Class No:* 677.07.5

[7083]

Directory to the furniture and furnishing industry, 1999. Tonbridge, Kent, Miller Freeman, 1998. vii, 484p. ISSN: 09548548.

Formerly *Directory to the furnishing trade;* incorporates *Carpet annual.*

Directory-type information for the UK and Eire. Sections: Furniture and furnishings - Carpets and floor coverings - Manufacturers' supplies and services - Brands and trade names - Overseas manufacturers and UK agents - Company data - Index to retail furnishers (alphabetical/ geographical) - Index to contract furnishers - Trade association and organizations. *Class No:* 677.07.5

[7084]

HEREFORD AND WORCESTER COUNTY LIBRARIES. Carpets and textiles: a complete list of the special collection in Kidderminster Library. Hereford and Worcester County Council. Libraries Dept, 1981. [i], [i], 54p. £1.

The catalogue of an extensive collection. *Class No:* 677.07.5

Textile Fibres

[7085]

HARDINGHAM, M. Illustrated dictionary of fabrics. London, Studio Vista, 1978. 159p. illus., facsims. ISBN: 0289708478.

Sections: Introduction - Wool, cotton, silk - Other plant fibres (Aida canvas ... Sisal) - Man-made fibres. Textile terms (Appliqué ... Yarn), p.130-51. List of obsolete fabrics, p.152-3. Bibliography, p.154-5. Index (small type), p.158-9. Quarto format. Covers' names and descriptions of fabrics we wear and use in our homes, as well as some used for industrial purposes' (*Introduction*). *Class No:* 677.1/.5

Jute

[7086]

GILL, C. The Rise of the Irish linen industry. Oxford, Clarendon Press, 1925. 359p. illus., tables, maps.

16 chapters. 4 appendices. Bibliography (grouped), p.344-9. Index, p.351-9. *Class No:* 677.13

Cotton

[7087]

BAINES, Sir E. History of the cotton manufacture in Great Britain; with a bibliographical introduction by W.H. Chaloner. 2nd ed. New York, A.M. Kelley; London, Cass, 1966. 544p. (*Reprints of economics classics.*)

Previous ed.: London, Fisher, Fisher & Jackson, 1835.

17 chapters (*e.g.* 6. The cotton manufacture in India; 7. The cotton manufacture in England; 12. Bleaching and calico printing; 13. Cotton-wool). No index, but full contents (p.11-18). *Class No:* 677.21

[7088]

FARNIE, D.A. The English cotton industry and the world market, 1815-1896. Oxford, Clarendon Press, 1979. [xi], 399p. illus., tables. ISBN: 0198224788.

3 parts (8 footnoted chapters): 1. The advent of a new economic order - 2. The main trends in production and trade - 3. The structure of the industry. Select bibliography, grouped, p.329-84. Detailed, analytical index, p.385-99. *Class No:* 677.21

Wool

[7089]

LEMON, H. How to find out about the wool textile industry. Oxford, etc., Pergamon Press, 1968. xiv, 217p. facsims.

6 chapters: 1. Education - 2. The principal organizations within the wool textile industry - 3. Other organizations of importance - 4. Research - 5. Wool processing (includes literature on; some textile dictionaries, etc.) - 6. Distribution of the wool textile industry. Appendices 1-3: Short reading lists; 4: Glossary of wool textile terms. Name and subject indexes. Whereas most other volumes in this series stress the literature, and organizations as information sources, this guide emphasizes organizations and technical processes. *Class No:* 677.31

[7090]

Wool trade directory of the world. 6th ed. Bradford, W. Yorks., World Textile Publications, 1996. 548p. £150. ISSN: 02683601.

Contents: The world's wool trade (A-Z by country) - Machinery and mill supplies - A-Z index - Categorised index. Data include contact details, activities (*e.g.* dyeing; weaving), products. *Class No:* 677.31

Silk

[7091]

FELTWELL, J. The Story of silk. London, Alan Sutton, 1990. xviii,233p. illus. (some col.), facsims. £16.95. ISBN: 0862996112.

11 chapters (1. The silk road: China to England ... 1. The industry today). 3 appendices (2. Museums - 3. Societies). Glossary. Bibliography and references (p.216-26). Index (tiny print). *Class No:* 677.37

Man-made Fibres

[7092]

Moncrieff's man-made fibres. McIntyre, J.E. 7th ed. Sevenoaks, Kent, Butterworth, 1988. 672p. ISBN: 0408005246.

6th ed. 1975 (1094p.).

Numerous sections, *e.g.* Fundamental concepts and terminology ... The synthesis of fibre-forming polymers ... Viscose fibres ... Nylon ... Non-woven fabrics - Dyeing and finishing - Identification and estimation of man-made fibres - Economic and social aspects - List of man-made fibres. Index. A classic work of reference on the structure, manufacture, dyeing, finishing and processing of man-made fibres. *Class No:* 677.4

[7093]

WINKLER, W., *comp.* **Fachwörterbuch Chemiefasern.** Deutsch-Englisch-Französich. Frankfurt-am-Main, Deutscher Fachverlag GmbH, 1979. 350p.

About 6,000 terms on man-made fibres, grouped and in 3 sequences: German-English-French; English-German-French; French-German-English. Genders are stated. *Class No:* 677.4

Carbon

[7094]

DONNET, J.B. *and* **BANSAL, R.C. Carbon fibers.** 2nd ed. New York, Marcel Dekker, 1990. xxii,470p. illus., graphs, tables. (*International Fiber Science and Technology, v.10.*) ISBN: 0824778650.

First published 1983.

7 chapters, closely subdivided: 1. Preparation - 2. Structure - 3. Surface treatment - 4. Surface properties - 5. Mechanical properties - 6. Electronic, magnetic and thermal properties - 7. Applications. Most chapters have extensive references (*e.g.* 135 for chapter 7). Author and subject indexes. *Class No:* 677.47

Cables & Ropes

[7095]

ASHLEY, C.W. The Ashley book of knots. London, Faber, 1944 (and reprints). xi, 620, 8p. illus. (pl.), diagrs.

First published 1944 (New York, Doubleday, Doran).

3,854 types of knots are described and illustrated. Bibliography of books; material on knots (p.593-6). Glossary of terms, p.597-605. The most comprehensive book on the subject. Reprinted with amendments by Geoffrey Budworth, 1993 (ISBN: 057109659x; £35). *Class No:* 677.7

[7096]

—BIGNON, M.M. *and* REGAZZINI, C. Guide to knots for sailing, fishing, camping and climbing. London, Century, 1988. 256p. illus. (col.). £8.95. ISBN: 0712623043.

Includes 647 col. illus. *Class No:* 677.7

[7097]

—GRAUMONT, R., *and others*. Encyclopedia of knots and fancy rope work. London, Conway Maritime Press, 1982. 690p. illus. £14.

332 illus.; a multi-purpose volume. *Class No:* 677.7

[7098]

—The Shell combined book of knots and ropework (practical and decorative). Newton Abbot, David & Charles, 1981. v.p. col. illus. ISBN: 0715381970.

First published as *The Shell book of knots and ropework* (1977).

95 knots are dealt with, each occupying 1-2 pages, plus col. illus. Part 1 (nos. 1-51): Knots - Rope slices - Decorative Knots - Wire splices - Part 2: Decorative knots - Plaits - Mats - Other knots and two toggles. Glossary. Index of knot numbers. Over 600 photographs. *Class No:* 677.7

Plastics & Rubbers (Polymers)

Bibliographies

[7099]

UNITED NATIONS. Industrial Development Organization. Information sources on the natural and synthetic rubber industry. New York, United Nations, 1979. xii, 108p. $4. (*UNIDO Guides to information sources, no. 34.*) ISBN: 9211061555.

11 sections: 1. Addresses of professional, trade and research organizations, learned societies and other economic periodicals - 2. Directories - 3. Sources of statistics and other periodicals ... 6. Current abstracting and indexing services - 7. Special documents; proceedings, papers and reports - 8. Monographs - 9. Specialized dictionaries and encyclopedias - 10. Bibliographies - 11. Films and film catalogues - 12. Other potential sources of information (A-L, *e.g.* A. Consulting and engineering services). 'Bibliographical services used in compiling the present guide', p.105-8. *Class No:* 678(01)

[7100]

YESCOMBE, E.R. Plastics and rubber: world sources of information. Barking, Essex, Applied Science Publishers; Philadelphia, Pa., International Ideas, 1976. xv, 547p.

A substantial, in-depth revision and enlargement of his *Sources of information on the rubber, plastics and allied industries* (Pergamon Press, 1968. ix, 253p.).

Nearly 7,000 references to the literature and notes on over 675 organizations. 7 parts: 1. Literature and information pattern - 2. Materials - 3. Polymer science - 4. Technology - 5. Safety and health (safety, industrial health, toxicity and fire hazards) - 6. Commercial aspects (commerce, economics, statistics, marketing and management) - 7. Organizations and institutions (international and national). Journals and abstract index, p.513-32. Abbreviations and anonyma index. Non-analytical subject index. 'Whether the user's interest is technical, commercial or statistical he will find advice and guidance to a wide variety of sources ...' (*Aslib proceedings*, v.29(5), May 1977, p.211). *Class No:* 678(01)

Handbooks & Manuals

[7101]

ASH, M. *and* **ASH, I.,** *comps.* **Handbook of plastic and rubber additives:** an international guide to more than 13,000 products by trade name, chemical, function and manufacturer. Aldershot, Hants., Gower, 1995. xvii, 1322p. ISBN: 0566075946.

About 13,000 trade name and chemical additive ingredients; 1,200 manufacturers and distributors. 4 sections: Trade name reference (A-Z) - 2. Chemical dictionary/cross reference - 3. Functional/cross reference - 4. Manufacturers directory (A-Z; contact information). *Class No:* 678(035)

[7102]

MURPHY, J. Reinforced plastics handbook. Oxford, Elsevier, 1994. xii, 541p. illus., diagrs., tables. ISBN: 1856172171.

Covers selection, design and processing of reinforced plastics, both thermosetting and thermoplastic. 5 sections: 1, Materials - 2. Machinery and equipment - 3. Design and applications - 4. Production - 5. Information (*e.g.* data sheets; trade names; manufacturers and suppliers, etc.). Acknowledgement is made to commercial firms who supplied illustrations and tables, and who have thus been allowed to advertise — rather like a theatre programme. *Class No:* 678(035)

Dictionaries

[7103]

LAMBERT, M. A Short Russian-English dictionary of terminology used in the Soviet rubber, plastics and tyre industries. London, Maclaren, 1963. [vii], 208p.

4,000 Russian words and phrases, A-Z by main word in a phrase. Relates to polymer chemistry and physics, rubber and plastics processing and machinery, and the tyre industry. Includes modern Soviet industrial and economic terms lacking in other dictionaries. Also lists 600 trade abbreviations (code designations of Soviet materials) and industrial organizations. Pocket-sized. *Class No:* 678(038)

[7104]

TEKNISKA NOMENKLATURCENTRALEN. Plast-och-gummi-teknisk ordlista. [Glossary of plastic and rubber terms.] Stockholm, the Centre, 1981. 356p. (*TNC 84.*) ISBN: 9171022128.

About 2,500 Swedish-base terms, plus explanations, with equivalents and indexes in English, French, German, Danish, Norwegian, Finnish. *Class No:* 678(038)

[7105]

—DORIAN, A.F., *comp*. Six-language dictionary of plastics and rubber technology: a comprehensive dictionary in English, German, French, Italian, Spanish and Dutch. London, Illife, 1965. [xii], 808p.

Provides 5,450 English-base terms, with definitions, plus equivalents and indexes in the other 5 languages. Genders are given. *Aslib book list* (v.31(4), April 1966, entry 197) notes 'some errors, misspellings and omissions'. *Class No*: 678(038)

Reviews & Abstracts

[7106]

RAPRA abstracts: the abstracts journal designed for rubbers and plastics producers, processors and users. Sawbury, Shrews., 1968-. 12pa. £1150pa. ISSN: 00336750.

RAPRA: Rubber and Plastics Research Association of Great Britain. Originally RABRM (Research Association of British Rubber Manufacturers) *Summary of current literature* (1923-51. v.1-29), then *Rubber abstracts* (1952-65. v.30-42), which divided into *Plastics: RAPRA abstracts* (1965-67) and *Rubbers: RAPRA* (1965-67).

About 20,000 abstracts and references pa. Main sections: General - Commercial and economic - Legislation - Industrial health and safety - Raw materials and monomers - Polymers and polymerization - Compounding ingredients - Intermediate and semi-finished products - Relating to particular industries and fields of use - Applications - Processing and treatment - Properties and testing. Detailed, analytical subject index per issue; annual author and subject indexes.

Online via DIALOG, ESA-IRS, STN International; CD-ROM. *Class No*: 678(048)

Progress Reports

[7107]

Progress in rubber and plastics technology: a quarterly review journal. Shawbury, Shrewsbury, Salop, RAPRA Technology, Ltd., 1985-. Quarterly. ISSN: 02667320.

Published jointly by the Plastics and Rubber Institute, and RAPRA. Issues usually include 3 or 4 well-documented review articles. Summary procedes each article. Biographical notes. *Class No*: 678(055)

Standards

[7108]

Specifications and standards for plastics and composites. Philadelphia, Pa., American Society of Testing and Materials; Hitchin, Herts., American Technical Publishers Ltd., 1990. 224p. £77. ISBN: 0871703965.

Over 2000 standards from a range of international organizations. *Class No*: 678(083.74)

Trade Names, Trade Marks, Brand Names

[7109]

RUBBER AND PLASTICS RESEARCH ASSOCIATION OF GREAT BRITAIN (RAPRA). RAPRA new trade names in the rubber and plastics industry. Davison, E., *ed*. Oxford, etc., Pergamon Press on behalf of RAPRA Technology, Ltd., [1988]. Annual. 603p. ISSN: 07474954.

First published 1962.

Trade name list - Company list - Classification list, p.171-542 (trade name categories, A-Z) - Company name and address - Journals and abbreviations. Also available online via Questel/ORBIT. *Class No*: 678(088.7)

[7110]

RUBBER AND PLASTICS RESEARCH ASSOCIATION OF GREAT BRITAIN (RAPRA). Trade names of rubbers, resins & plastics. Shawbury, Shropshire, the Association, 1949-61. 3v.

A complete listing of all the rubbers, plastics and resins collected since 1926. V.3 lists all the new materials in the synthetic rubber and plastics fields, 1955-59, describes each material, plus name and town of manufacturer. Earlier volumes have the title 'Annotated comprehensive list of trade names of synthetics'. *Class No*: 678(088.7)

Rubber

Handbooks & Manuals

[7111]

BLOW, C.M. *and* HEPBURN, C. Rubber technology and manufacture. London, Butterworth Scientific, for the Plastic and Rubber Institute, 1982. (Corrected reprint, 1985). 608p. illus., diagrs., graphs, tables. £38.50. ISBN: 0408005874.

51 contributors. 12 documented chapters (1. History - 2. Outline of rubber technology ... 4. Raw polymeric materials ... 6. Materials for compounding and reinforcement ... 10. Manufacturing techniques -

....(contd.)

11. Testing procedure; standards, specifications - 12. Organizations). Bibliography (general and by chapters), p.534-61. Literature and patent references. Index. *Class No*: 678.4(035)

[7112]

BOSTRÖM, S., *ed*. Kautschuk-Handbuch. Stuttgart, Verlag Berliner Union, 1959-62. 5v. & Supplement, illus., tables.

V.1 covers raw materials; v.2, synthetic rubbers, rubber compounding, and machinery; v.3, rubber technology, machinery and manufactured goods; v.4, rubber products and latex; v.5, physical and mechanical testing of rubber, with cumulative index to v.1-5. *Supplement,* 1961, covers techniques of measuring and control in the rubber industry. *Class No*: 678.4(035)

[7113]

HOFMANN, W. Rubber technology handbook. Munich, Hanser, 1989. xxv,611p. illus. £34; $85. ISBN: 0195207572.

Trans. from the German.

A highly technical treatment which includes extensive chapter bibliographies. Industrial buyer's guide (with German emphasis) appended. *Class No*: 678.4(035)

[7114]

Science and technology of rubber. Mark, J.E., *and others, eds*. 2nd ed. New York, etc., Academic Press, 1994. 751p. illus., diagrs., graphs, tables. $85 ISBN: 0124725252.

First published 1978.

Under the auspices of the Rubber Division of the American Chemical Society.

This new edition has been expanded by about 25 percent. 14 well-documented chapters by a number of different hands approach rubber from both a chemical and an engineering point of view. Author and detailed subject indexes. 'This simply marvelous treatise . . . Excellent!' (*Choice*, January 1995, p.821). *Class No*: 678.4(035)

[7115]

WEBSTER, C.C. *and* BAULKWILL, W.J. Rubber. Harlow, Essex, Longman, 1989. viii,[1],614p. illus., micrographs, graphs, tables. £54. ISBN: 0582404053.

8 contributors. 12 chapters (1. The history of natural rubber production ... 12. Organization and management of world rubber production). Chapter notes. 8 appendices (1. Literature of the history of rubber to 1045, p.539-40). References (c.1,000 authors, A-Z). Detailed, analytical index. *Class No*: 678.4(035)

Dictionaries

[7116]

HEINISCH, K.F. Dictionary of rubber. London, Applied Science Publishers, 1974. vi, 545p. tables.

Original German ed. as *Kautschuk-Lexikon* (Stuttgart, Gentner, 1966).

About 4,000 entries, including abbreviations and registered trade-names. 'Diberzthiazyl disulphide': 3 columns. Appended list of procedures and marketing organizations, p.535-45. *Class No*: 678.4(038)

[7117]

—AMERICAN SOCIETY FOR TESTING AND MATERIALS. Glossary of terms relating to rubber and rubber-like materials. Philadelphia, Pa., the Society, 1972. 122p. (*ASTM Special technical publications, no. 184.*)

Defines over 2,000 terms. Molecular structures are given. Appendix of trade names. *Class No*: 678.4(038)

[7118]

—BRITISH STANDARDS INSTITUTION. Glossary of rubber terms. London, BSI, 1980. 44p. £33.60. (*BS 3558: 1980(1996).*)

Defines terms used in the rubber industry in general, latex, rubber, properties and testing processes, machinery, and rubber products, including hoses, tyres, belts and footware. *Class No*: 678.4(038)

[7119]

RUBBER STITCHING. Elsevier's rubber dictionary in English/American, French, Spanish, Italian, Portuguese, German, Dutch, Swedish, Indonesian and Japanese. Amsterdam, etc., Elsevier, 1959. viii, 1537p. DFl.475. ISBN: 0444404996.

7,955 terms in English/American, with equivalents and indexes in the other 9 languages. Omission of Russian is a drawback. *Class No*: 678.4(038)

[7120]

YASHUNSKAYA, V.I. *and* FEIGIN, E.E. Anglo-russkiĭ slovar' po kắuchnuku, rezine i khimicheskim voloknam. 3. izd pereabotannoe i dopolnennoe. Moscow, Fizmatgiz, 1962. 260p.

Anglo-Russian dictionary of rubber, resin and chemical fibres. 11,000 English entry-words, with Russian word index, p.216-60. Abbreviations, p.208-15. *Class No*: 678.4(038)

Yearbooks & Directories

[7121]

Rubbicana: Europe, 1997. Shawbury, Shropshire, RAPRA, 1997. 500p. £85. ISBN: 1859570755.

A compendium on the rubber and polyerethene industries of Europe. Alphabetical company listing - Associations & societies - Classified listings (manufacturers; suppliers). Trade name index; Country classified index; Country code index; Advertisers index. *Class No:* 678.4(058)

Tables & Data Books

[7122]

Rubber statistical bulletin. London, International Rubber Study Group, 1946-. Monthly. tables.

Tables list gross exports of sheet rubber by grade; consumption, production and stocks of natural rubber; synthetic rubber; world synthetic rubber capacities. Includes annual data for the previous 5 years. *Class No:* 678.4(083)

Standards

[7123]

SMITH, L.P. The Language of rubber: an introduction to the specification and testing of elastomers. 2nd ed. Oxford, Butterworth-Heinemann, 1993. xiv, 257p. illus., diagrs., graphs. ISBN: 0750614137.

First published 1957.

In 3 parts. Parts 1 and 2 provide details of internationally accepted test methods used by the rubber industry for the selction and quality control of compounds. Part 3 comprises an eight-language (English; French; German; Italian; Spanish; Portuguese; Swedish; Dutch) vocabulary of the industry. *Class No:* 678.4(083.74)

Histories

[7124]

SCHIDROWITZ, P. and DAWSON, T.R., eds. History of the rubber industry. Compiled under the auspices of the Institution of the Rubber Industry. Cambridge, Heffer, 1952. xxiv, 406p. illus. (pl.).

6 sections, concerning origins of the industry, raw materials, scientific and technological developments, products of the industry, economic and social aspects. Annotated bibliography of rubber literature. Latex entries in the chronology are for 1948-49. *Class No:* 678.4(091)

Malaysia

[7125]

BARLOW, C. The Natural rubber industry: its development, technology, and economy in Malaysia. Kuala Lumpar, Oxford Univ. Press, 1978. xxiv, 500p. illus., graphs, tables, maps. £40. ISBN: 0195803140.

10 chapters (2. The early years - 3. Growth amidst difficulty - 4. The technologies of production - 5. The technology of processing - 6. The structure of the industry - 7. The economics of producing - 8. The rubber market - 9. The economics of institutional management - 10. The international context). Bibliography, p.460-486. Analytical index of subjects. Index of authors cited. Numerous tables. 49 plates. *Class No:* 678.4(595)

Plastics

Databases

[7126]

Plastec materials selection database. Yardley, Pa., D & S Data Resources.

Engineering and design data, chemical descriptions and trade names for over 11,500 grades of plastics materials. Updated monthly. Available on DIALOG, file 321. *Class No:* 678.5(003.4)

Encyclopaedias

[7127]

ROSATO, D.V. Rosato's plastics encyclopedia and dictionary. Munich, Hanser, 1993. lxvi, 817p. illus., diagrs., tables. ISBN: 3446164901.

About 11,000 entries and terms, some discussed at length (*e.g.* 'nylon plastic': 2p.). Abbreviations, conversion tables, chronology and references (6p.) precede. *Class No:* 678.5(031)

Handbooks & Manuals

[7128]

ASH, M. and ASH, I., comps. Handbook of plastic compounds, elastomers, and resins: an international guide by category, tradename, composition, and supplier. New York, VCH, 1992. xiv,872p. £132. ISBN: 1560815531.

Data on 15,000 tradename products. 4 parts: I. Tradename by category reference - II. Tradename cross reference - III. Chemical component cross reference - IV. Chemical manufacturer's directory. *Class No:* 678.5(035)

[7129]

BROWN, R.P., ed. Handbook of plastics test methods. 3rd ed. Harlow, Essex, Longman; New York, Wiley, 1988. xiv,442p. illus., diagrs., graphs, tables. £59. ISBN: 0582030153, UK; 0470211342, US.

First published 1971; 2nd ed. 1981.

21 documented chapters: 3. Preparation of test pieces ... 6. Polymer characterisation ... 10. Friction and wear - 11. Creep, relaxation and set - 12. Fatigue - 13. Electrical properties - 14. Optical properties - 15. Thermal properties ... 18. Fire testing of plastics ... 21. Testing products. Index, p.438-42. Emphasis is on testing of materials, not products. Tests related to 130 standards where possible. *Class No:* 678.5(035)

[7130]

BRYDSON, J.A. Plastics materials. 6th ed. Oxford, Butterworth-Heinemann, 1995. xxvii, 896p. diagrs., graphs, tables. £c £80. ISBN: 0750618647.

First published 1966. 5th ed. 1989.

The 6th ed. adds new chapters on polymer groups and materials selection. 32 documented chapters, closely subdivided, on properties, processes and applications of plastics materials. Includes recent production and consumption figures for the commercially important polymers. Detailed analytical index and contents list. *Class No:* 678.5(035)

[7131]

—GÄCHTER, R. and MILLER, H., eds. Plastics additives handbook: stablizers, processing aids. 2nd ed. Munich, etc., Hanser, 1983. xxxiv, 754p. graphs, tables, chemical structures.

The translated and rev. ed. of *Kunstoff industrie*. Detailed, analytical index, p.743-54. *Class No:* 678.5(035)

[7132]

HARPER, C.A., ed. Handbook of plastics, elastomers and composites. 2nd ed. New York, etc., McGraw-Hill, 1992. 960p. illus. £77.95. ISBN: 0070266867.

First published 1975.

Emphasis is on industrial techniques, developments and applications. Includes government (US) and commercial guidelines. Glossary of terms. *Class No:* 678.5(035)

[7133]

RUBIN, I.I., ed. Handbook of plastic materials and technology. New York, Wiley, 1990. xxv,1745p. illus., tables. £90. ISBN: 0471096342.

Over 100 contributors, most from industry. 119 chapters in 2 parts: 1. Materials (*e.g.* 'acetals'; 'nylons') - 2. Technology (*e.g.* 'blow molding'). 25 appendices. Detailed, analytical index, p.1729-45. A practical treatment which 'aims to make you more successful in your business' (*Preface*). *Class No:* 678.5(035)

Dictionaries

Polyglot

[7134]

A Glossary of plastics terminology in 5 languages: English, Deutsch, Français, Español, Italiano. Glenz, G., *ed.* 3rd ed. New York, Hanser Verlag, 1995. 304p. $24. ISBN: 3446184910.

1,383 English-base terms, A-Z, with equivalents in other languages. Indexes. Good value. *Class No:* 678.5(038)=00

[7135]

KALISKE, G. Fachwörterbuch kunstofftechnik: Englisch/Deutsch/ Französsich/Russisch. [Dictionary of plastics engineering: English/German/French/Russian.] 2nd ed. Berlin, Paris, Hatier, 1992. 646p. £102. ISBN: 3861170388.

First published 1982 by Elsevier.

About 16,000 English-based headwords, with equivalents and indexes in the other languages. Covers the range of plastics technology, from material, production and processing to applications. *Class No:* 678.5(038)=00

English

[7136]

Whittington's dictionary of plastics. Carley, J.F., *ed.* 3rd ed. Westport, Ct., Technomic Publishing Co., 1993. 568p. $85.

First published 1968; 2nd ed. 1978.

About 8,000 terms defined and explained, occasionally at length. Abbreviations and cross-references. 'Recommended for plastics collections' (*Choice*, April 1994, p.1279). *Class No: 678.5(038)=20*

German

[7137]

JUNGE, H.D., *ed.* **Dictionary of plastics technology,** English-German. [Wörterbuch Kunststofftechnologie, Englisch-Deutsch.] Weinheim (W. Germany), VCH, 1987. [v], 315p. £76. ISBN: 3527264329.

About 3,000 terms on the physics and chemistry of the high polymers. Many sub-entries, bringing gross total to c.20,000. 'Plant': 1½ columns; 'Unit': 7 columns. German genders given. At head of title page: 'Parat'. *Class No: 678.5(038)=30*

[7138]

WELLING, M.S., *comp.* **Dictionary of plastics and rubber technology.** 2nd ed. London, Pentech Press, 1994. 2v. (xi, 323p.; vi, 193p.). £42 each. ISBN: 0727304119, V.1; 0727304127, V.2.

First published 1985 as *German-English dictionary of plastics technology*.

V.1: German-English; v.2: English-German.

About 28,000 entries, concisely defined. Appendix of translation examples. *Class No: 678.5(038)=30*

[7139]

WITTFOHT, A. Plastics technical dictionary, English-German, German-English. New York, Macmillan, 1981. 3v. illus., tables.

German ed. as *Kunststofftechnisches Wörterbuch* (Munich, Hanser, 1978-81).

1. *Alphabetical dictionary, English-German.* 4th rev. ed. 1981. x, 550p.

2. *Alphabetical dictionary, German-English.* 1981. ix, 534p.

3. *Reference volume: illustrated systematic groups, English,-German, German-English.* 1981. ix, 508p.

About 40,000 entries in each of v.1-2, on processing, fabricating and using plastics. V.3 comprises 26 subject groups (Blow molding ... Welding), with numerous keyed illus. English and German subject indexes. *Class No: 678.5(038)=30*

French

[7140]

Dictionary: Plastics engineering. English/French. [Dictionnaire: Industrie des matières plastiques. Français/Anglais.] Widnau, Switzerland, Schnellmann Verlag, 1987. 114, [5]p. (*K.2.3.*)

About 1,500 terms, with equivalents, in each half of this dictionary. Appendix: 'Units'. *Class No: 678.5(038)=40*

Italian

[7141]

Dictionary: Plastics engineering. English/Italian. [Dizionario: Tecnica delle materie plastiche. Italiano/inglese.] Widnau, Switzerland, Schnellmann Verlag, 1985. 114. [5]p. (*K.1.3.*)

About 1,500 terms, with equivalents, in each half of this dictionary. Appendix: 'Units'. *Class No: 678.5(038)=50*

Russian

[7142]

GURARII, M.G *and* **IOFE, L.R. Anglo-russkiĭ slovar' po plastmassam.** Moscow, Fizmatgiz, 1963. 144p.

English-Russian plastics dictionary. About 5,000 English entry-words. Russian index, p.127-44. Abbreviations, p.123-6. *Class No: 678.5(038)=82*

Yearbooks & Directories

[7143]

The Plastics industry directory, 1992. Croydon, EMAP Vision, 1992. 196p. ISSN: 09562966.

10 sections: 1. Company information (2400 companies, A-Z) - 2. Materials - 3. Machinery - 4. Processing - 5. Moulds and dies - 6. Finished products ... 9. Trade names - 10. Glossary. *Class No: 678.5(058)*

Tables & Data Books

[7144]

SOCIETY OF THE PLASTICS INDUSTRY, Inc. **Plastics engineering handbook of the Society of the Plastics Industry, Inc.** Berins, M.L., *ed.* 5th ed. New York, etc., Van Nostrand Reinhold, 1991. 845p. illus., tables. $89.95. ISBN: 0442317999.

First published 1947 (*SPI handbook*); 4th ed. 1976.

Largely rewritten, with new illustrations and new terms in the glossary, for this edition. Extensive coverage of reinforced and cellular plastics and composites. 'An excellent source' (*Choice*, April 1992, p.1258). *Class No: 678.5(083)*

Histories

[7145]

The Development of plastics. Mossman, S.T.I. *and* Morris, P.J.T., *eds.* Cambridge, Royal Society of Chemistry, 1994. x, 120p. illus., tables. £35; $65. ISBN: 0851865755.

The proceedings of a Symposium on the History of Synthetic Materials at the Annual Chemical Congress, 1993. 9 chapters, by various hands, most with extensive references. Topics include Victorian plastics, Bakelite, polythene, acrylics, fibre reinforced composites, etc. Index. Selected by *Choice* as an outstanding academic book for 1995. *Class No: 678.5(091)*

[7146]

IMPERIAL CHEMICAL INDUSTRIES. Plastics Division. **Landmarks of the plastics industry.** Welwyn, Herts., ICI Plastics Division, [1962]. 126p. illus., diagrs.

Popular historical survey, particuary of more recent developments. Published to mark the centenary of A. Parke's invention of the world's first man-made plastic, Parkesine. *Class No: 678.5(091)*

Synthetic Polymers & Rubbers

Abbreviations & Symbols

[7147]

LOENING, K.L., *ed.* **List of standard abbreviations (symbols) for synthetic polymers and polymer materials.** Basic definitions of terms relating to polymers. Oxford, Pergamon, 1978. 20p.

Previously published in *Pure and applied chemistry*, v.40(3).

A. Abbreviations for synthetic polymer materials - B. Primary definitions. Secondary definitions. *Class No: 678.7(003)*

Bibliographies

[7148]

ADKINS, R.T., *ed.* **Information sources in polymers and plastics.** London, etc., Bowker-Saur, 1989. xii,313p. Tables. £40. (*Guides to Information Sources.*) ISBN: 040802027x.

In 3 parts, each with several sections. Part I covers published formats (serials, books, patents, standards, grey literature, online databases); Part II, materials (polymer structures, properties, adhesives, fibres, rubber, etc.); Part III, geographical areas and translations. 18 contributors. Subject index, p.303-13. A comprehensive guide to the literature. *Class No: 678.7(01)*

Encyclopaedias

[7149]

CORISH, P.J. Concise encyclopedia of polymer processing and applications. Oxford, Pergamon Press, 1992. 800p. illus. £140. ISBN: 0080370640.

A wide variety of articles. Emphasis is on practical handling and production aspects of polymers. Research level. Some material taken from *Encyclopedia of materials science and engineering* (*qv*) and the supplementary vols; other material is newly commissioned. *Class No: 678.7(031)*

[7150]

MARK, H.F., *and others, eds.* **Encyclopedia of polymer science and engineering.** 2nd ed. New York, etc., Wiley, 1985-90.

First published 1964-77 (16v. plus 2 suppt.) as *Encyclopedia of polymer science and technology*.

22v. with c.600 contributors. Articles are lengthy, signed and documented. V.1: A to Amorphous (843p.) has 27 contributions. That on 'Amorphous polymers' occupies p.789-843, with 260 references. Cross-references. The standard work on polymers. Available online via DIALOG (File 322) and on CD-ROM. *Class No: 678.7(031)*

[7151]

—**Polymers: fibers and textiles: a compendium.** Kroschwitz, J.I., *ed.* New York, Wiley, 1990. 950p. £66.20. ISBN: 0471512212.

Includes articles reprinted without change from the *Encyclopedia of polymer science and engineering*. Material on nomenclature, SI units and conversion factors had been added. *Class No: 678.7(031)*

[7152]

—Polymers: polymer characterization and analysis. Kroschwitz, J.I., *ed*. New York, Wiley, 1990. 984p. £66.20. ISBN: 0471513253.

Includes articles reprinted without change from the *Encyclopedia of polymer science and engineering*. Handy as a reference source and for libraries without the complete work. *Class No: 678.7(031)*

Handbooks & Manuals

[7153]

ALLEN, G. *and* BEVINGTON, J.C. **Comprehensive polymer science:** the synthesis, characterization, reactions and applications of polymers. Oxford, etc., Pergamon Press, 1988. 7v. (6000p.). illus. £1095. ISBN: 0080325157.

A treatise dealing in detail with polymer chemistry, characterization, physical properties and chemical reactions, concluding with processing, applications and nomenclature.

The first supplement (1992. £180) contains 21 chapters by various hands in 6 sections (4. 'Degradation of polymers').

Class No: 678.7(035)

[7154]

BRANDRUP, J. *and* IMMERGUT, E.H., *eds*. **Polymer handbook.** 3rd ed. New York, etc., Wiley, 1989. *c*.1870p. £115. ISBN: 0471812447.

First published 1966. 2nd ed. 1975.

About 80 contributors. 8 sections: 1. Nomenclature rules. Units - 2. Polymerization and depolymerization - 3. Physical properties of monomers and solvents - 4. Physical data of oligomers - 5. Physical constants of some important polymers - 6. Solid state properties (6.1 'Crystallographic data for various polymers', 208p. 1,946 references) - 7. Solution properties - 8. Abbreviations of polymer names. About 30% more data than previous ed. Concentrates on synthetic polymers, poly (saccharides) and derivatives and oligomers. Index lists only physical constants of polymers.

The 4th ed. is due for publication in 1999 (Wiley; £200; ISBN: 0471166286). *Class No: 678.7(035)*

[7155]

Handbook of polymer science and technology. Cheremisinoff, N.P., *ed*. New York, Dekker, 1989-. illus., graphs, tables, chemical structures.

V.1. *Synthesis and properties.*

V.2. *Performance properties of plastics and elastomers.*

V.3. *Applications and processing operations.*

V.4. *Composites and specialty applications.*

V.4 has 19 specialist contributors; 14 well-documented chapters. Each volume carries an index; further vols. 'In preparation'. *Class No: 678.7(035)*

[7156]

MARK, J.E. **Physical properties of polymers handbook.** New York, American Institute of Physics, 1996. 723p. tables. $120; £87.50. ISBN: 1563962950.

10 sections including theory; spectroscopy; mechanical properties; crystallinity and morphology; and electro-optical and magnetic properties. Numerous tables; extensive bibliographies. Also available on CD-ROM (£114.40; ISBN: 1563965984). *Class No: 678.7(035)*

Dictionaries

[7157]

ALGER, M.S. **Polymer science dictionary.** London, Elsevier, 1989. xii,531p. chemical formulas and structures. ISBN: 1851662200.

Some terms defined at length (*e.g.* 'Monosaccharide', 1p.). Excludes technology and 'polymer processing' (*Preface*). Appended: Units; Conversion factors; Physical constants; Relative atomic masses; Greek alphabet. Includes some tradenames. *Class No: 678.7(038)*

[7158]

DAWYDOFF, W. *and* HOWORKA, H. **Technical dictionary of high polymers.** Oxford, etc., Pergamon Press; Berlin, VEB Verlag, 1969. 959p.

About 10,000 technical terms and jargon in 4 sequences: English-German-French-Russian; German-English-French-Russian; French-English-German-Russian; Russian-German-English-French. Genders are stated. *Class No: 678.7(038)*

[7159]

WHELAN, T. **Polymer technology dictionary.** London, Chapman & Hall, 1994. viii, 555p. tables. ISBN: 0412581809.

A substantial dictionary with some terms defined and explained at length (*e.g.* 'Blow moulded container', 1½ cols.). Greek and numeric entries preced the main sequence, A-Z. 15 tables (15. 'Carbon black classification'). *Class No: 678.7(038)*

Reviews & Abstracts

[7160]

Additives for polymers. Shelton, J., *ed*. London, Elsevier, 1971-. Monthly. ISSN: 03063747.

A digest of *c*.20p., with some 60 entries per issue. Sections: Technical notes - Materials - Patents - Markets - Company news - Books - Publications - Diary. *Class No: 678.7(048)*

[7161]

Polymers/ceramics/composites alert. Metals Information. London, Institute of Metals; Metals Park, Ohio, American Society for Metals, 1985-. Monthly. £220pa. (EU).

300 abstracts per issue. Covers engineered materials industries, from ceramics to thermoplastics. One of 3 abstracts journals comprising the Materials Business File. Online database. *Class No: 678.7(048)*

Yearbooks & Directories

[7162]

Polymer yearbook. New York, Harwood Academic, 1984-. Annual. ISBN: 3718652633.

Contains reviews of topics of current interest and other newsworthy items, including a survey of recent publications in polymer science, a compendium of recent reviews (under topics), a tabulation of dissertation abstracts, a list of polymer journals, a calendar of forthcoming meetings, and much else. Includes contributions worldwide. 'A wealth of desk-top reference information' (*Science & technology libraries*, v.7(2), Winter 1986, p.1741).

Class No: 678.7(058)

Trade Names, Trade Marks, Brand Names

[7163]

FACHINFORMATIONSZENTRUM CHEMIE GmbH, Berlin. **Parat: Index of polymer trade names.** Junge, H.D., *ed*. 2nd ed. Weinheim, W. Germany, VCH, 1992. 2 computer disks. £150. ISBN: 3527283838.

First published 1987.

About 33,000 substances referred to by trade names in the literature. Names of producers are provided for about 13,000 and CAS registry numbers for over 21,000. *Class No: 678.7(088.7)*

Histories

[7164]

SEYMOUR, R.B., *ed*. **History of polymer science and technology.** New York, Dekker, 1982. 410p. ISBN: 0824713826.

Reports presented at a symposium sponsored jointly by the History, Organic Coatings and Plastics, Polymer and Rubber Divisions of the American Chemical Society at the 179th National Meeting, Houston, Texas, March 1980.

Coverage: history of adhesives, organometallic polymers, engineering thermoplastics, vinyl chloride polymers, natural rubber, synthetic rubber, reinforced plastics, natural fibres, and polyolefins. Index. *Class No: 678.7(091)*

PVC

[7165]

NASS, L.I. *and* HEIBERGER, C. **Encyclopedia of PVC.** 2nd ed., revised and expanded. New York, Dekker, 1980-. illus. diagrs., graphs, tables. ISBN: 0824774272.

1. *Resin manufacture and properties.*

2. *Compound design and additives.*

3. *Compounding processes, product design, and specifications.*

4. *Conversion and fabrication processes.*

5. *Safety and environmental concerns.*

V.1 (1985. 702p.) has 15 contributors, 11 documented sections, with author and subject indexes. The bibliography in v.5 runs to 323 references, plus an appended glossary of acronyms.

Class No: 678.743

[7166]

TITOW, W.V. **PVC plastics:** properties, processing, and applications. London, Elsevier, 1990. xxvii,902p. illus., diagrs., graphs, tables. £115. ISBN: 1851664718.

24 chapters, subdivided, with references and bibliography (3. PVC polymers ... 5. Plasticisers ... 7. Lubricants ... 13. Extrusion ... 16. Injection moulding ... 20. PVC Latices). 3 appendices (1. Material properties - 2. Quantities and units - 3. Abbreviations). Detailed, analytical index, p.881-902. Much of the material is drawn from the author's *PVC technology* (4th ed.). (*Preface*.). *Class No: 678.743*

Asbestos

[7167]

Asbestos management sourcebook. Lutherville, Md., Environmental Publications, 1990-. Annual. 145p. $20. ISSN: 10460438.

41 articles in sections: legal matters - financial considerations - inspection - insurance - asbestos abatement - asbestos management. Directories: professionals; government agencies. *Class No:* 679.867

[7168]

CHISSICK, S.S., *and others.* **Asbestos: properties, applications and hazards.** New York, etc., Wiley, 1979-83. 2v. illus., diagrs., graphs, tables. ISBN: 047199698x; 0471104892.

V.1, by L. Michaels and S.S. Chissick. 1979. xi, 553p.

V.2, by S.S. Chissick and R. Derricott. 1983. xiv, 652p.

V.1, has 22 contributors, with 16 documented chapters (chapter 9. 'Dealing with asbestos problems' p.279-304; 3p. of bibliography and references). V.2 has 9 contributors. 11 documented chapters concern the uses, abuses, dangers and benefits of asbestos. Each volume has a detailed, analytical index. *Class No:* 679.867

[7169]

—BRADFIELD, R.E.N. Asbestos: review of uses, health effects, measurement and control. Epsom, Surrey, Atkins Research and Development, 1977. iv, 101p.

A report describing the properties of asbestos fibres and how they have been exploited. Discusses health effects of occupational exposure to asbestos (used in over 3,000 products), and the evidence for, plus the risks associated with non-occupational exposure. *Class No:* 679.867

68 Industries, Trades & Crafts

Industries, Trades & Crafts

[7170]

Crafts Council web site. London, Crafts Council. URL: http:// www.craftscouncil.org.uk.

The Crafts Council promotes contemporary crafts in Great Britain. The free web site provides access to information about exhibitions and events, education and research, craft shops in the UK, services to crafts men and women and the public, buyer's guide, the *Crafts Magazine*, etc. *Class No:* 680

[7171]

Directory of European industrial and trade associations. Adams, R., *ed*. 6th ed. Beckenham, Kent, CBD Research, 1997. *c.*400p. £195. ISBN: 090024674x.

Editions 1-3 as part of *Directory of European associations* (1971, 1976, 1981), now split into the above and *Directory of European professional and learned societies.*

About 5,000 associations, A-Z, by title. Omits UK and Eire. Indexes: abbreviations; subjects. *Class No:* 680

[7172]

A Historical dictionary of American industrial language. Mulligan, W.H., *ed*. New York, Greenwood Press, 1988. 332p. $55. ISBN: 0313241716.

20 contributors. Over 3,000 terms, A-Z, on American industry prior to World War I, briefly defined. Cross-references. Appendix lists terms grouped by industry. Index of institutions and people mentioned in definitions. *Class No:* 680

Country Crafts

Great Britain

[7173]

COUNCIL FOR SMALL INDUSTRIES IN RURAL AREAS. Select list of books and information sources on trades, crafts and small industries in rural areas. London, the Council, 1973. [v], 80p.

About 1,500 titles. 14 sections: 1. General bibliography on 'country crafts' - 2. Clay and plaster - 3. Glass and crystal - 4. Horn - 5. Leather - 6. Metal - 7 Natural fibres - 8. Stone - 9. Reed and straw - 10. Underwood (basketry, etc.) - 11. Wood (furniture, wheelwrighting, etc.) - 12. Miscellaneous - 13. Folk collections in British museums and galleries - 14. Guilds, societies and trade associations (subjects, A-Z). Includes out-of-print books recognized as standard works on the subject. *Class No:* 680.0(410)

[7174]

HILL, J. The Complete practical book of country crafts. Newton Abbot, Devon, David & Charles, 1979. 254p. illus., diagrs., tables. ISBN: 071537706x.

22 sections: Materials - Tools and devices - Hurdle making - Clog making - Wood carving - Chair making - Coopering ... Blacksmithing ... Basket making - Thatch and straw - Rope making - Bricks and pottery - Hedging and walling. 2 appendices: 1. Further information, displays, courses; 2. Addresses of suppliers. Bibliography (grouped), p.249-52. Index, p.253-4. *Class No:* 680.0(410)

Scotland

[7175]

CARTER, J. and RAE, A. Chambers guide to traditional crafts of Scotland. Edinburgh, Chambers, 1988. 128p. illus. (incl. colour). ISBN: 0550200002.

8 wide-ranging chapters. 1: Land and sea (*e.g.* boat building) - 2. In the home (*e.g.* wood turning) ... 7. Industrial crafts. Select bibliography, p.123. Useful addresses. Index, p.125. Well illustrated. Necessarily selective. *Class No:* 680.0(411)

England

[7176]

Visiting craft workshops in the English countryside. Cole-Morgan, J., *ed*. Ashbourne, Derby, Moorland, 1992. 288p. illus. £5.95. ISBN: 0861901959.

Published in association with the Rural Development Commission.

Geographbical directory of English crafts, including furniture

....(contd.)

makers, gold and silversmiths, leather workers, spinners and weavers, toy makers, clock makers, glass engravers, potters, blacksmiths, etc. *Class No:* 680.0(420)

Clock & Watch Making

Bibliographies

[7177]

BAILLIE, G.H. Clocks and watches: an historical bibliography. London, N.A.G. Press, 1951. (Reprinted London, Holland Press, 1978). xxv, 388p. illus.

The period covered is 1344 - 1799; the arrangement of entries, chronological. Major works are analysed in detail (*e.g.* J.A. Lepaute's *Traité d'horlogerie* (1955) is alloted 2 pages, with 4 supporting diagrams). The bibliography 'is confined to mechanical timepieces and to everything connected with them' (*Foreword*). Name and subject indexes. The most important compendium of its kind. *Class No:* 681.11(01)

[7178]

BROMLEY, J., *comp*. The Clockmakers' Library: the catalogue of books and manuscripts in the Library of the Worshipful Company of Clockmakers. London, Sotheby Parke Bernet Publications, 1977. 136p. illus. (pl.), ports., facsims.

1,151 numbered items. Catalogue of printed books (p.1-62) - Catalogue of manuscripts (p.77-119); index - Concordance of Guildhall Library mansucript and catalogue numbers - Catalogue of portraits - Catalogue of prints, drawings, paintings (other than portraits) and photographs. 27 illus. No annotations, but a detailed inventory of manuscripts. Well produced. *Class No:* 681.11(01)

[7179]

—WORSHIPFUL COMPANY OF CLOCKMAKERS OF LONDON. The Catalogue of the Library ... preserved in the Guildhall Library. 2nd ed. London, Blades, East & Blades, 1898. v, 205p.

The predecessor of Bromley (*qv*) has 3 main sections: Books (by subjects, A-Z, including article offprints) - Manuscripts, patents, etc. - Prints, drawings, paintings, etc. *Class No:* 681.11(01)

Encyclopaedias

[7180]

BRITTEN, F.J. Britten's watch & clock maker's handbook, dictionary and guide. Good, R., *ed*. 16th ed. London, Eyre Methuen, in association with E. & F.N. Spon, 1978. viii, [1], 460p. illus., graphs, tables.

15th ed., 1955 (ix, 598p.).

'Dictionary and guide' (Abrasive ... Zodiac), p.1-355. 'Quartz crystal controlled watches', p.260-4; 'Repeating watches', p.267-76, with 23 line-drawings. Appendices: 1. Basic equipment for horological draughtsmen; 2. Tables; 3. Vocabulary (English, French, German, Spanish). Select bibliography, p.431-4. Over 700 good line-drawings. Index of illus. Analytical general index, p.440-60. *Class No:* 681.11(031)

[7181]

CURTIS, T. Clocks and watches. London, Lyle, Galashiels, 1993. 448p. illus. £14,95. ISBN: 086248149x.

Arranged by type of clock, A-Z, with current prices. Some 3,000 illus. Index of makers. *Class No:* 681.11(031)

[7182]

DE CARLE, D. Watch and clock encyclopedia. 3rd ed. Ipswich, Suffolk, N.A.G. Press, 1983. 326, [1]p. illus., diagrs., tables. £14.95. ISBN: 0719801702.

First published 1950.

Definitions of c.3,000 antiquarian, technical and commercial terms. No less than 31 appendices follow, including 'Chimes' (with music examples), 'Clock hands', 'English period styles', 'French period styles', 'Horological dates', 'Watch part nomenclatures in 6 languages'. Bibliography of 19 items. 1,350 small line-drawings. A mine of specialized information. *Class No:* 681.11(031)

Handbooks & Manuals

[7183]

The 'Country Life' international dictionary of clocks. Smith, A., *ed.*
London. 'Country Life' Books (distributed by Hamlyn), 1979. 352p.
illus. (incl. col.), ports.

By various hands. 5 sections, - on history and style of clocks,
mechanical parts, tools, materials and workshop methods, international
clock-making, and sundials and astronomical instruments.
Bibliography, p.339-42. 900 illus. 'This could become a standard work
for collectors, museum staffs, dealers and all interested in horology
and industrial history' (*Aslib book list,* v.44(12), December 1979, item
536). *Class No:* 681.11(035)

[7184]

FRIED, H.B. The Watch repairer's manual. 4th ed. Cincinnati, Oh.,
American Watchmaker's Institute Press, 1986. xii, 453p. illus., diagrs.
ISBN: 0918845114.

First published 1949; 3rd ed. 1976.

25 chapters on all aspects of watch cleaning and repair. 9 appendices
('Dictionary of trade terms', p.412-23). Detailed illustrations. Author
is the 'Dean of American Watchmakers'. *Class No:* 681.11(035)

Dictionaries

[7185]

BERNER, G.-A. Dictionnaire professionnel illustré de l'horlogerie:
français-allemand-anglais-espagnol. La Chaux-de-Fonds, La Chambre
Suisse de l'Horlogerie, 1961; London, Swiss Federation of Watch
Manufacturers, 1962. 1007p. illus.

4,103 numbered terms. French-based vocabulary, plus definitions in
French, with equivalents and indexes (on tinted paper) in German,
English and Spanish. If the number given to a term is underlined, there
is an illustration, with named parts, heading the page. Genders are
given. Small but clear type. *Class No:* 681.11(038)

[7186]

Dictionnaire horloger. Terminologie numérotation français - English -
russkiĭ - deutsch - español - italiano - portuges - [Japanese].
Neuchâtel, Switzerland, Ebauches SA, 1976. 493p. illus.

Dictionary of clock and watch terms in 8 languages. About 2,500
French-base entries, in sections, with English, Russian, Dutch,
Spanish, Italian, Portuguese and Japanese equivalents, and indexes for
each language. *Class No:* 681.11(038)

[7187]

MAUCH, C. and MAUCH, E. Horologisches Lexikon. [Horological
dictionary. Uhrenwörterbuch.] Tübinger, Universitäten Verlag
Tübinger, 1984. 2v. (728p.). ISBN: 9924895006.

1. *Deutsch-Englisch.* 2. *Englisch-Deutsch.*

V.1 (xv, 357p.) has *c.*15,000 German entry-words and sub-entries,
with English equivalents. German genders are given.
Class No: 681.11(038)

Trade Names, Trade Marks, Brand Names

[7188]

**KOCHMANN, K. Clock and watch trademark index European
origin:** Austria/England/France/Germany/Switzerland. Rev. ed.
Concord, Ca., Antique Clock Publishing, 1992. 967p. illus., diagrs.,
tables. ISBN: 0933396279.

Previous ed. 1989.

Over 35,000 trademarks and wordmarks. Arranged by country and
by watchmaker, A-Z. A brief history of watchmaking in that country
precedes each section. A wealth of information and a labour of love on
the part of the author. *Class No:* 681.11(088.7)

Histories

[7189]

BRITTEN, F.J. Britten's old clocks and watches, and their makers: a
history of styles in clocks and watches and their makers.
Baillie, G.H., *and others, eds.* 9th ed., rev. and enlarged by C.
Clutton. London, Methuen, in association with E. & F.N. Spon, 1982.
xxvii, 708p. illus., facsims. £60. ISBN: 0413397261.

First published 1875.

9 chapters: 1. Counting the hours, from the beginning to 1550 ... 4.
English supremacy *c.*1660-1750 ... 7. French clocks ... 9. Alarum,
striking and reporting mechanisms. 3 appendices (1. Records of
famous makers; 2. List of former clock and watch makers, p.345-654;
3. Hallmarks). Glossary. Select bibliography, p.675-81. Index, p.683-
708. 388 illus. (40 col.). A handsome quarto classic.
Class No: 681.11(091)

[7190]

—**BRUTON, E.M.** The History of clocks and watches. London, Orbis,
1979. 288p. illus. (incl. col.), facsims., ports.

11 sections: 1. The earliest clocks - 2. The advent of clockwork - 3.
Domestic clocks - 4. European mechanical clocks - 5. The time at sea -
6. The development of the watch - 7. Mass production - 8. The
technological age - 9. Watches for the people - 10. The science of time
- 11. Great clocks of the world. Glossary. Bibliography, p.278-80.
Illus. on every page. Index, p.281-7. A handsome quarto, for popular
consumption. *Class No:* 681.11(091)

Biographies

[7191]

BAILLIE, G.H. Watchmakers and clockmakers of the world. 3rd ed.
London, N.A.G. Press, 1951. xxv, 388p. maps.

First published 1929; 2nd ed. 1947 (xxv, 373p.).

The 3rd ed. reprints the 2nd ed's. 35,000 names, A-Z, 'Addenda' of
*c.*600 further makers. Brief entries state dates, location and type of
watch/clock made. Included are lists of place names, alternative
spellings, initials and marks. *Class No:* 681.11(092)

[7192]

—**LOONES, B.** Watchmakers and clockmakers of the world: Volume 2.
London, N.A.G. Press, 1976. xiii, 269p. £9.95.

Written as a supplement ot Baillie's *Watchmakers and Clockmakers*
(*qv.*) - 'to complement it, not to replace'. Arranged A-Z; entries state
name, location and dates. Gazetteer of lesser-known places. Tiny print.
Largely confined to UK. *Class No:* 681.11(092)

Equipment & Instruments

[7193]

DE CARLE, D. Clock and watch repairing, including complicated
watches. London, Pitman, 1959. viii, 312p. illus.

Covers all components of clocks and watches, how they can go
wrong, and how to repair them. All parts and tools are illustrated in
detail. Appended glossary of technical terms; also a section on Patak
Philippe Light Clock. *Class No:* 681.11:002.50

Museums

[7194]

TURNER, A. The Time Museum: catalog of the collection. Rockford,
Ill., Time Museum, 1984-. v.1-. illus. (incl. col.), facsims., map.

1. *Time-measuring machines.*

Pt.1: *Astrolabes. Astrolabe-related instruments.* 1985.

Pt.2: *Water-clocks. Sand-glasses. Fire clocks.* 1984.

V.1, pt.1 ([xv], 268p.) includes a glossary, bibliography of works
cited (p.243-60), concordance, and index. 137 figures. Pt. 2 ([xi],
183, [1]p.) includes a bibliography, p.163-73. Index, p.177-83.
Class No: 681.11:061:069

[7195]

**TYLER, E.J. Clock museums and collections visited by E.J. Tyler,
from 1971 to 1983.** Heathfield, E. Sussex, Watch & Clock Book
Society, 1983. 46p. illus. £4.75. ISBN: 090351236x.

Reprints of artices on clock collections visited. 19 illus.
Class No: 681.11:061:069

[7196]

**WARD, F.A.B. Descriptive catalogue of the collection illustrating
time measurement: Science Museum.** London, H.M. Stationery
Office, 1966. vii, 151p. illus. (pl.).

526 entries, with references appended. 16 sections: 1. Primitive and
other non-mechanical devices - 2. Sundials, nocturnal and perpetual
calendars ... 7. Chronometers ... 11. The atomic clock ... 15. Gas
controllers and time switches. List of the more important objects in the
reserve collection (R1-67). List of makers of watches included in the
catalogue. Index. *Class No:* 681.11:061:069

Sundials

[7197]

COUSINS, F.W. Sundials: a simplified approach by means of the
equatorial dial. London, J. Baker, 1969. 247p. illus., diagrs., graphs,
tables.

22 sections ending with 'Dialling scales'. Bibliography, p.214-22 (2
parts: 'Books on dialling before 1800', in chronological order; 'Works
on dialling after 1800', under authors, A-Z). Appendix: 'A note
concerning the accuracy of the tabulated values'. Name and subject
indexes. *Class No:* 681.111

Instrument Making

Bibliographies

[7198]
BRITISH SCIENTIFIC INSTRUMENT RESEARCH ASSOCIATION. **Catalogue of books in the Library** [Chiselhurst, Kent], BSIRA, 1966. 2v. mimeographed.
V.1, a U.D.C. classified list ([v], 170p.), - 'compiled with both librarians and general users in mind'. About 2,000 items. V.2: subject and author indexes (49p.). *Class No:* 681.2(01)

Encyclopaedias

[7199]
MILLS, J.F. **Encyclopaedia of antique scientific instruments.** London, Aurum Press, 1983. 255p. illus. (incl. col.), facsims., tables. ISBN: 0906053404.
More than 700 entries, A-Z, p.45-233 (*e.g.* 'Sextant': 2½ columns, 2 illus.). Includes biographies (*e.g.* 'Benjamin Franklin': over 1 column). Appendices: Care of the collection; Forgery and fakes; Table of events (to 1789); Museums (under countries, A-Z, p.251-9); Price guide. 'This book should have wide appeal' (*Library journal*, v.109(1), January 1984, p.76). *Class No:* 681.2(031)

Handbooks & Manuals

[7200]
EWING, G.W., *ed.* **Analytical instrumentation handbook.** New York, M. Dekker, 1990. 1088p. $195. ISBN: 0824781848.
Detailed descriptions of the major techniques of spectrochemical, electrochemical and chromotographic analysis, and other techniques (*e.g.* chapter of 73p. on nuclear magnetic resonance). This handbook can therefore 'serve as a one-volume resource in place of a number of monographs' (*Science and technology libraries*, v.11(1), Spring 1991, p.149). *Class No:* 681.2(035)

[7201]
The Instrument manual. Miller, J.T., *ed.* 5th ed. London, United Trade Press, 1975. [vii], 566p. illus., diagrs., tables.
First published 1949.
8 contributors. 23 sections (1. Automatic control ... 4. Measurement and control of viscosity - 5. Measurement of fluid flow ... 8. Techniques for measuring surface temperature (381 references) ... 13. Measurement and control of pressure ... 20. Analytical instrumentation - 21. Non-destructive testing - 22. Numerical control - 23. SI units). Section references. Analytical index. *Class No:* 681.2(035)

[7202]
Jones' instrument technology. Noltingk, B.E., *ed.* 4th ed. London, Butterworth, 1985-7. 5v. illus., diagrs., graphs, tables.
First published 1956.
1. *Mechanical measurements.* 1985. ix, 170p.
2. *Measurement of temperature and chemical composition.* 1985. [viii], 282p.
3. *Electrical and radiation measurement.* 1987. 220p.
4. *Instrumentation systems.* 1987. 168p.
5. *Automatic instruments and measuring systems.* 1986. 180p.
The 4th ed. reflects recent developments in electronics, gas analysis and other subjects. V.1 has 9 contributors, with 11 documented sections and a detailed subject index. *Class No:* 681.2(035)

[7203]
LIPTÁK, B.G., *ed.* **Instrument engineers' handbook.** 3rd ed. Oxford, Butterworth-Heinemann, 1995. 2v. (xxvii, 1391; xxvii, 1551p.) diagrs., graphs. £100 each. ISBN: 0750622547, v.1; 0750622555, v.2.
First published 1969-70 (2v.); supplement, 1972.
V.1. *Process measurement.* V.2. *Process control.*
V.2 comprises documented chapters on control theory, panels and displays, logic devices and PLCs, computer and distributed control, control of unit operations, etc. Index. *Class No:* 681.2(035)

[7204]
NACHTIGAL, C.L., *ed.* **Instrumentation and control:** fundamentals and applications. New York, etc., Wiley, 1990. xxii,890p. illus., diagrs., graphs, tables. (*Wiley series in mechanical engineering practice.*) ISBN: 0471880450.
20 chapters in 3 parts: I. General topics (system engineering concepts; instrument statics; electronic devices and data conversion, etc.) - II. Instrumentation (bridge transducers; temperature and flow transducers, etc.) - III. Control (closed-loop control system analysis; performance modification; controller design, etc.). Extensive chapter references. Analytical subject index, p.871-90. 46 contributors, both academic and industrial. *Class No:* 681.2(035)

Dictionaries

[7205]
CLASON, W.E. **Elsevier's dictionary of measurement and control** in six languages: English/American, French, Spanish, Italian, Dutch and German. Amsterdam, etc., Elsevier, 1977. 886p. £121.62. ISBN: 0444415823.
Almost 7,800 entries for terms in English, with equivalents in other languages. Alphabetical indexes in other languages refer to numbered entries in main section. Brief bibliography (p.885-6). Lack of Russian terminology a disadvantage. *Class No:* 681.2(038)

[7206]
RAMALINGOM, T. **Dictionary of instrument science.** New York, Wiley, 1982. 588p. ISBN: 0471863963.
More than 6,000 definitions of terms in control and instrumentation. Coverage includes chemical and process control instrumentation, optical electrical and electronics instrumentation, aerospace and remote-sensing instrumention, computer and data processing. Accessible to non-technical readers. *Class No:* 681.2(038)

Progress Reports

[7207]
Advances in instrumentation and control. Research Triangle Park, N.C., International Society for Measurement and Control, 1947-. Annual. illus., diagrs., graphs, chemical structures. ISSN: 10540032.
3 parts pa., usually. Includes papers presented at the Instrument Society of America's international conference, exhibition and training program. *Class No:* 681.2(055)

Festschriften

[7208]
Making instruments count: essays on historical scientific instruments presented to Gerard L'Estrange Turner. Anderson, R.G.W., *and others, eds.* New York, Variorum, 1993. 492p. illus. $89.95. ISBN: 0860783944.
Essays covering early instruments, instruments and art, instruments and science, British and Dutch instruments, optical instruments, and the instrument-making trade. Extensive references for each essay. Index. *Class No:* 681.2(082.20)

Histories

[7209]
BENNETT, J.A. **The Divided circle:** a history of instruments for astronomy, navigation and surveying. Oxford, Phaidon, Christie's, 1987. 224p. illus. (incl. col.). ISBN: 0714880388.
14 chapters covering historical periods: 1-5. Ancient to early modern - 6-9. Eighteenth Century - 10-13. Nineteenth century - 14. Twentieth century. Extensive bibliography; 3 indexes (makers; technical terms; general). A lavishly illustrated quarto. Includes 'a bibliography, an index of makers, an index of technical terms, and a general index, which make it an excellent reference as well as a fascinating book to read' (*Choice*, June 1988, p.1577).
Class No: 681.2(091)

[7210]
BILLMEIR, J.A. **Scientific instruments, 13th-19th century:** the collection of J.A. Billmeir, with supplement. Exhibited by the Museum of the History of Science, Oxford. 2nd ed. Oxford, the Museum, 1955-57. 2v.
First published 1954.
The 1955 catalogue lists 154 items in 7 classes, with brief notes on size, century, rarity, etc., followed by plates and index of inventors, designers and makers. The supplement provides much fuller notes on items in 9 classes: 1. Astrolabes; 2. Astronomical ring; 3. Globes; 4. Quadrants; 5. Sundials; 6. Nocturnals; 7. Astronomical compendia; 8. Topographical instruments; 9. Miscellaneous. Bibliographical note, p.9-12, and index. *Class No:* 681.2(091)

[7211]
DAUMAS, M. **Scientific instruments of the seventeenth and eighteenth centuries and their makers.** Translated and edited by M. Holbrook. London, Batsford, 1972. 361p. illus., diagrs.
3 parts (14 chapters): 1. Instrument-making industry in the seventeenth century - 2. Contributory factors in the evolution of the instrument-making industry - 3. The instrument-making industry in the eighteenth century. Chapter references and footnotes, p.295-340. Libraries, archives, collections, p.341. Bibliography (general works and periodicals), p.342-8. 142 plates; 151 illus. Index, p.349-61. *Class No:* 681.2(091)

[7212]

Instruments of science: an historical encyclopedia. Bud, R., *and others, eds.* London, Science Museum; New York, Garland, 1998. 709p. illus., diagrs. £110; $138. (*Garland encyclopedias in the history of science,* 2.) ISBN: 0815315619.

Edited by representatives from the Science Museum and the National Museum of American History, Smithsonian Institution, Washington, D.C.

About 250 contributors. 300 articles (A-Z; most between 2,000 and 3,500 words) cover Western scientific equipment and devices from ancient mathematics to modern science. Brief bibliographies; indexes: name; subject; instrument. 'A very important contribution to the literature of the history of science' ('Reference books bulletin', *Booklist*, June 1 & 15, 1998, p.1812). *Class No:* 681.2(091)

[7213]

SYDENHAM, P.H. Measuring instruments: book of knowledge and control. Stevenage, Herts., P. Peregrinus, in association with the Science Museum, London 1979. xvi, [1], 512p. ISBN: 0906068192.

6 sections: 1. Measurements for knowledge and control - 2. Science and technology of measuring instruments - 3. Ancient times to Middle Ages: birth of the first instruments - 4. Experimental science becomes established: Middle Ages - 1800 A.D. - 5. Growth of electrical methods - 6. The first half of the 20th century: 1900-1950. Bibliography (A-Z authors), p.456-81. 2 appendices: 1. Biographies relevant to instrument history; 2. Collections containing instruments. Detailed, analytical index, p.496-512. *Class No:* 681.2(091)

[7214]

TURNER, A. Early scientific instruments: Europe 1400-1800. London, Sotheby's Publications, 1987. 320p. illus. (incl. col.), ports. ISBN: 0856673196.

Describes what scientific instruments were available at given periods, explaining their origin and technical functions, and indicating the main lines of their development. Notes; bibliography, p.290-311. A lavishly illustrated large quarto. *Class No:* 681.2(091)

[7215]

TURNER, G.L'E. Antique scientific instruments. Poole, Dorset, Blandford Press, 1981. 165p. ISBN: 0713709235.

9 chapters: 1. Astronomy and time-telling - 2. Navigational instruments - 3. Surveying instruments - 4. Drawing and calculating instruments - 5. Optical instruments - 6. Philosphical instruments - 7. Weights and measures - 8. Medical instruments - 9. Practical advice on collecting. Bibliography (A-Z authors), p.160-2). Museums and collections p.163-4. Index (mostly non-analytical), p.165-8. Small format. A book that should have wide appeal. *Class No:* 681.2(091)

[7216]

TURNER, G.L'E. Nineteenth-century scientific instruments. London, P. Wilson, for Sotheby Pubns. 1987. 320p. illus. (incl. col.), facsims. ISBN: 0850671708.

16 chapters: 3. Weights and measures - 4. Mechanics - 5. Hydrostatics - 6. Pneumatics - 7. Heat - 8. Sound - 9. Light - 10. Magnetism - 11. Electricity - 12. Chemistry - 13. Meteorology - 14. Surveying and navigation - 15. Drawing and calculating - 16. Recreational science. Appended: 'Instrument makers exhibiting at the Great Exhibition of 1851'. Bibliography, p.311-3. Index, p.314-20. 377 illus. (32 col.). Quarto. *Class No:* 681.2(091)

Great Britain

[7217]

CLIFTON, G. Directory of British scientific instrument makers 1550-1851. London, Zwemmer, 1995. 331p. illus. £65. ISBN: 0302006346.

Includes those recorded as making or selling scientific, astronomical, drawing, measuring, or navigational instruments. About 5,000 full entries and 10,000 'apprentices' also listed.Indexes: name; geographical. *Class No:* 681.2(410)

USA

[7218]

SMITHSONIAN INSTITUTION. Early American scientific instruments and their makers. Bedini, S.A. Washington, the Institution, 1964. 196p. (*Bulletin 231.*)

A descriptive account. *Class No:* 681.2(73)

Museums

[7219]

HOLBROOK, M. and **ANDERSON, R.G.W.,** *and others, comps. and eds.* **Science preserved:** a directory of scientific instruments in collections in the United Kingdom and Eire. London, H.M. Stationery Office, 1992. 270p. illus. £35. ISBN: 0112900607.

A guide to some 3700 instruments in more than 200 publicly accessible collections in the museums, country houses and universities of the British Isles. *Class No:* 681.2:061:069

Computers

Abbreviations & Symbols

[7220]

MERKOW, M. Breaking through technical jargon: a dictionary of computer and automation acronyms. New York, Van Nostrand Reinhold, 1990. xviii,181p. £14.50. ISBN: 0442001517.

About 1,000 acronyms, A-Z (ABCD - Z-80). Strong North American bias (*e.g.* ANSI and ISO are present but not BSI). Some odd omissions, *e.g.* WIMP, WYSIWYG. *Class No:* 681.3(003)

[7221]

ROSENBERG, J.M., *ed.* **The McGraw-Hill dictionary of information technology and computer acronyms, initials and abbreviations.** New York, etc. McGraw-Hill, 1991. 240p. £24.95. ISBN: 0070539367.

Over 10,000 acronyms. *Class No:* 681.3(003)

[7222]

SOUTH, D.W. The Computer and information science and technology abbreviations and acronyms dictionary. Boca Raton, Fl., CRC Press, 1994. vii, 302p. £33; $39.95. ISBN: 0849324440.

About 9,000 entries, A-Z. Prelim. pages include 'Commonly used terms and prefixes'. 21 appendices (*e.g.* 'MS-DOS 6.0 command reference'). *Class No:* 681.3(003)

[7223]

TAVAGLIONE, D. Acronyms and abbreviations of computer technology and telecommunication. New York, Dekker, 1993. xi, 291p. ISBN: 0824787471.

About 7,000 entries, A-Z. Use and derivation occasionally given. 2 appendices: sources; recommended references (some very dated). *Class No:* 681.3(003)

[7224]

TOWELL, J.E. *and* **SHEPPARD, H.E.,** *eds.* **Computer & telecommunications acronyms.** Detroit, Mich., Gale, 1986. 391p. $60. ISBN: 0810324911.

A dictionary of *c.*25,000 acronyms, terms, etc., in the computer and telecommunications fields. Entries are selected from *Acronyms, initialisms & abbreviations dictionary* (9th ed. Gale, 1984). Added to many definitions are subject categories, geographical locations and citation of sources. *Class No:* 681.3(003)

[7225]

WENNRICH, P. International dictionary of abbreviations and acronyms of electronics, electrical engineering, computer technology, and information processing. München, Saur, 1992. 2v. (502; 458p.). ISBN: 3598109776.

Over 90,000 abbreviations, most of English-language derivation. *Class No:* 681.3(003)

Databases

[7226]

Computer database. Foster City, Ca., Information Access Company.

Covers computers, telecommunications and electronics with information on hardware, software, peripherals and services. About 450,000 records; updated weekly. Available on DIALOG (file 275) and Data-Star. *Class No:* 681.3(003.4)

[7227]

INSPEC. Stevenage, Herts., Institution of Electrical Engineers, 1969-.

INSPEC database provides online access to *Computer and control abstracts.* Available through various hosts and on CD-ROM. *Class No:* 681.3(003.4)

[7228]

RAITT, D. 'Computer and information science and technology'. *Manual of online search stategies.* Editors, C.J. Armstrong and J.A. Large, pp.309-56. 2nd ed. Aldershot, Ashgate, 1992. ISBN: 1857420071.

Extensive list of databases and host systems covering mainframes, micros, software, artificial intelligence, telecommunications, semiconductors, etc. *Class No:* 681.3(003.4)

CD-ROM

[7229]

Computing and communications. London, SilverPlatter, 1999. CD-ROM. 2pa.

About 30,000 bibliographic records from 6 databases. Covers popular computing, telecommunications, interactive and information science services. Emphasis in on Australian and New Zealand material and includes references to journal and newspaper articles, theses, research reports and conference proceedings. *Class No:* 681.3(003.40)

[7230]

The OCLC computer library. London, SliverPlatter, 1994. Annual. CD-ROM.

550,000 bibliographic records taken from the OCLC Online Union Catalog. Includes books, journals, newspapers, A-V materials, software. *Class No:* 681.3(003.40)

Internet

[7231]

Computer science collection. Bethesda, Md., Cambridge Scientific Abstracts. URL: http://www.csa.com or http://www.csa.sara.nl.

The web site provides access to a variety of bibliographic databases covering computers, microcomputers, information systems, electronics, communications, solid state technology, superconductors and ceramics technology applicable to electronics. About 775,000 records; 60,000 pa. Updated monthly, with backfiles to 1981. *Class No:* 681.3(003.41)

Bibliographies

[7232]

ACM guide to computing literature. New York, Association for Computing Machinery, 1978-. Annual. ISSN: 01491199.

Formerly *Computing reviews: bibliography and subject index of current computing literature*, 1963-76.

The 1996v. (xxiii, 1947p.) has about 24,000 references under 'Bibliographic listing' (books; journals; proceedings; doctoral theses; 'Computing reviews'). 6 indexes: Author; Keyword; Category; Proper noun subject; 'Computing reviews' reviewer; Source. *Class No:* 681.3(01)

[7233]

Computing information directory: a comprehensive guide to the computing literature. Hildebrandt, D.M., *ed.* 11th ed. Pullman, Wa., Computing Information Directory, 1994. 443p. $260 ISBN: 0933113196.

First published 1981 as *Computer science resources*.

Revised annually. Master subject index, with subheadings, by type of literature, *e.g.* current books; computer-related journals (including university computing centre newsletters); indexing and abstracting services; software resources; programming languages, etc. Well-produced and a valuable US-slanted source. *Class No:* 681.3(01)

Indexes

[7234]

CompuMath citation index: an international, interdisciplinary index to the literature of applied mathematics, computer science statistics, operations research and related disciplines. Phildealphia, Pa., Institute for Scientific Information, 1981-. 2pa. ISSN: 07306199.

CMCI consists of 5 indexes: Research front specialty index; Citation index; Corporate index; Source index; Permuterm subject index. Also, annual *Guide and list of source publications*. Available online as part of Scisearch. *Class No:* 681.3(014)

Encyclopaedias

[7235]

Encyclopedia of computer science and technology. Belzer, J., *and others, eds.* New York & Basle, Dekker, 1975-. illus., diagrs., tables. (v.34, supplement 19; 1996; 192p. $195). ISBN: 0824722515.

V.1-14 contain 277 documented articles, A-Z. V.13 (1979. vi, 507p., 'Reliability theory' ... 'USSR, computing in') has 23 contributors. 'Software engineering': p.216-44, carries 19 references. V.15, *Supplement* (1980) includes 12 contributors and one update. V.16 (viii, 192p.) provides author and subject indexes. V.34 has 17 articles covering fuzzy logic, computer performance, database theory, artificial intelligence in education, computer security, electronic music and other topics. The set provides a useful historical overview. *Class No:* 681.3(031)

[7236]

FREEDMAN, A. The Computer desktop encyclopedia. New York, AMACOM, 1996. 1005p. $39.95. ISBN: 0814400108.

About 8,500 brief entries coverings topics such as fundamentals, graphics and multimedia, communications, applications, programming, standards, compatibility, networking, etc. Includes acronyms and brief biographies. 'Knowledgeable, comprehensive, clear ... and easy to use' (*Choice*, February 1997, p.943). Also available on CD-ROM. *Class No:* 681.3(031)

[7237]

Macmillan encyclopedia of computers. Bitter, G.G., *ed.* New York, Macmillan, 1992. 2v. 1080p. illus., diagrs. $150. ISBN: 0028970454.

Over 200 articles with an emphasis on practical application. Numerous biographical entries. Appendix lists computing associations and computer manufacturers. Detailed, analytical index. Selected by *Choice* (January 1993, p.735) for its list of 'Outstanding academic books', 1993. *Class No:* 681.3(031)

[7238]

RALSTON, A. *and* **REILLY, E.D., *Jr., eds.* Encyclopedia of computer science.** 3rd ed. New York, Van Nostrand Reinhold; London, Chapman & Hall, 1993. xxv, 1558p. illus., diagrs., tables. $100; £72.50. ISBN: 0442276796, US; 0412497107, UK.

First published 1976; 2nd ed. 1983.

Over 300 contributors and about 500 signed articles, 175 of them new to this edition. Coverage: hardware; computer systems; information and data; software; mathematics and theory of computing; methodologies; applications; computing environments. Appendices (*e.g.* 'Glossary of major terms in five languages'); detailed, analytical index. The standard one-volume reference work on computers. *Class No:* 681.3(031)

Handbooks & Manuals

[7239]

The Computer science and engineering handbook. Tucker, A.B., *ed.* Boca Raton, Fa., CRC Press, 1996. *c.*2560p. illus., diagrs., graphs, tables. $129.95. ISBN: 0849329094.

Published in association with the Association for Computing Machinery. About 110 chapters in 10 sections: Algorithms and data structures - Architecture - Artificial intelligence - Computational science - Database and information retrieval - Graphics - Human-computer interaction - Operating systems and networks - Programming languages - software engineering. Extensive references; web sites; glossary. *Class No:* 681.3(035)

[7240]

TOOLEY, M. Newnes computer engineer's pocket book. 4th ed. Oxford, Butterworth-Heinemann, 1997. viii, 332p. illus., diagrs., tables. ISBN: 0750620951.

First published 1987; 2nd ed. 1991.

Covers a range of topics (*e.g.* Basic logic gates, Boolean algebra, ASCII control characters), devoting 1-2 pages to each (although 74 series has nearly 20 pages). Extensively illustrated; list of abbreviations; index (8p.). Small format. 'Aims to provide ... everyday information' in an accessible format (*Preface*). *Class No:* 681.3(035)

[7241]

VASSILIOU, M.S. *and* **ORENSTEIN, J.A. Computer professional's quick reference.** New York, McGraw-Hill, 1992. 266p. illus., diagrs., tables. $34.95; $24.95. ISBN: 0070672113; 0070672121, Pbk.

Includes common commands for 5 operating systems, UNIX, VMS, MVS, VM, MS-DOS, as well as networks and technical standards. Chapter bibliographies. Detailed, analytical index. *Class No:* 681.3(035)

Dictionaries

Polyglot

[7242]

Elsevier's dictionary of computer science and mathematics in English, German, French, and Russian. Peeva, K. *and* Delijska, B., *comps.* Amsterdam, etc., Elsevier, 1995. 785p. $220.50. ISBN: 0444818162.

9,594 English-base terms, followed by equivalents in the other languages. Index; appendix of mathematical symbols. *Class No:* 681.3(038)=00

English

[7243]

COLLIN, S.M.H. Dictionary of computing. 2nd ed. Teddington, Middlesex, Peter Collin, 1994. [iv], 304p. illus. ISBN: 0948549440.

First published 1988.

Produced in association with *Computing*, the IT weekly. About 6,000 headwords, briefly and simply defined. Supplementary explanations and quotations using terms in context. Appended section of illustrations, samples of programming languages, ASCII code, etc. *Class No:* 681.3(038)=20

[7244]

Dictionary of computer words. Rev. ed. New York, Houghton Mifflin, 1995. 332p. illus. $10.95. ISBN: 0395728347.

First published 1993.

About 12,000 terms, some defined at length. Cross references. Less technical than the *IBM dictionary of computing* (*q.v.*) and intended for lay persons rather than computer professionals. 'Recommended' (*Choice*, February 1996, p.927). *Class No:* 681.3(038)=20

[7245]

Dictionary of computing. Illingworth, V. *and* Pyle, I., *eds*. 4th ed. Oxford Univ. Press, 1996. [x], 550p. diagrs., tables. £25. ISBN: 0198538553.

First published 1983; 3rd ed. 1990.

Nearly 6,000 terms in computing. Includes technical terms in hardware and software, plus broader context of social and legal implications. Terms new to this ed. include ATM, freeware, Pentium, spam, URL. A major dictionary. *Class No:* 681.3(038)=20

[7246]

FREEDMAN, A. The Computer glossary: the complete illustrated desk reference. 7th ed. New York, AMACOM, 1993. 456p. illus. $36.95. ISBN: 0814402682.

About 5,000 terms, briefly and precisely defined; some include concise histories. Well-illustrated. Also available on computer disk. *Class No:* 681.3(038)=20

[7247]

A Glossary of computing terms. British Computer Society Schools Committee Glossary Working Party. 7th ed. London, Pitman for the British Computer Society, 1991. viii,150p. ISBN: 0273036459.

First published 1977; previous ed. 1987.

About 950 terms defined in simple language. Arrangement is by 15 broad headings (*e.g.* 'Applications'; 'Storage'; 'Truth tables and logic gates', etc.). Therefore, an index of terms is added. Includes 10 brief 'essays' on specific areas of computing and information technology. Recommended for schools and tertiary institutions. *Class No:* 681.3(038)=20

[7248]

GUNTON, T. A Dictionary of information technology and computer science. 2nd ed. Manchester, Oxford, NCC, Blackwell, 1993. vii, 343p. £25. ISBN: 1855543273.

First published 1991.

About 3,000 terms defined and explained, some at length (*e.g.* 'server': ½p.). Cross references. Appended: ASCII code chart. 'A comprehensive range of terms which are simple to understand and placed in well-considered context' (*Aslib information*, v.19(4), April 1991, p.143, on the 1st ed.). *Class No:* 681.3(038)=20

[7249]

IBM dictionary of computing. McDaniel, G., *ed*. 10th ed. New York, McGraw-Hill, 1994. 758p. diagrs. $39.50. ISBN: 0070314888.

Originally written for IBM personnel; this the first ed. to be published.

More than 20,000 terms, briefly defined, covering the entire field of computing. Many definitions are in the context of IBM hardware or operating systems. A substantial, comprehensive dictionary. *Class No:* 681.3(038)=20

[7250]

LYNCH, D.B. Concise dictionary of computing. London, Chartwell-Bratt, 1991. 380p. £9.95. ISBN: 0862382685.

Defines over 4,000 terms, A-Z. Comprehensive and non-technical reference source and guide for users of computers and IT in education and business. *Class No:* 681.3(038)=20

[7251]

Microsoft Press computer dictionary. Redmond, Wa., Microsoft Press, 1997. 540p. illus., diagrs., tables. $30. ISBN: 157231446x.

About 6,000 entries. Covers terms which are likely to appear in documentation, online help, computer manuals, marekting and sales material, the popular media and the trade press. Quarterly updates are available on the Microsoft Press web site. A good, standard dictionary. *Class No:* 681.3(038)=20

[7252]

The New hacker's dictionary. Raymond, E.S., *ed*. 3rd ed. Cambridge, Ma. and London, MIT Press, 1996. 547p. illus. $32. ISBN: 0262181789; 0262680920, Pbk.

First published 1983; 2nd ed. 1991.

More than 1,100 terms, A-Z. A dictionary of slang terminology, not technology. Introductory essay on the evolution of computer-hacking jargon. Brief, annotated bibliography. 'More than a typical dictionary ... Recommended' (*American reference books annual*, 1998, p.691). *Class No:* 681.3(038)=20

[7253]

Prentice Hall's illustrated dictionary of computing. Nader, J.C., *ed*. 2nd ed. New York, Prentice Hall, 1995. 691p. illus., diagrs. $24.95. ISBN: 0132057255.

First published 1992.

About 5,000 terms, some defined at length. Definitions frequently based on ISO standards. Includes 'Style manual' for correct use of computer terminology, covering acronyms, abbreviations, use of capital letters, form of numbers, etc. Criticized in *Choice* (December 1995, p.598) for poor illustrations, 'pompous self-quotation' and 'fluff'. *Class No:* 681.3(038)=20

[7254]

ROSENBERG, J.M. Business dictionary of computers. New York, Wiley, 1993. xii, 403p. £32.95. ISBN: 0471585750.

About 7,500 terms, most defined briefly (*e.g.* 'locator device': 4 lines). Cross references. *Class No:* 681.3(038)=20

[7255]

SIPPL, C.J. *and* **SIPPL, R.J. Computer dictionary and handbook.** 4th ed. Indianapolis, Ind., Sams, 1985. 962p. illus. $24.95. ISBN: 0672222051.

First published 1966. 3rd ed. 1980.

12,000 entries, including 1000 new to this ed. Cross-references; extensive appendices. For the advanced user. *Class No:* 681.3(038)=20

[7256]

SPENCER, D.D. Computer dictionary. 4th ed. Ormond Beach, Fl., Camelot Publishing, 1993. 459p. illus., facsims., ports. $24.95. ISBN: 0892182393.

Previous ed. 1986.

About 5,800 terms, briefly defined, with some cross references. Includes brand names. Primarily for non-specialists. *Class No:* 681.3(038)=20

[7257]

—**SPENCER, D.D.** Illustrated computer graphics dictionary. Ormond Beach, Fl., 1993. 305p. illus. $24.95. ISBN: 0892181176.

About 2,100 entries, most defined briefly, with 500 illustrations. 'Reference books bulletin' (*Booklist*, April 15, 1993, p.1532) commented that some definitions were misleading or confusing. *Class No:* 681.3(038)=20

[7258]

Webster's new world dictionary of computer terms. 3rd ed. New York, Simon & Schuster, 1988. vi,412p. £5.95. ISBN: 0139492313.

First published 1983.

About 4,500 terms, briefly defined (*e.g.* 'multipass sort': 3 lines). Small format. *Class No:* 681.3(038)=20

[7259]

WYATT, A.L. Computer professional's dictionary. Berkeley, Calif., Osborne McGraw-Hill, 1990. ix,352p. diagrs., tables. £22.95. ISBN: 0078817056.

About 2,500 terms, briefly defined (*e.g.* 1 parity': 10 lines). *Class No:* 681.3(038)=20

German

[7260]

COLLIN, S.M.H., *and others*. **Dictionary of computing and information technology: English-German.** Teddington, Middlesex, Peter Collin, 1991. [viii],410,[17]p. illus. ISBN: 0984859203.

About 5,000 English terms, briefly defined. Includes brief boxed quotations to illustrate use of a term. List of German words and their English equivalents. *Class No:* 681.3(038)=30

[7261]

FERRETTI, V. Dictionary of electronics, computing and telecommunication: English-German, German-English. [Wörterbuch der elektronik, datentechnik und der telekommunikation.] Berlin, Springer Verlag, 1992. 2v. (xxviii, 609p. + xxviii, 636p.) £58.50 each. ISBN: 3540541101, (G/E); 3540542027, (E/G).

About 60,000 entries in each half. Prelims. include 'Applied morphology of subject fields'. Bibliography, 5p. Also available on CD-ROM. *Class No:* 681.3(038)=30

[7262]

SCHULZE, H.H. Computer Englische: ein Fachwörterbuch. [Computer English: a dictionary.] Hamburg, Rowholt, 1991. 510p. ISBN: 3499181770.

About 18,000 terms in each language. *Class No:* 681.3(038)=30

French

[7263]
COLLIN, S.M.H., *and others*. Dictionary of computing and information technology: English-French; French-English. Teddington, Middlesex, Peter Collin, 1991. [x],323p. ISBN: 0948549246.

About 5,000 headwords in each language. Genders given. Distinguishes British and American usage. Includes brief boxed quotations to illustrate use of a term. *Class No:* 681.3(038)=40

[7264]
FISCHER, R. *and* KRUCHTEN, P. Dictionnaire informatique. Paris, Eyrolles, 1984-5.

Anglais-français. 3. éd., edited by R. Fischer and P. Kruchten. 1985. 375p.

Français-anglais; by R. Fischer. 1984. 480p.

About 15,00 terms and phrases. The work of a team of contributors. *Class No:* 681.3(038)=40

[7265]
INTERNATIONAL ORGANIZATION FOR STANDARDIZATION. Dictionary of computer science: the standardized vocabulary. Paris, ISO/AFNOR, 1997. xii, 612p. £40. ISBN: 2124869221.

About 30,000 entry words defined in English. Compiled by ISO/AFNOR and based on ISO/IEC 2382: Information technology vocabulary. French equivalents are provided, as well as an index in French, but essentially an English language dictionary. Authoritative. *Class No:* 681.3(038)=40

Spanish

[7266]
KAPLAN, S.M. Electrical and computer engineering dictionary: English - Spanish, Spanish - English. [Diccionario de ingenieria eléctrica y de computadoras: Inglés - Español, Español - Inglés.] New York, Wiley, 1996. viii, 792p. £45. ISBN: 0471010375.

About 50,000 entry terms in each half, with equivalents (usually one word or phrase) in the other language. *Class No:* 681.3(038)=60

Reviews & Abstracts

[7267]
Computer and control abstracts. Science abstracts. Section C. London, INSPEC, 1969-. Monthly. £1270. ISSN: 00368113.

Formerly *Control abstracts,* 1966-68.

About 100,000 abstracts pa. Classes, closely subdivided: 0000 General and management topics - 1000 Systems and control theory - 3000 Control technology - 4000 Numerical analysis and theoretical, computer topics - 5000 Computer hardware - 6000 Computer software - 7000 Computer applications. Author index per issue; Subject index, twice yearly; Subsidiary indexes, where appropriate; Bibliography index (for well-documented articles); Book index (for books received and abstracted); Corporate author index; Conference index. Indexes cumulated 2pa. and 4-yearly (*e.g.* 1987-1990). INSPEC database. CD-ROM. *Class No:* 681.3(048)

[7268]
Computer and information systems abstracts journal. Bethesda, Md., Cambridge Scientific Abstracts; New York, Engineering Information Inc., 1969-. Monthly. $1150 pa. ISSN: 01919776.

Formerly *Information processing journal* 1962-68.

About 71,600 abstracts pa. Sections: Civil engineering - Mining engineering - Mechanical engineering - Electrical engineering - Chemical engineering - General engineering. Detailed, analytical subject index and author index per issue. Cumulative index pa. Online as part of the *ELCOM* database and on the Internet (URL: http://www.csa.com). *Class No:* 681.3(048)

[7269]
—Computer abstracts. Bradford, MCB Press, 1961-. Monthly. $1,400 pa. ISSN: 00104469.

About 4,000 abstracts (averaging *c.*150 words apiece) pa. 13 sections: 1. General - 2. Computer theory ... 13. Applications (Aerospace ... Transport). Covers conference papers and US government reports as well as periodical articles and books. Annual subject and author indexes; list of journals abstracted. Also available on the World Wide Web (URL: http://www.anbar.com). *Class No:* 681.3(048)

[7270]
Computer literature index: a subject/author index to computer and data processing literature. Phoenix, Arizona, Applied Computer Research, Inc., 1981-. 4pa. ISSN: 02704846.

Formerly as *Quarterly bibliography of computers and data processing,* 1971-80.

About 2,500 briefly annotated entries per issue. Subject index (main sequence); author index; publisher index. Each issue covers the preceding quarter. Annual cumulation. *Class No:* 681.3(048)

[7271]
Computing journal abstracts. Stockport, Techgnosis Ltd., 1972-. Monthly. ISSN: 03098885.

Published in association with NCC.

About 2000 abstracts pa. Sections: Acquisitions - Case studies ... Languages ... Multimedia - Networks ... Software reviews ... Users and user interface. A current awareness service. Annual cumulative index. Also available on floppy disk (£250). *Class No:* 681.3(048)

[7272]
Computing reviews: review journal of the Association for Computing Machinery. New York, the Association, 1960-. Monthly. $145. ISSN: 00104884.

About 1,000 abstracts/reviews pa. Sections A-K: A. General literature - B. Hardware - C. Computer systems organization - D. Software - E. Data - F. Theory of computation - G. Mathematics of computing - H. Information systems - I. Computing methodologies - J. Computer applications - K. Computing milieux. Descriptors added. Preceding the abstracts section: Author index; Books and proceedings; Non-book literature. *Class No:* 681.3(048)

[7273]
Current papers on computers and control. Stevenage, Herts., Institution of Electrical Engineers, New York, Institute of Electrical and Electronic Engineers, 1974-. Monthly. £295 pa. ISSN: 00113794.

About 65,000 references pa. Main classes: 0000 General and management topics - 1000 Systems and control theory - 3000 Control technology - 4000 Numerical analysis and theoretical computer topics - 5000 Computer hardware - 6000 Computer software - 7000 Computer applications. A current awareness service; companion to *Computer and control abstracts.* Online INSPEC. *Class No:* 681.3(048)

Progress Reports

[7274]
Advances in computers. Orlando, Fl., Academic Press, 1962-. Annual. ISSN: 00652458.

V.39 (1994. 322p. illus.) is concerned with software products, active databases, operating systems and design of networks. Detailed, analytical index. *Class No:* 681.3(055)

Yearbooks & Directories

[7275]
The Computer users' year book, 1998. 29th ed. Oxford, Learned Information, 1997. 3v. ISSN: 02686821.

V.1.*IT suppliers and equipment book.*

V.2.*IT sites book.*

V.3.*IT services book.*

A mine of information. Covers company information, electronic information services, Internet/intranet and online services, network services, recruitment and consultants. Also available on CD-ROM. *Class No:* 681.3(058)

Histories

[7276]
AUGARTEN, S. Bit by bit: an illustrated history of computers. London, Unwin, 1985. 324p. illus. (incl. col.). ISBN: 0040010074.

9 chapters. 1. The first mechanical calculations - 2. The engines of Charles Babbage - 3. The invention of ENIAC ... 5. The stored-program computer - 6. The rise of IBM - 8. The integrated circuit - 9. The personal computer. Epilogue. Chronology. Bibliography and notes (by chapters), p.299-309. Detailed analytical index. Fully illustrated. *Class No:* 681.3(091)

[7277]
WILLIAMS, M.R. A History of computing technology. 2nd ed. New York, IEEE Computer Society Press, 1997. 530p. illus., facsims., ports., diagrs., chron. tables. $45. ISBN: 0818677392.

First published 1985.

Contents: In the beginning - Early aids to calculation - Mechanical calculating machines - The Babbage machines;- The analog animals - The mechanical monstoers - The electronic revolution - The first stored program electronic computers - Later developments. Appended chronology; detailed, analytical index. *Class No:* 681.3(091)

Biographies

[7278]
LEE, J.A.N. Computer pioneers. Los Alamitos, Ca., IEEE Computer Society Press, 1995. xiii, 816p. illus. $54 ISBN: 081866357x.

About 240 brief biographies (*e.g.* Vannervar E. Bush, 4p.) of those whose 'contributions have been central' and 'those who played supporting roles as enlightened managers, financiers or educators' (*Introduction*). Entries include education and experience, as well as brief bibliographies and 'quotation(s)' where appropriate. Information

....*(contd.)*
collected from published sources, obituaries and, where possible, interviews. A highly readable collection, but with some curious ommissions (*e.g.* Bill Gates). *Class No:* 681.3(092)

[7279]
MATTHEWS, C. 'Computer revolutionaries: a guide to the literature on pioneers in computing'. In *Science and technology libraries.* V.11(4), Winter 1991, p.43-74. ISSN: 0194262x.
Lists about 225 items, including periodical titles, indexing and abstracting services and organizations. *Class No:* 681.3(092)

Writing & Lecturing

[7280]
PERDUE, L. The High-technology editorial guide and stylebook. Homewood, Il., Business One Irwin, 1991. 194p. $32.50.
2 editions: Macintosh (ISBN: 1556235305); PC (ISBN: 0556235313).
About 3200 entries covering programming languages, corporations, hardware and software technical terms, publications. Includes floppy disk with all terms in ASCII format for incorporation into a word-processing spell checker. *Class No:* 681.3:001.81

Thesauri

[7281]
GOODMAN, A. Cambridge illustrated thesaurus of computer science. Cambridge Univ. Press, 1984. 262 + 10p. col. illus., diagrs. £5.50. ISBN: 0521262010.
19 sections/groups of associated words (*e.g.* Computers - Number systems ... Programs ... Electronics ... Memory ... Output devices ... Interfaces ... Files and operations). 10p. index. Over 500 illus., mostly in colour. Index has *c.*2,500 entries. A combined dictionary thesaurus, chiefly for the student in this field. *Class No:* 681.3:025.43

Classification Systems

[7282]
Classification 1995: a classification scheme for the INSPEC database. London, Institution of Electrical Engineers, 1995. ix, 136p. + index, 36p. ISBN: 0852969651.
A new version of the scheme designed for use with the INSPEC 2 version of the database. Includes classification codes (in order, A ... to D ...) and textual headings. Invaluable for a careful, structured search of the database or the printed indexes. *Class No:* 681.3:025.44

Data Processing

Encyclopaedias

[7283]
SAGE, A.P., *ed.* Concise encyclopedia of information processing in systems and organizations. Oxford, Pergamon, 1990. 548p. illus. £140; $225. ISBN: 008035954x.
68 articles, A-Z, on a range of topics (*e.g.* psychology, management, computer science, applied mathematics, systems engineering, decision sciences, industrial education). Some material taken from *Systems and control encyclopedia* (*qv*), but revised and updated. Cross-references; detailed, analytical index.
Class No: 681.31(031)

Handbooks & Manuals

[7284]
Handbook of theoretical computer science. Van Leeuwen, J., *ed.* Amsterdam, Elsevier; Cambridge, Mass., MIT Press, 1990. 2v. £185; $250 (set). ISBN: 0262220407, set.
V.A. *Algorithms and complexity.* xiv,978p. £92; $135. ISBN: 0262220385.
V.B. *Formal Models and semantics.* xiv,1273p. £109; $150. ISBN: 0262220393.
V.B. has 23 contributors. 19 documented, subdivided chapters (1. Finite automata ... 3. Formal languages and power series ... 6. Rewrite systems ... 11. Denotational semantics ... 14. Logics of programs ... 19. Operational and algebraic semantics of concurrent processes). Chapter 13, 'Algebraic specification': 111p., 9 sections, 186 references. Detailed, analytical index, p.1243-73. A theoretical, scholarly treatment, not for those new to the subject.
Class No: 681.31(035)

Dictionaries

Polyglot

[7285]
Dataordboken. Stockholm. SIS (Standardiseringscommission i Sverige), 1984. 187p. (*TNC 82. Svensk Standard SS 01 16 01.*) ISBN: 9171621717.
About 2,00 Swedish entry-words are defined, plus equivalents and indexes in English, French and German. *Class No:* 681.31(038)=00

[7286]
SCHULZ, E. Wörterbuch der Datentechnik: russisch-deutsch-englisch. Wiesbaden, Brandstetter, 1977. [xvi], 193 + 109 + 134p. ISBN: 3870970758.
About 4,000 terms in all. 3 sequences: Russian-German-English, German-Russian-English, English-Russian-German. Terms are categorized. *Class No:* 681.31(038)=00

[7287]
WITTMANN, A. *and* KLOS, J. Dictionary of data processing, including applications in industry, administration and business, in English, German, French. [Wörterbuch der datenverarbeitung mit anwendungsgebieten in industrie, verwaltung und wirtschaft. Dictionnaire du traitment de données, et de son application dans l'industrie, l'administration et l'economie.] 5th ed. Amsterdam, etc., Elsevier, 1987. xiii,357p. ISBN: 0444989471.
First published 1964; 4th ed. 1984.
About 6,000 terms in all, with some 300 new ones.. English base, with German and French equivalents and indexes. Terms are categorized. Genders given. *Class No:* 681.31(038)=00

English

[7288]
BRITISH STANDARDS INSTITUTION. Information technology: vocabulary. London, BSI, 1976-. Parts 1-8, 10-15, 18-23, 25-27. (*BS ISO/IEC 2382: 1976-.*)
Formerly *Data processing vocabulary.*
1. *Fundamental terms.* 1993. 44p.
2. *Arithmetic and logic operations.* 1976. 44p.
3. *Equipment technology.* 1987. 20p.
4. *Organization of data.* 1987. 28p.
5. *Representation of data.* 1989. 32p.
6. *Preparation and handling of data.* 1987. 24p.
7. *Computer programming.* 1989. 36p.
8. *Control, integrity and security.* 1986. 26p.
10. *Operation techniques and facilities.* 1979. 28p.
11. *Processing units.* 1987. 28p.
12. *Peripheral equipment.* 1988. 56p.
13. *Computer graphics.* 1984. 25p.
14. *Reliability, maintenance and availability.* 1978. 24p.
15. *Programming languages.* 1985. 24p.
18. *Distributed data processing.* 1987. 20p.
19. *Analog computing.* 1989. 24p.
20. *System development.* 1990. 28p.
21. *Interfaces between process computer systems and technical processes.* 1985. 28p.
22. *Calculators.* 1986. 28p.
23. *Text processing.* 1995. 36p.
25. *Local area networks.* 1992. 36p.
26.*Open systems interconnection.* 1993. 36p.
27. *Office automation.* 1994. 32p. *Class No:* 681.31(038)=20

[7289]
SIPPL, C.J. Macmillan dictionary of data communications. 2nd ed. London, Macmillan, 1985. [iv], 532p. £8.95. ISBN: 0333370724.
First published 1976.
About 9,000 entries, 'A and not B gate' ... 'Zoom'. Definitions and explanations of a wide range of terms, jargon, expressions and specific vocabulary used in data communication and data processing.
Class No: 681.31(038)=20

French

[7290]
CAMILLE, C. *and* DEHAINE, M. Harrap's French and English data processing dictionary. 3rd ed., rev. and updated. London, Harrap, 1985. 432p.
First published 1970. Pt.1: *English-French.* 223p. Pt.2: *French-English.* 194p.
Each part has *c.*2,000 entries, with massed sub-entries (*e.g.* 'Registrement' (recording): 2 columns). *Class No:* 681.31(038)=40

Histories

[7291]
CORTADA, J.W. Historical dictionary of data processing. New York, Greenwood Press, 1987. 3v.

[V. 1]. *Biographies.* xiii,321p. $50. ISBN: 0313256519.
[V. 2]. *Organizations.* x,309p. $45. ISBN: 0313233039.
[V. 3]. *Technology.* xix,415p. $55. ISBN: 0313256527.

Over 400 entries in the 3v., A-Z within each. Volume indexes. 'An important set' (*Choice,* February 1988, p.882) which provides a concise and accessible history of data processing.
Class No: 681.31(091)

Micros

Encyclopaedias

[7292]
Encyclopedia of microcomputers. Kent, A. *and* Williams, J.G., *eds.* New York, Dekker, 1988-96. 35v. illus., diagrs. ISBN: 0824727002.

Includes about 500 articles, and over 5000p. V.1 has 32 contributors, 26 articles. Well documented (*e.g.* 'Artificial intelligence'; p.283-324, with 62 references plus 3p. bibliography. V.5 (1990) has 20 contributors, 20 articles, but that on 'Display screens, touch sensitive' is based on an article published in 1986 and that for 'DOS' includes 49 references, nearly all pre-1985. 'Aimed to the needs of microcomputer hardware specialists, programers, system analysts, engineers, operation recorders, and mathematicians' (*Preface,* v.1). *Class No:* 681.31-181.4(031)

[7293]
McGraw-Hill personal computer programming encyclopedia. Birnes, W.J., *ed.* 2nd ed. New York, etc., McGraw-Hill, 1989. 752p. illus., tables. $95.

First published 1985.

Overviews of various programming languages and operating systems, as well as their operational differences. Sample programmes illustrate. Also, background articles on artificial intelligence, microcomputer graphics, etc. Glossary. Bibliography. Index to programming language keywords; subject index. *Class No:* 681.31-181.4(031)

Handbooks & Manuals

[7294]
BIRNES, W.J., *ed.* **Microcomputer applications handbook.** New York, etc., McGraw-Hill, 1989. x,645p. diagrs., tables. £65. ISBN: 0070053979.

30 contributors. 6 chapters: 1. Hardware systems - 2. MOS memory - 3. Operating systems - 4. Networked systems - 5. Applications systems - 6. High-level programming languages. Glossary (abend-Z-net), p.475-634. Detailed, analytical index, p.635-45. A basic, comprehensive guide to PCs. *Class No:* 681.31-181.4(035)

[7295]
Bowker's complete sourcebook of personal computing. New York, Bowker, 1985. 1030p. $19.95. ISBN: 0835219313.

First published 1984.

A guide to the microcomputer market, and related products and organizations. No less than 750 computers and 1,800 organizations are mentioned, plus profiles of machines, programmes, etc., and a list of 545 magazines apart from numerous reviews and review citations. 'This work is truly authoritative' (*Science and technology libraries,* v.7(1), Fall 1986, p.114). *Class No:* 681.31-181.4(035)

[7296]
CANTON, M.P. *and* **SANCHEZ, J. The McGraw-Hill PC programmer's desk reference.** New York, etc., McGraw-Hill, 1996. 470p.. $34.95. ISBN: 0070572046.

Covers the core programming information for C, BASIC, Pascal and Assembly languages for the IMB-PC and compatible machines, from 1981 to the present, as well as memory management, hardware architectures and chip programming. Entries, A-Z. 'Outstanding clarity ... highly recommended' (*Choice,* December 1996, p.646). *Class No:* 681.31-181.4(035)

[7297]
JONES, R., *ed.* **The Good hardware guide.** London, Kogan Page,1991. 286p. illus. £22.50. ISBN: 0749404639.

Covers disk drives, modems, monitors, PCs, plotters, printers and scanners. Data include model, price, manufacturer, product highlights, technical information and comment (sometimes pithy). A popular treatment for the lay person, which only occasionally slips into incomprehensible jargon. *Class No:* 681.31-181.4(035)

[7298]
LONGLEY, D. *and* **SHAIN, M. The Microcomputer users handbook:** the complete and up-to-date guide to buying a business computer. London, Macmillan Press, 1985. xvii, 405p. illus., charts, tables. ISBN: 0333368665.

Previous ed., 1984.

8 sections, closely subdivided (*e.g.* 2. Understanding a microcomputer; 3. Important applications; 5. Current trends in microcomputers; 6. Integrated software; 7. Microcomputer survey (with technical details on each type)). Appendix, A-J (J. Glossary, p.396-405). *Class No:* 681.31-181.4(035)

[7299]
MESSMER, H-P. The Indispensable PC hardware book: your hardware questions answered. 3rd ed. Harlow, Essex, Addison Wesley Longman, 1997. pp. xiv, 1384p. illus., diagrs., tables. £29.95 ISBN: 0201403994.

First published 1993; 2nd ed. 1995.

36 chapters in 6 parts: 1. Basics - 2. Processor and memory - 3. PC architectures - 4. Support chips - 5. Mass storage - 6. Externals and peripherals. Glossary, p.1311-62. A wealth of technical detail. *Class No:* 681.31-181.4(035)

[7300]
MONEY, S. A. Newnes microprocessor pocket book. Oxford, Heinemann Newnes, 1989. viii,252p. illus. £9.95. (*Pocket Book.*) ISBN: 0434912905.

A basic survey in 15 chapters (*e.g.* 1. Integrated circuits ... 6. 16/32 bit processors ... 9. Parallel input and output ... 15. System development). Appendices: Abbreviations (5p.); Useful addresses (UK and US). Index (4p.). Concentrates on 'popular microprocessors in current use' (*Preface*). Small format. *Class No:* 681.31-181.4(035)

Dictionaries

Polyglot

[7301]
MÜLLER, D. Dictionary of microprocessor systems: English, German, French, Russian. 2nd ed. Amsterdam, etc., Elsevier, 1990. 448p. £101. ISBN: 0444987819.

First published 1984.

About 12,000 English-base terms, with equivalents and indexes in the other 3 languages. *Class No:* 681.31-181.4(038)=00

English

[7302]
CHRISTIE, L.G. *and* **CHRISTIE, J. The Encyclopaedia of microcomputer terminology.** London, Unwin Paperbacks, 1985. 352p. illus., diagrs., tables. ISBN: 0040320014.

Over 4,000 microcomputer terms, A-Z, with definitions. 'Program generation': 11½ lines. Appendices A-N (N: Word-processing glossary, p.348-52). A sourcebook for business and professional people. *Class No:* 681.31-181.4(038)=20

[7303]
COLLIN, S.M.H. Dictionary of personal computing and the Internet. Chicago, Il., Fitzroy Dearborn, 1997. 205p. illus. $35. ISBN: 1579580165.

About 1,600 terms, covering the components and working of PCs, communication technology and the World Wide Web. Appendix lists HTML commands. *Class No:* 681.31-181.4(038)=20

[7304]
HORDESKI, M. The McGraw-Hill illustrated dictionary of personal computers. 4th ed. New York, etc., McGraw-Hill, 1995. 560p. diagrs. $24.95; £18.95. ISBN: 0070304106.

First published 1978; 3rd ed. 1990 as *The Illustrated dictionary of microcomputers.*

About 8,500 terms, covering both hardware and software. Includes jargon. Cross references and comparisons. Some helpful diagrams and charts. *Class No:* 681.31-181.4(038)=20

[7305]
LONGLEY, D. *and* **SHAIN, M. Macmillan dictionary of personal computing and communications.** London, Macmillan, 1986. [iv], 395p. illus. £6.95. ISBN: 0333390830.

About 5,000 entries and cross-references. 'Software protection': nearly 4 columns. *Class No:* 681.31-181.4(038)=20

[7306]
LOVEDAY, G. Microprocessor sourcebook. London, Pitman, 1986. viii,247p. diagrs., tables. ISBN: 0273021540.

Covers some 265 topics, A-Z, providing definitions and explanations, sometimes quite detailed (*e.g.* 8- and 16-bit processors cover *c.*50p.). Cross-references for most entries. No index, but the 'contents' is an alphabetical list of topics included. Intended for those working or studying 'in the service and test' areas of the microelectronics industry (*Preface*). *Class No:* 681.31-181.4(038)=20

[7307]

MARGOLIS, P.E. Hutchinson personal computer dictionary. London, Hutchinson, 1992. xv,512p. diagrs., tables. £9.99. ISBN: 0091773040.

About 1,500 terms, briefly defined (*e.g.* 'iteration': 5 lines). Cross references. Introduction includes 'categories of terms', *e.g.* communications systems; data storage; input devices; video, etc. *Class No:* 681.31-181.4(038)=20

[7308]

SINCLAIR, I.R. Collins dictionary of personal computing. Rev. ed. Glasgow, Harper Collins, 1991. [vi],424p. illus., diagrs. £6.99. ISBN: 0004343867.

First published 1988 as *Collins Dictionary of computing*.

About 3,500 terms, briefly defined (*e.g.* 'electronic mail': 5 lines). Covers hardware, programming languages, applications, networks and systems. For the layperson. *Class No:* 681.31-181.4(038)=20

[7309]

SIPPL, C.J. Macmillan dictionary of microcomputing. 3rd ed. London, Macmillan, 1985. [iv], 473p. illus. £8.95. ISBN: 0333370716.

First published 1975.

About 5,000 entries, 'A and not B gate' ... 'Zwitterion'. Coverage includes software, graphics, programming. 'Programmable calcuators': 1 column. A few line-drawings. Written specifically with the microcomputer in mind. *Class No:* 681.31-181.4(038)=20

Reviews & Abstracts

[7310]

Microcomputer abstracts. Medford, N.J., Database Services, 1980-. 4 pa + index $185 pa. ISSN: 10743995.

Formerly *Microcomputer index*.

About 17,000 descriptive abstracts pa. from some 50 microcomputer journals covering business, education and home computer uses. Author, subject indexes per issue. Also available on CD-ROM. *Class No:* 681.31-181.4(048)

Yearbooks & Directories

[7311]

BENNETT, S. *and* **FREIRMAN, R. Microcomputer marketplace:** the one-stop resource for industry information. London, Century Business, 1992. 620p. £26.99. ISBN: 0712655579.

Covers both hardware and software. Data: Companies, products, people, services, organizations. *Class No:* 681.31-181.4(058)

Tables & Data Books

[7312]

MONEY, S.A. Microprocessor data book. 2nd ed. Oxford, Blackwell Scientific, 1990. iv,316p. tables. ISBN: 0632020938.

Provides condensed data for most of the currently available microprocessor and microcomputer devices, with details of internal architecture, instruction set, electrical data and package details. 3 groups: 4-bit, 8-bit and 16-bit types. Also includes chapters covering input-output and other interfaces, peripheral control and support devices. Contains a directory of manufacturers (p.305-9) and glossary of terms. Useful as an aid to selecting appropriate device, to be followed up by consultation of manufacturers' data sheets and manuals. 'This is a useful volume for a wide range of practitioners' (*Electronics and Power*, v.29, Feb. 1983, p.181, of the first ed.). *Class No:* 681.31-181.4(083)

Microprocessor Applications

[7313]

Dictionary of CAD. Clarke, J. *and* Mayer, T., *eds.* Oxford, Butterworth Heinemann, 1991. 484p. illus. £40. ISBN: 0750612398.

About 2,500 a terms, most defined briefly. *Class No:* 681.31-181.4.004

[7314]

STOUT, D.F., *ed.* **Microprocessor applications handbook.** New York, etc., McGraw-Hill, 1982. xii, 448p. illus., diagrs., graphs. $35. ISBN: 0070617988.

16 contributors. 17 chapters. 1. Survey of microprocessor technology ... 4. Microprocessor-controlled color TV receiver ... 7. Programmable videogames ... 9. Microcomputer applications in telephony ... 11. Digital filters utilizing microprocessors ... 14. Voice recognition ... 17. Multiple microprocessors in small systems. Limited to the following microprocessors: 1802, 2650, 6800, 8080 and the following chips: 2920, 3870, 3872, 6801, 6802 and 8088.

'Focuses on immediately useful applications ... This authoritative resource examines design concepts, schematics, software and hardware for a wide range of microprocessor applications' (*SMPTE journal*, v.91, Mar 1982, p.306). *Class No:* 681.31-181.4.004

Computer Software

Databases

[7315]

Buyer's guide to micro software (SOFT). Weston, Conn., Online, Inc.

Directory of business and professional microcomputer software available in the US. Records include directory information, technical specifications, description, citations to reviews. About 7000 records. Available on DIALOG, file 237. *Class No:* 681.31.0(003.4)

[7316]

Microcomputer software guide. New York, Bowker.

Covers software and hardware, but excludes educational software. Data: ordering information, technical specification, subject classification, brief description. Over 18,000 records; monthly reloads. Available on DIALOG, file 278. *Class No:* 681.31.0(003.4)

Encyclopaedias

[7317]

Concise encyclopedia of software engineering. Morris, D. *and* Tamm, B., *eds.* Oxford, Pergamon Press, 1993. xiii, 400p. illus., diagrs., graphs, tables. £150; $300. (*Advances in systems control and information engineering*.) ISBN: 0080362141.

About 100 articles, A-Z, most 4-5p. Intended 'as a complementary companion' to *Systems and control encyclopedia* (*q.v.*) (*Introduction*), but 'comprising almost entirely new material specially commissioned' (*Preface*). 'European focus ... Makes a clear presentation of this developing field' (*Choice*, February 1994, p.912). *Class No:* 681.31.0(031)

[7318]

Encyclopedia of software engineering. Marciniak, J., *ed.* New York, Wiley, 1994. 2v. (xvii, 1453p.). diagrs., tables. $249. ISBN: 0471540013.

About 165 reviewed articles, A-Z, some fairly lengthy (*e.g.* 'Artificial intelligence in software engineering', 8p., 32 references). Detailed, analytical index, 19p. 'Informative ... recommended' ('Reference books bulletin', *Booklist*, July 1994, p.1974). *Class No:* 681.31.0(031)

[7319]

The Software encyclopedia 1998. New York, etc., Bowker, 199. 2v. $249.95, the set.

First published 1985.

V.1: Title index; V.2: System compatability/Applications index.

Within each system, software is arranged by specific applications (*e.g.* accounting; government; hobbies, etc). Publisher index. Covers all subject areas, including engineering, science and medicine.

The most up-to-date information appears in such online databases at the Microcomputer software guide (DIALOG file 278). *Class No:* 681.31.0(031)

Handbooks & Manuals

[7320]

Software engineer's reference book. McDermid, J.A., *ed.* Boston, Mass., Butterworth, 1990. v.p. illus., diagrs. $195. ISBN: 0750610409.

Stresses concepts and broad approaches. Extensive bibliography. 'Written for practitioners in the field, but appropriate for anyone with an understanding of computer science principles (*New technical books*, September/October, 1991, item 1179). *Class No:* 681.31.0(035)

[7321]

Software reliability handbook. Rook, P. London, Elsevier Applied Science, 1990. xix,542p. illus., diagrs., graphs, tables. £87. ISBN: 1851664009.

12 contributors. 12 chapters, closely subdivided: 1. Reliability issues ... 4. Fault tolerance - 5. Defect detection and correction ... 9. Quality management ... 12. Engineering environments. 4 appendices (D. software development cost models, p.487-517). References, p.519-32; detailed, analytical index, p.533-42. *Class No:* 681.31.0(035)

Yearbooks & Directories

[7322]

The Software users yearbook, 1999. 14th ed. Oxford, Learned Information Europe Ltd, 1998. 2v. (1191, 543p.) tables. ISSN: 02686708.

V.1. *Software products*.

V.2. *Companies*.

Includes 2,600 suppliers and 12,500 business software applications. Entry for a program includes title, description, hardware requirements. Index of products by manufacturer and industry. Reference tables indicate operating systems and prices of products. Also available on CD-ROM as *Computer software and services CD-ROM*; the disk includes selected information from the 'Services' vol. of *The Computers users year book*. *Class No:* 681.31.0(058)

[7323]
Text retrieval: a directory of software. Kimberley, R., *ed.* 2nd ed. Aldershot, Hants., Gower, 1987. v.p. Loose-leaf. ISBN: 0566053721.
At head of title-page: 'Institute of Information Scientists, Southern Branch'. First published 1983.
The directory: Packages featured - List of other packages. Appended check list; bibliography. Index of packages by operating system.
Class No: 681.31.0(058)

Standards

[7324]
IEEE standards collection software engineering: 1994 edition. New York, Institute of Electrical and Electronics Engineers, Inc., 1994. v.p. £245. ISBN: 155937442x.
27 standards on a range of software issues (*e.g.* glossary; test documentation; acquisition; maintenance; safety; quality management, etc.). The introduction provides a brief synopsis of each standard.
Class No: 681.31.0(083.74)

[7325]
MAGEE, S. *and* **TRIPP, L.L. Software engineering standards and specifications:** an annotated index and directory. New York, Global Professional, 1994. 228p. $79.50. ISBN: 0912702826.
Includes information on purpose, date, issuing organization and US distributor for 220 standards, technical reports and guidelines. Inadequate index. *Class No:* 681.31.0(083.74)

Patents

[7326]
HANNEMAN, H.W.A.M. The Patentability of computer software: an international guide to the protection of computer-related inventions. Deventer, Kluwer, 1985. 257p. £36.75. ISBN: 9065442251.
After chapters on general principles of protection of software and on the workings of a computer there are chapters on the situation in the USA, Canada, UK, Australia, France, Federal Republic of Germany, Austria, Switzerland, Japan, the Netherlands and in other countries and under the European Patent Convention. *Class No:* 681.31.0(088.8)

[7327]
—**BRETT, H.** *and* **PERRY, L.,** *eds.* The Legal protection of computer software. Oxford, ESC Publishing, 1981. xiv, 197p. £15.
Describes the protection available in Europe and US under the patent systems and by means of copyright and other laws. Proposals for protection of computer programs are discussed, and the World Intellectual Property Organization model provisions are given.
Class No: 681.31.0(088.8)

[7328]
MILLARD, C.J. Legal protection of computer programs and data. London, Sweet and Maxwell; Toronto, Carswell, 1985. xxvi, 239p. £24. ISBN: 0421334800.
The legal protection of software and data in the US, UK, Canada and other common law countries is discussed. Contains tables of cases and statutes. *Class No:* 681.31.0(088.8)

Laws

[7329]
BAINBRIDGE, D. Software copyright law. London, Pitman, 1992. 256p. illus. £45. ISBN: 0273038478.
Overview of European software copyright law. Covers computer programs, work stored and created, limits of the scope of legal protection. *Class No:* 681.31.0(094.1)

Security

[7330]
BAKER, R.H. The Computer security handbook. 2nd ed. Blue Ridge Summit, Pa., TAB Books, 1991. xx,416p. 35.80.
First published 1985.
Chapters include: Built-in security; Securing the network; The technology of passwords; Securing remote devices; Principles of network security; A system of network security. Index.
Class No: 681.31.004.4

[7331]
Encyclopedia of data protection. Chalton, S. *and* Gaskill, S., *eds.*
London, Sweet and Maxwell, 1988-. iv. Loose-leaf. £165.
Regular updates are planned. *Class No:* 681.31.004.4

[7332]
FLAHERTY, D.H., *ed.* **Privacy and data protection:** an international bibliography. London, Mansell, 1985. xxvi, 276p. £23.50. ISBN: 0720117194.
1,862 references to works, published and unpublished, on the need to protect individuals from misuse of computer-stored data concerning those individuals. 6 sections (4. Legal aspects of privacy and data protection: Canada, Federal Republic of Germany, France, Sweden, UK, US, International ... 6. Selected bibliographic materials, p.241-7). Author index. A valuable research tool. *Class No:* 681.31.004.4

[7333]
HIGHLAND, J. Computer virus handbook. Oxford, Elsevier, 1990. xvi,375p. illus., tables. £85. ISBN: 0946395462.
Definitions and descriptions of common viruses and technical evaluations of some 22 anti-virus software packages. Numerous references. *Class No:* 681.31.004.4

[7334]
JACKSON, K.M., *and others.* **Computer security reference book.** Oxford, Butterworth Heinemann, 1992. 800p. £90. ISBN: 0750603577.
In-depth treatment of the entire field, including computer crime, data protection, EFTPOS schemes, evaluation of security products, hacking, public key cryptography, and other topical aspects.
Class No: 681.31.004.4

[7335]
MADSEN, W. Handbook of personal data protection: national and international laws, standards and guidlines. London, Macmillan, 1992. 1250p. illus., diagrs. £85. ISBN: 0333569202.
Identifies differences among individual countries' legislation. Includes copies of national & international laws.
Class No: 681.31.004.4

[7336]
SLADE, R.M. Robert Slade's guide to computer viruses: how to avoid them, how to get rid of them, and how to get help. New York, Springer-Verlag, 1994. xvii, 472p. diskette, illus., tables. ISBN: 0387943110.
7 chapters on the effect of and protection against viruses. 11 appendices, including frequently asked questions, glossary (10p.) and reviews of 54 anti-viral products. A non-technical approach.
Class No: 681.31.004.4

[7337]
Vocabulary of computer security and viruses. [Vocabulaire de la sécurité et des virus informatiques.] Ottawa, Canada Communications Group, 1995. 333p. $38.95. (*Terminology bulletin, no.226.*) ISBN: 0660597918.
About 1,600 terms, briefly defined, in both French and English. Bibliography of sources. *Class No:* 681.31.004.4

Automation Technology

Abbreviations & Symbols

[7338]
BRITISH STANDARDS INSTITUTION. Graphical symbols for components of servo-mechanisms. London, BSI, 1960-64. 2v. diagrs. £28.90. (*BS 3238: 1960-1964.*)
Pt.1: *Transducers and magnetic amplifiers.* 1960. 16p. Pt.2: *General servo-mechanisms.* 1964. 32p.
Almost 100 symbols illustrated and annotated.
Class No: 681.5(003)

Bibliographies

[7339]
HAMILTON, L., *comp.* **Information pack including bibliography on advanced manufacturing technology.** London, Information and Library Service, Institution of Mechanical Engineers, 1986. vi,98p. £5. (*Information pack, 1.*) ISBN: 0852986041.
2 parts: 1. AMT information (abbreviations; contacts; products; open learning; abstracts and indexes, etc.), p. 1-45; 2. References (236 items) with abstracts (key reports; general articles; applications of AMT), p.47-98. Most from the mid-1980s. Good value.
Class No: 681.5(01)

[7340]
HAMILTON, L. *and* **HALLAM, L.,** *comps.* **Information pack on computer integrated manufacturing.** London, Information and Library Service, Institution of Mechanical Engineers, 1987. vi,89p. £12.50. (*Information pack, 4.*) ISBN: 0852986459.
2 Parts: 1. CIM information (abbreviations - standards), p.1-60; 2. CIM references (108 items) with abstracts, p.61-81. Indexes: author, subject, company name. A useful series. *Class No:* 681.5(01)

[7341]
SATTAR, T.P. 'Control engineering'. *Information sources in engineering*. K.W. Mildren and P.J. Hicks, eds. (3rd ed., 1996), p.389-409. 3rd ed. London, Bowker Saur, 1996. £80. ISBN: 1857390571.

A short discussion of various control systems is followed by sources of information, including abstracts and indexes, journals, databases and symposia. References, p.403-409. *Class No:* 681.5(01)

[7342]
TZAFESTAS, S.G. 'Information sources in systems and control'. *Systems and control encyclopedia*. Singh, M.G., *ed*. Oxford, Pergamon, 1987. v.8, p.5575-85.

Brief survey covering: guides, sourcebooks and services; encyclopedias and handbooks; dictionaries and glossaries; abstract and review sources; technical journals; international book series and conference proceedings; sources on people; other information sources; continuing education courses. *Class No:* 681.5(01)

Encyclopaedias

[7343]
GRAHAM, G.A. Encyclopedia of industrial automation. Harlow, Longman and Society of Manufacturing Engineers, 1988. [xvi],597p. illus. £48. ISBN: 058203566x.

US title: *Automation encyclopedia*.

About 700 entries, A-Z arrangement. Some definitions are very brief (*e.g.* 'comparator', 2 lines); others lengthy (*e.g.* 'numerical control', 31p.). Cross-references. Covers technologies, processes, techniques and applications. *Class No:* 681.5(031)

[7344]
SINGH, M.G., *ed*. Systems and control encyclopedia: theory, technology, applications. Oxford, etc., Pergamon, 1987. 8v. (5500p.). diagrs., graphs, tables. £1,600. ISBN: 0080287093, set.

29 subject editors; *c*.1,000 contributors. Truly encyclopaedic treatment with entries ranging from 2 or 3 lines to several pages, supported by illustrations, graphs, and bibliographies, all signed and arranged A-Z in v.1-7. V.8 contains a systematic outline of the *Encyclopedia*, alphabetical list of contents, list of contributors (from all continents), author citation index, subject index (p.5432-73), a list of acronyms and abbreviations and a guide to information sources (p.5575-85). 'Rarely is a major new encyclopedia published; this is one ... highly recommended' (*Choice*, April 1988, p.1226).

The publishers have produced 'Concise' editions, with revisions, of numerous of the subjects covered in the main work in a series *Advances in systems control and information engineering*. *Class No:* 681.5(031)

[7345]
—Concise encyclopedia of modelling and simulation. Atherton, D.P., *ed*. Oxford, Pergamon Press, 1992. 554p. £140. (*Advances in systems, control and information engineering, 5*.) ISBN: 008036201x.

172 newly commissioned and revised articles from the *Systems and control encyclopedia* (1987). Topics covered include model representation, simplification, validation, reduction techniques and algorithms, simulation, etc. *Class No:* 681.5(031)

Handbooks & Manuals

[7346]
Computer integrated manufacturing handbook. Teicholz, E. *and* Orr, J.N., *eds*. New York, McGraw-Hill, 1987. 434p. illus., diagrs., tables. ISBN: 0070477744.

21 contributors. 20 chapters in 4 parts: 1. Introduction - 2. Components - 3. Planning - 4. Implementation and management. Annotated bibliography of 125 items. Index. *Class No:* 681.5(035)

[7347]
CONSIDINE, D.M., *ed*. Standard handbook of industrial automation. London, etc., Chapman and Hall, 1987. xix, 460p. illus., diagrs., graphs, tables. £89. (*Advanced industrial technology series*.) ISBN: 0412008319.

Over 70 contributors. A practical handbook concentrating on the implementation of automation: designing, specifying, using, evaluating equipment and systems. 5 sections: 1. Backdrop to automation systems (including annotated brief glossary) - 2. Sensors and measuring systems - 3. Control systems - 4. Actuators and materials (with much emphasis on robots) - 5. Interfaces and communications (including Local Area Networks and communication standards). Ample illustration (445 diagrams and half-tones) and 57 tables complement an excellent index as aids to use of a wide-ranging work.

'... the Handbook represents the best we have come to expect from the American technical publishing houses. The editors and their 73 contributors are to be congratulated on their endeavors' (*Production engineeers*, v.66(8), Sept. 1987, p.9). *Class No:* 681.5(035)

[7348]
WESTPHAL, L.C. Sourcebook of control systems engineering. London, Chapman & Hall, 1995. pp. xx, 939. illus., diagrs., graphs, tables, formulas. ISBN: 0412484609.

'A resource book or survey of the elements/essentials of feedback control systems' (*Preface*). 34 chapters, closely subdivided: 3. Sensors and instrumentation ... 13. System performance indicators ... 16. Lyapunov stability testing ... 25. State observers ... 33. Robust control. 13p. of references; most before 1980. *Class No:* 681.5(035)

Dictionaries

[7349]
BODESTEDT, Olle. Dictionary of industrial automation and control. Bromley, Kent, Chartwell-Bratt, 1993. 455p. ISBN: 0862383390.

About 40,000 terms and definitions, covering automation within the process and manufacturing industries. Includes references to standards, regulations, etc. *Class No:* 681.5(038)

[7350]
BRITISH STANDARDS INSTITUTION. Glossary of terms used in automatic controlling and regulating systems. London, BSI, 1967. 42p. diagrs., graphs, tables. (*BS 1523: 1967*.)

Pt.1: *Process and kinetic control*, 1967. 42p. Basic definitions, classification, elements and characteristics of control systems, etc. About 180 terms defined in systematic order with alphabetical index. *Class No:* 681.5(038)

[7351]
CLASON, W.E. Elsevier's dictionary of measurement and control in six languages: English/American, French, Spanish, Italian, Dutch and German. Amsterdam, etc., Elsevier, 1977. 886p. £121.62. ISBN: 0444415823.

Almost 7,800 entries for terms in English, with equivalents in other languages. Alphabetical indexes in other languages refer to numbered entries in main section. Brief bibliography (p.885-6). Lack of Russian terminology a disadvantage. *Class No:* 681.5(038)

[7352]
JUNGE, H.D. Technische Kybernetik: Grundlagen und Anwendungen, Englisch-Deutsch, Deutsch-Englisch. Wiesbaden, Brandstetter; VEB Technik, 1983. 564p. DM85. ISBN: 3870971142.

24,000 terms, covering all aspects of automatic control, with equivalents in the second language, in each half of the dictionary. *Class No:* 681.5(038)

[7353]
Multilingual glossary of automatic control technology: English, French-German-Russian-Italian-Spanish-Japanese-Chinese. Prime, H.A. *and* Work, A., *eds*. New ed. Oxford, etc., Pergamon Press, for the International Federation of Automatic Control, 1995. xxv, 261p. £75.90. ISBN: 0080371922.

First ed. as *IFAC: Multilingual dictionary of automatic control terminology* (1967); rev. ed. 1981.

Adds Chinese equivalents to the 1981 ed. 1,645 English-base terms, with equivalents in the other languages presented across columns. Arranged in subject order. Indexes in each language lead to entries. *Class No:* 681.5(038)

Reviews & Abstracts

[7354]
Computer and control abstracts. Science abstracts. Section C. London, INSPEC, 1969-. Monthly. £1270. ISSN: 00368113.

Formerly *Control abstracts*, 1966-68.

About 100,000 abstracts pa. Classes, closely subdivided: 0000 General and management topics - 1000 Systems and control theory - 3000 Control technology - 4000 Numerical analysis and theoretical, computer topics - 5000 Computer hardware - 6000 Computer software - 7000 Computer applications. Author index per issue; Subject index, twice yearly; Subsidiary indexes, where appropriate; Bibliography index (for well-documented articles); Book index (for books received and abstracted); Corporate author index; Conference index. Indexes cumulated 2pa. and 4-yearly (*e.g.* 1987-1990). INSPEC database. CD-ROM. *Class No:* 681.5(048)

[7355]
Current papers on computers and control. Stevenage, Herts., Institution of Electrical Engineers; New York, Institute of Electrical and Electronic Engineers, 1974-. Monthly. £295 pa. ISSN: 00113794.

About 65,000 references pa. Main classes: 0000 General and management topics - 1000 Systems and control theory - 4000 Numerical analysis and theoretical computer topics - 5000 Computer hardware - 6000 Computer software - 7000 Computer applications. A current awareness service; companion to *Computer and control abstracts*. Online INSPEC. *Class No:* 681.5(048)

[7356]
Referativnyĭ zhurnal. 01. Avtomatika i vychislitel'naya tekhnika. Akademiya Nauk SSSR. Moscow, VINITI, 1987-. Monthly. R.299-40. ISSN: 02024098.

Formerly: *Referativnyĭ zhurnal avtomatika telemekhanika* (1963-1986).

3 parts: A. Automation and remote control - B. Computer science and computer hardware - V. Software. About 26,000 indicative and informative abstracts pa. (Part A contains almost 8,000), covering mainly periodicals worldwide and patents. Issue indexes of authors and patents. Annual author and subject indexes. English contents list. UDC numbers. *Class No:* 681.5(048)

Progress Reports

[7357]
Control and dynamic systems: advances in theory and applications. Orlando, Fl., etc., Academic Press, 1972-. v.9-. Annual. graphs. ISSN: 00905267.

Originally as *Advances in control systems: theory and applications*, v.1-8, 1964-71.

V.1-11 consisted of diverse contributions on significant topics within the field. From v.12 onwards each volume has contained lengthy articles written around a theme. V.75 (1996. xi, 411p. £70.) includes 8 contributions on 'Computer techniques and algorithms in digital signal processing'. *Class No:* 681.5(055)

Histories

[7358]
BENNETT, S. A History of control engineering, 1800-1930. London, P. Peregrinus, 1979. x, 214p. (*IEE Control engineering series, 8.*) ISBN: 0906048079; 0863410472, Pbk (1986).

Continues *The origins of feedback control*, by O. Mayr (MIT Press, 1970), which ends with the invention of the governor around 1800. Deals with the regulation of prime movers and development of steam and hydraulic servomechanisms and their use in the control of ships and, subsequently, aircraft. Later chapters cover electrical control systems and circuit analysis. Chapter references, bibliography and index give good support.

A History of control engineering, 1930-1955 was published in 1993. *Class No:* 681.5(091)

Cybernetic Technology

Artificial Intelligence. Expert Systems

Bibliographies

[7359]
Expert systems: a bibliography. London, Institution of Electrical Engineers, Library, 1983-86. 2v. ISBN: 085296272x; 0852963386.

1. *Expert systems: a bibliography*, by C.J. Biggar and J.W. Coupland. 1983. 74p. £12.

2. *Expert systems II: a bibliography on expert systems in electrical and electronic engineering*, by S.L. Penfold and J.W. Coupland. 1986. 103p.

V.1 carries 121 references from the INSPEC database, 1969-83, with author and keywords indexes. V.2 provides 194 references from the INSPEC database of English-language items since 1983. 6 sections. Author and keyword indexes. *Class No:* 681.51:007.510(01)

[7360]
GOMERSALL, A. Machine intelligence: an international bibliography, with abstracts of sensors in automated manufacturing. Bedford, IFS Publications; Berlin, New York, etc., Springer Verlag, 1984. vii, 232p. illus. £32. ISBN: 090360860x.

More than 1,300 items, with abstracts, covering journal and conference papers, 1972-84, extending and updating the sensors section in the author's *Robotics bibliography* (1981). The present work complements A. Gomersall and P. Fariner's *Robotics: an international bibliography* (qv). Emphasis (over 500 references) on vision sensors, plus tactile sensors; also, almost 500 items on industry and process applications. Classified arrangement, chronolgical within each section. Author index only. 'The abstracts, being truly informative in their own right, make this bibliography a must for all library bookshelves' (*Aircraft engineering*, v.56, April 1984, p.32). *Class No:* 681.51:007.510(01)

[7361]
—**BODEN, M.A. Artificial intelligence and natural man.** London, MIT Press, in conjunction with the British Psychological Society, 1987. 576p. ISBN: 0262022591.

Features an extensive bibliography, p.500-28. *Class No:* 681.51:007.510(01)

[7362]
—**SMITH, L.C. 'A Guide to information sources in artificial intelligence'.** *Science and technology libraries*, v.5(3), Spring, 1985. p.79-100.

Defines the scope and outlines development of AI before describing and discussing journals, conference proceedings, reports, theses, books, databases and abstracts covering the field. Appendix lists monographs discussed. *Class No:* 681.51:007.510(01)

[7363]
HANCOX, P.J., *and others*. Keyguide to information sources in artificial intelligence/expert systems. London, Mansell; Lawrence, KS, Ergosyst Associates, 1990. xii,300p. tables. ISBN: 0720120071, UK; 0916313182, US.

3 parts. I. Survey of artificial intelligence/expert systems and its literature (5 documented chapters, p.3-112). II. Bibliography (659 items): general sources, p.1133-55; component specialisms (automated theorem proving - robotics), p.155-84; applications (agriculture-space), p.184-212; directories and related sources, p.212-21. III. Organizations (includes research centres, online database hosts; international in scope), p.225-77. Detailed, analytical index, p.279-300. An authoritative survey. *Class No:* 681.51:007.510(01)

Encyclopaedias

[7364]
SHAPIRO, S.C., *ed*. Encyclopedia of artificial intelligence. New York, etc., Wiley, 1987. 2v. (1246p.). illus., diagrs., graphs, tables. £166.

More than 200 contributors. 450 documented articles (A-Z) cover all aspects of artificial intelligence and its applications over a wide field, embracing the sciences, arts and technologies, medicine, psychology and social issues. Over 5,000 literature references. Many cross-references, illus. and tables. List of abbreviations. 32-page index. *Class No:* 681.51:007.510(031)

Handbooks & Manuals

[7365]
Handbook of logic in artificial intelligence and logic programming. Gabbay, D.M., *and others, eds*. Oxford Univ. Press, 1993-98. 5 vols. diagrs., tables. £120 each.

V.1: *Logic foundations*. (1993. 534p. ISBN: 019853745x).

V.2: *Dedcution methodologies*. (1994. 526p. ISBN: 0198537468).

V.3: *Nonmonotomic reasoning and uncertain reasoning*. (1994. 548p. ISBN: 0198537476).

V.4: *Epistemic and temporal logics*. (1995. 628p. ISBN: 1098537913).

V.4: *Logic programming*. (1998. 814p. ISBN: 0198537921).

Provides an in-depth survey of the applications of logic. *Class No:* 681.51:007.510(035)

Dictionaries

Polyglot

[7366]
VOLLNHALS, O. A Multilingual dictionary of artificial intelligence: English, German, French, Spanish, Italian. London, Routledge, 1992. vii,423p. £75. ISBN: 0415074657.

About 3,500 English-base terms with equivalents and indexes in the other languages. Genders given. *Class No:* 681.51:007.510(038)=00

English

[7367]
Artificial intelligence terminology: a reference guide. Beardon, C., *ed*. Chichester, Ellis Horwood; New York, Halsted Press, 1989. xiii,283p. ISBN: 0745807186; 0745807631, Pbk; 0470216018, Halsted Press.

18 contributors. About 1,000 terms, A-Z, briefly defined (*e.g.* 'Horn clause': 7 lines). Most terms carry 'see also' terms and many include a bibliographic reference. *Class No:* 681.51:007.510(038)=20

[7368]
HUNT, V.D. Artificial intelligence and expert systems sourcebook. New York, London, Chapman & Hall, 1986. xi, 315p. diagrs., tables. £42. (*Advanced industrial technology series.*) ISBN: 0412012111.

An illustrated dictionary of definitions (p.41-277), many of them extensive and including acronyms and system names. Preceding it: a review of developments in artificial intelligence and expert systems. Appended: a brief directory of organizations, manufacturers and consultants; a list of acronyms; a bibliography of *c.*250 references and a short trademarks list. No index. Has more to offer than does Rosenberg's *Directory of artificial intelligence*. *Class No:* 681.51:007.510(038)=20

[7369]

—BAINS, W. *and* RAGGETT, J. A Glossary of artificial intelligence. London, Kogan Page, 1988. 200p. £14.95. ISBN: 1850915733.

'Aims to give clear meanings and explanations of the AI jargon in a simple, informal manner' (*British book news,* September 1988, p.657). *Class No:* 681.51:007.510(038)=20

[7370]

—ROSENBERG, J.M. Dictionary of artificial intelligence and robotics. New York, etc. Wiley, 1986. xi, 203p. ISBN: 0471849820.

Explains 4,000 terms, symbols, acronyms and abbreviations. Aims 'to specify the relationships among robotics, artificial intelligence and computer control terms' (*Preface*). Definitions are frequently at different levels of complexity, to assist the lay person as well as the professional. *Class No:* 681.51:007.510(038)=20

[7371]

MERCADAL, D. **Dictionary of artificial intelligence.** New York, Van Nostrand Reinhold, 1990. 334p. $29.95. ISBN: 0442004516.

Aims to define the 'large majority' of AI terms for both novices and professionals. Entries often provide examples and/or comparisons and many include brief bibliographies. Cross references. Appendix describes expert systems. References, p.318-34. *Class No:* 681.51:007.510(038)=20

[7372]

RAGGETT, J. *and* BAINS, W. **Artificial intelligence from A to Z.** London, Chapman & Hall, 1992. x,246p. illus. ISBN: 0412379503, UK; 0442312008, US.

About 200 AI terms defined in non-technical language: Abduction - Zero Sum. Definitions range 6 lines to 2p. Simple diagrams serve to illustrate points; some cross-references. Appendices: 'Benchmark'; AI programs; Languages and environments. Index, 6p. For the layperson and likely to be warmly welcomed. *Class No:* 681.51:007.510(038)=20

[7373]

SMITH, R. **Collins dictionary of artificial intelligence.** London, Collins, 1990. [vi],374p. diagrs. £5.95. ISBN: 0004343662.

First published 1989 as *The Facts on File Dictionary of artificial intelligence.*

About 2,000 terms, briefly defined (*e.g.* 'problem space': 9 lines). Cross references. Covers expert systems, problem solving, speech synthesis, robotics and knowledge representation. *Class No:* 681.51:007.510(038)=20

[7374]

THRO, E. **The Artificial intelligence dictionary.** San Marcos, Ca., Microtrend Books, 1991. xi,407p. diagrs. $24.94; £22.95. ISBN: 0915391368.

About 1,300 terms on AI and related fields, *e.g.* expert systems, robotics, data structures, etc., some with 'further reading'. Appendices, A-L (G. 'Research centres' (44 organizations), p.385-87). *Class No:* 681.51:007.510(038)=20

German

[7375]

JUNGE, H.D. **Dictionary of artificial intelligence and neurocomputers:** English-German/German-English. Weinheim, VCH, 1991. 238p. £34.

About 6,000 entries in each half. *Class No:* 681.51:007.510(038)=30

Reviews & Abstracts

[7376]

The Turing Institute abstracts in artificial intelligence and neural computing. London, Springer Verlag, 1986-. 6pa. £195 pa. ISSN: 02698862.

Lists material selected from the Turing Institute collection and includes research reports, journal articles, conference papers and some books. Subject arrangement. About 400 entries per issue. Author, title indexes per issue. *Class No:* 681.51:007.510(048)

Robots

Bibliographies

[7377]

GOMERSALL, A. *and* FARMER, P. **Robotics:** an international bibliography, with abstracts. Bedford, IFS, 1984. vii, 209p. illus. £36. ISBN: 0903608839.

Updates *Robotics bibliography, 1970-1981* (with its 1,800 references, spread thinly over the entire field). This update has 1,200 references covering 1982-1984, with more emphasis on industrial applications, management and socio-economic aspects. (Separate volume, *Machine intelligence,* for sensors, computer vision and artificial intelligence). Covers conference papers and reports, as well

....(contd.)

as periodical articles. Grouped entries (*e.g.* 'Design and performance'; 'Process applications'), helpfully annotated. Author index, but no subject index. *Class No:* 681.51:007.52(01)

[7378]

LANE, D. *and* ACLAND, J., *eds.* **Industrial robotics: a bibliography.** London, Institution of Electrical Engineers, 1981. [140]p. £17.

226 citations, in two sections: A. Introduction, reviews; B. Specific aspects and applications. Author and subject indexes. Items provide a selection of significant conference and periodical papers, 1960s-1980, with brief abstracts, mainly descriptive and drawn from the technical press. Languages other than English are normally stated. *Class No:* 681.51:007.52(01)

[7379]

—DAVIES, Z. Guide to information sources on industrial robotics. 3rd ed. Coventry, Warws., Coventry (Lanchester) Polytechnic, the Library, 1985. 41p.

First published 1981; 2nd ed. 1983.

Systematically covers all relevant types of published information sources held (*e.g.* handbooks, journals, reviews), and indicates external non-print sources. Separate chapters on general and industrial robotics literature, and robotics in mechanical and control literature. Intended primarily for students and staff of Lanchester Polytechnic. *Class No:* 681.51:007.52(01)

[7380]

McMASTER, R.S. *and* BOYLE, B.G. **'Robotics and automated manufacture'.** *Information sources in engineering.* K.W. Mildren and P.J. Hicks, eds. (3rd ed., 1996), p.378-88. 3rd ed. London, Bowker Saur, 1996. £80. ISBN: 1857390571.

Main sections: Journals - Organizations - Conference Proceedings - Reference works - Standards - Textbooks. *Class No:* 681.51:007.52(01)

Encyclopaedias

[7381]

International encyclopedia of robotics: applications and automation. Dorf, R.C., *ed.* New York, etc., Wiley, 1988. 3v. illus., diagrs., graphs, tables.

More than 250 contributors worldwide, About 250 lengthy articles (averaging 10p. and upwards of 50,000 words), with extensive bibliographies. Articles are arranged alphabetically under broad headings (sometimes inverted, but not consistently, *e.g.* 'Mining, Robots in', but 'Robotics in agriculture'). Subjects frequently overalp (*e.g.* 'Apparel industry, Robots in'; 'Garment and shoe industry, Robots in'). Some headings are imprecise and unsought (*e.g.* 'Issues in robotics'). At least one article, 'Medicine intelligence' does not itself use the term in the text, which is a review of artificial intelligence. There is much 'futurism', - overtly in 'Future applications', 'Factory of the future', etc., and inherently in many other artices. As a reference work, this *Encyclopedia* obviously suffers from a scatter of its subject content that can only be partly offset by a comprehensive index, v.3. *Class No:* 681.51:007.52(031)

[7382]

—Concise international encyclopedia of robotics: applications and automation. Dorf, R.C., *ed.* New York, etc., Wiley, 1990. xix,1190p. illus., diagrs., graphs, tables. $100. ISBN: 0471516988.

Treats 206 topics and includes shortened versions, 'updated where necessary', (*Preface*) of all the entries in the 3v. *International encyclopedia of robotics. Class No:* 681.51:007.52(031)

[7383]

The McGraw-Hill illustrated encyclopedia of robotics and artificial intelligence. Gibilisco, S. New York, McGraw-Hill, 1994. 420p., illus. $40. ISBN: 0070236135.

About 750 topics covered in short entries. Cross references. A popular treatment for the lay person. *Class No:* 681.51:007.52(031)

[7384]

TVER, D.F. *and* BOLZ, R.W. Robotics sourcebook and dictionary. New York, Industrial Press, 1983. vii, 258p. illus., diagrs. $32.50. ISBN: 0831111526.

Dictionary of types of industrial robot (with brief introduction); dictionary of applications (with descriptions). Glossary of robotics and computer-controlled terminology. List of *c.*80 US firms, with descriptions of selected products. '... this manual provides easy reference to the various robot types, applications, manufacturers and current market specifications' (*Robotics today,* v.8, December 1983, p.78). *Class No:* 681.51:007.52(031)

Handbooks & Manuals

[7385]

HODGES, B. *and* HALLAM, P. **Industrial robotics.** London, Heinemann, Newnes, 1990. 193p. illus., diagrs. $35. ISBN: 0434907820.

Material element of robotics - Drive systems - Robot sensors - Cost justification of robotics - Robot applications - The future of robotics. Chapter problems are included. *Class No:* 681.51:007.52(035)

[7386]

HUNT, V.D. **Industrial robotics handbook.** New York, Industrial Press, 1983. xiii, 432p. illus., diagrs., tables. $32.50.

10 introductory chapters on all aspects of robotics (*e.g.* 3. Sensor systems; 4. Tooling; 7. Robotic control systems; 10. Socioeconomic impact of robotics; 11: Specifications and illus. of 80 robotic systems from 25 manufacturers; 12: Brief surveys of developments in 8 major user-countries: 14: Forecasts of experts). Useful glossary (p.391-400). Bibliography, in 22 subject groups, p.401-17. Concise index. 'This rounded compilation of matter of diverse source and nature fills a volume of unexceptional size and weight, neatly produced' (*Scientific American*, v.249, October 1983, p.52F).
Class No: 681.51:007.52(035)

[7387]

HUNT, V.D. **Robotics sourcebook.** New York, Elsevier, 1988. 321p. illus., diagrs. $46.50. ISBN: 0444012982.

Focuses on the technology and industry of robotics, whereas the *International encyclopedia of robotics* addresses all areas of robotics. A book for 'both the management and the engineering student' (*Science and technology libraries*, v.11(1), Fall 1990, p.133).
Class No: 681.51:007.52(035)

[7388]

MILLER, R. **Industrial robot handbook.** New York, Van Nostrand Reinhold, 1989. 686p. illus., diagrs., tables. $82.95. ISBN: 0442237332.

A reprint of the 1987 Fairmont Press ed.

79 chapters, including case studies. 2 appendices: Robot manufacturers; Machine vision manufacturers.
Class No: 681.51:007.52(035)

[7389]

NOF, S.Y., *ed.* **Handbook of industrial robotics.** New York, etc., Wiley, 1985. xviii, 1358p. illus., diagrs., graphs, tables. £108. ISBN: 0471896845.

93 contributors, worldwide. 13 parts (77 documented chapters), arranged logically, from the development of industrial robots, through their mechanical design, control and intelligence systems, their implementation in society, to their applications (6 major areas: fabrication and processing; welding; material handling; assembly; inspection, quality control and repair; finishing, coatings and painting). Extensive glossary and index. 5 appendices, on robot markets, relevant organizations, manufacturers and journals. 'Professional engineers, managers and supervisors should ... find it to be a valuable aid for improving product quality and design as well as cutting safety hazards and labour costs' (*Automotive engineering*, v.93, November 1988, p.102); '... a major comprehensive reference' (*Chartered mechanical engineer*, v.32, December 1985, p.53). The 2nd ed. was published January 1999; $150; ISBN: 0471177830.
Class No: 681.51:007.52(035)

[7390]

Robot technology. London, Kogan Page, 1983-86. 8v. in 9.

1. *Modelling and control*, by P. Coiffet. 1983. ISBN: 0850385334. 156p. £25.

2. *Interaction with the environment*, by P. Coiffet. 1983. ISBN: 0850385342. 240p. £39.

3. *Teleoperation and robotics*, by J. Vertut and P. Coiffet. 1985. 2 parts. ISBNs: 0850385881; 0850389623. 332p; 256p. £65.

4. *Robot components and systems*, by F. Lhote and others. 1984. ISBN: 0850386497. 346p. £30.

5. *Logic and programming*, by M. Parent and C. Laurgeau. 1984. ISBN: 0850386500. 190p. £48.10.

6. *Decision and intelligence*, by J. Aleksander, H. Farrey and M. Ghallab. 1986. ISBN: 0850386519. 203p. £45.95.

7. *Performance and computer-aided design*, by A. Liegeois. 1985. ISBN: 0850386527. 268p. £44.90.

8. *Indexes and bibliography*. 1986. ISBN: 0850386977. 105p. £20.

'The series must constitute an essential element of any technical library worth its salt ... [and] ... will form an essential guide and reference source for all those in industry or research involved with robots and the related technology' (*Production engineer*, v.65(9) Oct. 1986, p.11). *Class No:* 681.51:007.52(035)

[7391]

TOEPPERWEIN, L.L., *and others.* **Robotics applications for industry:** a practical guide. Park Ridge, N.J., Noyes, 1983. x, 326p. diagrs. £46.15. ISBN: 0815509626.

An 'introduction to the basic concepts and techniques pertaining to the use of robotics technology for manufacturing and industrial applications' (*Foreword*), with special a section devoted to robotics in motor vehicle manufacture. Contains an extensive bibliography (about 300 references) classified under 21 headings (*e.g.* Manipulator design; Sensor technology and applications). Also a valuable glossary of terms (p.141-76), grouping almost 400 definitions under 14 headings. No index. *Class No:* 681.51:007.52(035)

Dictionaries

[7392]

BÜRGER, E. *and* KORZAK, G., *comps.* **Dictionary of robot technology** in four languages: English, German, French, Russian. Amsterdam, etc., Elsevier, 1986. 276p. £89.60. ISBN: 0444995196.

Over 6,100 English-language terms and phrases, cross-references and abbreviations/acronyms, identified by initial letters and consecutive numbers, with equivalents and indexes in the other three languages. No definitions. Letter-by-letter alphabetization.
Class No: 681.51:007.52(038)

[7393]

PALEY, S.M. **Illustrated dictionary of robotics:** English, German, French, Russian. Paris, La Maison du Dictionnaire, 1993. viii, 347p. illus. £35. ISBN: 2856080529.

About 4,800 terms grouped by subject (*e.g.* history; classification of robots; manufacturing; testing; control and programming, etc.). Indexes in each of the four languages. Useful schematic diagrams.
Class No: 681.51:007.52(038)

[7394]

WALDMAN, H. **Dictionary of robotics.** New York, Macmillan; London, Collier-Macmillan, 1985. viii, [1], 303p. illus. ISBN: 0029485304.

Concise, readable definitions of over 2,000 terms in robot systems, actions and hardware. Sequence: AA series CNC robots ... Zoom. 'Spot welding': ½p. Includes brief biographies. For students first exploring the subject, as well as for the researcher, the librarian and the business person. *Class No:* 681.51:007.52(038)

Reviews & Abstracts

[7395]

Referativnyĭ zhurnal. 37. Promyshlennye roboty i manipuliatory. Moscow, VINITI, 1983-. Monthly. diagrs. ISSN: 0208001x.

About 4,500 signed abstracts pa. covering industrial robots and manipulators. 9 sections (e.g., General - Theory, investigation and design of robots and manipulators - Construction and technical data - Robot and manipulator drives - Robot and manipulator control ... Applications ...). Illustrated with diagrams. UDC numbers. Annual subject index. English contents summary.
Class No: 681.51:007.52(048)

Progress Reports

[7396]

Developments in robotics. Rooks, B., *ed.* Bedford, IFS Publication, 1983-. illus., diagrs. ISBN: 0903608332.

Papers in the first volume (iv, 265p. £30) are grouped: applications; design and systems; sensors; drives, control and simulation. Intended to be an annual selection of previously unpublished papers emphasizing the latest developments and research in robotics.
Class No: 681.51:007.52(055)

Yearbooks & Directories

[7397]

World robotics, 1998: statistics, market analysis, forecasts, case studies and profitability of robot investment. Economic Commission for Europe *and* International Federation of Robotics. New York, United Nations, 1998. 240p. illus., maps. $120. ISBN: 9211007844. ISSN: 10201076.

Gives global industrial robot statistics for about 20 key industrialized nations. 5 parts: 1. Introduction (data collection methods, etc) - 2. Time series data (1981-1996) - 3. Comparative statistical date for 20 countries (North America; Europe; Asia) - 4. Forecasts (1997-2000) - 5. Articles (*e.g.* industrial activities; trends in packaging). Includes case studies. *Class No:* 681.51:007.52(058)

Teaching Materials

[7398]

PANTELIDIS, V.S. Robotics in education: an information guide. Metuchen, N.J., Scarecrow Press, 1991. 435p. $47.50. ISBN: 0810824663.

A bibliography of more than 1,500 items on robotics suitable for use in primary and secondary schools and for undergraduate education. 9 sections: 1. Reference sources - 2. General information - 3. Education robots - 4. Non-educational robots - 5. Social implications - 6. Economic implications - 7. Workplace impact - 8. Physical implications - 9. Nonprint media. Index. 'An amazing resource ... highly recommended' (*Choice*, September 1992, p.88). *Class No:* 681.51:007.52(072)

Trade Names, Trade Marks, Brand Names

[7399]

CUGY, A. and SIMPSON, J. Industrial robot specifications. Rev. ed. London, Kogan Page, 1984. 357p. diagrs., tables. £25. ISBN: 0850387698.

First published 1983.

Detailed specifications on over 300 robots manufactured and distributed under licence throughout Europe, covering output of over 90 companies. Part 1: an index of industrial applications in 3 groups (manufacturing and assembly robots; automated guided vehicles; vision systems) - Part 2: Technical specifications, grouped as in Part 1, and A-Z by firm - Part 3: Directory of manufacturers and distributors. Overlaps with *UK robots industry directory, 1984/8 (qv)*, but the data given complement rather than coincide with each other. *Class No:* 681.51:007.52(088.7)

Patents

[7400]

LAMMINEUR, P. and CORNILLIE, O. Industrial robots. Oxford, etc., Pergamon; E.E.C., 1984. viii, 154p. diagrs. £30. (*EPO Applied technology series, v.2.*) ISBN: 0080311431.

A classified bibliography of 170 patents on construction and applications of industrial robots (*c.*40 patents are Japanese; *c.*40, US; the rest from European countries). Detailed hierarchical classification (*e.g.* Part 1. Construction. Chapter 1.1: The manipulator arm; Section 1.1.1: Cartesian type; 1.1.1.2: with a suspended base; 1.1.1.2.1: Gantry-type). Each patent has a technical summary, plus diagram. A list of cited patents includes 'references to corresponding patents in other countries'. A-Z list of patentees and subject index. *Class No:* 681.51:007.52(088.8)

Typewriters

[7401]

BEECHING, W.A. Century of the typewriter. London, Heinemann, 1974. xii, 276p. illus., tables.

A survey from the beginnings up to 1973, in 8 chapters. Chapters 3-5. History of typewriter manufacture - 6. Electric and special-purpose typewriters ... 8. A compendium of typewriter history (in tabular form). Bibliography, p.266. Index. *Class No:* 681.612

Printing Machinery

Printers Devices

[7402]

McKERROW, R.B. Printers' and publishers' devices in England and Scotland, 1485-1640. London, Bibliographical Society, 1913. liv, 216p.

428 printers devices, p.1-160. Excludes devices of foreign printers for the English market. Introduction includes 'List of some books referred to' and 'Collections and libraries'. 5 indexes (1. Devices and compartments according to size; 2. Printers, booksellers, etc.). About 100p. of facsimiles. *Class No:* 681.626

[7403]

SILVESTRE, L.C. Marques typographiques; ou, Recueil des monogrammes, chiffres, ensignes, emblèmes, devises, rébus et fleurons des libraires et imprimeurs qui ont exercé en France, dupuis l'introduction de l'imprimerie, en 1470, jusqu'à la fin du seizième siècle ... Paris, Renou et Maulde, 1867. 2v. facsims.

Published anonymously, parts 1-13.

Records 1,310 typographical devices used by booksellers and printers operating in France, 1470-1599; also devices used by booksellers and printers of French books published outside France, during the same period. *Class No:* 681.626

Optical Apparatus

[7404]

LARIJANI, L.C. The Virtual reality primer. New York, McGraw-Hill, 1994. xxiii, 274p. illus. £24.95. ISBN: 0070364168.

Provides an overview of both the technology required and potential applications (*e.g.* in manufacturing, science and engineering, entertainment, etc). Appendices include a glossary (p.207-27) and directory of 'Places and players' (p.229-43). *Class No:* 681.7

[7405]

LATHAM, R. The Dictionary of computer graphics and virtual reality. 2nd ed. New York, Springer Verlag, 1995. xi, 169p. diagrs. ISBN: 0387944052.

First published 1991 as *Dictionary of computer graphics technology and applications*.

About 1,200 terms, briefly defined. Pronunciation indicated where necessary. Cross references and comparisons. *Class No:* 681.7

Sound & Video Recordings

Bibliographies

[7406]

KELLY, P., comp. Audio and video. London, Library Association, Public Libraries Group, 1983. 25p. ISBN: 0863700024.

169 numbered entries (1-149: Books; briefly annotated; 150-66: Periodicals). 'Audio' (nos. 1-94) covers historical background, basic general texts, construction, etc. 'Video' provides directories, home video, video film production, construction and repairs, games and videotext. Author index to each half. *Class No:* 681.8(01)

Encyclopaedias & Dictionaries

[7407]

LANGMAN, L. and MOLINARI, J.A. The New video encyclopedia. New York, Garland, 1990. xv,312p. illus., diagrs. ISBN: 0824082443.

About 2,400 brief entries (*e.g.* image sensor, ½ column). *Class No:* 681.8(03)

Handbooks & Manuals

[7408]

Audio engineer's reference book. Talbot-Smith, M., *ed.* Oxford, Butterworth-Heinemann, 1994. v.p. illus., diagrs., graphs, tables. £75. ISBN: 0750603860.

38 contributors, most from industry. 7 chapters: 1. Basic principles - 2. Acoustics and acoustic devices - 3. Recording and reproduction - 4. Digital equipment - 5. Studios and their facilities - 6. Distribution of audio signals - 7. Miscellaneous. Emphasis in on recording technology. Reprinted in paperback (1998. £50. ISBN: 0240515331). *Class No:* 681.8(035)

[7409]

BENSON, K.B., ed. Audio engineering handbook. New York, etc., McGraw-Hill, 1988. xxii,1040p. illus., diagrs., graphs, tables. £85. ISBN: 0070047774.

33 contributors. 17 chapters, most with references, beginning with principles of sound and hearing (1); digital audio (4); amplification (6); sound reproduction systems and techniques (7-13); post-production and noise reduction systems (14-15); tests and standards (16-17). The chapter on standards concentrates on the US. 21p. index. Extensively illustrated. 'Both practical and theoretical ... a major work in its field' (*Choice*, April 1989, p.1360, which found this more comprehensive than G. Ballou's *Handbook for sound engineers: The new audio cyclopedia*, 1987). *Class No:* 681.8(035)

[7410]

—**CAPAL, V. Newnes audio and hi-fi engineer's pocket book.** 3rd ed. Oxford, Butterworth-Heinemann, 1994. x, 323p. illus., diagrs., graphs, tables. £10.95. ISBN: 0750620013.

First published 1988; previous ed. 1991.

A basic survey in 11 parts: 1. Sound and acoustics ... 3. The gramophone ... 6. High quality radio ... 11. Facts and formulae. Small, handy format. *Class No:* 681.8(035)

[7411]
Newnes audio and hi-fi handbook. Sinclair, I.R., *ed*. 3rd ed. Oxford, Butterworth-Heinemann, 1998. 848p. illus., diagrs., graphs, tables. £50. ISBN: 075063636x.

First published 1989 as *Audio electronics reference book*; 2nd ed. 1993.

Contents include sound waves and acoustics; microphones; sound synthesis; digital principles; compact disc technology; other digital systems (DAT, NICAM, DCC, MD); noise reduction systems; the LP record; disc reproduction; tuners and radio receivers; valve amplifiers; loudspeakers; servicing. Comprehensive; a practical approach. *Class No:* 681.8(035)

[7412]
ROBINSON, J.F. Videotape recording: theory and practice. 4th ed. London, Focal Press, 1981. 256p. illus., diagrs., graphs, tables. £25.90.

First published 1975; 3rd ed. 1981..

17 chapters, each with references. Glossary, p.354-8. Detailed, analytical index. 'For the reader with a basic engineering knowledge and some experience in television' (*Preface*). *Class No:* 681.8(035)

[7413]
WEZEL, R. van. Video handbook. 2nd ed. London, Heinemann, 1987. viii, 455p. £25. ISBN: 0434921890.

First published Newnes, 1981. *Class No:* 681.8(035)

Dictionaries

[7414]
BRITISH KINEMATOGRAPH SOUND AND TELEVISION SOCIETY. Dictionary of image technology. 3rd ed. Oxford, Focal Press, 1994. [viii], 160p. diagrs. £19.95. ISBN: 0240513649.

First published 1983; 2nd ed. 1988.

Approx. 3,000 technical terms briefly defined. Acronyms and abbreviations included. *Class No:* 681.8(038)

[7415]
CLASON, W.E., *comp*. **Elsevier's dictionary of television and video-recording in six languages:** English/American-French-Spanish-Italian-Dutch-German. Amsterdam, etc., Elsevier, 1975. [viii], 608p. £156.90. ISBN: 0444412247.

Based on *Elsevier's Dictionary of television, radar and antennas* (1955), this polyglot version excludes terms on radar and antennas (other than for television); these will be found in *Elsevier's Telecommunications dictionary* (*qv*).

5,300 terms and phases are listed, numbered and defined in English, with equivalents in French, Spanish, Italian, Dutch and German. For each foreign language there is an A-Z index referring to the English section via the reference numbers. *Class No:* 681.8(038)

[7416]
WHITE, G.D. The Audio dictionary. Seattle, Wa., Univ. of Washington Press, 1988. x,291p. illus. $30; $15. ISBN: 0295965274; 0295965282, Pbk.

About 1,300 entries with clear definitions of about 1 paragraph. Cross references. Appendices: impedance; audio measurement; digital audio. Brief bibliography. 'Readable and informative' ('Reference books bulletin', *Booklist*, June 15, 1988, p.1715). *Class No:* 681.8(038)

Yearbooks & Directories

[7417]
AV market place, 1999. New York, etc., Bowker, 1999. Annual. 1600p. £135. ISBN: 0835240983. ISSN: 10440445.

First published 1984, continuing *Audiovisual market place*, 1969-83.
A directory of 1,250 products and services and 7,500 companies. Covers audio, AV, computer systems, film and video programming. Emphasis is on US and Canada. *Class No:* 681.8(058)

[7418]
The Directory of video, computer and audio-visual products, 1995-96. Fairfax, Va., International Communications Industries Association, 1995. 546p. ISSN: 08842124.

Buyers' guide. Contents: Consultants - Audio-video - A-V production - Computer/multimedia - Projection - Screens - Furniture - Related equipment - Trade names - Glossary - Index to contributors. *Class No:* 681.8(058)

Optical Discs

Handbooks & Manuals

[7419]
HELGERSON, L.W. CD-ROM: facilitating electronic publishing. New York, Van Nostrand Reinhold; London, Chapman & Hall, 1992. xxix,528p. diagrs. ISBN: 044200523 7.

28 chapters in 6 parts: I. Marketing - II. Product design - III. Production - IV. The Data - V. Now it begins - VI. Case studies.

....(contd.)
Appendix: Vendors of CD-ROM products and services (chiefly US). Glossary of CD-ROM terms, p.461-517. Detailed, analytical index, p.519-28. A practical treatment. *Class No:* 681.845(035)

[7420]
Rewritable optical storage technology. Roth, J.P. Westport, Ct., Meckler, 1991. x,172p. illus., diagrs. £28. ISBN: 0887365345.

Covers technology and applications in this rapidly developing area. Includes a directory of companies and organizations (p.24-56). 'Recommended readings' (p.142-56), 'glossary of terms and acronyms' (p.157-67). *Class No:* 681.845(035)

[7421]
SHERMAN, C., *ed*. **The CD-ROM handbook.** 2nd ed. New York, etc., McGraw-Hill, 1994. xxix, 579p. diagrs., tables. £55. ISBN: 0070566933.

First published 1988.

21 chapters in 6 parts: 1. Ancient history (1983-88) - 2. The CD-ROM format - 3. Storage and retrieval - 4. Creating a CD-ROM: the process - 5. Multimedia - 6. Resources. This new ed. emphasis advancements in multimedia hardware and software. The technical discussion (extensions, mastering process, etc.) is excellent and clearly presented. 'Highly recommended' (*Choice,* May 1989, p.1552) on the first ed.. *Class No:* 681.845(035)

Dictionaries

[7422]
FARACE, J. The Digital imaging dictionary. New York, Allworth, 1996. 223p. illus. $19.95. ISBN: 1880559463.

About 500 entries covering graphics, digital imaging and general computer terms. Appendixes: selecting an appropriate computer; companies mentioned in the dictionary. *Class No:* 681.845(038)

[7423]
HANSEN, B. The Dictionary of multimedia terms and acronyms. Wilsonville, Or., Franklin, Beedle, 1997. 343p. illus. $19.95. ISBN: 1887902147.

About 3,000 terms covering the wide range of the elements comprising multimedia: artistic; technical; computing; communication. Definitions are mostly brief, from 10 to 60 words; but some (*e.g.* copyright; MIDI; FireWire) are more extensive. Appendixes give an overview of HTML and DOS commands. 'A wide spectrum of information on a cross-disciplinary topic' (*American reference books annual*, 1998, p.688). *Class No:* 681.845(038)

[7424]
RICHTER, G. Fachwörterbuch optik, foto, video: Deutch-Englisch, Englisch-Deutsch. [Dictionary of optics, photography, video: German-English, English-German.] Gilching, Vfv verlag für foto, film und video, 1993. 429p. ISBN: 3889550630.

About 15,000 headwords in each half. A technical approach. *Class No:* 681.845(038)

Yearbooks & Directories

[7425]
International imaging source book including micrographics and optional imaging: 1994. Badler, M.M., *ed*. 2nd ed. Larchmont, N.Y., Microfilm Publishing, 1994. 440p. $122.50. ISBN: 091741408x.

First published 1992.

Directory-type information on electronic imaging sources and products, micrographics dealers, imaging software, CD-ROM and service bureaux. Data include manufacturer, model numbers, prices. List of consultants; index to associations. Bibliography. US bias. *Class No:* 681.845(058)

[7426]
Optical disk storage document image processing systems: a guide and directory. 2nd ed. Hatfield, Herts., Cimtech, 1990. 86p. £25. ISBN: 0852672772.

Information for the acquisition of systems to store and manipulate unstructured documents as digital images. Data: optical disk units, document image processing systems, data storage, computer output laser disk systems. Glossary; bibliography; address list. Covers UK availability only. *Class No:* 681.845(058)

Ironmongery & Hardware

[7427]
CLASON, W.E. Elsevier's dictionary of tools and ironware, in English/American, French, Spanish, Italian, Dutch and German. Amsterdam, etc., Elsevier, 1982. viii, 298p. £116. ISBN:

....(contd.)
0444420851.
2,578 English-base terms, with equivalents and indexes in the other 5 languages. Terms are categorized. *Class No:* 683

[7428]
DIY trade buyers' guide, 1995. Tonbridge, Kent, M-G Information Serices, Ltd., 1994. [viii], 369p. £62. ISSN: 09672257.
Formerly *Benn's Hardware and DIY buyers' guide.*
Main sections: Buyers' guide - Brands and trade names - Manufacturers and suppliers - Wholesalers - Retailers. *Class No:* 683

Locksmithing

[7429]
AMATT, L.K. Locks and lockmaking: an annotated bibliography. London, Library Association, 1973. [i], 392p.
Thesis submitted for Fellowship of the Library Association.
6 sections: A. General historical and descriptive works - B. History of locks and keys up to and including the eighteenth century - C. The age of invention in the nineteenth century - D. Security in the twentiety century - E. Practical locksmithing - F. Manufacture. 5 appendices (1. List of patent abridgement volumes, 1774-1965; 4. Notes on museum collections of locks and keys in Great Britain; 5. Annotated list of ten English and American journals). Author, title and subject indexes. *Class No:* 683.3

Furniture

[7430]
BRISTOW, P., *comp.* **Furniture literature:** a select bibliography on furniture and allied subjects. Stevenage, Herts., Furniture Industry Research Association, 1975-.
Furniture literature, 1986-1988 has *c.*2,000 entries, some with brief annotations. Sections: Adhesives - Computers - Ergonomics - Fastening - Finishing - Furniture - Hardware - Health hazards & safety - Machine tools - Hand tools - Management and organization - Mechanical handling - Packaging - Plastics - Robotics - Textiles - Timber - Woodworking - Miscellaneous. British Standards relating to furniture. 'This volume covers all relevant literature added to the stock of FIRA Library, between January 1986 and June 1988'. Includes books, pamphlets, journal articles and reports, but omits most trade literature. *Class No:* 684

[7431]
Directory to the furniture and furnishing industry, 1999. Tonbridge, Kent, Miller Freeman, 1998. vii, 484p. ISSN: 09548548.
Formerly *Directory to the furnishing trade*; incorporates *Carpet annual.*
Directory-type information for the UK and Eire. Sections: Furniture and furnishings - Carpets and floor coverings - Manufacturers' supplies and services - Brands and trade names - Overseas manufacturers and UK agents - Company data - Index to retail furnishers (alphabetical/geographical) - Index to contract furnishers - Trade association and organizations. *Class No:* 684

[7432]
JOYCE, E. The Technique of furniture making. 4th ed., revised by A. Peters. London, Batsford, 1987. [viii], 519p. illus. (incl. col.). ISBN: 071344407x.
First published 1970.
10 Parts: 1. Basic material - 2. Tools and equipment - 3. Basic techniques and joint construction - 4. Advanced areas of furniture construction - 5. Metal fittings, fasteners, and their application - 6. Advanced techniques - 7. Running a professional workshop - 8. Draughtsmanship and workshop geometry - 9. Furniture design and constructional details - 10. Restoration, repairs and wood finishing. Appendix: Costing and estimating. Detailed, analytical index, p.515-9. Profusely illustrated (307 photos, 288 line-drwings). Well produced and organized. *Class No:* 684

[7433]
LONDON COLLEGE OF FURNITURE LIBRARY, *comp.* **Periodicals list, 1988.** London, College of Furniture (A Faculty of the City of London Polytechnic), 1988. [iii], 18l.
Current titles taken by the Commercial Road Library features as both a classified list (14 headings, including 'Indexes & addresses') and an alphabetical list (*c.*500 titles, giving frequency and housing). Index to subjects precedes. The Tarrance Street Library 'Alphabetical list of current titles' has an appended list of Braille publications. Wide-ranging. *Class No:* 684

[7434]
UNITED NATIONS. Industrial Development Organization. **Information sources on the furniture and joinery industry.** Rev. ed. New York, United Nations. (*UNIDO Guides to information sources, no.4.*)
First published 1972.
698 items, in 12 sections: 1. Professional, trade and research organizations, learned societies and special information sources - 2. Directories - 3. Sources of statistics, marketing and other economic data - 4. Basic handbooks, textbooks and manuals - 5. Monograph series - 6. Current periodicals - 7. Current abstracting and indexing periodicals - 8. Proceedings, papers and reports of the United Nations and related bodies - 9. Specialized dictionaries and encyclopaedias - 10. Bibliographies - 11. Films and film catalogues - 12. Other potential sources of information (*e.g.* Fairs and exhibitions). *Class No:* 684

[7435]
'Which?' way to repair and restore furniture. London, Consumers' Association, and Hodder & Stoughton, 1980. 180p. illus. ISBN: 034025050x.
5 sections: 1. Starting (tools; sharpening chisels) -2. Structural repairs - 3. Cleaning, stripping and refinishing - 4. Upholstery (p.75-117) - 5. Materials and supplies (including list of specialist suppliers in UK.). Oblong format. Step-by-step approach. *Class No:* 684

Bedding & Upholstery

[7436]
BRITISH STANDARDS INSTITUTION. Terms relevant to the feather industry for fillings for bedding, upholstery and other domestic articles. London, BSI, 1988. 8p. (*PD 6522: 1988.*)
About 20 terms, some explained, in alphabetical order. *Class No:* 684.7

Footwear Boots & Shoes (Manufactures)

[7437]
PELLIZZARI, P. Multilingual footwear dictionary: English, French, Spanish, Italian, German. Padova, Edizioni Tradutec, 1989. 336p. illus. £39.95. ISBN: 8885158013.
About 17,000 English headwords, with equivalents. 130 labelled drawings. *Class No:* 685.3

[7438]
RAMA, L. Vocabulaire technique de l'industrie de la chaussure. [Footwear industry technical vocabulary: Français-English-Deutsch-Italiano-Español.] Paris, OECD, 1969. iv, 396p. £53.95.
5 sequences; French-German-English-Spanish-Italian, with definitions in French (p.3-125); English-French-German-Italian-Spanish, with definitions in English (p.127-263); etc. *Class No:* 685.3

[7439]
Shoe trades directory, 1998. 17th ed. London, Shoe and Leather News, 1998. 132p. ISSN: 13528858.
Main sections: A-Z company listing (manufacturers; services; associations) - Buyers' guide - Brand name listing - Overseas representation. *Class No:* 685.3

Bookbinding

[7440]
BRENNI, V.J., *comp.* **Bookbinding: a guide to the literature.** Westport, Conn., Greenwood Press, 1982. viii, 199, [1]p. £31.75. ISBN: 0313237182.
12 sections, 1,525 references, mostly periodical articles. 1. Reference works ... 3. Materials ... 5. Decoration - 6. History of bookbinding from ancient times to the present ... 8. Care and repair of bindings ... 10. Audiovisual aids - 11. Bookplates - 12. Book jackets. 3 Checklists of titles, - for university/college/medium-sized public library. List of binders, binding designers, and binding decorators, p.139-160. Book collectors. Glossary. Author index; detailed analytical subject index. *Class No:* 686

[7441]
JOHNSON, A.W. The Thames and Hudson manual of bookbinding. London, Thames & Hudson, 1978. 224p. illus. (incl. col. pl.). £7.95.
8 chapters. 1. A history of English bookbinding decoration - 2. Equipment - 3. Bookbinder's materials ... 5. Working procedures - 6. Binding styles - 7. Finishing ... 9. Changes in bookbinding construction (*e.g.* adhesive binding) - 10. Design. Glossary, p.211-8. 'Further reading', p.219. Analytical index. 258 clear line-drawings; 8p. of colour plates. 'This is the best manual of bookbinding to have

....(contd.)

been produced for around thirty years and it will, I believe, become the standard guide to all aspects of craft bookbinding' (*British book news*, June 1978, p.486). *Class No:* 686

[7442]
ROBERTS, M.T. *and* ETHERINGTON, D. **Bookbinding and the conservation of books:** a dictionary of descriptive terminology. Washington, Library of Congress, 1982. 296p. illus. (incl. col. pl.). ISBN: 0313237182.

Defines *c*.3,000 terms and expressions, drawn from 373 listed sources. Coverage: bookbinding history, papermaking, some bibliographical terms and, particularly, the techniques, processes, equipment and materials of hand and machine binding, plus conservation. 'Provides an authoritative, comprehensive dictionary for bookbinders and conservators' (*Reference books bulletin, 1983-1984,* p.57). *Class No:* 686

Clothing

Bibliographies

[7443]
UNITED NATIONS. Industrial Development Organization. **Information sources on the clothing industry.** New York, United Nations, 1974. [xii], 116, [1]p. $4. (*UNIDO Guides to information sources, no. 12.*)

876 items, in 12 sections: 1. Addresses of professional, trade and research organizations, learned societies and special information services - 2. Directories - 3. Sources of statistics and economic data - 4. Basic textbooks and manuals - 5. Monograph series - 6. Current periodicals - 7. Current abstracting and indexing periodicals - 8. Proceedings, papers and reports - 9. Specialized dictionaries and encyclopaedias - 10. Bibliographies - 11. Films - 12. Other potential sources of information (e.g., marketing, exporting and purchasing). Includes information on training facilities. 'Bibliographic sources used'. Items in some sections are annotated. *Class No:* 687(01)

Dictionaries

[7444]
GIOELLO, D.A. *and* BERKE, B. **Fashion production terms.** New York, Fairchild Books and Visuals, 1979. 340p. illus. (*Language of fashion series.*) ISBN: 0870052004.

Grouped headings (*e.g.* pattern layout; design control), covering both tools and techniques, and garment construction from design to completion. Each term is defined with photograph or line-drawing. Bibliography and index. 'An outstanding reference work for students or professionals in all facets of fashion' (*Choice*, v.16(7), September 1979, p.798). *Class No:* 687(038)

[7445]
PICKEN, M.B. **The Fashion dictionary:** fabric, sewing and apparel as expressed in the language of fashion. Rev. and enl. ed. New York, Funk & Wagnalls, 1973. ISBN: 0308100522.

First published 1939 as *The language of fashion.* Rev. ed. 1957.

More than 10,000 words, briefly defined, with pronunciation, concerning wearing apparel and accessories, and their manufacture. 100 group-terms (*e.g.* 'Linens'; 'Heels'). Over 750 illus. of stitches, weaves, laces and garments, including 200 half-tones. Includes obsolete terms. Adequate cross-references. A standard work in its field. *Class No:* 687(038)

[7446]
REBMANN, G. **Bekleidungs wörterbuch:** Deutsch-Englisch-Französich-Italienisch. [Dictionary of garment technology: English-German-French-Italian.] 2nd ed. Berlin, Schiele & Schön, 1990. xiv, 788p. £103.95. ISBN: 379490494x.

First published 1984.

In four parts: German, English, French, Italian. Indicates which terms accord with the Nomenclature of Garments. Designation of the Association Européenne des Industries de l'Habillement (AEIH). Names and address of German manufacturers appended. *Class No:* 687(038)

Yearbooks & Directories

[7447]
British clothing industry year book, 1998. Yardley, Birmingham, Kemps, 1998. v.p. ISBN: 0862593824.

Sponsored by the British Knitting & Clothing Export Council (BKCEC).

Contents: Features - Exhibitions - Trade names ... Menswear - Womenswear - Childrenswear ... Fabrics and textiles ... Serivces ... Buying offices - List of suppliers, A-Z. *Class No:* 687(058)

[7448]
The UK fashion handbook. London, Emap Fashion, 1997. [x], 272p. graphs, tables. £99. ISBN: 0952673053.

7 sections: 1. Overview - 2. Consumer behaviour and spending patterns - 3. Market sectors - 4. Manufacturing - 5. Retail - 6. Future of shopping (*e.g.* Internet) 7. Directory (retailers, manufacturers). *Class No:* 687(058)

Equipment & Instruments

[7449]
HALE, F.G. **The International history of the sewing machine.** London, Hale, 1982. 320p. illus. ISBN: 0709198260.

14 sections (2. The precursors ... 5. The commercial age, 1880-1900. Early automatics - 6. Twentieth century development, 1900-1950 - 7. The addition of other motive power, 1950- ... 11. Electricity and the sewing machine ... 13. Biographical section, p.214-79). Glossary (*c*.700 entries). Bibliography, p.316. Detailed, non-analytical index. 654 illus. *Class No:* 687:002.50

Hairdressing

[7450]
CORSON, B. **Fashions in hair:** the first five thousand years. 4th impression, with revised suppt. London, P. Owen, 1980. 719p. illus.

First published 1964.

14 chapters. Main feature: over 3,000 drawings, with text facing. (*e.g.* 19th-century women: 16 illus.). Sources, p.696-704 (museums and libraries; books and periodicals). Supplement, 1965-1978, p.678-95. Detailed, analytical index, p.705-19. A valuable source. *Class No:* 687.53

[7451]
COX, J.S. **An Illustrated dictionary of hairdressing & wigmaking.** London, Batsford, 1985. 312p. illus. £25. ISBN: 0713442085.

First published 1966 (xxiii, 359p.).

Over 4,000 concise definitions of British and American terms (some of them archaic and obsolete). 1,156 black-and-white illus. Extensive bibliography. Careful documentation of sources. The 1966 volume was a standard reference text for costume specialists and theatrical costumers. *Class No:* 687.53

Buttons

[7452]
ALBERT, L.S. *and* KENT, K. **The Complete button book.** Garden City, N.Y., Doubleday, 1949. xix, 409p. illus.

2 parts: 1. Methods of manufacture (13 chapters) - 2. Illustrations, p.80-401, with captions facing. Appendix : 'List of American button makers and outfitters, from pre-Revolutionary times to the 1890s'. *Class No:* 688.2

[7453]
—SQUIRE, G. Buttons: a guide for collectors. London, F. Muller, 1972. xi, 200p. illus. (pl.).

Concentrates on uniform buttons (Air Force ... Ambulance Service ... Hunt: Foxhounds ... Shipping lines - Police, transport, fire brigade ...). Nearly 3,000 are displayed on 100 plates, with text facing. British slant. *Class No:* 688.2

Toys

[7454]
DAIKEN, L. **World of toys:** a guide to the principal and private collections in Great Britain of period toys, dolls and dolls' houses, games, puppets and marionettes, toy soldiers, musical boxes and automata; also modern toys, toymakers and toyshops, puppets and marionette troupes, the British toy industry and toy trade press. London, Lambarde Press, 1963. xvi, 269p. illus. (pl.).

Ten short but highly informative chapters on a wide variety of topics, from dolls clubs and special exhibitions to hand-crafted toys and their makers, p.234-8. 'For further reading', p.241. Non-analytical index. *Class No:* 688.72

[7455]

KING, C.E. **The Encyclopedia of toys.** London, Hale, 1978. 272p. illus. (mostly col.), facsims. ISBN: 0707917269.

6 sections: 1. Miniature living (doll's houses, etc.) - 2. Toys principally for pleasure (*e.g.* music toys; automata) - 3. Wheeled toys & children's transport (prams, etc.) - 4. Metal toys (*e.g.* model soldiers) - 5. Board and table games - 6. Educational toys and pastimes (*e.g.* toy theatre; doll's dressmaking). Bibliography, p.266-7. Index, p.268-72. Quarto. *Class No:* 688.72

Dolls

[7456]

COLEMAN, D.S., *and others*. **The Collector's encyclopedia of dolls.** New York, Crown Publishers, 1968; London, Hale, 1970. vi, 697p. illus. (incl. col.), facsims.

Arranged A-Z, with entries for doll designers, trade names, etc. 'Chronology', p.138-55; 'Wooden dolls', p.656-66; 'Hands for dolls', p.280-2 (illus. 730-61). Many cross-references. Bibliography, in 6 sections, p.672-5. Non-analytical index; index of marks, p.689-97. 1,738 illus. and facsims.; 46 colour pl. *Class No:* 688.721

Amateur Hobbies & Crafts

Bibliographies

[7457]

LIBRARY ASSOCIATION. Public Libraries Group. **Handicrafts.** Compiled by the staff of the Kent County Library. 5th ed. London, the Association, [1975]. 43p. (*Readers' Guide no. 4.*)

About 400 unannotated entries, under subjects A-W (General - Basketry, Canework, rushwork and raffia work ... Block printing and lino cuts ... Flower making and pressing ... Knitting ... Leatherwork ... Needlework ... Plastic craft - Puppetry, marionette and model theatre ... Woodwork). *Class No:* 689(01)

[7458]

LOVELL, E.C. *and* HALL, R.M. **Index to handicrafts, model-making and workshop projects.** Boston, Mass., Faxon, 1936. 476p. Suppts. 1-5, 1943-75.

Largely concerned with material in books, but has some magazine references. *Fifth supplement* (1975. 650p.) covers 1968-73 and includes coverage of over 1,000 book titles and 15 periodicals not indexed in the *Reader's guide to periodical literature.* 'One of the most practical and useful indexes which has been published' (Barton, M., and Bell, M.V. *Reference books,* (7th ed., 1970, p.105). US slant. *Class No:* 689(01)

[7459]

SHIELDS, J.R. **Make it:** an index to projects and materials. Metuchen, N.J., Scarecrow Press, 1975. 485p. ISBN: 0810807728.

Indexes 475 how-to-do-it books. Part 1 concerns projects; part 2, materials. Coverage: weaving, plastics, ceramics, needlework, electronics, leather, metal, wood, and natural materials. *Class No:* 689(01)

[7460]

—Index to handicraft books, 1974-1984. Pittsburgh, Pa., Univ. of Pittsburgh, 1986. 413p.

Analyses *c.*1,000 know-how books, supplementing Shields (*qv*) and Lovell and Hall (*qv*). 'A valuable resource, even for libraries that do not own the Faxon series' (*Library journal,* July 1986, p.72). *Class No:* 689(01)

Indexes

[7461]

Clover index. Caldecote, Biggleswade, Beds., Clover Publications, 1975-. 4pa. £37 pa.

Title varies.

About 3,000 entries in each issue, A-Z. Draws upon 90 popular science magazines such as *Amateur gardening, Flight, New Scientist, Wireless World* and *Your model railway.* Titles of articles are occasionally given brief explanatory notes. Cheaply produced from typescript. To some extent supplements *Abstracts in new technologies and engineering* for public libraries. Annual cumulation. Available on CD-ROM and on the World Wide Web: URL: http://www.cloverweb.co.uk *Class No:* 689(014)

Encyclopaedias

[7462]

ANDREW, H.E.L. **The Batsford encyclopaedia of crafts.** London, Batsford, 1978. 431p. illus. (incl. colour).

As *The Arco encyclopaedia of crafts* (New York, Arco).

Covers 135 selected crafts, A-W, from Adhesives, Airbrush through Beads ... Casting ... Dyes ... Glass ... to Woodcuts. 'Table weaving', p.355-61, notes 12 items for further reading. Addresses of suppliers. 877 illus., with 27 in colour. 'Concentrates on the techniques of the various crafts as opposed to describing how to make a single item in a given craft' (*Introduction*).

1988 ed. 424p. 1101 illus. ISBN 0713462493. *Class No:* 689(031)

[7463]

TORBERT, L, *ed.* **The Encyclopedia of crafts.** New York, Scribner, 1980. 3v. (1032p.). ISBN: 0684164094.

Encyclopedic dictionary of *c.*50 major crafts from all over the world, with emphasis on techniques, materials, and equipment, plus brief historical summaries. Shorter entries for definitions of terms and minor crafts. Cross-references; well-captioned illus. 'A valuable pioneer in the field of craft reference' (*Library journal,* 15 January 1987, p.136). *Class No:* 689(031)

Handbooks & Manuals

[7464]

DIAGRAM GROUP. **Handbook of arts and crafts:** the encyclopedia of the fine, decorative and applied arts. London, Harrap, 1981. 320p. illus. ISBN: 0245538232.

18 chapters: 1. Writing and drawing - 2. Printing - 3. Making books ... 6. Clay and pottery ... 9. Cabinet making ... 11. Working with glass - 12. Fine metalwork ... 15. Weaving ... 18. Leatherwork, 'Stained glass', p.188-91: 41 terms defined and illustrated. Bibliography, by subject groups, p.310-1. Detailed, analytical index, p.313-20. Over 4,000 illus. in all, for more than 2,000 tools, their evolution, history, function and manner of use. *Class No:* 689(035)

69 Building Industry

Databases

[7465]

ICONDA Stuttgart, Fraunhofer-Gesellschaft

International bibliographic database, with abstracts, covering construction, civil engineering, urban and regional planning and architecture. 450,000 records from 1976. Subjects: structural engineering; construction equipment and materials; building maintenance, restoration and conservation; engineering geology; financial planning and project management. Online from CISTI, Questel SA, Questel/ORBIT, STN International. Also available on CD-ROM (SilverPlatter) and on the Internet. *Class No:* 69(003.4)

[7466]

RSWB. Stuttgart, Fraunhofer-Gesellschaft.

Bibliographic database of German and international publications on building and construction, including civil engineering. 550,000 records of which about 60% have abstracts in German. Available on STN International (updated monthly) and on CD-ROM (SilverPlatter, updated quarterly). *Class No:* 69(003.4)

Internet

[7467]

BRIDGES, A. The Construction net. London, Spon, 1996. 256p. illus., diagrs. 24.99. ISBN: 0419217800.

Indentifies, describes and evaluates online information sources (from commercial hosts and the World Wide Web) for the industry. *Class No:* 69(003.41)

[7468]

World wide web sites for chartered surveyors. 2nd ed. London, The Royal Institution for Chartered Surveyors, 1997. 54p. £5. ISBN: 0854068430.

Lists over 80 web sites of interest to chartered surveyors. Arranged by subject, A-Z (Arbritation - Transport) with a brief description and the URL. Appendixes list firms and property listing sites *Class No:* 69(003.41)

Bibliographies

[7469]

ADDIS, W. *and* **BUSSELL, M.** 'Construction engineering'. *Information sources in engineering.* K.W. Mildren and P.J. Hicks, eds. (3rd ed., 1996), p.519-45. 3rd ed. London, Bowker Saur, 1996. £80. ISBN: 1857390571.

Covers organizations, access to information (including search techniques), catalogues, indexes and electronic databases, periodicals, general reference works, construction materials (concrete, steel, stone, brickwork, timber, etc.), plant and equipment, and temporary works. *Class No:* 69(01)

[7470]

BUILDING CENTRE, LONDON. The Building Bookshop at the Building Centre, 1998 catalogue. London, the Centre, 1998. *c.*70p. illus. £1.

29 sections. Over 2,000 briefly annotated entries, with prices. Some major sections (*e.g.* Architecture; Building Services; Surveying) are subdivided. Title index of publications; author index. Some advertisements. *Class No:* 69(01)

[7471]

BUILDING RESEARCH ESTABLISHMENT. BRE publications guide. Garston, Herts., BRE, 1992-. Annual.

Includes a classified list of BRE publications. *Class No:* 69(01)

[7472]

Information sources in architecture and construction. Nurcombe, V.J., *ed.* 3rd ed. London, Bowker-Saur, 1996. xix, 489p. £68; $100. (*Guides to information sources.*) ISBN: 1857390946.

First published 1983.

22 contributors; 24 chapters, covering the standard information sources (*e.g.* libraries, periodicals, trade literature, official publications, etc.), IT applications, management of the design process, contracts and liability, conservation, landscape, interior design and architectural history. *Class No:* 69(01)

[7473]

RIBA list of recommended books, 1998. London, RIBA Publications, Ltd. 1998. 48p. Gratis.

First published 1969. Earlier title *RIBA Book list.*

Over 900 entries in 14 sections, closely subdivided: 1. Generalities - 2. Architecture and art ... 6. Building construction ... 9. Environment and energy ... 11. Landscape ... 14. Social sciences. New editions, new titles and out-of-print items are indicated. A valuable checklist; gives current prices, but not publishers. *Class No:* 69(01)

Encyclopaedias

[7474]

BROOKS, H. Encyclopedia of building and construction terms. 2nd ed. Englewood Cliffs., N.J., Prentice-Hall, 1983. [iv], 443p. illus., diagrs., charts. ISBN: 0132755114.

First published 1976.

Defines more than 2,800 terms, some at length (*e.g.* 'Solar collectors': nearly 3p.). 'Index by function' (24 functions/subject areas) precedes, p.7-38: 178 illus. etc. Four appendices: A. Construction centres (US); D. Conversion factors. 'This is one of the best encyclopedias covering the terminology associated with the building industry ...' (*Reference books bulletin, 1984/1985* (1986), p.21). *Class No:* 69(031)

Handbooks & Manuals

[7475]

Spon's construction resource handbook. Spain, B., *ed*. London, Spon, 1998. xvi, 596p. £75. ISBN: 0419236805.

Provides data for use in the preparation of analytical rates in the construction industry. 6 parts: 1. Building - 2. Civil engineering - 3. Landscaping - 4. Mechanical work - 5. Electrical work - 6. General information (*e.g.* useful addresses). *Class No:* 69(035)

Dictionaries

English

[7476]

HARRIS, C.M., *ed*. Dictionary of architecture and construction. 2nd ed. New York, etc. McGraw-Hill, 1993. 924p. illus. £40; $59.50 ISBN: 0070268886.

First edition 1975.

52 contributing editors; 20,000 entries illustrated by 2,000 line drawings. Includes terms from architectural design and construction and the building trades, as well as water supply, waste disposal and associated fields. *Class No:* 69(038)=20

[7477]

Means illustrated construction dictionary. Smit, K. *and* Chandler, H.M., *eds*. Kingston, Ma., Means, 1991. 691p. illus. ISBN: 087629218x.

About 14,000 terms defined briefly and clearly. Excellent illustrations. Means is a major US publisher in the construction field. *Class No:* 69(038)=20

German

[7478]

JUNGE, H.D. *and* **LUKHAUP, D. German dictionary of construction:** German-English, English-German. [Wörterbuch bauwesen: Deutsch-Englisch, Englisch-Deutsch.] London, Routledge, 1997. xxviii, 348p. £85. ISBN: 0415112427.

25,000 words in each language in common use in the industry. Includes specialized technical words and phrases. Cross-references and contexts of usage. Subjects covered include infrastructure and design, material properties, building accessories, structures, stone buildings, surface treatment, wastewater treatment, heating, ventilation and air conditioning, sound insulation, electrical engineering, building machinery, architecture and building planning, environmental issues, construction law. Also available on CD-ROM (£99; ISBN: 0415140293). *Class No:* 69(038)=30

Glossaries

[7479]

BRITISH STANDARDS INSTITUTION. **Glossary of building and civil engineering terms.** Oxford, Blackwell Scientific, 1993. xv, 624p. £45. ISBN: 0632028513.

Brings together some 9,000 buidling and civil engineering terms comprising BS6100. *Class No:* 69(038.1)

[7480]

STEIN, J.S. **Construction glossary:** an encyclopedic reference and manual. 2nd ed. New York, Wiley, 1993. xx, 1137p. £67; $95. ISBN: 047156933x.

16 sections: 1. General requirement - 2. Site work - 3. Concrete - 4. Masonry - 5. Metals - 6. Wood and plastics ... 9. Finishes ... 12. Furnishings ... 14. Conveying systems - 15. Mechanical - 16. Electrical. Also: A. Professional services; B. Construction categories; C. Technical-scientific and related data. Reference data sources. Appendices: 1. Abbreviations for scientific, engineering, and construction terms; 2. Weights and measures; Carpentry abbreviations. 'Sets the standard for clear communication' (*Choice*, June 1993, p.1611). *Class No:* 69(038.1)

Reviews & Abstracts

[7481]

Construction information file. Ascot, Berks., Chartered Institute of Building, 1976-. 6pa. £60.

Previous published as *Building management abstracts*

About 800 abstracts per issue. Subject fields: site and project organization, estimating and costs, building management. Coverage: periodical articles, books, conference proceedings, technical and law reports. Annual author, subject and legal case indexes. Abbreviated CIF. *Class No:* 69(048)

Tables & Data Books

[7482]

GREAT BRITAIN. Department of Environment, Transport, Regions. **Digest of data for the construction industry.** London, HMSO, 1998. 220p. tables. £45. ISBN: 011753465x.

Data tables covering all aspects of the construction industry in the UK. Includes price indices, output, commercial floorspace information, local authority expenditure and national lottery projects. *Class No:* 69(083)

Standards

[7483]

BRITISH STANDARDS INSTITUTION. **Construction standards manual.** London, BSI, 1995-. 5v. Loose-leaf + distribution packets. £680.

Replaces *BS handbook 3*, 1985 (4v. Loose-leaf).

CSMCSE: 1996. Civil and structural engineering. 260p.

CSMCS: 1996 Common standards [those across the construction sector]. 500p.

CSMI: 1996. Index (numerical, alphabetical and classified). 740p.

CCSMA: 1996. Architecture. 740p.

CSMBS: 1996. Building services. 1100p.

Volumes include summaries of standards of professional interest for all sectors of the construction industry. *Class No:* 69(083.74)

Films

[7484]

BRITISH INDUSTRIAL AND SCIENTIFIC FILM ASSOCIATION. **Guide to audiovisual material for the construction industry.** London, the Association, 1983. 73p.

Sponsored by the Building Centre Trust.

Subject list (based on UDC), p.5-9. Titles and descriptions, p.11-57. Annotated entries (mostly classified at 69, 71 and 72). Alphabetical title-index. List of distributors. *Class No:* 69(084.122)

Great Britain

Tables & Data Books

[7485]

GREAT BRITAIN. Department of the Environment, Scottish Office Environment Department, Welsh Office. **Housing and construction statistics, 1983-1993: Great Britain.** London, HMSO, 1994. Annual. xvi, [1], 165p. diagrs., graphs, tables, map. £45. ISBN: 0117518786.

15 sections of tables (General - Construction ... Structure ... Housebuilding ... Rent and rent regulations). Appended notes and definitions. Detailed, analytical index. *Class No:* 69(410)(083)

Laws

[7486]

House's guide to the construction industry: the regulations, recommendations, and statutory advisory bodies. Parlett, D.S., *ed.* 9th ed. Wokingham, Beds., VNR (UK), 1985. viii, 161p. ISBN: 0442306490.

First published 1968.

Directory of more than 1,000 organizations. 9 sections, covering bodies and information services, reports, forms of contract, building legislation and regulations. Section 9: Directory; classified index. Subject index. Late entries.

For the UK; companion volume: *Construction industry Europe.* *Class No:* 69(410)(094.1)

Information Management

[7487]

CIIG manual: a guide to good practice in construction industry information. Adderley, P. *and* O'Brien, A., *eds.* London, Construction Industry Information Group, 1994. 160p. ISBN: 0952392003.

Provides a comprehensive guide to the provision of information services to the industry. Identifies the information needs, discusses the management of an information service and describes in detail sources of information: the reference collection, external and internal sources. Also considers IT, day-to-day opeartions and quality assurance. Essential for those concerned with construction industry information. *Class No:* 69:025.4

[7488]

LANGFORD, D.A. *and* RETIK, A. **'Construction management'.** *Information sources in engineering.* K.W. Mildren and P.J. Hicks, eds. (3rd ed., 1996), p.569-88. 3rd ed. London, Bowker Saur, 1996. £80. ISBN: 1857390571.

Identifies the role of information within construction management and lists sources for this (*e.g.* statistics; forecasting; project-based information; journals; electronic databases; research organizations). *Class No:* 69:025.4

Classification Systems

[7489]

Uniclass: unified classification for the construction industry. Crawford, M., *and others, eds.*

A classification scheme intended to supercede CI/SfB and organize information to match the requirements of international standards. Includes CAWS and EPIC (Electronic Product Information Cooperation). *Class No:* 69:025.44

Information Services

[7490]

CONSTRUCTION INDUSTRY RESEARCH AND INFORMATION ASSOCIATION. **CIRIA guide to European Community and international sources of construction information.** Richardson, B., *comp.* 2nd ed. London, CIRIA, 1991. 236p. 309p. (*CIRIA special publication 66.*) ISBN: 0860173321.

First published 1989.

Data on over 200 (non-UK) EU and other international organizations of interest to the UK construction industry. Gives original name, with English translation if necessary. Subject, geographical and acronym indexes. *Class No:* 69:061:025.5

Building

Handbooks & Manuals

[7491]

CHANDLER, I. **Building technology.** London, Mitchell, for Chartered Institute of Building. 3v. ea. £9.95. ISBN: 0713451785, v.1.

1. *Site organization and method.* 1988.

2. *Performance.* 1988.

3. *Design, production and maintenance.* 1987.

V.1 (176p.) has 5 parts, concentrating on production services and systems installation, and the design/construction interface. Part 5 deals with 3 case studies. 'References and further reading'. p.172-7. Index. *Class No:* 69.0(035)

[7492]

MERRITT, F.S., *ed*. **Building design and construction handbook.** 5th ed. New York, etc., McGraw-Hill, 1994. v.p. illus., tables. $96.50 ISBN: 0070414963.

First published 1958; 4th ed. 1981.

19 documented sections, with the American civil engineer particulary in mind (*e.g.* structural theory; soil mechanics and foundations; building materials; the buidling team, etc.). Index. Lavishly illustrated. A highly practical treatment. *Class No:* 69.0(035)

[7493]

SZOKOLAY, S.V. Environmental science handbook for architects and builders. Lancaster, Construction Press, 1980. [vii], 572p. diagrs., graphs, tables.

6 parts, each with appended short bibliographies: 1. Space - 2. Light - 3. Sound - 4. Heat - 5. Resources - 6. Synthesis. Analytical index. Attractively produced. *Class No:* 69.0(035)

Dictionaries

Polyglot

[7494]

KORCHOMKIN, S.N. Dictionary of building and civil engineering: English, German, French, Dutch, Russian. London, etc., Kluwer, 1986. 935p. £81.75. ISBN: 2040157999.

14,000 English-base terms, with equivalents and indexes in German, French, Dutch and Russian. *Class No:* 69.0(038)=00

[7495]

The Multilingual dictionary of architecture and building terms. Grech, C., *ed*. London, Spon, 1998. xxi, 453p. £55 ISBN: 0419199209.

Languages: English, French, German, Italian, Spanish. 2,500 terms used in building, design and construction. Efficient and comprehensive, with a clear layout. *Class No:* 69.0(038)=00

[7496]

TEKNISKA NOMENKLATURCENTRALEN. Plan och byggtermer. [Glossary of planning and building terms.] Stockholm, the Centre, 1975. 198p. illus. (*TNC 58*.)

Replaces TNC 52 (Swedish monolingual glossary).

616 grouped Swedish entry-words (including compounds and expressions), plus Swedish definitions and English, French, German and Russian (transliterated) equivalents. Swedish, English, French, German and Russian (cyrillic) indexes. Issued by the Swedish Centre of Technical Terminology. *Class No:* 69.0(038)=00

[7497]

—**VAN MANSUM, C.J.** Elsevier's dictionary of building construction in English/American, French, Dutch, German. Amsterdam, etc., Elsevier, 1959 (5th reprint 1985). viii, 472p. DFl.250. ISBN: 0444406018.

5,328 English-base terms, with equivalents and indexes in French, Dutch and German. *Class No:* 69.0(038)=00

English

[7498]

BRETT, P. Building terminology: an illustrated reference guide for practitioners and students. Oxford, etc., Heinemann Newnes, 1989. [viii],339p. illus. £20. ISBN: 0434901768.

6 sections, each in alphabetical order: 1. Architectural style - 2. Building construction - 3. Documentation, administration and control - 4. General - 5. Materials and scientific principles - 6. Services and finishes. Index, p.321-39 (*c*.3,000 entries). Over 350 diagrams and photographs, so much superior in this respect to the *Macmillan dictionary of building* with its 12 appended pages of diagrams. *Class No:* 69.0(038)=20

[7499]

COWAN, H. *and* **SMITH, P. Dictionary of architectural and building technology.** 3rd ed. London, Spon, 1998. 280p. illus. £19.99. ISBN: 0419222804.

About 5,500 terms focusing on technical issues; for the profession. *Class No:* 69.0(038)=20

[7500]

MARSH, P. Illustrated dictionary of building. London & New York, Construction Press, 1982. [v], 256p. illus. £16.95. ISBN: 0860958485.

About 4,000 brief entries, rarely over 10 lines in length. 'Subsidence': 19 lines. Many small line-drawings (*e.g.* 'Roof': 6 types). Adequate cross-references. Highly practical, aiming to be reasonably comprehensive and intended for professionals. *Class No:* 69.0(038)=20

[7501]

—**McMULLAN, R.** Macmillan dictionary of building. London, Macmillan, 1988. [iv], 262p. diagrs. ISBN: 0333424395.

Concisely defines *c*.5,000 words drawn 'from the written material used in current building practice' (*Preface*). Cross-references. Appended diagrams (that would be better placed in the text): brickwork (8 types); doors; heating; masonry tools; mouldings; roof; roof truss; stairs; timber joints; windows; woodworking tools. *Class No:* 69.0(038)=20

[7502]

PHILBIN, T. The Illustrated dictionary of building terms New York, etc, McGraw-Hill, 1997. pp. v, 249. illus. £28.95. ISBN: 007049729x.

About 15,000 terms briefly defined. Includes [US] slang terms, *e.g.* 'horsefeathers' (fill-in materials used when preparing a roof for new roofing material). *Class No:* 69.0(038)=20

[7503]

SCOTT, J.S., *ed* **and MACLEAN, J. The Penguin dictionary of building.** 4th ed. Harmondsworth, Middx. Penguin Books, 1994. x, 516p. illus., diagrs. £7.99. ISBN: 014051239x.

First published 1964; 3rd ed. 1984.

Defines and categorizes over 5,000 building trade, tools and materials terms, with illus. US usage is differentiated. Cross-references to Penguin *Dictionary of civil engineering*. For both professional builder and do-it-yourself enthusiast. *Class No:* 69.0(038)=20

German

[7504]

BUCKSCH, H. Wörterbuch für Architektur, Hochbau und Baustoffe. [Dictionary of architecture, building construction and material.] Wiesbaden, Bauverlag GmbH, 1974-76. 2v. ISBN: 3762512019; 3762507147.

1. *Deutsch-Englisch*. 1974. (2. Auf. 1980. 942p.).

2. *Englisch-Deutsch*. 1976. 1137p.

V.1 has 65,000 German-English entries in its 2nd ed. V.2 has 75,000 English-German entries. Intended to complement the other Bucksch technical dictionaries published by Bauverlag. Lacks visual aids. *Class No:* 69.0(038)=30

[7505]

GELBRICH, U. Dictionary of architecture and building. Amsterdam, Elsevier, 1989. 418p. £75.95. ISBN: 0444988645.

About 30,000 terms. Distinguishes occasionally American and British usage. Genders given. Covers architecture, building, carpentry, joinery, heating, plumbing, lighting, materials, etc. *Class No:* 69.0(038)=30

French

[7506]

MACLEAN, J. Elsevier's dictionary of building construction: English-French. Amsterdam, etc., Elsevier, 1989. 2v.

V.1. English-French. [viii],389p. £99.90. (ISBN: 0444429662).

V.2. French-English. ix,345p. £99.90. (ISBN: 044442931x).

Covers 'the basic vocabulary of the industry, with particular emphasis on mechanical and electrical services' (*Preface*). Differentiates American and British English. Brief bibliography. *Class No:* 69.0(038)=40

[7507]

MONTAGUE, D. Dictionary of building and civil engineering. [Dictionnaire du bâtiment et du génie civil] London, Spon, 1996. xvii, 450p. £40 ISBN: 0419191101.

English and French; over 20,000 entries in each language. Appendix A lists 'False friends or faux amis'— words in one language that look like the same word in another, but that have other, related or completely different meanings in the second language. *Class No:* 69.0(038)=40

[7508]

MONTEAU, P. Dictionnaire du bâtiment: français-anglais, anglais-français. [Dictionary of building: French-English, English-French.] Paris, La Maison du Dictionnaire, 1994. 304p. £24.95. ISBN: 2856080677.

A glossary intended for prefessionals in the building trade. Single, equivalent words, for the most part. *Class No:* 69.0(038)=40

Russian

[7509]

PUSHKAREV, V.L. *and* **SHCHEGOLEVA, A.M. Anglo-russkii i russko-angliiskii arkhitekturnostroitel'nyi slovar'.** Pod red. L.S. Yampolskogo. Kiev, Gozisdat. Lit. po Straitel'stvu i Arkhiteklur. SSSR. 1961. 841, [3]p.

English-Russian dictionary, p.9-590; Russian-English dictionary (p.591-803) of building and architectural terms. Abbreviations, p.803-41; weights and measures. *Class No:* 69.0(038)=82

Reports Literature

[7510]

BUILDING RESEARCH ESTABLISHMENT. Building Research Establishment digests. London, HM Stationery Office, 1983. 4v. illus., diagrs., charts. ea. £15.

1. *Building structure and services.* 318p.
1. *Building components and materials.* 2284p.
3. *Building performance.* 308p.
4. *Design and site procedures: defects and repairs.* 226p.

Brings together in 4 self-contained volumes (but with cross-references between them) the numerous BRE *Digests* that review every aspect of building technology. Each volume has a detailed index.

Individual *Digests* (nos.4 ... 324) are available at £1.25 apiece (minimum order, £3). *Class No:* 69.0(047)

Reviews & Abstracts

[7511]

BUILDING RESEARCH ESTABLISHMENT. Overseas building notes. Garston, Herts., Publication Sales, BRE. ea. £1.25 (minimum order, £3).

A lengthy series, providing information on housing in tropical and sub-tropical countries. The October 1987 list records 39 titles in print (nos. 139-192), *e.g.* 143. *Building in earthquake areas;* 176. *Building materials in the Arabian Gulf - their production and use;* 192. *Solar energy applications. Class No:* 69.0(048)

[7512]

International building science and structural abstracts. Dublin, New York, CITIS Ltd., 1972-. 4pa. $325. ISSN: 0791492x.

About 1,600 abastracts pa. No subject arrangement, but keyword index. Also available on CD-ROM. *Class No:* 69.0(048)

Periodicals

[7513]

GRETES, F.C. Directory of international periodicals and newsletters on the built environment. New York, Van Nostrand Reinhold, 1986. xiv, 175p. £20.65. ISBN: 0442230036.

1,199 annotated, evaluated entries. 16 sections: 1. Architecture - 2. Office practice - 3. Building types ... 7. Planning, environmental design, housing and transportation planning ... 9. Building and construction (p.101-126) - 10. Building services and systems - 11. Engineering - 12. Real estate development and facility planning ... Appended 'Indexes and abstracts' (including databases). Alphabetical index; Geographical index (Argentina ... Zimbabwe); Non-analytical subject index. Aims 'to assist professionals who are involved in the planning, design, construction, and preservation of the built environment'. *Class No:* 69.0(051)

Yearbooks & Directories

[7514]

OPUS '98 Building services design file. London, Builder Group, 1998. 560p. £70.

Contents: A-Z guide to products - Product directories - OPUS Library - Suppliers and trade names - Importers and distributors - British, European and international standards - CIBSE publications - Useful addresses. *Class No:* 69.0(058)

Published Series

[7515]

Mitchell's building series. London, Mitchell, 1979-. 7v. illus., diagrs., graphs, tables.

Internal components, by A. Blanc. 1994. £18.99.
External Components, by M. McEvoy. 1994. £18.99.
Environment & services. 1988. £10.95.
Finishes, by Y. Dean. 1996. £17.99.
Materials, by A. Everett. 1994. £19.99.
Structure and fabric, by J. Foster. 1994. 2v., ea.c.£20.
Water, sanitary and waste services for buildings, by A. Wise. 1985. £12.95.

The *Materials* volume (320p.), first published 1970, has 17 sections. 1. Properties generally - 2. Timber ... 4. Stones ... 6. Bricks and blocks ... 8. Concrete - 9. Metals ... 12. Glass - 13. Plastics and rubbers - 14. Adhesives - 15. Mortars for joining ... 17. Sealants. Detailed analytical index. *Class No:* 69.0(082.1)

Tables & Data Books

[7516]

BLACK, L., ed. Builder's reference book. 12th ed. London, Northwood Books, 1985. 440p. illus., tables. £45. ISBN: 0419158901.

First published 1951; 11th ed. 1980..

22 sections: 1. General office information ... 4. The standard measurement of building works (SMME. 6th ed.) - 5. Standard data ...

.... (contd.)

10. The bricklayer - 11. The carpenter and joiner ... 18. The heating engineer ... 22. The glazier. Trade associations; professional associations; information sources. 'Designed for use in the office or on the site' (*Preface*). *Class No:* 69.0(083)

[7517]

NEUFERT, E. Architects' data. 3rd ed. Oxford, Blackwell, 1987. 433p. illus., diagrs., plans, tables. £21.50. ISBN: 0632023392.

The original *Bauentwurfslehre* (Berlin, Ullstein) had its 26th ed. in 1968 (471p.); first English edition 1970.

Provides data for the initial planning of a building project. Over 200 building types covered under broad headings (community, commerce, leisure, etc.). Bibliography (655 items); index. *Class No:* 69.0(083)

[7518]

Planning: the architect's handbook. Mills, E.D. 10th ed. London, Butterworths, 1985. 658p. diagrs., plans. £63. ISBN: 0408012137.

Basic data and information (with drawings) that are essential preliminaries before planning various types of buildings. Although geared to situations and conventions in the UK, the data are applicable wherever building design is under consideration. *Class No:* 69.0(083)

Standards

[7519]

SMITH, M., ed. Manual of British Standards in building construction and specification. 2nd ed. London, BSI, in association with Hutchinson, 1987. 334p. illus., tables. £25. ISBN: 0091707609.

First published 1985.

CI/Sf/B tables 0-4, further subdivided. 0. Physical environment - 1. Building elements - 2. Contractors, firms - 3. Materials - 4. Activities, requirements. Analysis of relevant standards, providing basic information. Index precedes. 213 tables. *Class No:* 69.0(083.74)

Histories

[7520]

BOWYER, J. History of building. London, Crosby Lockwood Staples, 1973. [vi], 275p. illus. ISBN: 0258968613.

5 parts (27 chapters): 1. Evolution of structure - 2. Historical development of building materials and components - 3. Building in the Middle Ages - 4. Growth, urbanization, industrialization and legislation - 5. The role of professionalism. Glossary, p.260-6. Detailed, analytical index, p.267-75. 142 small, neat line-drawings and plans. For building surveying and architectural students. No bibliography. *Class No:* 69.0(091)

Great Britain

Histories

[7521]

SALZMAN, L.F. Building in England, down to 1540: a documentary history. Oxford, Clarendon Press, 1952. xvi, 629p. illus., facsims. (Reprinted, with corrections and additions, 1967. xvi. 637p).

A scholarly account, with lengthy appendices of documents, arranged chronologically, apart from quotations in the text. Footnote references to sources. Index to persons and places.
Class No: 69.0(410)(091)

[7522]

—DAVEY, N. Building in Britain: the growth and organization of building processes in Britain, from Roman times to the present day. London, Evans, 1964. 191p. illus.

A concise account for candidates taking the examinations of the Institute of Builders and the City and Guilds of London Institute, 'but worthy of a wider audience' (*Aslib book list*, V.29(10), October 1964. Entry no. 583). *Class No:* 69.0(410)(091)

Laws

[7523]

Building and site development laws and procedures: a manager's guide. London, Gee, 1996-. Looseleaf. £97. ISBN: 186089058x.

Updated by supplements (11: December 1998).

11 chapters: 1. The construction site - 2. Planning ... 4. Working on the site - 5. Health, Safety and CDM ... 7. The construction contract ... 9. Polluting the environment ... 11. Buying and selling land. Also, glossary/useful addresses and index. Comprehensive.
Class No: 69.0(410)(094.1)

[7524]
The building regulations explained and illustrated. Powell-Smith, V. *and* Billington, M.J., *eds*. 10th ed. Oxford, Blackwell Science, 1995. 768p. £27.50. ISBN: 0632039337.

First published 1967.

Covers building control, regulations and approved documents, structural stability, insulation, draining and waste disposal, heating, conservation. *Class No:* 69.0(410)(094.1)

Writing & Lecturing

[7525]
CHAPPELL, D. Standard letters for building contractors. 2nd ed. Oxford, Blackwell Scientific, 1994. xviii, 286p. £35. ISBN: 0632034521.

First published 1987.

More than 200 standard letters for use with forms of building contract and sub-contract. The letters cover tendering, contract documents, insurance, site operations, payment, extensions of time, loss and/or expense, determination, arbitration and completion, and sub-contractors. *Class No:* 69.0:001.81

Thesauri

[7526]
ROBERTS, M.J. Construction industry thesaurus. 2nd ed. London, Dept. of the Environment, Property Services Agency, 1976. 419p.

First published 1972.

14,000 key-words; A-Z and classified sequences. The abridged ed. (1976), by M.J. Roberts and C.M. Kenwards, lists 3,000 key-words. *Class No:* 69.0:025.43

[7527]
—BUILDING RESEARCH ESTABLISHMENT. Building Research thesaurus. 2nd ed. Garston, Herts., BRE, 1975. vii, 270p.

Compiled by the library of the Building Research Establishment. *Class No:* 69.0:025.43

Information Services

[7528]
CONSTRUCTION INDUSTRY RESEARCH AND INFORMATION ASSOCIATION. The CIRIA UK construction information guide. Richardson, B. London, E. & F.N. Spon, 1989. xi,361p. £37.50. ISBN: 0419148906.

First published 1979.

Part 1: Alphabetical list of UK local authorities (but not identifying the relevant specific departments); part 2: Alphabetical list of UK construction information sources (p.39-283). No references to HMSO publications (including The Building Regulations); no mention of BRIX, etc. databases. Subject and acronym keys. Dated but still valuable. *Class No:* 69.0:061:025.5

Institutions & Associations

[7529]
ARMITAGE, J.S. Guide to international organizations of interest to the construction industry. London, Construction Industry Research and Information Association, 1982. (*CIRIA Special publication 24.*) ISBN: 0860171949.

32 international organizations: CICIND (International Committee on Industrial Chimneys) ... UIDC (International Union of Building Centres). Data on each include membership, aims, objectives and scope; activities; liaison with other bodies; publications. Appendices: 1. Sources of information - 2. Short guide to international organizations concerned with Standards. - 3. Glossary of acronyms used. Small format. *Class No:* 69.0:061:061.2

[7530]
International directory of building research, information and development organizations. International Council for Building Research, Studies and Documentation (CIB). Sebestyén, G. *and* Pollington, C.E. 5th ed. London, Spon, 1986. ISBN: 0419129901.

First published 1959.

2 main groups: International organizations; National organizations - (Argentina ... Zimbabwe). Data on each include status; main fields of work; total staff; name of director and chief executive; principal sources of finance; principal related bodies; publications. Covers 640 building research organizations in 54 countries. Organization index; Personnel index; Subject index. *Class No:* 69.0:061:061.2

[7531]
An International directory of building research organizations. United States. National Research Council. Washington, DC, National Academy Press, 1989. viii,228p. $27.95; £24.10. ISBN: 0309040272.

2 parts: 1. United States - 2. International (Argentina-Yugoslavia). Data include name; contact person; research focus; 'distinctive attributes'; publications. Indexes: organizations; subjects. *Class No:* 69.0:061:061.2

Research Projects

[7532]
GREAT BRITAIN. Department of the Environment *and* **DEPARTMENT OF TRANSPORT. Register of research, 1974-.** London, HQ Library, DOE/DTp, 1974-.

1. *Building and construction.*
2. *Environmental planning.*
3. *Roads and transport.*
4. *Environmental pollution.*

Part 1, *Building and construction,* for 1978 (the last to be published) had entries for c.1,000 research projects in this field in the UK. Based on data from a wide variety of organizations. Subject sections were followed by a list of research organizations, and indexes of research sponsors, research workers, and organizations. Detailed analytical subject index.

This valuable record of research is now online, ENREP (ECHO host) as part of a European Communities effort. *Class No:* 69.0:061:061.62.005

Metrication

[7533]
TUTT, P. *and* **ADLER, D. New metric handbook.** Rev. and exp. ed. London, Architectural Press, 1981, reprinted 1995. [viii], 504p. tables.

First published 1968 as *AJ metric handbook.*

48 sections. 1. Introduction - 2. Basic metric system and SI units - 3. Notation and drawing office practice ... 12. Factories ... 16. Offices ... 18. Hospitals ... 23. Theatres ... 25. Water sports and recreation ... 29. Church buildings - 30. Schools ... 32. Laboratories ... 34. Libraries - 35. Housing ... 39. Materials ... 41. Thermal comfort ... 43. Light ... 45. Structure ... 48. Window cleaning. Applied conversion factors and tables. Analytical index (small type), p.502-4. Attractively produced. *Class No:* 69.0:351.821

Machinery & Equipment

[7534]
CHABALLE, L.Y. *and* **VANDENBERGHE, J.-P. Elsevier's dictionary of building tools and materials,** in five languages: English/American, French, Spanish, German and Dutch. Amsterdam, etc., Elsevier, 1982. [xi], 722p. £155. ISBN: 0444420479.

5,853 English/American terms (with synonyms and variants), plus equivalents and indexes in the other 4 languages. Bibliography of sources precedes, p.[ix]-[x]. *Class No:* 69.0-1

Estimates

[7535]
GEDDES, S. Estimating for building and civil engineering works. 8th ed., edited by G. Chrystal-Smith. London, etc., Butterworths, 1985. viii, 424p. charts, tables. ISBN: 0408015578.

First published 1951.

30 sections (4. Costing the works of construction; 11. The working cost of plant; 13. Excavation earthwork below ground; 15. Brickwork and blockwork; 25. Drainage; 27. Plate laying; 30. Useful tables). 2 new sections: 5. Dayworks; 28. Landscaping. Numerous tables; explanatory notes; worked examples. Detailed, analytical index, p.415-24. *Class No:* 69.003.12

[7536]
Laxton's guide to budget estimating. Oxford, Butterworth-Heinemann, 1996. xvi, 238p. ISBN: 0750629673.

Provides guidance to budget estimating for construction project managers. Covers new building, refurbishment, civil engineering, landscaping and M&E systems. *Class No:* 69.003.12

[7537]
Laxton's national building price book, 1996. East Grinstead, West Sussex, Reed International, 1996. xli, 739p. tables, maps. £70. ISBN: 0611008890.

Sections: Major works - Small works - General information - Brands and trade names - Company information. Index precedes. Available on computer disk for pc. *Class No:* 69.003.12

[7538]
Means estimating handbook. Goldman, J.M. Kingston, Mass., Means, 1990. 905p. tables. $89.95. ISBN: 0876291779.

Tables and formulas for calculating construction costs using price information provided by the user. 3 sections: 1. Material type - 2. Equipment - 3. Internal building systems. Includes checklists, abbreviations, list of professional organizations. US slanted. *Class No:* 69.003.12

[7539]

Spon's architects' and builders' price book, 1999. 124th ed. London, Spon, 1998. xxvii, 912p. tables. £75. ISSN: 03063046.

First published 1873.

5 parts: 1. Fees and daywork - 2. Rates of wages - 3. Prices for measured work - 4. Approximate estimating - 5. Tables and memoranda. Numerous tables. Detailed, analytical index (p.1023-43). *Class No:* 69.003.12

Buildings

Handbooks & Manuals

[7540]

Historic floors: their history and conservation. Fawcett, J., *ed*. Oxford, Butterworth-Heinemann, 1998. x, 250p. illus., diagrs. £60. ISBN: 0750627654.

Published in association with the International Council on Museums and Sites, UK.

20 chapters covering important floors and methods for recording, preserving and restoring them. The emphasis is on floors in the UK, but the techniques for dealing with problems have wider application. Glossary; appendix ('Cathedral floor studies — identification of areas at risk and location of historic features'). Estensive reading list, p.229-35. *Class No:* 69.02(035)

[7541]

KNIGHT, J. *and* **JONES, P. Building services pocket book.** Oxford, Butterworth-Heinemann, 1995. x, 382p. diagrs., graphs, tables. £14.99. ISBN: 0750621486.

Covers energy, heating, air conditioning, automatic controls, fans pipework, fire protection, water services and drainage in 16 chapters. Small format; practical approach. *Class No:* 69.02(035)

[7542]

POWELL, M.J.V., ed. House builder's reference book. London, Newnes-Butterworth, 1979. [1120]p. illus., tables. ISBN: 0408003375.

59 contributors. Sections (64 subsections): Management - Design - Construction - Services - Finishes - General (subsection 64: Sources of building information: organizations; publications and bookshops; technical press). Subsection 45, Glazing (12p.) has five headings, with appended further information (trade associations; British Standards; other sources of information, *e.g.* BRE Digests). Index of 16p. *Class No:* 69.02(035)

[7543]

PYE, P.W. *and* **HARRISON, H.W. Floors and flooring:** performance, diagnosis, maintenance, repair and the avoidance of defects. London, Construction Research communications, 1997. vii, 304p. illus., diagrs. £39.50. (*BRE building elements*.) ISBN: 1860811736.

Describes the materials, production methods and criteria used in the construction of floors. 8 chapters, closely subdivided: 1. Basic function - 2. Suspended floors and ceilings - 2. Solid floors - 4. Screeds, underlays and underlayments - 5. Jointless floor finishes - 6. Jointed resilient finishes - 7. Jointed hard finishes - 8. Timber and timber products. References and further reading, p.285-94. *Class No:* 69.02(035)

Dictionaries

[7544]

Concise dictionary of house building terms. Lindsey, A.S., *comp*. Ferndown, Dorset, Hadley Pager, 1993. [iv], 240p. £25. ISBN: 1872739024.

In French and English, with about 10,000 terms in each half arranged by 14 trades: Architect - Foundations - Builder - Carpenter and joiner - Woods and Veneers - Roofer - Ironmonger - Metals - Plumber - Glazier - Electrician - Plasterer - Painter and decorator - Colours *Class No:* 69.02(038)

[7545]

KUT, D. Illustrated encyclopedia of building services. London, Spon, 1993. 355p. illus., diagrs. £70. ISBN: 0419176802.

More a dictionary than an encyclopedia. About 3,000 terms, briefly defined (*e.g.* 'fin drain': 12 lines). *Class No:* 69.02(038)

Standards

[7546]

Time-saver standards for building types. De Chiava, J. *and* Callender, J.H., *eds*. 3rd ed. New York, McGraw-Hill, 1990. xvii,1413p. illus. £74. ISBN: 0070162794.

First published 1973; 2nd ed. 1980.

Covers standards, procedures and devices for 11 types of buildings (residential; educational, etc.). Extensively illustrated. *Class No:* 69.02(083.74)

Equipment & Instruments

[7547]

STEIN, B. *and* **REYNOLDS, J.S. Mechanical and electrical equipment for buildings.** 8th ed. New York, Wiley, 1992. xxxi,1627p. illus., diagrs., graphs, tables. £54. ISBN: 0471525022.

First published 1937.

10 parts: 1. Energy overview - 2. Thermal control - 3. Water and waste - 4. Fire protection - 5. Electricity - 6. Illumination - 7. Signal equipment - 8. Transportation - 9. Acoustics - 10. Appendices (11 in all). Nearly 300 tables. Detailed, analytical index, p.1609-27. *Class No:* 69.02:002.50

Roofs

[7548]

WICKERSHAM, J.H. The David & Charles manual of roofing. Newton Abbot, Devon, David & Charles, 1987. 256p. illus., diagrs., graphs, tables. ISBN: 0715386980.

9 chapters: 1. Roofing and the spare-time builder - 2. Recreational and storage buildings - 3. Flat roofs - 4/6. Pitched roofs - 7. Ventilation, insulation and flashing - 8. Maintaining and repairing roofs - 9. Designing, constructing and repairing rainwater drainage systems. 2 appendices: 1. Tables; 2. Address list (British associations (products in bold) products), p.239-50. Detailed, analytical index, p.251-6. Fully illustrated (150 photographs). *Class No:* 69.024

Roof Coverings

[7549]

BRITISH STANDARDS INSTITUTION. Glossary of building and civil engineering terms. Part 1. General and miscellaneous. Section 1.3. Parts of construction works. Subsection 1.3.2 Roofs and roofing. London, BSI, 1989. 30p. AMD 7232. (*BS 6100: Subsection 1.3.2:1989(1997)*.)

Supersedes BS 2717: 1985.

Terms in systematic order. Sections: 1. Roof types - 2. Roof features - 3. General roofing - 4. Tile, slate and shale roofing - 5. Sheet roofing - 6. Thatch - 7. Properties - 8. Roofing joints and jointing products. Alphabetical index. *Class No:* 69.024.1

Building Materials

Bibliographies

[7550]

ADDERLEY, P. 'Executing the design: materials, structures, construction'. *Information sources in architecture and construction.* V.J. Nurcombe, ed. (3rd ed., 1996), p.277-316. 3rd ed. London, Bowker-Saur, 1996. £68; $100. (*Guide to information sources.*) ISBN: 1857390946.

Provides a comprehensive survey of the information sources in the field, including legislation, directories, dictionaries, data, official publications, specific materials, *e.g.* brick, etc. *Class No:* 691(01)

Handbooks & Manuals

[7551]

Construction materials reference book. Doran, D.K., *ed*. Oxford, Butterworth-Heinemann, 1992. v.p. illus., diagrs., tables. £95; $205. ISBN: 0750610042.

2 parts: 1. Metals - 2. Non-metals. Topics include cement, concrete, ceramics, timber, stone, aluminium, steel, etc. Chapters identify relevant British standards. Several hundred literature references. 'Recommended' (*Choice,* November 1992, p.500). *Class No:* 691(035)

[7552]

Green building handbook. Wooley, T., *and others, eds*. London, Spon, 1997. 224p. diagrs., graphs. £29.95. ISBN: 0419226907.

Considers the environmental issues which relate to the production, use and disposal of key building products and materials. Section on 'Best buys' ranks products from lowest to highest environmental impact. A useful survey of an increasingly important topic. *Class No:* 691(035)

[7553]

HUNTINGTON, W.C., *and others*. **Building construction materials and types of construction.** 3rd ed. New York, etc., Wiley, 1981. 471p. illus., diagrs., tables. ISBN: 0471053546.

10 chapters: 1. General data - 2. Sitework - 3. Concrete - 4. Masonry - 5. Metals - 6. Wood and plaster - 7. Thermal and moisture protection - 8. Doors and windows - 9. Finishes - 10. Acoustical control in buildings. References and recommended reading, p.436-46. Detailed, analytical index, p.447-70. Quarto. For students of architecture and building technology. *Class No:* 691(035)

[7554]

STULZ, R. *and* MUKERJI, K. **Appropriate building materials:** a catalogue of potential solutions. 3rd ed. St. Gallen, Switzerland, SKAT/Intermediate Technology, 1993. 434p. illus. £14.95. ISBN: 3908001447.

3 main parts: 1. General information on raw materials, the processing and use of building materials, design guidelines and protective measures - 2. Catalogue of traditional and experimental applications of building materials - 3. Practical implementation. Covers traditional (e.g. stone, concrete) as well as alternative (e.g. grasses, bamboo) materials. Appendix lists addresses for information on construction in various countries. Detailed, analytical index. *Class No:* 691(035)

[7555]

TAYLOR, G.D. **Construction materials.** London, Longman, 1991. 544p. £49.99. ISBN: 0582042992.

Covers properties of metals, concrete, ceramics, fibrous composites and siliceous materials. Includes standards. *Class No:* 691(035)

Dictionaries

[7556]

BIANCHINA, P. **Illustrated dictionary of building materials and techniques.** 2nd ed. New York, Wiley, 1993. xi, 238p. diagrs. ISBN: 0417576579.

First published 1986

Defines *c.*4,500 terms, covering building, plumbing, electrical writing, hardware, architecture, heating and ventilating. 500 line-drawings ('Window': 15 types). Nearly 60p. of appendices on conversions, abbreviations, hardware, etc. *Class No:* 691(038)

Tables & Data Books

[7557]

WADDELL, J.J. **Construction materials ready reference manual.** New York, etc., McGraw-Hill, 1985. 395p. illus., diagrs., charts. ISBN: 0070676496.

Properties and selection of materials - Rock and soils - Concrete - Masonry - Lath and plaster - Metals - Wood - Plastics - Paint - Roofing and asphalt - Pipes. 71 illus. Small format. *Class No:* 691(083)

Trade Names, Trade Marks, Brand Names

[7558]

Barbour Index building product compendium '99. Windsor, Barbour Index, 1999. 1011p. col. illus. £105. ISSN: 09689079.

25 sections (Buildings and building systems ... Formless materials). Covers more than 1,450 product ranges, illustrated in colour, plus captioned details - physical data plus performance characteristics. Index to products precedes. Appended: Manufacturers/Trade names (on blue-tinted paper). *Class No:* 691(088.7)

Histories

[7559]

DAVEY, N. **A History of building materials.** London, Phoenix, 1961. xiv, [5], 260p. illus. (incl. pl.), diagrs., plans, charts.

26 documented chapters (1. Stone - 2. Building in stone - 3. Earth walling ... 24. Water supply and sanitation - 25. Metals - 26. Modern trends). Appended 'Building tools', p.223-37 (selected traditional tools, with over 100 line-drawings). Analytical index to text. Profusely illustrated: 48p. of plates. Well produced. Examples are drawn almost entirely from Europe and the Near East. *Class No:* 691(091)

[7560]

Twentieth-century building materials: history and conservation. Jester, T.C., *ed.* New York, etc., McGraw-Hill, 1995. 352p. illus. ISBN: 0070325731.

Materials covered include metals, concrete, wood and plastics, masonry, glass, and products used for flooring, roofing, siding and walls. Provides historical information, identification of brand names, discussions of conservation issues and approaches, and guidance for research. Extensive notes and bibliography, p.272-332; sources for research, p.333-43. Focus is on buildings in the US. A beautiful book. *Class No:* 691(091)

Wood

[7561]

BRITISH STANDARDS INSTITUTION. **Glossary of terms relating to timber preservation.** London, BSI, 1985. 24p. (*BS 4261: 1985 (1997).*)

Defines 484 terms, in 6 sections: 1. General - 2. Attack by fungi - 3. Attack by insects and marine borers - 4. Preservative processes - 5. Terms associated with preservative treatments - 6. Miscellaneous. Index. *Class No:* 691.11

[7562]

Handbook of wood and wood-based materials for engineers, architects and builders. United States. Department of Agriculture. Forest Service. Forest Products Laboratory. Rev. ed. New York, Hemisphere, 1989. v.p. illus., diagrs., graphs, tables. $77. ISBN: 0891161244.

First published 1935 as *Wood handbook;* previous ed. 1974.

23 chapters of the properties, applications and treatments of wood. Numerous tables. Glossary, p. G1-G11. 12p. detailed, analytical index. Emphasis is on US. *Class No:* 691.11

[7563]

LAVERS, G.M. **The Strength properties of timber.** 3rd ed., revised by G.L. Moore. London, HM Stationery Office, 1983. 64p. £4.95. (*BRE Reports, 50 3.8.*) ISBN: 0116713569.

Physical and mechanical tests on over 200 hardwoods and softwoods (both seasoned and unseasoned): procedures and results. *Class No:* 691.11

[7564]

Wood engineering and construction handbook. Faherty, K.F. *and* Williamson, T.G., *eds.* New York, etc., Mc-Graw Hill, 1997. v.p. illus., diagrs., graphs, tables. $89.95 ISBN: 0070220700.

Information, formulas, procedures and examples for the design of wood structures or structural wood components. 13 contributors; 12 chapters: 3. Columns ... 6. Trusses ... 11. Wood foundation structures - 12. Adhesives. Appendices include 11 tables of reference data. Detailed, analytical index. *Class No:* 691.11

Stone

[7565]

SHORE, B.C.G. **Stones in Britain:** a practical guide to those in charge of valuable buildings. London, Hill, 1957. xii, 302p. illus., maps.

Thorough investigation of geological and chemical questions involved in the use of stone for building; also the stone-preservation problems. 4 main sections: care of ancient buildings; list of British building stones, their occurrence and structure; maintenance work, using stone; new buildings of stone, and stone for sculpture. Lavishly illustrated with fine photographs and maps. *Class No:* 691.2

Concrete

[7566]

BARKER, J.A. **Dictionary of concrete.** Lancaster, Construction Press, 1984. 124p. £16.

5,000 precise definitions. Includes major terms used in other countries, particularly the US. *Class No:* 691.32

[7567]

WADDELL, J.J. *and* DOBROWOLSKI, J.A. **Concrete construction handbook.** 3rd ed. New York, etc., McGraw-Hill, 1993. v.p. illus., graphs, tables. $92.50. ISBN: 0070676666.

First published 1968; 2nd ed. 1974.

18 contributors. Extensive references to relevant ASTM standards. The 3rd ed. includes new sections on architectural concrete and roller-compressed concrete. Well illustrated; detailed, analytical index. *Class No:* 691.32

Building Trades

Bricklaying

[7568]

BRICK DEVELOPMENT ASSOCIATION. **Bricks, their properties and use.** Lancaster, Construction Press, 1984. 251p. illus., diagrs., graphs, tables. ISBN: 0904406040.

Main sections: Basic information - Bricks in use - Technical information (p.91-248) ... Performance characteristics of perforated and solid bricks ... The stability of a five-storey brickwork cross-wall structure. Index. p.249-51. *Class No:* 693.22

[7569]
LLOYD, N. A History of English brickwork, with examples and notes of the architectural use and manipulation of brick, from medieval times to the end of the Georgian period. Woodbridge, Suffolk, Antique Collectors' Club, 1983. xi, 449p. illus., diagrs., tables. £25. ISBN: 0907482967.

First published 1926.

Text occupies p.1-100, the remainder being almost wholly illustrative, - photographs and measured drawings. Table of brick sizes. Data on prices, wages and output. 'Manipulation of brick' includes curved brick; stairs, vaulting, arcading; fonts, fireplaces, tables; pinnacles. Index. p.441-9. 360 illus. *Class No:* 693.22

Plastering

[7570]
BRITISH STANDARDS INSTITUTION. Glossary of building and civil engineering terms. Part 6. Concrete and plaster. Section 6.6 Products, applications and operations. Subsection 6.6.2 Plaster. London, BSI, 1990. 36p. (*BS 6100: Subsection 6.6.2: 1990(1997).*)

Supersedes BS 4049: 1966.

259 terms defined in systematic order. Alphabetical index. *Class No:* 693.6

Timber Construction & Carpentry

[7571]
RICHARDSON, B.A. Wood in construction. London, Construction Press, 1976. 220p. illus., facsims., tables.

Sections: 1. Wood as a material - 2. Converting trees to wood in service - 3. Wood protection - 4. Wood utilization - 5. Commercial woods and wood products. 3 appendices: Botanical classification of principal north temperate timber trees; Wood structure; Commercial woods. Index to common names, p.199-214. General index. *Class No:* 694.1

[7572]
TEKNISKA NOMENKLATURCENTRALEN. Träbyggnardsordlista. [Glossary of timber construction.] Stockholm, the Centre, 1973. 224p. illus. (*TNC 60.*)

725 Swedish entry-words and definitions; English, French and German equivalents. Classified arrangement; German, French, English and Swedish indexes. Swedish references p.10-11. Small line-drawings. A neat production. *Class No:* 694.1

Plumbing

[7573]
BRITISH STANDARDS INSTITUTION. Glossary of building and civil engineering terms. Part 3. Services. Section 3.3 Sanitation. London, BSI, 1992. 40p. (*BS 6100: Section 3.3: 1992(1998).*)

Supersedes BS 6100: Section 3.3: 1991.

444 plumbing and water supply terms defined in systematic order. Alphabetical index. *Class No:* 696.1

[7574]
HALL, E. The David & Charles manual of home plumbing. 2nd ed. Newton Abbot, Devon, David & Charles, 1992. 208p. illus., diagrs. ISBN: 0715300172.

Furst published 1982.

Covers taps, cisterns, lavatory suites, drains, hot water supply, frosts, handling plumbing materials. Project suggestions. Good, clear illustrations. *Class No:* 696.1

[7575]
JACOBSON, I.D., *ed.* Plumbing dictionary. 3rd ed. Cleveland, Ohio, American Society of Sanitary Engineering. [1], ix, 150p. illus.

First published 1971.

Over 3,000 definitions, giving pronunciation. Includes abbreviations. Cross references; tiny line-drawings. Bibliography, p.vi-viii. 'Wherever possible, non-technical language has been used' (*Foreword*). *Class No:* 696.1

[7576]
Plumbing engineering services design. Rev. ed. Hornchurch, Essex, Institute of Plumbing, 1988. [iv], 268p. diagrs., graphs, tables. ISBN: 0950167185.

First published 1977.

14 sections, A-N: A. Hot and cold water supplies ... D. Pumps and pumping ... G. Steam supplies ... I. Designing for the disabled - J. Legionnaires disease ... N. Conversion factors and miscellaneous data (*e.g.* glossary; useful addresses). Comprehensive and practical. *Class No:* 696.1

[7577]
TRELOAR, R.D. Plumbing encyclopaedia 2nd ed. Oxford, Blackwell Science, 1996. vi, 568p. illus., diagrs. £16.99. ISBN: 0632040564.

First ed. 1989, as *Mechanical engineering services: a plumbing encyclopaedia.*

About 1500 entries, A-Z. Covers water supplies, sanitation, drainage, oil and gas supplies, heating and general building science. *Class No:* 696.1

Heating & Ventilation

Bibliographies

[7578]
HASELER, A.E. District heating: an annotated bibliography. 2nd ed. Croydon, Surrey, Property Services Agency, 1977. xi, 130p.

660 numbered and annotated entries in 18 sections, subdivided and covering electricity environmental aspects, heating and cooling systems, architectural and building viewpoints, plus government policies and initiatives in both Britain and abroad. 'Brief history of district heating' precedes. Many cross-references. Geographical and name indexes. *Class No:* 697(01)

Handbooks & Manuals

[7579]
ASHRAE handbook. Atlanta, Ga., American Society of Heating, Refrigerating and Air-Conditioning Engineers, 1992-. 4v. ISSN: 10412344.

First published 1961. As *ASHRAE handbook and product directory,* 1974-77. 4v., now divided into *ASHRAE handbook* and annual *ASHRAE product information file. Fundamentals.* 1993. *Systems and Equipment.* 1992. *HVAC Applications.* 1995. *Refrigeration.* 1994.

Fundamentals, by various contributors, concerns basic principles, general engineering data, load calculations, duct and pipe sizing. Indexes. A detailed survey of US practice. *Class No:* 697(035)

[7580]
CIBSE guides. London, Chartered Institute of Building Services, 1986-97. 3v. £170, the set.

A. *Design data.* B. *Installation and equipment data.* C. *Reference data.* D. *Transportation systems in buildings.* E. *Fire engineering.*

Authoritative guides for designers planning heating, lighting and other installations in buildings. CIBS (Chartered Institute of Building Services) was formed by the amalgamation of the Institute of Heating and Ventilating Engineers and the Illuminating Engineering Society. For professionals. *Class No:* 697(035)

[7581]
WANG, S.K. Handbook of air conditioning and refrigeration. New York, McGraw-Hill, 1993. v.p. illus., diagrs. graphs. ISBN: 0070681384.

32 chapters, closely sub-divided, with references. Includes numerous case studies from a range of situations. Detailed, analytical index, 13p. A comprehensive treatment. *Class No:* 697(035)

Dictionaries

Polyglot

[7582]
International dictionary of heating, ventilating and air conditioning. Compiled by the Documentation Committee of the Representatives of European Heating and Ventilating Associations. 2nd ed. London, Spon, 1994. liii, 793p. £85. ISBN: 041915390x.

First published 1982.

Over 4,000 terms in 12 languages, - Dutch, English, French, German, Hungarian, Italian, Polish, Russian (entries in cyrillic), Spanish, Swedish, Danish and Finnish. English-base terms, with equivalents and indexes in the other languages. *Class No:* 697(038)=00

English

[7583]
BOOTH, K.M., *comp.* Dictionary of refrigeration and air conditioning. Amsterdam, etc., Elsevier, 1970. viii, 315p. . £21. ISBN: 044420069x.

More than 2,600 terms from both sides of the Atlantic are defined in entries ranging from a few words to more than 200. Copious cross-references. Author's Preface insists 'The book is a dictionary and not an encyclopedia'. Because of the impending changeover to use of SI units at the time of publication, metric equivalents to Imperial units are frequently given. Inevitably lacks terms relating to important recent developments (*e.g.* new refrigerants, use of computer and microprocessor control methods) but sound, descriptive definitions of fundamental material make this a brief dictionary of continuing importance in its field. *Class No:* 697(038)=20

[7584]

BRITISH STANDARDS INSTITUTION. Glossary of refrigeration, heating, ventilating and air-conditioning terms. London, BSI, 1984. 88p. (*BS 5643: 1984*.)

Supersedes BS 1584 and BS 5643: 1979.

Contains around 2,300 terms, of which more than one third are cross-references, many to noun/adjective forms from the alternative (*e.g.* dark smoke *see* smoke, dark), apparently assuming that the reader will overlook the clear explanation of policy in the Foreword! Concise definitions. *Class No:* 697(038)=20

[7585]

BRITISH STANDARDS INSTITUTION. Glossary of terms related to solid fuel burning equipment. London, BSI, 1968-94. 2pts. £17.90 + £11. (*BS 1846: 1968*.)

First published 1952.

Pt.1. *Domestic appliances.* 1994. 36p.

Pt.2. *Industrial water heating and steam raising installations.* 1968 (1984). 20p.

Pt.1 defines *c.*250 terms; pt.2, *c.*100, each with 10 sections and an index. *Class No:* 697(038)=20

Reviews & Abstracts

[7586]

International building services abstracts (IBSEDEX). Bracknell, Berks., Building Services Research and Information Association (BSRIA, formerly Heating and Ventilating Research Association), v.13(1), 1978-. 6pa. £90pa.

Formerly *Thermal abstracts,* 1966-77, v.1-12. Initially as *HVRF bulletin,* 1952-69, and then *HVRA library bulletin,* 1960-65.

About 2,000 abstracts pa. 21 sections (Building services in general - Heating - District heating and cooling ... Lighting - Instruments ... Building structures - Thermal insulation - Management and organization). On line, IBSEDEX. *Class No:* 697(048)

Tables & Data Books

[7587]

PARMLEY, R.O. HVAC design data sourcebook. New York, McGraw-Hill, 1994. 489p., graphs, tables. $49.50. ISBN: 0070485720.

Sections: Basic data and fundamentals - Heat loss estimating - Building materials properties - Heating fuel data and systems - Ventilating and air-conditioning systems - Piping design - Air distribution and duct design - Energy conservation - Climatic data - Standards and symbols - Metric data and conversion. Extensive tables and graphs. 'A wealth of information' (*Choice*, January 1995, p.821). *Class No:* 697(083)

[7588]

PORGES, F. HVAC engineer's handbook. 10th ed. Oxford, Butterworth-Heinemann, 1996. [vii], 278p. illus. tables. ISBN: 0750625945.

First published 1942; 9th ed. 1991 as *Handbook of heating, ventilating and air conditioning.*

17 sections, mainly tabular. 1. Abbreviations, symbols and conversions - 2. Standards for materials ... 4. Heat and thermal properties of materials ... 8. Heating systems ... 11. Ventilation - 12. Air conditioning ... 14. Sound - 15. Labour rates - 16. Bibliography (grouped) - 17. Standards. Detailed, analytical index. *Class No:* 697(083)

Europe

[7589]

LEWIS, O. The European passive solar handbook. London, Batsford, 1992. 304p. illus. £40. ISBN: 0713469188.

Design information on passive solar architecture. Review of the EC solar programme. *Class No:* 697(4)

[7590]

PALZ, W. *and* STEEMERS, T.C., *eds*. Solar houses in Europe: how they have worked. Compiled and written by W. Houghton-Evans. Oxford, etc., Pergamon Press, for the Commission of the European Communities. 303p. diagrs., graphs, tables, maps. ISBN: 0080267432.

Prepared within the framework of the European Communities Solar Energy Research and Development Programme.

7 chapters (2. How the buildings have performed - 3. Lessons from the survey - 4. Recommendations for design - 5. Statistical summaries - 6. Monitoring - 7. Reports on 31 projects (Denmark ... UK), p.80-303). Glossary. Location maps. *Class No:* 697(4)

Painting & Decorating

[7591]

FULCHER, A., *and others*. Painting and decorating: an information manual. 4th ed. Oxford Blackwell Science, 1998. 296p. illus., tables. £15.99. ISBN: 0632041595.

First published 1975.

Covers tools, equipment, scaffolding, surface coatings, glazing, colour, health and safety, etc. Includes guidance on specifying. Well illustrated, keyed line-drawings being a feature. *Class No:* 698.1

[7592]

GOODIER, J.H. Dictionary of painting and decorating, covering also allied industrial finishes. 3rd ed. London, C. Griffin, 1987. xi, 422p. £32.50. ISBN: 0852642792.

First published 1961.

About 1,500 entries (*e.g.* 'Metal spraying': 1p.; 'Lead paint - statutory regulations': 3p.). Conversion factors and tables precede. Cross-references. An encyclopaedic dictionary for craftsmen, students and teachers. *Class No:* 698.1

[7593]

JOHNSON, L. The Decorator's directory. London, M. Joseph, 1981. 318p. illus. (incl. col.). ISBN: 0718120036.

31 sections (*e.g.* Appliances & kitchen accessories; Architectural ornaments; Bathrooms; Bedrooms; Blinds; Carpeting; Kitchens ... Special furniture; Storage; Tables; Upholstered furniture; Wall coverings co-ordination). Useful addresses. Index of suppliers; index of catalogues. Subdivision under companies gives details and prices. Attractively produced. *Class No:* 698.1

Insulation

[7594]

BRITISH STANDARDS INSTITUTION. Glossary of terms relating to thermal insulation. London, BSI, 1981. 16p. (*BS 3533: 1981*.)

About 200 terms in a systematic order. Alphabetical index. *Class No:* 699.86

Author / Title Index

The index reference is to the running number given to each item. The running numbers are in one sequence throughout the volume and can be found at the top right-hand corner of the entry for each item.

This index is of authors and titles in one sequence. The names of the authors are printed in bold type. Where works are jointly authored, only the first name is indexed. All books and periodicals listed or mentioned in the text, except where cited as the source of review quotations or for purposes of comparison, are entered under the headings given. All entries in *Walford* have title entries in the index; where the main heading in *Walford* is under title, added entries to the index have usually been made for an editor or compiler.

Filing is word by word, with groups of initials counted as single words. Since *Walford* uses only initials and not forenames it may occasionally happen that titles by different authors with the same surname and initials are found grouped together.

The arrangement of entries under an author is alphabetically by title. To save space, most sub-titles have been omitted, and many lengthy titles have been shortened.

1:50,000 maps **1594**
100 modern reagents **1225**
100 statistical tests **656**
100 years in mathematics **581**
100 years of industrial property statistics **3183**
5001 hard-to-find publishers and their addresses **6222**
The A to Z of shopping by post **6031**
A to Z of thermodynamics **1074**
A-Z of clinical chemistry **2326**
A-Z of European brands **3130**
An A-Z of gynaecology **3895**
The A-Z of modern herbalism **3683**
The A-Z of nutritional health **3534**
An A-Z of offshore oil & gas **4800, 6767**
A-Z of sport's cars since 1946 **5321**
AA guide to hotels and restaurants in Britain and Ireland **5983**
AA hotel guide **5983**
Abbott, D.
The Biographical dictionary of scientists: chemists **1205**
The Biographical dictionary of scientists: engineers and inventors **3957**
The Biographical dictionary of scientists: physicists **978**
Mathematicians **589**
Abbott, R.T. *and* Dance, S.P.
Compendium of seashells **2788**
ABBR: abbreviations for scientific and engineering terms **33**
Abbreviations and acronyms in technology **3011**
Abbreviations dictionary **34**
Abbreviations used by FAO **5489**
ABC Biologie **2147**
ABC freight guide **6279**
Abel, E.L.
A Dictionary of drug abuse terms and terminology **3575**
Abell, G.O.
Exploration of the universe **684**
Abercrombie, M.
The New Penguin dictionary of biology **2162**
ABHB **6144**
Abkürzungen in der technik **3011**
Aboriginal tribes of Australia **2131**
ABPI compendium of patient information leaflets **3667**
Abramowitz, M. *and* Stegun, I.A.
Handbook of mathematical functions **626**
Abstract bulletin of the Institute of Paper Science and Technology **7042**
Abstract journal in earthquake engineering **1511, 5000**
Abstracting services **223**
Abstracts and abridgements of patent specifications **3170**

Abstracts and indexes in science and technology **225**
Abstracts (Graphic Arts Technical Foundation) **6193**
Abstracts in anthropology **2006**
Abstracts in biocommerce **2996**
Abstracts in German anthropology **2007**
Abstracts in new technologies and engineering **3046**
Abstracts of entomology **2818**
Abstracts of mycology **2649**
Abstracts on hygiene and communicable diseases **3524, 3863**
Academic Press dictionary of science and technology **115**
Academic Press dictionary of science and technology on CD-ROM **115**
Académie des Sciences. Paris
Index biographique des membres et correspondents de l'Académie des Sciences, du 22 décembre 1666 au 1 Octobre 1978 **382**
Academy of Natural Sciences of Philadelphia
Catalog of the Library. [Academy of Natural Sciences of Philadelphia] **2378**
Academy of the Hebrew Language
Dictionary of hydraulics **5082**
Access Russia - science and technology **386**
Accessible holidays in the British Isles 1999: a guide for disabled people **5989**
ACCIS guide to United Nations information sources on food and agriculture **5498**
The ACE directory, 1998/9 **3936**
Acetylene: its properties, manufacture and uses **6587**
Acid rain **5246**
Acid rain abstracts annual **5242**
Acid rain and the environment 1988-1991 **5243**
Ackerknecht, C.H.
A Short history of medicine **3401**
ACM guide to computing literature **7232**
Acoustics abstracts **1031**
Acoustics source book **1024**
Acronyms and abbreviations in molecular spectroscopy **1282**
Acronyms and abbreviations of computer technology and telecommunication **4488, 7223**
Acronyms, initialisms, and abbreviations dictionary: a guide to acronyms, abbreviations, contractions, alphabetic symbols, and similar condensed appellations **35**
The ACS style guide **1214**
Acupuncture: the modern scientific approach **3697**

Adamenko, P.A.
English-Russian dictionary of agriculture **5531**
Adams, F.D.
The Birth and development of the geological sciences **1571**
Adams, M.S.
Optical fibres and sources for communications **4528**
Adams, R.
Directory of European industrial and trade associations **7171**
Adams, T.R. *and* Waters, D.W.
English maritime books printed before 1901 **5366**
Adderley, P
'Executing the design: materials, structures, construction' **7550**
Adderley, P. *and* O'Brien, A.
CIIG manual **7487**
Addis, W. *and* Bussell, M.
'Construction engineering' **7469**
'Structural engineering' **4969**
The Addison-Wesley science handbook **95**
Additives for polymers **7160**
Adelman, G. *and* Smith, B.H.
Elsevier's encyclopedia of neuroscience **3832**
Adhesion and adhesives **6779**
Adhesive handbook **6781**
Adhesives and adhesion **6778**
Adhesives dictionary **6780**
Adhesives directory **6777**
Adkins, R.T.
Information sources in polymers and plastics **7148**
Admiralty list of lights and fog signals **6381**
The Admiralty list of radio signals **6379**
Admiralty manual of hydrographic surveying. 1965-73 **840**
Admiralty manual of navigation **806, 6366**
Admiralty manual of seamanship **6367**
Admiralty notices to mariners **806, 6366**
Adrian, J.
Dictionary of food and nutrition **3500, 6643**
Dictionnaire agro-alimentaire **6648**
Advanced materials CD-ROM **3981**
Advanced materials sourcebook **3993**
Advanced organic chemistry **1337**
Advanced surface coatings **4695**
Advances in agronomy **5541**
Advances in applied microbiology **2367**
Advances in atomic, molecular and optical physics **1091, 4191**
Advances in botanical research **2512**
Advances in catalysis **1267**
Advances in cereal science and technology **5737**
Advances in chemical engineering **6479**

Advances in chemical physics **1231**
Advances in chromatography **1296**
Advances in computers **7274**
Advances in cryogenic engineering **4589**
Advances in ecological research **2248**
Advances in electrochemical science and engineering **1242**
Advances in food and nutrition research **3539, 6652**
Advances in genetics **2308**
Advances in geophysics **1495**
Advances in heat transfer **1061**
Advances in heterocyclic chemistry **1367**
Advances in imaging and electron physics **1048**
Advances in inorganic chemistry **1306**
Advances in insect physiology **2822**
Advances in instrumentation and control **7207**
Advances in nuclear physics **1092, 4192**
Advances in nuclear science and technology **4193**
Advances in optical and electron microscopy **1043**
Advances in organometallic chemistry **1361**
Advances in oxygenated processes **1315**
Advances in parasitology **2322**
Advances in periglacial geomorphology **1641**
Advances in physical organic chemistry **1342**
Advances in printing science and technology **6158**
Advances in protein chemistry **1373**
Advances in quantum chemistry **1229**
Advances in solid-liquid separation **6498**
Advances in underwater technology, ocean science and offshore engineering **5101**
Advances in veterinary science **5840**
Adventurers afloat: a nautical bibliography **6324**
Advisory Committee for the Co-ordination of Information Systems
ACCIS guide to United Nations information sources on food and agriculture **5498**
Aeronautical and space serial publications **5404**
Aerospace and defense acronyms **4815, 5440**
Aerospace dictionary **5458**
Aerospace dictionary: English, French, German, Spanish **5449**
'Aerospace engineering' **5441**
Aerospace Europe **6394**
The Aerospace international directory of world airlines **6401**
Aerospace medicine and biology **3553**
Aerospace research index **5480**
Aerospace technology centres **5477**
Aerospace-Wörterbuch **5458**
Aérospatiale
Dictionnaire aérospatiale **5395**
AFRC Institute of Food Research
Home preservation of fruit and vegetables **6038**
African Academy of Sciences
Profiles of African scientific institutions **468**
African bibliographies **2069**
The African book world & press **6210**
African mining, '91 **4791**
Africa's ecology **2277**
Afro-American reference **2088**
AGA gas handbook **6539**
AGARD aeronautical multilingual dictionary **5397**
AGARD index of publications, 1952/1970- **5402**
Agarwal, R.K.
Chemistry: Who's who **1203**
AGDEX **5490**
AgECONCD **5494**
AgeInfo **3758**
AGELINE **3757**

Agence de Coopération Culturelle et Technique
Dictionnaire d'agriculture et des sciences annexes **5525**
Agence de Coopération Culturelle et Technique *and* Conseil International de la Langue Française
Vocabulaire de l'océanologie **1742**
Agents of chaos: earthquakes, volcanoes, and other natural disasters **1508**
Ager, D.V.
The Geology of Europe **1585**
Agha, Z.M.
Bibliography of Islamic medicine and pharmacy **3439**
The Agrarian history of England and Wales **5586**
AGREP: Permanent inventory of agricultural research projects in the European Communities **5604**
Agriasia **5594**
AGRICOLA **5491**
Agricultural and animal sciences journals and serials **5542**
Agricultural and veterinary sciences international who's who **5557**
An Agricultural atlas of England and Wales **5583**
An Agricultural atlas of India **5596**
An Agricultural atlas of Scotland **5582**
Agricultural compendium for rural development in the tropics and subtropics **5568**
Agricultural economics and rural sociology **5612**
Agricultural economics and rural sociology - multilingual thesaurus **5610**
Agricultural engineering **5670**
Agricultural engineering abstracts **5671**
Agricultural engineer's handbook **5663**
The Agricultural handbook **5518**
Agricultural history in Great Britain and Western Europe before 1914 **5572**
The Agricultural history review **5555**
Agricultural information resource centers **5603**
Agricultural insect pests of temperate regions and their control **5722**
Agricultural insect pests of the tropics and their control **5722**
Agricultural journal titles and abbreviations **5543**
The Agricultural notebook
See
Primrose McConnell's 'The agricultural notebook'
Agricultural plants **5729**
Agricultural research, 1931-1981 **5608**
Agricultural research centres **5607**
The Agricultural situation in the Community **5571**
The Agricultural systems of the world **5558**
Agricultural terms, as used in the Bibliography of Agriculture **5519**
Agricultural writers **5574**
Agriculture: a bibliographical guide **5501**
Agriculture and environment for developing countries **5566**
Agriculture catalogue 1996 **5573**
Agriculture in the tropics **5562**
The Agriculture of China **5592**
AgriGator **5492**
Agrindex **5535**
AGRIS **5493**
Agrisearch **5497**
Agroselekt **5540**
Agrovoc: multilingual agricultural thesaurus **5601**
Ahlberg, K.
AGA gas handbook **6539**
Ahlsved, K.-J.
Lexicon forestale **5625**

Ahrens, T.J.
Global earth physics **1498**
Mineral physics and crystallography **1853**
Rock physics and phase relations **1842**
AIDS abstracts **3868**
AIDS bibliography **3870**
The AIDS dictionary **3872**
The AIDS directory **3869**
Aids to geographical research **1665**
AIDSLINE **3870**
Ainbinder, M.I.
Anglo-russkiĭ meteorologicheskiĭ slovar' **1777**
Ainsworth & Bisby's dictionary of the fungi **2642**
Ainsworth, G.C.
Ainsworth & Bisby's dictionary of the fungi **2642**
Introduction to the history of medical and veterinary mycology **2654**
Introduction to the history of mycology **2653**
Ainsworth, G.C. *and* Sussman, A.S.
The Fungi **2648**
Ainsworth, J.
The Good food guide **6002**
AIP Style manual **986**
The Air & space catalog **714**
Air and space dictionary **5454**
Air-Conditioning and Refrigeration Institute
Refrigeration and air-conditioning **4582**
Air distances manual **6406**
Air navigation plans **809**
Air pollution **5244**
Air pollution control handbook **5245**
Air University Library index to military periodicals **4832**
Aircraft, engines and airmen **5389**
Aircraft of the Soviet Union **4891, 5425**
Aird, A.
The Good pub guide **6007**
The Airline bibliography **6402**
Airships: an illustrated history **5431**
Aitchison, L.
A History of metals **6881**
Aithgiorrachtaí móna **6555**
Aitken, A.
Fish handling and processing **6705**
A.J. Lohwater's Russian-English dictionary of the mathematical sciences **548**
Akehurst, B.C.
Tobacco **6622**
Akiner, S.
Islamic peoples of the Soviet Union **2053**
Akzhigtov, G.N.
Anglo-russkiĭ meditsinskiĭ slovar' **3346**
al-Hassan, A.Y. *and* Hill, D.R.
Islamic technology **3089**
Al-Khatib, A.Sh.
A New dictionary of scientific and technical terms, English-Arabic, with illustrations **191**
Albert, L.S. *and* Kent, K.
The Complete button book **7452**
Albert, R. *and* Hahnewald, H.
Eight-language dictionary of medical technology **3301**
Albion, R.G.
Naval & maritime history **6354**
Album of science **300**
Alcohol and the public health **3571**
Alderton, D.
The Handbook of cage and aviary birds **5897**
Aldous, K.
Who's who in the environment: England **5161**
Aldrich, U.
Automotive handbook **5271**

Alexander, B.A.
Journals with translations held at the Science Reference Library **239**

Alexander, F.G. *and* **Selesnick, S.T.**
The History of psychiatry **3859**

Alexandrov, P.S.
Anglo-russkiĭ slovar' matematicheskiĭ terminov **549**

Alexis Lichine's New encyclopedia of wines & spirits **6599**

Alfara Perez, T.
Diccionario marítimo y de construcción naval **5350**

Alford, M.H.T. *and* **Alford, V.L.**
Russian-English scientific and technical dictionary **180**

The Algae **2640**

Algebra in ancient and modern times **617**

Alger, M.S.
Polymer science dictionary **7157**

Ali, Salim *and* **Ripley, S.D.**
Handbook of the birds of India and Pakistan **2917**

All the US Air Force airplanes, 1907-1983 **4892**

All the world's battleships **4915**

Allaby, A. *and* **Allaby, M.**
The Concise Oxford dictionary of earth sciences **1465**

Allaby, M.
The Concise Oxford dictionary of botany **2501**
The Concise Oxford dictionary of ecology **2235**
The Concise Oxford dictionary of zoology **2722**
Illustrated dictionary of science **87**
Macmillan dictionary of the environment **2234, 2447**
The Oxford dictionary of natural history **2385**

Allan, B.
Guide to information sources in alternative therapy **3687**

Allan, B. *and* **Livesey, B.**
How to use *Biological abstracts, Chemical abstracts, Index chemicus* **2167**

Allen, C.W.
Astrophysical quantities **739**

Allen, D. *and* **Woolstenholmes, C.J.**
A Pictorial survey of railway signalling **6320**

Allen, G. *and* **Bevington, J.C.**
Comprehensive polymer science **7153**

Allen, G.E.
Life science in the twentieth century **2184**

Allen, J.L.
Aviation and space museums of America **5417**

Allen, J.P. *and* **Turner, E.J.**
We the people: an atlas of America's ethnic diversity **2084**

Allen, K.A. *and* **Neale, J.W.**
Principles of zoological micropalaeontology **1934**

Alley, E.R.
Air pollution control handbook **5245**

Allin, C.W.
International handbook of national parks and nature reserves **2433**

Allison, S.
The Cassell food dictionary **6062, 6644**

Alloys index **6893**

Altbach, P.G. *and* **Hoshino, E.S.**
International book publishing: an encyclopedia **6214**

'Alternative databases for anthropology searching' **1984**

The Alternative dictionary of symptoms and cures **3773**

Alternative energy sources. VII **4121**

Alternative fuels guidebook **6550**

Alternative medicine: a bibliography of books in English **3688**

Alternative medicine: a guide to natural therapies **3692**

Alternative medicine in Britain **3696**

Alternatives to laboratory animals **5813**

Altman, P.L. *and* **Dittmer, D.S.**
Biology data book **2178**

Altman, P.L. *and* **Katz, D.D.**
Human health and disease **3738**

'Aluminium' **6957**

Aluminium industry abstracts **6960**

Aluminum and its alloys **6959**

Aluminum: properties and physical metallurgy **6958**

Alvin, R.G. *and* **Smoots, V.A.**
Construction guide for soils and foundations **4993**

The Amateur astronomer's handbook **693**

Amateur astronomer's handbook **696**

Amateur radio call book **4546**

Amateur radio encyclopedia **4537**

Amatt, L.K.
Locks and lockmaking **7429**

Amdur, M.O.
Casarett and Doull's toxicology **3716**

American anthropologist **2011**

American Association of Petroleum Geologists
Index to films related to geology and energy exploration **1565**

American book trade directory **6211**

American Ceramic Society
Ceramic abstracts **6818**

American chemical industry **6469**

American Chemical Society
The ACS style guide **1214**
Chemical research faculties **1220**
Reagent chemicals **1226**

American Chemical Society. Committee on Professional Training
Directory of graduate research **1219**

American chemists and chemical engineers **1209**

American dental directory **3821**

American electricians' handbook **4275**

American engineers of the nineteenth century **3963**

American Geographical Society
Atlas of diseases **3743**
Research catalogue of the American Geographical Society **1660**

American Geographical Society. Department of Exploration and Field Research
Author/title, subject and geographic catalogs of the Glaciology Collection **1635**

American Geophysical Union
Antarctic research book series **1652**

American handbook of psychiatry **3844**

The American Heritage Stedman's medical dictionary **3290**

American Horticultural Society
North American horticulture **5759**
American Horticultural Society A-Z encyclopedia of garden plants **5781**

American Indian studies **2111**

American Indians **2104**

American Institute of Physics
AIP Style manual **986**
Glossary of terms frequently used in cryogenics **1069**
American Institute of Physics handbook **925**

American Kennel Club
The Complete dog book **5900**

American Medical Association
CMIT **3321**
The American Medical Association encyclopedia of medicine **3294**

American men and women of science 1998-99 **410, 2190**

American men and women of science. Editions 1-14 **411**

American Museum of Natural History
The New catalogue of the Library. [American Museum of Natural History] **2379**
Research catalog of the Library. [American Museum of Natural History] **2377, 2707**

American Museum of Natural History. Department of Library Services
Catalog of the American Museum of Natural History film archives **2396**

American National Standards Institute
Electrical and electronics graphic symbols and reference designations **4235, 4387**

American Paper and Pulp Association
The Dictionary of paper **7036**

American Petroleum Institute
Basic petroleum data book: petroleum industry statistics **6759**
Thesaurus. [American Petroleum Institute] **6760**

American Philosophical Society. Library
Catalog of books in the American Philosophical Society Library **284**
Catalog of manuscripts in the American Philosophical Society Library **361**

American Physiological Society
Handbook of physiology **3491**

American Psychiatric Association
Biographical directory of fellows & members of the American Psychiatric Association **3861**

American Psychiatric Association. Joint Commission on Public Affairs
A Psychiatric glossary **3849**

American Society for Metals
Alloys index **6893**
Aluminium industry abstracts **6960**
Aluminum: properties and physical metallurgy **6958**
ASM handbook **6852**
ASM handbook of engineering mathematics **529**
ASM metals reference book **6873**
Guide to materials engineering data and information **6872**
METADEX **6847**
Metals abstracts **6865**
Metals handbook; v.6. Welding, brazing and soldering **4683**
Metals handbook; v.7. Powder metallurgy **4663**
Metals handbook; v.9. Metallography and microstructures **4664**
Polymers/ceramics/composites alert **7161**
Source journals in metals and materials **6867**
Steels' alert **6922**
Woldman's Engineering alloys **6898**
Worldwide guide to equivalent irons and steels **6915**

American Society for Metals. International Handbook Committee
Engineered materials handbook **3994**

American Society for Testing and Materials
Annual book of ASTM standards **4022**
Annual book of ASTM standards. Section 10. Electrical insulation and electronics. Vols. 10.04 and 10.05 . Electronics **4440**
Compilation of ASTM standard definitions **4023**
Directory of testing laboratories **4024**
Glossary of terms relating to rubber and rubber-like materials **7117**

American Society of Civil Engineers
ASCE publications information **4949**

American Society of Heating, Refrigerating and Air-conditioning Engineers
ASHRAE handbook **7579**

The Anstey Weston guide to textile terms
7070
Antarctic bibliography **1653**
Antarctic earth science **1654**
Antarctic ecology **2279**
Antarctic meteorology and climatology **1824**
Antarctic research book series **1652**
Antarctic science **1655**
Antenna engineering handbook **4544**
Antenucci, J.C.
Geographic information systems **1706**
Anthony, K.
Medical equipment **3498**
Anthony, L.J.
Information sources in energy technology
4052
Anthony, P.
Patrick Anthony's international menu
dictionary **6064**
Anthropological bibliographies: a selected
guide **1985**
Anthropological bibliography of negro Africa
2071
An Anthropological bibliography of South Asia
2063-2064
Anthropological fieldwork **1993**
Anthropological index online **2008**
Anthropological index to current periodicals in
the Museum of Mankind Library **2008**
Anthropological literature: an index to
periodical articles and essays **2009**
Anthropological literature on disc **2009**
'Anthropology' **1996**
Anthropology Internet resources **1983**
Anthropology journals and serials: an
analytical guide **2014**
The Anthropology of Western Europe **2050**
Anthropometric standards for the assessment of
growth and nutritional status **2027**
The Anti-Corrosion handbook and directory
4701
Antique scientific instruments **7215**
Antoni, T
Wörterbuch antriebstechnic **4718**
Ap Simion, J.
The Total synthesis of natural products **1352**
Apes of the world **2978**
Apicultural abstracts **5921**
APILIT **6723**
APIPAT **6724**
Appleby, A.J. *and* Foulkes, F.R.
Fuel cell handbook **4355**
Applied botany abstracts **2621**
'Applied chemistry and chemical engineering'
6478
Applied geology for engineers **1519**
Applied mechanics reviews **4136**
Applied science and technology abstracts
3015
Applied science and technology index **3022**
Applied technology index **3081**
Appraisal: science books for young people
260
Appropriate building materials **7554**
Appropriate technology in Third World
development **3083**
Appropriate technology sourcebook **3082**
Aquaculture **5945**
Aquaculture desk reference **5933**
Aqualex: a glossary of aquaculture terms **5940**
Aqualine abstracts **1883, 5191**
Aqualine thesaurus 2 **5199**
The Aquarium encyclopedia **5966**
Aquatic microbiology **2371**
Aquatic plants in Britain and Ireland **2704**
Aquatic sciences and fisheries abstracts **1746,
2291**
Aquatic sciences and fisheries abstracts. Part 1:
Biological sciences and living resources
2854, 5941

**Arab League Educational, Cultural and
Scientific Organization**
Lexicon of botany: English, French, Arabic
2499
Lexicon of geology: English-French-Arabic
1554
Lexique de zoologie **2720**
**Arab Republic of Egypt. National
Information and Documentation Centre**
Directory of scientific and technical libraries
in the United Arab Republic **458**
Arabic dictionary of civil engineering **4947**
Arabic military dictionary: English-Arabic,
Arabic-English **4830**
Aranson, E.J.
Report series codes dictionary **3045**
Arbeitsgemeinschaft der Spezialbibliotheken
See
Germany. Federal Republic.
Arbeitsgemeinschaft der
Spezialbibliotheken
The Arboriculturalist's companion **5796**
Archaeological geology of North America
1609
The Archaeology of animals **2745, 5866**
Architects' and builders' price book **7539**
Architects' data **7517**
Archiv der Geschichte der Naturwissenschaften
299
Archive for history of exact sciences **313**
Archives of British men of science **371**
Archives of natural history **2380**
Arctic bibliography **1649**
Arctic Institute of North America
Arctic bibliography **1649**
Arctic Institute of North America Library
Catalogue. [Arctic Institute of North
America Library] **1650**
**Arctic Science and Technology Information
System**
ASTIS current awareness bulletin **1651**
**ARD [Arbeitsgemeinschaft der öffentlich
rechlichen Rundfunkanstalten der
Bundesrepublik Deutschland], *comp.***
Dictionary of radio and television terms,
English-German, German-English **4536**
Ardis, S.B.
A Guide to the literature of electrical and
electronics engineering **4241**
Arduini, P. *and* Teruzzi, G.
The Macdonald encyclopedia of fossils **1896**
Arem, J.E.
Color encyclopedia of gemstones **1423**
Arid zone geomorphology: process, form and
change in drylands **1702**
Aries, S.J.
Dictionary of telecommunications **4506**
Arieti, S.
American handbook of psychiatry **3844**
Arithmetical books **609**
The Arming and fitting of English ships of war
1600-1815 **4905**
Armitage, J.S.
Guide to international organizations of
interest to the construction industry **7529**
Armitage, P. *and* Colton, T.
Encyclopedia of biostatistics **2144**
Armstead, H.C.
Geothermal energy **1527**
Armstrong, C.J.
World databases in agriculture **5496**
World databases in chemistry **1108**
World databases in geography and geology
1444
World databases in medicine **3237**
World databases in patents **3155**
World databases in physics and mathematics
506, 911
Armstrong, C.J. *and* Fenton, R.R.
World databases in biosciences and
pharmacology **2135, 3637**

Armstrong, T.
Illustrated glossary of snow and ice **1640**
Armytage, W.H.G.
A Social history of engineering **3951**
Arnell, A.
Standard graphical symbols **44**
Arnett, R.H.
The Insect and spider collections of the
world **2799, 2830**
Arnold, E.N. *and* Burton, J.A.
A Field guide to the reptiles and amphibians
of Britain and Europe **2864**
Arnold, H.R.
Atlas of amphibians and reptiles in Britain
2865
Arntzen, C.J. *and* Ritter, E.
Encyclopedia of agricultural science **5507**
Arrigucci, M.
Trademarks **3126**
The ARRL handbook for the radio amateur
4538
The Art and history of book printing **6161**
Art, H.W.
The Dictionary of ecology and
environmental science **2237**
The Art of navigation in England in
Elizabethan and early Stuart times **816**
The Art of scientific writing **432**
Artificial intelligence and expert systems
sourcebook **7368**
Artificial intelligence and natural man **7361**
The Artificial intelligence dictionary **7374**
Artificial intelligence from A to Z **7372**
Artificial intelligence terminology **7367**
Asbestos management sourcebook **7167**
Asbestos: properties, applications and hazards
7168
Asbestos: review of uses, health effects,
measurement and control **7169**
ASCE publications information **4949**
ASE primary science teachers' handbook **264**
ASE secondary science teachers' handbook
263
ASFA
See
Aquatic sciences and fisheries abstracts
Ash, J.
Communication, storage and retrieval of
chemical information **1216**
Ash, L.
Subject collections: a guide to special book
collections and subject emphases **460**
Ash, M.
Handbook of industrial surfactants **4702**
Resins **6784**
Ash, M. *and* Ash, I.
Chemical manufacturers directory of trade
name products **6521**
Concise encyclopaedia of industrial chemical
additives **6520**
Gardner's chemical synonyms and trade
names **6460**
Handbook of cosmetic and personal care
additives **6719**
Handbook of food additives **6691**
Handbook of paint and coating raw materials
6846
Handbook of plastic and rubber additives
7101
Handbook of plastic compounds, elastomers,
and resins **6783, 7128**
Handbook of water treatment chemicals
5196
The Index of solvents **6499**
The Thesaurus of chemical products **6522**
What every chemical technologist wants to
know **6506**
Ashby, C.M. *and* Flesh, A.R.
Annotated acronyms and abbreviations of
marine science related international
organizations **1767**

Ashford, R.D.
Ashford's dictionary of industrial chemicals **6447**
Ashford's dictionary of industrial chemicals **6447**
The Ashley book of knots **7095**
Ashley, C.W.
The Ashley book of knots **7095**
ASHRAE handbook **7579**
Ashworth, W.
The Encyclopedia of environmental studies **2223, 5131**
Asimov, I.
Asimov's biographical encyclopedia of science and technology **328**
Asimov's chronology of science and discovery **281**
Asimov, I. *and* Shulman, J.A.
Isaac Asimov's book of science and nature quotations **267**
Asimov's biographical encyclopedia of science and technology **328**
Asimov's chronology of science and discovery **281**
Askew, C.
Thesaurus of consumer terms **6034**
Askim, P.
Engelsk-norsk maritim-teknisk ordbok **5347**
Norsk-engelsk maritim-teknisk ordbok **5348**
Aslib book guide **210**
The Aslib directory of information sources in the United Kingdom **451**
ASLIB. Motor Industry Information Group
Automotive engineering terms: a thesaurus **5295**
ASM Engineered materials reference book **3990**
ASM handbook **6852**
ASM handbook of engineering mathematics **529**
ASM materials engineering dictionary **4005**
ASM metals reference book **6873**
ASM specialty handbook: tool materials **4752**
ASME handbook **4142**
ASSET: abstracts of selected solar energy technology **4109**
Association for Computing Machinery
ACM guide to computing literature **7232**
Computing reviews **7272**
Association for Science Education
ASE primary science teachers' handbook **264**
ASE secondary science teachers' handbook **263**
Association française de normalisation
Dictionary of computer science **7265**
Association of Consulting Engineers
The ACE directory, 1998/9 **3936**
Association of Desk and Derrick Clubs
D&D oil standard abbreviator **6722**
Association of the British Pharmaceutical Industry
ABPI compendium of patient information leaflets **3667**
Association of Track Operating Companies
Railguide, 1997-98 **5039**
ASTIS bibliography **1651**
ASTIS current awareness bulletin **1651**
Astronauts and cosmonauts **5473**
The Astronomer's sourcebook **687**
The Astronomical almanac **812**
Astronomical centers of the world **747**
Astronomical dictionary **701**
Astronomical objects for southern telescopes **688**
Astronomical phenomena for the year 1999 **813**
The Astronomical telescope **751**
Astronomischer Jahresbericht **669**
Astronomy and aeronautics **673**

Astronomy and astrophysics: a bibliographical guide **671**
Astronomy and astrophysics abstracts **708**
The Astronomy and astrophysics encyclopaedia **678**
Astronomy before the telescope **720**
The Astronomy encyclopaedia **679**
Astronomy through the telescope **750**
Astrophysical formulae **740**
Astrophysical quantities **739**
Astrophysics of the sun **774**
At the farmer's service **5585**
ATHENA: mineralogy **1849**
Atherton, D.P.
Concise encyclopedia of modelling and simulation **7345**
Atherton, W.A.
From compass to computer: a history of electrical and electronics engineering **4288**
Atkins, P.W.
Physical chemistry **1234**
Quanta: a handbook of concepts **1230**
Atkins, S. *and* Woods, S.
The 'Which?' wine guide **6597**
Atkinson, B. *and* Mavituna, F.
Biochemical engineering and biotechnology handbook **2984**
Atkinson, D.W.
Weather **1818**
ATLA **5813**
Atlas and glossary of primary sedimentary structures **1633**
Atlas climatique de l'Europe **1814**
Atlas des grands gouffres du monde **1723**
Atlas for anthropology **2042**
Atlas narodov mira **2041**
Atlas of American agriculture **5689**
Atlas of amphibians and reptiles in Britain **2865**
Atlas of animal migration **2772**
Atlas of disease distributions **3742**
Atlas of diseases **3743**
An Atlas of distribution of the freshwater fish families of the world **2855, 5946**
Atlas of dog breeds of the world **5904**
Atlas of economic mineral deposits **1855**
The Atlas of endangered species **2450**
Atlas of environmental issues **2262**
Atlas of hardwoods **7002**
Atlas of human cross-sectional anatomy **3487**
Atlas of marine aquarium fishes **5959**
Atlas of meteorology **1786**
Atlas of North American Indians **2121**
Atlas of palaeobiogeography **1914**
An Atlas of past and present pollen maps for Europe 0-13000 years ago **1939**
Atlas of railway centres of Great Britain **5041**
An Atlas of renewable energy resources in the United Kingdom and North America **4105**
Atlas of the British flora **2565**
Atlas of the environment **2260, 5170**
Atlas of the great caves of the world **1723**
Atlas of the living resources of the seas **5953**
The Atlas of the living world **2397**
Atlas of the moon **758**
Atlas of the seas round the British Isles **1757**
Atlas of United States environmental issues **2261**
Atlas of world cultures **2038, 2043**
Atlas of zoogeography **2776**
Atlas sel'kogokhozyaistvo SSSR **5590**
Atlas van de europese vogels **2906**
Atomic data and nuclear data tables **4199**
Atomic energy level and Grotrian diagrams **4200**
Atomic gas laser transition data **4381**
Atomic, molecular, and optical physics handbook **1100**
The Atomic scientists **1101**

Attar, D.
A Bibliography of household books published in Britain, 1840-1914 **6091**
Attiyate, Y.H.
Wörterbuch der Mikroelektronik und Mikroechnertechnick **4463**
Atz, J.W.
Dean bibliography of fishes, 1968 **2849**
Audio and video **7406**
The Audio dictionary **7416**
Audio engineering handbook **7409**
Audio engineer's reference book **7408**
Audio, video and data telecommunications **4499**
'Audio-visual materials' **3389**
Audouze, J. *and* Israël, G.
The Cambridge atlas of astronomy **794**
The Audubon Society encyclopedia of animal life **2769**
The Audubon Society encyclopedia of North American birds **2921**
The Audubon Society field guide to North American fossils **1922**
The Audubon Society field guide to North American rocks and minerals **1419, 1844**
The Audubon Society field guide to North American trees **5653**
The Audubon Society field guide to North American wildflowers **2591**
Aufderheide, A.C. *and* Rodriguez-Martin, C.
The Cambridge encyclopedia of human paleopathology **1931**
Augarten, S.
Bit by bit: an illustrated history of computers **7276**
Auger, C.P.
Engineering eponyms **4125**
Information sources in grey literature **206**
Information sources in patents **3156**
Auger, P. *and* Rousseku, L.J.
Lexique anglais-français de l'industrie minière **4782**
Austin, M.
The ISTC handbook of technical writing and publication techniques **436**
Austin, R.M. *and* Nau, B.S.
Seal users handbook **4165**
Australia and the Pacific Islands **2427**
Australian men and women of science, engineering and technology **420, 3074**
Australian National University, Canberra. Department of Anthropology and Sociology
An Ethnographic bibliography of New Guinea **2100**
Australian native plants **5761**
Auszüge aus den Europäischen Patentanmeldungen **3171**
Author and classified catalogues. [Royal Botanic Gardens, Kew, Library] **2489**
An Author and permuted title index to selected statistical journals **636**
Author and subject catalogues of the Tozzer Library **1987**
Author catalog. [New York Academy of Medicine Library] **3264**
Author-title catalog ... for imprints through 1959. [Francis A. Countway Library of Medicine] **3248**
Author/title, subject and geographic catalogs of the Glaciology Collection **1635**
The Author's guide to biomedical journals **2176, 3360**
Auto sourcebook, 1991 **5291**
Automation encyclopedia **7343**
The Automobile **5310**
Automobile abstracts **5285**
Automobile Association
Book of the British countryside **2411**
Know your car **5303**
Automobile electronics **5273**

Beitz, W. *and* Küttner, K.-H.
Dubbel Handbook of mechanical engineering
4129
Bekleidungs wörterbuch 7446
Bekoff, M. *and* Meaney, C.A.
Encyclopedia of animal rights and animal
welfare **5860**
Belforte, D. *and* Levitt, M.
Industrial laser annual handbook **4380**
Bell, A.D.
Plant form **2683**
Bell, F.G.
Fundamentals of engineering geology **4986**
Ground engineer's reference book **4925**
Bell, G.H. *and* Rhodes, D.B.
A Guide to the zoological literature **2708**
Bell, M. *and* Boardman, J.
Soil erosion past and present **1668**
Bell, P.
Strasburger's textbook of botany **2498**
Bell, S.P.
A Biographical index of British engineers in
the 19th century **3961**
Belmonte, F.R.
Women and health **3239**
Belove, C.
Handbook of modern electronics and
electrical engineering **4398**
Bels-Koning, H.C. *and* Kuijk, W.M., van.
Mushroom terms **2658**
Belzer, J.
Encyclopedia of computer science and
technology **7235**
Benarde, M.A.
Global warning ... global warming **5228**
Bendall, S.
Dictionary of land surveyors and local map-
makers of Great Britain and Ireland, 1530-
1850 **838**
Bender, A.E.
A Dictionary of food and nutrition **3533**
Dictionary of nutrition and food technology
3533, 6645
Food processing and nutrition **6666**
Bender, A.E. *and* Bender, D.A.
Nutrition: a reference handbook **3541**
Bendiner, J. *and* Bendiner, E.
Biographical dictionary of medicine **3409**
Benedict, G.F.
Nontraditional manufacturing processes
4630
Benn, D.I. *and* Evans, D.J.A.
Glaciers and glaciation **1637**
Bennett, H.
The Chemical formulary **6458**
Concise chemical and technical dictionary
1135
Bennett, H.S.
English books & readers **6207**
Bennett, J.A.
The Divided circle **741, 7209**
Bennett, S.
A History of control engineering, 1800-1930
7358
Bennett, S. *and* Freirman, R.
Microcomputer marketplace **7311**
Bennett, W.R.
Atomic gas laser transition data **4381**
Bennigsen, A. *and* Wimbush, S.E.
Muslims of the Soviet empire: a guide **2054**
Benninghoff, H.
Index of chemicals used for the treatment of
metal surfaces **4703**
Bennington, J.L.
Saunders dictionary & encyclopedia of
laboratory medicine and technology **3445**
Benson, J. *and* Neville, R.G.
Bibliography of the British coal industry
6574
Benson, K.B.
Audio engineering handbook **7409**

Benson, K.B. *(contd.)*
Television engineering handbook **4558**
Benson, K.B. *and* Whitaker, J.G.
Television and audio handbook for
technicians **4557**
Bentham, G.
Handbook of the British flora **2567**
Benton, M.J.
The Fossil record 2 **1912**
The Penguin historical atlas of dinosaurs
1964
Vertebrate palaeontology **1950**
Berg, I.
The Guinness world car record **5307**
Berger, K.
Mykologisches Wörterbuch **2644**
Berger, P.
Goats: a bibliography **5882**
Bergey's manual of systematic bacteriology
2372
Bergteknisk ordlista 4984
Berins, M.L.
Plastics engineering handbook of the Society
of the Plastics Industry, Inc **7144**
Berkebile, D.H.
Carriage terminology **5267**
Berkovitch, I.
Energy sources and policy **4053**
Berkow, R.
The Merck manual of diagnosis and therapy
3772
Bernabo Silorata, M. *and* Picchi, F.
Grande dizionario di marina, italiano-
inglese, inglese-italiano **6347**
Bernal, I.
Bibliografia de arqueologia y etnografia:
Mesoamerica y norte de México, 1514-
1960 **2081**
Berner, G.-A.
Dictionnaire professionnel illustré de
l'horlogerie **7185**
Bernice P. Bishop Museum, Honolulu
Dictionary catalog of the Library of Bernice
P. Bishop Museum **2101**
Berra, T.M.
An Atlas of distribution of the freshwater
fish families of the world **2855, 5946**
Berrill, D.J.
Optoelectronics data book **4487**
Berry, M.J.
Science and technology in the USSR **17**
Bersch, E.
Shipbuilding, seafaring technical dictionary
5341
Bertin, L.
The New Larousse encyclopedia of the earth
1462
Bertino, J.R.
Encyclopedia of cancer **3729**
Berube, M.S., ed.
The American Heritage Stedman's medical
dictionary **3290**
Beryllium: its metallurgy and properties 6962
Bes, J.
Chartering and shipping terms **6336**
Besançon, R.M.
The Encyclopedia of physics **917**
Bespaloff, A.
The New encyclopedia of wine **6595**
Besson, A.
Thornton's medical books, libraries and
collectors **3396**
**Best science and technology reference books
for young people 70**
Besterman, T.
Medicine: a bibliography of bibliographies
3238
Physical sciences **55**
Betongteknisk ordlista 6833
Betteridge, W.
Nickel and its alloys **6937**

Bettex, J.
Lexique telecom lexicon **4502**
**Between covers: the rise and transformation of
book publishing in America 6235**
Bevan, J.
Your family doctor: the home medical
encyclopaedia **3295**
Bevan, S.C.
Concise etymological dictionary of chemistry
1136
Bever, M.B.
Encyclopedia of materials science and
engineering **3984**
'Beverages' 6591
Beydoun, Z.R.
The Middle East regional geology and
petroleum resources **1867**
Beyer, W.H.
CRC handbook of mathematical sciences
524
CRC handbook of tables for probability and
statistics **629**
Beyond broadcasting into the cable age 6137
Bezner, H.
Electrical machines dictionary **4326**
Fachwörterbuch industrielle electrotechnik,
energie- und automatisierungs-technik
4258
Bhatnagar, K.P.
Elsevier's dictionary of civil engineering
4946
Elsevier's dictionary of geosciences **1473**
Bhattacharya, S.K.
Elsevier's dictionary of civil engineering
4946
BI-Lexikon Rassekatzen 5905
Bianchina, P.
Illustrated dictionary of building materials
and techniques **7556**
Biass-Ducroux, F. *and* Napp-Zinn, K.
Glossary of genetics in English, French,
Spanish, Italian, German, Russian **2299**
Bibel, B.
'Medical reference sources' **3240**
**'Bibliografia botanica para América Latina'
2596**
**Bibliografia de arqueologia y etnografia:
Mesoamerica y norte de México, 1514-1960
2081**
Bibliografia Kopernikowska, 1509-1955 731
Bibliografiia izdanii Akademii Nauk SSSR 384
Bibliographia cartographica 852
Bibliographic guide for editors & authors 231
**Bibliographic guide to anthropology and
archaeology 1987 1990**
**Bibliographic guide to conference publications,
1975- 482**
Bibliographic guide to technology 3016
A Bibliographic history of the book 6146
**Bibliographical history of electricity &
magnetism 1078**
**A Bibliographical index of the British flora
2580**
**Bibliographical series. [International Atomic
Energy Agency] 4172**
**Bibliographical series. [Newberry Library
Center for the History of the American
Indian] 2108**
Bibliographical Society
[Dictionary of printers and booksellers in
England, Scotland and Ireland] **6164**
Bibliographical tools in apiculture 5922
Bibliographie astronomique 670
**Bibliographie de l'Afrique sud-saharienne,
sciences humaines et sociales 2074**
**Bibliographie der Islamischen Medizin und
Pharmacie 3439**
Bibliographie gastronomique 6047
Bibliographie générale de l'astronomie 668
**Bibliographie géographique internationale
1688**

Biographical encyclopedia of scientists 332
A Biographical index of British engineers in the 19th century 3961
Biographical index to American science 418
Biographical memoirs 419
Biographical memoirs of Fellows of the Royal Society 343
Biographical notes upon botanists 2534
'Biographical notices of historians of science: a checklist' 350
Biographien bedeutender Geowissenschaftler der Sowjetunion 1576
'Biographies of physicists' 982
Biographies of scientists: an annotated bibliography 352
Biographisches Lexikon der hervorragenden Ärzte aller Zeiten und Völker 3415
Biolexicon: a guide to the language of biology 2151
Biological abstracts 2169
Biological abstracts/RRM 2170
Biological and agricultural index 2171, 5537
Biological Council
Handbook of UK biological societies 2196
Biological journal of the Linnean Society 2311
Biological nomenclature 2181
Biological science 2149
Biological surveys of estuaries and coasts 2286
Biologie-Dokumentation: Bibliographie der deutschen biologischen Zeitschriftenliteratur, 1796-1965 2136
Biology data book 2178
Biology digest 2172
Biology of fresh waters 2287
Biomass handbook 4114
Biomedical, scientific & technical book reviewing 211
Biometrika tables for statisticians 651
BIOSIS PREVIEWS 2134
BIOSIS serial sources 2177
Biotechnology 2986
Biotechnology abstracts 3000
Biotechnology and genetic engineering reviews 3002
Biotechnology citation index 2980
The Biotechnology directory 3003
Biotechnology from A to Z 2991
Biotechnology glossary 2995
Biotechnology guide Japan, 1990-91 3007
Biotechnology guide U.S.A. 3008
Biotechnology in agriculture and forestry 2985
Biotechnology information sources 2981
The Biotechnology marketing sourcebook 3001
Biotechnology of waste treatment and exploitation 5212
Biotechnology: principles and applications 2989
Biotechnology research abstracts 2998
Bird conservation 3 2480
Bird, J.
The Major seaports of the United Kingdom 6382
Bird, J.O. and Chivers, P.J.
Newnes engineering and physical science pocket book 3918
Birds: a guide to the literature 2878
Birds: alternative names: a world checklist 2891
Birds in Europe: their conservation status 2475
The Birds of Africa 2918
Birds of prey 2934
Birds of prey of the world 2936
The Birds of South America 2925
The Birds of the British Isles 2908
The Birds of the Western Palearctic 2895
Birds of the Western Palearctic journal 2895
Birds to watch 2 2470
The Birdwatcher's dictionary 2884

The Birdwatcher's handbook 2900
The Birdwatcher's yearbook and diary 2888
Birkeland, P.W. and Larson, E.E.
Putnam's geology 1542
Birnes, W.J.
McGraw-Hill personal computer programming encyclopedia 7293
Microcomputer applications handbook 7294
Birren, J.E.
Encyclopedia of gerontology 3762
The Birth and development of the geological sciences 1571
The Birth of the British motor car 5315
Bishop, C.
The Encyclopedia of world sea power 4908
Bishop, W.J.
Bibliography of international congresses of medical sciences 3462
A Bio-bibliography of Florence Nightingale 3794
Bishop, Y.
The Veterinary formulary 5850
Bisio, A.
Encyclopedia of energy and the environmnet 4060
Bisio, A. and Boots, S.
Encyclopedia of energy technology and the environment 4059, 5132
Biswas, A.K.
History of hydrology 1885
Bit by bit: an illustrated history of computers 7276
Bitter, G.G.
Macmillan encyclopedia of computers 7237
Bitting, K.G.
Gastronomic bibliography 6044
Bitton, G.
Formula handbook for environmental engineers and scientists 5165
Bitumen 6581
Bituminous materials 6582
Bix, R.
Topics in geometry 618
Black Americans information directory 2089
Black, L.
Builder's reference book 7516
Black, M.H.
Cambridge University Press, 1584-1984 6166
Black, R.M.
The History of electric wires and cables 4336
Black studies on disc 2092
Black, W.T.
Thesaurus of terms in copper technology 6946
Blackburn, G.
The Illustrated dictionary of nautical terms 6340
The Illustrated encyclopedia of ships, boats, vessels and other water-borne craft 5332
Black's agricultural dictionary 5520
Black's medical dictionary 3274
Black's veterinary dictionary 5824
Blackwelder, R.E.
Guide to the taxonomic literature of vertebrates 2842
Blackwell, R.J.
A Bibliography of the philosophy of science, 1945-1981 57
Blake, E.R.
Manual of neo-tropical birds 2926
Blake, J.B. and Roos, C.
Medical reference works, 1679-1966 3262
Blake, L.S.
Civil engineer's reference book 4926
Blake, S.F.
Geographical guide to floras of the world 2550
Blakely, J. and Bade, D.H.
The Science of animal husbandry 5861

Blakemore, K.
The Retail jeweller's guide 6973
Blakiston's Gould medical dictionary 3275
Blakiston's Gould pocket medical dictionary 3275
Blamey, M. and Grey-Wilson, C.
The Illustrated flora of Britain and Northern Europe 2557
Blanchard, J.R. and Farrell, L.
Guide to sources for agricultural and biological research 5500
Blanco White, T.A.
Patents for invention 3204
Blanco White, T.A. and Jacob, R.
Kerly's law of trade marks and trade names 3121
Blaskett, D.R.
Lead and its alloys 6951
Blauvelt, C. and Nelson, F.R.T.
A Manual of orthopaedic terminology 3883
Blazer, A.M.
Index of generic names of fossil plants, 1966-1973 1935
Blinderman, C.
Biolexicon: a guide to the language of biology 2151
Bloch, C.C.
Coal information sources and databases 6556
Block, B.P.
Inorganic chemical nomenclature 1311
Blok, C. and Jezewski, W.
Illustrated automobile dictionary in six languages 5274
Six-language illustrated dictionary of the motor car 5275
Blood, D.C.
Veterinary medicine 5834
Blood, D.C. and Studdert, V.P.
Saunders comprehensive veterinary dictionary 5825
Bloomfield, J.E.
Textbook of science and medicine in sport 3560
The Bloomsbury encyclopedia of aromatherapy 3694
Bloor, D.
Encyclopedia of advanced materials 3986
Blow, C.M. and Hepburn, C.
Rubber technology and manufacture 7111
The Blue book of British broadcasting 6131
Blueprint electronic publishing glossary 6196
Blume, H.
Das Relief der Erde 1695
BMT [British maritime technology] abstracts 5352
BNF 3659
Boas, R.P.
A.J. Lohwater's Russian-English dictionary of the mathematical sciences 548
Boast, M.
Newnes refrigeration pocket book 4583
Bobsien, C.H. Fischer-
See
Fischer-Bobsien, C.H.
Bodechtel, J. and Gierloff-Emden, H.G.
The Earth from space 761
Boden, E.
Black's veterinary dictionary 5824
Boden, M.A.
Artificial intelligence and natural man 7361
Bodenham, D.
The Food dictionary 6646
Bodestedt, Olle
Dictionary of industrial automation and control 7349
Bodson, D. and Botez, D.
Electro-optical communications dictionary 4529
Boedijn, K.B.
Plants of the world: the lower plants 2636

British Standards Institution *(contd.)*
Specification for the presentation of research and documentation reports **430**
Symbols for machine tools **4750**
Terms relevant to the feather industry for fillings for bedding, upholstery and other domestic articles **7436**
Vacuum technology - graphical symbols **4575**
Vocabulary for reciprocating internal combustion engines **4567**
Welding **4689**
Welding terms and symbols **4685**
British steam locomotive, 1928-1965 **5387**
British Steel Corporation
The Sections book **4981**
Vocabulary of iron and steel terms: French/English, English/French **6909**
Vocabulary of iron and steel terms: German/English, English/German **6907**
Vocabulary of iron and steel terms: Italian/English, English/Italian **6910**
British television: the formative years **4559**
British Tourist Authority
Where to stay in Britain '96: Camping and caravanning parks **6015**
British transport **6270**
British Universities Film & Video Council
Discovery & invention **316**
British Valve Manufacturers Association
Valve users manual: a technical reference book on industrial valves for the control of fluids **4617**
British whales, dolphins and porpoises **2963**
Britten, F.J.
Britten's old clocks and watches, and their makers **7189**
Britten's watch & clock maker's handbook, dictionary and guide **7180**
Britten's old clocks and watches, and their makers **7189**
Britten's watch & clock maker's handbook, dictionary and guide **7180**
Broadcasting in the United Kingdom **6133**
Brobeck, S.
Encyclopedia of the consumer movement **6018**
Brock, W.H.
The Fontana history of chemistry **1198**
Brodie, P.R.
Dictionary of shipping and shipbroking terms, French/English, English/French **6346**
Dictionary of shipping terms **6338**
Illustrated dictionary of cargo handling **5106**
Brody, A.L. *and* **March, K.S.**
The Wiley encyclopedia of packaging technology **4707**
Bromley, J.
The Clockmakers' Library **7178**
Bronze age, Greek and Roman technology **3079**
Brook, G.
Smithells light metals handbook **6879**
Brook, R.J.
Concise encyclopedia of advanced ceramic materials **6808**
Brook, W.H.
Timbers of the world **7006**
Brooke, M. *and* **Birkhead, T.**
The Cambridge encyclopedia of ornithology **2885**
Brookes, J.K.A.
World directory and handbook of hard metals **4764**
Brooks, H.
Encyclopedia of building and construction terms **7474**
Brooks, J.R.V. *and* **Thomas, P.**
'A Selected bibliography of North Sea geology (up to 1974)' **1580**

Brothwell, D.R.
Digging up bones **2026**
Brouwer, N.J.
International register of historic ships **5361**
Brown, B.J.H.
Explorations in motoring history **6286**
Brown, C.D.
Dictionary of metallurgy **6859**
Brown, D.A.
The Geological evolution of Australia & New Zealand **1611**
Brown, E.H. *and* **Clayton, K.**
The Geomorphology of the British Isles **1705**
Brown, G.
OPEC, its member states and world energy market **6752**
Brown, J.
Farm tools and techniques **5673**
Brown, J.G.
Hydro-electric engineering practices **4316**
Brown, J.H. *and* **Gibson, A.C.**
Biogeography **2296**
Brown, J.R.
Foseco Foundryman's handbook **4656**
Brown, L. *and* **Amadon, D.**
Eagles, hawks and falcons of the world **2935**
Brown, L.H.
The Birds of Africa **2918**
Brown, L.M.
Twentieth century physics **985**
Brown, M.
Dictionary of medical equipment **3496**
Seals and sealing handbook **4163**
Brown, P.
Electronics and computer acronyms **4384**
Brown, R.
Tracks & signs of the birds of Britain and Europe **2907**
Brown, R.H.
Ground-water studies: an international guide for research and practice **1874**
Brown, R.P.
Handbook of plastics test methods **7129**
Brown, S.
Finding the source in sociology and anthropology **1992**
Brown, T.N.
Brown's nautical almanac; daily tide tables for 1999 **819**
Browne, E.
Table of radioactive isotopes **4221**
Browne, W.P. *and* **Cigler, A.J.**
U.S. agricultural groups: institutional profiles **5599**
Brown's flags and funnels of British and foreign steamship companies **6365**
Brown's nautical almanac; daily tide tables for 1999 **819**
Brown's star atlas **807**
Brownstone, D.
The Green encyclopedia **2226, 5227**
Bruce, K.
Science experiments on file **258**
Brücken: Ästhetik and Gestallung **5008**
Brundle, C.
Encyclopedia of materials characterization **3987**
Brunhuber, E.
Giesserei fachwörterbuch **4650**
Bruno, F.J.
The Family mental health encyclopedia **3840**
Bruno, L.C.
Science and technology breakthroughs: from the wheel to the world wide web **301**
Science & technology firsts **301**
The Tradition of science **302**

Bruno, T.J. *and* **Svornos, P.D.N.**
CRC handbook of basic tables for chemical analysis **1272**
Brunskill, R.W.
Traditional farm buildings of Britain and their conservation **5658**
Brush, S.G.
Resources for the history of physics **974**
Brush, S.G. *and* **Belloni, E.**
The History of modern physics **973**
Brush, S.G. *and* **Landsberg, H.E.**
The History of geophysics and meteorology **1500, 1787**
Bruton, E.
Diamonds **6978**
Bruton, E.M.
The History of clocks and watches **7190**
Bruun, P.
Port engineering **5105**
Bruzek, A. *and* **Durrant, C.J.**
Illustrated glossary for solar and solar-terrestrial physics **773**
Bryan, J.E.
Bulbs **5797**
Bryan, M.L.
Remote sensing of earth resources: a guide to information sources **845, 1522**
Bryant, E.
Natural hazards **1506**
Bryden, H.B.
A Scientific bibliography on the national parks of South Africa **2441**
Brydson, J.A.
Plastics materials **7130**
Bryon, R.V. *and* **Bryon, T.N.**
Maritime information **5368**
BSBI abstracts **2672**
BSI Standards Catalogue, 1998-99 **3054**
Buchan, A.
Atlas of meteorology **1786**
Büchner, W.
Industrial inorganic chemistry **6438**
Buchsbaum, W.H.
Encyclopedia of integrated circuits **4298**
Buckingham, J.
Dictionary of natural products **1369**
Dictionary of organic compounds **1329**
Buckler, J.M.H.
A Reference manual of growth and development **3505**
Bucksch, H.
Dictionnaire pour les travaux publics **4943**
Holz-Wörterbuch **6993**
Wörterbuch für Architektur, Hochbau und Baustoffe **7504**
Wörterbuch für Bautechnik und Baumaschinen **4939**
Buczacki, S.
Collins New Generation guide to the fungi of Britain and Europe **2662**
Buczacki, S.T. *and* **Harris, K.M.**
Collins' guide to the pests, diseases and disorders of garden plants **2609**
Bud, R.
Instruments of science **7212**
Instruments of science: an historical encyclopedia **442**
Budig, P.K.
Wörterbuch elektrotechnik und electronik **4255**
Budworth, G.
The Ashley book of knots **7095**
Buecken, F.J.
Vocabulário técnico **108**
Buettner, G.
The Audubon Society encyclopedia of animal life **2769**
Builder's reference book **7516**
Building and site development laws and procedures **7523**

Collin, S.M.H.
 Dictionary of computing **7243**
 Dictionary of computing and information
  technology: English-French; French-
  English **7263**
 Dictionary of computing and information
  technology: English-German **7260**
 Dictionary of personal computing and the
  Internet **7303**
Collins complete dog owner's manual **5902**
Collins dictionary of artificial intelligence
  7373
Collins dictionary of biology **2154**
Collins dictionary of environmental science
  5234
Collins dictionary of geology **1550**
Collins dictionary of mathematics **533**
Collins dictionary of personal computing **7308**
Collins field guide: spiders of Britain and
  northern Europe **2803**
Collins guide to butterflies **2834**
Collins' guide to dinosaurs **1965**
Collins' guide to the ferns, mosses and lichens
  of Britain and Northern and Central Europe
  2679
Collins' guide to the grasses, sedges, rushes
  and ferns of Britain and Northern Europe
  2693
Collins' guide to the pests, diseases and
  disorders of garden plants **2609**
Collins' guide to the rare mammals of the
  world **2947**
Collins' guide to the weather **1800**
Collins' guide to tropical plants **2556, 5736**
Collins, H.H.
 Harper & Row's complete field guide to
  North American wildlife. Eastern edition
  2422
Collins, M.
 The Last rain forests **2451**
Collins New Generation guide to the fungi of
  Britain and Europe **2662**
Collins, N.M.
 The Conservation atlas of tropical forests
  2458
Collins, P.
 British motorcycles since 1900 **5324**
Collins, P.M.
 Carbohydrates **1365**
Collins' pocket guide to stars and planets **778**
Collins, T.H.
 Analog electronics handbook **4400**
Collocott, T.C.
 Chambers diccionario cientifico y
  tecnológico i español / inglés / francés /
  alemán **167**
The Color atlas of galaxies **805**
The Color compendium **1056**
Color encyclopedia of gemstones **1423**
A Colour atlas of human anatomy **3488**
A Colour atlas of livestock breeds **5817**
A Colour atlas of poisonous fungi **2647**
A Colour atlas of poisonous plants: a handbook
  for pharmacists, doctors, toxicologists, and
  biologists **3724**
Colour atlas of the surface forms of the earth
  1695
A Colour guide to paleosols **1942**
The Colour handbook **6835**
Colour identification guide to moths of the
  British Isles **2838**
The Colour identification guide to the
  caterpillars of the British Isles
  (Macrolepidptera) **2837**
Colour identification guide to the grasses,
  sedges, rushes and ferns of the British Isles
  and north-western Europe **2697**
Colour index **1057**
Colour science **1059**
Colvin, M. *and* Reavey, D.
 A Directory for entomologists **2824**

Colwell, R.N.
 Manual of remote sensing **847, 1525**
Combes, S.
 Dictionary of cuisine **5973**
Combined membership list 1996-1997:
  American Mathematical Society **563**
Comet Halley **768**
Comets **772**
Comets: a descriptive catalogue **771**
**Comité International Du Film
 Ethnographique et Sociologique**
 Premier catalogue sélectif international de
  films ethnographiques sur l'Afrique noire
  2067
Comment choisir et cultiver vos plantes
  carnivores **2606**
Commentary on BS 7671: 1992 requirements
  for electrical installations **4343**
'Commercial aircraft of the world' **5423**
Commercial biotechnology **3009**
Commercial diving manual **5099**
Commercial timbers of the world **7004**
Commission Électrotechnique Internationale
 Electricity, electronics and
  telecommunications multilingual dictionary
  4248
 International electrotechnical vocabulary
  4249
Commission of the European Communities
 AGREP: Permanent inventory of agricultural
  research projects in the European
  Communities **5604**
 The Agricultural situation in the Community
  5571
 Directory of non-governmental agricultural
  organizations **5605**
 European directory of research centers in the
  fisheries sector **5942**
 Solvents in common use **6500**
 Veterinary multilingual thesaurus **5855**
**Commission of the European Communities.
 Directorate-General for Research, Science
 & Education**
 Agricultural economics and rural sociology -
  multilingual thesaurus **5610**
**Commission of the European Communities.
 Economic and Social Committee**
 Directory of European agricultural
  organizations **5606**
**Commission of the European Communities.
 Terminology Office**
 Glossaire nouvelles techniques de transport
  6255
**Commission on International Geographical
 Terminology**
 International geographical glossary **1679**
**Commission on Terminology of the
 International Cartographic Association**
 Multilingual dictionary of technical terms in
  cartography **871**
**Commission on Textile Documentation of the
 European Group for the Exchange of
 Experience on the Direction of Textile
 Research**
 Multilingual glossary of textile terminology
  7059
**Committee on Data for Science and
 Technology of the International Council of
 Scientific Unions**
 See
  CODATA
Common abbreviations in clinical medicine
  3222
Common, I.F.B.
 Moths of Australia **2841**
The Common names of North American
  butterflies **2840**

Commonwealth Bureau of Animal Health
 Controlled vocabulary for subject indexing
  in Veterinary bulletin, Index veterinarius,
  Animal disease occurrence, and Small
  animal abstracts **5827**
Commonwealth Forestry Institute
 Forestry Library list of serials **5631**
**Commonwealth of Scientific and Industrial
 Research Organization**
 CSIRO atlas of hardwoods **7002**
Communication, storage and retrieval of
  chemical information **1216**
Communications circuits ready-reference **4523**
'Communications engineering' **4493**
The Communications satellite **4551**
Communications satellite handbook **4550**
Communications standard dictionary **4512,
  6124**
Communications: the most comprehensive
  guide to the UK telecommunications industry
  4520
Compact data for navigation and astronomy
  1996-2000 **815**
The Compact dictionary of exact science and
  technology **137**
The Compact dictionary of food technology
  6647
Compact handbook **2917**
Compact Wörterbuch der exakten
  Naturwissenschaften und der Technik **137**
Companion encyclopedia of anthropology
  2002
Companion encyclopedia of the history and
  philosophy of the mathematical sciences **572**
Companion encyclopedia of the history of
  medicine **3399**
The Companion thesaurus to *Food science and
  technology abstracts* **6661**
Companion to psychiatric studies **3845**
Companion to the history of modern science
  322
A Companion to the physical sciences **128,
  915**
Comparative & veterinary medicine **5822**
Comparative plant ecology **2620**
Compendex **3904**
Compendex*Plus **3903**
Compendium of analytical nomenclature **1279**
A Compendium of armaments and military
  hardware **4819**
Compendium of chemical terminology **1193**
Compendium of seashells **2788**
A Compendium of the biographical literature
  on deceased entomologists **2825**
Compilation of ASTM standard definitions
  4023
Complementary medicine index **3686**
The Complete aquarium encyclopedia of
  tropical freshwater fish **5965**
The Complete book of Australian mammals
  2961
The Complete book of fruit **5765**
The Complete book of herbs **2632**
The Complete book of herbs, spices and
  condiments **6088**
The Complete book of mushrooms **2667**
The Complete book of self-sufficiency **5512**
The Complete book of spices **6087**
The Complete book of the greenhouse **5687**
The Complete book of tools **4753**
Complete British railway maps and gazetteers,
  1825-1985 **5037**
Complete British railways maps and gazetteers,
  1825-1985 **6302**
The Complete button book **7452**
The Complete catalogue of British cars **5314**
A Complete checklist of the birds of the world
  2889
The Complete dog book **5900**
Complete drug reference **3663**

Davis, B.
The Gardener's illustrated encyclopedia of trees and shrubs **5640, 5793**
Davis, B.J.
Information sources in transportation **6251**
Davis, D.
A History of shopping **6029**
Davis, E.B. *and* Schmidt, D.
Guide to information sources in the botanical sciences **2483**
Using the biological literature: a practical guide **2138**
Davis, G.
Who's who in engineering **3962**
Davis' handbook of applied hydraulics **5081**
Davis, H.B.O.
Electrical and electronic technologies: a chronology of events and inventors, 1940-1980 **4287**
Electrical and electronic technologies: a chronology of events and inventors from 1900 to 1940 **4286**
Electrical and electronic technologies: a chronology of events and inventors, to 1900 **4285**
Davis, J.G.
Cheese **5918**
Davis, J.R.
ASM materials engineering dictionary **4005**
ASM specialty handbook: tool materials **4752**
Davis, N.
Afro-American reference **2088**
Davis, P. *and* Brewer, R.C.
A Catalogue of natural science collections in North-East England **2431**
Davis, R.B.
Encyclopedia of American forest and conservation history **5636**
Davis, S.D.
Plants in danger **2453**
Davis, S.J.M.
The Archaeology of animals **2745, 5866**
Davison, E.
RAPRA new trade names in the rubber and plastics industry **7109**
Dawes, B.
A Hundred years of biology **2185**
Dawood, R.
Travellers' health **3523**
Dawson, E.
Directory of environmental abbreviations **2211**
Dawson, P.
Cruise ships **5373**
Dawson, R.M.C.
Data for biochemical research **2336**
Dawydoff, W. *and* Howorka, H.
Technical dictionary of high polymers **7158**
Day, L. *and* McNeill, I.
Biographical dictionary of the history of technology **3075**
Day, M.H.
Guide to fossil man **1978**
Day, R.A.
How to write and publish a scientific paper **431**
De Carle, D.
Clock and watch repairing **7193**
Watch and clock encyclopedia **7182**
De Chiava, J.
Time-saver standards for building types **7546**
De Coster, J.
Dictionary for automotive engineering **5276**
De Francis, J.
Chinese-English glossary of the mathematical sciences **552**
de Hamel, C.
A Guide to the published collections of spectral data held by the SRL **1052**

De Kerchove, R.
International maritime dictionary **6333**
De Morgan, A.
Arithmetical books **609**
De Oliveira, C.
Dicionário cartográfico **868**
De Pina Araújo, A.
De Pina's technical dictionary **175**
De Pina's technical dictionary **175**
De Robertis, E.D.P. *and* De Robertis, E.M.F.
Cellular and molecular biology **2319**
De Sitter, L.U.
Structural geology **1630**
De Sola, R.
Abbreviations dictionary **34**
De Vaucouleurs, G.
Second reference catalogue of bright galaxies **791**
De Vries, L.
French-English science and technology dictionary **150**
German-English science dictionary **132**
Wörterbuch der Chemie und der chemischen Vefahrenstechnik **1145**
De Vries, L. *and* Clason, W.E.
Dictionary of pure and applied physics **941**
De Vries, L. *and* Herrmann, T.M.
English-German technical and engineering dictionary **131**
German-English technical and engineering dictionary **133**
De Wit, H.C.D.
Plants of the world: the higher plants **2684**
De Zuane, J.
Handbook of drinking water quality **5178**
Dean, B.
A Bibliography of fishes **2848**
Dean bibliography of fishes, 1968 **2849**
Dean, N.
'Mathematics and statistics for engineers' **510**
Deblock, N.J.L.
Elsevier's dictionary of public health in six languages **3587**
DECHEMA Corrosion handbook
Corrosion handbook **4038**
The Decorator's directory **7593**
Deep-sea biology **2294**
The Deep sky observer **783**
Deer **2969**
Deer of the world **2968**
Deer, W.A.
Rock-forming minerals **1393, 1834**
Deeson, A.F.L.
The Collector's encyclopedia of rocks and minerals **1837**
Deev, G.N. *and* Losev, K.S.
Anglo-russkiĭ gidrologicheskiĭ slovar' **1882**
DeFelice, B.
Science and engineering conference proceedings: a guide to sources for identification and verification **477**
The Defining years in nuclear physics, 1932-1960s **1094**
Definitions of terms used in geodetic and other surveys **830**
Delacour, J.
The Waterfowl of the world **2930**
Delamare, J. *and* Delamare-Riche, T.
Dictionnaire français-anglais des termes de médecine **3334**
Delijska, B. *and* Manilova, P.
Elsevier's dictionary of communications **4504**
Dell, J.
'Electronics' **4391**
Delleur, J.W.
The Handbook of groundwater engineering **4930**
Delmar's automotive dictionary **5282**

Delves, P.J. *and* Roitt, I.M.
Encyclopedia of immunology **3800**
Demaison, H.
Complete multilingual dictionary of aviation and aeronautical terminology **5396**
DeMaw, M.F.
Ferromagnetic-core design and application handbook **4354**
Demos: internationale ethnographische und folkhistorische Informationen **2029**
Denbigh, K.
A Hundred British spas **3698**
Denffer, D. von
Strasburger's textbook of botany **2498**
Denk, R.
The Complete sailing handbook **6369**
Denney, R.C.
A Dictionary of chromatography **1293**
A Dictionary of spectroscopy **1285**
Dennis, J.G.
International tectonic dictionary: English terminology **1628**
Dennis, W.H.
A Hundred years of metallurgy **6890**
The Dent dictionary of measurement **999**
Dental abstracts **3819**
Denti, R.
Dizionario tecnico, italiano-inglese, inglese-italiano **159**
Dentistry: an illustrated history **3823**
The Dentists register **3822**
Denver Public Library
Catalog of the Conservation Library of the Denver Public Library **2443**
Department of Agriculture
See
United States. Department of Agriculture
Department of Defense
See
United States. Department of Defense
Department of Defense Dictionary of military and associated terms **4822**
Department of Health
See
Great Britain. Department of Health
Department of Health listings of research and development 1991 **3465**
Department of the Interior
See
United States. Department of the Interior
Department of the Interior.
See
United States. Department of the Interior
Department of the Navy
See
United States. Department of the Navy
Department of Trade
See
Great Britain. Department of Trade
Department of Trade and Industry.
See
Great Britain. Department of Trade and Industry
Derry, D.R.
World atlas of geology and mineral deposits **1566**
Derry, T.K. *and* Williams, T.I.
A Short history of technology, from the earliest times to AD 1900 **3066**
Derwent biotechnology abstracts **3000**
Derwent Publications
Thesaurus of agricultural organisms **5710**
Derwent veterinary drug file **5839**
Derwent world patents index **3151**
Desch, H.E.
Timber: its structure, properties and utilization **6988**
Descriptive catalogue of the collection illustrating time measurement: Science Museum **7196**
Desertification: a world bibliography **1718**

Dictionnaire de la chimie et de ses applications **1154**

Dictionnaire de la géographie **1686**

Dictionnaire de la technologie des corps gras en cinq langues **6708**

Dictionnaire de l'eau **5190**

Dictionnaire de l'ethnologie et de l'anthropologie **2036**

Dictionnaire de médecine Flammarion **3336**

Dictionnaire de physique **942**

Dictionnaire de science du sol **5679**

Dictionnaire de termes nouveaux des sciences et des techniques **114**

Dictionnaire des abréviations et acronymes scientifiques, techniques, médicaux, économiques, juridiques **40**

Dictionnaire des agents pathogenes des plantes cultivées **5721**

Dictionnaire des industries **3035**

Dictionnaire des mathématiques **545**

Dictionnaire des racines scientifiques **151**

Dictionnaire des sciences de la terre **1470**

Dictionnaire des sciences et techniques du pétrole **6742**

Dictionnaire des sciences et techniques nucléaires **4185**

Dictionnaire des sols **5680**

Dictionnaire des techniques et technologies modernes **3931**

Dictionnaire des télécommunications et de l'internet **4514**

Dictionnaire des termes techniques de médecine **3338**

Dictionnaire des termes techniques d'entomologie elementaire **2816**

Dictionnaire d'oto-rhino-laryngologie **3809**

Dictionnaire du bâtiment **7508**

Dictionnaire du bâtiment et du génie civil **4944, 7507**

Dictionnaire du forage et des puits **4769**

Dictionnaire du vin **6594**

Dictionnaire encyclopédique d'agrométéorologie **1778**

Dictionnaire encyclopédique d'électronique **4421**

Dictionnaire français-anglais, anglais-français des termes médicaux et biologiques **3335**

Dictionnaire français-anglais des termes de médecine **3334**

Dictionnaire français-anglais des termes relatifs à l'électronique, l'électrotechnique, l'informatique et aux applications connexes **4262**

Dictionnaire français de médecine et de biologie **3277**

Dictionnaire français et anglais de terminologie mathématique **546**

Dictionnaire français et anglais des aviateurs **5399**

Dictionnaire général d'acoustique et d'electroacoustique **1027**

Dictionnaire horloger **7186**

Dictionnaire: Industrie des matières plastiques. Français/Anglais **7140**

Dictionnaire informatique **7264**

Dictionnaire multilingue de la Fédération International de Géomètres **827**

Dictionnaire multilingue des poissons et produits de la pêche **5936**

Dictionnaire pétrolier des techniques de diagraphie, forage et production **6735**

Dictionnaire pour les travaux publics **4943**

Dictionnaire. Procédés et produits chimiques **6491**

Dictionnaire professionnel illustré de l'horlogerie **7185**

Dictionnaire technique anglais **158, 3036**

Dictionnaire technique de la marine **4825, 5087**

Dictionnaire technique de la mécanisation agricole **5667**

Dictionnaire technique de l'armement **4848**

Dictionnaire technique de l'hôtellerie **5974**

Dictionnaire technique des chemins de fer **5015**

Dictionnaire technique des industries graphiques **6187**

Dictionnaire technique illustré en six langues **1743**

Dictionnaire trilingue de la pomme de terre **5745**

Dictionnaires et vocabulaires à la bibliothèque de terminologie et références **5513**

The Diecasting book **4646**

Diesel engine reference book **4571**

Diesel engines of the world **4570**

Diesel generator handbook **4572**

Diet, nutrition and health **3546**

Dietel, W.
Seefahrts-Wörterbuch **6345**

The Digest of agricultural census statistics **5577**

Digest of data for the construction industry **7482**

Digest of environmental protection and water statistics **5168**

Digest of information and patent review **6801**

Digest of literature on dielectrics **4338**

Digest of United Kingdom energy statistics, 1998 **4093**

Digging up bones **2026**

Digital circuits ready-reference **4465**

The Digital imaging dictionary **7422**

The Digital signal processing handbook **4496**

Digital systems reference book **4480**

Diment, J.A.
Geological directory of the British Isles **1561**

DIN [Deutsche Industrie Normen]
Katalog für technische regeln **3055**

Dingley, P.
Historic books on veterinary science and animal husbandry **5819**

Dinosaur data book **1962**

Dinosaur tracks **1969**

Dinosaurs **1967**

Dinosaurs: a guide to research **1959**

Dinosaurs and their living relatives **1966**

Dinosaurs: the encyclopedia **1961**

D'inveno, R.A.
Introducing Einstein's relativity **1004**

Diodato, V. *and* Tolan, M.
'Mathematical biographies: profiles and sources of information on eighteen mathematicians' **595**

Directories held by the Science Reference and Information Service **3052**

Directory **834, 6236**

A Directory for entomologists **2824**

Directory for the environment: organisations, campaigns and initiatives in the British Isles **2250-2251**

A Directory of African wetlands **2266**

Directory of agricultural co-operatives and other farm-controlled businesses in the United Kingdom **5614**

Directory of American research and technology: 1998 **3101**

The Directory of appropriate technology **3084**

Directory of associations of inventors **3146**

Directory of audio-visual sources: history of science, medicine, and technology **317**

Directory of Australian professional associations, 1996 **473**

Directory of British fossiliferous localities **1921**

Directory of British geological museums **1616**

Directory of British postgraduate medical qualifications **3468**

Directory of British scientific instrument makers 1550-1851 **7217**

Directory of chemical producers: United States of America **6516**

Directory of chemical producers: Western Europe **6511**

Directory of chemistry software **1111**

Directory of Chinese agricultural and related organizations **5593**

Directory of collections of micro-organisms **2199**

Directory of consulting practices in chemistry and related subjects **1181**

Directory of consumer information sources **6023**

The Directory of continuing education for nurses, midwives and health visitors **3795**

Directory of courses in land-based industries 1999-2000 **5609**

Directory of current research on sheep and goats **5883**

Directory of energy databases **4049**

Directory of engineering education institutions **3972**

Directory of environment statistics **5169**

Directory of environmental abbreviations **2211**

Directory of European agricultural organizations **5606**

A Directory of European environmental organizations **2249**

Directory of European industrial and trade associations **7171**

Directory of European observatories **743**

Directory of European societies and associations: medicine **3456**

Directory of food and nutrition information services and resources **6663**

Directory of forestry research organizations **5633**

Directory of geo-analytical facilities in British universities, colleges, polytechnics and research institutions **1559**

Directory of geoscience libraries, North America **1486**

Directory of graduate research **1219**

Directory of health information resources in Scotland **3452**

Directory of information sources in Japan, 1986 **457**

Directory of international and national medical and related societies **3457**

Directory of international cooperation in science and technology **466**

Directory of international periodicals and newsletters on the built environment **7513**

Directory of iron and steel plants **6911**

Directory of Japanese scientific periodicals **396**

Directory of libraries and information centers of the Academies of Sciences of Socialist countries **446**

Directory of libraries and information centres in Ireland **454**

Directory of library and information facilities **5095**

Directory of low temperature research in Europe **4593**

Directory of medical and health care libraries in the United Kingdom and Republic of Ireland 1997-8 **3453**

Directory of mines and quarries **4790**

A Directory of mosses **2669**

Directory of national and regional industrial property offices **3192**

Directory of natural history and related societies in Britain and Ireland **2390**

Directory of non-governmental agricultural organizations **5605**

Directory of non-governmental environment and development organisations in OECD member countries **2256**

Directory of on-going research in cancer epidemiology, 1992 **3734**

Driver, A.H.
Catalogue of engraved portraits of the Library. [Royal College of Physicians of London] 3384

Driver, E.
Bibliography of cookery books, 1875-1914 6039
The Model maker's handbook 3950

Driving Standards Agency.
The Highway code 6292

Drought in Africa. 2 1794

Drozda, T.J.
Tool and manufacturing engineers handbook 4632

Druce, G.
'Kinematics, dynamics and machines' 1008

Drug companies and products world guide 3652

Drugs handbook, 1995-96 3670

Drummond, J.C. and Wilbraham, A.
The Englishman's food 3550

Drury, G.H.
Guide to North American steam locomotives 5383
Guide to tourist railroads and musuems 5051

Drury, S.A.
Images of the earth: a guide to remote sensing 1523

Dryden, I.G.C.
The Efficient use of energy 4064

Du Vall, N.
Domestic technology 6097

Dubbel Handbook of mechanical engineering 4129

Dubreuil, L.
World directory of map collections 881

Duckham, A.N.
Farming systems of the world 5559

Duckley, R.J.
History of tramways from horse to rapid transit 5056

Duda, R.
Minerals of the World 1414

Dudley, H.
The Presentation of original work in medicine and biology 3444

Dudley's gear handbook 4729

Dudszus, A.
Dictionary of ship types 5333

Duff, P.McL.D.
Holmes' principles of physical geology 1618

Duff, P.McL.D. and Smith, A.J.
Geology of England and Wales 1600

Duffey, E.
National parks and reserves of Western Europe 2435

Duke, J.A.
CRC handbook of medicinal herbs 3678

Dulbecco, R.
Encyclopedia of human biology 2146

Dumitrescu, D.
Dictionar tehnic: englez-român 164
Dictionar tehnic: român-englez 165

Dummer, G.W.A.
Electronic inventions and discoveries 4441

Dumper, L.
'Welding, brazing and soldering' 4679

Duncalf, W.G.
The Guinness book of plant facts and feats 2496

Duncan, A.S.
Dictionary of medical ethics 3473

Duncan, R. and Weston-Smith, M.
The Encyclopaedia of ignorance 85

Dunes of the European coasts 1713

Dunham, W.
Journey through genius 574
The Mathematical universe 525

Dunmore, J.
NSCA environmental glossary 5236
NSCA reference book 5232

Dunnill, P. and Rudd, M.
British biotechnology and British industry 3005

Dunning, F.W.
Mineral deposits of Europe 1861

Dunning, P.H.
Sources of information on alternative energy technology held at the Science Reference and Information Service 4117

Dunster, J. and Dunster, K.
Dictionary of natural resource management 2448

Dupayrat, J.
Dictionary of biomedical acronyms and abbreviations 2133, 3221

Durbin, R.T.
A Guide to the culture of science, technology and medicine 216

Durham, S.
Jane's international ABC aerospace directory 5464

Durney, L.J.
Electroplating engineering handbook 4358

Duval, C and Duval, R.
Dictionnaire de la chimie et de ses applications 1154

Duveen, D.I.
Bibliotheca alchemica et chemica 1114

Dwight, H.B.
Tables of integrals and other mathematical data 622

Dyakowski, T. and Brodowicz, K.
Heat pumps 4594

Dyer, J.C.
Vegetarianism: an annotated bibliography 3552, 6082

Dying, death and grief 3511

Dymshits, L.B.
Anglo-russkiĭ khimiko teknologicheskiĭ Slovar' 6450

Dyos, H.L. and Aldcroft, D.H.
British transport 6270

Eagle, S. and Deschamps, J.
Information sources in environmental protection 3602, 5127

Eagles, hawks and falcons of the world 2935

Eagleson, M.
Concise encyclopedia chemistry 1126

Eales, N.B.
Catalogue of books and pamphlets. [Cole Library of Early Medicine and Zoology] 3242

Early American scientific and technical literature 413

Early American scientific instruments and their makers 7218

'Early astronomical and mathematical instruments - a brief survey of sources and modern studies' 603

'Early astronomical and mathematical instruments: a brief survey of sources and modern studies.' 742

The Early history of metallurgy 6882

The Early history of palaeontology 1915

The Early history of veterinary literature and its development 5853

Early hominids of Africa 1979

The Early naturalists: their lives and work (1530-1789) 2401

Early physics and astronomy 971

Early radio wave detectors 4545

Early scientific instruments: Europe 1400-1800 7214

Earney, F.C.F.
Marine mineral resources 1860
Petroleum and hard minerals from the sea 1868

Earth and astronomical sciences research centres 733, 1487

The Earth from space 761

The Earth: its origin, history and physical constitution 1620

Earth online: an Internet guide for earth science 1443

The Earth sciences: an annotated bibliography 1484

Earth sciences reference 1467

Earthquake prediction 1504

East European peasantries: social relations 2049

Eastman, C.R.
A Bibliography of fishes 2848

Eastwood, B.
Directory of audio-visual sources: history of science, medicine, and technology 317

EBCC atlas of European breeding birds 2901

Ebel, H.F.
The Art of scientific writing 432

Ebied, R.Y.
Bibliography of mediaeval Arabic and Jewish medicine and allied sciences 3440

Ecce homo: an annotated bibliographic history of physical anthropology 1991

Eccles, H.
The Periodic table of elements compendium 1436

ECDB: (Electronic Components Data Bank) 4447

ECO directory of environmental databases in the United Kingdom 2213

ECODISC 2245

Ecolinking 5120

Ecological abstracts 2245

Ecological engineering 2229

Ecological terminology 2232

Ecology abstracts 2246

Ecology and biogeography in India 2275

The Ecology of fossils 1929

Ecology of North America 2278

The Ecology of river systems 2264

Economic Commission for Europe
Annual bulletin of steel statistics for Europe 6926

Economic Commission for Europe and International Federation of Robotics.
World robotics, 1998 7397

Economic Commission for Europe. Inland Transport Committee
Glossary for inland transport 6388

Economic mineral deposits 1851

Economics of shipping practice and management 6332

The Economist desk companion 996

Economist Intelligence Unit
World textile trade and production trends 7076

Ecosystems of the world 2263

EDAP 5720

Eden, P.
Dictionary of land surveyors and local cartographers of Great Britain and Ireland, 1550-1850 839

EDF-DOC 4303

EDI implementation and security 4530

Edible fungi cyclopedia 2660

Edinburgh Engineering Virtual Library 3908

Edmundson, R.S.
Dictionary of organophosphorus compounds 1366

Edney, A.
RSPCA complete cat care manual 5906

Edson, D.T.
Glossary of technical terms in computer assisted cartography 870

Edwards, E.H.
A Standard guide to horse and pony breeds 5878

European Communities Commission. Directorate - General Research, Science and Education. Nuclear Plant Safety Division
Nuclear standards **4206**

European Communities Commission. Terminology Office
Glossaire des normes de l'acier **6920**
Steel standards glossary **6925**

European Communities Commission. Translation Service
Biotechnology glossary **2995**

European Community Office for Official Publications.
EINECS-Plus **6504**

European Community shipping directory **5354**

European Conference of Ministers of Transport
European rules concerning road traffic signs and signals **6295**
European transport trends and infrastructural needs **6263**

European directory of agrochemical products **5720**

European directory of research centers in the fisheries sector **5942**

European electronics directory 1994 **4430**

European environmental information sourcebook **2272**

European environmental yearbook: nature conservation, protection of the environment, town and country planning in Belgium, Denmark, the Federal Republic of Germany, France, Greece, Ireland, Italy, Luxembourg, the Netherlands, Portugal, Spain and the United Kingdom, with special surveys on Australia, Japan, USA and USSR **2273**

European Foundry directory and register of forges **4654**

The European garden flora **2558**

European glass directory & buyers guide, 1997 **6803**

European guide to telecommunications standards **4524**

European handbook of plant diseases **5701**

European Inventory of Existing Commercial Substances **6504**

European paint and resin news **6845**

European Parliament
Ecological terminology **2232**

European Parliament. Terminology Office
Terminologie du secteur de la pêche **5937**
Terminology of new and renewable sources of energy **4102**

The European passive solar handbook **4112, 7589**

European patent bulletin **3172**
The European patent system **3202**
European patents handbook **3198**
European petroleum year book **6748**
European railway atlas **5030**
European research centres **490**
European rules concerning road traffic signs and signals **6295**
European sources of scientific and technical information **445**

European Space Agency
Recueil de terminologie spatiale **5460**

European technical consultancies **3094**
The European television directory 1994/95 **6136**
European transport trends and infrastructural needs **6263**
EuroPharm **3662**
Europump terminology **4623**
Evaluated Nuclear Structure Data File **4166**

Evans, A.
Glossary of molecular biology **2350**

Evans, D.
A History of nature conservation in Britain **2456**

Evans, D.S.
Under Capricorn **723**

Evans, G.
The Encyclopedia of drug abuse **3577**

Evans, J.G. *and* Williams, T.F.
Oxford textbook of geriatric medicine **3764**

Evans-Pritchard, E.E.
A History of anthropological thought **2020**

Everett-Heath, J.
British military helicopters **4890, 5435**

Everett, T.H.
The New York Botanical Garden illustrated encyclopedia of horticulture **5760**

Everitt, B.S.
The Cambridge dictionary of statistics **642**

Everywoman's medical handbook **3516**

Eves, H.
An Introduction to the history of mathematics **575**

Evetta, J.E.
Concise encyclopedia of magnetic and superconducting materials **4352**

Evolution **2316**
The Evolution of geomorphology **1700**
Evolution of tertiary mammals of North America **1971**
Evolution of the earth **1826**
The Evolution of the English farm **5587**
Evolution of the vertebrates **2843**
The Evolution of useful things **3148**

Ewer, R.F.
The Carnivores **2970**

Ewing, G.W.
Analytical instrumentation handbook **7200**

Excavation handbook **4997**
Excerpta botanica. Section B. Sociologica **2511**
Excerpta medica **3355**
Excerpta medica. 1. Anatomy, anthropology, embryology and histology **2010, 3484**
Excerpta medica. 3. Endocrinology **3825**
Excerpta medica. 5. General pathology **3739**
Excerpta medica. 7. Pediatrics and pediatric surgery **3756**
Excerpta medica. 8. Neurology and neurosurgery **3833**
Excerpta medica. 9. Surgery **3873**
Excerpta medica. 11. Oto-, rhino-, laryngology **3808**
Excerpta medica. 14. Radiology **3701**
Excerpta medica. 15. Chest diseases. Thoracic surgery and tuberculosis **3728**
Excerpta medica. 16. Cancer **3730**
Excerpta medica. 17. Public health, social medicine and hygiene **3588**
Excerpta medica. 18. Cardiovascular diseases and cardiovascular surgery **3805**
Excerpta medica. 20. Gerontology and geriatrics **3765**
Excerpta medica. 21. Developmental biology and teratology **3735**
Excerpta medica. 22: Human genetics **2306**
Excerpta medica. 23. Nuclear medicine **3702**
Excerpta medica. 24. Anesthesiology **3880**
Excerpta medica. 25. Hematology **3807**
Excerpta medica. 26. Immunology, serology and transplantation **3802**
Excerpta medica. 30. Clinical and experimental pharmacology **3649**
Excerpta medica. 31. Arthritis and rheumatism **3829**
Excerpta medica. 32. Psychiatry **3856**
Excerpta medica. 33. Orthopedic surgery **3884**
Excerpta medica. 35. Occupational health and industrial medicine **3611**
Excerpta medica. 40. Drug dependence, alcohol abuse and alcoholism **3580**
Excerpta medica. 46: Environmental health and pollution control **5158**
Excerpta medica. 48. Gastroenterology **3824**

Excerpta medica. 50. Epilepsy abstracts **3836**
'Executing the design: materials, structures, construction' **7550**
Exobiology: a research guide **2209**
Exotic tropical fishes **5960**
Exotica 4 international **5800**
Expert systems: a bibliography **7359**
Exploration of the universe **684**
Explorations in motoring history **6286**
Exploring the southern sky **796**
Extinct birds **2886**
Extinct species of the world **2468, 2748**
The Extra pharmacopoeia **3661**
The Extraterrestrial encyclopedia **2208**

Eylenbosch, E.
Elsevier's dictionary of pests and diseases in useful plants **5706**

Eyres, D.J.
Ship construction sketches and notes **5336**

Ezell, E.C. *and* Pegg, T.M.
Small arms of the world **4863**

Ezhela, V.V.
Particle physics: one hundred years of discoveries **1099**

The Faber medical dictionary **3288**

Facciola, S.
Cornucopia: a source book of edible plants **5728**

Fachinformation Bahn. Dokumentation der Fachliteratur **5019**

Fachinformationszentrum Chemie GmbH, Berlin
Parat: Index of polymer trade names **7163**

Fachwörterbuch akustick **1029**
Fachwörterbuch: Carbochemie. Petrochemie **6563, 6734**
Fachwörterbuch chemie und chemische **1149**
Fachwörterbuch Chemiefasern **7093**
Fachwörterbuch der Meereskunde-Meerestechnik **1744**
Fachwörterbuch für Bewässerung und Entwässerung **5083, 5692**
Fachwörterbuch industrielle electrotechnik, energie- und automatisierungs-technik **4258**
Fachwörterbuch kunstofftechnik **7135**
Fachwörterbuch mikroelektronik **4462**
Fachwörterbuch Optic und Optischer Gerätebau **1039**
Fachwörterbuch optik, foto, video **7424**
Fachwörterbuch papier **7038**
Fachwörterbuch technik und angewandte wissenschaften **3032**
Fachwörterbuch verpacking **4712**
FACT **5947**
The Facts-on-File dictionary of biology **2156**
The Facts-on-File dictionary of botany **2503**
The Facts on File dictionary of environmental science **5150**
The Facts on File dictionary of nautical terms **6342**
The Facts on File dictionary of telecommunications **4508**

Faherty, K.F. *and* Williamson, T.G.
Wood engineering and construction handbook **7564**

Fairbridge, R.W.
The Encyclopedia of atmospheric sciences and astrogeology **1769**
Encyclopedia of earth sciences **1453**
The Encyclopedia of geochemistry and environmental sciences **1514**
The Encyclopedia of geomorphology **1667**
The Encyclopedia of oceanography **1733**
The Encyclopedia of world regional geology **1578**

Fairbridge, R.W. *and* Bourgeois, J.
The Encyclopedia of sedimentology **1632**

Fairbridge, R.W. *and* Finkl, C.W.
The Encyclopedia of soil science **5677**

Fairbridge, R.W. *and* Jablonski, D.
The Encyclopedia of palaeontology **1897**

Fairchild's dictionary of textiles **7067**
The Fairplay book of shipping abbreviations **6323**
Fairplay world shipping directory **5355, 6352**
Fairpo, J.E.H. and Fairpo, C.G.
Heinemann dental dictionary **3816**
Falbe, J. and Regitz, M.
Römpp's Chemie-Lexikon **1128**
Familiar medical quotations **3373**
The Families of flowering plants **2687**
Family medical guide **3299**
The Family mental health encyclopedia **3840**
Family of man **2033**
Famous names in engineering **3958**
Fan engineering **4605**
Fanning, A.E.
Steady as she goes **6375**
FAO books in print **5499**
FAO documentation: current bibliography **5539**
FAO production yearbook **5549**
FAO quarterly bulletin of statistics **5549**
FAO trade yearbook **5654**
Farace, J.
The Digital imaging dictionary **7422**
Farago, F.T.
Handbook of dimensional measurement **4157**
Farber, E.
Great chemists **1204**
Farg-och lackteknisk ordlista **6843**
Farlow Reference Library of Cryptogamic Botany, Harvard, University
Catalog. [Farlow Reference Library of Cryptogamic Botany] **2637**
Farm buildings **5660**
Farm machinery **5664**
Farm management pocketbook **5657**
Farm tools and techniques **5673**
Farm tools through the ages **5673**
Farmer, R.H.
Handbook of hardwoods **7011**
The Farmer's tools **5674**
Farming systems in the tropics **5563**
Farming systems of the world **5559**
Farndon, J.
Concise encyclopedia earth **1457**
Farnie, D.A.
The English cotton industry and the world market, 1815-1896 **7088**
Farr, A.D.
Dictionary of medical laboratory sciences **3446**
Farrell, S.
International packaging information sources **4716**
World environmental research directory **5174**
The Fashion dictionary **7445**
Fashion production terms **7444**
Fashions in hair **7450**
Fasman, G.B.
CRC handbook of biochemistry and molecular biology **2335**
Fatigue data book **6894**
Faudouas, J.C.
Dictionnaire technique des industries graphiques **6187**
Faulks, R.W.
Bus and coach operation **6282**
Favati, F.
Dizionario di agricoltura: inglese-italiano, italiano-inglese **5526**
Fawcett, J.
Historic floors **7540**
Fayed, M.E.
Handbook of powder science and technology **4661**
Feast directory **6654**
Feather, J.
A Dictionary of book history **6145**

Feather, J. *(contd.)*
A History of British publishing **6227**
Fédération Dentaire Internationale
A Lexikon of English dental terms **3815**
Fédération Européenne des Fabricants des Produits Réfractaires
Vocabulaire: les produits réfractaires et leurs applications **6821**
Fédération Internationale de la Précontrainte
Multilingual dictionary of concrete **6832**
Fédération Internationale des Géomètres. Commission de Dictionnaire Technique
Dictionnaire multilingue de la Fédération International de Géomètres **827**
Fédération Nationale des Logis et Auberges de France
Logis de France **5986**
Feisenberger, H.A.
Sale catalogues of libraries of eminent persons **81**
Feldman, A. and Ford, B.
Scientists and inventors **338**
Felius, M.
Cattle breeds: an encyclopedia **5880**
Feltwell, J.
The Story of silk **7091**
Fenaroli, G.
Fenaroli's handbook of flavor ingredients **6694**
Fenaroli's handbook of flavor ingredients **6694**
Fenner, W.R.
Quick reference to veterinary medicine **5828**
Feret, B.L.
Gastronomical and culinary literature **6043**
Ferguson, E.S.
Bibliography of the history of technology **3068**
Ferguson, J.
Bibliotheca chemica **1115**
Ferguson, J.E.
The Heavy elements **1434**
Fermented foods of the world **6690**
Ferne, G.
Science and technology in Scandinavia **19**
The Ferns of Britain and Ireland **2682**
Ferretti, V.
Dictionary of electronics, computing and telecommunication **4419, 4513, 7261**
Ferrier, R.W.
The History of the British Petroleum Company **6757**
Ferro-alloy directory and databook **6895**
Ferromagnetic-core design and application handbook **4354**
Ferromagnetic materials **4353**
Fertilizer dictionary **5696**
Feutry, M.
Technological dictionary **110**
Ffloyd, T.
Croner's energy management **4095**
Fiala, I. and Fevre, F.
Dictionnaire des agents pathogenes des plantes cultivées **5721**
Fiber optics standard dictionary **4534**
Fichtner, N.
Nuclear standards **4206**
The Field artillery **4855**
Field crop abstracts **5734**
Field crop diseases handbook **5702**
Field, E.J. and Harrison, R.J.
Anatomical terms: their origin and derivation **3481**
Field engineer's manual **4929**
Field geology in the British Isles **1591**
A Field guide to birds of the USSR **2915**
A Field guide to caterpillars of butterflies and moths in Britain and Europe **2832**
The Field guide to geology **1541**
Field guide to mushrooms and toadstools of Britain and Europe **2663**

Field guide to orchids of Britain and Europe **2699**
A Field guide to rocks and minerals **1836**
Field guide to the birds of Australia **2929**
A Field guide to the birds of Britain and Europe **2902**
The Field guide to the birds of New Zealand **2928**
A Field guide to the birds of Southern Africa **2920**
A Field guide to the crops of Britain and Europe **5730**
A Field guide to the insects of Britain and northern Europe **2828**
Field guide to the insects of Britain and Northern Europe **2829**
A Field guide to the land snails of Britain and north-west Europe **2789**
A Field guide to the mammals of Africa, including Madagascar **2957**
A Field guide to the mammals of Central America and southeast Mexico **2960**
A Field guide to the reptiles and amphibians of Britain and Europe **2864**
Field guide to the rocks and minerals of the world **1403**
A Field guide to the stars and planets **780**
A Field guide to the trees of Britain and Northern Europe **5651**
Field, H.
Bibliography on Southwestern Asia **2060, 2588**
Fieldbook of natural history **2387**
Fieser, L.F.
Reagents for organic synthesis **1227**
Fifty famous liners **5372**
Les filigranes. Dictionnaire historique des marques du papier **7049**
Films for anthropological teaching **2018**
Filters and filtration handbook **4369**
'Financial Times' energy yearbook mining 1999 **4786**
'Financial Times' energy yearbook oil and gas 1999 **6749**
'Financial Times' who's who in world oil and gas **6751**
'Financial Times' world hotel directory 1999 **5977**
Finding answers in science and technology **75**
Finding the source in sociology and anthropology **1992**
Finding the source of medical information **3255**
Fine chemicals database **6503**
Finite element methods **3915**
Fink, D.G.
Standard handbook for electrical engineers **4277**
Finkel, H.J.
CRC handbook of irrigation technology **5691**
Finkelstein, L. and Grattan, K.T.V.
Concise encyclopedia of measurement and instrumentation **4348**
Finkl, C.W.
The Encyclopedia of applied geology **1537**
Encyclopedia of field and general geology **1538**
Finn, B.
The History of electrical technology **4291**
Fintel, M.J.
Handbook of concrete engineering **4976**
Fire-CD **3616**
Fire directory, 1996 **3617**
Fire sciences dictionary **3615**
Fire terms: a guide to their meaning and use **3613**
Firkin, B.G. and Whitworth, J.A.
Dictionary of medical eponyms **3412**
First aid manual **3634**

Firth, C.
World engine digest **4568**
Fischbeck, H.J. *and* **Fischbeck, K.H.**
Formulas, facts and constants **961**
Fischer-Bobsien, C.H.
International encyclopedia of textile finishing **7080**
Fischer, K.
Fachwörterbuch der Meereskunde-Meerestechnik **1744**
'Welding: a core list for community college libraries' **4680**
Fischer, R. *and* **Kruchten, P.**
Dictionnaire informatique **7264**
Fish catching methods of the world **5948**
Fish handling and processing **6705**
Fishbase 97 **2847**
Fisher, D.
Rules of thumb for engineers and scientists **653**
Fishermen's handbook **5950**
Fisher, Sir R.A. *and* **Yates, F.**
Statistical tables for biological, agricultural and medical research **2179, 3374, 5550**
The Fishes of the British Isles and North-west Europe **2859**
Fishes of the north-eastern Atlantic and the Mediterranean **2853, 5955**
Fishes of the world **2857**
Fitter, A.
New generation guide to the wild flowers of Britain and Northern Europe **2559**
Fitter, R. *and* **Fitter, A.**
Collins' guide to the grasses, sedges, rushes and ferns of Britain and Northern Europe **2693**
Fitzgibbon, T.
The Food of the western world **6058**
Fitzpatrick, J.J.
Encyclopedia of nursing research **3781**
Fitzsimons, V.F.M.
Snakes of southern Africa **2871**
Five centuries of map printing **899**
Five hundred years of nautical science, 1400-1900 **6356**
Five hundred years of technology in the home **6100**
Five language dictionary of surface coatings, plating, products, finishing, corrosion, plastics and rubber **6528**
Five-language technology dictionary **3030**
Fiziko-geograficheskiĭ atlas mira **1696**
Flags at sea **6364**
Flaherty, D.H.
Privacy and data protection **7332**
Flegg, G.
Numbers, their history and meaning **611**
Fleischer, M.
Glossary of mineral species **1412**
Flemming, E.
Encyclopaedia of textiles **7074**
Fletcher, A.
An Index of mathematical tables **663**
Fleury, B.E.
Dinosaurs: a guide to research **1959**
Fleutry, M.
Dictionnaire encyclopédique d'électronique **4421**
Flexible manufacturing systems handbook **4633**
Flick, E.W.
Cosmetics additives **6720**
Industrial solvents handbook **6501**
Flight and flying **5411**
'Flight International' Directory, part 1: United Kingdom and Ireland Directory **5406**
'Flight International' Directory, part 2: Mainland Europe and Ireland **5407**
Flindell, I.
'Noise as a pollutant' **5248**

Flint, V.E.
A Field guide to birds of the USSR **2915**
Flood hazard management **5109**
Flood studies report **5110**
Flood, W.E.
Scientific words, their structure and meaning **124**
Floods: a geographical perspective **1634**
Floors and flooring **7543**
Flora & fauna of localities **2544, 2777**
Flora Britannica **2575**
Flora europaea **2560**
Flora of Australia **2600**
Flora of Australia supplementary series **2600**
Flora of Great Britain and Ireland **2564**
Flora of New Zealand **2597**
Flora of North America **2592**
Flora of North America Editorial Committee
Flora of North America **2592**
Flora of Southern Africa **2590**
Flora of the British Isles **2572**
Flora of the British Isles: illustrations **2573**
Flora SSSR **2587**
'Floras great and small' **2569**
Flore complète illustrée en couleurs de France, Suisse et Belgique **2585**
Floristic regions of the world **2552**
Florkin, M. *and* **Stotz, E.H.**
Comprehensive biochemistry **2330**
Flour Milling and Baking Research Association abstracts **6688**
Flow measurement engineering handbook **4609**
Flower, R. *and* **Jones, M.W.**
One hundred years of motoring **5311**
Flowering plant index of illustration and information **2686**
Flowering plants of the world **2551**
Flowering plants of Wales **2584**
Flowers of Europe **2561**
Flowers of South-west Europe **2563**
Flügge, S.
Handbuch der Physik **926**
Fluid abstracts: civil engineering **5088**
Fluid abstracts: process engineering **4598, 5089**
Fluid flow measurements abstracts **1017**
'Fluid mechanics and fluid power systems' **4599**
Fluid power standards **4602**
Fluid sealing abstracts **4164**
FLUIDEX. BHRA Fluid engineering abstracts **4597, 5073**
Fluorine chemistry **1314**
F.O. Licht's Internationales zuckerwirtschaftliches Jahr- und Adressbuch... Weltzucker statistik **6681**
Fodor's railways of the world **6298**
Fogg, G.E.
A History of Antarctic science **1657**
Fogle, B.
The Encyclopedia of the cat **5908**
Foltz, R.D.
Protecting scientific ideas and inventions **3110**
The Fontana history of astronomy and cosmology **728**
The Fontana history of chemistry **1198**
Fontgalland, B.
The World railway system **5028**
Food additive user's handbook **6697**
Food additives handbook **6696**
Food and Agriculture Organization
Abbreviations used by FAO **5489**
Animal health yearbook **5844**
Directory of forestry research organizations **5633**
FAO books in print **5499**
FAO production yearbook **5549**
FAO trade yearbook **5654**

Food and Agriculture Organization *(contd.)*
International directory of marine scientists **1763**
Mammals in the seas **2952**
Manual for small veterinary libraries **5854**
Milk and milk products **5915**
Selected terms in fish culture **5939**
Soil map of the world **5683**
Technical conversion factors for agricultural commodities **5551**
Yearbook of fishery statistics **5944**
Yearbook of forest products **5638**
Food and Agriculture Organization *and* **Flood, R.C.**
A Selective annotated bibliography of fishery statistical publications **5943**
Food and Agriculture Organization. Fisheries Department
Atlas of the living resources of the seas **5953**
Food and Agriculture Organization. Terminology and Reference Section. Publications Division
Dictionaries and vocabularies **5513**
Food and food production encyclopedia **6632**
Food and nutrition bibliography **6629**
Food and nutrition encyclopedia **6635**
Food composition and nutrition tables **3543**
Food, cookery and diet **3528, 6050**
Food dehydration **6689**
Food dictionary **6644**
The Food dictionary **6646**
Food facts: the complete no-fads plain facts guide to healthy eating **3545**
Food focus **5688**
Food from your garden **5763**
Food industries manual **6641**
Food labelling data for manufacturers **6675**
Food microbiology **6669**
Food multilingual thesaurus **6662**
The Food of the western world **6058**
Food processing and nutrition **6666**
Food safety **6638**
'Food science' **6631**
Food science **6640**
Food science and technology abstracts **6650**
Food: the gift of Osiris **6658**
Food trades directory of the UK and Europe **6655**
Food - your miracle medicine: how food can prevent and treat over 100 symptoms and problems **3542**
Foods adlibra **6626**
Footwear industry technical vocabulary **7438**
Foraminifera **1948**
Forbes, J.R.
Dictionnaire des techniques et technologies modernes **3931**
Ford-Robertson, F.C. *and* **Winters, R.K.**
Terminology of forest science, technology, practice and products **5629**
Ford, T.D. *and* **Cullingford, C.H.D.**
The Science of speleology **1725**
Foreman, S.
Consumer monitor 2 **6016**
Forest encyclopaedia **5620**
Forest products abstracts **5639, 6995**
The Forester's companion **5622**
Forestry abstracts **5630**
Forestry and forest products vocabulary **5626**
Forestry handbook **5621**
Forestry Library list of serials **5631**
Forget, C.
Elsevier's dictionary of jewellery and watchmaking **6974**
Forging handbook **4647**
Forje, J.W.
Science and technology in Africa **26**
Forms and agreements on intellectual property and international licensing **3196**

Formula handbook for environmental engineers and scientists **5165**

Formulas, facts and constants **961**

Formulas for stress, strain, and structural matrices **4974**

Forrester, W.H.
Directory of medical and health care libraries in the United Kingdom and Republic of Ireland 1997-8 **3453**

Forscey, L.A.
Multi-lingual poultry dictionary **5891**

Fortescue, S.
Science policy in the Soviet Union **16**

Fortey, R.
Fossils: the key to the past **1900**

Forthcoming international scientific and technical conferences **475**

Fortress: a history of military defence **4838**

Foseco Foundryman's handbook **4656**

Fossil amphibians and reptiles **1958**

Fossil atlas: fishes **1956**

Fossil birds **1970**

The Fossil record 2 **1912**

Fossil vertebrates of Africa **1953**

Fossilen Atlas: Fische **1956**

Fossilium catalogus **1913**

Fossils for amateurs **1904**

Fossils, minerals and rocks **1899**

Fossils of the world **1901**

Fossils: the key to the past **1900**

Foster, W.D.
A History of parasitology **2323**

Foulkes, C.
Larousse encyclopedia of wine **6592**

Foundation engineering **4998**

Foundation engineering handbook **4999**

Founders of British physiology **3492**

Foundry dictionary **4650**

Foundry yearbook and casting buyer's directory **4655**

Four centuries of cat books, 1570-1970 **5909**

Four language encyclopaedic dictionary of terms in physical geography: Russian-English-German-French **1678**

Fourth report of the Independent Scientific Commmittee on Smoking and Health **3583**

Fowler, C.M.R.
The Solid earth **1492**

Fowler, M.E.
Zoo and wild animal medicine **2761, 5836**

Fowler, W. and Norris, J.A.
NBC: nuclear, biological and chemical warfare on the modern battlefield **4874**

Fox, D.M.
Nobel Laureates in medicine or physiology **3422**

Fox, M.F.
Bibliography on engine lubricating oil **4741**

Fox, P.F.
Cheese: chemistry, physics and microbiology **5920**

The Fragile contract: university science and federal government **27**

France. Centre National d'Études et d'Experimentation du Machinisme Agricole Tropical (CEEMAT)
Dictionnaire technique de la mécanisation agricole **5667**

France. Commisariat a L'Énergie Atomique
Dictionnaire des sciences et techniques nucléaires **4185**

Franceschetti, D.R.
Biographical encyclopedia of mathematicians **591**

Francis A. Countway Library of Medicine (Harvard Medical Library)
Author-title catalog ... for imprints through 1959. [Francis A. Countway Library of Medicine] **3248**

Francis, G.
The Penguin book of the motorcycle **5325**

Francis, P.
Volcanoes: a planetary perspective **1624**

Franck, I.
The Green encyclopedia **2226, 5227**

Frank, R.C.
Directory of food and nutrition information services and resources **6663**

Franklin, A.C.
J & P transformer book **4331**

Franklin & Andrews, International Property and Construction Consultants.
Spon's railways construction price book **5021**

Franks, F.
Water: a comprehensive treatise **1317**

Fraser, A.
The Gypsies **2103**

Fraser, F.C.
British whales, dolphins and porpoises **2963**

Fraser, G.
The Particle century **1098**

Frawley, G. and Thorn, J.
The International directory of civil aircraft 1995-96 **5408**
The International directory of military aircraft 1996-97 **4887**

Frazer, D.
Reptiles and amphibians in Britain **2866**

Frazier, W.C. and Westhoff, D.
Food microbiology **6669**

Fream, W.
Fream's principles of food and agriculture **5510**

Fream's principles of food and agriculture **5510**

Freedman, A.
The Computer desktop encyclopedia **7236**
The Computer glossary **7246**

Freeman, C.
A Guide to the literature of oceanography **1729**
Technology and the future of Europe **3086**

Freeman, C. and Tyrer, P.
Research methods in psychiatry **3862**

Freeman, H.G.
Taschenwörterbuch Eisen und Stahl **6908**
Wörterbuch technischer Begriffe **3033**

Freeman, H.M.
Industrial pollution prevention handbook **5229**

Freeman, R.B.
British natural history books, 1495-1900 **2382**

Freeman, R.L.
English-Spanish, Spanish-English dictionary of communications and electronic terms **4516**
Reference manual for telecommunications engineering **4522**

Freeman-Grenville, G.S.P.
The Islamic and Christian calendars AD 622-2222 (AH1-1650) **905**

Freight Transport Association
FTA Yearbook of road transport law **6280**

Freiser, H. and Nancollas, G.H.
Compendium of analytical nomenclature **1279**

Freitag, R.S.
Halley's comet: a bibliography **769**

Freiwillig, R.K.
Dictionary of physical metallurgy **6892**

French dictionary of telecommunications **4515**

French-English agricultural dictionary **5524**

French-English and English-French dictionary of technical terms and phrases **157, 3932**

French-English chemical terminology **1157**

A French-English dictionary for chemists **1155**

French-English horticultural dictionary with English-French index **5751**

French-English science and technology dictionary **150**

French glossary of food industry terms **6649**

French glossary of medical terms **3337**

French, M.J.
Invention and evolution **3216, 3975**

French, T.E.
Engineering drawing and graphic technology **3103**

French technical dictionary **158, 3036**

French's index of differential diagnosis **3770**

Frenot, G.H.
AGARD aeronautical multilingual dictionary **5397**

Fresenius, W.
Water analysis **5179**

Freshwater and aquaculture contents tables **5947**

Freshwater Biological Association, Cumbria
Catalogues of the Library of the Freshwater Biological Association **2281**

Freshwater fishes of the world **2858**

Freund, H. and Berg, A.
Geschichte der Mikroskopie **1045**

Frey, R.L.
Railroads in the nineteenth century **5049**

Frick, J.P.
Woldman's Engineering alloys **6898**

Frickhinger, K.A.
Fossil atlas: fishes **1956**

Friction wear, lubrication, tribology handbook **4745**

Friday, A. and Ingram, D.S.
The Cambridge encyclopedia of life sciences **2148**

Fried, H.B.
The Watch repairer's manual **7184**

Friedman, H.S.
Encyclopedia of mental health **3842**

Friedman, N.
The Naval Institute guide to world naval weapons systems **4895**
Navies in the nuclear age **4902**

Friedman, R.S.
An Illustrated examination of advanced technology warfare **4844**

Frimodt, C.
Multilingual illustrated guide to the world's commercial coldwater fish **5934**
Multilingual illustrated guide to the world's commercial warmwater fish **5935**

Frisancho, A.R.
Anthropometric standards for the assessment of growth and nutritional status **2027**

Frisch, M.
Directory for the environment: organisations, campaigns and initiatives in the British Isles **2250-2251**

The Fritzsche - D & O Library bulletin **6718**

Frodin, D.G.
Guide to standard floras of the world **2553**

Froelich, F.E.
The Froelich/Kent encyclopedia of telecommunications **4494**

The Froelich/Kent encyclopedia of telecommunications **4494**

Froes, F.H.
Titanium technology **6944**

Froggatt, P.
Fourth report of the Independent Scientific Commmittee on Smoking and Health **3583**

Frohne, D. and Pfänder, H.J.
A Colour atlas of poisonous plants: a handbook for pharmacists, doctors, toxicologists, and biologists **3724**

From CA to CAS online **1107**

From compass to computer: a history of electrical and electronics engineering **4288**

From Frege to Gödel **576**

From keel to truck: dictionary of naval terms **5339**

From mangle to microwave **6099**

Gingerich, O.
The Physical sciences in the twentieth century **984, 1213**

Ginsberg, G.L.
A User's guide to selecting electronic components **4449**

Ginsberg, M.
The Aerospace international directory of world airlines **6401**

Ginsburg, M.
The Illustrated history of textiles **7075**

Gioello, D.A. *and* **Berke, B.**
Fashion production terms **7444**

Gipe, P.
Wind energy comes of age **4318**

Gips-Wörterbuch **6822**

GIS world geodirectory **1481**

Giscard d'Estaing, V-A.
The Book of inventions and discoveries **3145**

Githens, J.
Guide to world cheeses **5917**

Gittus, J.H.
Uranium **6965**

Gjertsen, D.
The Newton handbook **377**

Glaciers and glaciation **1637**

Gladstone, W.J. *and* **Roche, P.**
Dictionnaire anglais-français des sciences médicales et paramédicales **3339**

Glaister, G.A.
Glaister's glossary of the book **6141**

Glaister's glossary of the book **6141**

Glasby, J.S.
Encyclopedia of antibiotics **2347**
Encyclopedia of the alkaloids **1372**

Glass engineering handbook **6793**

Glass-fibre directory and databook **6804**

Glass: nature, structure and properties **6794**

Glass science and technology **6795**

Glass technology (Section A: *Journal of the Society of Glass Technology*) **6802**

Glassfile **6785**

Glasstone, S.
Energy desk book **4062**
Nuclear reactor engineering **4212**

Gleason, V.E. *and* **Russell, H.H.**
Mine drainage bibliography, 1910-1976 **4813**

Gledhill, D.
The Names of plants **2516**

Glenn, J. *and* **Littler, G.**
A Dictionary of mathematics **536**

Glenn's complete bicycle manual **5329**

Glenz, G.
A Glossary of plastics terminology in 5 languages **7134**

Glick, D.M.
Glossary of biochemistry and molecular biology **2325**

Global earth physics **1498**

Global geomorphology **1675**

Global guide to medical information **3258**

Global marine pollution bibliography **5207**

Global patent services **3187**

Global warming **5238**

Global warning ... global warming **5228**

Globemac: the global military aircraft census **4888**

Glossaire de la terminologie acarologique **2798**

Glossaire de météorologie et de climatologie **1779**

Glossaire de zoologie **2721**

Glossaire des normes de l'acier **6920**

Glossaire des termes techniques en cartographie assistée par ordinateur **870**

Glossaire nouvelles techniques de transport **6255**

Glossaire systématique, anglais-français-espagnol-russe de la terminologie des methodes statistiques **641**

Glossaries for surveyors **828**

Glossario ceramico **6817**

Glossarium Europae avium **2903**

Glossary for gears **4727**

Glossary for horticultural crops **5753**

Glossary for inland transport **6388**

Glossary for radiologic technologists **3704**

Glossary for the food industries **6673**

Glossary of acarological terminology **2798**

Glossary of air pollution **3595**

Glossary of air pollution terms **3592**

Glossary of air treatment **3594**

A Glossary of artificial intelligence **7369**

Glossary of astronomy and astrophysics **700**

Glossary of bacteriological terms **2376**

Glossary of biochemistry and molecular biology **2325**

A Glossary of botanic terms **2505**

Glossary of building and bridge construction **4941**

Glossary of building and civil engineering terms **4948, 7479**

Glossary of building and civil engineering terms. Part 1. General and miscellaneous. Section 1.3. Parts of construction works. Subsection 1.3.2 Roofs and roofing **7549**

Glossary of building and civil engineering terms. Part 2. Civil engineering. Section 2.7 Public health. Environmental engineering **5219**

Glossary of building and civil engineering terms. Part 2. Civil engineering. Subsection 2.4.1 Highway engineering **5064**

Glossary of building and civil engineering terms. Part 3. Services. Section 3.3 Sanitation **7573**

Glossary of building and civil engineering terms. Part 6. Concrete and plaster. Section 6.6 Products, applications and operations. Subsection 6.6.2 Plaster **7570**

Glossary of cartographic terms **872**

Glossary of chemical terms **1139**

Glossary of coal preparation terms **4806**

A Glossary of computing terms **7247**

Glossary of corrosion terms in Scandinavian languages **4042**

Glossary of crop science terms **5731**

Glossary of electrotechnical, power, telecommunication, electronics, lighting and colour terms **4267**

Glossary of electrotechnical, power, telecommunication, electronics, lighting and colour terms. Part 2. Terms particular to power engineering. Group 10. Industrial electroheating terminology **4361**

Glossary of electrotechnical, power, telecommunication, electronics, lighting and colour terms. Part 3. Terms particular to telecommunications and electronics. Group 08. Acoustics and electroacoustics terminology **1030**

Glossary of electrotechnical, power, telecommunication, electronics, lighting and colour terms. Part 5: Terms particular to electromedical equipment **1081**

Glossary of electrotechnical, power, telecommunication, electronics, lighting and colour terms. Terms particular to electromedical equipemnt. Radiology and radiological physics terminology **3705**

Glossary of energy **4069**

Glossary of environmental terms **5144**

Glossary of forestry **5627**

Glossary of genetics: classical and molecular **2300**

Glossary of genetics in English, French, Spanish, Italian, German, Russian **2299**

A Glossary of geographical terms **1682**

Glossary of geology **1547**

Glossary of geotechnics **4991**

Glossary of health care terminology **3589**

Glossary of histopathological terms **3796**

Glossary of land resources **5516**

Glossary of leather terms **7023**

Glossary of maintenance management terms in terotechnology **4160**

Glossary of mapping, charting and geodetic terms **873**

Glossary of marine technology terms **5343**

Glossary of meteorology **1780**

Glossary of mineral species **1412**

Glossary of mining geology **4775**

Glossary of mining terms **4784**

Glossary of molecular biology **2350**

Glossary of municipal engineering **4936**

A Glossary of mycology **2645**

Glossary of navigation **811**

Glossary of oceanographic terms **1745**

Glossary of onshore and offshore pipelines **6762**

Glossary of organic chemistry **1341**

Glossary of packaging terms **4711**

Glossary of paint terms **6843**

Glossary of paper, board, pulp and related terms **7037**

Glossary of planning and building terms **7496**

Glossary of plant-pathological terms **2610**

Glossary of plant tissue culture **2206**

Glossary of plastic and rubber terms **7104**

A Glossary of plastics terminology in 5 languages **7134**

Glossary of Polish-English meteorological terms **1782**

Glossary of railway terms, English-French-German-Italian-Spanish-Swedish **5016**

Glossary of refrigeration, heating, ventilating and air-conditioning terms **4586, 7584**

Glossary of reliability and maintenance terms **3928**

Glossary of rheological terms **1014**

Glossary of rock engineering **4984**

Glossary of rubber terms **7118**

Glossary of Russian abbreviations and acronyms **38**

A Glossary of Russian technical terms used in metallurgy **6863**

A Glossary of sanitation engineering terms **5218**

Glossary of solid waste **5257**

A Glossary of space terms **5460**

'Glossary of technical terms for the sugar industry' **5747**

Glossary of technical terms in computer assisted cartography **870**

Glossary of terms and expressions used in well logging **4803**

Glossary of terms and symbols for measurement of fluid flow in closed conduits **4607**

Glossary of terms and symbols in thermionic conversion **1083**

Glossary of terms associated with fire **3612**

Glossary of terms for copper and copper alloys **6947**

Glossary of terms for cylindrical screw threads **4738**

Glossary of terms frequently used in cryogenics **1069**

Glossary of terms in heat transfer, fluid flow, and related topics **1062**

Glossary of terms: nuclear power and radiation **4183**

Glossary of terms related to solid fuel burning equipment **7585**

Glossary of terms relating to agricultural machinery and implements. AMD 1395. 1983 **5665**

Glossary of terms relating to mechanical vibration and shock **4029**

Glossary of terms relating to particle technology **4665**

Glossary of terms relating to refractory materials **6820**

Glossary of terms relating to rubber and rubber-like materials **7117**

Glossary of terms relating to thermal insulation **7594**

Glossary of terms relating to timber preservation **7013, 7561**

Glossary of terms, tests and drugs used in psychiatric practice **3851**

Glossary of terms used in automatic controlling and regulating systems **7350**

Glossary of terms used in materials handling **4733**

Glossary of terms used in non-destructive testing **4033**

Glossary of terms used in nuclear science and technology **4182**

Glossary of terms used in offset lithographic printing **6201**

'Glossary of terms used in physical organic chemistry' **1340**

Glossary of terms used in the gas industry **6541**

Glossary of terms used in the glass industry **6799**

Glossary of terms used in water pollution control **5202**

Glossary of textiles **7060**

Glossary of the Third World **2048**

Glossary of timber construction **6991, 7572**

Glossary of transport **6259**

Glossary of United Kingdom fishing gear terms **5949**

Glossary of water **1318, 1878**

Glossary of water supply and sewerage **5185**

Glossary of weather and climate **1803**

A Glossary of wood **6992**

Glossary of words and phrases used in radiology, nuclear medicine, and ultrasound **3700**

Glover, B.
CAMRA dictionary of beer **6609**
The World encyclopedia of beer **6606**

Glut, D.F.
Dinosaurs: the encyclopedia **1961**

Gmelin-Institut
GABCOM & GABNET: acronyms of compounds and methods in chemistry and physics **906, 1252**
Gmelin's Handbuch der anorganischen chemie **1303**
Gmelin's Handbuch der anorganischen chemie **1303**

Goats: a bibliography **5882**

Goats of the world **5884**

Goddard, S.
A Guide to information sources in the geographical sciences **1664**

Godfrey, L.E. and Redman, H.F.
Dictionary of report series codes **207**

Godman, A.
Longman chemistry handbook **1137**

Godman, A. and Denney, R.
Cambridge illustrated thesaurus of science & technology **443**

Godman, A. and Payne, E.M.F.
The Longman dictionary of scientific usage **126**

Godwin, Sir H.
The History of the British flora **2574**

Goedecke, W.
Wörterbuch der werkstoffprüfung **4009**

Gold **6931**

Gold: history and genesis of deposits **6929**

Gold, V.
'Glossary of terms used in physical organic chemistry' **1340**

Goldbeck, G.
Museen in Deutschland (West): Technische Museen **500**

The Golden century of oil, 1950-2050 **6728**

Golding, E.W.
The Generation of electricity by wind power **4319**

Goldman, J.M.
Means estimating handbook **7538**

Goldsmith, F.B. and Warren, A.
Conservation in progress **2446**

Goldsmith, M.
UK science policy **13**

Golze, A.R.
Handbook of dam engineering **5114**

Gomersall, A.
Lasers in materials processing **4372**
Machine intelligence **7360**

Gomersall, A. and Farmer, P.
Robotics **7377**

The Good beer guide **6006**

The Good code guide **6128**

The Good food guide **6002**

Good, G.A.
Sciences of the earth: an encyclopedia of events, people, and phenomena **1460**

The Good hardware guide **7297**

The 1995 Good hotel guide to Britain and Europe **5980**

'Good Housekeeping' every home should have one **6098**

Good Housekeeping household hints **6095**

'Good Housekeeping' microwave cookbook **6059**

'Good Housekeeping' new step-by-step cook book **6060**

The Good mail order guide **6032**

The Good pub guide **6007**

Good, R.
Britten's watch & clock maker's handbook, dictionary and guide **7180**

Good style: writing for science and technology **438**

Goodall, D.W.
Ecosystems of the world **2263**

Goodall, P.M.
The Efficient use of steam **4223**

Gooday, L. and Devine, J.
Sourcebook on green business **5172**

Gooders, J.
Larousse field guide to the birds of Britain and Europe **2904**

Goodier, J.
'Environmental technology and technology and the environment' **5128**

Goodier, J.H.
Dictionary of painting and decorating **7592**

Goodman, A.
Cambridge illustrated thesaurus of computer science **7281**

Goodman, W.L.
The History of woodworking tools **7014**

Goodsell, D.
Dictionary of automotive engineering **5280**

Goodwin, D.
Pigeons and doves of the world **2933, 5895**

Goodwin, P.
The Construction and fitting of the English sailing men of war, 1650 - 1850 **4904**

Göpel, W.
Sensors **997**

Gordon, R.E. and Anderson, J.N.
Conservation directory 1999 **2459**

Gorshkov, S.G.
World ocean atlas **1762**

Gotch, A.P.
Mammals - their Latin names explained **2946**

Gottstein, K.
Directory of international cooperation in science and technology **466**

Goudie, A.
The Encyclopaedic dictionary of physical geography **1681**

Goudie, A.S. and Brunsden, D.
The Environment of the British Isles: an atlas **2274**

Gough, B.E.
World environmental directory: North America **5171**

Gould, E. and McKay, G.
Encyclopedia of mammals **2938**

Gould, W.A.
Glossary for the food industries **6673**

Gourvish, T.R.
British railways, 1948-73 **6310**

Government publications. Sectional list 45, revised January 1996. British Geological Survey **1593**

Government reports announcements & index **208**

Government research directory **496, 3097**

Gowan, J.E.
Name index of organic reactions **1348**

Gowenlock, A.H.
Varley's practical clinical biochemistry **2332**

Gozmany, L.
Vocabularium nominum animalium Europae system linguis redactum **2728**

Gradshteyn, I.S. and Ryzhik, I.M.
Table of integrals, series, and products **621**

Graf, A.B.
Exotica 4 international **5800**
Tropica: color cyclopedia of exotic plants and trees from the tropics and subtropics **5801**

Graf, R.F.
Electronic databook **4435**
Modern dictionary of electronics **4413**

Graf, R.F. and Sheets, W.
Encyclopedia of electronic circuits **4450**

Graham, A.L.
The Catalogue of meteorites **1845**

Graham, G.A.
Encyclopedia of industrial automation **7343**

Graham, J. and Lowe, S.
The Facts on File dictionary of telecommunications **4508**

Graham, L.E.
Science in Russia and the Soviet Union: a short history **389**

Grallafent, R.J.
Intellectual property law and taxation **3208**

Grande dizionario di marina, italiano-inglese, inglese-italiano **6347**

Grandison, A.G.C.
Snakes - a natural history **2874**

Grant and Hackh's chemical dictionary **1138**

Grant, C. and Ballantyne, J.
Discovery & invention **316**

Grant, D.M. and Harris, R.K.
Encyclopedia of nuclear magnetic resonance **1085**

Grant, E.
Physical science in the Middle Ages **320**
A Source book in medieval science **320**

Grant, E.H.
Microwaves **4368**

Grant, R.L. and Grant, A.C.
Grant and Hackh's chemical dictionary **1138**

Graphic arts encyclopedia **6191**

Graphical symbols for components of servo-mechanisms **7338**

Graphics, design and printing terms **6188**

Grassé, P.-P.
Traité de zoologie **2717**

Grasselli, J.G. and Ritchey, W.M.
CRC atlas of spectral data **1053**

Grasses **2695**

Grasses, ferns, mosses and lichens of Great Britain and Ireland **2694**

Guilcher, A.
Coral reef geomorphology **1722**
The Guild handbook of scientific illustration **280**
Guinle, R.L.
A Modern Spanish-English and English-Spanish technical & engineering dictionary **169**
Guinness aircraft facts and figures **5422**
The Guinness book of astronomy **690**
The Guinness book of plant facts and feats **2496**
The Guinness book of ships and shipping facts and feats **5335**
The Guinness book of speed **1019**
The Guinness book of stamps facts and feats **6420**
The Guinness book of weather facts and feats **1799**
The Guinness guide to plants of the world **2496**
The Guinness railway fact book **6299**
The Guinness world car record **5307**
Gullberg, I.F.
Svensk-engelsk fackordbok för näringsliv, fövaltning, undevisning och forskning **146**
Gulliver, J.S. and Arndt, R.E.A.
Hydropower engineering handbook **4317**
Gunnel, J.A.
Standard catalog of American cars, 1946-1975 **5317**
Gunston, B.
Aircraft of the Soviet Union **4891, 5425**
Chronicle of aviation **5412**
The encyclopedia of world air power **4883**
The Guinness book of speed **1019**
An Illustrated guide to modern fighters **4884**
Jane's aerospace dictionary **5455**
World encyclopedia of aero engines **5419**
Gunstone, F.D.
The Lipid handbook **1370, 2340**
Guntau, M.
Biographien bedeutender Geowissenschaftler der Sowjetunion **1576**
Gunton, T.
A Dictionary of information technology and computer science **7248**
Gurarii, M.G and Iofe, L.R.
Anglo-russkiĭ slovar' po plastmassam **7142**
Gurnsey, J.
'Electronic publishing' **6197**
Gusev, B.V.
English-Russian dictionary of applied geophysics **1493**
Guston, D.H. and Keniston, K.
The Fragile contract: university science and federal government **27**
Gutiérrez, M.F.
Elsevier's dictionary of civil engineering in four languages **4934**
Elsevier's dictionary of machine tools and elements **4756**
Gutteridge, A.C.
Cambridge illustrated thesaurus of biology **2152**
Guy, N.G.
Pipe protection bibliography **4608**
Thesaurus for fluid engineering **4603**
Guyer, E.C.
Handbook of applied thermal design **4564**
Gyngell, J. and Poulter, A.
A User's guide to trade marks **3124**
The Gypsies **2103**
Gypsum and plaster dictionary **6822**
Haar, L.
NBS/NRC steam tables **1266, 4225**
Haas, M.L.
Indians of North America **2122**

Haas, R.
Dictionary of psychology and psychiatry **3855**
Haber, K.
Common abbreviations in clinical medicine **3222**
Haber, L.F.
The Chemical industries, 1900-1930 **6463**
The Chemical industry during the nineteenth century **6464**
Haberle, G.D.
Kurzlexikon der Elektrotechnik **4256**
Hackwood, S.
The Biotechnology directory **3003**
Hadfield, C.
The Canals of the British Isles **6391**
Hadfield's British canals **6390**
Hadfield's British canals **6390**
Haensch, G. and Haberkamp de Anton, G.
Dictionary of agriculture in six languages **5514**
Dictionary of biology **2150**
Hagemeijer, W.J.M. and Blair, M.J.
EBCC atlas of European breeding birds **2901**
Hague, D.B.
Lighthouses **5112**
Hague, H. and Jackson, M.
Core collection of medical books and journals **3245**
Hale, F.G.
The International history of the sewing machine **7449**
Hale, W.G.
Collins dictionary of biology **2154**
Halkin, P.
Dictionnaire technique de l'hôtellerie **5974**
Hall, C.W.
Encyclopedia of food engineering **6665**
Hall, C.W. and Olsen, W.C.
The Literature of agricultural engineering **5661**
Hall, E
The David & Charles manual of home plumbing **7574**
Hall, E.R.
The Mammals of North America **2959**
Hall, G.S. and Minter, D.W.
International mycological directory **2652**
Hall, P.S.
Radar **4877**
Hall, S.J.G. and Clutton-Brock, J.
Two hundred years of British farm livestock **5867**
Halla, C.W.
Dictionary of drying **6493**
Hallam, A.
Atlas of palaeobiogeography **1914**
The Geology of Africa **1606**
Planet earth: an encyclopaedia of geology **1622**
Halley, N.
The Wordsworth dictionary of drink **6085**
Halley's comet, 1755-1984: a bibliography **770**
Halley's comet: a bibliography **769**
Hallfasthetsoralista **4028**
Halpin, A.M.
Rodale's encyclopedia of indoor gardening **5802**
Halstead, B.W.
Poisonous and venomous marine animals of the world **2758**
Halstead, L.B. and Halstead, J.
Dinosaurs **1967**
Haltenorth, T. and Diller, H.
A Field guide to the mammals of Africa, including Madagascar **2957**
Ham, C. and Merry, P.
NHS handbook **3435**

Hamer, F. and Hamer, J.
The Potter's dictionary of materials and techniques **6809**
Hamill, T.
'Commercial aircraft of the world' **5423**
Hamilton, B. and Guidos, B.
MASA: medical acronyms, symbols and abbreviations **3226**
Hamilton, C.J.
Pest management: a directory of information sources. Volume 1: Crop protection **5700**
Pest management: a directory of information sources. Volume 2: Animal health **5823**
Hamilton, G.E.
Catalogue of the Translator's Library of the Department of Trade and Industry **101**
Hamilton, L.
Information pack including bibliography on advanced manufacturing technology **7339**
Hamilton, L. and Hallam, L.
Information pack on computer integrated manufacturing **7340**
Hamilton, R.J. and Bhatti, A.
Recent advances in chemistry and technology of fats and oils **6710**
The Hamlyn guide to edible and medicinal plants of Britain and Northern Europe **2634, 3682**
Hamlyn history of trains **5024**
Hammen, L. van der
Glossaire de la terminologie acarologique **2798**
Hammond, C.
Introduction to crystallography **1375**
Hammond, K.A.
The Sourcebook of the environment **2222**
Hammond-Tooke, W.D.
The Bantu-speaking peoples of Southern Africa **2073**
Hammond-Tooke, W.D. and West, M.
The Peoples of Southern Africa **2075**
Hampel, C.A. and Hawley, G.C.
Glossary of chemical terms **1139**
Han Ying i hsueh ta tzu tien **3352**
Han ying kung cheng chi shu tzu hui **197**
Hance, R.J. and Holly, K.K.
Weed control handbook **5726**
Hanchett, J.G. and Hasselberg, F.W.
Glossary of terms: nuclear power and radiation **4183**
Hancock, E.G. and Morgan, P.J.
A Survey of zoological and botanical material in museums and other institutions of Great Britain **2541, 2744**
Hancox, P.J.
Keyguide to information sources in artificial intelligence/expert systems **7363**
Handbok for nordisk träindustri **7007**
Handbook 1998/99. [Medical Research Council] **3464**
Handbook for astronomical societies **734**
Handbook for digital signal processing **4481**
Handbook for electronics engineering technicians **4402**
Handbook for engineering design using standard materials and components **3979**
A Handbook for naturalists **2429**
Handbook for scientific and technical research **429**
Handbook of acoustical measurements and noise control **5255**
Handbook of acoustics **1025**
Handbook of adhesives **6782**
Handbook of aerosol technology **1250**
Handbook of air conditioning and refrigeration **4584, 7581**
Handbook of air pollution analysis **3593**
Handbook of animal science **5863**
Handbook of applicable mathematics **526**
Handbook of applied chemistry **6441**
Handbook of applied hydraulics **5081**

Handbook of water treatment chemicals **5196**

Handbook of wood and wood-based materials for engineers, architects and builders **6989, 7562**

Handbook of world salt resources **1864, 6536**

A Handbook of writing for engineers **3968**

Handbook of writing for the mathematical sciences **601**

Handbook on semiconductors **4482**

Handbook on weaponry **4847**

[Handbook, Royal Life Saving Society] **3636**

Handbooks **4431**

Handbooks and tables in science and technology **64, 274**

Handbooks for the identification of British insects **2813**

Handbuch der Laubgehölze **5644**

Handbuch der Pflanzenanatomie **2616**

Handbuch der Physik **926**

Handbuch der Zoologie **2718**

Handguns and sub-machine guns **4867**

Handicrafts **7457**

Handmer, J.
Flood hazard management **5109**

Hanlon, J.F.
Handbook of packaging engineering **4708**

Hannah, L.
Electricity before nationalization **4315**
Engineers, managers and politicians **4314**

Hannay, N.B.
Treatise on solid state chemistry **1224**

Hanneman, H.W.A.M.
The Patentability of computer software **7326**

Hanniball, A.
Aircraft, engines and airmen **5389**

Hansen, B.
The Dictionary of multimedia terms and acronyms **7423**

Hansen, E.R.
A Table of series and products **627**

Hanson, A.A.
Practical handbook of agricultural science **5552**

Hanson, H.J.
The Cruising Association Library catalogue **6325**

Hanson, T.A.
'Electronic sources of engineering information' **3905**

Hanssen, M.
The New E is for additives **6693**

Harbord, J.B.
Glossary of navigation **811**

Harborne, J.B.
Phytochemical dictionary **2624**

Harborne, J.B. and Baxter, H.
Dictionary of plant toxins **3711**

Harding, D.
Weapons: an international encyclopedia, from 5000 BC to 2000 AD **4850**

Harding, K.A. and Welch, K.R.G.
Venomous snakes of the world **2872**

Hardingham, M.
Illustrated dictionary of fabrics **7085**

Hardup, P.
The Timetable of technology **3060**

Hardwick, W.A.
Handbook of brewing **6607**

Hardyment, C.
From mangle to microwave **6099**

Hargreaves, D. and Fromson, S.
World index of strategic minerals **6854**

Hargreaves, J.M.
Literature sources in toxicology: a survey **3708**

Hargreaves, V.
Fire directory, 1996 **3617**

Harland, J.
Seamanship in the age of sail **6357**

Harland, W.B.
Geologic time scale 1989 **1827**

Harmer, S.F. and Shipley, A.
The Cambridge natural history **2719**

Harper & Row's complete field guide to North American wildlife. Eastern edition **2422**

Harper & Row's complete field guide to North American wildlife. Western edition **2423**

Harper, C.A.
Electronic packaging and interconnection handbook **4473, 4709**
Handbook of electronic systems design **4405**
Handbook of plastics, elastomers and composites **7132**

Harper, C.A. and Miller, M.B.
Electronic packaging, microelectronics, and interconnection dictionary **4474, 4710**

Harper, C.A. and Sampson, R.N.
Electronic materials and process handbook **4401**

Harper, P.
Guide to the manuscript papers of British scientists **362**

The HarperCollins dictionary of electronics **4417**

Harper's wine and spirit directory **6602**

Harrap's French and English data processing dictionary **7290**

Harrap's French and English science dictionary **155**

Harrap's illustrated dictionary of science **120**

Harrap's illustrated history of the 20th century - Science **325**

Harrap's visual French-English dictionary **156**

Harré, R.
The Philosophies of science **98**
Scientific thought, 1900-1960 **326**

Harries, M.
Oxford textbook of sports medicine **3557**

Harrington, J.M. and Gill, F.S.
Occupational health **3607**

Harris, C.A.
Handbook of acoustical measurements and noise control **5255**

Harris, C.D.
Annotated world list of selected current geographical serials **1692**
Bibliography of geography **1666**
A Geographical bibliography for American libraries **1663**

Harris, C.D. and Fellmann, J.D.
International list of geographical serials **1691**

Harris, C.M.
Dictionary of architecture and construction **7476**
Shock and vibration handbook **1026**

Harris, J.
'Nuclear engineering' **4170**

Harris, J.G.
Plant identification terminology **2504**

Harris, J.W. and Stöcker, H.
Handbook of mathematics and computational science **655**

Harris, K.M.
Shorter guide to pests, diseases and disorders of garden plants **2609**

Harris, L.
Adhesives and adhesion **6778**

Harris, S.L.
Agents of chaos: earthquakes, volcanoes, and other natural disasters **1508**

Harris, T.
The Natural history of the Mediterranean **2408**

Harris, T.Y.
Wild flowers of Australia **2601**

Harrison, L. and Johnson, K.
UK hotel groups directory 1992/93 **5984**

Harrison, P.
The Cassell dictionary of physics **935**
The Cassell dictionary of science **129**

Harrison, P. *(contd.)*
Seabirds: an identification guide **2899**

Harrison, R.M. and Perry, R.
Handbook of air pollution analysis **3593**

Harry's cosmeticology **6713**

Hart, H.
Hart's rules for compositors and readers at the University Press, Oxford **6180**

Hartcup, G.
The Silent revolution **4845**

Hartman, H.L.
SME mining engineering handbook **4774**

Hartman, K.
Dictionary of process technology in four languages **6488**

Hartman, T.
The Guinness book of ships and shipping facts and feats **5335**

Hartmann, H.T.
Plant science **2497**

Hart's rules for compositors and readers at the University Press, Oxford **6180**

Hartung, E.J.
Astronomical objects for southern telescopes **688**

Harty, F.J.
Concise illustrated dental dictionary **3817**

Harvard encyclopedia of American ethnic groups **2079**

Harvard University
Catalogue of the Library of the Museum of Comparative Zoology **2713**
Gray Herbarium index **2673**

Harvard University. Peabody Museum of Archaeology and Ethnology. Library
Catalogue. [Peabody Museum of Archaeology and Ethnology, Library] **1988**
Index to subject headings. [Peabody Museum of Archaeology and Ethnology, Library] **1989**

Harvey, J.M.V.
Catalogue of manuscripts in the Entomology Library of the Natural History Museum **2827**

Harvey, N.
A History of farm buildings in England and Wales **5659**
The Industrial archaeology of farming in England and Wales **5584**

The Harwin chronology of inventions, innovations, discoveries **3147**

Haseler, A.E.
District heating **7578**

Haskell, D.C.
A Tentative check-list of early European railway literature, 1831-1848 **5026**

Haslam, J.M.
Writing engineering specifications **3965**

Hatch, J.E.
Aluminum: properties and physical metallurgy **6958**

Hathway, D.E.
Harrap's French and English science dictionary **155**

Haubrich, W.S.
Medical meanings **3324**

Haugen, C. and Durst, P.B.
Directory of selected tropical forestry journals and newsletters **5632**

Hausner, H.H.
Beryllium: its metallurgy and properties **6962**
Handbook of powder metallurgy **4662**

Haux, G.F.K.
Subsea manned engineering **5097**

Havard, C.
Medical eponyms **3414**

Hawke, N.
Encyclopedia of environmental health: law and practice **5134**

Hawkes, P.W.
Principles of electron optics **1035**
Hawking, S.F. and Israel, W.
Three hundred years of gravitation **1007**
Hawkings, D.T.
Railway ancestors **5047**
Hawkins, R.E.
Encyclopedia of Indian natural history **2421**
Hawksworth, D.L., and others, eds.
Ainsworth & Bisby's dictionary of the fungi **2642**
Hawksworth, D.L. and Seaward, M.R.D.
Lichenology in the British Isles, 1568-1978 **2668**
Hawley's condensed chemical dictionary **1140**
Haws, D.
The Maritime history of the world **5362**
Hay, R.K.M.
Science policies in Europe: unity and diversity **10**
Hay, W.W.
Railroad engineering **5012**
Hayes, M.H.
Veterinary notes for horse owners **5879**
Hayman, R.W.
A Field guide to the mammals of Africa, including Madagascar **2957**
Haynes, J.R.
Foraminifera **1948**
Haynes, W.
American chemical industry **6469**
Hayward, A. and Weare, F.
Steel detailers' manual **4980**
Hayward, P.J. and Ryland, J.S.
The Marine fauna of the British Isles and north-west Europe **2759**
Hazardous chemical data book **3629**
Hazardous chemicals desk reference **3630, 3722**
Hazardous chemicals handbook **3620**
Hazardous chemicals on file **3632**
Hazardous materials dictionary **3599, 3710**
Hazardous materials: sources of information on their transportation **3619**
Hazardous waste disposal guide **5214**
Hazardous waste management **5217**
Hazards in the chemical laboratory **3624**
Hazewinkel, M.
Encyclopaedia of mathematics **517**
HCIMA quarterly current awareness bulletin for hospitality management **5967**
He, J.
Internet resources for engineers **3910**
Headland, R.K.
Chronological list of Antarctic expeditions and related historical events **1658**
Headworth, H. and Staines, S.
Dictionary of environmental science and engineering **5152**
Health and safety at work **3604**
The Health and safety directory **3600**
Health and safety in biotechnology **2987**
Health and safety science abstracts **3601**
Health care buyers guide, 1996 **3366**
Health care of the elderly **3760**
The Health directory **3525**
Health education index **3371**
The Health information handbook **3249**
Health media review index **3387**
Health media review index 1984-1986 **3387**
Health science books, 1876-1982 **3250**
Health sciences information sources **3254**
'Health sciences supplement' **3251**
Health statistics **3376**
Hearn, P.
The Business of industrial licensing **3200**
Heastie, H.
A Course in elementary meteorology **1772**
The Heat pump **4596**
Heat pumps **4594**

Heat Transfer and Fluid Flow Service
HTFS digest **1063**
Heatflo **1063**
Heath, Everett- J.
See
Everett-Heath, J.
Heath, J. and others
The Moths and butterflies of Great Britain and Ireland **2836**
Heather, B.D. and Robertson, H.A.
The Field guide to the birds of New Zealand **2928**
Heath, Sir T.L.
A History of Greek mathematics **588**
Heaton, C.A.
The Chemical industry **6440**
Heaton, N.
Traditional recipes of the British Isles **6081**
The Heavy elements **1434**
Heawood, R. and Larke, C.
The Directory of appropriate technology **3084**
Hecht, J.
The Laser guidebook **4375**
Heck, A.
International directory of astronomical associations and societies **736**
International directory of professional astronomical institutions **737**
Hedberg, H.D.
International stratigraphic guide **1828**
Heftmann, E.
Chromatography **1290**
Heider, K.G. and Hermer, C.
Films for anthropological teaching **2018**
Heijenoort, J. van
From Frege to Gödel **576**
Heiken, G.
Lunar sourcebook **757**
Heilbron, J.L.
Electricity in the 17th and 18th centuries **1077**
Heilbron, J.L. and Wheaton, B.R.
Literature on the history of physics in the twentieth century **975**
Heiler, T.
Technisches Bildwörterbuch für spanende Werkzeuge zur 'Metallbearbeitung' **4757**
Heilpflanzenlexikon: Wirkungen, Verordnung, Selbstmedikation **3685**
Heinemann dental dictionary **3816**
Heinisch, K.F.
Dictionary of rubber **7116**
Heinzold, G.
Handbook of geometrical tolerancing **4634**
Heisler, S
The Wiley engineer's desk reference **3922**
Heistar, R.
Dictionary of abbreviations in medical sciences **3223**
Held, G.
Dictionary of communications technology **4509**
Heldman, D.R.
Handbook of food engineering **6637**
Helgerson, L.W.
CD-ROM **7419**
Hellemans, A. and Bunch, B.
The Timetables of science **282**
Heller, S.R.
The Beilstein system **1326**
Helmake, J.G.
Handbuch der Zoologie **2718**
Helminthological abstracts **2796**
Helping to care: a handbook for carers at home and in hospital **6119**
Hematology **3806**
Hemisphere handbook of heat exchanger design **4565**
Henbest, N. and Marten, M.
The New astronomy **795**

Henderson, A.
The Henston small animal veterinary vade mecum **5847**
Henderson, H.
Science tracer bullets: a reference guide to scientific, technological, health, and environmental information sources **222**
Henderson, I.F. and Henderson, W.D.
Henderson's dictionary of biological terms **2158, 2723**
Henderson's dictionary of biological terms **2158, 2723**
Hendricks, B.L.
International encyclopedia of horse breeds **2967**
Henley's formulas for home and workshop **6096**
Henrey, B.
British botanical and horticultural literature before 1800 **2484**
Henry, J.
The British Medical Association new guide to medicines and drugs **3668**
Henry, S.D.
Fatigue data book **6894**
The Henston large animal veterinary vade mecum **5846**
The Henston small animal veterinary vade mecum **5847**
Henston vade mecum **5846-5847**
The Herbaria of the world **2542**
Herbert, J.
Glossary of railway terms, English-French-German-Italian-Spanish-Swedish **5016**
Herbert, W.J.
Dictionary of immunology **3799**
Herbs: an indexed bibliography, 1971-1980 **3676**
Herbs, spices and flavorings **6090**
Herbst, S.T.
The New food lover's companion **6065**
Hereford and Worcester County Libraries
Carpets and textiles: a complete list of the special collection in Kidderminster Library **7084**
Hering, R.
Hering's dictionary of classical and modern cookery **6066**
Hering's dictionary of classical and modern cookery **6066**
Heritau, J. and Cathey, H.M.
The National Arboretum book of outstanding garden plants **5776**
Herland, L.
Dictionary of mathematical sciences **543**
Herman, H.
Treatise on materials science and technology **4003**
Hermann, A.
Lexikon Geschichte der Physik, A-Z **980**
Herring, S.D.
From the Titanic to the Challenger **3073**
Herrmann, D.B.
The History of astronomy from Herschel to Hertzsprung **725**
Hervey, J.D.
Submarines **4916**
Herzenberg, C.L.
Women scientists from antiquity to the present **356**
Hewett, C.A.
English historic carpentry **7018**
Hewitt, G.F.
Hemisphere handbook of heat exchanger design **4565**
Hewlett, J.
Keyguide to information sources in paramedical sciences **3257**
Hewlett, P.C.
Lea's chemistry of cement and concrete **6825**

The History of psychiatry **3859**
A History of refrigeration throughout the world **4592**
The History of roads, from amber route to motorway **5070**
A History of science **309**
History of science **315**
History of science and technology **292**
History of science and technology in India **402, 3438**
The History of science and technology in the United States **416**
History of science in the United States **415**
A History of scientific and technical periodicals **246**
History of Scottish medicine **3437**
History of sewage treatment in Britain **5206**
A History of shopping **6029**
History of staining **2204**
History of technology **3063**
A History of technology **3065**
History of technology **4289**
A History of technology and invention **3061**
History of technology index, 1991: journal articles in the Science Museum Library **3072**
The History of the barometer **1010, 1789**
The History of the British coal industry, **6576**
The History of the British flora **2574**
The History of the British Petroleum Company **6757**
A History of the British pig **5889**
History of the cotton manufacture in Great Britain **7087**
The History of the countryside **2416**
A History of the Institution of Electrical Engineers, 1871-1971 **4296**
A History of the life sciences **2186**
History of the life sciences: an annotated bibliography **2189**
'The History of the motor bus industry: a bibliographical survey' **5300**
A History of the Ordnance Survey **895**
A History of the Oxford University Press. v.1. To 1780 **6168**
The History of the retriangulation of Great Britain, 1935-1962.. **835**
History of the Royal Astronomical Society **735**
The History of the Royal Botanic Garden Library, Edinburgh **2535**
The History of the Royal Botanic Gardens, Kew **2536**
History of the rubber industry **7124**
The History of the ship **5365**
The History of the study of landforms **1699**
A History of the theories of aether and electricity **1079**
A History of the world's airlines **6404**
A History of the world's sports cars **5319**
History of tramways from horse to rapid transit **5056**
History of tribology **4749**
The History of tunnelling **5003**
The History of warships **4903**
The History of woodworking tools **7014**
HLAS online. **2095**
Hobson, G.D. *and* Tiratsoo, E.N.
  Introduction to petroleum geology **1871**
Hobson, L.
  Electroheat references **4360**
Hochenergiephysik index **1102**
Hochman, S.
  French-English science and technology dictionary **150**
Hochstim, A.R.
  Bibliography of chemical kinetics and collision processes **1240**
The Hodder stamp dictionary **6422**
Hodge, P.W.
  Galaxies **776**

Hodges, B.
  Industrial robotics **7385**
Hodges, E.R.S.
  The Guild handbook of scientific illustration **280**
Hodgkiss, A.G. *and* Tatham, A.F.
  Keyguide to information sources in cartography **854**
Hodgson, A.V. *and* Laming, D.J.C.
  Titles of research theses, 1960-1975: Geology of the British Isles and offshore areas **1592**
Hodgson, E.
  Dictionary of toxicology **3712**
Hodson, W.K.
  Maynard's industrial engineering handbook **3923**
Hoedeman, J.J.
  Naturalists' guide to fresh-water aquarium fish **5963**
Hoffman, D.
  New holistic herbal **3681**
  Thorson's guide to medical herbalism **3681**
Hoffmann, J.P.A.
  Fachwörterbuch verpacking **4712**
Hoffmann, R.K.
  Handbook of microwave integrated circuits **4363**
Hofmann, W.
  Rubber technology handbook **7113**
Hogarth, J.
  Glossary of health care terminology **3589**
Hogere planten **2684**
Hogg, I.V.
  The Encyclopedia of weaponry **4841**
  Fortress: a history of military defence **4838**
  The Illustrated encyclopedia of ammunition **4871**
  The Illustrated encyclopedia of artillery **4856**
Hogg, I.V. *and* Weeks, J.
  Military small arms of the 20th century **4865**
  Pistols of the world **4868**
Hohenadel, P. *and* Relton, J.
  A Modern textile dictionary **7068**
Hoiberg, A.J.
  Bituminous materials **6582**
Holbrook, M. *and* Anderson, R.G.W.
  Science preserved **7219**
Holden, U. *and* Mathez, E.A.
  The Encyclopedia of gemstones and minerals **1389**
Holdsworth, B.
  Digital systems reference book **4480**
Holford, I.
  The Guinness book of weather facts and feats **1799**
Holland, C.H.
  A Geology of Ireland **1599**
Holland, F.A.
  Thermodynamic design data for heat pump systems **4595**
Holland, R.C.
  Illustrated dictionary of microelectronics and microcomputers **4460**
Holland, W.W.
  Oxford textbook of public health **3591**
Holliday, P.
  A Dictionary of plant pathology **2611, 5707**
Hollingsworth, B.
  An Illustrated guide to modern trains **5381**
Hollingsworth, B. *and* Cook, A.
  The Great book of trains **5384**
Hollins, T.
  Beyond broadcasting into the cable age **6137**
Hollis, E.P.
  Bibliography of earthquake engineering **1503**

Hollister-Short, G.
  History of technology **3063, 4289**
Holloway, A.
  Information work with unpublished reports **209**
Hollyman, K.J.
  Extinct species of the world **2468, 2748**
Holm, L.
  World weeds: natural histories and distribution **5714**
Holmes, A.
  Holmes' principles of physical geology **1618**
  Holmes' principles of physical geology **1618**
Holmes, S.
  Outline of plant classification **2517**
Holmes-Siedle, A. *and* Adams, L.
  Handbook of radiation effects **4219**
Holmgren, P.K.
  The Herbaria of the world **2542**
  Index herbariorum **2542**
Holmstrom, J.
  Trilingual dictionary for materials and structures **4004, 4971**
Holography **1050**
Holz-Wörterbuch **6993**
Hom, K.
  Ken Hom's Chinese cookery **6078**
Homans, S.W.
  A Dictionary of concepts in NMR **1086**
Homburger, W.S.
  Transportation and traffic engineering handbook **6260**
Home medical encyclopedia **3295**
Home Office
  See
    Great Britain. Home Office
The Home planet **1483**
Home preservation of fruit and vegetables **6038**
Home, R.W.
  The History of classical physics **976**
The Homeowner's complete manual of repair & improvement **6102**
Honey bee science **5927**
Hongfu, Y.
  The Palaeobiogeography of China **1928**
Honigmann, J.J.
  Handbook of social and cultural anthropology **2003**
Hood, W.
  A-Z of clinical chemistry **2326**
Hoof, H. van
  Internationale Bibliographie der Übersetzung **423**
Hoofed mammals of the world **2966**
Hooker, Sir J.D.
  Handbook of the British flora **2567**
Hope, A. *and* Walch, M.
  The Color compendium **1056**
Hope, C.E.G.
  The Encyclopedia of the horse **5875**
Hope, R.
  A New history of British shipping **6358**
Hopkins, J.
  Glossary of astronomy and astrophysics **700**
Hopkins, N.J.
  The Numbers you need **612**
Hopkins, S.T. *and* Jones, T.E.
  Research guide to the arid lands of the world **1703**
Hopp, V.
  Handbook of applied chemistry **6441**
Hopwood, A.T. *and* Hollyfield, J.P.
  An Annotated bibliography of the fossil mammals of Africa (1742-1950) **1972**
Hora, B.
  The Oxford encyclopedia of trees of the world **5645**

Hunt, V.D. *(contd.)*
Dictionary of advanced manufacturing technology **4639**
Energy dictionary **4076**
Handbook of energy technology **4065**
Industrial robotics handbook **7386**
Robotics sourcebook **7387**
Windpower **4320**

Hunter, D.
The Diseases of occupations **3608**
Paper-making **7035**

Hunter, D.E. *and* **Whitten, P.**
Encyclopedia of anthropology **1998**

Hunter, R. *and* **Macalpine, I.**
Three hundred years of psychiatry, 1535-1860 **3860**

Hunter's tropical medicine **3751**
Huntia **2485**

Huntington, W.C.
Building construction materials and types of construction **7553**

Huntley, B. *and* **Birks, H.J.B.**
An Atlas of past and present pollen maps for Europe 0-13000 years ago **1939**

Huntley, I.D.
Mathematical modelling **570**

Huppmann, W.J. *and* **Dalal, K.**
Metallographic atlas of powder metallurgy **4670**

Hurlbut, C.S. *and* **Kammerling, R.C.**
Gemology **1427**

Hurle, D.T.J.
Handbook of crystal growth **1376**

Hurnik, J.F.
Dictionary of farm animal behavior **2764, 5811**

Hurt, C.D.
Information sources in science and technology **65**

Hurt, R.D. *and* **Hurt, M.E.**
The History of agricultural science and technology **5556**

Hüschke, R.E.
Glossary of meteorology **1780**

Hutchings, E.A.D.
A Survey of printing processes **6199**

Hutchinson, C.L.
The ARRL handbook for the radio amateur **4538**

The Hutchinson dictionary of science **125**
Hutchinson encyclopedia of the earth **1619**

Hutchinson, G.E.
A Treatise on limnology **2289**

Hutchinson, J.
The Families of flowering plants **2687**

Hutchinson personal computer dictionary **7307**
The Hutchinson world weather guide **1808**

Hutchison, C.S.
Geological evolution of south-east Asia **1605**

Huth, E.J.
Scientific style and format **435**

Huxley, A.
The New Royal Horticultural Society dictionary of gardening **5778**
Standard encyclopedia of the world's mountains **1711**
Standard encyclopedia of the world's oceans and islands **1709, 1736**

HVAC design data sourcebook **7587**
HVAC engineer's handbook **7588**

Hyam, R. *and* **Pankhurst, R.**
Plants and their names: a concise dictionary **2519**

Hyams, E.
Great botanical gardens of the world **2538**

Hyatt, E.
Keyguide to information sources in remote sensing **844, 1524**

The Hydraulic handbook **5078**
Hydraulics and hydraulic research **5094**

Hydraulics field manual **5079**
Hydro-electric engineering practices **4316**
Hydrogen **6546**
Hydrogen energy quarterly literature review **4113**

Hydrographic Department
See
Great Britain. Hydrographic Department$zOcean passages for the world

Hydrographic dictionary **1876**
Hydrological data United Kingdom **1887**
Hydropower engineering handbook **4317**

Hyman, C.J.
German-English, English-German astronautics dictionary **5459**

Hyman, C.J. *and* **Idlin, R.**
Dictionary of physics and allied sciences **940**

Hyman, L.H.
The Invertebrates **2781**

Hyne, N.J.
Dictionary of petroleum exploration, drilling and production **4794, 6737**

Hywell-Davies, J.
The Macmillan guide to British nature reserves **2437**

IARC
See
World Organization. International Agency for Research on Cancer

Ibeas, F.F.
Diccionario technologico inglés-español de electricdad, electronica, telecomunicacion y materias afines con la fisica, la optica y la quimica **4263**

IBM dictionary of computing **7249**
IC Master, 1987 **4302**
ICI colour atlas **1060**
ICO Library monthly entries - COFFEELINE **6617**
ICONDA **4921, 7465**
IDAAS 1990 **736**
The Identification of flowering plant families **2495**
The Identification of textile materials **7058**
IDPAI 1990 **737**

IEA Coal Research
International Conference on coal science **6568**

IEEE membership directory **4292**
IEEE standards collection software engineering **7324**

Ifrah, G.
Histoire universelle des chiffres **613**

Iglesia, M.E. de la
International catalogue of catalogues **6024**

Igneous rocks of the British Isles **1843**

Igoe, R.S.
Dictionary of food ingredients **6695**

Ilaco BV., Arnhem
Agricultural compendium for rural development in the tropics and subtropics **5568**

Ilic, J.
CSIRO atlas of hardwoods **7002**

Illingworth, V.
The Macmillan dictionary of astronomy **702**
The Penguin dictionary of physics **936**

Illingworth, V. *and* **Pyle, I.**
Dictionary of computing **7245**

Illumination engineering **5262**
Illustrated automobile dictionary in six languages **5274**
Illustrated chemistry laboratory terminology **1261**
Illustrated computer graphics dictionary **7257**
The Illustrated dictionary of boating terms **6343**
Illustrated dictionary of building **7500**

Illustrated dictionary of building materials and techniques **7556**
The Illustrated dictionary of building terms **7502**
Illustrated dictionary of cargo handling **5106**
Illustrated dictionary of dentistry **3818**
The Illustrated dictionary of electronics **4414**
Illustrated dictionary of equine terms **5876**
Illustrated dictionary of fabrics **7085**
An Illustrated dictionary of glass **6788**
An Illustrated dictionary of hairdressing & wigmaking **7451**
Illustrated dictionary of mechanical engineering **4133**
Illustrated dictionary of microelectronics and microcomputers **4460**
The Illustrated dictionary of nautical terms **6340**
Illustrated dictionary of robotics **7393**
Illustrated dictionary of science **87**
An Illustrated dictionary of word processing **6184**
An Illustrated dictonary of jewellery **6976**
The Illustrated directory of modern Soviet weapons **4853**
The Illustrated encyclopaedia of birds **2883**
The Illustrated encyclopaedia of shells **2795**
The Illustrated encyclopaedia of transportation **6257**
The Illustrated encyclopedia of ammunition **4871**
The Illustrated encyclopedia of artillery **4856**
The Illustrated encyclopedia of beekeeping **5928**
Illustrated encyclopedia of building services **7545**
Illustrated encyclopedia of dermatology **3827**
The Illustrated encyclopedia of dinosaurs **1963**
The Illustrated encyclopedia of general aviation **5391**
Illustrated encyclopedia of human histology **2775**
The Illustrated encyclopedia of mankind **2032**
The Illustrated encyclopedia of orchids **2701**
The Illustrated encyclopedia of ships, boats, vessels and other water-borne craft **5332**
The Illustrated encyclopedia of space technology **5445**
The illustrated encyclopedia of trucks and buses **5298**
Illustrated encyclopedia of wildlife **2716**
Illustrated encyclopedic dictionary of electronic circuits **4459**
An Illustrated examination of advanced technology warfare **4844**
The Illustrated field guide to ferns and allied plants of the British Isles **2680**
The Illustrated flora of Britain and Northern Europe **2557**
Illustrated glossary for solar and solar-terrestrial physics **773**
Illustrated glossary of snow and ice **1640**
An Illustrated guide to modern fighters **4884**
An Illustrated guide to modern trains **5381**
An Illustrated guide to rocks and minerals **1400**
Illustrated guide to the birds of southern Africa **2919**
Illustrated guidebook to electronic devices and circuits **4438**
The Illustrated history of canal and river navigation **5104**
The Illustrated history of textiles **7075**
The Illustrated petroleum reference dictionary **6738**
The Illustrated reference on cacti and other succulents **5806**
Illustrated Stedman's medical dictionary **3291**
Illustrated technical dictionaries in six languages **3031**

Information sources on the packaging industry 4706

Information sources on the paint and varnish industry 6840

Information sources on the pesticides industry 5724

Information sources on the petrochemical industry 6772

Information sources on the printing and graphics industry 6148

Information sources on the pulp and paper industry 7031

Information sources on the soap and detergent industry 6533

Information sources on the vegetable oil processing industry 6706

Information sources on woodworking machinery 7010

Information technology: vocabulary 7288

Information work with unpublished reports 209

The Infrared handbook 1042

Inglis, A.F.
Electronic communications handbook 4497

Ingold, T.
Companion encyclopedia of anthropology 2002

INIS Atomindex 4187

INIS (International Nuclear Information System) 4167

INIS: Thesaurus 4209

Inland transport statistics, Great Britain, 1900-1970 6265

Inland waterways 6387

Inland waterways of Europe 5102

Inland waterways series 6389

The Innovative engineer 3935

The Innovators handbook: 1988/89 3109

Inorganic chemical nomenclature 1311

Inorganic chemistry handbook 1304

Inorganic reacitons and methods 1301

Inpadoc/Family and legal status 3152

The Insect and spider collections of the world 2799, 2830

Insects: instructions for collectors 2812

Insects of the world 2814

Inskipp, T.
An Annotated checklist of the birds of the oriental region 2916

Inskipp, T. and Barzdo, J.
World checklist of threatened mammals 2466

INSPEC 220, 667, 909, 4238, 7227

INSPEC Thesaurus 988, 4294

Inspected hotels 5985

Institute of Electrical and Electronics Engineers
Electrical and electronics graphic symbols and reference designations 4235, 4387
IEEE membership directory 4292
Index to IEEE publications 4243
National electrical safety code handbook 4340
The New IEEE standard dictionary of electrical and electronic terms 4253

Institute of Geological Sciences
Regional geochemical atlases 1517

Institute of Marine Engineers
Glossary of marine technology terms 5343

Institute of Oceanographic Sciences
Serial holdings of UK marine and freshwater sciences libraries 1749

Institute of Paper Science and Technology graphic arts bulletin 6194

Institute of Petroleum
Standard methods for analysis and testing of petroleum and its products 6750

Institute of Physics
Research fields in physics 994

Institute of Scientific and Technical Communications
ISTC bibliography on technical communication 437

Institute of Water Pollution Control
Glossary of terms used in water pollution control 5202

Institution of Civil Engineers
CESMM3 4966

Institution of Civil Engineers. Library and Information Services
Catalogue of periodical publications 1665-1994 4951

Institution of Electrical Engineers
Computer and control abstracts. Science abstracts. Section C 7267, 7354
Current papers in electrical and electronics engineering 4268
Current papers on computers and control 7273, 7355
Electrical and electronics abstracts. Science abstracts. Section B 4269
A History of the Institution of Electrical Engineers, 1871-1971 4296
INSPEC 909, 4238, 7227
Key abstracts 4270
List of journals and other serial sources, INSPEC 4273
Physics abstracts. Science abstracts. Section A 950, 4189
Requirements for electrical installations BS 7671: 1992 4342
Science abstracts 220
Thesaurus 1999 988, 4294
Yearbook and list of members 4293

Institution of Engineering Designers
Official reference book and buyers' guide 3978

Institution of Fire Engineers
Dictionary of fire technology 3614

Institution of Highways and Transportation
Roads and traffic in urban areas 6278

Institution of Mechanical Engineers
Brief subject and author index of papers published in the *Proceedings*, 1847-1950 4127

Institution of Mining and Metallurgy
IMM abstracts 4785, 6864
IMMAGE Thesaurus 4793
Silver: exploration, mining and treatment 4810, 6935
Surface mining and quarrying 4811
Tunnelling 91 5006

The Institution of Naval Architects, 1860-1960 5360

Instructions for collectors. No. 10. Plants 2539

Instrument engineers' handbook 7203

The Instrument manual 7201

Instrumentation and control 7204

Instrumentation reference book 4350

Instruments of science 7212

Instruments of science: an historical encyclopedia 442

Integrals and series 623

Integrated circuits applications handbook 4299

Intel Corporation
Handbooks 4431

Intellectual mastery of nature 970

Intellectual property 3107, 3206

Intellectual property law and taxation 3208

Intellectual property law handbook 3108

Intellectual property rights 3184

Intellectual property rights and innovation 3207

Intellectual property world desk reference 3111

Inter-Press dictionary of science and engineering. English-Japanese; Japanese-English 200

Interavia ABC aerospace directory 5409

Interavia space directory 5467

Interdisciplinary dictionary of weed science 5713

Interdok
See
directory of published proceedings

International aerospace abstracts 5463

International Agency for Research on Cancer
See
World Health Organization. International Agency for Research on Cancer

International air/lift review 5057

International Air Transport Association
World air transport statistics 6398

International Air Transport Association *and* International AERadio, Ltd.
Air distances manual 6406

International airline phrase book in six languages, English, French, German, Italian, Portuguese and Spanish 6403

International Association of Volcanology
Catalogue of the active volcanoes of the world 1625

International Astronomical Union
Transactions of the General Assembly. Pt.A. Reports on astronomy. v.1- 738

International Atomic Energy Agency
Bibliographical series 4172
Catalogue: International Atomic Energy publications 4171
INIS Atomindex 4187
INIS: Thesaurus 4209
International nuclear information system multilingual dictionary 4180
Meetings on atomic energy 4210
Nuclear research reactors in the world 4213

International Bee Research Association
British bee books 5924

International bibliography of bibliographies in technology, science and economics 54

International bibliography of dictionaries, glossaries and terminological publications in forestry and related sciences 5616

International bibliography of social and cultural anthropology 1994

International bibliography of specialized dictionaries 103

International bibliography of standardized vocabularies 107

International bibliography of the book trade and librarianship 6205

International bibliography of translations 423

International bibliography of vegetation maps 2554

International book publishing: an encyclopedia 6214

International building science and structural abstracts 7512

International building services abstracts (IBSEDEX) 7586

International Cargo Handling Coordination Association
A Multilingual glossary of cargo handling terms 5107

International catalogue of catalogues 6024

International catalogue of scientific literature 66

International Civil Aviation Organization
Air navigation plans 809
Lexicon in English-French-Spanish-Russian 6395

International civil engineering abstracts 4950

International classification of impairments, disabilities and handicaps 3749

International classification of procedures in medicine 3300

International cloud atlas 1791

International Code of Botanical Nomenclature 2520

Israel. National Centre of Scientific and Technical Information
Directory of research institutes and industrial laboratories in Israel **495**
ISTC bibliography on technical communication **437**
The ISTC handbook of technical writing and publication techniques **436**
Ita, N.O.
Bibliography of Nigeria **2072**
ITS textile dictionary **7062**
Iturraldie, M.P.
Dictionary and handbook of nuclear medicine and clinical imaging **3703**
IUCN directory of neotropical protected areas **2434**
IUCN directory of protected areas in Oceania **2442**
IUCN directory of South Asian protected areas **2442**
1996 IUCN red list of threatened animals **2467**
1997 IUCN red list of threatened plants **2452**
IUPAC handbook 1998/99 **1218**
Ivanov, A.O.
Dictionary of shipping terms: Russian-English and English-Russian **6350**
IWSA yearbook **5192**
J & P transformer book **4331**
J + W international telefax **6126**
Jablonski, S.
Dictionary of medical acronyms and abbreviations **3224**
Illustrated dictionary of dentistry **3818**
Jablonski's dictionary of syndromes and eponymic diseases **3769**
Russian-English medical dictionary **3349**
Jablonski's dictionary of syndromes and eponymic diseases **3769**
Jackson, A.
The Complete book of tools **4753**
The Model maker's handbook **3950**
Jackson, A.A.
The Railway dictionary **5013**
Jackson, A.J.
British civil aircraft, 1919-1972 **5424**
Jackson, B.D.
A Glossary of botanic terms **2505**
Guide to the literature of botany **2488**
Jackson, G.
The History and archaeology of ports **6383**
Index to periodicals on agriculture held by the Science Reference Library **5544**
Jackson, J.A.
Bird conservation 3 **2480**
Jackson, K.G.
Dictionary of electrical engineering **4254**
Jackson, K.G. and Townsend, B.
Television and video engineer's reference book **4561**
Jackson, K.M.
Computer security reference book **7334**
Jackson, M.
The World guide to whisky **6613**
Jackson, M.H.
Environmental health reference book **5141**
Jackson, N
Civil engineering materials **4972**
Jacob, H.
A Pocket dictionary of publishing terms **6215**
Jacob, R. and Alexander, D.
A Guidebook to intellectual property **3112**
Jacobs, A.J.
Patents throughout the world **3194**
Trade marks throughout the world **3127**
Jacobsen, H.
Lexicon of succulent plants **5807**
Jacobson, C.A.
Encyclopedia of chemical reactions **1241**

Jacobson, I.D.
Plumbing dictionary **7575**
Jacolev, L.
German-English science dictionary **132**
Jaeger, E.C.
A Source-book of biological names and terms **2160**
Jaffe, J.H.
Encyclopedia of drugs and alcohol **3578**
Jaggi, O.P.
History of science and technology in India **402, 3438**
Jahns, H.M. and Massflink, A.K.
Collins' guide to the ferns, mosses and lichens of Britain and Northern and Central Europe **2679**
Jakobi, G.
Dictionary of washing **6532**
Jakubke, H-D. and Jeschkeit, H.
Concise encyclopedia chemistry **1126**
James, A.M. and Lord, M.P.
Macmillan's chemical and physical data **963, 1186**
James, D.E.
The Encyclopedia of solid earth geophysics **1489**
James, G. and James, R.C.
Mathematics dictionary **538**
James, L.
A Chronology of the construction of Britain's railways, 1778-1855 **5035**
James, L.K.
Nobel laureates in chemistry, 1901-1992 **1206**
James, N.D.G.
The Arboriculturalist's companion **5796**
The Forester's companion **5622**
James, P.
The Future of coal **6572**
James, V.U.
Africa's ecology **2277**
Jane's aerospace dictionary **5455**
Jane's aircraft recognition guide **5394**
Jane's airports, equipment and services **6399**
Jane's all the world's aircraft **5416**
Jane's ammunition handbook **4872**
Jane's armour and artillery **4857**
Jane's armour and artillery upgrades **4858**
Jane's avionics **4885**
Jane's defence glossary **4821**
Jane's dictionary of naval terms **4897**
Jane's encyclopedia of aviation **5392**
Jane's fighting ships **4909**
Jane's helicopter markets and systems **4889, 5436**
Jane's high-speed marine technology **5380**
Jane's index of indices **4817**
Jane's infantry weapons **4866**
Jane's international ABC aerospace directory **5464**
Jane's land-based air defence **4846**
Jane's merchant ships **5377**
Jane's military communications **4876**
Jane's military vehicles and logistics **4860**
Jane's naval weapon systems **4919**
Jane's radar and electronic warfare systems **4879**
Jane's space directory **5465**
Jane's underwater technology **5098**
Jane's underwater warfare systems **4851**
Jane's urban transport systems **6277**
Jane's world airlines **6405**
Jane's world railways **5029**
Jane's world sailplanes and motor gliders **5432**
Janis, C.M.
Evolution of tertiary mammals of North America **1971**
Jansonius, H.
Technish Engels woordenboek **140**
Japan chemical directory **6514**

Japan: Ministry of Education
Japanese-English scientific terms: chemistry **1166**
Japanese scientific terms: Seismology **1510**
Japan. Ministry of International Trade and Industry. Basic Industries Bureau. Chemical Products Safety Division
Handbook of existing and new chemical substances **1253, 6517**
Japan technology **3087**
The Japanese automobile industry **5316**
Japanese/English, English/Japanese glossary of scientific and technical terms **201, 3042**
Japanese-English scientific terms: chemistry **1166**
Japanese journals in English **399**
Japanese laws relating to industrial property **3213**
Japanese scientific and technical literature **397**
Japanese scientific terms: Seismology **1510**
Japanese Special Libraries Association
Directory of information sources in Japan, 1986 **457**
Japanese technical abstracts **3048**
Japan's high technology **3088**
Jarman, C.
Atlas of animal migration **2772**
Jaschek, C.
Data in astronomy **718**
Jaspert, W.P.
The Encyclopaedia of type faces **6174**
Jayawardene, S.A.
Reference books for the historian of science **291**
'Western scientific manuscripts before 1900: a check list of published catalogues' **363**
Jayawardene, S.A. and Lawes, J.
'Biographical notices of historians of science: a checklist' **350**
Jedraszko, S.
Slownik lekarski, angielsko-polski i polski-anglielski **3351**
Jedruch, J.
Nuclear engineering databases, standards and numerical analysis **4173**
Jefferson's welding encyclopedia **4681**
Jeffrey, C.
Biological nomenclature **2181**
Jeffreys, A.E.
Michael Faraday **375**
Jeffreys, Sir H.
The Earth: its origin, history and physical constitution **1620**
Jenkins, D.G. and Murray, J.W.
Stratigraphical atlas of fossil foraminifera **1949**
Jenkins, E.W.
References for chemistry teachers **1124**
Jenkins, G.
Oil economists' handbook **6730**
Jenkins, J.D.
Thesaurus of rock and soil mechanics terms **4990**
Jenkinson, K.A.
Preserved buses **5299**
Jenness, D.
The Indians of Canada **2119**
Jennett, S.
The Making of books **6139**
Jensen, M.L. and Bateman, A.M.
Economic mineral deposits **1851**
Jensen, R.D. and Smith, M.M.
Agricultural and animal sciences journals and serials **5542**
Jerde, J.
The Encyclopedia of textiles **7057**
Jermy, C. and Camus, J.
The Illustrated field guide to ferns and allied plants of the British Isles **2680**
Jerrard, H.G. and McNeill, D.B.
Dictionary of scientific units **276, 964**

Kuliev, A.S.
English - Azerbaijan - Russian dictionary on
oil field industry **6732**
Kulwiec, R.A.
Materials handling handbook **4734**
Kummel, B. *and* Raup, D.
Handbook of palaeontological techniques
1902
Kuo, C.
'Marine technology' **5074, 5331**
Kurian, G. T.
Global guide to medical information **3258**
Kurian, G.T.
Glossary of the Third World **2048**
Kurpis, G.P. *and* Booth, C.J.
The New IEEE standard dictionary of
electrical and electronic terms **4253**
Kürschners deutschen Gelehrten-Kalender 381
Kurtén, B.
Pleistocene mammals of Europe **1973**
Kurtén, B. *and* Anderson, E.
Pleistocene mammals of North America
1974
Kurtz, A.K. *and* Edgerton, H.A.
Statistical dictionary of terms and symbols
644
Kurtz, E.B.
Lineman's and cableman's handbook **4334**
Kurzlexikon der Elektrotechnik 4256
Kut, D.
Illustrated encyclopedia of building services
7545
Kut, R.
Dictionary of applied energy conservation
4071
Kuter, L.
The Anthropology of Western Europe **2050**
Kutz, M.
Mechanical engineer's handbook **4130**
Kuvshinoff, B.W.
Fire sciences dictionary **3615**
Kuznetsov, B.V.
Russian-English dictionary of scientific and
technical usage **181**
Kuznetsov, I.V.
Lycedi russkoĭ nauki **391**
Kverneland, K.O.
World metric standards for engineering
3949
KWIK index of international standards 3057
Kyang, R.K.
Periodicals current in mainland China held
by the Science Reference Library **393**
La Rocque, A.
Contributions to the history of geology **1574**
Labahn, O.
Cement engineers' handbook **6824**
Labarre, E.J.
Dictionary and encyclopaedia of paper and
paper-making **7032**
Labensky, S.
Webster's new world dictionary of culinary
arts **6068**
Laboratory animals 5814
The Laboratory companion 1257
Laboratory techniques in zoology 2743
Labrum, E.A.
Civil engineering heritage: Eastern and
Central England **4960**
Lackie, J.M. *and* Dow, J.A.T.
The Dictionary of cell biology **2320**
LaCourse, D.E.
Handbook of solid modeling **3976**
Ladbury, A.
The Dressmaker's dictionary **6111**
Ladd, H.S.
Treatise on marine ecology and
paleoecology. Volume 2: Paleoecology
1930
Ladies in the laboratory? 355
Ladybirds 2415

Laessøe, T. *and* Lincoff, G.
Mushrooms **2664**
Lafferty, P. *and* Rowe, S.
The Hutchinson dictionary of science **125**
Lagacé, R.O.
Sixty cultures **2046**
Lagere planten 2636
Lagowski, J.J.
Macmillan encyclopedia of chemistry **1130**
LaGrega, M.
Hazardous waste management **5217**
Laithwaite, E.R.
A History of linear electric motors **4328**
Lalande, J.J.F. de.
Bibliographie astronomique **670**
Lamb, E. *and* Lamb, B.
The Illustrated reference on cacti and other
succulents **5806**
Lamb, H.H.
Climate: present, past and future **1806**
Lambert, A.
Battleships in transition **4907**
Lambert, C.M.
Radioactive waste **5223**
Lambert, D.
Cambridge guide to prehistoric man **1981**
Lambert, D
The Ultimate dinosaur book **1962**
Lambert, D. *and* The Diagram Group
The Cambridge field guide to prehistoric life
1903
Lambert, D. *and* The Diagram Group
The Cambridge guide to the earth **1621**
Collins' guide to dinosaurs **1965**
Dinosaur data book **1962**
The Field guide to geology **1541**
Lambert, M.
A Short Russian-English dictionary of
terminology used in the Soviet rubber,
plastics and tyre industries **7103**
Lambrecht, K.
Palaeontologi. Catalogus bio-bibliographicus
1917
Lammineur, P. *and* Cornillie, O.
Industrial robots **7400**
Lampkin, N.
Organic farming **5655**
Lamps and lighting 5260
LAN Buyers' guide 4533
Lancaster Health Authority
Glossary of terms, tests and drugs used in
psychiatric practice **3851**
Lancaster, H.O.
Bibliography of statistical bibliographies **634**
'Problems in the bibliography of statistics'
633
Landau, L.D. *and* Lifshitz, E.M.
Course of theoretical physics **927**
Landau, S.I.
International dictionary of medicine and
biology **2159, 3317**
**Landmarks in American civil engineering
4964**
**Landmarks in the history of physical education
3565**
Landmarks of botanical history 2528
Landmarks of the plastics industry 7146
Landolf, H.H. *and* Börnstein, R.
Zahlenwerte und Funktionen aus
Naturwissenschaften und Technik **277**
Landsberg, H.E.
World survey of climatology **1813**
Landstrom, B.
The Ship **5363**
**Landwirtschaftliches Wörterbuch in acht
Sprachen 5515**
Landwirtschaftliches Zentralblatt 5540
Lane, D. *and* Acland, J.
Industrial robotics: a bibliography **7378**
Lang, K.R.
Astrophysical formulae **740**

Lang, K.R. *and* Gingerich, O.
A Source book in astronomy and
astrophysics, 1900-1975 **698**
Lange, K.
Handbook of metal forming **4644**
Langenkamp, R.D.
The Illustrated petroleum reference
dictionary **6738**
**Langenscheidt's Fachwörterbuch Wehrwesen
4823**
Langer, R.H.M. *and* Hill, G.D.
Agricultural plants **5729**
Lange's handbook of chemistry 1187
Langford, D.A. *and* Retik, A.
'Construction management' **7488**
Langley, G.
Telephony's dictionary **4510**
Langman, L.
An Illustrated dictionary of word processing
6184
The New video encyclopedia 7407
The Language of biotechnology 2994
The Language of rubber 7123
The Language of the foreign book trade 6203
L'Annunziata, M.F.
Handbook of radioactivity analysis **4218**
Lapedes, D.N.
Diccionario de términos cientificos y
técnicos **170**
McGraw-Hill dictionary of the life sciences
2161
McGraw-Hill encyclopedia of food,
agriculture and nutrition **5508**
Lapidus, D.F.
Collins dictionary of geology **1550**
Laplante, P.
Electrical engineering dictionary **4252**
Larijani, L.C.
The Virtual reality primer **7404**
Larn, R. *and* Wheeler, R.
Commercial diving manual **5099**
Larousse astronomy 689
Larousse des minéraux 1395
**Larousse des pierres précieuses, fines,
ornamentales, organiques 1424**
**Larousse dictionary of science and technology
129**
Larousse dictionary of scientists 339
Larousse encyclopedia of wine 6592
**Larousse field guide to the birds of Britain and
Europe 2904**
**Larousse field guide to the mushrooms and
toadstools of Britain and Europe 2665**
Larrauri, A.
Dictionnaire d'oto-rhino-laryngologie **3809**
Lasca, N.P. *and* Donahue, J.
Archaeological geology of North America
1609
The Laser guidebook 4375
Laser handbook 4376
Laser safety handbook 4377
Lasers 4378
Lasers in chemistry 4374
Lasers in materials processing 4372
Laskin, A.I. *and* Lechevalier, H.A.
CRC handbook of microbiology **2370**
Last, J.M.
A Dictionary of epidemiology **3754**
The Last rain forests 2451
Latham, R.
The Dictionary of computer graphics and
virtual reality **7405**
**Latin Americans: contemporary peoples and
their cultural traditions 2097**
Laudan, R.
From mineralogy to geology: the
foundations of a science, 1650-1860 **1572**
Launert, E.
Collins' guide to the ferns, mosses and
lichens of Britain and Northern and
Central Europe **2679**

The Literature of forestry and agroforestry **5617**

The Literature of gemstones **1422**

The Literature of lighting **5259**

The Literature of mineralogy **1387**

The Literature of soil science **5678**

The Literature of the life sciences **2141**

Literature on the history of physics in the twentieth century **975**

Literature sources in toxicology: a survey **3708**

The Lithographers manual **6202**

Litman, T.
Efficient electric motor systems handbook **4329**

Little, E.C.
The Audubon Society field guide to North American trees **5653**

The Little red book **6288**

Liu, H.
Wind engineering **4973**

Liungman, C.G.
Thought signs **39**

The Lives of the Fellows of the Royal College of Obstetricians and Gynaecologists, 1929-1969 **3900**

Lives of the Fellows of the Royal College of Surgeons of England, 1930-1951 **3877**

Lives of the Fellows of the Royal College of Surgeons of England, 1952-1964 **3878**

Lives of the Fellows of the Royal College of Surgeons of England, 1965-1973 **3879**

Livesey, B. *and* Strickland-Hodge, B.
How to search the medical sources **3450**

Living invertebrates **2782**

The Living isles-Safari UK **2413**

Lliboutry, L.
Traité de glaciologie **1638**

Lloyd, N.
A History of English brickwork **7569**

Lloyd's international marine equipment guide **5092**

Lloyd's maritime atlas **6384**

Lloyd's maritime directory **5356**

Lloyd's nautical year book **6353**

Lloyd's of London
Register of ships **5358**

Lloyd's ports of the world **6385**

Lo, Teh, C.
Handbook of solvent extraction **6502**

Lock, C.B.M.
Geography and cartography **1684**
Modern maps and atlases **861**

Lockard, D.
Coal: a memoir and critique **6578**

Locker, E.J.
Dictionary and encyclopaedia of paper and paper-making **7033**

Locket, G.H. *and* Millidge, A.F.
British spiders **2801**

Locks and lockmaking **7429**

Lockwood, W.B.
The Oxford dictionary of British bird names **2911**

Locquin, H. *and* Langeron, M.
Handbook of microscopy **1046, 2203**

Lodge, W.
Birds: alternative names: a world checklist **2891**

Loening, K.L.
List of standard abbreviations (symbols) for synthetic polymers and polymer materials **7147**

Loftness, R.L.
Energy handbook **4086**

Lofty, G.J. *and* Highley, D.E.
United Kingdom minerals yearbook **1408**

Logan, C.M. *and* Rice, M.K.
Logan's medical and scientific abbreviations **3225**

Logan's medical and scientific abbreviations **3225**

Logarithmetica Britannica **666**

Logic designer's handbook **4300**

Logie, G.
Glossary of land resources **5516**
Glossary of transport **6259**

Logis de France **5986**

Lohwater, A.J.
A.J. Lohwater's Russian-English dictionary of the mathematical sciences **548**

Loison, K.
Coke **6580**

Lomas, C.
Road construction and traffic directory 1994 **5069**

London College of Furniture Library
Periodicals list, 1988 **7433**

London School of Hygiene and Tropical Medicine. University of London
Dictionary catalogue. [London School of Hygiene and Tropical Medicine] **3260**

London University. Imperial College: King's College
Life sciences libraries in and around London **2193**

London University. Library
Union list of periodicals on mathematics and allied subjects in London libraries **558**

London University. Library Resources Co-ordinating Committee. Geography Sub-committee
A Guide to geography and map collections **898, 1707**

London weather **1815**

London's Underground **5055**

Longley, D. *and* Shain, M.
Macmillan dictionary of personal computing and communications **7305**
The Microcomputer users handbook **7298**

Longman chemistry handbook **1137**

Longman dictionary of environmental science **2242**

Longman dictionary of geography, human and physical **1680**

The Longman dictionary of scientific usage **126**

Longman illustrated animal encyclopedia **2750**

Longman illustrated dictionary of geology **1549**

Longman mathematics handbook **541**

Longshore, D.
Encyclopedia of hurricanes, typhoons, and cyclones **1790**

Longstaff, M.
Unlocking the atom **4207**

Longyard, W.H.
Who's who in aviation history **5414**

Longyear, M.
The McGraw-Hill style manual **439**

Loon, C.D. van *and* Heij, D.G. van der
Potato terms **5745**

Loones, D.
Watchmakers and clockmakers of the world: Volume 2 **7192**

Lorch, W.
Handbook of water purification **5200**

Lord, J.
Sizes: the illustrated encyclopedia **995**

Lord, M.P.
Macmillan dictionary of physics **937**

Lorenz, K.J. *and* Kulp, K.
Handbook of cereal science and technology **6670**

Lorenzini, J.A.
Medical phrase index **3318**

Loria, G.
Guida allo studio della storia delle matematiche **584**

Lösch, A.
World cars **5313**

Losee, J.
A Historical introduction to the philosophy of science **307**

Lötschert, W. *and* Beese, G.
Collins' guide to tropical plants **2556, 5736**

Loudon, I.
Western medicine: an illustrated history **3408**

Lourie, J.
Medical eponyms **3413**

Louros, N.C.
Obstétrique et gynécologie **3899**

Loveday, G.
Microprocessor sourcebook **7306**

Lovegrove, M.
Lovegrove's guide to Britain's North Sea oil and gas **6768**

Lovegrove's guide to Britain's North Sea oil and gas **6768**

Lovell, E.C. *and* Hall, R.M.
Index to handicrafts, model-making and workshop projects **7458**

Lovelock, Y.
The Vegetable book **6084**

Lowe, D.
The Transport manager's & operator's handbook **6283**

Lowenstein, M.Z.
Energy applications of biomass **4115**

Lowenthal, M.A.
Who's who in the history of cartography: the international guide to the subject **889**

Loyd, S.
The Heat pump **4596**

Lozet, J. *and* Mathieu, C.
Dictionnaire de science du sol **5679**

Lubell, C.
Textile collections of the world **7078**

Lubin, C.
Handbook of composites **3996**

Lubricants Europe **4748**

Lucca, J. de
Dictionnaire des télécommunications et de l'internet **4514**

Lucchesi, M.
Dizionario medico **3340**

Lück, E.C.
Bibliography of dictionaries and vocabularies on food, nutrition and cookery **6642**
The Compact dictionary of food technology **6647**

Luck, S.
Philip's nature encyclopedia **2386**

Ludwig Darmstaedter's Handbuch zur Geschichte der Naturwissenschaften **303**

Luedtke, J.R.
'Energy and the environment' **4050, 5226**

Lueger, O.
Lexikon der Technik **3025**

Luftbehandlingsordlista **3594**

Luginsky, Y.N.
Dictionary of electrical engineering **4251**

Lum, A.
'Palaeontology' **1895**

Lunar sourcebook **757**

Lund, H.F.
The McGraw-Hill recycling handbook **5231**

Lüning, K.
Seaweeds: their environment, biogeography, and ecophysiology **2641**

Luoyang Agricultural Machinery Academy
English-Chinese dictionary of agricultural machinery **5668**

Lura, A. Eggers-
See
Eggers-Lura, A.

Lusis, A.
Astronomy and aeronautics **673**

Luther, P.
Bibliography of astronomers **732**

McKetta, J.J.
Inorganic chemistry handbook **1304**
McKetta, J.J. *and* Cunningham, W.A.
Encyclopedia of chemical processing and
design **6485**
McKinlay, R.G.
Vegetable crop pests **5704**
McKitterick, D.
History of Cambridge University Press **6167**
McKnight, H.
The Shell book of inland waterways **5103,
6393**
MacKnight, N.
Space year 1991 **5448**
Macksey, K.
The Penguin encyclopedia of weapons and
military technology **4842**
Maclachlan, M.
An Introduction to marine drilling **4797**
McLean, A.C. *and* Gribble, C.D.
Geology for civil engineers **1520**
Maclean, J.
Elsevier's dictionary of building construction
7506
Maclean, N.
Macmillan dictionary of genetics & cell
biology **2304**
McLean, R.
The Thames and Hudson manual of
typography **6192**
Maclean, V.
A Short-title catalogue of household and
cookery books published in the English
tongue, 1701-1800 **6045**
McLellan, G.W.
Glass engineering handbook **6793**
McLelland, W.D.
Reviews of United Kingdom statistical
sources. V.22: Printing and publishing
6165
MacLeod, R.M. *and* Friday, J.R.
Archives of British men of science **371**
McMaster, R.S. *and* Boyle, B.G.
'Robotics and automated manufacture' **7380**
Macmillan dictionary of anthropology **1999**
The Macmillan dictionary of astronomy **702**
Macmillan dictionary of building **7501**
Macmillan dictionary of chemistry **1141**
Macmillan dictionary of data communications
7289
Macmillan dictionary of genetics & cell
biology **2304**
Macmillan dictionary of immunology **3798**
Macmillan dictionary of materials and
manufacturing **4008**
Macmillan dictionary of microcomputing **7309**
Macmillan dictionary of personal computing
and communications **7305**
Macmillan dictionary of physics **937**
Macmillan dictionary of the environment
2234, 2447
Macmillan encyclopedia of chemistry **1130**
Macmillan encyclopedia of computers **7237**
Macmillan encyclopedia of physics **923**
Macmillan encyclopedia of science **90**
Macmillan encyclopedia of the environment
2445
The Macmillan field guide to British
wildflowers **2576**
The Macmillan guide to British nature reserves
2437
The Macmillan guide to child health **3519,
6118**
Macmillan illustrated animal encyclopedia
2750
The Macmillan illustrated encyclopedia of
dinosaurs and prehistoric animals **1968**
The Macmillan nautical almanac **6370**
Macmillan's chemical and physical data **963,
1186**

McMinn, R.M.H.
A Colour atlas of human anatomy **3488**
McMullan, J.T.
'Energy technology' **4055**
McMullan, R.
Macmillan dictionary of building **7501**
McMurray, E.J.
Notable twentieth-century scientists **341**
McMurtrie, D.C. *and* Adamson, J.
The Invention of printing: a bibliography
6162
McNaught, A.D. *and* Wilkinson, A.
Compendium of chemical terminology **1193**
McNaughton, K.
'Chemical engineering' guide to pumps
4621
McNeil, M.
Earth sciences reference **1467**
McNeill, I.
An Encyclopedia of the history of
technology **3064**
McPartland, J.F. *and* McPartland, B.
McGraw-Hill National Electrical Code
handbook **4341**
Macpherson, A.
International telecommunication standards
organizations **4525**
Macrae, R.
Encyclopaedia of food science, food
technology and nutrition **6633**
McShane, C.
The Automobile **5310**
Macura, P.
Elsevier's dictionary of chemistry: Russian/
English **1163**
Russian-English botanical dictionary **2506**
Russian-English dictionary of
electrotechnology and allied sciences
4265
McVey, J.P.
CRC handbook of mariculture **5932**
Madden, J.S.
A Guide to alcohol and drug dependence
3573
Maddison, F.
'Early astronomical and mathematical
instruments - a brief survey of sources and
modern studies' **603**
'Early astronomical and mathematical
instruments: a brief survey of sources and
modern studies.' **742**
Maddox, G.L.
The Encyclopedia of aging **3761**
Madge, S. *and* Burn, H.
Wildfowl **2931**
Madisetti, V.K. *and* Williams, D.B.
The Digital signal processing handbook
4496
Madsen, W.
Handbook of personal data protection **7335**
Magalini, S.I.
Dictionary of medical syndromes **3768**
Magee, S. *and* Tripp, L.L.
Software engineering standards and
specifications **7325**
Magel, C.R.
Keyguide to information sources in animal
rights **5859**
Magie, W.F.
A Source book in physics **957**
Magill, F.N.
Magill's survey of science: applied science
series **91, 3026**
Magill's survey of science: earth science
series **1463**
Magill's survey of science: life science series
92
Magill's survey of science: physical science
series **924**
Nobel prize winners: chemistry **1207**
The Nobel prize winners: physics **981**

Magill, F.N. *and* Tobias, R.T.
USA in space **5446**
Magill's survey of science: applied science
series **91, 3026**
Magill's survey of science CD-ROM **52**
Magill's survey of science: earth science series
1463
Magill's survey of science: life science series
92
Magill's survey of science: physical science
series **924**.
Magner, L.N.
A History of the life sciences **2186**
Magnetism **1084**
Magyar-angol müszaki szótár **195**
Magyar-angol szótár **195**
Mahajan, S. *and* Kimerling, L.C.
Concise encyclopedia of semiconducting
materials and related technologies **4479**
Mahon, L.L.J.
Diesel generator handbook **4572**
Mahoney, R.
Laboratory techniques in zoology **2743**
Mahy, B.W.J.
A Dictionary of virology **2356, 3865**
Maichel, K.
Guide to Russian reference books. Volume
5: Science, technology and medicine **385**
Mail guide **6411**
Maintenance engineering handbook **4161**
Maitland, P.S.
Biology of fresh waters **2287**
Maize abstracts **5738**
Maizell, R.E.
How to find chemical information **1118**
Maizlish, A. *and* Tefft, W.
The World map directory, 1992-1993 **877**
Majerus, M.E.N.
Ladybirds **2415**
Major chemical and petrochemical companies
of Europe, 1991-1992 **6456**
Major chemical hazards **3625**
The Major seaports of the United Kingdom
6382
Make it **7459**
Makey, D.G.
ISIS world geographic and zoological
institution directory **2739**
Making instruments count **7208**
The Making of books **6139**
Makower, J.
The Air & space catalog **714**
Malclès, L.-N.
Les Sources du travail bibliographique **69**
Malinowski, S.
The Gale encyclopedia of Native American
tribes **2115**
Malinowsky, H.R.
Best science and technology reference books
for young people **70**
Reference sources in science, engineering,
medicine, and agriculture **72**
Mallick, P.K.
Composite materials technology **3997**
Mallow, A. *and* Chabot, L.
Laser safety handbook **4377**
Maltman, A.
Geological maps **1569**
Maludzinska, G.
Dictionary of analytical chemistry **1277**
Mammal evolution **2315**
Mammal species of the world **2944**
Mammalian paleofaunas of the world **1976**
Mammals **2937**
Mammals in the British Isles **2956**
Mammals in the seas **2952**
The Mammals of Britain and Europe **2954**
The Mammals of North America **2959**
Mammals of the neotropics **2951**
The Mammals of the Southern African
subregion **2958**

Miller, G.L. *(contd.)*
Zirconium **6945**
Miller, J.A.
The Island Press bibliography of
environmental literature **5129**
Miller, J.T.
The Instrument manual **7201**
Miller, J.Y.
The Common names of North American
butterflies **2840**
Miller, K.L. *and* **Weidner, W.A.**
CRC handbook of management of radiation
protection programs **3596**
Miller, M.A.
Birds: a guide to the literature **2878**
Miller, R.
Industrial robot handbook **7388**
Miller, R.W
Flow measurement engineering handbook
4609
Miller, S.A.
Acetylene: its properties, manufacture and
uses **6587**
Millero, F.J.
Chemical oceanography **1738**
Millodot, M.
Dictionary of optometry **3887**
Mills, D. *and* **Simpson, S.**
The Aquarium encyclopedia **5966**
Mills, D. *and* **Vevers, G.**
The Practical encyclopedia of freshwater
tropical aquarium fishes **5964**
Mills, E.D.
Planning: the architect's handbook **7518**
Mills, I.
Quantities, units and symbols in physical
chemistry **1238**
Mills, J.F.
Encyclopaedia of antique scientific
instruments **7199**
Mills, S.Y.
The A-Z of modern herbalism **3683**
Mills, W. *and* **Speak, P.**
Keyguide to information sources in the polar
and cold regions **1647**
Milne, P. H.
Underwater engineering surveys **5100**
Milne, T.A.
Source book of methods of analysis for
biomass and biomass conversion processes
4116
Milne-Thomson, L.M.
Russian-English mathematical dictionary
550
Milner, J.E.
The Green index **2255**
Milner, R.
The Encyclopedia of evolution **2314**
Milonni, P.W. *and* **Eberly, J.H.**
Lasers **4378**
Milovanov, E.V. *and* **Weizman, E.A.**
English-Russian dictionary of environmental
control **5155**
MIMS: monthly index of medical specialities
3671
Minasian, S.M.
The World's whales **2964**
Mind: the meetings index: Series SEMT **476**
Mine drainage bibliography, 1910-1976 **4813**
Miner, D.
Uranus **766**
Mineral deposits of Europe **1861-1862**
Mineral deposits within the European
Community **1416**
Mineral names: what do they mean? **1413,
1838**
Mineral physics and crystallography **1853**
'Mineral process engineering' **6850**
Mineral reference manual **1398**
Mineral resources **1859**
The Mineral resources of the sea **1415**

Mineralization in the British Isles **1417**
Mineralogical abstracts **1406, 6866**
Minerals handbook, 1996-97 **6874**
Minerals of the World **1414**
The Minerals yearbook **6884**
'Mining' **4772**
Mining and mineral industries **4773**
Mining annual review, 1994 **4787**
The Mining directory 1999 **4788**
Ministry of Agriculture, Fisheries and Food
See
Great Britain. Ministry of Agriculture,
Fisheries and Food
Ministry of Defence
See
Great Britain. Ministry of Defence
Ministry of Education, Japan
See
Japan, Ministry of Education
Minnick, R.
Glossaries for surveyors **828**
Minor metals survey **6964**
MinSys **4771**
Mintz, P.B.
Dictionary of graphic arts terms **6189**
Mirimanov, R.G.
Dictionary of electronics **4411**
The MIT guide to science and engineering
communication **3967**
Mitchell, A.
A Field guide to the trees of Britain and
Northern Europe **5651**
The Mitchell Beazley atlas of the oceans **1759**
The Mitchell Beazley pocket guide to the
seashores of Britain and Northern Europe
2271
Mitchell, H.C.
Definitions of terms used in geodetic and
other surveys **830**
Mitchell, M.
Library catalogue. [British Optical
Association] **1033**
Mitchell, R.S.
Dictionary of rocks **1838**
Mineral names: what do they mean? **1838**
Mitchell, R.S. *and* **Henry, J.R.**
Mineral names: what do they mean? **1413**
Mitchell's building series **7515**
Mitra, S.K.
Handbook for digital signal processing **4481**
Mitsch, W.J. *and* **Jorgensen, S.E.**
Ecological engineering **2229**
Mitton, J.
A Concise dictionary of astronomy **704**
The Penguin dictionary of astronomy **705**
Mitton, S.
The Cambridge encyclopaedia of astronomy
685
Observatories of the world **748**
Mladjenović, M.
The Defining years in nuclear physics, 1932-
1960s **1094**
Mochi, U. *and* **Carter, T.D.**
Hoofed mammals of the world **2966**
The Model engineer's handbook **5052**
The Model maker's handbook **3950**
Modelski, A.M.
Railroad maps of North America **6315**
Modern breeds of livestock **5862**
Modern British food **6074**
Modern cereal science and technology **6686**
Modern Chinese-English technical and general
dictionary **198**
Modern crystallography **1377**
Modern developments in powder technology
4668
Modern dictionary of electronics **4413**
A Modern dictionary of geography **1685**
Modern encyclopedia of typefaces 1960-90
6175

Modern English-Russian dictionary of
radioelectronics **4424**
A Modern herbal **3680**
Modern India and progress in science and
technology **23**
Modern maps and atlases **861**
Modern power station practice **4309**
A Modern Spanish-English and English-
Spanish technical & engineering dictionary
169
A Modern textile dictionary **7068**
Der Moderne Druck **6200**
Molho, E.
The Dictionary catalogue **102**
Moncrieff's man-made fibres **7092**
Money, S. A.
Newnes microprocessor pocket book **7300**
Money, S.A.
Microprocessor data book **7312**
Montague, D.
Dictionary of building and civil engineering
4944, 7507
Montague, J.
The A to Z of shopping by post **6031**
Monteau, P.
Dictionnaire du bâtiment **7508**
Montgomerie, G.
The Transport engineer's handbook **5061**
Monthly climatic data for the world **1807**
Monthly index of medical specialities
MIMS: monthly index of medical specialities
3671
Moo-Young, M.
Comprehensive biotechnology **2988**
Moon, M.
'Engineering' **3906**
Mooney, J.L.
Dictionary of American naval fighting ships
4914
Moorat, S.A.J.
Catalogue of Western manuscripts on
medicine and science in the Wellcome
Historical Medical Library **3429**
Moore, A.C.
How to clean everything **6115**
Moore, D.M.
Green planet: the story of plant life on earth
2527
The Marshall Cavendish illustrated
encyclopedia of plants and earth sciences
1459, 2494
Moore, J.
Warships of the Soviet Navy **4913**
Moore, P.
The Astronomy encyclopaedia **679**
The Guinness book of astronomy **690**
The International encyclopedia of astronomy
679
The Observer's year **691**
Patrick Moore's history of astronomy **722**
Philip's atlas of the universe **798**
Philip's guide to stars and planets **692**
Yearbook of astronomy **716**
Moore, R.C.
Treatise on invertebrate paleontology **1944**
Moores, E.M. *and* **Fairbridge, R.W.**
Encyclopedia of European and Asian
regional geology **1539-1540**
Móra, I.
Publisher's practical dictionary in 20
languages **6217**
Morchin, W.C.
Radar engineer's sourcebook **4555**
Morgan, B.
Keyguide to information sources in
agricultural engineering **5662**
Morgan, B.A.
'Maps and atlases as sources of agricultural
information' **5553**
Morgan, J. *and* **Richards, A.**
The Book of apples **5771**

Morgan, N.
Marine technology reference book 5093
Morgan, W.L. and Gordon, G.D.
Communications satellite handbook 4550
Moringo, F.P.
Aerospace and defense acronyms 4815,
5440
Moritz, H.
Technical dictionary of spectroscopy and
spectral analysis 1286
Moritz, R.E.
Memorabilia Mathematica 567
Morphologic encyclopedia of palynology and
illustrations of spore and pollen 2615
Morrell, R.
Handbook of properties of technical and
engineering ceramics 4018, 6812
Morris, D.
Cat world 5907
Morris, D. and Tamm, B.
Concise encyclopedia of software
engineering 7317
Morris, M.R.
Larousse astronomy 689
Morris, P.
The 'Country Life' book of the natural
history of the British Isles 2412
Morrison, G.
Britain's railways 1948-1993 5042
Morrow, C. and Perl, Teri
Notable women in mathematics 600
Morse, R.A. and Hooper, T.
The Illustrated encyclopedia of beekeeping
5928
Morskoǐ slovar' 5351
Morton, A.G.
History of botanical science 2529
Morton, B.
Halley's comet, 1755-1984: a bibliography
770
Morton, L.T.
Morton's medical bibliography 3395
Morton, L.T. and Godbolt, S.
Information sources in the medical sciences
3252
Morton, L.T. and Moore, R.J.
A Bibliography of medical and biomedical
biography 3418
A Chronology of medicine and related
sciences 3390
Morton, L.T. and Wright, D.J.
How to use a medical library 3263
Morton's medical bibliography 3395
Mosby's medical, nursing, and allied health
dictionary 3286, 3784
Moseley, C.
The Official World Wildlife Fund guide to
endangered species of North America
2481
Moses, A.J.
The Practicing scientist's tables 278
The Moss flora of Britain and Ireland 2670
Moss, T.S.
Handbook on semiconductors 4482
Mossman, S.T.I. and Morris, P.J.T.
The Development of plastics 7145
Mostert, F.J.A.
Medisch woordenboek 3333
Mothers and daughters of invention 3106
The Moths and butterflies of Great Britain and
Ireland 2836
Moths of Australia 2841
Motor application and maintenance handbook
4330
Motor industry of Great Britain 1995 5294
The Motor vehicle 5272
Motorcycles 5326
Motorcycles in magazines, 1895-1983 5323
Mottelay, P.F.
Bibliographical history of electricity &
magnetism 1078

Motz, L. and Nathanson, C.
The Constellations 777
Moulder, D.S.
Directory of library and information facilities
5095
Mountfort, G.
Rare birds of the world 2473
Moureau, M.
Dictionnaire des sciences et techniques du
pétrole 6742
Dictionnaire du forage et des puits 4769
Moy-Thomas, J.A.
Palaeozoic fishes 1957
Mucci, P.
Handbook for engineering design using
standard materials and components 3979
Mühlberg, H.
The Complete guide to water plants 2703
Mühle, P.
Dictionary of wood science and technology
6994
Muir, H.
Larousse dictionary of scientists 339
Muir, H. and Walker, P.M.B.
Larousse dictionary of science and
technology 129
Muir, R.
The National Trust rivers of Britain 1893
Muirden, J.
The Amateur astronomer's handbook 693
Amateur astronomer's handbook 696
Observational astronomy for amateurs 697
Mujundar, A.S.
Handbook of industrial drying 6494
Mulherin, J.
Spices and natural flavourings 6086
Mullard, Ltd
Mullard technical handbooks 4432
Mullard technical handbooks 4432
Mullens, W.H. and Swann, H.K.
A Bibliography of British ornithology 2912
Müller, D.
Dictionary of microprocessor systems 7301
Muller-Girard, C.
BI-Lexikon Rassekatzen 5905
Müller, P.M. and Lamparsky, D.
Perfumes 6714
Muller, W.
Dictionary of the graphic arts industry 6186
Mulligan, W.H.
A Historical dictionary of American
industrial language 7172
Multhauf, R.P.
The History of chemical technology 6465
Multi-lingual dictionary for photogrammetry
842
Multi-lingual dictionary of commercial
international trade and shipping terms 6334
Multi-lingual poultry dictionary 5891
The Multilayer printed circuit board handbook
4470
Multilingual dictionary of agronomic plants
5732
The Multilingual dictionary of architecture and
building terms 7495
A Multilingual dictionary of artificial
intelligence 7366
Multilingual dictionary of concrete 6832
Multilingual dictionary of fish and fish
products 5936
Multilingual dictionary of important terms in
molecular spectroscopy 1287
Multilingual dictionary of narcotic drugs and
psychotropic substances 3581
The Multilingual dictionary of printing and
publishing 6154
Multilingual dictionary of printing and
publishing terms 6156
Multilingual dictionary of publishing, printing
and bookselling 6216

Multilingual dictionary of remote sensing and
photogrammetry 848, 1526
Multilingual dictionary of technical terms in
cartography 871
Multilingual footwear dictionary 7437
Multilingual glossary 932
Multilingual glossary of automatic control
technology 7353
A Multilingual glossary of cargo handling
terms 5107
Multilingual glossary of heat treatment
terminology 6900
Multilingual glossary of textile terminology
7059
Multilingual illustrated dictionary of aquatic
animals and plants 2760
Multilingual illustrated guide to the world's
commercial coldwater fish 5934
Multilingual illustrated guide to the world's
commercial warmwater fish 5935
Multilingual list of vegetable names 5766
Multilingual technical dictionary on irrigation
and drainage 5083, 5692
Multilingual thesaurus of geosciences 1546
The Multimedia encyclopedia of mammalian
biology 2939
Mulvihill, J.
User guide to the Bibliography and index of
geology 1446
Mumby, F.A.
Mumby's publishing and bookselling in the
twentieth century 6228
Mumby's publishing and bookselling in the
twentieth century 6228
Munby, D.L.
Inland transport statistics, Great Britain,
1900-1970 6265
Mundy, B.P. and Ellerd, M.G.
Name reactions and reagents in organic
synthesis 1228
Munz, L.T. and Slauson, N.G.
Index to illustrations of living things outside
North America 2394, 2546, 2733
Muralidhara, H.S.
Advances in solid-liquid separation 6498
Murashkevich, A.M.
Anglo-russkiǐ aviatsionnyǐ slovar' 5401
English-Russian guided missiles and space
flight dictionary 5438
Murawski, H.
Geologisches Wörterbuch 1469
Murdin, P. and Allen, D.
Catalogue of the universe 781
Murdoch, J.B.
Illumination engineering 5262
Murdoch, G.P.
Atlas of world cultures 2038
Outline of cultural materials 2039
Outline of world cultures 2040
Murdock, G.P. and O'Leary, T.J.
Ethnographic bibliography of North America
2080
Murfin, D.
'Ceramics' 6806
Dictionary of ceramics 6814
Murith, J. and Bocabeille, J.-M.
Dictionnaire des abréviations et acronymes
scientifiques, techniques, médicaux,
économiques, juridiques 40
Murphy, J
Reinforced plastics handbook 7102
Murray, J
The Complete guide to whisky 6614
Museen in Deutschland (West): Technische
Museen 500
The Museum of Science and Industry basic list
of children's science books, 1973-1984 73
Mushroom terms 2658
Mushrooms 2664
Mushrooms and other fungi of Great Britain
and Europe 2666

Muslim peoples **2066**

Muslims of the Soviet empire: a guide **2054**

Mustoe, J.E.H.
An Atlas of renewable energy resources in the United Kingdom and North America **4105**

Myers, A.
Petroleum and marine technology information guide **5075, 6727**

Myers, P.A. and Martin, T.A.
Glossary for radiologic technologists **3704**

Mykologisches Wörterbuch **2644**

Myrants, G.
Protection of industrial designs **3220**

Mysterious universe **784**

Naas, H. and Schmid, H.L.
Mathematisches Wörterbuch **520**

Nachtigal, C.L.
Instrumentation and control **7204**

Nader, J.C.
Prentice Hall's illustrated dictionary of computing **7253**

Nadysev, M.A.
Russko-angliiskiĭ voehnotekhicheskiĭ slovar' **4829**

Naganagoudar, I.R.
World literature on patents (1900-1981) **3159**

Nagy, E.
Magyar-angol müszaki szótár **195**

Nagy, E. and Klar, J.
Angol-magyar müszaki szótár **194**

Nagy, P. and Tarján, G.
Elsevier's dictionary of microelectronics **4458**

Nairn, A.E.M. and Stehli, F.G.
The Ocean basins and margins **1739**

Nakao, S.
Tanaka's cyclopedia of edible plants of the world **2626**

Nakhimizhan, O.E.
Pyatiyazychnyĭ slovar' mineralogicheskikh nazvanii **1404**

Name index of organic reactions **1348**

Name reactions and reagents in organic synthesis **1228**

The Names of plants **2516**

Napier, J.R. and Napier, P.H.
A Handbook of living primates **2974**
The Natural history of the primates **2975**

Narrow gauge railways of the British Isles **5054**

The NASA atlas of the solar system **753**

Nasr, I. and Cordero, M.
Medical Spanish: an instant translator **3342**

Nasr, S.H.
An Annotated bibliography of Islamic science **404**
Islamic science **406**
Science and civilisation in Islam **407**

Nass, L.I. and Heiberger, C.
Encyclopedia of PVC **7165**

Nath, B.
Environmental management in practice **5140**

National Academy of Sciences of the United States of America
Biographical memoirs **419**

National Agricultural Library
See
United States. National Agricultural Library

The National Arboretum book of outstanding garden plants **5776**

National atlas of disease mortality in the United Kingdom **3745**

The National Childbirth Trust book of pregnancy, birth, and parenthood **3897**

National Climatic Data Center
World weather records, 1971-1980 **1811**

National Computing Centre
Handbook of data communications **4498**

National Council for the Conservation of Plants & Gardens
The National Plant Collections directory 1998 **2543**

National Council of Teachers of Mathematics
Handbook of research on mathematics, teaching, and learning **565**

National Electrical Code handbook **4341**

National electrical safety code handbook **4340**

National Federation of Consumer Groups
A Handbook of consumer law **6028**

National Fluid Power Association
Fluid power standards **4602**

The National formulary **3666**

National Information and Documentation Centre
See
Arab Republic of Egypt. National Information and Documentation Centre

National Library. Calcutta
Bibliography of Indology. v.1: Indian anthropology **2065**

National Library of Medicine
See
United States. National Library of Medicine

National Library of Medicine current catalog **3267**

National Maritime Museum
Catalogue of the Library. [National Maritime Museum] **6328**
Catalogue of the Library. v.3: *Atlases & cartography* **824**
Guide to the manuscripts in the National Maritime Museum **6326**
The Ship series **5357**

National Maritime Museum guide to maritime Britain **6363**

National Museum of Natural History. National Anthropological Archives
See
Smithsonian Institution. National Museum of Natural History. National Anthropological Archives

National parks and reserves of Western Europe **2435**

The National Physical Laboratory **992**

The National Plant Collections directory 1998 **2543**

National Reference Center for Bioethics Literature **3476**

National Society for Clean Air
NSCA environmental glossary **5236**
NSCA reference book **5232**

National Technical Information Service **3014**

National Testing Laboratories Accreditation Scheme
NATLAS year book **4025**

National Trust
The National Trust rivers of Britain **1893**
The National Trust book of bridges **5009**
The National Trust rivers of Britain **1893**

Nations within a nation: historical statistics of American Indians **2120**

'Native American reference sources' **2110**

Native Americans: an annotated bibliography **2105**

The Native peoples of Canada **2082**

NATLAS year book **4025**

NATO
See
North Atlantic Treaty Organization.

Natural Environment Research Council
Flood studies report **5110**

Natural gas **6540**

Natural hazards **1506**

Natural history atlas **2428**

Natural history manuscript resources in the British Isles **2406**

The Natural History Museum at South Kensington **2432**

A Natural history of Australia **2426**

The Natural history of Britain and Ireland **2414**

The Natural history of Britain and Northern Europe **2409**

The Natural history of China **2420**

The Natural history of domesticated mammals **5870**

The Natural history of North America **2424**

The Natural history of the Mediterranean **2408**

The Natural history of the primates **2975**

The Natural history of the USSR **2419**

The Natural history of Wales **2417**

Natural products updates **6510**

Natural resources **2228**

The Natural rubber industry **7125**

Naturalist's color guide **1058**

The Naturalists' directory and almanac (international) **2391**

Naturalists' guide to fresh-water aquarium fish **5963**

The Naturalist's lexicon **2182**

The Naturalized animals of the British Isles **2779**

Naturalized birds of the world **2897**

Naturalized fishes of the world **2856**

Naturalized mammals of the world **2948**

Nature **228**

Nature conservation in Britain **2457**

A Nature conservation review **2438**

The Nautical almanac **820**

Nautical Almanac Office
See
Great Britain. Nautical Almanac Office

Naval & maritime history **6354**

Naval electronic warfare **4920**

The Naval Institute guide to combat fleets of the world, 1998-1999 **4896**

The Naval Institute guide to world naval weapons systems **4895**

Naval Observatory Library, Washington
See
United States. Naval Observatory Library, Washington

Naval Oceanographic Office
See
United States. Naval Oceanographic Office

Naval phraseology **4899**

Naval technical dictionary **4825, 5087**

Naval terms dictionary **4898**

Navies in the nuclear age **4902**

Navigation dictionary **6373**

Nayar, A
The Metal databook **6875**

Nayler, G.H.F.
Dictionary of mechanical engineering **4134**

NBC: nuclear, biological and chemical warfare on the modern battlefield **4874**

NBS/NRC steam tables **1266, 4225**

NDE Handbook: non-destructive examination methods for condition monitoring **4026**

The NDT year book **4034**

Neale, M.J.
The Tribology handbook **4746**

Neave, H.R.
Statistical tables for mathematicians, engineers, economists and the behavioural and management sciences **650**

Neave, S.A.
Nomenclator zoologicus **2730**

Neaverson, E.
Stratigraphical palaeontology **1905**

Necker, C.
Four centuries of cat books, 1570-1970 **5909**

Needham, J.
Science and civilization in China **394**

The Needleworker's dictionary **6110**

Neiger, E.
  Gastronomisches Wörterbuch zur Übersetzung and Erklärung der Speisekarten 6069
Nelson, A.
  Dictionary of mining 4779
  Dictionary of water and water engineering 5188
Nelson, A. and Nelson, K.D.
  Dictionary of applied geology, mining and civil engineering 1521
Nelson, J.
  Fishes of the world 2857
Nelson, P.M.
  Transportation noise reference book 5251
Nelson's atlas of European birds 2906
Nentwig, K.
  Elsevier's dictionary of opto-electronics and electro-optics 4486
Neotropical rainforest mammals 2950
Network of African Scientific Organizations
  Profiles of African scientific institutions 468
Neu, J.
  ISIS cumulative bibliography, 1966-75 288
  ISIS cumulative bibliography, 1976-85 289
Neufeldt, S.
  Chronologie Chemie, 1800-1970 1197
Neufert, E.
  Architects' data 7517
Neutron activation tables 4202
Neutron cross sections 4203
Neville, H.H.
  A New German-English dictionary for chemists 1147
New and improved: inventors and inventions that have changed the modern world 3143
New and renewable sources of energy 4107
The New astronomy 795
The New atlas of breeding birds in Britain and Ireland 2913
New Cambridge statistical tables 649
The New cancer sourcebook 3732
The New catering repertoire 5970
New consultants 248
A New dictionary of birds 2882
A New dictionary of scientific and technical terms, English-Arabic, with illustrations 191
The New E is for additives 6693
The New encyclopedia of motorcars 5302
The New encyclopedia of wine 6595
New flora of the British Isles 2581
The New food lover's companion 6065
New generation guide to the wild flowers of Britain and Northern Europe 2559
A New German-English dictionary for chemists 1147
The New hacker's dictionary 7252
A New history of British shipping 6358
New holistic herbal 3681
The New IEEE standard dictionary of electrical and electronic terms 4253
The New illustrated science and invention encyclopedia : how it works 255
New international dictionary of refrigeration 4587
A New introduction to bibliography 6138
The New Larousse encyclopedia of animal life 2751
The New Larousse encyclopedia of the earth 1462
New Larousse gastronomique 6053
The New Macmillan guide to family health 3522
New metric handbook 7533
The New naturalist library 2415
The New naturalists 2415
The New organic grower 5788
The New 'Our bodies, ourselves' 3520
The New Oxford book of food plants 2631
The New Penguin dictionary of biology 2162
The New Penguin dictionary of geology 1552

The New Penguin dictionary of science 127
A New photographic atlas of the moon 759
The New physics 958
The New Royal Horticultural Society dictionary of gardening 5778
The New solar system 767
The New Sotheby's wine encyclopedia 6596
New technical books 218, 3049
New technologies and development 3051
The New video encyclopedia 7407
New York Academy of Medicine
  Illustration catalog of the Library 3381
  Portrait catalog of the New York Academy of Medicine. [New York Academy of Medicine] 3380
New York Academy of Medicine. Library
  Author catalog. [New York Academy of Medicine Library] 3264
  Subject catalog. [New York Academy of Medicine Library] 3265
The New York Botanical Garden illustrated encyclopedia of horticulture 5760
New York Botanical Garden. Library
  Biographical notes upon botanists 2534
  Catalog of the manuscript and archival collections and index to the correspondence of John Torrey 2532
New York Public Library
  Dictionary catalog of the Schomburg Collection of negro literature and history 2092
Newberry Library Center for the History of the American Indian
  Bibliographical series. [Newberry Library Center for the History of the American Indian] 2108
Newberry Library. Chicago
  Dictionary catalogue of the history of printing 6163
Newcomen Society for the study of the history of engineering
  Transactions, 1920/21-. [Newcomen Society] 3955
Newman, A.C.D.
  The Chemistry of clays and clay minerals 6813
Newman, H.
  An Illustrated dictionary of glass 6788
Newman, J. and Tilke, A.
  Sex education 3585
Newman, J.R.
  The World of mathematics 578
Newman, O. and Fisher, A.
  European environmental information sourcebook 2272
Newnes audio and hi-fi engineer's pocket book 7410
Newnes audio and hi-fi handbook 7411
Newnes computer engineer's pocket book 7240
Newnes electrical pocket book 4278
Newnes electronic circuits pocket book 4453
Newnes electronics assembly pocket book 4445
Newnes engineering and physical science pocket book 3918
Newnes engineering materials pocket book 3991
Newnes guide to satellite TV 4563
Newnes guide to TV and video technology 4562
Newnes instrumentation and measurement pocket book 4155
Newnes mechanical engineers' pocket book 4132
Newnes microprocessor pocket book 7300
Newnes radio and electronic engineer's pocket book 4436
Newnes refrigeration pocket book 4583
Newton and Newtoniana, 1672-1975 378

Newton, D.C.
  Trade names 3118
The Newton handbook 377
Newton, I.
  Birds of prey 2934
Newton, J. and Teece, P.
  The Guide to amateur astronomy 694
Newton, K. and Steeds, W.
  The Motor vehicle 5272
NGC 2000.0 790
NHS handbook 3435
NHS yearbook 1995/6 3436
Nibley, B.
  'Environmental reference sources' 2219
Nichol, S.W.
  The Torre-Bueno glossary of entomology 2817
Nicholas, R. and Nicholas, D.
  Immunology: an information profile 3797
  Virology: an information profile 2357
Nichols, D. and Cooke, J.A.C.
  The Oxford book of invertebrates 2783
Nicholson, R.
  Science and technology in the United Kingdom 12
Nicholson, T.R.
  The Birth of the British motor car 5315
  The World's motor museums 5296
Nickel and its alloys 6937
Nickel, E.H. and Nichols, M.C.
  Mineral reference manual 1398
Nickon, A.
  Organic chemistry: the name game 1347
Nicolosi, L.
  Terminology of communication disorders 3812
Nield, E.W. and Tucker, V.C.T.
  Palaeontology: an introduction 1906
Nierenberg, W.A.
  Encyclopedia of earth system science 1455
  Encyclopedia of environmental biology 2145
The Night sky 778
Nikkei Biotechnology
  Biotechnology guide Japan, 1990-91 3007
Nineteenth-century scientific instruments 7216
Nippes, E.F.
  Metals handbook; v.6. Welding, brazing and soldering 4683
Nissen, C.
  Die Botanische Buchillustration 2524
  Die Zoologische Buchillustration 2734
Nix, J. and Hill, P.
  Farm management pocketbook 5657
Nixon, J.M.
  Hotel and restaurant industries 5969
Nixon, M. and Whitely, D.
  The Oxford book of vertebrates 2846
Nobel, A.
  Dictionary of medical objects 3305
  Medical dictionary 3310
Nobel Foundation
  Nobel lectures including speeches and laureates' biographies. Physics 987
Nobel laureates in chemistry, 1901-1992 1206
Nobel Laureates in medicine or physiology 3422
Nobel lectures including presentation speeches and laureates' biographies. Chemistry 1215
Nobel lectures including speeches and laureates' biographies. Physics 987
Nobel prize winners: chemistry 1207
Nobel Prize Winners in medicine and physiology 3421
The Nobel prize winners: physics 981
Noble, L.
  Estuaries and coastal waters of the British Isles: an annual bibliography of recent scientific papers 1764
Nock, O.S.
  British locomotives of the 20th century 5385

Ocran, E.B. *(contd.)*
Ocran's acronyms **41**
Ocran's acronyms **41**
Odegard, G.
'Spectra: a bibliography of sources' **1055**
O'Dell, T.H.
Circuits for electronic instrumentation **4351, 4454**
O'Donoghue, M.
The Encyclopedia of minerals and gemstones **1399**
An Illustrated guide to rocks and minerals **1400**
The Literature of gemstones **1422**
The Literature of mineralogy **1387**
O'Dowd, M.J. *and* **Philipp, E.E.**
The History of obstetrics and gynaecology **3894**
Odum, E.P.
Fundamentals of ecology **2231**
OECD
See
Organization for Economic Cooperation and Development.
Office International des Epizooties
World animal health in 1997 **5857**
The Official ABMS directory of board certified medical specialists **3370**
Official and standardized methods of analysis **6461**
The Official driving manual **6293**
Official gazette of the United States Patent and Trademark Office: Patents **3182**
Official gazette of the United States Patent and Trademark Office: Trademarks **3137**
Official journal of the European Patent Office **3180**
Official journal (patents) **3181**
Official reference book and buyers' guide **3978**
'Official state lists of endangered, threatened, or rare species' **2482**
The Official United States fax directory **6127**
The Official World Wildlife Fund guide to endangered species of North America **2481**
'Offshore engineering' **4798, 6765**
Offshore oil and gas directory 1998/99 **6769**
Offshore petroleum engineering **4796, 6764**
Ogden, B.
Aviation museums **5418**
Ogilvie, M.B.
Women and science **358**
Women in science **359**
Oglesby, C.H. *and* **Hicks, R.G.**
Highway engineering **5062**
Oil and gas dictionary **6739**
Oil economists' handbook **6730**
Oil standard abbreviator
D&D oil standard abbreviator **6722**
Oilfields of the world **4805**
Olby, R.C.
Companion to the history of modern science **322**
Old age: a register of social research 1985-1990 **3766**
Old English farming books, 1523-1793 **5588**
Olea, R.A.
Geostatistical glossary and multilingual dictionary **1544**
O'Leary, T.J.
Ethnographic bibliography of South America **2096**
Oleson, J.P.
Bronze age, Greek and Roman technology **3079**
Olien, M.D.
Latin Americans: contemporary peoples and their cultural traditions **2097**
Oliver, J.E. *and* **Fairbridge, R.W.**
The Encyclopedia of climatology **1798**

Oliver, R.
Ordnance Survey maps: a concise guide for historians **896**
Oliver, R.L.
Antarctic earth science **1654**
Oliver, S. *and* **Ward, J.M.**
A Dictionary of genetic engineering **2301**
Ollier, C.
Ancient landforms **1671**
Olsen, W.C.
Agricultural economics and rural sociology **5612**
The Literature of crop science **5727**
Olsen's fisherman's nautical almanack, 1999 **821**
Olson, J.S.
An Ethnohistorical dictionary of China **2058**
The Peoples of Africa **2070**
The Olympic book of sports medicine **3555**
OMNI **3235**
On food and cooking **6061, 6639**
On the state of the public health **3590**
One hundred years of motoring **5311**
One hundred years of the motor car, 1882-1986 **5312**
Onisi, T.R.
Elsevier's dictionary of the cement industry **6827**
Online databases in the medical and life sciences **3236**
Online medical databases **3233**
Online patents trademarks and service marks databases **3153**
Onshore/offshore oil & gas multilingual glossary **6733**
OPEC, its member states and world energy market **6752**
Open Die Forging Institute. Metallurgical and Research Committee
Open die forging manual **4648**
Open die forging manual **4648**
Ophthalmic eponyms **3889**
Ophthalmic literature **3890**
Oppermann, A.
Wörterbuch der Elektronik **4420**
Optical disk storage document image processing systems **7426**
Optical fibre communication **1049**
Optical fibres **4532**
Optical fibres and sources for communications **4528**
The Opticians register **3891**
Optoelectronics data book **4487**
OPUS '98 Building services design file **7514**
Ordbok for petroleums-virksomhet **6766**
Ordbok for veg- og traffikk teknikk **5066**
Ordnance Survey
See
Great Britain. Ordnance Survey
Ordnance Survey guide to the waterways **6392**
Ordnance Survey maps: a concise guide for historians **896**
O'Reilly, W.
International directory to geophysical research **1502**
Organic agriculture worldwide **5656**
Organic chemistry: the name game **1347**
The Organic chemist's desk reference **1330**
Organic farming **5655**
Organic reactions **1349**
Organic syntheses **1351**
Organization for Economic Cooperation and Development
Annual oil and gas statistics, and main historical series **6753**
Basic science and technology statistics **270**
Megascience policy issues **3**
Reviews of national science and technology policy **5**
Science, technology and industry outlook **7**

Organization for Economic Cooperation and Development *(contd.)*
Science, technology and innovation policies: Federation of Russia **18**
Uranium: resources, production and demand **6966**
Organization for Economic Cooperation and Development. Joint ENEA-IAEA Liaison Group on Thermionic Electrical Power Generation
Glossary of terms and symbols in thermionic conversion **1083**
Organizing scientific meetings **474**
Organometallic compounds **1363**
Organometallics in synthesis **1364**
The Origin of medical terms **3323**
Origins in acoustics **1032**
The Origins of modern humans **1982, 2317**
Ornamental horticulture **5756**
Orne, J.
The Language of the foreign book trade **6203**
Orr, W.I.
Radio handbook **4539**
Orthwein, W.C.
Clutches and brakes **4730**
Orwin, C.S. *and* **Whetham, E.H.**
History of British agriculture, 1846-1914 **5579**
Orzagh, L.
Angol-magyar szótár **195**
Magyar-angol szótár **195**
O.S. Nock's Pocket encyclopaedia of British steam railways and locomotives **5032**
Osborn, H.
A Brief history of entomology **2826**
Osborn, P.D.
Handbook of energy data and calculations **4088**
Osler, Sir W.
Incunabula medica: a study of the earliest printed medical books, 1467-1480 **3427**
Ostroff, H. *and* **Nichols, T.**
Specialty cookbooks: a subject guide, v.1 **6048**
Otter, R.A.
Civil engineering heritage: Southern England **4962**
Ottley, G.
A Bibliography of British railway history **5043, 6305**
A Bibliography of British railway history. Supplement **5044, 6306**
Ottley's bibliography of British railway history. Second supplement 12957-19605 **5045**
Railway history **6311**
Ottley's bibliography of British railway history. Second supplement 12957-19605 **5045, 6307**
Our petroleum industry **6755**
Outlets for specialist new books in the UK **6238**
An Outline history of medicine **3406**
Outline of cultural materials **2039**
Outline of plant classification **2517**
Outline of world cultures **2040**
Outlines of entomology **2810**
Outlook on science policy **4**
Overmier, J.A.
The History of biology **2188**
Overseas building notes **7511**
Overseas geology and mineral resources **1579, 1856**
Ovio, G.
Storia dell'oculista **3893**
Owen, D.B.
Abstracts and indexes in science and technology **225**
Owen, K *and* **Coley, T**
Automotive fuels reference book **6589**

Patent Cooperation Treaty gazette **3178**
Patent information and documentation handbook **3190**
Patent information and documentation in Western Europe **3189**
Patent law fundamentals **3215**
Patent law of Europe and the United Kingdom **3203**
Patent licensing in Europe **3201**
Patent View: US patent information on CD-ROM **3186**
The Patentability of computer software **7326**
Patenting in the biological sciences **2183**
'Patents' **3154**
Patents and trademarks in Japan **3169**
Patents for invention **3204**
Patents handbook **3160**
Patents in chemistry and biotechnology **1196**
Patents throughout the world **3194**
Patents, trade marks and designs in information work **3188**
Paterson, G.
  The European patent system **3202**
Patrick Anthony's international menu dictionary **6064**
Patrick, D. and Patrick, M.
  The Hodder stamp dictionary **6422**
Patrick Moore's history of astronomy **722**
Patrick, P.K.
  Glossary of solid waste **5257**
Patrick, R.
  Rivers of the United States **2268**
Patten, M.
  Books for cooks **6049**
Patten, M.N.
  Information sources in metallic materials **6849**
Patterson, A.M.
  A French-English dictionary for chemists **1155**
  Patterson's German-English dictonary for chemists **1150**
Patterson, C.
  Evolution **2316**
Patterson, D.
  Commercial timbers of the world **7004**
  Patterson's German-English dictonary for chemists **1150**
Pattrick, R.A.D. and Polya, D.A.
  Mineralization in the British Isles **1417**
Paxton, J.R. and Eschmeyer, W.N.
  Encyclopedia of fishes **2850**
Paylore, P.
  Desertification: a world bibliography **1718**
PCT [Patent Cooperation Treaty] gazette **3178**
PDR **3662**
PDR for herbal medicines **2635**
PDR library on CD-ROM: physicians' desk reference library **3662**
Peacock, J.
  Book production **6140**
  Multilingual dictionary of printing and publishing terms **6156**
Pearce, E.A. and Smith, C.G.
  The Hutchinson world weather guide **1808**
  The World weather guide **1809**
Pearce, M.E.
  Medicines and poisons guide **3674, 3714**
Pearce's medical and nursing dictionary and encyclopaedia **3785**
Pearls: their origin, treatment and identification **6981**
Pears, N.
  Basic biogeography **2297**
Pearse, V.
  Living invertebrates **2782**
Pearson, B.
  Specialty chemicals **6508**
Pearson, B.C.
  Guide to the petroleum reference literature **6726**

Pearson, C.E.
  Handbook of applied mathematics **527**
Pearson, E.S. and Hartley, H.O.
  Biometrika tables for statisticians **651**
Pearson's chemical analysis of foods **6667**
Peat **6554**
Peat abstracts **6555**
Peattie, D.C.
  Green laurels **2402**
Pecht, M.
  Handbook of electronic package design **4403**
Pedersen, O. and Pihl, M.
  Early physics and astronomy **971**
Peel, J.
  The Lives of the Fellows of the Royal College of Obstetricians and Gynaecologists, 1929-1969 **3900**
Peeva, K. and Delijska, B.
  Elsevier's dictionary of computer science and mathematics in English, German, French, and Russian **532, 7242**
Pegler, D.
  Larousse field guide to the mushrooms and toadstools of Britain and Europe **2665**
Pěkarek, O.
  Velký anglicko-ceský technický slovník **189**
Pelczar, J. and Chen, E.C.S.
  Microbiology **2361**
Pélegrin, M. and Hollister, W.
  Concise encyclopedia of aeronautics and space systems **5390**
Pellant, C.
  Rocks, minerals and fossils of the world **1402**
Pelletier, P.A.
  Prominent scientists **351**
Pellizzari, P.
  Multilingual footwear dictionary **7437**
Pemberton, J.E.
  How to find out in mathematics **515**
  Who's who in ornithology **2894**
The Penguin book of curious and interesting puzzles **606**
The Penguin book of the bicycle **5330**
The Penguin book of the car **5305**
The Penguin book of the motorcycle **5325**
The Penguin dictionary of astronomy **705**
The Penguin dictionary of building **7503**
The Penguin dictionary of electronics **4415**
Penguin dictionary of mathematics **535**
The Penguin dictionary of physical geography **1683**
The Penguin dictionary of physics **936**
The Penguin encyclopedia of nutrition **3535**
The Penguin encyclopedia of weapons and military technology **4842**
The Penguin guide to the railways of Britain **5036**
The Penguin historical atlas of dinosaurs **1964**
The Penguin medical encyclopedia **3293**
Pennak, R.W.
  Collegiate dictionary of zoology **2726**
Pennington, J.A.T.
  Bowes and Church's food values of portions commonly used **3548, 6657**
Pennsylvania University
  Catalog of the Edgar Fahs Smith Memorial Collection in the History of Chemistry **1202**
The People's handbook of allergies and allergens **3767**
The Peoples of Africa **2070**
The Peoples of Southern Africa **2075**
Peoples of the world **2045**
Perdue, L.
  The High-technology editorial guide and stylebook **7280**
Peretz, A.A.
  Core collection in nursing and the allied health sciences **3777**

Perfect, C. and Rookledge, G.
  Rookledge's international type finder **6176**
Perfumes **6714**
Perfumes, cosmetics and soaps **6715**
Periglacial geomorphology **1642**
The Periglaciation of Great Britain **1644**
The Periodic table of elements **1437**
The Periodic table of elements compendium **1436**
Periodicals current in mainland China held by the Science Reference Library **393**
Periodicals in the library of the Royal Society of Chemistry **1175**
Periodicals list **4081**
Periodicals list, 1988 **7433**
Periodicals on chemistry held by the Science Reference Library **1174**
Perkampus, H.-H.
  Encyclopedia of spectroscopy **1283**
Perkins, C.F. and Parry, R.B.
  Information sources in cartography **855**
Perkins, L.
  A Bibliography of Soviet sources of medicine and public health in the USSR **3273**
Perkins, W.F.
  British and Irish writers on agriculture **5580**
Permanent International Association of Navigation Congresses
  Dictionnaire technique illustré en six langues **1743**
Perring, E.M. and Farrell, Ll.
  British red data books. 1. Vascular plants **2677**
Perring, F. and Walters, M.
  The Macmillan field guide to British wildflowers **2576**
Perring, F.H. and Sell, P.D.
  Critical supplement to the Atlas of the British flora **2566**
Perring, F.H. and Walters, S.M.
  Atlas of the British flora **2565**
Perrins, C.M.
  The Illustrated encyclopaedia of birds **2883**
Perrins, C.M. and Middleton, A.L.A.
  The Encyclopedia of birds **2881**
Perrot, P.
  A to Z of thermodynamics **1074**
Perrott, D.
  Ordnance Survey guide to the waterways **6392**
Perry, D.L. and Phillip, S.L.
  Handbook of inorganic compounds **1310**
Perry, R.H. and Green, D.W.
  Perry's chemical engineers' handbook **6476**
Perry's chemical engineers' handbook **6476**
Persch, F.
  Wörterbuch deutsch-englisch, englisch-deutsch: Erdöl und Erdgas **6741**
Personal computer dictionary **7307**
Pest and disease control handbook **5703**
PEST CABWeb **2168, 5708**
Pest management: a directory of information sources. Volume 1: Crop protection **5700**
Pest management: a directory of information sources. Volume 2: Animal health **5823**
The Pesticide manual **5723**
Peters, G.H. and Clark, K.R.
  Reviews of United Kingdom statistical sources. V.23: Agriculture **5578**
Peters, J.
  The Bookman's glossary **6142**
Peters, J.A.
  Dictionary of herpetology **2862**
Peters, U.H.
  Wörterbuch der Psychiatrie und medizinischer Psychologie **3848**
Petersen, D.
  Audio, video and data telecommunications **4499**

Plastics engineering handbook of the Society of
the Plastics Industry, Inc **7144**
The Plastics industry directory, 1992 **7143**
Plastics materials **7130**
Plastics technical dictionary **7139**
Platt, A.M.
Nuclear fact book **4204**
Pledge, H.T.
Science since 1500 **324**
Pleistocene mammals of Europe **1973**
Pleistocene mammals of North America **1974**
Plumbing dictionary **7575**
Plumbing encyclopaedia **7577**
Plumbing engineering services design **7576**
Plunkett, E.R.
Handbook of industrial toxicology **3633,
3715**
Plutonium handbook **6967**
Plywoods of the world **7019**
Pneumatic handbook **4574**
Pocket book of integrals and mathematical
formulas **625**
Pocket dictionary of laboratory equipment
1260
A Pocket dictionary of publishing terms **6215**
Pocket encyclopaedia of British steam railways
and locomotives **5032**
Pocket encyclopaedia of cacti in colour **5806**
A Pocket etymology of medical terms **3345**
The Pocket guide to wild flowers **2577**
Pocket guide: wildlife of Britain & Europe
2410
Pocock, R.F.
Nuclear power **4215**
Poggendorff, J.C.
Poggendorff's biographisch-literarisches
Handwörterbuch zur Geschichte der
exakten Wissenschaften **342**
Poggendorff's biographisch-literarisches
Handwörterbuch zur Geschichte der exakten
Wissenschaften **342**
Pohanish, R.P.
Rapid guide to trade names and synonyms of
environmentally regulated chemicals **6462**
Poirier, J.
Ethnologie régionale **2044**
Poisonous and venomous marine animals of the
world **2758**
Poisonous plants and fungi in Britain **3725,
5715**
Poisonous plants in Britain and Ireland **3726,
5716**
Poisonous snakes **2875**
Poisonous snakes of the world **2876**
Poissons de l'Atlantique du nord-est et de la
Méditerranée **2853, 5955**
Pokorný, V.
Principles of zoological micropalaeontology
1934
Poland, J.M.
A Guide to the literature of electrical and
electronics engineering **4241**
Poland, U.H.
World directory of biological and medical
sciences libraries **2194, 3455**
Polar and glaciological abstracts **1648**
Polar oceanography **1765**
Die Polarforschung **1646**
Polish-English dictionary of science and
technology **186**
Pollock, M. and Griffiths, M.
Royal Horticultural Society shorter
dictionary of gardening **5779**
Pollution abstracts **5237**
Polmar, N.
Guide to the Soviet navy **4912**
Polon, D.D.
Dictionary of mechanical engineering
abbreviations, signs and symbols **4122**

Polon, D.D. *(contd.)*
DPMA: Dictionary of physics and
mathematical abbreviations, signs and
symbols **908**
EESS/Encyclopaedia of engineering signs
and symbols **3902**
Polska Komitet Normalizacy
Vocabulary of mechanics in five languages
1006
Polunin, O.
Flowers of Europe **2561**
Polunin, O. and Smythies, B.E.
Flowers of South-west Europe **2563**
Polunin, O. and Walters, M.
A Guide to the vegetation of Britain and
Europe **2562**
Polyanin, A.D. and Zaitsev, V.F.
Handbook of exact solutions for ordinary
differential equations **620**
Polymer handbook **7154**
Polymer science dictionary **7157**
Polymer technology dictionary **7159**
Polymer yearbook **7162**
Polymers/ceramics/composites alert **7161**
Polymers: fibers and textiles **7151**
Polymers: polymer characterization and
analysis **7152**
Pomeranz, Y.
Functional properties of food components
6671
Modern cereal science and technology **6686**
Pond, G. and Raleigh, I.
A Standard guide to cat breeds **5910**
Ponting, K.G.
A Dictionary of dyes and dying **6836**
Poole, C.F.
Chromatography today **1291**
Poole, T.B.
UFAW handbook on the care and
management of laboratory animals **5815**
Pooley, R. and Patel, R.
Pooley's flight guide: United Kingdom 1998
6400
Pooley's flight guide: United Kingdom 1998
6400
Pope, S.
The Green book **2240**
Popular encyclopedia of plants **2629**
Popular physics and astronomy: an annotated
bibliography **676**
Porges, F.
HVAC engineer's handbook **7588**
Porkess, R
Dictionary of statistics **645**
Port engineering **5105**
Port statistics 1996 **6386**
Portable electronics data book **4393**
Porteous, A.
Dictionary of environmental science and
technology **5149**
Porter, F.
Zinc handbook **6954**
Porter, J.
The Colour identification guide to the
caterpillars of the British Isles
(Macrolepidptera) **2837**
Porter, M.R.
Handbook of surfactants **6527**
Porter, M.W. and Spiller, R.C.
The Barker index of crystals **1383**
Porter, R.
The Biographical dictionary of scientists **329**
The Cambridge illustrated history of
medicine **3403**
The Earth sciences: an annotated
bibliography **1484**
Porter, V.
Cattle: a handbook to the breeds of the world
5881
Goats of the world **5884**

Porter, V. *(contd.)*
Pigs: a handbook to the breeds of the world
5888
Portrait catalog of the New York Academy of
Medicine. [New York Academy of
Medicine] **3380**
Portraits of doctors and scientists in the
Wellcome Institute **3385**
Portraits of Nobel Laureates in medicine and
physiology **3383**
Postal addresses and index to postcode
directory **6411**
Postcode atlas of Great Britain and Northern
Ireland **6412**
Postcodes: the new geography **6413**
Potato abstracts **5744**
Potato terms **5745**
Potparic, O. and Gibson, J.
A Dictionary of sports injuries and disorders
3559
Potter, J.H.
Steam charts **4230**
Potter, N.N. and Hotchkiss, J.H.
Food science **6640**
The Potter's dictionary of materials and
techniques **6809**
Potts, L.W.
Quantitative analysis **1275**
Potts, P.J.
Geochemical reference material compositions
1515
Potts, P.J. and Tindle, A.G.
Directory of geo-analytical facilities in
British universities, colleges, polytechnics
and research institutions **1559**
Poucher, W.A.
Perfumes, cosmetics and soaps **6715**
Pough, F.H.
A Field guide to rocks and minerals **1836**
Poultry abstracts **5892**
Powder metallurgical materials and products
4666
'Powder metallurgy' **4660**
Powell, E.M. and Taylor, D.
Directory of rural organisations **5576**
Powell, M.J.V.
House builder's reference book **7542**
Powell, R.H.
Handbooks and tables in science and
technology **64, 274**
Powell-Smith, V. and Billington, M.J.
The building regulations explained and
illustrated **7524**
Power before steam **4152**
Power electronics handbook **4409**
Power from steam: a history of the stationary
steam engine **4232**
Power generation **4308**
Power hydraulics **5080**
The Power of steam **4231**
Power, Sir D'A.
Lives of the Fellows of the Royal College of
Surgeons of England, 1930-1951 **3877**
Plarr's lives of the Fellows of the Royal
College of Surgeons of England **3876**
Poynter, F.N.
A Catalogue of incunabula in the Wellcome
Historical Medical Library **3428**
Poynter, P.
The Parachute manual **5434**
Pozar, D.M.
Microwave engineering **4367**
Pozniak, G.I.
Russian-English dictionary of helminthology
and plant nematology **2797**
Practical electrical wiring **4337**
The Practical encyclopedia of freshwater
tropical aquarium fishes **5964**
A Practical guide to patent law **3210**
The Practical guide to patents, trademarks,
copyright, designs **3114**

Practical handbook of agricultural science **5552**

Practical handbook of environmental control **5167**

Practical handbook of marine science **2293**

Practical handbook of materials science **4016**

A Practical introduction to trademarks **3122**

Practical professional catering **5971**

Practical professional cookery **6056**

The Practicing scientist's tables **278**

Praeger, R.L.
Some Irish naturalists **2403**

Pratt, D.
Jane's world airlines **6405**

Precious metal databook **6933**

Precious metals **6932**

Preece, J.
The Good beer guide **6006**

Premier catalogue sélectif international de films ethnographiques sur l'Afrique noire **2067**

Prendergast, H.D.V.
Plants for food and medicine: proceedings of the joint conference of the Society for Economic Botany and the International Society for Ethnopharmacology, London, 1-6 July 1996 **2625**

The Prentice-Hall encyclopedia of mathematics **522**

Prentice Hall's illustrated dictionary of computing **7253**

The Presentation of original work in medicine and biology **3444**

Preserved aircraft **5427**

Preserved buses **5299**

Press, J.C.
American men and women of science. Editions 1-14 **411**

Pressure vessel design handbook **4671**

Pressure vessel handbook **4673**

Pressure vessels **4672**

Preston, A.
Warship 1998-1999 **4900**

Preston, C.D. and Croft, J.M.
Aquatic plants in Britain and Ireland **2704**

Preston-Mafham, R. and Preston-Mafham, K.
The Encyclopedia of land invertebrate behaviour **2768**
Spiders of the world **2802**

Pretz, B.
Dictionary of military and technological abbreviations and acronyms **4816**

Price, D.H.
Atlas of world cultures **2043**

Price, J.H.
The Shore environment **2269**

Price, V.
Dictionary of wines and spirits **6600**

Pridgeon, A.
The Illustrated encyclopedia of orchids **2701**

Primack, A.L.
Finding answers in science and technology **75**
Journal literature of the physical sciences **954**

Primates of the world **2976**

Prime, H.A. and Work, A.
Multilingual glossary of automatic control technology **7353**

Primrose McConnell's 'The agricultural notebook' **5511**

Princeton University. Plasma Physics Laboratory Library
Dictionary catalog **1021**

Principles and practice of infectious diseases.
Mandell, Douglas and Bennett's principles and practice of infectious diseases **3866**

Principles and practices for the safe processing of food **6672**

Principles of combustion engineering for boilers **6588**

The Principles of dairy farming **5911**

Principles of electron optics **1035**

Principles of powder technology **6524**

Principles of zoological micropalaeontology **1934**

The Print and production manual **6150**

Print buyers directory 1999/2000 **6159**

Printed circuits handbook **4468**

Printers' and publishers' devices in England and Scotland, 1485-1640 **7402**

Printing abstracts **6157**

Printing ink manual **6838**

Printing trades directory **6160**

Pritchard, D.E.
Important bird areas in the United Kingdom **2478**

Pritchard, M.E.
A Short dictionary of weaving **7081**

Pritzel, G.A.
Thesaurus litterata botanicae omnium gentium **2487**

Privacy and data protection **7332**

The Private press **6172**

Private presswork: a bibliographic approach to printing as an avocation **6173**

'Problems in anthropological bibliography' **1986**

'Problems in the bibliography of statistics' **633**

Proceedings in print **487**

Proceedings of the 2nd International Conference on Food Science and Technology Information **6664**

Process engineering data book **4642**

Proctor, C.E.
'The Engineer' index, 1856-1959 **3934**

Product finishing handbook and directory **4700**

Professions Supplementary to Medicine Act, 1960, section 2 (d) **3364**

Profiles of African scientific institutions **468**

Profiles of African scientists **409**

Progress in aerospace **5405**

Progress in contemporary cartography **875**

Progress in inorganic chemistry **1308**

Progress in low temperature physics **1071**

Progress in mathematics **561**

Progress in nuclear energy **4195**

Progress in optical communications **4531**

Progress in optics **1040**

Progress in physical geography **1693**

Progress in physical organic chemistry **1343**

Progress in powder metallurgy **4669**

Progress in rubber and plastics technology **7107**

Progress in the understanding and prevention of corrosion **4044**

Prominent scientists **351**

Properties and applications of diamonds **6982**

Properties and growth of diamonds **6980**

The Properties of gases and liquids **1313**

Properties of organic compounds **1357**

Properties of water and steam, in SI units **4229**

Protected areas of the world **2439**

Protected landscapes **2440**

Protecting scientific ideas and inventions **3110**

Protection of industrial designs **3220**

Protozoological abstracts **2785**

Proulx, J.-R.
Review of ethnohistorical research on the native peoples of Quebec **2083**

Provan, J.E. and Hunter, J.W.
Health media review index **3387**

A Provisional checklist of species for Flora North America **2593**

Prozesky, O.P.M.
A Field guide to the birds of Southern Africa **2920**

Prudnikov, A.P.
Integrals and series **623**

Pruett, N.J.
Keeping current with geoscience information **1485**

Prys-Roberts, C. and Brown, B.R.
International practice of anaesthesia **3881**

Prytherch, R. and Stanley, S.
Food, cookery and diet **3528, 6050**

PSTA **4705**

Psychiatric dictionary **3841**

A Psychiatric glossary **3849**

'Psychiatry' **3838**

Psychiatry: the state of the art **3857**

Public broadcasting for the 21st century **6134**

Publications catalogue, 1948-1989. [World Health Organization] **3272**

'Published portraits of anthropologists and workers in allied fields' **2024**

Publishers' catalogues home pages **6213**

Publishers directory, 1999 **6232**

Publishers, distributors & wholesalers of the United States **6233**

Publishers' international ISBN directory **6225**

Publishers' international ISBN directory plus. **6225**

Publisher's practical dictionary in 20 languages **6217**

Publishing and book development in sub-Saharan Africa **6230**

Publishing market place reference plus
Publishers, distributors & wholesalers of the United States **6233**

Puddephatt, R.J.,
The Periodic table of elements **1437**

Pugh, E.
Pugh's dictionary of acronyms and abbreviations **42, 3012**

Pugh's dictionary of acronyms and abbreviations **42, 3012**

Pulp and paper dictionary **7039**

Pump handbook **4619**

Pumping manual **4620**

Pumps and other fluids machinery abstracts **4624**

Pumps: selection systems and applications **4622**

Pure and applied science books, 1876-1982 **76**

Pushkarev, V.L. and Shchegoleva, A.M.
Anglo-russkiĭ i russko-angliĭskiĭ arkhitekturnostroitel'nyi slovar' **7509**

Putnam, P.A.
Handbook of animal science **5863**

Putnam, W.C.
Putnam's geology **1542**

Putnam's geology **1542**

PVC plastics **7166**

Pyatiyazychnyĭ slovar' mineralogicheskikh nazvanii **1404**

Pyatt, E.
The National Physical Laboratory **992**

Pybus, S.
Cutlery: a bibliography **6983**

Pye, P.W. and Harrison, H.W
Floors and flooring **7543**

Quanta: a handbook of concepts **1230**

Quantification in science **1001**

Quantitative analysis **1275**

Quantitative data file for ore minerals **1852**

Quantities and units of measurement **1000**

Quantities, units and symbols **37**

Quantities, units and symbols in physical chemistry **1238**

Quarterly bulletin of the International Association of Agricultural Librarians and Documentalists **5546**

Quarterly transport statistics **6268**

Que choisir? **6022**

Quémada, G.
Dictionnaire de termes nouveaux des sciences et des techniques **114**

The Quest for plants **2549**

Questionarium medicum **3306**

Referativnyĭ zhurnal. 51. Astronomiia **709**

Referativnyĭ zhurnal. 52. Geodeziia i aeros'emka **831**

Referativnyĭ zhurnal. 61. Nasosotroenie i Kompressorostroenie Kholodil'noe mashinostroenie **4625**

Referativnyĭ zhurnal. 63. Svarka **4686**

Referativnyĭ zhurnal. 64. Elektrosviaz **4518**

Referativnyĭ zhurnal. Fizika **952**

Referativnyĭ zhurnal. Geografiia **1690**

Referativnyĭ zhurnal. Khimiya **1173**

Referativnyĭ zhurnal. Matematika **557**

Reference books for the historian of science **291**

Reference data for engineers: radio, electronics, computer, and communication **3947**

The reference guide to famous engineering landmarks of the world **4970**

A Reference guide to practical electronic terms **4418**

Reference manual for telecommunications engineering **4522**

Reference sources in science, engineering, medicine, and agriculture **72**

'Reference sources on food and cooking' **6041**

References for chemistry teachers **1124**

'References to contemporary papers on acoustics' **1022**

Refrigeration and air-conditioning **4582**

The Refrigeration and air conditioning year book **4590**

Refrigeration pocket book **4583**

Regional geochemical atlases **1517**

A Regional history of the railways of Great Britain **6313**

Register of offshore units, submersibles & diving systems **4799**

Register of research, 1974- **7532**

Register of ships **5358**

Registers and directory **5842**

Registre mondial des barrages **5116**

Regulatory and technical reports **4186**

Regulatory Assistance Corporation
Directory of toxicological and related testing laboratories **3720**

Rehder, A.
The Bradley bibliography **5618**

Rehm, H.-J. and Reed, G.
Biotechnology **2986**

Rehm, S.
Multilingual dictionary of agronomic plants **5732**

Reich, W.T.
Encyclopedia of bioethics **3474**

Reid, B.C.
A Practical guide to patent law **3210**
A Practical introduction to trademarks **3122**

Reid, F.A.
A Field guide to the mammals of Central America and southeast Mexico **2960**

Reid, R.C.
The Properties of gases and liquids **1313**

Reineccius, G.
Source book of flavors **6698**

Reinforced concrete design **4979**

Reinforced concrete designer's handbook **4978**

Reinforced plastics handbook **7102**

Reiss, H.E.
Reproductive medicine: from A to Z **3509**

Das Relief der Erde **1695**

Remarkable animals: a unique encyclopaedia of wildlife wonders **2752**

Remote sensing and image interpretation **846**

Remote sensing of earth resources: a guide to information sources **845, 1522**

Remote Sensing On-Line Retrieval System
See
RESORS

The Remote sensing source book: a guide to remote sensing products, services, facilities, publications and other materials **849**

Remote sensing yearbook **850**

Rendall, D.
Jane's aircraft recognition guide **5394**

Rendle, A.B.
Handbook of the British flora **2567**

Rendle, B.J.
World timbers **7005**

Renewable energy and its environmental impact **4100**

Renewable energy bulletin **4103**

Renewable energy resources **4101**

Renewable energy technologies **4106**

Renewable sources of energy **4104**

Renner, E.
Grosse Molkerei Lexikon **5916**

Rennison, R.W.
Civil engineering heritage: Northern England **4961**

Renouil, Y. and Traversay, P. de
Dictionnaire du vin **6594**

Rensburg, W.C.J., van
Strategic minerals **1857**

Répertoire alphabétique et phonétique des marques internationales **3129**

Répertoire des organisations non gouvernementales dans les pays membres de l'OCDE pour l'environnement et le developpement **2256**

Répertoire du livre et de la presse en Afrique **6210**

Répertoire international d'associations et de sociétés astronomiques **736**

Répertoire international des institutions astronomiques professionnelles **737**

Repertorium commentationum a societatibus litterariis editarum **77**

Report of the Task Group on Reference Man **3485**

Report on United Kingdom Antarctic research **1659**

Report series codes dictionary **3045**

Reports on progress in physics **955**

Reproductive medicine: from A to Z **3509**

Reptiles and amphibians in Britain **2866**

Reptiles and amphibians of Australia **2869**

Reptiles of Australia **2870**

The Reptiles of North America **2867**

Requirements for electrical installations BS 7671: 1992 **4342**

Research and development in Russia **3100**

Research catalog of the Library. [American Museum of Natural History] **2377, 2707**

Research catalogue of the American Geographical Society **1660**

Research centers directory **470**

Research fields in physics **994**

Research guide to the arid lands of the world **1703**

Research in economic anthropology **2016**

Research in social anthropology, 1975 - 1980 **2005**

Research methods in psychiatry **3862**

Research topics in the life sciences 1996 **2198**

Resins **6784**

RESORS (Remote Sensing On-line Retrieval System) **843**

Resources for nursing research **3776**

Resources for the history of physics **974**

The Retail jeweller's guide **6973**

Retallack, G.J.
A Colour guide to paleosols **1942**

Retrospective index to theses of Great Britain and Ireland, 1716-1950 **205**

Retrospective index to theses of Great Britain and Ireland, 1716-1950. Volume 2: Applied sciences and technology **3043**

Retrospective index to theses of Great Britain and Ireland, 1716-1950. Volume 3: Life sciences **2166**

Reuss, J.D.
Repertorium commentationum a societatibus litterariis editarum **77**

Reverdin, A.
Katzarov's manual on industrial property **3197**

Review of agricultural entomology **2821, 5718**

Review of ethnohistorical research on the native peoples of Quebec **2083**

Review of medical and veterinary mycology **2651**

Review of plant pathology **5709**

Reviews of modern physics **953**

Reviews of national science and technology policy **5**

Reviews of United Kingdom statistical sources **6266**

Reviews of United Kingdom statistical sources. V.7: Road passenger transport; Road goods transport **6266**

Reviews of United Kingdom statistical sources. V.10: Ports and inland waterways; Civil aviation **6266**

Reviews of United Kingdom statistical sources. V.11: Coal, gas, electricity **6577**

Reviews of United Kingdom statistical sources. V.14: Rail transport; Sea transport **6266**

Reviews of United Kingdom statistical sources. V.22: Printing and publishing **6165**

Reviews of United Kingdom statistical sources. V.23: Agriculture **5578**

Rewritable optical storage technology **7420**

Reynard, K.W.
Data activities **3095**
Data activities: a guide to scientific and technical data collection in the United Kingdom **273**
UK materials information sources **4020**

Reynard, K.W. and Reynard, J.M.E.
The Aslib directory of information sources in the United Kingdom **451**

Reynolds, C.E. and Steedman, J.C.
Reinforced concrete designer's handbook **4978**

Reynolds, J.
Windmills and watermills **4579**

Rheinheimer, G.
Mikrobiologie der Gewässer **2371**

Rheinmetall
Handbook on weaponry **4847**

Rheology abstracts **1015**

Rhind, D.W. and Taylor, D.R.F.
Cartography, past, present and future **892**

Rhodes, C.P.
The Encyclopedia of beer **6605**

Rhodes, M.J.
Principles of powder technology **6524**

Rhodes, P.
An Outline history of medicine **3406**

Rhodes, P.H.
The Organic chemist's desk reference **1330**

The Rhododendron species **5808**

The RHS encyclopaedia of house plants **5799**

The RHS plant finder **5757**

RIBA list of recommended books, 1998 **7473**

Ricciuti, E.
The Natural history of North America **2424**

Rice abstracts **5739**

Rice almanac **5740**

Rice, R.P.
Spanish-English/English-Spanish illustrated agricultural dictionary **5527**

Richards Butler on copyright, designs and patents: the new law **3209**

Richards, J.M.
The National Trust book of bridges **5009**

Richards, O.W.
Imms' general textbook of entomology **2811**

Richardson, B.
CIRIA guide to European Community and international sources of construction information **7490**
The CIRIA UK construction information guide **4965, 7528**

Richardson, B.A.
Wood in construction **7571**

Richardson, M.L.
Dictionary of substances and their effects **1223**

Richey, C.B.
Agricultural engineer's handbook **5663**

Richling, C.
Wörterbuch der kabeltechnik **4335**

Richter, B. and Wenzel, D.
The Museum of Science and Industry basic list of children's science books, 1973-1984 **73**

Richter, G.
Fachwörterbuch optik, foto, video **7424**

Richter, H.P.
Practical electrical wiring **4337**

Ricker, W.E.
Russian-English dictionary for students of fisheries & aquatic biology **5938**

Rickerby, D.S. and Matthews, A.
Advanced surface coatings **4695**

Rickett, H.W.
Wild flowers of the United States **2594**

Rickman, W.S.
CRC handbook of incineration of hazardous wastes **5213**

RICS directory **834**

RICS Library Information Service abstracts and reviews **832**

RICS Library Information Service Weekly briefing: a digest of news selected from the press **833**

Rider, D.
Jane's airports, equipment and services **6399**

Rider, K.J.
History of science and technology **292**

Ridge, J.D.
Annotated bibliographies of mineral deposits in Africa, Asia (exclusive of the USSR) and Australasia **1858**
Annotated bibliographies of mineral deposits in Europe **1862**
Annotated bibliographies of mineral deposits in the Western Hemisphere **1863**

Ridgely, R.S.
The Birds of South America **2925**

Ridgway, S.H. and Harrison, R.J.
Handbook of marine mammals **2953**

Ridley, J.R.
Safety at work **3609**

Ridpath, I.
A Dictionary of astronomy **699**
The Encyclopaedia of astronomy and space **683**
The Night sky **778**
Norton's star atlas and reference handbook (epoch 2000.0) **797**

Ridpath, I. and Tirion, W.
Collins' pocket guide to stars and planets **778**

Riedman, S.R. and Gustafson, E.T.
Portraits of Nobel Laureates in medicine and physiology **3383**

Riegel, E.R.
Riegel's handbook of industrial chemistry **6442**
Riegel's handbook of industrial chemistry **6442**

Rieger, R.O.
Glossary of genetics: classical and molecular **2300**

Rigal, W.A.
The Inverted medical dictionary **3284**

Rigaux, F.
Les Observatoires astronomiques et les astronomes **749**

Rigby, M.
Bibliography of climate textbooks and studies **1796**

Rigden, J.S.
Macmillan encyclopedia of physics **923**

Rijsdijk, J.F. and Laming, P.B.
Physical and related properties of 145 timbers **6999**

Rimmington, A. and Greenshields, R.
Technology and transition **3006**

Rinaldi, A. and Tyndalo, V.
The Complete book of mushrooms **2667**

Ring, M.E.
Dentistry: an illustrated history **3823**

Rink, E.
Technical Americana **3018**

Rinzler, C.A.
The Complete book of herbs, spices and condiments **6088**

The Rise of early modern science: Islam, China and the West **306**

The Rise of the Irish linen industry **7086**

Ristić, S.
Rečnik techničkih 13 izrago srpskohrvatso-engleski, francuski-nemački **190**

Ristow, W.W.
Guide to the history of cartography **887**

Ritchie, D.
The Encyclopedia of earthquakes and volcanoes **1505**

Ritchie, L.A.
The Shipbuilding industry **5367**

Ritchie, W.
Surveying and mapping for field scientists **864**

Ritter, M.E.
Earth online: an Internet guide for earth science **1443**

Rittner, D.
Ecolinking **5120**

Riva, J.P.
World petroleum resources and reserves **6731**

Rivers of the United States **2268**

Rivers of the world **1888**

Rivkon, S.L.
Thermodynamic derivatives for water and steam **4226**

RLSD bibliography **4814**

Road construction and traffic directory 1994 **5069**

Road documentation for developing countries **6285**

Roads and traffic in urban areas **6278**

Roark, R.J.
Roark's formulas for stress and strain **4030**
Roark's formulas for stress and strain **4030**

Robb, C.
Metals databook **1320, 6876**

Robert, S. and Hay, T.
International directory of telecommunications **4527, 6120**

Robert Slade's guide to computer viruses **7336**

Roberts, F.
Medical terms, their origin and construction **3322**

Roberts, M.J.
Collins field guide: spiders of Britain and northern Europe **2803**
Construction industry thesaurus **7526**
The Spiders of Great Britain and Ireland **2804**

Roberts, M.T. and Etherington, D.
Bookbinding and the conservation of books **7442**

Roberts, R.B.
Encyclopedia of historic forts **4839**

Roberts, R.S.
Dictionary of audio, radio and video **4511**

Roberts, V.
British poultry standards **5890**

Roberts, W.L.
Encyclopedia of minerals **1391**

Robertson, B.
Aviation enthusiasts' data book **5410**

Robertson, J.D.
The Beer-taster's log **6611**

Robins, F.W.
The Story of water supply **5198**

Robinson, A.
Dictionary of aviation **5393**

Robinson, A.H.
Elements of cartography **860**
Marine cartography in Britain **894**

Robinson, E.
A Guide to geology libraries in London **1615**

Robinson, J.
The Oxford companion to wine **6593**

Robinson, J.F.
Videotape recording **7412**

Robinson, J.W.
CRC handbook of spectroscopy **1284**

Robinson, R.H.O.B. and LeFanu, W.R.
Lives of the Fellows of the Royal College of Surgeons of England, 1952-1964 **3878**

Robinson, W.D.
The Solid waste handbook **5258**

Robot technology **7390**

Robotics **7377**

'Robotics and automated manufacture' **7380**

Robotics applications for industry **7391**

Robotics in education **7398**

Robotics sourcebook **7387**

Robotics sourcebook and dictionary **7384**

Roche, L.J.
Physicists look back **972**

Rock-forming minerals **1393, 1834**

Rock physics and phase relations **1842**

Rockets into space **5439**

Rocks, minerals and fossils of the world **1402**

Rodale's encyclopedia of indoor gardening **5802**

Rodd, E.H.
Rodd's chemistry of carbon compounds **1319**
Rodd's chemistry of carbon compounds **1319**

Rodenwald, E. and Jusatz, H.J.
Weltkarten zur Klimakunde **1805**

Rodenwaldt, E.
The Welt-Seuchen Atlas **3744**

Rodes, B.K. and Odell, R.
A Dictionary of environmental quotations **2259, 5164**

Rodríguez, C.
Bilingual dictionary of the graphic arts **6190**

Rodríguez, M. García-
See
García-Rodríguez, M.

Rodwell, J.S.
British plant communities **2570**

Rogers, A.
The Student's companion to geography **1674**

Rogers, D.J.
A Bibliography of African ecology **2276**

Rogers, J.
The Encyclopedia of food and nutrition **3532, 6636**

Rogers, J.E.
The Shell book **2791**

Rogoyski, D.A.
Glossary of Polish-English meteorological terms **1782**

Rohsenow, W.M. and Hartnett, J.P.
Handbook of heat transfer applications **1064**

The Roll of the Royal College of Physicians of London **3419**

Roller, D.H.D. *and* **Goodman, M.M.**
The Catalogue of the history of science collections of the University of Oklahoma Libraries **293**

Rolling rivers **1894**

Rolt, L.T.C.
Tools for the job **4762**

Rom, W.N.
Environmental and occupational medicine **3606**

Romer, A.S.
Bibliography of fossil vertebrates, exclusive of North America, 1509-1927 **1951**
Notes and comments on vertebrate palaeontology **1954**
Vertebrate palaeontology **1954**

Rommetveit, N.
Norsk landbruksordbok **5517**

Römpp's Chemie-Lexikon **1128**

ROMULUS **233**

Ronan, C.
Encyclopedia of astronomy **686**

Ronan, C.A.
The Cambridge illustrated history of the world's science **308**
The Shorter 'Science and civilization in China' **395**

Ronayne, J. *and* **Boag, C.**
Science and technology in Australasia, Antarctica and the Pacific Islands **31**

Ronzio, R.A.
The Encyclopedia of nutrition and good health **3530**

Rook, P.
Software reliability handbook **7321**

Rookledge's international type finder **6176**

Rooks, B.
Developments in robotics **7396**

Room, A.
Dictionary of astronomical names **707**
Dictionary of trade name origins **3119**

Root, N.J.
Catalog of the American Museum of Natural History film archives **2396**

ROOT thesaurus **3091**

Roper, C. *and* **Silva, J.**
Science and technology in Latin America **30**

Roper, F.W. *and* **Boorkman, J.A.**
Introduction to reference sources in the health sciences **3253**

Rosaler, R.C.
Standard handbook of plant engineering **4162**

Rosato, D.V.
Rosato's plastics encyclopedia and dictionary **7127**
Rosato's plastics encyclopedia and dictionary **7127**

Roscher, N.M.
Women chemists, 1990 **1222**

Rose, A.H. *and* **Harrison, J.S.**
The Yeasts **2656**

Rose books **5804**

Rose Elliot's complete vegetarian cookbook **6083**

Rose, F.
Colour identification guide to the grasses, sedges, rushes and ferns of the British Isles and north-western Europe **2697**

Rose, J.W. *and* **Cooper, J.R.**
Technical data on fuel **6553**

Rosen, F.S.
Dictionary of immunology **3798**

Rosenberg, A.
Russian-English glossary of guided missile, rocket and satellite terms **5437**

Rosenberg, J.M.
Business dictionary of computers **7254**
Dictionary of artificial intelligence and robotics **7370**

Rosenberg, J.M. *(contd.)*
The McGraw-Hill dictionary of information technology and computer acronyms, initials and abbreviations **7221**

Rosenberg, P.D.
Patent law fundamentals **3215**

Rosenblum, J.
A Bibliographic history of the book **6146**

Roskill's directory of sources for metals and mineral data **6877**

Ross-Craig, S.
Drawings of British plants **2579**

Ross, I.A.
Medicinal plants of the world **3684**

Ross, J.P. *and* **Lefanu, W.R.**
Lives of the Fellows of the Royal College of Surgeons of England, 1965-1973 **3879**

Ross, R.B.
Handbook of metal treatments and testing **4645**
Metallic materials specification handbook **6855**

Rossdale, P.D.
Veterinary notes for horse owners **5879**

Rossdale, P.D. *and* **Wreford, S.M.**
The Horse's health, from A to Z **5877**

Roth, G.D.
Collins' guide to the weather **1800**

Roth, J.P.
Rewritable optical storage technology **7420**

Rothamsted Experimental Station
Soil maps **5681**

Rothamsted Experimental Station. Library
Catalogue of printed books and pamphlets on agriculture published between 1471 and 1840 **5503**

Rothbart, H.A.
Mechanical design handbook **4724**

Rothenberg, M.
The History of science and technology in the United States **416**

Rougemont, G.M. de
A Field guide to the crops of Britain and Europe **5730**

The Round the world air guide **6397**

Rousmaniere, J.
The Illustrated dictionary of boating terms **6343**

Les Routiers France 1997 **6005**

Routledge diccionario técnico inglés **171, 3039**

Routledge dictionary of medicine, Volume 1. German-English **3329**

Routledge dictionary of medicine, Volume 2. English-German **3331**

Routledge Dictionnaire technique anglais **158, 3036**

Routledge French technical dictionary **158, 3036**

Routledge German dictionary of electrical engineering and electronics **4255**

Routledge German dictionary of environmental technology **5151**

Routledge German technical dictionary **138, 3034**

Routledge Spanish dictionary of environmental technology **5153**

Routledge Spanish dictionary of telecommunications **4517**

Routledge Spanish technical dictionary **171, 3039**

Rowe, G.T.
Deep-sea biology **2294**

Royal Aircraft Establishment
The RAE table of earth satellites, 1957-1986 **5487**

Royal Anthropological Institute
Teachers' resource guide **2017**

The Royal Anthropological Institute Film Library catalogue **2019**

Royal Association for Disability and Rehabilitation
Accessible holidays in the British Isles 1999: a guide for disabled people **5989**

Royal Astronomical Society
Catalogue of the Library. [Royal Astronomical Society] **675**

Royal Automobile Club
Camping and caravanning: Great Britain & Ireland 1998 **6011**
Inspected hotels **5985**
One hundred years of motoring **5311**
RAC camping and caravanning in Europe **6014**
RAC hotels in Europe **5982**

Royal Botanic Gardens, Kew
List of periodical publications in the Library **2515**
Poisonous plants in Britain and Ireland **3726**
World plant conservation bibliography **2444**

Royal Botanic Gardens, Kew. Library
Author and classified catalogues. [Royal Botanic Gardens, Kew, Library] **2489**

Royal College of General Practitioners
Classification of diseases, problems and disorders **3750**

Royal College of Nursing
A Bibliography of nursing literature **3778**

Royal College of Physicians of London
Catalogue of engraved portraits of the Library. [Royal College of Physicians of London] **3384**
Portraits **3382**
Smoking or health **3584**
William Harvey, 1578-1657 **3420**

Royal College of Physicians of London. Joint Committee
The Nomenclature of disease **3741**

Royal College of Surgeons of England
A Catalogue of the portraits and other paintings and sculpture in the Royal College of Surgeons of England **3875**

Royal College of Veterinary Surgeons
Registers and directory **5842**

Royal Commission on Historical Manuscripts
The Manuscript papers of British scientists, 1600-1940 **380**

Royal Entomological Society of London
Catalogue of the Library. [Royal Entomological Society of London] **2808**
Handbooks for the identification of British insects **2813**

The Royal Greenwich Observatory and the Astronomers Royal, 1675-1976 **745**

Royal Horticultural Society
The Royal Horticultural Society colour chart **5750**
The Royal Horticultural Society A-Z encyclopedia of garden plants **5781**
The Royal Horticultural Society colour chart **5750**
The Royal Horticultural Society encyclopedia of gardening **5784**
The Royal Horticultural Society gardeners' encyclopedia of plants and flowers **5782**
Royal Horticultural Society shorter dictionary of gardening **5779**

Royal Institution of Chartered Surveyors
Directory **834**
RICS Library Information Service abstracts and reviews **832**
RICS Library Information Service Weekly briefing: a digest of news selected from the press **833**
Royal Institution of Chartered Surveyors directory **834**

Royal Life Saving Society. National Technical Committee
[Handbook, Royal Life Saving Society] **3636**

Royal Mail **6409**

The Royal Observatory at Greenwich and
Herstmonceux, 1675-1975 **744**
Royal Society
Biographical memoirs of Fellows of the
Royal Society **343**
Book catalogue of the library of the Royal
Society **78**
Catalogue of scientific papers, 1800-1900
79
Catalogue of scientific papers, 1800-1900.
Subject index **80**
Guide to the marine stations of the North
Atlantic and European waters **6378**
Quantities, units and symbols **37**
Report on United Kingdom Antarctic
research **1659**
Royal Society mathematical tables **665**
**Royal Society. Mathematical Tables
Committee**
Royal Society mathematical tables **665**
Royal Society of Chemistry
Chemicals and companies **6457**
Directory of consulting practices in
chemistry and related subjects **1181**
Index of chemistry films, 1984 **1195**
Isotopes: essential chemistry and applications
4222
Periodicals in the library of the Royal
Society of Chemistry **1175**
Specialist periodical reports: reviews of the
chemical literature **1178**
Royal Society of Chemistry. Working Party
Guidance on laboratory fume cupboards
1258
Royal Society of Medicine
Family medical guide **3299**
Roysden, C.
American engineers of the nineteenth century
3963
Rozenberg, M.B.
English-Russian dictionary of refrigeration
and low-temperature technology **4588**
RSPCA complete cat care manual **5906**
RSWB **4922, 7466**
RTD-Publications [Research and Technical
Developments Publications] **4168**
Rubash, J.
Master dictionary of food and wines **6601**
Rubatzky, V.E. and Yamaguchi, M.
World vegetables: principles, production,
and nutritive values **5767**
Rubber **7115**
**Rubber and Plastics Research Association of
Great Britain (RAPRA)**
Progress in rubber and plastics technology
7107
RAPRA abstracts **7106**
RAPRA new trade names in the rubber and
plastics industry **7109**
Trade names of rubbers, resins & plastics
7110
Rubber statistical bulletin **7122**
Rubber Stitching
Elsevier's rubber dictionary **7119**
Rubber technology and manufacture **7111**
Rubber technology handbook **7113**
Rubbicana: Europe, 1997 **7121**
Rubenstein, H.
The 1995 Good hotel guide to Britain and
Europe **5980**
Rubin, I.I.
Handbook of plastic materials and
technology **7133**
Rudkin, A. and Butcher, I.
A Book world directory of the Arab
countries, Turkey and Iran **6209**
Rudolph, J.R.
Energy **4056**
Rudzki, G.J.
Surface finishing systems **4693**

Ruffner, F.G. and Thomas, R.C.
Code names dictionary **121**
Ruffner, J.A.
Eponyms dictionaries index **116**
Ruffner, J.H.
Eponyms dictionaries index **337**
Ruiz, M.
One hundred years of the motor car, 1882-
1986 **5312**
Ruiz Torres diccionario de términos médicos
3343
Rükl, A.
Atlas of the moon **758**
Rules of thumb for chemical engineers **6481**
Rules of thumb for engineers and scientists
653
Runcorn, S.K.
International dictionary of geophysics,
seismology, geomagnetism **1491**
Ruokonen, M.
Forestry and forest products vocabulary
5626
Ruppert, E.E.
Invertebrate zoology **2784**
Rural transport and planning: a bibliography
with abstracts **6276**
Rushman, G.B.
A Short history of anaesthesia **3882**
Russell, C.A.
Recent developments in the history of
chemistry **1201**
Russell-Clark on copyright in industrial design
3217
Russell, G.E.
Biotechnology and genetic engineering
reviews **3002**
Russell, K.
The Principles of dairy farming **5911**
Russell, P.J. and Williams, A.
The Nutrition and health dictionary **3537**
Russell, R.W.
Patents and trademarks in Japan **3169**
Russell, Sir. E.J.
A History of agricultural science in Great
Britain, 1620-1954 **5581**
Russey, W.E.
Text and graphics in the electronic age **440**
Russian-English and English-Russian dictionary
of radar and electronics **4554**
Russian-English biological and medical
dictionary **2164, 3348**
Russian-English botanical dictionary **2506**
The Russian-English chemical dictionary **1161**
Russian-English dictionary for students of
fisheries & aquatic biology **5938**
Russian-English dictionary of chemistry and
chemical technology **1160**
Russian-English dictionary of
electrotechnology and allied sciences **4265**
Russian-English dictionary of helminthology
and plant nematology **2797**
Russian-English dictionary of modern terms in
aeronautics and rocketry **5400**
Russian-English dictionary of science and
technology **3040, 6449**
Russian-English dictionary of scientific and
technical usage **181**
Russian-English dictionary of the mathematical
sciences **548**
Russian-English English-Russian dictionary on
probability, statistics, and combinatorics
628
Russian-English/English-Russian glossary of
statistical terms **646**
Russian-English, English-Russian military
dictionary **4827**
Russian-English-French-German constructional
engineering dictionary **4935**
Russian-English-French-German kinematics
dictionary **1009**

Russian-English-German-French mining
dictionary **4777**
Russian-English glossary of guided missile,
rocket and satellite terms **5437**
Russian-English glossary of physics of fluids
and meteorology **1013**
Russian-English mathematical dictionary **550**
Russian-English medical dictionary **3349**
Russian-English medical dictionary phrasebook
3350
Russian-English military and technical
dictionary **4829**
Russian-English oil-field dictionary **1870,
4804**
Russian-English physics dictionary **944**
Russian-English scientific and technical
dictionary **180**
Russian-English space technology dictionary
5461
Russian-English translator's dictionary **184**
Russian research institutions and scientists
directory **492**
Russko-angliĭskiĭ geologicheskiĭ slovar' **1472**
Russko-angliĭskiĭ meditsinkiĭ slovar'-
razgovornik **3350**
Russko-angliĭskiĭ meditsinskiĭ slovar' **3347**
Russko-angliĭskiĭ nauchno-tekhnicheskiĭ slovar
perevodchika **184**
Russko-angliĭskiĭ politekhnicheskiĭ slovar' **182**
Russko-angliĭskiĭ slovar' knigovedcheskikh
terminov **6143**
Russko-angliĭskiĭ veterinaryĭ slovar' **5831**
Russko-angliĭskiĭ voehnotekhicheskiĭ slovar'
4829
Russo-anglo-nemetsko-frantsazki gorny slovar'
4777
Russo-English veterinary dictionary **5831**
Rutgers, A. and Norris, K.A.
Encyclopedia of aviculture **5896**
Ruthenberg, H.
Farming systems in the tropics **5563**
Rutten, M.G.
The Geology of Western Europe **1587**
Ryan, R.P. and Terry, C.E.
Toxicology desk reference **3719**
Rycroft, M.
The Cambridge encyclopedia of space **5443**
Ryder, J.D.
Engineers and electrons **4290**
Ryder, M.L.
Sheep and man **5885**
Rydnik, V.J.
Dictionary of physics in four languages **930**
Ryland's: the directory of the engineering
industry, 1993 **6871**
Rymdorlista: svensk-engelsk-fransk-tysk-rysk
5452
Sable, M.H.
Exobiology: a research guide **2209**
Sachet, M.H. and Fosberg, F.R.
Island bibliographies: Micronesian botany
2602
Sadler, M.
Encyclopedia of human nutrition **3529**
SAE dictionary of aerospace engineering **5456**
SAE glossary of automotive terms **5281, 5306**
SAE handbook **5292**
SAE motorcycle safety and environmental
terminology **5327**
Sáenz, A.L.
Noise pollution **5252**
Safe practices in chemical laboratories **3626**
Safe use of chemicals **1256**
Safety at work **3609**
Sage, A.P.
Concise encyclopedia of information
processing in systems and organizations
7283
Sagers, M.J.
The Chemical industry in the USSR **6468**

Sahrhage, D. and Lundbeck, J.
A History of fishing **5954**
Sahrmuller, R.
Mehrsprächiges Verzeichnis der
Gemüsenamen **5766**
Sailing directions (Pilots) **6377**
Saks, M.
Alternative medicine in Britain **3696**
Salaman, R.A.
Dictionary of leather-working tools, 1700-
1950 **7027**
Dictionary of woodworking tools **7016**
Sale catalogues of libraries of eminent persons
81
Salisbury, F.B.
Units, symbols, and terminology for plant
physiology **2605**
Saller, K.
Lehrbuch der Anthropologie in
systematischer Darstellung **2004**
Salter, R.J.
Highway design and construction **5063**
Salvadori, F.B. and Florio, P.L.
Wildlife in peril **2462**
Salvendy, G.
Handbook of industrial engineering **3924**
Salzano, F.M. and Callegari-Jacques, S.M.
South American Indians **2125**
Salzman, L.F.
Building in England, down to 1540 **7521**
Sambraus, H.
A Colour atlas of livestock breeds **5817**
Sambursky, S.
Physical thought from the Presocratic to the
quantum theory **959**
Sampling source book **6484**
Sampson, J.A.
Tropical fruits **5768**
Samson, P.
Glossary of bacteriological terms **2376**
Samsonov, G.V.
The Oxide handbook **1254**
Samuel, A.E.
Greek and Roman chronology **904**
Sanchez Monge y Parellada, E.
Diccionario de agronomia **5528**
Sandage, A. and Bedke, J.
The Carnegie atlas of galaxies **801**
Sanders, I.T.
East European peasantries: social relations
2049
Sanders, P.A.
Handbook of aerosol technology **1250**
Sandström, G.E.
The History of tunnelling **5003**
Santholzer, R.W. and Santholzer, C.
Five language dictionary of surface coatings,
plating, products, finishing, corrosion,
plastics and rubber **6528**
Santucci, R.
A Consumer's guide to home improvement,
renovation, and repair **6101**
Sardar, Z.
Science and technology in the Middle East
25
Sardegna, J. and Paul, T.O.
The Encyclopedia of blindness and vision
impairment **3888**
Sargent, F., II.
Human ecology: a guide to information
sources **2220**
Sargent, P.
'Materials information sources for engineers'
3983
Sarjeant, W.A.S.
Geologists and the history of geology **1575**
Sarton, G.
A History of science **309**
Horus: a guide to the history of science **286**
Introduction to the history of science **310**
SAS survival guide **3554**

Sattar, T.P.
'Control engineering' **7341**
Satzwörterbuch des Buch- und Verlagswesen,
Deutsch-Englisch **6219**
Saunders comprehensive veterinary dictionary
5825
Saunders dictionary & encyclopedia of
laboratory medicine and technology **3445**
Saunders pharmaceutical word book **3645**
Savage, D.E. and Russell, D.E.
Mammalian paleofaunas of the world **1976**
Savage, R.J.G. and Long, M.R.
Mammal evolution **2315**
Save the birds **2463**
Saveskie, P.N.
Radio propagation handbook **4541**
Savitskii, E.M.
Handbook of precious metals **6930**
Sawin, P.
A Literature guide to the hospitality industry
5968
Sax's dangerous properties of industrial
materials **3631, 3723**
Scanziani, P.
The British encyclopedia of dogs **5903**
Scarlett, J.A.
The Multilayer printed circuit board
handbook **4470**
Schaaf, W.L.
A Bibliography of recreational mathematics
605
Schalit, M.
Guide to the literature of the sugar industry
6678
Schaller, O.
Illustrated veterinary anatomical
nomenclature **5851**
Schapera, I.
Select bibliography of South African native
life and problems **2076**
Schapsmeier, E.L. and Schapsmeier, F.H.
Encyclopedia of American agricultural
history **5598**
Scharf, B.
Engineering and its language **3929**
Scheele, M. and Natalis, G.
Biologie-Dokumentation: Bibliographie der
deutschen biologischen
Zeitschriftenliteratur, 1796-1965 **2136**
Scherer-Brewer, J. and Wright, R.W.
Sex research **3586**
Scherz, H.
Food composition and nutrition tables **3543**
Schidrowitz, P. and Dawson, T.R.
History of the rubber industry **7124**
Schieferdecker, A.A.G.
Geological nomenclature: English-Dutch-
French-German **1563**
Schiffahrts-Wörterbuch **5340**
Schifftechnisches Wörterbuch **5346**
Schlachter, G.A.
Nuclear America **4174**
Schlebecker, J.T.
Bibliography of books and pamphlets on the
history of agriculture in the United States,
1607-1967 **5597**
Schlessinger, B.S. and Schlessinger, J.H.
The Who's who of Nobel Prize winners,
1901-1995 **346**
Schlomann, A.
Illustrated technical dictionaries in six
languages **3031**
Technologisches Wörterbuch **111**
Schlosser, M.
Organometallics in synthesis **1364**
Schmidt, A.
Chef's book of formulas, yields and size
6072
Schmidt, E.
Properties of water and steam, in SI units
4229

Schmitz, H.P.
Wörterbuch der druckbehälter- und
vohrleitungstechnik **4610**
Schneeweiss, R.
Dictionary of cereal processing and cereal
chemistry **6687**
Schneider, S.H.
Encyclopedia of climate and weather **1797**
Schniewind, A.P.
Concise encyclopedia of wood and wood-
based materials **6987**
Schobert, H.H.
Coal, the energy source of the past and
future **6559**
Schodek, D.L.
Landmarks in American civil engineering
4964
Schoenewald, T.S.
German-English medical dictionary **3330**
Scholze, H.
Glass: nature, structure and properties **6794**
Schomburg, D. and Salzmann, M.
Enzyme handbook **2341**
School science review **261**
Schreiber, H.
The History of roads, from amber route to
motorway **5070**
Schubert, J.
Dictionary of effects and phenomena in
physics **939**
Schulz, E.
Wörterbuch der Datentechnik **7286**
Wörterbuch der Optik und Feinmechanik
1037
Schulz, H. and Georgy, U.
From CA to CAS online **1107**
Schulze, H.H.
Computer Englische **7262**
Schumann, W.
Gemstones of the world **1431**
Schupp, J.F.
Environmental guide to the Internet **2214**
Schützsack, U.
Proceedings of the 2nd International
Conference on Food Science and
Technology Information **6664**
Schuwer, P.
Dictionnaire bilingue de l'édition: français-
anglais; English-French **6218**
Schvarts, V.V.
Illustrated dictionary of mechanical
engineering **4133**
Schwartz, H.L.
The Encyclopedia of beaches and coastal
environments **1716**
Schwartz, M.M.
Composite materials handbook **4001**
Handbook of structural ceramics **6811**
Schwartzberg, F.
Cryogenic materials data handbook **4591**
Schwartzman, S.
The Words of mathematics **553**
Schwarzbach, M.
Climates of the past **1801, 1926**
Schwarzenbach, R.P.
Environmental organic chemistry **1338**
Environmental organic chemistry: illustrative
examples, problems and case studies **1339**
Schweitzer, P.A.
Corrosion resistance tables **4045**
Handbook of separation techniques for
chemical engineers **6487**
Schwenkhagen, H.F. and Meinhold, H.
Wörterbuch elektrotechnik und elektronik
4259
Sci-tech libraries in museums and aquariums
461
'Sci-tech libraries serving zoological gardens'
2737
SCICAT **82**
Science abstracts **220**

The Shorter 'Science and civilization in China' **395**

Shreeve, C.M.
The Alternative dictionary of symptoms and cures **3773**

Shrier, L.L.
Corrosion **4037**

Shrum, W.
Science, technology, and society in the Third World **365**

Shugar, G.J.
Chemical technicians' ready reference handbook **1188, 6482**
The Chemist's ready reference handbook **1189**

Shugg, W.T.
Handbook of electrical and electronic insulating materials **4339**

Shurtleff, M.C. and Averre, C.W.
Glossary of plant-pathological terms **2610**

Shvarts, V.V.
Kratkiĭ illystrirovannyĭ russko-angliiskiĭ slovar' po mashinostroeniya **4135**

Sibilia, J.P.
A Guide to materials characterization and chemical analysis **1273**

Sibley, C.G.
A Supplement to distribution and taxonomy of birds of the world **2898**
A World checklist of birds **2898**

Sibley, C.G. and Monroe, B.L.
Distribution and taxonomy of birds of the world **2898**

Sibley, J.F.
Online patents trademarks and service marks databases **3153**

Sidders, P.A.
Guide to world screw threads **4737**

Side effects of drugs annual **3640**

Sides, C.H.
How to write and present technical information **3090**

Sidgwick, J.B.
Amateur astronomer's handbook **696**
Observational astronomy for amateurs **697**

Sidwick, J.M. and Holdon, R.S.
Biotechnology of waste treatment and exploitation **5212**

Sieber, N.
An Annotated bibliography on rural transport **6248**

Siegel, P.J.
Women in the scientific search **360**

Sigerist, H.E.
A History of medicine **3405**

Sigma-Aldrich handbook of stains, dyes and indicators **6837**

Sigmond, J. and Terpstra, M.
High-power lasers **4373**

Sigurdson, J.
Science and technology in Japan **22**

The Silent revolution **4845**

Silver: economics, metallurgy and use **6934**

Silver: exploration, mining and treatment **4810, 6935**

Silverstein, A.M.
A History of immunology **3803**

Silvestre, L.C.
Marques typographiques **7403**

Simkin, T.
Volcanoes of the world **1627**

Simmons, A.F.
Simmons' manual of fruit **5769**

Simmons, E.S.
'Patents' **3154**

Simmons, J.
The Railway in England and Wales, 1830-1914 **6314**

Simmons, J. and Biddle, G.
The Oxford companion to British railway history from 1603 to the 1990s **5046, 6312**

Simmons' manual of fruit **5769**

Simmons, N.
Railway modeling **5053**

Simon, A.L.
Bibliotheca gastronomica **6046**
Dictionary of gastronomy **6054**

Simon, J.T.
Herbs: an indexed bibliography, 1971-1980 **3676**

Simons, E.N.
A Dictionary of alloys **6896**
Dictionary of ferrous metals **6906**
Dictionary of foundry work **4651**
A Dictionary of metal heat treatment **6899**
Guide to uncommon metals **6856**

Simons, J.H.
Fluorine chemistry **1314**

Simpkins, N.S.
100 modern reagents **1225**

Simpson, K. and Day, N.
Field guide to the birds of Australia **2929**

Simpson, M.A.
Dying, death and grief **3511**

Simpson, N.D.
A Bibliographical index of the British flora **2580**

Sims, W.L.
Two hundred years of history and evolution of woodworking machinery **7017**

Sinclair, C.G.
International dictionary of food and cooking **6067**

Sinclair, I.
Illustrated guide to the birds of southern Africa **2919**

Sinclair, I.R.
Collins dictionary of personal computing **7308**
The HarperCollins dictionary of electronics **4417**
Newnes audio and hi-fi handbook **7411**

Sinclair, W.A.
Diseases of trees and shrubs **5646**

Singer, C.
A History of technology **3065**
A Short history of scientific ideas to 1900 **311**

Singer, C. and Underwood, E.A.
A Short history of medicine **3407**

Singer, L.
Russian-English-French-German kinematics dictionary **1009**

Singh, J.
An Agricultural atlas of India **5596**

Singh, M.G.
'Information sources in systems and control' **7342**
Systems and control encyclopedia **7344**

Singh, M.H.
Glossary of terms: nuclear power and radiation **4183**

Singleton, P. and Sainsbury, D.
Dictionary of microbiology and molecular biology **2365**

Sinkankas, J.
Gemstones and mineral data book **1432**

Sinnott, R.W.
NGC 2000.0 **790**

Sinnott, R.W. and Perryman, M.A.C.
Millennium star atlas **802**

Sippl, C.J.
Macmillan dictionary of data communications **7289**
Macmillan dictionary of microcomputing **7309**

Sippl, C.J. and Sippl, R.J.
Computer dictionary and handbook **7255**

Sittig, M.
Handbook of toxic and hazardous chemicals and carcinogens **3627, 3718**
Sodium: its manufacture, properties and uses **6970**

Sittig, M. and Kowalski, J.S.
Drug companies and products world guide **3652**

Sitwell, N.
The Shell guide to Britain's threatened wildlife **2479**

Sivetz, M. and Desrosier, N.W.
Coffee technology **6618**

Six-language dictionary of plastics and rubber technology **7105**

Six language dictionary of the confectionery industry **6682**

Six-language illustrated dictionary of the motor car **5275**

Six-language vocabulary of distillation terms **6496**

Six-languages dictionary of industrial properties **3164**

Sixty cultures **2046**

Sizes: the illustrated encyclopedia **995**

Skalak, R. and Chien, S.
Handbook of bioengineering **3499**

Skeist, I.
Handbook of adhesives **6782**

Skelly, C.J.
Dictionary of herbs, spices, seasonings, and natural flavorings **6089**

Skelton, R.A.
History of cartography **882**
Maps: a historical survey of their study and collecting **891**

Skempton, A.W.
British civil engineering literature, 1640-1840 **4924**

Skinner, B.
Colour identification guide to moths of the British Isles **2838**

Skinner, B.J. and Porter, S.C.
Physical geology **1623**

Skinner, D.
Cambridge textbook of accident and emergency medicine **3297**

Skinner, H.A.
The Origin of medical terms **3323**

Skoglista **5627**

Skolnik, H.
The Literature matrix of chemistry **1120**

Skoob directory of secondhand bookshops in the British Isles **6244**

Skorucak, A.
PhysLINK **912**

Skousen, P
Valve handbook **4618**

Sky and telescope **712**

Sky atlas 2000.0 **786, 800**

Sky catalogue 2000.0 **786**

Skypala, I.
What are you eating? **3549**

Slade, R.M.
Robert Slade's guide to computer viruses **7336**

Slama, C.C.
A Dictionary of photogrammetry **841**

Slater, K.
The Principles of dairy farming **5911**

Slauson, N.
Index to illustrations of the natural world **2395**

Sleep research **3569**

Slesser, M.
Dictionary of energy **4072**

Sliosberg, A.
Dictionary of pharmaceutical science and techniques **3647**
Elsevier's medical dictionary in five languages **3308**

Sokolov, V.E.
Piatiiazychnyi slovar nazvanii zhivotnykh. ryby **2851**
Solar energy in developing countries **4111**
Solar energy technology handbook **4110**
Solar houses in Europe **7590**
The Solar system **754-755**
Solar system log **5485**
The Solid earth **1492**
'Solid fuels' **6557**
Solid liquid flow abstracts **1016**
Solid state physics **1089**
Solid state physics literature guides **1087**
Solid state/superconductivity abstracts **1090**
The Solid waste handbook **5258**
Solomon, B.
Dictionnaire de la technologie des corps gras en cinq langues **6708**
Solubilities of inorganic and organic compounds **1255**
Solvents in common use **6500**
Some Irish naturalists **2403**
Somerville, S.M.
Dictionary of geotechnics **4989**
Sonnedecker, G.
Kremers and Urdang's history of pharmacy **3654**
Soothill, E. *and* Whitebread, P.
Wildfowl of the world **2932**
Sosa, M. *and* Malcolm, S.M.
'Science books & films' best books for children **71**
Soule, J.
Glossary for horticultural crops **5753**
Sound **1028**
Source book guide to food industry information **6628**
A Source book in astronomy and astrophysics, 1900-1975 **698**
Source book in bioethics **3477**
A Source book in chemistry, 1400-1900 **1182**
A Source book in chemistry, 1900-1950 **1183**
A source book in mathematics, 1200-1800 **577**
A Source book in medieval science **320**
A Source book in physics **957**
A Source-book of biological names and terms **2160**
Source book of flavors **6698**
Source book of methods of analysis for biomass and biomass conversion processes **4116**
Source journals in metals and materials **6867**
Sourcebook for out-of-school science and technology education **266**
Sourcebook of control systems engineering **7348**
The Sourcebook of the environment **2222**
Sourcebook on death and dying **3513**
Sourcebook on green business **5172**
Sources and effects of ionizing radiation **3597**
Les Sources du travail bibliographique **69**
Sources for the history of quantum physics **1005**
Sources for the history of science, 1660-1914 **323**
Sources of information for the literature of geology **1534**
Sources of information on alternative energy technology held at the Science Reference and Information Service **4117**
Sources of information on the geology of the continental EEC countries **1586**
[Sources of transport statistics] **6267**
Sourkes, T.
Nobel Prize Winners in medicine and physiology **3421**
Sousa Ferreira, K. de
Terminologie des Hoch- und Brückenbaues **4941**

South African Council for Scientific and Industrial Research
Scientific and technical societies in South Africa **469**
South American Indians **2125**
South, D.W.
The Computer and information science and technology abbreviations and acronyms dictionary **7222**
South, D.W. *and* Dwiggins, B.H.
Delmar's automotive dictionary **5282**
South, D.W. *and* Ewert, R.H.
Encyclopedic dictionary of gears and gearing **4731**
South-east Asian transport **6272**
Southampton University. Library
Catalogue of the Walter Frank Perkins Agricultural Library **5575**
Southon, I.W. *and* Buckingham, J.
Dictionary of alkaloids **1371**
Soviet cosmonautics, 1957-1969 **5476**
Soviet mathematical encyclopaedia
Encyclopaedia of mathematics **517**
Soviet merchant ships **5376**
Soviet Russian scientific and technical terms **183**
Soyabean abstracts **5743**
Spa-finders guide to spa vacations at home and abroad **3699**
Space almanac **717, 5447**
Space flight **5444**
Space industry international **5478**
Space satellite handbook **5488**
Space sciences dictionary **5450**
Space year 1991 **5448**
Spaceflight and rocketry **5469**
Spain, B.
Spon's construction resource handbook **7475**
Spanish cuisine: the gourmet's companion **6076**
Spanish-English dictionary of weed science **5711**
Spanish-English/English-Spanish illustrated agricultural dictionary **5527**
Spanish-English, English-Spanish medical dictionary **3341**
Spanish-English technical dictionary **172**
Spanish technical dictionary **171**
Sparks, B.W.
Geomorphology **1672**
Special Libraries Association. New York. Transportation Division
Transportation libraries in the United States and Canada **6273**
Special-purpose dictionary of civil engineering and architecture **4940**
Specialist periodical reports: reviews of the chemical literature **1178**
Specialty booksellers directory **6239**
Specialty chemicals **6508**
Specialty cookbooks: a subject guide, v.1 **6048**
Specialty handbook: tool materials **4752**
Specification for graphical symbols for general engineering. Part 1. Piping systems and plant **4606**
Specification for letter symbols for semiconductor devices and integrated microcircuits **4475**
Specification for quantities, units and symbols **36**
Specification for the presentation of research and documentation reports **430**
Specifications and standards for plastics and composites **7108**
'Spectra: a bibliography of sources' **1055**
Spedding, C.R.W.
Fream's principles of food and agriculture **5510**

Speight, J.G.
The Chemistry and technology of coal **6560**
Speiss, W.E.L.
Engineering and Food **6668**
Spencer, D.D.
Computer dictionary **7256**
Illustrated computer graphics dictionary **7257**
Key dates in number theory history **614**
Spencer, F.
Ecce homo: an annotated bibliographic history of physical anthropology **1991**
History of physical anthropology: an encyclopedia **2028**
Spencer, J.
The UFO encyclopedia **5484**
Spencer, R.F. *and* Johnson, E.
Atlas for anthropology **2042**
Spices and natural flavourings **6086**
The Spiders of Great Britain and Ireland **2804**
Spiders of the world **2802**
Spilker, B.
Medical dictionary in six languages **3309**
SPIN (Searchable physics information notices) **910**
SPINES thesaurus **32**
Splittstoesser, W.E.
Vegetable growing handbook **5770**
Spon's architects' and builders' price book **7539**
Spon's civil engineering and highway works price book, 1999 **4955**
Spon's construction resource handbook **7475**
Spon's mechanical and electrical services price book, 1999 **4148**
Spon's railways construction price book **5021**
Sports documentation monthly bulletin **3566**
Sports injuries: their prevention and treatment **3558**
Sportsearch **3567**
Spring designer's handbook **4158**
Spring manufacturing handbook **4159**
Spurgeon, K.
Renewable energy and its environmental impact **4100**
Spurr, H.
Fifth International directory of anthropologists **2023**
Squire, G.
Buttons: a guide for collectors **7453**
Stables, L.
Pest and disease control handbook **5703**
Stace, C.A.
New flora of the British Isles **2581**
Stacey, T.
Peoples of the world **2045**
Stafleu, F.A. *and* Cowan, R.S.
Taxonomic literature **2490**
Stainless steel databook **6924**
'Stainless steels' **6918**
Stammers, M.K.
Discovering maritime museums and historic ships **5370**
Stamp, Sir D. *and* Clark, A.N.
A Glossary of geographical terms **1682**
Stanaszek, M.J.
The Inverted medical dictionary **3284**
Stanbridge, H.H.
History of sewage treatment in Britain **5206**
Standard catalog of American cars, 1946-1975 **5317**
Standard encyclopedia of the world's mountains **1711**
Standard encyclopedia of the world's oceans and islands **1709, 1736**
Standard encyclopedia of the world's rivers and lakes **1890**
Standard graphical symbols **44**
A Standard guide to cat breeds **5910**
A Standard guide to horse and pony breeds **5878**

Talbot, C.H. *and* Hammond, E.A.
  The Medical practitioners in medieval
    England 3423
Talbot, D.E.
  Japan's high technology 3088
Talbot, F.H. *and* Stevenson, R.E.
  Oceans and islands 1708
Talbot-Smith, M.
  Audio engineer's reference book 7408
Tallarida, R.J.
  Pocket book of integrals and mathematical
    formulas 625
Talvitie, J.K.
  Suomalais-englantilainin teknikan ja kaupan
    sanakorjo 196
Tanaka, T.
  Tanaka's cyclopedia of edible plants of the
    world 2626
  Tanaka's cyclopedia of edible plants of the
    world 2626
Tang, T.B.
  Science and technology in China 21
The Tanker register 5379
Tanks 4859
Tanks of the World 4862
Tansley, A.G.
  The British islands and their vegetation
    2571
Tantalum and niobium 6942
Tapley, B.D.
  Eshbach's handbook of engineering
    fundamentals 3920
Tarassuk, L. *and* Balair, C.
  The Complete encyclopedia of arms and
    weapons 4843
Taschenbuch der Panzer 4862
Taschenwörterbuch Eisen und Stahl 6908
Tate, W.H.
  Handbook of the nautical rules of the road
    6372
Taton, R.
  A General history of the sciences 305
  Planetary astronomy from the Renaissance to
    the rise of astrophysics: Pt. A. Tycho
    Brahe to Newton 724
  Planetary astronomy from the Renaissance to
    the rise of astrophysics: the eighteenth and
    nineteenth centuries 724
Tattersall, I.
  Encyclopedia of human evolution and
    prehistory 2312
Taubert, S. *and* Weidhaas, P.
  The Book trade of the world 6204
Tavaglione, D.
  Acronyms and abbreviations of computer
    technology and telecommunication 4488,
    7223
Tawfik, E.S.
  Tierproduktion. Mehrsprachen-
    Bildwörterbuch 5812
Taxonomic literature 2490
Taxonomy of vascular plants 2676
Taylor, C.R.H.
  A Bibliography of publications on the New
    Zealand Maori 2128
  A Pacific bibliography 2102
Taylor, E.G.R.
  An Index to 'The mathematical practitioners
    of Hanoverian England, 1714-1800' 597
  The Mathematical practitioners of
    Hanoverian England, 1714-1800 598,
    817
  The Mathematical practitioners of Tudor and
    Stuart England 596, 818
Taylor, G.D.
  Construction materials 7555
Taylor, G.E.
  'Offshore engineering' 4798, 6765
Taylor, J.C.
  World survey of non ferrous smelters 4657

Taylor, J.L.
  Dicionário metalúrgico 6862
Taylor, L.E.
  World mineral statistics, 1990-94 1854,
    6885
Taylor, M.
  Brassey's world aircraft and systems
    directory 4886, 5421
Taylor, M. *and* Mondey, D.
  Guinness aircraft facts and figures 5422
Taylor, P.A.
  Dictionary of marine technology 5085
Taylor, R.J.
  History of the Royal Astronomical Society
    735
Taylor, V.
  The Woodworker's dictionary 7009
TDR. 3719
Tea: cultivation to consumption 6620
Teachers' resource guide 2017
Tebbel, J.
  Between covers: the rise and transformation
    of book publishing in America 6235
  History of book publishing in the United
    States 6234
Tebble, N.
  British bivalve seashells 2793
Technical Americana 3018
Technical conversion factors for agricultural
  commodities 5551
Technical data on fuel 6553
Technical dictionary, English-Italian, Italian-
  English 161, 3037
Technical dictionary for automotive
  engineering 5283
Technical dictionary of high polymers 7158
Technical dictionary of spectroscopy and
  spectral analysis 1286
Technical dictionary on dams 5115
Technical drawing 3104
Technical history of the beginnings of radar
  4556
'Technical literature' 3019
Technical literature abstracts 5288
Technical petroleum dictionary of well-
  logging, drilling and production terms 6735
Technical services in the United Kingdom
  3096
Technical translation bulletin 425
Technical vocabulary of arboriculture 5623
Technik-Wörterbuch Kristallographie 1378
The Technique of furniture making 7432
Techniques in electrochemistry, corrosion and
  metal finishing 1246, 4040, 4697
Technische Informationsbibliothek.
  Hannover
  Katalog der Technischen
    Informationsbibliothek (TIB) 3020, 3916
Technische Kybernetik 7352
Technisches Bildwörterbuch für spanende
  Werkzeuge zur 'Metallbearbeitung' 4757
Technisches Fachwörterbuch der Grundstoff -
  Industrien 4781
Technish Engels woordenboek 140
Technological dictionary 110
Technologisches Wörterbuch 111
Technology and culture 3071
Technology and the future of Europe 3086
Technology and transition 3006
Technology assessment 3102
Technology in action 3027
Technology in world civilization 3085
The Technology management handbook 3028
Tehnikon ellēno-agglikon kai agglo-ellēnikon
  lexikon meta proforas 177
Teich, A. *and* Pace, J.H.
  Science and technology in the USA 28
Teich, M. *and* Needham, D.M.
  A Documentary history of biochemistry
    1770-1940 2337

Teicholz, E. *and* Orr, J.N.
  Computer integrated manufacturing
    handbook 7346
Tekniska Nomenklaturcentralen
  Bergteknisk ordlista 4984
  Betongteknisk ordlista 6833
  Byggordsamling 4942
  Energiordlista 4069
  Farg-och lackteknisk ordlista 6843
  Geoteknisk ordlista 4991
  Hallfasthetsoralista 4028
  Kommunaltekniska ordlista 4936
  Korrosions-ordlista 4042
  Luftbehandlingsordlista 3594
  Miljöordlista 5144
  Pappersordlista 7041
  Plan och byggtermer 7496
  Plast-och-gummi-teknisk ordlista 7104
  Rymdorlista: svensk-engelsk-fransk-tysk-
    rysk 5452
  Skoglista 5627
  Textilordlista 7060
  Träbyggnardsordlista 6991, 7572
  Va-teknisk ord lista 5185
  Vattenordlista 1318, 1878
Telecom users handbook 6130
Telecommunications 4490
Telecommunications acronyms and
  organisations 4489
Telecommunications directory 1996-97 4521
Telecommunications engineer's reference book
  4500
TELEDOC 4491
Telephony's dictionary 4510
Television and audio handbook for technicians
  4557
Television and video engineer's reference book
  4561
Television engineering handbook 4558
Temple, P.
  Carnivorous plants 2607
Temple, S.
  100 years in mathematics 581
Tennant, B.
  Small animal formulary 5849
A Tentative check-list of early European
  railway literature, 1831-1848 5026
Terek, F.
  Scientific expeditions 503
Les termes pétroliers 6743
Terminologie des Hoch- und Brückenbaues
  4941
Terminologie des matériaux complexe 4010
Terminologie du secteur de la pêche 5937
Terminologie Forsteinrichtung/Waldinventur
  mit deutsch-russischem und russisch-
  deutschem Fachwörterbuch 5628
'Terminology for the theory of machines and
  mechanisms' 4719
Terminology of communication disorders
  3812
Terminology of forest management/forest
  inventory, with a German-Russian and
  Russian-German technical dictionary 5628
Terminology of forest science, technology,
  practice and products 5629
Terminology of new and renewable sources of
  energy 4102
Terminus: bauwessen und architektur 4940
Terms relevant to the feather industry for
  fillings for bedding, upholstery and other
  domestic articles 7436
Terrell on the law of patents 3211
Terres, J.K.
  The Audubon Society encyclopedia of North
    American birds 2921
Test 6022
Tester, J.W.
  Energy and the environment in the 21st
    century 4099

Voskoboynikov, B.S.
Dictionary of flexible manufacturing systems and robotics **4638**
Vreckový anglicko-slovenský a slovensko-anglický technický slovnik 188
Vsesoyuznyi Nauchno-Issledovatel'skii Geologicheskii Institut (VSE-GEI) Ministerstva Geologii i Okhrany Nedr SSSR
See
USSR. Vsesoyuznyi Nauchno-Issledovatel'skii Geologicheskii Institut (VSE-GEI) Ministerstva Geologii i Okhrany Nedr SSR
Vulkan, G.
Traffic noise **5249**
Waddell, J.J.
Construction materials ready reference manual **7557**
Waddell, J.J. and Dobrowolski, J.A.
Concrete construction handbook **7567**
WAERSA **5613**
Wagner and Abbott's standard catalog of shells **2794**
Wagner, R.J.L. and Abbott, R.T.
Wagner and Abbott's standard catalog of shells **2794**
Wailes, R.
The English windmill **4581**
Wakeley, Sir C.
The Faber medical dictionary **3288**
Waldman, C.
Atlas of North American Indians **2121**
Encyclopedia of native American tribes **2116**
Waldman, H.
Dictionary of robotics **7394**
The Dictionary of SDI [Strategic Defense Initiative] **4880**
Wales 1995: hotels, guest houses & farmhouses **5998**
Walker, C.
Astronomy before the telescope **720**
Walker, D.
Great engineers **3960**
Walker, H.T. and Graham, W.E.
The Evolution of geomorphology **1700**
Walker, J.F. and Jenkins, N.
Wind energy technology **4323**
Walker, J.M.
The Language of biotechnology **2994**
Walker on patents **3214**
Walker, P.M.B.
Chambers air and space dictionary **5454**
Chambers biology dictionary **2153**
Chambers materials science and technology dictionary **4006**
Chambers nuclear energy and radiation dictionary **4184**
Walker's mammals of the world **2949**
Wall, J.J.
Statistical data analysis handbook **639**
Wall, R.A.
Engineers' guide to product information **3969**
Wallingford, H.R. and Barr, D.I.H.
Tables for the hydraulic design of pipes, sewers and channels **4614**
Wallis, H.M. and Robinson, A.H.
Cartographical innovations **883**
Wallis, L.W.
Modern encyclopedia of typefaces 1960-90 **6175**
Wallis, P. and Wallis, R.
Newton and Newtoniana, 1672-1975 **378**
Walls, Ian G.
The Complete book of the greenhouse **5687**
Walrond-Skinner, S.
A Dictionary of psychotherapy **3706**
Walsh, J.
'Native American reference sources' **2110**

Walsh, N.
The Good mail order guide **6032**
Walsh, R.A.
McGraw-Hill machining and metalworking handbook **4636**
Walter, H.
Vegetationsmonographien der einzelnen Grossräume **2555**
Walter, H. and Lieth, H.
Klimadiagram Weltatlas **1804**
Walter, K.S. and Gillett, H.J.
1997 IUCN red list of threatened plants **2452**
Walters, B.
'Medical reference tools for the layperson' **3269**
Walther, R.
Dictionary of technology **139**
Walton, A.M.
Patent law of Europe and the United Kingdom **3203**
Walton, D.W.H.
Antarctic science **1655**
Walton, H.
Dictionary of psychiatry **3850**
Walton, J.
The Oxford medical companion **3287**
Wanderer, J.A.
Metallurgisches Wörterbuch **6861**
Wang, Chu-Kia
Reinforced concrete design **4979**
Wang, S.K.
Handbook of air conditioning and refrigeration **4584, 7581**
Wannack-Nunn, S.
Directory of scientific research institutes in the People's Republic of China **494**
War Department
See
United States. War Department
Ward, C.R.
Coal geology and coal technology **1865**
Ward, D.C.
Geologic reference sources **1448**
Ward, F.A.B.
Descriptive catalogue of the collection illustrating time measurement: Science Museum **7196**
Ward, R.
Floods: a geographical perspective **1634**
Wardle, D.
Vegetation of New Zealand **2598**
Warr, W.
Directory of chemistry software **1111**
Warr, W. and Suhr, C.
Chemical information management **1217**
Warren, K.S.
Coping with the biomedical literature **2137, 3244**
Warren, K.S. and Mahmoud, A.A.F.
Tropical and geographical medicine **3433**
Warrern, A.
Dansk-Engelsk teknisk ordbog **147**
Engelsk-dansk teknisk ordbog **148**
Warring, R.H.
Pumps: selection systems and applications **4622**
Warship 1998-1999 **4900**
Warships of the Soviet Navy **4913**
Warships of the world **4911**
Washino, S.
Automobile electronics **5273**
Wasserman, P. and Morgan, J.
Ethnic information sources of the United States **2087**
Wasserman, S.
Encyclopedia of physical sciences and engineering information sources **62**
Wasserwesen, Erd- und Grundbau **5086**
Waste and environment today **5211**
Waste management **5215**

Waste management research abstracts **5225**
Waste, recycling and environmental directory **5220**
Wastes in the ocean **5209**
'Wastes management' **5210**
Wastewater engineering **5205**
Watch and clock encyclopedia **7182**
The Watch repairer's manual **7184**
Watchmakers and clockmakers of the world **7191**
Watchmakers and clockmakers of the world: Volume 2 **7192**
Water **5197**
Water: a comprehensive treatise **1317**
Water analysis **5179**
Water and wastes **5193, 5221**
Water and water use terminology **1880**
The Water directory **5194**
The Water encyclopedia **1884**
Water plants of the world **2705**
[Water pollution]: literature review **5203**
Water quality and availability **5181**
Water Research Centre
Aqualine abstracts **1883, 5191**
Aqualine thesaurus 2 **5199**
Water resources abstracts **1872, 5175**
Water Resources Center Archives. University of California
Dictionary catalog. [Water Resources Center Archives] **1873, 5177**
Water resources engineering **5180**
Water treatment handbook **5201**
The Waterfowl of the world **2930**
Waterman, N.A. and Ashby, M.F.
Elsevier materials selector **3992**
Watermarks in paper in Holland, England, France **7050**
Waternet **5176**
Waters, A.W.
All the US Air Force airplanes, 1907-1983 **4892**
Waters, D.W.
The Art of navigation in England in Elizabethan and early Stuart times **816**
Watson, A.H.
Inland transport statistics, Great Britain, 1900-1970 **6265**
Watson, C.A.
Official and standardized methods of analysis **6461**
Watson, E.V.
British mosses and liverworts **2671**
Watson, J. and Hill, A.
A Dictionary of communication and media studies **6123**
Watson, L.
Whales of the world **2962**
Watson, R. and Gray, M.
The Penguin book of the bicycle **5330**
Watstein, S.B. and Chandler, K.
The AIDS dictionary **3872**
Watt, A.
Longman illustrated dictionary of geology **1549**
Watton, J.
'Fluid mechanics and fluid power systems' **4599**
Watznauer, A.
Dictionary of geosciences **1468**
Wauchope, R.
Handbook of Middle American Indians **2117**
Waveguide handbook **4370**
The Way things work **3925**
We the people: an atlas of America's ethnic diversity **2084**
The Wealth of India **4019**
Weapons: an international encyclopedia, from 5000 BC to 2000 AD **4850**
Wear control handbook **4747**
Wear resistant surfaces in engineering **4046**

Wind energy comes of age **4318**
Wind energy technology **4323**
Wind engineering **4973**
Wind engineering abstracts **4325**
Wind machines **4321**
The Wind power book **4322**
Windmills and watermills **4579**
Windpower **4320**
The Wines of France **6598**
Wingate, P. and Wingate, R.
 The Penguin medical encyclopedia **3293**
Wingrove, R.G. and Jammes, J.R.J.
 The Aviator's English and French dictionary
 5399
Winkler, W.
 Fachwörterbuch Chemiefasern **7093**
The Winning of nickel **6938**
Winship, I.
 Health and safety at work **3604**
Winslade, J.
 Dictionary of drug development **3648**
Winter, F.H.
 Rockets into space **5439**
Winter, R.
 The People's handbook of allergies and
 allergens **3767**
Winterkorn, H.F.
 Foundation engineering handbook **4999**
Winters, C.
 International dictionary of anthropologists
 2022
Winthrop, R.
 Dictionary of concepts in cultural
 anthropology **2037**
Wire industry yearbook **4677**
Wise, T.
 A Guide to military museums **4837**
Wiseman, C.H.
 The International countermeasures handbook
 4878
Wiseman, J.
 A History of the British pig **5889**
 SAS survival guide **3554**
Wistreich, G.A. and Lechtman, M.D.
 Microbiology **2363**
Witherby, H.F.
 The Handbook of British birds **2909**
Witte, G.
 'Glossary of technical terms for the sugar
 industry' **5747**
Wittering, S.
 French dictionary of telecommunications
 4515
Wittfoht, A.
 Plastics technical dictionary **7139**
Wittfoht, H.
 Building bridges **5010**
Wittmann, A. and Klos, J.
 Dictionary of data processing, including
 applications in industry, administration
 and business **7287**
 Dictionary of patent terms **3168**
WMO sea-ice nomenclature **1643**
Wohlauer, G.E.M. and Gholston, H.D.
 German chemical abbreviations **1104**
Wohlfarth, E.P.
 Ferromagnetic materials **4353**
Wold, H.O.A.
 Bibliography on time series and stochastic
 processes **652**
Woldman's Engineering alloys **6898**
Wolf, C.
 Indians of North and South America, second
 supplement **2113**
Wolf, C.E. and Chiang, N.S.
 Indians of North and South America **2112**
Wolfe, J.A.
 Mineral resources **1859**
Wolfe, W.L. and Zissis, G.J.
 The Infrared handbook **1042**

Wolfheim, J.W.
 Primates of the world **2976**
The Wolfson geochemical atlas of England and
 Wales **1518**
Wolman, B.B.
 International encyclopedia of psychiatry,
 psychology, psychoanalysis & neurology
 3843
Wolman, Y.
 Chemical information **1121**
Women and health **3239**
Women and science **358**
Women and technology **3105**
Women anthropologists: a biographical
 dictionary **2025**
Women chemists, 1990 **1222**
Women in chemistry **1211**
Women in chemistry and physics: a
 biobibliographic sourcebook **1212**
Women in medicine **3424**
Women in science **359**
Women in the biological sciences **2192**
Women in the scientific search **360**
Women of mathematics **599**
Women of science, technology and medicine
 357
Women scientists from antiquity to the present
 356
Wonder worker's complete book of cleaning
 6114
Wonders of creation: natural history drawings
 in the British Library **2393**
Wong, S.
 Dictionary of Chinese Communist
 agricultural technology **5534**
Wood, A.D.
 Plywoods of the world **7019**
Wood, C.A.
 An Introduction to the literature of vertebrate
 zoology **2844**
Wood, C.A. and Kienle, J.
 Volcanoes of North America **1626**
Wood, D.
 Trade names dictionary **3138**
 Trade names dictionary: company index
 3140
Wood, D.N.
 Information sources in the earth sciences
 1449
Wood engineering and construction handbook
 7564
Wood in construction **7571**
Wood, K. and McDonald, G.
 The Round the world air guide **6397**
Wood, R.A.
 Weather almanac **1823**
Woodburn, H.M.
 Using the chemical literature **1122**
Woodburn, J.
 The Royal Anthropological Institute Film
 Library catalogue **2019**
Woodman, R.
 The History of the ship **5365**
Woods Hole Oceanographic Institution
 Catalog of the Library of the Marine
 Biological Laboratory and the Woods Hole
 Oceanographic Institution **1732, 2283**
 Oceanographic index **1730**
Woods practical guide to fan engineering **4604**
Woods, R.S.
 The Naturalist's lexicon **2182**
Woodward, D.
 Five centuries of map printing **899**
The Woodworker's Bible **7008**
The Woodworker's dictionary **7009**
Woodworking machines in 4 languages **7015**
Wool trade directory of the world **7090**
Wooley, T.
 Green building handbook **7552**
Woolham, F.
 The Handbook of aviculture **5899**

Woollett, S.
 Environmental grants **2257**
Woordenlijst voor der tuinbouw in seven talen
 5752
Wootton, A.
 Insects of the world **2814**
Word processing dictionary **6183**
Words for birds: a lexicon of North American
 birds, with biographical notes **2924**
The Words of mathematics **553**
The Wordsworth dictionary of drink **6085**
Work manual **3123**
Work, M.N.
 A Bibliography of the negro in Africa and
 America **2093**
World aerospace **5468**
World agricultural economics and rural
 sociology abstracts **5613**
World air transport statistics **6398**
World aluminium **6961**
World animal health in 1997 **5857**
World archaeoastronomy **730**
World atlas of agriculture **5554**
The World atlas of cheese **5919**
World atlas of desertification **1719**
World atlas of epidemic disease **3744**
World atlas of geology and mineral deposits
 1566
The World atlas of wine **6603**
The World Book encyclopedia of science **100**
World cars **5313**
World cartography **876**
World catalogue of theses and dissertations
 about the Australian aborigines and Torres
 Strait islanders **2129**
World catalogue of very large floods **5111**
World cement directory **6828**
World ceramics abstracts **6819**
World checklist of birds. **2898**
The World checklist of conifers **5649**
World checklist of threatened amphibians and
 reptiles **2465**
World checklist of threatened mammals **2466**
World cocoa directory **6621**
World Conservation Monitoring Centre
 1996 IUCN red list of threatened animals
 2467
 Protected areas of the world **2439**
 World checklist of threatened mammals
 2466
 World plant conservation bibliography **2444**
World copper databook **6950**
World databases in agriculture **5496**
World databases in biosciences and
 pharmacology **2135, 3637**
World databases in chemistry **1108**
World databases in geography and geology
 1444
World databases in medicine **3237**
World databases in patents **3155**
World databases in physics and mathematics
 506, 911
World dictionaries in print, 1983 **106**
A World dictionary of livestock breeds, types
 and varieties **5865**
World directory and handbook of hard metals
 4764
World directory of biological and medical
 sciences libraries **2194, 3455**
World directory of collections of cultures of
 micro-organisms **2199**
World directory of crystallographers **1380**
World directory of energy information **4096**
World directory of environmental organizations
 2258
World directory of environmental testing,
 monitoring and treatment **5163**
World directory of fertilizer manufacturers
 5698
World directory of map collections **881**
World directory of mathematicians **564**

World directory of medical schools **3470**
World directory of mineral collections **1420**
World directory of mineralogists **1409**
World directory of modern military vehicles: unarmoured vehicles from 1970 **4861**
World directory of pesticide control organisations **5725**
The World directory of renewable energy suppliers and services **4084**
World directory of sources of patent information **3191**
The World electronics industry **4443**
World encyclopedia of aero engines **5419**
The World encyclopedia of beer **6606**
The World encyclopedia of fishes **2852**
World encylopedia of modern air weapons **4840**
World energy and nuclear directory **4097**
The World energy book **4070**
World energy CD-ROM **4051**
World Energy Council
 Energy dictionary **4068**
World engine digest **4568**
World environmental directory: North America **5171**
World environmental research directory **5174**
A World geography of human diseases **3747**
World geomorphology **1669**
The World guide to automobile manufacturers **5304**
World guide to environmental issues and organizations **5241**
World guide to scientific associations and learned societies **464**
The World guide to whisky **6613**
World Health Organization
 Animal health yearbook **5844**
 International classification of impairments, disabilities and handicaps **3749**
 International classification of procedures in medicine **3300**
 International digest of health legislation **3430**
 International nomenclature of diseases **3740**
 Lexicon of psychiatric and mental health terms **3853**
 Lexicon to alcohol and drug terms **3572**
 Manual of basic techniques for a health laboratory **3448**
 Manual of the international statistical classification of diseases, injuries and causes of death **3748**
 Mental disorders **3854**
 Publications catalogue, 1948-1989. [World Health Organization] **3272**
 World directory of medical schools **3470**
World Health Organization. International Agency for Research on Cancer (IARC)
 Directory of on-going research in cancer epidemiology, 1992 **3734**
World Health Organization. Regional Office for Europe
 Glossary of air pollution **3595**
World health statistics annual **3377, 3526**
A World history of physical education **3568**
World hotel directory **5977**
The World in perspective **859**
World index of strategic minerals **6854**
World list of agricultural serials **5545**
A World list of mammalian species **2942**
World list of scientific periodicals **244**
World literature on patents (1900-1981) **3159**
The World map directory, 1992-1993 **877**
World mapping today **856**
World maps of climatology **1805**
World medical periodicals **3363**
World meetings: Medicine **3461**
World meetings: outside United States and Canada **480**
World meetings: United States and Canada **481**

World Meteorological Organization
 International cloud atlas **1791**
 International glossary of hydrology **1879**
 International meteorological vocabulary **1783**
 WMO sea-ice nomenclature **1643**
World metric standards for engineering **3949**
World mineral statistics, 1990-94 **1854, 6885**
World mining: glossary of mining, processing and geological terms **4778**
World motor vehicle data **5308**
World motorcycles **5322**
World nuclear industry handbook, 1998 **4197**
World ocean atlas **1762**
The World of co-operative enterprise **5615**
The World of mathematics **578**
The World of model cars **5309**
The World of model[s] **5266**
The World of physics **977**
World of toys **7454**
The World of zoos **2742**
World Organisation for Animal Health
 World animal health in 1997 **5857**
World palaeontological collections **1923**
World patent information **3179**
World patents abstracts journal **3174**
World patents index **3151**
World patents index gazette **3175**
World petroleum resources and reserves **6731**
World plant conservation bibliography **2444**
World publishing monitor **6220**
World radio TV handbook 1999 **6135**
The World railway system **5028**
World register of dams **5116**
World report on palaeobotany, 1950/1974 **1937**
World resources 1998-99 **1848**
World Resources Institute
 World resources 1998-99 **1848**
World review of nutrition and dietetics **3540, 6653**
World road statistics, 1985-1989 **6287**
World robotics, 1998 **7397**
The World satellite almanac **4552**
World shipping statistics **6352**
World soils **5676**
World sulphur and sulphuric acid plant list and atlas **6535**
World surface coating abstracts **6530**
World surface coatings abstracts **6839**
World survey of climatology **1813**
World survey of non ferrous smelters **4657**
World technology policies **3078**
World textile abstracts **7072**
World textile trade and production trends **7076**
World textiles **7052**
World timbers **7005**
World tobacco directory **6625**
World translations index **428**
World truck handbook **5297**
World vegetables: principles, production, and nutritive values **5767**
The World weather guide **1809**
World weather records, 1971-1980 **1811**
World weeds: natural histories and distribution **5714**
The World wide web for scientists and engineers **3911**
World wide web sites for chartered surveyors **7468**
World Wildlife Fund guide to extinct species of modern times **2474**
World woods in colour **7003**
Worlds in the sky **729**
The World's lighthouses before 1820 **5113**
The World's motor museums **5296**
The World's whales **2964**
The Worldwide directory of agrobiologicals 1997/98 **5792**
Worldwide guide to equivalent irons and steels **6915**

Worldwide petrochemical directory **6775**
Wormleighton, A.
 The Encyclopedia of home furnishing techniques **6109**
Worrell, E.
 Reptiles of Australia **2870**
Worshipful Company of Clockmakers of London
 The Catalogue of the Library **7179**
Wörterbuch antriebstechnic **4718**
Wörterbuch bauwesen **7478**
Wörterbuch chemie **1151-1152**
Wörterbuch. Chemische Prozesse und Produkten **6490**
Wörterbuch der Chemie und der chemischen Vefahrenstechnik **1145**
Wörterbuch der dampferzeugungs technik **4224**
Wörterbuch der Datentechnik **7286**
Wörterbuch der datenverarbeitung mit anwendungsgebieten in industrie, verwaltung und wirtschaft. Dictionnaire du traitment de données, et de son application dans l'industrie, l'administration et l'economie **7287**
Wörterbuch der druckbehälter- und vohrleitungstechnik **4610**
Wörterbuch der Elektronik **4420**
Wörterbuch der elektronik, datentechnik und der telekommunikation **4419, 4513, 7261**
Wörterbuch der Fertigungstechnik **4640**
Wörterbuch der Holzwirtschaft **6994**
Wörterbuch der industriellen Technik **136**
Wörterbuch der industriellen Teknik **3930**
Wörterbuch der kabeltechnik **4335**
Wörterbuch der Medizin und Pharmazeutik, Deutsch-Englisch **3326**
Wörterbuch der Mikroelektronik **4464**
Wörterbuch der Mikroelektronik und Mikroechnertechnick **4463**
Wörterbuch der Optik und Feinmechanik **1037**
Wörterbuch der patent -und markenpraxis **3120, 3167**
Wörterbuch der Psychiatrie und medizinischer Psychologie **3848**
Wörterbuch der telekommunikations- technik **4505**
Wörterbuch der Veterinärmedizin **5832**
Wörterbuch der Wasserchemie **1316, 5187**
Wörterbuch der werkstoffprüfung **4009**
Wörterbuch der Wirtschaftswissenschaft: russisch, deutsch, englisch **1**
Wörterbuch des internationales Verkehrs: Deutsch-Englisch **6254**
Wörterbuch des Patentwesens in fünf Sprachen **3163**
Wörterbuch deutsch-englisch, englisch-deutsch: Erdöl und Erdgas **6741**
Wörterbuch elektrotechnik und electronik **4255**
Wörterbuch elektrotechnik und elektronik **4259**
Wörterbuch für Architektur, Hochbau und Baustoffe **7504**
Wörterbuch für Bautechnik und Baumaschinen **4939**
Wörterbuch für Physik und verwandter Wissenschafterv **940**
Wörterbuch Geowissenschaft **1468**
Wörterbuch Keramik und erden **6816**
Wörterbuch Kerntechnik **4181**
Wörterbuch korrosion und korrosionsschutz **4041**
Wörterbuch kraftfahrzeugtechnik **5284**
Wörterbuch Kunststofftechnologie **7137**
Wörterbuch lichtechnik **5263**
Wörterbuch messtechnik und einheiten **4349**
Wörterbuch numerische Steuerung und Werkzeugmaschinen **4763**
Wörterbuch Physik **931**
Wörterbuch technischer Begriffe **3033**

Subject Index

The index reference is to the running number given to each item. The running numbers are in one sequence throughout the volume and can be found at the top right-hand corner of the entry for each item.

The index is computer generated, thus terms for the index have been largely derived from the headings and sub-headings used throughout *Walford*, but many other entries have been added, including synonyms, inverted headings, and cross-references. Some form headings such as 'Bibliographies', 'Dictionaries', etc., are omitted as leading to too great a bulk.

The arrangement of the index is alphabetical and filing is word by word, with groups of initials counted as single words. Under each main heading printed in bold type in the index will be found a resumé of all the subject terms used under that heading and the numbers of the items to which they refer. Similarly, under each narrower sub-heading there is a list of terms used. Where the term in the index needs to be qualified by the broader term of which it is a sub-division, then the broader term is given in square brackets, *e.g.* **Africa** [Book Trade] or [Mammals].

Online and Database Services Index

The index reference is to the running number given to each item. The running numbers are in one sequence throughout the volume and can be found at the top right hand corner of the entry for each item. This index is of authors and titles in one sequence. The names of authors are printed in bold type. Filing is word by word with groups of initials counted as single words.

The titles appearing in this index have been published as electronic databases. The databases are available on subscription as online database services, as websites or in CD-ROM or disk formats. An indication of the names of some of the hosts from whom the online databases are available is given in the text.

Also from Library Association Publishing

A Guide to World Language Dictionaries

ANDREW DALBY

Sadly, most of the world's 5000 or more languages will be dead before anyone has had the time or energy to compile a full dictionary giving meanings, nuances, etymologies, etc. However, this unique new work looks worldwide at those languages for which in-depth research dictionaries do exist. It provides the first evaluative and critical bibliography of the dictionaries of 276 languages from Abkhaz to Zulu.

Organized in alphabetical order by language, the Guide appraises the main dictionaries, assessing the special value of each, its strengths and weaknesses and how different dictionaries complement one another. It includes comprehensive bibliographical details including up-to-date information on new editions and supplements and on the progress of multi-volume dictionary projects. There is also cross referencing to language families and comparative dictionaries. Its approach is unique as it:

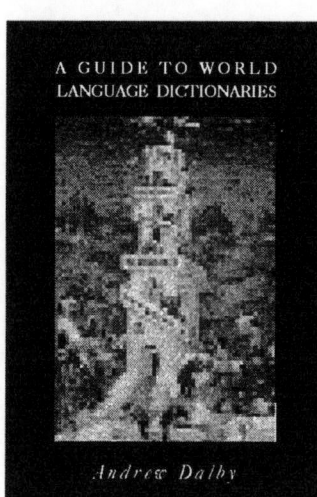

- gives detailed and critical annotation
- selects those dictionaries that are of long-term research use
- explores inside the dictionaries, approaching them as a user

- shows the script, transliteration and alphabetical order where needed
- traces history and publication dates fully
- includes dictionaries of slang, colloquialisms and dialects
- indicates the best source of word histories.

This is an indispensable guide for dictionary users and researchers who want to know the range of information sources available and how to use them. It is also essential as a tool to enable librarians and linguists to assess the strengths of their own reference collections, for enquiry desk work related to languages and foreign language study, and as a guide for library users.

1998; 480pp; hardback; 1-85604-251-0; £59.95

Also from Library Association Publishing

Outstanding Books for Children and Young People
The LA guide to Carnegie/Greenaway winners 1937–1997

KEITH BARKER

The Library Association's two children's book awards, the Carnegie Medal for outstanding writing for children, and the Kate Greenaway Medal for outstanding books in terms of illustration, are recognized the world over for their promotion of excellence in writing and illustration for children. The winners and commended books help to provide a microcosm of children's literature in the United Kingdom over the last half of the 20th century, and to identify trends, from forgotten writers and classics of the early period, through developments in the printing of illustrated material, to the gritty realism of recent winners.

Launched in the National Year of Reading, this book celebrates over 60 years of writing and illustration, and is introduced by a Foreword from the Rt Hon. David Blunkett MP, Secretary of State for Education and Employment. It presents a complete annotated list of winners, commended and highly commended titles, given in chronological order. The author supplies bibliographical details for each title, with ISBNs for those still in print, followed by a description of the story or illustration, and a critical evaluation of the book's relevance to today's children.

> 'Barker's book is an invaluable guide through the thickets of contemporary children's fiction'
> THE MAIL ON SUNDAY

Of considerable historical interest, this list of outstanding titles also has immense validity today. It is intended as an essential desktop companion for children's librarians and teachers who will find this book an ideal collection or curriculum development tool. It will also be a useful reference work for researchers in children's literature, publishers, library school students studying children's literature, and parents wishing to choose excellent reading material for their children.

1998; 152 pp; paperback; 1-85604-287-1; £15.95